**Hermeneia
—A Critical
and Historical
Commentary
on the Bible**

Romans

A Commentary

by Robert Jewett

Assisted by
Roy D. Kotansky

Edited by
Eldon Jay Epp

Fortress Press

Minneapolis

Romans
A Commentary

Images on endpapers: Romans 5:17—6:3 (Dublin, Chester Beatty papyrus II, folio 8, *verso*): photo © The Trustees of the Chester Beatty Library, Dublin; Romans 16:23—Hebrews 1:1-7 (Ann Arbor, Michigan papyrus inv. no. 6238, page MA = Chester Beatty papyrus II, folio 21, *recto*): digitally reproduced with the permission of the Papyrology Collection, Graduate Library, The University of Michigan.

Cover and interior design by Kenneth Hiebert
Typesetting and page composition by
The HK Scriptorium

Library of Congress Cataloging-in-Publication Data

Jewett, Robert.
    Romans : a commentary / by Robert Jewett ; assisted by Roy Kotansky ; volume editor, Eldon Jay Epp.
        p. cm. — (Hermeneia–a critical and historical commentary on the Bible)
    Includes bibliographical references and index.
    ISBN-13: 978-0-8006-6084-0 (alk. paper)
    ISBN-10: 0-8006-6084-6
    1. Bible. N.T. Romans—Commentaries. I. Kotansky, Roy David, 1953- II. Epp, Eldon Jay. III. Title.
    IV. Series.
        BS2665.53.J49 2006
        227'.1077—dc22

                              2006009375

The paper used in this publication meets the minimum requirements of American National Standard for Information Sciences—Permanence of paper for Printed Library Materials, ANSI Z329.48–1984.

Manufactured in the U.S.A.

10 09 08 07 06   1 2 3 4 5 6 7 8 9 10

■ In Memory of John William Colenso
(1814–1883)

The Author

Robert Jewett received his theological education at the
Federated Theological Seminary of the University of
Chicago and at the University of Tübingen. He is an
ordained United Methodist minister. After pastoral expe-
rience in three mid-western congregations, he taught at
Morningside College from 1966 to 1980 and at Garrett-
Evangelical Theological Seminary from 1980 to 2000.
At the seminary, he served on the doctoral program in
cooperation with Northwestern University. He is the
author of fifteen books and several hundred articles,
the editor of three volumes of biblical essays, and an
active member of the Society of Biblical Literature, the
Chicago Society of Biblical Studies, and the international
Society of New Testament Studies. Since 2000 Jewett has
served as a Guest Professor of New Testament at the
University of Heidelberg, where he directs an archive
project related to ecumenical research on Paul's letter
to the Romans.

Endpapers

The front and back endpapers of this volume present,
respectively, the first and last extant leaves of Romans in
P[46], dated ca. 200. The first leaf contains Romans
5:17–6:3 (Dublin, Chester Beatty papyrus II, folio 8,
verso); the latter has the final four words of Romans
16:23 plus Hebrews 1:1-7 (Ann Arbor, Michigan papyrus
inv. no. 6238, page MA = Chester Beatty papyrus II, folio
21, *recto*). P[46] is the oldest known manuscript of Romans.

Contents
Romans

■ **Commentary**

■ **End matter**

The name *Hermeneia*, Greek ἑρμηνεία, has been chosen as the title of the commentary series to which this volume belongs. The word *Hermeneia* has a rich background in the history of biblical interpretation as a term used in the ancient Greek-speaking world for the detailed, systematic exposition of a scriptural work. It is hoped that the series, like its name, will carry forward this old and venerable tradition. A second, entirely practical reason for selecting the name lies in the desire to avoid a long descriptive title and its inevitable acronym, or worse, an unpronounceable abbreviation.

The series is designed to be a critical and historical commentary to the Bible without arbitrary limits in size or scope. It will utilize the full range of philological and historical tools, including textual criticism (often slighted in modern commentaries), the methods of the history of tradition (including genre and prosodic analysis), and the history of religion.

Hermeneia is designed for the serious student of the Bible. It will make full use of ancient Semitic and classical languages; at the same time, English translations of all comparative materials—Greek, Latin, Canaanite, or Akkadian—will be supplied alongside the citation of the source in its original language. Insofar as possible, the aim is to provide the student or scholar with full critical discussion of each problem of interpretation and with the primary data upon which the discussion is based.

Hermeneia is designed to be international and interconfessional in the selection of authors; its editorial boards were formed with this end in view. Occasionally the series will offer translations of distinguished commentaries which originally appeared in languages other than English. Published volumes of the series will be revised continually, and eventually, new commentaries will replace older works in order to preserve the currency of the series. Commentaries are also being assigned for important literary works in the categories of apocryphal and pseudepigraphical works relating to the Old and New Testaments, including some of Essene or Gnostic authorship.

The editors of *Hermeneia* impose no systematic-theological perspective upon the series (directly, or indirectly by selection of authors). It is expected that authors will struggle to lay bare the ancient meaning of a biblical work or pericope. In this way the text's human relevance should become transparent, as is always the case in competent historical discourse. However, the series eschews for itself homiletical translation of the Bible.

The editors are heavily indebted to Fortress Press for its energy and courage in taking up an expensive, long-term project, the rewards of which will accrue chiefly to the field of biblical scholarship.

The editor responsible for this volume is Eldon Jay Epp, currently Visiting Professor of New Testament at the Harvard Divinity School.

Peter Machinist	*Helmut Koester*
For the Old Testament	For the New Testament
Editorial Board	Editorial Board

The English translation of the Letter to the Romans was provided by the author and reflects his exegetical decisions. Other biblical texts are usually from the New Revised Standard Version. Quotations from Latin and Greek authors, except where noted, follow the texts of the Loeb Classical Library or other standard editions; the translations, except where noted, are the author's.

Text-critical evidence has been compiled primarily by using the Nestle-Aland and UBS Greek New Testaments (see "Sources and Abbreviations"); Aland et al., *Ergänzungsliste;* Junack et al., *Das Neue Testament auf Papyrus. II: Die Paulinische Briefe, 1:1;* Metzger, *Textual Commentary* (both editions); and Swanson, *Vaticanus: Romans* (see "Works Cited").

That Romans was a missionary document aimed at overcoming the premises of imperial honor was first suggested by a missionary to Africa in 1863. This accounts for the dedication to the memory of Bishop John William Colenso on the frontispiece of this volume. Although he did not employ the categories of honor and shame as shaped by modern social theory, and despite his outdated grasp of the historical situation of the Roman audience, he was the first to suggest that Paul aimed to overcome prejudice against allegedly inferior peoples. By placing the argument of Romans in opposition to imperial claims of European colonists in South Africa, he showed that Paul defended the status of ancient inferiors comparable to the "Zulus and Kafirs" of nineteenth-century Africa and thus that the righteousness of God was impartial.[1]

Although unaware of Colenso's work until late in my twenty-six years' work on this commentary, I have followed in his footsteps by understanding Romans as intended to elicit support for a mission to the "barbarians" in Spain, which would only be credible if the churches in Rome ceased their imperialistic competition with one another under the premise that the gospel of impartial grace shatters all claims of superior status or theology. The rhetorical analysis developed in this commentary reveals a subtle interaction at many points with the cultural premises of imperialism as centered in the civic cult in Rome and expressed in the hostile relations between converted groups there. The rhetorical climax of the letter is therefore in the authentic portions of the *peroratio* of 15:14—16:16, 21-24 that alludes to this missionary project and urges the churches in Rome to welcome one another as equals in Christ, thus demonstrating the power of the gospel to overcome cultural barriers and conflicts. Although I remain faithful to the Hermeneia format by leaving the contemporary application up to my readers, I hope that the extraordinary relevance of Romans to the situation of cultural, religious, and imperial conflicts is easily discernible.

Intellectual and spiritual debts are owed to a great multitude of scholars from various traditions with whom I have interacted over the years. Their work has encouraged me to use all of the historical-critical techniques of exegesis and to take account, as far as possible, of the insights of interpreters beyond my own national and confessional boundaries. Inspired by Markus Barth at the Federated Theological Seminary of the University of Chicago in 1955–56, I wrestled night after sleepless night with his father's commentary on Romans. It brought me through a spiritual crisis similar to that experienced by many Europeans after 1914–18 in the discovery that the gospel challenged my dearest cultural premises. Attending Ernst Käsemann's lectures on Romans that were repeated twice in 1960–64 at the University of Tübingen was also formative. Although in later years I came to disagree with many aspects of Barthian and Käsemannian interpretation, their passionate advocacy of Paul's critique of widely accepted cultural values continues to guide my work. Immense debts are also owed to my colleague Peter Lampe here at the University of Heidelberg for his definitive analysis, first published in 1987, of the congregational situation in Rome, and to James D. G. Dunn,

---

1   Colenso, 195–96, as noted by Snyder, "Major Motifs," 54: Colenso's "attack on the British as the self-righteous Jews eventually brought his condemnation as a heretic."

whose commentary of 1988 has guided me throughout the gestation of my own work.

While valuable bibliographic assistance was rendered by Frank Witt Hughes, Keith Augustus Burton, Rainer Dahnelt, and Sebastian Kuhlmann, the greatest debt is owed to the classical scholar, Roy Kotansky, who has conducted innumerable searches through the *Thesaurus Linguae Graecae* and elsewhere and provided editorial corrections and counsel on every page of the commentary. I am also grateful to Eldon Jay Epp, who edited this volume as a member of the Hermeneia Board, and who encouraged me through the seemingly endless process of researching, writing, and revising this commentary. After my submission of the manuscript in August 2005, Eldon spent many hours correcting and augmenting the lists of witnesses in the text-critical notes. Olle Christopherson, Robert Gagnon, Frank Hughes, William Klassen, Troy Martin, David Mesner, Mark Reasoner, Stanley Stowers, and Peter Zaas also rendered significant help by critically reading sections of the manuscript. Beate Müller and James Cowey provided important assistance in checking references. Stanislaw and Aleksandra Burdziej with their friends, Jakub Jakalski, Ewa Chojnacka, Aleksandra Walkiewicz and Mateusz Wichary in Torun, Poland, helped me to create the index system. Thanks are owed to the proofreader Chuck John and to Michael West, Neil Elliott, Joshua Messner and their colleagues at Fortress Press for helping me to achieve a measure of stylistic consistency and to reduce the number of mistakes. Conversations with Peter Busch, Douglas Campbell, William Campbell, Terence Donaldson, Christian Eberhard, Kathy Ehrensperger, Neal Fisher, Ann Jervis, Peter Lampe, Hubert Locke, Harry Maier, Bernard Mutschler, Mark Nanos, Daniel Patte, David and Sandy Rhoads, William Schmidt, David deSilva, Lawrence Welborn, Annette Weissenrieder and many other colleagues contributed to the interpretation I have developed. I am indebted to Heike Goebel, Ellen Jewett and Husam Suleymangil, Paul and Judy Jewett, Janet Jewett and others for supporting the completion of this project and helping to sustain the larger hope of reconciling conflicts under the "God of peace" (Rom 15:33).

Heidelberg, 2006

Sources and Abbreviations

The following list does not include text-critical symbols, which follow those found in Nestle-Aland, *Novum Testamentum Graece*

AA	*Archäologischer Anzeiger*
AASF	Annales Academiae Scientiarum Fennicae. Series B
AB	Anchor Bible
ABD	*Anchor Bible Dictionary*
ABG	*Archiv für Begriffsgeschichte*
'Abod. Zar.	'Abodah Zarah (tractate)
'Abot	'Abot (tractate)
'Abot R. Nat.	'Abot of Rabbi Nathan
ABR	*Australian Biblical Review*
ABSA	Annual of the British School at Athens
AC	*L'Antiquité classique*
Achilles Tatius	
Leuc.	*Leucippe et Clitophon*
ACl	*Acta Classica*
AcPlTh	*Acts of Paul and Thecla*
Acts John	*Acts of John/Acta Joannis*
Acts Thom.	*Acts of Thomas/Acta Thomae*
Add. Esth.	Additions to Esther
Aeg	*Aegyptus: Rivista italiana di egittologia e di papirologia*
Aelian	
Nat. an.	*De natura animalium*
Var. hist.	*Varia historia*
Aelius Aristides	
Ἀθην.	Ὑπὲρ τῆς πρὸς Ἀθηναίους εἰρήνης
Ἀλλεξ.	Ἐπι Ἀλλεξάνδρῳ ἐπιτάφιος
Δημοσ.	Πρὸς Δημοσθένη περὶ ἀτελείας
Παν.	Παναθηναϊκός
Aelius Herodianus	
Παρων.	Περὶ παρωνύμων
Pros. cath.	*De prosodia catholica*
Συντάξ.	Περὶ συντάξεως τῶν στοιχείων
AER	*American Ecclesiastical Review*
Aeschines	
Ctes.	*In Ctesiphontem*
Epist.	*Epistulae*
Fals. leg.	*De falsa legatione*
Tim.	*In Timarchum*
Aeschylus	
Ag.	*Agamemnon*
Cho.	*Choephori*
Eum.	*Eumenides*
Pers.	*Persae*
Prom.	*Prometheus vinctus*
Sept.	*Septem contra Thebas*
Suppl.	*Supplices*
Aesop	
Fab.	*Fabulae*
Fab. Syn.	*Fabulae Syntipae philosophi*
Prov.	*Proverbia*
AGJU	Arbeiten zur Geschichte des antiken Jüdentums und des Urchristentums
AGS	Abhandlungen der Geistes- und Sozialwissenschaftlichen, Klasse 1
AGSU	Arbeiten zur Geschichte des Spätjudentums und des Urchristentums
AHPC	Academia de la historia. Publicaciones de la cátedra y becarios de la Fundación "Conde de Cartagena"
AJA	*American Journal of Archeology*
AJP	*American Journal of Philology*
AKG	Arbeiten zur Kirchengeschichte
ALBO	Analecta lovaniensia biblica et orientalia
Alciphron	
Ep.	*Epistulae*
Alexander Aphrodisiensis	
Fat.	*De fato*
Alexander Polyhistor	
Test.	*Testimonia*
ALL	*Archiv für lateinischen Lexikographie*
AMT	Abhandlungen zur Moraltheologie
ANAWSP	Abhandlungen der Nordrhein-Westfällischen Akademie der Wissenschaften, Sonderreihe Papyrologica Coloniensia
Anaximenes of Lampsacus	
Rhet. Alex.	*Rhetorica ad Alexandrum (Ars Rhetorica)*
AnBib	Analecta Biblica
Andocides	
Alc.	*In Alcibiadem*
Myst.	*De Mysteriis*
Pac.	*De pace*
Redit.	*De reditu suo*
Andronicus	
Pass.	*De passionibus*
ANET	*Ancient Near Eastern Texts Relating to the Old Testament*, ed. J. B. Pritchard. 3d ed. Princeton: Princeton Univ. Press, 1969
Ang	*Angelicum. Periodicum trimestre Pontificiae Studiorum Universitatis a Sancto Thoma Aquinate in Urbe*
AnGr	*Analecta gregoriana*

Anon. Arist.	*Anonymi in Aristotelis artem rhetoricam*	**Aratus**		
		Phaen.	*Phaenomena*	
Anon. Eth. Ni.	*Anonymi in Aristotleis Ethica Nichomachea paraphrasis*	*Arch*	*Archeology: A Magazine Dealing with the Antiquity of the World*	

Anon. Arist.   *Anonymi in Aristotelis artem rhetoricam*

Anon. Eth. Ni.   *Anonymi in Aristotleis Ethica Nichomachea paraphrasis*

Anonymus Epicureus
   V. Phil.   *Vita Philonidis*

Anonymus Iamblichi
   Frag.   *Fragmenta*

ANRW   *Aufstieg und Niedergang der römischen Welt*

ANTF   *Arbeiten zur neutestamentlichen Textforschung*

Antiphon
   Caed. Her.   *De caede Herodis*
   In nov.   *In novercam*
   Tetra.   *Tetralogia*

Anton   *Antonianum. Periodicum philosophico-theologicum trimestre*

ANVO   *Arhandlingen utgitt av det Norske Videnskaps-Akademi I Oslo*

APF   *Archiv für Papyrusforschung*

Apoc. Ab.   *Apocalypse of Abraham*

Apoc. Adam   *Apocalypse of Adam*

Apoc. Dan.   *Apocalypse of Daniel*

Apoc. El. (C)   *Coptic Apocalypse of Elijah*

Apoc. Ez.   *Apocalypse of Ezra*

Apoc. Mos.   *Apocalypse of Moses*

Apoc. Pet.   *Apocalypse of Peter*

Apoc. Sedr.   *Apocalypse of Sedrach*

Apocr. Ezek.   *Apocryphon of Ezekiel*

Apollodorus
   Biblio.   *Bibliotheca*

Apollonius Citiensis
   Hipp.   *In Hippocritis de articulis commentarius*

Apollonius Rhodius
   Argon.   *Argonautica*
   Cho. Frag.   *Choliambica Fragmenta*

Apollonius Sophista
   Lex. hom.   *Lexicon Homericum*

Apollonius Tyanensis
   Apol.   *Apotelesmata*
   Ep.   *Epistulae*

Apost. Con.   *Apostolic Constitutions/Didascalia Apostolorum*

APOT   *Apocrypha and Pseudepigrapha of the Old Testament*, ed. R. H. Charles. 2 vols. Oxford: Clarendon, 1913

Appian
   An.   *Annibaica*
   Bell. civ.   *Bella civilia*
   Hist. Rom.   *Historia Romana*
   Mithr.   *Mithridatica*
   Test.   *Testimonium*

Apuleius
   Flor.   *Florida*
   Metam.   *Metamorphoses*

Aratus
   Phaen.   *Phaenomena*

Arch   *Archeology: A Magazine Dealing with the Antiquity of the World*

Aristophanes
   Ach.   *Acharnenses*
   Av.   *Aves*
   Eccl.   *Ecclesiazusae*
   Eq.   *Equites*
   Frag.   *Fragmenta*
   Inc. fab.   *Incertum fabulorum*
   Nub.   *Nubes*
   Pax   *Pax*
   Plut.   *Plutus*
   Ran.   *Ranae*
   Thesm.   *Thesmophoriazusae*

Aristophanes Gramm.
   Epit.   *Aristophanis historiae animalium epitome*

Aristotle
   An.   *De anima*
   An. pr.   *Analytica priora*
   Eth. eud.   *Ethica eudemia*
   Eth. nic.   *Ethica nichomachea*
   Frag. var.   *Fragmenta varia*
   Gen. an.   *De generatione anamalium*
   Hist. an.   *Historia animalium*
   Mag. mor.   *Magna Moralia*
   Metaph.   *Metaphysica*
   Mir. ausc.   *De mirabilium auscultationes*
   Mund.   *De mundo*
   Phys.   *Physica*
   Pol.   *Politica*
   Rhet.   *Rhetorica*
   Rhet. Alex.   *Rhetorica ad Alexandrum*
   Top.   *Topica*

Arrian
   Anab.   *Alexandri anabasis*
   Cyn.   *Cynegeticus*
   Frag.   *Fragmentum*
   Ind.   *Historica Indica*
   Tact.   *Tactica*

ARSL   *Acta reg. societatis humaniorum litterarum Lundensis*

Artapanus
   Frag.   *Fragmenta*

Artemidoros Daldianus
   Onir.   *Onirocriticon*

ASAW   *Abhandlungen der (Königlich) Sächsischen Akademie der Wissenschaften, philologisch-historische Klasse*

Asc. Isa.   *Ascension of Isaiah/Martyrdom and Ascension of Isaiah*

ASE   *Annali di storia dell'esegesi*

ASH   *Ancient Society and History*

As. Mos.   *Assumption of Moses*

ASNU   *Acta seminarii neotestamentici upsaliensis*

ASP	American Studies in Papyrology	
ASRT	Ancient Society, Resources for Teachers	
AsSeign	Assemblées du Seigneur	
AThANT	Abhandlungen zur Theologie des Alten und Neuen Testaments	
Athenaeus		
Deipn.	Deipnosophistae	
Athenagoras		
Leg.	Legatio pro Christianis	
ATR	Anglican Theological Review	
Augustine		
Civ.	De civitate Dei	
C. Jul.	Contra Julianum	
Exp. quaest. Rom.	Expositio quarundum quaestionum in epistula ad Romanos	
Nup. concu.	De nuptis et concupiscentia	
Spir. lit.	De spiritu et littera	
AusBR	Australian Biblical Review	
AUSS	Andrews University Seminary Studies	
AzTh	Arbeiten zur Theologie	
b.	Babylonian Talmud	
BA	Biblical Archaeologist	
BAGD	W. Bauer, W. F. Arndt, F. W. Gingrich, and F. W. Danker, A Greek-English Lexicon of the New Testament and Other Early Christian Literature. 2d ed. Chicago: Univ. of Chicago Press, 1979	
BAGD (2000)	W. Bauer, W. F. Arndt, F. W. Gingrich, and F. W. Danker. A Greek-English Lexicon of the New Testament and Other Early Christian Literature. 3d ed. Chicago: Univ. of Chicago Press, 2000	
BAH	Bibliothèque archéologique et historique	
Bar	Baruch	
BAR	Biblical Archaeologist Reader	
2 Bar.	2 (Syriac) Baruch	
3 Bar.	3 (Greek) Baruch	
4 Bar.	4 Baruch (Paraleipomena Jeremiou)	
BARev	The Biblical Archeology Review	
Barn.	Epistle of Barnabas	
BBB	Bonner biblische Beiträge	
b.Ber.	Babylonian Talmud Berakoth	
BBET	Beiträge zur biblischen Exegese und Theologie	
BBH	Bible Bhashyam	
BBKW	Beitrage zur Begegnung von Kirche und Welt	
BBR	Bulletin for Biblical Research	
BCH	Bulletin de correspondance hellénique	
BDF	F. Blass and A. Debrunner, A Greek Grammar of the New	

	Testament and Other Early Christian Literature. Trans. R. W. Funk. Chicago: Univ. of Chicago Press, 1961	
BE	Bulletin épigraphique	
BEATAJ	Beiträge zur Erforschung des Alten Testaments und des antiken Judentums	
BECNT	Baker Exegetical Commentary on the New Testament	
Ber.	Berakot (tractate)	
Berossus		
Ant.	Antiquitates	
BETL	Bibliotheca ephemeridum theologicarum lovaniensium	
BEvTh	Beiträge zur evangelischen Theologie	
BFCTh	Beiträge zur Förderung christlicher Theologie	
BGU	Aegyptische Urkunden aus den Königlichen (later Staatlichen) Museen zu Berlin. Griechische Urkunden. 15 vols. Berlin, 1895–1983	
BHTh	Beiträge zur historischen Theologie	
Bib	Biblica	
BiBe	Biblische Beiträge	
BibInt	Biblical Interpretation: A Journal of Contemporary Approaches	
BibIntSer	Biblical Interpretation Series	
BibLeb	Bibel und Leben	
BibS(F)	Biblische Studien. Freiburg	
BibS(N)	Biblische Studien. Neukirchen	
Bijdr	Bijdragen. Tijdschrift voor philosophie en theologie	
BJRL	Bulletin of the John Rylands (University) Library of Manchester	
BK	Bibel und Kirche. Organ des katholischen Bibel-Werkes	
BLit	Bibel und Liturgie	
B. Mus. In.	A Collection of Ancient Greek Inscriptions in the British Museum	
BN	Biblische Notizen	
BNTC	Black's New Testament Commentary	
Bœ	Bibliothèque œcuménique	
BR	Biblical Research: Papers of the Chicago Society of Biblical Research	
BrAR	British Archaeological Reports	
BRev	Bible Review	
Bridge	The Bridge: A Yearbook of Judeao-Christian Studies	
BSac	Bibliotheca sacra	
BSem	Biblical Seminar	
BSt	Biblische Studien. Neukirchen-Vluyn	
BT	Bible Translator	

BTB	*Biblical Theology Bulletin*	
BT.B	Bibliothèque de Théologie. 3. Ser. Théologie biblique	
BThZ	*Berliner theologische Zeitschrift*	
BU	Biblische Untersuchungen	
Burg	Burgense. Collectanea scientifica	
BWANT	Beiträge zur Wissenschaft vom Alten und Neuen Testament	
BZ	*Biblische Zeitschrift*	
BZAW	Beihefte zur *ZAW*	
BZfr	Biblische Zeitfragen gemeinverständlich erörtert	
BZNW	Beiheft zur *ZNW*	

Caelius Aurelianus
  Morb. — *De morbis chronicis*

Calpurnius Siculus
  Ecl. — *Eclogue (Einsiedeln Eclogue)*

CaS — *Church and Society*

Cassius Dio
  Hist. Rom. — *Historiae Romanae*

CBET — Contributions to Biblical Exegesis and Theology

CBQ — *Catholic Biblical Quarterly*

CBQMS — Catholic Biblical Quarterly Monograph Series

CD — Damascus Document

Ceb. tab. — *Cebetis tabula*

Chariton
  Chaer. — *De Chaerea et Callirhoe*

CHL — Commentationes humanarum litterarum

CHM — *Cahiers d'Histoire Mondiale*

Chrysippus
  Frag. log. — *Fragmenta logica et physica*
  Frag. mor. — *Fragmenta moralia*

Cicero
  Arch. — *Pro Archia*
  Att. — *Epistolae ad Atticum*
  Cael. — *Pro Caelio*
  Clu. — *Pro Cluentio*
  Fam. — *Epistolae ad familiares*
  Fin. — *De finibus*
  Flacc. — *Oratio pro L. Flacco*
  Inv. — *De inventione rhetorica*
  Leg. — *De legibus*
  Mil. — *Oratio pro milone*
  Nat. d. — *De natura deorum*
  Off. — *De officiis*
  De or. — *De oratore*
  Parad. — *Paradoxa Stoicorum*
  Planc. — *Pro Plancio*
  Prov. cons. — *De provinciis consularibus*
  Quint. fratr. — *Epistulae ad Quintum fratrem*

CIG — *Corpus inscriptionum graecarum,* ed. A. Boeckh. 4 vols. Berlin, 1828–1877

CIGS — *Corpus inscriptionum graeciae septentrionalis,* ed. W. Dittenberger. Berlin, 1892

CIJ — *Corpus inscriptionum iudaicarum,* ed. J. B. Frey. 2 vols. Rome, 1936–52

CIL — *Corpus inscriptionum latinarum*

CJ — *Classical Journal*

CJT — *Canadian Journal of Theology*

CLat — Collection Latomus

Claudius Aelianus
  Frag. — *Fragmenta*

CLCAG.Sup — Corpus Latinum Commentariorum in Aristotelem Graecorum, Supplement

Cleanthes
  Frag. — *Fragmenta*

Clement of Alexandria
  Ex. The. — *Excerpta ex Theodoto*
  Paed. — *Paedagogus*
  Pro. — *Protrepticus*
  Stro. — *Stromata*

Clement of Rome
  1 Clem. — *Epistula i ad Corinthios*
  2 Clem. — *Epistula ii ad Corinthios*
  Hom. — Homiliae

Cleobulus
  Epig. — *Epigrammata*

Cleomedes
  Motu — *De motu circulari corporum caelestium*

ClW — *Classical Weekly*

CMech — *Collectanea mechliniensia*

CMRDM — *Corpus Monumentorum Religionis Dei Menis*

ColSB — Collection Sciences Bibliques

Con. Eph. — *Concilium universale Ephesenum anno 431*

ConBNT — Coniectanea biblica, New Testament Series

Conf. Asen. — *Confessio et precatio Aseneth*

ConJ — *Concordia Journal*

3 Cor. — *3 Corinthians*

Cornutus
  Nat. d. — *De natura deorum*

Corp. herm. — *Corpus hermeticum*

CP — *Classical Philology*

CPJ — *Corpus Papyrorum Judaicarum*

CPR — *Corpus Papyrorum Raineri*

CPSSV — Cambridge Philological Society Supplementary Volume

Cratinus
  Frag. — *Fragmenta*

CRINT — Compendia rerum iudaicarum ad Novum Testamentum

CSEL — *Corpus scriptorum ecclesiasticorum Latinorum*

CSS — Cursus Scripturae Sacrae

Ctesias
  Frag. — *Fragmenta*

CTJ — *Calvin Theological Journal*

CTM	Concordia Theological Monthly		DSD	Dead Sea Discoveries
CTOB	Cahiers de la traduction oecuménique de la Bible		DT(F)	Divus Thomas. Jahrbuch für Philosophie und spekulative Theologie
CUANTS	Catholic University of America New Testament Studies		EAC	Encyclopedia of Early Christianity. 2d ed. 1997
CurTM	Currents in Theology and Mission		Ecphantus	
CV	Communio viatorum		Frag.	Fragmenta
Damascius			EDNT	Exegetical Dictionary of the New Testament. Ed. H. Balz and G. Schneider. 3 vols. Grand Rapids: Eerdmans, 1990–93
Par.	In Parmenidem			
Vita. Is.	Vita Isidori			
DBH	A Dictionary of the Bible, ed. James Hastings. 4 vols. New York: Scribners, 1901–2.		EEC	Encyclopedia of Early Christianity. Ed. E. Ferguson. 2nd ed. New York, 1990.
Delph.	Fouilles de Delphes. Vol. 2. Épigraphie. Paris, 1909		EeC	Études et Commentaires
Demades			EEPS	Ἐπιστημονικὴ Ἐπετηρὶς τῆς φιλοσοφικῆς Σχολῆς τοῦ πανεπιστημίου Ἀθηνῶν
Frag.	Fragmenta			
Demetrius Phalereus			EFN	Estudios de Filología Neotestamentaria
Eloc.	De elocutione			
Frag.	Fragmenta		EHPhR	Études d'histoire et de philosophie religieuses
Demosthenes			EHS	Europäische Hochschulschriften. Reihe 23, Theologie
Cor.	De corona			
De pac.	De pace		EITRY	Ecumenical Institute for Theological Research Yearbook
Epist.	Epistulae			
Epitaph.	Epitaphius		EKK	Evangelisch-katholischer Kommentar
Erot.	Eroticus			
Fal. leg.	De falsa legatione		EKKNT	Evangelisch-katholischer Kommentar zum Neuen Testament
Mid.	In Midiam			
1 Olynth.	Olynthiaca i			
Orat.	Orationes			
2 Philip.	Philippica ii			
4 Philip.	Philippica iv		Empedocles	
Der. 'Er. Rab.	Derek 'Ereṣ Rabbah		Frag.	Fragmenta
Deut. Rab.	Deuteronomy Rabbah		Test.	Testimonia
Did.	Didache		1 En.	1 (Ethiopic) Enoch
Dinarchus			2 En.	2 (Slavonic) Enoch
Aristog.	In Aristogitonem		3 En.	3 (Hebrew) Enoch
Dem.	In Demosthenem		EncJud	Encyclopedia Judaica
Dio Chrysostom			EncR	Encyclopedia of Religion
2 Glor.	De gloria ii		Ep. Arist.	Epistle of Aristeas
Orat.	Orationes		Ep. Jer.	Epistle of Jeremiah
2. Tars.	Tarsica altera		Epictetus	
Diodorus Siculus			Diss.	Dissertationes
Hist.	Bibliotheca historica		Ench.	Enchiridion
Diogenes Laertius			Frag.	Fragmenta
Vitae philos.	Vitae philosophorum		Gnom.	Gnomologium
Diogn.	Epistle to Diognetus		Epicurus	
Diognetus Hist.			Dep.	Deperditorum librorum reliquiae
Test.	Testimonia		Ep. frag.	Epistolarum fragmenta
Dionysius Halicarnassus			Ep. Her.	Epistula ad Herodotum
Antiq. Rom.	Antiquitates Romanae		Epidauros	
Dionysius Periegeta			Frag. Gal.	Fragmentum ap. Galenum
Avi.	De Avibus		Epiphanius	
Dioscorides Pedanius			Adv. haer.	Adversus haereses
Eup.	Euporista		Eranos	Eranos. Acta philologica Suecana
DNTB	Dictionary of New Testament Background, ed. C. A. Evans and S. E. Porter. Downers Grove, IL: InterVarsity Press, 2000		EPRO	Études préliminaires aux religions orientales dans l'empire Romain
			ER	Ecumenical Review

Sim.	*Similitudes*	HThKNT	Herders theologischer Kommentar zum Neuen Testament
Vis.	*Visions*		
Hermogenes			
Prog.	*Progymnasmata*	*HTR*	*Harvard Theological Review*
Herodianus		HTS	Harvard Theological Studies
Mar.	*Ab excessu divi Marci*	*HUCA*	*Hebrew Union College Annual*
Herodotus		*HWP*	*Historisches Wörterbuch der Philosophie*
Hist.	*Historiae*		
Heron		Hyperides	
Bel.	*Belopoieca*	*Dem.*	*In Demosthenem*
HerTS	*Hervormde teologiese studies*	HZ.B	Historische Zeitschrift Beiheft
Hesiod		*I.Lamp.*	*Inschriften griechischer Städte aus Kleinasien VI. Die Inschriften von Lampsakos,* ed. P. Frisch. Bonn, 1978
Op.	*Opera et dies*		
Theog.	*Theogonia*		
Hesychius			
Lex.	*Lexicon*	*I.Magn.*	*Die Inschriften von Magnesia am Mäander,* ed. O. Kern. Berlin, 1900
HeyJ	*Heythrop Journal. A Quarterly Review of Philosophy and Theology*		
Hipparchus		*I.Milet.*	*Inschriften von Milet,* ed. A. Rehm. Berlin, 1997.
Hist. Rom.	*Historiae Romanae*		
Hippocrates		*I.Priene*	*Die Inschriften von Priene,* ed. H. von Gaertrigen et al. Berlin, 1906
Aphor.	*Aphorismata*		
Diaet. m.	*De diaeta in morbis acutis*		
Epist.	*Epistulae*	*I.Tyre*	*Inscriptions grecques et latines découvertes dans les fouilles de Tyr (1963–74) I. Inscriptions de la nécropole,* ed. J.-P. Rey-Coquais. Paris, 1977
Flat.	*De flatibus*		
Morb.	*De morbis*		
Off.	*De officina medici*		
Praec.	*Praeceptiones*		
Septim.	*De septimestri partu*	*IBS*	*Irish Biblical Studies*
Hippolytes		ICC	International Critical Commentary
Anti.	*De antichristo*		
Noet.	*Contra haeresin Noeti*	*I.Cos*	*Inscriptions of Cos,* ed. W. R. Paton and E. L. Hicks. Oxford, 1891
Trad. ap.	*Traditio apostolica*		
Hist	*Historia. Zeitschrift für alte Geschichte*		
		IDB	*Interpreter's Dictionary of the Bible*
Hist. Aug.	*Historia Augusta*	*IDBS*	*IDB Supplement*
Hist. Rech.	*History of the Rechabites*	*IG*	*Inscriptiones Graecae*
Historia Alexandri Magni		Ignatius	
Rec. β	*Recensio β*	*Eph.*	*To the Ephesians*
Rec. γ	*Recensio γ*	*Ep. interp.*	*Epistulae interpolatae et epistulae suppositiciae*
Rec. ϵ	*Recensio ϵ*		
Rec. byz.	*Recensio byzantina poetica*	*Mag.*	*To the Magnesians*
Rec. λ	*Recensio λ*	*Phld.*	*To the Philadelphians*
Rec. φ	*Recensio φ*	*Pol.*	*To Polycarp*
HKNT	Handkommentar zum Neuen Testament	*Rom.*	*To the Romans*
		Smyrn.	*To the Smyrneans*
HNT	Handbuch zum Neuen Testament	*IGRom*	*Inscriptiones graecae ad res romanas pertinentes,* ed. R. Cagnat and G. LaFaye. 4 vols. Paris: Leroux, 1906
HNTC	Harper's New Testament Commentaries		
Homer		*IJST*	*International Journal of Systematic Theology*
Il.	*Iliad*		
Od.	*Odyssey*	*IKZ*	*Internationale kirchliche Zeitschrift*
Horace		*Imm*	*Immanuel*
Carm.	*Carmina*	*Int*	*Interpretation. A Journal of Bible and Theology*
Ep.	*Epistulae*		
Sat.	*Satirae*	Irenaeus	
HSNT	Die Heilige Schrift des Neuen Testaments	*Adv. her.*	*Adversus haereses*

Isaeus
　Euph.　　　Pro Euphileto
　Orat.　　　Orationes
ISJ　　　Institución San Jerónimo
Isocrates
　Antid.　　　Antidosis (Orat. 15)
　Antipat.　　Ad Antipatrum (Epist. 4)
　Arch.　　　Archidamus (Orat. 6)
　Big.　　　De Bigis (Orat. 16)
　Callim.　　In Callimachum (Orat. 18)
　Dem.　　　Ad Demonicum (Orat. 1)
　Pac　　　De pace (Orat. 8)
　Ep.　　　Epistulae
　Euth.　　　In Euthynum (Orat. 21)
　Evag.　　　Evagoras (Orat. 9)
　Hel.　　　Helenae encomium (Orat. 10)
　Loch.　　　In Lochitum (Orat. 20)
　Nic.　　　Nicocles (Orat. 3)
　Paneg.　　Panegyricus (Orat. 4)
　Panath.　　Panathenaicus (Orat. 12)
　Phil.　　　Philippus (Orat. 5)
　Trapez.　　Trapeziticus (Orat. 17)
ITS　　　Indian Theological Studies
JAAR　　Journal of the American Academy of Religion
JAC　　　Jahrbuch für Antike und Christentum
JAC.E　　Jahrbuch für Antike und Christentum. Ergänzungsbände
JB　　　Jerusalem Bible
JBL　　　Journal of Biblical Literature
JBLMS　　JBL Monograph Series
JBTh　　　Jahrbuch für biblische Theologie
JCBRF　　Journal of the Christian Brethren Research Fellowship
JCE　　　Journal of Christian Education
JCSP　　　Journal of Classical and Sacred Philology
JDTh　　　Jahrbücher für deutsche Theologie
JE　　　Jewish Encyclopedia
JES　　　Journal of Ecumenical Studies
JETS　　　Journal of the Evangelical Theological Society
JHS　　　Journal of Hellenic Studies
JHSex　　Journal of the History of Sexuality
JITL　　　Jahresberichte der israelitisch-theologischen Lehranstalt
JJP　　　Journal of Juristic Papyrology
JLR　　　Journal of Law and Religion
JLW　　　Jahrbuch für Liturgiewissenschaft
John Chrysostom
　Hom Rom.　　Homiliae in epistulam ad Romanos
Jos. Asen.　　Joseph and Aseneth
Josephus
　Ant.　　　Antiquitates Judaicae (Jewish Antiquities)
　Bell.　　　Bellum Judaicum (Jewish War)
　C. Ap.　　Contra Apionem (Against Apion)
　Vita　　　Vita (Life)

JPGMJ　　J. P. Getty Museum Journal
JQR　　　Jewish Quarterly Review
JRE　　　Journal of Religious Ethics
JRH　　　Journal of Religious History
JRomS　　Journal of Roman Studies
JSNT　　Journal for the Study of the New Testament
JSNTSup　JSNT Supplement
JSOT　　Journal for the Study of the Old Testament
JSOTSup　JSOT Supplement
JSPSup　　Journal for the Study of the Pseudepigrapha Supplement
JSS　　　Journal of Semitic Studies
JTC　　　Journal for Theology and the Church
JTS　　　Journal of Theological Studies
JTSA　　Journal of Theology for Southern Africa
Jub.　　　Jubilees
Judaica　　Judaica: Beiträge zum Verständnis des jüdischen Schicksals in Vergangenheit und Gegenwart
Justin Martyr
　1 Apol.　　Apologia i
　Dial.　　　Dialogus cum Tryphone
Justinianus
　Cod. Just.　　Codex Justinianus
Juvenal
　Sat.　　　Satirae
KBANT　　Kommentare und Beiträge zum Alten und Neuen Testament
KD　　　Kerygma und Dogma
KEHNT　　Kurzgefasstes exegetisches Handbuch zum Neuen Testament
1-4 Kgdms　1-4 Kingdoms (LXX titles for 1-2 Samuel and 1-2 Kings)
KHAb　　Kölner historische Abhandlungen
KJV　　　King James Version
Klio　　　Klio: Beiträge zur alten Geschichte
KRS　　　Kirchenblatt für die reformierte Schweiz
Lactantius
　Inst.　　　Divinarum institutionum librii VII
　Opif.　　　De opificio dei
LAE　　　Literature of Ancient Egypt, ed. W. K. Simpson. New Haven, 1972
Lat.　　　Latin
Lat　　　Latomus. Revue d'études latines
LCL　　　Loeb Classical Library
LD　　　Lectio divina
Libanius
　Ep.　　　Epistulae
　Or.　　　Orationes
LingB　　Linguistica Biblica

Livy		*Epitr.*	*Epitreppontes*
Hist.	*History of Rome*	*Frag.*	*Fragmenta*
LOB	Leggere oggi la Bibbia	*Mon.*	*Monostichoi*
Longus		*Sent. Byz.*	*Sententiae e codicibus Byzantinis*
Daphn.	*Daphnis et Chloe*	*Sent. pap.*	*Sententiae e papyris*
LouvS	*Louvain Studies*	MeyerK	H. A. W. Meyer, *Kritisch-exegeti-*
LSJM	H. G. Liddell and R. Scott, *A*		*scher Kommentar über das Neue*
	Greek-English Lexicon, rev. H. S.		*Testament*. Göttingen:
	Jones and R. McKenzie. Oxford:		Vandenhoeck & Ruprecht
	Clarendon, 1968	*MGWJ*	*Monatsschrift für Geschichte und*
LSSt	Leipziger semitische Studien		*Wissenschaft des Judentums*
LTJ	*Lutheran Theological Journal*	MM	J. H. Moulton and G. Milligan,
LTPM	Louvain Theological and		*The Vocabulary of the Greek*
	Pastoral Monographs		*Testament*. 1930. Repr. Grand
Lucian of Samosata			Rapids: Eerdmans, 1985
Alex.	*Alexander (Pseudomantis)*	*Mn*	*Mnemosyne. Bibliotheca classica*
Cal.	*Calumniae non temere credendum*	MNTC	Moffatt New Testament
Demon.	*Demonax*		Commentary
Dial. mer.	*Dialogi meretricii*	Moffatt	James Moffatt, *A New Translation*
Dial. mort.	*Dialogi mortuorum*		*of the Bible* (1926)
Electr.	*De electro*	*MPTh*	*Monatsschrift für Pastoraltheologie*
Laps.	*Pro lapsu inter salutandem*		*zur Vertiefung des gesamten pfar-*
Lex.	*Lexiphanes*		*ramtlichen Wirkens*
Men.	*Menippus sive necyomantia*	MSU	Mitteilungen des Septuaginta-
Par.	*De parisito sive artem esse*		Unternehmens der Gesellschaft
	parasiticam	MT	Masoretic text
Phal.	*Phalaris*	MThS	Münchener theologische Studien
Pseudol.	*Pseudologista*	*MThZ*	*Münchener theologische Zeitschrift*
Sacr.	*De sacrificiis*	MTS	Marburger theologische Studien
LumVie(B)	*Lumière et vie. Abbaye de S. Andre*	Musonius Rufus	
LumVie(L)	*Lumière et vie. Revue de formation*	Τροφῆς	Περὶ τροφῆς
	doctrinale chrétienne	*NAB*	*New American Bible*
LV	*Lumen vitae. International Review*	*NASB*	*New American Standard Bible*
	of Religious Education	NBGZ	Die Neutestamentlichen Briefe
LXX	Septuagint		geschichtlich im Zusammenhang
Lycurgus			erklärt
Leoc.	*Oratio in Leocratem*	NCBC	New Century Bible Commentary
Lydus		*NDIEC*	*New Documents Illustrating Early*
Magistr.	*De magistratibus populi Romani*		*Christianity*, ed. G. H. R. Horsley.
Lysias			North Ryde, N.S.W.: Ancient
Orat.	*Orationes*		History Documentary Research
m.	Mishnah		Centre, Macquarie University,
MAAR	Memoirs of the American		1981–
	Academy in Rome	*NEB*	*New English Bible*
Macrobius		*Neot*	*Neotestamentica*
Sat.	*Saturnalia*	Nestle-Aland	Erwin Nestle and Kurt Aland,
MadF	Madrider Forschungen		eds. *Novum Testamentum Graece*.
Mak.	*Makkot* (tractate)		26th ed. 1979. 27th ed. 1993.
Marcus Aurelius			Stuttgart: Deutsche
Τὰ εἰς ἑαυτὸν	Τὰ εἰς ἑαυτὸν / *Meditations*		Bibelgesellschaft
Mart. Pet.	*Martyrium Petri*	NIBC	New International Bible
Mart. Pion.	*Martyrium Pionii presbyteri et*		Commentary
	sodalium	Nicander Colophonius	
Mart. Pol.	*Martyrium Polycarpi*	*Ther.*	*Theriaca*
Maximus Tyrius		*Nid.*	*Niddah* (tractate)
Phil.	*Philosophumena*	NIGTC	New International Greek
MBPS	Mellen Biblical Press Series		Testament Commentary
Menander		*NIV*	*New International Version*
Apsis	*Apsis*	*NJB*	*New Jerusalem Bible*

NJDTh	*Neue Jahrbücher für deutsche Theologie*
NKZ	*Neue kirchliche Zeitschrift*
NorTT	*Norsk Teologisk Tidsskrift*
NovT	*Novum Testamentum*
NovTSup	*NovT* Supplements
Nr.	Document number in collections of papyri, inscriptions, or ostraca
NRSV	New Revised Standard Version
NRTh	*La nouvelle revue théologique*
NSBT	New Studies in Biblical Theology
NStB	Neukirchener Studienbücher
NSTh	Nouvelle série théologique
NTAbh	Neutestamentliche Abhandlungen
NTD	Das Neue Testament Deutsch
NTGuides	New Testament Guides
NTOA	Novum Testamentum et Orbis Antiquus
NTS	*New Testament Studies*
NTT	*Nederlands theologisch Tijdschrift*
NTTS	New Testament Tools and Studies
NZSTh	*Neue Zeitschrift für systematische Theologie und Religionsphiloso-phie*
O. Amst.	*Ostraca in Amsterdam Collections*, ed. R. S. Bagnall et al. 1976
OBO	Orbis biblicus et orientalis
OBT	Overtures to Biblical Theology
OCD	*Oxford Classical Dictionary*, ed. N. G. L. Hammond and H. H. Scullard. 2d ed. Oxford: Clarendon, 1970
Odes Sol.	*Odes of Solomon*
OGIS	*Orientis Graeci Inscriptiones Selectae*, ed. W. Dittenberger. 2 vols. Leipzig, 1903–5. Repr. New York, 1970
OJRS	*Ohio Journal of Religious Studies*
Onasander	
Strat.	*Strategicus*
OrChr	*Oriens christianus*
OrChrA	Orientalia Christiana Analecta
Origen	
Cels.	*Contra Celsum*
Com. Joan.	*Commentarii in evangelium Ioannis*
Com. Rom.	*Commentarii in Romanos*
Exc. Ps.	*Excerpta in Psalmos*
Exp. Prov.	*Expositio in Proverbia*
Frag. Lam.	*Fragmenta in Lamentationes*
Orosius	
Hist.	*Historia adversus Paganos*
Orphica	
Frag.	*Fragmenta (=Orphicorum Fragmenta)*
ORPB	*Oberrheinisches Pastoralblatt.* Freiburg, 1899
OTP	*The Old Testament Pseudepigrapha,* ed. J. H. Charlesworth. 2 vols. Garden City: Doubleday, 1983–85
Ovid	
Metam.	*Metamorphosis*
Tris.	*Tristia*
O. Wilck.	*Griechische Ostraka aus Aegypten und Nubien.* O. Wilcken, ed. Two volumes. Leipzig/Berlin, 1899.
P. 'Abot	*Pirqe 'Abot*
P.Amh.	*The Amherst Papyri: Being an Account of the Greek Papyri in the Collection of the Right Hon. Lord Amherst of Hackney, F.S.A. at Didlington Hall, Norfolk.* B. P. Grenfell and A. S. Hunt, eds. 2 vols. London, 1900–1901
P.Col.	*Columbia Papyri, Greek Series,* vols. 3-4. New York: Columbia University Press, 1934–40
P.Flor.	*Papiri greco-egizii, Papiri Florentini.* 3 vols. Milan, 1906–1915
P.Fouad	*Le Papyrus Fouad,* ed. A. Bataille et al. Cairo, 1939
P.Giess.	*Griechische Papyri im Museum des oberhessischen Geschichtsvereins zu Giessen.* O. Eger, et al., eds. 3 vols. Leipzig/Berlin, 1910–1922
P.Grenf.1	B. P. Grenfell, ed. *An Alexandrian Erotic Fragment and Other Greek Papyri Chiefly Ptolemaic.* Oxford, 1896
P.Grenf.2	B. P. Grenfell and A. S. Hunt, eds. *New Classical Fragments and Other Greek and Latin Papyri.* Oxford, 1897
P.Herc.	*Herculanensium voluminum quae supersunt* I-XI. Naples, 1793–1885. *Herculanensium voluminum quae supersunt collectilo altera* I-XI. Naples, 1862–76. *Fragmenta Herculanensia,* Oxford, 1885
P.Hib.	*The Hibeh Papyri.* 2 vols. London, 1906–55
P.Köln.	*Kölner Papyri,* ed. B. Kramer et al. 4 vols. Cologne, 1976–82
P.Lips.	*Griechische Urkunden der Papyrussammlung zu Leipzig,* ed. L. Mittels. Leipzig, 1906
P.Lond.	*Greek Papyri in the British Museum.* 7 vols. London, 1893–1974
P.Mich.	*Michigan Papyri.* 15 vols. 1931–82
P.Oxy.	*The Oxyrhynchus Papyri,* ed. Bernard P. Grenfell et al. 70 vols. London: Egypt Exploration Fund. 1898–2006

P.Oxy.Hels.	*Fifty Oxyrhynchus Papyri*, ed. H. Zilliacus et al. Helsinki, 1979		Jos.	*De Iosepho*
P.Par.	*Notices et textes des papyrus du Musée du Louvre et de la Bibliothèque Impérial.* ed. A. Letronne et al. 1865		Leg.	*Legum allegoriarum libri i-iii*
			Legat.	*Legatio ad Gaium*
			Migr.	*De migratione Abrahami*
			Mos.	*De vita Mosis*
P.Petr.	*The Flinders Petrie Papyri*, ed. J. Mahaffy and J. Smyly. 3 vols. 1891–1905		Mut.	*De mutatione nominum*
			Opif.	*De opificio mundi*
			Plant.	*De plantatione*
P.Rein.	2 vols. 1 = *Papyrus grecs et démo-tiques recueillis en Egypte.* T. Reinach et al., eds. Paris, 1905. 2 = *Les Papyrus Théodor Reinach.* P. Collart, ed. Cairo, 1940		Post.	*De posteritate Caini*
			Praem.	*De praemiis et poenis*
			Prob.	*Quod omnis probus liber sit*
			QG	*Quaestiones in Genesin*
			Sobr.	*De sobrietate*
			Somn.	*De somniis*
P.Ryl.	*Catalogue of the Greek papyri in the John Rylands Library at Manchester*, ed. A. S. Hunt et al. 3 vols. 1911–38		Spec.	*De specialibus legibus*
			Virt.	*De virtutibus*
			Philodemus	
			Παρ.	Περὶ Παρρησίας
P.Tebt.	*The Tebtunis Papyri*, ed. B. P. Grenfell et al. 2 vols. London, 1902–7		Philol	*Philologus: Zeitschrift für das klassische Altertum.*
PapC	Papyrologica Coloniensia		Philostratus	
PAPS	*Proceedings of the American Philosophical Society*		Vit. Apoll.	*Vita Apollonii*
			Vit. soph.	*Vitae sophistarum*
ParPass	*La Parola del Passato. Rivista di studi classici/antichi*		PhJ	*Philosophisches Jahrbuch der Görres Gesellschaft*
Pausanius			Pindar	
Graec. descr.	*Graeciae descriptio*		Isthm.	*Isthmionikai*
PBTM	Paternoster Biblical and Theological Monographs		Nem.	*Nemeonikai*
			Oly.	*Olympian*
PelNTC	Pelikan New Testament Commentaries		Pyth.	*Pythionikai*
			Pittacus	
Periander			Epig.	*Epigramma*
Ep.	*Epistulae*		Plato	
Petronius			Alc. maj.	*Alcibiades*
Frag.	*Fragment*		Apol.	*Apology (Apologia Socratis)*
PG	*Patrologia graecae*, ed. J.-P. Migne. 162 vols. Paris, 1857–86		Clit.	*Clitophon*
			Crit.	*Crito*
PGM	*Papyri graecae magicae*, ed. K. Preisendanz. 2 vols. Leipzig, 1928–31		Def.	*Definitiones*
			Ep.	*Epistulae*
			Epin. Eryx	*Epinomis Eryx*
			Euthyd.	*Euthydemus*
Phalaridis			Gorg.	*Gorgias*
Ep.	*Epistulae*		Hipp. maj.	*Hippias major*
Phylarchus			Lach.	*Laches*
Frag.	*Fragmenta*		Leg.	*Leges*
Philo			Lys.	*Lysis*
Abr.	*De Abrahamo*		Men.	*Menexenus*
Cher.	*De cherubim*		Parm.	*Parmenides*
Conf.	*De confusione linguarum*		Phaed.	*Phaedo*
Cong.	*De congressu eruditionis gratia*		Phaedr.	*Phaedrus*
Cont.	*De vita contemplativa*		Phil.	*Philibus*
Dec.	*De decalogo*		Pol.	*Politicus*
Det.	*Quod deterius potiori insidiari soleat*		Prot.	*Protagoras*
			Resp.	*Respublica*
Ebr.	*De ebrietate ii*		Symp.	*Symposium*
Flacc.	*In Flaccum*		Theaet.	*Theaetetus*
Fug.	*De fuga et inventione*		Tim.	*Timaeus*
Gig.	*De gigantibus*		Plautus	
Heres	*Quis rerum divinarum heres sit*		Curc.	*Curculio*

Pliny		*Tu. san.*	*De tuenda sanitate praecepta*
Ep.	*Epistulae*	*Virt. mor.*	*De virtute morali*
Pliny the Elder		*Virt. vit.*	*De virtute et vitio*
Nat.	*Naturalis historia*	PNTC	Pillar New Testament
Plotinus			Commentary
Enn.	*Enneades*	Polemo	
Plutarch		*Decl.*	*Declamationes*
Adul. amic.	*De adulatore et amici*	Polyaenus	
Adv. Col.	*Adversus Coletem*	*Strat.*	*Strategemata*
Aem.	*Aemilius Paullus*	Polybius	
Aet. Rom.	*Aetia Romana et Graeca*	*Hist.*	*Historiae*
Ag. Cleom.	*Agis et Cleomenes*	Porphyry	
Amat.	*Amatorius*	*Abst.*	*De abstinentia*
Ant.	*Antonius*	Posidonius	
Arat.	*Aratus*	*Frag.*	*Fragmenta*
Brut.	*Brutus*	Posidonius Phil.	
Cat. Maj.	*Cato Major*	*Frag.*	*Fragmenta*
Cic.	*Cicero*	PR	Philosophy and Rhetoric
Cim.	*Cimon*	*Pr. Man.*	*Prayer of Manasseh*
Cohib. ira	*De cohibenda ira*	Protagoras	
Comp. Thes.	*Comparatio Thesei et Romuli*	*Frag.*	*Fragmenta*
Cor.	*Marcius Coriolanus*	PRS	Perspectives in Religious Studies
Curios.	*De curiositate*	*Ps. Sol.*	*Psalms of Solomon*
Def. orac.	*De defectu oraculorum*	PSBSup	Princeton Seminary Bulletin
Demetr.	*Demetrius*		Supplement
E Delph.	*De E apud Delphos*	Pseudo-Aristotle	
Fat.	*De fato*	*Mund.*	*De mundo*
Frag.	*Fragmenta*	*Oec.*	*Oeconomica*
Garr.	*De garrulitate*	*Physogn.*	*Physognomonica*
Gen. Socr.	*De genio Socratis*	*Probl.*	*Problemata*
Is. Os.	*De Iside et Osiride*	Pseudo-Clementine	
Luc.	*Lucullus*	*Hom.*	*Homilies*
Lyc.	*Lycurgus*	*Rec.*	*Recognitions*
Mor.	*Moralia*	Pseudo-Galen	
Non pos.	*Non posse suaviter viviserundum*	*De rem. par.*	*De remediis parabilibus libri iii*
	Epicurum	Pseudo-Hippocrates	
Num.	*Numa*	Ἑρμην.	Ἑρμηνεία περὶ ἐνεργῶν
Pel.	*Pelopidas*		λίθων
Phil.	*Philopoemen*	Pseudo-Lucian	
Phoc.	*Phocion*	*Am.*	*Amores*
Pomp.	*Pompeius*	*Asin.*	*Asinus*
Princ. iner.	*Ad principem ineruditum*	*Dem. enc.*	*Demosthenis encomium*
Publ.	*Publicola*	Pseudo-Philo	
Pyrrh.	*Pyrrhus*	*Lib. Ant.*	*Liber Antiquitatum Biblicarum*
Pyth. orac.	*De Pythiae oraculis*	Pseudo-Phocylides	
Quaest. conv.	*Quaestionum convivialum libri ix*	*Sent.*	*Sententiae*
Quo. adoles.	*Quomodo adolescens poetas*	Pseudo-Plato	
	audire debeat	*Def.*	*Definitiones*
Quo. adul.	*Quomodo adulator ab amico*	*Epin.*	*Epinomis*
	internoscatur	Pseudo-Plutarch	
Quo. quis	*Quomodo quis suos in virtute*	*Apoph. lac.*	*Apophthegmata laconica*
	sentiat profectus	*Flu.*	*De fluviis*
Rom.	*Romulus*	*Lib. ed.*	*De liberis educandis*
Sera	*De sera numinis vindicta*	PSI	*Papiri greci e latine. Pubbliacazioni*
Sol.	*Solon*		*della Società Italiana per la Ricerca*
Soll. an.	*De sollertia animalium*		*dei Papiri Greci e Latini in Egiito.*
Sull.	*Sulla*		15 vols. Florence, 1912–79
Thes.	*Theseus*		
Tim.	*Timoleon*		

PThS	Paderborner theologische Studien
Ptolemaeus (Claudius)	
Apotel.	*Apotelesmatica*
PVTG	Pseudepigrapha Veteris Testamenti graece
PW	A. F. Pauly and G. Wissowa, *Real-Encyclopädie der classischen Altertumswissenschaft.* Stuttgart: Metzler, 1893–1978
PWSup	Supplement to *PW*
Pythagoras	
Carm.	*Carmen Aureum*
Frag.	*Fragmenta*
Quintilian	
Inst.	*Institio oratoria*
1–11Q	Qumran Scrolls from Caves 1-11
1QapGen	*Genesis Apocryphon*
1QH	*Hodayot / Thanksgiving Psalms*
1QIsa[a]	*Isaiah[a]*
1QM	*Milhamah / War Scroll*
1QpHab	*Pesher Habakkuk*
1QPss[a]	*1Q10 / Psautier i*
1QS	*Serek Hayahad / Rule of the Community*
1QSa	Appendix A to *Rule of the Community*
1QSb	Appendix B to *Rule of the Community*
4Q177	*Catena*
4Q180-81	*Ages of the Creation*
4Q184	*Wiles of the Wicked Woman*
4Q178	Unclassified Fragments
4Q381	*Non-Canonical Psalms B*
4Q398	*Halakhic Letter*
4QCatena[a]	*Catena[a]*
4QDibHam	QP504 / *Words of the Luminaries*
4QFlor	*Florilegium*
4QMMT	*Halakhic Letter*
4QpIsa[c]	*Pesher Isaiah[c]*
4QpPs37	*Pesher Psalm 37*
4QpsDan	*Pseudo-Daniel*
4QTest	*Testimonia*
11QPs	*Psalm 151*
11QT	*Temple Scroll*
QD	*Questiones disputatae*
QJS	*Quarterly Journal of Speech*
QR	*Quarterly Review*
RAC	*Reallexikon für Antike und Christentum*
RB	*Revue biblique*
RBén	*Revue bénédictine de critique, d'histoire et de littérature religieuses*
RE	*Realencyklopädie für protestantische Theologie und Kirche*
RechBib	Recherches bibliques
RechSR	*Recherches de science religieuse*
REeL	*Revue ecclésiastique de Liège*
Res Gestae	*Res Gestae divi Augusti*
RestQ	*Restoration Quarterly. Studies in Christian Scholarship*
Rev	Revelation
RevExp	*Review and Expositor*
RevQ	*Revue de Qumrân*
RevScRel	*Revue des sciences religieuses. Faculté catholique de théologie*
RGG	*Religion in Geschichte und Gegenwart.* 3d ed. 1956-65. 4th ed. 1998-2005
RGRW	Religions in the Graeco-Roman World
Rhet	*Rhetorica: A Journal of the History of Rhetoric*
Rhet. Her.	*Rhetorica ad Herennium*
RhM	*Rheinisches Museum für Philologie*
RHPhR	*Revue d'histoire et de philosophie religieuses*
RivB	*Rivista biblica*
RNTS	Reading the New Testament Series
RP	Religious Perspectives
RQ	*Römische Quartalschrift für christliche Altertumskunde und Kirchengeschichte*
RSA	*Rivista storica dell'Antichità*
RSPhTh	*Revue des sciences philosophiques et théologiques*
RSV	*Revised Standard Version*
RTK	*Roczniki Teleologiczno-kanonizne: Annales Theologico-Canonici*
RTR	*Reformed Theological Review*
RV	*Revised Version*
RVV	Religionsgeschichtliche Versuche und Vorarbeiten
Šabb.	*Šabbat* (tractate)
Sal	*Salesianum. Pontificio ateneo salesiano.*
Sallust	
Bell. Jug.	*Bellum Jugurthinum*
SAmer	*Scientific American*
Sanh.	*Sanhedrin* (tractate)
SANT	Studien zum Alten und Neuen Testament
SB	*Sammelbuch griechischer Urkunden aus Aegypten,* ed. F. Preisigke et al. 14 vols. 1915–83
SBB	Stuttgarter biblische Beiträge
SBL	Society of Biblical Literature
SBLASP	*SBL Abstracts and Seminar Papers*
SBLDS	SBL Dissertation Series
SBLMS	SBL Monograph Series
SBLPS	SBL Pseudepigrapha Series
SBLSP	*SBL Seminar Papers*
SBLTT	SBL Texts and Translations
SBS	Stuttgarter Bibelstudien
SBT	Studies in Biblical Theology
SC	Sources chrétiennes

ScB	Sciences bibliques	SGKA	Studien zur Geschichte und Kultur des Altertums
ScE	*Science et Esprit*		
ScEc	*Science ecclésiastiques. Revue philosophique et théologique*	*SHAW*	*Sitzungsberichte der heidelberger Akademie der Wissenschaft Philosophisch-historische Klasse*
Sch. Arist.	*Scholia Aristophanem*		
Sch. Dem.	*Scholia in Demosthenem*	*Sib. Or.*	*Sibylline Oracles*
Sch. Iso.	*Scholia in Isocratem*	*SIG*	*Orientis Graeci Inscriptiones*
Sch. Opp.	*Scholia in Oppianum*		*Selectae: Supplementum Sylloges*
Sch. Pind.	*Scholia in Pindarum*		*Inscriptionum Graecarum*, ed. W.
Sch. Plat.	*Scholia in Platonem*		Dittenberger. 1915–24; repr.
SCJ	Studies in Christianity and Judaism/Études sur le christia-nisme et le judaïsme		Hildesheim: Olms, 1960
		SJ	Studia Judaica. Forschungen zur Wissenschaft des Judentums
ScrB	*Scripture Bulletin. Catholic Biblical Association of Great Britain*	SJLA	Studies in Judaism in Late Antiquity
Script	*Scriptura: Journal of Biblical Studies/Tydskrif vir Bybel-kunde*	*SJT*	*Scottish Journal of Theology*
		SJTOP	*SJT* Occasional Papers
		SkrifK	*Skrif en Kerk*
ScrTh	*Scripta Theologica. Facultad de teología de la universidad de Navarra*	SM	Scripta Minora
		SMB	Serie monografica di 'Benedictina,' sezione biblico-ecumenica
ScuolC	*La Scuola Cattolica. Revista di scienze religiose*	*SMSR*	*Studi e materiali di storia delle reli-gioni*
SD	Studies and Documents		
SDig	*Science Digest*	SNT	Schriften des Neuen Testaments neu übersetzt
SEÅ	*Svensk Exegetisk Årsbok*		
SEG	*Supplementum epigraphicum graecum*, ed. J. Hondius. Alphen, 1923–	SNTG	Studies in New Testament Greek
		SNTSMS	Society for New Testament Studies Monograph Series
Semonides		*SNTU*	*Studien zum Neuen Testament und seiner Umwelt*
Frag.	*Fragmenta*		
Seneca (the Elder)		SNTW	Studies in the New Testament and Its World
Con.	*Controversiae*		
Seneca (the Younger)		SNVAO	Skrifter utgitt av det Norske Videnskaps-Akademie i Oslo, Historisk-filosofisk Klasse
Ben.	*De beneficiis*		
Clem.	*De clementia*		
Ep.	*Epistulae morales*	*SO*	*Symbolae Osloenses. Norwegian Journal of Greek and Latin Studies*
Frag.	*Fragmenta*		
Ira	*De ira*	SO.S	Symbolae Osloenses Supplement
Marc.	*Ad Marciam de consolatione*	*Soc. Ep.*	*Socratis Epistulae*
Nat.	*Naturales quaestiones*	Solon	
Tro.	*Troades*	*Epig.*	*Epigrammata*
SeptArb	Septuaginta Arbeiten	Sophocles	
Septem Sapientes		*Aj.*	*Ajax*
Test.	*Testimonia*	*Ant.*	*Antigone*
Šeqal.	*Šeqalim* (tractate)	*El.*	*Electra*
Severus Iastrosophista		*Oed. col.*	*Oedipus coloneus*
Inst.	*De instrumentis infusoriis seu clysteribus ad Timotheum*	*Oed. tyr.*	*Oedipua tyrannus*
		Trach.	*Trachiniae*
Sextus Empiricus		Soranus	
Frag.	*Fragmenta*	*Gyn.*	*Gynaeciorum libri iv*
Math.	*Adversus mathematicos*	*SPAW*	*Sitzungsberichte der preussischen Akademie der Wissenschaften, Berlin. Philosophisch-historische Klasse*
Pyr.	*Pyrrhoniae hypotyposes*		
Sextus Phil.			
Sent.	*Sententiae Sextii*		
SF	Studia Friburgensia	SPB	Studia Post-biblica
SFF	Studien zur Friedensforschung		
SFSHJ	South Florida Studies in the History of Judaism		

SPCIC	Studiorum Paulinorum congressus internationalis catholicus. 2 vols. AnBib 17-18. Rome: Biblical Institute, 1963	Περὶ βλασ.	Περὶ βλασφημιῶν καὶ ἑκάστη
		SUNT	Studien zur Umwelt des Neuen Testaments
Speusippus		SupplMag	Supplementum Magicum. Ed. Daniel and Maltomini.
Frag.	Fragmenta		
SPGAP	Studien zur Problemgeschichte der antiken und mittelalterlichen Philosophie	SVF	Stoicorum Veterum Fragmenta
		SVTQ	St. Vladmir's Theological Quarterly
		SymBU	Symbolae biblicae Upsalienses
SR	Studies in Religion/Sciences Religieuses	Syntipas	
		Fab.	Fabulae romanenses Graece conscriptae
SSA	Schriften der Sektion für Altertumswissenschaft. Deutsche Akademie der Wissenschaft zu Berlin	Syrianus	
		t.	Tosephta
		T. Abr.	Testament of Abraham
SST	Studies in Sacred Theology	T. Adam	Testament of Adam
StBL	Studies in Biblical Literature	T. Job	Testament of Job
StBT	Studia Biblica et Theologica: Essays by the Students of Fuller Theological Seminary	T. Mos.	Testament of Moses
		T. Sol.	Testament of Solomon
		T. 12 Patr.	Testament of the Twelve Patriarchs
StCJ	Studies in Christianity and Judaism	T. Ash.	Testament of Asher
		T. Benj.	Testament of Benjamin
StCP	Studies in Classical Philology	T. Dan	Testament of Dan
StEv	Studia evangelica. Papers Presented to the . . . International Congress on New Testament Studies Held at Christ Church, Oxford, ed. F. L. Cross. Berlin: Akademie, 1959– (= TU 73, 87, 88, etc.).	T. Gad	Testament of Gad
		T. Iss	Testament of Issachar
		T. Jos.	Testament of Joseph
		T. Jud.	Testament of Judah
		T. Levi	Testament of Levi
		T. Naph.	Testament of Naphtali
		T. Reub.	Testament of Reuben
STL	Studia Theologica Lundenasia	T. Sim.	Testament of Simon
StNT	Studien zum Neuen Testament	T. Zeb.	Testament of Zebulun
Stobaeus		Tacitus	
Anth.	Anthologium	Ann.	Annales
StPat	Studia Patavinia. Rivista di filosofia e teologia. Padua, 1954–	Dial.	Dialogus de oratoribus
		Hist.	Historiae
STR	Studia Travaux de recherche	Tanh.	Tanhuma
Strabo		TANZ	Texte und Arbeiten zum neu-testamentlichen Zeitalter
Geogr.	Geographica		
Str-B	H. Strack and P. Billerbeck, Kommentar zum Neuen Testament aus Talmud und Midrasch. 6 vols. Munich: Beck'sche, 1926–28. 2d ed. 1963	TBAW	Tübinger Beiträge zur Altertumswissenschaft
		TBLNT	Theologisches Begriffslexikon zum Neuen Testament
		TDNT	Theological Dictionary of the New Testament, ed. Gerhard Kittel and Gerhard Friedrich. Trans. and ed. G. W. Bromiley. 10 vols. Grand Rapids: Eerdmans, 1964–74
StT	Studi e Testi. Biblioteca aposto-lica Vaticana		
StTh	Studia Theologica. Scandanavian Journal of Theology		
StTh(Riga)	Studia Theologica. Ordo theologo-rum universitatis Latviensis	TDOT	Theological Dictionary of the Old Testament, ed. G. J. Botterweck et al. Trans. D. E. Green et al. Grand Rapids: Eerdmans, 1974–
Suda			
Lex.	Lexicon		
Suetonius		TEH	Theologische Existenz heute. Eine Schriftenreihe
Aug.	Divus Augustus		
Cal.	Caligula	Teles	
Claud.	Divus Claudius	Rel.	Teletis reliquiae
Dom.	Domitianus		
Galb.	Galba		
Nero	Nero		

Terence
- *Ad.* — *Adelphi*

Tertullian
- *Apol.* — *Apologetus*

TEV — *Today's English Version*

TFPUB — Travaux de la Faculté de Philosophie et Lettres de l'université (libre) de Bruxelles

Tg. Neof. — *Targum Neofiti*

Tg. Onq. — *Targum Onqelos*

TGSS — Tesi Gregoriana Serie Spiritualità

ThA — Theologische Arbeiten

Thales
- *Epig. ded.* — *Epigramma dedicatrium*

ThBei — *Theologische Beiträge*

ThBl — *Theologische Blätter*

ThBT — Theologische Bibliothek Töpelmann

ThBü — Theologische Bücherei. Neudrücke und Berichte aus dem 20. Jahrhundert

Them — *Themelios*

Theod — Theodotion's Greek translation of the Old Testament

Theognis
- *Eleg.* — *Elegiae*
- *Frag. dub.* — *Fragmenta dubia*

Theok — *Theokratia. Jahrbuch des Institutum Judaicum Delitzschianum*

Théologie — Théologie. Études publ. sous la dir. de la faculté de théologie S. J. de Lyon-Bourvière

Theon
- *Prog.* — *Progymnasmata*

Theophilus Antiochenus
- *Autol.* — *Ad Autolycum*

Theophrastus
- *Caus. plant.* — *De causis plantarum*
- *Hist. plant.* — *Historia plantarum*

Theopompus
- *Frag.* — *Fragmenta*

ThF — Theologische Forschung

ThGl — *Theologie und Glaube. Zeitschrift für den katholischen Klerus*

ThHK — Theologischer Handkommentar zum Neuen Testament

ThLZ — *Theologische Literaturzeitung*

ThPh — *Theologie und Philosophie*

ThQ — *Theologische Quartalschrift*

ThR — *Theologische Rundschau*

ThRE — *Theologische Realenzyklopädie*

ThStK — *Theologische Studien und Kritiken*

ThSt(U) — *Theologische Studiën. Utrecht*

Thucydides
- *Hist.* — *Historiae*

ThV — *Theologische Versuche*

ThZ — *Theologische Zeitschrift*

TJT — *Toronto Journal of Theology*

TLG — *Thesaurus linguae graecae: Canon* of Greek Authors and Works, ed. L. Berkowitz and K. A. Squitier. 3d ed. Oxford, 1990

TLNT — C. Spicq, *Theological Lexicon of the New Testament.* Trans. and ed. J. D. Ernest. 3 vols. Peabody: Hendrickson, 1994

TPQ — *Theologisch-praktische Quartalschrift*

TR — Textus Receptus

TrinJ — *Trinity Journal*

TSAJ — Texte und Studien zum Antiken Judentum

TSt — *Teologiske Studier*

TT — Texts and Translations: Graeco-Roman Series.

TTh — *Tijdschrift voor Theologie*

TThZ — *Trierer theologische Zeitschrift*

TTKi — *Tidsskrift for Teologi og Kirke*

TTo — *Theology Today*

TU — Texte und Untersuchungen zur Geschichte der altchristlichen Literatur

TVGMS — Theologische Verlagsgemeinschaft, monographien und Studienbücher

Tyche — *Tyche. Beiträge zur alten Geschichte, Papyrologie und Epigraphie*

TynB — *Tyndale Bulletin*

TZTh — *Tübinger Zeitschrift für Theologie*

UBS — United Bible Societies Greek New Testament. 3d ed. 1983; 4th ed. 1993

UCantP — University of Canterbury Publications

UNT — Untersuchungen zum Neuen Testament

UPZ — *Urkunden der Ptolemäerzeit (Ältere Funde)*, ed. U. Wilckens. 2 vols. 1927, 1957

USFCJ — University of South Florida International Studies in Formative Christianity and Judaism

UUÅ — *Uppsala universitets årsskrift*

VD — *Verbum Domini. Commentarii de re biblica*

Velleius Paterculus
- *Hist.* — *Historiae Romanae*

VerV — Verkenning en Verklaring

Vettius Valens
- *Anth.* — *Anthologiarum libri ix*

VF — *Verkündigung und Forschung*

Vi. Ad. — *Vita Adae et Evae*

Vi. Aes. — *Vitae Aesopi*

Vi. Hom. — *Vitae Homer et Hesiodi*

VigC — *Vigiliae Christianae: Review of Early Christian Life and Language*

Virgil

   Aen.   *Aeneid*

   Ecl.   *Eclogue*

VoxEv   *Vox Evangelica*

VT   *Vetus Testamentum*

VTSup   VT Supplements

WBC   Word Biblical Commentary

WBTh   Wiener Beiträge zur Theologie

WF   Westfälische Forschungen

WMANT   Wissenschaftliche Monographien zum Alten und Neuen Testament

WTJ   *Westminster Theological Journal.*

WuD   *Wort und Dienst*

WUNT   Wissenschaftliche Untersuchungen zum Neuen Testament

WW   *Word and World*

WZ(J)   *Wissenschaftliche Zeitschrift der Friedrich-Schiller-Universität Jena*

Xenophanes

   Test.   *Testimonia*

Xenophon

   Ages.   *Agesilaus*

   Anab.   *Anabasis*

   Apol.   *Apologia Socratis*

   Cyr.   *Cyropaedia*

   Eq. mag.   *De equitum magisto*

   Hell.   *Hellenica*

   Mem.   *Memorabilia*

   Symp.   *Symposium*

ZAH   *Zeitschrift für Althebräistik*

ZAW   *Zeitschrift für die alttestamentliche Wissenschaft*

Zenodotus

ZEE   *Zeitschrift für evangelische Ethik*

ZKTh   *Zeitschrift für katholische Theologie*

ZNW   *Zeitschrift für die neutestamentliche Wissenschaft*

ZPE   *Zeitschrift für Papyrologie und Epigraphik*

ZPF   *Zeitschrift für philosophische Forschung*

ZRG   *Zeitschrift der Savigny-Stiftung für Rechtsgeschichte*

ZSTh   *Zeitschrift für systematische Theologie*

ZThK   *Zeitschrift für Theologie und Kirche*

Works Cited

Commentaries on Romans and other studies dealing with the entire letter are cited by author's name only. Frequently mentioned monographs or articles are cited by author and short title. The same procedure is occasionally used for a work cited within a series of notes on a single passage. In order to save space, full bibliographical information is provided only once, either in the first of such series or here for the most frequently cited items.

Aageson, *Biblical Interpretation*
Aageson, James W. *Written Also for Our Sake: Paul and the Art of Biblical Interpretation.* Louisville: Westminster/John Knox, 1993.

Aageson, "Scripture"
Aageson, James W. "Scripture and Structure in the Development of the Argument in Romans 9–11." *CBQ* 48 (1986) 265–89.

Aageson, "Typology"
Aageson, James W. "Typology, Correspondence, and the Application of Scripture in Romans 9–11." *JSNT* 31 (1987) 51–72.

Aasgaard, "Brothers in Brackets"
Aasgaard, Reidar. "Brothers in Brackets? A Plea for Rethinking the Use of [] in NA/UBS." *JSNT* 26 (2004) 301–21.

Aasgaard, *Siblingship in Paul*
Aasgaard, Reidar. *"My Beloved Brothers and Sisters!" Christian Siblingship in Paul.* JSNTSup 265. London: T. & T. Clark International, 2004.

Achtemeier
Achtemeier, Paul J. *Romans.* Interpretation: A Bible Commentary for Teaching and Preaching. Atlanta: John Knox, 1985.

Adams, "Abraham's Faith"
Adams, Edward. "Abraham's Faith and Gentile Disobedience: Textual Links between Romans 1 and 4." *JSNT* 65 (1997) 47–66.

Agnew, "Origin"
Agnew, Francis H. "The Origin of the NT Apostle-Concept: A Review of Research." *JBL* 105 (1986) 75–96.

Aland, *Entwürfe*
Aland, Kurt. *Neutestamentliche Entwürfe.* ThBü 63. Munich: Kaiser, 1979.

Aland and Aland, *Text*
Aland, Kurt, and Barbara Aland. *The Text of the New Testament: An Introduction to the Critical Editions and to the Theory and Practice of Modern Textual Criticism.* Trans. Errol F. Rhodes. Grand Rapids: Eerdmans, 1987.

Aland et al., *Ergänzungsliste*
Aland, Kurt, Annette Benduhm-Mertz, Gerd Mink, and Horst Bachmann, eds. *Text und Textwert der griechischen Handschriften des Neuen Testaments. II: Die paulinische Briefe. Band 1: Allgemeines, Römerbrief und Ergänzungsliste.* ANTF 16. Berlin: de Gruyter, 1991.

Aland et al., *Kurzgefasste Liste*
Aland, Kurt, Michael Welte, Beate Köster und Klaus Junack, eds. *Kurzgefasste Liste der griechischen Handschriften des Neuen Testaments.* 2d ed. ANTF 1. Berlin: de Gruyter, 1994.

Albl, *Scripture*
Albl, Martin C. *"And Scripture Cannot Be Broken": The Form and Function of the Early Testimonia Collections.* NovTSup 96. Leiden: Brill, 1999.

Aletti, "Argumentation"
Aletti, Jean-Noël. "L'Argumentation paulinienne en Rm 9." *Bib* 68 (1987) 41–56.

Aletti, "Rm 1,18—3,20"
Aletti, Jean-Noël. "Rm 1,18–3,20: Incohérence ou cohérence de l'argumentation paulinienne?" *Bib* 69 (1988) 47–62.

Aletti, "Romains 2"
Aletti, Jean-Noël. "Romains 2: Sa cohérence et sa fonction." *Bib* 77 (1996) 153–177.

Aletti, "Romans 7,7-25"
Aletti, Jean-Noël. "Romans 7,7-25: Rhetorical Criticism and its Usefulness." *SEÅ* 61 (1996) 77–95.

Alkier, *Wunder*
Alkier, Stefan. *Wunder und Wirklichkeit in den Briefen des Apostels Paulus.* WUNT 134. Tübingen: Mohr Siebeck, 2001.

Allen, "Old Testament Background"
Allen, Leslie C. "The Old Testament Background of (προ)ὁρίζειν in the New Testament." *NTS* 17 (1970–71) 104–8.

Allison, "Parallels"
Allison, Dale C., Jr. "The Pauline Epistles and the Synoptic Gospels: The Pattern of the Parallels." *NTS* 28 (1982) 1–32.

Althaus
Althaus, Paul. *Der Brief an die Römer übersetzt und erklärt.* NTD 6. Göttingen: Vandenhoeck & Ruprecht, 1966.

Anderson, "Sin Offering"
Anderson, M., and P. Culbertson. "The Inadequacy of the Christian Doctrine of Atonement in Light of Levitical Sin Offering." *ATR* 68 (1968) 303–28.

Anderson, *Paul*
Anderson, R. Dean, Jr. *Ancient Rhetorical Theory and Paul.* Rev. ed. CBET 18. Leuven: Peeters, 1999.

Anderson, *Glossary*
Anderson, R. Dean, Jr. *Glossary of Greek Rhetorical Terms Connected to Methods of Argumentation, Figures and Tropes from Anaximenes to Quintilian.* CBET 24. Leuven: Peeters, 2000.

Asmussen
Asmussen, Hans. *Der Römerbrief.* Stuttgart: Evangelisches Verlagswerk, 1952.

Atkins, *Egalitarian Community*
Atkins, Robert A., Jr. *Egalitarian Community: Ethnography and Exegesis.* Tuscaloosa: University of Alabama Press, 1991.

Attridge, *Hebrews*
Attridge, Harold W. *The Epistle to the Hebrews: A Commentary on the Epistle to the Hebrews.* Hermeneia. Philadelphia: Fortress Press, 1989.

Auguet, *Cruelty and Civilization*
Auguet, Roland. *Cruelty and Civilization: The Roman Games.* London: Routledge, 1994.

Aus, "Paul's Travel Plans"
Aus, Roger D. "Paul's Travel Plans to Spain and the 'Full Number of the Gentiles' of Rom xi.25." *NovT* 21 (1979) 232–62.

Austgen, *Motivation*
Austgen, Robert J. *Natural Motivation in the Pauline Epistles.* 2d ed. Notre Dame: University of Notre Dame Press, 1969.

Bachmann, "*Verus Israel*"
Bachmann, Michael. "*Verus Israel*: Ein Vorschlag zu einer 'mengentheoretischen' Neubeschreibung der betreffenden paulinischen Terminologie." *NTS* 48 (2002) 500–512.

Badenas, *Christ*
Badenas, Robert. *Christ the End of the Law: Romans 10:4 in Pauline Perspective.* JSNTSup 10. Sheffield: JSOT Press, 1985.

Bahr, "Subscriptions"
Bahr, Gordon J. "The Subscriptions in the Pauline Letters." *JBL* 87 (1968) 27–41.

Baker, "Motif of Jealousy"
Baker, Murray. "Paul and the Salvation of Israel: Paul's Ministry, the Motif of Jealousy, and Israel's Yes." *CBQ* 67 (2005) 469–84.

Balch, "Pauline House Churches"
Balch, David L. "Rich Pompeiian Houses, Shops for Rent, and the Huge Apartment Building in Herculaneum as Typical Spaces for Pauline House Churches." *JSNT* 27 (2004) 27–46.

Balch, "Zeus"
Balch, David L. "Zeus, Vengeful Protector of the Political and Domestic Order. Frescoes in Dining Rooms N and P in the House of the Vetii in Pompeii, Mark 13:12–13, and 1 Clement 6:2." Pp. 67–95 in A. Weissenrieder et al., eds., *Picturing the New Testament. Studies in Ancient Visual Images.* WUNT 193. Tübingen: Mohr Siebeck, 2005.

Bandstra, *Law and the Elements*
Bandstra, Andrew John. *The Law and the Elements of the World: An Exegetical Study in Aspects of Paul's Teaching.* Kampen: Kok, 1964.

Banks, *Community*
Banks, Robert. *Paul's Idea of Community.* Rev. ed. Peabody: Hendrickson, 1994.

Barclay, "Undermine the Law"
Barclay, John M. G. "'Do we undermine the Law?' A Study of Romans 14:1–15:6." Pp. 287–308 in J. D. G. Dunn, ed., *Paul and the Mosaic Law.* Tübingen: Mohr [Siebeck], 1996.

Bardenhewer
Bardenhewer, Otto. *Der Römerbrief des heiligen Paulus. Kurzgefasste Erklärung.* Freiburg: Herder, 1926.

Barr, *Semantics*
Barr, James. *The Semantics of Biblical Language.* Oxford: Oxford University Press, 1961.

Barr, *Time*
Barr, James. *Biblical Words for Time.* SBT 1/33. Naperville: Allenson, 1962.

Barrett, *Caligula*
Barrett, A. A. *Caligula: The Corruption of Power.* New York: Simon & Schuster, 1980.

Barrett
Barrett, Charles Kingsley. *A Commentary on the Epistle to the Romans.* 2d ed. BNTC/HNTC. London: Black; New York: Harper, 1991.

Barrett, *Adam*
Barrett, Charles Kingsley. *From First Adam to Last: A Study in Pauline Theology.* London: Black, 1962.

Barrett, "Boasting"
Barrett, Charles Kingsley. "Boasting (καυχᾶσϑαι, κτλ.) in the Pauline Epistles." Pp. 363–68 in *L'Apôtre Paul. Personalité, Style et Conception du Ministère.* BEThL 73. Leuven: Leuven University Press, 1986.

Barrett, *1 Corinthians*
Barrett, Charles Kingsley. *1 Corinthians.* BNTC. London: Black, 1968.

Bartchy, "Siblings"
Bartchy, S. Scott. "Undermining Ancient Patriarchy: The Apostle Paul's Vision of a Society of Siblings." *BTB* 29 (1999) 68–78.

Bartchy, "Slavery (Greco-Roman)"
Bartchy, S. Scott. "Slavery (Greco-Roman)." *ABD* 6 (1992) 65–73.

Barth
Barth, Karl. *The Epistle to the Romans.* Trans. E. C. Hoskyns. London: Oxford University Press, 1933.

Barth, *Shorter Commentary*
Barth, Karl. *A Shorter Commentary on Romans.* Richmond: John Knox, 1959.

Barth et al., *Foi et salut*
Barth, Markus et al., eds. *Foi et salut selon S. Paul (Épître aux Romains 1,16).* AnBib 42. Rome: Biblical Institute, 1970.

Barth, "Jews and Gentiles"
Barth, Markus. "Jews and Gentiles: The Social Character of Justification in Paul." *JES* 5 (1968) 241–67.

Barth, *People*
Barth, Markus. *The People of God.* JSNTSup 5. Sheffield: Sheffield Academic Press, 1983.

Bartsch, "Bekenntnisformel"
Bartsch, Hans-Werner. "Zur vorpaulinischen Bekenntnisformel im Eingang des Römerbriefes." *ThZ* 23 (1967) 329–39.

Bartsch, "Gegner"
Bartsch, Hans-Werner. "Die antisemitischen Gegner des Paulus im Römerbrief." Pp. 27–43 in W. P. Eckert, et al., eds., *Antijudaismus im Neuen Testament? Exegetische und systematische Beiträge.* Abhandlungen zum christlich-jüdischen Dialog 2. Munich: Kaiser, 1967.

Bartsch, "Historische Situation"
Bartsch, Hans-Werner. "Die historische Situation des Römerbriefes." *StEv* 4 (Berlin: Akademie-Verlag, 1968) 4.281–91.

Bassler, *Impartiality*
Bassler, Jouette M. *Divine Impartiality: Paul and a Theological Axiom.* SBLDS 59. Chico: Scholars Press, 1982.

Bauer, *Leiblichkeit*
Bauer, Karl-Adolf. *Leiblichkeit, das Ende aller Werke Gottes. Die Bedeutung der Leiblichkeit des Menschen bei Paulus.* StNT 4. Gütersloh: Gütersloher Verlagshaus, 1971.

Baumgarten, *Paulus*
Baumgarten, Jörg. *Paulus und die Apokalyptik.* WMANT 44. Neukirchen-Vluyn: Neukirchener Verlag, 1975.

Baumgarten-Crusius
Baumgarten-Crusius, Ludwig Friedrich Otto. *Commentar über den Brief Pauli an die Römer.* Ed. E. J. Kimmel. Jena: Maucke, 1844.

Baur, *Paul*
Baur, Ferdinand Christian. *Paul the Apostle of Jesus Christ: His Life and Work, His Epistles and His Doctrine.* Trans. E. Zeller and A. Menzies. 2 vols. London: Williams and Norgate, 1876.

Beard et al., *Religions of Rome*
Beard, Mary, John North, and Simon Rice. *Religions of Rome.* 2 vols. Cambridge: Cambridge University Press, 1998.

Beck
Beck, Johann Tobias. *Erklärung des Briefes Pauli an die Römer.* Ed. J. Lindenmeyer. 2 vols. Gütersloh: Bertelsmann, 1884.

Becker, *Auferstehung*
  Becker, Jürgen. *Auferstehung der Toten im Urchristentum*. Stuttgart: Katholisches Bibelwerk, 1976.
Becker, *Paul*
  Becker, Jürgen. *Paul: Apostle to the Gentiles*. Trans. O. C. Dean Jr. Louisville: Westminster/John Knox, 1993.
Beker, *Apocalyptic Gospel*
  Beker, J. Christiaan. *Paul's Apocalyptic Gospel: The Coming Triumph of God*. Philadelphia: Fortress Press, 1982.
Beker, *Paul*
  Beker, J. Christiaan. *Paul the Apostle: The Triumph of God in Life and Thought*. Philadelphia: Fortress Press, 1980.
Bell, *No One Seeks*
  Bell, Richard H. *No One Seeks for God: An Exegetical and Theological Study of Romans 1.18–3.20*. WUNT 106. Tübingen: Mohr Siebeck, 1998.
Bell, *Provoked to Jealousy*
  Bell, Richard H. *Provoked to Jealousy: The Origin and Purpose of the Jealousy Motif in Romans 9–11*. WUNT 63. Tübingen: Mohr (Siebeck), 1994.
Benecke
  Benecke, William. *An Exposition of St. Paul's Epistle to the Romans*. London: Longman, Brown, Green and Longmans, 1854.
Bengel, *Gnomon*
  Bengel, J. A. *Gnomon of the New Testament: A New Translation*. Trans. C. T. Lewis and M. R. Vincent. Philadelphia: Perkinpine & Higgins, 1864. 21:9–164.
Benko, *Early Christians*
  Benko, Stephen. *Pagan Rome and the Early Christians*. Bloomington: Indiana University Press, 1984. 79–102.
Benko, "Edict"
  Benko, Stephen. "The Edict of Claudius of A.D. 49 and the Instigator of Chrestus." *ThZ* 25 (1969) 406–18.
Berger, "Abraham"
  Berger, Klaus. "Abraham in den paulinischen Hauptbriefen." *MThZ* 17 (1966) 47–89.
Berger, "Apostelbrief"
  Berger, Klaus. "Apostelbrief und apostolische Rede: Zum Formular frühchristlicher Briefe." *ZNW* 65 (1974) 190–231.
Berger, *Formgeschichte*
  Berger, Klaus. *Formgeschichte des Neuen Testaments*. Heidelberg: Quelle & Meyer, 1984.
Berger, *Gesetzesauslegung Jesu*
  Berger, Klaus. *Die Gesetzesauslegung Jesu. Ihr historischer Hintergrund im Judentum und im Alten Testament. I. Markus und Parallelen*. WMANT 40. Neukirchen-Vluyn: Neukirchener Verlag, 1972.
Berger, "Gnade"
  Berger, Klaus. "'Gnade' im frühen Christentum." *NTT* 27 (1973) 1–25.
Berger, *Römerbrief*
  Berger, Klaus. *Gottes einzinger Ölbaum. Betrachtungen zum Römerbrief*. Stuttgart: Quell, 1990.
Bergmeier, *Gesetz*
  Bergmeier, Roland. *Das Gesetz im Römerbrief und andere Studien zum Neuen Testament*. Tübingen: Mohr [Siebeck], 2000.
Berkley, *Romans 2:17-29*
  Berkley, Timothy W. *From a Broken Covenant to Circumcision of the Heart: Pauline Intertextual Exegesis in Romans 2:17-29*. SBLDS 175. Atlanta: Society of Biblical Literature, 2000.

Best
  Best, Ernest. *The Letter of Paul to the Romans*. Cambridge Bible Commentary. Cambridge: Cambridge University Press, 1967.
Betz, *Galatians*
  Betz, Hans Dieter. *Galatians: A Commentary on Paul's Letter to the Churches in Galatia*. Hermeneia. Philadelphia: Fortress Press, 1979.
Betz, *Gesammelte Aufsätze IV*
  Betz, Hans Dieter. *Gesammelte Aufsätze. Band IV. Antike und Christentum*. Tübingen: Mohr-Siebeck, 1998.
Betz, *Greek Magical Papyri*
  Betz, Hans Dieter, ed. *The Greek Magical Papyri in Translation, Including the Demotic Spells*. Chicago: University of Chicago Press, 1986.
Betz, *Nachfolge*
  Betz, Hans Dieter. *Nachfolge und Nachahmung Jesu Christi im Neuen Testament*. BHTh 37. Tübingen: Mohr Siebeck, 1967.
Betz, *Paulinische Studien*
  Betz, Hans Dieter. *Paulinische Studien. Gesammelte Aufsätze III*. Tübingen: Mohr Siebeck, 1994.
Betz, *Sokratische Tradition*
  Betz, Hans Dieter. *Der Apostel Paulus und die sokratische Tradition*. BHT 45. Tübingen: Mohr [Siebeck], 1972.
Betz, *2 Corinthians 8 and 9*
  Betz, Hans Dieter. *2 Corinthians 8 and 9: A Commentary on Two Administrative Letters of the Apostle Paul*. Hermeneia. Philadelphia: Fortress Press, 1985.
Beyer, *Semitische Syntax*
  Beyer, Klaus. *Semitische Syntax im Neuen Testament*. Band 1: *Satzlehre*. Teil 1. SUNT 1. Göttingen: Vandenhoeck & Ruprecht, 1962.
Bindemann, *Hoffnung*
  Bindemann, Walther. *Die Hoffnung der Schöpfung. Römer 8:18-27 und die Frage einer Theologie der Befreiung von Mensch und Natur*. Neukirchen-Vluyn: Neukirchener Verlag, 1983.
Bindemann, *Theologie*
  Bindemann, Walther. *Theologie in Dialoge. Ein traditionsgeschichtlicher Kommentar zu Römer 1–11*. Leipzig: Evangelischer Verlagsanstalt, 1992.
Binder, *Glaube*
  Binder, Hermann. *Der Glaube bei Paulus*. Berlin: Evangelische Verlagsanstalt, 1968.
Bisping
  Bisping, August. *Erklärung des Briefes an die Römer*. Münster: Aschendorff, 1860.
Bitzer, "Rhetorical Situation"
  Bitzer, Lloyd F. "The Rhetorical Situation." *PR* 1 (1968) 1–14.
Bjerkelund, "Nach menschlicher Weise"
  Bjerkelund, Carl J. "'Nach menschlicher Weise rede ich.' Funktion und Sinn des paulinischen Ausdrucks." *StTh* 26 (1972) 63–100.
Bjerkelund, *PARAKALÔ*
  Bjerkelund, Carl J. *PARAKALÔ. Form, Funktion und Sinn der parakalô-Sätze in den paulinischen Briefen*. Bibliotheca Theologica Norvegica 1. Oslo: Universitetsvorlaget, 1967.
Black, "Death in Romans 5–8"
  Black, C. Clifton II. "Pauline Perspectives on Death in Romans 5–8." *JBL* 103 (1984) 413–33.

Black
Black, Matthew. *Romans.* 2d ed. NCBC. Grand Rapids: Eerdmans, 1989.

Blank, *Paulus*
Blank, Josef. *Paulus. Von Jesus zum Urchristentum.* Munich: Kösel, 1982.

Blaske, *Beschneidung*
Blaske, Andreas. *Beschneidung. Zeugnisse der Bibel und verwandter Texte.* TANZ 28. Tübingen: Francke, 1998.

Blumenfeld, *Political Paul*
Blumenfeld, Bruno. *The Political Paul: Justice, Democracy and Kingship in a Hellenistic Framework.* JSNTSup 210. Sheffield: Sheffield Academic Press, 2001.

Bockmuehl, *Revelation and Mystery*
Bockmuehl, Markus N. A. *Revelation and Mystery in Ancient Judaism and Pauline Christianity.* WUNT 36. Tübingen: Mohr Siebeck, 1990.

Bockmuehl, "Verb φανερόω"
Bockmuehl, Markus N. A. "Das Verb φανερόω im Neuen Testament: Versuch einer Neuauswertung." *BZ* 32 (1988) 87–99.

Boer, *Defeat of Death*
Boer, Martinus C. de. *The Defeat of Death. Apocalyptic Eschatology in I Corinthians 15 and Romans 5.* JSNTSup 22. Sheffield: JSOT Press, 1988.

Boers, *Justification*
Boers, Hendrikus. *The Justification of the Gentiles. Paul's Letters to the Galatians and Romans.* Peabody: Hendrickson, 1994.

Boers, "Romans 6:1-14"
Boers, Hendrikus. "The Structure and Meaning of Romans 6:1-14." *CBQ* 63 (2001) 664–82.

Bonda, *One Purpose*
Bonda, Jan. *The One Purpose of God: An Answer to the Doctrine of Eternal Punishment.* Trans. R. Bruinsma. Grand Rapids/Cambridge: Eerdmans, 1998.

Bonsirven, *Exégèse rabbinique*
Bonsirven, Joseph, S. J. *Exégèse rabbinique et exégèse Paulinienne.* Paris: Beauchesne et ses Fils, 1939.

Boobjer, "Thanksgiving"
Boobjer, George Henry. "'Thanksgiving' and the 'Glory of God' in Paul." Dissertation, University of Heidelberg, 1929. Printed Borna-Leipzig: Universitätsverlag Robert Noske, 1929.

Bornkamm, "Anakoluthe"
Bornkamm, Günther. "Paulinische Anakoluthe." Pp. 76–92 in *Das Ende des Gesetzes. Paulusstudien. Gesammelte Aufsätze.* 3d ed. Vol. 1. BEvTh 16. Munich: Kaiser, 1961.

Bornkamm, *Ende des Gesetzes*
Bornkamm, Günther. *Das Ende des Gesetzes. Paulusstudien. Gesammelte Aufsätze.* 3d ed. Vol. 1. BEvTh 16. Munich: Kaiser, 1961.

Bornkamm, *Experience*
Bornkamm, Günther. *Early Christian Experience.* Trans. P. L. Hammer. Philadelphia: Westminster, 1969.

Bornkamm, "Last Will and Testament"
Bornkamm, Günther. "The Letter to the Romans as Paul's Last Will and Testament." Pp. 16–28 in K. P. Donfried, ed., *The Romans Debate.* Rev. ed. Peabody: Hendrickson, 1991.

Bornkamm, *Paul*
Bornkamm, Günther. *Paul.* Trans. D. M. C. Stalker. New York: Harper & Row, 1971.

Bornkamm, "Revelation"
Bornkamm, Günther. "The Revelation of God's Wrath (Romans 1–3)." Pp. 47–70 in Bornkamm, *Experience.*

Bornkamm, "Sin, Law and Death"
Bornkamm, Günther. "Sin, Law and Death (Romans 7)." Pp. 87–104 in Bornkamm, *Experience.*

Bornkamm, *Studien*
Bornkamm, Günther. *Studien zum Neuen Testament.* Munich: Kaiser, 1985.

Bornkamm, "Theologie als Teufelskunst"
Bornkamm, Günther. "Theologie als Teufelskunst. Römer 3,1-9." Pp. 140–48 in vol. 4 of G. Bornkamm, *Geschichte und Glaube II. Gesammelte Aufsätze.* Munich: Kaiser, 1971.

Bouttier, *En Christ*
Bouttier, Michel. *En Christ. Étude d'exégèse et de théologie paulini-ennes.* EHPhR 54. Paris: Presses Universitaires de France, 1962.

Bouwman
Bouwman, Gijs. *Paulus aan de romeinen. Een retorische analyse van Rom 1–8.* Abjij Averbode: Werkgroep voor levensverdieping, 1980.

Bouwman, "Römer 1"
Bouwman, Gijs. "Noch einmal Römer 1, 21-32." *Bib* 54 (1973) 411–14.

Bowers, "Jewish Communities in Spain"
Bowers, W. P. "Jewish Communities in Spain in the Time of Paul the Apostle." *JTS* 26 (1975) 395–402.

Boyarin, *Radical Jew*
Boyarin, Daniel. *A Radical Jew: Paul and the Politics of Identity.* Berkeley: University of California Press, 1994.

Boylan
Boylan, Patrick. *St. Paul's Epistle to the Romans.* Dublin: Gill, 1934; repr. 1947.

Brandenburger, *Adam und Christus*
Brandenburger, Egon. *Adam und Christus. Exegetisch-religions-geschichtliche Untersuchungen zu Römer 5, 12-21 (1. Kor. 15).* WMANT 7. Neukirchen-Vluyn: Neukirchener Verlag, 1962.

Brandenburger, *Fleisch und Geist*
Brandenburger, Egon. *Fleisch und Geist. Paulus und die dualisti-sche Weisheit.* WMANT 29. Neukirchen-Vluyn: Neukirchener Verlag, 1968.

Brandenburger, *Frieden im Neuen Testament*
Egon Brandenburger, *Frieden im Neuen Testament. Grundlinien urchristlichen Friedensverständnisses.* Gütersloh: Mohn, 1973.

Brandenburger, "Paulinische Schriftauslegung"
Brandenburger, Egon. "Paulinische Schriftauslegung in der Kontroverse um das Verheissungswort Gottes (Röm 9)." *ZThK* 82 (1985) 1–47.

Brändle and Stegemann, "Formation"
Brändle, Rudolf, and Ekkehard W. Stegemann. "The Formation of the First 'Christian Congregations' in Rome in the Context of the Jewish Congregations." Pp. 117–27 in K. P. Donfried and P. Richardson, eds., *Judaism and Christianity in First-Century Rome.* Grand Rapids: Eerdmans, 1998.

Brandt, *Rhetoric of Argumentation*
Brandt, William J. *The Rhetoric of Argumentation.* Rev. ed. New York: Irvington, 1984.

Branick, *House Church*
Branick, Vincent P. *The House Church in the Writings of Paul.* Wilmington: Glazier, 1989.

Branick, *Introduction*
  Branick, Vincent P. *Understanding the New Testament and Its Message: An Introduction.* New York: Paulist Press, 1998.

Brauch, "Perspectives"
  Brauch, Manfred T. "Perspectives on 'God's Righteousness' in Recent German Discussion." Appendix pp. 523–42 in E. P. Sanders. *Paul and Palestinian Judaism: A Comparison of Patterns of Religion.* Philadelphia: Fortress Press, 1977.

Breytenbach, *Versöhnung*
  Breytenbach, Cilliers. *Versöhnung. Eine Studie zur paulinischen Soteriologie.* WMANT 60. Neukirchen-Vluyn: Neukirchener Verlag, 1989.

Bring, *Bedeutung des Gesetzes*
  Bring, Ragnar. *Christus und das Gesetz. Die Bedeutung des Gesetzes des Alten Testaments nach Paulus und sein Glauben an Christus.* Leiden: Brill, 1969.

Brinkman, "Creation I"
  Brinkman, B. R. "'Creation' and 'Creature'. I. Some Texts and Tendencies." *Bijdr* 18 (1957) 127–39.

Brinkman, "Creation II"
  "'Creation' and 'Creature'. II. Texts and Tendencies in the Epistle to the Romans." *Bijdr* 18 (1957) 359–74.

Brockhaus, *Charisma*
  Brockhaus, Ulrich. *Charisma und Amt. Die paulinische Charismenlehre auf dem Hintergrund der frühchristlichen Gemeindefunktionen.* Wuppertal: Rolf Brockhaus Verlag, 1972.

Brockmeyer, *Antike Sklaverei*
  Brockmeyer, Norbert. *Antike Sklaverei.* Ertrage der Forschung 116. Darmstadt: Wissenschaftliche Buchgesellschaft, 1979.

Brooten, "Junia"
  Brooten, Bernadette J. "'Junia . . . Outstanding among the Apostles' (Romans 16:7)." Pp. 141–44 in L. & A. Swidler, eds., *Women Priests: A Catholic Commentary on the Vatican Declaration.* New York: Paulist, 1977.

Brooten, *Love between Women*
  Brooten, Bernadette J. *Love between Women: Early Christian Responses to Female Homoeroticism.* Chicago: University of Chicago Press, 1996.

Brown, *Introduction*
  Brown, Raymond E. *An Introduction to the New Testament.* New York: Doubleday, 1997.

Brown and Meier, *Antioch and Rome*
  Brown, Raymond E., and John P. Meier. *Antioch and Rome: New Testament Cradles of Catholic Christianity.* New York: Paulist Press, 1983.

Bruce
  Bruce, Frederick F. *The Epistle of Paul to the Romans: An Introduction and Commentary.* 5th ed. TNTC. Grand Rapids: Eerdmans, 1985.

Bruce, *Paul*
  Bruce, Frederick F. *Paul: Apostle of the Free Spirit.* Exeter: Paternoster, 1977. American title: *Paul: Apostle of the Heart Set Free.* Grand Rapids: Eerdmans, 1977.

Brunt, "*Laus Imperii*"
  Brunt, P. A. "*Laus Imperii.*" Pp. 25–35 in R. A. Horsley, ed., *Paul and Empire: Religion and Power in Roman Imperial Society.* Harrisburg: Trinity Press International, 1997.

Bryskog, "Epistolography, Rhetoric and Letter Prescript"
  Bryskog, Samuel. "Epistolography, Rhetoric and Letter Prescript: Romans 1.1–7 as a Test Case." *JSNT* 65 (1997) 27–46.

Büchsel, "In Christus"
  Büchsel, Friedrich. "'In Christus' bei Paulus." *ZNW* 42 (1949) 141–58.

Bullinger, *Figures*
  Bullinger, Ernest W. *Figures of Speech Used in the Bible Explained and Illustrated.* London: Eyre and Spottiswoode, 1898. Rep. Grand Rapids: Baker, 1968.

Bultmann, "Adam"
  Bultmann, Rudolph. "Adam and Christ according to Rom 5." Pp. 143–65 in W. Klassen & G. F. Snyder, eds., *Current Issues in New Testament Interpretation. Essays in Honor of Otto A. Piper.* New York: Harper & Brothers; London: SCM, 1962.

Bultmann, "ΔΙΚΑΙΟΣΤΝΗ ΘΕΟΥ"
  Bultmann, Rudolf. "ΔΙΚΑΙΟΣΤΝΗ ΘΕΟΥ." *JBL* 83 (1964) 12–16.

Bultmann, *Exegetica*
  Bultmann, Rudolf. *Exegetica. Aufsätze zur Erforschung des Neuen Testaments.* Tübingen: Mohr Siebeck, 1967.

Bultmann, "Glossen"
  Bultmann, Rudolf. "Glossen in Römerbrief." Pp. 278–84 in Bultmann. *Exegetica.*

Bultmann, *Old and New Man*
  Bultmann, Rudolf. *The Old and New Man in the Letters of Paul.* Trans. K. R. Crim. Richmond: John Knox, 1967.

Bultmann, "Römer 7"
  Bultmann, Rudolf. "Römer 7 und die Anthropologie des Paulus." Pp. 53–62 in Bultmann. *Exegetica.* Tübingen: Mohr [Siebeck], 1967.

Bultmann, *Stil*
  Bultmann, Rudolf. *Der Stil der paulinischen Predigt und die kynisch-stoische Diatribe.* 1910. Repr. Göttingen: Vandenhoeck & Ruprecht, 1984.

Bultmann, *Theology*
  Bultmann, Rudolf. *Theology of the New Testament.* Trans. K. Grobel. 2 vols. New York: Scribner, 1955.

Burdick, "Οἶδα and Γινώσκω"
  Burdick, Donald W. "Οἶδα and Γινώσκω in the Pauline Epistles." Pp. 344–56 in R. N. Longenecker and M. C. Tenney, eds., *New Dimensions in New Testament Studies.* Grand Rapids: Zondervan, 1974.

Burger, *Jesus als Davidssohn*
  Burger, Christoph. *Jesus als Davidssohn. Eine traditions-geschichtliche Untersuchung.* FRLANT 98. Göttingen: Vandenhoeck & Ruprecht, 1970.

Burkert, *Mystery Cults*
  Burkert, Walter. *Ancient Mystery Cults.* Cambridge: Harvard University Press, 1987.

Burnett, *Individual*
  Burnett, Gary W. *Paul and the Salvation of the Individual.* Biblical Interpretation Series 57. Leiden: Brill, 2001.

Busch, *Testament Salomos*
  Busch, Peter. *Das Testament Salomos. Die älteste christliche Dämonologie, kommentiert und in deutscher Erstübersetzung.* TU 153. Berlin: de Gruyter, 2006.

Bussmann, *Missionspredigt*
  Bussmann, Claus. *Themen der paulinischen Missionspredigt auf dem Hintergrund der spätjüdisch-hellenistischen Missionsliteratur.* EHS 23.3. Bern: Lang, 1975.

Byrne
  Byrne, Brendan, S.J. *Romans*. Sacra pagina series 6. Collegeville: Liturgical Press, 1996.

Byrne, *Reckoning*
  Byrne, Brendan, S.J. *Reckoning with Romans: A Contemporary Reading of Paul's Gospel*. GNS 18. Wilmington: Michael Glazier, 1986.

Byrne, *Sons*
  Byrne, Brendan, S.J. *"Sons of God"–"Seed of Abraham": A Study of the Idea of the Sonship of God of All Christians in Paul against the Jewish Background*. AnBib 83. Rome: Biblical Institute, 1979.

Calvert-Koyzis, *Paul*
  Calvert-Koyzis, Nancy. *Paul, Monotheism and the People of God. The Significance of Abraham Traditions for Early Judaism and Christianity*. JSNTSup 273. London: T. & T. Clark, 2004.

Cambier
  Cambier, Jules. *L'Évangile de Dieu selon l'épître aux Romains: Exégèse et théologie biblique*. Vol. 1. *L'Évangile de la justice et de la grace*. Studia neotestamentica 3. Paris: Desclée de Brouwer, 1967.

Campbell, "Dying"
  Campbell, Alastair. "Dying with Christ: The Origin of a Metaphor." Pp. 273–93 in S. E. Porter and A. R. Cross, eds., *Baptism, the New Testament and the Church: Historical and Contemporary Studies in Honour of R. E. O. White*. JSNTSup 171. Sheffield: Sheffield Academic Press, 1999.

Campbell, *Quest*
  Campbell, Douglas A. *The Quest for Paul's Gospel: A Suggested Strategy*. London: T. & T. Clark, 2005.

Campbell, *Rhetoric of Righteousness*
  Campbell, Douglas A. *The Rhetoric of Righteousness in Romans 3.21-26*. JSNTSup 65. Sheffield: Sheffield Academic Press, 1992.

Campbell, "3.27–4.25"
  Campbell, Douglas A. "Towards a New, Rhetorically Assisted Reading of Romans 3.27–4.25." Pp. 355–402 in S. E. Porter and D. L. Stamps, eds., *Rhetorical Criticism and the Bible*. JSNTSup 195. Sheffield: Sheffield Academic Press, 2002.

Campbell, "*KOINΩNIA*"
  Campbell, J. Y. "*KOINΩNIA* and Its Cognates in the New Testament." *JBL* 51 (1932) 352–80.

Campbell, "Identity"
  Campbell, William S. "'All of God's Beloved in Rome!' Jewish Roots and Christian Identity." Pp. 67–82 in S. E. McGinn, ed., *Celebrating Romans: Template for Pauline Theology. Essays in Honor of Robert Jewett*. Grand Rapids: Eerdmans, 2004.

Campbell, *Paul's Gospel*
  Campbell, William S. *Paul's Gospel in an Intercultural Context: Jew and Gentile in the Letter to the Romans*. Studies in the Intercultural History of Christianity 69. Frankfurt: Lang, 1991.

Campbell, "Romans iii"
  Campbell, William S. "Romans iii as a Key to the Structure and Thought of the Letter." *NovT* 23 (1981) 22–40. Repr. pp. 251–64 in K. P. Donfried, ed., *The Romans Debate*. Revised and Expanded Edition. Peabody: Hendrickson, 1991.

Cantarella, *Bisexuality*
  Cantarella, Eva. *Bisexuality in the Ancient World*. Trans. C. Ó'Cuilleanáin. New Haven: Yale University Press, 1992.

Carr, *Angels and Principalities*
  Carr, Wesley. *Angels and Principalities: The Background, Meaning and Development of the Pauline Phrase hai archai kai hai exousiai*. SNTSMS 42. Cambridge: Cambridge University Press, 1981.

Carter, *Power of Sin*
  Carter, T. L. *Paul and the Power of Sin: Redefining 'Beyond the Pale.'* SNTSMS 115. Cambridge: Cambridge University Press, 2002.

Chae, *Paul*
  Chae, Daniel Jong-Sang. *Paul as Apostle to the Gentiles: His Apostolic Self-Awareness and Its Influence on the Soteriological Argument in Romans*. PBTM. Carlisle: Paternoster, 1997.

Champion, *Benedictions and Doxologies*
  Champion, L. G. *Benedictions and Doxologies in the Epistles of Paul*. Oxford: Kemp Hall, 1934.

Christensen, *Christus oder Jupiter*
  Christensen, Torben. *Christus oder Jupiter. Der Kampf um die geistigen Grundlagen des Römischen Reichs*. Trans. D. Harbsmeier. Göttingen: Vandenhoeck & Ruprecht, 1981.

Christiansen, *Covenant*
  Christiansen, Ellen Juhl. *The Covenant in Judaism and Paul: A Study of Ritual Boundaries as Identity Markers*. AGJU 27. Leiden: Brill, 1995.

Cineira, *Religionspolitik*
  Cineira, David Alvarez. *Die Religionspolitik des Kaisers Claudius und die paulinische Mission*. HBS 19. Freiburg: Herder, 1999.

Clarke, "Romans 16"
  Clarke, Andrew D. "Jew and Greek, Slave and Free, Male and Female: Paul's Theology of Ethnic, Social and Gender Inclusiveness in Romans 16." Pp. 103–25 in P. Oakes, ed., *Rome in the Bible and the Early Church*. Carlisle: Paternoster; Grand Rapids: Baker, 2002.

Colenso
  Colenso, John William. *Commentary on Romans*. Reprint of the 1861 edition. Edited, with an Introduction by Jonathan A. Draper. Pietermaritzburg: Cluster Publications, 2003.

Collins, *Diakonia*
  Collins, John N. *Diakonia: Re-interpreting the Ancient Sources*. New York: Oxford University Press, 1990.

Collins, "Jewish Source"
  Collins, Nina L. "The Jewish Source of Rom 5:17, 16, 10 and 9: The Verses of Paul in Relation to a Comment in the Mishnah at M. Makk 3.15." *RB* 112 (2005) 27–45.

Collins, "Wandering Doxology"
  Collins, Raymond F. "The Case of a Wandering Doxology: Rom 16,25–27." Pp. 293–303 in A. Denaux, ed., *New Testament Textual Criticism and Exegesis. Festschrift J. Delobel*. BETL 161. Leuven: Leuven University Press/Peeters, 2002.

Conzelmann, *1 Corinthians*
  Conzelmann, Hans. *1 Corinthians: A Commentary on the First Epistle to the Corinthians*. Trans. J. W. Leitch. Philadelphia: Fortress Press, 1975.

Conzelmann, "Theology or Anthropology"
  Conzelmann, Hans. "Paul's Doctrine of Justification: Theology or Anthropology." Pp. 108–23 in F. Herzog, ed., *Theology of the Liberating Word*. Nashville: Abingdon, 1971.

Cornely
  Cornely, Rudolf. *Commentarius in S. Pauli Apostoli epistolas. I, Epistola ad Romanos*. CSS 3.6. Paris: Lethielleux, 1896. 2d ed., 1927.

Corriveau, *Liturgy of Life*
　Corriveau, Raymond. *The Liturgy of Life: A Study in the Ethical Thought of St. Paul in His Letters to the Early Christian Communities.* Studia Travaux de recherche 25. Brussels: Desclée de Brouwer, 1970.

Cosby, "Paul's Persuasive Language"
　Cosby, Michael R. "Paul's Persuasive Language in Romans 5." Pp. 209–26 in Duane F. Watson, ed., *Persuasive Artistry: Studies in New Testament Rhetoric in Honor of George A. Kennedy.* JSNTSup 50. Sheffield: Sheffield Academic Press, 1991.

Cosgrove, *Elusive Israel*
　Cosgrove, Charles H. *Elusive Israel: The Puzzle of Election in Romans.* Louisville: Westminster/John Knox, 1997.

Cousar, *Theology of the Cross*
　Cousar, Charles B. *A Theology of the Cross. The Death of Jesus in the Pauline Letters.* OBT 24. Minneapolis: Fortress Press, 1990.

Cranfield
　Cranfield, C. E. B. *A Critical and Exegetical Commentary on the Epistle to the Romans.* 2 vols. ICC. Edinburgh: Clark, 1975–79.

Cranfield, *On Romans*
　Cranfield, C. E. B. *On Romans and Other New Testament Essays.* Edinburgh: T. & T. Clark, 1998.

Cremer, *Lexicon*
　Cremer, Hermann. *Biblico-Theological Lexicon of New Testament Greek.* Trans. W. Urwick. Edinburgh: T. & T. Clark, 1895.

Cullmann, *Confessions*
　Cullmann, Oscar. *The Earliest Christian Confessions.* Trans. J. K. S. Reid. London: Lutterworth, 1949.

Dabelstein, *Beurteilung*
　Dabelstein, Rolf. *Die Beurteilung der "Heiden" bei Paulus.* BBET 14. Bern: Lang, 1981.

Dabourne, *Purpose*
　Dabourne, Wendy. *Purpose and Cause in Pauline Exegesis: Romans 1.16–4.25 and a New Approach to the Letters.* SNTSMS 104. Cambridge: Cambridge University Press, 1999.

Dacquino, "In Christo"
　Dacquino, Pietro. "La formula paolina 'In Christo Jesù'." *Scuola cattolica* 87 (1959) 378–91.

Dahl, "Missionary Theology"
　Dahl, Nils A. "The Missionary Theology in the Epistle to the Romans." Pp. 70–87 in *Studies.*

Dahl, *Studies*
　Dahl, Nils A. *Studies in Paul: Theology for the Early Christian Mission.* Minneapolis: Augsburg, 1977.

Daniel and Maltomini, *Suppl. Mag. I, II*
　Daniel, Robert W., and Franco Maltomini, *Supplementum Magicum.* PapC 16.1–2. Paderborn: Schöningh, 1990–91.

Danker, *Benefactor*
　Danker, Frederick W. *Benefactor: Epigraphic Study of a Graeco-Roman and New Testament Semantic Field.* St. Louis: Clayton, 1982.

Danker, "Under Contract"
　Danker, Frederick W. "Under Contract: A Form-Critical Study of Linguistic Adaptation in Romans." Pp. 91–114 in E. M. Barth and R. E. Concroft, eds., *Festschrift to Honor F. Wilbur Gingrich, Lexicographer, Scholar, Teacher, and Committed Christian Layman.* Leiden: Brill, 1972.

Dassmann and Schöllgen, "Haus II (Hausgemeinschaft)"
　Dassmann, Ernst, and Georg Schöllgen. "Haus II (Hausgemeinschaft)." *RAC* 13 (1986) 801–905.

Daube, "Jewish Missionary Maxims"
　Daube, David. "Jewish Missionary Maxims in Paul," *Studia Theologica* 1 (1947): 158–69.

Dauge, *Barbare*
　Dauge, Yves Albert. *Le Barbare. Recherches sur la conception romaine de la barbarie et de la civilisation.* CLat 176. Brussels: Latomus, 1981.

Davies, *Faith and Obedience*
　Davies, Glenn N. *Faith and Obedience in Romans: A Study in Romans 1–4.* JSNTSup 39. Sheffield: Sheffield Academic Press, 1990.

Davies, *Paul*
　Davies, W. D. *Paul and Rabbinic Judaism: Some Rabbinic Elements in Pauline Theology.* London: SPCK, 1958.

Davies, "Paul and the People of Israel"
　Davies, W. D. "Paul and the People of Israel." *NTS* 16 (1969–70) 4–39.

Daxer, *Römer*
　Daxer, Heinrich. *Römer 1.18—2.10 im Verhältnis zu spätjüdischen Lehrauffassung.* Naumburg: Patz'sche, 1914.

Dehn, *Leben*
　Dehn, Günther. *Vom christlichen Leben. Auslegung des 12. und 13. Kapitels des Briefes an die Römer.* BibS(N) 6–7. Neukirchen-Vluyn: Neukirchener Verlag, 1954.

Deichgräber, *Gotteshymnus*
　Deichgräber, Reinhard. *Gotteshymnus und Christhymnus in der frühen Christenheit.* SUNT 5. Göttingen: Vandenhoeck & Ruprecht, 1967.

Deidun, *New Covenant*
　Deidun, Thomas. J. *New Covenant Morality in Paul.* AnBib 89. Rome: Biblical Institute, 1981.

Deissmann, *Light*
　Deissmann, Gustav Adolf. *Light from the Ancient East.* Trans. L. R. M. Strachan. Repr. Grand Rapids: Baker, 1965.

Deissmann, *Paul*
　Deissmann, Gustav Adolf. *St. Paul: A Study in Social and Religious History.* Trans. L. R. M. Strachan. London: Hodder & Stoughton, 1912.

Deissmann, *Studies*
　Deissmann, Gustav Adolf. *Bible Studies.* Edinburgh: T. & T. Clark, 1901.

Delling, *Studien*
　Delling, Gerhard. *Studien zum Neuen Testament und zum hellenistischen Judentum. Gesammelte Aufsätze 1950–1968.* Göttingen: Vandenhoeck & Ruprecht, 1970.

Delling, *Zeit und Endzeit*
　Delling, Gerhard. *Zeit und Endzeit. Zwei Vorlesungen zur Theologie des Neuen Testaments.* BibS(N) 58. Neukirchen-Vluyn: Neukirchener Verlag, 1970.

De Lorenzi, *Battesimo*
　De Lorenzi, Lorenzo, ed. *Battesimo e giustizia in Rom 6 e 8.* SMB 2. Rome: Abbazia S. Paolo, 1974.

De Lorenzi, *Dimensions*
　De Lorenzi, Lorenzo, ed. *Dimensions de la vie chrétienne (Rm 12–13).* SMB 4. Rome: Abbazia S. Paolo, 1979.

De Lorenzi, *Freedom and Love*
　De Lorenzi, Lorenzo, ed. *Freedom and Love: The Guide for Christian Life (1 Cor 8–10; Rom 14–15).* SMB 6. Rome: Abbazia S. Paolo, 1981.

De Lorenzi, *Israelfrage*
De Lorenzi, Lorenzo, ed. *Die Israelfrage nach Röm 9–11.* SMB 3. Rome: Abbazia S. Paolo, 1977.

De Lorenzi, *Law of the Spirit*
De Lorenzi, Lorenzo, ed. *The Law of the Spirit in Rom 7 and 8.* SMB 1. Rome: Abbazia S. Paolo, 1976.

De Lorenzi, *Paul de Tarse*
De Lorenzi, Lorenzo, ed. *Paul de Tarse: Apôtre du notre temps.* Rome: Abbazia S. Paolo, 1979.

De Lorenzi, *Romani*
De Lorenzi, Lorenzo. *Romani. Vivere nello Spirito di Cristo.* LOB 2.6. Brescia: Queriniana, 1983.

Denney
Denney, James. *Romans.* 2 vols. EGT. London: Hodder & Stoughton, 1900.

Denney, "Romans"
Denney, James. "St. Paul's Epistle to the Romans." Pp. 555–725 in vol. 2 of *The Expositor's Greek New Testament.* 1904. Repr. Grand Rapids: Eerdmans, 1970.

Denniston, *Particles*
Denniston, J. *The Greek Particles.* Oxford: Clarendon, 1934.

deSilva, *Honor*
deSilva, David A. *Honor, Patronage, Kinship and Purity: Unlocking New Testament Culture.* Downers Grove: InterVarsity Press, 2000.

deSilva, *Hope of Glory*
deSilva, David A. *The Hope of Glory: Honor Discourse and New Testament Interpretation.* Collegeville: Liturgical Press, 1999.

deSilva, *Introduction*
deSilva, David A. *An Introduction to the New Testament: Context, Methods, and Ministry Formation.* Downers Grove: InterVarsity Press, 2004.

de Wette
de Wette, Wilhelm Martin Leberecht. *Kurze Erklärung des Briefes an die Römer.* 4th ed. KEHNT 2.1. Leipzig: Wiedmann, 1847.

Dewey, "Σπανίαν"
Dewey, Arthur J. "Εἰς τὴν Σπανίαν: The Future and Paul." Pp. 321–49 in L. Bormann et al., eds., *Religious Propaganda and Missionary Competition in the New Testament World: Essays Honoring Dieter Georgi.* NovTSup 74. Leiden: Brill, 1994.

Dibelius, *Geisterwelt*
Dibelius, Martin. *Die Geisterwelt im Glauben des Paulus.* Göttingen: Vandenhoeck & Ruprecht, 1909.

Dibelius, "Vier Worte"
Dibelius, Martin. "Vier Worte des Römerbriefs, 5:5, 5:12, 8:10 und 11:30f." *SymBU* 3 (1944) 3–17.

Diehls and Kranz, *Vorsokratiker*
Diehls, H., and W. Kranz, *Die Fragmente der Vorsokratiker.* 2 vols. Berlin: Wiedmann, 1952.

Dietzfelbinger, *Berufung*
Dietzfelbinger, Christian. *Die Berufung des Paulus als Ursprung seiner Theologie.* WMANT 58. Neukirchen-Vluyn: Neukirchener Verlag, 1985.

Diezinger, "Unter Toten freigeworden"
Diezinger, Walter. "Unter Toten freigeworden. Eine Untersuchung zu Röm III–VIII." *NovT* 5 (1962) 272–98.

Dinkler, *EIRENE*
Dinkler, Erich. *EIRENE. Der urchristliche Friedensgedanke.* Heidelberg: Winter, 1973.

Dobbeler, *Glaube als Teilhabe*
Dobbeler, Axel von. *Glaube als Teilhabe: Historische und semanti-sche Grundlagen der paulinischen Theologie und Ekklesiologie des Glaubens.* WUNT 22. Tübingen: Mohr Siebeck, 1987.

Dodd, *Paul's Paradigmatic "I"*
Dodd, Brian. *Paul's Paradigmatic "I": Personal Example as Literary Strategy.* JSNTSup 177. Sheffield: Sheffield Academic Press, 1999.

Dodd
Dodd, C. H. *The Epistle of Paul to the Romans.* Rev. ed. MNTC. London: Collins, 1959.

Dodd, *New Testament Studies*
Dodd, C. H. *New Testament Studies.* Manchester: University of Manchester Press, 1953.

Donaldson, *Paul and the Gentiles*
Donaldson, Terence L. *Paul and the Gentiles: Remapping the Apostle's Convictional World.* Minneapolis: Fortress Press, 1997.

Donaldson, "Zealot and Convert"
Donaldson, Terence L. "Zealot and Convert: The Origin of Paul's Christ-Torah Antithesis." *CBQ* 51 (1989) 655–82.

Donfried, *Romans Debate*
Donfried, Karl P., ed. *The Romans Debate.* Rev. ed. Peabody: Hendrickson, 1991.

Donfried and Richardson, *Judaism and Christianity*
Donfried, Karl P., and Peter Richardson, eds., *Judaism and Christianity in First-Century Rome.* Grand Rapids: Eerdmans, 1998.

Doty, *Letters*
Doty, William G. *Letters in Primitive Christianity.* Philadelphia: Fortress Press, 1973.

Doughty, "Priority"
Doughty, Darrell J. "The Priority of χάρις." *NTS* 19 (1972–73) 163–80.

Douglas, *Purity and Danger*
Douglas, Mary. *Purity and Danger: An Analysis of Concepts of Pollution and Taboo.* London: Routledge & Kegan Paul, 1966.

Draper, "Colenso"
Draper, Jonathan A. "A 'Frontier' Reading of Romans: The Case of Bishop John William Colenso (1814–1883)." Pp. 57–82 in Khiok-Khng Yeo, ed., *Navigating Romans through Cultures: Challenging Readings by Charting a New Course.* London: T. & T. Clark International, 2004.

Du Plessis, *ΤΕΛΕΙΟΣ*
Du Plessis, Paul Johannes. *ΤΕΛΕΙΟΣ: The Idea of Perfection in the New Testament.* Kampen: Kok, 1959.

Dugandzig, *Ja Gottes*
Dugandzig, Ivan. *Das Ja Gottes in Christus. Studie zur Bedeutung des Alten Testaments für das Christusverständnis des Paulus.* FB 26. Würzburg: Echter Verlag, 1977.

Dunn
Dunn, James D. G. *Romans 1–8; Romans 9–16.* 2 vols. WBC 38a, 38b. Dallas: Word, 1988.

Dunn, *Christology*
Dunn, James D. G. *Christology in the Making: A New Testament Inquiry into the Origins of the Doctrine of the Incarnation.* Philadelphia: Westminster, 1980.

Dunn, "Covenant Theology?"
Dunn, James D. G. "Did Paul Have a Covenant Theology? Reflections on Romans 9:4 and 11:27." Pp. 3–19 in S. E. McGinn, ed., *Celebrating Romans: Template for Pauline Theology. Essays in Honor of Robert Jewett.* Grand Rapids: Eerdmans, 2004.

Dunn, *Jesus and the Spirit*
    Dunn, James D. G. *Jesus and the Spirit: A Study of the Religious and Charismatic Experience of Jesus and the First Christians as Reflected in the New Testament.* Philadelphia: Westminster, 1975.

Dunn, "Jesus Tradition"
    Dunn, James D. G. "Paul's Knowledge of the Jesus Tradition: The Evidence of Romans." Pp. 193–207 in K. Kertelge et al., eds., *Christus Bezeugen. Für Wolfgang Trilling.* Freiburg: Herder, 1990.

Dunn, "Paul's Epistle"
    Dunn, James D. G. "Paul's Epistle to the Romans: An Analysis of Structure and Argument." *ANRW* 2.25.4 (1987) 2842–90.

Dunn, "Perspective"
    Dunn, James D. G. "The New Perspective on Paul." *BJRL* 65 (1983) 95–122.

Dunn, *Theology of Paul*
    Dunn, James D. G. *The Theology of Paul the Apostle.* Grand Rapids: Eerdmans, 1998.

Dupont, *Gnosis*
    Dupont, Jacques. *Gnosis. La connaissance religieuse dans les épîtres de Saint Paul.* Paris: Gabalda, 1949.

Dupont, "Problème"
    Dupont, Jacques. "Le problème de la structure littéraire de l'Epître aux Romains." *RB* 62 (1955) 365–97.

Dupont, *Réconciliation*
    Dupont, Jacques. *La Réconciliation dans la théologie de Saint Paul.* ALBO 2.32. Bruges: Desclée de Brouwer, 1953.

Earl, *Age of Augustus*
    Earl, Donald. *The Age of Augustus.* New York: Crown, 1968.

Earnshaw, "Romans 7.1-4"
    Earnshaw, J. D. "Reconsidering Paul's Marriage Metaphor in Romans 7.1-4." *NTS* 40 (1994) 68–88.

Ebel, *Attraktivität*
    Ebel, Eva. *Die Attraktivität früher christlicher Gemeinden. Die Gemeinde von Korinth im Spiegel griechisch-römischer Vereine.* WUNT 178. Tübingen: Mohr Siebeck, 2004.

Eberhard, *Studien*
    Eberhard, Christian. *Studien zur Bedeutung der Opfer. Die Significanz von Blut- und Verbrennungsriten im kultischen Rahmen.* WMANT 94. Neukirchen-Vluyn: Neukirchener Verlag, 2002.

Ebner, *Peristasenkataloge bei Paulus*
    Ebner, Martin. *Leidenslisten und Apostelbrief: Untersuchungen zu Form, Motivik und Funktion der Peristasenkataloge bei Paulus.* FB 77. Würzburg: Echter Verlag, 1991.

Ebner and Heininger, *Exegese*
    Ebner, Martin, and Bernhard Heininger, *Exegese des Neuen Testaments. Ein Arbeitsbuch für Lehre und Praxis.* Paderborn: Schöningh, 2005.

Eckstein, *Syneidesis*
    Eckstein, Hans-Joachim. *Der Begriff Syneidesis bei Paulus.* WUNT 2.10. Tübingen: Mohr (Siebeck), 1983.

Edwards
    Edwards, James R. *Romans.* NIBC 6. Peabody: Hendrickson, 1992, 1995.

Ehrensperger, *Mutually Encouraged*
    Ehrensperger, Kathy. *That We May Be Mutually Encouraged: Feminism and the New Perspective in Pauline Studies.* London: T. & T. Clark, 2004.

Ehrman, *Historical Introduction*
    Ehrman, Bart D. *The New Testament: A Historical Introduction to the Early Christian Writings.* 2d ed. New York: Oxford University Press, 2000.

Ehrman, *Orthodox Corruption of Scripture*
    Ehrman, Bart D. *The Orthodox Corruption of Scripture: The Effects of Early Christological Controversies on the Text of the New Testament.* New York: Oxford University Press, 1993.

Eichholz, "Röm 1,8-15"
    Eichholz, Georg. "Der ökumenische und missionarische Horizont der Kirche. Eine exegetische Studie zu Röm 1,8-15." *EvTh* 21 (1961) 15–27.

Eichholz, *Umriss*
    Eichholz, Georg. *Die Theologie des Paulus im Umriss.* Neukirchen-Vluyn: Neukirchener Verlag, 1972.

Eisen, *Amtsträgerinnen*
    Eisen, Ute E. *Amtsträgerinnen im frühen Christentum. Epigraphische und literarische Studien.* FKDG 61. Göttingen: Vandenhoeck & Ruprecht, 1996.

Eisenbaum, "Genealogy in Romans"
    Eisenbaum, Pamela. "A Remedy for Having Been Born of Woman: Jesus, Gentiles, and Genealogy in Romans." *JBL* 123 (2004) 671–702.

Elliott, "Asceticism"
    Elliott, Neil. "Asceticism among the 'Weak' and 'Strong' in Romans 14–15." Pp. 231–51 in L. E. Vaage and V. L. Wimbush, eds., *Asceticism and the New Testament.* New York: Routledge, 1999.

Elliott, *Liberating Paul*
    Elliott, Neil. *Liberating Paul. The Justice of God and the Politics of the Apostle.* BSem 27. Maryknoll: Orbis, 1994.

Elliott, *Rhetoric of Romans*
    Elliott, Neil. *The Rhetoric of Romans: Argumentative Constraint and Strategy and Paul's Dialogue with Judaism.* JSNTSup 45. Sheffield: Sheffield Academic Press, 1990.

Ellis, *Paul's Use*
    Ellis, E. Earle. *Paul's Use of the Old Testament.* Grand Rapids: Eerdmans, 1957.

Ellis, *Prophecy*
    Ellis, E. Earle. *Prophecy and Hermeneutic in Early Christianity: New Testament Essays.* WUNT 8. Tübingen: Mohr Siebeck, 1978.

Ellison, *Mystery of Israel*
    Ellison, H. L. *The Mystery of Israel: An Exposition of Romans 9–11.* Grand Rapids: Eerdmans, 1966.

Engberg-Pedersen, "Reception"
    Engberg-Pedersen, Troels. "The Reception of Graeco-Roman Culture in the New Testament: The Case of Romans 7.7-25." Pp. 32–57 in M. Müller and H. Tronier, eds., *The New Testament as Reception.* JSNTSup 230; Copenhagen International Seminar 11. Sheffield: Sheffield Academic Press, 2002.

Engberg-Pedersen, *Stoics*
    Engberg-Pedersen, Troels. *Paul and the Stoics.* Edinburgh: T. & T. Clark, 2000.

Epp, *Junia*
    Epp, Eldon Jay. *Junia: The First Woman Apostle.* Minneapolis: Fortress Press, 2005.

Siker, *Disinheriting the Jews*
    Siker, Jeffrey S. *Disinheriting the Jews: Abraham in Early Christian Controversy*. Louisville: Westminster John Knox, 1991.

Slingerland, *Claudian Policymaking*
    Slingerland, H. Dixon. *Claudian Policymaking and the Early Imperial Repression of Judaism at Rome*. SFSHJ 160. Atlanta: Scholars Press, 1997.

Smallwood, *Jews*
    Smallwood, E. Mary. *The Jews under Roman Rule. From Pompey to Diocletian. A Study in Political Relations*. SJLA 20. Leiden: Brill, 1981.

Smiga, "Occasion of the Letter"
    Smiga, George. "Romans 12:1-2 and 15:30-32 and the Occasion of the Letter to the Romans." *CBQ* 53 (1991) 257–73.

Smiles, "Concept of 'Zeal'"
    Smiles, Vincent M. "The Concept of 'Zeal' in Second-Temple Judaism and Paul's Critique of It in Romans 10:2." *CBQ* 64 (2002) 282–99.

Smyth, *Grammar*
    Smyth, H. W. *Greek Grammar*. Rev. G. M. Messing. Cambridge: Harvard University Press, 1956.

Snyder, "Major Motifs"
    Snyder, Graydon F. "Major Motifs in the Interpretation of Paul's Letter to the Romans." Pp. 42–63 in S. E. McGinn, ed., *Celebrating Romans: Template for Pauline Theology. Essays in Honor of Robert Jewett*. Grand Rapids: Eerdmans, 2004.

Snyman, "Style"
    Snyman, A. H. "Style and the Rhetorical Situation of Romans 8.31-39." *NTS* 34 (1988) 218–31.

Söding, *Liebesgebot*
    Söding, Thomas. *Das Liebesgebot bei Paulus. Die Mahnung zur Agape im Rahmen der paulinischen Ethik*. NTAbh 26. Münster: Aschendorff, 1995.

Söding and Münch, *Methodenbuch*
    Söding, Thomas, and Christian Münch. *Wege der Schriftauslegung. Methodenbuch zum Neuen Testament*. Basel: Herder Freiburg, 1998.

Solin, *Beiträge*
    Solin, Heikki. *Beiträge zur Kenntnis der griechischen Personennamen in Rom*. Vol. 1. CHL 48. Helsinki: Societas Scientiarum Fennica, 1971.

Solin, "Juden und Syrer"
    Solin, Heikki. "Juden und Syrer im westlichen Teil der römischen Welt." *ANRW* II 29/2 (1983) 587–789.

Solin, *Namenbuch*
    Solin, Heikki. *Die griechischen Personennamen in Rom: Ein Namenbuch*. 3 vols. Berlin: de Gruyter, 1982.

Solin, *Sklavennamen*
    Solin, Heikki. *Die stadtrömischen Sklavennamen*. ForAS.B 2. Stuttgart: Steiner, 1996.

Song, *Diatribe*
    Song, Changwon. *Reading Romans as a Diatribe*. SBL 59. New York: Lang, 2004.

Stachowiak, *Chrestotes*
    Stachowiak, Lech Remigius. *Chrestotes. Ihre biblisch-theologische Entwicklung und Eigenart*. SF 17. Fribourg: Universitätsverlag, 1957.

Stählin, "Beteuerungsformeln"
    Stählin, Gustav. "Zum Gebrauch von Beteuerungsformeln im Neuen Testament." Pp. 115–43 in *Donum gratulatorium: Ethelbert Stauffer dem sechzigjahrigen in dankbarer Verehrung*. NovT 5.2–3. Leiden: Brill, 1962.

Stählin, *Skandalon*
    Stählin, Gustav. *Skandalon. Untersuchungen zur Geschichte eines biblischen Begriffs*. BFChTh 2.24. Gütersloh: Bertelsmann, 1930.

Stalder, *Werk*
    Stalder, Kurt. *Das Werk des Geistes in der Heiligung bei Paulus*. Zurich: EVZ Verlag, 1962.

Stambaugh, *Ancient Roman City*
    Stambaugh, John E. *The Ancient Roman City*. ASH. Baltimore: Johns Hopkins University Press, 1988.

Stanley, *Arguing*
    Stanley, Christopher D. *Arguing with Scripture. The Rhetoric of Citations in the Letters of Paul*. London: T. & T. Clark, 2004.

Stanley, *Scripture*
    Stanley, Christopher D. *Paul and the Language of Scripture. Citation Technique in the Pauline Epistles and Contemporary Literature*. SNTSMS 74. Cambridge: Cambridge University Press, 1992.

Stark, *Rise*
    Stark, Rodney. *The Rise of Christianity: A Sociologist Considers History*. Princeton: Princeton University Press, 1996.

Starnitzke, *Struktur*
    Starnitzke, Dierk. *Die Struktur paulinischen Denkens im Römerbrief. Eine linguistisch-logische Untersuchung*. BWANT 163. Stuttgart: Kohlhammer, 2004.

Stegner, "Midrash"
    Stegner, William R. "Romans 9:6-29—A Midrash." *JSNT* 22 (1984) 37–52.

Stendahl, *Final Account*
    Stendahl, Krister. *Final Account: Paul's Letter to the Romans*. Minneapolis: Fortress Press, 1995.

Stendahl, *Paul*
    Stendahl, Krister. *Paul Among Jews and Gentiles and Other Essays*. Philadelphia: Fortress Press, 1977.

Stöger, "Brüderliche Ordnung"
    Stöger, Alois. "Die brüderliche Ordnung unter Christen. Biblische Grundlegung." *TPQ* 117 (1969) 185–90.

Stowers, *Diatribe*
    Stowers, Stanley K. *The Diatribe and Paul's Letter to the Romans*. SBLDS 57. Chico: Scholars Press, 1981.

Stowers, *Letter*
    Stowers, Stanley K. *Letter Writing in Greco-Roman Antiquity*. Philadelphia: Westminster, 1986.

Stowers, *Rereading*
    Stowers, Stanley K. *A Rereading of Romans: Justice, Jews and Gentiles*. New Haven: Yale University Press, 1994.

Stowers, "Speech-in-Character"
    Stowers, Stanley K. "Romans 7.7-25 as a Speech-in-Character (προσωποποεία)." Pp. 180–202 in Troels Engberg-Pedersen, ed., *Paul in His Hellenistic Context*. Minneapolis: Fortress Press, 1995.

Strobel, "Begriff des 'Hauses'"
    Strobel, Adolf. "Der Begriff des 'Hauses' im griechischen und romischen Privatrecht." *ZNW* 56 (1965) 91–100.

Strobel, *Erkenntnis*
    Strobel, Adolf. *Erkenntnis und Bekenntnis der Sünde in neutestamentlicher Zeit*. Stuttgart: Calwer, 1968.

Strobel, "Röm 13"
    Strobel, Adolf. "Zum Verständnis von Röm 13." *ZNW* 47 (1956) 67–93.

Fridrichsen, "Paulusbriefen"
Fridrichsen, Anton. "Exegetisches zu den Paulusbriefen." *ThStK* 102 (1930) 291–301.

Friedrich, *Verkündigung*
Friedrich, Gerhard. *Die Verkündigung des Todes Jesu im Neuen Testament*. Neukirchen-Vluyn: Neukirchener Verlag, 1982.

Fritzsche
Fritzsche, Karl Friedrich August. *Pauli ad Romanos Epistola. Recensuit et cum commentariis perpetuis edidit*. 3 vols. Halle: Gebauer, 1836–43.

Fuchs, *Freiheit*
Fuchs, Ernst. *Die Freiheit des Glaubens. Römer 5–8 ausgelegt*. BEvTh 14. Munich: Kaiser, 1949.

Fuller, *Christology*
Fuller, Reginald H. *The Foundations of New Testament Christology*. New York: Scribner's, 1965.

Furnish, *Love*
Furnish, Victor P. *The Love Command in the New Testament*. Nashville: Abingdon, 1973.

Furnish, *Moral Teaching*
Furnish, Victor P. *The Moral Teaching of Paul*. Nashville: Abingdon, 1979.

Furnish, *Theology*
Furnish, Victor P. *Theology and Ethics in Paul*. Nashville: Abingdon, 1968.

Gager, *Origins*
Gager, John G. *The Origins of Anti-Semitism: Attitudes toward Judaism in Pagan and Christian Antiquity*. Oxford: Oxford University Press, 1983.

Gagnon, "Heart"
Gagnon, Robert A. J. "Heart of Wax and a Teaching That Stamps: τύπος διδαχῆς (Rom 6:17b) Once More," *JBL* 112 (1993) 667–87.

Gale, *Analogy*
Gale, Herbert Morrison. *The Use of Analogy in the Letters of Paul*. Philadelphia: Westminster, 1964.

Gamble, "Redaction"
Gamble, Harry Y., Jr. "The Redaction of the Pauline Letters and the Formation of the Pauline Corpus." *JBL* 94 (1975) 403–18.

Gamble, *Textual History*
Gamble, Harry Y., Jr. *The Textual History of the Letter to the Romans: A Study in Textual and Literary Criticism*. SD 42. Grand Rapids: Eerdmans, 1977.

Garlington, *Letter to the Romans*
Garlington, Don B. *Faith, Obedience, and Perseverance. Aspects of Paul's Letter to the Romans*. WUNT 79. Tübingen: Mohr-Siebeck, 1994.

Garlington, *Obedience*
Garlington, Don B. *'The Obedience of Faith': A Pauline Phrase in Historical Context*. WUNT 38. Tübingen: Mohr Siebeck, 1990.

Garlington, "Obedience of Faith"
Garlington, Don B. "The Obedience of Faith in the Letter to the Romans. Part II: The Obedience of Faith and Judgement by Works." *WTJ* 53 (1991) 47–72.

Gaston, *Paul*
Gaston, Lloyd. *Paul and the Torah*. Vancouver: University of British Columbia Press, 1987.

Gathercole, *Boasting*
Gathercole, Simon J. *Where Is Boasting? Early Jewish Soteriology and Paul's Response in Romans 1–5*. Grand Rapids: Eerdmans, 2002.

Gaugler
Gaugler, Ernst. *Der Römerbrief. 1 Teil. Kapitel 1–8*. Prophezei. Zurich: Zwingli, 1945. Repr. 1958. *2. Teil. Kapitel 9–15*. Prophezei. Zurich: Zwingli, 1952.

Gaugler, "Geist"
Gaugler, Ernst. "Der Geist und das Gebet der schwachen Gemeinde. Eine Auslegung von Röm. 8, 26–27." *IKZ* 51 (1961) 67–94.

Gaukesbrink, *Sühnetradition*
Gaukesbrink, Martin. *Sühnetradition bei Paulus. Rezeption und theologischer Stellenwert*. FB 82. Würzburg: Echter Verlag, 1999.

Gebauer, *Gebet*
Gebauer, Roland. *Das Gebet bei Paulus. Forschungsgeschichtliche und exegetische Studien*. TVGMS 349. Giessen: Brunnen, 1989.

Georgi, *Opponents*
Georgi, Dieter. *The Opponents of Paul in Second Corinthians*. Philadelphia: Fortress Press, 1986.

Georgi, *Remembering the Poor*
Georgi, Dieter. *Remembering the Poor. The History of Paul's Collection for Jerusalem*. Trans. I. Racz. Nashville: Abingdon, 1992.

Georgi, *Theocracy*
Georgi, Dieter. *Theocracy in Paul's Praxis and Theology*. Trans. D. E. Green. Minneapolis: Fortress Press, 1991.

Georgi, "Upside Down"
Georgi, Dieter. "God Turned Upside Down." Pp. 148–57 in R. A. Horsley, ed., *Paul and Empire: Religion and Power in Roman Imperial Society*. Harrisburg: Trinity Press International, 1997.

Gerleman, *Heidenapostel*
Gerleman, Gillis. *Der Heidenapostel. Ketzerische Erwägungen zur Predigt des Paulus zugleich ein Streifzug in der griechischen Mythologie*. SM 1987–1988: 2. Stockholm: Almqvist & Wiksell, 1989.

Gibbs, *Creation and Redemption*
Gibbs, John G. *Creation and Redemption: A Study in Pauline Theology*. NovTSup 26. Leiden: Brill, 1971.

Giblin, *God's Glory*
Giblin, Charles Homer. *In Hope of God's Glory: Pauline Theological Perspectives*. New York: Herder & Herder, 1970.

Giblin, "Written"
Giblin, Charles Homer. "'As It Is Written . . .'—A Basic Problem in Noematics and Its Relevance to Biblical Theology." *CBQ* 20 (1958) 327–53, 477–98.

Gibson, "Dying Formula"
Gibson, Jeffrey B. "Paul's 'Dying Formula': Prolegomena to an Understanding of Its Import and Significance." Pp. 20–41 in S. E. McGinn, ed., *Celebrating Romans: Template for Pauline Theology. Essays in Honor of Robert Jewett*. Grand Rapids: Eerdmans, 2004.

Gieniusz, "Rom 7,1-6"
Gieniusz, Andrzej. "Rom 7,1-6: Lack of Imagination? Function of the Passage in the Argumentation of Rom 6,1–7,6." *Bib* 74 (1993) 389–98.

Gifford
Gifford, Edwin Hamilton. *The Epistle of St. Paul to the Romans with Notes and Introduction*. Speaker's Commentary. London: Murray, 1881.

Gignac, *Romains 9–11*
  Gignac, Alain. *Juifs et Chrétiens à l'École de Paul de Tarse: Enjeux identitaires et éthiques d'une lecture de Romains 9–11*. ColSB. Montreal: Médiaspaul, 1999.

Gilmore, *Honor and Shame*
  Gilmore, David D., ed. *Honor and Shame and the Unity of the Mediterranean*. Washington: American Anthropological Association, 1987.

Glad, *Paul and Philodemus*
  Glad, Clarence E. *Paul and Philodemus: Adaptability in Epicurean and Early Christian Psychagogy*. NovTSup 81. Leiden: Brill, 1995.

Gloer, "Homologies and Hymns"
  Gloer, W. Hulitt. "Homologies and Hymns in the New Testament: Form, Content, and Criteria for Identification." *PRS* 11 (1984) 115–32.

Godet
  Godet, Fréderic. *Commentary on St. Paul's Epistle to the Romans*. Rev. and ed. T. W. Chambers. 1883. Repr. Grand Rapids: Kregel, 1977.

Goltz, *Gebet*
  Goltz, Eduard Alexander Freiherr von der. *Das Gebet in der ältesten Christenheit. Eine geschichtliche Untersuchung*. Leipzig: Hinrichs, 1901.

Goppelt, *Christologie und Ethik*
  Goppelt, Leonhard. *Christologie und Ethik. Aufsätze zum Neuen Testament*. Göttingen: Vandenhoeck & Ruprecht, 1968.

Goppelt, *Theology*
  Goppelt, Leonhard. *Theology of the New Testament*. Vol. 2. Grand Rapids: Eerdmans, 1982.

Goppelt, *Typos*
  Goppelt, Leonhard. *Typos: The Typological Interpretation of the Old Testament in the New*. Trans. D. H. Madvig. Grand Rapids: Eerdmans, 1982.

Gore
  Gore, Charles. *St. Paul's Epistle to the Romans: A Practical Exposition*. 2 vols. London: Murray, 1920.

Gorman, *Cruciformity*
  Gorman, Michael J. *Cruciformity: Paul's Narrative Spirituality of the Cross*. Grand Rapids: Eerdmans, 2001.

Grabbe, *Judaism*
  Grabbe, Leslie L. *Judaism from Cyrus to Hadrian*. Vol. 2. *The Roman Period*. Minneapolis: Fortress Press, 1992.

Gräbe, *Power of God*
  Gräbe, Petrus J. *The Power of God in Paul's Letters*. WUNT 2.123. Tübingen: Mohr Siebeck, 2000.

Grabner-Haider, *Paraklese*
  Grabner-Haider, Anton. *Paraklese und Eschatologie bei Paulus: Mensch und Welt im Anspruch der Zukunft Gottes*. NTAbh 4. Münster: Aschendorff, 1968.

Grappe, "Typologie adamique"
  Grappe, Christian. "Qui me délivera de ce corps de mort? L'Esprit de vie! Romains 7,24 et 8,2 comme éléments de typologie adamique." *Bib* 83 (2002) 472–92.

Greenlee, *Textual Criticism*
  Greenlee, J. Harold. *Introduction to New Testament Textual Criticism*. Grand Rapids: Eerdmans, 1964.

Grieb, *Story of Romans*
  Grieb, Katherine A. *The Story of Romans: A Narrative Defense of God's Righteousness*. Louisville: Westminster John Knox, 2002.

Griffin, *Nero*
  Griffin, Miriam T. *Nero: The End of a Dynasty*. New Haven: Yale University Press, 1984.

Grotius
  Grotius, Hugo (Huig van Groot). *Annotationes in Novum Testamentum*. 2 vols. 1644. Repr. Leipzig: Ptochotrophium, 1755–57.

Grundmann, "Stehen"
  Grundmann, Walter. "Stehen und Fallen in qumranischen und neutestamentlichen Schriftum." Pp. 147–66 in H. Bardtke, ed., *Qumran-Probleme*. SSA 42. Berlin: Deutsche Akademie der Wissenschaft, 1963.

Guerra, *Apologetic Tradition*
  Guerra, Anthony J. *Romans and the Apologetic Tradition. The Purpose, Genre and Audience of Paul's Letter*. SNTSMS 81. Cambridge: Cambridge University Press, 1995.

Guerra, "Romans 4"
  Guerra, Anthony J. "Romans 4 as Apologetic Theology." *HTR* 81 (1988) 251–70.

Gülzow, *Christentum und Sklaverei*
  Gülzow, Henneke. *Christentum und Sklaverei in den ersten drei Jahrhunderten*. Bonn: Rudolf Habelt, 1969.

Gundry, "Moral Frustration"
  Gundry, Robert H. "The Moral Frustration of Paul before His Conversion: Sexual Lust in Romans 7:7-25." Pp. 228–45 in D. A. Hagner and M. J. Harris, eds., *Pauline Studies: Essays Presented to Professor F. F. Bruce on His 70th Birthday*. Grand Rapids: Eerdmans, 1980.

Gundry, "Rhetoric of Surprise"
  Gundry, Robert H. "A Breaking of Expectations: The Rhetoric of Surprise in Paul's Letter to the Romans." Pp. 254–70 in S. K. Soderlund and N. T. Wright, eds., *Romans and the People of God: Essays in Honor of Gordon D. Fee on the Occasion of His 65th Birthday*. Grand Rapids: Eerdmans, 1999.

Gundry, *Sōma*
  Gundry, Robert H. *Sōma in Biblical Theology: With Emphasis on Pauline Anthropology*. SMTSMS 29. Cambridge: Cambridge University Press, 1976.

Güting and Mealand, *Asyndeton*
  Güting, Eberhard W., and David Mealand. *Asyndeton in Paul: A Text-Critical and Statistical Enquiry into Pauline Style*. SBEC 39. Lewiston: Mellen, 1998.

Gutjahr
  Gutjahr, Franz S. *Der Brief an die Römer*. 2 vols. Die Briefe des heiligen Apostels Paulus 2. Graz: Styria, 1923–27.

Gyllenberg, *Rechtfertigung*
  Gyllenberg, Rafael. *Rechtfertigung und Altes Testament bei Paulus*. Stuttgart: Kohlhammer, 1973.

Haacker
  Haacker, Klaus. *Der Brief des Paulus an die Römer*. ThNT 6. Leipzig: Evangelisches Verlagsanstalt, 1999.

Haacker, "Erwählung Israels"
  Haacker, Klaus. "Das Evangelium Gottes und die Erwählung Israels. Zum Beitrag des Römerbriefs zur Erneuerung des Verhältnisses zwischen Christen und Juden." *ThBei* 13 (1982) 59–72.

xlvi

Haacker, "Friedensmemorandum"
   Haacker, Klaus. "Der Römerbrief als Friedensmemorandum."
   NTS 36 (1990) 25–41.
Haacker, "Probleme"
   Haacker, Klaus. "Exegetische Probleme des Römerbriefs." *NovT*
   20 (1978) 1–21.
Hagen, "Deutero-Pauline Glosses"
   Hagen, Wayne H. "Two Deutero-Pauline Glosses in Romans 6."
   ExpT 92 (1980–81) 364–67.
Hahn, "Apostolat"
   Hahn, Ferdinand. "Der Apostolat im Urchristentum. Seine
   Eigenart und seine Voraussetzungen." *KD* 20 (1974) 54–77.
Hahn, "Gesetzesverständnis"
   Hahn, Ferdinand. "Das Gesetzesverständnis im Römer- und
   Galaterbrief." *ZNW* 67 (1976) 29–63.
Hahn, *Titles*
   Hahn, Ferdinand. *The Titles of Jesus in Christology: Their History
   in Early Christianity*. Trans. H. Knight and G. Ogg. New York:
   World, 1969.
Hahn, *Verständnis der Mission*
   Hahn, Ferdinand. *Das Verständnis der Mission im Neuen Testament*.
   Neukirchen-Vluyn: Neukirchener Verlag, 1963. Trans. *Mission in
   the New Testament*. Trans. Frank Clarke. SBT 1/47. London:
   SCM, 1965.
Hainz, *Ekklesia*
   Hainz, Josef. *Ekklesia. Strukturen paulinischer Gemeinde-Theologie
   und Gemeinde-Ordnung*. BU 9. Regensburg: Pustet, 1972.
Hainz, *Koinonia*
   Hainz, Josef. *Koinonia. "Kirche" als Gemeinschaft bei Paulus*. BU
   16. Regensburg: Pustet, 1982.
Haldane
   Haldane, Robert. *Exposition of the Epistle to the Romans: With
   Remarks on the Commentaries of Dr. MacKnight, Moses Stuart, and
   Professor Tholuck*. 3 vols. 1842. Repr. in 1 vol. *Commentary on
   Romans*. Grand Rapids: Kregel, 1988.
Halton, "Church"
   Halton, Thomas. "Church." *EEC* 1 (1997) 253–56.
Hamerton-Kelly, *Cross*
   Hamerton-Kelly, Robert G. *Sacred Violence: Paul's Hermeneutic of
   the Cross*. Minneapolis: Fortress Press, 1992.
Hamerton-Kelly, "Sacred Violence"
   Hamerton-Kelly, Robert G. "Sacred Violence and Sinful Desire:
   Paul's Interpretation of Adam's Sin in the Letter to the
   Romans." Pp. 35–54 in R. T. Fortna and B. R. Gaventa, eds., *The
   Conversation Continues. Studies in Paul and John. In Honor of J.
   Louis Martyn*. Nashville: Abingdon, 1990.
Hanson, *Interpretation*
   Hanson, Anthony T. *The New Testament Interpretation of Scripture*.
   London: SPCK, 1980.
Hanson, *Studies*
   Hanson, Anthony T. *Studies in Paul's Technique and Theology*.
   London: SPCK, 1974.
Hanson, *Wrath*
   Hanson, Anthony T. *The Wrath of the Lamb*. London: SPCK,
   1957.
Harder, *Gebet*
   Harder, Günther. *Paulus und das Gebet*. NTF 10. Gütersloh:
   Bertelsmann, 1936.

Harrill, *Slaves*
   Harrill, J. Albert. *Slaves in the New Testament: Literary, Social, and
   Moral Dimensions*. Minneapolis: Fortress Press, 2006.
Harrison, *Language of Grace*
   Harrison, James R. *Paul's Language of Grace in Its Graeco-Roman
   Context*. WUNT 172. Tübingen: Mohr Siebeck, 2003.
Harrisville
   Harrisville, Roy A. *Romans*. Augsburg Commentary on the New
   Testament. Minneapolis: Augsburg, 1980.
Hartman, "Baptism"
   Hartman, Lars. "Baptism." *ABD* 1 (1992) 587–88.
Harvey, *True Israel*
   Harvey, Graham. *The True Israel: Uses of the Names Jew, Hebrew,
   and Israel in Ancient Jewish and Early Christian Literature*. AGJU
   35. Leiden: Brill, 1996.
Harvey, *Listening*
   Harvey, John D. *Listening to the Text: Oral Patterning in Paul's
   Letters*. EThSt. Grand Rapids: Baker, 1998.
Hatch and Redpath, *Concordance*
   Hatch, Edwin, and Henry A. Redpath. *A Concordance to the
   Septuagint and the Other Greek Versions of the Old Testament*. 3 vols.
   Oxford: Clarendon, 1897.
Haußleiter, *Vegetarismus*
   Haußleiter, Johannes. *Der Vegetarismus in der Antike*. RVV 24.
   Berlin: Töpelmann, 1935.
Hay, *Glory at the Right Hand*
   Hay, David M. *Glory at the Right Hand: Psalm 110 in Early
   Christianity*. SBLMS 18. Abingdon: Nashville, 1973.
Hays, *Echoes*
   Hays, Richard B. *Echoes of Scripture in the Letters of Paul*. New
   Haven: Yale University Press, 1989.
Hays, "Righteous One"
   Hays, Richard B. "'The Righteous One' as Eschatological
   Deliverer: A Case Study in Paul's Apocalyptic Hermeneutics."
   Pp. 191–215 in J. Marcus and M. L. Soards, eds., *Apocalyptic and
   the New Testament*." Sheffield: JSOT Press, 1988.
Hays, "Romans 3"
   Hays, Richard B. "Psalm 143 and the Logic of Romans 3." *JBL*
   99 (1980) 107–15.
Hays, "Romans 3–4"
   Hays, Richard B. "Three Dramatic Roles: The Law in Romans
   3–4." Pp. 151–64 in J. D. G. Dunn, ed., *Paul and the Mosaic Law:
   The Third Durham-Tübingen Symposium on Earliest Christianity and
   Judaism*. WUNT 89. Tübingen: Mohr-Siebeck, 1996.
Heckel, *Segen*
   Heckel, Ulrich. *Segen im Neuen Testament. Begriff, Formeln, Gesten.
   Mit einem praktisch-theologischen Ausblick*. WUNT 150. Tübingen:
   Mohr Siebeck, 2002.
Heil, *Ablehnung der Speisegebote*
   Heil, Christoph. *Die Ablehnung der Speisegebote durch Paulus. Zur
   Frage nach der Stellung des Apostels zum Gesetz*. BBB 96. Weinheim:
   Beltz Athenäum, 1994.
Heil
   Heil, John Paul. *Paul's Letter to the Romans. A Reader-Response
   Commentary*. New York: Paulist Press, 1987.

Heiligenthal, *Werke*
　Heiligenthal, Roman. *Werke als Zeichen. Untersuchungen zur Bedeutung der menschlichen Taten im Frühjudentum, Neuen Testament und Frühchristentum.* WUNT 2.9. Tübingen: Mohr Siebeck, 1983.

Heine, *Leibhafter Glaube*
　Heine, Susanne. *Leibhafter Glaube. Ein Beitrag zum Verständnis der theologischen Konzeption des Paulus.* Vienna: Herder, 1976.

Hellholm, "Romans 6"
　Hellholm, David. "Enthymemic Argumentation in Paul: The Case of Romans 6." Pp. 119–79 in Troels Engberg-Pedersen, ed., *Paul in His Hellenistic Context.* Minneapolis: Fortress Press, 1995.

Hengel, *Atonement*
　Hengel, Martin. *The Atonement: The Origins of the Doctrine in the New Testament.* Trans. J. Bowden. London: SCM, 1981.

Hengel, *Crucifixion.*
　Hengel, Martin. *Crucifixion in the Ancient World and the Folly of the Message of the Cross.* Trans. J. Bowden. London: SCM, 1977.

Hengel, *Judaism and Hellenism*
　Hengel, Martin. *Judaism and Hellenism.* Trans. J. Bowden. 2 vols. Philadelphia: Fortress Press, 1974.

Hengel, *Juden, Griechen und Barbaren*
　Hengel, Martin. *Juden, Griechen und Barbaren. Aspekte der Hellenisieruing des Judentums in vorchristlicher Zeit.* SBS 76. Stuttgart: KBW, 1976.

Hengel, *Zealots*
　Hengel, Martin. *The Zealots: Investigations into the Jewish Freedom Movement in the Period from Herod I until 70 A.D.* Trans. D. Smith. Edinburgh: T. & T. Clark, 1989.

Hengel
　Hengel, Wessel Albert van. *Interpretatio Epistolae Pauli ad Romanos.* 2 vols. Silvae Ducis: Müller, 1855–59.

Hermann, *Kyrios und Pneuma*
　Hermann, Ingo. *Kyrios und Pneuma. Studien zur Christologie der paulinischen Hauptbriefe.* SANT 2. Munich: Kösel, 1961.

Herold, *Zorn*
　Herold, Gerhard. *Zorn und Gerechtigkeit Gottes bei Paulus. Eine Untersuchung zu Röm 1.16-18.* EHS 23.14. Bern/Frankfurt: Lang, 1973.

Hester, *Inheritance*
　Hester, James D. *Paul's Concept of Inheritance. A Contribution to the Understanding of Heilsgeschichte.* SJTOP No 14. Edinburgh: Oliver & Boyd, 1968.

Hill, *Greek*
　Hill, David. *Greek Words and Hebrew Meanings.* SNTSMS 5. Cambridge: Cambridge University Press, 1967.

Hock, *Social Context*
　Hock, Ronald F. *The Social Context of Paul's Ministry: Tentmaking and Apostleship.* Philadelphia: Fortress Press, 1980.

Hoffmann, *Toten*
　Hoffmann, Paul. *Die Toten in Christus. Eine Religionsgeschichtliche und exegetische Untersuchung zur paulinischen Eschatologie.* 3d ed. NTA 2. Münster: Aschendorff, 1978.

Hofius, "Adam-Christus-Antithese"
　Hofius, Otfried. "Die Adam-Christus-Antithese und das Gesetz. Erwägungen zu Röm 5,12-21." Pp. 165–206 in J. D. G. Dunn, ed., *Paul and the Mosaic Law: The Third Durham-Tübingen Research Symposium on Earliest Christianity and*

Judaism (Durham, September, 1994). WUNT 89. Tübingen: Mohr Siebeck, 1996.

Hofius, "Evangelium und Israel"
　Hofius, Otfried. "Das Evangelium und Israel. Erwägungen zu Röm 9–11." *ZThK* 83 (1986) 297–324.

Hofius, *Paulusstudien*
　Hofius, Otfried. *Paulusstudien.* WUNT 51. 2d ed. Tübingen: Mohr Siebeck, 1994.

Hofmann
　Hofmann, J. C. K. von. "Der Brief an die Römer." Pp. 1–633 in vol. 3 of *Die Heilige Schrift Neuen Testaments.* 11 vols. Nördlingen: Beck, 1868.

Holladay, *Critical Introduction*
　Holladay, Carl. R. *A Critical Introduction to the New Testament: Interpreting the Message and Meaning of Jesus Christ.* Nashville: Abingdon, 2005.

Holladay, *Orphica*
　Holladay, Carl R. *Fragments from Hellenistic-Jewish Authors.* Vol. 4. *Orphica.* SBLTT 40; SBLPS 14. Atlanta: Scholars Press, 1996.

Holladay, *Concise Hebrew and Aramaic Lexicon*
　Holladay, William L. *A Concise Hebrew and Aramaic Lexicon of the Old Testament.* Grand Rapids: Eerdmans, 1971.

Holloway, "Paul's Pointed Prose"
　Holloway, Paul A. "Paul's Pointed Prose: The *Sententia* in Roman Rhetoric and Paul." *NovT* 40 (1998) 32–53.

Holmberg, *Paul and Power*
　Holmberg, Bengt. *Paul and Power: The Structure of Authority in the Primitive Church as Reflected in the Pauline Epistles.* Philadelphia: Fortress Press, 1980.

Hommel, "7. Kapitel"
　Hommel, Hildebrecht. "Das 7. Kapitel des Römerbriefs im Licht antiker Überlieferung." Repr. with additions as pp. 141–73 in vol. 2 of H. Hommel. *Sebasmata. Studien zur antiken Religionsgeschichte und zum frühen Christentum.* Tübingen: Mohr [Siebeck], 1983–84.

Hooker, "Adam"
　Hooker, Morna D. "Adam in Romans 1." *NTS* 6 (1959–60) 297–306.

Hooker, *Paul*
　Hooker, Morna D. *From Adam to Christ: Essays on Paul.* Cambridge: University Press, 1990.

Horn, *Angeld des Geistes*
　Horn, Friedrich Wilhelm. *Das Angeld des Geistes. Studien zur paulinischen Pneumatologie.* FRLANT 154. Göttingen: Vandenhoeck & Ruprecht, 1992.

Horsley, "Personal News"
　Horsley, G. H. R. "Personal News and Greetings in a Letter." *NDIEC* 1 (1981) 54–56.

Horsley, *Paul and Empire*
　Horsley, Richard A., ed. *Paul and Empire: Religion and Power in Roman Imperial Society.* Harrisburg: Trinity Press International, 1997.

Horsley, *Paul and Politics*
　Horsley, Richard A., ed. *Paul and Politics: Ekklesia, Israel, Imperium, Interpretation: Essays in Honor of Krister Stendahl.* Harrisburg: Trinity Press International, 2000.

Hubbard, *New Creation*
　Hubbard, Moyer V. *New Creation in Paul's Letters and Thought.* SNTSMS 119. Cambridge: Cambridge University Press, 2002.

Hübner, *Gottes Ich und Israel*
Hübner, Hans. *Gottes Ich und Israel. Zum Schriftgebrauch des Paulus in Römer 9–11*. Göttingen: Vandenhoeck & Ruprecht, 1984.

Hübner, *Law*
Hübner, Hans. *Law in Paul's Thought*. Trans. J. C. G. Grieg. Edinburgh: T. & T. Clark, 1984.

Hübner, *Theologie des Paulus*
Hübner, Hans. *Biblische Theologie des Neuen Testaments*. Vol. 2. *Die Theologie des Paulus und ihre neutestamentliche Wirkungsgeschichte*. Göttingen: Vandenhoeck & Ruprecht, 1993.

Huby
Huby, Joseph. *Saint Paul. Épitre aux Romains. Traduction et commentaire*. Verbum Salutis 10. Paris: Beauchesne, 1940.

Hudson, "Diakonia"
Hudson, D. F. "Diakonia and Its Cognates in the New Testament." *ITJ* 14 (1965) 138–47.

Hultgren, *Gospel*
Hultgren, Arlan J. *Paul's Gospel and Mission: The Outlook from His Letter to the Romans*. Philadelphia: Fortress Press, 1985.

Hunter, *Predecessors*
Hunter, Archibald M. *Paul and His Predecessors*. 2d ed. London: SCM, 1961.

Hurtado, "Doxology"
Hurtado, Larry W. "The Doxology at the End of Romans." Pp. 185–99 in E. J. Epp and G. D. Fee, eds., *New Testament Textual Criticism: Its Significance for Exegesis: Essays in Honour of Bruce M. Metzger*. Oxford: Clarendon, 1981.

Hurtado, *Lord Jesus Christ*
Hurtado, Larry W. *Lord Jesus Christ: Devotion to Jesus in Earliest Christianity*. Grand Rapids: Eerdmans, 2003.

Hurtado, *One God*
Hurtado, Larry W. *One God, One Lord: Early Christian Devotion and Ancient Jewish Monotheism*. 2d ed. Edinburgh: T. & T. Clark, 1998.

Incigneri, *Gospel to the Romans*
Incigneri, Brian J. *The Gospel to the Romans: The Setting and Rhetoric of Mark's Gospel*. BibIntSer 65. Leiden: Brill, 2003.

Jaeger, *Paideia*
Jaeger, Werner. *Paideia: The Ideals of Greek Culture*. Trans. Gilbert Highet. 3 vols. New York: Oxford University Press, 1943–45.

Jameson, Jordan, and Kotansky, *Lex Sacra*
Jameson, M. H., D. R. Jordan, and R. D. Kotansky, *A Lex Sacra from Selinous*. GRBM 11. Durham: Duke University Press, 1993.

Jeffers, *Conflict at Rome*
Jeffers, James S. *Conflict at Rome: Social Order and Hierarchy in Early Christianity*. Minneapolis: Fortress Press, 1991.

Jeffers, "First-Century Rome"
Jeffers, James S. "Jewish and Christian Families in First-Century Rome." Pp. 128–50 in K. P. Donfried and P. Richardson, eds., *Judaism and Christianity in First-Century Rome*. Grand Rapids: Eerdmans, 1998.

Jeremias, *Abba*
Jeremias, Joachim. *Abba: Studien zur neutestamentlichen Theologie und Zeitgeschichte*. Göttingen: Vandenhoeck & Ruprecht, 1966.

Jeremias, *Central Message*
Jeremias, Joachim. *The Central Message of the New Testament*. London: SCM, 1965.

Jeremias, "Chiasmus"
Jeremias, Joachim. "Chiasmus in den Paulusbriefen." Pp. 276–90 in J. Jeremias, *Abba. Studien zur neutestamentlichen Theologie und Zeitgeschichte*. Göttingen: Vandenhoeck & Ruprecht, 1966.

Jeremias, "Gedankenführung"
Jeremias, Joachim. "Zur Gedankenführung in den paulinischen Briefen." Pp. 146–54 in J. N. Sevenster and W. C. van Unnik, eds., *Studia Paulina in honorem Johannis de Zwaan septuagenarii*. Haarlem: Bohn, 1953. Repr. pp. 269–72 in J. Jeremias. *Abba. Studien zur neutestamentlichen Theologie und Zeitgeschichte*. Göttingen: Vandenhoeck & Ruprecht, 1966.

Jeremias, "Röm 1:22-32"
Jeremias, Joachim. "Zu Röm 1:22-32." *ZNW* 45 (1954) 119–21.

Jeremias, "Römer 11.25-36"
Jeremias, Joachim. "Einige vorwiegend sprachliche Beobachtungen zur Römer 11.25-36." Pp. 193–203 in Lorenzo De Lorenzi, ed., *Die Israelfrage nach Röm 9–11*. SMB 3. Rome: Abbazia S. Paolo, 1977

Jervell, *Imago Dei*
Jervell, Jacob. *Imago Dei. Gen 1,26f im Spätjudentum, in der Gnosis und in der paulinischen Briefen*. Göttingen: Vandenhoeck & Ruprecht, 1960.

Jervell, "Letter to Jerusalem"
Jervell, Jakob. "The Letter to Jerusalem." Pp. 53–64 in K. P. Donfried, ed., *The Romans Debate*. Rev ed. Peabody: Hendrickson, 1991.

Jervis, "Commandment"
Jervis, L. Ann. "'The Commandment Which Is for Life' (Romans 7.10): Sin's Use of the Obedience of Faith." *JSNT* 27 (2004) 193–216.

Jervis, *Purpose*
Jervis, L. Ann. *The Purpose of Romans: A Comparative Letter Structure Investigation*. JSNTSup 55. Sheffield: Sheffield Academic Press, 1991.

Jewett
Jewett, Robert. *Romans*. Cokesbury Basic Bible Commentary 22. Nashville: Graded Press, 1988.

Jewett, "Ambassadorial Letter"
Jewett, Robert. "Romans as an Ambassadorial Letter." *Int* 36 (1982) 5–20.

Jewett, *Apostle to America*
Jewett, Robert. *Paul the Apostle to America: Cultural Trends and Pauline Scholarship*. Louisville: Westminster/John Knox, 1994.

Jewett, "Apportioned Spirit"
Jewett, Robert. "The Question of the 'Apportioned Spirit' in Paul's Letters." Pp. 193–206 in G. N. Stanton, B. W. Longenecker, and S. C. Barton, eds., *The Holy Spirit and Christian Origins: Essays in Honor of James D. G. Dunn*. Grand Rapids: Eerdmans, 2004.

Jewett, *Chronology*
Jewett, Robert. *A Chronology of Paul's Life*. Philadelphia: Fortress Press, 1979.

Jewett, "Conflicting Movements"
Jewett, Robert. "Conflicting Movements in the Early Church as Reflected in Philippians," *NovT* 12 (1970) 363–90.

Jewett, "Ecumenical Theology"
Jewett, Robert. "Ecumenical Theology for the Sake of Mission: Rom 1:1-17 + 15:14—16:24." Pp. 89–108 in vol. 3 of D. M. Hay and E. E. Johnson, eds., *Pauline Theology*. Minneapolis: Fortress Press, 1995.

Jewett, "Following the Argument"
Jewett, Robert. "Following the Argument of Romans." Pp. 265–77 in K. P. Donfried, ed., *The Romans Debate*. Rev. ed. Peabody: Hendrickson, 1991.

Jewett, "Gospel and Commensality"
Jewett, Robert. "Gospel and Commensality: Social and Theological Implications of Galatians 2.14," in *Gospel in Paul: Studies on Corinthians, Galatians and Romans for Richard N. Longenecker,* edited by A. Jervis and P. Richardson, JSNTSup 108 (Sheffield: Sheffield Academic Press, 1994), 240-52.

Jewett, "Homiletic Benediction"
Jewett, Robert. "The Form and Function of the Homiletic Benediction." *ATR* 51 (1969) 18-34.

Jewett, "Honor and Shame"
Jewett, Robert. "Honor and Shame in the Argument of Romans." Pp. 257–72 in A. Brown, G. F. Snyder, and V. Wiles, eds., *Putting Body and Soul Together: Essays in Honor of Robin Scroggs*. Valley Forge: Trinity Press International, 1997.

Jewett, "Law"
Jewett, Robert. "The Law and the Coexistence of Jews and Gentiles in Romans." *Int* 39 (1985) 341–56.

Jewett, "Love Feast"
Jewett, Robert. "Are There Allusions to the Love Feast in Rom 13:8-10?" Pp. 265–78 in J. V. Hills et al., eds., *Common Life in the Early Church: Essays Honoring Graydon F. Snyder*. Valley Forge: Trinity Press International, 1998.

Jewett, "Numerical Sequences"
Jewett, Robert. "Numerical Sequences in Paul's Letter to the Romans." Pp. 227–45 in D. F. Watson, ed., *Persuasive Artistry: Studies in New Testament Rhetoric in Honor of George A. Kennedy*. Sheffield: JSOT Press, 1991. "Numerical Sequences"

Jewett, "Rom 1:24-27"
Jewett, Robert. "The Social Context and Implications of Homoerotic References in Rom 1:24-27." Pp. 223–41 in D. Balch, ed., *Homosexuality, Science, and the "Plain Sense" of Scripture*. Grand Rapids: Eerdmans, 2000.

Jewett, "Romans since Barth"
Jewett, Robert. "Major Impulses in the Theological Interpretation of Romans since Barth." *Int* 34 (1980) 17-31.

Jewett, *Saint Paul at the Movies*
Jewett, Robert. *Saint Paul at the Movies: The Apostle's Dialogue with American Culture*. Louisville: Westminster/John Knox, 1993.

Jewett, *Saint Paul Returns to the Movies*
Jewett, Robert. *Saint Paul Returns to the Movies: Triumph over Shame*. Grand Rapids: Eerdmans, 1999.

Jewett, "Sexual Liberation"
Jewett, Robert. "The Sexual Liberation of the Apostle Paul." *JAAR Supplement* 47 (1979) 55–87.

Jewett, "Spanish Mission"
Jewett, Robert. "Paul, Phoebe, and the Spanish Mission." Pp. 144–64 in P. Borgen et al., eds., *The Social World of Formative Christianity and Judaism: Essays in Tribute to Howard Clark Kee*. Philadelphia: Fortress Press, 1988.

Jewett, "Tenement Churches"
Jewett, Robert. "Tenement Churches and Communal Meals in the Early Church: The Implications of a Form-Critical Analysis of 2 Thess 3:10." *BR* 38 (1993) 23-43.

Jewett, *Terms*
Jewett, Robert. *Paul's Anthropological Terms: A Study of Their Use in Conflict Situations*. AGJU 10. Leiden: Brill, 1971.

Jewett, *Thessalonian Correspondence*
Jewett, Robert. *The Thessalonian Correspondence: Pauline Rhetoric and Millenarian Piety*. FFac. Philadelphia: Fortress Press, 1986.

Jewett, *Tolerance*
Jewett, Robert. *Christian Tolerance: Paul's Message to the Modern Church*. Philadelphia: Westminster, 1982.

Joest, *Gesetz und Freiheit*
Joest, Wilfrid. *Gesetz und Freiheit. Das Problem des terius usus legis bei Luther und die neutestamentlilche Paränese*. Göttingen: Vandenhoeck & Ruprecht, 1951.

Johnson, *Function*
Johnson, E. Elizabeth. *The Function of Apocalyptic and Wisdom Traditions in Romans 9–11*. SBLDS 109. Atlanta: Scholars Press, 1989.

Johnson
Johnson, Luke Timothy. *Reading Romans: A Literary and Theological Commentary*. RNTS. New York: Crossroad, 1997.

Jones, *Freiheit*
Jones, F. Stanley. *"Freiheit" in den Briefen des Apostels Paulus. Eine historische, exegetische und religionsgeschichtliche Studie*. GThA 34. Göttingen: Vandenhoeck & Ruprecht, 1987.

Joubert, *Benefactor*
Joubert, Stephan. *Paul as Benefactor: Reciprocity, Strategy and Theological Reflection in Paul's Collection*. WUNT 124. Tübingen: Mohr Siebeck, 2000.

Judge, "Conflict of Educational Aims"
Judge, E. A. "The Conflict of Educational Aims in New Testament Thought." *JCE* 9 (1966) 32–45.

Judge, "Cultural Conformity"
Judge, E. A. "Cultural Conformity and Innovation in Paul: Some Clues from Contemporary Documents." *TynB* 35 (1984) 3–24.

Judge, *Rank and Status*
Judge, E. A. *Rank and Status in the World of the Caesars and St. Paul*. The Broadhead Memorial Lecture 1981. UCantP 29. Christchurch: University of Canterbury Press, 1982.

Judge, "Scholastic Community"
Judge, E. A. "The Early Christians as a Scholastic Community." *JRH* 1 (1960–61) 4–15, 125–37.

Jülicher
Jülicher, Adolf. "Der Brief an die Römer." Pp. 223–335 in *Die Schriften des Neuen Testaments*, vol 2. Göttingen: Vandenhoeck & Ruprecht, 1910. Rev. ed. 1917.

Junack et al., *Neue Testament auf Papyrus*
Junack, Klaus, E. Güting, U. Nimtz, and K. Witte, eds., *Das Neue Testament auf Papyrus. II: Die Paulinische Briefe. Teil 1: Röm., 1. Kor., 2 Kor.* ANTF 12. Berlin: de Gruyter, 1989.

Kähler, *Unterordnung*
Kähler, Else. *Die Frau in den paulinischen Briefen unter besonderer Berücksichtigung des Begriffes der Unterordnung*. Zurich: Gotthelf, 1960.

1

Kahn, "Greek Verb 'To Be'"
Kahn, Charles H. "The Greek Verb 'To Be' and the Concept of Being." *FLang* 2 (1966) 245–65.

Kamlah, *Form*
Kamlah, Ehrhard. *Die Form der katalogischen Paränese im Neuen Testament.* Tübingen: Mohr Siebeck, 1964.

Käsemann
Käsemann, Ernst. *Commentary on Romans.* Trans. G. W. Bromiley. Grand Rapids: Eerdmans, 1980.

Käsemann, *Exegetische Versuche*
Käsemann, Ernst. *Exegetische Versuche und Besinnungen.* Göttingen: Vandenhoeck & Ruprecht, 1960.

Käsemann, "Paul and Israel"
Käsemann, Ernst. "Paul and Israel." Pp. 183–87 in Käsemann, *Questions.*

Käsemann, *Perspectives*
Käsemann, Ernst. *Perspectives on Paul.* Trans. M. Kohl. London: SCM, 1971.

Käsemann, *Questions*
Käsemann, Ernst. *New Testament Questions of Today.* London: SCM, 1969.

Käsemann, "Rechfertigung"
Käsemann, Ernst. "Rechfertigung und Heilsgeschichte im Römerbrief." Pp. 108–39 in Käsemann, *Perspectives.*

Käsemann, "Righteousness"
Käsemann, Ernst. "'The Righteousness of God' in Paul." Pp. 168–82 in Käsemann, *Questions.* (A different translation appeared as "God's Righteousness in Paul." *JTC* 1 [1965] 100–110).

Kaye, *Chapter 6*
Kaye, Bruce N. *The Thought and Structure of Romans with Special Reference to Chapter 6.* Austin: Schola, 1979.

Kaylor, *Covenant Community*
Kaylor, R. David. *Paul's Covenant Community: Jew and Gentile in Romans.* Atlanta: John Knox, 1988.

Keck, *Paul*
Keck, Leander E. *Paul and His Letters.* Philadelphia: Fortress Press, 1979.

Keck, "Saints in Jewish Christianity and Qumran"
Keck, Leander E. "'The Poor among the Saints' in Jewish Christianity and Qumran." *ZNW* 57 (1966) 54–78.

Keck, "3:10-18"
Keck, Leander A. "The Function of Rom 3:10-18: Observations and Suggestions." Pp. 141–57 in J. Jervell and W. A. Meeks, eds., *God's Christ and His People: Studies in Honour of Nils Alstrup Dahl.* Oslo: Universitetsforlaget, 1977.

Keesmaat, *Paul*
Keesmaat, Sylvia C. *Paul and His Story: (Re)Interpreting the Exodus Tradition.* JSNTSup 181. Sheffield: Sheffield Academic Press, 1999.

Kegel, *Auferstehung*
Kegel, Günter. *Auferstehung Jesu–Auferstehung der Toten. Eine traditionsgeschichtliche Untersuchung zum Neuen Testament.* Gütersloh: Gerd Mohn, 1970.

Kelber, *Oral and the Written Gospel*
Kelber, Werner H. *The Oral and the Written Gospel: The Hermeneutics of Speaking and Writing in the Synoptic Tradition, Mark, Paul, and Q.* Philadelphia: Fortress Press, 1983.

Keller, *Gottes Treue*
Keller, Winfrid. *Gottes Treue–Israels Heil. Röm 11,25-27. Die These vom "Sonderweg" in der Diskussion.* SBB 40. Stuttgart: Katholisches Bibelwerk, 1998.

Kennedy, *New Testament Interpretation*
Kennedy, George A. *New Testament Interpretation through Rhetorical Criticism.* Chapel Hill: University of North Carolina Press, 1984.

Kertelge, *Rechtfertigung*
Kertelge, Karl. *"Rechtfertigung" bei Paulus. Studien zur Struktur und zum Bedeutungsgehalt des paulinischen Rechtfertigungsbegriffs.* 2d ed. NTAbh 3. Münster: Aschendorff, 1971.

Kertelge, "Verständnis des Todes Jesu"
Kertelge, Karl. "Das Verständnis des Todes Jesu bei Paulus." Pp. 114–36 in J. Beutler et al., eds., *Der Tod Jesu. Deutungen im Neuen Testament.* Freiburg: Herder, 1976.

Kettunen, *Abfassungszweck*
Kettunen, Markku. *Der Abfassungszweck des Römerbriefes.* AASF. Helsinki: Snomalainen Tiedeakatemia, 1979.

Kim, *Form*
Kim, Chan-Hie. *The Form and Structure of the Familiar Greek Letter of Recommendation.* SBLDS 4. Missoula: Scholars Press, 1972.

Kim, *Romans 9–11*
Kim, Johann D. *God, Israel, and the Gentiles: Rhetoric and Situation in Romans 9–11.* SBLDS 176. Atlanta: Scholars Press, 2000.

Kim, *Origin*
Kim, Seyoon. *The Origin of Paul's Gospel.* WUNT 2.4. Tübingen: Mohr Siebeck, 1981.

Kinneavy, *Greek Rhetorical Origins*
Kinneavy, James L. *Greek Rhetorical Origins of the Christian Faith.* New York: Oxford University Press, 1987.

Kirsch, *Titelkirchen*
Kirsch, Johann Peter. *Die römischen Titelkirchen im Altertum.* SGKA 9.1918. Repr. New York: Johnson, 1967.

Kitzberger, *Bau der Gemeinde*
Kitzberger, Ingrid. *Bau der Gemeinde. Das paulinische Wortfeld οἰκοδομή/(ἀπ)οικοδομεῖν.* FB 53. Würzburg: Echter Verlag, 1986.

Klaiber, *Rechtfertigung*
Klaiber, Walter. *Rechtfertigung und Gemeinde. Eine Untersuchung zum paulinischen Kirchenverständnis.* FRLANT 127. Göttingen: Vandenhoeck & Ruprecht, 1982.

Klauck, *Hausgemeinde*
Klauck, Hans-Josef. *Hausgemeinde und Hauskirche im frühen Christentum.* SBS 103. Stuttgart: Katholisches Bibelwerk, 1981.

Klauck, *Herrenmahl*
Klauck, Hans-Josef. *Herrenmahl und hellenistischer Kult. Eine religionsgeschichtliche Untersuchung zum Ersten Korintherbrief.* NTA 15. Münster: Aschendorff, 1982.

Klauck, "Kultische Symbolsprache"
Klauck, Hans-Josef. "Kultische Symbolsprache bei Paulus." Pp. 107–18 in J. Schreiner, ed., *Freude am Gottesdienst: Aspekte ursprünglicher Liturgie. Festschrift für Weihbischof Dr. Josef G. Plöger.* Stuttgart: Katholisches Bibelwerk, 1983.

Klauck, "Wortlose Seufzen"
Klauck, Hans-Josef. "Das wortlose Seufzen des Geistes in Uns. Das Unbewußte in der Sicht des Apostels Paulus." Pp. 79–95 in H.-J. Klauck, ed., *Vom Zauber des Anfangs. Biblische Besinnungen.* Franziskanische Impulse 3. Werl: Dietrich Coelde, 1999.

Klee

Klee, Heinrich. *Commentar über des Apostel Pauli Sendschreiben an die Römer*. Mainz: Kupferberg, 1830.

Klein, "Gottes Gerechtigkeit"

Klein, Günter. "Gottes Gerechtigkeit als Thema der neuesten Paulus-Forschung." Pp. 225–36 in *Rekonstruktion und Interpretation*. Munich: Kaiser, 1969.

Klein, "Paul's Purpose"

Klein, Günter. "Paul's Purpose in Writing the Epistle to the Romans." Pp. 29–43 in Karl P. Donfried, ed., *The Romans Debate*. Rev. ed. Peabody: Hendrickson, 1991.

Klein, "Römer 4"

Klein, Günter. "Römer 4 und die Idee der Heilsgeschichte." Pp. 145–69 in *Rekonstruktion und Interpretation*. Munich: Kaiser, 1969.

Kleinknecht, *Gerechtfertigte*

Kleinknecht, Karl Theodor. *Der leidende Gerechtfertigte. Die alttestamentlich-jüdische Tradition von 'leidenden Gerechten' und ihre Rezeption bei Paulus.* WUNT 2.13. Tübingen: Mohr Siebeck, 1984.

Klinzing, *Umdeutung*

Klinzing, Georg. *Die Umdeutung des Kultus in dem Qumrangemeinde und im Neuen Testament.* SUNT 7. Göttingen: Vandenhoeck & Ruprecht, 1971.

Klostermann, "Adäquate Vergeltung"

Klostermann, E. "Die adäquate Vergeltung in Röm 1:22-31." *ZNW* 32 (1933) 1–6.

Klumbies, *Rede von Gott*

Klumbies, Paul-Gerhard. *Die Rede von Gott bei Paulus in ihrem zeitgeschichtlichen Kontext.* FRLANT 155. Göttingen: Vandenhoeck & Ruprecht, 1992.

Knoche, "Römische Ruhmesgedanke"

Knoche, Ülrich. "Der römische Ruhmesgedanke." Pp. 420–45 in Hans Oppermann, ed., *Römische Wertbegriffe*. Darmstadt: Wissenschaftliche, 1983.

Knöppler, *Sühne*

Knöppler, Thomas. *Sühne im Neuen Testament. Studien zum urchristlichen Verständnis der Heilsbedeutung des Todes Jesu.* WMANT 88. Neukirchen-Vluyn: Neukirchener Verlag, 2001.

Knox, *Life*

Knox, John. *Life in Christ Jesus: Reflections on Romans 5–8.* Greenwich, CT: Seabury, 1961.

Knox

Knox, John, and Gerald R. Cragg. "Romans." Pp. 355–668 in vol. 9 of *The Interpreter's Bible*. New York: Abingdon, 1954.

Koch, "Beobachtungen"

Koch, Dietrich-Alex. "Beobachtungen zum christologischen Schriftgebrauch in den vorpaulinischen Gemeinden." *ZNW* 71 (1980) 174–91.

Koch, *Schrift*

Koch, Dietrich-Alex. *Die Schrift als Zeuge des Evangeliums. Untersuchungen zur Verwendung und zum Verständnis der Schrift bei Paulus.* Tübingen: Mohr Siebeck, 1986.

Koenig, *Charismata*

Koenig, John. *Charismata: God's Gifts for God's People.* Philadelphia: Westminster, 1978.

Köllner

Köllner, Wilhelm Heinrich Dorotheus Eduard. *Commentar zu dem Briefe des Paulus an die Römer.* Darmstadt: Diehl, 1834.

Könnecke, *Emendationen*

Könnecke, C. *Emendationen zu Stellen des Neuen Testaments.* BFChTh 12.1. Gütersloh: Bertelsmann, 1908.

Koppe

Koppe, J. B. *Novum Testamentum graece perpetua adnotatione illustratum . . . Volumen IV complectens epistolam Pauli ad Romanos.* 3d ed. rev. by C. F. Ammon. Göttingen: Dietrich, 1824.

Koskenniemi, *Studien*

Koskenniemi, Heikki. *Studien zur Idee und Phraseologie des griechischen Briefes bis 400 n. Chr.* AASF 102. Helsinki: Suomalainen Tiedeakatemia, 1956.

Kotansky, *Greek Magical Amulets*

Kotansky, Roy. *Greek Magical Amulets: The Inscribed Gold, Silver, Copper, and Bronze Lamellae*, Part I, *Published Texts of Known Provenance.* ANAWSP 22.1. Opladen: Westdeutscher Verlag, 1994.

Kotansky, "Jesus and Heracles in Cádiz"

Kotansky, Roy D. "Jesus and Heracles in Cádiz (τὰ Γάδειρα): Death, Myth, and Monsters at the Straits of Gibraltar (Mark 4:35–5:43)." Pp. 160–229 in A. Y. Collins, ed., *Ancient and Modern Perspectives on the Bible and Culture: Essays in Honor of Hans Dieter Betz.* Atlanta: Scholars Press, 1998.

Kramer, *Christ*

Kramer, Werner. *Christ, Lord, Son of God.* Trans. B. Hardy. SBT 1/50. Naperville: Allenson, 1966.

Kraus, *Heiligtumsweihe*

Kraus, Wolfgang. *Der Tod Jesu als Heiligtumsweihe. Eine Untersuchung zum Umfeld der Sühnevorstellung in Römer 3,25-26a.* WMANT 66. Neukirchen-Vluyn: Neukirchener Verlag, 1991.

Krehl

Krehl, August Ludwig Gottlob. *Der Brief an die Römer ausgelegt.* Leipzig: Kohler, 1849.

Kreitzer, *Striking New Images*

Kreitzer, Larry J. *Striking New Images: Roman Imperial Coinage and the New Testament World.* JSNTSup 134. Sheffield: Sheffield Academic Press, 1996.

Krentz, *Method*

Krentz, Edgar. *The Historical-Critical Method.* Philadelphia: Fortress Press, 1975.

Kruse, *Paul*

Kruse, Colin G. *Paul, the Law and Justification.* Peabody: Hendrickson, 1997.

Kühl

Kühl, Ernst. *Der Brief des Paulus an die Römer.* Leipzig: Quell & Meyer, 1913.

Kühner and Gerth, *Grammatik*

Kühner, Raphael, and Bernhard Gerth. *Ausführliche Grammatik der griechischen Sprache. Zweiter Teil: Satzlehre.* 2 vols. Darmstadt: Wissenschaftliche Buchgesellschaft, 1963.

Kümmel, *Introduction*

Kümmel, Werner G. *Introduction to the New Testament.* 17th ed. Nashville: Abingdon, 1975.

Kümmel, "Probleme"

Kümmel, Werner G. "Die Probleme von Römer 9–11 in der gegenwärtigen Forschungslage." Pp. 13–33 in L. De Lorenzi, ed., *Die Israelfrage nach Röm 9–11.* SMB 3. Rome: Abbazia S. Paolo, 1977.

Kümmel, *Römer 7.*
  Kümmel, Werner G. *Römer 7 und die Bekehrung des Paulus* (1929). UNT 17. Munich: Kaiser, 1974.
Kunst, "Wohnen"
  Kunst, Christiane. "Wohnen in der antiken Grossstadt. Zur sozialen Topographie Roms in der frühen Kaiserzeit." Pp. 2–17 in J. Zangenberg and M. Labahn, eds., *Christians as a Religious Minority in a Multicultural City. Modes of Interaction and Identity Formation in Early Imperial Rome.* London: T. & T. Clark, 2004.
Kürzinger
  Kürzinger, Josef. *Die Briefe des Apostels Paulus. Der Brief an die Römer.* Echter-Bibel NT. Hürzburg: Echter-Verlag, 1955.
Kuss
  Kuss, Otto. *Der Römerbrief übersetzt und erklärt.* 3 vols. Regensburg: Pustet, 1957–78.
Kuss, "Begriff des Gehorsams"
  Kuss, Otto. "Der Begriff des Gehorsams im Neuen Testament." *ThGl* 27 (1955) 695–702.
Laato, *Paul and Judaism*
  Laato, Timo. *Paul and Judaism: An Anthropological Approach.* Trans. T. McElwain. SFSHJ 115. Atlanta: Scholars Press, 1995.
Lagrange
  Lagrange, Marie-Joseph. *Saint Paul. Épître aux Romains.* ÉtBib. 1931. Repr. Paris: Gabalda, 1950.
Lamarche and le Dû, *Romains 5–8*
  Lamarche, Paul, and Charles le Dû. *Épître aux Romains 5–8. Structure littéraire et sens.* Paris: Centre National de la Recherche Scientifique, 1980.
Lambrecht, *Collected Studies*
  Lambrecht, Jan. *Collected Studies on Pauline Literature and on the Book of Revelation.* AnBib 147. Rome: Pontfical Biblical Institute, 2001.
Lambrecht, *Pauline Studies*
  Lambrecht, Jan. *Pauline Studies.* BETL 115. Leuven: Leuven University Press, 1994.
Lambrecht, *Wretched "I"*
  Lambrecht, Jan. *The Wretched "I" and Its Liberation: Paul in Romans 7 and 8.* LTPM 14. Grand Rapids: Eerdmans, 1992.
Lampe, "*Ktisis*"
  Lampe, Geoffrey William Hugo. "The New Testament Doctrine of *Ktisis.*" *SJT* 17 (1964) 449–62.
Lampe, "Family"
  Lampe, Peter. "The Family of New Testament Times." *CaS* 84.2 (1993) 18–38.
Lampe, "Konflikt"
  Lampe, Peter. "Der Konflikt zwischen Starken und Schwachen in Rome." Pp. 87–89 in C. Link et al., eds., *"Sie aber hielten fest an der Gemeinschaft. . . ." Einheit der Kirche als Prozess im Neuen Testament und heute.* Zurich: Benziger, 1988.
Lampe, "Paths"
  Lampe, Peter. "Paths of Early Christian Mission into Rome: Judaeo–Christians in the Households of Pagan Masters." Trans. M. B. Lampe. Pp. 143–48 in S. E. McGinn, ed., *Celebrating Romans: Template for Pauline Theology. Essays in Honor of Robert Jewett.* Grand Rapids: Eerdmans, 2004.
Lampe, *Paul to Valentinus*
  Lampe, Peter. *From Paul to Valentinus: Christians at Rome in the First Two Centuries.* Trans. M. Steinhauser. Foreword by R. Jewett. Minneapolis: Fortress Press, 2003.

Lampe, "Paulus–Zeltmacher"
  Lampe, Peter. "Paulus–Zeltmacher." *BZ* 31 (1987) 256–61.
Lampe, "Roman Christians"
  Lampe, Peter. "The Roman Christians of Romans 16." Pp. 216–30 in Karl P. Donfried, ed., *The Romans Debate.* Rev. ed. Peabody: Hendrickson, 1991.
Lampe, "Rome"
  Lampe, Peter. "Rome." *HBD*² 944–47.
Lampe, "Textgeschichte"
  Lampe, Peter. "Zur Textgeschichte des Römerbriefes." *NovT* 27 (1985) 273–77.
La Piana, "Foreign Groups"
  La Piana, George. "Foreign Groups in Rome during the First Centuries of the Empire." *HTR* (1927) 183–403.
Latto, *Star is Rising*
  Latto, Antti. *A Star is Rising: The Historical Development of the Old Testament Royal Ideology and the Rise of the Jewish Messianic Expectations.* USFCJ 5. Atlanta: Scholars Press, 1997.
Lausberg, *Handbuch*
  Lausberg, Heinrich. *Handbuch der literarischen Rhetorik.* 2d ed. Munich: Hueber, 1973.
Leenhardt
  Leenhardt, Franz-J. *The Epistle of Saint Paul to the Romans: A Commentary.* Trans. H. Knight. London: Lutterworth, 1961.
Légasse
  Légasse, Simon. *L'épitre de Paul aux Romains.* Paris: Cerf, 2002.
Lendon, *Empire of Honour*
  Lendon, J. E. *Empire of Honour: The Art of Government in the Roman World.* Oxford: Clarendon, 1997.
Leon, *Jews*
  Leon, Harry J. *The Jews of Ancient Rome.* Updated Edition with a new introduction by Carolyn A. Osiek. Peabody: Hendrickson, 1995.
Leske, "Righteousness"
  Leske, Adrian. "Righteousness as Relationship." Pp. 125–37 in W. Freitag, ed., *Festschrift: A Tribute to Dr. William Hordern.* Saskatoon: University of Saskatchewan Press, 1985.
Levick, *Government*
  Levick, Barbara. *The Government of the Roman Empire: A Sourcebook.* Totowa: Barnes & Noble Books, 1985.
Levinskaya, *Diaspora Setting*
  Levinskaya, Irina. *The Book of Acts in Its Diaspora Setting.* Vol. 5 of *The Book of Acts in Its First Century Setting.* Grand Rapids: Eerdmans, 1996.
Lewis, "Leitourgia"
  Lewis, Naphtali. "*Leitourgia* and Related Terms." *GRBS* 3 (1960) 175–84; 6 (1965) 227–30.
Lichtenberger, *Ich Adams*
  Lichtenberger, Hermann. *Das Ich Adams und das Ich der Menschheit.* WUNT 164. Tübingen: Mohr Siebeck, 2004.
Lichtenberger, "Jews and Christians in Rome"
  Lichtenberger, Hermann. "Jews and Christians in Rome in the Time of Nero: Josephus and Paul in Rome." *ANRW* 26.3 (1996) 2142–76.
Lietzmann
  Lietzmann, Hans. *An die Römer.* 3d ed. HNT 8. Tübingen: Mohr [Siebeck], 1928.

Lieu, *Neither Jew nor Greek*
Lieu, Judith. *Neither Jew nor Greek? Constructing Early Christianity.* Edinburgh: T. & T. Clark, 2002.

Lightfoot, "Caesar's Household"
Lightfoot, J. B. Excursus on "Caesar's Household." Pp. 171–78 in *Saint Paul's Epistle to the Philippians.* New York: Macmillan, 1903.

Lightfoot, *Notes*
Lightfoot, J. B. *Notes on Epistles of St. Paul.* London: Macmillan, 1895.

Lim, *Holy Scripture*
Lim, Timothy H. *Holy Scripture in the Qumran Community and Pauline Letters.* New York: Oxford University Press, 1997.

Lincoln, "Abraham"
Lincoln, Andrew T. "Abraham Goes to Rome: Paul's Treatment of Abraham in Romans 4." Pp. 163–79 in M. J. Wilkins and T. Paige, eds., *Worship, Theology and Ministry in the Early Church: Essays in Honor of Ralph P. Martin.* JSOTSup 87. Sheffield: Sheffield Academic Press, 1992.

Lindsay, *Josephus and Faith*
Lindsay, Dennis R. *Josephus and Faith:* Πίστις *and* Πιστεύειν *as Faith Terminology in the Writings of Flavius Josephus and in the New Testament.* AGJU 19. Leiden: Brill, 1993.

Lipsius
Lipsius, Richard Adelbert. *Briefe an die Galater, Römer, Philipper.* 2d ed. HKNT 2.2. Freiburg: Mohr, 1893.

Ljungman, *PISTIS*
Ljungman, Henrix. *PISTIS. A Study of its Presuppositions and its Meaning in Pauline Use.* ARSL 64. Trans. W. F. Salisbury. Lund: Gleerup, 1964.

Lohmeyer, *Probleme*
Lohmeyer, Ernst. *Probleme paulinische Theologie.* Darmstadt: Wissenschaftliche Buchgemeinschaft, 1954; Stuttgart: Kohlhammer, 1955.

Lohse, *Märtyrer*
Lohse Eduard. *Märtyrer und Gottesknecht. Untersuchungen zur urchristlichen Verkündigungen vom Sühntod Jesu Christi.* Göttingen: Vandenhoeck & Ruprecht, 1955.

Longenecker, *Eschatology and the Covenant*
Longenecker, Bruce W. *Eschatology and the Covenant: A Comparison of 4 Ezra and Romans 1–11.* JSNTSup 57. Sheffield: Sheffield Academic Press, 1991.

Longenecker, "Ancient Amanuenses"
Longenecker, Richard N. "Ancient Amanuenses and the Pauline Epistles." Pp. 281–97 in Richard N. Longenecker and M. C. Tenncy, eds., *New Dimensions in New Testament Study.* Grand Rapids: Zondervan, 1974.

Longenecker, *Paul*
Longenecker, Richard N. *Paul: Apostle of Liberty.* New York: Harper & Row, 1964.

Lorenzen, "Hauskirche"
Lorenzen, Thorwald. "Das christliche Hauskirche." *ThZ* 43 (1987) 333–52.

Louw
Louw, Johannes P. *A Semantic Discourse Analysis of Romans.* 2 vols. Pretoria: University of Pretoria Press, 1979.

Lovejoy and Boas, *Primitivism*
Lovejoy, Arthur O., and George Boas. *Primitivism and Related Ideas in Antiquity.* Vol. 1 of A. O. Lovejoy et al., eds., *A Documentary History of Primitivism and Related Ideas.* 1935. Repr. New York: Octagon, 1965.

Lübking, *Paulus*
Lübking, Hans-Martin. *Paulus und Israel im Römerbrief. Eine Untersuchung zu Römer 9–11.* EHS 260. Frankfurt: Lang, 1986.

Lucht, *Untersuchung*
Lucht, Hans. *Ueber die beiden letzten Kapitel des Römerbriefes. Eine kritische Untersuchung.* Berlin: Henschel, 1871.

Luedemann, *Chronology*
Luedemann, Gerd. *Paul, Apostle to the Gentiles. Studies in Chronology.* Trans. F. S. Jones. Philadelphia: Fortress Press, 1984.

Lührmann, *Glaube*
Lührmann, Dieter. *Glaube im frühen Christentum.* Gütersloh: Gütersloher Verlagshaus, 1976.

Lührmann, *Offenbarungsverständnis*
Lührmann, Dieter. *Das Offenbarungsverständnis bei Paulus und in paulinischen Gemeinden.* WMANT 16. Neukirchen-Vluyn: Neukirchener Verlag, 1965.

Lund, *Chiasmus*
Lund, Nils Wilhelm. *Chiasmus in the New Testament: A Study in the Form and Function of Chiastic Structures.* 1942. Repr. Peabody: Hendrickson, 1992.

Lütgert, *Römerbrief*
Lütgert, Wilhelm. *Der Römerbrief als historisches Problem.* BFCTh 17.2 Gütersloh: Bertelsmann, 1913.

Luz, "Aufbau"
Luz, Ulrich. "Zum Aufbau von Röm 1–8." *ThZ* 25 (1969) 161–81.

Luz, *Geschichtsverständnis*
Luz, Ulrich. *Das Geschichtsverständnis des Paulus.* BEvT 49. Munich: Kaiser, 1968.

Luz, "Mystic"
Luz, Ulrich. "Paul as Mystic." Pp. 131–43 in G. N. Stanton, B. W. Longenecker, and S. C. Barton, eds., *The Holy Spirit and Christian Origins: Essays in Honor of James D. G. Dunn.* Grand Rapids: Eerdmans, 2004.

Lyall, "Roman Law"
Lyall, Francis. "Roman Law in the Writings of Paul—Adoption." *JBL* 88 (1969) 458–66.

Lyonnet, *Étapes*
Lyonnet, Stanislas. *Les Étapes de l'histoire du salut selon l'Épître aux Romains.* Bœ8. Paris: Cerf, 1969.

Lyonnet, *Études*
Lyonnet, Stanislas. *Études sur l'épître aux Romains.* AnBib 120. Rome: Biblical Institute, 1989.

Lyonnet, "L'histoire"
Lyonnet, Stanislas. "L'histoire du salut selon le chaptire VII de l'Epître aux Romains." *Bib* 43 (1962) 117–51.

Lyonnet, *Message*
Lyonnet, Stanislas. *Le Message de l'épître aux Romains.* Paris: Cerf, 1971.

Lyonnet, "Notes"
Lyonnet, Stanislas. "Notes sur l'exégèse de l'Epître aux Romains. I. La structure littéraire de Rom 1,22-32." *Bib* 38 (1957) 35–61.

Lyonnet, *Quaestiones*
Lyonnet, Stanislas. *Quaestiones in epistulam ad Romanos: Prima series.* Rome: Biblical Institute, 1955; 2d ed. 1962. *Series altera* Rome: Biblical Institute, 1956. 3d ed. with suppl., 1975.

Lyonnet, *Storia*
Lyonnet, Stanislas. *La storia della salvezza nella lettera ai Romani.* Historia salutis 3. Naples: M. d'Auria, 1966.

Lyonnet, "Tu ne convoiteras pas"
Lyonnet, Stanislas. "'Tu ne convoiteras pas' (Rom 7:7)." Pp. 157–62 in W. C. van Unnik, ed., *Neotestamentica et Patristica: Eine Freundesgabe, Herrn Professor Dr. Oscar Cullmann zu seinem 60. Geburtstag überreicht.* NovTSup 6. Leiden: Brill, 1962.

Magnusson, *Verstehen*
Magnusson, Martin. *Der Begriff "Verstehen" in exegetischem Zusammenhang unter besonderer Berücksichtigung der paulinischen Schriften.* STL 8. Lund: Gleerup, 1954.

Maier
Maier, Adalbert. *Commentar über den Brief Pauli an die Römer.* Freiburg: Herder, 1847.

Maier, *Israel*
Maier, Friedrich W. *Israel in der Heilsgeschichte nach Röm 9–11.* BZfr 12.11-12. Münster: Aschendorff, 1929.

Maier, *Mensch*
Maier, Gerhard. *Mensch und freier Wille. Nach den jüdischen Religionsparteien zwischen Ben Sira und Paulus.* WUNT 12. Tübingen: Mohr (Siebeck), 1971.

Maier, "Imperial Iconography"
Maier, Harry O. "Barbarians, Scythians and Imperial Iconography in the Epistle to the Colossians." Pp. 385–406 in A. Weissenrieder et al., eds., *Picturing the New Testament. Studies in Ancient Visual Images.* WUNT 193. Tübingen: Mohr Siebeck, 2005.

Mainville
Mainville, Odette. *Un plaidoyer en faveur de l'unité: le lettre aux Romains.* ScB. Montreal: Médiaspaul, 1999.

Malherbe, "Ancient Epistolary Theorists"
Malherbe, Abraham J. "Ancient Epistolary Theorists." *OJRS* 5:2 (1977) 3-77.

Malherbe, "Μὴ γένοιτο"
Malherbe, Abraham J. "*Μὴ γένοιτο* in the Diatribe and Paul." *HTR* 73 (1980) 231–40. Repr. pp. 25–33 in *Paul and the Popular Philosophers.* Minneapolis: Fortress Press, 1989.

Malherbe, *Paul*
Malherbe, Abraham J. *Paul and the Popular Philosophers.* Minneapolis: Fortress Press, 1989.

Malherbe, *Paul and the Thessalonians*
Malherbe, Abraham. *Paul and the Thessalonians: The Philosophic Tradition of Pastoral Care.* Philadelphia: Fortress Press, 1987.

Malina, *New Testament World*
Malina, Bruce J. *The New Testament World: Insights from Cultural Anthropology.* Atlanta: John Knox, 1981.

Manson, "Romans—and Others"
Manson, Thomas Walter. "St Paul's Letter to the Romans—and Others." Pp. 1–15 in K. P. Donfried, ed., *The Romans Debate.* Rev. ed. Peabody: Hendrickson, 1991.

Marcus, "Circumcision and Uncircumcision"
Marcus, Joel. "The Circumcision and Uncircumcision in Rome." *NTS* (1989) 67–81.

Marcus, "Under the Law"
Marcus, Joel. "'Under the Law': The Background of a Pauline Expression." *CBQ* 63 (2001) 72–83.

Marguerat et al., *Introduction*
Marguerat, Daniel, with Corina Combet-Galland, Élian Cuvillier, Andreas Dettwiler, Jean-Daniel Kaestli, Yann Redalié, Jacques Schlosser, François Vouga, and Jean Zumstein. *Introduction au Nouveau Testament. Son histoire, son écriture, sa théologie.* Geneva: Labor et Fides, 2000.

Marshall, *Thessalonians*
Marshall, I. Howard. *1 and 2 Thessalonians.* NICNT. Grand Rapids: Eerdmans, 1983.

Martin, *Slavery as Salvation*
Martin, Dale B. *Slavery as Salvation: The Metaphor of Slavery in Pauline Christianity.* New Haven: Yale University Press, 1990.

Martin, *Antike Rhetorik*
Martin, Josef. *Antike Rhetorik. Technik und Methode.* Munich: Beck, 1974.

Martin, *Reconciliation*
Martin, Ralph P. *Reconciliation: A Study of Paul's Theology.* Atlanta: John Knox, 1981.

Martin, *2 Corinthians*
Martin, Ralph P. *2 Corinthians.* WBC 40. Waco. Word, 1986.

Mason, *Greek Terms*
Mason, Hugh J. *Greek Terms for Roman Institutions: A Lexicon and Analysis.* ASP 13. Toronto: Hakkert, 1974.

Mattern, *Verständnis*
Mattern, Lieselotte. *Das Verständnis des Gerichtes bei Paulus.* AThANT 47. Zurich: Zwingli, 1966.

Matthews, *Rich Pagan Women*
Matthews, Shelly. *First Converts: Rich Pagan Women and the Rhetoric of Missions in Early Judaism and Christianity.* Stanford: Stanford University Press, 2001.

Maurer, "A minore ad majus"
Maurer, Christian. "Der Schluss 'a minore ad majus' als Element der paulinischen Theologie." *ThLZ* 85 (1960) 149–52.

Mayer, *Gottes Heilsratschluß*
Mayer, Bernhard. *Unter Gottes Heilsratschluß. Prädestinationsaussagen bei Paulus.* FB 15. Würzburg: Echter Verlag, 1974.

McDonald, "Separate Letter"
McDonald, J. I. H. "Was Romans 16 a Separate Letter?" *NTS* 16 (1969–70) 369–72.

McGinn, *Celebrating Romans*
McGinn, Sheila E., ed. *Celebrating Romans: Template for Pauline Theology. Essays in Honor of Robert Jewett.* Grand Rapids: Eerdmans, 2004.

McGinn, "Feminist Approaches"
McGinn, Sheila E. "Feminist Approaches to Paul's Letter to the Romans." Pp. 165–76 in S. E. McGinn, ed., *Celebrating Romans: Template for Pauline Theology. Essays in Honor of Robert Jewett.* Grand Rapids: Eerdmans, 2004.

Meeks, "Judgment and the Brother"
Meeks, Wayne A. "Judgment and the Brother: Romans 14:1–15:13." Pp. 290–300 in G. F. Hawthorne and O. Betz, eds., *Tradition and Interpretation in the New Testament: New Testament Essays in Honor of E. Earle Ellis.* Grand Rapids: Eerdmans, 1987.

Meeks, *Urban Christians*
Meeks, Wayne A. *The First Urban Christians: The Social World of the Apostle Paul.* New Haven: Yale University Press, 1983.

Mehring
Mehring, Heinrich Johann Friedrich. *Der Brief Pauli an die Römer übersetzt und erklärt.* Erster Theil. Stettin: Nahmer, 1859

Meier, *Mystik*
Meier, Hans-Christoph. *Mystik bei Paulus: Zur Phänomenologie religiöser Erfahrung im Neuen Testament.* TANZ 26. Tübingen: Francke, 1998.

Meister, "Tugenden"
Meister, Karl. "Die Tugenden der Römer." Pp. 1–22 in H. Oppenheim, ed., *Römische Wertbegriffe.* Darmstadt: Wissenschaftliche Buchgesellschaft, 1983.

Merk, *Novum Testamentum*
Merk, Augustinus Mark, S.J., ed. *Novum Testamentum graece et latine, apparatus critico instructum.* 11th ed. Rome: Pontifical Biblical Institute, 1992.

Merk, *Handeln*
Merk, Otto. *Handeln aus Glauben. Die Motivierungen der paulinischen Ethik.* MTS 5. Marburg: Elwert, 1968.

Merklein, *Studien*
Merklein, Helmut. *Studien zu Jesus und Paulus II.* WUNT 105. Tübingen: Mohr Siebeck, 1998.

Mesner, "Rhetoric"
Mesner, David Earl. "The Rhetoric of Citations: Paul's Use of Scripture in Romans 9." Diss., Northwestern University, 1991.

Metzger, *Textual Commentary*
Metzger, Bruce M. *A Textual Commentary on the Greek New Testament. A Companion Volume to the United Bible Societies' Greek New Testament (Fourth Revised Edition).* 2d ed. Stuttgart: German Bible Society, 1994.

Metzger, *Textual Commentary (1975)*
Metzger, Bruce M. *A Textual Commentary on the Greek New Testament: A Companion Volume to the United Bible Societies' Greek New Testament (Third Edition).* Corrected ed. New York: United Bible Societies, 1975.

Meyer
Meyer, Heinrich August Wilhelm. *Critical and Exegetical Handbook to the Epistle to the Romans.* Trans. J. C. Moore. 3 vols. Edinburgh: Clark, 1876.

Michael, "Phenomenon"
Michael, J. Hugh. "A Phenomenon in the Text of Romans." *JTS* 39 (1983) 150–54.

Michel
Michel, Otto. *Der Brief an die Römer.* 14th ed. MeyerK 4. Göttingen: Vandenhoeck & Ruprecht, 1978.

Michel, *Bibel*
Michel, Otto. *Paulus und seine Bibel.* BFCTh 118. Gütersloh: Gütersloher Verlagshaus, 1929.

Middendorf, *Romans 7*
Middendorf, Michael Paul. *The "I" in the Storm: A Study of Romans 7.* St. Louis: Concordia Academic Press, 1997.

Miller, *Obedience of Faith*
Miller, James C. *The Obedience of Faith, the Eschatological People of God, and the Purpose of Romans.* SBLDS 177. Atlanta: Society of Biblical Literature, 2000.

van der Minde, *Schrift*
Minde, Hans-Jürgen van der. *Schrift und Tradition bei Paulus. Ihre Bedeutung und Funktion im Römerbrief.* PThS 3. Munich: Schöningh, 1976.

Minear, *Images*
Minear, Paul S. *Images of the Church in the New Testament.* Philadelphia: Westminster, 1960.

Minear, *Obedience*
Minear, Paul S. *The Obedience of Faith: The Purposes of Paul in the Epistle to the Romans.* SBT 2/19. London: SCM, 1971.

Mitchell, *Meaning of BRK*
Mitchell, Christopher Wright. *The Meaning of BRK "To Bless" in the Old Testament.* SBLDS 95. Atlanta: Scholars Press, 1987.

Moir, "Orthography and Theology"
Moir, Ian A. "Orthography and Theology: The Omicron-Omega Interchange in Romans 5:1 and Elsewhere." Pp. 179–83 in Eldon Jay Epp and Gordon Fee, eds., *New Testament Textual Criticism: Its Significance for Exegesis: Essays in Honour of Bruce M. Metzger.* Oxford: Clarendon, 1981.

Molland, "Διό"
Molland, Einar. "Διό". Einige Syntaktische Beobachtungen." Pp. 43–52 in H. Holst and H. Mørland, eds., *Serta Rudbergiana.* SO.S 4. Oslo: Brøgger, 1931.

Momigliano, *Claudius*
Momigliano, Arnaldo. *Claudius: The Emperor and His Achievment.* Oxford: Clarendon, 1934.

Momigliano, *Pagans*
Momigliano, Arnaldo. *On Pagans, Jews and Christians.* Middletown: Wesleyan University Press, 1987.

Mommsen, *Römisches Strafrecht*
Mommsen, Theodor. *Römisches Strafrecht.* Graz: Akademische Druck- und Verlagsanstalt, 1955.

Moo
Moo, Douglas J. *The Epistle to the Romans.* NICNT. Grand Rapids: Eerdmans, 1996.

Moores, *Wrestling*
Moores, John D. *Wrestling with Rationality in Paul: Romans 1–8 in a New Perspective.* SNTSMS 82. Cambridge: Cambridge University Press, 1995.

Morgan
Morgan, Robert. *Romans.* NTGuides. Sheffield: Sheffield Academic Press, 1995.

Morison
Morison, James. *A Critical Exposition of the Third Chapter of Paul's Epistle to the Romans.* London: Hamilton, Adams, 1866.

Morris
Morris, Leon. *The Epistle to the Romans.* PNTC. Grand Rapids: Eerdmans, 1988.

Mott, "Hellenistic Benevolence"
Mott, Stephen C. "The Power of Giving and Receiving: Reciprocity in Hellenistic Benevolence." Pp. 60–72 in G. F. Hawthorne, ed., *Current Issues in Biblical and Patristic Interpretation: Studies in Honor of Merrill C. Tenney Presented by His Former Students.* Grand Rapids: Eerdmans, 1975.

Moule, "Death"
Moule, C. F. D. "Death 'to Sin', 'to Law', and 'to the World': A Note on Certain Datives." Pp. 367–75 in A. L. Descamps and A. de Halleux, eds., *Mélanges bibliques en hommage au R. P. Béda Rigaux.* Gembloux: Duculot, 1970.

Moule, *Idiom Book*
Moule, C. F. D. *An Idiom Book of New Testament Greek.* Cambridge: Cambridge University Press, 1953, 1959.

Moulton, *Grammar I*
Moulton, James Hope. *Grammar of New Testament Greek.* Vol. I. *Prolegomena.* Edinburgh: T. & T. Clark, 1908.

Moulton and Howard, *Grammar II*
Moulton, James Hope, and Wilbert Francis Howard. *Grammar of New Testament Greek*. Vol. II. *Accident and Word Formation*. Edinburgh: T. & T. Clark, 1920.

Moulton and Turner, *Grammar III*
Moulton, James Hope, and Nigel Turner. *Grammar of New Testament Greek*. Vol. III. *Syntax*. Edinburgh: T. & T. Clark, 1963.

Moxnes, "Honour and Righteousness"
Moxnes, Halvor. "Honour and Righteousness in Romans." *JSNT* 32 (1988) 61–77.

Moxnes, *Theology in Conflict*
Moxnes, Halvor. *Theology in Conflict: Studies in Paul's Understanding of God in Romans*. NovTSup 53. Leiden: Brill, 1980.

Müller, *Gottes Gerechtigkeit*
Müller, Christian. *Gottes Gerechtigkeit und Gottes Volk. Eine Untersuchung zu Römer 9–11*. FRLANT 86. Göttingen: Vandenhoeck & Ruprecht, 1964.

Müller, "Zwei Marginalien"
Müller, Friedrich. "Zwei Marginalien im Brief des Paulus an die Römer." *ZNW* 40 (1941) 249–54.

Müller, "Qal Wachomer Schluss"
Müller, Heinrich. "Der rabbinische Qal-Wachomer-Schluss im paulinischer Typologie. Zur Adam-Christus-Typologie in Rm 5." *ZNW* 58 (1967) 73–92.

Müller, *Anstoß und Gericht*
Müller, Karlheinz. *Anstoß und Gericht. Eine Studie zum jüdischen Hintergrund des paulinischen Skandalon-Begriffs*. StANT 19. Munich: Kösel, 1969.

Müller, *Schluß*
Müller, Markus. *Vom Schluß zum Ganzen. Zur Bedeutung des paulinischen Briefkorpusabschlusses*. FRLANT 92. Göttingen: Vandenhoeck & Ruprecht, 1997.

Müller, "Glaube aus dem Hören"
Müller, Peter. "Der Glaube aus dem Hören. Über das gesprochene und das geschriebene Wort bei Paulus." Pp. 405–42 in L. Bormann et al., eds., *Religious Propaganda and Missionary Competition in the New Testament World: Essays Honoring Dieter Georgi*. NovTSup 74. Leiden: Brill, 1994.

Müller, *Prophetie*
Müller, Ulrich B. *Prophetie und Predigt im Neuen Testament*. SNT 10. Gütersloh: Gütersloher Verlagshaus, 1975.

Mullins, *Rome*
Mullins, Michael. *Called to be Saints: Christian Living in First-Century Rome*. Dublin: Veritas, 1991.

Mullins, "Disclosure"
Mullins, Terence Y. "Disclosure: A Literary Form in the New Testament." *NovT* 7 (1964) 44–50.

Mullins, "Formulas"
Mullins, Terence Y. "Formulas in New Testament Epistles." *JBL* 91 (1972) 380–90.

Mullins, "Greeting"
Mullins, Terence Y. "Greeting as a New Testament Form." *JBL* 87 (1968) 418–26.

Munck, *Christ*
Munck, Johannes. *Christ and Israel: An Interpretation of Romans 9–11*. Trans. I. Nixon. Foreword by K. Stendahl. Philadelphia: Fortress Press, 1967.

Munck, *Paul*
Munck, Johannes. *Paul and the Salvation of Mankind*. Trans. F. Clarke. Richmond: John Knox, 1959.

Munro, *Authority*
Munro, Winsome. *Authority in Paul and Peter and Paul: The Identification of a Pastoral Stratum in the Pauline Corpus and 1 Peter*. SNTSMS 45. Cambridge: Cambridge University Press, 1983.

Munro, "Interpolation in the Epistles"
Munro, Winsome. "Interpolation in the Epistles: Weighing Probability." *NTS* 36 (1990) 431–43.

Murphy-O'Connor, *Becoming Human*
Murphy-O'Connor, Jerome. *Becoming Human Together: The Pastoral Anthropology of St. Paul*. GNS 2. Wilmington: Glazier, 1982.

Murphy-O'Connor, *Paul*
Murphy-O'Connor, Jerome. *Paul: A Critical Life*. Oxford: Clarendon, 1996.

Murphy-O'Connor, *St. Paul's Corinth*
Murphy-O'Connor, Jerome. *St. Paul's Corinth: Texts and Archeology*. Wilmington: Glazier, 1983.

Murray
Murray, John. *The Epistle to the Romans: The English Text with Introduction, Exposition, and Notes*. NICNT. Repr. Grand Rapids: Eerdmans, 1997.

Nababan, "Bekenntnis"
Nababan, Albert E. S. "Bekenntnis und Mission in Römer 14 und 15." Diss., University of Heidelberg, 1963.

Nanos, *Mystery*
Nanos, Mark D. *The Mystery of Romans: The Jewish Context of Paul's Letter*. Minneapolis: Fortress Press, 1996.

Nash, "Interpolations"
Nash, Henry S. "Interpolations in the New Testament." Pp. 23–24 in vol. 6 of *The New Schaff-Herzog Encyclopedia of Religious Knowledge*. New York: Funk & Wagnalls, 1910.

Naveh and Shaked, *Magic Spells*
Naveh, J., and S. Shaked, eds. *Magic Spells and Formulae: Aramaic Incantations of Late Antiquity*. Jerusalem: Magnes, 1993.

Nebe, *Hoffnung*
Nebe, Gottfried. *"Hoffnung" bei Paulus. Elpis und ihre Synonyme im Zusammenhang der Eschatologie*. SUNT 16. Göttingen: Vandenhoeck & Ruprecht, 1983.

Neirynck, "Paul and the Sayings of Jesus"
Neirynck, Frans. "Paul and the Sayings of Jesus." Pp. 265–321 in A. Vanhoye, ed., *L'Apôtre Paul. Personalité, Style et Conception du Ministère*. BEThL 73. Leuven: Leuven University Press, 1986.

Neubrand, *Abraham*
Neubrand, Maria. *Abraham—Vater von Juden und Nichtjuden. Eine exegetische Studie zu Röm 4*. FB 85. Würzburg: Echter Verlag, 1997.

Neufeld, *Confessions*
Neufeld, Vernon H. *The Earliest Christian Confessions*. Grand Rapids: Eerdmans, 1963.

Neugebauer, *In Christus*
Neugebauer, Fritz. *In Christus/ΕΝ ΧΡΙΣΤΩ: Eine Untersuchung zum paulinischen Glaubensverständnis*. Göttingen: Vandenhoeck & Ruprecht, 1961.

Neuhäusler, "Entscheidende Augenblick"
Neuhäusler, Engelbert. "Der entscheidende Augenblick im Zeugnis des Neuen Testaments." *BibLeb* 13 (1972) 1–16.

Newman and Nida
    Newman, Barclay M., and Eugene A. Nida. *A Translator's Handbook on Paul's Letter to the Romans.* Stuttgart: United Bible Societies, 1973.

Newton, *Concept of Purity*
    Newton, Michael. *The Concept of Purity at Qumran and in the Letters of Paul.* Cambridge: Cambridge University Press, 1985.

Neyrey, *Paul*
    Neyrey, Jerome H. *Paul in Other Words: A Cultural Reading of His Letters.* Louisville: Westminster/John Knox, 1990.

Nieder, *Ethik*
    Nieder, Lorenz. *Die Motive der religiös-sittlichen Paränese in den paulinischen Gemeinde-Briefen. Ein Beitrag zur paulinischen Ethik.* MThS 12. Munich: Zink, 1956.

Niederwimmer, *Freiheit*
    Niederwimmer, Kurt. *Der Begriff der Freiheit im Neuen Testament.* ThBT 11. Berlin: Töpelmann, 1966.

Nielsen
    Nielsen, Rasmus. *Der Brief Pauli an die Römer entwickelt.* Leipzig: Michelsen, 1843.

Nissiotis, "νῦν"
    Nissiotis, Nikos A. "Der pneumatologische Ansatz und die liturgische Verwirklichung des neutestamentlichen νῦν." Pp. 302–9 in F. Christ, ed., *Oikonomia. Heilsgeschichte als Thema der Theologie: Oscar Cullmann . . . gewidmet.* Hamburg-Bergstedt: Reich, 1967.

Noack, "Current"
    Noack, Bent. "Current and Backwater in the Epistle to the Romans." *StTh* 19 (1965) 155–66.

Norden, *Agnostos Theos*
    Norden, Eduard. *Agnostos Theos. Uuntersuchungen zur Formgeschichte religiöser Rede.* Leipzig: Teubner, 1929.

Nygren
    Nygren, Anders. *Commentary on Romans.* Trans. C. C. Rasmussen. 1949. Paperback ed. Philadelphia: Fortress Press, 1975.

Oakes, *Rome*
    Oakes, Peter, ed. *Rome in the Bible and the Early Church.* Carlisle: Paternoster, 2002.

O'Brien, *Introductory Thanksgivings*
    O'Brien, Peter T. *Introductory Thanksgivings in the Letters of Paul.* NovTSup 49. Leiden: Brill, 1977.

O'Brien, *Philippians*
    O'Brien, Peter T. *Commentary on Philippians.* NIGTC. Grand Rapids: Eerdmans, 1991.

Oegema, *Israel und die Völker*
    Oegema, Gerbern S. *Für Israel und die Völker. Studien zum alttestamentlich-jüdischen Hintergrund der paulinischen Theologie.* NovTSup 95. Leiden: Brill, 1999.

Oeming, "Fürwahr"
    Oeming, Manfred. "'Fürwahr, er trug unsere Schuld.' Die Bedeutung der alttestamentlichen Vorstellungen von Sünde und Sündevergebung für das Verständnis der neutestamentlichen Abendmahlstraditionen." Pp. 1–36 in A. Wagner, ed., *Sühne, Opfer, Abendmahl. Vier Zugänge zum Verständnis des Abendmahls.* Neukirchen-Vluyn: Neukirchener Verlag, 1999.

Ollrog, "Abfassungsverhältnisse"
    Ollrog, Wolf-Henning. "Die Abfassungsverhältnisse von Röm 16." Pp. 221–44 in D. Lührmann and G. Strecker, eds., *Kirche:*

Festschrift Günther Bornkamm zum 75. Geburtstag. Tübingen: Mohr Siebeck, 1980.

Ollrog, *Mitarbeiter*
    Ollrog, Wolf-Henning. *Paulus und seine Mitarbeiter. Untersuchungen zu Theorie und Praxis der paulinischen Mission.* WMANT 58. Neukirchen-Vluyn: Neukirchener Verlag, 1979.

Olshausen
    Olshausen, Hermann. *Biblical Commentary on the New Testament Adapted Especially for Preachers and Students. Translated from the German by Clergymen of the Church of England. Containing the Epistle of St. Paul to the Romans.* Rev. ed. 1854. Repr. as *Studies in the Epistle to the Romans.* Minneapolis: Klock & Klock, 1983.

Oltramare
    Oltramare, Hugues. *Commentaire sur l'épître aux Romains.* 2 vols. 1843. Repr. Paris: Fischbacher, 1881–82.

O'Neill
    O'Neill, John C. *Paul's Letter to the Romans.* PelNTC. Harmondsworth: Penguin, 1975.

Ortkemper, *Leben*
    Ortkemper, Franz-Josef. *Leben aus dem Glauben. Christliche Grundhaltungen nach Römer 12–13.* NTAbh 14. Münster: Aschendorff, 1980.

Osiek, "Romans"
    Osiek, Carolyn. "Romans 'Down the Pike': Glimpses from Later Years." Pp. 149–61 in S. E. McGinn, ed., *Celebrating Romans: Template for Pauline Theology. Essays in Honor of Robert Jewett.* Grand Rapids: Eerdmans, 2004.

Osiek and Balch, *Families*
    Osiek, Carolyn, and David L. Balch. *Families in the New Testament World: Households and House Churches.* The Family, Religion, and Culture. Louisville: Westminster John Knox Press, 1997.

Osten-Sacken, *Evangelium*
    Osten-Sacken, Peter von der. *Evangelium und Tora. Aufsätze zu Paulus.* ThBu 77. Munich: Kaiser, 1987.

Osten-Sacken, *Römer 8*
    Osten-Sacken, Peter von der. *Römer 8 als Beispiel paulinischer Soteriologie.* FRLANT 112. Göttingen: Vandenhoeck & Ruprecht, 1975.

Overfield, "Pleroma"
    Overfield, P. D. "Pleroma: A Study in Content and Context." *NTS* 25 (1978–79) 384–96.

Pallis
    Pallis, Alexander. *To the Romans: A Commentary.* Liverpool: Liverpool Booksellers, 1920.

Palmer, "τί οὖν"
    Palmer, Micheal. "τί οὖν; The Inferential Question in Paul's Letter to the Romans with a Proposed Reading of Romans 4.1." Pp. 200–218 in S. E. Porter and D. A. Carson, eds., *Discourse Analysis and Other Topics in Biblical Greek.* JSNTSup 113. Sheffield: Sheffield Academic Press, 1995.

Parke-Taylor, "Romans i.5 and xvi.26"
    Parke-Taylor, Goeffrey H. "A Note on 'εἰς ὑπακοὴν πίστεως' in Romans i.5 and xvi.26." *ExpT* 55 (1943–44) 305–6.

Parunak, "Transitional Techniques"
    Parunak, Henry Van Dyke. "Transitional Techniques in the Bible." *JBL* 102 (1983) 535–48.

Pascher, *Rein und Unrein*
    Pascher, Wilfried. *Rein und Unrein. Untersuchung zur biblischen Wortgeschichte.* SANT 24. Munich: Kösel, 1970.

Patte, *Faith*
 Patte, Daniel. *Paul's Faith and the Power of the Gospel: A Structural Introduction to the Pauline Letters*. Philadelphia: Fortress Press, 1983.

Patterson, "Paul, Slavery and Freedom"
 Patterson, Orlando. "Paul, Slavery and Freedom: Personal and Socio-Historical Reflections." *Semeia* 83/84 (1998) 263–79.

Patterson, *Slavery and Social Death*
 Patterson, Orlando. *Slavery and Social Death: A Comparative Study*. Cambridge: Harvard University Press, 1982.

Paulsen, *Überlieferung*
 Paulsen, Henning. *Überlieferung und Auslegung in Römer 8*. WMANT 43. Neukirchen-Vluyn: Neukirchener Verlag, 1974.

Peace, *Conversion*
 Peace, Richard V. *Conversion in the New Testament: Paul and the Twelve*. Grand Rapids: Eerdmans, 1999.

Pedersen, *Israel*
 Pedersen, Johannes. *Israel: Its Life and Culture*. 4 vols. in 2. London: Oxford University Press, 1926–40.

Pedersen, "Agape"
 Pedersen, Sigfred. "Agape—der eschatologische Hauptbegriff bei Paulus." Pp. 159–86 in S. Pedersen, ed., *Die Paulinische Literatur und Theologie. Anlässlich der 50. jährigen Gründungs-Feier der Universität Aarhus*. Århus: Aros; Göttingen: Vandenhoeck & Ruprecht, 1980.

Pedersen, "Isagogik des Römerbriefes"
 Pedersen, Sigfred. "Theologische Überlegungen zur Isagogik des Römerbriefes." *ZNW* 76 (1985) 47–67.

Penna, *Paul the Apostle*
 Penna, Romano. *Paul the Apostle: Jew and Greek Alike. A Theological and Exegetical Study*. Vol. 1. Trans. T. P. Wahl. Collegeville: Liturgical Press, 1996.

Peristiany, *Honour and Shame*
 Peristiany, Jean G., ed. *Honour and Shame: The Values of Mediterranean Society*. London: Weidenfeld & Nicolson, 1966.

Pervo, "Panta Koina"
 Pervo, Richard I. "Panta Koina: The Feeding Stories in the Light of Economic Data and Social Practice." Pp. 163–94 in L. Bormann et al., eds., *Religious Propaganda and Missionary Competition in the New Testament World: Essays Honoring Dieter Georgi*. NovTSup 74. Leiden: Brill, 1994.

Pesch
 Pesch, Rudolf. *Römerbrief*. 3rd ed. Die Neue Echter Bibel, Kommentar zum Neuen Testament mit der Einheitsübersetzung 6. Würzburg: Echter Verlag, 1994.

Petersen, "House Churches"
 Petersen, Joan M. "House Churches in Rome." *VigC* 23 (1969) 264–72.

Peterson, *ΕΙΣ ΘΕΟΣ*
 Peterson, Erik. *ΕΙΣ ΘΕΟΣ. Epigraphische, formgeschichtliche und religionsgeschichtliche Untersuchungen*. FRLANT 41. Göttingen: Vandenhoeck & Ruprecht, 1926.

Pfammatter, *Kirche als Bau*
 Pfammatter, Josef. *Die Kirche als Bau. Eine exegetisch-theologische Studie zur Ekklesiologie der Paulusbriefe*. AnGr 110. Rome: Gregorian University, 1960.

Pfitzner, *Paul and the Agon Motif*
 Pfitzner, Victor C. *Paul and the Agon Motif: Traditional Athletic Imagery in the Pauline Literature*. NovTSup 16. Leiden: Brill, 1967.

Pfleiderer, *Paulinismus*
 Pfleiderer, Otto. *Der Paulinismus. Ein Beitrag zur Geschichte des urchristlichen Theologie*. 2d ed. Leipzig: 1890.

Philippi
 Philippi, Friedrich Adolph. *Commentary on St. Paul's Epistle to the Romans*. Trans. J. S. Banks. 2 vols. Edinburgh: Clark, 1878–79.

Pierce, *Conscience*
 Pierce, C. A. *Conscience in the New Testament*. SBT 1/15. London: SCM, 1955.

Pilch and Malina, *Biblical Social Values*
 Pilch, John J., and Bruce J. Malina, eds. *Biblical Social Values and Their Meanings: A Handbook*. Peabody: Hendrickson, 1993.

Piper, *Justification*
 Piper, John. *The Justification of God: An Exegetical and Theological Study of Romans 9:1-23*. Grand Rapids: Baker, 1983.

Pitta, "Strong"
 Pitta, Antonio. "The Strong, the Weak, and the Mosaic Law in the Christian Communities of Rome (Rom. 14.1–15.13)." Pp. 90–107 in J. Zangenberg and M. Labahn, eds., *Christians as a Religious Minority in a Multicultural City. Modes of Interaction and Identity Formation in Early Imperial Rome*. London: T. & T. Clark, 2004.

Pitt-Rivers, *Anthropology of the Mediterranean*
 Pitt-Rivers, Julian. *The Fate of Shechem or the Politics of Sex: Essays in the Anthropology of the Mediterranean*. Cambridge: Cambridge University Press, 1977.

Plag, *Israel's Wege*
 Plag, Christoph. *Israel's Wege zum Heil. Eine Untersuchung zu Römer 9 bis 11*. AzTh 40. Stuttgart: Calwer, 1969.

Plevnik, "Recent Developments"
 Plevnik, Joseph. "Recent Developments in the Discussion Concerning Justification by Faith." *TJT* 2 (1986) 47–62.

Plumptre, *Studies*
 Plumptre, E. H. *Biblical Studies*. London: Strahan, 1870.

Pobee, *Persecution*
 Pobee, John S. *Persecution and Martyrdom in the Theology of Paul*. JSNTSup 6. Sheffield: JSOT Press, 1985.

Pohlenz, "Stoa"
 Pohlenz, Max. "Paulus und die Stoa." *ZNW* 42 (1949) 69–104.

Popkes, "Aufbau"
 Popkes, Wiard. "Zum Aufbau und Charakter von Röm 1.18-32." *NTS* 28 (1982) 490–501.

Popkes, *Christus Traditus*
 Popkes, Wiard. *Christus Traditus. Eine Untersuchung zum Begriff der Dahingabe im Neuen Testament*. AThANT 49. Zürich: Zwingli, 1967.

Popper, *Conjectures and Refutations*
 Popper, Karl R. *Conjectures and Refutations: The Growth of Scientific Knowledge*. New York: Harper Torchback, 1968.

Porter, "Argument"
 Porter, Stanley E. "The Argument of Romans 5: Can a Rhetorical Question Make a Difference?" *JBL* 110 (1991) 655–77.

Porter, *Handbook*
 Porter, Stanley E., ed. *Handbook of Classical Rhetoric in the Hellenistic Period 330 B.C.–A.D. 400*. Leiden: Brill, 2001.

Porter, "Paul of Tarsus"
  Porter, Stanley E. "Paul of Tarsus and His Letters." Pp. 533–85
  in S. E. Porter, ed., *Handbook of Classical Rhetoric in the Hellenistic
  Period 330 B.C.–A.D. 400*. Leiden: Brill, 2001.
Porter, "Rhetorical Scribe"
  Porter, Stanley E. "The Rhetorical Scribe: Textual Variants in
  Romans and their Possible Rhetorical Purpose." Pp. 403–19 in
  S. E. Porter and D. L. Stamps, eds., *Rhetorical Criticism and the
  Bible*. JSNTSup 195. London: Sheffield Academic Press, 2002.
Porter, *Verbal Aspect*
  Porter, Stanley E. *Verbal Aspect in the Greek of the New Testament:
  With Reference to Tense and Mood*. New York: P. Lang, 1989.
Powers, *Salvation through Participation*
  Powers, Daniel Glenn. *Salvation through Participation: An
  Examination of the Notion of the Believers' Corporate Unity with
  Christ in Early Christian Soteriology*. CBET 29. Leuven: Peeters,
  2001.
Price, "Rituals"
  Price, S. R. F. "Rituals and Power." Pp. 47–71 in R. A. Horsley,
  ed., *Paul and Empire: Religion and Power in Roman Imperial
  Society*. Harrisburg: Trinity Press International, 1997.
Prümm
  Prümm, Karl. *Die Botschaft des Römerbriefes. Ihr Aufbau und
  Gegenwartswert*. Freiburg: Herder, 1960.
Prümm, "Dynamis"
  Prümm, Karl. "Dynamis in griechisch-hellenistischer Religion
  und Philosophie als Vergleichsbild zu göttlicher Dynamis im
  Offenbarungsraum. Streiflichter auf ein Sondergebiet antik-
  frühchristlicher Begegnung." *ZKT* 83 (1961) 393–420.
Prümm, "Dynamische"
  Prümm, Karl. "Das Dynamische als Grund-Aspekt der
  Heilsordnung in der Sicht des Apostels Paulus." *Greg* 42 (1961)
  643–700.
Quasten, *Music and Worship*
  Quasten, Johannes. *Music and Worship in Pagan and Christian
  Antiquity*. Trans. B. Ramsey. Washington: National Association
  of Pastoral Musicians, 1983.
Radermacher, *Neutestamentliche Grammatik*
  Radermacher, L. *Neutestamentliche Grammatik. Das Griechisch des
  Neuen Testaments im Zusammenhang mit der Volkssprache*. 2d ed.
  Tübingen: Mohr, 1925.
Radl, "Kult und Evangelium"
  Radl, Walter. "Kult und Evangelium bei Paulus." *BZ* 31 (1987)
  58–75.
Rahlfs
  Rahlfs, Alfred. *Septuaginta*. 2 vols. Stuttgart: Württembergische
  Bibelanstalt, 1935.
Räisänen, "ἐπιθυμία and ἐπιθυμεῖν"
  Räisänen, Heikki. "The Use of ἐπιθυμία and ἐπιθυμεῖν in
  Paul." Pp. 95–111 in *Jesus, Paul and Torah: Collected Essays*. Trans.
  D. E. Orton. JSNTSup 43. Sheffield: JSOT Press, 1992.
Räisänen, *Law*
  Räisänen, Heikki. *Paul and the Law*. WUNT 29. Tübingen: Mohr
  Siebeck, 1983.
Räisänen, "Paul's Word-Play"
  Räisänen, Heikki. "Paul's Word-Play on νόμος: A Linguistic
  Study." Pp. 69–94 in H. Räisänen, *Jesus, Paul and Torah: Collected
  Essays*. Trans. D. E. Orton. JSNTSup 43. Sheffield: JSOT Press,
  1992.

Räisänen, "Römer 9–11"
  Räisänen, Heikki. "Römer 9–11. Analyse eines geistigen
  Ringens." *ANRW* 2.25.4 (1987) 2891–2939.
Räisänen, *Torah*
  Räisänen, Heikki. *The Torah and Christ: Essays in German and
  English on the Problem of the Law in Early Christianity*. Publications
  of the Finnish Exegetical Society 45. Helsinki: Finnish Exegetical
  Society, 1986.
Rauer, *Schwachen*
  Rauer, Max. *Die "Schwachen" in Korinth und Rom nach den
  Paulusbriefen*. BibS(F) 21. Freiburg: Herder, 1923.
Reasoner, *The Strong*
  Reasoner, Mark. *The Strong and the Weak. Romans 14.1–15.13 in
  Context*. SNTSMS 103. Cambridge: Cambridge University Press,
  1999.
Reasoner, "The 'Strong' and the 'Weak' in Rome"
  Reasoner, Mark. "The 'Strong' and the 'Weak' in Rome and in
  Paul's Theology." Diss., University of Chicago, 1990.
Reiche
  Reiche, Johann Georg. *Versuch einer ausführlichen Erklärung des
  Briefes Pauli an die Römer, mit historischen Einleitung und exegetisch-
  dogmatische Excursen*. 2 vols. Göttingen: Vandenhoeck &
  Ruprecht, 1833–34.
Reicke, *Agapenfeier*
  Reicke, Bo. *Diakonie, Festfreude und Zelos in Verbindung mit der
  altchristlichen Agapenfeier*. UUÄ 5. Uppsala: Lundequistska, 1951.
Reid, "Consideration"
  Reid, Marty L. "A Consideration of the Function of Rom 1:1–15
  in Light of Greco-Roman Rhetoric." *JETS* 38 (1995) 181–91.
Reid, *Rhetoric*
  Reid, Marty L. *Augustinian and Pauline Rhetoric in Romans Five:
  A Study of Early Christian Rhetoric*. MBPS 30. Lewiston: Mellen,
  1996.
Rengstorf, "Christenheit"
  Rengstorf, Karl Heinrich. "Paulus und die älteste römische
  Christenheit." *StEv* 2 = TU 87 (1964) 447–64.
Reumann, *Righteousness*
  Reumann, John Henry Paul et al. *Righteousness in the New
  Testament*. Philadelphia: Fortress Press; New York: Paulist Press,
  1982.
Rhyne, *Faith*
  Rhyne, C. Thomas. *Faith Establishes the Law*. SBLDS 55. Chico:
  Scholars Press, 1981.
Richards, *Secretary*
  Richards, E. Randolph. *The Secretary in the Letters of Paul*. WUNT
  42. Tübingen: Mohr Siebeck, 1991.
Richardson, *Israel*
  Richardson, Peter. *Israel in the Apostolic Church*. SNTSMS 10.
  Cambridge: Cambridge University Press, 1969.
Ridderbos, *Theology*
  Ridderbos, Herman. *Paul: An Outline of His Theology*. Trans. J. R.
  DeWitt. Grand Rapids: Eerdmans, 1975.
Riedlinger et al., *Historisch-kritische Methode*
  Riedlinger, Helmut, Hermann Strasburger, Henning Graf
  Reventlow, Ferdinand Hahn, and Henri Cazelles. *Die historisch-
  kritische Methode und die heutige Suche nach einem lebendigen
  Verständnis der Bibel*. Freiburg: Katholische Akademie, 1985.

Robertson, *Grammar*
Robertson, A. T. *A Grammar of the Greek New Testament in the Light of Historical Research.* New York: Hodder & Stoughton, 1914.

Robinson, *Body*
Robinson, John A. T. *The Body: A Study in Pauline Theology.* SBT 1/5. Naperville: Allenson, 1952.

Robinson, *Wrestling*
Robinson, John A. T. *Wrestling with Romans.* London: SCM, 1979.

Robinson, *Criminal Law*
Robinson, O. F. *The Criminal Law of Ancient Rome.* London: Duckworth, 1995.

Roetzel, *Judgement*
Roetzel, Calvin J. *Judgement in the Community: A Study of the Relationship between Eschatology and Ecclesiology in Paul.* Leiden: Brill, 1972.

Roetzel, *Letters*
Roetzel, Calvin J. *The Letters of Paul: Conversations in Context.* Atlanta: John Knox, 1975.

Röhser, *Hamartia*
Röhser, Günter. *Metaphorik und Personifikation der Sünde. Antike Sündenvorstellungen und paulinische Hamartia.* WUNT 25. Tübingen: Mohr Siebeck, 1987.

Roller, *Formular*
Roller, Otto. *Das Formular der paulinischen Briefe. Ein Beitrag zur Lehre vom antiken Briefe.* Stuttgart: Kohlhammer, 1933.

Roloff, *Apostolat*
Roloff, Jürgen. *Apostolat-Verkündigung-Kirche. Ursprung, Inhalt und Funktion des kirchlichen Apostelamtes nach Paulus, Lukas und den Pastoralbriefen.* Gütersloh: Gütersloher Verlagshaus, 1965.

Romeo, "ΛΕΙΤΟΥΡΓΙΑ"
Romeo, Antonino. "Il termine ΛΕΙΤΟΥΡΓΙΑ nella grecità biblica (Settanta e Nuovo Testamento)." Pp. 467–519 in vol. 2 of *Miscellanea Liturgica in honorem L. Cuniberti Mohlberg.* Bibliotheca Ephemerides Liturgicae 23. Rome: Edizioni Liturgiche, 1949.

Rostovtzeff, *Empire*
Rostovtzeff, M. *The Social and Economic History of the Roman Empire.* 2d ed. Rev. P. M. Fraser. Oxford: Clarendon, 1957.

Rouland, *Pouvoir*
Rouland, Norbert. *Pouvoir politique et dépendance personelle dans l'Antiquité romaine. Genèse et rôle des rapports de clintèle.* CLat 166. Brussels: Latomus, 1979.

Rückert
Rückert, Leopold Immanuel. *Commentar über den Brief Pauli an die Römer.* 2d ed. 2 vols in 1. Leipzig: Volkmar, 1939.

Rudolf, *Gnosis*
Rudolf, Kurt. *Gnosis: The Nature and History of an Ancient Religion.* Trans. R. M. Wilson, P. W. Coxon, and K. H. Kuhn. Edinburgh: T. & T. Clark, 1983.

Rutgers, *Hidden Heritage*
Rutgers, Leonard V. *The Hidden Heritage of Diaspora Judaism.* CBET 20. Leuven: Peeters, 1998.

Sabatier, *Apostle Paul*
Sabatier, Auguste. *The Apostle Paul: A Sketch of His Doctrine.* Trans. A. M. Hellier. 5th ed. London: Hodder & Stoughton, 1903.

Sabou, "Between Horror and Hope"
Sabou, Sorin V. "Between Horror and Hope: Paul's Metaphorical Language of Death in Romans 6:1-11." Diss., Brunel University, 2001.

Safrai, "Home and Family"
Safrai, S. "Home and Family." Pp. 728–92 in S. Safrai et al., eds., *The Jewish People in the First Century: Historical Geography, Political History, Social, Cultural and Religious Life and Institutions.* Philadelphia: Fortress Press, 1976.

Safrai and Stern, *Jewish People*
Safrai, S., and M. Stern, eds. *The Jewish People in the First Century: Historical Geography, Political History, Social, Cultural and Religious Life and Institutions.* 2 vols. CRINT 1.1-2. Philadelphia: Fortress Press, 1974–76.

Sahlin, "Textemendationen"
Sahlin, Harald. "Einige Textemendationen zum Römerbrief." *ThZ* 9 (1953) 92–100.

Sampley, *Pauline Partnership*
Sampley, J. Paul. *Pauline Partnership in Christ: Christian Community and Commitment in Light of Roman Law.* Philadelphia: Fortress Press, 1980.

Sampley, *Walking*
Sampley, J. Paul. *Walking Between the Times: Paul's Moral Reasoning.* Minneapolis: Fortress Press, 1991.

Sampley, "Weak and Strong"
Sampley, J. Paul. "The Weak and the Strong: Paul's Careful and Crafty Rhetorical Strategy in Romans 14:1-15:13." Pp. 40–52 in L. M. White and O. L. Yarbrough, eds., *The Social World of the First Christians: Essays in Honor of Wayne A. Meeks.* Minneapolis: Fortress Press, 1995.

Sand, *Fleisch*
Sand, Alexander. *Der Begriff "Fleisch" in den paulinischen Hauptbriefen.* BU 2. Regensburg: Pustet, 1967.

Sanday and Headlam
Sanday, William, and Arthur C. Headlam. *A Critical and Exegetical Commentary on the Epistle to the Romans.* ICC. Edinburgh: T. & T. Clark, 1895.

Sanders, *Law*
Sanders, Ed P. *Paul, the Law, and the Jewish People.* Philadelphia: Fortress Press, 1983.

Sanders, *Paul*
Sanders, Ed P. *Paul and Palestinian Judaism: A Comparison of Patterns of Religion.* Philadelphia: Fortress Press, 1977.

Sandmel, *Paul*
Sandmel, Samuel. *The Genius of Paul.* 1958. Repr. Philadelphia: Fortress Press, 1979.

Sandnes, *Paul*
Sandnes, Karl Olav. *Paul—One of the Prophets? A Contribution to the Apostle's Self-Understanding.* WUNT 2.43. Tübingen: Mohr Siebeck, 1991.

Sänger, *Verkündigung*
Sänger, Dieter. *Verkündigung des Gekreuzigten und Israel. Studien zum Verhältnis von Kirche und Israel bei Paulus und im frühen Christentum.* WUNT 75. Tübingen: Mohr Siebeck, 1994.

Sansone, "Article in Greek"
Sansone, David. "Towards a New Doctrine of the Article in Greek: Some Observations on the Definite Article in Plato." *CP* 20 (1993) 191–205.

Sass, *Verheißungen*

' Sass, Gerhard. *Leben aus den Verheißungen. Traditionsgeschichtliche und biblisch-theologische Untersuchungen zur Rede von Gottes Verheißungen im Frühjudentum und beim Apostel Paulus.* FRLANT 164. Göttingen: Vandenhoeck & Ruprecht, 1995.

Satake, "Apostolat und Gnade"

Satake, Akari. "Apostolat und Gnade bei Paulus." *NTS* 15 (1968/69)

Schade, *Christologie*

Schade, Hans H. *Apokalyptische Christologie bei Paulus. Studien zum Zusammenhang von Christologie und Eschatologie in den Paulusbriefen.* GThA 18. Göttingen: Vandenhoeck & Ruprecht, 1981.

Schäfer, *Bruderschaft*

Schäfer, Klaus. *Gemeinde als "Bruderschaft." Ein Beitrag zum Kirchenverständnis des Paulus.* EHS 333. Frankfurt: Peter Lang, 1989.

Schäfer, *Judeophobia*

Schäfer, Peter. *Judeophobia: Attitudes toward the Jews in the Ancient World.* Cambridge: Harvard University Press, 1997.

Schattenmann, *Prosahymnus*

Schattenmann, Johannes. *Studien zum neutestamentlichen Prosahymnus.* Munich: Beck, 1965.

Schatzmann, *Charismata*

Schatzmann, Siegfried S. *A Pauline Theology of Charismata.* Peabody: Hendrickson, 1987.

Schenk, *Segen*

Schenk, Wolfgang. *Das Segen im Neuen Testament. Eine begriffs-analytische Studie.* ThA 25. Berlin: Evangelische Verlagsanstalt, 1967.

Schenke, "Aporien"

Schenke, Hans-Martin. "Aporien im Romerbrief." *ThLZ* 92 (1967) 882–88.

Schettler, *Durch Christus*

Schettler, Adolf. *Die paulinische Formel "Durch Christus" untersucht.* Tübingen: Mohr (Siebeck), 1907.

Schille, *Frühchristliche Hymnen*

Schille, Gottfried. *Frühchristliche Hymnen.* Berlin: Evangelischer Verlagsanstalt, 1965.

Schille, *Kollegialmission*

Schille, Gottfried. *Die urchristliche Kollegialmission.* AThANT 48. Zurich: Zwingli, 1967.

Schlatter

Schlatter, Adolf. *Romans. The Righteousness of God.* Trans. S. S. Schatzmann. Peabody: Hendrickson, 1995.

Schlatter, "Herz und Gehirn"

Schlatter, Adolf. "Herz und Gehirn im ersten Jahrhundert." Pp. 86–94 in Friedrich Traub, ed., *Studien zur Systematischen Theologie. Theodor von Häring zum siebzigsten Geburtstag (22. April 1918) von Fachgenossen dargebracht.* Tübingen: Mohr, 1918.

Schlier

Schlier, Heinrich. *Der Römerbrief.* HThKNT 6. Freiburg: Herder, 1977.

Schlier, *Besinnung*

Schlier, Heinrich. *Besinnung auf das Neue Testament: Exegetische Aufsätze und Vorträge.* Vol. 2. Freiburg: Herder, 1967.

Schlier, *Ende*

Schlier, Heinrich. *Das Ende der Zeit: Exegetische Aufsätze und Vorträge.* Freiburg: Herder, 1971.

Schlier, *Zeit*

Schlier, Heinrich. *Die Zeit der Kirche. Exegetische Aufsätze und Vorträge.* Freiburg: Herder, 1955, 1967, 1972.

Schmauch, *In Christus*

Schmauch, Werner. *In Christus. Eine Untersuchung zur Sprache und Theologie des Paulus.* NTF 9. Gütersloh: Bertelsmann, 1935.

Schmeller, *Diatribe*

Schmeller, Thomas. *Paulus und die "Diatribe." Eine vergleichende Stilinterpretation.* NtAbh 19. Münster: Aschendorff, 1987.

Schmid, *Gerechtigkeit als Weltordnung*

Schmid, Hans Heinrich. *Gerechtigkeit als Weltordnung. Hintergrund and Geschichte des altestamentlichen Gerechtigkeits-begriffes.* BHTh 40. Tübingen: Mohr Siebeck, 1968.

Schmidt

Schmidt, Hans Wilhelm. *Der Brief des Paulus an die Römer.* ThHK 6. Berlin: Evangelische Verlagsanstalt, 1963.

Schmidt, *Marcion*

Schmidt, Ulrich. *Marcion und sein Apostolos. Rekonstruktion und historische Einordnung der marcionitischen Paulusbriefausgabe.* ANTF 25. Berlin: de Gruyter, 1995.

Schmithals

Schmithals, Walter. *Der Römerbrief. Ein Kommentar.* Gütersloh: Mohn, 1988.

Schmithals, *Anthropologie*

Schmithals, Walter. *Die theologische Anthropologie des Paulus. Auslegung von Röm 7.17–8.39.* Stuttgart: Kohlhammer, 1980.

Schmithals, *Office of Apostle*

Schmithals, Walter. *The Office of Apostle in the Early Church.* Trans. J. E. Steely. Nashville: Abingdon, 1969.

Schmithals, *Römerbrief*

Schmithals, Walter. *Der Römerbrief als historisches Problem.* SNT 9. Gütersloh: Mohn, 1975.

Schmitt, *Paulus*

Schmitt, Rainer. *Gottesgerechtigkei-Heilsgeschichte-Israel in der Theologie des Paulus.* EHS 23.240. Frankfurt: Lang, 1984.

Schmitz, "Abraham"

Schmitz, Otto. "Abraham im Spätjudentum und im Urchristentum." Pp. 99–123 in K. Bornhäuser et al., eds., *Aus Schrift und Geschichte: Theologische Abhandlungen Adolf Schlatter zu seinem 70. Geburtstag dargebracht von Freunden und Schülern.* Stuttgart: Calwer Vereinsbuch, 1922.

Schnabel, *Law*

Schnabel, Eckhard J. *Law and Wisdom from Ben Sira to Paul. A Tradition Historical Enquiry into the Relation of Law, Wisdom, and Ethics.* WUNT 16. Tübingen: Mohr Siebeck, 1985.

Schneider, "Schwachen"

Schneider, Nélio. "Die 'Schwachen' in der christlichen Gemeinde Roms. Eine historisch-exegetische Untersuchung zu Röm 14,1–15,13." Diss., University of Wuppertal, 1989.

Schnider and Stenger, *Briefformular*

Schnider, Franz, and Werner Stenger. *Studien zum neutesta-mentlichen Briefformular.* NTTS 11. Leiden: Brill, 1987.

Schoeni, "Hyperbolic Sublime"

Schoeni, Marc. "The Hyperbolic Sublime as a Master Trope in Romans." Pp. 171–92 in S. E. Porter and T. H. Olbricht, eds., *Rhetoric and the New Testament: Essays from the 1992 Heidelberg Conference.* JSNTSup 90. Sheffield: JSOT Press, 1993.

Schott

Schott, Theodor Friedrich. *Der Römerbrief seinem Endzweck und seinem Gedankengang nach ausgelegt.* Erlangen: Deichert, 1858.

Schottroff, "Schreckensherrschaft"
  Schottroff, Luise. "Die Schreckensherrschaft der Sünde und die Befreiung durch Christus nach dem Römerbrief des Paulus." *EvTh* 39 (1979) 497–510.
Schrage, *Einzelgebote*
  Schrage, Wolfgang. *Die konkreten Einzelgebote in der paulinischen Paränese.* Gütersloh: Gütersloher Verlagshaus, 1975. Trans. D. E. Green. *The Ethics of the New Testament.* Philadelphia: Fortress Press, 1988.
Schreiner
  Schreiner, Thomas R. *Romans.* BECNT 6. Grand Rapids: Baker, 1998.
Schrenk, "Missionsdokument"
  Schrenk, Gottlob. "Der Römerbrief als Missionsdokument." Pp. 82–87 in *Studien zu Paulus.* Zurich: Zwingli, 1954.
Schubert, *Thanksgivings*
  Schubert, Paul. *Form and Function of the Pauline Thanksgivings.* BZNW 20. Berlin: de Gruyter, 1939.
Schulz, *Mitte der Schrift*
  Schulz, Siegfried. *Die Mitte der Schrift. Der Frühkatholizismus im Neuen Testament als Herausforderung an den Protestantismus.* Stuttgart: Kreuz, 1976.
Schumacher, *Letzten Kapitel*
  Schumacher, Rudolf. *Die beiden letzten Kapitel des Römerbriefes. Ein Beitrag zu ihrer Geschichte und Erklärung.* NTAbh 14. Würzburg: Aschendorff, 1929.
Schürer, *History*
  Schürer, E. *The History of the Jewish People in the Age of Jesus Christ (175 B.C.–A.D. 135).* Rev. G. Vermes et al. 3 vols. in 4. Edinburgh: T. & T. Clark, 1973–87.
Schürmann, "Gemeinde"
  Schürmann, Heinz. "Gemeinde als Bruderschaft." Pp. 61–73 in H. Schürmann. *Ursprung und Gestalt. Erörterungen und Besinnungen zum Neuen Testament.* Düsseldorf: Patmos, 1970.
Schütz, "Charisma"
  Schütz, John Howard. "Charisma IV. Neues Testament." *TRE* 7 (1981) 688–93.
Schweitzer, *Mysticism*
  Schweitzer, Albert. *The Mysticism of Paul the Apostle.* Trans. W. Montgomery. 1931. Repr. London: Black, 1953.
Schweizer, *Church Order*
  Schweizer, Eduard. *Church Order in the New Testament.* London: SCM, 1961.
Schweizer, *Erniedrigung*
  Schweizer, Eduard. *Erniedrigung und Erhöhung bei Jesus und seinen Nachfolgern.* Zurich: Zwingli, 1962.
Schweizer, "Hintergrund"
  Schweizer, Eduard. "Zum religionsgeschichtlichen Hintergrund der 'Sendungsformel' Gal 4,4 f.; Röm 8,3 f.; Joh. 3,16 f.; 1 Joh. 4,9," *ZNW* 57 (1966) 199–210; repr. pp. 83–95 in E. Schweizer, *Beiträge zur Theologie des Neuen Testaments: Neutestamentliche Aufsätze (1955–70).* Zurich: Zwingli Verlag, 1970.
Schweizer, *Neotestamentica*
  Schweizer, Eduard. *Neotestamentica. Deutsche und Englische Aufsätze 1951–1963. German and English Essays 1951–1963.* Zurich: Zwingli, 1963.
Schweizer, "Röm 15,1-13"
  Schweizer, Eduard. "Röm 15,1-13." Pp. 81–86 in *Neues Testament und heutige Verkündigung.* BSt 56. Neukirchen-Vluyn: Neukirchener Verlag, 1969.

Schweizer, "Sünde in den Gliedern"
  Schweizer, Eduard. "Die Sünde in den Gliedern." Pp. 437–39 in Otto Betz et al., eds., *Abraham unser Vater: Juden und Christen in Gespräch über die Bibel. Festschrift für Otto Michel zum 60. Geburtstag.* AGSU 5. Leiden: Brill, 1963.
Scott, *Adoption*
  Scott, James M. *Adoption as Sons of God: An Exegetical Investigation into the Background of ΥΙΟΘΕΣΙΑ in the Pauline Corpus.* WUNT 2.48. Tübingen: Mohr Siebeck, 1992.
Scramuzza, *Claudius*
  Scramuzza, Vincent M. *The Emperor Claudius.* Cambridge: Harvard University Press, 1940.
Scroggs, *Last Adam*
  Scroggs, Robin. *The Last Adam: A Study in Pauline Anthropology.* Oxford: Blackwell, 1966.
Scroggs, *New Day*
  Scroggs, Robin. *Paul for a New Day.* Philadelphia: Fortress Press, 1977.
Seeberg, *Katechismus*
  Seeberg, Alfred. *Der Katechismus der Urchristenheit.* ThBü 26. Munich: Kaiser, 1966.
Seesemann, *ΚΟΙΝΩΝΙΑ*
  Seesemann, Heinrich. *Der Begriff ΚΟΙΝΩΝΙΑ im Neuen Testament.* BZNW 14. Giessen: Töpelmann, 1933.
Segal, *Paul the Convert*
  Segal, Alan F. *Paul the Convert: The Apostolate and Apostasy of Saul the Pharisee.* New Haven: Yale University Press, 1990.
Segal, *Rebecca's Children*
  Segal, Alan F. *Rebecca's Children: Judaism and Christianity in the Roman World.* Cambridge: Harvard University Press, 1986.
Seifrid, *Christ, Our Righteousness*
  Seifrid, Mark A. *Christ, Our Righteousness: Paul's Theology of Justification.* NSBT 9. Downers Grove: InterVarsity Press, 2000.
Seifrid, *Justification*
  Seifrid, Mark A. *Justification by Faith: The Origin and Development of a Central Pauline Theme.* NovTSup 68. Leiden: Brill, 1992.
Sevenster, *Paul and Seneca*
  Sevenster, J. N. *Paul and Seneca.* NovTSup 4. Leiden: Brill, 1961.
Shantz, "Paul in Ecstasy"
  Shantz, Colleen. "Paul in Ecstasy: The Evidence for and Implications of Paul's Ecstatic Religious Experience." Diss., University of St. Michael's College, Toronto, 2003.
Sherwin-White, *Roman Society*
  Sherwin-White, A. N. *Roman Society and Roman Law in the New Testament.* Oxford: Clarendon, 1963.
Shum, *Paul's Use of Isaiah*
  Shum, Shiu-Lun. *Paul's Use of Isaiah in Romans: A Comparative Study of Paul's Letter to the Romans and the Sibylline and Qumran Sectarian Texts.* WUNT 156. Tübingen: Mohr Siebeck, 2002.
Siber, *Mit Christus*
  Siber, Peter. *Mit Christus Leben. Eine Studie zur paulinischen Auferstehungshoffnung.* Zürich: Theologischer Verlag, 1971.
Sickenberger
  Sickenberger, Joseph. *Die beiden Briefe des heiligen Paulus an die Korinther und sein Brief an die Römer.* 4th ed. HSNT 6. Bonn: Hanstein, 1932.
Siegert, *Argumentation*
  Siegert, Folker. *Argumentation bei Paulus gezeigt an Röm 9–11.* WUNT 34. Tübingen: Mohr Siebeck, 1985.

Siker, *Disinheriting the Jews*
   Siker, Jeffrey S. *Disinheriting the Jews: Abraham in Early Christian Controversy.* Louisville: Westminster John Knox, 1991.
Slingerland, *Claudian Policymaking*
   Slingerland, H. Dixon. *Claudian Policymaking and the Early Imperial Repression of Judaism at Rome.* SFSHJ 160. Atlanta: Scholars Press, 1997.
Smallwood, *Jews*
   Smallwood, E. Mary. *The Jews under Roman Rule. From Pompey to Diocletian. A Study in Political Relations.* SJLA 20. Leiden: Brill, 1981.
Smiga, "Occasion of the Letter"
   Smiga, George. "Romans 12:1-2 and 15:30-32 and the Occasion of the Letter to the Romans." *CBQ* 53 (1991) 257–73.
Smiles, "Concept of 'Zeal'"
   Smiles, Vincent M. "The Concept of 'Zeal' in Second-Temple Judaism and Paul's Critique of It in Romans 10:2." *CBQ* 64 (2002) 282–99.
Smyth, *Grammar*
   Smyth, H. W. *Greek Grammar.* Rev. G. M. Messing. Cambridge: Harvard University Press, 1956.
Snyder, "Major Motifs"
   Snyder, Graydon F. "Major Motifs in the Interpretation of Paul's Letter to the Romans." Pp. 42–63 in S. E. McGinn, ed., *Celebrating Romans: Template for Pauline Theology. Essays in Honor of Robert Jewett.* Grand Rapids: Eerdmans, 2004.
Snyman, "Style"
   Snyman, A. H. "Style and the Rhetorical Situation of Romans 8.31-39." *NTS* 34 (1988) 218–31.
Söding, *Liebesgebot*
   Söding, Thomas. *Das Liebesgebot bei Paulus. Die Mahnung zur Agape im Rahmen der paulinischen Ethik.* NTAbh 26. Münster: Aschendorff, 1995.
Söding and Münch, *Methodenbuch*
   Söding, Thomas, and Christian Münch. *Wege der Schriftauslegung. Methodenbuch zum Neuen Testament.* Basel: Herder Freiburg, 1998.
Solin, *Beiträge*
   Solin, Heikki. *Beiträge zur Kenntnis der griechischen Personennamen in Rom.* Vol. 1. CHL 48. Helsinki: Societas Scientiarum Fennica, 1971.
Solin, "Juden und Syrer"
   Solin, Heikki. "Juden und Syrer im westlichen Teil der römischen Welt." *ANRW* II 29/2 (1983) 587–789.
Solin, *Namenbuch*
   Solin, Heikki. *Die griechischen Personennamen in Rom: Ein Namenbuch.* 3 vols. Berlin: de Gruyter, 1982.
Solin, *Sklavennamen*
   Solin, Heikki. *Die stadtrömischen Sklavennamen.* ForAS.B 2. Stuttgart: Steiner, 1996.
Song, *Diatribe*
   Song, Changwon. *Reading Romans as a Diatribe.* SBL 59. New York: Lang, 2004.
Stachowiak, *Chrestotes*
   Stachowiak, Lech Remigius. *Chrestotes. Ihre biblisch-theologische Entwicklung und Eigenart.* SF 17. Fribourg: Universitätsverlag, 1957.
Stählin, "Beteuerungsformeln"
   Stählin, Gustav. "Zum Gebrauch von Beteuerungsformeln im Neuen Testament." Pp. 115–43 in *Donum gratulatorium: Ethelbert Stauffer dem sechzigjahrigen in dankbarer Verehrung.* NovT 5.2–3. Leiden: Brill, 1962.
Stählin, *Skandalon*
   Stählin, Gustav. *Skandalon. Untersuchungen zur Geschichte eines biblischen Begriffs.* BFChTh 2.24. Gütersloh: Bertelsmann, 1930.
Stalder, *Werk*
   Stalder, Kurt. *Das Werk des Geistes in der Heiligung bei Paulus.* Zurich: EVZ Verlag, 1962.
Stambaugh, *Ancient Roman City*
   Stambaugh, John E. *The Ancient Roman City.* ASH. Baltimore: Johns Hopkins University Press, 1988.
Stanley, *Arguing*
   Stanley, Christopher D. *Arguing with Scripture. The Rhetoric of Citations in the Letters of Paul.* London: T. & T. Clark, 2004.
Stanley, *Scripture*
   Stanley, Christopher D. *Paul and the Language of Scripture. Citation Technique in the Pauline Epistles and Contemporary Literature.* SNTSMS 74. Cambridge: Cambridge University Press, 1992.
Stark, *Rise*
   Stark, Rodney. *The Rise of Christianity: A Sociologist Considers History.* Princeton: Princeton University Press, 1996.
Starnitzke, *Struktur*
   Starnitzke, Dierk. *Die Struktur paulinischen Denkens im Römerbrief. Eine linguistisch-logische Untersuchung.* BWANT 163. Stuttgart: Kohlhammer, 2004.
Stegner, "Midrash"
   Stegner, William R. "Romans 9:6-29—A Midrash." *JSNT* 22 (1984) 37–52.
Stendahl, *Final Account*
   Stendahl, Krister. *Final Account: Paul's Letter to the Romans.* Minneapolis: Fortress Press, 1995.
Stendahl, *Paul*
   Stendahl, Krister. *Paul Among Jews and Gentiles and Other Essays.* Philadelphia: Fortress Press, 1977.
Stöger, "Brüderliche Ordnung"
   Stöger, Alois. "Die brüderliche Ordnung unter Christen. Biblische Grundlegung." *TPQ* 117 (1969) 185–90.
Stowers, *Diatribe*
   Stowers, Stanley K. *The Diatribe and Paul's Letter to the Romans.* SBLDS 57. Chico: Scholars Press, 1981.
Stowers, *Letter*
   Stowers, Stanley K. *Letter Writing in Greco-Roman Antiquity.* Philadelphia: Westminister, 1986.
Stowers, *Rereading*
   Stowers, Stanley K. *A Rereading of Romans: Justice, Jews and Gentiles.* New Haven: Yale University Press, 1994.
Stowers, "Speech-in-Character"
   Stowers, Stanley K. "Romans 7.7-25 as a Speech-in-Character (προσωποποιία)." Pp. 180–202 in Troels Engberg-Pedersen, ed., *Paul in His Hellenistic Context.* Minneapolis: Fortress Press, 1995.
Strobel, "Begriff des 'Hauses'"
   Strobel, Adolf. "Der Begriff des 'Hauses' im griechischen und romischen Privatrecht." *ZNW* 56 (1965) 91–100.
Strobel, *Erkenntnis*
   Strobel, Adolf. *Erkenntnis und Bekenntnis der Sünde in neutestamentlicher Zeit.* Stuttgart: Calwer, 1968.
Strobel, "Röm 13"
   Strobel, Adolf. "Zum Verständnis von Röm 13." *ZNW* 47 (1956) 67–93.

Strobel, *Verzögerungs-problem*
    Strobel, Adolf. *Untersuchungen zum Eschatologischen Verzögerungs-problem auf Grund der spät judisch-urchristlichen Geschichte von Habakuk 2,2ff.* NovTSup2. Leiden: Brill, 1961.

Strom, *Reframing Paul*
    Strom, Mark. *Reframing Paul: Conversations in Grace.* Downers Grove: InterVarsity Press, 2000.

Stuhlmacher
    Stuhlmacher, Peter. *Paul's Letter to the Romans: A Commentary.* Trans. S. J. Hafemann. Louisville: Westminster/John Knox, 1994.

Stuhlmacher, "Begriff des Friedens"
    Stuhlmacher, Peter. "Der Begriff des Friedens im Neuen Testament und seine Konsequenzen." Pp. 21–69 in vol. 4 of W. Huber, ed., *Historische Beiträge zur Friedensforschung.* SFF 4. Stuttgart: Klett, 1970.

Stuhlmacher, *Evangelium*
    Stuhlmacher, Peter. *Das paulinische Evangelium.* FRLANT 95. Göttingen: Vandenhoeck & Ruprecht, 1968.

Stuhlmacher, *Gerechtigkeit*
    Stuhlmacher, Peter. *Gerechtigkeit Gottes bei Paulus.* FRLANT 87. Göttingen: Vandenhoeck & Ruprecht, 1966.

Stuhlmacher, "Probleme"
    Stuhlmacher, Peter. "Theologische Probleme des Römerbriefpräskripts." *EvTh* 27 (1967) 374–89.

Stuhlmacher, "Purpose"
    Stuhlmacher, Peter. "The Purpose of Romans." Pp. 231–42 in Karl P. Donfried, ed., *The Romans Debate.* Rev. ed. Peabody: Hendrickson, 1991.

Stuhlmacher, *Reconciliation*
    Stuhlmacher, Peter. *Reconciliation, Law, and Righteousness: Essays in Biblical Theology.* Trans. E. R. Kalin. Philadelphia: Fortress Press, 1986.

Stuhlmacher, "Theme"
    Stuhlmacher, Peter. "The Theme of Romans." Pp. 333–45 in Karl P. Donfried, ed., *The Romans Debate.* Rev. ed. Peabody: Hendrickson, 1991.

Stuhlmann, *Eschatologische Maß*
    Stuhlmann, Rainer. *Das eschatologische Maß im Neuen Testament.* FRLANT 152. Göttingen: Vandenhoeck & Ruprecht, 1983.

Suggs, "Word"
    Suggs, M. Jack. "The Word Is Near You: Rom 10:6-10 within the Purpose of the Letter." Pp. 289–312 in W. R. Farmer, C. F. D. Moule, and R. R. Niebuhr, eds., *Christian History and Interpretation: Studies Presented to John Knox.* Cambridge: Cambridge University Press, 1967.

Sullivan, "ΕΠΙΓΝΩΣΙΣ"
    Sullivan, Kathryn. "ΕΠΙΓΝΩΣΙΣ in the Epistles of St. Paul." Pp. 405–16 in vol. 2 of *Studiorum Paulinorum congressus internationalis catholicus.* AnBib 18. Rome: Biblical Institute, 1963.

Synofzik, *Vergeltungsaussagen*
    Synofzik, Ernst. *Die Gerichts- und Vergeltungsaussagen bei Paulus. Eine traditionsgeschichtliche Untersuchung.* GThA 8. Göttingen: Vandenhoeck & Ruprecht, 1977.

Swanson, *Vaticanus: Romans*
    Swanson, Reuben J. *New Testament Greek Manuscripts: Variant Readings Arranged in Horizontal Lines against Vaticanus: Romans.* Wheaton: Tyndale House, 2001.

Tachau, *Einst*
    Tachau, Peter. *"Einst" und "Jetzt" im Neuen Testament. Beobachtungen zu einem urchristlichen Predigtschema in der neutestamentlichen Briefliteratur und zu seiner Vorgeschichte.* FRLANT 105. Göttingen: Vandenhoeck & Ruprecht, 1972.

Tamez, "Justification"
    Tamez, Elsa. "Justification as Good News for Women: A Re-reading of Romans 1–8." Trans. S. E. McGinn. Pp. 177–89 in S. E. McGinn, ed., *Celebrating Romans: Template for Pauline Theology. Essays in Honor of Robert Jewett.* Grand Rapids: Eerdmans, 2004.

Tannehill, *Dying*
    Tannehill, Robert C. *Dying and Rising with Christ: A Study in Pauline Theology.* BZNW 32. Berlin: Töpelmann, 1967.

Theissen, *Psychological Aspects*
    Theissen, Gerd. *Psychological Aspects of Pauline Theology.* Trans. J. P. Galvin. Philadelphia: Fortress Press, 1987.

Theissen, *Religion*
    Theissen, Gerd. *The Religion of the Earliest Churches: Creating a Symbolic World.* Trans. J. Bowden. Minneapolis: Fortress Press, 1999.

Theissen, *Social Reality*
    Theissen, Gerd. *Social Reality and the Early Christians. Theology, Ethics, and the World of the New Testament.* Trans. M. Kohl. Minneapolis: Fortress Press, 1992.

Theissen, *Social Setting*
    Theissen, Gerd. *The Social Setting of Pauline Christianity: Essays on Corinth.* Trans. J. H. Schütz. Philadelphia: Fortress Press, 1982.

Theobald
    Theobald, Michael. *Römerbrief.* 2 vols. Stuttgarter Kleiner Kommentar, Neues Testament 6.1-2. Stuttgart: Katholisches Bibelwerk, 1992–93.

Theobald, "Glaube und Vernunft."
    Theobald, Michael. "Glaube und Vernunft. Zur Argumentationen des Paulus im Römerbrief." *ThQ* 169 (1989) 287–301.

Theobald, *Gnade*
    Theobald, Michael. *Die überströmende Gnade. Studien zu einem paulinischen Motivfeld.* FB 22. Würzburg: Echter Verlag, 1982.

Theobald, "Gottesbild"
    Theobald, Michael. "Das Gottesbild des Paulus nach Röm 3,21-31." *SNTU* 6-7 (1981–82) 131–68.

Theobald, *Studien*
    Theobald, Michael. *Studien zum Römerbrief.* WUNT 136. Tübingen: Mohr Siebeck, 2001.

Therrien, *Discernement*
    Therrien, Gérard. *Le Discernement dans les écrits pauliniens.* ÉtBib. Paris: Gabalda, 1973.

Thielman, *Law*
    Thielman, Frank. *Paul & the Law: A Contextual Approach.* Downers Grove: InterVarsity Press, 1994.

Thielman, *Plight*
    Thielman, Frank. *From Plight to Salvation: A Jewish Framework to Understanding Paul's View of the Law in Galatians and Romans.* NovTSup 61. Leiden: Brill, 1989.

Thimmes, "Analogies"
Thimmes, Pamela. "'She Will be Called an Adulteress . . .':
Marriage and Adultery Analogies in Romans 7:1-4." Pp. 190–203
in S. E. McGinn, ed., *Celebrating Romans: Template for Pauline
Theology. Essays in Honor of Robert Jewett.* Grand Rapids:
Eerdmans, 2004.

Tholuck
Tholuck, Friedrich August Gottreu. *St. Paul's Epistle to the
Romans: With Extracts from the Exegetical Works of the Fathers and
Reformers.* Trans. R. Menzies. 2 vols. Philadelphia: Sorin and
Ball, 1824, 1844.

Thompson, *Clothed with Christ*
Thompson, Michael. *Clothed with Christ: The Example and
Teaching of Jesus in Romans 12.1–15.13.* JSNTSup 59. Sheffield:
Sheffield Academic Press, 1991.

Thomson, *Chiasmus*
Thomson, Ian H. *Chiasmus in the Pauline Letters.* JSNTSup 111.
Sheffield: Sheffield Academic Press, 1995.

Thorsteinsson, *Paul's Interlocutor*
Thorsteinsson, Runar M. *Paul's Interlocutor in Romans 2: Function
and Identity in the Context of Ancient Epistolography.* ConBNT 40.
Stockholm: Almqvist & Wiksell, 2003.

Thraede, *Brieftopoi*
Thraede, Klaus. *Einheit—Gegenwart—Gespräch: Zur
Christianisierung antiker Brieftopoi.* Bonn: Rheinische Friedrich-
Wilhelms-Universität, 1967.

Thraede, "Heiligen Kusses"
Thraede, Klaus. "Ursprünge und Formen des 'Heiligen Kusses'
im frühen Christentum." *JAC* 11–12 (1968–69) 124–80.

Thrall, *Greek Particles*
Thrall, Margaret. *Greek Particles in the New Testament: Linguistic
and Exegetical Studies.* NTTS 3. Leiden: Brill, 1962.

Thurén, *Derhetorizing Paul*
Thurén, Lauri. *Derhetorizing Paul: A Dynamic Perspective on
Pauline Theology and the Law.* WUNT 124. Tübingen: Mohr-
Siebeck, 2000.

Thurén, "Romans 7"
Thurén, Lauri. "Romans 7 Derhetorized." Pp. 420–40 in S. E.
Porter and D. L. Stamps, eds., *Rhetorical Criticism and the Bible.*
JSNTSup 195. Sheffield: Sheffield Academic Press, 2002.

Thüsing, *Per Christum*
Thüsing, Wilhelm. *Gott und Christus in der paulinischen
Soteriologie.* Vol. 1. *Per Christum in Deum. Das Verhältnis der
Christozentrik zur Theozentrik.* 3d ed. NTAbh 1. Münster:
Aschendorff, 1986.

Thyen, *Studien*
Thyen, Hartwig. *Studien zur Sündenvergebung im Neuen Testament
und seinen alttestamentlichen und jüdischen Voraussetzungen.*
FRLANT 96. Göttingen: Vandenhoeck & Ruprecht, 1970.

Tobin, *Paul's Rhetoric*
Tobin, Thomas H., S.J. *Paul's Rhetoric in Its Context: The
Argument of Romans.* Peabody: Hendrickson, 2004.

Tobin, "Romans 4"
Tobin, Thomas H. "What Shall We Say that Abraham Found?
The Controversy behind Romans 4." *HTR* 88 (1995) 437–52.

du Toit, "Dikaiosyne"
Toit, Andries B. du. "*Dikaiosyne* in Röm 6: Beobachtungen zur
ethischen Dimension der paulinischen Gerechtigkeitsauffassung," *ZThK* 76 (1979) 263–69.

du Toit, "Doxologische Gemeinschaft"
Toit, Andries B. du. "Die Kirche als doxologische Gemeinschaft
im Römerbrief." *Neot* 27 (1993) 69–77.

du Toit, "Persuasion"
Toit, Andries B. du. "Persuasion in Romans 1:1-17." *BZ* 33
(1989) 192–209.

Tomson, *Paul and the Jewish Law*
Tomson, Peter J. *Paul and the Jewish Law: Halakha in the Letters of
the Apostle to the Gentiles.* CRINT III.1. Minneapolis: Fortress
Press, 1990.

Trench, *Synonyms*
Trench, Richard Chenevix. *Synonyms of the New Testament.*
London: Kegan Paul, Trench, Trübner, 1906.

Trobisch, *Entstehung*
Trobisch, David. *Die Entstehung der Paulusbriefsammlung.* NTOA
10. Freiburg: Universitätsverlag; Göttingen: Vandenhoeck &
Ruprecht, 1989.

Troeltsch, *Social Teaching*
Troeltsch, Ernst. *The Social Teaching of the Christian Churches.*
New York: Macmillan, 1931.

Tuckett, *Interpretation*
Tuckett, Christopher M. *Reading the New Testament: Methods of
Interpretation.* London: SPCK, 1987.

Turner, *Insights*
Turner, Nigel. *Grammatical Insights into the New Testament.*
Edinburgh: T. & T. Clark, 1965.

Umbreit
Umbreit, Friedrich Wilhelm Carl. *Der Brief an die Römer, auf
dem Grunde des Alten Testaments ausgelegt.* Gotha: Perthes,
1856.

Unnik, "Reaktion der Nicht-Christen"
Unnik, Willem C. van. "Die Rücksicht auf die Reaktion der
Nicht-Christen als Motiv in der altchristlichen Paränese." Pp.
498–522 in F.-W. Eltester, ed., *Judentum, Urchristentum, Kirche.
Festschrift für Joachim Jeremias.* Berlin: Töpelmann, 1960.

Vanhoye, *L'Apôtre*
Vanhoye, Albert, ed. *L'Apôtre Paul: Personnalité, style et conception
du ministère.* BETL 73. Leuven: Leuven University Press, 1986.

Vanni, "Ὁμοίωμα in Paolo"
Vanni, Ugo. "Ὁμοίωμα (Rm 1,23: 5,14: 6,5: 8,3: Fil 2,7)
Un'interpretazione esegetico-teologica alla luce dell'uso dei
LXX—1ª Parte." *Greg* 58 (1977) 321–45; "2ª Parte." 431–70.

Vermes, *Dead Sea Scrolls*
Vermes, Geza. *The Dead Sea Scrolls in English.* 3d ed. London:
Penguin, 1987.

Viagulamuthu, *Offering*
Viagulamuthu, Xavier Paul B. *Offering Our Bodies as a Living
Sacrifice to God: A Study in Pauline Spirituality Based on Romans
12,1.* Rome: Pontifical Gregorian University, 2002.

Viard
Viard, A. *Saint Paul. Épître aux Romains.* 2d ed. Sources
bibliques. Paris: Gabalda, 1975.

Vielhauer, *Geschichte*
Vielhauer, Philipp. *Geschichte der urchristlichen Literatur.* Berlin:
de Gruyter, 1975.

Vielhauer, *OIKOΔOMH*
    Vielhauer, Philipp. *OIKOΔOMH. Das Bild vom Bau in der christlichen Literatur vom Neuen Testament bis Clemens Alexandrinus*. Karlsruhe-Durlach: Tron, 1939. Repr. pp. 1–168 in vol. 2 of G. Klein, ed., *Oikodome. Aufsätze zum Neuen Testament by Philipp Vielhauer*. Munich: Kaiser, 1979.

Vogt, *Kulturwelt und Barbaren*
    Vogt, Joseph. *Kulturwelt und Barbaren. Zum Menschheitsbild der spätantiken Gesellschaft*. AGS. Wiesbaden: Steiner, 1967.

Volf, *Paul and Perserverance*
    Volf, Judith M. Gundry. *Paul and Perserverance: Staying In and Falling Away*. Louisville: Westminster/John Knox, 1990.

Volkmar
    Volkmar, Gustav. *Paulus Römerbrief. Das älteste Text deutsch und im Zusammenhang erklärt. Mit dem Wordabdruck der vatikanischen Urkunde*. NBGZ 1. Zurich: Schmidt, 1875.

Vollenweider, *Freiheit*
    Vollenweider, Samuel. *Freiheit als neue Schöpfung. Eine Untersuchung zur Eleutheria bei Paulus und in seiner Umwelt*. FRLANT 147. Göttingen: Vandenhoeck & Ruprecht, 1989.

Vos, *Kunst der Argumentation*
    Vos, Johan S. *Die Kunst der Argumentation bei Paulus. Studien zur antiken Rhetorik*. WUNT 149. Tübingen: Mohr Siebeck, 2002.

Wagenvoort, *Roman Dynamism*
    Wagenvoort, H. *Roman Dynamism: Studies in Ancient Roman Thought, Language and Custom*. With an Introductory Note by H. J. Rose. Oxford: Blackwell, 1947.

Wagner, *Pauline Baptism*
    Wagner, Günter. *Pauline Baptism and the Pagan Mysteries: The Problem of the Pauline Doctrine of Baptism in Romans VI.1-11, in the Light of Its Religio-Historical "Parallels."* Trans. J. P. Smith. Edinburgh: Burns & Oates, 1967.

Wagner, *Heralds*
    Wagner, J. Ross. *Heralds of the Good News: Israel and Paul "in Concert" in the Letter to the Romans*. NovTSup 101. Leiden: Brill, 2002.

Wagner, "Heralds of Isaiah"
    Wagner, J. Ross. "The Heralds of Isaiah and the Mission of Paul: An Investigation of Isaiah 51–55 in Romans." Pp. 193–222 in W. H. Bellinger Jr. and W. R. Farmer, eds., *Jesus and the Suffering Servant: Isaiah 53 and Christian Origins*. Harrisburg: Trinity Press International, 1998.

Walker, *Interpolations*
    Walker, William O., Jr. *Interpolations in the Pauline Letters*. JSNTSup 213. Sheffield: Sheffield Academic Press, 2001.

Walters, *Ethnic Issues*
    Walters, James C. *Ethnic Issues in Paul's Letter to the Romans: Changing Self-Definitions in Earliest Roman Christianity*. Valley Forge: Trinity Press International, 1994.

Walters, "'Phoebe' and 'Junia(s)'"
    Walters, James C. "'Phoebe' and 'Junia(s)'—Rom 16:1-2,7." Pp. 176–90 in vol. 1 of C. D. Osburn, ed., *Essays on Women in Earliest Christianity*. Joplin: College Press, 1993.

Wanamaker, *Thessalonians*
    Wanamaker, Charles A. *The Epistles to the Thessalonians: A Commentary on the Greek Text*. NIGTC. Grand Rapids: Eerdmans, 1990.

Warnach, *Agape*
    Warnach, Viktor. *Agape. Die Liebe als Grundmotiv der neutestamentlichen Theologie*. Düsseldorf: Patmos, 1951.

Watson, *Agape*
    Watson, Francis. *Agape, Eros, Gender: Towards a Pauline Sexual Ethic*. Cambridge: Cambridge University Press, 2000.

Watson, *Paul*
    Watson, Francis. *Paul, Judaism, and the Gentiles: A Sociological Approach*. SNTSMS 56. Cambridge: Cambridge University Press, 1986.

Watson, "Two Roman Congregations"
    Watson, Francis. "The Two Roman Congregations: Romans 14:1–15:13." Pp. 203–15 in Karl P. Donfried, ed., *The Romans Debate*. Rev. ed. Peabody: Hendrickson, 1991.

Weaver, *Familia Caesaris*
    Weaver, P. R. C. *Familia Caesaris: A Social Study of the Emperor's Freedmen and Slaves*. Cambridge: Cambridge University Press, 1972.

Weaver, "Social Mobility"
    Weaver, P. R. C. "Social Mobility in the Early Roman Empire: The Evidence of the Imperial Freedmen and Slaves." Pp. 121–40 in M. I. Finley, ed., *Studies in Ancient Society*. London: Routledge & Kegan Paul, 1974.

Weber, *Beziehungen*
    Weber, Hans Emil. *Die Beziehungen von Röm 1–3 zur Missionpraxis des Paulus*. BFCTh 9. Gütersloh: Bertelsmann, 1905.

Webster, *Imperial Army*
    Webster, Graham. *The Roman Imperial Army of the First and Second Centuries A.D.* 2d ed. New York: Harper & Row, 1979.

Wedderburn, *Baptism and Resurrection*
    Wedderburn, A. J. M. *Baptism and Resurrection: Studies in Pauline Theology against Graeco-Roman Background*. WUNT 44. Tübingen: Mohr Siebeck, 1987.

Wedderburn, *Reasons*
    Wedderburn, A. J. M. *The Reasons for Romans*. SNTW. Edinburgh: T. & T. Clark, 1988.

Weder, *Kreuz*
    Weder, Hans. *Das Kreuz Jesu bei Paulus. Ein Versuch, über den Geschichtsbezug des christlichen Glaubens nachzudenken*. FRLANT 125. Göttingen: Vandenhoeck & Ruprecht, 1981.

Wegenast, *Tradition*
    Wegenast, Klaus. *Das Verständnis der Tradition bei Paulus und in den Deuteropaulinen*. WMANT 8. Neukirchen-Vluyn: Neukirchener Verlag, 1962.

Weima, "Epistolary Framework"
    Weima, Jeffrey A. D. "Preaching the Gospel in Rome: A Study of the Epistolary Framework of Romans." Pp. 337–66 in L. A. Jervis and P. Richardson, eds., *Gospel in Paul: Studies on Corinthians, Galatians and Romans for Richard N. Longenecker*. JSNTSup 108. Sheffield: Sheffield Academic Press, 1994.

Weima, *Neglected Endings*
    Weima, Jeffrey A. D. *Neglected Endings: The Significance of the Pauline Letter Closings*. JSNTSup 101. Sheffield: JSOT Press, 1994.

Weiss
    Weiss, Bernhard. *Der Brief an die Römer*. 9th ed. MeyerK 4. Göttingen: Vandenhoeck & Ruprecht, 1899.

Weiss, "Beiträge"
    Weiss, Johannes. "Beiträge zur Paulinischen Rhetorik." Pp. 165–247 in C. R. Gregory et al., eds., *Theologische Studien. Herrn Professor D. Bernhard Weiss zu seinem 70. Geburtstage dargebracht*. Göttingen: Vandenhoeck & Ruprecht, 1897.

Weiszäcker, "Römische Christengemeinde"
Weiszäcker, Carl. "Ueber die älteste römische Christen-gemeinde." *JDTh* 21 (1876) 248–310.

Welles, *Royal Correspondence*
Welles, C. Bradford. *Royal Correspondence in the Hellenistic Period.* 1934. Repr. Chicago: Ares, 1974.

Wengst, *Formeln*
Wengst, Klaus. *Christologische Formeln und Lieder des Urchristentums.* SNT 7. Gütersloh: Gütersloher Verlagshaus, 1972, 1973.

Wengst, *Pax Romana*
Wengst, Klaus. *Pax Romana and the Peace of Jesus Christ.* London: SCM, 1987.

Westcott
Westcott, B. F., and F. J. Hort. *The New Testament in the Original Greek.* 2d ed. Cambridge, 1896.

Westerholm, *Law*
Westerholm, Stephen. *Israel's Law and the Church's Faith: Paul and His Recent Interpreters.* Grand Rapids: Eerdmans, 1988.

Wetter, *Charis*
Wetter, Gillis P. *Charis. Ein Beitrag zur Geschichte des ältesten Christentums.* UNT 5. Leipzig: Hinrichs, 1913.

White, *Apostle*
White, John L. *The Apostle of God: Paul and the Promise of Abraham.* Peabody: Hendrickson, 1999.

White, *Body of the Greek Letter*
White, John L. *The Form and Function of the Body of the Greek Letter: A Study of the Letter Body of the Non-literary Papyri and in Paul the Apostle.* SBLDS 2. Missoula: Scholars Press, 1972.

White, "Epistolary Formulas"
White, John L. "Epistolary Formulas and Cliches in Greek Papyrus Letters." *SBLASP* 2 (1978) 289–319.

White, *Light*
White, John L. *Light from Ancient Letters.* Philadelphia: Fortress Press, 1986.

White, *Building God's House*
White, L. Michael. *The Social Origins of Christian Architecture.* Vol. 1. *Building God's House in the Roman World. Architectural Adaptation among Pagans, Jews and Christians.* Valley Forge: Trinity Press International, 1996.

White, *Texts and Monuments*
White, L. Michael. *The Social Origins of Christian Architecture.* Vol. 2. *Texts and Monuments for the Christian Domus Ecclesiae in Its Environment Texts and Monuments.* Valley Forge: Trinity Press International, 1996.

Whitsett, "Son of God"
Whitsett, Christopher G. "Son of God, Seed of David: Paul's Messianic Exegesis in Romans [1]:3-4." *JBL* 119 (2000) 661–81.

Wibbing, *Lasterkatalog*
Wibbing, Siegfried. *Die Tugend- und Lasterkataloge im Neuen Testament und ihre Traditionsgeschichte unter besonderer Berücksichtigung der Qumran-Texte.* BZNW 25. Berlin: Töpelmann, 1959.

Wick, *Gottesdienste*
Wick, Peter. *Die urchristlichen Gottesdienste. Entstehung und Entwicklung im Rahmen der frühjüdischenTempel-, Synagogen- und Hausfrömmigkeit.* BWANT 150. Stuttgart: Kohlhammer, 2002.

Wiederkehr, *Berufung*
Wiederkehr, Dietrich. *Die Theologie der Berufung in den Paulusbriefen.* SF 36. Fribourg: Universitätsverlag, 1963.

Wiefel, "Roman Christianity"
Wiefel, Wolfgang. "The Jewish Community in Ancient Rome and the Origins of Roman Christianity." Pp 95–101 in K. P. Donfried, ed., *The Romans Debate.* Rev. ed. Peabody: Hendrickson, 1991.

Wikenhauser, *Pauline Mysticism*
Wikenhauser, Alfred. *Pauline Mysticism: Christ in the Mystical Teaching of St Paul.* Trans. J. Cunningham. New York: Herder and Herder, 1960.

Wilckens
Wilckens, Ulrich. *Der Brief an die Römer.* 3 vols. EKKNT 6. Zurich: Benziger, 1978–82.

Wiles, *Paul's Intercessory Prayers*
Wiles, Gordon P. *Paul's Intercessory Prayers: The Significance of the Intercessor Prayer Passages in the Letters of St. Paul.* SNTSMS 24. Cambridge: Cambridge University Press, 1974.

Wilk, *Bedeutung des Jesajabuches*
Wilk, Florian. *Die Bedeutung des Jesajabuches für Paulus.* FRLANT 179. Göttingen: Vandenhoeck & Ruprecht, 1998.

Wilke, *Neutestamentliche Rhetorik*
Wilke, Christian Gottlob. *Die neutestamentliche Rhetorik. Ein Seitenstück zur Grammatik des neutestamentlichen Sprachidioms.* Dresden: Arnoldische Verlag, 1843.

Williams, *Paul's Metaphors*
Williams, David J. *Paul's Metaphors: Their Context and Character.* Peabody: Hendrickson, 1999.

Williams, "Identity of the Jewish Community"
Williams, Margaret H. "The Shaping of the Identity of the Jewish Community in Rome in Antiquity." Pp. 33–46 in J. Zangenberg and M. Labahn, eds., *Christians as a Religious Minority in a Multicultural City. Modes of Interaction and Identity Formation in Early Imperial Rome.* London: T. & T. Clark, 2004.

Williams, *Jesus' Death*
Williams, Sam K. *Jesus' Death as Saving Event: The Background and Origin of a Concept.* HDR 2. Missoula: Scholars Press, 1975.

Williams, "Righteousness"
Williams, Sam K. "The 'Righteousness of God' in Romans." *JBL* 99 (1980) 241–90.

Wilson, *Gnosis and the New Testament*
Wilson, Robert McL. *Gnosis and the New Testament.* Oxford: Blackwell, 1968.

Winger, *Law*
Winger, Joseph Michael. *By What Law? The Meaning of Νόμος in the Letters of Paul.* SBLDS 128. Atlanta: Scholars Press, 1992.

Wink, *Engaging the Powers*
Wink, Walter. *The Powers.* Vol. 3. *Engaging the Powers: Discernment and Resistance in a World of Domination.* Minneapolis: Fortress Press, 1992.

Wink, *Naming the Powers*
Wink, Walter. *The Powers.* Vol. 1. *Naming the Powers: The Language of Power in the New Testament.* Philadelphia: Fortress Press, 1984.

Winkel, "Argumentationsanalyse"
Winkel, Johannes. "Argumentationsanalyse von Röm 9–11." *LingB* 58 (1986) 65–79.

Winninge, *Sinners and the Righteous*
  Winninge, Mikeal. *Sinners and the Righteous: A Comparative Study of the Psalms of Solomon and Paul's Letters.* Stockholm: Almqvist & Wiksell, 1995.
Winter, "Romans 12–15"
  Winter, Bruce. "Roman Law and Society in Romans 12–15." Pp. 67–102 in P. Oakes, ed., *Rome in the Bible and the Early Church.* Grand Rapids: Baker, 2002.
Winter, *Seek the Welfare*
  Winter, Bruce. *Seek the Welfare of the City: Christians as Benefactors and Citizens.* Carlisle: Paternoster, 1994.
Wischmeyer, "ΑΓΑΠΗΤΟΣ"
  Wischmeyer, Oda. "Das Adjectiv ΑΓΑΠΗΤΟΣ in den paulinischen Briefen. Eine traditionsgeschichtliche Miszelle." *NTS* 32 (1986) 476–80.
Witherington
  Witherington, Ben, III. *Paul's Letter to the Romans. A Socio-Rhetorical Commentary.* Grand Rapids: Erdmans, 2004.
Witherington, *Triumph*
  Witherington, Ben, III. *Paul's Narrative Thought World: The Tapestry of Tragedy and Triumph.* Louisville: Westminster/John Knox, 1994.
Wlosok, "Vater"
  Wlosok, Antonie. "Vater und Vatervorstellungen in der römischen Kultur." Pp. 18–54 in II. Tellenbach, ed., *Das Vaterbild im Abendland I: Rom, frühes Christentum, Mittelalter, Neuzeit, Gegenwart.* Stuttgart: Kohlhammer, 1978.
Wobbe, *Charis-Gedanke*
  Wobbe, Joseph. *Der Charis-Gedanke bei Paulus. Ein Beitrag zur ntl Theologie.* NTAbh 13.3 Münster: Aschendorf, 1932.
Wolter, *Röm 5,1-11*
  Wolter, Michael. *Rechtfertigung und zukünftiges Heil. Untersuchungen zu Röm 5,1-11.* BZNW 43. Berlin: de Gruyter, 1978.
Wolter, "Verborgene Weisheit"
  Wolter, Michael. "Verborgene Weisheit und Heil für die Heiden. Zur Traditionsgeschichte und Intention des 'Revelationsschemas'." *ZThK* 84 (1987) 297–319.
Woyke, "Einst"
  Woyke, Johannes. "'Einst' und 'Jetzt' in Röm 1–3? Zur Bedeutung von νυνὶ δέ in Röm 3,21." *ZNW* 92 (2002) 185–206.
Wright, *Climax*
  Wright, N. Thomas. *The Climax of the Covenant: Christ and the Law in Pauline Theology.* Minneapolis: Fortress Press, 1991.
Wright, "Messiah"
  Wright, N. Thomas. "The Messiah and the People of God: A Study in Pauline Theology with Particular Reference to the Argument in the Epistle to the Romans." D. Phil. diss., Oxford University, 1980.
Wright, *People of God*
  Wright, N. Thomas. *The New Testament and the People of God.* Minneapolis: Fortress Press, 1992.
Wuellner, "Paul's Rhetoric"
  Wuellner, Wilhelm. "Paul's Rhetoric of Argumentation in Romans," *CBQ* 38 (1976) 330–51. Repr. pp. 128–46 in K. P. Donfried, ed., *The Romans Debate.* Rev. ed. Peabody: Hendrickson, 1991.
Wuellner, "Reading Romans"
  Wuellner, Wilhelm. "Reading Romans in Context." Pp. 106–39

in S. E. McGinn, ed., *Celebrating Romans: Template for Pauline Theology. Essays in Honor of Robert Jewett.* Grand Rapids: Eerdmans, 2004.
Wuellner, "Toposforschung"
  Wuellner, Wilhelm. "Toposforschung und Torahinterpretation bei Paulus und Jesus." *NTS* 24 (1978) 463–83.
Yavetz, "Living Conditions"
  Yavetz, Z. "Living Conditions of the Urban Plebs in Republican Rome." Pp. 500–517 in R. Seager, ed., *The Crisis in the Roman Republic: Studies in Political and Social History.* London: Heffer, 1969.
Yeo, "Messianic Predestination"
  Yeo, Khiok-Khng. "Messianic Predestination in Romans 8 and Classical Confucianism," in K. K. Yeo, ed., *Navigating Romans Through Cultures: Challenging Readings by Charting a New Course.* London: T. & T. Clark International, 2004.
Yeo, *Navigating Romans*
  Yeo, Khiok-Khng, ed., *Navigating Romans Through Cultures: Challenging Readings by Charting a New Course.* London: T. & T. Clark International, 2004.
Yinger, *Deeds*
  Yinger, Kent L. *Paul, Judaism, and Judgment according to Deeds.* SNTSMS 105. Cambridge: Cambridge University Press, 1999.
Zahn
  Zahn, Theodor. *Der Brief des Paulus an die Römer.* Kommentar zum Neuen Testament 6. Leipzig: Deichert, 1910.
Zanker, *Power of Images*
  Zanker, Paul. *The Power of Images in the Age of Augustus.* Ann Arbor: University of Michigan Press, 1990.
Zeev, *Jewish Rights*
  Zeev, Miriam Pucci Ben. *Jewish Rights in the Roman World. The Greek and Roman Documents Quoted by Josephus Flavius.* TSAJ 74. Tübingen: Mohr Siebeck, 1998.
Zeller
  Zeller, Dieter. *Der Brief an die Römer. Übersetzt und erklärt.* RNT. Regensburg: Pustet, 1985.
Zeller, *Juden*
  Zeller, Dieter. *Juden und Heiden in der Mission des Paulus. Studien zum Römerbrief.* 2d ed. FB 8. Stuttgart: Katholisches Bibelwerk, 1976.
Zerwick and Grosvener, *Grammatical Analysis*
  Zerwick, Maximilian, and Mary Grosvener. *A Grammatical Analysis of the Greek New Testament.* Rome: Pontifical Biblical Institute, 1981.
Ziesler
  Ziesler, J[ohn] A. *Paul's Letter to the Romans.* TPINTC. Philadelphia: Trinity Press International, 1989.
Ziesler, *Righteousness*
  Ziesler, John A. *The Meaning of Righteousness in Paul.* SNTSMS 20. Cambridge: Cambridge University Press, 1972.
Ziesler, "Romans 7"
  Ziesler, John A. "The Role of the Tenth Commandment in Romans 7." *JSNT* 33 (1988) 41–56.

Zimmermann, "Jesus Christus"
Zimmermann, Heinrich. "Jesus Christus, hingestellt als Sühne—zum Erweis der Gerechtigkeit Gottes." Pp. 71–81 in F. Groner, ed., *Die Kirche im Wandel der Zeit. Festsgabe seiner Eminenz dem hochwürdigsten Herrn Josef Kardinal Höffner, Erzbischof von Köln, zur Vollendung des 65 Lebenjahres am 24 Dezember 1971.* Cologne: Bachem, 1971.

Zimmermann, *Methodenlehre*
Zimmermann, Heinrich. *Neutestamentliche Methodenlehre: Darstellung der historisch-kritischen Methode.* 7th ed. Stuttgart: Katholisches Bibelwerk, 1982.

Zmijewski, *Paulus–Knecht*
Zmijewski, Josef. *Paulus–Knecht und Apostel Christi. Amt und Amsträger in paulinischer Sicht.* Stuttgart: Katholisches Bibelwerk, 1986.

Zuntz, *Text*
Zuntz, Günther. *The Text of the Epistles: A Disquisition upon the Corpus Paulinum.* British Academy Schweich Lectures, 1946. London: British Academy/Oxford University Press, 1953.

1. The Approach of the Commentary

This commentary employs all of the standard methods of historical-critical exegesis. This includes historical analysis; text criticism, form criticism, and redaction criticism; rhetorical analysis; social scientific reconstruction of the audience situation; an historical reconstruction of the situations in Rome and Spain, historical and cultural analysis of the honor, shame, and imperial systems in the Greco-Roman world; and a theological interpretation that takes these details into account rather than following traditional paths formed by church traditions. The basic idea in the interpretation of each verse and paragraph is that Paul wishes to gain support for a mission to the barbarians in Spain, which requires that the gospel of impartial, divine righteousness revealed in Christ be clarified to rid it of prejudicial elements that are currently dividing the congregations in Rome. In the shameful cross, Christ overturned the honor system that dominated the Greco-Roman and Jewish worlds, resulting in discrimination and exploitation of barbarians as well as in poisoning the relations between the congregations in Rome. The gospel offered grace to every group in equal measure, shattering the imperial premise of exceptionalism in virtue and honor. In the effort to follow Paul's attempt to persuade and transform the Roman congregations, one should bring to bear all of the available historical and cultural information. So the first matter on which an accounting should be given is the nature of the commentary's approach to the stubborn details of history and culture.

A. Practical Realism and Historical-Critical Methods

The interpretation of each verse in this commentary rests on a particular view of the historical situation of the letter and its recipients. Although the methods of historical-critical research are generally understood,[1] their use has come increasingly under criticism in recent decades.[2] Every branch of interpretive and historical study has had to confront these methodological issues. In *Telling the Truth about History*, Joyce Appleby, Lynn Hunt, and Margaret Jacob advocate a "democratic practice of history" that encourages "skepticism about dominant views, but at the same time sustains "trust in the reality of the past and its knowability."[3] They propose "practical realism" in the use of interpretive methods, an approach that aptly expresses the method of this commentary.[4] They acknowledge that there can never be a "precise fit between what is in the human head and what is out there" in the real world.[5] But they reject both the extremes of historical positivism and postmodernist relativism while criticizing the assumption that there must be an "enduring dichotomy between absolute objectivity and totally arbitrary interpretations of the world of objects."[6] Historians and interpreters must struggle for the truth while recognizing that each is "an agent who actually moulds how the past is to be seen."[7] Historical reconstruction is an essential dimension of interpretation.[8] Yet the stubborn contours of the evidence about the past must constantly be respected. Practical realism appreciates scientific advances because they reflect the awareness that the world does not always conform to our previously held convictions. Appleby, Hunt, and Jacob

---

1 See, e.g., Krentz, *Method*, 33–88; Zimmermann, *Methodenlehre*, 17–49, 77–84, 125–78, 215–37, 267–79; Riedlinger et al., *Historisch-kritische Methode*, 54–71; Tuckett, *Interpretation*, 41–187; Brown, *Introduction*, 3–47; Branick, *Introduction*, 5–19; Söding and Münch, *Methodenbuch*, 16–80, 221–304; Marguerat et al., *Introduction*, 139–58; Ehrman, *Historical Introduction*, 13–15, 260–75; Ebner and Heininger, *Exegese*, 1–24, 157–65, 205–18, 325–45, 347–59; Silva, *Introduction*, 219–26, 258–66, 370–77, 438–44, 463–71, 477–79, 508–17, 531–34, 578–85, 629–30, 703–13, 800–805, 831–38, 858–60, 879–81, 908–11; Holladay, *Critical Introduction*, 16–24, 39–57, 227–40, 263–81, 348–60.

2 See Krentz, *Method*, 78–88.

3 Joyce Oldham Appleby, Lynn Hunt, and Margaret

Jacob, *Telling the Truth about History* (New York: Norton, 1994) 11.

4 Ibid., 247–51.

5 Ibid., 248; see also Krentz, *Method*, 35–47; Riedlinger et al., *Historisch-kritische Methode*, 60–61.

6 Appleby, Hunt, and Jacob, *History*, 246; see also Riedlinger et al., *Historisch-kritische Methode*, 13–14.

7 Appleby, Hunt, and Jacob, *History*, 249.

8 See Söding and Münch, *Methodenbuch*, 38, 52–54, 275–94; Ehrman, *Historical Introduction*, 14.

advocate a "new theory of objectivity" that respects the fact that knowledge seeking always involves a lively process of "contentious struggle between diverse groups of truth-seekers."[9] They define historical objectivity as "an interactive relationship between an inquiring subject and an external object."[10] This resonates with David Hackett Fischer's critique of inductive as well as deductive reasoning in historical research; he proposes a form of adductive reasoning that accepts the constant interaction between the interpreter and historical evidence.[11]

Although Appleby, Hunt, and Jacob are critical of Karl Popper's tendency toward "metaphysical realism,"[12] I continue to accept his conviction that historical research is similar to scientific research in other fields in needing to rely on a system of conjectures and refutations, in which hypotheses "are not *derived* from observed facts, but *invented* in order to account for them."[13] The generalizations in this introduction, therefore, are "conjectures" and "hypotheses," despite the fact that they are widely accepted by reliable historians and commentators.[14]

A recognition of the tentative nature of all historical and interpretive work is particularly required for a commentary on Romans, because the tendency has been to burden each word and phrase in this letter with theological content held with absolute certainty by particular churches and groups. The result is that an anti-imperialistic letter comes to be overlaid with unacknowledged ideologies, with individual portions understood as embodying the theology of particular traditions, now reified under the canonical aegis of the apostle to the Gentiles, and hence rendered authoritative for all others. The transforming gospel about God's righteousness regaining control of all disobedient persons and institutions by overturning their guises of superior honor is thus domesticated into an ideology favoring one side or another in long-standing theological battles, with various kinds of culturally conditioned, hegemonistic agendas inserted into the interpretive process. The message of Romans is thus transformed into a new kind of theological law, producing bondage just as inexorably as Paul argues it always does.[15] At the same time, the distinctive historical and social background of the Roman audience and Paul's rhetorical purpose in addressing them are typically dealt with in the introductions to Romans commentaries but play virtually no role in the interpretive process.

The sociohistorical and rhetorical approach of this commentary[16] is designed to allow this process to come to light and to be overcome as far as possible. First, in eschewing a totally objective hermeneutic, I need to acknowledge my own methodological presuppositions to alert readers to the possibility of another biased reading of Romans. Second, by recovering the argument implicit

9   Appleby, Hunt, and Jacob, *History*, 254.

10   Ibid., 259; see also Brown, *Introduction*, 35; Krentz, *Method*, 47: "The historian has balance and humility. He knows and states, without apology, that his work does not have the objectivity of the natural sciences. He is as skeptical and critical of himself as he is of his sources, for he knows the gaps in the documents and his own tendency to ignore the data that do not fit his own reconstruction."

11   Fischer, *Historians' Fallacies*, xv, 38–39, 314–18. See also Krentz, *Method*, 46–47; Söding and Münch, *Methodenbuch*, 224–31.

12   Appleby, Hunt, and Jacob, *History*, 170.

13   Cited in Jewett, *Chronology*, 3, from Carl G. Hempel, *Philosophy of Natural Science* (Englewood Cliffs, NJ: Prentice-Hall, 1966) 15; see also Popper, *Conjectures and Refutations*, 15.

14   See Karl R. Popper, *The Logic of Scientific Discovery* (New York: Harper & Row, 1959) 277.

15   Thus the historical-critical method allows "the Scriptures to exercise their proper critical function in the church" (Krentz, *Method*, 65) and the interpretation of "theological insights" (Krentz, *Method*, 67).

16   The "sociorhetorical method" has been defined by Vernon K. Robbins in *The Tapestry of Early Christian Discourse: Rhetoric, Society and Ideology* (London: Routledge, 1996) and in *Exploring the Texture of Texts: A Guide to Socio-Rhetorical Interpretation* (Valley Forge: Trinity Press International, 1996). In contrast to Robbins's extensive and sophisticated employment of modern literary theories, my method makes more explicit use of historical and social evidence from the ancient world. His method seems more appropriate for the analysis of narrative materials from the Gospels than for epistolary documents such as Romans that reflect a unique rhetorical situation requiring historical and social reconstruction.

in larger pericopes and major proofs, supported by stylistic and rhetorical analyses, one can develop a counterweight against the traditional views of the theology of words, phrases, and verses. The bewildering array of exegetical options developed by generations of theological and historical-critical research on Romans can thus be sorted out on the basis of which alternative fits most smoothly into the larger argument of the proof and the letter as a whole. Third, the reconstructed audience situation is consistently used to provide criteria for deciding between exegetical options: if the argument of Romans was intended to be dialectical, the option that fits most closely into the reconstructed interaction between Paul and his audience is preferable. Finally, the search for appropriate historical-religious parallels and the investigation into the earlier phases of theological debates in early Christianity reflected in Paul's wording provide resources for eliminating inappropriate exegetical options and pointing toward likely connotations of words and phrases. The linguistic, intellectual, and religious horizon of the first century can thus be used to guard against imposing later ideological agendas back onto Romans. This hermeneutical principle promises a measure of accountability and testability in discerning Paul's intended argument; readers are offered a frankly acknowledged set of hermeneutical assumptions and methods to evaluate and correct. My goal is to sharpen the ancient horizon of the text so that it can enter into dialogue with the modern horizons of our various interpretive enterprises.

B. The Structure of the Sociohistorical and Rhetorical Commentary

The commentary on each pericope begins with a translation and extensive text-critical notes that evaluate and explain various readings. As section 2 will indicate, I have concluded that Romans was originally a sixteen-chapter letter, to which two interpolations were later attached. This text-critical work was done prior to starting the interpretive process, and it led to a number of deviations from the standard international Greek text available in the Nestle-Aland editions. The principle followed was to make text-critical decisions without allowing the interpretive consequences to influence the results. The translation is literal, aiming at offering precision rather than grace. It is not designed for liturgical use, and falls far short of the eloquence of Paul's text. The dynamic transference method would be preferable in a translation to be used in public worship or devotional reading.

A consensus crystallized in the activities of the Pauline Theology Seminars of the Society of Biblical Literature in the 1970s–90s that Romans should be viewed as a situational letter, and that historical circumstances should be taken into account just as in the other letters.[17] This commentary is a result of that consensus, as sections 3, 5-8 in the introduction show. I view the argument of this letter as an attempt to persuade Roman house and tenement churches to support the Spanish mission. Thus section 4 deals with the rhetorical means of persuasion reflected in the letter, designed to appeal to the audience that Paul believes on the basis of personal contacts and hearsay evidence to be present in Rome.[18] After a detailed analysis of the historical situation in Rome and of the congregations situated there in sections 5 and 6, I go on in section 7 to analyze the situation in Spain in order to clarify the conditions that Paul's mission would have had to fulfill. In contrast to many Romans commentaries that make no further use of such historical and cultural details after the introduction, I attempt to bring them into correlation with the persuasive formulation of the entire letter. This commentary therefore differs from the tradition that still dominates most scholarly studies on Romans, which continue an ancient legacy of overlooking the situational dimensions of the letter.[19]

17 That the other NT letters are occasional and reflect the background of audiences and senders is widely assumed; see Riedlinger et al., *Historisch-kritische Methode*, 65–67.

18 The methodological survey that comes the closest to describing the rhetorical method employed in this commentary is that of de Silva, *Introduction*, 111–44, 380–85, 438–44, 508–17, 572–74.

19 To give an example from 2004, the massive study by Dierk Starnitzke, *Struktur*, systematizes the entire argument of Romans under two aspects: the self-understanding of individual believers, and a theological, christological viewpoint (p. 7); nowhere in this 518-page book is there a discussion of the historical situation in Rome or the rhetorical situation of the letter.

There is room to disagree with the historical, social, and rhetorical premises on which this commentary rests, because "practical realism" recognizes that each interpreter actively molds the past by interpreting evidence in various ways. To put this in theological terms, we all "see through a glass darkly" and must recognize that all human knowledge is fragmentary and preliminary.[20] However darkly they have been grasped, these premises have led to an interpretation of the letter that differs from the one I was taught by my church and by the theological professors at Chicago and Tübingen. It is also different from the interpretation of Romans that I myself advocated through most of my teaching career. But difference is no proof of final adequacy, and the assessment of the results is left up to others. The readers of these pages are invited to enter into discussion about what Paul's gospel really meant for his time, and to go beyond this commentary in reflecting on the question of what it might mean today.

2. Text-Critical Issues in a Sixteen-Chapter Letter

The first task in this commentary is to deal with the issues related to the text of Romans, which are among the most complicated in the field of NT study. Although certainty is never achievable in this area, the conclusions drawn from text-critical analysis become the conjectures on which the subsequent tasks of translation, rhetorical analysis, historical reconstruction, and the exegesis of individual verses must depend. The priority of textual criticism is decisive, and it is certainly incorrect to believe that it "concerns itself with minutiae of little significance."[21] In the method followed in this commentary, interpretive options are not allowed to play a crucial role in making text-critical decisions.[22] Such decisions take priority over any interpretive theory or theological system. Here is an account of the major issues and the conjectures on which the commentary rests.

A. The Varied Forms of Romans

Text critics have discovered fifteen different forms of Romans, including one no longer extant that is described by the church fathers.[23] Marcion excised the final two chapters so that the letter would end with 14:23, a verse congenial to his theology.[24] We are informed by Origen that Marcion's edition of Romans lacked chaps. 15–16, which he "removed entirely" (*penitus abstulit*), including the doxology.[25] The text of Origen is as follows:

.

20 1 Cor 13:9-12; see Jewett, *Apostle to America,* 98–111.
21 J. K. Elliott, *Essays and Studies in New Testament Textual Criticism,* EFN 3 (Cordoba: Ediciones El Almendro, 1992) 17.
22 On the methodological issue of "factual verification," see Fischer, *Historians' Fallacies,* 40–63.
23 See Gamble, *Textual History,* 15–36; Aland, *Entwürfe,* 286–91; Lampe, "Textgeschichte," 273–77. For an earlier account of this textual variety, see Peter Corssen, "Zur Überlieferungsgeschichte des Römerbriefes," *ZNW* 10 (1909) 1–45, 97–102.
24 Donatien de Bruyne, "Les deux derniers chapîtres de la lettre aux Romains," *RBén* 25 (1908) 423–30; idem, "La finae marcionite de la lettre aux Romains retrouvée," *RBén* 28 (1911) 133–42; Corssen, "Überlieferungsgeschichte," 42–45; Adolf von Harnack, "Über I Kor. 14,32ff. und Röm. 16,25ff. nach der ältesten Überlieferung und der marcionitischen Bibel," in *Studien zur Geschichte des Neuen Testaments und der Alten Kirche. I. Zur neutestamentlichen Textkritik* (Berlin: de Gruyter, 1931)
  180–90; Zuntz, *Text,* 227–28; Manson, "Romans— and Others," 8–11; Karl P. Donfried, "A Short Note on Romans 16," in Donfried, *Romans Debate,* 50; John J. Clabeaux, *A Lost Edition of the Letters of Paul: A Reassessment of the Text of the Pauline Corpus Attested by Marcion* (Washington, D.C.: Catholic Biblical Association, 1989) 3; Walker, *Interpolations,* 198. The study by Alain Le Boulluec, "The Bible in Use Among the Marginally Orthodox," in P. M. Blowers, ed., *The Bible in Greek Antiquity,* Bible through the Ages 1 (Notre Dame: Univ. of Notre Dame Press, 1997) 199–200, provides an account of other Marcionite mutilations of the Pauline letters.
25 Bacon, "Doxology," 170.

Caput hoc Marcion, a quo scripturae evangelicae atque apostolicae interpolatae sunt, de hac epistula penitus abstulit: et non solum hoc, sed et ab eo loco ubi scriptum est "omne autem, quod non est ex fide, peccatum est" [Rom 14:23] usque ad finem cuncta dissecuit. In alilis vero exemplaribus, id est in his, quae non sunt a Marcione temerata, hoc ipsum caput diverse positum invenimus: in nonnullis etenim codicibus post eum locus quem supra diximus, hos est "ei autem, qui potens est vos confirmare" [Rom 16:25]; alli vero codices in fine id, ut nunc est positum, continent. ("This person Marcion, from whom gospel and apostolic scriptures have been falsified, took out the innermost part of this epistle: and not only this, but also from that place where it is written, 'because everything that is not from faith is sin' [Rom 14:23] up to the end, he cut out the whole thing. In other copies, furthermore, that is, in these that have not been corrupted by Marcion, we have discovered with this chapter a different situation: indeed, in not a few codices, following that place which we have spoken about above, this is written: 'But to him who is able to establish you' [Rom 16:25]; however, other codices, as in the present situation retain it at the end.")[26]

The question that arises from Origen's statement is whether the doxology was actually present in the version of Romans that Marcion mutilated. From the viewpoint of Origen's time period, and the texts available to him, the doxology was visible after 14:23 and 16:23, and thus he assumes that Marcion must have deleted it along with the rest of chaps. 15–16. However, Lietzmann's reading of the evidence remains plausible to many commentators in suggesting that the original form of Romans lacked the doxology, and that it was first added "by Mar-

cionite circles" to the fourteen-chapter letter, which at that time otherwise lacked an ending.[27] This matches the text-critical analysis by Peter Lampe, that the original form of Romans consisted of 1:1–16:23 + 16:24; that Marcion deleted chaps. 15–16 in their entirety; and that the new ending of 16:25-27 was added thereafter.[28] This explains why some texts have only 1:1–14:23 + 16:25-27 and why other text types have 16:25-27 in various locations.[29]

Kurt Aland provided a comprehensive analysis of the different forms of Romans and grouped them together as families that descended from one another in genealogical fashion.[30] His chart that shows the genealogy of the fifteen text types is printed below (see p. 6), employing the following symbols:

A = Rom 1:1–14:23
B = Rom 15:1–16:23
B¹ = Rom 15:1-33
B² = Rom 16:1-23
C = Rom 16:24
C¹ = Rom 16:24 (in abbreviated form)
D = 16:25-27

This chart shows that in contrast to earlier assessments, the Marcionite shortening of Romans is only one of three different strands of tradition present at the beginning of the second century. While it led to the complicated versions visible on the left arm of the genealogy, it cannot account for the full spectrum of variations. A weakness in Aland's genealogy was identified by Lampe,[31] namely that the original form is purely hypothetical, which is why Aland placed it in square brackets. No text of Romans currently extant consists of 1:1–14:23 + 15:1–16:23, and it is also odd that a Pauline

---

26 Origen *Com. Rom.* 10.43 (*PG* 14.1290 A-B); Lietzmann, 130, cites this as coming from 7,453 Lo.

27 Lietzmann, 131; see also Clabeaux, *Marcion*. For a discussion of the complex issue of the "original text," see Eldon Jay Epp, "The Multivalence of the Term 'Original Text' in New Testament Textual Criticism," *HTR* 92 (1999) 245–81, repr. in Epp, *Perspectives on New Testament Textual Criticism: Collected Essays, 1962-2004*, NovTSup 116 (Leiden: Brill, 2005) 551–93.

28 Lampe, "Textgeschichte," 273–75; for a similar hypothesis see Trobisch, *Entstehung*, 75–79.

29 This assessment corrects earlier views such as Manson, "Romans—and Others," 12, that the original form of the letter sent to Rome comprised chaps. 1–15 without the doxology. For a claim that Marcion was not responsible for the excision of the final chapters, see Schmidt, *Marcion*, 239–40.

30 Aland, *Entwürfe*, 287–91.

31 Lampe, "Textgeschichte," 273.

Aland's Textual Genealogy

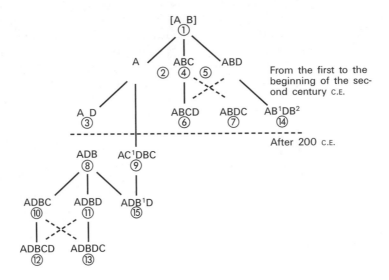

letter would end with 16:23. Lampe therefore suggests that the text form found in the family ABC, first appearing in the sixth century, but reflecting earlier forms of the same text, stands at the beginning of the genealogy.[32] The chart is as follows (see p. 7), with the explanation of the lower-case letters below:

Lampe's explains the development of the fifteen versions as follows:[33]

a = Marcion excises B and C (15:1–16:23)

b = A new conclusion D (16:25-27) is created and added

⑥ = The ending of AD is added to ABD, producing ABCD

c = The location of C (16:24) is shifted to the end to produce ABDC

d = Other texts delete C (16:24) because it seems out of place

e = The doxology (D) is moved to a position before B² (16:1-23)

⑩ = BC is taken from ABC and added to AD, producing ADBC

⑫ = Three possible sources: ⑩ + ③; or ⑩ + ⑥; or ③ + ⑥

f = C is excised because it seems out of place

g = C is placed at the end as in other Pauline letters

h = The second D is excised to eliminate the duplication in ADBD

i = B² is excised because the greetings seem irrelevant

⑨ = C is added to A and DBC is added from ⑩ to produce ACDBC

While the first witness to the reconstructed earliest form of Romans is from the sixth century, the Marcion text derived from it is around 150 C.E. and in all probability, the first forms of ②, ③, ⑤, ⑥, and ⑭ go back to the period around 200.[34] Neither Aland nor Lampe take account of the likelihood that 16:17-20 was a very early interpolation inserted into the text at the time of the publication of the letter corpus.[35] When this is taken into account, the likely earliest form of Romans consisted of 1:1–16:16 + 16:21-24, which is a slight modification of the Lampe hypothesis.

32   Ibid., 275.
33   Ibid., 274–76.
34   Ibid., 276.

35   See the discussion below on 16:17–20, in the section entitled "The Case for Interpolation."

Lampe's Textual Genealogy

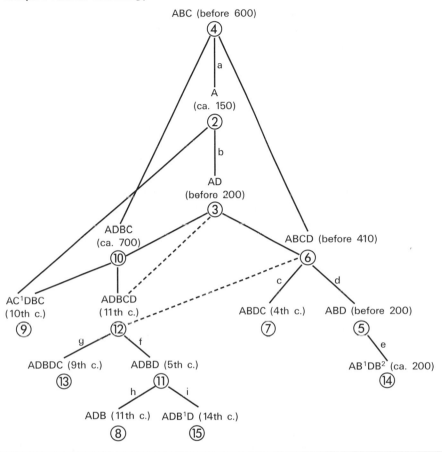

B. The Problem of the Benediction

The benediction is placed in different locations in the various families of texts: at 16:20b, 16:24, after 16:27, and in many texts both at 16:20b and 24. Harry Gamble has made a case that when "the intrusion of the doxology (16:25-27) is recognized as the *cause* of the omission of 16:24—and this is exactly what the alignment of the witnesses shows—then 16:24 has to be judged an original reading."[36] He concludes that the original form of Romans had the two benedictions, vv. 20b and 24, separated by the greetings of 16:21-23.[37] But this does not

take account of the interpolation of 16:17-20a, which distorted the flow of the greetings prior to the creation of the fourteen-chapter letter and the placement of the doxology in its various locations. When the interpolation of 16:17-20a is removed and the natural flow between the greetings of 16:3-16 + 21-23 is restored, the benediction of v. 20b appears to be out of place.[38] I therefore suggest that v. 20b was added after the insertion of the interpolation in vv. 17-20a, as a concluding comment thereto, which explains why some texts have the interpolation but lack the benediction at this location. This is the situ-

---

36 Gamble, *Textual History,* 130; Hurtado, "Doxology," 194–97, rejects Gamble's conclusion on the unconvincing ground that 16:24 is a later, secondary expansion of 16:20 to bring the letter to a more "impressive" (195) conclusion. Lampe, "Textgeschichte," 275–76, shows that the textual tradition concluding with 16:24 is the earliest form witnessed in D F G, from which all of the other fourteen text forms of Romans were derived. For an earlier argument for the originality of 16:24, see Corssen, "Überlieferungsgeschichte," 11–13, 31.

37 Gamble, *Textual History,* 132.

38 See Lagrange, 375; Byrne, 457.

ation with the Western text group of D F G m vg^ms Sedulius Scotus, which omit the doxology and have the benediction only at 16:24. This proposal also explains why the "Amen" was not attached to the blessing formula located at 16:20b,[39] which renders it unsuitable as a closing blessing in conformity with Pauline style at the end of all his other letters. Moreover, the formulation of the blessing at 16:24 is more suited to Romans because it includes πάντων ὑμῶν ("all of you"), which addresses the issue of a divided congregation just as in other letters confronting similar problems (1 Cor 16:24; 2 Cor 13:13; 2 Thess 3:18). Whether this proposal is judged more plausible than Gamble's, it remains likely that the textual decision of Nestle-Aland and UBS is in error in deleting v. 24 entirely and providing the benediction only at v. 20b.[40] Every other Pauline letter, including Ephesians, Colossians, and the Pastorals, concludes with a benediction and it is highly likely that the original form of Romans did as well. An examination of this evidence confirms Lampe's theory that the earliest published form of Romans was 1:1—16:23 + 16:24.[41]

C. The Problem of the Doxology

As visible in the charts produced by Aland and Lampe, the doxology of 16:25-27 (D in both charts) occurs in dif-

ferent locations in the manuscripts of Romans.[42] While one group of texts lacks the doxology entirely, others place it after 14:23, after 15:33, after 16:23, or after 16:24, and some texts add it twice, after 14:23, 15:33, or 16:23.[43] The most plausible explanation for its origin and use is related to Marcion's edition of Romans that ended with 14:23, "whatever is not of faith is sin."[44] The resultant fourteen-chapter letter had no appropriate ending, especially for liturgical purposes.[45] The doxology contains some elements congenial to Marcion's anti-Jewish bias, but as the doxological analysis below indicates, it was a three-step process that accounts for its redundant, lumbering style.[46] At any event, it will not be interpreted in this commentary as the ending Paul intended for his letter to the Romans.[47]

D. The Problem of Chapter 16: Rome or Ephesus

A widespread critical consensus that pertained until the late 1970s assumed that chap. 16 did not originally belong to Romans.[48] Either it was sent as a letter of greetings to the Ephesian church along with an extra copy of Romans,[49] or was part of a farewell letter to Ephesus sent from Rome that was mistakenly included in the editing of Romans,[50] or it was created at the time of the publica-

---

39 This anomaly is not discussed in current commentaries, all of which follow UBS and Nestle-Aland in viewing v. 20b as the concluding blessing formula that Paul originally intended.

40 For defenses of this elimination of 16:24, see Cranfield, 1:6, 3:804; Weima, *Neglected Endings*, 218. Scholars critical of Nestle-Aland's deletion of 16:24 include Jervis, *Purpose*, 138–39; Haacker, 330; Schreiner, 809.

41 Lampe, "Textgeschichte," 275.

42 See also Fitzmyer, 48.

43 See the schematic diagram in Lampe, "Textgeschichte," 275; also Collins, "Wandering Doxology," 295–97.

44 See Manson, "Romans—and Others," 11.

45 See Champion, *Benedictions and Doxologies*, 26–28, 96–97, 106.

46 See below in the "Doxological Analysis" section of 16:25-27.

47 See also Krentz, *Method*, 49.

48 See the complete listing of Ephesian advocates in Fitzmyer, 57, including many of the most influential figures in 20th-century scholarship: Bartsch, Bornkamm, Bultmann, Feine and Behm, Feuillet,

Friedrich, Georgi, Goodspeed, Harrison, Heard, Henshaw, Käsemann, Kinoshita, Koester, Lake, Leenhardt, McDonald, McNeile, T. W. Manson, Marxsen, Michaelis, Moffatt, Munck, Refoulé, Schenke, Schmithals, Schumacher, Scott, Suggs, Taylor, and Widman.

49 Paul Feine created a compelling form of this hypothesis in *Die Abfassung des Philipperbriefes in Ephesus, mit einer Anlage über Rm. 16, 3-20 als Epheserbrief,* BFChTh 20/4 (Gütersloh: Bertelsmann, 1916) 278–425; an account of the extensive early debate on this question is found in Rudolf Schumacher, *Die beiden letzten Kapitel des Römerbriefes: Ein Beitrag zu ihrer Geschichte und Erklärung* (Münster: Aschendorffer, 1929) 61–66; the foremost British and American advocates of this view were T. W. Manson, "St. Paul's Letter to the Romans—and Others," *BJRL* 31 (1948) 224–40, repr. in Donfried, *Romans Debate*, 3–16; and Edgar J. Goodspeed, "Phoebe's Letter of Introduction," *HTR* 44 (1950) 55–57; see also Willi Marxsen, *Introduction to the New Testament: An Approach to Its Problems*, trans. G. Buswell (Philadelphia: Fortress Press, 1968) 107–8; Gerhardt Friedrich, "Römerbrief," *RGG*³ 5 (1961)

tion of the letter in order to demonstrate Paul's close relations with the Roman church.[51] My initial adherence to a version of the Ephesian hypothesis[52] was undermined by the argument of Karl Donfried[53] and the text-critical studies by Harry Gamble[54] and Kurt Aland,[55] who made compelling cases that the textual history is best explained by an original letter of sixteen chapters and that the combination of recommendation and greetings is appropriate as an ending of an extended letter. Equally compelling was the argument of Wolf-Hennig Ollrog, that the greetings in Rom 16 are highly inappropriate for the Ephesian setting, or for any other church where Paul had ministered for a substantial length of time.[56] The personal details concerning some of the persons he greets are formulated as if the congregation as a whole did not recognize their accomplishments, which is strange if Paul's knowledge of them coincided with the congregation's knowledge. It sounds like Paul is introducing and recommending them as reliable leaders in a congregation where neither he nor they were very well known. Other persons are named without any personal reference or intimate detail whatsoever, which seems absurd if Paul had worked with them for almost three years, as was the case in Ephesus. This is a significant observation, it seems to me, when one reflects on how such a lack of social and political finesse would have

been received in a congregation like Ephesus where Paul should have known everyone intimately. The greetings of Rom 16 are therefore much more suitable for an audience where Paul had never functioned as a missionary. Ollrog also points out that Rom 16 refers neither to Paul's past experiences with the congregation nor to its future prospects, which is markedly in contrast with other letters addressed to congregations for which he felt responsible as a founder. These considerations require the recognition that the Ephesian hypothesis is far less adequate in explaining the peculiar content of Rom 16 than the assumption that it was originally directed to the Roman congregation. This text-critical decision has an enormous bearing on interpreting Romans, because it means that the congregational details in chap. 16 can be taken into account. The new phase of research signaled by the publication of the first edition of *The Romans Debate* in 1977[57] that popularized the idea of a situational letter derives to a significant degree from the abandonment of the Ephesian hypothesis.[58]

E. The Criteria for Evaluating Manuscripts

Since there are more than five thousand ancient Greek manuscripts of the NT either in its entirety or in part,[59] some method of weighing the evidence is required for the nonspecialist.[60] On the basis of information available

1138; Schmithals, *Römerbrief*, 138–47; Helmut Koester, *Introduction to the New Testament*, vol. 2, *History and Literature of Early Christianity* (Philadelphia: Fortress Press, 1982) 138–39; Marguerat et al., *Introduction*, 164–65.

50 J. J. MacDonald, "Was Romans xvi a Separate Letter?" *NTS* 16 (1969–70) 369–72, argues that the chapter matches several Greco-Roman paradigms for letters of recommendation; Hans-Martin Schenke, "Aporien im Römerbrief," *ThLZ* 92 (1967) 881–84; Hans-Martin Schenke and Karl M. Fischer, *Einleitung in die Schriften des Neuen Testaments* (Gütersloh: Gerd Mohn, 1978) 1:136–42, propose the provenance from Rome and suggest that the redactors mistakenly included it in with Romans.

51 See Knox, 365–68. Other versions of this scheme, though without the redactional motive suggested by Knox, include Paul Feine and Johannes Behm, *Einleitung in das Neue Testament*, 9th ed. (Heidelberg: Quelle & Meyer, 1950) 176; Bartsch, "Historische Situation," 282; and Johannes Müller-Bardorff, *Paulus. Wege zu didaktischer Erschließung der paulini-*

schen Briefe (Gütersloh: Gerd Mohn, 1970) 16–18.

52 Jewett, *Terms*, 41–42.

53 Donfried, "Short Note," in Donfried, *Romans Debate*, 44–52; idem, "False Presuppositions in the Study of Romans," in Donfried, *Romans Debate*, 102–25.

54 Gamble, *Textual History*, 31–95.

55 Aland, *Entwürfe*, 284–301.

56 Ollrog, "Abfassungsverhältnisse," 221–44; see also Schille, *Kollegialmission*, 51.

57 Karl P. Donfried, ed., *The Romans Debate* (Minneapolis: Augsburg, 1977); see esp. Donfried's article, "Short Note," in Donfried, *Romans Debate*, 44–52.

58 Among the prominent advocates of the sixteen-chapter letter are Stuhlmacher, "Purpose," 237; Donfried, "Short Note," 49–52; Fitzmyer, 61–65; Haacker, 18–19; Byrne, 29.

59 Elliott, *Textual Criticism*, 38.

60 See Eldon Jay Epp, "Issues in New Testament Textual Criticism: Moving from the Nineteenth Century to the Twenty-First Century," in D. A. Black, ed., *Rethinking New Testament Textual Criticism* (Grand Rapids: Baker, 2002) 34–44.

in Kurt and Barbara Aland's *Text of the New Testament* and elsewhere, evaluative lists of the manuscripts containing the text of Romans have been compiled.[61] The following tables rank these manuscripts according to their age, quality, and utilization in the currently standard critical Greek text of Romans. The "consistently cited witnesses" are cited regularly and explicitly throughout Romans in Nestle-Aland[27].[62] Since the UBS text does not provide a complete listing of variants, my decisions about individual readings rely primarily on the Alands' system, and I attempt to take their classification system into account. The classifications below reflect the Alands' categories:[63]

I = Manuscripts of a very special quality
II = Manuscripts of a special quality, but showing alien influences, particularly from the Byzantine text
III = Manuscripts with an independent text
IV = D text manuscripts
V = Manuscripts with a Byzantine text of secondary importance

The following manuscripts are consistently cited witnesses of the first order:

Century:	Manuscript:	Coverage of Romans:
ca. 200 C.E.	P[46]	5:17—6:3, 5-14; 8:15-25, 27-35; 8:37—9:32; 10:1—11:22; 11:24-33; 11:35—15:9; 15:11—16:27 (Free text, category I)
Third	P[27]	8:12-22, 24-37; 8:33—9:3, 5-9 (Strict text, category I)
Third	P[40]	1:24-27; 1:31—2:3; 3:21—4:8; 6:4-5, 16; 9:16-17, 27 (Free text, carelessly written, category I because of early date)
Third	P113	2:12-13; 2:29 (Category I)
Third	0220	4:23—5:3, 8-13 (Strict text, category I)
Fourth	P[10]	1:1-7 (Category I)
Fourth	ℵ (01)	1:1—16:27 (Text with numerous errors and singular readings, category I)
Fourth	B (03)	1:1—16:27 (Text with less quality in Pauline letters, Category I)
Fourth	0221	5:16-17, 19; 5:21—6:3 (Category III)
ca. 400 C.E.	P[99]	1:1 (Not categorized)
Fourth/fifth	0219	2:21-23; 3:8-9, 23-25, 27-30 (Category III)
Fifth	A (02)	1:1—16:27 (Uneven quality, category I)
Fifth	C (04)	1:4—2:4; 3:22—9:5; 10:16—11:30; 13:11—16:27 (Category II)
Fifth	048	13:4—15:9 (Category II)
Fifth	0172	1:27-30; 1:32—2:2 (Category II)
Fifth/sixth	P[94]	6:10-13, 19-22 (Not categorized)
Sixth	D (06)	1:8—16:27, with 1:27-30 as supplement (Category IV)

61 These lists are extensions of the compilations prepared for this commentary by Ernest W. Saunders. For complete details see "Codices Graeci" in Nestle-Aland[27], 684–714; Aland et al., *Kurzgefasste Liste*; Aland et al., *Ergänzungsliste*; Junack et al., *Neue Testament auf Papyrus*; Swanson, *Vaticanus: Romans*.
62 See Aland and Aland, *Text*, 239–41.
63 See ibid., 106–7. This categorization is not entirely adequate because the distinctions between categories I and II appear somewhat subjective and the definition of "independent" in category III is unclear. Nevertheless it appears useful to provide the Alands' characterization of each document in the following table. For other assessments of the texts, see Fitzmyer, 44–47; and Epp, "Issues," 39–44.

Sixth	0285	5:12-14; 8:37—9:5; 13:1-4; 13:11—14:3 (Not categorized)
ca. 600 C.E.	P[26]	1:1-16 (Category I)
Seventh	P[31]	12:3-8 (Category I)
Seventh	0209	14:9—15:2; 16:25-27 (Category III, influenced by Byzantine texts)
ca. 700 C.E.	P[61]	16:23-27 (Category II)
Seventh/eighth	0289	8:19-21, 32-35 (Not categorized)
Eighth/ninth	? (044)	1:1—16:27 (Category III)
Ninth	F (010)	3:20—16:27 (Category III)
Ninth	G (012)	1:6—2:15; 2:26—16:27 (Category III)
Ninth	0278	1:1-9, 24-30 (Not categorized)
Ninth	33	1:1—16:27 (Category I)
Tenth	1739	1:1—16:27 (Category I)
Fourteenth	1881	1:1—16:27 (Category II)

The following are consistently cited witnesses of the second order:

Ninth	K (018)	1:1—10:17 (Category V)
Ninth	L (020)	1:1—16:27 (Category V)
Ninth	P (025)	1:1—2:14; 3:6—8:32; 9:12—11:21; 12:2—16:27 (Category V)
Ninth	2464	1:1—11:28; 16:11-27 (Category II)
Tenth	1175	1:1—16:27 (Category II)
1044 C.E.	81	1:1—16:27 (Category II)
1087 C.E.	104	1:1—16:27 (Category III)
Twelfth	1241	1:1—16:27 (Category III)
Twelfth	365	1:19—7:17; 7:22—8:2; 8:32—16:27 (Category III)
Twelfth	1505	1:1—16:27 (Category III)
Twelfth/thirteenth	630	1:1—16:27 (Category III)
1320 C.E.	1506	1:1—16:27 (Category II)

Other manuscripts cited frequently in Nestle-Aland[27]:

Tenth	326	1:1—16:27 (Category III)
Eleventh	424	1:1—16:27 (Category V, corrected against a text of Category III)
Eleventh	945	1:1—16:27 (Category V)
Twelfth	323	1:1—16:27 (Category III)
Thirteenth	6	1:1—16:27 (Category III)
Thirteenth	614	1:1—16:27 (Category III)
Fourteenth	629	1:1—16:27 (Category III)
Fifteenth	2495	1:1—16:27 (Category III)

Several observations may be offered concerning these lists drawn from the Alands' work. A number of minuscules are categorized as having very high quality despite their late dates. This reflects in part the prodigious work of the Institute for New Testament Textual Research at Münster, which has devoted considerable energy to evaluating this type of manuscript. Among these, as noted in the preceding lists, are 33 and 1739,

11

which the Alands place in Category I, and nine others that fall into Category II (81, 1175, 1506, and 2464), or Category III (104, 365, 630, 1241, and 1505). A number of other minuscules are listed by the Alands[64] in the relatively high quality ranges of Categories II and III that are not cited consistently for variants in the text of Romans in Nestle-Aland[27], although most are cited in UBS[4]. These include the following, and they will be cited routinely in the commentary when information is available.

5, 61, 69, 88, 181, 218, 256, 263, 330, 436, 441, 442, 451, 459, 467, 621, 623, 700, 720, 915, 917, 1243, 1319, 1398, 1563, 1573, 1678, 1718, 1735, 1751, 1836, 1838, 1845, 1846, 1852, 1874, 1875, 1877, 1908, 1912, 1942, 1959, 1962, 2110, 2127, 2138, 2197, 2200, 2344, 2492, 2516, 2523, 2544, 2596, 2718

F. The Eclectic Method of Evaluating Variants

Modern textual criticism in the NT field began with the discovery and use of texts that were much older than the standardized Byzantine version, called the *Textus Receptus* (TR), that provided the basis for the translations of the sixteenth and seventeenth centuries.[65] Although scholars as early as Jerome in the late fourth century and Richard Bentley (1720), J. A. Bengel (1725–1734), and J. J. Griesbach (1775–1807) all gave weight to the more ancient manuscripts, it was Karl Lachmann's Greek New Testament of 1831 that made a decisive departure from the TR and asserted a firm reliance upon the older manuscripts. The discovery of Codex Sinaiticus by Constantin von Tischendorf and his monumental Greek New Testament of 1869–1872 set the stage for current views of textual criticism, followed by B. F. Westcott and F. J. A. Hort, whose two-volume critical edition, *The New Testament in the Original Greek* (1881–1882), was the culmination of 150 years of emphasis on the oldest manuscripts known at the time, notably Codex Vaticanus and Codex Sinaiticus, and on criteria for evaluating textual variants.[66] For several decades the Westcott and Hort text that they termed "neutral," that is, free from corruption as far as possible and allegedly providing the genealogical basis for later texts, was accepted as a kind of new TR. The Nestle-Aland and UBS texts currently in use are refinements of Tischendorf, Westcott and Hort, and other critical editions.

The arguments for evaluating the priority of readings have been divided into external and internal evidence. External evidence emphasizes the date, provenance, and character of manuscripts as manuscripts and assesses variants in terms of their support by the earliest manuscripts or those known to preserve early texts; or by the manuscripts evidencing careful copying or frequently offering readings judged to be prior to others; or by manuscripts with wide geographical distribution; or by groups of manuscripts of recognized antiquity and character. Some of these determinations of quality arise from internal evidence, which considers factors *within* the text of manuscripts— what would an author or scribe most likely write? Included are such questions as: Can a variant account for the rise of all others in the variation unit? Does a variant agree with the writer's literary style or theology? Is a reading "harder" than others—rougher or apparently unrevised? Is a variant shorter than others? If so, such a variant is likely to warrant adoption as the "original" or earliest reading, though recently it has become more of an open question whether scribes were more likely to add to their texts or to abbreviate them. Moreover, does a variant show signs of influence from a parallel passage, an OT text, liturgical usage, or from a theological or ideological viewpoint? If so, such a variant is likely to be secondary. It will be obvious, however, that these criteria cannot function as rigid rules, for often conflicting factors will be operative—a reading

---

64 See Aland and Aland, *Text*, 128–35.

65 See Z. C. Hodges and A. L. Faarstad, eds., *The Greek New Testament according to the Majority Text* (Nashville: Nelson, 1982); Leon Vaganay, *An Introduction to New Testament Textual Criticism*, trans. J. Heimerdinger; 2d ed. amplified and updated by C.-B. Amphoux and J. Heimerdinger (Cambridge: Cambridge Univ. Press, 1991) 129–45; Gordon D.

Fee, "The Majority Text and the Original Text of the New Testament," in E. J. Epp and G. D. Fee, eds., *Studies in the Theory and Method of New Testament Textual Criticism*, SD 45 (Grand Rapids: Eerdmans, 1993) 183–208.

66 See Epp, *Perspectives*, 130–59, 228–40; Elliott, *Textual Criticism*, 21; Vaganay, *Textual Criticism*, 149–51.

may be the harder reading but lack support from the older manuscripts, or may explain the other reading but fail to conform, for example, to Paul's theology. In such cases, after careful analysis of all relevant factors, the decision may have to be made on the basis of "the balance of probabilities"—judging which criteria appear to carry the most weight in the specific instance. So art and skill will be required for judicious text-critical decisions, for it is rarely a simple mechanical process.[67]

The procedures just described constitute the "Eclectic Method" in NT textual criticism—the consideration of both external and internal evidence when evaluating variant readings and deciding between or among them.[68] This method, as practiced by the majority of present-day textual critics, employs all relevant criteria—weighing them over against one another—and asks the simple question, What is the writer most likely to have dictated or written?[69] The eclectic method tends to be critical of the Westcott and Hort text and its successors on the grounds described by J. K. Elliott:

> that Codex Sinaiticus and Codex Vaticanus are not as trustworthy as was once thought, and that other manuscripts have an equal claim to contain original readings. . . . The text of early papyri, many discovered this century, can not be fitted into the neat theories of Westcott and Hort and others. . . . Hence the case for an eclectic approach to the problem of variants in the New Testament manuscripts, in which the cult of the best manuscripts gives way to the cult of the best readings.[70]

The eclectic method employs all of the standard tools of internal criticism, identifying involuntary mistakes of copyists such as additions and omissions, intentional variants such as corrections of grammar and style, improvements of quotations to agree with other biblical passages, and doctrinal corrections.[71] The external criteria involve evaluating the quality of witnesses, using some of the classifications of texts listed above. Two standard principles for evaluating the plausibility of textual variants are *brevio lectio probabilior* ("a shorter reading is preferable to a longer one") and *difficilior lectio potior* ("a more difficult reading is preferable to the simpler one"), although there are always exceptions to these rules.[79] Even more problematic is the effort to "select the variant which best fits with the general tendencies of the author,"[73] because in the case of a writing like Romans, this sometimes leads to preferring variants that conform to a particular theology that is allegedly Pauline but that conforms to a particular history of interpretation. My version of eclecticism also tends to be skeptical of textual emendations.

In the text-critical notes at the beginning of each chapter, I attempt to explain the implication and probable motivation for every variant reading.[74] In the process of working through this evidence, I noted an occasional decline in the clarity of text-critical method in Nestle-Aland[27] and UBS[4], visible in instances where a reading found in the TR is followed, although the ordinary application of the rules of textual criticism seems to favor other readings. There are many instances, of course, where Nestle-Aland and UBS depart from the TR, and

---

67 See Epp, *Perspectives*, 480–83, 490–93, 644–57.

68 See Eldon Jay Epp, "The Eclectic Method in New Testament Textual Criticism: Solution or Symptom," *HTR* 69 (1976) 211–57, repr. in Epp, *Perspectives*, 125–73.

69 See Epp, *Perspectives*, 125–29, 159–71, 265–68, 274–78.

70 Elliott, *Textual Criticism*, 27–28; see also Vaganay, *Textual Criticism*, 86–88, and the account of different versions of eclecticism in Michael W. Holmes, "Reasoned Eclecticism in New Testament Textual Criticism," in B. D. Ehrman and M. W. Holmes, eds., *The Text of the New Testament in Contemporary Research: Essays on the Status Quaestionis. A Volume in Honor of Bruce M. Metzger*, SD 46 (Grand Rapids: Eerdmans, 1995) 336–45. An important early critic

of the genealogical method was Ernest W. Colwell, *Studies in Methodology in Textual Criticism of the New Testament*, NTTS 9 (Leiden: Brill, 1969) 63–83.

71 Vaganay, *Textual Criticism*, 53–61.

72 Ibid., 80–81; see also Tuckett, *Interpretation*, 27–30; Ehrman, *Historical Introduction*, 447–48; Ebner and Heininger, *Exegese*, 39–42.

73 Vaganay, *Textual Criticism*, 83.

74 The external evidence under evaluation in the text-critical notes is drawn from Nestle-Aland[27]; Aland et al., *Kurzgefasste Liste*; Aland et al., *Ergänzungsliste*; Junack et al., *Neue Testament auf Papyrus*; and Swanson, *Vaticanus: Romans*.

in many cases after evaluating the evidence, I follow their judgment while indicating my reasons for doing so. I do not wish to exaggerate the implications of the instances in which the currently standard texts of Romans require reevaluation. In the instances in which Nestle-Aland[27] inserts brackets to indicate unusual difficulty in determining the correct text, and sometimes divided opinions on the editorial committee, I have weighed the evidence and made a decision one way or the other, thus eliminating ambiguity about the text I am to interpret. By explaining my reasons in each case, I enable critical evaluation by others. It still needs to be said that without the conscientious work of the text-critical center in Münster, where thousands of textual variants have been exhaustively catalogued and examined, little of this critical assessment would be possible. Moreover, the recent editions of Nestle-Aland contain an admirable incorporation of minuscule evidence.

G. Divergences from Nestle-Aland

I have followed the example of some other large-scale commentaries in evaluating the textual variants and giving reasons for my choices. As far as possible I attempt to explain the variants in the effort to identify the most likely reading. In 26 instances I have diverged from the Nestle-Aland text. My reasons for the decisions on these closely divided cases are provided in each instance in the notes to the translation. Since these decisions provide the basis for my interpretation of the letter, and since it is unusual for a contemporary commentator to depart from the international text prepared by Aland and the later associates in the Text Critical Institute at Münster, it is appropriate to provide an overview of the divergences:

4:11, τὸ λογισθῆναι αὐτοῖς ("reckoned to them") in place of the wording τὸ λογισθῆναι [καὶ] αὐτοῖς ("reckoned [also?] to them").

4:11, δικαιοσύνην ("righteousness") in place of the arthrous form: [τὴν] δικαιοσύνην ("[the?] righteousness").

4:22, ἐλογίσθη ("it was reckoned") in place of the reading that includes the "also" that Nestle-Aland places in brackets: [καὶ] ἐλογίσθη ("it was [also?] reckoned").

5:1, εἰρήνην ἔχωμεν ("let us have peace") in place of εἰρήνην ἔχομεν ("we have peace").

8:11b, ἐκ νεκρῶν Χριστὸν Ἰησοῦν ("from the dead, Christ Jesus") as in earlier Nestle-Aland editions, compared with the 27th edition, which follows the reading Χριστὸν ἐκ νεκρῶν ("Christ from the dead").

8:21, διότι ("because") in place of ὅτι ("that").

10:5, the absence of the article τοῦ ("of the") in front of νόμου ("of law"), which Nestle-Aland editions include in square brackets.

11:8a, καθάπερ ("as") in place of the more conventional formulation, καθώς ("as").

11:21b, οὐδὲ σοῦ φείσεται ("he will not spare you") as opposed to the less threatening formulation that Nestle-Aland places in brackets: [μή πως] οὐδὲ σοῦ φείσεται ("[perhaps?] he will not spare you").

11:25b, ἑαυτοῖς φρόνιμοι ("[wise-] minded [in relation to] yourselves") as a simple dative construction instead of [παρ'] ἑαυτοῖς φρόνιμοι ("[wise-] minded among, with yourselves") or ἐν ἑαυτοῖς φρόνιμοι ("[wise-] minded in yourselves");

12:14a, εὐλογεῖτε τοὺς διώκοντας ("bless the persecutors") in place of εὐλογεῖτε τοὺς διώκοντας [ὑμᾶς] ("bless those who persecute [you?]").

14:5a, ὃς μὲν κρίνει ("now the one person judges"), in place of ὃς μὲν [γὰρ] κρίνει ("for now the one person judges").

14:12, ἄρα ἕκαστος ἡμῶν ("so each one of us") in place of the reading with "therefore" that Nestle-Aland places in brackets: ἄρα [οὖν] ἕκαστος ἡμῶν ("so [therefore?] each one of us").

14:12, περὶ ἑαυτοῦ λόγον δώσει ("give account of himself") in place of the addition that Nestle-Aland again places in square brackets: περὶ ἑαυτοῦ λόγον δώσει [τῷ θεῷ] ("give account of himself [to God?]").

14:19, ἄρα οὖν τὰ τῆς εἰρήνης διώκομεν ("we therefore pursue what makes for peace") in place of the subjunctive reading, ἄρα οὖν τὰ τῆς εἰρήνης διώκωμεν ("let us therefore pursue what makes for peace").

15:5, Ἰησοῦν Χριστόν ("Jesus Christ") in place of the sequence, Χριστὸν Ἰησοῦν ("Christ Jesus").

15:14, πεπληρωμένοι πάσης γνώσεως ("filled with every kind of knowledge") in place of the reading with brackets, πεπληρωμένοι πάσης [τῆς] γνώσεως ("filled with all knowledge").

15:19, ἐν δυνάμει πνεύματος ("in the power of the spirit") in place of the formulation with brackets in recent editions of Nestle-Aland: ἐν δυνάμει πνεύματος [θεοῦ] ("In the power of [God's?] spirit").

15:21, ὄψονται οἷς οὐκ ἀνηγγέλη περὶ αὐτοῦ ("they shall see, who never have been informed about him") in place of the transposition of the verb to the end of the line: Οἷς οὐκ ἀνηγγέλη περὶ αὐτοῦ ὄψονται ("those who never have been informed about him shall see").

15:24, ἀφ᾽ ὑμῶν προπεμφθῆναι ("to be sent with your help") in place of ὑφ᾽ ὑμῶν προπεμφθῆναι ("to be sent by your help") as found in the TR.

15:26, εὐδόκησεν γὰρ Μακεδονία καὶ Ἀχαΐα ("for Macedonia was well pleased, also Achaia") in place of the plural verb εὐδόκησαν γὰρ Μακεδονία καὶ Ἀχαΐα ("for Macedonia and Achaia were well pleased").

15:28, σφραγισάμενος τὸν καρπὸν τοῦτον ("sealing this fruit") in place of the longer wording, σφραγισάμενος αὐτοῖς τὸν καρπὸν τοῦτον ("sealing this fruit to them").

16:6, Μαριάμ ("Mariam") in place of Μαρίαν ("Mary").

16:20b: As a later addition designed to conclude the interpolation of 16:17-20b, I delete ἡ χάρις τοῦ κυρίου ἡμῶν Ἰησοῦ μεθ᾽ ὑμῶν ("The grace of our Lord Jesus be with you.")

16:24: I restore the benediction that originally closed the letter, which NA[26/27] place in the text-critical footnotes: ἡ χάρις τοῦ κυρίου ἡμῶν Ἰησοῦ Χριστοῦ μετὰ πάντων ὑμῶν. ἀμήν. ("The grace of our Lord Jesus Christ be with you all. Amen.")

16:27, ἡ δόξα εἰς τοὺς αἰῶνας τῶν αἰώνιων ("glory for aeons of aeons") in place of the shorter formulation: ἡ δόξα εἰς τοὺς αἰῶνας ("glory for aeons").

H. Eliminating Ambiguous Brackets

On the premise that the responsibility of a commentator is to avoid ambiguity and make firm decisions that are

sufficiently clear that later researchers can find mistakes and correct them, I decided to eliminate the brackets employed by the Nestle-Aland and UBS texts.[75] Here is a list of the 21 instances in which I make decisions regarding readings that eliminate ambiguous brackets, with reasons provided in the textual notes for the various passages.

2:13a, παρὰ τῷ θεῷ ("before God") with the definite article in place of παρὰ [τῷ] θεῷ ("before [?] God").

3:2b, πρῶτον μὲν γὰρ ("for above all") in place of the brackets in Nestle-Aland: πρῶτον μὲν [γὰρ] ("[for?] above all").

3:12c, οὐκ ἔστιν ἕως ἑνός ("there is not a single one") in place of the brackets in Nestle-Aland: [οὐκ ἔστιν] ἕως ἑνός ("[there is?] not a single one").

3:25b, διὰ πίστεως ("through faith") removing "the," which Nestle-Aland places in brackets, διὰ [τῆς] πίστεως ("through [the?] faith").

4:19a, ἤδη νενεκρωμένον ("[already?] dead"), eliminating the ambiguous brackets in Nestle-Aland, [ἤδη] νενεκρωμένον ("[already?] dead").

5:2a, τὴν προσαγωγὴν ἐσχήκαμεν τῇ πίστει ("we have also gained access in faith"), in place of the brackets in Nestle-Aland: τὴν προσαγωγὴν ἐσχήκαμεν [τῇ πίστει] ("we have also gained access [in faith?]").

6:11a, εἶναι νεκροὺς μὲν τῇ ἁμαρτίᾳ ("on the one hand to be dead to sin") in place of the ambiguous brackets in Nestle-Aland: [εἶναι] νεκροὺς μὲν τῇ ἁμαρτίᾳ ("on the one hand [to be?] dead to sin").

7:20a, ὃ οὐ θέλω ἐγώ ("what I do not want") including the seemingly redundant pronoun "I", in place of the ambiguous brackets in Nestle-Aland: ὃ οὐ θέλω [ἐγὼ] ("what [I?] do not want").

8:34b, Χριστὸς ὁ ἀποθανών ("Christ who died") in place of Nestle-Aland's ambiguous brackets, Χριστὸς [Ἰησοῦς] ὁ ἀποθανών ("Christ [Jesus?] who died").

9:19b, Τί οὖν ("why then?") in place of the brackets in Nestle-Aland: Τί [οὖν] ("why [then?]?").

10:3, τὴν ἰδίαν δικαιοσύνην ζητοῦντες στῆσαι

---

75   My decision is supported by the recent appeal of Reidar Aasgaard in "Brothers in Brackets? A Plea for Rethinking the Use of [] in NA/UBS," *JSNT* 26 (2004) 301–21.

("seeking to validate their own righteousness"), a reading that Nestle-Aland places in brackets because other texts omit the word "righteousness": τὴν ἰδίαν [δικαιοσύνην] ζητοῦντες στῆσαι ("seeking to validate their own [righteousness?]").

10:5, τὴν δικαιοσύνην τὴν ἐκ τοῦ νόμου ("the righteousness that comes from the law"), in place of the ambiguous brackets τὴν δικαιοσύνην τὴν ἐκ [τοῦ] νόμου ("the righteousness that comes from [the?] law").

10:15c, τὰ ἀγαθά ("the good things") with the plural article that is found in the TR, as compared with Nestle-Aland's uncertain brackets: [τὰ] ἀγαθά ("[the?] good things").

10:20b, ἐν τοῖς ἐμὲ μὴ ζητοῦσιν ("among those not seeking me") in place of the ambiguous brackets in Nestle-Aland: [ἐν] τοῖς ἐμὲ μὴ ζητοῦσιν ("[among?] those not seeking me").

11:31b, νῦν ἐλεηθῶσιν ("they might now be shown mercy") in place of [νῦν] ἐλεηθῶσιν ("they might [now?] be shown mercy").

13:9f, ἀνακεφαλαιοῦται ἐν τῷ ("summed up in the [saying]"), for ἀνακεφαλαιοῦται [ἐν τῷ] ("summed up [in the?] [saying]").

13:12c, ἐνδυσώμεθα δὲ τὰ ὅπλα τοῦ φωτός ("and let us step into the armor of light") where Nestle-Aland employs brackets because other traditions omit the "and/but": ἐνδυσώμεθα [δὲ] τὰ ὅπλα τοῦ φωτός ("[and?] let us step into the armor of light").

14:22a, πίστιν ἣν ἔχεις ("the faith that you have") in place of Nestle-Alands brackets around the relative pronoun: πίστιν [ἣν] ἔχεις ("the faith [that?] you have").

15:17, ἔχω οὖν τὴν καύχησιν ("I therefore have the boast") in place of the Nestle-Aland brackets that reflect the deletion of the article in some texts: ἔχω οὖν [τὴν] καύχησιν ("I therefore have [the?] boast").

15:30, Παρακαλῶ δὲ ὑμᾶς, ἀδελφοί ("I urge you [brothers]") in place of the shorter reading found in P[46] B that led to placing ἀδελφοί in brackets by Nestle-Aland.

16:1, τὴν ἀδελφὴν ἡμῶν, οὖσαν καὶ διάκονον ("our sister who is also deacon") in place of the ambiguous brackets in Nestle-Aland that reflect the absence of "also" in the TR: τὴν ἀδελφὴν ἡμῶν, οὖσαν [καὶ] διάκονον ("our sister who is [also?] deacon").

I. Concluding Observations

At the Florence conference on rhetoric that occurred in 1998, Stanley Porter issued a call to analyze the rhetorical significance of textual variants.[76] Although most variants are "accidental and unconscious," some scribal alterations appear to be "conscious and intentional" and require a rhetorical method of explanation.[77] A few previous commentaries on Romans and Bruce Metzger's *Textual Commentary* have provided explanations of selected variants without such use of rhetorical methods. In the commentary below, I pursue this task systematically, distinguishing between accidental, stylistic, and theological factors that appear to be present. This is an essential step in weighing the value of textual variants.

In contrast to the modern commentary tradition, which has spent a disproportionate amount of time on the early chapters, the ancient scribes concentrated their energies on chaps. 14–16, with about twice as many variants per page of Nestle-Aland text as in the first eleven chapters. The interests of the later church are clearly reflected in some of these changes, thus providing further examples of "the text as window" to the life of the church, to use Bart Ehrman's expression.[78] Various doctrinal interests are reflected in the variants of 14:9, 12; 15:5, 19, 29, 32; 16:9, 26, some of which reflect the christological controversies that Ehrman discovered in textual variants elsewhere.[79] The request that God "fill" the audience with joy and peace is enhanced by a variant in 15:13 that employs the term for theological certainty: "give you full assurance in joy and peace." The same alteration appears in 15:29. The variants in 15:8 and 31 avoid the implication of the original text that Christ remains the servant of the Jews. The Jewish name "Miriam" is changed to "Mary" in 16:6, probably with a

76   Porter, "Rhetorical Scribe," 405–9.
77   Ibid., 405.
78   Bart D. Ehrman, "The Text as Window: New Testament Manuscripts and the Social History of Early Christianity," in Ehrman and Holmes, eds., *Text*, 361.
79   Ehrman, *Orthodox Corruption of Scripture*, 47–273.

similar motive. These variants fit the pattern that Eldon Epp discovered in the *Codex Bezae Cantabrigiensis,* which reveals an anti-Judaic bias.[80]

Some of the variants in these final chapters of Romans downplay the important role of women in leading early congregations. The role of Phoebe is diminished by the deletion of "and" in 16:1; by the reversal of "receive her" in 16:2; by eliminating the pronoun "she" in 16:2; and by the change from "patron" to "helper" in 16:2. In 16:3 several variants provide the diminutive form "Priscilla" in place of the polite, formal name, Prisca. Some medieval and modern scholars changed the feminine name of Junia to the masculine Junias in 16:7 to eliminate the impression that a woman was "outstanding among the apostles."[81] Some variants in 16:7 downplay the impression that Andronicus and Junia were converted before Paul. These variants fit the anti-feminine bias that text critics have discovered elsewhere.[82]

Some variants in the final chapters reflect concerns about church behavior. The claim of the church to embody the "good" surfaces in 14:16, and the exhortative need of the church to urge its members to seek "peace" led to the variant in 14:19. The doctrine that all things are clean in 14:20 is delimited by the moralistic variant, "to those who are clean." The many variants in 14:21 extend the urge not to cause a brother to "stumble" into the arenas of causing grief, scandalizing, weakening, and offending others in the church. The severity of the warning against heretics is augmented in 16:17 by the substitution of "firmly mark" for "look out;" by the variant with the aorist imperative "withdraw once and for all" in place of "keep withdrawing"; and by the replacement of "well-chosen words" with "glibness" in 16:18. Broadening the warning about heresy to all churches is achieved by variants in 16:19, and in 16:20 the future form "God will crush Satan under your feet" is changed to a prayer request, "may God crush Satan."

The variants that replace "us" with "you" in 15:2, 7, and 16:6 appear to bring Paul's apostolic authority to bear more directly on the later church and the addition of "all" in 15:4 reinforces the scope of his authority. The addition of "through my words" in place of "through me" in 15:18 concentrates Paul's authority in his doctrine and the change in 15:23 of "many years" to "sufficient years" with regard to Paul's hope to visit Rome augments his apostolic adequacy. Similarly the variant "for I perceive" in 15:29 eliminates the element of Paul's doubt about how he would be received in Rome. An effort to generalize Paul's message in Romans for the church as a whole is evident in the variants in 15:14 that delete "my" from "my brothers"; that omit "also yourselves" in reference to the Romans; and in the same verse, the change of "one another" to "others." The additions of "brothers" in 15:15 and 30 point in the same direction. These variants are similar to the well-known deletion of "in Rome" in 1:7 and 15, which has the effect of making Paul's message relevant to the church at large.[83] The opposite valence is visible in the addition of "I shall come to you" in 15:24, which concentrates Paul's mission on Rome in place of Spain.

In 15:11 the citation "let all the peoples praise him" is changed to "you should praise him," thus making clear that the church's praise alone is in view. In 15:16 the subjunctive in the clause, "that the offering of the nations might become," is changed to the aorist passive, "it became," which enhances the status of the later church. Similarly the variants that add "to be completed from Jerusalem" in 15:19 imply the success of the world mission that the church inherits. Finally, a vital interest in the names of early church leaders led to variants in the spelling of Ampliatus, Julia, Nereus, and Olympas in 16:15 and Tertius in 16:22.

The textual variants throughout the letter indicate the interest of the later church to bend Paul's challenging message in the direction of orthodox concerns, an interest that surfaced very early in the creation of the interpolations of 16:17-20a and 16:25-27 and in the deletion of chaps. 15–16 in some editions. Modern exegesis reveals some of the same tendencies to downplay the

---

80 Eldon J. Epp, *The Theological Tendency of Codex Bezae Cantabrigiensis in Acts,* SNTSMS 3 (Cambridge: Cambridge Univ. Press, 1966); see also Ehrman, "Text as Window," 366–67.
81 See Epp, *Junia,* 32–64.
82 See Ben Witherington III, "The Anti-Feminist Tendencies in the 'Western Text' of Acts," *JBL* 103 (1984) 82–84; Epp, "Romans 16,7," 227–91; Epp, *Junia;* Ehrman, "Text as Window," 367–68.
83 See Metzger, *Textual Commentary,* 446.

importance of chaps. 14–16 or even to assign them to a separate letter addressed to Ephesus. We can learn from this textual history but we are not bound to emulate its blind spots. This commentary rests on the conjecture that the original form of Paul's letter lacked both interpolations and consisted of 1:1–16:16 + 16:21-23 + 16:24. And as the rhetorical analysis will show, the material in 15:14–16:16 + 21-24 constitutes the peroration and thus the highpoint of the letter, whose ethos and argumentative power is substantially vitiated by the orthodox interpolations. This commentary will seek to interpret the letter not as the later church understood it, and especially not as the interpolations imply, but so far as possible as intended by the author who created a sixteen-chapter letter with the climax at the end.

3. Chronological and Compositional Circumstances

The historical-critical method requires "a firm chronological structure" because "chronology is the skeleton of history," in the formulation of Edgar Krentz.[84] There is a broad consensus that Paul dictated the letter from Corinth or its vicinity in the period immediately before departing on the final trip to Jerusalem to deliver the offering from the Gentile churches. While some commentators provide a precise date for writing the letter in 55,[85] 56,[86] 57,[87] 58,[88] or occasionally as late as 59,[89] others designate a broader period from 55 to 64.[90] The major exception to this broad consensus of a date in the middle to late 50s is Gerd Luedemann, who proposes 51/52 on the basis of a placement of the Edict of Claudius in 41 c.e. rather than 49,[91] but no Romans commentator has dealt with this as a serious alternative. The fluctuating dates require an examination of the various pieces of evidence on which the chronology of the latter part of Paul's career rests. In the case of the Edict of Claudius, its placement has a bearing both on the date for the composition of Romans and on the history of the Roman congregations prior to Paul's intended visit. When this and other data are weighed, the conclusion will emerge with a relatively high degree of probability that Romans was drafted in the winter of 56–57 c.e. or the early spring of 57.

A. The Date of the Edict of Claudius

In 41 Claudius extended Jewish rights "throughout the empire,"[92] but in the same year Dio Cassius reports that Claudius ordered the Jews, "while continuing their traditional mode of life, not to hold meetings" (*Hist. Rom.* 60.6.6). No explanation is provided for this remarkable order, but a consideration of the policy concerns of Roman administration suggests that an issue of orderly conduct in the Roman synagogues led to their closure and the prohibition of further meetings.[93] That Christian agitation in the synagogues resulting in violent conflicts led to this measure is likely in view of controversies reported elsewhere during this early period of evangelization.[94] Although some scholars suggest fusing the

---

84 Krentz, *Method*, 37.

85 Barrett, 5; Morris, 6–7.

86 Heil, 6, selects the winter of 55–56. Lagrange, xx; Cranfield, 1:16; Zeller, *Römer*, 15; and Dunn, 1:xliii, conclude it is either 55–56 or 56–57.

87 Leenhardt, 7; Bruce, 15–16; Byrne, 17; Schlier, 2: "most scholars assume 57 or 58"; Lagrange, xx; Cranfield, 1:16; Zeller, 15; and Dunn, 1:xliii, place the letter either in 55–56 or 56–57; Moo, 3: "the best alternative is probably A.D. 57."

88 Sanday and Headlam, xiii: "during the winter 57–58, or early in the spring of the year 58, according to almost all calculations"; Zahn, 20–21; Michel, 27–28; Bouman, 109; Black, 4–5; Harrisville, 15; Byrne, 9; Holladay, *Critical Introduction*, 278.

89 Meyer, 36; Godet, 47; Dodd, xxvi.

90 Best, 8: sometime between 55 and 59 c.e.; Achte-meier, 19: sometime between 55 and 64; Fitzmyer, 87: mid- to late 50s; Schreiner, 5, and de Silva, *Introduction*, 601: between 55 and 58.

91 Luedemann, *Chronology*, 173–75, 263.

92 Zeev, *Jewish Rights*, 328–30.

93 See Rutgers, *Hidden Heritage*, 184–89; Williams, "Identity of the Jewish Community," 38–39; Helga Botermann, *Das Judenedict des Kaisers Claudius: Römischer Staat und Christiani im I. Jahrhundert*, Herm.E 71 (Stuttgart: Steiner, 1996) 130; Cineira, *Religionspolitik*, 199–200. In contrast, Slingerland, *Claudian Policymaking*, 131–68, argues less plausibly for "the mental hostility of Claudius" against the Jews (149–50) as the motivation of the actions in 41 and later.

94 Zeev, *Jewish Rights*, 448–49, following Rutgers, *Hidden Heritage*, 197, and Botermann, *Judenedict*, 47–48,

two events,[95] a second quite different action is reported later in Claudius's administration by Suetonius, *Claud.* 25: *Iudaios impulsore Chresto adsidue tumultuantes Roma expulit* ("He expelled from Rome the Jews constantly making disturbances at the instigation of Chrestus"). Since the action reported by Suetonius is not dated, one is forced to rely on other data whose congruence is mutually supporting: Acts 18:2 reports that Prisca and Aquila had come to Ephesus because the Jews were expelled from Rome, an event that can be dated in the late 40s on the basis of the Gallio Inscription and other factors in Pauline chronology.[96] The fifth-century historian Orosius reports the date as follows:

> Josephus refers to the expulsion of Jews by Claudius in his ninth year. But Suetonius touches me more in saying, "Claudius expelled from Rome the Jews constantly making disturbances at the instigation of Chrestus." It cannot be determined whether he ordered only the Jews agitating against Christ to be restrained and suppressed, or whether he also wanted to expel Christians as being men of a related faith. (*Hist.* 7:6, 15-16)

This places the Edict of Claudius between January 25 of 49 C.E. and January 24 of 50 C.E.[97] Since currently available editions of Josephus lack this reference to Claudius's ninth year and since Orosius is sometimes inaccurate, skeptics tend to disallow this evidence,[98] but this leaves unexplained the remarkable congruence between two pieces of otherwise unrelated material. Hans-Werner Goetz's study of Orosius throws additional light on his aims and reliability; he viewed the Roman Empire as being used by God to allow the spreading of the Christian religion, so that the rise of Christian emperors in the fourth century is depicted as the goal of history and the promise of peace and prosperity.[99] Goetz shows that Orosius used two standards in evaluating Roman emperors: their relations toward Christians and their contributions to the empire.[100] For his own time, Orosius sought to unite Roman nationalism with Christian patriotism, but there is no indication that this might have influenced his understanding of Claudius in the first century.[101] In general, he appears to have been committed to the traditional requirement "of truth as the highest command of history."[102] Nevertheless, if the Orosius datum were the only indication of the date of the Edict of Claudius, most scholars would discount it. However, the coordination of this remarkable and unexplained datum with other details about Claudius's career lead most historians to take it into account and set the date for the edict in 49 C.E.[103]

Since Paul could not have met Prisca and Aquila until after this date (Acts 18:1-2), it must be correlated with the eighteen months of the Corinthian ministry (18:11) and Paul's departure from Corinth after the hearing before Gallio (18:12-18), datable on the basis of the Gallio Inscription to the twelve-month period July 1, 51 to July 1, 52.[104] When one calculates the subsequent events in his career, taking account of details in the letters and

---

134–35. Earlier support for this conclusion comes from Momigliano, *Claudius*, 20ff.; Smallwood, *Jews*, 210–16, esp. 211.

95   See, e.g., Murphy-O'Connor, *St. Paul's Corinth*, 130–37; Leon, *Jews*, 3–27; Luedemann, *Chronology*, 6–7, 165–70. Slingerland, *Claudian Policymaking*, 97, provides a comprehensive list of scholars fusing the two events.

96   See Jewett, *Chronology*, 36–40, 100–103.

97   See Jewett, *Chronology*, 37–38.

98   For example, Benko, "Edict," 406–18; Slingerland, *Claudian Policymaking*, 121–29.

99   Hans-Werner Goetz, *Die Geschichtstheologie des Orosius*, Impulse der Forschung 32 (Darmstadt: Wissenschaftliche Buchgesellschaft, 1980) 97; see also the appraisal of Orosius in Grabbe, *Judaism*, 2:560–61.

100   Goetz, *Orosius*, 96.

101   Ibid., 85–87, 114–17.

102   Ibid., 17.

103   See, e.g., Scramuzza, *Claudius*, 151, 287; Momigliano, *Claudius*, 37; Schürer, *History*, 3:77; Smallwood, *Jews*, 210; Jeffers, *Conflict at Rome*, 12–13; Grabbe, *Judaism*, 2:399; Williams, "Identity of the Jewish Community," 39; Solin, "Juden und Syrer," 689–90; Cineira, *Religionspolitik*, 208–14. Botermann, *Judenedict*, 135 notes that no date other than 49 can be documented, but that an earlier date is possible because it is hard to believe that the Roman government would have tolerated eight years of disturbances from 41 to 49.

104   See Jewett, *Chronology*, 38–40; Klaus Haacker, "Gallio," *ABD* 2 (1992) 901–3; Fritz Graf, "Gallio," *RGG*[4] 3 (2000) 461.

the realities of travel in the ancient world, this brings him to 56–57 C.E. as the final winter in Corinth (1 Cor 16:6) when the letter to the Romans was probably conceived and dictated.

B. *Termini a quo et ad quem* for Events after the Writing of the Letter

On the assumption that Paul could not have traveled to Jerusalem and subsequently, as a prisoner, to Rome until he finished and dispatched the letter, the various historical details relating to these travels need to be weighed to decide between the proposed dates for dictating Romans.[105] Since most of these details come from Acts, a work whose chronological framework of five Jerusalem journeys is demonstrably mistaken[106] but whose other details are often useful,[107] it is appropriate to weigh each detail separately, without seeking to harmonize them or to eliminate possible contradictions. In particular, it is methodically correct not to allow the conclusions reached above concerning the Edict of Claudius to influence the assessment of these details.

1. The Rebel from Egypt

In Acts 21:38 there is a report of the question posed by a Roman tribune, whether Paul was "the Egyptian who recently stirred up a revolt and led four thousand men of the Sicarii out into the wilderness."[108] In *Bell.* 2.261-63 Josephus describes how Felix reacted quickly against this threat, placing it after the death of Claudius in October 54 (*Ant.* 20.158ff). Since Paul did not arrive in Jerusalem until Pentecost (Acts 20:16), this places the earliest possible arrival in the spring of 55. In order to leave time for

the other events that Josephus places before the report of the Egyptian rebel (*Ant.* 20.158-65), the more likely terminus a quo is 56 C.E.[109]

2. The Hearing before Festus

In Acts 25:6, after being in prison for two years, Paul was brought before the newly appointed governor, Festus. Since this occurred "not more than eight or ten days" from the time Festus assumed office, it would provide a significant terminus ad quem for Paul's arrest in Jerusalem two years earlier. Some NT scholars argue that he assumed office in 54–56 C.E.[110] while historians set the date between 58 and 61.[111] The earlier date rests on the report of Josephus *Ant.* 182 that Felix's brother Pallas saved him from charges of misdeeds in office by influencing Nero after his term was over. Since Pallas was removed from office when Nero came to power, he presumably had no such influence. However, no historian shares this view, and there is considerable evidence that the immensely rich Pallas retained great influence among those who hoped to become his legatees.[112] It is likely that Festus took office either in July 59 or 60, and those who argue for the former appear to have a better case.[113] This would imply that Paul arrived in Jerusalem and was arrested in the spring of 57.

3. The Encounter with Ananias

When Paul was brought before the Sanhedrin after the riot in Jerusalem and declares his good conscience with regard to not having caused the disturbance, "the high priest Ananias commanded those who stood by him to strike him on the mouth" (Acts 23:2). If the date of his office could be determined, it could throw additional

---

105 The following sections are adapted from Jewett, *Chronology*, 40–44, 48–50.

106 See ibid., 89–94.

107 Ibid., 20–21, 25–62.

108 See Grabbe, *Judaism*, 2:441–42.

109 In "Sabbatical Chronomessianism and the Timing of Messianic Movements," *HUCA* 66 (1975) 216, Ben Zion Wacholder infers on the basis of sabbatical cycles that "Nisan of 56" was the likely date for the Egyptian's revolt.

110 Kirsopp Lake, *The Beginnings of Christianity* (London: Macmillan, 1933) 5:464–66.; Ernst Haenchen, *Die Apostlegeschichte* (Göttingen: Vandenhoeck & Ruprecht, 1961) 60–63; Hans Conzelmann, *Die Apostelgeschichte* (Tübingen: Mohr-Siebeck, 1963) 130.

111 Schürer, *History*, 1:465; Smallwood, *Jews*, 269; Grabbe, *Judaism*, 2:442–43; see the more complete listing in Jewett, *Chronology*, 129–30.

112 See Jewett, *Chronology*, 42–43; both Grabbe, *Judaism*, 2:442, and Joel B. Green, "Festus, Porcius," *ABD* 2 (1992) 795, concur.

113 See Daniel Plooij, *De Chronologie van het Leven van Paulus* (Leiden: Brill, 1918) 58ff.; G. B. Caird, "Chronology of the NT," *IDB* 1:604–5; William Mitchell Ramsay, *Pauline and Other Studies in Early Christian History* (London: Hodder & Stoughton, 1906) 103; Smallwood, *Jews*, 269; Green, "Festus, Porcius," 795, cites the Armenian version of the *Chronicle* of Eusebius, which sets the beginning of Festus's procuratorship in the tenth year of Agrippa II, which would be the summer of 59.

light on the date of this encounter. On the basis of details in Josephus *Ant.* 20.5.2; 20.6.2, Ananias ben Nedebaeus was appointed high priest in 47 c.e.[114] and sometime thereafter was sent as a prisoner to Rome in connection with a conflict with the Samaritans (Josephus, *Ant.* 20.125-33). The emperor judged in his favor so that Ananias could return to Jerusalem in early 52–53 (Josephus, *Ant.* 20.134-37) where he served until 58 or 59 (Josephus, *Ant.* 20.179).[115] Thus Paul could have encountered him anytime between 53 and 58 c.e.

4. The Single Prefect Receiving Paul

A textual variant in Acts 28:16 refers to the delivery of Paul and other prisoners to a single prefect upon their arrival in Rome. Two chronologists have used this detail to establish a terminus ad quem for Paul's arrival.[116] They argue that the last single prefect was Burrus, who died in January 62. After this, two prefects were assigned to the task by Nero.[117] This would imply that Paul's arrival in Rome must have occurred no later than the summer of 61.

5. The Departure from Philippi

In Acts 20 there are some precise travel details that have led scholars to calculate the alternative dates of 54 or 57 for Paul's departure from Philippi on his final trip to Jerusalem.[118] "But we sailed away from Philippi after the days of Unleavened Bread, and in five days came to them in Troas, where we stayed for seven days. On the first day of the week, when we were gathered together to break bread, Paul talked with them, intending to depart on the morrow" (Acts 20:6-7). Since Paul departed from Troas on a Monday that followed a seven-day visit, he must have arrived in Troas the preceding Tuesday, and since the trip from Philippi to Troas lasted five days, he must have departed from Philippi on the preceding Friday. On the basis that this day followed the end of the Feast of Unleavened Bread (i.e., the seven-day celebration that begins on the 15th of Nisan, the day after

Passover), astronomical tables were consulted to determine the years when the close of this festival fell on a Friday. The result was that this Friday must have been either April 19, 54, or April 15, 57. Objections to this reasoning have been raised by scholars who cannot fit either date into their chronology,[119] but no decisive flaw has been detected.

In summary, the assessment of these details supports the date of the winter of 56–57 for the writing of Romans. The mix-up between Paul and the rebel from Egypt could have occurred any time after 56; the hearing before Festus occurred in 59, after a two-year imprisonment; the encounter with Ananias could have occurred anytime between 53 and 58; the encounter with a single prefect in Rome after the shipwreck and the two-year imprisonment must have occurred no later than the summer of 61; and the departure from Philippi fell either in 54 or 57. Here is the result of the chronological reckoning that takes all of these factors into account:[120]

Winter 56–57	Dictation of Romans in Corinth
April 15, 57	Departure from Philippi
June 57–June 59	Two-year imprisonment in Caesarea
Mid-June, 59	Hearing before Festus
October 15, 59	Departure from Fair Havens
November 59– January 60	Three months on Malta
Early March 60	Arrival in Rome
March 62	Execution of Paul

C. Evidence of a Corinthian Setting for the Composition of Romans

There is conclusive evidence, drawn in part from primary evidence in the Pauline letters, that the letter to the Romans was created in Corinth. In Rom 16:23 Paul sends greetings from "Gaius, who is host to me and the whole

---

114 Schürer, *History,* 2:231, 233; Grabbe, *Judaism,* 2:389.

115 Schürer, *History,* 2:231, 233; R. Schmidt, "Ananias," *RE* 1:488; J. Büchler, "Ananias, Son of Nedebeus," *JE* 1 (1925) 558–59; Robert F. O'Toole, "Ananias," *ABD* 1 (1992) 225.

116 Karl Georg Wieseler, *Chronologie des apostolischen Zeitalters* (Göttingen: Vandenhoeck & Ruprecht, 1848) 83; Plooij, *Chronologie,* 81–83.

117 Plooij, *Chronologie,* 81–83, discusses Pliny *Ep.* 10.57,

and Philostratus *Vit. soph.* 2.32, in support of the customary reference to the office of prefects in the plural.

118 See William Mitchell Ramsay, "A Fixed Date in the Life of St. Paul," *Exp* 5th Series 3 (1896) 336–45; Plooij, *Chronologie,* 83–85; Jewett, *Chronology,* 49–50.

119 See the account in Jewett, *Chronology,* 50.

120 See Jewett, *Chronology,* 102.

church." There is a consensus that this is Gaius Titius Justus, who is mentioned in Acts 18:7 and 1 Cor 1:14 as a church leader in Corinth whose house was next door to the synagogue.[121] The greeting from "Erastus the city treasurer" in Rom 16:23 is widely assumed to be the official commemorated in a Corinthian inscription.[122] Paul greets Timothy, Lucius, Jason, and Sosipater in 16:21, and according to Acts 10:3-4 these were the delegates that rendezvoused in Corinth in preparation for the journey to Jerusalem.[123] In Rom 16:1 Paul recommends Phoebe, "the deacon of the church at Cenchreae," which is one of the ports of Corinth. Paul's knowledge of her travel plans confirms that he is in Corinth or its environs at the time of writing. This evidence has led Romans commentators, without exception as far as I know, to conclude that Paul wrote Romans in the area of Corinth.

D. The Role of the Secretary

The wording of Rom 16:21 makes clear that Paul used a secretary in writing this letter: "I, Tertius, the one who wrote this letter in [the service of the] Lord, greet you [pl.]." Although the detailed analysis of this verse will be taken up in the commentary below, here it is appropriate to describe the ancient rationale and methods of working with a trained scribe in writing letters. In view of the difficulty of writing with primitive pens on the less than perfectly smooth surface of the papyrus scrolls used for letters,[124] skilled secretaries were employed for public and much of the private correspondence.[125] Sometimes the dictation was syllable by syllable, a very slow process that approximated the painstaking process of ancient writing.[126] Pliny the Elder reported that Julius Caesar usually dictated from four to seven letters at a time to a group of secretaries who were using this method.[127] Highly trained secretaries could keep up with normal speech by writing in shorthand, but that required later deciphering to create a generally readable text,[128] which again was a time-consuming process. An Oxyrhynchus papyrus offers a vivid glance into the training of such scribes:

> Panechotes . . . to Apollonius, writer of shorthand (σημειογράφῳ), greetings. I have placed with you my slave Chaerammon to be taught the signs which your son knows, for a period of two years . . . and you will receive the second installment consisting of 40 drachmae when the boy has learned the whole system, and the third you will receive at the end of the period when the boy writes fluently in every respect and reads faultlessly.[129]

Secretaries also routinely refined the rough drafts of dictation or composed letters themselves on the basis of brief instructions.[130] In some instances the secretary acted as coauthor or wrote in behalf of more than one person.[131] Secretaries frequently became the trusted administrative assistants of their owners or employers.[132] But in every case, "the sender was held completely responsible for the content and the form of the letter."[133]

In the case of Romans, as the rhetorical analysis in the next chapter and the subsequent commentary will demonstrate, there is evidence of careful planning of the structure of the letter and attention devoted to making a varied and often elegant impression on hearers. It would have required weeks of intensive work during which Tertius must have been made available on a full-time basis. This expense is most easily explained by the detail Paul reveals in 16:2, that Phoebe "became a patroness to many and to myself as well." This is the only time in Paul's letters that he acknowledges having received fund-

---

121 Käsemann, 421; Cranfield, 3:807; Dunn, 2:910; Fitzmyer, 749; Moo, 935; Byrne, 460.
122 Fitzmyer, 750; Moo, 935–36; Byrne, 460; see the detailed discussion in the commentary below.
123 See particularly Ollrog, *Mitarbeiter*, 58; and Georgi, *Remembering the Poor*, 111, 122–23.
124 See Naphtali Lewis, *Papyrus in Classical Antiquity* (Oxford: Clarendon, 1974) 1–78; White, *Light*, 213–14.
125 Richards, *Secretary*, 15–67.
126 Ibid., 25–26.
127 Pliny the Elder, *Nat.* 7.25.91.
128 See the account of the scholarly debate over Latin and Greek shorthand methods in Richards, *Secretary*, 26–43.
129 Cited by Richards, *Secretary*, 38, from *P.Oxy.* 4. Nr. 724.
130 Richards, *Secretary*, 44–46, 49–56.
131 Ibid., 47–48, citing the study of Gordon J. Bahr, "Paul and Letter Writing in the First Century," *CBQ* 28 (1966) 476.
132 Richards, *Secretary*, 63–67.
133 Ibid., 67.

ing from a patron, and it is likely that this patronage was directly involved with the missionary project promoted by the letter. That Tertius was either her slave or employee is the conjecture that explains some of the extraordinary features of this letter, drafted in the winter of 56–57 in the area of Corinth. Since Tertius identifies himself in 16:22 as the secretary who is working "in the Lord," it seems likely to many scholars that he was well known to the believers in Rome.[134] As Phoebe's slave or employee, he reveals to the Roman audience that he is the proper one to read this letter when Phoebe delivers it to the congregations in Rome. Most commentators assume that Phoebe had agreed to be the letter bearer,[135] but a person of her social class would have her scribe read the letter aloud in her behalf. Phoebe and Tertius would then be in the position to negotiate the complex issue advanced by the letter in a manner typical for the ancient world. For example, a papyrus refers to a letter bearer as qualified to expand on the letter: "The rest please learn from the man who brings you this letter. He is no stranger to us."[136] As White explains, "The scribe was sometimes hired to deliver the letter as well as to write it. The messenger would have been somewhat more trustworthy in these cases—both as interpreter of the letter's content and as letter carrier—than messengers who merely happened to be travelling toward the letter's destination."[137] In view of the extraordinary refinement of the rhetoric of Romans, designed for oral presentation in interaction with a variety of groups in Rome, it is hard to believe that someone not involved in the creation of the letter would be in the position of presenting it effectively. In conclusion, this commentary rests on the conjecture that Tertius and Phoebe were engaged in the creation, the delivery, the public reading, and the explanation of the letter in the course of 57 C.E.

4. The Rhetoric of Romans: Evangelical Persuasion

While older commentaries and even some published recently view Romans "primarily as a repository of theology," this commentary follows the lead of recent developments that view the letter as "a work of Christian rhetoric, aiming to persuade."[138] In ancient rhetoric there were five means of persuasion: invention, arrangement, style, memory, and delivery, all of which are evident in Romans. But a sixth element needs to be taken into account: the audience. Ancient theorists assumed that speakers were acquainted with their audiences, and thus developed no theory to ascertain their nature and proclivities. Yet all of the components of rhetoric presuppose the need to use different means to persuade different audiences. The three standard genera of rhetoric pertain to three broad types of audience situations: the law court, the legislative assembly, and memorial occasions. The ancient epistolary handbooks also took account of the peculiar rhetorical requirements of letters to family members, friends, sovereigns, business associates, and patrons to whom recommendations and requests were addressed. Although the basic reality of the audience was assumed, it seems rarely to be taken into account as a decisive component of rhetorical analysis of NT texts. Since we do not have direct access to the audience of Romans, however, it is necessary to reconstruct a model of the audience to interpret the rhetorical devices Paul creates to persuade them. Hence the importance of what Bitzer has called "the rhetorical situation,"[139] which in coordination with "the historical situation" is the theme of sections 3, 5, 6, and 7 of this introduction. We begin our consideration with evidence of the first of the five classical means of persuasion.

---

134 See Zahn, 613; Schumacher, *Letzten Kapitel,* 102; Käsemann, 421; Cranfield, 3:806; Schreiner, 808; Richards, *Secretary,* 170.

135 For example, Godet, 488; Schmidt, 251; Michel, 473; Cranfield, 3:780; Schlier, 440; Wilckens, 3:131; Dunn, 2:886.

136 Cited by Eldon Jay Epp, "Papyrus Manuscripts and Letter Carrying in Greco-Roman Times," in B. A. Pearson et al., eds., *The Future of Early Christianity: Essays in Honor of Helmut Koester* (Minneapolis: Fortress Press, 1991) 46, from *P.Col.* 3.1. Nr. 6.15;

the full text of the letter is available in White, *Light,* 10–11.

137 White, *Light,* 216; he cites Chan-Hie Kim, "The Papyrus Invitation," *JBL* 94 (1975) 391–402, in which the scribe saluted the guests to be invited and then read out the invitation from the master's letter.

138 Byrne, 4; see also Witherington, 2–4; Tobin, *Paul's Rhetoric,* 1–15.

139 Bitzer, "Rhetorical Situation," 1–14.

A. Invention

Invention (Lat. *inventio*; Gk. εὕρεσις) is the rhetorical term for discovering the means of persuasion that are appropriate in particular rhetorical situations.[140] This includes some of the means that we shall discuss under the topic of arrangement: the *exordium* or prologue of a speech or letter, the narrative that provides the background of the case, the argument that consists of various kinds of proof, and the peroration or epilogue.[141] Some of the ancient rhetoricians divided the invention of proofs into two types, artificial and inartificial.[142] The latter includes testimony from witnesses, documents, citations from authoritative sources, and in the case of early Christian literature, appeals to shared religious experience. Among the most important of these for the argument of Romans are citations from early Christian creeds, hymns, and citations from Scripture. The identification of the hymnic and confessional material has resulted from form-critical analysis over the past decades. Artificial proofs are those created by the author, and in Romans these include midrashim, diatribes, speeches-in-character, and formal enthymemes and syllogisms. The following are examples of invention that play a prominent role in Romans.

1. Citations of Credal Formulations

Form-critical studies have identified credal elements that are embedded in the text of the NT, including many in Romans.[143] A Jewish Christian creed that had been expanded into a Hellenistic Christian creed is cited in 1:3-4. This composite creed sets the tone for the entire letter by finding common ground with various sides in Rome. In 3:30 Paul uses the formula "God is one" that was shared by Jewish, Orphic, and philosophical groups. A confessional formula probably used by the Roman churches is cited in 4:24, "faith in the one who raised Jesus our Lord from the dead." A close echo of widely used confessional formulas that were influenced by the Suffering Servant material of Isa 53 is constructed in

Rom 4:25 concerning Jesus, "who was handed over for the sake of our transgressions and was raised for the sake of our rightness." In 5:6 Paul uses an early Christian confession whose wording suggests provenance from the "strong" faction in Rome, and in 5:8 he cites the widely used formula, "Christ died on our behalf." In 7:4, 8:32 and 34, Paul cites confessional formulas that appear to have been used by all branches of early Christianity, that Jesus is "the one raised from [the] dead," that he "delivered up for us all," was "raised" and sits "at the right hand of God." In 10:9-10 Paul employs typical early Christian language about converts confessing "Lord Jesus!" and having faith that "God raised him from the dead." In 10:14 the formula that appears in Acts is employed, that converts "call upon him" as Lord. At the climax of the hymn of 11:33-36 is the formula widely employed in Greco-Roman and Hellenistic Jewish contexts, "from him and through him and unto him are all things." In 14:8-9 Paul adapts the traditional confessional formula about Christ dying and being raised up to maintain that "we belong to the Lord" and that he seeks to "be Lord over both the dead and the living." These citations reveal the rhetorical effort to find common ground with various groups of believers in Rome, and to avoid the impression that Paul's theology is eccentric in comparison with the faith held in common by other believers.

2. Citations of Hymns, Benedictions, and Doxologies

A wide variety of liturgical elements has been identified by form-critical methods,[144] including many in Romans. In 1:25 Paul breaks into the argument concerning the human assault against God with a typical Jewish doxology widely shared by early Christians, directed to God "who is blessed forever! Amen!" A fragment of a hymn that probably originated in the Hellenistic Christian milieu of Stephen is cited in 3:25-26a. In 6:17 Paul employs the formula "thanks be to God," a doxology

---

140   See Lausberg, *Handbuch*, §§260–442; Malcolm Heath, "Invention," in Porter, *Handbook*, 90.

141   Heath, "Invention," 103–18.

142   See Lausberg, *Handbuch*, §§351–426; Martin, *Antike Rhetorik*, 97–119.

143   See Bartsch, "Bekenntnisformel"; Cullmann, *Confessions*; Neufeld, *Confessions*; Burger, *Jesus als Davidssohn*; Hurtado, *Lord Jesus Christ*.

144   See the studies by Berger, *Formgeschichte;* Deichgräber, *Gotteshymnus;* Gloer, "Homologies and Hymns"; Schattenmann, *Prosahymnus;* Schille, *Frühchristliche Hymnen;* Heckel, *Segen;* Champion, *Benedictions and Doxologies;* Toit, "Doxologische Gemeinschaft."

widely used in Jewish, Greco-Roman, and early Christian piety. In 8:38-39 Paul creates a hymn with similarities to other early Christian hymns. In 11:33-36 he cites and amends a hymn that probably originated in Hellenistic Judaism and had been adapted for Christian use in Rome and elsewhere. This passage concludes with a doxology, "to him be glory forever! Amen," that is similar to the doxologies in the Psalms and in other early Christian letters. In 13:11-12 Paul cites and amends an agape hymn that was probably being used in baptismal contexts with the title, "The Critical Time." In 15:6 Paul alludes to typical early Christian doxologies, that "you might glorify the God and father of our Lord Jesus Christ." This is embedded in one of the two benedictions that Paul created to conclude the formal argument of Romans in 15:5-6 and 15:13. These homiletic benedictions are modeled after LXX wishes and blessings and serve to wrap up the argumentation of the letter in an ecstatic expectation of divine blessing that was probably typical for early Christian worship in Rome and elsewhere. These citations of hymns, doxologies, and blessings anchor Paul's discourse in the shared religious experience of early house and tenement churches while providing a measure of eloquent inspiration to his letter. These materials would have been effective because they resonated with the varied sides of Paul's audience in Rome.

3. Citations of Scripture and Scriptural Catenae

The intensive investigation in recent years of Paul's use of Scripture has resulted in a consensus about its central role in the argument of Romans.[145] A prominent emphasis in the opening of Romans is that the gospel about Christ was affirmed "in the holy scriptures" (1:2). That the Scriptures point to salvation by faith is argued in 1:17 and that the Scriptures were "written for our instruction,

in order that . . . we might have hope" is prominently stated in 15:4. Nowhere else in Paul's letters are there so many citations, which reveals his intent to rest the argument on a scriptural foundation. Dietrich-Alex Koch counts 28 citations from Isaiah, 20 from the Psalms, 15 each from Deuteronomy and Genesis, 6 from Exodus, 4 each from Leviticus and Hosea, 3 from Proverbs, 2 each from Habakkuk, 1 Kings, and Job, and one each from Malachi and Joel.[146] In Rom 3:10-18 Paul uses a scriptural catena that probably originated in a Jewish milieu, but which he alters to fit his argumentative purpose. In 9:25-29 and 15:9-12 there are additional catenae of citations, possibly assembled by Paul himself. In the commentary below, the source, framing, amending and use of each of these citations is analyzed in order to understand the argumentative weight that they are meant to carry.[147] Redaction-critical methods are employed to discern the intention of the framing and formulation of these alterations, and their rhetorical significance is assessed in the light of Paul's missionary project and the audience of the letter.

4. Diatribe

The most widely discussed technique of artificial invention in Romans is the diatribe. Earlier studies interpreted this as a combative argumentative technique, suitable for the refutation of contrary points of view and the defense of the author's viewpoint.[148] This was overturned by Stanley Stowers and others who showed that the classroom was the usual arena for diatribe, and that the teacher created imaginary interlocutors to voice the questions and misconceptions that push the discussion forward.[149] Unlike earlier treatments that viewed Romans as a judicial letter whose purpose was to defend the true faith, ancient rhetoricians viewed diatribe as particularly characteristic of the demonstrative genre,[150]

---

145 See Koch, *Schrift*, 88–91; Aageson, *Biblical Interpretation*, 73–127; and the studies by Michel, *Bibel*; Ellis, *Paul's Use*; Evans and Sanders, *Scriptures*; Stanley, *Scripture*; Hübner, *Gottes Ich und Israel*; Minde, *Schrift*; Hanson, *Interpretation*, etc.

146 Koch, *Schrift*, 33.

147 For a discussion of the rhetorical methodology required to pursue this task, see Stanley, *Arguing*, 9–21, 62–71.

148 See, e.g., Bultmann, *Stil*, passim; Käsemann, 53–61.

149 Stowers, *Diatribe*, 86–93; see also Schmeller, *Diatribe*; Song, *Diatribe*.

150 Aristotle *Rhet.* 2.17; Cicero *De or.* 2.50; 3.202-5; *Rhet. Her.* 4.42-58. See also George L. Kustas's citation of Hermogenes in "Diatribe in Ancient Rhetorical Theory," *Colloquy* 22 (1976) 7–11.

suitable for enhancing the ethos that an author or speaker wishes to sustain. In 2:1-16 there is a diatribe that sustains Paul's doctrine of impartial judgment that overturns the widespread assumptions of exceptionalism held by most of the groups in the Greco-Roman world. The imaginary interlocutor that Paul invents for this discussion is a bigot who claims exemption from divine judgment for himself while passing judgment on others for doing what he is doing. This depiction is meant to evoke the contempt of his audience for such hypocrisy and to establish the premise that divine judgment is impartial; only in the fourth proof with the argument concerning the weak and the strong in 14:1—15:13 does it become clear that the groups in Rome are behaving like the despised interlocutor. In 2:17-29 a diatribe establishes that Jews are not exempt from God's impartial judgment. In this case the interlocutor is a Jewish teacher who claims to be a guide to despised Gentiles while betraying ethical admonitions of his own tradition. The passage ends by maintaining that the true Jew is one who no longer seeks honor by claiming superiority over others. Again, the ultimate bearing of this diatribe on the audience does not become clear until chap. 14, where Paul deals with the tendencies of various groups in Rome to claim superior honor over others.

In 3:1-8 the interlocutor invented for the diatribe appears to accept Paul's argument on divine impartiality and then proceeds to find apparent flaws in Paul's argument. The pace through four diatribal exchanges in this passage is rapid and witty. In the diatribe of 3:9-20 the interlocutor poses the question in the light of Paul's compelling answers, "Are we [Jews] at a disadvantage" in comparison with Gentile believers? Paul answers with a resounding "No" and goes on to cite a catena of scriptural passages that demonstrate that all persons and cultural groups have sinned, and that none has an advantage in honor. In the diatribe of 3:27-31 Paul returns to this question of cultural advantage and poses the interlocutor's question in a way that includes all of the competitive groups in Rome. "Where then is *our* boasting?" This is followed by five additional questions that drive the argument to a conclusion that monotheistic faith means that God is the God of Gentiles as well as of Jews, and that consequently all boasting must cease. In the diatribe of 4:1-12, the interlocutor's questions in 4:1, 3, 9, and 10 reflect a less nationalistic point of view

and serve to drive the argument forward. The succinct questions allow Paul to respond rapidly and give the passage a lively, engaging tone.

It is unclear whether the three rhetorical questions in 5:15-16 indicate that this pericope (5:12-21) should be classified as a diatribe. In 6:1-14 the diatribal form is clearer and the interlocutor is a libertinist who draws a false conclusion from the doctrine of impartial grace, which gives Paul the opportunity to develop his doctrine of the death of the sinful self in baptism and the resultant new life in Christ. The same libertinistic interlocutor raises the rhetorical questions at the beginning of the next diatribe (6:15-23) and this provides the context for Paul's argument about living under the grace and lordship of Christ.

In 9:30—10:4 the diatribe features a friendly interlocutor who asks how it could be that Gentiles obtained righteousness without seeking it while Israel, which sought it, failed to find it. The answer that Paul provides is that misguided zeal led some Jews to oppose the Christ because they wished to "validate their own righteousness" (10:3). In the diatribe of 11:1-10, Paul casts himself as the imaginary interlocutor, beginning with "I say, therefore, 'God did not cast off his people, did he?'" The second diatribal exchange in this pericope begins again with Paul's question in 11:7, "What then?" This allows Paul to reiterate his doctrine that the Jews failed to find the righteousness they sought while the elect who relied on grace found it. In the next diatribe, Paul again plays the role of the imaginary interlocutor with the leading question in 11:11, "I say, therefore, 'They did not stumble as to fall, did they?'" After this question is answered in 11:19, a new interlocutor steps onto the stage, bragging that as a Gentile believer, he had displaced the Jewish branches of the sacred olive tree. Rather than repudiating this arrogant voice, Paul coolly responds with "Well said!" in 11:20 and goes right on to cite the traditional warnings against uppity mindedness. The pericope ends with the conviction that God is able to graft both Gentile and Jewish branches into the sacred tree.

In the final diatribe, Paul again plays the role of the imaginary interlocutor with the question in 13:3b, "Now, do you wish not to fear the authority?" Addressing an imaginary conversation partner who is fearful of the government, Paul urges compliance in order to avoid wrath and to satisfy the demands of conscience. These diatribes provide a lively, conversational quality to Paul's arguments. They evoke audience reactions with sharp involvement pro and con. The argumentative function is quite profound in the case of the early diatribes that lead the audience to make judgments against bigotry and pride that later are shown to lie at the root of the hostile competition between house and tenement churches.

5. Midrashim

A midrash is a Jewish argumentative form, usually consisting of a main text that is explained and interpreted by secondary texts.[151] Paul is a master of midrashic argument, usually combining it in a vibrant manner with diatribal elements that are intended to elicit responses from the audience. In 4:1-25 a two-part midrash is presented to prove that Abraham serves as the father of faith, not just for Jews but for believing Gentiles as well. The main text from Gen 15:6, "Abraham believed in God and it was reckoned to him as righteousness," is explained by a secondary text from Ps 31:1. In the second half of this midrash, Gen 17:5 is cited to prove that Abraham is the father of all believers, which is then buttressed by Gen 15:5, which proves that "his descendants" are those who live by faith. In this double midrash, portions of the main text from Gen 15:6 are again cited in Rom 4:9, 10, 22, and 23.

In 9:6-18 Paul develops a midrash with Gen 21:12 as the proof text that contains the catchwords "call" and "seed," which are elaborated by the secondary texts of Gen 18:10, 14; 25:23; Mal 1:2-3; Exod 33:19; and Exod 9:16, 26. This midrash is further developed in 9:19-29, which is again fused with diatribe. The theme of divine election, articulated in the first half by the proof text from Gen 21:12, is developed by secondary texts from Isa 29:16; Hos 2:25; and 2:1 that provide the catchwords "call," "beloved," and "sons," followed by citations from Isa 10:22-23 and 1:9 that pick up the catchwords "sons" and "seed." This elaborate midrash sustains the argument that God's election is righteous because it opens the path for the "children of the promise" who are the "remnant" that receives mercy in Christ. In Rom 11:1-6

there is another combination of diatribe and midrash in which the proof text comes from the virtually identical wording of 1 Sam 12:22 and Ps 94:24 that "God has not rejected his people." This is supported by citations from 1 Kgs 19:10 and 18 to show that the remnant is saved by grace alone. Then in Rom 11:7-10 there is a midrash with citations from Deut 29:4 and Ps 68:23 that shows the source of Israel's obtuseness. These midrashic arguments sustain Paul's case that his gospel rests on scriptural foundations and they are designed to appeal especially to those branches of the Christian movement in Rome that stand close to the Jewish tradition.

6. Speech-in-Character and Examples

Examples (Lat. *exemplum*; Gk. παράδειγμα) are a widely used means of argument,[152] based on the premise that what is true for one instance is true for similar cases elsewhere. In 1:26b-27 Paul provides the example of same-sex relations between men and women to confirm the presence of dishonorable relations mentioned in v. 26a. In 4:1-23 Abraham is presented as the example of achieving righteousness through faith. In 11:13-14 Paul presents himself as an *exemplum* of apostolic responsibility toward both Jews and Gentiles. In 12:4-5 Paul uses the example of the body to denote the social group of the church, but he goes beyond the political use of this example to place the church in the mystical union described as "in Christ." In 15:2-3 Christ is the example of building up the neighbor and not pleasing oneself. These examples have a direct argumentative force, because they are accepted as true by the audience.

A speech-in-character (Lat. *confirmatio;* Gk. προσωποποιία) is an elaborate example in which the writer creates a character who speaks in his own voice as an actor in the drama of the argument.[153] In 7:7-12 Paul presents himself as the character whose zealous obedience to the law was motivated by the desire to gain superior honor. This brought him into conflict with the Messiah's followers, and as the next pericope shows (7:13-25), sin corrupted the quest for the good so that the very good Paul sought to achieve in persecuting the

151 See Stegner, "Midrash," 37–52; M. Gertner, "Midrashim in the New Testament," *JSS* 7 (1962) 267–92; Gary Porton, "Defining Midrash," in Jacob Neusner, ed., *The Study of Ancient Israel I: Mishnah, Midrash, Siddur* (New York: Garland, 1981) 55–92.

152 See Lausberg, *Handbuch*, §§412–26; Anderson, *Glossary*, 87–88.

153 See Anderson, *Glossary*, 106–7; Stowers, "Speech-in-Character," 180–202; Thorsteinsson, *Paul's Interlocutor, passim.*

early Christians turned out to be evil. Zealotry for the law produced the opposite of its intended result because sin in the form of the desire for superior performance produced a body of death. Paul depicts himself as a violent zealot prior to his conversion because this speech-in-character has relevance for the Roman congregations, who are acting intolerantly toward one another and discrediting the gospel. In 11:17-21 Paul creates a smaller scale speech-in-character with a Gentile Christian interlocutor who brags about displacing the original Jewish branches of the olive tree.

7. Syllogisms, Enthymemes, and Lesser-to-Greater Arguments

A syllogism (Lat. *ratiocinatio*; Gk. συλλογισμός) is a fully developed logical argument with all parts present, usually with a major premise, one or more minor premises, and a conclusion.[154] While more frequently employed in philosophical writings, there are some examples in Romans. An elaborate syllogism is developed in 7:1-6 with the major premise in 7:1 about law having jurisdiction only during a lifetime and three minor premises in 7:2-3. Two inferences concerning Christians as dead to the law are drawn in 7:4 and an explanation is provided in 7:5-6. This powerful syllogism establishes that life in Christ is free from the law. In 10:14-21 an equally elaborate syllogism begins with a major premise in vv. 14-15 concerning hearing the gospel as the source of faith. After this premise is supported by a proof text from Isa 52:7, the minor premise is stated in Rom 10:16 that despite preaching, not all heed the gospel. The conclusion is drawn as an antithetical climax in 10:17 and the rest of the pericope applies the syllogism to the issue that Gentiles responded to the gospel but some Jews did not. Several proof texts are cited in this application, which makes this entire argument into a typically Pauline example of fusing scriptural proofs within the structure of a formal syllogism. It would have been far more persuasive for Paul's audience than a philosophical syllogism. In 14:7-9 Paul presents a syllogism dealing with life and death in Christ, with two premises in v. 7a and 7b and two counter-premises in v. 8a and 8b. The inference is drawn in l4:8 and a christological rationale for this inference is provided in 14:9.

An enthymeme (Gk. ἐνθύμημα) is a formal argument of the artificial type in which a major premise is sometimes supported by a minor premise and then a concluding inference is drawn.[155] It is usually an incomplete form of the syllogism, since either the major or the minor premise can be deleted on the assumption that the audience will supply it.[156] It is usually shorter than a syllogism, and thus often has more persuasive force. It establishes plausibility but cannot demonstrate final truth.[157] John D. Moores has shown that Paul's often confusing use of formal enthymemes in Romans can be clarified by the use of semiotic theory, in which the "recognition" of the premise Paul shares with his audience concerning the crucifixion and resurrection of Christ plays a crucial part of each argument.[158] He goes on to show that the background of Paul's argument is "Paul's recognition of the significance of the Crucifixion . . . in which the experience of a revelatory confrontation with the resurrected victim impinges on a network of attitudes and of beliefs drastically reshaping and expanding it."[159] Moving beyond the discussion of classical rhetoric used by Betz and the New Rhetoric advocated by Wuellner, Moores argues that Paul's argument depends on codes that the audience accepts, including a "nature transformed by the Holy Spirit (at work within them)," a new identification with the crucified and resurrected Christ, and an openness to the "truth of the Gospel."[160] On the basis of these codes, Paul explains the implications of the gospel in Romans by means of logical discourse that may at times appear arbitrary to a modern thinker not sharing the codes, but that reveals "his indomitable intellectual persistence."[161]

In 4:14 and 15 there are two enthymemes with premises in vv. 14a and 15a and inferences drawn in

154 Lausberg, *Handbuch*, §371; Martin, *Antike Rhetorik*, 242–43; Moores, *Wrestling*, 33–37.

155 See Martin, *Antike Rhetorik*, 102–6; Moores, *Wrestling*, 33–37; Anderson, *Glossary*, 45.

156 Lausberg, *Handbuch*, §371.

157 Martin, *Antike Rhetorik*, 103.

158 Moores, *Wrestling*, 3, 159; Gorman, *Cruciformity*, 15–49.

159 Moores, *Wrestling*, 9.

160 Ibid., 25.

161 Ibid., 32.

vv. 14b-c and 15b. In 5:15 there is an enthymeme that employs the "lesser-to-greater" argumentative scheme. The premise in 5:15b is that many died because of Adam's transgression, and the inference in v. 15c is that the grace of Christ will abound for many more. The enthymeme in 6:5-7 starts with two premises concerning being joined with Christ's death and having the promise of the resurrection in v. 5a and v. 5b. Four inferences are drawn from these premises in 6:6 7 to establish that those who have died with Christ are no longer in bondage to sin. The enthymeme in 6:8-10 begins with the premise just established, that believers have died with Christ. This is immediately followed by the inference in v. 8b that "we shall also dwell together with him." This is clarified in the following verses with maxims about life and death with Christ. The result of both enthymemes is then summarized in 6:11, and exhortations follow in 6:12-14 that those in Christ should live in the service of righteousness. In 11:6 there is an antithetical enthymeme with the premise of grace in v. 6a, an inference about the exclusion of works in v. 6b, followed by the consequence of not accepting the inference: that "grace would no longer be grace." In 11:12-15 there is an enthymeme that employs an *a minore ad maius* scheme similar to that found in 5:15. The premises are stated in 11:12a and b and the inference in v. 12c is "how much more wealth will their full total make." This is followed by a logical *exemplum* concerning Paul's responsibility to Jews and Gentiles. An unusual allegorical enthymeme appears in 11:16-21, with the wild olive tree used to show the continued priority of Israel. In 11:28-32 there is an elegant enthymeme on the topic of Israel's salvation that begins with a double premise in the form of a thesis about Israel's enmity benefiting Gentiles and the ultimate certainty of Israel's election. This thesis is clarified in vv. 29-31 and the conclusion is provided by the epigram of 11:32.

The *a minore ad maius* argument is typical for rabbinic as well as Greco-Roman discourse,[162] and it occurs several times in Romans. In 5:9 Paul writes, "much more, therefore, having been made righteous now by his blood, shall we be saved through him from the wrath." The same "much more" argument appears in 5:10, 15, 17. In 11:12, 15, and 24 the "how much more" scheme is employed in relation to the blessings to accrue from the future conversion of the Jews.

B. Arrangement

The second means of persuasion in classical rhetoric is arrangement (Lat. *dispositio*; Gk. οἰκονομία), by which the discourse is organized in a logical manner.[163] The basic structure is a beginning, a middle, and an end, which is elaborated in different ways for different genres of discourse. The introduction is called an *exordium*, whose purpose is to establish a relationship between the speaker or writer and his audience. The middle section is called the *probatio*, which provides the proof of the case being discussed. In the case of forensic rhetoric, this is also followed by a *refutatio*, the rebuttal of opposing views. Often the proof section is headed by a *propositio*, sometimes called a *partitio*, which provides a short statement of the thesis or an enumeration of the issues in the case. The conclusion is called a *peroratio*, which summarizes the argument and provides an emotional appeal to accept the viewpoint of the author or speaker. Some rhetorical systems recommend a *narratio* to be placed between the introduction and the proof, providing the background of the issue under discussion. These are only general guidelines, however, and every speech or letter requires a structure suited to its topic and audience.

Since the arrangement of the argument has always been a major theme in Romans research, there is an infinite variety of outlines for the letter. Many outlines use epistolographic terminology, referring to the introduction as the letter opening, to the proof as the body of the letter, divided into parts that correlate with the interpreter's understanding of the argument, followed by a letter closing. Since these categories are modern, this commentary uses the categories of classical rhetoric that would have been understood in the ancient world. The rhetorical categories are also more useful in tracing the persuasive intent of the letter.[164]

---

162 See Bonsirven, *Exégèse rabbinique*, 266–75; Müller, "Qal-Wachomer-Schluß," 73–92; Lausberg, *Handbuch*, §§396–97; Siegert, *Argumentation*, 190–91; see the discussion under Rom 5:9 in the commentary below.

163 See Lausberg, *Handbuch*, §§443–52.

164 See, e.g., Bryskog, "Epistolography, Rhetoric and Letter Prescript," 45–46.

A five-part arrangement is proposed in this commentary, and is visible in the table of contents: an *exordium* (1:1-12); a *narratio* (1:13-15); a *propositio* (1:16-17); a proof divided into four discrete arguments (1:18–4:25; 5:1–8:39; 9:1–11:36; and 12:1–15:13); and a peroration (15:14–16:16 + 16:21-23). Two parts of the letter are designated as interpolations: the warning against heretics in 16:17-20 and the concluding doxology of 16:25-27.[165] The parameters of the four proofs are widely accepted among current commentators, but some other aspects of this arrangement are controversial. In particular, the structure of each proof is similar in containing ten pericopes, a discovery that arose out of the semantic discourse analysis developed by J. P. Louw.[166] He provides a colon analysis of the Greek text and then organizes the cola into closely associated pericopes. The tenfold structure emerged when his scheme was correlated with the views of major commentators about the separation of the proofs into discrete pericopes. Since Louw does not use rhetorical categories to identify the large units of the argument, this scheme was not recognizable in his study. I altered his scheme by linking pairs of pericopes in the first proof, following his suggestions for the most part about the parallelism and thematic continuities in 1:18-32, 2:1-29, and 4:1-25. I abandoned his scheme of making a major division between 3:18 and 19 in favor of the widely shared opinion among commentators that 3:1-20 and 3:21-31 are discrete units with two pericopes each. I followed his analysis exactly in discerning the ten pericopes of the second and third proofs. I altered his outline at one point to produce the ten units of the fourth proof: I divided the first unit into the thesis statement of 12:1-2 and the material in 12:3-8, following Käsemann,

Harrisville, Dodd, Michel, Knox, Wilckens, and others at this point. I have also altered Louw's outline to produce the five pericopes in the final section, separating the recommendation of Phoebe in 16:1-2 from the greetings and commendations of 16:3-16, 21-23.[167]

There now appears to be a remarkable symmetry in the ten pericopes of second, third, and fourth proofs, each beginning with a formal introduction and ending with a formal, liturgical conclusion.[168] The correspondence with the ten pericopes of the first proof is also noteworthy although there is a more intricate structure in each group of paired pericopes in this section. My impression is that the formal disposition places Romans firmly within the arena of the discussion of the Jewish Torah, since series of fives and tens are not favored in Greco-Roman rhetoric.

C. Style

With the exception of the greetings at the end of Romans, the letter displays a wide range of stylistic features that would have made the hearing very engaging when the letter was declaimed in the early congregations. In the analysis section of each chapter there is an account of such devices. There are far too many for an exhaustive listing here:

Parallelismus membrorum—each line having parallel, though slightly differing features, a typical expression of Hebrew poetry[169] (e.g., Rom 4:17; 9:2; 10:1);
Synonymous parallelism—both lines with identical meaning[170] (e.g., 1:21; 7:7; 9:2; 7:13; 15:31; 16:2);

---

165 See the discussion of these post-Pauline interpolations in the commentary below; in contrast, 7:25b-c appears to have been interpolated during the dictation process

166 See Louw in list of works cited. For orientation to the recent discussion of discourse analysis, see the three essays in S. E. Porter and J. T. Reed, eds., *Discourse Analysis and the New Testament: Approaches and Results*, JSNTSup 170; SNTG 4 (Sheffield: Sheffield Academic Press, 1999): Eugene A. Nida, "The Role of Context in the Understanding of Discourse," 20–27; Jeffrey T. Reed, "The Cohesiveness of Discourse: Towards a Model of Linguistic Criteria for Analyzing New Testament Discourse," 28–46; and

Stanley E. Porter, "Is Critical Discourse Analysis Critical? An Evaluation Using Philemon as a Test Case," 47–70.

167 Louw, 2:141, provides support for this division of 16:1-16 into two pericopes.

168 The second proof is introduced by 5:1-11 and concluded with the exalted hymn in 8:31-39. The third proof is introduced by 9:1-5 and concludes with the hymn in 11:33-36. The fourth proof opens with 12:1-2 and closes with the hymnic catena of citations and the benediction in 15:7-13.

169 See Adele Berlin, "Parallelism," *ADB* 5 (1992) 155–62.

170 Ibid., 156.

Synthetic parallelism—a single thought conveyed by parallel members[171] (e.g., 4:25; 10:9-10);

Chain-link parallelism—sometimes called "staircase parallelism," where thought advances step by step[172] (e.g., 4:15; 5:20-21; 13:1-5);

Antithetical parallelism—two lines correspond with each other by opposing terms,[173] the most frequently used in Pauline corpus (extended, e.g., in 2:6-12, with chiastic development; 11:30; 8:10; 15:8-9, 16);

Anaphora—the repetition of initial words or syllables in closely related discourse[174] (e.g., 1:31 in the repetition of the alpha-negative; 3:5 = 3:7; the sixfold repetition of οὐκ ἔστιν ["there is not"] in 3:10-18; the fourfold repetition of τίς ["what?"] in 8:33, 34, 35, 39);

Antistrophe—the use of identical final words in succeeding sentences of clauses[175] (e.g., αὐτῶν ["their"] in 3:13a, 13c, and 18; πίστις ["faith"] in 3:27, 30, 31);

Homoioptoton—the repetition of the same case ending in successive words[176] (e.g., the genitive plural endings following the dental sounds of ν, δ, and τ in 1:23, πετεινῶν καὶ τετραπόδων καὶ ἑρπετῶν ["of birds and animals and serpents"]; 7:15-16, with four successive first person singular endings);

Homoioteleuton—similar sounding endings in close proximity[177] (e.g., the catalogue of vices in 1:29, with -ια and -ου endings: πάσῃ ἀδικίᾳ πονηρίᾳ πλεονεξίᾳ κακίᾳ, μεστοὺς φθόνου φόνου ἔριδος δόλου ["all manner of wrongdoing, evil, greed, badness, persons full of envy, murder, strife"]; 5:16, with play on sounds ending with -μα; 12:15, χαίρειν μετὰ χαιρόντων, κλαίειν μετὰ κλαιόντων ["rejoice with those who rejoice, weep with those who weep"];

Parechesis—assonance of different words in close proximity (e.g., 1:29, φθόνου φόνου ["envy, murder"]; 1:31, ἀσυνέτους ἀσυνθέτους ἀστόργους ἀνελεήμονας ["without understanding, without dutifulness,

without affection, without mercy"]; 14:17, οὐ . . . βρῶσις καὶ πόσις ἀλλὰ δικαιοσύνη καὶ εἰρήνη ["not food or drink but righteousness and peace"]);

Paronomasia—recurrence of the same word or word stem in close proximity[178] (e.g., 1:23, ἀφθάρτου θεοῦ . . . φθαρτοῦ ἀνθρώπου ["imperishable God . . . perishable human"]; ten repetitions of "sin" in 6:1-14; 12:3, with fourfold play on the stem, μὴ ὑπερφρονεῖν παρ᾽ ὃ δεῖ φρονεῖν ἀλλὰ φρονεῖν εἰς τὸ σωφρονεῖν ["do not be superminded above what you ought to be minded but set your mind on being soberminded"]).

Climax/*Gradatio*—key word of preceding clause or phrase taken up in the next member[179] (e.g., 5:3-5, "let us also boast in our afflictions, knowing that this affliction produces fortitude, and this fortitude approbation, and this approbation hope, and this hope does not cause shame;" 8:16-17, "those whom [God] foreknew, he also predestined . . .; and those he predestined, these he also called; and those he called, these he also made right; and those he made right, these he also glorified");

Paromoiosis—a figure with balanced clauses and similar sounding word endings[180] (e.g., 11:28).

Chiasm—the repetition in reverse sequence of words or ideas in succeeding sentences or clauses;[181] for example, 2:6-11:

    A God will judge according to works (2:6)
      B For those who do good, reward (2:7)
        C For those who do evil, punishment (2:8)
        C' For evil Jews and Greeks, punishment (2:9)
      B' For good Jews and Greeks, reward (2:10)
    A' God judges impartially (2:11)

(other examples of chiasm in 3:19; 11:12-15, 30-31);

---

171 Ibid.
172 Ibid., 156–57.
173 Ibid., 156.
174 See Lausberg, *Handbuch*, §§629–30; Anderson, *Glossary*, 19.
175 See Anderson, *Glossary*, 54
176 See Lausberg, *Handbuch*, 729–31; Anderson, *Glossary*, 78.
177 See Lausberg, *Handbuch*, 725–28; Anderson, *Glossary*, 79.

178 See Lausberg, *Handbuch*, 637.
179 See Lausberg, *Handbuch*, 623–24; Anderson, *Glossary*, 57–58.
180 See Siegert, *Argumentation*, 174; for definition see Anderson, *Glossary*, 91–92.
181 See Lausberg, *Handbuch*, 800–803; A. Di Marco, "Der Chiasmus in der Bibel. 1 Teil," *LingB* 36 (1975) 21–97; "3 Teil," 37 (1976) 49–68; "4 Teil," *LingB* 44 (1979) 3–70; Thomson, *Chiasmus*, 13–45.

Enumeratio—a coordinated series of terms listed next to each other, often with culturally significant numbers of references.[182] Considerable attention has been given to numerical sequences within the Bible, stressing the preference for series of ten, seven, five, and three.[183] The discussion of the "rhetorical use of numbers" in biblical literature by John J. Davis follows the lead of Wolfgang Roth, who analyzed the $x/x + 1$ formula as a climactic figure.[184] A classic example of this formula is Amos 1:3, "for three transgressions of Damascus, yea, for four, I will not turn away the punishment." This figure is often called a "priamel," as discussed by Bühlmann and Scherer[185] and others.[186] Occasionally the digit is named as in the Amos example, but more frequently "the rhetorical effect is achieved through a latent number, i.e., certain words or names occur a given number of times, although the actual figure is not specified."[187] The precedents of such series in the ancient Near East and the parallels in Greco-Roman culture, with its interest in tens, nines, sevens, fours, threes, and twos, have been explored.[188] Only at a few incidental points has such discussion touched the debate over Romans. The antithetical quality of the argument of Romans rests on multiple series of twos, of which there are scores of examples.[189] Rengstorf discussed the reference to the seven thousand faithful believers in Rom 11:4,[190] and Hauck pointed out the ten forms of demonic power in Rom 8:38-39,[191] while Dobschütz alluded to the triads in 1:24-26, 2:7-10, and 2:4.[192] No Romans commentary identifies further examples or explains the significance of such series, perhaps because there is no example of a numerical saying where the digit is supplied. The question of the rhetorical significance of such series in Romans has understandably not yet been raised in a commentary.[193]

1. Series of Tens

While the number ten was prominent in many ancient cultures,[194] probably relating to the number of fingers, it attained a peculiar significance in Hebrew culture because of its association with the commandments, the tithe, and the later requirement of ten males to constitute the quorum for a synagogue service.[195] As Hauck observes, in Judaism "the number is so fixed in this respect that the word *minyan* (number) may be used for it."[196]

182 See Lausberg, *Handbuch*, 660–74.
183 G. R. Driver, "Sacred Numbers and Round Figures," in F. F. Bruce, ed., *Promise and Fulfillment: Essays Presented to Professor S. H. Hooke in Celebration of His Ninetieth Birthday* (Edinburgh: T. & T. Clark, 1963) 62–90.
184 John J. Davis, *Biblical Numerology* (Grand Rapids: Baker, 1968) 93–102; Wolfgang M. W. Roth, *Numerical Sayings in the Old Testament: A Form-Critical Study*, VTSup 13 (Leiden: Brill, 1965); idem, "Ten Commandments, Twelve Apostles and One God," *Explor* 4/2 (1978) 4–11.
185 Walter Bühlmann and Karl Scherer, *Stilfiguren der Bibel: Ein kleines Nachschlagewerk*, BiBe 10 (Fribourg: Schweizerische Katholisches Bibelwerk, 1973) 60–62, with additional bibliography listed.
186 See U. Schmid, *Die Priamel der Werte im Griechischen von Homer bis Paulus* (Wiesbaden: Harrassowitz, 1964); Franz Dornseiff, "Das altorientalische Priamel," in *Antike und Alter Orient: Interpretationen* (2d ed.; Leipzig: Koehler & Amelang, 1959) 379–93.
187 Israel Abrahams, "Numbers, Typical and Important," *EncJud* 12:1255.
188 See, e.g., Eduard Wölfflin, "Zur Zahlensymbolik (Mit Probeartikel Septem und Novem)," *ALL* 9 (1896) 333–54, which discusses series of three, seven, nine, and ten in Greco-Roman culture.

189 See the classic study by Ernst von Dobschütz, "Zwei- und dreigliedrige Formeln: Ein Beitrag zur Vorgeschichte der Trinitätsformel," *JBL* 50 (1931) 117–47; also Jean Nélis, "Les antithèses littéraires dans les épîtres de Saint Paul," *NRTh* 70 (1948) 360–87.
190 Karl Heinrich Rengstorf, "ἑπτά κτλ.," *TDNT* 2 (1964) 627–35.
191 Friedrich Hauck, "δέκα," *TDNT* 2 (1964) 36–37.
192 Dobschütz, "Zwei- und dreigliedrige Formeln," 118–19, 123.
193 The following is adapted from Jewett, "Numerical Sequences," 227–45.
194 In "Numbers: An Overview," *EncR* 11:17, Annemarie Schimmel observes that "the Pythagoreans regarded ten as the perfect number."
195 See H. A. Brongers, "Die Zehnzahl in der Bibel und in ihrer Umwelt," in *Studia Biblica et Semitica . . . Festschrift T. C. Vriezen* (Wangeningen: Veenman, 1966) 30–45.
196 Hauck, "δέκα," 36; see also S. Krauss, "Minjan," *JITL* 37–39 (1933) 51–74; and H. Haag, "Die biblische Wurzeln des Minjan," in Otto Betz et al., eds., *Abraham Unser Vater . . . Festschrift für Otto Michel*, AGSU 5 (Leiden: Brill, 1963) 235–42, cited by Hauck.

The most prominent example in Romans is the one noted by Hauck, the ten forms of demonic power listed in 8:38-39:

For I am convinced that
1. neither death,
2.   nor life,
3.   nor angels,
4.   nor principalities,
5.   nor things present,
6.   nor things to come,
7. nor powers,
8.   nor heights,
9.   nor depths,
10.   nor any other creature . . .

Rhetorically, the series serves the purpose of amplifying the transcendent power of divine love through an accumulation of forces that were ordinarily thought to be capable of prevailing.[197] Given the subject matter of a people whose identity was so closely tied with the Ten Commandments, the tithe, and the ten men required for commencing a synagogue service, the length of this series was likely to have been noticeable.

Another example of a series of ten is found in 12:10-13, where five pairs of imperatival expressions serve to elaborate the injunction in 12:9, "let love be genuine!" Given the subsequent argument that love fulfills the entire law (Rom 13), the length of this series was probably not accidental. It conveys the theme of replacing the Torah-oriented ethic with a new, charismatic ethic based on love.

The last three examples are less easily discernible because they are embedded in larger pericopes rather than appearing in closely connected series. The diatribal exchange of 3:27—4:10 includes ten rhetorical questions. There are ten references to "sin" in a single pericope of 6:1-14, constituting a thematically significant reduplication. And there are ten quotations of Hebrew Scripture in the midrashic argument of 9:6-29, five in each of the two successive pericopes that carry out this argument.

2. Series of Fives

There is a considerably longer list of fivefold series in Romans, a datum that points decisively in the direction of Judaic cultural values as perceived in Paul's time. While series of tens were prominent in Greek culture, a preference taken over to a modest degree in Roman culture as well, series of fives appear to have emerged as more distinctively Jewish because of the association with the five books of the Torah and the later collection of the Five Megillot, the scrolls of Canticles, Ruth, Lamentation, Ecclesiastes, and Esther.[198] While there is little evidence of theological or rhetorical interest in the number five in the Hebrew Scriptures themselves,[199] later Jewish culture including the NT treat it as a favorite digit. Rabbinic Judaism developed the theory of the "five species" of plants in Israel to which the agricultural regulations of the Torah were to be applied,[200] but the different plants identified in various discussions of this issue suggest a numerical requirement. The Christian gospel with closest affinities to Jewish culture evinces a clear interest in this number by referring to the "five loaves of the five thousand" in the miraculous feeding story (Matt 16:9) and to the five wise and five foolish maidens and the five talents in Matthew's version of the parables (Matt 25:1-13, 15-30). These details are hardly coincidental because it has long been recognized that Matthew organizes his Gospel with five teaching discourses in an effort to emulate the five books of the Torah.[201]

The first example from Romans involves an impressive synthesis of style and content because the subject is Jews who are obedient to the law. In the diatribe concerning observant Jews in 2:17-23, we find three strophes of five lines apiece. In vv. 17-18 there are five examples of Jewish self-identity linked with καί ("and"); in vv. 19-20 there are five claims of Jewish superiority in an emphatic series marked by asyndeton; and in vv. 21-23 there are five moralistic injunctions matching the five

---

197 For a discussion of amplification through accumulation in classical rhetoric, see Lausberg, *Handbuch*, §§400–403.

198 See Bruce C. Birch, "Number," *International Standard Bible Encyclopedia* 3 (1986) 556–61.

199 Most of the standard articles on biblical numbers pass over "five" without comment, and there is no article in the *Theological Dictionary of the Old Testament* on *hāmēš*, the Hebrew word for "five."

200 See Jehuda Feliks, "Five Species," *EncJud* 6 (1971) 1332–33.

201 See Reginald H. Fuller, "Matthew," *HBC*, 951.

rhetorical questions concerning the consistency of Jewish principles and performance.

1. 17/ But if you call yourself a Jew
2. and support yourself on the law
3. and boast in God,
4. 18/ and know the will [of God]
5. and approve what is important because of being schooled out of the law,
1. 19/ and [if you] persuaded yourself that you are a guide of the blind,
2. a light of those in darkness,
3. 20/ a tutor of the foolish,
4. a teacher of the immature,
5. possessing the system of knowledge and of truth in the law—.
1a. 21/ The one who therefore teaches another,
1b. do you not teach yourself?
2a. The one who preaches not to steal,
2b. are you stealing?
3a. 22/ The one who says not to commit adultery,
3b. are you adulterous?
4a. The one who abhors idols,
4b. do you rob temples?
5a. 23/ The one who boasts in the law,
5b. do you dishonor God through transgressing the law?

This prominent pentadic structure is strongly evocative of the five books of the Torah, the chief foundation of Jewish piety. The basic issue of adhering to the standards of the Torah is amplified through the accumulation of superiority claims and rhetorical questions. The rhetorical effect of the pentadic structure is ironic and self-condemnatory in that the imaginary interlocutor who boasts in the Torah is shown to fall short of its full demands. The repetition of περιτομή ("circumcision") and ἀκροβυστία ("uncircumcision") in 2:25-29 would also have been noticed, the former being reduplicated six times and the latter four times. The argumentative impact of this discussion of circumcision is related to *expolitio*, the refining of a topic through variation and association with closely related thoughts.[202]

The same kind of noteworthy consistency between subject and style is present in 3:1-9, where there are five dialogical exchanges with Jewish conversation partners. They are as follows:

1. 3:1-2 "Therefore what advantage does the Jew have?"
2. 3:3-4 "So what if some were unfaithful. . . ?
3. 3:5-6 "If our wickedness demonstrates. . . ?
4. 3:7 "But if the truth of God abounds. . . ?
5. 3:8 "And why . . . should we not do evil. . . ?

A fourth instance of a pentadic series is found in the midrashic exegesis of 4:1-24, which contains five quotations from the OT, the last being a reiteration of the first. Once again, this stylistic feature is congruent with the argument, which suggests the primacy of faith on the basis of the story of Abraham.

1. 4:3 Gen 15:6
2. 4:7-8 Ps 31:1
3. 4:17 Gen 17:5
4. 4:18c Gen 5:5
5. 4:22 Gen 15:6

There are several other examples of pentadic series in midrashic sections of Romans. In Rom 9:6-18 there are five supplementary texts cited after the initial text in the extensive midrashic development. In the next pericope, which completes the midrash, there are five more texts cited referring to the "call" of the faithful, subordinate again to the initial text of Gen 21:12.[203] In Rom 10:5-13 there are five scriptural quotations, as also in 11:1-10. Finally, in the most visible instance of a pentadic series, Paul provides five quotations from the Ten Commandments in Rom 13:9. In each of these nine instances, the congruence between subject matter and the choice of a pentadic structure is clear, suggesting a conscious effort on Paul's part to honor Judaic stylistic preferences.

The last three examples appear to be unrelated to the debate concerning Jewish assumptions. In Rom 5:3-5a there is a fivefold climax with each line taking up motifs from the preceding:

---

202 For the use of *expolitio* in classical rhetoric, see the discussion in Lausberg, *Handbuch*, §§830–42.

203 See Stegner, "Midrash," 37–52.

1. 3/not only that, but we also boast in the afflictions,
2.   knowing that the affliction produces endurance,
3.   4/and endurance confirmation,
4.   and confirmation hope,
5.   5/and hope does not humiliate.

In 8:24-25 there are five brief lines in which "hope" or "to hope" are repeated five times, resulting in an effective paronomasia:

1. 24/For in this hope were we saved.
2.   But hope that is seen is not hope,
3.   for who hopes for what he sees?
4.   25/But if we hope in what we do not see,
5.   we wait in patience.

Given the prominence of the larger structuring principle of fives and tens in the organization of the pericopes of Romans, this large number of quinary and denary structures appears to signal an effort on Paul's part both to enter into conversation with Jewish partners, and also to legitimize Jewish Christian culture, which was being discriminated against in the Roman house churches. By using quinary sequences in these last several examples to describe crucial aspects of Christian life under the spirit, Paul allows a Judaic stylistic preference to predominate, thus indicating indirectly that the new life does not completely abrogate the Jewish tradition.

3. Series of Sevens

From the time of the formation of the Hebrew Scriptures down through later Jewish history, seven is the most distinctively Jewish number, representing "totality,"[204] "completeness and perfection."[205] It was associated with the creation story, the seven-day week, the sabbatical year cycle and the seven-branched menorah, "a paramount Jewish symbol, representing light and life eternal."[206] To a lesser degree, this number was valued in Greek culture, reflecting the seven-day periods in the four phases of the moon and later the seven planets.[207] It is the biblical legacy, however, that is reflected in Paul's reference to the seven thousand faithful ones who refused homage to Baal during the time of Elijah in Rom 11:4. The paradigm of seven abominable things that Yahweh hates in Prov 6:16-19 may well have provided the model for the seven scriptural quotations in the catena of condemnation in Rom 3:10-18. There is also a close parallel in the seven indictments of CD 5:13-17, which suggests a tradition of sevenfold catenae within Judaism.[208] The catena of condemnations in Romans contains the following seven quotations:

1. 3:10b   Eccl 7:20
2. 3:11-12   Ps 14:1-3
3. 3:13a   Ps 5:9
4. 3:13b   Ps 139:4
5. 3:14   Ps 10:7
6. 3:15-17   Isa 59:7-8, containing a tricola
7. 3:18   Ps 35:2, containing the inclusio for the catena

At the end of Rom 8, there are three similarly prominent series of sevens. The first is a sevenfold develop-

---

204 Rengstorf, "ἑπτά κτλ.," *TDNT* 2 (1964) 628.
205 Joel F. Drinkard Jr., "Numbers," *HDB*, 711; Johannes B. Bauer points out some Ugaritic parallels to the biblical symbol of completion in "Die literarische Form des Heptaemeron," *BZ* 1 (1957) 273–75.
206 Carol L. Meyers, "Lampstand," *HBD*, 546; see also Schimmel, "Numbers: An Overview," *EncR* 11:16; and Johannes Hehn, *Siebenzahl und Sabbat bei den Babyloniern und im Alten Testament*, LSSt 2.5 (Leipzig: Hinrichs, 1907). Philo provides an extensive discussion of "the perfecting power of the number 7" in *Opif.* 89-130, esp. 103.
207 Rengstorf, "ἑπτά κτλ.," 627; see also Wölfflin, "Zahlensymbolik," 342–51; H. Quiring, "Die 'heilige' Siebenzahl und die Entdeckung des

Merkur," *Altertum* 4 (1958) 208–14; see also Wilhelm Heinrich Röscher's extensive investigations of series of seven and nine in classical Greece: "Die Enneadischen Hebdomadischen Fristen und Wochen der ältestesten Griechen," *ASAW* 21:4 (1903) 1–92; "Die Sieben- und Neunzahl im Kultus und Mythus der Griechen," *ASAW* 24.1 (1904) 1–126; and "Die Hebdomadenlehren der griechischen Philosophen und Ärzte. Ein Beitrag zur Geschichte der griechischen Philosophie und Medizin," *ASAW* 24.6 (1906) 1–239.
208 The thematic parallel was identified by Leander Keck, who does not discuss the numerical parallelism in "3:10–18," 148–49.

ment ending with a climax on the theme of the glory manifested in Christians. When one eliminates the two theological comments of v. 28c and v. 29c, the stages of the development are as follows:

1. The premise in 8:28a: "those who love God"
2. The elaboration in 8:28b: "who are called according to his purpose"
3. The first synonym of calling in 8:29a: "those whom he foreknew"
4. The elaboration in 8:29b: "he also predestined"
5. The climax from "predestined" to "called" in 8:30a
6. The climax from "called" to "rightwised" in 8:30b
7. The climax from "rightwised" to "glorified" in 8:30c.

In the subsequent verses this rather covert developmental scheme is followed by a much more explicitly visible series of seven rhetorical questions:

1. 8:31a   "What then shall we say. . . ?"
2. 8:31b   "If God be for us, who is against us?"
3. 8:32   "how will he not also grace us. . . ?"
4. 8:33   "Who shall make a charge. . . ?"
5. 8:34   "who shall condemn?"
6. 8:35a   "Who shall separate us. . . ?
7. 8:35b   "Shall affliction. . . ?

The final question in 8:35b is then divided into seven forms of suffering, each linked with "or" to make an impressive series marked by epanaphora. The series amplifies the theme of Christian suffering through the accumulation of outward forms of tribulation that Paul had experienced:[209]

1. Shall affliction,
2.   or narrow scrapes,
3.   or persecution,
4.   or famine,
5.   or nakedness,
6.   or peril,
7.   or sword?

An equally impressive series is found in 12:6-8 in the listing of the gifts that mark the Christian community:
1.   whether prophecy—according to the analogy of faith,

2.   or service—in the serving,
3.   or the teacher—in the teaching,
4.   or the exhorter—in the exhortation,
5.   the sharer—with generosity,
6.   the leader—with diligence,
7.   the one showing mercy—with cheer.

The seven types of congregational service and leadership do not appear to be exhaustive, because several other types are listed elsewhere in Paul's letters. The choice of the sacred, rounded number of seven conveys the sense that these examples stand for the wide range of gifts, in which every member of the congregation was thought to participate.

In addition to these clearly visible series, there is reduplication within particular pericopes of Romans. In 6:2-13 there are seven references to "life" or "live." In 6:16-22 there are seven references to "slave." And in 9:30—10:4 there are seven references to "righteousness."

Only one of these numerical sequences of sevens is patterned directly after a Judaic literary paradigm and has a direct relevance for Gentile Christian/Jewish Christian relations. The others may reflect Greco-Roman as well as Judaic stylistic preferences and have no direct relationship to the relationship between such groups. Yet the indirect message of this large number of sevenfold series points to the legitimacy of Judaic preferences, a significant issue in a letter that seeks to overcome the prejudice of a Gentile Christian majority against a Jewish Christian minority.

4. Series of Threes

The prevalence of triads in all of the Pauline letters has been noted by earlier researchers. One thinks immediately of "faith, hope and love" in 1 Cor 13:13 and 1 Thess 1:3-4; 5:8; and the triadic priamel of 1 Cor 13:8.

as for prophecy, it will pass away;
  as for tongues, they will cease;
    as for knowledge, it will pass away.

The importance of such series for the OT, with prominent examples such as Aaronite Blessing of Num 6:24-26

---

209 See Dunn, 2:505.

and the threefold "Holy, holy, holy is the Lord of hosts" sung by the seraphim in Isa 6:3, has been discussed by Usener,[210] Stade,[211] and others.[212] This stylistic figure is found elsewhere in the Greco-Roman world,[213] often with mystical or magical significance,[214] so that the effort to discern a specific cultural implication is pointless. The rhetorical effectiveness of such triads in the Greco-Roman world is indisputable, however, often conveying completeness, perfection or the superlative in a series.[215]

For Romans, we begin by listing the simple threefold formulations that seem to conform to Paul's style elsewhere.[216] In the following nine examples, for the most part we have nouns linked with καί ("and").

1:23b	idols of "of birds and animals and serpents"
3:4	"the kindness and forbearance and patience" of God
2:7	the good seek "glory and honor and immortality"
2:10	the good receive "glory and honor and peace"
7:12	the law is "holy and righteous and good"
11:33	"the riches and wisdom and knowledge" of God
12:1	a "living, holy, and acceptable" sacrifice
12:2	the "good and acceptable and perfect" will of God
14:17	the kingdom of God is "righteousness and peace and joy"

There are at least eight reduplicative series of threes in Romans, including the repetition of παρέδωκεν ("he consigned") in 1:24, 26, and 28; the repetition of "baptism" in 6:3-4; the triple references to the "seed" of Abraham in 4:13-18 and 9:7-8; and the impressive paronomastic repetitions of κληρονόμοι and συν- in the climactic series of 8:17:

εἰ δὲ τέκνα, καὶ κληρονόμοι·
κληρονόμοι μὲν θεοῦ,
συγκληρονόμοι δὲ Χριστοῦ,
εἴπερ συμπάσχομεν
ἵνα καὶ συνδοξασθῶμεν.

The hymnic conclusion of the third proof is also marked by a triadic structure, with the "riches and wisdom and knowledge of God" in 11:33 replicated in chiastic order by the three questions with τίς ("who") in 11:34-35a.[217] The hymn closes in 11:36 with a prepositional triad with a repetition of αὐτός to elaborate the omnipotence of God.[218] Classical rhetoric used the term *polyptoton* to describe this type of repetition of a term with varied case endings:[219]

Because from him
and through him
and for him
are all things.

210 H. Usener, "Dreiheit," *RhM* 58 (1903) 1–362.
211 B. Stade, "Die Dreizahl im Alten Testament: Zum Gedächtnis Hermann Useners," *ZAW* 26 (1906) 124–28.
212 Dobschütz, "Zwei- und dreigliedrige Formeln," 120–41.
213 See Otto Weinreich, "Trigemination als sakrale Stilform," *SMSR* 4 (1928) 198–206; R. Mehrlein, "Drei," *RAC* 4 (1959) 269–310; Fritz Göbel, *Formen und Formeln der epischen Dreiheit in der griechischen Dichtung*, TBAW 26 (Stuttgart: Kohlhammer, 1935) 37–55.
214 Emory B. Lease, "The Number Three, Mysterious, Mystic, Magic," *CP* 14 (1919) 56–73; he speaks (70) of "the universality of the use of the mystic number 3" in ancient as well as modern cultures. In "Zwei- und dreigliedrige Formeln," 118, Dobschütz mentions well-known Greek sayings related to threefold

blessing, luck, unluck, etc.; in fact there are almost 200 Greek terms based in the τρι- stem or prefix according to my count in LSJM.
215 Gerhard Delling, "τρεῖς κτλ.," *TDNT* 8 (1972) 217; also W. Deonna, "Trois, superlatif absolu," *AC* 23 (1954) 403–28.
216 See Delling, "τρεῖς κτλ.," 222: "The triad [of faith, hope, and love] is firmly established in Paul. There is no evidence that he borrowed it"; 223: "The triad God - Lord - Spirit is also a fixed one in Paul, though the order varies."
217 Delling, "τρεῖς κτλ.," 224, observes this chiastic sequence.
218 See ibid.
219 See Lausberg, *Handbuch*, §§640–48; Rom 11:36 is mentioned in §646.

The triads in Romans do not appear to have a specific cultural reference, reflecting as they do the stylistic preferences of Jews as well as Greeks. The large number of examples signals, however, an interest on the part of the author to achieve stylistic sonority and completeness. The Roman audience would have taken pleasure in the rounded rhetoric that Paul so often achieves in this particular letter.

5. Series of Fours

The number four was prominent throughout the Mediterranean world, representing the four cardinal directions, the four winds, the four ages of the world, and so forth.[220] In the OT there are references to the four quarters of heaven, the four rivers of paradise, and the four world empires.[221] The Jewish tradition shared the perspective of the Greco-Roman world that four "signifies completeness and sufficiency."[222] The effort to create a "coordinated whole" is expressed with particular prominence in the graduated threefold to fourfold sayings in Prov 30:18-31.[223] Series of four appear in clearly recognizable form in Romans, though their relatively small number indicates a minor role as compared with fives and tens. The first example is in the comprehensive catalogue of evils in 1:29-31, constructed in series of fours with one alteration for rhyming purposes:

    29/ having been filled with all manner of
1.   wrongdoing,
2.   evil,
3.   greed,
4.   badness,
1.   persons full of envy,
2.   murder,
3.   strife,
4.   treachery,
5.   craftiness,
1.   whisperers, 30/ slanderers,
2.   haters of God, bullies,
3.   egotists, braggarts,
4.   inventors of evil, disobeyers of parents,

1.   31/ without understanding,
2.   without dutifulness,
3.   without affection,
4.   without mercy.

The use of the number four to denote comprehensiveness or roundedness[224] appears to be congruent with the content of this impressive group of quadruple series. The rhetorical effect is to amplify the picture of the reprobate mind of the human race by the accumulation of vices and evil types.

The next example appears relatively late in the letter (10:14-15), opening a pericope with four lines structured as a formal climax and marked by epanaphora in the opening word πῶς ("how") at the beginning of each line:

1.   14/ How therefore might they call upon one in whom they have not believed?
2.   And how shall they believe in one whom they have not heard?
3.   And how might they hear without someone preaching?
4.   15/And how will they preach if they have not been sent?

A similar quadruple series is found in 13:7, where parallel forms of civic obligation are listed with epanaphora in the identical opening word for each line, τῷ ("to the one") as well as internal reduplication within each line in the repetition of the terms for the four obligations:

1. taxes to whom taxes are due,
2.   custom taxes to whom the custom is due,
3.   fear to whom fear is due,
4.   honor to whom honor is due.

The next example (12:3) features paronomasia again, with an elaborate wordplay based on the stem widely used in philosophical discourse regarding proper self-assessment, φρον- ("be minded"):

---

220   Horst Balz, "τέσσαρες κτλ.," *TDNT* 8 (1972) 128–29.
221   Balz, "τέσσαρες κτλ.," 131–33.
222   Abraham, "Numbers," 1257; see also E. Kautsch, "Zahlen bei den Hebräern," *RE* 21:603.

223   See Roth, *Numerical Sayings*, 99; idem, "The Numerical Sequence x/x + 1 in the Old Testament," *VT* 12 (1962) 300–311.
224   Roth, *Numerical Sayings*, 131.

do not be super<u>mind</u>ed above what one ought to be <u>mind</u>ed,
but set your <u>mind</u> on being sober<u>mind</u>ed.

The final example is more elaborate, with three series of four admonitions grouped thematically, followed by a final series of four divided two by two. The first twelve items are listed in the admonitions of 12:14-19.

1. 14/ Bless the persecutors,
2.   bless and do not curse.
3.   15/ Rejoice with those who rejoice,
4.   weep with those who weep.
1. 16/ Be of the same mind toward one another.
2.   Do not set your minds on the heights
3.   but be drawn toward lowly people.
4.   "Never be [wise] minded in yourselves."
1. 17/ Do not pay back evil for evil.
2.   "Take thought for what is good before" all "persons."
3.   18/If possible, so far as you are able, be at peace with all persons.
4.   19/ Beloved, do not avenge yourselves, but give way to the wrath [of God].

The final series of four admonitions is as follows, with the explanatory material that breaks up the series placed in parentheses:

1. 20/ But if "your enemy is hungry, feed him;
2.   if he is thirsty, give him drink; (for by doing this you will pile up burning coals upon his head.")
3.   21/ Do not be conquered by the evil
4.   but conquer the evil with the good.

This impressive numerical series based on groupings of four serves as a comprehensive counterpart to the catalogue of evils that appears in chap. 1, conveying the sense that the universal evil of the fallen world is being overcome by the ethic followed by early Christians.

These numerical series appear to reinforce the argument of Romans. If the style of a discourse in classical rhetoric is supposed to be consistent with its content,[225] the large number of series associated with completeness

convey the comprehensive argument concerning the triumph of divine righteousness through the gospel. A large number of the series of threes, fours, and sevens aimed at comprehensive descriptions of the old life and the new, defined by the rightwising activity of God. In other instances, these series had a decorative, rounding effect that lifts the rhetoric of Romans to a level that would have been satisfying to the hearers in Rome, providing amplification and refinement. The prominent series of fives and tens along with one series of seven appear to reinforce other major goals of the letter. One of these is to interact critically with Jewish theological issues and the other is to lead the Gentile Christian majority to "welcome" the Jewish Christians into their assemblies, overcoming racial and theological tensions.

There is an ecumenical breadth in the appeal of so many different types of series in this letter, some of which would have resonated more strongly with one cultural group than another. The interest in respecting while transforming cultural distinctions, visible at many points in the argument of Romans, is congruent with this stylistic variety. The desire to communicate effectively with a culturally diverse audience is as clear in the style as in the argument. Finally, the unusual frequency of various numerical series indicates compositional forethought and/or careful editing. In Romans, the only Pauline letter addressing an audience that does not know Paul, he apparently took extraordinary care to create a rhetorically effective vehicle to convey the "apostolic parousia." Paul's perception of the importance and sensitivity of this particular mission to Rome manifests itself in these rhetorical details.

D. Delivery and Memory
The discovery of the remarkable array of stylistic and organizational devices in Romans calls attention to the crucial importance of the oral delivery to the various congregations in Rome. In view of the fact that ancient letters in Greek were written without spaces between words or punctuation, the discernment of the numerical sequences and other stylistic features would have been very difficult for anyone reading the letter aloud for the first time. Classical rhetoric taught the techniques of preparing texts for public delivery and for the actual

---

225 See *Rhet. Her.* 1.2.3, and Cicero, *Inv.* 1.7.9.

delivery itself, including the tone of voice and gestures suitable for different occasions.[226] In the Greco-Roman world, speaking without notes was preferred, and students were taught to memorize their speeches before delivering them. What moderns would view as prodigious memory was not unusual; Seneca the Elder claimed, for example that he could recite two thousand names in the same sequence that were spoken to him once, and Quintilian reported that his teacher could recite a vast quantity of poetry, even when he had heard it only once.[227] Various techniques of memorization were taught, including the creation of clearly organized presentations and practicing one unit at a time. This has an obvious bearing on the organizational structure that has been discerned for Romans. Although it would have to be read aloud as a letter coming from the apostle Paul, the reader would have had to virtually memorize the content for successful delivery.

Sound is the basic link between the speaker and the audience,[228] and ancient teachers gave detailed instructions about the different levels and intensities that are suitable for various parts of a speech. A soft tone typical for everyday speech was recommended for portions of a speech that portray past events as well as other parts that were intended to evoke laughter from the audience. A strong and argumentative voice was recommended for proofs and refutations. Intensification in a dramatic manner was considered suitable for perorations.[229] Gestures were recommended for each part of the speech, conveying different moods and evoking different audience reactions. At times the right hand was to be extended to signal points in a series, which again is relevant for the many numerical series in Romans.

Werner Kelber, in particular, has developed the relevance of Paul's use of "his first person singular authority in the manner of oral speech" and that his theology was "conceived as a theology of language. Centrally located in the apostle's theology is the issue of the Word of God in its oral and written dimension."[230] Since God "calls"

Jews and Gentiles into faith through the gospel (1:7; 9:24), and since Paul introduces himself as the one "called to be an apostle" (1:1), "It is fair to say that in Pauline theology the ear triumphs over the eye."[231] For Paul, "faith is from hearing" (10:17), which explains the dramatic climax of rhetorical questions, "And how might they have faith in someone of whom they have not heard? And how might they hear without someone preaching? And how might they preach if they have not been sent?" (10:14-15). This throws light on the central theme of Romans, because the "righteousness of God" in the thesis of 1:16-17 "manifests itself in divine power in the proclamation of the gospel."[232] Kelber cites a key emphasis of E. P. Sanders at this point, that "righteousness by faith and participation in Christ ultimately amount to the same thing."[233]

Kelber lifts up the participatory dimension of the Pauline approach:

> In view of the oral base of faith and gospel, one may call their sphere of influence an *auditory field.* "Standing" in this verbal space of the sounded gospel, one shares in the actuality of the dying and rising Christ. . . . The participatory élan distinguishes the Pauline gospel as a genuine oral proclamation, for behind every successful oral performer lies the ability to make hearers live the message. In short, what is implemented in the Pauline language of participation is the epistemological principle of orality that to know actuality is to participate in it.[234]

The key question in interpreting Paul's letter is therefore how it would have sounded to its intended hearers, and what kind of participation would it have evoked. The attention to the stylistic details of the text of Romans throughout this commentary is therefore not an exercise in rhetorical nomenclature but an effort to understand Paul's aim to make an oral impact on the congregations in Rome. An absolutely indispensable

226 See Kennedy, *New Testament Interpretation*, 13–14; Martin, *Antike Rhetorik*, 347–56.

227 Martin, *Antike Rhetorik*, 347.

228 See Margaret E. Dean, "The Grammar of Sound in Greek Texts: Toward a Method for Mapping the Echoes of Speech in Writing," *ABR* 44 (1996) 53–70.

229 Martin, *Antike Rhetorik*, 354.

230 Kelber, *Oral and the Written Gospel*, 140, 141.

231 Ibid., 143.

232 Ibid., 167.

233 Sanders, *Paul*, 506, cited by Kelber, *Oral and the Written Gospel*, 168.

234 Kelber, *Oral and the Written Gospel*, 150.

aspect of this quest is the hypothesis that it was presented in an effective oral form by Tertius, Phoebe's scribe.

E. Rhetorical Situation and Narrative World

In the classical definition of Lloyd Bitzer, the rhetorical situation is "a complex of persons, events, objects and relations presenting an actual or potential exigence which can be . . . removed if discourse . . . can so constrain human decision or action as to bring about the significant modification of the exigence."[235] An important modification of this theory was provided by A. Brinton, who showed that the interest pursued by the rhetor, that is, the exigence, is separate from the rhetorical situation in the audience.[236] George Kennedy and his followers use the terminology of rhetorical situation by dividing it into two components, the audience situation and the rhetorical task that the rhetor undertakes to achieve his purpose with this particular audience.[237] Kennedy uses the category of rhetorical situation to discover "the author's intent and . . . how that is transmitted through a text to an audience."[238] Further modifications have been suggested by Wilhelm Wuell-

ner, Elizabeth Schüssler-Fiorenza, Dennis Stamps, Johannes Vorster, and others, who advocate forms of entextualization that view the rhetorical situation as a literary construct in the text and tend to be skeptical about the possibility of historical reconstruction.[239] In this commentary I follow Kennedy's lead in taking account of a wide range of historical and cultural circumstances. In my view, the concept of the rhetorical situation provides a way of understanding the situation of the letter and its audience, viewed through the lens of the persuasion that the author is endeavoring to achieve.

Norman Petersen's study of the narrative situation is also helpful in conceptualizing the rhetorical situation of Romans.[240] There is a narrative behind each letter, and its reconstruction allows one to make use of social and historical information beyond the letter itself. In the case of Romans four interrelated narratives are visible in the letter that can be correlated with other information. The first is the narrative of each congregation's formation and development up until the time of receiving Paul's letter, which we shall attempt to piece together in section 6, including an account of the conflicts that currently divide these congregations into warring factions.

235 Bitzer, "Rhetorical Situation," 6.
236 A. Brinton, "Situation in the Theory of Rhetoric," *PR* 14 (1981) 246.
237 Kennedy, *New Testament Interpretation*, 35–36; see also Duane Frederick Watson, *Invention, Arrangement, and Style: Rhetorical Criticism of Jude and 2 Peter*, SBLDS 104 (Atlanta: Scholars Press, 1988) 8–9; idem, "The Contributions and Limitations of Greco-Roman Rhetorical Theory for Constructing the Rhetorical and Historical Situations of a Pauline Epistle," in S. E. Porter and D. L. Stamps, eds., *The Rhetorical Interpretation of Scripture: Essays from the 1996 Manibu Conference*, JSNTSup 180 (Sheffield: Sheffield Academic Press, 1999) 125–51; Clifton C. Black, "Rhetorical Criticism," in J. B. Green, ed., *Hearing the New Testament: Strategies for Interpretation* (Grand Rapids: Eerdmans, 1995) 256–77; Reid, *Rhetoric*, 258–59.
238 Kennedy, *New Testament Interpretation*, 12.
239 Wilhelm Wuellner, "Where Is Rhetorical Criticism Taking Us?" *CBQ* 49 (1987) 448–63; idem, "Death and Rebirth of Rhetoric in Late Twentieth Century Biblical Exegesis," in T. Fornberg and D. Hellholm, eds., *Texts and Contexts: Biblical Texts in Their Textual and Situational Contexts: Essays in Honor of Lars Hartman* (Oslo: Scandinavian Univ. Press, 1995) 917–30;

Elizabeth Schüssler-Fiorenza, "Rhetorical Situation and Historical Reconstruction in 1 Corinthians," *NTS* 33 (1987) 390–400; Dennis L. Stamps, "Rethinking the Rhetorical: The Entextualization of the Situation in New Testament Epistles," in S. E. Porter and T. H. Olbricht, eds., *Rhetoric and the New Testament: Essays from the 1992 Heidelberg Conference*, JSNTSup 90 (Sheffield: JSOT Press, 1993) 193–210; idem, "Rhetorical Criticism of the New Testament: Ancient and Modern Evaluations of Argumentation," in S. E. Porter and D. Tombs, eds., *Approaches to New Testament Study*, JSNTSup 120 (Sheffield: Sheffield Academic Press, 1995) 129–69; Johannes N. Vorster, "The Context of the Letter to the Romans: A Critique on the Present State of Research," *Neot* 28 (1994) 127–45.
240 Norman R. Petersen, *Rediscovering Paul: Philemon and the Sociology of Paul's Narrative World* (Philadelphia: Fortress Press, 1985) 1–32. See also Thurén, *Derhetorizing Paul*, 96–101.

The second is the narrative of Paul's previous ministry from the time of his preconversion activities down to the missionizing among the Gentiles "as far round as Illyricum" (15:19). The third is Paul's forthcoming situation, closing out the ministry in the east, delivering the Jerusalem offering, and organizing the mission to Spain, to which section 7 below will be devoted. The fourth narrative is the reading of the letter to each of the congregations in Rome, its transformative impact in resolving the conflicts between the congregations and clarifying the nature of impartial divine righteousness implied by the gospel, followed by their participation in the planning and preparation of the Spanish mission, which as section 8 will show, is the main purpose of the letter. Both of the last narratives are contingent on circumstances and the reactions of hearers of Paul's message, and as it turned out, neither was fulfilled as the letter hopes. To understand the bearing of Paul's argument on the four dimensions of the rhetorical situation requires a clarification of the rhetorical genre, which defines the relationship between the letter writer and the recipients.

F. The Genre of Romans in Relation to Its Epistolary Type

The collection of essays drawn together by Karl Paul Donfried in 1977 set forth the basic alternatives that had been considered on the question of the genre and purpose of Romans.[241] On the one side are those like Manson, Bornkamm, Karris, and to a degree also Klein, who treat Romans as a theological treatise or a circular letter. They are opposed by such scholars as Jervell, Wiefel, Minear, and Donfried, who insist that it is a situational letter with a relation to the audience that is basically similar to that of the other authentic Pauline letters. The conclusion one is inclined to draw from these valuable essays, which one could multiply many times with the inclusion of most of the classical commentators, including Nygren, Dodd, Cranfield, and Käsemann on the treatise side and writers like Bartsch, Harder, Rauer, and Gamble on the situational side, is that the conflict is irresolvable. Neither the treatise nor the situational theory is able to clarify the peculiar relation between Paul

and his audience that differentiates Romans from all of the other letters.

Generally speaking, scholars of both camps have tended consciously or unconsciously to assimilate Romans to one or the other of the two rhetorical genres into which the other Pauline letters fall. The deliberative genre of 1 Thessalonians and 1 Corinthians features advice offered by an authoritative figure to whom specific questions were posed or to whose attention problems were brought that he is uniquely in a position to answer. Paul speaks as the founder of the congregations and he refers repeatedly to the content of early instruction, the experiences of shared mission, and specific content of local controversies. The apologetic or forensic genre of Galatians and 2 Corinthians 10–13 features defense offered by an authoritative figure whose status has been threatened by competitors and accusers. The route of disentangling Romans from either alternative was suggested by Wilhelm Wuellner, and his contribution was generative for my own work on the letter.

Wuellner approaches the problem of Romans not through the traditional channels of "propositional theology" or epistolography but through rhetorical theory. To discover the *aptum*, this theory calls for an analysis of the relationship between speaker and speech content, the relationship between speaker and audience, and the relationship between speech content and audience.[242] Wuellner's analysis of the opening and closing of Romans and their relation to the intervening argument concludes that Paul's aim was to affirm communal values. Romans thus fits the epideictic, or demonstrative, genre which "tries to establish a sense of communion centered around particular values recognized by the audience (in Romans it is the faith stance and faith commitment of speaker and audience), and to this end he uses a whole range of means available to the rhetorician for purposes of amplification and enhancement."[243] In other words, the purpose of Romans as stated in 1:9-10 and elaborated in subsequent verses is to announce and prepare the way for an apostolic mission "by God's will" to visit the Christians in Rome.

---

241 Karl Paul Donfried, ed., *The Romans Debate* (Minneapolis: Augsburg, 1977); the citations in this commentary are drawn from the revised edition of 1991.

242 Wuellner, "Paul's Rhetoric," 140.

243 Ibid., 166; see also Wuellner, "Toposforschung," 476–79.

Several weaknesses in the development of Wuellner's hypothesis have to be overcome before it can attract wider support. His analysis rests on the difficult premise that Rom 1:13-15 is the *causa* which in a traditional *exordium* states the purpose which the letter or speech intends to achieve. It appears more likely that the *causa* is stated in 1:9-10 and is elaborated in vv. 11-12, while vv. 13-15 provide the background of this purpose,[244] namely Paul's repeated efforts to mount a mission to Rome and beyond. Wuellner rightly perceives the correspondence between the introduction and conclusion of Romans, suggesting that 15:14—16:23 constitute a *peroratio,* but is unable to make a convincing case that 15:30—16:23 is explainable by pathos whose components are "admiring love and despising hate." This fails to grasp the peculiar political function of the greetings and the commendation of Phoebe and overlooks the evidence concerning the interpolation of non Pauline material in 16:17-20. It is also difficult to support Wuellner's conclusion that 1:16-17 is a *transitus* leading to the main argument of 1:18—15:13. The consensus is fully justified that these two verses constitute the thesis developed in subsequent chapters.[245] Another problematic aspect of his work is that the content and style of Romans hardly seem to fit the traditional stereotype of epideictic literature as aiming for pleasing demonstrations of rhetorical skill. The question seems discussable only on the basis of a more precise identification of Romans as one of the subtypes of epideictic rhetoric that comes close to its style and content.

The definitive study of epideictic literature and oratory by Theodore C. Burgess provides a listing of a wide variety of subtypes, based on treatises by Menander and Dionysius of Halicarnassus. Since theological and historical studies related to the NT have usually been rather weakly related to classical rhetorical theory, a listing of the options will suggest ways to bring Wuellner's hypothesis into sharper focus. The 27 subtypes described by Burgess are: (1) Praise of a country; (2) Praise of a city; (3) Praise of a harbor; (4) Praise of a bay; (5) Praise of an acropolis; (6) Praise of a city's origin; (7) Praise of a city's pursuits; (8) Praise of a ruler; (9) Speech on disembarking; (10) Impromptu talk; (11) Speech to one departing; (12) Marriage hymn; (13) Talk that lulls to sleep; (14) Birthday speech; (15) Consolation speech; (16) Welcome speech; (17) Funeral oration; (18) Congratulatory speech; (19) Ambassador's speech; (20) Invitation speech; (21) Farewell speech; (22) Poetic plaint; (23) Sminthian hymn to Apollo; (24) Panegyric speech; (25) Parenetic speech; (26) Hortatory speech; and (27) Paradoxical encomium.[246]

Several of these categories seem quite close to aspects of Romans. Romans could be understood as a form of category 9, written in the time prior to Paul's departure to Jerusalem and thence to Rome and Spain, describing the purpose of his mission; much of Romans could fall under categories 25 and 26, with ethical and theological admonitions playing an important part in the argument; and category 19, the "Ambassador's speech," offers intriguing possibilities to comprehend the opening and closing chapters.

It is important to recognize that many of the speeches and writings in the demonstrative genre have much more than mere display of ornate style in view. Burgess observes that the philosophic essay and the popular diatribe derived from this genre, intending to convince and to teach as well as to delight the mind. "The element of persuasion or advice . . . was common in epideictic compositions. . . . Lysias, also, in the third section of the *Olympiacus,* says that he does not intend to trifle with words, like a mere sophist, but to offer serious counsel on the dangers of Greece."[247] The strength of Wuellner's suggestion rests on the principle, reaffirmed by modern rhetoricians like Lausberg, Perelman, and Olbrechts-Tyteca, that epideictic materials aim to "strengthen the disposition towards action by increasing adherence to the values it lauds."[248] It is the desire on the part of a writer or speaker to strengthen a particular ethos, there-

244 I am indebted to unpublished work by Hans-Dieter Betz for suggesting this organization of the opening verses of Romans.

245 See Cranfield, 1:87; Käsemann, 21, 32.

246 Theodore C. Burgess, "Epideictic Literature," *StCP* 3 (1902) 110–13.

247 Burgess, "Epideictic Literature," 96.

248 Wuellner, "Paul's Rhetoric," 139, cited from C. Perelman and L. Olbrechts-Tyteca, *The New Rhetoric: A Treatise on Argumentation* (Notre Dame: Univ. of Notre Dame Press, 1971) 50.

fore, rather than flowery style or congratulatory tone, that links the widely differing subtypes of the epideictic genre. This clears the way for a consideration of the possibility that Romans may fit somewhere in this genre.

The studies of diplomatic and administrative correspondence by Schubart, Welles, and Olshausen offer many parallels to Romans,[249] although quite naturally the specific content of Paul's message and mission are unparalleled. Burgess shows that the ambassadorial speech "states the special cause for the embassy and pictures the conditions which occasioned it. The speech admits of great variety."[250] Pseudo-Libanius includes the "diplomatic letter" among the forty-one types in his handbook, stating that it should be politely formulated and that it ordinarily makes a specific request. A brief sample letter requests the reader to "be constrained" by his "magnificent excellence" to comply with a particular diplomatic appeal.[251] This indirect style of appealing to common values is what places diplomatic rhetoric within the epideictic genre. There is a vivid example of ambassadorial speech in Euripides' play, *The Heracleidae,* in which the diplomat Copreus attempts to show why the refugees hated by the king of Argos should not be granted asylum. Copreus claims to have "authority for all I do or say," but he provokes the Athenians to resistance when he undiplomatically threatens "a total war" if they resist his demands.[252] An easily accessible example of diplomatic correspondence is contained in Philo's *Embassy to Gaius.* Although the ambassadors from Alexandria, including Philo, were frustrated in laying their case before the emperor in 40 c.e., the book contains a draft of Agrippa's letter to Gaius that fits the epideictic genre and provides interesting parallels to Romans.[253] Detailed studies of these documents from the perspective of the NT letters might provide valuable new insights, as proven by Carl Bjerkelund's use of such materials in the analysis of Paul's exhortation formulas.[254]

I suggest the following refinement of Wuellner's epideictic theory. Among the letters of Paul, Romans is a unique fusion of the "ambassadorial letter" with several of the other subtypes in the genre: the parenetic letter, the hortatory letter, and the philosophical diatribe. Its purpose is to advocate in behalf of the "power of God" a cooperative mission to evangelize Spain so that the theological argumentation reiterates the gospel to be therein proclaimed and the ethical admonitions show how that gospel is to be lived out in a manner that would ensure the success of this mission.

In the sections that follow I would like to set forth the evidence within the text of Romans itself that supports this hypothesis and then describe the rather wide-reaching consequences for interpreting the letter. But first I would like briefly to review the evidence concerning Paul's understanding of himself as an ambassador.[255] Paul's understanding of himself as "apostle" is closely related to the Greco-Roman world's understanding of "ambassador." In fact there are examples in which the term ἀπόστολος ("apostle") is used in the specific sense of a political ambassador as well as a special messenger of a king.[256] As K. H. Rengstorf pointed out in his classic article on "apostle," this term was used in connection with royal diplomacy in such a way as to make it clear that the officeholder carried the authority of the king himself. The apostle is the "representative of [his] monarch and his authority"[257] in the same way that a minister plenipotentiary or an ambassador functions in modern diplomacy. The study of Paul's apostolic authority by Bengt Holmberg concludes that when Paul

249 W. Schubart, "Bermerkungen zum Stil hellenistischer Königsbriefe," *APF* 6 (1920) 324–47; Welles, *Royal Correspondence,* passim; Eckart Olshausen, *Prosopographie der hellenistischen Königsgesandten* (Louvain: Nauwelaerts, 1974).

250 Burgess, "Epideictic Literature," 112.

251 Pseudo-Libanius, §76; cited by Abraham J. Malherbe, "Ancient Epistolary Theorists," *OJRS* 5 (1977) 74.

252 David Grene and Richmond Lattimore, eds., *The Complete Greek Tragedies* (Chicago: Univ. of Chicago Press, 1955) 1:122–23; "The Heracleidae," trans. R. Gladstone, lines 138, 160.

253 Philo *Legat.* 276, 329; see the introduction by F. H. Colson, *Philo* (Cambridge: Harvard Univ. Press, 1962), x, xiii, xxx, xxxi.

254 Bjerkelund, *PARAKALÔ,* passim.

255 This is a crucial factor in assessing Paul's motivation in writing Romans; on the methodological issues related to motivation and descriptions thereof, see Fischer, *Historians' Fallacies,* 187–215, 280–81.

256 BAGD 99.

257 K. H. Rengstorf, "ἀποστέλλω κτλ.," *TDNT* 1 (1964) 399.

"preaches it is God who really is the speaker," citing 2 Cor 5:18-20, "we are ambassadors for Christ, God making his appeal through us." Paul attaches this authority both to his doctrinal and to his ethical instruction, insisting that he is "bound to the service of Christ and His gospel as a slave to his lord (Gal 1:10, 1 Cor 9:16-23, Rom 1:1)."[258]

The development of this theme in 2 Corinthians has a direct bearing on the kind of self-understanding revealed in Romans. Under attack in Corinth from competitive missionaries, Paul defends his legitimacy as an apostle who extends God's power by himself remaining subordinate to it. Just as an ambassador in a political sense is capable of expressing the power of his sovereign only by submitting himself to it, becoming an extension of the monarch, so to speak, Paul states in 2 Cor 5:11-14, "Therefore, knowing the fear of the Lord, we persuade men; but what we are is known to God, and I hope it is known also to your conscience. . . . For the love of Christ controls us." The explicit claim of Paul and his missionary colleagues to be "ambassadors for Christ" is preceded by the summary of the "message of reconciliation" (2 Cor 5:19) with which they had been entrusted. As Ceslas Spicq points out, the ambassador is no greater than his message; he is in fact merely a channel through which the message, and thereby the foreign policy and the extension of political power, of the sovereign flows.[259] Günther Bornkamm spoke of the "authoritative and official expression" of ambassadorship that Paul uses in this passage,[260] while Spicq has provided extensive documentation concerning the political and bureaucratic horizon of Paul's usage. For example, the Greek term $\pi\rho\epsilon\sigma\beta\epsilon\acute{u}\tau\eta\varsigma$ was used in Roman administration to refer to imperial legates who stood at the pinnacle of the military and diplomatic hierarchy.[261]

The degree to which Paul had adopted the political flexibility of an ambassador is visible in 1 Cor 9:19-22. "For though I am free from all men, I have made myself a slave to all, that I might win the more. To the Jews I became as a Jew. . . . To those outside the law I became as one outside the law. . . . To the weak I became weak. . . . I have become all things to all men, that I might by all means save some." Bornkamm argues that this flexibility was a matter of abandoning all forms of preconditions for salvation imposed by the various religious traditions in the Greco-Roman world. "The whole of his concern is to make clear that the changeless gospel . . . empowers him to be free to change his stance." While Paul denies the validity of "the different standpoints of Jews and Gentiles" he accepts the significance of "the historical places" in which each is called. But Bornkamm is very uncomfortable with the political implications of this passage, denying "that the apostle played different roles in different places simply for the sake of the missionary effect. . . . To speak as if Paul Judaized it in one place and paganized it in another is wholly inaccurate."[262] Henry Chadwick offers a less defensive view of Paul's diplomatic capacities, arguing that the evidence in Galatians, Corinthians, and Colossians reveals "an astonishing elasticity of mind, and a flexibility in dealing with situations requiring delicate and ingenious treatment which appears much greater than is usually supposed."[263]

Another dimension of this internalization of the diplomatic role was discovered by Bjerkelund in his study of the background of $\pi\alpha\rho\alpha\kappa\alpha\lambda\hat{\omega}$, "I exhort you," and similar formulas in the Pauline letters. The parallels come almost exclusively from diplomatic and epistolary materials rather than from traditional ethics. He provides scores of examples of ambassadors or royal admin-

---

258 Holmberg, *Paul and Power*, 76.

259 Spicq, "$\pi\rho\epsilon\sigma\beta\epsilon\acute{u}\omega$," *TLNT* 3 (1994) 175; see also J.-F. Collange, *Enigmes de la deuxième épître de Paul aux Corinthiens. Étude exégètique de 2 Cor. 2:14—7:11*, SNTSMS 13 (Cambridge: Cambridge Univ. Press, 1972) 266–74.

260 Günther Bornkamm, "$\pi\rho\epsilon\sigma\beta\epsilon\acute{u}\omega$," *TDNT* 6 (1968) 682.

261 Spicq, "$\pi\rho\epsilon\sigma\beta\epsilon\acute{u}\omega$," 740–41.

262 Günther Bornkamm, "The Missionary Stance of Paul in I Corinthians 9 and in Acts," in L. E. Keck and J. L. Martyn, eds., *Studies in Luke–Acts: Essays*

Presented in Honor of Paul Schubert (Nashville: Abingdon, 1966) 196–97.

263 Henry Chadwick, "'All Things to All Men' (I Cor. ix.22)," *NTS* 1 (1954–55) 261–75.

istrators expressing commands to subordinates with this language, politely imploring their readers to comply with the wishes of the sovereign. "What is interesting about these letters is that παρακαλῶ ["I exhort"] appears in a carefully nurtured diplomatic style that remained unchanged through centuries . . . . It must be presupposed that it was known in the cities and territories through which Paul journeyed. It is very probable that Paul himself was well acquainted with this usage."[264]

The diplomatic background of the exhortation formulas used by Paul throws light on the disputed translation of Phlm 8-10: "Accordingly, though I am bold enough in Christ to command you to do what is required, yet for love's sake, I prefer to exhort you—I, Paul, an ambassador and now a prisoner also for Christ Jesus—I exhort you for my child, Onesimus." The term translated as "ambassador" could also mean "old man," because spelling variations in parallel passages allow either option. I would tend to concur with Bjerkelund, Suhl, and others[265] that the distinctive role of an ambassador is visible in this passage: empowered to issue commands because of his official status, Paul prefers diplomatic exhortation so that compliance can preserve the integrity of subordinates. It seems to me likely that Paul's reputation as a subtle and effective ambassador comes to expression in Ephesians, a product of the later Pauline school, which places in his mouth the words, "I am an ambassador in chains" (Eph 6:20). While none of these details proves that a particular letter like Romans fits the ambassadorial type, they serve to sustain the suggestion that the use of such rhetoric would be a natural expression of Paul's self-identity.

5. The Cultural Situation in Rome: The Pyramid of Honor

The interpretive method in this commentary is to understand the letter as far as possible within its cultural context, rather than treating it as an abstract theological document such as Paul's self-confession or the defense of some modern doctrinal stance. In view of the vast amount of information available about the city of Rome and the need to avoid duplicating details in the commentary, the principles of selection employed in this chapter are provided by the rhetorical analysis, the inferences drawn from the letter regarding the situation and location of the congregations, and what Paul as a well-informed and widely traveled citizen of the empire would have known about the situation in general, including what was known about the Jewish community from which Christianity emerged.[266] One of the dangers in this approach is that "potentially significant factors may be overlooked."[267] There is also an inevitable measure of circularity in this regard, because inferences drawn from evidence within the letter provides the screen by which other evidence is sifted and selected. Since final verification is not possible, the conclusions drawn in this chapter call for the "refutations" by other researchers who can examine whether they correlate adequately with the data within the letter and within the vast arena of cultural, archaeological, and historical studies on Rome.

A. The Historical Setting

The city of Rome within which the early congregations developed was decisively altered by Octavian's triumph over Mark Antony in the Battle of Actium in 31 B.C.E., which left Octavian as the sole master of the empire. He ceremonially turned power over to the Senate, receiving the title of "Augustus" in 27 for having restored the Republic, but in fact he ruled as the single head of state whose power derived from the oath of allegiance that the citizens of Rome and the governments of the provinces had granted him prior to the Battle of Actium. The populace thus became Octavian's private clientele with him, the emperor, as the master patron.[268] An effective propaganda campaign portrayed Augustus as the divinely appointed ruler who brought peace to a troubled world by restoring legitimate government based

---

264 Bjerkelund, *PARAKALÔ*, 110.
265 Ibid., 119; Alfred Suhl, "Der Philemonbrief als Beispiel paulinischer Paränese," *Kairos* 15 (1973) 272.
266 For the methodological issue see Jewett, *Thessalonian Correspondence*, 114; Krentz, *Method*, 36–37.
267 Jewett, *Thessalonian Correspondence*, 114.
268 Earl, *Age of Augustus*, 66, 193. See also Mullins, *Rome*, 32–38.

on the rule of law and the restoration of public virtue.[269] The *ludi saeculares* games and festivities were first celebrated in 18 B.C.E. to thank the gods for the Augustan peace, to purify the free citizens, and to enjoy days of celebration provided by the state.[270] An extensive building program paid by the emperor and his wealthy supporters transformed Rome into a gleaming city of marble that grew to house a million people. Under his loyal son-in-law Agrippa, a new aqueduct was built along with numerous public fountains; temples were restored; public gardens, baths, and theaters were erected; and the city administration was reorganized with fire brigades and police protection; enhanced grain deliveries to Roman citizens were also provided. All of these improvements served to demonstrate that the golden age of peace and plenty had finally arrived.[271] In place of the chaotic warren of streets and alleys that was difficult to administer, Augustus organized 265 neighborhoods with elected leaders and local shrines containing altars to the local Lares and to the emperor's genius,[272] thus linking leading craftsmen into his system of honorable governance. The beneficiaries of this vast program of renewal were the citizens of Rome but not the slaves and immigrants who made up the bulk of the early Christian congregations.

The successors of Augustus, Tiberius (14–32 C.E.) and Caligula (38–41 C.E.), were poor administrators who managed nonetheless to keep the precarious system of propagandistic dictatorship going.[273] Unlike Augustus, they no longer gave account of public funds, and the distinction between the immense personal wealth of the

emperor and public wealth disappeared,[274] a clear indication of dictatorship in fact if not in name. Of more direct relevance for the situation of Paul's Letter to the Romans were the reigns of Claudius (41–54 C.E.) and Nero (54–68 C.E.). Although plagued by conspiracies that resulted in the execution of 35 senators and 300 knights, Claudius continued the process of urban development with the creation of a new harbor for the grain trade, the improvement of the roads and aqueducts, the reorganization of the court system, and the creation of an imperial bureaucracy consisting of slaves and freedmen/women who administered the affairs of the empire in areas where the emperor had direct control.[275] Two of the leaders of this bureaucracy were the ex-slaves Pallas and Narcissus, who amassed vast powers and wealth, evoking the intense resentment of the Roman nobility.

Nero came to power with the pledge to restore the role of the Senate and the rule of law, and was celebrated for ushering in a golden age. He promoted Greek values with an aim of civilizing the Roman upper class and promised to cease the practice of issuing commands through imperial agents.[276] Pallas and Narcissus were deposed and were replaced by the Roman noblemen Seneca and Burrus, who led an exemplary administration,[277] until Nero began to deteriorate in 62 C.E., restoring the brutal practice of secret lese majesty trials with summary executions of political opponents,[278] including the eventual execution of the apostle Paul himself.[279] At the time Romans was written, however, the Nero administration was providing an exemplary form

269 See Ferrero, *Republic of Augustus*, 51–55, 76–82, 167–71.
270 See the vivid description in Ferrero, *Republic of Augustus*, 82–94; for earlier developments see John T. Ramsey and A. Lewis Licht, *The Comet of 44 B.C. and Caesar's Funeral Games* (Atlanta: Scholars Press, 1997).
271 See White, *Apostle*, 114–24, following Andrew Wallace-Hadrill, *Augustan Rome* (London: Bristol Classical Press, 1993) 10–24.
272 White, *Apostle*, 124.
273 For example, Barrett, *Caligula*, 56, cites Suetonius, *Cal.* 14.1, with regard to the emperor's meeting with the Senate on March 18, 37 C.E., which "granted to Caligula an awesome authority" (*ius arbitriumque omnium rerum*, "power and authority over all things.") On 57 Barrett observes that

Caligula thus became an emperor "not bound by the laws" (*princeps legibus solutus*).
274 Earl, *Age of Augustus*, 199.
275 See Brian W. Jones, "Claudius," *ABD* 1 (1992) 1054, building on studies by Momigliano, *Claudius;* and Scramuzza, *Claudius;* see also Barbara Levick, *Claudius* (London: Batsford, 1990).
276 See Miriam T. Griffin, "Nero," *ABD* 4 (1992) 1076–77, based on studies by Michael Grant, *Nero* (London: Weidenfeld & Nicolson, 1970), and Griffin's earlier book, *Nero: The End of a Dynasty* (New Haven: Yale University Press, 1987).
277 See Griffin, *Nero*, 67–82.
278 Ibid., 83–99.
279 Jewett, *Chronology*, 45–46, citing among other sources Will Durant, *Caesar and Christ* (New York: Simon & Schuster, 1944) 279.

of government and law enforcement,[280] despite the profligate personal habits of Nero himself—an aggressive bisexual who enjoyed stalking the streets of Rome with his crowd of sycophants demanding sexual services from passersby and "indulging in brawls and petty thieving."[281] The combination of Paul's denunciation of immorality combined with the command to respect governmental agents as the source of law and order may derive in part from these peculiar circumstances.

B. The Civic Cult

Recent research has suggested that the ideology of the ruler cult, especially with Augustan images, may well have influenced Paul.[282] In Rome, where people had traditionally hated the divinization of human beings, the ruler cult began with honoring the *Genius Populi Romani* in temples and house shrines. Octavius arranged for extravagant honors devoted to himself and for his statue to be placed next to the speaker's rostrum in the forum. He was called the "Son of the Divine Savior," and was initially depicted as a military redeemer, in nude pose, with his foot resting on a globe as universal ruler of the world. In his struggle with Mark Antony, who put himself forward as a prototype of Heracles and later of Dionysius, Octavian assumed the image of Apollo, in the role of a resister of tyranny. By adopting this self-limiting role, the victory over Antony at Actium was celebrated as a triumph of Apollo over a dangerous Dionysius. Following certain representations in the *Aeniad,* Octavian presents his struggle as that of humans fighting against wild beasts. With Octavian's victory over the alleged forces of barbarism, he is celebrated as the guarantor of peace and tranquility. In reality, however, Octavian had deposed a legitimately elected coregent in an aggressive campaign that followed the example of Julius Caesar in gaining sole access to dictatorial power.[283]

The sophisticated form of imperial propaganda developed by Octavian carried no overt elements of self-glorification but emphasized his Apolline role, now increasingly depicted in restored temples replete with traditional symbols of peace and tranquility.[284] Octavian reinforced the new mode of propaganda by melting down 60 silver statues of himself and ceremonially returning control to the Senate; this act of renouncing power allowed the Senate to save face, and to crown him as princeps, not king. While possessing unlimited power and authority, Augustus promoted the restrained values of the Republic and led Rome into what was celebrated as the Golden Age that embodied piety. *Pietas* was understood as respect for tradition, expressed in his renovating some 82 temples and building new temples with classical style and Roman elements where sacrifices were made to the god of peace. In these new temples Augustus as a symbol of Rome wears a veil with a toga, abandoning the Greek pose of an uncovered head. Augustus himself is no longer depicted as the half-nude divine hero, wearing a breastplate with honorific symbols, but is now shown in poses of piety. The performance of Augustus's religious duties was an essential part of this propaganda, and he assumed the high priestly office of *pontifex maximus* in 12 B.C.E. In temples and house shrines, the genius of Augustus wears the veil as a symbol of traditional Roman *pietas*.

It is clear that Paul criticizes and reverses the official system of honor achieved through piety on which the empire after Augustus rested. Paul offers a new approach to mercy, righteousness, and piety, one that avoided the propagandistic exploitation of the Roman imperial system. In the words of Dieter Georgi, "Here, in Romans, there is a critical counterpart to the central institution of the Roman Empire,"[285] that is, redemptive kingship (see Rom 1:1-3). Augustus is celebrated in the poetry of Virgil as the savior figure who ushers in "this glorious age"; he receives the prophetic tribute: "He shall have the gift of divine life, shall see heroes mingled with gods, and shall himself be seen of them. . . . Enter on thy high honors. . . . O thou dear offspring of the

---

280 See Griffin, "Nero," 176–77; for a description of the law enforcement system see Robinson, *Criminal Law,* 9–22.

281 Griffin, *Nero,* 111.

282 See Christensen, *Christus oder Jupiter,* 22–39; Ferguson, "Ruler-worship," 766–84; Fears, "Ruler Worship," 1009–26; White, *Apostle,* 124–29; Jeffers,

Greco-Roman World, 100–103; see particularly the essays in Horsley, *Paul and Empire* and *Paul and Politics.* Also Blumenfeld, *Political Paul,* 264–92.

283 See particularly Earl, *Age of Augustus,* 52–54.

284 See Beard et al., *Religions of Rome,* 1:318; White, *Apostle,* 124–29; Mullins, *Rome,* 33–38.

285 Georgi, *Theocracy,* 86.

gods, mighty seed of a Jupiter to be!" (Virgil, *Ecl.* 4.11.48). It is understandable that at Augustus's death in 14 C.E., he was voted *caelestes honores* ("eternal honors") by the Roman Senate. In Everett Ferguson's words, "Deification at Rome . . . was a conferring of status; cult was a supreme form of honor."[286] In a similar vein, Claudius was voted apotheosis by the Roman Senate when he died in 54 C.E. Nero, on his accession to the throne, was celebrated as the glorious leader who would usher in yet another Golden Age.[287] This follows the pattern established by Augustus, who developed this masterpiece of propaganda, with the regent holding unlimited power and ostensibly resisting divinization while receiving divine honors as the humble Apollo who restores peace to the world.

Several aspects of the civic cult are reflected in the way the argument of the Epistle to the Romans proceeds. It begins with a description of divine wrath against those who seek to suppress the truth (1:18) and worship the creature rather than the Creator (1:25), and it goes on to claim that all humans are liars (3:4) and none is truly righteous (3:19-10), all of which comprises the antithesis of official propaganda about Rome's superior piety, justice, and honor. The civic cult is also countered by Paul's depiction of Christ. That he alone is "Lord" with a name above every name, and that he subjects everything under his authority, fits the pattern of an imperial ruler. As Harry Maier observes, the visual depictions found everywhere in Rome were "designed to convince the inhabitants of the Roman Empire that they were governed by an order willed by the gods, with a divinely established ruler, indeed *divi filius* or υἱὸς θεοῦ, at its head."[288] In contrast to Julius Caesar, who seized authority as dictator, Augustus, his successors, and Christ all renounce tyranny and claim to bring peace through service; and the argument of Romans revolves around the question of which rule is truly righteous and which gospel has the power to make the world truly peaceful.

C. The Pyramid of Honor

J. E. Lendon has shown that a relatively small number of officials ruled the vast empire, using a combination of force, propaganda, and patronage that was held together by "the workings of honour and pride," which provided "the underpinnings of loyalty and gratitude for benefactions" that made the empire functional.[289] Although the threat of force and the desire for gain were always present, "the duty to 'honour' or respect officials, whether local, imperial, or the emperor himself, is vastly more prominent in ancient writings than the duty to obey. . . . The subject paid 'honour' to his rulers as individuals deserving of it in themselves, and, in turn, the rulers are seen to relate to their subjects by 'honouring' them. Subject and official were linked by a great network of honouring, and obedience was an aspect of that honouring. . . . As Cicero revealed, there was nothing specifically governmental in honouring people; it was an everyday social function."[290] This background is essential for understanding the argument of Romans, which employs honor categories from beginning to end. Lendon observes: "Honour was a filter through which the whole world was viewed, a deep structure of the Graeco-Roman mind . . . . Every thing, every person, could be valued in terms of honour."[291] At the peak of this pyramid of honor stood the emperor, who claimed to renounce honors while gathering them all to himself. Beneath him the intense competition for superiority in honor continued unabated on all levels of society.[292]

The competitive center of the ancient systems of shame and honor was what Paul called "boasting."[293] This was a much more blatant, socially acceptable form of behavior than is conceivable for most moderns, formed by often disingenuous traditions of public modesty. Not so for the shapers of the Greco-Roman world. As E. A. Judge observed, "Self-magnification thus became a feature of Hellenic higher education."[294] By eliminating the culturally endorsed motivation of seeking honor through teaching and learning, Paul in effect

---

286 Ferguson, *Backgrounds*, 197.
287 See Georgi, *Theocracy*, 87.
288 Maier, "Imperial Iconography," 386.
289 Lendon, *Empire of Honour*, 13.
290 Ibid., 22–23.
291 Ibid., 73; see also Earl, *Age of Augustus*, 13.
292 The material in this section is drawn in part from the first chapter of Jewett, *Saint Paul Returns to the Movies.*
293 See Malina, *New Testament World*, 51–70; Moxnes, "Honour and Righteousness," 61–77; Silva, *Honor*, 43–94; Jewett, "Honor and Shame," 257–72.
294 Judge, "Conflict of Educational Aims," 39. See also Strom, *Reframing Paul*, 64–67.

radically alters the Greco-Roman theory of education.[295] E. A. Judge makes a similar case concerning the broad cultural tradition of public service. The assumption was that the quest for honor was the only suitable goal for life. "It was held that the winning of honor was the only adequate reward for merit in public life. . . . It therefore became a prime and admired objective of public figures to enshrine themselves, by actually defining their own glory, in the undying memory of posterity" by publishing memorials of their accomplishments.[296]

The explicit concern in ancient Roman society with the issue of honor is visible in their creation of what Judge has called "an aristocracy of esteem."[297] They used the term *gloria* to describe the aura that "arises from a person's successfully exhibiting himself to others,"[298] particularly in victorious political or military leadership. Such glory was viewed as intrinsic to the heroic person, raising that person above the level of others. This was conveyed in expressions like "immortal glory" or "celestial glory" in that the superlative accomplishments would continue to resound after one's death. In contrast to Jewish thought, which reserved "glory" largely for descriptions of God, the Romans virtually restricted *gloria* to superior human accomplishments. Victorious military leaders were celebrated in religious processions, for example, that acknowledged the quality of immortal glory. Thus Ulrich Knoche contends "that the glorious man is raised up from the human to the eternal sphere: he does not become a [divine] hero but remains thoroughly human, indeed, remains a citizen."[299] Such glory depends, of course, on the recognition granted by other

citizens to its "great man" for performing public service. The glorious leader was thought to be capable of bringing the blessing of the gods upon the community; he was honored as the source of righteousness and prosperity. A sophisticated system of gradation in honor was established, in which the Roman Senate voted appropriate rewards, offices, and celebrations for various levels of accomplishment in the fields of philanthropy or military strategy. The ambition of Roman leaders, usually drawn from leading families, was to gain ever higher levels of honor.[300]

The competition for honor was visible in every city of the Roman Empire in which members of the elite competed for civic power through sponsoring games and celebrations, financing public buildings, endowing food distributions, and so on. The public life in the Roman Empire was centered in the quest for honor. There were inscriptions on every public building and artwork indicating to whose honor it should be attributed. Rome in particular was full of majestic public buildings such as temples, baths, fountains, and amphitheaters built to honor glorious leaders and triumphal occasions.[301] These ideas formed the center of the *Pax Romana* established by Augustus, whom Philo celebrated as the

first and greatest benefactor to whom the whole habitable world voted no less than celestial honors. These are so well attested by temples, gateways, vestibules, porticoes. . . . He received his honors . . . with the magnitude of so mighty a sovereignty whose prestige was bound to be enhanced by such tributes. That he

295 In ibid., Judge cites Tacitus, *Ann.* 4.38.20, "Disregard of fame leads to one's virtues being disregarded."

296 Judge, "Conflict of Educational Aims," 38–39; he cites Sallust *Bell. Jug.* 26, "Reticence would only cause people to mistake modesty for a guilty conscience."

297 E. A. Judge, "Roman Literary Memorials," *Proceedings of the Ninth Congress of the Australian Universities' Language and Literature* (Melbourne, 1964) 28.

298 Judge, "Roman Literary Memorials," 28.

299 Knoche, "Römische Ruhmesgedanke," 424.

300 See Hans Drexler, "*Honos*," in H. Oppermann, ed., *Römische Wertbegriffe* (Darmstadt: Wissenschaftliche Buchgesellschaft, 1983) 446–67, esp. 455; see also Earl, *Age of Augustus*, 13–14.

301 See particularly Halvor Moxnes, "'He saw that the city was full of idols' (Acts 17:16): Visualizing the World of the First Christians," in D. Hellholm, H. Moxnes, and T. K. Seim, eds., *Mighty Minorities? Minorities in Early Christianity–Positions and Strategies: Essays in Honour of Jacob Jervell on his 70th Birthday 21 May 1995* (Oslo: Scandinavian Univ. Press, 1995) 107–31, esp. the section on "Cities as Culture—Honour and Shame," 114–18.

was never elevated or puffed up by the vast honors given to him is clearly shown by the fact that he never wished anyone to address him as a god.[302]

The propagandistic *Res Gestae* that Augustus published and inscribed in Roman temples throughout the empire celebrates his glorious accomplishments in bringing peace to the Mediterranean world and consolidating his rule under the fiction of democracy. Here one can see the elaborate gradations of honors he boasts of having received:

In my sixth and seventh consulships, when I had extinguished the flames of civil war, after receiving by universal consent the absolute control of affairs, I transferred the republic from my own control to the will of the senate and of the Roman people. For this service on my part I was given the title of Augustus by decree of the senate, and the doorposts of my house were covered with laurels by public act, and a civic crown was fixed above my door, and a golden shield was placed in the Curia Julia whose inscription testified that the senate and the Roman people gave me this in recognition of my valour, my clemency, my justice, and my piety. After that time I took precedence of all in rank, but of power I possessed no more than those who were my colleagues in any magistracy.[303]

The claims of having restored power to the Senate and the Roman people, and of having only the collegial power of the magistracy were, of course, fictions. His position at the peak of the pyramid of honor rendered it logical that total power should be placed in his hands. His achievements are celebrated in the *Res Gestae* with language that is significant for the argument of Romans:

clementia = "mercies" in Rom 12:1; *justitia* = "rightwising, righteousness, etc."; *pietas* = "piety" that Paul finds lacking in 1:18. In every victory parade[304] and civic celebration in temple or coliseum, the Romans claimed superior honors for themselves and their rulers; they were firmly convinced that the gods had "exalted this great empire of Rome to the highest point yet reached on earth"[305] because of its superior virtue. In Cicero's memorable formulation, the Romans boasted of being *religione . . . multo superiores* ("with respect to religious observance far superior")[306] in comparison with the other nations they had incorporated into their empire. The argument about overturning this corrupt and exploitative honor system is found throughout Paul's Letter to the Romans.

D. Slaves and Barbarians

Largely exempt from the system of public honor were slaves and barbarians. They could vie for honor among themselves but never qualify for legitimate honor in the imperial system itself. A significant proportion of the inhabitants of the empire were slaves.[307] Jeffers reports, for example, that "something like 2 to 3 million of the 7.5 million inhabitants of Italy" were slaves.[308] There were five sources of slaves in Paul's time. The first and most important were enemies captured in warfare, which meant that the survivors of a Roman siege or campaign would be put on the auction block.[309] This also meant that slaves represented something of a cross section of Mediterranean society. The other four sources of slavery were equally indiscriminate, as far as racial stereotypes were concerned. The steadiest supply of slaves came from the offspring of slaves.[310] There were also persons who voluntarily sold themselves into slavery for economic reasons;[311] persons who fell into debt and

---

302 Philo *Legat.* 145–54.

303 *Res Gestae* 6.34.

304 See esp. Fears, "Cult of Jupiter," 1–141; "Theology of Victory," 737–826.

305 Velleius Paterculus *Hist.* 2.131.1.

306 Cicero *Nat. d.* 2.3.8., cited by Burkhard Gladigow, "Roman Religion," *ABD* 5 (1992) 815, with reference to the Roman claim to be the "most religious of mortals."

307 Gülzow, *Christentum und Sklaverei*, 78–80; Brockmeyer, *Antike Sklaverei*, 100–105, 150–53, 157–59; Bartchy, "Slavery (Greco-Roman)," 66.

308 Jeffers, *Greco-Roman World*, 221.

309 See Keith R. Bradley, "On the Roman Slave Supply and Slavebreeding," in M. I. Finley, ed., *Classical Slavery* (London: Cass, 1987) 43–46.

310 Bradley, "Slave Supply," 48–59.

311 In *MALLON CHRESAI: First Century Slavery and the Interpretation of 1 Cor 7:21*, SBLMS 36 (Missoula, MT: Scholars Press, 1985) 46, S. Scott Bartchy cites R. H. Barrow, *Slavery in the Roman Empire* (New York: Barnes and Noble, 1968) 12, on this point.

lost their freedom; and certain classes of criminals whose punishment was enslavement.

The legal status of slaves was more complicated than was the case in modern jurisprudence.[312] While both the ancient and the modern systems defined slaves as chattel and placed them under the absolute power of their master, in the ancient world the rights of a slave could be defended by his owner or some other benefactor in the courts. Roman legislation shortly before Paul's time restricted the right of owners to use slaves in combat with animals in the theaters and established the same trial procedures for slave criminals as for freedmen/women.[313] The courts also defined slaves as persons as well as things.[314] A different attitude from the modern is manifest in that ancient writers disputed whether slavery was "natural" and whether inner freedom was possible for slaves,[315] but no one opposed the legal system of slavery as such.[316] Slave revolts in the Greco-Roman world aimed at reversing the status of slaves and masters. Apparently no one, including the slaves themselves, could imagine an economic system that was not based on slavery. The historian Zvi Yavetz summarizes the current scholarly consensus on this point: "In the Greek and Roman world slavery was an uncontestable fact and the idea of a slaveless society was inconceivable."[317] The sheer size of the slavery system may have had an effect at this point; the usual estimate is that one-third of the population was slave; one-third consisted of freed slaves; so that only one-third of the population were not slaves, and even these could end up in slavery by a variety of means, as we have observed. Ferguson's figures are a little lower: 20 percent of the population the city of Rome were slaves.[318]

Unlike slavery in more recent centuries, the slave in Paul's time could expect to be manumitted after a cer-

tain number of years of service to his or her master.[319] There was a good chance of such manumission after slaves had served until they were 30 or 40 years old.[320] In some instances, particularly competent slaves were allowed to do work on the side, and were able to buy their own freedom. There were four legal components to a full writ of manumission for slaves, any one of which could be reserved to the owner, even in the interest of the well-being of the former slave: (1) the right to be a legal agent, which was sometimes less advisable than remaining under the protection of a powerful patron; (2) the right to refuse further enslavement by others; (3) the right to choose one's own employment, which was a mixed blessing at times because of the economic vulnerability of freed slaves; and (4) freedom of movement.[321] Many instances have been discovered of slaves being disadvantaged by their manumission, in some cases being thrown into abject poverty.[322]

Dale Martin's analysis of the social status of slaves throws light on the complexity of the Greco-Roman system. On the basis of surveying literary and inscriptional evidence, he concludes that many slaves enjoyed "a certain degree of social stability, and therefore power,"[323] despite their vulnerability to the power of their masters. While most slaves held menial positions, he discovered striking evidence of slaves holding "managerial and administrative positions" in Greece, Macedonia, and Asia Minor, where Paul's missionary activities were concentrated.[324] These "middle-level slaves" enjoyed a level of "independence, family life, financial abilities, and social power" that "belied their legal status as dispensable. They were by no means at the bottom end of the social pecking order," and insofar as they represented powerful owners, their status "would have appeared powerful, not weak."[325] Many of these slaves became

---

312 See William L. Westermann, *The Slave Systems of Greek and Roman Antiquity* (Philadelphia: American Philosophical Society, 1955) 102–17.
313 Ibid., 14.
314 Ibid., 104.
315 See Bartchy, *First-Century Slavery*, 63–67.
316 See Giuseppe Cambiano, "Aristotle and the Anonymous Opponents of Slavery," in M. I. Finley, ed., *Classical Slavery* (London: Cass, 1987) 39.
317 Zvi Yavetz, *Slaves and Slavery in Ancient Rome* (New Brunswick, NJ: Transaction Books, 1988) 117.
318 Ferguson, *Background*, 56.

319 See Bartchy, *First-Century Slavery*, 85–91.
320 Keith R. Bradley, *Slaves and Masters in the Roman Empire: A Study in Social Control*, REL (Brussels: Latomus, 1984) 81–112, esp. 96.
321 Ferguson, *Backgrounds*, 46.
322 Bradley, *Slaves and Masters*, 97–99.
323 Martin, *Slavery as Salvation*, 7.
324 Ibid., 14–15.
325 Ibid., 22.

upwardly mobile, "a recurring motif" within the popular novels and romances of the time, so that voluntary enslavement became appealing for some persons with no other prospects.[326] But upper-class persons held such mobility in contempt, reflecting the significant disparities in the culture between upper and lower levels of the population. "The terminology of slavery meant different things for different people because the social institution of slavery functioned differently for different people."[327]

These factors have to be taken into account in evaluating Paul's unusual discussions of slavery, rendering simplistic modern assessments implausible. Nevertheless, Orlando Patterson is correct in arguing that slaves were exempt from the public honor system of Greco-Roman culture.[328] No matter how successful a slave or former slave might become, the taint of slavery was never overcome.[329] Cicero refers to free people who are "just like slaves" in their lack of dignity and self-respect when they work with their hands (*Off.* 1.150). The hostility aroused by slaves and freedmen/women in the imperial bureaucracy related not to their efficiency but to the dishonor of reversing the role of slave and free.[330] As far as Roman law was concerned, any punishment for runaway slaves was legal, including even execution, which was characteristically done by crucifixion, to serve as a deterrent to others. The smoldering hostility between slaves and masters was a fixed reality in the culture, expressed in the popular proverb, "as many enemies as slaves."[331] Owners retained absolute power of life or death over their slaves, requiring their obedience by this final threat, which explains why the imperial bureaucracy consisted of "slaves of Caesar" who could be trusted to follow their regent's orders rather than being controlled by the competition for honor between noble families and their slaves.

Many slaves were considered barbarians when they derived from areas where either Greek or Latin was not spoken. They suffered a double disability in honor, neither of which could be fully overcome as far as Roman culture was concerned. Barbarians were considered subhuman and incapable of being civilized.[332] They were inherently violent and destructive, displaying the opposite of each of the Roman virtues.[333] It is significant that the ritualized battles in the theaters of the empire featured gladiators with barbaric costumes and weapons fighting with one another while Roman authorities decided which of them should die. Those exhibiting Roman virtues were allowed to live, while ferocious enemies of the empire were killed for the sake of peace. The empire of honor thus dominated the "circuses" that were an important strategy of maintaining the imperial system. Since Paul reverses the stereotype of "barbarians" in 1:14 and announces the plan to missionize in Spain (15:24, 28), a barbaric province par excellence, this prominent feature of the honor system is essential for understanding the letter.

E. The Housing Situation

A crucial element in understanding the situation of Christian congregations in Rome is the crowded urban environment. At the time of Paul's letter, most of the population in Rome lived in the upper levels of "multistory tenement houses" or in the rears of shops,[334] while the nobility and the wealthy citizens of Rome occupied lower floors of these buildings or in mansions in the better parts of the city.[335] Bruce Frier observes that the laws

---

326 Ibid., 35–42.

327 Ibid., 48–49.

328 Orlando Patterson, "Paul, Slavery and Freedom: Personal and Socio-Historical Reflections." *Semeia* 83/84 (1998) 263–79, summarizing findings in his study, *Slavery and Social Death: A Comparative Study* (Cambridge: Harvard Univ. Press, 1982).

329 See Harrill, *Slaves*, 36–52.

330 Bartchy, "Slavery (Greco-Roman)," 69.

331 Quoted from Seneca *Ep.* 47, by Peter Richardson, *Paul's Ethic of Freedom* (Philadelphia: Westminster, 1979) 47. See also Harrill, *Slaves*, 145–53.

332 Vogt, *Kulturwelt und Barbaren*, 6–12.

333 Dauge, *Barbare*, 472–544.

334 Jeffers, *Greco-Roman World*, 59; idem, "First-Century Rome," 131–33.

335 For general orientation see James E. Packer, *The Insulae of Imperial Ostia*, MAAR 31 (Rome: American Academy in Rome, 1971); A. G. McKay, *Houses, Villas and Palaces in the Roman World* (Ithaca: Cornell Univ. Press, 1975); John E. Stambaugh, *The Ancient Roman City*, ASH (Baltimore: Johns Hopkins Univ. Press, 1988); John R. Clarke, *The Houses of Roman Italy, 100 B.C.–A.D. 250: Ritual, Space, and Decoration* (Berkeley: Univ. of California Press, 1991).

regulating the lower-class housing in the upper floors of these tenement buildings, which "probably accommodated upwards of 90 percent of Rome's free population . . . was mostly of a criminal, administrative, or regulatory nature—intended above all to maintain the facade of public order."[336] The rights of privacy, of long-term tenure, of proper maintenance, and so forth that Frier discovered for upper-class apartment contracts in Rome were apparently irrelevant for tenement dwellers from the lower classes. Frier describes the "four- and five-story apartment blocks (*insulae*), constructed primarily in brick and concrete with vaults or wooden raftering" that was characteristic of Ostia and Rome.[337] The lower-class housing in Ostia is characterized by rooms of 100 to 115 square meters, divided by flimsy partitions into separate areas for each family. Frier explains:

> Because such partitions are easily swept away in the ruin of a building, their existence tends to be ignored by archeologists. Nonetheless, even the surviving walls confirm an impression of crowding and squalor: rows of rooms no longer easily distinguishable from one another in function, disposed along facades or lightwells, and often reached by long interior corridors. . . . The great majority of the free Ostian population, perhaps some 90-95 percent, occupied these dismal buildings.[338]

The luxury apartments had, in contrast, an

> astonishing modern look and "feel," especially in their standardized oblong apartment plan. . . . The plan consists of two large dayrooms . . . disposed at either end of a long axis running through a corridor-like central room. . . . All three rooms take light from large windows on the facade . . . on the inner side . . .

are a row of from two to five bedrooms . . . , which are directly lighted only on the rare occasions where the back wall is free to the air. . . . The apartment's entrance is almost without exception directly into, or through a vestibule-corridor. . . , which provides access to all the other rooms. . . . Their total floor area is normally 150-300 sq. m., thus very large.[339]

These buildings in Ostia analyzed by Frier were apparently patterned after those in Rome, so they provide models for the capital where too few buildings have remained to make a comprehensive view possible. In the case of Ostia, Frier estimates that the proportion of upper-class families living in such apartments as compared with private houses is about 3 to 1.[340] He describes the most completely surviving Roman *insula*, which has shops on the ground floor, with several large *cenacula* apartments above it. The upper floors, however, contain "a warren of tiny, squalid rooms, most of them not directly lighted and served by long interior corridors. Most rooms are very small (about 10 sq. m.), but it is still entirely probable that a small family could have occupied such humble quarters. The building obviously became more crowded and more lower-class in its upper stories."[341] It seems likely that house churches as normally conceived could not find space in the upper floors of such tenements when the rooms were that small. This kind of "vertical zoning" appears to have been typical, and the overall population density is estimated to be 300 per acre in the residential quarters of Rome, almost two-and-a-half times higher than modern Calcutta and three times higher than Manhattan Island.[342] The health conditions in these overcrowded buildings without toilet facilities or running water contributed to the plagues that periodically swept through Rome.[343]

The apartment buildings in Rome were owned by

---

336 Bruce W. Frier, *Landlords and Tenants in Imperial Rome* (Princeton: Princeton Univ. Press, 1980) xx.
337 Ibid., 3.
338 Ibid., 5.
339 Ibid., 5–6.
340 Ibid., 16.
341 Ibid., 15; see also Yavetz, "Living Conditions," 504, who reports in one instance that more than 16 persons "were huddled together in one flat." On 505 Yavetz concludes: "One thing is certain, namely,

that the inhabitants of the poorer quarters were crowded together in the upper storeys of the insulae, which were utterly unfitted for a normal and orderly family life." See also the description by Donald J. Watts and Carol Martin Watts, "A Roman Apartment Complex," *SAmer* 255.6 (December 1986) 132–39; and Kunst, "Wohnen," 4–12.
342 Stambaugh, *Ancient Roman City*, 337; Jewett, *Apostle to America*, 79; Stark, *Rise*, 149–50.
343 See Stark, *Rise*, 152–56.

investors and speculators willing to accept the high risks of loss through fire and deterioration in prospect of the high gains. There were two systems of renting housing. The first and most widespread method was to rent spaces within a building to individuals or families, often in the form of a lodging or rooming house run by a manager where servants or slaves fed tenants from a common kitchen.[344] The second method was to rent apartments, and this was done mainly for the upper-class luxury dwellings. Property was often managed through a middleman, and people frequently rented a portion of a building for subleasing it to tenants, along the lines of contemporary slum housing. The rental year was from July 1 to July 1. Middlemen paid in advance, usually in yearly installments, while apartment renters paid at the end of the period, usually every six months or a year. There was no quarterly or monthly rent system. These arrangements fit only upper-class housing, however. Frier assumes that the poor paid rent on a shorter term basis, but it is characteristic of the lack of legal protection that there is no evidence of such arrangements in the courts. One gains the impression that brutal rent collectors dealt with slum tenants directly and that the latter had no recourse but to pay or leave.

Young aristocrats, wealthy freedmen/women, and long-term visitors to Rome tended to rent the upper-class apartments, and Frier suggests that it was probably in such an apartment that Paul may have dwelled during his two-year stay in Rome: "his rent was presumably paid by the wealthy Christians at Rome, such as the traveling military provisioner Aquila and his wife Priscilla."[345]

However, since four of the five groups that Paul knows about in Rome consisted of slaves and former slaves residing in areas where *insula* buildings were most numerous, there is an urgent need to consider where such groups could have met, a theme taken up in the next section and pursued throughout the commentary.

F. The Situation of the Jewish Community

The large Jewish community in Rome had played a major role in the formation of the Christian congregations prior to the time of Paul's letter.[346] Jewish families that had arrived as part of the Diaspora[347] were augmented by Pompey, who brought large numbers of Jewish slaves from Jerusalem, which was captured in 63 B.C.E.[348] Most of them became Roman citizens upon their emancipation, and the community as whole numbered between 15,000 and 60,000 in the late 50s when Paul wrote.[349] They were concentrated especially in the Trastevere district of the city, according to Philo, *Legat.* 155-56, who reports: "He [Augustus] was aware that the great section of Rome on the other side of the Tiber was occupied and inhabited by Jews. . . . He knew therefore that they have houses of prayer and meet together in them, particularly on the sacred sabbaths when they receive training in their ancestral philosophy." Other literary sources indicate that the area around the Porta Capena was a popular gathering spot for Jews.[350] Judging from the grave inscriptions found in the Jewish catacombs as well as from references in non-Jewish sources, most members of the community were relatively uneducated and impoverished.[351] Most of the epitaphs (7 per-

344 Frier, *Landlords and Tenants,* 28.

345 Ibid., 43.

346 For an overview see Smallwood, *Jews,* 201–16; Leon, *Jews,* 1–45; Leonard V. Rutgers, *The Jews in Late Ancient Rome. Evidence of Cultural Interaction in the Roman Diaspora,* RGRW 126 (Leiden: Brill, 1995); Lichtenberger, "Jews and Christians in Rome," 2142–76; Nanos, *Mystery,* 41–75; Penna, *Paul the Apostle,* 19–47.

347 See Solin, "Juden und Syrer," 686.

348 Schürer, *History,* 3:75; Williams, "Identity of the Jewish Community," 34–35.

349 See the references to this enslavement in *Pss. Sol.* 2.6; 17.13-14; Philo *Legat.* 23; Josephus *Ant.* 14.77–79. Lampe, *Paul to Valentinus,* 84, refers to these estimates of the size of the Jewish community.

350 Lichtenberger, "Jews and Christians in Rome," 2157–59, refers to Juvenal, *Sat.* 3.10–18.

351 See Leon, *Jews,* 122–34; on 235 Leon notes that the various references to Jewish poverty "are to some extent borne out by the evidence of their graves . . . thousands of these are plain loculi, many of them marked, it seems, by no epitaph at all, others by a brief notice, crudely scrawled with paint or even just scratched on the stuccoed closures, or unskillfully carved with ill-shaped letters and in faulty grammar on pieces of discarded marble. The language of the inscriptions . . . points to a generally low degree of literacy."

cent) are in Greek and those in Latin commence after the third century C.E., which indicates that the Jewish community remained largely Greek speaking until well after the time of Paul's letter.[352] There are very few Hebrew inscriptions or epitaphs. Leonard Rutgers has analyzed these inscriptions in comparison with non-Jewish funerary inscriptions, showing close parallels that indicate a substantial degree of inculturation. Jewish families "chose names that were popular in contemporary non-Jewish society at large."[353]

Despite a fairly high level of "Judeophobia" in Rome,[354] the rights of the Jewish community were repeatedly recognized by the government. Cicero confirmed that there was "*de facto* recognition" of the Jewish right to collect from Jewish settlements all over the Roman Empire that allowed the collection of a yearly contribution to the temple in Jerusalem.[355] Julius Caesar granted the right of Jewish communities to follow their own laws, which was confirmed by the Senate in 44 B.C.E. and later by Augustus and Claudius.[356] The "right to live according to Jewish Laws and Customs" included permission to have meetings for worship and meals together, to organize a communal life, the right not to give bonds on the Sabbath, to have kosher markets, and to send funds to the Jerusalem temple.[357] A peculiar feature of Judaism in Rome was the habit of fasting on the Sabbath, which may reflect mourning over the fall of Jerusalem to Pompey in 63 B.C.E.[358]

As elsewhere in the Greco-Roman world prior to the destruction of the temple in Jerusalem, the Roman synagogues were primarily didactic in their function, and although there may have been occasional prayers, their function was not that of worship.[359] The synagogues apparently had the right to punish congregational members, reflected in Paul's earlier persecution of Christians prior to his conversion as well as his being punished five times in Diaspora synagogues with the traditional 39 stripes (2 Cor 11:24).

Evidence about synagogue life and organization comes in large part from the Jewish catacombs that have been found in Rome.[360] These underground cemeteries were mined out of the soft tufa clay and contain thousands of graves of members of particular synagogues. Until recently, the most critical assessment was that the Jewish catacombs originated in the second or third century and thus throw uncertain light on the rise of early Christianity and the construction of the similar Christian catacombs.[361] In 2002 one of the most important discoveries in recent biblical research was announced by Leonard Rutgers and his colleagues at the University of Utrecht, namely that carbon 14 dating techniques prove that the Jewish catacomb in the Villa Torlonia was started in the period from 50 B.C.E. to 50 C.E., and thus was in existence at the time of Paul's letter.[362] Since the catacombs appear to be related to specific synagogues to provide burial spaces for their members, this discovery

352   See Rutgers, *Jews in Late Ancient Rome*, 210–59; idem, *Hidden Heritage*, 73–96.

353   Rutgers, *Jews in Late Ancient Rome*, 161.

354   Schäfer, *Judeophobia*, 180–95, which details the hostility against Jewish separatism, the critique of the Sabbath as a sign of laziness, and horror about circumcision. He concludes (192–93): "The Romans disliked the Jews *because* they were afraid of them, and they were afraid of them because of their growing appeal to Roman society." Lichtenberger, *Ich Adams*, 7, cites Augustine's report in *Civ.* 6.11 of the situation during Nero's reign, that the Christians had a virulent hatred toward the Jews (*Christianos tamen iam tunc Iudaeis inimicissnos*).

355   Zeev, *Jewish Rights*, 411.

356   Ibid., 412–24.

357   Zeev, *Jewish Rights*, 430; Cineira, *Religionspolitik*, 161–70.

358   Williams, "Identity of the Jewish Community," 36;

fasting on the Sabbath is described by Suetonius, *Aug*, 76.2.

359   See Wick, *Gottesdienste*, 100.

360   For orientation see Leon, *Jews*, 46–66; Rutgers, *Hidden Heritage*, 45–72; A. Konikoff, *Sarcophagi from the Jewish Catacombs of Ancient Rome: A Catalogue Raisonné* (Stuttgart: Steiner, 1990); L. Hertling and E. Kirschbaum, *La catacombe Romane e i loro martiri* (Rome: Editrice Pontificia Universita Gregoriana, 1996); Jeffers, *Conflict at Rome*, 38–40. A convenient listing of publications related to each catecomb is provided by Solin, "Juden und Syrer," 655–58.

361   See the critical assessment of Rutgers, *Hidden Heritage*, 45–96, concluding on p. 70 that the earliest evidence comes from the "late second or early third century C.E."

362   Leonard V. Rutgers, Arie F. M. De Yong, and Klaas van der Borg, "Radiocarbon Dates from the Jewish Catacombs of Rome," *Radiocarbon* 44 (2002) 541–47.

makes inferences concerning their membership and social organization relevant for Paul's letter and it throws further light on the conflicts between traditionalists and messianic advocates as also involving burial rights. Although the carbon 14 tests have not yet been performed in the Christian catacombs, it is likely that they also originated in an earlier period than could previously be demonstrated, a period when members of early congregations were refused the right to bury in the Jewish catacombs where earlier members of their families had been interred.

Although there may have been others, there is solid evidence of at least eleven synagogues in Rome; the word συναγωγή may refer to congregations rather than buildings. In some instances on the basis of grave inscriptions, the names and districts associated with these congregations can be identified.[363] The Synagogue of the Agrippesians was probably located in Trastevere and was named either after the Agrippa who was Augustus's son-in-law or one of the two Jewish kings with this name. The Synagogue of the Augustesians, probably named after the emperor Augustus, who was perceived to be a patron, was also located in Trastevere.[364] Although the age of some other synagogues remains uncertain, those of the Agrippesians and Augustesians were certainly in existence in the first century C.E.[365] The Synagogue of the Calcaresians was probably located in Trastevere, although its name has not be satisfactorily clarified. The Synagogue of the Campesians was probably located somewhere in the Campus Martius, where Agrippa erected his most impressive buildings. The Synagogue of Elaea may have been located in a southeastern district of Rome because of the inscription found in the catacomb off the Via Appia, and it remains possible that the name refers to the olive tree, which would be relevant for Paul's argument in 11:17-24. The Synagogue of the Hebrews was probably the earliest to have been organized in Rome,[366] and it was associated with the Monte Verde catacomb, to the south of Trastevere, which suggests that the synagogue could well have been located in Trastevere itself. That there was a Synagogue of the Secenians is suggested by an inscription from the Nomentana catacomb but no satisfactory explanation of the name has been suggested. The Synagogue of the Siburesians probably derived its name from Subura, the dense district "populated by laborers and small shopkeepers"[367] that lies to the east of the Roman forum. The Synagogue of the Tripolitans was located in Trastevere and took its name either from the Tripoli in Phoenicia or the one in North Africa, both of which had Jewish communities from which this group could have emigrated. The Synagogue of the Vernaclesians was also located in Trastevere and derived its name from the Latin term *verna*, meaning native or indigenous. This implies either a membership of native-born persons converted to Judaism, or to an early group of Jewish emigrants who wished to distinguish themselves as having been born in Rome. The Synagogue of the Volumnesians was probably also located in Trastevere and was associated with the Latin name, Volumnius. There is some likelihood that this was the Volumnias who served as the tribune of Syria from 9 to 7 B.C.E. and who had supported Jewish interests.[368] The inscription referring to a Synagogue of Rhodians/Herodian is fragmentary and until recently there was no certainty either about its name or location.[369] It now appears likely that this synagogue was dedicated to Herod the Great.[370] The debate over the possibility of a Synagogue of Severus, of Arca, or of the Calabrians remains inconclusive.[371]

There were probably proselytes, God-fearers, and

363 For the following see Leon, *Jews,* 140–66; Rutgers, *Hidden Heritage,* 45–95; Peter Richardson, "Augustan-Era Synagogues in Rome," in K. P. Donfried and P. Richardson, eds., *Judaism and Christianity in First-Century Rome* (Grand Rapids: Eerdmans, 1998) 19–29.

364 Richardson, "Synagogues in Rome," 22.

365 See Lichtenberger, "Jews and Christians in Rome," 2160; Richardson, "Synagogues in Rome," 20–21.

366 Leon, *Jews,* 149; Lichtenberger, "Jews and Christians in Rome," 2160; Richardson, "Synagogues in Rome," 20.

367 Leon, *Jews,* 152.

368 Richardson, "Synagogues in Rome," 22–23.

369 See the account of the debate in Leon, *Jews,* 159–62.

370 Lampe, *Paul to Valentinus,* 178, accepts the completion of the inscription as "Herodians" and observes that there must have been other Herodian slaves brought to Rome who belonged to this group. The analysis of the inscription by Richardson, "Synagogues in Rome," 23–27, makes a dedication to Herod the Great very likely.

371 Leon, *Jews,* 162–65.

sympathizers in some of these synagogues,[372] and there is explicit evidence in Rome of conversions to Judaism.[373] An assessment of the appeal of these synagogues is provided by Seneca, the philosopher who served as a chief administrator in the period when Paul's letter was written: "The customs of the Jews, this accursed race, have gained such influence that they are accepted everywhere in the world. The Jews know about the origin and meaning of their rituals. But the largest part of the population take part in a ritual in which they don't know what they are doing."[374]

There is also solid evidence that conflicts within these synagogues had repeatedly come to the attention of the Roman authorities, in 41 and 49 C.E., as discussed above in section 3. Another piece of evidence suggests that the controversy in 41 was as related to Christian agitation as the event in 49 that led to the expulsion of Jewish and Jewish Christian leaders. Martin Hengel, followed by Herman Lichtenberger, draws an inference from Augustine's remark in *Ep.* 102.8 that the "Law of the Jews" arrived in Rome from Syria either during or shortly after Caligula's reign (37–41 C.E.), namely that this pertained to what was perceived to be a form of Judaism brought into the synagogues from the east.[375] The information that Augustine says came from Porphyrius's tract against the Christians is as follows: "longo post tempore lex Judaeorum apparuit ac viguit augusta Syriae regione, postea vero prorepsit etiam in fines Italos, sed post Caesarem Gajum aut certe ipso imperante." ("It was after a long time that the Jewish law appeared and flourished within the region of Syria, and after that, it gradually moved toward the coasts of Italy; but this was not earlier than the end of the reign of Caesar Gaius, or at the earliest, while he ruled.") Since Augustine had earlier contrasted the *lex Judaica vetus* with the *lex nova* of Christianity, and in view of the unlikelihood that Porphyrius believed that Judaism itself first arrived in Rome at this late date, he probably refers to a particular Jewish teaching derived from Syria, which was the area from which the first organized Christian mission movement is reported in Acts 13–14.

G. Implications for the Background of Paul's Letter

There is no evidence of a central organization of these synagogues in Rome similar to that in Alexandria; each synagogue apparently elected its own leaders and conducted its affairs without regard to other groups.[376] This absence of a central organization plays a key role in Wolfgang Wiefel's definitive reconstruction of the situation, because it enabled Christian evangelists to penetrate individual synagogues and made it impossible for Roman authorities to deal with disturbances arising therefrom by appealing to the Jewish community as a whole.[377] As shown in section 3 above, this resulted in the closing of synagogues in 41 and in the banning of Jewish and Christian agitators from Rome in 49, which had a dramatic effect on the shape of Christianity in Rome and the situation addressed by Paul's letter.

The earliest congregations in Rome developed in the context of synagogues; this situation correlates with the generalization made by Brown and Meier that the earliest form of Christianity in Rome consisted of "Christians who kept up some Jewish observances and remained faithful to part of the heritage of the Jewish law and cult."[378] If the closing of the synagogues in 41 related to conflicts over Christian agitation, which remains the most plausible explanation, then the origins of these messianic circles in the Roman synagogues originated in the 30s.[379] In the immediate aftermath of closing the synagogues in 41, some developments of church groups

---

372 Lichtenberger, "Jews and Christians in Rome," 2162; see the clarification of these terms in Bernd Wander, *Gottesfürchtige und Sympathisanten. Studien zum heidnischen Umfeld von Diasporasynagogen,* WUNT 104 (Tübingen: Mohr-Siebeck, 1998) 228–34.

373 See Rutgers, *Hidden Heritage,* 206–9.

374 Cited by Wander, *Gottesfürchtige,* 35 from Seneca, *De Superstitione,* found in Augustine, *Civ.* 6.11.

375 Hengel, *Geschichtsschreibung,* 91; Lichtenberger, *Ich Adams,* 5; idem, "Jews and Christians in Rome," 2161. The inference derives from Zahn, 8–9.

376 Leon, *Jews,* 167–94.

377 Wiefel, "Roman Christianity," 95–101; see also Brown and Meier, *Antioch and Rome,* 101.

378 Brown and Meier, *Antioch and Rome,* 104; see also Hultgren, *Gospel,* 149; Lampe, *Paul to Valentinus,* 9.

379 Fitzmyer, 29.

meeting outside synagogues probably evolved quickly. There is evidence of this in the case of Prisca (Priscilla) and Aquila whom Paul met in Ephesus after their banning in 49, because their establishment of a local house church probably followed a pattern they had followed in Rome.

With the banning of Jewish and Jewish Christian leaders in 49,[380] a dramatic development of house and tenement churches ensued. This explains why the majority of converts were Gentiles by the time of Paul's letter, less than a decade after these events. It explains how Paul could have become acquainted with so many Roman church leaders mentioned in chap. 16, and also why he urges that they be greeted and welcomed by all of the Roman congregations. After the Edict of Claudius was no longer enforced following the emperor's death in 54, the banned leaders apparently began moving back to Rome, but they soon found that they were no longer welcome as leaders in the congregations that had found new meeting places after 49. The conflicts between the "weak" and the "strong" in 14:1–15:7 are understandable as a result of these developments. Like all other conclusions drawn in this section, these conjectures are subject to refutation, despite the fact that they are supported by many researchers. In the case of this commentary, however, these conjectures provide the framework for interpreting the entire letter.

6. The History and Orientation of the Christian Communities in Rome

As we have seen, interpreting the rhetoric and argument of a letter requires a grasp of the "first audience" to which it is directed.[381] The author's understanding of the audience is an aspect of the "rhetorical situation," and since the modern interpreter is so much farther from that audience than is the author, the reconstruction of its situation needs to be augmented with relevant historical details. Information from sources beyond the letter must be correlated with evidence within the letter itself. In the case of Romans, we must exercise due care to respect the fact that the letter is not addressed to a congregation founded by Paul, and is not in the same genre as other Pauline letters that deal directly with congregational problems in an authoritative manner. Demonstrative rhetoric is as closely related to audience circumstances as deliberative or judicial rhetoric. However, we must draw inferences in a way that is consistent with the demonstrative genre, which deals with situations in abstracted, general terms. As we shall see, the evidence from both the rhetorical situation and the historical situation indicate a complicated variety of congregations in Rome. As shown in the previous section, there is an inevitable measure of circularity in reconstructing the history and orientation of these groups of believers, because evidence from the letter is used to draw a model of the audience, in relation to which the rhetoric of the letter is interpreted. I follow Thomas Carney in preferring homomorphic and descriptive models rather than isomorphic or normative ones.[382] The latter tend to claim too much in objectivity and to disregard the circularity inherent in all historical reconstructions, whose weaknesses can be dealt with only by transparency and a willingness to have the results examined by further tests against the rhetorical, historical, and cultural evidence. In the case of this commentary, the adequacy of the following model of the situation of the Christian communities in Rome can also be tested by its ability to explain the details of Paul's argumentation.

A. The History of Christianity in Rome

As noted in section 3 above, there is a likely allusion in the Roman historian Suetonius to the early development of Christianity in Rome. In his biography of Claudius, Suetonius reports that the emperor "expelled from Rome Jews who were constantly making disturbances at

---

380 See Solin, "Juden und Syrer," 690.

381 Krentz, *Method*, 39; on the methodological issue of developing models of historical groups, see Fischer, *Historians' Fallacies*, 216–42.

382 In *The Shape of the Past: Models and Antiquity* (Lawrence: Coronado Press, 1975) 10, Thomas F. Carney defines a "homomorphic model" as having "only the gross similarities, and not all of the detail of the thing modelled," whereas "isomorphic models" are perfect replicas or scale models. On p. 11 Carney defines "descriptive models" as providing "organizational frameworks for systematically gathering information about large and nebulous topics," in contrast to normative or static models. See the use of these categories in Jewett, *Thessalonian Correspondence*, 135–78.

the instigation of Chrestus" (*Iudaeos impulsore Chresto assidue tumultuantis Roma expulit*). Suetonius apparently believed that the disturbances were caused by a rabble-rouser named "Chrestus," a common slave name[383] that could easily be confused with "Christus" because of the tendency in Koine Greek to pronounce various vowels as *i*.[384] H. Dixon Slingerland argues that Chrestus was a Roman advisor who "caused Claudius to expel from Rome the continuously rebelling Jews,"[385] a highly unlikely translation of Suetonious in view of the absence of any other evidence of an official by this name in the Claudian period. It is also improbable that Chrestus was a Jewish zealot resident in Rome,[386] because it is unlikely that a single agitator could have evoked such massive Roman reaction, and moreover the name Chrestus does not appear among the hundreds of Jewish funerary inscriptions that have been assembled by Harry Leon.[387] Most historians infer that this is a reference to agitation in Roman synagogues concerning Jesus as the Christ,[388] and that the resultant exile should be correlated with the detail in Acts 18:2 concerning the expulsion of Priscilla and Aquila from Rome around 49 C.E.

While some scholars follow the detail in Acts that "all the Jews" were expelled, there is no necessity to read the Suetonius passage in this way, and it seems more likely that those responsible for the disturbance were expelled.[389] As we have seen, a similar episode occurred in 41 resulting in a prohibition of Jewish meetings that would have entailed closing the synagogues for a time. As noted in section 5 above, the detail from Augustine regarding the Jewish law coming to Rome from Syria either during or shortly after Caligula's reign sustains this impression. The history of the Christian movement prior to the 40s is shrouded in mystery. That there were Christians in Rome in the period prior to this is sug-gested by the reference in Acts 2:11 to "Jews and prose-lytes" from Rome being present in Jerusalem on the Day of Pentecost, but current scholarship on Acts views this Pentecost report as a later summary indicating how Christianity spread through the known world.[390] The penetration of Christianity via the "trade route" sketched by Lampe is based on the reference in Acts 28:13-14 to Paul encountering believers in the port of Puteoli,[391] but the history of Christianity in this city to the early 60s when Paul arrived as a prisoner is unknown. In a recent article, Lampe suggests that Jewish slaves and freedmen/women attached to Roman house-holds brought Christianity to Rome.[392] He shows that Valerius Biton, mentioned in *1 Clem.* 63.3 and 65.1 as a bearer of the letter from Rome to Corinth, was an old man who had been a believer since his childhood in the 30s or 40s; this can be correlated with grave inscriptions and other references to Jewish slaves of the Valerius gens. Although the evidence is unavailable to piece these details together in order to produce a coherent historical account, it is clear that Christianity had penetrated Rome from a variety of sources in the decades prior to the writing of Paul's letter. The sheer scale of Christian-ity in Rome along with the indications of diversity make a variety of avenues most likely.

Paul greets a large number of persons in Rom 16 whom he had met in previous missionary activities in the eastern half of the Mediterranean world. They are now back in Rome, which correlates with what we know about the Claudius Edict. The book of Acts indicates that Prisca and Aquila, whom Paul greets in Rom 16:3-5, were refugees forced out of Rome whom Paul met in Corinth when he arrived there in the winter of C.E. 50. Other likely refugees mentioned in chap. 16 are Epaine-tos, Miriam, Andronikos and Junia, Ampliatus, Urbanus,

---

383 For example, *CIL* 6:10233; 6390, 6402, 10046, 14756, 15757; *P.Grenf.1*. Nr. 49.11.

384 See Fitzmyer, 31; Cranfield, 1:16, notes that the confusion between "Christus" and "Chrestus" is also visible in Tertullian *Apol.*, 3 and Justin *1 Apol.* 4. Incigneri, *Gospel to the Romans*, 211, adds the refer-ence to Lactantius *Inst.* 4.7.5, who complains that opponents misspell Jesus' name in this way.

385 Slingerland, *Claudian Policymaking*, 228.

386 Benko, "Edict," 412–15.

387 Slingerland, *Claudian Policymaking*, 179–201.

388 Momigliano, *Claudius*, 33; Smallwood, *Jews*, 211–16; Benko, "Edict," 406–18; Wiefel, "Roman Christian-ity," 93; Levinskaya, *Diaspora Setting*, 181; Cineira, *Religionspolitik*, 204–5.

389 Lampe, *Paul to Valentinus*, 13–14; Dunn, 1:xlix; Cineira, *Religionspolitik*, 207.

390 See Brown and Meier, *Antioch and Rome*, 104.

391 Lampe, *Paul to Valentinus*, 7–10.

392 Lampe, "Paths," 143–48.

Incigneri, *Gospel to the Romans*, 211, notes the dis-parity in connection with Leon, *Jews*, 25.

Stachys, Apelles, Herodion, Tryphaina, Tryphosa, Persis, and Rufus and his mother. The most probable explanation for Paul's acquaintance with these early Christian leaders is that they met while in exile. Paul knows that they have returned to the capital of the empire during the peaceful, early years of the Nero administration[393] before he writes in the winter of 56–57 C.E. from Corinth.

The seemingly random greetings to this long list of Christians in Rome allow several inferences about their past and present relationships. As suggested by Wolfgang Wiefel,[394] it is appropriate to infer that the Christian groups originating inside the various Jewish synagogues in Rome had been deprived of their Jewish Christian leaders by Claudius's deportation order in 49 C.E. and that they continued as house congregations with Gentile leaders for the next five years. Four of the Christian groups mentioned in Romans 16 fit this generalization: the members of the households of Aristoboulus and Narkissos mentioned in 16:10 and 11, the "brothers" under the leadership listed in v. 14, and the "saints" led by the persons mentioned in v. 15. It is clear from the lack of personal references that Paul is not directly acquainted with the leaders of these four Christian groups. A fifth group, the only one named a "church," is identified with the household of Prisca and Aquila, which could not have been reestablished before their return sometime after 54 C.E. This may provide a significant clue as to why the word "church" was not mentioned in the address of Romans: Paul probably wanted to avoid the impression that he favored the Prisca and Aquila group that alone named itself with the word *ekklēsia*.[395]

Additional inferences can be drawn from the peculiar fact that twelve or thirteen of the persons whom Paul had likely met as Jewish refugees, or known through family and career connections, do not appear to be attached to any of the five groupings Paul identifies in Rome. These persons are also not grouped with one another in ways that indicate they formed leaders of groups in Rome. These former residents in Rome are apparently now being treated as interlopers by the congregations in Rome, a situation that correlates with the argument about Gentile Christians accepting Jewish Christians in Romans 14–15. Lampe connects this evidence with the later history of Christianity in Rome and concludes that separate and competitive development marks the churches there.[396] Sectarian splintering seems to have been characteristic of the recipients of Paul's letter.

B. The Size of the Christian Communities in Rome

The impression one gains from commentaries and specialized studies on Christianity in Rome is of a tiny movement at the time of Paul's letter. For example, Lampe concludes that there were "at least seven separate islands of Christianity,"[397] which would represent a total of only around two hundred believers. Rodney Stark estimates that the entire empire had only fourteen hundred Christians in the year 50,[398] of which Rome could surely have no more than several hundred. This impression cannot easily be correlated with the evidence from nonbiblical sources. Tacitus reports (*Ann.* 15.44.4) that Nero made the Christians into "scapegoats" after the great fire in July 64, and "had self-acknowledged members of this sect arrested.[399] Then, on their information, a tremendous crowd (*multitudo ingens*) were condemned."[400] This implies a "huge crowd"[401] or "tremendous crowd,"[402] which echoes πολὺ πλῆθος ἐκλεκτῶν ("great multitude of elect") in *1 Clem* 6:1.[403] In

393 See Griffin, *Nero*, 50–82.
394 Wiefel, "Roman Christianity," 95–101.
395 In "Pauline House Churches," 27–46, David Balch overlooks these details and does not include reference to Lampe's work in concluding that early congregations were exclusively "house churches."
396 Lampe, *Paul to Valentinus*, 359–412.
397 Ibid., 359. See also Mullins, *Rome*, 104–5.
398 Stark, *Rise*, 7.
399 Griffin, *Nero*, 132–33.
400 Incigneri, *Gospel to the Romans*, 219, observes that Tacitus also uses *ingens multiltudo* in *Ann.* 14.8 to describe the onlookers applauding Agrippina's escape from a sinking ship and concludes with regard to the persecution in 64, Tacitus's description "suggests that he had quite a large crowd in mind."
401 Halton, "Church," 253; see also J. Beaujeu, "L'Incendie de Rome en 64 et les Chrétiens," *Latomus* 19 (1960) 65–80, 291–311.
402 Lampe, *Paul to Valentinus*, 82.
403 A rejection of "exaggeration" in these references is present in Brown and Meier, *Antioch and Rome*, 99; and Lampe, *Paul to Valentinus*, 82.

view of the fact that Nero had the alleged arsonists wrapped in animal skins and used as torches in his gardens, a punishment that would have been illegal if they had been citizens, a status that most Jewish Christians would have possessed,[404] most of these victims were probably Gentile believers. Many Jewish Christians must have survived the persecution. At a minimum, the references in Tacitus and *1 Clement* indicate that several hundred victims must have been involved,[405] and since the Christian movement continued to increase in size after this event, many believers must have escaped. Yet, on the basis of the prevailing estimates of the size of Christianity in Rome, the movement should have been wiped out by Nero. It is also difficult to imagine that Nero would have felt it was feasible to scapegoat a movement so tiny that it could hardly be noticed in a city the size of Rome; the movement must have been sufficiently large to have become unpopular with a significant portion of the population to make scapegoating worthwhile.[406]

The reports by Tacitus and Suetonius about the events of 41 and 49 cannot be coordinated with a Christian movement that must have been much smaller in the 40s than in the 60s. If Stark is right that there were only a thousand Christians in the entire empire by the year 40, how could a tiny fraction of that number evoke official attention and sanctions twice in a decade? Finally, the large number of leaders and evangelists greeted in chap. 16 indicate more congregations than the usual estimate of five to seven. To think that Miriam, Andronikos and Junia, Ampliatus, Urbanus, Stacys, Apelles, Herodion, Tryphaina and Tryphosa, Persis, and Rufus and his mother all belong to one or two congregations would be totally uncharacteristic of churches elsewhere, which are referred to by the names of their leaders or patrons. On this premise, these names reflect

eight to ten separate congregations either in the past or at the time of Paul's letter.

These details point to a movement that had grown to several thousand adherents by the summer of 64 C.E.[407] With membership in early congregations ordinarily estimated between twenty and forty persons, there would have been dozens of groups at the time that Paul wrote his letter some seven years before the fateful fire, although he is able to identify only five of them. The later history of Christianity in Rome, involving many leaders whose activities can be traced by historical sources, indicates a large movement with substantial cultural and theological "fractionation" that prevented the development of a monarchical episcopacy until the latter part of the second century.[408] This variety in organization, orientation, and location was already present at the time of Paul's letter, and this explains many of its features.

C. The Location of Congregations in Rome

A significant breakthrough was achieved by Lampe's study of Christians at Rome, which first appeared in 1987.[409] Using a topographic method based on the coincidence between five different types of archeological and literary evidence, Lampe showed that two of the most likely areas for early Christian congregations were in Trastevere and the section on the Appian Way around the Porta Capena inhabited by the immigrants. Both Trastevere and the district around the Porta Capena were swampy areas where the poorest population of Rome lived. Lampe's vivid description follows:

Trastevere was a harbor quarter, a workers quarter. It accommodated harbor workers, who unloaded the ships' cargoes, porters of the many warehouses,

---

404 See Lampe, *Paul to Valentinus*, 82–84.
405 Jeffers, *Conflict at Rome*, 17: "Hundreds of Roman Christians, perhaps several thousand, lost their lives in this persecution."
406 Ibid. describes why the Christians had become unpopular because of their rejection of the Roman gods and their expectation of "the imminent destruction of the world by fire."
407 This correlates in a plausible fashion with the estimate of 7,000 Christians in Rome around the year 200, reported in Stark, *Rise*, 9, from Robert M.

Grant, *Early Christianity and Society: Seven Studies* (San Francisco: Harper & Row, 1977) 6.
408 See Lampe, *Paul to Valentinus*, 397–408; Osiek, "Romans," 149–59.
409 Peter Lampe, *Die stadtrömischen Christen in den ersten beiden Jahrhunderten: Studien zur Sozialgeschichte*, WUNT 18 (Tübingen: Mohr-Siebeck, 1987; 2d ed. 1989); English translation: *From Paul to Valentinus* (2003).

sailors, and also workers from the brickyards . . . . Storekeepers and small craftsmen were drawn by the harbor and its imported goods—ivory workers, cabinet makers, and potters. Millers from Trastevere ground the imported grains unloaded in the harbor . . . . Knacker and tanner operation spread a penetrating odor.[410]

Lampe found Roman population statistics that indicate Trastevere was the most densely populated section of the city with the highest proportion of apartment buildings (*insulae*).[411] He investigated the number of bakeries and found that Trastevere had the lowest number per square kilometer of any section of Rome, indicating very low socioeconomic conditions.[412] Trastevere was full of immigrants out of the east and was the site of mystery religion shrines and temples as well as the major center of the Jewish population. This section, which lay across the Tiber from the rest of Rome, was left untouched by the Roman fire, which may account in part for the later scapegoating of Christians by Nero.

The area around the Porta Capena was a damp valley with heavy traffic into the city. Lampe provides this description, beginning with Martial's quip that the Jewish beggars there were pressured by their mothers "to go begging" (12.57): "The Christians of the quarter could hardly have lifted themselves much above that social level; the quarter was populated by traders, craftsmen, and transport workers . . . . Hauling with carts was night work in Rome . . . . Just how low the social standing of transport workers, muleteers, and porters was is shown in the fact that almost no grave inscription . . . mentions their professions."[413] Lampe summarizes his finding: "The lowest social strata lived in the two regions, Trastevere and Via Appia/Porta Capena, so that it is not difficult to infer the social status of the Christians who dwelled there."[414]

Corresponding to the description of these slum districts where the bulk of the early Christians lived is Lampe's analysis of the social background of the names of persons greeted in chap. 16. Two-thirds of the names indicate Greek rather than Latin background, and hence confirm the immigrant status. After a careful and rather conservative estimate, he also concludes that of the 13 persons about whom something definite can be said, at least 9 point with great certainty to slave origins.[415] Here, as elsewhere in the early church, the bulk of the members consisted of slaves and former slaves, with the rest coming largely from lower-class handworkers.

Two other districts in Rome show evidence of early Christian population: Marsfield and the Aventine. Both districts reflect a potentially higher social status than Trastevere and Porta Capena. The area underneath the St. Prisca church in the Aventine has been excavated, revealing large patrician homes that date from the time Paul wrote Romans. One of them was later the residence of a wealthy friend of the emperor, Licinius Sura.[416] The Aventine area has aristocratic housing on the hills and poorer residents in the valleys. As Lampe observes, "The address list of the Aventine reads like a 'Who's Who in the Empire.'"[417] This is probably the area where the church of Prisca and Aquila was located; one of the buildings found under the St. Prisca church had been turned into a Mithraeum,[418] which may indicate that her house had been confiscated and put to non-Christian use. Whatever the precise fate of individual congregations, which probably waxed and waned over time, Lampe's discovery of the main districts where Christians were located is tremendously relevant for the interpretation of Romans. It helps explain why four of the five groups known to Paul according to chap. 16 lack patrons, and thus it requires a revision of the prevailing concept of house churches, because most of the population in these districts lived in crowded *insula* buildings.[419]

---

410 Lampe, *Paul to Valentinus*, 50.
411 Ibid., 51–52.
412 Ibid., 54.
413 Ibid., 56.
414 Ibid., 65.
415 Ibid., 182–83.
416 Ibid., 59.

417 Ibid.
418 Ibid., 63; see also M. J. Vermaseren and C. C. van Essen, *The Excavations in the Mithraeum of the Church of Santa Prisca in Rome* (Leiden: Brill, 1965).
419 See Kunst, "Wohnen," 4–19.

D. The Social Structure of House and Tenement Churches in Rome

One of the standard studies of house congregations and house churches by Hans-Josef Klauck opens with a citation from Heinz Schürmann, "The living space of the congregation is the house."[420] Another study rests on the same premise: "the earliest Christians met in private homes."[421] These studies investigate the references to houses as the meeting places of early Christian congregations and usually assume a freestanding building owned by the patron or patroness of a house church.[422] Although the term οἶκος can refer to a Roman atrium, a Greek peristyle house, a Hellenistic style of courtyard with adjoining rooms, or even an apartment building with shops on the ground floor,[423] the standard conclusion is: "Private houses were the first centers of church life."[424] Klauck remains more open than most scholars on this question, concluding that congregations of 10-40 members could function in any of the four options, but he does not entertain the possibility that a different structure of leadership and a different style of community life might result from meeting in a space not provided by a patron. Jerome Murphy-O'Connor's earlier calculation of the maximum size of 30-40 for a house church congregation rested on the premise of a freestanding villa.[425] His later work considers the possibility that the shop space on the ground floor of a tenement building might be used for a "house church" such as Prisca and Aquila sponsored in Corinth, Ephesus, and Rome; it might accommodate a group of 10-20 believers.[426] A number of earlier experts suggested the likelihood that even if Prisca and Aquila's church met in their private apartment, it was probably in a tenement building.[427]

Some details in the NT point indisputably in the direction of house churches presided over by patrons and patronesses, including references to "the church in the house" of particular patrons.[428] The model of a

420 Klauck, *Hausgemeinde*, 11; citation from Schürmann, "Gemeinde," 68.

421 Branick, *House Church*, 13.

422 See Floyd V. Filson, "The Significance of Early House Churches," *JBL* 58 (1939) 105–11; Werner Vogler, "Die Bedeutung der urchristlichen Hausgemeinden für die Ausbreitung des Evangeliums," *ThLZ* 107 (1982) 785–94; in "Hauskirche," 333–52, Lorenzen pursues this model of a private home as the setting for Christian groups from the early church to contemporary house churches.

423 See Klauck's discussion of the semantic range of οἶκος and οἰκία in *Hausgemeinde*, 15–20.

424 Murphy-O'Connor, *St. Paul's Corinth*, 153; see also Branick, *House Church*, 13. Treatments by scholars outside the NT field assume the existence of only one model of early Christian congregation, the house church that met in the home of a well-to-do patron, as stated by Karl-Heinrich Bieritz, "Rückkehr ins Haus? Sozialgeschichtliche und theologische Erwägungen zum Thema 'Hauskirche,'" *BThZ* 3 (1986) 118–21; Anton Weiser, "Evangelisierung im 'Haus,'" *BZ* 34 (1990) 64–77; Del Birkey, "The House Church: A Missiological Model," *Missiology* 19 (1991) 70–74; and Harry O. Maier, *The Social Setting of the Ministry as Reflected in the Writings of Hermes, Clement and Ignatius*, SR Dissertations 1 (Waterloo: Wilfrid Laurier Univ. Press, 1991) 15–39.

425 Murphy-O'Connor, *St. Paul's Corinth*, 156.

426 Jerome Murphy-O'Connor, "Prisca and Aquila," *BRev* 8.6 (1992) 49–50.

427 Willi Rordorf noted the evidence of ecclesiastical use of *insula* buildings on the basis of excavations of the later title churches in Rome; see "Was wissen wir über die christlichen Gottesdiensträume der vorkonstantinischen Zeit?" *ZNW* 55 (1964) 119–20. In "House-Churches," 270, Petersen surveys this evidence and concludes that while some of the archeological evidence points to "houses of wealthy persons," other locales used by early Christians appear to "have some connection with the world of craftsmen and artisans." On 266 she quotes the investigation by Richard Krautheimer, *Early Christian and Byzantine Architecture* (2d ed.; Harmondsworth: Penguin, 1975), showing that most of the title churches "incorporated into their walls or preserved below their floors are, almost without exception, the remnants of large tenement-houses . . . dating from the second or third centuries or at least from the period before Constantine." See the survey of the evidence and the scholarly debate by Paul Corby Finny, "Early Christian Architecture: The Beginnings (A Review Article)," *HTR* 81 (1988) 319–39.

428 Rom 16:5; 1 Cor 16:19; see also 1 Cor 1:11 and 16:15. See the extensive discussion of these and other details in Dassmann and Schöllgen, "Haus II (Hausgemeinschaft)," 801–905, which assumes throughout that the houses of early Christianity were provided by well-to-do patrons.

house church presupposes a patron or patroness who owns or rents the space used by the Christian community. A number of such persons are mentioned in the Pauline letters, including Phoebe, Erastos, Crispus, Stephanos, Gaius, Appia, and Philemon and his wife, Nympha. A house church is thus assimilated into the hierarchical social structure of the Greco-Roman world, in which heads of houses exercised legal and familial domination over their relatives and slaves.[129] In the words of Wayne Meeks, "The head of the household, by normal expectations of the society, would exercise some authority over the group and would have some legal responsibility for it. The structure of the *oikos* was hierarchical, and contemporary political and moral thought regarded the structure of superior and inferior roles as basic to the well-being of the whole society."[430] This model of a house church has led to the widely accepted theory of Gerd Theissen that such churches were marked by "love-patriarchalism" in which the hierarchical social order is retained while mutual respect and love are being fostered by patrons serving as leaders of the congregations in their houses.[431]

The question is whether church groups consisting entirely of members living in tenement buildings and lacking the sponsorship of a patron may have conducted their services within the *insula* itself, either using one of the workshop areas on the ground floor, or using temporarily cleared space used by Christian neighbors in upper floors.[432] In either case the church would not be meeting in space provided by patronage, but rather in rented or shared space provided by the members themselves. While there is evidence of the use of space in such buildings by patrons, is it possible to imagine congregations meeting in tenement buildings without the benefit of patrons?

The evidence in Rom 16 requires the hypothesis of nonpatriarchal groups that are creating a common life without the benefit of patronage. Four of the five groups

greeted in this chapter are operating without patrons, and I classify them as "tenement churches."[433] In 16:10 Paul greets "those belonging to Aristoboulus," an expression indicating that the patron is himself not a Christian but that some slaves and freedmen/women in his household are "in the Lord." The group greeted in 16:11 is "those belonging to Narkissos," indicating the slaves or employees of a patron who is himself not a believer. In the exegesis of 16:3-16, a case is made that these two groups are parts of the imperial bureaucracy, probably meeting in the building where they work. In 16:14 another group is identified as "the brothers," who are together with five named leaders. Since all five names are characteristic for slaves, freedmen, and lower-class Greeks, it is likely that this group consisted entirely of persons with low social status. The five persons named are probably the charismatic leaders of the community, and there is no indication that one of them is playing the role of patron. In the light of Lampe's research, this group is likely located in one of the tenement buildings of Trastevere or Porta Capena. In 16:15 Paul greets another group of "saints" that is led by five persons whose Greek names are associated with slavery. Again there is no indication of patronage in this early Christian cell that is probably meeting in an *insula* building.

No one of the five persons mentioned in these two groups appears to have a position of prominence over the others. If the persons named are the renters of family living spaces in the tenement building rather than charismatic leaders of the group, the social pattern still appears to be egalitarian. The leadership pattern appears to be collective rather than hierarchical. So who provides the economic support, the resources for the Lord's Supper, and the means for hospitality and charity characteristic for early Christianity in such a community? The system of love-patriarchalism would certainly not be relevant in a group of slaves and former slaves

429 See Strobel, "Begriff des 'Hauses,'" 91–100.
430 Meeks, *Urban Christians*, 76.
431 See Theissen, *Social Setting*, 11; also 107: "This love-patriarchalism takes social differences for granted but ameliorates them through an obligation of respect and love, an obligation imposed upon those who are socially stronger. From the weaker are required subordination, fidelity, and esteem."
432 Branick, *House Church*, 71, rejects this alternative in interpreting the evidence in Justin Martyr: "An apartment would not seem to be large enough to house a city-church."
433 See Jewett, "Tenement Churches," 23–43; idem, *Apostle to America*, 73–86, from which the material in this chapter is adapted.

residing in a densely packed tenement building. Some other system of support must be implicit in these references, perhaps one that has been overlooked by an interpretive tradition that is instinctively hostile to communalism and thus inclined to a euphemistic construal of the relevant terms. On the basis of the evidence in Romans, it is clear that the class structure of the groups greeted in 16:10, 11, 14, and 15 was one-dimensional. In contrast to house churches that have an upper- or middle-class patron along with his or her slaves, family, friends, and others, these four cells consisted entirely of the urban underclass, primarily slaves and poor freedmen/women. Lacking a patron who would function as a leader, the pattern of leadership appears to be egalitarian in tenement churches.

The path toward an alternative to the concept of love-patriarchalism in early Christian house churches has been available since the publication in 1951 of Bo Reicke's study of the early Christian systems of diaconal service and the love feast. He showed that the Eucharist was celebrated in the context of a common meal by a broad stream of early Christianity through the fourth century.[434] The explicit references to the "agape feast" in Jude 12 and Ignatius, *Smyrn.* 8.2, as well as the discussions of common meals in Acts 2 and 1 Cor 11, show that the eucharistic liturgy was combined with diaconal service, understood as serving meals in celebration with the faith community. Whereas researchers have often attempted to separate the Lord's Supper from a common meal, Reicke showed that early Christian sources, beginning with the biblical evidence, point toward the "single Christian sacrament of table fellowship."[435] The evidence justifies calling all such celebrations in the early church "love feasts." Such meals were marked by eschatological joy at the presence of a new age and of a Master who had triumphed over the principalities and powers. This joy was treated with ambivalence by early Christian writers because it tended toward excesses of zealous impatience with the continuation of a fallen world and sometimes resulted in licentious behavior. At times an overly realized eschatology in some of the agape meals led to Christian forms of the Saturnalia in Thessalonica[436] and to proto-gnostic excesses in Corinth.[437] The warning in Rom 13:13 appears to point in the same direction, as the commentary below demonstrates. Indeed, Reicke contends that the only NT passage that refers to such joyous celebrations as completely unambiguous is Acts 2:46. He does not take into account the likelihood that Paul cites an early agape hymn in Rom 13:11-12 and refers explicitly to "the agape" in 13:10, as the commentary demonstrates.[438]

The close association between "agape" and the communal meal documented by Reicke suggests that the frequent admonitions "to love the brothers" in the Pauline letters were intended to encourage support and participation in sacramental celebrations. In groups organized as house churches, the primary admonition would obviously be to the patrons, encouraging their involvement in love-patriarchalism. But in the context of groups organized as tenement churches, to whom would these admonitions of love be directed? Certainly not to patrons, because they are not present within the community itself. A second interpretive category is required alongside "love-patriarchalism," namely "agapaic communalism" as the ethical framework suitable for the early Pauline tenement churches. The provisions for the meal in that context would have to come from the sharing of the members. But this is all quite theoretical. Is there specific evidence anywhere in the Pauline letters for this kind of communal support for the love feast?

A passage in 2 Thessalonians provides just such evidence: "If anyone does not want to work, let [him/her] not eat" (2 Thess 3:10b). This points in the direction of a communally supported system of love feasts in the church at Thessalonica. However, the discussions of this verse in commentaries and other investigations tend to understand it as a general admonition to maintain a modern-sounding system of individual self-support.[439]

434 Reicke, *Agapenfeier,* 21–149.
435 Ibid., 14.
436 Ibid., 244–45.
437 Ibid., 282.
438 See below and Jewett, "Love Feast," 265–78.
439 See James Everett Frame, *A Critical and Exegetical Commentary on the Epistles of St. Paul to the Thessalonians* (New York: Scribner's, 1912) 304–5; Marshall, *Thessalonians,* 223–24; Wanamaker, *Thessalonians,* 285–86; for the typical perspective see also Christopher Rowland, *Christian Origins: An Account of the Setting and Character of the Most Important Messianic Sect of Judaism* (London: SPCK, 1985) 273. Neither Edgar V. McKnight, *What Is Form Criticism?*

One study even argues that the author wishes to "wean such persons from the welfare syndrome" of relying on a patron for economic support.[440] Such comments ignore the distinctive form and function of this saying as well as the relevant communal parallels in the ancient world.

The form of 2 Thess 3:10 is a typical example of casuistic law,[441] found in various settings in the ancient world.[442] The first half of the saying describes the nature of the offense and the second half provides the legal remedy or consequence.[443] Modified versions of this form are found elsewhere in the Pauline letters, setting forth general rules for congregational behavior (Rom 14:15; 15:27; 1 Cor 7:13, 15, 21; 8:13; 9:11; 11:6),[444] but there are no exact parallels in the letters to this classic legal form in which the offense is described in the conditional clause and the sanction in the second clause. Since the sanction implies communal discipline rather than some judicial punishment enacted by an official agency, this saying should be classified as a community regulation.

Instructive parallels to the content of this particular regulation have been found in the Qumran scrolls, where the sanctions for violating the rules of the community include exclusion from the table of the "pure," the reduction of food allotments, or excommunication from the community.[445] The regulations of Hellenistic and Greco-Roman guilds also prescribe penalties of exclusion from the common meal or from the guild itself for certain offenses, though the payment of fines is a more usual punishment.[446] Deprivation of food was also used in boarding schools to enforce proper academic performance.[447] It is significant that all of these parallels to 2 Thess 3:10 reflect settings in which communities are eating their meals together. Other examples sustain the generalization that social coercion through deprivation of food in the ancient world presupposed a communal system of some kind.[448] None of the parallels reflects the premise of independent self-support of individuals and families that dominates the interpretation of this verse in mainline churches and standard investigations.

The content of the offense in 2 Thess 3:10b relates to the unwillingness to work, not to the ability or availability of employment.[449] The verb "want" in this context implies conscious refusal to accept employment.[450] The

(Philadelphia: Fortress Press, 1969), nor Berger, *Formgeschichte*, 214–16, deals with 2 Thess 3:10.

440 Bruce W. Winter, "If Any Man Does Not Wish to Work . . . ." A Cultural and Historical Setting for 2 Thessalonians 3.6-16," *TynB* 40 (1989) 309; see also 314: "Christians were not only to command the respect of outsiders by being self-sufficient, but they were to seek the welfare of their city by having the wherewithal to do good to others." For a critique of this interpretation, see John S. Kloppenborg, "*PHILADELPHIA, THEODIDAKTOS* and the Dioscuri: Rhetorical Engagement in 1 Thessalonians 4.9-12," *NTS* 39 (1993) 276–77.

441 The classification of conditional legal material as "casuistic" by Albrecht Alt has been generally accepted; see Alt, "The Origins of Israelite Law," in *Essays on Old Testament History and Religion*, trans. R. A. Wilson (Oxford: Blackwell, 1966) 88–103.

442 See Bernard S. Jackson, "Law," *HBD*, 548–51, esp. 549.

443 See the standard studies by Hans Jochen Boecker, *Law and the Administration of Justice in the Old Testament and Ancient Near East*, trans. J. Moiser (Minneapolis: Augsburg, 1980) 150–55; and B. N. Kaye and G. J. Wenham, eds., *Law, Morality and the Bible* (Downers Grove, IL: InterVarsity Press, 1978).

444 See Berger, *Formgeschichte*, 214–15.

445 See 1QS 6:24–7:24.

446 A helpful listing of editions of some 17 penal codes from guilds and religious associations is available in Moshe Weinfeld, *The Organizational Pattern and the Penal Code of the Qumran Sect: A Comparison with Guilds and Religious Associations of the Hellenistic-Roman Period*, NTOA 2 (Göttingen: Vandenhoeck & Ruprecht, 1986) 9.

447 An example from Lucian of Samosata *Par.* 13 is provided by BAGD 313.

448 Even the imaginative portrayal of Aristophanes in *Eccl.* 665–66 indicates that the reduction of food as a social control was in the context of a utopian vision of a communist society. See the R. G. Ussher edition, *Aristophanes. Ecclesiazusae* (Oxford: Clarendon, 1973).

449 See Wanamaker, *Thessalonians*, 285–86.

450 See Gottlob Schrenk, "ϑέλω κτλ.," *TDNT* 3 (1965) 44–46; the odd disinterest in 2 Thess 3:10 among NT scholars is indicated by a lack of any reference in this standard dictionary article.

sanction is described with a two-word imperative: $\mu\eta\delta\grave{\epsilon}$ $\dot{\epsilon}\sigma\vartheta\iota\acute{\epsilon}\tau\omega$ ("let not eat!"), implying that deprivation of food as such is in view, not temporary exclusion from a particular meal. The form-critical method leads to the question of the type of social setting implicit in the sanction, because the sanction must be enforceable for the regulation to be effective. This means that the community must have had jurisdiction over the regular eating of its members, which would have been possible only if the community was participating in eating together on an ongoing basis. This inference is confirmed by the parallels from Qumran and the Greco-Roman world, all of which presuppose a situation of common meals organized by the community. It would be impossible to enforce this sanction if the members of the congregation ate all their meals in their own private homes or separate tenement spaces. The reference to eating in the absolute would also be overstated if the sanction merely related to exclusion from occasional sacramental celebrations. The formulation of this community regulation thus demands a love feast system organized on a regular, frequent basis.

Form-critical method seeks the *Sitz im Leben* of particular forms of social discourse, on the assumption that literary forms reflect specific types of settings.[451] In this instance the creation as well as the enforcement of this community regulation requires very specific conditions. The form-critical analysis of casuistic law in the OT and the ancient Near East indicates that the creation of such rules is the result of corporate jurisprudence rather than individual literary ingenuity.[452] Such sentences are abstracted and reformulated to make them universally valid. "These casuistic principles are therefore not, by origin, laws deliberately composed; their authority rests on tradition and custom; they are common law."[453] These considerations make it appear unlikely that the author of 2 Thessalonians composed this community regulation ex nihilo. If Paul was the author of 2 Thessalonians, an even stronger case can be made that he did

not create the regulation. As was noted above, the form of his policy advice on community issues never otherwise follows the precise casuistic form of a communal regulation. This particular casuistic regulation probably arose out of previous conflicts of a very specific type. The creation of the regulation required communities that were regularly eating meals together, for which the willingness or unwillingness to work was a factor of sufficient importance to require regulation, and in which the power to deprive members of food was in fact present. The same three conditions would be required for the author of 2 Thessalonians to advance this regulation in the particular context of conflicts in the Thessalonian churches. The form and content of this community rule, therefore, indicates the existence of such conditions both in earlier congregations and in the audience to which 2 Thessalonians was addressed—whether written by Paul in the early 50s or by a deutero-Pauline writer in the 90s. A system of Christian communes was required, in which regular commensality was supported by the sharing of members, and for which the refusal to work posed a significant threat.

Given the references to "brotherly love" (1 Thess 4:9) and "well doing" (2 Thess 3:13) in close proximity to the discussion of labor for bread, it appears likely that the food for the love feasts in Thessalonica was being provided by community members rather than by patrons. If the meals were being provided by patrons, it would be relatively immaterial whether particular guests were gainfully employed. Another social structure is implied by the form of this regulation, one in which food was being contributed by the members. In that kind of structure, the conscious refusal of able-bodied persons to add what they could to the common meal would present a morale problem of such a scale as to jeopardize the entire system. The form-critical assessment of the community rule thus points to the social structure of a "tenement church" rather than to the traditional "house church," not only in Thessalonica but in those other

---

451 See Gene M. Tucker, *Form Criticism of the Old Testament* (Philadelphia: Fortress Press, 1971) 15–17; and McKnight, *Form Criticism*, 20.

452 See Boecker, *Law*, 153.

453 Gerhard Liedke, *Gestalt und Bezeichnung alttestamentlicher Rechtssätze. Eine formgeschichtlich-terminologische Studie*, WMANT 39 (Neukirchen-Vluyn:

Neukirchener Verlaag, 1971) 56; cited by Boecker, *Law*, 153–54. Liedke shows that even in instances where Israelite law replicates ancient Near Eastern jurisprudence there is evidence of its reformulation in juridical situations; see the summary in *Studie*, 59.

early Christian communities where the regulation was formed into "common law."

The social importance of the regulation for the Thessalonian community is confirmed by the introductory comments in 2 Thess 3:10: "For when we were with you, we used to give you this command . . . ." The imperfect verbs point to repetitive instruction,[454] which would have been appropriate only if the instruction were actually crucial to the life of the community. If 2 Thessalonians is a pseudonymous letter, its author apparently wished to present this command as foundational in early Christian catechism. The introductory comments assume an even larger significance if Paul was the author of 2 Thessalonians, because the founding visit was cut off unexpectedly before the formation of the congregation was deemed complete. This community regulation must have been of primary relevance for the daily life of the congregation if it had been repeatedly stressed during so short a founding visit (1 Thess 2:17). In either case a tenement church structure in which communal meals were being provided by the members themselves is the only form of early Christian congregational life for which such instruction could be considered absolutely essential.

This evidence is highly relevant for the interpretation of Romans because it reveals the presence of a social system alongside house churches that enabled congregational groups to function without patrons. The climax of the letter that urges mutual welcome requires the context of meetings to which members and leaders from other groups could be invited and given the holy kiss of welcome to various agape meals (16:16). If the evidence of agapic communalism were taken seriously, it would be clear that at least in Rome and Thessalonica the numerical preponderance of groups fell in the category of tenement churches.

E. The Question of Title Churches

The so-called title churches offer an intriguing possibility of throwing additional light on the early history and social structure of Roman Christianity. The Latin term *titulus* indicates the house marker placed near the entrance with the name of the owner under whom property was registered in ancient Rome.[455] The churches that were built after the time of Constantine were located for the most part on the site of buildings that had been owned by Christian patrons and patronesses where house churches had earlier been established.[456] The name of René Vielliard is associated with the early effort to locate congregations in particular districts of Rome.[457] He began with the second and third century evidence and made no effort to push the history back into the first century, concluding that the *titulus* churches derived from private individuals giving real estate to the church.[458] Following the topography of the title churches, Vielliard suggested the idea of a crescent of Christian settlement from the northeast portion of the suburbs of Rome, from Gaius or St. Suzanne, down and around to Trastevere.[459] He made no distinction in this suggestion between the very earliest Christian locations and those of the fourth century. However, he commented on the antiquity of *titulus Fasciolae* and *titulus Crescentianae* near the beginning of the Appian Way as an indication that Christians were derived from merchants, artisans, and travelers from the Orient.[460] The three title churches in Trastevere should be counted among the most ancient in Rome.[461] Lampe notes that nine of the twenty-five title churches of later Roman history are associated with the names of leaders from the first and second centuries, but that the evidence for the most part is post-Constantinian.[462] A skeptical assessment of the relevance of this data for reconstructing the earlier history is

---

454 See Wanamaker, *Thessalonians*, 285.

455 Lampe, *Paul to Valentinus*, 362; Jeffers, *Conflict at Rome*, 42–45.

456 Kirsch, *Titelkirchen*, 134; Jeffers, *Conflict at Rome*, 45.

457 René Vielliard, *Recherches sur les origines de la Rome chrétienne: Les églises Romaines et leur rôle dans l'histoire et la topographie de la ville depuis la fin du monde antique jusqu'à la formation de l'état pontifical*, EUC (Rome: Edizioni di storia e litteratura, 1959).

458 Ibid., 34.

459 Ibid., 37.

460 Ibid., 47.

461 Ibid., 51; see the maps at the end of the volume that identify the locations of the earliest title churches and those that developed later. Map 3 shows the relation between these title churches and the great public buildings in Rome.

462 Lampe, *Paul to Valentinus*, 22–23, 360–65.

offered by Graydon Snyder and a less skeptical one by James Jeffers.[463] Many of these churches in time developed catacombs on property owned by patrons on the outskirts of Rome. In view of the innate conservatism of place names and addresses in a city like Rome and the continuity with Jewish burial practices that we now know originated before the Christian era, it seems likely that evidence will come to light that allows inferences about some of the early house churches. It seems highly unlikely, however, that the title churches can be associated with tenement churches, which lacked patrons with specific street addresses or with property outside Rome where catacombs could be developed. In any event, since most of the early Christians were associated with tenement churches, whose identity remained obscure in a class-oriented society where patrons are remembered while the names of their clients and of the slaves around them are mostly forgotten, further evidence about title churches will explain only a small fraction of the early Christian movement. Nevertheless, the locations of the nine title churches that have a possible link with the early history are revealing: two are in Trastevere, two in the Aventine, and the others elsewhere.[464]

F. The Ethnic Identity of Paul's Audience

In the early period of historical-critical research on Romans, scholars tended to follow F. C. Baur in the assessment that Paul's audience in Rome was entirely Jewish Christian.[465] However, in view of the address in 1:5 "among all the Gentiles" and the apology in 1:13 for not winning fruit among them "as among the rest of the Gentiles," it became clear by the 1870s that the audience was mostly Gentile.[466] In 11:13 the audience is explicitly placed among the Gentiles, and the wording of 15:14-19 makes it clear that most of the audience is indeed Gentile.[467] This assessment is accepted by all current commentators.[468] Nevertheless, it is clear that Christianity in Rome began with Jewish converts and that problematic relations between a Gentile majority and Jewish minority are in view throughout the letter.[469] The formulas, "to the Jew first and then to the Greek" (1:16; 2:9, 10) and "both Jews and Greeks/Gentiles" (3:9, 29-30; 9:24; 10:12), echo throughout the letter, and in 9:4-5 and 11:18 Paul emphasizes the Jewish origins of the messianic gospel. Yet it is clear from 14:1 and 11:17-24 that the Gentile majority was discriminating against the Jewish minority whom it was claiming to displace.[470] The "disputes over opinions" that Paul prohibits in 14:1 are obviously being dominated by the Gentile majority to the disfavor of the Jewish minority.[471]

The characterization of the factions in Rome as "weak" and "strong" in 14:1—15:13 has provoked such complicated debate that many scholars have concluded that no precise identification of the identity of these groups can be drawn.[472] Since I once stood within this group,[473] I realize that this assessment derives in part from the unacknowledged demonstrative genre of Romans, which required an indirect and diplomatically nuanced address to the issues in a congregation that Paul had not founded. Thus the audience situation

463 Graydon F. Snyder, *Ante Pacem: Archaeological Evidence of Church Life Before Constantine* (Macon, GA: Mercer Univ. Press, 1985) 82–87; Jeffers, *Conflict at Rome*, 44–45.

464 Lampe, *Paul to Valentinus*, 22–23.

465 See Weiszäcker, "Römische Christengemeinde," 248–49.

466 Ibid., 249–50, 263.

467 Ibid., 250–55.

468 See, e.g., Barrett, 22; Cranfield, 1:18; Dunn, 1:xlv; Haacker, 11; Schreiner, 13; Witherington, 7–8; Hans-Werner Bartsch, "Die Empfänger des Römerbriefes," *StTh* 25 (1971) 84–85; Brändle and Stegemann, "Formation," 124–25; an exception to the consensus is T. Fahy, "St Paul's Romans were Jewish Converts," *ITQ* (1959) 182–91.

469 Weiszäcker, "Römische Christengemeinde," 255–59; Lichtenberger, "Jews and Christians in Rome," 2166–68.

470 See particularly Bartsch, "Historische Situation," 285–87; idem, "Gegner," 40–41; Wiefel, "Roman Christianity," 95–101.

471 See Michel, 423; Cranfield, 3:701; Dunn, 2:798; Haacker, 278–80; Esler, *Conflict and Identity*, 349.

472 Elliott, "Asceticism," 243 n. 3, provides a convenient listing of scholars who reject a precise identification of the weak and strong, including Bornkamm, "Last Will and Testament," 16–28; Käsemann, 366; Robert J. Karris, "Romans 14:1–15:13 and the Occasion of Romans," in Donfried, *Romans Debate*, 65–84; Sampley, "Weak and Strong," 40–52; Meeks, "Judgment and the Brother," 290–300.

473 Jewett, *Terms*, 42–46.

appears very vague in comparison with the situations in Corinth, Thessalonica, Galatia, or Philippi. Another shortcoming in the previous discussion was that much of the evidence in the letter was not taken into account. For example, the composite confession in 1:3-4 reveals an interest in addressing both Jewish Christian and Gentile Christian concerns. The citations of credal formulas and hymnic fragments in 3:25-26; 4:24-25; 5:6-8; 8:32-34; 10.9, 11.33-36, and 13.11-12 are drawn from various traditions in the early church. Particularly the material in chap. 16 is often not taken seriously as evidence of the ethnic makeup of these groups.

When we take all this evidence into account, it becomes clear that the profile of the weak and the strong in 14:1–15:13 is abstractly drawn so as to depict extreme positions in opposite directions, within which a wide range of congregational viewpoints can be encompassed. In 14:2, for example, Paul writes that "the one has faith to eat everything, while the weak person eats leafy vegetables," but in fact no group in the ancient world was totally undiscriminating in food consumption, and no group was so extremely ascetic as to eat only lettuce. The exaggeration on both sides is humorous and rhetorically effective in supporting an argument that pertains to a wide range of controversial positions on diet and liturgy that divided the Roman congregations. In 14:5 Paul describes the controversial positions with regard to holy days in such generic terms that a wide range of alternative distinctions is encompassed: "Now the one person judges one day better than another, while the other judges all days [alike]." Rather than specifying that this formulation pertains to Sunday worship, Sabbath observances, Jewish festivals, fasting times, lucky days, or Roman feast days, the appropriate conclusion is that Paul intentionally formulated the matter so

that a number of controversies would be covered. In 14:14 it is clear that the controversies over food relate in part to kosher regulations.[474] The references to "despising" and "judging" in 14:3 and 10 are contrary strategies of mutual shaming, the one typical for legalists and the other for liberals, but the precise source of either law or freedom is intentionally left undefined. Hence the pejorative terms "weak" and "strong," which were obviously promoted by the group in the superior position, are generic terms that encompass theological as well as social diversity.[475] It is likely that the majority of the strong were Gentile believers, with Jewish liberals such as Paul and his close allies included in this group. It is also likely that the weak included Jewish adherents to the law, but this group probably included some Gentiles who had been close to synagogues before becoming believers, or those drawn to the movement when it was still meeting in synagogues, that is, prior to 49 C.E.[476] When the commentary below associates Jewish Christians with the weak and Gentile Christians with the strong, these are meant to be homomorphic and descriptive formulations that encompass a fairly wide range of ethnic and theological diversity.

An important alternative was developed by Mark Nanos in *The Mystery of Romans,* where he argues that the weak are unconverted Jews whom Paul wishes to draw into the circle of believers.[477] Among the positive contributions of this study is its countering of the abusive understanding of the weak as fundamentally deficient[478] and taking seriously Paul's interest in converting Jews, evident especially in chaps. 9–11.[479] While the aim of converting Jews is indisputable (11:14, 25-26), the argument in chaps. 14–15 directly counters any effort to convert the weak to the viewpoint of the strong.[480] In 14:13 and 21 Paul addresses both the weak and the strong as

---

474 See Pitta, "Strong," 99–102.

475 See Reasoner, *The Strong,* 45–63, 218; cf. Patte, *Paul,* 246–50.

476 That some groups of the "weak" consisted of Gentiles who had been God-fearers in the Roman synagogues prior to their acceptance of the messianic message about Jesus is suggested by Michele Murray, *Playing a Jewish Game: Gentile Christian Judaizing in the First and Second Centuries CE,* SCJ 13 (Waterloo: Wilfrid Laurier Univ. Press, 2004) 29–100.

477 See the summary statement in Nanos, *Mystery,* 143; an earlier advocate of this approach is the privately published study by Werner Eschner, *Der Römerbrief. An die Juden der Synagogen in Rom?* 2 vols. (Hannover: Werner Eschner, 1981).

478 Nanos, *Mystery,* 115–18.

479 Ibid., 151–59.

480 See particularly Jewett, *Tolerance,* 126–33.

believing "brothers" who should cease judging and scorning the other (ἀλλήλων) and should seek mutual edification rather than conversion to the other's point of view. The weak are consistently addressed as if they belonged to the believing community rather than to a group beyond the house and tenement churches in Rome. That both the weak and the strong who live and die τῷ κυρίῳ ("in relation to the Lord") in 14:8 are believers is indicated by the first person plural verbal forms, "we live . . . we die . . . we belong to the Lord." Both groups are described as "house slaves" of God in 14:4, and brothers of each other in 14:10, which must be understood as fellow believers. That "God has welcomed" both the weak and the strong is claimed in 14:4, and that each is called to "welcome one another" into their love feasts in 15:7 clearly implies that both groups are already within the believing community. Moreover, while Paul addresses the "weak" directly, there is no plausible way that Paul's letter could have been presented to Jewish synagogues hostile to the messianic message. Since these synagogues had experienced conflicts over the proclamation of Jesus as the Christ, and had been closed by the Edict of Claudius when the synagogue leaders were banned from Rome, it is extremely unlikely that they would have allowed the subversive message of Paul's letter to be delivered in any space under their authority. Furthermore, the substantial number of Jews addressed in chap. 16 are all identified as Christian believers or evangelists, who are to be greeted by the hearers of the letter but who would have been most unwelcome in Jewish synagogues. Finally, when one takes account of recent advances in understanding the "speech-in-character" created by Paul in 2:17-29, it is now clear that no nonbelieving Jew is addressed in second person style anywhere in the letter. When Paul speaks explicitly of his fellow Jews who have not yet accepted the gospel, he consistently uses the third person (e.g., 3:2; 9:3-5, 32; 10:1-3; 11:14, 20, 28-31; 15:31), which would have been perceived as impolite if they constituted the "weak" being addressed in the letter.

The ethnic diversity of the Roman congregations enhanced a combative tendency that was present throughout the culture. Despite their comparatively low social status, the house and tenement churches in Rome were engaged in fierce competitions with one another for superior honor. According to 14:1—15:7, the "weak" are judging their competitors for failing to live up to kosher food laws and to celebrate Christ on designated holidays, while the "strong" criticized their opponents for lacking freedom from the law. The very names they applied to each other, "weak/strong," "circumcised/uncircumcised," were honorific on differing scales of honor held by these groups. It may seem strange that persons and groups lacking honor in the society at large would vie with one another for honor, but nothing was more natural. Dio Chrysostom was not surprised to witness "fellow slaves wrangling with one another over glory and precedence,"[481] and Valerius Maximus observed: "There is no baseness so great that it cannot be touched by the sweetness of prestige . . . . Glory drags along the obscure no less than the nobly born bound to her shining chariot."[482] Lendon observes that such competition was "nowhere more evident than in the case of the slave and freedman assistants of the emperor,"[483] which is particularly relevant for understanding the situation in the Christian community in Rome because it is likely that two of the five groups were situated within the imperial bureaucracy.

G. The Religious Orientation of Roman Congregations

Since there were many congregations in Rome about which the letter gives no explicit information, to move beyond the parameters of the weak/strong identification requires the use of implicit details in the letter in coordination with generalizations about the Christian movement as a whole during its first generation. The likelihood that three of the congregations Paul knows about were associated with the strong[484] and two with the weak[485] sustains the impression gained elsewhere

---

481 Cited from Dio Chrysostom *2 Tars.* 34.51, by Lendon, *Empire of Honour*, 97.

482 Valerius Maximus *Columella* 11.1.19, cited by Lendon, *Empire of Honour*, 97.

483 Lendon, *Empire of Honour*, 102.

484 Since Paul had worked with Prisca and Aquila in Corinth and Ephesus, it is likely that they would have

been included in Paul's summary in 15:1, "Now we the strong are obliged to bear the weaknesses of the weak and not to please ourselves." The congregations associated with Narkissos (16:11) and the "brothers" (16:14) have no visible links with Judaism and therefore are likely part of the Gentile majority.

485 If the Aristoboulos of 16:10 was the grandson of

that the majority of the congregation was Gentile but adds little to the profile of the congregations beyond what has already been established. The other evidence indicates that the congregations shared the charismatic, apocalyptic piety typical of early Christianity elsewhere.

An important indication is that the word πνεῦμα ("spirit") is mentioned thirty times in Romans, revealing Paul's assumption about the nature of congregational life in Rome. In contrast to the modern perspective found in many commentaries, the predominant view of spirit in the ancient Jewish and Greco-Roman world was a wonder-working power that typically manifested itself in religious ecstasy.[486] This starting point is affirmed by Gerd Theissen, who concludes "that the 'Spirit' in early Christianity had nothing to do with the spirit of the modern world and of philosophy but was rather a power, envisioned as a fluid, that broke through the customary context of life and expressed itself in miracles and speaking in tongues."[487] This stands in contrast to classical Christian theology, which views "Spirit" as a person of the Trinity, often conceptualized on the model of the Stoic concept of a universal divine energy or substance that exists in the world or the model of a ghostly, angelic being. Greco-Roman popular religion tended instead to associate πνεῦμα with miracle working and with manic, enthusiastic inspiration that could sometimes lead to irrational, amoral actions. Except for

the view that the spirit of Yahweh was morally constrained, popular Jewish religion shared these characteristics. This ancient perspective was discovered a century ago by Hermann Gunkel, Heinrich Weinel, Martin Dibelius, Adolf Deissmann, and others,[488] who showed that πνεῦμα was viewed as "the cause ascribed to ecstatic experiences—a wonder-working, divine power."[489] The audience of Roman Christians probably shared the assumptions of other early Christians "that the Old Testament and Jewish expectation of the inspiring and vital πνεῦμα of the eschaton . . . has now been fulfilled. The reception of the πνεῦμα is discernable from external phenomena . . . esp. miraculous healings . . . ecstatic prayer . . . and prophetic speech."[490]

Paul's various discussions of the spirit in 1 Thess 5, 1 Cor 12–14, Rom 5, 8, 12, 14, and 15 presuppose a cultural situation in which ecstatic phenomena were primary constituents of religion.[491] Glossolalia was probably a typical aspect of most early Christian congregations.[492] However, these insights continue to be resisted in some strands of Romans research; the language employed in most commentaries on Rom 8 continues to assume the modern concept of trinitarianism as defined by two millennia of church tradition; with few exceptions, the standard commentaries resist any hint that "spirit" in Rom 8 is related to charismatic experiences of the Roman churches.[493] The long-standing hostility of

---

Herod the Great, his slaves would have been sympathetic to the Jewish point of view; see Lightfoot, "Caesar's Household," 174–75; Scott T. Carroll, "Aristobulus (Person)," *ADB* 1 (1992) 383. The group called the "saints" in 16:15 probably also have a Jewish orientation, consistent with Paul's reference in 15:26 to Christians in Judea with the term "saints."

486 See Jacob Kremer, "πνεῦμα," *EDNT* 3 (1993) 118.
487 Theissen, *Psychological Aspects*, 268.
488 Hermann Gunkel, *Die Wirkungen des Heiligen Geistes nach der populären Anschauung der apostolischen Zeit und der Lehre des Apostels Paulus. Eine biblisch-theologische Studie* (Göttingen: Vandenhoeck & Ruprecht, 1888; 3d ed., 1909); English trans. by R. A. Harrisville and P. A. Quanbeck II, *The Influence of the Holy Spirit* (Philadelphia: Fortress Press, 1979); Heinrich Weinel, *Die Wirkung des Geistes und der Geister im nachapostolischen Zeitalter bis auf Irenäus* (Tübingen: Mohr [Siebeck], 1899); Dibelius, *Geisterwelt;* Deissmann, *Paul,* 178ff., 297ff.

489 Jewett, *Terms,* 62.
490 Kremer, "πνεῦμα," 119.
491 See Karol Gabris, "Charismatische Erscheinungen bei der Erbauung der Gemeinde," *CV* 16 (1973) 147–62; Schatzmann, *Charismata,* 14–26; Koenig, *Charismata,* 168–69.
492 See Adolf Hilgenfeld, *Die Glossolalie in der alten Kirche, in dem Zusammenhang der Geistesgaben und des Geisteslebens des alten Christentums* (Leipzig: Breitkopf und Härtel, 1850); Dwight Moody Smith, "Glossalalia and Other Spiritual Gifts in a New Testament Perspective," *Int* 28 (1974) 307–20; Esler, *First Christians,* 35–51.
493 For example, Kaylor, *Paul's Covenant Community,* 148; "In its barest essential meaning, the Spirit is the presence of God effectively accomplishing God's will." He goes on to detail the Spirit's work without any reference to its links with charismatic experience. Willibald Pfister, *Das Leben im Geist nach Paulus. Der Geist als Anfang und Vollendung des christlichen Lebens,* SF 34 (Freiburg: Universitätsver-

mainstream theology against mysticism, enthusiasm, and various forms of charismatic exuberance usually leads to a leveling and domestication of Paul's revolutionary argument in this passage.

An exception to the trend of downplaying charismatic religion is Theissen, who perceives an argumentative relevance for the spiritual references in this pericope: "glossolalic experiences and behavior become the first sign of overcoming the conflict of flesh and spirit."[494] No criticism of charismatic religion is offered in this section; rather "the 'pledge of the Spirit,' the first experiential sign of an overcoming of the contradiction [i.e., between flesh and spirit, old age and new], shows itself in glossolalia."[495] Then in the next pericope, "Paul is concerned not with polemics against enthusiasm but rather with the integration of reality as a whole—including its negative aspects—into the ecstatic experience, and with a new view of reality on the basis of ecstatic experience."[496] In her recent study of "Paul in Ecstasy," Colleen Shantz maintains that Paul's interest is "not in ending ecstasy, but in maturing it."[497] In Philip Esler's words, "To receive the Spirit meant to have God within you. This overwhelming experience was frequently accompanied by charismatic gifts, such as prophecy, speaking in tongues, miracle working, visions, and auditions, and could result in feelings of euphoria among those involved . . . . Charismatic phenomena were fundamental to Paul's congregations."[498] There is every reason to conclude that this charismatic enthusiasm was characteristic not just of Pauline churches but of Roman Christianity as a whole, and this conjecture along with the other conclusions in this section will be followed throughout the commentary.

7. The Cultural Situation in Spain: Subjugated Barbarians

If Romans is an ambassadorial letter seeking support for a mission project in Spain, the obvious question is why such a letter was needed. There are no indications that similar letters were written in preparation of his ministries in Philippi, Corinth, Ephesus, or anywhere else. The obvious way to investigate this question is to examine the cultural situation in Spain, a task that no Romans commentator has thus far undertaken. This commentary rests on the premise that the situation in Spain throws decisive light on Paul's missionary strategy, evident throughout the letter.[499]

A. The Question of Jewish Population in Spain

The first matter on which significant information is available relates to the presence of Jewish population in Spain during the Julio-Claudian period. Käsemann and Cranfield assume the presence of Jewish communities in Spain, relying primarily on outdated information in Schürer and Michel.[500] Evidence of substantial Jewish settlement in Spain does not appear until the third and fourth centuries C.E., as W. P. Bowers has shown.[501] The indications of the practice of the Jewish religion in Spain are so sparse that it is not even included in the comprehensive survey of "oriental religions" by García y Bellido.[502] A trilingual inscription at Tortosa is cited by Michel as evidence of Jewish population, but this also appears to stem from the second century C.E. at the earliest.[503] The references to initial Jewish settlements in Spain found in the Talmud that were used by earlier researchers, according to Bowers, must "be traced back

---

lag, 1963), begins with references to the work of Gunkel et al. (pp. 1–2) but then treats the "spirit" in 8:1-11 and 12-17 in a traditional, ecclesiastical manner (29–48, 69–87). Shantz, "Paul in Ecstasy," 29–71, chronicles the account of exegetical resistance against mysticism and ecstasy.

494 Theissen, *Psychological Aspects*, 332.
495 Ibid., 334.
496 Ibid., 339.
497 Shantz, "Paul in Ecstasy," 257.
498 Esler, *Conflict and Identity*, 246; cf. Patte, *Paul*, 233–38.
499 This material is adapted from Jewett, "Spanish Mission," 144–64.
500 Käsemann, 398; Cranfield, 3:769; Michel, 369;

Schürer, *History*, 3:84–85. See the critique of this view in Dewey, "Σπανίαν," 324–27.
501 Bowers, "Jewish Communities in Spain," 400; John S. Richardson, *The Romans in Spain* (Oxford: Blackwell, 1996) 262, discusses the christianization of Spain in the context of the 2d and 3d centuries C.E.
502 Antonio García y Bellido, *Les religions orientales dan l'Espagne Romaine* (Leiden: Brill, 1967) 1–20.
503 Michel, 369, cites this as evidence of Jewish communities in Spain during the Pauline period, but Bowers, "Jewish Communities in Spain," 396–97, shows that the trilingual inscriptions both at Tortosa and Tarragona are dated by experts between the 2d and 6th centuries C.E.

to the massive disruptions and relocations of Judaism in A.D. 70–135."[504] Bowers further points out that in the various listings in Jewish literature of the lands to which the Diaspora had spread prior to these enforced migrations, it always "stops short of the western Mediterranean beyond Rome."[505] Paul appears to operate on the same assumption in Rom 10:18, that while "the proclamation to the Jewish people has been completed," there is still a need "for a pioneer mission to Spain," which implies that there was no Jewish population there.[506] There seems to be little doubt that commentators have often been led astray by outdated information on this issue.[507]

The lack of Jewish settlement in Spain would have posed several substantial barriers to Paul's previous missionary strategy. Not only would this eliminate the prospects of Jewish converts to the gospel, but it would also rule out finding a group of God-fearers or proselytes in the Spanish cities to recruit as the initial core of Christian churches. There would be no initial interest in a messianic proclamation prepared by devotion to the Septuagint. The evidence of the oriental religions in Spain, including the Semitic residue from Phoenician and later Punic colonization, shows no trace of Hebrew influence.[508] The absence of synagogues eliminated the avenues that Paul habitually used to establish a base of operations in the Greek cities of the east. There is a widespread consensus that despite the apologetic interests of the book of Acts, it is realistic to expect that wherever possible he would begin his missionary activities in local synagogues and move to an independent

base of operations after troubles erupted or patrons and patronesses emerged.[509] Without a synagogue as a starting point, the crucial contacts with appropriate patrons would be extremely difficult to make, especially for a handworker of Paul's social class.

The absence of synagogues would pose a related economic problem, because Jewish travelers often used such buildings as convenient hostels and places to develop business contacts. The studies by Ronald Hock and J. Paul Sampley reveal the role of these informal social contacts in providing the economic framework of Paul's self supporting missionary strategy.[510] In the case of Spain, prior arrangements for bases of operations and the recruitment of appropriate patrons would be required in the absence of the resources of local synagogues. Given the Roman domination of the economic resources in Spain and the high proportion of mines, industries, and estates directly owned and managed by the empire,[511] it would likely be necessary to approach this problem through persons close to administrators in Rome. The broad consequence of the lack of Jewish settlement is that the entire strategy of the Spanish mission needs to be reconceived.

B. The Cultural and Linguistic Situation in Spain

When one inquires about the nature of the Spanish cultural situation during the period of Paul's intended mission, the Romans commentators are silent. It is eloquent testimony to the preoccupation with Rome and Jerusalem that the Romans debate has never touched on what Paul states as the ultimate goal of his mission. But

504 Bowers, "Jewish Communities in Spain," 400.
505 Ibid., 401. The survey of Safrai in Safrai and Stern, *Jewish People*, 1:169–70, overlooks this lack of direct reference in Jewish sources and cites Rom 15:28 as evidence that "it may be assumed that there already was a Jewish settlement in Spain during the Julio-Claudian period." Stern observes, however, that there is no "concrete evidence of Jewish settlements . . . in the Latin provinces of the empire," which surely should include Spain. See also O. F. A. Meinardus, "Paul's Missionary Journey to Spain: Tradition and Folklore," *BA* 41 (1978) 61–63.
506 Bowers, "Jewish Communities in Spain," 402.
507 See, e.g., the commentaries written after Bowers's article: Harrisville, 243–44; Wilckens, 3.124, 128; Achtemeier, 228–33; Bryne, 443–46; Witherington, 365–66. In contrast, Zeller, 14; Fitzmyer, 717; Moo,

900; and Schreiner, 775, take the Bowers study into account.
508 See García y Bellido, *Religions orientales*, passim.
509 See Stanley Kent Stowers, "Social Status, Public Speaking and Private Teaching: The Circumstances of Paul's Preaching Activity," *NovT* 26 (1984) 68–73, for evidence suggesting that the homes of patrons were the primary locus of the Pauline mission.
510 Hock, *Social Context*, 29–42; Sampley, *Pauline Partnership*, 52–72, 81–87.
511 Rostovtzeff, *Empire*, 213–14. See also Jose Maria Blázquez, "Roma y la explotación económica de la Península Ibérica," in José Manuel Gómez-Tabanera, ed., *Las Raíces de España* (Madrid: Instituto Español de Antropología Aplicada, 1967) 253–81.

extensive information has long been available, most accessibly in Rostovtzeff's *Social and Economic History of the Roman Empire*.[512] He showed that the image of Spain as the most thoroughly latinized colony of Rome was in need of revision, that large portions of the Iberian peninsula were substantially untouched by the veneer of Roman civilization. The rural population in particular and the northern portions of Spain remained apart from Greco-Roman culture. In general, he concluded, "those who held Latin rights and were more or less romanized formed a small minority of the population of Spain, while the status of the rest remained the same as it had been before the 'thorough urbanization' of the country."[513]

On the decisive question of the language spoken in Spain, the barriers to a Greek speaker like Paul were rather high. While Latin was spoken in the major cities, at least in part, and at times rather poorly, the "Iberians and Celt-Iberians of Spain spoke their own languages."[514] A number of subsequent studies[515] and the extensive articles on the latinizing of Spain in *ANRW* confirm the general outlines of Rostovtzeff's summary.[516] At the time of the Roman conquest around 200

B.C.E., there were four main language groupings in Spain: the Indo-European languages in west-central and northwest Spain, the Iberian dialects in southern Spain and on the east coast, the Punic languages in the southern coastal area, and a wide range of primitive languages of obscure origin. In addition, in three small pockets Greek was used on the east coast where colonies had been established in an earlier period.[517] In the area around Cádiz the Phoenician language was still in use.[518] Faced with this bewildering variety of languages, the Romans made no effort to create a multilingual administration or even to develop a translation service; they simply imposed a Latin system that was more rapidly accepted in the south and east than in the west and north.

The most fully latinized area was *Hispania ulterior* or Baetica, where the native languages had largely been forgotten in the major cities by the Augustan period as indicated by the fact that non-Latin inscriptions as well as the minting of bilingual coins cease thereafter. It was this province that had attracted the largest group of Italian immigrants[519] and produced most of the impressive cultural, political, and military leaders who rendered

512 Rostovtzeff, *Empire*, 211–15.
513 Ibid., 215.
514 Ibid., 213.
515 Carol H. V. Sutherland, *The Romans in Spain 217 B.C.–A.D. 117* (London: Methuen, 1971); Francis Jowett Wiseman, *Roman Spain: An Introduction to the Roman Antiquities of Spain and Portugal* (London: Bell, 1956) 63: "it was only a small percentage of middle- and upper-class Spaniards who gained any direct contact with Rome and the Romans. It was only in the towns of Andalusia, the east coast and the Ebro valley that there was any marked transition to Roman manners and the Roman way of life, in the first century A.D." T. Robert S. Broughton, "The Romanisation of Spain: The Problem and the Evidence," *PAPS* 103 (1959) 645–51; idem, "Municipal Institutions in Roman Spain," *CHM* 9 (1965) 129–40; Pedro Bosch-Gimpera, "Les soldats ibériques agents de'hellénisation et de romanisation," in *Mélanges d'archéologie, d'épigraphie et d'histoire offerts à Jérôme Carcopino* (Paris: Hachette, 1966) 141–48; José Manuel Roldán Hervas, "De Numancia a Sertorio: Problemas de la romanización de Hispania en la encrucijada de las guerras civiles," in W. Eck, H. Galsterer, and H. Wolff, eds., *Studien zur antiken Sozialgeschichte: Festschrift*

Friedrich Vittinghoff, KHAb 28 (Cologne: Böhlau, 1980) 157–78.
516 Antonio García y Bellido, "Die Latinisierung Hispaniens," *ANRW* 1.1 (1972) 462–91; Antonio Tovar and José M. Blázquez Martínez, "Forschungsbericht zur Geschichte des römischen Hispanien," *ANRW* 2.3 (1975) 428–51.
517 Bellido, "Latinisierung Hispaniens," 463–66; the linguistic map he provides on 476 implies a larger importance for the Punic languages than in the earlier discussion. For a treatment of the cultural legacy of the Greek colonies, see Rhys Carpenter, *The Greeks in Spain* (1925; repr. New York: AMS Press, 1971), and Antonio García y Bellido, *Factores que contribuyeron a la helenización de la España prerromana*, AHPC 2 (Madrid: Tipografía de Archivos, 1934).
518 Kotansky, "Jesus and Heracles in Cádiz," 190–92, cites J. B. Tsirkin, "The Phoenician Civilization in Roman Spain," *Gerion* 3 (1985) 246–70.
519 See Alan John Nisbet Wilson, *Emigration from Italy in the Republican Age of Rome* (New York: Barnes & Noble, 1966) 22–40.

such conspicuous service to the empire. A senatorial province since the time of Augustus, Baetica was ruled by a proconsul of praetorian rank, frequently selected from senators with roots and experience in Spain, which indicates the cultural niveau and significance of the province to the empire.[520] It was the most heavily urbanized portion of Spain, with ninety municipalities boasting some level of Roman privilege.[521] The presence of several famous Greek teachers in Baetica indicates the level of cultural aspirations of the elite. Even here, the local languages retained their hold in smaller cities and rural areas, while the pre-Roman city names remained in circulation despite official renamings by Roman authorities.[522]

The other two provinces were latinized only along the coastal areas, in major river valleys, and in isolated military and mining colonies, which leads specialists like Galsterer to suspect an overstatement in Pliny's report that "all Spain" was given Roman citizenship under Vespasian.[523] *Hispania citerior*, often referred to as Tarraconensis, was the largest colony in the empire and was ruled by an imperial legate of high rank, indicating its importance and prestige.[524] Lusitania was the least urbanized portion of Spain, ruled by a legate of lower rank.[525] Continued resistance against Roman rule was evident in the destructive Cantabrian War of 29–19 B.C.E.[526] and in the refusal of a substantial portion of the population in Lusitania and Tarraconensis to abandon the worship of native deities in favor of the Roman pantheon. A large portion of the northern and western portions of the peninsula was not latinized until long after Paul's time. The Iberian alphabet and dialects remained in use in the inner regions of Spain until they were gradually displaced by Christian missionizing in

the sixth century and thereafter, with some regions retaining their linguistic distinctiveness until the Middle Ages.[527] The image of Spain correlates with the term Paul employs in 1:14, "barbarian." Strabo reported, for example, that the Spanish peninsula was "essentially incapable of supporting civilized life"[528] and that with the exception of a few coastal cities, the population resides "in villages, and are wild and uncivilized."[529] Cicero expressed the contempt felt by most Romans, that Spain lay "beyond the edge of the civilized world."[530]

C. Roman Administration of Spain

When Rome took over Spain after the Carthaginian Conflicts that lasted from 237 to 206 B.C.E. and devastated much of the peninsula, it conducted frequent campaigns against indigenous forces for much of the next two hundred years.[531] The area was divided between two military commanders appointed by the Senate, and Polybius comments on the never-ending Celtiberian War as the best example of a "fiery" war that could never be ended with a single decisive battle.[532] The Roman civil wars from 133 to 44 B.C.E. were particularly destructive. For example, T. Didius, who was consul in 98, sacked the town of Termantia after killing ten thousand of the inhabitants, and betrayed his agreement with another town and massacred men, women, and children.[533] In 81 B.C.E. the praetor Sertorius was forcibly evicted from office by his successor, and then was invited by the Lusitanians to be their supreme commander in the struggle for independence, which resulted in eight years of destructive sieges, battles, and guerrilla campaigns. The historian Florus describes the suffering of the Spanish population in these campaigns between Sertorius and

---

520 See Gésa Alföldi, *Fasti Hispanienses: Senatorische Reichsbeamte und Offiziere in den spanischen Provinzen des Römischen Reiches von Augustus bis Diokletian* (Wiesbaden: Steiner, 1969) 294.

521 See Hartmut Galsterer, *Untersuchungen zum römischen Städtewesen in Spanien*, MadF 8 (Berlin: de Gruyter, 1971) 65–68; Kotansky, "Jesus and Heracles in Cádiz," 190–92.

522 García y Bellido, "Latinisierung Hispaniens," 470–78.

523 Galsterer, *Untersuchungen*, 37–50.

524 See Alföldi, *Fasti Hispanienses*, 289–90.

525 Ibid., 293–94.

526 See Richardson, *Romans in Spain*, 133–34.

527 García y Bellido, "Latinisierung Hispaniens," 478–91. See also Kurt Baldinger, *Die Herausbildung der Sprachräume auf der Pyrenäenhalbinsel* (Berlin: Akademie Verlag, 1958) 43–51.

528 Richardson, *Romans in Spain*, 150.

529 Ibid., 151, referring to Strabo, *Geogr* 3.4.13.

530 Richardson, *Romans in Spain*, 126, referring to Cicero, *Planc.* 34.84; *Att.* 12.8.

531 See Richardson, *Romans in Spain*, 35–125.

532 Polybius, *Hist.* 35.1.1-6, cited by Richardson, *Romans in Spain*, 80.

533 Richardson, *Romans in Spain*, 85.

various Roman commanders.[534] For decades after Sertorius's assassination, Roman generals returned to Rome after repeated triumphs over resisting portions of Spain, accompanied by booty and slaves. The crucial battles between Julius Caesar and Pompey were fought in Spain, with each side exacting funds and soldiers from the areas they occupied. Richardson describes the result: The civil wars, both that against Sertorius and that between Caesar and the Pompeians, caused immense physical damage to the areas in which they took place. Pompeius, writing to the Senate in 74, described how that part of Hispania citerior which was not under the control of the enemy, had . . . been ravaged either by himself or by Sertorius. The destruction of towns by Caesar and his adversaries was also substantial, and has left its mark not only in the literary record but in the archaeological evidence of destruction.[535] Lands were confiscated and given to retiring legionnaires to establish colonies; survivors of sieges were enslaved; mines, vineyards, olive orchards, and industries were taken over by the government or given to Roman immigrants while their original owners were killed or enslaved. This pattern of local resistance, cultural conflict, and imperial exploitation had lasted for more than two and a half centuries before Paul began to make plans for a mission to Spain.

Gésa Alföldi's study of the careers of imperial administrators, officers, and jurists in Spain starting with the time of Augustus provides a basis for assessing the importance of the three provinces to the empire.[536] Significant clues are also available from this source about the differing strategies that would have been required for Paul to begin work in these three very different areas. Unfortunately none of the names of the legates or proconsuls during the period of Paul's intended missionizing is extant.[537] Alföldi describes the shift toward civilian administrators after 13 B.C.E. when the number of

legions was reduced from 6 to 4 and the area was reorganized into the three provinces.[538]

Hispania citerior, Tarraconensis, was ruled by royal legates selected by the emperor for three-year terms from leading senatorial families in Italy, never from Spain itself through the end of the first century C.E.[539] Judging from the promotion patterns, Alföldi argues that only the province of Syria had a higher prestige in the first and second centuries.[540] A younger but rapidly rising senator was usually appointed as juridical legate of Tarraconensis to deal with legal matters in distant portions of the province.[541] The distinction and competence of these administrators indicates the crucial importance of *Hispania citerior* for the empire as well as their relative insulation from local pressures. The military legates were selected from senators with less prestige or prospects of advancement, reflecting the lack of military threats in the three centuries after the Augustan settlement.[542]

Lusitania, the new province carved out of the west and northwest corner of Spain after the cessation of the Cantabrian War, was much less fully urbanized. Galsterer lists only nineteen urbanized centers in the province.[543] Since no legion was stationed in Lusitania and since the cultural niveau and economic significance of this colony were modest, a single imperial legate of low senatorial standing was usually selected.[544] In one instance, Nero appointed a prestigious senator to this post in order to remove him as far as possible from Rome,[545] which lends weight to the impression that Lusitania was a backwoods post. While the requirements for a Pauline mission in Lusitania would have to be arranged independently from a mission in Tarraconensis, the Roman bureaucracy would likely have been crucial in both instances.

The opposite impression is given by the administrative arrangements in the highly urbanized province of

---

534 Richardson, *Romans in Spain*, 100, refers to Florus, *Ep.* 2.10.22.8.
535 Richardson, *Romans in Spain*, 116–17.
536 Alföldi, *Fasti Hispanienses,* passim.
537 See the summary tables of imperial administrators in ibid., 303–10, which have gaps from the mid-30s and 40s to the early 60s, with the possible exception of Proculus, who was proconsul of Baetica sometime during the Julio-Claudian period.

538 Ibid., 286–87.
539 Ibid., 193–94.
540 Ibid., 290.
541 Ibid., 290–92.
542 Ibid., 292–93.
543 Galsterer, *Untersuchungen*, table in back of book.
544 See Alföldi, *Fasti Hispanienses,* 293–94.
545 Ibid., 294.

Hispania ulterior, or Baetica. The large number of latinized urban areas and the presence of the largest cities west of Rome can be correlated with evidence of an impressive number of senatorial families residing there. Hence Baetica was not administered as an imperial province, but was assigned by Augustus as a senatorial responsibility, with a proconsul selected yearly by lot from a list of qualified candidates. That so many of the proconsuls were senators who either stemmed from Spain or had experience in Spain leads to the impression that care was taken to deal with this prestigious colony with respect. The subordinate office of quaestor was appointed by the proconsul, which again reflects concern for local political pressures.[546] It is thus clear that the affairs in this colony were not being administered by a distant bureaucracy in Rome; Baetica was granted a much higher degree of autonomy than the rest of Spain because of the influential senatorial families dwelling there. An additional factor was undoubtedly the rich silver, gold, and copper mines in Baetica, which were so important a factor in the imperial budget that they were "exploited directly by the Roman state."[547] Paul's approach to *Hispania ulterior* would thus require patronage with connections to leading senatorial families in Rome as well as Spain.

D. Implications for Paul's Missionary Strategy

The situation in Spain presented Paul's missionary strategizing with formidable challenges both on the linguistic and political levels.[548] If he were to seek out the small remnants of Greek-speaking population, the mission would have little chance of spreading through the peninsula. Proclamation and instruction in Latin would be required, and there is no evidence that Paul was sufficiently fluent to carry this out without translators.

Indeed, such resources would be difficult to develop, because the Hebrew Scriptures were not yet available in Latin, and the first evidence we have of Latin-speaking churches is in the mid-second century.[549] Even the church in Rome remained Greek speaking until the mid-third century,[550] while elsewhere in the West the church was associated for centuries with Greek immigrants.[551] The translation of the kerygma, the liturgy, and the instructional traditions into another idiom would be a substantial undertaking, especially in light of the fact that a range of additional translation resources would be required to extend past the restricted circle of Latin civilization in Spain. Given the resistance against Roman culture in large portions of Lusitania and Tarraconensis, it would probably not have appeared either feasible or promising to rely entirely upon the language of the conquerors. Since the latinized urban centers functioned as outposts of Roman rule and civilization in ways quite different from the Greek-speaking portions of the empire where Paul had scored his earlier successes,[552] care would have to be taken to find local patrons who were not resented by the native population. Paul needed the aid and counsel of congregations in Rome with contacts in Spain to make these preparations. There are many indications that the Letter to the Romans was designed to prepare the ground for the complicated project of the Spanish mission, including the insistence that the impartial righteousness of God does not discriminate against "barbarians" such as the Spaniards, that all claims of cultural superiority are false, that imperial propaganda must be recognized as bogus, and that the domineering behavior of congregations toward one another must be overcome if the missional hope to unify the world in the praise of God is to be fulfilled (15:9-13).

---

546 Ibid., 294–95.

547 Richardson, *Romans in Spain*, 168; see also D. G. Bird, "Pliny and the Gold Mines of the North-west of the Iberian Penninsula," in T. F. C. Blagg, R. F. J. Jones, and S. J. Keay, eds., *Papers in Iberian Archaeology*, BrAR S193 (Oxford: British Archaeological Reports, 1984) 341–68; Dewey, "Σπανίαν," 328–29.

548 On the methodological problem of assessing causative factors, see Fischer, *Historians' Fallacies*, 164–86.

549 See William H. C. Frend, *The Rise of Christianity* (Philadelphia: Fortress Press, 1984) 340.

550 See William H. C. Frend, *Town and Country in the Early Christian Centuries* (London: Variorum, 1980) xiii, 126.

551 See ibid., xiii, 125–29.

552 See Werner Dahlheim, "Die Funktion der Stadt im Römischen Herrschaftsverband," in F. Vittinghoff, ed., *Stadt und Herrschaft: Römische Kaiserzeit und hohes Mittelalter*, HZ.B 7 (Munich: Oldenbourg, 1982) 48–55.

8. The Purpose of Romans in the Plan for the Spanish Mission

In 1969 Günter Klein articulated the issue of this section in a manner that has remained true for many: Romans "has thus far revealed less of the secret of its occasion than has any other authentic letter of Paul."[553] In 1991 Ann Jervis began her study of the *Purpose of Romans* with reference to the obscurity of this letter's purpose, an obscurity that had been acknowledged since the end of the nineteenth century.[554] A decade later Angelika Reichert surveyed the efforts in the past thirty years and concluded that the purpose of this letter had still not been clarified.[555] The "enigma of Romans" as articulated by A. J. M. Wedderburn is that despite its being the most intensely analyzed writing in Western literature, a variety of purposes continue to be maintained, including the suggestion that "no one, single reason or cause will adequately explain the writing of Romans."[556] While it is admirably tolerant to propose a multiplicity of "reasons" for Romans, since distinguished scholars have advanced each one in persuasive detail, the concept of exigency in relation to the rhetorical purpose of a letter renders this implausible. Letter writers usually have a central goal in writing, although subsidiary topics may be mentioned in passing. That no less than "six factors" constitute Paul's purpose is implausible despite its inclusive formulation by Wedderburn:

(1) *both* the letter-frame, the beginning and end of Romans which give it the formal characteristics of a letter, *and* the body of the letter which is contained between that opening and that ending, (2) *both* Paul's situation *and* that of the church to which he was writing, and (3) *both* the fact that Paul's arguments in the body of the letter seem to have Jewish criticisms of his message in mind *and* the fact that at times he plainly seems to be addressing himself to Christians who are not Jews.[557]

Many other scholars present complex forms of multiple motivations for the letter, which render it very difficult to understand.[558] The dominant tradition of interpreting Romans as a doctrinal treatise rather than a situational letter, reflected in Wedderburn's second pair of factors, also tends to divide the letter up into the sections congenial to one's theological orientation, which become the main point of the letter, while the other sections are considered secondary.

For the most part, however, this debate over the enigma of Romans has overlooked four of the most important factors in assessing its purpose: the peculiar rhetoric of the letter,[559] the form of the greetings at the end and their likely inclusion in the original form of the letter,[560] the cultural situation in Spain,[561] and the role that Phoebe was undertaking as the patron of the Spanish mission and presenter of the letter to the congregations in Rome.[562] This section advances the case that many of the valuable insights in previous studies can best be coordinated with the hypothesis that the letter seeks to elicit support for Paul's forthcoming mission to Spain.[563]

---

553 Klein, "Paul's Purpose," 29.

554 Jervis, *Purpose,* 11, referring to F. J. A. Hort, *Prolegomena to St. Paul's Epistles to the Romans and the Ephesians* (London: Macmillan, 1895) 5.

555 Angelika Reichert, *Der Römerbrief als Gratwanderung. Eine Untersuchung zur Abfassungsproblematik,* FRLANT 194 (Göttingen: Vandenhoeck & Ruprecht, 2001) 58.

556 Wedderburn, *Reasons,* 5; the expression "enigma" comes from 1–21; similarly, in *Story of Romans,* 14–16, Katherine Grieb lists eight reasons for writing Romans.

557 Wedderburn, *Reasons,* 5.

558 For example, Minear, *Obedience,* 1–35, lists a series of "purposes" for Romans; Cranfield, 1:23–24, lists the many factors that the "student of Romans" must bear in mind; Dunn, 1:lvii, argues for three "main

emphases and purposes"; in *Römerbrief,* 145, 217–18, 312, 321, Reichert proposes different purposes for each section of the letter.

559 The first commentaries that I have seen that present some type of the rhetorical point of view are by Byrne and Witherington.

560 See, e.g., Schmidt, 250–51; Käsemann, 409–16; Cranfield, 1:29; Fitzmyer, 100–101; Witherington, 22.

561 One of the few commentators to place the Spanish mission in a central place is Zeller, 15, but he provides no account of the peculiar cultural situation there.

562 I first proposed this in 1988 in "Spanish Mission," 144–64.

563 The viewpoint in this section is adapted from ibid.

A. Theological Apology, Last Will and Testament

Many commentators believe that Romans is a defense of Paul's gospel against misunderstandings by opponents.[564] On the premise that Romans is a polemical letter, scholars have perceived a critique of antinomians[565] as well as legalists.[566] The question is why such an apology was sent to Rome. Günther Bornkamm answers this question by declaring that the search for specific reasons in the Roman church situation is a "wrong track" that leads nowhere.[567] Assuming that chap. 16 was not part of the original letter to Rome, Bornkamm points to the parallels between passages in Romans and the earlier letters and observes that the apologetic sections and the theological argumentation are general and abstract.[568] "The previous actual and concrete references" that one finds in Paul's earlier letters "have disappeared" and now receive "a strongly universal meaning."[569] In contrast to earlier letters, Romans "expresses the world-wide program of the Pauline mission" so that even the effort to reconcile the quarrelling groups in chap. 14 climaxes in 15:7-13 in the hope of all nations uniting in the praise of God.[570] The letter is therefore to be explained as "the historical testament of the Apostle," which is aimed at preparing the way for "a great missionary endeavor in the West."[571] This concrete aim is virtually lost from sight, however, in the widely influential conclusion of Bornkamm's article: "This great document, which summarizes and develops the most important themes and thoughts of the Pauline message and theology and which elevates his theology above the moment of definite situations and conflicts into the sphere of the eternally and

universally valid, this letter to the Romans is the last will and testament of the Apostle Paul."[572]

While this viewpoint retained a central place for Romans in the era of dialectical theology,[573] it rested on an inadequate grasp of the text-critical evidence concerning the ending of the letter and it leaves unanswered why Paul would have thought that the Roman audience had need of such a testament. The rhetoric of the letter reveals detailed interaction with a specific audience that is very different from audiences in other Pauline churches.

B. A Circular Letter to Ephesus and Rome

Building on earlier suggestions that chap. 16 was originally directed to Ephesus,[574] T. W. Manson argued that two versions of the letter were created by Paul: a fifteen-chapter letter to Rome and a sixteen-chapter copy to Ephesus.[575] This explains why the explicit references to Rome are missing in some Greek and Latin versions of 1:7 and 15,[576] and also why Paul is able to greet so many leaders personally in chap. 16 when he had never visited Rome.[577] Taking account of the evidence of Corinthian provenance, Manson concludes that the letter sums up the controversies in earlier congregations and thus constitutes "a manifesto setting forth his deepest convictions on central issues, a manifesto calling for the widest publicity" to be achieved by creating multiple copies for different locations.[578] This hypothesis rests on an inadequate grasp of the text-critical issues and cannot explain why a general manifesto designed for the church at large contains advice in 14:1—15:13 for conflicts that are

---

564 For example, Käsemann, 71–84, 101–4; Stuhlmacher, 8–10; Grieb, *Story of Romans*, 19–43, views the letter as a defense of Paul's doctrine of God's righteousness.

565 Lütgert, *Römerbrief*, 69–78.

566 For example, Ferdinand Christian Baur, "Über Zweck und Veranlassung des Römerbriefs und die damit zusammenhängeenden Verhältnis der römischen Gemeinde. Eine historisch-kritische Untersuchung," *TZTh* 3 (1836) 59–178; Baur, *Paul,* 1.316–25; Gunther Harder, "Der konkrete Anlass des Römerbriefes," *ThViat* 6 (1959) 21; Stuhlmacher, "Theme," 337: Romans is "an apologetic, comprehensive description of the Pauline gospel in the face of Jewish-Christian objections to the preaching of Paul." See also Stuhlmacher, "Purpose," 236.

567 Bornkamm, "Last Will and Testament," 20.

568 Ibid., 26: Romans "still remains a polemical letter. But who is the opponent?"

569 Ibid., 25.

570 Ibid.

571 Ibid., 27.

572 Ibid., 27–28.

573 See also Nygren, 10, who maintains that Romans provides the "right perspective" on the Christian gospel.

574 See the discussion in section 2 above.

575 Manson, "Romans—and Others," 13–15.

576 Ibid., 5–6.

577 Ibid., 12–13.

578 Ibid., 15.

unique to Rome. Moreover, as we have seen in section 2 above, an Ephesian destination cannot be coordinated with the precise wording of the greetings in chap. 16.

C. Providing an Apostolic Foundation for Roman Churches

Günter Klein also accepts the theory of the Ephesian provenance of chap. 16, but he takes more seriously than others the "tension" between Paul's "intention to preach the gospel to the Romans" and "his principle of non-interference" in 15:20.[579] He is critical of the idea that Paul needed help from Roman churches for his mission further west because theology would thereby "be reduced to merely a means to an end; nothing but grist for his apostolic calling card . . . as a means to benefit his own prestige."[580] Such a conclusion would relativize the central Lutheran doctrine of justification by faith, which lends a measure of urgency to Klein's article. He notes that while the references to Spain in 15:24 and 28 seem vague, there are explicit references to Paul's goal to preach the gospel in Rome (1:15; 15:16-20). Klein is also critical of efforts to relate Paul's purpose to the conflicts between the weak and the strong in Rome, employing as his final trump card the noninterference clause that renders it unlikely that Paul intended to intervene in Roman conflicts.[581] Building his case on the wording of 15:20, Klein lifts up the importance of building a "foundation" through the preaching of the gospel, which was Paul's distinctive task. "Paul can consider an apostolic effort in Rome because he does not regard the local Christian community there as having an apostolic foundation."[582] This is supported by the facts that Romans has no co-sender (unlike most other Pauline letters), that in the extensive prescript there is an emphasis on the gospel, and that the word "church" is missing in the prescript and in the rest of the fifteen-chapter letter.[583] Returning to the central theme of Lutheran theology, Klein concludes that "the justification of the godless" is "the correct foundation for the church" that Paul alone was in the position to provide.[584] This interpretation requires the premise that the final chapter did not belong to the letter sent to Rome, because in 16:7 Paul greets Andronikos and Junia who "are outstanding among the apostles" and are currently working in Rome. It requires that one downplay 1:12, where Paul speaks of wanting "to be mutually encouraged by each other's faith," as well as 15:14, where Paul states his confidence that the Roman believers are "filled with every kind of knowledge, capable also to admonish one another."

A modified version of Klein's hypothesis that takes chap. 16 into account was worked out by Ann Jervis, that "Paul was chiefly exercising his apostolic mandate in the letter" to encourage them "to enter Paul's apostolic orbit . . . through hearing his preaching."[585] This is established through an analysis of the epistolary structures of opening formulas, thanksgiving, and apostolic parousia. In 1:1-5 Paul provides an apology "for his apostolic credibility by affirming the creed that he shares with his readers" and thereby creates a "bond between himself and his readers."[586] On the problematic premise that the thanksgiving extends from 1:8 to 1:15,[587] Paul's hope is to "exercise his apostolic obligation by preaching" to believers in Rome and thereby establishing his authority.[588] By viewing 15:14-32 as an apostolic parousia, Paul seeks "to involve them in his responsibilities" to deliver the Jerusalem offering and to become "partners" in the Spanish mission,[589] but in the final analysis she rejects the idea that Paul hoped to use Rome as the "staging area" for the trip to Spain.[590] Jervis believes that the establishment of an apostolic foundation for the believers in Rome is the ultimate goal of Paul's letter, but without following Klein's interpretation of 15:20, there is no adequate explanation of why Paul plans to violate his noninterference clause by ministering among the already converted in Rome.

---

579 Klein, "Paul's Purpose," 32.
580 Ibid., 33.
581 Ibid., 37.
582 Ibid., 39.
583 Ibid., 40–42.
584 Ibid., 43.
585 Jervis, *Purpose*, 163, 164; see the similar emphasis in Anton Fridrichsen, "The Apostle and His Message," *UUÅ* 3 (1947) 1–23, cited by Jervis on 26.
586 Jervis, *Purpose*, 85.
587 See the commentary below for the evidence that 1:8-12 constitutes the thanksgiving while 1:13-15 is the *narratio* of the letter.
588 Jervis, *Purpose*, 108–9; Kruse, *Paul*, 167.
589 Ibid., 130–31.
590 Ibid., 163.

D. Seeking Support for the Jerusalem Offering

Along with others,[591] Jakob Jervell[592] and Ulrich Wilckens[593] have made a case that Paul's concern about whether the Jewish Christians in Jerusalem might reject the offering from Gentile churches, out of anxiety about the reactions of Jewish zealots (Rom 15:30-31), is the most important factor in writing Romans.[594] Jervell shares the perspective of Bornkamm and Klein that the letter cannot be understood in the light of the congregational situation in Rome itself.[595] Nor can the letter be explained by a desire to missionize in Rome or Spain. The argument of Romans is related to the central issues raised by the Jerusalem offering, including the following:

> Israel's lack of faith and Israel's future as the people of God, the significance of the apostle of the Gentiles for Israel and their conversion, circumcision and the meaning of the law, Jews and Gentiles in their relationship to the final judgment and the righteousness of God. . . . The theme of Romans is this: the righteousness of God is revealed through faith apart from the law, first to the Jews, then to the Greeks, and at the end to all Israel.[596]

The style of Romans also reveals that Paul "is absorbed by what he is going to say in Jerusalem."[597] With its rapidly changing style, its diatribes, and its constant changes between first, second, and third person discourse, the letter has "the characteristics of a speech" that would be suitable as an apology in Jerusalem but not in Rome.[598] He shares the speech with the Roman congregations because they were "recognized within the entire church (1:8; 16:19)," and have taken up "a central position on behalf of the entire church."[599] Paul would like to claim that the Roman Christians are on his side in the forthcoming struggle with Jerusalem,[600] and his request for their prayers (15:30) can only result in full "solidarity" if the church in Rome understands the issues.[601] Jervell's thesis therefore is: "The essential and primary content of Romans (1:18-11:36) is a reflection on . . . the 'collection speech,' or more precisely, the defense which Paul plans to give before the church in Jerusalem. . . . Paul has only one objective: to ask the Roman congregation for solidarity, support, and intercession in his behalf."[602] It is revealing that when Jervell refers to the "primary content" of the letter, he disregards chaps. 12–16, which certainly would not have been suitable for a defense speech in Jerusalem. It is also hard to imagine that the argument about universal sin (1:18–3:20) would contribute to such a defense. Indeed, a more careful rhetorical analysis of the letter indicates that it is demonstrative rather than judicial, and thus inappropriate for an apology. But Jervell and Wilckens have developed a theme that is vitally important for the Spanish mission, as we shall see.

E. Preparation for a Mission

That Romans was in some sense a missionary letter has frequently been suggested,[603] and some have argued

591 See, e.g., Ernst Fuchs, *Hermeneutik* (4th ed.; Tübingen: Mohr [Siebeck], 1970) 191; Suggs, "Word," 289–95.
592 Jervell, "Letter to Jerusalem," 53–64.
593 Wilckens, 1:44–46; 3:129–30.
594 Although he does not develop the point in detail, Dahl, "Missionary Theology," 77, writes that the appeal for intercession in 15:30-31 "may, indeed, be a main reason why Paul wrote *this* letter to the Romans."
595 Jervell, "Letter to Jerusalem," 54–55, refers to the congregational route as "a dead end."
596 Ibib., 59.
597 Ibid., 60.
598 Ibid., 61.
599 Ibid., 63.
600 Ibid., 64; Wilckens, 1:46. Brown and Meier, *Antioch and Rome*, 110, stress that Paul needs Rome's help "because *the dominant Christianity at Rome had been shaped by the Jerusalem Christianity associated with James and Peter.*"
601 Jervell, "Letter to Jerusalem," 62; Dunn, 1:lvi, follows this reasoning by referring to Paul's confidence in "the importance and efficacy of prayer."
602 Jervell, "Letter to Jerusalem," 65. Wilckens, 1:46, dislikes this "letter to Jerusalem" formulation but in most regards follows Jervell's argument.
603 Schmidt, 2; Cranfield, 1:22–23; Schrenk, "Missionsdokument," 82–87; Georg Eichholz, "Der ökumenische und missionarische Horizon der Kirche. Eine exegetische Studie zu Röm. 1,8-15," in *Tradition und Interpretation. Studien zum Neuen Testament und zur Hermeneutik*, ThBü 29 (Munich: Kaiser, 1965) 85–98.

that as a Roman citizen Paul wanted to climax his missionary career by preaching in Rome.[604] Paul's theology of mission was worked out in detail by Nils A. Dahl, who maintained that his theology and missionary activity were "inseparable from one another."[605] In contrast, most commentators have explained Paul's theology as a body of thought separate from the day-to-day task of establishing and sustaining congregations. A proper approach would be to "characterize Paul's theology as a christocentric theology of mission with biblical history and eschatology as its framework."[606] The unparalleled expansions in the prescript set forth Paul's apostolic "credentials" and the conclusion of 15:14-33 is a model of "diplomatic tact and politeness" as Paul discusses his missionary plans.[607] The statement of indebtedness to Greeks and barbarians in 1:14 is particularly significant in revealing his sense of calling to preach the gospel "boldly to all men everywhere, even in Rome."[608] He sketches the argument of the letter as an example of missionary preaching and insists that "'justification by faith' is not in itself the theme of the letter but part of, and a criterion for, Paul's missionary theology."[609] A proper interpretation of the letter, in Dahl's view, would contribute to regaining "the unity of theology and evangelism, and of justification by faith and world mission."[610] In contrast to the views sketched above, this is an approach that allows the entire sixteen chapters of Romans to be taken into account. Scholars who have pursued this lead have elaborated Paul's purpose in at least five different ways.

1. A Mission to Urge Coexistence of the Weak and the Strong in Rome

A number of scholars have argued that Paul was seeking to reconcile the weak and the strong, whose conflicts threatened the unity of the church.[611] N. T. Wright, for example, has stressed that the missional statements of 10:14ff. and 11:13ff. seek to overcome Gentile arrogance against the Jews as no longer part of the covenant community, so that the exhortation to the strong to tolerate the weak in 14:1–15:13 constitutes "the climax of the entire epistle."[612] Wendy Dabourne agrees that 15:7-13 is "the climax of the letter" that introduces Paul to the Romans so he can "exercise his apostolic ministry among them."[613]

The most extensive exposition of this idea is found in the work of William S. Campbell.[614] The letter was written because "the liberal-minded Gentile Christian majority (the strong in faith) were unwilling to have fellowship with the conservative Jewish Christian minority (the weak in faith)."[615] Campbell argues that the theological center of Romans in chap. 3 deals with "problems within the Roman Christian community"[616] by stressing "the equality of Jew and Gentile in sin"[617] and under grace. Similarly the discourse in chaps. 4–15 is addressed "to a real situation in Rome where current anti-Judaism was threatening the unity of the church."[618] If Abraham is

---

604 Lipsius, 75; Zahn, 21–23.

605 Dahl, "Missionary Theology," 70; for a similar perspective see Eichholz, "Röm 1,8-15," 15–27.

606 Dahl, "Missionary Theology," 71.

607 Ibid., 75–76.

608 Ibid., 78.

609 Ibid., 82.

610 Ibid., 88.

611 Herbert Preisker, "Das historische Problem des Römerbriefes," WZ(J) 2 (1952-53) 25–32; Bartsch, "Historische Situation," 282–87; Minear, Obedience, 8–20; Jewett, Tolerance, 68–91, 126–33; Beker, Paul, 69–74; Smiga, "Occasion of the Letter," 262–69; Boers, Justification, 145–69, 221–24; Walters, Ethnic Issues, 88–92; Esler, Conflict and Identity, 339–52. Engberg-Pedersen, Stoics, describes the purpose of Romans "to prepare for a reasonably extended stay in Rome" (181) whose aim is "parenesis" (183).

612 Wright, Climax, 235.

613 Dabourne, Purpose, 72.

614 Among the extensive writings on this theme by William S. Campbell are "Why Did Paul Write Romans?" ExpT 85 (1973-74) 264–69; "The Romans Debate," JSNT 10 (1981) 19–28; "Revisiting Romans," ScrB 12 (1981) 2–10; "Romans iii," 251–64; "Paul's Missionary Practice and Policy in Romans," IBS 12 (1990) 2–25; "Identity," 67–82; Paul's Gospel, passim; "The Rule of Faith in Romans 12:1–15:13: The Obligation of Humble Obedience to Christ as the Only Adequate Response to the Mercies of God," in D. M. Hay and E. E. Johnson, eds., Pauline Theology (Minneapolis: Fortress Press, 1995) 3:259–86; "Favouritism and Egalitarianism: Irreconcilable Emphases in Romans?" SBLSP 37 (1998) 12–32.

615 Campbell, Paul's Gospel, 21.

616 Campbell, "Romans iii," 260.

617 Campbell, Paul's Gospel, 21.

618 Campbell, "Romans iii," 262.

"'the father of us all' (4:16) the implication is that there should be no division within this church."[619] In chaps. 10 and 11 Paul makes clear that election "is not a question of Jew *or* Gentile but of Jew *and* Gentile."[620] In 11:16-18 Paul opposes the "sectarian tendencies" of Gentiles to believe they had displaced Israel in the sacred olive tree.[621] Campbell has a particularly cogent grasp of the fact that "Paul in chapters 14–15 accepts the right of both 'the weak' and 'the strong' Christians to follow their own conscience . . . . They are to accept one another openly and without reservation as Christ has accepted them,"[622] an argument that reaches its high-point in 15:7.[623] Employing the terminology of contemporary missionary theory, Campbell says that Paul "accepts diversity as given and as an abiding reality."[624] The central theme of Romans is "the revelation of the righteousness of God in the Christ event which he depicts as being simultaneously (a) the confirmation of the covenant promises to Israel and (b) the opening up of its blessings to Gentiles also."[625] While this is an appealing exposition of the theology of Romans, it does not explain why Paul would break his noninterference principle (15:20) by intervening in Roman affairs; and like the other scholars mentioned in this section, he does not take account of the social information available in chap. 16 and in the research about Spain.

2. A Mission to Convert the Weak into Paulinists

Many have suggested that Paul's aim is to gain the allegiance of believers in Rome to his point of view with regard to faith as freedom from the law.[626] This approach is developed into a comprehensive theory by Francis Watson.[627] He infers from 14:1–15:13 that there were two congregations in Rome, "separated by mutual hostility and suspicion over the question of the law."[628] The legalists are mostly Jewish Christians who follow the precedents of Dan 1:8-16; Judg 12:1-4; and Esth 14:17 in avoiding nonkosher meat and wine and retaining the Jewish calendar. Watson does not grapple with the reference in 14:2 that is far more extreme than other forms of Jewish asceticism, that the weak "eat only lettuce." The Gentile Christians include some leaders whom Paul has met, so their congregation "may well have been founded by Paul's own converts and associates: *Gentile Christianity is therefore Pauline Christianity.*"[629] This is an effective way to avoid the contradiction between 1:13 and the noninterference clause in 15:20 but it is chronologically slippery, because Paul refers to Prisca, Aquila, Miriam, Andronicus, Junia, Urbanus, Tryphaina and Tryphosa, and Persis as persons who had worked as evangelists in Rome before he met them, probably sometime after their banning under the Edict of Claudius. As I noted in section 3 above, the churches in Rome had been founded in the 30s or early 40s, long before Paul had a chance to meet these leaders during their exile. Moreover, the only person greeted in chap. 16 for whose conversion Paul felt responsible and who could indisputably be classified as a "Paulinist" is Epainetos (16:5), but in contrast to others he is not identified as a congregational leader in Rome. In Watson's theory Paul's letter had "the aim of converting the Jewish Christians to his point of view so as to create a single 'Pauline' congregation in Rome."[630] Paul demands that the Jewish Christians "abandon the idea that the law is the authoritative, binding law of God" and that both sides must accept "the Pauline principle of freedom from the law."[631] Although Watson cites 14:1, where Paul recommends welcoming the weak "but not for disputes over opinions," he disregards this and other indications that Paul seeks coexistence between groups that retain their distinctive ethnic and theological integrity (14:4, 8, 10-12,

---

619 Campbell, *Paul's Gospel*, 21.
620 Ibid., italics in original.
621 Ibid., 141–42.
622 Ibid., 93.
623 Ibid., 22.
624 Ibid., 93; see also 101–6.
625 Ibid., 173.
626 See, e.g., Schmidt, 2–3; Wilckens, 1:40–42; N. Krieger, "Zum Römerbrief," *NovT* 3 (1959) 146–48, to win support for his Gentile mission from Jewish Christians; Brendan Byrne, "'Rather Boldly' (Rom

15,15): Paul's Prophetic Bid to Win the Allegiance of Christians in Rome," *Bib* 74 (1993) 83–96; idem, *Romans*, 18–19; Theobald, 1:21, in reference to Paul's aim of establishing a personal relationship with Roman believers.
627 Watson, *Paul*, 88–181, idem, "Two Roman Congregations," 203–15.
628 Watson, "Two Roman Congregations," 206.
629 Ibid., 209, italics in original.
630 Ibid., 207.
631 Ibid., 205, 207.

15-16, 19-23; 15:1-7).[632] In contrast to 1 Cor 8 and 10, in Rom 14:1–15:13 Paul prohibits mutual conversion of others to the point of view held by one's own group. Finally, Watson's repeated references to two congregations that should now become a "single" congregation[633] appears to imply a total number of believers far smaller than other evidence suggests if the average congregation had 20-40 members. Moreover, that two such groups could be expected to meet in a single location in an overcrowded *insula* building located in one of the slum districts identified by the early evidence is implausible.[634] Finally, in contrast to Watson's view, we shall see in the commentary below that there is evidence in every chapter of this letter that Paul seeks a respectful coexistence between the congregations in Rome, honoring the integrity of each side, but this must be coordinated somehow with the noninterference principle of 15:20.

Angelika Reichert develops a version of Watson's theory of conversion to Paulinism that contains the same shortcomings while suggesting different motivations for each section of the letter. Chapters 12–16 seek to convert the weak to the theological orientation of the strong, which is congenial to Paul, while encouraging the development of an outgoing disposition inclined to missionizing.[635] Chapters 9–11 advocate a "theocentric" perspective that Pauline theology alone can provide, which would allow Jews and Gentiles to live as equals in a Pauline congregation.[636] Chapters 1–8 establish Paul's status as the apostle to the Gentiles whose authoritative theology is able to unify the church.[637] It remains unclear in this complicated monograph why Paul violates his noninterference principle in seeking to extend his authority over the Roman congregations, but this indeed appears to be the theologically acceptable

"razor's edge" implied in Reichert's title. Why Paul needed the assistance of Roman churches in mounting the future mission to Spain also remains unclear, because the peculiar conditions there are not mentioned in her monograph.

3. A Mission to Include Gentiles as Legitimate Believers

Since neither of them deals explicitly with the purpose of writing Romans, the efforts of Lloyd Gaston and Terence Donaldson to place Paul's legitimation of the status of Gentile believers at the center of his theology must be treated here as an implicit alternative to other theories of Paul's mission. Gaston traces the theme of the inclusion of Gentiles throughout Romans, from 1:16-17 through 4:23-24 to 9:24 and 11:25.[638] The theme of divine impartiality in 2:11 pertains to Gentiles as well as Jews being under sin in equal measure as they now have equal access to grace, so that "inclusion of Gentiles does not mean exclusion of Jews."[639] Gaston places particular emphasis on 15:7-13, which recapitulates chaps. 3–4 and 9–11 by stressing "the inclusion of the Gentiles."[640] Gaston summarizes the central theme of Romans in a way that reveals his concern to avoid the residue of interpretive anti-Judaism: "at least in this letter the good news of Paul's gospel for Gentiles is not part of a polemic against Torah or Israel. Without at all excluding Jews, he is able to argue very effectively and very passionately that the inclusion of Gentiles was always the goal of the Torah, which has now been realized through the righteousness of God in the faithfulness of Jesus Christ."[641]

Donaldson provides a qualified version of Gaston's perspective, concluding that Paul struggles against the seeming impossibility of including Gentiles within "Israel" without denying the distinctive role granted to

---

632 See also the critique by Dunn, 1:lvii, citing my study, *Tolerance*, 41, 68–91.

633 Watson, "Two Roman Congregations," 206, 207, 209, 211, 212.

634 See section 6 above.

635 Reichert, *Römerbrief*, 312, 321.

636 Ibid., 217–18. In a similar manner Watson, *Paul*, 162, contends that Rom 9–11 maintains "the consistency of the Pauline view of God's activity with the OT Scriptures" so as to "convince his readers . . . to unite with the Roman Gentile Christians."

637 Reichert, *Römerbrief*, 145; see also Watson, *Paul*, 160, the "many and various" subjects discussed in

Rom 1–8 "are held together by a single purpose: to persuade Jewish Christian readers to accept the legitimacy of Pauline Gentile Christianity and to deny the claims of the synagogue."

638 Gaston, *Paul*, 118; see also idem, "Romans in Context: The Conversation Revisited," in J. C. Anderson et al., eds., *Pauline Conversations in Context: Essays in Honor of Calvin J. Roetzel*, JSNTSup 221 (Sheffield: Sheffield Academic Press, 2002) 125–41.

639 Gaston, *Paul*, 123.

640 Ibid., 133.

641 Ibid., 134.

the Jews.[642] Although he affirms the impartiality of God, Paul does not abandon "Jewish particularism," and in 15:7-13 Christ serves as the servant of Israel "in order that the Gentiles might glorify God for his mercy."[643] The argument concerning Abraham in chap. 4 claims "that uncircumcised Gentile believers enjoy full and legitimate status before God . . . on the basis of their faith" without fulfilling the "prerequisite" of circumcision.[644] In Rom 9–11 it becomes clear that the "Gentiles are present at the end of the race course . . . because the salvation accomplished by Christ is available . . . to all."[645] In particular 3:9-21 has "a leveling effect, putting Jew and Gentile on an equal footing,"[646] but since Donaldson does not extend his analysis into chaps. 14 and 16, it is impossible to be sure whether he would continue this argument about the inclusion of the Gentiles into the analysis of what Paul seeks with regard to the weak and the strong.

4. A Mission to Convert Nonbelieving Jews in Rome

In a section entitled "the impact of redefining the 'weak' and the 'strong' on the purpose and message of Romans," Mark Nanos makes a case that identifying the former as non-Christian Jews has a bearing on the entire letter.[647] Paul's goal is to change their Jewish faith into "faith in Jesus as the Christ."[648] This can be accomplished only when their loyalty to the Torah and to Jewish customs is respected, as suggested in 14:1-21, whereby Gentile Christians play the role of "righteous Gentiles" in refraining from nonkosher food.[649] However, the wording of 14:3, 4, 6, and 8-10 makes clear that both sides being addressed already serve the same Lord Christ.

More plausible is Nanos's claim that Paul's admonition to avoid giving offense to persons outside the circle of Christian groups (12:17-18) pertains "to the context of the Christian gentiles in Rome" in their effort to influence the large Jewish community in the city.[650] The wording of 11:12 and 25 should lead Gentile believers "to understand that Israel's suffering is vicariously for their gain," and therefore that humble recognition of historic Israel should be encouraged.[651] That Paul is deeply committed to the conversion of his fellow Jews is indisputable in the light of 9:1-5; 11:14-15; and 11:25-26, and it is clear that Paul's hope to missionize to the end of the known world is directly related to this commitment (11:11-14) and to the "mystery of Romans" that Nanos rightly derives from 11:25. But that the "weak" are nonbelieving Jews remains implausible.

5. A Mission to the Barbarians in Spain

Most commentators acknowledge that the references to Paul's travel plans to Spain in 15:24 and 28 are somehow related to the purpose of his letter.[652] The widely used introduction to the NT by W. G. Kümmel argued that Romans is an expression of "missionary politics" because Paul needed a "basis of operation" in Rome for his mission further west to Spain.[653] Similarly Peter Stuhlmacher argues that Paul "intends to visit the Christians in Rome, reach a consensus with them, and enlist their support for the missionary work he was planning in the West. He has no intention of engaging in such activity in somebody else's area. All he hopes for is Christian unity in respect of his gospel."[654] The dissertation by Markku Kettunen that Stuhlmacher sponsored comes to the same conclusion, that the Spanish mission is the "final purpose of the visit and the letter."[655] In comparison with the four approaches sketched above, this is the only one that avoids a violation of Paul's principle of noninterference, because Spain is virgin territory where Christ has not "already been named" (15:20).

---

642 Donaldson, *Paul and the Gentiles*, 305–6.
643 Ibid., 93, 97.
644 Ibid., 126.
645 Ibid., 130.
646 Ibid., 141; see also the similar arguments of Alfred Suhl, "Der konkrete Anlaß des Römerbriefes," *Kairos* 13 (1971) 119–30, esp. 127; and of Daniel Jong-Sang Chae, *Paul as Apostle to the Gentiles: His Apostolic Self-Awareness and Its Influence on the Soteriological Argument in Romans*, PGTM (Carlisle: Paternoster, 1997) 16, 46–71.
647 Nanos, *Mystery*, 159–65.
648 Ibid., 151.
649 Ibid., 160.
650 Ibid., 161.
651 Ibid.
652 See, e.g., Dodd, 7; Fitzmyer, 79; Haacker, 12–13; Stuhlmacher, 5–6.
653 Kümmel, *Introduction*, 305–7; see also Noack, "Current," 155–66; Vielhauer, *Geschichte*, 181–84; Aus, "Paul's Travel Plans," 232–62.
654 Stuhlmacher, "Theme," 237.
655 Kettunen, *Abfassungszweck*, 168, 138–41; see also Dewey, "Σπανίαν," 322–24.

Since Stuhlmacher and Kettunen take no account of the cultural situation in Spain, however, it remains unclear why Paul would have needed help from the congregations in Rome to missionize there.

As noted in section 7 above, the lack of Jewish population in Spain would have provided serious impediments to Paul's previous missionary strategy. He could not expect to find synagogues there to provide the initial basis for the messianic proclamation, to recruit converts and patrons, and also to make the business contacts that were necessary for a self-supporting mission supported by his own handwork. Even more serious were the linguistic barriers against missionizing in Koine Greek, the language of Paul's oral and written discourse and of the entire missional form of Christianity in the first generation,[656] because Greek was not widely known in Spain. The language of the Roman conquerors was used in the large urban areas, but the Celt-Iberian and other languages continued to be spoken by most of the population. For the first time in Christian history, as far as we know, a two-step process of translation was required: from Greek to Latin and then into the various local languages.

These financial and cultural barriers required the assistance of Roman congregations that had contacts with immigrants from Spain and with Roman bureaucrats charged with responsibilities there. To elicit this support, Paul needed to introduce his theology of mission, to dispel misunderstandings and allegations against his proclamation of the gospel, and to encourage the Roman congregations to overcome their imperialistic behavior toward one another, because it discredited the gospel of the impartial righteousness of God. If the Gentile and Jewish Christians continued to shame each other, they would carry a gospel to the barbarians in Spain that would continue the perverse system of honor on which the exploitative empire rested. Since the population in Spain continued to resist imperial exploitation, such a gospel would have no chance of success there. Therefore Paul attacked perverse systems of honor by dispelling the idea that some persons and groups are inherently righteous and by proclaiming the message that God honors sinners of every culture in an impartial

manner through Christ. Paul's indebtedness to "Greeks and barbarians, educated and uneducated" (1:14), led him to proclaim the boundless mercy of the one God of all peoples (3:29-30; 15:9-13), who alone is capable of evoking reconciliation and harmony in a world torn by exploitation and conflict (5:10-11; 15:5-6). This is why Rom 9–11 is crucial for the Spanish mission, because God does not abandon people even when they reject impartial righteousness (10:2-3), and in the end Paul's gospel proclaims that the Spaniards who are treated as shameful barbarians will stand alongside the Jews and every other nation in the recognition that "God has consigned all persons in disobedience that he might have mercy on all" (11:32). The climax of the letter is reached in the exhortation concerning mutual welcome between previously competitive groups (15:7; 16:3-16, 21-23) and the holy kiss that honors ethnic diversity within the new family of God (16:16). If the Roman house and tenement churches can overcome their conflicts and accept one another as honorable servants of the same master (14:4), they would be able to participate in a credible manner in the mission to extend the gospel to the end of the known world.

F. The Relation of Subsidiary Purposes to the Spanish Mission

With the exception of the Spanish mission hypothesis, the scholarly efforts to resolve the enigma of Romans have difficulty in accounting for all the evidence. Yet they provide a number of valid exegetical insights that can be incorporated into the missional goal that Paul has in mind. Here is a brief sketch of the points that will be developed in the commentary below.

It is the epideictic genre of the letter that gives the impression of a manifesto or a "testament," which sets forth Paul's convictions in a systematic manner. This was required to clarify his theology for the sake of gaining support of the Roman congregations, who had received distorted reports about him. There was a concrete reason for this particular presentation of Paul's theology. To be a credible leader of a mission to Spain, there is an urgent need to describe the kind of apostolic "foundation" he would provide—to pick up Klein's theme—in

---

656 Jeffers, *Conflict at Rome,* 7, states the consensus: "The lingua franca of earliest Christianity was Greek. Latin . . . did not supplant Greek among the

Christian churches of Rome until late in the second century."

Spain but not in Rome. The references to Spain are intentionally vague because the complication of the Spanish cultural situation required delicate negotiations that Phoebe could do only in person. Since a mission to those perceived to be "barbarians" in Spain would be jeopardized if the congregations in Rome continue to act in imperialistic ways toward one another, a resolution of the tensions between Gentile and Jewish Christians is essential. The issue posed by the Jerusalem offering is parallel to the conflicts among the Roman congregations, and both must be cleared away before the mission to Spain can be mounted. Although Romans is not a "letter to Jerusalem," the issue of the offering is crucial for Paul's missionary project. Moreover, the observations Jervell made about the oral style of Romans are confirmed throughout the commentary, and not only with regard to the first eleven chapters.

The dialectic between William Campbell and Francis Watson with regard to the question of coexistence or conversion has a direct bearing on the mission to the barbarians in Spain, because in contrast to the cultural bias in Rome, Paul wishes to reverse the imbalance of honor and insist on the impartial mercy of God that treats each group alike. As Gaston and Donaldson observe, Paul includes both Jews and Gentiles as equal in honor in God's realm, which sustains the promise that no one is classified by the gospel as an uncivilized and dangerous barbarian. And Nanos is certainly right that Paul retains a central place for the conversion of the Jews, coordinated with his commitment to the Gentile mission. Reichert and Klein are correct in highlighting Paul's claims to be an authoritative apostle, but he wishes thereby to qualify as the suitable agent to extend the gospel into Spain, not to take control of the Roman congregations themselves. Jervis's summary is still appropriate, except that she overlooks the noninterference clause in the final sentence:

> . . . the establishment of an apostolic relationship with the Roman readers is an important function of this

letter. Some of the terms of the relationship that it is this letter's function to establish seem to be: (1) the Roman Christians' acceptance of Paul's self-presentation as one with a particular God-given mission to evangelize Gentiles; (2) the reader's understanding that the mission Paul preaches is in accordance with what the faithful in Rome believe; and (3) the readers' recognition that Paul regards all Gentiles, even those in Rome, as falling under his leadership.[657]

The leadership Paul wishes to exercise is to lead the mission to Spain, not to establish Pauline congregations in Rome. This is why he explains his principle of noninterference in 15:20, and the Spanish mission hypothesis is the only one that takes this with full seriousness. But it should be clear in the light of the information now available about Spain that he needed the full resources of many of the congregations in Rome, none of which was accessible to him except through the ministrations of the woman who had agreed to be his patron.

G. The Crucial Role of Phoebe as Patron of the Spanish Mission

It is widely agreed among current commentators that the word προστάτις describing Phoebe's role in 16:2 is a technical term for an upper-class benefactor.[658] In contrast to his earlier reluctance to accept patronage (e.g., 1 Cor 9:3-23), Paul states that Phoebe "has been a patron to many and to myself as well," which indicates that she is "a person of some means, able to undertake business journeys with an entourage of some size"; she fits the class of "wealthy women . . . who acted as patrons for others."[659] The crucial element in reconstructing her role is the request in 16:2 that the congregations "provide whatever she needs from you in the matter (πράγματι)." In view of the impoverished status of congregations in Rome,[660] it is inconceivable that a woman of her social class could hope to gain help from them in her business, in a lawsuit, or in the provision of housing.[661] Paul's formulation provides a decisive clue

---

657 Jervis, *Purpose*, 159.
658 See the commentary below; for a recent survey of the social system of benefaction, see Joubert, *Benefactor*, 26–71.
659 Byrne, 447–48.
660 See section 6 above.

661 Michel, 378, and Dunn, 2:888, argue that Phoebe's matter was a lawsuit; Edgar J. Goodspeed, "Phoebe's Letter of Introduction," *HTR* 44 (1951) 55–57, imagines that she needs housing on a business trip.

about what is intended: "provide her whatever she needs in the matter, for she herself has been a patron to many and to myself as well" (16:2). The "matter" is her missionary patronage, which she has provided for many others and now is providing for Paul, and this help is what Paul requests from the Roman congregations.

In view of the practice of Greco-Roman epistolography, it is clear that the choice of a letter bearer was sometimes as crucial as the content of the letter. A trusted messenger would fill in the sensitive details and carry out the tasks envisioned in the letter. It is widely assumed that Phoebe was the bearer of Paul's Letter to the Romans.[662] Phoebe's primary task would thus be to present the letter to the various congregations in Rome and discuss its contents and implications with church leaders. Her scribe Tertius, who had written the letter, would read it on her behalf. As was customary for letter bearers, she would then attempt to achieve the aims of the letter, namely the unification of the Roman house churches so that they would be able to cooperate in the support of the Spanish mission. Given the diversity of the congregations alluded to in chap. 16, this would have required formidable political skills on Phoebe's part. In view of the complexity of the argument of the letter, it would have also required substantial interpretive skills.

Convincing the independent house churches that Paul was a trustworthy partner for the Spanish mission project would not have been easy, given his previous involvement in controversial projects and conflicts. Christians of various orientations would have had reason to question the advisability of working with Paul. Conservative, Jewish Christians would have known him as a radical advocate of the Gentile mission and a chief opponent of the Judaizers. They would have heard reports of Paul's harsh encounter with Peter at Antioch, in which Paul had denounced him as hypocritical for refusing to eat with Gentiles. They would have been suspicious of Paul's strategy of acting like a Jew to the Jews and a Gentile to the Gentiles, wondering if Paul was reliable.

The house churches close to Roman governmental circles (Rom 16:10-11) would have been concerned about Paul's history of difficulties with provincial authorities: his repeated imprisonments and the involvements with riots and other public disturbances in Pisidian Antioch, Iconium, Lystra, Philippi, Beroea, Corinth, and Ephesus. Cooperation with a controversial troublemaker might threaten the safety of the house churches in Rome or undermine the relationship of some of their leaders with other Roman authorities. These considerations would be particularly relevant in light of the crucial importance of Spain for imperial finances and the elements of resistance against Roman civilization in two of the three Spanish provinces. Although the repercussions about sponsoring subversive activities would have been felt most directly by Christians among the Narcissiani and the Aristobuliani who were administering imperial affairs in places like Spain, leaders of the other house churches in Rome would also have understood the risk.

Paul's sponsorship by an upper-class patroness like Phoebe would have gone far to answer the inevitable questions concerning Paul's reliability. Her wealth, social prestige, and legal status would serve as a kind of guarantee that his actions would remain within responsible limits and would afford him and the Roman church a measure of protection if he got into trouble. The churches at Rome could thus cooperate in the mission without undertaking its patronage, which meant that they would not become liable if Paul's history repeated itself. An additional mitigating factor that Phoebe would likely have pointed out was that the controversies related to Paul had largely been fomented by radical Jewish opposition to his mission, and the absence of a Jewish population in Spain might allow a less disruptive missional enterprise.

If Phoebe could succeed in the first two tasks, she would solicit the advice and counsel of the Roman house churches to find suitable resources for the mission in Spain. This would involve providing bases of operation in each of the three provinces for Paul and his missionary colleagues, finding logistical support for their travels and lodging, and recruiting translators capable of moving from Greek to Latin as well as other languages. The

---

662 See Cranfield, 3:780: "It is highly probable that Phoebe was to be the bearer of Paul's letter to Rome." Most commentators who believe chap. 16 originally belonged to the letter draw a similar conclusion.

most crucial decision, of course, would be the selection of the right contacts in Spain, because the lack of synagogues made it impossible for Paul to get acquainted with circles of Gentile God-fearers before recruiting appropriate patrons for house churches and leaders for tenement churches. In the Spanish context, the decisions would have to be made ahead of time and negotiations would be required to prepare the way before the arrival of Paul and his coworkers. If inappropriate local patrons were chosen, the entire mission would be jeopardized. These reflections about the practical exigencies of the Spanish mission are crucial for understanding the letter as a whole.

Commentary

1

The First Pericope

The Inauguration of Paul's Communication with Believers in Rome: Sender, Apostolic Credentials, Confession, Address, and Greeting

1/ **Paul, slave of Christ Jesus,[a] an apostle called [and] set apart for God's gospel, 2/ which he proclaimed beforehand through his prophets by the holy scriptures, 3/ concerning his son, who was**
  "born[b] from David's seed according to the flesh, 4/ appointed[c] God's son by power according to a spirit of holiness, by resurrecting from the dead," Jesus Christ our Lord, 5/ through whom we have received grace and apostleship [leading] to the obedience of faith among all the Gentiles, for the sake of his name, 6/ among whom you also are called of Jesus Christ; 7/ to all God's[d] beloved, called saints, who are in Rome.[e] Grace to you and peace[f] from God our Father and [the] Lord Jesus Christ.

a   The sequence "Jesus Christ" in P[26] ℵ A G K L P Ψ 0278 6 33 69 88 104 256 263 323 330 424 436 459 614 945 1175 1241 1243 1319 1505 1506 1573 1735 1739 1836 1852 1874 1881 1962 2127 2200 2344 2400 2464 2495 *Maj Lect* b d g o vg[cl] sy[p, h, pal] sa bo Ir[lat v.l.] (eth) geo slav Ir[lat mss] Or[1/3] Ps-Ath Bas GrNy Did Did[dub] Chr Severian Asterius-Amasea Cyr Hes Thret Ambst Faustinus Tyc Ambr[1/3] Hier Pel Aug[5/14] Quodvultdeus Vig is more widely attested than the "Christ Jesus" of P[10] B 81 *pc* ar mon vg[st, ww] Ir[lat] Or[2/3] Victorinus-Rome Ambr[2/3] Aug[9/14] that is favored by Nestle-Aland[26/27] and most current commentators. The latter is the more difficult reading in view of the frequent use of the sequence "Jesus Christ" in Rom 1:4, 6, 7, 8.

b   The minor variant γεννωμένου ("begotten") in 61* *pc* sy[p] Or appears to reflect later speculation about Christology.

c   The Latin versions, Ir[lat vid], and others have *praedestinatus* ("predestined") at this point, which leads Nestle-Aland[26/27] to include the Greek equivalent προορισθέντος as a textual variant, but as Cran-

field, 1:61, points out, there is no evidence of this in the Greek text.

d   The phrase ἀγαπητοῖς θεοῦ ("beloved of God") is omitted in D[abs1] 1915 and replaced by ἐν ἀγάπη θεοῦ in G ar d* g r Ambst *al.* Both the omission and the replacement are clearly secondary and may reflect efforts to downplay later claims of Roman precedence, since both would eliminate the implication that the Roman Christians deserve the title "beloved of God." Texts with the phrase "beloved of God" include P[10, 26] ℵ A B C K L P Ψ 6 33 69 81 88 104 181 330 424 436 451 614 629 630 945 1175 1241 1243 1319 1505 1506 1573 1735 1739 1836 1874 1877 1881 1962 2127 2344 2464 2492 2495 *Maj Lect* vg sy[p, h, pal] sa bo arm Or[gr, lat].

e   The absence of ἐν Ῥώμη ("in Rome") in G *pc* 1739[mg] 1908[mg] g Or[1739mg] is too weakly attested to be original, and according to Metzger, *Textual Commentary*, 446, was "probably . . . a deliberate excision, made in order to show that the letter is of general, not local, application." Following a suggestion by William Benjamin Smith, "Address and Destination of St. Paul's Epistle to the Romans," *JBL* 20 (1901) 1–21, Adolf von Harnack argues that the absence of "in Rome" was original, expressing Paul's intent to stress the "spiritual belongingness" of the congregation in "Zu Röm 1,7," *ZNW* 3 (1902) 85, but this assessment does not follow normal rules of text criticism. Theodor Zahn also made a case for the originality of G in his *Einleitung*, 268, 277–79, critiqued by Rudolf Steinmetz, "Textkritische Untersuchung zu Röm 1,7," *ZNW* (1908) 177–89. Zuntz, *Text*, 276–77, also argues that the original form of Romans lacked "in Rome" except as a marginal note, but this is not plausible in the light of Gamble's demonstration in *Textual History*, 29–33, that the absence occurs only in 14-chapter versions of the letter. The textual support for the inclusion of "in Rome" is very strong: P[10,26vid] ℵ A B C D[abs1] K L P Ψ 6 33 81 88 104 181 256 263 330 424 436 451 459 614 629 1175 1241 1319 1506 1573 1739 1852 1877 1881 1912[vid] 1962 2127 2200 2464 2492 *Lect* ar b d (mon) o vg sy[p, h, pal] sa bo arm eth geo slav Or[gr, lat] Chr Thret Ambst Pel Aug.

f   The widely attested order χάρις ὑμῖν καὶ εἰρήνη ("grace to you and peace") is shifted in sy[p] to the sequence εἰρήνη καὶ χάρις ὑμῖν ("peace and grace to you").

Analysis

The study of classical rhetoric reveals the crucial role of the *exordium* for the understanding of a subsequent argument. The *exordium* not only introduces the speaker in a manner calculated to appeal to the audience and lend credence to the speaker's cause, but it also frequently introduces the topics to be addressed in a speech.[1] When one compares this opening with Greco-Roman letters,[2] its length and complexity are unmistakable. If Paul had followed the typical form for a letter where the sender and recipient know each other, Romans would have begun as follows:

Sender: Παῦλος ("Paul")
Recipient: τοῖς οὖσιν ἐν Ῥώμῃ ("to those in Rome")
Greeting: χαίρειν ("greetings").

Even in comparison with the other Pauline letters, the opening of Romans is considerably expanded, as 2 Cor 1:1-2 indicates:

Sender: Παῦλος ἀπόστολος Χριστοῦ Ἰησοῦ διὰ θελήματος θεοῦ καὶ Τιμόθεος ὁ ἀδελφός ("Paul the apostle of Christ Jesus through the will of God and Timothy the brother")
Recipient: τῇ ἐκκλησίᾳ τοῦ θεοῦ τῇ οὔσῃ ἐν Κορίνθῳ σὺν τοῖς ἁγίοις πᾶσιν τοῖς οὖσιν ἐν ὅλῃ τῇ Ἀχαΐᾳ ("to the church of God that is in Corinth with all the saints in the whole of Achaia")
Greeting: χάρις ὑμῖν καὶ εἰρήνη ἀπὸ θεοῦ πατρὸς ἡμῶν καὶ κυρίου Ἰησοῦς Χριστοῦ ("Grace to you and peace from God our Father and the Lord Jesus Christ").

To understand Paul's relation to his audience and the purposes of his writing, we must examine the expansions that run from v. 1b through v. 6.[3] Calvin Roetzel draws a widely shared inference from these expansions that Paul desired to "establish the 'orthodoxy' of his gospel and the legitimacy of his apostleship" against suspicions that he was a "theological maverick" and an "interloper" in the Roman church.[4] To evaluate such inferences, a precise grasp of the Pauline expansions is required. In the opening verse, two themes (the "apostle" and the "gospel") are expanded and developed in reverse sequence, with the latter taking up vv. 2-4 and the former v. 5. The delay in addressing the issue of apostolicity is balanced out, as it were, by the initial threefold expansion in v. 1 concerning Paul's office as (1) "slave of Christ Jesus;" (2) his being "called" to the apostolic office; and (3) his being "set apart" by God for the task of proclaiming the gospel.[5] The "gospel" motif begins in v. 2 with a claim of scriptural foundation and is developed with an apparent credal formula in vv. 3-4 that Paul cites and emends. The elaboration of the "apostle" motif in v. 5 is developed in a fivefold manner, with (a) an insistence on its derivation from Christ; (b) its coordination with "grace"; (c) its role in promoting the "obedience of faith"; (d) its scope in the realm of the "Gentiles"; (e) and its ultimate purpose of augmenting the glory of Christ's "name" by bringing the world into subjection to him.

The address of the letter "to all those in Rome" is similarly expanded by a complex series of appellations that define the location and task of God's "beloved" among the Romans. The double reference to their "calling" as a matter of belonging to "Christ Jesus" and to their being the "saints" in 1:6-7 provides an inclusion with Paul's calling in 1:1. The careful description of their placement "among" the Gentiles evokes a distinctive role that correlates their destiny with Paul's own mission to "all the Gentiles." Finally, the greeting is expanded in the manner typical of the other Pauline letters, coordinating the means of eschatological salvation, "grace" and "peace" that rests in the intimate relation with God as "Father" and in the rulership of the "Lord

---

1   See Lausberg, *Handbuch*, 1:150–63; Kennedy, *New Testament Interpretation*, 23–24, 142, 153.

2   See the standard treatments of the prescript in Roller, *Formular*, 55–61; Koskenniemi, *Studien*, 155–61; Doty, *Letters*, 12–17; Berger, "Apostelbrief," 191–207; Kim, *Form*, 9–21.

3   Bullinger, *Figures*, 907, is thus on the wrong track when he identifies Rom 1:2-6 as a "parecbasis," a digression.

4   Roetzel, *Letters*, 20.

5   See Louw, 1:1.

Jesus Christ." The development of these themes in a single, elaborate sentence that runs from 1:1 through 1:7 is unified by paronomasia in the fourfold repetitions of "Jesus Christ" and "God," the threefold repetition of "called" and "holy," and the double references to "apostle," "all," and "grace."

As Samuel Bryskog observes, the audience would probably have understood this prescript "as a statement of the sender's credentials," and it would have established "Paul's right and authority to write or speak persuasively to the Romans."[6] There are close analogies in official governmental correspondence, in which the officeholder is announced in a formal way. Vincent Parkin has pointed to the similarities in form to the prescript of imperial correspondence, such as "Tiberius Claudius Caesar Augustus Germanicus Imperator, Pontifex Maximus, holder of the tribunician power, counsul designate, to the city of Alexandria, greeting."[7] More to the point are the parallels in diplomatic rhetoric, where the credentials of the ambassador are laid down in the *exordium*. For example, Dionysius Halicarnassus cites the letter that begins "Publius Valerius Labinius, Roman Consul, greetings to King Pyrrhus,"[8] and Philo cites the diplomatic correspondence from "Norbanus Flaccus, governor, greetings to the magistrates of the Ephesians."[9] Religious officials employed the same diplomatic form, for example, "Eleazar, chief-priest, to King Ptolemy, greetings."[10]

If the purpose of an epistolary opening is to establish a relationship between the recipients of a letter and the writer who is unable because of distance to speak his message in person,[11] this expanded prescript draws the Roman believers into Paul's vocation as an apostle authorized to preach to the Gentiles. Many themes of the subsequent argument come to initial expression here; this justifies the rhetorical identification of *exordium*. The apostolic motif is developed in 1:8-15 and 15:15-33 in relation to Paul's forthcoming visit to Rome to promote a mission among the nations. The content of Paul's "gospel" is elaborated from 1:16 through 8:39 with particular reference to its consistency with "holy scriptures" and the centrality of "faith." The motifs of lordship, the confession of the "name," the conversion of the Gentiles, and the tension between the fleshly realm of Jesus' origin as a Jew and the spiritual realm of his reign over all humankind are elaborated in 9:1–11:26. The themes of "holiness" and "sainthood" are picked up in 12:1–13:14. The triumph of the gospel among the nations climaxes the argument from 14:1 through 15:13. And the connection between apostolicity and world mission is restated in 15:14-33 with language strongly reminiscent of that used in 1:1-7.

A fairly wide consensus has crystallized that Paul is citing an early Christian confession in 1:3-4.[12] While studies differ in detail, a number of features have been cited as indications of the non-Pauline origin of this material. The cogency of these observations may be most easily grasped when the structure of the passage is made visible.[13]

3a	περὶ τοῦ υἱοῦ αὐτοῦ
3b	τοῦ γενομένου
3c	ἐκ σπέρματος Δαυίδ
3d	κατὰ σάρκα
4a	τοῦ ὁρισθέντος υἱοῦ θεοῦ
4b	ἐν δυνάμει
4c	κατὰ πνεῦμα ἁγιωσύνης
4d	ἐξ ἀναστάσεως νεκρῶν
4e	Ἰησοῦ Χριστοῦ τοῦ κυρίου ἡμῶν

6   Samuel Bryskog, "Epistolography, Rhetoric and Letter Prescript: Romans 1.1-7 as a Test Case," *JSNT* 65 (1997) 37, 40.

7   Cited by Vincent Parkin, "Some Comments on the Pauline Prescript," *IBS* 8 (1986) 96.

8   Dionysius Halicarnassus *Antiq. Rom.* 19.10.1; see also Plutarch, *Pyrrh.* 6.7.4; 21.3.3.

9   Philo *Legat.* 315.2; see also Josephus *A. J.* 14.225, 235.

10   Josephus *A. J.* 12.51; see also 12.148.

11   See Koskenniemi, *Studien*, 155–67. It is noteworthy that Paul uses here the language of speaking (e.g.,
   "I say" in Rom 7:1) and not of writing within the letter itself.

12   The following is a revision of my full-length study of the confession, "The Redaction and Use of an Early Christian Confession in Romans 1:3-4," in R. Jewett and D. E. Groh, eds., *The Living Text. Essays in Honor of Ernest W. Saunders* (Washington: University Press of America, 1985) 99–122.

13   This strophic analysis based on grammatical principles is adapted from Louw, 1:1.

The following observations have led researchers to the conclusion that Paul was citing traditional material in these verses: (a) The participial constructions in vv. 3b and 4a are typical for confessional materials found elsewhere in the NT.[14] (b) The position of the participles at the beginning of the subordinate clauses has been taken as an indication of the citation of traditional confessional material.[15] (c) The parallelism between vv. 3b and 4a, 3c and 4d, and 3d and 4c has indicated to a wide range of researchers the presence of careful, solemn composition typical of liturgical use.[16] (d) The lack of articles with many of the nouns has been suggested as a feature of traditional material here and elsewhere in the NT.[17] (e) The presence of non-Pauline terms like ὁρισθέντος ("appointed") and πνεῦμα ἁγιωσύνης ("spirit of holiness") lends itself to a theory of citation. The former appears in Acts 10:42 and 17:31, while the latter is found as an expression only in the *T. Levi* 18.11 and on a Jewish amulet.[18] (f) The expression ἐξ ἀναστάσεως νεκρῶν ("from resurrection of the dead") is used elsewhere in the Pauline letters for the resurrection of the dead in a general sense, in contrast to its use here in reference to Christ's resurrection.[19] (g) The terms σάρξ ("flesh") and πνεῦμα ("spirit") are used here in an uncharacteristic way compared with Paul's use elsewhere with an anthropological focus and a more clearly antithetical intent.[20] (h) Disparities with Pauline theology as visible elsewhere in the letters are quite striking. The reference to the Davidic origin of Jesus is not only unusual here but also stands in substantial tension with other references like that of 2 Cor 5:16.[21] (i) The lack of a reference to the cross or to Jesus' death seems very distant from Paul's usual emphasis, summarized in 1 Cor 2:2.[22] (j) The adoptionist tone of this confession is absent in other christological utterances of Paul's, who typically stresses preexistence.[23] (k) Paul introduces this material in Rom 1:1-2 as a summary of the "gospel" he had been preaching, which leads one to expect the citation of traditional material, as in 1 Cor 15:1-4.[24] (l) A primary indication of the presence of cited material is the smooth transition that would result if Rom 1:3a-4d were deleted: ". . . the gospel concerning his son, [delete 3a-4d] Jesus Christ our Lord, through whom we have received grace and apostleship. . . ."[25]

It is widely recognized that some of these observations carry more weight than others. Nevertheless, the impression made by these details is that 1:3-4 contains "a kind of potted creed," to use the expression that A. M. Hunter employed in 1940.[26] This is the hypothesis that is to be developed in the exegesis of 1:3-4.

The final words of the pericope are a stylized greeting, with a formal, poetic structure of three lines, each containing four words, while "the omission of the article emphasizes the rhythmic correspondence, pregnancy and loftiness of effect."[27] The structure is as follows:

χάρις ὑμῖν καὶ εἰρήνη ("grace to you [pl.] and peace")
ἀπὸ θεοῦ πατρὸς ἡμῶν ("from God our Father")
καὶ κυρίου Ἰησοῦ Χριστοῦ ("and [the] Lord Jesus Christ")

---

14 Wengst, *Formeln*, 112.
15 Ibid.
16 Neufeld, *Confessions*, 50.
17 Zimmermann, *Methode*, 198.
18 Kotansky, *Greek Magical Amulets*, 1.32.4-5.
19 See Becker, *Auferstehung*, 23–24.
20 See Brandenburger, *Fleisch und Geist*, 44–52; Jewett, *Terms*, 453–56.
21 The only other reference I know to the physical descent of Jesus in the Pauline letters is that of Rom 9:4, which does not mention the Davidic connection. The "son of David" title is found elsewhere in Matt 1:1; 2 Tim 2:8; Rev 5:5; and 22:16 and is supported by Matt 1:2-20; Luke 1:27, 32, 69; 3:4; 3:23-31; and Acts 2:30. See Burger, *Jesus als Davidssohn*, 25–41.
22 See Eduard Schweizer, "Römer 1,3f. und der Gegensatz von Fleisch und Geist vor und bei Paulus," *EvTh* 15 (1955) 563.
23 Kramer, *Christ*, 109–11.
24 See Vern S. Poythress's acknowledgment of "traditional material" being used in these verses, "Is Romans i.3-4 a Pauline Confession After All?" *ExpT* 87 (1976) 181–82.
25 See Heinrich Schlier, "Eine christologische Credo-Formel der römischen Gemeinde. Zu Röm 1,3f.," in H. Baltensweiler and B. Reicke, eds., *Neues Testament und Geschichte: Historisches Geschehen und Deutung im Neuen Testament: Oscar Cullmann zum 70. Geburstag* (Zurich: Theologischer Verlag, 1972) 208.
26 Hunter, *Predecessors*, 24.
27 Ernst Lohmeyer, *Probleme*, 14, followed by Schlier, 32.

This formula appears to have evolved from earlier greetings in the Pauline letters,[28] with the earliest example containing only "grace to you and peace" (1 Thess 1:1). 2 Thess 1:2 then moves to virtually the form found in the later letters, lacking only the "our" in connection with "Father." Col 1:2 has a shorter form, "Grace to you and peace from God our Father." In Gal 1:3; Phil 1:2; 1 Cor 1:3; 2 Cor 1:2; Phlm 3 we find the exact wording as in Romans that, with the exception of Eph 1:2, was not used in the later church tradition;[29] it remains a distinctive expression of Pauline rhetoric.

Rhetorical Disposition

1:1-12 I. The *Exordium*
1:1-7   A. The inauguration of Paul's communication with the believers in Rome
1:1   1. The name and status of the sender
1:1a   a. Name: "Paul"
1:1b-c   b. Official titles and status
              1) Ambassadorial title: "slave of Christ Jesus"
              2) Missionary title: "apostle"
              3) Evangelical vocation: "set apart for the gospel of God"
1:2-4   2. Confessional definition of the gospel
1:2   a. Scriptural warrant: proclaimed beforehand by God himself through the prophets
1:3-4   b. Citation of an early Christian confession
1:3a   1) Introductory formula
1:3b-4d   2) The early Christian confession
1:3b-d   a) Jesus' origin
1:3b-c   (1) Birth "from David's seed"
1:3d   (2) Interpretive qualification: "according to the flesh"
1:4a-d   b) Jesus' messianic appointment
1:4a   (1) Appointment as "Son of God"
1:4b   (2) Interpretive qualification: "in power"
1:4c   (3) Interpretative qualifications: "according to the spirit of holiness"
1:4d   (4) Basis of appointment: "resurrection"
1:4e   (5) The concluding Pauline formula
1:5   3. Paul's apostolic credentials
1:5a   a. Source of apostolicity in Christ and coordination with grace
1:5b   b. Goal of apostolic calling to gain "obedience of faith"
1:5c   c. The global scope of Paul's apostolic calling: "among all the nations"
1:5d   d. The ultimate purpose of Paul's apostolicity: to glorify Christ's "name"
1:6-7b   4. The address
1:6a   a. The crucial location of the Roman believers: among all the nations
1:6b   b. The first identification of addressees: "called of Jesus Christ"
1:7a   c. The second identification of addressees with an inclusive unification formula: "all those in Rome beloved of God"
1:7b   d. The third identification of addressees: "called to be saints"
1:7c   5. The salutation
            a. The content conveyed to Roman believers
              1) "grace"
              2) "peace"
            b. The ultimate source of the salutation:
              1) "God our Father"
              2) "[the] Lord Jesus Christ"

Exegesis

■ 1 The first word in Romans, typical for ancient letters, is Paul's name: Παῦλος is a Greek form of the Latin name *Paul(l)us*. Since it seems unlikely that *Paullus* could have been the apostle's cognomen (personal name) because of its use by noble senatorial families and because his original *cognomen* was apparently Saul,[30] it appears to have been a *signum* (nickname), as Colin Hemer has suggested. He cites a tombstone with the nickname "Neon," which resonates with the *cognomen* "Leo" in a manner parallel to Saul/Paul:[31] "To the spirits of the dead, Lucius Antonius Leo, also called Neon, son of Zoilus, by nation a Cilician, a soldier of the praetorian fleet at Misenum."[32] In place of the typical tripartite name of a Roman citizen, such as Gaius Julius Paulus, the apostle employs his official title, "slave of Christ Jesus, an apostle called." These expansions in the

---

28 See Gottlob Schrenk, "πατήρ κτλ.," *TDNT* 5 (1967) 1007.
29 See Käsemann, 16.
30 See Acts 7:58; 8:1, 3; 9:1, 4; 13:9, and the discussion of typical Roman names by G. A. Harrer, "Saul Who Also Is Called Paul," *HTR* 33 (1940) 19–34;

Sherwin-White, *Roman Society*, 153, cited by Murphy-O'Connor, *Paul*, 42.
31 Colin J. Hemer, "The Name of Paul," *TynB* 36 (1985) 179–83.
32 *CIL* 10.3377, cited also by Murphy-O'Connor, *Paul*, 43.

exordium fit exactly into the style of a cautiously diplomatic letter that introduces an ambassador with proper protocol before carefully setting forth the mission to be accomplished.

The second word of the letter, usually wrongly translated "servant" rather than the more accurate word "slave,"[33] is puzzling because its "degrading associations"[34] appear to contradict the elaborate claims about Paul as the one "called to be an apostle and set apart for the gospel of God" (1:1), and the one who has "received grace and apostleship for the purpose of the obedience of faith among all the Gentiles" (1:5). The usual explanation is that Paul's expression is patterned on the "slave of Yahweh," used in the OT for prophets (Amos 3:7; Jer 7:25; Dan 9:6), for Jewish worshipers (Neh 1:6, 11; Pss 19:11, 13; 35:23, etc.), and for Israel as a whole (Ps 135:22).[35] While the prophetic connotation would match the titular function required for this *exordium*,[36] it seems unlikely to be intended here; when Paul returns to this theme in 15:15-20 he describes his ministry in priestly rather than prophetic terms. Largely overlooked in the debate thus far is the local connotation of this expression,[37] which makes perfect sense in a letter to Rome, where influential slaves in imperial service proudly bore the title "slave of Caesar." More than four thousand slaves and freedmen associated with Caesar's household, his personal staff, and the imperial bureaucracy have been identified through grave inscriptions with this kind of title.[38] As P. R. C. Weaver points out, "The *Familia Caesaris*, the slaves and freedmen of the emperor's household, were the élite status-group in the slave-freedman section of Roman imperial society. . . . As assistants to the emperor in the performance of many of his manifold magisterial duties they had access to positions of power in the state which were totally inaccessible to other slaves and freedmen."[39] Indeed, their social and economic status was higher than most of the free population of the empire, with some slaves of Caesar rising to positions of immense power and wealth.[40] As Michael Brown points out, a slave of Caesar "could speak only on behalf of his master, but, given that his master was a son of a god and his word was backed by the full power of the Roman military establishment, the slave's word would be a powerful medium indeed."[41] Paul is therefore introducing his "*persona*"[42] with proper credentials as an agent of Christ Jesus, using the technical term for a "king's official" or an imperial bureaucrat.[43] This is the same title that members of the two churches within the imperial bureaucracy identified with Narcissus and Aristobulus (Rom 16:10-11) would have proudly carried. The proximity between "slave of Caesar" and "slave of Christ Jesus" sets an agenda pursued throughout the letter concerning whose power is ultimate, whose gospel is efficacious, and whose pro-

---

33 This section is adapted from Jewett, "Ambassadorial Letter," 5–20.

34 See Black, 19; Karl Heinrich Rengstorf's survey of Greek usage in "δοῦλος κτλ.," *TDNT* 2 (1964) 265, points out the scandal of any positive use of slavery in Greek and Hellenistic contexts where freedom is so highly valued.

35 See Sanday and Headlam, 3; Lagrange, 2; Dunn, 1:7–8.

36 See Sandnes, *Paul*, 146–53; Dunn, 1:7–8.

37 See the survey in Michael Joseph Brown, "Paul's Use of δοῦλος Χριστοῦ Ιησοῦ in Romans 1:1," *JBL* 120 (2004) 725–28, which finds the "slave of Caesar" connotation noted only by Kenneth S. Wuest, *Romans in the Greek New Testament for the English Reader*, Word Studies in the Greek New Testament for the English Reader 16 (Grand Rapids: Eerdmans, 1955) 12. Martin, *Slavery as Salvation*, 76, argues that Paul presents himself as "Christ's slave agent," and Combes, *Metaphor of Slavery*, 77, suggests the role of the household slaves. The earliest

38 Weaver, *Familia Caesaris*, 8–9, 17; the slave inscriptions are usually abbreviated as *Caes. ser.*, i.e., *Caesaris servus* ("slave of Caesar," pp. 75–76), the equivalent in Greek of Καίσαρος δοῦλος.

39 Weaver, "Social Mobility," 123.

40 Ibid., 129–30.

41 Brown, "Romans 1:1," 733.

42 See James D. Hester, "The Rhetoric of *Persona* in Romans: Re-reading Romans 1:1-12," in S. E. McGinn, ed., *Celebrating Romans: Template for Pauline Theology. Essays in Honor of Robert Jewett* (Grand Rapids: Eerdmans, 2004) 85–88, 98–101.

43 BAGD 205; see also Gerhard Sass, "Zur Bedeutung von δοῦλος bei Paulus," *ZNW* 40 (1941) 81–82; and Martin, *Slavery as Salvation*, 50–51, for evidence that "slave of Christ" is used here as "a title of leadership."

gram for global pacification and unification is finally viable.

The appellation κλητὸς ἀπόστολος is sometimes translated "a called apostle,"[44] "called an apostle,"[45] or "called to be an apostle,"[46] which seem inexact. Although some view κλητός as a technical term,[47] it remains an adjective modifying "apostle."[48] As we can see from the parallel passages in 1 Cor 1:1; 15:9; and Gal 1:15, Paul's apostolic office rests on the call of God rather than on human agencies or his own charismatic decision.[49] Believers are "called" by God to respond to the gospel by joining "in fellowship with his Son Jesus Christ" (1 Cor 1:9). The adjective in the expression κλητὸς ἀπόστολος in Rom 1:1 has the sense of perfect passive participle (κεκλημένος), modifying "apostle,"[50] a phrase that I translate "an apostle called," implying that his office rests on divine election. The word "apostle" itself means someone sent in behalf of someone else, in this instance, in behalf of Christ Jesus.

The background of ἀποστέλλω ("send"), a verb used for envoys who represent others, is attested in the political sphere, where ambassadors "are representatives of their monarch and his authority,"[51] and in the religious sphere, where philosophers are sent by the gods. For example, Epictetus describes Cynic philosophers as persons who must know that they are messengers sent by Zeus to humans (ὅτι ἄγγελος ἀπὸ τοῦ Διὸς ἀπέσταλται καὶ πρὸς τοὺς ἀνθρώπους), in order to show

people with regard to good and evil that they are in error.[52] This language appears in the LXX with great frequency in both secular and religious contexts, for example, in the famous calling of Isa 6:8 in which the one sent will be the prophetic messenger who bears the word of God: "And I heard the voice of the Lord, saying, 'Whom shall I send (τίνα ἀποστείλω), and who will go to this people?' And I said, 'Behold, I am here, send me (ἀπόστειλόν με).'" Later Judaism develops the institution of the Shaliach, the Hebrew equivalent of "apostle," in which authorized envoys represent their senders with specific commissions in a wide variety of circumstances. In Rengstorf's description, "the man commissioned . . . represents in his own person the person and rights of the [man who gives the commission]. The Rabbis summed up this basis of the שְׁלִיחַ [Shaliach, 'messenger'] in the frequently quoted statement: שלוחו של אדם כמותו, 'the one sent by a man is as the man himself' (Ber. 5,5)."[53] While this rabbinic material postdates the NT,[54] it seems that the sending-convention of the OT provides the most likely source of the NT concept.[55] There is a broad consensus concerning the distinctive development in early Christianity of this idea, reflected in Rom 1:1, that "the apostle is one who, through a vision of the risen Lord, has become an official witness to his resurrection and who has been commissioned by him to preach the gospel in a way fundamental to its spread."[56]

44 The translation "a called apostle" is proposed by Boylan, but as Morris, 38, points out, this implies that there are other apostles who are not called, which is not intended here.

45 Jost Eckert, "καλέω κτλ.," EDNT 2 (1991) 242; this formulation could be close to Apollonius Sophista Lex. hom. 100.7, who glosses "'called' (κλητούς): those who are called by name."

46 Supplying the words "to be" seems inexact and could imply that Paul was merely called and has not yet become an apostle.

47 Karl Ludwig Schmidt, "κλητός," TDNT 3 (1965) 494; Jost Eckert, "καλέω κτλ.," EDNT 2 (1991) 242.

48 Prosper Schepens, "Vocatus Apostolus (Rom i,1 - I Cor. i,1)," RechSR (1926) 40–42; Barrett, 16, suggests the translation "by divine call, an apostle."

49 See Schlier, 20; Morris, 38; Wiederkehr, Berufung, 153–68.

50 Smyth, Grammar, §358.b and §472.

51 Karl Heinrich Rengstorf, "ἀποστέλλω κτλ.," TDNT

1 (1964) 398, cites Dikaiomata ed. Graec. Hal. 1.124, "those sent (οἱ ἀπεσταλμένοι) by the king" as ambassadors.

52 Epictetus Diss. 3.22.23; see also 1.24.6; 3.22.69.

53 Karl Heinrich Rengstorf, "ἀποστέλλω κτλ.," TDNT 1 (1964) 415.

54 This has led critics such as Johannes Munck, "Paul, the Apostles, and the Twelve," StTh 3 (1949) 100, and Schmithals, Office of Apostle, 48–95, to reject the theory of a Jewish background for the NT concept of an apostle; for a full account of this debate, see Agnew, "Origin," 85–90.

55 Agnew, "Origin," 90–96, points to the decisive contributions of Birger Gerhardsson, "Die Boten Gottes und die Apostel Christi," SEÅ 27 (1962) 89–131; and Hahn, "Apostolat," 54–77.

56 Agnew, "Origin," 77, citing Raymond E. Brown, "The Twelve and the Apostolate," JBC 2 (1968) 789, and Hahn, "Apostolat," 56–60; see also Jan-Adolf Bühner, "ἀπόστολος," EDNT 1 (1990) 143.

Paul elaborates his apostolic calling with the expression ἀφωρισμένος εἰς εὐαγγέλιον θεοῦ ("set apart for God's gospel"), language he had used in Gal 1:15 to describe his conversion and apostolic calling: "But when he who had set me apart (ὁ ἀφορίσας με) before I was born, and had called me through his grace, was pleased to reveal his Son to me, in order that I might preach him among the Gentiles." The basic meaning of ἀφορίζω is to set apart, to separate,[57] which occurs in the OT most prominently in the context of separating the clean from the unclean (LXX Lev 13:11, 21, 26; 14:38, 46; 20:25). The classic reference is Lev 20:26: "And you shall be holy to me, because I the Lord your God am holy, who set you apart from all nations (ὁ ἀφορίσας ὑμᾶς ἀπὸ πάντων τῶν ἐθνῶν) to be mine." The use of this term to describe Paul's apostolic calling may have been influenced by Paul's Pharisaic background, because the word "Pharisee" itself appears to come from the same Hebrew root, פרוש ("to separate"), that lies behind the LXX occurrences of ἀφορίζω.[58] The ironic reversal is that while Paul's preconversion orientation required strict separation from unclean Gentiles, his postconversion calling was to preach to the very same Gentiles. While it does not seem likely that Paul intended a wordplay on this theme,[59] the choice of this term remains noteworthy. Paul's "separation" is described in positive rather than the ordinary negative terms:[60] the preposition εἰς ("to, for, toward") describes the goal of his commission. Instead of εὐαγγελίζεσθαι, which ordinarily would be expected after εἰς,[61] Paul uses the expression "God's gospel." This reference to God as the commissioner and thus the source of Paul's message appears again in 15:16 as well as in 2 Cor 11:7; 1 Thess 2:2, 8, 9.[62] Since the *exordia* in the other Pauline letters refer not to the gospel but to Paul's calling as an apostle "of Jesus Christ" (1 Cor 1:1; 2 Cor 1:1; Col 1:1), the formulation chosen in Romans requires further explanation. That the gospel derives from God resonates with the central theme that unites both the old and the new covenants[63] and this theme is particularly dominant in Romans. Compared with "law" (72 times), "Christ" (65 times), "sin" (48 times), "Lord" (43 times), or "faith" (40 times), the word θεός ("God") appears more frequently in this letter than any other theological term (153 times).[64] Halvor Moxnes shows that throughout Romans, Paul emphasizes "*the same God* acting both in the history of Israel and in Jesus." This emphasis has its primary bearing not in theoretical and theological issues but in "the conflict between Jews and Greeks, high and low, insiders and outsiders. Most of Paul's statements about God in Romans were related to this situation in which he attempted to achieve unity through conflict."[65] The bearing of this theme becomes clear in 3:29-30, where Paul insists that there is one God of both Jews and Gentiles. In 14:3–15:13 he shows that both the weak and the strong act out of reverence to the same God, whose praise will one day unite all peoples when the mission is fulfilled. With reference to 1:1, therefore, only if Paul's gospel is the "gospel of God" can it find common ground between the competing house and tenement churches in Rome and lead them to cooperate in the mission to the barbarians in Spain.

---

57 BAGD 127; see also Allen, "Old Testament Background," 104–8.

58 See Zahn, 31; Jan W. Doeve, "Paulus der Pharisäer und Galater 1:13-15," *NovT* 6 (1963) 170–81; Black, 20; Fitzmyer, 232. The critiques of this view by Hans Friedrich Weiss, "Φαρισαῖος," *TDNT* 9 (1974) 46 n. 211, and Betz, *Galatians*, 70 n. 134, are weakly argued.

59 Schlier, 1; Ulrich Kellermann, "ἀφορίζω," *EDNT* 1 (1990) 184.

60 See Morris, 40.

61 Michel, 68.

62 See Zahn, 33.

63 See Bernd Janowski, "Der eine Gott der beiden Testamente. Grundfragen einer biblischen Theologie," *ZThK* 95 (1998) 33–36.

64 See Morris, 20; also idem, "The Theme of Romans," in W. W. Gasque and R. P. Martin, eds., *Apostolic History and the Gospel: Biblical and Historical Essays Presented to F. F. Bruce on His 60th Birthday* (Exeter: Paternoster; Grand Rapids: Eerdmans, 1970) 249–63; idem, "The Apostle Paul and His God," in P. T. O'Brien and D. G. Peterson, eds., *God Who Is Rich in Mercy: Essays Presented to Dr. D. B. Knox* (Homebush: Lancer, 1986) 165–78; Moxnes, *Theology in Conflict*, 15–31.

65 Moxnes, *Theology in Conflict*, 288.

■ **2** That the gospel of God had been proclaimed beforehand by God is articulated with an aorist middle verb, προεπηγγείλατο, which has a reflexive meaning of an action by God "on his own behalf."[66] The divine authentication of the gospel that was detected in the last verse is reinforced here. The same stem ἀγγελ- appears here as in the word "gospel" in the preceding sentence, which suggests a narrower context than the secular connotation of "announce beforehand."[67] Here it is claimed that the prophets articulated the gospel of God in the period before Christ. This prophetic message provides consistency between the old and new covenants and confirms the authenticity of Paul's apostolic message. The expression "his [i.e., God's] prophets" appears otherwise only in the song of Zechariah (Luke 1:70), and it seems clear from the context that Paul has in mind all persons mentioned in the OT through whom God spoke,[68] such as Moses, David, Solomon, and others whom we otherwise would not classify as prophets.[69] The expression ἐν γραφαῖς ἁγίαις ("by the holy scriptures") is unparalleled in the NT and in Greek forms of Jewish writings; since 2 Tim 3:15 employs the associated terminology "sacred writings" (ἱερὰ γράμματα), the most precise parallel is the later rabbinic expression הקדש כתבי.[70] It therefore appears likely that this language derived from Hebrew tradition and that the reference is to the entire OT either in its Greek or in its Hebrew forms.[71] Since this is the only time that Paul claims prophetic and scriptural authentication of his gospel by employing this terminology, Michel and van der Minde have raised the question whether Paul is adapting liturgical tradition in

this verse.[72] Such an adaptation indeed appears likely, and the details point to an origin in the same kind of early Jewish Christianity that is evident in confession introduced in the next two verses. The effort to find common ground with conservative Jewish believers, who are being discriminated against in Rome, is signaled in these details.

■ **3-4** Having shown in the analysis above that these verses are in all probability cited from an early Christian creed, we must address the fact that this creed contains so many contradictory elements that hypotheses concerning its origin and implications have frequently been flawed. In the light of the criticisms mounted against the credal hypothesis,[73] it would appear to be a step in the wrong direction to suggest that the confession ought to be viewed as a unified creation of a single early church tradition without any redaction by Paul or anyone else. Yet this has often been proposed with elaborate argumentation by Dunn, who believes Paul added only the preface;[74] by Hahn, Stuhlmacher, Käsemann, and Wilckens, who believe Paul added both the preface and conclusion;[75] and by Hunter, Cullmann, Neufeld, Best, Bartsch, and Schneider, who assert that Paul added nothing whatsoever.[76] In whatever form one wishes to advance this option, it raises more problems than it solves. It requires advocates to downplay the tension between flesh and spirit to preserve the honor attached to the Davidic descent, to invent implausible explanations for the peculiar expression "spirit of holiness," and to provide alibis for the apparent heightening of adoptionism in the expression "in power." None of these hypotheses pro-

---

66 Dunn, 1:10, citing Moule, *Idiom-Book*, 24.

67 See Dio Cassius *Hist. Rom.* 36.39.1; 38.13.5; 38.41.2; 39.31.1; 42.33.3; 46.40.2; 59.21.2, where προεπαγγελίζω is employed for political announcements; a less clear example is Arrian *Anab.* 67.27.1.

68 Franz Schnider, "προφήτης," *EDNT* 3 (1993) 184.

69 See Michel, 69; Cranfield, 1:56; Rolf Rendtorff, "προφήτης κτλ.," *TDNT* 6 (1968) 803-4. This extended frame of reference for the "prophets" also occurs in Lukan material (Acts 2:30-31; 3:22).

70 See Moo, 44, citing Str-B 3.14; Gottlob Schrenk, "γράφω κτλ.," *TDNT* 1 (1964) 751.

71 See Dunn, 1:11; Hans Hübner, "γραφή, γράφω," *EDNT* 1 (1990) 263.

72 Michel, 70; van der Minde, *Schrift*, 39.

73 For example, Poythress, "Romans i.3-4," 182-83; Christopher G. Whitsett, "Son of God, Seed of David: Paul's Missionary Exegesis in Romans 1:3-4," *JBL* 119 (2000) 680.

74 Dunn, 1:5-6; idem, "Rom 1.3-4," 40-68.

75 Hahn, *Titles*, 246-52; Stuhlmacher, "Probleme," 374-89; Käsemann, 13; Wilckens, 1:56-61; Wilckens's position is somewhat difficult to determine, because he prints out the confession on p. 56 as if the phrase "in power" did not originally belong, but when discussing this detail he claims that "in power" stands parallel to "according to the spirit of holiness," which would seem to imply that it was original (65).

76 Hunter, *Predecessors*, 25-28; Cullmann, *Confessions*, 55-56; Neufeld, *Confessions*, 50-51; Best, 10-11;

vides a convincing historical *Sitz im Leben* for a pre-Pauline formula bearing all these contradictory features.

The conclusion I draw from this debate is that a three-level development of the confession emerges as the most likely option. On the basis of studies by Fuller, Schlier, and Becker,[77] this creed originated as a pre-Pauline expression of Jewish Christian theology:

1:3b τοῦ γενομένου
1:3c ἐκ σπέρματος Δαυίδ
1:4a τοῦ ὁρισθέντος υἱοῦ θεοῦ
1:4d ἐξ ἀναστάσεως νεκρῶν.

It is widely agreed that the motif of Davidic descent points to an origin in early Jewish Christianity.[78] Implying royal messianic descent,[79] the phrase ἐκ σπέρματος Δαυίδ ("from [the] seed of David") is a formula that originated "in Jewish Christian circles."[80] That the "seed of David" language appears in an ancient eucharistic creed cited by Ignatius[81] lends plausibility to the suggestion that the original context of this Jewish Christian creed may have been the Lord's Supper. Leslie C. Allen has shown that ὁρισθέντος ("appointed, designated") in 1:4 is derived from the royal decree language of Ps 2:7 with close analogues in the Aramaic section of Daniel.[82] In this context, the verb means "install" in the messianic office.[83] While there are also Greco-Roman parallels to ὁρίζω in a political context,[84] there is a strong likelihood

that this component in the confession derived from "the Aramaic-speaking primitive church,"[85] so it should be interpreted in light of the interests of that group. The same should be said for "son of God" as a royal title (cf. 2 Sam 7:14; Pss 2:7; 89:26-27; 1QSa 2:11-12; 4QFlor 1:10ff.).[86]

At the core of the original confession, therefore, is the affirmation of Jesus as the traditional Davidic Messiah, who was adopted and enthroned as the Son of God on the basis of his resurrection.[87] This theme is echoed in Rom 15:8-9 in which Christ is declared to be a "servant to the circumcised."[88] The popular Jewish expectation of a son of David as that found in *Ps. Sol.* 17:21 and elsewhere is reflected here with the traditional expectation of national restoration, victory over the Gentile nations, and governance of the world.[89] The potentially chauvinistic element in the first line of the credo is not diminished by the second line, which affirms the divine appointment of Jesus as the heavenly Son of God.[90] The adoptionist Christology of primitive Palestinian Christianity implied in Acts 2:36 and 13:33 surfaces in this formulation.[91] The famous parallel in *4 Ezra* 7.28-29 also reflects a Palestinian milieu:[92] "For my son the Messiah (*filius meus Christus*) shall be revealed with those who are with him. . . . And after these years my son the Messiah shall die, and all who draw human breath." It is clear that no diminution of authority is intended by this prim-

---

Bartsch, "Bekenntnisformel," 329–39; Bernadin Schneider, "Κατὰ πνεῦμα ἁγιωσύνης (Romans 1,4)," *Bib* 48 (1967) 360–69.

77 Fuller, *Christology*, 165–67; Schlier, "Röm 1,3f.," 207–18; Becker, *Auferstehung*, 20–31.

78 See A. J. B. Higgins, "The OT and Some Aspects of NT Christology," *CJT* 6 (1960) 200–202; Michel, 38; Burger, *Jesus als Davidssohn*, 28; Wilckens, 1:60.

79 See Dunn, 1:12–13.

80 Ulrich Kellermann, "σπέρμα," *EDNT* 3 (1993) 264.

81 *Epistulae vii genuinae* 4.7.2.

82 Allen, "Old Testament Background," 104–8.

83 Gerhard Schneider, "ὁρίζω," *EDNT* 2 (1991) 532.

84 Classical Greek literature has examples of this term in connection with "things decreed by law" (τὰ ὑπὸ νόμου ὁρισθέντ᾽ in Plutarch *Fat.* 570d9), "things decreed by the Romans" (ὑπὸ Ῥωμαίων ὁρισθέντων in Appian *Mithr.* 152.1) and loans "decreed by Caesar" (ὑπὸ τοῦ Καίσαρος ὁρισθέντα in Dionysius Halicarnassus *Antiq. Rom.* 42.22).

85 Allen, "Old Testament Background," 104–5.

86 See Georg Fohrer, "υἱός, υἱοθεσία," *TDNT* 8 (1972) 349–51; S. Morenz, "Sohn Gottes I. Religionsgeschichtlich," *RGG*³ 6 (1962) 118.

87 See Hurtado, *One God*, 95, citing Martin Hengel, *The Son of God: The Origins of Christology and the History of Jewish-Hellenistic Religion*, trans. J. Bowden (Philadelphia: Fortress Press, 1976) 60.

88 See Whitsett, "Son of God," 664–68.

89 Becker, *Auferstehung*, 29, cites Ps 2:8 and *Ps. Sol.* 17:3 in this connection. Cf. John J. Collins, *The Scepter and the Star. The Messiahs of the Dead Sea Scrolls and Other Ancient Literature* (New York: Doubleday, 1995) 49–67; Collins notes that becoming a messiah through resurrection "is without parallel in the Jewish sources" (204).

90 See Ferdinand Hahn, "υἱός," *EDNT* 3 (1993) 385: "Rom 1:3b, 4a associates divine sonship with the installation into the heavenly office of Messiah."

91 See Käsemann, 12; Dunn, 1:14, correctly points out an anachronistic element in the adoptionist identification but fails to eliminate the problem by contend-

itive formulation: the Son of God is emphatically appointed as ruler of the world.[93]

The precise implications of the phrase "from the resurrection of the dead" depend on whether one accepts Hans Lietzmann's suggestion that this is an aesthetically motivated abbreviation of a formula referring more precisely to Christ's resurrection.[94] However, in light of the compelling evidence Bartsch assembled to show that this reference to the general resurrection from the dead is typical of early Christian apocalyptic, there is no reason to provide a less than literal interpretation.[95] Käsemann writes, "The hymnic tradition does not isolate Christ's resurrection, but views it in its cosmic function as the beginning of general resurrection."[96] At the somewhat primitive level of the original credo,[97] no distinction is made between Christ's resurrection and the dawn of the age of the general resurrection. Both are apparently fused together as the event ushering in the new age.[98] This fusion leads to a significant conclusion: the original, Jewish Christian confession contained an emphasis on the apocalyptic hinge between the two ages even before the insertion of the clearly antithetical expressions, "according to the flesh/spirit."

Taking account of studies by Bultmann, Schweizer, Linnemann, and Theobald,[99] the second redacted level of the confession included the antithesis, "according to the flesh/spirit," which is underlined in this illustration:

1:3b τοῦ γενομένου
1:3c ἐκ σπέρματος Δαυίδ
1:3d κατὰ σάρκα
1:4a τοῦ ὁρισθέντος υἱοῦ θεοῦ
1:4c κατὰ πνεῦμα
1:4d ἐξ ἀναστάσεως νεκρῶν.

When the original confession was edited by the insertion of references to σάρξ and πνεῦμα, the implicit antithesis between the ages was developed in a radical direction. As Eduard Schweizer has pointed out, Hellenistic thought tended to conceive the flesh/spirit dualism in material terms, as counterposed realms of damnation/salvation.[100] Human destiny was thought to be determined by the realm to which one was subordinate. Bondage to the realm of the flesh could be overcome only by divine means. When flesh and spirit are combined with the preposition κατά, the thought of being

---

ing that "Paul would certainly see the earlier formula as congruent with his own Christology."

92 See Bruce M. Metzger, "The Fourth Book of Ezra," *OTP* 1 (1983) 520; the translation of the Latin text is drawn from Metzger, 537. In "'My Son the Messiah': A Note on 4 Esr 7,28-29," *ZNW* 66 (1975) 264–67, Stephen Gero argues that the Latin, Syriac, and Georgian versions of this verse probably derive from an obscure Hebrew antecedent, "my son the messiah." See also Wis 2:18.

93 See Anton J. Fridrichsen, *The Apostle and His Message* (Uppsala: Lundequistska, 1947) 10: "In other words, through His resurrection from the dead, Jesus, formerly the Messiah of the Jews, has been enthroned as Lord and Saviour of the whole world."

94 Lietzmann, 25.

95 Bartsch, "Bekenntnisformel," 330–35, shows the close parallels to Acts 26:23; Matt 27:51-53; and 1 Cor 15:20. Dunn, "Rom 1.3-4," 56, follows this approach, citing a number of scholars including S. H. Hooke, "The Translation of Rom. i.4," *NTS* 9 (1962–63) 370–71. In *Auferstehung*, 30–31, Becker overlooks this evidence in concluding that Rom 1:4 refers exclusively to Jesus' individual resurrection; see also Jacob Kremer, "ἀνάστασις κτλ.," *EDNT* 1 (1990) 92.

96 Käsemann, 12.

97 Schlier, "Röm 1,3f.," 214, speaks of "a certain archaic quality" in the wording of ἐξ ἀναστάσεως νεκρῶν, which appears elsewhere only in Acts 26:23. Cf. Latto, *Star Is Rising*, 317–54.

98 It therefore appears inappropriate to conclude with Ferdinand Hahn that the credo features "the de-eschatologization of the messianic office of Jesus" (*Titles*, 251). For a detailed critique on this point see Philipp Vielhauer, "Ein Weg zur neutestamentlichen Christologie? Prüfung der Thesen Ferdinand Hahns," *Aufsätze zum Neuen Testament* (Munich: Kaiser, 1965) 141–98, esp. 187.

99 Bultmann, *Theology*, 1:49; the first written expression of Bultmann's analysis appeared in "Neueste Paulusforschung," *ThR* 8 (1936) 11; Schweizer, "Römer 1,3f.," 563–71; Eta Linnemann, "Tradition und Interpretation in Röm 1,3f," *EvTh* 31 (1971) 264–75; Michael Theobald, "'Dem Juden zuerst und auch dem Heiden.' Die paulinische Auslegung der Glaubensformel Röm 1,3f.," in P.-G. Müller and W. Stenger, eds., *Kontinuität und Einheit. Festschrift für Franz Mussner* (Freiburg: Herder, 1981) 376–92.

100 Eduard Schweizer, "πνεῦμα, πνευματικός," *TDNT* 6 (1968) 392; idem, "σάρξ," 102–3.

limited or dominated by a particular sphere is strongly implied.[101] The philosophical expression ἡ κατὰ σάρκα ἡδονή ("the pleasure of the flesh")[102] conveys this sense of limitation. The antithesis thus has a negative as well as a positive set of implications. On the negative side, there is a clear deprecation of the significance of the Davidic origin of the Messiah and all that such derivation implied. The Hellenistic Christians who inserted this line probably stood close to the radicals refuted in 11:11-25 for vaunting their superiority as divinely grafted branches that displaced the original Jewish branches of the olive tree. They appear to have shared the outlook of the Corinthian radicals who devalued the fleshly, historical Jesus (1 Cor 12:3; 15:44-46). Insofar as Jesus descended from the fleshly seed of David, this insertion implies that he was bound to a realm of material bondage opposed to the power of salvation.

The positive implication of the phrase κατὰ πνεῦμα is that the redemptive power of Christ derives from his spiritual authority rather than from his Davidic origin. In place of the apocalyptic expectation of the dawn of the age of bodily resurrection, this phrase implies that the salvation brought by the Son of God is pneumatic and experiential. To belong to the sphere of the spirit was to be set free from bondage to the flesh, to partake in a superior world of divine power. In short, the insertions of the phrases κατὰ σάρκα and κατὰ πνεῦμα move the credo unmistakably in the direction of Hellenistic dualism with all its appeals, powers, and dangers.

The third level of the confession is marked below by double underlining and includes two Pauline insertions[103] and the epistolary framing of 1:3a and 1:4e,[104] thus producing the text as we find it in Romans:

1:3a   περὶ τοῦ υἱοῦ αὐτοῦ
1:3b   τοῦ γενομένου
1:3c   ἐκ σπέρματος Δαυίδ
1:3d   κατὰ σάρκα

1:4a   τοῦ ὁρισθέντος υἱοῦ θεοῦ
1:4b   ἐν δυνάμει
1:4c   κατὰ πνεῦμα ἁγιωσύνης
1:4d   ἐξ ἀναστάσεως νεκρῶν
1:4e   Ἰησοῦ Χριστοῦ τοῦ κυρίου ἡμῶν

I think that it was to contend with the dangers of the Hellenistic Christian redaction as well as of the original Jewish Christian wording of the credo that Paul inserted the phrase ἐν δυνάμει and the modifying term ἁγιωσύνη. The resultant expression, "the spirit of holiness," has no parallels in the OT or NT, but it appears in the vision of the tribe of Levi's future empowerment (T. Levi 18.11) and in a later amulet apparently referring to the "withdrawal of the spirit of holiness" (ἀνέχωρει τὸ ἁγιωσύν[ης πν]εῦμα) from the tabernacle.[105] Aside from the use in Rom 1:4, the only other NT uses of "holiness" are in two Pauline passages where ethical obligations are being stressed.[106] These passages provide an initial clue to Paul's intention here as well. The homiletic benediction that summarizes the argument of the first portion of 1 Thessalonians describes the action of God as establishing "your hearts unblamable in holiness before our God and Father, at the coming of our Lord Jesus with all his saints" (1 Thess 3:13). The specific reference of ἁγιωσύνη is developed in the succeeding section, which argues for sexual fidelity (1 Thess 4:1-8). A similar context is visible in 2 Cor 7:1, which refers to cleansing of "every defilement of body and spirit" so that "holiness" might be made "perfect in the fear of God." In both instances, congregational tendencies toward libertinism motivated by freedom in the Spirit are countered by the use of ἁγιωσύνη. One suspects a similar concern in Rom 1:4, because the belief in having transcended the realm of σάρξ by virtue of one's adherence to the realm of πνεῦμα could easily lead to a lack of concern over ethics and even to libertinistic excesses. The qualification of spirit as the "spirit of holiness" made clear that the divine power celebrated in the

---

101 See Bultmann, *Theology*, 1:236–37.
102 For example, Plutarch *Adv. Col.* 1125b3; Athenaeus *Deipn.* 7.11.4; 2.1.20; Sextus Empiricus *Math.* 11.47.
103 See Jewett, *Terms*, 136–39; Schlier, "Röm 1,3f.," 207–18; and Wengst, *Formeln*, 112–17.
104 See Dunn, "Rom 1.3-4," 40–68, for the argument that Paul added only the framing to a pre-Pauline confession.
105 See Kotansky, *Greek Magical Amulets* 1.32.4-5.
106 See Horst Balz, "ἅγιος κτλ.," *EDNT* 1 (1990) 18.

confession entailed moral obligations. Such obligations are developed at length in Rom 5–8, which shows that the new life involves righteousness, a repudiation of fleshly passions, and walking "according to the Spirit." Paul makes plain that the "spirit" given to Christian believers is the "Holy Spirit" (5:5), and that the law remains "holy" even for members of the new age (7:12). The key to the new ethic is giving oneself as a holy sacrifice for others (12:1). In this sense, the insertion of the term "holiness" prepares the reader for a major emphasis in the letter.

Paul's insertion of the phrase ἐν δυνάμει should be linked with "appointed" in an instrumental manner: Jesus was appointed through God's power.[107] This appears to be a correction of the Christology of the original confession, and thus to be directed more against the Jewish Christian than the Hellenistic Christian theology. It counters the adoptionism of the original confession by asserting that Christ was appointed by the "power" of God prior to the resurrection,[108] thus bringing the confession more nearly in line with Paul's typical interest in the doctrine of a preexistent κύριος ("Lord").[109] As the subsequent argument of Romans indicates, however, the interest in "power" is more than christological.[110] The thesis of Romans is that the gospel about Christ is "the power of God for salvation" (1:16). Insofar as Romans serves the task of world mission by aiming to elicit support for proclaiming the gospel in Spain, the entire letter can be understood as elaborating this thesis. It is consistent that the benediction wrapping up the formal argument of Romans reiterates this theme: "May the God of hope fill you with all joy and peace in believing, so that *by the power* of the Holy Spirit you may abound in hope" (15:13; cf. also 15:19). To return to the context of the confession, the insertion of "in power" therefore reiterates a motif that was implicit in the Hellenistic Christian insertion of the flesh/spirit dualism: the power of God resides not in Davidic descent but in the direct divine appointment of Christ as Son of God, so that the proclamation of the gospel about him can be the powerful means by which the "righteousness of God" is restored.

It would be a mistake, however, to interpret Paul's citation of the credo merely on the basis of relatively minor corrections. One needs to take into account the introductory and concluding formulations, and above all, in light of the purpose of the letter as a whole, one should reflect on the fact that Paul selected a composite creed.[111] The characteristic assumption of form and redaction criticism is that introductory and concluding formulas should be ascribed to redactors rather than to the original scope of cited material. That 1:3b, περὶ τοῦ υἱοῦ αὐτοῦ, was probably not part of the original credo has been assumed in this discussion. Klaus Wengst has pointed out that if this line belonged to the credo, the reference to appointed sonship in v. 4 would lose its emphatic quality through anticipation and redundancy.[112] By introducing the credo with these words, however, Paul thwarts adoptionist inferences and qualifies the Davidic sonship by stressing that Jesus was the Son of God prior to his earthly appearance.[113] The line that Paul provided to close the confession, Ἰησοῦ Χριστοῦ τοῦ κυρίου ἡμῶν, employs distinctively Pauline language that differentiates it from the cited material.[114] These words explicitly state the lordship theme that we detected both in the insertion of ἐν δυνάμει and ἁγιωσύνης. The preexistent Son of God celebrated in the credo is to be seen as the Lord of the world, a theme closely related with the thesis concerning the revelation of the "righteousness of God" (1:16-17) and the antici-

---

107 Godet, 79; Sanday and Headlam, 9; others such as Käsemann, 12; Barrett, 20; Cranfield, 1:62; Schlier, 24; Fitzmyer, 235, and Dunn, 1:14, link "in power" with "Son of God." In "δύναμις," *EDNT* 1 (1990) 357, Gerhard Friedrich points out that connection with θεοῦ would produce "Son of the powerful God." See also Hahn, *Titles*, 249–50.

108 See Schlier, "Röm 1,3f.," 210; Cullmann infers from the phrase "in power" that "Jesus is the 'Son of God' from the beginning" (*Christology*, 292).

109 See Burger, *Jesus*, 31–32; Wengst, *Formeln*, 114.

110 See Prümm, "Dynamische," 644–46.

111 Whitsett, "Son of God," 664–74, shows that the subsequent argument of Romans, recapitulated in 15:7-13, carries forward the Christology of the confession that proclaims Christ as a servant both to Jews and Gentiles.

112 Wengst, *Formeln*, 112; see also Käsemann, 10.

113 See Stuhlmacher, "Probleme," 382; Dunn, "Rom 1.3-4," 55–56.

114 See Schlier, "Röm 1,3f.," 208; Käsemann, 13–14; Bouwman, 128.

pated acknowledgment by the nations (15:10-12). In Käsemann's words, "For Paul the Kyrios is the representative of the God who claims the world and who with the church brings the new creation into the midst of the old world that is perishing."[115] With this introduction and conclusion, Paul effectively encloses the credo within the framework of his own theology.

The most significant feature of all, however, is that Paul selects a credo that bears the marks of both "the weak and the strong," the Gentile and the Jewish Christian branches of the early church. Despite the careful framing with typical Pauline language and the correcting insertions, the prominent location of this creed indicates Paul's acceptance of a common faith and his effort to be evenhanded. He is willing to cite the Jewish Christian affirmation of Jesus as coming from the "seed of David," despite his opposition to Jewish zealotism (10:1-3) and pride (2:17-24). He is willing to accept the Hellenistic Christian dialectic of flesh versus spirit, despite his subsequent effort to insist upon moral transformation (Rom 6–8) and to counter the results of spiritual arrogance (14:1–15:7). Yet none of these points is scored overtly; the credo is cited with respect, edited with skill, and framed effectively in language that various branches of the early church would have understood. The overwhelming impression one has after reflecting on the implications of Paul's use of the credo is his irenic approach. He is obviously seeking to find common ground by bringing the confession into the context of his ambassadorial strategy in the letter as a whole.

For this reason, I find it necessary to qualify Peter Stuhlmacher's formulation that Paul is attempting primarily to prove to the Romans that he shares an essentially salvation-historical Christology.[116] Schlier points out that the first-level editing of the formula had severely qualified this salvation-history point of view by the insertion of the "flesh/spirit" antithesis and that this edited credo was likely known in Rome. What Paul pro-

vides, in Schlier's perspective, is Paul's own edited version, which means that it functions as part of the firming up of their faith (1:11-12), an apostolic correction, so to speak. "He practices the spiritual relation between apostle and church,"[117] which, if understood in a traditional manner, might involve some rather authoritarian implications. It seems to me that Paul's use of the confessional formula transforms the features of both Stuhlmacher's and Schlier's perspectives. The christological parameters are drawn broadly enough to incorporate the insights both of the salvation-history advocates and the Hellenistic dualists. Apostolic authority is used here not to discredit theological options that Paul happens to dislike but rather to find common ground in the faith for a variety of cultural, theological, and ethical alternatives.

These considerations allow us to resolve the question of whether Paul was attempting to demonstrate his orthodoxy to the Romans by citing a creed in use there.[118] That this is a composite creed could lend precision to this suggestion. Insofar as it contains components contributed by branches of the early church that are in competition in Rome, the creed's use signals the intent to find common ground in the letter as a whole. The argument for early Christian pluralism that has been detected in 14:1—15:7 is thus integral to the letter as a whole, as the *exordium* makes plain.[119] Since the peroration was supposed to echo the *exordium* according to ancient rhetorical theory, it was appropriate that Paul returns to the theme of "the gospel for Jews and Gentiles alike" in 15:7-13.[120]

■ **5** With δι᾿ οὗ ("through whom") Paul links both grace and the apostolic ministry to the agency of the risen Christ, who had been celebrated in the preceding confession.[121] In view of the fact that Paul consistently uses the first person singular to refer to his apostolic mission from this point forward (see 1:9-16; 11:13-34; 15:15, 17-20, 23-32), there has been intensive discussion about why he uses the plural verb ἐλάβομεν ("we have received")

115 Käsemann, 14.
116 Stuhlmacher, "Probleme," 378–86.
117 Schlier, "Römer 1,3f.," 218.
118 See Neufeld, *Confessions*, 2, 51, citing Dodd, Bultmann, Michel, and Barrett; see also Kuss, 1:2, 8.
119 See Jewett, *Tolerance*, 121–41.
120 Bryskog, "Epistolography, Rhetoric and Letter Prescript," 44.
121 See Wobbe, *Charis-Gedanke*, 23; Dunn, 1:16.

here. Some have argued that Paul employs an epistolary plural that allows the "I" to remain in the background,[122] which seems to counter the requirements of establishing his ambassadorial credentials, visible throughout this *exordium*. That Paul wishes to include the twelve apostles may be overly specific,[123] but he certainly opens the door to some other apostles.[124] The detailed analysis of the "I" and "we" references in the Pauline letters by Otto Roller shows that exigent circumstances are the best explanation.[125] I infer that Paul wishes to convey solidarity with the apostles whose emissaries had established the house and tenement churches in Rome in the decades before the writing of this letter.[126] Whereas some of the twelve apostles restricted their mission to the land of Israel, remaining as leaders of the Jerusalem church,[127] the missionaries who reached Rome obviously shared Paul's calling to a Gentile mission. In 16:7, for example, Paul greets a married couple currently ministering in Rome by the names of Andronikos and Junia, who are "prominent among the apostles."

The reception of "grace and apostleship" has occasioned a debate over whether the former refers to Paul's conversion and the latter to his missionary calling,[128] or whether the two are more or less identical.[129] The latter would imply that χάριν καὶ ἀποστολήν constitute a hendiadys,[130] which is problematic because the plural "we received" would then suggest that other apostles received their calling at the moment of conversion just as Paul had. A more precise grasp has been worked out by Karl Olaf Sandnes on the basis of Gal 1:15-16 ("But when he who had set me apart before I was born, and had called me through his grace, was pleased to reveal his Son to me, in order that I might preach him among the Gentiles").[131] Here grace overcomes an insufficiency, thus making the call to service possible. Although Sandnes restricts grace to "God's forgiveness of Paul's prior life as a persecutor of the church,"[132] χάρις is clearly a broader category dealing with divine acceptance of persons with limitations and failures of various kinds.[133] It is a gift or favor given in an open, uncoerced manner,[134] and for Paul it is primarily a matter of being given access to God without having met any qualifications.[135] Given the overwhelming weight of the Augustinian tradition of interpreting the details of Romans under the assumption that justification by faith equals forgiveness, it is noteworthy that Paul selects a term here that deals with the wounds of shame rather than those of guilt.[136] One can speak here of the "priority of grace,"[137] which precedes an apostolic calling as well as the concept of faith; it is the most certain, commonly

---

122 K. Dick, "Der schriftstellerische Plural bei Paulus," diss., University of Halle, 1900, 151–66, followed by Lagrange, 10; see also Leenhardt, 38–39; Schlier, 28; Cranfield, 1:65. Michel, 75, refers to the "modesty" of this formulation.

123 Zahn, 43–44. Kuss, 1:9, dismisses this suggestion as "fantastic."

124 See Dunn, 1:16; Roller, *Formular*, 586 n. 494, concludes that Paul refers to the "Gesamtheit der Apostle," and that Zahn's suggestion should not be dismissed.

125 Roller, *Formular*, 151–87. An example of this plural usage in Josephus *Vita* 229: "Jonathan and those with him, to Josephus: greetings. We have reported to you (παραγγέλλομέν σοι). . . ."

126 An alternate view is suggested by Hester, "Persona," 100, that the epistolary plural conveys Paul's personal authority.

127 See Hans Dieter Betz, "Apostle," *ABD* 1 (1992) 310.

128 Lagrange, 10; Zahn, 44, referring to the link between "grace" and conversion in Rom 5:2; Gal 1:6.

129 Michel, 75; Dunn, 1:17; Wilckens, 1:66, noting that grace is viewed as the source of apostolic calling in

Rom 12:3; 15:15; Gal 2:9; 1 Cor 3:10. See also Satake, "Apostolat und Gnade," 106–7; Peace, *Conversion*, 33.

130 Kuss, 1:9–10; Cranfield, 1:66; Fitzmyer, 237.

131 Sandnes, *Paul*, 64–65, 150, relying on the work of Scott J. Hafemann that was later published as *Suffering and the Spirit* (Tübingen: Mohr-Siebeck, 1986), recalling that the call narratives of Moses (Exod 3:10), Isaiah (Isa 6:5), Jeremiah (Jer 1:6), and Ezekiel (Ezek 1:28–2:2) contain impediments that must be overcome by divine intervention before the prophetic message can be conveyed.

132 Sandnes, *Paul*, 64.

133 See Wobbe, *Charis-Gedanke*, 23, 40–41.

134 See Wetter, *Charis*, 12–18; Klaus Berger, "χάρις," *EDNT* 3 (1993) 457.

135 Berger, "χάρις," 458–59; Harrison, *Language of Grace*, 18, 88–89.

136 In "Gnade," 3–4, Klaus Berger shows that grace is primarily linked with election and has "no connection to forgiveness of sins." It functions primarily in the arena of human weakness (16).

137 See Doughty, "Priority," 163–80.

held foundation he shares with the varied churches in Rome.

The prepositional phrase εἰς ὑπακοὴν πίστεως ("leading to [the] obedience of faith") conveys the purpose of Paul's apostolicity and raises the question whether the genitive is objective (i.e., obedience in relation to faith or God's faithfulness),[138] subjective (i.e., obedience that faith produces or that faith requires),[139] or epexegetical (i.e., obedience that consists in faith).[140] Although the last seems most likely to the majority of commentators, the inference that faith and obedience are interchangeable terms for Paul seems problematic.[141] Since the expression "obedience of faith" is found only in 1:5 and 16:26 in the entirety of ancient literature,[142] it was most likely coined by Paul to fit the rhetorical exigency of this letter.[143] The grammatical options that have been discussed thus far are all aspects of the adnominal genitive, in which Smyth shows that "a substantive in the genitive limits the meaning of a substantive on which it depends."[144] Thus πίστεως ("faith") limits the meaning of ὑπακοήν ("obedience"). Whereas there are many forms of obedience, including obedience under the law, Paul speaks here of the special sort of obedience produced by the gospel. It is unnecessary to assume, however, with Don B. Garlington that the phrase "the obedience of faith" has a polemical and antithetical motivation in contrast to Jewish theology.[145] It appears more likely that it would have honored both Jewish Christian and Gentile Christian concerns in Rome, because, as Paul argues in the subsequent sections of this letter, obedience to the gospel leads to walking by the spirit and to the fulfillment of the law's demands to love and care for the neighbor.[146] Since "obedience" was a favored concept for Jewish theology[147] and "faith" was a favorite shibboleth for Gentile believers in Rome (14:1, 22, 23), the coordination of these two terms conveys an interest in finding common ground. There is not a hint of polemical intent in the wording of 1:5 or in its rhetorical echo of 15:18. The expression has a straightforward, missionary relevance: "the obedience of faith means acceptance of the message of salvation" that Paul intends to advance in this letter.[148] Paul's expression addresses a central feature of the honor system in the Greco-Roman world, because obedience carried the "stigma" of slavery and even the emperor preferred to phrase his directives "as suggestions and advice."[149] As J. E. Lendon observes, "the early and high empire simply avoided hierarchies of obedience as much as possible," preferring to speak of honoring persons in authority by complying with their wishes out of respect for their honorable character.[150] Cicero "placed duty to officials under the rubric of 'respect': 'The duty of respect requires us to reverence and cherish those outstanding because of age or wisdom, or office, or any other claim to prestige.' The duty to obey could be viewed as a subset of the wider duty to honour one's rulers."[151] Paul's

---

138 Lietzmann, 26; Michel, 75–76; Kuss, 1:10; idem, "Begriff des Gehorsams," 695–702; Gaston, *Paul*, 169, suggests "obedience to [God's] faithfulness." See the critique of this position by Käsemann, 14, that the object in this verse is "to spread his name."

139 Parke-Taylor, "Romans i.5 and xvi.26," 305–6.

140 Zahn, 45; Kühl, 13; Schlier, 29; Cranfield, 1:66–67; Käsemann, 14.

141 See Gerhard Friedrich, "Muss ὑπακοὴ πίστεως Röm 1:5 mit 'Glaubensgehorsam' übersetzt werden?" *ZNW* 72 (1981) 118–23, showing that if the faith and obedience are identical terms, the expression "obedience of faith" becomes a meaningless pleonasm, which should be replaced by a rather implausible translation "preaching of faith," on the grounds that for Paul the crucial form of obedience is apostolic preaching.

142 However, a similar expression is found in Acts 6:7, "a great many of the priests were obedient to the faith (ὑπήκουον τῇ πίστει)."

143 See Wolfgang Wiefel, "Glaubensgehorsam? Erwägungen zu Röm 1,5," in H. Benekert et al., eds., *Wort und Gemeinde. Festschrift für Erdmann Schott zum 65. Geburtstag* (Berlin: Evangelische Verlagsanstalt, 1967) 144.

144 Smyth, *Grammar*, §1290.

145 Garlington, *Obedience*, 1–4, 233; he derives from Michel's Romans commentary the assumption, typical of traditional European commentaries, that the formula is both antithetical and polemical.

146 See Miller, *Obedience of Faith*, 59–60.

147 See Garlington, *Obedience*, 11–13.

148 Käsemann, 15; see also Kinneavy, *Greek Rhetorical Origins*, 103–4; Binder, *Glaube*, 70.

149 Lendon, *Empire of Honour*, 20.

150 Ibid., 20–27.

151 Ibid., 23, citing Cicero *Inv.* 2.66.

qualification of "obedience" by "faith" removes the stigma of slavishness and inserts a large measure of honor, because the gospel to which one has freely responded in faith centers in the grace of God offered to the formerly shamed through Christ's death and resurrection in their behalf.

The scope of Paul's missionary calling is "among all the Gentiles," which refers to the non-Jewish groups within the Roman Empire. Two aspects of this formulation are noteworthy: the use of the prejudicial term "Gentiles" for the non-Jewish inhabitants of Rome and its empire,[152] and the sweeping inclusivity denoted by "all." Some prefer to downplay the former with the translation "nations,"[153] under the assumption that in this instance ἔθνη includes Israel among all the nations of the world.[154] This seems highly unlikely in view of Paul's description of his calling to be an apostle to the "Gentiles" (Gal 1:16; 2:8) and also in view of Paul's purpose in writing this letter, namely the mission to Spain, where there were as yet no Jewish settlements. But the inclusivity of the gospel remains startling. Not only does this imply mission to every nation in the entire known world, but also in Dunn's words it suggests "that Paul seriously contemplated this outreach being achieved within his own lifetime, as the last act before the end and the necessary preliminary to the salvation of Israel (1 Cor 4:9; Rom 11:13-27)."[155] This theme finds its echo in the climax of the theological argument in Rom 15:8-12 with all the Gentiles finding their unity in praising God. From the very opening words of this letter until its climax, therefore, Paul is inviting the Roman house and tenement churches into some form of participation in this global mission.

The formulation ὑπὲρ τοῦ ὀνόματος ("for the sake of his name") is not frequently found in secular Greek;[156] it is also found in Acts 5:41; 9:16; 15:26; 21:13; and 3 John 7, mostly in the context of Christian emissaries who proclaim Christ and suffer on his behalf.[157] In Hebrew thought the "name" of God "denotes the personal rule and work of Yahweh" and could "be used as an alternative term for Yahweh himself."[158] While Yahweh himself remains in his heavenly court, his name dwells among humans, is present in the temple, and extends divine lordship over the world.[159] In some OT passages the name of Yahweh is hypostasized as an acting subject worthy of honor in its own right, as in Ps 54:1, "O God, help me by your name, and establish justice for me by your strength," or as in Mal 1:11: "For from the rising of the sun to its setting my name is great among the nations, and in every place incense is offered to my name, and a pure offering; for my name is great among the Gentiles, says the Lord of hosts."[160] The name of Jesus Christ is "the foundation and theme of proclamation" in missionary contexts, both in Acts' account of Paul's mission to the Gentiles (Acts 9:15) and in the later reiteration of his mission to preach in places where Christ had not yet "been named" (Rom 15:20).[161]

■ 6 Ever since the nineteenth century, commentators have been divided over whether this verse should be translated as "among whom also you are called of Jesus Christ,"[162] or "among whom also you are, [the] called of

---

152 See Georg Bertram, "ἔθνος, ἐθνικός," *TDNT* 2 (1964) 368–69; Zahn, 46–48; Nikolaus Walter, "ἔθνος," *EDNT* 1 (1990) 382–83.

153 For example, Dabelstein, *Beurteilung*, 109–11; Dunn, 1:18; Leenhardt, 40; see the discussion of the 19th-century debate on this issue in Godet, 82–83. For recent advocacy of the translation "nations," see James LaGrand, "Gentiles in the New Revised Standard Version," *BR* 38 (1993) 44–54.

154 Zahn, 47. Michel, 76, weighs this option and decides that Paul's calling as a missionary to the Gentiles renders this implausible.

155 Dunn, 1:18.

156 The formulation ὑπὲρ τοῦ ὀνόματος occurs in Chrysippus *Frag. log.* 355.6, in reference to "quarreling over a name" (ἐρίζειν ὑπὲρ τοῦ ὀνόματος); the plural occurs in 24.7 and the expression occurs 37

times in Galen's writings, mostly in the plural. For the concept of the name of God, which does not occur in Greco-Roman sources, see Lars Hartman, "ὄνομα," *EDNT* 2 (1991) 520–21; however, the parallels he adduces at Ps 102:16 and Mal 1:11 do not include the preposition ὑπέρ.

157 See Hans Bietenhard, "ὄνομα κτλ.," *TDNT* 5 (1967) 273.

158 Ibid., 255.

159 Ibid., 256–57.

160 See also Pss 20:1, 5; 44:5; 118:10-12; Jer 10:6; Prov 18:10, cited by Bietenhard, "ὄνομα κτλ.," 257–58.

161 Ibid., 278. Cf. Hermann, *Kyrios und Pneuma*, 59–61.

162 See Meyer, 1:53–54, citing Lachmann, Tischendorf, Hofmann, and others. One could add Zahn, 49–50; Schlatter, 11.

Jesus Christ."[163] The advocates of the former reading argue that the latter is superfluous because the Roman believers know that they dwell among Gentiles,[164] but Godet reads this as a significant syllogism that places the Romans within the sphere of Paul's apostolic calling.[165] The major premise is

> Christ has made me the Apostle of the Gentiles; the minor: ye are of the number of the Gentiles; conclusion: therefore, in virtue of the authority of that Christ who has called you as He has called me, ye are the sheep of my fold. . . . The καί, *also,* from this point of view is easily explained: "of the number of whom (Gentiles) ye *also* are, ye Romans, falling consequently like the other Gentiles called by me personally to my apostolical domain."

Kühl argues that the placement of "and" before ὑμεῖς ("you") links it with the previous reference to the Gentiles and favors Godet's option,[166] which also seems most plausibly related to Paul's purpose in this *exordium.* Consistent with diplomatic caution, however, the formulation is subtly advanced, because Paul does not intend to claim a leadership role in Rome; as chap. 15 explains, his short visit is intended only to enlist their support for missionary activity in Spain. Far from implying that the Roman churches hitherto lacked a legitimate apostolic foundation[167] or that they should submit to his authority as part of his "domain," he is simply claiming diplomatic legitimacy in eliciting their assistance in an apostolic project to complete the circle of the Gentile world by missionizing in Spain. This reading also correlates with the expression κλητοὶ Ἰησοῦ Χριστοῦ ("called of Jesus Christ"), which is a predicate adjective related to "you are," and which therefore constitutes part of the address of the letter.[168] The genitive has been interpreted as possessive, "belonging to Jesus Christ,"[169] or of origin, "called by Jesus Christ."[170] Insofar as this is an address to the Roman believers, it seems unlikely that so fine a distinction would have been drawn. Rather, this is early Christian jargon that Paul employs in exact parallel to his self-appellation, "by divine call an apostle," and relates to the formulation in the next verse, "called saints." The use of this language reflects believers who appear to be using the name "Jesus Christ" as a personal name rather than as a peculiar messianic title, while Paul preferred the formula "Christ Jesus," in which the first word is "appellative."[171] As Schneider and Grundmann explain, "the strangeness of the Christ title ('Messiah' = 'anointed one') in the Gentile Christian churches probably required the transition to a double name."[172] In all likelihood, therefore, the appellation, "the called of Jesus Christ," would be natural for the Gentile Christian majority in Rome.[173] The Gentiles who boast in 11:18

---

163 Schlier, 29–30, cites Cornely, Gutjahr, Bardenhewer, Huby, Häring, Jülicher, Kühl, Lagrange, Barrett, Schmidt, Nygren, Althaus, Leenhardt. Others following this line are Cranfield, 1:67–68; Moo, 53–54.

164 The choice of the preposition ἐν ("in, among") rather than ἐκ ("from") is used by Schlatter, 11, to argue that Paul is not implying the church consists entirely of Gentiles; and Cranfield, 1:20, 68, takes this as a geographical indication of the placement of the Roman congregations "in the midst of the Gentile world."

165 Godet, 83, followed by Schlier, Cranfield, Moo, and most current commentators.

166 Kühl, 15.

167 Klein, "Paul's Purpose," 43.

168 Schlier, 30, citing Beck, 51.

169 Meyer, 1:54, citing "most modern commentators"; see also Sanday and Headlam, 12; Lagrange, 11; Kühl, 15; Barrett, 22; Schlier, 30; Dunn, 1:19; Wiederkehr, *Berufung,* 147. On p. 54 Moo opts for a predicative force, "called to belong to Jesus Christ,"

following Zerwick and Grosvener, *Grammatical Analysis,* 457; and A. Feuillet, "La vie nouvelle du chrétien et les trois Personnes divines d'après Rom. I-VIII," *RevThom* 83 (1983) 8–9.

170 Meyer, 1:54, cites Luther, Rückert, Mehring, and Hofmann as advocating this view; in the more recent period, see Murray, 14.

171 See S. V. McCasland, "'Christ Jesus,'" *JBL* 65 (1946) 377–83, esp. 382; Gerhard Schneider, "Ἰησοῦς," *EDNT* 2 (1991) 182: "While Ἰησοῦς Χριστός . . . is in most cases understood as a double name, Paul's preferred phrase Χριστὸς Ἰησοῦς . . . has more the sound of the titular sense ('the Messiah Jesus')."

172 Schneider, "Ἰησοῦς," 182; see also Walter Grundmann, "χρίω κτλ.," *TDNT* 9 (1974) 542.

173 I include the article in the translation "the called," because κλητοί ("called") is limited by the following genitive phrase, "of Jesus Christ."

that they had been elected to replace the Jewish branches in the divine olive tree of the chosen people would feel themselves included with this expression. I think it would have included at least three of the five congregations that Paul identifies in Rom 16. Insofar as the term "strong" in chaps. 14–15 refers to Gentile Christians, it would roughly correlate with this expression "called of Jesus Christ." Most scholars currently feel that such Gentile Christians formed the majority of the membership of the house churches at the time of the writing of Romans, and if this is true, it may explain why Paul uses this title first in his address.

■ **7** The formal address in the letter appears at the beginning of this verse with the dative clause, "to all God's beloved, called saints, who are in Rome." The place of emphasis is given to πᾶσιν ("to all"), which continues the theme of inclusivity noted in the earlier citation of the composite confession. This formulation includes both Gentile and Jewish Christians, both those whom he knows in Rome (16:3-16) and those he has not yet met.[174] Since this is the second reference to "all" in the *exordium*, the audience is prepared for the most extensive use of this term in any of the Pauline letters.[175] The discourse of Romans is carefully designed to include every branch of the splintered congregation in Rome. The cooperation and support of each group is required if the challenging Spanish mission is to have any chance of success. The definite article goes with "God's beloved" (τοῖς ἀγαπητοῖς θεοῦ) and with οὖσιν ἐν Ῥώμῃ ("to those in Rome") in the attributive position. The expressed κλητοῖς ἁγίοις ("called saints")

stands in apposition to "God's beloved." There are distant parallels to this formula for being loved by God, such as that found in Dio Chrysostom's advice that a wise king should seek to have "the love of men and gods instead of their hate" (*Orat.* 3.60) or when the Egyptian king is described as "beloved by the god Phtha."[176]

The link between God's calling of people and nations to be his beloved that we find in this *exordium*, however, has its roots in Judaism.[177] God elects and loves the patriarchs,[178] Abraham,[179] Joseph,[180] David,[181] Jerusalem,[182] and the entire people of Israel.[183] But it is important to note that this is the only time in the Pauline corpus, indeed in the entirety of ancient literature prior to Paul, that this exact formula is employed.[184] It signals a significant theme developed in the rest of Romans, that God pours out love for those who do not merit it (Rom 5:5-8; 8:31-39; 9:13). This gift of love comes to Jews who are "beloved on account of the patriarchs" (11:28),[185] as well as to Gentiles (8:35). All of the believers in Rome, no matter what their orientation, are recipients of this boundless love flowing from the Christ event. I think it is significant that Paul places this reference between the formulas "called of Jesus Christ" and "called saints" so that it serves as a unification formula. The wording is explicitly inclusive: "all God's beloved."[186] This phrase suggests the theological argument of the entire letter, namely that God's love is impartial.[187] No person on earth, whether Greek or Jewish, deserves such love, as 1:18–3:20 argues. Nevertheless, everyone receives such love in Christ, as 3:21–4:25 so eloquently shows. God is no respecter of persons, as 2:11 insists; all have made

174 See Godet, 84; Cranfield, 1:68. Schlier, 31, finds this improbable, for obscure reasons.

175 The word "all" appears 64 times in Romans; see B. Reicke, "πᾶς, ἅπας," *TDNT* 5 (1967) 893–96.

176 Cited by BAGD 5 from *SIG* 90.4.

177 See Wischmeyer, "ΑΓΑΠΗΤΟΣ," 477.

178 Wischmeyer refers to Josephus, *Ant.* 1.3.9 (§§104-6).

179 Wischmeyer cites Dan 3:35; Isa 41:8; *T. Abr.* A1; *3 En.* 44.10; CD 3:2-3.

180 *Jos. Asen.* 23.10.

181 Josephus *Ant.* 6.275-80.

182 Sir 24:11.

183 Wischmeyer points to *4 Ezra* 6.58; *Jub.* 2.20; the semantic field is also visible in Isa 44:2; see also Pss 59:7; 107:7, as noted by Schlier, 31.

184 The only parallel is the second-century Christian writing, *AcPlTh* 6.6, "through the love of God" (δι' ἀγάπην θεοῦ).

185 Wischmeyer, "ΑΓΑΠΗΤΟΣ," 477; see also Gerhard Schneider, "ἀγάπη κτλ.," *EDNT* 1 (1990) 10.

186 This nuance is overlooked by Garlington in *Obedience*, 241–42, who concentrates on the background in Isa 42–44 and Ps 108, arguing that Paul applies this "honorific title of Israel" to the Christian church.

187 See Bassler, *Impartiality*, 164–70.

themselves into God's enemies (5:10), but all are included in the sweep of divine love. The offering of salvation "to all who believe" epitomizes the argument of Romans (1:16; 3:22; 4:11; 10:4). In this sense, the opening address of Romans sets the tone for the entire letter, offering the most inclusive program for world unification found in the NT. If this gospel is understood and internalized, Paul suggests, the fragmented house churches of Rome would become unified in cooperation while preserving their distinctiveness. They would also be enabled to participate in a credible manner in completing the mission to the end of the known world, symbolized by Spain. When this unifying message is received in faith, the goal of history will be fulfilled and all the nations will praise God for God's mercy, as the climax of the formal argument in chap. 15 proclaims.

The expression κλητοῖς ἁγίοις ("called" or "elect saints") in this context seems "almost titular," similar to the self-identification used by the Essenes.[188] A prominent example is the Qumran War Scroll where the preparations for the holy war involve identifying the warriors with this title: "On the trumpets calling the congregation they shall write, 'The Called of God'" (קריאי אל; 1QM 3:2). Similarly 1QM 4:9-11 commands: "When they set out for battle they shall write on the first standard 'Congregation of God' . . . on the seventh standard, 'The Called of God' (קריאי אל)."[189] This titular use would best be captured by the translation "called saints" or "elect saints,"[190] because the usual translation "called to be saints" implies a moral agenda for salvation rather than the assured status implied by the title.

The repetition of "called" led Kühl to the impression that "another circle" of believers is being addressed in distinction to those mentioned in v. 6.[191] I believe this observation is correct and that there is evidence to support a more precise identification. When the term "saints" is used as a description of specific Christian groups in contrast to all Christians,[192] it refers to Jewish Christians, loyal to or associated with Jerusalem.[193] In the Roman context, I think this address would include many of those Jewish Christians banned under Claudius who have now returned to Rome, some of whom are being discriminated against by the Gentile Christian majorities in the house and tenement churches. This title would certainly include the group referred to in 16:15 that called itself "the saints." I think it might also include the Christian cell centered among the slaves and freedmen of Aristoboulus. The group stereotyped as "weak" in Rom 14–15 probably overlapped with such "saints." The expression would include those perceived to be "barbarian," to use the discriminatory term selected in 1:14 to depict those to whom Paul felt obligated. Those Jewish Christians whose Jewish accent remained prominent and who did not have enough education to be fully conversant with Greco-Roman culture would fall under this category, which overlaps to some degree with the expression "uneducated" in the same verse. The evidence from Leon's magisterial study, *The Jews of Ancient Rome,* is relevant here, because he discovered that several Jewish cemeteries contained a large proportion of virtually illiterate grave inscriptions, indicating that some of the Jewish synagogues served recent immigrants and lower class population with primitive educational standards.[194] Some of the Christians included among the "called saints" would probably come from such backgrounds. By employing this expression in apposition to "beloved," these Jewish Christians would feel themselves included among those addressed in the formula "all God's beloved . . . in Rome."

The greeting that closes the first pericope is found in

188 See Cranfield, 1:69; Wilckens, 1:68 n. 39.

189 See also 1QM 2:7; 14:5; 1QSa 1:27; 2:2, 11; CD 2:11; 4:3-4, noted by Dunn, 1:19. The translations are drawn from Cranfield, 1:69, cited from the Vermes version of the scrolls.

190 Karl Ludwig Schmidt, "κλητός," *TDNT* 1 (1964) 494.

191 Kühl, 16.

192 For example, Phil 1:1; Col 1:12; Rom 8:27. Stephen Woodward shows that the NT usage derives from Daniel and the Qumran literature but does not deal with the use of "saints" to refer to a particular group within the early church, in "The Provenance of the Term 'Saints': A *Religionsgeschichtliche* Study," *JETS* 24 (1981) 107–16.

193 For example, Rom 15:25, 26, 31; 1 Cor 16:1; see Wiederkehr, *Berufung,* 107; see also Horst Balz, "ἅγιος κτλ.," *EDNT* 1 (1990) 17.

194 Leon, *Jews,* 122–34, 233–38.

other Pauline letters, with slight variations (1 Cor 1:3; 2 Cor 1:2; Gal 1:3; 1 Thess 1:1; 2 Thess 1:2; Phil 1:2; Phlm 3). It consists of three lines of four words apiece, each line with eight syllables, and functions as a kind of blessing.[195]

χάρις ὑμῖν καὶ εἰρήνη
ἀπὸ θεοῦ πατρὸς ἡμῶν
καὶ κυρίου Ἰησοῦ Χριστοῦ

The "grace and peace" formula appears to be an early Christian adaptation of the Jewish epistolary greeting, "mercy and peace," as in *2 Bar.* 78.2, "Thus speaks Baruch, the son of Neriah, to the brothers who were carried away in captivity, '*Mercy and peace be with you.* I remember, my brothers, the love of him who created me.'"[196] Sometimes the peace wish is combined with the verb "be increased," as in King Darius's letter (Dan 6:22): "Peace be multiplied to you." In 2 Macc 1:1 we find a more conventional greeting such as appeared in most letters, "To the brethren, the Jews of Egypt, greeting (χαίρειν)," which was followed by the peace wish: "The brethren, the Jews in Jerusalem and throughout the land of Judaea, with you perfect peace." In comparison with all other greetings in the ancient world, Paul's combination of "grace and peace,"[197] as well as the elaboration of the source in "Christ and . . . God the Father," reflects a distinctive theological orientation.[198] That such greetings were used in early Christian worship is a possibility,[199] and insofar as the letters were read aloud in worship services, they certainly served a liturgical function on such occasions. Whereas the traditional Jewish blessing formula was "mercy and peace be with you,"[200] Paul appears to transform the Greco-Roman greeting with χαίρειν ("greeting"), used in correspondence and in meeting friends on the street,[201] into a distinctively Christian greeting with χάρις ὑμῖν ("grace to you [pl.]").[202] In his theology grace has priority as the essence of what Christ provides (Gal 2:21; 1 Cor 1:4; 2 Cor 6:1):[203] unmerited access to God for those who do not deserve it,[204] and thereby honor to those whom the world holds to be shameful. This theme is developed throughout the letter, showing that grace stands in opposition to the performance of legal requirements as the new means of gaining honor (Rom 4:14-16; 6:14). It also stands in contrast to grace as defined in the Roman civic cult, which had announced "an eschatological 'age of grace'. . . . The reign of Augustus represented a turning point in beneficence."[205] An official announcement of Nero's accession to power declares him to be "the hope of the world" and "the source of all good things. . . . Therefore we all ought to wear garlands and with sacrifices of oxen to give thanks to all the gods."[206]

That peace as well as grace is granted by God to the Christian recipients of the letter is also a theme that Paul develops in Romans. It is the more traditional half of a greeting, from the Jewish point of view,[207] whose content is defined in the OT primarily in terms of "peace from enemies and wild beasts," with attendant prosperity and contentment granted by Yahweh.[208] In Paul's thought, peace has the distinctive dimension of reconciliation with God, against whom human enmity had risen to its climax in the crucifixion of Christ.[209]

---

195 See Schlier, 32; Berger, "Apostelbrief," 191–207; idem, *Formgeschichte,* 245.

196 This translation from Syriac is provided by Charles, *APOT,* 2:521, but the recent translation by A. F. J. Klijn in *OTP* 1:648 uses the Pauline wording "grace and peace be with you."

197 Lieu, "Apostolic Greeting," 168–70.

198 Berger, "Apostelbrief," 202; Heckel, *Segen,* 281–84.

199 Lohmeyer, *Probleme,* 14–15.

200 Käsemann, 16; Dunn, 1:20. See also 2 Macc 1:1 ("peace and health") and the use of the "mercy and peace" formula in the NT at Gal 6:16 and Jude 2.

201 See Roller, *Formular,* 61; Hans Conzelmann, "χαίρω κτλ.," *TDNT* 9 (1974) 360, 394.

202 See Lieu, "Apostolic Greeting," 168–70.

203 See Doughty, "Priority," 172; Conzelmann, "χάρις κτλ.," 394.

204 Klaus Berger, "χάρις," *EDNT* 3 (1993) 458; see also H. Rongy, "La salutation de l'épître aux Romains," *REcL* 22 (1931) 228.

205 Harrison, *Language of Grace,* 213–14.

206 Cited by ibid., 87, from *P.Oxy.* 7. Nr. 1021.6-18.

207 For example, the typical greeting in the LXX is εἰρήνη σοι ("peace to you"), e.g., Judg 19:20; Dan 10:19, or in the pl. εἰρήνη ὑμῖν ἔσται, Tob 12.17. See Lieu, "Apostolic Greeting," 164–67.

208 Gerhard von Rad, "εἰρήνη κτλ.," *TDNT* 2 (1964) 404.

209 See Michel, 78.

This theme is developed in Gal 5:22 and Rom 5:1,[210] and the consequence in Romans for those who receive the gospel is a peaceful mindset (Rom 8:6) that is capable of finding peaceful solutions to social conflicts within the congregation (15:17-19).[211] In view of the performative element in a blessing like this, Michel is correct in perceiving that "in the greeting the content of the message of the blessing is given to the congregation," a content that is consistent with the rest of the thought of this letter.[212]

The power to grant the content of the blessing, "grace and peace," derives not from the person uttering the words as they are read aloud in the Roman house and tenement churches, but from the source of all blessing: "from God our Father and [the] Lord Jesus Christ." Although there are parallels to God as Father in the Greco-Roman as well as Jewish cultures,[213] this use of "our Father" resonates with the prayer taught by Jesus that begins with precisely the same words, πάτερ ἡμῶν (Matt 6:9).[214] This language combines patriarchy with intimacy and belongingness,[215] because in Christ believers are brought to know that God is indeed their loving parent as well as the source of their unity. Paul develops these themes later in Romans by noting that the Spirit utters the cry "Abba, Father" within the heart of believers (Rom 8:15), and that believers of many orientations should "with one voice glorify the God and Father of our Lord Jesus Christ" (15:6). The coordination of God with κυρίου Ἰησοῦ Χριστοῦ ("Lord Jesus Christ") is on a more equal level in the blessing than in 15:6. By using the copulative καί ("and"), the blessing makes clear that grace and peace derive from Christ as well as from God.[216] As Godet observes, "the conviction of Christ's divine nature can alone explain this construction, according to which His person and that of the Father are made alike dependent on one and the same preposition."[217] A distinctive feature of Paul's blessings is that the reference to "God our Father" is always followed by κύριος ("Lord"),[218] so this coordination is basic to his thought. The high Christology of the confession in 1:3-4 is reflected here and brings to an appropriate close the first pericope that establishes Paul's credentials as an apostle under the lordship of Christ.

---

210 See Rongy, "La salutation," 228; Werner Foerster, "εἰρήνη κτλ.," TDNT 2 (1964) 416.

211 See Foerster, "εἰρήνη κτλ.," 416–17.

212 Michel, 78.

213 See Gottlob Schrenk, "πατήρ κτλ.," TDNT 5 (1967) 945–82; G. Mensching, H.-J. Kraus, and J. Jeremias, "Vatername Gottes," RGG³ 6.1232–35; Wlosok, "Vater," 38–39.

214 See Dunn, 1:21.

215 See Schrenk, "πατήρ κτλ.," 983–85.

216 See Schlier, 32.

217 Godet, 85.

218 Schrenk, "πατήρ κτλ.," 1007.

1

The Second Pericope

Thanksgiving and *Causa*:
The Announcement and Rationale of
Paul's Forthcoming Visit

8/ **So first and foremost, I thank my God through Jesus Christ[a] concerning[b] all of you, because your faith is proclaimed through the whole world. 9/ For God is my[c] witness, whom I serve in my spirit in the gospel of his Son, how I ceaselessly make mention of you, 10/ always pleading in my prayers that if perhaps now at last I may be granted good passage, by the will of God, in coming to you. 11/ For I long to see you, in order that I might share some spiritual charisma with you that you may be strengthened, 12/ or to speak more properly, to be mutually encouraged among you[d] by each other's faith, both yours and mine.**

a   The phrase "through Jesus Christ" is missing in ℵ* 1270, probably a scribal omission.

b   In place of περί ("concerning") D^c G L P Ψ 0278 6 69 88 323 330 614 945 1175 1241 1243 1836 1874 2344 2464 *Maj* have ὑπέρ ("for the sake of"), which probably represents an effort at stylistic improve-ment in the coordination with the verb εὐχαριστῶ ("I give thanks"). The variant is not discussed by Cranfield, Zahn, Sanday and Headlam, or Wilckens. ℵ A B C D* K 33 81 104 424 1319 1505 1506 1573 1735 1739 1881 2495 *al* support the probably original inclusion of περί.

c   D* G Ψ 424 1319 1505 1506 1573 2495 *l* 249 *pc* have μοι ("for me") in place of the more solidly attested μου ("my") in ℵ A B C D^2 K L P 6 33 69 88 104 323 330 614 945 1175 1241 1243 1735 1739 1836 1874 1881 2344 2464, perhaps representing an effort at theological correction in avoiding the possessive in connection with God. Michel, 11, is the only commentator mentioning this variant, insisting it makes no substantive difference in meaning.

d   Though Nestle-Aland[26/27] does not mention it, referring only to Michelsen's conjecture ἐμέ ("me") in place of ὑμῖν ("you"), Cranfield, 1:81, discusses an unidentified variant of ἐν ὑμᾶς ("in relation to you") in place of the widely attested expression ἐν ὑμῖν ("among you"). This would produce the trans-lation, "that I be encouraged together with you." This conjecture is not discussed by any other commentator, but it seems redundant and also under-cuts Paul's careful diplomatic style.

Analysis

In Johannes Weiss's analysis, this pericope has little rhetorical color.[1] It is loosely organized in three sentences, the first of which contains a brief thanksgiving introduced by "first." Some commentators perceive a measure of rhetorical awkwardness in the lack of a "second,"[2] but this is a rather stereotypical Pauline epistolary feature that lifts up the main purpose of writing. In this instance the *causa* in 1:9-12 is firmly anchored within the thanksgiving. The subject of Paul's prayer concerning the Roman believers is that he be allowed by God to visit them, which is the fundamental cause for writing the letter. Wilhelm Wuellner's identification of the *causa* of Romans in these verses[3] is justified by the ancient rhetoricians' discussions of the function and placement of such an element in the exordium.[4] In this instance it is fused with the thanksgiving that continues through the end of v. 12. This section explains why Paul wants to visit Rome, thus justifying the letter as a whole.[5] Some analyses identify vv. 13-15 as also belonging to the thanksgiving,[6] but the disclosure formula in v. 13 and the content of these verses lead me to the identification of vv. 13-15 as a *narratio* that explains the background and rationale of Paul's forthcoming visit.

A closer analysis of the rhetoric of the pericope in vv. 8-12 reveals that the interplay between "me" and "you [pl.]" is carefully developed. Verse 8 has three sections with 11 beats apiece, the first ending with μου ("my")

---

1   Weiss, "Beiträge," 212.
2   Michel, 79.
3   Wuellner, "Paul's Rhetoric," 135.
4   See Lausberg, *Handbuch*, 152.
5   Reid, "Consideration," 187–89. Thorsteinsson, *Paul's Interlocutor*, 44–46, argues that 1:8 opens the body of the letter by presenting "the main purpose

of his writing," to preach the gospel "to gentiles in Rome" (p. 46).
6   Jervis, *Purpose*, 89–90; O'Brien, *Introductory Thanks-givings*, 201–2; Weima, "Epistolary Framework," 344–53; most commentators place 1:8-15 in a single pericope, e.g., Godet, 85–86; Sanday and Headlam, 18; Kühl, 21–22; Barrett, 23; Käsemann, 16–17;

and the second with ὑμῶν ("you [pl.]"). Each of the first two sections of v. 9 again contains μου and the third contains ὑμῶν. Verse 10 ends with πρὸς ὑμᾶς ("to you [pl.]"), and vv. 11-12a contain four additional references to "you [pl.]," and v. 12b concludes with "both yours and mine." With simple but effective rhetorical means, Paul establishes the relationship between himself and his audience within the framework of the inclusive gospel elaborated in the previous pericope.

Rhetorical Disposition

1:1-12	I. The *Exordium*
1:8-12	B. Thanksgiving and *causa* ("issue"): the announcement and rationale of Paul's forthcoming visit
1:8	1. The thanksgiving
1:8a	a. The expression of thanksgiving
	1) The introductory formula: "first, I give thanks"
	2) The deity to whom thanks are due: "my God"
	3) The agency of access to Deity: Christ
	4) The object of thanksgiving: "all of you"
1:8b	b. The reason for thanksgiving:
	1) The evangelical impact of Roman Christianity: "your faith is proclaimed"
	2) The ecumenical scope of the impact: "in the whole world"
1:9-12	2. The *causa* of the letter
1:9-10	a. The report of intercessory prayer to visit Rome
1:9a-b	1) The oath authenticating Paul's prayer
1:9a	a) The oath formula: "my witness is God"
1:9b	b) Paul's record of service to God
	(1) Service of spiritual devotion
	(2) Service in proclaiming "the gospel of his son"
1:9c-10	2) The content of Paul's intercessory prayer
1:9c	a) Paul's ceaseless intercession for Roman believers
1:10	b) Paul's petition to visit Rome
1:11-12	b. Paul's desire for a personal relationship with Roman believers
1:11	1) The consistency of Paul's personal wishes with his prayer to visit Rome
1:11a	a) The epistolary cliché: "I long to see you"
1:11b	b) The purpose of the visit: to strengthen the Roman believers by means of a "spiritual charisma"
1:1	2) The proviso of mutuality
1:12a	a) Strengthening defined as mutual encouragement
1:12b	b) The means of encouragement: faith
1:12c	c) The identification of whose faith is the source of encouragement: "both yours and mine"

Exegesis

■ **8** The opening words of the thanksgiving express the logical continuity with the foregoing greeting, with μέν used as a marker of continuation.[7] In order to emphasize the central importance of the thanksgiving that links Paul with the Romans, πρῶτον is used in the sense of "primarily," "in the first place," or "from the very outset."[8] Paul employs this idiom without the correlative δέ ("on the other hand") here as in 3:2 and 1 Cor 11:18, following the pattern of classical orators in giving emphasis to the main point of his discourse.[9] There is therefore no reason to believe that Paul "meant to make a further point in continuation, and then omitted to do so."[10] The audience of Romans would have perceived this idiom as lifting up the "main point" of Paul's letter, which correlates with Wuellner's identification of this pericope as the *causa* of Romans.[11]

The thanksgiving formula is a Pauline adaptation of forms that often appeared in the introductions of ancient letters.[12] For example, εὐχαριστῶ τῷ Σεράπιδι ("I give thanks to Sarapis") or εὐχαριστῶ τοῖς θεοῖς ("I give thanks to the gods") appear in letters of the first or second century C.E.[13] Paul Schubert showed that the

---

Kuss, 1:25; Ziesler, 55; Dunn, 1:26–27; Moo, 55–56; Schreiner, 47–48. Zeller, 39–41, appears close to my viewpoint, separating vv. 8-12 and 13-15.

7   BAGD (2000) 630.2; BDF §447.4.

8   BDF §447.4.

9   Demosthenes uses the idiom πρῶτον μέν some 225 times, usually without a following δέ ("but in the second place"), while Isocrates uses it 62 times and never follows it with a reference to a second topic.

10 Cranfield, 1:74; see also Weiss, 58; Meyer, 1:56–57; Morris, 55; and the rejection of this inference by Godet, 86, and Zahn, 55.

11 Wuellner, "Paul's Rhetoric," 135.

12 See Schubert, *Thanksgivings*, 31–33; Mullins, "Formulas," 380–83; O'Brien, *Introductory Thanksgivings*, 202–30; White, "Epistolary Formulas," 289–319; Schnider and Stenger, *Briefformular*, 45–49. Dunn, 1:27–28, and Byrne, 48, articulate the consensus that is attacked by Peter Arzt, "The 'Epistolary Introductory Thanksgiving' in the Papyri and in Paul," *NovT* 36 (1994) 26–46, and convincingly defended by Jeffrey T. Reed, "Are Paul's Thanksgivings Epistolary?" *JSNT* 61 (1996) 87–99.

13 Cited by Reed, "Are Paul's Thanksgivings Episto-

thanksgiving introduces "the main theme of the letter" and that the variations in form and complexity reflect "specific epistolary situations."[14] The expression εὐχαριστῶ τινί ("I give thanks to someone") also appears in inscriptions, as in one found in Ephesus during the imperial period that repeats the formula twice, followed by the names of the persons honoring the goddess: εὐχαριστῶ σοι, κυρία Ἄρτεμι ("I give thanks to you, Lady Artemis").[15] Paul employs the expression εὐχαριστῶ τῷ θεῷ in the opening thanksgivings of 1 Cor 1:4; 1 Thess 1:2; 2 Thess 1:3, while in Phil 1:3 and Phlm 4 the thanks is directed to "my God," just as here.

This is not an expression of the personal quality of his relationship[16] or of the "fervor of his devotion,"[17] but rather an indication of apostolic allegiance. Paul presents himself in this *exordium* as the ambassador of Christ, and the expression "my God" refers to the regent whom he serves. Far from claiming that God is Paul's possession, the "my" indicates the subordination of the servant to the master. The expression διὰ Ἰησοῦ Χριστοῦ ("through Jesus Christ") indicates that Christ is the "mediating causal agent of the thanksgiving,"[18] which again clarifies Paul's apostolic role as the "slave of Christ Jesus" (Rom 1:1).[19] More than in any other letter, the expression "through Jesus Christ/Christ Jesus" appears in Romans (1:8; 2:16; 5:21; 7:25; and in the interpolated doxology of 16:27) to convey the primacy of Christ's power as God's redemptive agent, of which Paul is the apostolic witness. The distinctive structure of "binitarian worship" in early Christianity,[20] in which prayers are offered to God "through Christ," is visible in this formulation. Both in writing this formula and at the moment of its being read to a Roman congregation, the prayer is being performed in a powerful manner, accompanied by Christ. Such prayers are, in effect, "performed utterances," in which the words dictated by Paul become an actual occasion of giving thanks in Rome.

The inclusive emphasis visible in Paul's formulation of the preceding seven verses is restated here as the subject for which he gives thanks: περὶ πάντων ὑμῶν ("concerning all of you"). He gives thanks for "all of God's beloved in Rome" (1:7), that is, all of the converts in Rome,[21] not just for those associated with the previous Pauline mission or for those inclined to accept his theological or cultural orientation.[22] In view of his previously adversarial relationship with believers advocating adherence to the Jewish law (see Galatians), this is a remarkable example of giving thanks for one's opponents. That the Romans' faith "is proclaimed" to others is an unusual formulation, because Paul ordinarily speaks of the gospel or Christ himself being proclaimed (1 Cor 9:14; 11:26; Phil 1:18). Very few pre-Christian occurrences of this present singular use of καταγγέλλεται ("it is proclaimed") are known; in one, Strabo reports that "Alexandrian rites are proclaimed and being consecrated there" (Ἀλεξάνδρεια καταγγέλλεται, συντελούμενος ἐνταῦθα), that is, at the sacred grove of the Chalcidians (Strabo *Geog.* 14.1.31). Paul's allusion to wide-ranging reports of the progress of the faith in Rome is similar to his report that the amazing growth of the Thessalonians' "faith" in the "word of God . . . has gone forth everywhere" (1 Thess 1:8). The word "faith" is used in these passages to refer not merely to theological doctrine[23] or the presence of believers in Rome,[24]

---

lary?" 92–93, from *SB* 6. Nr. 9017.23.2; *P.Mich.* 8. Nr. 465.13-14; 8. Nr. 473.29; 8. Nr. 476.25; *O.Amst.* 1. Nr. 29.5; *BGU* 14. Nr. 2418.9-10; *P.Lond.* 1. Nr. 42.11; additional examples are provided by MM 267.

14   Schubert, *Pauline Thanksgivings*, 180–81.

15   Cited by G. H. R. Horsley, "Giving Thanks to Artemis," *NDIEC* 4 (1987) 127–29, with discussions of other examples.

16   Schlier, 35; Morris, 56; O'Brien, *Introductory Thanksgivings*, 203.

17   Dunn, 1:28.

18   Meyer, 1:57; Hurtado, *Lord Jesus Christ*, 139, remains uncertain whether this formulation "alludes to actual prayer formulations . . . or merely

indicates the religious viewpoint that Christian prayer was always offered 'through' (as a result of) Jesus' redemptive work," but the latter seems most likely.

19   See particularly Jervis, *Purpose*, 107; Weima, "Epistolary Framework," 247; Schreiner, 49, stresses "apostolic authority."

20   See Hurtado, *Lord Jesus Christ*, 134–53.

21   See Eichholz, "Röm 1,8-15," 87–90.

22   See O'Brien, *Introductory Thanksgivings*, 206–7; Schreiner, 49.

23   O'Neill, 36; Morris, 56; Bruce, 75.

24   Schmidt, 24; Kuss, 1:16–17; Käsemann, 17; Cranfield, 1:75.

but to converts' participation in the charismatic process of proclamation, acceptance, transformation, and creation of new communities of faith.[25] The news about the creation of faith communities in Rome thus becomes an essential component of the triumph of the gospel ἐν ὅλῳ τῷ κόσμῳ ("through the whole world"). Although commentators often tone this down as mere hyperbole,[26] there are many examples of events in Rome being reported throughout the empire,[27] which in the Roman view comprised the entire world. That Jews and Christians had been banned from Rome by Claudius in 49 C.E., including many Christian leaders whom Paul mentions in Rom 16, renders it quite likely that the controversial success of the gospel there was widely known.[28] For Paul the apostle to the Gentiles, who aims to extend the reach of the gospel to Spain as the end of the known world, this formulation of the content of Paul's prayers with "mission terminology"[29] is integral to the letter and his forthcoming visit. The only other NT use of this expression "in the whole world" is in reference to the preaching of the gospel (Matt 26:13). When one takes the eschatological impetus of Paul's mission and the deep sense of interconnectedness of believers into account, it becomes clear that one should not reduce this formulation to the status of a mere *captatio benevolentiae*,[30] that is, flattery intended to gain favor with the audience.

■ **9** The truthfulness of Paul's claim to be bound in prayer to the Roman believers is confirmed by the highest possible authority: "God is my witness." As Hermann Strathmann observes, "Paul frequently calls upon God as a witness to processes and motives in his inner life" when "no other factual witnesses" are available.[31] In other letters Paul uses the same formulation of God as "my witness" (2 Cor 1:23; Phil 1:8; 1 Thess 2:5) to confirm that he is telling the truth (cf. 2 Cor 11:31; Gal 1:20). The background of this expression is judicial, with God playing the role of the supreme judge or king. Greek and Jewish writings provide examples of this locution, for example, Josephus *Bell.* 1.595, "Hear, O king, even with you is God my witness (ϑεὸς ὁ μάρτυς ἐμοί)."[32] While this asseveration of his truthfulness may counter a criticism that Paul had hitherto failed to honor Rome with a visit,[33] its primary function is to include Roman believers within the circle of his concern as the apostle to the Gentiles.[34] His oath conveys the point that this letter "is not a bolt from the blue but the expression of a long-standing sense of responsibility and desire to visit."[35] The God who witnesses to the truthfulness of Paul's concern is the one ᾧ λατρεύω ("whom I serve"). Since this verb is employed in the LXX predominantly in reference to cultic service,[36] it places Paul's missionary prayers within the context of "religious service" performed as "worship" of God.[37] This liturgical view of Paul's missionary activity recurs in 15:16, placing the entire project of the Spanish mission within the context of the worship that all believers owe to God.

25 See Rudolf Bultmann, "πιστεύω κτλ.," *TDNT* 6 (1968) 212: in such passages "πίστις is to be understood as acceptance of the Christian message"; O'Brien, *Introductory Thanksgivings,* 207; Dobbeler, *Glaube als Teilhabe,* 39; Kinneavy, *Greek Rhetorical Origins,* 106–41, deals with the persuasive element of "faith" but overlooks the communal dimension.

26 Meyer, 1:57; Godet, 86; Weiss, 59; Leenhardt, 49; Käsemann, 17; Cranfield, 1:75; Fitzmyer, 244; Moo, 57.

27 Haacker, 32, refers to events in Rome reported in "the whole world" as reported by Cicero *Mil.* 98; Seneca *Nat.* 6.25.3; Suetonius *Dom.* 16.

28 See Barrett, 24; Haacker, 32.

29 O'Brien, *Introductory Thanksgivings,* 209.

30 For example, see Käsemann, 17; Byrne, 49.

31 Hermann Strathmann, "μάρτυς κτλ.," *TDNT* 4 (1967) 491; see also O'Brien, *Introductory Thanksgivings,* 211.

32 See also 1 Sam 12:5-6; *T. Levi* 19.3; Philo *Ebr.* 139.2; *Plant.* 82 (§342); Polybius *Hist.* 11.6.4, as noted by Dunn, 1:28. For an assessment of the predominance of OT influence in this formula, see Stählin, "Beteuerungsformeln," 130–32.

33 See Barth et al., *Foi et salut,* 45–46; Meyer, 1:58; Haacker, 32; Moo, 58.

34 Wilckens, 1:78.

35 Byrne, 49.

36 Hermann Strathmann, "λατρεύω, λατρεία," *TDNT* 4 (1967) 59–61.

37 Ibid., 61; Corriveau, *Liturgy of Life,* 144–45; Kuss, 1:17; Cranfield, 1:76; O'Brien, *Introductory Thanksgivings,* 212.

Serving God "in my πνεῦμα in the gospel of his Son"[38] is one of the "most complex uses of πνεῦμα in the Pauline corpus," as Gordon Fee observes.[39] It is an unparalleled expression of Paul's self-identity, and in view of the connection with the verb "to serve" (λατρεύω), the parallel with Phil 3:3 strongly suggests that as one of the believers "who serve by the Spirit of God," Paul wishes to emphasize the source of his calling and effectiveness.[40] This metaphorical use of liturgical language such as "serve" is typical for Romans, and is echoed by 15:16 and 27.[41] In view of his premise that the "human spirit" is incapable of understanding God (1 Cor 2:11) and his insistence later in Rom 8:9 that those lacking the spirit of God do not belong to him, it is difficult to understand why he would wish to discredit his calling in 1:9. He makes plain in 8:26 that genuine prayer derives from God's Spirit, a premise developed in 1:8, where he describes his thanksgiving for the Roman believers "through Jesus Christ." An allusion to his "individual life-force and at the same time the place of his feelings,"[42] incapable of genuine prayer or service to the gospel, is precisely what he would not want to stress here. Instead, as part of laying out his credentials and clarifying the purpose of his letter, Paul emphasizes that his advocacy of the gospel derives from the apportioned Spirit, whereby God directly participates in his ministry.[43]

The gift of the Spirit places Paul in the structure of obedience to the gospel; although the Spirit is given to him in his conversion in such a manner that he can refer to it as "mine," he remains in dialogue with God's "witness" and he remains a servant to the Lord into whose service his conversion called him. The expression τῷ εὐαγγελίῳ τοῦ υἱοῦ αὐτοῦ ("gospel of his Son") appears here as a virtually verbal form, referring to the "preaching task that resulted in the founding of the church."[44] The peculiar kind of coparticipation in charismatic activity visible later in his letter emerges here, as the apportioned spirit within Paul serves God in apostolic service of the gospel.[45]

Paul's prayers for the Roman converts are described as ἀδιαλείπτως ("ceaselessly") being offered to God, an adverb that elsewhere in the NT is employed by Paul alone and exclusively for prayer (1 Thess 1:2; 2:13; 5:17). As Roland Gebauer observes, unceasing prayers of gratitude and intercession are the distinctive mark of Christian existence in Paul's view.[46] His charismatic view of the faith[47] is expressed by this reference to "prayer as a conscious, continuous state of mind."[48] To restrict the bearing of ἀδιαλείπτως to "prayer offered at frequent and regular intervals"[49] is an unwarranted restriction of Paul's mystical piety.[50] The expression μνείαν ποιεῖσθαι τινος ("to mention someone") occurs in early Christian literature only in the context of interces-

38   The argument in this section is adapted from Jewett, "Apportioned Spirit," 193–206.
39   Fee, *Empowering Presence*, 484–85.
40   See ibid., 485–86.
41   See Wick, *Gottesdienste*, 175–76.
42   Meier, *Mystik*, 252.
43   See Corriveau, *Liturgy of Life*, 147.
44   Georg Strecker, "εὐαγγέλιον," EDNT 2 (1991) 72; see also Wilckens, 1:78, who refers to other instances of "gospel" as a "verbum actionis" in Rom 1:1; 2 Cor 2:12; 8:18; 10:14; Phil 4:3; 1 Thess 3:2.
45   See Leenhardt, 43; O'Brien, *Introductory Thanksgivings*, 213; Jewett, "Apportioned Spirit," 194–95.
46   Gebauer, *Gebet*, 217–29.
47   See Heinrich Balz, "προσευχή κτλ.," EDNT 3 (1993) 168: "In Paul . . . [prayer is] the gift of the Spirit within believers to call on God steadfastly."
48   Earl J. Richard, *First and Second Thessalonians*, Sacra Pagina 11 (Collegeville, Minn.: Liturgical Press, 1995) 278. Following Harder, *Gebet*, 16, and Goltz, *Gebet*, 102–4, O'Brien, *Introductory Thanksgivings*,

21–22, believes that "ceaseless" is a Pauline "hyperbole" that refers to "his regular times of prayer."
49   O'Brien, *Introductory Thanksgivings*, 214, followed by Moo, 59, cites an example in MM 9, where ἀδιαλείπτως refers to coughing that was "intermittent but not continuous." Since this phenomenon derives from the link between coughing and breathing, a factor that does not influence prayer, O'Brien is making an unwarranted restriction of the semantic range of the adverb ἀδιαλείπτως. There are other examples of ἀδιαλείπτως in reference to activity that was indeed continuous, e.g., the uninterrupted services in the temple as described in *Ep. Arist.* 92 or "unceasingly making attacks on the walls" in Diodorus Siculus *Hist.* 5. See particularly Ceslas Spicq, "ἀδιαλείπτως," TLNT 1 (1994) 32–34, following Emile Delay, "ΑΔΙΑΛΕΙΠΤΟΣ," RThPh 47 (1950) 24–26, both of whom stress the "perpetual communion with God" implied by Paul's formulation.
50   See Schweitzer, *Mysticism;* Wikenhauser, *Pauline Mys-*

sory prayer.[51] "I make mention of you" (μνείαν ὑμῶν ποιοῦμαι) in ceaseless prayers means that Paul has long been connected with the Roman believers even though he has not seen their faces.[52] This expression occurs in the NT in other letter openings,[53] rehearsing the spiritual bond that links Paul with his congregations.[54] As Heinrich Balz observes, such "intercessory prayer is, after all, nothing other than a sharing of the struggle the apostle has to wage."[55] In keeping with the correspondence between the introduction and the conclusion in a well-designed letter or speech, Paul returns to this theme in 15:30-32, where he requests Roman intercession with regard to the dangers of his trip to Jerusalem.

■ **10** The punctuation of vv. 9-10 is a matter of debate, with some scholars preferring to link πάντοτε ἐπὶ τῶν προσευχῶν μου δεόμενος ("always pleading in my prayers") with the preceding verb ποιοῦμαι ("making") so as to avoid the unlikely inference that Paul's entire early ministry was preoccupied with the trip to Rome.[56] Since this renders "unceasingly" and "always" virtually tautologous and overlooks the distinction between intercession (v. 9c) and petition (v. 10), it is better to place a comma at the end of v. 9 to make clear that πάντοτε ἐπὶ τῶν προσευχῶν μου δεόμενος relates to the following petition.[57] Paul's habitual intercession for the Roman churches is conveyed by "always" (πάντοτε), as he goes

on to name the specific request that relates to the purpose of his letter. In the expression ἐπὶ τῶν προσευχῶν μου δεόμενος ("pleading in my prayers") the usual verb for a petition to God as found in the LXX and the NT (δέομαι) is employed with the meaning "to ask for something pleadingly."[58] The context "in my prayers" is sometimes taken to refer to the thrice-daily prayers of loyal Jews,[59] but it seems very unlikely in view of his admonition to "pray without ceasing" (1 Thess 5:17) that Paul felt himself restricted to the traditional rhythm. What Paul has regularly petitioned is that he be granted "good passage" to Rome, whereby the literal meaning of εὐοδόω, "be on a good path," seems more relevant than the metaphorical meaning, "have success."[60] This primary meaning is found in Tob 5:16, "prepare yourself for the journey and may you be granted a good journey (εὐοδωθείητε)."[61]

The uncertainties of travel and of God's inscrutable will are conveyed in the combined expression, εἴ πως ἤδη ποτέ ("if at long last") followed by ἐν τῷ θελήματι τοῦ θεοῦ ("in the will of God"). The first expression is an unprecedented combination of εἴ πως "(if perhaps/somehow"), as in Phil 3:11 and Acts 27:13, and ἤδη ποτέ ("now at last"), as in Phil 4:10.[62] The conditional expression εἴ πως conveys the uncertainty[63] that is appropriate to any petition offered to the sovereign

ticism; Luz, "Mystik"; Shantz, "Paul in Ecstasy," chap. 1.

51 See BAGD (2000) 654 and MM 414 for other examples such as *BGU* 2. Nr. 632.5, μνείαν σου ποιούμενος παρὰ τοῖς [ἐν]θάδε θεοῖς ἐκομισάμην [ἐ]ν ἐπι[σ]τόλιον . . . ("Making remembrance of you before the gods, I've gotten a single paltry letter . . ."); the expression is also found in Plato *Phaedr.* 254a6; *Prot.* 317e5, neither of which refers to prayer.

52 A parallel to this religious act in behalf of an addressee may be found in a papyrus of unknown provenance in which the writer makes "an act of worship for you (τὸ προσκύν[μ]ά σου ποιῶ) in the presence of the lords Dioskouri and in the presence of the lord Sarapis." See G. H. R. Horsley, "Deferential Greetings to a Patron," *NDIEC* 1 (1981) 56–57, citing Rea and Sijpesteijn, eds., *CPR* 5.2. Nr. 19.10-11.

53 Phil 1:3; 1 Thess 1:2; Phlm 4; cf. Eph 1:16; 2 Tim 1:3.

54 Gebauer, *Gebet*, 194–96, analyzes the "communicative function" of prayer that links Paul with the

recipients of his letters, providing a climate of mutual concern and trust.

55 Heinrich Balz, "προσευχή κτλ.," *EDNT* 2 (1993) 168.

56 For example, Lietzmann, 28; Schlier, 37; Cranfield, 1:77.

57 See Zahn, 58; Weiss, 61; Kühl, 24. Fitzmyer, 247, emphasizes this decision by starting a new sentence at the beginning of v. 10.

58 BAGD (2000) 218, referring to many NT examples.

59 See Dunn, 1:29, referring to Dan 6:11; Acts 3:1; 10:3.

60 Weiss, 61–62; Godet, 87; Dunn, 1:30, as opposed to Cranfield's unwarranted claim: "the thought of an actual journey is not present" (78).

61 See MM 263 for other examples of this "literal" reference to "a successful journey."

62 A TLG search yielded a single instance of εἴ πως ἤδη in Polybius *Hist.* 4.50.6, and several examples of πως ἤδη such as Xenophanes *Test.* 28, but the sequence of all four words, εἴ πως ἤδη ποτέ, occurs only in Rom 1:10.

63 Wilckens, 1:79.

God.[64] It is also well suited to a project that has long been delayed by adverse circumstances.[65] Many scholars have felt a note of frustration or impatience in the expression ἤδη ποτέ ("now at last"),[66] but these words simply compare "another time with the present," conveying "something long hoped for but delayed."[67] Paul's formulation has the epistolary function of indicating that at long last his plan to visit Rome may now be fulfilled; the unusual formulation honors Paul's audience by conveying his long-standing desire to see them, while at the same time forestalling potential criticism "for not coming sooner."[68] A similar prayer reflecting the uncertainties of travel is found in *Paralip. Jer.* 7.24: "My beloved son, don't slack off in your prayers (ἐν ταῖς προσευχαῖς), asking God in our behalf that he might grant our safe passage (ὅπως κατευοδόσῃ τὴν ὁδὸν) as far as we can leave this wicked king's jurisdiction."

That a successful passage to Rome would only be possible "by the will of God" is a theologically significant consideration that often recurs in Paul's letters (Rom 12:2; 15:32; 1 Cor 1:1; 2 Cor 1:1; 8:5; Gal 1:4; 1 Thess 4:3; 5:18; cf. Eph 1:1; 6:6; Col 1:1; 4:12). While "God willing" is a conventional motif throughout the ancient world,[69] Paul's frequent references make plain that he understands his apostolic calling and his subsequent activities as matters of obedience to God's will.[70] The rhetorical significance of this detail is that Paul presents himself as the servant of God whose "coming to you" will only be possible when and if God wills it, thus placing his relation to the Roman believers within the divine context with which they can easily identify, and thus sidestepping any differences of opinion that might divide the radical "apostle to the Gentiles" from various groups in Rome. That the infinitive expression, ἐλθεῖν πρὸς ὑμᾶς ("to come to you"), requires a metaphorical translation of the preceding verb εὐοδωθήσομαι as "I succeed" rather than "I am granted good passage"[71] undercuts the concrete reference to threatening travel conditions that only God can resolve.

■ **11** Paul's explanation of why he hopes to visit Rome is introduced by γάρ ("for")[72] and employs ἐπιποθεῖν ("to desire, long for"), which occurs frequently in various forms to express his "ardent desire"[73] to be in the presence of beloved members of his congregations.[74] While this terminology was sometimes employed in reference to familial feelings or personal friendship,[75] nowhere outside early Christianity does it appear in reference to bonds among group members. That such passionate bonding was expected of believers who were not personally acquainted is reflected in 2 Cor 9:14: the churches in Judea "long for you and pray for you, because of the surpassing grace of God in you." In connection with the infinitive ἰδεῖν ("to see") followed by the plural accusative ὑμᾶς ("you"), it is clear that this desire for sol-

64   Dunn, 1:29–30.
65   Weiss, 61.
66   Lietzmann, 28; Leenhardt, 43–44; Käsemann, 18; Schlier, 37; Wilckens, 1:79.
67   Meyer, 1:59; see also Weiss, 61; see also Deissmann, *Light*, 200. BAGD (2000) 434, refers to ἤδη ποτέ as a "marker of culmination."
68   Dunn, 1:29; du Toit, "Persuasion," 207.
69   See below on Rom 2:18 with regard to the Greek and Jewish formula, "if God wills," as discussed by Gottlob Schrenk, "θέλω κτλ.," *TDNT* 3 (1965) 45–47, and "will of God" in 53–54. It is likely that Paul's formulation is primarily shaped by the LXX, as in 1 Esdr 8:16; Sir 16:3; and in frequent references to "your will" when the antecedent is God. See also BAGD (2000) 447.
70   See particularly Sanday and Headlam, 2; Schlatter, 14; Michel, 82; O'Brien, *Introductory Thanksgivings*, 218–21; I. A. Allan, "The Will of God III: In Paul," *ExpT* 72 (1960–61) 142–45.
71   BAGD (2000) 410; Moo, 59.

72   See Kuss, 1:18; Murray, 21; Haacker, 23; the argument that γάρ in this context implies continuation or reiteration (Lietzmann, 28; Kühl, 24) remains unconvincing because "coming to you" at the end of v. 10 requires explanation in view of Paul's principle of missionizing only in areas where churches had not yet been established (Rom 15:10; 2 Cor 10:13-16).
73   Ceslas Spicq, "ἐπιποθέω," *TLNT* 2 (1994) 59.
74   The verb ἐπιποθέω is found in Phil 1:8; 2:26; 1 Thess 3:6; cf. 2 Tim 1:4. The nouns ἐπιπόθησις ("longing") and ἐπιποθία ("longing, desire") occur in 2 Cor 7:7, 11; Rom 15:23.
75   For example, Philo *Abr.* 195.3, with regard to parents doting on their late-born children, because "they have yearned (ἐπιποθοῦντος) for their births for a long period." See also Philo *Opif.* 10:4; Epictetus *Diss.* 3.24.8b. See Thraede, *Brieftopoi*, 50–52.

idarity in Christ includes not just the renewal of prior acquaintances[76] but all of the Roman believers who had been included in the formulation περὶ πάντων ὑμῶν ("for all of you") in 1:8. As Reid points out, this inclusive motif is a decisive clue about the motivation and purpose of Paul's letter, as stated in this exordium.[77] The importance of this personal bonding in Christ is confirmed by Paul's reiteration in 15:23, employing virtually the same language, "but having the desire to come to you for many years."

The extensive purpose clause introduced by ἵνα ("so that") is carefully formulated so as to avoid giving offense to Roman believers while at the same time conveying "the delicate matter of his real purpose in wanting to visit the Roman churches."[78] The effect of the rhetorically emphatic τι ("some, a kind of") prior to the expression μεταδῶ χάρισμα ὑμῖν πνευματικόν ("I might share some spiritual charisma with you") moderates Paul's reference to his charismatic contribution by not claiming too much.[79] The optative verb "may/might share"[80] is appropriately careful in conveying Paul's role in a collaborative, charismatic process in which the divine Spirit remains decisive.[81]

The unprecedented expression χάρισμα πνευματικόν sounds at first redundant, since early Christians considered the gifts of divine grace and individual grace-gifts to be spiritual.[82] Paul obviously felt the need to communicate as a charismatic with charismatics,[83] emphasizing the spiritual bond that linked all believers together with Christ who is "the Spirit" (2 Cor 3:17). It is therefore misleading to reduce χάρισμα πνευματικόν to the preaching of the gospel,[84] the gift of tongues or of prophecy,[85] the gift of the Spirit,[86] or to the gift of grace,[87] because the particle τι ("some, some kind of") leaves open the question of precisely what Paul seeks to contribute within the parameters of a charismatic gift. The hope that his spiritual charisma will serve "that you [pl.] may be strengthened" (εἰς τὸ στηριχθῆναι ὑμᾶς) is formulated in the passive voice, implying that divine action will be experienced.[88] This verb is used elsewhere in a metaphorical manner to describe Paul's work of "firmly establishing" and "making firm" the faith of his congregations in spite of afflictions and uncertainties (1 Thess 3:2, 13; 2 Thess 2:17; 3:5).[89] Close parallels to this usage are found in Qumran, where the equivalent term סמך refers to "strengthening" members with a

---

76 Fitzmyer, 248, following Rengstorf, "Christenheit," 453.

77 Reid, "Consideration," 189; that vv. 11-12 constitute a rhetorical *correctio*, as suggested by du Toit, "Persuasion," 207, overlooks the seamless rhetorical flow of this thanksgiving section that demonstrates Paul's relationship with the audience.

78 Weima, "Epistolary Framework," 349; while Weima believes Paul's purpose is simply "to preach the gospel to them," I maintain it is the larger task of the Spanish mission that surfaces in chap. 15.

79 Weiss, 62; Zahn, 60; Kühl, 24; BAGD (2000) 1008, where τίς/τι serves "to moderate an expression that is too definite."

80 The basic meaning of μεταδίδωμι is "give part of, give a share," according to LSJM 1111; see also BAGD (2000) 638. Michel, 82, refers to the collaborative nature of this communication, referring to the parallel in the use of μεταδίδωμι in 1 Thess 2:8. The translation "impart to you" (Sanday and Headlam, 19; Käsemann, 16; Murray, 18; Morris, 55; Weima, "Epistolary Framework," 350) implies a one-way form of authoritative communication that Paul avoids here.

81 Weiss, 62; Schmidt, 25.

82 See Wilckens, 1:79; Hans Conzelmann, "χαίρω

κτλ.," *TDNT* 9 (1974) 404; Klaus Berger, "χάρισμα," *EDNT* 3 (1993) 460–61; Michael N. Ebertz, "Charisma," *RGG*[4] 2.114; John Howard Schütz, "Charisma," *TRE* 7 (1981) 688–93.

83 Michel, 83; Wilckens, 1:79; Schütz, "Charisma," 689.

84 Käsemann, 19; Berger, "χάρισμα," 461; Weima, "Epistolary Framework," 350–51.

85 O'Brien, *Introductory Thanksgivings*, 221, cites J. K. Parratt, "Romans i.11 and Galatians iii.5—Pauline Evidence for the Laying on of Hands?" *ExpT* 79 (1967–68) 151–52, who concludes that the charismatic gifts Paul had in mind would have been conveyed by "the imposition of hands" in some kind of ordination process.

86 Schenk, *Segen*, 50.

87 Wetter, *Charis*, 168–69.

88 Meyer, 1:60: "wrought by means of the spirit"; Dunn, 1:31: "divine passive."

89 Günther Harder, "στηρίζω κτλ.," *TDNT* 7 (1971) 656; Gerhard Schneider, "στηρίζω," *EDNT* 3 (1993) 276.

"firm" and "established" mind.[90] As is appropriate in the introduction to a letter to congregations he has not founded, the shape of this strengthening is not specified until later, as in the conflicts between the "weak" and the "strong," that each "be fully convinced in his own mind" (Rom 14:5) while refraining from condemning others. What Paul wishes to convey in this opening section is that his spiritual charisma offers enrichment and consolidation for the faith of each congregation.[91]

Despite his reputation as a polemicist, Paul does not aim to take sides in Rome; his assurance is directed to "you all" ($\dot{\upsilon}\mu\hat{\alpha}\varsigma$), and as the following verse makes clear, he expects to gain as much from the Romans as they from him. In view of the complexity of the Spanish mission project, hope for decisive, charismatic, and logistical assistance is understandable. When the Roman letter is viewed as demonstrative discourse rather than as polemic against the viewpoints of others, the rest of the letter can be seen to conform to this cooperative rationale, and there is no need to conclude that the formulation of this pericope conveys Paul's "anxiety,"[92] "uncertainty,"[93] or "embarrassment."[94]

■ **12** The phrase $\tauο\hat{\upsilon}\tauο$ $\delta\acute{\epsilon}$ $\dot{\epsilon}\sigma\tau\iota\nu$ is often understood as merely introducing a qualifying repetition of the preceding verse, "that is to say."[95] This overlooks the antithetical $\delta\acute{\epsilon}$ ("but" or "however"), occurring in this expression for the only time in the NT,[96] which introduces the statement in v. 12 as "a certain modification and progress"[97] of the preceding explanation of Paul's purpose in visiting Rome. The verb $\sigma\upsilon\mu\pi\alpha\rho\alpha\kappa\lambda\eta\vartheta\hat{\eta}\nu\alpha\iota$ ("to be mutually encouraged, exhorted") in the aorist passive stands parallel to the aorist passive infinitive "to be strengthened" in the preceding verse,[98] which means that Paul wishes to qualify the process of apostolic strengthening. The verb "mutually encourage" occurs in classical texts[99] but is a hapax legomenon in the biblical tradition. Its probable meaning in this context is "encourage" rather than "exhort,"[100] and the element of mutuality conveyed by the prefix $\sigma\upsilon\mu$ ("with") is prominent throughout Romans.[101] Paul's goal of mutuality is reinforced by the wording of the rest of the verse. The phrase $\dot{\epsilon}\nu$ $\dot{\upsilon}\mu\hat{\iota}\nu$ that qualifies the passive verb "mutually encouraged" should be understood in a local sense, "among you,"[102] referring to the hope already expressed to "come to you" and "see you," during which time there would be an opportunity for Paul to receive as much encouragement as he provides. It comes $\delta\iota\grave{\alpha}$ $\tau\hat{\eta}\varsigma$ $\dot{\epsilon}\nu$ $\dot{\alpha}\lambda\lambda\acute{\eta}\lambda\upsilon\iota\varsigma$ $\pi\acute{\iota}\sigma\tau\epsilon\omega\varsigma$ $\dot{\upsilon}\mu\hat{\omega}\nu$ $\tau\epsilon$ $\kappa\alpha\grave{\iota}$ $\dot{\epsilon}\mu\upsilon\hat{\upsilon}$ ("by each other's faith, both yours and mine"). This reinforces the meaning Paul intended in employing the rare verb $\sigma\upsilon\mu\pi\alpha\rho\alpha\kappa\alpha\lambda\acute{\epsilon}\omega$, implying "a reciprocity by virtue of which his faith will act on theirs and theirs on his."[103] $\Pi\acute{\iota}\sigma\tau\iota\varsigma$ is used in this context not in the merely doctrinal sense of holding particular beliefs but rather to convey the full range of participation in the movement shaped by Christ.[104] This mutual enrichment through shared faith has theological, mystical, and communal connotations. Moores argues that $\sigma\upsilon\mu\pi\alpha\rho\alpha\kappa\lambda\eta\vartheta\hat{\eta}\nu\alpha\iota$ $\dot{\epsilon}\nu$ $\dot{\upsilon}\mu\hat{\iota}\nu$ should be interpreted as

90 Harder, "$\sigma\tau\eta\rho\acute{\iota}\zeta\omega$ $\kappa\tau\lambda$.," 655, refers to 1QS 4:5; 8:3; 1QH 1:35; 2:9; 7:6; 9:32.

91 See Kettunen, *Abfassungszweck*, 149.

92 Wilckens, 1:79.

93 Käsemann, 18.

94 Barrett, 25; O'Brien, *Introductory Thanksgivings*, 221.

95 Käsemann, 16; Murray, 22; Dunn, 1:31.

96 Cranfield, 1:80.

97 Godet, 88, suggesting the translation adopted above: "or to speak more properly"; see also Meyer, 1:61; Kühl, 25; Leenhardt, 44; Fitzmyer, 248: "or rather."

98 Kühl, 25; Schmidt, 25, as opposed to Zahn, 61, and Weiss, 63, who attach $\sigma\upsilon\mu\pi\alpha\rho\alpha\kappa\lambda\eta\vartheta\hat{\eta}\nu\alpha\iota$ to the verbal expression, "I long to see you" at the beginning of v. 11.

99 Cranfield, 1:81, observes that the classical meaning is usually "exhort together," or "invite at the same time." For example, Polybius *Hist.* 5.83.3 lists a

number of persons $\sigma\upsilon\mu\pi\alpha\rho\alpha\kappa\alpha\lambda\upsilon\acute{\upsilon}\nu\tau\omega\nu$ $\delta\iota\grave{\alpha}$ $\tau\grave{\upsilon}$ $\pi\alpha\rho^{`}\dot{\epsilon}\kappa\alpha\tau\acute{\epsilon}\rho\omega$ $\tauο\acute{\upsilon}\tauο\upsilon\varsigma$.

100 Meyer, 1:61; Godet, 88; Cranfield, 1:81; BAGD (2000) 958.

101 Dunn, 1:31, 313; Jewett, "Apportioned Spirit," 201, 204–5; see also Reid, "Consideration," 181, 189–90: "Paul's rhetoric of mutuality"; Ehrensperger, *Mutually Encouraged*, 177–79. In contrast, Kettunen, *Abfassungszweck*, 157, asserts that Paul expects to be encouraged not by the Romans' faith but only by God.

102 Cranfield, 1:81; BAGD (2000) 326–27, with the definition 1(d) "among."

103 Godet, 88.

104 See von Dobbeler, *Glaube als Teilhabe*, 315; a weakness in Kinneavy, *Greek Rhetorical Origins*, 101–50, is that he overlooks the participatory dimension of faith.

"encouragement arising from the way in which the semiotic dynamic of the Crucifixion . . . constrains such standard lexemes as 'law', 'righteousness' and 'death' to *express* the innovative *content* of the Pauline εὐαγγέλιον."[105] He goes on to show that Paul's mode of argument is "Recognition," based on the shared experience of faith, namely recognition "that the crucified Christ is risen and lives forever, with all that that entails."[106] It is this revolutionary starting point of a world-unifying mission that gives Paul's argument in the subsequent chapters its innovative, logical creativity.

---

105 Moores, *Wrestling*, 159; italics in original.

106 Ibid.

1

The Background of Paul's Missionary Project

13/ I do not wish[a] you to be ignorant, brothers, that many times I made plans to come to you, and have been hindered until now, in order that I might reap some fruit even among you just as also among the rest of the Gentiles. **14/** To both Greeks and barbarians, to both wise and foolish, I am under obligation; **15/** so the eagerness[b] on my part was also to preach the gospel to[c] you, the ones in Rome.[d]

a   The variant οὐκ οἴομαι ("I do not suppose") found in (D*,²) G b d g o Ambst Pcl is viewed by Metzger, *Textual Commentary*, 447, as a scribal modification limited to Western witnesses, while the variant οὐκ οἴσομαι ("I would not charge") is found only in D⁴ D^{abs1}. The change to οἴσομαι moves Paul's discourse toward good Attic style and possibly echoes Isocrates *Antid.* 19.4; 171.3; 299.1; *Arch.* 39.3; 103.3. An additional variant, οὐ θέλομεν ("we do not wish"), is weakly attested in 81 *l* 603. Metzger properly opts for the widely attested οὐ θέλω ("I do not want"), which is supported by ℵ A B C D^c K L P Ψ 6 69* 88 104 181 256 263 330 424 436 459 614 629 945 1175 1241 1243 1319 1506 1573 1735 1739 1836 1852 1874 1877 1881 1912 1962 2127 2200 2344 2464 2492 2495 *Maj Lect* ar mon vg sy^{(p),h} (sa) bo arm (eth) geo slav Or^{lat} Chr Theodore; Metzger

mentions the grounds of normal Pauline usage. I would add that the first two variants tone down any implication that the Roman congregation was ignorant, the avoidance of which might be the motivation for their creation.

b   The nominative ending πρόθυμος ("ready") as found in d vg^{mss} Or^{lat} Ambst produces a grammatical smoothing of the text by implying "[I am] ready." The more awkward, far more widely attested, and probably original πρόθυμον requires the expression κατ᾽ ἐμὲ πρόθυμον ("my readiness") to be held together as the subject of the sentence; see Cranfield, 1:85.

c   According to Cranfield, 1:86, the addition of ἐν ("among") by D* 440 b vg^{mss} may be an assimilation to the identical expression in 1:13. It is also potentially less offensive to Roman pride, implying that Paul would preach among them rather than to them. This variant, along with G's reading ἐπ᾽ ὑμῖν, is too weakly attested to be considered original.

d   The deletion of "those who are in Rome" by G g Orig^{lat 1/2} is consistent with these witnesses' deletion at v. 7; see the comment on v. 7. The inclusion of the phrase is strongly attested by P^{26vid} ℵ A B C D K L P Ψ 6 33 69 81 88 104 181 256 263 330 424 436 451 459 614 629 1175 1241 1319 1505 1506 1573 1735^c 1739 1836 1852 1877 1881 1912 1962 2127 2200 2464 2492 2495 *Maj Lect* ar b d mon o vg sy^{p,h, pal} sa bo arm (eth) geo slav Orig^{lat 1/2} Chr Ambr Pel Aug.

Analysis

This short pericope opens with the sense of starting "afresh"[1] with a typical, epistolary disclosure formula.[2] A straightforward rhetorical style marks the paragraph and a hint of the forthcoming eloquence in the letter is visible in the elegant repetition of τε καί ("and") linking the antithetical pairs in 1:14. While v. 13 seems almost "careless" in structure,[3] there is rhetorical balance between the second and third sentences (1:14-15).[4]

Taken as a whole, 1:13-15 constitutes a *narratio* section similar to the one Hans Dieter Betz identified in Paul's Letter to the Galatians.[5] Quintilian recommended that a *narratio* should convey "lucidity, brevity, and plausibility," and insisted that all other appeals including even the proof are dependent thereon.[6] This pericope provides the background for Paul's diplomatic visit to Rome, namely that he had repeatedly planned such a visit and had been hindered in carrying it out (1:13).[7] This verse reiterates the scope of Paul's mission,

---

1   Käsemann, 20.
2   See Mullins, "Disclosure," 44–50; Doty, *Letters*, 34–35.
3   Käsemann, 20.
4   Weiss, "Beiträge," 212, observes that vv. 14 and 15 each have the same number of syllables (22).
5   Betz, *Galatians*, 58–62; see also O'Banion, "Narra-

tion," 325–51. Less plausible is the suggestion by Weima, "Epistolary Framework," 346–53, that vv. 13-15 continue the thanksgiving from v. 8 and explain Paul's prayer report.
6   O'Banion, "Narration," 345.
7   See O'Banion, "Narration," 328: "*Narratio* was one's case proffered in the form of a story, a continuous

"among you as among the rest of the Gentiles," and the following verse elevates Paul's inclusive obligation "both to Greeks and to barbarians, both to wise and foolish." This inclusive reference picks up the theme of "obedience to the faith . . . among all the Gentiles" (1:5) and prepares the ground for the argument in the rest of Romans that the gospel is relevant for a pluralistic world.[8]

Rhetorical Disposition

1:13-15	II. The *Narratio* ("statement of facts")
1:13	A. The disclosure of the background of Paul's plan to visit Rome
1:13a	1. The disclosure formula
1:13b	2. Paul's past plans to visit Rome
1:13c	3. The previous hindrance of Roman travel plans
1:13d	4. The evangelical motivation for visiting Rome
	a. The hope to "reap some fruit" in Rome
	b. The comparison with fruit "among the rest of the nations"
1:14-15	B. The disclosure of Paul's missionary obligation
1:14	1. The scope of Paul's obligation
1:14a	a. To Greeks and barbarians
1:14b	b. To wise and foolish
1:15	2. The statement of eagerness to preach in Rome
1:15a	a. The formula of conditional readiness
1:15b	b. The aim in reaching Rome: "to preach the gospel"

Exegesis

■ **13** The pericope opens with a typical disclosure form, "I do not want you to be ignorant . . . ,"[9] that clarifies the background of Paul's forthcoming visit to Rome. We find similar forms in Rom 11:25; 1 Cor 10:1; 11:3; 12:1; 2 Cor 1:8; 1 Thess 4:13,[10] which employ the disclosure forms in standard letters. For example, a second-century B.C.E. letter from Egypt contains the disclosure, "I wish you therefore to know this ($\tau o\hat{v}\tau\acute{o}$ $\sigma\epsilon$ $\vartheta\acute{\epsilon}\lambda\omega$ $\gamma\epsilon\iota\nu\acute{\omega}\sigma\kappa\epsilon\iota\nu$) that I had given him orders to go to Takona."[11] The negative formulation employed by Paul of not wanting the congregation to be "ignorant, unaware" conveys information "of special importance"[12] that is essential to understanding Paul's embassy. As an outsider visiting Rome for the first time, Paul wishes to give the impression that there is nothing covert or underhanded about his project. He lays his cards on the table in addressing his audience as "brothers," the familial term for men and women[13] belonging to the Christian movement. While Jews typically referred to their compatriots as "brothers"[14] and members of Greco-Roman religious associations occasionally used comparable expressions,[15] the prior verses of Romans make clear that Paul is referring here to fellow believers in Christ.[16] As the succeeding argument of Romans explains, they constitute a

---

form that emphasized the sequence of events constituting the case." I therefore do not find plausible the suggestion by White, *Light*, 207, followed by Hester, "*Persona*," 93, that this disclosure formula constitutes the opening of the body of the letter.

8 The inclusive quality of this argument is particularly stressed by Wuellner, "Toposforschung," 476–79.

9 See Mullins, "Disclosure," 44–50.

10 See Meinrad Limbeck, "$\vartheta\acute{\epsilon}\lambda\omega$," *EDNT* 2 (1991) 138.

11 *P.Oxy.* 4. Nr. 743.27-29, cited by MM 286; see also *BGU* 1.276.5, $\gamma\iota\nu\acute{\omega}\sigma\kappa\epsilon\iota\nu$ $\sigma\epsilon$ $\vartheta\acute{\epsilon}\lambda\omega$ ("I want you to know").

12 Cranfield, 1:81; see also Walter Schmithals, "$\mathring{\alpha}\gamma\nu o\acute{\epsilon}\omega$ $\kappa\tau\lambda$.," *EDNT* 1 (1990) 21. In an epistolary context, Isocrates *Antipat.* 9 writes, "since I thought you were not unaware that . . . ($o\mathring{v}\kappa$ $\alpha\gamma\nu o\epsilon\hat{\iota}\nu$ $\mathring{o}\tau\iota$ . . .)."

13 See BAGD (2000) 18; Schäfer, *Bruderschaft*, 291.

14 For example, Moses is incensed when he sees an Egyptian is striking "a certain Hebrew of his brothers ($\tau\hat{\omega}\nu$ $\acute{\epsilon}\alpha\upsilon\tau o\hat{\upsilon}$ $\mathring{\alpha}\delta\epsilon\lambda\varphi\hat{\omega}\nu$) the children of Israel" (Exod 2:11); Jeremiah refers in 22:18 to the weeping

that would ordinarily attend the death of King Jehoiakim, $\mathring{\omega}$ $\mathring{\alpha}\delta\epsilon\lambda\varphi\acute{\epsilon}$ ("O, brother"). See Schelkle, "Bruder," 635, for additional references.

15 Schelkle, "Bruder," 631–32, shows that several references cited by earlier scholars in support of "brother" as a fellow member of a cult are actually to blood relatives. The term $\varphi\rho\acute{\alpha}\tau\rho\alpha$ ("brother") refers to cult members in a Syrian Baal cult and the initiates of the Mithras cult were called *fratres* (Latin for "brothers"), most with post-Christian evidence according to Schelkle, "Bruder," 634.

16 See Johannes Beutler, "$\mathring{\alpha}\delta\epsilon\lambda\varphi\acute{o}\varsigma$," *EDNT* 1 (1990) 30: the "prevailing sense" of "brother" in Paul's letters is "that of *fellow Christian*." Italics in original.

"spiritual brotherhood,"[17] the adopted children of the God revealed in Christ (Rom 8:15-23), bound to one another by love (12:9-10), joined by a common faith (chaps. 5–6, 14–15), and sharing their daily lives together in *koinonia* (12:13, 16; 15:26).[18] They are a fictive family whose membership includes Paul and whose loyalty since their conversion transcends blood lines and class distinctions.[19]

What Paul discloses is that πολλάκις ("many times, often, frequently")[20] he had made plans to visit Rome. His earnest desire to see them as expressed in the preceding pericope had issued in actual travel plans and scheduling decisions. His forthcoming embassy is therefore not a matter of recent whim but of long standing intent and planning. Paul employs the verb προ-τίθεσθαι ("to decide, make a decision")[21] rather than βούλεσθαι ("to want, be willing") or θέλειν ("to will")[22] to convey the seriousness of his endeavor. It seems possible that Paul had this visit in mind ever since the "second missionary journey," when he reached Troas, the transit point for the Egnatian Way that led to Rome.[23] Up to the time of writing Romans, ἄρχι τοῦ δεῦρο ("until the present"),[24] however, he explains that he had been "hindered."[25] This verb κωλύω is used elsewhere in the NT to refer to placing an obstacle in someone's way

or to resisting God's plans (e.g., 1 Thess 2:14-16).[26] The aorist passive ἐκωλύθην is employed here to indicate barriers imposed by outside forces and unfinished tasks that remain unspecified.[27] Paul makes no excuses for the delays but wishes only to convey by the aorist verb that the hindrances no longer prevail.[28] In cooperation with Phoebe, who brings the letter to the Roman house and tenement churches as the patron of the missionary project, his long-standing plans can now be put into effect.

After the parenthetical explanation of his delayed plans, Paul goes on to explain his purpose with wording that conveys little of the apologetic tone of v. 12. He boldly states his hope to "have some fruit" from Rome, an expression that came to be used for missionary resources in Phil 4:17, referring to the Macedonian gift that redounds to the benefit both of the givers and the recipients: "I seek the fruit (ἐπιζητῶ τὸν καρπὸν) that increases to your credit." Since "fruit" is also used in Phil 1:22 and Col 1:6 in the context of evangelistic success with Paul's referring to his apostolic vocation in agricultural terms (1 Cor 3:5-9; 9:7-12), Günter Klein is justified in referring to this term as "missionary language."[29] It seems less likely that Paul is thinking in terms of a Roman contribution to the Jerusalem offering, also described with the metaphor of "fruit" in

---

17 Hans Freiherr von Soden, "ἀδελφός κτλ.," *TDNT* 1 (1964) 145.

18 See Stöger, "Brüderliche Ordnung," 186–90.

19 See Atkins, *Egalitarian Community,* 171–90; Bartchy, "Siblings," 68–71.

20 BAGD 686. The adverb πολλάκις is often employed by orators in describing their relation to their audience, often referred to as "you" (ὑμᾶς) as here. Demosthenes uses this adverb 113 times and the fuller form ὅτι πολλάκις six times; Isocrates 32 times; Lysias 22 times. Examples are visible also in Aeschines *Tim.* 108.6; *Fals. leg.* 125.1; *Ctes.* 252; Andocides *Redit.* 23.1; Antiphon *In nov.* 3.4; *Caed. Her.* 46.2.

21 See, e.g., Isocrates *Nic.* 29.1, "Finally, then there are those matters concerning myself I decided (προεθέμην) to go over." Cf. Demosthenes *Cor.* 192.2.

22 See Cranfield, 1:82.

23 See Schlier, 39.

24 This is a term found in the Gospels (Matt 19:21; Mark 10:21; Luke 18:22), Acts 7:3, 34, and Rev 17:1; 21:9 but nowhere else in the Pauline corpus. While

ἄχρι τοῦ δεῦρο is a standard Greek expression (Josephus *Ant.* 10.265; Galen *Plac.* 6.5.8.1; 9.5.35.4; Aelius Aristides πρὸς Δημοσ. 24.18), the usual Pauline idiom is ἄχρι τοῦ νῦν ("until the present") in Rom 8:22; Phil 1:4.

25 Isocrates *Ep.* 6.1.1 similarly, in response to a request that he live abroad with friends, writes, "For many things hinder me, however, particularly my inability to travel."

26 See Simon Légasse, "κωλύω," *EDNT* 2 (1991) 332–33.

27 A similar passive sense of circumstantial hindrance is recorded in Dionysius Halicarnassus *Antiq. Rom.* 10.7.5.6: "intending to bring him to justice, I was prevented on account of the war (ἐκωλύθην διὰ τὴν πόλεμον)." See also Epictetus *Diss.* 4.1.89.

28 Fitzmyer, 249–50, refers to Schmithals, *Römerbrief,* for this inference, but I cannot locate the reference.

29 Klein, "Paul's Purpose," 38; see also Michel, 84; Zahn, 62; Hans-Theo Wrege, "καρπός," *EDNT* 2 (1991) 252. The expression is also used in nonreligious contexts, e.g., Cyrus's lament that people grow old before they "reap any fruits of their labor

15:28,[30] because the funds were already on their way by the time the Romans received this letter.

The most striking feature of Paul's formulation is the first person singular, "that *I* might reap some fruit." In contrast to the mutual benefit described in 1:12, here Paul implies that he seeks something from the Romans that is directly related to his own vocation as a harvesting apostle. The use of the indefinite pronoun τινα ("some, some kind of") signals that ordinary evangelistic fruit is not in view, that he does not intend to win converts in Rome as he had elsewhere, but that some other kind of fruit is in view.[31] As 15:24 and 28 go on to detail, Paul hopes to gain logistical and tactical support from Rome for his mission to Spain. The open-endedness of the indefinite pronoun is diplomatically appropriate, because Paul needs to clarify the theological foundations of his mission before suggesting the nature of the desired cooperation. A difference in the kind of fruit needed is also suggested by the following words, καὶ ἐν ὑμῖν ("and/on the one hand among you)," which cannot imply the conversion of Romans, because as Zahn points out the audience receiving this letter is already converted.[32] The καί . . . καθὼς καί construction employed here has the sense of "even . . . just as also,"[33] suggesting in a vague and somewhat crude[34] manner that the same kind of fruit is being sought in Rome as Paul seeks elsewhere, support for extending the gospel to the Gentiles, which Paul later explains involves a mission in Spain. With suitable diplomatic caution, Paul is laying the groundwork for chap. 15 that invites cooperation from the Roman house and tenement churches in organizing the Spanish mission, while making it clear from the outset that he does not intend to establish congregations of his own in Rome. His calling is to extend the gospel to the "rest[35] of the Gentiles,"[36] a stunningly sweeping scope whose rationale becomes clear when one realizes that Spain marked the end of the known world, the end of the "circle" (Rom 15:19) of the known world that ran from Jerusalem through Illyricum and Rome to the Pillars of Hercules. The expression "the rest of the Gentiles" refers to what remains of them rather than to "others" of them, thus implying a group that in Paul's view still remained to be evangelized.[37]

■ **14** Paul's calling as an apostle to the Gentiles is clarified in a remarkable formulation describing his "obligation" to the hostile poles of ethnicity, class, and education. Although its importance has rarely been recognized, this verse is in several respects the "key to Romans" and reveals the "situation of its composition."[38] Ἕλλησίν τε καὶ βαρβάροις is a stereotypical formula in which "Greeks" are typically mentioned first and "barbarians" second.[39] In the bilingual context of Rome, "Greek" means "Greco-Roman"[40] while "barbarian" refers to alien tribes who cannot speak Greek or Latin

(τινα καρπὸν . . . κομίσασθαι)" (Xenophon *Cyr.* 1.5.10; cf. 7.2.11). See also Demosthenes *Ora.* 50 61.4.

30 See M. A. Krüger, "*TINA KAPΠON*, 'Some Fruit' in Romans 1:13," *WTJ* 49 (1987) 167–73.

31 See BAGD 820 for τίνα as "serving to moderate or heighten," implying "some kind of" object. That Paul merely wished to "express a certain reserve and circumspection" (Cranfield, 1:82, based on Leenhardt, 45, does not convey the difference in kind that Paul's formulation implies).

32 Zahn, 63.

33 BDF §§444, 453.

34 Kühl, 26, and Schmidt, 26, refer to the formulation of καθὼς καί as "crude."

35 See BAGD (2000) 602; Anders Cavallin, "(τὸ) λοιπόν. Eine bedeutungsgeschichtliche Untersuchung," *Eran* 39 (1941) 121–44, argues against this translation but does not take account of the close parallels in *Jos. As.* 2.10; *Apoc. Mos.* 29; and Josephus *Ant.* 3.129. See also H. G. Meecham, "The

Meaning of (τὸ) λοιπόν in the New Testament," *ExpT* 48 (1936–37) 331–32, who does not deal with this passage but concentrates on the resumptive or inferential uses of λοιπόν in 1 Cor 7:29 and elsewhere.

36 In *Beurteilung*, 37, Dabelstein proposes the translation of ἔθνεσιν as "non-Jews," but the transforming power of the gospel to overcome ethnic distinctions is dulled when the abusive language is domesticated.

37 See Herodotus's reference in *Hist.* 8.73.5 to "the rest of the nations" (τὰ δὲ λοιπὰ ἔθνεα) that remain after an enumeration of tribes. Aristotle *Mir. ausc.* 841b 32 uses the same expression as Paul, "among those of the rest of the nations" (τῶν ἐν τοῖς λοιποῖς ἔθνεσι); see also Plutarch *Tim.* 26.2.

38 Pedersen, "Isagogik des Römerbriefes," 47.

39 See Isocrates *Callim.* 27.5; *Phil.* 121.3; *Hel.* 52.1; Demosthenes *4 Philip.* 69.40; Strabo *Geogr.* 1.4.9; Cicero *Flacc.* 24; etc.

40 Godet, 89, notes that Cicero in *Fin.* 2.15 joins

and are uncultured, wild, crude, fierce, and, in a basic sense, uncivilized.[41] Although there was a protest against this division of the human race by the geographer Eratosthenes (Strabo *Geogr.* 1.4.9), Joseph Vogt reports that the antithesis "Roman/barbarian" was so widely accepted that the Germans who established their kingdom within the empire referred to themselves as *barbari*.[42] The triumph of Rome over the barbarians was celebrated in public art and monuments, in victory parades, in the gladiatorial games, and on coins that reveal that this antithesis was basic to the imperial worldview. The comprehensive study of this phenomenon by Yves Albert Dauge shows that from the second century B.C.E. to the fifth century C.E., the Romans viewed barbarians as inherently "inhuman, ferocious, arrogant, weak, warlike, discordant . . . unstable, etc."[43] These character traits were seen as the polar opposites of Roman virtues.[44] For the safety of the world and of civilization itself, barbarians had to be subjugated by Rome, which received this appointed task from the gods. Particularly relevant to Paul's letter that prepared the way for a mission to Spain[45] is that the Spaniards were viewed as barbarians par excellence because so large a proportion continued to resist Roman rule, to rebel with frightening frequency, and to refuse to speak Latin or to use the Roman names for their cities, streams, or mountains.[46] Cicero, for example, classes the Spaniards along with the Africans and Gauls as one of the "uncivilized and barbarous nations (*immanibus ac barbaris nationibus*)"[47] In view of this profound cultural antipathy, it is amazing that Paul dared to link Greeks and barbarians with the connective $\tau\epsilon$ $\kappa\alpha\acute{\iota}$, used previously in 1:12 to imply an inclusion of opposites in the sense of "both and,"[48] and to use exactly the same connective with the next pair of opposites. He thereby conveys the sweeping inclusivity of the gospel of Christ crucified for all.[49]

The word $\sigma o\varphi o\acute{\iota}$ can be used to describe a wise, competent person or a philosopher,[50] but in this antithesis to $\dot{\alpha}\nu\acute{o}\eta\tau o\iota$ ("foolish, dull-witted")[51] rather than $\ddot{\alpha}\varphi\rho\omega\nu$ ("fool"), it has the connotation of the innately superior person shaped by Greco-Roman culture. It would be tempting to translate this antithesis as "both to philosophers and fools," but many wise people were not philosophers, and many uncultured people were not fools. The antithesis is closer to "sophisticates and rustics," and since the Greco-Roman educational system concentrated on linguistic and rhetorical competence in Greek and Latin, this antithesis roughly corresponds to "Greeks and barbarians."[52] There is no doubt that the negative pole, "foolish, dull-witted," carried an even heavier burden of opprobrium than it would today, because the Greeks had developed the idea that education created what Werner Jaeger described as

. . . a higher type of man. They believed that education embodied the purpose of all human effort. It was, they held, the ultimate justification for the existence of both the individual and the community. . . . And it was ultimately in the form of paideia, "culture," that the Greeks bequeathed the whole achievement of the Hellenic mind to the other nations of

---

Greece and Rome in antithesis to the *barbaria*; Hengel, *Juden, Griechen und Barbaren*, 90–93; Dierk Starnitzke, "'Griechen und Barbaren . . . bin ich verpflichtet' (Röm 1,14). Die Selbstdefnition der Gesellschaft und die Individualität und Universalität der paulinischen Botschaft," *WuD* 24 (1997) 188; on 192–93 Starnitzke places the term "Greek" in the context of Nero's effort to hellenize Roman culture.

41 Hans Windisch, "βάρβαρος," *TDNT* 1 (1964) 547–48; Vogt, *Kulturwelt und Barbaren*, 12; "in east and in west the view prevailed that the barbarians were excluded and that the civilized people of the *orbis Romanus* simply represented *genus humanum*. . . . All who lived outside of the border fortifications were called barbarians . . . they were to be opposed with every available means as enemies of

culture." See also Hengel, *Juden, Griechen und Barbaren*, 78–93.

42 Vogt, *Kulturwelt und Barbaren*, 8–9.

43 Dauge, *Barbare*, 472–73.

44 Ibid., 534–44.

45 See Pedersen, "Isagogik des Römerbriefes," 66.

46 See Dauge, *Barbare*, 175, 479, 489, 661, 733.

47 Cicero *Quint. fratr.* 1.1.27; see also Livy *Hist.* 25.33.2; 27.17.10; 28.33.2ff.; Florus 1.33-34; Caesar *civ.* 1.38.3; 1.44.2; Pliny *Ep.* 8.24.4.

48 See Fitzmyer, 250; Dunn, 1:32.

49 Starnitzke, "Griechen und Barbaren," 196–202.

50 Ulrich Wilckens, "σοφία, σοφός, σοφίζω," *TDNT* 7 (1971) 468–74; BAGD 760.

51 BAGD (2000) 64.

52 Kuss, 1:19; Kühl, 28–29.

antiquity. Augustus envisaged the task of the Roman empire in terms of Greek culture.[53]

The educational system developed by the Greek sophists and carried forward in Roman times for the Greco-Roman elite aimed at developing virtue and excellence needed for public service[54] with the corollary that the uncultured person was perceived to lack the capacity for either. A person called ἀνόητος was therefore not just unwise, irrational, and foolish,[55] but in the final analysis not fully human. To be classified as foolish in this social context is neither a deficit that can be overcome with more education nor a matter of what we would today refer to as "intelligence," because it pertains to the shameful being of outsiders. Barbarians are viewed as innately idiots, while Greeks are innately wise. Ἀνόητος shares with "barbarian" the contempt thought to be warranted for persons and groups capable of great mischief but inherently incapable of constructive contributions to the human enterprise. Moreover, since the relationship with the Divine was thought to be centered in knowledge, the "foolish" were viewed as profoundly impaired in religious capacity. For example, Philo can query those whose behavior blinds them to God, "Why is this evil plight, thou foolish one (ὦ ἀνόητε)" (Somm. 2.181). Titus 3:3 echoes this cultural commonplace when it describes the condition of humans prior to conversion as "foolish (ἀνόητοι), disobedient, led astray, slaves to various passions and pleasures."

As if the grouping of these two pairs of moral, ethic, and cultural opposites in a "both/and" syntax were not shameful enough, Paul employs the expression that he is "obligated" to all of the above. This term reflects an ethical system more prevalent in the Greco-Roman world than in the OT, where it is restricted to material indebtedness.[56] In his Leg. 417B Plato explains that piety requires gratitude to parents and the gods "to whom it is mete for the debter to pay back the first and greatest of debts (οἷς θέμις ὀφείλοντα ἀποτίνειν τὰ πρῶτά τε

καὶ μέγιστα ὀφειλήματα), the most primary of all dues, and that he should acknowledge that all that he owns and has belongs to those who begot and reared him." A first-century papyrus urges, "therefore we all are obligated (ὀφείλομεν) to give thanks to all the gods" (P.Oxy. 7. Nr. 102.14). This sense of ethical obligation was particularly prevalent in Rome, where officium ("obligation, duty") was required out of gratitude for gifts received from the gods, one's family, the state, or patrons.[57] Officials were bound to perform the duties of their officium, the technical term for a governmental post.[58] Cicero formulated the premise of this system in his essay De officiis ("The Duties, Obligations") 1.47: "For no obligation (officium) is more imperative than of proving one's gratitude."

The prominence of these ideas in Rome[59] and particularly their embodiment in two of the Christian cells situated within the bureaucracy (Rom 16:10-11) may explain why Paul uses "obligation" in Romans more than in any other letter. In this context it has a socially revolutionary implication, as Paul Minear explains:

Obligation to him who died [i.e., Christ] produces obligation to those for whom he died. This very "law" applies with special force to the particularity of Paul's call as an apostle. God's intention in bringing Paul to faith in Christ had been to send him as a "minister of Christ Jesus to the Gentiles" (15.16). To the extent that Paul was indebted to God for this call, to that very extent he was indebted to those Gentiles for whose sake God had called him.[60]

Thus, while the Greco-Roman ethic of reciprocity would require obligations to the Greeks and the educated who were perceived to have provided benefits for others, it was a complete reversal of the system of honor and shame to feel indebtedness to barbarians and the uneducated. As Lendon explains:

53   Jaeger, *Paideia*, 1:xvii; see also Ferrero, *Republic of Augustus*, 82, 93–94.
54   Jaeger, *Paideia*, 1:288–93.
55   Johannes Behm, "νοέω . . . ἀνόητος κτλ.," *TDNT* 4 (1967) 961.
56   See Friedrich Hauck, "ὀφείλω κτλ.," *TDNT* 5 (1967) 560–61.
57   See Reasoner, *The Strong*, 176–86.
58   Ibid., 181, cites A. E. R. Boak, "Officium," *PW* 34.2045–56, for this technical usage that provides the linguistic background for the modern concept of "official, office," etc.
59   See Lendon, *Empire of Honour*, 63–69, 154–60.
60   Minear, *Obedience*, 104.

When a great aristocrat peered down into society beneath him, there was a threshold beneath which, to his mind, honour did not exist; there were people, a great many people, without honour, and best kept that way. . . . This category of persons without honour in aristocratic eyes included those defined in the law . . . as "infamous"—brothel-keepers, actors, gladiators, convicted felons—persons whose conduct revealed that they had no sense of shame, and thus could have no honor. The slave is the archetype of the man without honor.[61]

That the barbarians and the uneducated resided underneath this threshold of honor is indisputable. Paul's formulation of indebtedness with the expression ὀφειλέτης εἰμί, which occurs in Romans and Galatians with the verb "to be" followed by the predicate nominative,[62] is found elsewhere in Sophocles *Ajax* 589–90, "Am I now brought low by the gods, as though it were not sufficient that I am still obligated (εἰμ᾽ ὀφειλέτης) to them?" The tone of regret and hostility against the unjust gods expressed by Sophocles, however, is absent from Paul, whose entire life appears to have been a joyful expression of an immeasurable obligation that now leads him to reverse the profoundest stereotypes of the ancient world in setting forth his "missionary motivation."[63]

■ **15** The result of Paul's global indebtedness is introduced by οὕτως ("so, in this manner")[64] followed by τὸ κατ᾽ ἐμὲ πρόθυμον, which has been translated in three different ways. The most plausible option is to take the words κατ᾽ ἐμέ ("on my part") as a restrictive qualification of the neuter term τὸ πρόθυμον ("the eagerness, readiness"), signifying that "as far as external circumstances" permit, his eagerness is to preach in Rome.[65] A second option is that the words τὸ κατ᾽ ἐμέ could be understood as the "subject of which πρόθυμον is the predicate," but this seems strained grammatically by leaving no subject for the predicate nominative "to preach."[66] A third option is to take πρόθυμον as the subject and τὸ κατ᾽ ἐμέ as a paraphrase for "I," resulting in a translation like "my readiness is to preach,"[67] but this erodes the element of "dependence on a higher Will"[68] that seems implicit in the formulation. Paul is willing and ready, but other circumstances, including the response of the Roman believers, may impinge on his missionary plans just as they have in the past.

Paul's reference to being πρόθυμον ("eager, ready"), appearing here in the neuter form indicating a concrete instance of the abstract noun προθυμία ("eagerness, readiness")[69] that he uses in 2 Cor 8:11, 12, 19, and 9:2 resonates with a wide range of Greco-Roman and Jewish references to willing and enthusiastic participation in a project. Passionate ardor in combat is extolled by Greek as well as Hellenistic Jewish writers.[70] In Spicq's words, the nuance of this term "ranges from simple goodwill to cordiality to devotion to zeal; but almost always there is an element of fervor, even enthusiasm."[71] The supreme

---

61   Lendon, *Empire of Honour*, 96.

62   See Michael Wolter, "ὀφειλέτης κτλ.," *EDNT* 2 (1991) 550, referring to Rom 8:12; 15:27; and Gal 5:3.

63   Minear, *Obedience*, 109.

64   BAGD 597; Lietzmann, 29, "dementsprechend" (i.e., "correspondingly"); Zahn's proposal (67) that οὕτως comprises the predicate is incomprehensible to me.

65   Godet, 89, following Fritzsche, Reiche, and Philippi, and although Godet understands him differently, also Meyer, 1:65. This is advocated by Kühl, 30, who understands κατ᾽ ἐμέ as an adverbial modifier placed between the article τό and the adjective πρόθυμον, resulting in a translation "the eagerness on my part." See the parallel expression in Demosthenes *Orat.* 8.25; 12.9.3; 13.1.7; 19.214.10; 19.268.4; 19.336.6; LCL 155, translated by C. A. Vince and J. H. Vince, as "on my part" in Demosthenes *Orat.* 12.180.

66   Cranfield, 1:85, describing an alternative he finds unlikely as proposed by Sanday and Headlam, 21; Lietzmann, 29; and others.

67   Cranfield prefers this option (85); it is more clearly explained by Godet, 90. See the critique of this option in Zahn, 67.

68   Meyer, 1:65.

69   See Karl Heinrich Rengstorf, "πρόθυμος, προθυμία," *TDNT* 6 (1968) 694, 697.

70   Ceslas Spicq, "προθυμία κτλ.," *TLNT* 3 (1994) 180–81. Judas Maccabeus encouraged his troops to be "even more eager" (προθυμοτέρους, 2 Macc 15:9).

71   Spicq, "προθυμία κτλ.," 181, citing Diodorus Siculus's description in *Hist.* 19.91.5 of Seleucus's ability to keep "his fellow adventurers ready and eager (εἶχε καὶ προθύμους) under every condition."

value of martial eagerness may be seen in Polemo's description of the martyred warrior Cynegirus, who was motivated by "independent valor and pure eagerness (καθαρᾷ προθυμίᾳ)" when he held the prow of a Persian ship, preventing its departure until both of his limbs were severed.[72] In contrast, Callimarchus, who remained upright after being pierced with many arrows, did not act "out of eagerness (ἐκ προθυμίας)," since the arrows held his body involuntarily upright after death. He thus receives less honor.[73] A new system of honor, however, surfaces in Paul's expression, in that "this eagerness to preach at Rome no less than elsewhere is the *consequence* of that debt to *all* which he feels lying upon him."[74]

Although many commentators see a contradiction between Paul's announcement of his readiness to preach in Rome and his principle stated in 15:20 never to build on someone else's foundation, the contradiction disappears entirely when the wording of v. 15 is read in the light of a precise interpretation of v. 13. The verbal form to be supplied in v. 15 must conform to the aorist tense of the verb προεθέμην ("I made plans") in v. 13.[75] Paul's earlier readiness with regard to Rome had not been to preach to the unconverted but to "you" believers who are in Rome, whether Jewish or Gentile in background. Paul had not intended to preach to the unconverted[76] in Rome, but now in this short visit he wishes to serve as the itinerant preacher in congregations already established by others.[77] While such preaching will be an expression of his obligation to treat the Greeks and barbarians, the wise and foolish alike, it will restrict itself to the diversity already contained in the house and tenement churches of Rome. Paul's hope is to gain a certain kind of evangelistic "fruit" in Rome, namely, the support of a daunting mission project to the distant barbarians in Spain, to persons beyond the range of Greco-Roman culture, thus transcending the boundaries of honor and shame.

---

72 Polemo *Decl.* A18.
73 Ibid. A24.
74 Godet, 90.
75 See Käsemann, 14; Zeller, 39; Kettunen, *Abfassungszweck,* 119–21; Stuhlmacher, "Purpose," 237.
76 See Schlier, 40, for the opposite view of this detail.
77 See Fitzmyer, 251; Moo, 63; Weima, "Epistolary Framework," 352, citing Munck, *Paul,* 298.

The Thesis about the Gospel as the Powerful Embodiment of the Righteousness of God

16/ **For I am not ashamed of the gospel,[a] for it is God's power for salvation[b] to all who have faith, both to the Jew first[c] and then to the Greek, 17/ for in it the righteousness of God is being revealed from faith to faith, as it has been written, "The one[d] who is put right [with God] shall live by faith."**

a   The addition of τοῦ Χριστοῦ by D^c K L P Ψ 69 88 104 323 330 424* 614 945 1175 1241 1243 1735 1836 1874 2464 *Maj* is clearly secondary and appears to have a "clarifying function, according to Cranfield, 1:87. The support for the text without this addition is overwhelming in P^26 ℵ A B C D* G (6) 33 81 424^c 1319 1505 1506 1573 1739 1881 2344 2495 *pc* lat sy cop.

b   The omission of εἰς σωτηρίαν ("for salvation") by G may be the result of a scribal omission.

c   The absence of πρῶτον in B G g sa Mcion^acc. to Tertul-^lian Ephraem may be due to the influence of Marcion.

d   The addition of μου ("my") by C* appears to be an assimilation to the LXX version of this quotation.

Analysis

That this passage contains the theme or thesis of Romans is almost universally accepted among commentators.[1] Several commentators identify vv. 16b-17 as the thesis,[2] but this artificially divides an integral syntactical unit in v. 16 and severs the issue of Paul's lack of shame in v. 16a from its natural antithesis in the power of God to create righteousness. A major issue among those who view the entirety of vv. 16-17 as the thesis or theme is how much of the subsequent argument of Romans is dominated thereby, that is, whether it involves the first five,[3] eight,[4] or eleven chapters.[5] On rhetorical as well as thematic grounds, I contend that all of the material through 15:13 carries out this proposition,[6] and that the subsequent *peroratio* in 15:14—16:24 takes up its practical enactment.[7] By identifying 1:16-17 as a *propositio*,[8] located in the rhetorically proper spot between the *narratio* and the *probatio*,[9] it is accorded its proper weight as the argumentative burden of the entire letter. It takes up the issue of Paul's intended missionary enterprise mentioned in 1:13-15 and sets forth a thesis that is confirmed in 1:18—4:25 and amplified in the subsequent three major argumentative sections of the letter. In view of the manner in which the theme in these two verses is elaborated and amplified in the argument of Romans, I prefer the term *propositio*, drawn from Quintilian,[10] to the term *partitio*, used by Cicero to describe a multifaceted thesis statement that divides up the subsequent argument.[11] Despite the complexity of the argument, there is a single theme in Romans: the gospel.

---

1   For example, Käsemann, 21–22; Cranfield, 1:87; Stuhlmacher, 29; Byrne, 51. Achtemeier, 35–36, argues that the grammatical subordination of v. 16 to v. 15, and the subsequent dependence of v. 17 on v. 16, and v. 18 on v. 17 as shown by the repetition of γάρ ("for") precludes the possibility that vv. 16-17 function as the theme of the letter. However, as Harrisville, 24, and Dunn, 1:38, point out, Paul uses γάρ throughout the letter to connect one section with another. See also Schlier, 42.

2   Cranfield, 1:87; Zeller, 42.

3   Godet, 98; Noack, "Current," 164; see Moo, 22–23, for a description of this concentration on the first five chapters.

4   See Luz, "Aufbau," 166; Kuss, 1:27; Cranfield, 1:102.

5   Meyer, 1:34; Zahn, 71; Fitzmyer, 253; Wilckens, 1:21; Haacker, 36; Grayston, 4–5; Byrne, 54; Theobald, 24–25.

6   Dunn, 1:37, argues that the thesis covers the first fifteen chapters; see also Best, 18; Edwards, 43–44.

7   Weiss, 69, 75: vv. 16-17 "express the fundamental thought of the entire letter." See Schlatter, 26–27; Michel, 92; Moo, 24, 65; Johnson, 24; Schreiner, 59.

8   See Theobald, *Studien*, 278–95.

9   See Lausberg, *Handbuch*, §346.

10   Quintilian *Inst.* 4.4.1–4.5.28; Haacker, 36, identifies Bengel as having used the term *propositio* for 1:16-17.

11   Cicero *Inv.* 1.22.31–1.23.33.

The rhetorical form of 1:16-17 sustains its identification as the *propositio* of the entire subsequent discourse. As Weiss pointed out,[12] there is a *parallelismus membrorum* in v. 16b-c and v. 17a-b, with two symmetrical statements about the "power of God" and the "righteousness of God," respectively, each providing a definition of the preceding contention about Paul not being ashamed of "the gospel." In this sense the subject of Romans is clearly Paul's gospel concerning the righteousness of God revealed in the Christ event and conveyed by the early Christian mission.[13] The reference to "all who have faith" in the first member is balanced by the reference "from faith to faith" in the second member,[14] thus relating the thesis to the establishment of faith communities. The entire statement is then sustained by the scriptural citation from Hab 2:4.

Rhetorical Disposition

1:16-17	III.	The *Propositio*: the thesis about the gospel as the powerful embodiment of the righteousness of God
1:16a		A. The contention about the gospel
		1. The actor in relation to the gospel: "I," Paul
		2. The attitude toward the gospel: "not ashamed"
1:16b-c		B. The gospel as a means of salvation
1:16b		1. The gospel as the "power of God"
		2. The purpose of the gospel: "for salvation"
		a. Access to salvation for "all who have faith"
1:16c		b. Access to salvation for Jews and Greeks
1:17a		C. The gospel in relation of righteousness
		1. The gospel as the revelation of the "righteousness of God"
		2. The vehicle of response to the gospel
		a. "From faith"
		b. "To faith"
1:17b-c		D. The scriptural proof
1:17b		1. The citation formula
1:17c		2. The citation from Hab 2:4
		a. The one set right shall live
		b. The means of gaining righteousness: "through faith"

Exegesis

■ **16** The reference to not being "ashamed of the gospel" (1:16) sets the tone for the entire letter. Michel, Barrett, Käsemann, and others understand Paul's formula in confessional terms along the lines of Mark 8:38 and parallels, as a negative formulation of "I confess."[15] Käsemann refers to a hypothetical "eschatological lawsuit" in which Paul hopes to prevail.[16] Weizsäcker and Lütgert perceive an apology for Paul's not having visited Rome earlier.[17] These interpretations correlate with the traditional misunderstanding of Romans as a defense of true doctrine, and it fails to explain why Paul chose not to employ ὁμολογέω ("I confess") in this verse as he does in 10:9-10. That shame in this context relates to Paul's perception that the Roman addressees belonged in the category of the "educated" (1:14) who might take offense at the gospel[18] overlooks the fact that this letter is addressed to believers who for the most part belonged to the social class of "uneducated" and "barbarian."[19] That the claim not to be ashamed was merely a "standard rhetorical device" that implies the forceful opposite that "I am mighty proud of the gospel"[20] sidesteps the precise social issues of shame or honor that orators sought to address in employing the "I am ashamed/not ashamed" formula. For example, when

12 Weiss, "Beiträge," 212–13.
13 See Dunn, 1:36: "the principal emphasis is actually on the saving power of the gospel."
14 Weiss, "Beiträge," 213, observes: "Only through taking account of the symmetrical rhythm can the quite remarkable, hardly explainable, in fact impossible ἐκ πίστεως εἰς πίστιν ('from faith to faith') be justified."
15 Michel, 86; Leenhardt, 46; Charles Kingsley Barrett, "I am Not Ashamed of the Gospel," in Barth et al., *Foi et salut*, 19–41; Käsemann, 22; Axel Horstmann, "αἰσχύνομαι," *EDNT* 1 (1990) 42; Wilckens, 1:82; Stuhlmacher, 28; Zeller, 42.
16 Käsemann, 22.
17 Weiszäcker, "Römische Christengemeinde," 280–92; Lütgert, *Römerbrief*, 36–38.
18 Weiss, 69; Meyer, 1:66; Sanday and Headlam, 23; Kühl, 35; Haacker, 37.
19 In "Von der Scham des Gläubigen. Erwägungen zu Röm i,14-17," *NovT* 4 (1960) 74–77, Otto Glombitza links the motif of shame in 1:16 with the reference to Greeks and barbarians in 1:14, but without developing the issue of social status.
20 Byrne, 51.

Isocrates states "concerning the choregoi, gymnasiarchs, and triararchs here, I am not ashamed to speak (οὐκ αἰσχύνομαι λέγειν),"[21] he is addressing a sensitive matter that touches the interests of these officeholders. When Aeschines defends his views in the debate over Philip of Macedon's encroachment in Greece, he states, "I am not ashamed of my words, but rather feel proud of them (οὐτ᾽ αἰσχύνομαι ἐπ᾽ αὐτοῖς, ἀλλὰ καὶ φιλοτιμοῦμαι)."[22] For Paul, the shameful issue of the letter is the gospel itself, which proclaimed Christ crucified and resurrected. Although the word "cross" is absent from Romans and the verb "crucified" appears only once (Rom 6:6), it is clear from 1 Cor 2:2 that Paul assumed the gospel was the message about "Jesus Christ and him crucified." Commentators frequently observe that when Paul employs τὸ εὐαγγέλιον ("the gospel") in the absolute, it is a nomen axionis that refers to "the act of proclamation."[23] What is not frequently grasped, however, is that "the words 'gospel' and 'apostle' are correlates, and that both are missionary terms."[24] As in the rest of this exordium, Paul announces himself as "the herald of the gospel, Christ's ambassador to the Gentiles . . . and all of this is part of his eschatological mission."[25] As the object of the verb αἰσχύνομαι ("ashamed"), it is very likely that the content of this missionary proclamation involves "the word of the cross" (1 Cor 1:18).[26] As one can see from the parallel text in 1 Cor 1:20-31, the gospel that Paul hopes to proclaim in Rome and thereafter in Spain was innately shameful as far as Mediterranean cultures were concerned.[27] The message about a redeemer being crucified was a "stumbling block to Jews and foolishness to Gentiles" (1 Cor 1:23).[28] A divine self-revelation on an obscene cross[29] seemed to demean God and overlook the honor and propriety of established religious traditions, both Jewish and Greco-Roman. Rather than appealing to the honorable and righteous members of society, such a gospel seemed designed to appeal to the despised and the powerless. To use the words of 1 Corinthians, "God chose what is foolish in the world to shame the wise; God chose what is weak in the world to shame the strong. God chose what is low and despised in the world . . . so that no one might boast in the presence of God" (1 Cor 1:27-29). There were deeply engrained social reasons why Paul should have been ashamed to proclaim such a gospel; his claim not to be ashamed signals that a social and ideological revolution has been inaugurated by the gospel.

At the center of the thesis of Romans in 1:16-17 is the paradox of power, that in this shameful gospel that would seem to lack the capacity to prevail, the power of God is in fact revealed in a compelling manner.[30] When Paul states that he is "not ashamed of the gospel" because it "is God's power," it seems most natural to take this in the context of weighing whether the sovereign an ambassador represents is capable of achieving the purposes of an embassy. The gospel is the "power of God," Paul contends,[31] echoing the formulation in 1 Cor 1:18, that the word of the cross "is God's power

21 Isocrates Big. 35.1; cf. Isocrates Antid. 272.7; Panath. 74.3; Isaeus Orat. 5; Phil. 39.7.
22 Aeschines Fals. leg., 69.16; cf. Aeschines Ctes. 217.6; Epist. 5:3; Tim. 120.13; 135.2-3.
23 Gerhard Friedrich, "εὐαγγελίζομαι κτλ.," TDNT 2 (1964) 729.
24 Dahl, Studies, 71, citing Anton Fridrichsen, "TO ΕΥΑΓΓΕΛΙΟΝ hos Paulus," NorTT 13 (1912) 153-70, 209-56; idem, The Apostle and His Message, UUÅ 3 (Uppsala: Lundequistska, 1947) 8-16.
25 Dahl, Studies, 73.
26 Schlier, 42; Morris, 66 n. 158; Zeller, 42.
27 See particularly Johnson, 25, and the analysis of the central role of honor for Romans in Lendon, Empire of Honour, 30-236. On 193 he describes the profound anxiety of officials about "loss of honour," citing Pliny Ep. 8.24.9, "it is more uglifying to lose, than never to get, praise." That shame in this context relates to the violation of unwritten customs in the Greek tradition, as argued by Blumenfeld, Political Paul, 311-12, seems unlikely.
28 See particularly Hengel, Crucifixion, 1-11, 84-90.
29 Crucifixion was primarily a ceremony of shame, designed to humiliate the most despised elements of society. It was the method employed for criminals, rebels, and slaves, and ordinarily could not be imposed on Roman citizens. See Hengel, Crucifixion, 39-63; Joseph Vogt, Sklaverei und Humanität. Studien zur antiken Sklaverei und ihrer Erfassung, Historia 44 (2d ed.; Wiesbaden: Steiner, 1983) 73-78. The obscenity of helpless, naked victims is disguised by Christian art that always supplies a loincloth, but the horror would have been extreme for Jews, who avoided any display of nudity.
30 See Ziesler, 68; Gräbe, Power of God, 176-77.
31 Schmidt, 26, notes that the rhetorical emphasis in 1:16-17 lies on the word "power."

($\delta\acute{v}\nu\alpha\mu\iota\varsigma\ \vartheta\epsilon o\hat{v}\ \dot{\epsilon}\sigma\tau\iota\nu$) for those who are being saved." Allusions to the power of God appear frequently in Jewish sources,[32] for example, to the "strength" of God's hand in the exodus (Exod 15:6; 32:11; Deut 9:26, 29; 26:8), to wisdom as the "breath of the power of God" (Wis 7:25); to Jerusalem as possessing "a certain power of God" ($\tau\iota\nu\alpha\ \vartheta\epsilon o\hat{v}\ \delta\acute{v}\nu\alpha\mu\iota\varsigma$, 2 Macc 3:38); or to the Torah as God's power.[33] In the Roman cultural context, it is important to recall that priestly, military, and administrative forms of power were celebrated as effective means of salvation. The priestly, sacrificial activities of the emperor and his local representatives constituted what Richard Gordon has described as a "veil of power" whose purpose was to legitimate imperial rule and "to maintain the power and wealth of the elite."[34] The imperial cult celebrated the "gospel" of the allegedly divine power of the emperor, viewing him, in the words of an official document from the province of Asia, as

. . . a savior ($\sigma\acute{\omega}\tau\eta\rho$) who put an end to war and will restore order everywhere: Caesar, by his appearing has realized the hopes of our ancestors; not only has he surpassed earlier benefactors of humanity, but he leaves no hope to those of the future that they might surpass him. The god's birthday was for the world the beginning of the gospel ($\epsilon\dot{v}\alpha\gamma\gamma\acute{\epsilon}\lambda\iota o\nu$) that he brought.[35]

The elaborate triumphs staged by emperors at the conclusion of military campaigns celebrated their allegedly divine power.[36]

This slant on the thesis of Romans not only enables one to explain the claim that "the gospel *is* God's power," but also allows access to the explanatory connection between 1:16a and b. The major point in the thesis statement, that the gospel is God's means of restoring righteous control over a disobedient creation, dovetails with Paul's understanding of his mission to extend that reign.[37] In effect, Paul presents himself in Romans as the ambassador of the "power of God," extending the sovereign's cosmic foreign policy through the preaching of the gospel.

The phrase $\epsilon\dot{\iota}\varsigma\ \sigma\omega\tau\eta\rho\acute{\iota}\alpha\nu$ ("for salvation") indicates the effect of divine power acting through the gospel.[38] Since Paul so frequently speaks of salvation in terms of preservation from divine wrath in the last judgment,[39] commentators are inclined to stress the eschatological dimension in this context.[40] But in view of 8:24, where salvation is described with a past tense verb, and the current verse dominated by a present tense verb "the power of God *is*,"[41] Käsemann is correct in concluding that salvation "already has become a present reality through Christ in the midst of the world and not just an anticipation 'in principle.'"[42] Deliverance from the present evil age and the restoration of wholeness are implied along

32   See Walter Grundmann, "$\delta\acute{v}\nu\alpha\mu\alpha\iota\ \kappa\tau\lambda.$," *TDNT* 2 (1964) 290–99.

33   Rabbinic examples provided by ibid., 297.

34   Richard Gordon, "The Veil of Power," in R. A. Horsley, ed., *Paul and Empire: Religion and Power in Roman Imperial Society* (Harrisburg: Trinity Press International, 1997) 126–37, esp. 132.

35   Letter of the Proconsul of Asia, Paulus Fabius Maximux, honoring Augustus, in *I. Priene* 105.35ff, cited by Ceslas Spicq, "$\sigma\acute{\omega}\zeta\omega\ \kappa\tau\lambda.$," *TLNT* 3 (1994) 353; and Price, "Rituals," 53; see also Georgi, "Upside Down," 150–51; Ferguson, "Ruler-worship," 766–84; Balch, "Zeus," 77, 88–89. For earlier developments of this theme, see Gail P. Corrington, "Power and the Man of Power in the Context of Hellenistic Popular Belief," *Helios* 13 (1986) 75–86; Lendon, *Empire of Honour*, 173–75.

36   Fears, "Theology of Victory," 737–826; see also Meister, "Tugenden," 5. A further example is Dio Cassius's claim in *Hist. Rom.* 61.34.4 that Claudius "received the greatest power of any man at that time" ($\mu\acute{\epsilon}\gamma\iota\sigma\tau o\nu\ \tau\hat{\omega}\nu\ \tau\acute{o}\tau\epsilon\ \dot{\alpha}\nu\vartheta\rho\acute{\omega}\pi\omega\nu\ \delta\upsilon\nu\eta\vartheta\epsilon\acute{\iota}\varsigma$).

37   See Alkier, *Wunder*, 268–70.

38   Godet, 92; Schlier, 42; Dunn, 1:39: "with the effect of bringing about salvation."

39   Rom 5:9-10; 13:11; 1 Cor 3:15; 5:5; Phil 1:28; 2:12; 1 Thess 5:8-9.

40   Kühl, 34; Zeller, 42; Zeisler, 69; Dunn, 1:39; Fitzmyer, 56; Byrne, 51; Schreiner, 61; Werner Foerster, "$\sigma\acute{\omega}\zeta\omega\ \kappa\tau\lambda.$," *TDNT* 7 (1971) 993; Karl Hermann Schelkle, "$\sigma\omega\tau\eta\rho\acute{\iota}\alpha$," *EDNT* 3 (1993) 327.

41   See also 1 Cor 1:18, "to us who are being saved," and 2 Cor 2:15; 6:2.

42   Käsemann, 22, countering Lietzmann, 30. The combination of future and present eschatology is also advocated by Schlier, 43; Moo, 67; Spicq, "$\sigma\acute{\omega}\zeta\omega\ \kappa\tau\lambda.$," 350.

with preservation from the wrath to come and the fulfillment of salvation when the new age is fully present. By implication, however, if such salvation comes as a result of the gospel that Paul proclaims about Christ crucified and resurrected, then salvation must not be present in the accoutrements of Roman rule that filled the city to which this letter was addressed. Germanicus had celebrated Augustus as "the true saviour and the benefactor of the entire race of men,"[43] and the Asian League had referred to "Providence" as having granting a "savior (σωτῆρα) for us and our descendants who brought an end to war and set all things in peaceful order."[44] Just as Augustus had been proclaimed as the "savior of the universe (σωτὴρ τῆς οἰκουμένης),"[45] Nero was celebrated as "the savior and benefactor of the universe (τῷ σωτῆρι καὶ εὐεργέτητι τῆ[ς] οἰκουμένης)."[46] Over against this politico-religious context, Paul contends that salvation is manifest now in the seemingly powerless communities of faith established by the gospel.

The contrast with Roman civic cult brings more clearly into focus the implications of Paul's thesis and its correlation with the rest of the *exordium* as well as the subsequent argument of the letter, because this gospel shatters the unrighteous precedence given to the strong over the weak, the free and well-educated over slaves and the ill-educated, the Greeks and Romans over the barbarians. If what the world considers dishonorable has power, it will prevail and achieve a new form of honor to those who have not earned it, an honor consistent with divine righteousness. All who place their faith in this gospel will be set right, that is, be placed in the right relation to the most significant arena in which honor is dispensed: divine judgment. Thus the triumph of divine righteousness through the gospel of Christ crucified and resurrected is achieved by transforming the system in which shame and honor are dispensed. The thesis of Romans therefore effectively turns the social value system of the Roman Empire upside down.[47]

Although πίστις ("faith") has already appeared three times in the *exordium*, marking the shared stance that links Paul with his audience, its verbal expression here in the participle τῷ πιστεύοντι ("to the one has faith") reinforces the identity of the group within which salvation is experienced. That Paul selects a present participle focuses attention "not solely on the initial act of faith but on faith as a continuing orientation and motivation for life."[48] More concretely, this refers to those who respond to the gospel by participating in faith communities.[49] The inclusive emphasis, with the word πᾶς—"to *all* who have faith"—is characteristic of Romans. Πᾶς appears already for the third time in Romans, marching toward a total of more than 75 times in the letter as a whole.[50] Commentators often note the universality of the gospel's range,[51] but the Roman context required particular emphasis because of the tendency for house and tenement churches to delegitimize one another. Moo observes that the formula "all who believe" occurs four other times in Romans, always in the context of tensions between Jewish and Gentile groups.[52] That the majority of "strong" or Gentile-oriented groups was discriminating against the minority of "weak" or Jewish-oriented groups is the most likely explanation for the explication of "all" as "both to the Jew first and then to the Greek." In keeping with the revolution in honor and

---

43 Cited by Harrison, *Language of Grace*, 228.

44 Cited by Spicq, *TLNT* 3 (1994) 353, from *I.Priene* Nr. 105.35-36.

45 Cited by Spicq, *TLNT* 3 (1994) 354, from *IG* 12.5, Nr. 557.3.

46 Cited by Spicq, *TLNT* 3 (1994) 354, from *APF* 2 (1902) 434 Nr. 24 = *OGIS* 2. Nr. 668.5.

47 Georgi develops this theme in "Upside Down," 148–57.

48 Dunn, 1:40.

49 See von Dobbeler, *Glaube als Teilhabe*, 188; in contrast Kinneavy, *Greek Rhetorical Origins*, 112, restricts the definition of πίστις in 1:16 to the "ethical" dimension, defined on 138 as "the argument from authority."

50 See particularly Gaston, *Paul*, 116–34.

51 Weiss, 70; Dodd, 9; Käsemann, 22; Cranfield, 1:90; Schlier, 43.

52 Moo, 68, suggests that Rom 3:22; 4:11; 10:4, 11 aimed to break down the "barriers between Jew and Gentile," which, however, broadens the issue in so abstract a manner that the conflicts between groups in Rome are no longer visible. Luke Timothy Johnson, "The Social Dimensions of *Sōtēria* in Luke-Acts and Paul," in E. H. Lovering Jr., ed., *Society of Biblical Literature 1993 Seminar Papers*, SBLSP 32 (Atlanta: Scholars Press, 1993) 531, writes that "God's plan for salvation . . . is not directed at scattered individuals but at social groups."

shame that the gospel entails, overturning the precedence of the Greco-Romans over the barbarians and the wise over the foolish, Paul seeks to correct the imbalance in Rome. Instead of the usual antithesis between Jews and Gentiles, Paul refers here to Ἕλληνες ("Greeks, Greco-Romans") and Ἰουδαῖοι ("Jews"), whereby the latter would correlate with the "barbarians" in the revolutionary antithesis of 1:14. Whereas Paul frequently employs the antithesis between Jews and Gentiles that was characteristic of Judaism, here and in 2:9-10; 3:9; and 10:12 he chooses to refer to "Greeks." Although most commentators interpret this antithesis as roughly equal with Jew/Gentile,[53] I believe it is preferable to seek the specific, rhetorical reason for selecting the word "Greek" in this context. I suggest that he felt it was politically wise in several contexts to avoid the use of the pejorative term "Gentiles" in referring to the groups currently dominating the Christian movement in Rome.[54] However, in response to the Greco-Roman majority that was inclined to believe it had displaced Jewish Christians in God's plan (cf. 11:17-24), Paul insists on the precedence of Jews in the history of the Christ movement, a theme developed in 9:1-5.[55] Nevertheless, the counterbalancing insistence is maintained here just as throughout the letter, that salvation is a matter of faith, to which all of the Christian groups in Rome have equal access.[56] In Colenso's words, salvation is "for all that believe, without any special favour or distinction."[57] The Greek churches experience salvation in their own right, not as second class non-Jews, which the epithet "Gentiles" would have implied. This sets the theme of the later argument for the equal accountability of Greeks and Jews in 2:9-10, for their joint involvement in sin in 3:9, and for the final abolition of any "distinction" between Greek and Jewish believers with regard to salvation through grace in 10:12. This inclusive orientation to salvation contrasts with Habakkuk, which employs the same terms to refer to saving the chosen people through "crushing" their enemies (3:13): "I will rejoice in God, a Savior to me (τῷ σωτῆρί μοι). God is a power to me (ὁ θεὸς δύναμις μοι)" (Hab. 3:18-19).[58] It also contrasts with Roman claims that the emperor and the Roman people possessed a kind of "monopoly" of fides = πίστις ("faith, faithfulness"),[59] which was so pleasing to the gods that the empire was granted to them. In the Acta Augusti 31-33, for example, the nations conquered by Rome said to have "discovered the πίστις of the Roman people" that justified their precedence. The Latin word fides assumes a central importance in imperial propaganda under Augustus, appearing frequently on coins and monuments created by him and his successors, implying that the emperors embodied this virtue in a preeminent and salvific manner.[60] In contrast, overturning all claims of cultural superiority, Paul claims that God's power for salvation

53   Hans Windisch, "Ἕλλην κτλ.," TDNT 2 (1964) 513–16, argues that although "Greek" refers to "Hellenistic elements of the Roman Empire (apart from the Jews)," in Romans there is an equation between "Greek = uncircumcised = Gentiles." Joachim Wanke, "Ἕλλην κτλ.," EDNT 1 (1990) 436, concurs that the meaning "Gentile" resonates" in Rom 1:16. Most commentators agree, e.g., Weiss, 71; Michel, 88; Kuss, 1:21; Murray, 28; Zeller, 43; Fitzmyer, 257; Moo, 68; Schreiner, 62.

54   For a discussion of the disparaging connotation of ἔθνος, see Karl Ludwig Schmidt, "ἔθνος, ἐθνικός," TDNT 2 (1964) 371; Dabelstein, Beurteilung, 21–37.

55   Hugolinus Langkammer, "πρῶτον," EDNT 3 (1993) 188, argues for temporal priority in that the first converts were Jews; Windisch concurs in "Ἕλλην κτλ.," 514. Käsemann, 23, argues for "precedence for the sake of continuity of the plan of salvation," which is accepted by Wilckens, 1:86; Fitzmyer, 257; etc., but this presupposes that Paul and his audience were privy to the modern debate over salva-

tion history. Theobald, 43, formulates the matter more aptly, referring to the fact that Jesus remains the Jewish Messiah according to 1:3-4, and that the question of whether Jewish unbelief means that God's Word has failed is the topic of Rom 9–11.

56   See particularly Dunn, 1:40; Zeller, 43; idem, Juden, 141–45; Wilckens, 84–86. For a predominantly individualistic interpretation of these details, see Burnett, Individual, 137–47; Starnitzke, Struktur, 61–69.

57   Colenso, 29.

58   Carter, Power of Sin, 138, accepts the idea of Hultgren, Gospel, 30–34, that LXX Ps 97:1-3 guided Paul's thought in the thesis statement, but that passage shares Habakkuk's bias that God's victory over the foreign powers is for the benefit of the "house of Israel."

59   Georgi, "Upside Down," 149.

60   See Georgi, "Upside Down," 149, citing Werner Eisenhut, "Fides," in Der kleine Pauly (Stuttgart: Druckenmüller, 1964) 2:545–46. The supreme value of πιστός/fides for the Romans is visible in the

exercises its transforming lordship over every group that responds in faith to the gospel of Christ crucified. This thesis is developed in every subsequent section of the letter, down to chap. 16, where the competing groups are admonished to welcome each other as members of the same family in Christ. Evangelical persuasion rather than political and military power is thus the means whereby the salvation of the world is now occurring.

■ 17 Although the expression, "the righteousness of God," has a rather wide semantic range,[61] it is best understood within the missional context already established in the first sixteen verses of this letter. The long battle between orthodox Protestant interpreters stressing forensic dimensions of imputed righteousness and Catholic, Calvinist, and pietistic interpreters stressing ethical transformation shaped by righteousness[62] failed to take account either of the apocalyptic background of Paul's language or the missional setting of Romans. These partisan controversies shared a mistaken premise that Paul's letter was a theological treatise aimed at refuting inadequate understandings of the doctrine of "justification by faith." A preliminary step out of the impasse was taken by Hermann Cremer, showing that

the biblical concept of righteousness was primarily relational, associated with covenantal loyalty, an insight that subsequent scholars have largely accepted.[63] Many subsequent scholars pointed to the social context of the interaction between Jews and Gentiles as a decisive framework for Paul's doctrine of divine righteousness.[64] A crucial contribution was made by Käsemann, who emphasized the apocalyptic understanding of the "righteousness of God," developed in response to the individualized, existential interpretation of imputed righteousness by his teacher, Rudolf Bultmann.[65] As Käsemann argued on the basis of apocalyptic parallels to 1:17, this phrase "speaks of the God who brings back the fallen world into the sphere of his legitimate claim."[66] The gift of righteousness brings the believer in obedience under the lordship of Christ, which overcame the classic conceptual dichotomy between justification and sanctification.[67]

The idea that the gospel is the means by which God establishes his righteous rule stands at the end of a long development. The early phases of OT faith conceived of Yahweh as demonstrating his righteousness by defending Israel and oppressed individuals (Deut 33:21; Judg

---

description of Domitius Corbulo, Nero's commander in Parthia and Armenia (64 C.E.), who showed "both justice and faithfulness towards all" ($\tau\grave{o}$ $\delta\acute{\iota}\kappa\alpha\iota\upsilon\nu$ $\tau\acute{o}$ $\tau\epsilon$ $\pi\iota\sigma\tau\grave{o}\nu$ $\grave{\epsilon}\varsigma$ $\pi\acute{\alpha}\nu\tau\alpha\varsigma$, Dio Cassius *Hist. Rom.* 62.19.2). Although some hoped that Domitius Corbulo would seize the sovereignty with his large army, he renounced this temptation because "he kept his faith with Nero" ($\acute{o}\tau\iota$ $\tau\grave{\eta}\nu$ $\pi\rho\grave{o}\varsigma$ $\tau\grave{o}\nu$ $N\acute{\epsilon}\rho\omega\nu\alpha$ $\pi\acute{\iota}\sigma\tau\iota\nu$ $\grave{\epsilon}\tau\acute{\eta}\rho\eta\sigma\epsilon\nu$, Dio Cassius *Hist. Rom.* 62.19.3–4).

61 See BAGD (2000) 247–49; Gottlob Schrenk, "$\delta\acute{\iota}\kappa\eta$ $\kappa\tau\lambda.$," *TDNT* 2 (1964) 192–225; J. J. Scullion, "Righteousness (OT)," *ABD* 5 (1992) 724–36; John Reumann, "Righteousness (Early Judaism)," *ABD* 5 (1992) 736–42; idem, "Righteousness (Greco-Roman World)," *ABD* 5 (1992) 742–45; idem, "Righteousness (NT)," *ABD* 5 (1992) 745–73. For the earlier development of *fides* as a national virtue, see Meister, "Tugenden," 6.

62 See Campbell, *Rhetoric of Righteousness*, 138–41, for an overview; also Wilckens, 1:223–33; Plevnik, "Recent Developments," 47–62; Brauch, "Perspectives," 523–42.

63 Hermann Cremer, *Die paulinische Rechtfertigungslehre im Zusammenhänge ihrer geschichtlichen*

Vorausetzungen (2d ed.; Gütersloh: Bertelsmann, 1900) 34–38, followed explicitly by later scholars such as Leske, "Righteousness," 125–37; Dunn, 1:40–41.

64 For example, Stendahl, *Paul*, 23–40; Dahl, *Studies*, 105–13; Barth, "Jews and Gentiles," 241–67; Boers, *Justification*, 95–109.

65 Bultmann, "$\Delta IKAIO\Sigma TNH$ ΘEOT," 12–16; idem, *Theology*, 1:270–329; prominent advocates of Bultmann's view include Bornkamm, *Paul*, 135–56; Conzelmann, "Theology or Anthropology," 108–23. For accounts of the debate see Jewett, "Major Impulses," 25; Hans Hübner, "Existentiale Interpretation der paulinischen 'Gerechtigkeit Gottes.' Zur Kontroverse Rudolf Bultmann-Ernst Käsemann," *NTS* 21 (1974–75) 462–88; and José M. Millás, "Justicia de Dios: Rudolf Bultmann intérprete de la teologia paulina de la justificacíon," *Greg* 71 (1990) 259–91.

66 Käsemann, 29; see also Seifrid, *Christ, our Righteousness*, 37–47, 76.

67 Käsemann, "Righteousness," 100–110; see also idem, "Justice for the Unjust," *Colloquium* 1 (1978) 10–16; idem, "Justification and Salvation History in the Epistle to the Romans," in *Perspectives*, 60–78.

5:11; 1 Sam 12:7; Pss 35:24; 50:6; 98:1-3; Mic 6:5), punishing evildoers (Pss 7:9; 9:3-4) and vindicating the righteous (Pss 5:8; 7:9; 9:5).[68] As Adolf Strobel showed, Jewish writings in the pre-Christian period had linked the triumphant righteousness of God with the fulfillment of messianic hopes.[69] In the expectation of Isa 46:13; 51:5, 6, 8; 62; Jer 23:5-6, a divinely appointed savior will bring God's "salvation" and "righteousness" to the earth. An example of this tradition in Qumran is visible at 1QH 4 (= Sukenik 17):20-21, "To you does righteousness belong, and blessing belongs to your name for ever. [Act according] to your righteousness and redeem [your servant] and may the wicked come to an end." One of the battle flags of the Sons of Light in the war against the Sons of Darkness is the "righteousness of God" (1QM 4:6).[70] Other writings tend to link the righteousness of God closely with the Torah[71] or refer to it as the criterion of divine judgment.[72] On the basis of apocalyptic parallels Käsemann and his followers argued that "righteousness of God" had become a technical term,[73] but subsequent studies showed this to be unlikely.[74] The evidence points rather to Paul's choice of one particular strand of the semantic tradition of the "righteousness of God" as "the act by which God brings people into right relationship with himself"[75] to develop his thesis.

Although Käsemann properly grasped the cosmic dimensions of Paul's usage, he did not take account of the establishment of new forms of communalism in faith communities formed by those who accepted this message about being set right in Christ. It is the inclusive gospel of Christ that equalizes the status of Greeks and barbarians, wise and uneducated, Jews and Gentiles, which offers new relationships in communal settings to all on precisely the same terms.[76] The early Christian mission is thus viewed as a decisive phase in the revelation of God's righteousness, restoring individuals, establishing new communities of faith, and ultimately restoring the whole creation. This missional context makes it likely that δικαιοσύνη θεοῦ should be taken as a subjective genitive referring to God's activity in this process of global transformation,[77] rather than as an objective genitive that would refer to the human righteousness bestowed by God.[78] The fact that "God's power" in 1:16 and "God's wrath" in 1:18 are both subjective genitives renders it likely that "righteousness of God" should be taken in the same way,[79] and commentators who believe that Paul intended both the subjective and objective genitive in 1:17 disregard this contextual and grammatical evidence.[80]

The evangelistic orientation of Paul's thesis explains why the key term ἀποκαλύπτεται ("is revealed") appears in the present tense. The phrase "in it," that is, in the gospel, specifies the agency wherein this revelation is occurring, and Paul returns to this theme of the

---

68 See Karl Kertelge, "δικαιοσύνη," *EDNT* 1 (1990) 328; J. J. Scullion, "Righteousness (OT)," *ABD* 5 (1992) 731: "God's saving action in behalf of his people."

69 Strobel, *Verzögerungs-problem*, 179–88.

70 In a similar manner the golden shield honoring Augustus mentioned in his *Res Gestae* 34 recognized his achievement of "righteousness" ([δ]ικαιοσύνη), "excellence" (ἀρετή), "piety" (εὐσέβεια), and "clemency" (ἐκείκεια).

71 *T. Dan* 6.10, "Forsake all unrighteousness and cleave to the righteousness of the law of God." Cf. 1QS 10:11-12; 11:2-3, 5. For a critique of Käsemann's claim that *T. Dan* 6.1 provides a key precedent for Rom 1:17, see Marion L. Soards, "Käsemann's 'Righteousness' Reexamined," *CBQ* 49 (1987) 265.

72 In *T. Abr.* 13.10 the angel "weighs the righteous deeds and the sins with the righteousness of God." Cf. 1QS 11:10-12. For a succinct critique of Käsemann's argument that 1QS 11 provides a link between divine righteousness and human justification, see Moo, 85. See also Soards, "Käsemann's 'Righteousness' Reexamined," 266–67.

73 Käsemann, "Righteousness," 172; Stuhlmacher, *Gerechtigkeit*, 142–75.

74 See particularly Seifrid, *Justification*, 42–46, 78–135; Campbell, *Rhetoric of Righteousness*, 147–60; Reumann, "Righteousness (NT)," 758; Moo, 85.

75 Moo, 74.

76 See Colenso, 29–34.

77 Dodd, 12; Schrenk, "δίκη κτλ.," 203–4; Barrett, 19; Kertelge, "δικαιοσύνη," 328; Cranfield, 1:96; Ziesler, 70–71; Fitzmyer, 257; Haacker, 41.

78 Lietzmann, 30; Lagrange, 19; Bultmann, "ΔΙΚΑΙΟΣΥΝΗ ΘΕΟΥ," 12–16; Kuss, 1:22; Klein, "Gottes Gerechtigkeit," 225–36; BAGD (2000) 247.

79 See particularly Cranfield, 1:96.

80 For example, Sanday and Headlam, 24–25; Morris, 69; Dunn, 1:41; Byrne, 60; Schreiner, 66.

triumphant spread of the gospel in 15:15-28. There is an important parallel in Ps 98:2, where it is clear that "reveal" implies divine action to achieve righteousness and salvation: "The Lord has made known his salvation, in the sight of the nations he has revealed his righteousness (ἐγνώρισεν κύριος τὸ σωτήριον αὐτοῦ, ἐναντίον τῶν ἐθνῶν ἀπεκάλυψεν τὴν δικαιοσύνην αὐτοῦ)."[81] Here as in Rom 1:17, revelation is more than cognitive;[82] it is historical,[83] and in Paul's case the verb refers to the spread of the gospel as the means by which the triumph of divine righteousness is now being achieved. The use of the passive voice, "is revealed," is an "indication of divine agency" both in Paul's ministry and in the triumph over unrighteousness.[84] The goal of divine righteousness is to establish salvation, which in the context of the expression "to all who have faith," implies the establishment of faith communities where righteous relationships are maintained.

It is essential at this point to recapture the social context of Paul's mission, rather than to allow our definition of salvation to be dominated by the later theological tradition. A correlative issue is to recapture the resonance these terms would have had for a Roman audience. Both in the missional program for the early church, and in Roman imperial propaganda, salvation implies the restoration of wholeness on a corporate as well as an individual level; its primary scope in biblical theology and in Roman civil religion is the group, that is, the nation and the world, rather than the individual. The stunning feature of Paul's thesis, therefore, is its contention that preaching the gospel to establish faith communities, rather than force of arms or apocalyptic military miracles, is the means by which such righteousness is restored. In the establishment of faith communities as far as the end of the known world, God will be restoring arenas where righteousness is accomplished, thus creating salvation. In place of the salvation of the *Pax Romana*, based on force, there is the salvation of small groups, cooperatively interacting with one another to extend their new forms of communality to the end of the world. The global offensive in behalf of divine righteousness envisioned by Romans is missional and persuasive rather than martial and coercive.

Dunn is on target in suggesting that "Paul's experience of evangelizing the Gentiles gives Paul firm confidence that in the gospel as the power of God to salvation such early converts are being given to see the righteousness of God actually happening, taking effect in their own conversion."[85] But I would rephrase this in social terms, to avoid the individualism that distorts Paul's apocalyptic vision. It is the conversion of tenement churches and house churches that will provide the beachheads of the new creation. Paul's hope in writing this letter is that this inclusive and restorative righteousness will be allowed to heal the divisions between the Roman groups of converts and thus enable them to participate in the campaign to missionize to the end of the known world, as far as the Pillars of Hercules in Spain, thus contributing to a nonimperialistic redemption of the world.

The divine righteousness that is revealed in the gospel as the power of God ushering in the time of salvation manifests itself in a progressive manner ἐκ πίστεως εἰς πίστιν ("from faith to faith"). The parallels to this sequence of prepositions make clear that a progression, transformation, or movement is intended.[86] For example, Ps 83:8 promises that the faithful shall move forward "from strength to strength" (ἐκ δυνάμεως εἰς δύναμιν),[87] whereas the wicked in Jeremiah's oracle (9:2) progress "from evil to evil" (ἐκ κακῶν εἰς κακά).

---

81 Haacker, 41, cites also Isa 46:13; 51:5; 56:1 as passages where divine righteousness is "revealed" or "disclosed" by God's actions.

82 Traugott Holtz, "ἀποκαλύπτω, ἀποκάλυψις," *EDNT* 1 (1990) 131; Morris, 71; Wilckens, 1:87–88.

83 See particularly Lührmann, *Offenbarungsverständnis*, 154–62; Schlier, 44–45; Murray, 29; Moo, 60; the effort by Stuhlmacher, *Gerechtigkeit*, 79ff., 238–39, to reduce the present tense verb to a disclosure of an apocalyptic triumph yet to come disregards the evidence about the currently visible missional context of this verse.

84 Bockmuehl, *Revelation and Mystery*, 138.

85 Dunn, 1:48.

86 See Charles L. Quarles, "From Faith to Faith: A Fresh Examination of the Prepositional Series in Romans 1:17," *NovT* 45.1 (2003) 6–7.

87 Ibid., 11. "Ps 83:8 either indicates physical movement from one place to another or progressive degrees of strength."

Paul uses this formula several times, "from death to death . . . from life to life" (2 Cor 2:16; cf. 3:18) and the classical parallels contain the same progressive element.[88] This rhetorical structure is violated by theologically motivated interpretations that define "faith" differently when following ἐκ as compared with εἰς,[89] or that take the expression as primarily decorative,[90] as an emphatic expression of the doctrine of *sola fidei*,[91] or as meaninglessly redundant.[92] In view of Paul's use of "faith" in 1:5, 8, 12, and 16 as appropriation of the gospel that allows cultural variations to stand side by side with equal validity, it is most likely that the progression in this verse refers to missionary expansion of the gospel, which relies on the contagion of faith.[93] This also brings the expression into consistency with the following citation from Habakkuk, which is altered by Paul to make plain to his audience that faith refers to acceptance of the gospel.

On syntactical grounds,[94] there is no question that "from faith to faith" qualifies the immediately preceding verb, ἀποκαλύπτεται ("is being revealed"),[95] rather than defining the distant expression "righteousness of God."[96] As an apostle to the Gentiles who wishes to elicit aid from the Roman believers in the project of the Spanish mission, Paul wishes to affirm that the revelation of divine righteousness in the gospel proceeds only on the basis of faith. Acceptance of the gospel of Christ crucified does not require conformity to a particular cultural tradition or to a specific theology. Although the faith of many Roman believers differs from Paul's, it serves equally well in advancing the gospel.

As scriptural confirmation of the principle "from faith to faith," Paul cites Hab 2:4, introduced by the traditional citation formula, καθὼς γέγραπται ("as it has been written").[97] Of the 29 citations in the Pauline letters introduced by the verb γράφειν ("to write"), the formula "just as it has been written" appears 18 times,[98] following the Jewish tradition found in 2 Chr 23:18 and

---

88   Anton Fridrichsen, "Aus Glauben zu Glauben, Rom 1,17," in *Walter Bauer Gottingensi viro de Novi Testamenti philologi optime merito sacrum*, ConBNT 12 (Lund: Gleerup, 1948) 54, cites Suetonius *Galb.* 14.1: in abandoning one imperial choice after the next after the death of Nero, "some demon" drove the soldiers "from treachery to treachery (ἐκ προδοσίας εἰς προδοσίαν)."

89   For an account of patristic suggestions of progressions from law to gospel, from the faith of preachers to the faith of hearers, from one article of faith to another, or God's faithfulness to human faith, see Meyer, 1:71–72; Schmidt, 28; Cranfield, 1:99; Kuss, 1:22–23. The widespread view of individual growth from initial appropriation of the gospel to mature belief or hope (e.g., Lagrange, 20; Sanday and Headlam, 28; Schmidt, 28; Kuss, 1:24) is countered by Paul's choice of the verb "reveal," as Godet, 97, showed. That "from faith" refers to God's faithfulness as opposed to human "faith" (e.g., Barth, 41–42; Arthur G. Hebert, "Faithfulness and 'Faith,'" *Theology* 58 [1955] 375; Gaston, *Paul*, 118–19; Dunn, 1:44; Douglas A. Campbell, "Romans 1:17—A *Crux Interpretum* for the Πίστις Χριστοῦ Debate," *JBL* 113 [1994] 227; Haacker, 43; Johnson, 28) is theologically appealing, but as Barrett, 31, points out, this requires differing definitions of πίστις within a single sentence. Quarles's advocacy of Chrysostom's antithetical interpretation, "from the faith of the old dispensation to the faith of the new" ("Faith to Faith ," 18–21) suffers

under the same weaknesses as well as the additional anomaly that the subsequent citation from Hab 2:4, which is clearly derived from the old dispensation, would thereby be rendered irrelevant in defining the new dispensation. Paul's contention, in contrast, is that faith in Christ is consistent with the OT as articulated by Habakkuk.

90   Lietzmann, 31; Ziesler, 71; Moo, 76; Schreiner, 72.

91   Fridrichsen, "Glauben zu Glauben," 54; Michel, 90; Schlatter, 24–25; Käsemann, 31; Zeller, 44; von Dobbeler, *Glaube als Teilhabe*, 154.

92   Pallas, 40; Michael, "Phenomenon," 151.

93   See Godet, 97; Wilckens, 1:88, refers to the universal outreach of the gospel.

94   See BDF §§472–74.

95   See Meyer, 1:71; Weiss, 73; Kühl, 42–43.

96   Weiss, 73, lists the Lutheran interpreters who violate this syntactical likelihood in order to insist that righteousness comes only through faith. Cranfield, 1:100, admits that the grammar indicates that "from faith to faith" was connected with the verb, but contends on theological grounds "that in Paul's thought it was linked rather" with "righteousness of God."

97   The formula appears also in Rom 2:24; 3:4, 10; 4:17; 8:36; 9:13, 33; 10:15; 11:8, 26; 15:3, 21. The verb γέγραπται is in the perfect passive, which most commentators and translators render in the present tense, "it is written," but I see no reason not to translate it accurately.

98   See Koch, *Schrift*, 25.

144

Dan 9:13 (Theodotion), καθὼς γέγραπται ἐν τῷ νόμῳ Μωυσῆ ("just as it has been written in the law of Moses"), and also in 4 Kgdms 14:6, καθὼς γέγραπται ἐν βιβλίῳ νόμων Μωῦσῆ ("just as it has been written in the book of Moses").[99] That the Hebrew equivalent of this expression occurs frequently in Qumran writings[100] leads me to conclude that Paul is following a widespread Jewish tradition of introducing a citation from authoritative Scripture.[101]

As one can readily see from the comparison below, Paul cites Hab 2:4 in a form that differs in significant ways from the Hebrew original, the LXX versions, and the parallel in Hebrews:

MT: וְצַדִּיק בֶּאֱמוּנָתוֹ יִחְיֶה ("The righteous one shall live by his faith/faithfulness")

LXX, codices S and W: Ὁ δὲ δίκαιος ἐκ πίστεως μου ζήσεται ("The righteous one shall live by my [i.e., God's] faith/faithfulness")

LXX, codices A and C: Ὁ δὲ δίκαιος μου ἐκ πίστεως ζήσεται ("My [i.e., God's] righteous one shall live by faith/faithfulness")

Heb 10:38: Ὁ δὲ δίκαιος μου ἐκ πίστεως ζήσεται ("My [i.e., God's] righteous one shall live by faith/faithfulness")

Rom 1:17; Gal 3:11: Ὁ δὲ δίκαιος ἐκ πίστεως ζήσεται ("The righteous one shall live by faith")

In contrast to the MT, which speaks of the faithfulness of the righteous believer in relation to God and the Torah,[102] the LXX codices S and W place the emphasis on God's faithfulness.[103] In these instances "faith" is understood primarily as "faithfulness." The same must be said of the version of Hab 2:4 in Hebrews, which conforms to LXX codices A and C, where "my righteous one" refers to the person who remains faithful to God despite the delay in the fulfillment of eschatological promises.[104] In a parallel manner "faithfulness" in the discussion of the Habakkuk oracle in 1QpHab 8:1-3 refers to "all observing the Law in the House of Judah, whom God will free from the house of judgment on account of their toil and their loyalty to the Teacher of Righteousness."[105] In the context of Heb 10:38, such "faithfulness" is an ethical matter, that is, "above all to follow Christ on the road to suffering that leads to heavenly glory."[106]

In contrast to these various efforts to construe faith in Hab 2:4 as "faithfulness," it is clear that Paul translated Hab 2:4 in an independent manner that eliminates this option.[107] The contexts of Rom 1:16-17 and Gal 3:6-14 and the deletion in each of the personal pronoun point indisputably in the direction of "faith" as a theological formula[108] for participation in the Christ movement. As we have seen, the word πίστις appears no less than six times in this short pericope prior to the citation of Hab 2:4, each time with the connotation of acceptance of the gospel and subsequent participation in the community of believers. That πίστις here refers to the faithfulness of God[109] or Christ[110] would more easily have been achieved by citing one of the LXX versions of Hab 2:4, which Paul obviously chose not to do.

The translation of Hab 2:4 has long been contested on the grounds that attaching the phrase ἐκ πίστεως

99   See also 1 Esdr 3:9.

100 Fitzmyer, 264, lists 1QS 5:17; 8:14; CD 7:19; 4QFlor 1-2 I 12; 4QpIsa^c 4-7 ii 18; 4Qcatena^a 10-11:1; 4Q178 3:2.

101 Koch, Schrift, 32, argues that Paul is following Hellenistic Jewish tradition while Fitzmyer, 264, stresses the "Palestinian Jewish tradition." See also Giblin, "Written," 327-53, 477-98; Ellis, Paul's Use, 22-49; Fitzmyer, "Old Testament Quotations," 297-333; Fred L. Horton Jr., "Formulas of Introduction in the Qumran Literature," RevQ 7 (1967-71) 505-14; Aageson, Biblical Interpretation, 19-69; R. R. Longenecker, "Prolegomena to Paul's Use of Scripture in Romans," BBR 7 (1997) 145-68.

102 See J. A. Emerton, "The Textual and Linguistic Problems of Habakkuk ii. 4-5," JTS 28 (1977) 10;

103 See Koch, Schrift, 127; Käsemann, 31; Dunn, 1:44-45.

104 See Strobel, Verzögerungsproblem, 79-177; Attridge, Hebrews, 302-3.

105 See Koch, Schrift, 128-29; Attridge, Hebrews, 303.

106 Attridge, Hebrews, 303; Eskola, Theodicy, 103-4.

107 See Koch, Schrift, 128; Eskola, Theodicy, 105-6.

108 Eskola, Theodicy, 106: "the quotation of Habakkuk is used as an argument for a proper understanding of faith."

109 Gaston, Paul, 118-19.

110 Hays, "Righteous One," 209-11; Campbell, "Romans 1:17," 281-85.

J. Gerald Janzen, "Habakkuk 2:2-4 in the Light of Recent Philological Advances," HTR 73 (1980) 62, 70-76; Dunn, 1:45.

("by faith") to the prior noun ὁ δίκαιος ("the righteous one, the one put right") concentrates on faith as the means by which justification is achieved. In general, advocates of this view have tended toward the classical Lutheran interpretation of Romans,[111] while those who advocate attaching the phrase to the following verb, "shall live," tend toward Catholic or pietistic views.[112] Rather than making this decision on the basis of one's theological preference, it is better to follow the normal rules of Greek grammar and connect ἐκ πίστεως with the verb ζήσεται. It is beyond the normal semantic range of the verb ζάω ("to live")[113] to refer to the process by which the status of righteousness is gained, for which Paul typically employs the verb λογίζειν ("to reckon"). As Zahn, Cavalin, Moody, and others have argued, if Paul had intended to say "the one who through faith is righteous shall live," he would have written ὁ δὲ ἐκ πίστεως δίκαιος ζήσεται.[114] Since the Hebrew original as well as the LXX translation of Hab 2:4 and the citation in 1 QpHab 7:17[115] link "faith" with the verb "live,"[116] it is likely that Paul's hearers in Rome would have understood it in this natural way rather than in the involuted fashion of post-Reformation interpreters.

Paul's altered citation of Hab 2:4 turns it into a confirmation of his particular emphasis on salvation by faith alone.[117] Since salvation for Paul was not a matter of innate righteousness or just behavior on the part of individuals or groups, the most adequate translation of ὁ δίκαιος is the one "who is put right with God."[118] The traditional doctrinal interpretation, however, does not take sufficient account of Paul's mission and the prior reference to "all who believe," referring to cultural groups rather than individuals. This provides a contex-

tual definition of ὁ δὲ δίκαιος ("but the righteous one, the one put right") in terms of persons emplaced within faith communities. The individual believer in the modern sense was not in view by Paul, even though the formulation from Habakkuk encourages an individualistic construal for the modern hearer. Moreover, the question of life should be understood as a matter of living together in faith communities rather than in the traditional theological sense of gaining eternal life on an individualistic basis. The proper question to be posed on the basis of Paul's argument in Romans is not, "Are you [sg.] saved?" but, "Are you all living together righteously in faith communities?"

The use of the passive verb, ἀποκαλύπτεται ("is being revealed"), is an "indication of divine agency" both in Paul's ministry and in the triumph over unrighteousness.[119] The goal of divine righteousness is to establish salvation, which in the context of the expression "to all who have faith" implies the establishment of faith communities where righteous relationships are maintained. It is essential at this point to recapture the social context of Paul's mission, rather than to allow our definition of salvation to be dominated by the later theological tradition. A correlative issue is to recapture the resonance these terms would have had for a Roman audience. Both in the missional program for the early church and in Roman imperial propaganda, salvation implies the restoration of wholeness on a corporate as well as an individual level; its primary scope in biblical theology and in Roman civil religion is the group, that is, the nation and the world, rather than the individual. The stunning feature of Paul's thesis, therefore, is its contention that preaching the gospel to establish faith

111 For example, Meyer, 1:72–73; Lietzmann, 30; Kühl, 44; Käsemann, 21; Barrett, 31; Nygren, 85–90; Schmidt, 28; Cranfield, 1:101–2; Morris, 70–72; Wilckens, 1:90.

112 See Godet, 93–94, for an account of the conflicted interpretation in the Reformation and the Council of Trent.

113 See BAGD (2000) 424–26: (1) "to be alive physically"; (2) "to live in a transcendent sense"; (3) "to conduct oneself in a pattern of behavior"; (4) "to be full of vitality"; and (5) "to be life productive."

114 Zahn, 85; H. C. C. Cavalin, "'The Righteous Shall Live by Faith.' A Decisive Argument for the Traditional Interpretation," ST 32 (1978) 33–43; R. M.

Moody, "The Habakkuk Quotation in Romans i.17," ExpT 92 (1980–81) 205–8, following the lead of Weiss, 75; Godet, 94–97; Sanday and Headlam, 28; Lightfoot, Notes, 250–51; Schlier, 46; Murray, 33; the translation linking "by faith" with the verb is currently accepted by Fitzmyer, 265; Haacker, 44; Schreiner, 74.

115 Schlatter, 26; Michel, 90–91.

116 See Binder, Glaube, 40–44, 76; Käsemann, 32.

117 Koch, Schrift, 276–77; Eskola, Theodicy, 106–10; Oegema, Israel und die Völker, 111.

118 Neuman and Nida, 21.

119 Bockmuehl, Revelation and Mystery, 138.

communities, rather than force of arms or apocalyptic military miracle, is the means by which such righteousness is restored. In the establishment of faith communities as far as the ends of the known world, God will be restoring arenas where righteousness is accomplished, thus creating salvation. In place of the salvation of the *Pax Romana,* based on military power and imperial administration, there is the salvation of small groups who believe in the gospel of Christ crucified. Paul's goal in this letter is to encourage their cooperation with each other to extend this new form of salvation to the end of the world. The global offensive in behalf of divine righteousness envisioned by Romans is missional and persuasive rather than martial and coercive. The implications of this audacious thesis are developed in the rest of this letter.

1:18—4:25 Part IVA. The First Proof: The Gospel Expresses the Impartial Righteousness of God by Overturning Claims of Cultural Superiority and by Rightwising Jews and Greeks through Grace Alone

1

The First Half of the First Pericope

The Revelation of Divine Wrath

a. Thesis and Rationale: The Exposure of Human Suppression of the Truth about God

18/ **For the wrath of God[a] is being revealed from heaven against all impiety and wrongdoing of humans who are suppressing the truth[b] by unrighteousness, 19/ because what can be known about God is manifest within them. For God has manifested [it] to them. 20/ For his invisible attributes are seen, becoming discerned from the creation of the world in the things made, namely his eternal[c] power and divinity, so that they are without excuse, 21/ because although they knew God, they did not glorify [God] as God or give [God] thanks, but they were made futile in their thinking, and their senseless heart was darkened. 22/ While claiming to be wise, they were made witless; 23/ and they changed[d] the glory of the imperishable God into a likeness of an image of a perishable human and birds and four-legged animals and reptiles.**

a   The lack of the word $\Theta\epsilon o\hat{v}$ ("of God") in 1908 *pc* and, according to Michel, 97, in Marcion is particularly understandable in the latter instance because of his ascription of wrath to the evil being worshiped by the Jews.

b   The addition of $\tau o\hat{v}\ \Theta\epsilon o\hat{v}$ ("of God") after "truth" in ar vg^{cl} sa Ambst, appearing occasionally elsewhere in Western theology since Hippolytes *De anti.* 64, according to Lietzmann, 31, is clearly a theological correction that is actually redundant if one follows Paul's argument closely.

c   The deletion of $\dot{\alpha}\dot{i}\delta\iota o\varsigma$ ("eternal") in L 1506* *pc* is probably a scribal error, not discussed in any of the commentaries.

d   The middle form of the verb, $\dot{\eta}\lambda\lambda\dot{\alpha}\xi\alpha\nu\tau o$ ("they gave in exchange, exchanged for themselves"), is found in K 6 88 630 *al* and conforms to LXX Ps 105:20. The active verb $\ddot{\eta}\lambda\lambda\alpha\xi\alpha\nu$ ("they exchanged") is the widely attested and probably original formulation.

Analysis

The first proof in Paul's argument opens with a rhetorical tour de force,[1] a beautifully balanced thesis statement about the revelation of wrath in 1:18,[2] which is followed by a rationale expressed in four periods with balanced lines. The two periods in this half of the pericope describe the shape of human sin requiring the response of divine wrath. The two in the next half of the pericope (1:24-32) describe the indications that humans are under divine wrath. While the two periods in 1:18-23 take up the themes of impiety and wickedness in 1:18 in chiastic order, the themes in 1:24-32 are discussed in the original order of 1:18.[3] The thesis in 1:18, identified as a "programmatic contention" by Michel,[4] is linked by chiasm with 1:17:[5]

1   See Wilckens, 1:96; for a discussion of the structural analysis see Popkes, "Aufbau," 490–501.

2   See Popkes, "Aufbau," 490–501, esp. 495; Aletti, "Rm 1,18–3,20," 48–49, suggests that 1:18 is a *"propositio"* rather than a thesis, followed by 1:18-32 as a *"narratio,"* 2:1–3:19 as a *"probatio,"* and 3:20 as a *"peroratio."* Aletti's analysis appears to confuse the arrangement of a discourse as a whole with the organization of a proof.

3   See Wilckens, 1:96. "Unrighteousness" is developed in 1:18b-21 and "impiety" in 1:22-23, the reverse of their order in 1:18a. In contrast "impiety" is developed in 1:25-27 and "unrighteousness" in 1:28-32.

4   Michel, 96.

5   See Harvey, *Listening*, 185.

δικαιοσύνη γὰρ θεοῦ ἐν αὐτῷ <u>ἀποκαλύπτεται</u> . . .
<u>ἀποκαλύπτεται</u> γὰρ ὀργὴ θεοῦ . . .

The thesis consists of three lines of 13 syllables apiece in which the last two are marked by assonance in the alpha negatives, reduplication in the use of "unrighteousness," and homoioteleuton, thus producing the following rhyme:

2. . . . ἀσέβειαν καὶ ἀδικίαν ἀνθρώπων
3. . . . ἀδικίᾳ κατεχόντων.[6]

The sentences beginning in 1:19 and 1:21 have identical opening conjunctions followed by "know" and "God" and are of roughly comparable length. There are several striking examples of paronomasia in 1:19-21, with γνωστόν ("known") in v. 19 echoed by γνόντες ("they knew") in v. 21, with φανερόν ("manifest") in v. 19a replicated by ἐφανέρωσεν ("he manifested") in v. 19b, and ἀόρατα ("invisible") in v. 20a replicated in antithetical form by καθορᾶται ("are made visible") in v. 20b. Διότι ("because") in v. 19 is duplicated by διότι in v. 21, while Θεός appears four times, echoing θειότης ("divinity") in v. 20. There is a synonymous parallelism between lines 1:21b and c in the second sentence,[7] while the next line has an elegant internal antithesis: "claiming to be wise, they were made fools." This antithesis is embodied in the next two lines by another example of paronomasia, with ἀφθάρτου θεοῦ ("immortal God") in v. 23a standing in opposition to φθαρτοῦ ἀνθρώπου ("mortal human") in v. 23b, while the final three nouns in v. 23c display homoioptoton in the genitive plural endings that contain the dental roots (ν-δ-τ): πετεινῶν καὶ τετραπόδων καὶ ἑρπετῶν ("of birds and animals and serpents"). So rhetorically rich and elegant is this mate-rial that Johannes Weiss suggested that Paul may have refined it in frequently repeated preaching on the wrath of God.[8]

A major issue concerns the scope of the first pericope (1:18ff.) with Klostermann, Jeremias, Dupont, and others arguing for the beginning of a separate pericope at 1:22,[9] but Wilckens and Cranfield arguing for a major break at 1:25.[10] Dunn divides the material from 1:18-32 into two pericopes, with the second beginning at v. 26.[11] Other commentators follow the division adopted here with the material from 1:18-32 viewed as a single discourse containing two pericopes, of which the second begins at v. 24.[12] The Nestle text and Louw's "semantic discourse analysis" also place a major break at v. 24.[13] Popkes weighs these alternatives and shows that there is wide agreement on v. 18 as an opening thesis and on v. 32 as a concluding remark. He has difficulty in assessing the flow of the argument in vv. 19-24, which he follows Wilckens in holding together.[14] I am impressed with the continuity between the mental and psychic disabling theme in v. 21 and the description of folly in vv. 22-23. The subject shifts from humans' changing the truth about God in vv. 18-23 to the divine response in v. 24 with the solemn declaration "therefore God delivered them . . . ," which requires a break at that point. The thrice-repeated παρέδωκεν in vv. 24, 26, and 28[15] leads me to place them in a separate pericope from the material in vv. 18-23. Nevertheless, the passage from v. 18 through v. 32 is so tightly woven together that many other links between various verses and subparagraph need to be acknowledged. Klostermann in particular has made a compelling case for a correspondence between deed and punishment; he links the assault on God's δόξα ("glory/honor") in v. 23 with the consignment to

6   See Weiss, "Beiträge," 214; Pallis, 40, deplores the obviousness of the reduplication, describing ἀδικίαν/ἀδικία as "an incredibly unskillful combination."

7   The synonymous parallelism consists of two lines of roughly equal length, with 16 and 15 syllables, respectively:

     1:21b—but they became futile in their thinking,
     1:21c—and their senseless heart was darkened.

8   Weiss, "Beiträge," 213.

9   Klostermann, "Adäquate Vergeltung," 1–6; Jeremias, "Röm 1.22-32," 119–21; Dupont, "Problème," 392;

     other literature listed in Lyonnet, "Notes," 35.

10   Wilckens, 1:95; Cranfield, 1:105.

11   Dunn, 1:52–53.

12   Lagrange, 21; Michel, 96–97; Kühl, 55.

13   Louw, 2:43.

14   Popkes, "Aufbau," 492, 499.

15   See Bouman, "Römer 1," 411.

dishonorable relationships in v. 24 and perceives similar correspondences that link the sections in the next pericope.[16] Taking all of the evidence into account, I think it is appropriate to consider vv. 18-32 a closely linked argument on the theme of the divine wrath, subdivided into two pericopes of roughly equal length with a thematic break at v. 24 with the first of three announcements of divine consignment.

Rhetorical Disposition

IV. The *Probatio*

1:18– 4:25	A. The first proof: The gospel expresses the impartial righteousness of God by overturning claims of cultural superiority and by rightwising Jews and Gentiles through grace alone
1:18-32	1. The gospel's revelation of divine wrath
1:18-23	a. Thesis and rationale: the exposure of human suppression of the truth about God
1:18	1) The thesis about divine wrath
1:18a	a) The current revelation of wrath in the gospel
1:18b	b) The form of human guilt: "impiety" and "wrongdoing"
1:18c	c) The action of guilty humans: suppression of "the truth"
1:19-20	2) The rationale: a description of the truth that humans suppress
1:19a	a) Divine knowledge is intrinsically available to humans
1:19b	b) The reason for the availability of truth: divine manifestation
1:20a	c) The invisibility of God since creation
1:20b	d) The visibility of God in the "things that are made"
1:20c	e) The clarification of "mental images" in terms of "power and deity"
1:20d	f) The consequence for humans: "no excuse"
1:21-23	3) The rationale: the manner in which humans suppress the truth about God
1:21a	a) The refusal to acknowledge God
	(1) The refusal to give God glory
	(2) The refusal to give God thanks
1:21b	b) The resultant futility of thought
1:21c	c) The resultant darkening of the heart
1:22	d) The resultant antithesis of claiming wisdom while acting the part of the fool
1:23a	e) The foolish exchange of imperishable glory
1:23b	f) The replacement of imperishable glory by facsimiles
	(1) Human being
	(2) Birds
	(3) Quadrupeds
	(4) Reptiles

Exegesis

■ **18** While most commentators understand the description of divine wrath within the traditional parameters of Jewish or Greco-Roman ideas of retribution,[17] the present tense of ἀποκαλύπτεται, which replicates the form used in 1:17, points toward a new understanding of wrath from the perspective of the gospel.[18] Rather than attempting to make Paul's argument conform to the traditional parameters, my effort here will be to follow the logic of the rhetorical premises already laid down in 1:1-17. Since Paul is writing to converted believers in Rome for whom the gospel of the death and resurrection of Christ is already understood and assumed, he does not reiterate the christological grounding of his theory here. As the subsequent argument shows, Paul is operating on the assumption that the gospel of Christ (1:17) reveals the shameful "secrets of the heart" (2:16; 1 Cor 14:25) that humans attempt to suppress. The cross of Christ reveals the unacknowledged tendency to stamp out the truth and to wage war against God so that humans and institutions can maintain their guise of superior virtue and honor. The resurrection of Christ exposed this vicious secret at the heart of the human endeavor, and reveals the shocking truth about the nature of the attempted reversal in the roles of humans and God. In their competition for honor, they claim a status due only to God and end up in shameful distortion. The present preaching of the gospel "reveals" this hidden reality.[19]

16 Klostermann, "Adäquate Vergeltung," 3–6.
17 See R. V. G. Tasker, *The Biblical Doctrine of the Wrath of God* (London: Tyndale, 1951); Synofzik, *Vergeltungsaussagen*, 79–80. For attempts to move beyond this framework, see G. H. C. Macgregor, "The Concept of the Wrath of God in the New Testament," *NTS* 7 (1960–61) 101–9; C. F. D. Moule, "Punishment and Retribution: An Attempt to Delimit Their Scope in New Testament Thought," *SEÅ* 30 (1966) 21–36; and Calvin R. Schoonhoven, *The Wrath of Heaven* (Grand Rapids: Eerdmans, 1966).
18 See Cranfield, 1:110, and esp. Wilckens, 1:102.
19 See Wilckens, 1:102, for an explanation of the apocalyptic tradition of using the word "reveal" to

Since "wrath" is redefined by the gospel, a present progressive translation of the present passive ἀποκαλύπτεται ("is being revealed") is appropriate.[20] This passive verb has significant implications for Paul's mission, because he is presenting the ongoing process of wrath (1:18), as well as eliciting "obedience of faith" as divinely guided and inspired.[21] The explicit reference to the revelation ἀπ᾽ οὐρανοῦ ("from heaven")[22] suggests the grounding of the entire edifice on the divinely authenticated witness "by the power of signs and wonders" (15:19)[23] to the death and resurrection of Christ. Following the premises laid down in the confession of 1:3-4, the resurrection "designated" Jesus as the "Son of God," thus revealing the "impiety and wickedness" (1:18) of those who crucified him. The "revelation of wrath" relentlessly exposes the awful truth that the human race constantly attempts to suppress about the true nature of its relationships. The gospel therefore reveals wrath, not simply by reminding of future punishment[24] or of "the inevitable process of cause and effect in a moral universe,"[25] but by indicating the culpability of the human race at so egregious a level as to make retribution morally necessary[26] and inevitable. Nevertheless, wrath is not the final word. Even though Paul expects further enactments of wrath to take place in the very near future,[27] the ultimate purpose of God is that all people will be saved (5:18; 11:26, 32; 14:9).[28] As the first proof in Romans goes on to show, the appropriate response to wrath is faithful acceptance of the grace of God (3:22-23).

This interpretation allows the γάρ ("for") of 1:18 to be taken with full seriousness. As a "marker of cause or reason,"[29] γάρ indicates that the discussion of wrath directly supports the thesis about the gospel in 1:16-17 rather than expressing its antithesis,[30] describing the deplorable state of human affairs evident without the perspective of the gospel,[31] or characterizing the era

---

describe the disclosure of future events that the seer conveys to his contemporary hearers: "In this sense the revelation of the wrath of God occurs in present proclamation." Since the verb means "to unhide" something, the concept presupposes that God's wrath has been hidden from general recognition.

20 While the present tense is often employed as a "present of anticipation" of future events (Smyth, *Grammar*, §1879), the reference to God's revelation "in the present time" in 1:17 requires that a present process be acknowledged in the verb of 1:18.

21 See Jonathan Draper's introduction to Colenso, 9.

22 See Hans-Joachim Eckstein, "'Denn Gottes Zorn wird vom Himmel her offenbar werden.' Exegetische Erwägungen zu Röm 1:18," *ZNW* 78 (1987) 83–86, for the construal of ἀπ᾽ οὐρανοῦ as a reference to the parousia, citing 1 Thess 1:9-10 and 2 Thess 1:7 along with Jewish apocalyptic texts. Similarly, Roetzel, *Judgement*, 81ff.; Herold, *Zorn*, 306ff.; and Käsemann, 38, opt for a futuristic, apocalyptic significance. Although the present tense can sometimes be employed for the future (Smyth, *Grammar*, §1879), the indications in this passage do not support this future interpretation. In addition to the present tense of the verb ἀποκαλύπτεται in 1:18, there is an explicit reference to a present revelation of the gospel in 1:17. The heavenly revelation of which Romans speaks is that of the gospel, with ἀπ᾽ οὐρανοῦ understood adverbially as defining "reveal," as Eckstein, "Denn Gottes Zorn," 79,

rightly insists. These details render improbable that "heaven" is merely a euphemism for God, indicating the divine origin of wrath as suggested by Michel, 97, and Cranfield, 1:111.

23 See Philippi, 21.

24 Eckstein provides a defense of the futuristic interpretation in "Denn Gottes Zorn," 82–89, resolutely disregarding the present tense of the verb.

25 See Dodd, 23.

26 For a discussion of "the settled and active opposition of God's holy nature to everything that is evil," without sharing the emphasis on the death and resurrection of Christ proposed here, see Morris, 76–77.

27 See Rom 2:5, 8; 5:9.

28 See Bonda, *One Purpose*, 79: "In Romans Paul does indeed speak of condemnation but he indicates in no way that this is God's final purpose for the condemned! On the contrary, all the remaining chapters of the letter focus on the *salvation* of condemned humanity (Rom. 5:18)." Italics in original. See also 257–61.

29 BAGD (2000) 189.

30 Stuhlmacher, *Gerechtigkeit*, 80–81, argues on the basis of OT parallels that the wrath of God must always be counterposed against the righteousness of God; this interpretation would be more plausible if Paul had used "but" rather than "for" in 1:18.

31 For instance, see Tholuck, 57; Weiss, 76; Zahn, 86–87; Bruce, 83.

before the proclamation of grace.[32] As Bornkamm showed, "the 'for' in 1.18 is not a 'simple transition particle'[33] but explicitly establishes what is said in 1.16f. about 'salvation.'"[34] Bornkamm explained this point by reflecting on the eschatological character of the gospel implicit in the present tense of the repeated "is revealed," which enhances the seriousness of the warning about the wrath.[35]

The target of divine wrath is against "all impiety and wrongdoing of humans," an encompassing description of what is wrong with the human race as a whole. Despite a later reference to characteristically pagan failures (1:23), the formulation with "all" indicates that Paul wishes to insinuate that Jews as well as Romans, Greeks, and barbarians are being held responsible.[36] "Impiety" (ἀσέβεια) and "wrongdoing" (ἀδικία) are not really synonyms[37] but distinct moral categories in the Greco-Roman world and to a lesser degree in the Jewish environment.[38] For Greeks and Romans, ἀσέβεια/impietas is the most heinous crime—the failure to respect deity,[39] especially in the civic cult.[40] In Greek-speaking Judaism, ἀσέβεια and its associated terms refer to impious actions rather than to attitudes or specifically proscribed crimes.[41] Paul's description of impiety in 1:21-23 that is specifically oriented to the Greco-Roman audience partially explains why this term that is so uncharacteristic of Paul[42] is used here. The term ἀδικία and its Latin equivalents are used with similar connotations of "wrongdoing," "injustice," and "lawbreaking" by the various cultural groups in the Mediterranean world.[43] The prominent repetition of this term in v. 18 signals its decisive link with the antithetical term δικαιοσύνη in the thesis of vv. 16-17 and suggests the opposition of humans against God.[44]

---

32 Lietzmann, 31; Jülicher, 233.

33 Advocated by Lietzmann, 31.

34 Bornkamm, "Revelation," 63.

35 Ibid., 62–63.

36 These details appear to be overlooked by commentators who construe 1:18-32 as a denunciation of pagans. For example, see Michel, 96–97; Käsemann, 36–38; Schlier, 48–50; Bruce, 81–82. See also Flückiger, "Rom. 1,18–2,3," 156–58. Perhaps following Zahn, 83, Cranfield is closer to the goal of Paul's argument when he says on 106: "So we understand these verses as the revelation of the gospel's judgment of all men, which lays bare not only the idolatry of ancient and modern paganism but also the idolatry ensconced in Israel, in the Church, and in the life of each believer." For arguments that Paul attacks the wickedness of both Jews and Gentiles in this passage, see Colenso, 37–39; Dabelstein, *Beurteilung*, 73–79.

37 See Käsemann, 38, and Wilckens, 1:104.

38 Fitzmyer, 278, notes both terms are used as a pair in LXX Ps 73:6 and Prov 11:5, but that "godlessness" is specifically linked to the "nations" in Deut 9:5.

39 See Erich Fascher, "Der Vorwurf der Gottlosigkeit in der Auseinandersetzung bei Juden, Griechen und Christen," in Otto Betz et al., eds., *Abraham unser Vater. Juden und Christen im Gespräch über die Bibel. Festschrift für Otto Michel*, AGSU 5 (Leiden: Brill, 1963) 78–93; also W. Nestle, "Asebieprozesse," *RAC* 1 (1950) 735–40; and D. Kaufmann-Bühler, "Euse-beia," *RAC* 6 (1966) 985–1052. Meister, "Tugenden," 7–8, shows that one of the three most important "pillars" of the Roman moral system was *pietas*, the sense of obligation to respect the gods, parents, and the state. Cicero *Nat. d.* 1.4 states, "When piety (*pietas*) goes, religion and sanctity go along with it. And when they are gone, there is anarchy and complete confusion in our way of life." Cited by Incigneri, *Gospel to the Romans*, 210.

40 Briefly noted by Dunn, 1:55; details in Josef Liegle, "Pietas," in Hans Oppermann, ed., *Römische Wertbegriffe* (Darmstadt: Wissenschaftliche Buchgesellschaft, 1983) 229–73, who shows that "piety" was understood as *the* Roman virtue, depicted on coins, celebrated in state propaganda, and embodied in laws related to the civic cult.

41 See Werner Foerster, "ἀσεβής κτλ.," *TDNT* 7 (1971) 187–89.

42 Aside from the quotation in 11:26, ἀσέβεια is not used elsewhere in the authentic Pauline letters, while ἀσεβής ("the impious person") is used only in 4:5 and 5:6. The interest in communicating with the unique Roman audience is signaled by this peculiar usage. See Blumenfeld, *Political Paul*, 319–23.

43 See BAGD, 17–18; Gottfried Quell, "δίκη κτλ.," *TDNT* 2 (1964) 174–78; Gottlob Schrenk, "δίκη," *TDNT* 2 (1964) 178–81; Schrenk, "ἀδικία," *TDNT* 1 (1964) 155.

44 See Dunn, 1:56; Adams, "Abraham's Faith," 51; Calvert-Koyzis, *Paul*, 124–26.

The essence of humankind's unrighteous design is to "suppress the truth" about God. The immediate context indicates that $\alpha\lambda\acute{\eta}\vartheta\epsilon\iota\alpha$ refers to the true status of God.[45] $K\alpha\tau\acute{\epsilon}\chi\omega$ in this context means to hold down, to take captive, and as the argument in v. 25 makes plain, to exchange position with God.[46] Cranfield suggests that the present participle $\tau\acute{\eta}\nu\ldots\kappa\alpha\tau\epsilon\chi\acute{o}\nu\tau\omega\nu$ requires the translation "try to suppress . . . ."[47] The conative sense, however, is more accurately captured with the progressive present: "are suppressing," and avoids Cranfield's value judgment concerning the ineffectual quality of such "trying." Such a value judgment may properly be derived from Paul's argument as a whole but not from this particular verbal form. What the gospel reveals is the ongoing human effort to suppress the truth. Persons and regimes constantly try to cover up the truth about themselves and their self-serving quests for superior honor, as revealed paradigmatically in the crucifixion of the Righteous One. His "resurrection from the dead" (v. 4), however, gives Paul confidence that divine truth is triumphant. The wrath of God sets limits that the human race incessantly tries to thwart, but Romans contends that the "wrath of God" is currently being "revealed" in the gospel message in such a way as to expose the "unrighteousness of humans."

■ **19** The conjunction $\delta\iota\acute{o}\tau\iota$ ("because") connects this verse with the final phrase of v. 18[48] and describes how humans suppress the truth. The phrase $\tau\grave{o}\ \gamma\nu\omega\sigma\tau\grave{o}\nu\ \tau o\hat{u}\ \vartheta\epsilon o\hat{u}$ should be translated "what can be known[49] about[50] God," similar to the classical usage as exemplified in Epictetus.[51] Paul is consistent at this point with Jewish writings that maintain God's self-revelation to be partial and elusive.[52] Whether this revelation occurs subjectively within each person's conscience[53] or publicly within each cultural group[54] is impossible to determine from the phrase $\acute{\epsilon}\nu\ \alpha\grave{u}\tauo\hat{\iota}\varsigma$.[55] I therefore make the ambiguous translation "within them." One point remains clear, despite the ambiguity: the link between $\alpha\grave{u}\tauo\hat{\iota}\varsigma$ and the plural reference to humans in v. 18 allows no discrimination between persons and groups. In contrast to the antinomies of alleged superiority mentioned in vv. 14-16, the knowledge of God is available to all.[56] A decisive

---

45   See Daxer, *Römer*, 8–20.

46   See esp. Wilckens, 1:105. Fitzmyer, 278, suggests the translation "stifle the truth." The significance of "banish" as found in the magical papyri does not seem to be in view here; see Käsemann, 38. Daxer, *Römer*, 17, overlooks Paul's aggressive formulation when he contends that failure to acknowledge the truth about God derives from "weakness of spirit, from foolishness."

47   Cranfield, 1:112, stresses the conative force of the present participle and cites BDF, p. 167 (§319), which discusses the present indicative "in [which] the durative present is bound up with the notion of incompleteness."

48   As suggested by Cranfield, 1:113; Morris, 79.

49   The translation "known," which would be consistent with other biblical usage (Sir 21:7; Luke 2:44; John 18:15; Acts 1:19; 17:23), would produce a tautology in that what is already understood is now being manifested; see Godet, 103; P. O. Schjött, "Eine Religionsphilosophische Stelle bei Paulus. Röm 1,18-20," *ZNW* 4 (1903) 76; Anton Fridrichsen, *Exegetical Writings. A Selection*, trans. and ed. C. C. Caragounis and T. Fornberg, WUNT 76 (Tübingen: Mohr-Siebeck, 1994) 160; Schlier, 51; Cranfield, 1:113; BAGD 164. For advocacy of the typical biblical usage, see Meyer, 78–79. Hellmut Rosin argues for "known" on dogmatic grounds in "To gnoston tou Theou," *ThZ* 17 (1961) 161–65. For philosophi-

cal background see Knut Kleve, *Gnosis Theon. Die Lehre von der natürlichen Gotteserkenntnis in der epikureischen Theologie*, SO.S 19 (Oslo: Universitetsforlaget, 1963).

50   The genitive is not to be understood in a partitive sense, "what can be known of God," but in an objective sense, "about God." For a discussion of the alternatives, see Rudolf Bultmann, "$\gamma\nu\omega\sigma\tau\acute{o}\varsigma$," *TDNT* 1 (1964) 719.

51   Epictetus, *Diss.* 2.20.4, refutes the thoroughgoing skeptic who claims $\acute{o}\tau\iota\ o\grave{u}\delta\acute{\epsilon}\nu\ \acute{\epsilon}\sigma\tau\iota\ \gamma\nu\omega\sigma\tau\acute{o}\nu$ ("that nothing is knowable").

52   Dunn, 1:56, cites in this connection Exod 33:20; Deut 4:12; Sir 43:31; *Sib. Or.* 3.17; Josephus *Bell.* 7.346; *C. Ap.* 2.167; Philo *Somn.* 1.65–66, 68–69; *Post.* 16-20. Philo *Leg.* 1.60–61, is typical in describing the elusive location where divine knowledge lies. For a discussion of the theological implications of this theme, see Samuel Terrien, *The Elusive Presence: Toward a New Biblical Theology*, RP 26 (San Francisco: Harper & Row, 1978).

53   See Godet, 103; Meyers, 79, cites the reference to "heart" and "conscience" in 2:15.

54   See Michel, 99; Cranfield, 1:113–14.

55   See Kuss, 1:36.

56   Ps 19:1-6 contains a similar assumption that the natural world "declares the glory of God," which presumably everyone who can see the stars can understand. However, the universal implication of

break with later Jewish theology is evident, for instance, in Paul's claim that the knowledge of God was available to every human, which obviously includes Gentiles and barbarians. As Bietenhard has shown, nowhere in Judaism was there an admission of a natural knowledge of God for Gentiles.[57] The contention of Hellenistic Judaism was the exact opposite of what we encounter in Romans:

> For by nature all men were foolish, and had no perception of God ($\vartheta\epsilon o\hat{v}\ \dot{\alpha}\gamma\nu\omega\sigma\acute{\iota}\alpha$),
>
> And from the good things to be seen had not power to know him ($o\dot{v}\kappa\ \ddot{\iota}\sigma\chi\upsilon\sigma\alpha\nu\ \epsilon\dot{\iota}\delta\acute{\epsilon}\nu\alpha\iota\ \tau\dot{\eta}\nu\ \ddot{o}\nu\tau\alpha$) that is, Neither by giving heed to the works did they recognize the artificer. (Wis 13:1)

In contrast to Gentiles, the Jews have access to the truth about God and are guaranteed access to the "root of immortality" (Wis 15:1-6). To admit genuine knowledge of God on the part of Gentiles would be to abandon the foundation of God's self-revelation to Israel through the Torah, which established Israel as the chosen nation.[58] Conversely, some Greco-Roman critics disputed access to genuine knowledge of God on the part of Jews.[59] Similarly, the presumption in Greco-Roman culture was that the educated have the possibility of knowing God, whereas fools and barbarians do not.

In view of the reluctance in the Greco-Roman world to grant legitimate knowledge of God to one's cultural inferiors, it is striking to observe how bluntly and unequivocally Paul speaks of divine manifestation to everyone. The play on the term "manifest" points to the interest in knowledge through divine disclosure that was characteristic of early Christianity, but that $\varphi\alpha\nu\epsilon\rho\acute{o}\omega$ ("manifest") is used synonymously with $\dot{\alpha}\pi o\kappa\alpha\lambda\acute{v}\pi\tau\omega$ ("reveal") and hence points to precisely the same phenomenon[60] seems unlikely because knowledge of God through the created order hardly derives from the gospel proclamation of the Christ event, which was the specific connotation of "reveal" both in vv. 17 and 18. The use of the aorist tense in $\dot{\epsilon}\varphi\alpha\nu\acute{\epsilon}\rho\omega\sigma\epsilon\nu$ ("has manifested") may imply a self-revelation of God to humankind at the time of the creation.[61] At any rate, the emphatic sentence "God manifested it to them" conveys an insistence on divine intentionality. While certain members of Paul's audience may have been inclined to dispute the innate capabilities of their competitors to "know God," they would hardly doubt God's power of self-manifestation. In contrast to most forms of natural theology in which qualified humans have access to divine knowledge, Paul relies on the classic biblical doctrine of divine self-disclosure to explain the truth that humans attempt to suppress.

■ **20** With rhetorical finesse, Paul fuses the biblical doctrines of revelation and creation with the Greco-Roman

---

this language is mitigated somewhat by the fusion with explicitly Jewish theologoumena concerning the "law of the Lord," "the decrees of the Lord," "the commandment of the Lord," and the "ordinances of the Lord" that the "servant" of God must follow (Ps 19:7-10).

57 Hans Bietenhard, "Natürliche Gotteserkenntnis der Heiden? Eine Erwägung zu Röm 1," *ThZ* 12 (1956) 275–88. Bussmann comes to a similar conclusion in *Missionspredigt*, 111–19.

58 Ibid., 288.

59 Josephus *C. Ap.* 2.80 refutes Apion's accusation that the Jews worship an ass's head, and in 2.148 Apollonius's charge that Jews are atheists. For a discussion of the hostile accusations against Jewish religion that were frequently expressed in Egypt, see M. Stern, "The Jews in Greek and Latin Literature," in Safrai and Stern, *Jewish People*, 2:1115–17. Stern, 1142, notes "a long-standing Graeco-Roman tradition" of viewing Jews as superstitious and cites Apuleius as viewing "the Jews as *superstitiosi* par

excellence." Stern cites Apuleius *Flor.* 6 in this connection, noting also that Cicero in *Pro Flacco* and *De provinciis consularibus* decried the Jewish religion as superstition (1144). As Gager points out in *Origins*, 39–88, these negative evaluations were not universally held.

60 See Dieter Lührmann and Rudolf Bultmann, "$\varphi\alpha\nu\epsilon\rho\acute{o}\omega$," *TDNT* 9 (1974) 4; and P.-G. Müller, "$\varphi\alpha\nu\epsilon\rho\acute{o}\omega$," *EDNT* 3 (1993) 413–14. The critique of the premise of synonymous use is developed by Bockmuehl, "Verb $\varphi\alpha\nu\epsilon\rho\acute{o}\omega$," 87–89, 93–96.

61 This suggestion rests on the reference to the creation in 1:20, but is not discussed by the commentators. Michel, 99, attributes the tense to the stylistic shifts between present and aorist that is characteristic of this passage, but this suggestion throws no light on its precise meaning here. In *Revelation and Mystery*, 141, Bockmuehl infers from this aorist verb that Paul wished to refer to God as having "already demonstrated" his deity at the time of creation.

doctrine of divinity visible in the natural world. The hostile debate between Protestant and Catholic scholars over the issue of natural revelation has skewed our understanding of this passage in polemical directions and obscured the straightforward synthesis that Paul achieved.[62] While the κτίσις κόσμου ("creation of the world") as an event in time about which one can say "since" is characteristically Judeo-Christian,[63] the rest of the language in this verse gives the impression of technical philosophical usage. Since the prepositional phrase ἀπὸ κτίσεως κόσμου ("since the creation of the world") and the dative expression τοῖς ποιήμασιν ("in the things that are made") must be construed with the participle νοούμενα ("discerned"), which supplements the verb καθορᾶται ("are made visible"),[64] I translate with the rather awkward expression, "are seen, becoming discerned."[65] The idea of τὰ ἀόρατα ("the invisible attributes") of God's being "made visible" (καθορᾶται) in the natural world is found in Stoicism[66] and adapted by Hellenistic Judaism.[67] The concept of attributes "discerned in the things that are made" (τοῖς ποιήμασιν νοούμενα) appears to be a Pauline adaptation of Platonic usage,[68] since no exact parallel has been found.[69] The peculiar combination of mental images with created objects rather than with abstract reflections of divine archetypes may be an effort to avoid Platonic idealism.[70]

In the syntax of v. 20, I understand the expression ἥ τε ἀΐδιος αὐτοῦ δύναμις καὶ θειότης to be in apposition to the subject, "God's invisible attributes." The word "namely" in my translation indicates such apposi-

62 For instance, see Edmund Schlink, "Die Offenbarung Gottes in seinen Werken und die Ablehnung der natürlichen Theologie," *ThBl* 20 (1941) 1–14; Kuss, 1:32–40; Käsemann, 39–44.

63 See Werner Foerster, "κτίζω κτλ.," *TDNT* 3 (1964) 1000–1035; Brinkman, "Creation II," 359. A similar expression is found in the *Apoc. El.* (C) 3.11-12, "Remember that the Lord instituted fasting *from his creation of the heavens* as a benefit to mankind."

64 See Smyth, *Grammar*, §§2088–89, 2110–12, 2094.

65 Meyer, 79, explains that "νοούμενα defines the *manner* in which the καθορᾶται takes place," and suggests the translation "the works are seen becoming discerned." Godet, 103, speaks of "intellectual perception."

66 Käsemann, 39, cites Pseudo-Aristotle *Mund.* 399a-b, which refers to God as ἀόρατος ὢν ἄλλῳ πλὴν λογισμῷ ("unseen except to the eye of reason"), "yet being invisible to every mortal he is seen through his deeds." Similarly Epictetus writes, "God brought in humankind to be a spectator of him and his works" (*Diss.* 1.6.19) and proceeds in 6.20 to argue that God "is already present in his own works" (ἀλλ᾽ ἔστιν ἤδη καὶ πάρεστιν τοῖς ἔργοις) that we are to "behold" (θεάσασθαι) and "perceive" (κατανοῆσαι). See also Erich Fascher, "Deus invisibilis," (1931) 41–77.

67 For instance, Wis 13:5; *Ep. Arist.* 132. According to Wilhelm Michaelis, "ὁράω κτλ.," *TDNT* 5 (1967) 368, Philo uses ἀόρατος more than 100 times and understands the human mind (νοῦς) as the organ capable of perceiving the divine archetypes in the created order. In *Spec. Leg.* 1.302 Philo speaks of the mind as perceiving "both the visible and the invisible and immaterial (ὁρατὸς καὶ ὁ ἀόρατος καὶ

68 ἀσώματος), the pattern of the visible heaven." Wilhelm Michaelis, "ὁράω κτλ.," *TDNT* 5 (1967) 380, shows that the participial construction νοούμενα καθορᾶται "is designed to show unambiguously that an intellectual process is in view," so that Paul is not claiming apprehension purely by sensory perception. The distinction between νοούμενον as a purely mental image and φαινόμενον as sensory perception goes back to Plato. H. Herring, "Noumenon/Phaenomenon," *HWP* 6.987, cites Plato *Resp.* 337c5; 517b8; 523b5; 596e4; 598b3; 602d8; *Parm.* 165c7; 166b6, for examples of νοούμενα. See also Dietmar Wyrwa, "Über die Begegnung des biblischen Glaubens mit dem griechischen Geist," *ZThK* 88 (1991) 49; and Wolfgang Wieland, *Platon und die Formen des Wissens* (Göttingen: Vandenhoeck & Ruprecht, 1982) 224–52. The suggestion by Schjött, "Röm 1,18-20," 77, to construe τὰ ἀόρατα as a simple adjective modifying νοούμενα and to translate as "the invisible thoughts of God" was refuted by Fridrichsen, *Selection*, 160–65.

69 See the rather distant Stoic parallels listed in Lietzmann, 31–32; and E. Würthwein, "νοέω κτλ.," *TDNT* 4 (1967) 950–51.

70 In the *Tim.* 92c, for example, Plato concludes, "For this very cosmos, having taken mortal and immortal creatures and having thus become fulfilled—a visible creature surrounding visible things—became an image of what can be conceived of, a God that can be perceived of (ζῷον ὁρατὸν τὰ ὁρατὰ περιέχον, εἰκὼν τοῦ νοητοῦ θεὸς αἰσθητός), greatest, best, most beautiful, and most perfect, being this single, only-begotten Heaven."

71 Smyth, *Grammar*, 1143.

tion, but the expression itself requires further explanation. When a single article is followed by two or more nouns connected by "and," this "produces the effect of a single notion."[71] In this case δύναμις ("power") and θειότης ("deity") are linked with καί ("and"), producing the odd expression "God-power."[72] This unique formulation combines the crucial terms "God" and "power" from the thesis statement in v. 16 with the classical Greek concept of ἀΐδιος ("eternity")[73] that occurs in Hellenistic philosophy of religion[74] and is found elsewhere only in Wis 18:9, where it refers to the divine origin of the law. The distinction popularized in medieval dogmatics between θειότης as pertaining to the divine nature and attributes and θεότης (Col 2:9) as the divine personality[75] was not reflected in Hellenistic usage and should not be read back into Romans.[76]

Verse 20 ends with a purpose phrase constructed out of the preposition εἰς ("so that, consequently") followed by the articular infinitive τὸ εἶναι ("to be") and the accusative αὐτοὺς ἀναπολογήτους ("they are without excuse"). The term ἀναπολόγητος ("without excuse") derives from Greek legal and rhetorical usage concerning defense speeches[77] and is used nowhere else in the Bible aside from 2:1. In view of the universal scope of Paul's argument as established in 1:18-19, which encompasses the social antimonies of Greeks/barbarians, wise/foolish, and Jews/Gentiles, it is clear that the αὐτούς ("they") who are without excuse includes everyone who is involved in suppressing the truth.[78] This clause in v. 20d should be taken as consecutive[79] rather than final,[80] which would place the rationale in the context of the last judgment. The argument focuses on the universal human dilemma currently visible in the light of the death and resurrection of Christ as proclaimed in the gospel.

■ 21 The verse beginning with διότι γνόντες τὸν θεόν ("because although they knew God") describes the manner in which humans suppress the truth. The straightforward acknowledgment of humankind's knowledge of God in v. 19 is reiterated without any derogatory implication about cultural qualifications. The shift from present tense verbs in vv. 18-20 to aorist verbs in vv. 21-23 signals a turn to the representatives of an archaic past[81] who turned away from the truth and imposed a grim future on their descendants. "The aorists are to be understood as gnomic; they express what pagans of all

---

72 Gräbe, *Power of God*, 188, notes the combination of these terms in 1:20 but provides neither an exact translation nor an explanation.

73 See Hermann Saase, "ἀΐδιος," *TDNT* 1 (1964) 168, for the use in Plato and Aristotle to depict what is without beginning or ending. It is also a favorite term for Philo; see *Plant.* 8, 18; *Spec. Leg.* 1.10; 2.166; for other references in Philo, see BAGD 22. Fitzmyer, 280, cites a Hellenistic Jewish adoption of these ideas in *Ep. Arist.* 132: "There is only one god, and his power is manifest through everything."

74 BAGD 354 lists Plutarch *Mor.* 398a; 665a; Lucian of Samosata *Cal.* 17; Hermotimus *Wr.* 9.1c; *SIG* 867.31; and Philo *Opif.* 172 v.1. Wilckens, 1:106, notes the expression δύναμις καὶ θειότης in Plato *Leg.* 691e. and the Latin parallel in Cicero *Nat. d.* 1.18.44. Diodorus Siculus *Hist.* 6.1.2 reports that ancient people "say that the gods are eternal and imperishable, for example, Sun and Moon and the other heavenly bodies." See also Diodorus Siculus *Hist.* 1.11.1; and Stobaeus *Anth.* 4.2.29.

75 For instance, Sanday and Headlam, 43–44.

76 See Henry S. Nash, "θειότης/θεότης, Rom. 1.20; Col. 2.9," *JBL* 18 (1899) 5–7.

77 See LSJM 207–8 on ἀπολογέομαι; parallels to ἀναπολόγητος ("without apology") are listed in

BAGD (2000) 71.

78 The effort by Hermann Langerbeck to narrow the focus of Paul's attack to contemporary philosophers is unconvincing: "Paulus und das Griechentum. Zum Problem des Verhältnisses der christlichen Botschaft zum antiken Erkenntnisideal," in *Aufsätze zur Gnosis* (Göttingen: Vandenhoeck & Ruprecht, 1967) 98–99. In "Stoa," 71–73, Pohlenz argues against any direct relationship between Paul's argument and Stoic philosophy.

79 Following Cornely, Gutjahr, Jülicher, Lietzmann, as noted by Kuss, 1:37, and followed by Lagrange, 24–25; Käsemann, 42; and Cranfield, 1:116.

80 With Kühl, 51, and Zahn, 92, as noted by Kuss, 1:37, and followed by Barrett, 36; Michel, 101; and Schmidt, 35.

81 See André Feuillet, "La connaissance naturelle de Dieu par les hommes d'apres Rom 1:18-23," *LumVie(B)* 14 (1954) 63–80; and D. M. Coffey, "Natural Knowledge of God: Reflections on Romans 1:18-32," *ThSt* 31 (1970) 675.

82 Fitzmyer, 282, following BDF §333. See also Bussmann, *Missionspredigt*, 64–65.

times have done."[82] The technical language for authentic knowledge of God as used in Hellenistic philosophy of religion, Judaism, and early Christianity is employed without apologies,[83] which is a considerable embarrassment to those who wish to enlist Paul in a campaign against natural theology. Paul's target is much broader than some theological doctrine; he is engaged in a missional endeavor that encompasses the entire human race that refuses to acknowledge God's preeminence.

Δοξάζειν ("to glorify") and εὐχαριστεῖν θεῷ ("to give thanks to God") are comprehensive descriptions of human obligations toward God, the failure of which were assumed to be signs of impiety.[84] To glorify God was the characteristic Judaic obligation,[85] established in the OT in the "demand to 'give' God כבוד ["glory"], i.e., to recognise the import of His deity."[86] To glorify God ὡς θεόν ("as God") means "according to the measure of His divine quality."[87] Such glorification is a recognition of the truth about the relative status of God and humankind.[88] This expression differentiates true worship from the worship of the images of humans, birds, and serpents (1:23). Leading the human race to this recognition in restoring the proper stance of humans in glorifying God is the goal of Paul's missionary project

that the entire letter seeks to advance, as 15:6 and 9 make plain. The reference in 4:20 to giving proper glory to God establishes Abraham as the ideal convert and the "positive foil" to those falling under wrath.[89]

In keeping with his rhetorical strategy of finding common ground with various social groups, Paul links the Judaic connotation of "glory" with the Greek usage shared by Jews and Gentiles alike of "giving thanks."[90] There are numerous indications that εὐχαριστέω was used in the religious context in the Greco-Roman world. It was generally assumed that the reception of a gift imposed the obligation of giving thanks.[91] Epictetus follows Plato in maintaining the need for every civilized person to have a "sense of gratitude" (τὸ εὐχάριστον)[92] and recommends that "we should be giving thanks to God for those things for which we ought to give Him thanks (ηὐχαριστοῦμεν τῷ θεῷ ἐφ᾽ οἷς δεῖ εὐχαριστεῖν)."[93] Particularly eloquent is Epictetus's argument that to be consistent with the nature of humankind, one must praise God: "If, indeed, I were a nightingale, I should be singing as a nightingale; if a swan, as a swan. But as it is, I am a rational being, therefore I must be singing hymns of praise to God (ὑμνεῖν μὲ δεῖ τὸ θεόν)."[94] A similar conviction lies at the heart of Roman

---

83 See Rudolf Bultmann, "γινώσκω," *TDNT* 1 (1964) 690–713; the excursus on "Knowledge of God by Heathen" in Kuss, 1:42–47; and Paolo Frassinetti, "Recenti contributi sulla γνῶσις θεῶν in Epicuro," *Athenaeum* 42 (1964) 214–22.

84 The common object for the verbs ἐδόξασαν ἢ ηὐχαρίστησαν ("glorify or give thanks") is θεὸν ("God"), even though the latter verb ordinarily requires the dative rather than the accusative. The rule in this instance is that the case of the object of two verbs is determined by the verb closest to the object, which in this instance is the verb "glorify," which requires an accusative object. See Smyth, *Grammar*, 1634–35. Therefore I supply "God" in brackets as the object of each verb in my translation.

85 Gerhard Kittel, "δόξα," *TDNT* 2 (1964) 237, 253–54, concludes that there is no Greek analogy for the distinctive biblical sense of "glory/glorify." According to Knoche, "Römische Ruhmesgedanke," 420–21, the Latin equivalent, *gloria*, pertains to social recognition and was not used in the religious arena. For Pauline usage see E. Lákatos, "El contenido teológico del "doxazein" en s Pablo," *RevBib* 26 (1965) 38–44, 89–93.

86 Gerhard von Rad, "כבוד in the OT," *TDNT* 2 (1964) 241, cites Jer 13:16; Ps 29:1-2; 96:7-8; and 115:1 as examples, of which the last is particularly relevant for Rom 1:21: "Not to us, O Lord, not to us, but to thy name give glory, for the sake of thy steadfast love and thy faithfulness!"

87 Meyer, 1:83; also Heinrich Schlier, "Doxa bei Paulus als heilsgeschichtlicher Begriff," *SPCIC* 1 (1963) 45–56; and Christine Mohrmann, "Note zur δόξα," *Sprachgeschichte und Wortbedeutung: Festschrift, Albert Debrunner gewidmet* (Bern: Francke, 1954) 321–28.

88 Du Toit, "Doxologische Gemeinschaft," 70.

89 Calvert-Koyzis, *Paul*, 129; see also Adams, "Abraham's Faith," 65.

90 Hans Conzelmann, "εὐχαριστέω κτλ.," *TDNT* 9 (1974) 407–11.

91 Ibid., 407; in particular the duty to give thanks to the gods as found in classical sources supports the use of εὐχαριστέω in the sense of "to pray"

92 Epictetus *Diss.* 1.6.1–2; the association with Plato was pointed out by Schubert, *Thanksgivings*, 132–42.

93 Epictetus *Diss.* 4.4.18; see also 4.1.105 and 4.4.29-32.

94 Epictetus *Diss.* 1.16.20.

religious sentiments.[95] Early Christianity gave particular prominence to this idea, not only in following the tradition of Hellenistic Judaism of giving thanks at mealtime but also in naming its principal ritual the "Eucharist."[96]

In view of this broad assent to the crucial necessity of being grateful to God, Paul could count on ready agreement that failure to do so was an indication of depravity. What would have been surprising, however, was so undifferentiated a claim of the failure of humans to give thanks. Nowhere else in the ancient world was so universal a failure decried. The closest parallels that have been found are in *2 Baruch*: "Because each of the inhabitants of the earth knew when he was transgressing. But my law they knew not by reason of their pride" (*2 Bar.* 48.40). Later in the writing, however, it becomes clear that the author has Gentiles rather than his own group of faithful Jews in mind with the denunciation of those who "deny the beneficence of God" (82.3-9). Although many commentators similarly assume that Paul is only targeting Gentiles in this passage, the inclusive reference in Rom 1:18 to "all impiety and unrighteousness of humans" eliminates this loophole. Paul's radicalized vision follows the logic of the cross of Christ that revealed the complicity of all parties in the attempt to suppress the truth he represented. The cross reveals a fundamental distortion of honor-shame systems in which a universal desire for superior status ends up in a hostile assault on God.

The verb ἐματαιώθησαν should be translated as a resultative aorist passive,[97] "they were made futile, vain," indicating the state into which humans are placed when they fail to honor God as God. The choice of this verb is influenced by the LXX, which uses the concept to depict the vanity of idolatry and the futility of ignorance.[98] Life that does not take account of the reality of God is doomed to the unreal world of self-deception. The verb ordinarily occurs in the passive in biblical usage and

means "to be delivered up to vanity."[99] The combination of "futility" and "thoughts" derives from Ps 94:11,[100] where foolish persons and nations fail to recognize the ultimate power of God and thus are doomed to frustration and defeat: κύριος γινώσκει τοὺς διαλογισμοὺς τῶν ἀνθρώπων ὅτι εἰσὶν μάταιοι ("The Lord knows the thoughts of humans that they are futile"). The psalm goes on to bless the wise person "whom you teach out of your law" (94:12), which provides an escape from human vanity into the certain triumph of divine righteousness. In Romans the emphasis is not on the futility of disregarding the Torah but on the more universal problem of suppressing the truth, a suppression that condemns the human mind to self-deceptive, scheming "thoughts"[101] that lead nowhere beyond the emptiness that conceived them.

The influence of the LXX and of Hebraic anthropology is manifest in the clause "their senseless heart was darkened" (v. 21d). LXX Ps 75:5-6 has a closely related formulation:

Φωτίζεις σὺ θαυμαστῶς ἀπὸ ὀρέων αἰωνίων.
Ἐταράχθησαν πάντες οἱ ἀσύνετοι τῇ καρδίᾳ
("You shine forth marvelously from eternal mountains. All the senseless in heart were thrown into confusion").

The argument in the psalm is parallel to that in Romans: whereas "God is known in Judah" (76:1), their enemies are frustrated and defeated (76:9-12), which proves they were "senseless" with regard to the ability of the "heart" to perceive reality. The term ἀσύνετος ("senseless, without understanding") is used in both places to indicate that the human ability to "bring together, perceive" (συνίημι) is disabled when God is unacknowledged. The darkening of the heart in Romans stands in antithesis to

---

95   See entries under *gratia* in Viktor Pöschl, *Grundwerte römischer Staatsgesinnung in den Geschichtswerken des Sallust* (Berlin: de Gruyter, 1940); Erik Wistrand, "*Gratus, grates, gradiosus,*" *Eranos* 39 (1941) 17-26.

96   See Conzelmann, "εὐχαριστέω κτλ.," *TDNT* 9 (1974) 411.

97   See Smyth, *Grammar*, 1926; Schlier, 56.

98   Otto Bauernfeind, "μάταιος," *TDNT* 4 (1967) 521-22.

99   Ibid., 523.

100   Ps 94:11 is employed by Paul in 1 Cor 3:20 in the context of warning against the presumption of being wise.

101   The NT tends to use διαλογισμοί ("thoughts") to depict the self-serving, scheming, manipulative aspect of mental activity; see Luke 5:22; 9:47; Rom

Yahweh's shining forth in the psalm (76:5). The aorist passive verb "was darkened" matches the passive formulation of the preceding clause and conveys a divinely imposed process of distortion already manifest in the experience of humans.[102] The idea of the deliberately darkened mind of pagans is found in *1 En.* 99.7-8 and *T. Levi* 14.4[103] in the context of repudiating the Torah and attachment to idolatry. The use of such language in close association with "vanity" leads commentators to assume that Paul is simply attacking idolatry in this pericope,[104] but the logical progression in Romans differs from the Judaic parallels. Rather than commencing with an attack on idolatry, a conventional line of argument that sustains the assumption of ethnocentric superiority, Paul builds his case here on the universal experience of suppressing the truth about God and describes a chain of consequences leading to idolatry in Rom 1:23.

As far as the anthropological assumptions in this passage are concerned, however, Paul's Judaic roots surface clearly in the use of καρδία ("heart"). While Hellenistic Judaism in reference to human reason tended to avoid this term and adopt Greek categories such as "mind" and "reason" in tension with "flesh" and "body,"[105] thinkers such as Paul who continued to use "heart" assume the essential unity of emotions, thoughts, bodily makeup, and attitude toward God.[106] The mixed audience we have perceived throughout Romans may well be involved in this synonymous parallelism: διαλογισμοί is language appealing to Greeks and καρδία to Hebrews. In any event the declaration that "their senseless heart was darkened" implies a comprehensive process of disabling and distortion that involves intellectual, emotional, and physical dimensions of the human being. In this divinely imposed distortion, the wrath of God is already manifest.

■ **22** The most obvious distortion of all is in the human self-image, although people are usually unable to recognize it for themselves or their institutions. Paul effectively copes with this distorted self-image by a witty and succinct formulation. The present participle φάσκοντες ("claiming, asserting"), a term often used in situations where unsubstantiated claims are being made,[107] participates in the action of the main verb, "they became witless." Thus I translate, "while claiming to be wise, they became witless." It is possible that an implication of "frequently claiming" is thereby conveyed.[108] While being wise provided supreme status in the ancient world,[109] suitable for frequently asserted ambition, it was widely assumed that one should never claim it for oneself. Socrates, for instance, was acknowledged as supremely wise because he never claimed it for himself, declaring instead that he knew nothing.[110] The claim here is precisely the opposite of the humble stance recommended by Greco-Roman and Judaic wisdom. These traditions would have made the expression ludicrous for Paul's hearers, particularly when combined so succinctly and effectively with its antithesis: ἐμωράνθησαν ("they were made witless/moronic"). The passive verb fits the pattern of the passives in the preceding verse, conforming to usage in the LXX, where "becoming a fool is

---

102 14:1; the verbal expression is found in Mark 2:6, 8; 9:33, etc. In Godet's words (105), "The term διαλογισμοί, *reasonings*, is always taken by the writers of the New Testament in an unfavorable sense; it denotes the unregulated activity of the νοῦς, *understanding*, in the service of a corrupt heart."

102 Godet, 105, suggests that the passive forms express "the conviction of a divine dispensation, though still under the form of a natural law, whose penal application has fallen on them." Cranfield, 1:117, rightly rejects any direct reference here to "God's judicial action."

103 *T. Reub.* 3.8 has a similar metaphor but without the passive form.

104 Schlier, 56; Dodd, 25; Wilckens, 1:107; Morris, 83–84.

105 See Schlatter, "Herz und Gehirn," 86–94.

106 Jewett, *Terms*, 309.

107 See Meyer, 1:84, and the hollow claims of financial status and accomplishment in MM 665.

108 Zahn, 94; Käsemann, 44.

109 See Ulrich Wilckens, "σοφία κτλ.," *TDNT* 7 (1971) 473; and Werner Gent, "Der Begriff des Weisen. Eine historisch-kritische Untersuchung," *ZPF* 20 (1966) 77–90.

110 See Plato *Apol.* 20c-23c; Socrates explains that he tried to show an Athenian with a reputation for wisdom that "he thought he was wise but was not," concluding that "neither of us really knows anything fine and good, but this man thinks he knows something when he does not, whereas I, as I do not know anything, do not think I do either" (21c-d). For a discussion of the distinction between loving wisdom and claiming to be wise, see B. Schnell,

obviously a divine judgment on men in their fancied superior wisdom."[111] The irony in Paul's memorable saying[112] resides in the quick juxtaposition between what is claimed and what is true. The formulation not only leads Paul's argument forward with a rhetorically effective turn but also casts one of the missional antitheses of 1:14 into a new light: the "wise" who claim superiority in this world are actually morons in the light of the gospel and the prospect of wrath.[113] They need the gospel as much as the "uneducated" if they are to recognize the truth about themselves.

■ **23** The height of folly is idolatry, which Paul depicts not as a silly mistake but as the ultimate expression of the human campaign to suppress the truth. The ironic vein of the preceding verse is continued with the words καὶ ἤλλαξαν . . . ("and they changed . . ."),[114] which picks up the theme of an active campaign to distort the truth that has been Paul's leitmotif since 1:18. The derivation of Paul's choice of the term "change" from Jer 2:11 and particularly Ps 106:20 is generally assumed,[115] but the aggressive intentionality that this wording would have conveyed to his audience has not been clearly per-

ceived.[116] The semantic overlap with the depiction of the golden calf episode of Ps 106:20 is particularly striking when the terms used in Rom 1:23 are underlined:

<u>καὶ ἠλλάξαντο τὴν δόξαν</u> αὐτῶν <u>ἐν ὁμοιώματι</u> μόσχου ἔσθοντος χόρτον ("<u>and they changed</u> their <u>glory into the facsimile</u> of a calf that eats grass").

There was no question of "exchanging" the glory for a preexisting "facsimile" in this psalm; the statue of the calf was fashioned by Aaron and his colleagues, making it the archetypal episode of idolatry in biblical literature. Paul avoids the LXX's ambiguity in the use of δόξα ("glory") by a formulation closer to the MT that suggests the "glory of God" as the target to be displaced by the idol.[117] The antithesis between ἀφθάρτου θεοῦ ("imperishable God") and φθαρτοῦ ἀνθρώπου ("perishable human")[118] in Paul's reworking of the psalmic allusion accentuates the preposterous level of self-delusion implicit in this act of idolatrous creation. The self-proclaimed exemplars of wisdom prove themselves incapable of making the most elementary kind of distinction. The phrase ἐν ὁμοιώματι is evidently cited

"Wie die Griechen lernten, was geistige Tätigkeit ist," *JHS* 93 (1973) 179.

111 Georg Bertram, "μωρός κτλ.," *TDNT* 4 (1967) 836, refers to Job 16:8, where Yahweh makes Job a "worn-out fool." Although the passive form is not used, there is also a parallel in Epictetus *Diss.* 2.15.15, "May I never have *a wise fool for a friend* (φίλον ἔχειν σοφὸν μωρόν)." Lucian of Samosata *Alex.* 40 probably coined the word μωρόνσοφος ("the wise-fool").

112 Zahn, 94, refers to this succinct verse as a "caption or motto, standing at the head of the depiction of the sentence" as an embodiment of the "wickedness" of 1:18, a suggestion properly rejected on rhetorical and argumentative grounds by Kühl, 53.

113 See Peter Fiedler, "μωρία," *EDNT* 2 (1991) 450.

114 Paul consistently uses ἀλλάσσω in the sense of "change" (1 Cor 15:51; Gal 4:20) rather than "exchange" as preferred by BAGD 39 and most translations and commentators. But Paul does not have a business transaction in view here, and the expression ἐν ὁμοιώματι εἰκόνος is rather strained when translated "*for* the facsimile of an image." See Ilmari Soisalon-Soininen, "*EN* für *EIΣ* in der Septuaginta," in Anneli Aejmalaeus and Raija Sollamo, eds., *Studien zur Septuaginta-Syntax* (Helsinki: Suomalainen Tiedeakatemia, 1987) 131–40.

115 Cranfield, 1:119; Wilckens, 1:107.

116 See the inadequate treatment of the issue in Friedrich Büchsel, "ἀλλάσσω," *TDNT* 1 (1964) 251. Schlatter, 41, infers that "the individual resists the truth," which implies an illicit choice between already existing alternatives. The usual translation "exchange" likewise tends to reduce the matter to a trade of one option for another. But the associations with the Eden and golden calf stories demand the recognition that the option of the false image was actively created by humans rather than merely being selected from preexisting alternatives. The intended aggressivity is glimpsed by Godet, 105–6, who refers to a "monstrous and debasing fetishism. The ungrateful heart did not stop short at not thanking God, it degraded and dishonored Him, by changing Him into His opposite."

117 See Weiss, 85; Fitzmyer, 283.

118 The antithesis between ἄφθαρτος and φθαρτός is typical in Hellenistic Judaism; Günther Harder, "φθείρω," *TDNT* 9 (1974) 96, 101–2, shows that the antithesis plays a key role in Philo's thought. Particularly clear examples are *Abr.* 243 and *Leg. All.* 3.36. The contrast in "perishability" is particularly stressed by Traugott Holtz, "φθείρω κτλ.," *EDNT* 3 (1993) 423.

directly from Ps 106[119] and bears the sense of "facsimile" or copy.[120] The counterfeit quality of the human production is emphasized by the addition of εἰκών, which results in the curious expression "facsimile of an image." The use of εἰκών in theological and christological contexts to depict the divine image[121] has led some commentators to see a juxtaposition between ὁμοίωμα and εἰκών, the former referring to the copy and the latter to the original or at least the form of the original.[122] It seems more likely that the two terms are practical synonyms in the context of Rom 1:23,[123] implying "a copy of a copy"[124] or more precisely, "the likeness of the image."[125] Paul depicts an image twice removed, a distortion[126] even of the proper shape of the creatures depicted in the idol. The choice of terms is ironic rather than merely pleonastic[127] and it serves to deepen the exposure of the witless fools of 1:22 who are now depicted as so stupid as to be oblivious of the discrepancies in their own counterfeits.[128]

The fourfold designation of idolatrous images "of a mortal human and of birds and four-legged animals and serpents" clearly moves the Pauline discourse beyond the parameters of the golden calf episode. Paul wishes to include more than Jewish idolatry in the scope of his argument,[129] intending instead to cover the entire sinful spectrum of human experience.[130] In keeping with this wider scope, which reaches back to the fall of the human race,[131] the fourfold designation is reminiscent of Gen 1:20-27.[132] Only a reference to the "fish of the sea" is missing. It is possible, however, that this omission allows the wider range of semantic reference in these idolatrous images to be suggested by Paul's argument. A remarkable parallel to this comprehensive listing of creatures has surfaced in a bilingual Aramaic-Greek magical text found in Egypt.[133] It describes an evil spirit's appearing or frightening the client "nor in any form" (לא בכל) "(either that) of a reptile, of a bird, of cattle, or in the form of a person (דמו ברדהש בעוף ברבעיר או ברמות ברנש)."[134]

---

119 Zahn, 95, showed that the alleged parallel to ἐν ὁμοιώματι in Sophocles *Ant.* 945 is inappropriate grammatically and that the phrase was quoted from Ps 106; for similar conclusions see Kühl, 54–55; Wilckens, 1:107. Fitzmyer, 283, suggests Deut 4:16-18, where idolatry is prohibited either in "likeness" or "image." He rightly rejects an allusion to Gen 1:26 as suggested by Niels Hyldahl, "A Reminiscence of the Old Testament at Romans 1:23," *NTS* 2 (1955–56) 285–88.

120 Johannes Schneider, "ὁμοίομα," *TDNT* 5 (1967) 191–92.

121 For instance, Gen 1:16-17 and Heb 10:1, as discussed by Gerhard Kittel, "εἰκών," *TDNT* 2 (1964) 392–97. Jervell, *Imago*, 325ff., argues that εἰκών alludes to the divine likeness in Gen 1:26, but as Käsemann, 45, points out, "εἰκών governs also the animals mentioned" in Rom 1:13. In "Adam," 304, Hooker comes to the same conclusion.

122 Gerhard Kittel, "εἰκών," *TDNT* 2 (1964) 395; Schlatter, 40; Cranfield, 1:120; Michel, 103.

123 See Trench, *Synonyms*, 47–51; Dunn, 1:61, notes that both ὁμοίωμα and εἰκών are used "as equivalents" in Deut 4:15-18.

124 Dunn, 1:61.

125 Fitzmyer, 283; this translation retains ὁμοίωμα as the larger category implying any "likeness," while the term εἰκών refers to the form of the calf in this context.

126 Barrett, 38, concludes that "the reduplication emphasizes the inferior, shadowy character of that which is substituted for God." See also Hooker, "Adam," 304-5.

127 See Lietzmann, 32.

128 It seems unlikely, therefore, that Kühl, 54, is on target in suggesting Paul uses ἐν ὁμοιώματι εἰκόνος to soften the attack on pagan cults by hinting they possessed some semblance of the original divine image. See the critique by Lagrange, 26–27.

129 In contrast, Wick, *Gottesdienste*, 176, limits this reference to the second commandment in Exod 20:4-5.

130 See Dabelstein, *Beurteilung*, 82.

131 See Jervell, *Imago Dei*, 321ff.; Hooker, "Adam," 301; idem, "A Further Note on Romans 1." *NTS* 13 (1966–67) 181–83.

132 See Hyldahl, "Reminiscence," 286–88; Käsemann, 45, also cites Louis Ligier, *Péché d'Adam und Péché du Monde*, Théologie 48 (Paris: Aubier, 1961) 2:172–73, as supporting this view. Ligier argues that the language of Genesis is used by Paul in Rom 1:23.

133 Roy Kotansky, J. Naveh, and S. Shaked, "A Greek-Aramaic Silver Amulet from Egypt in the Ashmolean Museum," *Le Muséon* 105.1-2 (1992) 5–24.

134 Ibid., 11, translated from lines 14-15. The editors' commentary on these lines (p. 16) does not mention Romans. The tablet dates from the 5th century c.e., although its text may be considerably earlier; see p. 7.

There are plenty of examples in Roman religion and politics of the adoration of humans, birds, four-legged animals, and serpents. The infusion of Egyptian shrines in Rome brought a wide variety of such figures.[135] Despite the skepticism of Greco-Roman philosophers that deities could be imagined to be like animals or humans,[136] the power of the iconic remained unbroken[137] on coins,[138] on the banners of the Roman legions,[139] and in the art and architecture of Rome and every other Greco-Roman city. While similar denunciations of idolatrous paganism in the Wisdom of Solomon[140] and other writings of Hellenistic Judaism[141] have led scholars to suppose that Paul was attacking only Egyptian religion, or non-Jewish religions in general,[142] it seems more likely that Paul was thinking as inclusively here as elsewhere in the pericope. As Dabelstein has demonstrated, there are ample precedents within Israelite history of sinful participation in idolatry,[143] including the golden calf episode that is explicitly in view in this pericope. Since every culture displays evidence of suppressing the truth by the adoration of perishable images, demonstrating that the perverse will to "change the glory of the imperishable God" is a universal problem, the gospel elaborated in this letter has an inclusive bearing.

---

135 Diodorus Siculus *Hist.* 1.12.9 describes the animal-forms of the Egyptian gods, which later came into vogue in Rome. See Alfonso Bartoli, "Tracce di culti orientali sul Palatino imperiale," *Rendiconti della Pontificia Accademia Romano di Archeologia* 24 (1956–57) 13–49; Franz Altheim, *La Religion romains antiques. Les éléments pré-romains - L'action des dieux Présages et vaticinations - Les apports grecs et orientau - Les oracles - La voix du peuple - Le culte solaire - L'avènement du christianne*, Bibliothèque Historique (Paris: Fayot, 1955); Momigliano, *Pagans*, 188; Michel Malaise, *Les conditions de pénétration et de diffusion des cultes Égyptiens en italie*, EPRO 22 (Leiden: Brill, 1972) 335–54. What Paul refers to as "birds" would imply the veneration of Ibis, of Isis with her vulture headdress, the goose figure Geb, Nehhbet or Mut with vulture's heads, and Horus or Re with the falcon head; the quadrupeds could include the cat figure Bast, the lion Sekhmet, the jackel Anubis, or Seth with a composite animal's body; and the reptiles could refer to Sebek the crocodile and to snakes used in Egyptian art.

136 See Xenophanes *Frag.* 23–26; Protagoras *Frag.* 4; Empedocles *Frag.* 134; Cicero *Nat. d.* 49, 105; Plutarch *E. Delph.* 388–89, 393.

137 See Zanker, *Power of Images, passim.*

138 A convenient illustration of the images of humans, birds, and quadrupeds on Roman coins is available in John Kent, "The Monetary System," in J. Wacher, ed., *The Roman World* (London: Routledge & Kegan Paul, 1987) 2:584–85.

139 See Webster, *Imperial Army*, 134–41, for a description of Roman standards that were held in great awe and used in religious ceremonies as well as battles. These standards depicted eagles, dragons, wolves, minotaurs, horses, boars, bulls, rams, images of the emperors, and a human hand. Some of the "standard-bearers wore animal skins over their uniform" or "heads of the animals" carried over their helmets (141). Lendon, *Empire of Honour*, 237–66, describes the honor system that explains why "the pride of units was invested particularly in their standards" (252); and Incigneri, *Gospel to the Romans*, 129, shows that such pride could rise to the level of worshiping the legion's standards.

140 See esp. Wis 11:15; 12:24; 13:10, 13-14; 14:8; 15:18-19.

141 Dunn, 1:61, lists *Ep. Arist.* 138; *Sib. Or.* 3; *T. Naph.* 3.2-4; *T. Mos.* 1.13; *1 En.* 91.4ff.; 99.2ff.; *2 Apoc. Bar.* 54.17-22.

142 See Klostermann, "Adäquate Vergeltung," 2–3; Jeremias, "Röm 1.22-32," 120; and Daxer, *Römer*, 17–24; Lagrange, 27, opts for general literary allusions rather than specific cultural allusions in the language of 1:23.

143 Dabelstein, *Beurteilung*, 82.

1

The Second Half of the First Pericope

The Revelation of Divine Wrath

b. Elaboration: Human Distortion as a Current Indication of Divine Wrath

24/ Therefore[a] God delivered them to the desires of their hearts for impurity of their bodies' being dishonored among themselves,[b] 25/ the very ones who exchanged the truth of God for their lie, and venerated and worshiped the creature rather than the Creator, who is blessed into the ages! Amen. 26/ For this reason, God delivered them [to the desires of their hearts] for passions of dishonor, for their females exchanged the natural use[c] for the unnatural,[d] 27/ and likewise also[e] the males, after they abandoned the natural use with females, were inflamed with their lust for one another, males who work up their shameful member in [other] males, and receive back[f] for their deception the recompense that is tightness in themselves.[g]

28/ And as they did not see fit to hold God in knowledge, God[h] delivered them to an unfitting mind to do the things that are improper, 29/ having been filled with all manner of

    wrongdoing,
        evil,[i]
            greed,
                badness,
        persons full of
            envy,
                murder,
                    strife,
                        treachery,[j]
                          malice,
    whisperers, 30/ slanderers,[k]
    haters of God, bullies,
        egotists, braggarts,
            inventors of evil designs,
            disobeyors of parents,
    31/ without understanding,
        without dutifulness,[l]
            without affection,
                without mercy.
32/ Though they[m] know[n] the righteous decree of God that those who practice such things deserve to die, they not only[o] do such things[p] but also applaud those who practice such things.

---

a   The witnesses for the inclusion of καί ("indeed"), D G K L P Ψ 6 69 88 323 326 330 365 424 614 945 1175 1241 1243 1505 1506 1735 1836 1874 2495

2464 *Maj* b sy[h], compete quite well with those lacking it, ℵ A B C 33 81 104 1319 1573 1739 1881 2344 *al* lat sy[p] cop Spec. While neither the recent commentators nor Metzger discuss the matter, most translators appear to follow the judgment of the Nestle text in not including καί, which when καί is mistakenly viewed as a conjunction rather than in this instance an adverb, is perceived to erode the sense that a new section begins in 1:24. Zahn, 96, accepts the inclusion of the καί on grounds of equal attestation, noting it is also reflected in Chr and Thret. However, the use of διὸ καί ("and therefore") in Luke 1:35; Acts 10:29; 24:26; Rom 4:22; 15:22; 2 Cor 1.20, 4.13; 5:9; Phil 2:9; Heb 11:12; 13:12 may indicate the likelihood of καί being added in assimilation to popular usage. Also, the slightly stronger attestation for its exclusion leads me to favor that option.

b   The reading ἑαυτοῖς ("to themselves") is weakly attested in D[1] G K L P Ψ 0278 6 33 69 326 330 365 424 614 945 1175 1241 1243 1319 1505 1506 1573 1739 1874 1881[c] 2344 2464 2495 *Maj* and thus should not be followed. Metzger is apparently among those reported in his *Textual Commentary*, (1975), 506, who "strongly preferred to use the rough breathing" in αὐτοῖς ("themselves") indicating a reflexive pronoun; see his discussion in *Textual Commentary* (1975), 615–16. The oblique case of αὐτός may be used instead of the reflexive pronoun "when the subordinate clause does not form a part of the thought of the principal subject" (Smyth, *Grammar*, §1229), as in this verse. The breathing must be inferred contextually, so about all that is relatively certain is that the original reading contained αὐτοῖς as supported by P[40vid] ℵ A B C D* 81 88 104 323 1735 1836 1881 *al*.

c   The reading of κτίσιν ("creation") by D* in place of χρῆσιν ("use, relation") appears to be a redactional improvement that emphasizes the charge of exchanging the natural creation for sexual use beyond the natural.

d   The variant χρῆσιν ("use, relation") found at this point in D* G appears to be a redactional change that correlates with the earlier reading of κτίσιν.

e   A reading with δέ ("but") widely attested in A D* G P Ψ 33 104 330 424 630 1505 1573 1739 1881 2344 2495 *pm* lat sy[h] Cl is found in place of the more likely original τέ (a virtually untranslatable connective) found in ℵ B D[c] K L 69 81 88 323 326 365 614 945 1175 1241 1243 1319 1735 1836 2464 *pm*. It is an understandable transcription error that ruins the connection (τέ. . . τέ) between vv. 26 and 27.

f   The minor variant ἀντιλαμβάνοντες ("they took part") is found in G in place of ἀπολαμβάνοντες ("they received back"). This variant is perhaps a stylistic improvement by conforming to $\dot{\alpha}\nu\tau\iota\mu\iota\sigma\vartheta\acute{\iota}\alpha\nu$ in v. 27.

g   In a variant that reverses the shift found in v. 24, B K 104* 323 1506 *pc* read $\alpha\dot{\upsilon}\tau o\hat{\iota}\varsigma$ ("to them") in place of the more broadly attested $\dot{\epsilon}\alpha\upsilon\tau o\hat{\iota}\varsigma$ ("to themselves"). Since reflexive pronouns are used "when they refer to the chief word (usually the subject) of the sentence or clause in which they stand," (Smyth, *Grammar*, §1218), $\dot{\epsilon}\alpha\upsilon\tau o\hat{\iota}\varsigma$ is properly used in this location.

h   The deletion of $\dot{o}\ \vartheta\epsilon\acute{o}\varsigma$ ("God") by ℵ* A 0172* 1735 appears to be an effort at stylistic improvement, to avoid the repeated use of "God" in a single sentence.

i   A series of textual variants presents itself here, clarified by Swanson, *Vaticanus: Romans*, 17, with D^supp2 L Ψ 0278^vid 88 (88 also adds $\kappa\alpha\acute{\iota}$ after each word, perhaps to avoid grammatical confusion) (104) 256 263 323 326 330 365 424* 436 451 (459) 614 1175 1241 1243 1319 1505 1573 1735 1874 1877 1962 2127 2200 2464 2492 2495 *Maj Lect* (ar b o vg) sy^h arm geo² slav (sy^p Ephr $\kappa\alpha\kappa\acute{\iota}\alpha\ \pi\lambda\epsilon o\nu\epsilon\xi\acute{\iota}\alpha$) Or^lat 1/6 Bas GrNy (Luc) (Ambst) (Pel) (Hier) inserting $\pi o\rho\nu\epsilon\acute{\iota}\alpha$ ("fornication") after $\dot{\alpha}\delta\iota\kappa\acute{\iota}\alpha$, and D^supp* G (P) 1852^vid d g (vg) Or^lat 2/6 inserting $\pi o\rho\nu\epsilon\acute{\iota}\alpha$ in the middle of a revised series of $\dot{\alpha}\delta\iota\kappa\acute{\iota}\alpha\ \kappa\alpha\kappa\acute{\iota}\alpha$, $\pi o\rho\nu\epsilon\acute{\iota}\alpha, \pi\lambda\epsilon o\nu\epsilon\xi\acute{\iota}\alpha$. 181 has $\dot{\alpha}\delta\iota\kappa\acute{\iota}\alpha$ ("unrighteousness") in place of $\pi o\nu\eta\rho\acute{\iota}\alpha$. Other traditions reverse the sequence without adding "fornication," with C D^supp2 33 81 1506 sa bo^(mss) eth (geo¹) (Or^lat 2/6) *pc* having "malice, evil, avarice," ℵ A bo^(mss) having "evil, malice, avarice," 104 (vg) having "evil, fornication, avarice, malice," P having "fornication, avarice, malice," and K (Or^lat 1/6) having a shortened list of "avarice, malice." The support for the sequence adopted by Nestle-Aland²⁷ and UBS⁴ and followed in my translation is B 0172^vid 6 424^c 1739 1881 *l* 596 *pc* Chr, but, as noted above, ℵ A C 33 81 1506 sa bo^(mss) eth etc. also omit "fornication," though with differing sequences of the terms. Metzger explains the addition of "fornication" by the TR (Byz) as a mistake resulting from the similar appearance of *ΠΟΝΗΡΙΑ* ("evil") to *ΠΟΡΝΕΙΑ* ("fornication") in the original text. Metzger argues against such an addition on the ground of redundancy, since all these evils derive "from the licentious practices of idolatry" (*Textual Commentary*, 447). I do not find this argument compelling, but the omission of $\pi o\rho\nu\epsilon\acute{\iota}\alpha$ in ℵ A and B seems sufficient reason to consider it secondary. The transposition of terms in the several traditions is easily accounted for by the poetically identical ending of -$\iota\alpha$ of each word in this first series of four evils. In *Textual Criticism*, 65, Greenlee discusses this explanation.

j   The deletion of $\delta\acute{o}\lambda o\upsilon$ ("treachery") by A may be a scribal error but would improve the poetic parallelism by reducing the second series of evils to four items to match the other series of fours or eight.

k   An apparent dictation error is manifest in D^supp that has $\kappa\alpha\kappa o\lambda\acute{\alpha}\lambda o\upsilon\varsigma$ ("revilers") in place of $\kappa\alpha\tau\alpha\lambda\acute{\alpha}\lambda o\upsilon\varsigma$ ("slanderers").

l   An additional evil, $\dot{\alpha}\sigma\pi\acute{o}\nu\delta o\upsilon\varsigma$ ("implacable"), is added to this series by ℵ² C D¹ K L P Ψ (transposed in 33) 81 104 256 263 365 424 436 459 1175 1241 1319 1573 1852 1881 1962 2127 2200 2464 *Maj Lect* vg sy^p, h arm geo slav Or^lat 1/2 Bas^1/2 GrNy Chr apparently as an assimilation to 2 Tim 3:3. The text without this addition is strongly supported by ℵ* A B D* G 6 1506 1739 *pc* ar b d g mon o vg^mss sa^ms bo Or^lat 1/2 Bas^1/2 Lcf Ambst Pel Aug Gildas.

m   An alternative verbal form $\dot{\epsilon}\pi\iota\gamma\nu\acute{\omega}\sigma\kappa o\nu\tau\epsilon\varsigma$ ("knowing") is found in B 1506 *pc*, but is probably a redactional effort to make the participle correspond to the other present time verbs in this verse.

n   The addition of $o\dot{\upsilon}\kappa\ \dot{\epsilon}\gamma\nu\acute{o}\eta\sigma\alpha\nu$ ("they did not understand") in D* (*pc*) latt and $o\dot{\upsilon}\kappa\ \acute{\epsilon}\gamma\nu\omega\sigma\alpha\nu$ ("they did not know") in G appear to be efforts at grammatical improvement, with the sense "knowing the righteous decree of God, they did not understand that those who do such things deserve to die." The result is to weaken Paul's argument considerably.

o   The addition of the particle $\delta\acute{\epsilon}$ ("and, but") by 1175 1241 1836 1874 *pc* b mon and $\gamma\acute{\alpha}\rho$ ("for") by D* appear to be secondary efforts to improve the syntax of this sentence in the versions that make the participle $\dot{\epsilon}\pi\iota\gamma\nu\acute{o}\nu\tau\epsilon\varsigma$ into a finite verb.

p   In place of the broadly attested $\alpha\dot{\upsilon}\tau\grave{\alpha}\ \pi o\iota o\hat{\upsilon}\sigma\iota\nu$ $\dot{\alpha}\lambda\lambda\grave{\alpha}\ \kappa\alpha\grave{\iota}\ \sigma\upsilon\nu\epsilon\upsilon\delta o\kappa o\hat{\upsilon}\sigma\iota\nu$ ("they do them, but also applaud"), B b vg^cl Lcf have the verbs in participial form, $\pi o\iota o\hat{\upsilon}\nu\tau\epsilon\varsigma$ ("doing") and $\sigma\upsilon\nu\epsilon\upsilon\delta o\kappa o\hat{\upsilon}\nu\tau\epsilon\varsigma$ ("applauding") while ar mon Ambst add the definite article $o\acute{\iota}$ ("the") to change the participles into predicate nominatives of the relative pronoun $o\acute{\iota}\tau\iota\nu\epsilon\varsigma$ with the verb "to be" ellipsed. Zuntz, *Text*, 219, observes that *1 Clem.* 35.6 indicates the variant reading was already present in the 1st century and suggests that the participles may have been influenced by the appearance of the two other participles in Rom 1:32.

Analysis

This second half of the first pericope provides an elaboration of the thematic statement in 1:18, with rhetorical finesse comparable to the first half of the pericope. The thematic links of terminological transplacement and paronomasia that hold the two halves of the first pericope together have been pointed out by Klostermann, Jeremias, Bouwmann, and Popkes.[1] The failure to honor God in 1:21-23 corresponds to the deliverance to dishonorable relationships in v. 24. The "exchanging" of truth for a lie in v. 25 corresponds to the "exchanging" of natural relations for unnatural in v. 26. Not seeing "fit" to acknowledge God in v. 28a corresponds to the deliverance to the "unfitting mind" of v. 28b. This link is solidified by the wordplay between ἐδοκίμασαν ("acknowledge, approve") and ἀδόκιμον ("not approved, unfitting").[2] The threefold reduplication of παρέδωκεν ("he delivered") serves as a forceful refrain[3] of deliverance to human distortion, first on the mental and religious level in the worship of the creature rather than the Creator (vv. 24-25), then on the sexual level in the form of perverted relationships (vv. 26-27), and finally on the public level in the form of criminal and sociopathic behavior (vv. 28-32).

The opening sentence in the first paragraph describes the divine deliverance to human degradation of those who suppress the truth.[4] This sentence is followed by four sentences marked by antithesis. The first in v. 25a-b is identified by Johannes Weiss with the Semitic concept of parallelismus membrorum,[5] which would be more adequately described as a rhetorical antithesis between "truth" and "lie" in v. 25a matched by an antithesis between "creature" and "Creator" in v. 25b. After the interruption of the doxology in v. 25c, there is a corresponding antithesis between "natural" and "unnatural" in v. 26b, while the final two pairs of lines in v. 27 describe unnatural relations between men.

The second paragraph (vv. 28-32) contains a brilliantly devised catalogue of evils introduced and concluded by symmetrical sentences with parallelism similar to that in the preceding section. There is an element of reduplication in that the key word "know" in relation to God occurs in vv. 28 and 32, the latter thus providing an inclusio. This is reminiscent of the preceding section (vv. 19, 21).[6] Verse 32 also features a repetition of the term "practice."

The catalogue of vices in vv. 29-31 is in the generic style with asyndeton, consistent with other vice catalogues in the Greco-Roman context.[7] The rhetorical effect of asyndeton is to make the items in the list appear to be "more numerous than they really are,"[8] which serves Paul's argumentative purpose. An enumeration like this provides a typical phase of amplification in classical rhetoric.[9] The first series in the catalogue contains four comprehensive vices marked by homoioteleuton, each word ending in -ια.[10] The second series contains four antisocial vices linked by parechesis, with an assonance of *o* sounds, ending with a fifth vice that rhymes with the preceding series.[11] The third series consists of four pairs of associated identifications of evil persons,[12] which is atypical for vice catalogues; this leads to my identification of the series as a "catalogue of evils." The fourth series of evil persons is marked by homoioteleuton in the first three word endings as well as anaphora in the beginning of each word, with the alpha negative that refers to the absence of virtues.[13] Each series is associated grammatically with the αὐτούς ("them") of 1:28, which produces a devastating description of fallen humanity as a whole.

---

1   Klostermann, "Adäquate Vergeltung," 6; Jeremias, "Röm 1.22-32," 119; Bouman, "Römer 1," 413; Popkes, "Aufbau," 499.

2   See Heil, 26.

3   Anderson, *Glossary*, 18; Lagrange, 28; Klostermann, "Adäquate Vergeltung," 5–6; see also Harvey, "Listening," 185–86.

4   Weiss, "Beiträge," 215, proposes a break after "impurity," but this does not appear warranted. The parallelism of the ἐν and εἰς phrases seems to be a typical example of Semitic poetic form.

5   See ibid.

6   See ibid.

7   See Wibbing, *Lasterkataloge*, 79.

8   Quintilian *Inst.* 9.3.50; see also Aristotle *Rhet.* 3.12.2.4.

9   See Bullinger, *Figures*, 437; Lausberg, *Handbuch*, §§669–74.

10 See Cranfield, 1:129; Wibbing, *Lasterkataloge*, 82.

11 Wibbing, *Lasterkataloge*, 82.

12 See Zahn, 103.

13 Wibbing, *Lasterkataloge*, 83.

IV.   The *Probatio*
1:18–   A. The first proof: The gospel expresses the impartial
4:25   righteousness of God by overturning claims of cultural superiority and by rightwising Jews and Gentiles through grace alone
1:18-32   1. The gospel's revelation of divine wrath
1:24-32   b. Elaboration: Human distortion as a current indication of wrath
1:24-27   1) The deliverance to sexual perversions
1:24   a) The basic statement of deliverance to wrath
                        (1) The agent: God
                        (2) Those being delivered: "them," i.e., those who suppress the truth
                        (3) The punishment: deliverance to impure desires
                        (4) Clarification of impurity: degradation of bodily relations
1:25a-b   b) Reiteration of the guilt of those punished by wrath
1:25a   (1) The exchange of the "truth" for a "lie"
1:25b   (2) Serving the "creature" rather than the "Creator"
1:25c   c) An interjection of a doxology to the Creator
1:26-27   d) The deliverance to dishonorable sexual relations
1:26a   (1) The renewed statement of deliverance to wrath
                        (a) The agent: God
                        (b) Those being delivered: "them," i.e., those who twist the truth
                        (c) The punishment: "dishonorable passions"
1:26b-27d   (2) The example of sexual perversion
1:26b   (a) Female perversion
                            i. Abandonment of the "natural" relation
                            ii. Adoption of an "unnatural" relation
1:27a-c   (b) Male perversion
1:27a   i. The abandonment of natural relations between men and women
1:27b   ii. The absorption in perverse passion
1:27c   iii. The shameful expression of male passion

1:27d   (c) Perverse sexual relations as recompense for deception
1:28-32   2) The deliverance to sociopathology
1:28   a) The introduction of the catalogue of vices and evil persons
1:28a   (1) The reiteration of the root cause of wrath: not recognizing God
1:28b   (2) The renewed statement of deliverance to wrath
                            (a) The agent: God
                            (b) Those being punished: "them," i.e., those not recognizing God
                            (c) The punishment
                                i. The "unfitting mind"
                                ii. Improper actions
1:29-31   b) The catalogue of evils
1:29a   (1) Four basic vices conducive to social pathology
1:29b   (2) Five antisocial vices
1:29b-30   (3) Four pairs of evil personal identifications
1:31   (4) Four references to persons lacking necessary virtues
1:32   c) The conclusion of the catalogue of evils
1:32a   (1) The knowledge that proves culpability
                            (a) The content of knowledge: the "righteous decree of God"
                            (b) The definition of the decree: that evildoers deserve death
1:32b   (2) The actions of social pathology
                            (a) "Practicing" vices
                            (b) Applauding those who "practice" vices

Exegesis

■ **24** The opening of this half-pericope with the inferential conjunction διό ("therefore")[14] indicates the logical connection with the preceding verses, which described the dishonoring of God by humans who seek to suppress the truth. Since continuity with the preceding argument is indicated, the aorist verb and preposition παρέδωκεν εἰς ("he delivered into") following διό ("therefore") suggests the deliverance by a judge to some form of retribution.[15] When παρέδωκεν is followed by a dative expression and then by an εἰς clause indicating the pur-

---

14   See BAGD 198, citing Molland, "Διό," 43–52.
15   The elaboration of this scheme by Schlatter, 42, has

been followed by Klostermann, "Adäquate Vergeltung," 3–6; Jeremias, "Röm 1.22-32," 120;

pose, it is a technical expression for the police or courts in turning someone over to official custody for the purpose of punishment.[16] This semantic field supports the translation with a formal expression such as "he consigned."[17] The explicit mention of the subject ὁ θεός ("God") indicates a decision on the part of God, moving beyond the vague passives in 1:21-22.[18] Paul insists that God became[19] directly[20] involved in the process of moral retribution in the period before the enactment of the final wrath, whereby the distorting and darkening of the heart (v. 21) result in God's confining the heart within the twisted circle of its desires (v. 24). Those who choose a dishonest heart are required to live out the life imposed by its twisted desires.[21] This formulation is a refinement of a favorite theme of a moral *lex talionis* in

Jewish and Greco-Roman ethics that is stated in classic form by Wis 11:16: "by what things a man sins, by these is he punished."[22] In this instance humans have no choice but to live out the consequences of their willful distortion of the truth by following "the desires of their hearts," a translation of a Hebrew expression for the motivational center of humankind (Deut 12:20 [A]; Ps 21:3 [S²]).[23] For example, Sir 5:2 provides an admonition with virtually the wording Paul uses in Romans: "Do not follow your soul and your strength, *to go in the desires of your heart*" (πορεύεσθαι ἐν ἐπιθυμίας καρδίας σου). In view of the typical formulation of consigning enemies to their victors or prisoners to their jailors reflected in this passage,[24] the preposition ἐν is not to be taken causally[25] or instrumentally,[26] but rather as indicating

---

Boumann, "Römer 1," 411; Bauer, *Leiblichkeit*, 140; and many others. An example of the formula used here appears in Job 16:11 (LXX): παρέδωκεν γάρ με ὁ κύριος εἰς χεῖρας ἀδίκου ("for the Lord delivered me into the hand of the wrongdoer").

16 Popkes, *Christus Traditus*, 83–85, with numerous examples; that Paul otherwise uses this technical expression is evident in 1 Cor 5:5, παραδοῦναι τὸν τοιοῦτον τῷ Σατανᾷ εἰς ὄλεθρον τῆς σαρκός ("deliver this man to Satan for the destruction of the flesh"). BAGD 614 lists as 1b "hand over, turn over, give up a person" in an official proceeding. However, Danker selects the translation "he abandoned" for Rom 1:24, which seems to overstate the element of ridding oneself of responsibility; see Cranfield, 1:121.

17 See esp. Popkes, "Aufbau," 496, and the comprehensive discussion of the term in idem, *Christus Traditus*, passim. Cranfield, 1:121, opts for "delivered up" with a vaguely judicial connotation.

18 Popkes, "Aufbau," 496, as opposed to Dunn, 1:62.

19 The aorist form of παρέδωκεν was probably not chosen merely for rhetorical effect, as Bauer, *Leiblichkeit*, 141, understands Michel, 102, to be suggesting. However, Bauer does not seem any closer to the temporal sense when he says the aorist emphasizes that the divine consignment continues on into the present, which would seem to be descriptive of the perfect tense. Schlier, 59, also understands παρέδωκεν in a perfect temporal sense. The aorist refers instead to a completed action in the past, which in this instance is visible in the perverse behavior of sinners.

20 Dodd discounts the subject of this active verb when he argues (p. 29) that evil in this passage "is pre-

sented as a natural process of cause and effect, and not as the direct act of God. . . . The act of God is no more than an abstention from interference with their free choice and its consequences." Hanson, *Wrath*, 85, concurs. Meyer, 1:86, and Moo, 111, have a more adequate sense of the "active role" of God in this process of judgment.

21 See Hamerton-Kelly, *Cross*, 152: "The wrath works by self-inflicted harm. God gives sinners up to the consequences of their self-destructive actions. . . . The wrath is the consequence of living willingly in the system of sacred violence." Heil, 25: "Vice is its own punishment."

22 See Klostermann, "Adäquate Vergeltung," 3–5, for additional references.

23 In *Terms*, 447–48, I concluded that "heart" was a typical term for Jewish anthropology, but it also appears in Greek texts as the center of "feeling and passion," according to LSJM 877. In the LXX the more frequent combination is between ἐπιθυμία and the closely associated term ψυχή ("soul") (Deut 12:20, 21; Pss 9:24; 20:2; Sir 18:31; Jer 2:24; 4 Macc 2:1).

24 For example, Judg 7:9, "I have delivered it [the Midian encampment] into your hands" (παρέδωκεν αὐτὴν ἐν τῇ χειρί σου); see also Judg 6:18; 2 Chr 36:17; 2 Esd 9:7; Ps 77(78):48; Hos 8:10; Isa 33:6; 36:15; 37:10; 1 Macc 5:50; Matt 20:19.

25 BAGD 261; MM 210, "because of the lusts of their hearts."

26 So Barrett, 38, "*by* the lusts of their own hearts."

the custody into which sinful humans are delivered as a consequence of their suppression of the truth. They are released from God's control and handed over to the control of their own desires. The choice of the plural form of ἐπιθυμία ("desire") makes clear that Paul does not share the Stoic assessment that desire is in and of itself a root cause of the human predicament as an expression of the lower nature.[27] Paul has in mind the LXX understanding of "the devices and desires of the heart" as the complex and devious cross-currents of human motivation that involve the entire person, not just one's bodily nature. According to the earlier portion of this pericope, the ultimate goal of the scheming heart encompasses the entire self and aims to suppress and distort the truth about the relative status of God and a human being.[28] Such wicked desires of the heart are the punitive custody into which God consigns sinners.

When humans live within the twisted prison of their desires, their inevitable direction according to this passage is "toward/for impurity,"[29] with the preposition εἰς used in a final sense.[30] Ἀκαθαρσία is used in the LXX to depict that which is ritually impure and thus fundamentally separated from the holy,[31] but it comes to be used in Hellenistic Judaism and the NT in a moral sense to denote behavior that "excludes man from fellowship with God."[32] Paul uses this term both in a moral[33] and a cultic sense with regard to food not being impure,[34] which reveals that instruction about purity/impurity comprised a fundamental part of instruction of converts (Rom 6:19; 2 Cor 12:21; Gal. 5:19; 1 Thess 2:3; 4:7). As we have come to learn from modern anthropologists, pollution is a state or action that is out of place and so inappropriate that it causes systems to become dysfunctional.[35] Although the ritual aspects of impurity were redefined and partially abandoned in the NT, the deep sense of revulsion about polluting behavior remains.[36]

The clause defining "uncleanness" is connected with a genitive that has been interpreted in a variety of ways. If it is understood as a genitive of purpose in a final or consecutive sense, "so that they might be dishonored,"[37] the idea would be that the goal of divine consignment is to a state of bodily perversion. If the genitive of the articular infinitive is understood to be epexegetic, "consisting in being dishonored," the implication would be that the term *dishonoring* "already constitutes the impurity itself, and does not merely attend it as a result."[38] It seems

---

27 See Friedrich Büchsel, "θυμός, ἐπιθυμία κτλ.," *TDNT* 3 (1965) 168–69. In "Natural and Unnatural Use in Romans 1:24-27: Paul and the Philosophic Critique of Eros," in D. Balch, ed., *Homosexuality, Science, and the "Plain Sense" of Scripture* (Grand Rapids: Eerdmans, 2000) 208, David E. Fredrickson argues in contrast for a Stoic understanding of this reference, without accounting for the plural form or the connection with "heart." Engberg-Pedersen, *Stoics,* 210, interprets Paul's argument as criticizing "a certain self-directedness" that is allegedly based on Stoicism.

28 In view of this previous argument, it is questionable whether "ἐπιθυμίαι in this context means 'antinomistic' desires," as argued by Räisänen, "ἐπιθυμία and ἐπιθυμεῖν," 106.

29 See Schlatter, 42: εἰς "thus designates the result arising from the domination of the lusts, namely, the fact that the individual has become impure."

30 This section is adapted from Jewett, "Rom 1:24-27," 223–41.

31 See Friedrich Hauck, "ἀκάθαρτος, ἀκαθαρσία," *TDNT* 3 (1965) 427; cf. also Helmer Ringgren, "טהר," *TDOT* 5 (1986) 287–96.

32 Hauck, "ἀκάθαρτος, ἀκαθαρσία," 428.

33 Ibid.

34 See Pascher, *Rein und Unrein,* 170–72.

35 See the pioneering work of Douglas, *Purity and Danger,* 35, where she defines "dirt" "as matter out of place. . . . Dirt is the byproduct of a systematic ordering and classification of matter, insofar as ordering involves rejecting inappropriate elements." She concludes on 40: "if uncleanness is matter out of place, we must approach it through order. Uncleanness or dirt is that which must not be included if a pattern is to be maintained. To recognise this is the first step towards insight into pollution."

36 For general orientation from a social-scientific point of view, see Jerome H. Neyrey, "Unclean, Common, Polluted, and Taboo: A Short Reading Guide," *Forum* 4.4 (1988) 72–82; Michael Newton takes a historical and descriptive approach in *Concept of Purity.*

37 Zahn, 98. Cranfield, 1:122, prefers the "consecutive" to the "final" sense, as does Schlier, 60.

38 Meyer, 1:88. See also Barrett, 38.

more likely that the articular infinitive should be understood as adnominal, which in the genitive has the effect of limiting the meaning of the substantive on which it depends.[39] Of the many types of uncleanness, Paul has in mind the specific form of dishonoring the body.

The verb is a middle or passive, with the latter being more likely here and reflecting the social dimension of honor.[40] In the context of $\tau\grave{\alpha}$ $\sigma\acute{\omega}\mu\alpha\tau\alpha$ $\alpha\grave{\upsilon}\tau\hat{\omega}\nu$ ("their bodies"), such dishonor could be achieved through perverse sexual relations,[41] which are undoubtedly the main focus in this verse. Paul assumes that there are "natural" bodily relationships that are normative for humans. A similar assumption appears in 1 Cor 6:18, where the reference to sinning against the body implies the abrogation of the rightful use of the body through union with Christ.[42] It should be noted, however, that the body is also involved in almost all the other forms of antisocial behavior listed in this pericope (Rom 1:29-30).[43] Although bodily dishonor was alleged to be particularly characteristic of polytheism as seen from the perspective of Judaism,[44] Paul does not limit the range of his argument to those parameters here.[45]

The final phrase $\acute{\epsilon}\nu$ $\alpha\grave{\upsilon}\tauo\hat{\iota}\varsigma$ can be interpreted in a variety of ways, that the dishonoring occurred "among them,"[46] which seems most likely in view of the nature of sexual intercourse, that the dishonoring was "in them," which seems overly privatistic, or that it affected "themselves,"[47] which seems rather self-evident. Others stress that the dishonoring came about "through themselves"[48] stressing personal responsibility for bodily actions. In view of the graphic description of perverse sexual intercourse in v. 27, the first of these alternatives appears probable.

■ **25** This verse reinforces and elaborates the leitmotif introduced in v. 18 and expressed in v. 23 as an aggressive campaign against God. The link between the relative pronoun $o\H{\iota}\tau\iota\nu\epsilon\varsigma$ ("the very ones who")[49] and the preceding verse is broken by those wishing to see a new paragraph[50] or a new sentence[51] beginning with v. 25, but the grammar demands a relative clause showing "a characteristic quality, by which a preceding statement is to be confirmed."[52] According to the final phrase of v. 24, the bodily dishonor for which persons are directly responsible is here connected with a reversal of the proper relationship between the creation and the Creator. It is unfortunate that the English term standing closest to the verb $\mu\epsilon\tau\acute{\eta}\lambda\lambda\alpha\xi\alpha\nu$ is the neutral-sounding verb "they exchanged," because the intensification of the word "change" as used in v. 23 with the addition of $\mu\epsilon\tau\acute{\alpha}$ implies an even more "odious" form of sin[53] and means

---

39 Smyth, *Grammar*, §§1290–91.

40 See Achatz von Muller, *Gloria Bona Fama Bonorum. Studien zur sittlichen Bedeutung des Ruhmes in der frühchristlichen und mittelalterlichen Welt* (Husum: Matthieseu, 1977), 22–38, for references to honor as a social concept in the Greco-Roman world; for the social-scientific point of view see Pitt-Rivers, *Anthropology of the Mediterranean*, 1–17; Gilmore, *Honor and Shame*, 2–21; Peristiany, *Honour and Shame*, passim.

41 Almost all commentators (e.g., Wilckens, 1:108–9; Dunn, 1:62) assume that the primary reference is sexual, since Paul takes up the sexual perversions first, and since there are Judaic parallels to connecting idolatry with sexual irregularities. See *Sib. Or.* 3.8-44; *T. Jos.* 4.5-6; Wis 14:24-27. In the context of slaves used for prostitution, Dio Chrysostom *Orat.* 7.132ff writes that they are "bearing the insult in [their] dishonored and slavish bodies ($\varphi\acute{\epsilon}\rho o\nu\tau\alpha\varsigma$ $\tau\grave{\eta}\nu$ $\epsilon\grave{\iota}\varsigma$ $\H{\alpha}\tau\iota\mu\alpha$ $\kappa\alpha\grave{\iota}$ $\deltao\hat{\upsilon}\lambda\alpha$ $\sigma\acute{\omega}\mu\alpha\tau\alpha$ $\H{\upsilon}\beta\rho\iota\nu$)" (7.138).

42 Jewett, *Terms*, 288; see also Gundry, *Sōma*, 70–75.

43 The reference in Wis 14:24-27 includes other forms of antisocial behavior and criminality along with sexual promiscuity, just as Paul does later in this chapter.

44 Michel, 104.

45 Dabelstein, *Beurteilung*, 83, cites *3 Ezra* 8.66 as evidence that Jews as well as Gentiles receive the accusation of impurity. See also Colenso, 47–51.

46 Sanday and Headlam, 46; Cranfield, 1:123; similar is an option mentioned by Michel, 104, "among themselves."

47 Kuss, 1:49; Lagrange, 28.

48 Barrett, 38; Käsemann, 48; Wilckens, 1:109.

49 Zahn, 98, stresses that $o\H{\iota}\tau\iota\nu\epsilon\varsigma$ in coordination with the preceding phrase $\acute{\epsilon}\nu$ $\alpha\grave{\upsilon}\tauo\hat{\iota}\varsigma$ implies that v. 25 describes not an additional class of sinners but the entire human race as described since v. 18.

50 Klostermann, "Adäquate Vergeltung," 1.

51 Cranfield, 1:123, argues against v. 25 as a relative clause that explains the cause of the action in v. 24 on grounds that the cause of v. 24 is already identified by the conjunction $\delta\iota\acute{o}$ as lying in vv. 22-23, but this presumes that Paul is incapable of redundancy.

52 BAGD 587; BDF §293.

53 Godet, 108; also Meyer, 1:89; *LSJM* 1113 lists "alter" and "substitute" as possible translations. Ceslas Spicq, "$\mu\epsilon\tau\alpha\lambda\lambda\acute{\alpha}\sigma\sigma\omega$," *TLNT* 2 (1994) 470: "radical . . . change is envisioned: it is a substitution." See

something like "travestied." As elsewhere in this pericope, the aorist tense refers to "the primal sin of rebellion against the Creator, which finds repeated and universal expression."[54]

The expression "the truth of God"[55] picks up the theme of v. 18 and makes unequivocally clear that it is not truth in general or some limited truth that humans wish to suppress but the truth of God's being as the Ultimate One disclosed by the creation. The choice of the term τὸ ψεῦδος ("the lie") as the antithesis to the truth of God emphasizes the intentionality of humans to distort and suppress the truth.[56] Conzelmann points out, "Lying cannot be viewed merely as the opposite of truth,"[57] because it contains an element of deception that differentiates it from mere falsehood. This is not simply "a lie" but "*the* lie,"[58] which involves the fundamental thrust of humans to replace God with themselves, a tendency visible from the fall to the crucifixion of Christ. The prophets had referred to idolators as speaking and trusting in "lies" about God (Hos 7:13; Jer 13:25; cf. Isa 59:13),[59] but the singular use of "the lie" in Romans implies an antecedent act from which all later lies about God derive, namely the primordial desire of humans to "be like God" and to define evil and good for

themselves (Gen 3:5). In the light of the gospel, Paul has radicalized the story of the fall by emphasizing the element of willful distortion.

The description of the means by which humans express their commitment to "the lie" is drawn from Greco-Roman and Jewish religion. Σεβάζεσθαι ("to venerate") is used here for the first and only time in the NT, perhaps because the term was so intimately associated with polytheistic religion and the Roman civic cult.[60] The verbal adjective σεβαστός ("the venerated one") was the exact equivalent of the Latin term "Augustus," which appeared in the calendar, the coins, the state propaganda, and the cultic honors paid to the Emperor Octavian and his successors.[61] In the *Res Gestae* 34.2, for example, Augustus claimed to have "surpassed all in respect of my prestige (*auctoritas*), but I had no more legal authority (*potestas*) than any others who were my colleagues in any magistracy." Thus, as Lendon remarks, "Augustus expected people to believe that he ruled the empire by virtue of his honour,"[62] which surpassed all others in a godlike manner.[63] Although commentators have not elaborated the political and ideological significance of this term,[64] its use obliquely suggests the false character of the veneration of the emperor that had

---

54   Käsemann, 47.

55   This expression could be translated as an objective genitive, "the truth about God," but the preceding discussion provides more support for the subjective genitive, "the truth of God." See Weiss, 89; Schlier, 60; Moo, 112. For a parallel to this expression in contrast to false worship, see *As. Mos.* 5.4.

56   The same antithesis, along with a form of the word "exchange," is found in Philo *Mos.* 2.167, which describes Moses' consternation at seeing the golden calf that represented "indeed how great a lie they had traded for so great a truth" (καὶ ὅσαν ψεῦδας ἀνθ᾿ ὅσης ἀληθείας).

57   Hans Conzelmann, "ψεῦδος κτλ.," *TDNT* 9 (1974) 595.

58   Fitzmyer, 284–85, refers to the "big lie. . . . the deception that smothers the truth." However, the article is probably the weak possessive, "their lie."

59   See Conzelmann, "ψευδός κτλ.," 598–99.

60   See BAGD 745–46; and Werner Foerster, "σέβομαι κτλ.," *TDNT* 7 (1971) 173–75; the latter argues that the associated term σέβομαι ("to worship, vener

also Friedrich Büchsel, "ἀλλάσσω κτλ.," *TDNT* 1 (1964) 259.

ate") is used only for non-Christian worship. Fitzmyer, 285, cites an exception in *Ep. Arist.* 139, where Israel is spoken of as "venerating the only powerful God instead of all creation" (τὸν μόνον θεὸν καὶ δυνατὸν σεβόμενοι παρ᾿ ὅλην τὴν πᾶσαν κτίσιν).

61   Foerster, "σέβομαι κτλ.," 174–75. See Chistensen, *Christus oder Jupiter*, 22–39; Bischoff discusses the calendric use of this term as an equivalent of the Latin, *Augustus*, in "Sebastos," *PW*, Series 2, 2:956–57.

62   Lendon, *Empire of Honour*, 129; the translation from the *Res Gestae* is also on this page.

63   Ibid.: "their own outlook encouraged aristocrats to imitate the emperor as the most honourable man in their world," citing Libanius *Or.* 18.156, "Whatsoever is scorned by our rulers is neglected by all; what is honoured by them, all practice."

64   The only exception I have found is Zahn, 99, who alludes indirectly to the civic cult and the adoration of heroes. Other commentators concentrate on explaining the apparent redundancy of using two similar terms for worship. Kühl, 57, explains that σεβάζεσθαι refers to "the pious honoring of

become so prominent a feature of Roman religion. The term "creature" cannot of course be restricted to emperor worship, since it refers to every human and animal and object that played a role in Greco-Roman worship. However, the countercultural quality of Paul's argument, detected already earlier in the letter, expresses itself here in a subtle manner, because Paul's audience could scarcely have missed this allusion to the most prominent form of "venerating the creature" in Rome.[65]

The second verb, λατρεύειν ("to worship"), is used broadly and positively in the LXX and the rest of the NT.[66] We noted Paul's use of the term for his own activity in 1:9. The selection of this term in coordination with σεβάζεσθαι indicates that Paul does not wish to isolate Roman polytheism as the only prominent expression of false worship. The universal scope of his argument includes all forms of worship and logically places Judaism on the same level as polytheism.[67] Every religion infected by the universal urge to suppress the truth can be involved in worshiping τῇ κτίσει παρὰ τὸν κτίσαντα ("the creature rather than the Creator"). The term κτίσις could mean the "creation" as a whole[68] or a particular "creature," of which the latter appears more probable to commentators in the light of the reference to "humans, birds, animals, and reptiles" in v. 23.[69]

The failure to worship God as Creator violates the foundational belief in the OT and in all later forms of Judaism, a belief shared by early Christianity.[70] Paul had reiterated the basis for such a belief in vv. 19-21. Now he creates the most memorable wordplay in the wide arena of discussion up to Paul's time, which articulates the distinction between the creature and the Creator. The rhetorical eloquence rests on a profound emotional and theological foundation,[71] which evokes an exclamation in the form of a traditional Jewish blessing.[72] Such blessings were used with meals and other family occasions as well as in religious services and were adopted and developed in early Christianity. Even to name the heretical act of worshiping the creature rather than the Creator evokes such a shudder in Paul and his audience that what some have called an "apotropaic blessing"[73] is required to set things right. To use the terminology of contemporary semantics, a biblical blessing is a performative utterance whose power resides not in the magical efficacy of the words themselves but in the authority of the speaker, the appropriateness of the situation, and the ultimate power of God to sustain the promised blessing.[74] All three conditions pertain here, as Paul breaks into the mood of prayer that has both an illocutionary and a perlocutionary force; that is, the prayer thanks God for the concrete blessing of the creation and invites "others to join the speaker in praising God."[75] Paul "blesses"[76] God "into the ages," a literal translation of

hearts" and λατρεύειν to "external action in cultic honoring." See the critique by Cranfield, 1:124, and Schlier's frank acknowledgment of the virtually identical meaning of the two verbs (61). Foerster argues in "σέβομαι κτλ.," 173, that the first term refers to worship in general, while the second refers to specific cultic acts.

65 Brinkman, "Creation II," 363–64, shows that "the *creation-creature* question is far from being general in this context," but he attaches the specificity to bodily perversion rather than to the civic cult.

66 See Hermann Strathmann, "λατρεύω, λατρεία," *TDNT* 4 (1967) 59–63.

67 For a less sweeping assessment see Dunn, 1:63.

68 Proposed by BAGD 456 on the basis of *Ep. Arist.* 139, which refers to worshiping God rather than "all creation" (τὴν πᾶσαν κτίσιν), but the omission of the word "all" is missing from Rom 1:25 erodes the basis for this choice. The LXX for Gen 1:1 and Acts 17:24, 26 would sustain the connotation of the "whole creation."

69 See Cranfield, 1:124; Lampe, "*Ktisis*," 449–62; and Brinkman, "Creation I," "Creation II."

70 See Werner Foerster, "κτίζω," *TDNT* 3 (1965) 1005–35; Lampe, "Ktisis," 21–24; for more recent approaches see Bernhard W. Anderson, ed., *Creation in the Old Testament* (Philadelphia: Fortress Press, 1984) 14–21, 102–17; and Karl Eberlein, *Gott der Schöpfer, Israels Gott: Eine exegetisch-hermeneutische Studie zur theologischen Funktion alttestamentlicher Schöpfungsaussagen*, BEATAJ 5 (Frankfurt: Lang, 1986) 253–63, 302–5.

71 See Schlatter, 43.

72 See Schenk, *Segen*, 97; Claus Westermann, *Blessing in the Bible and the Life of the Church* (Philadelphia: Fortress Press, 1978) 24–26; Heckel, *Segen*, 48–49.

73 See Schlier, 61; Wilckens, 1:109. Heckel, *Segen*, 51, refers to this as the "short blessing" typically used in Jewish writings after the mention of God's name.

74 Mitchell, *Meaning of BRK*, 173–76.

75 Ibid., 170; see also Wilckens, 1:109.

76 To "bless" God in the Judaic sense implied here is

the typical biblical formula that perceives the future as an endless series of time periods.[77] A profound antithesis is expressed in this phrase between the eternal Creator and the finite creatures who yearn for infinite status. Michel writes: "Paul praises the One whom the pagans blaspheme."[78] The "amen" at the end of the blessing[79] is the traditional Judaic manner of indicating something "is sure and valid" and continues the perlocutionary mood by inviting the audience's concurrence through responding in liturgical style with the same word.[80]

■ **26** In a second refrain-like[81] statement of divine response to the great lie, "God delivered them," meaning that God confirmed and sustained the twisted bondage to a chaotic world.[82] The introductory phrase διὰ τοῦτο ("for this reason")[83] explains the deliverance to dishonest relationships as the fitting response to the deceptive assault of humankind on the status of God.

The expression εἰς πάθη ἀτιμίας ("to dishonorable passions") resonates with the reference to "impurity" in 1:24. The term "passion" is a more distinctive term in Greco-Roman ethics than "desires."[84] Paul had combined both expressions in an unusual expression found in 1 Thess 4:5, ἐν πάθει ἐπιθυμίας ("in passions of desires").[85] Πάθος conveys the sense of an involuntary state that simply comes over a person.[86] Socrates, for instances, spoke of τὸ ἐρωτικὸν πάθος ("the erotic passion") as a kind of "madness," a "being led away."[87] Plato taught that a tyrannical person is ruled by an even more tyrannical force within called "passion."[88] Aristotle defined passion as an emotional state marked by pleasure or pain.[89] The Stoics developed an entire philosophy on the premise of passion, teaching that the expectation of pleasure therefrom is irrational so that the πάθη must be diagnosed as a sickness of the soul to be rooted out.[90] Hellenistic Judaism shared this view and

to acknowledge God as the source of all blessings, according to Hermann W. Beyer, "εὐλογέω," TDNT 2 (1964) 756: "The One who possesses and dispenses all blessings is God the Lord. This is the sacred knowledge underlying all OT statements concerning blessing."

77 Herman Sasse, "αἰών, αἰώνιος," TDNT 1 (1964) 199, shows that the plural formula used here, εἰς τοὺς αἰῶνας, is typical for religious doxologies with roughly identical meaning with the singular formula except that the former "presupposes knowledge of a plurality of αἰῶνες, of ages and periods of time whose infinite series constitutes eternity." For an assessment of the semantic issues see Barr, Time, 119–21; for a theological appraisal see Delling, Zeit und Endzeit, 49–56, 98–101.

78 Michel, 105.

79 In "Amen," ThRE 2 (1978) 386–87, Joachim Jeremias shows that the most frequent occasion for the formula in the OT is in connection with blessing and cursing.

80 Heinrich Schlier, "ἀμήν," TDNT 1 (1964) 336; see also Jeremias, "Amen," ThRE 2 (1978) 390; Heckel, Segen, 308–12.

81 Lagrange, 28.

82 Käsemann, 47.

83 For the use of διὰ τοῦτο as the beginning of a sentence see Meyer, 1:91; on the link with the foregoing argument see Zahn, 100.

84 See J. Hengelbrock, "Affect (πάθος, passio, Leidenschaft)," HWP 1:89–91; BAGD 602–3 shows the term is not used in the LXX with the connotation

of passionate desire, whereas LSJM 1285–86 lists a wide variety of classical and Hellenistic Greek usage, including the title of the Stoic Zeno's work, περὶ παθῶν ("Concerning the Passions"). See also A. Gilbert-Thirry, Pseudo-Andronicus de Rhodes "ΠΕΡΙ ΠΑΘΩΝ," CLCAG.Sup 2 (Leiden: Brill, 1977); Andronicus Pass. 1.1–15 defines passion as ἄλογος ψυχῆς κίνησις. . . καὶ παρὰ φύσιν ἢ ὁρμὴ πλεονάζουσα ("an irrational movement of the soul . . . and an unnatural or exaggerated impulse") of which there are four types: grief, fear, desire (ἐπιθυμίας), and pleasure. Gilbert-Thirry discusses numerous classical parallels on 273–319.

85 See Marshall, Thessalonians, 110, who translates 4:5 as "the passion of lust. The former word expresses an overpowering feeling . . . and the latter word reinforces the thought of sinful desire."

86 LSJM 1285: "that which happens to a person"; Wilhelm Michaelis, "πάθος," TDNT 5 (1967) 926: "The meaning 'mood,' 'feeling,' 'emotion' etc. is very common in both a good sense and a bad."

87 Plato Phaed. 265b. Fredrickson, "Natural and Unnatural Use," 209–11, argues that this erotic connotation is implied in Rom 1:26.

88 Plato Resp. 575a–c.

89 Aristotle Eth. nic. 1105b.

90 J. Hengelbrock and J. Lanz, "Affect (πάθος, passio, Leidenschaft)," HWP 1:90, citing Chrysippus, in SVF 1.121 and 3.443; for general orientation see B. Inwood, Ethics and Human Action in Early Stoicism (Oxford: Clarendon, 1985) 154–73.

urged the taming of the passions.[91] To be without unreasonable passion was true wisdom for the Stoics, while the Peripatetics and Skeptics taught the ideal of $\mu\epsilon\tau\rho\iota o$-$\pi\acute{\alpha}\vartheta\epsilon\iota\alpha$ ("moderate passion").[92] The noun $\grave{\alpha}\tau\iota\mu\acute{\iota}\alpha\varsigma$ ("dishonor")[93] and the context of 1:26b indicate that plural term $\pi\acute{\alpha}\vartheta\eta$ includes disreputable, erotic passions for Paul,[94] not the broader philosophical sense of emotions in general.[95] Paul's view is also far removed from the dominant social sense of dishonor as lack of respect, which often came from failing to conform to aristocratic standards.[96] To be confined within the realm of perverse passions apparently had a horrific connotation for Paul and his audience.

To substantiate the claim in v. 26a concerning dishonorable passions, Paul introduces with $\gamma\acute{\alpha}\rho$ ("for") the example of perverse sexual relations. The *exemplum* ("example") is a widely used means of proof in Greco-Roman rhetoric,[97] particularly suited for the epideictic genre that concerns itself with praise and blame of various types of behavior.[98] The most effective examples are drawn from everyday experience and derive their argumentative force from shared opinion or prejudice. Here we have the most egregious instance Paul can find to demonstrate his thesis about human distortion, the arena of sexual perversity that created wide revulsion in the Jewish and early Christian communities of his time.[99] There was also a widespread critique of effeminacy and homosexuality among traditional Romans, who castigated "Greek" behavior and found Nero objectionable in "dressing Greek" and publicly expressing bisexual impulses.[100] The depiction of a particularly unpopular example for the sake of an effective argument leads Paul to highly prejudicial language, particularly to the modern ear. It should be clear from the outset, however, that Paul's aim is not to prove the evils of perverse sexual behavior; that is simply assumed. The aim is to develop a thesis about the manifestation of divine wrath in the human experience of Paul's time. In contrast to traditional moralizing based on this passage, sexual perversion is in Paul's view "the result of God's wrath, not the reason for it."[101]

The same verb "exchange" is used for this type of sexual dishonor as had been used in v. 25 for religious dishonesty, which suggests a direct correspondence between the two.[102] Similar expressions were used in the denunciation of $\gamma\epsilon\nu\epsilon\sigma\acute{\epsilon}\omega\varsigma$ $\grave{\epsilon}\nu\alpha\lambda\lambda\acute{\alpha}\gamma\eta$ ("interchange of

---

91 Michaelis, "$\pi\acute{\alpha}\vartheta o\varsigma$," 927.

92 Hengelbrock, "Affect," 91.

93 Cranfield, 1:125, defines $\grave{\alpha}\tau\iota\mu\acute{\iota}\alpha\varsigma$ as a "genitive of quality, the meaning of the phrase being 'passions which bring dishonour.'" However, since genitives of quality usually occur in predicates, according to Smyth, *Grammar*, §1320, this is more likely a partitive genitive, since dishonor includes more than certain passions. Kühl, 57, suggests that dishonor in this context relates to the "perversion of the created order of the nature of humans, upon which their honor rests."

94 Michaelis, "$\pi\acute{\alpha}\vartheta o\varsigma$," 928, acknowledges the plural form but translates in the singular, "erotic passion." He properly repudiates Schlatter's translation (43), "passions that are a disgrace."

95 See Pohlenz, "Stoa," 82.

96 See Lendon, *Empire of Honour*, 50–51, 193–94.

97 For definition see Aristotle *Rhet.* 1.2.13; Quintilian *Inst.* 5.11.1; for general orientation see Hildegard Kornhardt, *Exemplum. Eine bedeutungsgeschichtliche Studie* (Göttingen: Noske, 1936); and Lausberg, *Handbuch*, §§412–26.

98 Lausberg, *Handbuch*, §245.

99 Typical denunciations of pagan homosexuality may be found in Philo *Abr.* 135; *Spec.* 1.50; 3.37–42; Wis

14:16. See also Jean-Claude Vilbert, "Aux origines d'une condamnation. L'homosexualité dans la Rome antique et l'église des premiers siècles," *LumVie*(L) 29 (1980) 15–28; and Wolfgang Stegemann, "Paul and the Sexual Mentality of His World," *BTB* 23 (1993) 161–66.

100 See Griffin, *Nero*, 119, 160–66.

101 Käsemann, 47.

102 Kuss, 1:50: "The 'exchange' as punishment follows the 'exchange' as guilt." See also Richard B. Hays, "Relations Natural and Unnatural: A Response to John Boswell's Exegesis of Romans 1," *JRE* 14 (1986) 192: "The deliberate repetition of the verb *metēllaxan* forges a powerful rhetorical link between the rebellion against God and the 'shameless acts' (1:27, *RSV*) which are themselves both evidence and consequence of that rebellion."

sexual roles") in the vice catalogue of Wis 14:26[103] and in *T. Naph.* 3.3-4:

Ἔθνη πλανηθέντα καὶ ἀφέντα Κύριον ἠλλιό-
ωσαν τὴν τάξιν αὐτῶν... Ὑμεῖς δὲ μὴ οὕτως,
τέκνα μου... ἵνα μὴ γένεσθε ὡς Σόδομα, ἥτις
ἐνήλλαξε τάξιν φύσεως αὐτῆς. ("Having gone
astray and forsaken the Lord, the Gentiles changed
their order. . . . But you shall not be so, my children
. . . so that you will not become as Sodom, which
changed the order of its nature.")

Paul uses the term "female" rather than "woman," which conforms to the usage in the LXX version of the creation story (Gen 1:27)[104] and the formula of Gal 3:28 that refers to biological rather than social differences.[105] In contrast to these and other examples, however, relations between females[106] are mentioned first by Paul, probably for rhetorical reasons.[107] The silence about lesbianism in the OT, the infrequent references to it in Greco-Roman literature,[108] and the deeply conservative and chauvinistic sexual climate of the post-Augustan age suggest that lesbianism was a sensitive topic for Paul and his audience.[109] Despite the appearance of lesbian scenes on the walls of Pompeii as reported by Luciana Jacobelli,[110] Dover refers to the "striking" element of male hostility in references to female homosexual behavior.[111] Bernadette J. Brooten has traced a broad pattern of such hostility in Greco-Roman literature including magical papyri, astrological texts, medical texts, and

103 See the translation by David Winston, *The Wisdom of Solomon,* AB (Garden City, NY: Doubleday, 1979) 26; and the discussion by James B. De Young, "A Critique of Prohomosexual Interpretations of the Old Testament Apocrypha and Pseudepigrapha," *BSac* 147 (1990) 442–45.

104 See Knut Holter-Stavanger, "A Note on the Old Testament Background of Rom 1,23-27," *BN* 69 (1993) 22.

105 See Betz, *Galatians,* 195.

106 Tomson, *Paul and the Jewish Law,* 94, argues for unnatural intercourse between men and women, but this would make v. 26 a doublet of v. 27.

107 The suggestion by Cornly, *Commentarius,* 99, and Murray, 47, that lesbian relations were perceived as more shocking than homosexuality provides the necessary social background for Paul's reversal of sequence. For other options see Cranfield, 1:125; and Dunn, 1:64.

108 For general orientation, including the use of abusive epithets, see W. Kroll, "Kinaidos," *PW* 11:1 (1921) 459–62. LSJM 1040 lists Aristophanes *Ran.* 1302, and Lucian of Samosata *Pseudol.* 28, as the only examples of λεσβιάζω ("act like a Lesbian woman"); Meyer, 1:92, adds Lucian of Samosata *Dial. mer.* 5.2, and Aelian, *Var. hist.* 3.12. Fitzmyer, 286, adds Pseudo-Lucian *Am.* 28, and Plutarch *Lyc.* 18, along with *Apoc. Pet.* 32. See also Kenneth James Dover, *Greek Homosexuality* (2d ed.; Cambridge: Harvard Univ. Press, 1989) 171–73. After an exhaustive search through the primary sources in *The New Testament and Homosexuality: Contextual Background for Contemporary Debate* (Philadelphia: Fortress Press, 1983) 115, Robin Scroggs concludes that the topic of lesbianism is "virtually absent" from Jewish and Greco-Roman ethical discussion; see the excursus,

"Female Homosexuality in the Greco-Roman World," 140–44. This assessment was refuted by Mark D. Smith, "Ancient Bisexuality and the Interpretation of Romans 1:26-27," *JAAR* 64 (1996) 238–43. A significant though distant allusion to lesbian relations appears in Philo *Spec.* 3.51.

109 In "Roman Attitudes toward Sex," in M. Grant and R. Kitzinger, eds., *Civilization of the Ancient Mediterranean: Greece and Rome,* 3 vols. (New York: Scribner's, 1988) 2:1265–78, Judith P. Hallett notes the tension between a puritanical view in older Roman thought and the permissive attitudes in the period from 220 B.C.E. to 150 C.E. She observes that "homosexual liaisons of women never received as much attention as those of men. This disregard seems related to the Romans' much more negative assessment of female homosexual activity than of male homoeroticism" (1266).

110 In "Why Unnatural? The Tradition behind Romans 1:26-27," *HTR* 90 (1997) 263–84, Roy Bowen Ward refers to Jacobelli's study, *Pitture erotiche delle Terme Suburbane di Pompei,* Soprintendenza archaeologica di Pompei, Monographie 10 (Rome: Bretschneider, 1995).

111 Dover, *Homosexuality,* 172. In *Bisexuality,* 166, Cantarelli concludes that for Romans, "homosexuality was the worst form of female depravity." In "The Practices of Romans 1:26: Homosexual or Heterosexual?" *NovT* 37 (1995) 6, James C. Miller also points out that Pseudo-Lucian in *Am.* 28 "broaches the double standard of accepting male homosexuality but despising female homosexuality." Lucian satirizes this double standard, and the humor would not have been effective without the hostility of his male readers toward same-sex relations among women.

guidebooks for interpreting erotic dreams.[112] She concludes that "the ancient sources nearly uniformly condemn sexual love between women."[113] There is evidence of frequent jokes in Greco-Roman culture about homosexual behavior but few about lesbians.[114] As seen in a writer like Horace,[115] there was appreciation for the eloquence of Sappho's poetry but contempt for her "masculine" qualities. By the first century, Sappho had become a stereotype for disreputable behavior.[116]

Paul's description of lesbian behavior as exchanging (μετήλλαξαν) "the natural use for the unnatural" (τὴν φυσικὴν χρῆσιν εἰς τὴν παρὰ φύσιν) employs philosophical language that gained particular prevalence among the Stoics.[117] They taught that proper use of objects is according to nature (κατὰ φύσιν) and that the

failure to follow common sense and the inner law of one's being was against nature (παρὰ φύσιν). The expression for heterosexual intercourse was "according to nature" (ἡ κατὰ φύσιν ἐπιπλοκή, Diodorus Siculus *Hist.* 32.10.4.9) and a homoerotic relationship was παρὰ φύσιν γάμος ("marriage against nature"; *Hist.* 32.10.9.3).[118] Plato describes the customary definition of these terms: "it is necessary to understand that the pleasure concerning these things according to nature (κατὰ φύσιν) is considered to be defined by the female nature and the nature of males that long for the partnership of procreation but [the pleasure concerning these things] contrary to nature (παρὰ φύσιν)."[119] Plutarch also uses "unnatural/beyond nature" to refer to female homoeroticism: "Women have no part in Ares at all but the

112 Brooten, *Love between Women*, 31–186. Roman writers after Augustus satirize women who do not conform to the passive role expected of women, while Greek writers in the same period "represent sexual love between women as masculine, unnatural, lawless, licentious, and monstrous," according to Brooten, 50.

113 Ibid., 359. She assumes that the basis for this condemnation was because lesbianism involved usurping the dominant place of men, but a further reason may have been the ancient preoccupation with procreation.

114 See Amy Richlin, *The Garden of Priapus: Sexuality and Aggression in Roman Humor* (New Haven: Yale Univ. Press, 1983) 132, 134, 220–26. In "Invective Against Women in Roman Satire," *Arethusa* 17 (1984) 77, Richlin observes that the "rare attacks on lesbians predictably focus on a woman's preemption of a male role in intercourse."

115 Brooten, *Love between Women*, 34, points to Horace's references to *mascula Sappho* in *Carm.* 4.9.10; *Ep.* 1.19.28. Plutarch *Pyth. orac.* 406A refers to the similarity of Sappho's love for women to Socrates' love for men. For the contrast with male-oriented erotic poetry, see Eva Stehle Stigers, "Sappho's Private World," in Helene P. Foley, ed., *Reflections of Women in Antiquity* (New York: Gordon and Breach, 1981) 45–61. John J. Winkler explores Sappho's celebration of a "world apart from men" (p. 83) in "Gardens of Nymphs: Public and Private in Sappho's Lyrics," in *Women in Antiquity*, 63–89. In *Constraints of Desire: Essays in the Anthropology of Sex and Gender in Ancient Greece* (New York: Routledge, 1990) 162–87, Winkler refers to the "mutilated and violent discourse which keeps cropping up around"

Sappho because her poetry was a "double violation of the ancient rules which dictated . . . that a proper woman accepted the administration and definition of her sexuality by her father and her husband" (163).

116 Dover, *Homosexuality*, 174, refers to Horace *Carm.* 2.13.5; Ovid *Tris.* 2.365; and *P.Oxy.* 1800 fragment 1, col. i 16-17, of which the last in particular has a critical view of Sappho's alleged homosexual behavior. Lucian develops the Sappho themes in *Dial. mer.* 5, which may indicate a change of attitude by the 2d century C.E. See Boswell, *Homosexuality*, 82–83. Brooten concludes in *Love between Women*, 36: "Thus, writers of the Roman period showed increased preoccupation with Sappho's love for women, often combined with disapproval of that love."

117 See Helmut Koester, "φύσις κτλ.," *TDNT* 9 (1974) 262–65, 273.

118 Ibid., 263, also cites Josephus *C. Ap.* 2.273–75 (see also 2.199), and the later Athenaeus *Deipn.* 13.84 (605d), as using the παρὰ φύσιν formula to describe homosexual relations. James B. De Young, "The Meaning of 'Nature' in Romans 1 and Its Implications for Biblical Proscriptions of Homosexual Behavior," *JETS* 31 (1988) 433, also cites *T. Naph.* 3.4-5 on homosexuals who "changed the order of nature." Using examples cited by Scroggs and Furnish, Hays, "Relations," 192–93, has recently discussed Dio Chrysostom *Orat.* 7.135.151–52, and Plutarch *Amat.* 751c, e, as using the "natural/unnatural" language to discuss homosexuality.

119 Plato *Leg.* 636c; citation noted by Ward, "Unnatural," 263–84.

possession by love induces [them] to dare [to do] something beyond nature (παρὰ φύσιν) and to die."[120] In a similar manner, Philo makes prominent use of the terminology Paul employs in this verse, describing the perversion of the Sodomites as a violation of "nature" (*Abr.* 135-37) and stigmatizing pederasty as ἡ παρὰ φύσιν ἡδονή ("an unnatural pleasure"; *Spec.* 3.39.2) while affirming the "natural use"[121] (τῆς κατὰ φύσιν χρήσεως) of heterosexual sexuality (*Mut.* 111-12).[122] Similarly, a Hellenistic Jewish writing roughly contemporaneously with Romans contains the admonishment: "Do not step beyond the marriage beds of nature (εὐνὰς φύσεως) into Cyprian lawlessness. Neither are male beasts pleased to bed with the same male beasts, nor should females imitate any marriage bed of husbands."[123]

It is clear from these and other references that "'natural' intercourse means penetration of a subordinate person by a dominant one," a female by a male.[124] One motif that Paul does not adopt from this philosophical tradition is ἡδονή ("pleasure"), referred to by Pseudo-Phocyclides as "Cyprian lawlessness."[125] Plato considered pleasure to be "natural" only when it resulted in legitimate childbearing.[126] There is no reference to parentage in Paul's discussion, either here or in other Pauline references to marriage, and there is a positive allusion to sexual attraction and pleasure between married partners in 1 Cor 7:4, 7.

In the light of these parallels, it is clear that Paul has in mind female homoeroticism in this verse, rather than women's engaging in oral or anal intercourse with males[127] or heterosexual women committing homoerotic acts.[128] There is a strikingly egalitarian note in Paul's treating same-sex intercourse among females as an issue in its own right and holding women to the same level of accountability as men.[129] It is nevertheless clear that Paul's choice and description of the lesbian example reflect confidence that his audience, shaped by a similar philosophical and religious heritage, "will share his negative judgment."[130]

---

120 Plutarch *Amat.* 761e; translation adapted from Edwin L. Minar Jr., E. H. Sandwich, and W. C. Helmbold, *Plutarch's Moralia,* LCL (Cambridge: Harvard Univ. Press, 1961) 9:383.

121 For parallels to χρῆσις to refer to sexual "use," see BAGD 886; this is the only use in the NT; see I. Opelt, "Euphemismus," *RAC* 6 (1966) 951. Fredrickson, "Natural and Unnatural Use," 199, shows that this term "does not refer to a relation carried out in the medium of sexual pleasure but the activity of the desiring subject, usually male, performed on the desired object, male or female."

122 See De Young, "Meaning of 'Nature,'" 434.

123 Pseudo-Phocyclides *Sent.* 190–93.

124 Brooten, *Love between Women,* 241; see also Winkler, *Constraints of Desire,* 36–43.

125 The reference to "Cyprian lawlessness" implies behavior influenced by Aphrodite whom tradition associated with Cyprus. On the importance of Pseudo-Phocyclides see Ward, "Unnatural," 23. He points out the flaw in Furnish's comment that "a Hellenistic Jew like Philo could just as well have written it" (*Moral Teaching,* 77), because "erotic acts between spouses without a procreative intent were forbidden by Plato, Philo and Pseudo-Phocyclides, but not by Paul" (25).

126 See the discussion of Plato *Phaedr.* 835c-e; 839a; 841d, by Ward, "Unnatural," 4–10.

127 See Miller, "Practices," 10: "Thus the similarity in function described in Romans 1:26 refers to non-coital sexual activities which are engaged by heterosexual women similar to the sexual activities of homosexual males. So females, described first, exchange natural function for unnatural, but an exchange of partners is not indicated." Fredrickson concurs in "Natural and Unnatural Use," 201: "Paul is not alluding to lesbianism in 1:26 . . . rather the reference is to inordinate desire within marriage."

128 See Klaus Wengst, "Paulus und die Homosexualität. Überlegungen zu Röm 1,26f," *ZEE* 31 (1987) 77–78; John J. McNeill, *The Church and the Homosexual* (3d ed.; Boston: Beacon, 1988) 53–56; Boswell, *Homosexuality,* 109, 112–13; Else Kähler, "Exegese zweier neutestamentlicher Stellen (Römer 1,18-32; 1. Korinther 6,9-11)," in T. Bovet, ed., *Probleme der Homophilie in medizinischer, theologischer und juristische Sicht* (Bern: Haupt, 1965) 31; A. M. J. M. Herman van de Spijker, *Die gleichgeschlechtliche Zuneigung. Homotropie: Homosexualität, Homoerotik, Homophilie–und die katholische Moraltheologie* (Freiburg: Walter, 1968) 82–83. The refutation of this option by Brooten, *Love between Women,* 242, is compelling.

129 See Brooten, *Love between Women,* 246: "the active verb (*metellaxan*) with a feminine subject . . . is striking." While Ward, "Unnatural," 27, affirms this egalitarian element in contrast to Stowers, he nevertheless suggests that 1:18-32 is placed in the mouth of the imaginary Jew of 2:1, 17, criticizing "the unnatural *pathos* of the Gentiles" with their "unpro-

In view of the complex variations of sexual inclination discussed in ancient astrological and medical sources,[131] the popular application of the modern concept of individual sexual orientation based on biological differences is anachronistic.[132] Such exegesis misreads Paul's argument as dealing with individual sins rather than the corporate distortion of the human race since Adam's fall.[133] However, Paul's argument is not without its problems. In Paul's usage there is no awareness of the weaknesses in the Greco-Roman concept of nature, which is culturally subjective and tends to threaten human freedom in that one is supposed to conform to whatever "nature," as defined by that cultural group, demands.[134] Paul is raising a cultural norm to the level of a "natural" and thus biological principle, which would probably have to be formulated differently today. Finally,

there may be an element of chauvinism or procreational preoccupation in the expression "their females,"[135] the only element in 1:26b that is not replicated in 1:27a.

There is no mistaking the direction of Paul's argument[136] or its consistency with all other known branches of ancient Judaism and early Christianity.[137] Convinced that heterosexuality was part of the divinely created order for humankind[138] and that sexual identity is essential to humans as $\sigma\hat{\omega}\mu\alpha$,[139] he presents deviations from traditionally Judaic role definitions as indicative of an arrogant assault on the Creator and as a sign of current and forthcoming wrath. The evidence in this verse is particularly damaging to the hypothesis by Scroggs that the critique of homosexuality in this pericope aims solely to attack pederasty and thus has no bearing on homoerotic relationships between consenting adults.[140]

---

creative acts, most obviously exemplified by same-sex acts by both women and men." This is most unlikely because the traditional Jew would not have argued as Paul does in this passage, dealing with female behavior as nonsubordinate to male behavior, and overlooking as he does the issue of procreation. The argument of Stowers also seems contrary to this and other passages in the Pauline letters; in *Rereading*, 94–95, he contends that Paul's argument in 1:26 was motivated by Paul's concern to retain "woman's status as inferior" by restricting sexual relations to the male dominance of penetrating females. This is implausible in view of the egalitarian sexual ethic of 1 Cor 7:4.

130 Hays, "Relations," 194.

131 See Brooten, *Love between Women*, 242–43; see also William Schoedel, "Same Sex Eros: Paul and the Greco-Roman Tradition," in Balch, ed., *Homosexuality*, 52–59, which analyzes Pseudo-Aristotle *Probl.* 4.26; Caelius Aurelianus *Morb.* 4.9.131–35; Lactantius *Opif.* 12–13. A discerning study of the Aurelianus text is provided by P. H. Schrijvers, *Eine medizinische Erklärung der männlichen Homosexualität aus der Antike. Caelius Aurelianus De morbis chronicis IV 9* (Amsterdam: Grüner, 1985).

132 Boswell, *Homosexuality*, 109; Furnish, *Moral Teaching*, 66; see the critique in Hays, "Relations," 200.

133 See Hays, "Relations," 200: "The charge is a corporate indictment of pagan society, not a narrative about the 'rake's progress' of particular individuals." See also the critique of Boswell in Fitzmyer, 286–88.

134 For a brief discussion of these dilemmas without

dealing directly with the issue of cultural relativity, see Koester, "φύσις κτλ.," 266.

135 The inclusion of αὐτῶν ("their") is unexplained in the commentaries, but clearly implies a view that females stand under the responsibility and jurisdiction of males. This view is typical of Greco-Roman and Jewish sexual ethics. In *Love between Women*, 241, Brooten claims that the reference to "their females" "is a logical term in male-dominated societies, in which women belong to men and are seen in relation to them."

136 For a critique of Boswell's specious argument (*Homosexuality*, 135) that there was "no general prejudice against gay people among early Christians," see Hays, "Relations," 202–4.

137 See Samuel H. Dresner, "Homosexuality and the Order of Creation," *Judaism* 40 (1991) 309–21.

138 See 1 Cor 7 and 11; Holter-Stavanger, "Rom 1,23-27," 21–23.

139 See Jewett, *Terms*, 268–71, 456; also Thomas J. Deidun, "Beyond Dualisms: Paul on Sex, *Sarx* and *Sōma*," *Way* 28 (1988) 201–4.

140 Scroggs, *Homosexuality*, 116; see particularly the critique by Peter von der Osten-Sacken, "Paulinisches Evangelium und Homosexualität," *BThZ* 3 (1986) 34; and Smith, "Ancient Bisexuality," 225–38, 243–44. The attempt by James C. Miller to answer these critiques is unconvincing: "Response: Pederasty and Romans 1:27: A Response to Mark Smith," *JAAR* 65 (1997) 861–66.

■ 27 Paul turns next to the example of male homoeroticism, the weaker case in his cultural setting because of its positive evaluation by some Greco-Roman writers[141] and its popularization among the Roman ruling class, including Emperor Nero.[142] This weakness is treated rhetorically by presenting male perversion as similar to the more disreputable female perversion: ὁμοίως τε καὶ ("and likewise also").[143] The language of "natural use" (τὴν φυσικὴν χρῆσιν) is consistent with the description of lesbianism in the preceding verse.[144] The link between the two sentences clarifies that both male and female homoeroticism are seen as evidence of the same πάθη ἀτιμίας ("passions of dishonor").[145] In the context of natural versus unnatural intercourse, the aorist participial ἀφέντες ("abandoning") is the rough equiva-lent of the term "exchange" in v. 26b. It implies a departure from a divinely intended, originally heterosexual relationship between males and females. Except for the missing "their" in v. 27a, this first clause is a characteristic example of the effort in Paul's later letters to equalize the roles and responsibilities of males and females.[146]

The rest of v. 27 continues the rhetorical effort to buttress the case about the despicable quality of homosexuality. To be "inflamed with their lust for one another" (ἐξεκαύθησαν ἐν τῇ ὀρέξει αὐτῶν εἰς ἀλλήλους) is rare and derogatory language in the NT,[147] but heat and flame are typically associated with sexual passion in Greco-Roman sources[148] and "appetite" is typically associated with eros.[149] This wording implies an

---

141 In "Greek Attitudes Toward Sex," Jeffrey Henderson notes that "homosexual sentiment [was] pervasive in Greek culture" and that it played a key role in the transition from childhood and adulthood, both for men and women, and that it does "not interfere with heterosexual enjoyment or with a happy marriage"; see Grant and Kitzinger, eds., *Civilization of the Ancient Mediterranean*, 2:1255. For similar assessments of Roman culture, see Vilbert, "L'homosexualité," 15–28; Hallett, "Roman Attitudes," 1265–78. Acknowledging that it is not always appropriate to use the modern term "homosexual" to describe Greco-Roman roles, Amy Richlin has shown that the social acceptance of males who penetrated other males was greatly in contrast to the prejudice against free adult males allowing themselves to be penetrated; such adult *cinaedi* ("queers") were viewed as abnormal or diseased and could be prosecuted under Roman law. See Richlin, "Not Before Homosexuality: The Materiality of the Cinaedus and the Roman Law against Love between Men," *JHSex* 3 (1993) 523–73.

142 See Boswell, *Homosexuality*, 82, 130; Richlin, "Not Before Homosexuality," 532, describes Nero as "a no-holds-barred omnisexual Sadeian libertine."

143 See Zahn, 100, and Michel, 105; for ὁμοίως as a commonly used term to indicate similarity or commonality, see Johannes Schneider, "ὅμοιος κτλ.," *TDNT* 5 (1967) 186–88.

144 Fredrickson, "Natural and Unnatural Use," 199, observes that scholars have been "remarkably incurious" about the meaning of χρῆσις, which implies "the instrumentality of the object of sexual desire" (202). He cites (200) Plutarch's description in *Amat.* 750e2 of Aristippus's using Laïs even though she did not love him: "He didn't imagine, he said, that wine or fish loved him either, *yet he used both with pleasure* (ἀλλ᾽ ἡδέως ἑκατέρῳ χρῆται)." Among other texts, Fredrickson cites Epictetus's references to intercourse as "use" in *Ench.* 33.8: "With regard to *aphrodisia*, maintain purity before marriage as far as you are able, and if you indulge, take only those privileges that are lawful. Do not become offensive or censorious to those who use, and do not comment frequently that you do not use (οὐ χρῆ)."

145 See Brooten, *Love between Women*, 253–55, for a compelling argument concerning the "parallel" between male and female actions in 1:26-27.

146 See Jewett, "The Sexual Liberation of the Apostle Paul," *JAAR* Sup (March, B) 47.1 (1979) 68–77; see also Scroggs, *Homosexuality*, 114–15, who comments that the complementarity of the female and male examples indicate "that the false world is lived in equally by women as well as men."

147 Both ἐκκαίω ("be inflamed") and ὄρεξις ("sexual desire, lust") are hapax legomena in the NT; see BAGD 240, 580; ὄρεξις is a technical term for sexual desire in Epictetus.

148 See Fredrickson, "Natural and Unnatural Use," 210–13. He refers to Plutarch *Amat.* 763a: "recall for us the ode in which the lovely Sappho describes how her voice is lost and her body burns (φλέγεσθαι τὸ σῶμα) when her beloved appears." Fredrickson, 211, notes that "Paul's use of ἐκκαίω in the passive voice reflects the idea bemoaned by philosophers and reluctantly celebrated by poets that the passion of love invades and overwhelms the individual." For example, Alciphron *Epistulae* 3.31 describes the flaming passion aroused by a beautiful girl in a procession: "I was so inflamed with love (ἐξεκαύθην εἰς ἔρωτα) that, forgetting who I was, I ran up and wanted to plant a kiss on her lips."

irrational bondage to an egoistic, empty, and unsatisfying expression of animalistic sexuality.[150] The next clause is usually translated with something like "males committing unseemly acts with males"[151] and interpreted in reference to the language of Lev 18:22 and 20:13 that prohibits "same-sex relations between males of all ages, not only pederasty."[152] The term ἀσχημοσύνη was used both for "unseemly deed" and for sexual organs,[153] whose privacy remained a matter of a substantial taboo in Judaism (e.g., Exod 20:26; Lev 18:6-18).[154] In this context the singular form of τὴν ἀσχημοσύνην following the plural reference to "males" indicates that the latter option is in view, which leads to my translation "shameful member." In this context, the participle κατεργαζόμενοι should be taken in the explicit sexual sense of "work up for use" or produce juices "in the body,"[155] which ancient medicine believed were reproductive fluids in the brain that were frothed up into semen at the moment of ejaculation. In the context of anal intercourse, the verb δεῖ has a special sense of "tighten," as in Hippocrates' explanation: "Friction is able to loosen, to tighten (δῆσαι), to increase, and to diminish. Hard friction (σκληρή) tightens (δῆσαι); soft friction loosens; much friction diminishes; moderate friction thickens."[156] Since male bodies were viewed as hard and nonabsorbent and female bodies were thought to be soft, loose, and absorbent, the latter were able to receive ejaculation whereas the former produced tightening, that is, soreness. The "recompense" that homosexual males therefore receive is this soreness that they experience ἐν ἑαυτοῖς ("in themselves"). The ancient sexual logic of this passage helps to explain why Paul employs this phenomenon of male homoeroticism as a prime instance of divine wrath that manifests itself in the act itself. Moreover, for Jewish hearers reared in an atmosphere of sexual modesty and for Greco-Romans that had been taught moderation, honor, and dutifulness, Paul's language served to remove any vestige of decency, honor, or friendship from same-sex relations. Neither distinguishing pederasty from relationships between adult, consenting males,[157] nor distinguishing between active and passive partners as Roman culture was inclined to do,[158] Paul simply follows the line of his Jewish cultural tradition by construing the entire realm of homosexual relations as evidence that divine wrath was active therein.

Plutarch *Amat.* 759b observes that "in erotic madness, when once it has really captured a human and set him or her afire" (διακαύσασαν) there is nothing that can restore him to calm. See also Philo *Decal.* 122; Chariton *Chaer.* 4.2.4-5; Longus *Daphn.* 1.11, 13, 14, 18, 23; 2.7, 8; *Anthologia Graeca* 5.10,75; 11.36; 12.46, 48, 63, 79, 99, 178. Text ed. H. Beckby, *Anthologia Graeca*, 2d ed., 4 vols. (Munich: Heimaran, 1965-68).

149 Fredrickson, "Natural and Unnatural Use," 213, cites Plutarch *Amat.* 750c-d, which associates ὀρέσις with ἔρως. *SVF* 3:181.21-22: "the Epicurians say that eros is an intense aphrodisian appetite" (τὸν ἔρωτα οἱ μὲν Ἐπικούρειοί φάσιν εἶναι σύντονον ἀφροδισίων ὄρεξιν). Often heat and desire are closely associated, as Fredrickson (214) points out with reference to Epictetus *Diss.* 2.14.22: αἱ ὀρέξεις σου φλεγμαίνουσιν ("your appetites are feverish"). Philo *Gig.* 34-35 also links "kindling the lusts" with "appetites."

150 See Wilckens, 1:110. See the similar expressions in Wis 14:2; 15:5; Sir 18:30; 23:6, pointed out by Brooten, *Love between Women*, 255.

151 Fitzmyer, 287.

152 Brooten, *Love between Women*, 256; she builds her case (61-62) on the work of Saul Olyan, "'And with a Male You Shall Not Lie the Lying Down of a Woman,'" *JHSex* 5 (1994) 179-206; and Daniel Boyarin, "Are There Any Jews in 'the History of Sexuality'?" *JHSex* 5 (1995) 333-55. For a discussion of other OT passages that condemn homoerotic relations between males, see James B. De Young, "The Contributions of the Septuagint to Biblical Sanctions against Homosexuality," *JETS* 34 (1991) 157-77.

153 BAGD 119.

154 Safrai, "Home and Family," 762, reports that a married partner had to be divorced after appearing in public in torn clothing or bathing together in public baths, following the Greco-Roman custom, because of the violation of the privacy custom.

155 LSJM 925, definitions II and III for κατεργάζομαι, with reference to Hippocrates *Praec.* 9, who described working up juice in the body.

156 Hippocrates *Off.* 17.1.

157 See Scroggs, *Homosexuality*, 115-17.

158 See Richlin, "Not Before Homosexuality," 532-40.

The final clause in v. 27 returns to the leitmotif of suppressing the truth that produces its twisted consequences, with the πλάνη of sexual misconduct being understood as an active "deception" about the created order.[159] Greco-Roman as well as Jewish sources associated πλάνη with sexual passion.[160] Rather than the bland translation of "error,"[161] perhaps even the sexually related term "seduction" might be appropriate here.[162] Such suppression of the truth necessitated an ἀντιμισθία ("recompense"), the "due penalty" whose divine origin[163] is emphasized by παρέδωκεν ("he delivered") in vv. 26 and 28. This term ἀντιμισθία ("recompense, reward") is exclusively Christian and reflects the "reciprocal nature" of the punishment[164] that comes in the form of injured "tightness." In this instance the dishonored relationships are themselves the punishment "received back" (ἀπολαμβάνοντες)[165] in return for the twisted "desires of their hearts" that had been led astray by deception about God and the created order.[166] These indications of divine involvement in the wrath are consistent with the thrice-repeated παρέδωκεν ("he delivered them").[167] The repetition of the pronouns αὐτῶν ("their") and ἑαυτοῖς ("themselves") serves to underscore the human responsibility for this primal deception and its social consequences. Since the participles κατεργαζόμενοι ("worked up") and ἀπολαμβάνοντες

("receive back") are connected syntactically with ἄρσενες ("males"), the scope of this responsibility does not include the females in v. 26.[168] Taken as a whole, this effort in vv. 26-27 to provide a theological approach to the issue of homoeroticism is unique in the ancient world.[169]

It remains puzzling why Paul assumes that his audience, consisting of a Gentile Christian majority coming from a background in which same-sex relations were often tolerated, would have accepted Paul's point of view without argument. While the Jewish background of Paul's heterosexual preference has been frequently cited as decisive by previous researchers, little attention has been given to the correlation between homosexuality and slavery.[170] The right of masters to demand sexual services from slaves and freedmen is an important factor in grasping the impact of Paul's rhetoric, because slavery was so prominent a feature of the social background of most of Paul's audience in Rome.[171] Werner Krenkel writes: "Intercourse between masters and their male slaves was normal and in accordance with the standards of a male-dominated society."[172] Krenkel cites Seneca the Elder as follows: *inpudicitia in ingenuo crimen est, in servo necessitas, in liberto officium* ("Sexual servicing is a crime for the freeborn, a necessity for a slave, and a duty for the freeman").[173] Paul Veyne reports that a "much

---

159 Herbert Braun, "πλανάω κτλ.," *TDNT* 6 (1968) 243; the other uses of πλάνη by Paul in 1 Thess 2:3 and 2 Thess 2:11 imply demonic deception rather than simple, human error.

160 Fredrickson, "Natural and Unnatural Use," 215, refers to Plato *Phaed.* 81a, which describes death as a state in which the soul is happy, "freed from deception and folly and fear and fierce loves and all other human ills" (πλάνης καὶ ἀνοίας καὶ φόβων καὶ ἀγρίων ἐρώτων καὶ τῶν ἄλλων κακῶν ἀνθρωπείων ἀπηλλαγμένη). *T. Reub.* 2.1 refers to the "seven spirits of deception" (ἑπτὰ πνευμάτων τῆς πλάνης) of which the last (2.8) is "the spirit of procreation and intercourse, with which through love of pleasure sins [occur]" (πνεῦμα σπορᾶς καὶ συνουσίας, μεθ᾽ ἧς συνέρχονταις διὰ τῆς φιληδονίας ἁμαρτίαι). See also *T. Reub.* 3.2; 4.6.

161 Dunn, 1:65; Morris, 93; Fredrickson, "Natural and Unnatural Use," 215.

162 See Zahn, 101.

163 Horst Balz and Gerhard Schneider, "ἀντιμισθία," *EDNT* 1 (1990) 110.

164 See BAGD 75, and H. Preisker, "μισθός κτλ.," *TDNT* 4 (1967) 702. This passage and 2 Cor 6:13 represent the first use of ἀντιμισθία in surviving Greek writings.

165 See Dunn, 1:65.

166 See Zahn's view (101) that the recompense is the "bodily deterioration" that comes upon those involved with sexual perversity.

167 Kühl, 58.

168 The issue of the antecedents is not explicitly discussed in any of the commentaries I have consulted.

169 Schlier, 62.

170 Vilbert points out this correlation, without connecting it with Paul's letter to the Christians in Rome, in "L'homosexualité," 19. As evidence he cites Plutarch *Aet. Rom.* 288a, and Plautus *Curc.* 23.

171 See the introduction above, and esp. the work of Lampe, *Paul to Valentinus*, 138–50, 170–83.

172 Werner A. Krenkel, "Prostitution," in M. Grant and R. Kitzinger, eds., *Civilization of the Ancient Mediterranean: Greece and Rome* (New York: Scribner's, 1988) 2:1296.

180

repeated way of teasing a slave is to remind him of what his master can demand of him, i.e., to get down on all fours."[174] Krenkel notes that in fourth-century Athens the minimum fee for a male prostitute was higher than that of females and that "to meet the demand for male prostitutes, beautiful boys were captured, imported . . . sold . . . and prostituted."[175] Krenkel describes the double standard in Greek culture in that it was considered superior for one male to dominate another but that to be "'the beloved boy' after reaching adulthood was frowned upon."[176] In contrast, the Romans forbade the passive sexual role for free males and enforced laws against pederasty when it involved the sons of citizens.[177] In general, sexual freedom was granted to freeborn males, with regard to all slaves, clients, and persons of lower standing so that sexual relations were clearly an expression of domination.[178] Observing that there are no firsthand accounts of the feelings of those being exploited, Krenkel cites the elder Seneca's words describing prostitution as *infelix patientia*—"unhappy and sterile submission."[179]

I suggest that Paul's rhetoric may provide entrée into the similarly unhappy experience of Christian slaves and former slaves who had experienced and resented sexual exploitation, both for themselves and for their children, in a culture marked by aggressive bisexuality.[180] Their countercultural stance as members of the new community of faith entailed a repudiation of such relationships and, from all the evidence available to us, a welcome restriction of sexual relations to married heterosexual partners. For those members of the Roman congregation still subject to sexual exploitation by slave owners or former slave owners who are now functioning as patrons, the moral condemnation of same-sex and extramarital relations of all kinds would confirm the damnation of their exploiters and thus raise the status of the exploited above that of helpless victims with no prospect of retribution.

■ **28** In the final paragraph of the first pericope, Paul explicitly names for the fifth time the leitmotif of suppressing the truth about God.[181] The choice of the verb δοκιμάζω ("test, approve, see fit") is influenced by Paul's desire for a wordplay with the expression "unfitting mind" (ἀδόκιμον νοῦν). The connotation of ἐδοκίμασαν ("see fit") in this context is "to regard as necessary,"[182] which conveys the same assault on divine truth that Paul has depicted repeatedly in this passage. In contrast to the Greek outlook, the flaw in the human race does not lie in ignorance that can be excused or modulated through education but rather in a direct and multifaceted campaign to disparage God and replace him/her with a human face or institution. The expression ἔχειν ἐν ἐπιγνώσει ("to hold in knowledge") has the connotation of proper recognition

173 *Con.* 4 preface 10; this view is similar to *Satyricon* 75.11.

174 Paul Veyne, "Homosexuality in ancient Rome," in P. Ariès and A. Béjin, *Western Sexuality* (Oxford: Oxford Univ. Press, 1985) 29, cited by Cantarelli, *Bisexuality*, 99. Winkler, *Constraints of Desire*, 211, cites Artemidoros, *Onir.* 78: "To have sex with one's own female slave or male slave is good, for slaves are the dreamer's possessions. . . . To be penetrated by one's house slave is not good. This signifies being despised or injured by the slave."

175 Krenkel, "Prostitution," 1296; Macrobius in *Sat.* 3.17.4 reports that in 161 B.C.E. "Most of the freeborn youths sold their modesty and freedom." In *One Hundred Years of Homosexuality and Other Essays on Greek Love* (New York: Routledge, 1990) 108–9, David M. Halperin discusses the high price of young male prostitutes. Cantarelli, *Bisexuality*, 102, notes that in Rome male prostitution became "a luxury item."

176 Krenkel, "Prostitution," 1297.

177 Cantarelli, *Bisexuality*, 97–186, 217–18; see also Hallett, "Roman Attitudes," 1268, 1272–78.

178 In *Bisexuality*, 217, Cantarelli concludes that the Roman male was socialized to be "an aggressive dominator," so that under a bas-relief of an erect phallus one reads the inscription *hic habitat felicitas* ("here dwells happiness"). See also Halperin, *Homosexuality*, 33.

179 Krenkel, "Prostitution," 1297; Halperin, *Homosexuality*, 96, observes: "Prostitution can be spoken of, especially in the case of males, as hiring oneself out 'for *hybris*' (*eph' hybrei*)—meaning, 'for other people to treat as they please.' . . . It was understood, for example, that a man went to prostitutes partly in order to enjoy sexual pleasures that were thought degrading to the person who provided them."

180 See esp. Cantarella, *Bisexuality*, 156–64.

181 Dunn, 1:66, notes 1:18, 21, 23, and 25 as the previous references.

182 Walter Grundmann, "δόκιμος κτλ.," *TDNT* 2 (1964) 259.

and response[183] to God as directly experienced by the human race.[184] Paul's formulation suggests the "critical distinction between knowing and *acknowledging*,"[185] because while humans may well admit the existence of God, they fail to acknowledge God's claim. Epictetus had a comparable failure in mind: "Receiving from nature measures and standards for recognizing the truth (εἰς ἐπίγνωσιν τῆς ἀληθείας), a person does not go further to augment and work out additional principles to fill in the gaps, but does exactly the opposite, attempting to remove and destroy whatever capacity he possesses to discover the truth."[186]

While Epictetus decries the failure to accept his naturalistic view of epistemology, Paul refers here to a much more direct assault on Deity itself. The persistence of the plural verbal forms and the aorist tense in this verse indicate that the story of Adam's fall remains in the background[187] and that the fall was radicalized by the gospel that viewed the crucifixion of Christ as expressing hostility against God. Rather than merely an act of disobedience, sin now takes the form of suppressing the truth.

The final sounding of the dreadful repetition of παρέδωκεν ("he delivered") follows the reiteration of the human campaign against God. Completing the wordplay with the term "see fit" and thus conforming to the premise that the punishment must match the crime,[188] Paul describes the deliverance of the human race to an "unfit mind" (ἀδόκιμος νοῦς).[189] This phrase does not have the connotation being "untested, without attestation,"[190] "void of discernment,[191] "incapable and useless,"[192] or lacking in measure and norm,[193] though

this last alternative is more accurate than the others. The meaning is closer to "reprobate instinct,"[194] a mindset that is perversely unfit for humane purposes. The context indicates "that such a mind does not simply lack in the power of discernment but instead perversely rejects that which it knows to be true."[195] In contrast with the Stoic theory of the "perverted mind" of unwise individuals who lack proper knowledge of natural obligations and appropriate discipline to maintain self-control through the avoidance of passion,[196] Paul's concept is both more intentional and more corporate in its orientation. The singular ἀδόκιμος νοῦς to which the human race is delivered involves a social network of procedures and prejudices constituting "a demonic, super-individual reality."[197] In modern parlance, Paul's concept of the "unfitting mind" evokes the disciplines of social psychology, political science, public administration, and sociology rather than of individual psychology.

The phrase that modifies the "unfitting mind" is ποιεῖν τὰ μὴ καθήκοντα ("to do the things that are improper"), which combines the widely shared assumption about mental processes as integrally linked to behavior with an expression adapted from Stoic ethics. Widely used in Greek culture to denote what is socially and religiously appropriate, the participle τὸ κατῆκον was used by the Stoic philosopher Zeno to denote a penultimate level of obligation that was binding so long as it was consistent with nature.[198] Epictetus taught that in addition to meeting physical needs, the wise person will find a way to fulfill such καθήκοντα as "citizenship, marriage, begetting children, reverence to God, care of

183 The intensive aspect of ἐπίγνωσις as compared with γνῶσις ("knowledge") has been picked up by Zahn, 104 ("willing and conscious recognition), and Kuss, 1:52 (not merely knowing about God but drawing the "absolutely necessary consequences"). See also Wolfgang Hackenberg, "ἐπίγνωσις," *EDNT* 2 (1991) 24.

184 Robert E. Picirelli presents an individualizing construal of this connotation, based on contemporary views of conversion in "The Meaning of 'Epignosis,'" *EvQ* 47 (1975) 91–92; for a treatment that is more aware of the corporate dimension Paul has in view here, see Sullivan, "ΕΠΙΓΝΩΣΙΣ," 406.

185 Johnson, 32.

186 Epictetus *Diss.* 2.20.21; see also Martin Dibelius, "Ἐπίγνωσις, ἀληθείας," in *Botschaft und*

Geschichte. Gesammelte Aufsätze, 2 vols. (Tübingen: Mohr [Siebeck], 1953–56) 2:1–13.

187 These details correlate with the case made by Hooker in "Adam," 300–303.

188 Klostermann, "Adäquate Vergeltung," 3–6.

189 The translation is suggested by Barrett, 39.

190 Grundmann, "δόκιμος κτλ.," 259; Kuss, 1:52.

191 Godet, 109.

192 Schlier, 63.

193 Michel, 69.

194 See Moffatt.

195 Jewett, *Terms,* 387.

196 See Maximilian Forschner, "Die pervertierte Vernunft: Zur stoischen Theorie der Affekte," *PhJ* 87 (1980) 258–80.

197 Jewett, *Terms,* 387; see also 375–78. Following the

parents."[199] In their dissertations entitled "Concerning Proper Things," Chrysippus and Panaetius raised this category to the highest level of moral obligation.[200] Hellenistic Judaism took over this terminology of social obligation and appropriateness.[201] The parallel Latin term *officium* was also prominent, with Cicero's writing of an ethical treatise under this title.[202] Since Philo used the expression τὸ μὴ καθῆκον to depict "an improper thing,"[203] an expression similar to the Stoic phrase τὸ παρὰ τὸ καθῆκον ("an improper thing"),[204] there is little point in downplaying Paul's adaptation of philosophical language here.[205] This language allows him to carry through the theme of what is "fitting" in the wordplay οὐκ ἐδοκίμασιν . . . ἀδόκιμον νοῦν. The reference to propriety suggests that God delivers the human race into a condition in which the most widely touted standards of behavior are consistently violated. There is a virtually contractual correlation between not "seeing fit" to acknowledge God, which produces the "unfitting mind," which in turn results in unfitting behavior.[206] The resultant picture of the human race is unremittingly bleak, as the following verses go on to document.

■ **29** The opening word in the catalogue of evils (1:29-31), which is carefully organized on rhetorical principles for the sake of effective oral presentation,[207] is πεπληρωμένους ("having been filled"),[208] implying the divine deliverance to a social orientation incapable of doing the right thing.[209] The connection with the following word "all" and the reiteration of this motif with μεστούς ("full") later in the sentence indicate Paul's intention to create an exclusively negative view of humankind. The literary model for Paul's catalogue is from Greco-Roman ethics, particularly in its Stoic form,[210] even though Hellenistic Judaism, Qumran, and early rabbinism developed such catalogues as well.[211] Paul's catalogue fuses elements from these several traditions in creating a comprehensive list of 21 vices and kinds of unrighteous persons. Since ψιθυριστής ("whisperers"), ὑβριστής ("bullies"), ἐφευρετής ("inventors"), and ἀνελεήμων ("unmerciful") are nouns, the other adjectives and participles in this list are substantivized.[212] The substantives are in apposition to the pronoun αὐτούς ("them") in v. 28 and list the improper things these people do.

Emulating the Greek tradition of four cardinal vices that stand as the opposites of the cardinal virtues,[213] par-

---

Greek concept of the individual mind, previous Romans commentators overlook the social dimension of Paul's usage here, e.g., Käsemann, 49; Cranfield, 1:128.

198 See Heinrich Schlier, "καθήκω (τὸ καθῆκον)," *TDNT* 3 (1965) 438; for general orientation see Gerhard Nebel, "Der Begriff des καθῆκον in der alten Stoa," *Herm* 70 (1935) 439–60; and Damianos Tsekourakis, *Studies in Terminology of Early Stoic Ethics*, Herm.E 32 (Wiesbaden: Steiner, 1974). W. Wiersma discusses Zeno in "τέλος und καθῆκον in der alten Stoa," *Mn* 5 (1937) 219–20.

199 Epictetus *Diss.* 3.7.25–26; see also 2.14.18; 3.2.2; 21.14; 4.10.12.

200 Schlier, "καθήκω (τὸ καθῆκον)," 438; R. Rieks, "Officium," *HWP* 6.1141.

201 See Schlier, "καθήκω (τὸ καθῆκον)," 439.

202 Rieks, "Officium," 1141, describes Cicero's *Off.*; see esp. 3.20; also Tacitus *Dial.* 10.

203 Philo *Cher.* 14.

204 See Diogenes Laertes *Vitae Philos.* 7.108; and Epictetus *Diss.* 1.7.21; 28.5.

205 Schlier, "καθήκω (τὸ καθῆκον)," 439–40; Käsemann, 49. Since the expression appears here for the only time in the NT (Acts 22:22 is an altogether difference usage), the likelihood that Paul derived it

206 See Danker, "Under Contract," 95–96.

207 While recognizing the rhetorical rationale of the catalogue, some scholars refer to the chaotic sequence of vices, symbolic of the chaos of evil itself; see Käsemann, 49; Kuss, 1:53.

208 Gerhard Delling, "πλήρη κτλ," *TDNT* 6 (1968) 291, shows the term πληρόω ("fill") sometimes "implies that a man is completely controlled and stamped by the powers which fill him. . . . There is in the term a strong element of exclusiveness or totality."

209 See Morris, 95: "*filled with* wickedness, showing that he does not think of them as half-hearted about their sin. They were wholly given over to it. Their exclusion of God left room for nothing else."

210 For general orientation see R. Hauser, "Lasterkatalog," *HWP* 5:37–39; and Burton Scott Easton, "New Testament Ethical Lists," *JBL* 51 (1932) 1–12; F. Varo, "El léxico del pecado en la Epístola de San Pablo a los Romanos," *ScrTh* 21 (1989) 99–116.

211 See esp. Kamlah, *Form,* 39–175; Wibbing, *Lasterkataloge,* 14–78; Bussmann, *Missionspredigt,* 120–21, 155–58.

212 See Smyth, *Grammar,* §§1021, 1130.

213 Wibbing, *Lasterkataloge,* 15–17, lists ἀφροσύνη ("foolishness"), ἀκολασία ("intemperance"),

alleled by the four passions in Stoicism,[214] Paul commences with four vices defined as broadly as possible by the term "all" that qualifies all four. Grammatically, the first four vices are subordinate to the participle "having been filled" in the accusative plural, which in turn stands in apposition to the accusative plural pronoun αὐτούς ("them") in v. 28. The next series of five vices is subordinate to the accusative plural μεστούς ("full"), which stands in apposition to the same pronoun "them" in v. 28. The twelve final vices are also accusative plurals that stand in apposition to "them" in v. 28 but not to "full of" in v. 29.[215] In contrast to the Greek tradition, Paul makes no effort to base the first four vices in a theory of virtues or of the individual human psyche.[216] Neither are the additional vices coordinated as derivative from a foundational group of four, as in the Greco-Roman catalogues.[217]

The source of all these evils is the human race as a whole, dominated by the "unfitting mind." Here we have a social pathology that is oriented not to the character flaws of individuals or groups but to the collective experience of the human race since the corruption of creation, viewed in the radical new light shed by the gospel. This catalogue undercuts in the most sweeping manner any potential claims of individual, group, or national exceptionalism. Pursuant to this aim, the 21 evils are drawn from Greek, Latin, and Jewish catalogues, no one of which tallies completely with Paul's scheme.[218] Paul's effort to find common ground between competitive cultural groups in Rome is eloquently expressed by the composite nature of this catalogue of evils.

The first four vices need to be construed as broadly as possible, taking account of the full semantic range that might be encompassed by πᾶς ("all, all manner of").[219] All four of these feminine abstract nouns formed from verbal roots[220] are dative complements of the participle πεπληρωμένους ("having been filled") and describe with what evils these persons are filled. In contrast to the Greco-Roman vice catalogues, Paul is not lifting up specific character flaws found in certain persons of weak will but broad-ranging characteristics of the entire human race since Adam. Ἀδικία encompasses a wide variety of objectively illegal and unjust actions done to others and is translated here as "wrongdoing" because of its antithesis to Paul's fundamental theme in Romans, the "righteousness of God."[221] Given Paul's avoidance of the genetic structure of the Greco-Roman vice catalogues, it is inappropriate to think of this as intended to include all the other vices within it because it is mentioned first.[222] The term πονηρία means "wickedness, baseness, maliciousness, sinfulness . . . evil-mindedness,"[223] and describes the defective state, will, and purpose[224] expressed in evil actions. Similar to the first term "injustice," "evil" is a widely comprehensive term.

Πλεονεξία is literally "a desire to have more"[225] and expresses itself in material covetousness, in grasping for power, in taking advantage of others, and in insatiable

ἀδικία ("wrongdoing"), and δειλία ("cowardice") as the cardinal evils, as found in Stobaeus Anth. 2.59.4.20, only one of which is exactly replicated by Paul.

214 Wibbing, Lasterkataloge, 17, lists ἐπιθυμία ("desire"), φόβος ("fear"), λύπη ("grief"), and ἡδονή ("pleasure") as the four passions according to Zeno, citing SVF 3.382–83.

215 See Cranfield, 1:129. Meyer, 1:95, suggests less plausibly that the last 17 vices are all in apposition to the participle πεπληρωμένους.

216 Engberg-Pedersen, Stoics, 210, argues in contrast that Paul agrees with the Stoics that "every social vice was seen to be derived from concern of the individual for him- or herself alone, to the exclusion of others." The issue for Engberg-Pedersen (214) is "selfishness."

217 See Wibbing, Lasterkataloge, 16–20.

218 See esp. Daxer, Römer, 48–55; for similar assess-

ments that do not proceed word by word through Paul's catalogue in 1:29-31, see Wibbing, Lasterkataloge, 86–108; and R. Hauser, "Lasterkatalog," HWP 5:37–38.

219 Cranfield, 1:105.

220 See Smyth, Grammar, §840a and 840a9.

221 See the discussion of ἀδικία in 1:18 above and the discussion in Dunn, 1:67–68.

222 Gottlob Schrenk, "ἀδικία," TDNT 1 (1964) 155, points to its primary quality and defines it more narrowly than Paul probably intended: "violation of the divine law and its norm"; the notion of a "comprehensive" category is suggested by Daxer, Römer, 48; and Morris, 195.

223 BAGD 690.

224 See Günther Harder, "πονηρία," TDNT 6 (1968) 562–65.

225 BAGD 667.

appetites for food, sex, and other pleasures.[226] While a philosopher like Dio Chrysostom viewed πλεονεξία as "the greatest evil" because of its antithesis to moderation,[227] Paul groups it with other vices that disqualify a person from fellowship in the church (1 Cor 5:11). Here it has a broadly comprehensive meaning related to the aggressive desire to have more,[228] so that "greed" or "greediness" are the best, though still inadequate, English equivalents. The final term in the first series is κακία, which has a negative connotation of lacking whatever is good.[229] Although more widely used in classical Greek and Greco-Roman culture than by NT writers and raised to a metaphysical principle by Plutarch and Plotinus,[230] it is occasionally employed by Paul and others to mean badness, depravity, wickedness, malice, and misfortune.[231] While exegetes have sought to draw sharp distinctions between πονηρία and κακία,[232] the contemporary consensus of their overlapping connotations is probably correct.[233] Although the English translation "badness" lacks the philosophical connotations of the Greek original, it is the best choice for this context.[234]

The "filled up" motif of v. 29a is reiterated with the term μεστός in v. 29b,[235] but the difference is worth pointing out. In v. 29a the perfect passive participle πεπληρωμένους ("having been filled") implies that their evil state is the result of God's consigning them to the "unfitting mind," while in v. 29b the adjective "full" simply implies there is no room for anything else but vice. The competition between vices and virtues, so typical of Greco-Roman and Hellenistic Jewish traditions, is thereby eliminated. Neither is there a dualistic tension between righteousness and unrighteousness as found in apocalyptic branches of Judaism.[236] In the entirety of v. 29, the vices have completely crowded out any virtues. The five vices that denote actions rather than states, as in the preceding four, are associated with social disruption. Several of the vices are linked in other contexts because of associations in sound and meaning. The sequence is associative rather than genetic. Φθόνος ("envy") and φόνος ("murder") appear as a wordplay in Euripides,[237] but there is no intention here of making envy the root of the other evil deeds.[238] Φθόνος should be understood as "malevolent envy" that is "aggressive and seeks to do harm" often through slander in the competitive environment of the Greco-Roman world.[239] Murder (φόνος) as an intentional taking of human life was prohibited by the sixth commandment of the Decalogue (Exod 20:15; Deut 5:18) and by all other legal codes of the ancient world. It was ordinarily punished by death.[240] The next vice, ἔρις ("strife"), is associated with φθόνος

---

226 Gerhard Delling, "πλεονέκτης κτλ.," *TDNT* 6 (1968) 266–67.

227 Delling, ibid., cites Dio Chrysostom *Orat.* 67.7 in this connection.

228 Delling, "πλεονέκτης κτλ.," 272.

229 Walter Grundmann, "κακός κτλ.," *TDNT* 3 (1965) 469.

230 Ibid., 470–84.

231 BAGD 397.

232 See Harder, "πονηρία," 565, for an account of various efforts to distinguish these two closely overlapping terms.

233 Ibid.; Cranfield, 1:130; Kuss, 1:54; Wilckens, 1:113.

234 See Dunn, 1:68.

235 The term means filled to the brim, saturating, sating, according to LSJM 1108, leading Godet, 110, to suggest the literal translation "stuffed."

236 The scholarly tradition of associating the catalogue with the Jewish two-path system begins with Daxer, *Römer*, 35–48, and continues with Wibbing, *Lasterkataloge*, 45–58, and Kamlah, *Form*, 40–50. It is accepted by contemporary exegetes who have not examined closely the implications of "filled" and

"all" in 1:29, e.g., Wilckens, 1:112; more cautiously, Käsemann, 50.

237 In Euripides *Tro.* 768–69, the Greeks invading Troy are accused of being the avenging curse "of envy, of murder and death" (εἶτα δὲ φθόνου φόνου τε θανάτου). A similar sounding alliteration is found in Appian *An.* 21: φόνος τε καὶ πόνος ἦν πολὺς ("there was a great slaughter and struggle"), which may be the reference alluded to in BAGD 864. See also Eiliv Skard, "Kleine Beiträge zum Corpus Hellenisticum Novi Testamenti," *SO* 30 (1953) 101–2.

238 As suggested by Godet, 110, and Cranfield, 1:130.

239 Ceslas Spicq, "φθόνος," *TLNT* 3 (1994) 434–35. A discussion of the visual images related to the ubiquitous "evil eye" in Greco-Roman household art, depicting "the malice that is inherent in *phthonos* rebounding upon the *phthoneros*," is discussed by Katherine M. D. Dunbar and M. W. Dickie, "Invidia Rumpantur Pectora: The Iconography of Phthonos/Invidia in Graeco-Roman Art," *JAC* 26 (1983) 7–37, esp. 9.

240 Horst Balz, "φοενύω," *EDNT* 3 (1993) 435.

by Appian,[241] just as the final vice of κακοήθεια ("malice") is associated with envy by Josephus[242] and Apollonius Tyanensis,[243] but again Paul is not interested in one vice causing another but in showing that all ultimately derive from the same primal lie. The fourth vice in the second series is δόλος, literally "bait for fish,"[244] and implies deceit, cunning, stratagem, or treachery,[245] of which the last is the more likely option in this listing of social misdeeds.[246] Its associations with the neighboring terms "strife" and "malice" are on the thematic level in that treachery involves elements of malignity that are characteristic of public strife.[247] The fifth vice, κακοήθεια, refers to "a general inclination toward evildoing," combining the elements of malice and deceit.[248] Aristotle defines it as "taking everything for the worse (τὸ ἐπὶ τὸ χεῖρον ὑπολαμβάνειν πάντα),"[249] so that it serves as a fitting climax for this series of vices.

It is the shocking sweep of evil that emerges most strongly from these expressions of social pathology. Since the first four of the second series are joined by parechesis in the repetition of the *o* sounds with φθόνου φόνου . . . δόλου making a particularly ominous wordplay, the fifth item κακοηθεία ("malice") springs out of the series by rhyming with the preceding series of four vices all ending in -ια.[250] This not only serves to reinforce the link with the first series that had been forged by the repetition of the "filled" motif, but by breaking

out of the traditional pattern of fours that characterize some Greco-Roman vice catalogues, it gives the impression that the series could go on and on to document ad infinitum the scope of social pathology since the fall of Adam.[251] It is not just a few bad types such as the vicious enemies of Israel or Rome, for instance, or even the antagonists of the churches in Rome that are in view here, but the entire human race.

A striking feature of this catalogue, unparalleled so far as I can determine in the Greco-Roman and Jewish vice catalogues, is that the last 12 of the 21 terms Paul selects to depict antisocial behavior refer to persons rather than vices. The antisocial types are listed in the accusative plural, associated grammatically with the αὐτούς ("them") of v. 28, which gives the impression that the earth is just as full of such persons as the collective "unfit mind" is full of vices. All eight types in the third series are thoroughly despicable, yet they are widely represented and at times even admired in the vicious environment of the Greco-Roman world. The ψιθυριστής, derived from the term "hiss, whisper," is a talebearer, gossip, character assassin, or political informant who avoids coming out in the open with rumors and accusations.[252] Paul probably means to include all of the above, so that a translation like "gossipers"[253] should be avoided as too specific and too petty to convey the sinister range of nuances that "whisperers" would have had in a city

---

241 Appian *Bell. civ.* 2.2.14.
242 Josephus *C. Ap.* 1.222 refers to vicious critics, "some out of envy and spite" (τινὲς μὲν διὰ φθόνον καὶ κακήθειαν) who attack persons of impeccable integrity.
243 Apollonius Tyanensis *Ep.* 43 demands that his students be "free from envy, craftiness, hatred, slander, hostility" (ἀπαθὴς εἶναι φθόνον κακοηθείας μίσους διαβολῆς ἔχρας).
244 LSJM 443.
245 BAGD 203.
246 The *NEB* chooses "treachery," as does Cranfield, 1:105.
247 See Godet, 110, and Kühl, 59.
248 Ceslas Spicq, "κακοηθεία," *TLNT* 2 (1994) 236.
249 Aristotle *Rhet.* 2.13, cited with approval by Spicq, "κακοηθεία," 236; Sanday and Headlam, 47; Lagrange, 32; Barrett, 40. Cranfield, 1:130, and Moo, 119, argue that this definition is too specialized, but it fits the context well.
250 There is also homoioteleouton that links the ending

of the last word of the series (κακοηθείας) with the first word of the next series (ψιθυριστάς).
251 Since vice catalogues are frequently organized on the principle of four cardinal vices or four desires, producing a pattern of fours that is followed for the rest of this catalogue, it is curious but hitherto unexplained that the second series contains five.
252 Tacitus *Ann.* 6.7 uses such language in connection with senatorial informers who "practiced even the based forms of denunciation, some with openness, many in private" (*infimas etiam delationes exercerent, alii propalam, multi per occultum*). See BAGD 892–93, and MM 698.
253 *RSV;* Morris, 97.

like Rome, which harbored a wide range of informers both political and domestic.[254]

■ **30** The associated term καταλάλος includes slanderers, defamers, detractors, or denouncers[255] who speak openly and even loudly[256] against others. In the setting of congregations that had suffered from the reports of hostile informants at the time of the Edict of Claudius,[257] and particularly among members who were slaves or employees vulnerable to denunciations, this rather neutral term would have included some sinister connotations that may not seem apparent for the contemporary audience from the translation "slanderers."

The second pair of terms is also internally associative, with ὑβριστής implying persons of insolence, pride, wantonness or violence[258] who are often related to the idea of θεοστυγής, in this instance, a person who hates God.[259] As N. R. E. Fisher has shown, the Greek tradition had developed the theme of hubris defined as a deliberate assault on the honor of others with the intent

of demonstrating one's superiority.[260] Hubris reflects contempt for the gods and for the law, leading always to divine nemesis,[261] a theme widely reflected in later literature.[262] The Greeks believed that persons of arrogance lacked a due sense of limits, which resulted in wanton behavior and violence that had disastrous social and political effects.[263] The OT taught that human pride and opposition to God were integrally related.[264] A Roman traditionalist such has Sallust viewed *superbia* ("pride, arrogance") as a crucial factor in Rome's political turmoil, since it violated the ancient republican ideal of modesty before the gods and one's fellow citizens.[265] In the NT the term carries the sense of outrageous treatment, usually violent, at the hands of arrogant people.[266] This sense may well be a connotation Paul intended here.[267] Since no English term carries the full range of meaning that ὑβριστάς implies, the translation "bullies" is the best alternative I can find.

The next pair of evil types violate the norms of social

254 Rostovtzeff, *Empire*, 398, 412, 513, refers to the hordes of secret police, the *frumentarii, stationarii, colletiones*, and *agentes in rebus* that dominated the later empire.

255 BAGD 412; see *PW* article on "*denunciatio.*"

256 LSJM 896 "talk, babble loudly . . . rail at."

257 Pallis, 47, notes that the early church found καταλάλοί ("denunciations") "particularly objectionable," perhaps because it rendered congregations vulnerable to outside pressures and persecution. See Jas 4:11 and *Herm. Mand.* 34.1-2; *Sim.* 103.7.

258 BAGD 832; Cranfield, 1:131; see also Fisher, *Hybris*, passim.

259 BAGD 358 and LSJM 792 note that classical Greek usage has a passive sense, "hated by a god," while the active sense appears intended here. It was used in the active sense by later Christian writers: *Pseudo-Clementine Hom.* 1.12 and *1 Clem.* 35.5. Arguing for the passive sense in Romans are Zahn, 103; Lagrange, 32–33; *NEB;* and Moffatt; but as Morris, 97, comments, hating God qualifies as a vice but being "hated by God does not."

260 Fisher, *Hybris*, 6: "a serious, often criminal, attack on the honour of another, typically committed gratuitously and for the pleasures of superiority," a definition that reflects Aristotle *Rhet.* 2.2.5–6: "The man committing *hybris* also slights: for *hybris* is causing injury and pain by which the victim incurs shame (αἰσχύνη), not in order that one may achieve anything other than what is done but simply

to get pleasure from it. . . . The cause of the pleasure for those committing *hybris* is that by harming others they think themselves more fully superior (ὑπερέχειν μᾶλλον). . . . Dishonor is characteristic of *hybris* (ὕβρεως δὲ ἀτιμία)." See also the discussion of the Latin equivalents, *contumelia/ iniuria*, in Lendon, *Empire of Honour*, 50.

261 Georg Bertram, "ὕβρις κτλ.," *TDNT* 8 (1972) 296–97, followed by Cranfield, 1:131; see also Jaeger, *Paideia*, 1:168; and C. del Grande, *Hybris, Colpa e castigo nell'espressione poetica e letteraria degli Scrittori della Grecia antica* (Naples: Ricciardi, 1947).

262 See Robert Payne, *Hubris, a Study of Pride* (New York: Harper, 1960).

263 See David Grene, *Man in His Pride: A Study of the Political Philosophy of Thucydides and Plato* (Chicago: Univ. of Chicago Press, 1950) 24–34, 86–92.

264 Bertram, "ὕβρις κτλ.," 299–302; see also Donald E. Gowan, *When Man Becomes God: Humanism and Hybris in the Old Testament* (Pittsburgh: Pickwick, 1975) 7–43.

265 Pöschl, *Sallust*, 59–60, 71, discusses the exposition of this motif in *Bell. Jug.* 40.3-5, 41-42, and 45.1.

266 Bertram, "ὕβρις κτλ.," 305–6, cites Matt 22:6; Acts 14.5, 27.10, 2 Cor 12.10; 1 Thess 2:2; and 1 Tim 1:13.

267 Wilckens, 1:114.

discourse. The ὑπερηφάνοι are persons who act haughtily and arrogantly, treating others disdainfully in an overbearing manner.[268] Since the basic meaning is "one who shines above others," perhaps the most appropriate contemporary translation would be "egotists," except that the nuance of acting arrogantly toward others may not be adequately conveyed thereby. The ἀλαζόναι are boasters, braggarts, loudmouths, quacks, and charlatans.[269] The two terms are associated in other vice catalogues,[270] and there seems to be a substantive link between the pair. The egotist seeks to attract admiration by bragging.

The final antisocial types are perverse in a notorious sense that brings the third series of eight evil kinds of persons to a deadly conclusion. Both types are wreckers of community, the first specializing in political and the second in domestic affairs. To be ἐφευρετὰς κακῶν ("inventors of evil") is a stock stereotype from the field of political propaganda[271] that accuses adversaries of being vicious and ingenious troublemakers who specialize in creating new recipes for disaster. Virgil uses the Latin equivalent *scelerum inventor* to describe an "evil contriver,"[272] and Tacitus applies the same expression to Sejanus.[273] A close Greek parallel is found in Philo, who calls one faction leader in the riots against the Jews a "contriver of evil" (κακῶν εὑρετής) and the chief agitator Flaccus an "inventor of novel iniquities" (ὁ καινῶν ἀδικημάτων εὑρετής).[274] Similarly, 2 Macc 7:31 refers to the dictator Antiochus Epiphanes as "having become the inventor of all evils against the Jews (πάσης κακίας εὑρετὴς γενόμενος εἰς τοὺς Ἑβραίους)." Given the scale of crimes committed by persons charged with this epithet, there is no doubt that its use here would have evoked shudders within the Roman house and tenement church members. Death was thought to be a penalty too light for such scoundrels.

Although it may not seem comparable to modern hearers,[275] the final group of "those disobedient to parents" (γενεῦσιν ἀπειθεῖς) was perceived by ancient Jews and Romans as profoundly dangerous. Deut 21:18-21 prescribed the death penalty for children who are disobedient to their mothers and fathers. While there are no indications that this law was enforced among Jews of the first century, there was frequent stress "on the honour and respect due to parents."[276] Roman law was even more severe, as Seneca the Elder reminded his readers of the ancient practice: "Remember, fathers expected absolute obedience from their children and could punish recalcitrant children even with death."[277] Seneca the Younger confesses such obedience to both parents: "I obeyed my parents; I deferred to their authority, whether it was fair or unfair or even harsh; I showed myself compliant and submissive."[278] The *patria potestas* ("the father's power") was broadly defined as life-long authority over one's family, including even at times the imposition of the death penalty.[279] Such authority was still an important factor in Roman family and political life in the first century.[280] The completion of this awful series of eight antisocial types with disobedience to parents drives home the impression that the world has literally been filled with people abandoned by God to their vices. No room seems to be left for justice and decency.

---

268 BAGD 841; LSJM 1864.
269 BAGD 34; LSJM 60.
270 Wilckens, 1:114, cites Stobaeus *Anth.* 95; 16; Wis 5:8; and *Herm. Mand.* 6.2.5. Daxer, *Römer,* 51, mentions also 2 Tim 3:2 and other early Christian catalogues where the two terms occur next to each other.
271 See BAGD 330 and Michel, 107.
272 Virgil *Aen.* 2.164.
273 Tacitus *Ann.* 4.11.
274 Philo *Flacc.* 20.73.
275 Wilckens, 1:114, says there is no visible connection between the last two types.
276 Safrai, "Home and Family," 2:771; 2:770 refers to the right of Jewish parents to apply physical discipline to their children.
277 Seneca the Elder, *Con.* 1.2; the distinctiveness of Roman law at this point is noted by Wlosok, "Vater," 19–28.
278 Seneca *Ben.* 3.38.2.
279 See Dionysius of Halicarnassus *Antiq. Rom.* 2.26–27.
280 See W. K. Lacey, "Patria Potestas," 121–44; and Beryl Rawson, "The Roman Family," 8, 16–17, both in Beryl Rawson, ed., *The Family in Ancient Rome* (Ithaca: Cornell Univ. Press, 1986); also Joseph Plescia, "Patria Potestas and the Roman Revolution," in Stephen Bertman, ed., *The Conflict of Generations in Ancient Greece and Rome* (Amsterdam: Grüner, 1976) 144–52.

■ **31** The rhetorical highpoint of the 21 vices and evil persons comes with four rhyming words that begin with the alpha negative, translated here as "without." The impression is that under the pervasiveness of the "unfit mind," the whole world is lacking in four of the attributes viewed as essential for humanity by Greco-Roman and Jewish thinkers. All four terms appear in other vice catalogues, which indicates a wide consensus about the importance of the positive form of these qualities in a civilized community. The pithy translation of the *NJB* captures the matter with appropriate rhetorical force: "without brains, honor, love or pity." The persons described as ἀσύνετοι are "senseless, without understanding," the same term that was used in v. 21 to describe the "senseless heart" of those who refuse to glorify God. The term is used to depict those lacking in intellectual and moral capacities[281] and is included in the vice catalogue by Dio Chrysostom.[282] Sir 15:7 states that the "senseless" cannot find wisdom. Aristophanes has the chorus in *The Birds* refer ironically to the "senseless wit" (φρενὸς ἀξυνέτου) of those unable to grasp the silly wisdom of the philosopher.[283] The crucial significance of good sense in Roman civil religion was evident in the cult of the Virtue *Mens,* authorized by the Sibylline Books.[284]

The similar sounding term ἀσυνθέντοι refers to those who break covenant, are faithless and undutiful.[285]

This is a term of supreme derogation for both Jewish and Greek writers. It is used repeatedly in LXX Jer 3:7-11 to describe "faithless Judah," and faithlessness is a connotation reflected in the *Lexicon* of Hesychius."[286] Demosthenes uses it to describe Athenian democracy that proved unfaithful to treaty obligations.[287] The opposite is a divine Virtue for the Romans, who deposited treaties in the temple of *Fides* ("faith").[288] Elsewhere, the term appears in the sense of "self-willed" or "difficult,"[289] so perhaps the best translation is "without dutifulness."[290] This term also appears in the vice catalogue of Ptolemaeus.[291]

The term ἄστοργος refers to someone's lacking in affection and love.[292] The verb στοργέω refers particularly to the ordinary affection between parents and children[293] and is viewed as a "natural" aspect of parental feelings toward their offspring.[294] The crucial importance of φιλοστοργία ("love of filial affection") in providing cohesion for society is evident in its role in the propaganda of Hellenistic and Roman monarchies.[295] Consequently, anyone who is ἄστοργος ("a person without affection") would have been viewed by typical members of Greco-Roman society as a threat to society. Both this and the following term appear also in the vice catalogue of 2 Tim 3:3.

The final term, ἀνελεήμων ("a person without mercy"), appears also in a Greek vice catalogue,[296] which

---

281 See esp. Lagrange, 33–34.
282 BAGD 118 cites Dio Chrysostom *Orat.* 2.75.; for further use within classical Greek, see LSJM 265.
283 Aristophanes *Av.* 456.
284 In "Cult of Virtues," 836, Fears explains that "*Mens* was regarded as a divine force of the greatest potency, capable of bestowing upon the Roman state and its leaders the supernatural and beneficent quality of practical intelligence—good sense—which alone could save the state." See also Fears, 853–57.
285 BAGD 118.
286 BAGD 118 cites Hesychius *Lex.*, μὴ ἐμμένων ταῖς συνθήκαις ("not remaining with treaties").
287 Demosthenes *Fal. leg.* 19.136: ὅς ὁ δῆμος ἐστιν ἀσταθημητότατον πρᾶγμα τῶν πάντων καὶ ἀσυνθετώτατον ("that the democracy is the most unstable and faithless thing of all").
288 Fears, "Cult of Virtues," 845; *fides* is defined as "a quality of trustworthiness and responsible behavior which manifests itself in the creation of secure and reliable bonds with another party." 863. See also Meister, "Tugenden," 6.
289 Anton Fridrichsen, "ΑΣΥΝΘΕΤΟΣ," *Coniectanea neotestamentica* 9 (1944) 47–48, quoted by Käsemann, 51.
290 See Dunn, 1:68.
291 Ptolemaeus (Claudius) *Apotel.* 3.35.4.
292 BAGD 118.
293 LSJM 1650.
294 See Demetrius Lacon *P.Herc.* 1012.44; see also Plutarch *Non pos.* 2.1100d: "love of parent for child" (γονέων πρὸς ἔκγονα στοργή). In *Att.* 10.8 Cicero uses the word στοργή to refer to his daughter's devotion to him.
295 See Fears, "Cult of Virtues," 850, 880–81, 892.
296 Ptolemaeus (Claudius), *Apotel.* 3.28.14.

suggests how widely the virtue of mercy was valued in the ancient world. Under Julius Caesar the Latin equivalent *clementia* became a divine virtue that celebrated his "mercy towards the vanquished, with a temple being dedicated in its honor."[297] It appears as a prominent motif on Roman coins and plays a crucial role in the political propaganda of Emperor Tiberius.[298] The Aphrodisias Sebasteion depicts the victorious Nero acting mercifully to Armenia by pulling her submissive body to its feet.[299] While ἔλεος ("mercy") as an emotion could play a role in legal justice for the Greek world, where it was associated with partiality toward those evoking sympathy,[300] for the OT and later Judaism mercy is an essential aspect of human solidarity that related more to actions than to feelings.[301] Philo emphasized the centrality of mercy in defining what is essentially human and referred to "mercy as that most vital of emotions and most nearly akin to the rational soul (τὸ ἀναγκαιότατον καὶ συγγενέστατον λογικῇ ψυχῇ πάθος ἐκτετιμημένον, τὸν ἔλεον)."[302] From this perspective, in which Philo characteristically epitomizes Greco-Roman and Jewish wisdom, "persons without mercy" lack the essential quality of a rational human soul and pose a mortal threat to human welfare.

■ **32** The final relative clause in the first pericope brackets off and completes the case for individual and corporate accountability.[303] The matter of recognizing God's will is reiterated from vv. 19-21 and v. 28, where cognate terms were used.[304] To specify what is known by all, the term τὸ δικαίωμα ("the righteous decree") is used here for the first time[305] and will appear later in 2:26 and 8:4 to refer explicitly to stipulations of the Jewish Torah. Since the content of the "decree" pertains to the penalty for vicious behavior, there has been discussion about whether the offenses Paul has named in the catalogue of evils literally entailed a death penalty. Zahn and Dupont have argued for an explicit reference to the death penalty in Jewish and Greco-Roman law,[306] while others note that not all of the offenses seem to be capital and either eliminate the phrase entirely[307] or suggest rather imprecise alternatives. Daxer, Wibbing, Schrenk, and Michel suggest the threat of death at the last judgment,[308] which is hardly germane since it would be effective only after death, and the expression ἄξιοι θανάτου εἰσίν ("deserving of death") clearly implies that only those committing such offenses are liable to death.[309] The language is in any event explicitly juridical.[310] There is insufficient basis in this sentence to suggest that sinful life stands under the power of death because it perverts the creation, as Schlatter, Käsemann, and Cranfield suggest.[311] Their interpretation is a theological inference from Paul's extensive argument in chaps. 5 and 6, which would not have been clear to the original hearers at the point of 1:32.

Somewhat more plausible, though still rather allusive for the original audience, is the suggestion that the

297 Fears, "Cult of Virtues," 886; for bibliography on this theme, see 842.

298 Fears, "Cult of Virtues," 890.

299 See Maier, "Imperial Iconography," 401–2.

300 Rudolf Bultmann, "ἔλεος," *TDNT* 2 (1964) 477–78.

301 Ibid., 480–82.

302 Partially cited by ibid., 482, from Philo *Virt.* 144.

303 See Popkes, "Aufbau," 498; and Lyonnet, "Notes," 37–39.

304 Felix Flückinger appears to overlook these elements of continuity in suggesting that while 1:18-31 deals with Gentile sins, 1:32 opens the accusation against Jews who alone allegedly could have been privy to the "righteous decree" of God; "Zur Unterscheidung von Heiden und Juden in Röm 1:18–2:3," *ThZ* 10 (1954) 156.

305 While δικαίωμα can mean a legal claim or "what is made right" in common Greek usage, the LXX uses it in the sense of "legal statute, requirement, commandment" (Gen 26:5; Exod 15:25-26; Deut 4:1, 5, 8, 40, etc.); see Karl Kertelge, "δικαίωμα," *EDNT* 1 (1991) 334–35. Gottlob Schrenk, "δικαίωμα," *TDNT* 2 (1964) 221, argues that Paul "goes beyond the LXX" in using this word in the singular and refers here "to the knowledge of God's statutes or ordinances which obtains among men." In *Law,* 169, Thielman notes that δικαίωμα "refers to the Mosaic law."

306 Zahn, 104; Dupont, *Gnosis*, 27–28.

307 O'Neill, 45.

308 Daxer, *Römer*, 62–63; Wibbing, *Lasterkataloge*, 117; Schrenk, "δικαίωμα," 221; Michel, 108.

309 See Werner Foerster, "ἄξιος κτλ.," *TDNT* 1 (1964) 379.

310 See Popkes, "Aufbau," 498.

311 Schlatter, 46; Käsemann, 52; Cranfield, 1:134.

Adam and Eve story is in view with reference to the words, "in the day that you eat of it you shall die" (Gen 2:17).[312] It is important to observe that the decree in Rom 1:32 is in the singular, which seems to imply an abstraction distinguished from the usual plural expression "decrees of the law"[313] employed in 2:26. The reference in 1:32 implies not some vague entity called "the one divine will,"[314] but rather a specific decree involving capital punishment that stands in a *pars pro toto* fashion for a wider practice of "such things" mentioned in the catalogue of evils, several of which were indeed subject to the death penalty.[315] What Paul contends is rhetorically but not logically conclusive, namely that everyone is "without excuse" because they do "such things" with full knowledge of the consequences.

This final verse in the pericope is the last plank in the rhetorical bridge called "suppression of the truth." It is rhetorically effective in large part because of the stunning list of social offenses and offenders that evoked many of the readiest stereotypes of the Greco-Roman and Jewish worlds. Paul would have no doubt after these 21 characterizations that his audience would nod in agreement with the sentiment that such persons "deserve" to die, even though not all of the evils were actually adjudicable in the courts and some of them were being routinely committed by the leaders and opinion makers of the era.

A rhetorically effective element of hyperbole is also present in the final line concerning the "approval" (συνευδοκέω) of evildoers. Moralistic interpreters have been bothered by the implication that applause is worse than the performance of an evil deed, with some attempting to tone down Paul's claim[316] and others providing additional reasons for it.[317] Given the fact that the formulation echoes a line from the *Testament of Asher*,[318] and that Paul's point is echoed by Seneca,[319] this detail functions as an effective rhetorical heightening to bring the pericope to a conclusion. The "not only . . . but also" formula points emphatically[320] toward the element of approval as the most egregious offense. Paul is neither setting forth a legal system here nor establishing ground rules for a social ethic for the Christian community. Rather, he is exploiting the ethical commonplaces of his time to make a case more radical than had ever been made before, namely that the human race was involved in a consciously vicious campaign to suppress the truth. The case is overwhelmingly strong on rhetorical grounds and can be understood as an outgrowth of Paul's reflection on the implications of the cross event. Yet neither here nor elsewhere in the early chapters of Romans is the argument watertight in a strictly logical sense. It is a matter of rhetoric driven by faith that was designed to be effective for the audience of Roman house and tenement churches in 57 C.E. Its persuasive power, measured against the social standards prevailing in that cultural setting, must be acknowledged as formidable.

---

312 Dunn, 1:69.
313 Schrenk, "δικαίωμα," 221, notes that "in the LXX the plural is preferred, and, even where the singular is used, it normally refers to one of many statutes."
314 Schrenk, "δικαίωμα," 221.
315 In Roman and Jewish law, "murder," civic "strife," political "treachery," "slander," "haters of God" (understood as atheism or impiety), "inventors of evil" (in a political sense), and "disobedience to parents" could be construed as capital offenses.
316 Barrett, 41.

317 Zahn, 104; Cranfield, 1:135.
318 *T. Ash.* 6.2 refers to the double-faced as being guilty of a "twofold sin," "because they practice evil and approve those practicing evil" (ὅτι καὶ πράσσουσι τὸ κακὸν καὶ συνευδοκοῦσιν τοῖς πράσσουσιν τὸ κακὸν).
319 Seneca *Ep.* 39.6 speaks of persons "who are not only attracted but even take pleasure in shameful things" (*turpia non solum delectant, sed etiam placent*); see Sevenster, *Paul and Seneca*, 126.
320 See Meyer, 1:99.

2

The First Part of the Second Pericope

The Righteous Judgment of
Greeks and Jews

**a. Diatribe concerning Impartial
Judgment according to Works**

1/ Therefore[a] you are without excuse,
O man/woman, whoever you are who
passes judgment. For by that which[b]
you judge the other, you are condemning yourself, for you, the one who
passes judgment, practice the same
things. 2/ But[c] we know that the judgment of God stands in truth against
those who practice such things. 3/ But
do you count on this, O man/woman,
who pass judgment on those who do
such things[d] and do them [yourself],
that you could escape the judgment of
God? 4/ Or do you scornfully presume
upon the riches of his kindness and his
forbearance and patience, not knowing
that the kindness of God is to lead you[e]
to repentance? 5/ But by your hardened and impenitent heart, you are
storing up for yourself wrath on the
day of wrath and[f] revelation[g] of the
righteous judgment of God.

6/ God "will recompense to each according
to his [or her] works": 7/ on the one
hand to those who by perseverance in
good work are seeking glory and honor
and incorruptibility, [he will recom-
pense] eternal life; 8/ on the other
hand to those who out of partisanship
not only disobey[h] the truth, but also
obey wrongdoing, [there will be] wrath
and fury, 9/ affliction and distress upon
every single person who brings about
evil, the Jew first and also the Greek,
10/ but glory and honor and peace to
everyone who does the good, to the
Jew first and also to the Greek. 11/ For
there is no partiality before God.

12/ For as many as have sinned outside the
law will also perish outside the law.
And as many as have sinned under[i] the
law will be judged by the law. 13/ For
it is not the hearers of law who are
righteous before[j] God, but the doers of
the law who shall be set right.[k] 14/ For
when Gentiles that do not have a law
by nature do the deeds of the law,
they—though not possessing a law—
are[l] a law unto themselves. 15/ Such
people demonstrate that the work of
the law is written in their hearts, their
conscience bearing witness, and the
thoughts[m] between them condemning
or even defending, 16/ [n]on a day when[o]
God judges[p] the secrets of people

through Christ Jesus,[q] according to
my[r] gospel.

a The conjecture by Anton Fridrichsen, "Der wahre
Jude und sein Lob: Rom 2:28f.," *SO* 1 (1922) 40,
and in "Quatre conjectures sur le texte du Nouveau
Testament," *RHPhR* 3 (1923) 440, that διό ("therefore") should be emended to δίς ("twice") rests on a
mistaken exegetical premise about the argument of
1:18-32 being directed only at Gentiles and 2:1-29
only at Jews.

b The addition of κρίματι ("in judgment") to the
phrase ἐν ᾧ by C*vid 69 88 104 1319 1573 1735 *pc*
syh** sa? may be a Hebraism similar to the formulation of Matt 7:2 and Rev 18:20. Cranfield, 1:142,
suspects an assimilation to the Matthew parallel.

c The textual evidence in A B Dgr G K L P Ψc 6 88
104 181 323 326 330 365 424 451 614 629 945 1175
1241 1243 1505 1506 1735 1739 1836 1874 1877
1881 2464 2495 *Maj Lect* arvid g sy(p),h Spec Tert Orlat
Ambst slightly favors δέ ("but") over γάρ ("for") in
ℵ C Ψ* 33 436 1573 1962 2127 2492 d vg, while
1827 1906 have neither. Since γάρ provides a
smoother transition with the preceding sentence,
the more difficult δέ should be preferred. Metzger
makes the same textual choice on syntactical
grounds (*Textual Commentary*, 507). Sahlin's proposal in "Emendationsvorschläge," 73, that οἶδα
μὲν ὅτι. . . ("now I say that . . .") was Paul's original
formulation that was later changed to the two versions currently available is not plausible in view of
the rhetoric of this passage that requires the first
person plural.

d There is a simplified version of the rather belabored and careful wording of the first eleven Greek
words in this sentence, but there is little likelihood
of the originality of the wording found in P,
νομίζεις οὖν ὁ ταῦτα πράσσων ("do you suppose,
therefore, the one who practices such things . . . ?").

e A minor variant in 33 has ἔναγει ("leads [you] in")
in place of σε ἄγει ("leads you"), probably a dictation or copying error.

f The variant found in A, ἀνταποδόσεως ("of retribution") appears to be a "not very perceptive
attempted improvement" of the difficult wording of
this verse, according to Cranfield, 1:145.

g The addition of καί ("also, and") in ℵ2 Dc K L P Ψ
33 88 104 326 330 365 424 614 1175 1241 1243
1319 1505 1735 1739 1836 1874 1881 2344 2464
2495 *Maj* syh appears to be a secondary effort to
smooth the text. It turns "on the day of wrath and
revelation of the righteous judgment" into "on the
day of wrath and revelation and righteous judgment
of God," i.e., creating three equal genitive modi-
fiers of "day of wrath." The text without the addi-

h The insertion of μέν ("on the one hand") at this point in ℵ² A Dᶜ K L P Ψ 6 33 69* 88 104 323 326 330 365 424 614 945 1175 1241 1243 1319* 1505 1506 1573 1735 1836 1874 2344 2464 2495 *Maj* syʰ is a later syntactical improvement to balance the second δέ, and its absence in ℵ* B D* G 1739 1881 *pc* latt is somewhat more strongly attested and should be accepted as the more difficult reading.

i The minor variant in *l* 44 that reads ἐννώμως ("lawfully") in place of ἐν νόμος ("under law") is understandable as a dictation or copyist's error.

j The absence of the definite article τῷ in B D* 056 1874* is a puzzling matter left undecided in Nestle-Aland²⁶/²⁷, because of the use of the ambiguous square brackets. It is not discussed by any of the recent commentators but is extensively treated in Moule, *Idiom-Book*, 115–16. There is stronger evidence for the inclusion of the article, with ℵ A Dᶜ G K L Ψ 6 33 69 88 104 323 326 424 614 945 1175 1241 1243 1319 1505 1506 1573 1735 1739 1836 1874ᶜ 1881 2344 2464 2495 *Maj.* It is possible that the deletion was caused by the typicality of the hebraizing expression, δίκαιοι παρὰ θέῳ ("justified ones before God"); see Michel, 117; and Moule, *Idiom-Book*, 117.

k A minor variant in G vgᵐˢˢ Spec inserts παρὰ θέῳ ("before God") after δικαιωθήσονται, a dittography caused by δίκαιοι παρὰ τῷ θεῷ. There is little likelihood of its originality.

l Another minor variant with G replaces οὗτοι νόμον ("these [not having] a law") with οἱ τοιοῦτοι νόμον ("such ones [not having] a law"), clearly an effort to improve the text.

m Once again G offers an improvement of the text, substituting διαλογισμῶν ("arguments") for λογισμῶν ("thoughts").

n The conjecture by Pohlenz, καὶ δικαιωθήσονται ("and they shall be justified") is inappropriate on text-critical grounds, but should be supplied on a contextual basis in modern translations, because this verse provides the conclusion of the discussion starting in v. 13, where δικαιωθήσονται appears; see Sanday and Headlam, 62.

o In place of the reading strongly attested in ℵ D G K L Ψ 6 33 69 104 323 326 330 365 424 614 945 1175 1241 1243 1315 1319 1505 1573 1735 1739 1836 1874 1881 2464 2495 *Maj* lat syʰ Spec, ἐν ἡμέρᾳ ὅτε ("on a day when"), B has the grammatically smoother reading ἐν ᾗ ἡμέρᾳ ("on which day"), and A 88 1506 *pc* have the latter two words in reverse order. I can find no discussion of the shift from the B reading in earlier editions of Nestle to the current text following ℵ, etc., in most recent commentaries or in Metzger, but the principles concerning stronger and broader evidence as well as preferring the more difficult text appear to be followed now. Käsemann, 67, follows Lietzmann, 42, in preferring the reading with the definite article because it emphasizes the eschatological reference, and Sahlin, "Textemendationen," 93–94, proposes that ἡμέρα was a secondary addition.

p The question of whether to accent κρινει as a future verb, κρινεῖ ("he will judge"), as in D² 33 69 88 104 323 326 365 614 945 1175 1241 1319 1505 1506 1573 1735 1739 1874 1881 2464 2495 *Maj* latt cop or as a present verb, κρίνει ("he judges"), as in B² Ψ 6 1241 1243 *pc*, followed by Nestle-Aland²⁶/²⁷, is complicated by the fact that most of the early texts have no accent at all: ℵ A B* D* G. In view of the logical difficulty in linking a present tense verb with the last judgment, it appears to me that the shift to a future tense verb is easier to explain as a correction, and therefore that the better reading is that advocated by Nestle-Aland²⁶/²⁷.

q The sequence "Jesus Christ" is found in ℵ¹ A K L Ψ 6 33 69 88 104 256 263 330 365 424 436 459 614 945 1175 1241 1243 1319 1505 1506⁽ᵃᶜᶜ· ᵗᵒ ˢʷᵃⁿˢᵒⁿ⁾ 1573 1735 1739 1874 1881 1962 2127 2200 2464 2495 *Maj Lect* latt syᵖ· ʰ cop arm eth geo² slav Orˡᵃᵗ Ad Serapion Chr Cyr John-Damascus Pel Aug Varimadum, (to which D 1852 ar b d mon o vgᵐˢˢ Ambst Prisc Ambr Nic Spec add "our Lord"), but the more likely original sequence is witnessed in ℵ*ᵛⁱᵈ B 81 1506⁽ᵃᶜᶜ· ᵗᵒ ᴳᴺᵀ⁾ geo¹ (Or) Rebaptism.

r The deletion of μου ("my") by 69 d* saᵐˢˢ appears to be secondary.

Analysis

The address to the imaginary interlocutor in 2:1 marks a vivid rhetorical shift into diatribe style,[1] which generalizes the application of the point made in the preceding pericope concerning the liability of those who practice evil. The links between this half-pericope and the foregoing are enhanced by multiple examples of paronoma-

---

1 See Stowers, *Diatribe*, 93–96, 110–112; Song, *Diatribe*, 92–94; Leenhardt, 75.

193

sia in the first paragraph, with πράσσειν ("practice"), which had been used twice in 1:32, repeated three times and κρίνειν ("judge") and its derivatives used seven times. Also, 2:1 may contain a miniature chiasmus[2] that features a wordplay between κρίνεις ("judge") and κατακρίνεις ("condemn"):

ἐν ᾧ γὰρ κρίνεις τὸν ἕτερον,
σεαυτὸν κατακρίνεις

The pattern of two-line sentences continues through the end of v. 5, which on rhetorical as well as semantic grounds is the end of the first paragraph.[3] In a compelling expression of accountability, several pairs of lines contain second person pronouns in the first line and "God" in the second line.[4] The additional examples of paronomasia help to confirm the structure of parallel lines, with κρίνων ("judging") in v. 3a matching κρίμα ("judgment") in v. 3b, χρηστότης ("kindness") in v. 4a matched by τὸ χρηστόν ("kindness") in v. 4b, and ὀργή ("wrath") in v. 5a picked up by ὀργή in v. 5b. In addition "penitence" in v. 4b stands in rhetorical juxtaposition to "impenitence" in v. 5a. The rhetorical flair of the paragraph is enhanced by the triad of "kindness," "forbearance," and "patience" in v. 4a.[5]

The second paragraph (vv. 6-11) contains a brilliantly devised chiasm framed by a matching introduction and conclusion and marked by antithetical parallelism and the repetition of the phrase "the Jew first and also the Greek."[6] In this paragraph the second person singular form of direct address shifts to a more objective third person form. The paragraph contains an extensive *merismos* or division, in which the aspects of the whole are enumerated after the whole—in this case the judgment

according to works—is mentioned.[7] The triad of "honor and glory and incorruptibility" in v. 7 is matched by the triad of "glory and honor and peace" in v. 10, making the chiastic structure more compelling:

A God will judge according to works (2:6)
   B For those who do good, reward (2:7)
      C For those who do evil, punishment (2:8)
      C' For evil Jews and Greeks, punishment (2:9)
   B' For good Jews and Greeks, reward (2:10)
A' God judges impartially (2:11)

The point of emphasis in the chiasm is at C and C[1], which state a universal accountability that includes both Jews and Greeks, based on actual performance of good and evil.[8] There is also a striking wordplay in C, with "disobey the truth" antithetically opposed to "obeying the injustice."[9] The concentration of three verbal ellipses in vv. 7b, 8b, and 9a[10] enhances the point of emphasis in the chiasm. Asyndeton enhances the rhetorical power of this passage.[11]

The third paragraph (vv. 12-16) commences with antithetical parallelisms reiterating the theme of universal accountability. The antithetical repetitions of "law" and "lawless" in vv. 12-13 are combined with homoioteleuton in the ending of the two lines in v. 12 (ἀπολοῦνται, "they will perish," and κριθήσονται, "they will be condemned"), producing a formal *sententia*.[12] There is a somewhat less parallel play on the word δικαιόω ("make righteous") in the antithetical *sententia* of v. 13.[13] In the middle of this paragraph (at 2:14) there is a shift to a more prosaic style[14] explaining the evidence of responsible moral reflection on the part of converted Gentiles. Even here, however, the verbal intensity is maintained by

---

2   See Harvey, *Listening*, 186.

3   See Louw, 2:45–46.

4   See Weiss, "Beiträge," 217, for the stylistic observations about this pericope.

5   Michel, 90.

6   See Weiss, "Beiträge," 179; Louw, 2:47; Kendrick Grobel, "A Chiastic Retribution-Formula in Romans 2," in E. Dinkler, ed., *Zeit und Geschichte. Dankgabe an Rudolf Bultmann zum 80. Geburtstag* (Tübingen: Mohr [Siebeck], 1964) 255–61; Wilckens, 1:126; Yinger, *Deeds*, 153, also accepts Grobel's chiastic structure.

7   See Bullinger, *Figures*, 435; Harvey suggests a more limited chiasmus in 2:6-10 in *Listening*, 186–87.

8   Moo, 135–36, perceives the emphasis in vv. 1 and 11.

9   Louw, 2:52, refers to this as "a chiastic pattern with regard to the positive/negative features of the items."

10   See Bullinger, *Figures*, 30; Güting and Mealand, *Asyndeton*, 2, 126.

11   See BDF §494.

12   See Holloway, "Paul's Pointed Prose," 51.

13   See ibid. Note, however, that the homoioteleuton is continued in v. 13c with the ending of δικαιωθήσονται ("they will be set right") that matches the ends of the lines in v. 12.

14   See Weiss, "Beiträge," 218.

the inversion of μὴ νόμον and νόμον μὴ in v. 14.[15] The pericope closes with a rhetorical flourish[16] by referring to Paul's gospel "through Christ Jesus."

Rhetorical Disposition

IV.	The *Probatio*
1:18– 4:25	A. The first proof: The gospel expresses the impartial righteousness of God by overturning claims of cultural superiority and by rightwising Jews and Gentiles through grace alone
2:1-29	2. The righteous judgment of Greeks and Jews
2:1-16	a. Diatribe concerning the impartial judgment according to works
2:1-5	1) The indictment of the imaginary interlocutor
2:1-2	a) Thematic statement of accountability
2:1a	(1) No human can contrive an alibi
2:1b	(2) Each human judging others condemns himself/herself
2:1c	(3) Each human commits the same evils that he/she condemns
2:2	(4) Divine judgment threatens all who practice evil
2:3	b) The rhetorical question about escaping divine judgment
2:3a	(1) The description of humans as accountable
2:3b	(2) The prospect of escaping divine accountability
2:4	c) The rhetorical question about presuming on divine forbearance
2:4a	(1) The description of human presumption of divine richness
	(a) Divine kindness
	(b) Divine forbearance
	(c) Divine patience
2:4b	(2) The description of the intent of divine kindness: to produce penitence.
2:5	d) The certain prospect of divine wrath
2:5a	(1) The prospects of the self-imposition of wrath
	(a) In response to hardness of heart
	(b) In response to impenitent heart
2:5b	(2) The eschatological context of wrath
	(a) The "day of wrath"
	(b) The revelation of "righteous judgment"
2:6-11	2) Impartial judgment according to works
2:6	a) The thesis about accountability, cited from Ps 62:12 and Prov 24:12
	(1) The one calling to account: "he," i.e., God
	(2) The scope of accountability "each" human
	(3) The standard of accountability: "works"
2:7	b) The reward for good works
	(1) The form of good behavior: patient good works
	(2) The motive of good behavior as gaining:
	(a) Glory
	(b) Honor
	(c) Incorruptibility
	(3) The reward of "eternal life"
2:8	c) The punishment of bad works
	(1) The form of bad works:
	(a) Factiousness
	(b) Disobedience of truth
	(c) The motive of bad behavior: "pursuing wrongdoing"
	(2) The punishment:
	(a) Wrath
	(b) Fury
2:9	d) The universal scope of punishment
	(1) The form of punishment:
	(a) Affliction
	(b) Distress
	(2) The scope of punishment:
	(a) Everyone doing evil
	(b) Both Jews and Greeks
2:10	e) The universal scope of reward
	(1) The form of the reward:
	(a) Glory
	(b) Honor
	(c) Peace
	(2) The scope of the reward:
	(a) Everyone doing good
	(b) Both Jews and Greeks
2:11	f) The conclusion about impartial divine judgment
2:12-16	3) The performance of the law rather than its mere possession leads to rightwising
	a) Law provides no exemption from judgment
2:12	(1) The situation of Greeks
2:12a	(a) Greeks sin "outside the law"
	(b) Greeks are punished "outside the law"
2:12b	(2) The situation of Jews

---

15 See Bullinger, *Figures*, 300.

16 See Käsemann, 68.

	(a) Jews sin "under the law"
	(b) Jews are punished "through the law"
2:13	b) Righteousness measured on performance of the law
2:13a	(1) Hearers of the law are not thereby righteous
2:13b	(2) Being set right comes only to performers of law
2:14-16	c) The explanation of Gentiles performing the law
2:14	(1) Converted Gentiles who lacked the law "by nature" now reveal an internal law
2:15	(2) Conscience and moral reflection among Gentiles reveals the presence of the law written on the heart
2:16	(3) Paul's gospel proclaims that the day of judgment will confirm those who have performed the law

Exegesis

■ **1** The pericope opens with an abrupt shift in style to that of direct, second person diatribe that is typical for Greco-Roman addresses to imaginary interlocutors.[17] The first word is the inferential conjunction διό ("therefore"), which we should understand in the full logical sense, drawing the inference from the preceding argument.[18] The reduction of the conjunction to a nonlogical transition[19] rests on a misperception of 1:18-32 as pertaining only to Gentiles, whereas it includes "*all* impiety and unrighteousness of humans who by unrighteousness are suppressing the truth" (1:18).[20] As Jouette Bassler has shown, the continuity of the argument from the first to the second chapter is marked by linguistic repetition, with πράσσειν ("practice" in 1:32 [twice]; 2:1, 2, 3), ποιεῖν ("do" in 1:28, 32; 2:3) and the important κριν- words ("judge-" in 2:1-3 [7 times]) bracketed by δικαίωμα ("righteous judgment" in 1:32) and δικαιοκρισία ("righteous judgment" in 2:5).[21] The διό ("therefore") signals "a further consequence" of the preceding argument,[22] that those who know God's decree cannot be excused by virtue of their being able to judge others when they themselves act in a similarly arrogant manner, suppressing the truth.[23] The expression ἀναπολόγητος εἶ ("you are without excuse") is drawn from 1:20, and reflects ethical discourse[24] or the courtroom language of a prosecutor.[25] The address ὦ ἄνθρωπε ("O human/man!") evokes the style of diatribe rather than that of the courtroom. Epictetus employs the vocative "Man!" some 64 times, though without the ὦ, as in *Diss.* 4.13.10, "Man (ἄνθρωπε), I did not invite your confidence. . . . If you were a babbler . . . do you also want me to be like yourself?" In the early Christian context, this address is suitable for unconverted outsiders, whereas one addresses insiders with the term "brothers."[26] Although there are more neutral, conversational contexts in classical literature in which ὦ ἄνθρωπε is used,[27] "O man!" has the feel of a missionary harangue[28] in reference to someone "who passes judgment."

The expression πᾶς ὁ κρίνων ("whoever you are who pass judgment") is inherently offensive in a tradition in which God alone is the final judge. The Jesus tradition that forbade judging or condemning one another (Matt

---

17 Stowers, *Diatribe*, 86–93; Dunn, 1:78; Thorsteinsson, *Paul's Interlocutor*, 152–53.

18 Meyer, 1:102; Sanday and Headlam, 55; Weiss, 100; Cranfield, 1:141; Fitzmyer, 298; Haacker, 60; Bassler, *Impartiality*, 133; Stowers, *Diatribe*, 217 n. 63.

19 Lietzmann, 39; Michel, 113; Käsemann, 54; and Schlier, 68, accept Molland's contention in "Διό," 43–44, that διό serves as a nonlogical transitional particle.

20 Thorsteinsson, *Paul's Interlocutor*, 165–88, overlooks this reference to "all impiety" in concluding that the argument in 1:18–2:29 is directed exclusively against Gentile believers. Leenhardt, 74–75, more properly concludes that the argument is relevant for both Jews and Gentiles.

21 Bassler, *Impartiality*, 131–32.

22 Bassler, *Impartiality*, 133.

23 Stowers, *Diatribe*, 110–12.

24 LSJM 117 refers to Polybius *Hist.* 12.21.10.

25 See BAGD (2000) 71.

26 This renders implausible the conclusion of Thorsteinsson, *Paul's Interlocutor*, 188–94, that Paul's interlocutor must have been a believing Gentile, and thus a member of the Roman congregation.

27 For example, Plato *Resp.* 329c2, 337b1, "O good sir," or "O mister." See also Plato *Apol.* 28b6; *Symp.* 200c8; *Prot.* 330d8; *Gorg.* 452b5; *Men.* 75a3.

28 Dunn, 1:79. Newman and Nida, 32, soften this to "my friend."

7:1-5; Luke 6:37) would surely have been known in Rome. In various locations (Rom 14:4, 10, 13; 1 Cor 4:5), Paul maintains the same principle: "Because judging is God's right alone, human judging is forbidden."[29] Paul's formulation depicts a censorious bigot who condemns everybody beyond himself. That this verb κρίνειν recurs in the context of Paul's critique of the judgmental spirit within Roman churches (14:3, 4, 5, 10, 13, 22) renders it likely that he is building a rhetorical argument here whose full relevance will emerge later. Since no one likes scolds and censors, Paul is certain to gain assent from all branches of the Roman churches.[30] This is reinforced by the present tense of the participle ὁ κρίνων ("the one who passes judgment," 2:1a, c), and the present tense verbs κρίνεις ("he passes judgment") and κατακρίνεις ("he is condemning"), which indicates habitual behavior,[31] in contrast to the considered verdict of a judge at the end of a trial that would normally require an aorist or perfect tense. The principle that one condemns oneself by the manner in which one judges others had been clearly enunciated by Jesus, and it is likely that Paul is dependent on the oral tradition of Matt 7:1-2:[32] Μὴ κρίνετε, ἵνα μὴ κριθῆτε· ἐν ᾧ γὰρ κρίματι κρίνετε κριθήσεσθε ("Judge not, that you be not judged. For with the judgment you pronounce you will be judged"). With rhetorical finesse, Paul formulates this idea in a neat chiastic structure that contains a wordplay between κρίνεις ("judge") and κατακρίνεις ("con-

demn").[33] Although the verb κατακρίνειν is ordinarily employed in the context of judicial condemnation,[34] its connotation here is determined by Paul's choice of the durative present tense and by the references to "the other" and passing judgment. This is the type of condemnation that occurs within the context of intergroup bigotry to which Paul plans to return in chap. 14.

It is significant that Paul employs the noun ὁ ἕτερος ("the other") as the object of the verb "judge," a word often employed by Paul to refer to the "neighbor" or other congregational members, as in 13:8.[35] While this term would not be appropriate in a judicial setting, it matches the congregational setting of Paul's discourse. In this connection it is worth observing that in the extensive debate about whether this pericope addresses the sins of Jews,[36] or of Gentiles and Jews alike,[37] or whether it makes a more general case about the impartiality of divine justice,[38] no reference to the congregational situation in Rome can be found in commentaries on this verse.[39] I wish to make the case here that the peculiarities of this passage can be explained by Paul's rhetorical goal of creating an argument that provides the premises for an ethic of mutual tolerance between the competitive house and tenement churches in Rome, which could enable them to participate with integrity in the Spanish mission.

The final line in v. 1 charges that the bigot who continually passes judgment on others practices the same things (τὰ γὰρ αὐτὰ πράσσεις). Many suggestions have

---

29 Mathias Rissi, "κρίνω, κρίσις," *EDNT* 2 (1991) 320. The contrast with *4 Ezra* 3.28-36, which "judges the nations to be morally inferior to Israel," is noted by Longenecker, *Eschatology and the Covenant*, 175.

30 In contrast, Heil, 28, says that the audience would "readily identify with the imaginary figure" and that Paul's aim is to "embarrass" the audience.

31 See the discussion of the "durative" dimension of the present tense in Greek in BDF §318; Moulton and Turner, *Grammar III*, 62.

32 Michel, 113; Dunn, 1:79-80.

33 See n. 2 above; BAGD (2000) 519.

34 BAGD (2000) 519: "pass a sentence after determination of guilt"; Friedrich Büchsel, "κατακρίνω, κατάκριμα, κατάκρισις," *TDNT* 3 (1965) 951-52.

35 See below on 13:8; Klaus Haacker discusses the use of "other" as "neighbor" in "ἕτερος," *EDNT* 2 (1991) 66.

36 Kuss, 1:60, lists Althaus, Gaugler, Gutjahr, Jülicher, Lagrange, Lietzmann, Lipsius, Nygren, Sanday and

Headlam, Sickenberger, and Weiss as advocates of Jews only as the target of 2:1-16; see also Nygren, 113; Dodd, 32; Cranfield, 1:136-40; Käsemann, 52-54; Murray, 54-56; Wilckens, 1:122; Zeller, 61-63; George P. Carras, "Romans 2,1-29: A Dialogue on Jewish Ideals," *Bib* 73 (1992) 183-207. If this alternative is correct, Räisänen aptly characterizes this passage as "propagandist denigration" in *Law*, 101.

37 Zahn, 104-7; Kühl, 66; Leenhardt, 74; Schlatter, 47-48; Barrett, 43; Stowers, *Diatribe*, 112.

38 Bassler, *Impartiality*, 121-31; Dunn, 1:77-78; Moo, 92. Käsemann, 53, entitles the section 2:1-11 "The Criterion of Eschatological Judgment," but perceives a polemic against "the Jewish tradition."

39 Carter, *Power of Sin*, 149-50, is exceptional in linking an identification of the interlocutor as Jewish with his congregational theory.

been made concerning what these sins might have been,[40] but Paul's rhetorical purpose requires that no precise definition be given at this point. He comes back to this matter in chap. 14, showing that both the weak and the strong are acting in a bigoted matter toward each other, but the basis for such specificity has not yet been fully established. In chap. 2 Paul's rhetorical purpose is to picture bigotry in such objectionable terms that condemnation from his hearers would be guaranteed: nothing is more infuriating than the hypocritical person who condemns others for the same sins that he/she him-/herself habitually commits.[41] In coordination with the address, "O man," this stereotype of the unconverted is enjoyable by insiders who assume that despite the second person style the target must be someone else. With brilliant rhetorical finesse, Paul prevents his audience from suspecting that the hypocritical bigots whose detestation they share in this verse would later turn out to be themselves.

■ **2** Paul provides immediate rhetorical reinforcement of his entrapment by placing his audience among the "we" converted believers who know about God's judgment against such wicked hypocrites. The particle in οἴδαμεν δέ should not be reduced to "and we know"[42] but rather translated as "but we know,"[43] which gently separates Paul's audience from the seeming targets of the harangue.[44] As Käsemann observes, "verse 2 aptly brings out the agreement between Paul and the partner in the conversation."[45] More specifically, in the Pauline letters the first person plural verb οἴδαμεν followed by ὅτι ("that") refers not to a single conversation *partner*

but to the audience of believers, as in 1 Cor 8:1, "for we know that (οἴδαμεν ὅτι) all of us possess knowledge," or 2 Cor 5:1, "for we know that (οἴδαμεν ὅτι) if the earthly tent we live in. . . ." Also in Rom 3:19; 7:14; 8:22, 28 οἴδαμεν ὅτι is a "formula to introduce a well-known fact that is generally accepted"[46] by fellow believers. While it is not an expression employed in other examples of diatribe, the verb "we know" conveys Paul's solidarity with his audience in the churches.[47] That converts know about τὸ κρίμα τοῦ θεοῦ ("the judgment of God") is self-evident for those who have decided to be saved "from the wrath to come" (1 Thess 1:10). The word κρίμα usually refers to the decision of a judge and since the verdict is ordinarily unfavorable, it carries the sense of "condemnation."[48] Thus in Acts 24:25 Paul's preaching to Felix and Drusilla is depicted as including an alarming message about "the future judgment" (τοῦ κρίματος τοῦ μέλλοντος). In view of the repeated refrain in the preceding pericope (Rom 1:24, 26, 28) that "God delivered them" to wrath, there would be no doubt in the minds of Paul's hearers that such condemnation would be directed "against those who practice such things." The participial phrase τὰ τοιαῦτα πράσσοντας ("those who practice such things") connects with the verb πράσσεις ("practice") in v. 1, so there is no ambiguity about whose behavior warrants such denunciation. This phrase occurs nowhere else in the NT but is typical for classical oratory. Lysias, for example, offers several parallels: οἱ νόμοι κελεύουσι τοὺς τὰ τοιαῦτα πράττοντας ("the laws order those who practice such things as these";[49] or οἱ γὰρ τὰ τοιαῦτα

40 For example, Minear, *Obedience*, 48–49, refers to false claims of wisdom; Barrett, 44, thinks of "man's ambition to put himself in the place of God"; Dunn, 1:80, thinks of "sins of pride and presumption." Longenecker, *Eschatology and the Covenant*, 176, cites *4 Ezra* 3.26, that Israelites "do in everything the things which Adam and his wicked descendants had done."

41 Haacker, 60, refers to Cicero *Fam.* 2.1; Valerius Max. 8.6; Seneca *Ira.* 2.7.3; 28.7–8; 3.26.4; *Clem.* 1.6.2; *Ben.* 8.28.3; *Ep.* 108.36; Marcus Antoniuis, 10.30.1; 11; 18.7; insincerity in relation to Nero described by Dio Cassius *Hist. Rom.* 61.

42 Dunn, 1:80; Godet, 115; and Moo, 131, prefer "now we know." Dodd, 31, eliminates the particle entirely.

43 For example, Käsemann, 53; Cranfield, 1:136; Schlier, 69.

44 Thorsteinsson, *Paul's Interlocutor*, 190, infers in contrast that those referred to in "we know" are the targets of the harangue, which makes no rhetorical sense.

45 Käsemann, 54.

46 BAGD (2000) 693.1e; Dunn, 1:80; see also Burdick, "Οἶδα and Γινώσκω," 344–47.

47 Stowers, *Diatribe*, 94; this solidarity between author and audience is rejected in an unconvincing manner by Haacker, 60.

48 Friedrich Büchsel and Volkmar Herntrich, "κρίνω κτλ.," *TDNT* 3 (1965) 942; Mathias Rissi, "κρίμα," *EDNT* 2 (1991) 317–18.

49 Lysias *Orat.* 1.27.2; other examples of this phrase or close equivalents in denunciatory contexts are found in Lysias *Orat.* 7.113.1 and 1.47.3; Isocrates

πράττοντες, ὁρῶντες οἷα τὰ ἆθλα πρόκειται τῶν τοιούτων ἁμαρτημάτων ("For those who practice such things, seeing such prizes presented for such errors as these").[50] Isocrates advises, "Never support to defend a bad cause, for people will suspect that you yourself do the things (καὶ αὐτὸς τοιαῦτα πράττειν) that you aid others in doing."[51]

The phrase κατὰ ἀλήθειαν ("according to/in truth") connects this condemnation with 1:18 and 25, where the human campaign to suppress the truth was denounced as warranting divine wrath. While the LXX can refer to God's judgment as "in the truth" (ἐν τῇ ἀληθείᾳ, Pss 53:5; 88:33; 95:13), Paul's unique expression employs the preposition κατά in the sense of "according to, in accordance with," thus indicating "the norm of judgment."[52] The formulation may be typically Pharisaic, because *P. 'Abot* 3.16 cites Rabbi Akiba as claiming that divine judgment "is a judgment according to truth." In a similar vein, *4 Ezra* 7.33-34 connects God's truth with divine judgment: "the Most High shall be revealed upon the seat of judgment, and compassion shall pass away, and patience shall be withdrawn, but judgment alone shall remain, *truth shall stand*, and faithfulness shall grow strong." CD 20:30 proclaims: "Righteousness and truth are your judgments over us."[53] That God's truth cannot be manipulated by pious bigots is here affirmed, and the audience of Roman converts would nod in agreement. Now that Paul has aligned his audience as belonging to the class of believers who are certain of divine judgment against such hypocrites, they can take pleasure in the subsequent harangue under the illusion that it does not pertain to them.

■ **3** Certain that he has now ensured the entrapment of his audience, Paul returns to the second person style of diatribal harangue to pose a rhetorical question that his audience must now believe to be an attack on an incorrigible outsider. Once again the particle δέ is used in the sense of "but"[54] to distinguish between the audience and the outsider addressed by ὦ ἄνθρωπε ("O Man"), whose hypocrisy Paul exposes. The word τοῦτο ("this") is dropped from most translations of v. 3, but a few scholars incorporate it either as a forecast of the forthcoming illusion that "you could escape the judgment of God"[55] or as a reference back to the certainty of divine judgment mentioned in v. 2, as in Barrett's translation, "But, knowing this, do you think, my man, that you. . . ."[56] It is necessary to treat τοῦτο as the emphatic object of the verb λογίζῃ ("you count, reckon, think"), whereby the content of "this" is specified by the ὅτι clause at the end of v. 3. There is a broad semantic range in the verb λογίζομαι, including count, credit, reckon, think, devise, have an opinion, imagine or consider,[57] and I believe that a translation such as "do you count on this" or "do you imagine this" is appropriate.

The following reiteration of the identity of Paul's rhetorical target employs exactly the same terms as in the preceding two verses. The person counting on exemption from divine evaluation is ὁ κρίνων τοὺς τὰ τοιαῦτα πράσσοντας καὶ ποιῶν αὐτά ("the one who passes judgment on those who do such things and does them [himself]"). The reiteration reinforces the identification of this bigoted hypocrite as different from the audience, but there is a subtle shift that needs to be taken into account. While the expression "those who do such things" in v. 2 referred to actions of the bigots themselves, now it serves to designate the actions of those whom the bigots judge. This rhetorically heightens the moral outrage because it describes bigots who denounce bigotry, yet engage in its pursuit in the conviction that they are exempt from divine judgment. The rel-

---

Panath. 2.2; Demosthenes *Orat.* 19 (336.6), (214.10), 268.4); 12 (9.3); 13 (1.7; 8 (25); *4 Philip.* 33.8, etc.

50   Lysias *Orat.* 1.47.3; other examples of "such things" referring to dishonorable deeds are Xenophon *Ages.* 5.6-7; Isocrates *Euth.* 8.3.

51   Isocrates *Demon.* 37.7-9.

52   Käsemann, 55; see BAGD (2000) 512.5a.

53   See Schlier, 69, for other examples of this association; for background see Klaus Haacker, "Wie redet die Bibel von Wahrheit," *ThBei* 10 (1979) 13-15.

54   Meyer, 1:104; Barrett, 44; Haacker, 57. However, most commentators and translators either delete this δέ (Sanday and Headlam, 53; Käsemann, 53; Schlier, 67; Dunn, 1:81; Fitzmyer, 300) or translate with "and" (Cranfield, 1:136; Murray, 54), which in either case assumes that the (usually "Jewish") target of v. 2 continues in vv. 3-12.

55   Meyer, 1:104.

56   Barrett, 44.

57   BAGD (2000) 597-98; Hans-Werner Bartsch, "λογίζομαι," *EDNT* 2 (1991) 354-55.

evance of this tiny detail will be made plain only when Paul reaches chap. 14, where the verb κρίνειν ("judge") is again employed with reference to bigotry between the weak and the strong, but there is no hint at this point that the target might include the audience of believers in Rome, for good rhetorical reasons.

The pretentious bigot's illusion of moral exceptionalism is succinctly described by the clause ὅτι σὺ ἐκφεύξῃ τὸ κρίμα τοῦ θεου ("that you could escape the judgment of God"). The σύ in connection with the verb ἐκφεύξῃ is emphatic, "you, of all people!"[58] The person who is capable of judging others should surely have known that no one can escape from God's wrath. The verb ἐκφεύγω ("escape")[59] was used along with the word κρίμα ("judgment") in the *Ps. Sol.* 15.8: "And those who do lawlessness shall not escape the Lord's judgment" (καὶ οὐκ ἐκφεύξονται οἱ ποιοῦντες ἀνομίαν τὸ κρίμα κυρίου).[60] In another context, Demosthenes used this verb to denounce someone who thinks "he might prove worthy of escaping indictment (ἐκφεύγειν ἀξιοίη) because of these things."[61] The formulation makes clear that Paul wishes to depict this illusion as actually being held.[62] As Barrett observes, Paul's formulation indicates that "the objector doubtless did suppose this, and not without reason, for the visible handing over to reprobate mind and behavior (i. 24, 26, 38) which was the token of God's wrath upon Gentile sinners, did not apply to him."[63] Thus the rhetorical question is meant to be answered by the imaginary conversation partner in

the affirmative,[64] while the audience says to themselves, "those hypocrites think they are exempt from wrath, but we know better!" It is a brilliant rhetorical trap.

■ **4** In this verse the "pretentious and arrogant" dimensions of the imaginary that Stowers perceives in the entire section comes to explicit expression.[65] But with rhetorical sophistication, Paul disguises the motif of arrogance until the thirteenth word in this sentence when the verb καταφρονεῖν finally appears. Since modern interpreters know the whole sentence and often translate it with the verb placed early in the sentence as in this commentary, the impact of the word order on the original audience has not been noticed. By beginning with ἤ ("or"), which was a typical way to introduce a new theme in diatribal discourse,[66] Paul at first appears to draw attention away from the previous topic of wrath against bigots.[67] The prayer-like[68] combination of three familiar attributes of God in the next eleven words that are joined in a formal sequence of genitive constructions makes it appear that Paul is describing a belief in God's bounty that the audience of believers would approve. The πλοῦτος ("fullness, riches") of God's gifts is a characteristic theme in Paul (1 Cor 1:5; 4:8; 2 Cor 8:2; 9:8-12; Phil 4:19) and in the gospel tradition (Mark 4:24; Luke 8:38).[69] The converts in Rome could easily have thought this word alluded to their own experience of divine grace. The word χρηστότης ("kindness/goodness") is ordinarily used in the LXX with regard to God,[70] and this motif is carried forward by Hellenistic Jewish writ-

---

58   Sanday and Headlam, 55.

59   BAGD (2000) 312, "run away, escape, avoid."

60   Schlier, 70, also points to parallels in Luke 11:36; 1 Thess 5:3; Heb 2:3; 12:25.

61   Demosthenes *Orat.* 22.27.3; see also 22.28.3 and *De pac.* 2.7, "and concerning which affairs you are planning to escape (ἐκφεύγειν ὑμᾶς)."

62   Jülicher, 238; and Weiss, 104, speak of the "Wahn" ("illusion, obsession") of the imaginary conversational partner. See also Zahn, 108.

63   Barrett, 44.

64   Commentators (e.g., Kuss, 1:62; Murray, 57) assume that the rhetorical question requires a negative response, on the mistaken premise that Paul is denouncing Jewish sins not being performed by the audience.

65   Stowers, *Diatribe*, 110–12.

66   See Epictetus *Diss.* 3.23.37 ("Or, tell me, who is lis-

tening to you reading"), cited by Stowers, *Diatribe*, 106; see also Epictetus *Diss.* 1.6.32, ἢ τί οἴει ὅτι ὁ Ἡρακλῆς ἂν ἀνέβη. . . ("Or, what do you suppose Heracles would have amounted to . . .").

67   Godet, 116; Murray, 58. Cranfield, 1:144, points to 1 Cor 9:6 as an example of argumentative discourse beginning with "Or."

68   Cranfield, 1:144. Michel, 114, points to *4 Ezra* 7.132ff. as an example of listing divine attributes in the context of prayer.

69   See Friedrich Hauck and Wilhelm Kasch, "πλοῦτος κτλ.," *TDNT* 6 (1968) 325–26; Helmut Merklein, "πλούσιος κτλ.," *EDNT* 3 (1993) 116.

70   Josef Zmejewski, "χρηστότης," *EDNT* 3 (1993) 475, refers to Pss 24:7; 83:12; 84:12; 118:65; 144:7; see also Stachowiak, *Chrestotes*, 8–18.

ers.[71] The Jesus tradition accentuates this motif, that God "is kind (χρηστός ἐστιν) to the ungrateful and self-ish" (Luke 6:35) and that the divine yoke is "kind/gentle" (χρηστός, Matt 11:30).[72] In combination with πλοῦτος, the neuter noun[73] χρηστότης in Rom 2:4 has the primary connotation of "kindness,"[74] referring to God's benevolent attitude toward his wayward children.[75] There are references to the ἀνοχή ("forbearance") of God in the LXX (Isa 42:14; 64:12), but the only other time this expression appears in the NT is in Rom 3:26. Here it has the sense of divine forbearance or restraint,[76] which Paul's hearers in Rome would have affirmed. The third divine attribute, μακροθυμία ("patience"), appears in the LXX with reference to God's restraint in expressing wrath to humans who deserve punishment.[77] In apocalyptic literature the patience of God is associated with his decision to delay the day of wrath in order to allow time for repentance.[78] Although Paul employs the theme of patience only as an attribute of the transformed moral life of believers (1 Cor 13:4; 2 Cor 6:6; Gal 5:22; 1 Thess 5:14), there is no doubt that here it is a familiar attribute of God, which leads me, as in the case of the previous attribute, to translate the definite article with "his."[79]

The verb καταφρονέω appears only here in all of Romans, with the connotation "to despise/disparage," with the object in the genitive, as usual.[80] Since Paul had employed the related derogatory stereotypes, θεοστυγεῖς ("haters of God"), ὑβριστάς ("arrogant ones"), ὑπερηφάνους ("egotists"), and ἀλαζόνας ("braggarts") in 1:30,[81] and since he evidently wished to depict the bigoted interlocutor in the worst possible terms, it is inappropriate to translate this verb as "think lightly, disregard."[82] To despise God was for the Greco-Roman and Jewish worlds an unspeakable offense. Hosea 6:7 contends that when people break covenant, καταφρόνησέν μου ("they despise me [Yahweh]"), and Euripides, Bacch. 199 has Cadmus state in company with the blind prophet Teirisias, "Mortal-born, I do not think lightly of the gods" (οὐ καταφρονῶ 'γὼ τῶν θεῶν θνητὸς γεφώς).[83] This is behavior that was even more outrageous than believing that one could escape from the judgment of God. This point is invisible when one assumes, as most commentators have, that Paul is polemicizing against self-righteous Jews at this point.[84] From the perspective of a Christian audience in Rome, converted by a gospel concerning the mercy of God, it was far worse to despise "the richness of God's kindness and his forbearance and his patience" than to maintain an illusion of exemption from wrath. While this verse would have aroused a shudder among pious hearers, who could not have dreamed that it applied to their behavior, this theme has a specific relevance for the Roman congregational situation, as we shall see when Paul turns in 14:3 to denounce the strong who are "despising" the weak for abstaining from certain foods.

The participial clause that follows the verb "despise" serves to heighten the outrageous behavior of the bigot by alleging an incredible level of ignorance.[85] Although he "passes judgment" on others, he is ἀγνοῶν ("unknowing") that God's "kindness" aims to evoke "repentance." The present tense verb "lead" is employed

---

71 Ceslas Spicq, "χρηστεύομαι κτλ.," *TLNT* 3 (1974) 512, refers to Philo *Mut.* 15ff.; *Det.* 46; *Leg.* 3.73, 215; Josephus *Ant.* 4.180, 237; 6.144; 20.90, 144; *Ps. Sol.* 9.11.

72 See esp. Konrad Weiss, "χρηστός κτλ.," *TDNT* 9 (1974) 487.

73 Ibid.

74 Stachowiak, *Chrestotes*, 77–79; Zmejewski, "χρηστότης," 475–76; Cranfield, 1:136; Dunn, 1:82.

75 Morris, 112; Markos A. Siotis, "La 'CHRESTOTES' de Dieu selon l'Apôtre Paul," in De Lorenzi, *Paul de Tarse*, 217–20.

76 Heinrich Schlier, "ἀνέχω, ἀνεκτός, ἀνοχή," *TDNT* 1 (1964) 359–60; Morris, 112, translates with "tolerance."

77 See Harm W. Hollander, "μακροθυμία κτλ.," *EDNT* 2 (1991) 380.

78 See Strobel, *Verzögerungs-problem*, 198–200; key texts are *Apoc. Ez.* 2.8; Sir 5:4-7; 1QH 16:16; 17:17-18; *4 Ezra* 3.18.

79 See, e.g., Zahn, 110; Schmidt, 41; Murray, 58.

80 Carl Schneider, "καταφρονέω κτλ.," *TDNT* 3 (1965) 361–62; BAGD (2000) 529.1; Ceslas Spicq, "καταφρονέω κτλ.," *TLNT* 2 (1994) 280.

81 See Stowers, *Diatribe*, 110–11.

82 Dunn, 1:81–82.

83 Cited by Spicq, "καταφρονέω κτλ.," 280; see also *PSI* 1337.17.

84 See, e.g., Weiszäcker, "Römische Christengemeinde," 248, 280–92; Schreiner, 108, 111–14.

85 Weiss, 105.

here with a conative sense that implies an attempt that is not yet complete.[86] God's mercy "is intended to lead"[87] to repentance. Wis 11:23 has a similar idea, that God's mercy "overlooks people's sins towards repentance" (παρορᾷς ἁμαρτήματα ἀνθρώπων εἰς μετάνοιαν). By using the word "repentance" that refers in the LXX, intertestamental literature, and early Christianity to conversion[88] as a matter of turning away from sin and toward God,[89] Paul evokes the formative experience of believers in Rome to cast the bigot in the worst possible light. The audience would not feel threatened by this formulation, because in contrast to the bigot[90] they had responded positively to the conveyance of divine kindness in the gospel and through repentance had gained a new life. They will not realize until chap. 14 that their own bigotry toward one another is another form of treating God's kindness with contempt, and that another stage of repentance is now required.[91]

■ **5** The harangue against the arrogant interlocutor continues with terminology typical for the LXX and intertestamental literature. Many warnings against "hardness of heart" reflect a "topos of the deuteronomistic-prophetic" tradition of conversion,"[92] which surfaces in passages such as Deut 10:16: "circumcise the hardness of your heart" (περιτεμεῖσθε τὴν σκληροκαρδίαν ὑμῶν).[93] Pharaoh in particular is stigmatized by "hardness of heart."[94] In 1QS 4:11 hardness of heart (כובוד לב) is listed along with other vices belonging to the "spirit of deceit." The adjective "impenitent" (ἀμετανόητος) is not found elsewhere in the biblical tradition, but *T. Gad* 7.5 employs this rare philosophical term[95] with a distinctively Judaic connotation that matches Paul's use here: "the impenitent one receives eternal punishment." To be stigmatized as not only having a hard heart but also being unwilling to repent spells doom, which Paul announces with typical biblical language: "you are storing up for yourself wrath on a day of wrath." While the verb θησαυρίζω ("store") is often employed in reference to good works safeguarded in the heavenly storehouse,[96] evil deeds are also stored up and recorded for future wrath. For example, Prov 1:18 proclaims that "those who deal in murder store up evils for themselves" (θησαυρίζουσιν ἑαυτοῖς κακά).[97]

The elaboration of formulas for divine judgment bring this verse to a powerful, rhetorical climax: "the day of wrath and revelation of the righteous judgment of

---

86 Moulton and Turner, *Grammar III*, 63; Sanday and Headlam, 56; Moule, *Idiom-Book*, 8.

87 See Udo Borse, "ἄγω," *EDNT* 1 (1990) 25; the only other occurrence of ἄγω in Romans is 8:14, in which believers "are led by the Spirit of God."

88 Johannes Behm "μετανοέω, μετανοία," *TDNT* 4 (1967) 989–1006.

89 See Helmut Merklein, "μετάνοια, μετανοέω," *EDNT* 2 (1991) 416, 418.

90 Dunn, 1:82: Paul's rhetorical goal was to "turn one of the Jewish interlocutor's own key beliefs against him."

91 Stowers, *Diatribe*, 112, therefore draws a premature conclusion that "the indictment of 2:1-5 . . . appeals to the reader to give up pretentiousness and arrogance and to repent." By depicting the bigot in terms that the audience deplores, Paul sets a trap that will have the effect Stowers perceives only by the time of the reading of chap. 14.

92 See Peter Fiedler, "σκληροκαρδία κτλ.," *EDNT* 3 (1990) 254; σκληροκαρδία and the adjective σκληροκάρδιος also occur in Jer 4:4; Ezek 3:7; Sir 16:9-10; Prov 17:20; Matt 19:8; Mark 16:14.

93 Later parallels are in *1 En.* 16.3; *T. Sim.* 6.2; CD 2:17-18; 3:5, 11-13; 8:8, 19; 20:9; 1QS 1:6; 2:14; 3:3; 5:4, etc. See Michel, 114.

94 See Ceslas Spicq, "σκληροκαρδία κτλ.," *TLNT* 3 (1994) 261–62, referring to God's hardening Pharaoh's heart in Exod 4:21; 7:3; 9:12; 10:1, 20, 27; 11:10; 14:4, 8; and Pharaoh hardening his own heart in Exod 7:22; 8:15; 9:35; 13:15.

95 BAGD (2000) 53 refers to the meaning "irrevocable" in Lucian, Plotinus, etc. In the only other relevant first-century occurrence of this philosophical term, Epictetus *Frag.* 24.4 (= Stobaeus *Anth.* 3.20.67) refers to one having conducted one's life without having "to repent (ἀμετανόητος) or be summoned to account."

96 Dieter Zeller, "θησαυρίζω κτλ.," *EDNT* 2 (1991) 150–51, cites *1 En.* 38.2; 2 Esd 6:5; 7:7; 8:33; *2 Bar.* 14.12; 24.1; *2 En.* 50.5, as well as later rabbinic parallels.

97 Zeller, "θησαυρίζω κτλ.," 150–51, refers also to Prov 16:27; Philo *Leg.* 3.105–6; and a series of Qumran references to the divine storehouse of wrath.

God." The two concepts are ordinarily kept separate. The ἡμέρα ὀργῆς is the technical term for the day of judgment that prophetic and apocalyptic writings expected at the end of time. Although Paul had referred to wrath as a current experience in 1:18-32, here he returns to the classic doctrine of the last judgment.[98] In the context of divine vengeance the "day of wrath" awaits those in Jerusalem who "despise the things committed to them" (καταφρονοῦντας τὰ φυλάγματα αὐτῶν), according to Zeph 1:12, which employs the same verb that Paul used to decry the arrogance of the religious bigot in v. 4. Zephaniah goes on: "A mighty day of wrath (δυνατὴ ἡμέρα ὀργῆς) is that day, a day of affliction and destruction, a day of gloominess and darkness, a day of cloud and vapor, a day of the trumpet and cry against the strong cities, and against the high towers" (Zeph 1:15-16; see also 2:3). This is clearly a description of punishment for evildoers.

In contrast to the "day of judgment" on which merits as well as demerits are measured out, Paul selects here a strictly negative expression to drive home the negative stereotype of the bigoted interlocutor. He balances it with a unique expression that lifts up the standard of divine righteousness by which sinners as well as the righteous are measured. The ἀποκαλύψεως δικαιοκρισίας τοῦ θεοῦ ("revelation of the righteous judgment of God") is closely paralleled in apocalyptic literature by the *T. Levi* 3.2, "the day determined by God's righteous judgment," and 15.2, "you shall receive scorn and eternal humiliation through the righteous judgment of God." The word δικαιοκρισία ("righteous judgment") also appears in later papyri that petition a judge,[99] and in a collection of gnomic sayings, "righteous judgment (δικαιοκρισία) is primary among excellent things."[100] In Paul's context, the term ἀποκαλύψεως ("revelation") sets the tone. As we saw in the thesis statement (1:17) and the opening sentence of the first proof (1:18), God's righteousness is presently being revealed through the gospel, and will be confirmed at the end of time. Paul's idea, according to Käsemann, is that both wrath and righteousness are combined in the gospel:

The solution of the dialectic is that with the revelation of righteousness in the gospel the destiny of wrath, which rules and may be detected already, is manifested in its eschatological orientation, namely as the hidden epiphany of the final Judge and the anticipatory execution of his sentence on a rebellious world. . . . On the other hand, the righteousness of God as salvation remains a gift which can be received only in faith. Unbelief as disobedience to the offer does not cancel the gift and certainly does not set aside the Lord who expresses himself therein. Yet the disdained Lord, since he does not give up his claim to creation or relativize the salvation consisting in his Lordship, can reveal himself only as Judge and that to our destruction.[101]

What Käsemann and other commentators do not explain, however, is why this dialectic is developed in a diatribe against religious bigotry and how it is related to the rhetorical situation of the letter. By combining the "righteous judgment of God" with divine "wrath" against a bigot currently depicted as separate from the believing congregations in Rome, Paul opens a way to overcome cultural and religious bigotry by means of righteousness through faith in Christ crucified. To achieve this by the end of the letter and thus prepare the way for an effective mission to the despised barbarians in Rome, Paul must show that all humans have sinned and that no group is exceptional and thus superior to other groups; that all are saved by grace alone; and therefore that each group is obligated to accept others as equally beloved by God. The elaborate rhetorical trap for both the weak and the strong in Rome being prepared in these verses cannot function unless the audience's resentment against the arrogant bigot is fully developed and the thesis of impartial righteousness is driven home.

■ **6** In the next six verses, Paul continues his diatribe in a more objective third person style. The transition is accomplished smoothly, in the very middle of a long sentence that began in v. 5, so that the argument concern-

---

98 See Rudolf Pesch, "ὀργή," *EDNT* 2 (1991) 530; Gerhard Delling, "ἡμέρα," *TDNT* 2 (1964) 951-52.

99 See G. H. R. Horsley, "δικαιοκρισία," *NDIEC* 1 (1981) 83; and MM 161.

100 *Comparatio Menandri et Philistionis* 1.51; see also the scholium on *Iliad* 18.

101 Käsemann, 56.

ing impartiality in vv. 6-11 appears to be directed against the bigot rather than against the audience whose detestation has been aroused. Yet by agreeing with Paul's apparent critique of bigotry, they are being led to the denouement in chaps. 14–16 in which their own bigotry will be exposed and overcome.

Paul begins by citing a widely accepted principle of the biblical faith, that God "will recompense to each according to his [or her] works."[102] With a slight variation in the tense of the verb in order to match the eschatological context, this is an exact citation from Prov 24:12, ὃς ἀποδίδωσιν ἑκάστῳ κατὰ τὰ ἔργα αὐτοῦ ("he recompenses each according to his [or her] works." The future tense occurs in LXX Ps 61:13b, σὺ ἀποδώσεις ἑκάστῳ κατὰ τὰ ἔργα αὐτοῦ ("you will recompense each according to his [or her] works"), but the second person address was unsuited to Paul's context.[103] In this instance Paul does not introduce the citation with a formula or otherwise indicate its origin, probably because it was so widely accepted as a premise of divine judgment.[104] According to Jouette Bassler, Paul is arguing for "the exact correspondence between deed and reward or punishment."[105] While the reference to "each" person being held accountable appears to refer to the bigot whose despicable profile Paul has drawn in vv. 1-5, the point is now universalized in a manner that will ultimately lead to a new awareness on the part of the audience in Rome. As Colenso observes, "the Apostle is seeking to shatter by repeated blows, in all manner of ways this fond notion of their being *favourites* with God."[106]

■ **7** Paul's thesis about "each" person being accountable to God is elaborated first on the positive side with μέν ("on the one hand"), to be matched with "on the other hand" in the following verse. Paul's generalizing effort is conveyed in the subtle shift from the single bigot, addressed as "O man/woman" in vv. 1 and 3, to the third person plural "those." The expression τοῖς μὲν καθ᾽ ὑπομονὴν ἔργου ἀγαθου ("to those who persevere in good work") is formulated in so honorific a manner that the audience of believers in Rome must consider it a description of themselves,[107] in contrast to the despicable bigot. There are many references in early Christian writings to believers performing "good work,"[108] and the importance of this theme in Romans is indicated by the 21 later occurrences of ἀγαθός ("good") in Romans. Although some have argued that the singular formulation ἔργον ἀγαθόν ("good work") as performed by the righteous stands in contrast to "works" performed by those wishing to justify themselves,[109] the use of the plural "works" in v. 6 and the singular "good" in v. 10 appear to reflect roughly interchangeable meaning.[110]

The term ὑπομονή is used here in the active sense of "perseverance,"[111] and should not be rendered as "patience," as most translators and commentators carelessly suggest. The context demands a vigorous form of moral endeavor, conducive to the performance of "good work," rather than a passive waiting for divine intervention. The classical Greek definition of ὑπομονή as an aspect of manliness and courage in maintaining one's place in a line of battle is reflected here.[112] As Hauck points out, "Unlike patience, [ὑπομονή] has an active

---

102 See Heiligenthal, *Werke*, 186.

103 See Koch, *Schrift*, 111.

104 See Friedrich Büchsel, "δίδωμι κτλ.," *TDNT* 2 (1964) 167–68; Dunn, 1:85, notes the formulation of this principle of exact retribution in Job 34:11; Jer 17:10; Hos 12:2; Sir 16:12-14; *1 En.* 100.7; *Jos. Asen.* 28.3; Pseudo-Philo *Lib. Ant.* 3.10. For a comprehensive discussion of such parallels see Heiligenthal, *Werke*, 172–76.

105 Bassler, *Impartiality*, 129; see also Heiligenthal, *Werke*, 185–86.

106 Colenso, 59.

107 Murray, 63–64; Dunn, 1:85: "Paul here seems deliberately to choose language of broad appeal," and I assume he also has in mind appeal to Paul's audience.

108 Jörg Baumgarten, "ἀγαθός," *EDNT* 1 (1990) 5, describes the "special accent" the expression "good work" has among believers, as evident in Eph 2:10; Acts 9:36; 1 Tim 2:10; 2 Cor 9:8; 2 Thess 2:17; Col 1:10; 1 Tim 5:10; 2 Tim 2:21; Titus 1:16; 3:1.

109 Zahn, 112; Mattern, *Verständnis*, 141–51.

110 Yinger, *Deeds*, 24–26, 159, shows that "the easy interchange between singular and plural 'work(s)' . . . was . . . characteristic of Jewish literature."

111 Friedrich Hauck, "ὑπομονή κτλ.," *TDNT* 4 (1967) 587; Ceslas Spicq, "ὑπομένω, ὑπομονή," *TLNT* 3 (1994) 419, provides the translation "with endurance" for Rom 2:7.

112 See Spicq, "ὑπομένω, ὑπομονή," 414, for a discussion of Plato *Lach.* 192–93; see also Festugière, "ΥΠΟΜΟΝΗ," 477–86.

content. It includes active and energetic resistance to hostile power."[113] The ethical context of this first appearance of the term helps to provide a rhetorical framework for its use later in the letter.

The motivation of perseverance in good work is described in terms that the audience would find flattering. The verb ζητέω ("seek") is often employed in the context of moral endeavor on the part of believers,[114] and it appears here as a present participle that denotes "a sustained and deliberate application"[115] rather than a merely momentary pursuit of the good. The triad of δόξα καὶ τιμὴ καὶ ἀφθαρσία ("glory and honor and incorruptibility") evokes many qualifying comments among commentators who are intent to preserve selfless ethical motivation and avoid justification by works,[116] but Paul is deliberately employing honorific categories that will appeal to his audience. The first two terms in the triad appear in the same sequence in Pss 8:5; 29:1; 96:7; Job 37:22; 40:10; 1 Macc 14:21; 2 Macc 5:16, and in the opposite sequence in Exod 28:2; Dan 2:37; 4:27, so that in view of their appearance together in Greco-Roman literature, they constitute a traditional "combination."[117] Both glory and honor are central motivations in the culture of the ancient Mediterranean world, where young people were taught to emulate the behavior of ideal prototypes. As Cicero remarked, "A few men—a handful—great in honor and glory (*honore et gloria amplificati*) can either corrupt or correct the morals of the city."[118] That one should seek such honor and glory was simply assumed in Rome, the capital of what J. E. Lendon has aptly called "the Empire of Honour."[119] The third item, ἀφθαρσία, could be translated either "immortality" or "incorruptibility,"[120] and I prefer the latter because it avoids redundancy with "eternal life" and because "immortality" does not fit the category of a "good work."[121] Since this word is never otherwise linked in a series with glory and honor, Paul must have had a specific reason for its employment here. While these three terms are inadequate in constituting an authentically Christian ethic as set forth in Rom 12–16,[122] they are an apt description of the motivations present in the Roman situation, as our congregational reconstruction suggests. Not only were these groups intent to maintain precedence in glory and honor compared with others (14:1), and to act in a manner to give "honor" to the Lord (14:6), but it is also clear that some of them (the weak) were involved in ascetic avoidance of corruption. At the end of chap. 3 Paul will make a case that no boasting in the honor of one's own group is allowed, and in chap. 7 he will show that obedience to the law with the motive of gaining honor will not produce the good. Yet there is no hint of disapprobation in Paul's formulation of good works in 2:7, because all who perform such deeds receive "eternal life." The expression ζωὴ αἰώνιος that occurs for the first time in Dan 12:2[123] and surfaces in later Jewish writings[124] appears here as the direct object of the verb "recompense" in v. 6.[125] As in this verse in Romans, ζωὴ αἰώνιος is a reward for good deeds in passages like *Ps. Sol.* 3.12, "those who fear

---

113 Hauck, "ὑπομονή κτλ.," *TDNT* 4 (1967) 582.

114 See Edvin Larssen, "ζητέω κτλ.," *EDNT* 2 (1991) 102.

115 Dunn, 1:86.

116 For example, Godet, 119–20; Barrett, 46–47; Morris, 116–17; Kuss, 1:64–65; Dunn, 1:86.

117 BAGD (2000) 1005, citing classical parallels in Dio Chrysostom *Orat.* 4.116; 27 [44].10; Appian *Bell. civ.* 3.18.388; Arrian *Ind.* 11.1; Plutarch *Mor.* 486b. In contrast, Hans Hübner, "τιμή," *EDNT* 3 (1990) 358, believes that "honor and glory" was not an "idiomatically fixed henidiadys" in the LXX, but that it became so in the NT.

118 Cited by Lendon, *Empire of Honour*, 47, from Cicero *Leg.* 3.32. For an analysis of the all-encompassing motivation of the "love of honor" (φιλοτιμία), see ibid., 85–88, 166–68.

119 See Lendon, *Empire of Honour*, 13–29, 235–36, and the summary on 173: "The emperors and the historians were brought up in the same school, in a society in which the protection and expansion of renown were enormously important, in which renown was seen as significant in all areas of life, and in rulership especially. Honour exists only in the mind, depending for its existence on a widespread conspiracy of the imagination. But if everyone, including the emperor, partly shared in this conspiracy, honour was a reality to them, and played a real role in politics."

120 BAGD (2000) 155; LSJM 289.

121 See Günther Harder, "φθείρω κτλ.," *TDNT* 9 (1974) 104–5.

122 See Weiss, 108–9; Kuss, 1:64–65.

123 Rudolf Bultmann, "ζάω κτλ.," *TDNT* 2 (1964) 856.

124 See ibid., 859.

125 Cranfield, 1:147.

the Lord shall rise up to eternal life."[126] Later in Romans, Paul will link "eternal life" more closely with grace in Christ (Rom 5:21; 6:21-22),[127] thus removing it from the framework of a reward for good behavior. But there is no hint of this clarification in 2:7, which simply conforms to what Paul perceives to be the orientation of his audience. The Roman believers still have no inkling that in the later course of the letter, the problematic dimension of their motivation and its bigoted social consequences will come to light.

■ **8** The negative side of divine judgment is introduced with δέ ("on the other hand"), and once again it evokes the stereotype of the bigot who "judges" others (2:1) by means of a complex triad of characteristics that correspond to the positive triad in the preceding verse. Since commentators do not relate this passage to the congregational situation in Rome, Paul's choice of the first term ἐριθεία ("partisanship, selfishness") remains "puzzling."[128] The debate over the etymology of this rare word, used prior to the NT only by Aristotle to describe political intrigue, has been resolved in favor of ἐριθεύομαι ("work for hire") rather than ἔρις ("strife").[129] But this does not support the individualistic, moralistic translation "selfishness" favored by many commentators,[130] because all of the NT references as well as those in Aristotle carry the "connotations of intrigue, disputation, and chicanery" in the pursuit of "honor and wealth."[131] Aristotle describes the possibility of constitutional subversion "through political intrigues" (διά τε τὰς

ἐριθείας, *Pol.* 1303a16) and the soliciting of votes "through intrigue" (δι᾽ ἐριθεία, *Polit.* 1302b4). Aristotle also employs the verb ἐριθεύομαι in political contexts for "hiring paid canvassers and promoting party spirit."[132] This factional connotation is particularly clear in Phil 1:17, where Paul charges that rival evangelists "preach Christ out of partisanship,"[133] and other references can have a similar translation (Phil 2:3; 2 Cor 12:20; Gal 5:20).[134] Although the expression ἐξ ἐριθείας ("out of partisanship") aptly describes the behavior of the Roman house and tenement churches, and is directly countered by the argument of chaps. 14–16, Paul disguises the trap by embedding the phrase in a participial construction that seems to point to the unbelieving bigot described in vv. 1-5. The stereotype is further disguised by a καί . . . δέ ("not only . . . but also") syntax[135] that heightens the sinfulness of those deserving wrath, thus further separating them from the believers in Paul's audience. The expression καὶ ἀπειθοῦσι τῇ ἀληθείᾳ ("not only those who disobey the truth") appears to add rejection of the gospel[136] to the fault of partisanship, thus reducing the possibility that the congregations will prematurely see themselves under attack. The artful repetition of the stem πειθ- in the third segment of the triad, πειθομένοις δὲ τῇ ἀδικίᾳ ("but also those who obey the wrongdoing") further serves to draw attention to outrageous and unrepentant evildoers who not only disobey the truth but are also persuaded and convinced in their loyalty to injustice.[137]

---

126 See Horst Balz, "αἰώνιος," *EDNT* 1 (1990) 47–48, referring also to *Ps. Sol.* 13.1; Wis 5:15; Mark 10:17 par.; 10:30 par.

127 Balz, "αἰώνιος," 47.

128 Cranfield, 1:148.

129 See Meyer, 1:110–11; Ceslas Spicq, "ἐριθίζω κτλ.," *TLNT* 2 (1994) 70; Heinz Giesen, "ἐριθεία," *EDNT* 2 (1991) 52; BAGD (2000) 392.

130 For example, Kühl, 74; Barrett, 47–48; Schlier, 73; Dunn, 1:86–87; Moo, 138.

131 Spicq, "ἐριθίζω κτλ.," 70; see also Lietzmann, 39; Murray, 65.

132 See Sanday and Headlam, 57. A second-century B.C.E. decree mentions "mischievous canvassing" (ἠρειθεῦσθαι ἐπὶ κακοσχολίᾳ, *Delph.* 3(1).362.i.31).

133 Spicq, "ἐριθίζω κτλ.," 71, cites standard studies of anti-Pauline opposition in favor of the "spirit of factionalism and rivalry."

134 Although Giesen, "ἐριθεία," 52, favors the translation "selfishness," he admits that "intrigues could be in mind" in Gal 5:20 and 2 Cor 12:20.

135 While not taking the rhetorical implications into account, the καί . . . δέ syntax is discussed by Zahn, 116, and Kühl, 74; the syntax is otherwise overlooked in recent commentaries and translations. See BDF §447.9.

136 Godet, 119; Dunn, 1:87. Schlier, 73, refers to Rom 11:30-32 and Gal 5:7 to support the connotation of disobedience in relation to the gospel. Rudolf Bultmann, "πειθώ κτλ.," *TDNT* 6 (1968) 11, observes that "disobedience" often stands in antithesis to "having faith." Thorsteinsson, *Paul's Interlocutor*, 194–95, overlooks this implication in maintaining that the interlocutor is a believing Gentile and a member of the Roman church.

137 The middle or passive voice of πειθομένοις has the connotation of "be prevailed on, won over, per-

In view of such incorrigibility, the divine recompense of "wrath and fury" seems entirely justified. The nominative case of ὀργὴ καὶ θυμός ("wrath and fury") along with its emphatic position at the end of a participial expression and the lack of a finite verb justify an exclamation point: "[there shall be] wrath and fury!"[138] The two terms ὀργή and θυμός often occur together in the LXX[139] and in pagan magical curses.[140] Josephus employs precisely the same formulation that Paul selects to depict a state of supreme moral outrage: "On the fourth day of the festival, one of the soldiers uncovered his genitals and exhibited them to the multitude—an action which created wrath and fury (ὀργὴ καὶ θυμός) in the onlookers, who said it was not they who had been insulted, but that it was a blasphemy against God."[141] In the context of Paul's argument, it is the incorrigibility of such bigots that evokes this expression of divine outrage, and again, at this point in the discourse, no one in the audience of converted believers in Rome would realize that their own bigotry could bring them under such condemnation.[142]

■ 9 Paul's rhetorical strategy to generalize the implications of God's impartial judgment continues in vv. 9-10, beginning again with the fate of evildoers. As in the previous verse with "wrath and fury," a formula from the LXX is employed to describe the human impact of judgment. The formula θλῖψις καὶ στενοχωρία ("affliction and distress") occurs in the LXX (Deut 28:53, 55, 57; Esth 1:1; Isa 8:22; 30:6),[143] and in view of its appearance in Rom 8:35 and 2 Cor 6:4, it appears to constitute a formula for divine wrath.[144] In this context the formula depicts the manner in which divine wrath is experienced.[145] In biblical sources, for example, θλῖψις is employed for afflictions such as political hostility (Isa 11:13; Pss 31:7; 53:7; 54:3), military defeat (Hos 7:12; Obad 12), foreign oppression (Deut 28:57; Ps 107:12), slavery (Ps 80:7), natural disasters (Ps 45:1), persecution (1 Macc 5:16; 9:27; Mark 13:10 par.; 1 Thess 3:3-4), financial pressures (1 Cor 7:23-25), ill health (Ps 90:15), imprisonment (Gen 42:21; Phil 1:17), poverty (Pss 24:17; 33:6; 43:24; 106:40; Rev 2:9), anxiety (Ps 141:2; 2 Cor 2:4), or the threat of death (Ps 114:3).[146] There are passages in which θλῖψις itself has the connotation of divine judgment, for example, LXX Ps 77:49: "He sent out against them [the Egyptians] the fury of his anger, wrath, and indignation, and affliction (θυμὸν καὶ ὀργὴν καὶ θλῖψιν)." The word στενοχωρία refers to a tight spot in which one is threatened by disaster,[147] and is employed in the LXX to refer to inescapable oppression (Jer 37:7; 3 Macc 2:10), unavoidable anxiety (1 Kgs 13:6), unrelieved famine (Job 18:11; Isa 8:22), unavoidable military conflict (1 Macc 13:3; 2 Macc 2:11), inescapable military reverses and sieges (Deut 28:53, 55, 57), or hopeless imprisonment (1 Macc 2:53). The two

---

suaded," according to LSJM 1354; BAGD (2000) 792.3, a detail picked up by Dunn, 1:87, but rejected by Bultmann, "πειθώ κτλ.," 4, on theological rather than grammatical grounds.

138 Godet, 119; supplying a verb as proposed by Wilckens, 1:127, weakens the emphasis that Paul intended.

139 See Friedrich Büchsel, "θυμός κτλ.," TDNT 3 (1965) 168. H. W. Hollander, "θυμός," EDNT 2 (1991) 160, lists Deut 9:19 ("fury and wrath . . . of God); Ps 2:5 ("in his wrath . . . in his fury"); Hos 13:11 ("I gave them a king in my wrath . . . in my fury").

140 For example, "restrain the anger, the wrath of Paomios" (κατάσχετε τὴν ὀργήν, τὸν θυμὸν Παωμίου; Daniel and Maltomini, Suppl. Mag. II.57.4); see also Suppl. Mag. II.57.30, 31, 35, 49; 79.255.

141 Ant. 20.108, noted by Büchsel, "θυμός κτλ.," 167.

142 For an interpretation of this passage that does not take the congregational situation or the rhetorical aim of Paul's argument into account, see Hanson, Wrath, 85–89.

143 In view of the varied locations where "affliction and distress" appear, it seems inappropriate to single out Deuteronomy as the crucial passage for interpreting Paul's argument, as proposed by Berkley, Romans 2:17-29, 161–63.

144 Georg Bertram, "στενός, στενοχωρία, στενοχωρέω," TDNT 7 (1971) 605; Jacob Kremer, "θλίψις, θλίβω," EDNT 2 (1991) 152, referring to 2 Thess 1:6; Rev 2:22. The formula also appears in Epictetus Diss. 1.25.26. In verbal form the two cognates occur in Epictetus Diss. 1.25.28, "For in general recall this that we afflict ourselves, we distress ourselves (ἑαυτοὺς θλίβομεν, ἑαυτοὺς στενοχωροῦμεν); that is, our fixed ideas afflict and distress us (θλίβει καὶ στενοχωρεῖ)."

145 Schlier, 74.

146 See Heinrich Schlier, "θλίβω, θλῖψις," TDNT 3 (1965) 140–43; Pobee, Persecution, 13–46.

147 BAGD (2000) 943: "narrowness"; Bertram, "στενός, στενοχωρία, στενοχωρέω," 604–5.

terms are not synonyms,[148] nor do they refer to the outward and inward aspects of distress.[149] While θλῖψις refers to afflictions in general, στενωχορία conveys the unavoidability of divinely imposed disaster.[150] There is no escape for anyone, which means that the illusion of the bigot that he could "escape the judgment of God" (2:3) is strongly reaffirmed.

The generalizing emphasis is reinforced by the expression ἐπὶ πᾶσαν ψυχὴν ἀνθρώπου ("upon every single person"), which occurs in the LXX (Num 19:11; Isa 13:7) with the sense of "every single man."[151] The emphasis here is on the word πᾶς ("every"), which is repeated in the following verse,[152] so that no precedence is granted to any privileged group.[153] Anyone who "brings about evil," whether he is Jew or Greek and regardless of any presumed superiority or inferiority in social rank, will be punished. The compound verb κατεργάζομαι is employed here with the sense of "bring about, accomplish," referring to the end result of one's deeds.[154] The reiteration of the phrase found in Rom 1:16, "of the Jew first and also of the Greek," confirms the impartiality of divine judgment. Although most commentators interpret this expression as if Paul used "Gentile" rather than "Greek,"[155] it is likely that he selected the latter in order to address each house and tenement church in Rome on its own terms. The formula Ἰουδαίου τε πρῶτον καὶ Ἕλληνος is a genitive in agreement with ἀνθρώπου ("of person"), indicating that every single person among either Jews or Greeks who performs evil is subject to this punishment. That the word "Jew" comes first in this formula, following a tradi-

tional biblical concept, should not be taken to mean that Jews in particular are under attack here.[156] While Jews are "the first among equals" because of their early conversion to Christ, their continued covenantal status, and their having given birth to the Messiah (Rom 9:4-5), and while Paul attempts throughout the letter to equalize their inferior status in the competition with Greek believers in Rome, they retain no privilege with regard to divine judgment.[157] Paul is making a case that God will treat Jews and Greeks "equally and not on the basis of membership in one group or another," as Stowers shows.[158]

■ 10 As noted in the analysis above, the triad of "glory and honor and peace" provides an effective rhetorical echo to "glory and honor and incorruptibility" in v. 7. The antithetical δέ distinguishes the recipients of these blessings from the damned in the preceding verse. The problematic implications of the former triad, noted above, are covered here by a more theologically appropriate formulation of divine blessings given to those who instead of "seeking glory," and so on (2:7), actually "do the good." In contrast to the compound verb κατεργάζομαι ("bring about, accomplish") in the preceding verse, here we have the simple verb ἐργάζομαι ("do, perform").[159] That God grants "honor and glory" to humans is affirmed in the classic formulation of Ps 8:5, "You made humans a little less than the angels and crowned them with glory and honor (δόξα καὶ τιμή)," a formulation echoed in Job 40:10.[160] There are also biblical precedents for "peace" as a gift of God that is tanta-

148 Bertram, "στενός, στενοχωρία, στενοχωρέω," 607: "it is well nigh impossible to differentiate between θλῖψις and στενοχωρία in R. 2:8f."

149 Cranfield, 1:149, following Aquinas, Calvin, and Barth; also Wilckens, 1:127; however, see the critique by Morris, 119–20.

150 Weiss, 111; Käsemann, 60.

151 Michel, 116, discusses this Semitic formula for "every single person"; see also Jewett, Terms, 356.

152 Dunn, 1:88.

153 Kuss, 1:66; see also Aletti, "Romans 2," 164–68; Yinger, Deeds, 150.

154 See Horst Balz , "κατεργάζομαι," EDNT 2 (1991) 271; Georg Bertram, "κατεργάζομαι," TDNT 3 (1965) 635; Zahn, 116–17; Sanday and Headlam, 58: "carry to the end."

155 Kuss, 1:67; Cranfield, 1:150; Murray, 67; Dunn, 1:88; Wilckens, 1:127; Stuhlmacher, 41.

156 Dunn, 1:68; Yinger, Deeds, 152–53, argues that Jewish Christians are the target of Paul's attack in this formulation.

157 Wilckens, 1:127; Horst Kuhli, "Ἰουδαίος," EDNT 2 (1991) 195.

158 Stowers, Diatribe, 113; see also Bassler, Impartiality, 136.

159 For the distinction between accomplishment and ongoing performance of actions as conveyed by these two verbs, see Zahn, 116–17; Meyer, 1:92–93; BAGD (2000) 389.2a and 531.1.

160 See Johannes Schneider, "τιμή," TDNT 8 (1972) 172, who also notes that "honor and glory" often appear together in Josephus, as for example in Ant.

mount to salvation.[161] For example, Jer 36:11 hears God's promise to bring the exiles back from Babylon, "And I will devise for you a device of peace ($\lambda o \gamma \iota \sigma \mu \grave{o} \nu$ $\epsilon \grave{\iota} \rho \acute{\eta} \nu \eta \varsigma$), not evil, to bestow upon you these good things." The parallelism between "peace" and "salvation" in Ps 84:8-9 suggests that the two terms can be virtually interchangeable.

What the commentators do not explain, however, is why Paul selected $\epsilon \grave{\iota} \rho \acute{\eta} \nu \eta$ ("peace") if he really meant to convey the idea of $\sigma \omega \tau \eta \rho \acute{\iota} \alpha$ ("salvation").[162] The answer is contained in 14:17, 19, where peace is described as a mark of authentically transformed congregations that stop fighting over "food and drink" and take up the tasks of mutual "upbuilding." God is the "God of peace" (15:33) who grants peace to his people when they accept this transforming message (15:13).[163] Although the Roman house and tenement churches cannot realize the precise implications of Paul's triad until later in the letter, it seems clear that he is preparing the way here. The reiteration of the formula, "to the Jew first and also to the Greek," as in 1:16 and 2:9, maintains divine impartiality in salvation as well as wrath, because it redresses the deficit in honor from which the Jews are suffering in the Roman congregations.

■ **11** The conclusion of the first phase of the diatribe is succinct and undeniable in the light of the preceding argument: "for there is no partiality before God." Although the theme of divine impartiality is widely dispersed in biblical and postbiblical writings, the abstract noun $\pi \rho o \sigma \omega \pi o \lambda \eta \mu \psi \acute{\iota} \alpha$ occurs only in Christian writings and in the roughly contemporaneous *T. Job* 43.13,

"Righteous is the Lord, true are his judgments. With him there is no favoritism ($\pi \rho o \sigma \omega \pi o \lambda \eta \mu \psi \acute{\iota} \alpha$); he will judge us all together."[164] The word is based on the LXX adaptation of the Hebrew expression for lifting up, "as a sign of appreciation, the face of one who has prostrated himself in greeting."[165] When one raises one's face to someone in a biased manner, this would be acting contrary to God's impartial judgment, as described, for example, in Sir 32:12-13:[166] "For the Lord is judge, and with him there is no respect of persons ($\delta \acute{o} \xi \alpha$ $\pi \rho o \sigma \acute{\omega} \pi o \upsilon$). He will not lift up his face against a poor man ($o \grave{\upsilon} \lambda \acute{\eta} \psi \epsilon \tau \alpha \iota \pi \rho \acute{o} \sigma \omega \pi o \nu \grave{\epsilon} \pi \grave{\iota} \pi \tau \omega \chi o \hat{\upsilon}$), but will hear the prayer of the oppressed." In Deut 10:18 the basic statement of this theme is articulated without the verb $\lambda \alpha \mu \beta \acute{\alpha} \nu \epsilon \iota \nu$ ("take, choose"), that "the great and strong and terrible God does not respect persons ($o \grave{\upsilon} \theta \alpha \upsilon \mu \acute{\alpha} \zeta \epsilon \iota$ $\pi \rho \acute{o} \sigma \omega \pi o \nu$), nor will he accept a bribe." The social implication is stated in Deut 16:19, "You shall not pervert justice; you shall not show partiality ($o \grave{\upsilon} \delta \grave{\epsilon} \grave{\epsilon} \pi \iota \gamma \nu \acute{\omega} \sigma o \nu \tau \alpha \iota$ $\pi \rho \acute{o} \sigma \omega \pi o \nu$); and you shall not take a bribe, for a bribe blinds the eyes of the wise and subverts the cause of the righteous." As Jouette Bassler shows, the LXX and later literature developed a view of impartial judgment "as an axiomatic attribute of God,"[167] but nowhere is this developed in a universalistic manner that undermines the distinction between Jews and Gentiles.[168]

Prior to Romans, the primary framework of this semantic field was social equality between members of the Jewish community.[169] In the context of Paul's argument, however, this restricted definition of partiality is overcome. Paul declares that "God recompenses all men

12.118. On 174-75 Schneider writes that the combination of these words is "a familiar one in Hellenistic thought and usage."

161 See Werner Foerster, "$\epsilon \grave{\iota} \rho \acute{\eta} \nu \eta$ $\kappa \tau \lambda$.," *TDNT* 2 (1964) 407-8.

162 Cranfield, 1:150, claims the two words are "more or less equivalent" in 2:10; also Byrne, 86.

163 See the analysis of the congregational dimensions of peace in Victor Hasler, "$\epsilon \grave{\iota} \rho \acute{\eta} \nu \eta$," *EDNT* 1 (1990) 396. For an account of Paul's strategy of encouraging reconciling conversations within congregations, see Strom, *Reframing Paul,* 169-97.

164 See also *T. Job* 4.8, "the Lord is impartial ($\grave{\alpha} \pi \rho o \sigma \omega$-$\pi \acute{o} \lambda \eta \mu \tau o \varsigma$)—rendering good things to each one who obeys." Eduard Lohse, "$\pi \rho \acute{o} \sigma \omega \pi o \nu$ $\kappa \tau \lambda$.," *TDNT* 6 (1968) 780, makes a plausible case that the noun

$\pi \rho o \sigma \omega \pi o \lambda \eta \mu \psi \acute{\iota} \alpha$ probably was taken over by early Believers from Hellenistic Judaism, which accounts for its use in traditional "Household Tables," Eph 6:9; Col 3:25.

165 Klaus Berger, "$\pi \rho o \sigma \omega \pi o \lambda \eta \mu \psi \acute{\iota} \alpha$," *EDNT* 3 (1990) 179.

166 See also the idiom $\pi \rho \acute{o} \sigma \omega \pi o \nu \lambda \alpha \mu \beta \acute{\alpha} \nu \epsilon \iota \nu$ in Ps 81:2; Sir 4:27; 35:13; 1 Esd 4:39; Mal 1:8.

167 Bassler, *Impartiality,* 43.

168 Bassler, *Impartiality,* 44; later rabbinic writings sometimes extend the impartiality of God to Gentiles (72-76); Philo did not follow the universal direction in a consistent manner (118-19).

169 See Berger, "$\pi \rho o \sigma \omega \pi o \lambda \eta \mu \psi \acute{\iota} \alpha$," 179-80.

impartially according to a strict but neutral standard of merit."[170] No claim of exemption can stand before this impartial tribunal, so there is no chance that the arrogant bigot who judges other people can "escape the judgment of God" (2:1, 3). By employing traditional biblical language to draw this conclusion, Paul assures the assent of his audience, which cannot yet perceive that this principle of impartiality will have a bearing on the conflicts between the weak and the strong.[171]

■ **12** In the next five verses, Paul makes a case that performance rather than mere possession of the law is assessed by God's impartial justice. With two parallel ὅσοι ("as many as, whoever") clauses, Paul places Jews and Greeks in the same position.[172] The description of Greeks as those who "sin outside the law" (ἀνόμως ἥμαρτον) matches the Jewish definition of non-Jews, employed only once in the LXX (2 Macc 8:17) but closely associated with the adjective ἄνομος ("lawless") that epitomized Gentiles.[173] That non-Jews could be said

to "sin," even though they do not have the Torah, was not unusual, as the absolute use of the verb ἁμαρτάνω in classical literature shows.[174] There are also many references to sinning in the papyri that do not appear to be influenced by Jewish or Christian traditions.[175] This is the first appearance of the technical term for "sin" in Romans, and it appears to have the same connotation for everyone in the Greco-Roman and Jewish environments, namely the "failure to meet a standard," to "miss the mark," or to "transgress."[176]

The verb ἀπόλλυμι can be translated as "destroy, perish, lose, be ruined,"[177] and in this instance death appears to be in view.[178] That death was considered the appropriate penalty for sin was characteristic for the entire culture, as the examples in Greco-Roman[179] and Jewish literature[180] attest. The succinct formula ἀνόμως καὶ ἀπολοῦνται ("will also perish outside the law") means that impartial judgment takes no account of cultural or religious background.[181] Klaus Haacker explains

170 Bassler, *Impartiality*, 137; Käsemann, 60–61; see also Riemer A. Faber, "The Juridical Nuance in the NT Use of προσωπολημψία," *WTJ* 57 (1995) 304–5.

171 The extensive debate over the disparities between this passage and a pure doctrine of justification by faith has been conducted without regard to Paul's rhetorical purpose and therefore remains unresolvable. See, e.g., Cranfield, 1:151–53; Wilckens, 1:127–31; Moo, 139–43; Schreiner, 114–15, who grapple with proposals by Herbert Braun, *Gerichtsgedanke und Rechtfertigungslehre bei Paulus*, UNT 19 (Leipzig: Hinrichs, 1930) 90–99; Mattern, *Verständnis*, 130–38; Sanders, *Law*, 123–35; Russell Pregeant, "Grace and Recompense: Reflections on a Pauline Paradox," *JAAR* 47 (1979) 73–96; Klyne R. Snodgrass, "Justification by Grace—to the Doers: An Analysis of the Place of Romans 2 in the Theology of Paul," *NTS* 32 (1986) 72–93, etc.

172 See Bassler, *Impartiality*, 138; BAGD (2000) 729.2.

173 For example, Esth 4:17; *3 Macc* 6.9; *Ps. Sol.* 17.11; 18.19; 1 Cor 9:21; see Hermann Kleinknecht and Walter Gutbrod, "νόμος κτλ.," *TDNT* 4 (1967) 1087: "a common term for the Gentiles."

174 BAGD (2000) 49; LSDJ 77 cites Homer *Il.* 5.501, where religious rituals turn away the wrath of the gods "whenever anyone transgresses or sins (ὅτι κέν τις ὑπερβήῃ καὶ ἁμάρτῃ); Semonides *Frag.* 7.111; Aristotle *An. pr.* 262; Sophocles *El.* 1207. In Aeschylus *Prom.* 267–68, Prometheus unabashedly claims, "I sinned knowingly; willingly, willingly, I

sinned and won't deny it (πράσσοντ᾽ ἐγὼ δὲ ταῦθ᾽ ἡπιστάμεν ἑκὼν ἑκὼν ἥμαρτον, οὐκ ἀρνήσομαι)."

175 MM 25 refers to a private letter during the time of Augustus that claims, οὐδὲ γὰρ ἡμάρτηκά τι εἰς σέ ("nor did I wrong you in the matter," *BGU* IV.114.14ff.). Another example is Antonius Longus's rather illiterate letter to his mother begging for reconciliation, "furthermore I know what I have brought upon myself. Punished I have been as I ought. I know that I have sinned (οὐθὲν ἁμάρτημα ἔνει)" (*BGU* III.846).

176 Peter Fiedler, "ἁμαρτία κτλ.," *EDNT* 1 (1990) 66.

177 BAGD (2000) 115–16; Armin Kretzer, "ἀπόλλυμι," *EDNT* 1 (1990) 135.

178 Weiss, 113; Godet, 121; Morris, 122; Schlier, 76; Moo, 146.

179 The most common reference is to the death penalty for civil "sin," but the Greeks did not share the Judeo-Christian idea of moral wrong punishable by death. Plutarch *Sol.* 17.1 reports that the extreme laws of Draco had prescribed the death penalty even for idleness: "One . . . penalty, death, was assigned to all sinners" (μία . . . ἅπασιν ὥριστο τοῖς ἁμαρτάνουσι ζημία θάνατος).

180 Dunn, 1:96, refers to LXX Ps 36:20 ("for sinners will be destroyed, οἱ ἁμαρτωλοὶ ἀπολοῦνται); Ps 67:2 ("so let sinners be destroyed [ἀπόλοιτο οἱ ἁμαρτωλοί] from before the Lord").

181 Bassler, *Impartiality*, 139–40.

this bare reference to perishing as an expression of the inherent destructiveness of sin that Paul had established in 1:18-32 and reiterates again in 5:13-14.[182] The second half of the parallel sentence makes the same point. "As many as have sinned under the law" clearly refers to Jews who have violated the Torah.[183] While the verb "sin" is employed for Jews as well as Greeks in this sentence, the form of punishment differs. In place of the destruction that threatens sinners without the law, there is the phrase διὰ νόμου κριθήσονται ("they will be judged by the law"). This is a traditional belief within Judaism, stated in classic form by *2 Bar.* 48.46-47: "You, O Lord . . . commanded the dust one day to produce Adam; and you knew the number of those who were born from him and how they sinned before you. . . . And concerning all of those, their end will put them to shame, and your Law which they transgressed will repay them on your day." The passive form of the verb κριθήσονται ("they will be judged by the law") clearly implies that God is the source of judgment, which reflects a tradition starting in the OT "in which God was regarded as both legislator and legal partner" who defended the weak and punished those who violated the Torah.[184] The link between divine judgment and the Law was one of the "cardinal articles of faith" in the Judaism out of which Christianity in Rome sprang, namely that God "upholds with punishments and rewards His holy Law and its demands and prohibitions, that He enforces it irresistibly in face of those who despise it. This belief, whose roots go back to the very early days of Israelite religion, was inseparably related to the Law, and was transmitted with it."[185]

Although Paul formulates the principle differently for those "under the law" as compared with those "outside the law," the end result is the same. While each of the groups in Rome thought of itself as exceptional and superior, they are in fact equally accountable. Although the hearers of Paul's letter still assume that this argument exposes the illusions of the religious bigot, the later portions of the letter will show the relevance of this

principle for the Roman house and tenement churches. It is significant that the only other place in Romans that the verb ἀπόλλυμι ("perish") appears is in 14:15, where Paul warns the "strong" not to cause the destruction of the "weak" by encouraging them to eat foods they consider unclean. Correspondingly, the verb κρίνειν ("judge"), which appears seven times in chap. 2, recurs in another cluster of eight appearances in chap. 14 in connection with the inappropriate judging of the "strong" by the "weak." The elaborate rhetorical trap entangles both sides, sentence by sentence ever more effectively, but its persuasive energy must first be gathered by its seeming critique of the straw man who appears to stand outside the circle of the converted, that is, the bigot who "passes judgment" and yet does the very same things him-/herself.

■ **13** Divine impartiality is proven by the lack of privilege accorded to υἱ ἀκροαταὶ νόμου ("the hearers of law,") a unique Pauline expression that resonated with references to the Jewish people as those who heard God's law read aloud. Although the precise expression is not found in Deuteronomy, Israel's encounter with God was viewed as an acoustic phenomenon. For example, Moses reports that Yahweh commanded him, "Gather the people to me and let them hear my words (ἀκουσάτωσαν τὰ ῥήματά μου)" (Deut 4:10). Israel receives the command, "Draw near and hear all that the Lord our God shall say" (Deut 5:27). The famous Shema repeated on a daily basis by loyal Jews[186] begins with the words, "Hear, O Israel (ἄκουε Ἰσραήλ), the Lord our God is one" (Deut 6:4). In Sirach's words, "an attentive ear (οὖς ἀκροατοῦ) is the desire of a wise man." Attentive hearing of the law was a cultural feature of Jews, about which they were justifiably proud, so that "hearers of the law" naturally refers to Jewish worshipers who participate in public readings on the Sabbath.[187] In contrast, *Sib. Or.* 3.70 refers to Gentiles as "the lawless ones who have never heard God's Word," and Josephus (*Ant.* 5.107, 132) refers to sinners as those who fail to hear

182 Haacker, 63.
183 The suggestion by Sanday and Headlam, 58, that ἐν νόμῳ in this instance refers to law in general is refuted by Zahn, 120; Cranfield, 1:154; cf. Westerholm, *Law*, 106–9. Betz, *Galatians*, 146, also understands "by law" to mean "by the Jewish Torah."
184 Volkmar Herntrich, "κρίνω κτλ.," *TDNT* 3 (1965) 924.
185 Friedrich Büchsel, ibid., 935.
186 Safrai and Stern, *Jewish People*, 800–801, discusses the requirement to repeat the Shema twice daily.
187 See Meyer, 1:115; Michel, 117.

God's law. The problem that Paul addresses here is that religious exercise such as hearing the Torah read easily expands into a claim of an assured status with God, expressed for example in Bar 4:3-4: "Do not give your glory to another, or your advantages to an alien people. Happy are we, O Israel, for we know what is pleasing to God." That Israel enjoys a permanently favored status is proclaimed by Bar 5:1-4 in terms that appear to be directly countered by Paul's wording:

> Take off the garment of your sorrow and affliction,
>   O Jerusalem,
>   and put on for ever the beauty of the glory
>   from God.
> Put on the robe of the righteousness that comes from
>   God;
>   put on your head the diadem of the glory of the
>   Everlasting;
> for God will show your splendor everywhere under
>   heaven.
>   For God will give you evermore the name,
>   "Righteous Peace, Godly Glory."

Dunn suggests that the distinction between hearing and doing the law drives "a wedge between the interconnected elements of Jewish self-understanding,"[188] but this is performed with rhetorical finesse. As far as the listeners of Rom 2 are concerned, the bigot who knows God's will but fails to perform it is under attack here.[189] Paul's assertion that hearing the law does not make one "righteous before God" counters the claim of superior status made by the bigot, and would have been supported by some important rabbis. Wilckens reports that Rabbi Johannai (30 B.C.E.) taught his disciples, "Make the study of Torah into something solid: speak little but do

much. . . . The main thing is not studying but doing."[190] Paul's denial is categorical: participation in synagogue worship or reciting the Shema provides the religious bigot no guarantee of assured status before God.

Paul's antithesis is that only "the doers of the law" will be accounted righteous. The future tense of $\delta\iota\kappa\alpha\iota\omega\vartheta\dot{\eta}\sigma\sigma\nu\tau\alpha\iota$ ("they shall be set right") is probably eschatological[191] rather than gnomic;[192] at the last judgment each person's status before God will be assessed, and no exceptionalism of any kind will be allowed, as v. 11 had made plain. This verse reiterates the point of v. 7, that those who actually accomplish good works will gain eternal life. At first glance this appears to contradict the main argument of Romans, that no flesh will be set right by works of the law and that salvation comes only through faith in God's grace (3:20-24). However, the underlying issue is that actions motivated by the desire for superior honor, in Paul's view, pervert obedience and frustrate the purpose of divine law. Only those who abandon claims of superiority can fulfill the law, which required both Jews and Gentiles to change their motivational systems.[193] In the formulation of Klyne Snodgrass, "'Works righteousness' is excluded, but saving obedience in response to God's grace is not."[194] Garlington maintains that "Paul has in mind *a different kind of 'doing the law,'* a doing . . . commensurate with 'the obedience of faith.'"[195]

■ **14** The seeming contradiction with Paul's main thesis about the universal failure to attain salvation by lawful obedience has led to a wide variety of approaches to the last three verses in this pericope. Most exegetes take the Gentiles embodying the law to be pagans, arguing that (a) Paul wants to confirm their accountability when they are condemned at the last judgment,[196] or (b) Paul wants to show that there are righteous Gentiles who even with-

188 Dunn, 1:97; cited with approval by Garlington, *Letter to the Romans,* 59.
189 Heil, 30, argues in contrast that this verse is a direct attack on the audience's belief that "they might receive some sort of favored treatment from God."
190 Wilckens, 1:132, citing *'Abot R. Nat.* 1.15; 3.9.
191 Käsemann, 62.
192 Bultmann, "$\Delta IKAIO\Sigma TNH$ $\Theta EO\Upsilon$," 15.
193 The "complete moral reorientation" required by faith is stressed by Watson, *Paul,* 119.
194 Snodgrass, "Doers," 84.
195 Garlington, *Letter to the Romans,* 59.
196 See, e.g., Meyer, 1:116; Rolf Walker, "Die Heiden und das Gericht: Zur Auslegung von Römer 2,12-16," *EvTh* 20 (1960) 302–14; Friedrich Kuhr, "Römer 2:14f und die Verheissung bei Jeremia 31,13ff," *ZNW* 55 (1964) 243–61; Kuss, 1:68–71; Fitzmyer, 311.

out having responded to the gospel "stand a better chance of acquittal at the final judgment than many Jews,"[197] or (c) Paul refers to pre-Christian Gentiles whose later conversion confirms that God's law had indeed been inscribed on their hearts.[198] A minority view is that Paul refers here to previously converted Gentile Christians whose fulfillment of the law will be confirmed at the last judgment.[199] While some allow the seeming discrepancy to stand as an example of Pauline inconsistency,[200] others vitiate the problem by asserting that these verses are a parenthetical aside[201] or a hypothetical argument as if the gospel had not yet come[202] or as if such Gentiles actually existed.[203] The most likely of these views from a rhetorical point of view is that Paul is here describing the status of converted Gentiles. Having assented that wrath is already evident among unconverted Gentiles (1:18-31) and that Jews are not exempt from God's impartial judgment (2:1-13), the audience consisting mainly of converted Gentiles would assume that their current situation is described in these verses, which provide a preliminary form of Paul's strategy of touting Gentile conversion in order to provoke Jewish conversion through jealousy (11:11-14). The alleged contradiction between these verses and chap. 3 is removed if one takes the latter as claiming that all unconverted Gentiles and Jews have sinned and fallen short of the glory of God, and that salvation is by grace alone for Jews as well as Gentiles.

The $\gamma\acute{\alpha}\rho$ ("for") of v. 14 indicates an argumentative connection with the foregoing thesis concerning the impartial judgment of God in v. 11.[204] It is significant that Paul refers here to $\check{\epsilon}\vartheta\nu\eta$ ("Gentiles") without the article, implying that some but not all Gentiles are in view.[205] The expression $\tau\grave{\alpha}\ \mu\grave{\eta}\ \nu\acute{o}\mu o\nu\ \check{\epsilon}\chi o\nu\tau\alpha$ ("those that do not have the law") refers to the absence of the Jewish Torah within the cultural tradition of Gentiles,

197 Dunn, 1:104; see also Barrett, 41–52, 58; Schlatter, 59; Jules-M. Cambier, "Le jugement de tous les hommes par Dieu seul, selon la vérité, dans Rom 2,1–3,20," *ZNW* 66 (1975) 187–213; Johannes Riedl, "Salus paganorum secundum Rom 2," *VD* 42 (1964) 61–70; Peter Bläser, *Das Gesetz bei Paulus* (Münster: Aschendorffsche Verlagsbuchhandllung, 1941) 195–97; Snodgrass, "Doers," 72–93.

198 See Davies, *Faith and Obedience,* 53–67; Simon J. Gathercole, "A Law unto Themselves: The Gentiles in Romans 2.14-15 Revisited," *JSNT* 85 (2002) 29 n. 9, refers to Anabaptist interpretations as moving in the same direction.

199 Zahn, 122; Wilhelm Mundle, "Zur Auslegung von Röm 2:13ff," *ThBl* 13 (1934) 249–56; Felix Flückiger, "Die Werke des Gesetzes bei den Heiden (nach Röm 2. 14ff.)," *ThZ* 8 (1952) 17–42; Barth, *Shorter Commentary on Romans,* 36–39; J. B. Souçek, "Zur Exegese von Röm 2, 14ff.," in *Antwort: Karl Barth zum siebzigsten Geburtstag am 10. Mai 1956* (Zurich: Evangelischer Verlag, 1956) 99–113; Cranfield, 1:155–63; Adrio König, "Gentiles or Gentile Christians? On the Meaning of Romans 2:12-16," *JTSA* 15 (1976) 53–60; A. Salas, "Dios premia según las obras (Estudio exegetico-teólogico de Rom.2,6-11)," in *La idea de Dios en la Biblia XXVIII semana biblica española (Madrid 23–27 sept. 1968* (Madrid: Consejo Superior de Investigaciones Cientificas, 1971) 265–86; Bergmeier, *Gesetz,* 31–102; Watson, *Paul,* 118–22; N. Thomas Wright, "The Law in Romans 2," in J. D. G. Dunn, ed., *Paul and the Mosaic Law*

(1996; repr. Grand Rapids: Eerdmans, 2000) 131–50; Gathercole, "Law unto Themselves," 27–49.

200 Joest, *Gesetz und Freiheit,* 169–76; Räisänen, *Law,* 101–9; Sanders, *Law,* 123–35. Pfleiderer, *Paulinismus,* 281, viewed this argument as an "unexpurgated and unnecessary fragment" of Paul's previously Pharisaic view on divine judgment, according to Snodgrass, "Doers," 73. In *Paul and Judaism,* 83, Laato tries to refute the inconsistency theory by maintaining that no Gentiles fulfill the Torah but nevertheless "do at least a little good."

201 Weiss, "Beiträge," 219–20 n. 1, observing that Wilke and Blass perceived a later marginal gloss by Paul himself. For other such suggestions see Meyer, 1:114–15.

202 Martin Kähler, "Auslegung von Kap. 2,14-16 im Römerbrief," *ThStK* 47 (1874) 274, 277; Lietzmann, 13; Bornkamm, *Studien,* 110; Knox, 409, 418; Kuss, 1:64–68; Harrisville, 43–50; Thorsteinsson, *Paul's Interlocutor,* 195.

203 John W. Martens, "Romans 2.14-16: A Stoic Reading," *NTS* 40 (1994) 61–63.

204 See Gathercole's critique of Kuhr, "Römer 2.14f.," 260–61, in "Law unto Themselves," 32–34.

205 See Meyer, 1.117, Wilckens, 2:133. Dabelstein, *Beurteilung,* 37, suggests "non-Jew" as the translation for $\check{\epsilon}\vartheta\nu\eta$ in this verse, which would be less abusive from a modern point of view, but Paul's argument requires "Gentiles" in this instance as commentators generally agree.

whereby the word φύσις should be taken as qualifying their identity[206] rather than their behavior.[207] It refers to Gentiles whose birthright lacked exposure to the Torah. Yet they do the "deeds of the law,"[208] a claim that in the experience of the Roman audience could only have referred to converted Gentiles.

That those Christian Gentiles who fulfill the law "are a law" expands the moral tradition of Aristotle, who argued that suicide is a criminal act because it willingly does harm "against the law" (παρὰ τὸν νόμον βλάπτῃ).[209] The Stoics developed this theme in the direction of a common law (νόμος κοινός) embedded in nature and in enlightened humans, as claimed in Diogenes Laertius *Vitae philos.* 7.87–89. But, as John Martens points out, only the enlightened sage was considered capable of following such a law by choosing the right course of action in complex situations.[210] In contrast to the philosopher-kings of Aristotle and the elite sages who embody Stoic ideals, Paul boldly claims that the rank and file of Gentile converts have so internalized the law of God that its performance is instinctive. Their renewed nature is so infused by the divine Spirit that the gap between knowing and doing has been overcome. In other writings Paul formulates this idea with language such as "we have the mind of Christ" or "the spirit that you have." As the following verse documents, this embodiment of law through conversion fulfills the prophetic hope that had initially been articulated concerning the future transformation of Israel itself.

■ **15** Paul's explanation of the phenomenon of the righteous Gentiles continues with οἵτινες ("such people"), which, as in 1:25 and 32, is a relative pronoun with a mildly confirmatory sense that picks up the thread from the preceding sentence.[211] The converted Gentiles' behavior of doing by nature the things of the law "demonstrates" the condition of their heart. The verb ἐνδείκνυμι is employed here in the sense to "cause something to become known, show, demonstrate,"[212] and may have a "forensic sense"[213] that is close to the classical expression used by Antiphon 5.2, κακοῦργος ἐνδεδειγμένος ("informed crime," i.e., a crime identified by an informer).[214] The context in Romans fits best with the sense of public demonstration, as in Isocrates' advice, "Demonstrate good will towards me in works rather than in words (τὴν εὔνοιαν τὴν πρὸς ἡμᾶς ἐν τοῖς ἔργοις ἐνδείκνυσθε ἢ ἐν τοῖς λόγοις)."[215]

The phrase "work of the law" (τὸ ἔργον τοῦ νόμου) is a collective expression as in v. 7[216] that avoids the negative connotation of "works of the law," used elsewhere by Paul in polemical contexts (Rom 3:20, 28; Gal 2:16; 3:2, 5, 10).[217] Bornkamm and Heiligenthal insist that this expression implies that in different forms both Jews and Gentiles possess a fundamental awareness and obligation to God's law.[218] The content of this "work" remains

206 See Cranfield, 1:156–57; Achtemeier, 45; P. Maertens, "Une étude de Rm 2.12-16," *NTS* 46 (2000) 510; Bergmeier, "Das Gesetz im Römerbrief," 53; Gathercole, "A Law unto Themselves," 36–37, citing parallels in Rom 2:27; 11:21; Gal 4:8; Eph 2:4; Wis 13:1; Ignatius *Eph.* 1.1; Josephus *Ant.* 8.142.

207 This exegetical decision renders irrelevant the immense debate over natural law with regard to this verse; see for example C. H. Dodd, "Natural Law in the New Testament," in *New Testament Studies* (Manchester: Manchester Univ. Press, 1953) 129–42; Stanislas Lyonnet, "Lex naturalis et iustificatio Gentilium," *VD* 41 (1963); J. L. McKenzie, "Natural Law in the New Testament," *BR* 9 (1964) 3–13, 238–42; David Greenwood, "Saint Paul and Natural Law," *BTB* 1 (1971) 262–79; A. F. Johnson, "Is There a Biblical Warrant for Natural-Law Theories?" *JETS* 25 (1982) 185–99; Mark A. Seifrid, "Natural Revelation and the Purpose of the Law in Romans," *TynB* 49 (1998) 115–29.

208 See Fitzmyer, *According to Paul*, 19–24; a parallel expression occurs in 1QS 1:7, "to do the statutes of God" (לעשות חוקי אל).

209 Aristotle *Eth. nic.* 1138A; Greenwood, "Saint Paul and Natural Law," 264, advocates the Aristotelian link.

210 Martens, "Romans 2.14-16," 64–66.

211 Schlier, 78.

212 BAGD (2000) 331.

213 Käsemann, 64.

214 See LSJM 558.

215 Isocrates *Nic.* 61; see also Aeschines *Ctes.* 12.3.

216 See Weiss, 118; Kühl, 81; Kuss, 1:69; Roman Heiligenthal, "ἔργον," *EDNT* 2 (1991) 50.

217 See Dunn, 1:100.

218 Bornkamm, *Ende des Gesetzes*, 99–101, discussed by Heiligenthal, *Werke*, 282–83.

undefined at this point,[219] although the subsequent reference to what God has "written" on the hearts of converted Gentiles points toward the theme developed in 13:10, that "the love" is law's fulfillment. That such work is "written in their hearts" (γραπτὸν ἐν ταῖς καρδίαις αὐτῶν) is a deliberate echo of LXX Jer 38:33, to which Paul also appears to have alluded in 1 Cor 11:25; 2 Cor 3:2, 3, 6, 14: "For this is my covenant which I will make with the house of Israel; after those days, says the Lord, I will put my laws into their mind and write them on their heart (καὶ ἐπὶ καρδίας αὐτῶν γράψω αὐτούς); and I will be to them a God and they shall be to me a people."[220]

Some scholars reject this echo on grounds that the eschatological fulfillment scheme associated with the Jeremiah prophecy seems to be missing here and that Paul speaks of the "work of the law" rather than the plural "laws" as in Jeremiah.[221] The first objection is viable only if the Gentiles in this passage are not Christian, and the second falsely presupposes that Paul is polemicizing against Jewish legalists. Paul is implying that the Jeremiah prophecy has been fulfilled in an unexpected manner as the gospel recruits Gentiles to become the heirs of the divine promise who perform the "work of the law" in their love feasts. The rhetorical impact of this allusion to Jeremiah is to cement the contrast between the seeming target of Paul's polemic, the legalistic bigot, and the audience consisting predominately of Gentile Christians who consider themselves the recipients of Jeremiah's eschatological promise of a new covenant. This detail also brings the Gentile Christians into close proximity to the Jewish Christians, in that both have a law written on their hearts, though in differing manners.

The next two clauses are usually taken as if v. 15b ("their conscience bearing witness") were explained by v. 15c ("their thoughts condemning or even defending"), even though the latter contains plural participles and the former is a singular genitive absolute.[222] This approach requires that the καί ("and") between the two clauses has an explicative connotation,[223] which requires an inappropriate definition of conscience as consisting of competing thoughts.[224] The simple solution of two separate genitive abstract constructions connected by "and" was developed by Godet[225] and is increasingly accepted today.[226] This allows the word "conscience" to carry its ordinary connotation of an autonomous witness as to whether a particular action is consistent with the internalized standard.[227] In contrast to modern usage that is shaped by the Stoic view of conscience as the guiding

---

219 See Heiligenthal, *Werke*, 283–84, who argues that Paul's intent is not to define the work but merely point to the presence of the law within Gentiles, alongside conscience; cf. Binder, *Glaube*, 55.

220 See Zahn, 124; Lietzmann, 41; Souçek, "Röm 2, 14ff.," 101–2; Cranfield, 1:159; Dunn, 1:100; Fitzmyer, 311; see also Hays, *Echoes*, 45, 128–32. Overlooking the allusion to Jeremiah, Engberg-Pedersen, *Stoics*, 215, interprets heart in a Stoic manner as "a certain *inner state of mind*, one that ensures that he actually does what he knows needs doing because he (now) wishes to do it for himself," having overcome "his self-directedness."

221 Käsemann, 64; Schlier, 78; Christian Wolff, *Jeremia in Frühchristentum und Urchristentum*, TU 119 (Berlin: Akademie, 1976) 196–97, Wilckens, 1:134; Koch, *Schrift*, 46.

222 See Jewett, *Terms*, 442–43, criticizing the approach of Zahn, 128–30; Lagrange, 51; Lietzmann, 40; Althaus, 20; Dodd, 36; Barrett, 53; Michel, 83–85, Kuss, 1:69; Kühl, 81; Schmidt, 48; Bornkamm, *Studien*, 111; Fitzmyer, 311; Byrne, 87.

223 See BAGD (2000) 495.1c. Kuss, 1:69, and Byrne, 93, explicitly support the explanatory meaning of "and," and Christian Maurer, "σύνοιδα, συνείδησις," *TDNT* 7 (1971) 917, views the "accusing and excusing thoughts" as the expressions of conscience. Bo Ivar Reicke's hypothesis in "Syneidesis in Röm 2,15," *ThZ* 12 (1956) 157–61, that τῶν λογισμῶν ("the reasonings") is an objective genitive attached to συνείδησις ("conscience") cannot account for this "and" and results in a problematic translation of συνείδησις "feeling for something."

224 In "The Objective Witness to Conscience: An Egyptian Parallel to Romans 2:15," *ERT* 18 (1994) 206, Ramez Atallah assumes that the conflicting thoughts are an expression of conscience, which will be tested on judgment day. For a critique of this view, see Jewett, *Terms*, 443; Dunn, 1:102.

225 Godet, 125.

226 Sanday and Headlam, 54; Moule, 64; Schlatter, 62; Eckstein, *Syneidesis*, 165–67; Dunn, 1:102; Moo, 152.

227 See Jewett, *Terms*, 411, 425, 444, accepted by Eckstein, *Syneidesis*, 313–14.

voice of God,[228] Paul views συνείδησις as an anthropological phenomenon of the knowledge one has "with oneself" that "marks any transgression against the individual's accepted code."[229] This correlates with C. A. Pierce's discovery of the "moral bad" and "moral bad absolute" connotations of συνείδησις in popular usage, in which the very presence of conscience was considered painful, because it marked a transgression against an internalized standard.[230] Only in a secondary sense, therefore, was conscience thought to be "guiding," because one's advanced knowledge of which actions to avoid could lead one to act in such a way as to avoid such painful knowledge of transgression. Thus in this passage the conscience of the Gentiles "bears witness with" (συμμαρτυρέω)[231] them to confirm that they have a law within.[232] The function of conscience as an autonomous witness, an irrepressible knowledge about whether an act is consistent with one's norm, explains why it can be employed here as the subject of the verb συμμαρτυρέω ("bears witness") as if it were somehow separate from the person.[233]

The autonomous function of conscience is confirmed by the following clause that refers to the rational process of conflicting thoughts: καὶ μεταξὺ ἀλλήλων τῶν λογισμῶν κατηγορούντων ἢ καὶ ἀπολογουμένων ("and the thoughts between them condemning or even defending"). The expression μεταξὺ ἀλλήλων ("among/between themselves") could refer to debate between different Gentiles[234] or conflicting thoughts within an individual.[235] The contradistinction between ἀλλήλων ("themselves") and the preceding αὐτῶν in the expression "their conscience" understood as belonging to each one individually,[236] along with the use of μεταξύ in biblical and secular texts, leads me to prefer the more public alternative. Typical examples of μεταξύ occur in Matt 18:15, "between you and him"; Acts 12:6, "between two soldiers"; Acts 15:9, "between us and them"; and P.Rein 44.16, "between him and Isidoros."[237] The most graceful translation of this public alternative in English was proposed by Barrett, "their inward thoughts in mutual debate accuse or else excuse them."[238] The word λογισμοί refers to thoughts, plans, or rational reflections that were typical features of Greco-Roman life, including business calculations, political debate, formal argumentation, and diatribe.[239]

The negative potential of such reasoning is visible in the only other occurrence in the Pauline letters, "for the weapons of our warfare are not fleshly but have divine power to destroy strongholds, destroying thoughts (λογισμοὺς καταιρούντες) and every proud obstacle to the knowledge of God" (2 Cor 10:4-5). The background to this negative appraisal of human thoughts is visible in

---

228 For an account of the history of research, see Jewett, *Terms,* 402–21; Eckstein, *Syneidesis,* 35–104; Eckstein notes that Cicero insisted that *conscientia* was the inner voice of the gods, as, e.g., in Cicero *Clu.* 58.159, *conscientiam mentis suae, quam ab dis immortalibus accepimus* ("the consciousness of his spirit, which we receive from the immortal gods"). Seventester, *Paul and Seneca,* 91, concludes: "By saying that God has entered into man Seneca evidently wishes to express the belief that the divine part of man makes itself heard in the conscience. Hence it is incorrect to say that above the conscience there is the supreme authority of the godhead," cited in part by Eckstein, *Syneidesis,* 101.

229 Jewett, *Terms,* 425.

230 Pierce, *Conscience,* 21–28.

231 Hermann Strathmann, "ἐπιμαρτυρέω κτλ.," *TDNT* 4 (1967) 508–9, cites Plutarch *Comp. Thes.* 6.4.2 (I,39b), "even the deeds [of Romulus] bear witness to him" (συμμαρτυρεῖ καὶ τὰ ἔργα). See also Plato *Hipp. maj.* 282b, "I must agree with you (συμμαρτυρήσαιδέ σοι) that you are right."

232 See Eckstein, *Syneidesis,* 163, 179.

233 Jewett, *Terms,* 444, citing Bornkamm, *Antike,* 112, and Schlatter, 62. It is therefore a mistake to contend that conscience "is the person functioning in the realm of moral discrimination and judgment" (Murray, 75).

234 Meyer, 1:121; Sanday and Headlam, 61; Kühl, 82–83; Schmidt, 48; Schlatter, 62–63; Barrett, 53; Murray, 76; BAGD (2000) 641; Horst Balz, "μεταξύ," *EDNT* 2 (1991) 419.

235 Zahn, 126; Jülicher, 240; Godet, 125; Michel, 125; Käsemann, 66; Schlier, 79; Cranfield, 1:162; Wilckens, 1:136–37; Fitzmyer, 311; Moo, 153.

236 See particularly Meyer, 1:121; Murray, 76.

237 See MM 404; LSJM 1115.II, "between," with numerous examples.

238 Barrett, 53.

239 Hans-Wolfgang Heidland, "λογίζομαι, λογισμός," *TDNT* 4 (1967) 284–86.

biblical writings[240] that castigate "self-glorious reason apart from God."[241] The verbal combativeness of Greco-Roman culture is captured by Paul's reference to those whose reasoning leads them to "condemning" (κατηγορούντων) "or also defending" (ἢ καὶ ἀπολογουμένων) one another. These terms were used in a variety of contexts, including interpersonal arguments, the courtroom, or God's tribunal.[242] This public discourse that is shaped by a constant controversy between condemnation and defense is employed by Paul to prove something that at first glance would seem to remove all ambiguity, that is, the law written on the heart.

The full implications of this depiction become clear later in the letter, when the controversies between the "weak" and the "strong" are discussed more openly. At that point it will become clear that this depiction of moral ambiguity even for those whose righteous behavior demonstrates a law written on the heart provides the basis for mutual understanding and sympathy. While both sides in the Roman churches are acting as if they have access to total truth and that their competitors must be "judged" or "held in contempt," they are all subject to human ambiguity. The insight of 1 Cor 13 is evident here, that believers continue to see through a glass darkly, and that all human knowledge, even that of prophets and charismatics, is partial. Paul's rhetorical strategy requires, however, that no hint of disapprobation is struck in Rom 2:15. Paul knows that he cannot achieve his rhetorical purpose by attacking either camp in a direct manner, so he constructs a rhetorical trap that by the end of the letter will "wound from behind," to employ Kierkegaard's famous expression.

■ **16** This verse brings to conclusion the sentence that began in v. 14, but does so in a manner that has given rise to unending controversy. The present tense of the verb ἐκδείκνυνται ("they demonstrate") in the previous verse seems inconsistent with the reference to the day of judgment in v. 16[243] and the tense of the verb κρίνει ("he judges") is present, which also seems odd in reference to the final judgment.[244] Scholars have observed that a seemingly more logical place for this reference to the day of judgment would be after v. 13,[245] or even v. 10.[246] Others argue that vv. 14-15 constitute a parenthesis[247] or a gloss,[248] while Bultmann argued that v. 16 is itself a gloss.[249] Sanday and Headlam note that the thought of this verse "goes back to δικαιωθήσονται in ver. 13,"[250] while Michel and others supply "all this will be made plain on the day of judgment."[251] That Paul himself supplied no such verb at the beginning of v. 16 indicates that he wanted to convey the idea that the final assessment of behavior, conscience, and reasoning belongs to God alone.[252] The idea that God is able to expose the secrets of the heart was widely affirmed in Scripture.[253] *Ps. Sol.* 14.8 follows this line in declaring

240 For example, Sir 1:3, "unscrupulous thoughts separate people from God"; 1:5, "thoughts without understanding"; 9:14, "the thoughts of mortals are miserable"; 11:15, "the foolish thoughts of their wrongdoing"; 12:10 "the thoughts [of the ungodly] would never be changed"; see also Sir 17:12; 19:3; and Ezek 38:10, where Gog is warned "that things shall come up into your heart and you shall think evil thoughts (λογιῇ λογισμοὺς πονηρούς)."

241 Heidland, "λογίζομαι, λογισμός," 286.

242 See BAGD (2000) 533 on κατηροέω ("bring charges against, condemn, accuse, reproach") and 116–17 on ἀπολογέομαι ("speak in one's defense, defend oneself").

243 Käsemann, 67, reports efforts to resolve this apparent contradiction by interpreting the "day" as the current moment of encounter with God's word, or the moment of conversion.

244 Haacker, 66, therefore proposes that ἡμέρα has the sense of "court" rather than the day appointed by a court, but this appears to be a strained translation

(see BAGD [2000] 438 on the translation of 1 Cor 4:3).

245 Dodd, 35, following the Moffatt translation; Fitzmyer, 311.

246 In *Emendationen*, 22–23, Könnecke argues that this verse is out of place, and that it would be better placed after v. 10.

247 Meyer, 1:123, following Lachmann; Kuss, 1:71, rejects this option on grounds that the proposed parenthesis would be too long.

248 Weiss, "Beiträge," 218; Bultmann, *Theology*, 1.217.

249 Bultmann, "Glossen," 282–84, followed by Watson, *Paul*, 116–17; Schulz, *Mitte der Schrift*, 128.

250 Sanday and Headlam, 62.

251 Michel, 126; Schlier, 81, cites Jülicher, Huby, Leenhardt, and others in favor of this general option of a mediating thought that introduces v. 16.

252 See Käsemann, 67–68.

253 On the basis of Dan 2:22; Sir 39:19; Jer 16:17; 23:24; Job 34:22; and other passages, Albrecht Oepke and Rudolf Meyer, "κρύπτω κτλ.," *TDNT* 3

that God "knows the secrets of the heart before they happen."[254] In the expression "the secrets of humans" Paul employs the term ἄνθρωπος that appeared in 2:1 and 3 to address the legalistic bigot, in contradistinction to Paul's audience. This conveys a hint that along with the bigot the audience might find its own secrets exposed. The hint is elaborated in 14:4 and 10 that neither the "weak" nor the "strong" should presume upon God's right to judge. It is perhaps for this reason that ἡμέρα ("day") appears here as in 2:5 without the article, referring to God's judgment that can occur at any time, in the present as well as in the final judgment.[255]

The significance of the final prepositional phrases has been particularly difficult to define, in part because κατὰ τὸ εὐαγγέλιόν μου ("according to my gospel") appears elsewhere only in 2 Tim 2:8 and in the deutero-Pauline benediction of Rom 16:25. That Paul's gospel is the "criterion" of divine judgment[256] seems to claim too much, and since it was widely believed that God judges secretive thoughts and behavior,[257] this could not be presented as a distinctive aspect of Paul's gospel. That the distinctive feature of his gospel was criticism of Jewish self-righteousness[258] is an outmoded expression of anti-Judaism that is particularly distant from this discussion of the behavior of Gentiles. It seems evasive to contend

that the "my" in this phrase refers simply to "the gospel which he preached together with other Christian preachers."[259] Some feature of Paul's preaching appears to be in view here. It is frequently asserted that the phrase κατὰ τὸ εὐαγγέλιόν μου ("according to my gospel") should be attached to the verb "judge," thereby indicating that Christ is the agency of final judgment, as in 1 Cor 4:4 and 2 Cor 5:10.[260] However, the word order of the prepositional phrases suggests that "through Christ Jesus" defines Paul's gospel.[261] None of these suggestions that are oriented to the construction of a consistent theology takes account of the peculiar rhetorical situation in this passage, and indeed, in the letter as a whole. The two prepositional phrases seem intended to raise nagging doubts in the minds of Paul's audience concerning divine assessment of the heart, thus opening the door to the later argument of the letter. If God will judge the secrets of every heart, what is peculiar about Paul's gospel? In what way is Paul's approach to divine judgment consistent with Christ Jesus? Not until the hearer of Romans comes to 14:1—15:13 do these questions receive a direct answer, in a distinctively Pauline advocacy of cooperative coexistence between formerly competitive house and tenement churches based on Christ's acceptance of them all.

(1965) 967, state, "The OT takes God's omnipresence and omniscience more seriously than any religion." See also Hans-Joachim Ritz, "κρύπτω κτλ.," *EDNT* 2 (1991) 324.

254 The "Egyptian Parallel to Romans 2:15" discussed by Atallah from the *Papyrus of Ani* II, "Heart of my mother . . . my breast . . . rise not up as a witness against me" on the day of judgment does not feature God as the one who exposes the secrets of the heart.

255 See Dunn, 1:102: "That final judgment is in view is not to be doubted." Delling, "ἡμέρα," 952–53, insists that "nowhere is there any suggestion that this day . . . is already present or reaches into the present," but Rom 2:16 may be an exception.

256 Schlier, 81; Dunn, 1:103.

257 Cranfield, 1:162–63, and Moo, 154, cite references to divine exposure of secrets in 1 Sam 16:7; Ps 139:1-2; Jer 17:10; Matt 6:4, 6, 18.

258 Schmidt, 49; Murray, 77; Schlatter, 64.

259 Cranfield, 1:163.

260 For example, Morris, 129; Zeller, 70; Zeisler, 89; Fitzmyer, 312.

261 Cranfield, 1:163; Robinson, *Wrestling,* 29, notes that the emphatic position of "through Christ Jesus" at the end of the sentence distinguishes what Paul's gospel contains.

2

The Second Part of the Second Pericope

The Righteous Judgment of Gentiles and Jews

b. Diatribe concerning the Nonexemption of Jews from Impartial Judgment

17/ But if[a] you call yourself a Jew
  and find your comfort in [the] law
    and boast in God,
      18/ and know God's will
        and approve the things that
        are important,
          being educated in the law;
19/ and have convinced yourself that
you are a guide of the blind,
  a light of those in darkness,
    20/ a tutor of fools,
      a teacher of the simple,
      possessing the embodi-
      ment of knowledge and of
      truth in the law;
21/ the one therefore who teaches the
other, do you not teach yourself?
  the one who preaches not to steal,
  do you steal?
    22/ the one who says not to
    commit adultery, do you commit
    adultery?
      the one who abhors idols, do
      you rob temples?
    23/ you who boast in [the] law, do
    you dishonor God through trans-
    gressing the law?
24/ "For the name of God is blasphemed
among the Gentiles on account of you,"
as it has been written.
25/ For on the one hand circumcision is
  advantageous if you do[b] the law. But
  on the other hand if you are a transgressor of law, your circumcision has
  become uncircumcision.
  26/ If therefore "the uncircumcision"
  observes the righteous requirements of
  the law, will not[c] his uncircumcision be
reckoned as a circumcision? 27/ And
will [not] "the physical uncircumcision"[d] who satisfies the law judge
you, law's transgressor, notwithstanding [your possession of] letter and circumcision? 28/ For not the public [Jew]
is a Jew, nor is public[e] [circumcision],
by flesh, circumcision; 29/ rather, the
hidden Jew [is a Jew], and circumcision of the heart, in spirit rather than
letter, [is circumcision]; [he is a Jew]
whose praise is not from people but
from God.

a   In place of εἰ δέ ("but if"), broadly attested by ℵ A B D* K Ψ 81 88 104 630 1506 1836 *al* latt syᵖ cop Cl, manuscripts D² L 6 33 69 323 326 330 365 424 614 945 1175 1241 1319 1505 1573 1735 1739 1874 1881 2464 2495 *Maj* syʰ have ἴδε ("behold"), proba- bly the result of an itacism, since in dictation the εἰ and ι would have sounded alike. See Nestle- Aland²⁶/²⁷ and Metzger, *Textual Commentary*, 448.

b   A minor variant in D* latt substitutes φυλάσσῃς ("you observe") for the less technical term πράσσῃς ("you do, accomplish"), which is so widely attested that it is clearly original.

c   The more strongly emphatic οὐχί ("not") is found in D G K L 6 33 69 88 104 323 326 330 365 424 614 945 1175 1241 1243 1319 1505 1573 1739 1874 1881 2344 2464ᶜ 2495 *Maj* in place of the better, though not more broadly, attested οὐχ ("not") found in ℵ B Ψ 945 1506 1735 *pc*, which is clearly original.

d   The deletion of the next four Greek words by G appears to be a scribal error.

e   The suggestion by H. Sahlin, "Textemendationen," 95–96, to delete the reduplicated phrase ἐν τῷ φανερῷ ("outward, in outward appearance"), is unnecessary and would erode the eloquent elliptical style of this concluding antithesis.

Analysis

Paul returns to the style of diatribe in 2:17-24 with rhetorical accusations and questions to an imaginary interlocutor. In an effective apostrophe, the interlocutor is emphatically addressed as "you" in vv. 17-27,[1] replicat- ing the style of vv. 1-5. The first two verbs contain an alliterative wordplay: ἐπονομάζῃ καὶ ἐπαναπαύῃ ("call yourself and find your comfort"). In this first paragraph, three sentences of five lines each are artfully con- structed,[2] with each sentence ending with an explicit ref- erence to the law. The series is introduced by the

---

1   See Bullinger, *Figures*, 904; Aletti, "Romans 2," 168.
2   Bengel, *Gnomon*, 36–37; see Weiss, "Beiträge," 219, for a recognition of the "fine and effective struc- ture" of this passage, but an unconvincing effort to force the first two sentences into three lines each; Weiss more properly identifies the five lines in the

expression Εἰ δέ ("But if") that leads the audience to expect a main clause that never appears,[3] although some have tried to see it in v. 24.[4] The logical progression is that if the interlocutor behaves with such arrogant disobedience (vv. 17-23), it follows that "the name of God is blasphemed among the Gentiles on account of you" (v. 24). The first sentence contains five typical examples of Jewish self-identity linked by καί ("and"). The second incomplete sentence or protasis has a series of five superiority claims in the accusative singular, requiring separation by commas. The first two sentences precisely correspond with each other, the first describing Jewish self-identity based on the law and the second describing relations to those outside the law.[5] The third sentence contains five moral injunctions followed by rhetorical questions about whether the imaginary interlocutor lives up to the law. The figure of polyptoton in the repetitions of διδάσκων . . . διδάσκεις ("teach"), κλέπτειν κλέπτεις ("steal"), μοιχεύειν μοιχεύεις ("commit adultery"), and νόμῳ . . . νόμου ("law") in vv. 21-23[6] renders the questions more emphatic and condemnatory. The prominent pentadic structure of this passage, evocative of the five books of the law,[7] is capped by a citation in v. 24 from Isa 52:5 that confirms the dishonoring of God among the Gentiles by Jewish disobedience.

The second paragraph (2:25-29) of this half-pericope also appears to have a pentadic structure, with five pairs of somewhat unbalanced lines followed by a rhetorical clausula[8] that concludes the series just as effectively as the citation from Isaiah does in 2:24. The first pair is in the form of antithetical parallelism, with chiastic development.[9] The fourth and fifth pairs are synonymous parallels that stand in antithetical parallelism to each other.[10] The ten references to "circumcision" and "uncircumcision" are rendered more emphatic by

antanaclasis,[11] the repetition of terms in the same sentence with different meanings in that both words are used to denote the persons as well as the conditions.

Rhetorical Disposition

IV.	The *Probatio*
1:18–4:25	A. The first proof: The gospel expresses the impartial righteousness of God by overturning claims of cultural superiority and by rightwising Jews and Gentiles through grace alone
2:1-29	2. Diatribe concerning the righteous judgment of Gentiles and Jews
2:17-29	b. The nonexemption of Jews from impartial judgment
2:17-24	1) The betrayal of Jewish prerogatives
2:17-18	a) Five claims of the interlocutor calling himself a Jew (2:17a)
2:17b	(1) Taking comfort in a law
2:17c	(2) Boasting in God
2:18a	(3) Claiming to know God's will
2:18b	(4) Approving what is important
2:18c	(5) Being educated from the law
2:19-20	b) Five claims of Jewish prerogatives
2:19a	(1) A guide to blind Gentiles
2:19b	(2) A light to Gentiles in darkness
2:20a	(3) A tutor of foolish Gentiles
2:20b	(4) A teacher of immature Gentiles
2:20c	(5) A connoisseur of legal truth
2:21-23	c) Five betrayals of Jewish admonitions
2:21a	(1) Teaching others but not oneself
2:21b	(2) Preaching against stealing but doing it
2:22a	(3) Speaking against adultery but doing it
2:22b	(4) Abhorring idols but robbing temples
2:23	(5) Boasting in the law but dishonoring it
2:24	d) The Scripture proof
2:24a	(1) The citation formula
2:24b	(2) The citation and emendation of Isa 52:5 concerning God being blasphemed among the Gentiles because of Israel's sin

---

third sentence (2:21-23) but draws no conclusion about the link between the pentadic structure and the theme of the law.

3   Weiss, 122.

4   See Godet, 127, 129, following Hofman's commentary.

5   Bullinger, *Figures*, 370, refers to vv. 17-20 as an "extended alternation," a form of correspondence.

6   See Bullinger, *Figures*, 271; polyptoton is wordplay with the same opening syllable and different endings, according to Anderson, *Glossary*, 103.

7   See Jewett, "Numerical Sequences," 227–45.

8   See Weiss, "Beiträge," 189 n. 1. For a discussion of the clausula technique of bringing a colon to conclusion, see Lausberg, *Handbuch*, §§985–1052.

9   Harvey, *Listening*, 187, lifts up a chiastic development in this verse: "circumcision . . . law . . . law . . . circumcision," without noting the parallelism. Perhaps one might more accurately describe this as parallelism with chiastic development.

10   Louw, 2:55, suggests that the five pairs of lines constitute a ring composition, but this is hard to discern.

11   See Bullinger, *Figures*, 290.

Exegesis

■ **17** This half-pericope opens with the same kind of diatribe that we encountered in 2:1-6. As Stowers observes, "If the reference to a Jew were changed to a Stoic . . . , then this text would be a classic example of indictment of the pretentious philosopher."[12] In an elegant manner that Paul's audience would have enjoyed, Paul augments the previous depiction of the pretentious bigot with a series of boasts that exaggerate well-known Jewish claims. As in the previous half-pericope, Paul's target is ostensibly far from his audience.[13] They are invited to join Paul's indictment of an insufferably arrogant bigot, not realizing that similar pretensions will later be exposed in their own behavior toward one another. The sentence opens with a subordinate clause, εἰ δὲ σὺ Ἰουδαῖος ἐπονομάζῃ ("but if you call yourself a Jew"), which requires a subsequent main clause that some have found in v. 21,[14] or in v. 24 where Paul cites Isa 52:5 that God's name is blasphemed among the nations because of the behavior of the Jews.[15] Strictly speaking, this sentence remains incomplete, as Weiss and Bornkamm have shown.[16] The first three words also appear in Epictetus, "but if you are not able to do this . . . (εἰ δὲ σὺ μὴ δύνασαι . . .)" (*Diss.* 1.25.5); such emphatic, diatribal use of σὺ ("you") occurs more than 250 additional times in Epictetus. The verb ἐπονομάζῃ can be translated either in the passive ("you are called")[17] or middle voice ("you call yourself").[18] The emphatic pronoun "you" and the dynamics of diatribe make the latter more likely.[19] The topos of claiming cultural identity that one does not sincerely follow is well known in philosophical circles. Epictetus raises the issue this way:

> Why, then, do you call yourself a Stoic (τί οὖν Στωικὸν λέγεις σεαυτόν), why do you deceive the multitude, why do you act the part of a Jew when you are a Greek (τί ὑποκρίνῃ Ἰουδαῖον ὢν Ἕλλην)? Do you not see in what sense men are severally called Jew (πῶς

12   Stowers, *Diatribe*, 112.

13   See Tobin, *Paul's Rhetoric*, 117. If Thorsteinsson is correct in *Paul's Interlocutor*, 197, that the interlocutor is "a Gentile who wants to call himself a Jew," the Gentile audience in Rome would feel itself under attack in this diatribe. The traditional view advanced by Watson, *Paul*, 113, that this is an "attack" on Jewish teachers in the congregation overlooks the indirection of diatribe.

14   Meyer, 1:125; Kühl, 88; Cranfield, 136; Dunn, 108; Moo, 158–59.

15   Godet, 127.

16   Weiss, 122; Bornkamm, "Anakoluthe," 76–78; Käsemann, 69.

17   Meyer, 125; Dunn, 109.

18   Zahn, 135–36; Kuss, 1:84; Käsemann, 68–69; Cranfield, 164; Schlier, 81–82; Fitzmyer, 315.

19   See Thorsteinsson, *Paul's Interlocutor*, 197–98.

ἕκαστος λέγεται Ἰουδαῖος), Syrian, or Egyptian? For example, whenever you see a man halting between two faiths, we are in the habit of saying, "He is not a Jew, he is only acting the part" (οὐκ ἔστιν Ἰουδαῖος, ἀλλ᾽ ὑποκρίνεται). But when he adopts the attitude of mind of the man who has been baptized and has made his choice, then he both is a Jew in fact and also called one (τότε καὶ ἔστι τῷ ὄντι καλεῖται Ἰουδαῖος). So we also are counterfeit "baptists," ostensibly Jews, but in reality something else, not in sympathy with our own reason, far from applying the principles which we profess, yet priding ourselves upon them as being men who really know them.[20]

The link that Paul develops between the law and the proud name, Ἰουδαῖος ("Jew"), reflects a designation that had become widely accepted during the later Hellenistic period.[21] The Jew is "one who identifies with beliefs, rites, and customs of adherents of Israel's Mosaic and prophetic tradition."[22] The Jew was an "adherent to the religion and member of the 'nation of the Jews.'"[23] Josephus refers to the details of the Torah as τῶν παρὰ Ἰουδαῖος νομίμων ("many points of Jewish law," *C. Ap.* 1.165). Paul's formulation of "calling yourself a Jew" recalls the Roman propagandist's appeal not to burn down the temple at the climax of the First Jewish-Roman War: "Who would not bewail and lament for the city at this amazing inversion, when aliens and enemies rectify your impiety, while you a Jew, nurtured in her laws (σὺ δ᾽ ὁ Ἰουδαῖος, ὁ τοῖς νόμοις ἐντραφεὶς), treat them more harshly even than your foes?"[24]

In combination with this proud title, Paul's choice of the compound verb "to apply a name/call by a name" (ἐπονομάζεσθαι)[25] in the middle voice alludes to the public claim by such a person as matching the title.[26] The name Ἰουδαῖος was sometimes placed on gravestones,[27] and Acts 22:3 places the typical formulation in Paul's mouth, "I am a Jew, born at Tarsus in Cilicia." Every detail of this initial identification of the imaginary interlocutor evokes the feeling of cultural superiority.[28] In the five clauses that follow, Paul elaborates in a succinct and witty manner the arrogance of this bigot whom the audience has already been led to despise.

That "you find your comfort in [the] law" (ἐπαναπαύῃ νόμῳ) conveys a sense of self-satisfaction and contentment.[29] The verb in the middle voice implies finding such comfort for oneself; it appears in the LXX of Mic 3:11 to depict the illusory assurance of the false prophets who "rested in the Lord (ἐπὶ τὸν Κύριον ἐπανεπαύοντο) while saying, 'Does not the Lord rest among us? no evil will come upon us.'" In other contexts this verb conveys leaning on someone for support (4 Kgdms 5:18; 7:2, 17; Ezek 29:7; 1 Macc 8:12; Philo *Trypho* 194; Epictetus *Diss* 1.9.9), but nowhere else does it appear in connection with the Torah. In the context of this diatribe, where Paul has already depicted the bigot in highly derogatory terms, this comfort in "a law," as if there were no other law in the world, is a transparent claim of cultural and religious superiority.[30] It matches the mood of *2 Bar.* 48.22-24 that similarly places trust in the possession of the "one law" that sets Jews apart from Gentiles: "In you we have put our trust, because, behold, your Law is with

---

20   Epictetus *Diss.* 2.9.19–21; translation W. A. Oldfather, 2 vols., LCL (London: Heinemann, 1926–28) 1:272.

21   Karl Georg Kuhn and Walter Gutbrod, "Ἰσραήλ κτλ.," *TDNT* 3 (1965) 363, 369–71; Horst Kuhli, "Ἰουδαῖος," *EDNT* 2 (1991) 194; Fitzmyer, 316; Peter J. Tomson, "The Names Israel and Jew in Ancient Judaism and in the New Testament," *Bijdr* 47 (1986) 123–25.

22   Cited from Schürer, *History*, 3:87–91. See BAGD (2000) 478.

23   Tomson, "Names Israel and Jew," 125.

24   Josephus *Bell.* 6.102. Elsewhere in Josephus, claims of Jewishness occur with the phrase γένος (ὢν) Ἰουδαῖος ("being Jewish by race") in *Ant.* 11.207; cf. 17.324; 18.103; 20.117; *Vita* 6.3; *C. Ap.* 179; *Bell.* 2.101.

25   See LSJM 676; this verb appears nowhere else in the NT but 36 times in the LXX, with formulations such as God "called his name Adam (ἐπωνόμασε τὸ ὄνομα Ἀδάμ)." See Hans Bietenhard, "ὄνομα κτλ.," *TDNT* 5 (1967) 264, 282.

26   For example, Thucydides *Hist.* 7.69, "and they, laying claim to name on the father's side (πατρόθεν τε ἐπονομάζων), by both their name and tribe."

27   Schlier, 82, lists *CIG* 9919, 9916; *CIJ* 530, 643 as examples.

28   Murray, 81, "a name associated . . . with all on which he prided himself." See also Wilckens, 1:147.

29   LSJM 607, "rest one's hopes on"; BAGD (2000) 358, "to find well-being or inner security, find rest, comfort, support . . . rely on."

30   See Kühl, 87; Kuss, 1:84.

us, and we know that we do not fall as long as we keep your statutes. We shall always be blessed; at least, we did not mingle with the nations. For we are all a people of the Name; we, who received one Law from the One. And that Law that is among us will help us, and that excellent wisdom which is in us will support us."[31] In view of the conflicts the congregations had experienced in Jewish synagogues prior to the Edict of Claudius, there is no doubt that they would have been inclined to perceive the arrogance in this form of "taking comfort in the law." As the letter develops, however, the problematic dimensions of their own imposition of the law on other groups will become clear (7:7-25; 10:1-4; 14:1-23).

Except for the polemical context of this diatribe, the next clause, καὶ καυχᾶσαι ἐν θεῷ ("and boast in God"), could be understood in a positive sense.[32] For example, Jeremiah contrasts human boasting with a conviction that Yahweh alone is the ruler of all: "Let not the wise man boast (μὴ καυχάσθω) in his wisdom, and let not the strong man boast in his strength, and let not the rich man boast in his wealth; but let him that boasts boast in this, the understanding and knowing that I am the Lord (ἐν τούτῳ καυχάσθω ὁ καυχώμενος, συνίειν καὶ γινώσκει ὅτι ἐγώ εἰμι κύριος)" (Jer 9:22-23). The formula "boasting in God" is unique to Paul,[33] and in this context it would have sounded like an overly audacious claim of superiority,[34] as if God could always be counted on to act in favor of the bigot. At the end of chap. 3, Paul returns to this theme and flatly prohibits boasting that God belongs to one cultural group or another (Rom 3:27-30).

■ **18** The third characterization of the pretentious bigot is "you know God's will" (γινώσκεις τὸ θέλημα), which follows a Jewish idiom in the absolute use of the noun.[35] To repeat the Hebrew or Aramaic formula "May it be the will!" expresses a hope that God's mysterious purpose will bless an endeavor, but the verbal form of the adage makes clear that one can never be sure. There are many examples of the formula "to do your will" or "to do God's will,"[36] but nowhere can I find a precise parallel to "knowing" God's will.[37] Although pious Jews could exclaim, "Happy are we, Israel, because we know what is pleasing to God" (Bar 4:4; see also Wis 15:2-3), it is quite a different manner to claim knowledge of God's inscrutable will. Paul's formulation contains an element of presumption that would have been immediately apparent to the Roman audience that expects a continuation of the ironic diatribe. The audience's delight involves a trap for themselves, however, because later in the letter they will discover that their certainty about what God wills for others places a "stumbling block or hindrance in the path of a brother" (14:13).

In a witty change of pace, Paul shifts from Jewish to philosophical jargon in the fourth expression of the bigot's self-identity. To "approve things that are important" (δοκιμάζεις τὰ διαφέροντα) employs a verb that was characteristic of a culture that placed emphasis on public testing and examination of ideas and qualifications.[38] For example, Plato "envisages δοκιμάζεσθαι of those nominated to office."[39] The concept of approval through testing was a hallmark of popular moral philosophy; for example, Epictetus Diss. 1.7.6; 1.7.8 refers to

---

31 Cited by Wilckens, 1:148, and Dunn, 110; translation here from *OTP* 1:636.

32 See Schmidt, 51; Wilckens, 1:148.

33 See the elaboration of Paul's extensive use of the boasting motif in Josef Zmijewski, "καυχάομαι κτλ.," *EDNT* 2 (1991) 276–79, and the references in Phil 3:3; 1 Cor 1:31; 2 Cor 10:17; Rom 5:2, 11; a somewhat distant parallel is *Ps. Sol.* 17.1, "Lord, you are our king forevermore, for in you, O God, does our soul take pride."

34 See Rudolf Bultmann, "καυχάομαι κτλ.," *TDNT* 3 (1965) 649; Dunn, 110–11; Stowers, *Diatribe*, 112: "The 'Jew' here pretends to have a special relationship with God."

35 Zahn, 136; see also Michel, 128; Gottlob Schrenk, "θέλω κτλ.," *TDNT* 3 (1965) 54; Schlier, 83, cites

1QS 8:6, "the elect of the will," and other Qumran references to the will of God.

36 See Schrenk, "θέλω κτλ.," 53–54, for numerous examples including Pss 39:9; 49:8; 102:21; 143:10; 2 Macc 1:3; 4 Macc 18:16.

37 Philo *Leg.* 3.197 refers to Abraham's obedience to the "will of God" (τῷ θεοῦ θελήματι), but there are no parallels to "knowing God's will."

38 See Therrien, *Discernement*, 15; Walter Grundmann, "δόκιμος κτλ.," *TDNT* 2 (1964) 256; BAGD (2000) 255: "to make a critical examination of something . . . to draw a conclusion about worth on the basis of testing."

39 Grundmann, "δόκιμος κτλ.," 256, citing Plato *Leg.* 754a.

the inherent "power of discernment" (δύναμις δοκι-μαστική) and regularly calls his followers to discern what is true or false (e.g., *Diss.* 1.27.7; 2.12.20; 2.18.25; 2.23.7-8). Hellenistic Jewish authors employed δοκιμάζω in the same manner to describe public testing of what is true or false, for example, Josephus's description of the testing of Abraham (*Ant.* 1.233.3, 15) and Asher's claim that "I have demonstrated all these things in my life, and have strayed from the Lord's truth" (*T. Ash.* 5.4). The participle διαφέροντος is an equally significant Hellenistic expression for what is different, what matters, or what is important.[40] Paul Wendland reports that this term refers to "what is of moral interest" to the philosopher, while its opposite ἀδιάφορα refers to what is "morally indifferent."[41] For example, Andocides *Alc.* 19.5 asks "if anyone knowingly dares to transgress important matters (τὰ διαφέροντα)." In the explanation provided in Diogenes Laertius *Vitae philos.* 7.61.14, the Stoic Zeno taught that some things are good, some not good, some are bad, but some are merely "indifferent" (τὰ ἀδιάφορα). Paul employs both the verb δοκιμάζω and the participle διαφέροντα in his prayer on behalf of the Philippians, that they "might approve what is important" (εἰς τὸ δοκιμάζειν ὑμᾶς τὰ διαφέροντα, Phil 1:10). There is a difference, however, between praying that a congregation might gain such a perception and the claim by an individual already to possess it. In the context of this diatribe concerning a Jewish bigot, Paul's formulation conveys a transparent pretense to know what is really important.[42] Later in the letter Paul exposes this trait within the congregation itself, which seems willing to "destroy the work of God" by squabbling over the proper food in the Lord's Supper (14:20).

The fifth and climactic characteristic of being a Jew is "being educated in the law." It is likely that Paul selects the verb κατηχέω because it was already being used as in-group jargon for religious schooling, instruction, or catechizing of Christian converts.[43] In Gal 6:6 Paul refers to a convert as "one who is taught the word" (ὁ κατηχούμενος τὸν λόγον), and Acts 18:25 refers to Apollos has having been "instructed in the way of the Lord" (κατηχημένος τὴν ὁδὸν τοῦ κυρίου). While there is no explicit evidence that Jewish instruction employed this expression,[44] the pious perceive wondrous things "out of your law" (ἐκ τοῦ νόμου σου, LXX Ps 118:18), and Judas Maccabeus exhorts his troops "from the law and the prophets" (ἐκ τοῦ νόμου καὶ τῶν προφητῶν, 2 Macc 15:9).[45] Other writers often refer to matters being extracted "from the law," for example, Isaeus, *Orat.* 111.22.9, "to know readily from the law" (ἐκ τοῦ νόμου γνῶναι ῥᾴδιον).[46] For an audience acquainted with these legal traditions, Paul's combination of "educated" (κατηχούμενος) with the phrase "from the law" (ἐκ τοῦ νόμου) provides a succinct and wittily arrogant depiction of the source of Jewish indoctrination: it is not a mere matter of human teaching, but of instruction from the divine law itself.

40 See Konrad Weiss, "φέρω κτλ.," *TDNT* 9 (1974) 62–63.

41 Cited by ibid., 62, from Paul Wendland, "Zu Theophrasts Charakteren," *Philol* 57 (1898) 115; this antithesis was picked up by Lietzmann, 43; Dunn, 111; Fitzmyer, 316; and others.

42 Paul's ironic formulation was discerned by Godet, 128, in reference to "legal casuistry," such as the debate between the schools of Shammai and Hillel about whether it was lawful to eat an egg laid on the Sabbath.

43 BAGD (2000) 534; A. Knauber, "Zur Grundbedeutung der Wortgruppe κατηχέω-catechizo," *ORPB* 68 (1967) 301; A. Garcia del Moral, "'Catequizar' según Pablo y Lucas," *Studium* 24 (1984) 57–110; Ceslas Spicq, "κατηχέω," *TLNT* 2 (1994) 292–94. Gerhard Schneider, "κατηχέω," *EDNT* 2 (1991)

273, argues that even the second-century occurrences do not reflect a technical connotation of catechesis, but every Pauline use is in the context of Christian instruction, as Hermann Wolfgang Beyer observes in "κατηχέω," *TDNT* 3 (1965) 638–39.

44 Beyer, "κατηχέω," 639.

45 The phrase "from the law" does not occur in Philo and only twice in Josephus (*Ant.* 13.78; *C. Ap.* 2.173) in contexts extraneous to Rom 2. But is is possible that Käsemann, 70, is right that the early Christian use of this verb in a catechetical sense derived from Judaism.

46 See also Demosthenes *Orat.* 19.70.3; 21.26.8; 22.33.6; 23.27.7; 39.39.7; Aeschines *Tim.* 79.7. Pseudo-Plutarch *Apoph. Lac.* 214b4 refers to Spartan deserters as being "liable to disgrace, as provided by law" (ταῖς ἐκ τοῦ νόμου ἀτιμίαις).

■ **19** The second group of five Jewish traits relate to a superior role in relation to others, particularly with regard to Gentiles.[47] The transparent arrogance of this stance is conveyed in the opening words, πέποιθάς τε σεαυτὸν ("and you have convinced yourself"). The verb πείθω refers ordinarily to convincing someone of a particular point of view by evidence or force of argument. For example, Dionysius Halicarnassus *Antiq. Rom.* 12.2.6 urges, "If you're convinced (πέποιθας) you've done no wrong, go and tell the just deeds about yourself to a real patriot!" To "convince yourself" (πέποιθας σεαυτόν) is felt to be evidence of cocksuredness, as in Aristophanes *Eq.* 770. In Paul's witty formulation, the object of persuasion is oneself. With this formulation, all five of the exalted allusions that follow, regardless of their religious sources, become a matter of "pretensious assurance" and naïve self-confidence.[48] To be a "guide of the blind" (ὁδηγὸν τυφλῶν) is probably an allusion to a proverbial claim that is also attacked in Matt 15:14, "they are blind guides" (τυφλοί εἰσιν ὁδηγοί) who claim to be able to guide the blind (see also Luke 6:39; Matt 23:16, 24; John 9:40-41).[49] *1 En.* 105.1 has God proclaim that faithful Jews are the "guides" for the "children of the earth." The Sibylline Oracles employ the same term to predict that "the people of the great God will again be strong who will be guides in life for all mortals" (3.194-95). That Israel was called to be a leader of other nations was widely believed. For example, Josephus claimed that "we have introduced to the rest of the world" the most beneficial ideas and laws (*C. Ap.* 2:291-95), and Philo argued that Israel, which is the "nation dearest of all to God . . . has received the gift of priesthood and prophecy on behalf of all mankind" (*Abr.* 98).

In view of these parallels and the rhetoric of this diatribe, it seems likely to many commentators that those in darkness that the bigot believes need to be guided are Gentiles.[50] However, the prophets frequently employ the metaphor of blindness in reference to the Israelites who refuse to follow God (Zeph 1:17; Isa 43:8; 56:10; 59:9-10),[51] and it seems likely that Paul intentionally employs a formulation that could refer to either Jews or Gentiles.[52]

The second prerogative is to be "a light to those in darkness," which echoes Isa 42:6-7, where God calls Israel to be "a light of the Gentiles, to open the eyes of the blind." Paul otherwise employs the word σκότος ("darkness") to symbolize unconverted status (Rom 1:21; 2 Cor 4:6), sinful behavior in general (1 Cor 4:5), and the works of the old age (Rom 13:12),[53] all of which would pertain to Jews as well as Gentiles. This usage was typical of sectarian groups such as the Dead Sea community that called its members the "children of light" and nonmembers "the children of darkness" (1QS 1:9; 2:16; 3:13, 24-25; 1QM 1:1, 7, 11, 13-15, etc.). The "children of light" are called by God "to detest all of the children of darkness" (1QS 1:10) and to wage war against them with mottos such as "God had struck all the sons of darkness" (1QM 3:9). That the house and tenement churches in Rome harbored similar feelings about each other is evident in Rom 14:1—15:13, which may explain why Paul's formulation here is not restricted to Gentiles. But as in the rest of this diatribe, Paul does not tip his hand. As far as the Roman audience is concerned, he is still describing the detestable bigot who claims not just to be a man of light but to be the light itself.[54] Once again, his insufferable arrogance is succinctly expressed.

47 Wilckens, 1:148; Zeller, 71; Deissmann, *Paul*, 96, suggests that this and the following verse express the "proud self-consciousnesss" that Paul had prior to his conversion.

48 Godet, 128; Michel, 129.

49 See Schlier, 84; Haacker, 68; Michel, 129, notes that the precise background of this polemic has not yet been discovered, but that Paul's formulation presupposes a specific tradition known to the audience. Among other sources, Berkley, *Romans 2:17-29*, 123–24, suggestrs that Isa 42:6-7 is echoed here.

50 Schlier, 84; Michel, 129; Gerhard Schneider, "τυφλός," *EDNT* 3 (1993) 377; BAGD (2000) 1021.

51 See Wolfgang Schrage, "τυφλός κτλ.," *TDNT* 8 (1972) 281–82.

52 There is also a reference to going "to God as a guide (ἐπὶ τὸν θεὸν ἔρχεσθαι ὡς ὁδηγόν)" in Epictetus *Diss.* 2.7.11.

53 See Hans Conzelmann, "σκότος κτλ.," *TDNT* 7 (1971) 441–42.

54 Ceslas Spicq, "φῶς κτλ.," *TLNT* 3 (1994) 478–86, notes that early Christian writers tended to emphasize that God or Christ is the light and that believers receive their light from this source. In view of this tradition, to claim to be the "light to those in darkness" would have appeared arrogant.

■ **20** To be a παιδευτής ("tutor, teacher") was a supreme accomplishment in Greek and Hellenistic Jewish culture,[55] and the coordination with ἀφρόνων ("of fools") conveys an immeasurable sense of superiority claimed by the tutor over his charges. That fools were in fact considered ineducable was frequently stated by Greek as well as Jewish writers,[56] but it was the duty of tutors (παιδογωγαί) to try their best to overcome this barrier. Since tutors were expected to beat their charges in order to convey a modicum of good sense, they readily became objects of resentment,[57] a cultural inclination that Paul expects to evoke with this succinct, ironic formulation. The irony is continued in the next clause, in which "children" (genitive, νηπίων) are the wards of the διδάσκαλος ("teacher, master"), a term that was sometimes employed for an instructor of older youth or adults[58] and was used to describe the instructional activity of the god Hermes or of Jesus.[59] The supreme religious leader in the Qumran community was called "the Teacher of Righteousness," and his pupils were definitely not children. The term "teacher/rabbi" conveyed a sense of greatness and high social status in every branch of the Jewish community,[60] and Jesus' repudiation of this title as a false form of respect (Matt 23:7-12) must have been known to Paul's audience. A combination of ridiculous arrogance and audience resentment is therefore evoked by Paul's formulation, because this bigot who claims to be able to instruct everyone else does not appear to know the precise connotation of the titles he arrogates to himself, and he views his wards as fools and infants, which places the audience in a position of absolute, imputed inferiority. There is still no hint that this humorous depiction conveys a warning about the audience's behavior, because not until chaps. 14–15 can they be led to see that the efforts of the weak and the strong to instruct each other in the truth are equally arrogant and conducive of resentment.

A similar treatment of someone who claims to be a teacher of fools is found in Philo's *Legat.* 53, where the emperor speaks about his erstwhile supporter, Macro; this passage demonstrates how readily this topos could be used to poke fun at would-be educators:

> Here present is the teacher (ὁ διδάσκαλος) of one no longer needing to be taught, the tutor (παιδαγωγός) of one who is no longer a child, the censor of one more prudent, the one who thinks that an emperor should obey his subject, who prescribes himself (παιδευτὴν ἑαυτὸν γράφει) as one accustomed to the art of government . . . but from whom he learned the principles of ruling I am unaware.

That Paul's bigot actually possesses "the embodiment of knowledge and of truth in the law" is transparently false. The participle ἔχοντα ("having, possessing") conveys a false relationship between a teacher and the law, as if the former rather than the latter were paramount; a proper rabbi in the Jewish tradition stood under the supreme authority of the law, and if anything, the law possessed him rather than becoming a human possession. The word μόρφωσις carries the sense of "embodiment" or "impression" that emerged with Koine usage, as compared with "form," "outline," or "structure" in classical Greek.[61] The irony is that this arrogant bigot whose behavior violates the intention of the divine law

---

55 See Georg Bertram, "παιδεύω κτλ.," *TDNT* 5 (1967) 597–617. The noun παιδευτής ("tutor, teacher") appears first in Plato (*Protag.* 324 b6; *Resp.* 492d5; 493c8; *Leg.* 812e10; 835a3; 964c4) and is found in Philo *Prob.* 143.2; *Legat.* 53.4; in Diodorus Siculus *Hist.* 9.1.2; 17.110.3; Dionysius Halicarnassus *Antiq. Rom.* 2.59.3; Strabo *Geogr.* 16.2.10; Plutarch *Lyc.* 12.4.3; Dio Chrysostom *Orat.* 4.132.

56 The chorus in Sophocles *Aj.* 162–63 sings, "But it is not possible to teach the foolish wisdom in such matters (ἀλλ᾽ οὐ δυνατὸν τοὺς ἀνοήτους τούτων γνώμας προδιδάσκειν)."

57 See Norman H. Young, "The Figure of the *Paidagōgos* in Art and Literature," *BA* 53 (1990) 80–86.

58 Karl Heinrich Rengstorf, "διδάσκω κτλ.," *TDNT* 2 (1964) 148–49.

59 See ibid., 136, 153–57.

60 In describing the widespread use of this term in Jewish circles, Eduard Lohse, "ῥαββί, ῥαββουνί," *TDNT* 6 (1968) 961–63, observes that the word *rab* meant "great."

61 See Käsemann, 70–71; Johannes Behm, "μορφή κτλ.," *TDNT* 4 (1967) 754; BAGD (2000) 660; Dunn, 113; Wolfgang Pöhlmann, "μορφή κτλ.," *EDNT* 2 (1991) 444.

at every point claims to possess its "moulding"[62] in the form of "knowledge and truth." In a biblically shaped tradition in which knowledge "has an element of acknowledgment" of what God has revealed rather than claiming "the possession of information,"[63] the bigot's claim is ridiculous. Even more absurd is his claim to embody the "truth" (ἀλήθεια), a key biblical term implying integrity and actual correspondence with reality.[64] That knowledge and truth were revealed in the Torah was widely assumed, which lends a measure of plausibility to Paul's almost sarcastic depiction. For example, that God "reveals all the paths of knowledge (πᾶσαν ὁδὸν ἐπιστήμης) and has given it to Jacob his servant and to Israel his beloved" was claimed by Bar 3:36. In *2 Bar.* 44.14 the pious Jews who have "prepared for themselves treasures of wisdom and stores of insight" are affirmed to have "preserved the truth of the law." Sirach echoes this claim, that God "gave them (the Jews) knowledge and the law of life (ἐπιστήμην καὶ νόμον ζωῆς)" for an inheritance (Sir 17:11; cf. 45:5). In Johannes Behm's words, the entire formulation "is stated with obvious irony by Paul."[65] With this climactic, fifth claim of superior status the pretension of the bigot becomes truly laughable. Yet there is still no hint in this depiction of the arrogant nonbeliever that similar pretensions are evident within the Roman house and tenement churches.

■ **21** The third series of five forms of Jewish boasting begins in v. 21 with an effective change of form. Since the previous portrayal of the imaginary interlocutor has reached a ludicrous extreme in the disparity between claim and performance, each of these five rhetorical questions in vv. 21-23 requires an answer from the audience that condemns the hypocritical behavior. Yet each rhetorical question is formulated in second person style,

so that the audience is forced to condemn itself, as it were, in the condemnation of the detestable bigot. This happens so quickly and is formulated in such a compelling style that the full implications are not immediately apparent. The many parallels in ancient literature to this kind of diatribe[66] would have rendered this feature unobjectionable to the audience, which continues to assume that the bigot rather than themselves was under attack. It is only when one follows Paul's rhetoric to the end of the letter that one discovers the bearing of this series of questions on the in-group. Despite superficial appearances, Paul is not engaged in "propagandistic denigration" of Jews, in Räisänen's provocative formulation,[67] but rather in the rhetorical demolition of claims of cultural superiority whose continuation would have sabotaged the mission to the so-called barbarians in Spain.

The protasis of the first question takes up the preceding five claims of being a superior teacher of subordinates. "The one who therefore teaches the other" (ὁ οὖν διδάσκων ἕτερον) employs the same stem employed in v. 20b, "the teacher" whose wards are infants. Godet catches the irony of this first question: "The term *teach* includes all the honorable functions toward the rest of the world which the Jew has just been arrogating. . . . Thou, the so called great teacher!"[68] Both the philosophical and the rabbinic traditions contain similar critiques of "the one who teaches others but has not yet learned how to live what he teaches."[69] In Epictetus *Diss.* 3.7.17 Arrian records a similar warning about not teaching oneself: "If you wish to be a philosopher as one ought, if really a perfect one, be one who follows your own dogmas; but if not, you would seem no better than we so-called 'Stoics,' for even we ourselves say one thing but do another." With regard to students of the Torah, Rabbi

62 Cited by Pöhlmann, "μορφή κτλ.," 444, from Schlatter's *Gottes Gerechtigkeit*, 103; in contrast, the discussion by Schlatter in his commentary (69) is obscure.

63 Rudolf Bultmann, "γινώσκω κτλ.," *TDNT* 1 (1964) 698.

64 Gottfried Quell, "ἀλήθεια κτλ.," *TDNT* 1 (1964) 232-37; Klaus Haacker, "Wie redet die Bibel von Wahrheit?" *ThBei* 10 (1979) 13-18.

65 Behm, "μορφή κτλ.," 754; this assessment is rejected by Cranfield, 167, who along with most

commentators appears to be oblivious to the humor in this passage.

66 See, e.g., Stowers, *Rereading*, 144-53; and Anton Fridrichsen, "Das wahre Jude und sein Lob: Rom. 2:28f.," in *Exegetical Writings. A Selection*, trans. and ed. C. C. Cargounis and T. Fornberg, WUNT 76 (Tübingen: Mohr-Siebeck, 1994) 186-94; both cite numerous examples from Epictetus.

67 Räisänen, *Law*, 101, cited by Dunn, 114.

68 Godet, 128.

69 Stowers, *Rereading*, 148.

Saul ben Nannos observed: "You have many a man . . . who teaches others but does not teach himself. . . . How, for example? A man who learns a piece of teaching twice or thrice, then teaches it to others, and then concerns himself with it no further, but forgets it; that is the one who teaches others but does not teach himself."[70]

Paul's formulation of this issue is much more succinct and compelling. In the light of the previous depiction of the bigot's hypocrisy, the question, "do you not teach yourself?" requires the audience to reply, "Obviously not!" There can be no ambiguity on this point, because the fundamental requirement of humility before God (e.g., Ps 35:13; Mic 6:8) has been violated by every component in the bigot's self-advertisement. This unequivocal starting point helps to make the other points in Paul's final, fivefold series plausible.

The choice of the participle ὁ κηρύσσων ("the one who preaches") in the second query exaggerates the disparity between advocacy and action with regard to stealing. The verb κηρύσσω is associated with the herald (κῆρυξ) who makes public announcements such as the coming of the king or the opening of a sacred festival.[71] In the early church this verb was employed in reference to the preaching of the innovative gospel about Jesus as the Christ.[72] Since the law about stealing was traditional and categorical, none of the other biblical references to theft or to the Eighth Commandment employ the verb "preach." The typical formulations are "You shall not steal" (Exod 20:15) or "Neither shall you steal" (Deut 5:19).[73] To "preach" against stealing therefore conveys an inappropriate exaggeration, with a whiff of self-righteousness, that stands in obvious tension with the question that appears to require an affirmative answer, "Do you steal?" Having already established that the bigot who condemns everybody's sins "does the very same

things" (Rom 2:1), there is no need to adduce examples from contemporary Jewish history about the prevalence of theft.[74] Rather than decrying an alleged low state of Jewish morality, as many commentators assume,[75] Paul is continuing his dialogue with an imaginary interlocutor with the goal of demolishing the premise of cultural exceptionalism.

■ 22 The third query has the same structure as the second, and deals with the Seventh Commandment, about adultery. In this instance a less exaggerated participle is selected, ὁ λέγων μὴ μοιχεύειν ("the one who *says* not to commit adultery"), but the allusion to the commandment in Exod 20:14 and Deut 5:18 is clear. In the light of 1 Cor 6:9-20, it is likely that by the time of writing Romans Paul shared the intensified definition of adultery characteristic of early Christianity, in which both the husband and wife were held to the same standard.[76] In the light of Jesus' words to the Pharisees concerning the stoning of the adulteress, "Let him who is without sin among you be the first to cast a stone at her" (John 8:7), a memorable saying that may have already circulated in oral form in Rome, the stark question, μοιχεύεις; ("do you commit adultery?"), would have been perceived as an unassailable challenge.

The fourth query follows the same form, but moves beyond the context of the Ten Commandments: "The one who abhors idols, do you rob temples?" To hold idols in contempt could be understood as an expression of the Second Commandment not to make "a graven image" that you "bow down" and worship (Exod 20:4-5). The participle ὁ βδελυσσόμενος refers to someone who abhors something as "utterly offensive or loathsome."[77] Philo writes of God "hating and abhorring iniquity" (θεὸς ἀδικίαν βδελύττεται καὶ μεμίσκε, *Heres* 163.1), and Plutarch speaks of one "abhorring depravity" (βδε-

70 *'Abot R. Nat.* 29 (8a), cited by Dodd, 38–39, and Cranfield, 168.

71 See Gerhard Friedrich, "κῆρυξ κτλ.," *TDNT* 3 (1965) 683–700.

72 Ibid., 703–14.

73 The standard moral injunction also in Greco-Roman culture was "do not . . . ," as in the formula of Pythagoras, "Don't overdo it!" (μὴ παραβαίνειν, Diogenes Laertius *Vitae philos.* 8.9).

74 For example, Cranfield, 168, cites the first-century Rabbi Johanan ben Zakkai in *T. Sota* 14.1 and the

second-century Rabbi Simlai in *Deut. Rab.* 2 *ch (198a) about the prevelance of theft and adultery.

75 Weiss, 126; Jülicher, 240; Schmidt, 52; Dodd, 39; Moo, 163–65.

76 See Friedrich Hauck, "μοιχεύω κτλ.," *TDNT* 4 (1967) 733–34; for an analysis of Paul's development on this point from early to later letters, see Jewett, "Sexual Liberation," 55–87, which was updated in chap. 4 of *Apostle to America*, 45–58.

77 BAGD (2000) 172; see also Werner Foerster, "βδελύσσομαι κτλ.," *TDNT* 1 (1964) 598–600.

λυττομένῳ τὴν μοχθηρίαν, *Quo. Quis* 82c6). The object of such loathing in Paul's diatribe is τὰ εἴδωλα ("the idols"), which clearly refers to non-Jewish cult images.[78] Nevertheless, the link with temple robbery is puzzling because it does not appear to violate the abhorrence of idolatry; indeed, contempt for the falsity of Greco-Roman deities could easily rationalize temple theft on the grounds that the alleged owner is nonexistent.[79] Moreover, the following query in 2:23 appears to link temple robbery with dishonoring God.[80] Don Garlington argues that the ἱεροσυλεῖν in view is "Israel's idolatrous attachment to the law itself . . . its tenacious insistence that the Torah is God's definitive provision for eternal life and, therefore, its clinging to the law as an object of trust to the exclusion of Christ."[81] However, this view cannot account for 3:31, "Rather, we establish the law."[82] Edgar Krentz follows J. B. Barber and Gerhard Delling in suggesting the background of a Hellenistic Jewish tradition that advocated respect for non-Jewish religion.[83] In *De Spec. Leg.* 1.53, Philo argues that Moses "counsels them that they must not . . . deal in idle talk or revile with an unbridled tongue the gods whom others acknowledge, lest they on their part be moved to utter profane words against Him Who truly is." In *De vita Mosis* 2.2053, Philo contends that "we must refrain from speaking insultingly of these [i.e., idols of wood and stone], lest any of Moses' disciples get into the habit of treating lightly the name 'god' in general, for it is a title worthy of the highest respect and love." Josephus follows this tradition in his admonition: "Let none blaspheme the gods which other cities revere, nor rob foreign temples, nor take treasure that has been dedicated in the name of any god" (*Ant.* 4.207). In the light of this tradition, Krentz concludes that for Paul, "Temple robbery means there is no respect for the concept, the name, the honor of God."[84] In this way, the fourth query leads directly to the climactic question in the following verse.

■ **23** Although most exegetes and some translators consider this verse to be a declaration rather than a question,[85] its word order matches the preceding four questions, and it closes, just as they do, with a second person singular verb that can be translated as an interrogative, ἀτιμάζεις ("do you dishonor?"). On rhetorical as well as grammatical grounds,[86] I prefer to take this as the fifth and climactic question in the final series whose function is to sum up the preceding queries by a specific reference to the Torah. In place of the participial expressions in the first four questions, here we have a finite form of the key word καυχᾶσαι ("you boast"), which had been used in 2:17. Rather than honoring the law and conforming to its guidance, the bigot is employing the law as a means of achieving superiority over others.[87] Social competition rather than justice lies at the core of this mistaken approach to the Torah. The boast-

---

78 Terry Griffith, "*ΕΙΔΩΛΟΝ* as 'Idol' in Non-Jewish and Non Christian Greek," *JTS* 53 (20035) 95–101, explains that the normal Greek meaning of this term was statue, image, or symbol and that Jewish and early Christian usage writings applied "the term εἴδωλον to the deity itself" (101) because its derivation from εἴδεσθαι ("to appear") allowed the connotation of idolatry. For example, Polybius reports in *Hist.* 30.25.13–15 that at the games celebrated by Antiochus IV, there were "sacred images (ἀγαλμάτων) for statues (εἴδωλα) of all beings who are said or are held to be gods (θεῶν). . . . They were followed by images (εἴδωλον) of Night and Day, Earth and Heaven, and Dawn and Noon." Dionysius Halicarnassus *Antiq. Rom.* 1.68.2 reports, "We have seen many other statutes also of these gods (εἴδωλα τῶν θεῶν) in ancient temples." In contrast, the polemical use appears in Jewish sources, e.g., 1 Chr 16:26, "For all the (θεοί) of the Gentiles are idols (εἴδωλα)."

79 Gottlob Schrenk, "ἱερός κτλ.," *TDNT* 3 (1965) 256; Wilckens, 1:150; Moo, 164.

80 See Edgar Krentz, "The Name of God in Disrepute: Romans 2:17-29," *CurTM* 17 (1990) 433–35.

81 Garlington, *Letter to the Romans*, 39, 40.

82 Garlington, *Letter to the Romans*, does not discuss this verse, and it is not listed in his index.

83 Krentz, "Romans 2:17-29," 436–37, referring to Lightfoot, *Notes*, 262–63; and Gerhard Delling, "Josephus und die heidnischen Religionen," in *Studien*, 45–52.

84 Krentz, "Romans 2:17-29," 437.

85 Weiss, 127, rejects the view of earlier commentators that this verse constitutes a question; so also Meyer, 1:130; Schlier, 86; Cranfield, 170; Dunn, 115. Moo, 165, notes that *NEB* and *JB* translate as a declaration while *KJV, NASB, RSV, NIV,* and *TEV* translate it as a question.

86 Godet, 129, translates v. 23 as a question because of the grammatical structure of the material from v. 17 onward, dependent on εἰ δὲ . . . ("but if. . .").

87 See Dunn, 115, "boasting . . . becomes a cause of boasting over those who do not have the law." In

ing of the imaginary interlocutor to possess "knowledge and truth in the law" (2:20) and to having been "schooled out of the law" (2:18) has been shown at every decisive junction to have been false because of the failure to live up to the law. Now Paul can pose the final question that requires a strongly affirmative answer, "do you dishonor God through transgressing the law?" Although the expression παραβάσις τοῦ νόμου ("transgression of the law") is not found in the LXX, there are many associated formulations such as "transgress the word of the Lord" (Num 14:21; 22:18; 24:13; Deut 1:43), "transgress the commandments" (Deut 17:20), "transgress the covenant of the Lord" (Josh 7:11, 15; 23:16), "those who have transgressed against me" (Isa 66:24), or "to transgress against the Holy God" (3 Macc 7:10).[88] Since Josephus refers repeatedly to "transgressing the law" (*Ant.* 3.218; cf. 8.129; 9.243; 14.167; 18.81; 18.268), Paul employs this expression (Rom 4:15; 5:14; Gal 3:19), and other NT passages use it (1 Tim 2:14; Heb 2:2; 9:15), it seems likely that it had become a conventional expression in Hellenistic Jewish circles. The use of the verb ἀτιμάζω ("dishonor") brings the behavior of the proud interlocutor into the same arena as the pagans in Rom 1:21-27 whose refusal to honor God as God led to the dishonoring of their own bodies.[89] Since a primary obligation of faithful Jews was to give honor and glory to God (Pss 28:1; 95:7),[90] this rhetorical question about dishonoring God would have evoked a shudder. That transgressing God's law would dishonor God himself is a self-evident premise in Jewish thought.[91] That the bigot who was intent on demonstrating his superiority over Gentiles ends up dishonoring the very God he claims to serve is the clear implication of this climactic rhetorical question. The audience is given no chance to ponder whether this is so, because the point is driven home by the scriptural citation in the next verse.

■ **24** Paul selects a citation from the LXX that precisely fits his rhetorical purpose. While the original meaning of Isaiah's remark in 52:5 was that God's name was reviled by the Gentiles on account of Israel's captivity, in Paul's context it is made to refer to Israel's transgression against the law.[92] Paul alters the sequence in order to bring the crucial phrase into the emphatic position.[93] The LXX wording of Isa 52:5 is as follows:

δι᾽ ὑμᾶς διὰ παντὸς τὸ ὄνομά μου βλασφημεῖται ἐν τοῖς ἔθνεσιν ("on account of you my name is continually blasphemed among the Gentiles")

Paul places the phrase "the name of the Lord" at the beginning of the citation and adds "for" to connect the citation tightly to the preceding verse.[94] This shifts the emphasis to the honor of God's name, onto which Jewish unbelief "casts aspersions."[95] In order to provide an uninterrupted transition between the final rhetorical question and the citation, the formula "as it has been written" is postponed until the end of the sentence.[96] Paul also substitutes the "my" of the Isaiah citation with τοῦ θεοῦ ("of God"), which connects the citation more tightly with the word "God" in Rom 2:23.[97] He deletes the phrase διὰ παντός ("continually, through everything"), which is irrelevant in the new context.[98] Here is the result of Paul's slight but highly effective alteration:

τὸ γὰρ ὄνομα τοῦ θεοῦ δι᾽ ὑμᾶς βλασφημεῖται ἐν τοῖς ἔθνεσιν ("For the name of God is blasphemed among the Gentiles because of you")

"καυκάομαι κτλ.," *TDNT* 3 (1965) 649, Rudolf Bultmann restricts boasting to individual trusting in achievements, and Cranfield, 170, argues that boasting is not used "simply in a bad sense" here.

88 Some of the examples are provided by Johannes Schneider, "παραβαίνω κτλ.," *TDNT* 5 (1967) 738.

89 See Hans Hübner, "ἀτιμάζω κτλ.," *EDNT* 1 (1990) 177.

90 See Johannes Schneider, "τιμή κτλ.," *TDNT* 8 (1972) 172.

91 See Zahn, 140–41; Michel, 131.

92 See Schmidt, 52; Michel, 131; Cranfield, 141; Winninge, *Sinners and the Righteous*, 259–60; Shum, *Paul's Use of Isaiah*, 179.

93 Koch, *Schrift*, 105.

94 See Berkley, *Romans 2:17-29*, 137.

95 Stanley, *Scripture*, 84–85.

96 Weiss, 127, observes that this is the only time that Paul provides the citation formula after the citation rather than before. For the traditional Jewish background of the formula, "as it has been written," see on 1:17.

97 Stanley, *Scripture*, 85–86; Wilk, *Bedeutung*, 49.

98 Koch, *Schrift*, 116; Stanley, *Scripture*, 86. Wagner, *Heralds*, 177, suggests that this deletion softens the criticism of Israel.

The citation does more than to provide confirmation that the final rhetorical question in the preceding verse must be answered in the affirmative: "Yes, the bigot in fact dishonors God!" The plural "you" in the Isaiah formulation δι᾿ ὑμᾶς ("because of you [pl.]") serves to generalize Paul's point by confirming the universal sinfulness of all (3:9).[99] It is also significant that while Paul could have selected many passages to confirm that transgressions dishonor God, he selects a citation that brings the Gentiles into the equation.[100] If the motivation of the bigot was to prove superiority over Gentiles, the consequence of such a religion is that they despise the God who is allegedly being touted by such behavior. The implications of this point become clear later in the letter when Paul refers to blasphemy in the context of competition between Jewish and Gentile Christians (14:16), behavior that could discredit any effort to evangelize the Gentiles in Spain. Paul's goal is to make clear that no boasting in cultural or religious superiority is allowable (3:37), and his hope is that when the gospel is rightly understood, all nations will come to glorify God rather than themselves (15:9-12).

■ **25** The second section of the diatribe opens with measured argument, but the questions of Jewish exceptionalism and the assertion of superiority remain central. The issue in this second section is whether circumcision provides a status for Jews that "Gentiles, however righteous, simply lack," to employ John Barclay's formulation.[101] Some have found the transition to this section so abrupt that a new pericope is considered to begin with v. 25,[102] but since the rhetorical questions typical for diatribe continue in vv. 26 and 27, most commentators accept the continuation of a single pericope encompassing vv. 17-29. The substantive continuation of Paul's argument is clear when one understands his assault on the bigot's claim of cultural superiority over Gentiles. Michel observes that v. 25 has the form of a thesis that is presented in a formal manner with μέν . . . δέ ("on the one hand . . . on the other hand").[103] The crucial term in this discourse concerning social and religious superiority is the verb ὠφελέω, which has the semantic range of providing assistance, aid, benefit, or advantage.[104] The antithetical syntax in v. 25 brings a comparative nuance to the fore: benefit or advantage compared with what?[105] While some commentators assume that the advantage in view is salvation,[106] membership in the Jewish covenant is more likely in view,[107] with particular reference to the superior position circumcision provides over against the Gentiles.[108] In the words of *Jub.* 15.26, "Anyone . . . whose own flesh is not circumcised on the eighth day is not from the sons of the covenant which the Lord made for Abraham since (he is) from the children of destruction." A typical expression of emotional revulsion against uncircumcised persons is expressed in the Additions to Esther, where the heroine prays, "you know that I hate the splendor of the wicked and abhor the bed of the uncircumcised and of any alien" (βδελύσσομαι κοίτην ἀπεριτμήτων καὶ

99 See Berkley, *Romans 2:17-29*, 141. Koch, *Schrift*, 260–61, overlooks this detail in claiming that the citation does nothing beyond confirming the point of 2:23. Wagner has a clear grasp of the argumentative thrust that all humans sin, in "Heralds of Isaiah," 214–15.

100 In *Beurteilung*, 37, Dabelstein confirms that the context of this citation demands that the term ἔθνη be translated as "pagan/heathen/Gentile." This citation renders highly implausible Thorsteinssen's hypothesis in *Paul's Interlocutor*, 196–231, that the interlocutor in this section is a Gentile pretending to be a Jew. Isaiah plainly states that Jewish behavior causes God to be dishonored among the Gentiles.

101 John M. G. Barclay, "Paul and Philo on Circumcision: Romans 2.25-9 in Social and Cultural Context," *NTS* 44 (1998) 544.

102 For example, Kühl, 91; Schmidt, 52–53; Käsemann,

71–72; Ziesler, 92; Dunn, 118–19; Fitzmyer, 319–20; Stuhlmacher, 48; Moo, 166.

103 Michel, 132.

104 BAGD (2000) 1107–8; Monika Rutenfranz, "ὠφελέω," *EDNT* 3 (1993) 511.

105 For example, Epictetus *Diss.* 2.24.25, "And what does the purple benefit (ὠφελεῖ) the robe?" See also 3.20.10-11.

106 Schlier, 88; Moo, 167; Rutenfranz, "ὠφελέω," 511; however, the references to salvation and its antithesis of wrath in 2:2-16 center on the question of comparative advantage between Jews and Gentiles and do not set forth Paul's doctrine of salvation through grace, which comes in 3:21-26.

107 Weiss, 128; Murray, 85; Cranfield, 171; Dunn, 119–20.

108 Wilckens, 1:154; Seifrid, *Justification*, 65, "a claim of religious preeminence."

παντὸς ἀλλοτρίου, Add. Esth. C 14:15).[109] During the period of the Maccabean struggle, circumcision assumed a crucial role as a "mark of Jewish national distinctiveness,"[110] "an essential expression of the national religion."[111] The Hasmoneans decreed that Gentiles could remain within the territory of Israel only "so long as they had themselves circumcised and were willing to observe the laws of the Jews" (Josephus *Ant.* 13.257 318–19, 397; 1 Macc 2:46). Marriages with uncircumcised partners were forbidden (Josephus *Ant.* 20.139, 145) because Gentiles bring "shame" and "defilement" (*Jub.* 30.7-12). Along with others, the Qumran community taught that circumcision frees adherents from the demonic powers (CD 16:4-6). The good angels, in contrast, were created as already circumcised, and Israel was enabled because of its circumcision to be sanctified, to share in their perfection and to participate in their heavenly worship (*Jub.* 15.27).[112]

On the basis of surveying all the relevant texts, Andreas Blaschke concludes that "the high estimation of circumcision corresponds to the low estimation of uncircumcision," which is "a synonym for what is lawless, alien, hateful and detestable."[113] The innovation of Paul's argument, therefore, is that the "advantage" of circumcision accrues only "if you observe the law" (ἐὰν νόμον πράσσῃς). In view of the supreme position of the Torah, this contention would have been difficult to refute. That faithful Jews were required not just to possess but also to obey the law was stated in classic form by Eleazar to the convert Izates of Adiabene: "you ought not merely to read the law but also, and even more, to do what is commanded in it."[114] But while Eleazar states this principle in support of the absolute necessity of circumcision even for a royal convert, Paul makes circumcision dependent on lawful praxis. He employs the verb πράσσω ("accomplish, do") that had been employed in 1:32; 2:1, 2, 3 with reference to performing evil deeds that warrant punishment, while the context in 2:26 requires the sense of "observe the law."[115] It is roughly synonymous with ποιεῖν νόμον ("do the law," 2:14), τὸν νόμον φυλάσσειν ("observe the law," 2:26), or τελεῖν τὸν νόμον ("observe the law," 2:27), all of which reiterate the premise that lawful performance is an absolutely binding requirement.

The radical inference is stated in the "on the other hand" clause of v. 25, that "if you are a transgressor of law," the imaginary interlocutor loses the potential advantage that circumcision offers. To fall into the status of a παραβάτης νόμου ("transgressor of law") requires that the violations be more than occasional or accidental.[116] This technical usage surfaces in Gal 2:18, "I become a transgressor,"[117] a state of being that can lead only to damnation. Since Paul has created such an elaborate denunciation of the bigoted interlocutor, the audience is prepared to view him as a transgressor in this comprehensive sense. The denouement is thus compelling, "your circumcision has become uncircumcision." In view of the primary meaning of the terms περιτομή and ἀκροβυστία as epithets hurled between Jews and Gentiles, Joel Marcus provides the appropriately shocking translation, "your circumcised glans becomes a foreskin."[118] This formulation would have evoked the

---

109 See Blaske, *Beschneidung*, 130–31.

110 Dunn, 119; see also Robert G. Hall, "Circumcision," *ABD* 1 (1992) 1027–28; Robert Goldenberg, "Beschneidung. IV. Judentum," *RGG⁴* 1:1358.

111 Rudolf Meyer, "περιτέμνω κτλ.," *TDNT* 6 (1968) 77.

112 See Isaac Kalimi, "'He was born circumcised': Some Midrashic Sources, Their Concept, Roots and Presumably Historical Context," *ZNW* 93 (2002) 4–5; Blaske, *Beschneidung*, 133–39.

113 Blaske, *Beschneidung*, 321.

114 Josephus *Ant.* 20.44, cited also by Wilckens, 1:154; and Blaske, *Beschneidung*, 411.

115 BAGD (2000) 860; Christian Mauer, "πράσσω κτλ.," *TDNT* 6 (1968) 635, notes that most of the NT references are in the context of doing evil deeds.

116 Haacker, 72, argues that παραβάτης implies something "habitual, fundamental."

117 Betz, *Galatians*, 121, refers to παραβάτης as a "legal term, here with special application to the Jewish Torah." See also Johannes Schneider, "παραβαίνω κτλ.," *TDNT* 5 (1967) 741. The use in classical sources is similar: Aeschylus *Eum.* 553 contrasts a transgressor (παρβάταν) with a righteous man (δίκαιος ὤν).

118 Marcus, "Circumcision and Uncircumcision," 75; see also Barclay, "Romans 2.25-9," 544. The use of these epithets renders implausible the hypothesis of Thorsteinssen, *Paul's Interlocutor*, 226–27, that the circumcised interlocutor is a Gentile.

practice of *epipasmos,* the surgical restoration of the foreskin practiced by Jews who wished to assimilate into Gentile culture.[119] This practice was viewed with horror by adherents of the Torah, as in *As. Mos.* 8.1-3, where a sign of the "second visitation and wrath" is present when Jews "shall be operated upon by physicians in order to bring forward their foreskins."[120]

This background enhances the extraordinary reversal of honor that Paul's argument evokes. The potential privilege that circumcision offers to Jews in comparison with Gentiles turns into its opposite, and the bigot becomes the very object of derision that he had habitually decried. The claim that disobedience cancels the privilege of circumcision is reminiscent of the Sicarii, who viewed fellow citizens who tolerated the rule of Gentiles as having lost their Jewish status and therefore being similarly suited for revolutionary violence.[121] However, Paul's argument aims to expose and overcome the cultural prejudices that provoke such violent consequences, because the argument of chap. 2 leads to the proclamation of salvation of Jews and Gentiles by grace alone in chap. 3 and to the advocacy of tolerant coexistence between believers of different cultural and theological orientation in chaps. 14–16.

■ **26** The first inference in the form of a rhetorical question that Paul draws from his thesis statement in v. 25 is that if uncircumcised persons observe the law, do they not gain the privileged status of being circumcised? Although most Jewish teachers in Paul's time would have denied this possibility,[122] the Christian audience that has followed this diatribe since the beginning of chap. 2 would naturally answer in the affirmative. Paul's formulation is shrewdly designed to evoke this response. It is not only that a question with οὐκ ("not") requires an affirmative response.[123] The condition he describes is that uncircumcised Gentiles "observe" (φυλάσσῃ) the "righteous requirements of the law" (τὰ δικαιώματα τοῦ νόμου), employing technical terminology of legal conformity from the LXX.[124] This terminology occurs throughout the LXX, for example, in Exod 15:26, where Moses promises prosperity "if . . . you observe all his righteous requirements (ἐὰν . . . φυλάσσῃς πάντα τὰ δικαιώματα αὐτοῦ)."[125] The possibility of such exemplary obedience on the part of Gentiles was established in Rom 2:14-16, and there is no indication in Paul's formulation that this is merely hypothetical.[126]

The apodosis of the rhetorical question is formulated with the logical future, "will not his uncircumcision be reckoned as circumcision?" The future verb λογισθήσεται ("it will be reckoned, counted") is required by the syntax of the "if" clause,[127] and should not be interpreted in reference to the eschatological judgment,[128] which is extraneous to this discussion of one group gaining a social or religious advantage over another. This

---

119 Dunn, 121, mentions this possibility, and Blaschke, *Beschneidung,* 139–44, discusses all of the relevant texts, beginning with *Jub.* 15.34, "they made their members like the Gentiles"; 1 Macc 1.15, "they made foreskins (ἀκροβυστίας) for themselves"; etc. See also Hall, "Circumcision," 1029.

120 See Blaschke, *Beschneidung,* 321; he also discusses early rabbinic sources that view *epipasmos* as one of the worst sins that a Jew can commit.

121 Haacker, 72, refers to Josephus *Bell.* 7.254-55: "For the Sicarii contrived against those who wanted to obey the Romans and began to treat them, in every way, as enemies (ὡς πολεμίοις προσεφέροντο), seizing their belongings, harassing them, and setting fire to their dwellings; for they would claim they were nothing more than foreigners (οὐδὲν γὰρ ἀλλοφύλων)."

122 See Dodd, 41; Michel, 133; Dunn, 122.

123 Cranfield, 173.

124 See Georg Bertram, "φυλάσσω, φυλακή," *TDNT* 9 (1974) 237-39; Gottlob Schrenk, "δικαίωμα,"

TDNT 2 (1964) 220; nowhere else does Paul employ the plural of δικαίωμα.

125 Other examples of this technical formulation are in Deut 4:40; 6:2; 7:11; 26:17; 28:45; 30:10, 16; 3 Kgdms 2:3; Pss 104:45; 118:5, 8; Prov 2:8; Mic 8:16; Ezek 11:20; 18:9; 20:13, 18, 19, 21; 43:11.

126 For example, Käsemann, 73; Cranfield, 173; and others maintain the purely hypothetical nature of this argument in order to prevent a contradiction with Paul's conclusion in 3:9 that "both Jews and Greeks are under the power of sin." Barrett, 58, is correct in arguing that "the 'when' of the parallel in v. 14 suggests that the possibility is not merely hypothetical."

127 Kühl, 92; Moulton and Turner, *Grammar III,* 115–16; Meyer, 1:132, refers to this as the assessment of "older expositors."

128 Meyer, 1:132; Zahn, 143; Weiss, 130; Lagrange, 56; Kuss, 90; Schlier, 26; Wilckens, 1:155.

would be rendered more clearly if Marcus's translation were followed, with the abusive term ἀκροβυστία translated as "foreskin," a derogatory term for Gentiles.[129] Paul's point is that if Gentiles obey the law of God, they suffer no disadvantage in comparison with circumcised Jews. As John Barclay points out, "that non-Jews could be counted as 'circumcised' merely on the basis of 'keeping the just requirements of the law' is an astonishing claim."[130] Yet for the Christian audience of this brilliant rhetorical argument, assent to this rhetorical question is ineluctable, and thereby Paul establishes a crucial foundation not only for the rest of this pericope, but also for the later argument (in chaps. 12–16) in favor of equalizing honor between members of the Christian community despite their differences in culture and social status.

■ 27 Paul's second inference from the antithesis in v. 25 concerns a remarkable role reversal. Whereas the bigot had judged the Gentiles as infinitely inferior, now they perform the law in such a way that they become the symbolic judges of the bigot. He refers to such an exemplary Gentile as ἡ ἐκ φύσεως ἀκροβυστία τὸν νόμον τελοῦσα ("the one from physical uncircumcision who satisfies the law"), which takes up the point of the preceding verse that obedience of the law can be reckoned as equivalent to circumcision without a physical change. The retention of the physical foreskin renders this as a kind of title for Gentiles, signaled in my translation by quotation marks.[131] The verb τελέω is a rough equivalent of φυλάσσω in the preceding sentence, although lacking the religious resonance noted above; here it appears for the only time in Paul's letters in a legalistic

context[132] with the connotation of "fulfill" or "satisfy."[133] That faithful believers would participate in "judging" sinners at the final assize was widely assumed in Judaism[134] and early Christianity,[135] and the surprising reversal between Gentiles and Jews appears also in the Jesus tradition (Matt 12:41-42; Luke 11:31).[136]

Whether this judgment by righteous Gentiles is direct or symbolic remains unclear, but the target of the diatribe is unequivocal: "you," the bigot, "law's transgressor." That the bigot had failed to obey the law was established in Rom 2:1-5, and the expression "transgressor of law" (παραβάτης νόμου) was employed in reference to the bigot in 2:25, but the precise meaning of the phrase διὰ γράμματος καὶ περιτομῆς ("by/through letter and circumcision") remains a matter of debate. The well-grounded, nineteenth-century approach to διά as referring to attendant circumstances leads to the plausible interpretation of the bigot "who transgresses the law notwithstanding letter and circumcision."[137] To translate διά in an instrumental manner imposes an antithesis between spirit and letter that matches the thought in 2 Cor 3 but is inappropriate for this diatribe against the bigot.[138] Paul is not arguing that the bigot as a representative of Judaism "focused too much on the outward rite,"[139] but that despite the possession of a written law and circumcision, he nevertheless fails to obey. This leads to the astounding reversal in which the uncircumcised Gentile stands in judgment of the circumcised Jew whose actions reveal him to be "law's transgressor."

129 Marcus, "Circumcision and Uncircumcision," 74–78.
130 Barclay, "Romans 2.25-9," 545.
131 See Helmut Koester, "φύσις κτλ.," *TDNT* 9 (1974) 272; Kühl, 92.
132 Noted by Cranfield, 59.
133 Hans Hübner, "τελέω," *EDNT* 3 (1993) 346; BAGD (2000) 997.
134 For example, see Dan 7:22; Wis 3:8; *1 En.* 91.12; 98.12; *Apoc. Ab.* 29.19-21; 1QHab 5:4-5.
135 For example, see 1 Cor 6:2; Rev 2:26; 20:4, discussed by Mathias Rissi, "κρίνω, κρίσις," *EDNT* 2 (1991) 320; Michel, 133–34.
136 See particularly Lagrange, 56. Wilckens, 1:156, is skeptical that Paul knew the Synoptic tradition at this point, but an oral form of this tradition does not seem unlikely.
137 Meyer, 1:134; Weiss, 131; Sanday and Headlam, 67; this view was followed by later commentators such as Kühl, 1:92–93; Lagrange, 56; Lietzmann, 44; Schmidt, 55; Kuss, 90; Käsemann, 74; Cranfield, 174; Morris, 141; Murray, 87; BAGD (2000) 224.3c; Stuhlmacher, 50; Moo, 172–73.
138 Gottlob Schrenk, "γράμμα," *TDNT* 1 (1933) 765: "It is precisely through what is written and through circumcision that the Jew is a transgressor." See also Hans Hübner, "γράμμα," *EDNT* 1 (1990) 258; Schlatter, 73; Dunn, 123.
139 Dunn, 123.

■ **28** Paul explains the reversal by an eloquent, elliptic antithesis that some interpreters view as the climax of this pericope.[140] For rhetorical reasons, the honorific terms "Jew" and "circumcision" are the predicates in v. 28 and the subjects in v. 29, while the reduplicated subjects are missing from v. 28 and the predicates are missing from v. 29a-b, while the subject "Jew" is again elided in v. 29c.[141] While perfectly understandable in Greek, the translation of this antithetical sentence requires the addition of the missing subjects and predicates, which I place in brackets.[142]

The antithesis between $\dot{\epsilon}\nu\ \tau\hat{\omega}\ \varphi\alpha\nu\epsilon\rho\hat{\omega}$ ("in public, in outward appearance") in v. 28 and $\dot{\epsilon}\nu\ \tau\hat{\omega}\ \kappa\rho\upsilon\pi\tau\hat{\omega}$ ("hidden, in a hidden manner") in v. 29 is used here with the same social implication as in Matt 6, which criticizes the perversion of religious works into means of status acquisition. Rather than acting so as to be "praised by men" (Matt 6:2) or "seen by men" (Matt 6:5), Jesus recommends giving alms and praying $\dot{\epsilon}\nu\ \tau\hat{\omega}\ \kappa\rho\upsilon\pi\tau\hat{\omega}$ ("hidden, in secret," Matt 6:4, 6). The TR adds the Pauline formula to the end of Matt 6:4, "your father who sees in secret ($\dot{\epsilon}\nu\ \tau\hat{\omega}\ \kappa\rho\upsilon\pi\tau\hat{\omega}$) will reward you openly/publicly ($\dot{\alpha}\pi\sigma\delta\acute{\omega}\sigma\epsilon\iota\ \sigma\sigma\iota\ \dot{\epsilon}\nu\ \tau\hat{\omega}\ \varphi\alpha\nu\epsilon\rho\hat{\omega}$),"[143] but this shifts the antithesis away from the issue of status acquisition that both Jesus and Paul had in view.[144] A similar antithesis occurs in Isocrates *Nic.* 30.5, who maintains that the truest praises come not in the public eye ($\dot{\epsilon}\nu\ \tau\hat{\omega}\ \varphi\alpha\nu\epsilon\rho\hat{\omega}$) but when one is alone with oneself ($\pi\alpha\rho$' $\alpha\dot{\upsilon}\tau\sigma\hat{\iota}\varsigma\ \ddot{\sigma}\nu\tau\epsilon\varsigma$). There is a more distant parallel in Epictetus, who criticizes those who love the appearance of being prestigious Stoics but lack the inner conformity to Stoic doctrine (Epictetus *Diss.* 2.19-28).[145] In the context of Paul's diatribe, the expression the "public Jew"[146] as defined in 2:17-23 is the one who boasts in his superiority over Gentiles and in his possession of the law.[147] Similarly the "public circumcision" is that which is openly claimed to be "advantageous" in comparison with others who remain uncircumcised (2:25). This social dimension is overlooked by commentators who stress the allegedly superior spirituality of the Christian as opposed to the Jewish faith, which in effect establishes a new honor system that undercuts Paul's diatribe.[148] His creation of the bigot as the imaginary interlocutor aims to undercut every claim of cultural and religious superiority, as I have repeatedly shown by reference to the conclusion of Paul's argument in chaps. 12–16.

The term $\sigma\dot{\alpha}\rho\xi$ appears to be used here in the sense of the physical organ that is circumcised.[149] Cranfield lifts up the parallels in *Exod. Rab.* 19 (81c), which states: "If the seal of Abraham is not in your flesh, you may not eat (of the meal)." Also *Targum Cant.* 3:8 "and every one of them had the seal of circumcision in his flesh, as it was sealed in the flesh of Abraham." In contrast to these traditional sources, however, Paul denies that such fleshly circumcision is genuine without accompanying obedience or when it becomes a matter of status acquisition.[150] In both instances, the bigot's behavior disqualifies him.

---

140 See Kühl, 93; Käsemann, 74; Cranfield, 175; Dunn, 123; Blaschke, *Beschneidung*, 411.

141 See particularly the clear analysis in Godet, 131, and Käsemann, 74.

142 My translation of vv. 28-29 largely follows the succinct formulation of Barrett, 59–60.

143 See Rudolf Bultmann and Dieter Lührmann, "$\varphi\alpha\nu\epsilon\rho\acute{\sigma}\varsigma$," *TDNT* 9 (1974) 3.

144 A further shift in the antithesis is visible in John 7:4 in reference to the need for public recognition: "no man works in secret ($\dot{\epsilon}\nu\ \kappa\rho\upsilon\pi\tau\hat{\omega}$) if he seeks to be known openly ($\dot{\epsilon}\nu\ \pi\alpha\rho\rho\eta\sigma\acute{\iota}\alpha$). If you do these things, show yourself outwardly to the world ($\varphi\alpha\nu\acute{\epsilon}\rho\omega\sigma\sigma\nu\ \sigma\epsilon\alpha\upsilon\tau\grave{\sigma}\nu\ \tau\hat{\omega}\ \kappa\acute{\sigma}\sigma\mu\omega$)."

145 See the discussion in Anton Fridrichsen, "Der wahre Jude und sein Lob: Röm 2:28f, " in *Exegetical Writings. A Selection*, trans. and ed. C. C. Cargounis and T. Fornberg, WUNT 76 (Tübingen: Mohr-Siebeck, 1994) 191.

146 Other classical examples of $\dot{\epsilon}\nu\ \tau\hat{\omega}\ \varphi\alpha\nu\epsilon\rho\hat{\omega}$ with the connotation of "public" are Xenophon *Hell.* 6.4.16; *Mem.* 1.1.10.

147 See also Bachmann, "*Verus Israel*," 504.

148 For example, Zahn, 144; Dodd, 42; Schreiner, 142–44. Murray, 88, contends that "the outward has no spiritual significance except as the sign and seal of that which it represents."

149 See Zeller, 74; Cranfield, 175.

150 See Barrett, 60: "The 'outward Jew' . . . externalizes his religion and esteems his membership of the people of God as a visible privilege which he can parade before the world." In *Terms*, 140, I stressed that in the light of Paul's earlier discussions in Gal 6:13ff. and Phil 3:3ff., Rom 2 "rejects the circumcision which is openly visible in the flesh because it has become the source of boasting for the nomist and because on the basis of such boasting, the nomist rejects the revelation of God's righteousness

■ 29 The antithesis to the public boasting of the bigot's status and accomplishment is that "the hidden Jew [is a Jew]," whereby the expression ἐν τῷ κρυπτῷ refers to the person who makes no such display. Picking up the line of argument from the Jesus tradition, this is a matter of giving alms in secret and praying in the privacy of one's closet (Matt 6:1-8), not because inward religion is inherently superior to external practice[151] but rather to avoid the ulterior motive of performing religious acts as a means of status acquisition.

In v. 29b Paul extends the metaphor of outward and hidden manifestations in even more provocative directions that have come to dominate the exegesis of this passage to the point that the social dimension is usually lost from sight. The reference to "circumcision of the heart" stands in place of hidden circumcision, evoking a series of biblical associations.[152] "Circumcise the foreskin of your heart!" is the admonishment in Deut 10:16, with echoes in Deut 30:6; Lev 26:41; Jer 4:4; 6:10; 9:25; Ezek 44:7, 9 and later literature, referring to the need to obey God's law with a purified heart.[153] The force of Paul's argument about the hidden Jew performing the law relies on this tradition, but there is an innovation in his critique of using circumcision as a means of status acquisition.[154] The Jew with a circumcised heart, whether of Jewish or Gentile lineage,[155] performs the law out of a transformed heart, without regard to reputa-

tion. The word καρδία ("heart") in this context refers to "a transformed person, turned towards obedience," a theme developed in Rom 6:17, and "towards faith," which is developed in 10:8-10.[156]

The reference to "spirit" is also associated in the Jewish tradition with the circumcision of the heart, for example, in *Jub.* 1.23: "But after this they will return to me in all uprighteousness and with all of their heart and soul. And I shall cut off the foreskin of their heart and the foreskin of the heart of their descendants. And I shall create for them a holy spirit, and I shall purify them so that they will not turn away from following me from that day and forever."[157] Once again, Paul's argument gains strength from this tradition, but he develops it in an innovative, antithetical manner. The antithesis between spirit and letter is a Pauline innovation[158] that appears for the first time in 2 Cor 3:6 in the context of a controversy over the proper hermeneutical method. Although the commentators ordinarily follow the lead of 2 Corinthians in defining the antithesis in Romans in a strictly theological manner,[159] here it is the social dimension that is central, even though πνεῦμα in this context clearly refers to the divine rather than the human spirit.[160] To act in the spirit according to this diatribe is the opposite of using the law as a means to gain advantages over others.

The relevance of Paul's concluding reference to the

---

in Christ which ushered in the new aeon." This reference to boasting as a theological issue goes only part way in clarifying the dimension of social competition that Paul is countering in this diatribe.

151 See, e.g., Albrecht Oepke, "κρύπτω κτλ.," *TDNT* 3 (1965) 977; Hans-Joachim Ritz, "κρύπτω κτλ.," *EDNT* 2 (1991) 324; Dunn, 124.

152 See particularly Eduard Schweizer, "'Der Jude im Verborgenen . . . , dessen Lob nicht von Menschen, sondern von Gott kommt.' Zu Röm 2,28 f. und Matt 6,1-18," in J. Gnilka, ed., *Neues Testament und Kirche für Rudolph Schnackenburg* (Freiburg: Herder, 1974) 118–19.

153 In *Romans 2:17-29*, 147–49, Berkley unnecessarily narrows this intertextual reference down to Jer 9:25-26. This theme of the circumcised heart is continued in Qumran, "For he did not circumcise the foreskin of his heart" (1QS 5:5; see also 1QpHab 11:13; 4Q 177, 184); there are also close parallels in *Jub.*1.23; *Odes Sol.* 11.1-3; Acts 7:51.

154 Barclay, "Romans 2.25-9," 552, refers to the sharp-

ness of Paul's "antithesis between the two sorts of circumcision" that results in "declaring that Jew and Gentile can equally count as circumcised."

155 See Schlier, 89; Blaschke, *Beschneidung*, 414.

156 Barclay, "Romans 2.25-9," 553; see also Jewett, *Terms*, 333, where καρδία is defined as "the center of man which is encountered by God."

157 See also *Odes Sol.* 11.1-3.

158 See Blaschke, *Beschneidung*, 412.

159 For example, Schmidt, 55; Schweizer, "Jude im Verborgenen," 122; and Wilckens, 1:157, interpret the antithesis as a critique of works righteousness and an affirmation of justification by faith; Schlier, 90, argues that the Spirit makes the fulfillment of the law possible, and Lagrange, 57, claims that the realm of the Spirit transcends the literal commandments of the law; Murray, 89, refers to the "impotence which belongs to law as mere law" and to the Spirit as "life-giving power."

160 Haacker, 73, argues that an explicit reference to the Holy Spirit would break out of the context of this

proper source of praise has long puzzled scholars,[161] evoking some implausible interpretations.[162] A series of commentators suggest a wordplay between the Hebrew words for "Jew" and "praise,"[163] but as Käsemann remarks, such an arcane reference "would hardly have been intelligible to the Roman community."[164] Käsemann and others argue on the basis of 1 Cor 4:5 that ἔπαινος refers to an eschatological reward,[165] but how such a reward could have been thought to come ἐξ ἀνθρώπων ("from people") remains thereby unexplained. Fridrichsen points to the parallels in Matt 6:1-8 and in Stoic teachings about living according to an internal standard rather than conforming to the opinions of others.[166] Barclay suggests a "concrete social correlation" between this final clause and conflicts between Gentile and Jewish Christians in Rome, with particular reference to tensions arising from Paul's argument about circumcision.[167] This would fit the classical understanding of ἔπαινος as "approval" or "applause," which correlates with the competitive social context that Paul exploits throughout this diatribe.[168] It is significant that this pericope ends on the question of gaining honor. While the seeking of praise from fellow humans lies at the root of the perversion of Jewish—and Gentile—advantages, those who receive the gift of the circumcised heart rely on God's praise alone.[169] This prepares the way for Paul's proclamation of grace that comes to all, without reference to achievement or status (3:21-31), and that Christ welcomes all, Gentile and Jew alike, into his realm (15:7-12).

---

diatribe, but there is no likelihood that Paul refers here to the human spirit; see Jewett, *Terms*, 197. In *Holy Spirit*, 113–15, Ervin makes an implausible case that the spirit of the law stands here in contrast to the letter of the law.

161 See Fridrichsen, "Wahre Jude," 192; Barclay, "Romans 2.25-9," 546; Käsemann, 77, speaks of the "surprising introduction of the motif of ἔπαινος."

162 See Fridrichsen, "Wahre Jude," 192.

163 The wordplay between יְהוּדָ־ ("Jehuda") and יָדָה ("praise") is found in Gen 29:35 and 49:8. According to Murray, 89, this wordplay hypothesis goes back to Haldane, Gifford, and Sanday and Headlam; it is advanced by Godet, 131; Schmidt, 55; Barrett, 60; Cranfield, 175; Morris, 142.

164 Käsemann, 77.

165 Käsemann, 77; Wilckens, 1:158; Otfried Hofius, "ἔπαινος, ἐπαινέω," *EDNT* 2 (1991) 17; Schreiner, 144, defines the eschatological reward as "eternal life."

166 Fridrichsen, "Wahre Jude," 191–92, based on citations from Epictetus *Diss*. 4.8.17, who reports that the philosopher Euphrates did everything for himself and God. Marcus Aurelius Τὰ εἰς ἐαυτὸν 4.19.1 remarks that since immortality comes only through memoralized deeds, "what then is praise in respect to the living? (ἀλλὰ πρὸς τὸν ζῶντα τί ὁ ἔπαινος)." In 12.11.1 Marcus Aurelius says, "So great a right does no person have to do other than that which God will praise (ὁ θεὸς ἐπαινεῖν)."

167 Barclay, "Romans 2.25-9," 548.

168 Herbert Preisker, "ἔπαινος," *TDNT* 2 (1964) 586, referring to such applause as "a characteristic goal in antiquity," and citing Hegel's reference to "the restless urge of individuals to display themselves, to show what they can make of themselves, and thus to enjoy their standing with their fellows."

169 In contrast, Heil, 32–33, argues that this verse forces Paul's "audience to dismiss any previously held beliefs that the Jews will be be favored in God's judgment because they possess and know his Law. . . . Paul has stunned his audience with this penetrating attack."

3

The First Part of the Third Pericope

The Evidence of Universal Sin

a. Diatribe Refuting Objections to Impartial Judgment

1/ 'Therefore what benefit does the Jew have? Or what is the[a] usefulness of circumcision?'
2/ [The benefit] is huge in every respect. Primarily [the benefit is huge] for[b] indeed they were entrusted with the oracles of God.
3/ 'What then if some were unfaithful? Will their unfaith abrogate[c] the faithfulness of God?'
4/ By no means! But let[d] God show himself to be true but "every person [show himself to be] a liar!" Just as[e] it has been written, "That you may be righteous in your words and shall be victorious[f] when you judge."
5/ 'But if our wrongdoing proves God's righteousness, what shall we say?[g] Wouldn't God who inflicts wrath be unjust?'
(I speak in a human[h] manner.) 6/ By no means! Otherwise how will[i] God judge the world?
7/ 'But[j] if the truth of God by my falsehood gains benefit to his glory, why then should I be judged as a sinner?'
8/ [Why should we] also not [be judged as sinners] just as we are slandered [to be] and[k] just as some allege us to say, 'Let us do bad things[l] in order that good things might come?'[m] Their condemnation is well deserved.

a   The elimination of the article ἡ by ℵ* G 323 1241 1505 2495 pc is not widely enough attested to be original, and may have resulted from a dictation error or haplography since a single η without the rough breathing was used immediately before: ἤ τίς ἡ ("or what [is] the"). Another possibility is that τίς was understood as an interrogative adjective modifying ὠφέλεια ("advantage") rather than as an interrogative pronoun and the subject of the sentence. The inclusion of the article is supported by ℵc A B D K L Ψ 33 6 69 88 104 326 330 365 424 614 945 1175 1319 1506 1573 1735 1739 1836 1874 1881 2344 2464 Maj.
b   Several variants arose in response to Paul's expression that implies both a continuation of a series and an antithesis of some sort: πρῶτον μὲν γὰρ ὅτι (lit. "first, on the one hand, for, that") as found in ℵ A D² K L 33 69 88 104 323 326 330 424* 614 945 1175 1241 1243 1505 1735 1836 1874 2464c 2495

Maj syh cop, with strong claims to originality. The γάρ ("for") is deleted by B D* G Ψ 81 365 1319 1506 1573 2344 2464* pc latt syp bomss and the entire expression is replaced by πρῶτοι γάρ ("for [the] first one") by 6 1739 (424c) Eus.
c   Tischendorf suggests an emendation of καταργήσει ("he will abrogate") to the subjunctive, καταργήσῃ ("he may abrogate"), because both would have sounded the same and the future seems odd in this context, but his suggestion has not evoked adherence; see Lagrange, 63, and the commentary below.
d   In place of the theologically problematic but widely attested and undoubtedly original term γινέσθω ("let him be/become"), G has the reading ἔστω ("let him be"). For the discussion of the awkward theological implications among the older theologians, see Cranfield, 1:181.
e   A difficult but fortunately inconsequential choice must be made between καθώς ("just as") found in A D G K L 6 33 69 88 104 323 326 330 365 424 614 945 1175 1241 1243 1319 1505 1506 1573 1735 1739 1836 1874 1881 2344 2464 2495 Maj and καθάπερ ("just as") in ℵ B Ψ. Nestle-Aland[26/27] shifted to the former, which seems reasonable, but the question is not discussed by recent commentators or by Metzger. The comparative function of καθώς (BAGD 391) seems slightly awkward in the context of the citation it introduces and thus should be preferred as the more difficult reading. The substitution by καθάπερ may also have been motivated by the desire to avoid undue repetition of the word used twice in v. 8 and again in v. 10.
f   The use of the subjunctive νικήσῃς ("you may prevail") in B G L Ψ 69 323 330 365 614 945 1175 1241 1243 1505 1573 1735 1739 1836 1874 1881 2344 2495 pm is the easier reading that follows the LXX, compared with νικήσεις ("you shall prevail") in ℵ A D K 6 81 88 104 326 424 1319 2464 pm (33 1506 uncertain). Since the pronunciation of both forms would have been identical, this variant may be a very early dictation error. I shall take up below the question, not dealt with by earlier commentators, of whether Paul's argument favors an intentional change to the indicative. For an assessment favoring the Nestle-Aland[26] preference for νικήσεις see Cranfield, 1:182.
g   Nestle-Aland[25] (1963) cites Paul W. Schmiedel's conjecture ("Ein paar Konjekturen zum Text des Neuen Testaments," in Festgabe Adolf Kaegi von Schülern und Freunden dargebracht [Zurich: Frauenfeld, 1919] 181) that v. 7 originally followed at this point, which would bring the two "but if . . ." sentences next to each other. This conjecture seems

implausible since God's judging the world in v. 5b does not lead naturally to the question in v. 7 about whether God's truth can be advanced by falsehood. Schmiedel's suggestion, however, signals an odd parallelism in the text that needs to be taken into account.

h   A variant weakly attested by 1739 ^{mg} sa (Or$^{mss\ Graeca\ apud\ Or^{lat}}$) places "human" in the plural at this point, which would result in the translation "according to the people." The entire expression κατὰ ἄνθρωπον λέγω ("Over against a human I say") is deleted by Cl, although this is not noted in NA^{27}.

i   Just as in Rom 2:16, there is a difficult choice to be made between the present and the future tense of "judge." K^c Ψ 6 69 88 104 323 326 330 365 614 424 945 1175 1241 1319 1505 1735 1739 1836 1874 1881 2344 2495 *Maj* latt cop have the accent indicating future κρινεῖ while B^2 D^2 K* 365 629 1243 1506 *pc* have the present κρίνει; ℵ A B* D* G L P 33 1573 2464 have no accents. It is evident from the fact that the first manuscripts with extensive punctuation are from the 6th and 7th centuries that the decision about accenting this word probably occurred very late; although the intonation of either reading would have differed, we have no direct evidence that an independent oral tradition was handed down. So the decision has to be made on the basis

of context. The wide consensus of commentators should probably be followed that the future is required here.

j   There is strong evidence in B D G K L P Ψ *Maj* 6 33 69 88 104 323 326 330 424 436 451 459 614 629 945 1175 1241 1243 1319^c 1505 1962 1735 1739 1836 1874 1881 1962 2200 2344 2464 2492 2495 *Lect* ar b d g mon o vg sy^{p,h} sa eth slav Or^{lat} Ambst Chr Pel Aug$^{1/4}$ for γάρ ("for") in place of δέ ("but") found in ℵ A 81 256 263 365 1319* 1506 1573 1852 2127 *pc* vg^{mss} bo Aug$^{3/4}$. Metzger, *Textual Commentary*, 448, reports that the committee decided on the latter on argumentative grounds that are also compelling to me.

k   The absence of καί ("and") in B K 326 629* *pc* may have derived from a dictation error with words having the same opening sound following each other: καὶ καθώς. This omission may also be a conscious decision to relate the second καθώς ("also") clause to βλασφημούμεθα ("we are slandered").

l   The absence of the article before κακά ("evil") in D* 1646 is an error that was appropriately corrected by a later scribe of the D manuscript.

m   The addition of the words ἐφ᾽ ἡμᾶς ("upon us") in 0219 69 81 330 1735 *pc* ar bo may be an attempt to provide theological precision.

Analysis

In the last two pericopes Paul made a case that Jewish descent provides no exemption from the impartial judgment of God that is based on works actually performed rather than status allegedly inherited. This raises the question of whether the divine election of Israel as a chosen people had been abrogated. If so, this would imply that God's Word was invalid, a question that Paul takes up in explicit detail in 9:6ff. Does not the argument about impartial judgment invalidate the divine promises to Israel? How can one say that, when confronted with Christ, Israel violates the righteousness of God? Paul makes use of the diatribe device of the imaginary interlocutor to pose four pairs of questions[1] to deal with these crucial issues and to drive home his underlying argument about the universal sinfulness of humankind. The doubling of the questions gives the impression of satisfying completeness and matches the stylistic inclination of Greco-Roman rhetoric.[2] The diatribal exchanges[3] are organized as doubled answers to

---

1   See Bornkamm, "Theologie als Teufelskunst," 142–46; Song, *Diatribe*, 94–95; Tobin, *Paul's Rhetoric*, 118–21; Alain Gignac, "Procès de l'human ou procès de Dieu? Le jeu intertextuel entre Rm 3,1-9 et Ps 50 (LXX)," *RB* 112 (2005) 46–62. My translation uses single quotes in vv. 1, 3, 5, 7, and 8 to designate the questions of the imaginary interlocutor. Paul's replies are indented. The single quotation marks in v. 8 also indicate a libertinistic slogan slanderously imposed by people like the Jewish interlocutor onto Paul's ministry.

2   See Fridrichsen, "Paulusbriefen," 291–94.

3   I have adapted this category from Stowers's use of "dialogical exchange" in *Diatribe*, 164–65, to describe the interaction between Paul and the friendly interrogator in 3:27ff. Stowers distinguishes between that more friendly dialogue and the sharper dialectic involving the false conclusions drawn by the interrogator in passages like 3:1-8, but this contrast is less compelling to me in the light of recent work on 3:1-8. Schmeller, *Diatribe*, does not deal with this pericope.

these questions, with citations in 3:4.[4] Each of these questions could plausibly be drawn from the argument of the preceding two pericopes, so that Paul is really dealing in this section with logical objections to the impartial judgment of God.[5] Each set of questions is succinctly and vehemently answered before the next set begins, which pattern produces a vivid impression of a dialogue between Paul and the imaginary interlocutor. The viewpoint of the interlocutor shifts in this diatribe as if he were convinced by Paul's previous argument and has given up the pose of the bigoted teacher who is fundamentally superior to the rest of humankind.[6] Now he takes up the Pauline doctrine of divine impartiality and seeks to expose its inner contradictions. This technique allows Paul to deal with questions while avoiding "any direct confrontation with the Roman Christians."[7] The pace is rapid and witty, marked by frequent elisions, with the interlocutor cleverly finding apparent flaws in Paul's argument and Paul quickly replying to each query. The final line of the pericope is Paul's indignant comment about those who allege that his doctrine of impartial judgment and grace results in libertinism.

The logical connections between this pericope and the rest of Romans have been a matter of debate. Some have argued that this is a diversion from the main flow of the argument[8] or that it provides a transitional bridge to later chapters (such as chaps. 6–7, 9–11).[9] Godet perceives the argumentative flow to be "the most difficult, perhaps, in the Epistle,"[10] and Dodd assesses the flow of thought as "obscure and feeble."[11] Räisänen contends that Paul loses track of his argument in this pericope out

of excessive zeal,[12] and Lietzmann senses that this passage drifts away from the main theme of his letter.[13] Stowers clarifies these obscurities by a theory of diatribal dialogues with the interlocutor posing four questions in double form,[14] while Romano Penna suggests that 3:1-4 provides a "prism" for the later development of 9:1—11:36 and 3:4-8 does the same for 6:1—8:39.[15]

Joachim Jeremias proposed a chiastic structure with the references to divine "truth" and "righteousness" in v. 4 taken up in reverse order in the rhetorical questions of vv. 5 and 7-8.[16] Some of the links between questions and answers are enhanced by alliteration at the ends and beginnings of sentences, with $\tau\rho\acute{o}\pi ov/\pi\rho\hat{\omega}\tau ov$ in v. 2 and $\gamma\acute{e}vot\tauo/\gamma\iota v\acute{e}\sigma\vartheta\omega$ in v. 4. There is a striking resonance in the anaphora between vv. 5 and 7:

$$\epsilon\grave{\iota}\ \delta\grave{\epsilon}\ \acute{\eta}\ \grave{\alpha}\delta\iota\kappa\acute{\iota}\alpha\ \acute{\eta}\mu\hat{\omega}v\ \vartheta\epsilon o\hat{v}\ldots$$
$$\epsilon\grave{\iota}\ \delta\grave{\epsilon}\ \acute{\eta}\ \grave{\alpha}\lambda\acute{\eta}\vartheta\epsilon\iota\alpha\ \tauo\hat{v}\ \vartheta\epsilon o\hat{v}\ldots$$

There is a potentially ironic paronomasia between $\pi\epsilon\rho\iota\sigma\sigma\acute{o}v$ ("benefit, advantage") in v. 1 and $\grave{\epsilon}\pi\epsilon\rho\acute{\iota}\sigma\epsilon v\sigma\epsilon v$ ("provide benefit, advantage") in v. 7. There are wordplays in vv. 2-3 between "faithfulness" and "unfaithfulness" with the $\pi\iota\sigma\tau$- stem employed four times, and in v. 5 between "unrighteousness" and "righteousness" with the $\delta\iota\kappa$- stem reiterated three times.[17] The $\delta\iota\kappa$- stem recurs in the final verse that brings this lively passage to a satisfying oral conclusion when read aloud in the Roman congregations.

4   See Weiss, "Beiträge," 220.

5   See Stowers, *Diatribe*, 149: "The section 3:1-9 functions as an indictment of false inferences from and objections to his indictment of both Jews and Gentiles in 1:18—2:29." See also Tobin, *Paul's Rhetoric*, 118–19.

6   Stanley K. Stowers, "Paul's Dialogue with a Fellow Jew in Romans 3:1-9," *CBQ* 46 (1984) 717, maintains that the interlocutor now affirms "exactly what is at the heart of Paul's argument: Whatever happens in history, God is righteous."

7   Tobin, *Paul's Rhetoric*, 119; in "Procès," 51–59, Gignac's thesis about a lawsuit with a series of indictments implies a much more combative tone.

8   Jülicher, 242; Dodd, 48; Kuss, 1:99; Schlier, 176; Black, 62; Käsemann, 78; Zeller, 77.

9   Campbell, "Romans iii," 23; Dunn, 1:129–30; Pesch, 11, 37.

10 Godet, 131; David R. Hall, "Romans 3:1-8 Reconsidered," *NTS* 29 (1983) 183, also describes this as "one of the most puzzling passages in the epistle."

11 Dodd, 46.

12 Heikki Räisänen, "Zum Verständis von Röm 3,1-8," in *Torah*, 185, cites Jülicher, 242, on this point.

13 Lietzmann, 45.

14 Stowers, *Rereading*, 165–75, modifying the analysis in Stowers, "Romans 3:1-9," 715.

15 Romano Penna, "The Structural Function of 3:1-8 in the Letter to the Romans," *Paul the Apostle*, 1:88–89.

16 Jeremias, "Chiasmus," 155.

17 See Dunn, 1:134.

Rhetorical Disposition

Exegesis

■ **1** If the true Jew has circumcision of the heart rather than in the flesh, and consequently may not share Jewish ethnicity as the last pericope argued, then it is logical to ask τί οὖν τὸ περισσόν ("what therefore is the benefit") of being a Jew.[18] While it is clear that the words τί οὖν introduce an "inferential question" arising from the preceding pericope,[19] commentators have not explained why the first question is posed by τί and the second by τίς. Smyth explains, "τίς asks a question concerning the class, τί concerning the nature of a thing."[20] Paul's interlocutor is therefore inquiring about the nature of the advantage that Jews enjoy. Cleverly taking over what he understands to be Paul's viewpoint, the interlocutor speaks of the Jews in the third person, as if he were not one.[21] The context of the expression τὸ περισσόν is unique in the NT, because it otherwise refers to the superabundance of the new age.[22] Paul refers to the verbal form of this term in 5:20 and 2 Cor 7:4 to refer to the surpassing grace and comfort of Christ, while Matt 5:20 uses it to refer to the surpassing righteousness of the kingdom of God, and John 10:10 uses it to refer to

---

18 This rhetorical question renders implausible the
    suggestion by Thorsteinsson, *Paul's Interlocutor*,
    197–231, that the interlocutor is a Gentile claiming
    to be a Jew.
19 Meyer, 1:138; Stowers, *Rereading*, 166; Palmer, τί
    οὖν, 201–2.
20 Smyth, *Grammar*, §1265.
21 See Thorsteinsson, *Paul's Interlocutor*, 237–38.
22 See Friedrich Hauck, "περισσεύω κτλ.," *TDNT* 6
    (1968): 59–61.

abundant life. The verbal adjective περισσός is used in classical sources to describe "unusual, noteworthy" persons, as in Hippolytus's question to Theseus, whether he views himself "as a noteworthy man (ὡς περισσὸς ὢν ἀνήρ)."[23] The interlocutor's question is comparable to Epictetus in *Diss.* 1.17.13, "What therefore is [your] admirable" occupation (τί οὖν τὸ θαυμαστόν ἐστιν)?" Although Paul's question relates to "the extra"[24] that Jews have over others, it sounds neither polemical nor ironic; the interlocutor simply pursues the logical inference from the preceding pericope. The parallel question about the value of circumcision makes a similar impression. The word ὠφέλεια, found only here in Paul, refers to usefulness or profitability.[25] For example, an Egyptian papyrus (*P.Oxy.* 12. Nr. 1409.11) contains the line that everyone "is aware of the usefulness" (γεινομένην ὠφ[ελί]αν) of repairing the dikes.

A comprehensive range is conveyed when the first question is couched in terms of comparative advantage and the second in terms of utility. The second question pursues the logical inference that if circumcision is ultimately a matter of the heart, of disposition (Rom 2:28-29), what use is its physical enactment? If God's election of the Jewish people and the sign of circumcision are set aside, neither the witness of Scripture nor the "credibility of God" can survive. The questions Paul constructs for his imaginary interlocutor are anything but "frivolous,"[26] either in and of themselves or with regard to the larger purpose that they serve, namely to demonstrate that Jews participate along with Gentiles in sin as suppression of the truth.[27] Although the interlocutor is the

same as in the preceding chapter, the tone is objective and respectful,[28] as if the interlocutor had now taken over Paul's viewpoint and wants to test its logical coherence. By this ingenious device, Paul avoids offending the Jewish Christians in Rome who wish to defend their cultural prerogatives. In any case, this diatribe is not intended for a non-Christian Jewish audience.

■ **2** In a certain sense, Paul's answer that the benefit is "huge in every respect" is surprising. As Dodd observes, "the logical answer on the basis of Paul's argument would seem to be 'None whatever!'" Dodd perceives that the basis of Paul's positive answer is nothing but nationalistic prejudice.[29] Paul's concentration on Israel's task to be a light to the Gentiles (2:17-24; 15:8-13) and the missional purpose of this letter, however, lead to the sweeping use of πολύ ("huge, much, many")[30] and κατὰ πάντα τρόπον ("in every way, every respect).[31] Cranfield concludes that this expression does not mean "much of every sort," but "much in every way" as defined in the subsequent reference to the "oracles of God"; Cranfield summarizes this advantage: "God's special choice of Israel, the fact that it is through this nation that God's covenant with mankind has been made, the fact that it is in Jewish flesh that the redemption of the world was to be, and now has been, accomplished."[32] However, the neuter πολύ functions as an adjective modifying τὸ περισσόν ("the benefit") in 3:1 rather than the feminine expression ὠφέλεια τῆς περιτομῆς ("usefulness of circumcision"), which means that the nature of the benefit of Jewish identity is in view.[33] In view of the contempt for Jewish Christians expressed by

---

23   Euripides *Hipp.* 948.
24   Penna, "Structural Function of 3:1-8," 75.
25   BAGD 900.
26   Cranfield, 1:176–77.
27   See Bornkamm, "Theologie als Teufelskunst," 142, 147.
28   See Stowers, *Rereading*, 162–66.
29   Dodd, 43.
30   See BAGD (2000) 847–48; πολύς appears frequently in Luke–Acts (e.g., Luke 7:47; 12:48; Acts 18:27; 27:14) but nowhere else in Paul aside from a textual variant in 2 Cor 8:22. Following LSJM 1442.I.2, "of size, degree, intensity, *much, mighty*," I translate "[the benefit] is huge."
31   See BAGD (2000) 1017. This idiom occurs in Xenophon *Anab.* 6.6.30, to ask Kleander "by all

means (κατὰ πάντα τρόπον) to release the two men" held prisoner. Cf. Plato *Resp.* 589b8; Aristotle *Gen. an.* 736a32; 30 times in Polybius; in the LXX only at Num. 18:7. *Ep. Arist.* 215 urges King Ptolemy, "In every way (κατὰ πάντα τρόπον), Your Majesty, you must make piety the objective of whatever you say and do." This idiom, which struck Zahn, 146–17, and Kühl, 97, as a hyperbole, is found nowhere else in the NT.
32   Cranfield, 1:177.
33   Weiss, 135, contends in contrast that the neuter πολύ modifies both "benefit" and "usefulness."

the majority of Gentile Christians in Rome (14:1–15:13), Jewish identity rather than the usefulness of circumcision is the central issue.

Many commentators state that Paul's listing of the oracles of God with πρῶτον ("in the first place, above all, chiefly")[34] indicates that he intended a further enumeration, but breaks off in a distracted manner and postpones the further listing of Jewish advantages until 9:3-5.[35] The enumeration theory overlooks how ἐπιστεύθησαν ("were believed, entrusted") defines and delimits the sense of τὰ λογία τοῦ θεοῦ ("the oracles of God"),[36] which in other sources can refer to the messianic promises,[37] the promises to Abraham and the patriarchs,[38] the commandments of the Torah,[39] or even the whole of Scripture.[40] While the passive is common in secular Greek texts with the sense of "entrusted,"[41] it seems likely that Paul intended a wordplay with the πιστ- stem, which he employs four times in this pericope[42] and has used since the *exordium* of Romans as a technical term for response to the gospel. Sam K. Williams has shown that Paul always uses the passive of πιστεύω in the context of responsibility for the gospel (Gal 2:7; 1 Thess 2:4; 1 Cor 9:17), so that in Romans he "means that since the promises were given to Abraham, Israel has been and is now the trustee of the divine word that God wills the salvation of all peoples on the basis of faith."[43] For Paul this is the issue of "chief importance" because of its decisive bearing on his missionary project, because the "oracles of God" given in faith to the Jews contained "good news to the gentiles," as Stowers explains.[44] The verb ἐπιστεύθησαν appears here with the connotation of "entrusted,"[45] with Jews in the plural as the assumed subject. I also translate μέν in this context as "indeed."[46] The question of faithfulness to this calling is picked up in the next round of diatribal questions, which reveals that Paul has not lost track of his argument about the failure of all humans despite the impression made on many commentators. My transla-

---

34 According to BAGD (2000) 894, the neuter πρῶτον is used adverbially to indicate numerical sequence, "first," or degree, "above all, especially." For example, Josephus *Ant.* 10.213 reports that King Nebuchadnezzar "summoned the chief men (τοὺς πρώτους) from all the lands over which he ruled." Paul employs the word in this sense of primary importance in 2 Cor 8:5, "they gave themselves first of all (πρῶτον) to the Lord, and then to us." The sense of πρῶτον in Rom 3:2 as "chiefly" or "above all" was advocated by Godet, 132.

35 See, e.g., Tholuck, 94; Meyer, 1:139; Schlier, 92; Kuss, 1:100; Morris, 153; Fitzmyer, 326.

36 The use of this formula as a "formal Hellenistic expression" (Michel, 137) is traced by J. W. Doeve, "Some Notes with Reference to ΤΑ ΛΟΓΙΑ ΤΟΥ ΘΕΟΥ in Romans III 2," in J. N. Sevenster and W. C. van Unnik, eds., *Studia Paulina in honorem Johannes de Zwaan septuagenarii* (Haarlem: Bohn, 1953) 113–21, which evaluates Greco-Roman and Jewish sources. Τὰ λόγια, usually appearing in the plural, refers to ancient oracles as in Euripides *Heracl.* 405, "oracles of old (λόγια παλαιά), salvific to this land." The expression is used frequently by Philo, Plutarch, and others to refer to divine oracles.

37 See Meyer, 1:139; Sanday and Headlam, 170; Godet, 133.

38 Lietzmann, 45.

39 Cranfield, 1:179; Zeisler, 96.

40 Lagrange, 60; Wilckens, 1:164; Fitzmyer, 326; J. W. Doeve, "Some Notes," 121; Hall, "Romans 3:1-8," 185.

41 For example, Polybius *Hist.* 31.18.17: "and he was entrusted (ἐπιστεύθη) with the care of everything by the king"; Posidonius *Frag.* 13.222, "he was entrusted (ἐπιστεύθη) with preparation of gifts"; Claudius Aelian *Frag.* 114.4, "he was entrusted (ἐπιστεύθη) with authority over royal properties"; Appian *Test.* 2b, 156 T. 2.10, "he was entrusted (ἐπιστεύθη) with political rulerships"; *Acts John* 113.21, "now when I was entrusted (ἐπιστεύθην) with a stewardship by you."

42 See Michel, 138; Dunn, 1:131.

43 Williams, "Righteousness," 267–68, building on the foundation of Thomas Walter Manson, "Appendix 1. ΛΟΓΙΑ in the Greek Versions of the O.T.," 87–96; "Appendix 2. ΛΟΓΙΑ in N.T.," in *Studies in the Gospels and Epistles* (Manchester: Manchester University Press, 1962) 87–104, showing that the "oracles of God" refer primarily to the promises of God. Williams's view is accepted by Stowers, *Rereading*, 166–67.

44 Stowers, *Rereading*, 167; he relates this interpretation of Rom 3:2 to Philo's reference to the "unfalsifiable witness of the holy oracles" (*Somn.* 2.220) either of pagan or Jewish origin.

45 Dunn, 1:130.

46 See BAGD (2000) 629, "for indeed."

tion of πρῶτον with "primarily" is an effort to follow this central theme.

■ **3** Punctuating the questions in this verse is difficult. The standard Nestle-Aland text and the commentators follow the parallel in Phil 1:18 and take τί γάρ ("for what, so what?") as a separate question, but some classical parallels[47] favor connecting τί γάρ with the following words to create a single question, "So what if some were unfaithful, does their faithlessness abrogate the faithfulness of God?"[48] The problem with this reading is that if τί γάρ introduces a single question containing the entirety of v. 3, it would require an answer that explains how their unfaithfulness would abrogate the faithfulness of God. However, "By no means!" in v. 4 answers a yes/no question, which must begin with μή ("not"),[49] as in the middle of v. 4: μὴ ἡ ἀπιστία αὐτῶν τὴν πίστιν τοῦ θεοῦ καταργήσει; ("Does their unfaith not abrogate the faithfulness of God?"). While the logic of this question seems to demand the answer "Yes," the use of μή prepares the audience for the negative answer[50] that Paul provides with a vehement denial. I therefore translate the first question as "What then if some were unfaithful," which brings it directly into relationship with Paul's answer in v. 2 about the oracles of God being given in faith to the Jews. The interlocutor pounces on a seeming contradiction between the contention of Jewish faith with regard to the oracles of God and the charge in Paul's preaching that Jews who reject the gospel are exhibiting unfaith in such oracles. Rather than answering this contradiction, Paul has his interlocutor move on to what seems to be an even more serious contradiction.

The second question by the interlocutor allows Paul to block an invalid conclusion that might be drawn from the fact that τινες ("some") but not all Jews have shown themselves to be unfaithful in regard to the oracles of God.[51] This theme recurs later in Rom 11:17, where Paul states that "some of the branches" of the olive tree were broken off because of unbelief. The use of the πιστ-stem in the threefold wordplay in this question points away from the nuance of being "untrustworthy"[52] and toward the explicitly Christian sense of responding in faith to the gospel.[53] In contrast to Jewish and Greco-Roman sources, the NT uses "faith" as "the central and comprehensive designation for one's relationship to God," implying "an indissoluble relationship to Jesus as the crucified and exalted Lord of the Church."[54] Meyer explains that faith and unfaith "are by the context necessarily referred to the λογία τοῦ θεοῦ; the unbelief on a part of the Jews in the promises manifested itself, namely, by their rejecting the Messiah who had appeared according to the promise."[55] The aorist tense also points to a specific act of unbelief such as rejecting Jesus as the Messiah.[56] Only if "their unfaith" is understood as "unbelief in Jesus" does the question of abrogating the faithfulness of God make sense, because "if God spurns Torah-faithful Jews" who reject Jesus, then one could make the case that God "has broken covenantal faith."[57] In Paul's view, however, to be entrusted with the oracles of God is the "chief" component in Israel's covenant, which means that God is justified in condemnation. A favorite Pauline verb, καταργέω is used here in the sense of "to nullify,"[58] as in Andocides *Pac.* 38.7, "and

---

47 See Epictetus *Diss.* 4.1.10, τί γάρ, εἰ ἐκεῖνοι μὲν γενναῖοι ἦσαν, σὺ δ᾽ ἀγενής; ("For what [is this to you] if these were high-born but you were low-born?") We find the same sequence in Demosthenes *Orat.* 37.26.6, τί γάρ, εἰ κατέστησεν Εὔεργος ἐγώ σ᾽ ἀδικῶ; ("For why am I treating you unjustly if Euergus stationed [the slave]?"). There are, however, parallels to the succinct question τί γάρ; as in Epictetus *Diss.* 1.12.18.

48 See the discussion in Cranfield, 1:179–80.

49 Smyth, *Grammar*, §§2642, 2651.

50 Moulton and Turner, *Grammar III,* 283; Smyth, *Grammar*, §2651.

51 Godet, 133.

52 See Schlier, 92–93; Bruce, 95–96; Morris, 154; Rudolf Bultmann, "πιστεύω κτλ.," *TDNT* 6 (1968)

178, shows that classical sources do not support the translation of ἀπιστέω as "untrustworthy, unreliable" but rather in the sense of "distrustful, unbelieving." On 205 he favors the translation of Rom 3:3 as "to be unfaithful."

53 See Sanday and Headlam, 71; Käsemann, 79; Cranfield, 1:180; Black, 54; Räisänen, *Torah*, 189–90.

54 Gerhard Barth, "πίστις, πιστός," *EDNT* 3 (1993) 93.

55 Meyer, 1:140.

56 Räisänen, *Torah*, 190.

57 Charles H. Cosgrove, "What If Some Have Not Believed? The Occasion and Thrust of Romans 3:1-8," *ZNW* 78 (1987) 97–98.

58 See Gerhard Delling, "ἀργός, ἀργέω, καταργέω," *TDNT* 1 (1964) 453; Hans Hübner, "καταργέω," *EDNT* 2 (1991) 267–68.

having overpowered the enemy we nullified the rule of the Hellenes (τὴν ἀρχὴν τῶν Ἑλλήνων κατηργασάμεθα)."[59] The future tense is employed here, although it is rendered as a present or past tense in standard translations and many commentaries as a kind of "logical future."[60] I prefer a straightforward future: "Will their unfaith abrogate the faithfulness of God?" This formulation casts an eye to the future of God's dealing with Israel that is discussed in Rom 9–11.

■ **4** Paul answers the question with a forceful μὴ γένοιτο ("By no means!"),[61] the first of ten times in Romans, more than anywhere else in the NT. The only other author in whom it appears as a denial standing by itself is Epictetus.[62] As Dunn points out, the force of this denial rests on Paul's premises of God's abiding covenant with Israel, of the current failure of Israel to understand this covenant properly, and of the continuity of Paul's gospel with God's promises.[63] The denial is followed immediately by a pungent exclamation, "Let God show himself to be true but every person a liar!" The imperative γινέσθω ("let it be/let it become") seems to imply that God is not yet true, which has occasioned several explanations and translations. Meyer, Godet, and others suggest, "Let God's theodicy come to pass."[64] Zahn, Morison, Hodge, and others propose, "Let God be recognized as true."[65] Sanday and Headlam, Schlier, and others refer to God's becoming the truthful being

that he already is.[66] Cranfield and Moo take this in a confessional manner, "We confess rather that God is true."[67] O'Neill proposes in a similar manner that the imperative relates to human rather than to divine action: "you must recognize that God remains true."[68] Schlatter and Käsemann seem more congruent with the rest of the argument of Romans in stressing the apocalyptic dimension of this statement: "From the perspective of the end of history: . . . May it become true and attest itself so."[69] This alternative of letting God demonstrate God's self to be true correlates nicely with the juridical and legal use of the imperative γινέσθω in reference to laws or conditions that should exist by virtue of the force behind them or their inherent validity. For example, Josephus *Ant.* 12.418 cites the Roman treaty that contains the provision: "And if the Jewish nation wishes either to add anything to, or remove anything from, this treaty of alliance, this shall be done (γινέσθω) with the concurrence of the Roman people, and whatever is added shall be valid."[70] My translation therefore follows Käsemann: "Let God show himself to be true but "every person [show himself to be] a liar!"

What needs to be confirmed as true, of course, are "the oracles of God," which are the crucial issue as far as Paul is concerned. The confirmation of these oracles requires an eschatological horizon, and the hope with which the formal argument of Romans ends is that the

---

59   See also Lysias *Orat.* 2 47.3.

60   For example, the *RSV* and *NRSV* have the present tense; Dunn, 1:129, has the past tense. Commentators acknowledging the future include Zahn, 150; Fitzmyer, 327. Kuss, 1:101, and Käsemann, 80, take the future in a "logical" sense. Cf. Smyth, *Grammar*, §1914: "the future may express a general truth."

61   That v. 4 should be understood as the reply of the interlocutor, as argued by Stowers, "Romans 3:1-9," 715–17, is rightly refuted by Tobin, *Paul's Rhetoric*, 119; the "by no means" is definitely in Paul's voice.

62   In "Μὴ γένοιτο," 26, Malherbe lists many occurrences in Epictetus (we count 32 on the basis of a *TLG* search) and shows that both Paul and the philosopher follow the denial with argument. For example, in *Diss.* 1.29.1–8, Epictetus answers the question about whether he teaches students to despise kings, "by no means (μὴ γένοιτο)! Which one of us teaches you to dispute their claim to the things over which they have authority?" Other writers who employ μὴ γένοιτο in prohibitions include

Euripides *Ion* 731; *Heracl.* 714; Aeschylus *Ag.* 1249; Herodotus *Hist.* 5.111.

63   Dunn, 1:132.

64   Meyer, 1:143; Godet, 134.

65   Zahn, 151; Morison, 36; and others noted by Moo, 16.

66   Sanday and Headlam, 71; Schlier, 93.

67   Cranfield, 1:181; Moo, 186.

68   O'Neill, 61.

69   Käsemann, 80; see Schlatter, 77, and Leander E. Keck, "The Moral Integrity of God and the Human Situation," in *Paul and His Letters*, Proclamation Commentaries (Philadelphia: Fortress, 1979) 120–22.

70   Dionysius Halicarnassus *Antiq. Rom.* 8.11.2 uses γινέσθω in reference to laws that should exist, and Euclid *Elem.* 10.2.17 and other similar passages employ γινέσθω in reference to what mathematical laws should stand.

promise of blessing to all the nations will be fulfilled as the converted come to praise their maker with one voice (Rom 15:6-13). The following quotation from Euripides provides a striking parallel to Paul's reference γινέσθω δὲ ὁ θεὸς ἀληθής ("but let God be true") and demonstrates the link between divine reliability and the validity of prophetic oracles that would have been readily understood by Paul's audience, when Ion states, in a questioning manner, to his mother Creusa: ὁ θεὸς ἀληθής, ἢ μάτην μαντεύεται ("The god is true, or he prophesies falsely").[71]

The second half of Paul's exclamation is a quotation from Ps 115:2, "I said in my amazement, every person is a liar (πᾶς ἄνθρωπος ψεύστης)."[72] This continues the theme from 1:18, 25, that in the light of the Christ event, which discloses the truth about God, humans are shown to be chronically suppressing the truth and exchanging truth for lies.[73] While classical sources can refer to "men's fashioning lies, which one might not even see" (ἄνθρωπος ψεύδεά τ' ἀρτύνοντας ὅθεν κέ τις οὐδὲ ἴδοιτο)[74] and the Hebrew Scriptures can decry false witnesses (e.g., Exod 20:16; Deut 19:16; Prov 21:28), only Paul systematically develops the claim that all men and women of every culture are liars.[75] Even the psalmist, whom Paul quotes, assumes a distinction between the righteous and the wicked, so the citation has a more sweeping bearing in Paul's argument than in the original. In order to counter the superiority claims that dominate Rome and threaten to discredit the mission to the barbarians in Spain, Paul allows no exceptions.[76]

The citation formula, καθὼς γέγραπται ("just as it has been written")[77] suggests the argumentative function of the following quotation from Ps 50:6, confirming the reliability of divine words.[78] Except for a significant alteration of νικήσῃς ("you may prevail") to νικήσεις ("you shall prevail"), the citation is verbatim from the LXX. This alteration shifts the citation into the mode of an apocalyptic contest in which God's words are vindicated against human opposition.[79] It is clear that the Hebrew text would have been less suited to Paul's argumentative purpose, as the following illustration indicates:

Hebrew Ps 51:4b: "that you are righteous in your sentence
   and blameless in your judgment."
LXX Ps 50:6b: "That you may be righteous in your words
   and may be victorious when you judge."
Rom 3:4b: "That you may be righteous in your words
   and shall be victorious when you judge."

In the Hebrew text the psalmist acknowledges that God is "righteous" and "blameless" in judging the sinner, but according to the LXX the psalmist prays that God *may* prove himself righteous and *may be* "victorious" in the competition with humans and the gods who challenge his rule.[80] Simple changes in mood and voice suffice to effect these alterations. Even more significant is that in the context of Rom 3:4, the word "righteous" takes on a meaning synonymous with "truthful" used earlier in the

---

71 Euripides *Ion* 1537; Jewish references to God's truth are in *Sch. Plat.* 382a2; *Act. John* 76.22; Josephus *Ant.* 11.55; and many places in Philo where "the true God" is used in the sense of the one and only God.

72 See Cranfield, 1:182; Dunn, 1:133, noting that ψεύστης appears elsewhere in the LXX only at Prov 19:22 and Sir 15:8; 25:2.

73 See Hans Conzelmann, "ψεῦδος κτλ.," *TDNT* 9 (1974) 601.

74 Homer *Od.* 11.365-66; see also Aesop *Fab.* 21.1; Lucian of Samosata *Electr.* 2.1; Aristotle *Metaph.* 1025a2.

75 See Heinrich Balz, "ψεύστης," *EDNT* 3 (1993) 499.

76 See Bornkamm, "Theologie als Teufelskunst," 143: the argument deals with whether there is an "exceptional" place for Israel in the judgment of the

world, making a case "against the Jews who consider themselves absolved from judgment."

77 The expression "just as it has been written" occurs in CD Ms. A 7:19 and elsewhere: כאשר כתוב.

78 A sketch of the traditional Jewish background of the formula for citing authoritative Scripture, "as it has been written," appears above on 1:17.

79 Käsemann, 81. Although the future indicative occurring after ὅπως ("so that") can have the sense of the subjunctive, according to Smyth, *Grammar*, §2203, Paul's change of the subjunctive to the future tense of this verb needs to be taken into account, as Käsemann does.

80 Bruce, 96, and others take κρίνεσθαι as a middle rather than passive, so that it refers to God "entering into judgment."

verse[81] and "your words" resonate with the reference in 3:2 to the "oracles of God" concerning the messianic promise. Moreover, in the competition in which God is being tested and judged,[82] Paul alters the LXX citation to proclaims that God "*will be* victorious."[83] Käsemann has the clearest grasp of the implications of this remarkably transformed citation: "In this struggle for vindication the issue is who is truthful and constant and who is the liar, or the victim of illusion and falsehood. . . . Paul already knows the outcome and wishes it almost in the form of an incantation. . . . God's truth . . . manifests itself eschatologically and the struggle for it is the content, center, and meaning of world history."[84] This verse therefore develops a leitmotif that was initially suggested by the formulation of the thesis of Romans: the public "revelation" of divine righteousness occurs in the gospel (1:17) and its public "demonstration" occurs in the atoning death of Christ (3:25-26); its final enactment will occur when all nations unite in response to the gospel mission by glorifying God for his truthfulness and mercy (15:8-9).[85]

■ **5** The third pair of questions posed by Paul's interlocutor springs from the citation of Ps 50 and develops a wordplay on the δικ- stem. If God is "righteous" in judging the wicked, as the psalm insists, is it not logical to infer that "our wrongdoing proves God's righteousness?"[86] The possessive pronoun ἡμῶν ("our") and the plural question that follows, "what shall we say," suggests that the interlocutor believes that Paul must share this view.[87] The form of the question introduced with εἰ δέ ("but if") introduces a condition assumed to be an incontrovertible fact: human injustice falls under divine wrath and thus demonstrates God's righteousness. The verb συνίστημι is used here in the sense of "prove" or "demonstrate,"[88] as in Philo *Heres* 258: "it is not merely this experience [of ecstasy] that proves (συνίστησι) him a prophet." A victory charm probably from Roman Arabia contains the words, "Prove him strong (σύστησον αὐτὸν κραταιόν); make him a victor over everyone."[89] The object of such proof in Rom 3:5 is similar to the *Rule of the Community* of Qumran, whose priests "report the righteousness of God (צדקות אל) along with its wondrous works (1QS 1:21)." The rhetorical question posed by the interlocutor, "what shall we say?" implies that Paul must share the inference about to be drawn. Seeking to preserve a measure of exceptionalism for his people in face of Paul's charge that "every person is a liar,"[90] the Jewish interlocutor seeks to make Paul admit that his doctrine contains a fatal contradiction. Admitting for the sake of argument that Paul is correct in exposing Jewish "unrighteousness," the teacher cleverly suggests that Paul's doctrine implies that such wickedness serves to prove divine righteousness and that therefore Paul must believe that "God is unrighteous to carry out his wrath."[91] The issue of the righteousness of God entails divine faithfulness to the promises of salvation,[92] as well as a willingness to defend the right by means of ἡ ὀργή ("the wrath"), both in the present and

---

81   In "Romans 3," 110, Hays points out that "righteousness of God" in 3:5 stands in parallel to "faithfulness of God" in 3:3-4 and the "truth of God" in 3:7, so that "these expressions function interchangeably in this passage and therefore interpret one another."

82   See Gignac, "Procès," 55–56.

83   See Müller, *Gottes Gerechtigkeit*, 65–67; Stuhlmacher, *Gerechtigkeit Gottes*, 85; Kertelge, *Rechtfertigung*, 66; Stanley, *Scripture*, 87.

84   Käsemann, 81; for a critique of this interpretation, see Williams, "Righteousness," 269–70.

85   This missional horizon is overlooked in discussions of this passage by Tobin, *Paul's Rhetoric*, 118–23; and Gignac, "Procès," 57–61.

86   Stowers, "Romans 3:1-9," 715–17, places this verse in Paul's voice, but Tobin, *Paul's Rhetoric*, 120, is correct in placing the questions in the interlocutor's voice and the answers in Paul's.

87   The only NT examples of the question τί ἐροῦμεν are in Romans. Similar formulations occur in other oratorical materials such as in Demosthenes *Orat.* 8.37.5; 20.38.3, τί πρὸς θεῶν ἐροῦμεν ("what, by the gods, shall we say . . . ?"). See also Dinarchus *Dem.* 66.1; 68.7.

88   Wilhelm Kasch, "συνίστημι, συνιστάνω," *TDNT* 7 (1971) 897-98; Käsemann, 83; Hall, "Romans 3:1-8," 189.

89   Text published by Kotansky, *Greek Magical Amulets*, 1.58, 22-23.

90   See Stowers, *Rereading*, 169; Räisänen, *Torah*, 196: "The 'we' of v. 5 is undoubtedly the unbelieving Jew."

91   Godet, 228, and Hall, "Romans 3.1-8," 190, however, argue that 3:5b is a Pauline comment.

92   See Dennis Charles Gaertner, "'The Righteousness of God' in Light of the Theocentric Message of Romans" (diss., Southern Baptist Theological Semi-

in the final judgment.[93] As Schlier explains, wrath does not stand as an antithesis to the righteousness of God: "it is so to speak the reverse side of the righteousness of God, which is the truth of its abiding covenant loyalty."[94] It follows that the interlocutor's challenge to Paul's doctrine is potentially fatal. If Paul does undermine the wrath of God, divine righteousness itself is jeopardized. The seriousness of this challenge probably explains why Paul introduces the question in v. 5b with μή ("not"), which expects a negative answer.[95] Despite the insinuation of the interlocutor that Paul is caught in an irresolvable contradiction, and therefore that his doctrine of impartial judgment is false and Jewish prerogatives remain intact,[96] the question evokes a negative response from the audience: "No, God is not unjust in inflicting wrath on evildoers."

The blasphemous challenge to the righteousness of God posed by the interlocutor is so insidious that Paul feels compelled to explain parenthetically, "I speak in a human manner." This remark constitutes "a parenthetical apology for the blasphemous thought of God as unjust."[97] A similar expression appears in 6:19 and was used in earlier Pauline letters (Gal 3:15; 1 Cor 9:8), but exact parallels have not been discovered either in Jewish[98] or Greco-Roman materials.[99] The formulation appears to derive from Paul's own sense of the antithesis between human and divine logic as revealed in the

Christ event (see 1 Cor 2:6-16). The statement implies the presence of strictly human and worldly reasoning that has no claim on divine authorization.[100] Particularly if the preceding rationalization was perceived to have derived from an authoritative Jewish teacher in the voice of the interlocutor,[101] Paul's parenthetical remark has a disqualifying effect. Despite the sophisticated logic, human lies and evasions are at work in the interlocutor's questions.[102]

■ 6 For the second time in this pericope Paul utters the forceful denial, μὴ γένοιτο ("By no means!"), confirming that the distorted, human logic of the preceding rationalization cannot be allowed to stand. In typical diatribal fashion, Paul provides the reason for the denial in the statement that follows.[103] The conjunction ἐπεί is employed in the sense of "otherwise,"[104] as in a second century B.C.E. papyrus: "For otherwise you would not be so unreasonable" (ἐπεί οὐκ ἂν οὕτως ἀλόγητοι ἦτε).[105] So "otherwise," that is, if the logic of the preceding alibi is accepted, "how will God judge the world?" With the verb κρίνειν ("judge") we confront an axiom of Jewish and early Christian belief,[106] as Büchsel explains: "It is one of the cardinal articles of faith in Judaism that God judges, that He does not just let evil occur without resisting it, that He upholds with punishments and rewards His holy law and its demands and prohibitions, that He enforces it irresistibly in face of

nary, 1986) 137–43, who follows the commentaries by Bruce, Barrett, and Leenhardt.

93   See Wilhelm Pesch, "ὀργή," *EDNT* 2 (1991) 530; Dunn, 1:135.

94   Schlier, 96.

95   Smyth, *Grammar*, §2651.

96   See particularly Watson, *Paul*, 126.

97   Dunn, 1:135.

98   See Str-B 3:136–39; David Daube, *The New Testament and Rabbinic Judaism* (London: Athlone, 1956) 394–400.

99   Betz, *Galatians*, 155, refers to distant parallels in Aeschylus *Ag.* 351; *Sept.* 425; *Eum.* 310; Sophocles *Ajax* 761, 777; *Oed. Col.* 598; Plato *Phil.* 62 a-b; Aristides *Or.* 19 (vol. 2, p. 16); Athenaeus *Deipn.* 10.444B; Diodorus Siculus *Hist.* 16.11.2; Porphyry *Abst.* 2.2. Although the verb λέγω ("I say") is not used, the closest parallel found in a *TLG* search is Marcus Aurelius Τὰ εἰς ἑαυτὸν 9.3.1.6, "This, therefore, on the one hand, is reasoned on human terms (κατὰ ἄνθρωπον ἐστι λελογισμένον)." The

phrase κατὰ ἄνθρωπον appears frequently with the comparative ἤ, meaning more than that accorded a person. For example, Xenophon *Hell.* 3.3.1, "he received a burial more august than that accorded man (ἤ κατὰ ἄνθρωπον ταφῆς)"; see also Xenophon *Cyr.* 8.7.1; Galen *Hipp. prog.* 3.18b 315.2.

100   See Bjerkelund, "Nach menschliche Weise," 67, 94–99; Joachim Jeremias, "ἄνθρωπος, ἀνθρώπινος," *TDNT* 1 (1964) 364: "κατὰ ἄνθρωπον . . . expresses . . . the limited nature of human thinking and conduct in contrast to God and His revelation."

101   See Stowers, "Romans 3:1-9," 707–22.

102   Heil, 35, aptly observes: "Here Paul rhetorically presents a perverted bit of reasoning to be ridiculed and rejected by his audience."

103   See Malherbe, "Μὴ γένοιτο, " 29–30.

104   See BAGD 284.

105   Cited by BAGD 284 from *Urkunden der Ptolemäerzeit*, ed. U. Wilckens, 110.204.

106   See Dunn, 1:135. Michel, 139, suggests that an Ara-

those who despise it. This belief, whose roots go back to the very earliest days of Israelite religion, was inseparably related to the Law, and was transmitted with it."[107] Provided my decision about the future accent of κρινεῖ is correct,[108] Paul is referring in this context to the final judgment that will encompass the entire κόσμος ("world").[109] There are similar formulations in 1 Cor 6:2 and 11:32[110] that suggest Paul is employing a standard doctrine shared by Judaism and early Christianity. In the words of 1 Kgs 2:10, the Lord executes "judgment and justice in the midst of the earth (κρίμα καὶ δικαιοσύνην ἐν μέσῳ τῆς γῆς)." Since the Jewish teacher who serves as interlocutor in this passage would never deny this axiom,[111] the alibi of the insinuation of the verse that aimed to maintaining Jewish exception from condemnation is seen to be fundamentally contradictory.[112] Since the question in this verse can only be answered in the negative, the Christian audience of Paul's diatribe would readily concur and with this stroke, the matter should be closed. Yet the next verse moves on without a hitch to reformulate the claim of exemption with similarly inventive insidiousness, which would have elicited exasperation from Paul's audience that had already drawn the logical conclusion from this rhetorical question.

■ **7** The imaginary interlocutor formulates the next question in direct response to the preceding two verses, indicated by εἰ δέ ("but if"), that is, to the foregoing demonstration of the all-too-human absurdity of charging God with unrighteousness for inflicting wrath. In a first person singular style acknowledging not only himself but also all people as liars, the interlocutor poses the slyest question of all: "But if the truth of God gains benefit to his glory, by my falsehood, why then should I be judged as a sinner?" This question does not merely duplicate the question in v. 5,[113] and the ψεῦσμα ("lie") does not refer to "unreliable conduct,"[114] to "fundamental human dishonesty,"[115] or a general failure to live up to divine expectations.[116] The reference to "*my* lie" points unmistakably to the preceding verses where Paul showed that the interlocutor was engaged in "falsehood" in the evasive rationalization concerning the righteousness of God.[117] Here the interlocutor shrewdly accepts the force of Paul's argument in vv. 4-6 and flatly admits his "falsehood." Nevertheless, he claims that the lie really serves an ameliorating purpose: it has redounded to God's glory and thus should not provide a basis for his condemnation! The first person singular form of the query expresses self concern for the maintenance of superior status, with the emphatic κἀγώ . . . κρίνομαι:[118] "Why then should *I* be judged as a sinner?" Perhaps the best dynamic translation of these words would be "Why am I of all people still being judged . . . ?"

The wording of v. 7 shows that the interlocutor is attempting to evade the classification of himself ὡς ἁμαρτωλός ("as a sinner").[119] Mikael Winninge explains the significance of this language by pointing to the distinction between the action of sinning and the status of being a sinner: "Whereas sinful action could be found in the life of anyone, the designation 'sinner' (רשע or ἁμαρτωλός) was only applicable to the radically sinful in the Hebrew Bible and the Apocrypha. In fact, already

maic dictum about God judging the world probably lies behind Paul's statement; he cites later rabbinic sayings from Str-B 3:139.

107 Friedrich Büchsel, "κρίνω κτλ.," *TDNT* 3 (1965) 935.
108 See note i above.
109 See, e.g., Meyer, 1:146; Cranfield, 1:184; Fitzmyer, 329.
110 See Hermann Sasse, "κόσμος κτλ.," *TDNT* 3 (1965) 892.
111 See Zahn, 156–57.
112 See Moxnes, *Theology in Conflict*, 39.
113 See Käsemann, 83; Morris, 160; Fitzmyer, 329; Moo, 192–93; Räisänen, *Torah*, 198, who argue for simple duplication. Meyer, 1:147; Godet, 137; and Schlier, 96, deny duplication but fail to attach the details

directly with the foregoing verse that showed the deceitful human quality of the interlocutor's questions in v. 5.
114 Black, 55.
115 Balz, "ψεύστη," 499.
116 Morris, 160.
117 Stowers, *Rereading*, 173, comes close to this insight by suggesting that "the rhetorical first-person singular aims to highlight the absurdity of someone like the teacher questioning God's plan."
118 Meyer, 1:148, reports efforts of earlier scholars to capture the nuance with "even I still" or "just I," observing that "there lies in the expression something of boldness and defiance."
119 See Watson, *Paul*, 127.

on a terminological level ἁμαρτωλός is a considerably stronger word than ἁμαρτία, ἁμαρτάνειν and ἁμάρτημα."[120] In the Psalms, for example, "sinners" are a "definite religious type . . . the opposite of the pious, righteous and godly."[121] Ps 49:16-19 is typical in having God speak "to the sinner" (τῷ δὲ ἁμαρτωλῷ) and challenge his mouthing of divine ordinances when he consorts with thieves and adulterers and when his mouth "multiplies wickedness" and his tongue has "framed deceit." The Pharisaic definition of those not adhering to their program of oral law as "sinners"[122] that held them responsible for the ongoing presence of divine wrath and the postponement of the reign of God[123] intensified this characterization in the first century. The impulse to distinguish oneself from sinners was satirized by Jesus' illustration of the Pharisee who prays in the temple, "I thank you that I am not like other men, extortioners, unjust, adulterers, or even like this tax collector" (Luke 18:11). Given this background, the formulation of this question by the Jewish interlocutor is so transparently evasive, and its language so familiar to the audience in Rome that was shaped by synagogue experience, that it required no rebuttal.[124] It would instead probably have provoked contemptuous laughter and hearty repudiation.

The issue here is lying for seemingly good reasons and with the best of motives, that is, to advance the glory of God. There is an ironic paronomasia in the verb employed here, ἐπερίσσευσεν ("it abounded, gained benefit"), which picks up περισσόν ("augmentation, advantage") from 3:1. It is as if the advantage of being a Jew were epitomized by glorifying God through prevarications intended to maintain religious superiority. The aorist tense ἐπερίσσευσεν entails an arrogant claim that such glorification had occurred. False testimony against Jesus at his trial and against his followers in later controversies is hereby claimed to be justified because it served the larger purpose of benefiting God's glory in warding off perceived threats to divine dignity and lawful obedience. To an audience scarred by synagogue controversies and also surfeited with imperial propaganda in which the most brutal and exploitative policies were routinely advanced to glorify Rome and to satisfy the Roman gods, this discourse would have seemed quite familiar and transparent but, above all, infuriating.

■ 8 A wonderful piece of rhetorical jujitsu brings the diatribe to a conclusion. It begins with the words that could be translated, "and not" or "also not." To what does the conjunction καί ("also/and") connect? It certainly does not connect Paul's response to the evasive rationalization of v. 7, as if Paul agreed with its logic. The question in the preceding verse began with μή ("not") that requires a reason rather than a yes/no response.[125] The conjunction καί connects grammatically equivalent constructions. Therefore the καὶ μή that opens Paul's response signifies an ellipse of the entire previous verse, which I translate as follows: "[Why should we] not also [be judged as sinners] just as we are slandered [to be]." The logic of Paul's response is as follows: the interlocutor asks why he is still being judged as a sinner since his lie benefits God's glory. Paul responds with a question that shrewdly brings his audience into the dialogue: "And why should we believers also not be judged to be sinners as we are slandered to be?" Paul includes the Christian audience in Rome in the "we" who are slandered as advocating such views in consequence of the doctrine of freedom from the law. As noted with regard to 2:24, βλασφημεῖν ("to slander, blaspheme") has both a secular meaning of "disparage, slander, defame," and a religious connotation of dis-

---

120 Winninge, *Sinners and the Righteous*, 235.

121 Karl Heinrich Rengstorf, "ἁμαρτωλός, ἀναμάρτητος," *TDNT* 1 (1964) 321.

122 See Joachim Jeremias, "Zöllner und Sünder," *ZNW* 30 (1931) 294; Rengstorf, "ἁμαρτωλός, ἀναμάρτητος," 322–23; Winninge, *Sinners and the Righteous*, 125–26, notes that *Ps. Sol.* 1.8; 2.3, 11, 16; 8.9-10, 22; 17.19 refer to the inhabitants of Jerusalem as οἱ ἁμαρτωλοί engaged in cultic and sexual sins and bringing Israel under the control of foreigners.

123 See Joseph P. Healey, "Am Ha'arez," *ABD* 1 (1992) 169, for an account of how "people of the land" gained "a pejorative meaning" of "the ignorant, the impious, the nonobservant, etc." Healey does not take account of the Pharisaic contribution as described by Anthony J. Saldarini, "Pharisees," *ABD* 5 (1992) 298–303.

124 Many commentators have noted that Paul makes no reply to the evasive question in v. 7, e.g., Leenhardt, 94; Fitzmyer, 330; Moo, 193.

125 Smyth, *Grammar*, §§2638, 2642.

paraging God. It appears that both are present to some degree in this verse,[126] in that the allegation that believers advocate libertinism is not only objectively false but also disparages the gospel itself. The passive first person plural form ("we are slandered, blasphemed") indicates that group disparagement is in view. Paul includes the Roman audience alongside himself as the previous targets of such abuse.

The key to this passage, however, is that those who advocate such slanders are the very legalists represented by the interlocutor,[127] which inserts a large measure of hypocrisy into the interlocutor's side of the diatribe. The classic legalistic accusation is that the gospel of salvation by grace and of freedom from the law constitutes a sly form of libertinism. The interlocutor's lies, which were admitted in v. 7, are here extended into the area of social prejudice and abuse. Paul cleverly draws the audience on his side against those who spread such slander, counting on the audience's past experiences with such smear tactics in the conflicts that occurred in Roman synagogues prior to the Edict of Claudius. It is not that the legalistic interlocutor's doctrine is itself libertinistic[128] but rather that the slanderous accusation about believers advocating libertinism comes from the very same legalists who are represented by the morally evasive interlocutor. As a question beginning with $\mu\acute{\eta}$, the citation of the motto requires a negative answer from the audience[129] that places them firmly on Paul's side against the insidious interlocutor. It is a stunning denouement.[130]

The motto, "Let's do bad things in order that good things might come," appears to be a citation of an actual accusation that Paul himself advocated libertinism. The semantics of the motto seem to be non-Pauline. He never otherwise uses $\tau\grave{\alpha}\ \kappa\alpha\kappa\acute{\alpha}$ ("bad things") or $\tau\grave{\alpha}\ \mathring{\alpha}\gamma\alpha\vartheta\acute{\alpha}$ ("good things") in the plural, with the exception of the citation in Rom 10:15. In 2:9, for example, we encountered "the evil" and in 2:10 "the good," both in the singular. Furthermore, the reference to $\kappa\alpha\grave{\iota}\ \kappa\alpha\vartheta\acute{\omega}\varsigma$ $\varphi\alpha\sigma\acute{\iota}\nu\ \tau\iota\nu\epsilon\varsigma\ \mathring{\eta}\mu\hat{\alpha}\varsigma\ \lambda\acute{\epsilon}\gamma\epsilon\iota\nu$ ("just as some allege us to say") makes clear that this is a slander that Paul and others had actually experienced from Jewish legalists who were outraged at the abandonment of the Torah.[131] Zeller refers to the slogan as a caricature that pretends to be a Pauline maxim, whereby the "good" is obviously not grace but divine judgment.[132]

The passage ends with a "condemnation" ($\kappa\rho\acute{\iota}\mu\alpha$), a formal judicial decision by the divine judge,[133] against those involved in such prevarications. While the interlocutor claims to be serving the cause of divine righteousness and truth, what is actually "right"[134] is his condemnation along with others who participate in such lies. All the moral force of the Judeo-Christian tradition of a righteous God who maintains the right in God's

---

126 Otfried Hofius, "$\beta\lambda\alpha\sigma\varphi\eta\mu\acute{\iota}\alpha\ \kappa\tau\lambda$.," *EDNT* 1 (1990) 220. Hermann Wolfgang Beyer, "$\beta\lambda\alpha\sigma\varphi\eta\mu\acute{\epsilon}\omega$ $\kappa\tau\lambda$.," *TDNT* 1 (1964) 622–24, argues in contrast that "the concept of blasphemy is controlled throughout by the thought of violation of the power and majesty of God."

127 See Zahn, 160; Zeller, 79; Watson, *Paul,* 127.

128 As advocated by Hall, "Romans 3:1-8," 193–96.

129 See Cranfield, 1:187.

130 For accounts of earlier efforts to penetrate the logical connections between vv. 7 and 8 without the use of rhetorical method, see Meyer, 1:149–50, and Cranfield, 1:185–87. Paul J. Achtemeier, "Romans 3:1-8: Structure and Argument," in A. J. Hultgren and B. Hall, eds., *Christ and His Communities: Essays in Honor of Reginald H. Fuller,* ATRSup 11 (Cincinnati: Forward Movement Publications, 1990) 85–87, seeks to understand vv. 7-8 in exact parallel to the earlier rhetorical questions and answers, not taking account of the pause between vv. 7 and 8 or the introductory formula "and not."

131 Meyer. 1:150; Kühl, 101; Schlier, 97; Haacker, 78.

132 Zeller, 79.

133 See Büchsel , "$\kappa\rho\acute{\iota}\nu\omega\ \kappa\tau\lambda$.," *TDNT* 3 (1965) 942; Mathias Rissi," $\kappa\rho\acute{\iota}\mu\alpha$," *EDNT* 2 (1991) 317–18; BAGD 450, "mostly in an unfavorable sense, of the sentence of condemnation," as in Rom 2:2-3 and Polybius *Hist.* 23.1.12, "and some, as victims of perversions of justice, brought charges against them in the courts ($\tau\acute{\iota}\nu\epsilon\varsigma\ \delta$' $\mathring{\epsilon}\gamma\kappa\alpha\lambda\sigma\hat{\upsilon}\nu\tau\epsilon\varsigma\ \tauο\hat{\iota}\varsigma\ \kappa\rho\acute{\iota}\mu\alpha\sigma\iota\nu$ $\mathring{\omega}\varsigma\ \pi\alpha\rho\alpha\beta\epsilon\beta\rho\alpha\beta\epsilon\upsilon\mu\acute{\epsilon}\nu\sigma\iota$)." In other passages $\kappa\rho\acute{\iota}\mu\alpha$ has the sense of the court case itself, as in Aeschylus *Suppl.* 397, "the case is not easy to try" ($ο\mathring{\upsilon}\kappa\ ε\mathring{\upsilon}\kappa\rho\iota\tau\sigma\nu\ \tau\grave{\sigma}\ \kappa\rho\acute{\iota}\mu\alpha$). In Dionysius of Halicarnassus *Antiq. Rom.* 4.12.3.6, $\kappa\rho\acute{\iota}\mu\alpha$ has the sense of a decree or judgment: "to ratify the decrees of the people ($\mathring{\epsilon}\pi\iota\kappa\upsilon\rho\hat{\omega}\sigma\alpha\iota\ \tau\grave{\alpha}\ \tauο\hat{\upsilon}\ \delta\acute{\eta}\mu\sigma\upsilon\ \kappa\rho\acute{\iota}\mu\alpha\tau\alpha$)."

134 This is the only occurrence of $\mathring{\epsilon}\nu\delta\iota\kappa\sigma\varsigma$ in the Pauline letters; BAGD 262, "based on what is right, hence just, deserved."

judgment lies behind this short final sentence.[135] The scope of such judgment encompasses both the libertinists and the legalistic calumniators, including the interlocutor whose voice was heard in the first five questions. This brings to conclusion an exciting and forceful diatribe that was both entertaining and compelling. By showing that a tenacious, law-abiding Jewish teacher can be plausibly depicted as participating in the shield of lies with which the entire human race seeks to disguise its situation before God, Paul exposes the illusion of moral and cultural superiority on the part of Jewish members of his audience.

A close reading of this diatribe, using the methods of rhetorical criticism and taking account of the cultural context, shows it to be a brilliant tour de force, more compressed than any Socratic dialogue and equally effective. Paul's target, however, is not persons like the imaginary interlocutor. He is demonstrating to a Christian audience that in the reaction to the righteousness of God as revealed in the cross and resurrection of Christ, even the most brilliant and legally loyal interlocutor responds with evasions and lies, ultimately showing himself to be a hypocrite who wishes to avoid accountability by claiming to advance his understanding of divine glory while smearing others with falsehoods. This diatribe achieves the most difficult part of Paul's proof that "all have sinned and fallen short of the glory of God." The diatribe is obviously the product of Paul's engagement with synagogue disputations before and after his conversion, that is, for almost twenty-five years. Its wit and cogency would have delighted the Roman audience that had been shaped and scarred by such controversies that had led in 49 C.E. to the riots and the banning of Roman church leaders. Given Paul's grasp of both sides of this argument, it could well be that no Jewish leader had ever argued precisely this way.[136] Paul conducts both sides of the dialogue, but his aim is not to convince Jewish teachers themselves. The key to the effectiveness of the diatribe is not the objective accuracy of his depiction of the imaginary interlocutor but its plausibility to the audience. My reading suggests that he succeeded in demonstrating to the mixed Christian audience of Rome that there is a similarity between Gentiles and Jews when confronted with the righteousness of God revealed in Christ. What 1:18-32 did in showing Gentile suppression of the truth, 3:1-8 accomplishes in showing that Jews also participate in falsehood and lies. Since the interlocutor has been shown to admit his evasions that were designed to defend the superiority of his ethnic group and its self-serving version of righteousness, Paul hopes that the Jewish Christians in his audience will acknowledge that they also have no basis to claim exemption.[137] The path to demonstrating the solidarity of the human race in the reign of lies is now paved and ready for traffic.

---

135 This is why I find to be implausible Dodd's critique of Paul's response on 46: "Paul had no right, having challenged the debate, to close it in this cavalier fashion." In a diatribe, in contrast to a debate, the assumptions of the audience are being used by the teacher to carry the day.

136 See Bornkamm, "Theologie als Teufelskunst," 142.

137 See ibid., 142, 147–48.

3

The Second Part of the Third Pericope

The Evidence of Universal Sin

b. Diatribe and Catena of Quotations Demonstrating Universal Sin

9/ 'What then? Are we at a disadvantage?'[a]
Not at all![b] For[c] we have already established[d] that both Jews[e] and Greeks are all under sin. 10/ Just as it has been written,

> "A righteous human does not exist
> and neither is one human righteous;
> 11/ a human who[f] understands does not exist,
> a human who[g] seeks[h] God does not exist."
> 12/ "All humans turned aside;
> at one and the same time, [all] were corrupted;
> A human who[i] does what is proper does not exist;
> not even one [who does what is proper] exists.[j]
> 13/ Their throat is a grave that has been opened;
> with their tongues they continue deceiving.
> A poison of asps is under their lips,
> 14/ whose[k] mouth is full of cursing and bitterness.
> 15/ Their feet are swift to shed blood;
> 16/ ruin and misery are in their paths;
> 17/ and a path of peace they do not know.
> 18/ A fear of God does not exist before their eyes."

19/ Now we know that whatever the law says, it speaks to those within the law, in order that every mouth might be stopped and all the world might be under indictment to God. 20/ Therefore all flesh shall not be set right before him from works of the law, for an acknowledgment of sin [is] through law.

a The series of textual variants at this point witness to the ambiguity of Paul's expression. The best-attested variant is προεχόμεθα ("we have advantage") found in ℵ B (D[c]) K 0219[vid] 6 33 69 81 88 181 323 326 (330 προσευχόμεθα) 365 424 436 451 614 629 630 945 1175 1241 1243 1319 1573 1739 1836 1877 1881 1962 2344 2464 2492 *Maj* (vg) sy[hmg] cop?. P has the same reading but deletes the two following words οὐ πάντως ("not in every respect"). A L have προεχώμεθα ("might we have advantage?"); D* G (Ψ) 104 (1505) 1735 (2495) *pc* it (sy[p, h**]) bo

Ambst have προκατέχομεν περισσόν ("do we have excessive possession?"). All of these variants are easily understandable improvements of the difficult and probably original wording προεχόμεθα οὐ πάντως.

b Although Nestle-Aland[27] indicates that L contains the words οὐ πάντως ("not at all"), Nils A. Dahl argues that their omission by P constitutes an original "Antiochene" reading since its addition is easier to explain than its omission; see "Romans 3:9: Text and Meaning," in M. D. Hooker and S. G. Wilson, eds., *Paul and Paulinism: Essays in Honour of C. K. Barrett* (London: SPCK, 1982) 184–204. He is followed by Dunn, 1.144–45. This is an improbable reading of the evidence.

c The absence of γάρ ("for") in D* 1611 appears to be a scribal error that was properly corrected.

d The minor variant ἠτιασάμεθα ("we have established") is found in D* G 104 1505 2495 *pc* latt, but the more broadly attested reading προητιασάμεθα ("we have established before") is to be preferred. Cranfield, 1:191, suggests the possible influence of the Latin tradition on this variant.

e The addition of πρῶτον ("first") by A may be an extension of Pauline rhetoric used in Rom 1:16, 2:9, 10, but it also conveys the nasty sense that Jews are more sinful than Greeks. There is no chance that this was an original part of Paul's formulation.

f According to Cranfield, 1:192, the absence of the definite article ὁ in A B G 81 1241 *pc* is probably an assimilation to the LXX. The inclusion of the article is more strongly attested by ℵ D K L P Ψ 6 33 69 88 104 323 326 330 424 365 614 945 1175 1243 1319 1505 1573 1735 1739 1836 1874 1881 2344 2495 *Maj* Mar[Ir].

g The absence of the article ὁ in B G, as in the earlier part of this verse, is probably an assimilation to the LXX.

h A minor variant is found in B which has ζητῶν ("seeking") in place of ἐκζητῶν ("seeking out"), perhaps representing the influence of the citation of Isa 65:1 in Rom 10:20.

i As in v. 11, ὁ is missing at this point in A B G K L P Ψ 6 69 33 88 104 323 330 365 424 614 945 1175 1241 1243 1319 1505 1573 1735 1739 1836 1874 1881 2344 2464 2495 *Maj*. Although different textual traditions are involved, this omission appears once again to be an assimilation to the LXX. The inclusion of the article by ℵ D 81 326 *pc* appears to be original.

j The expression οὐκ ἔστιν ("there is not") disappears in B 6 424[c] 1739 *pc* sy[p] Or, which would make the text differ from the LXX. Οὐκ ἔστιν is included in ℵ A D G K L P Ψ 5 33 61 69 81 88 104 181 218

256 263 323 326 330 365 424* 436 441 451 459 467
614 621 623 629 720 915 917 945 1175 1241 1243
1319 1398 1505 1506 1563 1573 1678 1718 1735
1751 1836 1838 1845 1852 1874 1875 1877 1881
1908 1912 1959 1962 2110 2127 2138 2197 2200
2344 2464 2492 2495 2516^{sup} 2523 2544 2718 *Maj*
Lect ar b d g mon o vg sy^h sa bo arm eth geo slav

Or^{lat} Chr^{lem} (Cyr) Ambst Pel and is probably original. See Metzger, *Textual Commentary*, 448–49.

k   The minor variant αὐτῶν ("their") in B 33 88 1646 brings the formulation into consistency with the twice-repeated αὐτῶν in the preceding verse.

Analysis

These verses present the fifth and climactic dialogue between the imaginary interlocutor and Paul. In this instance the issue of superior advantage touched on in 3:1-2 is reiterated and answered with a statement of universal sin in 3:9. The diatribal exchange is organized in two double sentences matching those in 3:1-8, with a double question by the interlocutor in v. 9a-b and a double answer by Paul in v. 9c-d. The exchange is followed by a carefully constructed catena of scriptural citations in vv. 10-18[1] that draws together themes from earlier portions of the argument of Romans and makes a compelling case that all persons including the chosen people are under the power of sin.[2] The catena probably originated in a Jewish milieu,[3] and with the exception of the slight redaction of LXX Ps 13:1-2 in vv. 3:10-11, the rest is found verbatim in several manuscript traditions of LXX Ps 13:3.[4] Paul reframes the catena by eliminating references to the "fool" in Ps 13:1 and omitting 13:4-7, which refer to "my people," "the righteous generation," and God's "people" who are to be brought back from captivity. Paul thus eliminates the psalm's contrast between the righteous and the wicked. The catena is woven together out of other psalm citations with great sophistication; the catena is marked by anaphora in six lines beginning with οὐκ ἔστιν ("there is not") and by antistrophe in four lines ending with αὐτῶν ("their"), in addition to two instances of medial αὐτῶν. There is an internal ring composition in vv. 10-12 with οὐδὲ εἷς ("not one") in the beginning and ἕως ἑνός ("not a single one") in the final verse. The cited material conveys bodily involvement in sin by reference to "throat . . . tongue . . . lips . . . mouth . . . feet . . . eyes,"[5] with a clever juxtaposition of singular nouns of body parts and path references with their plural pronouns. All of these details reinforce the impression that every individual and all groups are engaged in evildoing.[6]

---

1   The single quotation marks around vv. 10b-11 in the translation above indicate Paul's paraphrasing of the catena; the double quotation marks around vv. 12-18 indicate verbatim quotation from LXX Ps 13:3 and allusions to other Psalms and Isaiah.

2   See Cranfield, 1:191–92; Bornkamm, "Theologie als Teufelskunst," 147.

3   Albl, *Scripture*, 172–74, presents compelling reasons to believe that Paul did not compose this catena and that the material in Ps 13 did not originate in Christian circles. (1) The catena is internally coherent and "makes complete stylistic and thematic sense as it stands"; (2) the catena is attested in all three of the oldest LXX streams of Psalms as well as in Syriac and Vulgate versions, which is hard to explain on the basis of influence from Romans; (3) there are no christological aspects of the catena, nor for that matter, any distinctively Christian traits; (4) as argued by Robert A. Kraft, "Christian Transmission of Greek Jewish Scriptures: A Methodological Probe," in A. Benoit et al., eds., *Paganisme, Judaïsme,*

Christianisme: Influences et affrontements dans le monde antique: Mélanges offerts à Marcel Simon (Paris: Boccard, 1978) 219–20, Ps 13 does not reflect the precise wording of Rom 13:10b-11, which is hard to explain if Christian copyists took over this material from Romans. Koch, *Schrift*, 181–83; Stanley, *Scripture*, 88–89; and Shum, *Paul's Use of Isaiah*, 181–84, argue instead that Paul composed the catena of citations prior to the composition of Romans.

4   See Albl, *Scripture*, 174–77, drawing primarily on the work of Kraft, "Christian Transmission," 220–21.

5   Albl, *Scripture*, 172.

6   Carter, *Power of Sin*, 155–62, offers a less plausible interpretation of the catena on the premise that the word "'heart' is found in all four of the original contexts of these citations from the psalms" (157), which leads to his supposition that Gen 6:5 links the key word "heart" with Isa 59, thus comprising "the hidden verse which holds the key to the catena as a whole. Gen 6:5 was a key verse for the Jewish doc-

The catena as revised by Paul opens with a topical sentence followed by six lines marked by anaphora in the first and third pair of lines expressing the divine assessment of the universal corruption of the human race (3:11-12).[7] The catena continues with a quatrain with a kind of chiastic development that demonstrates the universal corruption of human speech (vv. 13-14).[8] A tricola follows to describe the violence that marks the universal corruption of humankind (vv. 15-17), with three references to motion away from peace: feet . . . paths of misery . . . path of peace. The catena closes with an inclusio that picks up the universal theme of the topic sentence in v. 10b as well as matching it with anaphora. The inclusio charges a universal lack of respect for God (v. 18). Both the recast opening and the choice of the closing line in the catena are closely related to Paul's argumentative context and reflect the kind of careful redactional work found in Paul's other citations. The meaning of the catena is interpreted in vv. 19-20 by means of a powerful conclusion that drives home the contention of pericopes 5 and 6 concerning universal sin. The rhetorical force of v. 19 is heightened by chiastic development,[9] but the most prominent features in this construction are the continuation of the metaphor of the mouth and the paronomasia with the word "all," which recurs yet a third time in the final sentence of the pericope with "all flesh." Here is the proposed chiasm:

ἵνα ("in order that")
   A πᾶν στόμα ("every mouth")
      B φραγῇ ("might be stopped")
         C καὶ ὑπόδικος ("and indictment")
      B' γένηται ("might be")
   A' πᾶς ὁ κόσμος ("all the world")
τῷ θεῷ· ("to God")

The final sentence in the pericope uses the themes of setting right the ungodly and the incapacity of legal works to provide righteousness as a springboard for the subsequent argument of the letter. A citation adapted from LXX Ps 142:2 draws the pericope to a close in a manner congruent with the catena by maintaining that no person can be set right before God through legal conformity.

Rhetorical Disposition

IV.	The *Probatio*
1:18– 4:25	A. The first proof: The gospel expresses the impartial righteousness of God by overturning claims of cultural superiority and by setting right Jews and Gentiles through grace alone
3:1-20	3. The evidence of universal sin
3:9-20	b. A diatribe and catena of quotations demonstrating universal sin
3:9-18	1) The issue of advantage, stated in universal terms
3:9	a) The diatribal exchange on the question of excuse
3:9a	(1) The question of whether Jews are at a disadvantage
3:9c	(2) The contention: "not at all!"
3:9d	(3) The explanation in terms of universal unrighteousness
	(a) The reiteration of previous argument
	(b) The scope of sin encompasses
	i. All Jews
	ii. All Greeks
3:10-18	b) A scriptural catena proving universal unrighteousness
3:10a	(1) The citation formula
3:10b	(2) The topic sentence adapted from Eccl 7:20 declaring universal unrighteousness
3:11-12	(3) Three doublets declaring universal corruption by the citation, abbreviation, and emendation of LXX Ps 13:1-3
3:13-14	(4) A quatrain declaring the universal perversion of human communication by the citation of Pss 5:9; 139:4; and the emendation of Ps 10:7
3:15-17	(5) A tricola declaring the violent consequences of universal unrighteousness by the citation and abbreviation of Isa 59:7-8
3:18	(6) An inclusio concerning the universal failure to fear God in the citation of Ps 35:2

---

trine of the evil *yetzer,* the principle in the heart of humanity that lies behind the universal tendency to sin." However, since neither "heart" nor Gen 6:5 appears in the catena, Carter's theory is not convincing.

7   This analysis is adapted from Keck, "3:10-18," 142–46.

8   See Käsemann, 86.

9   See Fitzmyer, 337, followed by Harvey, "Listening," 187.

Exegesis

■ **9** The opening of this pericope bristles with problems, the first of which is whether v. 9 should be attached to the end of the preceding pericope[10] or whether it initiates a new one.[11] The formula τί οὖν gives the impression of transition to a new section that matches the opening of the preceding pericope. However, those who hold v. 9 to be the conclusion of vv. 1-8 can view it as an inclusio. The punctuation and transla-

tion of the five words τί οὖν + προσεχόμεθα + οὐ πάντως are involved in this decision and there is a good reason why the Nestle-Aland text provides a question mark after τί οὖν and again after προσεχόμεθα. The interrogative τί ("what") cannot be followed by a yes/no response, which is precisely what would be given in οὐ πάντως ("not at all") if προσεχόμεθα ("we have an advantage") were not a separate question that immediately precedes the answer, "not at all." Translations such as "What then do we plead in our defense?"[12] are therefore inadvisable. The more difficult aspect of the puzzle is whether the second question should be translated "do we have an advantage?" or "are we at a disadvantage?"

There are two keys to this puzzle, the meaning of προεχόμεθα and of οὐ πάντως. The verb προεχόμεθα is a middle or passive form of the verb προέχω, meaning "to stand out, be prominent."[13] If this verb is taken as a passive, it would mean "are we surpassed/at a disadvantage?" and imply that Jews are now inferior to Greeks.[14] Most interpreters and modern translators believe this is a middle verb. An implausible alternative is to translate the middle voice in terms of something put forward "in our defence."[15] Most translators and commentators offer a translation of the middle voice as an active form with the translation "have we an advantage?"[16] Although

---

10   Bornkamm, "Theologie als Teufelskunst," 140–41; Stowers, *Rereading Romans*, 165–75; Fitzmyer, 325–26, 30–31.

11   Weiss, 148–40; Kühl, 101–2; Schlier, 97; Käsemann, 85; Wilckens, 1:170–71; Bouwman, 171–72; Morris, 162–63; Dunn, 1:144–45.

12   Dunn, 1:144; Haacker, 79.

13   Christian Maurer, "προέχομαι," *TDNT* 6 (1968) 692; the glossator Hesychius (*Lex. Π-Ω πι*.3444.1) explains προεχόμεθα with προβαλλόμεθα, evidently implying the sense of "do we surpass/excel." See also LSJM 1479–80.

14   Colenso, 72; Sanday and Headlam, 74–75. As reported by Cranfield, 1:189, Olshausen, Vaughan, and Liddon take the passive to mean that Jews have an advantage over Gentiles, which presupposes that the "we" in 9:1 is Paul and his Gentile audience. Stowers, *Rereading*, 174, reformulates the passive option by saying "that it makes good sense for him [the Jewish interlocutor] to ask whether he as a sinner stands in a worse position than Gentiles. Thorsteinsson, *Paul's Interlocutor*, 239–40, properly selects the passive alternative, but on the assump-

tion that the interrogator is a Gentile, the question is whether Gentiles are at a disadvantage. This seems very unlikely.

15   See Meyer, 1:151–52, listing Benecke, Fritzsche, Krehl, Ewald, Morison, Schott, and others as supporting this translation; Weiss, 149, adds Volkmar, Luther, and others to this list. The modern discussion of this option was instigated by Nils A. Dahl, "Romans 3:9: Text and Meaning," in M. D. Hooker and S. G. Wilson, eds., *Paul and Paulinism: Essays in Honour of C. K. Barrett* (London: SPCK, 1982) 184–204; and Gaston, *Paul*, 121.

16   Weiss, 149; Maurer, "προέχομαι," 693, following Lietzmann, 47; Lagrange, 67–68; Dodd, 46–47; Michel, 140–41; Schlier, 97; see the extensive discussion in Morris, 163–66. There are examples of the middle voice of προέχω in reference to objects put forward, e.g., Dionysius Halicarnassus *Antiq. Rom.* 1.58.41, "concerning us, offering our hands (χεῖρας προεχομένων)" with garlands and supplications. See also *Antiq. Rom.* 7.32.1; 10.31.1.3; Homer *Il.* 17.355; Apollonius of Rhodes *Argon.* 1.512; Sophocles *Ant.* 30; Thucydides *Hist.* 1.140.4, the

there are examples of middle forms being taken as actives,[17] it is difficult to explain why Paul did not simply use the proper active form προέχομεν if this were intended.[18] The most serious weakness with this popular solution is that the diatribal logic is thereby destroyed, because the Jewish interlocutor could hardly think of himself sharing an advantage after the condemnation of v. 8 and indeed, the result of the entire preceding diatribe in vv. 1-8.

The more likely alternative is that προεχόμεθα should be taken as a passive with the meaning "are we excelled? i.e. are we in a worse position (than they)?"[19] This passive use is similar to Plutarch *Mor.* 1038d, "of the philosopher whose majesty is not excelled by that of Zeus (οὐδὲν προέχεθαι ὑπὸ τοῦ Διός)." This alternative has been preferred by Lightfoot, Sanday and Headlam, Stowers, and Fitzmyer, and it functions as the "climactic question in Paul's dialogue with the Jewish interlocutor."[20] Having admitted in 3:5 that he was "unrighteous" and in v. 7 that he had been advocating a "falsehood," and having heard the assessment in v. 8, "their condemnation is well deserved," it is logical that the interlocutor should ask the question whether Jews actually stand at a disadvantage in comparison with Gentiles.[21]

There is no difficulty in coordinating a passive reading of προεχόμεθα with a proper translation of οὐ πάντως. In the context of diatribes, it means "not at all" or "by no means." For example, Epictetus *Diss.* 4.8.2–3, "Is he doing something bad? By no means (οὐ πάντως)!"[22] In this sequence, οὐ πάντως can mean "not at all," but in the reverse sequence it would mean "altogether not."[23] The connotation of "nothing at all" or "altogether not" appears in Diognetus Hist. *Test.* 9.1; Epictetus *Ench.* 1.5; and Theognis *Eleg.* 305, while the Vulgate translates with *nequaquam* ("not at all").[24] On the basis of this evidence, Black proposes the translation "absolutely not."[25] Since commentators have construed Paul's use of οὐ πάντως in 1 Cor 5:10 to mean "not in the absolute sense,"[26] "not at all,"[27] or "not in general,"[28] it appears that a contextual decision is required.

I therefore conclude that in response to the interlocutor's question, "Are we [Jews] at a disadvantage?" Paul's reply, "Not at all!" advances his case that all groups have sinned and no group has an inherent superiority before God. In Colenso's words, "there is no favouritism."[29] It is also significant that the Jewish interlocutor has now accepted the results of the previous diatribe in giving up the pose of superiority. It is clear from this reading that Stowers is correct in viewing diatribe as a conversation with a tractable interlocutor. In this case a dramatic change of opinion has taken place: Paul's Jewish conversation partner, despite his previous wiliness, is shown to be anything but incorrigible. This change provides encouragement for Paul's Christian audience in Rome to give up their own claims of cultural and religious superi-

---

only other relevant examples found in a *TLG* search. As BAGD (2000) 869 observes, the meaning "have an advantage" is "not found elsewhere for the middle" voice.

17   Cited by Lagrange, 69; also BDF §316 (I).
18   See Cranfield, 1:189; however he overturns this objection in accepting the translation "Do we *Jews* have an advantage?" on p. 137. See the critique of the "middle as active" option in Stowers, *Rereading Romans*, 173.
19   BAGD (2000) 869.
20   Fitzmyer, 331, who lists the aforementioned commentators as supporting the passive interpretation.
21   See Watson, *Paul*, 128.
22   See also Philo *QG* 1.32.2. A *TLG* search found οὐ πάντως 21 times in Clement of Rome; 16 times in Aristotle; 7 times in Chrysippus, Soranus Ephesius, and Dio Chrysostom; 5 times in Theophrastus and Euclid; 4 times in Philo and Tryphon Gramm.; 3 times in Apollonius Sophista and Plutarch; twice in Plato, Epictetus, Theon; and once in Aristophanes Gramm., Dionysius Thrax, and Ignatius.
23   See Cranfield, 1:188–89; the connotation "perhaps" suggested by G. M. Lee on the basis of Coptic and Syriac translations does not seem relevant for this context. See "Πάντως 'perhaps'?" *ZNW* 64 (1973) 152; idem, "Further on Πάντως 'perhaps'?" *NovT* 19 (1977) 240.
24   See Cranfield, 1:189; BDG §433.2; Moule, *Idiom-Book*, 168; Francis C. Synge, "The meaning of προεχόμεθα in Romans iii.9," *ExpT* 81 (1969–70) 351.
25   Black, 56.
26   See Barrett, *1 Corinthians*, 130.
27   Fee, *1 Corinthians*, 220.
28   Conzelmann, *1 Corinthians*, 95.
29   Colenso, 72.

ority and to recognize that their groups also participate in the lies that mark the whole human race.

Paul provides the rationale for his negative answer in a collaborative form: "for *we* have already established. . . ." As Stowers explains, "the plural is a dialogical 'we,' that is, 'I, Paul, and you, the interlocutor, in our discussion have already concluded.'"[30] The verb προητιασάμεθα may have the connotation "to previously allege, establish" rather than "accuse beforehand" or "demand in advance."[31] Paul again employs the inclusive τε καί to claim that "both Jews and Greeks" are under the power of sin. Rolf Dabelstein downplays the distinction between Jews and Greeks in this sentence and suggests instead that the Christian congregation is perceived to stand over against "a 'world' within which ethnic . . . identity has become meaningless (Rom 3:9)."[32] However, this interpretation confuses the outcome of Paul's argument with the discourse leading to that outcome, which requires the sharp distinction between ethnic groups to remain. It is significant in this context that for the fourth time in the letter, Paul uses the word Ἕλληνας ("Greek") rather than ἔθνεσιν ("Gentile"),[33] thus holding each group accountable in its own terms. He does not wish to have his audience, consisting mainly of Greco-Roman groups calling themselves "strong," absolve themselves from accountability on the grounds that Paul employs the abusive epithet, "Gentile."

While commentators have wondered exactly where Paul has made the case that all have sinned[34] or commented on the "gross exaggeration" of Paul's inclusive claim,[35] my reading of the previous diatribe indicates the ground for including both Jews and Greeks in this generalization. By inducing an arrogant, self-righteous interlocutor to acknowledge that his evasive behavior places him in the class of "sinners," Paul has made a strong rhetorical case that Jews as well as Greeks are under sin.[36] It is a rhetorical tour de force, but not a logically compelling argument.[37] It would be impossible to maintain that all Jews, without exception, or that all Gentiles, without exception, are sinners. Yet Paul is required by the rhetorical situation of competing superiority claims in Rome to make precisely this case and he does so effectively. As Esler has shown, this doctrine of universal sin "knocks away the respective foundations each group has for harboring feelings of ethnic superiority over the other that would get in the way of their accepting the value of the new common group identity" of oneness in Christ.[38]

For the first time in the letter, Paul refers to "sin" with the striking formulation "under sin," which is unparalleled either in Paul's other letters or in other early Christian literature. As is typical for Paul in contrast to other early Christian writers, ἁμαρτία ("sin") is used here in the singular in an "almost hypostatizing fashion" as the "power of sin."[39] The investigation by Günter Röhser recommends the concept of "personification" rather than hypostatizing to describe this phenomenon in Pauline thought,[40] but Röhser does not feel that the formulation in 3:9 or its immediate context provides any indications of such personification.[41] However, I believe that Walter Grundmann is correct in concluding:

30 Stowers, *Rereading Romans*, 180.
31 BAGD (2000) 865; LSJM 1467; the word does not appear elsewhere in extant Greek literature apart from later patristic references to this passage; see MM 537. However, Godet, 140, and Morris, 166, note that the stem αἰτία implies an indictment and thus the latter translates "we have already made the charge"; see also BAGD (2000) 31, which lists Acts 23:28; John 18:38; 19:4, 6 as examples where αἰτία appears with the sense of a legal charge or complaint.
32 Dabelstein, *Beurteilung*, 118.
33 Most commentators fail to observe this distinction, interpreting this verse as if Paul really meant "Gentile." See Weiss, 150–51; Michel, 141; Cranfield, 1:191; Murray, 102; Dunn, 1:147–48; Moo, 201; Stuhlmacher, 53; Schreiner, 161, 163.
34 Zeller, 99–100; Räisänen, *Law*, 99.
35 Sanders, *Law*, 125.
36 See also Carter, *Power of Sin*, 154.
37 Vos, *Kunst der Argumentation*, 77–78, concludes that Paul employs sophistic techniques of argument to support this claim.
38 Esler, *Conflict and Identity*, 144.
39 Käsemann, 86; see also Michel, 141–42. The rare plural employment of "sins" occurs in Rom 4:7; 7:5; 11:27; see Dunn, 1:149; and Peter Fiedler, "ἁμαρτία," *EDNT* 1 (1980) 67.
40 Röhser, *Hamartia*, 131–81.
41 Ibid., 167–68.

"For Paul sin does not consist only in the individual act. Sin is for him a state which embraces all humanity."[42] This clearly goes beyond the traditional sense of sin as transgression of the law,[43] and it moves beyond any other ancient source in placing "Jews and Greeks" at a point of emphasis as a predicate nominative before the expression "be under sin." This sweeping declaration that "all" ($\pi\acute{\alpha}\nu\tau\alpha$) are under this evil power means that they participate in various cultures of lies from which they do not seem able to escape without outside exposure and intervention.

■ **10** It is widely accepted today that a carefully constructed catena of LXX quotations was used in 3:10-18. Otto Michel suggests the presence of an "early Christian psalm . . . which has been drawn together out of multiple individual citations into an artful unity." He also claims that "the new psalm as such has gained authority as divine accusation for Paul and his readers."[44] Leander Keck concurs in this assessment and shows that "the catena was not composed for this place in the letter, but has integrity of its own."[45] He believes that it arose in Jewish apocalyptic circles.[46] As noted above, the recent study by Martin C. Albl shows that the catena derived from a Jewish setting similar to that producing the *Psalms of Solomon,* which maintains that among the Jews in Jerusalem who opened the gates to the invading Romans, "there was no one among them . . . who acted with mercy or truth . . . who practiced righteousness or justice" (*Ps. Sol.* 17.15, 19).[47] The connection of the catena with the earlier argument of Romans leads Keck to the plausible conclusion that it provided "the theological starting-point for Paul's reflection."[48] When one recognizes that the alteration of the LXX citation in the opening verse (3:10b) reflects a specifically Pauline

interest in righteousness[49] and that neither the opening in vv. 10-11 nor the closing in vv. 19-20 belonged to the original catena,[50] our attention must turn to Paul's redactional work as a clue to his intentions.

The formula for citing authoritative Scripture appears frequently in Romans, $\kappa\alpha\vartheta\grave{\omega}\varsigma\ \gamma\acute{\epsilon}\gamma\rho\alpha\pi\tau\alpha\iota$ ("as it has been written").[51] The opening line of the catena was rather forcibly derived from a combination of Ps 13:1 and Sir 7:20, as the following quotations indicate:

Ps 13:1c: $o\grave{\upsilon}\kappa\ \acute{\epsilon}\sigma\tau\iota\nu\ \pi o\iota\grave{\omega}\nu\ \chi\rho\eta\sigma\tau\acute{o}\tau\eta\tau\alpha,\ o\grave{\upsilon}\kappa\ \acute{\epsilon}\sigma\tau\iota\nu\ \acute{\epsilon}\omega\varsigma\ \acute{\epsilon}\nu\acute{o}\varsigma$ ("a human doing good does not exist, not even one")

Sir 7:20a: $\acute{o}\tau\iota\ \acute{\alpha}\nu\vartheta\rho\omega\pi o\varsigma\ o\grave{\upsilon}\kappa\ \acute{\epsilon}\sigma\tau\iota\nu\ \delta\acute{\iota}\kappa\alpha\iota o\varsigma\ \acute{\epsilon}\nu\ \tau\grave{\eta}\ \gamma\grave{\eta}$ ("that a righteous person does not exist on earth")

Rom 3:10b: $o\grave{\upsilon}\kappa\ \acute{\epsilon}\sigma\tau\iota\nu\ \delta\acute{\iota}\kappa\alpha\iota o\varsigma\ o\grave{\upsilon}\delta\grave{\epsilon}\ \epsilon\grave{\hat{\iota}}\varsigma$ ("a righteous human does not exist; neither [is] one human [righteous]")

The Pauline redaction replaces the motif of "goodness" in Ps 13 with "righteous" from Ecclesiastes, a theme that resonates with his previous discussion and with the thesis of Romans.[52] Paul also deletes the reference to the "fool" in Ps 13:1,[53] thus eliminating the traditional distinction between the wise, righteous person and the foolish, wicked one. In the compressed formulation of Rom 3:10, $o\grave{\upsilon}\kappa$ is an adverb that modifies the verb "is" ($\acute{\epsilon}\sigma\tau\iota\nu$), thus denying the existence of something. Since $o\grave{\upsilon}\delta\acute{\epsilon}$ is a conjunction that connects the two clauses, the ellipses implied must be filled in, so I translate the verb $o\grave{\upsilon}\kappa\ \acute{\epsilon}\sigma\tau\iota\nu$ ("does not exist") and not $\epsilon\grave{\hat{\iota}}\varsigma$ ("a righteous human").[54] Paul's reformulation eliminates the existence of any righteous person. All of humanity is now captured in this denunciation.[55] The resultant opening of

---

42 Walter Grundmann, "$\acute{\alpha}\mu\alpha\rho\tau\acute{\alpha}\nu\omega\ \kappa\tau\lambda$.," *TDNT* 1 (1964) 309.

43 For an attempt to reduce sin to legal transgression see Merklein, *Studien,* 316–56, esp. 317.

44 Michel, 143.

45 Keck, "3:10-18," 147.

46 Ibid., 148–49.

47 Albl, *Scripture,* 174–77.

48 "The Function of Rom 3:10-18," 153.

49 See Barrett, 69.

50 See the strophic analysis of the Greek text in Keck, "3:10-18," 142–43, and the detailed analysis of the

poetic structure below. In addition, Justin *Dial.* 27.3 reflects an abbreviated form of the Romans catena that must have existed independently, but without equivalents to Rom 3:10b and 18. Cf. Keck, "3:10-18," 150.

51 See the discussion of the traditional Jewish background of the formula in relation to 1:17.

52 Stanley, *Scripture,* 90.

53 See Koch, *Schrift,* 119.

54 For the logic of these ellipses see Smyth, *Grammar,* §§2688a and 2932.

55 Stanley refers to stylistic reasons for Paul's reformu-

the redacted catena sets the theme that Paul wishes to develop, namely, that the human race finally has no exceptions in the tendency toward wickedness. There are parallels in Qumran to this bleak assessment[56] such as 1QH 12:31, which proclaims "that righteousness does not belong to man nor to a son of Adam a perfect path." The catena in the Pauline redaction goes farther than this, however, and eliminates the typical distinction in the Qumran literature between "the just and the wicked" (e.g., 1QH 12:38).

■ **11** The second line of the catena is cleverly adapted by Paul from LXX Ps 13:2, which depicts God's looking "down from heaven upon the sons of men to see if there were any that understood, or sought after God ($\tau o\hat{v}$ $\mathring{\iota}\delta\epsilon\hat{\iota}\nu$ $\epsilon\mathring{\iota}$ $\mathring{\epsilon}\sigma\tau\iota\nu$ $\sigma\upsilon\nu\acute{\iota}\omega\nu$ $\mathring{\eta}$ $\mathring{\epsilon}\kappa\zeta\eta\tau\hat{\omega}\nu$ $\tau\grave{o}\nu$ $\vartheta\epsilon\acute{o}\nu$)."[57] With the removal of the theme of the fool, this reference to God's inquiring gaze in Ps 13:2a becomes irrelevant,[58] and Paul can augment the anaphoric parallelism with two additional $o\mathring{v}\kappa$ $\mathring{\epsilon}\sigma\tau\iota\nu$ references that serve to comprise a series of five, counting the two in the following verse.[59] The words $\mathring{o}$ $\sigma\upsilon\nu\acute{\iota}\omega\nu$ ("one who understands") and $\mathring{o}$ $\mathring{\epsilon}\kappa\zeta\eta\tau\hat{\omega}\nu$ $\tau\grave{o}\nu$ $\vartheta\epsilon\acute{o}\nu$ ("one who seeks God") are taken from the psalm and enhanced with parallel articles that accentuate the stress on "not even one" person's performing these righteous acts.[60] The resultant poetry resonates with the earlier sections of Romans. Keck observes that the motif "no one understands" (3:11a) matches the allegation of twisted intellect in 1:22, and that "no one seeks God" (3:11b) sums up the argument of 1:21 and 25.[61] In the context of the original catena in the psalm, not "understanding" is rather ambivalent because it is "not a faculty native to man as such. It is the gift of God," as Hans Conzelmann explains, yet "one has to seek it. Lack of understanding is a fault and is punished."[62] On the other hand, within Qumran, which may be closer to the sectarian orientation of the original catena, "understanding is the prerequisite for acceptance into the sect,"[63] so this lack results in exclusion and damnation. For example, 1QS 5:21 describes how a potential member is to be examined "in respect of his insight and of his deeds in law." The expression $\mathring{\epsilon}\kappa\zeta\eta\tau\acute{\epsilon}\omega$ $\tau\grave{o}\nu$ $\vartheta\epsilon\acute{o}\nu$ ("seek God") in a book like 2 Chronicles is a technical reference to Yahwist devotion (14:4, 7; 15:2; 17:4; 19:3; 20:4; 26:5; 30:19; 31:21), and the same verb depicts the absence of such devotion (12:14; 15:13; 16:12) or replacement by idolatry (25:20; 28:23). $\mathring{E}\kappa\zeta\eta\tau\acute{\epsilon}\omega$ $\tau\grave{o}\nu$ $\vartheta\epsilon\acute{o}\nu$ also appears frequently in LXX Pss 30:23; 33:4, 10; 52:2; 68:32; 76:2; 118:2, 10. Within this frame of thought, not to seek God is to take one's place among God's sworn enemies and to participate in betraying the faith.

■ **12** This verse is drawn verbatim from LXX Ps 13:3, which in turn appears to have been adapted from Ps 52:3-4, with the change of a single word.[64] Here are the two versions, for comparison:

> Ps 13:3 and Rom 3:12: $\pi\acute{a}\nu\tau\epsilon\varsigma$ $\mathring{\epsilon}\xi\acute{\epsilon}\kappa\lambda\iota\nu\alpha\nu$ $\mathring{a}\mu\alpha$ $\mathring{\eta}\chi\rho\epsilon\acute{\omega}\vartheta\eta\sigma\alpha\nu\cdot$ $o\mathring{v}\kappa$ $\mathring{\epsilon}\sigma\tau\iota\nu$ $\mathring{o}$ $\pi o\iota\hat{\omega}\nu$ $\chi\rho\eta\sigma\tau\acute{o}\tau\eta\tau\alpha,$ $o\mathring{v}\kappa$ $\mathring{\epsilon}\sigma\tau\iota\nu$ $\mathring{\epsilon}\omega\varsigma$ $\mathring{\epsilon}\nu\acute{o}\varsigma$ ("All turned aside; at one and the same time [all] were corrupted; a human who does what is *proper* does not exist; not even one exists")
> Ps 52:3-4: $\pi\acute{a}\nu\tau\epsilon\varsigma$ $\mathring{\epsilon}\xi\acute{\epsilon}\kappa\lambda\iota\nu\alpha\nu$ $\mathring{a}\mu\alpha$ $\mathring{\eta}\chi\rho\epsilon\acute{\omega}\vartheta\eta\sigma\alpha\nu\cdot$ $o\mathring{v}\kappa$ $\mathring{\epsilon}\sigma\tau\iota\nu$ $\mathring{o}$ $\pi o\iota\hat{\omega}\nu$ $\mathring{a}\gamma\alpha\vartheta\acute{o}\nu,$ $o\mathring{v}\kappa$ $\mathring{\epsilon}\sigma\tau\iota\nu$ $\mathring{\epsilon}\omega\varsigma$ $\mathring{\epsilon}\nu\acute{o}\varsigma$ ("All turned aside; at one and the same time [all] were corrupted; a human who does what is *good* does not exist; not even one exists")

With the inconsequential alteration from "proper" to "good," both psalms retain the traditional distinction between the "fool" (52:1) and "God's people . . . Israel" (52:6) that the catena abandons. Since this portion of the catena was probably derived from a Pharisaic Jewish source, and was cited twice as Scripture along with other psalms being created in the first century before the canon was finalized,[65] the condemnation includes the Pharisees themselves. Dunn observes that the psalm citations in this catena "presuppose an antithesis between

---

lation in *Scripture*, 91, but a significant theological point is thereby being scored.

56 Noted by Schlier, 99.
57 This motif from Ps 13 appears to be cited from LXX 52:2.
58 Koch, *Schrift*, 119.
59 Stanley, *Scripture*, 91.

60 Ibid., 92.
61 Keck, "3:10-18," 151–52.
62 Hans Conzelmann, "$\sigma\upsilon\nu\acute{\iota}\eta\mu\iota$ $\kappa\tau\lambda.$," *TDNT* 7 (1971) 890.
63 Ibid., 891.
64 See Dunn, 1:150.
65 See Albl, *Scripture*, 174–75, who shows not only that

the righteous (the faithful member of the covenant) and the unrighteous. The implication is that when that pre-supposition of favored status before God is set aside, the scriptures serve as a condemnation of *all* humankind."[66] In the light of the parameters established in Rom 1:14 and developed in 1:18-32, this aspect of the catena undercuts the superiority claims of any group to gain honor through performance or ethnic status. The motifs in this verse also echo earlier material in Romans: Keck notes that the clause all "turn aside" (3:12a) seems to match the twistedness described in 1:23,[67] and I would add that the references to corruption in 3:12b and impropriety in 3:12c-d provide an effective summary of 1:26-31. It is as if the earlier condemnation of the Gentiles were now extended to the Jews, thereby making the case for universal sin. In the original context of the catena, ἐκκλίνω ("turn aside") may have the connotation of perversion of justice (Deut 24:17; 27:19) or of turning away from God (Deut 29:18; Sir 2:7) and his laws (Deut 31:29). This would be close to LXX Ps 118:21, "Cursed are those who turn aside (οἱ ἐκκλίνοντες) from your commandments," an action that leads to the total per-version of life. In combination with ἄμα ("at one and the same time") the verb ἠχρεώθησαν has the connota-tion of a kind of corruption[68] that people engage in together.[69] The noun χρηστότης with reference to humans has a broader connotation of honest, respectable, kind behavior, although it can be used to refer to proper marital relations.[70] We encountered this word in Rom 2:4 in relation to God's kindness, but the context in the catena seems to favor the connotation of

propriety[71] or usefulness.[72] All three references could as easily relate to heresy as viewed by a sectarian group: turning aside from true doctrine or law; being mutually corrupted by false teaching; and promoting improper things. The final line of 3:12 claims that "not a single person" performs a proper act, which is an awful indica-tion of the universal corruption of the human race, whether the intended context was moral or theological violations.

■ **13-14** This quatrain is drawn verbatim from LXX Ps 13:3c-f, which in turn quotes 5:10 in the first two lines and 139:4 in the third but adapts 9:28 in the fourth.[73] The adaptation is as follows:

LXX Ps 9:28a: οὐ ἀρᾶς τὸ στόμα αὐτοῦ γέμει καὶ πικρίας καὶ δόλου ("of which cursing his mouth is full and bitterness and deceit")

LXX Ps 13:3e-f; Rom 3:14: ὧν τὸ στόμα ἀρᾶς καὶ πικρίας γέμει ("whose mouth is full of cursing and bitterness")

The change of the singular relative pronoun οὗ ("of which") to the plural pronoun ὧν ("of whom") and the omission of αὐτοῦ ("his") brings the formulation into consistency with the "all" who have "turned aside" in v. 12.[74] The shift in the position of the accusative noun ἀρᾶς ("cursing") to its more graceful position in the sequence with "bitterness" improves the style of the cita-tion.[75] The deletion of the third noun in the sequence, καὶ δόλου ("and deceit"), eliminates a possible redun-dancy with ἐδολιοῦσαν ("they deceive") in v. 13b.[76] The

---

the book of Psalms was being expanded but also that the Qumran community was composing new psalms from citations of older ones and that 11QPs containing such material was viewed by its users as canonical.

66   Dunn, 1:145.
67   Keck, "3:10-18," 151.
68   LSJM 297, referring to Apollonius Citiensis *Hipp.* 1.9, ἐπεὶ γὰρ ἔνιοι δι᾽ ἀπειρίαν τινῶν ἠχρειώ-θησεν ("Since some have, through inexperience, been corrupted by certain ones.")
69   In contrast, Murray, 103, takes "together" to mean everyone is corrupted, which would be correct if ἄμα were used as a preposition with the dative; here it functions as an adverb meaning "at the same time." See BAGD (2000) 49.

70   Konrad Weiss, "χρηστός . . . χρηστότης," *TDNT* 9 (1974) 489, mentions Plutarch *Ag. Cleom.* 17.2 (802d), referring to a "wife's propriety and devotion (ἐπὶ τῇ χρηστότητι καὶ φιλοστοργίᾳ τῆς γυναικός) in standing by her husband's misfor-tunes."
71   BAGD 886: "do what is right."
72   Josef Zmijewski, "Χρηστότης," *EDNT* 3 (1993) 476.
73   See Dunn, 1:150; Stanley, *Scripture*, 93–95; Koch, *Schrift*, 109. Albl, *Scripture*, 171, derives this citation from a textual variant of Ps 13:3 that appears to have been influenced by Rom 3:13-14.
74   Stanley, *Scripture*, 93–94.
75   Ibid., 94.
76   Koch, *Schrift*, 116; Stanley, *Scripture*, 94.

verb γέμει ("it is full") to the position at the end of the sentence brings this citation into stylistic conformity with the other verbs in vv. 10-18, which are all at the end of their clauses.[77] As in the earlier citations, all three psalms (5, 9, 139) make distinctions between the righteous and the wicked that the catena drops (5:5, 12; 9:1-4, 12-14; 139:4, 13).[78]

The throat of sinners in v. 13 is described as a "grave that has been opened." The anarthrous τάφος ("grave") is a predicate nominative followed by a perfect passive participle, ἀνεῳγμένος ("it has been opened"), which leads to my translation, "Their throat is a grave that has been opened." Since an open grave allowed pollution to spread, this metaphor may refer to corrupt and filthy speech. It is also possible that the metaphor of an open grave reflects the ancient view of Mot, the god of death, whose gigantic maw had an "insatiable . . . voracious appetite" to swallow up the living.[79] In that case, the metaphor relates to death-dealing words and indicates the likely future of those who participate in this kind of speech. In the second line of the quatrain, the tongue participates by its deceit in the universal lies of the human race. The imperfect verb ἐδολιοῦσαν ("they were deceiving") implies a continually repeated behavior.[80] In the third line the deadly poison of asps is spewed out by lethal words that destroy others as well as one's self. The reference to poison ὑπὸ τὰ χείλη αὐτῶν in this phrase with the accusative[81] implies that the poison lies "under their lips" ready to strike the victim. In the final line the mouth utters words of cursing and bitterness against the world. These metaphors are vivid descriptions of unrighteous communication, the "sins of the mouth."[82] These motifs also resonate with earlier sections of Romans, with the deceit in 3:13b echoing the theme of guile in 1:29[83] and with the open grave, poisoned lips, cursing, and bitterness echoing the details of 1:29-30. Once again Jews and Greeks are joined without exception in sinful patterns of behavior.

■ **15-17** This tricola is adapted from Isa 59:7-8 and Prov

1:16.[84] The similarities and changes can be visualized as follows:

> Rom 3:15: ὀξεῖς οἱ πόδες αὐτῶν ἐκχέαι αἷμα ("their feet are swift to shed blood")
> Isa 59:7a: οἱ δὲ πόδες αὐτῶν ἐπὶ πονηρίαν τρέχουσιν ταχινοὶ ἐκχέαι αἷμα ("but their feet are swift to shed blood with those who run to wickedness")
> Prov 1:16: οἱ δὲ πόδες αὐτῶν ἐπὶ κακίαν τρέχουσιν καὶ ταχινοὶ τοῦ ἐκχέαι αἷμα ("but their feet are swift to shed blood with those who run to badness")

While all three passages refer to "the feet" of those who "shed blood," the catena is more vivid in using the adjective ὀξύς ("swift") in place of the cumbersome Hebraism "run quickly to wickedness/evil." This detail suggests that the creators of the original catena had a well developed sensitivity to Greek style. It seems likely that the association between feet and bloodshed derived from stalking others (LXX Prov 1:11-16; 6:18).

> Rom 3:16 and LXX Ps 13:3h: σύντριμμα καὶ ταλαιπωρία ἐν ταῖς ὁδοῖς αὐτῶν ("ruin and misery are in their paths")
> Isa 59:7c: σύντριμμα καὶ ταλαιπωρία ἐν ταῖς ὁδοῖς αὐτῶν ("ruin and misery are in their paths")

Here the psalmist exactly quotes Isaiah, who laments that Israel's sins have brought such social disaster upon the population.

> Rom 3:17 and LXX Ps 13:3i: καὶ ὁδὸν εἰρήνης οὐκ ἔγνωσαν ("and a path of peace they do not know/comprehend")
> Isa 59:8a: καὶ ὁδὸν εἰρήνης οὐκ οἴδασι ("and a path of peace they do not know/are not acquainted")

---

77   Stanley, *Scripture*, 95.
78   Noted by Dunn, 1:150.
79   Theodore J. Lewis, "Mot," *ABD* 4 (1992) 923.
80   Godet, 141. The form ἐδολιοῦσαν has the aorist third person plural ending but the imperfect contraction of the vowels. See BDF §84.3.
81   See BAGD (2000) 1036.
82   Keck, "3:10-18," 151.
83   Ibid.
84   See Fitzmyer, 336; Koch, *Schrift*, 119; Stanley, *Scripture*, 95–98.

Except for the use of two different verbs of knowing, both texts are identical. The difference is subtle but significant, because the LXX of Isaiah can imply a simple nonacquaintance[85] for which one may not be responsible, while the catena employs the verb γινώσκω, which can have the connotation of comprehension[86] that in this context implies a refusal to comprehend. This willful abandonment of the path of peace echoes the material in Rom 1:29-32 that depicts the violent consequences of unrighteousness.[87]

■ **18** Except for one significant alteration, the final verse of the catena comes verbatim from LXX Ps 35:2.[88] The singular reference in the psalm to "his eyes" is changed to τῶν ὀφθαλμῶν αὐτῶν ("their eyes"), bringing this reference in line with all of the other plurals in the catena that serve to generalize and universalize responsibility for evil.[89] Again in contrast to Ps 35, where the distinction between the righteous (35:7-10) and the unrighteous (35:1-4, 11-12) is explicitly made, the catena in Paul's context extends the condemnation to all people. As Dunn observes, in the view of modern interpretive techniques, only two of these citations could "on any straightforward reading be applied to the Jews as a whole." Nevertheless, Paul recontextualizes the catena in line with first-century methods "as a turning of the tables on Jewish overconfidence in their nation's favored status before God."[90] The absence of "fear of God" is a typical expression for impiety in the OT and the wisdom literature.[91] While the righteous, reliable person fears and honors God (Exod 18:21; Deut 6:2, 24; 10:12, 20; Ps 111:10), a false person "withholds kindness from a friend, forsakes the fear of the Almighty" (Job 6:14). In the wisdom literature "fear of God" is the basis of wisdom (Prov 9:10), which produces genuine knowledge and insight and manifests itself in the avoidance of immorality.[92] In Prov 14:2, for example, "he who walks in uprightness fears the Lord, but he who is devious in his ways despises him." These themes are carried forward in the *Testaments of the 12 Patriarchs*, where Simeon reports, "For two years of days I afflicted my soul with fasting in the fear of the Lord (ἐν φόβῳ κυρίου); and I learnt that deliverance from envy comes through the fear of God (διὰ φόβῳ κυρίου)" (*T. Sim.* 3.4). Such fear is the basis of moral behavior according to *T. Gad* 5.4-5: "the fear of God (ὁ φόβος κυρίου) overcomes hatred. For fearing (φοβούμενος γάρ) that he should offend the Lord, he does not want to do anything wrong to a man, even in thought." The Qumran community is composed of those "who fear God" (1QH 12:3).[93] Since Gentile sympathizers drawn to the moral and spiritual legacy of Judaism were called "God-fearers,"[94] to be entirely lacking in fear places the Jewish person below the worst of Gentiles.

The metaphor of fear "before their eyes" is typical of the OT, where "eyes" appears around 700 times and the human attitude toward God is depicted as having eyes turned toward God.[95] For example, LXX Ps 24:15 has the righteous person confess, "My eyes (οἱ ὀφθαλμοί μου) are continually toward the Lord." Job 42:5 uses the metaphor of the eyes to depict a personal relationship with God: "I had heard of you by the hearing of the ear, but now my eye sees you." That there is no fear "before their eyes" gives the impression of incorrigible impiety.[96]

Thus the catena ends with an inclusio to the opening lines concerning the lack of righteousness, insight, and seeking after God. The catena declares a complete betrayal of Israel's religious heritage on the part of those who should be the first to embody it. Since the

85 BAGD (2000) 693 (1), "to have information about"; Axel Horstmann, "οἶδα," *EDNT* 2 (1991) 494, "know, be acquainted with."
86 This distinction is suggested by Koch, *Schrift*, 143, and Stanley, *Scripture*, 98. See BAGD (2000) 200 (3), "to grasp the significance or meaning of something, *understand, comprehend.*"
87 See Keck, "3:10-18," 151.
88 See Dunn, 1:151; Stanley, *Scripture*, 99.
89 Stanley, *Scripture*, 99.
90 Dunn, 1:151.
91 Günther Wanke, "φοβέω κτλ.," *TDNT* 9 (1974) 201–3.
92 See ibid., 204.
93 Ibid., 206.
94 See K. Romaniuk, "Die 'Gottesfürchtigen' im Neuen Testament. Beitrag zur neutestamentlichen Theologie der Gottesfurcht," *Aeg* 44 (1964) 66–91; F. Siegert, "Gottesfürchtige und Sympathisanten," *JSJ* 4 (1973) 109–64; T. M. Finn, "The God-Fearers Reconsidered," *CBQ* 47 (1985) 75–84.
95 See Wilhelm Michaelis, "ὁράω . . . ὀφθαλμός κτλ.," *TDNT* 5 (1967) 376.
96 Murray, 105, refers to "unqualified ungodlessness."

catena was probably created by Jewish sectarians, and was intended to buttress their claims against other groups whom they considered to be heretics, Paul has taken this weapon out of their hands and turned it back on its creators. With Paul's elimination of the distinction between the righteous and fools, the catena relegates all Jews along with all Gentiles to the category of sinners and traitors, placing them on same level as enemies of God.[97]

■ **19** An abrupt change of style marks the end of the poetic catena and the beginning of Paul's theological conclusion. As in 2:2, the formula οἴδαμεν δὲ ὅτι ("now we know that") appeals to the "common knowledge" shared by Paul, his audience, and also his interlocutor concerning the validity of the law for those ἐν τῷ νόμῳ ("within the law").[98] Burdick shows that the basic sense of οἶδα from classical to NT times relates to "something that was universally known or that was known assuredly."[99] The first person plural usage in "we know" is a standard rhetorical formula, for example, Antiphon *Tetra.* 1 1.2.7, "For we surely know (οἴδαμεν) the fact about the whole city being polluted by him."[100] The expression ὅσα ὁ νόμος λέγει . . . λαλεῖ ("whatever the law says . . . it speaks") is inclusive because of the choice of the correlative ὅσος ("as much as, everything"),[101] and it reflects the notion that the law "speaks" directly to its adherents.[102] This carries forward the theme of

oral utterance in the quatrain of 3:13-14, but the basic concept of the law as an oral phenomenon is found throughout the OT. One thinks of the scene in Nehemiah when Ezra reads the law aloud and "all the people wept when they heard the words of the law" (Neh 8:9; see also 13:3). There was thought to be a responsibility to "hear" the law as it directed its message to individuals: "If one turns away his ear from hearing the law, even his prayer is an abomination" (Prov 28:9). The LXX of Isa 1:10 catches this sense of oral encounter in its warning: "Hear the word of the Lord, you rulers of Sodom; listen to the law of God (νόμον θεοῦ), you people of Gomorrah." It is clear from the context that "law" is being used here in the inclusive sense of all Scripture[103] and that it refers back to the previously cited catena drawn from the Psalms and Isaiah. This catena is therefore binding on Jewish people who are "within the law"[104] as well as to all others. In view of the references to "every mouth," "all the world," and "all flesh" in vv. 19-20, Paul's formulation allows no evasions to stand.

The ἵνα clause in v. 19b is more likely final (i.e., purposive) than consecutive or resultative;[105] it shows the goal toward which the speaking of the law was intended.[106] There are two goals: stopping mouths and indicting the wicked. The biblical metaphor of shutting mouths follows the logic of the previous references to sinful throats, tongues, lips, and mouths, found in the

97 See Watson, *Paul,* 128–30.

98 Dunn, 1:151–52. In contrast to those in Gal 4:21 who are ὑπὸ νόμου ("under law"), referring to those wishing to follow the Torah (Betz, *Galatians,* 241), the phrase in Rom 3:19 refers to all persons encompassed by the law. See Murray, 105–6.

99 Burdick, "Οἶδα and Γινώσκω," 344, 347; see also Horstmann, "οἶδα," 493–94.

100 See also *Apoc. Ez.* 25.10, "for we know (οἴδαμεν) that you are merciful." Other examples are in Demosthenes *Orat.* 21.82.7; 21.93.5; 21.121.7, 13; Epictetus *Diss.* 2.24.12.

101 BAGD 586.

102 For the distinction between "say" and "speak," see Godet, 143; Hans Hübner, "λαλέω," *EDNT* 2 (1991) 335–36.

103 Cranfield, 1:195, refers to 1 Cor 14:21; John 10:34; 15:25; and rabbinic usage as background for this inclusive reference; however, the comprehensive survey of biblical, Hellenistic Jewish, and rabbinic usage by Walter Gutbrod, "νόμος κτλ.," *TDNT* 4

(1967) 1036–59, provides no examples of this inclusive usage.

104 See Kuss, 1:108; Morris, 170; Winger, *By What Law,* 104, cited with approval by Hays, "Romans 3–4," 153. Murray, 106, in contrast, argues that the law addresses "the whole world," i.e., both Jews and Greeks.

105 Lietzmann, 48; Kühl, 104; Cranfield, 1:196; Morris, 170, in line with BDF §369 describing ἵνα followed by the subjunctive. Moulton and Turner, *Grammar III,* 100–104, describe the purpose clause as the predominate syntax of ἵνα followed by the subjunctive. Fitzmyer, 337, argues for a result clause on the basis of BDF §391.5, which describes the "infinitive of result"; but the subjunctive rather than an infinitive is used in 3:19b. Lagrange, 71, and Schlier, 99, suggest a consecutive reading, implying that v. 19b simply follows v. 19a rather than describing the purpose thereof, but this seems less likely.

106 Meyer, 1:159.

catena. Since the στόμα/פֶּה ("mouth") is the "organ of speech" in the OT and Judaism,[107] to stop it up is to bring human talking to a halt. In Greco-Roman as well as biblical sources φράσσειν στόμα is an idiom for shutting the mouth and silencing speech.[108] But the adjective πᾶς ("all, every") in connection with στόμα ("mouth") is explainable on the basis of OT precedents.[109] In every instance in which God shuts the mouths of humans, it is to silence unrighteous words and actions. Job 5:11 has God's intervening on behalf of the weak, so "the poor have hope and injustice shuts her mouth." LXX Ps 62:12 celebrates the time when the "mouth of those speaking wicked things have been stopped up." Similarly Ps 107:42 expresses hope for God's reversal of status by bringing down princes and raising up the needy, so that "all wickedness stops its mouth." Paul uses this biblical metaphor to draw together the earlier argument of the chapter, including the citation of the catena. Since "all persons are liars," it follows that every evil mouth must be shut. I will trace the later development of this motif through the letter, because at the end Paul utters a prayer that the converted "with one mouth" will glorify God (15:6) and that when the world mission is completed, every "tongue" will confess Christ as Lord (15:16). The chronic perversion of human speaking will be at an end.

The second purpose toward which the law speaks is to bring all the world under divine indictment.[110] The word ὑπόδικος, which appears here for the only time in the NT or LXX, is a term widely used in Greco-Roman legal practice and means "under judgment or indictment" and therefore "answerable, accountable."[111] For example, Plato Leg. 954a: "The broker in a sale shall act as security for the seller should the latter have no real right to the goods sold or be quite unable to guarantee their possession; the broker shall be legally liable (ὑπόδικος) equally with the seller." In combination with the verb γίνομαι ("come about, become") as in Paul's formulation, Plato refers to a verdict: "let him be guilty (ὑπόδικος γιγνέσθω)."[112] When Paul states that all the world is under indictment τῷ θεῷ ("to God"), this refers to the injured party, who has a right to initiate legal proceedings. There are no exact parallels to Paul's reference to indictment to God, although the idea without the use of the Greek legal term is found throughout the Hebrew Scriptures.[113] In this case "all the world" is brought before God's judgment seat.[114] The point is that the scriptural legacy of Israel places the chosen people "firmly 'in the dock' along with everyone else."[115]

■ **20** The final sentence of the pericope is introduced with the conjunction διότι ("because, therefore"), ordinarily used at the beginning of causal clauses within sentences rather than as the opening word.[116] It draws the entire final sentence into relationship to the earlier discourse of the pericope, providing the underlying reason for the divine action of silencing human evasions and holding all to be accountable. That Paul changed the wording of LXX Ps 143:2b from πᾶς ζῶν ("all life") to πᾶσα σάρξ ("all flesh") is widely acknowledged by commentators,[117] but the reason for the change is a matter of debate. The influence of the wording of *1 En.* 81.5 is occasionally suggested,[118] and Isa 66:23 contains the words πᾶσα σάρξ ἐνώπιον μου ("all flesh before me"), but the consensus is that Paul was working primarily with the psalm text. It does not seem plausible that the

---

107 Konrad Weiss, "στόμα," *TDNT* 7 (1971) 695–97.
108 BAGD 865 cites Galen *Script. Min.* I p. 73.17; *Sib. Or.* 8.420; 2 Macc 9:55.
109 The LXX has πᾶν στόμα ("every mouth") in 3 Kgdms 19:18; Sir 19:1; Isa 9:16.
110 See Hays, "Romans 3–4," 155–58.
111 BAGD 844; see the many examples in LSJM 1880 and MM 657.
112 Plato *Leg.* 868d5, which refers to the verdict of being guilty of impiety. See also *Leg.* 878d3; 907e5; and elsewhere; also Lysias *Orat.* 10.9.4; 11.4.5; Isocrates *Loch.* 2.7; see LSJM 1880.
113 For example, Gen 30:6; Exod 12:12; Job 22:4; Sir 11:9; Pss 9:7-8; 76:8-9; Isa 3:14. These similarities

lead Jülicher, 244, to express the suspicion that Paul is citing a "lost piece of OT speech" in v. 19b.
114 Cranfield, 1:197.
115 Dunn, 1:152.
116 See BAGD 199; BDF §456.1.
117 While the citation is assumed by most commentators, it is denied by Koch, *Schrift*, 18, 145. In *Paul's Use*, 153, Ellis lists Rom 3:20 as an instance of an OT allusion rather than a direct quotation. Other specialists in the quotation of OT material assume an alteration of Ps 143:2 at this point: Michel, *Bibel*, 76; van der Minde, *Schrift*, 54–58.
118 Käsemann, 82; the most extensive discussion is found in Jewett, *Terms*, 97.

alteration came from quoting the psalm from memory[119] because precisely the same wording is found in Gal 2:16, written years earlier than Romans. Despite the rough semantic equivalence of the two expressions, it hardly seems appropriate to say that the alteration is meaningless[120] when a term as laden with polemical significance as "flesh" is selected. As Betz showed in analyzing the parallel passage in Gal 2:16, Paul's theological interpretation is visible in the alteration of the quotation.[121] At a minimum one can say that while $\pi\hat{\alpha}\varsigma\ \zeta\hat{\omega}\nu$ is a neutral expression for humans, $\pi\hat{\alpha}\sigma\alpha\ \sigma\acute{\alpha}\rho\xi$ provides a reminiscence through Gen 6:12 of creaturely limitations[122] or opposition to God.[123] Given the original setting of the saying in the circumcision crisis reflected in Galatians, I believe it is more plausible to suggest that Paul "wished to counter the Judaizer's claim that circumcised <u>flesh</u> was acceptable as righteous to God."[124] This connotation is strongly suggested also for the Romans setting because of Paul's prior use of the term $\sigma\acute{\alpha}\rho\xi$ ("flesh") in the context of circumcision (Rom 2:28).

If there is a citation here from Ps 143, the more important alteration is the addition of the phrase "from works of the law." This expression has elicited an enormous discussion.[125] Dunn has moved the discussion of this verse beyond the denunciation of Jewish law popularized by the interpretive tradition undergirded by the Reformation to what he has called "the function of the law as an identity factor, the social function of the law as marking out the people of the law in their distinctiveness." The discovery of the rough Hebrew equivalent of

the expression "works of the law" in 4Q398 14-17 ii 3 (מעשי התורה), lends strength to Dunn's analysis.[126] The problem is that "works of the law" served as an identity marker for those "whom God has chosen and will vindicate," providing a method of "maintaining his status within that people."[127] However, Dunn does not link these insights with the systems of gaining honor and avoiding shame in the Mediterranean world, which linkage would allow a broader grasp of Paul's argument. It is not just the Jewish law that is in view here, but also law as an identity marker for any culture. $\Sigma\acute{\alpha}\rho\xi$ in this verse was not selected by Paul to expose "the equation of covenant membership with physical rite and national kinship" on the part of Jews only,[128] but because it includes the entirety of the human race. In the face of the impartial righteousness of God, no human system of competing for glory and honor can stand.

The knowledge that traditional systems of achieving honor and avoiding shame are sinful and must be abandoned is in view with the final clause of this pericope. The intensive form of knowledge, $\dot{\epsilon}\pi\acute{\iota}\gamma\nu\omega\sigma\iota\varsigma$, is used here as in 1:28 to refer to "knowledge directed towards a particular object, perceiving, discerning, recognizing."[129] For example, a papyrus letter directs that actions be taken $\pi\rho\grave{o}\varsigma\ \tau\grave{o}\ \mu\grave{\eta}\ \breve{\epsilon}\kappa\alpha\sigma\tau\alpha\ \dot{\epsilon}\pi'\ \dot{\epsilon}\pi\acute{\iota}\gamma\nu\omega\sigma\iota\nu\ \dot{\alpha}\chi\vartheta(\hat{\eta})\nu\alpha\iota$ ("in order to prevent the details being recognized").[130] In Romans the law allows a precise recognition of sin, which fatally poisons all systems of achieving superior status through performance. In Morris's words, "no one will be accepted before God on account of his obser-

119 So Cranfield, 1:198.

120 Wilckens, 1:173, citing Sand, *Fleisch*, 150.

121 Betz, *Galatians*, 118–19.

122 Zahn, 169; his discussion of the parallel text in Gal 2:16 was somewhat stronger, referring to the corruptibility of humankind. See also Theodor Zahn, *Der Brief des Paulus an die Galater*, 2d ed. (Leipzig: Deichert, 1907) 123.

123 See Michel, 144–45.

124 Jewett, *Terms*, 98.

125 Significant literature is listed in Josef Blank, "Warum sagt Paulus: 'Aus den Werken des Gesetzes wird niemand gerecht'?" *EKK Vorarbeiten* 1 (1969) 79–107; Rafael Gyllenberg, "Die paulinische Rechtfertigungslehre und das AT," *StTh(Riga)* 1 (1935) 35–52. See also Westerholm, *Law*, 15–101, 116–21.

126 Dunn, 1:159. See Fitzmyer, *According to Paul*, 19–24;

Martin G. Abegg Jr., "4QMMT C27,31 and 'Works of Righteousness,'" *DSD* 6 (1999) 139–47. Abegg, 140, concludes: "it appears highly likely that Paul was reacting to a position that was espoused in 4QMMT by the Qumran covenanters, namely that a person was reckoned righteous by keeping 'works of the law'" (4Q398 14-17 ii 3 = 4QMMT C 27.31).

127 Dunn, 1:159.

128 Dunn, 1:160.

129 Robert E. Picirelli, "The Meaning of 'Epignosis,'" *EvQ* 47 (1975) 89, citing from J. Armitage Robinson, *St. Paul's Epistle to the Ephesians* (London: Macmillan, 1903) 254.

130 Cited from MM 237; see also Diodorus Siculus *Hist.* 3.56.5, which refers to the honors given to Uranus because of "his knowledge of the stars ($\tau\grave{\eta}\nu\ \tau\hat{\omega}\nu\ \breve{\alpha}\sigma\tau\rho\omega\nu\ \dot{\epsilon}\pi\acute{\iota}\gamma\nu\omega\sigma\iota\nu$)."

vance of the law."[131] This pertains as much to Greeks as to Jews.[132] It is not a matter of failure to perform the law,[133] but as Rom 7 will explain in detail, a matter of sinful competition that turns conformity to law into a means of status acquisition. While Paul's conversion led to his acknowledgment of this dilemma along with the bloodshed that such fanatical obedience always entails, here he insists that the law itself conveys the truth for everyone: whether Jew or Gentile, barbarian or Greek, educated or uneducated, "weak" or "strong." Every boastful mouth must be closed in view of the righteousness of God, a requirement that has a direct bearing on the missional purpose of this letter. For until the superiority claims of the Roman house and tenement churches are abandoned, their participation in a mission to the barbarians in Spain will be one more form of cultural imperialism, and thus a violation of the righteousness of God as revealed in the cross of Christ.

---

131 Morris, 171. Byrne, 118, restricts this insight unduly: "the law reveals to Jews that they, like the Gentiles, stand as sinners before God, liable to condemnation." Most other commentators follow this restricted view that the argument pertains mainly to Jewish self-righteousness, e.g., see Godet, 143–44; Barrett, 71.
132 See Wilckens, 1:180.
133 For example, Ziesler, 106; Moo, 210; Theobald, 92–95.

3

The First Part of the Fourth Pericope

The Righteousness of God and Setting Right of All by Faith Alone

a. Thesis and Rationale concerning the Triumph of Righteousness in Christ

21/ But God's righteousness that was attested by the law and the prophets has been manifested apart from the law, 22/ that is, God's righteousness [has been manifested] through faith in[a] Jesus[b] Christ, in regard to all[c] who have faith, (for there is no distinction, 23/ for all sinned and fall short of the glory of God, 24/ being set right freely by his grace) through the redemption that is in Christ Jesus,
> 25/ "whom God put forth as a mercy seat"
> through[d] faith "in his blood"
> for a demonstration of his righteousness
> "because of the passing over[e] of sinful actions previously committed
> 26/ by the forbearance of God";

to demonstrate his righteousness in the present critical time, so that he is righteous and[f] makes righteous the one who has faith in Jesus.[g]

a   The uncial A has the wording πίστεως ἐν Χριστῷ Ἰησοῦ, noted by Sanday and Headlam, 84, and Porter, "Rhetorical Scribe," 416–17, but not by Nestle-Aland. Porter makes a good case that this was "a conscious change" that rejects the subjective genitive interpretation made possible by the original wording, πίστεως Ἰησοῦ Χριστοῦ. The change in A from "Christ Jesus" to "Jesus Christ" points in the same direction of stressing Christ as the agent of salvation, in whom faith should be placed (Porter, "Rhetorical Scribe," 418).

b   The absence of "Jesus" in B Marcion is too weakly attested to be considered original. The presence of the name is overwhelmingly attested by P[40] *rell*.

c   In place of εἰς πάντας ("for all"), strongly attested by P[40] ℵ* A B C P Ψ 5 6 81 88 104 263 424ᶜ 436 459 630 915 1506 1739 1875 1881 1908* 2110 2200 *l* 60 *l* 598 *l* 599 *l* 617 syᵖᵃˡ sa bo arm Cl Orˡᵃᵗ ⁵/⁶ Apollinaris Did Cyr Aug, a minor variant is found in vgˢᵗ· ʷʷ Ambst Pel, ἐπὶ πάντας ("upon all"). A conflated version of both readings is found in ℵ² D F G K L 33 61 69 181 218 256 323 326 330 365 424* 441 451 467 614 621 623 629 720 917 945 1175 1241 1243 1319 1505 1563 1573 1678 1718 1735 1751 1836 1838 1845 1852 1874 1877 1908ᶜ 1912 1959 1962 2127 2138 2197 2344 2464 2492 2495 2516ˢᵘᵖ

2523 2718 *Maj Lect* ar b d f g mon (o) vgᶜˡ syᵖ·ʰ geo slav Orˡᵃᵗ ¹/⁶ Didᵈᵘᵇ Chr Ambst Chromatius; cf. Metzger, *Textual Commentary*, 449.

d   The rather evenly balanced evidence for and against the inclusion of the definite article τῆς in the expression "through faith/through the faith" is manifest in Nestle-Aland²⁶,²⁷, which places it in square brackets, while the earlier editions of the Nestle text deleted it. In favor of deletion are ℵ C* D* F G 0219ᵛⁱᵈ 6 88 104 365 424ᶜ 436 459 1319 1505 1506 1573 1739 1881 1962 2495 Or Eus Did Cyr Hes¹/² , while texts including the article are P⁴⁰ᵛⁱᵈ B C³ D² K L P Ψ 33 69 81 181 263 323 326 330 424* 451 614 945 1175 1241 1243 1735 1836 1874 1877 1912 2200 2344 2464 2492 *Maj Lect* Chr Severian Hes¹/² . It seems more likely that the article would be added than deleted, as shown particularly by its presence in the corrected version of D² (though D¹ lacks the artcle) and in the vast majority of other manuscripts, so I believe a firm decision should be made for its exclusion. The addition by a later scribe may reflect an understanding of faith such as one finds in the Pastorals, where ἡ πίστις refers to "the faith" in a credal sense. The lack of discussion in recent commentaries may reflect the tendency to view the expression διὰ πίστεως ("through faith") as a favorite theological formula. As for the omission of the entire expression, "through the faith," by A and 2127, the best assessment is Metzger's word in *Textual Commentary*, 449, that it was "accidental," although Porter, "Rhetorical Scribe," 413, suspects a rhetorical motive in emphasizing "the sacrificial imagery . . . rather than imposing 'faith' as an intermediary."

e   Several minor and late variants appear to be aimed at theological clarification of the text. In place of the widely attested original διὰ τὴν πάρεσιν ("because of the remission"), 1908 has διὰ τὴν πάρεσιν ἐν τῷ νῦν αἰῶνι ("because of the remission in the present aeon"), while 1875 provides the reading ἐν τῷ νῦν καιρῷ διὰ τὴν πώρωσιν ("in the present time because of the hardening").

f   The absence of καί ("and") in F G 796 it Ambst may represent an effort at syntactical improvement by changing the participle δικαιοῦντα from a compound predicate adjective to a circumstantial participle of means that explains how God is righteous: "so that he is righteous in setting right the person from faith in Jesus."

g   The widespread witness for the reading Ἰησοῦ ("of Jesus") in ℵ A B C K P 6 81 88 104 323 365 424 1175 1241 1243 1505 1735 1739 1836 1874 1877 1881 1962 2495 *Maj l* 598, 599, 603 ar d* vgˢᵗ vgʷʷ syʰ sa boᵐˢˢ indicates its originality as compared with Ἰησοῦ Χριστοῦ ("of Jesus Christ") in 629 *pc* it vg^{cl} bo, or "our Lord Jesus Christ" in sy^p. Metzger, *Textual Commentary*, 449, suggests that the omission of Ἰησοῦ in F G 336 g and the shift to the accusative case Ἰησοῦν in D^{gr} L Ψ 33 326 330 436 451 614 945 1319 1506 1573 1881 2127 2344 2464 2492 *Lect* Cl, which makes God the subject who makes Jesus righteous, are understandable copyists' blunders while transcribing a continuous text, but the matter remains unclear. Metzger's suggestion might also explain the variant of Ἰησοῦν Χριστόν ("Jesus Christ") found in 1984.

Analysis

The impression of semantic and rhetorical obscurity[1] or complexity[2] in this pericope is caused partially by the citation of a confessional or liturgical fragment in 3:25-26a, partially by the compact use of Pauline theological formulas, but primarily by a stylistic shift that has not been understood until relatively recently. As Douglas A. Campbell demonstrates, this pericope departs from the intermediate style of the preceding sections of Romans and moves into the grand or elegant style, with "extended periodic syntax" that fuses the entire pericope into a single sentence.[3] "The grand or elevated style used rounded periods and long members, a complex diction, variable connectives (with frequent use of asyndeton) and was considered proper to the exposition of a vivid and elevated subject matter. As Cicero says, it is 'magnificent, opulent, stately and ornate . . . the kind of eloquence which rushes along with the roar of a mighty stream.'"[4]

Verse 21 opens the pericope with an antithesis marked by paronomasia in the use of νόμος ("law"), which provides a wordplay on two slightly different definitions of the term.[5] From this point on, however, the typical Pauline antithesis gives way to a broad and interconnected synthesis. The theme of divine righteousness is elaborated by three clauses marked by anaphora in the use of διά ("through") and separated from vv. 22d-24a by a rhetorical parenthesis.[6] There is also a citation of a pre-Pauline christological formula in vv. 25a-26a[7] followed by a resumption of the phrase "to demonstrate his righteousness."[8] This provides an isocolic reduplication in the use of ἔνδειξιν ("demonstration") in v. 25a and v. 26a, separated by the fourth διά ("through") clause dealing with the remission of sins. The passage contains other paronomastic series, with the key terms "righteousness" appearing seven times and "faith" appearing four times. The sweeping interconnectedness of this passage serves to incorporate a range of allusions to atonement theories and to views of faith favored in branches of early Christianity that are distinct from the Pauline churches. Under the rubric of "manifesting" and "demonstrating" the "righteousness of God," Paul celebrates the theological breadth of early Christianity with an inclusivity that is explicitly stressed in v. 22c-d with "no distinction" being made among "all who have faith."

1   See Weiss, "Beiträge," 221–23; Käsemann, 92.
2   See Theobald, "Gottesbild," 133; Kraus, *Heiligtumsweihe*, 15
3   Campbell, *Rhetoric of Righteousness*, 81; a brief evaluation of Campbell's theory is provided by Anderson, *Paul*, 199–201. See also Kuss, 1:102–3, and Campbell, *Paul's Gospel*, 26, for sketches of the solemn, proclamatory style of this pericope. The investigation by Reinhard Wonneberger, "Römer 3,21-26," in *Syntax und Exegese. Eine generative Theorie der griechischen Syntax und ihr Beitrag zur Auslegung des Neuen Testaments, dargestellt an 2. Korinther 5,2f und Römer 3,21-26*, BBET 13 (Frankfurt: Lang, 1979) 214–70, attempts to explain the passage with syntactical means and downplays the issue of style (esp. 269–70).
4   Campbell, *Rhetoric of Righteousness*, 82, citing Cicero *De or.* 97.
5   See Campbell, *Rhetoric of Righteousness*, 83–86.
6   See ibid., 175–89; he incorporates only the first three διά clauses in the analysis, but there is no reason not to include the fourth as well, even though the fourth has διά with the accusative while first three are διά with the genitive.
7   See Kraus, *Heiligtumsweihe*, 16–20, 92–167; for discussion of details see notes on relevant verses below.
8   See Bullinger, *Figures*, 206.

This addresses the audience situation in Rome that was marked by tension between ethnic groups of believers.[9] The grand style lifts the hearers into a performative experience of the triumph of divine righteousness reinforced by the repetition of $\nu\hat{\nu}\nu$, the "now" in v. 21a and the "present time" in v. 26c. The passage concludes with a ringing clausula in v. 26d-e that drives home the theme of the "righteousness of God" by using $\delta\iota\kappa$- terms twice in connection with $\pi\iota\sigma\tau\iota\varsigma$ ("faith").[10]

The indications that a pre-Pauline formula is cited in vv. 25-26 have been assembled by a series of authoritative studies.[11] (a) There are three hapax legomena in this section: $\iota\lambda\alpha\sigma\tau\eta\rho\iota\sigma\nu$ ("expiation"), $\pi\acute{\alpha}\rho\epsilon\sigma\iota\varsigma$ ("remission"), and $\pi\rho\sigma\gamma\epsilon\gamma\sigma\nu\acute{\sigma}\tau\alpha$ $\dot{\alpha}\mu\alpha\rho\tau\dot{\eta}\mu\alpha\tau\alpha$ ("previously committed sins"); (b) two terms appear with uncharacteristic definitions: $\pi\rho\sigma\tau\acute{\iota}\vartheta\eta\sigma\vartheta\alpha\iota$ ("put forth")[12] and $\alpha\hat{\iota}\mu\alpha$;[13] (c) there are two indications of the intrusion of typically Pauline expressions into formulations that seem self-contained: $\delta\iota\dot{\alpha}$ $\pi\iota\sigma\tau\epsilon\omega\varsigma$ ("through faith"), since the phrase "expiation in his blood" belongs together,[14] and "in order to demonstrate his righteousness" breaks the natural link between expiation and remission of sins;[15] (d) and the relative pronoun $\ddot{\sigma}\varsigma$ appears at the beginning of this as in other christological formulas and hymns cited in the NT (Phil 2:6; Col 1:15; etc.).

Various hypotheses have been proposed about the lines of demarcation between the original hymn and Pauline additions. Bultmann, followed by Käsemann and others,[16] proposed that the material in parentheses was added by Paul:

> justified (by his grace as a gift)
> through the redemption which is in Christ Jesus,
> whom God put forward as an expiation by his blood
>   (to be received by faith);
> this was to show God's righteousness,
> because in his divine forbearance he had passed over
>   former sins.

Since the opening two lines are typical Pauline formulations lacking in hymnic style, Eduard Lohse limited the citation to the following:[17]

> whom God put forward as an expiation by his blood,
> this was to show God's righteousness,
> because in his divine forbearance he had passed over
>   former sins.

On grounds that the second line of the citation is typically Pauline and that it is echoed in v. 26, Wolfgang Kraus and others have concluded that the probable wording of the pre-Pauline hymnic fragment is as follows:[18]

---

9   See Campbell, "Romans iii," 31–33.

10   See Campbell, *Rhetoric of Righteousness*, 99; Holloway, "Paul's Pointed Prose," 47.

11   For an account of early insights into the peculiar style and content of this material, see Alfons Pluta, *Gottes Bundestreue. Ein Schlüsselbegriff in Röm 3,25a*, SBS 34 (Stuttgart: Katholisches Bibelwerk, 1969) 40–41; Käsemann, *Exegetische Versuche*, 96–100; Heinrich Zimmermann, *Jesus Christus–Geschichte und Verkündigung* (Stuttgart: Katholisches Bibelwerk, 1973) 71–81; Marie-Louise Gubler, *Die frühesten Deutungen des Todes Jesu. Eine motivgeschichtliche Darstellung aufgrund der neueren exegetischen Forschung*, OBO 15 (Freiburg: Universitätsverlag, 1977) 224–29; Theobald, "Gottesbild," 131–68; Hans-Jürgen van der Minde, "Wie geht Paulus mit der Tradition um?" *BK* 37 (1982) 6–13; Hultgren, *Gospel*, 47–72; Ben F. Meyer, "The Pre-Pauline Formula in Rom 3:25-26a," *NTS* 29 (1983) 198–208; Dunn, 1:163–64; Kraus, *Heiligtumsweihe*, 14.

12   See Käsemann, *Exegetische Versuche*, 96; Kraus, *Heiligtumsweihe*, 16.

13   While "blood" appears also in Rom 5:9 and, in connection with the tradition of the Lord's Supper, in 1 Cor 11:25, Paul ordinarily refers to the "cross" rather than to the "blood." See Bultmann, *Theology*, 1:46; Kraus, *Heiligtumsweihe*, 16.

14   See Dunn, 1:164, 172; Käsemann, *Exegetische Versuche*, 100.

15   See Kraus, *Heiligtumsweihe*, 18–20.

16   Bultmann, *Theology*, 1:46; Käsemann, *Exegetische Versuche*, 96–100; Hunter, *Predecessors*, 120–22. Charles H. Talbert argues for the later interpolation of this material in "A Non-Pauline Fragment at Romans 3:24-26?" *JBL* 85 (1966) 289–90.

17   Lohse, *Märtyrer*, 149–50, followed to a large extent by Wengst, *Formeln*, 87–90, and Meyer, "Pre-Pauline Formula," 204.

18   Kraus, *Heiligtumsweihe*, 20, 92; on 18 Kraus summarizes the analysis of Hugolinus Langkammer, "Ekspiacyjna formula wiary w Rz 3, 2-26" [The Atonement Formula in Rom 3:2-26], *RTK* 23 (1976) 33, 38, which comes to a similar conclusion. See also Theobald, *Gottesbild*, 153; Zimmermann, *Jesus*

v. 25a: whom God put forward as a mercy seat (ὃν προέθετο ἱλαστήριον)

v. 25b: in his blood (ἐν τῷ αὐτοῦ αἵματι)

v. 25d: because of the remission of previously committed sins (διὰ τὴν πάρεσιν τῶν προγεγονότων ἁμαρτημάτων)

v. 26a: in the forbearance of God (ἐν τῇ ἀνοχῇ τοῦ θεοῦ).

Pauline redaction is therefore visible in the framing of the hymn, the insertion of the phrases "through faith" in v. 25b and "in order to demonstrate his righteousness" in v. 25c.

This pericope sums up, advances, and eloquently climaxes the preceding argument of the letter, which begins with the "righteousness of God" (cf. 1:17; 3:5) manifest "apart from the law" (cf. 3:20) and moves on to the lack of distinction (cf. 2:6-16) and the universality of sin (cf. 1:18–3:20). The performative aspect of the grand style also conveys "spiritual charisma" in Paul's preaching that had been suggested in 1:11. In contrast to the exegetical tradition of isolating and debating each detail in this passage, a procedure that turns it into an obscure discussion "about" an abstractly conceived "righteousness of God," the passage was intended to lift its original hearers into an immediate "demonstration" of divine power to set right a culturally diverse world. Rather than reifying favored theological concepts as various interpretive traditions have tended to do, Paul celebrates the righteousness manifest in Christ that "now" promises to complete the conversion of the known world. This eloquent argument abolishes the distinctions that sustain claims of cultural, ethnic, and religious superiority. While traditional interpretation has been preoccupied with doctrinal debates on the doctrine of "justification," the bearing of this passage on the missionary expedition to Spain is evident in the stress on impartial atonement "for all who have faith."

Rhetorical Disposition

Christus, 73; van der Minde, *Schrift*, 61–62. For an analysis of the hymnic quality of this material see Schattenmann, *Prosahymnus*, 22–23; for a critique of the citation theory see Campbell, *Rhetoric of Righteousness*, 45–57.

Exegesis

■ **21** The new pericope opens with the adverbial expression νυνὶ δέ ("but now"), a characteristically Pauline formulation[19] that implies either a contrast with a previously mentioned time period[20] or a logical contrast with a preceding argument.[21] The latter seems most likely here because in place of an explicit reference to a previous time period, there is a logical antithesis, "apart from the law," that contrasts with "works of the law" in the preceding verse.[22] The main theme of Romans, "God's righteousness," which was announced in 1:16 and reiterated in 3:5, appears primarily in the sense of God's saving activity in the crucified Christ that sets the world right.[23] This phrase is similar to the Hebrew expression צדקות אל ("the righteous deeds of God") in Qumran (1QS 1:21), which the priest is to report in recounting God's wondrous deeds and acts of love. In Diogenes Laertius *Vitae philos.* 3.79, Plato is attributed with claiming that "righteousness is the law of God" (τὴν δικαιοσύνην θεοῦ νόμον) since it encourages people to act righteously and imparts fear of punishment after death. This link with human virtue is typical for classical culture, as in the sixth-century B.C.E. maxim attributed to Theognis *Eleg.* 1.47, or Phocyclides *Sent.* 10:1: "By righteousness, in sum, is every virtuous thing" (ἐν δὲ δικαιοσύνηι συλλήβδην πᾶς᾽ ἀρετή ἐστι).[24] *Virtus* ("virtue") was one of the three most important moral principles in Roman culture, with a primary connotation of martial manliness and courage.[25]

A dynamic, cosmic grasp of divine righteousness has emerged in the wake of Käsemann's work: "δικαιοσύνη θεοῦ is for Paul God's sovereignty over the world revealing itself eschatologically in Jesus. . . . It is the rightful power with which God makes his cause to triumph in the world which has fallen away from him, and which yet, as creation, is his inviolable possession."[26] Käsemann's starting point is further developed by Peter Stuhlmacher, who explains that the righteousness of God refers to the power by which the Creator's right over his creation is expressed.[27] The glory of the creation is restored thereby by a new creation.[28] The participatory and transformational aspects of Paul's view were developed by E. P. Sanders and Axel von Dobbeler,[29] and the social implications for the inclusion of Gentiles were raised by Krister Stendahl, Nils Dahl, James Dunn, Lloyd Gaston, and others.[30] Attention to the underlying framework of Christ's reversal of systems of honor and shame to create new communities by grace alone would help to hold these recent insights together. However, the subject of divine righteousness remains God himself,[31] whose dynamic activity is proclaimed by the gospel. The genitive in δικαιοσύνη θεοῦ should therefore be taken as subjective,[32] with God's action being defined as righ-

19 See Rom 7:6, 17; 15:23, 25; 1 Cor 12:18; 13:13; 15:20; 2 Cor 8:22; Phlm 9, 11; among the Attic Orators, νυνὶ δέ is used by Demosthenes 15 times, by Lysias 13 times, Aeschines 11 times, and Isaeus 4 times, but never as an introduction to a new paragraph. Johannes Woyke's analysis of this expression in the LXX, Philo, and Josephus ("Einst," 189–96) indicates that context alone determines whether the contrast is temporal or logical.

20 For example, Walter Radl, "νῦν, νυνί," *EDNT* 2 (1991) 481; Leenhardt, 98; Dunn, 1:164; Moo, 221, and the overwhelming majority of interpreters.

21 Godet, 146; Kühl, 107; Woyke, "Einst," 206.

22 Meyer, 1:163; Woyke, "Einst," 97.

23 See the discussions on 1:16 and 3:5 and the histories of research by Brauch, "Perspectives," 523–42; Seifrid, *Justification,* 1–75; John Reumann, "Righteousness (Early Judaism, Greco-Roman World, NT)," *ABD* 5 (1992) 736–73; Dieter Lührmann, "Gerechtigkeit. III. Neues Testament," *TRE* 12 (1980) 416–17.

24 Δικαιοσύνη appears some 199 times in Aristotle and is regularly associated with ἀρετή ("virtue").

25 Meister, "Tugenden," 6–7.

26 Käsemann, *Questions,* 180; see also idem, "Justice for the Unjust," *Colloquium* 1 (1978) 10–16; idem, *Perspectives,* 60–78.

27 Stuhlmacher, *Gerechtigkeit,* 87–89.

28 Stuhlmacher, *Reconciliation,* 81.

29 Sanders, *Paul,* 474–523, 549; von Dobbeler, *Glaube als Teilhabe,* 166–70; 239–80.

30 Stendahl, *Paul,* 3–5, 23–28; Dahl, *Studies,* 107–12; Gaston, *Paul,* 116–23.

31 Karl Kertelge, "δικαιοσύνη," *EDNT* 1 (1990) 238: "The use of δικαιοσύνη θεοῦ presupposes the question, Who is God? The God that Paul proclaims is the God who has revealed himself in abiding faithfulness to himself and to his people in Jesus Christ." For the consistency of this emphasis with Judaism, see Asher Finkel, "Gerechtigkeit. II. Judentum," *TRE* 12 (1982) 412–13.

32 See Barrett, 29: "On God's side, salvation means

teous. Since the modern terms "righteousness," "justice," and "justification" are used to render forms of the same δικ- stem, in this commentary I select translations based on the English stem "right," so that the integration of personal and cosmic transformation, the restoration of the divinely intended order, the achievement of justice, and the character of divine righteousness can be articulated. The decisive OT background for the concept of the righteous God, which dominates this pericope by no less than five references, is visible in LXX Ps 97.[33] The cosmic scope of Yahweh's actions as "the King of creation"[34] is celebrated by all nations as well as by the physical and animal kingdoms:

> Let the sea be moved, and all that fills it;
> the world and those who dwell in it!
> Let the rivers clap their hands;
> let the hills sing for joy together
> for he comes to rule the earth.
> He will judge the world with righteousness (ἐν δικαιοσύνῃ),
> and the peoples with uprightness (ἐν εὐθύτητι).
> (Ps 97:7-9)

In biblical history God intervenes repeatedly to counter injustice and to restore the order of creation and of human society that have been corrupted by sinful human activity.[35] John Scullion comments, "the creator God, the prime orderer, is the one who restores order in society, who demands proper order in worship, and who acts in his restoring, saving way to effect this."[36] By acting in this manner, Paul claims that God publicly "demonstrates his righteousness," to use the wording of Rom 3:26. When the social and cosmic dimensions of this divine activity are taken into account, it becomes clear that "setting right" or "making upright" is much broader than the usual idea of "justification." It is not so much the individual soul that is at stake in the revelation of divine righteousness that occurred in Christ and the subsequent preaching of the gospel, but rather the restoration of the entire cosmic order, including each group and species distorted by sin.

To claim that divine righteousness "has been manifested" (πεφανέρωται) means that it became visible historically in the Christ event. This formulation moves beyond the claim of 1:17, with which this verse is often identified.[37] The idea of the invisible becoming visible is illustrated in *Jos. Asen.* 12.2: Κύριε ὁ θεὸς . . . ὁ ποιήσας τὰ πάντα καὶ φανερώσας τὰ ἀφανῆ ("Lord God . . . who created the universe and manifested the things in secret").

The place of emphasis[38] in this opening sentence is the unusual phrase χωρὶς νόμου ("apart from law"). Since it is dependent on the verb "manifested" rather than the noun "righteousness,"[39] the phrase describes

---

the operation of his righteousness, which is not simply his property or attribute of being right, or righteous, but also his activity in doing right, and (as we say) seeing right done; thus his righteousness issues in his vindicating—those whom it is proper that he should vindicate." See also Fitzmyer, 344.

33 See Mark A. Seifrid's unpublished paper, "The Righteousness of God: The Theme of Romans," 4–15; his book, *Justification*, did not develop this theme.

34 Seifrid, "Righteousness of God," 5; see also Hans Heinrich Schmid, "Rechtfertigung als Schöpfungsgeschehen. Notizen zur alttestamentlichen Vorgeschichte eines neutestamentlichen Themas," in J. Friedrich et al., eds. *Rechtfertigung Festschrift für Ernst Käsemann zum 70. Geburtstag* (Tübingen: Mohr [Siebeck], 1976) 403–14.

35 See Schmid, *Gerechtigkeit als Weltordnung*, passim.

36 John J. Scullion, "Righteousness (OT)," *ABD* 5 (1992) 735.

37 In "φαίνω κτλ.," *TDNT* 9 (1974) 4, Rudolf Bultmann and Dieter Lührmann have argued for synonymous definition with ἀποκαλύπτω ("reveal") in the thesis of Rom 1:17, an assessment with which most commentators agree. Paul-Gerd Müller reduces the claim to "almost synonymously" in "φανερόω," *EDNT* 3 (1993) 413, but Bockmuehl has provided a more precise assessment in "Verb φανερόω," 95–96. The perfect tense of the verb in 3:21 and the choice of φανερόω point to the "historical salvation event in Jesus Christ." The use of φανερόω in Heb 9:26 is similar.

38 See Godet, 146.

39 Zahn, 172, argues that since "apart from law" precedes "righteousness," it cannot define it and must be attached to the verb; Cranfield, 1:201, agrees. Interpreters dominated by the classical doctrine of justification by faith alone tend to link χωρὶς νόμου with δικαιοσύνη θεοῦ, e.g., Wilckens, 1:185: "Die Offenbarung der Gottesgerechtigkeit schließt die Wirksamkeit des Gesetzes im Sinne von 3,20 aus." Morris, 174, comments that grammatically "apart

not the "process by which people are made right with God,"[40] but rather the method that God has chosen to reveal herself.[41] The preposition is used here with the sense of without relation to something, independent of something,[42] and the parallels in Greco-Roman literature tend to refer to independence from persons[43] or their activities.[44] Objects being excluded tend to be material, such as "excluding the tax of an artaba on each field (χωρὶς τῆς κατ᾽ ἄρουραν ἀρταβιῆας)" (P.Amh. 2. Nr. 85.9-10 from 78 C.E.) or "the lessee may sow and gather whatever crops he chooses apart from woad and coriander (χωρὶς ἰσάτεως καὶ ὀχομενίου)" (P.Oxy.1. Nr. 101.10-12 from 142 C.E.)." While the use of the preposition χωρίς with an abstraction such as "law" does not occur elsewhere in the ancient world,[45] Paul uses this phrase in Rom 7:8-9 to indicate the law's absence, and a similar phrase "apart from works of law" in 3:28 and "apart from works" in 4:6. Since the anarthrous use of νόμος here could extend its semantic field to every kind of law,[46] it seems unlikely that Paul wishes to restrict the argument to Israel's law.[47] The gen-

itive construction remains ambiguous, as Lohmeyer and Gaston have shown,[48] so long as one tacitly inserts the idea of "works of the law" as found elsewhere in Paul's letters, including the preceding verse (3:20).[49] It appears that it is the law itself rather than its works that are in view in v. 21. Whereas no form of law is able to place its adherents in a right relationship with God, the righteousness of God is manifested in a revolutionary manner through Christ. It is essential, therefore, to universalize the scope of Dunn's summary: "'Without the law' then means outside the national and religious parameters set by the law, without reference to the normal Jewish hallmarks."[50]

The participial clause headed by μαρτυρουμένη ("attested, witnessed") has a contrasting relationship to the preceding clause,[51] but there is no conjunction or particle to raise this to the level of an antithesis. The verb "witness" appears in its typical legal and argumentative connotation,[52] although this is the only time Paul employs it in reference to the witness of Scripture.[53] The theme was enunciated in 1:2, which refers to the

---

from law" belongs with the verb "but most agree that it is better taken with the noun." See also Michel, 147–48; Kühl, 107; Schlier, 105. Meyer, 1:163, mentions Reiche, Winzer, Klee, and Mehring as supporting the link between χωρὶς νόμου and δικαιοσύνη θεοῦ.

40 Moo, 223.

41 Kühl, 107; Kuss, 1:113; Fitzmyer, 344.

42 BAGD 891, meaning 2δ.

43 BAGD 890 refers to Vi. Hom. 2, "apart from everyone (χωρὶς πάντων)," and 1 Cor 11:11, "apart from us (χωρὶς ἡμῶν) you have already become kings." MM 696 refers to P.Oxy. 6. Nr. 932.10 from the late 2d century C.E.: "do not sell the young pigs without me (χωρὶς μοῦ)."

44 For example, BAGD 890 refers to Dionysius Periegeta Avi. 33.13, that the phoenix comes into being "apart from father and mother (πατρός τε καὶ μητρὸς χωρίς)."

45 A TLG check indicates the closest parallel is to the verbal cognate of the preposition in Aristotle's reference in Pol. 1253a32 to humankind's "being separated from law and justice" (χωρισθεὶς νόμου καὶ δίκης).

46 Zahn, 172.

47 See Fitzmyer, 344; Morris, 174.

48 Lohmeyer, Probleme, 31–74; Gaston, Paul, 100–106.

49 See Campbell, Rhetoric of Righteousness, 178–79.

50 Dunn, 1:165.

51 See Campbell, Rhetoric of Righteousness, 83–86.

52 See Hermann Strathmann, "μάρτυς κτλ.," TDNT 4 (1967) 476–81, referring to the discussion of witnesses in Aristotle's Rhet. 16-17 and the "almost inexhaustible number of examples of solemn witness in every possible kind of written agreement and record," found in inscriptions and papyri. A TLG search confirms the juridical use of μαρτυρουμένη as "testified to" as in Antiphon Tetra. 1 3.9.5: "nor by witnesses is this one now being cross-examined (μήτε τῶν μαρτυρουμένων οὗτος νῦν ἐλέγχεται)." Cf. Demosthenes Orat. 57.24.2, and Anaximenes of Lampsacus Rhet. Alex. 12.3.5. For a use with the preposition ὑπό ("by"), see Chrysippus Frag. log. 902.48: ἐναργῶς καταμαρτυρουμένους ὑφ᾽ ὧν ἐπικαλοῦνται μαρτύρων ("those manifestly witnessed against by the witnesses they summon"). The juridical use appears frequently in the LXX (Strathmann, 483), e.g., Deut 19:15, 18; Sus 40 ("these things we do testify [ταῦτα μαρτυροῦμεν]"). See also Acts 10:22; 22:12; Heb 11:4.

53 See Fitzmyer, 344; Allison A. Trites, The New Testament Concept of Witness, SNTSMS 31 (Cambridge: Cambridge University Press, 1977).

promise of the gospel "through his prophets in the holy scriptures," but here Paul employs the traditional formula, "the law and the prophets," for the entirety of Scripture.[54] Although specific scriptural passages have been cited in the earlier sections of Romans from the Law, the Prophets, and the Writings,[55] Paul is content with a generalization here.[56] In a letter that has more scriptural citations and allusions per page than anywhere else in the Pauline corpus, Paul is making a broad generalization[57] that the divine righteousness in Christ is affirmed by Scripture as a whole. There are some exceptions and inconsistencies, particularly with the claim of salvation "apart from the law,"[58] but it makes a potent rhetorical point that God's righteousness remains reliable and true.

■ **22** In 3:22 an explication of the preceding verse is offered, with δέ used in an explanatory sense, "that is."[59] The nature of "God's righteousness" is defined as coming "through faith in Jesus Christ" and being available "to all who have faith." It therefore seems preferable to assume that an objective genitive is employed here as in the preceding verse. It is "righteousness deriving from God" that is imparted to all humans, both Jews and Gen-

tiles, who respond to the gospel with faith.[60] God's righteousness is manifested in Christ[61] in such a way that it shatters ordinary definitions of righteousness as conformity to a particular culture's norms. In Christ divine righteousness acts to counter the arrogance of dominant groups and the shame of subordinates.[62] God's righteousness expresses the OT expectation of salvation of the "poor, the oppressed, the widow, the orphan."[63] Whereas earlier forms of salvation had been achieved when divine righteousness was thought to triumph over the enemies of the beleaguered faithful (Pss 35, 71), or of Israel as a nation (Pss 97–99, 145), restoring Jerusalem to its former glory (Isa 45–46), now this is being accomplished through the preaching of a gospel that offers equal access to the members of the ancient covenant as well as to Gentiles.

Paul's conception of impartial righteousness differed substantially from the partisan tendencies of contemporary culture. In Qumran the theme of the righteousness of God is employed to depict Yahweh's judgment in behalf of the Essene community (1QS 10:25; 11:12; 1QM 4:6).[64] In Greco-Roman sources, the gods were not noted for their righteous qualities, but they could be

54 The formula appears in 4 Macc 18:10; 2 Macc 15:9; and numerous NT passages: Matt 5:17; 7:12; 11:13; 24:14; Luke 16:16; John 1:45; Acts 13:15; 24:14; 28:23; and with variations in 1QS 1:3; 8:15-16; CD 5:21–6:1; 4QDibHam (= 4Q504) 1-2 iii 12-13, indicating that the "writings," the third division of the LXX and Hebrew Bible, were in a secondary place, except for Sirach, Prologue 8-9, which refers to "law and prophets and writings." See also Helmut Krämer et al., "προφήτης κτλ.," TDNT 6 (1968) 832; Alexander Sand, Das Gesetz und die Propheten, BU 11 (Regensburg: Pustet, 1974); Milner S. Ball, "Law and Prophets, Bridges and Judges," JLR 7 (1989) 1-20; Wolfgang Beilner, "Gesetz und Propheten erfüllen. Zum Gesetzesverständnis Jesu," in F. V. Reiterer, ed., Ein Gott, eine Offenbarung. Beiträge zur biblischen Exegese, Theologie und Spiritualität. Festschrift für Notker Füglister OSB (Würzburg: Echter, 1991) 439–60.

55 See the list of scriptural references and allusions in Nestle-Aland[27] that reaches far beyond Hab 2:4; Gen 15:6; and Ps 142, which are often adduced (Campbell, Rhetoric of Righteousness, 180), or the Isaiah passages dealing with divine righteousness (46:13; 51:5-8; see Moo, 223). In Echoes, 52–53, Hays thinks of the promise of divine righteousness in

LXX Ps 142 as the primary allusion, although that would be outside the "law" by any version of the division of Scripture.

56 See Hays, "Romans 3–4," 158–63.

57 See Kuss, 1:113.

58 See Räisänen, Law, 69–73.

59 BAGD (2000) 213.2; BDF §447.8; Schlier, 105; Cranfield, 1:147.

60 This is the dominant interpretation of Protestant orthodoxy, e.g., Meyer, 1:163: "the righteousness of God as being imparted to the believer without the law." It is represented more recently by Schlier, 105; O'Neill, 70–72; Moo, 226; Edwards, 99–101; Burnett, Individual, 154–58, 171–72.

61 See Williams, "Righteousness," 271–72.

62 See Josef Scharbert, "Gerechtigkeit I. Altes Testament," TRE 12 (1983) 410.

63 Scullion, "Righteousness (OT)," 726; see also D. J. Smit, "In a special way the God of the destitute, the poor, and the wronged," in G. Cloete and D. J. Smit, eds., A Moment of Truth: The Confession of the Dutch Reformed Mission Church (Grand Rapids: Eerdmans, 1984) 53–65.

64 The most prominent reference is 1QS 11:12-14, "my vindication is with the righteousness of God (צדקת אל) which stands forever. . . . By the righ-

induced to intervene in behalf of justice for their favorites. While the ancient Romans did not refer to the righteousness of their deities, the god *Iustitia/Δικαιοσύνη* ("righteousness") surfaces in the Augustan period in celebrations of the Roman imperial cult.[65] The Roman gods promoted "justice/righteousness" by rewarding Rome with the privileges of empire in response to its surpassing virtue and piety. This system allowed no real equality between provincials and Rome; righteousness entailed imperial submission.[66] The magical papyri also define righteousness as favoritism for those employing the formulas accepted by the gods, as in *PGM* III. 157: "Come to me, hearken [to me], most righteous (δικαιότατε) one of all, steward of truth, the one who establishes righteousness (δικαιοσύνης)."

Richard Hays has identified as the most important parallel to Paul's rhetoric in this passage, the LXX wording of Ps 142 to which Rom 3:20 had already alluded.[67] Here we find the typical OT sense of Yahweh as the righteous one who will vindicate the faithful:

> O Lord . . . hear me in your righteousness (ἐν τῇ δικαιοσύνῃ σου). And do not enter into judgment with your servant, for in your sight shall no one be set right (δικαιωθήσεται). For the enemy has persecuted my soul; he has brought my life down to the ground. . . . Deliver me from my enemies, O Lord, for I have fled to you for refuge. . . . In your righteousness (ἐν τῇ δικαιοσύνῃ σου) you shall bring my soul out of affliction. And in your mercy you will destroy my enemies and destroy all those that afflict my soul, for I am your servant. (142:1-3, 9, 11-12)

While the claim that the final reference to "righteousness" in 142:11 is used instrumentally may be somewhat strained,[68] there is no doubt that divine power is expected to save the faithful. A notable aspect of this citation is that God's righteousness is expected to set a believer "right" in the sense of preservation from threat; the forensic dimension of entering into judgment rescues people from enemies. As noted in connection with 3:20, moreover, there is acknowledgment that not even the servant of God deserves such divine favor. Yet the psalmist hopes that the righteous believer will indeed be rescued. Paul's wording in Rom 3 can easily be seen to have evolved as a transformation from this set of ideas, removing the last vestiges of privilege granted to the "servant of God," and opening salvation through faith to groups that lack any qualifications. While the psalm expects God's righteousness to destroy the servant's enemies, Paul affirms that righteousness entails equal acceptance of Jews and Gentiles alike through faith in Christ.

Paul's need to overcome the barriers of shame explains why "faith" appears twice in this sentence to indicate that participation in righteousness is available to all groups regardless of their status or ethnicity. The distinctive early Christian use of πίστις followed by a reference to Jesus Christ is evident here, a use that implies "an indissoluble relationship to Jesus as the crucified and exalted Lord of the Church."[69] Unfortunately, this faith is usually thought of as an individualized phenomenon.[70] Since πίστις described the response of converts to the gospel, however, it functions as what Axel von Dobbeler describes as a *Schwellenphänomen* that inaugurates participation as citizens in the realm of God's redeeming and righteous activity and simultaneously their entrance into the "spiritual fellowship of believers."[71] Since faith has a social function related to

---

teousness of his truth (וכצדקתו) he will judge me." See Seifrid, *Justification*, 103, and for a discussion of other passages, 99–107.

65 Albrecht Dihle, "Gerechtigkeit," *RAC* 10 (1978) 283; Fears, "Cult of Virtues," 937, notes the sparsity of references to the worship of *Iustitia* in the west, but the frequency of rites dedicated to *Dikaiosyne* in the eastern part of the empire.

66 See Brunt, "Laus Imperii," 21–35.

67 See Hays, "Romans 3," 113–15.

68 Seifrid, *Justification*, 107–8, shows that a modal sense "of God responding in covenant faithfulness" is equally likely.

69 Gerhard Barth, "πίστις, πιστός," *EDNT* 3 (1993) 93; Dieter Lührmann, "Faith," *ABD* 2 (1992) 753: "in the connection *pistis Christou* the genitive always designates the content of faith." Some earlier commentators defined faith as trust in Christ as savior, e.g., Weiss, 160.

70 Kühl, 109; Zahn, 175. Moo, 224: "faith as the means by which God's justifying work becomes applicable to individuals."

71 Von Dobbeler, *Glaube als Teilhabe*, 95; see also the ecclesiastical emphases by Neugebauer, *In Christus*, 164–71; and Klaiber, *Rechtfertigung*, 174–82.

conversion and participation in a new community, it entails more than an individual's intellectual,[72] emotional,[73] or existential stance.[74] The recent resurgence of interest in the subjective genitive "faith of Jesus Christ"[75] is in part an effort to overcome the shortcomings of an intellectualized and dogmatized conception of faith, but it also tends to lose sight of the social dimension of very early Christian usage[76] in which πίστις / πιστεύω functioned as broadly defined jargon for participation in the community of the converted. Given that "not all genitives can easily be forced into the scheme established by grammarians"[77] and that "there is no reason why a gen. in the author's mind may not have been both subjective and objective,"[78] it seems precarious to erect a theology on the interpretation of a case ending. Both the subjective or objective theories as currently presented have loopholes, and therefore a high degree of certainty should not be claimed in deciding between them. It may be that a simple association between "faith" and "Jesus," perhaps in a formulaic manner as used by early believers, may have been intended, and that neither of the strict construals matches what the original audience

72 Von Dobbeler, *Glaube als Teilhabe*, 95–86, 166–70. For examples of viewing πίστις Ἰησοῦ Χριστοῦ as referring to the "object of faith" in which one believes, see Meyer, 1:164; Schmidt, 66; Murray, 111.

73 Dodd, 56: faith is "the attitude of pure receptivity in which the soul appropriates what God has done." Leenhardt, 99: "this inner spiritual attitude is faith." Dunn, 1:166: "Faith is the human condition or attitude which is set in contrast to 'works of the law.'" Käsemann, 94: "Faith is basically human receptivity, as actively as it may express itself in obedience." See the critique of this emotional approach in Wilckens, 1:188.

74 See Rudolf Bultmann, "πιστεύω κτλ.," *TDNT* 6 (1968) 219–20, who stresses "man's absolute committal to God . . . a radical decision of the will in which man delivers himself up." See also Schlier, 105–6. Barrett, 74, stresses the new relationship of "trust."

75 P. Valloton, *Le Christ et la foi. Étude de théologie biblique*, Nouvelle série théologique 10 (Geneva: Labor & Fides, 1960) 47; Markus Barth, "The Faith of the Messiah," *HeyJ* 10 (1969) 363–70; D[onald] W. B. Robinson, "'Faith of Jesus Christ'–A New Testament Debate," *RTR* 29 (1970) 71–81; John J. O'Rourke, "Πίστις," *CBQ* 36 (1973) 188–94; Sam K. Williams, "The 'Righteousness of God' in Romans," *JBL* 99 (1980) 272–78; George Howard, "On the 'Faith of Christ,'" *HTR* 60 (1967) 459–65; idem, "Faith of Christ," *ABD* 2 (1992) 758–60; idem, "The Faith of Christ," *ExpT* 85 (1974) 212–15; Luke T. Johnson, "Romans 3:21-26 and the Faith of Jesus," *CBQ* 44 (1982) 77–90; Richard B. Hays, *The Faith of Jesus Christ*, SBLDS 56 (Chico: Scholars Press, 1983) 170–77; idem, "ΠΙΣΤΙΣ and Pauline Christology: What Is at Stake?" in E. H. Lovering Jr., ed., *SBLSP 30* (Atlanta: Scholars Press, 1991) 714–29; Gaston, *Paul*, 58; Campbell, *Rhetoric of Righteousness*, 58–69; and the full monograph devoted to this theory by Ian G. Wallis, *The Faith of Jesus Christ in Early Christian Traditions*, SNTSMS 84 (Cambridge: Cambridge University Press, 1995) 65–102. There were earlier advocates of the subjective interpretation: Godet, 147 (refers to Benecke for the definition of fidelity to God); Johannes Haussleiter, *Der Glaube Jesu Christi und der christliche Glaube. Ein Beitrag zur Erklärung des Römerbriefes* (Erlangen: Deichert, 1891) 109–45; idem, "Der Glaube Jesu und der Christliche Glaube," *NKZ* 2 (1891) 109–45; Gerhard Kittel, "Πίστις Ἰησοῦ Χριστοῦ bei Paulus," *ThStK* 79 (1906) 419–36; Arthur G. Hebert, "Faithfulness and 'Faith,'" *RTR* 14 (1955) 33–40; Barry R. Matlock, "Detheologizing the ΠΙΣΤΙΣ ΧΡΙΣΤΟΥ Debate: Cautionary Remarks from a Lexical Semantic Perspective," *NovT* 42 (2000) 1–23. Holladay, *Critical Introduction*, 367, accepts the subjective genitive that views Jesus "as an active participant with God in the act of salvation."

76 This broad and relatively undefined usage is the strength of the theory advanced by Deissmann, *Paul*, 140–43, followed by Asmussen and Leenhardt, that the genitive construction is both subjective and objective genitive in a mystical sense. An adjectival construal of "Christ-faith" as proposed by Sam K. Williams, *Jesus' Death*, 48; idem, "Again Πίστις Χριστοῦ," *CBQ* 9 (1987) 431–47, could also be understandable as community jargon.

77 Kühner-Gerth, *Grammatik*, 1:334.

78 Moulton and Turner, *Grammar III*, 210; Robinson, "Faith of Jesus Christ," 76, cited with approval by Matlock, "Detheologizing," 3.

would have understood. I wonder whether the ambiguity may have been intentional on Paul's part so as to encompass the variety of house and tenement churches in Rome that may well have been using the formula of πίστις Χριστοῦ with a variety of connotations. I am struck that the entire discussion seems to revert to the premise that Romans is a doctrinal treatise, which must be internally consistent, whereas it should be viewed as a situational letter written to a mixed audience with an aim of finding common ground. Even though various interpretations of the genitive construction are grammatically possible, the reiteration of the inclusive social scope of "all who have faith" in 3:22 suggests that Paul is focusing on the faith of believers rather than the faithfulness of Christ.[79] "Faith" is used here to denote a group's assent to and participation in the gospel of Christ crucified and resurrected, a gospel that reveals the righteousness of God as transcending the barriers of honor and shame. God's righteousness is manifested διὰ πίστεως, with the preposition bearing the sense of "by means of, through."[80]

The expression in 3:22 that emphasizes universal access to the righteousness of God is almost always translated and interpreted as if the πιστ- stem were no longer present: "for all who believe,"[81] rather than more properly, "for all who have faith."[82] Although it is understandable that such translations seem apt because English and the Romance languages lack a current, verbal

form for "faith,"[83] the shift to "belief" too easily supports the traditional misconception that a particular belief system offers sole access to God. Thus only those believing the right doctrine of justification by faith are acceptable. Paul's point is stood on its head when overly precise definitions of belief shaped by dogmatic conflicts centuries after the writing of Romans are allowed to undercut the remarkable inclusivity of Paul's formulation.[84] Paul relies on distinctively early Christian usage in this formula, since only there is πιστεύειν combined with εἰς ("for, in reference to").[85] Since the expression "in regard to all who have faith"[86] modifies the ellipsed "manifested," it is clear that divine self-revelation in the gospel does not conform to the assumptions of chosen peoples that they alone qualify for divine favor.[87] Salvation is equally available to Gentiles and Jews, Greeks and barbarians, because divine impartiality does not conform to their systems of assigning honor and shame. The stress on God's righteousness manifesting itself in equal measure "to all" (εἰς πάντας) is what distinguishes Paul's view of being made right in Christ.[88] In Colenso's words, this is "a righteousness which *all* must receive as an act of mere favour, but which God will bestow freely 'upon all' them that believe. Thus every pretense of privilege and favouritism is struck away."[89]

While exact precedents for the expressions "through faith" and "in regard to all who have faith" have not been located,[90] there are examples of close association

79 See Arlan J. Hultgren, "The πίστις Χριστοῦ Formulation in Paul," *NovT* 22 (1980) 248–63; James D. G. Dunn, "Once More, *Pistis Christou*," in Lovering, ed., *SBLSP 30,* 733–44; C. E. B. Cranfield, "On the Πίστις Χριστου Question," in *On Romans,* 81–97.

80 BAGD 180.

81 For example, Godet, 146; Käsemann, 91, 94; Cranfield, 1:201; Morris, 176; Dunn, 1:167; Fitzmyer, 346.

82 I acknowledge that this translation also has its weakness because it gives the false impression that Paul views faith as a human possession or achievement.

83 See Dieter Lührmann, "Faith," *ABD* 2 (1992) 749–50, noting that Latin translations and discussions also distinguish between *fides* (= πίστις, "faith") and *credere* (= πιστεύειν, "belief"). This terminological confusion influences the entire discussion of "justification by faith."

84 See the warning on this point by Kuss, 1:132.

85 Dieter Lührmann, "Faith," *ABD* 2 (1992) 752; examples of πιστεύω εἰς are found in Rom 10:14; Gal 2:16; Phil 1:24.

86 The preposition εἰς is translated on the basis of the LSJM 491 definition IV, "to express relation, towards, in regard to." See also BAGD (2000) 291.5, listing Rom 8:28 as an example, "I say this not with reference to these days."

87 See Dunn, 1:166; the limit of Dunn's insight, however, is that such faith pertains only to Israel's view of itself as "members of the covenant" and thus "recipients of his righteousness."

88 See Georg Strecker, "Befreiung und Rechtfertigung," in J. Friedrich et al., eds., *Rechtfertigung. Festschrift für Ernst Käsemann zum 70 Geburtstag* (Göttingen: Vandenhoeck & Ruprecht, 1976) 507–8.

89 Colenso, 77 (italics in original).

90 See Lührmann, "Faith," *ABD* 2 (1992) 750–52; von Dobbeler, *Glaube als Teilhabe,* 283–304; Joseph P. Healey, "Faith. Old Testament," *ABD* 2 (1992) 744–49.

between words based on the δικ- and πιστ- stems. An inscription from the first century B.C.E. includes these words in a series of virtues that describe the honoree: "proving to have been a good man and one who excelled in faith (πίστει) and virtue and righteousness (δικαιο-σύνη) and piety".[91] Other texts decry the decline from the high ethical standards of the Golden Age, which include "righteousness" and "faithfulness."[92] In judicial usage, one finds the formula πιστεύω τῷ δικαίῳ, "I have faith in my innocence" while his accusers are shameful,[93] but this frame of reference is foreign to Paul's argument in Rom 3. In Hab 2:4, which we discussed in relation to Rom 1:16, and in Gen 15:6, which we shall discuss in connection with Rom 4:3, there are important precedents for this early Christian association of faith and righteousness. There was also a widespread use of words with the πιστ- stem in Greco-Roman religion, referring to faith in the gods,[94] belief in miracles,[95] and belief in revelation,[96] so that it is clear that Paul's use of "faith" in this passage would have been readily understood as missionary discourse.[97]

The parenthesis identified by Douglas Campbell opens with the insistence that there is no διαστολή ("distinction"), a comparatively rare term meaning "summons, incision, separation."[98] There is an LXX passage where this sense of "separation" is found, in which Yahweh informs Pharaoh with regard to a plague: "I will place a separation (διαστολήν) between my people and your people" (Exod 8:23). The background of the use of διαστολή here and in Rom 10:12 is that "God shows no partiality" (2:11; Acts 10:34).[99] Disregarding the honor/shame distinctions that humans claim in competition with one another, God treats all persons fairly while holding each equally accountable. That all humans and all groups sin and fall short means that the exemptions claimed by those in superior positions, such as the superiority of Romans over all other ethnic groups, are disallowed. The stress on impartiality has a crucial bearing on the purpose of Romans that aims to formulate the gospel in such a manner as to overcome the presumption of inferiority on the part of the "barbarians" in Spain.

■ 23 The rationale that "all have sinned" is a further refinement of the contention in 3:9, specifying the arena in which "no distinction" can be made between nations or persons. The formulation in v. 23, that "all have sinned and fallen short of the glory of God," makes clear that this includes all believers, because πάντες ("all") is modified by the attributive participle δικαιούμενοι ("being set right") in v. 24a. No participant in any Christian group, including Paul himself, can claim exemption from this generalization.[100] Paul's argument has a bearing on the Jewish and Greco-Roman systems of shame and honor that scholars have not noticed . The distinctively Pauline combination of πᾶς ("all") and ἁμαρτάνω ("sin")[101] eliminates all claims of honorable superiority, including those that were developing within the church itself. It reflects a paradigm shift made by Paul that abandons "the reinstitution of law as the path to life"[102] and thus maintains the absolute priority of grace.

91 SIG 2. Nr. 438.8.
92 Marcus Aurelius Τὰ εἰς ἑαυτὸν 5.33.3; Theognis Eleg. 1.135ff. Von Dobbeler, Glaube als Teilhabe, 107–11, suggests that the association between "righteousness" and "faith" in this Greek tradition is due to the background of the friendship ethic.
93 Demosthenes Orat. 35.40-41; 47.45; see von Dobbeler, Glaube als Teilhabe, 112–14.
94 For example, Thucydides Hist. 4.92.7; Aelius Aristides Πρὸς Δημοσ. 1.155.
95 For example, Epidauros Frag. Gal. W3 (Herzog, 8–10); Lucian of Samosata Pseudol. 10.
96 For example, Xenophon Mem. 1.1.15; Plutarch Mor. 398e; 402e; 549b.
97 Von Dobbeler, Glaube als Teilhabe, 295–98.
98 Karl Heinrich Rengstorf, "διαστολή," TDNT 7 (1971) 592; MM 154 reports: "We are unable to illustrate the NT use of this word" with the connotation "distinction."
99 In Mos. 2.158 Philo refers to a "distinction (δια-στολή) between holy and profane, between things human and divine"; see also Philo Spec. 1.100.
100 In contrast, Hays, "Romans 3–4," 158, argues that Paul "is seeking to destabilize an entrenched position that associates the Law with the privileged status of the elect Jewish people."
101 Winninge's analysis of parallels in Sinners and the Righteous, 209–12, indicates no exact replication of Paul's formulation. Röhser, Hamartia, 17, lists the passages where Paul combines "all" with "sin": Gal 3:22; Rom 3:4, 9, 12, 19, 12; 5:12.
102 Zeller, 82, developed by Merklein, Studien, 2:335–38.

The reference to falling short of "the glory of God" also has a bearing on the issue of competition for honor. That Adam and Eve were originally intended to bear the glory of God but lost it through the fall is widely acknowledged.[103] Adam's words in *Apoc. Mos.* 20.2 are frequently cited, "Why have you done this to me and deprived me of my glory?"[104] Nevertheless, the use of the verb ὑστερεῖν has not been sufficiently explained, since neither this nor comparable terms are employed in any of the Jewish parallels that claim universal sinfulness. Ὑστερεῖν is a comparative term relating to the failure to reach a goal, to be inferior to someone, to fail, to come short of something.[105] The basic connotation is that of "deficit, which consists either in remaining below the normal level, or in being behind others,"[106] which are failures that place one in a position of deserving shame. An important parallel in Pauline usage is 2 Cor 11:5 and 12:11, "to be inferior to someone," an expression that reflects the competition between Paul and the superapostles.[107] To fall short is an honor issue and it resonates with the competition for honor within and between groups in the Greco-Roman world. It echoes the wording of Rom 1:18-32 in terms of refusing to grant honor to God by choosing to worship the creature rather than the Creator. Despite the claims of Jews and Greeks to surpass each other in honor and despite their typical claims that the other groups are shameful because of their lack of wisdom or moral conformity, Paul's claim is that *all* fall short of the transcendent standard of honor. Dunn comes close to seeing this issue: Paul "reduces the difference between Jew and Gentile to the same level of their common creatureliness."[108] If all persons and groups including believers in Rome had been equally involved in sin and thereby had fallen short of the ultimate standard of honor that they were intended to bear, that is, "the glory of God," then none has a right to claim superiority or to place other groups in positions of inferiority.

To be "set right" in the context of the "righteousness of God,"[109] and with reference to humans who fall short of the "glory of God," is to have such glory and honor restored, not as an achievement but as a gift. This perspective follows up on Käsemann's contention about the "correspondence of δόξα and δικαιοσύνη τοῦ θεοῦ. . . . To put it more precisely, the δόξα τοῦ θεοῦ is δικαιοσύνη within the horizon of the restoration of paradisaical perfection, while conversely δικαιοσύνη is the divine δόξα within the horizon of controversy with the world."[110]

■ **24** While commentators continue to translate δικαιούμενοι as "being justified"[111] and thus to disguise the link with the dominant theme of the "righteousness of God,"[112] it is essential to render it with something like "being set right."[113] The syntactical link that has puzzled

---

103 See Hofius, "Adam-Christus-Antithese," 182–84.

104 Dunn, 1:168, claims that Paul refers here "*both* to the glory lost in man's fall *and* to the glory that fallen man is failing to reach in consequence" (italics in original). Fitzmyer, 347, properly repudiates such a direct reference; it would be better to speak of the Jewish references (1QS 4:23; CD 3:20; 1QH 17:15; *3 Bar.* 4.16) to humans participating in the "glory of God" as general background of Paul's reference.

105 See BAGD 849; Ulrich Wilckens, "ὕστερος κτλ.," *TDNT* 8 (1972) 592–601.

106 See Godet, 148.

107 Paul's word choice reflects common Greek usage as found in Plato *Resp.* 539e.

108 Dunn, 1:168.

109 For the translation "set right," see Newman and Nida, 67.

110 Käsemann, 95.

111 For example, Dunn, 1:168; Moo, 227; Stuhlmacher, 60.

112 See Michel, 149.

113 See A. J. Mattill Jr., "Translation of Words with the Stem Δικ- in Romans," *AUSS* 9 (1971) 89–98, who points to the earlier advocacies of translations using the English stem "right" by Horace Bushnell, *The Vicarious Sacrifice* (New York: Scribner's, 1883) 406–22, and by Kendrick Grobel's translation of Bultmann's *Theology*, 2:253, 271, 264, 278, using the Middle English term "rightwise," which Mattill prefers (p. 97). Another translation alternative ("rectify") is suggested by J. Louis Martyn, "God's Way of Making Right What Is Wrong," in *Theological Issues in the Letters of Paul* (Nashville: Abingdon, 1997) 141–56. See also Campbell, *Rhetoric of Righteousness*, 183. My translation catches the nuance of the OT use of ṣedeq. According to George A. F. Knight, "Is 'Righteous' Right?" *SJT* 41 (1988) 4, "those who have been put right, acquitted, by God."

previous scholars[114] has been resolved by Douglas Campbell's theory of a parenthesis from v. 22d through v. 24a that elaborates the theme of "all who have faith."[115] There is a fundamental lack of distinction between believers either in shame or honor, because all fall short and all are set right as a sheer gift. Just as in LXX Ps 142, where the δικ- stem was used in the passive (δικαιωθήσεται) to depict rescue from enmity, the passive participle δικαιούμενοι appears here for the only time in the Pauline corpus in reference to "God's gracious reversal and recreation of humanity's fallen condition."[116] The participle δικαιούμενοι ("being set right") modifies the inclusive πάντες ("all") in v. 23,[117] a point that remains undeveloped by commentators, perhaps out of concern that it might imply universal salvation.[118] Paul is literally claiming that "all will now be saved."[119] While advocates of a forensic doctrine of justification point to the frequent use of δικαιόω and its Hebrew equivalent צדק in the sense of "acquit, justify, declare right, vindicate,"[120] this connotation usually appears in the context of social justice where God or the judge takes the side of the weak. For example, LXX Ps 81:1-3 uses the δικ- stem to refer to just and unjust treatment: "God stands in the divine council; and in the midst of them he holds judgment: 'How long will you [people] judge injustice (κρίνετε ἀδικίαν) and show partiality to the wicked? Pause. Judge the orphan and the poor; do right (δικαιώσατε) to the lowly and needy.'" The theme of reversing shameful status that is implicit in all such passages where God takes the side of the lowly rather than the privileged is explicitly noted in LXX Ps 30:1-2: "I have hoped in you, O Lord; let me never be put to shame (μὴ καταισχυνθείνην); deliver me in your righteousness (ἐν τῇ δικαιοσύνῃ σου). Incline your ear to me; make haste to rescue me."

In view of this background, to be "set right freely by his grace" could be understood in terms of the restoration of honor. "Righteousness," "honor," and "glory" can be used as virtually synonymous terms, a point whose relevance can be grasped only if the traditional English translation for δικαιούμενοι, "being justified," is replaced with its more adequate verbal equivalent, "being set right" or "declared upright."[121] Paul is not suggesting that believers gain a comparative form of honor and glory, so that they can continue to compete with others who remain shameful. Rather, in Christ they are given an honorable relationship that results in what 2 Cor 3:18 describes as an actual transformation derived from the mirror image of Christ in which believers change "from one degree of glory to another," but not because of their superiority to one another. In being honored by God through Christ who died for all, the formerly shamed are integrated into the community of the saints in which this transformation process occurs, under the lordship of Christ. This issue of overcoming shameful status could be correlated with the work of Stuhlmacher, Hays, Campbell, and others who argue that the righteousness given to the converted Jews and Gentiles is understood "primarily in terms of the covenant relationship to God and membership within the covenant community."[122] In place of a largely abstract construct elaborated by some biblical theologians, Paul has in mind a new social reality:[123] within the community of the shamed made right by the death and resurrection of Christ, the manifestation of divine righteousness disallows any "distinction" (Rom 3:22) in honor.

Paul's crucial contention is that the rightful status of humans before God cannot be achieved on the basis of any human effort. The threefold reference in Rom 3:24

114 Sanday and Headlam, 85; Cranfield, 1:205; Käsemann, 95; Dunn, 1:168; Moo, 227.

115 Campbell, *Rhetoric of Righteousness*, 86–92, 182–83.

116 Ibid., 183; see also Murray, 114: "the fact of universal sinfulness bears directly upon the other fact that there is no discrimination among believers—they are all beneficiaries of the righteousness of God."

117 See Sanday and Headlam, 85–86, following Vaughan and Ewald.

118 See the careful wording of Wilckens, 1:188–89.

119 Kuss, 1:114; see also Colenso, 78–79.

120 Scullion, "Righteousness (OT)," 726, referring to Exod 23:7; Deut 25:1; 2 Sam 15:4; Prov 17:15.

121 BAGD 197 draws this translation from Goodspeed, *Problems*, 143–46; idem, "Some Greek Notes III: Justification," *JBL* 73 (1954) 86–91.

122 Richard B. Hays, "Justification," *ABD* 3 (1992) 1131; see Stuhlmacher, 31; Campbell, "Identity," 67–82.

123 See Barth, "Jews and Gentiles," 252–59; Warren C. Carter, "Rome (and Jerusalem): The Contingency of Romans 3:21-26," *IBS* 11 (1989) 58–63.

to the "free gift," to divine "grace," and to "redemption" through Christ makes plain that no one gains this honorable, righteous status by outperforming others or by privilege of rank, wealth, or ethnicity. The term δωρεάν means "without payment, as a gift; undeserved,"[124] and its derivation from δίδωμι may well have evoked reminiscences of Jesus' self-giving in the Last Supper (Mark 14:22) and in death (Mark 10:45 and parallels; Gal 1:4). The word δωρεά always occurs in the singular in the NT, referring to the gift of the Spirit (Acts 2:38; 8:20; 10:45; 11:17; Heb 6:4), the grace of God expressed in Christ (Rom 5:15; 2 Cor 9:15; Eph 3:7; 4:7), the gift of righteousness (Rom 5:17), or simply a gift from God (John 4:10). The contrast between this early Christian viewpoint and Greco-Roman attitudes has been pointed out by James Harrison: "Paul's emphasis on the unilateral nature of divine grace was directed against the idea that God was compelled by acts of human piety to reciprocate beneficently."[125] The Roman believers would have experienced a reinforcement of this basic idea of a supreme gift every time they participated in the Lord's Supper together, hearing the words: "This is my body that is for you . . . the new covenant in my blood" (1 Cor 11:24-25). In the context of Rom 3:21-26, the gift par excellence beyond all deserving is Christ's shameful death freely given in behalf of the shamed.

The dative expression τῇ αὐτοῦ χάριτι ("by/in his grace") reiterates the nature of the gift of the new relationship of "being right" before God as explicitly derived from the giver. The antecedent of "his" is God in the preceding sentence,[126] the one whose righteousness comes to expression in the Christ event. A "distinctive new meaning" is present in this usage as compared with other occurrences of "grace" in the Pauline letters,[127] namely an antithesis to salvation through law.[128] Conzelmann states, "If God's favor is identical with the crucifixion, then its absoluteness is established. We are saved by grace alone."[129] Such grace is usually understood primarily as forgiveness of sins,[130] but this is not suggested by this context, in which equal access to divine favor is in view. In contrast to the hyper-competitive environment of the Greco-Roman world, including its Jewish component, God grants this new status to groups and persons that have failed, to those whose shame is evident. By its very nature, honor granted through grace alone eliminates the basis of human boasting, as Paul goes on to show in 3:27: "Where is the boast? It is excluded!" Once again, it is ethnic boasting that is primarily in view: the one God of all the nations "will set right the circumcised by faith and the uncircumcised through faith." In Moxnes's words, this argument aims "to exclude false claims to honour."[131]

While the means by which humans were set right were by "his grace," the agency of being set right is the "redemption that is in Christ Jesus."[132] Ἀπολύτρωσις is used to depict (a) deliverance of a group from any form of captivity,[133] (b) ransoming captives by paying the

124 Gerhard Schneider, "δωρεά, δωρεάν," *EDNT* 1 (1990) 364.

125 Harrison, *Language of Grace*, 18.

126 Morris, 178.

127 Hendrikus Boers, "Ἀγάπη and Χάρις in Paul's Thought," *CBQ* 59 (1997) 706–7; he sees Gal 1:6; 2:21; 5:4; Rom 4:16; 6:14-15; 11:6 as further examples of this "specialized use." What he calls "traditional usage" is consistent with Aristotle's definition of χάρις as "that according to which the one who has it is said to render favor to the one who needs it, not for something [in return], nor for the sake of the one who renders it, but for the sake of the other (*Rhetoric* 2.7.2)," as cited by Boers, 703.

128 See Klaus Berger, "χάρις," *EDNT* 3 (1993) 459.

129 Hans Conzelmann, "χαίρω κτλ.," *TDNT* 9 (1974) 394. See also Gorman, *Cruciformity,* 155–77.

130 For example, see Gore, 132–35; Wobbe, *Charis-Gedanke*, 37–39.

131 Moxnes, "Honour and Righteousness," 71. Unfortunately Moxnes goes on to claim: "It is the particular boasting of the Jew, not something which is common to Jews and Gentiles, which Paul attacks. . . . Paul sees a direct connection between boasting and the Jewish Law." This overlooks the clear implication of the earlier argument of Romans, which makes plain that all humans are involved in seeking honor that belongs to God alone, and that they all thereby forfeit their share of the "glory of God."

132 The preposition διά with the genitive expresses "agency," as suggested by BAGD (2000) 225, A.4; see Kühl, 110.

133 Zahn, 179–80; Dodd, 77–78; Wilckens, 1:189; Schlier, 108–9; Dodd, 53–54; Black, 59; Campbell, *Rhetoric of Righteousness,* 119–30; Elpidius Pax, "Der Loskauf. Zur Geschichte eines neutestamentlichen Begriffes," *Anton* 37 (1962) 239–78. Although the noun ἀπολύτρωσις does not appear with this con-

price of exchange,[134] (c) freeing a slave either by legal writ of manumission or by purchase,[135] and, most frequently, (d) a specialized theological concept of salvation through forgiveness of sins.[136] Even though there is no basis in Romans for option (d), assuming the references to "passing over previously committed sins" (3:25) refer to divine forbearance for Gentile behavior in the period before Christ according to the Kraus hypothesis,[137] the word "redemption" would have had a wide resonance with Paul's audience.[138] The precise connotation of ἀπολύτρωσις in this pericope cannot be resolved by background studies that have raised several equally plausible alternatives. Choices between them tend to be made on the grounds of contemporary theological preferences to the detriment of sound practice in the interpretation of ancient texts. Dunn wisely makes the point that "the distinctively Christian note" of redemption in Paul's expression is "in Christ Jesus,"[139] a note that shows the direction we should take, because the very next verse explicates the distinctive shape of Christ's sacrifice in blood. Redemption through Christ differs from other concepts of redemption, which discriminated in favor of chosen peoples by offering them escape at the price of the death of others, by offering ransom for the privileged while others remain in captivity, or by freeing favored slaves while others remain in bondage. In some later Christian theories of forgiveness, atonement was effectively restricted to those favoring a particular creed or sect. As we shall see, the "mercy seat" provided by Christ was marked first and foremost by its undiscriminating generosity to all.

■ **25-26** The material marked with quotation marks in the translation above is cited from a hymnic fragment, as noted in the introductory analysis of this pericope.[140] Our interpretive effort must therefore distinguish between the original significance and provenance of this material and its meaning in the context of Paul's letter. The hymnic fragment begins with an affirmation of divine action, ὅν προέθετο ὁ θεός ("whom God put forth"), with the verb employed differently from 1:13 to imply in the context of 3:21-25 a kind of public manifestation.[141] This sense of public display is reflected in a first-century contract, "subject to your consenting a copy of this lease be displayed (προετεθ(ῆ)ναι τῆσδε μισθώσεως ἀντίγραφον) for the legal period of ten

---

notation in the LXX, λυτρόω frequently appears in discussions of the exodus (e.g., Deut 7:8, "the Lord brought you out with a strong hand, and the Lord redeemed [λυτρώσατο] you from the house of bondage, out of the hand of Pharaoh"), of individual rescue from danger (e.g., LXX Ps 30:5, "Into your hands I will commit my spirit; you have redeemed [ἐλυτρώσω] me, O Lord God of truth"), and of Israel's rescue from Babylonian captivity (Isa 43:1, "O Israel, fear not, for I have redeemed [ἐλυτρωσάμην] you").

134 Godet, 149; Sanday and Headlam, 86; Barrett, 76; Murray, 116; Moo, 229. *Ep. Arist.* 12 refers to the "redemption (ἀπολυτρώσεως) of those who had been carried away from Judea by the king's father." Josephus *Ant.* 12.27 reports, "they said that the cost of redeeming (τῆς ἀπολυτρώσεως) them would be more than four hundred talents."

135 Deissmann, *Light*, 322–34; Lietzmann, 49. In the LXX the verb ἀπολυτρουν occurs in Exod 21:8, but the example more widely discussed was adduced by Deissmann, 327. For a critique of the Deissmann hypothesis, see Wilfred Haubeck, *Loskauf durch Christus. Herkunft, Gestalt und Bedeutung des paulinischen Loskaufmotivs*, TVG 317 (Giessen: Brunnen, 1985) 164–65.

136 Karl Kertelge, "ἀπολύτρωσις," *EDNT* 1 (1991) 138; Wilckens, 1:189–90. Deutero-Isaiah linked forgiveness with redemption in 44:21-22, "I have blotted out your transgressions as a cloud and your sin as darkness, and I will redeem you (καὶ λυτρώσομαί σε)"; see also Isa 50:1-3.

137 See the discussion of Kraus, *Heiligtumsweihe*, in the Analysis section above, and the detailed discussion of v. 25 below.

138 Leenhardt, 101–2, argues, for example, that both deliverance from Egypt and emancipation of slaves would have been on the minds of Paul and his Roman audience.

139 Dunn, 1:169; for discussions of the phrase "in Christ Jesus," see Schmauch, *In Christus*, 68–103; Büchsel, "In Christus," 147–49; Dacquino, "In Christo," 282–85; Wikenhauser, *Pauline Mysticism*, 21–33, 50–65; Bouttier, *En Christ*, 136–39; Fritz Neugebauer, *In Christus*, 101–2, 133–47. See the discussion under 8:1-17.

140 See the Analysis section above.

141 Christian Maurer, "προτίθημι, πρόθεσις," *TDNT* 8 (1972) 166; the connotation of "purpose, intend, foreordain" has been proposed by Lagrange, 75; Cranfield, 1:208–9; Pluta, *Gottes Bundestreue*, 59–62; Dieter Zeller, "Sühne und Langmut. Zur Traditions-

days."[142] The head of the executed traitor Trebonius was "publicly displayed (προετεθῆναι) on the praetor's chair where Trebonius was accustomed to transact public business" (Appian *Hist. Rom.* 2.26). To view this usage as a cultic technical term because προτίθεσθαι appears in the LXX descriptions of offering the bread of the Presence (Exod 29:23; 40:23; Lev 25:8; 2 Macc 1:8, 15)[143] seems strained because this verb does not really function elsewhere in the LXX as a technical term,[144] and the sense of public display is absent from the description of presenting such bread before the altar in the Holy of Holies.[145] While the wording may imply a contrast between the public character of Jesus' ministry and the unseen activity of the high priest in the Holy of Holies,[146] a straightforward claim of God's public provision of a new means of atonement seems as relevant for the original formula[147] as for Paul ("in order to demonstrate his righteousness," 3:25).[148]

The word ἱλαστήριον has been extensively investigated[149] with the conclusion that in the LXX it refers either to the gold plate on the ark of the covenant above which the invisible presence of God was thought to hover and where blood was sprinkled on the Day of Atonement,[150] or to purification, propitiation, and expiation in a more general sense.[151] In the context of the Day of Atonement that the reference to blood in 3:25 implies, the mercy seat was the center of the temple where God dwelled, and all of the temple activities aimed at celebrating God's presence and restoring relationships with the invisible, transcendent Deity that had been broken by sin. The most decisive parallel is Lev 16:15-22:

"And he [Aaron] shall kill the goat . . . and shall bring in from its blood within the veil and shall do with its blood as he did with the blood of the calf and shall sprinkle its blood on the mercy seat, opposite the face of the mercy seat (ἐπὶ τὸ ἱλαστήριον, κατὰ πρόσωπον τοῦ ἱλαστηρίου). And he shall make atonement for the sanctuary from the impurity of the children of Israel and from their unjust acts concerning all of their sins;

geschichte von Röm 3:2-26," *ThPh* 3 (1968) 57–58; and others. See the critique of this option in Schlier, 109–10; Dunn, 1:170; Kraus, *Heiligtumsweihe*, 157.

142 *P.Amh.* 2. Nr. 85.19, cited by MM 554.

143 See Pluta, *Gottes Bundestreue*, 59–62; Wilckens, 1:192.

144 See Kraus, *Heiligtumsweihe*, 158, citing Haubeck, *Loskauf*, 173.

145 See Kraus, *Heiligtumsweihe*, 158.

146 See Thomas Walter Manson, "ΙΛΑΣΤΗΡΙΟΝ," *JTS* 6 (1945) 5; Stuhlmacher, "Zur neueren Exegese," 321–28; idem, *Romans*, 60.

147 Kraus, *Heiligtumsweihe*, 158–59.

148 See Schlier, 110.

149 The most comprehensive listing of parallel passages is found in Romuald Alphonse Mollaun, *St. Paul's Concept of ΙΛΑΣΤΗΡΙΟΝ according to Rom. III,25: An Historico-Exegetical Investigation*, CUANTS 4; SST 21 (Washington, D.C.: Catholic University of America, 1923) 45–89; see also Adolf Deissmann, "ΙΛΑΣΤΗΡΙΟΣ und ΙΛΑΣΤΗΡΙΟΝ. Eine lexikalische Studie," *ZNW* 4 (1903) 193–212; C. H. Dodd, "ΙΛΑΣΤΗΡΙΟΝ, Its Cognates, Derivates, and Synonyms in the Septuagint," *JTS* 32 (1930–31) 352–60; Thomas Walter Manson, "ΙΛΑΣΤΗΡΙΟΝ," *JTS* 6 (1945) 1–10; Friedrich Büchsel and Johannes Herrmann, "ἱλαστήριον," *TDNT* 3 (1965) 318–23; Hultgren, *Gospel*, 47–72; Campbell, *Rhetoric of*

Righteousness, 107–13; Kraus, *Heiligtumsweihe*, 21–31; idem, "Der Jom Kippur, der Tod Jesu und die 'Biblische Theologie': Ein Versuch, die jüdische tradition und die Auslegung von Röm 3,25f einzubeziehen," in I. Baldermann et al., eds., *Altes Testament und christlicher Glaube*, JBTh 6 (Neukirchen-Vluyn: Neukirchener Verlag, 1991) 157–61. Daniel P. Bailey provides an exhaustive discussion of the parallels in "Jesus as the Mercy Seat: The Semantics and Theology of Paul's Use of *Hilasterion* in Romans 3:25" (diss., University of Cambridge, 1999) 15–75.

150 Exod 25:7-22; 30:6; Lev 16:2; Num 7:89; Amos 9:1; *T. Sol.* 21.2; Philo *Cher.* 25; *Fug.* 100; *Mos* 2.95; see Wilckens, 1:191; Jürgen Roloff, "ἱλαστήριον," *EDNT* 2 (1991) 186. The Symmachus translation of Gen 6:15 refers to Noah's ark as a ἱλαστήριον, a place of expiation. See Bernd Janowski, *Sühne als Heilsgeschehen. Studien zur Sühnetheologie der Priesterschrift und zur Wurzel KPR im Alten Orient und im Alten Testament*, WMANT 55 (Neukirchen-Vluyn: Neukirchener Verlag, 1982) 361–62; Kraus, *Heiligtumsweihe*, 25; Paul Fiebig, "Miscellen: Kappôres," *ZNW* 4 (1903) 341–43.

151 Ezek 43:20; 4 Macc 17:21-22; Aelius Herodianus *Pros. cath.* 3.1, 365.24; *P.Oxy.* 16. Nr. 1985.11; *I.Cos* Nr. 81.4; 347.2-3; Dio Chrysostom *Orat.* 11.121.40; see BAGD 375; Deissmann, "ΙΛΑΣΤΗΡΙΟΣ," 207–8; 196; Kraus, *Heiligtumsweihe*, 23–32.

and thus he shall do in the tabernacle of witness, which has been established among them in the midst of their uncleanness . . . and he shall make atonement for himself and his house and for all the congregation of the children of Israel. . . . And he shall finish making atonement for the sanctuary and for the tabernacle of witness and for the altar. . . . And Aaron shall lay his hands on the head of the live goat, and he shall declare over him all the iniquities of the children of Israel. . . . And the goat shall bear upon itself their unrighteousness . . . into the wilderness."

Research on this passage makes clear that the Atonement Day ritual served primarily to remove priestly and national sins that pollute the altar and thereby render the temple service ineffective.[152] The remaining sins were laid on the scapegoat to be driven out into the wilderness.[153] In contrast to most interpreters influenced by Christian doctrines of the atonement,[154] the effective forms of atonement offered in the temple were the burnt offerings, whose smoke reestablished relationships with Yahweh.[155] The killing of animals was merely a prerequisite for burnt offerings, with the exception for grain offerings in which blood played no part. As the citation from Lev 16 makes plain, the Atonement Day ritual employed blood as a means to purify the mercy seat and the rest of the temple.[156] Several inconclusive arguments have been developed against associating ἱλαστήριον in Romans with the "mercy seat," such as that the lack of an article as found in the LXX points to expiation in general,[157] that the Roman audience would not have understood the allusion to the ark,[158] or that it seems illogical for a person to be both the location and means of atonement.[159] There is no doubt, however, that the hymn cited by Paul identifies Christ as the ἱλαστήριον.[160]

In view of the need for temple purification on the Day of Atonement when the "mercy seat" was approached by the high priest, it appears that a kind of renewed temple was thereby created. In a way parallel to the Qumran community, which hoped for an eschatological temple to replace the corrupt temple in Jerusalem,[161] the hymn celebrates the death of Jesus as having established a new "place of atonement, epiphany, and the presence of God."[162] This understanding of the hymn renders unnecessary elaborate theories about the typological,[163] functional, or metaphorical interpretation of Christ as the mercy seat.[164] Since blood had a cleansing rather than a directly atoning function with regard to the mercy seat, the long-standing debate about propitiation[165] or expiation is largely irrelevant for the inter-

---

152 See particularly Kraus, *Heiligtumsweihe*, 45–69. Eberhart, *Studien*, 237–38; Gaukesbrink, *Sühnetradition*, 230–45; and Knöppler, *Sühne*, 113–17, disregard the evidence concerning the cleansing of the sanctuary.

153 See Kraus, *Heiligtumsweihe*, 45–59, for a survey of investigations on this issue.

154 See, e.g., the influential study by Janowski, *Sühne*, 103–81, and his recent reiteration of the blood atonement theory in "Sühne. II," *RGG*⁴ 7 (2004) 1844. Anderson, "Sin Offering," 312–22, is apt.

155 See Eberhard, *Studien*, 70–76.

156 Anderson, "Sin Offering," 312–15; Kraus, *Heiligtumsweihe*, 59; Eberhart, *Studien*, 159–69.

157 Lohse, *Märtyrer*, 149–54; Leon Morris, "The Meaning of ΙΛΑΣΤΗΡΙΟΝ in Romans iii,25," *NTS* 2 (1955–56) 40; Käsemann, 97.

158 Werner Georg Kümmel, *Heilsgeschehen und Geschichte* (Marburg: Elwert, 1965) 265; Schlier, 111; Käsemann, 97; Stowers, *Rereading*, 210.

159 Käsemann, 97.

160 See particularly Bailey, "Jesus as the Mercy Seat," 170, 173: "God made Christ to be ἱλαστήριον . . . accessible to all through faith."

161 See B. Gärtner, *The Temple and the Community in Qumran and the New Testament: A Comparative Study in the Temple Symbolism of the Qumran Texts and the New Testament*, SNTSMS 1 (Cambridge: Cambridge University Press, 1965) 1–46, cited by Kraus, *Heiligtumsweihe*, 76.

162 Kraus, *Heiligtumsweihe*, 163.

163 See, e.g., Wilckens, 1:190–96; Janowski, *Sühne*, 350–55; Merklein, *Studien*, 33–34.

164 Campbell, *Rhetoric of Righteousness*, 109–13, building on Deissmann, "ΙΛΑΣΤΗΡΙΟΣ," 103–211. See also Bruce, 106; Cranfield, 1:106; Dunn, 1:171. For a critique of the typological interpretation see Stowers, *Rereading*, 209–10.

165 See Dodd's vigorous argument for expiation rather than propitiation for the biblical material in *Bible and the Greeks*, 82–95; and "ΙΛΑΣΚΕΣΘΑΙ, Its Cognates, Derivates, and Synonyms in the Septuagint," *JTS* 32 (1930–31) 352–60. His critics include Morris, *Apostolic Preaching*, 125–85; Roger R. Nicole, "C. H. Dodd and the Doctrine of Propitiation," *WTJ* 17 (1954–55) 117–57; idem, "'Hilaskesthai' Revisited," *EvQ* 9 (1977) 173–77; Norman H. Young,

pretation of this verse.[166] The central claim in the hymn is that Christ provided a new means of access to God that reached beyond the sins of Israel.[167] In view of Paul's other statements about atonement, moreover, it seems unlikely that he shared an expiatory theory, which concentrates so exclusively on the matter of forgiveness, a matter of decidedly secondary interest in his theology. Propitiation also seems far from Paul's intent.[168] The likely alternative is found in 2 Cor 5:19, 21, reiterated in Rom 5:10, where we find a distinctively Pauline formulation of atonement as reconciliation: ὡς ὅτι θεὸς ἦν ἐν Χριστῷ κόσμον καταλλάσσων ἑαυτῷ. . . . τὸν μὴ γνόντα ἁμαρτίαν ὑπὲρ ἡμῶν ἁμαρτίαν ἐποίησεν, ἵνα ἡμεῖς γενώμεθα δικαιοσύνη θεοῦ ἐν αὐτῷ ("Because in Christ God was reconciling the world to himself. . . . For our sake he made him who knew no sin to be sin, in order that in him we might become the righteousness of God.") This form of atonement aims not at assuaging divine wrath or repairing damage to divine justice, but at overcoming human enmity against God and restoring humans to righteousness "in him," that is, in the new community of faith. While traditional interpreters construe this passage as "putting away of God's wrath against human transgressions," exhausting "the effects of divine wrath against sin,"[169] Frank Matera wisely observes that "there is no need for God to be reconciled to humanity as appears in 2 Macc 1:5; 7:33; and 8:29. To the contrary, humanity stands in need of reconciliation with God."[170] The situation resolved by the death of Christ was the massive human assault on the righteousness of God, an assault that dominates the

argument of Romans from 1:18 through 3:20 and is reiterated in 3:23.

The designation of a person as a mercy seat is similar to 4 Maccabees, where the national sins of Israel are atoned by the death of the martyrs: "for they became a ransom for the sin of our nation, and through the blood of these pious ones and their atoning death (διὰ τοῦ αἵματος τῶν εὐσεβῶν ἐκείνων καὶ τοῦ ἱλαστηρίου τοῦ θανάτου αὐτῶν) divine providence saved Israel . . . by the blood of these pious ones and their propitiatory death (προκακωθέντα)" (17:22). The exhaustive analysis of historical-religious parallels by Wolfgang Kraus concludes that pre-Christian Jewish literature provides no closer parallel, "especially when the author's declaration is understood as the 'answer' to Eleazar's plea at 6:29. . . . Eleazar prays that God will make his blood their purification, that is, that He will accept it, regard it as such. That, in different terminology, is exactly what the pre-Pauline formulation says that God has done in response to the death of Jesus."[171]

What Kraus and other researchers overlook, however, is that 4 Maccabees delimits the scope of this atonement to "our nation." While some are inclined to view martyrdom as an alternative to mercy seat in assessing the background of ἱλαστήριον,[172] there are sound reasons to view the latter as foundational. As Lohse, Stuhlmacher, and others point out, 4 Maccabees assumes that the martyrdom of the righteous will assuage God's wrath against Israel, the hymnic fragment in Rom 3 proclaims God as providing atonement for all humans.[173] What 4 Macc 17 offers is a precedent for replacing the

"C. H. Dodd, 'Hilaskesthai' and His Critics," *EvQ* 48 (1976) 67–78.

166 See Christopher M. Tuckett, "Atonement in the NT," *ABD* 1 (1992) 519.

167 See Kraus, *Heiligtumsweihe*, 166–67.

168 Mollaun, *ΙΛΑΣΤΗΡΙΟΝ*, 95; Morris, *Apostolic Preaching*, 125–85; in *Cross*, 81, Hamerton-Kelly offers a provocative version of this theory, that the wrath that fell on Jesus was not divine wrath against human sin, but "human vengeance dissembled through the Sacred." Christ became the victim of human zealotism and thus "bears the wrath for us, to disclose and thus disarm it."

169 I. Howard Marshall, "The Meaning of 'Reconciliation,'" in R. A. Guelich, ed., *Unity and Diversity in New Testament Theology: Essays in Honor of George E.*

Ladd (Grand Rapids: Eerdmans, 1978) 123; see also Martin, *2 Corinthians*, 154–55.

170 Frank J. Matera, "Reconciliation," *HBD* (1985) 856; see also Knöppler, *Sühne*, 116.

171 Kraus, *Heiligtumsweihe*, 41 (underlining in original; my translation).

172 See Williams, *Jesus' Death*, passim; and the critique by Bailey, "Jesus as the Mercy Seat," 118–42.

173 Lohse, *Märtyrer*, 150–53; Stuhlmacher, *Reconciliation*, 101–2; Kraus, *Heiligtumsweihe*, 42–43; Gaukesbrink, *Sühnetradition*, 241; see also Jan Willem van Henten, "Das jüdische Selbstverständnis in den ältesten Martyrien," in J. W. van Henten, ed., *Die Entstehung der jüdischen Martyrologie*, SPB 38 (Leiden: Brill, 1989) 127–61.

Day of Atonement ritual with a martyr's death, making clear that the hymn proclaims Jesus' blood as a new institution of atonement. It is an early Christian version of the expectation found in the Temple Scroll (11QT) and *Jub* 1.29; 4.24-26, that in the final days God will provide a purified temple. For example, "And I will sanctify my temple with my glory. I will cause my glory to dwell over it until the day of creation when I create my temple anew, establishing it for myself for all time according to the covenant which I have made with Jacob in Bethel" (11QT 29:8-10). Both in 11QT and *Jubilees,* a new, purified temple is anticipated, reflecting sectarian dissatisfaction with the Jerusalem temple in the hands of the Sadducees. A similar critique is found in early Hellenistic Christianity represented by Stephen, whose denunciation of the temple led to his stoning (Acts 7:47-53). This leads to the most likely provenance of the hymnic fragment being the Hellenistic Christian circle that viewed Stephen as a decisive leader in his critique of the Jerusalem temple.[174]

The theory of a hymnic citation needs to be taken into account while analyzing the expression "through faith in his blood," because we are assuming that δια πίστεως was added by Paul.[175] This phrase has long been considered intrusive in the context of a "mercy seat in his blood."[176] That blood was associated with the "mercy seat" is widely recognized, and it is clear that the Atonement Day ritual used blood to atone for priestly and national sins that polluted the altar (Lev 16:16).[177] Ezek 43:20-27 and 45:18-20 also employ blood in this pri-

mary sense of purifying the sanctuary whose efficacy was lost through pollution.[178] It follows that "the forgiveness which is provided through the blood ritual on the ἱλαστήριον is related to the purification of the sanctuary" and that a fundamental distinction needs to be recognized "between personal sins and sins against the sanctuary."[179] The phrase ἐν τῷ αὐτοῦ αἵματι ("in/by his blood") should therefore be taken in the original hymnic fragment to refer to the provision of a new system of atonement available to all rather than to "an antidemonic means of purification and protection" and "atonement" as found in the OT[180] or to an "interchange" between sinners and a spotless victim as found in both the OT and the NT.[181] Kraus explains, "since the impurity of the people disable the cult, the sanctuary must first be purified, before further offerings may be brought."[182] Hence the reference to Jesus becoming a "mercy seat" refers not to the placing of the sins of the people on the goat sent out into the wilderness but rather to the provision of a new institutional vehicle for atonement. The hymn proclaims that God made Jesus into "the new place of atonement, epiphany, and divine presence."[183] This blood covers both shameful discrimination and the guilt of groups as well as persons because Christ's death overcame the ethnic and religious boundaries that barred access to atonement for Gentiles.

Paul's view of the effectiveness of the blood of Christ is visible in his addition of δια πίστεως ("through faith"), an expression that is "singular in the New Testament" because nowhere else do we find faith "in the

174 See Stuhlmacher, *Reconciliation*, 104; Kleinknecht, *Gerechtfertigte*, 188; Kraus, *Heiligtumsweihe*, 232–34; this hypothesis fits the generalization of the early NT atonement statements made by Martin Hengel in *Atonement*, 47: "the one common root of all this multiple tradition is probably to be discovered where there had been a fundamental break with the atoning and saving significance of sacrifice in the worship of the temple in Jerusalem." In *Gottes Bundestreue*, 92–104, 109–10, Alfons Pluta develops an alternative thesis that the citation derives from a eucharistic prayer shaped by OT expectations.

175 See Käsemann, 98; Zimmermann, "Jesus Christus," 73; Kraus, *Heiligtumsweihe*, 18. For an appraisal of "through faith" as belonging to the cited hymn, see Pluta, *Gottes Bundestreue*, 34–42; von Dobbeler, *Glaube als Teilhabe*, 80–84, and Bruce W. Longe-

necker, "ΠΙΣΤΙΣ in Romans 3.25: Neglected Evidence for the 'Faithfulness of Christ?'" *NTS* 39 (1993) 478–80.

176 See Michel, 150; Wilckens, 1:194; Käsemann, 97–98.

177 Kraus, *Heiligtumsweihe*, 45–59.

178 See ibid., 59–65.

179 Ibid., 69 (my translations of all Kraus material); see also Anderson, "Sin Offering," 312–15.

180 Otto Böcher, "αἷμα," *EDNT* 1 (1990) 37.

181 See Morna D. Hooker, "Interchange and Atonement," *BJRL* 60 (1978) 62–81.

182 Kraus, *Heiligtumsweihe*, 91.

183 Ibid.

blood" or even followed by the preposition ἐν ("in") itself.[184] There are distant parallels elsewhere to an association between faith and atonement or blood, but none that fully clarifies this verse.[185] The strange wording is explained by Paul's redactional insertion. To view "through faith" as a parenthesis,[186] as a reference to God's covenant faithfulness,[187] or as an allusion to "the cost/price of his blood"[188] provides no coherent grasp of Paul's redactional motive, which probably aimed to emphasize that access to this new institution of atonement through the blood of Christ was available to everyone through faith.[189] While the former institution of atonement in the temple was restricted to Jews and did not require a particular act of faith on the part of recipients, the new spiritual sanctuary marked by those who participate in the meal of the "blood of the new

covenant" is open to "all who have faith" (Rom 3:22).[190] In contrast to expiation, which functions regardless of the behavior or attitude of recipients, atonement in the Pauline sense of reconciliation of those who declared war against God is effective only for those who respond to the good news in faith.

The Pauline insertion of the clause, "for a demonstration of his righteousness," echoed in the following verse, integrates the hymnic fragment into the thesis of the letter. The word ἔνδειξις is used here in the sense of "proof, demonstration,"[191] with the latter connotation allegedly supported by Aeschines Ctes. 2.219.1.[192] However, the effort to distinguish sharply between "proof" and "demonstration"[193] cannot be supported by the linguistic evidence.[194] On the basis of Douglas Campbell's

184 Käsemann, 98.

185 Jan Willem van Henten, "The Tradition-Historical Background of Rom 3:25: A Search for Pagan and Jewish Parallels," in M. de Boer, ed., *From Jesus to Paul: Essays on Jesus and New Testament Christology in Honour of Marinus de Jonge*, JSNTSup 84 (Sheffield: JSOT Press, 1993) 108–9, points to Plutarch *Sera* 560 c-d, "But . . . consider whether in your opinion our own god of this place [Apollo Pythios], knowing that when men die their souls perish immediately, exhaled from the body like vapour or smoke, nevertheless prescribes many appeasements (ἱλασμούς πολλούς) of the dead and demands for them great honours and consideration, deluding and cheating those who put faith in him (τοὺς πιστεύοντας)." Henten's search of medical, erotic, and literary texts was "almost completely negative" in finding appropriate parallels to Rom 3:25. On pp. 110–27, Henten discusses the closer parallels in the martyrdom texts of 2 Macc 7:37–8:5, 4 Macc 6–7, and LXX Dan 3:39-40, but concludes on 126, "the way in which Paul has assimilated these traditional conceptions must be investigated further."

186 Käsemann, 98; Dunn, 1:172.

187 Arthur G. Hebert, "Faithfulness and 'Faith,'" *Theology* 58 (1955) 376; Pluta, *Gottes Bundestreue*, 105–7; see the critique by Barr, *Semantics*, 161–87.

188 Williams, *Jesus' Death*, 47, follows Turner in taking the "in" as "a curious instrumental dative of price"; see Moulton and Turner, *Grammar III*, 253. This would bring the Romans passage close to 4 Maccabees, where God responds favorably to the martyr's endurance unto death and accepts it as a means of purification, delivering Israel. Thus it is really the faithfulness demonstrated by Jesus that saves.

189 See von Dobbeler, *Glaube als Teilhabe*, 84.

190 See Gaukesbink, *Sühnetradition*, 242; Knöppler, *Sühne*, 119.

191 See Henning Paulsen, "ἐνδείκνυμαι, ἔνδειξις," *EDNT* 1 (1990) 450. In "Romans 3:26b: A Question of Translation," *JBL* 87 (1968) 203, Cyril Blackman suggests that ἔνδειξις was employed in preference to "reveal" in 1:17 and "manifest" in 3:2 "because it seemed stronger evidentially and logically."

192 See Werner Georg Kümmel, "Πάρεσις und ἔνδειξις. A Contribution to the Understanding of the Pauline Doctrine of Justification," *JTC* 3 (1967) 4–5, but the passage in Aeschines *Ctes.* 219 is quite ambiguous on the distinction Kümmel wishes to make: ἀπηνέχθη γὰρ ἡ κατὰ τοῦδε τοῦ ψηφίσματος γραφή, ἣν οὐχ ὑπὲρ τῆς πόλεως ἀλλ᾽ ὑπὲρ τῆς πρὸς Ἀλέξανδρον ἐνδείξεώς με φῂς ἀπενεγκεῖν . . . πῶς ἂν οὖν ἐγὼ προενεδεικνύμην Ἀλεξάνδρῳ. ("For the indictment concerning this decree was submitted, an indictment you allege that I submitted not on behalf of the city but in behalf of the writ of indictment against Alexander . . . how therefore can I exhibit myself before Alexander?")

193 Schlier, 111–12; Kümmel, "Πάρεσις und ἔνδειξις," 5.

194 See the critique of Kümmel by John Piper, "The Demonstration of the Righteousness of God in Rom 3:25, 26," *JSNT* 7 (1980) 2–32; repr. in S. E. Porter and C. A. Evans, eds., *The Pauline Writings*, Biblical Seminar 34 (Sheffield: Sheffield Academic Press, 1995) 183–91; also Campbell, *Rhetoric of Righteousness*, 189–91.

analysis,[195] the point is "not so much that God's righteousness has been manifested for the purpose of display,"[196] but that Christ is the definite means and vehicle of its revelation. This "demonstration" carries forward the leitmotif of divine triumph over human opposition expressed in the psalm citation in 3:4. That divine righteousness needs to be displayed openly is assumed by the OT,[197] so that even "the heavens declare his righteousness (τὴν δικαιοσύνην αὐτοῦ), for God is judge" (LXX Ps 49:6), and so that "the heavens proclaim his righteousness (τὴν δικαιοσύνην αὐτοῦ); and all the peoples behold his glory" (LXX Ps 96:6). The *Pseudo-Clementine Rec.* 3.38.5 claim that the "righteousness of God" will be displayed as sinners are judged and the righteous are blessed at the last judgment: *ita in die iudicii, cum iusti introducentur in regnum dei, iniusti autem abicientur foras, tunc enim iustitia dei ostendetur* ("Thus in the Day of Judgment, when the just are brought into God's Kingdom, the unjust will indeed be brought low, and then truly God's justice will be manifested").[198]

The question Paul addresses with the insertion of the expression "for a demonstration of his righteousness" is whether the provision of the new system of atonement through Christ crucified was a violation of divine righteousness. How can divine faithfulness to covenant partners be demonstrated in this disgraceful manner? How can the boundaries of shame be so egregiously violated? Dunn alludes to the revolutionary implications of Paul's claim: "That the shameful death of crucifixion should be thus presented as an expression of God's saving grace is

a classic example of the gospel's transformation of normal human values."[199] This is a theme that is carried through the entire letter (esp 1:14; 12:1-21; 14:1–15:13). As in Jer 9:12-26,[200] divine righteousness surfaces here in the form of fairness to all, impartial judgment, and the refusal to be a "respecter of persons" by placing some groups above others.[201] The new "mercy seat" is effective for all in equal measure.

The third line in the cited hymn has provided crucial support for the individualistic misunderstanding of "justification" as "forgiveness." The phrase διὰ τὴν πάρεσιν τῶν προγεγονότων ἁμαρτημάτων ("because of the passing over [or remission] of previously committed sins") has often been taken as referring to individual pardon or forgiveness as the main arena for atonement,[202] even though the usual technical term ἄφεσις, common in the Gospels, is not used here. In fact, ἄφεσις is used only once in the entire group of Pauline letters, and then in a quotation (Rom 4:7). Πάρεσις is found only in nonbiblical writings[203] that refer to remission of debts[204] or dismissal of charges, as in the following example: "But from the tribunes, in spite of many entreaties, they were unable to obtain a complete dismissal (ὁλοσχερῆ πάρεσιν) of the charges against Marcius, although they did get a postponement of his trial for as long as they asked" (Dionysius Halicarnassus *Antiq. Rom.* 7.37.2).[205]

In the four instances where the verbal equivalent of πάρεσις is found in conjunction with sins,[206] transgres-

---

195 Campbell, *Rhetoric of Righteousness*, 195.

196 As in Piper, "Demonstration," 201–2.

197 See Scullion, "Righteousness (OT)," 731.

198 Klaus Berger provides this reference in "Neues Material zur 'Gerechtigkeit Gottes,'" *ZNW* 68 (1977) 268–69, and also discusses *Pseudo-Clementine Rec.* 3.42.2; Philo *QG* 1.10; and other passages, showing that divine righteousness and holiness reacts against evil and rewards virtue.

199 Dunn, 1:173; also Strom, *Reframing Paul,* 58–69.

200 See Josef Scharbert, "Gerechtigkeit I. Altes Testament," *TRE* 12 (1983) 409.

201 See Schmid, *Gerechtigkeit als Weltordnung*, 89–91.

202 See Kümmel, "Πάρεσις und ἔνδειξις," 1–2, 9–10; K. Karner, "Rechtfertigung, Sündenvergebung und neues Leben bei Paulus," *ZSTh* 16 (1939) 548–61; Rudolf Bultmann, "ἀφίημι . . . πάρεσις," *TDNT* 1

(1964) 513; Stanislas Lyonnet, "Notes sur l'exégèse de l'Epître aux Romains. II. Le sens de πάρεσις en Rom 3,25," *Bib* 38 (1957) 50–54; Stuhlmacher, 57. A complete history of interpretation is offered by Mansetus Rath, who shows the domination of the forgiveness construal: "De Conceptu 'Paresis' in Epistola ad Romanos (3,25)" (Ph.D. diss., University of Jerusalem, 1965), conveniently summarized by Kraus, *Heiligtumsweihe*, 96–97.

203 The most complete discussion of parallels is available in Kraus, *Heiligtumsweihe*, 98–102.

204 Phalaridis *Ep.* 81.1; *BGU* 2. Nr. 624.31 "remission of debt."

205 See J. M. Creed, "Πάρεσις in Dionysius of Halicarnassus and in St. Paul," *JTS* (1940) 28–30.

206 Xenophon *Eq. mag.* 7.10.39; Dionysius Halicarnassus *Antiq. Rom.* 2.35.4.42; Josephus *Ant.* 15.48; Sir 23:2-3.

sions are left unpunished and passed over but not pardoned.[207] Paul's unusual expression $\pi\rho o\gamma\epsilon\gamma o\nu\acute{o}\tau\omega\nu$ $\dot{\alpha}\mu\alpha\rho\tau\eta\mu\acute{\alpha}\tau\omega\nu$[208] refers to sinful actions[209] committed in the period up to the time of Christ.[210] What commentators call the "puzzle" of this usage[211] has been convincingly explained by Wolfgang Kraus as a reference to God's having overlooked sins not covered by the temple cult. The reference is retrospective rather than prospective, showing why the new system of atonement was required. The preposition $\delta\iota\acute{\alpha}$ with the accusative thus has its normal causative meaning,[212] because prior to the cross event, God had merely shown forbearance for sins not covered by temple rites, which would have included all transgressions outside Israel's ethnic boundaries. This situation was finally overcome by Christ's death, which replaced the temple as a means of reconciliation with God.[213] The issue here was not access to individual forgiveness but the provision of an institution of atonement for groups and nations beyond the scope of the Jerusalem temple. Henceforth a restoration to the status of righteousness is available through Christ's death to "all who have faith" (3:22) throughout the entire world. Christ is viewed here as the replacement of the temple in Jerusalem,[214] which functioned to restore Israel to righteousness. The wording thus reveals the new social identity of converts outside the range of the Jewish temple, an identity as the redeemed in Christ.[215] Whereas the temple sought to offer honorable atonement for Jews and left others in a status of shame, Christ's death restores honor to the whole human race. The puzzling language therefore points to discriminated groups overcoming their shameful status through "faith in Christ." Individualistic concerns about forgiveness to overcome bad conscience that have dominated the discussion of this reference in the post-Augustinian tradition[216] are therefore a diversion from the point of the hymnic fragment in its original context and also in Paul's letter.

■ **26** The final line of the cited hymn is $\dot{\epsilon}\nu\ \tau\hat{\eta}\ \dot{\alpha}\nu o\chi\hat{\eta}$ $\tau o\hat{\upsilon}\ \vartheta\epsilon o\hat{\upsilon}$ ("by the forbearance of God"), which has been taken to refer to God's readiness to forgive[217] or to divine restraint in the sense of postponement of punishment.[218] Epictetus refers to having "some respite from these threats" ($\tau\iota\nu\alpha\ \dot{\alpha}\nu o\chi\dot{\eta}\nu\ \dot{\alpha}\pi\grave{o}\ \tau o\acute{\upsilon}\tau\omega\nu$) of retribution from the government (*Diss.* 1.29.62) and Josephus refers to Aristobulus's being given a brief "respite from war" ($\dot{\alpha}\nu o\chi\dot{\eta}\nu\ \tau o\hat{\upsilon}\ \pi o\lambda\acute{\epsilon}\mu o\upsilon$) before the Romans captured

---

207 See Kraus, *Heiligtumsweihe*, 102–3; also Williams, *Saving Death*, 28.

208 This is the only occurence of $\pi\rho o\gamma\acute{\iota}\nu o\mu\alpha\iota$ ("happen before, occur previously") in the NT, but there is a close parallel in Apollonius Rhodius *Cho. Frag.* 4.411-13. The expression "previously committed sins" employing $\dot{\alpha}\mu\alpha\rho\tau\acute{\iota}\alpha$ rather than $\dot{\alpha}\mu\acute{\alpha}\rho\tau\eta\mu\alpha$ is found in a political context as an explanation of the motive of conspirators against King Philip of Macedonia: "Leontias, Megaleas, and Ptolemaeus, still hoping to intimidate Philip and free themselves in this manner from their earlier sins ($\lambda\acute{\upsilon}\sigma\epsilon\iota\nu\ \tau\hat{\omega}$ $\tau o\iota o\upsilon\tau\hat{\omega}\ \tau\rho\acute{o}\pi\hat{\omega}\ \tau\grave{\alpha}\varsigma\ \pi\rho o\gamma\epsilon\gamma\epsilon\nu\eta\mu\acute{\epsilon}\nu\alpha\varsigma\ \mathring{\eta}$ $\dot{\alpha}\mu\alpha\rho\tau\acute{\iota}\alpha\varsigma$), spread among the . . . troops . . . suggestions that they were in risk of losing all their advantages" (Polybius *Hist.* 5.25.1; see also Eunapius *Vit. soph.* 10.1.13).

209 With regard to translating $\dot{\alpha}\mu\acute{\alpha}\rho\tau\eta\mu\alpha$, I follow Smyth, *Grammar*, §841.2, in viewing morphemes marked with $-\mu\alpha$ as the result of actions, whereas -$\iota\alpha$, as in $\dot{\alpha}\mu\alpha\rho\tau\acute{\iota}\alpha$ refers to the abstract state.

210 Kraus, *Heiligtumsweihe*, 104–8; his analysis of the use of $\dot{\alpha}\mu\acute{\alpha}\rho\tau\eta\mu\alpha$ indicates it refers to sins in a comprehensive sense, which includes those prior to Sinai and thus indicates a "universal horizon" (112) that reaches beyond the Jewish law.

211 See Dunn, 1:174.

212 BDF §222; BAGD 181: "to indicate . . . the reason why something happens, results, exists"; Kraus, *Heiligtumsweihe*, 93, 103.

213 Kraus, *Heiligtumsweihe*, 95–104.

214 Ibid., 233.

215 Ibid., 234.

216 See, e.g., John Reumann, "Righteousness (Early Judaism, Greco-Roman World, NT)," *ABD* 5 (1992) 766; Karl Kertelge, "$\delta\iota\kappa\alpha\iota\acute{o}\omega$," *EDNT* I (1990) 332. For a more adequate view, see Patte, *Paul*, 254.

217 Dieter Zeller, "Sühne und Langmut. Zur Traditionsgeschichte von Röm 3:24-26," *ThPh* 3 (1968) 62; Schmidt, 69; Morris, 183–84; the association of "long forbearance" and forgiveness is suggested by CD Ms A 2:4-5, "long forbearance is with him and manifold forgiveness, so as to atone for those who repent of rebellions and sin."

218 Heinrich Schlier, "$\dot{\alpha}\nu\acute{\epsilon}\chi\omega,\ \dot{\alpha}\nu\epsilon\kappa\tau\acute{o}\varsigma,\ \dot{\alpha}\nu o\chi\acute{\eta}$," *TDNT* 1 (1964) 360; Williams, *Jesus' Death*, 28; see the exhaustive discussion of parallels in Kraus, *Heiligtumsweihe*, 112–49.

him (*Bell.* 1.173). *Ep. Arist.* 194.5 comes closer to the usage in Romans: "for God also, by granting forbearances (ἀνοχάς) and displaying his sovereign power, implants awe into every mind." Sam Williams points out that the theme of divine restraint in Isa 64:10-12, 63:15, and 42:14 relates to "inactivity, his failure to act on behalf of his people."[219] A similar idea is found in apocalyptic literature and in 2 Macc 6:12-17, where God's long-suffering forbearance, in Williams's view, ". . . is not an act of clemency nor the divine attribute of mercy. It is rather the divine inactivity, the failure to intervene, which allows sin to run its natural course until the day of judgment when finally God will indeed act. And from whom does God hold back punishment so that sins pile up? Again it is other nations, other peoples. To his own people God demonstrates his mercy by early chastisement, but the Gentiles he leaves alone until their sins have accumulated beyond the breaking point. Not Jews but Gentiles are the present beneficiaries of God's long-suffering in II Maccabees 6."[220] As Kraus points out, there is no indication either in Romans or in the parallel passages that the "forbearance of God" is a term for salvation; it describes a period in which God refrains from wrath.[221] It describes the situation prior to the cross event.

Therefore Rom 3:25-26 refers mainly to God's having previously overlooked Gentiles' sins, and now giving them a chance for reconciliation that they had never before enjoyed. I therefore contend that Paul was able to include the Hellenistic-Christian hymnic fragment in Rom 3 because the reversal of the honor-shame system embodied in the cross of Christ constitutes a new system of atonement. The focus here is not on individual confession and forgiveness of sins, but the provision of an institution that places competing groups on the same level before God. A discriminatory form of forgiveness was symbolized by the Jewish temple, where women and Gentiles were placed in separate courts that were more distant from God than the court for Jewish males. In the new system with Christ as the mercy seat, traditional distinctions in honor are abrogated by divine impartiality. All groups without exception have access to this atonement. However, this does not mean that in Paul's view forgiveness itself is the sum total of Christ's work on the cross. It is the elimination of invidious distinctions in the availability of divine favor, the access to salvation for "all who have faith," that stands at the center here.

Paul's interpretation of the hymnic fragment is visible in the reduplicated clause that follows: "it was to demonstrate his righteousness in the present time" (3:26b). This demonstration refers back to the establishment of the new system of atonement in Christ. The formulation of πρὸς τὴν ἔνδειξιν in v. 26 is equivalent to εἰς ἔνδειξιν in the preceding verse, since πρός with the accusative can have the same meaning as εἰς with the accusative.[222] The duplication of virtually the exact clause from the preceding verse reinforces Paul's main point concerning this new system as a public exhibition of the righteousness of God.[223] It reinforces the leitmotif of divine triumph first developed in 3:4. There is no intent here to separate different epochs of salvation[224] or to offer a correction of the christological hymn.[225]

The expression ἐν τῷ νῦν καιρῷ is used here in the sense of "the now existing time,"[226] as contrasted with the period before the coming of Christ when divine forbearance overlooked sins beyond the scope of temple ceremonies. This is usually taken as the epoch beginning with Christ and extending to the time of writing Romans,[227] which would be consistent with the νῦν in 3:21. Yet this also includes the present moment in which the gospel of the righteousness of God is being preached, and thus has a direct bearing on the missional purpose of this letter, because as the thesis of Romans states, the gospel "is the power of God for salvation,"

---

219 Williams, *Jesus' Death*, 29 (underlining in original).
220 Ibid., 32.
221 Kraus, *Heiligtumsweihe*, 148.
222 Smyth, *Grammar*, §1686d; see Campbell's discussion of "isocolic reduplication" of the expression "to demonstrate" in *Rhetoric of Righteousness*, 95–99.
223 Kraus, *Heiligtumsweihe*, 184–85.
224 Ibid., 185, cites Cambier, *Évangile*, 122–24; Zimmermann, *Jesus Christus*, 222.
225 Käsemann, 100.
226 Jörg Baumgarten, "καιρός," *EDNT* 2 (1991) 232; Gerhard Delling, "καιρός," *TDNT* 3 (1965) 459–60.
227 See Baumgarten, *Paulus*, 192; Moo, 241; Neuhäusler, "Entscheidende Augenblick," 1. The correlation with Eastern Orthodox theology is worked out by Nissiotis, "νῦν," 303–9.

revealing the righteousness of God (1:16-17). I therefore translate, "the present critical time," to capture this sense of eschatological urgency.

The final clausula in v. 26d-e designates the purpose of God's demonstration of righteousness through the atoning death of Jesus. The εἰς τὸ εἶναι αὐτὸν δίκαιον construction is a purpose phrase[228] that draws a conclusion from the entire pericope.[229] In contrast to the preceding phrase dealing with the public demonstration of divine righteousness, this final emphasis is on "God's *being* righteous."[230] The surpassing quality of divine righteousness is consistently affirmed in biblical thought. As Hannah exclaims in 1 Sam 2:2, "there is none holy as the Lord, and there is none righteous as our God (οὐκ ἔστι δίκαιος ὡς ὁ θεὸς ἡμῶν)." The psalmist typically affirms, "Righteous is the Lord in all his ways (Δίκαιος Κύριος ἐν πάσαις ταῖς ὁδοῖς) and holy in all his works" (LXX Ps 144:17). This theme echoes throughout the Psalms and Isa 40–66 as well as other biblical[231] and intertestamental contexts.[232] While there were excellent reasons both within Judaism and Greco-Roman religion and ethics to question whether God's provision of this new system of atonement through the shameful death of Christ placed God's

honor in disrepute, Paul affirms God's "absolute faithfulness always to act for his name's sake and for the preservation and display of his glory."[233]

There has been a tangled debate over whether the καί in v. 26d is (a) copulative, indicating that God both shows his righteousness and sets people right and that the two acts are not contradictory;[234] (b) intensive, ascensive, or concessive, indicating that God maintains righteousness even while setting right the wicked;[235] (c) instrumental, insisting that God maintains righteousness by means of setting people right;[236] or (d) explicative, either showing how God can accept sinners without polluting his justice, thus reflecting the classic dilemma of Anselmian atonement theory,[237] or explaining "that God is right within the very act of rightwising" the faithful because he "reaches out . . . to draw the believer" into the realm of righteousness.[238] While it seems problematic to build theological constructs on the slim foundation of a single conjunction, some version of the explicative construal of καί seems most plausible for this pericope, where the main theme is God's righteousness that establishes a new, inclusive system of atonement. In "setting right" those who have "faith in Jesus,"[239] God breaks through the barriers of honor and

---

228 BDF §402.2; Moulton and Turner, *Grammar III*, 143: "expresses purpose or result."

229 See Campbell, *Rhetoric of Righteousness*, 166; the contention of Bultmann, "ΔΙΚΑΙΟΣΥΝΗ ΘΕΟΥ," *JBL* 83 (1964) 12–16; Käsemann, 101; Müller, *Gottes Gerechtigkeit*, 110–13; Stuhlmacher, *Gerechtigkeit*, 90; and others that this verse serves as a corrective to the cited confession is indicated neither by the form nor the content of this clausula; see Kuss, 1:161.

230 Cranfield, 1:213; emphasis in the original.

231 See Scullion, "Righteousness (OT)," 731–34, mentioning Pss 5; 7; 22; 32; 33; 35; 36; 40; 50; 71; 88; 89; 97; 98; 103; 119; 143; 145.

232 See Reumann, "Righteousnes (Early Judaism)," 739–42.

233 Piper, *Justification*, 130; see also Stuhlmacher, *Gerechtigkeit*, 90–91.

234 BAGD 391–92; Godet, 158–59.

235 BAGD 393, II.2; Cyril Blackman, "Romans 3:26b: A Question of Translation," *JBL* 87 (1968) 203–4; Wolfgang Schrage, "Römer 3,21-26 und die Bedeutung des Todes Jesu Christi bei Paulus," in P. Rieger, ed., *Das Kreuz Jesu. Theologische Überlegungen*, Forum 12 (Göttingen: Vandenhoeck

& Ruprecht, 1969) 87; Williams, "Righteousness," 277–78; Moo, 242.

236 This category is used by Moo, 242, and seems more apt than the "explicative sense" claimed by Käsemann, 101: "The Giver himself makes himself known in the gift. He makes himself known as the Almighty who intervenes in righteousness." See also Wilckens, 1:198: "that God is just in that he justifies every sinner on the basis of faith."

237 BAGD 393, I.3; see Campbell, *Rhetoric of Righteousness*, 167–68, for an explication of the theodicy and atonement issues that dominate some of the older commentators such as Meyer, 1:179–81. A protest against the domination of atonement theory in the interpretation of 3:26d was registered by Gustav Adolf Fricke, *Der paulinische Grundbegriff der ΔΙΚΑΙΟΣΥΝΗ ΘΕΟΥ erörtert auf Grund von Röm. 3,21-26* (Leipzig: Böhme, 1888), cited by W. F. Lofthouse, "The Righteousness of God," *ExpT* 50 (1938–39) 445.

238 Campbell, *Rhetoric of Righteousness*, 170.

239 Morris, 184, discusses the unusual expression of ἐκ πίστεως preceded by τόν, which is found only here in the NT and possibly in all of classical Greek. See

shame that separated individuals and groups from one another and from God.[240] Faith is the sole requirement, and here it means accepting the message about Jesus' shameful death in behalf of the shamed and joining the community of the shamed that is now being honored by God. Distinctions between the "inherent righteousness"[241] of believers and "imputed righteousness"[242] granted to those who remain sinners seem very distant from Paul's discourse; God's very being as a righteous God is expressed as she makes groups righteous by faith. The use of "Jesus" in the absolute at the end of the pericope probably refers, as elsewhere in the Pauline corpus according to John Pryor, to "the events of his life, chiefly to his death and resurrection."[243] Faith in the person of

Jesus, probably an objective genitive because of the connection with the stance of those being set right, is the great equalizer, leveling all distinctions of ethnic, economic, social, religious, or sexual status. Thus the righteousness of God manifests itself in the restoration of the fallen world in the small communities of faith whom Paul wishes to enlist in the project to carry this gospel of the crucified Lord to the end of the known world. By fusing his missionary theology with the atonement hymn, Paul has created a firm bond between himself and the various congregations in Rome, establishing a persuasive basis for a jointly sponsored mission in behalf of the impartial righteousness of God.

Moulton and Turner, *Grammar III*, 260, referring to the "character" of the persons in question.

240 See Zahn, 198: "that in this connection there might be no distinction among believers." In "The Revelation of Christ to Paul on the Damascus Road and Paul's Doctrine of Justification and Reconciliation. A Study of Galatians I" (trans. J. M. Owen), in R. Banks, ed., *Reconciliation and Hope: Essays on Atonement and Eschatology Presented to L. L. Morris on His 60th Birthday* (Grand Rapids: Eerdmans, 1974) 102, Günther Bornkamm concludes that in this passage "God has shown himself to be the God of all men, Jews and Gentiles, and has shown both groups on an equal footing the only way to salvation." See also

Tamez, "Justification," 184: "God offers the opportunity to transform this upside-down world—which excludes those who are discriminated against because of their gender, race or class—by raising up the One who was condemned for his practice of justice."

241 Weiss, 172, argues against this distinction.

242 Nygren, 161.

243 W. Pryor, "Paul's Use of Ἰησοῦς—A Clue for the Translation of Romans 3:26?" *Colloquium* 16.1 (1983) 40–41, on the basis of analyzing Rom 8:11; 10:9; 1 Cor 9:1; 12:3; 2 Cor 4:5-14, 11:4; Gal 6:17; Phil 2:10; 1 Thess 1:10; 4:14.

3

The Second Part of the Fourth Pericope

The Righteousness of God and Setting Humans Right by Faith Alone

b. Diatribe Affirming the One God of Jews and Gentiles

27/ 'Where then is our[a] boasting?'
It is excluded!
'Through what kind of law? That of works?'
No! But [it was excluded] through the law of faith! 28/ For[b] we reckon[c] a human[d] to be set right by faith without works of law.

29/ 'Or [does] God [belong] only[e] to Jews? Doesn't [God] also [belong] to Gentiles?'
Yes, [God] also [belongs to] Gentiles, 30/ if indeed[f] "the God is one" who will set right the circumcision from faith and the uncircumcision through this faith.

31/ 'Are we then neutralizing law through this faith?'
By no means! Rather we establish law [through this faith].

a The addition of σου ("your") in F G *pc* it vg[ww] appears to be a later effort to accentuate the personal emphasis in a manner similar to 2:1-5.

b There is a fair probability for the reading γάρ ("for"), supported by ℵ A D* F G Ψ 81 256 263 323 326 365 436 630 945 1319 1506 1573 1739 1852 1881 1962 2127 2200 2492 ar b d f g o vg sy[pal] sa bo

arm eth Or[lat] Cyr Ambst Ambr Pel Aug[3/7] as compared with οὖν ("therefore") in B C D[c] K L P 6 33 69 88 104 181 330 424 451 459 614 629 1175 1241 1243 1505 1735 1836 1874 1912 2344 2464 2495 *Maj* mon sy[p.h] Chr Theodore; see Metzger, *Textual Commentary*, 450. There is no likelihood that *Lect* bo[mss] slav[ms] Aug [4/7] Hier are correct in simply omitting the γάρ.

c A minor and late variant in K P 049 1175 2464 *al* has λογιζώμεθα ("let us reckon"), probably the result of a dictation error since ω and ο would sound the same.

d The rather abbreviated though widely attested expression δικαιοῦσθαι πίστει ἄνθρωπον ("a human set right by faith") is replaced in F G lat with δικαιοῦσθαι ἄνθρωπον διὰ πίστεως ("a human set right through faith"), an apparent attempt to make the formula consistent with 3:21-22, where διὰ πίστεως contrasts with χωρὶς νόμου.

e The adverb μόνον ("only) is changed by D into the nominative singular μόνος, which would imply "God alone" and by B 88 323 330 945 1739[c] *pc* Cl to the genitive plural μόνων, nicely coordinated as "only Jews." The adverbial reading should stand as the most widely attested reading.

f The variant ἐπείπερ ("since indeed"), found in ℵ[2] D* F G (K) L P Ψ 33 69 88 104 323 326 330 424 614 945 1175 1241 1243 1505 1735 1836 1874 1881 2344 2464 2495 *Maj* Ir[lat] Eus is a stylistic improvement with no claim to originality as compared with εἴπερ ("if indeed") found in ℵ* A B C D[1] 6 365 1319 1573 1506 1739 *pc* Cl Or.

Analysis

This passage represents an abrupt change in style from the elevated "grand style" of 3:21-26 to a crisp, dialogical exchange between Paul and an interrogator.[1] The elliptical style requires the inclusion of the ellipsed materials in an English translation, as supplied above within square brackets. A skillfully constructed series of six rhetorical questions is arranged in an A-B-B'-A' sequence with the first and last questions answered emphatically and the middle pairs supplied with potent supportive arguments. The οὖν ("therefore") in 3:27 links the initial question about boasting to a previous discussion, including the references to boasting in 2:17 and 23.[2] In 3:28 the argument is stated as a succinct Pauline thesis reiterating the premise of the argument in vv. 21-26. In v. 30b-c there is a striking parallelism in successive phrases with antistrophe in the repetition of πίστις ("faith") and antithesis in the references to "circumcision" and "uncircumcision."[3] The final verse, 31, responds to the accusation of v. 8 that Paul undermines the law.[4] The paronomastic series of five refer-

---

1 See Michel, 147; the category "dialogical exchange" is suggested by Stowers, *Diatribe*, 164–67. In *Diatribe*, 96–97, Song refers to this section as a "dialogue."

2 See Richard W. Thompson, "Paul's Double Critique of Jewish Boasting: A Study of Rom 3,27 in Its Context," *Bib* 67 (1986) 521–23.

3 Weiss, "Beiträge," 223, notes the thesis quality of 3:28 and refers to a "hebraicizing double expression" almost amounting to synonymous parallelism in 3:30.

4 See Wilckens, 1:244.

ences both to "faith" and to "law" provide a measure of continuity with the terminology of the preceding pericope, and χωρίς ("apart from, without") in v. 28 provides a potent echo of v. 21.[5]

Rhetorical Disposition

Exegesis

■ **27** The opening question in Paul's dialogical exchange draws an inference from the preceding argument:[6] if all humans are under the power of sin (3:9) and all have fallen short of the glory God intended for them (3:23), then boasting such as that mentioned in 2:17 and 23 is out of place. To ask "Where then is our καύχησις (boasting)?"[7] is to raise a question about the legitimacy of boasting itself, which was a radical step in a cultural setting in which boasting was the normal means of maintaining one's honor in the face of competition.[8] Paul himself uses καυχάομαι in its socially acceptable connotation in 1 Cor 15:10; 2 Cor 7:4, 14; 8:24; 9:2-3; Rom 5:11; 15:17; and elsewhere.[9] Here, however, a negative assessment of boasting is implied.[10] While the question of Jewish boasting dominates the interpretation of this passage,[11] which correlates with the previous identity of the interlocutor as a Jewish intellectual,[12] it is ordinarily overlooked that Rome was the boasting champion of the ancient world, filled with honorific monuments and cel-

---

5   See ibid.

6   While Käsemann, 102, denies that this pericope is inferential, most commentators agree with Richard Thompson in "Rom 3:27 in Its Context," 521, that the particle οὖν in connection with "boasting" suggests taking "the whole argument of 2,17 up to 3,26 into account when deciphering Rom 3,27."

7   Since καύχησις is a verbal noun, I translate it as such in English with "boasting." See BAGD (2000) 537, "act of taking pride in something, boasting."

8   See Moxnes, "Honour and Righteousness in Romans," 70; Esler, *Conflict and Identity,* 168.

9   See Klaus Berger, *Exegese des Neuen Testaments,* 144–56, confirmed by Josef Zmijewski, "καυχάομαι κτλ.," *EDNT* 2 (1991) 276–79.

10 While Paul uses καύχησις only here and in 15:17, the negative connotation is consistent with LXX usage (Sir 31:10; Prov 16:31; etc.). There is also a philosophical tradition of criticizing "sophistic boasting from the mouth" (ἡ ἀπὸ τοῦ στόματος καύχησις σοφιστική; Epicurus *Ep. frag.* 93.13). In *Cong.* 107.6 Philo also links boasting with οἴησις ("vain conceit"), and *Herm. Mand.* 38.3 includes καύχησις in a vice list with ὑψηλοφροσύνη ("haughtiness") and ὑπερηφανία ("arrogance").

11 For example, Meyer, 1:181; Michel, 154–55; Wilckens, 1:244; Dunn, 1:185; Haacker, 92; Kruse, *Paul,* 191–92.

12 Thorsteinsson, *Paul's Interlocutor,* 240, properly assumes that the interlocutor in 3:27-31 is identical with the one in 2:1–3:9. While he argues that the

ebrations of imperial glory. While earlier Greco-Roman moralists had warned against self-glorying,[13] they were not averse to imperial boasting. There was no criticism of Rome's proudly displayed power and superiority in a massive propaganda system incorporating the art and entertainment of the entire Mediterranean world. I noted allusions in 1:18-32 to this pervasive effort to "worship the creature rather than the Creator," which correlated with the discrimination against "barbarians" and the "uneducated" (1:14) that Paul wished to overcome in the presentation of the gospel in his mission to Spain. Neither of the two schools of interpretation that dominate the construal of the boast in this verse takes this broader social context into account. The "Protestant" construal in the neo-orthodox period generalized the boasting of the Jewish community as characteristic of religious persons everywhere, who rely on their own piety and virtue for salvation.[14] The "Jewish ethnicity" construal insists that the boasting and works in this passage relate "to the way of life in the Jewish community, and to that alone,"[15] certainly not to any moral or spiritual failure. However, the form of the interlocutor's question is basic and cannot be restricted to a particular group within the ancient world.[16] The preceding argument about salvation by grace alone renders all boasting problematic. I therefore take the earlier references to Jewish boasting in 2:17 and 23 as illustrating a universal phenomenon in Paul's social environment; while the references to "works" and "doing the law" (3:27) clearly imply that if Jewish boasting is illegitimate, so is Gentile boasting. By its very nature, honor granted through grace alone eliminates the basis of all human boasting; in Moxnes's words, the result of Paul's argument here is "to exclude false claims to honour."[17] I therefore translate the definite article in the expression ἡ καύχησις as "our boasting,"[18] which includes the Jewish interlocutor, Paul, and everyone else.

Paul's forceful answer to the initial question is in the aorist passive, implying exclusion by the atoning event described in the preceding pericope.[19] The verb ἐξεκλείσθη ("it is excluded, shut out") can mean literally to have the "door shut in one's face," as in the humiliating exchange recounted in Epictetus *Diss.* 2.6.6: ἀλλ᾽ ἐξεκλείσθης– διὰ θυρίδος γὰρ οὐκ ἔμαθον εἰσέρχεσθαι ("But you were shut out"–"Because I haven't learned to enter through a window"). Paul uses the verb in this sense in Gal 4:17, "They want to exclude you (ἐκκλαῖσαι)." With the provision of a new system of atonement available to Jews and Gentiles alike, the door is firmly barred against any kind of competitive boasting. As Harrison observes, "Paul's up-ending of the honour system excluded all human boasting."[20] The question of what sustains this exclusion is formulated succinctly with διὰ ποίου νόμου ("through what kind of

interlocutor is a Gentile attempting to gain proud Jewish identity, I think it is more plausible to view the interlocutor as a Jew.

13 See Bultmann, "καυκάομαι κτλ.," 646.

14 For instance, Käsemann, 102, insists that Paul is attacking "the religious person" in general rather than any particular tendency in "Jewish Christianity." Dunn, 1:185, cites Bornkamm, *Paul*, 95, as contending that "the Jew symbolizes man in his highest potentialities; he represents the 'religious man' whom the Law tells what God requires of him . . . and who refuses to admit that he has failed to measure up to God's claim on him . . . who prides himself on being religious." The classic statement of this approach is provided by Bultmann, "καυχάομαι κτλ.," 648–49: "For Paul καυχᾶσθαι discloses the basic attitude of the Jew to be one of self-confidence which seeks glory before God and which relies on itself. . . . Faith implies the surrender of all self-glorying."

15 Watson, *Paul*, 133. Dunn, 1:185, speaks of "the self-

16 See Neil Elliott's critique in *Rhetoric of Romans*, 205–17, of interpreting 3:27 as directed to a perverse Jewish opponent: Paul intends "an exclusion of *all* boasting, not only that of the Jew who is under the law" (p. 215, italics in original).

17 Moxnes, "Honour and Righteousness," 71. Unfortunately Moxnes goes on to claim: "It is the particular boasting of the Jew, not something which is common to Jews and Gentiles, which Paul attacks. . . . Paul sees a direct connection between boasting and the Jewish Law." Moxnes overlooks the clear implication of the earlier argument of Romans, which makes plain that all humans are involved in seeking honor that belongs to God alone and that they all thereby forfeit their share of the "glory of God."

18 See Smyth, *Grammar*, §1121.

19 See Michel, 154; Wilckens, 1:244.

20 Harrison, *Language of Grace*, 219.

law?"), in which ποῖος takes the place of τίς ("what?"), as is usually the case in classical Greek.[21] The rhetorical force of this question may be assessed by numerous parallels in classical oratory. In each case the formulation presumes that the audience knows the answer to be in the orator's favor. In *Orat.* 10 21.2, for example, Isaeus asks with incredulity, "According to what laws (κατὰ ποίους νόμους) was he introduced into the tribe?" In *Orat.* 39.9.5 Demosthenes poses the sarcastic question, "According to what law (κατὰ ποῖον νόμον) might this additional rule be tacked on?"[22]

The debate over whether the distinction between a "law of works" or a "law of faith" is merely rhetorical[23] and whether "law" has the connotation of "principle,"[24] "order of salvation,"[25] or "religious system"[26] rather than "Torah"[27] cannot be resolved on the basis of whether the article is used with νόμος. As Friedrich has shown, there are places where Paul uses νόμος both with and without the article in a single sentence (Rom 2:14, 23, 27; 3:21), and many instances in the LXX and Romans in which νόμος without the article clearly refers to the Torah.[28] Moreover, as David Sansone has suggested, the article indicates topicality while its absence indicates focality.[29] In this instance the topic is boasting while the law is the specific agency through which boasting is achieved.[30] Unfortunately the scholarly debate on this verse has tended to make νόμος the topic, which diverts attention from Paul's principal concern. The effort to render "law of works" and "law of faith" as synonymous since Paul has made a case that salvation by faith was supported by his interpretation of the Torah[31] undercuts the clearly intended antithesis punctuated by the forceful "No!" in 3:27e. In view of these difficulties, interpretations of these problematic details tend to follow previously established views of Paul's critique of "works" and his view of "faith."[32] The most compelling resolution was worked out by Johannes Sijko Vos, who proposed that Paul employs here the rhetorical technique ἐκ τοῦ ποσαχῶς, a form of linguistic dissociation that distinguishes between components that had previously been joined.[33] The Jewish concept of law is thus rendered ambivalent. Having distinguished in 2:17-24 between true and false uses of the law and in 3:21 between the law as a power that demands righteousness that humans cannot achieve and law as Scripture that affirms righteousness through faith, Paul now creates a distinction between the "law of works" that demands good works but produces only the awareness of sin, and the "law of faith" derived from Christ.[34] This is a distinction between an interpretation of law that enhances boasting and an interpretation of law that excludes boasting. The full contours of the latter are developed in chaps. 4, 7, and 8, which develop the contrast between the "law of the spirit of life" and the "law of sin and death" in 8:2. The former is defined

---

21 BDF §298.2 recognizes that the equivalence is not always required, and in this instance ποῖος retains its proper force, "of what kind," as in BAGD (2000) 834.

22 See also Aeschines *Fals. Leg.* 160/2-3; Demosthenes *Orat.* 44.33.2; 46.12.5; 46.27.2; Plato *Leg.* 683b; Xenophon *Mem.* 4.4.13.

23 See Lietzmann, 52; Martin Dibelius, "Synthetische Methode in der Paulus-Forschung," *ThBl* 3 (1924) 62.

24 Dodd, 63; Sanders, *Law*, 33; Räisänen, *Law*, 50–52; Räisänen, "Paul's Word-Play," 91–92; Watson, *Paul*, 131; Theobald, *Studien*, 178–82; Westerholm, *Law*, 122–26.

25 Weiss, 173; Kühl, 121.

26 Sanday and Headlam, 95; Barrett, 83.

27 Cremer, *Lexicon*, 433–34; Gerhard Friedrich, "Das Gesetz des Glaubens Römer 3,27," *ThZ* 10 (1954) 409–11.

28 See Friedrich's references in "Röm. 3,27," 403–4, to Wis 6:4; Sir 19:14; 21:11; 32:1, 24; 33:2; 34:8; 35:1; Rom 2:12-14, 17, 23, 25, 27; 3:20-21; 5:13, 20; 10:5.

29 Sansone, "Article in Greek," 199–201.

30 The semantic function of the article in τῶν ἔργων therefore points to the preceding reference in 3:20 to the Jewish law whose "works" cannot provide salvation.

31 See Friedrich, "Röm. 3,27," 409–15; Cranfield, 1:220; that Paul made a coherent case against boasting in 2:17–3:20 is confirmed by Thompson, "Boasting," 525–27.

32 See Dunn, 1:186–87.

33 Johannes Sijko Vos, "*Legem statuimus.* Rhetorische Aspekte der Gesetzesdebatte zwischen Juden und Christen," in J. van Emersfort and J. Cort, eds., *Juden und Christen in der Antike* (Kampen: Kok, 1990) 45–46. See also Vos, *Kunst der Argumentation,* 67–72. The rhetorical technique is discussed in Aristotle *Metaph.* 1028a5; *Rhet.* 1398a28; *Top.* 105a23.

34 Vos, "*Legem statuimus,*" 47–49.

in 8:3-11 as "a law of God that is fulfilled and leads to life through the power of the spirit received by believers on the basis of the death and resurrection of Christ."[35]

What remains clear from this complex debate is that Paul needs all three terms, "law," "works," and "faith," to provide a basis for his thesis in 3:28. He wishes to render "law" ambivalent and to eliminate all forms of boasting as inconsistent with faith in Christ crucified. It is clear that Paul wished to repudiate the traditions of boasting in the possession of superior honor and in conformity to a superior law, tendencies as characteristic of Jewish as of Roman and Greek culture.

■ **28** Paul defines the "law of faith" (3:27)[36] as follows: "For we reckon a human to be set right by faith without works of law." It is noteworthy that only here in the Pauline letters is λογίζομαι used in the first person plural, which suggests an appeal to "the common opinion among all the Christian communities."[37] This reference to reasoning or reckoning[38] that is widely shared by early believers is a testimony to Paul's effort to find common ground. God's activity in Christ to set right a fallen world is relevant to all humankind as implied by the choice of the generic term ἄνθρωπος ("a person, human").[39] I prefer the translation of δικαιοῦσθαι with "to be set right" rather than "to be justified,"[40] in order to convey an association with honor and avoid a legalistic theory of salvation.[41] The issue in this pericope is not whether humans can be justified despite their violations of the law but whether boasting is legitimate. God's

granting of righteousness through faith in the crucified Christ counters the seemingly universal tendency to claim honor on the basis of performance or social status. It eliminates claims of cultural or ethnic superiority. The dative formulation of πίστει ("by faith") refers to the positive response of believers to the gospel message rather than to divine faithfulness.[42] The stress on human response continues the theme of human "faith" from 3:22, 25, 26 and 27, but it is not intended to be restrictive as in later dogmatic interpretations that limit justification to those holding a precise doctrinal commitment. Since the new atonement system provided by the blood of Christ overturns the distinctions in honor and shame between ethnic and religious groups, to have "faith" in this message is to abandon any claim of special status.

With the words χωρὶς ἔργων νόμου ("without/apart from works of law"), Paul drives home the separation between the new honor system in Christ and the traditional achievement of honor through performance or social privilege. The point of emphasis is the opposition between the law of faith and the law of works.[43] Aspects of this opposition appear throughout Romans. The expression "apart from law" appears in 3:21; 7:8, 9, and "apart from works" in 4:6. That χωρίς appears nowhere else in the NT in connection with law or works aside from Jas 2:26,[44] which appears to counter Pauline doctrine, confirms that this is a theme distinctive to Romans. These expressions of apartness are all generic, lacking the article, so it appears that not only the Jewish

---

35   Ibid., 50.

36   I follow Wilckens, 1:245–46, in the translation "law" by which Paul is carrying out his contention that the Hebrew Torah itself shows that being set right is only possible through faith.

37   Dunn, 1:187; see also Cranfield, 1:220–21.

38   See Hans-Werner Bartsch, "λογίζομαι," *EDNT* 2 (1991) 354–55, for a discussion of the LXX background of Paul's use; and Hans-Wolfgang Heidland, "λογίζομαι, λογισμός," *TDNT* 4 (1967) 284, for the philosophical background of λογίσεσθαι as logical reasoning; e.g., Plato *Phaed.* 65c: "Thus, in reasoning (ἐν τῷ λογίσεσθαι) something of the realities becomes clear to it [i.e. the soul]? Yes. But it reasons (λογίζεται) best when none of these things troubles it, neither hearing nor sight, nor pain nor any pleasure."

39   See George Howard, "Romans 3:21-31 and the

Inclusion of the Gentiles," *HTR* 63 (1970) 232; for a general survey see also Sand, "ἄνθρωπος," 100–104. In contrast, Starnitzke, *Struktur*, 159, interprets ἄνθρωπος as an individual person who needs to be set free from guilt.

40   See Cremer, *Lexicon*, 194–97, for the traditional translation "justify"; Newman and Nida, 71: "he will put . . . right."

41   For a comprehensive discussion of Pauline usage that employs the traditional language of "justification," see Schrenk, "δίκη, δίκαιος κτλ.," 215–18; and Kertelge, "δικαιόω," 330–34.

42   As in Barth, noted by Dunn, 1:187.

43   See Michel, 156; for the Qumranic background of the expression "works of the law" see Fitzmyer, *According to Paul*, 19–24.

44   See Johannes B. Bauer, "χωρίς," *EDNT* 3 (1993) 493.

Torah but all other forms of law or works of law are eliminated as means of access to the new form of honor in Christ.[45]

■ **29** The form of the interlocutor's question beginning with ἤ ("or") indicates the alternative that would hold if the preceding verse were not true.[46] Being set right "by works of law" would imply that the God who established the Torah given to the Jewish people is in effect "their God" alone. There were voices in ancient Judaism that came close to the claim that Paul opposes.[47] For example, Deut 32:8-9 refers to ἀγγέλων θεῶν ("angels of God") that rule over the Gentile nations "while the Lord's own portion is his people, Jacob his allotted heritage." Hos 2:21-22 claims that Israel was the only nation to whom Yahweh had espoused himself eternally. *Jub.* 15.31 claims that God "chose Israel to be his people" while all other nations have been placed under angelic forces "that they might lead them astray from following him." One of the rabbis of the second century interprets Yahweh's commitment to a unique relation with Israel as follows: "I am God over all who come into the world, but my name have I united only with you: I have not called myself the God of the nations of the world, but the God of Israel."[48]

While exponents of Jewish sectarianism probably advocated this line of thought in Paul's time or before, his formulation of the interlocutor's question in v. 29a prevents such an inference. The rhetorical form of question beginning with "or" requires a negative response from anyone who had followed the preceding argument. The second question by the interlocutor in v. 29 requires an affirmative answer, since it opens with οὐχὶ καί ("not also"). The same formula is used in Rom 8:32 and 1 Thess 2:19, both requiring an affirmative reply. A classical example of diatribe that uses οὐχὶ καί in coordina-

tion with ναί ("yes") is Epictetus *Diss.* 4.1.107: "Yes (ναί), but I want my children and wife to be with me. For are they yours? Do they not belong to the One who gave them? Do they not indeed belong to the One who has made you? (οὐχὶ καὶ τοῦ σὲ πεποιηκότος;)." Paul contends that the relationship of the "Gentiles"[49] and "Jews" to God is now exactly the same as conveyed by the parallel genitive constructions; God is the God of both ethnic groups. The revolutionary equality of all nations before God that flows from the Christ event is emphatically stated by Paul's response to the interlocutor's question: ναὶ καὶ ἐθνῶν ("Yes, [God] also [belongs to] Gentiles").[50] The particle ναί ("yes, certainly") leaves no room for doubt, as one may see in Paul's famous discourse on "yes, yes" as opposed to "no, no," in which the affirmation is grounded in the gospel and the truthfulness of God (2 Cor 1:17-20). The consequence for missionizing in an imperialistic environment was firmly grasped by Colenso: "The idea of this brotherhood of all mankind, the great family on earth, implies that all men have certain ties with us, and certain rights at our hands. The truest way, in which we can regard them, is as they appear in the sight of God, from whom they can never suffer wrong, nor from us, when we think of them as His creatures equally with ourselves. There is yet a closer bond with them as our brethren in the Gospel. No one can interpose impediments of rank, or fortune, or colour, or religious opinion, between those who are one in Christ."[51]

■ **30** The conjunction εἴπερ, used mainly by Paul in the NT (Rom 8:9, 17; 1 Cor 8:5; 15:15; a variant reading in 2 Cor 5:3), introduces the great Jewish confession of the oneness of God. Stowers observes that the translation of εἴπερ as "since" as in the *RSV* reflects the influence of the textual variant ἐπείπερ ("seeing that"), while εἴπερ

---

45 Most interpreters continue to interpret the polemic here as if it were directed solely against Jewish legalism (e.g., Erich Grässer, "'Ein einziger ist Gott' (Röm 3,30). Zum christologischen Gottesverständnis bei Paulus," in N. Lohfink, ed., *"Ich will euer Gott werden": Beispiele biblischen Redens von Gott*, SBS 100 (Stuttgart: Katholisches Bibelwerk, 1981) 202–3) or the Jewish definition of its ethnic boundary, as in Dunn, 1:188.

46 See Cranfield, 1:221.

47 See Dunn, 1:188; Grässer, "Ein einziger ist Gott," 201–5.

48 Cranfield, 1:222, citing Rabbi Simeon ben Jochai from *Exod. Rab.* 29:4.

49 Dabelstein, *Beurteilung*, 37, prefers the translation of ἐθνῶν with "non-Jew" in this verse. This would eliminate the abusive implication of "Gentiles" as inherently inferior to Jews, but would also undermine the thrust of Paul's argument.

50 See Heil, 43.

51 Colenso, 88–89.

allows the answer of v. 29c to stand alone and v. 30a to begin a new sentence. He suggests the translation: "If he really is [the God of the gentiles], he is the one God who will justify the circumcised by faith and the uncircumcised through faith."[52] Along with most commentaries,[53] Stower's translation overlooks the syntactical function of εἴπερ to introduce the protasis presented as a fact in v. 30,[54] which supplies the premise of the apodosis of v. 29.[55] Stowers's translation has the disadvantage of appearing to make the confession of the oneness of God dependent on Paul's argument that God is the God of Gentiles. It has rather the force of a theological premise that supports the claim that God belongs also to the Gentiles in v. 29.[56] The entire construction supports Paul's larger case about honor granted impartially to all by the one God of all people.

The confessional formula about the oneness of God cited in v. 30a reflects a tradition held in common[57] by ancient Orphic religion,[58] Greek magical texts,[59] the OT,[60] Hellenistic Judaism,[61] and early Christianity.[62] The εἷς θεός formula appears in various ways in 1 Cor 8:4, 6; Gal 3:20; and it appears also in the deutero-Pauline tradition (Eph 4:6; 1 Tim 2:5). The distinctive Pauline approach to monotheism in Romans may be gauged by comparing it with the interpretation of the Shema of Deut 6:4, which was recited twice a day by loyal Jews: "Hear, O Israel, the Lord your God is One (κύριος εἷς ἐστιν), and you shall love the Lord your God with all your heart and with all your soul and with all your strength."[63] Even though universal in its implications, this confession tended to be understood to be a Jewish prerogative in Paul's time. The recitation of the Shema marked the line between the practicing Jew and idolators. Unlike Christian orthodoxy, however, the later rabbinic consensus did not develop this line of argument into a rigid claim that all Gentiles were damned. Alan Segal comments, "The consensus in Rabbinic Judaism shortly became not merely that some righteous would have a place in paradise but that all righteous Gentiles would also enjoy the felicities of the world to come."[64] The Greco-Roman theory of religion tended to favor the unity of God and to be critical of the popular polytheism manifest in various temples and shrines.[65] This was sometimes acknowledged even in the Jewish community, for example, by Pseudo-Orpheus, who was a Hellenistic Jewish writer of the second or third century B.C.E. and claimed that the best of the Greeks share the belief in the oneness of God: "Thearidas, in his book *On Nature* writes: 'There was then one really true beginning of all that exists—one. For that Being in the beginning is one and alone.' Nor is there any other except the Great King, says Orpheus. In accordance with whom, the comic poet Diphilus says very sententiously, 'The One who is of all.'"[66]

---

52 Stowers, *Diatribe,* 165.

53 For example, Meyer, 1:184–85; Lagrange, 80; Käsemann, 104; Fitzmyer, 355–56.

54 See Smyth, *Grammar,* §2298.

55 See Schlier, 102, 118; Cranfield, 1:222; Dunn, 1:188–89.

56 See Dunn, 1:189; Christoph Demke, "'Ein Gott und viele Herren.' Die Verkündigung des einen Gottes in den Briefen des Paulus," *EvTh* 36 (1976) 475.

57 For an overview of monotheistic preferences in Paul's time, see Klumbies, *Rede von Gott,* 13–32; Shum, *Paul's Use of Isaiah,* 186–87, argues for an explicit "intertextual relation" between Rom 3:29–30 and Isa 45:21-22, but this is not compelling.

58 In *Galatians,* 172, Betz cites Orphica *Frag.* 31, line 23; 168, lines 6-7; 239; 245, line 8; 247, line 10.

59 See Peterson, *ΕΙΣ ΘΕΟΣ,* 91–129. For example, one of the magical amulets affirms, "There is but one God (εἷς ϑ(εό)ς) who heals every illness." *Suppl. Mag.* 1.33 R.2-4, in Daniel and Maltomini, 97. See also C. Bonner, *Studies in Magical Amulets,* *Chiefly Graeco-Egyptian* (Ann Arbor: University of Michigan Press, 1950) 174–75.

60 See Ethelbert Stauffer, "εἷς," *TDNT* 2 (1964) 435; John J. Scullion, "God (OT)," *ABD* 2 (1992) 1042-43.

61 See Hans Dieter Betz, "εἷς, μία," *EDNT* 1 (1990) 399; S. S. Cohen, "The Unity of God: A Study in Hellenistic and Rabbinic Theology," *HUCA* 26 (1955) 425–79; Peterson, *ΕΙΣ ΘΕΟΣ,* 276–99.

62 Jouette M. Bassler, "God (NT)," *ABD* 2 (1992) 1050–51.

63 See Marvin R. Wilson, "The *Shema* in Early Jewish Teaching," *Jerusalem Perspective* 4 (1991) 9–10, adapted from idem, *Our Father Abraham: Jewish Roots of the Christian Faith* (Grand Rapids: Eerdmans, 1989) 122–25, who shows from Deut 6:7, the *Epistle of Aristeas,* and the Mishna (*Tamid* 4:3; 5:1) that the Shema was in use prior to the NT period.

64 Segal, *Rebecca's Children,* 168.

65 See Betz, "εἷς, μία," 969–70.

66 Translation by Holladay, *Orphica,* 127, lines 1-2 from

Nevertheless, Paul does not follow this line of argument that grants access to Gentiles on the basis of their conformity to monotheistic belief. By correlating the oneness of God with righteousness through faith, Paul erects an impenetrable barrier against boasting of either ethnic or theological superiority. Erich Grässer explains: "Henceforth the line of demarcation no longer ran between Jews and Gentiles, but between law and gospel. . . . The resurrected one is in fact the inaugurator of a new humanity."[67] Even more clearly, Klumbies concludes from Paul's argument: "The previously binding assumptions of a relationship of humans with God are set aside and the existing barriers between diverse groups of humans are leveled. Even the Gentiles, which previously had no access to God because they stood outside the law, are included in the confession of the one God. Only by acting in the same way toward both groups, Jews as well as Gentiles, can he be identified as the one God of all people."[68]

The final references to faith in Rom 3 reveal the social and ethnic equality that faith in the Crucified One produces. That the "circumcised" are set right "from faith" and the "uncircumcised through faith" places each on a comparable footing before God. The entirety of the human family has access to righteousness through Christ. When the Jew performs the law "from faith," and when the Gentile comes to God "through faith," both are set right. It is possible that the formula ἐκ πίστεως may have been favored by Jewish Christians because of its association with Hab 2:4[69] and that διὰ τῆς πίστεως was a locution employed by Gentile Christians.[70] It is also possible that the article in the second reference was intended to consolidate the two forms of faith. Howard states, "God justifies the circumcision by faith (ἐκ πίστεως) and the uncircumcision through the *same* faith (διὰ τῆς πίστεως)."[71] Although no certainty can be attached to these suggestions, particularly in view of the fact that in 3:22, 26, and 27 both prepositions are applied to both groups, it remains clear that the variety of formulations used by Paul provides no support for later efforts to require doctrinal conformity with regard to faith, an effort that has undercut Paul's argument by erecting new boundaries of honor and shame.[72] Paul accepts several formulations of faith, which were probably intended to appeal to various components in his audience.[73]

The multicultural inference is more clearly visible in the abusive, ethnic epithets discovered by Joel Marcus.[74] The references to the "circumcision" and "uncircumcision" are polite translations of lewd epithets that were probably being hurled between groups in Paul's time, with Gentiles calling the Jews the περιτομή ("circumcised penis") and Jews calling Gentiles the ἀκροβυστία ("uncircumcised foreskin").[75] Paul counters the shameful implications of such epithets by insisting that God is the Lord of both groups, and that both will be "set right" by their acceptance of the gospel. This corresponds to Moxnes's assessment that Paul's purpose in 3:27-31 was to address the "problem of divisions between Jews and non-Jews within Christian communities. . . . In this context, 'God is one' served as an argument for the inclusion and co-existence of both Jews and non-Jews in the

---

Clement of Alexandria *Stromata*; see also pp. 135–43.

67 Grässer, "Ein einziger ist Gott," 204–5; see also Demke, "Ein Gott," 475, who points out the distinctive Pauline emphasis on God being the "same God for Jews and Gentiles."

68 Paul-Gerhard Klumbies, "Der Eine Gott des Paulus—Röm 3,21-31 als Brennpunkt paulinischer Theologie," *ZNW* 85 (1994) 204.

69 See Dunn, 1:189. However, the study by Bruno Corsani, "Ἐκ πίστεως in the Letters of Paul," in vol. 1 of W. C. Weinrich, ed., *The New Testament Age: Essays in Honor of Bo Reicke* (Macon: Mercer University Press, 1984) 87–93, finds no such pattern.

70 See Godet, 165–66; Stanley K. Stowers, "Ἐκ πίστεως and διὰ πίστεως in Romans 3:30," *JBL* 108 (1989) 665–74.

71 Howard, "Rom. 3:21-31," 233.

72 See Bonda's critique of viewing faith in 3:30 as a "limitation," *One Purpose*, 90–92.

73 See esp. John M. G. Barclay, "'Neither Jew nor Greek': Multiculturalism and the New Perspective on Paul," in M. G. Brett, ed., *Ethnicity and the Bible*, Biblical Interpretation Series 19 (Leiden: Brill, 1996) 197–214.

74 Marcus, "Circumcision and Uncircumcision," 67–81.

75 Ibid., 78–79; the epithet "foreskin" is the equivalent of the abusive modern epithet "dickhead." For another view of this terminology see J. N. Adams, *The Latin Sexual Vocabulary* (Baltimore: Johns Hopkins University Press, 1982) 13.

same community, on the basis of faith."[76] Moxnes points out that the argument in these verses concerning the oneness of God as God of the uncircumcised as well as the circumcised constitutes "a conscious effort to include" the less popular Jewish Christians in a hostile Gentile Christian majority in Rome. In sum, "The confession that 'God is one' was meant to serve as a bond of unity between Christians."[77]

■ **31** The conclusion of Paul's comments about the oneness of God and the inclusive quality of God's righteous activity in Christ is the inferential question, "Are we then neutralizing law through this faith?"[78] The undeniable premise of v. 30a establishes a rhetorical requirement of a negative answer to this question of whether Paul and his fellow believers are antinomians. The verb καταργέω is used here in the sense of "thwart, neutralize, render inactive," as in the hitherto unrecognized parallels in *Testament of Solomon,* where wicked angels or demons are neutralized or thwarted by good angels wishing to build the temple.[79] Solomon puts the question to seven evil angels and receives a similar reply from each:

> "Tell me what you do." He responded, "I am Deception. I plot deception and I devise the most evil heresies. But I have one who neutralizes me (ἀλλ᾽ ἔχω τὸν καταργοῦντον με), the angel Lamechiel."
>
> The second said, "I am Strife. I cause strife by making available clubs, pellets, and swords, my implements of war. But I have an angel who neutralizes me (ἀλλ᾽ ἔχω ἄγγελον τὸν καταργοῦντον με), Baruchiel." (*T. Sol.* 6.5-6)

Later Solomon asks the demon of discord,

> "By what name are you neutralized (ἐν ποίῳ ὀνόματι καταργεῖσαι;)?" He responded, "The name of the archangel Azael." Then I placed my seal on the demon and commanded him to pick up stones and hurl them up to the heights of the Temple for the workmen; compelled, the demon complied with his orders. (*T. Sol.* 7.7-8)

That καταργέω functions in these citations as the equivalent of an alleged Aramaic technical term לתב ("make to cease"), which stands in antithesis to ἰστάνω/ מוק ("establish"),[80] has been disproved by Hans Hübner[81] and Richard W. Thompson[82] on grounds that לתב does not appear as an exegetical term during the Tannaitic period; that it never appears with מוק; and that the key supporting text in *m. 'Abot* 4:9 is actually unrelated to the theme of Rom 3:31.[83] A stronger case can be made that the second verb employed by Paul (ἰστάνομεν, "we uphold, establish/make to stand upright") reflects biblical and later Jewish discussions of the law.[84] For example, "These are the words of the covenant, which the Lord commanded Moses to establish (στῆσαι) with the children of Israel" (LXX Deut 28:69; cf. 2 Chr 35:19; Jer 42:14, 16). A textual variant of LXX 1 Sam 15:11[85] has Yahweh saying, "I repent that I established (ἐστήσεν) Saul as king." The legal context is reflected in the Markan logion: "You have a fine way of rejecting the commandments of God, in order to uphold (στήσητε) your tradition!" (Mark 7:9). Idomeneus *Test.* 2.35,

---

76 Moxnes, *Theology in Conflict,* 223.

77 Ibid., 224.

78 Many translations and some commentators understand 3:31 as an independent sentence, even as the opening of the next proof. See Meyer, 1:185–86; Lagrange, 80; Achtemeier, 77.

79 See Dennis C. Duling, "Testament of Solomon," *OTP* 1:768–69; Busch, *Testament Salomos,* 131–35.

80 This technical usage was proposed by Zahn, 211; Schlatter, 105; Michel, 157, followed by many others.

81 Hans Hübner, *Law,* 113–18, 137–44, followed up in his article, "καταργέω," *EDNT* 2 (1991) 267–68.

82 Richard W. Thompson, "The Alleged Rabbinic Background of Rom 3.31," *EThL* 63 (1987) 136–48.

83 *'Abot R. Nat.* 4.9 is as follows: "Rabbi Johanan said: He that fulfills (měqayyēm) the Law in poverty shall in the end fulfill (lěqayyěmāh) it in wealth; and he that neglects (měbaṭṭēl) the Law in wealth shall in the end neglect (lěbaṭṭēlāh) it in poverty."

84 See Michael Wolter, "ἵστημι, ἰστάνω," *EDNT* 2 (1991) 207; Thompson, "Rabbinic Background," 141–42.

85 The Rahlfs edition lists this variant as AL+, noted by Wolter, "ἵστημι, ἰστάνω," 207.

reflects this usage: στήσασθαι ἤθεα τε καὶ νόμους ("to establish both customs and laws").

While the terms chosen by Paul would have been readily understood by Jewish members of his audience in Rome, these terms also have a more general bearing. Of particular significance is that νόμος ("law") is used both times in v. 31 without the article, which suggests that law in general may be in view.[86] Greco-Romans as well as Jews were at times passionate advocates of the sanctity of their laws, so Paul's argument allows an appeal to a mixed audience in Rome. While no law can provide salvation and while honor should no longer be attached to its compliance, Paul upholds law in a transformed and clarified state by faith in Christ crucified.[87] While some exegetes from the strict Protestant tradition continue to feel that v. 31 is inconsistent with his earlier critique of law,[88] Dunn is correct when he concludes, "When it is taken as 'the law of faith,' when it is seen as speaking to Gentiles as well, it [law] is established and its validity confirmed."[89] Since it is not the law itself but rather boasting about performance under the law that is excluded by Christ, faith in him is not only affirmed by the Jewish law but also upholds law. Faith in Christ inspires a new, critical form of moral and legal responsibility that Paul elaborates not just in the final chapters but also throughout the Letter to the Romans. Paul's aim is neither simply to influence the thinking of the Roman house and tenement churches nor to teach a new doctrine of law but more importantly to guide and motivate their action. With regard to the mission to Spain, which some may have feared would be likely to provoke complications with Roman law concerning the administration of that crucial province, Paul's claim is forthright: "we uphold law," whether it be Jewish or Roman. When compliance with the law is removed from the arena of boasting, its capacity to support hostile competition is diminished and tolerant adherence to a new law of faith "without works" becomes possible. This is an essential component of the gospel that Paul wishes now to extend to the end of the known world.

---

86 Winger, *Law*, 80–81, argues in contrast that νόμος refers here to the Torah only.

87 See the case by Thomas R. Schreiner, "The Abolition and Fulfillment of the Law in Paul," *JSNT* 35 (1989) 59–65, who argues that Paul distinguishes in other passages between elements of the moral law that continue to be binding and elements of ceremonial law that do not. Schreiner, 53, accepts the conclusions of Schrage and Deidun that "concrete external commandments are still binding for Paul"; see Schrage, *Einzelgebote*, 129–40; Deidun, *New Covenant*, 188–217.

88 See, e.g., Hahn, "Gesetzesverständnis," 40–41; Räisänen, *Law*, 50, 69, 71.

89 Dunn, 1:193, contends that when law is no longer taken as an "identity and boundary marker" for the Jewish community, it is rendered useful. My point is broader, that law's involvement in systems of honor and shame, within any culture, renders it problematic, and that this is precisely what was changed by the cross event. See also Schreiner, "Abolition," 65–66; Robinson, *Wrestling*, 51.

4

The First Part of the Fifth Pericope

Abraham and the Righteousness That Comes through Faith

a. Diatribe and the First Part of a Midrash Showing That Abraham Received Righteousness by Faith before He Was Circumcised

1/ 'Therefore what shall we say that Abraham our forefather[a] found[b] according to flesh?' 2/ For if Abraham was set right through works, he has a boast, but not in reference to God. 3/ 'For what does the scripture say?'
"Now Abraham believed in God and it was reckoned to him as righteousness."
4/ Now to the one who works, his pay is not reckoned as a gift but as an obligation, 5/ but to the one who does not work yet has faith in the one who sets right the impious, his faith is reckoned as righteousness. 6/ Just as[c] also David pronounces the blessing upon the person to whom God reckons righteousness apart from works:
7/ "Blessed are those whose iniquities have been forgiven
and whose sins have been covered up;
8/ blessed is the man whose[d] sin the Lord will in no wise reckon."
9/ 'Is this blessing therefore upon the circumcision[e] or also upon the uncircumcised foreskin?' For we say [that][f] "the faith was reckoned to Abraham as righteousness." 10/ 'How therefore was it reckoned? While he was in (the state of) circumcision or in uncircumcised foreskin?' Not in circumcision but in uncircumcised foreskin! 11/ And he received a sign of circumcision,[g] a seal of [h] the righteousness through faith [that he had] while in uncircumcised foreskin, that he might become the father of all who have faith while in foreskin, that righteousness[i] might be reckoned[j] to them, 12/ and the father of circumcision, not only to those who are circumcised, but also to those[k] who walk in the steps of the uncircumcised foreskin faith of our father Abraham.

a   The replacement of the unusual word προπάτορα ("forefather") by πατέρα ("father") in ℵ[1] C[3] D F G K L P Ψ 6 33 69 88 104 323 326 424 436 459 614 629 945 1175 1241 1243 1319[c] 1505 1573 1735 1739 1836 1852 1874 1881 1912 1962 2200 2344 2464

2495 *Maj Lect* ar b d f g mon o vg (eth) geo slav Or[lat] Chr[lem] Ambst Pel Aug is an understandable effort to achieve a more traditional formulation, since Abraham was so frequently called by this term. The word προπάτορα ("forefather") is strongly attested by ℵ[*.2] A B C[*] 81 256 263 330 1319[*] 1506 2127 sy[(p),pal] sa bo? arm Or[gr lem] Cyr. 365 has both terms.

b   The varying locations of εὑρηκέναι ("has found") prior to "Abraham" in ℵ[*. 1. 2] A C[*. 3] D F G Ψ 81 256 263 330 365 629 1319[*. c] 1506 1573 1852 2127 ar b d f g mon o vg sy[p, pal] sa bo? arm slav geo Or[gr lem] Or[lat] Cyr Ambst Pel Aug, or after the expression "our father" in K L P 33 69 88 104 323 326 424 436 459 614 945 1175 1241 1243 1505 1735 1836 1874 1881 1962 2200 2344 2464 2495 *Maj Lect* (eth) Chr[lem] as well as the deletion of εὑρηκέναι in B 6 1739, reflect the grammatical incompleteness of this sentence. Whether a textual emendation is required at this point should be explored. At the present time the least problematic option is the first one mentioned above, which is more broadly supported.

c   Although the witnesses are somewhat differently divided in 3:4, the confusion between the widely attested καθάπερ ("just as") and καθώς ("just as") in D F G surfaces here again. In this instance, the former is to be preferred.

d   The grammatically awkward but strongly attested genitive form οὗ ("of whom") in P[40vid] ℵ[*] B D[*] G 1506 1739 is improved by ℵ[2] A C D[c] F K L P Ψ 33 104 323 326 365 424 614 945 1175 1241 1505 1573 1735 1874 1881 2464 2495 *Maj* with ᾧ ("to whom"), but the difficult reading is to be preferred.

e   The addition of μόνον ("only") in D it vg[cl] Ambst has an explanatory function, and is clearly secondary; see Lietzmann, 51. Schlier, 126, argues for the inclusion of "only" on logical grounds, thus shifting Paul's argument in the direction of Gentiles replacing Jews as the only legitimate children of Abraham.

f   The supplying of the logically necessary ὅτι ("that") by A C D[c] F G K L P Ψ 6 33 69 88 104 323 326 330 365 424 614 945 1175 1241 1243 1319 1505 1506 1573 1735 1836 1874 2344 2464 2495 *Maj* appears to be a grammatical improvement of the awkward but original wording lacking "that" in ℵ B D[*] 630 1739 1881 *pc*.

g   The variant of the accusative form περιτομήν ("circumcision") in A C[*] 6 424 1506 1739 1881 *pc* sy is puzzling because it would create the third accusative form in this sentence, which is quite impossible in Greek: "he received a sign—a seal of the righteousness." Whether this accusative form constitutes the more difficult reading that was later corrected by most other texts is a matter that should be investigated by an expert. In the meanwhile, I follow Nestle-Aland[26/27], but without a large measure of confidence.

h   The provision of the preposition διά ("through") in F G is an attempted grammatical improvement of the text.

i   The expression εἰς δικαιωσύνην ("for righteousness") in A 424* 1319 1881 pc lat in lieu of τὴν δικαιοσύνην appears to be an assimilation of the expression in 4:5. The evidence concerning whether the definite article τήν should be included before "righteousness" is so evenly divided that the Nestle-Aland[26/27] square brackets are understandable, while the lack of a discussion in Metzger's Textual Commentary is disappointing. ℵ C² D* 6 365 424ᶜ 1506 1739 pc lack the article, while B C* D² F G K L P Ψ 33 69 88 104 323 326 945 1175 1241 1243 1505 1735 1836 1874 2344 2464 2495 Maj have it. 424* has both: εἰς τήν. The deletion of the article is more difficult to explain than its addition, so I would prefer to eliminate it.

j   The appearance of καί ("and, also") at this point in ℵ² C D F G K L P 69 88 104 323 326 365 424* 614 945 1175 1241 1319 1505 1573 1735 1836 1874 2127 2344 2495 Maj lat sy sa is more than counterbalanced by its absence in ℵ* A B Ψ 6 81 330 424ᶜ 630 1243 1506 1739 1881 2464 al vgᵐˢˢ bo and the fact that the addition is easily understandable as an improvement of the argument, provided καί is understood as "also." The shift from the earlier absence of καί in Nestle editions to its inclusion in square brackets in Nestle-Aland[26/27] seems unwarranted. See Metzger, Textual Commentary, 450–51, who also refers to an additional variant of λογισθῆναι αὐτόν ("he was reckoned [as righteous]") supported only by 451 and not listed in Nestle-Aland[26/27].

k   The conjecture by Hort that αὐτοῖς should replace τοῖς would result in the translation "to those who themselves walk." Another approach is to delete the "superfluous" (BDF §276.3) article τοῖς as suggested by Beza, which in effect has been followed by all modern translations. See Lietzmann, 52, and the exegesis below.

Analysis

The diatribe in the preceding pericope is continued in this half-pericope with questions from the interrogator in 4:1, 3, 9, and 10 that I have enclosed in single quotation marks in the translation.[1] The substantive questions in vv. 1 and 9 require negative responses from the audience that are presupposed by the following explanations appended in Paul's voice, whereas the question in v. 10 is provided with an emphatic answer. The key words in the passage are "work" (ἐργάζεσθαι, "to work," 3 times; ἔργον, "work," once) in vv. 1-8 and "circumcision" (περιτομή, "circumcision," 6 times; ἀκροβυστία, "uncircumcision," 6 times) in vv. 9-12.[2] The passage is organized as an uneven series of parallel lines, with the balance between members distended by the addition of qualifying material. For instance, in vv. 4-5 the symmetry of an antithetical parallelism describing those who work and those who do no work is interrupted by the clause in v. 5a, having "faith in the one who sets right the impious."[3] In vv. 11b-12 the symmetry is distorted by the explanatory antithesis in v. 12a, "not only to those who are circumcised."[4]

The diatribe is skillfully fused with a midrashic exegesis consisting of a main text from Gen 15:6 in Rom 4:3b and 4:22 that is interpreted by a secondary text from LXX Ps 31 in Rom 4:7-8.[5] Each text is introduced and interpreted to provide a distinctively Pauline answer to the questions of the nature of Abraham's righteousness and the identity of his true descendants. The rabbinic

---

1   Stowers, Rereading, 165, suggests the dialogical exchange continues only through 4:2, while mistakenly including the rhetorical question introducing the citation in 4:3a within this verse. To suggest a break after 4:3a results in severing the introduction of the citation in 4:3a from the citation itself in 4:3b. See also Campbell, "3.27–4.25," 357–91.

2   Harvey, Listening, 188.

3   See Weiss, "Beiträge," 175.

4   See ibid., 224.

5   See Michel, 160–61; Jeremias, "Gedankenführung,"

271–72; H.-J. van der Minde, Schrift, 78–83, argues that Paul cites an early Christian midrash, but there is stronger support for Moxnes's view in Theology in Conflict, 130–64, that Paul composed the midrash with traditional Jewish methods; see Dunn, 1:197. Without reference to van der Minde, Lou H. Silberman identified the same rabbinic form in "Paul's Midrash: Reflections on Romans 4," in J. T. Carroll, C. H. Cosgrove, and E. E. Johnson, eds., Faith and History: Essays in Honor of Paul W. Meyer (Atlanta: Scholars Press, 1990) 99–104.

method of drawing inferences through analogy employed in 4:4-5 is augmented by the seventh rule of Hillel in 4:10-11,[6] drawing inferences from context, in showing that the later provision of circumcision in Gen 17 proves that Abraham had performed no religious work at the time of the promise in Gen 15:6. Dietrich-Alex Koch also shows that beginning with a text from the Pentateuch (Gen 15:6 in Rom 4:3) and then following with a text from the rest of Scripture (Ps 31; Rom 4:7-8) fits a rabbinic pattern.[7] Moreover, the method of providing an *exemplum* ("example, illustration") such as the authoritative figure of Abraham conforms to the rules of Greco-Roman rhetoric, as Stowers has shown.[8] The passage is designed to appeal to each of the groups in Rome, whether Greco-Roman or Jewish in background, whether "weak" or "strong."

Rhetorical Disposition

IV.	The *Probatio*
1:18–4:25	A. The first proof: The gospel expresses the impartial righteousness of God by overturning claims of cultural superiority and by rightwising Jews and Gentiles through grace alone
4:1-25	5. Abraham and the righteousness that comes through faith
4:1-12	a. Diatribe and the first part of a midrash showing that Abraham received righteousness by faith before he was circumcised
4:1-5	1) Setting Abraham right through faith
4:1-2	a) The first dialogical exchange concerning Abraham's rightwising
4:1	(1) The question about what Abraham found "according to the flesh"
	(2) The unspoken answer: "Nothing!"
4:2	(3) The rationale:
4:2a	(a) The unreal condition of righteousness through works
4:2b	(b) The impossible consequence of possessing a "boast"
4:2c	(c) The theological reason for the impossibility: "not before God"
4:3-5	b) The first proof text
4:3a	(1) The rhetorical question as a formula of citation
4:3b	(2) The citation of Gen 15:6 concerning Abraham's faith reckoned as righteousness
4:4-5	(3) The interpretation of the text
4:4	(a) Works require wages as an obligation rather than a gift
4:5	(b) Faith in God is reckoned as righteousness without works
4:6-12	2) Abraham as the father of the faithful whether circumcised or not
4:6-8	a) The second proof text
4:6	(1) The interpretive introduction to the text
	(a) The speaker: David
	(b) The utterance: a blessing
	(c) The recipient: a man reckoned righteous by God
	(d) The qualification of righteousness: "apart from works"
4:7-8	(2) The citation of Ps 31:1
4:7a	(a) Blessing upon the forgiven person
4:7b	(b) Blessing upon the person whose sins are covered
4:8	(c) Blessing upon the person whose sins are not "reckoned"
4:9	b) The second dialogical exchange on whether the recipient of the blessing was circumcised
4:9a	(1) The question whether the recipient was circumcised
	(2) The unspoken answer: "Not circumcised!"
4:9b	(3) The rationale: on the basis of Gen 15:6, Abraham had faith alone
4:10-12	c) The third dialogical exchange on whether the reckoning of Abraham's righteousness required circumcision
4:10a-b	(1) The questions
4:10a	(a) General question: how was righteousness reckoned?
4:10b	(b) Specification: in circumcision or not?
4:10c	(2) The emphatic answer: "In uncircumcised foreskin!"
4:11-12	(3) The rationale
4:11a	(a) Abraham received circumcision as a sign of righteousness already received
4:11b-12	(b) The purpose: to become the father of the faithful
4:11b-c	i. The uncircumcised faithful
4:12	ii. The circumcised faithful

---

6   See Koch, *Schrift*, 221–24.

7   Ibid., 223; Aageson, *Biblical Interpretation*, 85–86.

8   Stowers, *Diatribe*, 155–74; see also Schmeller, *Diatribe*, 418–23; Neubrand, *Abraham*, 174–77.

Exegesis

■ **1** The opening verse in this pericope seems grammatically incomplete because the question "what then shall we say?" that recurs from 3:5 is not followed by "that" and because the infinitive εὑρηκέναι ("has found, to have found") followed by the accusative Ἀβραὰμ τὸν προπάτορα ἡμῶν ("Abraham our forefather") has no proper object. In the other instances where the question τί οὖν ἐροῦμεν ("what then shall we say?") appears in Romans (7:7; 8:31; 9:14, 30), the rhetorical question is followed by a statement and an answer or a second rhetorical question.[9] Although it is clear from οὖν ("therefore") that this pericope carries forward the thought of the preceding sections of the first proof,[10] any further rendition of this verse remains a matter of exegetical choice. Two translation problems in particular have been debated, whether "according to the flesh" goes with "Abraham" or with the verb "found," and whether the infinitive construction functions as the subject of the sentence. The flexible word order in Greek allows the first question to be answered either way, and while most exegetes have opted for "our forefather according to the flesh" because it fits the conventional view of σάρξ,[11] the formula remains odd for Abraham, who is depicted here as the honorific parent of all believers, explicitly including those unconnected to his physical lineage. It is strange that restricting Abraham to being the forefather of Jews, who alone would qualify as sharing his fleshly lineage,[12] would serve Paul's purpose of depicting Abraham as the forefather of Gentile con-verts, as explicitly stated in 4:11, that Abraham "might become the father of all who have faith while in foreskin." This option also produces an egregious conflict with Paul's later argument that Abraham's "children of the promise" rather than his "fleshly children" are the legitimate "children of God" (9:9). The translation "forefather according to the flesh" provides no link either to the preceding pericope or to the following sentence that begins with εἰ γάρ ("for if"), thus providing the reason for the negative answer required in the opening question.

In another version of this theory, Richard B. Hays has argued that the infinitive construction provides the subject of the sentence with a first person plural connotation, resulting in the translation, "Have we found Abraham (to be) our forefather according to the flesh?"[13] To supply the first person connotation to an infinitive construction is grammatically possible, although it is odd that the subject remains unexpressed.[14] Hays's hypothesis requires an overly subtle argument that must insert the word "only" to make a link between the rhetorical question and the more immediate context of 4:2-10: "Look, do you think that we Jews have considered Abraham our forefather only according to the flesh?"[15] Thus instead of arguing against a conventional picture of Abraham, who could boast of having earned righteous status through conformity to the law, Paul wants to show "that Judaism itself, rightly understood, claims its relation to Abraham not by virtue of physical descent . . . but by virtue of sharing his trust in the God who made the promises."[16] This inter-

---

9   See Micheal Palmer, "τί οὖν; The Inferential Question in Paul's Letter to the Romans with a Proposed Reading of Romans 4.1," in S. E. Porter and D. A. Carson, eds., *Discourse Analysis and Other Topics in Biblical Greek*, JSNTSup 113 (Sheffield: Sheffield Academic Press, 1995) 202–7. For classical examples of the question, "What shall we say," see the examples in n. 87 at Rom 3:1-8.

10   Meyer, 1:189; Dunn, 1:198; Neubrand, *Abraham*, 150.

11   See Schmidt, 76–77; Lietzmann, 50; Kuss, 1:179–80; Wilckens, 1:261; Dunn, 1:199; Byrne, 148; Neubrand, *Abraham*, 184–87; etc.

12   Gottlob Schrenk, "πατήρ κτλ.," *TDNT* 5 (1967) 976, supported by Davies, *Land*, 177, who is cited by Dunn, 1:199, as saying that "even proselytes were not allowed to call Abraham 'our father.'"

13   Richard B. Hays, "'Have We Found Abraham to Be Our Forefather according to the Flesh?' A Reconsideration of Rom 4:1," *NovT* 27 (1985) 81, following the lead of Zahn, 212–18, and also adopted by Neubrand, *Abraham*, 184.

14   See Thomas H. Tobin, "What Shall We Say that Abraham Found? The Controversy behind Romans 4," *HTR* 88 (1995) 443.

15   Hays, "Rom 4:1," 87; see also Seifrid, *Christ Our Righteousness*, 68.

16   Hays, "Rom 4:1," 87–88; in this attempt to downplay the conflict between Paul and what is ordinarily called "Judaism," Hays skips the abrasive topic of boasting that links 3:27 with 4:2.

pretation requires a jarring shift from what "we find" to what "Judaism" finds, and it should logically require Paul to cite Jewish interpreters, whereas in the subsequent argument he cites only Gen 15:6 and Ps 31. Hays concludes that Abraham becomes not just "an exemplar of Christian believing but also . . . a typological foreshadowing of Christ, the 'one man' (Rom 5:19) through whose obedience 'the many were constituted righteous.'"[17] Thus in the end it is Abraham's Christlike virtue of "faithfulness"[18] that allegedly proves redemptive, but this opens the door to the kind of religious boasting that Paul shows the Abraham story forbids.

In view of the negative connotations of Paul's phrase κατὰ σάρκα ("according to flesh"), denoting the competitive, self-reliant propensity of humans to boast in fleshly achievements, of which circumcision was the most influential example,[19] the better choice is to attach this prepositional phrase to the verb so that the question turns on what Abraham found on the basis of his fleshly capacities.[20] This corresponds to Paul's use of κατὰ σάρκα ("according to flesh") in an adverbial rather than an adjectival sense thirteen out of sixteen times in his authentic letters, and it provides a cogent link to the following discourse, which deals with the question of whether Abraham performed works of the law prior to being set right by God. Specifically, the question turns on whether Abraham had circumcised his flesh before or after being declared righteous. While persons acquainted with the biblical tradition might supply

"grace" or "favor" (Gen 18:3, in connection with the Abraham story; Gen 30:27; 33:8, 10, 15; Luke 1:30; Acts 7:46) to the verb εὑρίσκειν ("find"),[21] the immediate context suggests that Paul had in mind the closely associated word δικαιοσύνην ("righteousness"), employed in 3:30 and 4:2.[22] The question is whether Abraham was granted a righteous status by God on the basis of the works of his flesh.[23] In view of the preceding pericope that proves no one is made righteous, that is, acceptable to God by "works of the law," such a question requires a negative response from Paul's audience: "No, Abraham cannot have been set right on the basis of fleshly accomplishment!" This leads smoothly into the following discourse about whether Abraham found a basis for boasting in the works of his flesh, which basis Paul denies. This logical connection was clearly understood by a number of earlier commentators.[24]

Within the Hebrew Bible, Abraham "was regarded as the nation's progenitor. . . . Israel's claim to Canaan rested on the promises made to him, and the God worshipped by Israel was preeminently the God of Abraham."[25] In later Judaism Abraham is "the celebrated national and religious hero of his people. . . . Descent from Abraham is the pride of Israel."[26] As the model of monotheism and piety, Abraham provided Israel its "shining mark of identity."[27] Maria Neubrand and Philip Esler have shown that Abraham served as a "prototype of group identity" that guaranteed a unique and superior

---

17 Ibid., 98.

18 Ibid., 92. Silberman offers a similar summary in "Paul's Midrash," 103: "Abraham 'our forefather' is an exemplar of that trust that brings in its wake divine acceptance."

19 See Jewett, *Terms*, 95–98, where I analyze Paul's critique of the Judaizers' boast in circumcised flesh (Gal 6:13).

20 See Jewett, *Terms*, 142–44; Luz, *Geschichtsverständnis*, 174; Dobbeler, *Glaube als Teilhabe*, 134. A step in this direction was taken by Campbell, "3.27–4.25," 386–90, who translates (388): "'Did Abraham obtain paternity for us, the Gentiles, *in relation to flesh?*' Read in this manner the phrase κατὰ σάρκα can be understood to be signaling the matter of circumcision." See also Stowers, *Rereading*, 234, 242; Colenso, 91; Starnitzke, *Struktur*, 164.

21 Weiss, 182; Michel, 161; Cranfield, 1:227; Schlier, 122; Wilckens, 1:261; see Sigfred Pedersen,

"εὑρίσκω," *EDNT* 2 (1991) 83–84. The proposal by R. R. Williams, "A Note on Romans iv. 1," *ExpT* 63 (1951–52) 91–92, to change εὑρηκέναι ("to find") to ἔργασθαι ("to do") is appropriately judged to be "improbable" by Fitzmyer, 371.

22 For earlier advocates of this view see Meyer, 1:190; Klein, "Römer 4," 151; Zeller, 99; Schmithals, *Römerbrief*, 135.

23 See Kuss, 1:180; Wilckens, 1:261; Dunn, 1:198; Fitzmyer, *According to Paul*, 19–24.

24 See Meyer, 1:191, who details the extensive nineteenth-century discussion of this issue; followed by Philippi, 125–27; Hodge, 163; Godet, 168.

25 Alan Ralph Millard, "Abraham," *ABD* 1 (1992) 35.

26 Joachim Jeremias, "Ἀβραάμ," *TDNT* 1 (1964) 8; see also Otto Betz, "Ἀβραάμ," *EDNT* 1 (1990) 2.

27 William Baird, "Abraham in the New Testament: Tradition and the New Identity," *Int* 42 (1988) 369.

status for his descendants.[28] In *Ps. Sol.* 9.8 the author gives thanks for this status: "For you chose the descendants of Abraham above all the nations, and you put your name upon us, Lord, and it will not cease forever." In contrast to the view that Paul develops, this identity was primarily oriented to Abraham's performance of the law.[29] With paradigmatic heroism Abraham was depicted as withstanding temptations, resisting idolatry, and obeying the precise details of Israel's later laws.[30] He thus became the model for all loyal Jews to follow. Paul's question is whether Abraham's heroism can properly be said to have derived from his fleshly achievement.

■ **2** The reason for the negative answer supplied by Paul's audience to the opening rhetorical question is provided in a coherent sentence beginning with εἰ γάρ ("for if"). The unreal condition indicated by "if," namely that Abraham's virtue provided a legitimate basis for his boasting,[31] was claimed in numerous Jewish writings available during Paul's time.[32] Sirach uses the term "flesh" that Paul had just employed in raising the question of Abraham's virtue prior to receiving the blessing: "Abraham was a great father of many nations, and no one was found like him in glory, who kept the law of the Most High, and entered into covenant with him, and established the covenant in his flesh, and was found faithful in testing. Therefore the Lord assured him by an oath that the nations would be blessed through his posterity."[33] In 1 Macc 2:52 there is an opposite claim to Paul's

argument, citing the same verse from Genesis that he employs in Rom 4:3-5: "Was not Abraham found faithful in temptation and it was reckoned to him as righteousness? (καὶ ἐλογίσθη αὐτῷ εἰς δικαιοσύνην)."[34] That such virtue provided the basis for boasting is clear from the speech that *Jub.* 21.1-3 places in the mouth of Abraham: "Behold, I am a hundred and seventy-five years old, and throughout all of the days of my life I have been remembering the Lord, and sought with all my heart to do his will and walk uprightly in all his ways. . . . I have offered my heart and spirit so that I might be careful to do the will of the one who created me."

In the social environment that pertained throughout the Greco-Roman and Jewish world, such virtue was a natural basis for boasting,[35] according to Sirach, who tells the "righteous man" who is "blameless" and "perfect": "Then let him boast!" (Sir 31[34]:5-9).[36] In *Spec.* 4.164 Philo claims that the summary of the law that he has written is "my incomparable boast and glory (καύχημα καὶ κλέος ἀνανταγώνιστον), a sign of sovereignty that none can challenge, formed in the image of its archetype the kingship of God."

The basis for Abraham's potential boast, in Paul's formulation, is drawn from the tradition of legal requirements that Paul had exposed in the preceding chapter. The expression ἐξ ἔργων ἐδικαιώθη ("he was set right through works") picks up the formulation in 3:28, " set right . . . without works of law."[37] Representatives of the

28 Neubrand, *Abraham*, 291–94; Esler, *Conflict and Identity*, 171–94; see also Siker, *Disinheriting the Jews*, 15–27. In "Aeneas und Abraham. Paulus unter dem Aspekt der Latinität?" *ZNT* 5 (2002) 40–42, Dieter Georgi shows that Abraham and Aeneas were viewed as founder figures who under divine guidance defined the national mission and global destiny of their cultures.

29 Michel, 162. In "Abraham in Graeco-Roman Paganism," *JSJ* 18 (1987) 188–208, Jeffrey S. Siker shows that non-Jewish sources also portray Abraham as a wise and righteous hero, e.g., Berossus *Ant.* 1.158; Alexander Polyhistor *Test.* 1.170-71. See also Calvert-Koyzis, *Paul*, 134–36.

30 See Schmitz, "Abraham," 100–116.

31 See Michel, 162; Cranfield, 1:227; Kuss, 1:180–81; Schlier, 123; Morris, 195; Berger, "Abraham," 65; Schmithals, *Römer*, 136; Moo, 260. Jan Lambrecht, "Why Is Boasting Excluded? A Note on Rom 3,27 and 4,2," *EThL* 61 (1985) 366–67, argues that the

"if" clause designates an unreal condition while the "not before God" clause states the real situation.

32 See particularly Luz, *Geschichtsverständnis*, 177–80; Ferdinand Hahn, "Genesis 15:6 im Neuen Testament," in H. W. Wolff, ed., *Probleme biblischer Theologie. Gerhard von Rad zum 70. Geburtstag* (Munich: Kaiser, 1971) 97–100; Gathercole, *Boasting*, 235–42; Dunn, 1:200–201.

33 Sir 44:19-21; see also *Jub.* 17.15-18; 19.8-9; 23.9-10; CD 3.2-4; Philo *Abr.* 192; Josephus *Ant.* 1.223-25.

34 Sir 44:20 makes almost precisely the same claim, also using Gen 15:6.

35 See Josef Zmijewski, "καυχάομαι κτλ.," *EDNT* 2 (1991) 278.

36 Cited by Gathercole, *Boasting*, 241.

37 See Roman Heiligenthal, "ἔργον," *EDNT* 2 (1991) 50; Dunn, 1:200. In contrast, Neubrand, *Abraham*, 193–96, seeks to reduce the bearing of this formulation to an emphasis on God's free act, in an effort to eliminate any semblance of anti-Judaism.

"New Perspective" deny that Paul is "opposing a view of a legalistic Abraham" whose virtues legitimate boasting.[38] Maria Neubrand provides a sophisticated version of this perspective in arguing that the common theme in all of Paul's references to "works" is that God's mercy alone suffices for justification,[39] and that in this verse no polemic against Jewish "works-righteousness" is intended.[40] Yet the antithesis between Paul's view of Abraham and that of Jewish religionists in his period cited above is sharply delineated by the wording of 4:2, and it fails to do justice to the explicit references to boasting and justification by works by substituting a politically correct emphasis on God's mercy. Paul intends to say that if indeed Abraham had been set right on the basis of such works, he would have a legitimate basis for boasting. But the preceding sections of Paul's argument show that all human beings have fallen short in the glory required for boasting, and that a new basis for righteousness has been created through Christ, so that boasting in any human accomplishment has been excluded by divine action.[41] A new system of honor and shame has been erected by Christ that overturns the universal human impulse to boast. Even the traditional boast of Israel's supreme religious prototype, Abraham, is therefore excluded. Thus Paul declares: "but not before God,"[42] whose righteousness was "demonstrated" in the Christ event (3:25). Godet offers a typical misunderstanding of Paul's point: "In comparing himself with men less holy than he, Abraham might have some cause for glorying; but the instant he put himself before God, his righteousness vanished."[43] As Paul shows in subsequent verses, since Abraham was declared righteous by God, honored by the gift of a new relationship based on grace alone, there was no more need for boasting, either before God or before fellow humans. To reiterate the dialogical exchange from the preceding pericope: "Where then is the boast? It is excluded!" (3:27).[44]

■ **3** As confirmation of divine resistance against boasting,[45] even with regard to Israel's paradigmatic hero, Abraham, Paul has the interlocutor ask what the γραφή ("scripture") says.[46] In contrast to the plural formulation of "scriptures" found in the early Christian confession of 1:2 and to the Hebrew Bible's reference to the "writings," here Paul refers in his typical manner to the authoritative writings as a "unity."[47] The same singular usage is visible in Hellenistic Jewish writings such as *Ep.*

38 Gathercole, *Boasting*, 232, referring to the downplaying of legalistic boasting in Dunn, 1:200; Sanders, *Law*, 33; Michael Cranford, "Abraham in Romans 4: The Father of All Who Believe," *NTS* 41 (1995) 71–88; Räisänen, *Law*, 170–71; Gaston, *Paul*, 49–63; Stowers, *Rereading*, 242–43; Elliott, *Rhetoric*, 218.

39 Neubrand, *Abraham*, 192–95.

40 Ibid., 190–91.

41 See particularly Erich Gräßer, "Der ruhmlose Abraham (Röm 4,2). Nachdenkliches zu Gesetz und Sünde bei Paulus," in M. Trowitzsch, ed., *Paulus, Apostel Jesu Christi. Festschrift für Günter Klein zum 70. Geburtstag* (Tübingen: Mohr-Siebeck, 1998) 15–22.

42 The expression καύχημα . . . προς θεόν ("boast . . . in reference to God") is unique to this passage; this preposition followed by the accusative often has the sense of "in reference to, in respect of, touching," according to LSJM 1498. A classical parallel to the preposition πρός in relation to boasting is in Aelius Aristides Ἀλλεξ. 81.25, "no small boast in reference to the Greeks (οὐ μικρὸν καύχημα πρὸς τοὺς Ἕλληνας)."

43 Godet, 170; for an analysis of the logic behind Paul's remark, see Murray, 130.

44 See Campbell, "3.27–4.25," 364–67. Although a unique theology of boasting is an important Pauline theme (1 Cor 5:6; 9:15-16; 2 Cor 1:14; 5:12; 7:14; 9:3; Gal 6:4; Phil 1:26; 2:16), other ancient authors also raise this issue. In Plutarch *Aem.* 27.4, students are advised to limit their "boast and hubris" (τὸ καύχημα καὶ τὴν ὕβριν) in view of life's uncertainties, because "empty insolence" and "pride of victory" can bring the "jealous displeasure" of the divine.

45 Calvert-Koyzis, *Paul*, 134–35, shows that "one of the major early Jewish traditions about Abraham was that he was obedient to the law even before it was given," citing *Jub.* 16.20-23; 22.1-2; Philo *Migr.* 129–30; Sir 44:19-20; Josephus *Ant.* 1.154–56.

46 The use of the verb λέγω ("say, speak") is another confirmation of the ancient premise that Scripture was read aloud, as Paul's letter is being read, so that it "speaks" to its hearers. See Hans Hübner, "λέγω," *EDNT* 2 (1991) 347.

47 Gottlob Schrenk, "γράφω κτλ.," *TDNT* 1 (1964) 754; other references with the same singular word "scripture" are in Rom 9:17; 10:11; 11:2; Gal 4:30; see also Hans Hübner, "γραφή, γράφω," *EDNT* 1 (1990) 260–64; Schlier, 123; Dunn, 1:202.

Arist. 155, "So we are exhorted through scripture." In this instance the proof text from Gen 15:6 in Paul's midrash is slightly altered from the LXX by the replacement of καί ("and, also") with δέ ("but, now"), thus giving rhetorical emphasis to the antithesis between the Scripture and the human tendency to boast.[48] In addition the name Ἀβράμ ("Abram") is expanded to Ἀβραάμ ("Abraham"), which was Abraham's longer spelling given after the sealing of the covenant in Gen 17; this alteration may allude to the promise he received,[49] which was crucial to Paul's argument that he was the father of all believers: "Behold, my covenant is with you and you shall be the father of a multitude of nations. No longer shall your name be Abram, but your name shall be called Abraham" (Gen 17:4-5).

Paul's citation from Genesis needs to be read in its present argumentative context, with these tiny but significant alterations and with the prior use of the key terms in view. The verb πιστεύειν ("believe") and the nouns δικαιοσύνη ("righteousness") and θεός ("God") were redefined in the first three chapters of Romans to describe a new means of overcoming hostility against God and becoming righteous through faith in the gospel.[50] Without this argumentative context, the citation "Abraham believed in God and it was reckoned to him as righteousness" could easily have been understood as an expression of traditional piety cited in the explanation of v. 2 above, that Abraham's virtuous obedience to God earned the reward of righteousness.[51] The original Hebrew formulation stands closer to this traditional view, because וְהֶאֱמִן ("and he was faithful") conveys a sense of abiding loyalty that is lacking in the Greek translation by the aorist verb ἐπίστευσεν ("and he believed"), which points to the inceptive moment in which Abraham believed God's promise.[52]

A half century ago, Gerhard von Rad opened a new way to interpret the expression "reckoned to him as righteousness," namely that the ancient Hebrew priest had the responsibility to accept or reject the worshiper as he presented a sacrifice at the altar or performs some other religious service (e.g., Lev 7:18).[53] The expression in Gen 15:6 is a "declaration of acceptance,"[54] similar to that found in Pss 15, 24, and Ezek 18, in which only righteous persons are deemed acceptable before God. Although the subsequent discussion proved that the technical use of "reckon as righteousness" by priests employs the niphal form of the verb rather than the simple qal form used in Gen 15:6,[55] the latter appears in 2 Sam 19:19 and Ps 32:2 in the context of reckoning sins.[56] There are also parallels to the use of "faith" in the context of Yahweh's promised deliverance (e.g., Exod

---

48 Koch, *Schrift*, 133, argues for an intentional alteration at this point to convey an antithesis with a more traditional view of Abraham as a patriarch who was justified by law. This is more plausible than Stanley, *Paul*, 100, and Neubrand, *Abraham*, 197, who argue that the similar wording in Jas 2:23 indicates Paul employed an already altered form of Gen 15:6.

49 See Dunn, 1:202; the same expanded form, "Abraham," occurs in Gal 3:6; see Koch, *Schrift*, 106; Oegema, *Israel und die Völker*, 88.

50 See Aageson, *Biblical Interpretation*, 85.

51 See Schmitz, "Abraham," 108–13; Zeller, 99; Wilckens, 1:262. Gaston, *Paul*, 45–63, argues that since the original Hebrew text could be translated as if Abraham declared God righteous, this was Paul's reading of Gen 15:6, which would bring him in line with some later rabbinic exegesis. Although Gaston is able to disentangle Paul's argument with anti-Judaistic hermeneutics, he cannot explain the wording of 4:6, 9, or the argument in the next pericope (particularly 4:13, 17, 21-22), which makes plain that righteous status was being imputed to Abraham.

52 See Godet, 170; Haacker, 100–101; Neubrand, *Abraham*, 201–3. In "Ist Gen 15,6 ein Beleg für die Anrechnung des Glaubens zur Gerechtigkeit?" *ZAW* 95 (1983) 196, Manfred Oeming concludes that Paul's interpretation is simply false when compared with the original Hebrew text. Dirk U. Rottzoll, "Gen 15,6—Ein Beleg für den Glauben als Werkgerechtigkeit," *ZAW* 106 (1994) 21–27, develops a moderating position, while Achin Behrens, "Gen 15,6 und das Vorverständnis des Paulus," *ZAW* 109 (1997) 327–41, legitimates Paul's exegesis.

53 Gerhard von Rad, "Faith Reckoned as Righteousness," in *The Problem of the Hexateuch and Other Essays,* trans. E. W. Trueman Dicken (New York: McGraw-Hill, 1966) 125–30 (German original 1951)

54 John Van Seters, *Abraham in History and Tradition* (New Haven: Yale University Press, 1975) 257.

55 Oeming, "Ist Gen 15,6 ein Beleg," 185–90; accepted by Behrens, "Gen 15,6," 329.

56 See Behrens, "Gen 15,6," 329.

4:31; 14:31), while "righteousness" often appears as an ascribed status rather than an intrinsic quality (e.g., Deut 24:10-13).[57] Gen 15:6 therefore declares that Abraham's faith in God's promise sufficed to declare him righteous, that is, acceptable to God. Although this provides the clearest explanation of the peculiar expression in Gen 15:6, it has not found its way into Romans commentaries,[58] perhaps because it does not fit the Augustinian framework of forgiveness or the definition of righteousness as a matter of accepting a particular doctrine of justification.[59] But it fits precisely within the theory of ascribed honor that in Paul's view is granted to the undeserving. It was possible, however, to understand this ascription within a framework of religious boasting. The verb וַיַּחְשְׁבֶהָ ("and he reckoned") was also a commercial term that had already been applied to Abraham by 1 Macc 2:52, cited above,[60] as if the righteous status given to him were a payment for good deeds.[61] In contrast Paul had signaled by his prior use of the Greek equivalent λογίζομαι ("reckon, calculate, conclude") in 2:3, 26, and 3:28 that a new system of ascribing righteousness had been established by the grace of Christ.[62] In its present context, Paul employs Gen 15:6 as if it flatly denied the possibility of human boasting on the basis of "works" and therefore provides the basis for reinterpreting Abraham as the father of all believers, including Gentiles who lacked the honor of physical descent.[63] For Paul, righteousness is the gift of a new relationship with God that comes when humans stop competing for honor and accept the grace that they could never earn.[64] To be "reckoned as righteousness" is to be accepted by the God of righteousness and therefore to be granted honor that overturns shameful status.

■ **4** Since the key issue is whether righteousness can be earned by pious works, Paul begins his exposition of the main proof text by defining λογίζομαι ("reckon") in the light of his previous argument in favor of salvation by grace alone. The logic is drawn from the world of everyday experience in the economic realm. The verb ἐργάζομαι is employed with its usual connotation of active work, such as Paul did with his hands on a daily basis in making tents and awnings (1 Thess 2:9; 1 Cor 4:12).[65] The realm of work for wages is most naturally in view with the noun μισθός, which should be translated as "pay" or "wages,"[66] without reference to its metaphorical use elsewhere in the NT in terms of a religious "reward" (e.g., Mark 9:41; Matt 5:12, 46; Luke 6:35).[67] Similarly, the verb λογίζεται should be translated as a technical

57   See Rottzoll, "Gen 15,6," 26; Behrens, "Gen 15,6," 331.
58   For instance, von Rad's article is not cited by Kuss in his comprehensive discussion, 1:179–81; although listed in Dunn's bibliography, it is not mentioned in his discussion of Rom 4:3 on 1:202–3 or 227–28. Despite von Rad's prominence, his contribution on this issue is overlooked by other large-scale commentators such as Schlier, 123–24; Michel, 162–63; Murray, 130–32; Wilckens, 1:260–62; Fitzmyer, 373–74; Byrne, 144–48. Moo, 262, lists von Rad in n. 35, but does not follow the logic of his contribution, and there is no evidence of this research in Richard Holst, "The Meaning of 'Abraham Believed God' in Romans 4:3," *WTJ* 59 (1997) 319–26.
59   See, e.g., Hofmann, 134–35; Westerholm, *Law*, 141–65.
60   "Was not Abraham found faithful in temptation and it was reckoned to him as righteousness?" (καὶ ἐλογίσθη αὐτῷ εἰς δικαιοσύνην;)."
61   See Wilckens, 1:262.
62   See Schmidt, 78.
63   In "Romans 4," 262–63, Anthony Guerra explains this universalizing motif as trumping "Jewish apologetic."
64   See Morris's emphasis on grace, 197.
65   Roman Heiligenthal, "ἐργάζομαι κτλ.," *EDNT* 2 (1991) 48.
66   Rudolf Pesch, "μισθός," *EDNT* 2 (1991) 432–33; he shows (433) that this word group "has no specific theological significance in Paul," and that payment for work remains dominant. Xenophon *Hell.* 6.2.16 refers to "those mercenaries who remained, he owed two months pay (ὤφειλε τὸν μισθόν)." Similarly Xenophon *Anab.* 1.2.11 and 7.7.14 speak of μισθός owed to soldiers. Epictetus *Diss.* 3.26.27 asks, "And the paymaster will not come up short (οὐ λείπει ὁ μισθοδοτῶν) for the good soldier or the worker or cobbler, will he?"
67   It is therefore inappropriate to refer to the "religious use" of this term (Dunn, 1:203). Herbert Preisker, "μισθός κτλ.," *TDNT* 4 (1967) 700, refers to "Paul's concept of reward" as if the argument in Rom 4 were identical with the inherent meaning of μισθός itself. P. C. Böttger makes the same semantic mistake in "μισθός," *TBLNT* 2 (1972) 915.

term for charging a bill, calculating a debt, or counting out wages earned for work performed.[68] For example, a first-century C.E. account states that "the due amounts in money and corn are reckoned (λογίζεται) here."[69] The price of wine to be charged to a buyer is described as follows: "reckoning (λογιζομένου) the wine to him at sixteen drachmae per monochore."[70] The analogical argument also requires a neutral definition of χάρις as "gift" or "favor"[71] rather than as the technical term "grace" that plays such an important role in Paul's theology elsewhere (e.g., 1:5; 3:24).[72] The antithesis between gift and obligation (ὀφείλημα) that Paul uses here was widely assumed in the ancient environment, and is explicitly stated in Thucydides *Hist.* 2.20.4,[73] where Pericles in his funeral oration of 431/430 B.C.E. compares the Athenians' sense of goodwill and freedom with others who owe Athens a favor and therefore act "not out of grace but out of a sense of obligation (οὐκ ἐξ χάριν, ἀλλ᾽ ἐς ὀφείλημα)." If a person has performed work, appropriate remuneration was an absolutely binding obligation that was not only universally accepted but also reinforced by law throughout the Greco-Roman world.[74] Paul is certain to gain assent for the first part of his development of the midrash on Gen 15:6.

■ **5** The antithesis to v. 4 begins with the parallel formulation marked by μὴ ἐργαζομένῳ ("to the one who does not work"), whereby the commercial logic of wages paid

for work performed remains dominant. Yet with the next word, πιστεύοντι ("believes"), Paul steps beyond the commercial realm of his analogy toward the central category of early Christianity. As Murray observes, "The antithesis is not simply between the worker and the non-worker but between the worker and the person who does not work *but believes*."[75] That Abraham performed no religious "work" prior to the reference to his faith in Gen 15:6 is detailed in vv. 9-10 below, so in a sense the claim in v. 5 is something of a forecast. Yet its argumentative force for the hearers has been firmly established by the preceding chapter,[76] where the early Christian experience of faith was elaborated by use of an early Christian confession that was probably known in Rome. In this sense the argument rests not simply on Paul's experience of faith,[77] but also on the various congregations' experience of faith as participation in the realm of grace.[78]

The content of Abraham's faith in τὸν δικαιοῦντα τὸν ἀσεβῆ ("the one who sets right the impious") is drawn from the preceding pericopes, but the formulation would have appeared paradoxical to persons schooled in the Jewish tradition.[79] This phrase appeared in Exod 23:7 and Isa 5:23 in reference to "those who give unjust judgments because of bribes."[80] That Abraham argued that God should not destroy the righteous along with the ἀσεβής (Gen 18:23, 25) hardly provides a

---

68 See the examples provided by Hans-Wolfgang Heidland, "λογίσθαι, λογισμός," *TDNT* 4 (1967) 284. Hans-Werner Bartsch, "λογίζομαι," *EDNT* 2 (1991) 354, states that Paul's usage in this verse is "derived from commerce." For example, Plutarch *Phoc.* 22.2 describes "as much as Harpalos was charged . . . for the work (ὅσα τῷ Ἁρπάλῳ λογισθῆναι . . . εἰς τὸ ἔργον)."

69 Cited by MM 377 from *P.Oxy.* 12. Nr. 1434.8.

70 Cited by MM 377 from *P.Flor.* 2. Nr. 123.7-10.

71 See BAGD 877.2, "favor, grace, gracious care or help"; Dunn, 1:205.

72 Klaus Berger overlooks this distinction and views Rom 4:4 as a matter of "God's saving grace" in "χάρις," *EDNT* 3 (1993) 458; Hans Conzelmann talks about *sola gratia* in "χαίρω κτλ.," *TDNT* 9 (1974) 394; and many commentators follow this line, e.g., Meyer, 1:196-97; Michel, 163; Morris, 197; Stuhlmacher, 72.

73 Noted by Friedrich Hauck, "ὀφείλω κτλ.," *TDNT* 5 (1967) 565; see also Aristotle *Eth. nic.* 1165a3.

74 See Édouard Will, "Notes zur μισθός," in J. Bingen et al., eds., *Le Monde grec. Hommages à Claire Préaux,* TFPUB 62 (Brussels: Éditions de l'Université, 1975) 426-38; see also Walther Bienert's description of the obligation within Jewish ethics for fair payment of wages in *Die Arbeit nach der Lehre der Bibel. Eine Grundlegung evangelischer Sozialethik* (Stuttgart: Evangelisches Verlagswerk, 1954) 94-98. Pay for labor accomplished is a common agrarian maxim, as in 'Abot R. Nat. 5.6, "According to the labor is the reward"; and Matt 10:10, "the laborer is worth his hire."

75 Murray, 132 (italics in original).

76 See Weiss, 189; Kühl, 135.

77 See Kuss, 1:182.

78 See Dobbeler, *Glaube als Teilhabe,* 167-70.

79 Käsemann, 111; Morris, 198-99; Stuhlmacher, 73.

80 See Anitra Kolenkow, "The Ascription of Romans 4:5," *HTR* 60 (1967) 228, citing Dodd, *Bible and the Greeks,* 57.

precedent for Paul's formulation,[81] because the wicked in Sodom and Gomorrah were indeed punished. The general pattern in the Hebrew Scriptures and subsequent Judaism is that God justifies only those who obey the law. Something radically new is in view here,[82] even though Abraham is employed as the precedent, namely that God in Christ restores a right relationship with those who have not earned it. It was Abraham's faith in such a God, rather than any virtuous action on his own part, that opened the door to this paradoxical view that counters "the more normal interpretation of Abraham as a model of covenant righteousness."[83]

In view of Paul's prior use of $\dot{\alpha}\sigma\epsilon\beta\epsilon\dot{\iota}\alpha$ in 1:18 and his subsequent use of $\dot{\alpha}\sigma\epsilon\beta\dot{\eta}\varsigma$ in the confessional citation of 5:6, both of which refer to a universal human condition of arrogant rebellion against God,[84] it seems inappropriate to construe it here as "idolatry"[85] or "sinner" in the technical sense of violating the Torah.[86] Either of these options would restrict the bearing of Abraham's example to either the Gentile Christian or the Jewish Christian side of the Roman congregations.[87] In view of the central of issue of boasting that was dividing these churches into competitive factions, the word $\dot{\alpha}\sigma\epsilon\beta\dot{\eta}\varsigma$ clearly refers to the person "who has no ground of boasting before God."[88] In Paul's interpretation the God in whom Abraham believed is the same as the father of Jesus Christ who accepts and honors those who have no basis for honor, either in their religious accomplishments, their wisdom, or their social status.

Abraham's faith was reckoned by God, according to the citation from Genesis, $\epsilon\dot{\iota}\varsigma$ $\delta\iota\kappa\alpha\iota\sigma\sigma\dot{\upsilon}\nu\eta\nu$ ("as righteousness"), in which the preposition is employed to produce a predicate nominative.[89] An example of this usage is Wis 3:17, $\epsilon\dot{\iota}\varsigma$ $\sigma\dot{\upsilon}\vartheta\dot{\epsilon}\nu$ $\lambda\sigma\gamma\iota\sigma\vartheta\dot{\eta}\sigma\sigma\nu\tau\alpha\iota,$ that the offspring of adulterers will "be reckoned as nothing."[90] The formulation has to do with ascription of status, in the instance of Abraham, declaring someone to be something he was not. Most commentators sidestep this peculiar formulation and point to some form of human behavior that produces righteousness: belief in a doctrine of justification of faith,[91] an attitude of trust[92] or faith,[93] but every such explanation constitutes a potential new form of religious boasting that Paul wishes to exclude.

The formulation of this clause within the Pauline context should be interpreted as a matter of God pronouncing people to be righteous even though they were impious, as Käsemann saw with unusual clarity.[94] The "declaratory element" is crucial, in which "God makes the ungodly person a new creature; he really makes him righteous."[95] But Käsemann overlooked the communal

81   Kolenkow, "Romans 4:5," 228–30.
82   See Stuhlmacher, *Gerechtigkeit*, 227; Wilckens, 1:263. The effort by Cranford, "Abraham," 79–82, and Neubrand, *Abraham*, 207–12, to downplay this radicalism in order to avoid anti-Judaism is not convincing.
83   Dunn, 1:205; see also Stuhlmacher, 72–73.
84   The apocalyptic background of $\dot{\alpha}\sigma\epsilon\beta\dot{\eta}\varsigma$ suggested by Alexander Sand, "Die Polemik gegen 'Gesetzlosigkeit' im Evangelium nach Matthäus und bei Paulus," *BZ* 14 (1970) 121–22, is not visible in this verse.
85   Meyer, 1:197, reports that Reiche and a number of earlier scholars advocated this view. Edward Adams, "Abraham's Faith and Gentile Disobedience: Textual Links between Romans 1 and 4," *JSNT* 65 (1997) 55–62, makes the case that Abraham is relevant because he overcame idolatry. In the Psalms the idea of "evildoers" is primarily associated with Gentiles as a class, according to Harris Birkeland, *Evildoers in the Book of Psalms*, ANVO 2.2 (Oslo: Almqvist & Wiksell, 1955) 93–94, but this restrictive view is not carried over into Romans.
86   Wilckens, 1:263; Werner Foerster, "$\dot{\alpha}\sigma\epsilon\beta\dot{\eta}\varsigma$ $\kappa\tau\lambda.$," *TDNT* 7 (1971) 190.
87   The suggestion by Haacker, 102, that Abraham was impious in violating the value of honoring one's parents and homeland also seems overly restrictive in the light of the argument in Romans.
88   Käsemann, 112; see also Peter Fiedler, "$\dot{\alpha}\sigma\epsilon\beta\dot{\eta}\varsigma$ $\kappa\tau\lambda.$," *EDNT* 1 (1990) 169.
89   BAGD 230.8γ, "under Semitic influence, which has strengthened Greek tendencies in the same direction."
90   See also Wis 2:16; Acts 19:27; Xenophon *Cyr.* 3.1.33 speaks of 3,000 talents left "when reckoned in silver ($\epsilon\dot{\iota}\varsigma$ $\dot{\alpha}\rho\gamma\dot{\upsilon}\rho\iota\sigma\nu$ $\lambda\sigma\gamma\iota\sigma\vartheta\dot{\epsilon}\nu\tau\alpha$)."
91   Wilckens, 1:236.
92   Godet, 170; Weiss, 189; Cranfield, 1:231.
93   Kühl, 136; Murray, 133–34.
94   See Käsemann, 112: "What is meant is pronouncing righteous. This is an eschatological act of the Judge at the last day which takes place proleptically in the present."
95   Käsemann, 112–13.

dimension of faith as the early church experienced it: faith was the response of converts to the message that Christ died for the impious, and it led to their joining small communities of faith in which righteousness became a social reality as the dishonored were restored to honor, that is, to "righteousness." This was grasped with unparalleled clarity by Colenso in the context of the interaction between Africans and Europeans, that "the blessings of salvation has been given in Christ to all humankind in solidarity with him."[96] Moo's formulation captures a portion of this idea, without grasping the social dimensions of the shamed being treated as righteous: "Paul has in mind a creative act, whereby the believer is freely given a new 'status.'"[97] This occurred in the mystery of conversion in response to the gospel.[98] The Spirit was understood to evoke positive responses to the gospel, making persons know in the depth of their despair and dishonor that together they could call God "Abba" and live as honored "children of God" (Rom 8:15-16). Faith is therefore "participation" in this new reality, as Axel von Dobbeler has shown.[99] Philip Esler describes God's rightwising activity as "the ascription of honor by God to the sinner [which makes] . . . the person so honored actually righteous."[100] Without any accomplishment whatsoever, converts who responded to the gospel of unconditional grace became participants in "righteousness" that God alone is in the position to ascribe, and it is this dynamic process that Paul reads out of the citation from Gen 15:6.

■ **6** The secondary text in Paul's midrash is framed by an unusually elaborate introduction that begins with a typical citation formula, $\kappa\alpha\vartheta\acute{\alpha}\pi\epsilon\rho$ ("as, just as"),[101] followed by $\kappa\alpha\acute{\iota}$ ("also").[102] David is identified as the voice that speaks in the Psalm,[103] a traditional claim reflected in that more than half of the Psalms contain superscriptions identifying him as the author.[104] The LXX identifies Ps 31, cited here, as "of David, a psalm of understanding."[105] In the context of a $\mu\alpha\kappa\alpha\rho\iota\sigma\mu\acute{o}\varsigma$ ("the blessing"), a formal utterance that has performative power deriving from the divine realm,[106] the verb $\lambda\acute{\epsilon}\gamma\omega$ should be translated as "pronounce."[107] The recipient of David's blessing is identified with the terminology Paul had employed in explaining the primary text of Gen 15:6: "the person to whom God reckons righteousness apart from works." Paul wishes to stress God's merciful action toward those who have no claim on honorable achievement, and he subsumes the references to forgiveness in the psalm citation under this category. In contrast to the mainstream of commentators who understand justification as forgiveness of sins, following the Augustinian legacy,[108] Paul retains a stress on the new relationship of honor that God chooses to "reckon" to those who do not deserve it. This is congruent with the idea of blessing, for as Kent Richards observes, "The

---

96   Colenso, 90, 202, cited by Draper, "Colenso," 71.

97   Moo, 264; see also Calvert-Koyzis, *Paul*, 119–23, 137.

98   See Kuss, 1:183.

99   Dobbeler, *Glaube als Teilhabe*, 132–45, 275–77; while participation in the community of the elect and the centrality of conversion in response to the gospel are clearly grasped, von Dobbeler makes no use of the granting of honor, which was the social form of righteousness in the Pauline communities.

100   Esler, *Conflict and Identity*, 187.

101   "Just as" is a typical Pauline introduction for quotations, used also in 3:4; 9:13; 10:15; and 11:8, and appearing in the NT only in the Pauline letters and Hebrews. See BAGD 387. Godet, 172, suggests the translation "exactly as" to indicate "an intrinsic and striking agreement."

102   Wilckens, 1:263, suggests that the "also" indicates the two texts stand "side by side" in proving justification by faith.

103   See Helmut Merkel, "$\Delta\alpha\nu\acute{\iota}\delta$," *EDNT* 1 (1990) 277.

104   David M. Howard Jr., "David," *ABD* 2 (1992) 47, also observes that 11QPs^a col. 1 claims David wrote no less than 4,050 psalms.

105   Fitzmyer, 375.

106   See the discussion of the dynamistic interpretation of blessings by Kent Harold Richards, "Bless/Blessing," *ABD* 1 (1992) 754–55; also William J. Urbock, "Blessings and Curses," *ABD* 1 (1992) 756.

107   So Byrne, 149; Moo, 265. An example of "speak" in connection with a macarism is available in *Sib. Or.* 13.117, "The living, speaking from their mouths, shall utter a macarism ($o\acute{\iota}\ \zeta\tilde{\omega}\nu\tau\epsilon\varsigma\ \mu\alpha\kappa\alpha\rho\iota\sigma\mu\grave{o}\nu\ \grave{\alpha}\pi\grave{o}\ \sigma\tau\acute{o}\mu\alpha\tau\omega\nu\ \grave{\epsilon}\nu\acute{\epsilon}\pi o\nu\tau\epsilon\varsigma\ \varphi\vartheta\acute{\epsilon}\gamma\xi o\nu\tau\alpha\iota$)."

108   For example, Meyer, 1:198, citing Augustine; Schmidt, 79–80, excursus 7 on justification and forgiveness of sins; Cranfield, 1:233; Murray, 134; Stuhlmacher, 73; Byrne, 146; Moo, 266; Schlier, 126. Dunn, 1:206, cites Jeremias, *Central Message*, 66: "justification is forgiveness, nothing but forgiveness."

primary factor of blessing is the statement of relationship between parties," rather than the concrete benefit itself.[109] In this instance Paul signals in advance that the secondary text from Ps 31 should be understood as confirming[110] that God grants righteous status to the undeserving and thus establishes a new relationship between God's self and the community of those who accept grace without any claim of having earned it.

■ **7** The citation from Ps 31:1-2 is identical with the LXX because it fits Paul's purpose so precisely. In the light of the introduction provided by v. 6, the emphasis is on the blessed status of those whose former alienation has been overcome by the reckoning of righteousness.[111] The aorist passive verbs ἀφέθησαν ("they have been forgiven")[112] and ἐπεκαλύφθησαν ("they have been covered up")[113] point to a single event that is now completed, which would probably have been understood by an early Christian audience as the moment of conversion. In place of the traditional emphasis on the process of repentance, restitution, and forgiveness, the psalm in Paul's interpretation refers to the new status of blessedness that God imparts to those God chooses to make righteous. No longer are they defined by their former

"iniquities" (ἀνομίαι)[114] or "sins" (ἁμαρτίαι)[115] that rendered them unfit for acceptance by decent communities or by a righteous God. Without any achievement or virtue to earn honorable status, they have been accepted unconditionally by Christ and now enjoy the status of righteousness in communities of faith that honor one another as blessed children of God. In the context of Paul's argument, this text from Ps 31 has been completely recontextualized and redefined. In Kuss's formulation, "Paul transforms the message of the psalm: in place of the person who gains forgiveness from God on the basis of remorseful repentance, there emerges a person whose absolute lostness before God has been overcome by an absolutely new beginning through the salvific act of God through Jesus Christ."[116] Yet in Paul's view this innovative perspective is contained within the precise wording of the psalm itself.

■ **8** The citation from Ps 31 continues with the blessing on the "person whose sin the Lord will in no wise reckon," which retains the focus on the new status ascribed to the person. Once again, the current situation of sin is not in view. Instead the future tense of the verb λογίσηται ("he will reckon") says that God[117] will not

109 Richards, "Bless/Blessing," 754. In this light the stress in Schlatter, 88, and Friedrich Hauck, "μακάριος κτλ.," *TDNT* 4 (1967) 369, on the content of "salvation" seems misplaced.

110 Meyer, 1:198; Murray, 133. Koch, *Schrift*, 222, and Neubrand, *Abraham*, 213, point to the confirmatory function of Ps 31 in this context.

111 See esp. Kuss, 1:183.

112 Herbert Leroy, "ἀφίημι, ἄφεσις," *EDNT* 1 (1990) 183, observes that the words "forgive" and "forgiveness" "do not belong to the theological language of Paul." See also Cranfield, 1:233; Käsemann, 113.

113 As Cranfield, 1:234, observes, ἐπικαλύπτειν ("cover up") appears here for the only time in the NT, and that it is drawn from the Hebrew idea of being "covered in respect to sin" by atoning blood and ritual.

114 For example, Ps 5:4-5 declares that God hates iniquity (ἀνομία) and will not dwell with those who "work iniquity"; see also 44:7; 50:9. The antithesis between iniquity and righteousness lies behind the prayer that God "add iniquity to their iniquity and let them not come into your righteousness" (Ps 68:27). Ps 6:8 states that the righteous will not live together with "those who work iniquity (οἱ ἐργαζό-μενοι τὴν ἀνομίαν)." Walter Gutbrod, "ἀνομία,

ἄνομος," *TDNT* 4 (1967) 1087, notes that οἱ ἄνομοι was the "common term for Gentiles" whose sinful behavior required faithful Jews to separate themselves. See also Meinrad Limbeck, "ἀνομία κτλ.," *EDNT* 1 (1990) 106; Birkeland, *Evildoers*, 31-40, 93-94.

115 That sin alienates people from God is basic to biblical thought, according to Robin C. Cover, "Sin, Sinners (OT)," *ABD* 6 (1992) 36-39. In "Sin, Sinners (NT)," *ABD* 6 (1992) 43, E. P. Sanders writes: "'Sinners' as the enemies of God, and thus of the 'righteous,' are prominent in the Psalms" and other Jewish writings; see also Sanders, *Paul*, 342-60. For example, Ps 108:1-20 describes the social alienation and misfortune that should befall sinners; see also Ps 140:4-10. In *Sinners and the Righteous*, 128-30, 186-87, Winninge provides examples of persons whose sins stereotype them as outsiders to be shunned.

116 Kuss, 1:183.

117 The word κύριος should be understood as "God" in this passage, as with other citations from the LXX; see Joseph A. Fitzmyer, "κύριος, κυριακός," *EDNT* 2 (1991) 330; L. Cerfaux, "Le nom divin 'Kyrios' dans la Bible grecque," *RSPhTh* 20 (1931) 27-51.

allow sin to disqualify this person from blessedness. The occurrence of this verb is crucial for Paul's argument, constituting the second exegetical rule of Hillel, the appearance of an equal term as found in the primary text.[118] The double negative οὐ μή is emphatic,[119] giving assurance that the Lord will under no circumstance act differently than promised in v. 6 and throughout the preceding argument, namely that God ascribes righteousness to whom God chooses, apart from one's works. In contrast to the Augustinian tradition of interpreting justification as forgiveness, there is no reference in this verse to the process of repentance, restitution, and forgiveness.[120] Sin in this verse is simply not "counted,"[121] because God "who sets right the impious" (4:5) chooses to accept this person unconditionally into the relationship of righteousness and honor. It is not the human experience of forgiveness that is blessed, according to this citation from Ps 31, but the person him-/herself is blessed in having received the amazing gift of an assured relationship with God, despite his/her previous dishonor.

■ **9** In the first half of this verse Paul returns to his diatribe style by posing the question about whether the blessing is available to both Jews and Gentiles. Whereas the citation from Ps 31 had employed past and future tenses, the verb to be supplied in v. 9a must be in the present tense, matching the present tense verb λέγομεν ("we say") in v. 9b, which serves to relate the question to the current circumstances in the Roman house and tenement churches.[122] The expression ὁ μακαρισμός . . . οὗτος, which I translate as "this blessing," identifies the topic of the question with the three previous references to blessing and οὖν ("therefore") links the question with the preceding citation from Ps 31.[123] There would have been no question that the blessing applies to "the circumcision," a metonymic reference to the Jewish people.[124] Moreover, in view of the use of Ps 31 in the Day of Atonement ritual,[125] it is likely that most Jews would have understood the blessing to be available only to themselves and not to Gentiles. Several commentators[126] have cited the Talmud, which articulates a view that was prevalent in Paul's time:[127]

> On the Day of Atonement God cleanses Israel and atones for its guilt, as it is written, "For on this day shall atonement be made for you, to cleanse you" (Lev 16:30). And if you would say, "Another nation too [he cleanses, know that] it is not so, but it is only Israel, for so spoke the prophet Micah (7:18): "Who is a God like unto you, who pardons iniquity, and passes by the transgression of the remnant of his heritage?" It is only Israel that he forgives. When David saw how God forgives the sins of the Israelites and has mercy upon them, he began to pronounce them blessed and to glorify them: "Blessed is he whose transgression is forgiven. (Ps 33:1)"[128]

While not denying that the blessing comes to the "circumcised,"[129] Paul diplomatically poses the question with ἢ καὶ ἐπὶ τὴν ἀκροβυστίαν ("or also upon the circumcised foreskin").[130] He uses the same categories employed in 2:25-27 and 3:30 that had probably been

---

118 See Jeremias, "Gedankenführung," 271–72; Koch, *Schrift*, 221–22.
119 See BDF §365; BAGD 517.D.2; Cranfield, 1:234.
120 Zahn, 222; Kühl, 137; Wilckens, 1:264; Zeller, 100; Zeisler, 127. Murray, 135, speaks of the "virtual identification" of forgiveness and justification; in view of the weight of this Augustinian tradition, it is misleading to claim with Dunn, 1:207, that "reckon righteous = forgive acts of lawlessness = cover sins = not reckon sins."
121 Morris, 200.
122 Zeller, 100, refers to the generalizing effect of the present tense in this verse.
123 See Weiss, 191; Neubrand, *Abraham*, 216.
124 Wilckens, 1:264; Neubrand, *Abraham*, 216.
125 Michel, 165, citing *b. Yoma* 86b; *Pesiqta* 45 (185b and 186a). In *Heiligtumsweihe*, 45–91, Kraus shows that the Day of Atonement ritual restored the purity of Israel's temple, but there is no indication that the temple dealt with Gentile sins; see also David P. Wright, "Day of Atonement," *ABD* 2 (1992) 72–76.
126 Michel, 166; Schlier, 126; Cranfield, 1:234.
127 Stuhlmacher, 73, observes that Paul had already struggled in the Galatian crisis against the view that Gentiles "could participate in the blessings of the Abrahamic covenant only through circumcision."
128 Quotation adapted from Cranfield, 1:234, who cites *Pesiqta* 45 (185b).
129 See note e above.
130 See Dunn, 1:208; in "Romans 4," 451, Tobin observes that in comparison with the parallel discussion in Galatians, which is much more polemical

abusively hurled back and forth between Jews and Gentiles in Rome.[131] Since Paul had already shown that God was the God of both Jews and Gentiles (3:29-30), his audience would have been willing to affirm the logic of this question and answer yes to extending the blessing to non-Jews.

The affirmative answer is confirmed by a striking rhetorical shift to the first person plural, "for we say [that] 'the faith was reckoned to Abraham as righteousness.'" Here Paul assumes the assent of his Roman audience in the interpretive process,[132] using the early Christian terminology of "the faith"[133] while reiterating the theme of Gen 15:6 concerning Abraham's having been reckoned as righteous. At the same time, in effect the text from Ps 31 that is applied to Abraham, whose faith in the God "who sets right the impious," is employed to extend the blessing beyond the circle of the circumcised.[134] Thus while the focus shifts to the "apart from works" dimension of the issue, which was explicitly supported by neither text, Paul builds a case for Abraham as the father of both Jewish and Gentile Christians.[135] From this point the argument drives toward the conclusion of vv. 11-12.[136]

■ **10** With two successive questions, Paul moves toward his conclusion with a tempo that sweeps his hearers forward. The interlocutor's question, "How therefore was it reckoned?"[137] refers back to the situation of Abraham at the time the promise of Gen 15:6 was given.[138] Was he circumcised at the time or not? The biblical account in Genesis makes the sequence plain; the birth of Ishmael when Abraham was 88 years old (Gen 16:16) came between the promise of Gen 15 and the sign of circumcision that was given after his 99th birthday (Gen 17:1). The rabbinic tradition calculated 29 years between the promise of Gen 15:6 and Abraham's circumcision.[139] Paul therefore does not wait for the audience to respond to the rhetorical questions: there is absolutely no doubt on this point that Abraham's reckoning of righteousness came when he was "not in circumcision but in uncircumcised foreskin." The conclusion is inescapable that, in Käsemann's words, "circumcision is not an indispensable presupposition of justification."[140] No religious act gave Abraham his "standing before God."[141] Since Abraham's status of righteousness was granted at a time when he was in the situation of Gentiles,[142] against whom the epithet "foreskin" could be employed,[143] the logical implication is that he is the forefather of all persons of faith, regardless of their ethnic background.[144]

■ **11** In a skillful paraphrase of Gen 17, Paul makes the case that circumcision was not only performed long after Abraham's reckoning as righteous, but also that it was merely a "seal" of the righteous status that he had already received.[145] That Abraham received a $\sigma\eta\mu\epsilon\hat{\iota}o\nu$ ("sign") is drawn from Gen 17:11, that circumcision

---

against Jewish Christians, the Abraham of Romans is the "father of both Jews and Gentile believers."

131 See Marcus, "Circumcision and Uncircumcision," 73–81; see also Dunn, 1:208, for a review of circumcision as a boundary marker between Jews and Gentiles.

132 Meyer, 1:199: "The *plural* assumes the assent of the readers" (italics in original). See also Neubrand, *Abraham*, 218. Lietzmann, 51, and Schmidt, 81, reduce the significance of the first person plural to "I repeat," which misses the rhetorical effect.

133 See Dobbeler, *Glaube als Teilhabe*, 166–70, 315–16.

134 Jülicher, 252, observes that Ps 31 gives no hint that the blessing comes upon those who have performed no righteous deeds. That link is supplied entirely by Paul's argument.

135 See Heil, 47; Stowers, *Rereading*, 227; Eisenbaum, "Genealogy in Romans," 686–87; Hays, "Romans 4:1," 93.

136 See Neubrand, *Abraham*, 218–20.

137 The form of the question with $\pi\hat{\omega}\varsigma\ o\hat{\upsilon}\nu$ ("how there-

fore?") appears elsewhere in all of the epistles only at Rom 10:14, although it occurs frequently in classical diatribes, 35 times in Epictetus and 41 times in Demosthenes.

138 See Meyer, 1:199; Neubrand, *Abraham*, 219.

139 Michel, 166; Kuss, 1:183; Dunn, 1:208.

140 Käsemann, 114; also Murray, 137.

141 Morris, 202.

142 Godet, 173.

143 Marcus, "Circumcision and Uncircumcision," 77–78: "From the very beginning, then, $\dot{\alpha}\kappa\rho o$-$\beta\upsilon\sigma\tau\dot{\iota}\alpha$ was a derogatory word for a part of the body that was shameful to Jewish eyes . . . the term eventually became an ethnic slur designating the whole Gentile person."

144 See Jülicher, 252; Neubrand, *Abraham*, 220.

145 Berger, "Abraham," 67, argues that this point is derived from 2:25-29, that circumcision has validity only on the basis of righteousness already received.

"shall be a sign of the covenant between you and me (καὶ ἔσται ἐν σημείῳ διαθήκης ἀνὰ μέσον ἐμοῦ καὶ ὑμῶν)." In place of circumcision as a "sign of the covenant," which would retain the premise of Israel's preeminent position as Yahweh's sole covenant partner, Paul speaks of circumcision as the sign of something else, that is, the "righteousness through faith" that was ascribed to Abraham while he was still an uncircumcised Gentile.[146] In this context σημεῖον refers to a distinctive mark[147] or sign.[148] The words ἀκροβυστία ("foreskin") and περιτομή ("circumcision") are drawn from the same passage in Gen 17, but without reference to covenant or to the physical offspring and slaves of Abraham:

καὶ περιτμηθήσεσθε τὴν σάρκα τῆς ἀκροβυστίας ὑμῶν. . . . περιτομῇ περιτμηθήσεται ὁ οἰκογενὴς τῆς οἰκίας σου καὶ ὁ ἀργυρώνητος, καὶ ἔσται ἡ διαθήκη μου ἐπὶ τῆς σαρκὸς ὑμῶν εἰς διαθήκην αἰώνιον. ("And you shall be circumcised in the flesh of your foreskin. . . . He that is born in your house and he that is bought with money shall surely be circumcised, and my covenant shall be on your flesh for an everlasting covenant.") (Gen 17:11, 13)

Paul contends that circumcision served as a "seal" (σφραγίς) that confirms the validity of a reality already present,[149] that is, righteousness through faith.[150] In the ancient world seals were used to certify documents and mark the possession of objects.[151] In this case the seal functions as confirmation[152] or authentication[153] of an already existing condition, Abraham's having been accepted as righteous before God. That this word alludes in some way to Christian baptism[154] seems highly unlikely.[155]

The two purpose clauses of v. 11 draw conclusions that are genuinely "radical,"[156] because in contrast to the long-standing tradition of viewing Abraham as the forefather of the Jewish people, he now becomes the "prototype" of a new group of believers who remain "in uncircumcised foreskin." Abraham is the "father" not just of Jews but also of Gentiles who share his faith.[157] As a parenthetical remark in the middle of the first purpose clause concerning Abraham's paternity, which continues into v. 12, Paul inserts the clause, "that righteousness might be reckoned to them," that is, to the Gentiles. It is unclear whether this is a purpose clause[158] or a result clause[159] or whether it has exactly the same function as the main purpose clause,[160] but its bearing is evident in any case. Abraham's example legitimates the acceptability of Gentiles who have responded to the message of unconditional grace in Christ. They become righteous and are honored before the throne of grace.

■ **12** The parallel to Abraham's paternity of Gentile

146 See Käsemann, 114–15; Klein, "Römer 4," 154–55; Berger, "Abraham," 67; Neubrand, *Abraham*, 222.
147 Ceslas Spicq, "σημεῖον," *TLNT* 3 (1994) 249–50.
148 For example, in the magical papyri, as in *PGM* 4.1263, "But another version has an amulet were there is this sign (τὸ σημεῖον τοῦτο). See also *PGM* 10.22.
149 See BAGD 796.d.2.a; Tim Schramm, "σφραγίς," *EDNT* 3 (1993) 317.
150 See Esler, *Conflict and Identity*, 189. That σφραγίς had been associated with circumcision in the Jewish tradition (see Sanday and Headlam, 107; Michel, 166; Cranfield, 1:236) is visible only in texts from a much later period, as shown by Gottfried Fitzer, "σφραγίς κτλ.," *TDNT* 7 (1971) 949. There is no parallel even from the later period to Paul's contention that circumcision is a seal of "righteousness through faith."
151 Fitzer, "σφραγίς κτλ.," 940–42.
152 See Schlier, 127.
153 Murray, 138.
154 Käsemann, 115; Wilckens, 1:265. The background of later Christian references to baptism as a seal is analyzed by William Heitmüller, "*Sphragis*," in *Neutestamentliche Studien Georg Heinrici zu seinem 70. Geburtstag (14. März 1914)* (Leipzig: Hinrichs, 1914) 40–59.
155 See Dunn, 1:210.
156 Esler, *Conflict and Identity*, 190; see also Adams, "Abraham's Faith," 63–65.
157 For the role of fathers in shaping the identity of their children, see Otto Michel, "πατήρ," *EDNT* 3 (1993) 53–57.
158 Käsemann, 116; Cranfield, 1:237; Wilckens, 1:264–65; Moo, 270; Calvert-Koyzis, *Paul*, 136–37.
159 Godet, 173; Kühl, 139–40; Dunn, 1:210.
160 Neubrand, *Abraham*, 226.

believers in the preceding verse is introduced with καὶ πατέρα περιτομῆς ("and the father of circumcision"), clearly referring to a group with Jewish identity. The sentence is structured by "not only . . . but also," which divides this group of Jews into two parts, and thereon hangs an exegetical impasse. As observed in note k above, translators and commentators silently eliminate the seemingly redundant article in the expression τοῖς στοιχοῦσιν ("to those walking") in v. 12b.[161] James Swetnam argues in contrast that the article is intentional and points to two groups: Jewish Christians whose circumcision was real and Gentile Christians who were granted "circumcision of the heart."[162] This seems implausible because it would require circumcision to be employed in two different senses within the same sentence; moreover, the allusion to circumcision in the last half of v. 12 is the potentially abusive word ἀκροβυστία ("uncircumcised foreskin") rather than a spiritual περιτομὴ καρδίας ("circumcision of the heart," 2:29)[163] that would fit Swetnam's explanation. Maria Neubrand has provided support for the two-group interpretation by showing that the postponed position of "not" in v. 12a, which in ordinary Greek style would precede the dative article τοῖς, is a typical feature of Paul's flexible style, as in 4:4 and 23.[164] Furthermore, in every instance where Paul uses

the "not only" formula, it is followed by the antithesis "but also," which in v. 12 clearly implies two groups with opposing characteristics.[165] Paul contends therefore that Abraham is the father of both groups: those "who are circumcised," that is, Jews, and those "who walk in the steps of the foreskin faith," that is, Gentile believers.[166] While it remains ambiguous in the light of the rest of Paul's argument in Romans that he wishes to emphasize the continued sonship of nonbelieving Jews,[167] it is clear that the main thrust of this argument is to show that believers in Christ are legitimate children of Abraham.[168] Neubrand is consistent in arguing that both groups in v. 12 must be Jewish, because Abraham is here identified as the "father of circumcision," just as he had been identified in the preceding verse as the "father of all who have faith while in uncircumcised foreskin."

However, in view of the epithet "foreskin" employed in v. 12b, whose connotation Neubrand overlooks,[169] there is a need to explain what Jewish Christians in Rome were intended to infer. The reference to the definitive footprints (τοῖς ἴχνεσιν)[170] of Abraham might have been intended to turn the attention of Jewish Christians away from the primacy of circumcision, which established a competitive group identity, and toward the primacy of faith, which would establish a unified group

---

161 See Weiss, 196–99; Sanday and Headlam, 108; Schlier, 128; Cranfield, 1:237; Byrne, 151.

162 James Swetnam, "The Curious Crux at Romans 4:12," *Bib* 61 (1980) 110–15, following Lucien Cerfaux, "Abraham 'père en circoncision' des Gentils (Rom IV,12)," in *Mélanges E. Podechard. Études de sciences religieuses offertes pour son emeritat au doyen honoraire de la Faculté de Theologie de Lyon* (Lyon: Facultes Catholiques, 1945) 57–62; repr. in *Recueil Lucien Cerfaux. Etudes d'exégèse et d'histoire religieuse de Monseigneur Cerfaux réunies à l'occasion de son soixante-dixième anniversaire*, BETL 6-7 (Gembloux: Duculot, 1954, 1962) 2:333–38. Other advocates of a distinction between two groups in 4:12 include Käsemann, 116; Gaston, *Paul*, 124; Fitzmyer, 381–82.

163 See also Neubrand, *Abraham*, 234, 238.

164 Ibid., 234–35.

165 Ibid., 235–36; she also refutes the contention of exegetes (e.g., Cranfield, 1:238; Schlier, 128) who reduce the force of "but" (ἀλλά) to a clarification, because nowhere else in Paul's letters does it have such a limited connotation.

166 See Stowers, *Rereading*, 243–44. Klein, "Römer 4," 157–58, overlooks the social reality of the Roman churches in arguing that Paul wishes to argue against the modern doctrine of salvation history, that is, there is no historical continuity between Abraham and the later emergence of salvation by faith, which means that "the history of Israel is radically desacralized and paganized." See also Klein, "Heil und Geschichte nach Römer IV," *NTS* 13 (1966–67) 45. For a critique of this view see Wilckens, 1:121–23; and Berger, "Abraham," 75–76.

167 It is at any rate clear that Käsemann, 116, misconstrues the thrust of the argument as "only the Christian is the true Jew." See also Godet, 173. Klein, "Römer 4," 156, argues that Paul radically desacralizes both circumcision and Jewish self-identity.

168 Neubrand, *Abraham*, 240–42.

169 Ibid., 242–43.

170 Murray, 139: "we walk, not abreast, but in file, following in the footprints left by Abraham." G. H. R. Horsley discusses the parallel formulation in an altar dedication to the god Men set up "on the footprints (ἐπὶ τὰ ἴχνη) made by the god in the place

identity,[171] thus providing the basis for ameliorating the conflicts between groups in Rome. The concluding words of the pericope sustain this thrust, lifting up the "faith of our father Abraham," whereby the first person plural pronoun would have been understood to include all of the members of the separated house and tenement churches in Rome.[172] In Dunn's formulation, "because faith is the crucial factor, all those who believe as he did are his children, whether circumcised or uncircumcised."[173] The formulation "our father Abraham" seals the new "in-group identity"[174] of those who accept the message that God was and remains the God of the ungodly. Whether they are Jews or Gentiles and no matter what form of boasting they had previously followed, they are now Abraham's children and recipients of the righteousness that comes through faith alone.

where the epiphany occurred" ("τὸ θεῖον," NDIEC 3 [1983] 68, from CMRDM 1. Nr. 85 from the 2d century C.E.).
171 See Colenso, 95.
172 See Dunn, 1:232–33; Murray, 139.
173 Dunn, 1:232–33.
174 Esler, *Conflict and Identity,* 194.

The Second Part of the Fifth Pericope

Abraham and the Righteousness That Comes through Faith

b. **Expansion of the Midrash Showing That Abraham's Promise Comes to Those Who Are Righteous through Faith**

13/ For it was not through a law [that] the promise to Abraham or his offspring [came] that he should inherit the world, but through righteousness of faith. 14/ For if those of the law are the heirs, his faith has been invalidated and the promise was nullified. 15/ For the law produces wrath. But[a] where there is no law, neither [is there] transgression. 16/ Because of this [it is] by faith, in order that[b] according to grace, that the promise might be guaranteed to all the descendants, not only to those of the law but also to those of the faith of Abraham, who is the father of us all, 17/ just as it has been written:
"I have appointed you a father of many nations"
—in the presence of the God in whom he had faith, who gives life to the dead and calls that which does not exist into existence. 18/ In hope beyond hope who had faith that he should become a father of many nations, as he had been told, "So shall your descendants be."[c] 19/ Also not having weakened in[d] faith, he[e] considered his own body already[f] dead, since he was about a hundred years old, [he] also [considered] the deadness of Sarah's womb. 20/ Yet with regard to the promise of God, no doubt made him waver in unfaith, but he was empowered in his faith, giving glory to God, 21/ and[g] fully convinced that the one who had promised is capable also to do [it]. 22/ For this reason "it was[h] reckoned to him as righteousness." 23/ But it was not written, "it was reckoned to him,"[i] for his sake alone 24/ but also for our sake, who were about "to be reckoned" as those having faith in the one who raised Jesus our Lord from the dead,

25/ who was handed over for the sake of our transgressions and was raised for the sake of our rightness.

a In place of δέ ("but") in אֵ* A B C 81 104 436 945(acc. to N-A) 1506 1852 pc vgmss sa bo syhmg arm eth geo Orlat6/7 Thretlem Ambr Aug2/30 Julian-Eclanum Prim, γάρ ("for") appears in אֵ² D F G K L P Ψ 6 69

88 256 263 323 326 330 365 424 459 945(acc. to Swanson) 1175 1241 1243 1319 1505 1573 1735 1739 1836 1874 1881 1912 1962 2127 2200 2344 2464 2495 *Maj Lect* ar b d f g mon o vg syp, h slav Orlat1/7 Chr Cyr Ambst Tyc Aug28/30 Pel. The evidence for the former is considerably stronger, and it is likely that the series of γάρ in preceding verses was assimilated here.

b The provision of the subjunctive verb ᾖ ("it might be"; cf. Moulton and Howard, *Grammar II*, 204 n. 1, for irregular forms of the subjunctive of εἰμί found in the papyri) in A 1505 2495 *pc* is a secondary improvement of the text.

c The completion of the citation from Gen 15:5 in F G 205 209c ar, "as the stars of heaven and the sand of the sea," is clearly the result of later editorial activity.

d The provision of the preposition ἐν ("in") by D* F G is a redundant, editorial improvement, but the English translation requires that we supply an "in" to express the dative of the original text τῇ πίστει ("in/by faith").

e The presence of the negative οὐ by D F G K L P Ψ 33 69 88 104 323 326 330 424* 436 451 459 945 1505 1735 1175 1241 1243 1319c 1852 1874 1881 1912 1962 2200 2344 2464 2492 2495 *Maj Lect* ar b d f g mon² o vgcl syh geo slav Orlat 2/3 Meth Asterius Bas Chr3/4 Ambst Pel Beda, resulting in the translation "he did not consider his body," may be a secondary and inappropriate attempt to improve on the more widely attested version without a negative in אֵ A B C 6 81 256 263 365 424c 1319* 1506 1573 1739 1836 2127 *pc* mon* vgst. ww syp sa bo fay (arm) eth Or gr. lat 1/3 CyrJ Chr1/4 Julian-Eclanum. Cf. Metzger, *Textual Commentary*, 451. The apparent addition of ἀλλά ("but") in sypal is too weakly attested to be considered seriously.

f The absence of ἤδη ("already") in B F G 630 1739 1881 2200 *pc* ar b d f g vg syp, pal sa eth geo1 Orlat 1/4 Meth Asterius Chr Ambst Pel would be difficult to explain if original; on the other hand, "the presence of ἤδη gives the impression of a certain heightening of the account" (Metzger, *Textual Commentary*, 451), suggesting its secondary nature. The square brackets in Nestle-Aland26/27 indicate "the conflict between external evidence and internal considerations" (ibid.), making a choice difficult. Yet the broader textual evidence supports its inclusion in אֵ A C D K L P Ψ 6 33 69 81 88 104 256 263 323 326 330 365 424 436 459 945 1175 1241 1243 1319 1506 1573 1735 1836 1852 1874 1912 2127 2344 2464 2495 *Maj Lect* mon o syh** bo arm geo2 slav Orgr. lat 3/4 Bas CyrJ Epiphvid Julian-Eclanum Beda.

g The absence of καί ("and") in F G latt appears to be an effort to smooth out the text.

h   The presence of καί ("also, and") in ℵ A C D¹ K L P Ψ 6 33 69 81 88 104 256 263 323 326 330 365 424 436 451 459 945 1175 1241 1243 1319 1505 1573 1735 1739 1836 1852 1874 1881 1912 1962 2127 2200 2344 2464 2495 *Maj Lect* ar vg syʰ eth Orˡᵃᵗ Bas Pel Julian-Eclanum is counterbalanced by its absence in B D* F G 365 *pc* b f g mon o syᵖˑ ᵖᵃˡ sa bo arm, with the result that Nestle-Aland²⁶/²⁷ places it in square brackets. That the quotation from Gen 15:6 contains the καί in 4:3 leads one to suspect the word was also assimilated here. See Cranfield, 1:250. *Καί* is also extraneous in the context of 4:22. For these reasons I feel that the absence of καί is more likely to be original.

i   The completion of the citation by the words "for righteousness" in D² 1241 *pc* vgᶜˡ syᵖ is a weakly attested effort to improve the text.

Analysis

The midrashic exegesis that commenced in 4:1-12 continues in vv. 13-25, with citations from Gen 17:5 and 15:5. The center of attention shifts from Abraham to the recipients of the promise[1] given to his descendants. Whereas the key words in the preceding pericope were "work," "circumcision," and "uncircumcision," the theme here shifts to the "promise" (ἐπαγγελία, 4 times; "to promise," ἐπαγγέλλομαι, once) of an "inheritance" (κληρονόμος, twice) granted to Abraham and his "seed/offspring" (σπέρμα, 3 times) regardless of their relation to the "law" (νόμος, 5 times).[2] The themes of "righteousness" (δικαιοσύνη, twice) granted to "all" (πᾶς, twice) who have "faith" (πίστις, 5 times; "having faith," πιστεύειν, 3 times) are continued from the previous pericope. The argument is structured around a thesis statement in 4:13[3] that is developed negatively by two enthymemes in vv. 14-15 and positively on the basis of scriptural citations in vv. 16-22. The conclusion that Christ believers are the recipients of Abraham's promise is then drawn in vv. 23-25.

There are occasional rhetorical flourishes in this pericope, including the Hebraic parallelism in v. 14b-c, the polyptoton in the phrase "in hope beyond hope" in v. 18,[4] the antithetical correspondence between "weakening in faith" in v. 19a and "strengthened in faith" in v. 20a, the symmetrical balance of vv. 23, 24a, and 24b, the parallelism in v. 14b and c as well as v. 25a and b,[5] and the paronomastic series with "promise" in vv. 13, 14, 16, 20, and 21.[6] There is also an effective homoioteleuton in the genitive plural endings of the final three lines of this passage (vv. 24b, 25a, 25b). In addition to the clausula in v. 25[7] with synthetic parallelism between two passive verbs followed by διά phrases,[8] these rhetorical features provide a compelling conclusion to the first proof that began in 1:18.[9]

There is considerable debate about how this pericope should be divided, with Kühl, Lagrange, Schlatter, Nygren, and Wilckens arguing for vv. 13-16 as an independent section, while Barth, Schmidt, Michel, Kuss, and Louw hold vv. 13-17 together and Käsemann argues for a break in the middle of v. 17.[10] Many other commentators discern no break at all between vv. 12 and 13, and prefer to view the entire chapter as a single pericope.[11] I would contend instead that the section of vv. 13-25 constitutes a single pericope[12] that elaborates the theme of Abraham's promise, with vv. 14-15 arguing against the law as the key to the promise and vv. 16-22 arguing for faith as the key to the promise. The conclusion about Christ believers as the true recipients of Abraham's promise, the main contention of this pericope, is developed in vv. 23-25. This section serves as a kind of *transitus* from the first proof to the second proof

---

1   See Käsemann, 118.
2   See Neubrand, *Abraham*, 246.
3   See Schmidt, 83; Schlier, 128; Kuss, 1:188.
4   See Bullinger, *Figures*, 282.
5   See Weiss, "Beiträge," 224–25.
6   See Harvey, *Listening*, 188. Less convincing are the suggestions of rhythmic and chiastic structures in 4:16-10 by J. Smit Sibinga, "*Serta Paulina.* On Composition Technique in Paul," *FilN* 10.19-20 (1997) 40–44.
7   See Holloway, "Paul's Pointed Prose," 47–48.
8   See Popkes, *Christus Traditus*, 93–94; Dodd, 70; Michel, 174–75; Dunn, 1:225.
9   See Weiss, "Beiträge," 172.
10 See Käsemann, 118, for an identification of this disagreement. See also Sass, *Verheißungen*, 386–88.
11 Dunn, 1:196–98; Murray, 127, 140: "At verse 13 there is no break in the argument."
12 See also Jülicher, 253; Byrne, 152; Fitzmyer, 383–84; Haacker, 105–6; Neubrand, *Abraham*, 246–47. Moo, 271–73, argues that vv. 13-22 constitute a single pericope.

that begins in 5:1.[13] The pericope closes with a confessional formulation that brings to a climax the entire first proof, confirming the thesis of 1:16-17 that the gospel of Christ crucified and resurrected conveys the righteousness of God.

Rhetorical Disposition

IV.	The *Probatio*
1:18–4:25	A. The first proof: The gospel expresses the impartial righteousness of God by overturning claims of cultural superiority and by setting right Jews and Gentiles through grace alone
4:1-25	5. Abraham and the righteousness that comes through faith: part two
4:13-25	b. Expansion of the midrash showing that Abraham's promise comes to those who are righteous through faith
4:13	1) The thesis about the promise given to Abraham
	a) Not through the law
	b) But through faith
4:14-15	2) The negative qualification of the scriptural promise
4:14	a) The first enthymeme
4:14a	(1) The unreal condition of law adherents as inheritors
4:14b-c	(2) The impossible consequences
4:14b	(a) The faith emptied
4:14c	(b) The promise voided
4:15	b) The second enthymeme
4:15a	(1) The premise of law producing wrath
4:15b	(2) The inference: no law, no transgression
4:16-22	3) The positive qualification of the scriptural promise
4:16a	a) The positive contention: "from faith"
4:16b	b) The clarification of faith in relation to the promise
4:16c	(1) Definition of faith as consistent with grace
4:16d-e	(2) The promise to all of Abraham's descendants
4:16d	(a) Jewish descendants under the law
4:16d	(b) Gentile descendants sharing Abraham's faith
4:16e	(3) The definition of Abraham as "father of us all"
4:17a-b	c) The Scripture proof
4:17a	(1) The citation formula
4:17b	(2) The citation of Gen 17:5 concerning Abraham as "father of many nations"
4:17c-18a	d) The clarification of Abraham's faith
4:17c-e	(1) Abraham's relation to God
4:17c	(a) Abraham's faith in God
4:17d	(b) God defined as resurrecting the dead
4:17e	(c) God defined as creating from nothing
4:18a	(2) The quality of Abraham's faith
	(a) Abraham's "hope beyond hope"
	(b) Abraham's faith that he would become a "father of many nations"
4:18b-c	e) The Scripture proof
4:18b	(1) The citation formula
4:18c	(2) The citation of Gen 15:5 concerning Abraham's "descendants"
4:19-22	f) The strength of Abraham's faith
4:19	(1) No weakening because of old age
4:20-21	(2) No doubt that God was capable of fulfilling the promise
4:22	(3) The consequence drawn from Gen 15:6 concerning the reckoning of "righteousness"
4:23-25	4) Conclusion that Christ believers are the recipients of Abraham's promise
4:23	a) The negative contention: the reckoning of righteousness was not intended for Abraham alone
4:24a	b) The positive contention: the reckoning was for the sake of Christ believers
4:24b-25	c) The credal definition of faith
4:24b	(1) Faith in God who raised Jesus
4:25a	(2) Faith in Jesus, who died for transgressions
4:25b	(3) Faith in Jesus' resurrection to make right

Exegesis

■ **13** With a formulation that begins in the same way as the thesis statement of 1:16-17, οὐ γάρ ("for not"),[14] Paul articulates an antithetical thesis about Abraham's promise.[15] Four crucial terms appear in this thesis that had not been mentioned in the preceding pericope, but

---

13   Campbell, "3.27–4.25," 373.
14   The expression οὐ γάρ ("for not") appears 17 times in Romans, but never elsewhere than in 1:16 and 4:13 to introduce a thesis. The phrase is common in rhetoric, appearing almost 500 times in Demosthenes alone.
15   So far as I can tell, Schlier, 128, is alone among commentators in correctly identifying this statement as a thesis, but he does not show the development of the thesis through to the end of the chapter, perceiving a break at v. 17a.

that arise from the Abraham example that Paul wishes to develop: "law," "promise," "seed," and "inheritance." It is therefore not plausible to explain the "for" as if Paul were simply substantiating a point from the preceding argument.[16] The contention that Abraham's promise did not come διὰ νόμου ("through a law")[17] implies an antithesis between legalistic obedience and righteousness through faith that reaches back to 3:27-31[18] and indeed clear back to the dominant thesis of the letter in 1:16-17. Byrne accurately discerns the logical requirement of this pericope in the development of Paul's first proof: "Paul has to cut the nexus between promise and obedience"[19] that was presupposed in the traditional view of Abraham as the father of those committed to the Torah.[20]

The word ἐπαγγελία appears for the first time in Romans to refer to the "promise" given to Abraham. Although Paul consistently employs this term in reference to God's "promises granted to the patriarchs" (Rom 15:8; see also Rom 9:4, 8-9; Gal 3:14, 16, 18-29; 4:23, 28), the OT does not employ this term at all.[21] It originates as a Greek term for announcing something, offering to do something, or claiming to have carried out what was announced,[22] and develops as a technical term for divine promises within Hellenistic Jewish writings. For example, 3 Macc 2:10-11 refers to the faithfulness of God in the following manner: "And out of love

for the house of Israel, you promised (ἐπηγγείλω) that should we fall away from you and become afflicted and then come to this house and pray, you would hear our prayer. Verily you are faithful and true." Ps. Sol. 12.6 prays, "And may the Lord's devout inherit the Lord's promises (κληρονομήσαισαν ἐπαγγελίας)." The context of patriarchal promises is illustrated by T. Jos. 20.1, "God will work vengeance on your behalf and will lead you into the promises made to your fathers."

The content of Abraham's promise is formulated with seemingly grandiose dimensions: "that he should inherit the world." Klaus Haacker notes how astounding this would have sounded in Rome, which claimed rule over the entire world, but that there were precedents in the Sermon on the Mount for a "nonpolitical and at any event nonmilitary" form of imperialism: "blessed are the meek, for they shall inherit the earth" (Matt 5:5).[23] Most commentators either spiritualize this grandiosity by reference to the eschatological future[24] or explain it as an expression of Jewish messianic hopes,[25] but there are indications elsewhere in Paul's letters that a new form of inheriting the world was in view. The present tense verb in 1 Cor 3:21-23 makes clear that he considers this inheritance to be a matter of current experience among converts: "For all things are yours (πάντα γὰρ ὑμῶν ἐστιν), whether Paul or Apollos or Cephas or the world (εἴτε

---

16 Schmidt, 82; Morris, 205.
17 The anarthrous prepositional phrase διὰ νόμου ("through a law") occurs elsewhere in Rom 2:12; 3:27; 7:7; Gal 2:19, 21; and in the odd expression διὰ νόμου ἐλευθερίας ("through a law of freedom") in Jas 2:12. The only example in pre-Christian literature is in Sch. Dem. 24.8.2.
18 See Wilckens, 1:268; Campbell, "3.27–4.2," 370.
19 Byrne, 152; Gaston, Paul, 45–63, rejects this interpretation.
20 See Schmitz, "Abraham," 99–116. A Stoic form of this traditional view is advocated by Engberg-Pedersen, Stoics, 220–21, that salvation is gained by "the proper kind of directedness towards God" that overcomes selfishness and generates "proper 'ethical' behavior" (italics in original).
21 Julius Schniewind and Gerhard Friedrich, "ἐπαγγέλλω κτλ.," TDNT 2 (1964) 579: "This word has no preliminary history in the OT."
22 Ibid., 576–79; BAGD (2000) 356.
23 Haacker, 106. Dunn, 1:213, speaks of the "a-territor-

ial" definition of inheritance, referring to Davies, Land, 179. Kenneth E. Bailey takes the same line in "St. Paul's Understanding of the Territorial Promise of God to Abraham. Romans 4:13 in Its Historical and Theological Context," NESTR 15 (1994) 68–69. O'Neill, 8, admits: "The inheritance of the world is extraordinarily difficult" (italics in original).
24 Käsemann, 120: "The earthly promise is applied apocalyptically to the future world." See also Weiss, 199; Kühl, 143; Schmidt, 83; Zeller, 101; Wilckens, 1:269–70; Morris, 206.
25 Michel, 168; Schlier, 129; Moo, 274; Murray, 142. Stuhlmacher, 73, cites Jub. 22.14, that Abraham's descendants "will rule over all nations as they desire." Rudolf Pesch follows this line in "Erbe der Welt' (Röm 4,14). Zur Weitung der Landverheißung im Neuen Testament," in C. Mayer, K. Müller, and G. Schmalenberg, eds., Nach den Anfängen Fragen. Herrn Prof. Dr. theol. Gerhard Dautzenberg zum 60. Geburtstag am 30. Januar 1994, GSTR 8 (Giessen: Fachbereich Evangelische Theologie und Katholische Theologie

---

κόσμος) or life or death or the present or the future, all are yours, and you are Christ's, and Christ is God's."[26]

In Rom 8 Paul will claim that the entire creation waits with eager longing for the "revelation of the sons of God," who as we shall see would take responsibility for the polluted world. "May God's kingdom come" was part of the prayer every early Christian probably prayed daily, in the firm belief that the new social order in their love feasts was the harbinger thereof. Their inheritance of the world had ready begun, "but through righteousness of faith." The ἀλλά ("but") in this formulation needs to be taken with full seriousness, not merely as a theological antithesis between justification by faith and justification through works,[27] but as an allusion to a new social reality of a community that is granted righteous status by faith in the gospel.[28] This inheritance comes "not through the law" but "through righteousness of faith," which defines the new basis on which the community of inheritors functions. Gentile believers as well as Jewish believers qualify as inheritors in equal measure[29] within this new community based on grace rather than law. Paul and other early Christian thinkers are really articulating a new social order, based not on force but on persuasion, not on dominance but on cooperation, with an ethic of responsibility rather than of exploitation. This powerful thesis is developed and substantiated through the rest of the pericope.

■ **14** In an "if clause" indicating what would logically follow provided the condition were real,[30] Paul opens an enthymeme that shows the promise could not have been restricted to those obeying the law. The negative defini-tion of the κληρονόμοι ("inheritors") is taken up first, with good reason. The Jewish interpretation of the Abrahamic inheritance concentrated on adherence to the law, and it is likely that the phrase οἱ ἐκ νόμου ("those of the law") is the technical expression in Judaism for "the sons of the Torah" (בני התורה).[31] As cited above, *Ps. Sol.* 12.6 makes a typical claim that the pious alone will be the inheritors of the promise.[32] Philo's treatise on *Who Is the Heir?* contends that Abraham received the inheritance because he neglected none of the commandments[33] and that the wise ones will share this inheritance through adherence to the Torah[34] and the attainment of higher wisdom accessible in the scripture.[35] Since Gentile proselytes could also become "sons of the law," it is inappropriate to conclude that Paul's primary interest here is to overcome the ethnic prerogative with regard to the promise.[36]

If adherents to the law are the heirs, Paul argues, two negative consequences would follow. These are drawn as inferences from the "if" clause at the beginning of this short enthymeme. In contending that the faith would be emptied, Paul employs the perfect passive verb κεκένωται ("has been invalidated") in combination with the definite article attached to the subject, both of which make clear that Abraham's faith is in view.[37] I therefore translate ἡ πίστις with a weak possessive as "his faith," which would be rendered empty if Abraham had qualified for righteousness by performing works of the law.[38] The verb κενόω appears here with the sense of "reduce to nothing,"[39] as in the second-century C.E. astronomer, Vettius Valens *Auth.* 90.7: "The ruler over acquisition

---

	und deren Didaktik, 1994) 514–19. See also *Jub.* 17.3; 32.19; Sir 44:21; *1 En.* 5.7; *4 Ezra* 7.59; for general background see Hester, *Inheritance*, 22–36.
26	See Cranfield, 1:240; Bandstra, *Law and the Elements*, 54.
27	Kuss, 1:188; Wilckens, 1:270.
28	See von Dobbeler, *Glaube als Teilhabe*, 137, 143–45.
29	Neubrand, *Abraham*, 254–56.
30	See BDF §372; BAGD (2000) 277; Moo, 274.
31	Michel, 168; Dunn, 1:213. Moo, 275, overlooks this background.
32	See Werner Foerster, "κλῆρος κτλ.," *TDNT* 3 (1965) 779–85; Johannes H. Friedrich, "κληρονόμος," *EDNT* 2 (1991) 298, cites LXX Dan 12:13; *1 En.* 39.8; 71.16.
33	Philo *Her.* 9.
34	Philo *Her.* 161–93.
35	Philo *Her.* 313–16.
36	Dunn, 1:213–14, refers to the "ethnic force" of the expression "those of the law." See also the similar views of Klein, "Römer 4," 158–59; van der Minde, *Schrift*, 88; Watson, *Paul*, 141–42; and the refutation of this ethnic interpretation by Neubrand, *Abraham*, 258–61.
37	Dunn, 1:214: "The reference to Gen 15:6 is clear." See also Wilckens, 1:270. Most commentators, however, simply eliminate the article, thus generalizing the point about faith; Meyer, 1:206; Sanday and Headlam, 109; Barrett, 94; Morris, 205; Zeisler, 130; Fitzmyer, 385; Stuhlmacher, 74; Byrne, 151; Moo, 275.
38	See Campbell, "3.27–4.2," 371; also Albrecht

standing in diametrical opposition to acquisitions brings possessions to nought ($\tau\hat{\omega}\ \pi\epsilon\rho\iota\pi\sigma\iota\acute{\eta}\mu\alpha\tau\iota\ \kappa\epsilon\nu\sigma\hat{\iota}\ \tau\grave{\alpha}\varsigma\ \acute{\nu}\pi\acute{\alpha}\rho\xi\epsilon\iota\varsigma$)." This verb is a favorite of Paul,[40] who argues elsewhere that eloquent preaching would "empty ($\kappa\epsilon\nu\omega\vartheta\hat{\eta}$) the cross of Christ" (1 Cor 1:17) and who insists that "no one will invalidate ($\sigma\grave{\nu}\delta\epsilon\grave{\iota}\varsigma\ \kappa\epsilon\nu\acute{\omega}\sigma\epsilon\iota$)" his claim of having preached the gospel free of charge (1 Cor 9:15).[41] In Phil 2:7 he cites the hymn that proclaims the self-emptying ($\grave{\epsilon}\alpha\nu\tau\grave{\sigma}\nu\ \grave{\epsilon}\kappa\acute{\epsilon}\nu\omega\sigma\epsilon\nu$) of Christ's transcendent status in the incarnation. In the context of this extended midrash, what is emptied is nothing less than the faith that God ascribed as righteous in the citation from Gen 15:6.

There is no doubt that "the promise" in Paul's statement of the second negative consequence is that given to Abraham and his heirs (4:13) who are accepted by God as righteous regardless of their qualifications.[42] The verb $\kappa\alpha\tau\alpha\rho\gamma\acute{\epsilon}\omega$ is used here as in 3:3 and 31 with the sense of "nullify" or "render inactive."[43] While no other example of this verb in connection with "promise" has been found,[44] Stowers offers the translation, "God's promise is unkept,"[45] and Godet explains that the promise would "be paralyzed in its effects."[46] If the

promise were restricted to those who conform to the Torah, it would no longer be valid for "the ungodly" (4:5) whom Abraham's God wished to welcome. The predominance of grace would then be abrogated,[47] a theme to be elaborated in detail later in this pericope.

■ **15** The second enthymeme begins with a premise concerning the law, followed by an inference about the absence of the accusation of transgressions when law is absent. The article with law ($\acute{o}\ \gamma\grave{\alpha}\rho\ \nu\acute{\sigma}\mu\sigma\varsigma$) points clearly to the Torah,[48] and it is equally clear that the $\grave{\sigma}\rho\gamma\acute{\eta}$ ("wrath") is God's wrath,[49] just as in the earlier references in 1:18; 2:5, 8; 3:5. Having shown in 1:18-32 and 2:5-6 that God's wrath is directed against those who perform evil works, Paul states his major premise in a highly condensed manner that functions as a kind of "combat slogan" in opposition to the premise of Judaism that law produces life.[50] That law "produces" ($\kappa\alpha\tau\epsilon\rho\gamma\acute{\alpha}\zeta\epsilon\tau\alpha\iota$)[51] wrath effectively covers the minor premise that is missing in this enthymeme: first comes the law, then the transgression, then the response of divine wrath.[52] The absent minor premise would have been presupposed by Paul's audience. It is stated in typical form in Greek text of *Apoc. Mos.* 14.3, in which Adam tells Eve, "Call all our

Oepke, "$\kappa\epsilon\nu\acute{o}\varsigma\ \kappa\tau\lambda.$," *TDNT* 3 (1965) 662: "if the people of the Law are heirs, this logically implies the invalidation of faith as a principle of salvation."

39 Ceslas Spicq, "$\kappa\epsilon\nu\acute{o}\varsigma$," *TLNT* 2 (1994) 309; this connotation is related to the basic meaning of $\kappa\epsilon\nu\acute{o}\omega$ "to empty, evacuate" as in emptying a city of its inhabitants (Josephus *Bell.* 1.355; *Ant.* 2.457) or a cistern of its water (Josephus *Ant.* 3.186). See also Michael Lattke, "$\kappa\epsilon\nu\acute{o}\varsigma$," *EDNT* 2 (1991) 281.

40 See Spicq, "$\kappa\epsilon\nu\acute{o}\varsigma$," 308–9.

41 In "'Vergeblich' als Missionsergebnis bei Paulus," in J. Jervell and W. A. Meeks, eds., *God's Christ and His People. Essays in Honor of Nils Alstrup Dahl* (Oslo: Universitetsforlaget, 1977) 179–83, Carl J. Bjerkelund points to Isa 29:8; 45:18; 65:23; Hab 2:3 as important precedents to Paul's use of "empty" in missionary contexts, but there is no evidence that "eschatological seriousness" (188) is emphasized in Rom 4:14.

42 Meyer, 1:207; Neubrand, *Abraham*, 260.

43 See Gerhard Delling, "$\grave{\alpha}\rho\gamma\acute{o}\varsigma,\ \grave{\alpha}\rho\gamma\acute{\epsilon}\omega,\ \kappa\alpha\tau\alpha\rho\gamma\acute{\epsilon}\omega$," *TDNT* 1 (1964) 453; Hans Hübner, "$\kappa\alpha\tau\alpha\rho\gamma\acute{\epsilon}\omega$," *EDNT* 2 (1991) 267–68; MM 331; Kenneth W. Clark, "The Meaning of $\grave{\epsilon}\nu\epsilon\rho\gamma\acute{\epsilon}\omega$ and $\kappa\alpha\tau\alpha\rho\gamma\acute{\epsilon}\omega$ in the New Testament," in *The Gentile Bias and Other Essays* (Leiden: Brill, 1980) 191: "to render powerless."

44 Other verbs are employed to convey the idea of voiding promises, such as Polybius's description in *Hist.* 30.3.7 of the Senate's "having broken its promise ($\grave{\alpha}\vartheta\epsilon\tau\eta\sigma\alpha\sigma\alpha\ \tau\grave{\eta}\nu\ \grave{\epsilon}\pi\alpha\gamma\gamma\epsilon\lambda\acute{\iota}\alpha\nu$)," or Epictetus's reference in *Diss.* 4.8.6 to someone who did "not fulfill the promise ($\tau\grave{o}\ \mu\grave{\eta}\ \pi\lambda\eta\rho\sigma\hat{\nu}\nu\ \tau\grave{\eta}\nu\ \grave{\epsilon}\pi\alpha\gamma\gamma\epsilon\lambda\acute{\iota}\alpha\nu$)" of being a philosopher.

45 Stowers, *Rereading*, 246, cited with approval by Neubrand, *Abraham*, 260.

46 Godet, 177; see also Schlier, 130.

47 See Barrett, 95; Morris, 206; Westerholm, *Law*, 113.

48 See Godet, 177; Dunn, 1:214–15. That $\acute{o}\ \nu\acute{o}\mu\sigma\varsigma$ at this point refers to law in general is unconvincingly argued by Zahn, 228; Weiss, 201–2; and Winger, *Law*, 83–84, 162.

49 Meyer, 1:207; Murray, 143; Fitzmyer, 385.

50 Michel, 169; see also Rudolf Pesch, "$\grave{\sigma}\rho\gamma\acute{\eta}$," *EDNT* 2 (1991) 530.

51 See Georg Bertram, "$\kappa\alpha\tau\epsilon\rho\gamma\acute{\alpha}\zeta\sigma\mu\alpha\iota$," *TDNT* 3 (1965) 635; the present tense of the verb in this verse has a "gnomic sense" that describes what law "generally" accomplishes, according to Moo, 276.

52 Kuss, 1:188; Michel, 169; Käsemann, 121. Murray, 143, and Moo, 276–77, attempt to fill in the missing step or steps in this argument, focusing attention on the issue of universal wrath or the function of the

children and our children's children, and tell them how we transgressed."[53] Paul is not interested in developing a comprehensive doctrine of the law at this point.[54] His interest centers on the question in v. 13 whether the promise comes through law or through faith.[55]

The antithetical premise of the inference in the second enthymeme is indicated by δέ, which in this context has the sense of "but" rather than "and" or "now."[56] Paul employs the technique of "contrary argument" (ἐναντία),[57] which was defined by Aristotle as follows: "One topic of enthymemes is that from opposites (ἐκ τοῦ ἐναντίων); for one should look to see if the opposite [predicate] is true of the opposite [subject], [thus] refuting the argument if it is not, confirming it if it is."[58]

Rather than drawing an inference from the presence of the law, as might have been expected from v. 15a, Paul formulates its logical opposite in v. 15b, "where there is no law," to draw the conclusion he desires. With elegant brevity that marks an effective enthymeme, he infers that where law is absent, "neither" is there "transgression" (οὐδὲ παράβασις). As in 2:23, "transgression" is the violation of law, which follows the usage of Hellenistic Judaism.[59] For example, Josephus speaks of

"transgressing the laws" (παράβασις τῶν νόμων) or "transgressing the laws of the fathers" (παράβασις τῶν πατρίων νομίμων).[60] The argumentative bearing of this inference is not the "truism" that there can be no transgression if there is no law.[61] Paul's point concerns the heirs of Abraham's promise: if legal obedience were required, then "ungodly" Gentiles (4:4, 11-12) would by definition be excluded. As Fitzmyer says, Paul is contending that "the world needs a dispensation independent of law."[62] The dispensation of grace promised to Abraham's heirs overcomes transgressions and places both Jewish and Gentile believers on the same footing.[63]

■ 16 Paul turns to the positive definition of Abraham's promise as the logical consequence of the two preceding enthymemes. The transitional phrase διὰ τοῦτο ("because of this") refers to the preceding argument,[64] with the preposition employed as a "marker of something constituting cause, the reason why something happens, results, exists."[65] In a shorthand formulation without subject or verb that is nevertheless perfectly understandable within the context of this argument, Paul contends that the fulfillment[66] of Abraham's promise (which is the subject of this paragraph in 4:13)

---

law rather than the question of who inherits the promise.

53 Cited by Michael Wolter, "παράβασις κτλ.," *EDNT* 3 (1991) 14.

54 Dunn, 1:215.

55 Neubrand, *Abraham*, 261; Dunn, 1:215.

56 BAGD (2000) 213.4d, "introducing an apodosis after a hypothetical or temporal protasis." For an argument in favor of "and," see Godet, 177, and Moo, 276, neither of whom appears to understand the contrary argument employed here.

57 See Anders Eriksson, "Contrary Arguments in Paul's Letters," in S. E. Porter and D. L. Stamps, eds., *Rhetorical Criticism and the Bible*, JSNTSup 195 (Sheffield: Sheffield Academic Press, 2002) 338–45.

58 Aristotle *Rhet.* 2.23.1, cited by Eriksson, "Contrary Arguments," 341. See also Brandenburger, *Adam und Christus*, 183, on Paul's use of *argumentum e contrario*.

59 Wolter, "παράβασις κτλ.," 14; Johannes Schneider, "παραβαίνω κτλ.," *TDNT* 5 (1967) 738–39.

60 Josephus speaks in an historical context of Onias's being blamed for the "sin and transgression of the law (τὴν ἁμαρτίαν καὶ τὴν τοῦ νόμου παράβασιν)" in *Ant.* 13.69. In *Ant.* 18.268 the concept of transgression of law (παράβασιν τοῦ νομίμου) is

combined with incurring God's wrath (ἅμα πολλὴν ὀργὴν τοῦ θεοῦ). See also *Ant.* 3.218; 9.243; 18.81, etc.

61 See Moo, 277; Schmidt, 84. The Latin formula sometimes cited to illustrate this point, *nulla poena sine lege* ("no punishment without law"), is a principle first enunciated by legal scholars during the European Enlightenment, as shown by Brandenburger, *Adam und Christus*, 195.

62 Fitzmyer, 385; see also Weiss, 202.

63 See Neubrand, *Abraham*, 262–64.

64 As Cranfield, 1:241–42, observes, two-thirds of the διὰ τοῦτο phrases in the Pauline letters refer to the previous argument; Weiss, 292, Kuss, 1:189, Moo, 277, and others properly see this as a reference to 4:14-15. O'Neill, 88, and Neubrand, *Abraham*, 266, see a reference to 4:13-15, while Meyer, 1:208, Wilckens, 1:271, and Murray, 144, limit the reference to 4:15. That διὰ τοῦτο refers forward to the "in order that" clause of v. 16 (Cranfield, 1:241; Moo, 277) is highly unlikely in view of the argumentative structure of this pericope.

65 BAGD (2000) 225.B.2, describing διά with the accusative.

66 See Godet, 178; Kühl, 145; Wilckens, 1:271; Fitzmyer, 385. Following Käsemann, 121, Moo, 277,

comes ἐκ πίστεως ("by faith"). This formula harks back to the thesis of Romans drawn from Hab 2:4, that "the righteous shall live ἐκ πίστεως (1:17), which was elaborated in 3:25-30 and 4:5-12. As a formula, this phrase is distinctively Pauline. While πίστις and its Latin equivalent *fiducia* were used to refer to acceptance of religious propaganda,[67] no other examples of Paul's formulaic use have been found.[68] Early Christianity shared with Paul the "missionary language" that featured "πιστ- as a central term in the sense of conversion,"[69] so the succinct formula employed here without a full sentence structure would have been easily understood. The preposition ἐκ occurs here as a "marker denoting origin, cause, motive, reason," and in this case more specifically, "the reason which is a presupposition for something."[70] "By faith" is not an abstract theological principle,[71] but rather a reference to conversion as the origin of a new, honorable status, of which Abraham in this chapter is cited as the prime example.[72] The formula alludes to the path whereby believers can be declared righteous and join the community of the elect in accordance with Abraham's promise.[73] As we have seen throughout Romans, faith has to do with participation in a new spiritual and social reality through acceptance of the gospel of God's righteousness made present in the Christ event.[74]

The purpose clause that again lacks a verb or subject, ἵνα κατὰ χάριν ("in order that according to grace") explains the preceding word, "faith,"[75] and should be understood in a final, purposive sense.[76] Faith is not a virtue or, despite the tendencies of the interpretive tradition, a theological accomplishment. It is defined by grace, that is, by access to God that is granted without prior conditions.[77] The promise given to Abraham was a matter of sheer grace, which came without any virtuous preparation on his part, and the heirs of his promise gain access to God's righteous presence only through grace. Their faith is nothing more than the acceptance of this unearned honor. With this thought, Paul reinterprets the Abraham story in the light of salvation through grace as experienced by believers in Christ.[78]

If faith remains the main characteristic of Abraham's promise, it seems likely that the next clause should also be understood as final[79] rather than consecutive.[80] The nature of faith is such that "that the promise might be guaranteed (εἰς τὸ εἶναι βεβαίαν τὴν ἐπαγγελίαν) to all the descendants." The word "promise" is com-

---

refers to the "promised inheritance." Meyer, 1:208; Sanday and Headlam, 112; Lagrange, 94; Barrett, 95–96; and Cranfield, 1:242, believe that the divine purpose of salvation is the subject.

67 See Rudolf Bultmann, "πιστεύω κτλ.," *TDNT* 6 (1968) 181–82; for example, when Lucius is initiated into the Isis mysteries, he says, "I was illumined by the nocturnal mysteries of the foremost god, and in full faith (*plena iam fiducia*) practiced the holy service of this religion" (Apuleias *Metam.* 11.28). *Odes Sol.* 34.6 assures converts, "Grace is revealed to your redemption. Believe, and you shall live and be redeemed."

68 With a completely different connotation, ἐκ πίστεως was used by the second-century C.E. philosopher Sextus Empiricus in *Pyr.* 2.141.4 and *Math.* 3.308 in reference to "those who think they depend upon trust (ἐκ πίστεως) and memory."

69 Dieter Lührmann, "Faith," *ABD* 2 (1992) 753; see also Bultmann, "πιστεύω κτλ.," 208–20, dealing with, inter alia, faith as "Acceptance of the Kerygma."

70 BAGD (2000) 296–97.

71 Bultmann, "πιστεύω κτλ.," 213; Schlier, 131: "the principle of divine action," criticized by Wilckens, 1:271.

72 Lührmann, "Faith," 754.

73 Neubrand, *Abraham*, 267.

74 See von Dobbeler, *Glaube als Teilhabe*, 138, 275–77.

75 See Meyer, 1:298; Murray, 144: "faith and grace cohere; law and the promised inheritance are contradictory."

76 Wilckens, 1:271; Dunn, 1:216; Neubrand, *Abraham*, 267; see BDF §269.

77 See Klaus Berger, "χάρις," *EDNT* 3 (1993) 458–59; also Gary S. Shogren, "Grace," *ABD* 2 (1992) 1087: "grace must be undeserved."

78 See Dieter Sänger, "Gnade/Gnade Gottes. III. Neues Testament," *RGG⁴* 3 (2000) 1026, referring to Rom 3:24 as a key to understanding 4:16.

79 See Zahn, 230; Michel, 170; Dunn, 1:216; Albrecht Oepke, "εἰς," *TDNT* 2 (1964) 430; Neubrand, *Abraham*, 268.

80 Käsemann, 121, proposes a consecutive sense, "offering a conclusion" for the argument; see also Wilckens, 1:271. This has the effect of making v. 16c-f the main point of Paul's discourse, rather than understanding it as a further elaboration of "faith" in v. 16a.

bined here with an expression that forms the opposite to "nullify" in v. 14.[81] The word βέβαιος could have the meaning "firm in the sense of being solidly grounded,"[82] but the sense of a "legally guaranteed security" as suggested by Deissmann seems more appropriate.[83] In a first-century contract, for example, the typical legal language is employed: "the lease may remain guaranteed [βεβαία] to us for a period of five years without change."[84] In a political context a similar formulation appeared in Emperor Claudius's letter to the Alexandrians: "I guarantee to the ephebes the right to the Alexandrine city."[85] There are numerous examples of this formulation that guarantees the reliability of commitments and promises.[86] In Spicq's explanation, this verse contends that "the divine promise is not only firm and immutable, not only assured for all posterity, but it is guaranteed to them."[87] Only a system of salvation by grace alone can provide such a guarantee, because if "those of the law are the inheritors" (4:14), the fulfillment of the promise is dependent upon their performance. The promise to Abraham's descendants, however, rests with God and not with human frailties. In Philo's view this kind of reliability is characteristic of all of God's promises: "it is because of God that the oath is guaranteed (ὁ ὅρκος βέβαιος)."[88]

The innovation in Paul's interpretation is that the promise was not merely guaranteed by God, which would conform to the conviction of Philo and most other adherents of the biblical faith, but "to *all* the descendants."[89] That Abraham's promise remained valid for the Jewish people was widely believed. For example, even after Israel violated its covenant by worshiping the golden calf, Moses was able to appeal successfully to God's abiding promise:[90] "Remember Abraham, Isaac, and Israel, your servants, to whom you swore by your own self, and said to them, 'I will multiply your descendants . . . and all this land that I have promised, I will give to your descendants, and they shall inherit it forever.' And the Lord repented of the evil that he thought to do to his people" (Exod 32:13-14). Despite some interpreters who believe that Paul eliminates Jews from Abraham's promise,[91] Paul's revolutionary stress is on πᾶν τὸ σπέρμα ("all the descendants"), which in one way or another includes Jewish as well as Gentile believers.[92] Grace is thereby "democratized."[93]

The word πᾶς ("all") is crucial for Romans, having been employed nineteen times already in the letter, including the close parallel in 4:11 referring to Abraham as the "father of all who believe." The opening lines of the letter feature this inclusive emphasis, addressed to "all those in Rome beloved of God" (1:7), praying for "all of you" (1:8), and serving a mission aimed at the obedience of faith among "all the Gentiles" (1:5), that offers salvation "to all who believe" (1:16). So in this chapter the "righteousness of faith" (4:13) in Abraham's promise establishes an inclusivity of all faithful people, no matter what their ethnic or religious status might be. This is driven home by the "not only . . . but also" phrases that follow in v. 16.

The antithesis between "those of the law" and "those

81 See Schmidt, 84; Wilckens, 1:271; Dunn, 1:216; Neubrand, *Abraham*, 268.

82 Heinrich Schlier, "βέβαιος κτλ.," *TDNT* 1 (1964) 602; see also Alfred Fuchs, "βέβαιος κτλ.," *EDNT* 1 (1990) 211.

83 Deissmann, *Bible Studies*, 104–9, cited by MM 107 and accepted by Dunn, 1:216.

84 *P.Amh.* 2.85.21 cited by MM 107; see also *BGU* IV.1116.34; 1127.16; *OGIS* 669.25.

85 *P.Lond.* 1912.54, cited by Ceslas Spicq, "βέβαιος κτλ.," *TLNT* 1 (1994) 281.

86 See Spicq, "βέβαιος κτλ.," 280–81. For example, Diodorus Siculus *Hist.* 1.5.3, declares that "we shall undertake to make good the promise in the writing (τὴν ἐπαγγελίαν τῆς βεβαιοῦν ἐγχειρήσομεν)." See also Dio Cassius *Hist. Rom.* 43.19.1; 68.22.2.

87 Spicq, "βέβαιος κτλ.," 281.

88 Philo *Sacr.* 93.

89 See Zahn, 230 (italics in original); Schmitz, "Abraham," 120. Kühl, 145, observes that the previous discussion, including v. 13, would lead one to expect "the descendants" but not all the descendants; Alexander Sand, "ἐπαγγελία κτλ.," *EDNT* 2 (1991) 15: "Abraham is now as the recipient of the promise a type for all believers, Jews and well as Gentiles." For general orientation on "all," which occurs almost 1,300 times in the NT, see Hugolinus Langkammer, "πᾶς," *EDNT* 3 (1993) 47–49.

90 Neubrand, *Abraham*, 268, cites the following: Lev 26:42; Deut 9:27; Ps 105:8-9, 42, etc.

91 Moo, 278–79; Schreiner, 231.

92 Schmidt, 84; Theobald, 1:130.

93 Harrison, *Language of Grace*, 224.

of the faith of Abraham" is somewhat odd, and has given rise to considerable controversy. Most interpreters have taken the former as a reference to Jewish Christians,[94] based on the parallel in 4:12. However, the use of "those of the law" in v. 14 in reference to nonbelieving Jews leads others to believe that the expression in v. 16 points in the same direction.[95] Although it produces some inconsistencies in Paul's argument, particularly in v. 13 where the Abrahamic promise is not given "through the law," it seems likely that the word choice in v. 16d refers to Jews, whether believing or not. This has an immediate implication for the congregational situation in Rome, where the Gentile majority were excluding Jewish Christians as weak in faith. If the guarantee of Abraham's promise remains valid for "those of the law," such prejudice appears illegitimate. What remains unclear with this interpretation is why Paul chose a formulation that appears to retain law-observant Jews within the realm of Abraham's promise even if they do not, or do not yet, share his faith.[96] By not excluding nonbelieving Jews from Abraham's inheritance, Paul places on the table for future discussion the issue he takes up in the third proof, Rom 9–11, and follows through with the controversial formula used three times in the letter thus far, that salvation as well as wrath come "to the Jew first and also to the Greek."

The expression "those of the faith of Abraham" in 4:16e is also difficult to define in relation to v. 16d. The "not only . . . but also" syntax places emphasis on the second element;[97] whereas it was traditionally believed

that "those of the law" were Abraham's heirs, Paul's emphatic innovation is to maintain that the heirs included "those of the faith of Abraham." Although most commentators interpret this expression as a reference to Gentile Christians,[98] which he could easily have expressed by using οἱ ἐν ἀκροβυστίᾳ as in vv. 11-12, both Gentile and Jewish believers actually fit within this rubric.[99] Both groups have responded in faith to the gospel and have received the grace of God conveyed by Christ. Rather than the neat antithesis between Gentile Christians and Jewish Christians, Paul's formulation implies overlapping groups, with the Jewish Christians included both in the "not only" and the "but also" sides of the equation. Although it appears to produce logical inconsistencies with the rest of Paul's argument, this formulation subtly achieves the equality in honor that we have perceived throughout Romans. While the semantic emphasis is on the inclusion of all believers in v. 16e, including both Jewish Christian and Gentile Christian groups,[100] v. 16d retains a legitimate status for "those of the law" who are being treated with contempt by other groups in Rome.

The final line of v. 16 carries through with the inclusion of "not only those of the law" and "also those of the faith of Abraham." To refer to Abraham as πατὴρ πάντων ἡμῶν ("the father of us all") includes all of Paul's fellow believers, no matter which cultural and theological tendency they represent.[101] Interpreters have pointed to the "solemnity" of this language, marked not only by the ὅς ἐστιν ("who is") formula used in christological

94 Zahn, 231; Sanday and Headlam, 112; Schmidt, 84; Käsemann, 121; Kuss, 1:189; Morris, 207; Wilckens, 1:272; Cranfield, 1:242–43; Moo, 278–79.
95 Weiss, 203–5; Kühl, 147; Murray, 144–45; Dunn, 1:216; Neubrand, Abraham, 270–72.
96 Dunn, 1:216, makes an effort to explain this with a distinction between "a member of the Jewish people" and those who claim "the merit of self-achievement," but this inappropriate terminology seems far from the rhetoric of this passage. Neubrand, Abraham, 274–75, sees in this verse the basis of a nondiscriminatory attitude toward unbelieving Jews.
97 See Neubrand, Abraham, 273, following Mussner, "Same," 162. Kühner-Gerth, Grammatik, 2:257, discusses οὐ μόνον . . . ἀλλὰ καί under the rubric of "Gradation," in which a less important matter is sometimes linked with a more important matter.
98 Meyer, 1:209; Zahn, 230–32; Godet, 179; Schmidt,

85; Barrett, 96; Michel, 170; Käsemann, 121; Schlier, 131; Kuss, 1:189; Klein, "Römer 4," 160; Zeller, 102; Cranfield, 1:242; Moo, 279.
99 Weiss, 203–5; Kühl, 147; Neubrand, Abraham, 274, cites Klein, "Römer 4," 160; Mussner, "Same," 162; Friedrich Emanuel Wieser, Die Abrahamvorstellungen im Neuen Testament, EHS 23.317 (Bern: Lang, 1987) 75; von Dobbeler, Glaube als Teilhabe, 137, among other advocates.
100 See particularly Aageson, Biblical Interpretation, 75, "Paul's gospel of inclusion"; Eisenbaum, "Genealogy in Romans," 691; Sass, Verheißungen, 394–97.
101 See Tobin, "Romans 4," 438–42, 449, for a discussion of the contrast between this argument and the treatment of Abraham in Galatians. On 454 he concludes, "The Abraham of Romans 4 is the father of both Jews and Gentile believers."

confessions[102] but also by the poetic paramoiosis in the repetition of $\pi\alpha$- sounds. The inclusive $\pi\hat{\alpha}\varsigma$ ("all") is reiterated from v. 16c, creating a single group identity for each house and tenement church in Rome as well as for Paul himself.[103] As we saw with regard to the use of "father" in vv. 1, 11-12, it forms a new group identity that transcends the differences between Gentile and Jewish believers. An opposite kind of group identity is expressed in 1 Maccabees when Mattathias speaks of Phineas as the father of those who zealously "fight the battle of Israel (1 Macc 3:2): "Phineas our father ($\Phi\iota\nu\epsilon\grave{\alpha}\varsigma$ $\acute{o}$ $\pi\alpha\tau\grave{\eta}\rho$ $\acute{\eta}\mu\hat{\omega}\nu$), because he was zealous with zeal, received the covenant of everlasting priesthood" (1 Macc 2:54).[104] There is a parallel expression in Qumran, in which such familial language is used with regard to "all" in which God is addressed as the father of sectarian members: "Because you are father to all the sons of your truth (בני] אמתכה‎ כי אתה אב לכול [בנ). You rejoice in them like her who loves her child, and like a wet-nurse you take care of all your creatures on your lap."[105]

Hellenistic Jewish voices are more inclusive in viewing God as the "father of all" ($\pi\acute{\alpha}\nu\tau\omega\nu$ $\pi\alpha\tau\acute{\eta}\rho$),[106] and philosophers such as Pythagoras describe the one God as the "first cause of all, radiance in heaven, and father of all ($\grave{\alpha}\rho\chi\grave{\alpha}$ $\pi\acute{\alpha}\nu\tau\omega\nu$, $\grave{\epsilon}\nu$ $o\grave{\upsilon}\rho\alpha\nu\hat{\omega}$ $\phi\omega\sigma\tau\grave{\eta}\rho$ $\kappa\alpha\grave{\iota}$ $\pi\acute{\alpha}\nu\tau\omega\nu$ $\pi\alpha\tau\acute{\eta}\rho$)."[107] Most commentators assume that the "us all" includes only fellow believers,[108] but there is no reason

to exclude nonbelieving Jews in this formulation, since Paul plans to refer to them as part of the "we" of 9:3, his "brothers" and "kinsmen," to whom patriarchs such as Abraham belong (9:5). It is possible that this expression, along with the odd antithesis in v. 16d-e, prepares the way for the third proof in Paul's letter, chaps. 9–11.

■ **17** The third proof text in the midrash that began in 4:1 is drawn verbatim from Gen 17:5, introduced by the $\kappa\alpha\vartheta\grave{\omega}\varsigma$ $\gamma\acute{\epsilon}\gamma\rho\alpha\pi\tau\alpha\iota$ ("as it has been written")[109] formula employed in 1:17; 2:24; 3:4; 3:10; and elsewhere,[110] which connects the citation closely with the preceding argument concerning Abraham as the father of Gentiles as well as Jews.[111] The divine promise, "I have made you a father of many nations," follows the LXX, which translated Heb. *gôyim* with $\grave{\epsilon}\vartheta\nu\hat{\omega}\nu$, both of which have the discriminatory connotation "Gentiles." Although the translation convention leads all commentators that I have consulted to render this with "nations," some have argued that in this context Paul really means "Gentiles."[112] This would restrict Paul's reference to "all nations in distinction from Israel," that is, as the goyim ("heathen, Gentiles").[113] However, the preceding formulation that this citation substantiates refers to Abraham as the "father of us all," which in the Roman context would definitely include Jewish Christians as well as Gentile Christians. To categorically eliminate all Jews from Abraham's paternity might be consistent with a

---

102 Cranfield, 1:243, citing the analysis of formulas beginning with $\acute{o}\varsigma$ $\grave{\epsilon}\sigma\tau\iota\nu$ in Norden, *Agnostos Theos*, 168ff. See also Michel, 170; Neubrand, *Abraham*, 276.

103 See Aageson, *Biblical Interpretation*, 79; Neubrand, *Abraham*, 276; Esler, *Conflict and Identity*, 193–94.

104 See Hamerton-Kelly, *Sacred Violence*, 75, for an analysis of the "sacred violence" that in contrast to Abraham's paternity stood in opposition to Christ and sought to exclude "gentiles."

105 1QH 17:35-36, cited by Otto Michel, "$\pi\alpha\tau\acute{\eta}\rho$," *EDNT* 3 (1993) 54.

106 Josephus *Ant.* 1.20; cf. also 1.230; Philo *Opif.* 74.1; *Cher.* 49.9; *Decal.* 64.4.

107 Pythagoras *Frag.* 186.16; see also Pindar *Oly.* 2.17; Chrysippus *Frag. log.* 1021; Plutarch *Pel.* 21.5.

108 For example, Weiss, 205; Kuss, 1:189; Cranfield, 1:243; Dunn, 1:216; Moo, 279.

109 BAGD (2000) 493.

110 For the traditional Jewish background of the formula, "as it has been written," see on 1:17.

111 See Koch, *Schrift*, 261; Neubrand, *Abraham*, 277, citing BDF §453.2 that $\kappa\alpha\vartheta\grave{\omega}\varsigma$ sometimes carries the sense of "since."

112 Käsemann, 121: "$\grave{\epsilon}\vartheta\nu\acute{\eta}$ incontestably means the Gentile"; similarly Zeller, 102. Dunn, 1:217, translates with "nations" but says "Gentiles" are "part of Paul's argument, but at the implicit rather than explicit level." Fitzmyer, 386, also translates with "nations" but states that Paul "understands 'many nations' as a term for Gentiles in general." See Nikolaus Walter's analysis of Paul's distinctive definition of "Gentiles" in "$\check{\epsilon}\vartheta\nu o\varsigma$," *EDNT* 1 (1991) 382–83.

113 Karl Ludwig Schmidt, "$\check{\epsilon}\vartheta\nu o\varsigma$, $\check{\epsilon}\vartheta\nu\iota\kappa o\varsigma$," *TDNT* 2 (1964) 369–70, referring particularly to Rom 15:11. See also Neubrand, *Abraham*, 277, citing Walter, "$\check{\epsilon}\vartheta\nu o\varsigma$," *EDNT* 1 (1991) 382–83.

radical interpretation of v. 14a, but would not fit the references in v. 16c, e, or the inclusive argument in the rest of Romans. It is probable that the meaning of πολλῶν ἐθνῶν in this citation is close to the original connotation in Genesis, something like a "plurality of nations" including Israel.[114] Paul's citation therefore resonates with the promise given twice to Abraham (Gen 12:3; 28:14) that in him shall "all of the tribes of the earth (πᾶσαι αἱ φυλαὶ τῆς γῆς)" be blessed.[115] The perfect tense of the verb τέθεικα ("I have made") in the citation from Gen 17:5 sustains the inclusive implication, because it signifies, in Dunn's words, "a status and fulfillment already established and operative before the issue of circumcision arose, with the 'many nations' referring to the rapidly growing Gentile mission."[116] The entire citation fits not only Paul's argument about Abraham but also drives forward his project of the mission to the end of the known world, Spain.

The expression κατέναντι οὗ ἐπίστευσεν θεοῦ ("in the presence of God in whom he believed")[117] defines the context in which Abraham received the promise cited in v. 17a.[118] An alternate translation links κατέναντι with the words of the promise rather with the person of God.[119] In either instance we have a typical Hebraicism that Paul uses elsewhere,[120] employing one of the Greek terms that translates לִפְנֵי ("in the presence of").[121] Paul echoes the context of the many-nation promise in which Yahweh appears to Abraham with the words, "I am your God. Be well-pleasing before me (לְפָנַי, ἐνώπιον ἐμοῦ), and be blameless" (Gen 17:1).[122] In the presence of this Deity, Abraham had faith (ἐπίστευσεν), the verb employed in the main text of this extended midrash, drawn from Gen 15:6.[123] It is clear from this formulation that faith is a relational term,[124] describing the proper stance that persons and groups should take in response to divine grace. The definition of this faith has to do with persuasion, as Kinneavy has shown: Abraham was convinced that God's promise was valid, and this conviction placed him in the right relationship with God.[125]

In v. 17c-d, Paul goes on to delineate the nature of God in whom Abraham had faith, employing liturgical sounding language that may have originated in Hellenistic synagogues.[126] The participial expression τοῦ ζῳοποιοῦντος τοὺς νεκρούς ("who gives life to the dead") appears to be drawn from the second benediction in the Eighteen Benedictions used by many Jews on a daily basis, "Blessed be you, Lord, who gives life to the dead."[127] That this belief was a firmly established feature in the Pharisaic tradition that shaped Paul's early beliefs is confirmed by Josephus Ant. 18.14-15: "The Pharisees believe that souls have power to survive death and that there are rewards and punishments under the earth for those who have led lives of virtue or vice: eternal impris-

---

114 Schmidt, "ἔθνος, ἐθνικός," 367; see also Kuss, 1:190.
115 See Godet, 179.
116 Dunn, 1:217.
117 For a discussion of the grammatical phenomenon of attraction in this expression, see Meyer, 1:210–11; Kühl, 149–50; BDF §294. In "Aporien," 886, Schenke infers from the seemingly loose syntax that the text must be corrupt at this point; this does not appear plausible.
118 See Godet, 179; Käsemann, 121.
119 Campbell, "3.27–4.25," 381–83: "in the presence of which [i.e. that declaration], he trusted the God who makes alive the dead."
120 2 Cor 2:17; 12:19, "in the presence of God (κατέναντι θεοῦ) we speak in Christ," as in Exod 32:11, "And Moses prayed in the sight of the Lord God (ἔναντι Κυρίου τοῦ Θεοῦ)"; Ps 5:5, "neither shall transgressors continue in the sight of your eyes (κατέναντι τῶν ὀφθαλμῶν σου)"; Sir 50:19, "their prayers before the Merciful One (κατέναντι ἐλεή-

μενος)." See Michel, 171; BDF §214; BAGD (2000) 530.
121 See BDF §214; Meyer, 1:210.
122 See Sanday and Headlam, 113; Wilckens, 1:274.
123 Wilckens, 1:274; Dunn, 1:217.
124 Gerhard Barth, "πίστις," EDNT 3 (1993) 93: "the central and comprehensive designation for one's relationship to God."
125 Kinneavy, Greek Rhetorical Origins, 133–35.
126 See Michel, 171; Wilckens, 1:274.
127 Cited by Michel, 171. Haacker, 108, observes that this prayer would have been part of Paul's Pharisaic tradition but that recent research indicates it was not universally employed in synagogal worship during the first century. S. Safrai, "The Synagogue," in Safrai and Stern, Jewish People, 2:922–26, shows that although Rabbi Gamaliel was reported to have insisted that the Eighteen Benedictions should be recited daily, its precise text cannot be reconstructed with certainty in the period before 70 C.E. See also Rudolf Bultmann, "νεκρός κτλ.," TDNT 4

onment is the lot of evil souls, while the good souls receive an easy passage to a new life. Because of these views they are, as a matter of fact, extremely influential among the townsfolk; and all prayers and sacred rites of divine worship are performed according to their exposition."

Belief in God's power to resurrect the dead was widely shared after the postexilic period in Israel.[128] Wis 16:13 affirms that God has "the power of life and death," while Dan 12:2 promises that the righteous will be awakened by God "from their sleep in the dust of the earth." In 2 Macc 7:23 the mother of the seven martyred sons assures them that the "Creator of the world . . . will also of his mercy give you breath and life again." In Rom 8:11 Paul cites a christianized version of this belief,[129] that "the one raising Christ Jesus from the dead will also give life to your mortal bodies," but in 4:17 the formulation remains within the context of Hellenistic Jewish faith.[130]

The second participial phrase, "who calls that which does not exist into existence" (καλοῦντος τὰ μὴ ὄντα ὡς ὄντα), is likewise a typical expression of Jewish faith,[131] stated in 2 Baruch with the same terminology employed by Paul: "You who created the earth, the one who fixed the firmament by the word and fastened the height of heaven by the spirit, the one who in the beginning of the world called that which did not yet exist and they obeyed you" (2 Bar. 21.4); "And with the word you bring to life that which does not exist" (2 Bar. 48.8). The

combination between God's word and creation from nothing is an important theme for Philo, whose formulation in *Spec. leg.* 4.187 is almost identical with Paul's:[132] "God . . . wills the good only. This is shown both in the creation and in the ordering of the world. He called that which does not exist into existence (τὰ γὰρ μὴ ὄντα ἐκάλεσεν εἰς τὸ εἶναι) and produced order from disorder . . . equality from inequality and light from darkness." Another Hellenistic Jewish parallel to Paul's celebration of Abraham's faith in the God who creates ex nihilo is found in Pseudo-Orpheus, which speaks of God as the "master of the universe. He is one, self-generated; all things have been brought forth as the offspring of this one."[133] In another fragment Pseudo-Orpheus refers to God's creative power: "He is one, self-proceeding; and from Him alone all things proceed."[134]

As one can see from these and other parallels, there is nothing distinctively Christian about either of these traditional formulations.[135] While interpreters have drawn profound connections within the context of Christian theology between creation and justification,[136] between conversion and creation,[137] the latter with particular reference to the inclusion of converted Gentiles,[138] there is no indication in the text itself that Paul wishes to do more than provide a widely acceptable framework for interpreting the story of the seemingly impossible progeny from "the deadness of Sarah's womb" (4:19). That framework is the divine Creator whose power to overcome death and nothingness abides

(1967) 892. Shum, *Paul's Use of Isaiah*, 187, suggests an allusion here to Isa 48:13, but the theme of resurrection is absent there and the reference to creation lacks the ex nihilo emphasis.

128 See George W. E. Nickelsburg, "Resurrection (Early Judaism and Christianity)," *ABD* 5 (1992) 685; also Rudolf Bultmann, "ζάω κτλ.," *TDNT* 2 (1964) 856–61.

129 See Paulsen, *Überlieferung*, 51–55, and the discussion below of 8:1-17.

130 Dunn, 1:218; Haacker, 108–9.

131 See Arnold Ehrhardt, "Creatio ex nihilo," in *The Framework of the New Testament Stories* (Cambridge: Harvard University Press, 1964) 200–204, 214–20.

132 Dunn, 1:218, refers also to Philo *Opif.* 81; *Leg.* 3.10; *Migr.* 183; *Her.* 36; *Mut.* 46; *Somn.* 1.76; *Mos.* 2.100, 267.

133 Pseudo-Orpheus 105, lines 8-10 (Holladay, *Orphica*, 127; see also p. 111).

134 Pseudo-Orpheus 115, line 10 (Holladay, *Orphica*, 127).

135 Guerra, "Romans 4," 264, argues that this verse's congruity with Jewish theology reflects "Paul's apologetic affirmation of the continuity of God's activity." Kahn, "Greek Verb 'To Be,'" 245–65, surveys the use of expressions like τὰ ὄντα to show that the modern antithesis between the "existential and copulative" (247) is not found in ancient writers, who assumed an "intrinsically stable and lasting character of Being" (255) in their use of the verb "to be."

136 Käsemann, 122–24; Stuhlmacher, 74; idem, *Gerechtigkeit*, 236–37.

137 Wilckens, 1:274–75; Moxnes, *Theology in Conflict*, 241–53.

138 Neubrand, *Abraham*, 278–80.

forever,[139] as indicated by the present tense of the participles ζῳοποιοῦντος and καλοῦντος.[140]

■ **18** As proof that Abraham responded appropriately to God's unlimited power, Paul turns to the nature of his faith.[141] The liturgical style is continued with the pronoun ὅς ("who") providing the subject as in 4:16e.[142] The expression παρ᾽ ἐλπίδα ἐπ᾽ ἐλπίδι ("beyond hope in hope") is a rhetorically impressive combination of two well-known expressions. In *Vit. Mos.* 1.250 Philo describes a victory in battle whose easy victory was παρ᾽ ἐλπίδα in the sense of being unexpected,[143] but there are no other examples in ancient literature of these two prepositional phrases appearing together as in Paul's rhetorically effective formulation: "in hope beyond hope." The paradox is that in this situation beyond all hope,[144] Abraham continues "in hope" to believe in God's promise. The expression ἐπ᾽ ἐλπίδι is a favorite Pauline formula, used again in 5:2 and 8:20 as well as in 1 Cor 9:10 where Paul cites the line from Sir 6:19, that "the ploughman should plow in hope (ἐπ᾽ ἐλπίδι) and the thresher thresh in hope (ἐπ᾽ ἐλπίδι) of a share in the crop." This is a typical biblical expression, for example, Ps 4:8, "for you, Lord, only caused me to dwell in hope (ἐπ᾽ ἐλπίδι)," or Ps 15:9, that in the Lord "my flesh shall rest in hope (ἐπ᾽ ἐλπίδι)."[145] In a situation beyond all human hope, long past the time in which Abraham or Sarah could normally produce a child,

Abraham continued to believe "in hope" that God's promise would be fulfilled, thus exemplifying this biblical stance of trusting in God.[146] The relation between faith and hope in this instance is that Abraham continued to have faith in God, to be firmly related to God, in the hope that the promise would somehow be fulfilled. In Murray's words, "Apparently what is meant by 'believed in hope' is that Abraham's faith was exercised in the confident hope which the promise of God engendered."[147]

The infinitive clause that follows the verb "he had faith" can be taken in either of two basic ways. The expression εἰς τὸ γενέσθαι αὐτὸν πατέρα πολλῶν ἐθνῶν could refer to the content of his faith that he should become the "father of many nations,"[148] or that the result or consequence of his faith was that he became such a father.[149] The latter is favored by those wishing to concentrate on God's purpose of demonstrating the power of faith or creating the community of faith including Jews and Gentiles, but Paul's interest here is in clarifying the nature of Abraham's faith, as the following citation and the argument in vv. 19-20 show. He does not come to the matter of the current embodiment of Abraham's faith until vv. 23-25. It is more natural grammatically to view the εἰς clause with the articular infinitive as the object of the verb ἐπίστευε-

---

139 See Alkier, *Wunder*, 275–78.

140 Schlier, 133.

141 In *Rereading*, 246–47, Stowers appropriately observes that v. 18 does not open a "new section" but is a continuation of a sentence that began in v. 16 and continues until v. 22.

142 See Meyer, 1:213.

143 For the interpretation of παρά as "beyond" see Cranfield, 1:245; BAGD (2000) 758 prefers to interpret παρά with the accusative as "against, contrary to," but the connotation "more than, beyond" (757) seems more appropriate. For other parallels see Josephus *Bell.* 3.183; Aeschylus *Ag.* 899; Pindar *Oly.* 13.83.

144 Rudolf Bultmann, "ἐλπίς κτλ.," *TDNT* 2 (1964) 531, refers to the "paradox" of this verse.

145 Koch, *Schrift*, 42, cites also Judg 18:7, 10; Zeph 2:15 as instances in which the LXX uses ἐπ᾽ ἐλπίδι to render לבטח or בטח. Michel, 172, refers to ἐπ᾽ ἐλπίδι as a "Hellenistic formula" that occurs in *T. Benj.* 10.11. See also Thucydides *Hist.* 4.103. It also

appears in Hos 2:18; Acts 2:26; 26:6; Titus 1:2; and *1 Clem.* 57.7. This formula was employed long before the Hellenistic period and occurs in Pseudo-Plato *Epin.* 974c8; Lysias *Orat.* 6.23.1; Demades *Frag.* 87.17.6 ("in hope of freedom"); Diodorus Siculus *Hist.* 13.21.7 ("in hope of deliverance"); Strabo *Geogr.* 12.3.34.12; Plutarch *Rom.* 8.4.6; Dio Chrysostom *Orat.* 38.2.2; Josephus *Ant.* 4.36; 6.26; *Bell.* 1.44.

146 See esp. Schlier, 133; Murray, 147–48.

147 Murray, 148.

148 Godet, 181. Meyer, 1:213–14, cites Reiche, Köllner, Baumgarten-Crusius, Krehl, Mehring, and Hofmann as advocating this view, with which Meyer himself disagrees on grounds that it is "quite contrary to the usage of the N. T." Other advocates include Weiss, 209; Zahn, 236–37; Kühl, 152; Bultmann, "πιστεύω κτλ.," 206; Kuss, 1:192; Murray, 148; Fitzmyer, 387; Byrne, 154.

149 The clause is construed as the final result of Abraham's faith by Sanday and Headlam, 114; Schmidt, 86; Dunn, 1:219; Neubrand, *Abraham*, 280–81; it is

σεν,[150] describing the content of what was believed, whereas the final or consecutive interpretation absolutizes the verb by leaving it without an object. This may be appealing theologically, but it allows πιστεύειν to become a kind of theological work that is rewarded by the fulfillment of the promise, resulting in conflicts over faith that had already emerged in the Roman churches, in which the "strong" are accusing their opponents of being "weak in faith." By understanding the infinitive clause as a clarification of the content of Abraham's faith, the reiteration of the phrase "father of many nations" in v. 18a, drawn from the citation from Gen 17:5 in v. 17, makes sense. The object of Abraham's hope was the fulfillment of this promise.

By introducing the following citation from Genesis with the words, κατὰ τὸ εἰρημένον ("as he had been told"), Paul again evokes the face-to-face encounter with God that we noted in v. 17b. Abraham's faith is a proper response to this encounter with God's promise, cited here verbatim from Gen 15:5, Οὕτως ἔσται τὸ σπέρμα σου, which draws the conclusion from the preceding message from Yahweh, "Look up now to heaven and count the stars, and if you can number them, *so shall your descendants be.*" The citation confirms the content of Abraham's promise reiterated in v. 18a, "that he should become a father of many nations." By reaching back to this verse from Gen 15, prior to the instructions about circumcision in chap. 17, Paul once again drives home the thesis from the opening verse in this pericope, that the promise did not come "through the law" (4:13).[151] The effect of this citation, as Cranfield points out,[152] is

to subsume the material from Gen 17 under the rubric of God's promise in Gen 15. That Abraham's descendants would become a vast multitude from many nations rested solely on the power of God's word rather than on anything Abraham's himself could accomplish.

■ **19** The next four verses continue the description of Abraham's faith in terms of its lack of doubt. The expression μὴ ἀσθενήσας τῇ πίστει ("not having weakened in faith") stands in antithesis to ἐνεδυναμώθη τῇ πίστει ("being strengthened in faith") in v. 20.[153] The basic meaning in either case has to do with the "measure of certainty" in persuasion.[154] While there are some distant parallels to this use of "weakness" to describe a moral condition,[155] it is likely that the formulation here was influenced by the polemical context within the churches of Corinth and Rome where alleged weaknesses in conscience (1 Cor 8:11-12) and faith (Rom 14:1) were under dispute.[156] In view of Paul's later effort to counter the prejudicial treatment of those stigmatized as "weak in faith" (14:1–15:7), however, it remains puzzling that the antithesis between weak and strong in faith would be used here. This formulation would certainly have been welcomed by the majority of Gentile Christians in Rome, because in that controversial situation it would have appeared that they conformed more fully to Abraham's example than did the Jewish Christians who bore the insulting title, "the weak in faith."

The paradox of hope that is beyond hope (4:18a) is illustrated by Abraham's avoiding weakness of faith while at the same time "he considered his own body already dead (κατενόησεν τὸ ἑαυτοῦ σῶμα ἤδη

---

consecutive result in the interpretation of Meyer, 1:213 (citing earlier advocates Rückert, Tholuck, Philippi); Lagrange, 95; Schlier, 133; Cranfield, 1:246; Käsemann, 124; Morris, 210; Zeller, 103; Moo, 283.

150 See BDF §402.2; Moulton and Turner, *Grammar III*, 143, citing Rom 12:3; 1 Cor 8:10; 11:22 as examples of this construction following finite verbs.

151 See Dunn, 1:219. For a clarification of the argumentative function of this citation, see Koch, *Schrift*, 261; and Hays, *Echoes*, 56.

152 Cranfield, 1:246–47.

153 Michel, 172–73.

154 Kinneavy, *Greek Rhetorical Origins*, 137–38.

155 Gustav Stählin, "ἀσθενής κτλ.," *TDNT* 1 (1964) 492, cites *Ps. Sol.* 17.38 that "the blessing of the

Lord will be with him [the Messiah] in strength, and he will not weaken, His hope (will be) in the Lord." In several contexts Epictetus uses ἀσθενής in the sense of moral weakness: the soul, just like the body, can be weak (ἀσθενὴς ψυχή, *Diss* 2.15.20), and things that are "not under control" are characterized as "weak, servile, and hindered" (ἀσθενῆ, δοῦλα, κωλυτά, *Ench.* 1.2.3). In *Diss.* 1.8.8 he seems to couple the "uneducated and morally weak" (τοῖς ἀπαιδεύτοις καὶ ἀσθενέσι)" in a statement warning that proper faculties in the hands of such as these can cause conceit and arrogance.

156 See Stählin, "ἀσθενής κτλ.," 492; Josef Zmijewski, "ἀσθένεια κτλ.," *EDNT* 1 (1990) 171; Jewett, *Terms*, 426–30; Reasoner, *The Strong*, 133–34, 200–220.

νενεκρωμένον).” This is a rather sober allusion to the Abraham story,[157] in which he responded to the promise by falling on his face with laughter while saying “in his heart, ‘Shall there be a child to one who is a hundred years old, and shall Sarah who is ninety years old, bear?’” (Gen 17:17). As far as Abraham’s and Sarah’s capacities to produce a child were concerned, he considered them nothing less than dead. The verb νεκρόω is a typical expression for death, as in a Roman epitaph for Rufinius, who “died (νεκρωθείς) and gave his soul back to the sky, his body to the earth.”[158] As Schlier observes, Abraham’s hope did not overlook the reality of his concrete situation but was not deterred by its ridiculous prospect.[159] He could laugh at human weakness but refused to give up hope in the superior power of God.

■ **20** The final reference to Abraham’s promise in this pericope is formulated in an adversative style, marked by δέ (“yet”)[160] and coordinated with “unfaith” and “faith.” The verb διακρίνω appears here with the distinctively early Christian connotation of doubt in a matter of faith, as in Mark 11:23: “And Jesus answered them, ‘Have faith in God. Truly, I say to you, whoever says to this mountain, ‘be taken up and cast into the sea,’ and does not doubt in his heart, but believes (μὴ διακριθῇ ἐν τῇ καρδίᾳ αὐτοῦ ἀλλὰ πιστεύῃ) that what he says will

come to pass, it will be done for him.”[161] Michel argues for active disbelief in the object of faith,[162] which seems to be followed by Synge, who interprets this verb as “decide that a thing is impossible.”[163] The aorist passive verb requires a translation such as that suggested here: “no doubt made him waver.” While laying the basis for the discussion of doubt in 14:23,[164] Paul is doubtless formulating this verse with a view of the final outcome of the Abraham story, which stands in contrast with his open disbelief expressed in Gen 17:17.[165] Jewish sources turn this embarrassing laughter into an expression of faithful joy[166] or certainty,[167] while Moo’s commentary admits “momentary hesitations” while denying a “deep-seated and permanent attitude of distrust.”[168]

Sidestepping the details of Gen 17, Paul’s concentration here is entirely on the power of the divine promise to evoke faith, that is, to elicit persuasion.[169] As in 2 Cor 1:20 and Gal 3:21, Paul employs the expression ἡ ἐπαγγελία τοῦ θεοῦ (“the promise of God”) to emphasize that it is “dependent on God alone.”[170] Cranfield explains the relevance of this reference to “the divine promise. It is the promise on which it rests which is its power. It exists because a man has been overpowered, held and sustained by God’s promise.”[171]

The expression ἐνεδυναμώθη τῇ πίστει (“empow-

157 See William Baird, “Abraham in the New Testament: Tradition and the New Identity,” *Int* 42 (1988) 377.
158 Cited by G. H. R. Horsley, “A Judicial Career Cut Short,” *NDIEC* 4 (1987) 35–38, from *IG* 14, Nr. 1976.6-7; see also Rudolf Bultmann, “νεκρός κτλ.,” *TDNT* 4 (1967) 894; Deissmann, *Light*, 94, 97, cited by MM 424: “O man, pass not by my body, now dead (ἄνθρωπε . . . μὴ μου παρέλθῃς σῶμα τὸ νεν[ε]κρ[ω]μένον),” drawn from *IG* 3.2, Nr. 1355.3-4.
159 Schlier, 133–34.
160 See Schmidt, 86; Barrett, 97; Morris, 212; Wilckens, 1:272; Zeller, 96.
161 See MM 150; BAGD (2000) 231; Sanday and Headlam, 115; Schlier, 134; other examples of the link between faith and the verb διακρίνειν are Matt 21:21; Jas 1:6; Jude 22.
162 Michel, 173.
163 F. C. Synge, “Not Doubt But Discriminate,” *ExpT* 89 (1977–78) 203–5; cited and rejected by Moo, 285.
164 Lincoln, “Abraham,” 174.
165 See Fitzmyer, 387.

166 *Jub.* 16.19 claims that after receiving assurance from the divine messengers, both Abraham and Sarah “rejoiced very greatly.”
167 Philo *QG* 3.55, “Rightly did he laugh in his joy over the promise, being filled with great hope and in the expectation that it would be fulfilled, and because he had clearly received a vision, through which he knew more certainly Him who always stands firm, and him who naturally bends and falls.”
168 Moo, 285.
169 Kinneavy, *Greek Rhetorical Origins*, 102–6. The background of this concept in the field of rhetoric is sketched by Kinneavy, 33–100.
170 Schniewind and Friedrich, “ἐπαγγέλλω κτλ.,” 552. There is a close parallel in Josephus, who refers in *Ant.* 3.24 to “the promises that are from God (ταῖς ἐπαγγελίαις ταῖς παρὰ τοῦ θεοῦ)”; see also *Ant.* 2.219.
171 Cranfield, 1:248.

ered in his faith") employs one of the favorite stems in Pauline literature,[172] stated in memorable form in the motto of Phil 4:13, "I can do all things in him who empowers me (ἐν τῷ ἐνδυναμοῦντί με),"[173] and playing a decisive role in the argument of Romans, as we have seen with the word δύναμις ("power").[174] The aorist passive voice of the verb should be understood as a reference to being strengthened by God,[175] which clearly assumes that the source of faith does not lie within human power. The dative expression with the article (τῇ πίστει) should be understood "with respect to his faith"[176] rather than in a causal sense, "because of his faith."[177] Here we find the typical Pauline premise that God alone has the power to evoke faith, as stated in the thesis of the letter (1:16-17) and in other Pauline passages (e.g., 1 Cor 12:3).[178]

The final line of v. 20 harks back to the opening two verses in the midrash, namely whether Abraham found a basis for boasting in his own fleshly accomplishments. The expression δοὺς δόξαν τῷ θεῷ ("giving glory to God") is the opposite of giving glory to oneself, and it is possible in the radical sense of the expression only for those who recognize that their own power to accomplish is "dead," to use the language of 4:19. Among commentators of the modern period, Käsemann offers the best explanation of the connection between faith as evoked by the gospel and the phenomenon of a proper doxology: "Faith . . . is reception of the word. If we let ourselves be bound to this alone, the power of God grasps us and makes possible the doxology which the Gentiles did not raise according to 1:21. God is given the glory only when we let him be God, omnipotent and sovereign. Constantly . . . the believer stands in such a doxology when he looks away from himself and in doing so responds to the promise."[179] The congregational relevance of this point is developed in 15:5-9, where both sides in Rome are urged to glorify God together.[180]

■ **21** In 4:21 the rare verb πληροφορέω is used in a passive form to describe the full conviction that Abraham had in the divine promise. There are no parallels in Jewish materials to this description of Abraham or of any other patriarch, because πληροφορέω ("be fully convinced") and its substantive πληροφορία ("full conviction, assurance") appear primarily in early Christian materials describing certitude of belief.[181] For example, Ignatius *Mag.* 8:2 does not hesitate to employ this distinctive Christian preference for πληροφορέω in the passive to describe the prophets' conversion of unbelievers to monotheism: "The divine prophets lived according to Jesus Christ. Therefore they were also persecuted, being inspired by his grace, so that the unbelievers might be fully convinced (πληροφορηθῆναι) that there is only one God, who manifested himself through Jesus Christ his son."

The object of Abraham's confidence is (ὃ ἐπήγγελται), with the verb in the perfect passive that lends "an air of permanence"[182] to "what had been

---

172 Meyer, 1:216, observes that this verb does not occur in Greek authors outside the LXX; this is confirmed by LSJM 559–60 and MM 212; see also Walter Grundmann, "δύναμαι κτλ.," *TDNT* 2 (1964) 286.

173 This becomes a decisive term for the deutero-Pauline literature (Eph 6:10; 1 Tim 1:12; 2 Tim 2:1; 4:17). Col 1:11 intensifies this emphasis on power, "May you be strengthened with all power (ἐν πάσῃ δυνάμει δυναμούμενοι), according to his glorious might."

174 See Rom 1:4, 16, 20; 8:38; 9:17; 15:13, 19. The closely related word δυνατός appears in 4:21; 9:22; 11:23; 12:18; 15:1.

175 Michel, 126; Käsemann, 124–25; Cranfield, 1:248–49. Henning Paulsen, "ἐνδυναμόω," *EDNT* 1 (1990) 451, appears to overlook this aorist passive in his explanation, "Faith is thus not thought of as the cause of the strengthening, but as a more precise definition of it."

176 BDF §197; Weiss, 211; Schmidt, 86–87; Murray, 150.

177 Zahn, 237; Sanday and Headlam, 115; Moo, 285.

178 See von Dobbeler, *Glaube als Teilhabe*, 54–71.

179 Käsemann, 124–25.

180 See particularly Calvert-Koyzis, *Paul*, 137.

181 Luke 1:1; 1 Thess 1:5; Col 2:2; 4:12; 2 Tim 4:5, 17; Heb 6:11; 10:22; *1 Clem.* 42.3; Ignatius *Smyrn.* 1.1; Hegesippus in Eusebius *Hist.* 2.23.14; *Mart. Pion.* 4.17. See Gerhard Delling, "πληροφορέω," *TDNT* 6 (1968) 309; Joachim Becker, "Zu πληροφορεῖσθαι in Röm 14,5," *Bib* 65 (1984) 364; idem, "Quid πληροφορεῖσθαι in Rom 14,5 significet," *VD* 45 (1967) 11–18; Ceslas Spicq, " πληροφορέω, πληροφορία," *TLNT* 3 (1994) 120–23.

182 Morris, 213.

promised,"[183] "what He had promised,"[184] or "that which had been promised."[185] If the last translation is selected, the nominative neuter article ὅ must refer back to the neuter expression "what he had been told" (τὸ εἰρημένον, v. 18) regarding the gift of progeny from "many nations." The object of Abraham's conviction is that God "is also able to do (it)" (δυνατός ἐστιν καὶ ποιῆσαι). This claim that God is powerful enough to accomplish God's righteous purposes in history is fundamental to the OT, to other forms of Hebrew and Hellenistic Jewish literature, as well as to the NT.[186] In Philo's discussion of the Abraham story, the question of the believability of divine power plays a similarly important role:

But to Abraham and Sarah the thing seemed incredible (τὸ πρᾶγμα ἄπιστον), and therefore they did not pay serious regard even to the promises of the three [angelic messengers]. For as they had passed the years of parenthood their great age had made them despair of the birth of a son. So the scripture says that the wife first laughed at the words and afterwards when they said, "Is anything impossible with God (μὴ ἀδυνατεῖ παρὰ τῷ θεῷ πᾶν ῥῆμα)?" was ashamed and denied her laughter, for she knew that all things were possible with God (πάντα γὰρ ᾔδει θεῷ δυνατά), a truth which she had learnt long ago, and even from the cradle.[187]

That God was powerful enough to fulfill the promise, even when it was beyond all hope, was the key to Abraham's faith,[188] which is why this motif immediately precedes the reiteration of the main text from Gen 15:6.

■ **22** Just as in the two earlier instances where διό ("for this reason, therefore") occurs (Rom 1:24; 2:1), here a logical inference is drawn from the preceding argument.[189] The ascription of righteous status that we analyzed in connection with 4:3 was based only on Abraham's faith in the power of God to fulfill the promise, despite his human inability.[190] Abraham had no virtue to display, and had not conformed to the law. Even his faith was evoked and sustained by God's power rather than his own. Therefore not even faith itself counts as a qualification for righteousness. Abraham was honored by God because he allowed the divine promise to have its way, being fully convinced that God was capable of carrying through with the purpose of creating descendants who similarly lacked any qualifications. He receives the status of righteousness not as an achievement but as a gift. He stands now "in the presence of God" and under the power of God's promises, enjoying a relationship he has not earned. With this affirmation, the negative and positive descriptions of the Abrahamic promise come to their appointed end, and the way is open for Paul to describe how Christ believers become the descendants of this great example of faith.

---

183 This translation retains the strict syntactical link between ὅ ("what") in the nominative requiring that it be the subject of the passive verb ἐπήγγελται ("had been promised"); normally, however, the verbal form in such a construction would be a participle, rather than a finite verb as in this instance.

184 This translation rests on taking the deponent verb as in the middle voice, preferred by Meyer, 1:217; Weiss, 213; Kuss, 1:193; Schlier, 135; Käsemann, 118; Wilckens, 1:272; Morris, 213; Murray, 151, but nowhere is this vague translation argued in detail. A formulation with the relative pronoun in the accusative seems presupposed by this popular translation, such as found in Esth 4:7, "and the promise that he had promised (καὶ τὴν ἐπαγγελίαν ἣν ἐπηγγείλατο)."

185 According to BAGD (2000) 725–26, the relative pronoun occasionally has a concealed demonstrative sense, which in this instance gives the easiest translation, "that which had been promised." See Moul-

ton and Turner, *Grammar III*, 324: "The Greek relative, unlike the English, includes in itself the demonstrative idea," producing "compressions" such as Luke 9:36 and Matt 10:40.

186 See Grundmann, "δύναμαι κτλ.," 290–317; Wilckens, 1:276.

187 Philo *Abr.* 111-12, noted by Dunn, 1:221, along with other passages from Philo.

188 See William Neil, "Paul's Certainties. I. God's Promises Are Sure—Romans iv. 21," *ExpT* 69 (1957–58) 146–48.

189 BAGD (2000) 250, referring to the study by Molland, "Διό," 43–52.

190 This verse is particularly damaging to Gaston's thesis in *Paul*, 45–63, that the ascription of righteousness was directed to God rather than to Abraham.

■ **23** The fourth and final paragraph in this pericope—and in the first proof—begins with a "not only . . . but also" formula, parallel to the ones we analyzed in vv. 12 and 16. The verb ἐγράφη clearly refers to the scriptural promise from Genesis cited in the preceding verse, "it was reckoned to him as righteousness." In the phrase δι' αὐτόν ("for his sake") the preposition with the accusative has the connotation "because of, for the sake of,"[191] so Paul is claiming that the Scripture was not written only for Abraham's sake.[192] Kuss observes that it remains unclear what "for his sake" meant in Abraham's case,[193] while Dunn suggests that Abraham's memory was thereby preserved and moreover that Paul wishes to lift the story up to the level of an "historical event."[194] Käsemann discusses "the problem of Pauline typology" whereby past events prefigure current events and point to the eschaton, but it remains unclear what Abraham himself would have derived from this subsequent hermeneutical process.[195]

Compared with such floundering, several earlier scholars saw clearly what was at stake, that ἐγράφη δι' αὐτόν meant "written *to his honor*."[196] In a midrashic exegesis that began with the question of what Abraham gained in terms of boasting and honor, and in which the ascription "reckoned to him as righteousness" had the primary significance of providing honorable status to those who had not earned it, it would have been self-evident to ancient hearers what this prepositional phrase implied. In an honor-shame society, the divine ascription of acceptable status was the ultimate honor that one could receive, not only transforming one's status but

also giving promise of guaranteeing the fulfillment of Abraham's hope of progeny that would be as many as the stars in heaven. While the point of emphasis in a "not only . . . but also" formula lies on the second half, which falls in vv. 24-25, Paul's argument requires that Abraham gained something of immense value for himself from the ascription of righteousness. In order for him to function as a prototype of the new group identity of Christ believers,[197] Abraham must remain a supreme example of faith's bounty.[198]

■ **24** With the expression ἀλλὰ καὶ δι' ἡμᾶς ("but also for our sake") "the epistolary audience comes explicitly into view" for the first time since 1:1-15.[199] This verse contains what many interpreters view as the main point of chap. 4.[200] For example, Wilckens describes the "future, eschatological directionality" of the Abraham story that provides the foundation of the Christian doctrine of justification by faith.[201] Following the tradition of Jewish hermeneutics,[202] the idea of Scripture as guidance for contemporary behavior was stated by Paul in reference to scriptural episodes from the exodus period:[203] "Now these things are warnings for us, not to desire evil as they did. . . . Now these things happened to them as a warning, but they were written down for our instruction, upon whom the end of the ages has come" (1 Cor 10:6, 11). This idea of Scripture's contemporary relevance is reiterated toward the end of the fourth proof in Romans (15:4), "for whatever was previously written was written for our instruction, in order that through the steadfastness and through the encouragement of the scripture we might have the hope." In

191 BAGD (2000) 225.B.2.
192 Classical examples of διά followed by a pronoun are Thucydides *Hist.* 1.41, "on account of us Peloponnesians (δι' ἡμᾶς Πελοποννησίους)"; Xenophon *Anab.* 7.7.7, "since you have become our friends on account of us, with the help of the gods" (δι' ἡμᾶς συν θεοῖς)"; see also Xenophon *Hell.* 6.3.17.
193 Kuss, 1:193.
194 Dunn, 1:222; earlier suggestions along these lines were made by Weiss, 213; Cranfield, 1:250; Zeller, 103.
195 Käsemann, 125–26; see also Goppelt, *Typos*, 163–81.
196 Godet, 183, dismisses this suggestion by Beza and Tholuck, while preferring the theory that the event belonged not only "to Abraham's history" but also

to the later history of believers. Schmitz, "Abraham," 121, and Wilckens, 1:277, also dismiss the idea that "for his sake" referred to Abraham's *Ruhm* ("honor, reputation").
197 See Esler, *Conflict and Identity*, 193–94; Neubrand, *Abraham*, 286–89.
198 See Dunn, 1:222: the "not only" expression "should be given due weight."
199 Stowers, *Rereading*, 247.
200 Neubrand, *Abraham*, 287, cites van der Minde, *Schrift*, 100; Theobald, 1:135.
201 Wilckens, 1:277.
202 See Koch, *Schrift*, 322–27; Moshe Goshen-Gottstein, "Scriptural Authority (Judaism)," *ABD* 5 (1992) 1017–21.
203 See Aageson, *Biblical Interpretation*, 50–51.

this context the preposition διά should be rendered "on behalf of, for the sake of," just as in the reference to Abraham in the preceding verse, which points to the benefit gained by Paul and his fellow believers from the scriptural promise of ascribed righteousness.[204] The precise nature of their honor is described in the phrase that follows.

There is a significant controversy about how the words οἷς μέλλει λογίζεσθαι should be interpreted. The translation "are going to 'be reckoned'" takes μέλλω in a futuristic sense, usually taken as referring to eschatological salvation[205] or the day of judgment.[206] The translation "who must certainly 'be reckoned'" takes the verb μέλλω followed by the infinitive to be an indication of inevitability, destined by a divine decree.[207] However, the examples adduced for the latter translation all have a future dimension (e.g., Matt 17:12, "destined to suffer"; 17:22, "destined to be delivered"; Rev. 1:19, "those who are to inherit salvation"; Heb 1:14, "those destined to obtain salvation"),[208] and the other four instances of μέλλω in Romans (5:14; 8:13, 18, 38), and those in the other Pauline letters (1 Cor 3:22; Gal 3:23; 1 Thess 3:4; see also Col 2:17) retain basic futurity.[209] A crucial observation was made by Kühl that μέλλω in this context was future from the standpoint of the Genesis account of Abraham but present for believers in the Messiah.[210] The aorist verb ἐγράφη ("it was written") in v. 23 establishes the temporal reference for the other verbal forms in this sentence, so that the intended meaning for οἷς μέλλει λογίζεσθαι was "those who were about to be 'reckoned.'" There is certainly no place for

allusions to the last judgment or eschatological fulfillment in this discussion of current belief in Christ's resurrection and atonement (4:24-25), which is followed in 5:1 and 9 by references to justification as an accomplished fact.[211]

The correspondence between Christ believers and Abraham continues by referring to them as "those having faith in the one who raised Jesus our Lord from the dead." While the words "faith" and "reckon" link them to the Abraham story, the content of their faith differs substantially.[212] Abraham believed in God, "who gives life to the dead" (4:17c), and thus had the power to produce an heir from a couple too old to have children, but Christ believers have a very specific form of this belief that has nothing to do with progeny. Paul alludes here to a widely used confessional formula in connection with the present participle τοῖς πιστεύουσιν ("those who believe").[213] Here are some examples of this formula:[214]

Rom 4:24: ἐπὶ τὸν ἐγείραντα Ἰησοῦν τὸν κύριον ἡμῶν ἐκ νεκρῶν ("in the one raising Jesus our Lord from the dead")

Acts 3:15; 4:10: ὅν ὁ θεός ἤγειρεν ἐκ νεκρῶν ("whom God raised from the dead")

Acts 13:30: ὁ δὲ θεός ἤγειρεν αὐτὸν ἐκ νεκρῶν ("But God raised him from the dead")

Rom 8:11: ὁ ἐγείρας τὸν Ἰησοῦν ἐκ νεκρῶν ("the one who raised Jesus from the dead")

The points of commonality are the use of the verb ἐγείρω ("waken, raise"),[215] the word "Jesus" or a pro-

---

204 Guerra, "Romans 4," 264–65, argues for "continuity" with Judaism as the main point of this verse, overlooking that the "us" are Christ believers who are reckoned to be righteous on a completely different basis than Abraham.

205 Michel, 127; Schlier, 134; Käsemann, 128.

206 Schlatter, 117; Barrett, 99.

207 BAGD (2000) 628.2a, advocated by Weiss, 214; Meyer, 1:217–18; Kühl, 155; Schmidt, 88; Kuss, 1:193; Cranfield, 1:250.

208 See Walter Radl, "μέλλω," *EDNT* 2 (1991) 404.

209 LSJM 1099 says with regard to the definition of μέλλω as "to be destined or likely to," that it indicates "an estimated certainty or strong probability in the past, present, or future," since probabilities for the future can be described as having been calculated at any time.

210 Kühl, 135, followed with hesitation by Wilckens, 1:277; more clearly by Luz, *Geschichtsverständnis*, 113.

211 See Cranfield, 1:250.

212 Stowers, *Rereading*, 247–48, shows that Christ believers are "justified" in a different way than Abraham demonstrated.

213 Michel, 174, sees this present form as an allusion to confessional practice, "We believe. . . ."

214 See Paulsen, *Überlieferung*, 51–55; Kramer, *Christ*, 20–26; Wengst, *Christologische Formeln*, 21–23; Rese, "Formeln," 87–93. A complete listing of parallels is provided in the introduction to 8:1-17.

215 See Jacob Kremer, "ἐγείρω," *EDNT* 1 (1990) 375–76.

noun for him in the accusative, and the phrase ἐκ νεκρῶν ("from the dead"). In contrast to many of these other confessional formulas, the object of faith is God rather than Christ,[216] perhaps to correlate the formulation more closely with the Abraham story.[217] Paul's use of a traditional formula that was probably employed by all of the Roman churches as well as his reference to "Jesus our Lord" serves to include both the weak and the strong in Rome.[218] As Paul explains in detail elsewhere (1 Cor 15), and assumes that every believer understands, the starting point of faith in Christ is faith in his resurrection. If the Crucified One had not been resurrected, there would have been no proof that he was indeed the Messiah. That Gentiles are now included among the descendants of Abraham depends on their having shared this faith.

■ **25** With compact and persuasive parallelism, Paul brings the proof to a conclusion by affirming the redemptive work of Jesus. While the terminology is largely traditional in confessions of the early church,[219] the style is distinctively Pauline.[220] For example, ὃς παρεδόθη ("he was handed over") employs a verb associated with Jesus' being delivered up for execution,[221] his being handed over by Judas,[222] the willingness of Jesus to "give his life as a ransom for many,"[223] but only here and in Rom 8:32 is there reference to being delivered up by God, as the passive verb in this instance implies.[224]

There is a consensus that this widespread use of παραδίδωμι in early Christian confessions was influenced by the Suffering Servant song in Isa 53, where it appears three times:

> And the Lord delivered him up for our sins (καὶ κύριος παρέδωκεν αὐτὸν ταῖς ἁμαρτίαις ἡμῶν). . . . Therefore . . . he shall divide the spoils of the mighty because his soul was delivered up to death (ἀνθ' ὧν παρεδόθη εἰς θάνατον ἡ ψυχὴ αὐτοῦ), and he was numbered among the lawless and he bore the sins of many and was delivered up for the sake of their iniquities (καὶ διὰ τὰς ἁμαρτίας αὐτῶν παρεδόθη) (53:6, 12)

Both the passive verb employed by Paul (παρεδόθη, "he was handed over," Rom 4:25) and the choice of the preposition in the phrase διὰ τὰ παραπτώματα ἡμῶν ("for the sake of our transgressions") echo this passage from Isaiah.[225] In other contexts Paul follows the tradition of early christological confessions in using ὑπέρ ("for"),[226] but the choice of διά ("for the sake of") not only follows Isa 53 but also echoes the use of this preposition in Rom 4:23-24, where the benefit of being set right was in view. In place of "sins" as in Isa 53, Paul employs the nearly synonymous term παράπτωμα ("transgressions").[227] Although this term does not

---

216 Neubrand, *Abraham*, 287, cites with approval Hays, *Echoes*, 84–87, who maintains that the focus here is "theological" rather than "christological."

217 Dunn, 1:223.

218 See Campbell, "3.27–4.25," 372.

219 See Wegenast, *Tradition*, 80–82; Popkes, *Christus Traditus*, 193–94; Wengst, *Christologische Formeln*, 101–3; Gaukesbrink, *Sühnetradition*, 177–79; Lietzmann, 56; Michel, 174; Schlier, 136; Käsemann, 128; Dunn, 1:224.

220 See Kuss, 1:194–95.

221 Mark 9:31 par.; 10:33 par.; 15:1 par., 10 par., 15 par.; John 19:16; Acts 3:13; see Popkes, *Christus Traditus*, 153–68.

222 Mark 14:10, 21, 41; Matt 10:4; John 19:11; see Popkes, *Christus Traditus*, 174–89.

223 Mark 10:45 par.; see also Gal 1:4; 2:20; Eph 5:2, 25; see Popkes, *Christus Traditus*, 169–74.

224 See Meyer, 1:213; Weiss, 214; Schlier, 236; Käsemann, 128; Dunn, 1:224; Popkes, *Christus Traditus*, 193–95; Norman Perrin, "The Use of (Para)didonai

in Connection with the Passion of Jesus in the New Testament," in *A Modern Pilgrimage in New Testament Christology* (Philadelphia: Fortress Press, 1974) 94–103.

225 Popkes, *Christus Traditus*, 194–95, 221; Michel, 175; Dunn, 1:224–25; Albl, *Scripture*, 166; Shum, *Paul's Use of Isaiah*, 189–93. For an unconvincingly skeptical assessment of the influence of Isa 53, see Koch, *Schrift*, 237–38, followed by Powers, *Salvation through Participation*, 128–30.

226 See Harald Riesenfeld, "ὑπέρ," *TDNT* 8 (1972) 508–12.

227 Popkes, *Christus Traditus*, 221, 233–35, suggests that the choice of "transgressions" may have been Pauline rather than traditional, but that the Targum may provide a precedent, despite its later provenance. Wilhelm Michaelis, "παραπίπτω, παράπτωμα," *TDNT* 6 (1968) 172, contends that "transgressions" is simply the equivalent of "sins" in Rom 4:25; see also Michael Wolter, "παράπτωμα," *EDNT* 3 (1991) 33. That "transgressions" is derived

appear in early Christian confessions, it occurs in a prominent place in the Gospels (Matt 6:14-15; Mark 11:25-26) and would have been widely used in recitations of the Lord's Prayer. The word "transgressions" fits Paul's rhetorical purpose by encompassing violations both of Jewish and Greco-Roman norms as described in 1:18–3:25[228] and also by providing a connection to the six occurrences of παράπτωμα in the subsequent discussion of Adam's transgression (5:15-20).[229] On the basis of Paul's citation of the hymn in 3:25-26 that celebrated Christ's blood as the new means of atonement for Jews and Gentiles alike, the claim here is that Christ's shameful death overcame the shame of "our transgressions." Whether one's declaration of war against God had occurred as a Jew or a Gentile, it was exposed and overcome by the cross of Christ. Christ's shameful death in behalf of the shamed conveyed in a new way the divine "grace" that Paul had identified as the key to Abraham's promise (4:16b)

In a similar way to Paul's editing of the atonement hymn in 3:25-26, he concludes here on the note of divine righteousness. The second half of the synonymous parallelism employs another passive verb and the same preposition as in the first half: καὶ ἠγέρθη διὰ τὴν δικαίωσιν ἡμῶν ("and was raised for the sake of our rightness"). While the verb ἐγείρω ("raised") was typical for early Christian confessions, as I showed in connection with the preceding verse, neither the preposition διά ("in behalf of") nor the noun δικαίωσις ("rightness, justification") was employed. The word δικαίωσις can refer to the "act of executing" righteous judgment,[230] and is typically translated as "justification,"[231] "acquittal,"[232] or "vindication,"[233] but I prefer the word "rightness" to correlate with the imputation scheme from Gen 15:6 that is dominant in this midrash. In Paul's view it is Christ's resurrection that proves the validity of the gospel that in Christ's death there is a conveyance of grace for all. When converts accept the gospel in faith, they are "reckoned" to be right before God and are placed in a community in which honor is dispensed according to a new principle of equality. It is not just the weak, or only the strong, who are recipients of this new status of honor, because it is a matter διὰ τὴν δικαίωσιν ἡμῶν ("on account of our rightness"). This "our" encompasses both the Jewish and the Gentile believers for whom the gospel's power is effective for righteousness, according to the thesis of the letter (1:16-17). They are all heirs of Abraham's promise, sharing his faith that God is the one who "who gives life to the dead and calls that which does not exist into existence."[234]

228 Michaelis, "παραπίπτω, παράπτωμα," 170, refers to Polybius *Hist.* 9:10.6-7, "if any might say it was a blunder (παράπτωμα) of the doers." Similarly Diodorus Siculus *Hist.* 19.100 employs παράπτωμα as a blunder leading to defeat, "on account of the defeat (παράπτωμα) that occurred." See also *Hist.* 15.23.5; 16.20.5; and Ps 18:13, "who will understand his transgressions?" as examples of cross-cultural employment of this term. Philo *Migr.* 170 refers to "great errors" (μεγάλα . . . παραπτώματα) caused by lack of knowledge and boldness.

from an independent translation of Isa 53:12 is argued on the basis of 1QIsa^a, b by Hermann Patsch, "Zum alttestamentlichen Hintergrund von Römer 4,25 und I. Petrus 2,24," *ZNW* 60 (1969) 277–78.

229 Powers, *Salvation through Participation*, 127, argues that the appearance of παράπτωμα is an indication of Pauline authorship of this confession.
230 Gottlob Schrenk, "δικαίωσις," *TDNT* 2 (1964) 223.
231 Spicq, "δίκαιος κτλ.," 344–45; Meyer, 1:218; Barrett, 99; Cranfield, 1:226; Käsemann, 118, 129; Wilckens, 1:273; Murray, 155–56; Morris, 215; Moo, 288; Byrne, 152.
232 BAGD (2000) 250: "justification, vindication, acquittal."
233 Dunn, 1:255.
234 See particularly Gaukesbrink, *Sühnetradition*, 178.

5:1-11 The Second Proof

5

The First Pericope

Introduction: Righteousness in Christ Requires a New System of Boasting

1/ Therefore, having been made righteous "by faith," let us have[a] peace with God through our Lord Jesus Christ, 2/ through whom we also have gained access in the faith[b] to this grace in which we have stood; let us also boast in hope of the glory of God; 3/ not only that,[c] but let us also boast in our afflictions, knowing that this affliction produces fortitude, 4/ and this fortitude approbation, and this approbation hope, 5/ and this hope does not cause shame, because the love of God has been poured into our hearts through [the] Holy Spirit that was given to us.

6/ "For[d] while we were still weak, still[e] Christ died at that time on behalf of the ungodly." 7/ "For scarcely[f] on behalf of a righteous [person] will someone die!" "For perhaps on behalf of the good [person] someone might dare to die!" 8/ But God[g] demonstrates to us his own love in that while[h] we were yet sinners "Christ died on our behalf." 9/ Much more, therefore,[i] having been put right now by his blood, shall we be saved through him from the wrath. 10/ For if while we were enemies we were reconciled to God through the death of his Son, much more, having been reconciled, shall we be saved by his life, 11/ not only that,[j] but also boasting[k] in God through our Lord Jesus Christ,[l] through whom we have now received this reconciliation.

a The subjunctive ἔχωμεν is found in ℵ* A B* C D K L 33 61ᶜ 69 81 181 436 614 621 630 720 915 945 1175 1243 1398 1678 1735 1739* 1838 1874 1912 1942 1962 2197 2516ˢᵘᵖ *l* 846 *pm* Lectᵖᵗ b d f g mon o vg bo arm eth Marcionᵃᶜᶜ· ᵗᵒ ᵀᵉʳᵗ Orˡᵃᵗ GrNy Chr Theodore Hes Cyr¹/⁵ Thretˡᵉᵐ Ambst Pel Julian-Eclanum Aug and thus has "far better external support" (Metzger, *Textual Commentary*, 452) than the indicative ἔχομεν in ℵ¹ B² F Gᵍʳ P Ψ 0220ᵛⁱᵈ 5 6 61* 88 104 218 256 263 323 326 330 365 424 441 451 459 467 623 629 917 1241 1319 1505 1506 1563 1573 1718 1739ᶜ 1751 1836 1845 1846 1852 1875 1877 1881 1908 1959 2110 2127 2138 2200 2344 2464 2492 2495 2523 2544 2718 *pm* Lectᵖᵗ·ᴬᴰ ar vgᵐˢˢ sa geo slav Bas GrNyᵐˢˢ Didᵈᵘᵇ Epiph Cyr⁴/⁵. Additional support for the indicative is adduced by W. H. P. Hatch, "A Recently Discovered Fragment of the Epistle to the Romans," *HTR* 45 (1952) 83. Although many interpreters and the text-critical committees controlling UBS³ and Nestle-Aland²⁶/²⁷ believe the context favors the indicative, particularly with the indicative ἐστήκαμεν in the second half of the sentence (5:2), the more strongly attested subjunctive form should be accepted. The assessment of what the context requires is highly subjective, resting on an exegetical legacy that has always stressed the doctrinal objectivity of Romans and downplayed its situational orientation. Stanley E. Porter has made a compelling case for the subjunctive in "Argument," 662–65. Advocates of the subjunctive reading include older exegetes discussed by Weiss, 217, along with Sanday and Headlam, 120; Lagrange, 101; Neugebauer, *In Christus*, 61; Dinkler, *RAC* 3:463–64; Dodd, 72. Kuss, 1:201–2, argues on grounds of the intermixing of indicative and imperative in a later passage (Rom 6:12-23) for the originality of the subjunctive, bearing the sense "let us maintain peace." Most commentators opt for the traditional indicative: Lietzmann, 58; Käsemann, 133; Barrett, 102; Cranfield, 1:257; Wolter, *Röm 5,1-11*, 89–94; Wilckens, 1:288–89. Aland and Aland, *Text*, 286; Metzger, *Textual Commentary*, 452; and others suggest that an early dictation error accounts for a substitution of the subjunctive for the indicative, but this argument throws no light on which version was originally intended. While it is likely that the Greek *omega* and *omicron* were pronounced in virtually identical fashion by first-century speakers, just as in Hellenistic, Byzantine, and modern Greek, the confusion could have gone either way. In reporting on his computerized study of such confusion ("Orthography and Theology," 179–83), Ian A. Moir finds many instances where scribes intended to write *omega* and instead wrote *omicron* and vice versa. Wilckens, 1:288–89, cites Karl-Hermann Schelkle, *Paulus–Lehre der Väter* (Düsseldorf: Patmos, 1956), who showed that most church fathers interpreted this verse as exhortative.

b The words τῇ πίστει ("in faith") are not in B D F G 0220 d* f g sa Orˡᵃᵗ³/⁵ Bas Ambst Julian-Eclanum Aug, probably deleted for stylistic reasons; see Wolter, *Römer 5,1-11*, 105. However, Lietzmann, 58, refers to the deletion as arbitrary. The inclusion of "in faith" is strongly supported in ℵ*,² C K L P Ψ 5 6 33 61 69 81 104 181 218 256 263 323 326 330 365 424 441 436 451 459 467 621 623 629 630 720 917 945 1175 1241 1243 1319 1398 1505 1506 1563 1573 1678 1718 1735 1739 1751 1836 1838 1852 1874 1875 1877 1881 1908 1912 1942 1959 2110 2127 2138 2197 2200 2344 2464 2492 2495 2516ˢᵘᵖ 2523 2718 *Maj Lect* ar b d² mon o vg syᵖ, ʰ, ᵖᵃˡ bo arm eth geo slav Orˡᵃᵗ²/⁵ Chr¹/² Cyr. Some less significant variants include ἐν τῇ πίστει ("in the faith") in ℵ¹ A 88 915 1962 1845 1846 2544 *l* 597 vgᵐˢˢ Chr¹/² Hes.

c D* ar adds τοῦτο ("this") to smooth out the elliptical phrase, but commentators appear to agree that it is secondary.

d A complicated jumble of textual variants at this point has been sorted out by Wilckens, 1:294, although he does not include all the witnesses: (1) B 945 vgᵐˢˢ sa (bo) (syᵖ, ᵖᵃˡ) [see (3) below] Aug provide εἰ γε ("if indeed") with ἔτι five words later; (2) ms 201, 1852, vgᵐˢˢ bo provide εἰ γὰρ γε ("for if indeed"); (3) the Peshitta supports εἰ δέ ("but if"); (4) ℵ A C D* 81 104 256 263 365 424 459 1241 1319 1506 1573 2127 *pc* syʰ Marcᵃᶜᶜ. ᵗᵒ ᴱᵖⁱᵖʰ provide the reading ἔτι γὰρ ("for still") with a second ἔτι five words later; (5) ἔτι γὰρ ("for still") without a second ἔτι, as in D² K P Ψ 6 33 69 88 323 326 330 436 614 945 1175 1243 1505 1735 1739 1836 1874 1881 1912 1962 2200 2344 2464 2495 (syᵖ) arm eth geo slav Orˡᵃᵗ Apollinaris Chr; (6) F G ar b d f g mon (o) vg Irˡᵃᵗ Ambst Faustinus Pel provide εἰς τί γάρ ("for to what") with the later ἔτί, while D¹ omits the ἔτι (though Swanson, *Vaticanus: Romans*, 66, disagrees). Wilckens concurs with Nestle-Aland²⁶/²⁷ that the fourth option is most likely original, with options 1-3 as transcription errors and options 5-6 as conscious corrections of the awkward duplication of ἔτι. Cranfield, 1:263, suggests that all the options except for the fourth originated in efforts to eliminate the duplication of ἔτι. This appears more likely, since multiple and varied transcription errors at the same spot are improbable and since the deletion of the second ἔτι in the sentence also occurred. See also Michael, "Phenomenon," 152.

e The word ἔτι ("still") was not in D² K P L Ψ 6 33 69 88 323 326 330 436 614 945 1175 1243 1505 1735 1739 1836 1874 1881 1912 1962 2200 2344 2464 2495 (syᵖ) arm eth Orˡᵃᵗ Apollinaris Chr, probably deleted to eliminate the redundancy with the first word in v. 6. See Wilckens, 1:294. A possibility to be considered is whether the ἔτι/ἔτι doublet signals a marginal gloss of κατὰ καιρόν introduced

erroneously into the text; the intended emendation was to be ἔτι γὰρ < κατὰ καιρὸν > Χριστὸς ὄντων ἡμῶν ἀσθενῶν ὑπὲρ ἀσεβῶν ἀπέθανεν ("For while we were weak, Christ <at the right time> died for the ungodly").

f ℵ* 1739 *pc* and Or read μόγις ("hardly") instead of μόλις ("scarcely"), an understandable confusion of two closely related and virtually synonymous terms, according to Sanday and Headlam, 127.

g The words ὁ θεός ("God") appear before εἰς ἡμᾶς ("to us") in D F G L 629 1241 2197 *pc* lat Irˡᵃᵗ and are deleted in B. Wilckens, 1:297, suspects a correction for christological consistency in the deletion, and prefers the placement of "God" after "to us" as in ℵ A C K P Ψ 5 6 33 61 69 81 88 104 181 218 256ᶜ 263 323 326 330 365 424 436 441 459 467 614 621 623 630 720 915 917 945 1175 1243 1319 1398 1505 1506 1563 1573 1678 1718 1735 1739 1751 1836 1838 1845 1846 1852 1874 1875 1877 1881 1908 1942 1959 1962 2110 2127 2138 2200 2344 2464 2492 2495 2516 2523 2544 2718 *Maj*.

h Before the word ἔτι ("while"), D¹ F G it syᵖ Cyp Ambst provide the reading εἰ ("if"), a secondary addition that appears to downplay the universality of sin as argued in these verses. I find no discussion of this in the commentaries.

i The term οὖν ("therefore") is missing in D* F G *pc* it Irˡᵃᵗ Ambst, resulting in a smoother reading since it disturbs the idiomatic expression πολλῷ μᾶλλον. The absence is not discussed in any of the standard commentaries.

j Just as in 5:3, D* F G it Ambst add τοῦτο ("this") for stylistic reasons. It is not likely to have been original, since the reading is rougher without it.

k A few late texts (L 69 104 330 365 630 945 1241 1319 1573 1735 2344 2464 *al* latt) provide the first person plural form καυχώμεθα ("we boast"), and F G have the ending -ωμεν in place of the strongly attested participial form καυχώμενοι ("boasting, we boast"). These variants should be seen as secondary grammatical improvements of Paul's awkward habit of using participles where finite verbs might be anticipated. Cranfield, 1:268, cites 2 Cor 5:12; 7:5; 8:4; and Phil 3:4 as examples.

l The word Χριστοῦ ("Christ") is absent from B 1739 1881ᶜ *pc*, probably an "accidental omission" according to Cranfield, 1:268. It may have resulted from haplography with the similar sounding expression that follows: δι᾽ οὗ. The inclusion of Χριστοῦ is strongly supported by ℵ A C D F G K L P Ψ 6 33 69 88 104 323 326 330 365 424 614 945 1175 1241 1243 1319 1505 1506 1573 1735 1836 1874 1881*ᵛⁱᵈ 2344 2464 2495 *Maj* lat sy.

Analysis

It is widely recognized that this pericope provides both an introduction to the themes of Rom 5–8 and a development of the preceding argument.[1] It develops and extends the preceding argument while answering questions and objections. In 5:1-2 Paul opens the argument with a classic *transitio*, defined by the *Rhetorica ad Herennium* as "a figure which briefly recalls what has been said, and likewise briefly sets forth what is to follow next."[2] Two exhortative theses are stated in this transition concerning the nature of righteousness through faith,[3] and the powerful rhetorical momentum beginning with v. 2 tends to blur the lines between having peace with God in the present (vv. 1-2b) and boasting in future glory (vv. 2c-5).[4] These two themes are recapitulated in chiastic order in v. 11,[5] providing an effective conclusion to this introductory pericope. The repetition of the refrain διὰ τοῦ κυρίου ἡμῶν Ἰησοῦ Χριστοῦ, δι᾽ οὗ ("through our Lord Jesus Christ, through whom") in vv. 1-2a and 11 seals this conclusion, and is replicated by similar phrases in later pericopes (5:21; 6:23; 7:25; 8:39) that constitute the second proof of the letter.[6] Other terms reduplicated to provide thematic unity in the passage are δικαιωθέντες ("having been set right") in 5:1 and 9; ἐλπίς ("hope") in vv. 2, 4, 5; ἀποθνῄσκω ("die") in vv. 6, 7-8; and καταλλάγω-γή ("reconcile") in vv. 10-

11.[7] Parallelism between lines of roughly equal length begins with vv. 1-2a, enhanced by the reduplication of ἔχω ("we have")[8] and homoioteleuton in the perfect tense endings in v. 2: ἐσχήκαμεν ("we have gained") and ἑστήκαμεν ("we have stood"). The reduplication of καυχώμεθα ("let us boast/we boast") in vv. 2b and 3a leads into an effective rhetorical climax (*gradatio*) with the repetition of key words in four parallel phrases in vv. 3b-5a.[9] The climax reaches its apex in v. 5a with the third reduplication of ἐλπίς ("hope") from vv. 3c and 4b.[10] The statement of the two major theses is completed in v. 5b with a coda concerning the love of God and the gift of the Spirit that provides the experiential grounding of both theses. When the introductory line to the climax in v. 2b is counted, this coda completes the colon with a total of seven lines, reflecting the Hebraic rhetorical preference for the number representing totality, completeness, and perfection.

The christological rationale for peace and hope is provided in vv. 6-11, consisting of two sections marked by sporadic parallelism and by several chiastic developments.[11] The first is vv. 6-8 in which Louw has pointed to a chiastic pattern on the thematic level in vv. 6 and 8, referring to the death of Christ, while v. 7a and b refer in parallel fashion to humans dying for someone else, resulting in an A, B, B', A' sequence.[12] The chiasm is held together by the fourfold reduplication of ὑπέρ ("on

---

1   See Dahl, *Studies*, 82, 88–90; Luz, "Aufbau," 178. Wilckens, 1:286–87, in particular, points out the significant connections between 5:1-11 and the preceding four chapters. Elliott, *Rhetoric of Romans*, 226, contends that "Romans 5 is the pivot on which the letter's argument turns," because it channels the argument of the preceding four chapters into the new life described in succeeding chapters. Patricia M. McDonald, "Romans 5:1-11 as a Rhetorical Bridge," *JSNT* 40 (1990) 81–96, sees a bridge of a different sort, between Paul and his audience.

2   *Rhet. Her.* 4.26.35; cited by Cosby, "Paul's Persuasive Language," 213. See also Reid, *Rhetoric*, 94.

3   Louw, 2:68–69, identifies the semantic separation of the material in 5:1-2b and 5:3-5 but does not speak of "theses." Weiss, "Beiträge," 225, refers to 5:1 as a "basic thesis with full clausula," but does not similarly identify 5:2c as the statement of a second thesis. Wilckens, 1:288, refers to two separate theses in this passage, and Lamarche and le Dû, *Romains 5–8*, 22–23, overlook the *transitus* in proposing a less

plausible, parallel structure for the pericope: 1-2 // 5; 3-4 // 11; 6-9 // 10.

4   See Michel, 176–77.

5   Käsemann, 132, observes the chiastic pattern in v. 11 but associates it only with vv. 1-2 rather than with the two theses developed in vv. 1-2b and 2b-5.

6   See Harvey, *Listening*, 189–90.

7   See ibid., 191.

8   Noted by Cosby, "Paul's Persuasive Language," 213.

9   See ibid., 214–15; Reid, *Rhetoric*, 103. Augustine, followed by Wolter, *Röm 5,1-11*, 149–50, understood v. 5a as an *ambitus sive circuitus*, commenting on the climax by referring back to v. 2b.

10 See Reid, *Rhetoric*, 104.

11 Ibid., 91–115.

12 Louw, 2:69.

behalf of"), the threefold reduplication of the verb $\overset{\backprime}{\alpha}\pi o$-
$\vartheta\nu\acute{\eta}\sigma\kappa\omega$ ("die") in vv. 6-8,[13] and the duplication of $\overset{\backprime}{\epsilon}\tau\iota$
("still"). It has been proposed that the first three lines of
this chiasm (vv. 6-7b) are placed in the mouth of an
imaginary interlocutor,[14] with v. 6 in particular understood as a rhetorical question.[15] But since the formulation of v. 6 does not conform to interrogatory style,
containing both a genitive absolute and the argumentative conjunction "for," it is better to take it as a citation
from or an allusion to an early Christian creed.[16] Moreover, it makes good sense out of an otherwise contradictory discourse to take v. 7a and b as comments by
imaginary interlocutors,[17] who are answered by the
restatement of a christological creed in v. 8.

The final paragraph (vv. 9-11) contains a "lesser to
the greater" argument with an effective parallelism[18] in
lines that are not of precisely comparable length.[19] The
reduplication of $\nu\hat{\upsilon}\nu$ ("now") in vv. 9 and 11 provides an
eschatological intensity to this final paragraph, which
concludes with a recapitulation of the themes of boasting and reconciliation.[20] First person plural forms dominate this paragraph, just as in the rest of the pericope,[21]
and link Paul with the Roman audience in the same
experience of righteousness and reconciliation.

Rhetorical Disposition

IV.   The *Probatio*
5:1–   B. The second proof: Life in Christ as a new system of
8:39   honor that replaces the quest for status through con-
        formity to the law
5:1-11   1. Introduction: righteousness in Christ requires a new
           system of boasting
5:1-5   a. Two implications resulting from righteousness
            through faith
5:1-2a   1) *Transitio* into the first implication: the appro-
              priateness of having peace with God
5:1a   a) The recapitulation of the premise concern-
                ing righteousness through faith
5:1b   b) The exhortation to have peace with God
                through Christ
5:2a   c) The clarification of the role of Christ in
                providing access to grace
5:2b-5a   2) *Transitio* into the second implication: the
             appropriateness of boasting in the hope of the
             glory of God
5:2b   a) The exhortation to boast in the hope of
              glory, concluding the *transitio*
5:3a 5a   b) The climax of boasting in the face of afflic
             tions
5:3a   (1) The exhortation to boast in affliction
5:3b   (2) Affliction produces endurance
5:4a   (3) Endurance produces confirmation
5:4b   (4) Confirmation produces hope
5:5a   (5) Hope does not disappoint
5:5b   3) The experiential grounding of the implica-
            tions concerning peace and hope
            a) The ground of peace and hope in the love
             of God experienced in the heart
            b) The means by which love is communi-
             cated: through the Spirit apportioned to
             believers
5:6-11   b. The christological rationale of righteousness as
          current reconciliation and future salvation
5:6-8   1) The chiastic discussion concerning the death
            of Christ for the undeserving
5:6   a) The credal declaration about the "weak"
             receiving the benefits of Christ's death
5:7   b) Rhetorical comments by imaginary
             interlocutors from common sense
5:7a   (1) The unlikelihood of someone dying for
             the sake even of a righteous person
5:7b   (2) The possibility of someone dying for a
             "good" person
5:8   c) The response to the interlocutors by
             reasserting the formula about Christ's
             death for sinners
5:9-10   2) The syllogism concerning future salvation of
            sinners
5:9   a) Salvation from wrath
5:9a   (1) The christological premise of righteous-
             ness through the blood of Christ
5:9b   (2) The inference from the greater to the

---

13   See Cosby, "Paul's Persuasive Language," 216.
14   See Porter, "Argument," 666–67.
15   See ibid., 666, who builds on the work of Michael,
      "Phenomenon," 150–54; and Black, 76–77.
16   See Michel, 134–35; Wengst, *Formeln*, 78; for a
      reconstruction of the original confessional citation,
      see the exegesis below.
17   Reid, *Rhetoric*, 108–9, argues that 5:7 is part of a syl-
      logism "that progresses from the universal to the

particular," but most commentators find this illogical.
18   Reid, *Rhetoric*, 110.
19   Weiss, "Beiträge," 226, suggests that the phrase "by
      him from the wrath" in 5:9 might be struck for styl-
      istic purposes, but this is an instance where theolog-
      ical clarity took precedence over symmetry.
20   See Reid, *Rhetoric*, 113–14.
21   See McDonald, "Romans 5.1-11," 88–91.

	lesser: more certain is salvation from wrath
5:10	b) Salvation in the form of reconciliation
5:10a	(1) The christological premise of reconciliation through the death of Christ
5:10b	(2) The inference from the greater to the lesser: more certain is salvation for believers
5:11	c) The chiastic recapitulation
5:11a	(1) The appropriateness of boasting in God through Christ
5:11b	(2) The christological basis of receiving reconciliation

Exegesis

■ **1** After summing up the burden of the preceding proof in the clause, "having been set right by faith," Paul turns to an elaboration of the implications. In an effective transition in v. 1a, he picks up the theme of righteousness through the death of Christ in 4:25.[22] By employing the nominative plural of the aorist passive participle, he clearly refers to an event in the past, an event that extended righteousness to all believers, with reference perhaps to the moment of baptism[23] or more broadly to the acceptance of the gospel in conversion.[24] The righteousness thereby gained is a matter of divine gift, as indicated by the passive voice. This clause sums up the argument in the first proof that no person or group can stand before God on the basis of achievements or prior status but only on the basis of grace. By citing again the ἐκ πίστεως ("by faith") formula derived from Hab 2:4, and employed earlier at Rom 1:17; 3:26, 30; 4:16, Paul insists that such righteousness never comes through works but only by faith in the gospel. The believers have been surpassingly honored, but not on the basis of their achievements.

The text-critical decision in favor of the more strongly supported subjunctive, "let us have peace,"[25] was made without consideration of the interpretive implications. Nevertheless, it has a significant affect on the understanding of this entire pericope,[26] indeed of the entire second proof. Most commentaries reject the subjunctive on theological grounds by affirming that "peace . . . is the gift of God which no one can merit or earn,"[27] or by rejecting the implication that "a man who has been justified may thereafter freely choose whether or not he will be at peace with God."[28] The house and tenement churches in Rome are acting in so combative a manner against one another, however, that it is clear that they have not yet embodied the peace that Paul has in mind. Stated more generally, Paul is saying, "Now that God has provided the opportunity to be in right relationship with him, let us make the necessary response and take advantage of his offer" by entering into "harmonious communion."[29] It is clearly peace πρὸς θεόν ("with, toward God"), but it has significant social implications. Rather than a triumphalist argument about the current possession of peace and hope by Christian believers that the indicative interpretation has traditionally assumed,[30] the subjunctive produces an admonition about the concrete embodiment of faith in the life of the congregation. The formulation in the first person plural includes all the members of Paul's audience as well as Paul and his colleagues in a common obligation.[31] The theme of obligation carries through when the exhortative subjunctive in 5:1 is translated in similar ways in vv. 2, 3, and 11.

Given the argument in the first proof concerning the aggressive campaign of the human race to suppress the truth about God and to enter into competition with the Creator[32] that resulted in social discord and alienation (1:18-32), the issue of "peace with God" should be

22 See Reid, *Rhetoric*, 93–94.
23 Schlier, 140.
24 Zeller, 108.
25 BDF §363 refers to the subjunctive bearing the sense of "volition or obligation," closely related to the imperative; §364 describes the "hortatory subjunctive," which "supplements the imperative."
26 See Elliott, *Rhetoric of Romans*, 227–28; Stowers, *Rereading*, 249; Seifrid, *Justification*, 223: Rom 5:1-11 is hortatory, either implicitly or explicitly.
27 Martin, *Reconciliation*, 148; so also Leenhardt, 132.

28 Cranfield, 1:102. Hofmann, 163–67, is exceptional in accepting the subjunctive reading.
29 Theodore Pulcini, "In Right Relationship with God: Present Experience and Future Fulfillment: An Exegesis of Romans 5:1-11," *SVTQ* 36 (1992) 67.
30 See Meyer, 1:221–22; Kühl, 160; Byrne, 165.
31 See McDonald, "Rhetorical Bridge," 81–84, 87–90; Pulcini, "Right Relationship," 64–65; Reid, *Rhetoric*, 96–97.
32 See Elliott, *Rhetoric of Romans*, 228.

understood as introducing the theme of reconciliation found in 5:10-11.[33] Its social antithesis in this passage is "boasting," in which groups claim honor for themselves alone while denigrating others[34] and, ultimately, making war on God. Although εἰρήνην ἔχειν ("to have peace") is a common, political expression,[35] in this context it has a comprehensive implication that includes the relationship with God as well as the rest of creation, including one's fellow humans. The term εἰρήνη refers explicitly to difficulties within the congregation in 14:19.[36] Erich Dinkler has shown that "peace" has this kind of comprehensive implication;[37] Egon Brandenburger stresses the cosmic horizons of Paul's conception[38] but does not touch on the concrete embodiment of this conception in the congregational situation. Michael Wolter on the other hand wishes to restrict εἰρήνη to the relationship with God,[39] as if this term had no social dimension. The comprehensive range of "peace" must be kept in view, if Paul's apocalyptic theology and missional goals are allowed their natural scope.[40]

The phrase "through our Lord Jesus Christ" defines the means by which peace with God is achieved, but since so many commentators understand the context as indicative rather than exhortative, the tendency is to relate this phrase to justification and reconciliation already achieved and to consider it identical in reference to the following verse.[41] Although he also favors the indicative, Godet observes that the past tense verbal forms in vv. 1a and 2a refer to redemptive work already completed, whereas the formulation of v. 1b implies "a present and permanent taking in possession" through the power of Christ currently active in believers.[42] Their activities under the lordship of Christ are in view here; he is the one who sustains the ongoing task of living within the peace of God as believers respond to the imperative: "let us have peace!" Christ is the lord of the church, and as 14:3-12 makes clear, to hold other Christian groups in contempt or to judge them as lawless is to disregard that lordship. Any peace with God that is achieved through the lordship of Christ has a necessary social correlate, if we take into account the argument of this letter as a whole.

■ **2** The second διά ("through") phrase in the pericope carries forward the theme of the work of Christ, who granted "access in the faith to this grace in which we have stood." The noun προσαγωγή ("access"), employed here for the only time in the authentic Pauline letters (also in Eph 2:18; 3:12), typically appears in the context of entree to kings, dignitaries, and shrines. The LXX employs the verbal form of this term with reference to approaching the altar with an offering,[43] as in the command that "the congregation bring (προσάξει) an unblemished calf of the herd for a sin offering, and they shall bring (προσάξει) it to the doors of the tabernacle of witness" (Lev 4:14). Only those qualified and unblemished can approach God in this way (e.g., Exod 29:4, 8; Lev 21:18-19; Num 8:9-10), a theme extensively developed by the Essenes, who believed that their community

---

33   Hasler, "εἰρήνη," 396; Stuhlmacher, "Begriff des Friedens," 33–37; Reid, *Rhetoric*, 96–97. That the combination of "righteousness" and "peace" in 5:1 is derived from Isa 32:17, as argued by Shum, *Paul's Use of Isaiah*, 193–96, is not convincing.

34   Enno Heyken, "ἔχωμεν oder ἔχομεν," *MPTh* 41 (1952) 94–98, perceives a narrow focus on the tendency within Judaism to boast in its conformity with the law. In view of 14:1–15:13, both the Jewish and Gentile Christians appear to be involved in different forms of boasting.

35   Andocides *Pac.* 33.2; Xenophon *Hell.* 3.4.6.7; Demosthenes *Orat.* 12.22.8; Polybius *Hist.* 21.41.8.1; etc.

36   Dunn, 1:247, refers to peace implying an "outworking" in the life of the congregation, but instead of developing this, he turns to the theological issue of the connection between peace and the Jewish covenant.

37   Dinkler, *EIRENE*, 34–35, citing Ps 34:15, "Let us seek peace and follow it." See also Martin, *Reconciliation*, 148.

38   Brandenburger, *Frieden im Neuen Testament*, 51–60.

39   Wolter, *Röm 5,1-11*, 99–102.

40   See Haacker, "Friedensmemorandum," 30; Findeis, *Versöhnung*, 321, 327.

41   Meyer, 1:222; Cranfield, 1:258; Fitzmyer, 395; Wolter, *Römer 5,1-11*, 91–95; Thüsing, *Per Christum*, 184–86.

42   Godet, 187; see also Kuss, 1:203. Schettler, *Durch Christus*, 19, proposed a reference to both present and past activity of Christ.

43   See Karl Ludwig Schmidt, "ἀγωγή κτλ.," *TDNT* 1 (1964) 131; Wolter, *Röm 5,1-11*, 107–9.

349

alone enjoyed access to God (e.g., 1QH 12:20-26).[44] There are verbal similarities in Greek religious references to πομπὰς καὶ προσαγωγάς ("processions and approaches") to the sanctuary.[45] The same language is employed in approaching a king; for example, Xenophon reports that if any wished to obtain an audience with the Persian emperor Cyrus, "they were to court favor as my friends for access (τοὺς ἐμοὺς φίλους δεομένους προσαγωγῆς)."[46] G. P. Wetter argues in this connection that προσαγωγή reflects the contemporary imperial cult.[47] This background throws light on two details in Paul's formulation: this access is to "grace," and it comes "by faith," both of which reverse the cultural expectation that approaching either God or the emperor requires a high level of purity and clout. This is an unqualified access, open to the shamed as well as the honored without regard to their performance. These details need to be interpreted in the light of the preceding proof, which showed that divine χάρις ("grace") is conveyed by Christ to the undeserving and that the righteousness required for access to God comes by means of πίστις ("faith") rather than by performance. The dative expression τῇ πίστει ("in faith") refers back to the preceding verse, which summarized the message of the first proof that righteousness comes "by faith" in Christ rather than by works of the law. That proof reached its climax in the treatment of Abraham's faith, which was reckoned as righteousness and becomes the model of Christian believers (4:16-25).[48]

Two verbs are employed here in the perfect tense, "we have gained" (ἐσχήκαμεν) and "we have stood" (ἐστήκαμεν), to reflect a status gained by believers in the past and continued to the present.[49] The expression "to stand in grace" sounds odd in Greek and conveys the impression that grace is a sphere into which one enters and remains.[50] The background of this usage is the LXX, which employs ἵστημι in the context of the priest's or congregation's "standing before God," for example, in Lev 9:5, "all the congregation drew nigh,

and they stood (ἔστησαν) before the Lord."[51] The Levites are appointed "to stand before him [the Lord] to minister" (στῆναι ἐναντίον αὐτοῦ λειτουργεῖν, 2 Chr 29:11). On the question of who "will stand" (στήσεται) in his holy place, the famous passage from LXX Ps 24:3-4 declares, "He who has clean hands and a pure heart, who has not lifted up his soul to vanity, nor sworn deceitfully to his neighbor." This language is prominent in Qumran documents, which promise that God will "raise up the son of your handmaid to stand everlastingly (להתיצב) in your presence" (1QS 11:16-17).[52] Paul routinely uses expressions such as "to stand in faith" (1 Cor 15:1; 16:13; 2 Cor 1:24), "to stand in the Lord" (Phil 4:1), or "to stand in one Spirit" (Phil 1:27). It seems clear that he conceives the situation of believers as standing in a "collective realm of salvation and power."[53] Unlike traditional religion and politics, however, entrance to this realm is completely free to everyone, regardless of their previously shameful status. By setting one's faith in the grace of Christ, one gains access to God's love in a completely impartial form. Equal access renders competition between groups of believers in Rome fundamentally inappropriate. Paul employs first person plural verbs, "we have gained access" and "we have stood" in this realm together, to include himself and the rest of the early church in all its varieties in an indivisible solidarity. All have a direct access to the throne of grace, to use the expression from Heb 4:16, an access gained "through our Lord Jesus Christ" (Rom 5:1).

This reference to standing before God has a direct bearing on the congregational situation, as indicated by the use of the verbs στήκειν and ἵστημι in 14:4 that deal with the question of the legitimacy of believers' not belonging to one's own group. Paul states, "It is in relation to his own Lord that he stands (στήκει) or falls. He will be made to stand (σταθήσεται) because the Lord has the power to enable him to stand (στῆσαι)." It therefore constricts Paul's point to connect these verses exclu-

44   See Wolter, *Röm 5,1-11*, 113–16.
45   Herodotus *Hist.* 2.58.
46   Xenophon *Cyr.* 7.5.45.
47   Wetter, *Charis*, 18, cited by Wolter, *Röm 5,1-11*, 124.
48   See Dunn, 1:248.
49   See Godet, 188; Schlier, 142; Murray, 219.
50   Wobbe, *Charis-Gedanke*, 80; Dunn, 1:248.

51   See Walter Grundmann, "στήκω, ἵστημι," *TDNT* 7 (1971) 643; Wolter, *Röm 5,1-11*, 121, cites Deut 29:9; 1 Kgs 8:14; 2 Chr 18:18; 29:11; Zech 3:7; idem, "ἵστημι," *EDNT* 2 (1991) 207.
52   In "Stehen," 147–66, Grundmann also discusses 1QH 4:21-22, 28, 33, 35-56, etc.
53   Wolter, *Röm 5,1-11*, 125.

sively to the matter of Gentile access,[54] which had already been established in the preceding proof and which is rendered implausible by the first person plural forms throughout this pericope. Paul is here addressing all branches of early Christianity in Rome, celebrating their common relationship under the lordship of Christ.

In 5:2c the verb καυχώμεθα can either be translated as an indicative, which most commentators prefer, or as a hortatory subjunctive, matching the finite verb in the preceding verse.[55] The indicative is particularly inappropriate in this instance, because it places both Paul and the Romans in the position of continuing to act contrary to his previous critique of boasting (2:17, 23; 3:27; 4:2). If the verb is in the subjunctive, it clearly indicates that he is recommending a revolutionary new form of boasting to replace the claims of honorable status and performance that mark traditional religion in the Greco-Roman world. While boasting was criticized in 2.17 and excluded because of divine impartiality in 3:37, it is now allowed in a reversed form, not in what the groups in Rome claim as their superiority over one another but "only in what God has accomplished through Christ."[56] Rather than boasting in present status and past achievements, Paul recommends a form of boasting consistent with the realm of grace that concentrates on two things: in "hope of the glory of God," and in the next verse, "in our afflictions." Neither was a suitable basis for boasting in the honor-shame systems of the first century.

In Greco-Roman culture boasting was oriented to one's own glory or the glory of one's family or group;[57] it was an essential aspect of the social competition by which the "dyadic personality" defined itself.[58] The contrast with boasting in God's glory is visible in E. A. Judge's description of the prevailing social attitudes:[59]

By New Testament times the predominant Stoic school of philosophy had raised the estimate [of the value of glory] to a very high level, apparently in response to the cult of glory among the Roman nobility. It was held that the winning of glory was the only adequate reward for merit in public life, and that, given the doubt as to the state of man after death, it was the effective assurance of immortality. It therefore became a prime and admired objective of public figures to enshrine themselves, by actually defining their own glory, in the undying/memory of posterity. What was more, a man was thought the meaner for not pursuing this quest for glory. . . . Self-magnification thus became a feature of Hellenic higher education, and by means merely a caricature of its aims.[60]

In the Corinthian correspondence, Paul had worked out the contrast between Greco-Roman/Jewish boasting and the new orientation required by faith in Christ. Since the entire system of honor and shame has been reversed (1 Cor 1:26-28), it follows that the only legitimate form of boasting is to "boast in the Lord" (1 Cor 1:30).[61] In this instance the boast concentrates on the hope of God's future revelation of glory. Michael Wolter distinguishes between ἐλπίς ("hope") in the absolute, as in 1 Cor 13:13 and Rom 15:13, and hope that is defined by a specific object, as in Rom 5:2. The former is a characteristic of Christian existence, as Bultmann showed,[62]

54 Ibid., 126. In taking Eph 2:18, Justin *Dial.* 11.5, and *Apost. Con.* 7.36 as the closest parallels, Wolter in effect is reading Romans through the lens of the interpolation of Rom 16:25-27, which claims that Paul's message is that Gentiles now have sole access to the divine secret.

55 So Kuss, 1:200, 203; Pulcini, "Right Relationship," 68–69.

56 Reid, *Rhetoric*, 100; see also Schoeni's description of the "outrageous" nature of this admonition, in "Hyperbolic Sublime," 178.

57 For a discussion of ancient approaches to comparison and self-praise, see Christopher Forbes, "Comparison, Self-Praise and Irony: Paul's Boasting and the Conventions of Hellenistic Rhetoric," *NTS* 32 (1986) 2–10.

58 Malina, *New Testament World*, 51–70.

59 Judge, "Conflict of Educational Aims," 38–39.

60 See also Earl, *Age of Augustus*, 13: "to the Roman noble the pursuit of power and glory, position and prestige was paramount."

61 See Barrett, "Boasting," 367; Rudolf Bultmann, "καυχάομαι κτλ.," *TDNT* 3 (1965) 649: "faith implies the surrender of all self-glorying." See also Josef Zmijewski, "καυχάομαι κτλ.," *EDNT* 2 (1991) 278–79.

62 Rudolf Bultmann, "ἐλπίς κτλ.," *TDNT* 2 (1964) 532, followed by Bernhard Mayer, "ἐλπίς κτλ.," *EDNT* 1 (1990) 438–39.

but the latter is oriented toward a specific form of eschatological salvation,[63] similar to the phrase found in one of the variants of *1 En.* 98.14, ἐλπὶς σωτηρίας ("hope of salvation").

It is significant, however, that Paul does not refer here to the hope of salvation but to the hope of "God's glory," which draws attention away from the future status of one's self or group.[64] The formulation is consistent with the Abrahamic stance: "he grew strong in his faith as he gave glory to God" (Rom 4:20). It is a mistake to orient this reference primarily to "the salvation . . . of fallen humanity"[65] or even to "the eschatological future of salvation."[66] In the context of a dialectic over human boasting that addresses groups inclined to claim that they would participate in the final glory of God while others would not, Paul draws attention to ἡ δόξα τοῦ θεοῦ ("the glory of God") in and of itself.[67] To boast in God's glory is to share the OT awe at the כבוד יהוה ("glory of Yahweh") that was manifest in radiant holiness and in transcendent power to create and redeem; only divine glory is perceived to be worthy of the highest possible honor.[68] In the NT, which follows this usage, the δόξα τοῦ θεοῦ refers to "'divine honour,' 'divine splendour,' 'divine power' and 'visible divine radiance,'"[69] which is worthy of admiration regardless of whether it involves the redemption of one's group. Paul's admonition to boast in God's glory[70] echoes the insistence in 3:27-31 that human boasting in achievements or status that exalt one group over another is excluded because God is not the possession of any one group. God's glory transcends the entire created order, and the hope of that glory relates to its final manifestation at the end of time when heaven and earth are restored to the condition God intended. To boast in that transcendent hope is to abandon any effort to claim superior honors for oneself or one's group.[71]

■ **3** The formulation that opens this verse, οὐ μόνον δέ, ἀλλὰ καί ("not only so, but also"), is used frequently by Paul (2 Cor 8:19; Rom 5:11; 8:23; 9:10) and except for the particle δέ ("but, so") is identical with the expression found in classical prose.[72] The elliptic parallel between the two admonitions[73] is highlighted by the repetition of καυχώμεθα ("let us boast") that focuses this time on experiences within the human realm that would never otherwise provide grounds for boasting.[74] The phrase ἐν ταῖς θλίψεσιν ("in the/our afflictions") designates the ground of boasting,[75] as in 2 Cor 12:9, where Paul evidently developed this idea in opposition to the super-apostles: "I will all the more gladly boast in my weaknesses (ἐν ταῖς ἀσθενείαις μου), that the power of Christ may rest upon me."

The formulation is noteworthy in several regards. First and foremost, some Greco-Roman and Jewish attitudes toward honor and shame, success and adversity,

63 Wolter, *Röm 5,1-11*, 131.

64 In contrast, Carter, *Power of Sin*, 167, argues that the "hope that the distinctive values of the group will one day be proved right gives the group the determination required to persevere through the present adversity, while the expectation of future vindication reinforces the group's separation from the world."

65 Dunn, 1:249; see also Meyer, 1:225; Morris, 220; Zeisler, 138; Byrne, 170; Moo, 302.

66 Wolter, *Röm 5,1-11*, 133; see also Nebe, *Hoffnung*, 126–27; Fitzmyer, 395.

67 See Kühl, 161; Fuchs, *Freiheit*, 13; Schlier, 144; Murray, 162.

68 See Gerhard von Rad, "δοκέω κτλ.," *TDNT* 2 (1964) 239–42.

69 Gerhard Kittel, "δοκέω κτλ.," *TDNT* 2 (1964) 247; see also Harald Hegermann, "δόξα, δοξάϑω," *EDNT* 1 (1990) 346.

70 The uniqueness of this admonition is visible in the fact revealed by a *TLG* search that the first person plural imperative form of καυχάομαι is unparalled in Greek literature until patristic writers cite this verse.

71 See Watson, *Paul*, 144–47.

72 Xenophon *Cyr.* 8.7.10; Plato *Gorg.* 449b2; *Resp.* 607d8; *Leg.* 789b7; Plutarch *Mor.* 479e3, 4, etc. The phrase with δέ, just as Paul employs it here, may reflect Koine usage and is found in later writers such as Dio Cassius *Hist. Rom.* 8; *Ceb. tab.* 31.5; Justin *1 Apol.* 49.5; Vettius Valens *Anth.* 9.338.9; Damascius *Vita Is.* 100.6.

73 See BDF §479.1; Wolter, *Röm 5,1-11*, 137.

74 See Schoeni, "Hyperbolic Sublime," 178.

75 So Godet, 188–89; Schlier, 146; Cranfield, 1:260; Murray, 163; Wolter, *Röm 5,1-11*, 138–39. On the other hand, Weiss, 220; Zahn, 245; and Dodd, 72–73, interpret the phrase as referring to the conditions within which one nevertheless boasts.

are reversed here. This reversal continues to reflect a congregational situation of competitive boasting, which was culturally consistent with such attitudes.[76] Rather than boasting in superior virtue and status, Paul recommends boasting in "afflictions," that is, hardships, persecutions, eschatological troubles, or daily trials,[77] that unite all believers in "covenantal mutuality"[78] under the lordship of the Crucified One. The definite article attached to "afflictions" is also noteworthy and should be translated either with "the" or "our."[79] Whereas commentators tend to generalize afflictions as if there were no specifying article,[80] Paul evidently has specific hardships in mind that are known to himself and the Roman congregation. The difficulties related to the expulsion of Jewish Christian leaders under Claudius and their return from exile after 54 C.E. would certainly be included along with whatever portion of Paul's own sufferings that were known in Rome. The idea of boasting in sufferings is so remarkable in its social context and the reference to experiences known to the congregation is so specific that direct relevance for the experience of that congregation must be inferred. In the extreme version of an honor/shame environment present in Rome, where triumphs over enemies were celebrated on every side, to boast in a group's adversities not only is countercultural in the general sense but also probably counters specific interpretations of such adversities by the competing churches in Rome.

The formulation of 5:3b continues to reflect Paul's extraordinary effort to detach boasting from any arena of human accomplishment. It initiates a climax that has a structure reminiscent of the saying attributed to Maximus of Tyre: τὴν ἀρετὴν διδόασιν οἱ λόγοι, ("Words [enable] virtue") τοὺς δὲ λόγους ἡ ἄσκησις, ("and training [gives] words") τὴν δὲ ἄσκησιν ἡ ἀλήθεια ("and truth [enables] training") τὴν δὲ ἀλήθειαν ἡ σχολή (and [scholastic] leisure [gives] truth").[81] The contrast in content between this understanding of how virtue is attained through discipline and Paul's discourse is quite striking. Whereas the Greco-Roman and Jewish cultures viewed perseverance and tested character as virtues about which one could legitimately boast, Paul removes them from human causation and employs the formula εἰδότες ὅτι ("knowing that") to introduce experiential material known to the congregation.[82] It is "sufferings" that "produce fortitude," whereby the verb κατεργάζομαι has the sense of "complete, accomplish, bring about," or "produce,"[83] without reference to the human factor. Following Calvin, Cranfield demonstrates the problems caused by reading καυχώμεθα as an indicative by faulting Paul's formulation on the grounds that tribulations often lead people to "murmur against God, and even to curse him."[84]

Even though the wording of Phil 2:12-13 may be more satisfactory in accounting for both the divine and the human factors, Paul has a specific rhetorical goal in mind here. By eliminating human participation in the creation of ὑπομονή ("fortitude, patience, perseverance"),[85] he is able to carry through with his argument that ordinary boasting is disallowed before God. In Greco-Roman ethics ὑπομονή is the virtue of manly resistance to contrary pressure, thought to be necessary

---

76 See Reid, *Rhetoric*, 101: "the *rhetorical exigence* involving the question of status and position within the Roman congregation(s)," possibly involving the expulsion under Claudius.

77 See Jacob Kremer, "θλῖψις, θλίβω," *EDNT* 2 (1991) 152-53; Wilckens, 1:291; see also A. J. Mattill Jr., "The Way of Tribulation," *JBL* 98 (1979) 535-39.

78 Reid, *Rhetoric*, 101.

79 See Fitzmyer, 379; Smythe, *Grammar*, §1121.

80 Kuss, 1:204; Morris, 220; Dunn, 1:250; Moo, 302-3; Byrne, 170.

81 Maximus Tyrius *Phil.* 16.3b, cited by Reid, *Rhetoric*, 102.

82 Käsemann, 134; Nebe, *Hoffnung*, 129; Dunn, 1:250; Burdick, "Οἶδα and Γινώσκω," 344, 347: οἶδα

implies "something that was universally known or that was known assuredly."

83 Horst Balz, "κατεργάζομαι," *EDNT* 2 (1991) 271; Georg Bertram, "κατεργάζομαι," *TDNT* 3 (1965) 634-35.

84 Cranfield, 1:261.

85 In "ὑπομένω, ὑπομονή," *TDNT* 4 (1967) 587, Friedrich Hauck misses this point in reasserting the human element into this passage: "Tribulation, piously endured, accomplishes as its result . . . in the Christian highly estimable ὑπομονή."

for the soldier or citizen.[86] Socrates converses with Laches about assessing the courage of a soldier who despite disadvantageous circumstances "is willing to persevere and endure" (ἐλέθοντα ὑπομένειν δὲ καὶ καρτερεῖν, Plato *Lach.* 193a). Plato extends this virtue to the arena of philosophical debate, in which courageous persons "are willing to have fortitude (ὑπομεῖναι) for a while like men and do not run away like cowards" (*Theaet.* 177b). With the Stoics, Philo valued the capacity of the virtuous person to "bear, resist, hold fast, fortify one's resolution and barricade it with firmness and fortitude (καρτερία καὶ ὑπομονή) drawn from within, the most potent of virtues."[87] This theme is picked up by 4 Macc 5:23, that virtue "demands of us courage that will cause us to endure (ὑπομένειν) willingly all sorts of woes." There is no doubt that this strain of Greco-Roman and Hellenistic Jewish material places a supreme value on fortitude and endurance, which makes it all the more striking that Paul eliminates the element of human volition in his argument that "this[88] affliction produces perseverance." He returns to this theme in the more direct admonition of 12:12, τῇ θλίψει ὑπομένοντες ("fortitude in affliction"). In the context of afflictions, and in the light of the linguistic background sketched above, I prefer the translation "fortitude," which conveys the quality of "manly courage" that is less prominent in "patience" or "perseverance."

■ **4** As in the first member of the climax, Paul again uses the article in ἡ ὑπομονή, which I render as "this fortitude" produced by afflictions suffered in the context of Christian commitment.[89] The word δοκιμή,

appearing here for the only time in Romans and nowhere else in the entirety of Greek literature prior to the Pauline letters, has been difficult to translate, with "character," "confirmation," "authentication," "proof," "trial," "test," "ordeal," and so on, suggested as partially satisfactory substitutes.[90] The key to its meaning in this context is the testing of qualifications by performance in battle or public life.[91] For example, in *Leg.* 754d Plato speaks of magistrates "appointed and tested according to the law (κατὰ νόμους καταστᾶσαι τε δοκιμασθῶσι)." Similarly a gloss or variant reading on Aesop's Fables has the line, "whenever they received a trial and testing" (δοκιμήν, *Fab.* 274.17). In *Bell.* 2.138 Josephus reports that a novice was not admitted as a full member in the Essene community until "his character was tested (τὸ ἦθος δοκιμάζεται)" for two years.

It is highly significant that these terms show up in the Corinthian controversy, where Paul responds to the congregation's desire for "authentication (δοκιμήν) that Christ is speaking in me" (2 Cor 13:3), because the superapostles had brought letters authenticating their record of success and were claiming that Paul's weaknesses disqualified him.[92] He uses the same terms to claim that the Corinthians needed to test themselves (δοκιμάζετε, 2 Cor 13:5) in terms of their own progress in the faith to determine whether Paul was unqualified (ἀδόκιμος, 2 Cor 13:6), because they should recognize that his conformity to Christ crucified proved that he and his colleagues were indeed fully qualified (δόκιμοι, 2 Cor 13:7).[93] This rare word δοκιμή also shows up in 2 Cor 2:9; 8:2; 9:13; and Phil 2:23, which was probably

---

86   See ibid., 581–82; Ceslas Spicq, "ὑπομένω, ὑπομονή," *TLNT* 3 (1994) 414–15.

87   Philo *Cher.* 78, cited by Spicq, "ὑπομένω, ὑπομονή," 415.

88   The use of the article in the reduplicated members of the climax is translated as "this," reflecting the origin of the article in Greek as a demonstrative pronoun (BDF §§249, 252), referring back to an item just mentioned. Most translations and commentators simply skip the article in ἡ θλῖψις, thus implying that any affliction produces fortitude, but Paul has the specific, aforementioned affliction in mind.

89   See n. 79 above; for examples of commentators dropping the article, see Barrett, 104; Dunn, 1:251; Fitzmyer, 397; Moo, 296, 303; Byrne, 170.

90   See BAGD 202; Walter Grundmann, "δοκιμός κτλ.," *TDNT* 2 (1964) 255–60; Gerd Schunack, "δοκιμάζω κτλ.," *EDNT* 1 (1990) 341–43; Ceslas Spicq, "δοκιμάζω κτλ.," *TLNT* 1 (1994) 353–61; Gerard Therrien, *Discernement*, 154–58.

91   An alternative explanation is developed by Wolter, *Röm 5,1-11*, 139–40, that δοκιμάζειν is a technical term for testing saints through undeserved suffering, which fails to explain why δοκιμή appears only in the Pauline letters. It also provides no link to the issue of boasting.

92   Georgi, *Opponents*, 235: Whereas the Corinthians looked in vain for the δοκιμή of the Christ speaking in Paul, the opponents apparently could demonstrate it in a verifiable manner." See also Schunack, "δοκιμάζω κτλ.," 343.

written during the same period. It is therefore highly likely that the term δοκιμός derived from the super-apostolic controversy in Corinth and that its meaning in Rom 5:4 is close to "approbation," that is, a faith that has been tested and found to be authentic. Paul's point, as in the Corinthian controversy, is that no one should claim such approbation for oneself, since it ultimately comes from Christ alone. To make it a matter of boasting in themselves and of negative comparisons with others, as the superapostles did, was a violation of the gospel's transformation of the honor system. So Paul contends here that approbation comes not from human effort but from "this fortitude" that in turn had been produced by Christian "affliction." The curious formulation bears the clear stamp of the Corinthian controversy and suggests that Paul knows of voices like those of the superapostles active in Rome. It is clear from 14:1–15:7 that Christian groups in Rome were attempting to disqualify each other because of differences in liturgy and ethics, so his argument here has cogency for the rhetorical situation.

That "this approbation produces hope" sounds at first like a circular argument since ἐλπίς ("hope") had been mentioned in v. 2 with reference to boasting in the hope of the glory of God.[94] It does not appear that Paul is implying that approbation evokes more confident hope[95] or hope for a restoration of good fortune after the deprivations of affliction[96] but rather simply that it produces new hope,[97] because in Barrett's words, "He has learnt to look not to himself but to God."[98] Barrett's words are congruent with the Corinthian background of this line of thought and the formulation of the climax. This particular hope does not arise from the emotional resources of the saint as if it were a result of an optimistic disposition.[99] It arises instead from the approba-

tion that comes from God's providential working and thus eliminates another form of human boasting. To set one's hope in God's glory rather than in claims of professional superiority is the logical consequence of this revolutionary new stance in "grace" (5:2).

■ **5** The conclusion of the climax in v. 5a reiterates the theme of hope and claims that it "does not put to shame" (οὐ καταισχύνει), a formulation that provides a satisfying correlation with boasting in vv. 2c-3a. If the normal goal of boasting is to achieve honor and avert shame, here it is claimed that the avoidance of shame is accomplished in a revolutionary manner. The theme of shame in the context of the hope of deliverance is clearly articulated with the verb καταισχύνω, drawn from the language of the Psalms.[100] In LXX Ps 21:6, for example, the Israelite forebears "cried to you and were saved; they hoped in you and were not put to shame (οὐ κατῃσχύνθησαν)." In Ps 24:20 the righteous believer prays, "Keep my soul, and deliver me; let me not be ashamed (μὴ καταισχυνθείην), because I have hoped in you."[101] In these examples the faithful worshipers hope for a concrete restoration of fortune and a relief from adversity. When they triumph over their enemies, it becomes clear that they have not been put to shame. Their honor requires Yahweh's victory over their adversaries or, at least, the compensation of a blessed life after death,[102] a theme that provides the basis for much commentary on Rom 5:5.[103] Compensation, whether worldly or otherworldly, is conspicuously absent from 5:1-11, and herein lies part of the remarkable revolution. By employing what should be read as a present tense verb, "does not cause shame,"[104] Paul points to the overcoming of shame in the present experience of righteousness by faith, in the current stand of believers in grace. Käsemann explains that Paul's "concern is for the eschatolog-

---

93 See Georgi, *Opponents*, 237, 289.
94 Murray, 164.
95 Kuss, 1:205; Michel, 180; Morris, 221.
96 Wolter, *Röm 5,1-11*, 142, referring to Job 42:11-17.
97 Schlier, 148.
98 Barrett, 104.
99 See Therrien, *Discernement*, 157.
100 See Rudolf Bultmann, "αἰσχύνω κτλ.," *TDNT* 1 (1964) 189–99; Cranfield, 1:262; Dunn, 1:252; Reid, *Rhetoric*, 104.
101 See also Pss 30:2; 70:1; Jer 31:13; Prov 11:7, noted by Wolter, *Röm 5,1-11*, 150.
102 Similarly, Nebe, *Hoffnung*, 55–57, 129–30, argues that the reference to shame in 5:5a implies the final judgment, but the present tense of the verb καταισχύνω points in another direction.
103 For example, Godet, 189: "This hope will not be falsified in the end by the event." See also Weiss, 221; Schmidt, 91; Schlier, 149; Zeisler, 129; Dunn, 1:252.
104 Meyer, 1:227, and Kühl, 162, report that the commentator Hofmann accented this verb as a future, καταισχύνει, which is accepted by no modern commentator or critical Greek text so far as I have read.

ical miracle of the humanization of man which is prefigured by the crucified Christ and in which the coming of the new world takes place."[105] In this case, however, the eschatological fulfillment is in the present, because the verb καταισχύνει is in the present tense. The background of this revolutionary doctrine of shame is visible in 1 Cor 1:27-30: "God chose what is foolish in the world to shame the wise; God chose what is weak in the world to shame the strong. God chose what is low and despised in the world, even things that are not, to bring to nothing things that are, so that no human being might boast in the presence of God. . . . 'Let him who boasts, boast in the Lord.'"[106]

The reason for Paul's confidence that the deficit of shame is being filled in the current experience of believers is stated in v. 5b, which opens with the explanatory ὅτι ("because").[107] It is often overlooked what reasons are *not* supplied in this sentence. There is no reference to triumph over adversaries, to overcoming suffering, or even to the final victory of Christ at the parousia. Indeed, the link between the outpouring of divine love in v. 5b and the first half of this verse relating to the overcoming of shame remains largely unexplained in the commentaries because of doctrinal preoccupation with the certainty of eschatological salvation.[108] The reference to love's being "poured out" (ἐκχύννω) is highly evocative[109] because of the associations of this verb with the shedding of blood in murder (Gen 9:6; Ezek 18:10; Matt 23:34; Acts 22:20; Rom 3:15) and in the Lord's Supper (Mark 14:24; Matt 26:28; Luke 22:20), while the Pentecost traditions in Acts 2:16-17 linked the gift of the Spirit with the prophecy in Joel 3:1 that "I will pour out (ἐκχέω) my Spirit upon all flesh" (see also Acts 10:45).[110] In this instance the verb is in the perfect tense

and refers to the event of conversion or baptism when God's love was first experienced in its fullness.[111]

While the "love of God" is an expression found in *T. Gad* 5.2 and in a variant of *T. Job* 5.1, it becomes a central category for Pauline and Johannine Christianity,[112] both of which stress that ἀγάπη derives from God rather than being a natural human capacity.[113] The closing benediction of 2 Cor 13:14 refers to the "love of God," and there are similar references in 2 Cor 9:7; 13:11; Gal 2:20; 1 Thess 1:4; and later in Rom 5:8; 8:37; and 9:13. While Paul also speaks of the "love of Christ" (2 Cor 5:14), John 3:16 and especially 1 John 4:7-12 develop the theme of "God's love" very extensively. In Rom 5 it comprises what Ralph Martin describes as "the heart" and "centrepiece" of Paul's message.[114] Divine love addresses shame at its deepest level and reveals the motivation behind "peace" and "reconciliation."

That the outpouring of divine love flows "into our hearts" reflects a Judaic conception of the human person, in which the καρδία functions not as a physiological organ but as "the seat of understanding, knowledge, and will."[115] When Jeremiah envisions the new covenant, for example, God states, "I will put my law within them, and I will write it upon their hearts, and I will be their God, and they shall be my people" (Jer 31:33). This idea of the "heart" as the location for encountering God was developed in 1 Thess 3:11-13; 2 Thess 2:16-17; 3:5. A particularly close parallel to Rom 5:5 occurs in Gal 4:6, that God "has sent the Spirit of his Son into our hearts" (εἰς τὰς καρδίας ἡμῶν; see also 2 Cor 1:22; 4:6). Schlier comments that the reference to love poured into the hearts of believers "grasps humans at the innermost center of their selfhood, which is visible only to God and the spirit,"[116] thus addressing the hidden wounds of

---

105 Käsemann, 135.

106 See Wolter, *Röm 5,1-11*, 152, citing also Jer 12:13; on 153 he interprets 5:5a as a reference to eschatological salvation, which disregards the present tense of the verb.

107 See Wolter, *Röm 5,1-11*, 153.

108 For example, while most commentators glide over the problem, the most extensive discussions in Schlier, 150–51, and Wolter, *Röm 5,1-11*, 153–54, argue that divine love assures future hope. No commentator discusses overcoming shameful status.

109 Cosby, "Paul's Persuasive Language," 215: the use

of "shed" serves "to increase the vividness of his expression" in a lavish direction.

110 See Johannes Behm, "ἐκχέω, εκχύν(ν)ω," *TDNT* 2 (1964) 467–69; Franz Georg Untergassmair, "ἐκχέω, ἐκχύννω," *EDNT* 1 (1990) 424.

111 See Kühl, 163; Schlier, 150.

112 See Wolter, *Röm 5,1-11*, 154–55; Gerhard Schneider, "ἀγαπή κτλ.," *EDNT* 1 (1990) 10–11.

113 See Warnach, *Agape*, 199–205.

114 Martin, *Reconciliation*, 142, 145.

115 Alexander Sand, "καρδία," *EDNT* 2 (1991) 250; see also Jewett, *Terms*, 309.

shame that otherwise provoke them to engage in a boastful war with God.

God's love is conveyed "through the Holy Spirit given to us,"[117] whereby the object of the preposition διά should be understood as the agent enabling this communication.[118] The Spirit conveys God's love "to us," a formulation that overcomes any distinction between Jewish and Gentile believers.[119] Michael Wolter opposes this interpretation of διά on the grounds that it leaves a vague impression of the Spirit's role; he proposes instead that the preposition conveys the "particular way and means, the perceptible form or shape" in which the Spirit is conveyed.[120] While this swerves beyond Paul's precise argument in this passage, the formulation remains puzzling to others because the aorist participle δοθέντος states that the Holy Spirit has been "given" to believers.[121] This formulation is an example of the "apportioned Spirit" of God that is parceled out to all believers, comprising their new center, as in Phil 4:23; 1 Cor 5:4-5; 14:14; 2 Cor 2:13; 7:3; Rom 1:6; 8:10.[122] In every detail it is clear that Paul has selected language in this verse that has very wide resonance in early Christianity, and Paul assumes also in Rome.[123] Nevertheless, his goal is not merely to sustain eschatological hope,[124] which is a secondary concern in this passage, but to rest his case about overcoming shame and transforming the shape of boasting on the foundation of the widely shared experience of the unconditional love of God that is conveyed by the gift of the Spirit.

To reiterate, the material in vv. 3-5 does not form a general maxim, valid at all times and circumstances, as the traditional indicative reading suggests; rather it is counterintuitive at many points, especially in the ancient context. Instead Paul provides a fresh and creative admonition about how to live out the "peace with God," namely by changing the form of one's boasting in the light of salvation by grace alone. Given the mind-set produced by Greco-Roman and Jewish cultures, he cannot eliminate boasting altogether; it is bred in the bone, so to speak. Nevertheless, he hopes to change its form into a celebration of the glory of God and of the love of Christ that sustains believers through every adversity. The traditional forms of boasting are no longer needed to gain and sustain their honor in the face of a hostile world. Christ's blood that was shed for the undeserving fills that need, and its consoling message is conveyed by the Spirit directly to the vulnerable hearts of believers who thereby are enabled to live in confident hope no matter how badly they are treated. In Christ, adversity has lost its power to shame.

■ 6 In the second half of the pericope, Paul sets forth in more detail the christological and experiential foundations of the new form of boasting. The chiastic argument of vv. 6-8 employs traditional credal formulations interspersed with rhetorical comments. Verse 6 bristles with problems despite its seeming adaptation of the well-known formula embedded in v. 8, Χριστὸς ὑπὲρ ἡμῶν ἀπέθανεν ("Christ died on behalf of us").[125] The subject and the verb are placed at points of emphasis at the beginning and end of the sentence,[126] with an oddly formulated genitive absolute, "while we were still weak," which is introduced by ἔτι ("still, yet") that seems to have a somewhat different nuance ("yet") when it is reduplicated five words later ("still").[127] Several unique phrases, whose precise meaning is difficult to ascertain[128] and even more difficult to accommodate within

116 Schlier, 150.
117 This section is adapted from Jewett, "Apportioned Spirit," 193–206.
118 BAGD 180, III.2a; see also Weiss, 222; Murray, 165; Fitzmyer, 398.
119 See Reid, *Rhetoric*, 105.
120 Wolter, *Röm 5,1-11*, 164; followed by Dunn, 1:253.
121 See Wiard Popkes, "δίδωμι," *EDNT* 1 (1990) 321. Bultmann, *Old and New Man*, 21, accepts the idea that the Spirit is "a supernatural but substantial power which then dwells within man" after baptism.
122 Jewett, *Terms*, 197, 451–53; idem, "Apportioned Spirit," 193–206.
123 See Wolter, *Röm 5,1-11*, 166.
124 Wolter, *Röm 5,1-11*, 166; Dunn, 1:252–54, 265–66.
125 Wengst, *Formeln*, 78; see also Kramer, *Christ*, 26–27; Michel, 134–35; the anomalies in vv. 6-7 are on such a scale that Leander E. Keck follows Fuchs, *Freiheit*, 16–17, in arguing that they are a later interpolation: "The Post-Pauline Interpretation of Jesus' Death in Rom 5,6-7," in C. Andresen and G. Klein, eds., *Theologia Crucis–Signum Crucis. Festschrift für Erich Dinkler zum 70. Geburtstag* (Tübingen: Mohr [Siebeck], 1979) 237–42.
126 Dunn, 1:254.
127 See ibid.
128 See Wolter, *Röm 5,1-11*, 169–71.

the usual parameters of Paul's theology, appear here. This is the first time "Christ" appears by itself in Romans, possibly echoing the doctrinal formula that is cited in v. 8. There is disagreement whether "that time" should be connected with the genitive absolute "while we were still weak,"[129] or with the verb "he died" at the end of the sentence.[130] The latter alternative seems more consistent with the word order. Even more baffling is the use of ἀσθενής ("weak"),[131] appearing here for the only time in Romans but associated with the verb ἀσθενέω, which later appears in 14:1, 2, 21 to refer to a group within the congregation.[132] Ἀσθενής appears in 1 Cor 8:7, 9, 10 to describe the "weak conscience" of the former pagans who fear eating meat offered to idols. In 1 Cor 4:20 it describes the low social status of most early Christian converts. It seems problematic that Paul would use the same term here to describe all humans prior to Christ, especially in a sentence where it stands parallel to "ungodly," implying that both conditions are overcome by the atonement. Some commentators avoid this obvious dilemma by linking this verse to the use of ἀσθένεια ("weakness") in 1 Cor 15:43, referring to human susceptibility to death.[133] This linkage creates a further tension with the earlier argument of Romans that describes the human situation prior to salvation as marked by rebellion and hostility against God rather than by weak finitude. In addition, the use of ἔτι ("still") would then imply that finite status has been overcome by Christ, thus producing the absurd implication that Christians somehow become immortal.

The phrase κατὰ καιρόν ("at that time") remains peculiar because Paul otherwise uses καιρός with the prepositions ἐν ("in," Rom 3:26; 11:5; 2 Cor 8:14; 2 Thess 2:6), πρό ("before," 1 Cor 4:5), πρός ("for," 1 Cor 7:5; 1 Thess 2:17), or περί ("concerning," 1 Thess 5:1). Only in the citation of Gen 18:10 in Rom 9:9 does Paul use κατά with καιρός in a context demanding the translation "about this time," which supports the rendition of the phrase in 5:6 as "at that time"[134] rather than the theologically loaded "at the right time."[135]

The phrase ὑπὲρ ἀσεβῶν ("for the sake of the godless") is also unparalleled, although Paul employed the noun in 4:5 in the expression "set right the ungodly."[136] When one takes into account the parallelism between v. 6a and 6b, it becomes clear that "weakness" is made the equivalent of "godless."[137] Such a connection was advanced by the superapostles in 2 Corinthians, which provoked Paul's striking boast in his own weaknesses (2 Cor 11:30; 12:5-10) and his insistence that Christ was "crucified in weakness" (13:4). How Paul could have now abandoned this powerful theological insight based on his theology of the cross remains unanswered by the commentators.

The puzzle is deepened by the twice-repeated adverb ἔτι, which normally implies a period of time extending up until the moment of the action,[138] in the first occurrence referring to the status of weakness that persisted until the moment of salvation, after which the condition would be overcome.[139] This first use of ἔτι makes Pauline provenance even more difficult to maintain, because he had struggled in Corinth against the assumption that afflictions and bodily weaknesses were incom-

129 See Weiss, 224; Schmidt, 93; Bultmann, "Adam," 428; Wilckens, 1:295.

130 Michel, 181; Kuss, 1:208; Wolter, *Röm 5,1-11*, 169; Fitzmyer, 399.

131 See Josef Zmijewski, "ἀσθενής κτλ.," *EDNT* 1 (1990) 170–71.

132 For an effort to relate this reference to Rom 14, see Pulcini, "Romans 5:1-11," 73.

133 BAGD 115: "morally weak"; Dunn, 1:254: "the human condition as such"; Wolter, *Röm 5,1-11*, 170.

134 BAGD 395; Dunn, 1:254; Cousar, *Theology of the Cross*, 44.

135 Meyer, 1:230; Cranfield, 1:264.

136 Peter Fiedler, "ἀσεβής κτλ.," *EDNT* 1 (1990) 168, points out that in the LXX ἀσεβής is characteristically used to refer to sinners.

137 See Moo, 306; this is denied by many exegetes on purely theological grounds, without explaining the syntactic parallelism, e.g., Barrett, 105; Wolter, *Röm 5,1-11*, 170–71. A link between weakness and impiety is implicit in LXX Prov 24:16, "the righteous shall fall seven times and get up, but the impious will grow weak (οἱ δὲ ἀσεβεῖς ἀσθενήσουσιν) with evil deeds."

138 See BAGD 315; Horst Balz and Gerhard Schneider, "ἔτι," *EDNT* 2 (1991) 67.

139 In the textual suggestion in note e above, the possibility is weighed that κατὰ καιρόν was a marginal correction introduced by ἔτι, to signal where it belonged in the text, viz., right after the initial ἔτι γάρ. Therefore its intended position was before Χριστός, and not in its present position in the

mensurate with life in the new age. This array of difficulties makes v. 6 difficult to defend as a Pauline composition.[140]

All of these anomalies could be explained by a theory of Pauline citation of an early Christian confession that may have been employed in Rome. Heinrich Schlier took the first step in this direction by observing that a poetic completion is in view with the formulation: ἔτι ὄντων ἡμῶν ἀσθενῶν ("still while we were weak") ἔτι κατὰ καιρὸν ὑπὲρ ἀσεβῶν ("still at that time for ungodly").[141] The poetic balance is interrupted, however, by γὰρ Χριστός ("for Christ") in the first member. If "for" had been added by Paul to incorporate the citation into the argument of Romans, and if the word "Christ" was intentionally moved to a position earlier in the sentence,[142] the following ending of the original confession can be inferred: Χριστὸς ἀπέθανεν ("Christ died"). This produces a coherent confessional formula translated above with quotation marks that contains two lines of roughly equal length, followed by a line with two beats. The reconstructed confession contains an elegant parallelism with anaphora in the opening of the first two lines and homoioptoton in the closing of these lines. The orientation of the confession seems to reflect that of the "strong" in Rome, who view weakness as a condition that should have been overcome by the new life in Christ. The confession clearly implies that the condition of the ἀσθενεῖς ("the weak ones") that continued up to the time of Christ ought to have been overcome along with godlessness. The concern to transcend the condition of weakness is consistent with Paul's opponents in 2 Corinthians and his critics in Ephesus. If this hypothesis is accepted, it follows that Paul's adaptation of this confession is an expression of his attempt to find common ground by using a formula that appears to support the prejudicial attitude of the strong against the weak. The same effort would be manifest if he formulated this verse himself and accommodated the ideas of a group in Rome whose behavior he seeks to influence throughout this letter. This dialogue is rendered plausible by having eliminated the prejudicial implications of boasting in 5:1-5 and by having affirmed the ongoing relevance of suffering. Moreover, Paul's placement of the subject "Christ" toward the beginning of the sentence enhances his lordship over both the weak and the ungodly. If, as seems likely, the formula was being used in Rome, its rhetorical force would be greatly enhanced, and there would be no need to bend its wording into conformity with Pauline theology.

■ 7 As shown in note f above, the text-critical evidence suggests the possibility that this verse was a later gloss or perhaps two glosses. Another option is that Paul may here be formulating comments by imaginary interlocutors. At the very least, the verse needs to be taken as parenthetical.[143] The evidence leading to these options is quite extensive. The word μόλις ("hardly") in v. 7a never appears elsewhere in Paul's letters, and seems most at home in Hellenistic Judaism.[144] The prepositional combination ὑπὲρ ἀσεβῶν ("for ungodly") occurs only one other time in all of Greek literature.[145] The word δικαίου ("righteous") is used here in a typically Judaic manner,[146] contradicting Paul's earlier argument in 1:18–3:23 that no one, in fact, is righteous. Wolter takes v. 7a as a comment based on Prov 11:31, dealing with the problem of the premature death of the righteous:[147] "If the righteous can scarcely be saved, where shall the

---

canonical text. If this possibility is accepted as plausible, the emended text should read ἔτι γὰρ <κατὰ καιρὸν> Χριστὸς. . . ἀπέθανεν ("for at the right time Christ died"). The second ἔτι would therefore become superfluous.

140 See Keck, "Rom 5,6-7," 238–48; Kertelge, "Verständnis des Todes Jesu," 116; Gaukesbrink, Sühnetradition, 120–23.

141 Schlier, 152.

142 For a discussion of earlier efforts to shift the location of "Christ," see Weiss, 223.

143 Johannes Schneider, "μόλις, μόγις," TDNT 4 (1967) 735.

144 Schneider, ibid., notes that the term has no single Hebrew equivalent, and appears only in Prov 11:31; Wis 9:16; Sir 21:20; 26:29; 29:6; 35:7; 3 Macc 1:23; 5:15.

145 Diodorus Siculus Hist. 23.1.4.13, describes the outset of the First Punic War, "But if they were to enter upon a war of such magnitude over the most impious of people (ὑπὲρ ἀσεβεστάτων). . . ."

146 See Gottlob Schrenk, "δίκη κτλ.," TDNT 2 (1964) 183–86; Winninge, Sinners and the Righteous, 135–36; Yehezkel Landau, "Martyrdom in Paul's Religious Ethics: An Exegetical Commentary on Romans 5:7," Imm 15 (1982–83) 30–32.

147 Wolter, Röm 5,1-11, 173–74.

ungodly and the sinner appear? (εἰ ὁ μὲν δίκαιος μόλις σώζεται, ὁ ἀσεβὴς καὶ ἁμαρτωλὸς ποῦ φανεῖται;)." While this parallel demonstrates the likely source of several key terms, it is unrelated to the decisive idea of one person's dying for another.

It is generally agreed that v. 7b is a correction of v. 7a,[148] in a rather ambiguous manner. The concept of the "the good man" in v. 7b appears to be roughly synonymous with "the righteous" in v. 7a,[149] although many efforts have been made to distinguish between them so as to rescue some semblance of logical development.[150] The most plausible distinction is that ὁ ἀγαθός in Greek society refers to the benefactor,[151] but this raises the question about why Paul would insert a social concept in the midst of a discussion of the atonement. However this debate is resolved, the concept of a "good man's" dying for others stands in tension with 1:18–3:23 and with 7:18-19, which deny that goodness lies within the grasp of humans.[152] Classical Greek thought, on the other hand, provides examples of daring to die for others.[153] The rest of v. 7b appears more congruent with Pauline thought and style, with τάχα ("perhaps") employed in v. 7b as in Phlm 15 without the usual optative verb,[154] and τολμάω ("dare") appears in a typical manner.[155]

Taking this evidence into account, Lietzmann saw this verse as containing a secondary doublet, providing contradictory reflections on v. 6.[156] Although the usual indications of citation are absent, it may be more satisfactory to take these remarks as coming from imaginary interlocutors, which would account for the distinctive style and vocabulary of each half of this verse. The first remark takes up the extraordinary theme in v. 6b of dying for the ungodly, with "lesser-to-greater" reasoning: if it is so unusual to die for a righteous person, how much more so for godless persons?[157] The second interlocutor offers a correction, in the light of classical references to heroic benefactors dying for their cities and for righteous causes.[158] The target of such benefaction would be among the class of upright citizens,[159] and thus worth saving, but to die for the "godless," as in v. 6b, would be unthinkable. While contradicting each other, both comments agree on the main point: dying for shameful, unworthy people is unprecedented. This sets up the confessional statement that Paul expands in the following verse.

■ **8** This verse opens with an adversative δέ ("but, yet")[160] that signals a response to the voices in the preceding verse. The verb συνίστημι is employed here as in 3:5 in the sense of "prove, make known, demonstrate,"

148 Kuss, 1:209; Leenhardt, 136; Wilckens, 1:296; Barrett, 106; Käsemann, 137.

149 See Meyer, 1:232; Walter Grundmann, "ἀγαθός κτλ.," *TDNT* 1 (1964) 13–15; Kuss, 1:208–9; Bultmann, "Adam," 428; Bruce, 117; Murray, 167–68; Wolter, *Röm 5,1-11*, 174–75; Frederik Wisse, "The Righteous Man and the Good Man in Romans v.7," *NTS* 19 (1972-73) 92–93.

150 Godet, 192, cites distinctions suggested by Olshausen, De Wette, Hodge, Ewald, Philippi, and Tholuck; other examples include Zahn, 251–52; Sanday and Headlam, 128; Lagrange, 103; Schlatter, 123; Dunn, 1:255; Landau, "Romans 5:7," 33; for a more recent account of such efforts see Andrew D. Clarke, "The Good and the Just in Romans 5:7," *TynB* 41 (1990) 128–32.

151 See Clarke, "Romans 5:7," 138–40, followed by Pulcini, "Romans 5:1-11," 75.

152 See Grundmann, "ἀγαθός κτλ.," 16; Jörg Baumgarten, "ἀγαθός," *EDNT* 1 (1991) 5–6.

153 Euripides *Alc.* 644 has Admetus exclaim to Pheres, "you were not willing nor daring to die (οὐκ ἠθέλεσας οὐδ᾽ ἐτόλμησας θανεῖν) for your

child"; Isocrates *Pac.* 143 recalls that Spartans "not daring to die in battle (οἱ μὴ τολμῶντες ἐν ταῖς μάχαις ἀποθνήσκειν)" were held in greater dishonor than deserters.

154 See BAGD 806.

155 See Michael Wolter, "τολμάω," *EDNT* 3 (1993) 365.

156 Lietzmann, 59, followed by Sahlin, "Textemendationen," 96–97; see also Kümmel, "Interpretation of Romans 5:1-11," 55.

157 See Wisse, "Romans v.7," 93.

158 Isocrates *Arch.* 107 states that "if we are willing to die for righteous things (ἢν μὲν γὰρ ἐθέλωμεν ἀποθνήσκειν ὑπὲρ τῶν δικαίων), not only will we be approved of, but it shall also in the future be permitted to live most securely." On dying for various ideals and causes: Lycurgus *Leoc.* 86.2 (for the salvation of those governed); Philo *Agr.* 156.3 (for the common salvation); Diodorus Siculus *Hist.* 9.2.6.3 (for freedom).

159 Clarke, "Romans 5:7," 142.

160 See Godet, 194; Reid, *Rhetoric*, 109. Meyer, 1:235, rejects the adversative reading, arguing that v. 8 simply carries the argument forward.

almost in the sense of "bring to light."[161] The present tense refers to the ongoing demonstration of the gospel in the church's proclamation and celebration of the Lord's Supper. It is God's "own love" that is demonstrated "to us" ($\epsilon\grave{\iota}\varsigma\ \dot{\eta}\mu\hat{\alpha}\varsigma$), whereby the pronoun $\dot{\epsilon}\alpha\upsilon\tau\acute{o}\varsigma$ ("his own") has an emphatic sense contrasted with human love at its best, which is described in the preceding verse.[162] This formulation reaches back to "the love of God" in 5:5 and makes clear that the message of unmerited acceptance poured into the heart of believers is the message about Christ crucified on behalf of sinners.

In a formulation parallel to 5:6, Paul explains that this event occurred "while we were yet $\dot{\alpha}\mu\alpha\rho\tau\omega\lambda o\acute{\iota}$" ("sinners"), a term used here as a virtual synonym of $\dot{\alpha}\sigma\epsilon\beta\acute{\eta}\varsigma$ ("godless").[163] The abusive term $\dot{\alpha}\mu\alpha\rho\tau\omega\lambda\acute{o}\varsigma$ refers to those whose behavior demonstrates that they are "radically sinful,"[164] belonging to a class of people who are the "opposite of the pious, righteous, and godly;" sinners engage in "social oppression," and stand in opposition to God.[165] In contrast to Greco-Roman culture and particularly to the Roman civic cult, where the hero dies for the honored fatherland,[166] Jesus died for undeserving sinners.[167] In 1:18–3:23, Paul contended in effect that every human being belongs to this class, a contention that is clearly implied here with the first person plural form, "while *we* were yet sinners." Nevertheless, the term still carries a burden of social discrimination, which is visible in its employment as an epithet of contempt in the Gospels (e.g., Mark 2:15-16; Matt 11:19; Luke 7:34), where the remedy is Jesus' forgiveness. The theme of forgiveness is conspicuously absent here, where the context is defined by God's love. Despite the weight of the Augustinian tradition that construes salvation primarily as individual forgiveness,[168] Paul's concern is with overcoming the shameful status of "sinner" through divine love that accepts each person and group without qualification as demonstrated on the cross of Christ.

There is a case to be made that the final four words of v. 8 are either cited from an early Christian confession[169] or reflect formulaic language employed elsewhere:[170] $X\rho\iota\sigma\tau\acute{o}\varsigma\ \dot{\upsilon}\pi\grave{\epsilon}\rho\ \dot{\eta}\mu\hat{\omega}\nu\ \dot{\alpha}\pi\acute{\epsilon}\vartheta\alpha\nu\epsilon\nu$ ("Christ died on our behalf"). A comparison with similar formulas in other Pauline letters indicates the basis of these judgments:

I delivered to you as of first importance what I also received, that Christ died for our sins ($\ddot{o}\tau\iota\ X\rho\iota\sigma\tau\grave{o}\varsigma\ \dot{\alpha}\pi\acute{\epsilon}\vartheta\alpha\nu\epsilon\nu\ \dot{\upsilon}\pi\grave{\epsilon}\rho\ \tau\hat{\omega}\nu\ \dot{\alpha}\mu\alpha\rho\tau\iota\hat{\omega}\nu\ \dot{\eta}\mu\hat{\omega}\nu$) in accordance with the scriptures (1 Cor 15:3)

Do not let what you eat cause the destruction of one for whom Christ died ($\dot{\upsilon}\pi\grave{\epsilon}\rho\ o\hat{\upsilon}\ X\rho\iota\sigma\tau\grave{o}\varsigma\ \dot{\alpha}\pi\acute{\epsilon}\vartheta\alpha\nu\epsilon\nu$) (Rom 14:15)

For God has not destined us for wrath, but to obtain salvation through our Lord Jesus Christ, who died for us ($\tau o\hat{\upsilon}\ \dot{\alpha}\pi o\vartheta\alpha\nu\acute{o}\nu\tau o\varsigma\ \dot{\upsilon}\pi\grave{\epsilon}\rho\ \dot{\eta}\mu\hat{\omega}\nu$) (1 Thess 5:9-10)

And so by your knowledge this weak man is destroyed, the brother for whom Christ died ($\dot{o}\ \dot{\alpha}\delta\epsilon\lambda\phi\grave{o}\varsigma\ \delta\iota'\ \ddot{o}\nu\ X\rho\iota\sigma\tau\grave{o}\varsigma\ \dot{\alpha}\pi\acute{\epsilon}\vartheta\alpha\nu\epsilon\nu$) (1 Cor 8:11)

For the love of Christ controls us, because we are convinced that one has died for all ($\ddot{o}\tau\iota\ \epsilon\hat{\iota}\varsigma\ \dot{\upsilon}\pi\grave{\epsilon}\rho\ \pi\acute{\alpha}\nu\tau\omega\nu\ \dot{\alpha}\pi\acute{\epsilon}\vartheta\alpha\nu\epsilon\nu$); therefore all have died (2 Cor 5:14)

The common elements in these formulas are the verb $\dot{\alpha}\pi o\vartheta\nu\acute{\eta}\sigma\kappa\omega$ ("die") in the aorist, the preposition $\dot{\upsilon}\pi\acute{\epsilon}\rho$

---

161 Wilhelm Kasch, "$\sigma\upsilon\nu\acute{\iota}\sigma\tau\eta\mu\iota,\ \sigma\upsilon\nu\iota\sigma\tau\acute{\alpha}\nu\omega$," *TDNT* 7 (1971) 897–98; Armin Kretzer, "$\sigma\upsilon\nu\acute{\iota}\sigma\tau\eta\mu\iota,\ \sigma\upsilon\nu\iota\sigma\tau\acute{\alpha}\nu\omega$," *EDNT* 3 (1993) 308.

162 Godet, 194; Cranfield, 1:265.

163 Wolter, *Röm 5,1-11*, 176; see Karl Heinrich Rengstorf, "$\dot{\alpha}\mu\alpha\rho\tau\omega\lambda\acute{o}\varsigma,\ \dot{\alpha}\nu\alpha\mu\acute{\alpha}\rho\tau\eta\tauo\varsigma$," *TDNT* 1 (1964) 320–27; Peter Fiedler, "$\dot{\alpha}\mu\alpha\rho\tau\acute{\iota}\alpha\ \kappa\tau\lambda.$," *EDNT* 1 (1991) 66.

164 Winninge, *Sinners and the Righteous*, 235.

165 Rengstorf, "$\dot{\alpha}\mu\alpha\rho\tau\omega\lambda\acute{o}\varsigma,\ \dot{\alpha}\nu\alpha\mu\acute{\alpha}\rho\tau\eta\tauo\varsigma$," 321.

166 See Gibson, "Dying Formula," 28–39.

167 Harrison, *Language of Grace*, 225: "the death of Christ surpasses in scope all contemporary Graeco-Roman beneficence precisely because it was conditioned by $\dot{\alpha}\gamma\acute{\alpha}\pi\eta$ rather than by reciprocity," i.e., it came to the undeserving.

168 J. Michl, "Sündenvergebung in Christus nach dem Glauben der frühen Kirche," *MThZ* 24 (1973) 25–35; idem, "Sündenbekenntnis und Sündenvergebung in der Kirche des Neuen Testament," *MThZ* 24 (1973) 189–207; Thyen, *Studien*, 60, 171, 194–95, 203.

169 Michel, 181–82; Wengst, *Christologische Formeln*, 78–82; Black, "Romans 5–8," 420.

170 Kramer, 33; Dunn, 1:257; Werner Bieder, "$\vartheta\acute{\alpha}\nu\alpha\tauo\varsigma,\ \dot{\alpha}\pi o\vartheta\nu\acute{\eta}\sigma\kappa\omega$," *EDNT* 2 (1991) 130.

("for"),[171] the name of Χριστός ("Christ") without "Jesus" or "Lord," and in several instances the genitive pronoun ἡμῶν ("our"). In view of this evidence, Karl Kertelge points to the broad terminological and substantial agreement between Paul and pre-Pauline traditions in interpreting Jesus' death as a vicarious sacrifice.[172]

As Daniel Powers has shown, however, the widely used formula of Christ dying in behalf of others should be understood "in terms of representation and not in terms of substitution."[173] It seems likely that Paul is citing a well-established formula at the end of v. 8, integrating it into his larger argument that Christ's death for sinners expresses God's love[174] that overcomes their shameful status, and thus provides the basis for a revolutionary new form of boasting. Since the formula was apparently so widely employed and was so close to the words of institution recited in the frequent love feasts of the house and tenement churches, that Christ's death is ὑπὲρ ὑμῶν ("on your behalf"), the expression "on our behalf" conveys a sense of "participationism and solidarity"[175] that Paul wishes to be felt to include everyone in the various branches of the community, and even Paul himself. As suggested in 1:7, God's love unites them all, draws them together with the same experience of unmerited grace, and produces a "peace with God" that entails peaceful relations with each other.[176] All of this, however, remains implicit in chap. 5, which seeks to find common ground; the social implications of this powerful argument will be drawn in explicit detail in the final three chapters of the letter, which is why "welcome one another" and "greet so and so" should be taken as the climax of the letter and the goal toward which this discourse leads.

■ **9** This verse opens with the first use of a hermeneutical formula that appears four times in this and the following pericope: πολλῷ μᾶλλον ("much more").[177] In Greco-Roman rhetoric this is the *a minori ad maius*/τόπος ἀπὸ τοῦ ἐλάττονος ("from lesser to greater") inference,[178] which is the equivalent of Heb. קל וחמר (*Qal waḥomer*, "light and heavy") argument.[179] The procedure is to compare two realities, showing that if the lesser is true, it is more likely that the greater will also be true. The argument can also go the opposite direction: if the greater is true, how much more so the lesser.[180] It is a form of enthymeme in which the premise is provided in what has already been accepted as true and the inference is drawn to what has not yet been accepted as true.[181] There is evidence that this procedure was developed on the Jewish side in pre-Christian times, and it is listed as one of the seven exegetical rules promoted by Hillel.[182] Since Paul uses the *Qal waḥomer* argument repeatedly (Rom 5:9, 10, 15, 17; 2 Cor 3:9, 11; Phil 1:23; 2:12), it seems likely to have been part of his rabbinic training.[183]

171   See the discussion of the "ὑπέρ formula" in Hermann Patsch, "ὑπέρ," *EDNT* 3 (1993) 397.
172   Kertelge, "Verständnis," 123–24.
173   Powers, *Salvation through Participation*, 233.
174   See Pedersen, "Agape," 172–73.
175   Powers, *Salvation through Participation*, 108.
176   See McDonald, "Romans 5.1-11," 90–91; Gibson, "Dying Formula," 39: "I would suggest that in using this 'dying formula' Paul was engaged in a profound polemic against the prevailing values of his day with respect to what ordinarily was thought to produce personal and public 'salvation.' The one whose death Paul proclaims as salvific is the very antithesis of those who in the secular instances of the 'dying formula' are known, proclaimed, and honored as having brought about peace and security through their deaths. . . . Instead of dying for his own, he dies for his enemies."
177   See Gottfried Nebe, "πολύς," *EDNT* 3 (1993) 131–32; Michael Wolter, "μᾶλλον," *EDNT* 2 (1991) 382.
178   See Wilke, *Neutestamentliche Rhetorik*, 315; Lausberg,

Handbuch, §§396–97. The "lesser-to-greater" rhetorical figure, which is attested at least 1,048 times in *TLG,* is conveniently illustrated in the fragment of Epicurus in Diogenes Laertius *Vitae philos.* 91, referring to the appearance and size of the sun: "For he states, 'If size decreases on account of distance, how much more (πολλῷ μᾶλλον) its intensity."
179   Str-B 3:223–25, citing *t. Sanh.* 7.
180   See Wolter, *Röm 5,1-11,* 178; Bonsirven, *Exégèse rabbinique,* 83.
181   For general orientation see Moores, *Wrestling,* 16–28, 68–86.
182   See Müller, "Qal-Wachomer-Schluß," 78, following David Daube, "Rabbinic Methods of Interpretation and Hellenistic Rhetoric," *HUCA* 22 (1949) 239–64; F. Maas, "Von den Ursprüngen der rabbinischen Schriftauslegung," *ZThK* 52 (1955) 139–40; see also Burton L. Visotzky, "Hermeneutics, Early Rabbinic," *ABD* 3 (1992) 154–55; Collins, "Jewish Source," 28–33.
183   See Bonsirven, *Exégèse rabbinique,* 266–75, 317;

In this case the premise or "lesser" point on which all agree is "having been put right now by his blood." The aorist passive participle δικαιωθέντες ("having been put right, made righteous")[184] is reiterated from 5:1, and the references to Christ's atoning death in the credal statements of vv. 6 and 8 are picked up with ἐν τῷ αἵματι αὐτοῦ ("by his blood"),[185] and this prepositional phrase echoes the theme of 3:25.[186] According to chap. 3, the blood of Christ provides a new system of atonement that is open "now" (νῦν; cf. 3:26) to Jews and Gentiles alike,[187] by which their shameful status is overcome. As in other Pauline passages where Christ's blood is mentioned (1 Cor 10:16; 11:25, 27), it overcomes barriers between honored and shameful groups; his death conveys righteousness as a gift that restores and equalizes all.[188] Nowhere does Paul link the blood of Christ with remission of sins, as some maintain.[189]

No matter how one explains the significance of Christ's blood,[190] some commentators feel it is too crucial to comprise the "lesser" part of Paul's argument.[191] Michael Wolter prefers to describe Rom 5:9-10 as an *a fortiori* ("from the greater") argument in which justification is the greater point and salvation from wrath is the minor.[192] Since the comparative point remains undeniable in πολλῷ μᾶλλον ("how much more"), which should be attached to the finite verb "we shall be saved" rather than to the subordinate participle "made righteous,"[193] Wolter's preference should be rejected, although it raises an important issue that is muffled in most commentaries.

In what sense is being saved from wrath the "greater" point in comparison with righteousness through the blood of Christ? As a purely theological proposition it is difficult to defend, but as an argumentative ploy within the Roman rhetorical situation it makes sense. While Paul counts on agreement from all congregations concerning the archetypal significance of the death of Christ, there is no similar agreement about who is damned and who is not, as demonstrated by 14:1—15:13. When ἡ ὀργή is used in the absolute, it refers to the context of the last judgment[194] in which some are condemned and others accepted.[195] In this regard vv. 9-10 develop the future dimension of v. 5a, that "love does not put us to shame,"[196] the ultimate shame being the last judgment if one falls short. The emphatic location of "wrath" at the end of v. 9 indicates clearly where the issue lies.

However, the amazing feature of Paul's formulation is the unqualified future verb and its modifying phrase, "we shall be saved through him" (σωθησόμεθα δι' αὐτοῦ).[197] The future tense is all the more heightened by the emphatic position of νῦν ("now"). Schlier protests

---

Müller, "Qal-Wachomer-Schluß," 73, 80–92; Maurer, "A minore ad majus," 149.

184 Newman and Nida, 99: "we are now put right with God."

185 See Otto Böcher, "αἷμα," EDNT 1 (1990) 38–39.

186 This reference to well-developed earlier discourse about Christ renders implausible Collins's theory in "Jewish Source," 40–42, that Rom 5:9-10 was patterned after the later text m. Mak. 3.15, "If the sinner of one sin causes his death, is it not logical to assume that a meritorious deed of one man causes his life to be given?"

187 Walter Radl, "νῦν," EDNT 2 (1990) 480, citing Luz, Geschichtsverständnis, 88; see also Tachau, Einst, 81–82; Neuhäusler, "Entscheidende Augenblick," 2–3.

188 For an alternative theory that features Christ's identification with the human condition "so that he might return us to God," see Edward F. Siegman, "The Blood of Christ in St. Paul's Soteriology," in M. R. Ryan, ed., Contemporary New Testament Studies (Collegeville, Minn.: Liturgical Press, 1965) 365–66.

The articles by Dennis J. McCarthy, "The Symbolism of Blood and Sacrifice," JBL 88 (1969) 166–76, and "Further Notes on the Symbolism of Blood and Sacrifice," JBL 92 (1973) 205–10, deal with ancient Near Eastern background.

189 Johannes Behm maintains this traditional view "of the death of Christ as the guarantee of remission" in "αἷμα κτλ.," TDNT 1 (1964) 174.

190 See Davies, Paul, 232–84.

191 Meyer, 1:236; Godet, 194; Kuss, 1:210; Moo, 310.

192 Wolter, Röm 5,1-11, 179–80, following Bonsirven, Exégèse rabbinique, 83–88. See also Murray, 169–71; Schoeni, "Hyperbolic Sublime," 180.

193 See Barrett, 107; Käsemann, 138; Fitzmyer, 401.

194 See Gustav Stählin, "ὀργή, in the NT," TDNT 5 (1967) 423–24; Wilhelm Pesch, "ὀργή," EDNT 2 (1991) 529–30; Wolter, Röm 5,1-11, 180.

195 Murray, 171.

196 Wolter, Röm 5,1-11, 177.

197 Werner Foerster, "σῴζω κτλ.," TDNT 7 (1971) 992–93, presents "salvation" as eschatological deliverance from wrath, primarily related to the "last

that Paul could not have meant that those made righteous by faith "were no longer responsible," because many other passages refer to believers remaining accountable to God (Rom 14:10; 2 Cor 5:10; 1 Cor 3:14-15, etc.).[198] The "eschatological reservation" is supposed to accompany any such future promise of salvation, yet such a reservation is not provided anywhere in Rom 5:1-11. Paul eliminates the human factor entirely in claiming that salvation is "through him," that is, through Christ.[199] This lack of the eschatological reservation reflects a rhetorical situation very different from that found in the Thessalonian and Corinthian letters. The problem now lies in a different quarter, namely in Christian groups' damning one another because of disagreements over liturgy and ethics and the outcome of divine wrath. In this situation Paul finds it necessary to insist that measuring up to societal standards will be irrelevant at the last judgment. It will be as much a matter of pure grace as righteousness itself. In a stunning formulation Fitzmyer writes that the "consummation is guaranteed."[200] Believers are therefore to abandon all boasting and make no claims. In effect, Paul is urging the Roman Christians to be prepared to say at the last judgment, "We are unprofitable servants" (Luke 17:10) and cast ourselves entirely upon your mercy!

■ **10** In a manner analogous to v. 9, the "lesser-to-greater" argument moves in v. 10 from the present state of reconciliation to the even higher certainty of future salvation. The terminology heightens the preceding reference to "wrath" and thus pushes the argument forward: the "godless" and "sinners" are here revealed to have made themselves into "enemies" of God; the "unrighteous" are now declared to be "reconciled."[201] The term ἐχϑρός ("enemy") evokes the human war against God, as described in 1:18–3:23. While it is possible to understand ἐχϑροὶ ὄντες ("being enemies") in a passive sense, that is, hated by God and thus standing under wrath,[202] the theme of God's hatred is alien to this passage, which has repeatedly stressed divine grace, love, sacrifice, and salvation from wrath. It is much more logical to accept the active sense of human hostility against God[203] that expresses itself in the boasting against which this passage struggles. To view "enemies" as both objective and subjective[204] is to confuse modern interpretive options with Paul's intention and to bend his wording into an abstract discourse that satisfies contemporary theological needs. In his most explicit discussion of human enmity and reconciliation, Paul appeals to human volition, "We beseech you, in behalf of Christ, be reconciled to God" (2 Cor 5:20); this passage opens with the appeal, "let us have peace with God" (Rom 5:1). The atoning death of Christ did not aim at assuaging divine wrath, since "God was in Christ reconciling the world to himself, not counting their trespasses against them" (2 Cor 5:19), a viewpoint echoed throughout this pericope: Christ died "on our behalf" (Rom 5:8), for "the ungodly" (5:6), to demonstrate "God's love" (5:6, 8), not to prompt a transformation of divine wrath into love. To turn this into a drama of assuaging God's anger or counterbalancing divine justice is to impose later theories of the atonement onto a passage where they do not belong.

---

judgment." See also Walter Radl, "σῴζω," *EDNT* 3 (1993) 321. Wolter, *Röm 5,1-11*, 191, concludes that Christ replaces the law as the standard at the last judgment, saving believers by standing at their side. But he does not comment on the lack of the "eschatological reservation."

198 Schlier, 155; see also Dunn, 1:258.

199 Synofzik, *Vergeltungsaussagen*, 98, notes that viewing the final judgment through "justification and atonement is without analogy in the early Christian kerygma."

200 Fitzmyer, 400; see also Volf, *Paul and Perseverance*, 53.

201 See Wolter, *Röm 5,1-11*, 193–94.

202 Meyer, 1:226; Weiss, 229; Lietzmann, 60; Jacques Dupont, *La Réconciliation dans la théologie de Saint Paul*, ALBO 2.32 (Bruges: Desclée de Brouwer, 1953) 26–27; Bultmann, "Adam," 429; Murray, 172; Wolter, *Rechtfertigung*, 86; idem, "ἐχϑρός, ἔχϑρα," *EDNT* 2 (1991) 93; Martin, *Reconciliation*, 144; N. S. L. Fryer, "Reconciliation in Paul's Epistle to the Romans," *Neot* 15 (1981) 52–53.

203 See Colenso, 108; Deissmann, *Paul*, 147–48; Wilhelm Foerster, "ἐχϑρός, ἔχϑρα," *TDNT* 2 (1964) 814; Schmidt, 94; Sanday and Headlam, 129; Kuss, 1:211; Michel, 136; Käsemann, 130.

204 Cranfield, 1:267; Dunn, 1:258; Fitzmyer, 401; Moo, 312.

In the NT the καταλλαγ- terms are found only in the Pauline tradition, although the idea is conveyed with similar language elsewhere (e.g., Matt 5:34, διαλλάγηθι, "be reconciled").[205] The word "reconcile," or "exchange one thing for another," is drawn from spheres of conflict, in which warring groups,[206] quarrelling citizens,[207] or alienated marital partners[208] make peace. Victors claim to be able to impose reconciliation, as illustrated by Alexander the Great's grandiose claim to be διαλλάκτης τῶν ὅλων ("reconciler for the whole world," Plutarch *Mor.* 329c). This background has led Martin Hengel and Ferdinand Hahn to suggest that the Greco-Roman ruler cult was a source of Paul's concept of reconciliation.[209] Käsemann, followed by Dieter Lührmann and Egon Brandenburger, perceived a cosmological tradition in Col 1:15-20 and 2 Cor 5:19 that influenced the anthropological strand of atonement found in Rom 5.[210] A crucial issue in this regard is whether 2 Cor 5:19 is a pre-Pauline formula, which seems unlikely, although it remains beyond the scope of the present study.[211] Leonhard Goppelt made a strong case that 2 Cor 5 and Rom 5 do not reflect a pre-Pauline tradition of reconciliation applied to Christian atonement; his conclusion seems considerably more plausible than the Käsemann theory that requires a hypothetical tradition reaching behind Colossians.[212]

"Reconciliation" appears in explicitly religious contexts prior to the NT only in the form of God's turning from wrath.[213] Thus 2 Macc 1:5 hopes that God might "hear your prayers and be reconciled with you (καταλλαγείη ὑμῖν) and never forsake you in time of trouble."[214] Wolter has pointed out the link between atonement and reconciliation in the very structure of 2 Maccabees: while God's wrath lay against Israel because of its sins (2 Macc 3:1—7:42), the martyrdom of Eleazar and the seven brothers makes it possible for God to show mercy again (2 Macc 8:29), which results in Judas Maccabeus's triumphs in 8:1—12:36.[215] These references lead to the proposal that Hellenistic Judaism provided the source of NT usage, but the appeal to human transformation has no precedent there. Otfried Hofius suggests Deutero-Isaiah as the source, although

---

205 See I. Howard Marshall, "The Meaning of 'Reconciliation,'" in R. A. Guelich, ed., *Unity and Diversity in New Testament Theology: Essays in Honor of George E. Ladd* (Grand Rapids: Eerdmans, 1978) 118–21; Stanley E. Porter, Καταλλάσσω *in Ancient Greek Literature, with Reference to the Pauline Writings*, EFN 5 (Cordoba: Ediciones el Almendro, 1994).

206 Aristophanes *Av.* 1588, "We are envoys from the gods for reconciliation concerning war (περὶ πολέμου καταλλαγῆς)"; see also Plato *Resp.* 566e5, on the reconciliation of enemies. In the imperial context Dio Cassius *Hist. Rom.* 39.6 refers to Antony's desire to be reconciled to Caesar (ἠθέλησε καταλλαγῆναι τῷ Καίσαρι); 55.21, of Caesar wishing to be reconciled to Fulvius and Lucius; 64.9.3.15, of Otto wishing to be reconciled to Vitellius.

207 Thucydides *Hist.* 4.61.2 refers to "common citizen with common citizen to be reconciled (καταλλαγῆναι) and city with city"; see also Dio Chrysostom *Orat.* 40.16; Thucycides *Hist.* 4.59.4; Josephus *Ant.* 6.353; Dio Chrysostom *Orat.* 38.21, on "no longer holding hope for a reconciliation" (μηδέποτε σχεῖν ἐλπίδα καταλλαγῆς).

208 Josephus *Ant.* 7.185, 196; 11.195; *P.Oxy.* 1. Nr. 104.26, ἐὰν ἀπαλλαγῇ τοῦ ἀνδρὸς . . . καταλλαγῇ ("as if in deliverance of the man . . . in reconciliation").

209 Martin Hengel, "Der Kreuzestod Jesu Christi als

Gottes souveräne Erlösungstat. Exegese über 2.Korinther 5,11-21," in *Theologie und Kirche. Reichenau-Gespräch der Evangelischen Landessynode Württemburg* (Stuttgart: Calwer, 1967) 75; Ferdinand Hahn, "'Siehe, jetzt ist der Tag des Heils.' Neuschöpfung und Versöhnung nach 2. Korinther 5,14–6,2," *EvTh* 33 (1973) 247.

210 Ernst Käsemann, "Some Thoughts on the Theme 'The Doctrine of Reconciliation in the New Testament,'" in J. M. Robinson, ed., *The Future of Our Religious Past: Essays in Honour of Rudolf Bultmann* (New York: Harper & Row, 1971) 52–64; Wolter, *Röm 5,1-11*, 46, lists advocates of Käsemann's theory as including Dieter Lührmann, "Rechtfertigung und Versöhnung. Zur Geschichte der paulinischen Tradition," *ZThK* 67 (1970) 437–52.

211 See Merkel, "καταλλάσσω," 262.

212 Goppelt, "Versöhnung durch Christus," in *Christologie und Ethik*, 148–54.

213 See Friedrich Büchsel, "ἀλλάσσω κτλ.," *TDNT* 1 (1964) 254; Wolter, *Rechtfertigung*, 42–43; Helmut Merkel, "καταλάσσω κτλ.," *EDNT* 2 (1991) 261–62.

214 See also 2 Macc 7:33; Josephus *Ant.* 6.143; G. H. R. Horsley, "θλίβω," *NDIEC* 4 (1987) 155.

215 Wolter, *Röm 5,1-11*, 44–45.

the reconciliation terminology is not found there.[216] Cilliers Breytenbach has made a compelling case that Paul drew the reconciliation language from the political sphere of creating peace between warring parties, showing that diplomacy in particular employed this terminology.[217] Seyoon Kim argues that Paul's conversion provides the likely location for the development of the concept of reconciliation. Paul's former enmity against God was transformed by divine love, and he thereupon took up the task of bearing a reconciling gospel to the hated Gentiles.[218] While some of the antecedents of the reconciliation concept suggested by previous research may have contributed, the decisive innovation of understanding an atoning death as causing humans to be reconciled with God is plausibly related to Paul's conversion. Kim's suggestion also has the advantage of explaining why reconciliation remains limited to the Pauline tradition.

None of these discussants observes the way reconciliation is embedded in an argument dominated by shame and boasting in Rom 5:1-11. Ralph Martin seems more accurate when he insists that Paul himself is employing the term καταλλαγή ("reconciliation") to explain the atonement and to provide a larger context for righteousness, one that easily extends to the reconciliation with fellow humans.[219] Paul insists that we are "reconciled to God through the death of his Son." Martin observes that whereas Paul employs traditional atonement language without explanation in 3:24-25 and 5:6, 8, only with the introduction of the word καταλλαγή ("reconciliation") in 5:10 does he move into an explanatory mode.[220] Nevertheless, Martin does not take the framework of honor, shame, and boasting into account. John Fitzgerald's argument for a paradigm shift in Paul's use of the reconciliation language could provide an avenue to take

account of this terminology, because in contrast to the usual view that the offending party must take the first step toward peace, Paul makes "God, the offended party, the one who takes the initiative in reconciliation."[221] The human dilemma revealed in the cross of Christ is the quest for honor that worships the creature rather than the Creator, that finds it necessary to kill the Messiah rather than allow one's hypocrisy and hostility to be exposed. Christ's love for shameful sinners, tax collectors, and even Gentiles led to his death, but in so dying he conveyed divine love in an unconditional form. This love overcomes shameful status and renders unnecessary further boasting and other forms of competition for honor. When this gospel is internalized, reconciliation is achieved because the latent hostility against God has been exposed and overcome. By revealing the truth about the human condition, and by the power of divine love to fill the otherwise insatiable yearning for honor, the death of Christ makes peace possible, both with God and with the human race.

Verse 10b draws the heightened conclusion: how "much more, having been reconciled," Paul writes, "shall we be saved by his [the son's] life." The argument from the lesser to the greater points to a future fulfillment that will transcend current difficulties, with "death" in v. 10a contrasted with "life" in v. 10b.[222] While the expression ἐν τῇ ζωῇ αὐτοῦ ("by his life") is unprecedented, it sets the theme for subsequent pericopes that describe the new life in Christ (5:15, 17, 18, 21; 6:2, 4, 10, 11, 13, 22, 23; 7:1, 2, 3, 9, 10; 8:2, 6, 10, 12, 13, 38).[223] The closest analogy is 2 Cor 4:10, which describes the paradox of life in the midst of death and blessing in the midst of tribulations: "Always carrying in the body the death of Jesus, so that the life of Jesus (ἡ ζωὴ τοῦ Ἰησοῦ) may also be manifested in our bod-

---

216 Otfried Hofius, "Erwägungen zur Gestalt und Herkunft des paulinischen Versöhnungsgedankens," *ZThK* 77 (1980) 196–99; see the critique in Merkel, "καταλλάσσω," 262. Equally implausible is Anthony Bash's effort in *Ambassadors for Christ. An Exploration of Ambassadorial Language in the New Testament*, WUNT 92 (Tübingen: Mohr Siebeck, 1997), to derive the reconciliation concept from Jewish descriptions of Moses.

217 Breytenbach, *Versöhnung*, 40–104.

218 Kim, *Origin*, 13–20, 312–15.

219 Martin, *Reconciliation*, 148.

220 Ibid., 152.

221 John T. Fitzgerald, "Paul and Paradigm Shifts: Reconciliation and Its Linkage Group," *Cracks in an Earthen Vessel*, 253.

222 See Dunn, 1:260; this interpretation answers Fuchs's question in *Freiheit*, 17, about the motivation of the transition between vv. 10 and 11.

223 See Luise Schottroff, "ζῶ, ζωή," *EDNT* 2 (1991) 106–7; Dodd, 77.

ies."[224] Instead of relieving them from the burdens of finitude as the superapostles in Corinth had proclaimed, Jesus' life sustains the faithful while they are suffering and dying, and this sustenance is the fundamental reason they are enabled to boast therein, as 5:3 urges. Heinrich Schlier[225] is therefore correct that in the context of this paragraph the life of Jesus is not primarily related to the resurrection, as most commentators assert.[226] The resurrection theory disregards how the thought of v. 10 reaches its syntactical conclusion in v. 11. While the new life shared with Christ will climax in "eternal life" (v. 21), its redemptive power is experienced by the faithful as they are enabled to boast in a transformed manner in the very midst of their tribulations,[227] in every future event both good and ill between the $\nu\hat{\upsilon}\nu$ ("now," v. 11) and the parousia.[228]

■ **11** The "not only, but also" formula reappears from v. 3 and makes clear that this sentence belongs with the foregoing. While most modern commentators and translators make v. 11 into a separate sentence, it is syntactically subordinated to the preceding sentence.[229] One has a choice of linking it with the preceding participle, $\kappa\alpha\tau\alpha\lambda\lambda\alpha\gamma\acute{\epsilon}\nu\tau\epsilon\varsigma$ ("being reconciled," v. 10), which produces the meaning "not merely, however, as reconciled, but also as those who glory,"[230] that is, "boast in God." More likely is the proposal developed by Godet that subordinates the participle to the last finite verb, $\sigma\omega\vartheta\eta\sigma\acute{o}\mu\epsilon\vartheta\alpha$ ("we shall be saved," 5:10), producing the meaning: "we shall be saved, and that not only as reconciled but also as glorying."[231] With this interpretation, which seems consistent with the thrust of the entire

paragraph, the participle $\kappa\alpha\upsilon\chi\acute{\omega}\mu\epsilon\nu\omega\iota$ ("boasting") defines the context in which the "life" of Christ achieves its future salvation (v. 10). The recapitulation of v. 11 echoes v. 1, with "peace" picked up here as reconciliation. Since false boasting declares war against God, and engages in battles with God's rightful children, the gift of reconciliation through Christ produces a veritable new form of life. The innovative contours of Paul's approach are clearly visible when compared with Greco-Roman philosophers who agreed, in Lendon's words,

that the quest for honor was vain. . . . Yet however bristly his beard, however intimidating his stare, he could not escape honour. Greeks and Romans could not take off the spectacles of honour, and thus the admiration contemporaries felt for philosophers' virtue, freedom from convention, free speeches, or miracles . . . was necessarily expressed with honour. . . . Philosophers were doomed to be honoured for their scorn of honor.[232]

While accusing one another of harboring $\varphi\iota\lambda\sigma\tau\iota\mu\acute{\iota}\alpha$ ("love of honor"), philosophers competed with one another for superior honor in a variety of ways. As Cicero observed, "philosophers inscribe their own names on those very books in which they write that glory should be scorned."[233] For Paul, however, the quest for human honors is past. As in 5:9, the situation "now" contrasts with the former time before Christ was known.[234] To boast "in God through our Lord Jesus Christ," also echoing v. 1, is to abandon all prior human

---

224 See Käsemann, 139.
225 Schlier, 156.
226 Jülicher, 257; Kuss, 1:212; Wilckens, 1:299–300; Murray, 174; Morris, 226; Dunn, 1:260–61; Zeisler, 142–43.
227 See Fuchs, *Freiheit*, 16–17.
228 For a more abstract and individualized interpretation, see Findeis, *Versöhnung*, 276–86, 338–39.
229 See Meyer, 1:238; Godet, 197–98; Weiss, 231–32; Lietzmann, 60; Kuss, 1:200. Dunn, 1:261, cites BDF §468.1 in support that this participle should be taken as a finite verb, but this is more likely a standard example of a "finite verb" followed by "coordinated participles," as also in BDF §468.1.
230 Meyer, 1:239.
231 Godet, 198; see also Pulcini, "Romans 5:1-11," 81.

232 Lendon, *Empire of Honour*, 90–91; he cites Dio Chrysostom *2 Glor.* 67.3, the philosopher is a man who "will bid adieu to honours and dishonours and to the praise and blame of foolish persons, whether they be many, or few but powerful and rich. Repute he will regard as no different than a shadow."
233 Cited by Lendon, *Empire of Honour*, 92, from Cicero *Arch.* 26.
234 See Tachau, *Einst*, 82, 115; Neuhäusler, "Entscheidende Augenblick," 8–9; Nissiotis, "$\nu\hat{\upsilon}\nu$," 306–7.

claims of virtue, status, or superiority. It definitely does not mean boasting that God is on the side of an ethnic group, as in 2:17 ($\kappa\alpha\nu\chi\hat{\alpha}\sigma\alpha\iota\ \dot{\epsilon}\nu\ \vartheta\epsilon\hat{\wp}$, "boasting in God"), because 3:27-31 has closed that door forever. God is not the possession of either Jews or Gentiles, weak or strong, barbarian or Greek. To boast "through our Lord Jesus Christ" is to take up the revolution he inaugurated, in which the first are last and the last first, in which the greatest is servant of all, in which the weak and unseemly are honored with the rest, and in which the needs that elicit boasting have finally been met. His blood is the source of the grace in which believers stand, and this grace eliminates all need for boasting, except to boast in the Deity whose boundless love was expressed in the Crucified One. This is the basis of the "reconciliation" that believers have now "received," the "peace with God" (5:1) that this pericope encourages all of the groups in Rome to internalize and to enjoy.

5

The Second Pericope

Abundant Grace in Christ Overwhelms Adam's Reign of Death

12/ On account of this, as indeed through one person sin came into the world, and through sin [came] death, and thus death[a] reached[b] to all people, on which [world] all sinned—. 13/ For prior to law, sin was in [the] world, but sin is not chalked up[c] [against them] where law does not exist. 14/ But death reigned from Adam until Moses, even over those who did not[d] sin in[e] the likeness of the transgression of Adam, who is a type of the one to come. 15/ But [is] not the grace-gift just like[f] the trespass? For if by the trespass of the one the many died, how much more did the grace of God and the gift by[g] grace of the one person Jesus Christ abound for the many? 16/ And [is] not the gift just like the one's sinning[h]? For on the one hand, the judgment from one [led] to condemnation, but on the other hand the grace-gift from many trespasses [led] to a righteous decree.[i] 17/ For if by[j] the trespass of one, death reigned through that one, how much more shall those receiving the abundance of grace and of the gift[k] of righteousness[l] reign in life through the one, Jesus Christ[m]?

18/ Therefore, indeed, as through the one[n] trespass[o] condemnation [came] to all people, so also through the one act[p] of setting right for all people [leads] to rightness of life. 19/ For just as through the disobedience of one person many were made to be sinners, so also through the obedience of one[q] many shall be made righteous. 20/ But law encroached in order that the trespass might increase; but where the sin increased, the grace increased to the superlative degree, 21/ in order that just as sin reigned in death, so also this grace might reign through righteousness [leading to] life eternal through Jesus Christ our Lord.

---

a The deletion of ὁ θάνατος ("the death") by largely Western readings D F G 1505 2495 *pc* it Cl Ambst is difficult to explain as a transcription error. It may reflect the Greek tendency for economy of words, because θάνατος was mentioned in 5:12b and would clearly be the subject of the verb διῆλθεν if it were not repeated in v. 12c. The inclusion of "the death" is convincingly attested by ℵ A B C K L P Ψ 6 33 69 88 104 323 326 330 365 424 614 945 1175 1241 1243 1319 1506 1573 1735 1739 1836 1874 1881 2344 2464 *Maj Lect* vg.

b In place of the widely attested διῆλθεν ("it reached, came"), the verb εἰσῆλθεν ("it came into") appears in 1881, probably an assimilation to the use of εἰσῆλθεν earlier in the verse. A reversal of sequence between the verb and the subject is weakly attested in Ψ arm Chr Thret John-Damascus, according to UBS[3]. Neither of these variants, however, is included in Nestle-Aland[26 or 27] or in UBS[4], and, due to the revisions made in UBS[4] regarding patristic witnesses, the testimony of the latter as given in UBS[3] cannot be assumed to be certain; see UBS[4], 30*–31*.

c A series of minor variants arises in connection with the use of the commercial term ἐλλογέω ("charge to an account"). ℵ[1] 1881 provide the spelling ἐλλογᾶται, related to the confusion of inflectional systems, according to BAGD 252. The readings ἐνελογεῖτο ("it was charged") by ℵ* it vg[cl] and ἐνελογεῖται ("it is charged") in ℵ[2] D F G appear to be secondary. The reading ἐλλογᾶτο ("it was charged") in A (-εῖτο 1505 2495) *pc* seems to be an effort to make the verb conform more fully to the context, according to Sanday and Headlam, 135. Other spellings may be observed in Swanson, *Vaticanus: Romans*, 71, where the problem of itacism also is illustrated.

d That μή was deleted by 6 385 424[c] 614 1739* 2495* *pc* d* mon Or[pt] Aug[v.l.] Ambst as a theological "improvement" (Cranfield, 1:283) is generally assumed.

e The replacement of ἐπί ("in, on") by ἐν ("in") by B 365 1505 1573 1735 2495[c] *pc* Ir[lat] Or[lat] appears to be a stylistic alternative.

f The omission of καί ("and, also") in B sy[p] appears to be a removal of a perceived redundancy, although Cranfield, 1:284, suggests that the omission may be original. BAGD 393 discusses the seemingly pleonastic use of καί in sentences of comparison.

g The deletion of ἐν ("by, in") by F G may be due to haplography with ἑνός.

h The reading of ἁμαρτήματος ("[through] sin") in D F G mon vg[cl] sy[p] in place of ἁμαρτήσαντος ("[through the one] sinning") appears to be a Western style improvement of a difficult reading; see Cranfield, 1:286.

i The addition of the word ζωῆς ("of life") by D* vg[mss] is a secondary assimilation of this verse to the expression "rightness of life" in v. 18. See Cranfield, 1:286.

j   The awkward but well-attested reading τῷ τοῦ ἑνός ("of the one's [transgression]") is probably original, while the options ἐν ἑνός ("in one") 1739 1881 *pc* mon vg^st Or, ἐν ἑνί ("in one") A F G, and ἐν τῷ ἑνί ("in the one") D may be efforts to improve the correspondence with "in life" later in the verse, as suggested by Cranfield, 1:287.

k   The deletion of τῆς δωρεᾶς ("of the gift") by B sa Ir^lat Ambst appears to be an effort at stylistic improvement. There is strong support for the inclusion of both "grace" and "gift of righteousness" in P⁴⁶ (P⁴⁶ not extant until the word "gift") ℵ A C D F G K L P Ψ 6 33 69 104 323 326 330 365 424 614 945 1175 1241 1243 1319 1505 1506 1573 1735 1739 1836 1874 1881 2344 2464 2495 *Maj Lect.* However, some manuscripts render "gift" in the less likely accusative form (τὴν δωρεάν), as found in 6 104 424 *pc*. The accusative reading makes δωρεάν coordinate with περισσείαν. The addition of καί ("and") after "gift" in Ψ 0221 330 365 1319 1505 1573 1735 2495 *pc* lat sy appears to serve the same end.

l   The absence of the broadly attested τῆς δικαιοσύνης ("of righteousness") in C appears to be an instance of accidental omission.

m   The reversal of the words "Jesus" and "Christ" by B may be a stylistic improvement by avoiding an exact duplication of the sequence in v. 15.

n   The addition of ἀνθρώπου ("of a person") by ℵ* 1836 *pc* appears to be a clarifying or stylistic improvement.

o   The reading τὸ παράπτωμα ("the transgression") in F G (69) 1836 cop? appears to be a grammatical improvement by making "transgression" the subject of the sentence.

p   The reading of τὸ δικαίωμα ("the righteous decree") in D (F) G 69 cop? appears to be an attempt at grammatical improvement.

q   The addition of ἀνθρώπου ("of a person") by D* F G Ir is a secondary stylistic improvement to provide a closer correspondence with the first half of the sentence.

Analysis

Commentators widely assume that 5:12-21 is a separate pericope, opened by the transitional formula, "on this account" in v. 12 and closed with a christological clausula, "through Jesus Christ our Lord" in v. 21.[1] The role and appropriateness of this pericope in the argument of Romans have been debated for a long time, but I conclude that the main theme is how Christ's life (v. 10) defines the future destiny of believers just as Adam's life defined the future of his descendants. The primary goal of the passage is not to set forth a doctrine of Adam's sin but to demonstrate the scope of the overflowing dominion of grace (vv. 15-17, 20-21) in the "life" of all believers (vv. 17-19, 21). The comparison between the realms of Adam and Christ dominates the passage and is expressed in various ways no less than eight times.[2] The verb "rule over" is therefore a key to the passage, employed for Adam, Christ, and finally for believers reigning through Christ in the fivefold paronomasia of vv. 14, 17, 21. The themes of the "one" (12 times) and the "many/all" (9 times) are also emphasized by extensive paronomasia. The abstract nouns ending with –μα appear 12 times in vv. 16-18, producing an impressive oral impact through homoioteleuton.[3] The logical development is somewhat difficult to follow because the initial comparison between Adam and Christ in v. 12 is interrupted by historical and theological clarifications before it is resumed.[4] The organization of this pericope has appeared to be quite complicated,[5] with parallel lines in vv. 12-14b being interrupted in v. 14c, with v. 15a corresponding to v. 16a, v. 15b corresponding with v. 17b, and v. 15c corresponding with v. 17c. In the case of v. 13, there is a chiastic structure: law . . . sin; sin . . . law. Ian Thomson has proposed a much more elaborate chiastic structure encompassing the entire pericope,[6] but his proposal is difficult to support in every detail.[7] Gijs Bouwman proposes that vv. 12-14 be understood as

---

1   See Reid, *Rhetoric*, 117; Lamarche and le Dû, *Romains 5–8*, 25; Richard J. Erickson, "The Damned and the Justified in Romans 5.12-21: An Analysis of Semantic Structure," in S. E. Porter and J. T. Reed, eds., *Discourse Analysis and the New Testament: Approaches and Results*, JSNTSup 170; SNTG 4 (Sheffield: Sheffield Academic Press, 1999) 287–88.

2   De Boer, *Defeat of Death*, 157.
3   See Hofius, "Adam-Christus-Antithese," 171.
4   See Bullinger, *Figures*, 723; Wilckens, 1:307–8.
5   See Weiss, "Beiträge," 226–28.
6   Thomson, *Chiasmus*, 190–91.
7   Thomson, *Chiasmus*, 200–204, argues that v. 12 = A and v. 21 = A', but only v. 21a actually matches the

a diatribe, with v. 12 answering an implicit question about why evil still exists in the new age of reconciliation celebrated in v. 11.[8] However, the introductory words in v. 12, διὰ τοῦτο ("on this account"), do not seem appropriate as a diatribal response. Bouwman seeks to explain the anacoluthon of v. 12d with a theory of an interruption by the interlocutor,[9] but v. 13a does not provide this voice but rather the voice of Paul stating his thesis concerning sin being in the world prior to the law. The antitheses in vv. 13-14 could be explained with this theory, with the interlocutor's voice in the second half of each verse, but it is precarious to erect a diatribal theory on the basis of voices not found directly in the text.

I am inclined to see a structure of four paragraphs (vv. 12, 13-14, 15-17, 18-21), with the first organized as a ὥσπερ. . . οὕτως construction, and the second and fourth organized in double clauses.[10] Verse 15 opens a paragraph commencing with "but" and the next paragraph begins with "therefore" in v. 18.[11] While the suggestion that v. 13b is an objection by an imaginary interlocutor seems improbable in view of its chiastic coherence,[12] compelling reasons have been set forth by Chrys Caragounis to punctuate vv. 15a and 16a as rhetorical questions requiring an affirmative answer.[13] The answer to the first questions is provided by a

"lesser-to-greater" inference in v. 15b + 15c and the answer to the second question in v. 16b + 16c constitutes a straightforward example of antithetical parallelism. These details concerning vv. 15-17 strongly suggest that these verses should be held together by the interpreter. John D. Harvey suggests the presence of a somewhat inexact anaphoric ring composition that links vv. 12 and 18:[14] ὥσπερ δι᾽ ἑνὸς . . . καὶ οὕτως εἰς πάντας ἀνθρώπους . . . ὡς δι᾽ ἑνός . . . οὕτως καὶ . . . εἰς πάντας ἀνθρώπους. At the center of the composition, a section appears to be structured in an ABA' pattern with "through the trespass of one, how much more" in v. 15 reiterated in "by the trespass of one . . . much more" in v. 17.[15] Verse 16 has a prominent homoioteleuton in the fivefold repetition of the ending -μα, which corresponds with three occurrences in v. 15, one in v. 17, and three in v. 18;[16] it also contains a wordplay on κρίμα ("judgment") and κατάκριμα ("punishment"); v. 16b-c actually embodies symploce, with τό . . . τό ("the . . . the") at the beginning of each line and -μα . . . -μα at the ending of each sentence.[17]

The comparison between Adam and Christ continues in v. 18 with the antithetical parallelisms of vv. 18a + 18b and 19a + 19b,[18] the latter enhanced by paregmenon in the derivation of παρακοῆς ("of disobedience") and

---

thought of v. 12. That v. 13 = B and v. 20 = B' (p. 200) and v. 15a = D and v. 18 = D' (pp. 196–98) and v. 15b = E and v. 17 = E' (pp. 194–96) seems more plausible, but that v. 14 = C and v. 19 = C' (pp. 198–200) is not convincing. The Thomson analysis requires that v. 16 be the central element in the chiasm (pp. 193–94), which makes little sense because it is closely paralleled in structure to v. 15 and the decisive motif of "life" that binds this pericope to the foregoing is missing.

8 Gijs Bouwman, "'Zonde wordt niet aangerekend, wanneer er geen wet is.' Een onderzoek naar de structuur van Rom. 5, 12-14," *TTh* 17 (1977) 137–39.

9 Ibid., 140–41.

10 See the similar structure in the forthcoming study by David Hellholm, "Universalität und Partikularität. Die amplifikatorische Struktur von Römer 5,12-21," in D. Sänger and U. Mell, eds., *Johannes und Paulus*, WUNT (Tübingen: Mohr Siebeck, 2006), cited below with temporary page numbers.

11 Erickson, "Semantic Structure," 288; that a new

paragraph begins with v. 20 is a less plausible element in the Erickson analysis.

12 See Porter's discussion in "Argument," 672, 674, of the interlocutor proposal by B. Engelzakis, "Rom 5:12-15 and the Pauline Teaching on the Lord's Death: Some Observations," *Bib* 58 (1977) 233; and Bouwman, "Zonde," 138–44.

13 Chrys C. Caragounis, "Rom 5:15-16 in the Context of 5:12-21: Contrast or Comparison?" *NTS* 31 (1985) 142–45; Porter, "Argument," 673–74, adds the stylistic observation that ἀλλ᾽ οὐκ ("but not") is typical in diatribal questions posed by interlocutors, while the γάρ ("for") in vv. 15b and 16b would be typical for the speaker's answer to the question.

14 Harvey, *Listening*, 192.

15 Ibid., 192–93.

16 Ibid., 193; Tobin, *Rhetoric of Paul*, 183–84.

17 Schoeni, "Hyperbolic Sublime," 182–83.

18 See Bullinger, *Figures*, 716; and Cosby, "Paul's Persuasive Language," 223–24. Reid, *Rhetoric*, 144, provides further analysis of v. 19 as an "elegant isocolon."

ὑποκοῆς ("of obedience") from the same root.[19] A word-play on "increased" (πλεονάζω) appears in v. 20a + 20b and an antithetical parallelism appears in v. 21a + 21b, with a clausula concluding the pericope in v. 21c. The passage is linked with extensive paronomasia, beyond the "one" and the "many," mentioned above. Παράπτωμα ("trespass, blunder") appears six times and its virtual synonym παράβασις ("transgression") appears once; ἁμαρτία ("sin") and δικαιο- stem terms ("right-") appear six times each; χάρις ("grace") and χάρισμα ("grace-gift") seven times; θάνατος ("death") five times; and ζωή ("life") three times. This extensive repetition reflects an argument aimed at demonstrating the dimensions and implications of the contrasting realms of Adam and Christ, with the primary interest remaining in the latter.

Rhetorical Disposition

Exegesis

■ **12** The formula διὰ τοῦτο ("on this account") is commonplace in Paul (Rom 1:26; 4:16; 13:6; 15:9, etc.) but never otherwise appears in combination with the comparative conjunction ὥσπερ ("just as"). The combination is found in Plato *Eryx.* 400c5, "on account of this, exactly

---

19   Bullinger, *Figures*, 305.

as" (διὰ τοῦτο, ὥσπερ γε), and a few other writings.[20] Commentators are divided[21] about whether διὰ τοῦτο refers backward to 5:11,[22] 5:1-11,[23] or to the entire argument from 1:17 onward.[24] Others find the matter so ambiguous that no logical link with the foregoing is implied.[25] Since the main theme of vv. 12-21 is the "unity of *the many in the one*,"[26] both in Adam and in Christ, the strongest case is the description in the preceding pericope of the new stance in grace, of the status of righteousness through the blood of Christ, and of salvation "by his life."[27] Since Paul has dismissed the human factor in salvation while retaining an important role for human volition in living it out, he needs to establish the basis of the all-encompassing relationship between Christ and believers, a relationship that stands in contrast to the dominion of Adam. In either realm Paul needs to make case that "all" are included.[28] This pericope elaborates the thought first expressed in 1 Cor 15:22, "For just as in Adam *all* die, so also in Christ shall all be made alive" (ὥσπερ γὰρ ἐν τῷ Ἀδὰμ πάντες ἀποθνήσκουσιν, οὕτως καὶ ἐν τῷ Χριστῷ πάντες ζωοποιηθήσονται). As in this verse, it is widely assumed that a comparative clause beginning with ὥσπερ ("just as") demands a main clause beginning with οὕτως ("so also"). Whereas v. 12c has καὶ οὕτως ("and as") that draws an implication rather than a comparison, most scholars view this verse as an anacolouthon.[29] In an

effort to overturn this consensus about the incomplete sentence, John T. Kirby suggests that v. 12a-c is a "complete rhetorical syllogism."[30] This leads to a translation of v. 12c as the conclusion of the syllogism, "*so too [sc. through one man, Adam] death came to all men*."[31] A problem with this proposal, as Cosby points out, is that v. 12d is thereby eliminated from the syntax of the verse.[32] But even if one fuses v. 12c and d into a single thought, "in the same way death came to all men because all sinned,"[33] the sentence does not leave the impression of completeness because the ὥσπερ ("just as") in v. 12a "clearly is intended to introduce the first half of a contrast which is not in fact completed until v 18."[34] We have here a rhetorical comparison rather than a logical syllogism.

The expression δι᾽ ἑνὸς ἀνθρώπου ("through one person") appears here for the only time in biblical material. Classical parallels refer to evil caused by a single person, such as: "I have suffered injustices by a single wicked person (ὑφ᾽ ἑνὸς ἀνθρώπου πονηροῦ), even having presented his case in our presence."[35] While commentators agree that the reference here is to Adam, the figure in biblical history by whom sin originated (Gen 3:1-24), the precise phrase εἰς τὸ κόσμον ("into the world") is not characteristically employed in the Adamic narratives. Prior to the NT period, when it becomes a stock phrase in the Johannine tradition relating to the

20 A *TLG* search turns up examples in Aristotle *Hist. an.* 618a 27; Dio Cassius *Hist. Rom.* 66.2.4; Dinarchus *Dem.* 96.2; Porphyry *Abst.* 3.17.11.

21 A useful survey is provided by S. Lewis Johnson Jr., "Romans 5:12—An Exercise in Exegesis and Theology," in R. N. Longenecker and M. C. Tenney, eds., *New Dimensions in New Testament Study* (Grand Rapids: Zondervan, 1974) 300–302.

22 Meyer, 1:240; Morris, 228.

23 Godet, 202, cites Hofmann and Schott, and Meyer, 1:240, refers to others who supported this option. See also Sanday and Headlam, 131; Weiss, 233; Michel, 186; Cranfield, 1:271; Dahl, *Studies*, 90; Johnson, "Romans 5:12," 300–301; de Boer, *Defeat of Death*, 145–46; Fitzmyer, 411; Moo, 317.

24 Meyer cites Tholuck, Rückert, Reiche, Köllner, Holsten; see also Godet, 202; F. Ghislain Lafont, "Sur l'interprétation de Romains V, 15-21," *RechSR* (1957) 511–12; Wilckens, 1:307; Beker, *Paul*, 85; Dunn, 1:272.

25 Lietzmann, 60–61; Schlier, 159. Bultmann, "Adam," 153, argues that "therefore" in this verse is "no more than a transitional expression."

26 Gifford, 115, cited by Johnson, "Romans 5:12," 301, italics in original.

27 See Hofius, "Adam-Christus-Antithese," 176–79.

28 See ibid., 178.

29 See Bornkamm, "Anakoluthe," 81–82; Bultmann, "Adam," 152; Brandenburger, *Adam und Christus*, 158; Cranfield, 1:272–73; Dunn, 1:271; Fitzmyer, 411.

30 John T. Kirby, "The Syntax of Romans 5:12: A Rhetorical Approach," *NTS* 33 (1987) 284. Reid, *Rhetoric*, 125–28, supports Kirby's conclusions, as do Erickson, "Semantic Structure," 290; Denis Biju-Duval, "La traduzione di Rm 5,12-14," *RivB* 38 (1990) 361–62; and Tobin, *Paul's Rhetoric*, 177–78.

31 Kirby, "Syntax of Romans 5:12," 284, italics in original.

32 Cosby, "Paul's Persuasive Language," 220.

33 Ibid.

34 Dunn, 1:272.

35 Dinarchus *Dem.* 49.4; see also Hippocrates *Epist.*

incarnation of Christ's "coming into the world,"[36] the closest parallel is found in the LXX: Wis 2:24 reports that "by envy because of the devil, death entered the world" (εἰσῆλθεν εἰς τὸ κόσμον; see also 14:14). Egon Brandenburger has commented about the lack of speculative, metaphysical details in Paul's formulation,[37] which does not refer to the devil's wiles,[38] to Eve's seduction of Adam,[39] to angelic corruption of Eve[40] or her descendants,[41] to the perverse heart of Adam,[42] to the cosmic powers,[43] or to materiality itself as in later Gnostic speculations.[44] Paul also does not follow the tradition of viewing Adam as the "first father of Israel"[45] or as the "image of and promise for eschatological humanity."[46] He simply explains that through Adam's sin, death came "to all persons."[47] That death came as a result of Adam's fall is integral to the biblical narrative (Gen 3:3-4, 19, 22), and Paul refers to it here as a kind of "epidemic" sweeping over the world as a result.[48] It is a destiny that afflicted all of the descendants of Adam, without exception, placing all under the powers of sin and death.[49] This is a significant point in the Roman context, because the tendency to claim cultural superiority had infected the relationship between the house and tenement churches. In contrast to intertestamental discussions of Adam,[50] both death and sin[51] appear to function here as cosmic forces under which all humans are in bondage.[52] The language of "personification" does not do justice to the apocalyptic worldview within which Paul is operating.[53] To speak of sin as "entering" the world and death as "reaching"[54] all persons clearly implies that neither

11.9; Plutarch *Cim.* 2.1.3; Plato *Men.* 92e3; *Resp.* 462c10.

36 See Horst Balz, "κόσμος," *EDNT* 2 (1991) 312; the phrase εἰς τὸ κόσμον appears in John 1:9; 3:17, 19; 6:14; 8:23, 26; 9:39; 10:36; 11:27; 12:46; 16:21, 28; 17:18; 18:37; 1 John 4:1, 9; 2 John 7; in the *Historia Alexandri Magni*, the phrase appears 65 times; and Plotinus *Enn.* 2.9.12 speaks of "images of souls entering into this world (ἐλθόντας εἰς τὸν κόσμον τόνδε)."

37 Brandenburger, *Adam und Christus*, 159; see also Dunn, 1:272, and Martin Meiser, "Die paulinischen Adamsaussagen im Kontext frühjüdischer und frühchristlicher Literatur," in H. Lichtenberger and G. S. Oegema, eds., *Jüdische Schriften in ihrem antik-jüdischen und urchristlichen Kontext. Studien zu den jüdischen Schriften aus hellenistisch-römischer Zeit 1* (Gütersloh: Gütersloher Verlagshaus, 2002) 386-87.

38 Wis 2:24; *Vi. Ad.* 9.1–11.3; see John R. Levison, *Portraits of Adam in Early Judaism: From Sirach to 2 Baruch*, JSPSup 1 (Sheffield: JSOT Press, 1988) 51-52, 176-78.

39 Sir 25:24: "the beginning of sin is from a woman and on account of it we are all dying"; *Apoc. Adam* 21.1, Eve says to Adam, "Rise, come to me and I will show you a great mystery"; see also *2 En.* 30.17-18; see Levison, *Portraits of Adam*, 168.

40 *1 En.* 69.6, "Gaderel . . . who misled Eve."

41 *1 En.* 6.2–10.12; *Jub.* 4.22; 5.1-14; 7.21-25; see Levison, *Portraits of Adam*, 89–97.

42 *4 Ezra* 4.21, "For the first Adam, burdened with an evil heart, transgressed and was overcome, as were also all who were descended from him." See also 4:30, "For a grain of evil seed was sown in Adam's heart from the beginning, and how much ungodli-

ness it has produced until now." See Levison, *Portraits of Adam*, 113–27.

43 See Brandenburger's discussion of the magical papyri and Hermetic writings in *Adam und Christus*, 77–83.

44 See ibid., 83–109.

45 Scroggs, *Last Adam*, 22–23, citing Sir 49:16; *2 En.* 33.10; 58.1-2, and other passages. See also Jervell, *Imago Dei*, 33–34.

46 Scroggs, *Last Adam*, 22–29.

47 The universal scope of this "all" is elaborated by Hofius, "Adam-Christus-Antithese," 180, but he remains on the abstract level and does not explain the relevance of this emphasis for the audience.

48 Werner Bieder, "θάνατος, ἀποθνήσκω," *EDNT* 2 (1991) 130.

49 See Brandenburger, *Adam und Christus*, 162–65.

50 See Levison, *Portraits of Adam*, 47–48, 61–62, 96–97, 125–27, 142–44, 155–56, 187–88.

51 Since the definite articles with "death" (ὁ θάνατος) and "sin" (ἡ ἁμαρτία) denote "an entire class as distinguished from other classes," according to Smyth, *Grammar*, §1122, the article remains untranslated in English.

52 Brandenburger, *Adam und Christus*, 164–65; Wilckens, 1:315.

53 Cranfield, 1:274; Röhser, *Hamartia*, 157–61; Hofius, "Adam-Christus-Antithese," 172. For the apocalyptic dimension see Käsemann, 141–43.

54 See Ulrich Busse, "διέρχομαι," *EDNT* 1 (1990) 323, for διῆλθεν followed by the preposition εἰς as conveying the sense of "reach, arrive at."

was present prior to Adam's act.[55] However one explains the background of this thought,[56] it remains clear that Paul depicts Adam's act as decisively determining the behavior of his descendants. A social theory of sin appears to be implied here in which the actions of forebears determine those of their descendants.

The situation is much less clear with the final clause, ἐφ᾽ ᾧ πάντες ἥμαρτον (v. 12d), which is usually translated "because all sinned."[57] Many different interpretations have been proposed, reflecting the extensive discussion of "original sin" by later theologians:[58]

—One can understand ᾧ as a masculine pronoun referring back to an implied law;[59] to "the death";[60] to "one man," Adam, who passed hereditary depravity to his descendants;[61] to the entire preceding sentence describing the circumstances under which humans sinned.[62]

—One can take ᾧ as neuter so that the phrase ἐφ᾽ ᾧ gains the conjunctive sense of "because"[63] or "so that"[64] and refers to the involuntary participation of humans in Adam's sin,[65] to their inheriting his corrupt nature,[66] to their being imputed sinful because their representative, Adam, sinned,[67] or to independent human actions following the example of Adam.[68]

Progress in this debate dominated by complicated theories of original and imputed sin that arose long after Paul's time was made by Fitzmyer, who showed that although "because" is not supported as a translation of ἐφ᾽ ᾧ in texts prior to the sixth century c.e.,[69] several passages appear to support the consecutive sense of "so that, with the result that."[70] One example that does not support Fitzmyer as well as he would like is the report by Diogenes Laertius that the philosopher Cleanthes while leading his students to a public ceremony "was exposed by the wind and seen to be without an undergarment upon which he was honored with applause by the

---

55 Brandenburger, *Adam und Christus*, 63–64.

56 See A. J. M. Wedderburn, "The Theological Structure of Romans v.12," *NTS* 19 (1972–73) 340–54.

57 See Newman and Nida, 102.

58 For overviews see Kuss, 1:228–32; Cranfield, 1:274–75; Johnson, "Romans 5:12," 303–5. Kuss and Johnson are particularly valuable in describing the extensive discussion of "original sin" within systematic theology.

59 Frederick W. Danker, "Rom V.12: Sin under Law," *NTS* 14 (1967–68) 428. This option seems quite distant from the context.

60 Schmidt, 98–99; Schlier, 159–63; Bultmann, "Adam," 153. This option creates unsupportable redundancy and seems quite problematic.

61 Johnson, "Romans 5:12," 303, and Reid, *Rhetoric*, 74–75, refer to the Augustine passages but do not subscribe to his interpretation. According to Cranfield, 1:276, modern supporters include Manson, *Notes*, 159, and Turner, *Insights*, 116–18. The difficulty is that if Adam were in view, ἐν ("in") would seem more appropriate than ἐπί ("upon"). This objection is taken into account with the translation "because of Adam," advocated by Lucien Cerfaux, *Christ*, 178; J. Cambier, "Péchés des hommes et péché d'Adam en Rom v. 12," *NTS* 11 (1964–65) 246–46, 253.

62 Zahn, 261–67.

63 Johnson, "Romans 5:12," 305, states that this "has the overwhelming support of the commentators."

See Sanday and Headlam, 133; Murray, 1:182–87, with a penetrating evaluation of the alternatives. Fitzmyer, 415, provides an exhaustive list of commentators favoring this general option and argues that "there are almost no certain instances in early Greek literature wherein *eph hô* is used as the equivalent of causal *dioti*." See LSJM 622 B.III.3.

64 Fitzmyer, 416; idem, "The Consecutive Meaning of ἐφ᾽ ᾧ in Romans 5.12," *NTS* 39 (1993) 321–39.

65 Cranfield, 1:277, lists Lagrange, 106–7; Prat, *Theology*, 1:214–17; Huby, 190–91; Bruce, 129–30; this is Cranfield's preferred view, 1:279.

66 Cranfield, 1:278, identifies this as the view of Cyril of Alexander.

67 Johnson, "Romans 5:12," 312–13; Murray, 185–86.

68 Cranfield, 1:277, identifies this as Pelagius's view, which he rejects as not taking vv. 18-19 sufficiently into account. Commentators favoring this option include Denney, "Romans," 627–28; Barrett, 111; Zeisler, 147.

69 See Fitzmyer's critique of BAGD references in support of the alleged causal sense in "Romans 5.12," 331–32.

70 Ibid., 332–38; accepted by Hellholm, "5,12-21," 14.

Athenians (ἐφ᾽ ᾧ κρότῳ τιμηθῆναι ὑφ᾽ Ἀθηναίων)"
(*Vitae philos.* 7.169.4–6). In *Arat.* 44.4.1 Plutarch says that
a Sicyonian statesman fell into disrepute after lawlessly
mistreating a suspect: "having tortured Aristomachus on
the rack in Cenchraea, they drowned him in the sea, for
which reason (ἐφ᾽ ᾧ) Aratus enjoyed an especially bad
reputation." Neither of Fitzmyer's examples supports a
strictly consecutive sense that implies "the sequel to
Adam's baleful influence on humanity by the ratifica-
tion of his sin in the sins of all individuals."[71]

The more likely alternative is that ἐφ᾽ ᾧ refers to the
realm in which humans were sinning, that is, the κόσμος
("world") that is mentioned in vv. 12 and 13. That
humans are responsible for spread of sin throughout the
world is clearly implied by the expression πάντες ἥμαρτον ("all sinned"), although this creates inconsistencies
with the later argument of the pericope, which consistently stresses Adamic causation of later actions.[72] Paul
would then be advancing a paradoxical combination of
fateful influence from Adam and individual responsibility for sins.[73] As Käsemann observed, there is precedent
for this paradox in Jewish materials such as *2 Bar.* 54.15,
19: "For although Adam sinned first and has brought
death upon all who were not in his own time, yet each of
them who descended from him has prepared for himself
the coming torment. . . . Adam is, therefore, not the
cause, except only for himself, but each of us has
become our own Adam."[74] While certainty about Paul's

theory is hardly possible, this line of interpretation
would imply that each person in v. 12d replicates Adam's
fall because of his or her own free will.[75] In the light of
v. 12a-c, however, each is sufficiently determined by the
social poison of sin that choices of evil deeds remain
inevitable.[76]

■ **13** The interruption of Paul's comparison between
Adam and Christ begins with the parenthetical explanation that "sin was in the world" prior to the development
of law under Moses.[77] This reference tends to confirm
the interpretation of ἐφ᾽ ᾧ in the preceding verse as a
reference to the world in which sin had spread. While
ἄχρι γάρ ("for prior/up to the time of") appears also in
2 Cor 3:14 and 10:14, the phrase ἦν ἐν κόσμῳ ("was in
[the] world") is unique in all of Greek and biblical literature until a few patristic writers quote this passage. The
γάρ ("for") clearly indicates that this verse relates to the
foregoing, but the connection remains murky and widely
debated.[78] The most plausible explanation suggested
thus far is that Paul's contention in 4:15 ("where there is
no law, neither [is there] transgression") seems to contradict both Adamic causation and individual responsibility for sin in the period between Adam and Moses.[79]
Here Paul answers the potential objection by insisting
that sin was actually in the world during that period
(v. 13a), "but" (δέ)[80] according to the usual interpretation that it was "not put to account, chalked up" in the
heavenly record[81] until after the time of Moses (v. 13b).

71   Fitzmyer, 416; see also idem, "Romans 5.12,"
     338–39; and Erickson, "Semantic Structure," 303–4.

72   Hofius, "Adam-Christus-Antithese," 184–86, rejects
     the traditional reading that "all sinned" on the
     grounds that καὶ οὕτως ("and so") must be under-
     stood in a modal sense, that "through Adam" sin
     came to the whole world.

73   See Dibelius, "Vier Worte," 5–8; Bornkamm,
     "Anakoluthe," 84, 89; Schlier, 162–63; Branden-
     burger, *Adam und Christus*, 175–80; Wedderburn,
     "Romans v. 12," 351–54; Robinson, *Wrestling*,
     61–63; Dunn, 1:274; Esler *Conflict and Identity*, 200.

74   Käsemann, 148; see also Levison, *Portraits of Adam*,
     124; Schäfer, "Adam," 73.

75   Meiser, "Die paulinischen Adamsaussagen," 392,
     observes that this contention is consistent with Rom
     1:18–3:20, which holds each person accountable for
     actively choosing sin.

76   See Jewett, "A *Separate Peace* with Adam's Fall," in
     Saint Paul at the Movies, 43–53.

77   See Hellholm, "5,12-21," 16–17.

78   See Bultmann, *Theology*, 1:252; Brandenburger,
     Adam und Christus, 180–81; Morris, 232–33.
     O'Neill, 103, finds the argument so murky that he
     suspects a non-Pauline gloss.

79   Brandenburger, *Adam und Christus*, 183–84.

80   Hofius, "Adam-Christus-Antithese," 172, argues that
     in this context δέ should be translated as "freilich"
     ("certainly") or "nur" ("merely"), following Dennis-
     ton, *Particles*, 165, but this does not express the
     antithesis suggested by the rhetoric of 5:13-14. See
     Kühl, 178, and other commentators who translate
     this properly with "but."

81   The translation "chalked up" is proposed by Käse-
     mann, 149. According to Herbert Preisker, "ἐλλο-
     γέω," *TDNT* 2 (1964) 516–17, this is a commercial
     term found in papyri meaning to charge something
     on one's account, as in Phlm 18. For example, a
     second-century c.e. papyrus (*P.Ryl.* 2. Nr. 243.11)
     requests a steward to "charge to our account

Otfried Hofius makes a compelling case, however, that ἐλλογεῖν refers to sending someone a bill rather than reckoning a credit on his account.[82] A clear example of this usage is Phlm 8: if Onesimus "owes you anything, charge it to my account (τοῦτο ἐμοὶ ἐλλόγα)." In other words, prior to the law,[83] God chose not to hold evildoers accountable.[84]

This explanation does not account for why this question would be sufficiently crucial to break off the comparison at this point. Whether sin in this context was in the form of general Adamic influence,[85] of unconsciously performed evil,[86] or of concrete, personal deeds[87] remains unclear. It seems likely that a concrete congregational issue was addressed in this peculiar parenthesis.[88] As Thomas Tobin points out, the "all" who have sinned in v. 12 includes "both Jews and Gentiles," but since the latter lacked the guidance of the patriarchs in the period from Adam to Moses, "the Gentiles would have come perilously close to having no morality at all."[89] Since 14:14 reveals that the "weak" were "judging" the "strong" for violations of kosher food laws, it is apparent that these legalists were maintaining the permanent validity of the Torah even after the dawn of the messianic age. The Jewish Christian conservatives in Rome probably agreed with Jewish sectarians who maintained that the law is eternally valid (Bar 4:1; *Jub.* 2.33; 6.4), comprising a universally applicable guide for Jews and Gentiles alike (*Sib. Or.* 3.757), and that the law existed prior to Moses (*Jub.* 24.11) and was involved in the creation itself (*m. 'Abot* 3.14).[90] This idea of the eternality of the law meant that sin was defined exclusively

as legal violation. Paul undermines this entire construct by arguing that sin existed prior to the law's promulgation for the first time in the era of Moses. It therefore follows that Adam's sin cannot be reduced to violation of Jewish laws. It is deeper and more pervasive, infecting even those who conform to the Torah. The priority of sin over law also implies that no law can be granted universally applicable validity. When Paul returns to this problem in Rom 14, he defends the integrity of the "weak" in conforming to the kosher rules but rejects their effort to damn others for nonconformity. His argument thus requires the demolition of the dogma that the law is eternal.

■ **14** However one conceives the form of sin in the period between Adam and Christ, Paul insists that "death reigned" (ἐβασίλευσεν ὁ θάνατος) at that time. The crucial term βασιλεύω ("be king, reign") appears here for the first of five times in this pericope with the sense of "dominion"[91] exercised by death as a cosmic power.[92] The lack of parallels in Greek and biblical literature to the idea of death's exercising kingly powers illustrates the distinctiveness of Paul's view. In the Roman imperial context in particular, this verb with its Latin equivalent *regnere* implies irresistible coercive power.[93] Paul "is not speaking primarily of [individual] act and punishment but of ruling powers which implicate all people individually and everywhere determine reality as destiny."[94] The lack of exception to this dominion of sin is emphasized by v. 14b, which insists that it extends even over those who did not sin in precisely the same manner of Adam's transgression. Some have

(ἐνλόγησον ἐπὶ λόγου) everything you expend on the cultivation of the holding." (See also a papyrus from 237 C.E., *P.Grenf. 2.* Nr. 67.18; see also *P.Lond.* 2. Nr. 359.4.) For the argument that a principle of Jewish law is enunciated here, see Gerhard Friedrich, "Ἁαρτία οὐκ ἐλλογεῖται, Röm. 5,13," *ThLZ* 77 (1952) 525–27.

82 See Hofius, "Adam-Christus-Antithese," 196, citing Deissmann, *Light,* 84; MM 204b.

83 While most interpreters assume that νόμος refers to the Torah, Winger, *Law,* 4, 162, argues for a generic sense.

84 See Hofius, "Adam-Christus-Antithese," 197.

85 Lipsius, 112; Zahn, 271; Althaus, 47.

86 Preisker, "ἐλλογέω," 517.

87 Brandenburger, *Adam und Christus,* 186–87; Kuss, 1:232–33; Käsemann, 149–50; Fitzmyer, 417.

88 Reid, *Rhetoric,* 130, takes a step in this direction by insisting that "both Jews and Gentiles commit acts of sin."

89 Tobin, *Paul's Rhetoric,* 180–81.

90 For later rabbinic development of this theme see Str-B 1:245ff.

91 Peter Lampe, "βασιλεύς, βασιλεύω," *EDNT* 1 (1990) 208.

92 Bieder, "θάνατος," 130, death as a "domain of sovereignty."

93 See Weiss, 242. Karl Ludwig Schmidt, "βασιλεύς κτλ.," *TDNT* 1 (1964) 564–93, deals with Hellenistic and Jewish perceptions of kingship, but overlooks the Roman imperial background.

94 Käsemann, 150.

argued for a distinction between "sin" as an "inward disposition" and "transgression" as a breach of a particular command such as Adam had received (Gen 2:16-17).[95] Josephus employs the term to refer to "God's displeasure at violating the laws (ἐπὶ τῇ παραβάσει τῶν νόμων)" (*Ant.* 3.218). The syntax of v. 14 suggests that "transgression" and "sin" are not synonymous, because all sinned but not in the likeness of Adam's transgression. Since παράπτωμα ("trespass") appears six more times in reference to Adam's actions as well as those of his descendants, however, the distinctions between these forms of violation remain murky. The noun ὁμοίωμα appears to be used here with the simple sense of "similarity, resemblance,"[96] certainly not implying identity in an ontological sense.[97] To probe for subtle implications in the use of this term seems inappropriate at this point because Paul's intent is not to develop a consistent doctrine of sin but simply to close a loophole so his comparison of the dominions of Adam and Christ remains plausible.

That Adam constitutes "a type of the one to come" has occasioned much debate over Christ as the "second" or "last" Adam,[98] with minor disputes over the unlikely suggestions that the "one to come" (τοῦ μέλλοντος) might be Moses[99] or that it might be taken as a neuter and refers to an event yet to come.[100] The basic meaning of τύπος is the hollow impression made by a flow or a form, with a wide range of subsequent meanings such as a mold for producing a shape, a seal to make engravings, or a model for subsequent copies.[101] Paul employs this term in a similar manner in 1 Cor 10:6 and in the context of moral example in 1 Thess 1:7; 2 Thess 3:9; Phil 3:17. In the context of OT characters or events providing the τύπος for characters and events in the new age, some have proposed the temporal sense of "an advance presentation" or a prefiguring of future events,[102] while others suggest that Adam provided a kind of outline, a preliminary sketch,[103] or a model[104] of Christ. The translation "type" has been proposed to capture this sense,[105] but its scope needs to be delimited by the argument of the passage. In view of the contrast developed later in the passage, Adam has been viewed as the "antithetical correspondent" to the coming Christ,[106] but such an antithesis does not seem inherent in the term itself.

Since the exact expression ὅς ἐστιν τύπος ("who is a type") does not appear elsewhere in the entirety of Greek literature, the exegetical question is how Paul delimits the typology. His primary interest appears to be in the idea of dominion:[107] both Adam and Christ determine the fate of their subjects (βασιλεύω in vv. 14, 17 [twice], 21 [twice]). In other regards, as the pericope

95   Barrett, 112; see Johannes Schneider, "παραβαίνω κτλ.," *TDNT* 5 (1967) 739-40; Michael Wolter, "παράβασις κτλ.," *EDNT* 3 (1991) 14; Dunn, 1:276.

96   BAGD 567.1; Traugott Holtz, "ὁμοίωμα, ὁμοίωσις," *EDNT* 2 (1991) 513.

97   See Betz, *Nachfolge*, 172.

98   Among the scores of books and articles on this theme, the most frequently cited are C. Bruston, *La Parallèle entre Adam et Jésus-Christ. Étude exégétique sur Romains V,12-21* (Paris: Fischbacher, 1894); Karl Barth, *Christ and Adam. Man and Humanity in Romans 5*, trans. T. A. Smail, SJTOP 5 (Edinburgh: Oliver & Boyd, 1956); Matthew Black, "The Pauline Doctrine of the Second Adam," *SJT* 7 (1954) 170-79; Bultmann, "Adam," 143-65; Brandenburger, *Adam und Christus*, 9-14; Barrett, *Adam*, 15-17, 70-76; Scroggs, *Last Adam*, i-xxiv; A. J. M. Wedderburn, "Adam in Paul's Letter to the Romans," in E. A. Livingstone, ed., *Studia Biblica 1978. III. Papers on Paul and Other New Testament Authors*, JSNTSup 3 (Sheffield: Sheffield Academic Press, 1980) 413-30; Ole Davidsen, "The Structural Typology of Adam and Christ: Some Modal-Semiotic Comments on the Basic Narrative of the Letter to the Romans," in P. Borgen and S. Giversen, eds., *The New Testament and Hellenistic Judaism* (Aarhus: Aarhus University Press, 1994) 244-62.

99   Robinson, *Body*, 35; Scroggs, *Adam*, 81; Haacker, "Probleme," 16-19.

100   Meyer, 1:258, reports this suggestion by Bengel and Koppe; see also Godet, 212; Biju-Duval, "5,12-14," 372.

101   Leonhard Goppelt, "τύπος κτλ.," *TDNT* 8 (1972) 246-47; Ceslas Spicq, "τύπος," *TLNT* 3 (1994) 384-85.

102   Goppelt, *Typos*, 155-56; idem, "τύπος κτλ.," 252; Cranfield, 1:283; Wilckens, 1:321.

103   Spicq, "τύπος," 385-86.

104   Byrne, 184.

105   Käsemann, 151; Dunn, 1:277.

106   Gerd Schunack, "τύπος κτλ.," *EDNT* 3 (1993) 375; Hofius takes a similar line in "Adam-Christus-Antithese," 168-69, 180-81.

107   See Godet, 213, citing Ewald.

goes on to show, Adam and Christ are more antithetical than similar. The historical-religious background of this comparison between Adam and Christ remains problematic. Despite claims that Paul's view develops primarily on Judaic soil,[108] there is no credible evidence that Jewish thinkers ever viewed the Messiah as a kind of second Adam.[109] The idea of the original man as a redeemer figure surfaces in later Gnosticism and is a controversial issue in 1 Cor 15:45-47, which sustains the likelihood that Paul derived this comparison from Gnostic[110] or proto-gnostic[111] sources close to early Christianity. However, no trace of polemic against an original spiritual Adam is visible in Romans,[112] and Paul appears to employ the idea solely as a means to elaborate the dominion of Christ over believers.

■ **15** Following Caragounis and Porter,[113] I take v. 15a as a rhetorical question posed by Paul to the audience, requiring the answer, "Yes, it is!" This resolves the tension between v. 15a and v. 15b-d that arises from conceiving the former as a negative comparison between the results of Adam and Christ,[114] since "how much more" in v. 15c requires an argument of similarity. This also removes the difficulty in combining "not" and "also" in the same sentence[115] and eliminates the need to view vv. 15-17 as a vague and "virtually incomprehensible"[116] parenthesis that swerves from Paul's main line of argument.[117] Since ἀλλ᾿ οὐχ ("but not") is a typical

opening for a rhetorical question in a diatribe,[118] I understand the question "But [is] not the grace-gift just like the trespass?" as aiming to show that "the free gift affects all men in the same way as [Adam's] sin did."[119] This rhetorical question develops the positive comparison between the effects of Adam and Christ that was implicit in the incomplete opening sentence of this pericope. just as the transgressions of subsequent generations derived from Adam's act, so also the "grace-gift" comes through Christ's redemptive work with the power to overcome the Adamic legacy.

The term παράπτωμα ("trespass, blunder") appeared in the confessional formula of 4:25 and becomes the dominant term for Adam's deed in the rest of this pericope. In contrast to παράβασις ("transgression"), παράπτωμα does not necessarily entail a violation of law;[120] as in the Lord's Prayer, it can be translated as "wrongs" or "debts" (Mark 11:25). It is sometimes used to depict minor offenses, as in Gal 6:1, *Ps. Sol.* 3.7; 13.5, 10. In the case of Adam, however, his sin clearly entailed an overstepping of the direct command of God,[121] so a fine distinction between "transgression" and "trespass" makes no sense. In this passage both are roughly synonymous with ἁμαρτία ("sin").[122] The choice of παράπτωμα may have been purely rhetorical, since it would provide homoiouteleuton with the other -μα endings in the passage (χάρισμα, δώρημα, κρίμα, κατάκριμα,

108 Davies, *Paul*, 36–57; Scroggs, *Last Adam*, 1–58; Dunn, 1:279.

109 See Scroggs, *Last Adam*, 55–56; Zeller, 118; see also the survey by Peter Schäfer, "Adam in der jüdischen Überlieferung," in W. Strolz, ed., *Vom alten zum neuen Adam. Urzeitmythos und Heilsgeschichte* (Freiburg: Herder, 1986) 69–93. Meiser, "Adamsaussagen," 380–81, sees the possibility of metaphoric messianism in *1 En.* 85.3–90.42, but this requires later targumic evidence and does not come close to a "second Adam" speculation.

110 Bultmann, "Adam," 154; Brandenburger, *Adam und Christus*, 117–31; Käsemann, 144; Wilckens, 1:308–10; Kurt Rudolf, "Gnosticism," *ABD* 2 (1992) 1037.

111 See Hans Martin Schenke, "Die neutestamentliche Christologie und der gnostische Erlöser," in H. W. Tröger, ed., *Gnosis und Neues Testament* (Gütersloh: Gütersloher Verlagshaus, 1973) 205–29; Wilson, *Gnosis and the New Testament*, 31–59; Kurt Rudolf, "'Gnosis' and 'Gnosticism'–The Problems of Their Definition and Their Relation to the Writings of the New Testament," in A. H. B. Logan and A. J. M. Wedderburn, eds., *The New Testament and Gnosis: Essays in Honour of Robert McL. Wilson* (Edinburgh: T. & T. Clark, 1983) 24–27.

112 Zeller, 118.

113 See n. 13 above.

114 For example, Dunn, 1:279; Fitzmyer, 418.

115 See Caragounis, "Rom 5.15-16," 144: the normal Greek style for a declarative statement would be ἀλλὰ τὰ χάρισμα οὐκ ἐστιν ὡς τὰ παράπτωμα ("but the grace-gift is not like the transgression").

116 Theobald, *Gnade*, 69.

117 So Brandenburger, *Adam und Christus*, 219–24.

118 Porter, "Argument," 674, cites Teles *Rel.* 2.89 (SH), 207 (19H); 3.24 (25H), 108, 115 (26H) as examples.

119 Caragounis, "Romans 5.15-16," 145.

120 Michael Wolter, "παράπτωμα," *EDNT* 3 (1991) 34; Dunn, 1:279.

121 See Michel, 188.

122 See Wilhelm Michaelis, "παραπίπτω, παρά-

$\delta\iota\kappa\alpha\acute{\iota}\omega\mu\alpha$).[123] This terminological fuzziness is a clear sign that Paul has no interest in developing a consistent doctrine of sin or even of Adam's fall; his main concern is to show the all-encompassing and surpassingly glorious effect of Christ on those who belong to him, and the Adamic comparison merely serves that end.[124]

Paul's choice of the term $\chi\acute{\alpha}\rho\iota\sigma\mu\alpha$ ("charismatic gift, grace-gift") is rather surprising,[125] since this term was used to depict the charismatic gift that Paul wished to share with the Roman congregation (1:11); later in 12:6 and in the other letters, this term refers to the charismatic gifts granted to each member of the Christian community (1 Cor 7:7; 12:4-7). Since $\chi\acute{\alpha}\rho\iota\sigma\mu\alpha$ has no charismatic connotations in non-Christian usage but refers simply to a gift,[126] the special usage visible in the NT letters likely arose in early Christianity and bears the stamp of its charismatic enthusiasm. Although most studies maintain that the proper translation here would be something like "grace-gift" or "God's gift,"[127] referring to the entirety of salvation as in 2 Cor 1:11, there is no reason to suppress the charismatic component of this term.[128] Although one cannot speak of this word as a technical term,[129] the NT usage suggests that Paul's audience would have shared his view that the gift of salvation and the granting of charismatic gifts were inseparable. The choice of this term resonates with the charismatic terminology in the preceding pericope (v. 5) as well as with the pericopes that end this proof (8:1-39). While the results are antithetical, the future influence of the two figures of Adam and Christ is similarly encompassing: "the act of each is considered to have determinative

significance for those who 'belong' to each,"[130] and with regard to those belonging to Christ, their charismatic endowment remains inseparable from their salvation. In the context of a letter to Rome this reference to the "grace-gift" has a significant political resonance, because in the words of the proconsul to the Asian League, "it is difficult to return for (Augustus') many great benefactions thanks in equal measure ($\kappa\alpha\tau$' $\acute{\iota}\sigma o\nu$ $\epsilon[\grave{\upsilon}\chi\alpha\rho\iota\sigma]\tau\epsilon\hat{\iota}\nu$)."[131] The Julio-Claudian dynasty rested on the foundation of what Germanicus claimed concerning his father, Augustus, as "the true saviour and the benefactor of the entire race of men."[132]

In support of the audience's positive response, "Yes it is!" that was required by the form of the rhetorical question in v. 15a, the rest of the verse provides the substantiation of this "Yes," beginning as usual with the inferential $\gamma\acute{\alpha}\rho$ ("for"). Here is a properly grammatical lesser-to-greater argument, matching the form of v. 10 with the protasis introduced by "if," and the apodosis by "how much more."[133] Verse 15b simply restates the thought of v. 12 that the trespass of "one" person, Adam, led to the death of "the many." In this instance, $o\dot{\iota}$ $\pi o\lambda\lambda o\acute{\iota}$ ("the many") is "practically equivalent" to the "all" who died in vv. 12 and 18.[134] To draw inferences from this use of virtually synonymous terminology[135] is to lose sight of Paul's main thread, which does not provide a consistent doctrine of Adam's sin but draws inferences about the "coming one" and his saints. The bare formulation of v. 15b stands in striking contrast to the plerophorastic expansion of v. 15c-d,[136] where the third $\pi o\lambda\lambda\hat{\omega}$ $\mu\hat{\alpha}\lambda\lambda o\nu$ ("how much more") figure in chap. 5 is

---

$\pi\tau\omega\mu\alpha$," *TDNT* 6 (1968) 172; Schlier, 168; Brandenburger, *Adam und Christus*, 219.

123 See Barrett, 113; Dunn, 1:179; Hellholm, "5,12-21," 23; see also n. 7 above.

124 See Theobald, *Gnade*, 74; Aageson, *Biblical Interpretation*, 111–12, 114.

125 Gundry, "Rhetoric of Surprise," 257, notes that "righteousness" would seem to be a better counterpart to "trespass."

126 For example, the first attested use of the term is *Sib. Or.* 2.54, "for every soul among humankind is God's gift of grace ($\vartheta\epsilon o\hat{\upsilon}$ $\acute{\epsilon}\sigma\tau\iota$ $\chi\acute{\alpha}\rho\iota\sigma\mu\alpha$)."

127 Hans Conzelmann, "$\chi\alpha\acute{\iota}\rho\omega$ $\kappa\tau\lambda$.," *TDNT* 9 (1974) 404; Klaus Berger, "$\chi\acute{\alpha}\rho\iota\sigma\mu\alpha$," *EDNT* 3 (1993) 460–61; Michael N. Ebertz, "Charisma," *RGG4* 2:114.

128 See Brandenburger, *Adam und Christus*, 219; also Schütz, "Charisma," 689–91; Dunn, 1:279.

129 Ebertz, "Charisma," 114.

130 Moo, 334.

131 Cited by Harrison, *Language of Grace*, 228.

132 Ibid.

133 See Hellholm, "5,12-21," 23–24.

134 Cranfield, 1:285; see also Joachim Jeremias, "$\pi o\lambda\lambda o\acute{\iota}$," *TDNT* 6 (1968) 540–41; Gottfried Nebe, "$\pi o\lambda\acute{\upsilon}\varsigma$," *EDNT* 3 (1993) 132–33.

135 For example, Meyer, 1:263, rejects the view of Grotius that "the many" was employed to leave the exception of Enoch, who in biblical narratives is reported not to have died.

136 Theobald, *Gnade*, 93; Müller, "Qal-Wachomer-Schluß," 81. Collins, "Jewish Source," 38, suggests

employed to draw attention to how the "grace of God" surpassingly "abounded for the many."[137] There is a similar stress on the excess of benefaction in the claims of the civic cult.[138]

Paul's language is repetitive, rich, and resonant, particularly in view of the charismatic piety of first-generation believers. The χάρις τοῦ θεοῦ ("grace of God") is depicted in tandem with ἡ δωρεὰ ἐν χάριτι ("the gift by grace"), the latter alluding to the charismatic dimension of the Spirit's gift in v. 5[139] as well as to the gift of righteousness in 3:24. In this verse as well as the other Pauline letters (1 Cor 1:4; 3:10; 15:10; 2 Cor 1:12; 6:1; 8:1; 9:14; Gal 2:21; 2 Thess 1:12), "the grace of God" is granted to the undeserving through Christ's life, death, and resurrection.[140] The "gift by grace" refers both to the gift of salvation and the specific gifts of God's mercy and calling into his gratifying service,[141] given without regard to whether one has fulfilled the requirements of the law.[142]

Paul frequently uses the verb περισσεύειν ("to abound, surpass") with the sense of *Entgrenzung*,[143] the removal of boundaries or limitations in the description of the gifts of the new age. The idea that the future age would reinstate the plenitude of paradise is conveyed in Isa 25:6-8; 27:6; 65:17-25; Amos 9:13; Ezek 47:9-12, and picked up in later descriptions of the messianic period.[144] For example, 4 Ezra 8:52 promises that when "Paradise is opened, the tree of life is planted, the age to come is pre-

pared, plenty is provided (*praeparata est habundantia*), a city is built, rest is appointed, goodness is established and wisdom perfected beforehand." The verb περισσεύω is clearly a "characteristic" expression[145] of Paul's overflowing charismatic piety. He believed that with the dawn of the new age, paradisal plenitude was flowing out into the world.[146] The aorist tense of the verb ἐπερίσσευσεν ("it abounded") conveys the idea that this age has already begun[147] and is being experienced by the Roman churches. Paul had linked this idea with grace in 2 Cor 9:14, "because of the surpassing grace of God in you." Here the "lesser-to-greater" figure conveys the capacity of grace brought by "the one person Jesus Christ" to overturn the Adamic legacy of trespasses.[148] Paul's formulation implies a theology of "superabundance."[149] Overflowing grace is granted εἰς τοὺς πολλούς ("to the many," v. 15d), which provides a fitting match with "the many" (v. 15b) who died because of Adam's trespass. Similarly, the "one person" Jesus Christ matches the "one" person of Adam by whom the many died. By enhancing the parallelism and dissonance between Adam and Christ, Paul renders more powerful his argument that the lesser is surpassed by the greater.[150]

■ **16** Again following Caragounis and Porter,[151] I take v. 16a as a rhetorical question posed by Paul that carries forward the logic of the antithesis between the sin of Adam and the grace of Christ. The introductory καὶ οὐχ ("and not") again requires an affirmative response

---

that Paul's formulation was derived from *m. Mak.* 3.15, "If the sinner of one sin causes his death, is it not logical to assume that a meritorious deed of one man causes his life to be given?" While the "how much more" logic is in both texts, the Mishnah text does not deal either with Adam or the Messiah's action in bringing "life" to others. Collins also cannot account for the plerophorastic expansion of "the grace of God" and "the gift by grace of the one person Jesus Christ," which is clearly derived from early Christian piety rather than from the Mishnah.

137 Commentators are divided about whether the "much more" refers to the quantity of blessings (Meyer, 1:323, cites Rückert, Reiche, Köllner, Nielsen, Baumgarten-Crusius, Maier, Hofmann; other advocates include Alford; Barrett, 113–14; Murray, 193), to the intensity of the blessings (Kühl, 184), or to the certainty of their being granted (Meyer, 1:263, cites Fritzsch and Philippi along with himself; see also Sanday and Headlam, 140;

Theobald, *Gnade*, 95–96; Moo, 337). The first option is more congruent with the rhetoric of v. 15.
138 Harrison, *Language of Grace*, 231.
139 Gerhard Schneider, "δωρεά, δορεάν," *EDNT* 1 (1990) 364; Dunn, 1:280.
140 See Wobbe, *Charis-Gedanke*, 20–26.
141 Ibid., 63–74.
142 See Doughty, "Priority," 174–75.
143 Theobald, *Gnade*, 40–52.
144 Friedrich Hauck, "περισσεύω κτλ.," *TDNT* 6 (1968) 59; Theobald, *Gnade*, 58–61.
145 Gerhard Schneider, "περισσεύω," *EDNT* 3 (1993) 77.
146 Hauck, "περισσεύω κτλ.," 60.
147 Kuss, 1:235.
148 Wilckens, 1:323.
149 Theobald, *Gnade*, 95–99.
150 See Michel, 189–90.
151 See n. 13 above.

from Paul's audience. The comparative ὡς ("as") is repeated from v. 15a, but not the οὕτως ("so too"), which needs to be supplied by the hearers. The question is again oppositional, with elisions filled in from the context: "And [is] not the gift just like the one's sinning?" Here the verb ἁμαρτάνειν ("to sin") picks up the previous terms, "trespass" and "transgression," in describing Adam's act of rebellion against God, showing again that the three terms are intended to function as virtual synonyms in this pericope. The word δώρημα ("gift") picks up the motif of the "gift in grace" in the preceding verse,[152] referring to the result of Christ's ministry. Philo provides an example of this word, found nowhere else in the Pauline letters: "rational speech was bestowed on humans by God as the best gift (δώρημα κάλλιστον, *Somn.* 1.103)." *Epistle of Aristeas* 276 claims that the capacity for impartial judgment is "a good gift of God (δώρημα καλόν ἐστιν)." Paul's rhetorical question invites the audience to reflect on the antithetical consequences of Adam's and Christ's acts,[153] which are elaborated in the explanation of v. 16b-c, introduced by the explanatory γάρ ("for") and held together by the formula, μέν ("on the one hand") . . . δέ ("on the other hand").

The wordplay with κρίμα ("judgment, verdict")[154] and κατάκριμα ("punishment, condemnation") conveys the doleful process that led from the verdict against Adam (Gen 3:13-14)[155] to the punishment that affected all of his descendants (Gen 3:14-19).[156] While κρίμα refers to the verdict of a judge,[157] κατάκριμα is the punishment that ensues from the negative verdict.[158] In this instance the punishment is death for all (vv. 12, 14-15)[159] and also, implicitly, damnation for all.[160]

The succinct formulation of v. 16c, again lacking a verb, is understandable in the context of the previous argument. The χάρισμα ("grace-gift") mentioned in v. 15 appears here again as the symbol of Christ's work of redemption and charismatic endowment for believers. It leads to δικαίωμα, which most interpreters view either as identical in meaning with δικαίωσις, that is, "justification, the state of being declared right,"[161] or "sentence of justification/decree of righteous status."[162] However, the first and, to a lesser degree, the second option are special translations suggested by the context and theological considerations, rather than choices of connotations within the normal semantic range of the term, which is the result of the action of making righteous, thus "regulation," "ordinance," "decree," "requirement," "righteous deed," "right punishment," and so on.[163] I think it would be semantically more methodical to select a translation such as "righteous decree" or "righteous deed"; since the latter would become redundant in view of the reference to Christ's "grace-gift" earlier in this verse, the translation "righteous decree" is preferable. Condemnation is therefore juxtaposed with God's righteous decree of salvation in Christ; a new regimen of salvation, a new "law of the spirit of life in Christ Jesus," which Paul will clarify in 8:2, has been enacted that overcomes the legacy "of the trespasses of many."[164] The translation of "from many trespasses" (ἐκ πολλῶν παραπτωμάτων) in v. 16c[165] preserves the echo with "many" in v. 15, which will appear twice more in v. 19.

152 See Gerhard Schneider, "δώρημα, δωρέομαι," *EDNT* 1 (1990) 365.

153 Brandenburger, *Adam und Christus*, 224–25; Caragounis, "Romans 5.15-16," 145; Dunn, 1:280.

154 Mathias Rissi, "κρίμα," *EDNT* 2 (1991) 317–18.

155 Hofius, "Adam-Christus-Antithese," 174, correctly rejects the suggestion that "from one" in this context refers to sin, as proposed by Lietzmann, 62–63; Schmidt, 101; Barrett, 114–15. The "one" in this context is Adam.

156 Byrne, 184, refers to the wordplay but, following most current commentators, turns it into redundancy with the translation "judgment . . . condemnation."

157 Friedrich Büchsel, "κρίνω κτλ.," *TDNT* 3 (1965) 942.,

158 Ibid., 951–52; Wolfgang Schenk, "κατακρίνω κτλ.,"

EDNT 2 (1991) 259–60; BAGD 412, noting the wordplay; also Danker, "Under Contract," 105–6.

159 Weiss, 250.

160 Synofzik, *Vergeltungsaussagen*, 100; Büchsel, "κρίνω κτλ.," 952; Lafont, "Sur l'Interprétation de Romains V, 15-21," 485–86.

161 Meyer, 1:263; Barrett, 115; Käsemann, 154; Fitzmyer, 419; Reid, *Rhetoric*, 138; Moo, 338.

162 Weiss, 251; Godet, 218; Zahn, 276; Kühl, 184–85; Schmidt, 101; Schlatter, 130; Gottlob Schrenk, "δικαίωμα," *TDNT* 2 (1964) 222; Schrenk admits that this is a "rather uncommon application of the term."

163 Schrenk, "δικαίωμα," 221–22; Karl Kertelge, "δικαίωμα," *EDNT* 1 (1990) 334–35; however, Kertelge also adopts the translation "justification."

164 See Brandenburger, *Adam und Christus*, 226.

While the sense does not appear to be that the "righteous decree" springs from these sins, coming rather as a divine response thereto, the precise connotation of the preposition ἐκ ("from") remains unexplained by commentators.[166] With a formulation as compressed as this, the best one can do is to interpret the details as far as possible in the light of the context.

■ **17** This verse provides a syllogism with the fourth "lesser-to-greater" figure in chap. 5, showing that Adam's reign of death is surpassed and overturned by the new reign of those receiving grace and righteousness in Christ.[167] The puzzle is how to define the role of γάρ ("For").[168] Does it clarify that the "righteous decree" in v. 16 will be confirmed by future righteousness,[169] that the decree overcomes the deadly transgressions of the many by authorizing the many to "reign in life,"[170] or that it clarifies the two forms of kingly reign?[171] Current commentators skip over the question, which remains unresolved because of entanglement with special translations of δικαίωμα itself. As in v. 15, the "lesser-to-greater" argument is properly introduced by an "if" clause that correlates closely with the preceding argument. On account of the "trespass of the one," that is, Adam, "death reigned through that one," as the previous argument has shown. The repetition of δι᾿ ἑνός ("through one") "underscores again the antithetical correspondence of the two bearers of destiny," as Käsemann explains.[172] In this sense Paul's employment of the "lesser-to-greater" figure moves well beyond the rabbinic method.[173] The same verb, βασιλεύω ("to rule, have kingly dominion"), is employed here as in v. 14 and implies that death's irresistible power is derived and continued from Adam's act. The surprising feature of v. 15 is that the "how much more" figure is attached to the subject, "those receiving the abundance of grace and the gift of righteousness," rather than to Christ. It is the believers who "will reign."[174] This detail confirms that Paul's interest is not in developing a doctrine of Adam's sin but rather to employ the Adamic material as a foil to explain the abundant life in Christ that overturns the legacy of sin and death. The rare noun περισσεία ("abundance, excess") picks up the theme of abounding grace from v. 15; in its employment in 2 Cor 8:2 and 10:15 as well as here, it conveys "the superabundant fullness of the time of salvation."[175] This excess pertains both to χάρις ("grace") and to the δωρεᾶς τῆς δικαιοσύνης ("gift of righteousness").[176] While some commentators believe that the second reference is identical in content with the first,[177] thus absorbing grace into justification, the connecting καί ("and") and the repeated article[178] indicate that Paul has two distinct though equally superabundant realities in view. "Grace" refers to the

---

165 See Godet, 218, citing 2 Cor 1:11 and Luke 2:35 as examples.

166 Gundry, "Rhetoric of Surprise," 259: the preposition "from" implies that "the gracious gift of God's righteousness came not just in answer to our many transgressions, but—strikingly and mysteriously—through them, by way of them, out of them." This observation takes account of the parallel between ἐκ πολλῶν παραπτωμάτων and the preceding reference to ἐξ ἑνός.

167 See Gibbs, *Creation and Redemption*, 50; Hellholm, "5,12-21," 26–27.

168 For an intricate analysis of nineteenth-century debate on this point, see Godet, 219–21.

169 Meyer, 1:269.

170 Godet, 220–21.

171 Brandenburger, *Adam und Christus*, 227–28.

172 Käsemann, 155; see also Müller, "Qal-Wachomer-Schluß," 81, 87.

173 Müller, "Qal-Wachomer-Schluß," 92; Müller's work is not cited by Collins, "Jewish Source," 27–45, and it seems highly unlikely that Paul "adapted the mish-

naic statement [from *m. Mak.* 3.15, cited in n. 136 above] to serve his own cause" (36). The statement in the Mishnah deals with God's judgment of individual sinners while Paul is dealing with the effects of Adam and Christ, so it is hard to imagine that Paul is following the wording of the Mishnah, even in the unlikely case that this second-century C.E. text were available in oral form in his time.

174 See Gundry, "Rhetoric of Surprise," 259.

175 Hauck, "περισσεύω κτλ.," 63. A *TLG* search confirms that περισσεία does not occur in literary materials prior to the Pauline letters, but it is frequently used by LXX Ecclesiastes (1:3; 2:11, 13; 3:9; 5:8, 15; 6:8; 7:11, 12; 10:10, 11) in the sense of "gain" or "advantage." It appears in inscriptions referring to "surplus" funds (*CIG* 1:1378; *BCH* 21 [1897] 65 Nr. 75), as noted by MM 508.

176 Murray, 198.

177 Schlier, 172; Wilckens, 1:323; Dunn, 1:281–82; Schütz, "Charisma," 689.

178 See Smyth, *Grammar*, §§1143–44.

unconditional love conveyed by Christ that overcomes shame by granting access to God (v. 2). It also refers to the vocational commission of believers (1:5; 12:3; 15:15) that has a particular bearing on the missional purpose of this letter.[179] The gift of righteousness is the new status of honor granted to believers through the sacrifice of Christ. As the earlier chapters of Romans demonstrated, this righteous status is not gained by conformity to the law but is a sheer gift offered to everyone through Christ. God makes believers "right" through their acceptance of the gospel of Christ crucified and resurrected.[180] Paul's point is that both grace and righteousness have been "received" ($\lambda\alpha\mu\beta\acute{\alpha}\nu o\nu\tau\epsilon\varsigma$) by believers in such overflowing measure that the legacy of Adam has been overcome, thereby establishing a realm of abundant life.[181]

Since the believers in Rome have already "received" this gift, Paul asks, "how much more will they reign in life through the one, Jesus Christ?" This rhetorical question requires an affirmative answer from the audience: "Much, much more!" The verb $\beta\alpha\sigma\iota\lambda\epsilon\acute{\nu}\epsilon\iota\nu$ ("to reign as king") is employed here for the third time in the pericope to depict the antithetical realms of Adam and Christ. Using the future tense with an eschatological implication,[182] although the reference to "life" might imply its force in the immediate future as well,[183] the "how much more" figure renders this kingly rule of the saints infinitely more powerful than the reign of death.[184] That the saints will share in the rule of the messianic age is a stock motif in apocalyptic literature.[185] Paul had apparently taught this in Corinth (1 Cor 6:2)

and later chastised them for turning it into a basis for arrogance (1 Cor 4:8).

The crucial point is that this rule is $\dot{\epsilon}\nu$ $\zeta\omega\hat{\eta}$ ("in life"), a unique expression that picks up the theme of life from the preceding pericope, but it is not found anywhere else in the NT. There is no indication that "reigning in life" was intended as a negative qualification, that is, not rule over the Gentiles, as in Jewish messianic expectation.[186] Rather, in contrast to Adam's reign of death, to reign in life refers to "a new, holy, inexhaustible, and victorious vitality" that will make believers kings in life,[187] in the here and now. In contrast to the Roman civic cult that celebrates the rule of a single Caesar, here we have "the sovereignty of all."[188] However, this revolutionary form of sovereignty occurs only "through the one, Jesus Christ," with particular reference to his future parousia.[189] The future verb makes clear that such a reign will not occur on the basis of any inherent power of life that renders believers immortal or invulnerable, because as the preceding pericope urged, believers learn to boast in their adversities, knowing that God's grace sustains them whether they live or die.[190]

Paul's wording allows no distinctions between believers to remain intact, because all without exception will share in the kingly rule with Christ; this verse effectively undercuts the "invidious pretensions to superiority" that some in Rome were making in comparison with others.[191] This verse reflects the center of Paul's interest, and it has a situational bearing as well. He uses the Adam comparison to prepare the foundation for the argument in 8:31-39 that no one can impeach believers

---

179 Berger, "$\chi\acute{\alpha}\rho\iota\varsigma$," 457–58.

180 Karl Kertelge, "$\delta\iota\kappa\alpha\iota o\sigma\acute{\nu}\nu\eta$," *EDNT* 1 (1990) 326–27.

181 Gottlob Schrenk, "$\delta\iota\kappa\alpha\iota o\sigma\acute{\nu}\nu\eta$," *TDNT* 2 (1964) 209.

182 See Schlier, 172; Dunn, 1:282; Reid, *Rhetoric*, 141. Thüsing, *Per Christum*, 212, argues for an exclusively eschatological interpretation.

183 Murray, 1:198: "the certainty and security of the reign in life rather than its futurity"; followed by Moo, 340.

184 See Brandenburger, *Adam und Christus*, 229–31; Schoeni, "Hyperbolic Sublime," 183.

185 Schmidt, "$\beta\alpha\sigma\iota\lambda\epsilon\acute{\nu}\varsigma$ $\kappa\tau\lambda$.," 590; see, e.g., Dan 7:22, 26-27; Wis 3:8; 5:15-16; 1QM 12:14-15; 1QpHab 5:4-5; Matt 19:28; Rev 20:4, 6.

186 Dunn, 1:282.

187 Godet, 223.

188 Georgi, *Theocracy*, 98.

189 See Thüsing, *Per Christum*, 213–14.

190 See Rudolf Bultmann, "$\zeta\acute{\alpha}\omega$ $\kappa\tau\lambda$.," *TDNT* 2 (1964) 868–69.

191 Minear, *Obedience*, 59. For this reason I do not find Carter's contention plausible that Paul's goal in this pericope is "establishing and strengthening the boundaries around the group" (*Power of Sin*, 169), which would tend to intensify the conflicts between the weak and the strong that Paul is trying to overcome.

and separate them from the love of Christ, or from their destined role as rulers of the world. This verse provides an essential theological foundation for chaps. 14–15, which deal directly with the efforts of Christian groups in Rome to dispute the legitimacy of other groups.

■ **18** The final paragraph in the pericope begins with the inferential ἄρα οὖν ("so then, consequently"), characteristic of Pauline style but in classical Greek never otherwise employed at the beginning of a sentence.[192] This inferential opening does not have the function of summarizing the material from vv. 12-17[193] but rather in that light draws the consequence in the following comparison between Adam and Christ.[194] On the basis of the clarifications in vv. 12d-17, Paul resumes the straightforward comparisons between the "one" Adam and the "one" Christ.[195] Adam's "trespass" is reiterated and followed by two εἰς ("to") phrases in clauses marked by ὡς ("as") and οὕτως ("so also") clauses for which verbs such as "came," "became," or "led to" must be supplied. Whereas Adam's trespass led to κατάκριμα ("condemnation") for all people, Christ's δικαίωμα ("righteous deed, decree") led to salvation. The terminology has all been employed earlier in the argument, but δικαίωμα in this context has the nuance of an act rather than a law or decree, that is, an act that matches the requirement of a divine command.[196] Paul proceeds in the next verse to refer to Christ's "obedience," and in the Philippian Christ hymn he had described Christ's refusal to claim high status and

his willingness to be "obedient unto death, even death on the cross" (Phil 2:6, 8).

The most striking feature of v. 18 is the exact parallelism between Adam's damnation that came εἰς πάντας ἀνθρώπους ("to all people") and Christ's redemption that comes εἰς πάντας ἀνθρώπους. As Colenso showed, the "all" in this verse "must be the whole race, the whole family of man," including alleged barbarians as well as those viewing themselves as civilized.[197] Bonda has lifted up the universalistic implications of Paul's wording "that the salvation God has realized in Christ encompasses all humanity from the beginning."[198] In the context of Romans, however, the concern is not so much whether salvation is universal in a theoretical sense, a question shaped by later theories of predestination, but whether all believers stand within its scope.[199] This verse strongly suggests that Adamic damnation has been overturned by Christ's righteous act and that the scope of righteousness in Christ includes all believers without exception, both now and at the parousia. This has a powerful bearing on the issues of mutual condemnation between Christian groups that surface in 14:1–15:6.

In this verse salvation comes in the form of δικαίωσις ζωῆς, a unique expression that picks up the theme of "life" from 5:10 and 17. The rare word δικαίωσις implies the "act of executing" righteous judgment,[200] and is often translated "justification,"[201] "acquittal,"[202] or

---

192 BAGD 103–4; see also Rom 7:3, 25; 8:12, 9:16, 18; 14:12, 19. Only in Gal 6:10 is it followed by the comparative ὡς ("as") as in this verse.

193 Lipsius, 114; Weiss, 253; Michel, 191.

194 Brandenburger, *Adam und Christus*, 232; Esler, *Conflict and Identity*, 202.

195 See Brandenburger, *Adam und Christus*, 232; Murray, 199. Tobin, *Rhetoric of Paul*, 184–85, identifies this as *paria ex paribus* ("comparison between equals"). See also Hellholm, "5,12-21," 30–33.

196 Zahn, 281; Schmidt, 102; Schlier, 173; Kertelge, "δικαίωμα," 335: "righteous deed (as fulfillment of the requirement of God)"; Murray, 201; Moo, 341. Godet, 224, and Morris, 239, prefer "sentence of justification."

197 Colenso, 114, cited by Draper, "Colenso," 73.

198 Bonda, *One Purpose*, 97; he goes on in 103–7 to critique the commentators who restrict salvation to believers while insisting that the fall encompasses everyone.

199 Kuhl, 187; Minear, *Obedience*, 60; Moo, 343.

200 Gottlob Schrenk, "δικαίωσις," *TDNT* 2 (1964) 223. A *TLG* search indicates the first attestation of δικαίωσις is in Thucydides *Hist.* 1.141, "acquittal . . . before a court (δικαίωσις . . . πρὸ δίκης)"; 8.66, "neither a judicial enquiry nor, if they would suspect, an acquittal occurred (δικαίωσις ἐγίγνετο)." In Dionysius Halicarnassus *Antiq. Rom.* 1.58, a nonjudicial sense of "justice" seems to be in view when Aeneas is condemned for "by-passing the sense of justice with all men (παρελθὼν τὴν ἁπάντων ἀνθρώπων δικαίωσιν)." In *Antiq. Rom.* 7.59, Dionysius Halicarnassus refers to "the just claim of life and of freedom (ἡ τοῦ βίου καὶ τῆς ἐλευθερίας δικαίωσις)."

201 Brandenburger, *Adam und Christus*, 233; Barrett, 116; Cranfield, 1:289; Wilckens, 1:326; Murray, 1:202; Morris, 239.

202 BAGD 198; Black, 84.

"vindication,"[203] almost always in reference to the fate of individuals. Since it qualifies "life" and functions in this sentence as the counterpart of "condemnation," I prefer "rightness," implying the state of righteousness produced by Christ's grace that will assure the new form of life in groups of believers both now and in the future.[204] Once again, it is striking that this future judgment does not take human qualifications or performance into account in any way. Thus any effort by believers to condemn their fellow believers on the basis of nonperformance of law is undercut.

■ **19** The second comparison in the final paragraph clarifies the nature of the "trespass" and "righteous deed" of the preceding verse. Adam's sin consisted in παρακοή ("disobedience, turning a deaf ear")[205] in that he and Eve violated an explicit command not to touch the tree of life (Gen 2:16-17; 3:4-7, 14). This theme is picked up by the *Apoc. Ez.* 2.12, "Since he who established disobedience [i.e., Satan] made this (man) sin." The consequence was that οὐ πολλοί ("the many") became sinners, which is the same discriminatory term (ἁμαρτωλός) as in v. 8.[206] In view of Paul's contention in v. 13 that sin preceded the law, this wording implies that one becomes a sinner without violating specific laws later set down by Moses. Again, this broad definition of sin has a significant implication for the congregational situation, in that the conservative factions in Rome were maintaining that the law was eternal and that those not conforming thereto were sinners.

In contrast to the effect of Adam, Paul maintains that Christ demonstrated an "obedience" (ὑπακοή) that made all believers righteous, regardless of their conformity to the Torah. Although some commentators have suggested that this obedience entailed Christ's entire life,[207] the comparison with Adam's single act of obedience suggests that Christ's obedience unto death is implied.[208] The verb καθίστημι ("make, cause") is employed here twice in the passive, and while some have argued that it has the legal sense of "bring before a judge,"[209] it seems more likely that it bears the nontechnical sense of "take," "appoint," or "become."[210] While the aorist tense of κατεστάθησαν ("they were made to be") is assumed to refer to the status of "sinner" imposed upon Adam's descendants, scholars debate about whether the future κατασταθήσονται ("they shall be made to be") should be interpreted as "logical" and thus refer to the certainty of justification,[211] or as an eschatological future that echoes the future verb δικαιωθήσονται ("they will be made righteous") in 2:13.[212] In support of the properly future construal, one could cite 1 Cor 15:49, "Just as we have

203 Dunn, 1:225, 283.
204 Thüsing, *Per Christum*, 215, argues for an exclusively eschatological construal of this expression: "the eschatological decree of righteousness." For an interpretation that combines the present with the eschatological future, see Lafont, "Sur l'interprétation de Romains V, 15-21," 491–92.
205 Gerhard Kittel, "παρακούω, παρακοή," TDNT 1 (1964) 223: "bad hearing . . . unwillingness to hear"; see also Ceslas Spicq, "παρακοή," TLNT 3 (1994) 28–29.
206 See Winninge, *Sinners and the Righteous*, 235.
207 Michel, 191; Käsemann, 157; Cranfield, 1:291; Fitzmyer, 421.
208 Gerhard Kittel, "ὑπακοή, ὑπακούω," TDNT 1 (1964) 224–25; Ceslas Spicq, "εἰσακούω . . . ὑπακοή," TLNT 1 (1994) 451; Wilckens, 1:326; Dunn, 1:284; Moo, 344.
209 Danker, "Under Contract," 106, citing *P.Oxy.* 2. Nr. 281.24, in which an abandoned wife asks the judge to bring her husband to account: "I therefore beg you to order him to stand (καταστῆσαι) before you." See also Jan-Adolf Bühner, "καθίστημι, καθιστάνω," EDNT 2 (1991) 225–26.

210 BAGD (2000) 492; Albrecht Oepke, "καθίστημι κτλ.," TDNT 3 (1965) 445, suggests the meaning "to make someone something." Oepke retains a judicial component, "make righteous," because he advocates a judicial theory of justification; for a nonjudicial interpretation see Brandenburger, *Adam und Christus*, 161–62. MM 313 cites *P.Rein.* 1. Nr. 18.40 as an example of passive use of καθίστημι.
211 Weiss, 258; Zahn, 284–85; Sanday and Headlam, 142; Lagrange, 112; Schmidt, 102; Bultmann, *Theology*, 1:274; Cranfield, 1:291; Brandenburger, *Adam und Christus*, 234; Murray, 1:206; Moo, 346. Whether a "gnomic future" (BDF §349; Moulton and Turner, *Grammar III*, 86) is present here seems doubtful in view of the comparative syntax of 5:19; no grammar identifies 5:19 as an example of the "gnomic future"; the main reason to adduce the special category of "logical future" is theological, to bring v. 19b into conformity with vv. 17, 21.
212 Meyer, 1:274, cites Reiche and Fritzsche in support of his future construal; see also Godet, 226; Kühl, 190; Michel, 126; Bultmann, "Adam," 159; Käsemann, 157–58; Kuss, 1:239; Wilckens, 1:328; Klaiber, *Rechtfertigung*, 119; Dunn, 1:285.

borne the image of the man of dust, we shall also bear the image of the man of heaven."

The idea of one person's obedience making "many righteous" appears to echo the Hebrew text of Isa 53:11, "the righteous one, my servant, shall make many to be accounted righteous." In Shum's words, "what Paul draws on from the Suffering Servant song is not simply (Second) Isaiah's language, but the prophet's concept of a *one-many-solidarity-relationship*."[213] Since this pericope interacts repeatedly with congregational impulses in Rome to damn opposing groups because of nonconformity with the Torah, the reference to "many" is defined as believers being made righteous. The context denies "the limited nationalism of the normal Jewish hope"[214] that restricts the number of the "righteous" to those following the Torah. The πολλοί ("many") in this context as in 5:15 includes all those who have accepted the gospel,[215] both Jewish and Gentile in background, both "weak" and "strong," without regard to their adherence to the law.[216] Bonda assumes that the "all" of v. 18 carries over into this verse, so that the purpose of God is "that all may be made righteous" because God "has no other purpose, and never had any other purpose, than that all might inherit the life for which he created them."[217] While some have taken the "many" of v. 19 to "imply a restriction: many people, but not all," Bonda insists that the same universal implication of "many" should be understood here as in v. 15. The "many" who die through Adam's trespass also contain no exceptions according to v. 12.[218] In view of Paul's concern with congregational issues rather than with doctrinal questions such as universalism, however, it seems more likely that "many" in this context refers to believers.

■ **20** Paul's effort to demote the role of law is continued with his choice of the derogatory expression νόμος δὲ παρεισῆλθεν ("but law slipped in, encroached"),[219] not to guide the faithful to life but to increase the scale of sin. The only other occurrence of παρεισέρχομαι ("I slip in stealthily, sneak in") in the Scriptures is in Paul's description of the "false brothers . . . who slipped in (τοὺς παρεισάκτους) to spy out our freedom" in the context of the apostolic conference (Gal 2:4). Since this verb is so frequently employed in contexts of unwanted, illegitimate entry or of the insertion of an object into an area where it would not ordinarily belong,[220] there is no reason to accept a specialized translation here that softens the derogatory note to preserve as far as possible a positive appraisal of law.[221] One should note that Paul does not employ the article with νόμος ("law") in this verse, thus allowing the scope of his argument to extend to all law everywhere.[222] Especially in view of the Jewish dogma of the law as eternal and involved in the very creation of the universe,[223] however, both this verb and the entirety of v. 20a would have been felt to be derogatory.[224] To say that law's purpose was "in order to increase the trespass" is a shocking denial of the positive function of the law to guide the faithful in righteousness.[225] The verb πλεονάζω refers to growth in size,[226]

213 See Shum, *Paul's Use of Isaiah*, 199; parenthesis and italics in original; cf. Latto, *Star Is Rising*, 343–44.

214 Dunn, 1:285.

215 Nebe, "πολύς," 132–33; Klaiber, *Rechtfertigung*, 118.

216 Kaylor, *Covenant Community*, 104–14.

217 Bonda, *One Purpose*, 102.

218 Ibid., 106.

219 Sanday and Headlam, 139; Leenhardt, 149; Brandenburger, *Adam und Christus*, 249–50, following Bornkamm, "Anakoluthe," 88–89; with qualifications, also Käsemann, 158; Schlier, 177; Hofius, "Adam-Christus-Antithese," 199–200.

220 The nuance is perfectly captured in Polybius *Hist.* 2.55.3: "He slipped inside these walls secretly at night (παρεισῆλθε διὰ τούτων λάθρα νυκτὸς ἐντὸς τειχῶν)." See also Polybius *Hist.* 1.7.3; 3.18.11; Plutarch *Gen. Socr.* 596a; *Cor.* 23.1; *Publ.* 17.2; *Soll. an.* 980b; Lucian of Samosata *Call.* 28; *Dial. meretr.* 12.3; Philo *Abr.* 96; *QG* 3.21.6.

221 Meyer, 1:276; Cranfield, 1:292: insert something "alongside of"; Horst Balz, "παρεισέρχομαι," *EDNT* 3 (1991) 37, citing Jüngel's reference to the law as "a provisional regulation between Adam and Christ that is theologically necessary for the Adam-Christ correspondence." See also Wilckens, 1:329; Hofius, "Adam-Christus-Antithese," 200–201.

222 Overlooking this detail, most commentators relate this verse only to the Jewish Torah; see, e.g., Kühl, 192; Schmidt, 103; Cranfield, 1:293; Beker, *Paul*, 86–87; Dunn, 1:286.

223 See Schlier, 177.

224 De Boer, *Defeat of Death*, 167–68.

225 See Boyarin, *Radical Jew*, 161–62.

226 Gerhard Delling, "πλεονάζω, ὑπερπλεονάζω," *TDNT* 6 (1968) 264–65.

often in a negative sense of going too far or being out of control. For example, πλεονάζω is used in reference to a river overflowing its banks (Dio Cassius *Hist. Rom.* 54.25.2; 57.14.8), a regent committing excesses in violence (Dio Cassius *Hist. Rom.* 69.23.3), or victors increasing in pride (Dio Cassius *Hist. Rom.* 44.29.2). The problematic increase of the trespass is a matter that Rom 7:5 explains more explicitly,[227] namely that human passion turns law into a competition for honor, thereby widening the extent of the perversion.[228] Even the performance of law with the intention to produce the good as God intends will be twisted and turned into its opposite when used to gain honor. Here Paul moves beyond Gal 3:21-25, where law "cannot make alive" because it serves as a kind of custodian until Christ sets believers free.[229] To increase the trespass is to take up and intensify Adam's plight, to deepen the legacy of his enmity against God,[230] thus echoing themes in the preceding proof (vv. 8-11). Rather than lessening the human tendency to sin and thus ameliorating the Adamic legacy, law inflames the trespass and makes it ever more vicious and pervasive, as the crucifixion of Christ revealed.[231]

It is clear that ἁμαρτία ("sin") in v. 20b is used interchangeably with παράπτωμα ("trespass") in v. 20a,[232] showing again that "Paul is not concerned with minor distinctions among grades of evil."[233] Where "the sin increased," referring to a specific location,[234] probably the climactic event of the crucifixion of the Messiah,[235]

God's grace "abounded to a superlative degree." Paul selects the verb ὑπερπερισσεύω rather than its synonym ὑπερπλεονάζω, which would have correlated even more closely with v. 20a, because the latter has a negative connotation of increasing "too much."[236] In what may be the first use in the Greek language, certainly the first that has been identified in a written document,[237] Paul employed ὑπερπερισσεύω in 2 Cor 7:4, "with all our afflictions, I am abounding to a superlative degree in joy." The use of ὑπερπερισσεύω in Rom 5:20 reflects the sense of eschatological superabundance that characterizes Paul's charismatic piety.[238] In this verse the verb is in the aorist, referring to a single moment in the past when "the grace" abounded in this magnificent, overflowing manner, referring undoubtedly to the cross event.[239] As Godet observes, "Golgotha, that theatre where human sin displayed itself as nowhere else, was at the same time the place of the most extraordinary manifestation of divine grace."[240] At the very moment when the distortion of the law reached its climax of hostility against God, ἡ χάρις ("the grace") overflowed to cure that hostility, conveying unconditional acceptance to those whose yearning for acceptance had led them into so horrific an act. The verb ὑπερπερισσεύω ("abound superabundantly") is the transcendent climax of this remarkable series of references to the "much more . . . abounded" (v. 15), "much more . . . abundance" (v. 17) of grace in Christ.[241] Paul's formulation reaches beyond the scope of

227 See Cranfield, 1:293.

228 In contrast, Garlington, *Letter to the Romans*, 108, maintains that "*it was the very possession of the Torah which engendered the spirit of idolatry*" (italics in original).

229 See Brandenburger, *Adam und Christus*, 250.

230 Luz, *Geschichtsverständnis*, 206–7.

231 Schmidt, 103.

232 Dunn, 1:287. Brandenburger, *Adam und Christus*, 250, tries in vain to distinguish between "sin" and "trespass."

233 Morris, 241.

234 Godet, 228, notes that οὐ has the sense of "where . . . in a strictly local and limited sense" rather than of "where ever" as in the case of a general maxim.

235 Godet, 228. In contrast, Meyer, 1:277, and Wilckens, 1:329, identify the location as the "world"; Cranfield, 1:293, identifies it as "in Israel." Neither option correlates well with the aorist verb in v. 20b

that refers to a single aspect of the abounding of grace.

236 Delling, "πλεονάζω, ὑπερπλεονάζω," 263. Theobald, *Gnade*, 117, also observes that Paul did not wish to make the realms of Adam and Christ exactly parallel, because the latter is qualitatively different.

237 The Latin text of *4 Ezra* 4.50 refers metaphorically to the "far greater quantity" (*superabundavit*) of days yet to come before the arrival of the new age; although this is cited as a parallel to Rom 5:20 (Hauck, "περισσεύω κτλ.," 60; Dunn, 1:287), it does not refer to an increase in blessings as in the Pauline letters.

238 Hauck, "περισσεύω κτλ.," 62.

239 De Boer, *Defeat of Death*, 168.

240 Godet, 228; see also Theobald, *Gnade*, 124.

241 See Cranfield, 1:294; Schoeni, "Hyperbolic Sublime," 184.

human logic to a spiritual reality in Christ that remains indescribable in its abundance, fullness, and joy.

■ **21** By locating the event in which grace abounded in the crucifixion of Christ, the peculiar wording of the purpose clause that concludes this pericope may be taken into account. It is not just sin and death in general, but ἡ ἁμαρτία ("sin") that reigned ἐν τῷ θανάτῳ ("in death"), namely the climactic human sin of the crucifixion of the Messiah and the death of that Messiah, that reveal the superabundance of grace. Most commentators assume that the articles with "sin" and "death" signify generic references[242] and that this verse harks back to v. 18 in referring to the single deed of Christ that brought "rightness of life to all people." Since it was the Christ event that brought the overwhelming victory of grace,[243] the reign of sin ended there and the new reign of grace began. In Brandenburger's words, "an all-encompassing change of kingly rule" occurred as a result of the obedience of Christ, and the new reign of grace is incommensurate with the old reign of death and sin.[244] The aorist subjunctive verb βασιλεύσῃ ("it might reign") is explained by Dunn as containing an "eschatological note"[245] and by Käsemann as a "logical future,[246] but under no circumstances can it be viewed as an expression of an unreal circumstance. As a conditional clause determined by v. 21a, the reign of superabundant grace is as real as the reign of sin since Adam's fall. The new kingly rule in Christ exercises its dominion "through righteousness for life eternal." We encountered the phrase διὰ δικαιοσύνης ("through righteousness") in 4:13, in reference to Abraham's descendants who would inherit the promises not through law but "through righteousness of faith." The phrase does not occur elsewhere in the NT. While the word "life" appeared in vv. 10, 17, 18, and comprises one of the leitmotifs of this pericope, the exact phrase εἰς

ζωὴν αἰώνιον ("for life eternal") does not appear elsewhere in the Pauline letters and seems most at home in John's Gospel (John 4:14, 36; 6:27; 12:25).[247] That eternal life is the exact equivalent of "for rightness of life" in v. 18 seems doubtful,[248] but the dimension of eternality is indeed linked with the gift of righteousness; as Godet explains, "it comprehends the holiness which from this time forward should flow from the state of justification."[249] All who are in Christ are granted the ultimate honor of righteousness that assures them both now and in the future access to eternal life.[250] The social implication of Paul's formulation is that the mutual damnation that has marked the Roman house and tenement churches is completely out of bounds, because grace's reign does not require righteousness in the form of conformity with law.[251] All boastings and mutual damnations are eliminated in this reign of grace that unites believers of every ethnic and theological group before God's throne of grace.[252] In Colenso's words, "the gift is bestowed freely upon the whole human race."[253]

As the final clausula ("through Jesus Christ our Lord") rehearses, grace, righteousness, and life eternal are expressions of the lordship of Christ. This theme of lordship recurs in 14:4-12, which suggests the scope of its relevance here as well. Christ is here proclaimed as "our Lord," the regent of the entire church with all its diversity, and in the context of "eternal life," the Lord of the last judgment.[254] Paul places himself under the rule of this mediator of grace and unity, whose lordship makes it possible for groups and leaders to live in harmony without agreeing on particular issues such as those reflected in the later chapters of the letter.[255] Where God's grace abounds and is received, no further honor is required and the shameful competition that marks the reign of sin should be at an end.

242 Meyer, 1:278; Kühl, 193; Cranfield, 1:294; Schlier, 178; Zeisler, 152; Dunn, 1:287; Moo, 349. See Smyth, *Grammar*, §1122.
243 Brandenburger, *Adam und Christus*, 254.
244 Ibid.
245 Dunn, 1:287.
246 Käsemann, 158.
247 See Luise Schottroff, "ζῶ, ζωή," *EDNT* 2 (1991) 108.
248 Dunn, 1:287.
249 Godet, 229; see also de Boer, *Defeat of Death*, 175–78.
250 See Hellholm, "5,12-21," 49.
251 See Minear, *Obedience*, 61.
252 See Erickson, "Semantic Structure," 301.
253 Colenso, 118; it is therefore problematic to limit the significance of this argument to a defense of Paul's doctrine of justification as in Hübner, *Theologie des Paulus*, 245; and Hellholm, "5,12-21," 50–51.
254 Thüsing, *Per Christum*, 218–19.
255 See Reid, *Rhetoric*, 149.

6

The Third Pericope

Diatribe and Enthymemes Concerning the Death of the Sinful Self and the New Life in Christ

1/ What then shall we say? "Let us remain[a] in sin, so that grace might abound?" 2/ No way! How shall we who are such that died to sin still live[b] in it? 3/ Or do you not know that as many of us as were baptized into Christ Jesus[c] were baptized into his death? 4/ We were therefore[d] co-buried with him through our baptism into his death, in order that as Christ was raised from [the] dead through the glory of the father,[e] so also we might walk in newness of life.

5/ For if we have been joined together with the likeness of his death, we shall indeed[f] be [joined in the likeness] of his resurrection, 6/ [g]since knowing this, that our obsolete self was co-crucified [with him] in order that its sinful body might be destroyed, so that we are no longer being enslaved to sin; 7/ for he who died has been declared right [= free] from sin. 8/ Now[h] if we died with Christ, we have faith that we shall also co-dwell[i] with him,[j] 9/ knowing that after Christ was raised from [the] dead, no longer does he die; his death no longer has lordship [over him]. 10/ For in respect to that he died, he died once for all to sin, but in respect to that he lives, he lives to God. 11/ So also you are considering yourselves to be[k] on the one hand dead to sin but on the other hand living to God in Christ Jesus.[l]

12/ Therefore do not let this sin reign in your mortal body, so that you obey its[m] desires. 13/ Neither continue to yield your members to [the power of] sin as weapons of wrongdoing, but yield yourselves to God as made alive[n] from [the] dead, and your members to God as weapons of righteousness. 14/ For sin will not rule over you, for you are not under law but under grace.

a   Commentators agree that the subjunctive form ἐπιμένωμεν ("let us remain"), strongly attested by A B C D F G (L) Ψ (33) 81 (88) 104 326 424ᶜ (630) 1241 1506 (1735) 1836 1874 *pm* ar sa bo Ambst, takes precedence over the variants ἐπιμενοῦμεν ("we shall remain") in 69 323 614 945 1505 2495 *al* lat or ἐπιμένομεν ("we remain") in ℵ K P (6) 330 (365) 424* 1175 1243 1319 (1573) (1739) 1874ᶜ

(1881) 2464 *pm* boᵐˢ Tert. Moir suggests in "Orthography and Theology," 171, that the frequent interchange between omega and omicron indicates that manuscripts with ἐπιμένομεν are to be read as the subjunctive ἐπιμένωμεν.

b   The indicative ζήσομεν ("we shall live") is strongly supported by ℵ A B D K P 0221 6 69 323 424 614 945 1175 1241ᵃᶜᶜ· ᵗᵒ ˢʷᵃⁿˢᵒⁿ 1319 1505 1573 1739 1881 2495 *Maj* latt Cl. The variant ζήσωμεν ("we should live") in P⁴⁶ C F G L Ψ 33 81 88 326 365 1243 1506 1735 1836 1874 2464 *al* appears to be a secondary assimilation to the subjunctive form of ἐπιμένωμεν in 6:1; see Cranfield, 1:298.

c   The word "Jesus" is lacking in B 104ᶜ 326 *pc*.

d   The slightly attested reading of γάρ ("for") in place of οὖν ("thus/therefore") in 1506ᵛⁱᵈ ar b mon o r vg Orᵍᵏ, ˡᵃᵗ ⁴/⁸ GrNy Cyr²/⁶ Ambr Chromatius¹/³ Gaudentius Hier¹/³ Pel Aug⁴/¹⁵ is not discussed by the commentators. Its effect would be to make the content of v. 4 provide the reason for the contention in v. 3. The omission of οὖν in syᵖ boᵐˢ arm geo Orˡᵃᵗ ⁴/⁸ Marcus-Eremita Hier²/³ Aug³/¹⁵ may be due to uncertainty about relating v. 4 to v. 3 (Metzger, *Textual Commentary*, 453).

e   The deletion of the phrase "through the glory of the father" in Irˡᵃᵗ Tert Spec (not in Nestle-Aland²⁷) appears to be a secondary smoothing of the text by eliminating a motif not usually linked with the resurrection motif. This variant is not discussed by the commentators.

f   The replacement of the expression ἀλλὰ καί ("but also/no less so/also certainly") by ἅμα καί ("and at the same time") in F G latt appears to result from scribal misreading of uncial letters, as Aland suggests in Aland and Aland, *Text*, 283.

g   The addition of καί ("and") before "this" in B is weakly attested.

h   The reading of γάρ ("for") in P⁴⁶ F G 945 *pc* ar o vgᵐˢˢ (syᵖ) Julian-Eclanum, if not original, may reflect an effort to match the wording of the preceding sentence. Cranfield, 1:311, calls this "an instance of parablepsis."

i   The subjunctive reading συζήσωμεν ("we might live") in C K P 104 326 330 614 1735 1836 1874 2464 2344 *l* 249 *al* is similar to the secondary variant discussed in 6:2 and may reflect an effort to create verbal forms consistent with ἐπιμένωμεν ("let us remain") in 6:1.

j   In place of the well-attested αὐτῷ ("in him"), D* F G b vgˢᵗ (syᵖ) provide τῷ Χριστῷ ("Christ"), which appears to be a secondary clarification. It is not discussed by the commentators.

k   The omission of εἶναι ("to be") by P⁴⁶ᵛⁱᵈ A D*,ᶜ F G 33ᵛⁱᵈ 2344 *l* 249 *pc* Tert al, though rather strongly attested, produces an effective ellipse and as the smoother reading, ought to be rejected. The inclusion is strongly supported by P[94vid] ℵ* B C 81 104 365 1319 1506 1573 1739 1881 *pc*. The verb "to be" is placed after νεκροὺς μέν in ℵ[2] D[1] K L P Ψ 6 69 88 323 326 330 614 424 945 1175 1241 1243 1505 1735 1836 1874 2464 2495 *Maj* lat, and this variant is discussed neither by the commentators nor by Metzger but nevertheless is placed within square brackets after ἑαυτούς by Nestle-Aland[26,27].

1 The addition of the words "our Lord" after "Christ Jesus" by P[94vid] ℵ C K L P 5 6 33 61 69 81 88 181 218 256 263 323 326 330 365 424 436 441 451 459 467 614 621 623 720 915 917 945 1175 1241 1243 1319 1398 1505 1506 1563 1573 1678 1718 1735 1739[c] 1751 1836 1838 1845 1846 1874 1875 1877 1881 1908[c] 1912 1942 1959 1962 2110 2127 2138 2197 2344 2464 2492 2495 2523 2544 2718 *Lect Maj* vg[cl] (sy[p, pal]) bo arm (eth) geo[2] slav Or[lat 1/11] Did[dub] Chr Ambst Aug[1/14] appears to be a secondary stylistic improvement that brings v. 11 to a more solemn conclusion, as in 5:21 and 6:23. See Wilckens, 2:19. A similar variant reflecting the same motivation is ἐν Χριστῷ τῷ κυρίῳ ἡμῶν ("in Christ our Lord") in 104 459. The absence of "our Lord" is more strongly attested by P[46] A B D F G Ψ 629 630 1739* 1852 1908* 2200 *pc* ar b d f g mon o vg[st. ww] sy[h] sa geo[1] Or[gr, lat 1/11]Bas Cyr Thret Tert[1/2 (1/2)] Hil Pel Aug[8/14] Spec, while the entire phrase "in Christ Jesus our Lord" is lacking in r Ir[lat] Or[lat 9/11] Ambr Hier Aug[5/14].

m Several textual variants appear as attempted improvements of the expression ταῖς ἐπιθυμίαις αὐτοῦ ("its desires"), strongly supported by P[94] ℵ A B C* 6 61* 81 256 263 326 330 365 424 436 451 623* 630 1319 1506 1573 1739 1852 1881 1908 1942 1962 2110 2127 2200 *al* ar d[2] mon r vg sy[p] sa bo arm eth slav Or[(gr), lat 6/7] Meth Did Cyr Ambr Hier Pel Aug. The problem is that "its" (αὐτοῦ) is neuter, whereas "sin" is feminine, although it is possible to construe αὐτοῦ with σώματι, "so that you may obey the body's desires." Accordingly P[46] D F G 1919 2516 b d* f g o Ir[lat] Or[1/7] Tert Ambst Julian-Eclanum Spec Victor-Tunis, which lack the expression ταῖς ἐπιθυμίαις αὐτοῦ, replace it with the feminine pronoun αὐτῇ (obey "her" [sin] instead of "its [the body's] desires.") As Wilckens, 2:20, concludes, the first variant above is an artificial smoothing of the text. The *Maj* text along with C[3] K L P Ψ (33 323 1751 1912 2344 2718* αὐτοῦ for αὐτῇ) 5 61[c] 69 88 104 181 218 441 459 467 614 621 623[c] 629 915 917 945 1175 1241 1243 1398 1505 1563 1678 1718 1735 1836 1838 1874 1875 1877 1959 2138 2464 2492 2495 2523 2544* 2718[c] (*Lect*) sy[h] geo Chr conflate both readings: "obey her with its passions," or "obey her [i.e., sin] and her desires" as in 720 1845 2197 *al*. See Cranfield, 1:317; Metzger, *Textual Commentary*, 454.

n The nominative form of ζῶντες ("those made alive") supplied by P[46] D* F G is not discussed by the commentators, but it would destroy the agreement with ἑαυτούς ("yourselves"), making it an independent clause modifying παριστάνετε as subject: "as if (you are) living from [the] dead." The widely attested reading of ζῶντας ("enlivened") is probably original.

Analysis

The length of this pericope is a matter of dispute, with some commentators believing that it contains vv. 1-12,[1] while others find that it continues through the end of v. 15.[2] The recent analyses of the argument by David Hellholm and of the structure by Hendrikus Boers make the extension of the pericope through v. 14 highly probable.[3] In a persuasive rhetorical shift, Paul moves into first person plural style with vivid diatribal elements from vv. 1-11 and then into exhortative style for the rest of the pericope. The pericope opens with a diatribal exchange consisting of a double question, an answer, followed by two rhetorical questions that initiate the argument.[4] The substantive, libertinistic question in v. 1b poses a false conclusion, arising from 5:20b, that grace abounds more than the increase of sin.[5] Verse 2 answers the question emphatically and then poses the first coun-

---

1 See Kuss, 2:382; Käsemann, 171–72; Dunn, 1:335; Fitzmyer, 444; Kaye, *Chapter 6*, 24–28; Andries B. du Toit, "*Dikaiosyne* in Röm 6: Beobachtungen zur ethischen Dimension der paulinischen Gerechtigkeitsauffassung," *ZThK* 76 (1979) 263–69, provides a structural analysis that holds the entirety of chap. 6 together, but he perceives a new paragraph beginning with v. 12.

2 Kühl, 194–98, 216–17; Schlier, 190–205; Cranfield, 1:316–21; Moo, 396–97; Haacker, 124–27, 131; Esler, *Conflict and Identity*, 192–98.

3 Hellholm, "Romans 6," 138; Boers, "Romans 6:1-14," 664–82.

4 Hellholm, "Romans 6," 138–41; Boers, "Romans 6:1-14," 676.

5 See Stowers, *Rereading*, 148–49.

terquestion in the form of a contrary *sententia*[6] concerning the inconsistency of living in the realm just transcended. It requires a negative response: "No, we cannot continue in sin." The second counterquestion in v. 3 concerning the shared experience of baptism requires a positive response: "Yes, we know we were baptized into Christ's death." The questions and the emphatic answer are arranged in nicely balanced sentences in the first three verses of the pericope,[7] in which there is a rhyming homoioteleuton in the endings of the first two verses. There is a chiastic formulation in the diatribal question of v. 3:[8]

A ἐβαπτίσθημεν
   B εἰς Χριστὸν Ἰησοῦν
   B' εἰς τὸν θάνατον αὐτοῦ
A' ἐβαπτίσθημεν

A paronomastic series of references to ἁμαρτία ("sin") begins in the second line of v. 1 and extends to a total of seven occurrences by the end of the pericope. Another series of six references to "life" or "live" begins in v. 2. A third paronomastic series of three baptismal references occurs in close proximity in vv. 3-4. A fourth such series of references to death in various verbal and substantive forms begins in v. 2 and reaches a total of thirteen occurrences by v. 13. Finally, there are four recurrences of the prefix σύν- in compounds such as "buried with" and one expression with the preposition in the phrase "with Christ."[9] These series signal the thematic unity of the passage consistent with the "extensive argumentative progression" throughout chaps. 5–8.[10]

Verse 4 is a deductive inference[11] organized in three clauses of roughly equal length, with the final line containing homoioteleuton in the same first person plural ending as in v. 3. Verse 4 explains the principle of inconsistency between life in sin and baptism, showing that in baptism believers experienced the death of Christ and are set free to participate in a new life with Christ. This theme is developed in two subparagraphs, each of which opens with an "if" clause.[12] The first subparagraph (6:5-7) contains a coherently organized enthymeme[13] and contains a prominent concentration of paronomasia in the recurrence of ἁμαρτία ("sin") in verses 6-7. The contention of this enthymeme is that since believers are joined with Christ's death, it is inappropriate to revert to the realm of sin. The second enthymeme (6:8-10) contains homoioteleuton in the endings of verses 8 and 9 and also with anaphora in the form of the relative pronoun ὁ at the beginning of each sentence in verse 10.[14] The adverb οὐκέτι ("no longer") occurs twice in v. 9, lending emphasis to the overcoming of death by Christ and believers. The emphasis in this enthymeme is that the fusion with the death of Christ means that the dominion of death has been broken, opening up the possibility of a new life with God. Verse 11 draws both enthymemes together with a reminder that the Roman believers already view themselves as dead to sin and alive to God. The phrase "in Christ Jesus" provides a brief clausula that concludes the pericope at the end of v. 11. Hendrikus Boers argues for a chiastic structure in vv. 4-11, which I illustrate as follows:[15]

A 6:4, ". . . as Christ was raised from the dead through the glory of the father, so also we might walk in newness of life"
   B 6:5, "For if we have been joined together with the likeness of his death, we shall certainly also be [joined in the likeness] of his resurrection"

---

6   Holloway, "Paul's Pointed Prose, " 50.
7   Weiss, "Beiträge," 228.
8   In *Listening*, 194, Harvey identifies four chiasms in this passage, but only v. 3 would likely have been identifiable by a listening audience. See also Holloway, "Paul's Pointed Prose," 51.
9   The last two series were observed by Harvey, *Listening*, 194.
10   Elliott, *Rhetoric of Romans*, 236, refers to Berger's discussion of symbouleutic ("advisory") argumentation in *Formgeschichte*, 93–101.
11   Hellholm, "Romans 6," 138, 155–58.

12   While not pointing out the stylistic or strophic elements in vv. 5-7 and 8-10, Wilckens, 2:7, refers to "two parallel structured thoughts" in these brief paragraphs; Louw, *Romans*, 2:75–77, suggests in contrast paragraph breaks at v. 3 and v. 8, while holding the material from v. 8 through v. 11 together. Tobin, *Paul's Rhetoric*, 194–95, shows that vv. 1-7 and vv. 8-11 have a parallel structure.
13   Weiss, "Beiträge," 228; Hellholm, "Romans 6," 160–64.
14   See also Michel, 201, for further structural parallels between these two paragraphs.

C 6:6a-c, "We know this, that our obsolete self was co-crucified [with him] in order that the sinful body might be destroyed . . ."

    D 6:6d, ". . . for the purpose of our no longer being enslaved to sin"

C' 6:7, "for he who died has been declared right from sin."

  B' 6:8-9a, "Now if we died with Christ, we have faith that we shall also co-dwell with him, knowing that . . ."

A' 6:9b-11, ". . . Christ having been raised from [the] dead does not die again; death no longer has lordship over him. For the death which he died, he died once for all to sin, but the life he lives, he lives to God. So also you consider yourselves to be on the one hand dead to sin but on the other hand living to God in Christ Jesus."

This chiasm works fairly well on the thematic level, with the exception that C does not match C' and the centerpiece of D is a sentence fragment that would not have been discernible to hearers as a discrete unit. Moreover, the argumentative structure discerned by Hellholm is not taken into account.[16]

Verses 12-14 maintain the previous second person plural and imperative style of v. 11 to draw theological and ethical implications about repudiating the realm of sin and death and participating in the new realm of life with God. There is effective parallelism in the exhortations "do not let this sin reign . . . neither . . . yield . . . but yield yourselves to God" and in the expressions "your members . . . as weapons of wrongdoing" . . . "and your members to God as weapons of righteousness."[17] The exhortations draw this discourse into line with the thesis in 1:16-17, urging action as agents of divine righteousness. These verses continue the pattern of double lined sentences and feature a striking continuation of paronomasia in the fourfold recurrence of ἁμαρτία ("sin"), bringing the series to the round number of ten. Verse 13 contains the final recurrence of the stem "live,"

bringing that paronomastic series to the similarly round number of seven. The conclusion in v. 14 provides reassurance that sin's reign is truly broken for believers, reiterating the motifs of sin and grace from 6:1 and leading to the diatribe that follows.

Rhetorical Disposition

IV.	The *probatio*
5:1–8:39	B. The second proof: Life in Christ as a new system of honor that replaces the search for status through conformity to the law
6:1-14	3. The death of the sinful self and the new life in Christ
6:1-4	a. A diatribal exchange concerning remaining in sin after sharing in Christ's death
6:1	1) The questions about the implications of grace that increases in proportion to sin
6:1a	a) The introductory question of general inference
6:1b	b) The question by the imaginary interlocutor about remaining in sin so grace may abound
6:2a	2) Paul's emphatic denial
6:2b-3	3) Paul's counterquestions about the implications of having died with Christ
6:2b-c	a) The first question concerning the contradiction of living in sin after having died to it
6:3	b) The second question about baptism as participation in Christ's death
6:4	4) The doctrinal explanation of baptism
6:4a	a) Baptism as burial with Christ
6:4b-c	b) The resultant participation in Christ's resurrection
6:4b	(1) Christ was raised by means of divine glory
6:4c	(2) The divine provision of new life for believers
6:5-11	b. The enthymemes concerning sin and the new life in Christ
6:5-7	1) The first enthymeme about persons in Christ being free from sin
6:5	a) The premises concerning incorporation in Christ
6:5a	(1) Joined into the "likeness" of Christ's death

---

15   Boers, "Romans 6:1-14," 676–81.

16   Hellholm, "Romans 6," 138, identifies vv. 4, 6-7, and 9-11 as deductive inferences and vv. 5 and 8 as *argumentum*. Esler, *Paul's Rhetoric*, 194–95, suggests

that vv. 5-7 and vv. 8-11 are parallel sentences, which takes account of the structural similarities.

17   See Harvey, *Listening*, 194.

Exegesis

■ **1** The diatribal exchange begins with an opening question that involves the hearers: "What then shall we say?" This friendly inclusion of the hearers in an expression that is uniquely Pauline[18] continues in the nondenunciatory style that had commenced in the diabribal exchange of 4:1-2. As in 3:5; 7:7; and 9:14, this question sets up a false inference that could be drawn from the preceding argument.[19] The rhetorical question about remaining "in sin" reflects a Christian premise about converts' undergoing genuine transformation and does not presuppose a Jewish antagonist.[20] In other contexts, the idea of remaining in corruption is depicted with the same verb that Paul selects. For example, Philo *Sobr.* 69 refers to a slave who chooses to "remain in his iniquity" (ἠ ἐπιμένων τῷ ἀδικεῖν) despite chastisement, and Marcus Aurelius maintains that, "The one who continues (ὁ ἐπιμένων) in his own deception and ignorance hurts himself."[21] Some commentators find the subjunctive verb ἐπιμένωμεν ("let us remain/persist")[22] unexpected in connection with sin,[23] so much so that they ordinarily fail to translate it as a properly hortatory form.[24] This wording in the mouth of an imaginary interlocutor would likely strike the Christian audience in Rome as risible, unless a serious antinomian threat were present in the congregations, which seems unlikely. The incongruity between the exhortative verb and the topic of sin makes transparent the flimsy contrivance and evokes the

---

18   See Stowers, *Diatribe*, 134.

19   See Palmer, "τί οὖν," 202, 15; Tobin, *Paul's Rhetoric*, 192.

20   Elliott, *Rhetoric of Romans*, 238, makes this point in opposition to Beker's insistence in *Paul*, 85–86, that Paul is replying here to criticism of his theology by synagogue authorities. Alastair Campbell, "Dying," 284–85, reiterates the idea of "the outraged Jewish moralist." Hellholm follows this line in "Romans 6," 143–45.

21   Marcus Aurelius Τὰ εἰς ἑαυτόν 6.21.1.3. Another example of such usage is provided by MM 242 in *P.Tebt.* 2. Nr. 424.4–5, εἰ μὲν ἐπιμένις σου τῇ ἀπονοίᾳ, συνχέρω σοι ("if you continue in your madness, I may ruin it for you").

22   See Horst Balz and Gerhard Schneider, "ἐπιμένω," *EDNT* 2 (1991) 31.

23   Dunn, 1:306.

24   On the hortatory subjunctive, see BDF §364; the only commentator who takes this as hortatory is Fitzmyer, 432; Godet, 236, renders the subjunctive with "*should we* continue in sin [italics in original]?"

levity that earlier commentators could not perceive, because diatribe was thought to be solely a denunciatory style, aimed at refuting "opponents."[25] The humor involves sinning with allegedly good intentions, slyly claiming to help God out in the work of augmenting grace. The subjunctive πλεονάσῃ ("might increase, augment")[26] repeats the verb used in 5:20, "where sin *increased*, grace abounded to the ultimate degree."[27] Neil Elliott points out that the wording of Paul's counterquestion implies a proportionality between grace and sin, "the magnitude of one being measured by the gravity of the other."[28] As we shall see in this pericope, the issue of proportionality lies at the heart of some of the misunderstanding of sin in Rome. By posing the libertinistic option in so ridiculous and insidious a form, Paul effectively opens the issue of the incongruity of persons saved by grace who fail to live the new life. The implied answer to this rhetorical question is "that it is impossible" to live in what has already died.[29]

■ **2** The denial μὴ γένοιτο could be translated several ways, such as "Never!" or "By no means!" or "Certainly not!" I prefer the colloquial "No way!" to signal the laughable quality of this diatribal exchange. As in other instances of Pauline use, this formula introduces the following substantiation.[30] The first counterquestion in v. 2a-b is carefully constructed to evoke a thoughtful response.[31] In place of the more ordinary relative pronoun, Paul opens the question with οἵτινες, referring to those sharing an essential quality,[32] in this instance that of having died with Christ.[33] To capture this nuance, I translate "we who are such that died." The aorist verb ἀπεθάνομεν ("we died") harks back to the singular, punctiliar moment in the life of believers when they appropriated the death of Christ for themselves. For a first-generation audience of converts, this moment is usually assumed to be each individual's conversion event associated with baptism.[34] It is significant, however, that Paul refers here not to baptism but to death. The idea of sharing in Christ's atoning death is basic here,[35] having been mentioned repeatedly in the prior argument of the letter. The basic idea behind this formulation is stated in 2 Cor 5:14, "we are convinced that one has died for all; therefore all have died." In other words, "I have been crucified with Christ," as Paul explains in Gal 2:20; by sharing the shameful death of Christ, who died in their behalf, their shameful status and selfhood was replaced by a new status as God's beloved and a new selfhood of Christ living in them. Paul states in Gal 2:20, "It is no longer I who live, but Christ lives in me." The formulation in Rom 6:2 indicates that Paul assumes that the audience knows that they belong to this class of persons who have died to sin,[36] referring back to "sin" in the preceding sentence and to sin as a hostile power in the preceding pericope. The dative expression τῇ ἁμαρτίᾳ is one of respect, that is, in relation to the sin that had functioned as a controlling power ever since Adam's fateful deed.[37] Since in Christ they had died to this destructive force, Paul's question is forcefully stated:

---

25   For example, Michel, 204–5; Schlier, 191; Wilckens, 2:8–9; Hellholm, "Romans 6," 142–45; Søren Agersnap, *Baptism and the New Life: A Study of Romans 6.1-14* (Aarhus: Aarhus University Press, 1999) 235–36. Elliott, *Rhetoric of Romans*, 238, offers the first reference I have seen to Paul's "use of the technique of ridicule" in this section.

26   Gerhard Delling, "πλεονάζω, ὑπερπλεονάζω," *TDNT* 6 (1968) 265.

27   See Kaye, *Chapter 6*, 23.

28   Elliott, *Rhetoric of Romans*, 250.

29   Tobin, *Paul's Rhetoric*, 193.

30   Malherbe, "Μὴ γένοιτο," 32–33.

31   Smyth, *Grammar*, §2663, shows that questions with πῶς ("how") require an explanatory response.

32   BAGD 587.2; Moule, *Idiom Book*, 123–24; BDF §293 argues that the distinction between ὅς and ὅστις is no longer "clearly distinguished in the NT," but a case can be made that it indeed functions here.

33   Barrett, 121: "We who in our essential nature, i.e., just because we are Christians, died."

34   Meyer, 1:280; Weiss, 264; Werner Bieder, "Θάνατος, ἀποθνήσκω," *EDNT* 2 (1991) 131.

35   Colenso, 121. Godet, 236, writes that 6:2 depicts believers' "appropriation of our Lord's expiatory death." Dunn, 1:308: "baptism is not the subject of the passage. The theme is one of death to sin and life under grace . . . ."

36   That the expression "dying to" sin is "a syntactical novelty" is confirmed by Moule, "Death," 151, and it should be classified as a dative of relation, conveying the idea "that you cannot pay more than your life; and therefore, when you have parted with your life, you are quit" (152).

37   Godet, 236; Kuss, 1:296; Moo, 357.

"How shall we still live in it?" I take the prepositional phrase ἐν αὐτῇ ("in it") to refer to the location of sin's realm.[38] Robert Tannehill argues that this formulation reflects the basic idea developed by Ernst Käsemann, of conversion as "a change of masters."[39] Tannehill contends that this theme is implicit in the dative construction of v. 2, "died to sin," in which the dative of respect is in relation to powers functioning as "slave masters who rule over men." The formulation of v. 2 "makes clear that for Paul dying with Christ means a change of lordship."[40] The expression "live in it," that is, "in sin" in v. 2 implies being in "a power field. It is the sphere in which a power is at work."[41] Paul's assumption, like that of the rest of the NT, is imperial: no one can serve two empires or masters simultaneously. Dying to the realm of sin means living in the realm of Christ; the two realms are as incommensurate as the antithesis between "life" and "death." Although the implications of this antithesis in terms of "sinlessness"[42] remain controversial,[43] Paul's starting point of Christ's atoning death remains clear. The movement is from this starting point to baptism, not vice versa.

■ **3** The opening formula of this verse is typical of a diatribe, suggesting in a gently reprimanding manner a reality that the foolish suggestion in v. 1 had overlooked. "Or do you [pl.] not know" (ἢ ἀγνοεῖτε), used elsewhere in the NT only in Rom 7:1, implies by the disjunctive particle (ἤ) that the following material "surely" should be understood[44] but apparently is not fully grasped because the matter of living by grace and thereby abandoning sinful impulses still remains a problem in and between the Roman house and tenement churches. Although almost all commentators take this expression to imply relatively complete knowledge on the part of the audience,[45] the classical parallels point toward material that the audience does not yet fully comprehend as the speaker or writer thinks they should.[46] Interpreters who have perceived a polite reprimand in this formulation[47] are more readily in the position to acknowledge that although some views of baptism were certainly present in Rome, there is no evidence that the link between baptism and the death of Christ or the symbolic death of believers was explicitly developed even by Paul himself prior to the writing of Romans.[48] In the previous Christian adaptation of John the Baptist's ritual of eschatological repentance and

---

38   BAGD 258.I: the dative of place, "the space within which something is found."

39   Tannehill, *Dying*, 17.

40   Ibid., 18.

41   Ibid., 19; Campbell, "Dying," 285, overlooks this dimension of competing power spheres in suggesting that death with Christ refers primarily to the hostility and "public shame" aroused by converts no longer sharing the life of their "old associates."

42   Hans Windisch, "Das Problem des paulinischen Imperativs," *ZNW* 23 (1924) 280, rejected by Dunn, 1:307, for theological reasons.

43   See Godet's discussion (235–36) of the theories of sanctification and sinlessness; also Cranfield, 1:298–300.

44   Walter Schmithals, "ἀγνοέω κτλ.," *EDNT* 1 (1990) 21.

45   Weiss, 265; Barrett, 121–22; Michel, 205; Murray, 214; Cranfield, 1:300; Käsemann, 165; Wilckens, 2:11; Tannehill, *Dying*, 12–14; Hartman, "Baptism," 587–88; Leenhardt, 152, suggests knowledge that the congregation may have forgotten. None of these commentators explains the disjunctive particle, which adds the mild corrective to the verb ἀγνοεῖν ("to be unknowing / unaware").

46   The verb ἀγνοέω is used by rhetoricians to bring pointed attention to a salient point, as in Isocrates *Pac.* 114.1: "which you see in respect of the others, but these things in respect of you yourselves are unaware (ἐφ᾽ ὑμῶν αὐτῶν ἀγνοεῖτε)." Similar examples are in Demosthenes *Orat.* 7.13.6; 49.14.1; 56.48.1; Aeschines *Tim.* 111.2; Dinarchus *Aristog.* 6.1; Lycurgus *Leoc.* 20.2; Demades *Frag.* 87.6.7; Plato *Clit.* 407b1; Pseudo-Plutarch *Reg. imp.* 190 Cl; *Apoph. lac.* 219 D8; Plutarch *Quaest. conv.* 723 C6; Epictetus *Diss.* 4.8.27.

47   Günter Wagner, *Pauline Baptism and the Pagan Mysteries. The Problem of the Pauline Doctrine of Baptism in Romans VI. 1-11, in the Light of its Religio-Historical "Parallels"* (trans. J. P. Smith; Edinburgh: Oliver and Boyd, 1967) 278; Hubert Frankemölle, *Das Taufverständnis des Paulus: Taufe, Tod und Auferstehung nach Röm 6* (SBS 47; Stuttgart: Katholisches Bibelwerk, 1970) 40; Franz Mussner, "Zur paulinischen Tauflehre in Röm 6,1-6: Versuche einer Auslegung," in F. Mussner, *Praesentia Salutis: Gesammelte Studien zu Fragen und Themen des Neuen Testaments* (KBANT; Düsseldorf: Patmos-Verlag, 1967) 278–79.

48   Rudolf Schnackenburg, *Baptism in the Thought of St Paul: A Study in Pauline Theology* (trans. G. R. Beasley-Murray; Oxford: Blackwell; New York: Herder & Herder, 1964) 33–34; Hans Dieter Betz,

pardon,[49] the formula "baptized into the name of the Lord Jesus" was apparently coined by the Palestinian church and later translated literally into Greek, which produced the odd expression found in Acts 8:16; 19:5; cf. Matt 28:19; 1 Cor 1:13, 15.[50] This formula differentiated Christian baptism from that of John and related the recipient in some way to the Lordship of Christ, but it did not suggest an explicit association with a dying of the baptized convert. The language Paul employs in Rom 6:3b, "baptism into (εἰς) Christ Jesus," echoes formulations in his earlier letters (1 Cor 12:13; Gal 3:37) and points metaphorically[51] to a mystical and corporate reality of the new community "in Christ,"[52] but none of these references explicitly links baptism to Christ's death or to the symbolic death of baptizands.[53] Dunn maintains that baptism "*was not* an obvious symbol for death" in the ancient world,[54] but this overlooks that initiation in the cult of Isis and Osiris also involved baptism, in which the believer "identified with the god Osiris, whose

death in the Nile was one of the central myths of the Isis cult."[55] This cultural background may be one of the reasons that Paul appears to have assumed a measure of agreement with the audience that their baptism was some form of incorporation into Christ,[56] and therefore, that "as many of us" (ὅσοι)[57] who have undergone that experience have been "baptized into his death."[58] Here, the verb "baptized" is employed for the second time in this sentence, matching the aorist passive form of other early Christian references, to convey the act performed on baptizands by others.[59] As Hans Dieter Betz observes, baptism "into his death" was a logical development from Paul's earlier references to being crucified with Christ (Gal 2:20) and being "conformed to his death" (Phil 3:10). The sequence of the argument from Rom 6:2 to 6:3 confirms that Paul viewed such a death on the part of the converted as occurring prior to baptism.[60] Betz interprets the development of this innovative doctrine of baptism as evidence of Paul's role as a founder figure in

---

"Transferring a Ritual: Paul's Interpretation of Baptism in Romans 6," in Troels Engberg-Pedersen, ed., *Paul in His Hellenistic Context* (Minneapolis: Augsburg Fortress, 1995); repr. in H. D. Betz, *Paulinischen Studien. Gesammelte Aufsätze III* (Tübingen: Mohr (Siebeck), 1994) 110.

49 See Hartwig Thyen, "Johannes der Täufer," *EKL* 2 (1989) 834–35; Otto Böcher, "Johannes der Täufer," *TRE* 17 (1988) 172–81; Hartman, "Baptism," 583–84.

50 Hartman, "Baptism," 586, summarizing his work in *"Into the Name of the Lord Jesus": Baptism in the Early Church* (SNTW; Edinburgh: Clark, 1997). See also Joel B. Green, "From 'John's Baptism' to 'Baptism in the Name of the Lord Jesus': The Significance of Baptism in Luke-Acts," in S. E. Porter and A. R. Cross, eds., *Baptism, the New Testament and the Church: Historical and Contemporary Studies in Honour of R. E. O. White* (JSNTSup 171; Sheffield: Sheffield Academic Press, 1999) 168–72.

51 See Dunn, *Baptism*, 109–13, 139–46; idem, "'Baptized' as Metaphor," in S. E. Porter and A. R. Cross, eds., *Baptism, the New Testament and the Church: Historical and Contemporary Studies in Honour of R. E. O. White* (JSNTSup 171; Sheffield: Sheffield Academic Press, 1999) 294–310. For an informed approach to interpreting metaphors, see Sabou, "Between Horror and Hope," 53–67.

52 See Frankemölle, *Taufverständnis*, 41–53; Tannehill, *Dying*, 22, 42; Dunn, 1:311; idem, *Baptism*, 112, 140;

Betz, "Baptism in Rom 6," 108. Newman and Nida, 112, translate "we were baptized into union with Christ Jesus."

53 See Dunn, 1:311–12; idem, *Baptism*, 144.

54 Dunn, 1:312, italics in original.

55 Brook W. R. Pearson, "Baptism and Initiation in the Cult of Isis and Sarapis," in S. E. Porter and A. R. Cross, eds., *Baptism, the New Testament and the Church: Historical and Contemporary Studies in Honour of R. E. O. White* (JSNTSup 171; Sheffield: Sheffield Academic Press, 1999) 51.

56 See Wedderburn, *Baptism and Resurrection*, 54–60.

57 BAGD 586.2, "all who," referring to examples such as Josephus, *Ant.* 12.399, which describes how Judas Maccabeas "put to death as many as (ὅσους) who sided with the enemy."

58 Agersnap, *Baptism*, 265: "the baptized are drawn into Christ's death, so that they share in its effects."

59 Luke 11:38; Acts 2:41; 9:18; 16:15, 33; 19:5; 1 Cor 1:13, 15; 12:13; Gal 3:27; see Albrecht Oepke, "βάπτω, βαπτίζω κτλ.," *TDNT* 1 (1964) 537–38; Werner Bieder, "βαπτίζω κτλ.," *EDNT* 1 (1990) 192–95.

60 Betz, "Baptism in Rom 6," 111–12; see also Wedderburn, *Baptism and Resurrection*, 49–50.

revising a ritual that would effectively transfer believers into the new cult.[61] This is an important generalization concerning Paul's career, but throws no light on this letter, because Paul explicitly has renounced the founder role with regard to Rome (1:11-13; 15:20). I believe that Paul's goal in this pericope is to convince the combative house and tenement churches that there is a solid basis for overcoming sin and pursuing a new life in Christ without the imposition of divisive laws. To be baptized into Christ's shameful death is to quit the life of sin.[62] The divisive competition for honor is exposed and laid to rest by the cross. If the Roman believers can understand the deeper meaning of their incorporation into Christ's death, which they had experienced in an ecstatic manner,[63] they will be able to welcome each other as fellow children of God despite their differences and will be in a position to cooperate in mounting the Spanish mission.

■ **4** On the basis of participating in Christ's death as reviewed in v. 3, Paul proceeds to develop an innovative consequence. Paul claims that believers "were co-buried with him," employing the verb συνθάπτω, which apart from here and in Col 2:12, always refers literally to being buried in a shared grave[64] or to participants joining together in burying the deceased.[65] Although Paul's employment of this term is clearly metaphorical,[66] it conveys the idea of a "real death,"[67] since burial is the

climactic moment in the ritual of dying, the point of no return. Rom 6:4 is the first instance of religious use of this term in Greco-Roman or Jewish culture; it belongs along with the large number of σύν-compounds that Paul employs[68] and in some instances that he invents or redefines to convey the idea of "communality in Christ."[69] There is no evidence that anyone employed the co-burial language in connection with baptism prior to this passage in Romans. That Christ was buried after his crucifixion was an integral part of the early kerygma (1 Cor 15:4), but to connect this burial with baptism was anything but obvious.[70] While both baptism and burial entail being covered over, the metaphor is strained because permanent submersion in water produces death rather than new life.[71] The co-burial reference is clearly an argumentative inference from the preceding verse, which is why Paul includes οὖν ("therefore") as the second word in this remarkable sentence. The finality of burial shuts the door against the frivolous question in v. 1: if one is truly both dead and buried to the life of sin, continuing therein is impossible. Paul contends that co-burial occurs "through our baptism," taking διά ("through") as instrumental and translating the article in τοῦ βαπτίσματος as an unemphatic possessive pronoun.[72] This formulation fits Paul's argument that the death with Christ that occurs at the time of conversion

61 Betz, "Baptism in Rom 6," 86–107, 116–18.

62 See Hellholm, "Romans 6," 153–57.

63 See Shantz's explanation of the neurological basis of this experience in "Paul in Ecstasy," 180.

64 For example, Aelian *Nat. an.* 7.40.10, of being cast "in a tomb and buried with someone (ἐς τὴν θήκην τοῦ νεκροῦ καὶ συνετάθη)"; see also Diodorus Siculus *Hist.* 12.22.8; Lycurgus *Leoc.* 50.5; Herodotus *Hist.* 5.5.7.

65 Examples of active use include Aeschylus *Sept.* 1032: "If any other be not willing to join in burying him (ἢν μή τις ἄλλος τόνδε συνθάπτειν θέλῃ), I shall bury him." See also Euripides *Hel.* 1545; Sophocles *Aj.* 1378; Plato *Leg.* 909c5; Josephus *Ant.* 10.48; Plutarch *Lyc.* 27.1.9; *Sull.* 38.4.1; Dio Chrysostom *Orat.* 13.1.7.

66 Dunn, "'Baptized' as Metaphor," 299–300; Agersnap, *Baptism,* 269–70.

67 See Walter Grundmann, "σύν-μετά κτλ.," *TDNT* 7 (1971) 790, citing E. Stommel, "'Begraben mit Christus' (Römer 6, 4) und der Taufritus," *RQ* 49 (1954) 6–8, 9–11. See also Nieder, *Ethik,* 25–26.

68 Grundmann, "σύν-μετά κτλ.," 786–87, deals with fourteen σύν- compounds associated with the theme of "with Christ"; Dunn, 1:313, counts forty σύν- compounds in all.

69 Dunn, 1:313; the translation "co-buried" is suggested by Fitzmyer, 434.

70 It is possible, however, that there is a link with Mark 10:38–39; Luke 12:50, where Jesus speaks of his forthcoming death as a baptism.

71 βαπτίζω in the passive means "to be drowned," as in Epictetus *Gnom.* 47.2, or for ships to be sunk (Polybius *Hist.* 1.51.7; 8.6.4; 16.6.2). Divination through drowning is an Egyptian concept derived from the drowning of Osiris in the Nile, after which he is ritually reborn, according to Betz, *Greek Magical Papyri,* 18.

72 See Smyth, *Grammar,* §1121.

precedes baptism, which is presented here as a ritual reenactment of incorporation into that death.[73]

While v. 4a reiterated Paul's distinctive doctrine of baptism as incorporation into Christ's death, v. 4b employs a traditional formula of Christ's resurrection that appears also in 4:24; 8:11; 10:9 with the verb ἐγείρω ("waken, raise") and the phrase ἐκ νεκρῶν ("from [the] dead").[74] The purpose of being buried with Christ is explained in the ἵνα clause, in which the correlative syntax of ὥσπερ ("as") . . . οὕτως ("so") in 4b-c draws a parallel between the divine passive of Christ's being raised (ἠγέρθη) and the behavior of believers, which makes it clear that the latter no less than the former is a matter of divine causation.[75] This explains the peculiar formulation "through the glory of the father," which otherwise is neither connected with resurrection formulae in biblical or patristic texts[76] nor appears elsewhere in Pauline writings.[77] The preposition διά should be taken as designating the efficient cause in the resurrection and the new life.[78] Although δόξα ("glory") is viewed by many commentators as synonymous with δύναμις ("power") in this context[79] or as referring only to the glory to be revealed at the end of time,[80] the distinctive wording suggests reference to past and present realities: the glory visible in the resurrection of Christ and the new life of believers is that of God the father "who alone creates life."[81] Once again, Paul makes clear that there is no room for boasting in human glory, even with regard to the most marvelous ethical achievements, except to boast in the God whose glory is therein manifest.

That believers are enabled through their burial in Christ's death to "walk in newness of life" is not an expression of Paul's eschatological caution, as Käsemann suggests.[82] The formulation of v. 4c articulates Paul's central point that a new form of behavior is made possible by God through Christ,[83] and that this is given to "the whole brotherhood of Man," in the words of John Colenso.[84] The verb περιπατέω is Paul's characteristic term for ethical behavior, a usage that is unparalleled in classical Greek,[85] and the aorist subjunctive implies "a decisive transition to a new lifestyle" in contrast to OT references to walking in the statutes of God.[86] "Newness of life" echoes Paul's idea that believers "in Christ" constitute a "new creation" (2 Cor 5:17; Gal 6:15).[87] The formulation with the emphatic "so also we" (οὕτως καὶ

---

73 Powers, *Salvation through Participation*, 158: "The notions of participationism and unity with Christ are strikingly visible in this verse."

74 See Paulsen, *Überlieferung*, 51–55, following studies by Kramer, *Christ*, 18; Wengst, *Formeln*, 21ff., and others; for a complete listing of the parallel forms, see the introduction to 8:1-17.

75 Käsemann, 166.

76 This was confirmed by a *TLG* check. Dunn, 1:315, explains the "glory of the father" formula as an effort "to avoid attributing Christ's resurrection to the Spirit," a theological concern that is suggested nowhere in this passage.

77 The closest parallels are Matt 16:27 = Mark 8:38, where the Son of Man returns "in the glory of his Father." The exact phrase appears in Arrian *Anab.* 2.15.4: "to the memory of the glory of the father (μνήμῃ τῆς δόξης του πατρός)"; see also *AcPlTh* 63; Irenaeus *Adv. haer.* 1.1.1.30. Käsemann, 166, suggests that the phrase is a pre-Pauline formula, "since it speaks of the Father with no further definition and δόξα is identified with δύναμις or πνεῦμα." With no further examples surfacing, the case for a traditional formula is fatally weak, and there is no real evidence that "glory" here is used synonymously with "power" or "spirit."

78 BAGD (2000) 224 (d), "of efficient cause, through;" Meyer, 1:284; Weiss, 268; Murray, 1:217; Black, 88.

79 Sanday and Headlam, 167; Fuchs, *Freiheit*, 29; Schlier, 194; Käsemann, 166; Zeller, 124; Byrne, 196.

80 Barrett, 123.

81 Otto Michel, "πατήρ," *EDNT* 3 (1993) 55.

82 Käsemann, 166.

83 See Agersnap, *Baptism*, 273–74.

84 Colenso, 124, cited by Draper, "Colenso," 72.

85 Georg Bertram and Heinrich Seesemann, "πατέω κτλ.," *TDNT* 5 (1967) 941, 944; see also Roland Bergmeier, "περιπατέω," *EDNT* 3 (1993) 75–76.

86 Dunn, 1:316, referring to Exod 16:4; Lev 18:3-4; Deut 28:9; Josh 22:5; Jer 44:23; Ezek 5:6-7; Dan 9:10; Mic 4:2. Jörg Baumgarten, "καινός κτλ.," *EDNT* 2 (1991) 230: "The newness of life stands in antithesis to pre-Christian life."

87 Johannes Behm, "καινός κτλ.," *TDNT* 3 (1965) 449, 51. The noun καινότης ("newness") is employed to describe a novelty in speech, as in Thucydides *Hist.* 3.38.5, "speech of a new strain," or Philo *Cont.* 63.4, "enticing the ears with the newness (τῇ καινώτητι) of a notion or idea." It becomes a more popular term in the first centuries B.C.E. and C.E., with Plutarch using it some fourteen times.

ἡμεῖς) places Paul and all of his hearers in the position of having already participated in this new ethic that displays the glory of God.[88] The central issue being addressed here is whether the new life in Christ with ethical and liturgical manifestations that vary from group to group can be pursued without evoking new claims of superiority in honor that have hitherto divided the Roman churches.

■ **5** That baptism is not the subject of this pericope[89] is confirmed by the shift to the metaphor of fusion in this verse and the fact that the rest of the pericope reverts to the basic theme of dying and rising with Christ without any further, explicit references to baptism.[90] The enthymeme[91] concerning incorporation into Christ that begins in this verse and runs through v. 7 opens with an "if" clause in which εἰ has the sense of "since," because "an actual case is taken as a supposition,"[92] namely, that believers have indeed been united together by the death of Christ. The adjective σύμφυτος appears here for the

only time in the NT; it is used in a wide variety of secular contexts, including horticultural references to grafting or growing together,[93] biological references to knitting together the edges of a wound or the ends of broken bones,[94] and social references to citizens clustering around their leader[95] or sharing a particular ethos.[96] In view of these wide-ranging references, I prefer a generic translation such as "joined together" or "united together,"[97] which implies that believers share an indivisible, organic unity with Christ.[98] The perfect verb γεγόναμεν ("we have become") supports the idea of a new relationship inaugurated in the past, but whose effects continue through the present. This verbal form comports well with the baptismal context of this passage.

The dative expression τῷ ὁμοιώματι τοῦ θανάτου αὐτοῦ ("in the likeness of his death") in Rom 6:5 can be understood as the instrumental means by which the believer is united with Christ[99] or, as seems more likely, the one with whom believers are joined.[100] Albert

---

88   See Tobin, *Paul's Rhetoric*, 194.

89   See Dunn, 1:317.

90   See particularly Sabou, "Between Horror and Hope," 98.

91   For the argumentative structure, see Hellholm, "Romans 6," 160–63.

92   BAGD 219.III.

93   According to Dunn, 1:316, the horticultural metaphor rests on the premise that σύμφυτος derives from συμφυτεύω ("plant together, graft"), but Ceslas Spicq, "σύμφυτος," *TLNT* 3 (1994) 322 argues that the agricultural usage is also connected with συμφύω as in Luke 8:7. LSJM 1689 derives σύμφυτος from συμφυτέω, but notes a wide range of references beyond the horticultural. The horticultural interpretation is advocated by Black, 88–89; O'Neill, 114; Leenhardt, 160; Murray, 218; Spicq, "σύμφυτος," 322; Fitzmyer, 435; Betz, "Baptism in Rom 6," 112. Plato *Tim.* 42a6 taught that God has "sown" each soul into a star, where it can "grow" and then be "implanted" into bodies where they "have joined (σύμφυτον γίγνεσθαι) the same nature" sharing the violent passions common to all.

94   Dunn, 1:316, advocates the interpretation "knitting together" on the basis of a "general agreement" that σύμφυτος derives from συφύω. One example of this usage with a verbal form appears in Hippocrates *Aphor.* 6.24, "If one of the intestines gets cut off, it does not unite/mend (οὐ συμφύεται)."

95   For example, Plutarch reports in *Lyc.* 25.3 that the Greek political leader Lycurgus used the verb συμ-

φύω in urging citizens to be "just like bees that are ever of one nature (τῷ κοινῷ συμφύεις ὄντας ἀεί) for the common good."

96   For example, Pindar *Isthm.* 3.13–14, "not disgracing the kindred virtue of men (ἀνδρῶν δ᾽ ἀρετάν/ σύμφυτον οὐ κατελέγχει)."

97   See Horst Balz and Gerhard Schneider, eds., "σύμφυτος," *EDNT* 3 (1993) 290.

98   An opposite form of unity appears in a grave curse reported by Dorottya Gáspar, "Eine griechische Fluchtafel aus Savaria. Tafel 4," *Tyche* 5 (1990) 13–16, which consigns a corpse to remain always with the demon responsible for his unfortunate death: "since you [i.e., the corpse whose name was 'Adiektos'] are dead, so should that one [i.e., the demon] live with you, for eternity (ὡς σὺ νεκρὸς εἶ, οὕτως κἀκῖνος μετὰ σοῦ, εἰς ὁπόσον χρόνον, ζῇ)."

99   Meyer, 1:286, lists Fritzsche, Krehl, Baumgarten-Crucius, Maier, and van Hengel as supporting this instrumental option; see also Weiss, 269; Godet, 243; Michel, 206; Lagrange, 146; Kühl, 204; Cranfield, 1:307; Fitzmyer, 435. Since this interpretation requires the translator to supply αὐτῷ ("to him") as the object of "joined together," it lacks plausibility.

100   Meyer, 1:286, advocates this view, because it does not require separating "likeness" from the foregoing "uniting with." He refers to Koppe, Tholuck, Rückert, Reiche, Olshausen, De Wette, Philippi and others as agreeing. See also Käsemann, 167–68; Wilckens, 2:13; Black, 88; Dunn, 1:316; Francis A.

Schweizer follows the latter in suggesting that Paul thinks of believers as having been mystically and bodily "grafted into Christ's death."[101] However, a hostility against mysticism[102] and an interest in sacramentalism lead most scholars to view baptism as the means by which Christ's death is appropriated by believers[103] despite Paul's shifting of the metaphor from baptism to organic unity.[104] This shift has a decisive bearing on the understanding of ὁμοίωμα, a term that as we noted with regard to 1:23 and 5:14 can mean "image," "copy," "likeness," or "form."[105] Sorin Sabou suggests an additional possibility of taking ὁμοίωμα as "representation," based on his translation of passages in Plato and Aristotle.[106] If baptism is understood as a ritual reenactment of a conversion experience that has already occurred, Paul's references to dying or being crucified with Christ rise to the forefront, and the connotations of "form" or "likeness" become likely. Robert Tannehill and others have argued that ὁμοίωμα in this verse reflects the idea of conformation to Christ, "that Christ's death and resurrection are continuing aspects of the 'form' of Christ . . . so that believers take on the same 'form.'"[107] Since believers are not themselves literally crucified or resurrected and since the theme of conformation is not taken up until 12:1-2, it seems more probable that "likeness" is in view, as in 5:14.[108] Paul's point is that life in Christ rests on the premise of the death of the old self and of

former relationships.[109] Converts acknowledge that the universally human quest for honor led to Jesus' death, that his death was for their sake, and that by his death their own former lives distorted by such a quest are now dead and a new life based on unconditional grace has begun. As Alastair Campbell points out, the "likeness of his death" also entails "social rejection" and signing a "death warrant so far as acceptance by this world is concerned" as believers sever old relationships and become part of the new, persecuted community of faith.[110]

The apodosis following the "if" clause is opened by ἀλλὰ καί, which in this syntactical context has the emphatic sense of "forthwith, certainly, indeed,"[111] which leads to my translation, "we shall indeed be" joined in the likeness of Christ's resurrection.[112] Although for stylistic reasons Paul refrains from reiterating "joined together with the likeness of" from v. 5a, commentators are agreed that it should be supplied as an ellipse in v. 5b. It seems clear from the context that τῆς ἀναστάσεως should be rendered "his [Christ's] resurrection"[113] as in 1:4. As we observed with regard to v. 5a, believers do not participate in the exact form of Christ's resurrection, which occurred before the end of time, but in "the likeness of his resurrection," which refers to the general resurrection at the end of time. The future tense of the verb has been a matter of debate, with advocates of the sacramental interpretation

---

Morgan, "Romans 6:5a: United to a Death like Christ's," *EThL* 59 (1983) 273-76; Moo, 368; Betz, "Baptism in Rom 6," 115.

101 Schweitzer, *Mysticism*, 119.

102 For example, see Johannes Schneider, "ὅμοιος κτλ.," *TDNT* 5 (1967) 195. For a recent account of scholarly resistance against mysticism and ecstasy in Paul, see Shantz, "Paul in Ecstasy," 21–71.

103 For example, Barrett, 123–24; Schlier, 195–96; Kuss, 1:302. Traugott Holtz, "ὁμοίωμα, ὁμοίωσις," *EDNT* 2 (1991) 512–13, opts for "form" in connection with baptism. See also Ervin, *Holy Spirit*, 110–12.

104 This is the major problem with Betz's suggestion that ὁμοίωμα refers to the baptismal ritual itself as a *similitudo* that "makes mythic realities present in symbolic fashion"; see "Baptism in Rom 6," 115. The syntax of this verse requires that σύμφυτος ("joining together") rather than βάπτισμος ("baptism") is the subject of the "likeness of his death."

105 BAGD 567–68; Schneider, "ὅμοιος κτλ.," 191–95.

106 Sabou, "Between Horror and Hope," 92–94; see

also Sorin Sabou, "A Note on Romans 6:5: The Representation (Ὁμοίωμα) of His Death," *TynB* 55 (2004) 226–29. However, the references in Aristotle *Pol.* 1340a-b and Plato *Leg.* 812b could just as easily be translated with "forms."

107 Tannehill, *Dying*, 38–39; see also Ludovít Fazekaš, "Taufe als Tod in Röm 6,3ff," *ThZ* 22 (1966) 311; Moo, 369–70.

108 Agersnap, *Baptism*, 287: "Although the main point is the correspondence between Christ and the Christians, one cannot ignore that ὁμοίωμα expresses that there is also a difference and a distance."

109 See Hubbard, *New Creation*, 92, 97–103.

110 Campbell, "Dying," 287.

111 BDF §448.6; Smyth, *Grammar*, §2782; Godet, 243.

112 Dunn, 1:318.

113 See Meyer, 1:287; Wilckens, 2:15; Jacob Kremer, "ἀνάστασις κτλ.," *EDNT* 1 (1990) 92.

of this passage tending to favor a "logical future," implying that a spiritual resurrection of believers has already occurred[114] or should now occur in the moral effort of believers.[115] As Dunn observes, however, either of these ideas would more easily have been conveyed by a past or present tense verb.[116] The future tense in connection with the resurrection thus should be understood with its fully eschatological dimension: while believers have already participated in the death of Christ, their joining in his resurrected state will occur at the end of time.[117] The "eschatological reservation" remains intact, although in a nonpolemical form. Paul refrains from treating the present moment of faith as if the threats of the principalities and powers had already been overcome. As Tannehill observes,

> The believer participates in the new life in the present, but Paul is careful to make clear that it does not become the believer's possession, as indicated by the expression "we have been grafted together." It is realized through a continual surrender of one's present activity to God, a *walking* in newness of life, and at the same time it remains God's gift for the future. Both of these aspects make clear that the new life remains in God's control, and the future verbs in Rom. 6:5 and 6:8 play their part in bringing this out.[118]

The reason for this caution, however, is not concern over spiritual enthusiasm such as Paul had countered in 1 Corinthians but an interest in dissociating the new life in Christ from particular forms of ethical and sacramental behavior that were dividing the Roman house and tenement churches. It is God's activity in Christ that alone legitimates believers. So regardless of whether they belong to the "weak" or the "strong," their death with Christ and their future share of his resurrection are assured.

■ **6** This verse and the following conclude the first enthymeme by drawing inferences concerning the freedom from sin enjoyed by believers.[119] The first person plural participle γινώσκοντες ("knowing") is employed to indicate that both Paul and his audience already share or should share the knowledge of what death with Christ implies.[120] Although the material that follows was probably not fully understood by Roman believers,[121] Paul presents it as a matter of shared understanding drawn from the conversion experience of believers, which leads to the translation "knowing this."[122] The object of knowledge is that "our obsolete self was co-crucified [with Christ]." While some have suggested that the expression παλαιὸς ἄνϑρωπος ("obsolete man") is derived from a pre-Pauline Adam/Christ typology, for which there is no direct evidence,[123] Paul's creative development of the "old/new" antithesis between the old age and the new, with "mutually exclusive" forms of behavior appropriate to each (1 Cor 5:7-8; 2 Cor 3:6, 14; Gal 6:15; also Col 3:9),[124] and his use of "newness of life" in Rom 6:4 point to a distinctively Pauline concept. While παλαιὸς ἄνϑρωπος means "the aged person" in classical Greek,[125] here it is the obsolete human in the generic

114 Zahn, 301; Fitzmyer, 435; Johannes Schneider, *Die Taufe im Neuen Testament* (Stuttgart: Kohlhammer, 1952) 47; Kühl, 204–5; Schlier, *Zeit*, 48; Porter, *Verbal Aspect*, 422–23; Bo Frid, "Römer 6:4-5: εἰς τὸν ϑάνατον und τῷ ὁμοιώματι τοῦ ϑανάτου αὐτοῦ als Schlüssel zu Duktus und Gedankengang in Röm 6,1-11," *BZ* 30 (1986) 198–99.
115 Kuss, 1:304; Cranfield, 1:308.
116 Dunn, 1:318.
117 Tannehill, *Dying*, 10–12; Käsemann, 166–67; Wilckens, 2:15; Powers, *Salvation through Participation*, 159–60.
118 Tannehill, *Dying*, 12, italics in orginal; see also Agersnap, *Baptism*, 290–94.
119 Moo, 372; Hellholm, "Romans 6," 160–63.
120 Godet, 244; Walter Schmithals, "γινώσκω κτλ.," *EDNT* 1 (1990) 248; Schlier, 196–97, emphasizes the imperative dimension of this formulation: "this you

should know," but I cannot find confirmation of this in the standard grammars.
121 Dunn, 1:318.
122 A translation of the participle γινώσκοντες that subordinates it to the preceding verb ἐσόμεϑα ("we shall be") at the end of v. 5 is rejected by Meyer, 1:288, and Kühl, 205, because a future verb cannot logically be followed by a subordinate present participle. In addition, the content of v. 6 connects more closely with v. 4 than with v. 5. These considerations lead all recent commentators and the Nestle-Aland text to understand v. 6 as an independent sentence.
123 Käsemann, 169, followed by Gerhard Schneider, "παλαιός," *EDNT* 3 (1993) 7. For classical parallels to παλαιός, see on 7:1-6 below.
124 Heinrich Seesemann, "πάλαι, παλαιός κτλ.," *TDNT* 5 (1967) 719.

sense, with all of its corrupt relationships, that is put to death with Christ.[126] The "obsolete self" is the one that "belongs to the old aeon, the self dominated by sin and exposed to wrath."[127] This old "self" should not be interpreted in an individualistic manner, as almost all commentators have done.[128] The same must be said about the singular expression τὸ σῶμα τῆς ἁμαρτίας ("the sinful body") in v. 6b, which refers to the human body[129] that stands in the generic sense "under the rule of sin and death."[130] As Tannehill observes, "these phrases do not refer to the 'old man' and 'body' of each individual, but to a collective entity which is destroyed in the death of Christ."[131] This collective viewpoint is expressed by the plural pronoun placed between the singular elements in the expression ὁ παλαιὸς ἡμῶν ἄνθρωπος ("*our obsolete self*"). This expression is linked with the Adam/Christ terminology, in which each establishes a dominion. Therefore the "body of sin" and "our old man," in Tannehill's words,

refer to the old dominion as a corporate entity. When the believers were in slavery to sin, they were part of this inclusive "old man"; their existence was bound up with his. Therefore the destruction of the "old man" in the cross of Christ meant the death of the believers as men of the old aeon. Paul is not speaking of the death of individual believers one by one. He is speak-

ing of the destruction of the dominion of sin, of which all believers were a part. . . . When Paul speaks of dying and rising with Christ, and associates it, as he does here, with the end of the old dominion and the foundation of the new, it is clear that he is thinking of the death and resurrection as eschatological events. And because they are eschatological events, affecting the old dominion as a whole, they are also inclusive events.[132]

What Tannehill and others have not been able to explain, however, is why this collective discourse was selected by Paul and how it addressed the situation in Rome. By speaking in generic terms, Paul is able to include all of the believers in Rome regardless of their varying understandings of conversion, baptism, and the new life in Christ. What unites all believers, including Paul himself, is their having died with Christ.

The verb συσταυρόω ("co-crucify"), appearing here in the aorist passive, which probably reflects the moment of initiation into faith however that may have occurred in the various Roman congregations,[133] is found only in the NT and later Christian writings. This verb refers to Jesus being crucified with thieves and, in this passage and Gal 2:19, to believers dying with Christ.[134] Interpreters have lifted up the sacramental,[135] historical,[136] mystical,[137] and social[138] dimensions of this formulation

---

125 For example, Homer *Il.* 14.106, "But now there but be one who would utter better counsel than I, whether he be young or old (ἢ νέος ἠὲ παλαιός)"; and *Od.* 1.395 speaks of kings "both young and old."

126 See Moo, 373–75, for a critique of the misunderstanding of this verse in terms of an old, Adamic nature that stands in tension with a new nature granted to believers, a misunderstanding suggested by Eph 4:22-24 and developed by Murray, 219–20, and others.

127 Fitzmyer, 436.

128 See, e.g., Agersnap's defense of the traditional individualism in *Baptism*, 320–23.

129 See Jewett, *Terms*, 291–92, and Gundry, *Sōma*, 29–31; Eduard Schweizer, "σῶμα," *EDNT* 3 (1993) 323, although all three are flawed by a too-individualistic construal of this verse. The suggestion that "the body of sin" refers to the mass of sin (D. E. H. Whiteley, *The Theology of St. Paul* [Philadelphia: Fortress, 1972] 42) lacks lexical support as

noted by Moo, 375. Nygren, 234, and Schmidt, 111, suggest that this expression personifies sin as a cosmic power in the old age, but this does not comport with the references to human involvement in the rest of this verse.

130 Dunn, 1:320, following Michel, 207, and Gaugler, 167.

131 Tannehill, *Dying*, 24.

132 Ibid., 30.

133 Interpreters such as Kuss, 1:304; Schlier, 197; and Wilckens, 2:16, who perceive baptism as the dominant motif in this passage relate the aorist passive to the moment of baptism.

134 Heinz-Wolfgang Kuhn, "συσταυρόω," *EDNT* 3 (1993) 313.

135 For example, Schlier, 197; Egon Brandenburger, "Σταυρός, Kreuzigung Jesu und Kreuzestheologie," *WuD* 10 (1969) 40.

136 Weder, *Kreuz*, 175–82.

137 Schweitzer, *Mysticism*, 101–40, 302.

138 Campbell, "Dying," 287–88, explains being "co-

of dying with Christ, but it is significant that Paul does not further specify what he has in mind. By remaining on the generic level, he disallows any qualitative advantages in how the competitive churches interpret their relationship with Christ. What unites them is that they have been co-crucified with him so that the sinful form of bodily existence could be overcome. In this context the first article in the expression τὸ σῶμα τῆς ἁμαρτίας functions as a weak possessive referring back to the collective entity "the obsolete self," which leads to my translation "its sinful body." Paul's choice of the verb καταργέω ("destroy") is congruent with this generic sense, employed here in the passive to indicate the divine abrogation of bodily existence dominated by sin.[139] As in 1 Cor 6:13; 15:24, 26 and in contrast to Rom 3:3, 31; 4:14, where the sense of disablement was dominant, καταργέω in this context has the connotation of "abolish, wipe out, bring an end to."[140] The ἵνα clause ("in order that") indicates that this abolition of the sinful form of life was the purpose of co-crucifixion with Christ that all believers have undergone.

In apposition to v. 6b,[141] the final clause makes clear that the purpose of co-crucifixion is liberation from the power of sin. Since the infinitive δουλεύειν ("to be enslaved") is a verbal noun that fulfills a nominal function when used with the definite article,[142] translation as a gerund in English is appropriate: "for the purpose of our no longer being enslaved to sin." This clarifies that the human plight is caused not by bodily existence itself but by sin, which exercises its dominion over the entire human race outside of Christ.[143] Such enslavement is

"no longer" (μηκέτι)[144] in force for believers as indicated by ἡμᾶς ("we"), a pronoun that includes both Paul and the entirety of the Roman congregations. The forceful verbs employed in this sentence indicate that Paul does not wish to imply "that the possibility of the believer's *continuing* to serve sin is very real."[145] The burden of his argument throughout this pericope is that persisting in sin is a logical and relational contradiction for those in Christ. Freed from bondage to the cosmic power of sin, Paul is contending that believers "cannot sin"[146] because they are under the lordship of Christ.

■ **7** The first enthymeme ends with a gnomic saying about the status of one who has died through co-crucifixion with Christ. The formulation of ὁ ἀποθανών ("he who died") is again generic and refers to everyone who has died.[147] It is possible that Paul has adapted an early version of rabbinic sayings such as "when a man is dead he is freed from fulfilling the law"[148] or a more specific reference to the effect of martyrdom, that "all those who die by their death make expiation."[149] The formulation δικαιοῦσθαι ἀπὸ τῆς ἁμαρτίας ("declared right from the sin") is similar to Sir 26:29, "a huckster shall not be declared right from sin (δικαιωθήσεται κάπηλος ἀπὸ ἁμαρτίας)" and to *T. Sim.* 6:1, "I have told you everything, so that I might be righteous with regard to your sin (δικαιωθῶ ἀπὸ τῆς ἁμαρτίας ὑμῶν)." In the light of these parallels, which employ δικαιοῦσθαι ("to be set right") in a nontechnical sense differentiated from Paul's use elsewhere, one could take the generalization to mean that a dead person can no longer serve the pur-

---

crucified with Christ" as abandoning the old social networks and sharing as believers the sufferings of Christ. In a more abstract manner, Sabou, "Between Horror and Hope," 99–105, notes that Greco-Roman material associated punishment, revenge, terror, and especially "horror" with crucifixion, but he does not develop the theme of believers' sharing Christ's abusive fate.

139 Käsemann, 159; Hans Hübner, "καταργέω," EDNT 2 (1991) 267; Gerhard Delling, "ἀργός, ἀργέω, καταργέω," TDNT 1 (1964) 453.

140 BAGD 417; Dunn, 1:319.

141 Schlier, 198.

142 Moulton and Turner, *Grammar III*, 140–42; Weiss, 272.

143 Jewett, *Terms*, 292.

144 BAGD 518.

145 Dunn, 1:320, italics in original.

146 Schlier, 198; Nieder, *Ethik*, 25–26.

147 In contrast, Conleth Kearns, "The Interpretation of Romans 6,7," SPCIC 1 (1963) 303–7, suggests that "the one who died" is Christ, but this decontextualizes v. 7 and results in the odd notion that the process of making righteous pertains to Christ rather than to believers.

148 Str-B, 3.232, citing *b. Šabb.* 151b *Baraita*; a citation is proposed by Karl Georg Kuhn, "Röm 6,7: ὁ γὰρ ἀποθανὼν δεδικαίωται ἀπὸ τῆς ἁμαρτίας," ZNW 30 (1931) 305–10, but decisively criticized by Cranfield, 1:310–11.

149 Kuhn, "Röm 6,7," 310, citing *Sifre Num* §112, critiqued by Pallis, 86, and Kearns, "Romans 6,7," 1.302–3.

poses of sin[150] or that death pays all debts.[151] This approach allows the γάρ ("for") in this verse to have its full argumentative sense but is unable to explain the article attached to sin (τῆς ἁμαρτίας), which appears to refer to enslaving sin mentioned in the preceding verse. Only death with Christ frees people from such enslavement, a framework that provides an understanding of δικαιοῦσθαι ("to be set right") in the technical, Pauline sense.[152] In this line of interpretation, "he who died" would refer either to someone's experiencing symbolic death in baptism[153] or, in a nonsacramental sense, to a believer's being co-crucified with Christ. This interpretation views "made righteous" as being set free from the power of sin and being set right before God. Since this line of interpretation renders v. 7 virtually a redundant restatement of the preceding verse and weakens the argumentative force of γάρ, however, it appears that no fully satisfactory solution is currently available.

■ **8** The second enthymeme begins with the premise established in the preceding verses, with εἰ δέ ("now if/since") followed by the indicative verb "we have died" implying "a condition thought of as real."[154] The particle δέ is transitional, "without any contrast intended,"[155]

introducing the new enthymeme, which makes a point consistent with the preceding. The basic reality of the new existence is described as dying σὺν Χριστῷ ("with Christ"), a phrase that in Romans appears only here. The preposition σύν was used to connect believers with Christ in Paul's first letter (1 Thess 4:14, 17; 5:10) and occasionally thereafter (2 Cor 4:14; 13:4; Phil 1:23; also Col 2:13, 20; 3:3, 4); the earliest of these instances presupposes that the phrase is known by Paul's audience.[156] Not found in the LXX or the NT, the formula "with God" appears frequently in Hellenistic Jewish writings,[157] classical Greek writers,[158] in magical tablets,[159] and later mystical writings.[160] While the analogy to the identification assumed by the mystery religions may have rendered this phrase understandable,[161] Paul's formulation lacks the individualistic flavor of initiation into the mysteries. The first person plural verbs in this sentence make it clear that he operates within "a communal or corporate mysticism"[162] in which all believers share a charismatic experience of life and death with Christ. He died a shameful death in their behalf, and they recognize that their former life has now died with him, which enables a new life under his grace and lordship to

150 Godet, 246; Kühl, 207; Kuss, 1:304.

151 Cranfield, 1:310.

152 Stanislas Lyonnet, "'Qui enim mortuus est, iustificatus est a peccato' (Rom 6,7)," *VD* 42 (1964) 17–21; Robin Scroggs, "Romans vi. 7: ὁ γὰρ ἀποθανὼν δεδικαίωται ἀπὸ τῆς ἁμαρτίας," *NTS* 10 (1963–64) 104–8; Fitzmyer, 437.

153 Cranfield, 1:311.

154 BAGD 219.I; also BDF §372; for the argumentative structure, see Hellholm, "Romans 6," 164–65.

155 BAGD 171.2.

156 See Ernst Lohmeyer, "Σὺν Χριστῷ," in *Festgabe für Adolf Deissmann zum 60. Geburtstag 7. November 1926* (Tübingen: Mohr [Siebeck], 1927) 229.

157 Philo *Somn.* 1.158; *Abr.* 18.3; Josephus *Bell.* 6.411.

158 For example, Homer *Il.* 9.49 cites the claim of Diomedes and Sthenelus, "we have come with the help of a god (σὺν γὰρ θεῷ εἰληλούθμεν)." Hesiod *Theog.* 444 reports that Hecate "is excellent in the plumbs, with the help of Hermes (σὺν Ἑρμῇ) to increase the cattle." Pindar *Nem.* 8.17 claims that when something "has been planted with god's help (σὺν θεῷ γάρ τοι φυτευθείς), it is a long-lasting boon for humankind." See also Lohmeyer, "Σὺν Χριστῷ," 226–28.

159 MM 600, cites *IG* 3.3. Nr. 108, δήσω ἐγὼ κείνην . . .

σὺν δ᾽ Ἑκάτ(η)ι χθονίαι καὶ Ἐρινύσιν ("For I shall bind that [woman] . . . with the help of both Chthonian Hekate and the Erinyes"). See also Deissmann, *Light*, 303.

160 For example, *Odes Sol.* 5:14-15, "And when what is visible disappears, I will not die, because the Lord is with me and I am with him. Halleluja!"

161 Winfried Elliger, "σύν," *EDNT* 3 (1993) 292; the repudiation of any influence whatsoever by Wagner, *Pauline Baptism*, 283–85, and Wedderburn, *Baptism and Resurrection*, 342–48, seems extreme, although they have made a compelling case against direct derivation of early Christian usage from mystery religions. Walter Burkert's summary in *Mystery Cults*, 101, is convincing: "there is a dynamic paradox of death and life in all the mysteries associated with the opposites of night and day, darkness and light, below and above, but there is nothing as explicit and resounding as the passages in the New Testament, especially in Saint Paul. . . ."

162 F. F. Bruce, "Was Paul a Mystic?" *RTR* 34 (1975) 67; see Deissmann, *Paul*, 140–43, 159–60.

emerge. The shared death leads to Paul's confident claim: "we have faith that we shall also live together with him." The verb πιστεύομεν occurs here for the first time in Romans with the connotation of a shared faith "that" something is true as, for example, in 1 Thess 4:14, "since we have faith that (πιστεύομεν ὅτι) Jesus died and rose again, even so, through Jesus, God will bring with him those who have fallen asleep."[163] The only other time πιστεύειν ὅτι ("to believe that") occurs in the Pauline letters is Rom 10:9, but it is a typical formula for other NT writings[164] and usually refers to saving faith in the kerygma of Christ's death and resurrection.[165] By employing a formula that was widely used in the early church, Paul is certain of finding common ground with the Roman audience.

The interpretation of the first person plural future verb συζήσομεν ("we shall live") has been widely debated, with many commentators taking it as a logical future referring to life with Christ as a current experience that is certain to continue into the future.[166] The argumentative context clearly favors this view, because the apodosis draws the logical inference from the protasis of dying with Christ.[167] To restrict συζήσομεν to an eschatological future[168] is unduly to limit the effect of dying with Christ, which in Paul's theology determines the nature of life from the moment of conversion until the end of time (2 Cor 4:10-11; 6:17). The eschatological interpretation also undercuts the exhortative conclusion of this pericope, which urges believers to be "living to God in Christ Jesus" (6:11b) in the present as well as the future. The choice of the verb συζάω ("live with") confirms that a logical future is in view, because a purely

eschatological reference would more naturally be combined with death or rapture. Συζάω is ordinarily employed for sharing everyday life or work with someone else,[169] but here, as in 2 Tim 2:11, it refers to the shared life between believers and their Lord. It is a striking expression of corporate mysticism involving solidarity with Christ in the entirety of human life.[170] Its context is not the isolated soul of individual believers but their corporate life together in the fictive families of house and tenement churches that made up the early church.[171] These groups shared decisive moments of life together from the birth of infants to the burial of the dead, from sharing meals to caring for the infirm, thus encompassing the entire range of bodily and spiritual experiences (see 1 Cor 6:13b, 17). Their entire life as a community of believers is "with him" (αὐτῷ), from the moment of their conversion until the eschaton and beyond. It therefore follows that believers cannot simultaneously live in sin. Rom 6:8b expands the theme of "life" from 5:10, 17, and 21 and provides the final answer to the interlocutor's question in 6:1.[172]

■ 9 In vv. 9-10, Paul provides additional clarifications about why dying and living with Christ eliminate the possibility of living in the ongoing death that is sin. Both verses function on the basis of the mystical "with Christ" in the preceding verse: what is true for Christ is also true for believers. The first clause opens with εἰδότες ὅτι ("knowing that"), referring to knowledge shared in common by all early believers.[173] The verb εἶδον refers to sense perception and often bears the sense of "to experience something"[174]—in this case, the believers' experience with the resurrected Christ. Knowing with certainty

---

163 See also Agersnap, *Baptism*, 326–27.
164 For example, Luke 1:45; John 4:21; Acts 27:25; Heb 11:6; Jas 2:29; 1 John 5:1, 5; see Gerhard Barth, "πίστις, πιστός," *EDNT* 3 (1993) 92.
165 See Rudolf Bultmann and Artur Weiser, "πιστεύω κτλ.," *TDNT* 6 (1968) 209–10.
166 Meyer, 1:292; Weiss, 293; Kühl, 207; Lagrange, 148; Murray, 223; Cranfield, 1:312–13; Morris, 254.
167 For a partial analysis of this syllogistic argument, see Moores, *Wrestling*, 83–86.
168 Zahn, 305–6; Schlier, 199; Kuss, 1:305; Käsemann, 170; Dunn, 1:322; Moo, 377.
169 Paul employs the verb in this way in 2 Cor 7:3; see also Demosthenes *1 Olynth.* 14.1. The verb συζάω is also employed metaphorically as in Josephus *Ant.*

16.212, "and may your conscience live (συζήσειεν) with you!"
170 Agersnap, *Baptism*, 328, lists some advocates of the mystical interpetation but retains the skeptical distance typical of mainline European scholarship.
171 See Atkins, *Egalitarian Community*, 171–90; Bartchy, "Siblings," 68–71.
172 In Agersnap's exhaustive discussion of v. 8 in *Baptism*, 325–42, its argumentative function in relation to 6:1 is overlooked.
173 Burdick, "Οἶδα and Γινώσκω," 344, 47, 50.
174 BAGD (2000) 280.

that Christ had been raised from the dead, it follows that Christ "dies no longer" (οὐκέτι ἀποθνῄσκει). The same adverb occurs in the next clause, "death no longer (οὐκέτι) has lordship over him,"[175] which lends emphasis to the uni-directionality of resurrection life that pertains both for Christ and for his people. Since the parallel between believers and Christ is not complete, inasmuch as they must still face their own physical deaths, the wording of this verse remains concentrated on Christ's closure with death. The power of death referred to in 5:14 and 17 has been broken by Christ, which implies that those who are "with him" are also no longer subject to that power. The implication is that the "life eternal" mentioned in 5:21 is shared by Christ and his followers, which provides a firm foundation for the inference of v. 8b concerning faith that all believers share in continuing to "co-dwell" with him.

■ **10** The second enthymeme closes with an antithetical maxim that begins in a manner similar to the gnomic saying that concluded the first enthymeme in v. 7. Although the first three words are identical with v. 7 except for the inflection of the finite form of the verb ἀπέθανεν ("he died"), the grammatical structure is marked by ὅ, which serves twice as a kind of accusative of respect: "In respect to that he died . . . in respect to that he lives."[176] Both halves of the maxim are dative constructions that clarify the relationality of Jesus' death

and life. To "die to this sin" exactly replicates the wording of 6:2, which described the status of believers,[177] and Paul does not spell out the differing forms of relationship to sin: while believers had been under the power of sin in performing its actions, Christ had been subject to the murderous consequences of such actions while remaining sinless himself.[178] The emphasis here is not on the atonement[179] but on the unrepeatable dimension of Christ's life and death. His death in relation to sin was ἐφάπαξ ("once for all"), an adverb constructed out of the components ἐπί + ἅπαξ ("upon + once").[180] This word is illustrated by Pseudo-Lucian *Dem. enc.* 18.6, "if you would turn your view to the whole matter of Demosthenes once and for all (ἐπὶ τὸ Δημοσθένην ὅλον ἐφάπαξ)"[181] and it gains a technical sense in Heb 7:27; 9:12; 10:10.[182] While Christ's crucifixion was an unrepeatable moment of being subjected to the power of sin, his current life, indicated by the present tense verb ζῇ ("he lives") is in relation to God. The two forms of existence are diametrically opposed, both in time and effect. Again, what is claimed for Christ in terms of death to sin and life to God pertains in equal measure for believers,[183] a parallelism established by the "with Christ" language of this pericope as well as the gnomic quality of the verse itself. He died to sin "once for all" and so do believers; their life "to God" eliminates the possibility of living on under the power and lure of sin. These mutu-

---

175 *Epistle of Barnabas* 8.2 has a similar sequence with οὐκέτι repeated twice; Polyaenus *Strat.* 1.41.2 has a threefold sequence.

176 For the accusative of respect, see Smyth, *Grammar*, §1600–1. Fitzmyer, 438, argues for a cognate accusative, citing BDF §154, which seems less plausible because the verbs "to die" and "to live" are intransitive and cannot take an accusative object. See also Meyer, 1:293, for a summary of the older exegetical discussion of the use of ὅ as an accusative in a grammatical construction that also appears in Gal 2:20b, "For in respect to that I now live (ὃ δὲ νῦν ζῶ) in the flesh, I live by faith . . ."

177 See Moule, "Death," 151–52.

178 See Weiss, 275.

179 For example, the atonement is stressed by Godet, 248; Wilckens, 2:19; Cranfield, 1:314.

180 Gustav Stählin, "ἅπαξ, ἐφάπαξ," *TDNT* 1 (1964) 383, citing BDF §12.3.

181 See also Dio Cassius *Hist. Rom.* 66.17.5.5; 69.8.2.3; S211.4; S246.12; ἐφάπαξ has the sense of "alone"

in Eupolis Comic *Frag.* 175 and of "one at a time" in Aristophanes Gramm. *Epit.* 2.439.

182 Stählin, "ἅπαξ, ἐφάπαξ," 383; however, that ἐφάπαξ is a "technical term for the definitiveness and therefore the uniqueness or singularity of the death of Christ and the redemption thereby accomplished" in Rom 6:10 is an unwarranted claim for a single occurrence of this adverb. Ceslas Spicq, "ἅπαξ, ἐφάπαξ," *Lexicon* 1 (1994) 142, is on more solid ground in viewing ἐφάπαξ as a synonym of ἅπαξ, both of which refer to an unrepeatable event.

183 Barrett, 126–27; this argumentative link between believers and Christ is overlooked by Agersnap, *Baptism*, 344, who maintains that vv. 9-10 are "purely Christological." On 348, Agersnap admits that these verses emphasize "this accord between Christ and the Christians."

ally exclusive realms with their inherent characteristics provide the ultimate reason why the libertinistic question in 6:1 must be answered negatively. This leads to the exhortation in the following verse.

■ **11** Both enthymemes are drawn to conclusion by this verse, which reinforces the answer to the rhetorical question in 6:1. The opening three words οὕτως καὶ ὑμεῖς ("so also you") are argumentative, explicitly drawing the inferences from Christ to believers: what the two enthymemes argued is true for him is true for them as well. The μέν . . . δέ ("on the one hand . . . on the other hand") syntax points also to argumentative rather than exhortative discourse. These argumentative links with the foregoing suggest that the verb λογίζεσθε ἑαυτούς should be taken as an indicative ("you are considering yourselves") rather than an imperative ("consider yourselves!), as most commentators have preferred.[184] The indicative is more consistent with the participle εἰδότες ("knowing") in v. 9, which refers to the experience with Christ that all of the congregations share, whereas the imperative would imply that some congregations are falling short of proper life with Christ. The indicative reading allows Paul to conclude his argument by referring back to the Roman believers' experience of dying with Christ (6:3-6) and their anticipation of living with him (6:8). The final plank in his argument is the transformed experience of the Romans themselves, not the logic of his enthymemes. Having turned away from the sinful systems of honor and shame that distorted their former lives, thus becoming "dead to sin," the Roman believers are experiencing the converted life of being "alive to God in Christ Jesus." This is a pregnant expression of corporate mysticism in which "living to God" is extended from individual martyrs[185] or spiritual paragons[186] into the entire community of those who are "in Christ Jesus." In their quests for honor and sustenance, guidance, and comfort, believers share a directionality "to God" that replaces their former orientation "to sin." This all-encompassing[187] mystical relationship is grounded and sustained by the corporate life "in Christ Jesus"[188] as the communities of faith in Rome share their sacramental love-feasts and their daily lives together. Paul is including all of the Christian groups in Rome in this concluding statement; no distinctions between the "weak" and the "strong," with their varying interpretations of the law, are allowed to surface here, which would indeed occur if the imperative reading were intended. The unifying experience with Christ provides the final answer to the question that opened this pericope. The death and new life in Christ shared by them all is the indicative on which the imperative of the paragraph is based.[189]

■ **12** Two negative and one positive admonition open this paragraph in vv. 12-13. The practical consequence of the preceding pericope is drawn by the prohibition introduced by μὴ οὖν ("don't, therefore"), which occurs only here in the authentic Pauline letters.[190] When employed with a present imperative, it is a forcible expression of "a command that is generally valid."[191] Having been set free from the power of sin by the death and resurrection of Christ, believers have the responsibility of refusing sin's further domination. The verb

---

184 Every commentator except for Bengel and Hofmann assumes the imperative here, but none account for the precise nuance of οὕτως καὶ ὑμεῖς ("so also you"). For an extensive development of the conventional interpretation, see Thüsing, *Per Christum*, 67–93.

185 Dunn, 1:324, refers to the martyrs who "as our forefathers, Abraham, Isaac, Jacob, live to God (ζῶσι τῷ Θεῷ, 4 Macc 7:19); in 16:25 it is said that such martyrs "who die for God, live to God (ζῶσιν τῷ Θεῷ)."

186 Dunn, 1:324, refers to Philo *Mut.* 213, "For the life of virtue, which is life in its truest form, is shared by few . . . only those to whom it is granted to escape the aims that engross humanity and to live for God alone (Θεῷ μόνῳ ζῆσαι)"; *Heres* 111, "if with all parts of his being one is able to live for God rather than for himself (ζῆσαι Θεῷ μᾶλλον ἢ ἑαυτῷ) . . . he will live a happy and blessed life."

187 Thüsing tends to reduce "living to God" to the matter of obedience in *Per Christum*, 67, 89–93.

188 See Bouttier, *En Christ*, 132–33; Büchsel, "In Christus," 147; Dacquino, "In Christo," 281–85; Wikenhauser, *Pauline Mysticism*, 21–33, 50–65; Neugebauer, *In Christus*, 101–2, 133–47.

189 See Godet, 249; Dunn, 1:333.

190 This expression is typical for deutero-Pauline materials, as, e.g., Eph 5:7; Col 2:16; 2 Tim 1:8; it appears frequently in Matthew (6:1; 8:31, 34; 10:26, 31). See also Exod 5:5 and Ep Jer 22.

191 BDF §513.III.2.

βασιλεύω ("rule") harks back to 5:21, which refers to sin's deadly rule. Paul's choice of the present imperative form of βασιλεύω has led interpreters to infer that actions persisting until the present must now be terminated,[192] that the effort of resistance should be continuous,[193] or that sin continues to dominate the world so that believers must resist the old age with the power of the new age.[194] The effort to resolve this on purely grammatical grounds[195] fails because Paul's prohibitive imperatives do not always carry the connotation of ceasing an action,[196] but the context, the situation, and the use of μὴ οὖν ("do not, therefore") suggest that Paul believes that the actions of the Roman believers reflect the ongoing effect of sin. The reference to "your mortal body" as the arena of such domination implies the entire arena of human relatedness, since as Käsemann as shown, the σῶμα for Paul is the basis of relationships.[197] Bodily relations are certainly included, but the adjective θνητός ("mortal") does not invite speculation about physicality or sensuality as the source of sin.[198] It refers instead to sin's death-dealing dominance over bodily relations, which results in the wrath described in 1:18-32 and the curse of Adam's death in 5:18-21. To obey the ἐπιθυμίαι ("desires") of the body is to continue to aspire to relationships of domination that were endemic in the honor-shame culture of the ancient Mediterranean world.[199] These compulsions were so powerful that Paul refers to humans obeying such desires as being completely dominated by sin. The expression εἰς τὸ ὑπακούειν ("for obedience") is a hapax legomenon in the NT, thus reflecting Paul's distinctive view of sin's domination of the old age. In Ulrich Wilckens's words, humans confront the "either-or of slavery under sin or slavery under obedience."[200] The fault lies not in the inherent nature of sexual and other bodily relationships[201] but in their sinful misuse in the pursuit of honor and power, in various campaigns of human boasting. In the context of the Roman believers, the indications are that such desires for dominance were expressed in mutual contempt and judging (Rom 14–15) rather than in sensual excesses.

■ **13** The second negative admonition introduced by μηδέ ("neither") employs the language of standing before or alongside someone or something.[202] In the context of standing before a commanding power, παρίστημι has the sense of being "at the disposal of"[203] or "yielding oneself to" a regent.[204] To stand alongside the power of sin or the command of God in this context means to serve the purposes of another power, to become a willing instrument in its system of domination.[205] The present imperative μὴ παριστάνετε of subordinating oneself to the power of sin ("don't continually yield your members") stands in contrast to the aorist imperative παραστήσατε employed to depict placing oneself once and for all in the service of God.[206]

---

192 Godet, 250; Cranfield, 1:316; Fitzmyer, 44.
193 Dunn, 1:336.
194 Kuss, 2:382–83; Käsemann, 176.
195 See Moulton and Turner, *Grammar III*, 76.
196 See Johannes Louw, "On Greek Prohibitions," *ACl* 2 (1991) 43–57, cited by Moo, 382.
197 See the discussion of Käsemann's view in *Exegetische Versuche*, 32, in Jewett, *Terms*, 216–19.
198 Godet, 250, provides an account of the extensive nineteenth-century discussion of the connotation of "mortal body," with Philippi stressing the malignant character of the body, Flatt referring to the transient quality of bodily pleasures, Grotius stressing the brevity of bodily pleasures, and Godet himself stressing the "egotistical instinct of the soul."
199 See Moo, 383: "the desire to have our own way, the desire to possess what other people have . . . , the desire to have dominance over others." The repudiation of Käsemann's interpretation in terms of "self-will and self-assertion" (177) by Räisänen, "ἐπιθυμία and ἐπιθυμεῖν," 107–8, is compelling.

200 Wilckens, 2:34, cited by Gerhard Schneider, "ὑπακοή, ὑπακούω," *EDNT* 3 (1993) 395.
201 See Hans Hübner, "ἐπιθυμία κτλ.," *EDNT* 2 (1991) 27.
202 See BAGD (2000) 778; LSJM 1341; e.g., Homer *Od* 1.335 employs παρίστημι in the sense of standing alongside.
203 Käsemann, 177, citing Polybius *Hist.* 3.109.9d in reference to "presenting oneselves for battle" (οὕτως ἑαυτοὺς παραστήσεσθε πρὸς τῆς μάχην).
204 Suggested by Bo Reicke, "παρίστημι, παριστάνω," *TDNT* 5 (1967) 840, as in 3 Kgdms 10:8, which refers to the royal servants standing before Solomon, ready to do his bidding.
205 See Schlier, 203.
206 See Schmidt, 113.

Paul employs the plural form of $\mu\acute{\epsilon}\lambda o\varsigma$ ("member"), often translated broadly as "faculties"[207] or "capabilities,"[208] but referring more specifically to limbs and organs with which humans carry out tasks and enter into relationships with others.[209] For example, Dionysius Halicarnassus *Antiq. Rom.* 5.18.12 refers to $\tau\grave{\alpha}\ \mu\acute{\epsilon}\lambda\eta\ \tau o\hat{v}\ \sigma\acute{\omega}\mu\alpha\tau o\varsigma$ ("parts of the body") and 17.83.9 refers to the mangling of limbs with $\sigma\upsilon\gamma\kappa o\pi\grave{\eta}\ \mu\epsilon\lambda\hat{\omega}\nu$.[210] An Egyptian papyrus complains that an opponent "belabored me with blows on every limb of my body ($\epsilon\grave{\iota}\varsigma\ \pi\hat{\alpha}\nu\ \mu\acute{\epsilon}\lambda[o]\varsigma\ \tau o[\hat{v}\ \sigma]\hat{\omega}\mu\alpha\tau o\varsigma$)."[211] It is therefore likely that Paul has actual bodily parts in mind that can serve as "instruments of wrongdoing by sinning." The term $\ddot{o}\pi\lambda o\nu$ ("tool, instrument, weapon") correlates with human limbs rather than with "faculties" or "capabilities." While the precise connotation is open to debate,[212] Paul's use of the metaphor of weapons in 2 Cor 6:7 and 10:4 and the use of $\ddot{o}\pi\lambda o\nu$ to refer to military armor in Rom 13:12 suggest the translation of "weapon" in this verse.[213] To allow oneself to be used as a "weapon of wrongdoing,"[214] placing one's members in the service of sin, needs to be understood in the context of military domination, which was central for the Roman empire and for the audience of this letter. Rome used its weapons to dominate others and, if they refused to be subjugated, to destroy them. Wicked systems of gaining dominance lead people to behavior they might not engage in individually; people become weapons in the hands of such systems, committing evil deeds. It is clear from the use of "desires" in the preceding verse and $\mu\acute{\epsilon}\lambda\eta$ ("members") in this verse that

sexual misbehavior as well as other destructive actions are in view; the references to the "mortal body" in v. 12 and to God's making believers "alive from the dead" in v. 13b make it clear that all such behavior participates in the realm of death. This formulation counters the Roman civic cult in a decisive manner, because it celebrates military domination as producing peace and preserving human life.

The dative $\tau\hat{\eta}\ \dot{\alpha}\mu\alpha\rho\tau\acute{\iota}\alpha$ ("to sin") refers to the power that seeks to take over the body and its members in the campaign against God.[215] That sin functions as a cosmic power that rules the world outside of Christ was established in 5:21, and the audiences' former enslavement to this power was recalled in 6:6.[216] To place oneself "at the disposal" of sin would be to participate willingly in the war against God and to deny the redemption experienced in Christ. In the "eschatological struggle for power" over the control of the world, believers are called to make a choice between serving sin and serving God.[217]

After the two negative admonitions in v. 12a and v. 13a, Paul strikes the positive note in v. 13b, urging believers to "yield yourselves to God." In contrast to the earlier admonitions formulated in present imperatives, here Paul employs the aorist imperative $\pi\alpha\rho\alpha\sigma\tau\acute{\eta}\sigma\alpha\tau\epsilon$, which has an ingressive sense of commencing conduct that contrasts with earlier conduct.[218] Rather than continuing to place themselves at the disposal of sin in its deadly human and institutional manifestations, believers are admonished to lend themselves to the service of God as persons "made alive from the dead."[219] The

---

207 Barrett, 128; Dunn, 1:337.

208 Käsemann, 177; Cranfield, 1:317; Moo, 384.

209 Meyer, 1:297; Zahn, 311; Dodd, 94; Johannes Horst, "$\mu\acute{\epsilon}\lambda o\varsigma$," *TDNT* 4 (1967) 555–56, notes the classical parallels to $\mu\acute{\epsilon}\lambda o\varsigma$ as members and bodily parts, but in his explanation of Paul's usage (561–62), he concentrates solely on the theological issue of human domination by higher powers.

210 See BAGD (2000) 628 for additional examples.

211 Cited by MM 396, from *P.Tebt.* 2.331.11.

212 F. S. Malan, "Bound to Do Right," *Neot* 15 (1981) 123, prefers the sense of "instruments."

213 See Albrecht Oepke and K. G. Kuhn, "$\ddot{o}\pi\lambda o\nu\ \kappa\tau\lambda.$," *TDNT* 5 (1967) 294; Dunn, 1:337; Fitzmyer, 447; Agersnap, *Baptism*, 366–69.

214 As elsewhere in Romans, $\dot{\alpha}\delta\iota\kappa\acute{\iota}\alpha$ has the sense of performing acts of injustice or wrongdoing; see LSJM 23.

215 See Weiss, 279; Schlier, 203.

216 See Lohmeyer, *Probleme*, 79–81; Schottroff, "Schreckensherrschaft," 499–500; Fitzmyer, 447.

217 Käsemann, 177; see also Moo, 384.

218 BDF §337(1); Moulton and Turner, *Grammar III*, 76; Schlier, 203; Dunn, 1:338; see Moo, 385, for other references and his rejection of any contrast with the present imperative.

219 This appeal for a voluntary decision on the part of the audience is the main consideration Wayne Hagen advances to classify v. 13 as a gloss in "Deutero-Pauline Glosses," 364–65. The contextual evidence for a gloss is weak: the use of second person plural verbs, and an alleged disruption of the flow of the argument from v. 12 to v. 14.

particle ὡσεί is employed here for the only time in the Pauline letters with a connotation that is interchangeable with ὡς ("as");[220] believers are to view themselves not as the helpless tools of evil powers but as weapons in the hands of the living God. The particle and the sentence should be taken to depict not a fictional condition but rather the reality of believers who have been given new life in Christ.[221] Paul's formulation picks up the theme of Christ's gift reigning for believers "in life" (5:17) and in "life eternal" (5:21), of believers walking "in newness of life" (6:4) and considering themselves "alive to God in Christ Jesus" (6:11). In contrast to some interpreters who wish to restrict the gift of life to its eschatological dimension,[222] Paul wants believers to act in God's behalf as persons already redeemed from the realm of deadly domination. He goes on with "weapons of righteousness" to create a truly striking metaphor, whose military connotation remains intact; "righteousness" is personified here as the force wielding the weapons.[223] That such weapons are to be yielded "to God" prevents this from becoming an expression of crusading zealotism; a significant observation in this regard is that Paul develops an antithesis not between God and the devil but between God and sin.[224] Yet the martial implications should not be disguised by euphemistic translations, because weapons engage in risky combat. To become a weapon of righteousness is to become even more vulnerable than before; the risks are alluded to in Rom 8. That one's hands and feet and other bodily organs are to constitute such weapons is picked up in chaps. 14–16, where reaching out one's arms in welcoming members of other groups is advocated, where eating the food offered by others is in view, where new forms of noncompetitive speech are enjoined, and where the holy kiss is to be extended to all. In the situation of tension between early

Christian groups, and in the context of the Greco-Roman environment, where one did not ordinarily share food with outsiders, the righteous gestures enjoined in chaps. 14–16 carried significant social risks. Such risks are counterbalanced by the idea of being a weapon in the hand of another, in this case the hand of God, which provides the impetus and courage for unprecedented forms of hospitality and other actions of love. It is interesting, however, that the slavery language that would seem to be congruent with this usage is not employed until the next pericope. There is nothing servile in this admonition to employ one's limbs and organs to serve God as "weapons" in the new, nonviolent campaign to restore righteousness in a corrupted world.

■ **14** The rationale that concludes the series of admonitions is thoroughly reassuring. While it is possible to understand the future verb κυριεύσει as hortatory, "sin is not to have lordship over you,"[225] or a conditional statement, "if you stop obeying sin, it will have no mastery over you,"[226] neither option seems likely in view of the explanatory γάρ ("for").[227] This is a genuine future of the verb "to be or become Lord,"[228] indicating that the reign of sin is surely at an end for believers.[229] The verb κυριεύω is reiterated from 6:9, where it was claimed that death no longer has lordship over believers. In v. 15 it continues the theme of domination in which underlings in the Greco-Roman world routinely placed themselves at the disposal of higher powers. The additional reassurance is required because wherever believers looked in their cultural environment, the sway of sin seemed unbroken. This future promise is directed at "you," the believers, and it is followed by an additional explanation that brings the discussion back into the framework of freedom from law. It is not only that every form of law in the Greco-Roman world required the sub-

220 BAGD 899; BDF §453 (3).
221 Schlier, 203–4.
222 Zahn, 312; Schmidt, 113; Barrett, 128; Käsemann, 177; Dunn, 1.338; Wilckens, 2:21–22, rightly protests against this overinterpretation of the particle ὡσεί.
223 See du Toit, "Dikaiosyne," 272–73. A related philosophical idea was expressed by Diogenes Laertius *Vitae philos.* 6.12.4, "Virtue is a weapon that can't be taken away (ἀναφαίρετον ὅπλον ἡ ἀρετή)."
224 See Dunn, 1:338.

225 Jülicher, 266; O'Neill, 116; Fitzmyer, 447, citing BDF §362.
226 Dodd, 95.
227 Schreiner, 325.
228 See Gottfried Quell and Wilhelm Foerster, "κύριος κτλ.," *TDNT* 3 (1965) 1097, referring to Polybius *Hist.* 2.11.14. G. H. R. Horsley points to a parallel use of κυριεύω with an object in the genitive in "A Gymnasiarchal Law from Beroia," *NDIEC* 2 (1982) 105.
229 Kühl, 210; Dunn, 1:339; Moo, 387.

mission of common people, but also that law itself had been perverted by the universal quest for honor and status.[230] Submission to law's commands was usually motivated in part by the desire to gain honor as a decently submissive citizen or slave, a decent respecter of the gods, or in the Jewish case, a proper God-fearer. The system of domination erected by sin was itself motivated by the quest for power and honor for those in charge. To be set free from the compulsion to gain honor through adherence to the law was therefore the essential first step in breaking away from the habit of lending one's weight to the system of domination, whether one was a Jewish or a Gentile Christian. To become an instrument of righteousness therefore required the confidence that sin's realm was broken, despite all of the social, political, and economic evidence to the contrary. Thus, the reassuring verse ends with a statement in the present tense: "you are not under law but under grace."[231] This statement, whose cogency is enhanced by the lack of definite articles attached to either "law"[232] or "grace,"[233] would make no sense if the first part of v. 14 were either hortatory or conditional. For believers, grace abounding (5:17, 20; 6:1) is the transforming basis of the new life in which they "stand" (Rom 5:2). As conveyed in the life, death, and resurrection of Christ, grace frees believers from the compulsion to obey the law their culture promotes as a means of gaining honor.[234] They now have another obligation, to which Paul calls for willing assent in these verses, to serve the purposes of grace by yielding their bodies as weapons employed by the God and Father of Jesus Christ, serving their fellows in righteousness. Precisely how they are to perform such service is left open. In Käsemann's words, "Christian obedience is not to be equated with obedience under the Torah, for as standing in grace it is also freedom."[235] The ethic of free responsibility developed in chaps. 12–16 flows directly out of this series of admonitions.

---

230 Dunn, 1:339, followed by Moo, 387–88, restricts law to the Jewish Torah, which fails to account for the lack of a definite article; in the context of Rom 6, it must include law in every form available to Paul's audience in Rome. For an account of the widespread disregard of "constitutional niceties" in the Roman empire, which was dominated by desires for honor and power, see Lendon, *Empire of Honour*, 8–9.

231 In all of Greek literature, not counting later patristic sources, this expression ὑπὸ χάριν ("under grace") appears only in Rom 6:14, 15.

232 In "'Under the Law': The Background of a Pauline Expression," *CBQ* 63 (2001) 72–83, Joel Marcus has made a case that the expression ὑπὸ νόμον arose from the Galatian crisis and expressed the viewpoint of Judaizing opponents arguing for the necessity of obeying the Torah on the basis of Exod 19:17 and Deut 4:11.

233 See Kühl, 211.

234 The implications of this statement for feminist theology are developed by Tamez, "Justification," 185–87.

235 Käsemann, 178.

6

The Fourth Pericope

Diatribe Concerning Living to God under the Grace and the Lordship of Christ

15/ What then? "Let us sin[a] because we are not under law but under grace?" No way! 16/ [b]Do you not know that to whatever you yield yourselves in obedience as slaves, you are slaves to what you obey, either to sin resulting in death[c] or to obedience resulting in righteousness? 17/ But thanks be to God that you were slaves of this sin [[you obeyed from (the) heart[d] the imprint stamped by teaching, to which (imprint) you were handed over,]] 18/ but having been freed from sin, you were enslaved to righteousness. 19/ (I am speaking in human terms because of the weakness of your flesh.) For just as you yielded your members as enslaved[e] to impurity and to lawlessness resulting in anarchy,[f] so now yield your members as enslaved[g] to righteousness resulting in sanctification.

20/ For when you were slaves of sin, you were liberated in respect to the righteousness. 21/ Consequently what fruit were you having then? Things of which you are now ashamed, for the[h] outcome of those things is death! 22/ But now, having been set free from sin and having become slaves to God, you have your fruit resulting in sanctification, and the outcome is life eternal. 23/ For the remuneration of sin is death, but the free gift of God is life eternal in Christ Jesus our Lord.

a   In place of the aorist subjunctive, 6 323 424 614 629 630 945 1319 1505 1881 2495 *pm* ar t vg[cl] provide the future form $\dot{\alpha}\mu\alpha\rho\tau\dot{\eta}\sigma o\mu\epsilon\nu$ ("we shall sin"), which appears to be secondary. An additional variant $\dot{\eta}\mu\alpha\rho\tau\dot{\eta}\sigma\alpha\mu\epsilon\nu$ ("we have sinned"), which Cran-

field, 1:321, terms "nonsensical," is found in F G lat Ambst. This past construal, however, seems to place sinning as an act of a former mode of life for which the readers feel themselves presently accountable. This final variant appears to be a simple scribal error.

b   D* F G vg[mss] sa[ms] bo add $\ddot{\eta}$ ("or") at the beginning of v. 16 appears to be an effort to make it correspond to the formulation of Rom 6:3; 7:1.

c   The deletion of $\epsilon\dot{\iota}\varsigma$ $\vartheta\dot{\alpha}\nu\alpha\tau o\nu$ ("unto death") by D 1739* d r vg[st] sy[p] sa Ambst appears to be "accidental"; see Metzger, *Textual Commentary*, 454. The inclusion of the phrase is surely original, on the basis of ℵ A B C F G K L P Ψ 6 69 33 81 88 104 181 323 326 330 365 424 436 451 614 629 945 1175 1241 1243 1319 1505 1506 1573 1735 1739[mg] 1836 1874 1877 1881 1962 2127 2344 2464 2492 2495 *Maj* ar g sy[h,pal] bo eth *al.*

d   The addition of $\kappa\alpha\vartheta\alpha\rho\tilde{\alpha}\varsigma$ ("pure") to $\kappa\alpha\rho\delta\dot{\iota}\alpha\varsigma$ ("heart") by A is a moralistic improvement that is clearly secondary.

e   The replacement of $\delta o\tilde{\upsilon}\lambda\alpha$ ("enslaved") by the infinitive $\delta o\upsilon\lambda\epsilon\dot{\upsilon}\epsilon\iota\nu$ by F G latt (sy[p]) is a stylistic improvement.

f   The absence of $\epsilon\dot{\iota}\varsigma$ $\tau\dot{\eta}\nu$ $\dot{\alpha}\nu o\mu\dot{\iota}\alpha\nu$ ("unto lawlessness") in B *pc* 1912 sy[p] appears to be a stylistic simplification.

g   Several efforts at stylistic improvement are visible at this point: F G latt (sy[p]) replace $\delta o\tilde{\upsilon}\lambda\alpha$ with $\delta o\upsilon\lambda\epsilon\dot{\upsilon}\epsilon\iota\nu$ ("to be enslaved") as earlier in this verse, and A replaces it with $\ddot{o}\pi\lambda\alpha$ ("instruments") as in Rom 6:13. Neither variant is plausible.

h   The addition $\mu\dot{\epsilon}\nu$ by P[94vid] ℵ[2] B D*,[1] F G 1505 2495 *pc* sy[h] appears to be a stylistic improvement, bringing out the antithesis with the $\delta\dot{\epsilon}$ in the next sentence. See Zuntz, *Text*, 197, who speaks of the Byzantine fondness for "Attic polish." The absence of $\mu\dot{\epsilon}\nu$ is supported by ℵ* A C D[2] K L P Ψ 6 33 69 88 104 323 326 330 365 424 614 945 1175 1241 1243 1319 1506 1573 1735 1739 1836 1874 1881 2344 2464 *Maj* Cl.

Analysis

While commentators disagree about whether the new pericope begins with v. 12[1] or with v. 15,[2] the $\tau\dot{\iota}$ $o\dot{\upsilon}\nu$ ("what then?") at the beginning of v. 1 and v. 15 indicates the beginnings of discrete sections. Verse 15 states a false conclusion arising out of the formulation of v. 14 that believers "are not under law but under

---

1   See Kuss, 1:382; Käsemann, 171–72; Dunn, 1:335; Fitzmyer, 444; du Toit, "*Dikaiosyne*," 263–69, provides a structural analysis that holds the entirety of chap. 6 together, but he perceives a new paragraph beginning with v. 12.

2   Kühl, 194–98, 216–17; Schlier, 190–205; Cranfield, 1:316–21; Moo, 396–97; Haacker, 124–27, 131; Hellholm, "Romans 6," 138; Hendrikus Boers, "The Structure and Meaning of Romans 6:1-14," *CBQ* 63 (2001) 664–82.

grace."[3] The question is denied by a counterquestion in v. 16 reminding Christians of the exchange of lordship they had experienced in their conversion and subsequent baptism. This diatribal exchange is organized in sentences of three lines each, matching the beginning of the preceding pericope and continuing to v. 19a.[4] There is a striking wordplay in the two εἰς ("unto") phrases "sin unto death"/"obedience unto righteousness" in v. 16c. In v. 17b-c, however, there is material concerning obedience to doctrine that breaks into the flow of the argument and may constitute a gloss, to be discussed in the exegesis below. If this material is removed, a well-developed antithesis emerges between being slaves of sin in v. 17a and being freed from sin in v. 18a and enslaved to righteousness in v. 18b.

In the new paragraph beginning with v. 19b the style shifts to sentences of two lines each,[5] providing an exhortative syllogism supporting the paradoxical expression "slaves of righteousness." There is an elaborate parallelism between v. 19b and c, with "members" and "slaves" repeated in each line and antitheses between the two lines involving "impurity/righteousness" and "lawlessness/holiness." Verse 20 also contains a neat antithetical parallelism opposing "slave" to "free" and "sin" to "righteousness."

Verses 21-23 shift back to diatribe style to lift up the consequences of the two lordships, the one leading to shame and death and other to holiness and life. This dialogical exchange is initiated by a three-line sentence that matches the structure of v. 15. The theological rationale and conclusion in vv. 22-23 are organized in two-line sentences matching the preceding paragraph and marked by antithetical parallelism: "free from sin/slaves of God" in v. 22 and "death/life" in v. 23. The final verse juxtaposes the results of the two realms of sin and Christ, picking up the motif of the wages of death from v. 21 and of eternal life from v. 22, signaling its concluding function by a clausula in v. 23c matching the one that closed the pericope of 5:12-21.[6]

Rhetorical Disposition

IV.	The *probatio*
5:1–8:39	B. The second proof: Life in Christ as a new system of honor that replaces the search for status through conformity to the law
6:15-23	4. Diatribe concerning living to God under the grace and the lordship of Christ
6:15-19a	a. A diatribal exchange concerning remaining in sin
6:15a-b	1) The questions
6:15a	a) The introductory question of general inference: "What then?"
6:15b	b) The question of sinning since the law is no longer binding
6:15c	2) The emphatic answer
6:16	3) The counterquestion about slaves being obedient to the kind of lord they have
6:16a	a) Submission to a lord implies slavery
6:16b	b) One becomes a slave to the lord one obeys
6:16c	c) The alternative lords
	(1) Slavery to sin leads to death
	(2) Slavery to obedience leads to righteousness
6:17-19a	4) The explanation on the basis of Christian experience
6:17	a) Doxology concerning slaves now bound to a new Lord
6:17a	(1) The expression of thanks concerning former slaves
6:17b	(2) The current state of former slaves: obedient to new Lord
6:17c	(3) The criterion of obedience: the new Christian "teaching"
6:18a-19a	b) The current status of former slaves
6:18a	(1) Restatement of the premise: freed from sin
6:18b	(2) The new status of slaves to righteousness

---

3   See Stowers, *Rereading*, 148–49.

4   Weiss, "Beiträge," 229, suggests the three-line sentences in vv. 16 and 17-18, but in making v. 18 into the third line of the second sentence, he disregards its natural antithesis between freed from sin and enslaved to righteousness, which seems to require two lines. He also identifies v. 19a as a freestanding interjection, thus not incorporating it into the strophic pattern. Louw, 2:79, suggests that vv. 17-20 provide a chiastic expansion that contrasts the new

lordship with the old, but his scheme takes account neither of v. 19a nor of the precise wording of the passage.

5   Weiss, "Beiträge," 229, notes the pattern of two-line sentences at this point and observes that the seemingly redundant phrase "unto lawlessness" in 6:19b distorts the symmetry of the lines.

6   See Weiss, "Beiträge," 189, 229; Harvey, *Listening*, 195.

Exegesis

■ **15** With the diatribal question "What then?" Paul takes up a false inference that could be drawn from his previous sentence.[7] In the aorist subjunctive voice, which I take as exhortatory, following the pattern of 6:1 and 13, ἁμαρτήσωμεν ("let us sin") no longer carries the slightly humorous air of 6:1. The sly, even outrageous suggestion[8] of augmenting the realm of grace by additional sinning finds no echo here; the ὅτι ("because") clause appears to provide a straightforward, legalistic rationalization for sin. The formulation ὑπὸ νόμον ("under law") matches Plato's description of "the mass of people bound by the same law" (ὑπὸ νόμον τὸν αὐτόν),[9] whereas the parallel expression ὑπὸ χάριν ("under grace") appears nowhere in Greek literature except here and in the following verse. "Under law" probably originated as a slogan coined by Judaizers in the Galatian crisis who followed an early rabbinic interpretation of Exod 19:17 and Deut 4:11 to the effect that the law was suspended in a threatening manner over their heads.[10] The use of the expression seems more generalized here. The rationalization is straightforward: "If there's no law against it, go ahead and do it!" In the light of the previous argument, this diatribal statement now appears as an egregious violation of grace itself, evoking the response "No way!" that the audience probably also echoes. For it was the grace of Christ, not the reign of law, that conquered the realm of sin. Grace also provides a powerful restraint, as Paul articulated in an earlier letter:

> The love of Christ constrains us, because we are convinced that one has died for all; therefore all have died. And he died for all, that those who live might live no longer for themselves but for him who for their sake died and was raised. (2 Cor 5:14-15)

However, the rhetorical question about continuing in sin is useful because it provides a foil for Paul's argument about the "two mutually exclusive *spheres of dominion* that comprehensively determine human existence," in Elliott's words.[11] The question also has a genuine though politely distant bearing on the situation in the Roman house and tenement churches because, although they appear to lack principled antinomian impulses, they are continuing to act in discriminatory ways toward each other. Their "judging" and "condemning" of each other (14:3-10) indicate that the constraint of mutual love still has not produced a thorough transformation of typical social hostilities. The diatribe that includes voices as extreme as this verse allows Paul to build a theological and ethical argument that addresses such issues in a basic manner without offending his audience.

■ **16** The argument opens with a rhetorical question, "Do you not know that," which will recur at 11:2 with a

---

7   See Esler, *Paul's Rhetoric,* 208.
8   Dunn, 1:341.
9   Plato *Def.* 415c3.

10   Marcus, "Under the Law," 80–82.
11   Elliott, *Rhetoric of Romans,* 240, italics in original.

scriptural citation. In this instance it is possible that Paul is alluding to traditional teaching, perhaps derived from the Jesus tradition about no person being able to serve two masters (Matt 6:24)[12] or sinners becoming slaves to sin (John 8:34),[13] but it seems more likely in view of the precise point being made that Paul refers to the widely understood reality of slavery.[14] The argument turns not on the question of serving God or mammon or even serving sin, but rather that those who "yield themselves as slaves" actually become slaves. As Kühl observes, the placement of $\hat{\omega}$ ("to whom") in front of "yield" and "obey" places the emphasis on the theme of slavery as completely subordinate to a particular master.[15] The verb $\pi\alpha\rho\iota\sigma\tau\acute{\alpha}\nu\omega$ ("yield oneself, place oneself at the disposal of") recurs from v. 13, but here in the context of $\delta o\acute{\nu}\lambda o\upsilon\varsigma$ $\epsilon\grave{\iota}\varsigma$ $\grave{\upsilon}\pi\alpha\kappa o\acute{\eta}\nu$ ("in obedience as slaves"), which requires voluntary placement of oneself at the disposal of another. The expression quite literally means "to stand by the side of someone as a slave," indicating readiness to serve the needs of the master. One thinks of the expression in Epictetus *Diss.* 1.25.23, "I have given myself away as a slave ($\delta o\hat{\nu}\lambda o\nu$ $\acute{\epsilon}\mu\alpha\upsilon\tau\grave{o}\nu$ $\pi\alpha\rho\alpha\delta\acute{\epsilon}\delta\omega\kappa\alpha$)" or the typical request that magical deities should "stand by me" ($\pi\alpha\rho\acute{\alpha}\sigma\tau\alpha$ $\mu o\iota$) in the performance of a service.[16] Studies of slavery in the ancient world indicate that somewhere between one- and two-thirds of the population were either slaves or former slaves, and that among the significant avenues of replenishing the supply of slaves, who were often manumitted after reaching the age of thirty or forty,[17] were the enslavement of debtors and voluntary selling of oneself as a slave.[18] Severe economic necessity was the usual motive of selling oneself, although there were cases of selling oneself or one's family members into particular forms of slavery such as imperial service or service to a distinguished patron in the hope of economic and social advancement.[19] This social reality is the basis of the comparison Paul draws with service to sin:[20] those who voluntarily place themselves into the position of slavery in fact become actual "slaves to what you obey." Once the step into slavery was made, there was legally no escape except for death or manumission at the discretion of the owner. The owner literally had the power of life and death over his slaves; he could discipline them or execute them at will, with no legal jeopardy. They were simply his property, and whatever rights they may previously have enjoyed were eradicated. This social reality forms the background of Luise Schottroff's provocative essay "Die Schreckensherrschaft der Sünde" in Rom 6.[21]

A stark choice thus lies before Paul's audience: "whether" ($\acute{\eta}\tau o\iota$)[22] to return to their former situation of being slaves of sin or to live out their new situation as slaves of Christ. Paul insists, "you are slaves ($\delta o\hat{\nu}\lambda o\acute{\iota}$ $\acute{\epsilon}\sigma\tau\epsilon$) to what you obey," reminiscent of Epictetus's reminder of menial status, "You are a slave ($\delta o\hat{\nu}\lambda o\varsigma$ $\epsilon\hat{\iota}$) of a wretched maid-servant—even of a cheap one! Why do you then still say you are free?"[23] Ernst Käsemann is correct in observing the vast difference between Paul's view and the "idealistic heritage" of Western thought, which assumes that human freedom is basic: "It is presupposed here as elsewhere that a person belongs constitutively to a world and lies under lordship," either to God or to evil powers.[24] Following this lead, Neil Elliott observes that Paul's wording shows that "there are no pockets of neutral independence, no 'freedom' from one that is not immediately and necessarily fealty to the

12   Kaye, *Chapter 6*, 120–29.
13   Moo, 398.
14   Tobin, *Paul's Rhetoric*, 208, observes that Paul "expects their immediate agreement." See also Harrill, *Slaves*, 28.
15   Kühl, 217.
16   *PGM* 1.Nrs. 2.79; 4.2501, 2503; 12.95, etc.
17   See Géza Alföldy, "Die Freilassung von Sklaven und die Struktur des Sklaverei in der römischen Kaiserzeit," *RSA* 2 (1972) 114–15, 119–20.
18   See Alföldy, "Freilassung," 125–26; Gülzow, *Christentum und Sklaverei*, 78–80; Brockmeyer, *Antike Sklaverei*, 100–5, 150–53, 157–59; Bartchy, "Slavery (Greco-Roman)," 65–73.

19   See Dale B. Martin's discussion of "slavery as upward mobility" in *Slavery as Salvation*, 30–42.
20   See Schlier, 206; Haacker, 132.
21   Dunn, 1:342; Schottroff, "Schreckensherrschaft," 500–507; see also G. H. R. Horsley, "Dedications to 'The Most High God,'" *NDIEC* 1 (1981) 28–29.
22   BAGD 342 1.b, found only here in the NT but occurring in classical sources as "either. . . or" ($\acute{\eta}\tau o\iota$ . . . $\acute{\eta}$).
23   Epictetus *Diss.* 4.1.21.
24   Käsemann, 179.

other."[25] However, the antithesis to "sin resulting in death," an association well prepared by 5:20-21 and 6:12, seems oddly worded with "to obedience resulting in righteousness." The word "obey" was associated with slavery to sin in v. 16b, and now in v. 16c with the new relationship to "righteousness." It would seem to have produced a more symmetrical parallelism to contrast "sin resulting in death" with "righteousness leading to life."[26] Since none of the explanations of this oddity in formulation is fully satisfactory,[27] it may be that one should consider the possibility of dittography in the inadvertent repetition of ὑπακοή ("obedience"). However, as Fitzmyer remarks, "the parallel is not perfectly expressed, but the sense is clear."[28] The new life in Christ requires obedience to the righteous norm of grace;[29] its structure and motivation are different from obedience to law. Yet it remains central for Paul's apostolic mission to the Gentiles to teach the "obedience of faith" (1:5), and the phrase εἰς ὑπακοήν ("for obedience") found four times in Romans (1:5; 6:16; 15:18; 16:26) occurs only one other time (1 Pet 1:2) in the entirety of Greek literature.

■ **17-18** The theme of obedience is prominently inserted into v. 17, just as in the previous verse, seemingly disturbing what would have been a neat rhetorical antithesis between the "slaves of sin" (v. 17a) being "freed from sin" and "enslaved to righteousness" (v. 18). This has led some exegetes to the conclusion that a non-Pauline gloss was inserted in v. 17b.[30] The vocabulary and thought of this possible gloss are similar to that of 16:17-20, where similar questions of heterodoxy are implied. The evidence in support of the post-Pauline provenance of 16:17-20 is adduced in the relevant chapter below. The evidence is less convincing here, but the discrepancies are problematc. There is a threefold repetition of δέ

("but"), the last two standing in illogical antithesis to v. 17b; the syntactical link is between ἐλευθερωθέντες δέ ("but having been set free") and v. 17a rather than v. 17b where it would seem more logical. Even more problematic is the tension between v. 17b and the argument in the rest of this chapter, to be discussed below. All of these irregularities would be removed if the original text lacked v. 17b. But the case is not ironclad, as Robert Gagnon has shown.[31] Although he was unable to answer the question about v. 17b's disruption of the parallelism between v. 17a and v. 18,[32] Gagnon provides a convincing translation of this difficult verse: "you obeyed from the heart the imprint stamped by teaching, to which [imprint] you were handed over."[33]

Verse 17 opens with thanksgiving to God for the liberation from slavery to sin that the Roman believers have already experienced, with χάρις δὲ τῷ θεῷ ("but thanks [be] to God") as an elliptical form of χάρις ἔστω τῷ θεῷ ("thanks be to God") such as that found in Epictetus *Diss.* 4.4.7 and in the plural form, "thanks [be] to the gods," in papyri since the third century B.C.E.[34] Since Paul employs the same elliptical form of thanksgiving in 2 Cor 2:14 and 9:15, it appears to be a conventional expression of gratitude for divine benefaction. In this instance Paul expresses thanks for the drastic change in status from when "you were slaves of this sin," with the definite article in τῆς ἁμαρτίας referring to the death-dealing sin mentioned in the preceding verse. The contrast between this new obedience and their former status that had been produced by their conversion is nicely conveyed by juxtaposing the imperfect verb ἦτε ("you were") slaves to sin with the aorist participle ἐλευθερωθέντες ("having been set free") and the aorist verb ἐδουλώθητε ("you were enslaved") to righteousness in v. 18. The syntax of ἐλευθερωθέντες . . . ἀπό ("hav-

25 Elliott, *Rhetoric of Romans*, 251.
26 Proposed by Weiss, "Beiträge," 181, noted by Käsemann, 180; Dodd, 97, refers here to an inadvertence in Paul's dictation; O'Neill, 116, proposes that ὑπακοή ("obedience") was a gloss.
27 See Käsemann, 180; Dunn, 1:342; Moo, 399.
28 Fitzmyer, 448.
29 See du Toit, "*Dikaiosyne*," 278-89.
30 Bultmann, "Glossen," 202, followed by Fuchs, *Freiheit*, 44; Tachau, *Einst*, 117; Schlier, 208-10; Furnish, *Theology*, 197-98; O'Neill, 116-17; Schmithals, 199-200; Zeller, 127-28; see the inadequate critique

by Käsemann, 181; other more recent exegetes brush aside the problem without adequate consideration.
31 Gagnon, "Heart," 667-87
32 Gagnon, "Heart," 671-72, proposes a chiasm involving vv. 17b-18, but A (v. 17b) does not really match what he conceives to be A' (v. 18c), nor does "type of teaching" in v. 17b really match "freed from sin" in v. 18a.
33 Ibid., 687.
34 BAGD 878.5, citing BDF §128.6.

ing been set free. . . from") is found only in Romans (6:22; 8:21) and alludes to being liberated by a superior force after enslavement. Pausanias employs the same language in referring to the "Corinthians, having been set free from the Macedonians (ἀπὸ Μακεδονίων ἐλευθερωθέντες),"[35] and Herodotus describes how "the Athenians were set free (ἐλευθερώθησαν) from the Tyrants."[36] Paul's expression of "enslavement to righteousness" is reminiscent of a similar sociopolitical background. Herotodus reports that "the Carians were enslaved (ἐδουλώθησαν) by Harpagus,"[37] and Josephus reports that the Israelites "were enslaved" (ἐδουλώθη, *Ant.* 11.300) by the Persians. In the highly politicized context of Rome, where military conquest was so crucial a provider of slaves and victims for theaters, this language was unmistakable. So with the elimination of the possible interpolation, the two verses would read as follows:

17/ But thanks be to God that you were slaves of this sin,
  18/ but having been freed from the sin,
    you were enslaved to righteousness.

The syntax is still not completely satisfactory, because there is no temporal adverb or conjunction in v. 17a to mark the contrast between v. 17a and v. 18 more clearly. A μέν ("on the one hand") in v. 17a to match the δέ ("on the other hand") in v. 18a would be most suitable, but there is no evidence in the textual history that it ever was part of v. 17. The consequence is that v. 17 initially sounds as if Paul were thanking God that the Roman Christians had previously been slaves of sin, whereas the obvious intent is to praise God for freedom

from sin and the new enslavement to righteousness. This discrepancy reduces the likelihood of the hypothesis of a gloss in v. 17b.

The possible gloss of v. 17b refers to converts obeying ἐκ καρδίας ("from heart"), an expression found elsewhere only in 1 Pet 1:22 and 1 Tim 1:5, referring in a typically Judaic manner to the whole person engaged without reservation in obedience.[38] Nowhere else does Paul employ "heart" in connection with belief or obedience, nor does he ever employ it anarthrously following a preposition in this manner. It is significant, however, that the theme of "heart" is prominent in the interpolation of chap. 16, which castigates heretics who "deceive the hearts of the simple," thus implying that sincere belief does not suffice, because it can so easily be misled by false leaders with malicious intent (16:18).

To whom or what the obedience of believers should be directed remains a matter of controversy, with most commentators taking εἰς ὃν παρεδόθητε τύπον διδαχῆς as "to the type of teaching to which you were given."[39] James D. G. Dunn argues on theological grounds that Christ is the "type" or "pattern" for Paul, from whom teaching is derived, so he offers the translation, "to the pattern of teaching to whom you were handed over."[40] This is an appealing reading, although on grammatical grounds it seems difficult to avoid attaching the accusative singular ὄν ("to which or whom") to the accusative singular masculine word, τύπον ("type").[41] The word τύπος itself has plausibly been explained by Gagnon[42] as the imprint made on the mind by divine teaching, such as Philo's idea that Moses "stamped upon their minds as with a seal deep imprints of understanding (βαθεῖς τύπους ταῖς διανοίαις),"[43] and that at creation, "the invisible deity stamped on the

---

35 Pausanius *Graec. descr.* 7.9.3.
36 Herodotus *Hist.* 5.62.4.
37 Ibid. 1.174.2.
38 See Jewett, *Terms*, 60, where I expressed an unwarranted skepticism about Bultmann's suggestion of a gloss; Fitzmyer, 449; Alexander Sand, "καρδία," *EDNT* 2 (1991) 250, misses the nuance of wholehearted sincerity in the expression "from heart" in his comment that καρδία is the "place" where persons encounter God.
39 Meyer, 1:305; Godet, 256, following Tholuck, De Wette, and Philippi; see also Zahn, Kuss, 2.388; Cranfield, 1:320; Fitzmyer, 450; Moo, 396.
40 Dunn, 1:343–44; Wilckens, 2:36–37, weighs the patristic evidence that might support this possibility, but retains the traditional translation of believers being delivered to the doctrinal instruction, with the theological suggestion that such teaching contains "its original reality in the person of the resurrected one."
41 See the additional grammatical problems in the Dunn reading pointed out by Gagnon, "Heart," 676–77.
42 Gagnon, "Heart," 682–87.
43 Philo *Spec.* 1.5.30; see also Plato *Resp.* 677b; *Leg.* 681b.

invisible soul the imprints of itself ($\tau o \dot{\nu} \varsigma \; \dot{\epsilon} \alpha \upsilon \tau \hat{\eta} \varsigma \; \tau \dot{\upsilon} \pi o \upsilon \varsigma$)."[44] These parallels, however, do not indicate proximity to Pauline teaching. The interpolation of Rom 16 also refers to "teaching that you learned," which the heretics are now disturbing, a formulation that is widely recognized to be the closest parallel to the formulation in v. 17b.[45] It seems clear that both in v. 17b and 16:17, $\delta\iota\delta\alpha\chi\dot{\eta}$ refers to "firmly established . . . definite traditions of faith that one is to learn."[46] Not only "learn"— one should add—but also subordinate oneself in an absolute manner. The context of slavery, within which this possible gloss was placed, strongly suggests that $\pi\alpha\rho\alpha\delta\dot{o}\vartheta\eta\tau\epsilon$ ("you were handed over") means that believers are absolutely bound by this teaching, subject to it as slaves to their master.[47]

When the full implications of v. 17b in its context are weighed, its disparity from Paul's line of argument as well as from the situation in Rome becomes more pronounced. This pericope warns against returning to the former state of slavery to sin by showing that there are only two alternatives available: slavery to sin or to Christ. The issue of specific doctrinal instruction is not only extraneous but also adds another criterion, that is, whether persons or groups are conforming to a certain set of teachings. This criterion is consciously avoided throughout the theological argument of Romans, because the Weak and the Strong are divided in their teachings about worship and ethics, reflecting the various forms of apostolic preaching that formed the earliest congregations in Rome.[48] Paul seeks to make a case that will unite them, which is why he concentrates on their common experience of a new life in Christ, and their common experience of slavery in sin prior to the conversion. Thus, v. 18 concludes with the theme of being

enslaved to righteousness, which is personalized as a power of God in Christ[49] that sets all persons and groups right before God and provides a new basis for their unity beyond cultural and theological conformity.

In conclusion, although I recognize that the case remains somewhat ambiguous, it seems likely to me that v. 17b was not originally drafted by Paul but was added later by the authors of the interpolation in 16:17-20. It is therefore printed in the translation above with double brackets.

■ **19** The raw political and social background of Paul's references to enslavement and liberation lead to his apology of speaking about holy realities in such terms.[50] Enslavement either through voluntary decision or through military conquest was an unhappy topic to those who had experienced it, or had to face its aftermath, as many in the Roman house and tenement churches had certainly done.[51] To speak "in human terms" is to take frailty and suffering into account, as the use of this term by Epictetus suggests:

Someone else's child or wife has died. But there's no one who might say, "It's only human!" ($o\dot{\upsilon}\delta\epsilon\dot{\iota}\varsigma \; \dot{\epsilon}\sigma\tau\iota\nu \; \ddot{o}\varsigma \; o\dot{\upsilon}\kappa \; \ddot{\alpha}\nu \; \epsilon\ddot{\iota}\pi o\iota \; \ddot{o}\tau\iota, \; "\dot{\alpha}\nu\vartheta\rho\dot{\omega}\pi\iota\nu o\nu.")$ But whenever one's own dies, immediately, "Woe is me—wretched man am I."[52]

Plato also speaks of "holding in low esteem human weakness ($\tau\dot{\eta}\nu \; \dot{\alpha}\nu\vartheta\rho\omega\pi\dot{\iota}\nu\eta\nu \; \dot{\alpha}\sigma\vartheta\dot{\epsilon}\nu\iota\alpha\nu \; \dot{\alpha}\tau\iota\mu\dot{\alpha}\zeta\omega\nu$)."[53] There may also have been Jewish parallels to this statement, but the available evidence comes from a much later period.[54] The word $\sigma\dot{\alpha}\rho\xi$ ("flesh") appears to be used here to depict a "merely worldly" understanding of reality.[55] Although the apology was probably necessary, and

---

44 Philo *Det.* 24.86.

45 See Meyer, 1:304; Kühl, 219; Cranfield, 1:324; Fitzmyer, 450.

46 Hans-Friedrich Weiss, "$\delta\iota\delta\alpha\chi\dot{\eta}$," *EDNT* 1 (1990) 20.

47 Moo, 401: "becoming a Christian means being placed under the authority of Christian 'teaching. . . .'" See also Schreiner, 335–36.

48 Meyer, 1:303, appears to be alone among exegetes in recognizing that various "distinct expressions" of the gospel had been influential in forming the Roman congregations, and that this needs to be weighed in deciding how the expression "type of teaching" should be understood.

49 See du Toit, "*Dikaiosyne*," 276–77.

50 See Gale, *Analogy*, 182–89; Tobin, *Paul's Rhetoric*, 209; Esler, *Paul's Rhetoric*, 209.

51 Schottroff, "Schreckensherrschaft," 510, properly insists that the social reality of slavery in its various forms needs to be taken into account in interpreting this passage.

52 Epictetus *Ench.* 26.1.8.

53 Plato *Phaedr.* 107b1.

54 See Bjerkelund, "Nach menschlicher Weise," 68–81, 99–100; see also Fitzmyer, 451.

55 Alexander Sand, "$\sigma\dot{\alpha}\rho\xi$," *EDNT* 3 (1993) 231; Lietzmann, 71; Barrett, 132; see also Jewett, *Terms*,

similar apologies are found in Rom 1:11; 3:5; 1 Cor 9:8; and Gal 3:15, only here is the blame, in effect, placed on the audience. The reference to the limitations of the flesh could hardly have been taken as honoring the spiritual and intellectual acumen of the churches in Rome.[56] If "flesh" implied a warning against backsliding,[57] or an indication of the inadequate faith of Gentile believers,[58] the insult to the congregation would be even more severe. In several regards, the tone of his more polite formulation of 1:11 would have been preferable.

Like a bull in a china closet, Paul rushes ahead to compound his rhetorical problem by reiterating his argument in such a manner as to imply that the former corruption of believers in Rome was responsible for this alleged failure to understand.[59] He connects his reiteration with the foregoing by ὥσπερ γάρ ("for just as"), making clear that the material in v. 19b-c explains why Paul had to speak in "human terms." In a syllogism employing a "no-less-than" scheme, Paul returns to the language of "yielding your members as slaves (παρεστήσατε τὰ μέλη ὑμῶν δοῦλα)" as employed in vv. 12, 13, 16, to describe the preconversion state of the Roman believers in a thoroughly pagan manner. Although ἀκαθαρσία ("impurity") was used by Greco-Roman writers to depict dirtiness, ceremonial impurity, or depravity,[60] its use in Rom 1:24 and its frequent employment in Jewish critiques of Gentile behavior[61]

lend support to Friedrich Hauck's assessment that "Paul adopts ἀκαθαρσία from Judaism as a general description of the absolute alienation from God in which heathenism finds itself."[62] It included ritual as well as ethical impurity, as revealed in the section of 2 Corinthians rejecting believers being joined with unbelievers (2 Cor 6:14–7:1). The use of the expression ἀνομία εἰς ἀνομίαν ("lawlessness resulting in lawlessness") to describe the prior behavior of the Roman converts also reflects typical Hellenistic Jewish critiques of paganism.[63] The word ἀνομία can be used to indicate a lawless state or the product of lawlessness,[64] both of which may be present in the expression Paul uses here.[65] In Conf. 108, for example, Philo describes "mob-rule, which takes inequality for its ideal, and in it wrongdoing and lawlessness are dominant (ἐν ᾗ ἀδικία καὶ ἀνομία καταδυναστεύουσιν)." In Acts 2:23 and 1 Cor 9:21, "lawless" is employed to depict the characteristic behavior of Gentiles. Philo refers to the "the old lawlessness" (παλαιὰν ἀνομίαν) of Israel that the scapegoat cleanses on the Day of Atonement (Spec. 1.188). Walter Gutbrod explains, in Rom 6:19 "ἀνομία for the individual act is found along with ἀνομία for the general condition which is the result of such acts."[66] Thus, Fitzmyer apropriately translates, "iniquity which led to anarchy."[67]

In v. 19c, Paul carries through with the no-less-than figure that began with ὥσπερ γάρ ("for just as") and

---

154–55, where the proto-Gnostic implications are lifted up, in that the physical nature of the flesh appears to prevent understanding of spiritual matters.

56 Hagen, "Deutero-Pauline Glosses," 366, would resolve this dilemma by excising v. 19 as an interpolation, but the basis for such excision is not convincing.

57 Kühl, 220.

58 Kaye, Chapter 6, 28; similarly Engberg-Pedersen, Stoics, 235–386, interprets v. 19a as suggesting that the congregation members need "a little reminding" (236; italics in original) about their former enslavement to selfishness and the requirement to internalize the proper orientation to God.

59 Käsemann, 182, places a theological spin on this statement, that "the flesh desires autonomy and thus rejects the idea of slavery as too much to demand," which may touch modern ethical issues but is hard to correlate with anything we know about the Roman house and tenement churches.

60 See Hippocrates Morb. 6.3.1; Demosthenes Orat. 21.19.4; Dionysius Halicarnassus Antiq. Rom. 19.5.2.

61 E.g., Ep. Arist. 166 describes Gentiles as "unclean"; see also 3 Macc 2:17 and Philo Leg. 2.29.

62 Friedrich Hauck, with Rudolf Meyer, "καθαρός κτλ.," TDNT 3 (1965) 428; see also Hartwig Thyen, "καθαρός κτλ.," EDNT 2 (1991) 220. See also Kühl, 221; Fitzmyer, 451, comments that impurity and lawlessness "may seem to be typically pagan vices, but Qumran Essenes repudiated the same in their Jewish confrères (1 QS 3:5; 4:10, 23–24)."

63 See particularly Dunn, 1:346–47.

64 BAGD (2000) 85.

65 Käsemann, 184; See Alexander Sand, "Die Polemik gegen 'Gesetzlosigkeit' im Evangelium nach Matthäus und bei Paulus," BZ 14 (1970) 122.

66 Walter Gutbrod, with Hermann Kleinknecht, "νόμος κτλ.," TDNT 4 (1967) 1085.

67 Fitzmyer, 451; the translation of ἀνομία as anarchy also seems appropriate for Pisias's criticism of self-

now continues with οὕτως νῦν ("so now"). The past tense verb in v. 19b stands in contrast with the "now" of v. 19c.[68] The logic of the syllogism is that if v. 19b is true, what is claimed in v. 19c is equally true. With impressive symmetry Paul employs the same expression, "yield your enslaved members," but this time τῇ δικαιο-σύνῃ εἰς ἁγιασμόν ("to righteousness resulting in sanc-tification"). The antithesis anticipated since v. 16 is now articulated, and it is interesting to observe that the matter of obedience is no longer in view. The striking metaphor developed in v. 13c, that one's bodily parts should serve as weapons of righteousness, surfaces again. To be a slave of righteousness is to use one's human energies for the sake of the new creation, the body of Christ in which the new age is being embodied in the world. The new form of community created and sustained by the crucified one is the location where most of this energy is to be expended, if the rest of the clues throughout the letter are followed. New forms of hospitality and philanthropy are called for, along with a more generous form of group interaction than was typi-cal for the competitive Greco-Roman and Jewish envi-ronments. An ethic of genuine love, spelled out later in 12:9-21, provides the guideline for this new type of righ-teousness. The consequence of such righteous slavery is ἁγιασμός ("sanctification")," which appears here for the first time in Romans. Although it is ordinarily inter-preted as an individual virtue,[69] the second person plural imperatives throughout this pericope point to a new form of social life as the primary embodiment of holiness.[70] Paul views the church as the new, holy temple of God (1 Cor 3:16-17), filled and directed by the Holy Spirit (Rom 5:5; 14:17; 15:13; 2 Cor 13:14), and called upon to exhibit holiness in its social relations (Rom 12:1; 1 Thess 4:3). He had addressed the Corinthian church as "those sanctified in Christ Jesus, called to be saints together with all those who in every place call on the name of our Lord Jesus Christ" (1 Cor 1:2). In Horst Balz's words, "God's gift of holiness becomes reality in the whole, new people of God, which is the holy temple (1 Cor 3:17), and in mutual διακονία (Rom 15:25, 31), κοινωνία (1 Cor 12:13), and ἀγάπη (Eph 1:15)."[71]

■ **20** This verse has an explanatory function, as indi-cated by γάρ ("for"), but precisely what is explained remains a matter of dispute. Meyer sees this verse as pro-viding a rationale for the discourse in vv. 21-22, explain-ing the tragic fact that slaves of sin remain "independent" of the demands of righteousness.[72] Mur-ray and Cranfield suggest that v. 20 explains v. 19 as well as vv. 21-22,[73] while Moo contends that "for" introduces vv. 20-23 as "the ground of the command in v. 19b."[74] That "for" introduces subsequent material, particularly when the following verse contains οὖν ("consequently"), seems quite unlikely. Kuss seems more justified in taking v. 20 to explain v. 19b-c, with ἐλεύθεροι ("liberated, free") having an ironic tone compared with the matter of liberation from sin in v. 18.[75] To be liberated "with respect to righteousness"[76] is to be free for anything but life itself; to live under the bondage of sin is to experi-ence an abstract kind of freedom that disallows a rela-tionship with the only thing that matters, the righteousness of God.[77] This verse therefore posits two

government leading εἰς ἀνομία, as reported by Plutarch *Amat.* 755B ll.

68 See Tachau, *Einst,* 119–20; Neuhäusler, "Entschei-dende Augenblick," 9–11.

69 Godet, 259, describes the nineteenth-century con-sensus that holiness is "the progressive amelioration of the individual resulting from his moral self-disci-pline," and he prefers an emphasis on the divine gift of "an inward disposition" of holiness. Cran-field, 1:327: holiness "denotes God's work in the believer, his ethical renewal." Horst Balz, "ἅγιος κτλ.," *EDNT* 1 (1990) 20, largely continues the indi-vidualistic tradition by describing "the holiness of those who believe . . . the sanctification of their lives (Rom 6:19, 22)."

70 See Wilckens, 2:39.

71 Balz, "ἅγιος κτλ.," 20.

72 Meyer, 1:308–9.

73 Murray, 234; Cranfield, 1:327.

74 Moo, 405.

75 Schlier, 212; Kuss, 2:392; similarly Godet, 260, understands v. 20 to provide an explanation of the degrading state of unbelievers described in v. 19b.

76 The dative expression is of respect, following BDF §197; Moule, *Idiom Book,* 46; Dunn, 1:347; Moo, 406.

77 See Wilckens, 2:39; Moo, 405–6; Jones, *Freiheit,* 113–14.

contrary forms of freedom, freedom from sin, which is at the same time a life under the constraint of righteousness, and freedom from righteousness itself, which is inevitably caught in the bondage to sin and destined for death. In a daring move, Paul implicitly places the various forms of freedom touted in his time—the Cynics' escape from societal conventions, the Stoics' self-sufficiency under all circumstances, the citizens' access to the privileges of empire, and the zealots' release from compulsion under Rome and concomitant right to enforce the rules of holiness—under the rubric of "freedom with respect to righteousness." These other forms of freedom rely on compulsion against others, even enslaving others while retaining claims of superior virtue that counter the righteousness that Christ inaugurates; they maintain the competition for honor and superior status for oneself and one's group that corrupts all relationships and sustains social conflict. In Kurt Niederwimmer's words, to be "liberated from the tyranny of sin's power . . . as well as from the concealed fallenness and self-alienation under which all achievement-oriented piety stands" is the only form of freedom that is consistent with righteousness.[78]

■ **21** The final dialogical exchange in this pericope opens with τίνα οὖν καρπόν ("consequently what fruit?"), whereby the particle οὖν[79] introduces the consequence of the preconversion status of freedom from righteousness. The punctuation of this verse, following Theodore of Mopsuestia and the Nestle-Aland, UBS printings, places a question mark after "then" and understands the subsequent line (v. 21b) as Paul's answer.[80] The alternative punctuation follows the Vulgate and takes vv. 21a-b as the question, evoking the audience's negative response and Paul's comment in v. 21c.[81] This allows "fruit" to have the positive meaning it usually con-

tains in the Pauline letters,[82] but, as Godet observes, it removes the vivacity from the diatribe and creates a lumbering question with v. 21a-b; the alternate punctuation disguises the neat contrast between the fruit of freedom from righteousness in v. 21a and the fruit of freedom from sin in v. 22 and creates a grammatical problem, since v. 21a provides no proper antecedent for the dative plural, ἐφ᾽ οἷς ("things of which").[83] It is also more natural to place the "then" of v. 21a in a separate sentence from the "now" of v. 21b. A third alternative of reading v. 21 is proposed by Jeffrey Reed, that τίνα, ordinarily punctuated as an interrogative pronoun, should be read as an enclitic, indefinite pronoun, τινα, modifying "fruit." This would result in the translation, "consequently, you were having a certain kind of fruit of which you are now ashamed. . . ."[84] However, the placement of τίνα οὖν at the beginning of the sentence points toward understanding it as an interrogative pronoun.[85]

The word καρπός ("fruit") is frequently used in philosophical and moral discourse as well as in the LXX to refer to the result or gain from actions, whether good or ill.[86] For example, Marcus Aurelius Τὰ εἰς ἑαυτὸν 9.10.1 explains that nature "bears fruit (φέρει καρπὸν)—even man and God and the cosmos too!" Philo's *Fug.* 176 uses fruit in a figurative fashion to represent virtue: "vineyards and olive orchards represent progress and growth and the yield of fruits; and the fruit of knowledge (καρπὸς δ᾽ ἐπιστήμης) is the life of contemplation." In Jer 17:10, Yahweh promises "to give to everyone according to his ways, and according to the fruits (κατὰ τοὺς καρπούς) of his endeavors." This figurative use predominates in the NT, as reflected in this verse.[87] As Godet points out, the verbs φέρειν ("bear") and ποιεῖν ("make") would ordinarily be expected with "fruit," but Paul employs the imperfect form of "you

78 Kurt Niederwimmer, "ἐλεύθερος κτλ.," *EDNT* 1 (1990) 433.
79 See BAGD 593.1c.
80 See Kuss, 2:392–93; Cranfield, 1:328; Moo, 406–7.
81 According to Kuss, 2:393, this punctuation was advocated by Bardenhewer, Bengel, Gutjahr, Kürzinger, Sanday and Headlam, 169–70; recent advocates include Schreiner, 339.
82 See Hans-Theo Wrege, "καρπός, ἄκαρπος," *EDNT* 2 (1991) 252.
83 Godet, 260; see also Moo, 407.
84 Jeffrey T. Reed, "Indicative and Imperative in Rom

6,21-22: The Rhetoric of Punctuation," *Bib* 74 (1993) 251, 256.
85 See BDF §298 for τίς as an interrogative pronoun.
86 Friedrich Hauck, "καρπός κτλ.," *TDNT* 3 (1965) 614.
87 Wrege, "καρπός, ἄκαρπος," 251.

(pl.) have"[88] to indicate that they "possess and keep" such fruit as part of their lives, "that they drag it with them as forming part of their own moral life."[89] The adverb τότε ("then, at that time") makes clear that the question relates to the former life of the Roman converts, when their entire existence was determined by enslavement to sin. This is not a threatening question for this congregation of first-generation converts, who knew full well the dismal shape of their former lives and, if they were similar to contemporary converts, would have been happy to admit the sordid details because of their tremendous sense of liberation therefrom.

Paul's answer to the question refers to "things of which you are now ashamed," taking ἐφ᾽ οἷς, literally "things of which," to function as the object of the verb ἐπαισχύνεσθε ("you are ashamed"). The placement of νῦν ("now") before the verb makes clear that the current attitude of converts toward their former behavior is in view.[90] The usual interpretation is that conversion results in a sensitized conscience and an awareness of universal depravity; it is ordinarily thought to be the product of ethical instruction.[91] The underlying dynamic, however, has to do with the deeper issue of shameful status. When society treats persons as nobodies—and this was the status of most of the Roman converts—they naturally treat others with the same cruelty and contempt. As "weapons of wrongdoing" wielded by evil forces (6:13), they had injured, dominated, and exploited others without compunction. If their lives were worthless, then the lives of others were also worthless, and no empathy was required. The only semblance of honor left was to follow commands related to being "weapons of wrongdoing" without compunction. This entire heartless system, which Paul in an earlier letter had described as "devouring one another" (Gal 5:15), was overcome by the gospel of Christ's death in behalf of the lowly, of divine grace thereby expressed that honors each person in equal measure. Receiving the gospel meant accepting the message that Christ died for oneself

and one's group, but also for all others as well, and thus that each now has immeasurable value. As this is internalized, converts begin to realize that if their lives are valuable in God's sight, so are the lives of other humans whom they had routinely and heartlessly mistreated. They begin to grasp the true dimension of their former behavior as "weapons of wrongdoing"; deeds that had seemed natural, that expressed the will of superiors, and that were widely accepted socially are now seen to have injured others and thus to have violated the ethos created by the cross of Christ. It was not through the preaching of a new law, but through the healing of their shameful sense of nothingness that such converts gained the capacity to become ashamed of their former behavior. Although the same verb ἐπαισχύνομαι ("be ashamed") is employed here as in the thesis of 1:16,[92] this provides the obverse side of the powerful dynamic of shame in early Christianity: the shameful gospel, of which Paul declared himself not to be ashamed, is capable of evoking new, responsible forms of shame in those who receive it.

In v. 21c, Paul provides a reason for the newly awakened feeling of shame on the part of converts, "for the outcome of those things is death." The word τέλος is used here to refer to "the result emerging necessarily from a certain manner of existence,"[93] which is usually taken to be eschatological wrath.[94] But this hardly explains the phenomenon of shame now felt for former deeds.[95] Since the reign of death has frequently been mentioned in preceding pericopes (5:14, 17, 21; 6:16), it seems more natural to understand v. 21c as describing the awareness of the converted that their former deeds were part and parcel of Adam's legacy, compounding its effect by serving as instruments of wrongdoing. They now know that they had willingly participated in the culture of death, which in many ways had reached its apex in Rome's glorifying of its violent history, in the brutal duels and executions in the public theaters and arenas sponsored by patrons to honor Rome's superiority, and

---

88   Contemporary commentators appear always to translate this as an aorist verb, with the simple past tense, "did you have," because the imperfect of "to have" is awkward in English.
89   Godet, 260.
90   See Neuhäusler, "Entscheidende Augenblick," 8–9.
91   Moo, 406, citing Calvin.

92   See Axel Horstmann, "αἰσχύνομαι," *EDNT* 1 (1990) 42.
93   Hans Hübner, "τέλος," *EDNT* 3 (1993) 348.
94   Dunn, 1:348; Moo, 407.
95   See Murray, 236; Schlier, 212.

in the vicious policies of military expansion, occupation, and economic exploitation. The gospel of Christ crucified exposes the culture of death and leads to a shaming awareness of universal complicity in its enactment.

■ **22** In a rhetorically impressive antithesis that opens with the eschatological νυνὶ δέ ("but now") as in 3:21, [96] Paul sets forth the exchange of lordship that the converts in Rome have experienced. In contrast to the "then" of v. 21 when sin's terrible reign produced its shameful fruit, the eschatological present[97] is now at hand, in which liberation from sin has been achieved and is being experienced in a new kind of fruitfulness. As Cranfield points out, the temporal designation should be attached to the finite verb "you have fruit" rather than to the participles "set free" and "become slaves."[98] The present tense of the verb ἔχετε ("you have") stands in contrast to the imperfect εἴχετε ("you were having") in v. 21, with reference to the shameful fruit of sin.[99] In v. 22 Paul employs the aorist passive participle, ἐλευθερωθέντες ("having been set free"), just as in 6:18 to designate the divine provenance of this liberation, a point further enhanced by the replacement of "slaves to righteousness" in 6:18 by "slaves to God" in this verse.[100] As Dunn observes, this replacement confirms that "for Paul δικαιοσύνη is essentially the self-manifestation of God in effective power to reclaim and support his sinful people and fallen creation."[101] To be a slave of God is to be bound to divine righteousness or, in the metaphor developed in 6:13, to become a "weapon of righteousness." The result of this new status that resulted from the believers' response to the gospel is that "you have your fruit resulting in sanctification." Again Paul employs the verb "you have" (ἔχετε) rather than "bear" or "make," indicating how integral a role the new "fruit" plays in their new group identity. In fact, Paul goes further to identify this as τὸν καρπὸν ὑμῶν ("your fruit"), in contrast to the deadly fruit produced

under their slavery to sin. Commentators balk at the present tense of this verb on grounds that it fails to preserve the tension between the "already" and "not yet" of Christian life,[102] and they usually do not provide an explanation for the second person plural pronoun used in this sentence.[103] Despite Paul's idea that God's Spirit works within believers (Rom 8:28) and his consistent claim that humans are not set right by their works, he continues to display an interest in human work, the fruits of which define who one is. With regard to his own labors, for example, Paul contends in 1 Cor 3:13-14:

> each person's work will become manifest; for the Day will disclose it, because it will be revealed with fire; the fire will test what sort of work each one has done. If the work which any person has built on the foundation survives, he will receive a reward. If any one's work is burned up, he will suffer loss, though he himself will be saved, but only as through fire.

The issue here is one of accountability and personal identity: although believers are not saved by the quality of the fruit they produce, they are defined thereby, and their work will be evaluated at the end of time. Although their work no longer earns honor or status and is now performed out of a sense of gratitude and vocation, its fruit remains a matter for accountability.

The assurance in this verse is that the fruit of one's work as a weapon of righteousness will result in "sanctification," a term that, as we noted with regard to v. 19, had primarily a social connotation related to the new community of faith. This is a stunning claim, that the fruit of human work will result in communal holiness. The background of the OT concept of holiness provides a key to understanding this verse. Johannes Pedersen defined holiness as "the force on which life depended and from which it was renewed,"[104] derived ultimately

---

96   See Walter Radl, "νῦν, νυνί," *EDNT* 2 (1991) 480; Käsemann, 185; Dunn, 1:348.

97   See Luz, *Geschichtsverständnis*, 88; Radl, "νῦν," 480; Neuhäusler, "Entscheidende Augenblick," 1–16; Nissiotis, "νῦν," 302–9.

98   Cranfield, 1:328.

99   That ἔχετε should be read as an imperative, as proposed by Reed, "Indicative," 255–56, seems implausible in view of the word order; in the imperative,

the verb would normally be placed at or close to the beginning of the sentence; see BDF §387.

100 See Cranfield, 1:328.

101 Dunn, 1:348.

102 See ibid..

103 If anything, there is a tendency to reject any idea that human activity produces holiness; see, e.g., Wilckens, 2:39–40.

104 Pedersen, *Israel III-IV*, 295.

from Yahweh, the God of holiness. "What is holy has its value in itself by virtue of its sovereign power," Pedersen goes on to argue. "But it is not immutable; holiness can be acquired and lost, just as it can deteriorate and be renewed. If all holiness vanished, life would perish because the blessing draws its nourishment from holiness. But it is in man's power to contribute to the renewal of holiness."[105] In Israel's life, the cult was the primary avenue of achieving such renewal. In place of the holy priesthood and the holy temple, the NT views the converted community as the new locus of holiness. As we have seen, Paul refers to the members of the new community as "the saints" and understands their being made righteous in terms of access to divine holiness. The "Holy Spirit" now dwells in the new community as well as in each believer, without distinction of rank or status. As Robert Hodgson has shown, holiness defines the group identity of the new movement, ensures its boundaries against outsiders, and explains the vitality that the community experiences.[106] In view of the OT precedents, this vitality includes a sense of wholeness, material and spiritual well-being, moral uprightness, harmonious relationships, and some form of fecundity.[107] As members contribute to the community's common life—economically and spiritually—the fruit of their labor is holiness in this broader sense of the term.[108] Holiness is certainly not to be reduced, as in modern thought forms, to moralistic strictures.

In contrast to the deadly outcome of slavery to sin, Paul describes the final τέλος ("outcome, result")[109] of slavery to God as "eternal life." Just as in 2:7 and 5:21, ζωὴ αἰώνιος refers to life after death, which has an unending horizon. This expression appears frequently in the Johannine literature, and there are four occurrences in Romans and one in Galatians, not counting the references in the interpolated Rom 16:25-27. The connota-

tion of "life eternal" here and in the next and final verse of this pericope is fullness of existence for the saints in the present that continues on into the future.[110] This reaches beyond the matters of holiness as the fruit of one's labors in the here and now. To refer again to Paul's discussion in 1 Cor 3, each person's work will be tested on the day of judgment, but even if it falls short, divine grace will bring the faithful into the blessed life: the saints will be "saved" in the eschatological sense, "but only as through fire" (1 Cor 3:15). This τέλος ("end, outcome") lies beyond the scope of human effort, remaining entirely in the hands of the gracious God who liberates her beloved children from the power of sin and death. It is on the theme of this promised gift that the pericope closes.

■ 23 In a memorable formulation that concludes the pericope, Paul sets off the antithesis between the realms of sin and grace. He uses the slang term ὀψώνιον, which originally referred to buying cooked fish and was popularized by military usage to refer to wages or rations given as remuneration for services performed.[111] For example, Polybius Hist. 4.60.20 reports, "The Achaeans proved negligent in the payment of their wages to the mercenaries," and 1 Macc 3:28 reports that "Antiochus opened his treasury and distributed wages (ὀψώνια) for a year to the soldiers." In the familiar words of John the Baptist, soldiers are exhorted "to be content with your wages" (τοῖς ὀψωνίοις ὑμῶν, Luke 3:14). The word came to be used more broadly for the regular remuneration of teachers, officials, secretaries, guardians, musicians, farmers, workmen, and even slaves.[112] Since other Pauline usages (1 Cor 9:7; 2 Cor 11:8) reflect both the general sense of remuneration and the more specialized sense of a soldier's wage, it is unwise to assume that Paul is picturing sin "as a commanding general paying a wage to its 'soldiers.'"[113] The metaphor is of sin, which had ear-

105 Ibid., 299.
106 Robert Hodgson, Jr., "The Social Setting of Holiness in Intertestamental Judaism and Early Christianity," in S. Burgess, ed., Reaching Beyond: Studies in the History of Perfectionism (Peabody: Hendrickson, 1986) 65–91; see also idem, "Holiness (NT)," ABD 3 (1992) 249–54; Michael Lattke, "Heiligkeit. III. Neues Testament," TRE 14 (1985) 703–8.
107 See Pedersen, Israel I-II, 182–212.
108 See Jülicher, 267–68, as discussed by Kühl, 221.
109 See Hans Hübner, "τέλος," EDNT 3 (1993) 348.
110 Horst Balz, "αἰώνιος," EDNT 1 (1990) 47.
111 Ceslas Spicq, "ὀψώνιον," TLNT 2 (1994) 600–601; Hans Wolfgang Heidland, "ὀψώνιον," TDNT 5 (1967) 591–92.
112 See Spicq, "ὀψώνιον," 602; Cranfield, 1:329; A. L. Connolly, "A Troublesome Worker," NDIEC 4 (1987) 95–99.
113 Moo, 408; see also Käsemann, 185; Wilckens, 2:40.

lier appeared as a slavemaster or ruler, providing remuneration to its underlings in the form of death. While the ὀψώνιον in ordinary usage provided sustenance for life, this wage provides its opposite—death.[114] Since wages are paid in increments as well as at the end of a task, the death that Paul has in mind is a present reality that will extend into the future. The most striking feature of this sentence, however, is the contrast between ὀψώνιον and the χάρισμα τοῦ θεοῦ ("free gift of God").[115] Whereas the remuneration is paid in return for services rendered, the χάρισμα is a sheer gift provided to those who have performed no service at all, to those in fact who have made themselves God's enemies. The gift could be related to the *donativum* ("donation") given by the "largess" of a regent, often at the time of his ascension to power.[116] It could also be possible to think of this as the gift provided by a victorious general to his soldiers after a great victory.[117] But in view of the way χάρισμα was used earlier in the letter to depict the gift of unmerited love granted through Christ to "the many" who deserve nothing (Rom 5:15-16),[118] it is better to define this as Paul and early Christians would. They perceived the death and resurrection of Christ as granting shamefully undeserving people the gift of salvation as well as specific gifts of God's mercy and calling into his gratifying service.[119] In Paul's view, these gifts were granted without regard to whether or not one has fulfilled the requirements of the law.[120] In Rom 4:4, this was connected to the matter of wages in a manner that provides the premise for 6:23: "to one who works, his wages are not reckoned as a gift but as his due."[121] In contrast to earning death as a result of enslavement to sin, therefore, Paul counterposes the "free gift of God," which is "life eternal." In his view there is nothing whatsoever that anyone can do to deserve such a gift; life eternal is the very opposite of the death the children of Adam have earned. This antithesis strikes at the heart of much of the religious motivation in Paul's time. That life eternal could be assured by proper initiation into the mysteries or by faithful observance of the law was a commonplace assumption. The latter is illustrated, for example, by the Jewish mother in 4 Macc 15:3 who held to the law despite the threat to her seven sons, and thus whose faithfulness "according to God saves to life eternal (σώζουσαν εἰς αἰώνιον ζωὴν κατὰ Θεόν)."[122] In the *Psalms of Solomon,* the righteous "will rise to eternal life" (3.16) while sinners are doomed to "eternal destruction" (3.13).[123] *Second Baruch* promises that "the righteous will be freed from the limitations of this age and transformed into glory like the stars and the angels with whom they will inherit paradise in the age to come," while the wicked will face eternal torment.[124] This entire system of religious debits and credits is left behind with Paul's dramatic formulation.

The final *clausula* reiterates the theme of sheer grace, because life eternal is defined as being "in Christ Jesus our Lord." To be ἐν Χριστῷ ("in Christ") is to reside in the realm where grace rules,[125] where Christ the slave (Phil 2:7) functions as Lord of all, and thus where the ordinary rules of honor and accomplishment, of wages and recompense, are no longer in effect. The church resides in this realm in the present, which accounts for its revolutionary social structure, where the first are last, and the last are first—where the greatest is servant of all. This social embodiment is perceived to be a proleptic expression of "life eternal," when the old age is at an end, the powers of darkness and death are finally dispelled, and the new relationship between believers and Christ is unimpeded by adverse circumstances. This realm of eternal life, however, has the same structure as

114 Heidland, "ὀψώνιον," 592.
115 See Schütz, "Charisma," 689.
116 Spicq, "ὀψώνιον," 603; see also Heidland, "ὀψώνιον," 592; Dunn, 1:349; Moo, 408.
117 This alternative is rejected by Kuss, 2:394, who argues that χάρισμα is employed here in its usual Pauline sense of an unmerited, divine gift; see also Klaus Berger, "χάρισμα," *EDNT* 3 (1993) 461.
118 See Schlier, 213.
119 Wobbe, *Charis-Gedanke,* 63–74.
120 See Doughty, "Piority," 174–75.

121 Berger, "χάρισμα," 461.
122 See George W. E. Nickelsburg, "Resurrection (Early Judaism and Christianity)," *ABD* 5 (1992) 686: "eternal life is God's reward for obedience" in 4 Maccabees. See also *T. Ash.* 5.2.
123 See also *Pss. Sol.* 13.9-10; also Nickelsburg, "Resurrection," 687.
124 Nickelsburg, "Resurrection," 687; see *2 Bar.* 30.1-5; 44.14-15; 49–52.
125 Bouttier, *En Christ,* 132–33.

the current life in Christ: it is dominated by grace rather than law; it equalizes the honor of all its participants, who stand in equal closeness to their Lord; and it demonstrates the freedom of those who no longer rely on what they have accomplished. With the free gift replacing remuneration, a new age has truly dawned, which in Paul's promise will extend into eternity.

7

The Fifth Pericope

Syllogism Concerning Life in Christ as Freedom from the Law

1/ Or do you not understand, brothers—for I am speaking to those who know law—that "the law rules over a person as long as he [or she] lives? 2/ For a married woman is bound by law while the husband is alive. But if the husband dies, she is released from the law concerning the husband. 3/ Accordingly, while the husband is alive she shall be declared an adulteress if she has relations with another husband. But if the husband dies, she is emancipated from the law[a] and thus she is not an adulteress if she has relations with another man."

4/ Consequently, my brothers, you were also put to death with respect to the law through the body of Christ, so you can have relations with another—with the one raised from [the] dead, in order that we might bear fruit for God. 5/ For when we were in the flesh, [our] sinful passions that [came] through the law were at work in our members in bearing fruit to death. 6/ But now we have been released from the law, having died[b] to that by which we were confined, so that we[c] might serve as slaves in newness of spirit and not in the obsolescence of letter.

a A minor variant found in 330 629 2344 *pc* mon vg^{ww} includes the words τοῦ ἄνδρος ("of the husband"), clearly an explanatory addition.

b The support for the participle ἀποθανόντες ("having died") in ℵ A B C K L P Ψ 6 33 69 88 104 181 323 326 330 365 424 436 451 614 629 945 1175 1241 1243 1319 1505 1506 1573 1735 1739 1874 1877 1881 1962 2127 2344 2464 2492 2495 *Maj* vg^{ww} is too overwhelming to allow in its place the reading τοῦ θανάτου ("of death"), supported by D F G it vg^{cl} Or$^{lat mss}$ Ambst. As Metzger points out in Metzger, *Textual Commentary (1975),* 524, the latter is also the easier reading, since it would allow a phrase "from the law of death" without the awkwardness of the subsequent participle.

c The pronoun ἡμᾶς ("we") is missing in B F G 629 and changed to ὑμᾶς ("you") in 1505 2495 *pc,* neither of which has so strong a claim as the inclusion of "we" in ℵ A C D K L P Ψ 6 33 69 88 104 323 326 330 365 424 614 945 1175 1241 1243 1319 1506 1573 1735 1739 1836 1874 1881 2344 2464 *Maj.*

Analysis

Once again Paul opens a new pericope with a diatribal exchange in an opening sentence that has a three-line structure typical of earlier exchanges. Verse 1c lays down the premise of a syllogism[1] on the topic of the law that was announced in 6:14 and developed in a subsidiary sense in 6:15-23. The argument of exchange of lordship or jurisdiction from the preceding section is continued in the thesis stated in the form of a rhetorical question. Verses 2-3 continue the syllogism with two-line sentences.[2] Here Paul states the premise of marital law to establish the point that jurisdiction does not continue after a death has occurred. There are antithetical developments in these verses that convey the essential argument, the first in chiastic form: "bound"–"lives" : "dies"–"released" (7:2), and the second in sequentially parallel form: "lives"–"adulteress" : "dies"–"not an adulteress" (7:3).[3] The term "law" recurs six times in 7:1-6, providing thematic unity in the pericope.[4]

Verses 4-6 draw the conclusion of the syllogism,[5] applying the principle of release through death for

---

1 Bullinger, *Figures,* 167–68; Gieniusz, "Rom 7,1-6," 397–98. While most interpreters view this passage as allegorical or analogical, which produces serious logical problems, Kümmel, *Römer 7,* 36–39, correctly analyzed the logical development in which the inference in 7:4 is drawn from premises laid down in vv. 1-3. In "Römer 7,2-3 im Kontex," in B. Kollman et al., eds., *Antikes Judentum und Frühes Christentum: Festschrift für Hartmut Stegemann zum 65. Geburtstag* (Berlin/New York: de Gruyter, 1999) 448, Christoph Burchard properly identifies this passage as a syllo-

gism. Chul Woo Lee makes a similar case in "Understanding the Law in Rom. 7:1-6: An Enthymemic Analysis," *Scriptura* 88 (2005) 127–32. The analogical approach is unconvincingly reasserted by Joyce A. Little, "Paul's Use of Analogy: A Structural Analysis of Romans 7:1-6," *CBQ* 46 (1984) 82–90, and Earnshaw, "Romans 7.1-4," 68–88.

2 See Weiss, "Beiträge," 229.

3 Louw, 2:82, mistakenly claims that both antitheses are developed chiastically.

4 Harvey, *Listening,* 195.

believers who have died to the law in experiencing the shift in lordship through Christ. Under Christ a new bondage in the Spirit is established, providing a climactic juxtaposition with bondage to the law. This paragraph continues the pattern of two-line sentences[6] and parallels the development of 7:1-3 in that it opens with an address to the brothers [and sisters] followed by an inference statement and supporting explanations of equal length.[7] According to my analysis, there are four double-lined sentences in the paragraph that develop the conclusion of the syllogism.

Rhetorical Disposition

---

5   Lee, "Enthymemic Analysis," 135–36, argues instead that three separate enthymemes are contained in 7:4-6, which undercuts the coherence of Paul's argument.

6   Weiss, "Beiträge," 230, suggests that "consequently, my brothers" at the beginning of 7:4 falls outside of the symmetrical pattern, but he is forced to posit an extraordinarily long line in what I am calling v. 4c-d in order to bring the verse into comformity with a two-line pattern.

7   See Wilckens, 2:63.

Exegesis

■ **1** The pericope opens in diatribe style with ἢ ἀγνο-εῖτε . . . ὅτι ("or, do you not understand . . . that"), which appeared first in 6:3. The formulation is gently reprimanding, introducing material the author fears is not sufficiently understood by the audience,[8] addressed here as Christian "brothers," which softens the reprimand. That this includes all members of the communities, including woman, is self evident. In this instance, as the following words indicate, Paul assumes they know the content he wishes to convey from the Jewish Torah.[9] The rhetorical question is intended to elicit the answer, "Of course!" The interjection, "for I am speaking to those who know the law," is a terse expression for which the article τοῖς would be sometimes expected to appear before the dative plural participle, γινώσκουσιν ("to those knowing"). The choice of the verb λαλῶ ("am speaking") is taken to be a progressive present, reflecting the fluid boundary between writing and speaking in the Greco-Roman world;[10] when the audience in Rome hears the letter read aloud to them, they have the impression that Paul is addressing them directly. In this instance, all those who are acquainted with the Torah are addressed: clearly including the "weak" of Rom 14–15 but also a large portion of the "strong." The similarity to 1 Cor 7:39 clearly indicates the paraphrased material, which derives in part from the LXX, but is formulated by Paul in a manner that serves his argumentative purpose. Note the overlap between these two Pauline passages:

1 Cor 7:39: <u>Γυνὴ δέδεται ἐφ᾽ ὅσον χρόνον ζῇ ὁ ἀνὴρ αὐτῆς· ἐὰν δε κοιμηθῇ ὁ ἀνήρ, ἐλευθέρα ἐστὶν ᾧ θέλει γαμηθῆναι</u> . . . ("A wife is bound to her husband as long as he lives. If the husband dies, she is emancipated to be married to whom she wishes. . . .")

Rom 7:1: ὁ νόμος κυριεύει τοῦ ἀνθρώπου ἐφ᾽ ὅσον χρόνον ζῇ; <7:2> ἡ γὰρ ὕπανδρος γυνὴ τῷ ζῶντι ἀνδρὶ δέδεται νόμῳ· ἐὰν δὲ ἀποθάνῃ ὁ ἀνήρ, κατήργηται ἀπὸ τοῦ νόμου τοῦ ἀνδρός. <7:3> ἄρα οὖν ζῶντος τοῦ ἀνδρὸς μοιχαλὶς χρηματίσει ἐὰν γένηται ἀνδρὶ ἑτέρῳ· ἐὰν δὲ ἀποθάνῃ ὁ ἀνήρ, ἐλευθέρα ἐστὶν ἀπὸ τοῦ νόμου . . .

The first statement, "that the law masters a person as long as he [or she] lives," is formulated as a general principle of Jewish law, with the corollary that death frees people from the law being explicitly worked out by later rabbinic sources.[11] The expression "as long as he/she lives" is found both in 1 Cor 7:39 and in this verse and may be cited from traditional material, although the exact expression is found only in Christian sources.[12] Part of this expression also appears in Gal 4:1 in a legal context: "the heir, as long as (ἐφ᾽ ὅσον χρόνον) he is a child, is no better than a slave, though he is the owner of all the estate." The verb κυριεύω ("rule, have mastery") does not appear in these parallels, however, and is derived from Paul's earlier references to believers' being set free from the reigns of death (6:9) and sin (6:14). This verbal choice signals that Paul intends to place law in a parallel category as a force from which believers have been freed. This statement provides the major premise in the formal syllogism, namely, that law has jurisdiction only during a lifetime. By formulating this premise in the form of a question designed to evoke an "Of course!" from his audience, Paul hopes to gain assent to a plausible generalization of the Torah, but one that was actually explicitly found nowhere therein.[13] In

8 Zahn, 327. See n. 45 in the previous chapter, which cites the parallels in rhetorical literature.

9 See Zahn, 328–29; Godet, 263–64; Schlatter, 153; Schmidt, 120; Schlier, 215; Wilckens, 2:63; Dunn, 1:359; Moo, 411–12; the passage does not correlate well with "a general principle of law" (Colenso, 147; Knox, 448; Käsemann, 187) and the details of Roman law do not appear to be in view, as proposed by Weiss, 293–94; Jülicher, 269; Kühl, 224.

10 See also 1 Cor 9:8; 15:34; 2 Cor 11:17, 23.

11 See Wilckens, 2:64, citing Rabbi Johanan in *b. Šabb.* 30a, "as soon as a man dies, he is free from the law and the commandments." See also *b. Nid.* 61b; *Pesiq. R.* 51b; *y. Kil.* 9.3. That this later tradition was present in Paul's time is argued by Diezinger, "Unter Toten freigeworden," 271–74, on grounds that it surfaces in Job 3:19 and LXX Ps 87:5 and the subsequent rabbinic discussion of these verses.

12 The phrase ἐφ᾽ ὅσον χρόνον ζῇ ("as long as he/she lives") also appears in Mark 2:19; Josephus *Ant.* 3.32, "for as long as (ἐφ᾽ ὅσον χρόνον) they were in the wilderness."

13 See Burchard, "Römer 7,2-3," 447.

view of the thrust of Paul's argument, it is understandable that no advocate of obedience to the Torah in the ordinary sense of the term would have an interest in formulating matters this way. Nevertheless, this statement offers the foundation of Paul's basic point, argued in the second half of this pericope, that believers who have died to sin are released from the law.[14]

■ **2** The first of three minor premises provided by the Jewish legal tradition is that a wife is bound to her husband only during his lifetime. The reference to a wife as ἡ γὰρ ὕπανδρος γυνή echoes Prov 6:24, 29 and Sir 9:9; 41:23 (ὕπανδρος, "married," with γυνή, "woman"), while the classical parallels tend to use ὕπανδρος as a noun. For example, an Aristotelian fragment complains that "the immoderate married women (αἱ ὕπανδροι) resorted to aphrodisiacs."[15] In the Jewish context, as Pamela Thimmes has shown, ὕπανδρος indicates that "the woman is understood solely in terms of her husband," as "'chattel' who lacks power, rights or duty under the law."[16] While the exact expression Paul employs is not found in the LXX legal materials, the rule he cites appears to derive from Deuternomy, that only males have the right to divorce.

Deut 24:1-4 [1]When a man takes a wife and marries her (Ἐὰν δέ τις λάβῃ γυναῖκα καὶ συνοικήσῃ αὐτῇ), if then she finds no favor in his eyes because he has found some indecency in her, and he writes her a bill of divorce and puts it in her hand and sends her out of his house, and she departs out of his house [2]and if she goes and becomes another man's wife (γένηται ἀνδρὶ ἑτέρῳ) [3]and the latter husband dislikes her and writes her a bill of divorce and puts it in her hand and sends her out of his house, or if the latter husband dies, who took her to be his wife, [4]then her former husband, who sent her away, may not take her again to be his wife, after she has been defiled. . . .

This description of male rights certainly does not match Roman divorce law, which allowed either partner to divorce the other.[17] Moreover, as Dunn points out, Roman law did not release a wife from obligations at the moment of her spouse's death, because she was obligated to mourn his death and to remain unmarried for a year under the jeopardy of losing her inheritance.[18] As for the formulation τῷ ζῶντι ἀνδρὶ δέδεται νόμῳ ("is bound by law while the man is alive"), it is not found in Jewish sources, and the close parallel in 1 Cor 7:39 to the use of "bound" (δέδεται) to the law[19] points to a distinctive formulation of what Paul takes to be the principle implicit in the Torah. The corollary of the first minor premise is that the death of the married partner releases the wife from the law requiring her subordination to him. Again the close parallels to Paul's formulation in 1 Cor 7:39 and the distance from explicitly stated legal material within the Jewish tradition point to a Pauline paraphrase of what he takes to be an implication of the Torah.[20]

With the exception of shifting to a verb with similar meaning, the formulation ἐὰν δὲ ἀποθάνῃ ὁ ἀνήρ ("but if the husband dies") is found in both Pauline texts. However, the choice of wording in κατήργηται

---

14 See Hubbard, *New Creation*, 105: "And for all the confusion that the marriage analogy and its application has generated, in point of fact, it is particularly well calculated to make Paul's point. Paul required a death-life scenario in which death somehow liberates a person who remains alive. . . . Paul draws only one conclusion from this illustration: death severs the relationship."

15 Aristotle *Frag. var.* 7.39.285.8 ib. p. 97,6, in response to Dunn's contention (1:360) that "ὕπανδρος hardly appears in nonbiblical literature," see also Aristophanes Gramm. *Epit.* 1.104; Polybius *Hist.* 10.26.3; Posidonius *Frag.* 85.48 = Diodorus Siculus *Hist.* 32.10.4; Plutarch *Pel.* 9.4.5.

16 Thimmes, "Analogies," 200, citing Judith Romney Wegner, *Chattel or Person? The Status of Women in the Mishnah* (New York/Oxford: Oxford University Press, 1988) 13.

17 See *OCD*, 650.

18 Dunn, 1:360.

19 There are no close parallels to this use of δέδεται in the Pauline letters, although Plato's reference in *Resp.* 567d1 to being "bound by necessity" (ἀνάγκῃ δέδεται) provides a distant parallel; see also Plato *Gorg.* 508e7; Pindar *Nem.* 11 45f; Euripides *Hipp.* 160.

20 For a succinct discussion of the relation between Greco-Roman and Jewish marriage laws, see Jeffers, "First-Century Rome," 138–43.

ἀπὸ τοῦ νόμου τοῦ ἀνδρός ("she is released from the law concerning the husband") reflects the specific argumentative purpose of Romans. The verb καταργέω was used in 3:31; 4:14 in the sense of "neutralize, render inactive, release,"[21] with the connotation here being that the wife is released from the law's obligation. The expression "law concerning her husband" is also unique to this letter,[22] producing some bafflement by commentators.[23] In this instance, the formulation of the minor premise of the syllogism is designed specifically to provide a basis for Paul's inference in 7:4 concerning believers being freed from the law by Christ. Although Paul's use of a traditional Jewish view of marriage could be understood "as an example that reinscribed gender hierarchy in the community,"[24] his intent was to support freedom from the law that pertained to all believers.

■ **3** The second minor premise is stated in v. 3a-b, that adultery is defined only during the lifetime of a husband. Since it is inferred from the first minor premise,[25] this minor premise is introduced by the conjunctive expression ἄρα οὖν ("therefore, accordingly"), which Paul uses more frequently in Romans than anywhere else.[26] Repeating the expression "while the husband is alive" from v. 2, Paul states in typical Jewish fashion that "she shall be declared an adulteress (μοιχαλὶς χρηματίσει)." The word "adulteress" is rare outside of the Jewish Christian literature, appearing repeatedly in the LXX but never in the context of a verb such as χρηματίζω ("call, name"). It evokes a social situation of extreme moral severity, when a person could be given so shameful a title, such as is reflected in the episode of the woman caught in adultery in John 8:1-11. Neither of these terms is used by Paul outside of Romans, but one suspects that they would have been within the vocabulary readily employed by Paul the zealous Pharisee prior to his conversion. Adultery, of course, would only be defined from the act itself, and Paul's formulation is a reference thereto. A literal translation of ἐὰν γένηται ἀνδρὶ ἑτέρῳ is "if it happens with another man," or taking γίνομαι in its frequent use as "beget," the translation would be "if she begets with another man." Another option is to follow the clue of an ostracon with the words τὸ γινόμενόν μοι ("it belongs to me," O. Wilck. 2. Nr. 1530),[27] which would produce the translation "in becoming another man's."[28] However, in view of the wording of Deut 24:2, which Paul follows in the wording of γένηται ἀνδρὶ ἑτέρῳ, his locution should be identified as septuagintal, because this is the only example found thus far where the clause has an explicitly sexual connotation. The same locution appears again in v. 3d.

This brings us to the third minor premise, the obverse side of v. 3a-b that is stated in v. 3c-d, that if her husband dies, her relations with another man do not constitute adultery. The formulation is quite striking: she is "free" (ἐλευθέρα ἐστίν) not merely from her husband, but ἀπὸ τοῦ νόμου ("from the law") itself.[29] This sleight of hand was enabled by the formulation at the end of v. 2, "the law concerning the husband," and it obviously has a tremendous significance as far as Paul was concerned.[30] With the death of the husband, her relations with another man cannot be classified as adultery. Although there are no Jewish precedents for this

21 See on 3:31 above, referring to *T. Sol.* 6.5-6; 7.7-8.
22 The Greek title of a Aristotelian work extant only in Latin translation, was Νόμοι ἀνδρὸς καὶ Γαμετῆς ("Laws Concerning Husband and Marriage," mentioned in Aristotle *Frag. var.* 4.28), obviously employed "law" in a sense different from that required by the Pauline expression.
23 Lietzmann, 72; Barrett, 135–36. Moo, 412, follows Moulton and Turner, *Grammar III*, 212, in translating this as an objective genitive, "the law directed towards the husband."
24 Thimmes, "Analogies," 201.
25 Gieniusz, "Rom 7,1-6," 393.
26 The expression ἄρα οὖν ("accordingly, so then") appears seven times in Romans and no more than once each in other letters.

27 See BAGD 160, II.3.
28 Dunn, 1:361.
29 Burchard, "Römer 7,2-3," 452–53, seeks to reduce the scope of this freedom by observing that the woman is only freed from the marital law, but Paul draws a much more sweeping inference here, one that Burchard notes (456) is the point of the passage: "freedom from a failed obedience to the Torah."
30 Jones, *Freiheit*, 119–22, makes a case for an advance in Paul's doctrine of freedom as compared with 1 Cor 7:39. For a skeptical assessment of Paul's argument from a feminist point of view, see Thimmes, "Analogies," 200–204.

final premise, or indeed for the precise way Paul summarizes the Jewish law in most of this passage, there is a relevant episode in Achilles Tatius's novel *Leucippe et Clitophon,* in which the death of a husband exonerates a woman whose sexual license had become a subject of gossip in Ephesus. The narrator reports in 8.10.11–12:

> Therefore, if he has died, she is free of accusation (ἀπήλλαξαι τῆς αἰτίας), because the person suffering the adultery (τὴν μοιχείαν) does not exist, nor is the marriage, which no longer has a husband, insulted. But if wedlock to the married man who is still living is not annulled (ὁ γάμος τῷ τὸν γήμαντα ζῆν οὐκ ἀνήρηται), the married woman, if she is corrupted by another, is ruined.

Although this ancient novel has the *deus ex machina* scheme in which the heroine is exonerated against all expectations, which is a world removed from Paul's thought, a case could made that in other respects it is quite close to the premises set forth in 7:1-3. Nevertheless, it remains clear that Paul's doctrine of Christian freedom derives from experience with Christ. Although it was forged by the Judaizer crisis of the late 40s C.E., Paul's conviction did not originate from a legalistic argument. The syllogism in this pericope is compelling only for persons who are already believers, who are ready enough to hear an argument seemingly based on the Torah. However, Torah advocates not sharing the believers' viewpoint and experience probably would not find this argument compelling.

■ **4** The first of two inferences in the syllogism is introduced by ὥστε ("consequently")[31] followed by ἀδελφοί μου ("my brothers [and sisters]"), a diatribal reference that places Paul's audience on the same level as himself:[32] all are members of the new fictive family in Christ.[33] As in other references, confirmed in this instance by the warm greetings to female leaders in chap. 16, the term "brothers" refers to congregational members, whether male or female. The premise of death freeing people from the law leads to the inference that was confirmed by the conversion experience of early believers: καὶ ὑμεῖς ἐθανατώθητε τῷ νόμῳ ("you were also put to death with respect to law").[34] The aorist passive verb points to a single event in the past life of believers, either to their conversion or their baptism. This formulation picks up the theme of 6:2 in which believers have died to sin, thus confirming that it is not merely baptism but the entire process of ending a former existence that is in view.[35] The passive verbal form places a strong emphasis on divine initiative, and θανατόω ("put to death") is arguably a forceful expression of intentional execution,[36] thus making a subtle distinction between the death of a husband and the death of believers to the old age.[37] In contrast to 6:2 and 10, however, this death is "with respect to the law," with νόμος ("law") referring primarily to the Jewish Torah.[38] The means by which this liberating death occurred for believers is described by the prepositional phrase διὰ τοῦ σώματος τοῦ Χριστοῦ ("through the body of Christ"). In the light of 6:2-6, the word "body" appears to refer to the crucified body of Christ, into which believers have been bap-

---

31 BAGD (2000) 1007, 1A, cites Xenophon *Anab.* 1.7.7 as an example, "Therefore (ὥστε), it was not for this reason that I was afraid. . . ." LSJM 2041 B.II.2, "at the beginning of a sentence, to mark a strong conclusion"; see also BDF §391.

32 Schäfer, *Bruderschaft,* 348.

33 See Atkins, *Egalitarian Community,* 171–90; Bartchy, "Siblings," 68–73.

34 Moule, "Death," 154, suggests the translation "with reference to law."

35 See Dunn, 1:361, in contrast to Schlier, 217; Käsemann, 188.

36 Rudolf Bultmann, "θάνατος κτλ.," *TDNT* 3 (1965) 21, refers to passages such as Exod 21:12, "And if any man strikes another and kills him, let him be certainly put to death (θανάτῳ θανατούσθω)."

Xenophon *Anab.* 2.6.4, "for this reason he was put to death by (ἐθανατώθη ὑπό) the Spartan troops." However, no examples of metaphorical use of this verb aside from Romans have been found.

37 See Dunn, 1:361; this is a puzzling feature in a syllogism, which should move logically from premises to conclusions, leading Lietzmann, 73; Gale, *Analogy,* 192–96; and Räisänen, *Law,* 61, to refer to the muddled nature of Paul's argumentation.

38 Fitzmyer, 458; Byrne 211.

tized and buried.[39] While the same expression appears in 1 Cor 10:16-17 with reference to Christ's body regularly experienced in the Eucharist, the combination with the aorist passive verb "were put to death" points to the initial incorporation of believers into the event of Christ's death on their behalf.[40] That incorporation released them from bondage to law, which had dominated life in the old age,[41] leading them into perverse forms of competition for honor. His death exposed and overcame law's perversion, revealing its deadly though disguised hostility to God and demonstrating a new path to righteousness through the acceptance of divine grace to the undeserving that comes through Christ's life and death. Those who accept this message become members of the church as the "body of Christ" (1 Cor 12:5), but the vehicle of the transformation that Paul describes here is not ecclesiastical.[42] It is the power of God acting through the death and resurrection of the "body of Christ" that brings the reign of law to an end and ushers believers into a new realm of grace dominated by Christ himself.

The new relationship created by the grace of Christ is described with the same marital language that appeared in the premises of the syllogism: "so you can have relations with another ($\epsilon\dot{\iota}\varsigma\ \tau\dot{o}\ \gamma\epsilon\nu\acute{\epsilon}\sigma\vartheta\alpha\iota\ \dot{\nu}\mu\tilde{\alpha}\varsigma\ \dot{\epsilon}\tau\acute{\epsilon}\rho\omega$)." Rather than being wedded, body and soul, to the all-encompassing system of competition for honor, believers are now wedded to Christ.[43] This is a stunning metaphor for religious transformation, reflecting the theme of psychosexual unity between believers and Christ that appeared in 1 Cor 6:13-20:

[13]The body is not meant for immorality, but for the Lord, and the Lord for the body. . . . [15]Do you not know that your bodies are members of Christ? Shall I

therefore take the members of Christ and make them members of a prostitute? Never! [16]Do you not know that he who joins himself to a prostitute becomes one body with her? For, as it is written, "The two shall become one flesh." [17]But he who is united to the Lord becomes one spirit with him. . . . [19]Do you not know that your body is a temple of the Holy Spirit within you, which you have from God? You are not your own; [20]you were bought with a price. So glorify God in your body.

While it remains unclear why Paul chose to stress this somatic relationship in the context of the Roman letter, which unlike 1 Corinthians does not otherwise reflect a congregational situation in which bodily relations are at issue,[44] there is no doubt that Paul is using a marital metaphor to describe the relation between believers and Christ. The same conception is found also in 2 Cor 11:2. There are precedents in the OT for speaking of the relationship between God and Israel in marital terms (Isa 54:5-6; 62:4-5; Jer 2:2; 3:14; Ezek 16:7-8; Hos 1:2; 2:19),[45] but the Pauline writings are the only NT documents to apply the concept to the relationship of believers. This physical mysticism is a distinctive contribution of Pauline theology, carrying forward an OT legacy, but one that has had scant impact because of misperceptions of Paul's view of flesh and spirit, of marriage and sexuality in other passages. The implications are clear and straightforward, even though not usually picked up by commentators.[46] The relationship between believers and Christ established by the death of Christ is as totally encompassing as the relationship between a husband and wife. It is a distinctive form of physical mysticism in which mind, heart, spirit, and other "spiritual dimensions" of the human psyche are completely integrated

---

39   See Schlier, 217; Jewett, *Terms*, 300.

40   Schmidt, 121: "sacramental participation in Christ's death." See also Haacker, 138, and particularly Earnshaw's analysis of Paul's "participationist soteriology" in "Romans 7.1-4," 71, 88.

41   See Jewett, *Terms*, 299–300.

42   Cf. Dodd, 102; Robinson, *Body*, 47.

43   See John Duncan Martin Derrett, "Romans vii.1-4: The Relationship with the Resurrected Christ," in J. D. M. Derrett, *Law in the New Testament* (London: Darton, Longman & Todd, 1970) 463–70.

44   See Jewett, *Terms*, 300–301.

45   See Dunn, 1:362, and Derrett, "Romans vii.1-4," 465–68.

46   For example, Dunn, 1:362, argues that Paul in fact did not intend "to apply the illustration of vv 2-3 in a complete way to believers." Richard A. Batey, *New Testament Nuptial Imagery* (Leiden: Brill, 1971) 19, concludes that the "the relation of this passage to nuptial symbolism is at the most only remote." Gieniusz, "Rom 7,1-6," 399–400, provides a more sympathetic reading of the marriage metaphor.

with physical, sexual dimensions. That Christ is the partner in the new Christian marriage between believers and their Lord is confirmed by Paul's explanatory clause, τῷ ἐκ νεκρῶν ἐγερθέντι ("with the one raised from [the] dead"). This formulation employs the same terminology as that of 4:24; 6:4; 8:11; 10:9 and probably derives from an early Christian confession.[47] As always in Pauline theology, the resurrection of Christ lies at the foundation of faith. Christ's death as a victim of legal fanaticism would have meant little without the resurrection that confirmed that he was indeed the Messiah. So to be married to the resurrected one, which goes a step farther than 6:4, where only union with Christ's death was claimed,[48] constitutes the epitome of being freed from the law. This reference to the resurrection claims common ground for Paul's innovative doctrine of freedom from law, thus addressing the Roman situation in an effective manner. The house and tenement churches reflecting the theological and social tendencies of the "weak" and the "strong" were relying on different interpretations of law to make their cases for supremacy over the others. Yet each claimed a common relationship with Christ crucified and resurrected; they encountered him in their love feasts and experienced him in their daily prayers and struggles. Nevertheless, the relationship that each group enjoyed was not an end in itself, as the final line of this verse makes plain.

The "in order that" clause refers to productive transformation on the part of those who have died with Christ: ἵνα καρποφορήσωμεν τῷ θεῷ ("in order that we might bear fruit for God"). This verb appears only in this and the following verse in all of the indisputable Pauline letters, and is found also in Col 1:6, 10. None of the NT occurrences of this verb shares the legal context of *4 Ezra* 9.31, "For lo, I sow in you my law, and it shall bring forth in you the fruits of righteousness."[49] While some interpreters have faulted Paul for seeming to shift his metaphor to the agricultural realm,[50] a good case can be made that a figurative form of productivity in a general sense including childbearing is in view.[51] Matthew Black infers that "the believer is free to contract a new union with his Risen Lord, and obtain new progeny through this fresh 'marriage.'"[52] This provides an excellent correlation with the missional purpose of Romans, because Paul hopes that by acknowledging the marriage between Christ and each of the house and tenement churches, they will discover their commonality and cease the competition that would discredit the gospel to the barbarians in Spain. Paul places the purpose of their joint marriage with Christ in the first person plural, because he hopes to join with the Roman churches in planning and mounting this mission to bear God further fruit of converts. When the Spaniards hear the gospel, they will discover that despite the contempt in which they had formerly been held, especially by their Roman conquerors, they along with all others are rightful children of God. But this can happen only if the Roman house and tenement churches realize that their marriage to Christ means they have died to the law, because their continued insistence on the priority of particular laws was the motivation for their discrimination against each other. This persistence of the social habits of judging and contempt, typical for honor-shame societies,[53] would inevitably carry over into their attitude toward the barbarians in Spain, and thus erode the credibility of the gospel. If the house and tenement churches of Rome could grasp the true dimension of their marriage to Christ, they would be enabled to share in Paul's mission to restore "to God" his rightful children in Spain, thus completing the task of bringing the Gentiles as an offering to God (Rom 15:16), which Isaiah had hoped would usher in the end of the age (Isa 66:20). However, "bearing fruit" is too generic a formulation to be restricted to this missional context. Paul assumes that believers will recover the Adamic responsibility to care for the creation, a theme that is developed in chap. 8. Their conversion is not an end in itself, but serves the larger purpose of recovering the role of co-creators with

---

47 See Paulsen, *Überlieferung*, 51–55, following Kramer, *Christ*, 18; Wengst, *Formeln* 21ff., and others; a complete listing of the parallel forms will be discussed in the introduction to 8:1-17.
48 Dunn, 1:362.
49 Cited by Friedrich Hauck, "καρπός, ἄκαρπος, καρποφορέω," *TDNT* 3 (1965) 616.
50 Dunn, 1:362–63.
51 Sanday and Headlam, 174; Barrett, 137; Bruce, 146; Gale, *Analogy*, 197–98; Derrett, "Romans vii. 1-4," 471. Cranfield, 1:337, refers to this explanation as "altogether grotesque."
52 Black.
53 See Lendon, *Empire of Honour*, 30–106.

God. Whatever their form of work, whether as slaves or self-employed handworkers, whether as widows engaged in congregational work or even as patrons who are directing their energies toward productive congregational enterprises for the first time, their goal is no longer the attainment of honor but service to God.

■ **5** The γάρ ("for") at the beginning of this verse indicates an explanation of the syllogism, in this instance by reference to the religious experience of the congregation, both prior to and after their conversion. Alongside the previous antitheses between sin and righteousness, law and grace,[54] Paul announces in this and the following verse an antithesis between flesh and spirit that receives its fullest development in chap. 8. The antithesis marked by ὅτε γάρ . . . νυνὶ δέ . . . ("for when, at one point . . . but now . . .") places the era dominated by the flesh in the past and the new era of the Spirit in the present.[55] A negative view of the flesh as a power in the old age is indicated by the associations in this verse with passions, sin, law, and death. While Paul sometimes refers to life ἐν τῇ σαρκί ("in the flesh") in neutral terms (2 Cor 4:11; 10:2; Gal 4:14; Phil 1:22, 24; Phlm 16), here it appears to have a meaning identical to κατὰ σάρκα ("according to the flesh"), implying that "existence in the flesh is automatically sinful."[56] The associations with sin, passions, law, and death demand an interpretation of flesh as the power that drives perverted systems of honor and shame, leading captives into lives of unrelenting competition to gain advantage over other persons and groups. In the Roman environment, the tone was set by what Lendon describes as the "aristocrats' yearning for contests over honour with clear winners and losers. . . . In a world where posts were perceived to go to the candidate who enjoyed the greatest aristocratic esteem, to gain them was to prove to the world that you had honour greater than those you defeated. . . ."[57] The παθήματα τῶν ἁμαρτιῶν τὰ διὰ τοῦ νόμου ("sinful passions that came through the law") are therefore to be differentiated from sensual passions or human weak-

nesses, because the allusions to Paul's own previous experiences as a competitively zealous Pharisee and an opponent of the church seem so clear.[58] How else is one to explain the extraordinary role of law in promoting sinful passions rather than, as traditionally believed, holding them in check?[59] In Gal 1:14 Paul explained how "I advanced in Judaism beyond many of my own age among my people, so extremely zealous was I for the traditions of my fathers," leading to his sinful behavior in persecuting the church (Gal 1:13). In Phil 3:5-6, he again links this zealous legalism to surpassing performance of the law and opposition to the messianic movement: "as to the law a Pharisee, as to zeal a persecutor of the church, as to righteousness under the law blameless." In this light, the "sinful passions" in Rom 7:5 are the yearnings for honor in conforming to the law and in coercing compliance with its norms. In the light of his conversion, Paul recognizes that such religious "passion" was motivated by "the flesh," that is, the desire to surpass others in honor, which engaged a highly religious person to enter into sinful opposition to God's will. This entire process operated "through the law," by which in Paul's case the Torah had become traduced into an instrument of gaining honor. By generalizing this analysis through reference to the "we" who are in the flesh in this sense, and by referring to τὰ παθήματα ("the passions"), which I translate as "our passions," Paul transforms his experience into comprehensive analysis of the situation of the believers in Rome. Even those who had not come from a zealously Pharisaic environment, he argues, had been engaged in comparable competitions for honor. They had misused their religious and ethical norms as vehicles to triumph over other persons and groups;[60] in view of the similar thrust of 6:12, they had allowed their passions for superior status to provoke destructive behavior. Παθήματα, appearing usually in the plural in the NT, is used here as in Gal 5:24 in the sense of passions or impulses,[61] but unlike the classical parallels, there is no hint that they derive from "uncontrolled

---

54   See Schmidt, 121.
55   BAGD (2000) 731; Tachau, *Einst*, 126–27.
56   Jewett, *Terms*, 153.
57   Lendon, *Empire of Honour*, 191.
58   See Dunn, 1:363.
59   Philo *Heres* 268; *Abr.* 164.
60   See Dunn's warning (1:363) against viewing flesh

"in merely individual terms"; however, on 1:364 it becomes clear that Dunn conceives of this as a peculiarly Jewish problem.
61   See Wilhelm Michaelis, "πάθημα," *TDNT* 5 (1967) 930–31.

emotionalism"[62] or the "lower nature" of human sensuality.[63] In the context of the argument in Romans, these passions are associated as much with the mind as with the body; indeed in this instance the desires to surpass others in obedience to the law and in other forms of competition for honor are viewed as always "sinful" because they inevitably damage others and challenge the surpassing honor of God.

The social consequences of degenerate systems of honor and shame are depicted in the final words of v. 5, which refers to human actions and picks up the theme of "fruit" from the preceding verse. As in 6:13, Paul refers to bodily limbs and organs that were energized by competitive passions that $\grave{\varepsilon}\nu\eta\rho\gamma\epsilon\hat{\iota}\tau o\ \grave{\varepsilon}\nu\ \tau o\hat{\iota}\varsigma\ \mu\acute{\varepsilon}\lambda\epsilon\sigma\iota\nu\ \acute{\eta}\mu\hat{\omega}\nu$ ("were at work in our members"). Unlike in Hellenistic parallels, Paul does not imply that the passions have their seat in bodily parts, but rather that "the states of passion brought about by sins were given expression by means of our members."[64] Paul employs the imperfect tense to imply that this was a continuously present circumstance prior to conversion, implying in the choice of the verb $\grave{\varepsilon}\nu\epsilon\rho\gamma\acute{\varepsilon}\omega$ ("work, effect") that passion deriving from the power sphere of death, rather than human volition, was responsible for what occurred.[65] No matter what good was intended, such passions produced death. The evil consequences implied by the consecutive construction $\epsilon\grave{\iota}\varsigma\ \tau\grave{o}\ \kappa\alpha\rho\pi o\varphi o\rho\hat{\eta}\sigma\alpha\iota$ ("in order to bear fruit")[66] came as a consequence of humans' yielding their "members as weapons of wickedness with respect to sin," to use the formulation of 6:13. In contrast to the new form of creative endeavor of the converted, fulfilling their God-given destiny in caring for the creation, such behavior produces fruit $\tau\hat{\omega}\ \vartheta\alpha\nu\acute{\alpha}\tau\omega$ ("to death"). It

destroys others and brings death upon the doers. Like some of the brutal performances in the Roman theaters, all of the competitors in the struggle for honor lie bloodied and dead at the end. The social chaos described in 1:29-32 surfaces here again, and the penalty of divine wrath that is already visible will be executed at the end of time. Death is the requisite fruit of the conventional competition for honor, with regard to both its present consequences and its ultimate divine penalty exacted against all who assault the glory of God.

■ **6** The turn of the new creation is indicated by $\nu\nu\nu\grave{\iota}\ \delta\acute{\varepsilon}$ ("but now"),[67] the eschatological present in which believers enjoy a new form of life no longer dominated by the performance principle or the obsessive competition for honor. The key to this new life is release from the law,[68] expressed here with the aorist passive $\kappa\alpha\tau\eta\rho\gamma\acute{\eta}\vartheta\eta\mu\epsilon\nu$ ("we were released"), which refers to a single moment in the past of believers in which they accepted the gospel of Christ crucified and resurrected and became part of the new community of faith. With regard to v. 2, we observed the same verb in the peculiar expression "released from the law concerning the husband," which was obviously intended to lead to v. 6. To define salvation so explicitly in terms of freedom from the law represents a radical break from traditional Judaism as Paul had experienced it.[69] Since Christ died as a victim of the law, revealing the lethal implications of its perversion into a system of gaining precedence over others, to accept this gospel is simultaneously to be set free from the compulsion to perform and to compel others to conform. It is to abandon any further efforts to gain honor through meeting law's demands. Under the aegis of grace, the need for honor has been met and the compul-

62   Haacker, 138.
63   E.g., Plutarch *Quaest. conv.* 745EF refers to the "soul's ears" being stopped up not with wax but with "carnal obstructions and passions ($\sigma\alpha\rho\kappa\acute{\iota}\nu o\iota\varsigma$ $\grave{\varepsilon}\mu\varphi\rho\acute{\alpha}\gamma\mu\alpha\sigma\iota\nu\ \kappa\alpha\grave{\iota}\ \pi\acute{\alpha}\vartheta\epsilon\sigma\iota\nu$)." For additional parallels, see Eduard Schweizer, "Die hellenistische Komponente im neutestamentlichen *Sarx*-Begriff," in Schweizer, *Neotestamentica*, 40–44.
64   Johannes Horst, "$\mu\acute{\varepsilon}\lambda o\varsigma$," *TDNT* 4 (1967) 562, cited from Schlatter.
65   See Georg Bertram, "$\grave{\varepsilon}\nu\epsilon\rho\gamma\acute{\varepsilon}\omega\ \kappa\tau\lambda.$," *TDNT* 2 (1964) 654; BAGD 265 observes that this verb always has an "impersonal subject" in early Christian literature.
66   The consecutive understanding of the purpose clause is advocated by Schlier, 218; Kuss, 2:438; Cranfield, 1:338; Moo, 420, in contrast to the final or purposive interpretation proposed by Godet, 268–69; Kühl, 226; Schmidt, 122, because unlike "desires" in 6:12, "passions" do not imply intentionality.
67   Walter Radl, "$\nu\hat{\upsilon}\nu,\ \nu\upsilon\nu\acute{\iota}$," *EDNT* 2 (1991) 480; Luz, *Geschichtsverständnis*, 88; Neuhäusler, "Entscheidende Augenblick," 1–16; Nissiotis, "$\nu\hat{\upsilon}\nu$," 302–9.
68   See Burchard, "Römer 7,2-3," 456.
69   See Dunn, 1:365.

sion to obey the law, in whatever form it appears, is removed from its motivating power. By participating in the death of Christ, believers have "died to that by which we were confined." The bondage of their former life is fittingly described with κατειχόμεθα, the same verb we encountered in 1:18 under the translation "suppress." While the basic meaning of the verb κατέχω is "to hold down, hold fast,"[70] Paul employs it in 1:18 and 6:6 in the sense of "holding illegally"[71] or restraining by superior force. It is typically used to refer to the police arresting someone[72] or to being detained by unavoidable circumstances.[73] A later Christian amulet employs the verbs of this verse, requesting that God "restrain (κατάσχησον) and destroy (κατάργησον) him who is approaching upon little Sophia. . . ."[74]

It is therefore surprising that Paul employs the language of slavery to depict the status of believers: ὥστε δουλεύειν ἡμᾶς ("that we might serve as slaves"). The premise here is that all people are slaves. None is absolutely free. Liberation from conformity to a particular law never leaves people neutral.[75] At this point Pauline theology corrects a crucial illusion in some later views of freedom, including some allegedly influenced by the letters themselves. Paul views the Christian life in what Godet describes as "a new *servitude* of the noblest and most glorious nature, which alone indeed deserves the name of liberty."[76] So the question of life for Paul is whom shall groups serve? They can either serve under the traditional mastery of law in its various forms, leading to death, or under the new lordship of Christ that leads to life. The former is dominated by the performance principle, in which one's honor and the honor of

one's group are earned by conformity to social expectations. Or one accepts the regime of grace, but this new regime also involves a Lord and a system of obedience in which one follows the logic of grace not in order to gain honor but to express one's gratitude for being set free from the competition that leads to death.

The alternatives that Paul describes are to serve the "obsolete letter" or to live "in newness of spirit." The expression ἐν καινότητι πνεύματος echoes "in newness of life" in 6:4 and conveys the innovative quality of salvation "in comparison with the worthlessnes of their former condition."[77] The only NT use of the noun καινότης ("newness") is in Romans, reflecting Paul's preoccupation with the new life in Christ "in antithesis to pre-Christian life,[78] which rests on the eschatological foundation of the "now" at the beginning of v. 6, in contrast to the "then" of the old age.[79] The combination with "Spirit," in contrast to the parallel passage in 2 Cor 3, which deals with hermeneutical issues, suggests the new structure of obedience[80] that replaces legal compulsion for the sake of honor. Believers serve Christ "as slaves," according to this sentence, but in an entirely new manner of following the Spirit[81] who calls them to serve others rather than to be served.[82] The new ethos brought by this ethic was delineated in Gal 5:22-23 in terms of the "fruits of the spirit" that mark the new community: "love, joy, peace, patience, kindness, goodness, faithfulness, gentleness, self control." Although Paul postpones describing this ethos in detail until chaps. 12–15, his wording in this verse suggests that the fruits of humane mutuality produced by the Spirit of Christ replace the culturally conditioned products of prestige.

70 LSJM 926.

71 Hermann Hanse, "κατέχω," *TDNT* 2 (1964) 529.

72 MM 336 cites *P.Flor.* 1. Nr. 61.60 from 85 C.E.

73 MM 337 cites *PSI* 5. Nr. 525.9 and *BGU* 4. Nr. 1205.27.

74 *SupplMag* I 13,8; Deissmann, *Light*, 308, notes the use of the compound θυμοκάτοχον in the sense of "cripple" and notes that the verb κατέχω appears in an ostracon concerning "Kronos, who cripples (ὁ κατέχων) the anger of all people" (cf *PGM* 1. Nr. 5. 363; Daniel and Maltomini, *Suppl. Mag.* 1. Nr. 13.7,12–15, 19–20).

75 See Käsemann, 190.

76 Godet, 269, italics in original; see also Gieniusz, "Rom 7,1-6," 395.

77 Johannes Behm, "καινός κτλ.," *TDNT* 3 (1965) 431.

78 Jörg Baumgarten, "καινός κτλ.," *EDNT* 2 (1991) 230.

79 See Wilckens, 2:69–70; Schmidt, 122; Haacker, 138–39.

80 See Dunn, 1:373–74; Haacker, 138.

81 See particularly Hubbard, *New Creation*, 109–12.

82 See the section entitled "Spirit as Openness for God and One's Neighbor," by Eduard Schweizer, "πνεῦμα, πνευματικός," *TDNT* 6 (1968) 430–32.

The obsolete code[83] could be the OT, or the Pharisees' oral law, or the mores of Roman society.[84] The language of παλαιὸς γράμμα ("obsolete code, letter") appears to echo the discourse of 2 Cor 3:6, that the "new covenant" appeared "not in a written code but in the Spirit; for the written code (τὸ γὰρ γράμμα) kills, but the Spirit gives life." This expression calls to mind Paul's references in earlier letters to the "the old covenant" (ἡ παλαιὰ διαθήκη, 2 Cor 3:14) and "the old leaven" (ἡ παλαιὰ ζύμη, 1 Cor 5:7), which are defined by their opposition to the new revelation in Christ,[85] holding both mind and body of their adherents in bondage. In the context of Romans, this reference picks up the theme of the παλαιὸς ἄνθρωπος ("old man, obsolete self") that was crucified with Christ (Rom 6:6), which was a corporate expression for humans bound by corrupt relationships. Here it becomes clear that life under the law was a matter of the "obsolete letter," in which the intended purpose of the law had been perverted by the "flesh" (7:5).[86] Its obsolete quality was demonstrated by the Christ event, which ushered in the era of "newness of Spirit," whereby the intended purpose of the law is followed because the wicked involvement of the "letter" in systems of earning honor and advantages over others has been eliminated.

---

83 Cranfield, 1:339–40, draws the contrast between the "newness" of the spirit and the "oldness" of the letter that "the legalist is left with as a result of his misunderstamding and misuse of the law. It is the letter of the law in separation from the Spirit."

84 See Dunn, 1:373, for a reading that restricts Paul's message to "the law as the 'works' done by devout Jews."

85 Heinrich Seesemann, "παλαιός κτλ.," TDNT 5 (1967) 719–20. According to LSJM 1290 the term παλαιότης can mean "obsoleteness," as in the case of an outdated means of deliverance in Euripides Hel. 1056 or agedness in the case of a person's literal age (Aeschines Fals. leg. 42.2) or the age of seeds in Theophrastus Hist. plant. 7.1.6.2. Frequently the term refers to past times in the sense of "antiquity," as in Hecataeus Abderita Frag. 3a 264 F25 1175 [= Diodorus Siculus Hist. 1.77.1.3]; Arrian Frag. 2b 156f 32.2; Josephus Ant. 1.16; Herennius Philo Frag. ec 790 Fl.29; Suetonius Περὶ βλασ. 8.6.

86 See Dunn, 1:373.

7

The Sixth Pericope

Speech-in-Character Concerning the Moral Status of the Law

7/ **What then shall we say? [Is]ᵃ the law sin? Certainly not! Nevertheless I did not know the sin except through law, for I also did not know about coveting except [that] the law was saying, "You shall not covet!" 8/ But, finding opportunity through the commandment, sin was working in me every manner of coveting, for apart from law sin [is]ᵇ dead. 9/ Now I was once living apart from law, but when the commandment came, the sin came to life again, 10/ but I died, and it was found with respect to me [that] the commandment that was for life, thisᶜ was for death. 11/ For the sin, finding opportunity through the commandment, deceived me, and through it slayed [me]. 12/ So on the one hand the law [is] holy, and the commandment [is] holy and righteous and good . . .ᵈ**

a   A variant attested by 33 88 1175 *al* Mcion^Tert places ὅτι ("that") before "the law," which introduces a direct quotation (with ὅτι recitativum). It seems clearly to be a secondary improvement of the text.

b   The use of ἦν ("was") in F G (K before νεκρά) latt syᵖ bo intends to replace the present tense implicit in the copula ("is") with the past tense ("was"), making sin's deadness comply with the past tense of the previous verb κατειργάσατο ("was working").

c   Griesbach suggested a soft breathing that would result in αὐτή ("it," referring to ἐντολή, following BAGD [2000] 153.2), but this does not seem to be supported by Ambst vg^cl, who have the demonstrative pronoun "hoc esse ad mortem" ("it is toward death").

d   A minor variant in 1908 replaces the widely attested ἀγαθή ("good") with θαυμαστή ("wonderful"), either an effort to elevate the status of the law or an ancient variant arising from a scribal confusion of similarly written letters.

Analysis

The formulation of Rom 7:5 concerning sinful passions being aroused by the law could easily lead to the objection that law would thereby fall into the moral status of sin. This is the false conclusion that Paul denies in the diatribal exchange of 7:7 and goes on to explain with the idea of law making humans conscious of sin.[1] The status of the law is so crucial for the development of Paul's case that it is inappropriate to view the material from 7:7-25 as an excursus,[2] even though the motifs in 7:6 recur for full development in chap. 8. Nor is the identification of 7:7-25 as an "apology for the law" fully adequate,[3] because Paul's concern is not to develop an abstract doctrine of the law but rather to clarify its bearing on the situation of the Roman church. The term "law" appears no fewer than six times in this short pericope, while "commandment" appears five times;[4] the question in v. 1 whether the law is sin is answered by the reprise in v. 12 concerning the law being holy and the commandment "holy and righteous and good." Paronomasia is also provided by the fourfold repetition of "sin," while "I" (or "me") is repeated five times, the motif of death four times, and of life three times. Verse 8 interprets the commandment cited in vv. 7-8, showing that sin merely found a "foothold" in the law, leading to covetousness. The shift to the past tense in this verse continues through the end of v. 11, contrasting with the present tense description of being discharged from the law at the end of the last pericope, thus signaling a shift in focus to "the time and the human condition *before* the deliverance."[5] Verses 8-11 constitute a ring-composition with "finding opportunity through the commandment" in v. 8 echoed with "finding opportunity through the commandment" in v. 11, and the term "commandment" employed twice more in vv. 9 and 10.[6] This first paragraph is organized in three triple-line sentences that match the form of several earlier diatribal exchanges in Romans.

---

1   See Stowers, *Diatribe*, 148–49.

2   Barrett, 142; Beker, *Paul*, 85; Moo, 424; those rejecting the excursus hypothesis include Fitzmyer, 462; Dunn, 1:377.

3   Kuss, 2:441; Schmidt, 123; Wilckens, 2:74; Kümmel, *Römer 7*, 8–13; Bultmann, *Old and New Man*, 41.

4   Noted by Harvey, *Listening*, 196.

5   Lambrecht, *Wretched "I,"* 34, italics in original.

6   See Harvey, *Listening*, 196.

There is a shift to double-line sentences in 7:9, continuing down through v. 12.[7] Here Paul brings his pre-Christian experience to bear on the question of the effect of the legal commandment. The paragraph of 7:9-12 is also held together by paronomasia, with the repetition of "commandment" in each verse, and the repeated antitheses between "life" and "death" in vv. 9-11. Verse 12 concludes with an anacoluthon in which μέν ("on the one hand") is not followed by the usual δέ ("on the other hand"). Here Paul states the principle implicit in his earlier denial of the sinful quality of the law in 7:7, namely, that the commandment is "holy and righteous and good." This threefold affirmation linked with the repetitive "and" provides an effective clausula that concludes the pericope.[8]

The Rhetorical "I" in 7:7-25

The remarkable shift to "I" as the subject of the verbs in this and the succeeding pericope is a stylistic feature that determines how both pericopes should be interpreted. In the immense scholarly debate about this feature,[9] two separate questions have remained entangled: Is the "I" autobiographical or not? And which aspect of Paul's life or some other life is in view? Although the first question has recently been resolved by rhetorical analysis, the second has not yet been satisfactorily answered, and a tentative hypothesis is suggested in the exegesis below.

Against a widely accepted autobiographical view of the preconversion Paul as afflicted by bad conscience because of an alleged inability to perform the law,[10] W. G. Kümmel published two books in 1929 that provided a watershed in the debate.[11] He argued against the prevailing autobiographical interpretation on the grounds that Phil 3:6 claims that prior to his conversion, Paul has been "blameless" in performing the law.[12] While this contention remains solid despite subsequent efforts to sidestep the evidence,[13] it does not really sustain Kümmel's conclusion that all autobiographical theories should be abandoned. As with his subsidiary argument that nowhere else does Paul speak of a life "apart from the law" (7:9),[14] these details could be coordinated with some other version of autobiographical self-reference.

Another widely popular alternative is to take these verses as a reference to the postconversion Paul or to the typical Christian who experiences justification in the context of ongoing sinfulness, understood as the inability to perform the law.[15] This carries forward Luther's famous motto, *simul iustus et peccator*, that the justified believer remains a sinner until the day he dies.[16] In Cranfield's formulation, this passage depicts "the inner conflict characteristic of the true Christian" whose conscience is sensitive to the sinful egotism that yet remains in his thoughts and behavior.[17] Dunn reformulates this as a situation of "eschatological tension" between the spirit and the flesh in which the power and possibility of sin remain in force and require constant struggle.[18] This

7   Weiss, "Beiträge," 231, speaks of the "fine correspondence" in these verses and provides a detailed analysis (232).

8   Weiss, "Beiträge," 231, refers to the sense of exaltation that 7:12 produces, pointing out the Hebraic parallelism and the three concluding adjectives, but not identifying them as a clausula.

9   The earlier phase of this debate is covered by Kuss, 2:462–68; more recent views are surveyed in Mark A. Seifrid, "The Subject of Rom 7:14-25," *NovT* 34 (1992) 313–33; Juan Miguel Díaz-Rodelas, *Pablo y la ley: La novedad de Rom 7,7-8,4 en el conjunto de la reflexión paulina sobre la ley* (ISJ 28; Estella: Verbo Divino, 1994).

10   E.g., Godet, 272–80; Paul Althaus, "Zur Auslegung von Röm 7:14ff.: Antwort an Anders Nygren," *ThLZ* 77 (1952) 475–80.

11   Kümmel, *Römer 7*; idem, *Das Subjekt des 7. Kapitels des Römerbriefs* (Altenburg: Pierer, 1929).

12   Kümmel, *Römer 7*, 111–17.

13   E.g., J. M. Espy, "Paul's 'Robust Conscience' Reexamined," *NTS* 31 (1985) 161–88.

14   Kümmel, *Römer 7*, 67–90, 118–32.

15   E.g., Zahn, 337–71; Ronald Y. K. Fung, "The Impotence of the Law: Towards a Fresh Understanding of Romans 7:14-25," in W. W. Gasque and W. S. LaSor, eds., *Scripture, Tradition and Interpretation: Essays Presented to Everett F. Harrison* (Grand Rapids: Eerdmans, 1978) 34–48; Winger, *Law*, 171–72; Laato, *Paul and Judaism*, 109–45; Jervis, "Commandment," 193–216; Thurén, *Derhetorizing Paul*, 117–26.

16   For a defense of this traditional interpretation, see Theobald, *Studien*, 250–76.

17   Cranfield, 1:341–42; also 369–70.

18   Dunn, 1:411–12; see also Dunn, "Rom 7:14-25 in the Theology of Paul," *ThZ* 31 (1975) 257–73; repr. in P. Elbert, ed., *Essays on Apostolic Themes: Studies in Honor of Howard M. Erwin* (Peabody: Hendrickson,

interpretation gives the appearance of ethical realism but is impossible to coordinate with the details of Rom 5–6, which clearly state Paul's view that the converted have "died to sin."

A further alternative is to see Adam as the representative figure speaking in the first person as "I" in Rom 7, as Stanislas Lyonnet,[19] Lichtenberger,[20] and others[21] have argued. Although there are some potential allusions to the Genesis story in 7:9-13, the issue of the law that dominates chap. 7 was not part of the original Adam story.[22] The conflict between the intention to achieve the good and the contrary result of producing evil is also absent from the Adam story, either in its original form in Genesis or in its later development in Jewish literature.[23] There is even less likelihood that the "I" refers to the people of Israel,[24] because that would entail the same imposition of an "introspective conscience" that was troubled by the inability to obey the law, which was not in fact characteristic of first-century Judaism. Both of these views are problematic, since it is difficult to find good parallels to a group being referred to by the first person pronoun, especially in the absence of any introductory clause or literary device that would signal a peculiar use.

None of these theories has proven fully satisfactory, and the effort of some recent studies to combine them merely muddles the issue. While taking account of the diatribal style of the passage, Brian Dodd adopts a "composite" theory that is almost bizarre in its complexity: "The 'I' of Romans 7 incorporates elements of Adam's story, elements of Paul's experience, and is somehow intended to relate to the experience of Jewish, and perhaps Christian, believers."[25] A similar confusion is evident in the work of Gerd Theissen, who nevertheless provides a useful categorization of Paul's use of the first person singular in three ways: the personal (e.g., 1 Cor 15:8), the typical (e.g., Gal 2:20), and the fictive (e.g., 1 Cor 10:29).[26] In the first, unique personal experiences are in view, while in the second, such experiences are presented as paradigmatic for others. In the fictive mode, a hypothetical case is made without resort to specific personal experiences. Theissen argues that the "I" in Rom 7 "combines personal and typical traits."[27] However, he links this with an acceptance of an Adamic identification of the "I," which sounds very much like a "fictive" use; in the end there is an ambivalent picture of the "I" as referring both to Adam and to Paul himself, and "somehow intended to relate to the experience of Jewish, and perhaps Christian, believers."[28] Many contemporary commentators offer similar "composite proposals,"[29] which offer scant hope to make progress in understanding this passage.

1985). Middendorf, *Romans 7*, 171, concludes that the "'I' is Paul, a man who formerly took great pride in his observance of the Law." Paul's purpose is "*to inform* his addressees in an indirect manner *about the interrelationship between the Law, sin, and death* (237, italics in original)." Consistent with Lutheran doctrine, Middendorf states Paul's belief that all people are sinners "when they are confronted with the full impact of the Law" (239), which is "a generally applicable truth about how sin is able to misuse the Law to provoke sin, to deceive and to kill . . ." (241).

19   Lyonnet, "L'histoire"; idem, "Quaestiones ad Rom 7,7-13, *VD* 40 (1962) 165–83; idem, "'Tu ne convoiteras pas,'" 157–65.

20   Lichtenberger, *Ich Adams,* 107–86.

21   Käsemann, 195–98; Stuhlmacher, 106–7, 111; Hofius, *Paulusstudien II*, 104–54; Grappe, "Typologie adamique," 472–92.

22   See the critiques of this option by Brian Dodd, *Paul's Paradigmatic 'I': Personal Example as Literary Strategy* (JSNTSup 177; Sheffield: Sheffield Academic Press, 1999) 225; and Lambrecht, *Wretched "I,"* 63–64. Lichtenberger, *Ich Adams,* 205–41, reviews

intertestamental and rabbinic sources that understood the Adam story as if Adam possessed the law, but Paul states categorically in Rom 5:13 that the law was not in existence in Adam's time.

23   The surveys in Grappe, "Typologie adamique," 473–79, and Lichtenberger, *Ich Adams,* 205–41, provide no parallels to the internal conflict described in Rom 7:15, 18-20.

24   Moo, 426, lists advocates of this view, including Mark W. Karlberg, "Israel's History Personified: Romans 7:7-13 in Relation to Paul's Teaching on the 'Old Man,'" *TrinJ* 7 (1986) 65–74; and Jan Lambrecht, "Man Before and Without Christ: Rom 7 and Pauline Anthropology," *LouvS* 5 (1974) 18–33, reiterated by Lambrecht, *Wretched "I,"* 64–65. Moo himself advocates this view on 430–31.

25   Dodd, *Paul's Paradigmatic 'I,'* 230.

26   Theissen, *Psychological Aspects*, 191.

27   Ibid., 201.

28   Ibid., 230.

29   See Lambrecht, *Wretched "I,"* 67–71; Lichtenberger, *Ich Adams,* 163; Bandstra, *Law and the Elements,* 135–36.

A path leading to a potential resolution was opened by Jan Lambrecht. In contrast to a major stream of scholarship that has followed W. G. Kümmel in rejecting autobiographical construals of the "I" in Rom 7, Lambrecht contends that "Paul has depicted his pre-Christian, not his Christian situation."[30] While avoiding a technical discussion of the rhetoric of Romans, Lambrecht insists that "a rhetorical 'I'" appears in Rom 7 where Paul exaggerates in suggesting "that all the 'I' does is (always) sin."[31] This contradicts Paul's earlier argument in 2:14 concerning the righteous Gentiles who perform the law, but it accurately conveys an existential reality. Lambrecht follows Ziesler's view that Paul's use of the commandment concerning covetousness in Rom 7:7 implies that "inner desires and secret cravings" exist even in those who obey the law. Paul is speaking autobiographically in admitting that "notwithstanding his outward radical religious stand and zeal for the law, his inner desires were not without sinful covetousness."[32] But this insight was possible only "*after* his conversion. Only through justification has he achieved the correct insight into the actual tragic condition of his pre-Christian existence as a Jew. . . . Paul re-reads the past through the prism of faith."[33] While I would prefer a more nuanced and more historically grounded formulation that avoids a psychological theory of covetousness, Lambrecht selects the most plausible of the basic approaches to the enigma of Rom 7. Troels Engberg-Pedersen has recently confirmed this autobiographical approach as one of the important exegetical advances made in recent years:

It may be taken as established that Paul is describing an experience of living under the Mosaic Law as seen from the Christ-believing perspective. . . . It is one of the very real advances of twentieth-century scholarship to have established this point beyond reasonable doubt, and scholarship should never go back on it.[34]

This advance should be combined with the rhetorical clarification provided in the recent work of Stanley Stowers,[35] Jean-Noël Aletti,[36] and Jean-Baptiste Édart,[37] who point to the Greek convention of $\pi\rho\sigma\omega\pi\sigma\pi\sigma\epsilon\iota\alpha$, a "speech-in-character."[38] This was a widely used technique in Greco-Roman rhetoric in which an imaginary person or type is allowed to speak in the first person in order to make an emotionally effective argument. Quintilian's rhetorical handbook explains this aspect of $\pi\rho\sigma\omega\pi\sigma$-$\pi\sigma\epsilon\iota\alpha$ as follows:

The bare facts are no doubt moving in themselves but when we pretend that the persons concerned are speaking, the personal note adds to the emotional effect. . . . it is rendered to some extent more effective when it is, as it were, put into their mouth by their advocate: we may draw a parallel from the stage, where the actor's voice and delivery produce greater emotional effect when he is speaking in an assumed role than when he speaks in his own character.[39]

There are, moreover, striking parallels between Rom 7:7-12 and passages from Epictetus where *prosopopoeia* is employed in an illustrative manner. The "I" material is usually in the present tense, serving a rather gnomic purpose, but it can also be an anecdote from events in a speaker's past. For example in *Diss.* 1.10.7–9 the philosopher writes:

What then ($T\iota\ o\mathring{v}\nu;$)? Do I say that the living creature is unsuited to do anything? Certainly not ($\mu\grave{\eta}$ $\gamma\epsilon\nu\sigma\iota\tau\sigma$)! But how can you say that we don't do any-

---

30 Lambrecht, *Wretched "I,"* 90.

31 Ibid., 74, parenthesis in original.

32 Ibid., 78.

33 Ibid., 86, italics in original.

34 Engberg-Pedersen, "Reception," 37; see also Engberg-Pedersen, *Stoics*, 243–44; Räisänen, *Law*, 109.

35 Stowers, "Speech-in-Character," 180–202; Stowers's initial assessment in *Rereading*, 269, identifies this stylistic feature as $\epsilon\nu\alpha\lambda\lambda\alpha\gamma\eta$ or $\mu\epsilon\tau\alpha\beta\sigma\lambda\eta$; see also Lausberg, *Handbuch*, §257.2b; 509. An earlier effort in rhetorical clarification was provided by Kümmel, *Römer 7*, 126–31.

36 Jean-Noël Aletti, "Romans 7,7-25: Rhetorical Criticism and Its Usefulness," *SEÅ* 61 (1996) 77–95, taking up Stowers's theory on 90.

37 Jean-Baptiste Édart follows Stowers's lead in "De la nécessité d'un sauveur: Rhétorique et théologie de Rm 7, 7-25," *RB* 105 (1998) 359–64.

38 This is adopted by deSilva, *Introduction*, 620. Thurén develops an implausible critique of this theory in *Derhetorizing Paul*, 118–20.

39 Quintilian *Inst.* 6.1.25–26, cited by Stowers, "Speech-in-Character," 185–86.

thing? Take me first (αὐτὸς ἐγὼ πρῶτος). Whenever day comes, I bring my mind a little something that I must read over. Then I immediately [say] to myself, "What does it matter to me how so-and-so reacts? I must first get my sleep."

Whether the anecdote is true or not is less relevant for the argument than the argumentative point itself. In *Diss.* 1.18.15–16, for example, Epictetus recalls for argument's sake a past event in which a thief broke into his home and stole a lamp. His reference to this event again in 1.29.21 shows that the theft really occurred, but Epictetus's use of this element of *prosopopoeia* serves to substantiate a philosophical argument that in and of itself had nothing in common with thievery. The argumentative framework of *prosopopoeia* is strikingly parallel to Romans, as seen below:

Rom 7:7	*Diss.* 1.12
Τί οὖν ἐροῦμεν;	Τί οὖν;
("What then shall we say?")	("What then?")
ὁ νόμος ἁμαρτία;	ἀπόνοιά ἐστιν ἡ ἐλευθερία;
("Is the law sin?")	("Is freedom madness?")
μὴ γένοιτο·	μὴ γένοιτο·
("Certainly not!")	("Certainly not!")
+	+
1st Person Anecdote	1st Person Anecdote
+	+
Argumentative inference:	Argumentative inference:
ὥστε ὁ μὲν νόμος ἅγιος	οὐκ οἶδας, ὅτι τι καλόν τι ἐλευθερία
καὶ ἡ ἐντολὴ ἁγία καὶ δικαία καὶ ἀγαθή	ἐστί καὶ ἀξιολόγον
("so that the law is holy and the commandment holy and just and good")	("Do you not know that freedom is a thing that is good and worthy?")

In the analysis of *prosopopoeia*, therefore, the argumentative point is as important as the source of the example and the identity of the person. In the case of the rhetorical "I" that Paul employs in Rom 7, both dimensions need to be kept in mind.

In the debate over *prosopopoeia* in Rom 7, the identity and situation of the character remain unresolved. Stowers combines his hypothesis with a problematic theory of the identity of the fictitious person as "Gentiles who try to live by works of the law."[40] Édart returns to a more conventional hypothesis in identifying the character of Paul as a Jew who had been incapable of fulfilling the law.[41] Aletti refines this somewhat by showing that "it is surely Paul, as a disciple of Christ, that lets speak the Saul who was subject to the law, as if he had been conscious at that time of the contradictions surfaced in Rom 7."[42] In our exegesis below, we go a step farther to define this contradiction in terms of religious zealotism that failed to achieve the good that Paul had believed he could bring about by persecuting the followers of Christ.[43] While fulfilling the law in a zealous manner, he found himself opposing God's Messiah, whose coming he had hoped his violence would advance.[44]

I suggest that Paul's speech-in-character is artificially constructed in the light of his preconversion experience as a zealot,[45] but with an eye to the current situation in the Roman churches. It is formulated in such generic terms that persons outside of Paul's circle of experience can apply the argument to themselves. The discourse is paradigmatic, but in a negative sense, because by the time chap. 14 is reached, it becomes clear that both the weak and the strong have acted toward each other with the same competitive zeal that had corrupted Paul's pre-Christian experience with the law. With the exception of the closing verse of chap. 7, this speech demonstrates the counterproductivity of acting in the hostile, competitive manner that marked the Roman house and tene-

40   Stowers, *Rereading*, 273.
41   Édart, "Rm 7, 7-25," 394–95; Harrill identifies the fictitious person as Paul himself, understood to be a slave of Christ (Rom 1:1) who had formerly been captured by the demonic power of sin, which ends up as "bland moral polarity of good and bad and . . . an artificial construction serving Roman slave-holding ideology" (Harrill, *Slaves*, 33). What Harrill cannot explain with this view is the tendency of the enslaved self to achieve the opposite of the intended good (Rom 7:15-20).
42   Aletti, "Romans 7,7-25," 90.
43   This interpretation evolved from Jewett, *Terms*, 146–47, and received support from Schmithals, *Anthropologie*, 52–54. See also Leenhardt, 181; Donaldson, "Zealot and Convert," 668–82; and Smiles, "Concept of 'Zeal,'" 293–99.
44   This hypothesis lends precision to the view of

ment churches. They have been acting in a preconversion manner, although they are now in a postconversion situation, and Paul can only make the contradiction plain by a dramatic depiction of his own preconversion impasse as revealed in his encounter with the risen Christ.[46]

The crucial question that remains concerns the identity of the character that Paul depicts with the first person singular pronoun in Rom 7. Despite the fact that the depiction does not fit any of the stock characters known to Greco-Roman rhetoric, Paul nevertheless assumes that his hearers in Rome will have an instant grasp of who this character is. The most obvious alternative is that this character is Paul himself. Although most of the Roman converts had never met Paul, he has good reason to assume that they share the hearsay information of others who "only heard it said, 'He who once persecuted us is now preaching the faith he once tried to destroy'" (Gal 1:23). Paul has decided to couch his argument concerning zealotism with *prosopopoeia* drawn from his own life, because it was rhetorically more effective than to mount a direct attack on similar problems in Rome itself. If Paul can convince his audience that zealous prejudice had been counterproductive for himself as a paradigmatic convert, he will be in a position to address the remnants of this legalistic tendency in the later sections of his letter. The hypothesis of the "I" as Paul the zealot prior to his conversion will be developed in the exegesis below.

Rhetorical Disposition

IV.	The *probatio*
5:1–	B. The second proof: Life in Christ as a new system of
8:39	honor that replaces the quest for status through conformity to the law
7:7-12	6. Speech-in-character concerning the moral status of the law
7:7-8	a. The status of the law and the problem of covetousness
7:7a-c	1) The diatribal exchange concerning the moral status of the law
7:7a-b	a) The questions about the moral status of the law
7:7a	(1) The introductory question of general inference
7:7b	(2) The question whether the law is a sin
7:7c	b) The emphatic denial
7:7d-8	2) The doctrinal explanation of law leading to death
7:7d	a) Generalization: a law provides knowledge of sin
7:7e	b) The rationale that the Torah brings covetousness to awareness
7:7f	c) The scripture proof from Exodus 20:17
7:8a	d) Sin's opportunity provided by the commandment
7:8b	e) Sin evokes coveting
7:8c	f) The rationale that sin is dead without the law
7:9-12	b. The explanation of sin's deception by means of a law that remains holy
7:9-11	1) The commandment designed for life actually led to death
7:9a	a) Paul once lived without the law
7:9b	b) Sin revived after the commandment was given
7:10a	c) In his resultant death Paul discovered the paradox of the commandment intended for life
7:10b	d) The commandment led paradoxically to death rather than life
7:11a	e) Sin found an opportunity through the commandment
7:11b	f) Through deceit sin used the commandment to kill humans
7:12	2) The conclusion, with a final *clausula*
7:12a	a) The law is holy
7:12b	b) The threefold designation of the commandment as holy and righteous and good

Exegesis

■ **7** As in 3:5 (without οὖν, "therefore") and in 6:1, Paul poses the inferential question τί οὖν ἐροῦμεν ("what then shall we say?") in a form that brings the audience along with Paul into the diatribe.[47] This inclusive formulation with the first person plural verb does not sustain

Burnett, *Individual*, 200–205, that Rom 7 deals with the "danger of falling back into law observance." He cites as predecessors W. K. Grossouw, "De verscheurde mens van Romeinen zeven," in *Vriendengave Barnadus Kardinaal Alfrink aangeboden* (Utrecht, 1964) 80; and A. A. Hoekema, *The Chris-*

tian Looks at Himself (Grand Rapids: Eerdmans, 1975) 62.

45 Lambrecht, *Wretched "I,"* 90.

46 See Johnson, 110–13.

47 The exact phrase "What then shall we say?" is found in Greek literature first here in Paul, but only in

the usual inference that Paul is citing the critique of Jewish Christian or Jewish opponents.[48] The question is formulated in a compressed manner that reflects the oral quality of the letter: ὁ νόμος ἁμαρτία; ("the law, a sin?"), required the reader to provide the copula to be understandable.[49] A proper reading of the text would have made this plain. This is one of many indications that the rhetor on Phoebe's staff who provided the reading of the letter for the various house and tenement churches in Rome was intimately acquainted with its content and probably was also involved in the creation of Romans. The formulation is radical in the extreme, asking whether the law is an instance of sin, with the article attached to "law" indicating topicality, and the absence of the article with the word "sin" indicating a specific instance of sin. While some interpreters overlook this distinction in viewing sin and law as equivalent,[50] it seems more appropriate to conclude that the question suggests that the Torah[51] is an example of sin, that is, "something bad in itself, contrary to the essence and will of God, and consequently malignant."[52] Such an inference could have been drawn from Paul's earlier argument that sinful passions "came through the law" (7:5) and that the law had "encroached in order that the trespass might increased" (5:20). The formulation of the question, however, is so radical that it seems preposterous, rendering plausible Paul's flat denial, μὴ γένοιτο ("no way! certainly not!"), which appears here for the sixth time in the letter (3:4, 6, 31; 6:2, 15). In this instance the less colloquial form— "Certainly not!"— seems appropriate.[53]

The theological explanation of Paul's denial begins with ἀλλά, which in this instance has the sense of "nevertheless/rather." It retains the force of the denial ("Certainly not!") while clarifying the intention of Paul's critical view of the law.[54] Reiterating the terms of the question, Paul neatly reverses the placement of the articles, with "sin" now carrying the article, and "law" not: ἀλλὰ τὴν ἁμαρτίαν οὐκ ἔγνων εἰ μὴ διὰ νόμου ("nevertheless I did not know *the sin* except through [*a*] *law*"). The article with "sin" implies the topic or subject of sin, which would not have come to Paul's attention except for the limit posed by the concept of law. The anarthrous wording of "a law" implies an intellectual and emotional process of a matter coming to awareness, and the second aorist verb in the first person singular strongly suggests that Paul is here explaining his earlier moral development. I am therefore disinclined to translate this simple aorist form as a conditional subjunctive on the basis of the εἰ μή ("except, unless not") construction: "I *would* not have known the sin. . . ."[55] The verb γινώσκω refers to knowledge gained through experience, thus implying that without the presence of a law, he would have been unaware of sin.[56] The generalizing effect of Paul's formulation is conveyed by the anarthrous term "law,"[57] implying that although his own experience was with the Torah, the same awareness would have emerged if Paul's law had been Roman or barbarian, weak or strong. Moreover, Paul has stated unequivocally in 2:12-16 that Gentiles without the Torah still obey a law of conscience written on their hearts.

Romans in the NT (4:1; 6:1; 7:7; 8:31; 9:14; 9:30). The earliest attestation thereafter is in the second century, Aelius Herodianus Παρων. 3.2,866.43.

48   Wilckens, 2:75; Moo, 432; Hommel, "7. Kapitel," 152.

49   Dunn, 1:378.

50   Schlier, 220; Dunn, 1:378.

51   That νόμος in this context refers to the Torah rather than to law in a generic sense is confirmed by Winger, *Law,* 162–66.

52   Godet, 272.

53   Malherbe, "Μὴ γένοιτο," 32–33.

54   BAGD (2000) 44.1a; Kümmel, *Römer 7,* 47; Cranfield, 1:347; Moo, 432, argues for the restrictive connotation of ἀλλά in this context as opposed to the strictly adversative connotation translated by "but."

55   Fuchs, *Freiheit,* 55; Schlier, 220; Moulton and Turner, *Grammar III,* 92; Dunn, 1:378; Fitzmyer, 466; Moo, 433; the literal translation of the past tense verb is favored by Sanday and Headlam, 179; Barrett, 140–41.

56   Schmithals, "γινώσκω κτλ.," 250; Kuss, 2:442; Zeller, 139. The effort by Kümmel, *Römer 7,* 45; Bornkamm, "Sin, Law and Death," 102; Dunn, 1:378, and others to extend the meaning of γινώσκω as in 2 Cor 5:21 beyond the noetic to actually committing or at least experiencing sin seems inappropriate for this context; see Moo, 434.

57   In contrast, Dunn, 1:378-79, contends that "the absence of the definite article is of no consequence."

The issue here is not whether Paul had sinned prior to knowing the law,[58] but whether he would have been capable of conscious awareness of sin's reality without some form of law. Paul's point is quite different from a contention made about Adam, who was given a positive and negative command in the Garden (Gen 2:15-17) and thus, according to some rabbis, was called "to busy himself with words of Torah."[59]

Paul documents the claim about the awareness of sin coming through law by citing the Tenth Commandment concerning coveting. With the formulation $\tau\epsilon$ $\gamma\acute{\alpha}\rho$, which is an elegant, Attic equivalent of $\kappa\alpha\grave{\iota}$ $\gamma\acute{\alpha}\rho$ ("for also, indeed")[60] Paul draws v. 7e-f into an explanatory connection with v. 7d.[61] "I also did not know about coveting except [that] the law was saying . . . ," Paul explains, using $\mathring{\eta}\delta\epsilon\iota\nu$ ("to know, be aware"), a verb whose pluperfect carries an imperfect meaning.[62] In view of the lack of an aorist form of this verb "to know" ($o\mathring{\iota}\delta\alpha$, $\epsilon\mathring{\iota}\delta\acute{\epsilon}\nu\alpha\iota$) in Greek, this word has a meaning roughly synonymous with $\mathring{\epsilon}\gamma\nu\omega\nu$, the preceding verb.[63] Not to "know sin" in this context means that Paul was not able to recognize that a particular act or deed was wrong until it was pointed out as such. This applies to

any concept of law; it is only "wrong" when one knows a law has forbidden it.

There is a broad consensus that the citation $\mu\grave{\eta}$ $\mathring{\epsilon}\pi\iota\vartheta\upsilon\mu\acute{\eta}\sigma\epsilon\iota\varsigma$ ("you shall not covet"), stated here as coming from the law, would have been perceived as an abbreviation of the last of the Ten Commandments:[64]

You shall not covet ($o\mathring{\upsilon}\kappa$ $\mathring{\epsilon}\pi\iota\vartheta\upsilon\mu\acute{\eta}\sigma\epsilon\iota\varsigma$) your neighbor's wife; you shall not covet ($o\mathring{\upsilon}\kappa$ $\mathring{\epsilon}\pi\iota\vartheta\upsilon\mu\acute{\eta}\sigma\epsilon\iota\varsigma$) your neighbor's house, or his manservant, or his maidservant, or his ox, or his ass, or anything that is your neighbor's. (Exod 20:17; Deut 5:21)

Paul's formulation of this command with $\mu\acute{\eta}$ instead of $o\mathring{\upsilon}\kappa$ appears to follow a Hellenistic Jewish tradition reflected in 4 Macc 2.6, "For instance, the law says, 'You shall not covet ($\mu\grave{\eta}$ $\mathring{\epsilon}\pi\iota\vartheta\upsilon\mu\acute{\eta}\sigma\epsilon\iota\varsigma$) your neighbor's wife, nor anything that belongs to your neighbor.'"[65] The verb $\mathring{\epsilon}\pi\iota\vartheta\upsilon\mu\acute{\epsilon}\omega$ and its cognate forms appeared in a variety of contexts in the Greco-Roman world, ranging from desiring good things such as beauty or freedom[66] to desiring sensual pleasures such as food, alcohol, or sex.[67] For philosophers, $\mathring{\epsilon}\pi\iota\vartheta\upsilon\mu\acute{\iota}\alpha$ was associated with the bestial

---

58 Meyer, 2:6, rejects Fritzsche's proposal that knowing sin was in fact to be engaged in sin.

59 Cited by Scroggs, *Last Adam*, 42–43, from *Pirqe R. El.* 12; see also Dunn, 1:379, who refers to *Tg. Neof.* Gen 2:15. Lichtenberger, *Ich Adams*, 163, claims that Rom 7:7-11 is "streng als Auslegung von Gen 2f. begriffen," despite the fact that nothing in Genesis or the Jewish tradition echoes Paul's point that he would not have known about sin without the law.

60 The expression $\tau\epsilon$ $\gamma\acute{\alpha}\rho$, found also in 1:26 and 14:8, is common in Attic rhetoric (e.g., twenty-three times in Demosthenes), but occurs nowhere else in the NT except Heb 2:11.

61 See BDF §443; BAGD 807; the translation "for indeed" and the punctuation with a semicolon are suggested by Barrett, 138. Nestle-Aland and UBS both provide a period in place of a semicolon, thus separating the thought into two sentences.

62 See Dunn, 1:379, "I would not have come to that experience of covetousness which I still have."

63 Moo, 433.

64 Käsemann, 194; Wilckens, 2:80; Ziesler, "Romans 7," 47; Moo, 434. Lyonnet, "'Tu ne convoiteras pas,'" 157–65, suggests that this verse is drawn from the Adam story in Genesis, but as Moo, 435, points out, none of the cognates for $\mathring{\epsilon}\pi\iota\vartheta\upsilon\mu\acute{\iota}\alpha$ ("desire")

appear in this section of Genesis. That such cognates occur in Ps 106:14 to describe the illicit desires of the desert generation as noted by John G. Strelan, "A Note on the Old Testament Background of Romans 7:7," *LTJ* 15 (1981) 23–25, does not explain the wording of Rom 7:7 in the form of a commandment.

65 Friedrich Büchsel, "$\vartheta\upsilon\mu\acute{o}\varsigma$ $\kappa\tau\lambda$.," *TDNT* 3 (1965) 171; for a survey of sources dealing with the prohibition of desire, see Berger, *Gesetzesauslegung Jesu*, 346–49.

66 E.g., Epictetus *Diss.* 1.6.24 describes the desire evoked by seeing Pheidias's statue of Zeus at Olympia, "will you not desire to behold these things and to contemplate them ($\tau\alpha\mathring{\upsilon}\tau\alpha$ $\delta\grave{\epsilon}$ $\vartheta\epsilon\acute{\alpha}\sigma\alpha\sigma\vartheta\alpha\iota$ $\kappa\alpha\grave{\iota}$ $\kappa\alpha\tau\alpha\kappa\sigma\mathring{\eta}\sigma\alpha\iota$ $o\mathring{\upsilon}\kappa$ $\mathring{\epsilon}\pi\iota\vartheta\upsilon\mu\acute{\eta}\sigma\epsilon\tau\epsilon$)?" BAGD (2000) 372 cites Diodorus Siculus *Hist.* 11.36.5, "desire for freedom ($\mathring{\epsilon}\pi\iota\vartheta\upsilon\mu\acute{\iota}\alpha$ $\tau\mathring{\eta}\varsigma$ $\mathring{\epsilon}\lambda\epsilon\upsilon\vartheta\epsilon\rho\acute{\iota}\alpha\varsigma$)," while Lysias *Orat.* 13.16.3; 20.3.1 refers to peace or oligarchy as objects of desire. Hans Hübner, "$\mathring{\epsilon}\pi\iota\vartheta\upsilon\mu\acute{\iota}\alpha$ $\kappa\tau\lambda$.," *EDNT* 2 (1991) 27, argues that the LXX employs this term most often in "an ethically neutral sense."

67 E.g., Epictetus *Diss.* 4.9.3 warns against desiring a neighbor's sexy wife: "(If) another (has) a shapely wife, you should not covet a shapely wife ($\sigma\grave{\upsilon}$ $\tau\grave{o}$ $\mu\grave{\eta}$

side of human nature, which should be held in check by the mind; Stoicism listed ἐπιθυμία as one of the four chief passions that must be subdued.[68] It was therefore not unusual both in Judaism and in Hellenism for desires to be considered evil in and of themselves,[69] which is reflected in the two earlier references in Rom 1:24 and 6:12. One thinks of the words of *Apoc. Mos.* 19.3, "desire (ἐπιθυμία) is the origin of every sin."[70] There was in fact "a tendency to see the essential element of the law in the prohibition of covetousness," as Gerd Theissen shows.[71] *4 Macc* 2.6 summarizes the law with the formula μὴ ἐπιθυμεῖν ("you shall not covet"), and Philo refers to coveting as the "fountain of all evils" (ἀπάντων πηγὴ τῶν κακῶν τῶν κακῶν, *Spec.* 4.84) and "desire is the passion to which name 'originator of evil' can truly be given" (τὸ γὰρ ἀψευδῶς ἂν λεχθὲν ἀρχέκακον πάθος ἐστὶν ἐπιθυμία, *Spec.* 4.85).[72]

The interpretations of ἐπιθυμία suggested by commentators for this passage have taken a variety of approaches to the context of the Tenth Commandment, reflected in my translation as "covetousness." The classical psychological approach developed by Augustine concentrates on the seductive power of forbidden fruit to awaken "concupiscence" that rebels against God.[73] Augustine, of course, interpreted concupiscence as involuntary sexual desire. There is support in the ancient texts for understanding ἐπιθυμία as "paradigmatically sexual" as proposed by Watson, along with Gundry, Räisänen, and others.[74] A few classical parallels support the interpretation of sexual desire. In *Opif.* 152, Philo explicitly links the story of Adam and Eve with sexual lust, but the word ἐπιθυμία does not appear there. However, the critique of this interpretation by Ziesler renders implausible an exclusive reference to sexual sins.[75] Not only does Paul fail to cite the explicit prohibition of adultery in this verse, following Deuteronomy and Exodus, but he lists the commandments about adultery, murder, theft, and coveting in Rom 13:9 as if covetousness were not primarily sexual.

Nor have psychological theories proved fully satisfactory in explaining Paul's intention in summarizing the commandments with "Do not covet." The Freudian dynamic of the superego that resists and simultaneously internalizes parental authority, whereby coveting is expressed with murderous Oedipal energy, has been suggested by Scroggs, Theissen, and myself in earlier work.[76] Robert Hamerton-Kelly uses this verse to construct his theory of "the deformation of desire" by "mimetic rivalry," in which Adam's sin consisted of "divine envy" that resulted in "sacred violence."[77] Other interpreters employ the modern category of "selfishness" in explaining ἐπιθυμία as "desire for self, for self-satisfaction."[78] It is questionable, however, whether any of these psychological and self-theories are adequate to explain a text written prior to their emergence. Similarly problematic is the outmoded theory of Paul's inability to perform the law, which still has its echoes in references to ἐπιθυμία as "sluggish moral conscience."[79]

That ἐπιθυμία in this verse includes "nomistic desire" has been argued by Bultmann, Bornkamm, and others[80] on the basis of connections to Rom 12:2-3 and

---

ἐπιθυμεῖν)." Desiring property, goods, and materials is discussed with this term in Lucian of Samosata *Phal.* 1.11.7. See other examples in BAGD (2000) 372.

68 Büchsel, "θυμός κτλ.," 168, cites Zeno's list from Diogenes Laertius *Vitae philos.* 7.110.

69 Büchsel, "θυμός κτλ.," 169.

70 See also *Apoc. Abr.* 24.10.

71 Theissen, *Psychological Aspects*, 205.

72 See also Philo *Spec.* 4.130–31.

73 E.g., Lietzmann, 73; Dodd, 109–10; Barrett, 141; Bruce, 149; Best, 81; Morris, 280; the Augustinian position is stated in his *Spir. lit.* 22; *Nup. concu.* 1.6–8, 24, 27; 2.14, 53.

74 Watson, *Agape*, 154; see also Gundry, "Moral Frustration," 228–45; Räisänen, "ἐπιθυμία and ἐπιθυμεῖν," 96–104.

75 Ziesler, "Romans 7," 44–46, pointing to "all kinds of covetousness" in Rom 7:8b, which makes it clear that Paul has a variety of forms of coveting in mind, consistent with that of the Tenth Commandment. The connotation of ἐπιθυμία in this verse is thus broader than 1 Thess 4:5 which refers to sexual infidelity as acting "in the passion of desire (ἐν πάθει ἐπιθυμίας) like Gentiles who do not know God."

76 Theissen, *Psychological Aspects*, 245; Scroggs, *New Day*, 12–13; Jewett, *Apostle to America*, 87–97.

77 Hamerton-Kelly, *Cross*, 90, 97.

78 Dunn, 1:380; Engberg-Pedersen, *Stoics*, 245, presents a Stoic form of this theory that "what accounts for sinning on the part of a person living under the law is a *perspective*, the I-perspective" (italics in original).

79 Fitzmyer, 466.

80 Bultmann, *Old and New Man*, 33–48; Bultmann,

Phil 3:4-6, where Paul discusses the problem of legalistic zealotism. Bultmann shows that ἐπιθυμία is associated with "flesh" (Gal 5:16-17; Rom 6:12; 13:14), which in turn is employed in connection with zealous fulfillment of the law (Gal 3:3; Phil 3:3-7).[81] But rather than speaking of "nomistic desire," which is too subjective, individualistic, and anti-Judaic, I prefer to keep the context of the Tenth Commandment in the forefront; it is not desire as such that is forbidden, but coveting what belongs to others. Paul refers here to a distortion in interpersonal relations such as we have traced in the earlier sections of Romans. The sin of asserting oneself and one's group at the expense of others[82] fits the intensely competitive environment of Greco-Roman and Jewish culture. This interpretation contains the aggressive connotation that Scroggs, Hamerton-Kelly, Dunn, and others have intuited; it would include the Jewish alternative of desiring superior performance of the law, which was part of Paul's own past, but it would also include distinctively Gentile forms of competition for honor.[83]

■ **8** Sin is the active agent in this sentence, causing evil behavior that Paul as a paradigmatic human proved unable to resist. The idiom ἀφορμὴν λαμβάνειν ("to take opportunity") first appears with the Greek orators in the context of trade, agriculture, and war.[84] In one such example, Andocides (*Pac.* 37.4) uses this idiom with the same verb, κατεργάζομαι ("work, bring about"), that Paul employs in this verse:

ταύτην δὲ λαβόντες ἀφορμὴν οἱ πατέρες ἡμῶν καρηργάσαντο τῇ πόλει δύναμιν τοσαύτην . . .

("But having taken this opportunity our fathers exercised so great a force in the city . . .")

There is also an example of this idiom in Philo, where the deeds elicited are explicitly evil, as in this verse of Romans: in support of the accusation that the Alexandrian prefect Flaccus encouraged mob violence against the Jews, Philo observes that "if the unruly crowd takes such an opportunity to commit wrong doings (ἀφορμὴν λάβῃ τῶν ἁμαρτημάτων) they do not stop there but pass on from one act to another, always engaging in new forms of violence" (*Flacc.* 35.7). Elsewhere in the Pauline letters (2 Cor 5:12; 11:12; Gal 5:13) such "opportunities" or "occasions" are not in themselves bad,[85] except when misused by others to advance their agendas. Thus, in this verse, rather than providing a barrier against sin, as the rabbis taught,[86] the ἐντολή ("commandment") was misused by sin to produce the opposite of its intended purpose.

In the case of Paul's preconversion experience under review here, sin took the form of the competitive urge to "advance in Judaism beyond many of my own age among my people, so extremely zealous was I for the traditions of my fathers" (Gal 1:14).[87] This context correlates closely with the particular commandment in view here, namely, the prohibition of coveting as cited in the previ-

Theology, 1:247–48; Bornkamm, "Sin, Law and Death," 87–104; Furnish, *Theology,* 141–43.

81 Bultmann, *Theology,* 1:240–41; the critique of Bultmann's logic by Räisänen, "ἐπιθυμία and ἐπιθυμεῖν," 99–100, does not eliminate the implication of these associations. Some interpreters continue to view this passage as directed against Jewish legalism, as for example Carter, *Power of Sin,* 183, who entitles his discussion of this passage "A Torah-observant Jew as a sinful outsider."

82 See Käsemann, 194: ἐπιθυμία is "the passion to assert oneself against God and neighbor." See also Patte, *Paul,* 265–74.

83 Johnson, 113, comes close to this view in referring to a "desiring disease . . . that applies to all craving" which expresses "the idolatrous impulse that lies at the heart of sin. Coveting is that need to have, to possess, to acquire, in order to secure being and worth." While this is potentially related to Johnson's grasp of Paul's conversion from Jewish zealotism

(109–11), his employment of medical terminology associated with addiction fails to take the ancient honor system into account, which allowed Paul to universalize his experience in this passage.

84 E.g., Isocrates *Evag.* 28.3; *Paneg.* 61.4; see Georg Bertram, "ἀφορμή," *TDNT* 5 (1968) 472.

85 Bertram, "ἀφορμή," 473.

86 Michel, 227, describes the rabbinic teaching that the "good urge" makes use of the law to oppose the impulses of the "evil urge."

87 In view of the specificity and cogency of this autobiographical comment from Galatians, references to the power of "forbidden fruit" (Godet, 274), to "native mulishness" (Morris, 280), or to the Adam story (Dunn, 1:381; Haacker, 143) seem quite speculative.

ous verse,[88] not the entire νόμος, as many commentators assume.[89] The word order of the sentence, as well as the peculiar role of the Tenth Commandment, suggests that the phrase "through the commandment" is attached to the participial expression "taking opportunity."[90] The fault lies not with the commandment itself but with its misuse by sin, which elicited in Paul's prior life "every manner of coveting." In the competitive environment of the Greco-Roman and Jewish worlds, the desire to surpass others and to achieve honor had invaded the arena of religion, perverting it into a means of achieving superiority. This situation is presented as paradigmatic, because the Roman house and tenement churches are behaving in a similar manner toward one another, and if given the opportunity, will certainly extend this competitive zeal into the mission to Spain, where it would have equally fatal consequences.

The congregational situation, viewed afresh from Paul's own past experience, leads to the radical conclusion of this verse, that "apart from law sin is dead." The adjective νεκρός appears here with the sense of "lifeless,"[91] incapable of achieving its object.[92] In contrast to the corollary from 1 Cor 15:56, "the power of sin is the law," here both "law" and "sin" are anarthrous, thus broadening Paul's claim to include every form of law.[93] This adapts his point to the congregational situation in Rome,[94] where varying forms of law are dividing the house and tenement churches into competitive factions. But while the rhetorical force of Paul's formulation is undeniable, particularly in view of its audience, its logical force remains weak; the mere fact that sin finds opportunity in law does not mean that it lacks the capacity to act as an evil force in other circumstances. Paul's argument is aimed at a specific rhetorical situation and cannot bear the weight of logical discourse valid for all times and circumstances.

■ 9 Employing the first person pronoun ἐγώ for the first time in the letter, to be followed by seven more references in this chapter, Paul points explicitly to his own personal experience.[95] That he was living "once[96] apart from law" is most plausibly linked with the typical experience of a Jewish boy who was not required to obey the Torah until he was initiated as a "son of the commandment."[97] Critics of this view refer to early training in the

---

88 Käsemann, 194; Reinhard Weber, "Die Geschichte des Gesetzes und des Ich in Römer 7,7–8,4: Einige Überlegungen zum Zusammenhang von Heilsgeschichte und Anthropologie im Blick auf die theologische Grundstellung des paulinischen Denkens," NZSTh 29 (1987) 156–58; Fitzmyer, 467.

89 Kümmel, Römer 7, 48–49; Gottlob Schrenk, "ἐντολή," TDNT 2 (1964) 550; Schlier, 223; Dunn, 1:380.

90 This is argued by Kühl, 231; Lagrange, 169; Kümmel, Römer 7, 44; Schlatter, 159; Wilckens, 2:81, and especially Schmidt, 124; also Fitzmyer, 466; that "through the commandment" should be attached to the verb κατειργάσατο ("it worked") is preferred by Lipsius, 126; Sanday and Headlam, 179–80; Zahn, 339; Schlier, 222–23; Cranfield, 1:350; Dunn, 1:380.

91 Rudolf Bultmann, "νεκρός κτλ.," TDNT 5 (1967) 893.

92 Michel, 227; Kuss, 2:444; Cranfield, 1:351.

93 Most commentators and translations add the article at this point: e.g., Dunn, 1:381, writes "apart from the law sin is dead," thus limiting the bearing of Paul's argument to "the typical Jewish prizing of the law." Among modern commentators, Schlier, 220, Barrett, 143, and Wilckens, 2:73, respect the anarthrous use of "law" in this verse.

94 Jervis, "Commandment," 197, shows that the formulation "apart from the law" requires the context of the congregation's "life in Christ."

95 See the discussion in "Analysis" above; Theissen, Psychological Aspects, 195, 201, shows that ἐγώ "combines personal and typical traits." Dodd, Paul's Paradigmatic 'I,' 230, extends this reference to "elements of Adam's story, elements of Paul's experience, and is somehow intended to relate to the experience of Jewish, and perhaps Christian, believers." However, see below for the evidence that a reference to Adam is unlikely.

96 According to BAGD 695, ποτέ has the sense of "once, formerly," as in Josephus Bell. 7.112, describing Titus revisiting the ruins of Jerusalem and contrasting it with "the former splendor of the city (τῇ ποτε τῆς πόλεως λαμπρότητι)."

97 See Davies, Paul, 24–25; Michel, 228; Barrett, 143–44; the reference in 'Abot R. Nat. 5.24 from around 150 C.E. is that at the age of thirteen a boy is made a bar-mitzwah ("son of commandment"). Deissmann, Paul, 94–95, cites the rabbinic teaching that children know nothing about sin until the "evil urge" awakens at the age of nine.

law provided to Jewish boys[98] and to their love of the law,[99] but this does not address the question of the age when a boy was required to live under its authority. The popular interpretive alternative is that Paul refers here to himself in the role of Adam,[100] which labors under the burdens of having to assume a complicated shift in roles that is not explicitly mentioned in the text and also of reading the Genesis account in a manner that no ancient Jew would have done, that is, assuming a period prior to Gen 2:16 when Adam and Eve lived without the commandment.[101] Following the hypothesis of an autobiographical reference, the imperfect verb ἔζων ("I was living") would refer to a period in Paul's early life when he was not obligated and thus defined by law. This imperfect form appears here for the only time in the NT and is reminiscent of the dying Alcestis's lament to her husband, bewailing the fact that she must leave a bereaved husband and motherless children, κἀγώ τ' ἂν ἔζων ("but had I lived on . . . ," Euripides *Alc.* 295) and Sinorix's explanation for suicide because she was unable to live with her husband, σοῦ χωρὶς ἔζων ἀνιαρῶς ("for apart from you I was living grievously," Plutarch *Amat.* 768D). In both of these instances, the quality of life is determined by an all-encompassing circumstance, comparable to the law that defines the Jewish person once he has undertaken its burden and joy. In this case, Paul's early life was defined as χωρὶς νόμου ("apart from law"), which as in Rom 3:21, 28; 7:8 refers not to the mere awareness of law but to law as that which had not yet determined his relation to God and fellow humans.

The genitive absolute construction that follows in v. 9b has a temporal sense defined by the imperfect verb in v. 9a, referring to a point in Paul's past when "the commandment came" (ἐλθούσης δὲ τῆς ἐντολῆς). Following the hypothesis of Paul's teenage experience, this would be the moment of the *bar-mitzwah,* when the commandment shifted from a written text to an obligation. It was at this point for the first time in his experience that "the sin came again to life." The verb ἀναζάω ("revive, come to life again") contains a clear reference to Adam's sin that produced the fateful legacy for every subsequent human.[102] This formulation cannot literally relate to Adam's own sin, which is a further reason to reject the hypothesis that the "I" in this passage plays the role of Adam. Scholars have averted this implication by suggesting an "inchoate" interpretation of the prefix ἀνα-, resulting in the translation "sprang/came to life,"[103] but no evidence has been adduced in support of this connotation.[104] Sin, appearing here with the definite article to indicate the active subject of the action, emerged to pervert the purpose of the commandment, turning it into an instrument for gaining honor in competition with Paul's fellows. Paul refers explicitly to this experience of his earlier life in Gal 1:14-15, that "I advanced in Judaism beyond many of my own age among my people, so extremely zealous was I for the tradition of my fathers." It was this competitive subversion of the commandment, emerging at the very moment when Paul took up the burden of the Torah, that produced his destructive zealotism, which led to the persecution of the early church and to the dilemma analyzed in the rest of this chapter.

---

98 Dunn, 1:382, refers to descriptions of Jewish education in Philo *Legat.* 210; Josephus *C. Ap.* 2.178.

99 Theissen, *Psychological Aspects*, 251, refers to a Roman epitaph published by Harry J. Leon in *AJA* 28 (1924) 251–52, "Here lies Eukarpos, a child hallowed, a friend of the law (φιλονόμος). Your sleep is in peace."

100 See Lyonnet, "L'histoire," 130–42; Käsemann, 195–96; Scroggs, *Last Adam*, 33, 42–43; Theissen, *Psychological Aspects*, 251–60; Dunn, 1:381–83.

101 The dogma that the Torah was eternal prevented Jewish interpreters from reading the Genesis account in terms of an early period of innocence followed by the obligation to obey the law.

102 See Lambrecht, *Wretched "I,"* 24; Moo, 438.

103 Meyer, 2:11, cites Tholuck, Rückert, Fritzsche, Baumgarten-Crusius, de Wette, Maier, and Hofman as supporting the translation "came to life;" among more recent commentators, Cranfield, 1:352; Morris, 28; Franz Schnider, "ἀναζάω," *EDNT* 1 (1990) 80.

104 LSJM 104; BAGD 53; MM 32; in discussing this composite verb, Moulton and Howard, *Grammar II,* 295, provides no option apart from "live again, revive" as found in the other biblical example (Luke 15:24) and the close parallels (Rom 14:9; Rev 20:5). Meyer, 2:11, showed that there was not a single example of "came to life" in ancient literature.

■ **10** The sentence describing Paul's youthful experience with the law continues with the forceful expression "but I died," with the personal pronoun "I" at the point of emphasis at the beginning of the sentence: ἐγὼ δὲ ἀπέθανον. There can be little doubt that this second occurrence of the personal pronoun refers to Paul's personal experience, viewed in the light of his conversion.[105] The antithesis to "I was once living" is stark, preparing the way for the contradiction described in the rest of this verse.[106] Although interpreters have suggested an allusion to the threat of Adam's death in Gen 2:17b,[107] this seems unlikely, because this threat was not carried out after eating the forbidden fruit, and Adam was thought to have had a natural death in old age (Gen 5:5). It is more likely that Paul has in mind the death that always results from sin, as stated in Rom 5:12, 15, 17, 21 and climaxing in 6:23, "the wages of sin is death."[108] In Paul's autobiography, of course, the awareness of this sin and its fatal consequence did not emerge until his conversion, when he discovered that his zealous obedience to the law had brought him into conflict with God and the Messiah.

The ironic reversal of the traditional expectation of law's potential is that "the commandment that was for life, this was for death." The passive expression εὑρέθη μοι ("was found with respect to me"), a Hebraism not found otherwise in Greek literature,[109] depicts the surprising discovery[110] as something derived not from his own insight or from traditional wisdom but from divine disclosure.[111] The traditional view that was overturned by Paul's conversion is stated in Lev 18:5, referring to obeying the commandments as that "by doing which a man shall live in them (ἃ ποιήσας ἄνθρωπος ζήσεται ἐν αὐτοῖς)."[112] In the light of the Christ event, Paul confesses the opposite consequence, that legal observance when corrupted by the sinful energy of covetousness brings death rather than life. The emphatic αὕτη ("the same") heightens the sense that "even the same" commandment that was intended to produce life resulted in death.[113] As Michel observes, this sentence would have sounded blasphemous to those holding the traditional view of the Torah.[114]

■ **11** While repeating the thought of v. 8, Paul adds the element of deception to his account of sin's perversion of the law. He selects the compound verb ἐξαπατάω, which has the same connotation as the simple verb ἀπατάω ("deceive"),[115] which occurs in the account of Adam's alibi: "the serpent deceived me and I ate" (Gen 3:13). An allusion to the Genesis account is likely,[116] but the shape of the deception and the manner of its discovery are radically different. While the deception of Adam and Eve related to the assurance given by the snake that they would not in fact die from eating the forbidden fruit but would become "like the gods, knowing good and evil" (Gen 2:5), Paul's deception was in believing that superior performance of the law would earn honor

---

105 See Theissen, *Psychological Aspects*, 201.
106 Jervis, "Commandment," 200, contends that "sin's revival (7.9) must occur in the life of one in whom it has previously been defeated," that is, believers, but the emphatic ἐγὼ points to Paul's personal experience.
107 Dunn, 1:383.
108 Cranfield, 1:352; Schlier, 224.
109 A *TLG* search located only a few, late theological works that employ this Hebraic formulation; see BAGD 325.2 for more distant parallels; Michel, 228, and Schlier, 225, cite the Hebrew expression נמצא as lying behind this formulation.
110 Godet, 276.
111 See Paul's formulation in Gal 1:12-16 of divine disclosure at the time of his conversion.
112 See also Deut 4:1, "do the commandments that you may live"; *Ps. Sol.* 14.1-2, "the Lord is faithful . . . to those who live in the righteousness of his commandments in the law, which he has commanded for our

life." See also Gen 2:17; Deut 6:24; Prov 6:23; Sir 17:11; 45:5; Bar 3:9; *4 Ezra* 14.30.
113 Schlier, 225, followed by Dunn, 1:384. That "the death about which Paul speaks in 7.9-10 also has a beneficial result" because it reveals the nature of sin and the holiness of the law (Jervis, "Commandment," 198) is an accurate assessment of the consequences of Paul's conversion, but it swerves away from the point of this passage, which is that the quest for honor through zealous observance of the law leads to death rather than life.
114 Michel, 228.
115 Armin Kretzer, "ἀπάτη, ἀπατάω, ἐξαπατάω," *EDNT* 1 (1990) 117; see 1 Cor 3:18; 2 Cor 11:3; 2 Thess 2:3.
116 See Meyer, 2:12; Godet, 277; Schlier, 225–26; Michel, 228–29; Dunn, 1:384–85.

452

both from fellow humans and from God and that such obedience would ultimately usher in God's kingdom. His zealous adherence to this illusion was broken only by conversion; its lethal consequences could not have been understood from the Genesis account.[117] This explains the personal formulation: the commandment "deceived me" and "sin killed me." It is Paul's own experience, drastically shaped by his encounter with the risen Lord, that is herein presented as the paradigmatic "character" for the congregations in Rome, not the experience of Adam. It is not the sin of disobedience, as in the Genesis account, but the sin of legalistic zealotism that leads to the death Paul has in mind. This new approach to sin has a bearing on the squabbling house and tenement churches in Rome and on the mission to Spain, a bearing that the Genesis account entirely lacks.[118] When law is employed in the effort to dominate others and to earn superior status before God, its holy purpose is perverted and it leads to death rather than to life.

■ 12 Here Paul returns to the theme with which the pericope opened, whether or not the law is sin. The sentence remains an anacoluthon because it begins with "so on the one hand the law . . . (ὥστε ὁ μὲν νόμος)" but lacks the "other hand."[119] Günther Bornkamm's study of Pauline anacoluthon showed that it documents "the hiatus between subject and expression, thought and language, and thereby is an apt expression" of a paradoxical situation.[120] Paul's experience with the law, its perversion, and the revelation of its dilemma in the cross of Christ produces an almost unspeakable gulf between the divine essence of the Torah and its actual impact under the power of sin. Both the law as a whole and the particular commandment about coveting are "holy," partaking of the holiness of God and therefore

worthy of "respect, reverence, and awe."[121] This was a conventional view of the law, as, for example, the "holy law" in 2 Macc 6:23, 28. A comparable expression of the paradox is expressed in *4 Ezra* 9.37: "For we who have received the law and sinned will perish . . . ; the law, however, does not perish but remains in its glory." The supreme ethical value of the law is expressed by the rest of the threefold expression that comprises the clausula ending this pericope. That the law is δίκαιος ("righteous") echoes the claim of Deut 4:8, "and what manner of nation is so great, which has righteous ordinances and right judgments (δικαιώματα καὶ κρίματα δίκαια) according to all this law, which I set before you this day." In contrast Romans argues that the righteousness of God is revealed in the process of making people right by faith in Christ (1:17; 3:26; 5:19), rather than in strict obedience to the law (3:20). The standards of equity and impartiality that marked Israel's conception of righteous law had been newly minted in the earlier argument of the letter, with the grace of Christ that comes to all without consideration of merit. This eliminates any vestige of Deuteronomy's claim that the gift of a righteous law makes Israel greater than all other nations. The final term that describes the nature of the law is "good," referring to the absolute moral quality of the law.[122] This formulation echoes Prov 4:2, "for I give you a good gift (δῶρον ἀγαθόν), forsake not my law."[123] Yet the contradiction that finds expression in Romans, portrayed in the four additional references to "the good" in this chapter (vv. 13 [twice], 18, 19), is that when any person or group pursues it in the zealous quest for honor, the achievement is always evil. The pericope thus ends in a manner that leads directly into the rest of this explosive chapter.

117 See Kuss, 2:448–49.
118 None of the commentaries I have consulted links this passage in any way with the congregational situation.
119 Godet, 278, observes that although the corresponding δέ ("on the other hand") is missing, v. 13b provides the appropriate sense. See also Meyer, 2:12–13.
120 Bornkamm, "Anakoluthe," 76; his study does not cover this particular example, however.
121 Horst Balz, "ἅγιος κτλ.," *EDNT* 4 (1987) 111, mentions a fragmentary inscription that refers to the Roman law as "holy."
122 See Kühl, 232; Michel, 229; Dunn, 1:386; Fitzmyer, 469; Jörg Baumgarten, "ἀγαθός," *EDNT* (1990) 6.
123 Walter Grundmann, "ἀγαθός κτλ.," *TDNT* 1 (1964) 14.

7

The Seventh Pericope

Speech-in-Character Concerning the Effect of the Law

13/ Did the good, therefore, cause my death? By no means! But the sin, in order that it might be shown to be sin, was bringing about my death through the good, in order that the sin might become sinful beyond measure through the commandment. 14/ For we know[a] that the law is spiritual, but I am fleshly,[b] having been sold under the sin. 15/ For I do not know what I bring about. For what I don't want—this I practice, but what I hate—this[c] I do. 16/ But if what I don't want—this I do, I agree with the law that [it is] excellent.[d] 17/ Now surely it is not I [who] brings it about, but the sin dwelling[e] in me. 18/ For I know that excellence[f] does not dwell in me, that is in my flesh. For wishing it lies within my reach, but bringing about what is excellent does not.[g] 19/ For I don't do the good that I want, but the bad that I don't want[h] —this I practice. 20/ Now if what I[i] don't want—this I do, it is no longer I who bring it about but the sin dwelling in me.

21/ Thus I discover that while my will is directed to the law in order to do what is excellent, the bad lies within my reach. 22/ For with respect to my inner self, I share pleasure in the law of God,[j] 23/ but I see another law in my members, warring against the law in my mind and captivating me by[k] the law of the sin that exists in my members.[l] 24/ How wretched a person I [am]! Who will rescue me from this body of death? 25/ But thanks [be] to God[m] through Jesus Christ our Lord! [n]Thus, left to myself, I am a slave to God's law in my mind, but in my flesh [I am a slave] to sin's law.

a   A minor variant in 33 *l* 883 slav (Hier[1/10]) *pc* has the text οἶδα μέν ("I know on the one hand") in place of the widely attested οἴδαμεν ("we know"), and several older commentators have argued for this reading. Metzger refers in *Textual Commentary (1975)*, 514, to Reiche and Hofmann; and Zahn, 347, refers to the strangeness of Paul's describing his own personal experience prior to the Damascus conversion by an obtrusive "we." There is little doubt that the plural form should be preferred here.

b   א² K L P 88 104 323 326 330 365 614 945 1175 1241 1243 1319 1505 1573 1735 1836 1874 2464 2495 *Maj* have the softer term σαρκικός ("belonging to a fleshly realm") in place of σαρκινός ("made of flesh") strongly attested by א* A B C D F G Ψ 6 33 69 81 424 1506 1739 1881 *al* Meth. The alteration probably had the motivation of reducing the theological difficulty of saying Paul was fleshly in a comprehensive physical sense.

c   The omission of τοῦτο ("this") in D F G mon appears to be a stylistic improvement, eliminating the repetition of a parallel phrase in 7:15b and the redundancy caused by ὅ and τοῦτο. See Cranfield, 1:358.

d   A minor variant in F G t supplies καλόν ἐστίν ("it is good") for καλός ("good"), but this looks very much like an attempted clarification of the text.

e   In place of οἰκοῦσα ("dwelling") found in A C D F G K L P Ψ 6 33 69 88 104 323 326 330 365 424 614 945 1175 1241 1243 1319 1505 1506 1573 1735 1739 1836 1881 1874 2464 2495 *Maj* lat Cl [630 *lacking due to homoioteleuton*], ἐνοικοῦσα ("indwelling") appears in א B 1270 vg^mss Ambst, a reading previously preferred by Nestle-Aland[25]. The latter looks like an effort to improve the text, and should be regarded as secondary despite Sanday and Headlam's argument (182) about appropriateness to context.

f   The provision of the article τό ("the") in F G appears to be a grammatical improvement.

g   The abrupt and undoubtedly original conclusion of the sentence with οὔ ("not") in א A B C 6 81 424^c (acc. to Swanson) 436 1739 1852 1881 1908 2200 *pc* sa bo goth arm Meth Did Cyr^comm Hier[2/5] Aug[18/38] Greek mss^acc. to Aug evoked several efforts at stylistic improvement. D F G K L P Ψ 5 33 61 69 88* 104 181 218 323 326 330 424* 451 459 467 614 623 629 720 915 917 945 1175 1241 1243 1398 1505 1506 1563 1678 1718 1735 1751 1836 1838 1845 1846 1874 1875 1877 1912 1942 1959 1962 2110 2138 2197 2344 2464 2492 2495 2516 2523 2544 2718 *Maj Lect* (ar) b d f g mon o vg sy^p, h eth geo² slav Ir^lat Or^lat Bas Chr Cyr^lem Ambst Hier[3/5] Pel Aug[20/38] supply οὐχ εὑρίσκω ("I do not find"), and 88^mg 256 263 441 621 1319 1573 2127 *pc* supply οὐ γινώσκω ("I do not know"). Metzger, *Textual Commentary*, 455, gives the force of the eth as "is not in me."

h   In place of the broadly attested οὐ θέλω ("I do not want"), F *pc* vg^s have μισῶ ("I hate"), a logical but obvious improvement of the text.

i   The lack of ἐγώ ("I") is broadly attested by B C D F G 104 256 263 436 1241 1243 1319 1506 1573 1735 1852 2127 2464 *pc* ar d f g mon o vg sa arm eth geo slav Meth Macarius/Symeon Theodore Ambst Ambr Hier[2/4] Pel Aug[7/15], but the inclusion of this seemingly redundant term in ℵ A K L P Ψ 6 33 69 81 88 323 326 330 424 459 614 945 1175 1505 1739 1836 1874 1881 1912 1962 2200 2495 *Maj Lect* sy[h] bo Cl Or[lat] Bas Chr Cyr Hier[2/4] Aug[8/15] is so hard to explain that it is likely original. Its force is to intensify the subject, "I." Nestle-Aland[26/27] use the square brackets for this reading, which is explained by Metzger, *Textual Commentary*, 455, as a consequence of "rather evenly balanced" evidence (see also Nestle-Aland[27] 49*-50*; UBS[4] 2*). The sequence ΘΕΛΩΕΓΩ ("I want") could have caused the similar ending of ΕΓΩ to drop out due to haplography.

j   A minor variant in B uses νοός ("of mind") in place of θεοῦ ("of God"), probably a simple case of dittography caused by the scribe's eye dropping to the next line (v. 23): τῷ νόμῳ τοῦ νοός ("the law of my mind"); Cranfield, 1:363, suggests an assimilation to the wording of the next verse. Whatever its original cause or motivation, this variant weakens and confuses the argument.

k   The preposition ἐν ("by, in") is found in a compelling array of texts: ℵ B D F G K P Ψ 33 69 88 181 424* 1735 1175 1836 1874 1881 *pm* latt Cl. It is deleted by (A) C L 6 81 104 323 326 330 365[acc. to Swanson] 424[c] 436 451 614 629 630 945 1241 1243 1319 1505 1506 1573 1739 1962 2127 2344 2464 2495 sy[p]. The deletion may be an effort at stylistic improvement or, as Metzger suggests in *Textual Commentary (1975)*, 515, a harmonization of the expression τῷ νόμῳ earlier in the verse.

l   Venema conjectures that this was the original location of v. 7:25b, a matter that cannot be resolved without the analysis below.

m   Several alternatives appear to have been developed by the early church to replace the probably original exclamation χάρις δὲ τῷ θεῷ ("but thanks be to God") found in ℵ[1] C[2] (C* *illegible up to 8:3*) Ψ 33 81 88 104 256 (263) 365 436 459 1319 1506 1573 1852 2127 2344 *pc* bo arm geo[1] Meth[ms] Did[1/3] Cyr. B sa Or Meth Epiph Hier[1/6] delete the δέ ("but"), probably in accordance with liturgical use (Metzger, *Textual Commentary*, 455). D ar b d mon o vg *al* Or[lat 2/3] Thret Ambst Ambr Hier[4/6] Pel Aug Varimadum have ἡ χάρις τοῦ θεοῦ ("the grace of God"). F G f g have ἡ χάρις κυρίου ("the grace of [the] Lord"), and ℵ* A K L P 6 69 323 326 330 424 451 614 945 1175 1241 1243 1505 1739 1836 1874 1877 1881 1912 1962 2200 2464 2492 2495 *Maj Lect* sy[p,h] geo[2] (slav) Did[2/3] Macarius/Symeon (Chr) Marcus-Eremita Cyr[lem] Hier[1/6] have εὐχαριστῶ τῷ θεῷ ("I give thanks to God"). Metzger suggests that the latter arose from a transcriptional error and that the other two variants are pedantic answers to the question, "Who will deliver me?"

n   The omission of μέν in ℵ* F G latt, although not wide enough to prevail, is evidence of the logical and textual confusion at the end of this chapter in that v. 25b-c does not follow smoothly on v. 25a. Venema places v. 25b-c after v. 23 and the Michelsen conjecture listed in Nestle-Aland deletes v. 25b-c as an interpolation. Zuntz, *Text*, 16, refers to this as a "marginal gloss . . . inserted into the text." See the discussion in the exegesis below.

Analysis

This pericope continues the "speech-in-character"[1] in which Paul's preconversion zealotism is depicted. This passage opens with a diatribal exchange organized in double-line sentences.[2] The intense, first person discourse marked by a high level of pathos characteristic of προσωποποεία ("speech-in-character") that began in 7:7 is continued through the pericope. The juxtaposition of death by means of the deceit of the law in v. 11 and the traditional affirmation of the goodness of the law in v. 12 give rise to the question of v. 13a concerning the effect of the law.[3] The paronomastic series of nine recurrences of "law" in this passage clearly indicates the topic.[4] The diatribal question is answered in v. 13c-f with the thesis of sin invading the law to produce death. The crucial role of sin is emphasized by the fourfold repetition of ἁμαρτία ("sin") and ἁμαρτωλός ("sinful") in the thesis statement, a forceful instance of paronomasia that holds the opening verse together. The two matching ἵνα ("in order that") clauses provide an instance of synonymous parallelism in this impressive thesis statement.[5]

---

1   The rhetorical analysis by Stowers, "Speech-in-Character," 180–202, is discussed in the section entitled "The Rhetorical 'I'" in 7:7-25" in the preceding chapter. See also Tobin, *Paul's Rhetoric*, 238–45.

2   For a less regular strophic analysis, see Weiss, "Beiträge," 232.

3   See Stowers, *Diatribe*, 149.

4   Räisänen, "Paul's Word-Play," 89–94, develops the idea of a wordplay primarily between the occurrences of "law" in 7:23.

5   See Weiss, "Beiträge," 232.

The thesis in v. 13c-f is sustained by the subsequent argument, organized primarily in double-line sentences, showing how sin prevents a person from achieving the desired good. Each paragraph ends with a triple-line sentence marking the end of the coherent units of argument. The parallelism in v. 14a + b is marked by the antithesis between "spiritual" and "fleshly," while vv. 15a-16a is marked by homoioptoton in four successive first person singular endings. These verses also contain the first two of seven reduplications of the verb "want" in this pericope, expressing the contradiction between wanting and achieving. The concluding line of this paragraph refers back effectively to the word "good" in the opening rhetorical question.

The paragraph of vv. 17-20[6] shows that sin is responsible for the actions of the frustrated self. It is organized as a ring-composition with "it is not I [who] brings it about, but the sin dwelling in me" in v. 17 echoed by "it is no longer I who brings it about but the sin dwelling in me" in v. 20.[7] The paragraph is marked by homoioteleuton in the o- or ov-type endings (vv. 17a, 18a, 18b, 19a, 19b, 20a, 20b) as well as by the repetition of "sin" and "good" as the final words in lines 17b + 20c and 18a + 19a respectively. The three pairs of double lines followed by a concluding triple-line sentence are exactly matched by the next paragraph, which describes the "law of sin" that struggles against the good intentions of the mind (7:21-23). A well-developed antithetical parallelism contrasts the "good" of v. 21a with the "evil" of v. 21b, the "inner self" of v. 22 with the "members" in v. 23a, and the "mind" of v. 23b with the "members" of v. 23c. The

crucial significance of "law" in this paragraph is indicated by the repetition of νόμος in vv. 21a, 22, 23a, 23b, and 23c. Each of the final three lines in the paragraph concludes with μου ("my"), an impressive example of homoioptoton.

The ejaculation in vv. 24-25a about the wretchedness of the human plight and the blessedness of the grace of Jesus Christ, who saves humans from this plight, provides a powerful triple-line expression to conclude the argument. A recapitulation of the argument follows in v. 25b-c, interrupting the flow of argument in such a way that some form of textual intrusion has long been suspected.

The Question of Interpolation

Since a significant number of scholars have proposed that all or part of this pericope resulted from an interpolation,[8] the question must be assessed before we can turn to exegesis. On the assumption that an interpolation is a later insertion into a document with the intent to change its meaning,[9] several of the criteria required to identify such an interpolation appear to be lacking in v. 25b-c.

(a) The material in v. 25b-c does in fact disturb the triumphant flow of discourse from 7:25a to 8:1.[10] It reaches back in a rather pedantic manner to reiterate the argument that had come to a rhetorically effective climax in v. 25a. This has led various scholars to suggest an originally intended sequence of 7:22, 23, 25b-c, 24, 25a, 8:1, or the sequence 8:2, 1, 3.[11] Placing v. 25b-c

---

6   That a new paragraph begins in v. 17 with νυνὶ δέ is argued by Wilckens, 2:87, and Engberg-Pedersen, "Reception," 46–47.

7   See Harvey, *Listening*, 196.

8   See the listing of interpolation proposals in nn. n and 11.

9   See the discussion in the chapter below devoted to the likely interpolation in Rom 16:17-20a; the most recent theoretical discussion is available in Walker, *Interpolations*, 1–90.

10 As Keuck, "Röm 7:25b," demonstrated, this verse has long troubled interpreters.

11 See the Venema and Michelsen textual emendations in n. n above. In *Emendationen*, 24–25, Könnecke argued for an emendation by Paul himself that should have been placed between v. 23 and v. 24.

Scholars wishing to resolve the difficult transition with a theory of interpolation include Weiss, "Beiträge," 232–33; J. Wilson, "Romans vii. 24–viii. 2: A Rearrangement," *ExpT* 4 (1892–93) 192; Jülicher, 279; Dodd, 104; Käsemann, 211–12; Wilckens, 2:96–97; O'Neill, 131–32; Schlier, 235, following Fuchs, *Freiheit*, 82–83; Bauer, *Leiblichkeit*, 159; Schulz, *Mitte der Schrift*, 127–28. Other prominent advocates include Bultmann, "Glossen," 198–99; Schmithals, *Anthropologie*, 81–82; Paulsen, *Überlieferung*, 23–24; Kuss, 2:461, following Lipsius, Bultmann, and Müller. In "Zwei Marginalien," 249–52, Müller opts for a marginal correction written by Paul himself that was inserted into the wrong location instead of between v. 23 and v. 24. Lichtenberger, *Ich Adams*, 150–60, concludes that an

between v. 23 and v. 24 is not unobjectionable, however, because v. 23 already contains an adequate transition to v. 24,[12] so no improvement is achieved by the addition. The proposal to interpret v. 25b-c as a question, "Is it really true that I remain a slave to the law of sin?"[13] could provide a relatively smooth transition to chap. 8, albeit one that is inferior to a direct transition between v. 25a and 8:1. However, the translation as a question is grammatically problematic,[14] and it lacks a denial such as "No longer!" or "By no means!" which should immediately follow.[15]

(b) A contradiction with the earlier argument of the pericope has been proposed by Bultmann in that the alleged interpolation replaces agreement with the law with "serving the law."[16] This is not convincing because Paul depicts himself in this pericope as a Jewish zealot who "shares delight" in the law (7.22) with other like-minded religionists. In the context of first-century zealotism, the verb "serve" is perfectly appropriate. Hermann Lichtenberger perceives a contradiction with the previous argument in the insistence of v. 25b-c that the entire self, despite its inner division, serves the law of sin.[17] Käsemann argues virtually the opposite, that a non-Pauline anthropological dualism between the mind and the flesh is implied here.[18] The formulation is understandable, however, so long as one keeps the dilemma of the religious zealot in view, because while his inner person delights in the law of God, his violent deeds serve the law of sin in opposing the new revelation of divine righteousness in Christ (7.22-23). Rom 7:25b-c aptly recapitulates the previous argument in a clarifying manner, and unlike other interpolations in the Pauline letter corpus, there is no substantive element of refutation.

(c) An interpolation should feature vocabulary and style that differentiate it from the surrounding material written by a different author. No matter how assiduously a later writer attempts to emulate the style and word usage of an earlier author, tiny discrepancies remain visible. Yet every word in this sentence, as well as its style, is typically Pauline. The key terms in this pericope, "I myself," "mind," "law of God," "flesh," and "law of sin" are embedded in a typically Pauline antithesis. The inferential expression ἄρα οὖν ("so then") is a distinctive expression of Pauline style, employed eleven other times in Paul's letters, indeed, seven other times in Romans.[19] The sentence rings true, but remains rhetorically disruptive in its current location.

(d) Until recently, no advocate of interpolation had proposed a redactional motivation for the insertion of this sentence. Lichtenberger now proposes that v. 25b-c in its present location serves to relate the preceding argument to the situation of believers as marked by the continued presence of sin in the full Lutheran sense of *simul iustus et peccator*.[20] If this is convincing, the verse refutes both chap. 7 and chap. 8 and sets a long tradition of misinterpretation in motion. However, the entire case rests on the fragile premises that vv. 22-23 contain a dualistic anthropology and do not reflect the situation of the religious zealot. If the refutation in section b (above) is correct, it remains implausible to suggest that a later redactor sought to alter the thrust of Paul's argument. Moreover, Lichtenberger makes no effort to situate the theological correction allegedly visible in this interpolation in the late first century when the Pauline letters were being edited.[21]

Scholars who have inferred a Pauline correction or

unknown editor who misunderstood Paul added v. 25b and thereby provided the foundation for the *simul iustus et peccator* doctrine. In "Glosse, Interpolation, Redaktion und Komposition in der Sicht der neutestamentlichen Textkritik," in *Studien zur Überlieferung des Neuen Testaments und seines Textes* (ANTF 2; Berlin: de Gruyter, 1967) 53–55, Kurt Aland rejects both the marginal correction and interpolation options.

12 See Jülicher, 279; Wilckens, 2:86.

13 Zahn, 372, followed by Keuck, "Röm 7:25b," 279.

14 BDF §440; 451, makes clear that ἄρα can be interrogatory when it stands alone, but in combination with οὖν as in v. 25b, it has a resumptive sense.

15 See Lichtenberger, "Röm 7,25b," 286.

16 Bultmann, "Glossen," 198; see Jewett, *Terms*, 388.

17 Lichtenberger, "Röm 7,25b," 292–94; idem, *Ich Adams*, 157–58.

18 Käsemann, 211.

19 See Dunn, 1:282.

20 Lichtenberger, "Röm 7,25b," 294.

21 Lichtenberger, *Ich Adams*, 159–60, deals with the later history of interpretation, which he feels was led toward the *simul iustus et peccator* and the two kingdom doctrines by this verse, but these are not evident among the theological interests of the post-Pauline period responsible for distributing the Pauline letter corpus.

"second thought," perhaps in conjunction with a pause in dictation, are more likely on the right track.[22] Paul's motivation may well have been to close the door against a dualistic construal of the preceding argument: both the mind and the flesh of the zealot remain as doomed aspects of the person "left to himself," for without the transforming revelation of the righteousness of God on the Damascus road, Paul would never have seen the light. The addition of this sentence, probably in the margin of Paul's final draft of the letter, reflects a dictation process in conversation with others in the Corinthian arena. This included Tertius (16:22) and the people around him, as well as Phoebe (16:1-2), who probably not only invested the funds required for the drafting of this extensive letter but also served as its first interpreter in the Roman house and tenement churches. In view of her probable involvement in the redactional process related to Paul's dictation, the precise placement of this sentence would not have been a matter of concern, because she and her secretarial staff would have understood the genesis and hence the original motivation of the gloss. It was only with the later copying and publication of Romans, which had not been envisioned by Paul, who believed that history would come to its appointed end with a successful Spanish mission, that v. 25b-c came to pose so formidable a problem.

Rhetorical Disposition

IV.	The *probatio*
5:1–	B. The second proof: Life in Christ as a new system of
8:39	honor that replaces the search for status through conformity to the law
7:13-25	7. Speech-in-Character Concerning the effect of the law
7:13	a. A diatribal exchange concerning the goodness of the law in relation to sin
7:13a	1) The question whether the good law caused death
7:13b	2) The emphatic denial
7:13c-f	3) The thesis about sin acting through the law to produce death
7:13c	a) The active agent: "sin"
7:13d	b) The purpose of sin's action: to reveal its true nature
7:13e	c) Sin's action of producing death by means of the good law
7:13f	d) The purpose of sin's action: to become sinful beyond measure
7:14-16	b. An explanation about how the law remains spiritual and good while humans are caught in the contradiction of sin
7:14	1) The antithesis between the spiritual law and the fleshly self
7:14a	a) The shared assumption that the law is spiritual
7:14b	b) The declaration of fleshliness as bondage to sin
7:15-16	2) The dilemma of achieving what one really intends
7:15a	a) The "I" has no understanding of its actions
7:15b	b) The "I" does not do what it wants
7:15c	c) The "I" does what it hates
7:16a	d) Restatement of the premise that the "I" does not do what it wants
7:16b	e) Conclusion that the law remains good
7:17-20	c. An explanation about how sin is responsible for the actions of the divided self
7:17	1) The contention of sin's action
7:17a	a) The "I" does not intend the evil consequences of zealous behavior
7:17b	b) The sin that dwells within the self is dominant in producing evil consequences
7:18-19	2) The proof that the performance of the good is frustrated by sin
7:18a	a) The good does not dwell in the fleshly "I"
7:18b	b) The "I" wants to perform the good but is unable to do so
7:19a	c) Reiteration that the "I" does not do what it wants
7:19b	d) Reiteration that the "I" performs the evil it does not want
7:20	3) The concluding proof that sin contradicts the intention of the "I"
7:20a	a) The premise: the "I" does not achieve what it wants
7:20b	b) The inference that the "I" is not acting in its own behalf
7:20c	c) The contrary inference that "sin" is acting to produce evil consequences
7:21-25a	d. An explanation about how the law of sin captures the self by countering the law of the mind
7:21	1) The discovery of a new law of human behavior
7:21a	a) The condition of the new law: whenever the "I" wishes to accomplish the good

---

22   Könnecke, *Emendationen,* 24–25; Lietzmann, 78; Jewett, *Terms,* 388–89; Müller, "Marginalien," 251–52; Zeller, 145.

7:21b		b) The action of the new law: evil lies ready to act
7:22-23	2)	The proof of the action of the malevolent new law
7:22		a) The "inner self" delights in God's law
7:23a		b) A new law is at work in the "members"
7:23b		c) The action of the new law: to counter the "law of my mind"
7:23c		d) The consequence of captivity to the "law of sin"
7:24	3)	The lamentation of the doomed self
7:24a		a) The wretchedness of the "I"
7:24b		b) The need of deliverance from the "body of death"
7:25a	4)	The thanksgiving
		a) The one to whom thanks are due: God
		b) The means by whom one gives thanks: Christ
7:25b-c	e.	A recapitulation of the antithesis between the "law of God" and the "law of sin"
7:25b	1)	The mind serves the law of God
7:25c	2)	The flesh serves the law of sin

Exegesis

■ **13** The rhetorical question that opens this pericope picks up the category of "the good" from the end of v. 12 in reference to the law, which is similar to Prov 4:2-4:

I give you a good gift (δῶρον γὰρ ἀγαθόν):
    do not forsake my teaching . . .
my father . . . taught me, and said to me,
    "Let your heart hold fast my words;
keep my commandments, and live. . . ."

In a similar vein, Epictetus refers to the "laws of God" dwelling within him as "the good" (τὸ ἀγαθόν) that he was obligated to keep, in every respect.[23] "Was it the good law that caused my death?"[24] asks Paul, reiterating in a more radical manner the thought of v. 11. If the fault lies in the law itself, then it must be revised or abandoned. This simplistic answer has always been available, and apparently had some foothold in the Roman

congregations in which the "strong" were criticizing the "weak" for their adherence to the law. But if the problem lies elsewhere, the human dilemma must be probed more deeply and the resolution is not so simple. It cannot be framed in a liberal/conservative polarity that lends superiority to one side or the other. The problem is much more basic; indeed, it is universal in its scope. So Paul flatly denies this possibility: "By no means!" he declares, which establishes the theme of the pericope. This is the seventh time μὴ γένοιτο ("by no means") has appeared in Romans, conveying a flat repudiation of what was probably a popular view in the majority of Roman churches.

The counter-thesis is stated in a rather rambling manner, without a finite verb but with two ἵνα ("in order that") clauses, contending that "the sin" misused the good law to produce death and thereby proved to be sin beyond measure. The first "in order that" clause refers to sin manifesting itself as sin: ἵνα φανῇ ἁμαρτία ("that it might be shown to be sin"), with the verb φαίνομαι ("manifest, show oneself") appearing here for the only time in Romans.[25] The expression is rare, with the only occurrences in the pre-Pauline period found in LXX *Ps. Sol.* 2.17, ἵνα φανῇ τὸ κρίμα σου ("in order that your judgment might appear"), and Herodotus *Hist.* 3.137.22, reporting that Democedes acted "in order to seem worthy in Darius' eyes (ἵνα φανῇ πρὸς Δαρείου ἐών . . . δόκιμός)." "The sin" appears here with the article to denote the subject of the sentence; the article refers back to the definition in the previous pericope: sin as covetousness, desiring what belongs to another, that is, that spirit of competition for honor that had corrupted the law and turned it into a means of status acquisition. The problem was that such competition was so ingrained in the Greco-Roman and Jewish cultures that it seemed perfectly benign and thus remained unacknowledged as sin. It required the crucifixion and resurrection of Christ to expose this lethal competition for what it was; it was "unmasked" not by the law[26] but by

---

23 Epictetus *Diss.* 4.3.11–12; Michel, 229, refers also to later rabbinic writings that identify the law as "the good": *Ber.* 5a; *'Abot.* 6.3; *'Abod. Zar.* 19b.

24 The idiom ἐμοὶ ἐγένετο θάνατος probably means "cause my death," as illustrated in Aristotle *Frag. var.* 8.44.552 in reference to the Thracian Leibethians, "since by their hands the death of Orpheus

occurred (ἐπειδὴ παρ᾽ αὐτοῖς ὁ τοῦ Ὀρφέως ἐγένετο θάνατος)." See Godet, 278; Cranfield, 1:354.

25 See Rudolf Bultmann and Dieter Lührmann, "φαίνω κτλ.," TDNT 9 (1974) 2: "to become visible . . . for spiritual perception."

26 Käsemann, 198; Dunn, 1:386.

459

the cross, which revealed the full, evil potential of religious zeal acting to defend itself and to prove its superiority. Indeed, the cross contradicts every human campaign to achieve honor through superior performance. The true character of sin was disclosed, according to this verse, by bringing about "my death through the good," that is, through the law. The participle κατεργαζομένη is used here with the connotation of "bringing about, producing"[27] to convey how sin accomplishes this perversion of the good. Sin takes the law, which was intended to guard peace and justice, and turns it into an instrument for claiming superiority over others. Once again, what Paul has in mind is understandable in the light of his preconversion experience of having opposed the gospel because of his own competitive righteousness,[28] which brought him into conflict with God's Messiah and therefore under wrath. The death he had been living and promoting was exposed and overcome by the encounter with the risen Christ.

The second ἵνα ("in order that") clause "discloses in rhetorical crescendo the point of the first,"[29] exclaiming that this perversion of the original purpose of the law reveals sin as becoming "sinful beyond measure." The verb γένηται ("become, occur") is employed to produce an idiom first found in Plato *Theaet.* 193c4, "in order that recognition might occur (ἵνα γένηται ἀναγνώρισις)," and occurs elsewhere in the NT (Matt 10:25; 23:26; Luke 4:3; Rom 15:16; 1 Cor 3:18; Col 1:18). However, the thought that "sin" achieves the epitome of sinfulness in its twisting of the "commandment" into a vehicle of gaining honor is uniquely Pauline. Rengstorf observes that this verse poses "some difficulty," but that it can be explained with the premise that a personified sin "becomes aware of itself and its power" through the commandment.[30] However, for Paul to speculate about sin's awareness of itself seems far from the concern of this letter. Moo proposes that sin "becomes worse" when

it rises to "deliberate violation of God's good will for his people,"[31] but this is surely true for all sin. What Paul finds so outrageous as an expression of sin's inherent nature is that it perverts the finest dimension of religion into a system of dominating others and demonstrating the superior virtue of one's own group, whatever that might be. The expression καθ᾽ ὑπερβολήν ("beyond measure") appears in the authentic Pauline letters (1 Cor 12:31; 2 Cor 1:8; 4:17; Gal 1:13) and is a favorite of the Attic orators.[32] In the light of Paul's experience, the immeasurable capacity of sin and its inherent perversity were most clearly demonstrated in turning his passion to be more righteous than others into a campaign against the Messiah and his people, so that the commandment that God gave to sustain and protect life resulted instead in death. In Godet's words, "sin wrought death by goodness, that it might become as sinful as possible."[33]

■ **14** Paul's explanation of the thesis begins with the unparalleled claim that the law is "spiritual" (πνευματικός). While he had earlier referred to the spiritual blessing of the gospel (Rom 1:11), a theme to which he will return in 15:27, and while he frequently referred to other features of the new age as "spiritual" (eleven times in 1 Corinthians; once in Galatians),[34] never did he or anyone else prior to this moment, as far as I can tell, ever connect the word "law" with the adjective "spiritual."[35] In the OT and intertestamental literature, prophetic and wisdom literature are thought to be expressions of the divine Spirit,[36] but it was not until the early rabbinic period that a spiritual origin was claimed for the entire Jewish Scripture.[37] Early Christians were making similar claims about their sacred writings (Matt 22:43; Mark 12:36; Acts 1:16; 4:25; 28:25; 2 Pet 1:21), but without using the terms Paul employs here. The later talmudic viewpont is visible in *Sanh.* 10.1, that whoever says "that the law is not from heaven" has no place in the

---

27   See Cranfield, 1:354; Wilckens, 2:84.

28   See Middendorf, *Romans 7*, 174.

29   Käsemann, 198.

30   Karl Heinrich Rengstorf, "ἁμαρτωλός, ἀναμάρτητος," *TDNT* 1 (1964) 329.

31   Moo, 453.

32   Demonsthenes *Erot.* 7.9; 20.4; 33.2; Isocrates *Antid.* 147.7; *Phil.* 11.5; *Panath.* 123.5, etc. It appears some twenty-two times in the Aristotelian corpus.

33   Godet, 279.

34   See Jacob Kremer, " πνευματικόι, πνευματικώς," *EDNT* 3 (1993) 122–23.

35   Philo claims that "the nature of angels is spiritual" (πνευματική) in *QG* 1.92, but never claims this attribute for the Torah.

36   Erik Sjöberg, "πνεῦμα, πνευματικός . . . in Palestinian Judaism," *TDNT* 6 (1968) 381–82.

37   Ibid., 382.

world to come. There is little doubt, therefore, about the likely assent of at least a portion of the Roman audience with Paul's contention even though it was formulated in an innovative manner, couched with the formula, "for we know," as in Rom 2:2; 3:19. In this context it seems likely that Paul intends to imply that the Torah was created, activated and authorized by the Spirit.[38]

The antithesis is formulated with ἐγώ ("I") in the emphatic position, contrasting with the "we" who know that the law is spiritual.[39] That the "I" is σάρκινός ("fleshly") picks up the theme from v. 5, "when we were in the flesh," which we showed to be a matter of living under the power of perverse systems of honor and shame, in which the will to surpass others destroys the good that one wants to achieve. While σάρκινός in secular usage referred to obesity,[40] to human limitation,[41] and to susceptibility to corruption,[42] both the earlier formulation in Rom 7:5 and the use of this word in 1 Cor 3:1-3, referring to a carnal, worldly orientation closed off to the Spirit, suggest a specifically Pauline definition. The closest non-Pauline parallel is *T. Jud.* 19.4,[43] but there the fault lies in susceptibility to a demonic force rather than in a human revolt against God: "The prince of error blinded me, and I was ignorant—as a human being, as flesh, in my corrupt sins (ὡς σάρξ ἐν ἁμαρτίαις φθαρείς) until I learned of my own weakness after supposing myself to be invincible." For Paul, to be

"fleshly" refers not primarily to the material nature of humans but to opposition against God, for it was precisely in his own zealous advocacy of the law that Paul found himself in such opposition. In his striving to demonstrate his righteousness under the law, he found himself caught in the throes of sin.[44]

An extensive *TLG* search indicates that the expression "sold under sin" (πεπραμένος ὑπὸ τὴν ἁμαρτίαν) appears here for the first time in Greek literature, and thereafter is entirely restricted to patristic writers dependent on this verse. The verb πιπράσκω ("sell") occurs in a variety of commercial contexts including slavery,[45] as, for example, in Lev 25:39, "and if your brother is humiliated and sold to you (πραθῇ σοί) he shall not serve you with the servitude of a slave." In Isa 50:1, being sold into the slavery of captivity is associated with Israel's sins, but there is no suggestion that sin itself is the slaveholder: "Behold, you are sold on account of your sins (ταῖς ἁμαρτίαις ὑμῶν ἐπράθητε), and for your iniquities have I put your mother away."[46] A particularly striking parallel occurs in a Hellenistic lead inscription from Asia Minor in which the slave Antigone is to be "sold from among her fellow slaves" (πεπρημένα ἐξ ὁμολοδούλ[ων]) and given over to the power of Demeter, an infernal deity who will "not be propitious to her."[47] Paul's formulation is also unique in employing the article in the expression "sold under *the* sin," refer-

38 See Schlier, 229; Cranfield, 1:355; Winger, *Law*, 172–73. As Jervis points out ("Commandment," 201), this "foreshadows the thought of 8.4 that the just requirement of the Law is fulfilled by those who walk according to the Spirit."

39 It is possible that "we know" should be understood as a "plural of modesty," according to Smyth, *Grammar*, §1008–12. E.g., Xenophon *Cyr.* 1.1.1, ἔννοιά ποθ᾽ ἡμῖν ἐγένετο ("the reflection once occurred to me"). See also Plutarch *Rom.* 15.2. In this case, however, commentators who discuss the matter are agreed that the plural includes Paul's audience; see Schlier, 229; Cranfield, 1:355; Dunn, 1:387; Wilckens, 2:85; Moo, 453.

40 Eupolis Comic *Frag.* 387, "a corpulent woman" (σαρκίνη γυνή); see also Anonymus Iamblichi *Frag.* 7.53.

41 Aristophanes *Inc. Fab.* 26.1, "not as another man of flesh (ἄνδρα σάρκινον)"; see also Hipparchus (Stobaeus *Anth.* 4.960.15H = *Sib. Or., Frag.* 1.1); Aristotle *Eth. nic.* 1117b 3; Polybius *Hist.* 38.8.6.

42 Epicurus *Dep.* 16.1, "what is of flesh is capable of corruption (τὸ σάρκινον φθορᾶς εἶναι δεκτικόν)."

43 See Jörg Frey, "Die paulinische Antithese von 'Fleisch' und 'Geist' und die palästinisch-jüdische Weisheitstradition," *ZNW* 90 (1999) 66, 72–76.

44 This interpretation is adapted from Robert Jewett, "The Basic Human Dilemma: Weakness or Zealous Violence (Romans 7:7-25 and 10:1-18)," *ExAud* 13 (1997) 96–109. For a recent restatement of the *simul iustus et peccator* interpretation that "sin remains a problem in believers' lives," see Jervis, "Commandment," 202.

45 See MM 513–14, and Herbert Preisker, "πιπράσκω," *TDNT* 6 (1968) 160.

46 See Marc Philonenko, "Sur l'expression 'vendue au péché' dans l'Épître aux Romains,'" *RHR* 203 (1986) 45–51.

47 C. T. Newton, *A History of Discoveries at Halicarnassus, Cnidus, and Branchidae* (London: Day & Son, 1863) vol. 2, part 2, no. 81, pp. 725–27.

ring back to "the sin" in 7:13c, which was defined as the perverse spirit of competition for honor that had turned the law into a system of status acquisition. In Gal 3:22 an anarthrous form of this expression occurs, that "scripture consigned all things under sin (ὑπὸ ἁμαρτίαν)." Sin functions in Paul's expression as the alien power that enslaves its helpless victims, which would have been an emotionally powerful metaphor for Paul's audience that consisted mostly of slaves and former slaves with first-hand experience of slavery's abuse and degradation.[48] It is all the more striking that Paul applies this metaphor not to a sinner defined in terms of violating the law but to himself as the epitome of legal righteousness prior to his conversion.

■ **15** Verses 15-16 clarify what it means to be "sold under sin." Taking the formulation of this sentence in the Greek word order, ὃ γὰρ κατεργάζομαι ("for what I bring about, accomplish") refers simply "to that which is accomplished by one's activity."[49] What is striking, however, is that this same verb was employed in 7:8 and 13 with sin as the subject.[50] A kind of cosponsorship of evil is evidently in view, in which human action is at the same time performed by sin as an alien power, so that no evasion of responsibility is possible.[51] What Paul had intended to bring about in his zealous advocacy of the law, ending up in the persecution of early Christians, was the messianic reign of righteousness and peace.

What he actually achieved was the opposite, the direct thwarting of God's Messiah and the new community of those who accepted his lordship.[52]

That Paul did not understand the contradiction between his intent and his accomplishment is conveyed by the verb γινώσκω, which is often taken in the Augustinian sense of "I do not approve,"[53] which fits the classic doctrine of Rom 7 as descriptive of the sins of believers.[54] No linguistic parallels have been adduced for this special translation of a word that has the basic definition of "experience, know, or understand,"[55] so this option should be rejected as "forced."[56] The more serious exegetical choice is whether οὐ γινώσκω implies basic lack of knowledge and awareness of the contradiction, as in 7:7,[57] or whether it implies a failure to understand the contradiction and its consequences.[58] The example of Medea, who murders her children as vengeance against her unfaithful husband, is frequently cited in support of this latter alternative:[59]

I can no longer, as such, gaze upon you; rather I am vanquished by evils (ἀλλὰ νικῶμαι κακοῖς), and I learn what sort of wicked things I intend to do, but passion has gotten the better of my plans (θυμὸς δὲ κρείσσων τῶν ἐμῶν βουλημάτων), and such is the reason for the greatest of evils to mortals. (Euripides *Medea* 1077b–80)

---

48 See Harrill, *Slaves*, 29–33.
49 Horst Balz and Gerhard Schneider, "κατεργάζομαι," *EDNT* 2 (1991) 271; see also BAGD 421.2, "bring about, produce, create."
50 See Schlier, 240; Wilckens, 2:86.
51 Zahn, 353.
52 Although he acknowledges these details, Middendorf, *Romans 7*, 243, insists that Paul's purpose is "*to inform* his readers about the role and activity of the Law in the Christian life" (243, italics in original), which is explained in terms of classical Lutheran doctrine (244–52).
53 Fitzmyer, 474, identifies the source of this view in Augustine's *Exp. quaest. Rom.* 36 (*CSEL* 84.19).
54 See Weiss, 316, for an account of earlier advocates of this interpretation, followed in recent times by Barrett, 148; Cranfield, 1:359; Moo, 457; etc. An extensive argument to this effect is available in Magnussen, *Verstehen,* 157–99.
55 Rudolf Bultmann, "γινώσκω κτλ.," *TDNT* 1 (1964) 689, 703–4; BAGD 160–61; Walter Schmithals, "γινώσκω κτλ.," *EDNT* 1 (1990) 248–51.

56 Godet, 284.
57 BAGD 160.1; Lietzmann, 77; Schmidt, 130; cf. Johnson, 110–12.
58 BAGD 161.2; Weiss, 316; Lagrange, 175; Hommel, "7. Kapitel," 165–67; Kuss, 2:453; Schlier, 230; Haacker, 146; Schreiner, 373; most other commentators.
59 Haacker, 146, Hommel, "7. Kapitel," 160–61; Theobald, 212; Robert Renehan, "Classical Greek Quotations in the New Testament," in D. Neiman and M. Schatkin, eds., *The Heritage of the Early Church: Essays in Honor of the Very Reverend Georges Vasilievich Florovsky* (OrChrA 195; Rome: Pontificium Institutum Studiorum Orientalium, 1973) 24; Klauck, "Wortlose Seufzen," 87; Lichtenberger, *Ich Adams*, 177–86. See the discussion of the Greek philosophical background of the premise that people always seek to accomplish the good but sometimes have "the wrong idea of what is good," in Strom, *Reframing Paul,* 49; cf. 48–57.

On closer analysis, however, this classic expression of the contradiction between reason and passion is quite different from the lack of knowledge claimed by Paul. Nor does the philosophical discussion of ἀκρασία ("lack of self control, weakness of will") match Paul's insistence on prior unawareness.[60] Moreover, if the model of Paul the zealot is employed, the matter of previous understanding seems less plausible; unlike Medea, Paul was completely unaware of the contradiction between his actions and their consequences until after his conversion, which means that a lack of basic knowledge is more likely in view here. This brings the use of γινώσκω as "know" in this verse into consistency with v. 7 and the earlier usages in Rom 1:21; 2:18; 3:17; 6:6; and 7:1.[61]

The contradiction that Paul discovered on the Damascus road is explained by parallel clauses, in which "what I don't want" and "what I hate" are matched with "this I practice" and "this I do." The first of seven reduplications of θέλειν in this pericope appears here with the connotation of "want," understood with the negative οὐ ("not") as the will not to disobey the law.[62] This is intensified by the verb μισῶ, used here for the only time in the Pauline letters. It appears with the connotation of "hate,"[63] because what Paul the zealous Pharisee deplored most of all was disobedience to the oral and written Torah. His own "blameless" conformity with the law (Phil 3:6) was an expression of this profound antipathy. The two verbs for action have roughly synonymous meaning.[64] Πράσσω has the sense of "intensive occupation with the matter at hand,"[65] and was used in 2:25 in the expression "practice the law," to which 7:15 comprises the ironic antithesis. Ποιέω means to act or do, which appeared in 2:13 as "doers of the law," and has the connotation here of performing a specific action,[66] which again has an ironic resonance. It is not that Paul proved unable to obey the law, but that his very obedience achieved the opposite of its intended effect[67] because rather than pleasing God and advancing the cause of God's realm, Paul's had opposed the Messiah. This dilemma of misguided religious zealotism was very different from classical expressions of human contradiction, and it had a much more direct bearing on the actual behavior of the Roman house and tenement churches toward each other. For example, Euripides places these words in the mouth of Phaedra:[68]

During long nights I have often thought about what so wrecks our human life, and I realized that lack of understanding is not the root of all evil (οὐ κατὰ γνώμης φύσιν πράσσειν κάκιον)—most people lack nothing in insight, so the cause must lie elsewhere: we know and recognize the good but we do not do it (τὰ χρήστ᾽ ἐπιστάμεσθα καὶ γιγνώσκομεν. οὐκ ἐκπονοῦμεν δ᾽), some from sloth and others preferring pleasure over duty. . . . (Euripides Hipp. 375–82)

Ovid's epigrammatic formulation of Medea's dilemma fits this classic conflict between reason and passion or pleasure: "I see and approve the better course, but I follow the worse" (Metam. 7.21).[69] Epictetus comes closer to Rom 7 in arguing that "every sin involves a contradiction. For since he who sins does not wish to sin, but to

60 See Ronald V. Huggins, "Alleged Classical Parallels to Paul's 'What I Want to Do I Do Not Do, but What I Hate, That I do' (Rom 7:15)," WTJ 54 (1992) 158–61. Engberg-Pedersen, "Reception," 47, 54–56, appears to overlook the disparity with ἀκρασία, as does Carter, Power of Sin, 191.

61 Lichtenberger, Ich Adams, 163–64, proposes that the commandment in Gen 2:17, "of the tree of the knowledge of good and evil you shall not eat," is the source of what the speaker "does not know" in this verse, but the link is purely on the verbal level, because Adam now knows that he should not eat from the tree while the speaker is described as being unaware of the consequences of his actions. So far as I can tell, the two situations are entirely different.

62 Gottlob Schrenk, "θέλω κτλ.," TDNT 3 (1965) 50; the effort to develop a special connotation for θέλω as trans-subjective desire to achieve life (Bultmann, Old and New Man, 33–48; idem, Theology, 248) is overly specific and too existentialist to be plausible in ancient usage.

63 Otto Michel, "μισέω," TDNT 4 (1967) 692.

64 Barrett, 147.

65 Christian Maurer, "πράσσω κτλ.," TDNT 6 (1968) 632.

66 Walter Radl, "ποιέω," EDNT 3 (1993) 125.

67 See Schmidt, 130.

68 Cited by Theobald, 212; Theissen, Psychological Aspects, 212–13.

69 See Renehan, "Classical Greek Quotations," 25.

be right, it is clear that he is not doing what he wishes" (πᾶν ἁμάρτημα μάχην περίεχει. ἐπεὶ γὰρ ὁ ἁμαρτάνων οὐ θέλει ἁμαρτάνειν, ἀλλὰ κατορθῶσαι, δῆλον ὅτι μὲν θέλει οὐ ποιεῖ, *Diss.* 2.26.1–2). However, the contradiction described by Epictetus could be overcome by enlightenment, whereas for Paul the situation of being "sold under sin" involved an unacknowledged hostility against God and thus required a much more fundamental cure. Epictetus continues:

> He, then, who can show to each man the contradiction which causes him to err, and can clearly bring home to him how he is not doing what he wishes, and is doing what he does not wish, is strong in argument, and at the same time effective both in encouragement and refutation. For as soon as anyone shows a man this, he will of his own accord abandon what he is doing. (*Diss.* 2.26.4–5)

That the human dilemma is more than cognitive[70] is conveyed by Paul's following verse.

■ **16** The mysterious conflict between willing and achieving the good, in which Paul again employs θέλω ("will") and ποιέω ("do") as in the preceding verse, cannot be clarified by increased knowledge of and adherence to the law. "If what I don't want—this I do" points to a deeper dilemma than Paul's Pharisaic teachers of the law had imagined. Paul's adherence to the law, both in spirit and in deed, is affirmed by means of a unique formulation for the NT, one that appears in philosophic usage: σύμφημι with the dative ("I agree with . . ."). Plato uses this expression, σύμφημι σοι, ἔφη ("'I agree with you,' he said").[71] That the law is καλός ("excellent, beautiful") reiterates the thrust of 7:12[72] and makes it clear that Paul's dilemma was not inadequate adherence to the law or some hidden conflict or weakness in performing its demands.[73] This verse confirms the problem with the classic explanations of Rom 7 in terms of human weakness.[74] Fréderic Godet provides a classic

statement of this mistaken theory that Rom 7 describes the conflict between "the Jew such as he ought to be . . . [and] the real Jew, such as he shows himself in practice."[75] Sanday and Headlam's influential commentary suggests that the dilemma of Rom 7 had been

> felt most keenly when he was a "Pharisee of the Pharisees." Without putting an exact date to the struggle which follows we shall probably not be wrong in referring the main features of it especially to the period before his Conversion. It was then that the powerlessness of the Law to do anything but aggravate sin was brought home to him.[76]

The theory of Paul's bad conscience as a Jew unable to obey the whole law has been refuted by Krister Stendahl,[77] E. P. Sanders,[78] and a host of others. It is contradicted by the references in Rom 7:13-16 and 9:1-5 to the Jewish law as holy and good; it is even more sharply refuted by Paul's statements in Phil 3:4-6 and Gal 1:14 about his having excelled in the performance of the Jewish law, even to the point of being "blameless." The idea that he nevertheless had a bad conscience was a figment of the introspective conscience of the West and of liberal Protestantism of the last century, a view whose vicious stereotype of Jewish religiosity has evoked widespread criticism in the wake of the studies by Stendahl and Sanders.

Another problematic alternative is the psychological theory of an unconscious conflict with the law prior to Paul's conversion. C. H. Dodd builds his case on Rom 7:8, where "the command gave an impulse to sin," following Augustine's confession that "the desire to steal was aroused simply by the prohibition of stealing."[79] He goes on to explain as follows:

> It is one of the most important teachings of modern psychology . . . that the attempt to repress an instinctive desire directly, seldom succeeds in its object. If

70   See Theissen, *Psychological Aspects*, 216.
71   Plato *Resp.* 608 b9; see also 403c8; 526c7; 608b3.
72   That καλός is used here as a "near synonym" of ἀγαθός in 7:12-13 is suggested by Dunn, 1:390, and Jörg Baumgarten, "ἀγαθός," *EDNT* 1 (1990) 6.
73   See Schmidt, 130; Murray, 263.
74   Heil, 77: "this common weakness of the human condition."
75   Godet, 280.
76   Sanday and Headlam, 186.
77   Stendahl, *Paul*, 78–96.
78   Sanders, *Paul*, 443, 494, 504.

the desire is repressed, it is likely to form a "complex" below the threshold of consciousness, and to break into the conscious life in fresh and perhaps even more deleterious forms.[80]

The psychological approach has been further developed by Gerd Theissen.[81] His viewpoint rests on an exegesis of the "I" in Rom 7 that is widely accepted today, that it "combines personal and typical traits."[82] It is Paul's own ego that is being described, and in view of the past tense forms of the verbs and the contrast with current Christian experience described in Rom 8, Theissen finds it very likely that Paul's pre-Christian past is in some sense being described. Looking back on his life, Paul detects an "unconscious conflict with the law,"[83] a conflict of which he became aware only after his conversion.[84] It was not that he had been unable to perform the law as some of the earlier psychological theories had suggested, but that there was internal resistance within him that expressed itself through hostility to others. Theissen writes:

> Christ became to him a symbol of his negative identity, that is, of all those aspects he did not wish to perceive in himself and from which he consciously wished to distance himself. Instead of seeing and addressing in himself repressed incapacity to fulfill the law and anxiety at the demands of the law, he persecutes them in a small group that deviated from the law.[85]

Later Theissen uses Freudian categories to understand this unconscious civil war: "Destructive and libidinus

drives of the id overpower the superego and influence the ego from above in threatening and promising manners."[86]

The problem is that there is not a hint of such a conflict in Paul's description of his former life as a Pharisee. Theissen has simply provided an internalized variety of the old theory of Paul's introspective conscience, based not on an actual incapacity to obey the law but on an inner anxiety that he might be unable to do so. But the theory's only evidence is Rom 7 itself, and it is contradicted by the rest of the evidence from the Pauline letters and by our knowledge of ancient Judaism.

A similarly problematic theory relates to Paul's allegedly suppressed sexual tension and his inability to control his desires, suggested by Robert Gundry,[87] Holger Tiedemann,[88] and Francis Watson.[89] The only indication, however, that Paul was bothered by the "awakening of sexual desire at the very time his obligation to the law matured"[90] in some first century Bar Mitzvah is the reference to the "law in my members" (Rom 7:23). However, $\tau\grave{\alpha}$ $\mu\acute{\epsilon}\lambda\eta$ was used twice in 6:13 to refer to human capacity in general,[91] and in 12:4-5 the phrase refers to individual members of the body of Christ, in neither case with any sexual overtones. Moreover, there is not a hint in Paul's other letters that he had had an unsuccessful "confrontation with the tenth commandment";[92] indeed, this would seem to be contradicted by Paul's claim in Phil 3:6 to have been "unblemished" in his obedience to the law prior to the conversion. It is also contradicted by 1 Cor 7:7, where a particular sexual inclination to marry or not to marry is described as a divine charisma. The same objections pertain with regard to Watson's claim that "[s]exual desire—Augus-

---

79 Dodd, 109.
80 Ibid., 110.
81 Theissen, *Psychological Aspects*, 179–201, 211–60.
82 Ibid., 201.
83 Ibid., 231.
84 Ibid., 235.
85 Ibid., 243.
86 Ibid., 245; for a similar analysis, see Klauck, "Wortlose Seufzen," 88–90, and Michael Reichardt, *Psychologische Erklärung der paulinischen Damaskusvision? Ein Beitrag zum interdisziplinären Gespräch zwischen Exegese und Psychologie seit dem 18. Jahrhundert* (SBB 42; Stuttgart: Katholisches Bibelwerk, 1999) 329–34.

87 Gundry, "Moral Frustration," 228–45; Gundry, *Sōma*, 137.
88 Holger Tiedemann, *Die Erfahrung des Fleisches: Paulus und die Last der Lust* (Stuttgart: Radius, 1998) 287–304.
89 Watson, *Paul*, 151–53, and *Agape*, 171–82.
90 Gundry, "Moral Frustration," 233.
91 See Käsemann, 177; Dunn, 1:337, following the lead of Schweizer, "Sünde in den Gliedern," 437–39.
92 Gundry, "Moral Frustration," 234.

465

tine's *concupiscentia*—is for Paul the paradigmatic instance of the desire the law prohibits." It entails "a reorganization of the body around the genitals."[93]

That Paul was skeptical about the human capacity to live the transformed life even after conversion remains typical of Lutheran and Calvinist exegesis. In the classic formulation of Anders Nygren, Rom 7 describes "the tension which exists, in the Christian life, between will and action, between intention and performance. . . . The will to do the right is always present in him; but he steadily falls short in performance."[94] The reason for this failure is that "the Christian belongs at the same time to both the new and the old aeons,"[95] and the constant lures of the latter cause weakness in performance. This interpretation is now becoming more popular because of the collapse of other interpretive alternatives. An example of this is James D. G. Dunn, who concludes his discussion as follows:

> It is not Paul the pious Pharisee who speaks here, but Paul the humble believer. . . . Evidently conversion for Paul means becoming aware as never before of the power of sin in his own life . . . not just as a power now broken insofar as he had died with Christ, but as a power still in play insofar as he was still a man of flesh. . . .[96]

The main barriers to this exegesis are the contradictions in Rom 6:4, 7, 11-14, 17-19, and chaps. 12–16 as well as the ethical sections in other letters, none of which hints that Paul believed the Christian ethic was incapable of fulfillment. Honesty about the dilemmas of current Christian ethics should not be allowed to override the evidence in Paul's own letters of an expectation of ethical transformation.

An approach derived from French literary criticism is employed in Robert Hamerton-Kelly's provocative study, *Sacred Violence: Paul's Hermeneutic of the Cross*. Building on the scapegoat and mimesis theories developed by

René Girard, he interprets the death of Christ as "an epiphany of sacred violence."[97] To accept the gospel therefore commits one to resist the principalities and powers that encourage "exclusiveness and scapegoating" and to join "the new community of freedom and mutual acceptance."[98] The Pauline doctrine of original sin is reinterpreted as a manifestation of "mimetic rivalry within the system of sacred violence,"[99] since it focuses so intensively on the elements of covetousness and desire that corrupt the law. Hamerton-Kelly interprets the dilemma of a representative religious person in Rom 7, "caught in the coils of the Sacred" that instruct him in zealous obedience.[100] "Sin used the Law to deceive him, by constructing the sacred community of sin and death within which his desire for God was deformed continuously into the service of self. His will was not weak but warped by mimeseis, the deviated desire that dwelt in his religious identity as a Jew." By zealous conformity to the law, there is created "a sphere of sacred violence within which good intentions have bad outcomes."[101] Although he does not provide an extensive discussion of Rom 7, Hamerton-Kelly suggests in a footnote, "Looking back on his Jewish life from the other side of his conversion, he saw the moral numbness caused by the system and confesses it ironically. . . . Now he understands that he really did not know what he was doing (Romans 7:15a)."[102] Although this theory gives too little attention to the social context of Paul in the first century, it moves in the right direction, despite ferocious criticism about the alleged anti-Semitism it implies.[103] There is a grain of truth in this critique, because Paul's analysis of the human plight generalizes from his Jewish experience, suggesting that all groups have the same zealous tendencies.

The wording of 7:16 suggests that the details match Paul's experience of frustration as a zealot, a frustration only manifest at the moment of his conversion.[104] The dilemma of zealous religion, however, is recurring within the church as ethnic conflicts between house and tene-

93 Watson, *Agape*, 177–78.
94 Nygren, 293.
95 Ibid., 296.
96 Dunn, 1:407.
97 Hamerton-Kelly, *Cross*, 63.
98 Ibid., 87.
99 Ibid., 111.

100 Ibid., 107.
101 Ibid., 108.
102 Ibid., 122 n. 11.
103 See especially Boyarin, *Radical Jew*, 214–19.
104 This section is adapted from chap. 7 of my book *Apostle to America*. See also *Saint Paul at the Movies*, 21–25, 126–33. Cf. Patte, *Paul*, 275–77.

ment churches arise. Paul needs to expose this fundamental problem in order to provide a basis for cooperation and to clarify the task of the mission to Spain, lest it become one more zealous, imperialistic exercise similar to the efforts Rome had long made to dominate Spain.

■ 17 The next four verses explain how sin causes an objective kind of contradiction between willing and achieving the good. There is wide agreement that νυνὶ δὲ οὐκέτι has a logical and inferential rather than a temporal sense;[105] there is also a contrasting connotation in this expression that introduces a new argument,[106] so I translate it with "Now surely it is not . . . ." In view of the agreement of the ego with the law, which produces perfect performance thereof, how can one explain that the very opposite of the law's object is achieved? Paul reiterates the theme of v. 14, that the ego is "sold under the sin," claiming here that sin rather than the ego "brings about" (κατεργάζομαι, as in v. 15) the awful contradiction inherent in religious zealotism. This could be taken as a denial of human responsibility for evil consequences, but it seems clear from the expression "the sin dwelling in me" (ἡ οἰκοῦσα ἐν ἐμοὶ ἁμαρτία) that sin and the self are inextricably tangled and thus are mutually responsible for such consequences.[107] Walter Grundmann claimed that this expression implies that the person in Rom 7 "is possessed by demonic power," having been sold under sin.[108] Commentators have noted a close parallel to this idea in *T. Naph.* 8.6, "The one who does not do the good . . . the devil will inhabit him as his own instrument." But it is questionable whether demonic possession is the appropriate model for Paul's argument, because human assent to sin is the necessary precondition to being enslaved by it. Exorcism would not

suffice in this situation, because the sinful distortion of the motivation to obey the law is so willingly endorsed by the ego that seeks the honor of superior performance. Both Greco-Roman and Jewish cultures provided elaborate support for this distortion, so that Paul's first person singular discourse was truly paradigmatic. Although it was the very opposite of the intention of the religious zealot to oppose God's will, this indwelling sin transforms obedience into a means of status acquisition and thus produces the disastrous contradiction between what is intended and what is actually achieved.

■ 18 The next two verses explain how the motivation to achieve the "good" is frustrated by sinful distortion. The first person singular verb "I know" (οἶδα) opens the sentence as in the succeeding vv. 21, 22, and 23, making clear that the failure to perform the "good" (ἀγαθός) is an insight derived from Paul's personal experience with the law. In the preceding pericope Paul had made the claim that "the commandment is holy and righteous and good (ἀγαθός)" (7:12) and the same word is used in reference to the law in the opening verse of the present pericope (τὸ ἀγαθόν, 7:13). The cryptic formulation in this verse, that the good does "not dwell in me, that is in my flesh," is usually mistranslated as "nothing good dwells within me,"[109] but as Leander Keck has shown, the "not" immediately precedes what is negated, that is, "dwells in me" (οὐκ οἰκεῖ ἐν ἐμοί).[110] The question here is not how much good resides in the self but rather the "non-residence of the good," because as long as sin dominates, the good is entirely absent.[111] This contention refers again to the capacity of the flesh to transform the law into a system of status acquisition, and thus totally to frustrate its capacity to produce the good. The will to

105 BAGD 546.2; 592.2; Weiss, 318; Meyer, 2:20; Godet, 285; Kuss, 2:454; Käsemann, 204; Moo, 457; Dunn's effort (1:390) to retain "the eschatological overtone" despite the "primarily logical" function of this expression is semantically illogical and unconvincing.
106 See Engberg-Pedersen, "Reception," 46–47.
107 Moo, 458.
108 Walter Grundmann, "ἁμαρτάνω κτλ.," *TDNT* 1 (1964) 311, followed by Käsemann, 204; Otto Michel, "οἰκέω," *TDNT* 5 (1967) 135; Zeller, 141.
109 Godet, 285; Lietzmann, 76; Lagrange, 176; Kuss, 2:451; Michel, 223; Schmidt, 126; Barrett, 148; Dunn, 1:390; Stuhlmacher, 108; Ziesler, 197;

Fitzmyer, 475; Byrne, 224; Haacker, 140; Schreiner, 372; Witherington, 196.
110 Leander E. Keck, "The Absent Good: The Significance of Rom 7:18a," in S. Maser and E. Schlarb, eds., *Text und Geschichte: Facetten theologischen Arbeitens aus dem Freundes- und Schülerkreis Dieter Luhrmann zum 60. Geburtstag* (MTS 50; Marburg: Elwert Verlag, 1999) 73–74. Commentaries providing an accurate translation include Weiss, 319; Zahn, 354–55; Schlier, 228; Cranfield, 1:340; Käsemann, 199; Zeller, 126; Moo, 458; Newman and Nida, 139.
111 Keck, "Absent Good." 74.

perform the good "lies ready at hand for me" (παρά-κειταί μοι), an expression that appears here and in 7:21 but nowhere else in early Christian literature. Sir 31:16 uses this term in the admonition "Eat like a human being what is set before you (τὰ παρακείμενά σοι)," which fits the basic meaning of "lie ready . . . at disposal."[112] Paul's entire Pharisaic education had prepared him for a life under the law—the ultimate good—which was as natural as eating the food laid on the table before him. Yet "bringing about the good" (τὸ κατεργάζεσθαι τὸ καλὸν)[113] did not lie ready at hand, because Paul discovered on the Damascus road that he had been opposing the Messiah, whose advent he believed his zealous violence would advance.

■ 19 This verse reiterates 7:15b-c, using the language of good and evil: "For I do not do the good that I want, but the bad that I do not want—this I practice." The good that Paul wished to achieve as a persecutor of the church was to advance adherence to the Torah as a means to usher in the messianic age. He sought to follow the will of God but discovered through the encounter with the risen Lord that he was in fact opposing the will of God as exemplified in the Messiah Jesus. What v. 19 describes is not an inability to perform the violent deeds that Paul was taught were right, but rather the objective failure of zealous obedience to produce the good. The last thing he desired was to oppose the Messiah, and this is precisely what he ended up doing. This is a different dilemma from the classical parallels. Epictetus describes the contradiction of a person lacking reason and thus acting in ignorance against his better interest: "what he wants he does not do, and what he does not want he does" (Diss. 2.26.4). In a similar vein Ovid depicts the dilemma of the weak-willed person who says, "I perceive what is better and approve of it, but I pursue what is worse" (Metam. 7.20–21). In either case the problem is nonperformance of what the actor should know is the right thing to do. A proper philosophical education will presumably resolve this dilemma. But in Paul's formula-

tion, the problem is the objective reversal of good and evil, namely, that the very good one aims to accomplish turns out to be evil in the enactment thereof. This is precisely the dilemma of Paul the former persecutor of the church, pursuing "zeal without knowledge" (Rom 10:2).

■ 20 This verse reiterates 7:17-18, which explained the role of sin in causing moral contradiction. Paul employs here the metaphor of "the sin dwelling in me" (ἡ οἰκοῦσα ἐν ἐμοὶ ἁμαρτία), which has a distant parallel in Philo Leg. 1.78.5: "Now the overall intelligence that indwells the wisdom of God (ἡ οἰκοῦσα τὴν τοῦ θεοῦ σοφιάν) and his house is beautiful, for it is imperishable and abides in an imperishable house." In the light of Rom 1, Paul views such sin as the human desire to be godlike in an effort to suppress the truth about shameful status. Culturally twisted systems of competing for honor lead individuals and groups to challenge the honor of God. In this case, the sinful competition for honor dwelling in Paul's zealous behavior was frankly acknowledged in Gal 1:14, the verse that immediately follows his description of persecuting the church: "I advanced in Judaism beyond many among my people of the same age, for I was far more zealous for the traditions of my ancestors." Competition in zeal promised social honor and divine approbation. The shocking discovery on the Damascus road was that such competition was a demonstration of the power of "sin," acting at the very heart of religious devotion. There is no doubt that sin is used here to refer to a cosmic force that leads people to act in certain ways. A demonic social power[114] deriving from a distorted system of honor and shame that had infected religion as well as the political realm, had been internalized by Paul so that it "dwelled" within him and led him to act as he did. The frustration consisted not in the ability to perform the zealous deeds he felt were justified, but in the inability of such deeds, motivated by a sinful system of competition for honor, to achieve the good. Such zeal, in fact, had led him into conflict with the very God he wanted to serve.

---

112 Friedrich Büchsel, "κεῖμαι κτλ.," *TDNT* 3 (1965) 656; G. H. R. Horsley provides a more distant example from the first century, referring to "their appended letters" (αἱ παρακείμεναι ἐπιστολαι αὐτῶν) in "Petition Concerning Ephesian Mysteries," *NDIEC* 4 (1987) 94–95.

113 Here as in 7:16 and 19, καλός appears as a virtual

synonym of ἀγαθός; see Meyer, 2:21–22; Kuss, 2:454; Dunn, 1:391; BAGD 400.

114 Schottroff, "Schreckensherrschaft," 501–2, deals with sin as demonic power that exercises a reign of terror, but she does not deal with the issue of competition for honor.

■ **21** The final argument in this pericope, comprising the next five verses, explains the role of the Torah in the contradiction between willing the good and actually performing it. Paul announces his discovery by means of εὑρίσκω ("I find, discover"),[115] which implies a new insight that had been unavailable to Paul prior to his conversion. The controversy in interpreting this verse centers on "the law," which most interpreters view as a general rule rather than as an explicit reference to the Torah.[116] Dunn points out, however, that most of the previous occurrences of νόμος in Romans refer to the Jewish Torah, and there is no semantic indication of a changed connotation here; that nowhere else in the NT does νόμος mean "rule"; and that the argumentative function of this verse synthesizes the preceding argument concerning the Torah.[117] Failing to take the intense grammatical discussion of nineteenth-century commentators into account, however, Dunn does not offer an adequate translation, which weakens his case. By taking τὸν νόμον τῷ θέλοντι ἐμοι as "my will is directed to the law," whereby θέλειν followed by the accusative τὸν νόμον indicates the object of willing, and with ποιεῖν τὸ καλόν understood as an infinitive of purpose, "in order to do the good," H. A. W. Meyer has provided a viable translation of this verse with the Torah in view:[118] "it results to me, therefore, that, while my will is directed to the law in order to do the good, the evil lies before me." This translation effectively brings v. 21a into congruence with the preceding argument and provides a smooth transition into vv. 21b-23.[119]

The statement "the bad lies within my reach" employs the same terminology as vv. 18-19, ὅτι ἐμοὶ τὸ κακὸν παράκειται. The self-evident pattern of enforcing conformity with the law, shaped by a competitive religious tradition of nomistic zealotism, is herein expressed. While Paul intended to achieve the good in persecuting the early Christians, he found that the behavior that appeared so natural and good was actually bad. Again, the contradiction between wanting and actually achieving the good is in view; not the capacity to obey the law, but the surprising consequence that such obedience led Paul into conflict with God's Messiah.

■ **22** Paul explains the contradiction by means of an expression not found elsewhere in biblical Greek, συνήδομαι γὰρ τῷ νόμῳ τοῦ θεοῦ, which I translate "for I share pleasure in the law of God."[120] The verb συνήδομαι is used by classical writers to convey rejoicing together with others,[121] as in Plato's explanation of the ideal state in which all will "share the pleasure or the pain" (ἢ ξυνησθήσεται ἅπασα ἑαυτῆς εἶναι τὸ πάσχον) of each individual citizen (*Resp.* 462e). Contemporary commentators avoid the social dimension of such joy and provide translation guesses such as "joyfully agree,"[122] "delight/rejoice in,"[123] or "agree with,"[124] without citing precise semantic parallels. The social dimension was suggested in the nineteenth century but dropped as "foreign" to the context.[125] To the contrary, the pleasure shared with fellow Pharisees in the performance of the law is exactly appropriate for the context of social zealotism. The joy shared by the obedient conformed to a biblical paradigm: "the precepts of the Lord are right, rejoicing the heart" (Ps 19:8); "Blessed is the

---

115   See Herbert Preisker, "εὑρίσκω," *TDNT* 2 (1964) 769.

116   BAGD 542.2; for examples from the last century, see Meyer, 2:23; Godet, 286–87. Other advocates include Sanday and Headlam, 182; Kühl, 239; Lagrange, 177–78; Käsemann, 205; Schlier, 233; Cranfield, 1:362; Kuss, 2:455–56; Murray, 264–65; Ziesler, 197; Zeller, 142; Moo, 460; Thielman, *Law,* 200.

117   Dunn, 1:392–93.

118   Meyer, 2:25–26.

119   Meyer, 2:26.

120   That νόμος refers here to the Jewish Torah is shown by Winger, *Law,* 186–87.

121   LSJM 1715; Weiss, 323; see also Philo *Conf.* 7, "community of languages led them to impart to each other their pleasures and discomforts (συνήδετο καὶ συναηδίζετο)." Xenophon *Symp.* 8.18 refers to friends "sharing a common joy in life's pleasures (συνήδεσθαι δὲ ἐπὶ ταῖς καλαις πράξεσι)."

122   BAGD 789; Schlier, 233; Wilckens, 2:74; Zeller, 136.

123   Zahn, 359; Cranfield, 1:362; Murray, 294; Ziesler, 197; Fitzmyer, 476; Moo, 461.

124   Kühl, 241; Schmidt, 132; Michel, 223; Kuss, 2:456; Dunn, 1:393.

125   Meyer, 2:26, citing van Hengel, who proposed "joy over the law, shared with others." Nor has Meyer's suggestion of a personified law, whose joy is shared by performers, been followed, because nowhere in the Hebrew Scriptures is the law's own joy described.

man who fears the Lord, who greatly delights in his commandments! His descendants will be mighty in the land; the generation of the upright will be blessed (Ps 112:1-2); "May we shout for joy over your victory, and in the name of our God set up our banners!" (Ps 20:5)

As the choice of the preposition κατά suggests,[126] the location of the shared joy in the law is specified as Paul's "inner self/person." This concept has been extensively investigated in recent decades,[127] with the realization that although Paul uses a Platonic concept here, his anthropology is not dualistic.[128] While the expression appears to have developed in the context of the Corinthian correspondence,[129] Paul was the first to have used the "inner/outer man" terminology, apparently coining these words to articulate Middle Platonic ideas in a radically innovative manner.[130] In 2 Cor 4:16-18, the inner man is being renewed by the spirit while the outer man is subject to persecution and other forms of deterioration that will ultimately lead to death. The very different use in Romans is neatly captured by Nikolaus Walter and others as what "the individual should be, in distinction from what he actually is."[131] This can easily be coordinated with the hypothesis of this "speech-in-character," with Paul as the zealot whose deeds achieved the opposite of his original intent to serve "the law of God."

■ 23 The antithesis to the joy shared with other zealous followers of the law is stated in terms that could easily be interpreted as an expression of Hellenistic dualism.[132] "Another law in my members" and "the law of sin in my members" stand in stark antithesis to the "law of my mind," which could be understood as a virtually Gnostic expression of the material side of humankind holding the spiritual side in bondage.[133] In the context of Paul's argument in this pericope, however, the ἕτερον νόμον ("another law") is identical with "the law of sin" that twists performance of the law into a means of status acquisition (see 7:5, 7-8, 11, 13-14). This functions ἐν τοῖς μέλεσίν μου ("in my members"), repeated twice in this sentence in reference to the human limbs required for action.[134] In this context, bodily "members" are the means of zealous action that reveal a bondage to the foreign power of sin. The good the law is intended to achieve, that is, the "the law of the mind" of Paul the zealot hoped to advance, is captured by this alien force. Paul uses military verbs for making war against an enemy (ἀντιστρατεύομαι)[135] and for being taken captive after a defeat in war (αἰχμαλωτίζω),[136] which carried none of the benign features that moderns associate with prisoners of war. In the Roman Empire, defeat implied subsequent slavery, death in an imperial theater, or if a prisoner was particularly important or attractive, he would be executed in honor of Jupiter at the end of a victory parade.[137] For example, at the end of the

126 The prepositional phrase "qualifies the first person singular of the verb" (Cranfield, 1:363), and category 6 for κατά with the accusative, "denoting relationship" (BAGD 407) leads to my translation, "with respect to my inner self."

127 See Christoph Markschies, "Innerer Mensch," *RAC* 18 (1997) 266–312; A. van den Beld, "Romans 7:14-25 and the Problem of *Akrasia*," *RelS* 21 (1985) 495–515; repr. *Bijdr* 46 (1985) 39–58; Theo K. Heckel, *Der Innere Mensch: Die paulinische Verarbeitung eines platonischen Motivs* (WUNT 53; Tübingen: Mohr-Siebeck, 1993); Hans Dieter Betz, review of Heckel, *Der Innere Mensch* in *ThLZ* 119 (1994) 133–35.

128 See Alexander Sand, "ἄνθρωπος," *EDNT* 1 (1990) 102; Markschies, "Innerer Mensch," 279–82; Schmithals, *Anthropologie*, 41–42.

129 See Jewett, *Terms*, 396–99; Heckel, *Innere Mensch*, 141–47; Betz, review of Heckel, 133–35.

130 See Heckel, *Innere Mensch*, 146–47; Markschies, "Innerer Mensch," 280.

131 Nikolaus Walter, "ἔσω, ἔσωθεν, ἐσώτερος," *EDNT* 2 (1991) 65; see also Hofius, *Paulusstudien*, 59; Markschies, "Innerer Mensch," 281.

132 Zeller, 142–44.

133 See Jewett, *Terms*, 400; the dualistic anthropology of Gnosticism is explained by Rudolf, *Gnosis*, 88–112, and is developed by Fuchs, *Freiheit*, 77–78; see also Schmithals, *Anthropologie*, 146–52.

134 See the analysis of 6:13 and Johannes Horst, "μέλος," *TDNT* 4 (1967) 561–63; Martin Völkel, "μέλος," *EDNT* 2 (1991) 404, stresses the service of humans either to the power of sin or of God.

135 See BAGD 75; an example is Xenophon *Cyr.* 8.8.26, which reports that no state can get along without Greek mercenaries, "neither when they make war against one another, nor when the Greeks make war against them (ὅταν οἱ Ἕλληνες αὐτοῖς ἀντιστρατεύωνται)."

136 See BAGD 27; a parallel figurative use of this verb is found in Dio Chrysostom *Orat.* 32.90, who describes "ransoming" the soul as "captivity, slavery,

Jewish–Roman war, Josephus reports that, of the ninety-seven thousand, those who had borne arms should be executed immediately after their capture, that the "tallest and most handsome of the youth" were reserved for the triumphal parade in Rome, while the rest were either enslaved or "presented by Titus to the provinces, to be destroyed in the theaters by the sword or by wild beasts."[138] Since the majority of the members of the early house and tenement churches in Rome were either slaves or former slaves, many of whom had been prisoners of war or were descended therefrom, this formulation would have a particularly powerful resonance. However, this "battle for world domination"[139] did not in Paul's view require heroic resistance on the part of believers, but rather a sober recognition that their martial inclinations were themselves the evidence of having already been taken prisoner by sin. The impulse to crusade against others in behalf of one's view of the law was in this sense "the law of sin at work in my members." Yet by maintaining the first person possessive μου ("my"), Paul maintains the "speech-in-character" that dramatizes his own experience with the law, thus avoiding any direct accusation against the groups in Rome.[140] Only at the end of this letter does it become evident that another form of human interaction, "welcoming one another as Christ has welcomed you" (Rom 15:7), should replace zealous crusading. Before that can be understood, however, the awful dilemma of the law corrupted by sin needs to be grasped.

■ 24 The exclamation "How wretched a person I [am]" is the appropriate response to Paul's dilemma of frustrated zealotism. The wording has parallels in early Attic,[141] Hermetic,[142] Stoic,[143] Cynic,[144] and Hellenistic Jewish[145] sources where the adjective ταλαίπωρος ("wretched, miserable") appears, but the context of frustrated zeal for the law in Paul's discourse is quite different from these dualistic treatments of a fatal conflict between the mind and the flesh, or between love's passion and fate's cruelty. Paul's exclamation cannot refer to the tension between the two aeons[146] or to a yearning for resurrection,[147] which reflect the experience of believers rather than of the pre-Christian Paul. The sentiment of hopeless misery resonates with Paul's admission in 1 Cor 15:9, "For I am . . . unfit to be called an Apostle, because I persecuted the church of Christ."

The rhetorical question about who can deliver such a

---

dragging away (αἰχμαλωσία, δουλεία, ἀπαγωγή)."

137 Auguet, *Cruelty and Civilization*, 184–99; Fears, "Cult of Jupiter," 1–141; Fears, "Theology of Victory," 737–826.

138 Josephus *Bell.* 6.414–19. Kreitzer, *Striking New Images*, 136–38, observes that Roman coins struck after the victory over Jerusalem feature dejected Jewish prisoners with their hands bound.

139 Käsemann, 207; see also Zahn, 360.

140 In contrast, Carter, *Power of Sin*, interprets Rom 7:7-25 in the context of "high group/low grid anthropology of the good inside and the evil outside" (193), which identifies "the Jew under the law as a sinful outsider, one who is excluded from the righteous eschatological in-group (197)." Both the "weak" who continue as believers to follow the law and the Jews who reject the messianic message would be included in this exclusion, which fundamentally distorts the message of the letter as a whole.

141 Aeschylus *Prom.* 233; 595; Demosthenes *Cor.* 121.3; Plato *Euthyd.* 302b7.

142 Edgar W. Smith, Jr., "The Form and Religious Background of Romans 7:24-25a," *NovT* 13 (1971) 128 points to a Hermetic version of despair of life in the body deprived of access to truth in *Corp. herm.* 34–37: "For we wretched ones have been condemned, and seeing was not granted to us directly, etc."

143 Dunn, 1:396, points to Epictetus *Diss.* 1.3.5–6, "'For what am I? A miserable, paltry man,' (ταλαίπωρον ἀνθρωπάριον) say they, and 'Lo, my wretched, paltry flesh.' Wretched indeed, but you have also something better than your paltry flesh," that is, reason and intelligence. See also *Diss.* 1.4.1; 1.28.9; 3.3.17; 3.26.3; 4.4.4; 4.16.18; etc.

144 When Diogenes the Cynic, in Diogenes Laertius *Vitae philos.* 6.66.7, encounters a man suing a courtesan, he remarks, "Why, O miserable man (ὦ ταλαίπωρε), are you at such pains to win your lawsuit, when you are better off to lose it?"

145 Smith, "Romans 7:24-25a," 129, cites *Conf. Asen.* 6.7.2, where the lovelorn cries out after ruining her chance to marry Joseph, "Woe to me the miserable one. . . . I am wretched and foolish (ταλαίπωρος ἐγὼ καὶ ἄφρων), because I have spoken wicked words to my father."

146 Dunn, 1:396; see Zeller, 144.

147 See Robert J. Banks, "Romans 7:25a: An Eschatological Thanksgiving?" *ABR* 26 (1978) 34–42.

miserable person is posed in such a way as to require the answer, "Nobody can!"[148] In this context, the "body of death" in 7:24 links most closely with Paul's own involvement in the persecution and death of early Christians.[149] The question of whether to translate with "the body of this death"[150] or "this body of death"[151] is relatively clear grammatically. The word sequence may favor the first alternative, but the connection between v. 24 and the reference to the "members" in the preceding verse leads Kühl, Kuss, and others to connect "this" in a substantive manner with the body doomed to death.[152] Schlier observes that "this" cannot be attached to the word "death" because, in contrast to "body," it was not developed in the previous argument.[153] The easiest way to convey this in English is the formulation, "this body of death." Although some commentators assume that the death being specified by "this" is a spiritual death, the wording would function equally well in reference to the death-dealing quality of Paul's former action as a Jewish zealot, which we have traced through the rest of Rom 7. There is a vague, metaphorical quality of explanations in terms of "spiritual death,"[154] which seems to reflect modern views. The death probably in view here is Paul's involvement in violent persecutions prior to his conversion: "I was violently persecuting the church of God and was trying to destroy it" (Gal 1:13). It was of course only after his conversion that Paul was able to discern his

body as a body of death,[155] imposing death on others and doomed to a divine sentence of death as punishment for murder. The theme of death picks up Paul's replication of the theme of the fall of Adam in 7:11, "sin . . . deceived me, and through it slayed me."

That Paul cannot be speaking here of the current condition of believers, following the *simul iustus et peccator* interpretation,[156] was shown by Godet on the basis of two details in this rhetorical question. The first is the use of the indefinite pronoun τίς ("who"): "A Christian may find himself in distress; but he knows at least the name of his deliverer."[157] The second is the future tense of the verb "will deliver me," which places the speaker at a point prior to experiencing salvation through Christ. The status of the current believer is properly formulated in 8:2: God "has set you free from the law of sin and death." The rhetorical question in 7:24 therefore relates to the preconversion Saul, caught in an awful contradiction between the good he sought to advance and the evil that he actually achieved.

■ 25 In answer to the rhetorical question, Paul breaks forth in a "joyful shout"[158] that reiterates the ecstatic cry of 6:17, thanking God for deliverance that would otherwise be impossible: "But thanks be to God (χάρις δὲ τῷ θεῷ)!"[159] In addition to 6:17, there are four similar thanksgivings in the Corinthian correspondence (1 Cor 15:57; 2 Cor 2:14; 8:16; 9:15), of which the first is the

---

148 Morris, 297.
149 Grappe, "Typologie adamique," 473–75, argues that the "body of death" in Rom 7:24 is drawn from *4 Ezra* 3.4-5 (". . . Adam, a lifeless body [*Adam corpus mortuum*]? Yet he was the workmanship of your hands, and you breathed into him the breath of life, and he was made alive in your presence"). But there is no hint in *4 Ezra* that the not-yet-enlivened body of Adam was dead because of sin.
150 Godet, 290, prefers this translation, citing Meyer that "the sigh for deliverance does not arise from the fact that the body is *this* earthly, but from the fact that the body is the instrument of *this* state of death in which the soul is sunk (ver. 11)." According to Käsemann, 209, this view is adopted by Schlatter, Bardenhewer, Gaubler, Murray, Kümmel, and Schmidt. Barrett, 151, rightly comments that "'the body of this death' is grammatically possible but scarcely makes sense."
151 Käsemann, 209, citing Kühl, Lietzmann, and Lagrange. Moo, 466, adopts this view because of

the references to "flesh" in 7:18 and to "members" in 7:23.
152 Kühl, 242; Kuss, 2:459, following Gutjahr, Dodd, and Jülicher.
153 Schlier, 235, following Hommel, "7. Kapitel," 146–47.
154 See Moo, 466, and Gundry, "Moral Frustration," 239.
155 Hommel, "7. Kapitel," 146, argues on grammatical grounds that this phrase should be translated "von diesem Todesleib."
156 See James D. G. Dunn, "Rom 7:14-25 in the Theology of Paul," *ThZ* 31 (1975) 68, cited with approval by Garlington, *Letter to the Romans*, 112.
157 Godet, 290.
158 Morris, 297.
159 Smith, "7:24-25a," 134, cites the parallel formulation in Epictetus *Diss.* 4.4.7 that refers to the philosopher's enlightenment as having overcome his former preoccupation with external success: "There was a time when I too made mistakes, but

closest parallel: "but thanks be to God ($\tau\hat{\omega}$ δὲ θεῷ χάρις) who gives us the victory through our Lord Jesus Christ."[160] Although some commentators and translators drop the δέ, in part under the influence of text-critical confusion,[161] the adversative sense of "but" should be retained[162] to express the antithesis between the hopeless situation of the "body of death" and the release from that bondage by the power of Christ. The context in Romans is reminiscent of χάριτι δὲ θεοῦ εἰμι ὅ εἰμι ("by the grace of God I am who I am"), which Paul appended to his sad admission about having persecuted the church (1 Cor 15:10). If the dilemma of zealotism was a trap that captured the most devoted of religious fanatics, only a divine agency could possibly provide release from the impasse. The extraordinary redemption Paul and other early believers had experienced requires the full christological formulation, "through Jesus Christ our Lord." It is only "through" (διά) the agency of Christ's redemptive activity that they had been released from the hopeless misery of sin. This differentiates Paul's thanksgiving from other Greco-Roman formulations, such as "I give thanks to you, Lady Artemis" in an official inscription found in Ephesus.[163] There is a significant shift in Paul's formulation of the plural "our" Lord, from the singular "I" that had been dominant throughout the earlier portion of this pericope. Although the reason for his former misery was unique, he shared the experience of unmerited grace with all other believers.

Having concluded above that v. 25b-c is a marginal gloss added by Paul himself that was probably intended to be placed between v. 23 and v. 24, the implications of this recapitulation should be sought. Taking ἄρα οὖν in an inferential sense, the expression αὐτὸς ἐγώ refers to the self restricted to its own resources,[164] translated aptly by Dodd as "Thus, left to myself."[165] Without the intervention of Christ, the νοῦς of the zealot believes that he serves the "law of God" but as a consequence of misunderstanding the "righteousness of God" (see Rom 10:2), the deeds of his flesh actually serve the "law of sin." The human dilemma lies not in some kind of ontological dualism posed between allegedly higher and lower aspects of the self, as a misinterpretation of vv. 22-23 could have been taken to imply. Insofar as the entire pericope concentrates on Paul's paradigmatic situation before his conversion, and in view of the fact that temporal categories are absent from v. 25b-c, the effort to see therein a reference to the "eschatological tension" between the already and not yet of faith[166] is misguided. Neither did Paul intend to imply "that the Christian, so long as he remains in this present life, remains in a real sense a slave of sin."[167] The originally intended climax of v. 25a should provide the parameters of our interpretation, which leads directly into 8:1, regardless of the afterthought (v. 25b-c) that Paul added in the margin. It is the grace of Christ that reveals and overcomes the destructive zealotism that had marked Paul's former life and that was reemerging in the conflicts between the weak and the strong in Rome. By using himself as the paradigmatic example of such misunderstanding, thus avoiding the evocation of divisive accusations between groups in Rome, Paul sought to clarify a profound dilemma at the heart of religion.

now no longer, thanks be to God (χάρις τῷ θεῷ)." That thanks were due to God or the gods was a common belief in the Greco-Roman and Jewish worlds, as the exegesis of 1:21 demonstrates. See also BAGD 878.5; Alfred Stuiber, "Eulogia," *RAC* 6 (1966) 909, suggesting dependency on the Hellenistic Diaspora; and Klaus Berger, "χάρις," *EDNT* 3 (1993) 459.

160 See Banks, "Romans 7:25a," 38–39.

161 See note n above. Commentators dropping "but" include Weiss, 327; Lietzmann, 76–77; Michel, 223; Kuss, 2:451, 460; Barrett, 151; Cranfield, 1:367; Wilckens, 2:74, 95; Ziesler, 199; Fitzmyer, 476; Theobald, 218–19; Moo, 466; Byrne, 233.

162 Zeller, 136; Stuhlmacher, 112–13.

163 See G. H. R. Horsley, "Giving Thanks to Artemis," *NDIEC* 4 (1987) 127–29.

164 Meyer, 2:33; Godet, 291–92; Zahn, 370; Kümmel, *Römer 7*, 66; Wilckens, 2:97; Lichtenberger, "Röm 7,25b," 287–88.

165 Dodd, 104.

166 Dunn, 1:411–12.

167 Cranfield, 1:370.

8

The Eighth Pericope

Thesis and Rationale Concerning the Cosmic Struggle Between Flesh and Spirit

we are suffering jointly [with him] in order that we might also° be glorified jointly [with him].

1/ So now[a] [there is] no punishment for those in Christ Jesus.[b] 2/ For the law of the Spirit of the life in Christ Jesus has freed you[c] from the law of sin and death. 3/ For the law [being] powerless, in that it was weak on account of the flesh, "God, having sent his own son in the likeness of sinful flesh" and concerning sin,[d] condemned sin in the flesh, 4/ in order that the righteous requirement of the law might be fulfilled[e] among us who do not walk according to flesh but according to Spirit.

5/ For those who exist according to flesh set their minds on the things of the flesh, but those who exist according to Spirit [set their minds] on the things of the Spirit. 6/ For the mind of the flesh is death, but the mind of the Spirit is life and peace. 7/ Because the mind of the flesh is hostile to God, for it does not submit itself to the law of God, for it isn't even able. 8/ And those who exist in the flesh are unable to please God.

9/ But you do not exist in flesh but in Spirit, since indeed God's Spirit dwells among you (pl). But if someone does not have Christ's Spirit, that one is not his. 10/ But if Christ is in your midst, though the body [be][f] dead because of sin, the Spirit [is] life because of righteousness. 11/ But if the Spirit of "the one who raised Jesus[g] from the dead" dwells in your midst, "the one raising Christ Jesus[h] from the dead" will also[i] give life to your mortal bodies through his Spirit[j] dwelling in your midst.

12/ So then, brothers, we are obligated ones, not to the flesh to live according to flesh; 13/ for if you (pl.) live according to flesh, you are going to die; but if by Spirit you (pl.) put to death the practices of the body,[k] you (pl.) will live. 14/ For all those who are being led by God's Spirit, these are sons of God.[l] 15/ For you did not receive a Spirit of slavery resulting again in fear; rather you received a spirit of sonship by which we cry out, "Abba, the Father!"[m] 16/ The[n] Spirit itself bears witness with our spirit that we are God's children, 17/ and if children, also heirs, on the one hand God's heirs, but on the other hand Christ's joint heirs, since indeed

a   The absence of νῦν ("now") in D* 205 517 1908[mg] syᵖ appears to smooth out the text of 8:1, which commences with an overabundance of conjunctions and adverbs.

b   A phrase found also in 8:4 appears in the text at this point in A D¹ Ψ 81 256 263 (365 has τοῖς for μή) 629 1243 1319 1573 1852 2127 *pc* d² f mon² vg syrᵖ goth armᵐˢ Chr Victorinus-Rome Hier Pel Spec: μὴ κατὰ σάρκα περιπατοῦσιν ("who do not walk according to flesh"). The phrase appears with the rest of the quotation, ἀλλὰ κατὰ πνεῦμα ("but according to spirit"), in ℵ² D² K L P 5 33^vid 61 69 88 104 181 218 323 326 330 424* (436 *omits* μή) 441 451 459 467 614 621 623 720 915 917 945 1175 1241 1398 1505 1563 1678 1718 1735 1751 1836 1838 1845 1846 1874 1875 1877 1908ᶜ 1912 1942 1959 1962 2138 2197 2200 2464 2492 2495 2516 2523 2544 2718 *Maj Lect* ar o syʰ geo² slav Cyrˡᵉᵐ. The witnesses without these two phrases, ℵ* B C² (C* illegible up to 8:3) D* (F G with space for addition) 6 424ᶜ 1506 1739 1881 1908* 2110 *pc* b d* g mon* sa bo armᵐˢ (eth) geo¹ Mcionᵃᶜᶜ· ᵗᵒ ᴬᵈ Orˡᵃᵗ Ath Diodore Did Cyr Ambst Aug, are sufficiently broad and ancient to claim priority.

c   One reading with σε ("you" [singular]) is supported by ℵ B F G 1506* 1739* ar b f g o syᵖ geo¹ Tert¹ᐟ² Victorinus-Rome Ambst Pel Aug¹⁰ᐟ¹³ Spec Varimadum. The alternative pronoun, με ("me"), appears in A Cᶜ D K L P 6 69 81 88 104 181 256 263 323 326 330 365 424 436 451 459 614 629 945 1175 1241 1243 1319 1505 1506ᶜ 1573 1735 1739ᶜ 1836 1852 1874 1877 1881 1912 1962 2127 2200 2464^vid 2492 2495 *Maj Lect* d mon syʰ sa arm geo² slav Cl Orˡᵃᵗ Ath Evagrius Did Did^dub Macarius/Symeon Chr Severian Theodore Marcus-Eremita Cyr Thret Tert¹ᐟ² Ambr Hier Faustus-Nilevis Aug³ᐟ¹³; ἡμᾶς ("you" [pl.]) appears in Ψ syᵖᵃˡ bo eth Mcionᵃᶜᶜ· ᵗᵒ ᴬᵈ Meth Bas Fulg. No pronoun at all appears in Orᵖᵗ armᵐˢˢ. The last two options are less strongly attested and may represent efforts to apply Paul's argument to everyone, as in 8:4. The broader support for σε and its awkwardness in the context indicate its priority. See Metzger, *Textual Commentary*, 455–56.

d   The deletion of the awkward phrase "and on account of sin" in 1836 1912 *pc* is an understandable effort to smooth out the text.

e   An important but apparently hitherto unnoticed variant on πληρωθῇ ("be fulfilled") occurs in Hip-

474

polytus *Noet.* 15.5.5, which substitutes "manifested" (φανερωθῇ) for "fulfilled."

f   The provision of the copula ἐστίν ("it is") by F G, transposed in 629 *pc*, lat Ambst Spec represents a later effort to improve the text.

g   The omission of the article τόν before "Jesus" in ℵ² C D F G K L P Ψ 33 88 69 104 323 326 330 424 614 945 1175 1241 1243 1319 1506 1573 1735 1836 1874 2464 *Maj* Cl Meth appears to be a stylistic improvement of the probably original wording with the article found in ℵ* A B 6 630 1505 1739 1881 2495 *pc*.

h   Several variants apparently arose in response to the puzzling parallelism in the expression "Jesus/or/Christ from the dead," used twice in this sentence. The most broadly attested and probably most reliable version, followed in the earlier editions of Nestle²⁴ᐟ²⁵, is ἐκ νεκρῶν Χριστὸν Ἰησοῦν ("from [the] dead, Christ Jesus") found in ℵ* A (C 5 81 623 have "Jesus Christ") 630 1243 1506 1739 1852 1881 1908 2110 2200 *pc*. The same words are found in the sequence "Christ Jesus from [the] dead" in D* 441 1942 (104 467 1838 1959 lat sy^p have "Jesus Christ") bo, but the support for this is too narrow to be plausible. The traditional reading found in ℵ² K L P Ψ 6 33 61 69 88 181 218 323 326 330 424 451 614 720 915 917 945 1175 1241 1398 1505 1563 1718 1735 1751 1836 1845 1846 1874 1875 1877 1912 2138 2197 2344 2492 2495 2523 2544 2718 *Maj* Lect, τὸν Χριστὸν ἐκ νεκρῶν ("the Christ from [the] dead") is unlikely to be original because it so closely resembles the wording earlier in the sentence. Although Metzger observes that the inclusion of the article in this traditional reading "is probably a scribal parallelization to the preceding τὸν Ἰησοῦν," he calls this option "the least unsatisfactory reading" (*Textual Commentary (1975)*, 516). The indication in *GNT³* concerning the status of the article in f g mon sa eth^pp Ir^lat Tert Or^lat Ambst Hil may recognize that Latin has no definite article. The wording of Nestle-Aland²⁶ᐟ²⁷ is derived from B D² F G 256 263 1319 1573 2127 2516 *l* 249 pc mon sa Mcion^Tert Ir^lat Spec, Χριστὸν ἐκ νεκρῶν ("Christ from [the] dead"). This appears to be an instance when the recent text-critical work reflected in Nestle-Aland²⁷ regresses to a less certain and less broadly attested variant.

In addition to these variants listed in Nestle-Aland, Metzger explains the omission of ἐκ νεκρῶν ("from [the] dead") in 103 Chrys and the deletion of the entire clause "the one raising . . . from [the] dead" in 436 629 ar as resulting from scribal blunders. The minor variants Ἰησοῦν ἐκ νεκρῶν ("Jesus from dead") in 621 *l* 809 Tert CyrJ; Ἰησοῦν Χριστὸν ἐκ νεκρῶν ("Jesus Christ from dead") in

104 467 1838 1959 lat (sy^p, our Lord Jesus Christ); and ἐκ νεκρῶν Ἰησοῦν Χριστόν ("from dead Jesus Christ") in C 5 81 623 are not covered by Metzger, either in the 1975 or the 1994 edition.

i   The omission of καί ("and, also") in ℵ Λ 326 630 1739 1881 *pc* Epiph^pt appears to reflect an authoritative Alexandrian effort to smooth out the text. There is more weight for the inclusion of καί.

j   An expression using the accusative case, διὰ τὸ ἐνοικοῦν αὐτοῦ πνεῦμα ("because of his indwelling spirit") found in B D F G K L P* Ψ 6 33 181 323 330 424 451 459 (614) (629) 720 917 945 1175 1241 1398 1678 1739 1751 (1836) 1845 1846 2516 1874 (1877) 1881 1908 (1912 omits αὐτοῦ) 1942 2138 2197 2200 2344 2464 2492 2523 2544 2718 *Maj* Lect ar b d g o vg sy^p, (pal) Ir^lat Hipp^sy Or^gr,lat Meth^1/2 Did^lat 1/2 Chr Tert Hil Ambst Ambr^1/3 Hier^2/3 Pel Niceta Aug^15/43 Spec mss & Heretics^acc. to Ps-Athanasius appears to be an expression of grammatical preference over the more widely attested expression in the genitive construction translated with "through his indwelling spirit," found in ℵ A C^c, (* *has* αὐτοί) P^c 5 (61) 69 81 (88) 104 218 256 263 326 436 441 467 621 623 915 1243 1319 1505 1506 1563 1573 1718 1735 (1838) 1852 1875 1959 1962 2110 2127 2495 *l* 249 *al* f mon sy^h sa bo arm eth geo slav Cl Hipp Meth^1/2 Ath Ps-Ath mss^acc. to Ps-Ath Bas CyrJ Apollinaris Did^lat 1/2 Did^dub Macarius/Symeon Epiph Cyr Victorinus-Rome Ambr^2/3 Prisc Hier^1/3 Aug^28/43 Ps-Vig Varimadum Vig Beda. See Metzger, *Textual Commentary*, 456. Other minor variants are διὰ τὸ ἐνοικοῦν αὐτῷ πνεῦμα ("because of the spirit that dwells in him") in 614 1836 plus four other minuscules, and διὰ τὸ οἰκοῦν αὐτοῦ πνεύμα ("because of his dwelling spirit") in 1877 and five others.

k   The replacement of the widely attested expression "of the body" by τῆς σαρκός ("of the flesh") in D F G 630 *pc* latt Ir^lat is clearly an effort to eliminate a major interpretive problem in the wording of this text.

l   While I know of no explanation for the various sequences of the final three words in this sentence, the one followed by Nestle-Aland²⁶ᐟ²⁷ and *GNT*³ᐟ⁴, υἱοὶ θεοῦ εἰσιν ("sons of God are"), is strongly supported by ℵ A C D 81 88 630 1319 1506 1573 1739 *pc* ar b Ambst Spec. This evidence is stronger than that followed by earlier editions of Nestle supporting the sequence υἱοὶ εἰσιν θεοῦ (B F G mon vg^sl Or Pel), a sequence that Cranfield, 1:395, evidently prefers because it provides stress on "sons" that is consistent with his view of the argument. The third option, εἰσιν υἱοὶ θεοῦ in K L P Ψ 6 33 69 104 323 330 424 614 945 1175 1241 1243 1505 1735 1836 1874 1881 2464 2495 *Maj* vg^cl Ir^lat Cl is even less likely; cf. εἰσιν θεοῦ υἱοί in 326.

m   Beza conjectured that the original text did not include the Greek translation ("the Father") of the Aramaic expression "Abba." This does not seem very plausible since the phrase "Abba the Father" appears in Gal 4:6 and Mark 14:36, the only examples of "Abba" in the NT, thus indicating the presence of a traditional formula.

n   The provision of the conjunction ὥστε ("for this reason") by D (sy^p) appears to be a secondary effort to strengthen the argument.

o   The omission of καί ("and, also") in P^{46} vg^{ms} sa^{ms} is too weakly attested to be original, and may be an effort to smooth out the text.

Analysis

The rough transition between 7:25 and 8:1 has elicited proposals to place 8:1 after 8:2[1] or to consider v. 1 a non-Pauline marginal gloss.[2] Wilckens argues that the first option is rendered implausible by the tight connection between v. 2 and v. 3[3] and that a gloss is rendered unlikely by the Pauline diction in v. 1 as well as by the links between "punishment" in v. 1, the powerlessness of the law in 8:2-4, and the captivity under the law in 7:7-25.[4] However, a serious and hitherto unresolved transmission issue remains with these verses, especially with the textual variants in the pronouns, the awkward wording of 8:3, and the fact that only 7:25a prepares the reader for the "so now" of 8:1, which otherwise harks back either to 7:6[5] or to the conclusion of 5:12-21.

The form of 8:1 is that of a dogmatic thesis,[6] formulated without a verb,[7] drawing the conclusion that believers have been set free from sin and death,[8] which was the burden of the argument in the previous sections of 5:1—7:25. This thesis is elaborated in the rest of this pericope as well as in the final pericope of this proof (8:31-39). The following verse reverts to the double-line sentence pattern of Pauline explanation in an effective instance of antithetical development with the "law of the Spirit of life in Christ Jesus" in v. 2a contrasted with the "law of sin and death" in v. 2b.[9] This is followed by a pos-sible chiastic development in vv. 3-4,[10] marked by weak parallelism between C and C' and by the reversal of the expected sequence of A' and B':

A   For the *law* [being] powerless (v. 3a)
  B   in that it was weakened by the *flesh* (v. 3b)
    C   *God* having sent his own Son (v. 3c)
      D   in the likeness of *sinful* flesh,
      D'   and concerning *sin* (v. 3d)
    C'   [*God*] condemned *sin* in the flesh (v. 3e)
  A'   in order that the righteous requirement of the *law* might be fulfilled among us (v. 4a)
B'   who do not work according to the *flesh* but according to the Spirit (8:4b)

The spirit/flesh antithesis at the end of v. 4 is developed in the next paragraph (vv. 5-8) by means of double-line sentences of which v. 5 and 6 are antithetical parallels and vv. 7 and 8 constitute an extended synthetic parallel.[11] Both v. 5 and v. 6 present the antithesis between "flesh" and "spirit" in successive lines, while v. 6 also contains the antithesis between "death" and "life." Cognates with the element φρον- appear four times in vv. 5-7.[12] The homoioteleuton in the -ται verbal endings at the ends of the last three lines of the synthetical parallelism of vv. 7-8, combined with the actual

1   Müller, "Zwei Marginalien," 249–54.
2   Bultmann, "Glossen," 197–202.
3   While other commentaries support Wilckens's claim, it appears that not everyone senses a tight connection at this point, as indicated by the provision of an open sequential space between these verses in Nestle-Aland^{27}.
4   Wilckens, 2:119.
5   Godet, 296; Barrett, 154.
6   Käsemann, 214.
7   Wilckens, 2:120.
8   See Louw, 2:87–88.
9   Bengel, *Gnomon*, 89, identifies this as an example of *epanalepsis*, by which the same word ("law") is at the beginning and the end of the clause.
10   Weiss, "Beiträge," 234, refers to the elegant structure of 8:3-4 but does not identify the chiastic structure, which I illustrate below.
11   Weiss, "Beiträge," 234, suggests that 8:8 stands alone, but it fits quite well as a synonymous parallel to 8:7c. Bullinger, *Figures*, 716, identifies only v. 5 as an antithesis.
12   See Harvey, *Listening*, 197.

paronomasia of the repeated δύναται ("can, be able"), enhances the parallelism in thought.

The next two paragraphs (8:9-11, 12-17) alternate between antithetical or synthetic parallelism and repeated climax structures, in which motifs from preceding lines are picked up and qualified in succeeding lines. So "Spirit" in 8:9a is picked up by the stipulation about the "Spirit" dwelling in believers in v. 9b while "someone" and "Christ" in v. 9c are picked up by "that one" and "him" in v. 9d. The climactic element is combined in this verse with an antithetical parallelism between the two successive sentences beginning with "but if" clauses, in which being "in the Spirit" in v. 9a is contrasted with not having the Spirit in v. 9c. The sequence of "but if" clauses continues in vv. 10 and 11, completing a fourfold anaphoric series of εἰ δέ ("but if"). In v. 10 there is a double apodosis containing a brilliantly devised antithetical parallelism in which each word in sequence is contrasted with its corresponding word in the next line:

> τὸ μὲν σῶμα νεκρὸν διὰ ἁμαρτίαν ("the body dead through sin")
> τὸ δὲ πνεῦμα ζωὴ διὰ δικαιοσύνην ("the Spirit life through righteousness").[13]

In v. 11 a traditional, early Christian formula[14] is cited twice with slight variations, printed out below, followed by other early Christian passages that employ the same terminology.[15]

> Rom 8:11a τοῦ ἐγείραντος τὸν Ἰησοῦν ἐκ νεκρῶν ("the one who raised Jesus from the dead")
> Rom 8:11b ὁ ἐγείρας Χριστὸν ἐκ νεκρῶν ("the one raising Christ Jesus from the dead")
> Rom 4:24 τὸν ἐγείραντα Ἰησοῦν τὸν κύριον ἡμῶν ἐκ νεκρῶν ("the one who raised Jesus our Lord from the dead")
> Rom 6:4b ὥσπερ ἠγέρθη Χριστὸς ἐκ νεκρῶν ("as Christ was raised from the dead")

> Rom 10:9 ὁ θεὸς αὐτὸν ἤγειρεν ἐκ νεκρῶν ("God raised him from the dead")
> Gal 1:1 τοῦ ἐγείραντος αὐτὸν ἐκ νεκρῶν ("the one who raised him from the dead")
> 1 Thess 1:10 ὃν ἔγειρεν ἐκ νεκρῶν ("whom he raised from the dead")
> Eph 1:20 ἐγείρας αὐτὸν ἐκ νεκρῶν ("he raised him from the dead")
> Col 2:12 τοῦ ἐγείραντος αὐτὸν ἐκ νεκρῶν ("the one who raised him from the dead")
> Acts 3:15; 4:10 ὃν ὁ θεὸς ἤγειρεν ἐκ νεκρῶν ("whom God raised from the dead")
> Acts 13:30 ὁ δὲ θεὸς ἤγειρεν αὐτὸν ἐκ νεκρῶν ("but God raised him from the dead")
> 1 Pet 1:21 θεὸν τὸν ἐγείραντα αὐτὸν ἐκ νεκρῶν ("God who raised him from the dead")
> Polycarp 2.1 τὸν ἐγείραντα τὸν κύριον ἡμῶν Ἰησοῦν Χριστὸν ἐκ νεκρῶν ("the one who raised our Lord Jesus Christ from the dead")
> Polycarp 2.2 ὁ δὲ ἐγείρας αὐτὸν ἐκ νεκρῶν ("he who raised him from the dead")
> Polycarp 12.2 qui resuscitavit eum a mortuis ("who raised him from the dead")

In each of these instances the same verb, ἐγείρω ("waken, raise"), is followed by a reference to Jesus in the accusative with the anarthrous prepositional phrase ἐκ νεκρῶν ("from [the] dead"), confirming the formulaic nature of these references. They do not all appear to have come from the same kind of context, reflecting instead a broad variety of traditions in early Christianity.[16]

Romans 8:11 also contains a recurrence of the phrase οἰκεῖ ἐν ὑμῖν ("he dwells among you") from v. 9, and since ἐν ὑμῖν appeared also in v. 10, this phrase is reiterated three times. The verse ends with a clausula that breaks out of the parallel structure, concluding the paragraph with "through his Spirit dwelling in you." The clausula does not, however, signal the conclusion of a pericope.[17] The theme of struggle between flesh and

---

13   See Weiss, "Beiträge," 180.
14   See Paulsen, *Überlieferung*, 51–55, following Kramer, *Christ*, 24–25; Wengst, *Formeln*, 21ff., and others.
15   See also additional passages listed by Paulsen, *Überlieferung*, 52 n. 150.
16   See Kramer, *Christ*, 32–38; Paulsen, *Überlieferung*, 53.

17   Wilckens, 2:120, observes that most exegetes separate vv. 1-11 from vv. 12-17; he cites Michel, Kuss, Käsemann, Cranfield, Schlier, and Balz.

Spirit is continued in vv. 12-17, and the announcement of the next theme of suffering does not occur until v. 17. So there is good reason to hold the material in vv. 1-17 together.[18]

The alternation between parallelism and climax continues through vv. 12-17. The expression "obligated to the flesh" in v. 12a is defined climactically in v. 12b by living "according to the flesh." There is a structural parallelism in the sentences of 8:12-15, with protases of normal length[19] and very short apodoses.[20] The parallelism in 8:13 is antithetical,[21] producing a paradoxical *sententia*,[22] while the next verse is in climactic form, with "these" in v. 14b picking up "as many as" in v. 14a. Verse 15 is also in the form of antithetical parallelism[23] in which "spirit of slavery" is contrasted with "spirit of sonship," while the same verb ἐλάβετε ("you received") is used for each member, enhancing the antithesis through paronomasia. Finally, vv. 16-17 contain a more elaborate climax[24] in which "children" of v. 16 is picked up by "children" in v. 17a, "heirs" in v. 17a is repeated in v. 17b, and then heightened by the term "joint heirs" in v. 17c. The climax is marked by the fourfold repetition of verbal forms beginning with συν- ("joint"), providing both paronomasia and anaphora.[25] The pericope is thus brought to a powerful conclusion that effectively states the theme of suffering for the sake of glory that is dominant in the following pericope.

Rhetorical Disposition

IV.	The *probatio*
5:1–	B. The second proof: Life in Christ as a new system of
8:39	honor that replaces the search for status through conformity to the law
8:1-17	8. Thesis and rationale concerning the cosmic struggle between flesh and Spirit
8:1	a. The thesis concerning freedom from condemnation for believers
8:2-4	b. The first argument, that Christ frees believers to fulfill the law through the Spirit
8:2	1) The law of Christ frees believers from the law of sin and death
8:2a	a) The specification of Christ as embodying the "law of the Spirit of life"
8:2b	b) Freedom from "the law of sin and death"
8:3-4	2) Christ overcomes the dilemma of the law and enables believers to fulfill its just requirement
8:3a	a) The powerlessness of the law
8:3b	b) The cause of powerlessness: the "flesh"
8:3c	c) God overcomes such powerlessness through his son
8:3d	d) Christ represented "sinful flesh" and acted in relation to "sin"
8:3e	e) Christ condemned sin in the "flesh"
8:4a	f) The purpose of enabling believers to fulfill the law
8:4b	g) Believers walk by the Spirit rather than the flesh
8:5-8	c. The second argument, distinguishing life according to the flesh from life according to the Spirit
8:5	1) The consistent mind-sets of flesh and Spirit
8:5a	a) Those living "according to the flesh" set their minds on flesh
8:5b	b) Those living "according to the Spirit" set their minds on Spirit
8:6	2) The doom and promise of the two mind-sets
8:6a	a) The mind of the flesh is toward death
8:6b	b) The mind of the Spirit is toward life and peace
8:7-8	3) The antipathy between flesh and God
8:7a	a) The mind of the flesh is hostile toward God
8:7b	b) The mind of the flesh does not submit to God's law
8:7c	c) The mind of the flesh cannot submit to God
8:8	d) Those determined by flesh cannot please God
8:9-11	d. The third argument, that belonging to Christ involves possession of the Spirit

---

18 See Wilckens, 2:120; Louw, 2:88–91.

19 The protases in these parallel sentences have eight to twenty beats.

20 The apodoses have three to six beats.

21 See Bullinger, *Figures*, 716.

22 Holloway, "Paul's Pointed Prose," 50.

23 Bullinger, *Figures*, 719, identifies the antithesis in 7:15 as an enantiosis in which an affirmation is made by contrary contentions.

24 See Weiss, "Beiträge," 235; Harvey, *Listening*, 197; Bullinger, *Figures*, 255, contends that the expression "if children also heirs: heirs of God" constitutes an anadiplosis, which is a repetition of the same word at the end of one sentence and at the beginning of the next. This overlooks the larger rhetorical unit of the climax, in which such repetition would be natural.

25 See Fee, *Empowering Presence*, 562.

8:9	1) The thesis concerning the correlation between flesh and Spirit and belonging to Christ
8:9a-b	a) The positive statement of the thesis
8:9a	(1) The address to those who are "in Spirit" rather than "in flesh"
8:9b	(2) The promise that the Spirit really dwells within the Roman churches
8:9c-d	b) The negative statement of the thesis
8:9c	(1) The reference to someone not possessing the Spirit
8:9d	(2) Such a person does not belong to Christ
8:10	2) The effect of the indwelling Christ on body and spirit
8:10a	a) The premise of Christ dwelling in believers
8:10a	b) The contrary condition of the body dead through sin
8:10b	c) The Spirit produces life through righteousness
8:11	3) The christological assurance of new life in the Spirit
8:11a	a) The necessary condition of the indwelling Spirit
	(1) The specification of the Spirit as divine
	(2) The action of the divine Spirit in the resurrection of Jesus
8:11b-c	b) The assurance of Christ's resurrection
	(1) The specification of God as the one raising Jesus
	(2) The action of God in enlivening the bodies of believers
8:11c	(3) The vehicle of God's action: the indwelling Spirit
8:12-17	e. The fourth argument, that possession of the Spirit implies a new relationship with God
8:12-13	1) The relation of believers to the flesh
8:12	a) The thesis regarding nonobligation to the flesh
8:13	b) The parenetic rationale
8:13a	(1) Life according to the flesh leads to death
8:13b	(2) Life in the Spirit that repudiates the "practices of the body" leads to life
8:14-17	2) The relation of believers to God
8:14	a) The thesis regarding those led by the Spirit as "sons of God"
8:15-17	b) The experiential rationale
8:15	(1) The clarification of Spirit in relational terms
8:15a	(a) The Spirit is not that of fearful slavery
8:15b	(b) The Spirit is one of sonship, as exhibited in the "Abba" cry
8:16-17	(2) The amplification of the relational implications of the Spirit
8:16	(a) The Spirit witnesses to the new status as "children of God"
8:17	(b) The climax of the new relationship
8:17a	i. Childhood implies inheritance
8:17b	ii. Inheritance comes from God
8:17c	iii. Joint heirs with Christ
8:17d	(c) The proof of jointly suffering
8:17e	(d) The goal of jointly being glorified

Exegesis

■ **1** The thesis of 8:1 is introduced by οὐδὲν ἄρα νῦν κατάκριμα ("so now, [there is] no punishment") with the initial negative οὐδὲν/κατάκριμα ("no/punishment") carrying the emphasis.[26] For those in Christ the condemnation of sin and the flesh, whose destructive force was the subject of the preceding pericope, has no more effect. The inferential particle ἄρα, appearing elsewhere in Romans in combination with οὖν (5:18; 7:3, 25; 8:12; 9:16, 18; 14:12, 19) appears here with the connotation "so, then, consequently,"[27] reaching back to pick up the thread of the argument from 7:6 that had been interrupted by 7:7-25.[28] The expression ἄρα νῦν also appears in Plato,[29] but in Romans it has an eschatological bearing, referring to "the time of salvation begun through Christ."[30] In contrast to the era in which death reigns through sinful distortion of the law, producing the "body of death" from which humans yearned to be liberated, the new era offers the possibility of a "new life of the Spirit" (7:6). The era of condemnation and doom is over. We encounter the word κατάκριμα ("punishment, condemnation") for the second time in the letter (see 5:16), and it is probably used here in the sense of a sentence of guilt, to judge from the verbal cognate

---

26 See Newman and Nida, 144; Weiss, 390; Kühl, 251.
27 BAGD 103; BDF §451.2.
28 See Godet, 295; Schlier, 237; Barrett, 154; Cranfield, 1:373; Moo, 471-72; this view is repudiated by Käsemann, 214-15, but he does not work out an alternative.
29 Plato *Alc. maj.* 106e1; *Lys.* 212d1; *Hipp. maj* 281d9; 295e5; *Resp.* 438d12.
30 Walter Radl, "νῦν, νυνί," *EDNT* 2 (1991) 480, cited from Luz, *Geschichtsverständnis*, 88; see also Tachau, *Einst*, 127; Neuhäusler, "Entscheidende Augenblick," 4-6; Nissiotis, "νῦν," 305.

κατακρίνειν, which has the sense of "condemn, deem guilty of";[31] κατάκριμα can also be used to convey a sense of "doom,"[32] a sentence "imposed in a criminal proceeding,"[33] "a judgment to pay overdue taxes,"[34] or "penal servitude,"[35] such as is found in Dionysus Halicarnassus, χρεῶν ἀποκοπὰς καὶ κατακρίματων ἀφέσεις ("termination of debts and remissions of punishments," *Antiq. rom.* 13.5.1). The setting of such punishment in the context of a legal decision is visible in the following decision from 83-84 C.E.:

... καθαρὰ ἀπὸ παντὸς ὀφειλήματος ἀπὸ μὲν δημοσίων τελεσμάτων πάντων καὶ ἑτέρων εἰδῶν καὶ ἀρταβίων καὶ ναυβίων καὶ ἀριθημητικῶν καὶ ἐπιβολῆς κώμης καὶ κατακριμάτων πάντων καὶ παντὸς εἴδους ("... shall be cleared of all debt and all public taxations and [other pay]ments, *artaba*-taxes, *naubia*-taxes, land-taxes, village fine, and all judgments and all payment").[36]

Paul's point is that, since the epoch of Adam's doom has been ended by Christ, those who are "in Christ Jesus" are free from the punishment that came upon the entire human race after the fall. The phrase τοῖς ἐν Χριστῷ Ἰησου ("those in Christ Jesus") appears nowhere else in the NT except in 1 Pet 5:14: "Peace to all you who are in Christ." The ἐν ("in") at this point needs to be taken in a local rather than an instrumental sense,[37] referring to the ecclesiastical realm created and ruled by Christ,[38] a mystical, ecstatic realm of the Spirit in which believers participate.[39] As Paul showed in 5:15-

18, the gift of grace in Christ frees believers from the burden of sin and sets them right before God. The paralysis caused by the reign of sin was so eloquently and terribly portrayed in the preceding pericope that the contrast with the new age needed to be forcefully stated. Paul's previous development of the distinction between the "dispensation of death, of condemnation" and the "dispensation of the Spirit, of righteousness" in 2 Cor 3:7-11 seems to be reflected here.[40] But it is possible that Paul overstates the contention that for believers there is "no punishment," because he elsewhere insists that each believer faces judgment according to works (2:6, 13; see also 1 Cor 3:13-15); moreover, the effects of Adam's fall are still felt as the principalities and powers continue to struggle against the adherents of the new age (Rom 8:12, 35-39). The peculiar rhetorical situation of Romans may account for this seeming anomaly, because the congregations were condemning each other as if God wished to punish their alleged wickedness. This may account for the accurate assessment of Braun and Synofzik that a fully systematic coordination between "justification" and "judgment" is not present in Paul's theology.[41]

■ **2** The first argument in support of the thesis concerning the end of the legacy of doom develops the idea of Christ granting freedom from "the law of sin and death." The contrast between this law and the "law of the Spirit of life in Christ Jesus" has engendered a huge debate over whether the latter refers to the Torah.[42] While many have rejected this identification,[43] arguing that νόμος is used in v. 2 in the sense of "principle" or

31 LSJM 896, *s.v.* 2, citing Aristotle *Rhet. Alex.* 1423b and other references.
32 BAGD 412.
33 Danker, "Under Contract," 105; Thomas Kruse, "Katakrima—Strafzahlung oder Steuer?" *ZPE* 124 (1999) 166–68.
34 Kruse, "Katakrima," 168–90.
35 Deissmann, *Studies*, 164–65; Bruce, 159.
36 Cited by MM 327, from *CPR* 1:15ff.
37 See Wilckens, 2:121.
38 The word order of ἐν Χριστῷ Ἰησοῦ ("in Christ Jesus"), which we have already encountered in 3:24 and 6:11, 23, is noteworthy because Paul always uses the sequence "Christ Jesus" with the preposition ἐν, whereas the sequence "in Jesus Christ" never appears in Paul and occurs once in Rev 1:19. Con-

versely, the sequence "Jesus Christ" is favored with the preposition διά in Rom 1:8; 2:16; 3:22; 5:1, 11, 17, 21; 7:25; 15:30. See Büchsel, "In Christus," 146–54; Dacquino, "In Christo," 282–85; Neugebauer, *In Christus*, 101–2, 133–47.
39 See Deissmann, *Paul*, 121–35; Schmauch, *In Christus*, 158–60; Bouttier, *En Christ*, 132–33; Wikenhauser, *Pauline Mysticism*; Shantz, "Paul in Ecstasy," 163–65.
40 See Fitzmyer, 482.
41 Synofzik, *Vergeltungsaussagen*, 9, citing Herbert Braun, *Gerichtsgedanke und Rechtfertigungslehre bei Paulus* (UNT 19; Leipzig: Hinrichs, 1930) 14–31, 89–92. Synofzik's monograph does not deal with Rom 8:1.
42 Grappe, "Typologie adamique," 477–78, discusses

"rule,"[44] a number of scholars have argued that Torah appears here in both its perverted and restored forms.[45] Whether the phrase ἐν Χριστῷ Ἰησοῦ ("in Christ Jesus") belongs with the preceding reference to the "law of the Spirit"[46] or with the following reference to emancipation[47] is also debated. The latter is preferred by those who find theological difficulties with the idea of the law, in whatever form, setting people free, but the fact remains that νόμος ("law") is the subject of the verb ἠλευθέρωσεν ("has set free"). Despite the problems it may cause, the entire subject of this sentence, "the law of the Spirit of life in Christ Jesus," needs to be kept together on syntactical grounds. Paul coined this lumbering phrase "to make clear that the resolution coincides precisely with the portrayed dilemma."[48] My conclusion from this intricate debate, taking the previous argument of Romans into account, is that under the power of sin and flesh, the law was distorted and became an instrument of gaining honor for oneself and one's group. But in Christ the law regains its proper spiritual function, which leads to genuine life (Rom 7:10-14; 8:4). Thus, v. 2a refers to the Torah derived from the "Spirit of life in Christ Jesus," a spiritual law that func-tions in the domain of Christ,[49] setting believers free from the compulsion to compete for honor by misusing the law as a means of gaining status.[50] There is a wider measure of agreement about the "law of sin and death," referring to the Torah in the Adamic period (Rom 5:12-20) and particularly to the power of sin to distort the Torah (Rom 7:5-12, 23).[51] As Keck explains, "'The law of sin' is a structure of power, which one inevitably obeys. It is not really a matter of 'the bondage of the will' but of the bondage of the self which is free enough to will but not free enough to achieve what is willed."[52]

The aorist tense of the verb, "has set you free," has evoked suggestions that it may be taken as a gnomic present, which would eliminate the potential contradiction with the future of this verb in v. 21. Dunn wishes to read this aorist with "circumspect cautions and warnings" visible elsewhere in Paul,[53] which implies that in this context the aorist is to be read with fingers crossed. If one does not wish to engage in the effort to improve Paul's formulations, the past tense should be taken literally here, as a reference to the conversion of the Romans, the event that marked their participation in the turning of the ages brought by the Christ event. The

the parallels to "spirit of life" in the intertestamental writings (*T. Abr.* 18.11; *T. Reub.* 2.4; *Jos. Asen.* 16.14; *1 En.* 61.7), none of which has the connotations that Paul has in mind by combining it with the expression "in Christ Jesus."

43 Meyer, 2:41; Cranfield, 1:375–76; Moo, 474–65; Fitzmyer, 482.
44 Dodd, 119; Ziesler, 202; Leenhardt, 201; Räisänen, *Law*, 52; Räisänen, "Paul's Word-Play," 90.
45 Schmidt, 136; Wilckens, 2:122; Hübner, *Law*, 144–49; Osten-Sacken, *Römer 8*, 226–27; Räisänen, *Law*, 51, mentions Friedrich, Fuchs, Lohse, Hahn, Stuhlmacher, Gaston, Meyer, and Berger as taking "law" literally as the Torah in Rom 8:2; see also Dunn, 1:416–18.
46 Godet, 296; Kühl, 251; Lagrange, 101, Schlatter, 173; Dodd, 118-19; Kuss, 2:490; Schlier, 238–39.
47 Kuss, 2:490, lists Bardenhewer, Bisping, Cornely, Gutjahr, Julicher, Kuhl, Reithmayr, Sanday and Headlam, and Weiss as advocating this view; see also Meyer, 2:142; Cranfield, 1:374–75; Zeller, 152; Dunn, 1:418.
48 Leander E. Keck, "The Law and 'The Law of Sin and Death' (Rom 8:1-4): Reflections on the Spirit and Ethics in Paul," in J. L. Crenshaw and S. Sandmel, eds., *The Divine Helmsman: Studies on God's Control of Human Events, Presented to Lou H. Silberman* (New York: Ktav, 1980) 49.
49 See Schlier, 239; Georgi, *Theocracy*, 100: the law of the spirit "is not a demand, a norm, or an authority. It is, rather, an environment of loyalty and solidarity, of fidelity and confidence, of spirit and community." Paul's expression thus stands in contrast to LXX Bar 3:9, "Hear, O Israel, commandments of life (ἐντωλὰς ζωῆς); listen to know understanding (φρώνησιν)." Newman and Nida, 145, translate "life in union with Christ Jesus."
50 A shortcoming in Hubbard, *New Creation*, 121, is that he disconnects the "spirit of life" formulation from the issue of the misuse of the law, arguing instead that "in this passage, 'life' and 'Spirit' are interchangeable," which is far from Paul's argument.
51 See Schlier, 238–39; Dunn, 1:418-19; Jones, *Freiheit*, 125.
52 Keck, "Law," 49.
53 Dunn, 1:418.

language of this verse takes up the theme of Rom 6:6, 11, that the believer experiences a baptismal death that liberates "from the tyranny of sin's power."[54] Freedom in this context can be compared with Cicero's formulation,[55] which lacks the ominous sense of release from bondage to a dominating power: "Then what is freedom? The power to live as you wish. (*Quid est enim libertas? Potestas vivendi, ut velis.*) Who actually lives as he wishes if not the one . . . who submits to the law not out of fear but honors and obeys it because he believes it is advantageous" (*Parad.* 34). The content of freedom in Paul's context seems primarily negative, "free from external dominance," but in view of sin's impact as described in chap. 7 in preventing people from accomplishing what they wish, F. Stanley Jones argues that the Cicero citation conveys Paul's concept.[56] Samuel Vollenweider stresses the context of the "power of the Spirit" that achieves this freedom,[57] so in contrast to the philosophical theory of individual autonomy,[58] it is really a question of which Lord shall be dominant. Käsemann's notion of freedom as an exchange of lordship seems quite suitable here.[59]

■ **3** The awkwardness of this verse is widely recognized, but Leander Keck has suggested a plausible reason for the lack of syntactical coherence, that Paul incorporates a traditional christological model that "God sent his own son" to redeem the world.[60] The close parallel with Gal 4:4 indicates that Paul substituted the wording "likeness of sinful flesh" in place of "born of a woman, born under the law," to bring the material into closer relation to the context. It seems appropriate to speak here of a

"pattern"[61] rather than a citation of a fully developed christological formula,[62] because the parallels are restricted to the sending language and sonship: ὁ θεὸς τὸν ἐαυτοῦ υἱὸν πέμψας ("God having sent his own son," Rom 8:3) as compared with ἐξαπέστειλεν τὸν υἱὸν αὐτοῦ ("he sent forth his son," Gal 4:4; see also "God sent (ἀπέστειλεν) his son" in John 3:17 and "God has sent (ἀπέσταλκεν) his only begotten son" in 1 John 4:9).

The sentence in vv. 3-4 begins with "for," indicating that the christological content sustains the claim in v. 2 concerning being set free from sin and death.[63] The syntax of v. 3a-b must be explained either on the basis of a nominative or an accusative absolute in apposition to the rest of the sentence.[64] The former seems more plausible, because it brings the clause in apposition to God's action of condemning the flesh and thus provides a substitute for the absent main verb, to which the participle πέμψας ("sent") can be subordinate.[65] The probable meaning of τὸ ἀδύνατον is the active sense of being "powerless, impotent"[66] as taken by the church fathers,[67] rather than the passive sense of "being made powerless" and thus translated with "impossible," as preferred by most commentators and translators on theological and stylistic grounds.[68] Since Paul otherwise uses δύνατος in the sense of power and capability,[69] and since the passive reading requires the supplying of a passive verb, it should be rejected.

---

54 Kurt Niederwimmer, "ἐλεύθερος κτλ.," *EDNT* 1 (1990) 433; for a nonpersonified interpretation, see Röhser, *Hamartia*, 166–67.

55 See Jones, *Freiheit*, 125.

56 Ibid., 125–26.

57 Vollenweider, *Freiheit*, 368–69.

58 See Engberg-Pedersen, *Stoics*, 247–53.

59 Käsemann, 216; see Niederwimmer, *Freiheit*, 85–102.

60 Keck, "Law," 43–44; the case is based on Eduard Schweizer, "Zum religionsgeschichtlichen Hintergrund der 'Sendungsformel' Gal 4,4 f.; Röm 8,3 f.; Joh. 3,16 f.; 1 Joh. 4,9," *ZNW* 57 (1966) 199–210; repr. pp. 83–95 in E. Schweizer, *Beiträge zur Theologie des Neuen Testaments: Neutestamentliche Aufsätze (1955–70)* (Zurich: Zwingli, 1970). See also Kramer,

Christ, 111–15; Käsemann, 216–17; Osten-Sacken, *Römer 8*, 144–45; Lichtenberger, *Ich Adams*, 192–93.

61 Keck, "Law," 44.

62 See Paulsen, *Überlieferung*, 43–44.

63 See Kühl, 252; Keck, "Law," 45.

64 Sanday and Headlam, 191–92.

65 See Cranfield, 1:378–79.

66 BAGD 19.

67 See Sanday and Headlam, 192; Cranfield, 1:378–79.

68 For the arguments in favor of "impossible," see Cranfield, 1:378–79. This majority viewpoint is reflected in Gerhard Friedrich, "ἀδύνατος," *EDNT* 1 (1990) 33–34. Morris, 302; Dunn, 1:419; and others leave the question open.

69 See Josef Zmijewski, "δύνατος," *EDNT* 1 (1990) 359.

The explanation of powerlessness is formulated with ἐν ᾧ ("in that, because")[70] followed by the verb ἠσθένει ("it became weak, sick"), an expression ordinarily referring to someone becoming ill.[71] In this instance, it is the law that became "weak on account of the flesh," a phrase unique to the NT that recapitulates the argument of the preceding chapter about human arrogance and the quest for honor, which corrupt the law and destroy its capacity to achieve the good. The powerlessness of the law is therefore not inherent in the law itself but is the consequence of its involvement in the sinful legacy of Adam's fall.[72] Σάρξ ("flesh") is "weak" not because of its frailty or sensuality but because of its capacity to pervert the law into an instrument of status acquisition, which is a universal human phenomenon. Hamerton-Kelly reduces the scope by the translation "Jewish way of life" for every use of σάρξ in this pericope,[73] implying "Jewish religious attitudes, whether legalism or exclusionism," in contrast with the quality of life in the Christian community.[74] While the Pauline doctrine of the flesh arose in the controversy over the status of the Jewish law with regard to the circumcised flesh,[75] it now functions as a universal symbol for the crippling competition for honor that distorts every human endeavor.

The so-called sending formula alluded to in this verse is widely attested in Greco-Roman,[76] Jewish,[77] and early Christian sources,[78] as Eduard Schweizer demonstrated. But Paul's allusion to the formula in Romans does not necessarily imply that a fully developed theory of Christ's preexistence was entailed by the formula itself.[79] It suffices to recognize that Paul alludes here to a formula that was probably familiar to Roman believers, thus providing a christological grounding for his theory of the struggle between Spirit and flesh. Christ was sent "in the likeness of sinful flesh" to overcome "sin in the flesh" and thus to open up the possibility of a new life in the Spirit. The implications of this language have been hotly debated, both in exegetical and dogmatic circles, concerning incarnation, docetism, sinlessness, and the atonement brought by Christ.[80] We encountered the word ὁμοίωμα ("likeness") in 1:23; 5:14; 6:5 with the connotation of close similarity but not full identity. In a classic statement that reflects dogmatic concerns, Johannes Schneider argues that the ambiguity in ὁμοίωμα

indicates two things, first the likeness in appearance, and secondly . . . [w]ith this body the intrinsically sinless Christ became the representative of sinful mankind. Hence God, by giving up Christ to death, could condemn sin by destroying His body, and thus cancel it. Christ took the likeness of σάρξ ἁμαρτίας in order that God in Christ might achieve the liberation of mankind from sin.[81]

---

70   See BDF §219 (2); Lagrange, 192–93; Cranfield, 1:379.

71   See Xenophon *Anab.* 1.1.1, "Now when Darius lay sick (ἠσθένει)" and 6.2.19 "because Cheirisophus was sick (ἠσθένει)," a locution found in John 1:12 "whose brother, Lazarus, was sick (ἠσθένει)."

72   See Lichtenberger, *Ich Adams*, 192–94.

73   Hamerton-Kelly, *Cross*, 121; see also 123, 148.

74   Ibid., 122.

75   See Jewett, *Terms*, 95–101.

76   For example, a North African inscription from the first century C.E. proclaims Hermes as the "logos whom the gods sent (ἀπέστειλαν) to us from heaven" (Cornutus *Nat. d.* 16; see also Diogenes Laertius *Vitae philos.* 8.1.36 [49]). An inscription from Halicarnassus declares that "the eternal and immortal nature of the universe has sent us Caesar . . ." (*B. Mus. In.* 4.1. Nr. 894.4–6). Both passages are cited by Schweizer, "Hintergrund," 199–201.

77   Schweizer, "Hintergrund," 201–6, notes that the LXX frequently refers to Moses (15 times), the prophets (53 times), and angels (18 times) being sent by God. Artapanus *Frag.* 3.169 refers to God as "the one who sends (πέμψας)" Moses, while Wis 9:10, 17 refers to God sending wisdom and spirit to humans. Philo speaks of God sending angels to heal and redeem (*Heres* 205; *Somn.* 1.69).

78   John's Gospel refers to John the Baptist (1:6; 3:28) and Jesus (1:33) as sent by God, while Jesus is quoted as saying that God is the "one who sent me" (Matt 10:40; Mark 9:37; Luke 9:48; 10:16). Mark 12:1-9 implies the sending of God's son; explicit references to God sending his own son are restricted to John 3:16-17; Rom 8:3-4; Gal 4:4–5; 1 John 4:9. See Schweizer, "Hintergrund," 206–10.

79   See Dunn's critique (1:420–21 and *Christology*, 38–45) of Schweizer's contention that the formula presupposes a preexistent Christology.

80   See Kuss, 2:490–98; Cranfield, 1:379–82; Wilckens, 2:124–28.

81   Johannes Schneider, "ὁμοίος κτλ.," *TDNT* 5 (1967) 196.

There is a serious semantic problem here, because the capacity of ὁμοίωμα to convey similarity in some contexts and identity in others is here compounded as if both were present in a single reference. Ugo Vanni has argued in contrast that in the LXX and Paul's letters, ὁμοίωμα means "the perceptible expression of a reality" rather than a mere likeness.[82] Vincent Branick concurs that ὁμοίωμα is the "full expression of that sinful flesh. . . . Sinful flesh is fully visible in the flesh of Christ," allowing no distinction to be made between Christ and sinful flesh.[83] Ulrich Wilckens comes close to this position in insisting that ὁμοίωμα implies that Christ takes on the "concrete form" of human nature as in Phil 2:7, entering into the sphere of sinful humanity; but he retains the dogmatic concern by insisting that Christ did not engage in sinful actions.[84] Florence Morgan Gillman argues in contrast that a measure of ambiguity is implicit in Paul's use of the word "likeness." Whereas Rom 1:23; 5:14; and 6:5 imply "similarity-yet-difference," Phil 2:7 probably implies "full identity."[85] Since the word ὁμοίωμα vacillates between "total identity and mere similarity,"[86] the argumentative context needs to be taken into account.[87] If "sinful flesh" is understood as the perverse quest for honor that poisons every human endeavor, it is clear that Christ entered fully and without reservation into that social arena with all its evil consequences, at the cost of his own life. His extraordinary exhibition and proclamation of a noncompetitive lifestyle in the awareness that the Abba's love filled all need for honor and set him free for generous love provoked the opposition that led to his crucifixion. Christ's life and death "condemned sin in the flesh" by exposing the hostility against God entailed in the quest for honor on the basis of competitive achievement. The antinomy of this verse is therefore contained not in the word ὁμοίωμα itself but in Christ's fully participating in the realm of sinful flesh[88] in order to replace it with a new lifestyle based on the Spirit. Traugott Holtz confirms the conclusion that σαρκὸς ἁμαρτίας ("sinful flesh") does not address the traditional "problem of the sinlessness of the Son,"[89] while the oddly appended phrase καὶ περὶ ἁμαρτίας ("and concerning sin"), which echoes LXX references to atonement rituals,[90] makes clear that Christ's mission was to overcome sin. Whether or not Bradley H. McLean is correct in perceiving the background of an expulsion ritual in which the burden of sin was thought to be transferred to Christ as the "scapeman,"[91] the consequence of sin's divine condemnation expressed by the verb κατακρίνειν remains the point of emphasis.[92] Christ's death brings to an end the "whole epoch" of sin's domination,[93] offering a new possibility of living according to the Spirit rather than the flesh.

82   Vanni, "Ὁμοίωμα in Paolo," 2:468.

83   Vincent P. Branick, "The Sinful Flesh of the Son of God (Rom 8:3): A Key Image of Pauline Theology," *CBQ* 47 (1985) 250.

84   2:125–26.

85   Florence Morgan Gillman, "Another Look at Romans 8:3: 'In the Likeness of the Sinful Flesh,'" *CBQ* 49 (1987) 599.

86   An example of likeness is available in Aesop *Fab. Syn.* 15.2 of a doe "seeing in the water the likeness of its own body (τὸ τοῦ ἰδίου σώματος ὁμοίωμα)." Porphyry *In Arist.* 4.1.66.27 seems closer to "likeness" when he explains, "because it is the likeness/image of a living person (ὅτι ὁμοίωμα ἐστι τοῦ ζῶντος ἀνθρώπου)."

87   Gillman, "Another Look," 600, 601–4; she interprets the argument as basically supporting Branick's view.

88   See Paulsen, *Überlieferung*, 59.

89   Traugott Holtz, "ὁμοίωμα, ὁμοίωσις," *EDNT* 2 (1991) 513; Kuss, 2:493, wisely concedes that this passage does not provide solutions for problems addressed by later christological debates; Patte, *Paul*, 281–86.

90   Wilckens, 2:126–28, points to περὶ ἁμαρτίας in the LXX of Lev 4:3, 14, 28, 35; 5:6, 7, 8, 10, 11, 13, etc., and the adaptation of this language in other references to Christ's atoning death "for our sins" (1 Cor 15:3; Heb 13:11; 1 John 2:2; etc.). Dunn, 1:422; Michel, 251; Stuhlmacher, and others concur that this expression comes from "as a sin offering," thus alluding to Jesus' sacrificial death. Paulsen, *Überlieferung*, 58–59, remains skeptical of the relevance of this LXX background.

91   Bradley H. McLean, *The Cursed Christ: Mediterranean Expulsion Rituals and Pauline Soteriology* (JSNTSup 126; Sheffield: Sheffield Academic Press, 1996) 140–45.

92   See Mattern, *Verständnis*, 91–96; Synofzik, *Vergeltungsaussagen*, 104; Wolfgang Schenk, "κατακρίνω κτλ.," *EDNT* 2 (1991) 260; Sanday and Headlam, 193, referring to Rom 6:7-10; Kuss, 2:494–95.

93   Dunn, 1:422; see also Osten-Sacken, *Römer 8*, 251.

■ **4** The purpose of the redemptive action depicted in v. 3 is here set forth with a typical ἵνα ("so that") clause.[94] The τὸ δικαίωμα τοῦ νόμου refers to a fixed form of righteousness, in this case the requirement of the Mosaic Law conceived in its unity.[95] In the LXX, δικαιώματα is employed to refer to statutes and requirements but not for commandments;[96] for example, the divine promise given to Isaac was granted "because Abraham your father hearkened to my voice, and kept my injunctions, and my commandments, and my requirements, and my statutes" (τὰ προστάγματά μου, καὶ τὰς ἐντολάς μου, καὶ τὰ δικαιώματά μου, καὶ τὰ νόμιμά μου, Gen 26:5). In secular usage, δικαίωμα typically appears in legal settings to refer to a claim, legal principle, judgment, or decree,[97] but the only exact parallel to the expression "requirement of the law" is found in LXX Num 31:21, where Eleazar the priest establishes a ruling of holy war concerning the distribution of booty: "This is the ordinance of the law which the Lord has commanded Moses."[98] In general, the LXX uses this term for an ordinance, so that the singular refers to a specific ordinance.[99] But while the singular is preferred by Paul, in contrast to the LXX preference for the plural of δικαίωμα,[100] efforts to provide a narrow definition are unconvincing.[101] Cranfield properly concludes that the singular implies "that the law's requirements are essentially a unity," and I would add in the

light of the rest of the argument of Romans, "the fatherly will of God for his children."[102] While the verb πληρωθῇ ("it might be fulfilled") would be unsuited for restricted forms of the righteous requirement of the law,[103] it is naturally combined with a broader understanding of the "essential requirement . . . which lies behind the individual requirements" of divine law.[104] That those set right by faith and thus freed from the law would be involved in fulfilling the Mosaic Law seems contradictory,[105] standing in tension with earlier Pauline letters,[106] but this verse is consistent with the effort throughout the rest of Romans to demonstrate "the continuity of God's purpose in the law and through the Spirit."[107] It is also important to observe that Paul retains a barrier against self-salvation by the passive formulation of "be fulfilled"; as Knox explains, "Paul speaks not of our fulfilling the just requirements of the law, but of its being fulfilled in us."[108] When Paul returns to this theme in 13:8, he explains that "the love" evoked by the Spirit within Christian communities "is law's fulfillment."

It follows that the appropriate explanation of the arena of this fulfillment, ἐν ἡμῖν, should be taken as "among us,"[109] that is, within house and tenement churches, rather than "in us" in some individualistically spiritual or existential manner.[110] The distinctively Pauline antithesis between walking according to the Spirit or the flesh specifies what is at stake in the distinc-

94 See BDF §369.
95 Gottlob Schrenk, "δικαίωμα," *TDNT* 2 (1964) 219, 221; Karl Kertelge, "δικαίωμα," *EDNT* 1 (1990) 335.
96 See Schrenk, "δικαίωμα," 220.
97 See the survey by Hubert Waltherus Maria van de Sandt, "An Explanation of Rom. 8,4a: The Legal Claim of the Law," *Bijdr* 37 (1976) 256–60.
98 See ibid., 261.
99 See J. A. Ziesler, "The Just Requirement of the Law (Romans 8:4)," *ABR* 35 (1987) 78–79.
100 See Sandt, "Explanation," 265.
101 For example, Meyer, 2:48–49, reports that Köllner restricted this to the "justifying sentence of the law," which is close to Schlatter, 176, while Fritzsche, Philippi, and Ewald restricted it to the "verdict of the law" against sinners; Ziesler, "Just Requirement," 79–81, and Watson, *Paul*, 157, argue for the law of coveting mentioned in Rom 7:7, while Dunn, 1:421, closely following Sanders, *Paul*, 100–102, argues for "something more or other than . . . circumcision, sabbath, food laws, etc."

102 Cranfield, 1:384.
103 See Godet, 301; Murray, 1:283.
104 Dunn, 1:423; see also Gerhard Delling, "πλήρης κτλ.," *TDNT* 6 (1968) 292.
105 See Käsemann, 423–24, pointing to the proximity to Matthew's concept of fulfilling the law in 5:17-20.
106 For example, 2 Cor 3:6; Gal 3:13; on this issue see Räisänen, *Law*, 64–73.
107 Dunn, 1:423. In *Derhetorizing Paul*, 133, Thurén denies that "the actual commands of the Mosaic law" are implied by Rom. 8:4, prefering a modified form of the *simul iustus et peccator* doctrine.
108 Cited by Dunn, 1:424; I cannot find the reference in Knox's Romans commentary. See also Fee, *Empowering Presence*, 535.
109 Meyer, 2:49; Weiss, 339; Kühl, 258; Schlier, 243.
110 Meyer, 2:49, and Weiss, 339, refer to Reiche, Klee, Hofmann, and Beck's arguments for the "inward fulfilling of the law" by Christian individuals while Fuchs, 91, refers to the existential decision that can only be made alone.

tive fulfillment enacted by Christian congregations. As in 6:4, περιπατέω ("walk, behave, conduct oneself") is used in the moral sense that is unparalleled in classical Greek,[111] but a portion of this formulation echoes the language of the Essene community, which taught that God "created man to rule the world and placed within him two spirits so that he would walk with them until the moment of his visitation: they are the spirits of truth and of deceit" (1QS 3:17-19; see also 4:6, 12, 24). In the light of the previous argument of Romans, consistent with the earlier Pauline letters (2 Cor 10:2; 2 Thess 3:6), Paul's language describes the avoidance by the converted community of fleshly behavior aimed at gaining honor for one's group in competition with others, and its replacement by following the Spirit of Christ. This entails a noncompetitive, cooperative style of behaving, guided by love and aimed at mutual upbuilding. The law could be fulfilled in its intention and scope only by communities set free from the compulsion to compete for honor, because the ultimate form of honor had already been granted in the form of unmerited, divine grace. Walking κατὰ πνεῦμα ("according to the Spirit") has an indisputably charismatic quality,[112] involving encouragement, guidance, and inspiration by the Spirit, experienced within early Christian groups in their ecstatic worship services and in their life together. The Spirit also conveys the basis of the new approach to ethics by meeting the need for acceptance (Rom 5:5), so that the needs of others can be addressed without fleshly motives. Rather than treating other members of the community as means to gain honor, which was the typi-cal style of the old age of the flesh, the community in which divine law is being fulfilled acts out of genuine love. The agent of this transformation, according to the rhetoric of 8:3-4, is God, who sent his son to inaugurate a new form of community by his life, death, and guiding Spirit.

■ **5** The realms of flesh and Spirit create two distinct mind-sets and modes of behavior. The theme of walking according to the flesh (8:4) is here qualified as an "existence according to the flesh," in which the participle οἱ ὄντες has the sense of "those who exist," referring more to their being than to their behavior.[113] We encountered the neutral form of this expression in 4:17, "the things that do not exist," and a classic formula for God uses the same participle in the singular: ὁ ὤν ("the one who is").[114] In this instance Paul is describing two classes of people, believers and nonbelievers, whose very being is determined by the realm to which they belong.[115] In contrast to some modern interpreters who prefer a less radical disjunction between these realms,[116] favoring an anthropology that interprets Rom 7 as a description of the inability of believers to perform the good,[117] Paul allows no admixture. Those whose being is shaped by σάρξ ("flesh") have a mind-set determined thereby. He uses the verb φρονέω as in earlier Pauline letters to depict a "basic orientation,"[118] "mind-set or attitude."[119] For example, Phil 2:5 advocates the mind-set demonstrated by Christ's self-emptying love, which stands in contrast to τὰ ἐπίγεια φρονοῦντες ("those who are earthly minded," Phil 3:19); the former renounces honor and high status, while the latter seeks to gain glory

111 See Georg Bertram and Heinrich Seesemann, "περιπατέω," *TDNT* 5 (1967) 944.
112 See Käsemann, 218–19.
113 See Weiss, 340; Kuss, 2:498; Horst Balz, "εἰμί," *EDNT* 1 (1990) 393. Kahn, "Greek Verb 'To Be,'" 250–51, argues that the basic meaning of εἶναι is "to be so, to be true," referring to the "necessary connection between truth and fact" (252). Cranfield, 1:385, and Dunn, 1:425, downplay the sense of being and argue for synonymous meaning with "walk according to the flesh."
114 Exodus 3:14; Philo *Abr.* 12; Josephus *Ant.* 8.350; see Friedrich Büchsel, "εἰμί, ὁ ὤν," *TDNT* 2 (1964) 398; Balz, "εἰμί," 393.
115 See Lietzmann, 79–80; Moo, 486; Carter, *Power of Sin*, 178–88; Schlier, 244, refers, perhaps too explic-itly, to the baptized; Fee, *Empowering Presence*, 540, refers to "those who belong to Christ and those who do not."
116 For example, Dunn argues that Christian are similar to adherents of Essenism, who refer to "the spirits of truth and injustice" that feud in the "heart of man" (1QS 4:23), but it remains clear that the Essenes use this expression to refer to their status before joining the community (see 1QS 4:22—5:13).
117 See Kühl, 258–59.
118 Georg Bertram, "φρήν κτλ.," *TDNT* 9 (1974) 232.
119 Moo, 486; see, e.g., the first-century *P.Ryl.* 2. Nr. 128.8–12, "Soueris . . . changed her attitude (ἀλλό-τρια φρονήσασα), left the mill, and departed." In *Die Phronesis in der Philosophie Platons vor dem Staate* (Philol. Sup 25.1; Leipzig: Dieterich, 1932) 12–17,

through behavior shaped by the old age. A similar contrast is implied in Rom 8:5 between those who set their minds on the flesh and those who set their minds on the Spirit. Two completely antithetical orientations to gaining honor are in view here, as the earlier argument of Romans made clear. To gain honor through performance or by virtue of allegedly superior status is the way of the flesh, shaped by the dominant culture both Greco-Roman and Jewish. To receive the gift of honor as a result of Christ's dying for the ungodly, without making any claim of merit, is the way of the Spirit. Thus, the mind-sets of flesh and Spirit are radically and unalterably opposed because they derive from different starting points. The source of honor and the method of overcoming shame determine the orientation of the person as well as the group. As the use of $\gamma \acute{\alpha} \rho$ ("for") at the beginning of this verse implies, Paul's purpose at this point is to explain, not to exhort.[120]

■ **6** The profound consequences of the antithetical mind-sets of flesh and Spirit are further explained in this sentence also containing "for."[121] The nominal form of $\varphi \rho o \nu \acute{\epsilon} \omega$ ("be minded") is employed here for the first time in the Pauline letters, and indeed in the NT. $\Phi \rho \acute{o} \nu \eta \mu \alpha$ has a meaning identical with the infinitive "to be minded," namely, the mind-set or orientation itself.[122] The expression "the mind of the flesh" is reminiscent of Aeschylus's description of the "presumptuous pride and impious thoughts ($\kappa \grave{\alpha} \vartheta \acute{\epsilon} \omega \nu \ \varphi \rho o \nu \eta \mu \acute{\alpha} \tau \omega \nu$)" of the Persian invaders who suffered disaster because they ravaged

temples.[123] The mind of the Spirit, on the other hand, reminds one of Euripides, whose chorus tells Electra that she has "changed her mind ($\varphi \rho \acute{o} \nu \eta \mu \alpha \ldots \mu \epsilon \tau \alpha$-$\sigma \tau \acute{\alpha} \vartheta \eta$)" and is "now thinking holy thoughts ($\varphi \rho o \nu \epsilon \hat{\iota} \varsigma$ $\gamma \grave{\alpha} \rho \ \grave{o} \sigma \iota \alpha \ \nu \hat{\upsilon} \nu$)."[124] But while $\varphi \rho \acute{o} \nu \eta \mu \alpha$ appears with increasing frequency by the first century B.C.E.,[125] there are no examples of the neat antithesis Paul develops here between the mind of the flesh and the mind of the Spirit. The one orientation is inherently a matter of "death"[126] and the other a matter of "life and peace," a claim based on the preceding argument of Romans (5:12–7:24). There are numerous parallels to the antithesis between death and life in Greco-Roman and Jewish culture,[127] but the addition of "peace" inserts a new element. While "life" has functioned as a leitmotif since 1:17,[128] the addition of "peace" is rather puzzling, because it muddles the neat contrast between death and life required by the antithetical parallelism in this verse. While none of the commentaries explains this detail, it does serve to emphasize the social, relational quality of mind of the Spirit, erecting a barrier against individualistic, proto-Gnostic understandings of life in the Spirit.[129] Even more significant is the bearing of this detail on the congregation, which stands in need of peace (Rom 14:17, 19; 15:13). Paul's argument is that while the mind of the flesh intends to achieve life, it results in death (Rom 7:10). The quest for honor corrupts all good intentions and relationships, bringing conflict, despair, and death. The mind of the Spirit, on the other hand, con-

186–88, Johannes Hirschberger shows that $\varphi \rho o \nu \acute{\epsilon} \omega$ and associated terms refer to assumptions and attitudes related to specific goals.

120 See Barrett, 147; Fee, *Empowering Presence*, 540.

121 Lagrange, 190, finds this use of $\gamma \acute{\alpha} \rho$ problematic, but Meyer, 2:51, properly understands it as "explicative."

122 Bertram, "$\varphi \rho \acute{\eta} \nu \ \kappa \tau \lambda$.," 232; BAGD 866.

123 Aeschylus *Pers.* 808; see also *Cho.* 191, 324.

124 Euripides *El.* 1201–4; see also Josephus *Bell.* 4.358, which describes Gurion, who was murdered by the Zealots, as a person "filled with the thought of freedom ($\varphi \rho o \nu \acute{\eta} \mu \alpha \tau o \varsigma \ \grave{\epsilon} \lambda \epsilon \upsilon \vartheta \epsilon \rho \acute{\iota} o \upsilon \ \mu \epsilon \sigma \tau \acute{o} \varsigma$)."

125 A *TLG* search lists $\varphi \rho \acute{o} \nu \eta \mu \alpha$ in Philo 47 times; Diodorus Siculus 51 times; Dionysius Halicarnassus 50 times; Dio Cassius 88 times; and Plutarch 207 times.

126 In contrast to Newman and Nida1, 49, who supply

the verb "results in," Morris, 305–6, opposes the addition of verbs such as "results in death," "spells death," or "leads to death," insisting that "to be bounded by the flesh is itself death."

127 See J. Nélis, "L'antithèse littéraire *ZΩH–ΘANATOΣ* dans les épîtres pauliniennes, *EThL* 20 (1943) 22–30, who cites the metaphysical formula of Sextus Empiricus *Frag.* 62: $\grave{\alpha} \vartheta \acute{\alpha} \nu \alpha \tau o \iota \ \vartheta \nu \eta \tau o \acute{\iota}, \ \vartheta \nu \eta \tau o \grave{\iota}$ $\grave{\alpha} \vartheta \acute{\alpha} \nu \alpha \tau o \iota, \ \zeta \hat{\omega} \nu \tau \epsilon \varsigma \ \tau \grave{o} \nu \ \grave{\epsilon} \kappa \epsilon \acute{\iota} \nu \omega \nu \ \vartheta \acute{\alpha} \nu \alpha \tau o \nu, \ \tau \grave{o} \nu \ \delta \grave{\epsilon}$ $\grave{\epsilon} \kappa \epsilon \acute{\iota} \nu \omega \nu \ \beta \acute{\iota} o \nu \ \tau \epsilon \vartheta \nu \epsilon \hat{\omega} \tau \epsilon \varsigma$ ("immortal mortals, mortal immortals, living the death of one and dying the life of other). See also Epictetus *Diss.* 1.29.60; *Pseudo-Clementine Rec.* 2.15.17. Eccl 3:2 refers to a "time to be born and a time to die"; see also Philo *Heres* 109.

128 See Nygren, 306.

129 See Nygren's critique of the "individualistic point of view" (306).

487

firms God's love for the undeserving (Rom 5:5) and halts the quest for honor that produces enmity with God (Rom 1:18–3:20; 5:10). This produces a new kind of life (Rom 1:17; 6:5-13, 22-23), as well as peace with God (Rom 5:1). There is no middle ground here, no possibility of successfully combining these contrary orientations. Paul intends to draw the distinctions as starkly as possible, so it can become clear in 11:17-25 and 14:1-15:13 that the habits of the old age of the flesh still visible in the arrogant and discriminatory behavior of competitive congregations toward one another entail serious consequences.

■ **7** With διότι ("because")[130] Paul explains why "the mind of the flesh" is oriented to death. That such a mind-set is "hostility toward God (ἔχθρα εἰς θεόν)" is a striking declaration even though its basis was prepared by the earlier argument of the letter. The ancient Greeks could conceive of the god "Death" being "hostile to the immortal gods (ἐχθρὸς δὲ καὶ ἀθανάτοισι θεοῖσιν)"[131] and ancient Israel thought of its adversaries as those against whom God declared hostility (Exod 23:22) as "enemies of the Lord" (ἐχθροὶ τοῦ Κυρίου, LXX Ps 26:20).[132] Paul can speak of opponents who are "enemies of the cross of Christ" (Phil 3:18) and of the principalities and powers as "enemies" whom Christ will place under his feet (1 Cor 15:25-28). But for people to adopt an orientation of active hostility[133] to God would have appeared to ancients as the height of folly. Paul conveys here the discovery of the true nature of his original piety, marked by the fleshly drive to excel ("confidence in the flesh" in Phil 3:3-6; Gal 1:14), which evoked hostility to the cause of Christ. The religion that seeks superior honor is actually hostile to the God it feigns to

love. By absorbing this hostility on the cross, Christ exposed and overcame the mind of the flesh that Paul is here seeking to explain.

As proof of human hostility to God, Paul argues that the "mind of the flesh" does not "submit itself" (ὑποτάσσεται) to God's law. This verb in the middle voice has a reflexive sense of voluntarily submitting oneself,[134] usually to a superior authority.[135] This verse reiterates the thought of 8:3-4 that the function of the Torah is distorted by the fleshly quest to excel in honor. Although the law may well be obeyed, even with surpassing punctilliousness as in the case of Paul's claim of blameless performance as a zealous Pharisee (Phil 3:6), there is no willing submission to the divine intent.[136] This is a matter not of inherent human weakness[137] or lack of willpower to do the law, but of bondage under "the law of sin" energized by the flesh (Rom 7:25).[138] So long as the motivation is dominated by the "mind of the flesh," which twists every endeavor into a means of attaining glory for oneself or one's group, no genuine good can be achieved. Thus Paul adds "for it isn't even able," a translation that understands οὐδὲ γάρ to mean "not either"[139] or "not even,"[140] and δύναται as "able."[141] No human cunning or energetic adherence can extricate someone from this fundamental incapacity. So long as the mind of the flesh is the motivating force, law's performance remains a travesty, and the war against God continues to rage.

■ **8** The incapacity of the flesh extends to the crucial issue of pleasing God, a central idea for Paul that is widely shared with the rest of the Greco-Roman and Jewish world.[142] In 1 Thess 4:1 Paul refers to the converted congregation as having learned how "to please God"

---

130 BAGD 199.

131 Hesiod *Theog.* 766.

132 See Werner Foerster, "ἐχθρός, ἔχθρα," *TDNT* 2 (1964) 812.

133 Weiss, 342, observes that the noun ἔχθρα is a stronger formulation than the adjective would have been, denoting the character of enmity that campaigns directly against God. Kühl, 272, and Schlier, 245, lift up the active hostility implied by this formulation.

134 See Ceslas Spicq, "ὑποτάσσω," *TLNT* 3 (1994) 424; Gerhard Delling, "ὑποτάσσω," *TDNT* 8 (1972) 40–41, following Kähler, *Unterordnung,* 172–83.

135 For example Josephus *Ant.* 13.88 refers to the lack

of submission to the king (οὐχ ὑποτασσώμενον τῷ βασιλεῖ). See also Onasander *Strat.* 1.17; Plutarch *Pomp.* 64.5.

136 See Leenhardt, 206.

137 Weiss, 343, cites Lipsius as advocating this explanation; see also Zahn, 387–88.

138 See Weiss, 343.

139 BDF §452.3.

140 Meyer, 2:52.

141 Gerhard Friedrich, "δύναμαι," *EDNT* 1 (1990) 355.

142 See Werner Foerster, "ἀρέσκω κτλ.," *TDNT* 1 (1964) 455.

(ἀρέσκειν θεῷ), and in 1 Cor 7:32-34 the basic criterion of ethics is "how you might please the Lord (πῶς ἀρέση τῷ κυρίῳ)." A very serious matter is to displease God (1 Thess 2:15) or instead to seek to please humans (Gal 1:10).[143] Theopompus describes a view widely shared among Greco-Romans, "the wish to please the gods (τὸ βούλεσθαι τοῖς θεοῖς ἀρέσκειν),"[144] while Ecphantus uses the formula "he does things pleasing to god (ποιεῖ τὰ ἀρέστα τῷ θεῷ)."[145] The LXX frequently employs the compound "well pleasing" to describe successful piety, as in εὐηρέστησε δὲ Ἐνὼχ τῷ Θεῷ ("And Enoch was well pleasing to God").[146] The idea is that if one pleases God, good fortune will follow, but the one not pleasing God will face misfortune and wrath. Baruch 4:4 proclaims, "Blessed [are] we, Israel, because the things pleasing to God (ὅτι τὰ ἀρεστὰ τῷ θεῷ) are known to us." Paul's contention is that those whose very being is defined by flesh (οἱ ἐν σαρκὶ ὄντες)[147] are incapable of achieving the most basic goal of ancient religion and ethics: to please God. Such persons are in a hopeless situation, from which they have no capacity to extricate themselves.[148]

■ 9 This verse begins the third argument in support of the thesis in 8:1, showing that belonging to Christ involves possession of the Spirit.[149] The emphatic form, ὑμεῖς δέ ("but you [pl.]"), appears for the only time in Romans to open the sentence. It signals a reassuring shift to the situation of the audience as members of the realm of Christ. Their very being is shaped by Spirit rather than flesh, because their conversion set them free from the compulsion to conform to the world's method of gaining honor through competition with others or by reliance on some allegedly superior status. While they remain human and therefore vulnerable, they are no longer ἐν σαρκί ("in flesh") in the sense developed since Rom 7:5, "when we were in the flesh, our sinful passions that [came] through the law were at work in our members in bearing fruit to death."[150] The formulation simply assumes that all of the believers in Rome, in contrast, are ἐν πνεύματι ("in Spirit"),[151] implying an undeniably charismatic description of the community.[152]

Whether the next clause, "if indeed/since indeed God's Spirit dwells among you," is intended as a warning, a condition, or as assurance has long been debated.[153] The conjunction εἴπερ can be read either as "since" or "if indeed."[154] Since those who see a warning or condition[155] are unable to explain why the verb οἰκεῖ ("it dwells") is in the indicative rather than the subjunctive,[156] and why Paul did not select εἴγε ("if at least") rather than εἴπερ ("if indeed"),[157] Paul's formulation is more likely intended to provide assurance.[158] A translation with "since indeed" is also more consistent with the formulation of v. 9a, which flatly states that believers "are" in the Spirit. That God's Spirit dwells "among," "within," or "in the midst of" (ἐν)[159] the congregation, rather than merely within the heart of individuals,[160] seems likely in view of the second person plural address, which matches Paul's reference in 1 Cor 3:16 to what was apparently a typical component in early cate-

---

143 See Gerhard Schneider, "ἀρέσκω," *EDNT* 1 (1990) 151.

144 Theopompus *Hist. Frag.* 2b115 [*Frag.* 344.6 Jac.]. See also Josephus *Ant.* 13.289–90; 6.164.

145 Ecphantus *Frag.* 82.82, in Stobaeus *Anth.* 6.65.

146 See also Gen 5:24; 6:9; 17:1; 24:40; 39:4; 48:15; Ps 26:3; 35:14; 56:13; 116:9; Sir 44:16, cited by Foerster, "ἀρέσκω κτλ.," 455.

147 See Weiss, 343; Godet, 303.

148 See Moo, 489.

149 This section is adapted from Jewett, "Apportioned Spirit," 193–206.

150 See Schlier, 246.

151 See Sanday and Headlam, 197; Kühl, 273; Schlier, 246; Barrett, 158.

152 See Fee, *Empowering Presence*, 547; Fitzmyer, 490; Dunn, 1:428, attempts to qualify the "enthusiastic"

dimension of this distinction by insisting that "the flesh is still a factor."

153 See Kuss, 2:500–501 for a listing of patristic and more recent views.

154 See BAGD 200.11; BDF §454.2; Newman and Nida, 150, suggest "if indeed," which stresses conditionality.

155 For example, Weiss, 344; Fuchs, *Freiheit*, 96; Dunn, 1:428.

156 See Kuss, 2:501.

157 See Godet, 304.

158 Kuss, 2:501, cites others such as Schlatter, 178, and Leenhardt, 206–7, who see assurance for other reasons. See also Morris, 308; Moo, 490.

159 See BAGD 258, "among."

160 The individualistic construal is widely represented in the commentaries: Godet, 304; Cranfield, 1:388;

chesis,[161] "Do you not know that you [pl.] are God's temple and that God's Spirit dwells in your midst (ἐν ὑμῖν οἰκεῖ)?" There are Greco-Roman parallels to this idea, as for example Seneca's assurance to his friend Lucilius:

God is near you, he is with you, he is within you (*intus est*). This is what I mean, Lucilius: a Spirit indwells within us (*sacer intra nos spiritus sedet*), who marks our good and bad deeds, and is our guardian.[162]

It is likely, however, that Paul's conceptual framework and that of early Christianity in this regard was drawn from Judaism.[163] The Hebrew text of Exod 29:45-46 has Yahweh promise, "And I will dwell among the people of Israel, and will be their God . . . that I might dwell among them; I am the Lord their God." This theme reappears in *T. Levi* 5.2, where God promises, "I shall come and dwell in the midst of Israel (κατοικήσω ἐν μέσῳ τοῦ Ἰσραήλ)."[164] This is also stated in an individualistic form in *T. Zeb.* 8.2, that whenever God finds a compassionate person, "in that person he will dwell (ἐν αὐτῷ κατοικεῖ)."[165] Later Judaism develops the concept of the Shekinah, based on the Hebrew root "to dwell," to refer to God's presence.[166] It is consistent with this tradition that Paul refers here, for the first time in Romans, to "God's Spirit," which stands parallel to the "Spirit of Christ" in v. 9b.[167] The idea of the Spirit dwelling in the midst of the Christian community was widely shared,[168] reflecting a charismatic view of the church (1 Cor 12–14), whose common life in the love feast featured Christ as the Lord of the feast, ushering in God's kingdom by granting God's Spirit to all believers.

In contrast to the assuring, collective language of v. 9a-b, Paul refers to the antithetical circumstance in v. 9c with an individual expression: "but if anyone"[169] does not have the Spirit, that person does not belong to Christ. In contrast to later, noncharismatic understandings of the church, Paul here clearly states that possession of the Spirit is a *sine qua non*. He does not hesitate to use the language of "possession," employed both for demonic forces and for the Spirit of God.[170] A striking feature of this formulation is the mutuality of possession: the person not having the Spirit is therefore not had by Christ: οὗτος οὐκ ἔστιν αὐτοῦ ("such a one does not belong to him"). That v. 9c-d originated as a formula of exclusion allegedly used at the Lord's Supper, as Michel and others suggest,[171] seems unlikely because the language of anathama is not employed (see 1 Cor 16:22; *Did.* 10.6) and the formulation is so consistent with the vocabulary and style of the preceding verses. Belonging to Christ is as typical a Pauline formula (1 Cor 3:23; 15:23; Gal 5:24) as "having" the Spirit (1 Cor 7:40; 2 Cor 4:13) and being "in Christ." This language reflects Paul's charismatic view of the faith, as Käsemann explains: "Nevertheless the reciprocity in the use of the formulae makes sense only if they are derived from pneumatology and understood in the light of it. By the Spirit Christ seizes power in us, just as conversely by the Spirit we are incorporated into Christ."[172] Although many exegetes remain uncomfortable with this dimension, Paul's language throughout this passage is charismatic and "mystical";[173] it reflects a collective type of charismatic mysticism in which God's Spirit was thought to enter

---

Wilckens, 2:131; Murray, 1:228; Moo, 490; see also Otto Michel, "οἰκέω," *TDNT* 5 (1967) 135.

161 See Michel, "οἰκέω," 135.

162 Seneca *Ep.* 41.1–2; see Sevenster, *Paul and Seneca*, 89, 129; Zeller, 158.

163 See Paulsen, *Überlieferung*, 48–51, relying on the work of Brandenburger, *Fleisch und Geist*, 136–38.

164 See also *T. Dan* 5.1.

165 See also *T. Jos.* 10.2-3; *T. Benj.* 6.4.

166 See Anthony J. Saldarini, "Shekinah," *HarperCollins Bible Dictionary* (San Francisco: HarperCollins, 1996) 1009.

167 See Fee, *Empowering Presence*, 547–48.

168 Paulsen, *Überlieferung*, 50.

169 See Sanday and Headlam, 197, for an appreciation of the "vague and general force" and "characteristic

delicacy" of Paul's expression in v. 9b, which refrains from saying that the Roman believers do not have the spirit.

170 Dunn, 1:429, refers to Matt 11:18; Acts 16:16; 1 Cor 7:40; 2 Cor 4:13, etc., where persons "have" the spirit or a demon.

171 Michel, 253; Paulsen, *Überlieferung*, 37, 47; Wilckens, 2:131.

172 Käsemann, 222; see also Dunn, 1:429–30.

173 See Leenhardt, 208; Black, 112; Wilson, *Gnosis and the New Testament*, 49, remarks that "the spirit-ruled Christians of I Cor. 3.16 and Rom. 8.9 'look like' the Gnostic *pneumatikoi*."

and energize the community as well as each member.[174] Its primary arena of manifestation, in contrast to most later Christianity, was not individual ecstasy but social enthusiasm, speaking in tongues, prophecy, and joyous celebration in the context of the common meal that united the formerly shamed from different families and backgrounds into a single family honored and chosen and hallowed by God.

■ **10** The "but if" that opens this sentence stands in antithesis to v. 9c and picks up the tone of assurance from v. 9a-b.[175] Christ is in fact "among you/in your midst" ($\dot{\epsilon}\nu$ $\dot{\upsilon}\mu\hat{\iota}\nu$), which is a classic instance of the "democratization of mysticism."[176] Although many scholars are uncomfortable with the seeming identification of Christ and the Spirit of God reflected in this parallel use of $\dot{\epsilon}\nu$ $\dot{\upsilon}\mu\hat{\iota}\nu$ in 8:9-10, since it raises problems for later trinitarian thought,[177] there seems little doubt "that Christ and Spirit are perceived in experience as one"[178] in the circle Paul represents. In the overpowering enthusiasm of the love feast in which the Spirit was perceived to be ushering in God's new age, the sharp distinctions made by later christological controversies were not necessary.

The real problem in this compact verse is how to understand the antithesis between $\sigma\hat{\omega}\mu\alpha$ $\nu\epsilon\kappa\rho\grave{o}\nu$ $\delta\iota\grave{\alpha}$ $\dot{\alpha}\mu\alpha\rho\tau\acute{\iota}\alpha\nu$ ("body [is] dead through sin") and $\pi\nu\epsilon\hat{\upsilon}\mu\alpha$ $\zeta\omega\grave{\eta}$ $\delta\iota\grave{\alpha}$ $\delta\iota\kappa\alpha\iota\sigma\acute{\upsilon}\nu\eta\nu$ ("Spirit [is] life through righteousness"). Whereas the antithesis in the earlier verses of

Rom 8 was between "flesh and Spirit" as cosmic forces and modes of behavior, now we suddenly confront "body and spirit" in an anthropological sense. A bewildering variety of interpretive suggestions has been proposed, among which the most frequently advocated is that the body is dead since Adam's sin produced its lethal consequence,[179] while "spirit" refers to the human spirit enlivened by Christ.[180] Others insist that both the context and the reference to "life" require that only God's Spirit be in view here,[181] but this is a false dichotomy because Paul frequently speaks of the apportioned divine Spirit given to believers as if it were now a human possession.[182] The interpretation of $\sigma\hat{\omega}\mu\alpha$ $\nu\epsilon\kappa\rho\acute{o}\nu$ as referring to Adam's mortal curse "does not do justice either to the introductory 'but if Christ is in you . . .', or to the theme of new life which dominates Rom. 8."[183] It seems likely that the expression $\sigma\hat{\omega}\mu\alpha$ $\nu\epsilon\kappa\rho\acute{o}\nu$ alludes to the destruction of the sinful body in baptism, as described in 6:6-11, where both terms appear.[184] The difficulty with this option is that $\delta\iota\grave{\alpha}$ $\dot{\alpha}\mu\alpha\rho\tau\acute{\iota}\alpha\nu$ ("on account of sin") might then seem to imply that sin, rather than Christ, was the agent of overcoming the body of death.[185] One way to take this phrase is as a reiteration of 6:6, where "the sinful body" was destroyed in baptism, which makes clear that it is because of sin and not because of the materiality of the body that participation in Christ's death was required.[186] While the bap-

---

174 See Luz, "Mystik," 137: "the gift of the spirit seems to me to be the experiential basis of Christ-mysticism." See also Shantz, "Paul in Ecstasy," chap. 4.

175 See Dunn, 1:430.

176 Luz, "Mystic," 139, citing Daniel Marguerat, "La mystique de l'apôtre Paul," in Association Catholique Française pour l'étude de la Bible, ed., *Paul de Tarse* (LD 165; Paris: Cerf, 1996) 327.

177 See Kuss, 2:502; Cranfield, 1:389; Fee, *Empowering Presence*, 548–49; Moo, 491.

178 Dunn, 1:430.

179 Kuss, 2:502, lists Bardenhewer, Bisping, Cornely, Gutjahr, Kühl, Kürzinger, Lagrange, Sanday and Headlam, Weiss, and Zahn; more recently Morris, 309; Dunn, 1:431; and Moo, 491, have joined this group.

180 Kuss, 2:502, lists Bardenhewer, Bisping, Cornely, Gutjahr, Kühl, Lagrange, Sanday and Headlam. One could add Hodge, Hunter, Godet, 305; Fitzmyer, 491, to this list.

181 See Hermann, *Kyrios und Pneuma*, 65–66; Barrett, 159; Michel, 254; Murray, 1:289; Morris, 309; Cranfield, 1:390; Fee, *Empowering Presence*, 550–51; Moo, 492.

182 Jewett, *Terms*, 198, referring to Rom 1:9 and 8:16, along with 1 Cor 5:5; 7:34; 2 Cor 2:13; 7:1, 5. See also Jewett, "Apportioned Spirit," 195–98.

183 Jewett, *Terms*, 296; see Kuss, 2:503.

184 See Rudolf Bultmann, "$\nu\epsilon\kappa\rho\acute{o}\varsigma$ $\kappa\tau\lambda$.," *TDNT* 4 (1967) 894; Kuss, 2:502-4; Jewett, *Terms*, 296-97; Barrett, 159; Käsemann, 224; Osten-Sacken, *Römer 8*, 239; Rolf Dabelstein, "$\nu\epsilon\kappa\rho\acute{o}\varsigma$," *EDNT* 2 (1991) 461.

185 In order to avoid this implication, both Kuss, 2:503, and Wilckens, 2:132, are forced to cumbersome reformulations of Paul's thought.

186 See Jewett, *Terms*, 297.

tismal reading remains most probable, no completely satisfactory explanation of all the details is currently available, and one is inclined to accept Lietzmann's comment that the verbal parallelism in this verse is more strict than the thought itself.[187]

The baptismal reading of v. 10 implies that the indwelling Christ allows believers to live within the tensions between body and spirit, sin and righteousness, death and life. At the terminological level these three antitheses are compelling, and the resonances with being buried with Christ and raised to new life are sufficient to avert questions about the precise relationships, at least for the original hearers, who would not have had time in an oral presentation for detailed analysis. In that context, this verse is a rhetorical tour de force, showing the anthropological impact of the Spirit. While the "body of death" (7:24) that suffered under the condemnation due to sin ($\delta\iota\grave{\alpha}\ \dot{\alpha}\mu\alpha\rho\tau\acute{\iota}\alpha\nu$, "on account of sin" in 8:10b) has been buried with Christ, the Spirit apportioned to believers results in a new kind of life because of the gift of righteousness. Shameful humans are granted honor and made right[188] in new communities of faith by the gift of divine grace in Christ, the entire process being symbolized by baptism and supported by the gifts and manifestations of the Spirit within both the individual and the community.

■ **11** The final "if" formula opens v. 11 in a manner parallel to v. 10, bringing to conclusion the argument that began in v. 9 concerning the presence of the Spirit $\dot{\epsilon}\nu$ $\dot{\nu}\mu\hat{\iota}\nu$ ("in your midst"). That it is once again conceived as God's Spirit as in v. 9 is evident in the christological formula that Paul cites twice in this verse. The Spirit of God is the "one who raised Jesus from the dead," or, in the second version—clearly with a Pauline formulation not found elsewhere in the tradition, as visible in the

analysis section above—"the one raising Christ Jesus from the dead." Nowhere else in the early Christian tradition do we find the formula repeated in such close proximity. A reason for this double reference is not explained by commentators; Morris perhaps comes close to providing an explanation with his observation that "the Spirit is not usually linked with resurrection."[189] Here the Spirit of God that resurrected Jesus is not only the very Spirit animating the churches in Rome but also the basis of their future hope.[190] The divine action holding both present and future together is resurrection. As Paul had argued in 1 Cor 6:14; 15:12-19; and 2 Cor 4:14, the basis of both the present Christian faith and the future hope is the resurrection of Christ; without that everything is "vain."[191] The context for these references in Corinthian controversies is fairly well understood, but why this emphatic link between resurrection and Spirit was required by circumstances in Rome is yet to be fully explained.

The future promise is that God will "make alive" ($\zeta\omega\sigma\pi\sigma\iota\acute{\eta}\sigma\epsilon\iota$) the mortal bodies of believers, which most current commentators understand as a reference solely to the eschatological resurrection.[192] What this interpretation cannot explain is why Paul selected $\zeta\omega\sigma\pi\sigma\iota\acute{\eta}\sigma\epsilon\iota$ ("he will enliven") rather than $\dot{\epsilon}\gamma\epsilon\rho\hat{\epsilon}\iota$ ("he will raise up"), why he shifts from "dead body" in v. 10 to "mortal bodies" ($\tau\grave{\alpha}\ \vartheta\nu\eta\tau\grave{\alpha}\ \sigma\acute{\omega}\mu\alpha\tau\iota$) in v. 11,[193] and why he associates this process with the ongoing work of the indwelling Spirit (v. 11d).[194] The verb $\zeta\omega\sigma\pi\sigma\iota\acute{\epsilon}\omega$, which appeared earlier in 4:17, alludes in other Pauline letters to enlivening activity with regard both to restoring the dead and to enhancing the quality of life for those currently in Christ.[195] The broad sense of God as the source of life in every form is reflected in LXX usage. God is the one who preserves life in the midst of afflictions (Ps

187 Lietzmann, 80; see also Dibelius, "Vier Worte." 10.
188 For an account of the tangled debate on how to understand "justification" in this verse, see Kuss, 2:503; also Dibelius, "Vier Worte," 12–13.
189 Morris, 310; see also Käsemann, 225; Jacob Kremer, "$\dot{\epsilon}\gamma\epsilon\acute{\iota}\rho\omega$," *EDNT* 1 (1990) 376, observes that "further reflection," presumably by Paul, since this is the only place it is found, led to the link between resurrection and the spirit.
190 See Paulsen, *Überlieferung*, 53.
191 See ibid., 53–54.
192 See Cranfield, 1:391; Michel, 193–94; Kuss, 2:505;

Wilckens, 2:133; Dunn, 1:432; Morris, 310–11; Murray, 1:291–92; Moo, 493; Powers, *Salvation through Participation*, 164–66.
193 Rudolf Bultmann, "$\vartheta\nu\eta\tau\acute{o}\varsigma$," *TDNT* 3 (1965) 21–22, makes clear that this term refers to the mortal quality of human nature, not the status of being dead; Werner Bieder, "$\vartheta\nu\eta\tau\acute{o}\varsigma$," *EDNT* 2 (1991) 153: "*mortal* body . . . attesting the awakening power of God on the mortal person at the present time."
194 See Meyer, 2:58–59.
195 See Rudolf Bultmann, "$\zeta\acute{\alpha}\omega\ \kappa\tau\lambda.$," *TDNT* 2 (1964) 874–75; in Rom 4:17; 1 Cor 15:22, 36 it refers to

70:20, "you turned and made me alive [ἐζωοποίησάς με]") while "the excellence of wisdom will give life (ζωοποιήσει) to him who has it" (Eccl 7:13). This comprehensive scope is captured by *Corp. herm.* 11.4, which asserts that the divine soul "surrounds the universe and brings it to life (ζωοποιοῦσα τὸ πᾶν)."[196] It appears to me that Lietzmann is correct in interpreting this reference as an extension of "life because of righteousness" in v. 10.[197] As Dodd observes, "It was in this spiritual body that Christ was raised; and the same power of which He was raised is at work for those who are in Him."[198] The reference in the clausula at the end of v. 11 to the Spirit currently dwelling in the midst of the congregation points to forms of anticipatory enlivenment in the present, which transform the body and its activities. This formulation may be intended to point toward 12:1-2, where bodily transformation in the ethical behavior of congregations is indeed in view.

■ **12** With ἄρα οὖν ("so then")[199] Paul introduces the fourth argument in support of the thesis in 8:1, showing that the Spirit/flesh dichotomy instituted by Christ involves obligations and relationships that are mutually exclusive. Two opposing theses are established to develop this idea, the first being stated in this verse. In view of the preceding argument, Paul appeals to his Christian "brothers,"[200] members of house and tenement churches in Rome both male and female, who are part of the larger Christian family extending throughout the world,[201] to recognize that they and he have no further obligation to the realm of the flesh. The expression ὀφειλέται ἐσμέν ("we are the obligated ones") is the same noun as was employed in 1:14, describing Paul's reversal of the social obligations of the Greco-Roman world. He always employs this term as a predicate nominative with the verb εἰμί ("to be"),[202] reflecting a social status of having received patronage and being required to render reciprocal service.[203] In the Roman legal context "obligation" is defined as follows:

Obligationum substantia non in eo consistit, ut aliquod corpus nostrum aut seruitutem nostram faciat, sed ut alium nobis obstringat ad dandum aliquid uel faciendum uel praestandum ("The essence of obligations does not consist in that it makes some property or a servitude ours, but that it binds another person to give, do, or perform something for us").[204]

Roman ethicists taught that such obligations are owed to everyone in one's social sphere, to parents, friends, and patrons; a "gradation of duties" (*gradus officiorum*) placed obligations to the gods first, to country second, to parents third, etc.[205] Although commentators consistently overlook this social background in interpreting v. 12,[206] to be obligated τῇ σαρκί ("to flesh") would entail the entire range of social and religious obligations in the Roman environment. Paul's wording is quite intriguing because he qualifies the admonition with the clause τοῦ κατὰ σάρκα ζῆν ("to live according to flesh"), whose nuance was caught by Meyer: "according to the rule and standard of σάρξ so that σάρξ is the regulative principle."[207] The regulative principle for Christian family members is the Spirit of Christ, which redefines all social obligations, at times with considerable cost and pain. Paul does not admonish the Roman believers to withdraw completely from their previous obligations to patrons and family, but to redefine those

---

resurrecting the dead, while in 1 Cor 15:45; Gal 3:21; and 2 Cor 3:6 it involves "the present . . . life made possible by Christ," according to Luise Schottroff, "ζωοποιέω," *EDNT* 2 (1991) 110.

196 See Bultmann, "ζάω κτλ.," 874.

197 Lietzmann, 80; see also Leenhardt, 210; Schlier, 248; Barrett, 160: "even our *mortal* bodies . . . are transformed and quickened."

198 Dodd, 125; see also Osten-Sacken, *Römer 8,* 241–42.

199 BAGD 104 notes that ἄρα οὖν at the beginning of a sentence should be translated "so, as a result, consequently."

200 Schäfer, *Bruderschaft,* 348, points to the element of commonality: their obligation is also his obligation.

201 See Aasgaard, *Siblingship in Paul,* 166–84.

202 See Michael Wolter, "ὀφειλέτης κτλ.," *EDNT* 2 (1991) 550.

203 See Reasoner, *The Strong,* 176–86.

204 *Digest of Justinium* 44.7.3, cited by Reasoner, *The Strong,* 181.

205 The Roman moralist Panaetius, according to Cicero *Off.* 1.160, cited by Reasoner, *The Strong,* 182.

206 See, e.g., Cranfield, 1:394; Wilckens, 2:134; Dunn, 1:448; Zeller, 159; Fitzmyer, 492; Moo, 493–94.

207 Meyer, 2:61.

obligations so that the society no longer determines what one should do or be. This was a particularly difficult issue for early believers, whose love feasts caused them to withdraw from family meal patterns and often provoked serious discord with patrons. The obligatory patterns of society had been broken by Christ; henceforth they are to live as family members of God, as v. 14 will go on to argue. The use of the term "flesh" implies that this entails a new mode of "living," defined not by the competitive drive for individual and familial and national honor but by the Spirit of Christ, which conveys an unconditional form of honor through grace and leads one into new forms of obligation motivated by love.[208]

■ **13** In support of the contention that believers have no further "obligation" to the flesh, Paul reminds them of its ultimate dimensions with regard to life and death. By means of a *sententia ex inopinato*, a paradoxical formula,[209] Paul reminds them that "to live" according to the flesh is to "die," whereas putting to death the "deeds of the body" will lead to life. Dying is the result of flesh whereas living is the result of Spirit. This paradoxical formulation develops themes from earlier parts of Romans: that sin leads to death-dealing behavior (1:28-32); that it stands under divine wrath (1:18–2:16); and that Adam's sin led to condemnation and death (5:12-21), whereas Christ's grace leads to "eternal life" (5:21). The idea that evil deeds result in death imposed by divine decree, stated earlier in 7:9-10, was widely assumed in Jewish and Greco-Roman materials.[210] The innovation in this verse is to place the paradox within

the context of the cultural and cosmic conflict between flesh and Spirit. It is therefore problematic to restrict this struggle to the arena of the individual soul, as most interpreters have done.[211] The verbal forms are all second person plural, indicating that communities of Christian "brothers" (v. 12) rather than isolated individuals are in view. This communal orientation is evident in Paul's adaptation of a traditional formula in "you (pl.) are about/bound to die," which appears as an individual reminder in the Orphic gold tablets directed to someone on the verge of dying, being buried, and becoming divine in the afterlife: "This is the tomb of Memory, when one is about to die (ἐπεὶ ἂν μέλλησι θανεῖσθαι)."[212] The death that Paul has in mind is collective; the fleshly mode of behavior shaped by traditional obligations of honor, by a chronic suppression of the truth, and by lethal competition is like a plague that destroys a house or tenement church and everyone in it. In Paul's formulation, the consequence of death is inevitable only on the condition that the community actually conducts its life κατὰ σάρκα ("according to the flesh"); εἰ ("if") followed by the indicative verb ζῆτε ("you [pl.] live") indicates "a simple conditional assumption with emphasis on the reality of the assumption (not of what is being assumed): the condition is considered 'a real case.'"[213] As the letter goes on to document in chaps. 14–15, there are in fact dimensions of the competitive relations between Roman churches that reveal the ongoing power of the flesh.[214] While his formulation is neutral and nonaccusatory, Paul leaves no doubt that the consequences are real and unavoidable if such behavior

---

208 See Minear's formulation of this theme in less social terms in *Obedience*, 105–6.
209 See Holloway, "Paul's Pointed Prose," 50.
210 See Black, "Death in Romans 5–8," 415; J. B. Burns, "The Mythology of Death in the Old Testament," *SJT* 26 (1973) 327–40. For example, *T. Abr.* (A) 8.25–30, "Do you not know that all those from Adam and Eve died (πάντες ἀπέθανον), and not one of the prophets escaped death, and not one of the kings is immortal and not one of the forefathers escaped the mystery of death." LXX Bar 4:1-2 proclaims that "This is the book of the Ordinances of God and the Law that endures forever. All who hold on to it will live (οἱ κρατοῦντες αὐτὴν εἰς ζωήν), and all who abandon it, will die (ἀποθανοῦνται)."

211 See, e.g., Kuss, 2:598–99; Michel, 258; Leenhardt, 211; Murray, 1:294; Fitzmyer, 492; Moo, 494–95; see also Black, "Death in Romans 5–8," 426–28.
212 See Giovanni Pugliese Caratelli, "*OΡΦΙΚΑ*," in *ParPass* 29 (1974) 135–44; Hans Dieter Betz, *Gesammelte Aufsätze* IV. *Antike und Christentum* (Tübingen: Mohr-Siebeck, 1998) 226 n. 16, for additional references.
213 BDF §371.1.
214 In contrast, Werner Bieder, "θάνατος, ἀποθνήσκω," *EDNT* 2 (1991) 130, relates this threat to unbelievers who reject the gospel and thus "hasten the process of decay."

continues. The contrast with the simple future verb employed at the end of the sentence, "you (pl.) shall live," reinforces the impression that Paul believes the Roman churches are in fact able to renounce fleshly forms of behavior and continue to enjoy their new life in the Spirit.

An unresolved problem in Paul's formulation is the apparent substitution of σῶμα ("body") for σάρξ ("flesh") in the expression "put to death the deeds of the body," which alters the antithesis between flesh and Spirit that has hitherto dominated the argument of chap. 8. The formulation "works of the flesh" (ἔργα τῆς σαρκός) employed in Gal 5:19 is cited by commentators to interpret this verse,[215] but this does not explain the substitution. Others brush the problem aside by simply reinserting "flesh" as the interpretive key,[216] with explanations such as "deeds worked out through the body under the influence of the flesh."[217] Earlier formulations in Romans, such as "sinful body" (6:6) and "body of death" (7:24) echo in this verse, with the last reference in particular suggesting that the deeds in question have a sinful quality of distorting the law in a zealous manner in order to gain honor. In 1971 the suggestion was made that the substitution of σῶμα for σάρξ in this verse and elsewhere in Romans was motivated by a desire to "provide a basis for the unique systematic portrayal of ethics as worship in which the body is sacrificed in daily obedience,"[218] but this is not fully satisfactory. Even less satisfactory is the attempt to resolve the odd formulation by arguing that πράξεις has the inherent connotation of "machinations,"[219] since it is probably the context rather

than the normal semantic range of the word itself that allows this pejorative connotation.[220] What remains clear about Paul's remarkable formulation is that bodily actions of a certain type are to be "put to death" by the congregation, and in view of the previous argument of Romans, this would include not only the deeds enumerated in 1:29-32 but also the bigotry described in chap. 2 and the misdeeds described in chaps. 3, 5, and 7. The radical response envisioned here is far from the moderation implied in a warning not to become bound "more tightly to that which is corruptible and perishable," avoiding "undue dependence on satisfying merely human appetites and ambitions."[221] No gradations are in view here.[222] Morris is correct in observing that Paul's formulation implies "killing off" such deeds, "getting rid of them entirely. But the tense is present, which indicates a continuing activity,"[223] such as that demanded of the congregation by 12:1-2, not to be conformed to this world in its bodily service. A cosmic struggle to the death is here envisioned within the community and between the community and the world. Under the power and guidance of the Spirit, with "Spirit" appearing here in the dative,[224] the community through its discernment and ethical choices is to kill the actions of the old age as they crop up as alternatives ever and again. This is very different from "mortification" by individual ascetics who renounce bodily desires as if they were inherently evil.[225] Given the context Paul has provided in the earlier argument in this letter, the "deeds of the body" are more likely social than sensual, which is confirmed by the plural verbs employed in this pericope.

---

215 See Zeller, 159; Dunn, 1:449.

216 For example, see Kühl, 283, and Fee, *Empowering Presence*, 558–59.

217 Gundry, *Soma*, 39, cited with approval by Moo, 495.

218 Jewett, *Terms*, 159, following Käsemann, "Worship in Everyday Life," in *Questions*, 188-95.

219 Meyer, 2:62, followed by Lagrange, 200; Wilckens, 2:134.

220 See Weiss, 352; BAGD 698 provides other examples of "evil or disgraceful deed," as determined by context; see also Gerhard Schneider, "πράξις," *EDNT* 3 (1993) 145. Christian Maurer, "πράξις," *TDNT* 6 (1968) 643, argues that the term itself "has a strong inclination to the ethically negative side," but this again seems entirely a matter of context.

221 Dunn, 1:448.

222 See Räisänen, *Law*, 113.

223 Morris, 312.

224 See Moule, "Death," 157, in reference to a dative of reference or relation.

225 Zeller, 159, notes the proximity of this language with that of Plato *Phaed.* 67a, "we shall be nearest to knowledge when we avoid, so far as possible, intercourse and communion with the body (τῷ σώματι) . . . freeing ourselves from the foolishness of the body (τῆς τοῦ σώματος ἀφροσύνης) and being pure we shall be with the pure and shall know of ourselves all that is pure, and perhaps the truth." See the similar formulation in Philo *Sobr.* 70: "Therefore we shall kill our 'brother,' not a man, but the soul's brother, the body, that is we shall dissever the passion-loving and mortal element from the virtue-loving and divine."

■ **14** The conjunction γάρ ("for") at the head of this sentence indicates that it provides a reason for the foregoing, namely, that the promise of life reflects the new status as "sons of God."[226] The correlative ὅσοι has a restrictive force of "only those who" for some interpreters,[227] but an inclusive force of "all those who" for others,[228] which is the option that fits best with the context and the earlier use of ὅσος to describe inclusive groups in 2:12 and 6:3. Dunn believes that a deliberate ambiguity was intended, which seems unlikely because there are no rhetorical indications of ambiguity in this context.[229] The reference to "being led" by the Spirit is a distinctively Pauline formulation, found in Gal 5:18, reflecting an "enthusiastic" understanding of believers being "carried away" by a spiritual force.[230] In 1 Cor 12:2 Paul uses the same verb, ἄγω, to refer to the pagan experience of being carried away by "dumb idols," which reflects the sense dominant in the Greco-Roman world of spiritual forces overpowering humans and leading them this way and that. The notion of a spirit "leading" someone is particularly common in magical texts, where ἄγειν is the technical term for gods, spirits, or ghosts of the dead, who are commanded to supernaturally "lead" a targeted person to act in a way that the practitioner desires.[231] It is therefore appropriate to explain Paul's formulation of being led by the Spirit as "being constrained by a compelling force, of surrendering to an overpowering compulsion,"[232] which implies divine intervention into the decision-making process of the community, led by inspired leaders and tested by the inspired and transformed minds of the members (12:1-2). Interpreters are usually skittish about this language and seek to temper it by insisting on the noncompulsory decision of believers to follow Christ[233] and on Paul's issuing a "license for uninhibited ecstasy,"[234] but no such reminders are actually included here. The suspicion of charismatic excess typical of the modern interpreter has no part in this letter. The role of prophetic and charismatic factors in perceiving this kind of divine guidance in the early house and tenement churches needs to be kept in view; this was probably not the quiet deliberation of the modern seminar room or church council meeting and, unlike modern ethical discourse, it was certainly not centered in the individual believer grappling with a personal decision.[235]

The word οὗτοι ("these") has a resumptive sense in v. 14b, giving "special emphasis" to something previously mentioned,[236] namely, those led by the Spirit of God. One could translate "these very ones are God's sons." This is the first reference in Romans to the υἱοὶ θεοῦ ("sons of God"), an expression with broad resonance in the Greco-Roman and Jewish environments.[237] Heroes and rulers were celebrated as individual sons of God,[238] and this formulation had a particular resonance

---

226 See Meyer, 2:62; Godet, 308; Cranfield, 1:395; Murray, 295.

227 Lagrange, 201, 259.

228 BAGD 586; Kühl, 285–86; Cranfield, 1:395; Moo, 562–63.

229 Dunn, 1:450; for an earlier suggestion along these lines, see Zahn, 393.

230 Betz, *Galatians*, 281; see also Zahn, 392; Jülicher, 282; Godet, 309; Käsemann, 226. The classification of this usage as "figurative" by BAGD 14 is apparently intended to prevent this enthusiastic reading.

231 For example, *PGM* I.97–99 refers to a divine "aerial spirit" (πνεῦμα ἐστιν ἀέριον) that, upon command, "straightaway accomplishes the task. It sends dreams, leads women (ἄγει γυναῖκας) [and] men (for sexual gratification) without [using] magical material." See also Daniel and Maltomini, *Suppl. Mag.* I. 45.6, 11, 29, 43, in reference to spirits (δαίμονες) of the dead adjured to awaken and "lead" (ἄξατε) a woman. Plutarch reports in *Gen. Socr.* 581e that disaster resulted when comrades "disre-

garded Socrates' daimon (τοῦ Σωκράτους δαιμονίου) by taking a path other than what he had led (οὐχ ἦν ἐκεῖνος ἦγε) in retreat from battle." In 586a Plutarch remarks that "while the paths of life are myriad, few indeed are the paths on which divine spirits lead people (ὀλίγαι δὲ ἃς δαίμονες ἀνθρώπους ἄγουσιν)."

232 Dunn, 1:450; Schäfer, *Bruderschaft,* 43; see also Colenso, 174, for the observation that the "stress" in this verse is on "God's Spirit."

233 Käsemann lists Sanday and Headlam; Kühl, Gutjahr, Lagrange, Dodd, Kuss, Stalder, Bultmann, and Schrage in this regard; see also Deidun, *New Covenant,* 71; Moo, 563.

234 Dunn, 1:450; see also Morris, 313.

235 See the reference to the individual "Christian" in Cranfield, 1:395; see also Leenhardt, 213; Murray, 295. For corrective, see Keesmaat, *Paul,* 55–59.

236 BAGD 596.

237 See the comprehensive survey by Jarl Fossum, "Son of God," *ABD* 6 (1992) 128–37.

in the Roman environment because of the civic cult. The Pergamon Altar celebrated Augustus as the "son of a god" (υἱὸν θεόν),[239] and he is elsewhere called the son of Apollo,[240] while Nero was celebrated as "Son of the greatest of the gods (τὸν υἱὸν τοῦ μεγίστου θεῶν), i.e., Tiberius Claudius."[241] The extension of this title to larger groups was also possible. Epictetus taught that humans are sons of God if they recognize their participation in the divine *logos*, as in *Diss.* 1.3.1–3. The *Corp. herm.* 13.2 claims that every initiate can become "a god, a child of God" (θεὸς παῖς θεοῦ). In the Hebrew Scriptures, Israel is referred to as Yahweh's son (Exod 4:22; Hos 2:1; 11:1), which was originally understood in terms of kinship with Yahweh who had established a covenant that included a wide range of people in a new kinship system that entailed mutual obligations.[242] A typical statement of this system is Deut 14:1-2, which forbids ritual disfigurement popularized by other ancient Near Eastern religions:[243] "You are sons of the Lord your God (υἱοί ἐστε κυρίου τοῦ θεοῦ ὑμῶν); you shall not cut yourself . . . for the dead. For you are a people holy to the Lord your God and the Lord has chosen you to be a people for his own possession." In Sir 4:10 the one who performs the righteous works of the law is promised, "you shall be as the son of the most high (ὡς υἱὸς ὑψίστου)" and the *Ps. Sol.* 17.26-27 promise that when God separates the righteous from sinners, the elect will "all be sons of their God (πάντες υἱοὶ θεοῦ εἰσιν αὐτῶν)." The restored Israel "will do according to my commandments, and I will be their father and they shall be my sons, and they shall all be called sons of the living God" (*Jub.* 1.24-25).[244] As long as they remain righteous, God's sons will be protected from evil (Wis 16:10; *As. Mos.* 10.3).

The innovation in Romans is to redefine sonship as derived from having received the Spirit of God,[245] a theme that is driven home in the next verse. Sonship is thus christianized and broadened beyond ethnic, familial, imperial, legalistic, and educational barriers. Whether this link between Spirit and divine sonship developed in pre-Pauline Christian baptismal rituals,[246] or whether it is a distinctive contribution of Pauline theology, remains unclear. But it defines the varied groups of believers in Rome as God's family, adopted by him through the Spirit into a position of extraordinary honor.

■ **15** The contrast between the new, pneumatic sonship offered in Christ and traditional sonship, which entailed performance of covenantal obligations, is articulated by v. 15, linked to the foregoing sentence with the explanatory γάρ ("for"). Believers, who are still addressed with the plural forms used since the reference to the "brothers" in v. 12, have not received[247] "a Spirit producing slavery unto fear." In the context of the previous argument of Romans, this expression must be understood in terms of slavery to sin (6:17-20), which transformed the law into a perverse system of gaining status (7:7-20). The construction of πνεῦμα δουλείας should be taken as a "genitive of direction and purpose,"[248] indicating that the Spirit does not produce the result of slavery. As in Gal 4:25 and 5:1,[249] δουλεία refers to slavery in relation to the law, which has been twisted in this manner.[250] The

238 Ibid., 132–33.
239 See Deissmann, *Light*, 347.
240 Fossum, "Son of God," 133, cites Suetonius *Aug.* 94.4 and Dio Cassius *Hist.* 45.1.2.
241 Deissmann, *Light*, 347.
242 See Frank Moore Cross, "Kinship and Covenant in Ancient Israel," in *From Epic to Canon: History and Literature in Ancient Israel* (Baltimore: Johns Hopkins University Press, 1998) chap. 1.
243 See Byrne, *Sons*, 15.
244 See ibid., 30–32.
245 See Dunn, 1:451.
246 This connection is suggested by Gal 3:26-27, according to Betz, *Galatians*, 210, but Paulsen, *Überlieferung*, 86, concludes that the origin of "the connection between spirit and sonship cannot be more precisely defined."

247 For an explanation of ἐλάβετε ("you received") as a virtually technical term for early Christian reception of the spirit, see Dunn, 1:451, referring to 2 Cor 11:4; Gal 3:2; John 7:39; 14:17; 20:22; Acts 1:8; 2:33, 38; 8:15, 17, 19; 10:47; 19:2; 1 John 2:27; see also Gerhard Delling, "λαμβάνω κτλ.," *TDNT* 4 (1967) 7; Armin Kretzer, "λαμβάνω," *EDNT* 2 (1991) 337.
248 See BDF §166; Godet, 309–10; Meyer, 2:63, cites Köllner, Rückert, Baumgarten-Crusius, and Hofmann as supporting this view; a recent proponent is Fee, *Empowering Presence*, 565.
249 See Betz, *Galatians*, 246, 58.
250 Schlier, 252–53; Wilckens, 2:136; Schäfer, *Bruderschaft*, 44–46; see also Alfons Weiser, "δουλεύω κτλ.," *EDNT* 1 (1990) 350.

φόβος ("fear") in view here is not a proper respect for God (Rom 3:18)[251] but a "fear of failing to come up to the mark of acceptability" that the competitive approach to the law entailed,[252] and thus fearing "again" (πάλιν) to fall under wrath.[253] This is emphatically not what believers have received in the gift of God's Spirit; as Paul had shown in 2 Cor 3:17, "where the Spirit of the Lord is, there is freedom."

The parallel expression in this antithetical formulation is that "you received a Spirit producing sonship," once again taking the genitive construction as one of purpose.[254] Francis Lyall tried to show that υἱοθεσία ("sonship, adoption") in the legal sense was available only in Roman laws concerning the *adoptio* or *adrogatio* of someone to become the child of a new *paterfamilias*.[255] However, G. H. R. Horsley has shown that this term appears in Greek sources before and after the development of the Latin terminology, referring for example to a petition from Isidora, "the adopted child of Dionysios (τεκνοθεσίαν Διονυσίο[υ])."[256] Despite the lack of comparable legal terminology in Jewish sources, there are some links here with the ethos of ancient Israel, in which Yahweh was thought to have adopted the people of Israel as his kinfolk.[257] It appears that Paul is drawing on a widely available concept of adoption in formulating his thesis, which anchors the charismatic Spirit in the familial community of the early church by referring to adoption as "sons" and "children" of God.[258] This provides "a fictive kinship relationship offering the advantages of privileges of future inheritance and present status. . . . There is a commonality in the background of those who enter this fictive kinship."[259]

The confirmation of this extraordinarily high status granted to believers is drawn from the widely shared experience of charismatic language being used in the early house and tenement churches.[260] Just as in Gal 4:6, Paul refers to an acclamation that "we cry out" (κράζομεν), apparently referring "to a worship situation"[261] in which unison prayer is heard. Such prayer is thought to be an indication of the presence of the Spirit, which explains the formulation ἐν ᾧ κράζομεν ("in which we cry out"). The verb is similar to the English word "croak," implying a rough or raucous sound,[262] with a semantic range from "cry out, scream, shriek" to "call out."[263] It can depict "the screaming baby" (τὸ παιδίον κεκραγός),[264] a call to the gods of the underworld in a

251 See Horst Balz, "Furcht vor Gott? Überlegungen zu einem vergessenen Motiv biblischer Theologie," *EvTh* 29 (1969) 626–44.

252 Dunn, 1:452, citing Gal 1:14 and Phil 3:6.

253 Schlier, 252; Horst Balz, "φοβέομαι κτλ.," *EDNT* 3 (1993) 433: believers "have nothing further to do with the slavish anxiety of those who fear the imperious judging God." See also Hans-Josef Klauck, "Religion without Fear. Plutarch on Superstition and Early Christian Literature," *SkrifK* 18 (1997) 122–23.

254 See Kuss, 2:601, following Bardenhewer, Bisping, Huby, Lietzmann, Sickenberger, Zahn; W. Twisselmann, *Die Gotteskindschaft der Christen nach dem Neuen Testament*, BFCTh 41.1 (Gütersloh: Bertelsmann, 1939) 264; Dunn, 1:452. Weiss, 355; Kühl, 286; and Byrne, 100, prefer a possessive genitive, that is, "genitive of origin and relationship" (BDF §162) resulting in the idea that the spirit "goes with" or "pledges" sonship, but this seems rather vague and somewhat less likely.

255 Lyall, "Roman Law," 66, referring to Gaius *Inst.* 1.97–107, 134–35; 3.83–84.

256 G. H. R. Horsley, "Petition to a Prefect," *NDIEC* 3 (1983) 16–17; Horsley, "καθ᾽ υἱοθεσίαν," *NDIEC* 4

(1987) 173, notes that this phrase occurs nine times in *IGRom*, referring to adopted sons.

257 Fossum, "Son of God," 129; see also Daniel J. Theron, "'Adoption' in the Pauline Corpus," *EvQ* 28 (1956) 6–7. In *Paul*, 60–74, Keesmaat shows that both sonship and being led by God are linked in the exodus tradition.

258 Scott, *Adoption*, 55, translates υἱοθεσία as "adoption as son"; and Byrne, *Sons*, 79–80, prefers "sonship." Trevor J. Burke proposes "adoptive sonship" in "The Characteristics of Paul's Adoptive Sonship (Huiothesis) Motif," *IBS* 17 (1995) 62–74.

259 Atkins, *Egalitarian Community*, 190.

260 Burke, "Adoptive Sonship," 66–70, deals with the gift of the spirit in theological terms as an "eschatological blessing."

261 See Käsemann, 272; Herbert Fendrich, "κράζω," *EDNT* 1 (1990) 313.

262 Walter Grundmann, "κράζω κτλ.," *TDNT* 3 (1965) 898.

263 BAGD 447–48; see also Paulsen, *Überlieferung*, 94–96.

264 MM 357.

pagan ritual,[265] or a public declaration: "Thus the hierophant has proclaimed aloud ($\kappa\acute{\epsilon}\kappa\rho\alpha\gamma\epsilon$) the great mysteries of Eleusis" (Hippolytus *Ref* 5.8). In the biblical tradition, this verb is used for fervent prayer (LXX Pss 4:3; 16:6; 21:24; 27:1; 30:22; etc.), for impassioned weeping before God (LXX Ps 31:3), for the uncontrolled shrieking of the insane (Mark 5:5), for the complaints of demons (Mark 9:26; Luke 9:39), for the outcries of mobs (Acts 19:28, 32, 34), and for Jesus' death cry (Matt 27:50). This potentially "violent verb"[266] leads some interpreters to think of the words "Abba, the Father" as an ecstatic "acclamation."[267] Grundmann, Cranfield, Dunn, Fendrich, and others reject the idea that this acclamation was "ecstatic,"[268] but this rejection seems to reflect a misconception of the nature of early Christian worship, which was much more enthusiastic and participatory than many modern churches that provide a tacit frame of reference for interpreters.[269] In view of the raucous verb $\kappa\rho\acute{\alpha}\zeta\omega$ that is employed here, the noisy and ecstatic quality of this acclamation is highly likely.[270]

The word "Abba" is Aramaic, a transliteration of אבא, which was being used in the first century as the direct, vocative address to a father, as the noun "the father," and also as the first person possessive form, "my father."[271] Although Joachim Jeremias and others popularized the widely accepted idea that "Abba" was an informal, childish word for the male parent, to be translated with a term such as "Daddy,"[272] this has now been recognized as only partially true because "Abba" was the regular Aramaic word for a male parent used both by adults and children.[273] Käsemann rejects the proposal that "Abba" refers to the Lord's Prayer,[274] since that does not contain the Aramaic original followed by a Greek translation. But the odd use of an Aramaic word followed by a Greek translation is most easily explained by the presence of the Aramaic form of the Lord's Prayer in the community along with Greek speakers, who used the prayer in Greek.[275] At the very least, a liturgical context is implied by this Aramaic term that "we" cry out together.[276] Käsemann rejects the idea that this is an early confession or a baptismal formula,[277] "let alone glossalalia," although the proximity to such ecstatic speech is palpable.[278] The question of the original setting of the acclamation has been taken up by Henning Paulsen, who concludes that the translation suggests a setting in "Hellenistic Jewish Christianity" and that the

---

265 Grundmann, "$\kappa\rho\acute{\alpha}\zeta\omega$ $\kappa\tau\lambda$.," 899, cites Lucian of Samosata *Men.* 9, "And the magician . . . no longer in a quiet voice but really loudly, such as he was, crying out ($\mathring{\alpha}\nu\alpha\kappa\rho\alpha\gamma\acute{\omega}\nu$) to all the demons at once, began shouting to the Avengers and Furies. . . ."

266 Barrett, 164.

267 Käsemann, 228, following Peterson, *ΕΙΣ ΘΕΟΣ*, 191–93; Kuss, 2:603–4; Dodd, 145, 260–61; Schlier, 253–54; Horn, *Angeld des Geistes*, 411; Paulsen, *Überlieferung*, 90–91, 95: "a spirit filled acclamation"; Betz, *Galatians*, 210: "the term has the ring of ecstasy." See particularly Shantz, "Paul in Ecstasy," 156–58, 163–64.

268 Grundmann, "$\kappa\rho\acute{\alpha}\zeta\omega$ $\kappa\tau\lambda$.," 903; Cranfield, 1:399; "Fendrich, "$\kappa\rho\acute{\alpha}\zeta\omega$," 314; Dunn, 1:453; E. A. Obeng, "Abba, Father: The Prayer of the Sons of God," *ExpT* 99 (1987–88) 365, views 8:15 as a short prayer but not "a glossolalic utterance"; J. A. Grassi, "Abba, Father," *TBT* 21 (1983) 321–22, views this verse as "a cry of obedience" with no reference to its ecstatic quality.

269 See Shantz, "Paul in Ecstasy," 22–71, 194–252, citing Esler, *First Christians*, 35–51.

270 See Meeks, *Urban Christians*, 88.

271 James Barr, "'Abba' Isn't Daddy," *JTS* 39 (1988) 40; Betz, *Galatians*, 211, understands the word in contrast as emphatic and vocative, not as a nominative meaning "the father."

272 See Joachim Jeremias, *Abba: Studien zur neutestamentlichen Theologie und Zeitgeschichte* (Göttingen: Vandenhoeck & Ruprecht, 1966) 15–67; idem, "Dio Abba-Patro," *BibR* 18 (1982) 19–30.

273 Barr, "'Abba' Isn't Daddy," 35–40; Dieter Zeller, "God as Father in the Proclamation and in the Prayer of Jesus," in A. Finkel and L. Frizzell, eds., *Standing Before God: Festschrift J. M. Oesterreicher* (New York: Ktav, 1981) 122–25.

274 Gerhard Kittel, "$\mathring{\alpha}\beta\beta\mathring{\alpha}$," *TDNT* 1 (1964) 6; Zahn, Dodd, Leenhardt, Lietzmann, Barrett, Black.

275 See Zahn, 395–97; Wilckens, 2:137.

276 See Byrne, *Sons*, 100.

277 Seeberg, *Katechismus*, 240–43; Zahn, 395; T. M. Taylor, "'Abba, Father' and Baptism," *SJT* 11 (1958) 2; Georg Braumann, *Vorpaulinische christliche Taufverkündigung bei Paulus*, BWANT 82 (Stuttgart: Kohlhammer Verlag, 1962) 62–74; Paulsen, *Überlieferung*, 88–93; Meeks, *Urban Christians*, 87–88, 155–56.

278 Käsemann, 227–28.

connection both with Spirit and with sonship found in Galatians and Romans was probably derived from that setting.[279] Since the Spirit impels believers to utter their prayers directly to their Abba, this is a powerful, experiential confirmation of their status as children of God.[280] Since the Spirit confirms that they belong to God, there is no longer any basis for anxiety about their status. Their need for honor has been fully met by their relationship with the heavenly parent who loves them unconditionally according to the earlier argument of Romans (5:8, 15; 6:23).[281]

■ **16** The final two verses in the pericope amplify the relational implications of the congregations' charismatic experience. The lack of a particle or conjunction between this and the preceding verse indicates, in Godet's words, "profound emotion,"[282] while making clear that this verse reiterates and clarifies the thought of the preceding verse.[283] The expression αὐτὸ τὸ πνεῦμα ("the Spirit itself") has a resumptive sense, referring with emphasis to the theme of the preceding sentence.[284] The Abba cry is confirmation of sonship, not merely in the reception of the "Spirit producing sonship" but in the actual status as sons and daughters of God. The use of the verb συμμαρτυρέω ("bear witness with") in connection with "our spirit" has occasioned considerable discussion.[285] If "our spirit" is understood as the human spirit in an anthropological sense,[286] then it would have no independent knowledge of divine destiny (see 1 Cor 2:11); but if this is the "apportioned Spirit" of God granted to believers,[287] then the verb seems to imply the theologically awkward conundrum

that God's Spirit witnesses to God's self. Some commentators have avoided such problems by following Strathmann in eliminating the συν- ("with") component of the verb and translating it simply as "bear witness."[288] This is inadmissible because this verb is in fact typically used to depict co-witnessing of some sort,[289] as, for example, Plato's assurance, "I am able to testify with you (συμμαρτυρῆσαι δέ σοι) that you are telling the truth."[290] Plutarch maintains that working together with a friend requires that they "should witness together, not deceive together (συμμαρτυρεῖν μὴ συνεξαπατᾶν)."[291] Others suggest that Paul really meant to say that God's Spirit witnesses *to* our spirit, which also effectively eliminates the element of co-witnessing.[292] In view of the fourfold reiteration of the συν- component of verbs in these two verses, revealing explicit authorial intent to emphasize the mutuality produced by the Spirit, it is inappropriate to reduce the semantic range of συμμαρτυρέω ("bear witness with") for apologetic reasons. It is preferable to accept Paul's idea that both the apportioned Spirit granted to believers and the "Spirit itself" confirm that believers are "children of God,"[293] despite the "logical difficulties in conceptualizing this in modern terms."[294] Paul's goal is not to produce a doctrine of the Spirit or a consistent anthropology but to convince the Roman believers that their charismatic experience bears witness that they are τέκνα θεοῦ ("children of God").

This is the first occurrence of τέκνον in Romans, with a connotation at first glance virtually synonymous with "sons of God" (8:14, 19).[295] Some have observed that this expression explicitly includes women as well as

279 Paulsen, *Überlieferung*, 92–96.
280 Schäfer, *Bruderschaft*, 46–47.
281 That the term "father" carried connotations of tender care as well as authority was as true for Latin (Wlosok, "Vater," 25–37) as for Jewish culture (Otto Michel, "πατήρ," *EDNT* 3 [1993] 53–57).
282 Godet, 310.
283 See Kuss, 2:604, following Gutjahr, Jülicher, Kühl, and Lietzmann.
284 See BAGD 123.2.
285 See Hermann Strathmann, "μάρτυς κτλ.," *TDNT* 4 (1967) 509; Kuss, 2:604–5.
286 See Cranfield, 1:402–3; Dunn, 1:454; Fee, *Empowering Presence*, 568; Moo, 503.
287 See Schlatter, 181; Lagrange, 202; Eduard Schweizer, "πνεῦμα, πνευματικός," *TDNT* 6 (1968)

436; Paulsen, *Überlieferung*, 100–101; Jewett, *Terms*, 198–99.
288 Strathmann, "μάρτυς κτλ.," 509.
289 LSJM 1677, "to bear witness *with* or *in support of* another."
290 Plato *Hipp. maj.* 282b1; see also Plato *Leg.* 680d4; Plutarch *Quaest. conv.* 724c.
291 Plutarch *Adul. amic.* 64c13; see also Isocrates *Trapez.* 41.8; *Paneg.* 31.8; Dionysius Halicarnassus *Antiq. Rom.* 3.73.3.1; Josephus *Ant.* 19.154.
292 See Godet, 311; Leenhardt, 215; Cranfield, 1:403; Morris, 316.
293 See Black, 114: "Two witnesses, according to the OT injunction, establish the truth of any witness."
294 Jewett, *Terms*, 199.
295 Gerhard Schneider, "τέκνον," *EDNT* 3 (1993) 341,

men,[296] which may correlate with Paul's commendations in chap. 16 of the remarkably large number of feminine church leaders. Τέκνα θεοῦ ("children of God") appears as a technical formula for Christian believers in the Johannine tradition (John 11:52; 1 John 3:1, 2, 10; 5:2),[297] which might suggest an effort on Paul's part to extend the range of his discourse to include various groups present in Rome. A measure of inclusivity is certainly conveyed by Paul's reference to himself along with other believers in the verbal claim "that we are children of God."[298] No distinctions of status among believing groups are allowed by this formulation, a point consistent with 3:27-31 and developed in full detail with reference to the situation in the Roman congregations in 14:1–15:13. This solidarity also implies that "there is no gender which can be considered inferior."[299] The implication of the shift from "sons of God" to "children of God," which remains on the implicit level in v. 16, becomes clear in the very next verse.

■ **17** The rhetorical climax that concludes this pericope expands the significance of the status of believers as "children of God." Paul stands in the mainstream of Jewish and most Greco-Roman law in claiming that if believers are children (of God), then they are also "heirs" (κληρονόμοι),[300] a term we encountered in 4:13-14, where Paul claimed that Christian believers are the heirs of Abraham's promise. Here the claim is more sweeping; they are heirs not just of promises but also of the divine patrimony in its fullest sense. As Schlatter explains, "from the union of life arises the union of possession; the son becomes the heir."[301] A threefold expansion of the inheritance is expressed rhetorically: first "heirs" in an absolute sense, without qualification; then "heirs of God," making clear the source of their patrimony; and finally "joint-heirs with Christ," which clarifies the spiritual and relational nature of the inheritance.[302] Werner Foerster and Johannes Herrmann have shown that in the OT the term κληρονόμος is never attached to the ownership of "movable property" but only to "real property or goods" considered "essential" to the patrimony of a household.[303] In this pericope it is not so much ownership of property "as relationship that he has in mind," as Morris points out.[304] So in the case of the children of God in Paul's discourse, every promise and possession once granted to Israel are now granted in a new and symbolic sense to each and every believer and to each believing community.[305] Once this is understood, Paul's reason for shifting from "sons" to "children" becomes

---

claims exactly synonymous meaning; see also Gerhard Delling, "Lexikalisches zu τέκνον: Ein Nachtrag zur Exegese von I. Kor. 7,14," in G. Delling, *Studien zum Neuen Testament und zum hellenistischen Judentum: Gesammelte Aufsätze 1950 68* (Göttingen: Vandenhoeck & Ruprecht, 1970) 275; Schäfer, *Bruderschaft*, 48.

296 See Weiss, 357; Zeller, 160. Dunn, 1:455, observes correctly that "sons of God" also includes women, but the point remains that "children of God" is more explicit on this point. See Bartchy, "Siblings," 68–78.

297 The only other examples of the expression τέκνα θεοῦ are in mythological contexts in which Hesiod *Theog.* 240 refers to "children of the goddesses" (τέκνα θεάων) and in *Theog.* 366 to the "glorious children of the goddesses" (θεάων ἀγλαὰ τέκνα). In these instances, however, the mythological offspring are given other specific parents; see M. L. West, *Hesiod. Theogony* (Oxford: Clarendon Press, 1978) 237. A later Orphic tablet from Rome addresses an initiate as "Zeus's glorious child" (Διὸς τέκος ἀγλαά). See Kotansky, *Greek Magical Amulets*, 110–11, for a discussion of the problem of interpreting this evidence.

298 See Byrne, *Sons*, 99–101.

299 Tamez, "Justification," 188.

300 See Werner Foerster and Johannes Herrmann, "κλῆρος κτλ.," *TDNT* 3 (1965) 768–69; Johannes II. Friedrich, "κληρονόμος," *EDNT* 2 (1991) 298.

301 Schlatter, 182; note, however, that Schlatter shifts the terminology from "children" back to "sons."

302 See Hester, *Inheritance*, 88; Kuss, 2:606; Friedrich, "κληρονόμος," 298.

303 Foerster and Herrmann, "κλῆρος κτλ.," 769.

304 Morris, 317; see also Godet, 311: "rightly taken His inheritance is Himself."

305 See Dunn, 1:455, who lists the references to inheritance that comprised "a basic datum of Jewish self-understanding": Deut 32:9; Judg 13:5; 1 Kgs 8:51, 53; 2 Kgs 21:14; Pss 33:12; 74:2; Isa 63:17; Jer 10:16; Mic 7:18; Sir 24:8, 12; *Jub.* 1.19–21; 22.9–10, 15; 33.20; 3 Macc 6:3; *2 Bar.* 5.1; Pseudo-Philo *Lib. Ant.* 12.9; 21.10; 27.7; 28.2; 39.7; 49.6. Paul L. Hammer offers the cautionary observation in "Inheritance (NT)," *ABD* 3 (1992) 415, that "unlike the OT, he [Paul] never refers to the land of Canaan as Abraham's inheritance."

obvious.[306] It is not only that primogeniture granted larger or sometimes exclusive shares to eldest sons, or that favored sons could arbitrarily be given precedence, according to Roman law.[307] In biblical history as well as throughout the Greco-Roman world, the struggles between sons for shares of their inheritance are celebrated, with guile, treachery, and murder as leitmotifs. From Jacob and Esau (Gen 25:29-34) to Romulus and Remus (Plutarch *Rom.* 9–11), triumphs in inheritance by the cleverer or more violent sons were told and retold. This dominant cultural legacy is sidestepped by Paul's choice of τέκνα θεοῦ as the key to inheritance, because now each member of the new community of faith, whether male or female, Gentile or Jew, Greek or barbarian, slave or free, child or adult, shares equally in the patrimony.

The pre-Pauline examples of συγκληρόνομος refer to parties who share an inheritance. For instance, an inscription from the imperial period refers to Eutychis as "co-heir of P. Umphuleius Bassus (συ[γ]κληρονό[μου αὐτ]οῦ)."[308] In the later *Acts of John* 106.4, there is a reference to "brothers and fellow-slaves and fellow-heirs (συγκληρόνομοι) and fellow sharers in the Lord's kingdom."[309] "Joint heirs" belongs with a group of at least fourteen συν- compounds that Walter Grundmann has identified as expressing the dimensions of the "with Christ" language developed by Paul,[310] and, like many of

the other examples, it appears in materials written by Christians after the time of Romans.[311] Although there are no other references in Paul's letters to Christ as the heir of God,[312] it appears that the genitive construction is dependent on the preposition συν- ("with") in συγκληρόνομος ("joint-heir") and that the proper translation is "joint-heirs with Christ."[313] This is confirmed by the εἴπερ clause that rounds out the sentence by referring to suffering with Christ and being glorified with him. This compound preposition can be translated "if indeed, if after all, since," or "provided that,"[314] evoking a range of suggestions by commentators, reflecting their understanding of the pericope and the letter as a whole. Those who understand Romans as an admonitory treatise take εἴπερ as a condition yet to be fulfilled or an indirect warning, "provided that."[315] The more plausible alternative in view of the explanatory function of the argument in 8:14-17 is to translate εἴπερ as "since indeed," just as in 8:9.[316] The Roman congregation continues to experience suffering in the aftermath of the Edict of Claudius and thus requires no admonition about the necessity of endurance. Moreover, the verb συμπάσχομεν is in the present tense, "we suffer together with," which appears to refer to ongoing experiences rather than a future condition, as Michel observes: "The present suffering with Christ (i.e. for the sake of

---

306 G. H. R. Horsley provides an example of "children" rather than "sons" in connection with "inheritance" in "συγκληρόνομος," *NDIEC* 2 (1982) 97, citing *P.Mich.* 13. Nr. 659.58–60, which contains the line "Victor and Senouthes undertake business for Apollos, Paul and Maria, children and inheritors (τέκνων καὶ κληρονόμων) of John of pious memory."

307 See Francis Lyall, "Legal Metaphors in the Epistles," *TynB* 32 (1981) 94.

308 *B. Mus. In.* 3. Nr. 633, p. 249; BAGD (2000) 952 include Philo *Spec.* 2.73.4; *Legat.* 28.3; 29.3; 68.1; 75.5; 87.3; Aelius Herodianus Συντάξ. 3.2.400; *Conf. Asen.* 24.9.2; *Sch. Arist., Scholia in aves* 1653.3; see also 1656.8 for the verbal form.

309 See the inscription from Commodus's reign cited in Foerster and Herrmann, "κλῆρος κτλ.," 768. A parallel in a later Christian letter contains the line "If I assault Tithoes next time I make an attack on my very self . . . since he is joint-heir with me

(συ[ν]κληρονόμος μοῦ)" (G. H. R. Horsley, "A Christian Complains about an Assault," *NDIEC* 1 [1981] 134–35). The editors are unsure whether this is a reference to their Christian status or to their being heirs of the same property.

310 Walter Grundmann, "σύν-μετά," *TDNT* 7 (1971) 786–87; see also Deissmann, *Paul*, 173–76.

311 Eph 3:6; Heb 11:9; 1 Pet 3:7; *Herm. Mand.* 55.7.5; 55.8.2; Justin *Dial.* 14.1.5; Irenaeus *Adv. Haer.* 1.4.1.23.

312 See Foerster and Herrmann, "κλῆρος κτλ.," 782, lines 2–6.

313 See BDF §181; Horst Balz and Gerhard Schneider, eds., "συγκληρονόμος," *EDNT* 3 (1993) 283.

314 See BAGD 220 (VI.11).

315 Weiss, 358; Godet, 311; Kuss, 2:607; Wilckens, 2:138; Murray, 299; Dunn, 1:456; Fitzmyer, 502; Moo, 505.

316 Kühl, 290; Zahn, 398; Jülicher, 282–83; Lagrange, 203; Michel, 262; Newman and Nida, 156; Cranfield, 1:407; Black, 114.

Christ) is the basis of the future glorification."[317] In classical sources the compound verb συμπάσχειν can mean "suffer with,"[318] or "sympathize with," as in Polybius *Hist.* 4.7.3, "the Achaeans . . . sympathized with (συμπάσχοντες) the Messenians in their misfortune."[319] But in this passage in Romans, it clearly has the sense of believers suffering with Christ, in behalf of Christ.[320] Paul had developed this idea in Phil 3:10, of sharing Christ's "sufferings, becoming like him in his death" in order to participate in his resurrection.[321] To be a child of God in the Christian sense, to live according to the Spirit, is to take up one's cross.[322] In Käsemann's memorable words, "the Spirit who makes Christ present on earth is the very one who imposes on them a pilgrim theology. . . . Only he who participates on earth in the passion of the Kyrios will participate in his glory."[323]

The rare verb συνδοξάζω appears in classical sources only in the active voice, joining others in praising or approving something as in Aristotle *Pol.* 1310a.13, "of the most beneficial laws also jointly approved by the citizens (νόμων καὶ συνδεδοξασμένων ὑπὸ πάντων τῶν πολιτευομένων)."[324] Only Paul uses this verb in the passive voice, in this single passage, and the subjunctive mood and punctiliar nature of the aorist συνδοξασθῶμεν ("that we might be glorified") in the ἵνα ("in order that") clause points toward a fulfillment[325] that is granted but never becomes a permanent possession.

This formulation provides a reprise of the entire pericope. While walking according to the flesh was a matter of the perverse quest to earn and retain glory at the expense of others and in opposition to God, walking by the Spirit brings one into participation with the dishonored, crucified Lord whose glory was granted as a gift from the God of glory (Rom 6:4; see also Phil 2:9-11). By sharing suffering with the dishonored Christ, believers receive the promise of a divine reversal, sharing in his glory. While some commentators insist that this is purely a future promise,[326] even constituting a kind of "eschatological reservation,"[327] nothing in Paul's formulation demands this. The future passive is not employed here. In 2 Cor 4:18, Paul employs a similarly passive formulation indicating that the gift of glory is both a present and a future bonus: "And we all, with unveiled face, beholding the glory of the Lord, are being changed into his likeness from one degree of glory to another; for this comes from the Lord who is the Spirit." Although a measure of glorification is currently visible among the saints, in partial and vulnerable forms, those who persist in living according to the Spirit will participate in its fulfillment now and at the end of time. It comes only as a gift of grace, however, and only in the context of suffering with Christ. This sets the theme for the next pericope while bringing to a ringing climax this discussion of what it means to walk by the Spirit and to enjoy the imparted dignity of adoption as the children of God.

---

317 Michel, 262.
318 BAGD (2000) 958, as in Epictetus *Diss.* 1.14.2 or Philo *Spec.* 3.194, "the eyes suffer with the soul's passions (τοῖς τῆς ψυχῆς πάθεσιν συμπάσχουσιν οφθαλμοί)."
319 See also Plutarch *Demetr.* 38.3; Pseudo-Aristotle *Physogn.* 805 a6; Aristotle *An.* 427b 21, "Whenever we entertain something dreadful or fearful, we immediately sympathize (συμπάσχομεν)." The sense of "feeling together" or "operating together" appears frequently in medical texts such as Soranus *Gyn.* 3.20.1.3; Severus Iastrosophista *Inst.* 31.6.
320 Wilhelm Michaelis, "συμπάσχω," *TDNT* 5 (1967) 925–26, reduces this to "Christ leads them to suffering" in order to avoid any connotation of mystical participation in Christ's sufferings. Pobee, *Persecu-*

tion, 112, is correct in suggesting that "Christ is with the Christian both in his suffering and in his eventual glorification."
321 See Michel, 262–63; see also 2 Cor 4:10.
322 See Deissmann, *Paul,* 174–75.
323 Käsemann, 229; it is clear from his formulation, however, that he takes the εἴπερ clause in a rather conditional sense.
324 A *TLG* search turned up no other relevant examples.
325 See Gerhard Kittel, "δοξάζω, συνδοξάζω," *TDNT* 2 (1964) 253–54; Horst Balz and Gerhard Schneider, eds., "συνδοξάζω," *EDNT* 3 (1993) 299.
326 See, e.g., Weiss, 358; Wilckens, 2:138; Fitzmyer, 502; Dunn, 1:457.
327 Moo, 505.

8

The Ninth Pericope

Thesis and Rationale Concerning the Hopeful Suffering of the Children of God

18/ For I reckon that the sufferings of the present critical time cannot compare with the coming glory to be revealed to us. 19/ For the eager expectation of the creation[a] awaits the revelation of the sons of God. 20/ For the creation was subjected to futility, not voluntarily[b] but rather on account of the one who subjected it—in[c] hope— 21/ because[d] the creation itself will[e] also be set free from its enslavement to corruption to obtain liberation [consisting] of the glory for the children of God. 22/ For we know that the whole creation groans together and travails together[f] until now, 23/ and not only [the creation] but even ourselves[g] who have the firstfruits of the Spirit, even we ourselves,[h] groan within ourselves as we await[i] the redemption of our body.

24/ For in this hope were we saved. Now a hope seen is not hope, for who[j] can hope[k] for what one sees? 25/ But if we hope in what we do not see, we await [it] with perseverance. 26/ In a similar way the Spirit also lends assistance in our weakness,[l] for the [question], "What should we to pray for, as is required?" We do not know! But the Spirit itself intercedes[m] with unspoken groans. 27/ But the one searching the hearts knows what the intention of the Spirit [is], that by God it intercedes for the sake of saints.[n] 28/ But we know that for those who love God, in all things[o] it cooperates[p] for good,[q] with those who are called according to a purpose,

29/ because those whom [God] foreknew,

he also predestined to be conformed to the image of his son, in order that he might be the firstborn among many brothers;
30/ and those he predestined,[r] these he also called;
and those he called, these he also made right;
and those he made right, these he also glorified.

b In place of the widely attested οὐχ ἑκοῦσα ("not willingly"), F G (D* is illegible) Ir^lat have οὐ θελοῦσα ("not desiring"), perhaps a visual, scribal error or an effort at clarification through replacing the less common adjective.

c The variant found in P^27 A B^2 C D^2 K L P Ψ^(acc. to Swanson) 6 33 69 88 104 323 326 330 424 614 945 1175 1241 1243 1319 1505 1506 1573 1735 1739 1836 1874 1881 2464 2495 *Maj* Cl^ex Theod with ἐπ᾽ appears to be a correction of the more strongly attested ἐφ᾽ found in P^46 ℵ B* D* F G, which presupposes a false aspiration ἑλπίς in lieu of ἐλπίς.

d There is an uncritical consensus that ὅτι ("that") in P^46 A B C D^2 K L P Ψ 0289 6 33 69 81 88 104 181 256 263 323 326 424 436 459 614 629 945^(acc. to Swanson) 1175 1243 1319 1505 1506 1573 1735 1739 1836 1852 1874 1877 1881 1912 1962 2200 2464 2492 2495 *Lect Maj* sy^p arm eth geo slav^ms Cl^ex Theodotus Or Meth Eus Marcellus Diodore Chr Severian Thret is replaced by διότι in ℵ D* F G 330 945^(acc. to N-A) 2127 *pc* sy^h, pal slav^ms, as a result of dittography, according to Metzger, *Textual Commentary*, 456. The reading ὅτι is accepted by Nestle-Aland^26/27; *GNT*^3/4; Dunn, 1:471; Fitzmyer, 509; Byrne, 261; Moo, 516; Schreiner, 440. Chang, *Die Knechtschaft*, 74–75, follows Cranfield, 1:414–15, and Wilckens, 2:155, to make a compelling case that haplography would more likely drop the prefix δι- than add it; that διότι should be preferred as the more difficult text; and that the causal sense of διότι is better suited to the argumentative context. Neither word appears in 1241 *l* 895*.

e In place of the widely attested future passive form, P^27c vid vg^ms have a present middle passive form ἐλευθεροῦται ("it is freed"), probably to conform with the other present tenses in this passage. The variant is too weakly attested to be original.

f A minor variant in F G ar has ὀδύνει ("suffers pain") in place of the widely attested word for suffering agony together, συνωδίνει. It could be a dictation error because of the similar sounding last syllables.

g Several variants indicate an interest in clarifying the awkward grammar of the broadly attested καὶ αὐτοί ("even ourselves"). D F G lat have καὶ ἡμεῖς αὐτοί ("also we ourselves") and 88 104 630 1243 have καὶ αὐτοὶ ἡμεῖς οἱ ("even we ourselves who"), while P^46 lacks the entire expression.

h The extension of the confusion noted in the earlier portion of this verse is manifest in the variants to ἡμεῖς καὶ αὐτοί ("also we ourselves") convincingly attested by P^46 ℵ A C 5 81 436 623 1506 1739 1852 1881 1908 1962 2110 *pc*, whereas K L P 6 33 61^c 69 181 323 326* 330 424 451 614 629 720^c 917 945 1175 1241 1398 1505 1678 1735 1751 1836 1845 1846 1874 1875 1877 1912 2138 2197 2200 2344

a An understandable scribal error in 69 2464 *pc* produced πίστεως ("faith") in place of κτίσεως ("creation").

2464 2492 2495 2516 2523 2544 2718 *Maj* (sy^h) have the altered sequence καὶ ἡμεῖς αὐτοί; B 88 104 441 459 467 621 915 1243 1838 1959 *pc* lat Meth have καὶ αὐτοί ("also we"); Ψ d* g Ambst have ἡμεῖς αὐτοί ("we ourselves"); and D F G *pc* vg^ius have αὐτοί alone ("ourselves").

i The absence υἱοθεσίαν ("adoption") in P^46 vid D F G 614 d f g o t Ambst should be classified as a "Western non-interpolation," and thus may have a claim of originality, although no commentary or critical text claims it as such; see Metzger, *Textual Commentary*, 457. There is support for the inclusion of "adoption" in ℵ A B C K L P Ψ *Maj* 5 33 61 69 81 88 104 181 218 256 263 323 326 330 424 436 441 451 459 467 621 623 629 630 720 915 917 945 1175 1241 1243 1319 1398 1505 1506 1563 1573 1678 1718 1735 1739 1751 1836 1838 1845 1846 1852 1874 1875 1877 1881 1908 1912 1942 1959 1962 2110 2127 2138 2197 2200 2344 2464 2492 2495 2516 2523 2544 2718 *Lect* ar b mon vg sy^p,h sa bo arm eth geo slav Or^lat Meth Apollinaris Diodore Chr Theodore^lat Cyr Ambr Pel Aug, but the addition of this word is easier to explain than its deletion. Moreover, the addition produces a discrepancy with 8:12-14 where the gift of sonship is a present possession of faith whereas this verse postpones it until the future.

j A complicated series of variations presents itself here, with the older Nestle^25 text (1963) following ℵ^2 A C K L P Ψ 6 33 69 81 88 104 256 263 323 326 330 424 436 451 614 629 945 1175 1241 1243^c 1319 1505 1506 1573 1735 1836 1852 1881 1912 1962 2127 2200 2464 2492 2495 *Maj Lect* b sy^h sa arm^ms (eth) geo slav^ms Cl GrNy Did Chr Thret Ambr^1/2 Aug^9/51 in the wording ὃ γὰρ βλέπει τίς, τὶ καὶ ἐλπίζει ("for what someone sees, why does he also hope for it?"). The more terse form of this question, ὃ γὰρ βλέπει, τίς ἐλπίζει ("for who hopes for what he sees?") is supported by weighty witnesses in P^27vid, 46 B* 1739^v.l. 1908^mg mon* bo and is followed by Nestle-Aland^26/27 and Metzger, *Textual Commentary*, 457. Two other forms of the questions surface in the tradition: ὃ γὰρ βλέπει τίς, τὶ ἐλπίζει ("for what someone sees, why does he hope for it?") in B^1 D F G 1874 1877 *pc* ar d f g mon^2 o vg (sy^p) slav^ms Or^gr, lat Cyp Ambst Ambr^1/2 Pel Aug^42/51 and ὃ γὰρ βλέπει τίς καὶ ἐλπίζει ("for what one sees he also hopes for") in ℵ* 459 1243* 1739^txt arm^ms. It is likely that the terse form followed by Nestle Aland^27 was the original.

k In place of the widely attested ἐλπίζει ("he hopes"), ℵ* A 1739^mg sy^p sa bo provide ὑπομένει ("he perseveres"), clearly a secondary anticipation of the motif of perseverance in the next verse. The reading "he hopes" is supported by P^46 ℵ^c B C D F G K L P Ψ 6

33 69 81 88 104 181 256 263 323 326 330 424 436 451 459 614 945 1175 1241 1243 1319 1505 1506 1573 1735 1739* 1836 1852 1874 1877 1881 1912 1962 2127 2200 2464 2492 2495 *Lect* ar b d f g mon o vg sy^h bo^ms arm eth geo slav Cl Or^gr,lat GrNy Did Chrys Thret Cyp Ambst Ambr Pel Aug.

l In place of the singular form of "the weakness" convincingly attested in ℵ A B C D* 69 81 104 218 330 451 459 630 1563 1718 1739 1838 1852 1881 1908 2110 2200 *pc* vg sy^p cop, the plural ταῖς ἀσθενείαις ("the weaknesses") is found in K L P Ψ 5 6 33 61 88 181 256 263 323 326 424 441 467 614 621 623 629 720 915 917 945 1175 1241 1243 1319 1398 1505 1573 1678 1735 1751 1836 1845 1846 1874 1875 1877 1912 1942 1959 1962 2127 2138 2197 2344 2464 2492 2495 2516 2544 2718 *Maj* sy^h. F and G have τῆς δεήσεως ("of prayer"), while it Ambst have the conflated form, τῇ ἀσθενείᾳ τῆς δεήσεως ἡμῶν ("the weakness of our prayer"). All of these variants give the impression of attempted clarifications.

m The addition of ὑπὲρ ἡμῶν ("for our sake") in ℵ^2 C K L P Ψ 33 69 88 104 181 323 326 330 424* 436 451 459 614 945^(acc. to Swanson) 1175 1241 1243 1505 1735 1836 1852 1874 1877 1912 1962 2464 2492 2495 *Maj Lect* ar d^2 f mon o vg sy^h sa bo eth geo slav Or^lat Eus (Diodore) Did^lat Did^dub (Macarius/Symeon) (Severian) Epiph^3/4 Chr (Theodore) (Cyr) (John-Damascus) Nov Hil Ambst Gregory-Elvira Ambr Hier Pel Maximinus Aug^3/17 appears to be an intended improvement of the text. There is strong support for the version without "for our sake" in ℵ* A B D F G 6 81 256 263 424^c 945^(acc. to N-A) 1319 1506 1573 1739 1881 2127 *pc* b d* g arm (Or) Epiph^1/4 Aug^14/17. Additional minor variants are ὑπὲρ ἡμῶν ἐντυγχάνει in 2200 Varimadum and ἐντυγχάνει ὑπὲρ ἡμῶν in 629, which appear to be assimilations to the wording of the next verse.

n The replacement of the widely attested "saints" by ἡμῶν ("us") in 33 *pc* may be a visual error, with ΑΓΙΩΝ read as ΗΜΩΝ.

o The replacement of the widely attested neuter plural πάντα ("all things") by the singular πᾶν ("everything") in P^46 is too weakly supported to be considered original. The conjecture that πνεῦμα ("spirit") was mistakenly changed to πάντα by the original scribe, suggested by James P. Wilson, "Romans viii,28: Text and Interpretation," *ExpT* 60 (1948–49) 111, followed by Matthew Black, "The Interpretation of Rom 8:28," in *Neostestamentica et Patristica: Eine Freundesgabe, Herrn Professor Dr. Oscar Cullmann zu seinem 60. Geburtstag Überreicht* (NovTSup 6; Leiden: Brill, 1962) 166–72; and E. H. Daniell, "Romans viii, 28," *ExpT* 61 (1949–50) 59, is unlikely on text-critical grounds and would violate

Paul's normal practice of referring to $\pi\nu\epsilon\hat{\nu}\mu\alpha$ with the article. See Wilckens, 2:163.

p The older Nestle[25] text (1963), following P[46] A B 81 sa eth, adopted the reading $\acute{o}$ $\vartheta\epsilon\acute{o}\varsigma$ ("God"), though in spare brackets, which supplies a subject for the verb, but there is broader support for the version lacking this detail: ℵ C D F G K L P Ψ 6 33 69 88 104 256 263 323 326 330 424 436 451 459 614 629 945 1175 1241 1243 1319 1505 1506 1573 1735 1739 1836 1852 1874 1877 1881 1912 1962 2127 2200 2464 2492 2495 *Maj Lect* ar b d f g mon o vg sy[p,h] bo arm geo slav Cl Or[gr. lat] Eus CyrJ Diodore (GrNy) Did Macarius/Symeon Chr Cyr Hes Thret Lcf Ambst Ambr Hier Pel Aug. See Metzger, *Textual Commentary*, 458.

q The provision of the definite article $\tau\acute{o}$ in L 945 *pm* Cl appears to be a secondary improvement.

r In place of the widely attested "predestined," A has $\pi\rho o\acute{\epsilon}\gamma\nu\omega$ ("he foreknew"), an unlikely variant harking back to the $\pi\rho o\acute{\epsilon}\gamma\nu\omega$ of the earlier part of v. 29.

Analysis

While commentators agree that this is a separate pericope, its links with the preceding pericope as well as with 5:1-11 are obvious. The theme of sonship in 8:14-15 is carried forward in vv. 19 and 23; the glorification scheme in 8:17 is picked up in vv. 18, 21, 30; and the theme of the Spirit continues throughout chap. 8. Just as at the beginning of the last pericope, this one opens with a thesis concerning suffering in the light of future glory (8:18), which elaborates the two themes announced at the end of the preceding verse.[1] The thesis is developed in two major sections: vv. 19-27 dealing with the motif of suffering, and vv. 28-30 with the motif of glory. A series of key terms found in 5:1-11 reappears here and in the following pericope, bringing the second proof to an effective thematic unity. Harvey has developed this list, elaborating observations by Douglas Moo:[2]

5:5, 8	"love"	8:35, 39
5:1, 9	"make right"	8:30, 33
5:2	"glory, glorify"	8:18, 21, 30
5:2, 4, 5	"hope, to hope"	8:20, 24
5:3	"suffering"	8:35
5:9, 10	"save"	8:24
5:3, 4	"patience"	8:25

Other commentators have noted that this pericope also provides the climactic elaboration of the themes of creation, corruption, and glorification announced in the first proof of the letter as well as the themes of Adam, suffering, and glorification announced in the first two pericopes of the second proof.[3] The stylistic unity of the passage is enhanced by eight verbs that are compounds with $\acute{\alpha}\pi o$-,[4] nine verbs that are $\sigma\nu\nu$- compounds,[5] and five words that are $\pi\rho o$- compounds.

In contrast to the double-line sentences of earlier sections of Romans, this pericope is marked by larger thought units and extensive climaxes. Theodor Zahn suggested that the thesis in 8:18 was developed in three concentric circles of argument, vv. 19-22, 23-25, and 26-27,[6] which overlooked the correspondence between v. 22 and v. 23.[7] As Johannes Weiss showed, the eight lines of vv. 19-23 appear to be organized in two corresponding sentences of roughly equal length. "Creation" is the subject in the first line of each sentence (8:19, 22), while the second lines each have a "not . . . but" structure (vv. 20, 23a) and the third lines have "the creation itself" (v. 21) matching "we ourselves" (v. 23b).[8] There is a thematic parallelism between the fourth lines in that the "glorious liberation of the children of God" in v. 21b corresponds to "the redemption of our body" in v. 23c. Verse 22 also contains an elegant reduplication of $\sigma\nu\nu$- ("together, with") in the expression "groans together and travails

---

1 Chang, *Die Knechtschaft*, 77.
2 Harvey, *Listening*, 194.
3 Rom 5:1-11 + 12-21; 8:1-17 + 18-30; see particularly Osten-Sacken, *Römer 8*, 124–28, and Dunn, 1:467.
4 Harvey, *Listening*, 197.
5 Theissen, *Psychological Aspects*, 333; Klauck, "Wortlose Seufzen," 92.

6 See also Chang, *Die Knechtschaft*, 79.
7 Zahn, 400; see also Käsemann, 231.
8 See Weiss, "Beiträge," 237; his observation about the corresponding repetition of the "creation" motif is mitigated by the additional uses of this term in the second and third lines of the first sentence (v. 20f.).

together." Verses 19, 20, 21, and 22 are held together by a γάρ-chain, each translated with "for" and providing the reason for the preceding claims.[9] This extensive unit is followed in vv. 24-25 with a kind of climax in which hope is clarified in five rather brief successive lines in which the terms "hope" or "to hope" are repeated five times, providing an appealing instance of paronomasia. Since "hope" appears both at the beginning and at the end of v. 24b, the repetition creates *epanadiplosis*.[10] The verb ἀπεδέχομαι ("await") is also repeated three times in this pericope (vv. 19, 23, 25), and joins with its near cognate ἀποκαραδοκία ("eager expectation") in v. 19 to reinforce the stance of hopeful waiting. This clarification of hope is followed by five more extensive lines that explain the role of the Spirit in the context of groaning and suffering creatures (vv. 26-27).[11]

The pericope concludes with a much more formal, fivefold climax declaiming the glory manifest in believers.[12] The first two stages in the climax are thematic developments (8:28-29), interrupted twice by theological comments (v. 28b and v. 29c). Stage 1 is a succinct *sententia*[13] stating the premise concerning those who love God (v. 28a), who are identified as consisting of those called by God (v. 28c). Stage 2 picks up the first synonym of calling, "foreknowledge" (v. 29a), elaborating this with reference to predestination in conformity with Christ (v. 29b). The first two stages are linked with a paronomastic series with the prefix προ-, πρόθεσιν . . . προέγνω . . . προώρισεν ("purpose . . . foreknew . . . predestined"). The final three stages[14] each form an anaphora with v. 29a, οὓς προέγνω, καὶ προώρισεν, and contain the reduplication characteristic of a climax, with "called" in v. 30a picked up in v. 30b, while "set right" in v. 30b is picked up in v. 30c. The final word in the pericope, "he glorified" (v. 30c), provides an effective reprise of "the coming glory to be revealed to us" in the thesis statement of v. 18.

Rhetorical Disposition

IV.	The *probatio*
5:1–8:39	B. The second proof: Life in Christ as a new system of honor that replaces the quest for status through conformity to the law
8:18-30	9. Thesis and rationale concerning the hopeful suffering of the children of God
8:18	a. The thesis concerning present suffering in view of future glory
	1) The formula for a statement of a thesis
	2) The subject of present sufferings
	3) The contention of incomparability with future glory
	4) The locus of glory in the future status of believers
8:19-27	b. The explanation of hopeful suffering in the context of a groaning creation
8:19-23	1) The cosmic context of suffering
8:19-21	a) The yearning of creation for redemption
8:19	(1) The creation yearns for human redemption
8:20	(2) The incompleteness of creation itself
	(a) The creation subjected to futility
	(b) The rationale of divine subjection in hope
8:21a	(3) The creation itself will be redeemed
8:21b	(4) The creation will ultimately contribute to the glory of human liberation
8:22-23	b) Human suffering as part of the creation's yearning for redemption
8:22	(1) Humans are aware of their inclusion in the groaning of creation
8:23a	(2) Even Spirit-filled believers participate in suffering
8:23b	(3) Believers groan for the "redemption of our body"
8:24-25	2) The clarification of hope in an unredeemed world
8:24a	a) Believers are saved in hope
8:24b	b) Hope is defined by the unseen
8:24c	c) Rhetorical question confirming that hope requires lack of sight

---

9   Chang, *Die Knechtschaft*, 81.
10 For this duplication (*epanadiplosis*), see Bullinger, *Figures*, 249.
11 Weiss, "Beiträge," 237, prints out the five lines but does not comment on the correspondence with the preceding sequence.
12 The traditional punctuation of a period at the end of v. 28 hinders the grasp of the larger unit of thought contained in this fivefold climax discerned

by Michel, 276. A period at this point also has the disadvantage of isolating v. 28 from its eschatological context.
13 Paul Holloway identifies this verse as a formal *sententia* in "Paul's Pointed Prose," 50.
14 Harvey, *Listening*, 197, limits the climax to the verbal reiterations of vv. 29-30.

Exegesis

■ **18** The climactic, argumentative phase of the second proof is introduced by λογίζομαι γάρ, translated as "For I reckon" and implying the result of an "act of thought according to strict logical rules."[15] Although used elsewhere in Romans, this is the only occurrence in the first person singular.[16] In this case, Paul offers the "judgment of faith,"[17] conveying "a firm conviction reached by rational thought on the basis of the gospel."[18] Although some commentators tend to depreciate or qualify the rational implications of this usage,[19] Paul is operating out of the restored rationality provided by Christ, which overcomes the deluded reasoning of the old age (Rom 1:21-22). Such reasoning in the classical Greek tradition includes comparing and contrasting, in this instance by means of the logical term ἄξιος ("weighing as much as, equivalent, worth").[20] For example, Agamemnon berates his Greek warriors: νῦν δ᾽ οὐδ᾽ ἑνὸς ἄξιοί εἰμεν Ἕκτορος ("we together are not the worth of one Hector!").[21] For Paul, the sufferings experienced by the believers "are not equivalent in comparison with the glory" yet to be revealed, for the weight of such glory is incalculably immense.

The reference to the sufferings "of the present critical time" employs the expression found in 3:26, τὸ νῦν καιρός, representing the eschatological period inaugurated by Christ.[22] Although commentators note that the sufferings to be experienced by the saints in the escha-

15 Hans-Wolfgang Heidland, "λογίζομαι, λογισμός," *TDNT* 4 (1967) 284.

16 The expression appears several times in Demosthenes *2 Philip.* 20.6, εἰ μὲν ὀρθῶς λογίζομαι ("if I reckon correctly"), and *2 Philip.* 6.8, ἐγὼ τοίνυν, ὦ ἄνδρες Ἀθηναῖοι λογίζομαι ("I accordingly, O Athenian men, am taking into consideration"); see also Demosthenes *Orat.* 15.11.3; 19.59.1; 23.2.5; also Aeschines *Tim.* 152.10; Isocrates *Ep. 4* 9.1.

17 Heidland, "λογίζομαι, λογισμός," 288.

18 Cranfield, 1:408.

19 See Barth, 303; Dunn, 1:468.

20 See Werner Foerster, "ἄξιος κτλ.," *TDNT* 1 (1964) 379–80; Balz, *Heilsvertrauen*, 93–95, argues that the expression ἄξιος πρός appeared infrequently in classical literature and reflects Hebraic usage and later rabbinic terminology. However, a *TLG* search

indicates that while there are no parallels in the LXX, there are significant classical Greek parallels to the idiom ἄξιος πρός ("worthwhile in respect of"), including Plato *Leg.* 850b6, "if he happens to be worthy in respect of (ἀξίῳ πρός) doing good for the city"; Plutarch *E Delph.* 319e9, "it is not worthy in respect of these matters (οὐκ ἄξιον πρός ταῦτα) to argue too precisely"; Plutarch *Luc.* 33.2.7, "he thought them not equivalent (ἄξιος πρός) as compared with himself"; also Aristotle *Mun.* 391b2; Herodotus *Hist.* 5.20.17; Strabo *Geogr.* 1.2.1.33; Posidonius *Frag.* 127.9; Dio Chrysostom *Orat.* 1.57.2; 11.150.5; Dio Cassius *Hist. Rom.* 37.10.1.2; Epictetus *Ench.* 36.1.2, 4.

21 Homer *Il.* 8.234.

22 See Neuhäusler, "Entscheidende Augenblick," 4–8; Jörg Baumgarten, "καιρός," *EDNT* 2 (1991) 233.

ton was a traditional motif,[23] they tend to overlook the contextual implications this formulation would have had for the Roman believers who had already experienced harassment and deportation and whose everyday life as members of the Roman underclass was anything but idyllic.[24] Paul's formulation simply assumes, without arguing the point, that the Caesarean view about the presence of a peaceful, magically prosperous golden age is illusory. In the *Fourth Eclogue* 11–41 a regent had been prophesied who would restore the golden age of paradise, when the earth would produce its plenty without any human work, and when the blight of human impiety would no longer pollute the earth.[25] In the light of Virgil's later support of Augustus, this prophecy was thought to have been fulfilled when he assumed a virtually "messianic" role:[26]

> And in your consulship . . . shall this glorious age begin . . . under your sway, any lingering traces of our guilt shall become void, and release the earth from its continual dread. . . . But for you, child, shall the earth untilled pour forth. . . . Uncalled, the goats shall bring home their udders swollen with milk, and the herds shall fear not huge lions. . . . The serpent, too, shall perish, and the false poison-plant shall perish; Assyrian spice shall spring up on every soil. . . . the earth shall not feel the harrow, nor the vine the pruning-hook; the sturdy ploughman, too, shall now loose his oxen from the yoke.

In Virgil's *Aen.* 6.789–94, the link with the reigning Augustus becomes explicit: "here is Caesar and all of Iulus' progeny, coming beneath the revolving heaven. This man, this is he, whom you often hear promised to you, Augustus Caesar, son of a god, who will establish once more . . . the Golden Age in the fields once ruled by Saturn." Calpurnius Siculus, whose *Eclogue* was composed in Neronian times, provides a similarly idyllic vision:

> Rejoice, first of all, dwellers in the forests, rejoice, O my people. Though all your flocks wander without a guardian, and the shepherd neglect to close them in at night . . . , yet no thief shall lay his traps near the sheep-fold nor loosen the tethers of the beasts of burden to drive them off. The golden age of untroubled peace is born again, and kindly Themis returns to earth freed from stain and rust. The happy times are ruled by a youth [i.e. Nero] who won the victory while still in his mother's arms. When he shall himself reign as a god. . . . Peace will appear . . . and clemency has broken in pieces the weapons of madness. . . . Full peace will come upon us, a peace that . . . shall bring back a second reign of Saturn.[27]

---

23 See, e.g., Schlier's discussion (257) based on *4 Ezra* 13.16-19; *2 Bar.* 25.1-3; *2 Thess* 1:4. Dunn, 1:468–69, provides an extensive response to Sanders's contention that the doctrine of the suffering of the saints prior to the arrival of the reign of God is rare prior to 135 C.E. Dunn cites Dan 7:21-22, 25-27; 12:1-3; *Jub.* 23.22-31; *T. Mos.* 5–10; 1QH 3:28-36; *Sib. Or.* 3.632-56 and Matt 3:7-12 and parallels in support of the contention that "Paul is taking over an earlier eschatological schema" in this verse. Walther Bindemann's claim in *Die Hoffnung der Schöpfung: Römer 8,18-27 und die Frage einer Theologie der Befreiung von Mensch und Natur* (NStB 14; Neukirchen: Neukirchener Verlag, 1983) 82–95, that Paul is polemicizing here against an apocalyptic scheme stressing the distance of God seems strained.

24 Dieter Georgi, "Upside Down," 155, states that Rom 8 differs from Roman views of the "idyllic" quality of nature.

25 Andreas Anföldi, "Der neue Weltherrscher der vierten Ekloge Vergils," *Herm* 65 (1930) 369–85, esp. 369, analyzed the propaganda of the divine ruler who will emerge to redeem Rome from its decline and restore paradisiacal conditions of plenty on the earth.

26 Hildebrecht Hommel, "Vergils 'messianisches' Gedicht," in H. Hommel, *Sebasmata: Studien zur antiken religionsgeschichte und zum frühen Christentum* (Tübingen: Mohr Siebeck, 1983) 1:267–72, shows that the poem was written in 41 B.C.E. during the period of uncertainty and revolution and that the redeemer child born in the poem was originally the son of the consul Asenius Pollio, Virgil's patron (303); apparently it was only later that it was applied to Augustus.

27 Calpurnius Siculus *Ecl.* 1.33–99; see also Aratus *Phaen.* 100-36; Ovid, *Metam.* 1.89–112.

Paul cuts through this propagandistic nonsense to refer directly to the παθήματα ("passions, sufferings") suffered by the Roman believers, employing the plural form typical of Pauline usage (2 Cor 1:5, 6, 7; Gal 5:24; Phil 3:10; Col 1:24), referring to the sufferings that believers should expect in following a suffering Christ.[28] This wording follows up on the idea of suffering together with Christ that I analyzed in 8:17. While the entire fallen world is subject to τὰ παθήματα τῶν ἁμαρτιῶν ("sinful passions") of 7:5, these particular sufferings are a sign of eschatological solidarity with Christ.

The expression τὴν μέλλουσαν δόξαν should be translated in the adjectival sense of "the future glory" rather than linking the participle with the verb to depict the close proximity of "about to be revealed."[29] Paul used a similar expression in Gal 3:23, τὴν μέλλουσαν πίστιν ἀποκαλυφθῆναι ("the future faith to be revealed"), indicating that such faith became available only in the future.[30] To follow Chrysostom in speculating about the degree to which such glory was already present, albeit in concealed form,[31] or to infer from the typical use of μέλλειν to substitute for future verbal forms that Paul implies some degree of certainty in the eschatological fulfillment,[32] would read too much into this simple expression of futurity. I find it particularly significant, however, that Paul uses the expression "to be revealed" in a manner parallel to the thesis of Romans,[33] conveying an apocalyptic disclosure of the triumph of God over adversity and the corruption of the cosmic order. Despite the illusions of the Roman civic cult, the originally intended glory of the creation shall yet be restored, including specifically the glory humans were intended to bear.

The phrase εἰς ἡμᾶς, which ends the verse, could be translated "for us," implying that the glory is "to be bestowed upon us, so that we become the actual partakers; it is not a glory of which we are to be mere spectators,"[34] and in contrast to imperial claims, it is not a glory that shines from the head of Caesar alone.[35] The concept of "glory" implied in this passage is quite distant from the classical Greek sense of opinion, reputation, or renown ascribed by public opinion; it is closely related to the Hebrew sense of כבוד/δόξα as innate weightiness, honor, beauty, fiery presence, splendor, or power.[36] As in Roman usage, glory had a "physical realness" and was "sharply reified."[37] This term is comparable to what moderns refer to as "stardom," the innate capacity some people have to perform with inspiration, to be intensely attractive, and to shine beyond others. The Hebrew term plays a crucial role in OT thought,[38] being used two hundred times to portray such themes as royal or divine power (Isa 14:18; Hos 9:11; Pss 24:8; 29:3), the fiery radiance flowing from the tent of meeting (Exod 40:34; Lev 9:23-24), from Mount Sinai (Exod 24:16-17), or from the temple (2 Chr 7:1; Isa 6:3-4; Ezek 10:4; 43:2). The "glory of God" therefore has the concrete meaning of "a fiery phenomenon issuing from radiance and brilliance, and an abstract meaning of honor, worthiness, and majesty."[39] Human beings were created to reflect such glory (Ps 8:1, 5-6), which is particularly visible in the wise, and is symbolized throughout the ancient Near East by the royal crown or diadem.[40] When persons or nations become corrupt and fall, they lose their glory (Hos 4:7; 9:11; Jer 2:11; Ezek 24:25), but when Yahweh redeems them, their glory is restored (Isaiah 35:1-2). The connection in Rom 8:18 between "revelation" and the restoration of "glory" is derived from a major stream of prophetic and postexilic expectations. Isa 24:23 foresees

28   See Wilhelm Michaelis, "πάθημα," TDNT 5 (1967) 930–34.
29   BAGD, 501.
30   See Betz, Galatians, 176. In a similar vein, though in the distant past, Josephus Ant. 1.202.3 refers to the warning to Lot of "the future destruction (τὴν μέλλουσαν ἀπώλειαν) by God of the Sodomites"; see also Ant. 11.233.5; Bell. 2.288.1.
31   See Cranfield, 1:409–10.
32   See Wilckens, 2:151; Dunn, 1:468.
33   See Dunn, 1:470.
34   Murray, 1:301; also Newman and Nida, 157.

35   Anföldi, "Weltherrscher," 376–77, describes coins in which Caesar with light streaming from his head stands with his foot on the globe while he holds in his hands the symbols of the "return of the golden age," including the cornucopia, the symbol of magical, earthly plentitude.
36   See Gerhard Kittel, "δόξα," TDNT 2 (1964) 233–51, esp. 247; Keesmaat, Paul, 98–102.
37   Lendon, Empire of Honour, 47.
38   See Weinfeld, "כבוד," TWAT 4 (1982) 23–40.
39   Ibid., 38.
40   Ibid., 30–31.

the time "when the Lord will reign on Mount Zion and in Jerusalem, and before his elders he will reveal his glory." As Weinfeld has shown, this expectation reflects Exod 24:9-10, where Yahweh revealed himself to the elders at Mount Sinai.[41] Deutero-Isaiah foresaw a universal extension of this idea in 40:5, "then the glory of Yahweh shall be revealed, and all flesh shall see it together." The revelation of divine radiance and glory, to be seen by all the nations, is also expressed in Isa 60:1-3, which reiterates the theophanic vision of Deut 33:2 and Hab 3:3-4, a vision that will one day "fill the whole world" (Isa 6:3; Num 14:21; Ps 72:19), thus demonstrating God's triumph over evil.[42]

In the light of this background and of Paul's argument concerning the present experience of faith in the midst of suffering, it seems inappropriate to restrict "glory" in this passage to a future state of "immortality" to be enjoyed by the saints.[43] As will become clear in v. 30 with the past tense verb "he glorified," Paul intends the beleaguered believers in Rome to discern in the growing triumph of the gospel the initial evidence of this glory, which will one day fill the creation. In the glowing faces around the circle of early Christian love feasts, the proleptic evidence of this restoration could be seen.

■ **19** Paul explains the cosmic scope of divine glory by reintroducing the concept of κτίσις ("creation"), probably referring primarily to the various nonhuman components of the universe.[44] In contrast to Greco-Roman views of the eternal Mother Earth,[45] the word implies purposeful creation of the natural order by God at a particular moment in time. The biblical creation stories are in view, but in contrast to Genesis, there is a striking measure of personification that may have been influenced by the Roman depictions such as the great Ara Pacis monument in Rome in which the earth is depicted as a female figure sitting with "two children and pomegranates, grapes and nuts on her lap; in front of her a cow and a sheep."[46] The personified image Paul employs is given the mood of ἀποκαραδοκία ("eager expectation"), also employed for humans in Phil 1:20. This word, attested for the first time in Paul,[47] conveys a positive connotation of "confident expectation,"[48] very much in contrast to the reclining depictions of Mother Earth in the Augustan Altar of Peace, which was emulated all over the empire.[49] The attitude is contrasting, but the personification is similar.[50] This personification of creation is also parallel to what Olle Christoffersson has detected in an apocalyptic treatment of the flood tradition (*1 En.* 7.6) where the earth takes on human quali-

41   Ibid., 36.

42   See ibid., 37.

43   See Byrne, *Sons*, 107, following Siber, *Mit Christus*, 150f. Similarly, Fitzmyer, 506, restricts glory to that which will occur "in the *eschaton*."

44   In Rom 1:20-25 κτίσις referred to all created things, including birds, reptiles, and humans. But Wilckens, 2:152–53, and Cranfield, 1:411–12, advance compelling arguments that neither non-Christian believers nor the angelic forces are implied in the formulation of 8:19. See also Brinkman, "Creation II," 367–68, and Chang, *Die Knechtschaft*, 85–90. Gibbs, *Creation and Redemption*, 40, argues that κτίσις in v. 19 refers to "all of creation," including human beings.

45   See Ilona Opelt, "Erde," *RAC* 5 (1962) 1136–38, who shows that depictions of "Mother Earth" came to center stage on coins and altars in the period of Augustus and his successors.

46   Beard et al., *Religions of Rome*, 204, discussing fig. 4.6; see also David Castriota, *The Ara Pacis Augustus and the Imagery of Abundance in Later Greek and Early Roman Imperial Art* (Princeton: Princeton Univ. Press, 1995) 141–44.

47   See Georg Bertram, "Ἀποκαραδοκία," *ZNW* 49 (1958) 138–40, confirmed by Hae-Kyung Chang, "(ἀπο)καραδοκία bei Paulus und Aquila," *ZNW* 93 (2002) 271–73.

48   D. R. Denton, "Ἀποκαραδοκία," *ZNW* 73 (1982) 139, in contrast to Bertram's problematic argument from etymology (138–40) that the term carries a sense of anxious waiting. Bertram's case was accepted by Schlier, 259, and Wilckens, 2:152. As noted by Deissmann, *Light*, 374 n. 5, a verbal form of the word that lacks any sense of anxiety appears in Polybius *Hist.* 18.31, "to expect earnestly (ἀποκαραδοκεῖν) the arrival of Antiochus." Chang, "(ἀπο)καραδοκία," 270–71, confirms Denton's stress on confidence.

49   See Beard et al., *Religions of Rome*, 331.

50   Chang, *Die Knechtschaft*, 100, notes the significant element of personification in Paul's use, but draws no comparison with the Roman civic cult.

ties as it lays accusation against its abusers:[51] τότε ἡ γῆ ἐνέτυχεν κατὰ τῶν ἀνόμων ("then the earth made accusation against the outlaws"). This idea of the natural world eagerly awaiting its own redemption reflects an ancient view of the world as a living organism. Paul implies that the entire creation waits with baited breath for the emergence and empowerment of those who will take responsibility for its restoration, small groups of the υἱοὶ τοῦ θεοῦ ("sons of God")[52] which the mission envisioned by Romans hopes to expand to the end of the known world, that is, to Spain. These converts take the place of Caesar in the imperial propaganda about the golden age,[53] but they employ no weapons to vanquish foes. When Paul speaks of their "revelation/unveiling," there is a clear reference to God's glory advancing in the world, in this instance, through the triumph of the gospel. As the children of God are redeemed by the gospel, they begin to regain a rightful dominion over the created world (Gen 1:28-30; Ps 8:5-8); in more modern terms, their altered lifestyle and revised ethics begin to restore the ecological system that had been thrown out of balance by wrongdoing (1:18-32) and sin (Rom 5–7). In contrast to the civic cult, Paul does not have a magical transformation of nature in view. For example, David Castriota describes the imagery on the Altar of the Augustan Peace created by Augustus in Rome as symbolizing "the return of this lost age of bounty and goodness" that had pertained in the mythical "golden age."[54] In Paul Zanker's view, the altar portrays a supernatural world in which plants are larger than life and animals live in peace with one another.[55] This magical new world

had allegedly been ushered in by Caesar Augustus's triumph over his enemies.

The background of Paul's idea of the fall and redemption of nature is surveyed by Donald Gowan, who shows that the apocalyptic writers remain largely within the biblical parameters.[56] Like other biblical scholars, Gowan does not take account of the peculiar kind of Roman new age ideology that provides the foil for Romans. In Paul's case the avenue of divine action is the conversion of humans rather than their colonization under a ruler pretending to be a god. In Paul's case the avenue of divine action is the conversion of humans. So what the creation awaits with eager longing is the emergence of this triumph of divine righteousness (cf. Rom 1:17), which will begin to restore a rightful balance to the creation once again, overcoming the Adamic legacy of corruption and disorder that fell as a calamitous curse upon the ground (Gen 3:17-19). Paul concentrates on the transformed children of God rather than on specific actions and policies they may be led to follow in carrying out the ethic of transformation (Rom 12:1-2); he assumes that the renewed mind of such groups will be able to discern what God wills for the ecosystem. So the eager longing of the creation awaits the appearance of such transformed persons,[57] knowing that the sources of ecological disorder will be addressed by them in due season. Here as in many other portions of this letter, scholars have refrained from thinking through the implications of Paul's argument because they failed to take the missional context into account. The very barbarians that Rome believed it must subdue in order to bring

---

51   Olle Christoffersson, *The Earnest Expectation of the Creature: The Flood-Tradition as Matrix of Romans 8:18-27* (Stockholm: Almqvist & Wiksell, 1990) 120.

52   Fitzmyer, 507, states the widely shared consensus: "'the revelation of the sons of God' refers to glorified Christians. . . ." Chang, *Die Knechtschaft*, 101–8, concentrates on the gathering of believers in the eschaton. Christoffersson's suggestion in *Earnest Expectation*, 120–24, that the "sons of God" are the angelic powers widely discussed in apocalyptic literature does not comport well with the references to the "sonship" of believers in Rom 8:15 and 23. His study helps to highlight the fact that Paul places believers in the role of the redemptive angels of *1 En.* and elsewhere. Mark D. Baker and J. Ross Wagner, "'The righteousness of God' and Hurricane Mitch: Reading Romans in Hurricane-

Devasted Honduras," in Khiok-khng Yeo, ed., *Navigating Romans Through Cultures: Challenging Readings by Charting a New Course* (New York/London: T.&T. Clark International, 2004) 118, report that Honduran Christians inferred "that God holds human beings responsible in the here and now for how they take care of creation."

53   See, e.g., Maier, "Imperial Iconography," 403–6.
54   Castriota, *Ara Pacis Augustus*, 125.
55   Zanker, *Power of Images*, 178, 182.
56   Donald E. Gowan, "The Fall and Redemption of the Material World in Apocalyptic Literature," *HBT* 7 (1985) 83–103.
57   See Bindemann, *Hoffnung*; and Vögtle, *Zukunft*, 193–96; idem, *Röm 8:19-22: eine schöpfungstheologische oder anthropologisch-soteriologische Aussage?* (Gembloux: Duculot, 1970) 351–66. For a skeptical

about the golden age are the persons to whom Paul feels "obligated" (Rom 1:14) in this proclamation of the new form of world transformation.

■ **20** The explanation of creation's yearning for redemption is provided by allusion to the Genesis story, where the perversion of the originally good and glorious garden commenced. In this myth, it is the progenitor of the entire human race who was responsible for the corruption of the garden, not the enemies of Roman imperialism. The use of the divine passive, ὑπετάγη ("was subjected"), points to God's action in response to Adam's fall.[58] A magical spell apparently influenced by Jewish ideas uses this same language: "I adjure you by the [holy] and honored name to whom all creation is subjugated (ἡ πᾶσα κτίσις [ὑ]πόκειται)."[59] In the Genesis account, the divine curse upon the ground resulted in its producing "thorns and thistles," causing chronic frustration symbolized by the "sweat" on the face of Adam's descendants (Gen 3:17-19). In this powerful symbolization, humans trying to play God ended up ruining not only their relations with each other but also their relation to the natural world. The Roman myth system claimed the exact opposite: that a ruler who plays god can restore the world to a paradisiacal condition by his piety and military dominance.

Paul's choice of the term ματαιότης ("emptiness, vanity, fruitlessness") in the emphatic position at the head of the sentence[60] to depict this situation would have led his hearers to think of the somber dictum of Ecclesiastes, which portrays this same dilemma: ματαιότης ματαιοτήτων, εἶπεν ὁ Ἐκκλησιαστής, ματαιότης ματαιοτήτων, τὰ πάντα ματαιότης ("'Vanity of vanities,' says the Preacher, 'vanity of vanities, all is vanity,'" Eccl 1:2).

This dilemma is more basic than the resultant "corruption" to be mentioned in Rom 8:21.[61] Given the use of ματαιόω ("make vain, empty") in Rom 1:21 to describe the frustration and destructiveness of persons or groups who suppress the truth and refuse to recognize God, it seems likely that Paul has in mind the abuse of the natural world by Adam and his descendants.[62] The basic idea is that the human refusal to accept limitations ruins the world.[63] By acting out idolatrous desires to have unlimited dominion over the garden, the original purpose of the creation—to express divine goodness (Gen 1:31) and reflect divine glory (Ps 19:1-4)—was emptied.[64] As in Eccl 2:1-17, it is the drive for fame, prestige, and immortal achievement that evacuates the goodness and glory of the creation and piles up endless frustrations in the human interaction with the natural environment, symbolized in Genesis by the "thorns and thistles" (Gen 3:18). With such clear allusions to this biblical tradition, Paul's audience could well have thought about how imperial ambitions, military conflicts, and economic exploitation had led to the erosion of the natural environment throughout the Mediterranean world, leaving ruined cities, depleted fields, deforested mountains, and polluted streams as evidence of this universal human vanity. That such vanity, enhanced by the Roman civic cult, was promising the restoration of the "golden age," "the age of Saturn," appears utterly preposterous in the light of this critical, biblical tradition.

---

appraisal of the significance of the cosmological dimension of Paul's argument, see Baumgarten, *Paulus*, 171–74.

58   See the discussion in Wilckens, 2:154; Murray, 1:303, refers to this verse as "Paul's commentary on Gen. 3:17, 18." Dunn, 1:470, observes that there is "now general agreement" on this point.

59   *PGM* XII.85; see also XIII.745. A clear indication of Jewish influence in this magical spell is the use of κτίσις for creation, a term normally restricted to the colonization of cities. In Naveh and Shaked, *Magic Spells*, Nr. 16, pp. 43–49, the verb כבש, the exact equivalent of the Greek verb ὑποτάσσομαι ("subdue"), refers to seasonal barrenness, which apparently was thought to derive from the curse following Adam's fall.

60   Newman and Nida, 159.

61   See Schlier's critique (260–61) of the exegetical consensus of most ancient and modern commentators who argue for the essential identity of "vanity" and "corruption." He mentions Ambrosiaster, Theodoret, Augustine, Aquinas, Bisping, Schmidt, Althaus, Lietzmann, and Michel; to this list one could add Chrysostom, Jülicher, Lipsius, Zahn, Kühl, and others; see Kuss, 3.626.

62   Gibbs, *Creation and Redemption*, 42–43.

63   Chang, *Die Knechtschaft*, 110–12, argues for "nothingness" and "perishability" in the physical sense, but the degree to which humans are responsible for this remains unclear.

64   Cranfield, 1:413, refers to the creation "not being able properly to fulfill the purpose of its existence."

The somewhat awkward qualification that the futility of the nonhuman creation was οὐχ ἑκοῦσα ("not willingly, voluntarily") makes clear that Paul does not subscribe to a gnostic view of the world as innately frustrating and evil.[65] The fall of nature was "not through its own fault,"[66] because it is the human race that remains responsible for the defacing of the ecosystem.[67] Paul had used this classic term for free will in Phlm 14, describing his preference for the slave-owner to act voluntarily rather than under compulsion: "in order that your good deed might not be done out of necessity but out of free will (κατὰ ἑκούσιον)." Here Paul continues the personified manner of speaking about nature, as if it would have preferred not to participate in the sinful futility caused by Adam and Eve and their descendants. The contrast with "voluntarily" is διὰ τὸν ὑποτάξαντο, ἐφ' ἐλπίδι ("on account of the one who subjected it—in hope"), clearly referring to God's curse against the land in response to human sin.[68] We find the same idea derived from Genesis in *4 Ezra* 7.1, "And when Adam transgressed my statutes, what had been made was judged." A later rabbi expressed the same idea: "Although things were created in their fullness, when the first man sinned they were corrupted, and they will not come back to their order before Ben Perez (the Messiah) comes."[69] The curse thus remains provisional, awaiting the dawn of a new age when nature will be restored to its original beauty and glory. The expression ἐφ' ἐλπίδι ("in hope/anticipation") was used by Paul in Rom 5:2 with specific reference to overcoming suffering. The "hope" in this passage, to be elaborated in 8:21, is

that the human race, which had defaced the world, would be redeemed and would begin to participate in removing the curse from the land.[70] Paul's wording makes it absolutely clear that such redemption is a matter of future hope and not a present political reality, as the Roman civic cult was maintaining.

■ **21** In view of the causal διότι ("because") that introduces this sentence, it explains why the entire creation was marked by "hope."[71] That the realm of nonhuman creation "itself will also be set free"[72] from the Adamic distortion was a significant theme in Jewish prophetism and apocalypticism,[73] which articulate in a contrasting manner some of the themes in the Roman expectation. Isaiah's vision of a messianic future includes both a king who will restore righteousness among humans (Isa 11:4-5) and a restoration of Edenic conditions between animals and humans (Isa 11:6-9; 65:17, 25; 66:22). *Jubilees* envisions the time when "the heavens and the earth shall be renewed" (1.29). *1 Enoch* speaks of regaining access to the "fragrant tree" on the seventh mountain, which restores the joy and long life of Eden (chaps. 24–25; see also 91.16-17), while the *Testament of Levi* anticipates a messianic priest who "shall open the gates of paradise, and shall remove the threatening sword against Adam. And he shall give to the saints to eat from the tree of life, and the spirit of holiness shall be on them" (18.10–11). *4 Ezra* 13.26 expects the messianic "Man from the Sea" to "deliver his creation" from the perils of violence. The *Sibylline Oracles* predict a time after the day of judgment and the arrival of a just empire when the earth will once again become "the uni-

---

Schlier's explanation (260) is so subtly existential, with the creation absolutizing itself just as humans do, that the causative link between human sin and ecological futility is rendered obscure.

65 Wilson, *Gnosis and the New Testament,* 49, appears to leave this question open.

66 Cranfield, 1:414; Chang, *Die Knechtschaft,* 113–14.

67 See Brinkman, "Creation II," 369.

68 It is implausible to suggest that either Adam or Satan may be identified as the "one subjecting it in hope," because neither can be understood as acting "in hope." See Kuss, 3:627–28; Chang, *Die Knechtschaft,* 113–25.

69 Cited by Käsemann, 233, from *Gen. Rab.* 12.6.

70 See Leenhardt, 125–26.

71 Chang, *Die Knechtschaft,* 127.

72 The emphatic καὶ αὐτή ("also itself") explicitly includes nature in the redemptive process, rendering implausible Barrett's comment (165) that Paul "is not concerned with creation for its own sake." Colenso, 180, restricts his attention to the human dimension of creation, that "the faithful and true of all ages, all lands, all religions, will be 'revealed,' will receive their 'glorious freedom' in the Kingdom of their Lord."

73 Gowan's survey in "Fall and Redemption," 100–102, concludes that apocalyptic literature echoes but does not extensively develop the biblical theme.

versal mother who will give to mortals her best fruit in countless store of corn, wine and oil. . . . And the cities shall be full of good things and the fields rich" (*Sib. Or.* 3.744–45, 750–51). The *Oracles* reiterate Isaiah's vision of wolves and lambs eating grass together, with no creature harming others (*Sib. Or.* 3.788–95).

Paul's version of this Edenic hope features the converted "children of God" (Rom 8:19) in place of the righteous king, priest, or empire whose ministration would overturn the Adamic curse. Although the future tense of the verb Paul selects, ἐλευθερωθήσεται ("it will be freed"), clearly correlates with the "revelation of the sons of God" in v. 19,[74] the inference is rarely drawn concerning the means by which God intends to restore the natural world. Schlier is exceptional in referring to the "responsibility that Christians have not only for themselves but also for the realm of pure creatureliness."[75] Overcoming ecological disorder is depicted here as a divine gift enacted as a result of God's restoration of humanity to its position of rightful dominion, reflecting God's intended glory. In the place of the single figure of a glorious Caesar, the glory proclaimed by Paul will be shared by every converted person, whether slave or free, male or female, Roman or barbarian. As Michel points out, "bondage stands in opposition to freedom, corruption to glory"[76] in this passage. The term φθορά ("corruption, decay, destruction") refers to the conse-

quence of the perverse "vanity" of the human race, namely, the disruption and death of natural ecological systems.[77] This occurs in a process that takes a course of its own, thwarting human efforts at dominion and producing a veritable "bondage to corruption."[78]

A correlative inference is drawn in v. 21b, that the restored creation will serve the purpose of the liberation of the children of God. This is a puzzling reversal, because on the basis of v. 19, it had appeared that the revelation of such liberation on the part of the redeemed would become the divinely appointed agency for the restoration of nature. But if the achievement of τὴν ἐλευθερίαν τῆς δόξης ("liberation consisting of glory")[79] is understood in terms of humans regaining a proper dominion over the creation, participating responsibly in the "righteousness of God," whose scope is cosmic (see Rom 1:17), this corollary is understandable. For Paul it is inconceivable that humans could exercise any absolute form of liberation related only to themselves.[80] Freedom must be responsibly embodied in the real world as the "new creation" manifests itself in the lives and actions of believers.[81] Paul's premise is that humans and the creation are interdependent and that human fulfillment is contextual and cosmic.[82] Murray states the theological corollary that "the glory of the people of God will be in the context of the restitution of all things" (cf. Acts 3:21).[83] Despite the interpretive diffi-

---

74 Cranfield, 1:415.

75 Schlier, 262–63, restricts this responsibility to the arena of a proper existential attitude toward nature, refraining from any discussion of ethical responsibility.

76 Michel, 268.

77 Traugott Holtz, "φθείρω κτλ.," *EDNT* 3 (1993) 422–23, shows that φθορά can convey corruption or destruction and that in Rom 8:21, the emphasis is on "perishability." "Corruption" is preferred by Meyer, 2:77; Schlier, 262; "decay/corruption" in Cranfield, 1:415, Fitzmyer, 504, and Dunn, 1:465, 472.

78 I take the second genitive in the phrase ἀπὸ τῆς δουλείας τῆς φθορᾶς as an objective genitive, "from the bondage to corruption," following Lipsius, 139, who refers to corruption as "a ruling power." For arguments in favor of a genitive of quality, see Günther Harder, "φθείρω κτλ.," *TDNT* 9 (1974) 104; and Morris, 322.

79 See Cranfield's argument (1:415–16) against the

adjectival construal of τῆς δόξης ("of glory"); he wishes to preserve the correspondence with the phrase "bondage to corruption" in v. 21a and to retain the dependence of the genitive τῶν τέκνων ("of the children") on the adjacent word "glory" rather than on the more distant word "freedom." The genitive "of glory" thus becomes epexegetical, "liberty-resulting-from-glory." Newman and Nida, 160, suggest instead "the glorious freedom."

80 See Vollenweider, *Freiheit*, 331–36, 402–6.

81 See Vollenweider's argument in *Freiheit*, 386–88, that freedom in this passage is both a present and a future reality.

82 Gibbs, *Creation and Redemption*, 41. See also Chang, *Die Knechtschaft*, 140, who concludes "that in any event the redemption of humans cannot be conceived without the redemption of the non-human creation."

83 Murray, 1:305.

culties in understanding v. 21b, it provides a barrier against the chronic individualizing of salvation that has marked the tradition of Pauline theology just as it stood against the glorification of Caesar.

■ **22** In vv. 22-23 Paul moves on to place human suffering in the context of the creation's groaning for redemption. As Gerd Theissen observes, "Whereas elsewhere Paul always emphasizes the contradiction between nature and the new man, here he uncovers a profound correspondence—a common longing that joins 'nature' and the Spirit."[84] The wording οἴδαμεν γὰρ ὅτι ("for we know that"; see 2:2; 3:19) makes clear that Paul assumes that the Roman believers are acquainted with the idea of nature's corruption. It had played a decisive role in the Roman civic cult[85] and was explained in another way by the Genesis story. The expression πᾶσα ἡ κτίσις ("the whole creation") includes the entire range of animate and inanimate objects on earth and in the heavens. The personification of creation noted earlier is continued in this verse by the metaphors of groaning and travailing.[86] Once again, the personification stands parallel to Roman usage, but in place of nature's joy at its deliverance through Augustus and his succes-

sors,[87] Paul hears only agonized groans. The verb στενάζω ("cry out, groan"), used here in the compound form of συστενάζω ("cry out, groan together"), appears with a similar meaning in Job 31:38-40, where the link established in Gen 3:17-18 between human sin and the groaning of nature provides the basis for Job's protestation of innocence: "If at any time the land has groaned (ἐστέναζεν) against me, and if its furrows also have mourned together (ἔκλαυσαν ὁμοθυμαδόν), and if I alone have eaten its yield without payment, and if I have grieved the soul of the owner by expropriation, let nettle grow up instead of wheat, brambles instead of barley!" The idea that the earth "languishes," "mourns," and suffers "pollution" under the burden of human exploitation also appears in Isa 24:4-7; Hos 4:1-3; and *4 Ezra* 7.1-4. In the Roman context, it is important to observe that the mourning Paul describes is a present reality. Nothing whatsoever remains of the illusion that the golden age has already arrived and that the whole world rejoices in Caesar's victories.[88]

---

84 Theissen, *Psychological Aspects*, 333.

85 In Hesiod *Op.* 109–201 a theory of decline from an idyllic beginning is sketched, in which human failure is linked with nature's corruption. In contrast to the idyllic golden age, the later ages of silver, bronze, and iron are marked by increasing levels of violence and impiety, when humans lose their superior mental and moral qualities. "The Golden Race disappears for no assigned cause; the Silver because of *hybris* and impiety; the Bronze by internecine war; the Heroes by external war; the Iron by exhaustion, or perhaps because of their evil-doing," as described by Lovejoy and Boas, eds., *Primitivism*, 31. In Virgil *Ecl.* 4.11.41 a regent is prophesied who would restore the golden age of paradise, when the earth would produce its plenty without any human work, and when the blight of human impiety would no longer pollute the earth. Caesar Augustus was thought to have fulfilled this prophecy about the removal of earth's corruption, which would restore earth's magical fecundity:

> And in your counsulship . . . shall this glorious age begin . . . under your sway, any lingering traces of our guilt shall become void, and release the earth from its continual dread. . . . But for you, child, shall the earth untilled pour

forth. . . . Uncalled, the goats shall bring home their udders swollen with milk, and the herds shall fear not huge lions. . . . The serpent, too, shall perish, and the false poison-plant shall perish; Assyrian spice shall spring up on every soil . . . the earth shall not feel the harrow, nor the vine the pruning-hook; the sturdy ploughman, too, shall now loose his oxen from the yoke.

See the discussion of this idea in Castriota, *Ara Pacis Augustus,* 139.

86 See Brinkman, "Creation II," 373.

87 See the note above with the citation from Calpurnius Siculus *Ecl.* 1.33–99, in which Nero's reign calls for global rejoicing: "Rejoice, first of all, dwellers in the forests, rejoice, O my people . . . . The golden age of untroubled peace is born again. . . ." An earlier parallel was identified by Hildebrecht Hommel, "Das Harren der Kreatur (Röm 8,14-25)," in H. Hommel, *Sebasmata: Studien zur antiken Religionsgeschichte und zum frühen Christentum* (Tübingen: Mohr Siebeck, 1983), 1:137, in Virgil *Ecl.* 4.50–52, "See how the arched weight of the universe waves and swings: lands, waves of the sea and the deeps of heavens above! See how everything joyfully awaits the coming world!"

88 See Maier, "Imperial Iconography," 398–99.

The theme of birth pangs is frequently employed as a metaphor for the painful prospect of divine judgment (Isa 13:8; 21:3; 26:17-18; Jer 4:31; 22:23; Hos 13:13; *1 En.* 62:4; 1 Thess 5:3). Both the inevitability of punishment and the happy outcome of the establishment of divine justice, sometimes in the form of the messianic era (Mark 13:8; John 16:21), may be conveyed by this metaphor. A Greco-Roman writer can also refer to the regeneration of nature after the groaning of winter's dormancy: "the groaning earth gives birth in travail to what has been formed within her (ἐπειδὰν ἡ μεμυκυῖα γῆ τὰς κυοφορουμένας ἔνδον ὠδῖνας ἐκφήνῃ)."[89] Paul's usage at this point is somewhat reminiscent of the later rabbinic concept of the "messianic woes,"[90] except that such woes were expected to be intensified in the period just prior to the coming of the messiah, and they were anticipated to fall upon humans rather than on the creation as a whole. The exclusive concentration on humans is also visible when birth pangs are used to depict the suffering of the innocent at the hands of the wicked (1QH 3:7-18) or the painful birth of Israel (Isa 66:7-8).

Paul moves beyond this familiar range of usage in two ways: by imagining nature as a whole undergoing such birth pangs, and by the anaphoric reduplication of συν- ("with"), which brings the expression συστενάζει καὶ συνωδίνει ("groans together and travails together") into a rhetorically unified expression.[91] The first of these verbs recalls Euripides *Ion* 935: ὡς συστενάζειν γ᾽ οἶδα γενναίως φίλοις ("Indeed, I genuinely know now to groan with friends"). In Paul's formulation "together" refers to the shared experience of believers and the creation as a whole, both yearning for the future restoration. There is an unparalleled coherence in this expression that combines the suffering of creation from the time of Adam with a metaphor of hope—travail, the agony that leads to a new birth. In Schlier's words, "All of the pain of the creature in the entire world . . . , is not a proclamation and beginning of death, but of salvation, and all the sighs of the entire world . . . signify its glorification, the glorification of the 'children of God' in the glory of Christ."[92] Paul views the creation as a holistic, interdependent system with a life and development of its own, yet anticipating appropriate human intervention to counter Adam's fall. If the groaning really lasts "until now," this would exclude the Augustan premise that the golden age had been inaugurated by the Saecular Games of 17 B.C.E.,[93] or that Nero had ushered in a "golden age of untroubled peace."[94] The emphatic reference to the "whole" creation and the unique use of the compound verbs with συν- points to the option preferred by Origen, Athanasius, Schlatter, Asmussen, and Lipsius,[95] that human beings along with the rest of creation appear to be included in this groaning; perhaps it would be better to say that these clues provide rhetorical hints at human participation, which becomes explicit in v. 23.[96] The mainstream interpretation rejecting this option[97] aims to improve the logic of Paul's argument by making the wording of v. 22 consistent with v. 19, at the expense of denying its rhetorical suggestiveness for the audience. That the groaning lasts ἄχρι τοῦ νῦν ("until now") echoes the eschatological emphasis of v. 18[98] while

---

Although Chang, *Die Knechtschaft*, 172, does not take the civic cult into account, he aptly observes that believers know that the world is not in order as the creator intended.

89 BAGD 793, from Heraclitus Stoicus *Quest. Hom.* c. 39 p. 58, cited by Fitzmyer, 509, with reference to A.-M. Dubarle, "Le gémissement des créatures dans l'ordre divin du cosmos (Rom 8,19-22)," *RSPhTh* 38 (1954) 445-65.

90 See Schlier, 263–64; Cranfield, 1:416.

91 See particularly Chang, *Die Knechtschaft*, 157–61.

92 Schlier, 264, referring to Paul Claudel's discussion in *Conversations dans le Loir-et-Cher* (Paris: Gallimard, 1935) 255.

93 Beard et al., *Religions of Rome*, 1:203, show that the games organized by Augustus in 17 B.C.E. "marked the birth of a new age" in which the "fertility of Mother Earth" was seen to be restored and "guarded by the Fates and the Goddesses of Child-birth."

94 Cited from Calpurnius Siculus *Ecl.* 1.33–99. See Balch, "Zeus," 72, for a description of Nero's Domus Aurea in which the emperor "represented himself as the Sun, the initiator of a new golden age." See also Griffin, *Nero*, 87–96.

95 See the refutation in Kuss, 3:629.

96 See F. R. Montgomery Hitchcock, "'Every Creature,' Not 'All Creation' in Romans viii. 22," *ExpT* 8 (1916) 372–83.

97 See Kuss, 3:629–36; Dunn, 1:472.

98 Barrett, 166, and Dunn, 1:473, move beyond a verbal echo to contend that this expression conveys a

including the suffering presently experienced and witnessed in the natural world within the painful legacy of the fall.[99]

■ **23** That believers are included in the suffering of creation, the theme of Rom 8:18, is developed with the contrasting formula οὐ μόνον δέ, ἀλλὰ καί ("not only, but also"),[100] which serves to eliminate any exceptionalism for those who have the supreme gift of the Spirit. I take the participle ἔχοντες in the simple attributive sense of believers "having" the firstfruits of the Spirit, rather than in a strictly causal[101] or concessive[102] sense. The elimination of any exception is emphatically driven home by the repeated αὐτοὶ . . . καὶ αὐτοί ("ourselves . . . even ourselves"), closing the door to the kinds of Christian enthusiasm Paul had earlier encountered in Thessalonica and Corinth, which understood the gift of the Spirit as a form of divinization, rendering believers invulnerable to suffering. This concern probably also explains the expression τὴν ἀπαρχὴν τοῦ πνεύματος ("firstfruits of the Spirit"),[103] a unique Pauline combination of the concept of the firstfruits of the harvest to be dedicated to God[104] and the Christian concept of the

Spirit as the identifying mark of believers.[105] The odd feature of this expression is that "the relationship of giver and recipient is reversed,"[106] since it is not humans who give the firstfruits to God, but God who bestows them on believers. Although the expression "firstfruits of the Spirit" is highly evocative, with numerous implications,[107] Paul's point is that no matter how charismatically they may be endowed, believers continue to participate in the suffering to which the entire world has been subjected as a result of sin. Believers also "groan," with the expression ἐν ἑαυτοῖς specifying the arena as being "within ourselves," in the inner life of individual believers where the tension between the already and the not yet, between the hope of righteousness and the weight of corruption, is most intensely felt. Paul had referred in Rom 5:5 to the heart as the locale of the Spirit's action and in 7:21-24 to the inner conflict that will not be completely set aside until the eschaton; he will go on in 8:26-27 to describe how the Spirit sustains believers in the meanwhile in the secret places of their hearts. By associating the charismatic Spirit with human vulnerability,[108] Paul effectively eliminates any project of

---

unique eschatological emphasis. Chang, *Die Knechtschaft*, 176, moves beyond the semantic range by maintaining that the expression ἄχρι τοῦ νῦν implies "the eschatological dialectic" of the "already" and the "not yet."

99 See Cranfield, 1:417; Wilckens, 2:156.

100 This expression is a favorite of Paul, used in Rom 5:3, 11; 9:10; 2 Cor 7:7; 8:19.

101 Kuss, 3:638, argues for the causal sense, "because we have the firstfruits," following Gutjahr and Bernard Weiss. Dunn, 1:473, follows this course.

102 Käsemann, 237, follows Jülicher's line in arguing that "Christians do not sigh because they do not yet have the Spirit totally but in spite of the fact that they have him. . . ."

103 I feel that the context favors the possessive genitive here, in which the spirit remains the active force of God within believers, a theme elaborated in 8:26-27. Käsemann's advocacy of an epexegetical genitive (237) has a similar implication. The active role of the Spirit is downplayed by the theories of the partitive genitive advocated by Bardenhewer, Bisping, and Lietzmann, implying that the firstfruits are only partially represented by the work of the Spirit; also of a genitive of apposition advocated by Gutjahr, Kühl, Michel, Weiss, Zahn, and Kuss, which identifies the present experience of the spirit as constituting the firstfruits.

104 See the extensive discussion in Dunn, 1:473, citing Deut 12:6; Exod 22:29; 23:19; Lev 2:12; 23:10; Num 15:20; 18:12, 30; Deut 26:2; 2 Chr 31:5; Neh 10:37, 39; Mal 3:8; Judg 11:13. Whether the association of firstfruits with Pentecost, and of Pentecost with the gift of the Spirit, influenced this expression is possible but not demonstrable. See also Ceslas Spicq, "ἀπαρχή," *TLNT* 1 (1994) 151.

105 For the somewhat more distant Greco-Roman parallels to the use of ἀπαρχή ("firstfruit"), see Arrian *Cyn.* 33.1; Theopompus Hist. *Frag.* 2b.115 [F.334.29]; Cornutus *Nat. d.* 55.8; Aelius Aristides Παν. 105.30; 128.1; 188.26; etc.; Porphyry *Abst.* 2.5.6; 2.6.17; etc. See Fitzmyer, 510; Spicq, "ἀπαρχή," 145–46, cites other examples. See also C. C. Oke, "A Suggestion with Regard to Romans 8:23," *Int* 11 (1957) 455–60; and H. Stuart Jones, "ΣΠΙΛΑΣ–ΑΠΑΡΧΗ ΠΝΕΥΜΑΤΟΣ," *JTS* 23 (1922) 282–83. The latter infers from the legal use of ἀπαρχή in Egyptian papyri that it is "the birth-certificate of a free person." The parallels are discussed in Jameson, Jordan, and Kotansky, *Lex Sacra*, 24, 38–39, 64, 69.

106 Gerhard Delling, "ἀπαρχή," *TDNT* 1 (1964) 486.

107 See Dunn, 1:473–74.

108 See Klauck, "Wortlose Seufzen," 92; Schade, *Christologie*, 102–4.

apotheosis such as he had confronted in Corinth. This is highly relevant for the Roman context, whose civic cult centered on the apotheosis of Caesar.

It is rather puzzling at first glance that Paul would refer to "awaiting sonship" as a future fulfillment when he had spoken so clearly in 8:15 of the Spirit confirming the sonship of believers as a present experience. The clue is in his repetition of ἀπεκδέχομαι ("await"), which had been used in v. 19 to refer to awaiting the "revelation of the sons of God."[109] The content of the future hope is that the full and undistorted dominion of God's children will one day manifest itself in the context of a restored creation. Thus, the phrase Paul selects to explain this restoration is τὴν ἀπολύτρωσιν τοῦ σώματος ἡμῶν ("the redemption of our body"), since body is the basis of communicating and interacting with the world.[110] Paul does not hope for "redemption from the body,"[111] or as the peculiar singular reference to "body" seems to suggest, for a resurrection of the body in some individualistic sense of being detached from the creation and its corruptibility,[112] but for a socially transformed corporeality within the context of a transformed creation that is no longer subject to "corruption."[113] Paul's verb ordinarily has a military connotation, referring to the redemption of captives or prisoners of war either by victory or paying a ransom.[114] Whereas in the Roman context only persons with status and means could hope for that kind of redemption, here Paul speaks of all members of the community who share in the groaning as well as in the future release.[115]

The "new creation" of 2 Cor 5:17 and Gal 6:15 is clearly in view here, but not merely in the traditional form of an inaccessible theological ideal, because the guiding metaphor is provided in Rom 8:19, where the disclosure of rightful, future dominion is announced. The sons and daughters of God demonstrate their status by exercising the kind of dominion that heals rather than destroys. Although the tension between the "already" and the "not yet" will not be overcome until the parousia, Paul's purpose is to encourage the Roman believers to begin enacting their sonship and daughtership right now, in refusing to conform to the fallen age, and resolutely acting rightly toward the groaning creation, of which their bodies are a part. The arena for such action was narrower for the members of Roman house and tenement churches than for later Christian communities, probably consisting mainly of the spheres of bodily responsibility in work, family, and congregational life—and, given the purpose of Romans, the sphere of mission. By participating in the Spanish mission, Paul is offering the Romans a concrete opportunity to enact their rightful belongingness to God's family and to contribute to the ultimate restoration of the creation. Given the presumption of powerlessness on the part of

109 This is an instance where the literal language of "sonship" needs to be preserved despite its chauvinistic implications, because if the less offensive term "adoption" is used in 8:15 and 23 as in the NRSV and Dunn, 1:452, 474, the link with "the revelation of the sons of God" in v. 19 is rendered obscure. The translation "adoption" is in any case a secondary choice, since adoption places a person in the category of sonship. For a discussion of the use of υἱοθεσία in the sense of legal adoption, see G. H. R. Horsley, "καθ᾿ υἱοθεσίαν," NDIEC 4 (1987) 173; the reflections of Greek legal practice render implausible Francis Lyall's contention in "Roman Law," 458–66, that Paul's usage reflects an exclusively Roman practice. In "Petition to a Prefect," NDIEC 3 (1982) 16–17, Horsley discusses an alternate term for adoption not used by Paul, τεκνόθεσις, indicating the adoption of a girl.

110 See Jewett, Terms, 218–19; 254–79.
111 See Lietzmann, 85.
112 See the discussion of individual resurrection without the cosmic context in Morris, 324. Some of the older commentaries by Beck, Zahn, Nygren, and Schmidt stress the redemption of individual believers from temptation, corruption, and mortality. See the critique in Schlier, 266.
113 See Ziesler, 222.
114 See Friedrich Büchsel, "ἀπολύτρωσις," TDNT 4 (1967) 351: "to set free for a ransom"; Karl Kertelge, "ἀπολύτρωσις," EDNT 1 (1990) 138: redemption "of prisoners and slaves." The military context is clear in Posidonius Phil. Frag. 213.20; Diodorus Siculus Hist. 37.5.3.
115 Kertelge, "ἀπολύτρωσις," 139, offers an abstraction in place of a contextual explanation that might have arisen out of the consideration of the Roman context: "The completed form of redemption is given when this mortal body is 'further clothed' with that new corporeality which God has prepared for his own (2 Cor 5:1-5; cf. 1 Cor 15:37f)."

the underclass represented by most of the Roman house and tenement churches, such prospects would have appeared grandiose and utterly unrealistic—without the foundation of eschatological hope. However, compared with believing that the Roman gods had already ushered in the golden age through a grandiose world ruler, this hope could lead to a far more realistic form of collective responsibility for the creation.

■ **24** Having established the cosmic context of hopeful suffering, Paul moves on in vv. 24-25 to clarify the nature of hope itself. The expression with a definite article, τῇ γὰρ ἐλπίδι ("for in the hope"), refers to the hope just mentioned in the preceding verse, thus justifying the translation "in this hope,"[116] that is, the hope of fulfilled adoption as children of God and the final redemption of the creation. The use of the aorist passive verb ἐσώθημεν ("we have been saved") is surprising, given Paul's usual reticence in passages such as Rom 5:10; 13:11; 1 Cor 3:15; 5:5; 1 Thess 5:8, where salvation is explicitly reserved for the future.[117] The problem is mitigated, as Dunn argues, by the dialectic between the already and the not yet in the expression "saved in hope,"[118] implying that while salvation has already occurred, its fulfillment remains in the future. But the forthright reference to the salvation of the Roman believers as an accomplished event, probably referring to their response to the gospel,[119] indicates that the theory of an attack on "enthusiasm" is off target.[120] There is no hint of polemic in this passage.[121] To the contrary, the thrust of these two verses is to assure the Roman believers that despite the lack of publicly visible evidence in altered political, economic, or ecological conditions, the rightful dominion of the "children of God" over the creation is coming to pass. Their salvation entails such a hope.

The very definition of hope, Paul argues, requires that its object remain invisible. Recent studies have clarified the apocalyptic background of ἐλπὶς βλεπομένη ("hope seen") as referring to what is currently visible in historical and cosmic circumstances as compared with the future world, which has not yet appeared.[122] What remains unclear is why Paul initiates this discussion of hope, posing the rhetorical question, "for who hopes for what he sees?"[123] which demands the answer, "No one!" The argument seems too self-evident and uncontroversial to be polemical;[124] it seems rather gratuitous as a substantiation of the already proven point that even believers must wait for a future fulfillment.[125] I think that Paul appeals to the understanding of hope shared by Roman believers in order to render more plausible his contention that current sufferings are part of the longing of the creation for the "revelation of the sons of God" in a proper form of dominion over a new creation. Admittedly such dominion is not yet visible, but the Christian stance of hopeful waiting should take this into account even when current experiences of suffering appear to invalidate faith in the triumph of Christ over the principalities and powers.

116 Morris, 324, who refers to a similar translation in the *NIV*. The translation with an instrumental dative, "saved by or through hope," proposed by Zahn and Schlatter, has been refuted by Käsemann, 238; the dative of advantage, "saved for the sake of hope," proposed by Kühl, is also rejected by Käsemann, whose argument in favor of a dative of modality is followed by most current interpreters.

117 See Georg Fohrer, "σώζω," *TDNT* 7 (1971) 992: "Primarily, then, σωτηρία is for Paul a future, eschatological term. . . ."

118 Dunn, 1:475.

119 See Fohrer, "σώζω," 994; Schlier, 266; Moo, 520.

120 Käsemann, 238, resorts to the traditional Lutheran critique of "enthusiasm"; Dunn feels that Käsemann is too "confident" in stressing this point, but follows anyway (1:475); Schade, *Christologie*, 103–4.

121 See Bindemann, *Hoffnung*, 30.

122 See Vögtle, *Zukunft*, 204, for the contrast with the typical Greek concept of hope as uncertain expectation. Nebe points to the apocalyptic background in *Hoffnung*, 51–60, 82–94, followed by Dunn, 1:476.

123 The translation depends, of course, on which of the complicated text-critical options one follows; see note j above. I follow Cranfield, 1:420, in placing an acute accent on τίς, which then reads "who" rather than "someone" (τις), thus producing a rhetorical question.

124 Baumgarten, *Paulus*, 176–77, infers from the difference between Paul's insistence on the invisible future as compared with precise descriptions offered in apocalyptic writings that this passage is "antiapocalyptic," which confuses the issue by inserting an element of polemic in a clearly non-polemical passage.

125 Schlier, 266.

■ **25** The conditional clause, "but if we hope in what we do not see," assumes a negative answer by the audience to the rhetorical question at the end of v. 24, that is: "No, of course no one hopes for what he/she already sees." Paul is confident that the premise of his argument will arouse the assent of the Roman audience. And he had already established in 5:3-5 that the Spirit sustains perseverance in response to persecution, thus producing a firm "character" that remains hopeful because it is certain of God's love in the most adverse of circumstances. Now Paul uses the verb ἀπεκδέχομαι ("await") for the third time in this pericope, indicating that persons of faith remain in the same state of eager anticipation as does the creation, in this case awaiting with a firm and persevering expectation concerning the future that God will provide. In the context of this argument, the word ὑπομονή should be translated as "perseverance" rather than as the largely attitudinal term "patience." There is a close parallel to this prepositional phrase in Heb 12:1: δι᾽ ὑπομονῆς τρέχομεν τὸν προκείμενον ἡμῖν ἀγῶνα ("let us run with endurance the race that is set before us ...").[126]

Although it is appealing to modern interpreters who favor a theology of Christian resignation,[127] Paul had no need to encourage a passive form of waiting for his audience in Rome; indeed the letter as a whole proposes audacious forms of ethical behavior, including joint sponsorship of the mission to Spain. The first use of this term in 2:7 implied the active sense of "persevering [in] good works,"[128] and a similar definition is presupposed in 5:3-4, as I have shown. In the context of a creation groaning for the human race to reassert a righteous form of dominion, ὑπομονή refers to the brave resistance against evil and firm perseverance in doing good that believers demonstrate as they strive toward the goal that God will one day cause to be fully achieved—the "revelation of the sons of God" in a new creation.

■ **26** The active construal of "awaiting with perseverance" in v. 25 provides the basis of the comparison that opens the next subparagraph.[129] "In a similar way also" (ὡσαύτως δὲ καί)[130] does not imply that the Spirit "groans" in futility along with the creation (8:22-23)[131] and does not simply refer back to the Abba cry in vv. 15-16,[132] but is defined by the active verb συναντιλαμβάνεται ("lends assistance"),[133] which occurs elsewhere in the NT only in Luke 10:40. The Spirit "in a similar way also" stands alongside the saints as they persevere, guiding their most decisive intervention into the fallen world, namely, their prayer.[134] While this verb is used in the LXX to refer to humans taking up a portion of each other's work (Exod 18:22; Num 11:17),[135] there is a close parallel to Paul's expression in Ps 89:21, where Yahweh offers to provide aid to his people Israel: ἡ γὰρ χείρ μου συναντιλήψεται αὐτῷ ("my hand will lend him aid").

126 Attridge, *Hebrews*, 355, suggests that this wording implies "that the race is more marathon than short sprint." He notes the use of this term in the martyrological context by 4 Macc 17:10, 12, 17.

127 See Kuss's citation (3:641) of Bardenhewer; Murray, 1:310, amplifies on the virtues of "patient waiting," contrasting it with impatience, which "spells dispute and dissatisfaction with God's design." See also J. Giblet, "De patientia christiana iuxta S. Paulum," *CMech* 40 (1955) 28–30; Th. Deman, "La Thèologie de l'ΥΠΟΜΟΝΗ biblique," *DT*(F) (1932) 2–20.

128 Friedrich Hauck, "ὑπομένω κτλ.," *TDNT* 4 (1967) 587.

129 The argument in this section is adapted from Jewett, "Apportioned Spirit," 193–206.

130 BAGD 899 refers to Strabo *Geogr.* 10.3.10 for an exact parallel to this expression; see also 1.3.10; 3.2.4. The expression occurs twenty-one times in Sextus Empiricus *Math.*; nine times in Plato; twenty times in Pausanias, as well as in Mark 14:31; Luke 20:31.

131 That the verb στενάζω ("groan") should be supplied is advocated by Schlier, 268, and Cranfield, 1:421, but its absence from v. 26a and the awkwardness of placing the divine spirit under the curse of futility render this option implausible.

132 See Lietzmann, 86: "Just as the spirit cries 'Abba' within us, so also it intercedes in prayer for our weakness." For a critique of this view along with other advocates, see Schlier, 268.

133 Deissmann, *Light*, 83, refers to the use of this verb in the LXX, in Josephus, and in inscriptions such as in the temple of Apollo at Delphi (*SIG* 2.250.7), "to lend assistance (συναντιλήψεσθαι) in things profitable unto the city." See also *P.Hib.* 1. Nr. 82.18.

134 See Wink, *Engaging the Powers*, 304–13.

135 See Balz, *Heilsvertrauen*, 71; Schlier, 268, and Wilckens, 2:161.

For Paul, the necessity of such aid is described by the phrase "in our weakness" ($\tau\hat{\eta}\ \dot{\alpha}\sigma\vartheta\epsilon\nu\epsilon\dot{\iota}\alpha\ \dot{\eta}\mu\hat{\omega}\nu$), referring to the vulnerable position of believers caught between the two ages and thus involved in the "suffering" referred to in v. 18. They know enough of the coming new age to yearn for it, along with the rest of the creation, but they continue to be assaulted by the principalities and powers of the old age of the flesh.[136] Given the use of the derogatory term "weak" to refer to groups of Roman believers, it is significant that Paul attaches the possessive pronoun to this term in v. 26 ("in *our* weakness"), making clear that he and all other believers share this vulnerable status. He refuses to accept the premise held by some in the early church that the gift of the Spirit lifts believers above weaknesses, and thus above each other. All believers participate in the groaning of v. 23.

In v. 26b-c, Paul explains how the Spirit lends assistance to believers caught between the two ages. The two lines need to be kept together as a coherent antithesis, because v. 26b taken by itself is so sweepingly stated and so atypical for both Paul and early Christianity as a whole that serious misunderstandings have arisen.[137] The clause beginning with $\tau\grave{o}\ \gamma\acute{\alpha}\rho$ ("for that") is usually thought to provide the object of the verb "we do not know,"[138] but this is provided by the next word $\tau\acute{\iota}$, referring to "what" should be prayed for rather than "how"[139]

or "what things."[140] The neuter article $\tau\acute{o}$ serves to introduce the entire question or topic,[141] as in 1 Thess 4:1, "finally then, brothers, we ask you and exhort you by Lord Jesus, [in order that] just as you received from us, the ($\tau\acute{o}$) [instructions], how you ought to walk and please God. . . ." The phrase $\kappa\alpha\vartheta\grave{o}\ \delta\epsilon\hat{\iota}$ is associated with the verb "we pray" and is best translated "as we ought,"[142] referring to divine compulsion.[143] The resultant translation of v. 26b, "What are we to pray for, as we ought?" We do not know!" helps to clarify the exegetical options.[144] It is not that believers are fundamentally incapable of praying,[145] are too ignorant to pray as particular exigencies demand,[146] or lack the visionary capacity to see into the eschatological future.[147] Käsemann suggests that v. 26b expresses Paul's critique of ecstatic prayer and speaking in tongues, which is actually evident nowhere in this pericope.[148] When the second half of the antithesis in v. 26c is taken into account, referring explicitly to the Spirit's prayerful intercession in behalf of believers, Paul's view may be seen as consistent with his premise of co-responsibility with the divine Spirit as the mark of proper discipleship. "I will pray with the Spirit, but I will pray with the mind also" (1 Cor 14:15); "for it is God who is at work in you, enabling you both to will and to work for his good pleasure (Phil 2:13; also 1 Cor 12:6, 11; Gal 3:5). It would be consistent to maintain, therefore, that even believers, who have the Spirit,

---

136 Julius Schniewind, "Das Seufzen des Geistes," in J. Schniewind, *Nachgelassene Reden und Aufsätze* (Berlin: Töpelmann, 1952) 83, 92. See also Pierre Bonnard, "Faiblesse et puissance du Chrétien selon St. Paul," *ÉThR* 33 (1958) 61–70.

137 See Käsemann, 239–40, following Kurt Niederwimmer, "Das Gebet des Geistes, Röm 8:26f.," *ThZ* 20 (1964) 255–59.

138 See Sanday and Headlam, 213, and Lagrange, 211, followed by Dunn, 1:477.

139 See Cranfield, 1:421, for a rebuttal of the popular construal followed by Sanday and Headlam, Lagrange, the *RV, NEB,* and *NRSV.*

140 See Dunn, 1:477.

141 See LSJM 1195, VIII.B.5: "in neut. before any word or expression which itself is made the object of thought . . . and so before whole clauses," as in Plato *Resp.* 431e, "the opinion . . . about the question $\pi\epsilon\rho\grave{\iota}\ \tau o\hat{\upsilon}\ o\ddot{\upsilon}\sigma\tau\iota\nu\alpha\varsigma$ ('who ought to rule')."

142 See Godet, 320, and BAGD 172.2; a secular use of the phrase is found in the third-century B.C.E. histo-

rian Phylarchus *Frag.* 2a, 81, T. 73.4, "even as it is necessary ($\kappa\alpha\vartheta\grave{o}\ \delta\epsilon\hat{\iota}$) to sail for Sicily."

143 BAGD 172 refers to the parallels in 2 Macc 6:20; 4 Macc 7:8; 2 Tim 2:6, 24.

144 Newman and Nida, 164: "we do not know how we ought to pray."

145 See Schniewind, "Seufzen des Geistes," 85, 92; Niederwimmer, "Das Gebet des Geistes," 255–56. Harder, *Gebet,* 161, posited a cultural crisis in the Greco-Roman world that followed the breakup of a naive belief that the gods answer prayer.

146 See Murray, 1:311, and Morris, 327, along with Jülicher and Schmidt.

147 See Bindemann, *Hoffnung,* 80, followed by Gebauer, *Gebet,* 167.

148 Käsemann, 239–41; see the critique by Cranfield, 1:422.

cannot pray without it; yet with it, they have aid, as v. 26a asserted. They do not pray alone, but the "Spirit himself intercedes ($\dot{v}\pi\epsilon\rho\epsilon\nu\tau\nu\gamma\chi\acute{a}\nu\epsilon\iota$)" in their behalf. Paul apparently coined this word by adding the prefix $\dot{v}\pi\acute{\epsilon}\rho$ ("for, in behalf of") to the familiar word $\dot{\epsilon}\nu\tau\nu\gamma\chi\acute{a}\nu\epsilon\iota\nu$ ("meet, converse with, appeal to"), since the first appearance of this double compound verb in Greek writings is in this pericope.[149] It conveys his distinctive view of the Spirit as both apportioned out to believers and as the Spirit of God and/or Christ acting within them and beyond them.[150] Although the motif of humans[151] and angels[152] interceding for others appears in the OT and intertestamental literature,[153] there are no references to the Spirit interceding in behalf of humans prior to this reference in Romans. Olle Christoffersson has detected a substantive parallel in *1 En.* 7.6, where the angels converse about the need to intercede for the suffering people threatened by the flood:[154] "The spirits and the souls of the people groan and intercede ($\dot{\epsilon}\nu\tau\nu\gamma\chi\acute{a}\nu\alpha\nu\tau\alpha$) saying, 'bring our cause before the Highest and our destruction before the Majesty of glory. . . .'" The parallel references to the Spirit's activity in Mark 13:11 and to the Paraclete's work in John 15:26f. and 16:8ff. indicate that the general idea of divine intercession was known in Paul's time, but he remains "the first to speak clearly of the Spirit as an intercessor. . . ."[155] It is clearly "a Pauline novelty."[156]

There is widespread disagreement about the reference to the $\sigma\tau\epsilon\nu\alpha\gamma\mu o\hat{\iota}\varsigma$ $\dot{\alpha}\lambda\alpha\lambda\acute{\eta}\tau o\iota\varsigma$ ("unspoken groans") by which the Spirit conveys its intercession. Käsemann[157] has popularized the idea suggested by Origen and Chrysostom[158] that this expression refers explicitly to the kind of glossology evident in 1 Cor 14,[159] while others suggest the "inarticulate aspiration" of believers.[160] Since there is no evidence elsewhere of such aspirations in early Christianity,[161] this option is not compelling.[162] While the rare adjective $\dot{\alpha}\lambda\acute{\alpha}\lambda\eta\tau o\varsigma$ implies wordless groans, sighs,[163] or silence,[164] the closely associated adjective $\ddot{\alpha}\lambda\alpha\lambda o\varsigma$ refers to unintelligible speech in references such as Plutarch's description of the oracle at Delphi as possessed by "an unspeaking and bad spirit ($\dot{\alpha}\lambda\acute{\alpha}\lambda o\nu$ $\kappa\alpha\grave{\iota}$ $\kappa\acute{\alpha}\kappa o\nu$ $\pi\nu\epsilon\acute{\nu}\mu\alpha\tau o\varsigma$)."[165] While some form of charismatic expression is implied,[166] a direct link with glossolalia may be unlikely.[167] But if Paul intended a merely metaphorical construal unrelated to human prayer of any kind, it is unclear what its referent

149 Balz, *Heilsvertrauen*, 75f.
150 See Jewett, *Terms*, 172–200, 451–53; Shantz, "Paul in Ecstasy," 165–66.
151 See the survey by E. A. Obeng in "The Origins of the Spirit Intercession Motif in Romans 8:26," *NTS* 32 (1986) 621; Obeng refers to Gen 18:22-32; 20:17; Exod 8:8, 12, 28-30; 9:28, 33; 10:17, 18; Lev 16:21; Num 6:23-29; 2 Sam 12:16; 1 Kgs 8:22-54; 2 Kgs 19:15-19; 2 Chr 30:18, 19; Ezra 6:10.
152 Obeng, "Origins," 621, refers to Gen 21:17; 2:11.
153 Obeng, "Origins," 621–22, cites Tob 12:12; *3 Bar.* 11.4, 9; 12.1-5; 14:2; *T. Lev.* 3.5, 6; *T. Jud.* 20.1-5; 2 Macc 15:12-16; *As. Mos.* 11.14, 17; 12.6; Wis 1:6-9; 9:17-18.
154 See Christoffersson, *Earnest Expectation*, 117.
155 Obeng, "Origins," 630.
156 Fitzmyer, 518.
157 Käsemann, 240–41.
158 Cranfield, 1:423, provides the references: Origen *PG* col. 1120; Chrysostom *PG* col. 533.
159 A charismatic construal of "inexpressible groans" is also favored by Zahn, 412–13; Hunter, 84; Althaus, 84; Balz, *Heilsvertrauen*, 80; Paulsen, *Überlieferung*, 122–23; Zeller, 163; Theissen, *Psychological Aspects*, 315–20.
160 Dodd, 135; Godet, 321; in a similar vein, O'Neill,
142, refers to "inarticulate prayer"; Schlier, 269; and others listed by Käsemann, 240.
161 See Schniewind, "Seufzen des Geistes," 86–91; Gaugler, "Geist," 71–74.
162 See the citation of the James Montgomery poem about prayer as "the soul's sincere desire" in Bruce, 175.
163 BAGD 34.
164 Theognis *Frag. dub.* 6.2 refers to $\pi o\lambda\lambda$ $\dot{\alpha}\lambda\acute{\alpha}\lambda\eta\tau\alpha$ ("many unspoken things"), with a slightly different version in Stobaeus *Anth.* 3.36.1.3; the *Anth.* 5.4.1 names "a witness of things unspoken ($\dot{\alpha}\lambda\alpha\lambda\acute{\eta}\tau\omega\nu$)."
165 Cited by Theissen, *Psychological Aspects*, 315, from Plutarch *Def. orac.* 438b, which describes a reluctant Pythian priestess who responded to a request like a "labored ship."
166 See Theissen, *Psychological Aspects*, 317: "Paul is seeking . . . to make the boundary between glossolalia and intelligible speech more fluid [in 1 Cor 14]. What the Spirit inspires is to be understood simultaneously with the mind. Sharp distinctions between glossologic and normal linguistic 'sighs' tend to disappear for him as long as it is a matter of utterances caused pneumatically—and that is the case in Rom. 8:26."
167 See the critiques of the glossolalia hypothesis in

might be in the experience of the Roman believers.[168] What remains relatively unexplored is the unusual idea of wordless, silent prayer, since most prayers in the ancient world were spoken out loud.[169] There may be a link here with the "sighing or groaning which precedes or accompanies" prayer on some occasions in the OT.[170] Roland Gebauer explains: "In this passage the spirit comes before God with a sigh that requires no language . . . because God as the one who knows both the human heart and the impulse of the spirit, receives and understands the sighs of the spirit without language."[171] Colleen Shantz explains these inarticulate sighs as typical aspects of the neurology of ecstatic experience, in which the right hemisphere of the brain experiences the ineffable in a manner that the linguistic capacity located in the left hemisphere cannot articulate.[172] To formulate this in theological terms, the Spirit of God interacts with the inner sighs (8:23) in the human heart (8:27), bringing them before God in unspoken intercession.

Paul is clearly suggesting that the "weakness" of believers is addressed and sustained by the Spirit's intervention, so it is fair to conclude that he understands all prayer as arising from an inarticulate realm that expresses human vulnerability at its depth.[173] Glossolalia could well arise from such experience, but there is nothing like an explicit polemic here against either the practice or the theology of speaking in tongues. His point is

a positive one, that the inarticulate groans of believers, whether of glossology, frustration, or pain, are taken up by the Spirit's silent intercession in behalf of the children of God, whose dominion over a fallen world is not yet fully realized. By associating charismatic experiences with human weakness rather than strength, it "becomes a vehicle to make one sensitive to the sufferings of all creatures" while impeding grandiosity on the part of charismatics.[174]

■ 27 That the Spirit's intercession, even in the most unintelligible form, is understandable by God provides the conclusion of Paul's argument. He resorts to typical OT usage in referring to God[175] as ἐραυνῶν τὰς καρδίας ("the one who searches the hearts").[176] The wording is reminiscent of examples like Prov 20:27, "The light of the Lord is the spirit of humans, who searches the inmost parts of the innards (ὃς ἐρευνᾷ ταμίεια κοιλίας)" or 1 Sam 16:7, "for man looks at the face, but God looks at the heart (εἰς καρδίαν)."[177] The "heart" is the typical Hebraic expression for the inner center of a human being, the source of will, emotion, and intentionality,[178] and in this instance, the arena where the "silent groans" of Rom 8:26 are heard. The potentially threatening invasion of divine oversight is transformed here by a penetrating grace that accepts and sustains the deepest levels of human consciousness and unconsciousness.[179]

What God knows is τί τὸ φρόνημα τοῦ πνεύματος,

Dunn, 1:478–79, and Osten-Sacken, *Römer 8*, 272–75.

168 George W. MacRae, "Romans 8:26-17," *Int* 34 (1980) 291.

169 See Johannes Herrmann and Heinrich Greeven, "εὔχομαι κτλ.," *TDNT* 2 (1964) 779–84, esp. 786: "In the Ps. esp. though also elsewhere, prayer is described as calling . . . and open prayer seems to have been so much the rule that the silent prayer of Hannah in 1 S. 1 was obviously strange to Eli the priest."

170 Herrmann and Greeven, "εὔχομαι κτλ.," 786, referring to Pss 6:6; 31:10; 38:9; 102:5; Lam 1:22. The evidence is elusive because none of these references explicitly refers to groans preceding prayer.

171 Gebauer, *Gebet*, 169.

172 Shantz, "Paul in Ecstasy," 125–35, 165.

173 See Gaugler, "Geist," 69–80; Wink, *Engaging the Powers*, 305–6.

174 Theissen, *Psychological Aspects*, 339–40.

175 George W. MacRae's proposal that "spirit" rather

than "God" is the antecedent of the verb "search" reduces the complexity of communication within aspects of divinity, but provides a poor basis to understand the reference to the interceding before "God" in v. 27b. See "A Note on Romans 8:26-27," *HTR* 73 (1980) 227–30.

176 BAGD 306 refers to the standard grammars of the LXX in assessing this typical usage. Gerhard Delling, "ἐρευνάω, ἐξερευνάω," *TDNT* 2 (1964) 655, notes that the first appearance of the variant spelling ἐραυνάω used in Romans was in the LXX.

177 Other parallels noted by Zeller, 163, are 1 Kgs 8:39; 1 Chr 28:9; 29:17; Ps 7:10; 17:3; 26:6; 44:22; 139:1-2, 23; Prov 15:11; 17:3; 24:12; Jer 11:20; 12:3; 17:10; 20:12; Wis 1:6; Sir 42:18.

178 See Jewett, *Terms*, 305–13, 333.

179 See Klauck, "Wortlose Seufzen," 90–95.

which should be translated as "the spirit's intention," "the spirit's thinking," or "the spirit's aspiration."[180] The intentionality and modus operandi of the Spirit are in view here, not the objective content of its "mind,"[181] because the context deals with the Spirit's activity within the human heart. With a line of thought similar to 1 Cor 2:11, "no one understands the things of God except the Spirit of God," Paul is insisting not only that God knows and intercedes at the point of the deepest human confusion[182] but also that God communicates with God's self[183] through the groans that humans share with the rest of the fallen creation. To place this in the context of the argument beginning in v. 18, even the "sufferings" that cause human groaning are being drawn by the Spirit into "the future glory revealed to us," the glory of a dialogue within deity itself. That glory also discloses itself in ecstatic language such as glossolalia,[184] where the weakness and vulnerability of the creature are expressed with sounds that only the Spirit can interpret. This is a "cognitive restructuring of ecstatic experience" as "an impulse toward human transformation."[185]

The final clause in v. 27 concerning the Spirit's intercession opens with ὅτι ("because, that"), which may be taken either as causative, explaining how or why God knows the intention of the Spirit,[186] or as explicative, describing "the nature of the Spirit's intercession."[187] The decision depends in part on how one takes the following phrase, κατὰ θεόν, either as "according to God"[188] or "before God/with respect to God."[189] The former favors the causative meaning on the grounds that whatever is according to God "cannot remain unintelligible to Him."[190] But the latter seems more likely, because it avoids making the superfluous contention that whatever God does must be according to God's will. What this phrase explains is that the intercession[191] of the Spirit[192] is between God and the groaning "saints," a point that was not explicit in v. 26. The word "saints" without the article refers to believers in general,[193] not merely to Jewish Christians with a Palestinian background who are sometimes referred to as οἱ ἅγιοι ("the saints").[194] The holiness of believers thus entails an ongoing intervention of the Spirit, maintaining their relationship as children of God through the inarticulate groans they utter as well as their "Abba" acclamations as described in vv. 15-16.

---

180 BAGD 866 refers to classical and intertestamental references as well as to Josephus *Bell.* 1.204 and 4.358, where the expression φρόνημα ἐλευθερίου ("aspiration for freedom") appears. See Godet, 321, "aspiration of the spirit," and Dunn, 1:479.

181 The translation "mind" is found in the *RSV* and *NRSV* as well as in many commentaries.

182 See Käsemann, 242: "He sees through human beings and even grasps what they are not able to recognize on their own."

183 See Michel, 273; Dunn, 1:479–80.

184 See Käsemann, 242.

185 Theissen, *Psychological Aspects*, 337, 320.

186 See Käsemann, 242; Schmidt; and Wilckens, 3:161, following B. Weiss, Godet, and Kühl.

187 Sanday and Headlam, 214, following Meyer, Hofmann, Lipsius, Oltramare, Lagrange, Bisping, Cornely, Gutjahr, Zahn, and Moule, and followed by Gaugler, "Geist," 90; Balz, *Heilsvertrauen*, 80–81; Kuss, 3:644, and Cranfield, 1:424, as well as Michel and Black.

188 BAGD 407.5a relating to "the norm, of similarity, homogeneity," with parallels in Rom 15:5, κατὰ Χριστὸν Ἰησοῦν ("according to Jesus Christ"); 2 Cor 11:17, κατὰ κύριον ("according to [the] Lord"). The parallel in *Soc. Ep.* 14.5, κατὰ θεόν,

could be translated either "according to God" or "in relation to God." The option "according to God" is selected by BAGD and the commentaries I have consulted.

189 BAGD 406, "direction toward, to, up to," with parallels in Gal 2:11, κατὰ πρόσωπον ("to [his] face"); 2 Cor 10:1, κατὰ πρόσωπον ταπεινός ("humble [when face] to face"), and Luke 2:31; Acts 3:13, κατὰ πρόσωπον Πιλάτου ("in the face of Pilate").

190 Godet, 322.

191 Paul uses the more usual term ἐντυγχάνειν ("meet, converse with, appeal to") in place of the double compound word used in 8:26.

192 Christoffersson, *Earnest Expectation*, 119–20, has pointed to the parallel in *1 En.* 4.6, where the seer hears the voice of the angel Gabriel before God's throne: "And the third voice I heard interceding and praying on behalf of those who dwell upon the earth and supplicating in the name of the Lord of the Spirits." In Romans, of course, it is the spirit itself that conducts the intercession.

193 See Schlier, 270.

194 See Rom 15:25-26, 31; 1 Cor 16:14; 2 Cor 8:4; 9:1, 12; see the discussion above of 1:7. Morris draws a broader, less contextual inference that the "force" of the word "saints" without the article "will be that

■ 28 Paul initiates the climactic celebration of the thesis concerning the hopeful suffering of the children of God by reviewing what "we know"[195] as persons who "love God." The language of this verse reflects Paul's adaptation of traditional Jewish teaching.[196] Although loving God is a typical description of believers in Judaism,[197] and is used elsewhere by Paul,[198] the context of the Spirit's intervention within the hearts of believers suggests that this particular love derives from the process referred to in 5:5: "because God's love has been poured into our hearts through the Holy Spirit that has been given to us." This love is confirmed by the Abba acclamation (8:15-16), which the Spirit evokes in Christian believers, expressing their profound sense of acceptance and belongingness as "children of God" despite their vulnerability. The love of God that they have is thus a response to the event of their salvation, sustained by ongoing spiritual experiences that continue in the midst of suffering. The reference to their love of God is thus not honorific, as if such love originated from the good will of believers, or were grounded in their obedience. But the reference clearly implies appropriately loving action on the part of believers, who are motivated by God's love shown in the Christ event. The effect of beginning the climactic elaboration of the glory to be manifest in believers is therefore restrictive: the divinely intended goodwill come out of sufferings and other forms of evil, "for those who love God" in this active sense.

As one can infer from the density of text-critical variants,[199] the theological comment, $\pi\acute{\alpha}\nu\tau\alpha$ $\sigma\upsilon\nu\epsilon\rho\gamma\epsilon\hat{\imath}$ $\epsilon\grave{\imath}\varsigma$ $\grave{\alpha}\gamma\alpha\vartheta\acute{o}\nu$ ("in all things it cooperates for good") in v. 28b, has long provoked difficult translational and interpretive problems. Given the text-critical likelihood of the shorter text being original, there are three options for translating this clause. If $\pi\acute{\alpha}\nu\tau\alpha$ is understood as the subject of the verb ("all things cooperate for good"),[200] Paul is turned into an advocate of what Dodd aptly described as a congenial modern theory that the universe contains "a natural tendency towards progress."[201] While it seems more appropriate on substantive grounds to construe $\pi\acute{\alpha}\nu\tau\alpha$ as an accusative of specification, "in all things,"[202] it remains unclear why Paul did not provide a preposition such as $\kappa\alpha\tau\grave{\alpha}$ $\pi\acute{\alpha}\nu\tau\alpha$, which would have removed all possibility of ambiguity. If the translation "in all things" is followed, there are two options for

they are being prayed for because of their quality as 'saints,' not because they belong to 'the' saints as a group."

195 The $o\check{\imath}\delta\alpha\mu\epsilon\nu$ ("we know") formula was last used in 8:22 to refer to knowledge shared by believers. It has now been used seven times beginning with 2:2. Given the discussion of the content of this particular knowledge in 5:5, Cranfield, 1:424 suggests that Paul "is deliberately incorporating a piece of traditional teaching."

196 See Michel, 273; Zeller, 163–64, and Oda Wischmeyer, "*ΘΕΟΝ ΑΓΑΠΑΝ* bei Paulus: Eine Traditionsgeschichtliche Miszelle," *ZNW* 78 (1987) 143. She rightly rejects Johannes B. Bauer's contention that Paul polemically altered the Jewish tradition of the saints loving God in ". . . *ΤΟΙΣ ΑΓΑΠΩΣΙΝ ΤΟΝ ΘΕΟΝ*. Röm 8,28 (1 Cor 2,9; 1 Cor 8,3)," *ZNW* (1959) 106–12.

197 See Michel, 275; Cranfield, 1:424; and Dunn, 1:480–81, who refer, among numerous other passages, to the formulaic references to $\grave{\alpha}\gamma\alpha\pi\hat{\omega}\nu\tau\epsilon\varsigma$ $\tau\grave{o}\nu$ $\vartheta\epsilon\acute{o}\nu$ ("those who love God") in *Ps. Sol.* 4.29; 6.9; 10.4; 14.1 and to $\tauo\hat{\imath}\varsigma$ $\grave{\alpha}\gamma\alpha\pi\hat{\omega}\sigma\iota$ $\mu\epsilon$, $\kappa\alpha\grave{\imath}$ $\tauo\hat{\imath}\varsigma$ $\phi\upsilon\lambda\acute{\alpha}\sigma\sigma o\upsilon\sigma\iota$ $\tau\grave{\alpha}$ $\pi\rho o\sigma\tau\acute{\alpha}\gamma\mu\alpha\tau\acute{\alpha}$ $\mu o\upsilon$ ("to those who love me and keep my commandments") in Exod 20:6; Deut 5:10; Dan 9:4; etc. Dunn feels that it is

significant that Paul uses only the first part of the latter formula, "thereby both evoking Christianity's Jewish inheritance while at the same time separating it from its more distinctively Jewish devotion to the Torah."

198 1 Corinthians 8:3, "but anyone who loves God ($\grave{\alpha}\gamma\alpha\pi\hat{\alpha}$ $\tau\grave{o}\nu$ $\vartheta\epsilon\acute{o}\nu$) is known by him"; see also 1 Cor 2:9 and other NT references to the commandment to love God, such as Matt 22:37.

199 See notes o, p, and q above; also the extensive discussion of the eight interpretive options involving both the shorter and longer readings in Cranfield, 1:425–29.

200 This option is favored by the *KJV* and *AV*, and by modern commentators like Barrett, 169; Käsemann, 243; Wilckens, 2:163; Dunn, 1:481; also Mayer, *Gottes Heilsratschluß*, 138–42.

201 Dodd, 138.

202 Cranfield, 1:427, notes that Baur cites Alexander Aphrodisiensis *Fat.* 31 for $\pi\acute{\alpha}\nu\tau\alpha$ used as an accusative of respect; in BAGD 632–33 other instances are cited but not this particular one.

construing the subject of the verb. The path most frequently taken is to supply "God" as the subject, which follows the logic of the early textual variant that added ὁ θεός.[203] This is stylistically awkward because the immediately preceding clause ends with the word God in the accusative, τὸν θεόν,[204] and it requires an unexplained and unstated change of subject from "the Spirit," which was the subject of the third person singular verbs since the beginning of v. 26. The most likely option is that Paul intended τὸ πνεῦμα ("the Spirit") to be supplied by the reader in v. 28b,[205] because this requires no change of subject from the end of v. 27. This option is strongly suggested by the repetition of the prefix συν- in συνεργεῖ ("it cooperates with"), following συναντιλαμβάνεται ("it lends assistance with") in v. 26, where the subject "the Spirit" is explicitly supplied. The same subject is also stated for the next verb in v. 26, ὑπερεντυγχάνει ("it intercedes"), and must be supplied for the final verb in the immediately preceding v. 27, ἐντυγχάνει ("it intercedes"). The objection that this option leads to an unexplained change of subject between v. 28 and v. 29 from "Spirit" to "God"[206] overlooks the fact that otherwise there would be an unexplained subject change from "Spirit" in vv. 26-27 and "God" in v. 28. In either case, one is compelled to admit that Paul is not always entirely consistent and clear in his syntax and logic. The content and rhetoric of vv. 29-30 will make it sufficiently clear that God, rather than the Spirit, must now become the subject, but to extrapolate this awareness backward to v. 28 is not only rhetorically implausible, since the flow of the oral argument is forward rather than backward, but it also deflects Paul's intended concentration in vv. 26-28b on the work of the Spirit with and among believers, which continues despite their weakness and suffering.

As the introductory formula "for we know" implies, Paul can count on his audience in Rome giving assent to the premise widely held in the ancient world of divine activity leading to good even in the midst of trouble. Socrates' famous confidence in Plato's *Apol.* 41d was "that no evil can come to a good man (οὐκ ἔστιν ἀνδρὶ ἀγαθῷ κακόν) either in life or after death, nor do the gods neglect such matters." In the Jewish tradition Paul's formulaic statement is similar to Josephus's premise "that men who conform to the will of God and do not transgress laws that have been excellently laid down, prosper in all things beyond belief."[207] The somewhat later comment by Rabbi Aqiba is even closer: "Everything that the Almighty does, He does for good."[208] The saying of Issachar in a pre-Christian Aramaic papyrus reflects a similar confidence in the divine capacity to aid believers: "The righteous among men, all who [or all things that] meet him are for his help."[209] The use of the verb συνεργεῖν ("works with, cooperates with") brings Paul's formula close to the apocalyptic perspective of the *Testament of the Twelve Patriarchs*,[210] but I have been unable to find any parallel that matches the precise thrust of Paul's compressed formula. It claims a divine–human synergism in the midst of disadvantageous circumstances, because the Spirit works "with" those who love God. In the tangled discussion about the translation and appropriate parallels for v. 28, the συν- of the verb συνεργεῖν has tended to drop out of consideration.[211] Paul's wording implies divine and human co-responsibility in the face of adversity, and in the context of this letter, the "good" to be accomplished by this cooperation includes the daily work and congregational formation in behalf of the Roman house and tenement churches as well as the risky mission to Spain that they will be asked to support. The thrust of the argument is

203 This is found in *RSV, NIV, NJB*, Denney, Lagrange, Knox, Dodd, Gaugler, Bruce, Byrne, *Reckoning*, 173; Kuss, Paulsen, *Überlieferung*, 152–54.

204 See Black, 118.

205 This option is followed by the *NEB*, by James P. Wilson, "Romans viii, 28: Text and Interpretation," *ExpT* 60 (1948–49) 110–11; Black, 118; and Robinson, *Wrestling*, 104–5.

206 Cranfield, 1:425–26, is followed on this point by subsequent commentators.

207 Josephus *Ant.* 1.14.

208 *B. Ber.* 60b.

209 Cited by Bauer, "Rm 8.28," 106, from A. Cowley, *Aramaic Papyri of the Fifth Century B. C.* (Oxford: Oxford University Press, 1923) 218.

210 See Michel, 275, and Dunn, 1:481, who refers to *T. Iss.* 3.7 ("And the Lord increased the good things through my hands; and also Jacob knew that God worked together with my integrity"); also *T. Reub.* 3.6; *T. Dan* 1.7; *T. Gad* 4.5, 7.

211 Cranfield, 1:428, explicitly repudiates the translation "work together with" in favor of the more

encouraging: despite adversity and the ongoing weakness of the congregation, the Spirit labors alongside believers in such tasks.[212]

The clause in v. 28c, τοῖς κατὰ πρόθεσιν κλητοῖς οὖσιν ("with those called according to a purpose"), elaborates the theme of believers loving God in v. 28a. Referring to believers as the "called" picks up the language of 1:1 and 6, where Paul referred to himself as "a called apostle" and the Roman believers as the "called of Jesus Christ." The term "purpose," used here for the first time in the Pauline corpus, appears to be the rough equivalent of the Hebrew term עצה. A characteristic example is Isa 46:10, where Yahweh proclaims his divinity: "My purpose shall stand, and I will fulfill my intention."[213] This becomes a prominent term for the Essene community, which gives thanks for being the "men of your purpose" who stand with the angels before the throne of God.[214] We will encounter a similar use of πρόθεσις in Rom 9:11. In the context of this pericope, the "purpose" of God relates to the establishment of the new creation, in which the "sons of God" will be "revealed" in a properly responsible role. The whole passage is intended to encourage the saints in their cooperation with the Spirit, working in all things toward the good. This larger thrust of the argument coheres with the grain of truth in the patristic construal of πρόθεσις as referring to the "good choice" of believers to place themselves in the service of

God.[215] Something more concrete than a doctrine of "the certainty of hope"[216] is at stake here, therefore, because the future "glory to be revealed to us" (8:18) will soon be referred to in the past tense (8:30), as it is manifest in the transformed life of Roman believers, who reveal by their actions that they are pursuing the divine calling.

■ **29** The second phase of the fivefold climax begins with ὅτι ("because"), which connects the last two verses of the pericope with the entirety of v. 28.[217] The climactic development in this verse specifies the "purpose" of v. 28c, namely, the recovery of true sonship, with its attendant impact on the groaning creation. The verbs προγινώσκω ("know beforehand") and προορίζω ("destine beforehand") reduplicate the prefix from the key term πρόθεσις at the end of v. 28, confirming the connection to the theme of divine purpose. The term προγινώσκω will be used in 11:2 in connection with God's relation to Israel. In earlier letters Paul referred to God as knowing Christian believers (Gal 4:9; 1 Cor 8:3; 13:12) who were elected beforehand (1 Cor 2:7). By including these ideas under the rubric of what "we know" (8:28), Paul assumes that the biblical themes of divine foreknowledge[218] and election[219] were familiar to the congregations in Rome, perhaps through their use in baptismal homilies or ceremonies.[220] It is especially the wording σύμμορφους τῆς εἰκόνος τοῦ υἱοῦ αὐτοῦ ("conformed to the image of his son")[221] that points to a

bland translation "assist, help on, profit," which is consistent with a Calvinist perspective hostile to synergism.

212 See Yeo, "Messianic Predestination," 268.

213 See also Ps 33:11; Prov 19:21; Isa 14:26; 19:17; 25:1; Jer 49:20; 50:45; Mic 4:12, but note that the LXX never translates עצה with πρόθεσις.

214 1QH 6:11-13; see also 1QS 3:6. 1QS 1:13 refers to the "perfection of His ways and . . . the purpose of His righteousness," while 1QH 4:13 speaks of "Your purpose" to defeat the plans of Belial.

215 Origen PG 14, col. 1126. See also the references to Chrysostom, Theodoret, and Oecumenius as well as to their rebuttal by Augustine in Cranfield, 1:429.

216 Cranfield, 1:431.

217 See ibid.

218 See Gen 18:19; Hos 13:4; Pss 38:18; 139:1-16; 1QH 9:29-30 and As. Mos. 1.14. In Amos 3:2 Yahweh addresses Israel with the words, "You only have I known of all the families of the earth . . ."; and in Jer 1:5 Yahweh tells the young Jeremiah, "Before I

formed you in the womb I knew you. . . ." See P. J. Jacobs and H. Krienke, "Vorsehung (προγινώσκω)," TBLNT 3 (1972) 1334-35.

219 Although the Hebrew Bible speaks of God determining events in advance (2 Kgs 19:25; Isa 22:11), the word προορίζω does not appear in the OT. It is found in Acts 4:28; 1 Cor 2:7; Eph 1:5, 11. See Ernst von Dobschütz, "Prädestination," ThStK 106 (1934-35) 9-19; and Rudolf Liechtenhan, Die göttliche Vorherbestimmung bei Paulus und in der Posidonianischen Philosophie (FRLANT 18; Göttingen: Vandenhoeck & Ruprecht, 1922) 17-50.

220 See Jervell, Imago Dei, 272; Käsemann, 244.

221 See Josef Kürzinger, "Σύμμορφους τῆς εἰκόνος τοῦ υἱοῦ αὐτου (Röm 8:29)," BZ 2 (1958) 294-99, esp. 296f.; A. R. C. Leaney, "'Conformed to the Image of His Son' (Rom 8:29)," NTS 10 (1963-64) 470-79. The only occurrence of σύμμορφος prior to its use in the NT is by Nicander of Colophon (third century B.C.E.) who contrasts two kinds of snakes: "You might easily recognize the body of the

process of transformation that begins in baptism, in which an old self is buried and a new person arises out of the water to live henceforth in Christ, who was himself the image of God.[222] The transformation is currently manifest, at least in part, as believers cooperate with the Spirit to achieve the good (Rom 8:28);[223] to restrict the bearing of this passage to future transformation in the resurrection[224] overlooks the significance of the aorist verbs and the context of current suffering.[225]

The idea of humans bearing the image of God in Gen 1:27; Ps 8:6-7; and Sir 17:2-4 was derived from ancient kingship ideology, in which the ruler was thought to represent divine sovereignty and glory.[226] Paul joins the OT tradition of democratizing this ideology by extending the restoration of sovereignty and glory to all those conforming to Christ's image.[227] Paul's aim here is not to establish an abstract doctrine of predestination or sonship, or to invite "reflection on the classic problems of determinism and free will,"[228] but to reassure the vulnerable, harried believers in Rome that their lives and work have significance in the grand plan of God for the restoration of the creation through the recovery of "sonship" by conforming to the image of Christ.[229] That the "many brothers" in this verse already share the sonship with Christ is consistent with the argument concerning believers as joint heirs in 8:17.[230] As elsewhere in Romans, "brothers" refers to female as well as male believers. Since Christ demonstrated the recovery of the divine image by acting as the true child of God, he became the πρωτότοκος ("firstborn"), the preeminent[231] of "many brothers," that is, the converted church members, siblings both male and female.[232] The liturgical parallels in Col 1:15-18 and Heb 1:1-6 indicate that both the creation and the resurrection of Christ are involved in his status as "firstborn." In this context the siblings of the "first born" are to cooperate with the Spirit to exercise a proper dominion in a corrupted world. To extend this circle of "many" brothers and sisters is the goal of the mission project that this argument serves, which means that cooperating with the plans set forth in Rom 15:15-21 will constitute a way to embody such conformity to Christ. Given the purpose clause at the end of v. 29 (εἰς τὸ εἶναι αὐτόν, "in order that he might be"), the mission will also serve to fulfill Christ's destiny to

---

'putrefaction' serpent, another that in its form is *of the same shape as* (συμμόρφον) the 'blood-flowing' serpent" (*Ther.* 320–21).

222 See Jervell, *Imago Dei*, 197–256, for the evidence that the early Christian baptismal materials understood the ceremony as restoring the image of God that was lost in the fall, in that baptism joined the believer with Christ, who was that image. This context for Rom 8:20 is supported by Balz, *Heilsvertrauen*, 113; Käsemann, 244, and Wilckens, 2:164.

223 Cranfield, 1:432, speaks of "a progressive conformity to Christ" as an aspect of sanctification; see also Yeo, "Messianic Predestination," 270.

224 See Lietzmann, 87; Sanday and Headlam, Knox, Gutjahr, Huby, Gaugler; Edvin Larsson, "Christus als Vorbild," *ASNU* 23 (1962) 115–27; Heinrich Schlier, "Das, worauf alles wartet: Eine Auslegung von Römer 8,18-30," in H. Kuhn et al., eds., *Interpretation der Welt: Festschrift für Romano Guardini* (Würzburg: Echter Verlag, 1965) 613; Byrne, *Sons*, 117–18.

225 See Käsemann, 244.

226 Balz, *Heilsvertrauen*, 111–12, points to the significant study of this background by H. Wildberger, "Das Abbild Gottes: Gen 1,26-30," *ThZ* 21 (1965) 245–59, 481–501.

227 See Brian K. Blount, "Cultural Studies and Intersubjective Work," in Khiok-khng Yeo, ed., *Navigating Romans Through Cultures: Challenging Readings by Charting a New Course* (New York/London: T.&T. Clark International, 2004) 293.

228 Dunn, 1:486.

229 In *Sons*, 118, Byrne restricts this to "participation in his heavenly, glorious way of being, which will come about when we arrive at the same state." Scott, *Adoption*, 252–58, appropriately interprets "firstborn" in the context of the messianic promises of Ps 89:28 and Ps 2:7-8 so that the believers as sons "enter into the inheritance of the Son at the Parousia" (254).

230 See Schäfer, *Bruderschaft*, 57.

231 See Wilhelm Michaelis, "πρωτότοκος," *TDNT* 6 (1968) 877, who argues on the basis of the rights of the firstborn in Jewish culture that the term in Rom 8:29 suggests that Christ is "like them but above them in rank and dignity, since He remains their Lord." See also A. Durand, "Le Christ premierené," *RechSR* 1 (1910) 56–66; F. Wulf, "Der Erstgeborene unter vielen Brüdern, R 8,29," *GuL* 43 (1970) 466–69; and Wilhelm Michaelis, "Die biblische Vorstellung von Christus als dem Erstgeborenen," *ZSTh* 23 (1954) 137–57; Schäfer, *Bruderschaft*, 63.

232 Byrne, *Sons*, 118–19. Scott, *Adoption*, 248–58, mentions only males as inheritors.

restore the image of God to a fallen human race. In other words, Paul's global mission is christologically grounded.[233]

■ **30** After the brief expansion of the second climactic elaboration in the preceding verse, Paul returns to the style of a classic climax to provide the last steps in the symmetrical chain. In οὓς δὲ προώρισεν, τούτους καὶ ἐκάλεσεν ("and those whom he predestined, these he also called") he picks up both themes in the initial step of the chain in v. 28, "called" and "purpose." The verb tense continues in the aorist through the end of the chain, with "predestined . . . called . . . set right . . . and glorified." While the sovereign action of God provides the impetus, the repeated τούτους ("them") places the emphasis on the recipients, the "many brothers" who are being conformed to the image of Christ. All persons whom God had predestined to join this company of believers had experienced invitations[234] to respond to the gospel and to exercise transformed dominions in various arenas of responsibility.[235] All such persons "he made righteous" (ἐδικαίωσεν) with a new relationship with God and the world,[236] thus becoming products and agents of the δικαιοσύνη θεοῦ ("righteousness of God").

The climax ends with the startling claim that all such persons whom God set right were also "glorified." Since glory was referred to in the opening sentence of this pericope as a future gift, exegetes have struggled to explain the past tense verb in v. 30. Paul elsewhere refers to the gift of heavenly glory at the parousia, so many scholars regard the aorist verb at this point as anticipatory,[237] as an expression of the hymnic source of the passage,[238] or as an expression of "an enthusiastic baptismal tradition."[239] The first two options require the final verb, "glorified," in the climactic sequence to be taken in a different sense from the four prior aorists, which is problematic. I believe the latter option is the most satisfactory, particularly in the light of the stress on the process of formation into the image of God in the earlier verses of this pericope. Believers are in the process of being glorified according to the image of Christ, as in 2 Cor 3:18, made radiant with righteousness.[240] The point of the climactic series is to confirm the status of believers, reassuring them that despite present suffering, and in the face of their vulnerability as house and tenement church members in Rome, their status of being called, set right, and glorified is already visible. The glory that will yet be revealed in a definitive form in the children of God (8:18-19) will one day overcome the ambiguity of life in a fallen world. But in the work that the Spirit already cooperates in accomplishing in Rome,[241] and the work that they will soon perform for the Spanish mission, this glory has become—and will become—partially visible.

233 See Schäfer, *Bruderschaft*, 76–80.

234 See the analysis of the invitation from God characteristic of Pauline thought in Wiederkehr, *Berufung*, 32–35. He finds this emphasis on a divine invitation also in Rom 8:28-30; see p. 163.

235 See particularly Werner Bieder's stress on concrete arenas of responsibility in *Die Berufung im Neuen Testament* (AThANT 38; Zurich: Zwingli, 1961) 55–104.

236 See Newman and Nida, 167: "those that he called he also put right with himself."

237 Käsemann, 245, lists Lietzmann, Kühl, Gutjahr, Lagrange, Bardenhewer, Leenhardt, Gaugler, Michel, Bultmann, *Theology*, 1:348-49; Thüsing, *Per Christum*, 123–30. Among more recent exegetes, one could mention Mayer, *Gottes Heilsratschluß*, 163–65, and Dunn, 1:486.

238 Schille, *Frühchristlichen Hymnen*, 89–90; Wilckens, 2:165.

239 Käsemann, 245, following F.-W. Eltester, *Eikon im Neuen Testament* (BZNW 23; Berlin: Töpelmann,

1958) 24–25, 165; Peter Schwanz, *Imago Dei als christologisch-anthropologisches Problem in der Geschichte der Alten Kirche von Paulus bis Clemens von Alexandrien* (Göttingen: Vandenhoeck & Ruprecht, 1970) 18; [Bp.] Cassien, "Le fils et les fils, le frère et les frères," in P. I. Bratsiotis, ed., *Paulus-Hellas-Oikumene: An Ecumenical Symposium* (Athens: Student Christian Association, 1951) 42; Balz, *Heilsvertrauen*, 113.

240 BAGD 204.2, "clothe in splendor, glorify." Although most of the NT instances of this usage refer to "the glory that comes in the next life," the past tense verb in 8:30 clearly alludes to the present process of glorification: "And we all, with unveiled face, beholding the glory of the Lord, are being changed into his likeness from one degree of glory to another . . . (2 Cor 3:18)."

241 Luz, "Mystic," 141–42, refers to 8:30 as a reflection of "a mystical experience of the Spirit" on the part of believers.

8

The Tenth Pericope

Conclusion: The Status of the Elect Based on Divine Love

31/ What then shall we say in view of these things? If God [is] for us, who [is] against us? 32/ [He] who surely did not spare even his own son[a] but delivered him up for us all, how will he not also with him graciously give us the universe?

33/ Who shall impeach God's elect? Shall God—who sets [us] right? 34/ Who will be the condemner?[b] [c] "Christ[d] who died"?[e] But even more so, "was raised,[f] who" not only[g] "is at the right hand of God," "who" also "intercedes for us"?

35/ Who shall separate us from the love of the Christ?[h]
    Affliction,
        or distress,
            or[i] persecution,
                or hunger,
                    or nakedness,
                        or peril,
                            or sword?
36/ Just as it has been written, "For your sake we are being put to death all the day long, we are reckoned as sheep for slaughter." 37/ But in all these things we are supervictors through him who loved[j] us.

38/ For I have become convinced that
        neither death,[k]
            nor life,
                nor angels,[l]
                    nor rulerships,[m]
                        nor things present,
                        nor things to come,
                            nor powers,[n]
                                39/ nor height,
                                    nor depth,
                                        nor any other[o] kind of creature
will have power to separate us from the love of God which is in Christ Jesus our Lord.

---

a   In place of the broadly attested wording γε τοῦ ἰδίου υἱοῦ οὐκ ἐφαίσατο ("who surely did not spare even his own son"), D (F G) (sy^p) have οὐδὲ τοῦ ἰδίου υἱοῦ οὐκ ἐφαίσατο ("nor who spared his own son"), which appears to be a minor stylistic improvement.

b   The evidence for accenting the participle is slim, with 1506 pc supporting the future form, κατακρινῶν ("will condemn"), and the rest supporting the present tense form, κατακρίνων. Unfortunately P^{46} ℵ A B* C D F G lack accents. The

future form is more appropriate for the context; see Cranfield, 1:438.

c   The minor variant ἅμα δέ ("but at the same time") in P^{46} ar d* o Ir^{lat} appears to be an editorial addition to introduce the brief sentence more effectively.

d   The omission of "Jesus" by B D K 0289 69 88 263 323 326 330 424* 459 614 945 1175 1241 1506 1735 1739 1836 1874 1881 1912 2200 2464 Lect Maj ar d^2 mon sy^p sa slav Ir^{lat} CyrJ Chr Severian Hil Ambst Ambr Aug$^{1/4}$ has broad support in the Alexandrian, Western and Palestinian traditions. The addition of "Jesus" is explained by Ehrman, Orthodox Corruption of Scripture, 150–51, as an effort to combat gnostic claims that only Jesus—not Christ—was subject to death, which might explain why so many texts support it: P^{46vid} ℵ A C F G L Ψ 6 33 81 104 256 365 424^c 436 1243 1319 1505 1573 1852 1962 2127 2495 al b f g vg sy^h bo arm eth geo^2 (geo^1) Or^{lat} Did^{dub} Cyr Pel Aug$^{3/4}$ Varimadum. The use of the square brackets around "Jesus" indicating "evenly balanced" evidence in Nestle-Aland^{26,27} is understandable in this instance, according to Metzger, Textual Commentary, 458. I believe the evidence supports the omission.

e   The addition of καί ("and"), missing in Nestle-Aland$^{26/27}$ but noted by Ehrman, Orthodox Corruption of Scripture, 152, is found in P^{46} D F G K L Ψ 6 69 88 104 181 218 256 263 330 365 424 451 459 614 629 630 915 917 945 1175 1241 1319 1398 1505 1563 1573 1735 1739 1751 1836 1838 1845 1846 1874 1875 1877 1881 1908 1942 1959 1962 2127 2138 2200 2464 2492 2495 2516 2523 2544 2718. Ehrman 152 explains this as an "orthodox" addition to make plain that Jesus both died and was raised.

f   The presence of ἐκ νεκρῶν ("from [the] dead") in ℵ* A C Ψ 0289^{vid} 33 81 88 104 326 330 436 441 451 467 621 915 1243 1506 1838 1942 1959 1962 2110 2344 pc sa bo al is more than counterbalanced by the evidence for its omission in P^{27vid,46} ℵ^2 B D F G K L 5 6 69 181 218 256 263 323 365 424 459 614 623 629 630 720 917 945 1175 1241 1319 1398 1505 1563 1573 1678 1718 1735 1739 1751 1836 1845 1846 1874 1875 1877 1881 1908 1912 2127 2138 2197 2200 2464 2492 2495 2516 2523 2544 2718 Maj Lect latt sy$^{p.h}$ Ir^{lat}. The shorter text is to be preferred, and the addition is plausibly explained by Ehrman, Orthodox Corruption of Scripture, 152, as confirmation of the doctrine that Christ went to the place of the dead.

g   The omission of καί ("and" but in this context of καί . . . καί, "not only . . . but also") by ℵ* A C 0289^{vid} 81 323 424 629 945 1506 1836 pc it vg^{ww} bo

Ir^{lat} (1739 1881 lack it due to *homoioteleuton*) appears to reflect the tendency of the Alexandrian tradition toward stylistic improvement, in this case eliminating the first in a seemingly redundant and repetitive series of "and . . . and." The evidence for the inclusion of καί in P²⁷·⁴⁶ ℵ² B D F G K L Ψ 6 33 69 88 104 326 330 365 614 1175 1241 1243 1319 1505 1573 1735 1874 2464 2495 *Maj* b vgst sy^h sa is too broad to be denied.

h In place of "Christ," which is convincingly attested by C D F G K L Ψ 6 33 69 81 88 104 181 256 263 323 424 436 459 614 629 945 1175 1241 1243 1319 1505 1573 1739 1836 1852 1874 1877 1881 1912 1962 2127 2200 2464 2492 2495 [A *is illegible*] *Maj Lect* ar b d f g mon o vg sy^{p,h} bo arm eth geo Or^{gr,} ^{lat3/11} Or^{dub} Meth Eus^{1/4} Ath Bas CyrJ Diodore Did^{1/8} Amphilochius Macarius/Symeon^{2/3} Chr^{2/3} Severian Marcus-Eremita Cyr Proclus Hes Thret Tert Nov Cyp Hil^{1/3} Luc Ambst Ambr^{7/9} Gregory-Elvira Gaudentius Hier^{6/7} Pel Aug^{24/25} Quodvultdeus^{1/2}, the reading θεοῦ ("of God") appears in ℵ 326 330 365 451 1506 *pc* t sa slav Hipp Or^{gr mss, lat3/11} Eus^{3/4} Did^{5/8} Macarius/Symeon^{1/3} Chr^{1/3} Hil^{1/3} Aug^{1/25} Quodvultdeus^{1/2}, while a phrase, apparently influenced by Rom 8:39, appears in B Or^{lat4(1)/11} GrNy Did^{2/8} (Hil^{1/3}): θεοῦ τῆς ἐν Χριστῶ Ἰησοῦ ("of God which is in Christ Jesus"). See Metzger, *Textual Commentary*, 458.

i The omission of ἤ ("or") by P⁴⁶ D* F G seems to be a scribal error. The inclusion of "or" is adequately supported by ℵ A B C D² K L Ψ 6 33 69 88 104 323 326 330 365 424 614 945 1175 1241 1243 1319 1505 1506 1573 1735 1739 1836 1874 1881 2464 2495 *Maj* lat sy cop Cyp.

j A variant in D F G latt preserves the participle "loved us" in the accusative, making the phrase read, "on account of him who loved us."

k Pseudo-Justin Martyr reads here for "neither death nor life" the following: οὔτω ζωὴ οὔτε κόσμος οὔτω θάνατος ("neither life nor world nor death"), which is unlikely to be original.

l The singular form ἄγγελος ("an angel") appears in

D F G b Ambst, and unlike other "Western" readings, it does not look like an intentional alteration and perhaps should be accepted as the more difficult and hence, more original reading. Remaining uncertain, I follow the Nestle-Aland preference for the majority reading of the plural "angels."

m In place of ἀρχαί ("principalities"), which stands alone in a wide range of texts, D has ἐξουσία οὔτε ἀρχαί ("an authority nor principalities") and C 81 104 256 263 330 459 1735 1836 *al* vg^{cl} sy^{h**} bo^{mss} (Or^{lat2/9}) (Hil) have ἀρχαὶ οὔτε ἐξουσίαι ("principalities nor authorities"). Similar formulations are found in Eph 1:21; 6:12; Col 1:16; 2:10, 15, which may have influenced these variants. Neither variant has much likelihood of being original.

n A variant now attested in Nestle-Aland²⁷ is the placement of οὔτε δυνάμεις ("or powers") between ἀρχαί ("rulerships") and ἐνεστῶτα ("things present") in K L Ψ 6 33 88 323 326 (330) 424 (436) 614 945 1175 1241 (1735) (1836) (1852) 1874 1912 2200 (2344) 2464 *Maj* Lect^{pt, AD} b mon sy^p geo² Or^{lat2/9} Chr Theodore^{vid} Thret (Ambst) Ambr^{2/3} Aug^{1/8}, but the strong contrary evidence in P²⁷vid, ⁴⁶ ℵ A B C D F G 0285 69 81 104 256 263 459 365 1243 1319 1505 1506 1573 1739 1881 1962 2127 2495 *pc* ar d f g o vg^{(cl),ww,st} syr^{h with*} sa bo arm eth slav Or^{lat2(2)/9} Eus Cyr Hier^{1(6)/7} (Hil) Pel (Aug^{5/8}) *al* supports the location after "things to come." See Metzger, *Textual Commentary*, 458–59. In place of "angels nor rulerships," Pseudo-Justin Martyr has οὔτε ἄγγελοι οὔτε δυνάμεις οὔτω ἀρχαί ("nor angels nor powers nor rulerships").

o The omission of the indefinite pronoun τίς ("any, any other") in P⁴⁶ D F G 1505 2495 lat sy is counterbalanced by the broad evidence for its inclusion: ℵ A B C K L Ψ 0285 6 33 69 88 104 323 326 330 365 424 614 945 1175 1241 1243 1319 1506 1573 1735 1739 1836 1874 1881 2344 2464 *Maj* (t) Cl, leading Nestle-Aland²⁶/²⁷ to an unequivocal decision for inclusion. This appears to be the fourth example of peculiar variants in this pericope associated with what used to be called the "Western" text.

Analysis

This pericope not only provides the conclusion of chap. 8, dealing finally with the issue concerning the condemnation of believers mentioned in 8:1, but also constitutes the peroration of the entire second proof, which began

in 5:1.[1] The rhetorical or even hymnic qualities of this passage have often been observed,[2] but efforts to discern citations from pre-Pauline liturgical or catechetical materials in vv. 31-32 or 38-39 have not been successful.[3] That early kerygmatic material is cited in v. 34b-e, however, seems quite likely because of the parallel formula-

---

1 See Dahl, *Studies*, 88–90; Andreas H. Snyman uses the proper rhetorical term, "peroration," for this section in "Style and Meaning in Romans 8:31-9,"

Neot 18 (1984), 227; his analysis also confirms that this pericope is epideictic (228). With the exception of Tobin, *Paul's Rhetoric*, 300–317, who views 8:31-

tions elsewhere, the relative clauses beginning with ὅς ("who"), and the presence of atypical terminology.[4] Henning Paulsen proposes an early Hellenistic, Jewish Christian kerygma in v. 34, which I would reduce to the following:[5]

Christ who died [and] was raised,
who is at the right hand of God,
who intercedes for us.

Throughout this pericope, a noteworthy Hebraic preference for series of sevens and tens needs to be taken into account.[6] An *erotesis*[7] containing ten rhetorical ques-

tions is arranged in three sections (8:31-32, 33-34, 35-37),[8] of which the last contains seven forms of suffering in a rhetorically effective series linked with "or" (v. 35).[9] This reflects a Hebraic numerical preference for seven as the number that connotes completeness.[10] Three of the questions begin with τίς ("who"), producing a rhetorically pleasing anaphora in vv. 33a, 34a, and 35a,[11] echoed by a final τίς in v. 39. The questions are all formulated in the future tense, while the answers are in the present tense.[12] A fourth section of roughly equal length (vv. 38-39)[13] contains a development of ten forms of adverse power in a series linked with "nor" (vv. 38-39c). This has an almost hymnic quality,[14] in which eight of

39 as the opening of the proof that extends to 11:36, recent commentaries view this as the concluding pericope of the preceding several chapters; see Cranfield, 1:434; Achtemeier, 148; Dunn, 1:497; Stuhlmacher, 138–39; Moo, 537–38; Theobald, 253–54; Schreiner, 456–57; Haacker, 173; Byrne, 247–75.

2 See Weiss, "Beiträge," 195f.; Gaugler, 342; Balz, *Heilsvertrauen*, 116–17; Michel, 213; Kuss, 2:487; Käsemann, 246.

3 Osten-Sacken's proposal of a catechetical formula of questions and answers in *Römer 8*, 20–47, requires the inversion of v. 31b and c and the excision of vv. 35b-37, rendering it implausible. While accepted by Synofzik, *Vergeltungsaussagen*, 102–4, the critique by Dunn, 1:497, is convincing. The comprehensive survey of similar proposals by Paulsen, *Überlieferung*, 137–51, results in the proposal of a two-strophe hymn cited in vv. 31-34, but the poetic structure is not compelling and the lack of non-Pauline language or ideas renders the theory of citation implausible.

4 See Norden, *Agnostos Theos*, 201–7, 273; Paulsen, *Überlieferung*, 168–72, following suggestions by Seeberg, *Katechismus*, 77ff.; Kramer, *Christ*, 29; Schweizer, *Erniedrigung*, 110–11.

5 Paulsen, *Überlieferung*, 171; Balz, *Heilsvertrauen*, 119–20. I eliminate the word "Jesus" on text-critical grounds, and "rather" on rhetorical grounds, discussed below. I also eliminate the καί . . . καί ("not only . . . but also") syntax, which serves Paul's rhetorical purpose but not that of the original confessional material.

6 See Jewett, "Numerical Sequences," 230, 237–38. Dunn, 1:499, comments on the "strongly Jewish character" of this passage, but does not refer to the Jewish numerical preferences for series of sevens and tens. Osten-Sacken, *Römer 8*, 21–47, argues for

a four-question-and-answer structure taken over by Paul in 8:31-35, counting only the questions beginning with τίς ("who"). Snyman, "Style," 220–21, offers an alternative analysis that the first three rhetorical questions in vv. 31-32 are followed by three *dialektika*, consisting of vv. 33-34a, 34b-c, and 35-39.

7 Bullinger, *Figures*, 950, classifies this series as an *erotesis* (= an interrogation with animated questions) in affirmative negation, in which the questions are put in the affirmative, but the answers must be supplied by the audience in the emphatic negative.

8 See Lamarche and le Dû, *Romains 5–8*, 77–79; in "Numerical Sequences," 237, I followed the Nestle-Aland punctuation of the questions in vv. 31-35, resulting in a series of seven. But closer examination based on Barrett, 172, and Fitzmyer, 533, adds three questions to this series, resulting in a series of ten.

9 See the discussion of the parallel passage of 2 Cor 1:7-8 by C. F. G. Heinrici, *Der zweite Brief an die Korinther* (Göttingen: Vandenhoeck & Ruprecht, 1900), 65–68; see also Ferrari, *Peristasenkatalogen*, 287; Ebner, *Peristasenkataloge bei Paulus*, 371.

10 See Jewett, "Numerical Sequences," 236; Gottfried Schille, "Die Liebe Gottes in Christus. Beobachtungen zu Rm 8:31-39," *ZNW* 59 (1968) 236.

11 Bullinger, *Figures*, 202; Snyman, "Style," 221–22.

12 See Snyman, "Style," 223–26.

13 A four-strophe pattern was suggested by Weiss, "Beiträge," 195; see also Lamarche and le Dû, *Romains 5-8*, 79.

14 Schille, "Rm 8:31-39," 238.

the forces are listed as correlative pairs: "death/life," "angels/rulers," "things present/things to come," and "height/depth."[15] The discrepancy in pairing caused by the insertion of "powers"[16] at the end of v. 38 and "any other creature" in v. 39 may be motivated by Paul's desire to end the series of ten with an inclusive category for which no pairing was available.

The four sections in this pericope are arranged in two closely linked pairs. Each of the first two sections contains five lines, the first beginning on the theme of God being for us (v. 31b) and the second concluding on the note of Christ's intercession (v. 34d). The third section begins with "who can separate us from the love of the Christ" (v. 35a) and the fourth ends with nothing being "able to separate us from the love of God" (v. 39d), which produces a kind of ring-composition.[17] A striking paronomasia links the final two verses, with the "powers" (δυνάμεις) not being sufficiently "powerful" (δυνήσεται) to separate believers from God. The reiteration of ὑπὲρ ἡμῶν ("on behalf of us") in vv. 31, 32, and 34 echoes in the wordplay with ὑπερνικῶμεν ("we are supervictors") in v. 37. The passage concludes with an effective clausula, "which is in Christ Jesus our Lord." It is a wonderful, exultant example of Pauline inspiration, driving artistic prose as far as possible in the direction of poetry[18] and providing the "emotional appeal to the audience" required in a proper peroration.[19]

Rhetorical Disposition

IV.		The *probatio*
5:1– 8:39	B.	The second proof: Life in Christ as a new system of honor that replaces the quest for status through conformity to the law
8:31-39		10. Conclusion: The status of the elect based on divine love
8:31-32		a. The first *Erotesis*: rhetorical questions concerning divine favor
8:31a		1) The first rhetorical question: A question of general inference from the preceding argument
8:31b		2) The second rhetorical question
		a) The premise of God's favor
		b) The question whether any power is capable of impeaching the elect
		c) The implied answer: "None!"
8:32		3) The third rhetorical question
8:32a-b		a) The christological premise
8:32a		(1) God did not spare Christ
8:32b		(2) God allowed Christ to die for all
8:32c		b) The inference that God will give believers "the all" in league with Christ
		c) The implied answer: "Yes!"
8:33-34		b. The second *Erotesis*: Rhetorical questions about whether believers can be disqualified
8:33a		1) The fourth rhetorical question about a charge against the elect
8:33b		2) The fifth rhetorical question
		a) The absurd possibility that the rectifying God impeaches his own elect
		b) The implied answer: "No way!"
8:34a		3) The sixth rhetorical question about who condemns
8:34b		4) The seventh rhetorical question
		a) The absurd possibility that the Christ is the condemner
		b) The implied answer: "No way!"
8:34c-e		5) The eighth rhetorical question
		a) The absurd possibility that the resurrected, interceding Christ is the condemner
		b) The implied answer: "No way!"
8:35-37		c. The third *Erotesis*: Rhetorical questions concerning suffering as separation from Christ
8:35a		1) The ninth rhetorical question about who can separate the elect from Christ
8:35b		2) The tenth rhetorical question about seven forms of suffering unable to separate the elect from Christ
		a) Affliction
		b) Narrow scrapes
		c) Persecution

---

15 See Friedrich Hauck, "δέκα," *TDNT* 2 (1964) 37; Jewett, "Numerical Sequences," 230.

16 Paulsen, *Überlieferung*, 148–51, discusses the efforts by Könnecke, *Emendationen*, 25; Dibelius, *Geisterwelt;* and Schille, "Rm 8:31-39," 237–38, to restore a consistent pairing either by deleting "powers" or shifting its location. Paulsen concludes that the canonical text should be preserved.

17 See Weiss, "Beiträge," 196; Harvey, *Listening*, 197, argues for a ring-composition in the reiteration of "separate from the love of Christ . . . God." Pieter J. Maartens's proposal of a chiastic order in verses 32-34 is less plausible; see "The Vindication of the Righteous in Romans 8:31-39: Inference and Relevance," *HerTS* 51 (1995) 1060–61.

18 See Käsemann, 246–47.

19 Snyman, "Style," 227.

	d) Famine
	e) Nakedness
	f) Peril
	g) Sword
8:36	3) The Scripture proof
8:36a	a) The citation formula
8:36b-c	b) The citation of Ps 44:22 concerning believers being slaughtered
8:37	4) The interpretation: Believers are super victors through Christ's love
8:38-39	d. *Enumeratio*: Paul's conviction that no force is able to separate the elect from Christ
8:38	1) The formula of conviction
8:38-39a	2) Ten references to forces
	a) Death
	b) Life
	c) Angels
	d) Rulers
	e) Things present
	f) Things to come
	g) Powers
	h) Heights
	i) Depths
	j) Any other creature
8:39b	3) The contention of nonseparation
	a) None has sufficient power to divorce believers from God
	b) Those threatened by separation: "us"
	c) The center from which separation threatens: "the love of God"
	d) The clausula elaborating the mediation of divine love: "in Christ Jesus our Lord"

Exegesis

■ **31** The pericope opens with the rhetorical question, τί οὖν ἐροῦμεν ("What then shall we say?"), an inferential formula that I discussed in 4:1; 6:1; and 7:7. It conveys "the processibility of the discourse," leading the hearer from the previous argument to this peroration in a smooth manner without any hint of censure.[20] In this instance, the formula is augmented by the prepositional phrase πρὸς ταῦτα ("in view of these things"). A similar formula occurs in Plato *Crito* 50b5, "What shall we say (τί ἐροῦμεν), O Crito, in view of these things and other such things? (πρὸς ταῦτα καὶ ἄλλα τοιαῦτα)." There is a consensus that πρός should be translated "in view of,"[21] but the reference to "these things" has been widely debated. It could relate to the immediately preceding vv. 28-30,[22] but they do not contain the themes of suffering, condemnation, or the atoning death of Christ. A reference to the entire preceding pericope seems more plausible because it contains the themes of suffering, creation, intercession, love, and the future glory,[23] but the theme of Christ's death is also absent, which would be included if Paul were referring to the entire preceding chapter.[24] To suggest that 8:31-39 provides a peroration for the entire argument of the letter beginning with 1:16[25] is too wide ranging; many of the themes in the first proof are missing here. The strongest case is made by those who see a peroration of the entire second proof that begins in 5:1-11,[26] because 8:31-39 provides such extensive echoes to that first pericope in the second proof:[27]

set right	5:1, 9	8:33
suffering	5:3	8:35-37
God's love	5:5, 8	8:35, 39
Christ's death	5:6, 10	8:34
Saved from wrath	5:9	8:31-34
Christ's resurrection	5:10	8:34
Rejoicing in God	5:11	8:31-39

The rhetorical question thus asks the audience to reflect on the burden of the entire second proof. The

---

20 Palmer, "τί οὖν," 205–6; see also Moores, *Wrestling*, 118.

21 Moule, *Idiom Book*, 53, followed by Cranfield, 1:435; Dunn, 1:499; Moo, 539.

22 Weiss, 381; Jülicher, 287; Kühl, 306; Michel, 279.

23 Peter Fiedler, "Röm 8:31-39 als Brennpunkt paulinischer Frohbotschaft," *ZNW* 68 (1977) 33–34; Zeller, 165; Dunn, 1:499.

24 Lipsius, 142.

25 Cranfield, 1:435, followed vaguely by Dunn, 1:499; Morris, 334.

26 Zahn, 422; Käsemann, 236; Barrett, 171; Dodd, 146; Nygren, 225–26, 251 (German edition); Schlier, 276; Osten-Sacken, *Römer 8*, 47–60; Wilckens, 2:172; Fitzmyer, 530; Moo, 539.

27 See Dahl, *Studies*, 88–90; also Osten-Sacken, *Römer 8*, 50–60, 310–11; Maartens, "Vindication," 1057–58, creates a comparable list of correlative language from 4:22 to 5:11.

answer is formulated in language shaped by the atonement of Christ: "If God is for us (ὑπὲρ ἡμῶν), who is against us?"[28] Since there are no exact antecedents in the OT for this formula of God's activity, the use of this preposition draws the memory of the hearers back to 5:5-8, where God demonstrated his love in that Christ "died for the ungodly" (ὑπὲρ ἀσεβῶν), which, as we noted, was followed by three additional occurrences of ὑπέρ related to Christ's atoning death. This is reiterated in 8:27, where Christ intercedes ὑπὲρ ἁγίων ("for the saints"). The next verse (v. 32) employs the formula again in an explicitly christological context. This usage echoes the language of the Eucharist: "This is my body which is for you" (ὑπὲρ ὑμῶν, 1 Cor 11:24); "the blood of the covenant poured out for many" (ὑπὲρ πολλῶν, Mark 14:24).[29] In Käsemann's words, Paul has in mind here "not a concept of God but the saving act centered in the death of Jesus characterizes the God for us."[30] Christ's shameful death in behalf of the shamed bestows the ultimate honor of God's favor on those who deserve nothing.

The second rhetorical question, "who is against us?" reflects the premise of biblical monotheism and the situation of believers facing antagonism or martyrdom. If the one God of the universe is "for us," nobody can finally thwart that favor.[31] The "who" remains unspecified[32] and thereby inclusive, implying that no power or person can prevail against the one true God. It is not that believers lack adversaries, as this pericope will go on to elaborate,[33] but that none of them will ultimately prevail. An example of this confidence is Isa 50:9, which

conveys the monotheistic confidence in the face of opposition by reduplicating Yahweh's name, "the Lord, the Lord will help me; who will harm (τίς κακώσει) me?" The succinct formula καθ' ἡμῶν ("against us") appears with its antithesis in Mark 9:40, "for whoever is not against us (καθ' ἡμῶν) is for us (ὑπὲρ ἡμῶν)." As a summary of the second proof, this first question makes it clear that the traditional understanding of justification in terms of individual forgiveness is too narrow.[34] To participate in divine righteousness, as this entire proof has demonstrated, is to be brought by grace under God's favor and protection. The deepest concern of shame is here addressed: whether we are valued and loved, despite the precarious situation of being assaulted by forces superior to our puny powers. If God is "for us," the lives of the slaves and handworkers as well as the patrons and the clients in the Roman house and tenement churches have a divinely imparted significance that no other power can remove no matter what they decide to do "against us."[35]

■ 32 The opening of the third rhetorical question with the relative pronoun ὅς ("who") is reminiscent of hymnic citations elsewhere in the NT (Phil 2:6-11; Col 1:15-20), and the expression "delivered up for us all" appears formulaic, but the form and style of this sentence do not appear to be hymnic and the language is typically Pauline.[36] The particle γέ has the intensive meaning of "even" in this context,[37] and thus is argumentative rather than hymnic. It is the reference to God's not "sparing (ἐφείσατο) his own son" that has attracted the most attention in this sentence. Abraham is promised a bless-

---

28 See Gerhard Delling, "Die Entfaltung des 'Deus pro nobis' in Röm 8,31-39," *SNTU* 4 (1979) 76–96.

29 See Jeremias, *Abba*, 206, 213; Hermann Patsch, "ὑπέρ," *EDNT* 3 (1993) 397.

30 Käsemann, 247, referring to Luz, *Geschichtsverständnis*, 371; Balz, *Heilsvertrauen*, 118; see also Popkes, *Christus Traditus*, 195–96.

31 See Dunn, 1:500.

32 This is a significant feature of the demonstrative rhetoric evident in the fourfold repetition of τίς ("who") in this passage; the references are on the level of generality that avoids attacking persons. Demonstrative rhetoric does not name names.

33 Morris, 335.

34 See Moores, *Wrestling*, 121–22.

35 See Maartens's contention in "Vindication,"

1065–66, about the "alternative community of believers" that Paul's discourse was intended to sustain.

36 A hymnic citation is proposed by Osten-Sacken in *Römer 8*, 20–47, discussed in n. 3 above; Fuchs, *Freiheit*, 116–18, suggests the citation of traditional, confessional materials; the critique of the hymnic theory is found in Wengst, *Formeln*, 55–56, 61; Paulsen, *Überlieferung*, 161–62. Schille, "Rm 8:31-39," 232–35, notes that the language is thoroughly Pauline.

37 BAGD 152.

ing since "you did not spare your beloved son" (οὐκ ἐφείσω τοῦ υἱοῦ σου τοῦ ἀγαπητοῦ, Gen 22:16), which led to the later development of the Aqedah, the rabbinic and haggadic term for the binding of Isaac as an atoning sacrifice.[38] In 1946 Hans Joachim Schoeps proposed that the Aqedah provided the precedent for understanding the atoning death of Jesus,[39] which had a wide impact on the subsequent discussion.[40] Several careful evaluations of the evidence adduced by Schoeps and his advocates showed, however, that the atoning dimensions of the Isaac story arose in Judaism only after the second century C.E. and thus could not have stimulated the development of Christian atonement materials.[41] Paulsen concludes that there is probably a traditional allusion to Gen 22 in Rom 8:32, but that the goal and precise scope of this tradition are no longer accessible and Paul never develops the Aqedah motif.[42] Others flatly deny any allusion to Gen 22.[43] This skeptical conclusion tallies with the fact that there are other LXX passages that employ the same terminology. For example, David commands Joab, "Spare for my sake (φείσασθέ μοι) the young man, Absalom" (2 Sam 18:5); and David "spared" (ἐφείσατο) Mephibosheth while other hostages were "given" (ἔδωκεν) to the Gibeonites to be hanged to redeem them from the famine, thought to be God's punishment for the unavenged blood of their kinsmen killed earlier by Saul (2 Sam 21:7, 9).[44] There is nothing unusual about this terminology in a world in which the vanquished often fell to the mercy of victors.[45] The refusal to spare one's own children, for example, is expressed in Brutus's words to his treacherous co-consul, "Since I, not having spared my own children, shall spare you, O Collatinus . . . (ἔπειτ᾽ ἐγὼ τῶν ἐμῶν οὐ φεισά-μενος τέκνων, σοῦ φείσομαι, Κολλατῖνε. . . , Dionysus Halicarnassus Antiq. rom. 5.10.7).[46] This Republican consul had executed his conspiratorial sons but now spares his equally treacherous co-consul. Nor is the link between "sparing" and "handing over" that we find in this verse unusual; for example, Diodorus Siculus reports that the Spartan admiral Callicratidas conquered Methymne but "sparing the men, he handed over the city to the Methymnaeans" (τῶν δ᾽ ἀνδρῶν φεισάμενος, ἀπέδωκε τοῖς Μηθυμναίοις τὴν πόλιν, Hist. 13.76.5). While the vocabulary is ordinary, the event to which Paul alludes is extraordinary and arresting. "Not even to spare his own son" is the ultimate act

38 See P. R. Davies and B. D. Chilton, "The Aqedah: A Revised Tradition History," *CBQ* 40 (1978) 514–15.

39 Hans Joachim Schoeps, "The Sacrifice of Isaac in Paul's Theology," *JBL* 65 (1946) 385–92.

40 Earlier commentators such as Zahn, 422, pointed to the Genesis parallel; the influence of the Schoeps hypothesis is visible in Cranfield, 1:208; Wilckens, 2:173; Zeller, 166; Moo, 540; J. E. Wood, "The Isaac Typology in the New Testament," *NTS* 14 (1968) 583–89; Nils A. Dahl, "The Atonement—An Adequate Reward for the Akedah? (Ro 8:32)," in E. E. Ellis and M. Wilcox, eds., *Neotestamentica et Semitica: Studies in Honour of Matthew Black* (Edinburgh: T.&T. Clark, 1969) 15–29; Max Wilcox, "'Upon the Tree'—Deut. 21:22-23 in the New Testament," *JBL* 96 (1977) 98–99; Robert J. Daly, "The Soteriological Significance of the Sacrifice of Isaac," *CBQ* 39 (1977) 67; Popkes, *Christus Traditus*, 195; L. W. Hurtado, "Jesus' Divine Sonship in Paul's Epistle to the Romans," in S. K. Soderlund and N. T. Wright, eds., *Romans and the People of God: Essays in Honor of Gordon D. Fee on the Occasion of His 65th Birthday* (Grand Rapids/Cambridge: Eerdmans, 1999) 231–32; Powers, *Salvation through Participation*, 137.

41 See Davies and Chilton, "Aqedah," 545–46; Alan F. Segal, "'He Who Did Not Spare His Own Son . . .': Jesus, Paul and the Akedah," in P. Richardson and J. C. Hurd, Jr., eds., *From Jesus to Paul: Studies in Honour of Francis Wright Beare* (Waterloo, Ont.: Wilfrid Laurier University, 1984) 169–84; Barrett, *Adam*, 27–30; Fitzmyer, 531–32.

42 Paulsen, *Überlieferung*, 167.

43 Kuss, 3:652; Schlier, 277; Fitzmyer, 532.

44 See Daniel R. Schwartz, "Two Pauline Allusions to the Redemptive Mechanism of the Crucifixion," *JBL* 102 (1983) 264–66. This episode is taken up by Hamerton-Kelly in *Cross*, 79, to suggest that Paul understands the death of Jesus as "an inversion of sacrificial violence" that aimed to stop the cycle of vengeance, showing that "God does not need to be appeased like the Gibeonites."

45 For example, Diodorus Siculus *Hist* 14.75.8; Josephus *Ant.* 1.340; Plutarch *Cic.* 18.1. Paul also employs the verb φείδομαι within its normal semantic range in Rom 11:21; 1 Cor 7:28; 2 Cor 1:23; 12:6; 13:2, according to BAGD 854.

46 See also Dionysus Halicarnassus *Antiq. Rom.* 8.79.3; Pseudo-Plutarch *Flu.* 23.112 (sparing one's daughters).

that a father could perform in behalf of others; its pathos, especially in the ancient context, which assumed an ineradicable, emotional bond between father and son, is unmistakable. Nothing could more clearly demonstrate that "God is for us."

The second line in this section, that "God delivered him up (παρέδωκεν) for us all," employs the verb of 4:25, "delivered up for our transgressions." There is wide agreement that this formula is pre-Pauline,[47] and it seems likely that it echoes the language of Isa 53:6, 12.[48] The ὑπὲρ ἡμῶν ("for us, on our behalf") formula recurs from the preceding verse but with an addition that was not a part of the traditional formula:[49] the "all" reflects Paul's particular concerns for the inclusivity of the gospel.[50] Christ's atoning death encompasses Jews as well as Gentiles, weak as well as strong. Here Paul places himself among the "us all," along with all of the Roman believers, as well as all who have not yet heard the gospel, thus bringing this formulation in line with the confessional citation in Rom 3:25-26. The death of Christ offers universal atonement, moving beyond the boundaries of traditional cultic activities in the ancient world, including the Day of Atonement ceremonies in the Jerusalem temple. It conveys divine love for the entire human race, overcoming the deficits of shame that have corrupted history since Adam's fall.

The final line of the third question begins with πῶς οὐχί ("how not"), an unusual combination that Paul employs in 2 Cor 3:8. The interrogative particle with a negative produces the sense of "surely, most certainly,"[51] completing in this instance a "lesser to greater" argument.[52] This rather awkward formulation[53] conveys "forcibly the unthinkableness of the opposite."[54] Since the incredible gift of Jesus' atoning death has already been granted, it is all the more certain that God will grant believers everything. The same form of argument was used in 5:9-10.[55] The verb χαρίζομαι ("to give, bestow grace") is used here for the only time in Romans, echoing the concept of χάρις ("grace"), which has appeared so frequently thus far in the letter (1:5, 7; 3:24; 4:4, 16; 5:2, 15, 17, 20, 21; 6:1, 14, 15, 17; 7:25). Χάρις refers to the gifts of divine favor granted through Christ to the undeserving, a leitmotif in Paul's argument.[56] The verb should therefore be translated in a manner that reflects this connection in English, which means that "give" or "grant" without an adverbial clarification remain inadequate.[57] I follow Morris in translating, "graciously give us the universe."[58] That τὰ πάντα ("the all") refers to the entire creation[59] rather than the totality of salvation[60] is indicated by the article[61] and suggested by the previous argument that believers inherit the promise to Abraham that his descendants should "inherit the world" (4:13). This promise was reiterated in 8:17, that believers are "joint heirs with Christ." With or without the article, πᾶς often has an expansive, cosmological sense in Paul's letters.[62] In 1 Cor 3:21-23 Paul elaborated on the boundless, cosmological gift already granted to believers, although here πάντα is anarthrous: "For all

---

47   See Popkes, *Christus Traditus*, 251–53; Paulsen, *Überlieferung*, 163; Dunn, 1:500; Fitzmyer, 532.

48   See Kazimierz Romaniuk, "De Themate Ebed Jahve in Soteriologia Sancti Pauli," *CBQ* 23 (1961) 15; Fitzmyer, 532; Moo, 650; Shum, *Paul's Use of Isaiah*, 200–201.

49   See Rom 4:25; 5:8; 2 Cor 5:21; Gal 3:13; 1 Thess 5:10, along with later NT references such as Eph 5:2; Titus 2:14; 1 John 3:16.

50   See Dunn, 1:501; Byrne, 275–76; Powers, *Salvation through Participation*, 137–38.

51   BAGD 732.

52   Meyer, 2:98–99.

53   Fitzmyer, 532, refers to this as an anacoluthon, but it appears to be a complete sentence.

54   Murray, 1:326.

55   See Cranfield, 1:436.

56   It is a mistake to limit this gift to "forgiveness," as proposed by Schlatter, 195.

57   Klaus Berger insists on "give, grant" in "χαρίζομαι," *EDNT* 3 (1993) 456.

58   Morris, 336.

59   See Berger, "χαρίζομαι," 456; Wilckens, 2:173–74; Dunn, 1:502; Byrne, 276; BAGD 631: "everything."

60   Black, 120; Morris, 336; Murray, 1:326; Fitzmyer, 532.

61   BAGD 633, as, for example, Plato *Ep.* 6. p. 232d, "God of all things" (τῶν πάντων θεός); *Corp. herm.* 13.17, "having created the universe" (κτίσαντα τὰ πάντα); Philo *Spec.* 1.208; *Her.* 36; *Somn.* 1.241. Paul uses τὰ πάντα to refer to the universe in 1 Cor 8:6; 15:28; Phil 3:21; it is also found in Eph 3:9; 4:10; Col 1:16-17.

62   See Hugolinus Langkammer, "πᾶς," *EDNT* 3 (1993) 48; Dunn, 1:502, also lists Rom 11:36; 1 Cor 8:6; 11:12; 15:27-28; Phil 3:21; Col 1:16-17, 20; Eph 1:10-11, 23; 3:9; 4:10 as having this cosmological sense.

things ($\pi\acute{\alpha}\nu\tau\alpha$) are yours, whether Paul or Apollos or Cephas or the world or life or death or the present or the future, all are yours ($\pi\acute{\alpha}\nu\tau\alpha$ $\acute{\upsilon}\mu\hat{\omega}\nu$); and you are Christ's, and Christ is God's."

This is a reconfiguration of imperialism, because the gift of the world is constrained by a hierarchy of belongingness in which one's proximity to worldly power and prestige no longer plays a role. As Barrett points out, as free lords of all things "the Christians' sovereignty over the world . . . takes place only through and in Christ. The moment Christians seek to escape from the sovereignty of Christ they lose their own partially recovered status among God's creatures."[63] They are coming into ownership of the universe, but only as Christ owned it, through suffering love rather than through imperial domination and exploitation. And unlike traditional imperialism, this eliminates all claims of superiority on the part of the recipients of grace. In this new form of responsible sovereignty over the universe, the "revelation of the sons of God" (8:19) and their recovery of "glory" (8:17-18, 30) are occurring both in the present and in the future. The future tense $\chi\alpha\rho\acute{\iota}\sigma\epsilon\tau\alpha\iota$ ("he will graciously give") has the function of celebrative assurance,[64] not postponement.[65] The gift of transformed sovereignty that believers have already received will continue and be fulfilled in the eschaton. This renders it likely that the phrase $\sigma\grave{\upsilon}\nu$ $\alpha\grave{\upsilon}\tau\hat{\omega}$ ("with him") in v. 32 refers to their joint inheritance under the lordship of Christ, rather than the sacramental gift of Christ.[66] The one crucified for the sake of others thus shares and shapes the churches' sovereignty over the world.

■ 33 The second series of rhetorical questions deals with whether the saints can be disqualified from their participation in the glorious new form of sovereignty over the world. The legal term $\grave{\epsilon}\gamma\kappa\alpha\lambda\epsilon\hat{\iota}\nu$ ("to impeach, bring charges against"), used elsewhere in the NT only in public trials depicted in Acts 19:38, 40; 23:29; 26:2, 7, is ordinarily thought to evoke the scene of the final judgment in the divine court.[67] But this shifts attention away from the immediate context of the sovereignty of the saints over the universe and their glory in the midst of adversity. Nowhere else in the OT, the NT, or associated literature is this verb employed in connection with eschatological judgment.[68] Moreover, when one places vv. 33-34 in the context of the last judgment, the element of impartial, divine evaluation of performance on which Paul insists in Rom 2:1-16 and in his other letters is drastically curtailed.[69] It would be as if believers were exempt from accountability simply because they are the elect, which is far from Paul's point. Moreover, none of the adverse experiences listed in vv. 35 and 38 could count as indictments against the saints in the last judgment. The issue here is whether anyone can disqualify the elect from their inheritance, which was a highly relevant question in the light of the mutual damning between the churches in Rome. The form of the rhetorical question requires the response, "No one!"[70] Although the verb $\grave{\epsilon}\gamma\kappa\alpha\lambda\epsilon\hat{\iota}\nu$ was widely used in court situations,[71] it is wrong to assume modern court conditions. In Greek and Roman law, a public official or a private citizen could be charged/impeached on vague indictments of malfeasance or lack of credentials.[72] In Rome, a censor

---

63 Barrett, *1 Corinthians*, 96.
64 See Snyman, "Style," 223–25.
65 Fitzmyer, 532: "eschatological salvation."
66 Schmidt, 153.
67 See Leenhardt, 237, and Barrett, 173, for the suggestion that Satan would be the one making this accusation, an interpretation rightly rejected by Käsemann, 248, and Fitzmyer, 533; the last judgment scheme is advocated by others such as Synofzik, *Vergeltungsaussagen*, 103; Schlier, 277; Dunn, 1:502; Stuhlmacher, 138; Moo, 541.
68 There is a brief article by Karl Ludwig Schmidt, "$\grave{\alpha}\nu\tau\iota$-, $\grave{\epsilon}\gamma\kappa\alpha\lambda\acute{\epsilon}\omega$ $\kappa\tau\lambda$.," *TDNT* 3 (1965) 496, with a conventional view of "accuse," and only the briefest reference in *EDNT;* all of the examples provided by BAGD 215 and those listed in Hatch-Redpath (Exod

22:9; Prov 19:3; Zech 1:4; Sir 46:19; 2 Macc 6:21) deal with humans making charges against their fellows. Wis 12:12 refers to humans attempting to impeach God.
69 This problem appears to be overlooked by Synofzik, *Vergeltungsaussagen*, 102–4; Volf, *Paul and Perseverance*, 66–69.
70 Newman and Nida, 171.
71 A *TLG* search produced over twenty-two hundred examples, mostly from the legal sector.
72 See Alan Watson, "Roman Law," in M. Grant and R. Kitzinger, eds., *Civilization of the Ancient Mediterranean: Greece and Rome* (New York: Scribner, 1988) 1:607–30.

possessed "unlimited discretionary power" to issue moral censures, which "could practically destroy a man politically and socially."[73] As in Rom 8:33, Dio Chrysostom *Orat.* 52.5.7 refers to indicting or impeaching a group, in this instance for vague reasons: "so that anyone might happen to indict those who don't love the man (ὥστε τυχόν ἄν τις ἐγκαλέσαι τῶν οὐ φιλούντων τὸν ἄνδρα)." Similarly vague charges appear to be in view with regard to Diogenes, "Concerning the philosophers, he impeaches them all (πᾶσιν ἐγκαλεῖ), particularly the Seven."[74] References to bringing charges against the gods also come close to the sense of impeachment,[75] because no law was binding on them and no earthly court could adjudicate their indictment.[76]

The issue of impeachment and possible disqualification is evident in Paul's choice of the expression "God's elect." While this is the only time Paul refers to believers as the ἐκλεκτοὶ θεοῦ,[77] the stem is directly related to the previous passage, which proclaimed that "those whom he predestined, these he also called (ἐγκάλεσεν, 8:30).[78] As Schrenk observes, this formulation "sums up emphatically all that has been said in 8:14f. about the bearers of the Spirit, the υἱοὶ θεοῦ ['sons of God'], the ἀγαπῶντες τὸν θεόν ['those loving God']."[79] It is their status, not their performance, that is in question here. Given the marginal social circumstances of most of the believers in Rome and their ongoing troubles with persecution, poverty, and conflict, how could anyone imagine that they would inherit the earth? In fact, there are indications in 11:17-25 and 14:1—15:13 that Christian groups in Rome were questioning each other's legitimacy. While the question about who shall impeach God's elect had a direct relevance for the Roman situation, the identifica-

tion of the elect as belonging to God renders the question moot. Especially in the Roman context, the person at the top defines the law—and, in a sense, is the law.[80] The emperor's rescripts become law for future generations. Similarly in the Christian context, God has an absolute power to determine one's status. This leads to the next rhetorical question.

There is an issue concerning the punctuation of v. 33b, with Nestle-Aland and most commentaries opting for the tradition developed by the church fathers, who understood "God who sets right!" as the answer to the rhetorical question in v. 33a.[81] The problem is that if "God who sets right!" is an answer to the question about who makes a charge, then it must be understood as ironic. That is, the one who impeaches God's elect is God herself, a claim that makes so little sense that it must be rejected as ironic. This seems quite heavy-handed and, given the importance and development of the δικ- stem in Romans, both confusing and unnecessary. The solution was put forward by C. K. Barrett, that vv. 33-34 contain a series of four rhetorical questions, translated as follows:[82] "Who can bring a charge against God's elect? God—who justifies us? Who condemns us? Christ Jesus—who died, or rather was raised, who is at the right hand of God, who actually is interceding on our behalf?" Joseph Fitzmyer has suggested a final refinement of this hypothesis—that v. 34b-e actually consists of two rhetorical questions, the last beginning with the otherwise peculiar μᾶλλον ("rather").[83] So, remaining with the wording of Barrett, the revised punctuation appears as follows: "Christ Jesus—who died? Rather was raised, who is at the right hand of God, who actually is interceding on our behalf?" This new hypothesis pro-

---

73   Hans Julius Wolff, *Roman Law: An Historical Introduction* (Norman: University of Oklahoma Press, 1951) 35.

74   *Septem Sapientes Test.* 1.3; see Diehls and Kranz, *Vorsokratiker,* 61, Nr. 10.1–4.

75   Dio Chrysostom *Orat.* 38.20.1–2: "Now whenever there's a plague or earthquake, we bring charges against the gods (τοῖς θεοῖς ἐγκαλοῦμεν)." See also Epictetus *Diss.* 1.6.39; 2.5.12; 3.5.16; 3.22.12.

76   In part for this reason Aristotle comments in *Eth. eud.* 1238 b27, "for it's laughable, if any were to bring a charge against god (εἴ τις ἐγκαλοίη τῷ θεῷ)."

77   The only other occurrence in the indisputable

Pauline letters is Rom 16:13, where Rufus is called "elect in the Lord." The term "elect" is used frequently in the Synoptic Gospels; see Jost Eckert, "ἐκλεκτός," *EDNT* 1 (1990) 417.

78   See Michel, 281; Eckert, "ἐκλεκτός," 417–18.

79   Gottlob Schrenk, "ἐκλεκτός," *TDNT* 4 (1967) 189.

80   See Barrett, *Caligula,* 57, 266.

81   See Meyer, 2:99–101, for an account of the nineteenth-century discussion; Weiss, 383; Lagrange, 219–20; Dunn, 1:503; etc.

82   Barrett, 172–73, followed only by Fitzmyer, 533, but anticipated in part by Barth, 328.

83   Fitzmyer, 533.

vides a straightforward approach to vv. 33-34,[84] with each question beginning with τίς ("who") followed by obviously absurd queries that correlate nicely with the wording of the initial questions. If it is God who chooses the "elect," this comprises a close correlate to "God who sets right." By placing "God who sets right?" in the form of a question, its absurdity requires the audience to respond with a negative answer, "No way!" This correlation also confirms the line I have been following throughout this commentary, that righteousness is a matter of status rather than of forgiveness. Through the death of Christ, God rectifies the relationship between God's self and humans, transforming those who accept the gospel into God's elect. Paul has established such a firm foundation for this central theme in the previous chapters of Romans that the rhetorical question in v. 33b would have been very effective. The effectiveness may well have been enhanced by rather distant echoes between vv. 33b-34a and Isa 50:7-9.[85]

■ **34** Following the hypothesis developed by Barrett and Fitzmyer, the rhetorical question in v. 34a is coordinated with two succeeding questions about Christ's actions in v. 34b-e, each understood as showing the absurdity of fearing that anyone can disqualify the elect. The participle can be either present or future,[86] depending on the context; the parallelism with v. 33a suggests that the future was intended: "Who will be the condemner?"[87] The formulation harks back to the thesis in 8:1, that "there is no condemnation for those in Christ Jesus," so the succeeding question about the role of Christ makes perfect rhetorical sense. Again, there is a definite link between the choice of this verb and the congregational situation, since κρίνειν is employed in 14:3-4 to depict groups condemning the behavior of others who do not conform to their eating patterns.[88]

The counterquestion, "Christ who died?" (Χριστὸς ὁ ἀπέθανεν) in v. 34b is formulated in a traditional manner that echoes 5:6-8. In 1 Cor 15:3, the same verb appears in a confessional formula that Paul claims he received from the early Christian tradition: ὅτι Χριστὸς ἀπέθανεν ὑπὲρ τῶν ἁμαρτιῶν ἡμῶν ("that Christ died for our sins"), which sustains the impression that this is a pre-Pauline formula well known to the Roman churches. Even without the phrase "for us" or "for our sins," the redemptive significance of Christ's death was so widely shared in early Christianity[89] that the bare reference to it would have conveyed the sense of the atoning sacrifice. But that Christ who died for the sake of others should now become a "condemner" is so preposterous that it would evoke the response from believers in Rome, "No way!"

In v. 34c-e Paul goes on to heighten the absurdity by recalling the intercessory activity of the risen Christ. The question begins with μᾶλλον, which is often taken as a mild amendment or corrective ("rather"),[90] but here it has the sense in combination with δέ of "even more so."[91] A similar comparative sense was seen in each of the preceding appearances of μᾶλλον in 5:9, 10, 15, 17. As the beginning of a rhetorical question, following the Fitzmyer reading, this adverb makes excellent sense, but it remains unprecedented and contradictory in the middle of a kerygmatic formula as traditionally translated.

---

84   The critique of Barrett's proposal by Cranfield, 1:437–38, simply reiterates the traditional view, without recognizing its problems. Moo, 541, lists further options in punctuating these verses, but returns to the traditional punctuation without explaining why.

85   See Michel, 281; Osten-Sacken, *Römer 8*, 43–45, and Wilk, *Bedeutung des Jesajabuches*, 280–84, who suggest that 8:33-34 is an intentional resumé of Isa 50:7-9. That passage contains the words ὁ δικαιώσας ("the one who set right"), τίς ("who"), and κρινόμενος ("judge"). The echo seems quite faint, because Isaiah refers to enemies attempting to put the faithful to shame while God defends them, whereas in Rom 8, the question is whether God himself will disqualify the elect.

86   The accent, which of course is an editorial decision, would be on the third syllable in the present, κατακρίνων, and on the final syllable in the future, κατακρινῶν.

87   See Fitzmyer, 533, citing BDF §251.2.

88   See also the use of κατακρίνειν in 14:23.

89   See Kertelge, "Verständnis des Todes Jesu," 123–24.

90   Meyer, 2:102–3; Godet, 331; Murray, 1:328; Dunn, 1:503; Michael Wolter, "μᾶλλον," *EDNT* 2 (1991) 382.

91   BAGD 489.1–2: "to a greater degree, for a better reason, more surely." See also Zahn, 424; Kuss, 3:654; Cranfield, 1:434, 439.

As a corrective, it implies that there was a deficit in Christ's death, and as a simple comparative, it presents the resurrection as superior to the crucifixion.[92] The point of the comparison is not to contrast the resurrection with the crucifixion but to show how much more preposterous it would be to consider the resurrected, interceding Christ as the condemner; one could even translate, "Even more absurd," which would convey the vapidity of asserting that the risen, interceding Christ now condemns the elect. The verb ἐγείρω ("raise"), which appeared frequently in the earlier chapters of Romans in connection with Christ's resurrection, occurs also in 1 Cor 15:4, which Paul received from the tradition. Both verbs appear next to each other in other traditional formulas, such as 2 Cor 5:15, "who for their sake died and was raised (ἀποθανόντι καὶ ἐγερθέντι)." When ἐγερθείς is used in the passive, as in this instance, it has "a technical sense known to the readers,"[93] explicitly referring to Christ. Similarly to be "at the right hand of God" is a technical expression, in this instance for being at "the highest place of honor."[94] This expression is never otherwise employed by Paul, although it is typical for early Christian confessional and liturgical material (Eph 1:20; Col 3:1; Heb 1:3; 8:1; 10:12; 12:2; 1 Pet 3:22), influenced by Ps 110:1, which in the LXX has the famous line addressed by God to his son, κάθου ἐκ δεξιῶν μου ("sit at my right hand").[95] The καὶ . . . καί syntax of v. 34d-e, which was probably not part of the kerygmatic material Paul cited here, should be translated "not only . . . but also,"[96] enhancing the rhetorical absurdity that Paul is developing. Not only

is Christ seated at God's right hand, but he also intercedes for the saints, which renders the notion of his playing the role of the condemner all the more absurd.

The verb ἐντυγχάνειν ("to intercede") in v. 34c is picked up from vv. 26-27, where the Spirit is identified as the intercessor. Never elsewhere is Christ's intercession mentioned by Paul, although it is an important motif in Heb 7:25, and with different terminology in 1 John 2:1 and John 6:26; 17:1-26.[97] The word belongs in "the conceptual world of the ruler's court,"[98] where accusations and requests are heard and the person closest to the throne usually has the most influential word. An example of effective intercession is provided by Polybius *Hist* 4.76.9; Aratus, one of King Philip's influential advisors, approached him on behalf of some injured parties and "[w]hen they interceded with the king about these matters (ἐντυγχόντων δ᾽ αὐτῶν τῷ βασιλεῖ περὶ τούτων), Philip listened intently to what had happened, and encouraged the lads to take heart."[99] Ἐντυγχάνειν can also be used in the sense of petition as in this appeal to the emperor Diocletian, "making a petition (ἐντευξομένη) and requesting that through your attention the slave may be compelled to pay the income owed by him and be ordered to remain in our service."[100] In the religious context, there is a close parallel to Paul's wording in a second-century C.E. letter with the reassurance, ἰδότες ὅτι νυκτὸς καὶ ἡμέρας ἐντυγχάνω τῷ θεῷ ὑπὲρ ὑμῶν ("knowing that night and day I interceded to God on your behalf").[101] Paul's point, in this context, is that if Christ intercedes in behalf of the saints, it is utterly preposterous to fear that anyone can impeach

---

92 I find no discussion of these conundrums in the commentaries, but they are identified by Schweizer, *Erniedrigung*, 210–11; Paulsen, *Überlieferung*, 169; Balz, *Heilsvertrauen*, 119, refers explicitly to Paul's insertion of rhetorical terms such as μᾶλλον and καί.

93 Jacob Kremer, "ἐγείρω," *EDNT* 1 (1990) 375; see Kegel, *Auferstehung*, 12–25, for an analysis of this early, kerygmatic formula.

94 Peter von der Osten-Sacken, "δεξιός," *EDNT* 1 (1990) 286.

95 Ibid.; Hay, *Glory at the Right Hand*, 59–90; Paulsen, *Überlieferung*, 169–70; see also Martin Hengel, "Psalm 110 und die Erhöhung des Auferstandenen zur Rechten Gottes," in C. Breytenbach and H. Paulsen, eds., *Anfänge der Christologie: Festschrift*

für Ferdinand Hahn zum 65. Geburtstag (Göttingen: Vandenhoeck & Ruprecht, 1991) 43–73.

96 BAGD 393.6.

97 See Käsemann, 248, referring to Johannes Behm, "παράκλητος," *TDNT* 5 (1967) 811–14.

98 See Otto Bauernfeind, "ἐντυγχάνω," *TDNT* 8 (1972) 243; Horst Balz, "ἐντυγχάνω," *EDNT* 1 (1990) 461.

99 See also 1 Macc 8:38; 11:25; 2 Macc 2:25.

100 A. L. Connolly, "A Slave's Bid for Freedom," *NDIEC* 4 (1987) 100–104, cited from *P.Oxy.Hels.* Nr. 26.15–18.

101 *BGU* 1. Nr. 246.13–14, cited by MM 219.

their status. The audience in Rome can only answer "No way!" to this question, which brings the second series of *erotesis* to a close.

■ **35** The third series of rhetorical questions begins again with τίς matching the form of vv. 33a and 34a, although since the subsequent listing of seven forms of adversity are all neuter in English, the translation "what" is required.[102] The point of emphasis, in view of the word order, is on ἡμᾶς ("us"), a matter that has been noted but not explained by commentators.[103] The "us" is the first clue that the forms of adversity to be listed in this sentence have all been experienced by Paul and the Roman congregations, and there are reasons to suspect that such adversity was being used as the basis of discrimination against fellow believers in Rome, just as it was in Paul's earlier experiences in Ephesus and Corinth. The emphatic position of ἡμᾶς is a clear indication that separation from Christ because of the implications of adversity was a genuine issue,[104] not a rhetorical ploy. The vital question in this verse is not whether such adversity should hold "terrors for the believer,"[105] but whether it should constitute evidence for some groups to discredit the status of other groups on the premise that the elect should be exempt from misfortune. The verb χωρίζω ("divide, separate") points in this direction. It is used to describe the severance of

personal relationships, as in divorce (Mark 10:9; Matt 19:6; 1 Cor 7:10, 11, 15).[106] While the concept of the love of God derives from the OT (e.g., LXX Jer 38:3; Zeph 3:17), the "love of Christ" is a distinctively Pauline concept,[107] which articulates everything believers have received from him.[108] It is clearly a subjective genitive, referring to the love Christ shows to the undeserving. To be separated from this love implies alienation, breach of relationship, and severance from the community of the saints. While it may imply some form of legal separation,[109] it definitely would involve the loss of salvation.[110] Since "the love of God implies election," as Stauffer observes,[111] separation from that love means damnation, falling again under wrath.[112] So the question Paul poses here is whether anyone will be able to disqualify and thus sever the elect from Christ's love, a theme developed in 5:5-8 and reiterated in 8:37. Leaving unanswered the question of precisely "who" might wish to impose such separation on others, Paul moves instead to list the forms of adversity that some were in fact probably citing to delegitimize other house and tenement churches.

The catalogue of seven forms of adversity is similar to other tribulation lists in Greco-Roman and Jewish sources,[113] but the variety of details and the distinctive Pauline framework in this particular letter render it

102 Meyer, 2:103, suggests that this detail serves the rhetorical purpose of reiterating the openings of 33a and 34a. Godet, 333, proposes that Paul wished to suggest that each adversity was "an enemy bearing a grudge," but no indications of personification are in fact present.

103 See Cranfield, 1:439; Dunn, 1:504. Ebner, *Peristasenkataloge bei Paulus*, 372–73, appears to have this detail in mind when he argues that Paul selected dangers that he himself as well as other believers had experienced.

104 Gibbs, *Creation and Redemption*, 47.

105 Dunn, 1:512; similarly Schlatter, 197.

106 See Johannes B. Bauer, "χωρίζω," *EDNT* 3 (1993) 492.

107 See Oda Wischmeyer, "Traditionsgeschichtliche Untersuchung der paulinischen Aussagen über die Liebe (ἀγάπη)," *ZNW* 74 (1983) 235.

108 See Schlier, 278.

109 See Balz, *Heilsvertrauen*, 121, rejected for unclear reasons by Käsemann, 249.

110 See Gerhard Schneider, "ἀγάπη κτλ.," *EDNT* 1 (1990) 10.

111 Gottfried Quell and Ethelbert Stauffer, "ἀγαπάω κτλ.," *TDNT* 1 (1964) 49.

112 See Warnach, *Agape*, 517–29.

113 The classic study by Bultmann, *Stil*, 71–72, was followed up by many investigations of the lists in the Corinthian letters, surveyed and evaluated in John T. Fitzgerald's comprehensive study, *Cracks in an Earthen Vessel*, 7–31. Studies of tribulation lists related to Romans include Daniel Fraiken, "Romains 8:31-39: la position des églises de la gentilité" (diss., Harvard University, 1975); Wolfgang Schrage, "Leid, Kreuz und Eschaton. Die Peristasenkataloge als Merkmale paulinischer theologia crucis und Eschatologie," *EvTh* 34 (1974) 142–50; Ferrari, *Peristasenhatalogen*, 83–107; Robert Hodgson, "Paul the Apostle and First Century Tribulation Lists," *ZNW* 74 (1983) 59–80; Ebner, *Peristasenkataloge bei Paulus*, 161–69.

likely that he formulated this with a specific rhetorical situation in mind.[114] John Fitzgerald, in particular, has shown that Paul "adopts and adapts these materials for his own purposes" in a "highly creative manner" shaped by his understanding of the cross.[115] The following comparison between the major Pauline examples of tribulation lists shows a modest level of overlapping, with 2 Cor 11:23-29 and 1 Cor 4:10-13 each replicating three of the hardships mentioned in Romans. But the widely differing styles and content of these lists confirm Fitzgerald's conclusion.

Rom 8:35	2 Cor 6:4-5	2 Cor 11:23-29	2 Cor 12:10	1 Cor 4:10-13	Phil 4:12
1. θλίψις ("affliction")	θλίψεσιν	—	—	—	—
2. στενοχωρία ("distress")	στενοχωρίαις	—	στενοχωρίαις	—	—
3. διωγμός ("persecution")	—	—	διωγμοῖς	διωκόμενοι	—
4. λιμός ("hunger")	—	λιμός	—	πεινῶμεν καὶ διψῶμεν	πεινᾶν
5. γυμνότης ("nakedness")	—	γυμνότης	—	γυμνιτεύομεν	—
6. κίνδυνος ("peril")	—	κίνδυνος	—	—	—
7. μάχαιρα ("sword")	—	—	—	—	—
	seven additional forms of distress	twenty-three additional forms of distress	three additional forms of distress	seven additional forms of distress	two additional forms of distress

The list in Rom 8:35 belongs to the first of seven types of peristasis catalogues, the "catalogues of human hardships."[116] A classical example that comes relatively close to the form in Rom 8:35 is found in Dio Chrysostom's discussion of pain and distress of spirit; the Greek terms that overlap with verse 35 are provided in parentheses:

For instance, either (ἤ) the death of a relative, or (ἤ) the illness of one of them or (ἤ) of oneself, may occur, and besides these, loss of reputation, a financial reverse, complete or partial failure in some undertaking, pressure of affairs, danger (κίνδυνος), and all the countless other misfortunes which occur in life. . . .[117]

A brief catalogue of hardships in Philo's treatise *On the Virtues* (5) demonstrates that the peristasis theme was also important for Hellenistic Judaism: "Further there are many other conditions in human life admittedly hard to bear, poverty and disrepute and disablement and sickness in its manifold forms, in the face of which those of little wit all grow craven-hearted, lacking the valour even to raise themselves." In the later *Sayings of the Fathers (Pirqê 'Abôt)* 5.1, seven woes are attributed to seven types of sins, as follows:[118]

1. Drought (רעב אל בצרת) comes for partial tithing;
2. Panic and drought (רעב של מהומה ושל בצרת) come for not tithing at all;
3. Destruction (רעב של כליה) comes for not offering dough cake;
4. Plague and pestilence (דבר) come for failure to punish crime;
5. Sword (חבר) comes for delay of justice;

114 According to Paulsen, *Überlieferung*, 172–73, only Gerhard Münderlein, "Interpretation einer Tradition: Bemerkungen zu Röm 8:35f," *KD* 11 (1965) 136–42, has attempted to make a case for literary dependency on Deut 28:48, 53-57, which has not proven convincing.
115 Fitzgerald, *Cracks*, 207; Gorman, *Cruciformity*, 284–88.
116 Fitzgerald, *Cracks*, 47; Gorman, *Cruciformity*, 51–52, 285.
117 Dio Chrysostom *Orat.* 16.3.
118 Cited from Joseph H. Hertz, ed., *Sayings of the Fathers* (West Orange: Behrman House, 1945). As Ebner, *Peristasenkataloge bei Paulus*, 383, points out, Sir 40:8 also refers to "sevenfold" punishment for sinners, but Sir 40:9 actually lists eight tribulations: "death, bloodshed, strife, sword, calamities, famine, tribulation, and the scourge."

6. Wild Beasts (חיה רעה) come for perjury and profanation;
7. Captivity (גלות) comes for idolatry, immorality, and bloodshed.

A Latin example that reflects the Roman cultural environment is found in Seneca's letter of consolation to Marcia:[119] "But there, too, will be found a thousand plagues, banes of the body as well as of the mind, wars, robberies, poisons, shipwrecks, distempers of climate and of the body, untimely grief for those most dear, and death—whether an easy one or only after pain and torture no one can tell." The purpose of these catalogues in Stoic, Epicurean, and Cynic circles was to demonstrate the virtues of a sage[120] and, in the case of religious competition, to demonstrate "divine power" to overcome adversity and thus confirm the legitimacy of a philosopher or apostle.[121] But as Hans Dieter Betz showed, Paul rejects the tradition of self-praise[122] and, particularly in 2 Corinthians, employs the catalogues of hardship to demonstrate his congruence with the suffering Christ. He is the foolish, righteous sufferer who truly lives under the shadow of the cross.[123] The key to understanding Rom 8:35, which contains nothing of the traditional claim of the virtuous sage, is that in Ephesus and Corinth, Paul's weaknesses, poverty, imprisonments, and other forms of adversity were used by opponents to show that he was not "qualified" (2 Cor 2:6, 16; 3:5) to be an apostle.[124] The superapostles claimed exemption

from hardships while arguing that no one whose career was as troubled as Paul's could possibly embody the power of Christ. In this respect, they were apparently close to the OT tradition of the Deuteronomic Principle, which promised success and prosperity to the righteous and disasters to the wicked (Deut 30:15–31:22).[125] We find this reiterated in a Qumran fragment[126] that describes God's wrath, which will overtake evildoers, as involving "severe disease, famine, thirst, pestilence, and sword," a catalogue of hardships in which two elements overlap with Rom 8:35.[127] The seven punishments in *Pirqê 'Abôt* 5.1 "come into the world" in response to sins, several of which also overlap with Rom 8:35.[128] What all of these catalogues have in common are the issues of honor, shame, and qualification, which provide the immediate background for understanding the seven forms of hardship that Paul claims cannot separate the faithful from the love of Christ. By a detailed examination, we shall see that these seven forms of hardship could have provided the basis for critics within the early church to delegitimize sufferers, a possibility that Paul wished to counter.

The first two forms of tribulation, "affliction and distress," are reiterated from 2:9, reflecting LXX usage (Deut 28:53, 55, 57; Isa 8:22; 30:6). Since the terms appear in the same sequence also in the catalogue of 2 Cor 6:4, it appears that this constitutes a formula for divine wrath.[129] In other contexts, and without the combination with στενοχωρία ("distress"), θλῖψις ("afflic-

---

119 Seneca *Marc.* 18.8.
120 See Fitzgerald, *Cracks*, 107: "the suffering sage is clearly worthy of the highest praise."
121 Georgi, *Opponents*, 157.
122 Betz, *Sokratische Tradition*, 74–89.
123 Fitzgerald, *Cracks*, 206.
124 See Georgi, *Opponents*, 231–42; Jewett, "Conflicting Movements," 369. This background is overlooked by Ferrari, *Peristasenkatalogen*, 287–89, and Ebner, *Peristasenkataloge bei Paulus*, 371–74.
125 Ebner, *Peristasenkataloge bei Paulus*, 384–86, employs this material to argue that Paul's point is to demonstrate "the validity of his doctrine of justification of the godless" (385).
126 4Q504, frag. 2, col. 3, line 8.
127 Another Jewish voice roughly contemporaneous with Paul's is *2 Enoch*, which lists the six virtues and eight hardships that sustain and test the true chil-

dren of Enoch; this list contains most of the items listed by Paul in Rom 8:35: "Walk, my children, in long suffering, in meekness, in affliction, in distress, in faithfulness, in truth, in hope, in weakness, in derision, in assaults, in temptation, in deprivation, in nakedness, having love for one another, until you go out from this age of suffering, so that you may become inheritors of the never-ending age. How happy are the righteous who shall escape the Lord's great judgment. . . ." *2 En.* 66.6 is discussed by Hodgson, "Tribulation Lists," 68; this material was first brought into the discussion by Schrage, "Leid," 144–45.
128 *Pirqê 'Abôt*, 5.11 in Hertz, *Sayings*.
129 Georg Bertram, "στενός, στενοχωρία, στενοχωρέω," *TDNT* 7 (1971) 605; Jacob Kremer, "θλῖψις, θλίβω," *EDNT* 2 (1991) 152, referring to 2 Thess 1:6; Rev 2:22; and Jean Carmignac's discus-

545

tion") can refer to the eschatological woes suffered by the saints (Mark 13:19, 34; Matt 24:9; 1 Cor 7:26) or the troubles accompanying the apostolic preaching (1 Thess 3:3-4; Acts 20:23).[130] It is thus clear that everything depends on how a particular experience of tribulation is interpreted.[131] This is crucial for understanding Rom 8:35, because these first two terms played a crucial role in Paul's struggles with the Corinthian superapostles, who interpreted his experiences of "affliction and distress" as signs of divine wrath and thus as disqualifications for apostolicity.[132] In 2 Cor 1:4-6, 8; 6:4; and 12:10 Paul acknowledges such afflictions but claims that they are consistent with true discipleship under the cross of Christ.[133] In Phil 1:17 Paul replies to Christian opponents in Ephesus, the probable location of his imprisonment at the time of writing that letter, who seek to "afflict" him in his imprisonment by asserting that it impeded the Christian mission and failed to reflect the triumphant status of being "in Christ" (Phil 1:13).[134] Paul responds by defining true discipleship as a matter of sharing Christ's sufferings (Phil 3:10)[135] and expresses appreciation for the support shown by the Philippians "sharing my affliction" by sending Epaphroditus with a financial contribution (Phil 4:14). The alternative ways of understanding affliction are also addressed in 1 Thess 1:6; 3:3, 7, where Paul responds to the congregation's perception that their troubles alienated them from Christ and the new age.[136]

My hypothesis is that Paul's discourse reflects a rhetorical situation in which voices were being raised in Rome against the "weak" who consisted predominantly of Jewish Christians whose leaders had been expelled from Rome by the Edict of Claudius. These critics suggested that the "affliction and distress" suffered by believers should be interpreted as divine disfavor and inadequate faith. Paul is insisting that such afflictions suffered by believers do not imply a separation from Christ's love, and that those who make any such allegation are wrong.

Διωγμός ("persecution") is used here for the only time in Romans, although it appears in nominal and verbal forms in 1 Cor 4:12; 2 Cor 4:9; 12:10; and 2 Thess 1:4 in contexts that are similar to those discussed above. Particularly in 2 Cor 4:9, Paul seems to be contrasting his views with those who claim to possess transcendent power that allows them to avoid persecution.[137] What the Jewish Christians in Rome suffered under the Edict of Claudius would certainly be classed as "persecution,"[138] and Paul is here claiming its congruence with the strand of the early Christian tradition that viewed such adversity as a mark of discipleship.[139] Paul's understanding of martyrdom fits the pattern of intertestamental Judaism that viewed a martyr as a "devotee" and "witness to God" whose courageous action constitutes "a missionary endeavor."[140] Paul's contention is that such persons should not be discredited with the insinuation that their persecution was a sign of alienation from Christ.

sion of Qumranic parallels, "La théologie de la souffrance dans les hymnes de Qumrân," *RevQ* 9 (1961) 366-86. Θλῖψις by itself often has the sense of divine wrath, as, for example, in LXX Ps 77:49: "He sent out against them [the Egyptians] the fury of his anger, wrath, and indignation, and affliction (θυμὸν καὶ ὀργὴν καὶ θλῖψιν)."

130 See Heinrich Schlier, "θλίβω, θλῖψις," *TDNT* 3 (1965) 143; Kremer, "θλῖψις," 152; Pobee, *Persecution*, 93-118. For a discussion of Matthean use of "affliction" and "hardship," see A. J. Mattill, Jr., "The Way of Tribulation," *JBL* 98 (1979) 531-46, esp. 542.

131 Schrage, "Leid," 149-50, points out the disparity between the Pauline use of "affliction" and "hardship" in comparison with Epictetus, who makes victims responsible for suffering because they are concerned with external pressures.

132 See Georgi, *Opponents*, 280; Jewett, *Saint Paul at the*

Movies, 77-81; idem, "Paul's Dialogue with the Corinthians . . . and Us," *QR* 13.4 (Winter 1993) 89-112; the "superapostles" are mentioned in 2 Cor 11:5; 12:11.

133 See Schrage, "Leid," 171-75.

134 See Jewett, "Conflicting Movements," 364-71.

135 See Barnabas Mary Ahern, "The Fellowship of His Sufferings (Phil 3:10): A Study of St. Paul's Doctrine on Christian Suffering," *CBQ* 22 (1960) 28-32.

136 See Jewett, *Thessalonian Correspondence*, 93-96.

137 See Jewett, *Saint Paul at the Movies*, 92.

138 Robert Lee Williams, "Persecution," *EAC* 2 (1997) 896; D. S. Potter, "Persecution of the Early Church," *ABD* 5 (1992) 231-35.

139 See Otto Knoch, "διώκω, διωγνός," *EDNT* 1 (1990) 338-39.

140 Pobee, *Persecution*, 33; see also Albrecht Oepke, "διώκω," *TDNT* 2 (1964) 229.

The fourth and fifth tribulations, "hunger" and "nakedness," also appear here for the only time in Romans. Λιμός ("hunger")[141] occurs elsewhere in the Pauline letters only in the catalogue of 2 Cor 11:27, where Paul boasts of his vulnerabilities, in contrast to the superapostles' claims of spiritual and material success. In 2 Cor 11:27 it is connected with the γυμνότης ("nakedness"): Paul's ministry was "in hunger and thirst, often without food, in cold and nakedness." This is the only other time "nakedness" occurs in the Pauline letters, and there is no doubt that it refers to destitution.[142] On several other occasions, Paul refers to the poverty caused by his missionary activities (Phil 4:11-12; 1 Thess 2:9; 1 Cor 4:11-12; 2 Cor 6:10). That the exile imposed by the Edict of Claudius would have placed such burdens on some of the Jewish Christians is highly likely, and Rom 12:13 urges "sharing in the needs of the saints," probably referring to these exiles, who are now returning to Rome to take up their lives again. There are excellent grounds in Deuteronomy and Proverbs to expect that prosperity rather than poverty should attend the righteous, so it is understandable that "hunger and nakedness" could be adduced by critics as signs of separation from Christ. But in Paul's view, neither form of adversity suffered by the saints is a sign of divine displeasure.

The sixth tribulation, κίνδυνος ("danger"), is echoed elsewhere in the Pauline corpus only in the verb κινδυνεύσομεν ("we are in danger") in 1 Cor 15:30 and in the striking catalogue of hardships in 2 Cor 11:26, where it is repeated eight times as part of the fool's discourse that differentiates Paul's career from that of the allegedly always successful superapostles. Most of the eight dangers are related to travel, a risky undertaking in the Roman world made riskier still by the "danger from false brothers."[143] It is conceivable that all eight would have been faced by the Jewish Christian leaders exiled from Rome in 49 C.E., but the bare reference in Rom 8:35 adequately conveys the thought. In contrast to the magical spells such as a Jewish one invoking divine protection from "fear and every danger presented to me (ἀπὸ παντὸς κυνδίνου τοῦ ἐνεστῶτός μου),"[144] the emphasis here is on status rather than courage or protection. Does danger divorce believers from God's love? Paul insists not.

The climactic tribulation in Paul's catalogue is capital punishment, referred to here as μάχαιρα, the short sword or dagger[145] as opposed to the long sword (ξίφος).[146] In Rev 13:10; Matt 10:34, 38f.; Acts 12:2; Heb 11:34, 37, this word refers to execution by the sword,[147] the ultimate punishment imposed by the state. The word "sword" appears in a catalogue of Sib. Or. 8.119, "neither strife, nor varied wrath, nor sword (οὐδὲ μάχαιρα)." Another instance of "sword" in the absolute referring to various manners of perishing occurs in Epictetus Diss. 2.6.18: "Now the method of destruction is either a sword (μάχαιρα), or rack, or sea, or tile, or tyrant." Bar 2:25 reports that exiled Jews "died by grievous pains, by famine, sword and banishment." The word "sword" does not appear in the earlier Pauline letters, but there are references to deadly dangers from the state (Phil 1:20-21; 1 Cor 15:32; 2 Cor 11:32) to which his superapostolic adversaries evidently believed themselves immune. And that the sword was regularly employed in Rome in the enforcement of its decrees, such as the Edict of Claudius, hardly needs to be recalled. This reference brings the series of seven tribulations to a striking climax. But again, this is a rhetorical question, and the only answer the audience can give, in view of the earlier argument of Romans, is "No! No adversity or critic can

---

141 In the singular and in this context, it is probably "hunger" rather than "famine." Examples of the former are Luke 15:17 and Aeschylus Pers. 491: "many perished of thirst and hunger (δίψῃ τε λιμῷ); of the latter are Acts 7:11; 11:28; Rev 6:8; 18:8; and Aristophanes Plut. 31: "there was a famine (λιμοῦ) in Greece." Λιμός in the plural refers to "famines," anticipated among the tribulations of the end times (Matt 24:7; Mark 13:8); see BAGD 475.

142 See BAGD 168, referring to T. Zeb. 7.1, "I saw a man suffering from nakedness (ἐν γυμνότητι) in the wintertime and I had compassion on him." See

Horst Robert Balz, "γυμνός, γυμνότης," EDNT 1 (1990) 265.

143 See Josef Zmijewski, Der Stil der paulinischen "Narrenrede": Analyse der Sprachgestaltung in 2 Kor 11, 1-12, 10 als Beitrag zur Methodik von Stiluntersuchungen neutestamentlicher Texte (BBB 52; Cologne/Bonn: Hanstein, 1978) 254–59, 317–19.

144 PGM XIII.1049; see also XII.160, 260.

145 See Pindar Nem. 4.59; Herodotus Hist. 6.75, etc.

146 See LSJM 1085, s.v. 1.

147 See Wilhelm Michaelis, "μάχαιρα," TDNT 4 (1967)

in fact separate us and our fellow believers from Christ's love! We remain God's elect, no matter what befalls us! Our position is secure, even if our life is not!"

■ **36** Following the citation formula, "just as it has been written that," which appeared in 1:17, Paul provides a scriptural proof. The threat of capital punishment links this citation from LXX Ps 43:23 with the final line in the preceding rhetorical question: "For your sake we are being put to death all the day long, we are reckoned as sheep for slaughter." This verse suits Paul's needs so exactly that it is cited verbatim, yet its function needs to be clarified.[148] That suffering was predicted by Scripture[149] is hardly germane, since Paul does not seem to be addressing the question of whether it was expected or not, as in 1 Thess 3:3-4. Some have suggested that Paul simply follows the Jewish tradition in applying this verse to the situation of persecution,[150] but the evidence for this in Strack-Billerbeck comes from a period centuries after the writing of Romans.[151] And the citation makes no sense at all if Paul's point in this passage was to provide subjective courage to face persecution. While confirming that the dangers in the preceding catalogue are real and life-threatening,[152] the main purpose of the citation is conveyed by the opening words, ἕνεκεν σοῦ ("for your sake"), which stands in the emphatic position and indicates that the tribulations suffered by believers are for Christ's sake.[153] Paul makes the same point in his own words in 2 Cor 4:11, "we are always being given up to death for Jesus' sake."[154] Yet why scriptural proof on this point was required—indeed why the point was not self-evident and thus redundant—remains unexplained, either in the commentaries or in the specialized studies of affliction catalogues. This citation makes full sense only if there were contrary voices that Paul wished to counter, arguing, as I have suggested in the preceding verse, that Paul's sufferings and those of the Jewish Christian exiles in Rome were not for Christ's sake, but rather disqualified them as genuine disciples. That is, if they were genuinely righteous and filled with the Spirit, they would be blessed with success and prosperity rather than cursed with afflictions.[155] The citation answers the rhetorical need by affirming that believers' "death all the day long," being slaughtered "as sheep," demonstrates their solidarity with Christ. Ulrich Luz correctly identifies this as an example of "Pauline passion-mysticism."[156] Christ died for their sake, and they die for his. No one can therefore claim that their suffering divorces them from Christ and his cross.

■ **37** The concluding interpretation of suffering draws the seven tribulations together with the fatal details in the psalmic citation: "But in *all* these things. . . ."[157] The claim that believers are "supervictors,"[158] a literal translation of ὑπερνικάω, brings Paul's discourse within the scope of divinely inspired warriors and kings who win

---

526; Eckhart Plümacher, "μάχαιρα," *EDNT* 2 (1991) 397; Käsemann, 249.

148 Kühl, 309, remarks that this citation does not warrant a detailed explanation; Moo, 543, finds the citation to be "an interruption in the flow of thought."

149 Barrett, 173.

150 Leenhardt, 238; see also Dunn, 1:505-6.

151 See Str.-B., 4:259; that 2 Macc 7 shows the application of this psalm to the situation of persecution (Michel, 283; Ziesler, 230) also remains undemonstrated, because the psalm is not cited there. These martyrs die for the law (2 Macc 7:9, 11), but the distinctive preposition ἕνεκεν ("for the sake of") in the psalm is not found here. Paulsen, *Überlieferung*, 174, points to the difficulty of proving a pre-Pauline, Christian use of Ps 44:23 and concludes that this is Paul's selection.

152 See Werner Bieder, "θανατόω," *EDNT* 2 (1991) 133; Luz, *Geschichtsverständnis*, 376; Morris, 339. Koch, *Schrift*, 264, shows that the "we" who are

being led to slaughter are the same as the "us" of v. 35.

153 Zahn, 425; Osten-Sacken, *Römer 8*, 314–15; Koch, *Schrift*, 264; Schmidt, 154; Käsemann, 249; Wilckens, 2:175; Murray, 1:331; Ebner, *Peristasenkataloge bei Paulus*, 375. That "for your sake" refers to God rather than Christ is suggested by Meyer, 2:104, and Michel, 283, but the closest antecedent in Romans is v. 35a, "the love of Christ."

154 See Zeller, 167; Sanday and Headlam, 222, also point to the close parallel in 1 Cor 15:31.

155 See Morris, 339: "Christians might be tempted to think that because the love of Christ is so real and so unshakable they need not fear that they will run into trouble."

156 Luz, "Mystic," 141.

157 See Meyer, 2:105, italics in original. Bruce, 181, proposes the translation "in spite of these things," but this seems unlikely. See Cranfield, 1:440–41.

158 Zeller, 167. Fitzmyer, 534, and Sanday and Headlam, 222, refer to Tertullian and Cyprian conveying

total victories over their foes.[159] A variant of Menander's maxim, καλὸν τὸ νικᾶν, ὑπερνικᾶν δὲ κακόν ("To be victorious is good, but to be super-victorious is bad")[160] was a prudential assessment of the dangers of crushing one's enemies completely. But in other contexts this compound verb refers simply to decisive victory,[161] which would support the traditional translation, "prevail." I prefer the translation "supervictor" because it correlates with the peculiar wording of v. 35, whose details pointed to interaction with superapostolic forms of early Christianity. It also resonates with the wordplay on "supermindedness" in 12:3. Here is a claim of supervictory, but without the traditionally associated claim in ancient and modern superheroic discourse that the victors are thereby super, in some sense more than human, or at least, definitely superior to the vanquished.

The particular victory Paul has in mind is won through love rather than competition, and it is won "through him who loved us," in which διά followed by the genitive has the sense of agency, "through, by means of, through the agency of."[162] Since the present form of the verb is used (ὑπερνικῶμεν, "we are supervictors"), it is a victory currently visible in the lives of the suffering saints,[163] achieved through Christ's supreme expression of love in his sacrificial death (8:32).[164] The word ἀγαπήσαντος ("the one who loved us") is an aorist participle, pointing to a single act of love.[165] This supervictory therefore derives not from the skill and strategy of combatants[166] but from the power of the gospel, which declares the love of God shown on the cross of Christ. And in Volf's words, "to remain in Christ's love is nothing else than to continue in salvation."[167] Living "according to the Spirit" results in supervictories that are vastly different from Roman imperialism, as embodied in the goddess "Victoria"[168] and in the ceremonies of victory parades, triumphal arches, and gladiatorial games that feature the vanquishing of barbarians.[169] Rather than a victorious general leading the vanquished in

this concept with the Latin term *supervincimus*. For an account of attempts to paraphrase this expression without taking account of the superheroic background, see Morris, 340.

159 For example, *Historia Alexandri Magni Rec.* γ 21.45 has Alexander the Great report that on one occasion he was unable to win the expected supervictory: "When I came into the land of wild men, a great many rose up against me and prevented my being supervictorious over them (ὑπερνικήσαντά με)." See also *Rec.* ε 15.2.18; *Rec. byz.* 21.

160 Menander *Sent. Byz.* 419; *Sent. pap.* 9 r.7; the wording καλὸν τὸ νικᾶν, ὑπερνικᾶν δὲ σφαλερόν, appears in Menander *Mon.* 1.299.

161 For instance, Hippocrates *Septim.* 50.17 employs ὑπερνικάω as the natural process (ὑπερνικᾷ γὰρ τὸ φυσικόν) of prevailing over diseases such as fever in the summer and dropsy in the winter. See also Empedocles *Test.* 66.8; Diodorus Siculus *Hist.* 9.14.2; *Anon. Arist.* 18.33; *Sch. Pind.* Ol. 13.17–24.3; *Anon. Eth. Ni.* 86.33. Ebner, *Peristasenkataloge bei Paulus*, 376–77, sketches the use of νικᾶν to depict victory in athletic and philosophical contexts, but refers to ὑπερνικᾶν as a Pauline creation of a new term that expresses the transcendent quality of the Christ event. He overlooks the earlier use of ὑπερνικᾶν by Menander and others and Paul's wordplay on this theme in Rom 12:3.

162 BAGD, 180, III.f; see Schettler, *Durch Christus*, 32–33; Thüsing, *Per Christum*, 221.

163 Thüsing, *Per Christum*, 219–20.

164 See Gerhard Delling, *Der Kreuzestod Jesu in der urchristlichen Verkündigung* (Göttingen: Vandenhoeck & Ruprecht, 1972) 18–19. Sam K. Williams, *Jesus' Death*, 242, argues that Hellenistic Christians were familiar with the idea of redemptive suffering from the Greek funeral oration and drama as well as from 4 Maccabees. Paul was familiar with the latter, as shown in Rom 8:37 which is "reminiscent of the fundamental motiv of IV Maccabees that the martyrs conquer through suffering endured on behalf of their religion, especially in 1:11, 6:10, 7:4, 9:30, 16:14."

165 Thüsing, *Per Christum*, 221; Cranfield, 1:441, referring back to Rom 5:6-8; Volf, *Paul and Perseverance*, 63; Moo, 544. Morris, 340, frankly observes that this aorist verb "is not quite what we expect of a love that goes on and on." The solution is that it refers to the crucifixion, as seen by Murray, 1:331–32.

166 Meyer, 2:105, conveys more than a whiff of traditional Christian imperialism, with its usual claim of superiority: v. 37 conveys "*a holy arrogance of victory* [italics in original], not selfish, but in the consciousness of the might of Christ." See also Schmidt, 154.

167 Volf, *Paul and Perseverance*, 63.

168 See Fears, "Theology of Victory," 740–52.

169 See Meister, "Tugenden," 5.

triumph and receiving the lion's share of the glory, here is a community of victors whose glory is shared equally. Their glory remains reflected rather than innate, because the victories of love are won through Christ. And with supervictory comes empire; these victors, as v. 32 declared, inherit "the all," but only in the midst of their ongoing vulnerability and suffering in behalf of Christ. It follows that these supervictors must eschew any claim of being above finitude because they have discovered that they are loved despite their flaws and limitations. So they experience a transformed type of imperialism, based on victories of inclusion under the aegis of love. And this all has an obvious bearing on the goal of Paul's letter, to win support of, and to clarify the gospel for, the barbarians in Spain.

■ **38** The final section in this pericope contains an enumeration of ten factors that are unable to divorce believers from God's love. It opens with an assurance formula, $\pi\acute{\epsilon}\pi\epsilon\iota\sigma\mu\alpha\iota$ in the perfect passive with the meaning, "I have become convinced,"[170] with the implication that the conviction continues into the present.[171] Examples of this usage are Herodotus *Hist.* 9.88, who reports that some Greeks held for trial "were convinced ($\grave{\epsilon}\pi\epsilon\pi\sigma\acute{\iota}\vartheta\epsilon$-$\sigma\alpha\nu$) that they would defeat the indictment by bribery," but were executed nevertheless.[172] Employing this verb in the perfect is characteristic of Paul (Rom 2:19; 14:14; 15:14; 2 Cor 1:9; 2:3; 10:7; Gal 5:10; Phil 1:6, 14, 25; 2:24; 3:3; 2 Thess 3:4; with other tenses in 2 Cor 5:11; Gal 5:7), which perhaps explains why he shifts to the first person singular in this final sentence of the pericope.[173] There remains a substantial dispute over whether all ten are astrological[174] or supernatural forces,[175] whether they are strictly finite forces,[176] or

whether, as seems more likely, the list contains a mixture of earthly and cosmic forces that are currently thought to be capable of impinging on the elect.[177] The syntax of the list is dominated by the tenfold repetition of the adverb $o\check{\upsilon}\tau\epsilon \ldots o\check{\upsilon}\tau\epsilon$ ("neither . . . nor . . . nor"), which has a correlative rather than disjunctive sense in this context;[178] the forces are not placed over against each other but are correlated in pairs to make a cumulative impression of comprehensiveness.[179] The closest parallel to this comprehensive list appears in Epictetus *Diss.* 1.11.33: "And simply put, it is neither death nor exile nor pain nor any other of these things ($o\check{\upsilon}\tau\epsilon \ \vartheta\acute{\alpha}\nu\alpha\tau o\varsigma$ $o\check{\upsilon}\tau\epsilon \ \varphi\upsilon\gamma\acute{\eta} \ o\check{\upsilon}\tau\epsilon \ \pi\acute{o}\nu o\varsigma \ o\check{\upsilon}\tau\epsilon \ \check{\alpha}\lambda\lambda o \ \tau\iota \ \tau\hat{\omega}\nu \ \tau o\iota o\acute{\upsilon}\tau\omega\nu$) that is the reason for our doing or not doing something." In view of the innate ambiguity of Paul's words describing the ten powers, it is wise to interpret them as far as possible within the framework of Paul's theology and prior usage[180] rather than opening the door to the entire semantic range of these terms.

The first pair of terms, "death" and "life," picks up major themes of the second proof as well as of 8:35-36.[181] The connection with the immediately preceding verses explains the reversal of the normal sequence of "life and death," as, for example, in 1 Cor 3:22. Death has a wide range of connotations, as a "personified power" in Rom 5:1, 14, 17, 21; 6:21; 7:5; 1 Cor 15:26, 56,[182] as a symbolic event of dying with Christ in 6:2-5, 7-8, 10-11; and as a "biological reality" in Rom 6:6; 7:2-3; 8:11.[183] While some interpreters prefer to think of $\vartheta\acute{\alpha}\nu\alpha\tau o\varsigma$ ("death") in this verse solely as a cosmic power,[184] C. Clifton Black, Jr., argues against any "monolithic understanding of death" and shows that Paul's "perspectives on death are rich and many-sided, at many

170 See Rudolf Bultmann, "$\pi\epsilon\acute{\iota}\vartheta\omega$ $\kappa\tau\lambda$.," *TDNT* 6 (1968) 6–7; Alexander Sand, "$\pi\epsilon\acute{\iota}\vartheta\omega$," *EDNT* 3 (1993) 63.
171 Moo, 544; see also Fuchs, *Freiheit*, 122; Käsemann, 250; Moores, *Wrestling*, 122–23.
172 See also Sophocles *Aj.* 769, and for more extensive parallels, see commentary on 2:19.
173 The singular usage is discussed by Meyer, 2:106.
174 Barrett, 174.
175 Dibelius, *Geisterwelt*, 110–13; Wink, *Naming the Powers*, 47–50.
176 Carr, *Angels and Principalities*, 112–14.
177 Kuss, 3:657; Ziesler, 230–31.
178 See Osten-Sacken, *Römer 8*, 307; Carr, *Angels and*

Principalities, 112; BAGD 596. Note that the parallel catalogue in 1 Cor 3:22 is inclusive rather than correlative.
179 See Volf, *Paul and Perseverance*, 57.
180 The proposal by Paulsen, *Überlieferung*, 174–75, that the tenfold list is traditional, stemming from Hellenistic Christianity, lacks plausibility and has attracted no support in subsequent commentaries.
181 See Dunn, 1:506–7.
182 Bieder, "$\vartheta\acute{\alpha}\nu\alpha\tau o\varsigma$, $\grave{\alpha}\pi o\vartheta\nu\acute{\eta}\sigma\kappa\omega$, $\vartheta\alpha\nu\alpha\tau\acute{o}\omega$," 130.
183 Black, "Death in Romans 5–8," 429.
184 Schlier, 280; Käsemann, 251; Wink, *Naming the Powers*, 48.

points lying in tension with one another," particularly in Rom 5–8.[185] The only parallel to Paul's formulation refers to physical death along with other forms of suffering: Epictetus *Diss.* 1.11.33 argues that "it is neither death (οὔτε θάνατος) nor exile nor pain nor any other of these things (οὔτε ἄλλο) that is the reason for our doing or not doing something . . . ." It is understandable, particularly in the light of the references to capital punishment and the implied danger of being cut off from Christ in the preceding verses of this pericope, that death in its various forms could be viewed as an adversary and a threat.

It remains somewhat puzzling that ζωή ("life"), the connotations of which seem positive in Paul's letters, could be paired in this verse with death as a potentially threatening reality.[186] Godet tries to explain by alluding to "*life* with its distractions, its interests and seductions,"[187] but this remains quite vague because ζωή does not appear in passages such as 1 Cor 7:25-35, where such matters are discussed, and earlier in this chapter of Romans Paul refers to such matters under the rubric of "walking according to the flesh" without employing either ζάω or ζωή on the negative side of the equation. A similar explanation is offered by Michel, that life in 2 Cor 5:8-9 and Phil 1:23 remains separated from God, but ζωή is not explicitly mentioned in either verse, and Phil 1:21 expresses the hope that "Christ will be honored in my body, whether by life or by death." Others resort to extraordinarily broad generalizations, that life and death paired together imply that "nothing at all in human experience" can separate us from God's love,[188] but this overlaps with "things present and things to come" later in this verse, and in the only other location where Paul uses these terms together, they are joined with words describing further dimensions of human life (1 Cor 3:21-22).

No one thus far has suggested a situational explanation of this peculiar use of "life," but it could reflect Paul's effort to counterbalance the claims of each group in Rome against others. If the "strong" were critical of the "weak" because of their involvement in persecution and death, as we have suggested, then the "weak" could also have been critical of the "strong" for failing to demonstrate solidarity with Christ by participation in tribulation. In 14:1-23 Paul takes great pains to equalize the moral imperative to both groups, counteracting each group's tendencies to judge and show contempt for others. There is evidence elsewhere in the Pauline letters for an enthusiasm for martyrdom that appeared to favor death over life: "if I deliver my body to be burned" (1 Cor 13:3).[189] If this background were taken into account, Paul's point would be that neither life nor death, in whatever dimensions they appear, can grant priority or separate believers from Christ's realm. But there is no evidence from the earlier letters or elsewhere that the word "life" was employed in this connection. The plausibility of this suggestion thus remains at the comparative level: the reader will have to judge whether it makes more sense than previous explanations.

Since "angels" and "rulers/principalities" appear here for the only time in Romans, we are dependent on usage elsewhere and contextual considerations to assess their meaning. In Paul's letters, the word ἄγγελος[190] refers to otherworldly messengers sent by God (Gal 1:8; 4:14) to supervise the human scene (1 Cor 4:9) and at times to inflict punishment on those who resist Christ (2 Thess 1:7). Angels have a distinctive language that humans emulate in glossolalia (1 Cor 13:1). Some angels are fallen and thus pose a threat to humans (1 Cor 6:3; 11:10; 2 Cor 12:7); the angelic capacity to deceive, transforming demonic forces into the appearance of "angels of light" (2 Cor 11:14), poses a particular threat to

---

185 Black, "Death in Romans 5–8," 429; see also Leander E. Keck, "New Testament Views of Death," in L. O. Mills, ed., *Perspectives on Death* (Nashville: Abingdon, 1969) 61–80.

186 See Dunn, 1:507.

187 Godet, 334, italics in original; similarly Leenhardt, 239; Morris, 340.

188 Ziesler, 231; similarly Luise Schottroff, "ζῶ, ζωή," *EDNT* 2 (1991) 106.

189 See Pobee, *Persecution*, 116–17; Conzelmann,

1 Corinthians, 222–23; Erwin Preuschen, "'Und liesse meinen Leib brennen' 1 Kor 13,3," *ZNW* 16 (1915) 127–98.

190 See Walter Grundmann, Gerhard von Rad, Gerhard Kittel, "ἄγγελος κτλ.," *TDNT* 1 (1964) 83–86; Ingo Broer, "ἄγγελος," *EDNT* 1 (1990) 14; Duane F. Watson, "Angels, New Testament," *ABD* 1 (1992) 253–54.

believers. Paul evidently anticipates that even these demonic angels will ultimately be brought to their knees by Christ (Phil 2:10), but at present they continue their threatening activities. Although some commentators infer that Paul has the good angels in mind here,[191] thus assuming an antithetical pairing of a good and a bad force, it remains questionable that divinely obedient angels could be thought to pose a potential threat to divorce believers from Christ. Others insist that both good and bad angels are in view here,[192] but it seems more likely in the context of this passage that Paul has only fallen angels in mind.[193]

The situation is equally difficult with regard to the term $\dot{\alpha}\rho\chi\alpha\dot{\iota}$: although it can refer to earthly authorities in other writings,[194] there remains a debate whether earthly or cosmic forces are implied in 1 Cor 15:24, where Christ is expected "to destroy every principality/ruler and authority and power." Although some commentators appear certain that $\dot{\alpha}\rho\chi\dot{\eta}$ in this 1 Corinthian passage implies cosmic powers,[195] Barrett makes a more compelling case that it refers to earthly rulers, since the related term, $\ddot{\alpha}\rho\chi\omega\nu$, in 1 Cor 2:6, 8 refers to political authorities who oppose Christ.[196] Eph-

esians and Colossians employ both $\dot{\alpha}\rho\chi\dot{\eta}$ and $\ddot{\alpha}\rho\chi\omega\nu$ in reference to cosmic forces,[197] but the uncertain provenance of these letters renders them less relevant for interpreting Romans. Nevertheless, the combination of $\ddot{\alpha}\gamma\gamma\epsilon\lambda o\iota$ $o\ddot{\upsilon}\tau\epsilon$ $\dot{\alpha}\rho\chi\alpha\dot{\iota}$ leads most commentators to assume that both are superhuman forces, but nowhere is this argued in detail.[198] In order to prevent redundancy with the seventh term in this series, $\delta\upsilon\nu\dot{\alpha}\mu\epsilon\iota\varsigma$ ("powers"), which refers quite clearly to spiritual forces, it seems likely to me that the rulers in view are political. This would support Phillips's arresting translation: "neither messenger of heaven nor monarch of earth,"[199] which captures the pairing of opposites. But the fuzzy nature of the evidence and of the scholarly discussion precludes certainty in this assessment. What remains clear is that Paul denies that any powers can succeed in severing the relationship between believers and God.

The participles $\dot{\epsilon}\nu\epsilon\sigma\tau\ddot{\omega}\tau\alpha$ ("things present")[200] and $\mu\dot{\epsilon}\lambda\lambda o\nu\tau\alpha$ ("things coming")[201] appear in the same sequence in 1 Cor 3:22, the only difference being that in Romans the valence is negative because either can be thought to separate believers from Christ. This is a conventional way of referring to the present and the future,

---

191 Meyer, 2:106, cites Tholuck, Philipp, Fritzsche, Hofmann, and others, on the grounds that when Paul refers to angels with a qualifying adjective, they are always good; see also Godet, 334; Murray, 1:333; Morris, 341; Moo, 545. Carr, *Angels and Principalities*, 112–13, concludes that the entire company of angels is in view.

192 Weiss, 388, listing Bengel, Koppe, van Hengel, Lipsius. Fitzmyer, 535, says it remains unclear whether they are good or bad angels.

193 See Käsemann, 249–51: "a universe detached from God" (251). Whether a general rivalry between angels and humans was assumed in Paul's time remains to be debated; Peter Schäfer, *Rivalität zwischen Engeln und Menschen: Untersuchungen zur rabbinischen Engelvorstellung* (SJ 8; Berlin: de Gruyter, 1975) 235, concludes that the first certain evidence is from the third century C.E., although oral tradition of such rivalry based on Psalm 8 may have emerged earlier.

194 Konrad Weiss, "$\dot{\alpha}\rho\chi\dot{\eta}$," *EDNT* 1 (1990) 162, refers to Luke 12:11; 20:20; Titus 3:1 for governmental authorities.

195 Conzelmann, *1 Corinthians*, 271–72, and Fee, *1 Corinthians*, 754, assume a demonic or spiritual definition of $\dot{\alpha}\rho\chi\dot{\eta}$, but cite Rom 8:38 as primary evidence. See also Wink, *Naming the Powers*, 49.

196 Barrett, *1 Corinthians*, 357; Wesley Carr, "The Rulers of this Age—I Corinthians II.6-8," *NTS* 23 (1976–77) 20–35; Carr, *Angels and Principalities*, 118–20. LSJM 252, II.4, list "authorities, magistrates" as a possible translation.

197 Ephesians 1:21; 2:2; 3:10; 6:12; Col 1:16; 2:15; see Weiss, "$\dot{\alpha}\rho\chi\dot{\eta}$," 162; the assessment by Gerhard Delling, "$\dot{\alpha}\rho\chi\dot{\eta}$ $\kappa\tau\lambda$.," *TDNT* 1 (1964) 483–84, is based primarily on the deutero-Pauline evidence.

198 Schmidt, 154; Leenhardt, 239; Lietzmann, 88; Black, 121; Schlier, 280; Michel, 284; O'Neill, 144; Cranfield, 1:442.

199 Cited by Morris, 341.

200 Albrecht Oepke, "$\dot{\epsilon}\nu\dot{\iota}\sigma\tau\eta\mu\iota$," *TDNT* 2 (1964) 544, suggests the meaning of "present," but provides no further insights.

201 See Walter Radl, "$\mu\dot{\epsilon}\lambda\lambda\omega$," *EDNT* 2 (1991) 404; this term is frequently used by Paul to refer to the future, discussed earlier under 5:14 and 8:18; see also Gal 3:23; 1 Thess 3:4.

as, for example, *Barn.* 1.7a, "For the Lord has made known to you through the prophets things past (τὰ παρεληλυθότα) and things present (τὰ ἐνεστῶτα), and of things to come (τῶν μελλόντων). . . ."[202] That these are technical terms referring to the sway of the astrological powers has been suggested,[203] but this interpretation remains unconvincing, although Vettius Valens employs them in the general context of astrological prognostication: "and it is necessary to foresee the present and future times (τοὺς ἐνεστῶτας καὶ μέλλοντας χρόνους) and to examine them closely.[204] The suggestion that they refer to the power of the present age in contrast to a future utopia[205] also remains unproven. That these terms functioned to convey the burden of the Greek concept of fate (μοῖρα, εἱμαρμένη; Latin, *fatum*) in which the gods arbitrarily determined both the present and the future of each person and nation, an idea developed into a philosophical doctrine by the Stoics,[206] seems more likely. But since Paul nowhere defines what he has in mind with these categories, all we can say for certain is that they represented realities that could be thought capable of separating believers from God's love.[207]

The term δυνάμεις ("powers") appears to interrupt the sequence of paired forces at the end of v. 38, which has led interpreters to assess this as an "emendation,"[208] an "afterthought,"[209] or the result of "spontaneous dictation."[210] Bernhard Weiss proposed that "powers" stands in a triad with "things present" and "things to come,"[211] an intriguing suggestion that later scholarship has not pursued. This term appears to refer to spiritual powers

in 1 Cor 15:24, consistent with references to the heavenly forces of Mark 13:25 that fit the distinctively Jewish usage of Isa 34:4; LXX Pss 102:21; 148:2; etc.[212] For example, *1 En.* 82:8 refers to the "powers in heaven which revolve in their circular chariots," and 40:9 identifies the angel Gabriel, "who is set over all the powers." Philo describes the "forces" in the air that cannot be seen but form a hierarchical structure in the heavens (*Plant.* 14). Its solitary placement as the seventh item in the tenfold series of 8:38-39 calls attention to the paronomasia in the succeeding verse, the wordplay on the word "to be able/empowered." It also allows Paul to end his series in v. 39 with a solitary item that had no proper parallel or antithesis, but which has a substantial relevance to Paul's argument that the gospel is the "power of God" (1:16) and that his mission has been sustained "by the power of signs and wonders, by the power of the Holy Spirit" (15:19). Rhetorical considerations thus explain why "forces" appears alone, and there is no need to think of this as an impenetrable mystery.[213]

■ **39** Regarding the final pair of forces, it is frequently claimed that they are astrological, although this would be the only time in Paul's undisputed letters that such an idea appears. While ὕψωμα is used in 2 Cor 10:5 with the connotation of prideful opposition that "rises up" in opposition to Christ, its combination with βάθος ("depth") in Rom 8:39 leads most scholars to the conclusion that the former describes the "apogee of the planets" and the latter refers to the "lowest point in the planet's course,"[214] both of which are critical in assessing astrological fates. But since the usual astrological pair is

202   See also *Historia Alexandri Magni, Rec. byz.* 512–16, which describes Nectanebo's divinatory powers: "For he learned the future (τὰ μέλλοντα) in respect of the present situation (πρὸς τούτοις ἐνεστῶτα)," informing Olympia, "For you yourself will overcome your present condition (τὴν ἐνεστῶσαν φύσιν)."

203   Barrett, 174.

204   Vettius Valens *Anth.* 9.252.25; for nonastrological parallels, see Isocrates *Antid.* 33.3; 167.4; Polybius *Hist.* 3.102.8; Diogenes Laertius *Vitae philos.* 7.141.2; *Historia Alexandri Magni Rec. byz.* 512–16.

205   Schlier, 280.

206   See John M. Dillon, "Fate, Greek Conception of," *ABD* 2 (1992) 776–78.

207   Wilckens, 2:176, warns against assuming these are cosmic powers that oppose the saints, but he provides no other explanation.

208   Könnecke, *Emendationen*, 25.

209   Cranfield, 1:443.

210   Dunn, 1:498.

211   Weiss, 388.

212   See Walter Grundmann, "δύναμαι κτλ.," *TDNT* 2 (1964) 295–96, 307–8; Gerhard Friedrich, "δύναμις," *EDNT* 1 (1990) 58; Carr, *Angels and Principalities*, 113, maintains that δύναμις is never used by Paul to refer to a demonic power, but he fails to mention 1 Cor 15:24.

213   Moo, 546: "Why the word occurs on its own is impossible to know."

214   Dunn, 1:508; see Lietzmann, 89; Georg Bertram, "ὕψωμα," *TDNT* 8 (1972) 613–14; Adolf Strobel,

ὕψωμα/ταπείνωμα[215] and Paul's word βάθος is only found once in an astrological text as an equivalent to ταπείνωμα,[216] one has to conclude either that he did not know the technical term or that he for some reason chose to avoid it.[217] Some connection with astrological forces seems to be assumed because they have the power to determine earthly life in fateful manners and thus could be thought capable of separating believers from divine love as revealed in Christ. Paul denies that this is so.

The final threat is inclusive and cumulative, relating to all nine previous items and providing a fitting conclusion for the series. The expression τίς κτίσις ἑτέρα is usually translated "any other creature,"[218] but Fitzmyer argues that the adjective ἑτέρα implies "any other kind of creature."[219] The noun κτίσις appears here in the sense of individual creature, as in 1:25, rather than as the entire creation, as in 8:19-22.[220] This same sense of individual creatures is found in Tob 8:5, 15, where "all your creatures" (κτίσεις σου) are expected to praise God. The word τίς is employed here adjectively, matching the masculine singular of κτίσις. This expression includes any other cosmic factors not implied by the previous nine categories, and also any human voices. This inclusion of both human and nonhuman actors is at the point of emphasis at the conclusion of the series. No creaturely voice, whether coming from the weak or the strong, from Gentiles or Jews, barbarians or Greeks, angels or principalities, can disqualify the elect, no matter what arguments are raised concerning the causation of their tribulations. Moreover, this formulation has the function of relativizing all of the powers;[221] they are all creatures, just as humans are, and no creature has the power to contend with God. This is the point of the wordplay on the δυν- stem, that even the cosmic powers that appear so immense compared with the puny reach of humans nevertheless lack the power to contend with the Creator.

In the clausula, "the love of God which is in Christ Jesus our Lord," this exultant passage is brought to a satisfying conclusion. It is Christ who reveals and defines the love of God.[222] The lordship of Christ extends over all the powers, in heaven and on earth, and its motivating center is love. So, to cite Ernst Käsemann, who faced such powers in Gestapo cells, "even when inferno threatens the Christian on all sides, he is marked by the Lord, who is present for him . . . he finds even in the midst of painful experience that the claim of the powers to dominion is illusory."[223] With this assurance, the second proof climaxes on the note of the secure status of all those who are loved, set right, and chosen as the elect in Christ.[224] Their honorable status depends entirely on divine love. But that is enough, even in the face of human malice or cosmic adversity.

"βάθος," *EDNT* 1 (1990) 190; Heinrich Schlier, "βάθος," *TDNT* 1 (1964) 517-18; Lagrange, 223; Schlier, 280; Kuss, 3:657-58; Fitzmyer, 535. Voices dissenting from the astrological interpretation include Cranfield, 1:443; Zeller, 168; Carr, *Angels and Principalities*, 113; Moo, 546.

215 See Carr, *Angels and Principalities*, 113.

216 Vettius Valens *Anth.* 9.241.26.

217 The extensive use of ταπεινός ("lowly"), ταπεινόω ("make humble"), ταπείνωσις ("humility"), and ταπεινοφροσύνη ("humble-mindedness") in early Christian writings may have led to the avoidance of the astrological term. For general orientation, see Heinz Giesen, "ταπεινός κτλ.," *EDNT* 3 (1994) 333-35.

218 See BAGD 455, "beings created, creature, created thing."

219 Fitzmyer, 535; see BAGD 315.2: "another, different from what precedes." See also Godet, 335.

220 See Gerd Petzke, "κτίζω, κτίσις," *EDNT* 2 (1991) 326; BAGD 455.1a; Brinkman, "Creation," 359-74; Schille, "Rm 8:31-39," 240, argues that this clause is non-Pauline, because κτίσις is used for "creature" rather than "creation," but this does not seem justified.

221 Wink, *Naming the Powers*, 50; Volf, *Paul and Perseverance*, 57; Dunn, 1:508.

222 Meyer, 2:108; Cranfield, 1:444; see the extended discussion of the argumentative basis for this conclusion in Moores, *Wrestling*, 122-29.

223 Käsemann, 251.

224 See Dunn, 1:508, 513.

9:1—11:36 Part IVC. The Third Proof: The Triumph of
Divine Righteousness in the Gospel's Mission to Israel
and the Gentiles

9:1-5 The Third Proof

9

The First Pericope

Introduction: The Tragic Riddle of Israel's Unbelief

1/ **I am telling the truth in Christ,[a] I am not lying, my conscience bearing me witness in [the] Holy Spirit, 2/ that my sorrow is great and a pain in my heart [is] unceasing. 3/ For I used to pray that I myself be banned from[b] the Christ for the sake of my brothers,[c] my compatriots by flesh 4/ who are Israelites,[d]**

   **whose [are] the sonship
      and the glory
         and the covenants[e]
         and the lawgiving
            and the worship
               and the promises,[f]
                  5/ whose [are] the fathers
   and out of whom [is] the Christ, insofar as the flesh is concerned,[g] who[h] is God over all, blessed forever, amen!**

---

a   The addition of Ἰησοῦ by D* F G ar vg[s] appears to be secondary.

b   D G 1505 have ὑπό ("by") and Ψ provides ὑπέρ ("on behalf of") in place of the appropriately severe, and undoubtedly original ἀπό ("from"). Cranfield, 2:458, suspects the influence of the Latin translation *a Christo*, which contains the ambiguity as to whether it is "by" or "from." Another explanation is that the Semitic construction ἀνάθεμα εἶναι ἀπὸ τοῦ Χριστοῦ ("to be accursed from Christ") was felt by D and G to be too awkward.

c   The possessive pronoun μου ("my") is missing after τῶν ἀδελφῶν ("the brothers") in P[46], while the entire phrase "of my brethren" is absent from B*. Cranfield, 2:458, properly refers to these variants as "accidental."

d   The deletion of the rest of this verse by A, not noted by Nestle-Aland, is explained by Porter, "Rhetorical Scribe," 414, as an "attempt to link Christ more closely with the Jewish people"; this explanation lacks cogency.

e   The singular ἡ διαθήκη ("the covenant") is strongly supported by P[46] B D[gr] F G 1852 ar b vg[cl] sa bo[mss] eth Theodore Cyr Hes Cyp Hil[1/2] Hier[3/7] Aug[1/6], but the plural form as found in ℵ C K Ψ 0285 6 33 69 81 88 104 181 256 263 323 326 330 365 424 436 451 459 614 629 945 1175 1241 1243 1319 1505 1506 1573 1735 1739 1836 1874 1877 1881 1912

(1962 omits αἱ) 2127 2200 2344 2464 2492 2495 *Maj* (A omits by *homoioteleuton*) *Lect* d f g mon o vg[ww, st] sy[p,h,(hgr)] bo arm geo slav Or[lat] Bas Diodore Epiph Chr Proclus Hil[1/2] Ambst Tyconius Hier [4/7] Pel Aug[5/6] is more likely because it breaks out of the pattern of singular nouns in the series and in view of the predominance of the singular in the biblical tradition, the plural is the more difficult reading. The theological difficulties the plural posed for the early church would have easily motivated a change, according to Metzger, *Textual Commentary*, 459. Christiansen, *Covenant*, 220–28, argues for the originality of the singular because "in the Old Testament *Berith* is never used in the plural" (28), a point she derives from James Barr, "Some Semantic Notes on the Covenant," in H. Donner et al., eds., *Beiträge zur alttestlamentlichen Theologie: Festschrift für Walter Zimmerli zum 70. Geburtstag* (Göttingen: Vandenhoeck & Ruprecht, 1977) 30–31, who in fact does not extend this claim to the Greek portions of Scripture. The plural occurs in Wis 18:22; 2 Macc 8:15, and Sir 44:18. See Michel, 295, for evidence that Jewish sources often referred to plural covenants.

f   P[46vid] D F G ar bo[mss] provide the singular form ἐπαγγελία ("promise"), though D also has the article (ἡ ["the"]). These variations are spurious for the reasons noted in the previous note.

g   Cuthbert Lattey, "The Codex Ephraemi Rescriptus in Romans ix. 5," *ExpT* 35 (1923–24) 42–43, shows that this codex (C) contains a small cross at this point that designates some form of a stop, which the NA text reflects with a comma.

h   For discussions of the punctuation problem as well as the conjectured emendations suggested at this point, see Metzger, *Textual Commentary*, 459–62; idem, "The Punctuation of Rom 9:5," in B. Lindars and S. S. Smalley, eds., *Christ and Spirit in the New Testament: In Honour of Charles Francis Digby Moule* (Cambridge: Cambridge University, 1973) 95–112. Since the decision on punctuation must be made on contextual and theological grounds, the discussion thereof is found in the exegesis below. Hans-Werner Bartsch, "Rom 9:5 und 1 Clem 32:4: Eine notwendige Konjektur im Römerbrief," *ThZ* 21 (1965) 401–09, advocates the emendation by Jonasz Schlichting in 1665-68, changing ὁ ὢν ἐπὶ πάντων θεὸς ("of whom is God over all things") to ὢν ὁ ἐπὶ πάντων θεὸς ("whose is the God over all things"), which makes God the possession of Israel; see Cranfield, 2:466–67; Haacker, 187; W. L. Lorimer, "Romans 9:3-5," *NTS* 13 (1966–67) 385–86.

Analysis

This artfully constructed pericope provides an introduction[1] to the third proof, which is the counterpart of the concluding section, 11:33-36.[2] It begins in first person singular style[3] with a solemn, threefold asseveration of Paul's sorrow, three witnesses as it were, in hierarchical order.[4] The description of Paul's pain in v. 2 is in the form of synonymous parallelism with an artful chiastic pattern, λύπη + μεγάλη : ἀδιάλειπτος + ὀδύνη ("sorrow" + "great" : "unceasing" + "pain").[5] Verse 3 continues the pattern of double-line sentences with two lines of approximately equal length.[6] The pathos that marks these opening verses serves Paul's argumentative purpose[7] by showing that although he is the apostle to the Gentiles, he not only lacks anti-Jewish feelings,[8] but also is profoundly troubled about the opposition to the gospel by legalistic zealots. The pathos aims to evoke *exsuscitatio*, the arousal of similar sympathies on the part of the audience,[9] moving the largely Gentile Christian audience "to share his profound and anxious compassion *for the Jews* who have not yet embraced the fulfillment of what is properly *their* destiny."[10] The continued opposition of zealous Jews places a question mark about the power of the gospel, which is the premise of Paul's missionary project that the letter seeks to promote. The central issue in the third proof, the faithfulness and reliability of God,[11] is thus effectively introduced with pathos suitable to the tragic aspect of the issue.

The rhetorical cadence of 9:4-5 is both formal and solemn,[12] with a listing of seven attributes of Paul's fellow Jews followed by two further attributes introduced by relative pronouns, the second of which is defined by a further relative clause, making a formal series of ten.[13] The first item in the series, "who are Israelites," is the generic reference that "embraces the items which follow."[14] In v. 4 there is a threefold pattern of homoioteleuton, with -θεσία, -α, -αι / -θεσία, -α, -αι endings in sequence.[15] There is an impressive paronomasia in the repetition of ὧν ("of whom") in v. 4b followed by ὧν in v. 5a, b and ὧν in v. 5c.[16] The sixfold repetition of καί ("and") produces emphasis through polysyndeton.[17] The pericope ends with a doxology to Christ as God that corresponds to the doxology of 11:36, sealing the cohesion between the introduction and the conclusion of the third proof.

Rhetorical Disposition

IV.	The *probatio*
9:1–11:36	The third proof: The triumph of divine righteousness in the gospel's mission to Israel and the Gentiles
9:1-5	1. Introduction: The tragic riddle of Israel's unbelief
9:1-2	a. Paul's sorrow about unbelieving Israel

---

1   Kim, *Romans 9–11*, 116, 121–23, employs the term "exordium" for this introduction, but I prefer to reserve this formal designation to 1:1-12.

2   See Käsemann, 257.

3   Kim, *Romans 9–11*, 99.

4   Michel, 291.

5   See Weiss, "Beiträge," 238; Louw, 2:97; Siegert, *Argumentation*, 122.

6   See Weiss, "Beiträge," 238.

7   Kim, *Romans 9–11*, 122, cites Quintilian *Inst.* 6.2.34 in connection with forensic rhetoric, that pathos "is the emotional power that dominates the court, it is this form of eloquence that is the queen of all." Although I do not follow Kim in judging Rom 9–11 to be forensic, this comment about the argumentative force of pathos is equally valid for demonstrative discourse.

8   Schlier, 284; Siegert, *Argumentation*, 121, cites 1 Thess 2:15 and Acts 18:6 as well as the denial in Rom 3:8 as indications that Paul may have been conscious of allegations that he was hostile to his Jewish kinsfolk.

9   Elliott, *Rhetoric of Romans*, 261–62; see also Anderson, *Glossary*, 49.

10   Elliott, *Rhetoric of Romans*, 263, italics in original; also cited by Kim, *Romans 9–11*, 123.

11   Kim, *Romans 9–11*, 110, following the consensus summarized by Räisänen, "Römer 9–11," 2930–36; Wright, *Climax*, 236; Dunn, *Theology of Paul*, 501. See also Davies, "Paul and the People of Israel," 13; Dahl, *Studies*, 143.

12   Michel, 290.

13   Jewett, "Numerical Sequences," 230–31; Haacker, 183.

14   Cranfield, 2:460.

15   Siegert, *Argumentation*, 122; Moo, 561–62; Sass, *Verheißungen*, 427.

16   Siegert, *Argumentation*, 122.

17   Bullinger, *Figures*, 224.

9:1		1) The threefold asseveration about Paul's sorrow
9:1a		a) The witness of Christ to the truth of Paul's sorrow
9:1b		b) Paul's oath of honesty
9:1c		c) The independent witness of Paul's conscience about the presence of his sorrow
9:2		2) The scope and content of Paul's sorrow
9:2a		a) The scale of pain: "great"
9:2b		b) The scope of sorrow: "unceasing"
9:3-5		b. Paul's preference for personal damnation in place of his Jewish compatriots
9:3		1) The expression of the impossible prayer
		a) To be "accursed"
		b) To be cut off from Christ
		c) For the sake of Paul's "brethren"
9:4-5		c. The ten glorious attributes of the Jewish people
9:4a		1) The generic description: "Israelites"
9:4b		2) The "sonship"
9:4c		3) The "glory"
9:4d		4) The "covenants"
9:4e		5) The "lawgiving"
9:4f		6) The "worship"
9:4g		7) The "promises"
9:5a		8) The "fathers"
9:5b		9) The "Christ"
9:5c		10) The doxology to Christ

Exegesis

■ **1** The third proof opens with a threefold attestation of Paul's sorrow about the continued unbelief of many of his fellow Jews. This calls into question the power of the gospel (1:16) concerning God's impartial grace expressed in Christ, which should come to Jews first and then to Greeks (1:16; 2:9, 10). If believers are the true heirs of Abraham (4:11-17) and the adopted children of God (8:14-17), what becomes of Israel's status as a chosen people?[18] Does Paul's theology require the abandon-ment of Israel? Paul takes up these difficult questions by asserting the sincerity of his commitment to Israel: ἀλή-θειαν λέγω ("I am telling [the] truth") is a formula frequently employed in classical oratory[19] that Paul used also in 2 Cor 12:6, "I shall not be a fool, for I shall be speaking the truth (ἀλήθειαν γὰρ ἐρῶ)." That the claim in Rom 9:1 is made ἐν Χριστῷ ("in Christ") differentiates Paul's stance from classical rhetoric, and in this context it expresses both the fact that he is a member of the mystical body of the church[20] and that what he says is authorized and authenticated by Christ himself.[21] To question Paul's truthfulness in this circumstance is to question the truth of Christ, for as he says in 2 Cor 11:10, "the truth of Christ is in me."[22] Skepticism about Paul's truthfulness would also contradict the belief that believers share this mystical union with Christ, as stated in 2 Cor 1:21, "it is God who establishes us with you in Christ."

The second claim of truthfulness is formulated in the negative, "I am not lying," which forms a kind of "sandwich" with "in Christ" in the middle. This expression appears also in classical texts such as Aeschines *Tim.* 99.8, "I am not lying (οὐ ψεύδομαι) . . . I shall call witnesses." The same denial is found in 2 Cor 11:31 and Gal 1:20, where Paul is countering slanderous accounts of his behavior. J. Lionel North suggests that the denial may "imply that some Jews believed that in identifying Jesus as the Messiah and preaching this to Gentiles, Paul had severed himself from his Jewish heritage and lost all affection for Jews and Judaism."[23] He criticizes J. Paul Sampley's contention that Paul is employing a Roman legal practice called *iusiurandum voluntarium,* an oath that he is willing to go to court to prove his contention, because it is unlikely that a Roman court would "take cognizance of what these particular litigants wanted to debate."[24] A metaphorical use of the denial of lying

---

18   See Moo, 549; Esler, *Conflict and Identity,* 269–73.

19   The expression ἀληθῆ λέγω appears in Isocrates *Euth.* 14.1, and the plural form is used by Demosthenes *Orat.* 13.3.9, τἀληθῆ λέγω ("I am telling truths"); cf *Orat.* 14.6; *4 Philip.* 6.4; 54.5. As Siegert, *Argumentation,* 120, observes, such claims of truthfulness were widely accepted in the ancient world.

20   Neugebaur, *In Christus,* 126; Dacquino, "In Christo," 281; Murray, 2:1, "union with Christ"; Schlier, 284; Kuss, 3:670; Fitzmyer, 543.

21   Sanday and Headlam, 227; Käsemann, 257; Dunn, 2:523.

22   See Schlier, 284.

23   J. Lionel North, "Paul's Protest That He Does Not Lie in the Light of His Cilician Origin," *JTS* 47 (1996) 441.

24   North, "Paul's Protest," 445, with regard to J. Paul Sampley, "'Before God I Do Not Lie,'" *NTS* 23 (1977) 477–82.

seems more probable, and the slur that all Cilicians were liars provides the more appropriate background. North surveys classical sources to confirm the tradition that Cilicians were dishonest and unreliable, and Paul's repeated reference that he does not lie "is explained, at least in part, by his opponents' sneering at his origins."[25] I believe that the context of Romans provides a more solid basis to assess this statement. Although Rom 3:4 had maintained that all persons are liars, thus requiring that all accept the gospel of salvation by grace alone, the immediately preceding reference to speaking "in Christ" authenticates this "solemn protestation" in 9:1.[26] While it is natural to assume that this denial responds to charges that Paul was disloyal to Israel,[27] the effort to work this out by assuming that every detail in vv. 1–5 polemicizes against correlative charges by his enemies has not been persuasive.[28] The polemical and defensive approaches overlook the rhetorical feature of evoking sympathy for Israel's plight through *exsuscitatio*[29] and wrongly assume that Romans is a judicial letter in defense of Paul's gospel. The asseveration of his anguish at the continued unfaith of many of his fellow Jews introduces a proof that concentrates on the faithfulness and power of God to overcome resistance to the gospel and ultimately to have mercy on "all" (11:32).

The clause in the genitive absolute, "my conscience bearing me witness in the Holy Spirit," provides independent confirmation of the foregoing double claim of truthfulness.[30] This threefold sequence gains rhetorical force by conforming to the biblical rule that "two or three witnesses" (Deut 17:6; 19:17) are required in dis-

puted cases, a rule that Paul cites in 2 Cor 13:1.[31] The clause is connected syntactically with the preceding verbs[32] rather than with the subsequent reference to Paul's pain and sorrow.[33] The verb συμμαρτυρεῖν ("to bear witness with") was used in connection with "conscience" in 2:15 just as here, conveying the idea that it functions as an autonomous witness to the consistency of behavior and internalized norm.[34] Unlike most modern conceptions, conscience for Paul was neither the voice of God nor a guiding moral agency but rather the irrepressible knowledge one has "with oneself" that an action is consistent or inconsistent with one's ethical norm.[35] This explains why conscience could be presented here as an independent witness, distinguished from the "I" of the preceding verbs, "telling the truth" and "not lying," and witnessing "to me" (συμμαρτυρούσης μοι) that the truth is being told. "The autonomous nature of the conscience is nowhere more apparent than in this verse . . . yet at the same time Paul does not hesitate to refer to the conscience as his own" ("my conscience," συνειδήσεώς μου).[36] A unique feature of this reference to conscience, when compared with other Pauline passages, is the link with the Holy Spirit. The anarthrous expression ἐν πνεύματι ἁγίῳ ("in [the] Holy Spirit")[37] has been interpreted as if the conscience were acting in behalf of God's Spirit[38] or that it is directly controlled[39] or guided by the Spirit,[40] but these explanations are grammatically problematic[41] and overlook the fact that for Paul conscience is a fallible human instance of judgment, shaped by "custom" rather than by God (1 Cor 8:7, 10, 12).[42] In this instance, since con-

25 North, "Paul's Protest," 462.

26 Hans Conzelmann, "ψεῦδος κτλ.," *TDNT* 9 (1974) 601.

27 For example, see Lietzmann, 89; Kühl, 312; Barrett, 175–76; Dunn, 2:523; Byrne, 285; Moo, 554.

28 Minear, *Obedience*, 75.

29 See Elliott, *Rhetoric of Romans*, 261–63, as discussed above.

30 Eckstein, *Syneidesis*, 186; Philip Bosman, *Conscience in Philo and Paul: A Conceptual History of the Synoida Word Group* (WUNT 166; Tübingen: Mohr Siebeck, 2003) 253–54.

31 See Kühl, 312; Schmidt, 155.

32 Meyer, 112; Weiss, 392; Godet, 339.

33 As implied by Barrett, 174–76, but refuted by Cranfield, 2:452.

34 See Jewett, *Terms*, 445.

35 See particularly Pierce, *Conscience*, 21–28.

36 Jewett, *Terms*, 445–46; Dunn, 2:523, qualifies this claim with "a semi-autonomous faculty (not wholly autonomous)." See also Ziesler, 235.

37 The same anarthrous form occurs in Rom 14:17; 1 Cor 12:3; 2 Cor 6:6; 1 Thess 1:5, all of which appear to reflect a Semitic idiom, "by Holy Spirit" (1QSb 2:24).

38 Zahn, 429.

39 Christian Maurer, "σύνοιδα, συνείδησις," *TDNT* 7 (1971) 916; Schreiner, 479.

40 Käsemann, 257; Kuss, 3:670.

41 Weiss, 392, followed by Eckstein, *Syneidesis*, 188, and Bosman, *Conscience*, 255, observes that "in Holy Spirit" cannot be linked adjectively with "con-

science can give false testimony, "the veracity of the witness of his conscience is certified by the Holy Spirit."[43] This completes the most extensive affirmation of Paul's truthfulness in any of his letters, strongly suggesting his conviction that at least some members of the audience are inclined to doubt the sincerity of his devotion to Israel.

■ **2** The dependent clause introduced by ὅτι ("that") in this verse specifies the emotional state that Paul affirms. The chiastic figure of λύπη + μεγάλη : ἀδιάλειπτος + ὀδύνη ("sorrow" + "great" : "unceasing" + "pain")[44] employs nouns that are closely associated in classical and biblical texts. Demosthenes *Epist.* 2.16 refers "to rather being grieved most painfully about everything" (εἰς δὲ τὸ μᾶλλον λυπεῖσθαι πάντων ὀδυνηρότατον), and other texts refer to the heavy weight of sorrow.[45] Prov 31:6 advises, "Give strong drink to those in grief and wine to those in pain" (δίδοτε μέθην τοῖς ἐν λύπαις καὶ οἶνον πίνειν τοῖς ἐν ὀδύναις). Isa 35:10 and 51:11 promise that when the exiles return to Israel "pain and grief and groaning" (ὀδύνη καὶ λύπη καὶ στεναγμός) will cease.[46] The term λύπη has a wide semantic range, including "pain of mind or spirit, grief, sorrow, affliction,"[47] and the connotation that is most likely here is

sorrow.[48] Paul does not "grieve," as if his fellow Israelites were dead, but he suffers from disappointment and regret. In Paul's case, the sorrow is described as "great" (μεγάλη) in the sense of being "deep"[49] and profoundly felt.[50]

There is also a relatively wide semantic range for the word ὀδύνη, including physical pain, suffering, woe, distress, and sorrow.[51] In this context, pain and/or distress is primarily in view,[52] as the parallels in medical literature indicate.[53] The "pain of mind"[54] that Paul feels is ἀδιάλειπτος ("unceasing"), implying that "his emotional response is neither superficial nor transitory but remains with him as a chronic condition."[55] Paul had employed the adverbial form of this word (ἀδιαλείπτως) in 1:9 in reference to his ceaseless prayers for the Roman congregations. The location of this pain is "in my heart," referring in traditional Judaic fashion to the center of one's "will, emotion, thoughts and affections."[56] This reference has led Godet to posit a threefold gradation of intensity between "great," "continually," and "heart,"[57] but this seems implausible in view of the chiastic structure of this verse. Although heartsick and profoundly sorrowful, Paul does not yet specify why, which renders the emotional shift from the

science" without a repetition of the article after the noun.

42 Jewett, *Terms*, 421–30, 459–60; Schreiner, 479.

43 Murray, 2:2; see also Schlier, 284; Jewett, *Terms*, 446; Eckstein, *Syneidesis*, 189; Bosman, *Conscience*, 256.

44 See the reference above to Weiss, "Beiträge," 238; Louw, 2:97; Siegert, *Argumentation*, 122.

45 Isocrates *Panath.* 20.1; 216.2; 232.2; *Phil.* 22.5; *Antid.* 153.2.

46 Cited by Dunn, 2:523.

47 BAGD (2000) 604.

48 Horst Balz, "λύπη," *EDNT* 2 (1991) 363, "great sorrow and unending pain"; see also Rudolf Bultmann, " λύπη κτλ.," *TDNT* 4 (1967) 320; Godet, 339; Sanday and Headlam, 227; Schlier, 285; Murray, 2:2; Fitzmyer, 544. BAGD (2000) 605, offers "I am greatly pained," but provides parallels that mostly refer to grief and sorrow; Cranfield, 2:453, denies that "any clear distinction" can be made between λύπη and ὀδύνη.

49 Michel, 292; Otto Betz, "μέγας," *EDNT* 2 (1991) 400.

50 Johnson, 144.

51 BAGD (2000) 692; Friedrich Hauck, "ὀδύνη, ὀδυνάομαι,"*TDNT* 5 (1967) 115.

52 Sanday and Headlam, 227; Hauck, "ὀδύνη, ὀδυνάομαι," 115; Schlier, 285; Fitzmyer, 544.

53 For example, Galen *Constit.* 1.249.16, "whether there might be pain in the head (ὀδύνη κεφαλῆς) or any other part," and Galen *Plac.* 1.8.7, "to have pain in the heart (καρδίαν ὀδυνᾶσθαι)." See also Galen *San.* 6.296.4. That both "sorrow" and "pain" are mentioned in LXX Isa 35:10 and 51:11 (see Dunn, 2:523) is less relevant for this context, because the "sorrow and pain and groaning (ὀδύνη καὶ λύπηκαι στενογμός)" that "will pass away" were related to the anticipated end of Israel's exile rather than to anguish over her continuing alienation. See Moo, 557: "It is unlikely . . . that Paul's use of the two terms owes anything to these two texts in Isaiah."

54 LSJM 1199.2.

55 Johnson, 144.

56 Jewett, *Terms*, 448; Alexander Sand, "καρδία," *EDNT* 2 (1991) 250.

57 Godet, 339, accepted by Kühl, 312.

glorious, joyous certainty of 8:37-39 all the more stark. Although many commentators hasten to suggest reasons for Paul's agonized feelings,[58] the fact remains that he gives no hint in the first two verses of this pericope that his anguish relates to Israel, and even in the next verse, the precise reason remains rather unclear. His strategy to evoke *exsuscitatio* begins with arousing sympathy on the part of the audience, which must be wondering while listening to vv. 1-2 why Paul is so distressed. Since the expression of excruciating sorrow invites sympathy on the part of hearers, Paul evidently expects that he can later extend such personal sympathy to the larger dilemma of Israel's continued rejection of the gospel and its bearing on the missional project that this letter seeks to advance.

■ **3** Paul provides the reason for his anguish by a complex construction introduced by the imperfect verb ηὐχόμην ("I was praying, wishing"),[59] which has "the force of throwing this wish into the past, and into a past that remains always unfinished, so that this expression takes away from the wish all possibility of realization."[60] Paul avoids the subjunctive formulation with ἄν ("if") because this would render the wish itself unreal and thus awaken the suspicion that Paul in fact had never wished such a thing.[61] To translate this as "I would pray that I

myself be accursed . . ." implies that the prayer was "unattainable or impermissable"[62] and therefore unlikely to have actually been made by Paul, in which case the preceding threefold assertion of his truthfulness is reduced to claiming good intentions.[63] The subjunctive translation would also render the emphatic αὐτὸς ἐγώ ("I myself") insincere and unconvincing, because Paul would have actually failed to place his future in jeopardy. It is better in this context to translate, "I used to pray that I myself be banned . . ."[64] implying actual prayer requests made sometime before the moment of writing,[65] requests that God had thus far chosen not to fulfill.[66] This brings Paul's prayer in line with the extraordinary dialogue between Yahweh and Moses in Exod 32:31-33:[67] "Alas, this people have sinned a great sin; they have made for themselves gods of gold. But now, if you will forgive their sins—and if not, blot me, I pray you, out of your book which you have written." But the Lord said to Moses, "Whoever has sinned against me, him will I blot out of my book." To pray to be ἀνάθεμα is an apt expression of being blotted out of the book of life, that is, "something delivered up to divine wrath, dedicated to destruction and brought under a curse."[68] The function of this curse is to ban someone from a religious congregation,[69] which is its

---

58 For example, Zahn, 429; Murray, 2:3; Morris, 346; Zeller, 172; Cranfield, 2:453–54; Moo, 557.

59 BAGD (2000) 417 observes that εὔχομαι can be rendered either "pray" or "wish." Johannes Hermann and Heinrich Greeven, "εὔχομαι κτλ.," *TDNT* 2 (1964) 775–808, concentrate exclusively on passages in which this verb refers to prayer. Although Horst Balz, "εὔχομαι, εὐχή," *EDNT* 1 (1990) 89, prefers the translation "wish," he observes that "this can only be accepted with certainty where God is not named as the addressee." But who, apart from God, would be in the position of granting this wish? In the only other uses of this term in the Pauline letters (2 Cor 13:7, 9), εὔχομαι clearly refers to prayer, and in view of the religious context of this discussion, the translation "I prayed" is likely here. See Cranfield, 2:454–55; Dunn, 2:524; Haacker, 181. Wilckens, 2:186, observes that unfulfilled wishes are expressed by Paul with ὄφελον (1 Cor 4:8; 2 Cor 11:1; Gal 5:12), ἤθελον (Gal 4:20), or ἐβουλόμην (Phlm 13), rather than by εὔχομαι.

60 Godet, 339; see also Kühl, 312; BDF §359.2.

61 Weiss, 393.

62 Cranfield, 2:455.

63 The same considerations render unlikely Zahn's suggestion (431) that Paul may have offered a temporary, earthly separation from Christ in behalf of his people, a theory rejected by Godet, 339; Kühl, 313; Michel, 292; Käsemann, 258.

64 See Colenso, 213: "I was wishing to be myself accursed from Christ." See also Hays, *Echoes*, 62, 206.

65 Smyth, *Grammar*, §1891, observes, "The imperfect of verbs of *sending, going, saying, exhorting*, etc., *which may imply continuous action*, is often used where we might expect the aorist of concluded action" (italics in original), which might be translated in this instance as "I prayed."

66 Sanday and Headlam, 228: "St. Paul merely states the fact of the wish without regard to the conditions which made it impossible." See also Gaugler, 2:8.

67 See Michel, 293; Cranfield, 2:454.

68 Johannes Behm, "ἀνάθεμα κτλ.," *TDNT* 1 (1964) 354; see also Douglas Stuart, "Curse," *ABD* 1 (1992) 1218–19.

69 Wilhelm Rees, "Anathema," *RGG*⁴ 1 (1998) 458.

primary meaning here, because separation from Christ means "reversing the integration into Christ accomplished in baptism."[70] This formulation may reflect Paul's internalization of the anathemas expressed against himself in synagogal disputes[71] in which he claims to have received the penalty of thirty-nine lashes on five separate occasions (2 Cor 11:24). The banning ἀπὸ τοῦ Χριστοῦ ("from the Christ") includes the article that makes clear that separation from the Messiah and his community are at stake.[72] Christ is also referred to later in v. 5 with the article, referring to the messiah of Israel.[73] The rhetorical force of this reference to Paul's willingness to be banned from Christ is enhanced by its juxtaposition with the triumphant conclusion of the second proof, that nothing in the entire creation can "separate us from the love of God in Christ Jesus our Lord" (8.39).

As in the case of Moses' offer cited above, the risk of being separated from Christ was undertaken ὑπὲρ τῶν ἀδελφῶν μου ("for the sake of my brothers"), a formulation that has led commentators to search for parallels in the atonement and expiation theologies of the ancient world.[74] There are reasonable objections to Paul's thinking of himself as playing the role of Moses, the Suffering Servant of Isa 53, one of the Maccabean martyrs, or Christ himself,[75] so the only certain inferences that can be drawn from this compressed formulation are that in some sense Paul offered his own damnation in behalf of his fellow Jews and that his prayer was rejected. It is noteworthy, moreover, that he refers to non-Christian Jews as "my brothers," thus avoiding any sense that his feeling of solidarity with them is in any way diminished. The further elaboration of "my compatriots by flesh" was required because the formulation "brothers" was so frequently employed to refer to fellow believers, whether Jews or Gentiles.[76] The word συγγενής appears here with the meaning "compatriots," fellow Jews.[77] The formulation expresses a close identification of Paul with his fellow Israelites,[78] which is a further expression of solidarity[79] that serves the purpose of *exsuscitatio*, inviting his audience, part of which is inclined to prejudicial feelings against nonbelieving Jews with whom conflicts had erupted in previous years, to share his sympathy.[80]

■ **4** The sequence of ten attributes of Paul's compatriots begins with οἵτινές εἰσιν Ἰσραηλῖται ("inasmuch as they are Israelites").[81] This is the name given to Jacob by Yahweh according to Gen 32:29 and used to describe the tribal confederacy[82] in one of the earliest examples of Hebrew poetry, the Song of Deborah: Yahweh is the "God of Israel" (Judg 5:2) and Deborah is the "mother of Israel" (Judg 5:7). The psalms echo this usage: "O that deliverance for Israel would come from Zion! When God restores the fortunes of his people, Jacob will rejoice and Israel will be glad" (Ps 53:6; see also 25:22; 130:7-8). The designation "Israel" is particularly employed in the period before the exile, while the word "Jews" becomes more prominent thereafter. Horst Kuhli observes that Josephus uses the term "Israelite" 188 times in the early portion of the *Antiquities* down to the period of the Maccabees, and thereafter he uses "Jews" in reference to more contemporary history.[83] Thus, when Paul employs the present tense verb, "who *are*

---

70 Käsemann, 158; see also Ziesler, 236; Schmidt, 156. This is rejected by Cranfield, 2:458, on the unconvincing grounds that separation from the church would be less serious than separation from Christ and salvation. For Paul, to be separated from the church is to be separated from Christ and salvation.

71 Argued by Lyder Brun, *Segen und Fluch in Urchristentum* (Oslo: I Kommisjon hos Jacob Dybwad, 1932) 127–28, on the basis of 1 Thess 2:15 and 1 Cor 4:12.

72 See Käsemann, 258; cf. Latto, *Star Is Rising*, 317–54.

73 See Dunn, 2:525.

74 See Michel, 294; Dunn, 2:525; Siegert, *Argumentation*, 121.

75 Käsemann, 258.

76 Schmidt, 156.

77 Wilhelm Michaelis, "συγγενής, συγγένεια," *TDNT* 7 (1971) 741; BAGD (2000) 950.

78 See Michael Cranford, "Election and Ethnicity: Paul's View of Israel in Romans 9.1-13," *JSNT* 50 (1993) 30.

79 See Moo, 559.

80 Elliott, *Rhetoric of Romans*, 263.

81 Dunn, 2:526; BDF §293; οἵτινες is used "where the relative clause expresses a general quality." See also Moule, *Idiom Book*, 123–24; Käsemann, 258: "οἵτινες is explanatory."

82 Gerhard von Rad, Karl Georg Kuhn, and Walter Gutbrod, "Ἰσραήλ κτλ.," *TDNT* 3 (1965) 356–57.

83 Horst Kuhli, "Ἰσραηλίτης," *EDNT* 2 (1991) 205; see also Fitzmyer, 545.

Israelites," he "evokes the blessings (v. 4b) that were given to the people in the past and reinforces the abiding validity of their place as the people of God."[84] There is an honorific aspect to the title "Israelite,"[85] as one can see in 1 Maccabees where Israel is "the name the people uses for itself," whereas non-Jews consistently refer to them as "Jews."[86] Official correspondence, even when written by Jews and directed to foreign rulers, always employs the title "Jews" rather than Israelites.[87] Greco-Roman writers also employ the terms "Jew" or "Jews" rather than "Israelite."[88] Dunn therefore infers that this reference to "Israelites" employs "his people's own view of themselves, as himself an insider rather than as one looking in from outside."[89] The blessings cited by Haacker from the *Memar Marqah* 2.12 convey this honorific dimension, which the Samaritans desired to share:

> Blessed are you, Israel, for Yahweh is your God!
> Blessed are you, Israel, for the right ancestors are your fathers!
> Blessed are you, Israel, for Mount Gerizim is your sanctuary!
> Blessed are you, Israel, for Moses ben Amram is your prophet!
> Blessed are you, Israel, for the holy law is your scripture!
> Blessed are you, Israel!
> Who is like you, the redeemed people!

Dunn is correct in concluding that the terms "Israel" and "Israelite," which occur twelve times in chaps. 9–11 in contrast to "Jews" in the earlier chapters, are "therefore deliberately chosen by Paul to evoke his people's sense of being God's elect, the covenant people of the one God."[90] As Gutbrod observes, "Israel is not just the totality of its individual members; it is the bearer of the promise and the recipient of its fulfillment."[91] This sets the stage for the argument of the third proof, that God's promise has not failed (9:6), that God has not abandoned Israel (11:1), and that in the end "all Israel will be saved" (11:26). While there is no hint in this reference of implicit criticism of Israel—that its current behavior contradicts its status as God's chosen people[92]—the juxtaposition with the previous description of Paul's anguish conveys the "tension that Paul seeks to resolve" in this third proof.[93] The chauvinistic impulse of many Gentile converts was to resolve this tension by abandoning the Jews to their fate. But Paul's purpose in this *exsuscitatio* is to arouse a sympathetic understanding of Israel's crucial role in the future salvation of the world through the gospel.

The possessive pronoun ὧν makes clear that the following six attributes belong to Israel. The resultant exegetical task, which has not hitherto been clearly addressed in the commentaries, is to discern the argumentative bearing of this possession in the *exsuscitatio* designed for this particular rhetorical situation and audience. The first attribute, ἡ υἱοθεσία ("the sonship, adoption"), has evoked puzzlement, because nowhere in the LXX and only once in other ancient Jewish literature[94] is this concept mentioned, and because Paul developed an explicitly Christian use of this term in Rom 8:15, 23. Although the term "sonship/adoption" is largely absent from Jewish writings, the concept is certainly present in the biblical accounts of Israel's election. In Exod 4:22, Pharaoh is told by Yahweh that "Israel is my firstborn son," and Isa 1:2 has Yahweh say, "Sons have I reared and brought up, but they rebelled against me." Jer 31:9 repeats this idea in Yahweh's words, "for I am a father to Israel, and Ephraim is my firstborn." As a consequence, Israelites are "sons of the living God" (Hos 1:10).[95] We noted in connection with the use of υἱοθεσία in 8:15 that Paul appeared to build on this tra-

---

84 Kuhli, "Ἰσραηλίτης," 205.
85 Michel, 295; Kuss, 3:672.
86 Von Rad, Kuhn, and Gutbrod, "Ἰσραήλ κτλ.," 360.
87 Ibid., 366–61.
88 Ibid., 371–72.
89 Dunn, 2:526.
90 Ibid.
91 Von Rad, Kuhn, and Gutbrod, "Ἰσραήλ κτλ.," 387.
92 Jülicher, 291; Kühl, 314; Schmidt, 156.
93 Moo, 561.
94 Eduard Schweizer, "υἱοθεσία," *TDNT* 8 (1972) 399, notes that the only exceptions are Philo's references to the wise as the adopted sons of God, but a *TLG* search turns up no instances of υἱοθεσία in Philo.
95 See also Hos 11:1; Deut 1:31; 8:5; 14:1; Isa 43:6; Wis 9:7; *Jub.* 1.24-25.

dition of Israel's having been chosen by God as his children.[96] This is definitely confirmed by 9:4, which makes it clear that sonship, which had earlier been promised to believers, belongs first and foremost to Israel. Access to this status through faith and the gift of the Spirit, as in 8:15, 23, is therefore valid only if Israel's sonship remains intact.[97] This explains why the article is attached to υἱοθεσία in this context: "the sonship" discussed in 8:15, 23 belongs first to Israel. Believers who do not have Jewish blood become sons and daughters of God (8:15, 23; 2 Cor 6:18) and thus enter into the family of Israel. Eldon J. Epp properly infers from 9:4 "the continuity of the one people of God,"[98] which would be weakened if υἱοθεσία were reduced to "adoption."[99] This theme is developed in the next pericope, where Paul maintains that the "children of the promise" are the true "children of God" (9:8), whether Jews or Gentiles (11:30-32). But this entire argument would collapse if Israel's sonship were invalidated.

In a way similar to the term "sonship," Israel's δόξα ("glory") is the manifestation of divine radiance and honor that believers in Christ come to bear, according to the argument of the preceding second proof (5:2; 8:17, 18, 21, 30).[100] The use of the article with glory (ἡ δόξα), when not part of a genitive construction such as "the glory of the Lord," "his glory," or "the glory of the temple," is unprecedented in Jewish sources,[101] and in this case it refers back to the topic introduced in the preceding discussion,[102] namely, "the glory to be revealed in us" (8:18) as the "sons of God" are "revealed" (8:19).[103] Commentators overlook this function of the article, disregarding the connection with the immediately preceding chapter and referring instead to ancient Israel's concept of glory.[104] This misses the point that Paul wanted to make, namely, that the glory revealed in believers is part of Israel's glory. The possessive pronoun ὧν ("whose") pertains to glory as well as to sonship. Thus, to hold Israel in contempt and fail to recognize that such glory belongs to her are to undermine "the glory to be revealed" in believers. As in the references to "Israelites" and "the sonship," this reference to "the glory" is a crucial step in Paul's *exsuscitatio*, showing that sympathy for Israel is demanded by the nature of eschatological salvation as experienced by the audience.

The plural reference to "the covenants" has elicited considerable discussion, although it is not at all unusual in Jewish texts.[105] It seems clear that this reference alludes to the theme of the "covenants of the fathers" from Judaism,[106] to which Paul referred in 4:18 with regard to the covenant with Abraham that he should "become the father of many nations." Other covenants possibly covered in this formulation are with Noah (Gen 9:8-17), with Josiah (2 Kgs 23:3) and with Nehemiah (Neh 9–10), the covenants enacted at Mount Sinai (Exod

---

96   Byrne, *Sons*, 84; Byrne, *Romans*, 250–53.
97   See Atkins, *Egalitarian Community*, 173; Tobin, *Paul's Rhetoric*, 304.
98   Eldon J. Epp, "Jewish-Gentile Continuity in Paul: Torah and/or Faith? (Romans 9:1-5)," *HTR* 79 (1986) 82.
99   Scott, *Adoption*, 61–117, maintains the problematic view that all references to υἱοθεσία, including Rom 9:4 (pp. 148–49), imply adoption rather than sonship, which tends to undercut the continuing legitimacy of Israel's status as sons of God. In fact, the technical phrase for adoption is not employed by Paul; see the listing of nine examples of καθ᾽ υἱοθεσίαν in G. H. R. Horsley, "καθ᾽ υἱοθεσίαν," *NDIEC* 4 (1987) 173, and the discussion of this issue in Horsley, "Petition to a Prefect," *NDIEC* 3 (1983) 16–17.
100 See Tobin, *Paul's Rhetoric*, 304.
101 Cranfield, 2:462, citing Str-B, 3:262, and followed by Michel, 295; Dunn, 2:526; and Fitzmyer, 546. See also Gerhard Kittel, "δοξάζω, συνδοξάζω," *TDNT* 2 (1964) 237–47.

102 BDF §252, where the article designates "the known, particular, previously mentioned" reference.
103 See Harald Hegermann, "δόξα, δοξάζω," *EDNT* 1 (1990) 346–47. Dunn, 2:526, followed by Moo, 563, overlooks this contextual implication in suggesting that the article with glory is "motivated by stylistic concerns" to bring the expression into correspondence with "the sonship."
104 See Cranfield, 2:462; Michel, 295; Morris, 384; Murray, 2:5; Schlier, 287; Kuss, 3:673–74; Wilckens, 2:188; Dunn, 2:526; Fitzmyer, 546; Haacker, 184; Moo, 536; Byrne, 287; Schreiner, 484.
105 Cranfield, 2:462, and Dunn, 2:527, refer to Wis 18:22; Sir 44:11, 18; 2 Macc 8:15; 4 Ezra 3.22, 5.29.
106 See Johannes Behm, "διαθήκη," *TDNT* 2 (1964) 130; that the covenants made with the fathers have continued validity for Paul is argued by Harald Hegermann, "διαθήκη," *EDNT* 1 (1990) 300, citing Rom 11:29.

19:5), at Moab (Deut 29:1), at Mount Ebal and Mount Gerizim (Josh 8:30-35), and the covenant with David (2 Sam 23:5).[107] I see no good reason to exclude any of these covenants from the plural reference in 9:4. As far as Paul's audience is concerned, however, this plural reference would also include the new covenant, which stands in contrast to the old, as in 2 Cor 3:6, 14; Gal 4:24,[108] because it is clear from the words of institution cited in 1 Cor 11:25 that the "new covenant" was a widely shared aspect of early Christianity.[109] In view of the fact that this "new covenant" was announced in Jer 31:31-34, there is a basis for Paul's claim that even this belongs to Israel. Therefore, to lack respect and sympathy for Israel is to call into question the legitimacy of believers' participation in the Abrahamic covenant discussed in Rom 4 as well as the "new covenant" celebrated in every sacramental meal shared by the congregations in Rome. Although Paul later makes clear that "obtuseness" has come over Israel (11:7-10, 25), which will ultimately be overcome (11:26-32), the shoe is on the other foot here. There is no hint in 9:4 that the continuity between Gentile believers and Israel has been "broken,"[110] because the covenants by which believers share a transformed life still belong to Israel.[111] The covenantal relationship is open to Gentile believers, to be sure, but Paul never states that it belongs to them; instead, they have a share in what belongs to Israel, a point developed in 11:18.

The fourth attribute is ἡ νομοθεσία ("lawgiving, legislation"), which appears here for the only time in the NT. It is found in 2 Macc 6:23 in reference to "the holy and God-given legislation" honored by Eleazar, who in his martyrdom extols the νομοθεσίας ἐπιστήμη ("science of lawgiving," 4 Macc 5:35). Such martyrs should be admired as "champions of true lawgiving/ legislation (τοὺς τῆς ἀληθείας νομοθεσίας ἀθλητάς)" according to 4 Macc 17:16. Νομοθεσία can mean either lawgiving or legislation, but in view of the fact that the latter is referred to as νόμος, δικαίωμα, διαταγή, διάταγμα, ἐντολή, ἐπίταγμα or κέλευσμα, the former seems more appropriate.[112] The translation "legislation" offers a conventional link with Paul's earlier references in Romans to the law,[113] but overlooks the decisive argument in 4:13-14 that the law was given *after* Abraham's act of faith in the divine promise; indeed, as Paul calculated in Gal 3:17, the law was given to Moses 430 years later. The law that Paul believes he has "established" (3:31), and that witnesses to righteousness through faith (3:21), is therefore not eternal,[114] but was given to Israel as part of a long history of salvation to which non-Jewish believers are now indebted. How can one be certain about this gospel, therefore, if the lawgiving experience of Israel is held in contempt? Once again, sympathy with Israel and its tragic plight is evoked by this formulation.

The fifth honorific attribute of the Israelites is ἡ λατρεία ("the worship, sacrificial service"). That this refers specifically to the sacrificial system is widely maintained,[115] with Exod 12:25-26 describing the sacrifice of passover as a λατρεία and Josh 22:27 employing this term in reference to "our burnt-offerings and our meat-offerings and our peace-offerings." Since Judaism at this

---

107 See George E. Mendenhall and Gary A. Herion, "Covenant," *ABD* 1 (1992) 1179–1202. As Calvin J. Roetzel points out in "Διαθῆκαι in Romans 9:4," *Bib* 51 (1970) 379–84, and *Judgement*, 100–101, such covenant ceremonies involved decrees, statutes, and ordinances, but that is no reason to translate διαθῆκαι as "commandments," "oaths," or "decrees" in this verse ("Διαθῆκαι," 389–90).

108 Epp, "Jewish-Gentile Continuity," 83.

109 Mendenhall and Herion, "Covenant," 1197–99.

110 Epp, "Jewish-Gentile Continuity," 83; Dunn, "Covenant Theology?" 15–16.

111 Tobin, *Paul's Rhetoric*, 305.

112 Meyer, 2:116; Godet, 341; Weiss, 395; Sanday and Headlam, 231; Jülicher, 291; Lietzmann, 88; Kühl, 314; Schmidt, 157; Michel, 295; Käsemann, 259;

Murray, 2:6; Morris, 349; Kuss, 3:677; Zeller, 173; Ziesler, 237; Haacker, 184–85; Luz, *Geschichtsverständnis*, 272, and Epp, "Jewish-Gentile Continuity," 85–89.

113 Advocated by Cranfield, 2:463; Wilckens, 2:188; Fitzmyer, 546; Moo, 563–64; Byrne, 287; see also Walter Gutbrod, "νομοθεσία," *TDNT* 4 (1967) 1089.

114 Epp, "Jewish-Gentile Continuity," 89, is therefore correct in discerning in the choice of νομοθεσία a rejection of the dogma of the eternal law, which allowed him to "diminish its otherwise logically preeminent place among the factors of continuity for God's people, though without diminishing the 'good' and 'holy' nature of Torah."

115 Hermann Strathmann, "λατρεύω, λατρεία,"

time restricted worship to the temple in Jerusalem, this is likely intended here.[116] However, the two earlier occurrences in Romans that are decisive for the interpretation of 9:4 both refer to worship in a more general sense, which also reflects LXX usage.[117] In 1:9, Paul worships God "in my spirit in the gospel of his son," and in 1:25 sinners are depicted as "worshiping the creature rather than the creator." The later references to worship are in the same vein (12:1; 15:16), and it seems clear on other grounds that λατρεία would be understood by the Roman audience as referring to worship in general, including temple sacrifices, home services, the observation of the Sabbath, the recitation of the Shema,[118] and also the Lord's Supper and other forms of early Christian worship. In Phil 3:3 Paul refers to various forms of early Christian services with the verb λατρεύω ("worship"); "For we are the true circumcision, who worship God (θεοῦ λατρεύοντες) in spirit and glory in Christ Jesus. . . ." There is no reason to believe that Christian forms of worship were not also included in the reference to "the worship" in 9:4. The implication is that even the liturgies of early house and tenement churches, in their various forms, are part of Israel's worship. This was a well-grounded assertion, because all of the elements in early Christian worship appear to have derived from Judaism, including the rituals of baptism and Lord's Supper,[119] and the use of Aramaic formulas such as "Abba" and "Maranatha."[120] Therefore, to deny the importance of Israel's legacy is to delegitimize Christian worship. This points forward to the hope that the global mission will result in Gentile and Jewish voices joining together in worshiping God (15:9-12).

The sixth honorific attribute of Israel is αἱ ἐπαγγελίαι ("the promises"), a word that appeared in the singular four times in chap. 4 in reference to Abraham's promise to inherit the world (4:13), which made him "the father of all who have faith" (4:11). It appears that the plural was intended to include promises made to the other fathers because Paul refers explicitly to τὰς ἐπαγγελίας τῶν πατέρων ("the promises to the fathers") in 15:8. This would include promises to Isaac (Gen 26:3-5), Jacob (Gen 28:13-15), and to other "outstanding men of God in Scripture and right up to the present time,"[121] in later Jewish sources.[122] The plural formulation of "the promises" could also include promises made to Sarah, David, and the Jewish people, as well as specific promises such as salvation, eternal life, and the coming of the Messiah.[123] Paul's own usage reflects this wider reference, as in 2 Cor 7:1, where he speaks of the "promises" by God to dwell with his people (2 Cor 6:18) and treat them as his "sons and daughters" (2 Cor 6:18). The broad reference of αἱ ἐπαγγελίαι ("the promises") in 9:4 does not "distract from the primary thrust of Paul's argument,"[124] because he has more than "Messianic salvation"[125] in view. When the possessive pronoun ὧν ("whose") is taken into account,[126] the

TDNT 4 (1967) 65, and Heinrich Balz, "λατρεύω, λατρεία," EDNT 2 (1991) 345, both point to "sacrificial service" as the dominant connotation in biblical sources. None of the commentators advocating this interpretation (Godet, 341; Schmidt, 157; Käsemann, 259; Dunn, 2:527–28; Fitzmyer, 547; Moo, 564; Schreiner, 484) provides an explanation of why the Jewish maintenance of temple worship would be relevant at this point in Paul's argument.

116 See Wick, Gottesdienste, 67–81, 179.
117 Balz, "λατρεύω, λατρεία," 344, points to Deut 24:48 and 3 Macc 4:14 as referring in more general terms to service to God.
118 Cranfield, 2:463.
119 See Luke T. Johnson, "Gottesdienst: 4, Neues Testament," RGG⁴ 3 (2000) 1182.
120 See Wick, Gottesdienste, 244–366.
121 Gottlob Schrenk and Gottfried Quell, "πατήρ κτλ.," TDNT 5 (1967) 976; Sass, Verheißungen, 427.
122 For example, Sir 44:1–50:26 extends the list of

fathers from Enoch to the high priest Simon; see also 4 Macc 13:17.
123 Julius Schniewind and Gerhard Friedrich, "ἐπαγγέλλω κτλ.," TDNT 2 (1964) 580; Cranfield, 2:464; Byrne, 287.
124 Dunn, 2:528.
125 Schniewind and Friedrich, "ἐπαγγέλλω κτλ.," 583.
126 Among commentaries I have surveyed, Kühl, 314; Barrett, 178; Murray, 2:6; Morris, 349; Stuhlmacher, 146; Fitzmyer, 547; Moo, 564; Witherington, 251; and Schreiner, 485, allude to this matter of possession in connection with "the promises." Commentators who appear to forget this possession include Meyer, 2:116; Weiss, 395; Godet, 341; Sanday and Headlam, 231; Schmidt, 157; Lietzmann, 89; Schlier, 287; Dodd, 152; Michel, 295; Käsemann, 259; Kuss, 3:677; Ziesler, 238; Wilckens, 2:188; Zeller, 173; Haacker, 185; Dunn, 2:528; Johnson, 146; Byrne, 287.

point is that all of the promises received by the congregations in Rome belong first and foremost to Israel.[127] Sympathy with Israel's tragic plight is therefore required by the multitude of divine promises on which the life of these congregations depends.[128]

■ **5** After the listing of six attributes qualified by ὧν ("whose") in the early part of v. 4, two additional relative clauses are contained in v. 5, each beginning again with ὧν. This gives particular emphasis to the final items in the tenfold sequence.[129] There is a close association beween the previously mentioned "promises" and the "fathers" here in v. 5a, because they were the chief recipients of divine assurances.[130] As we noted above, the list of the fathers is headed by Abraham, Isaac, and Jacob, but includes the entire sequence of Israel's important forebears. In the context of Romans, however, it is Abraham's role that is given the largest billing, in chap. 4. In the next pericope in the third proof, for which these references in 9:1-5 provide an introduction, Abraham is mentioned along with Isaac and Jacob (9:6-13). Since both the OT and the NT refer to God as the God of the fathers, there is no possibility of separating off the Christian God from its roots in Israel's history.[131] Paul refers repeatedly in his letters to Abraham as the patriarch who set his faith in the divine promise and becomes the prototype for Christian believers (Rom 4:11; 2 Cor 11:22; Gal 3:6-9; 4:21-31). He returns to this theme in 15:8-9, making clear that Gentiles as well as Jews share in the promises made to "the fathers."[132] The continuity between Christian believers and the ancestral faith of Israel has not been destroyed, even despite Israel's current resistance, for which Paul mourns.[133] Therefore, to lack sympathy for Israel's situation is to jeopardize this redemptive legacy, which could potentially unite the human race (15:9-13).

That Christ descended from Israel and was promised by its prophets was declared in the confession that opens Romans (1:2-3), but here the reference is arthrous: ὁ Χριστός ("the Christ"), which accents his messianic status.[134] That the Messiah came from "the Israelites," both in expectation and in fulfillment,[135] is affirmed by the expression ἐξ ὧν ("from whom"), which simply expresses derivation.[136] No matter how hostile some of the house and tenement churches in Rome were to Judaism and Jewish Christian believers, the fact of Jesus' birth in a Jewish family and the weight of his cultural background as an Israelite were undeniable. Yet there is a curiously critical note in the very next phrase, τὸ κατὰ σάρκα, which should be translated in a delimiting sense such as "insofar as the flesh is concerned."[137] In 1971 I discussed this reference under the category of the polemical use of flesh, suggesting that it sets the stage for 9:6-13, where the descendents of Isaac are the recipients of the promise, while the "children of flesh"

127 See Tobin, *Paul's Rhetoric*, 304.

128 Gignac, *Romans 9–11*, 178–79, argues in contrast that Paul's purpose in this pericope is to render Israel's election problematic.

129 Moo, 564.

130 Kühl, 315.

131 Haacker, 185, makes this point while listing as examples Gen 26:24; 28:13; 31:42, 53; 48:15; Exod 3:6, 15, 16; 4:5; 1 Kgs 8:26; 1 Chr 29:18; 2 Chr 30:6; Tob 7:15; Mark 12:26 and parallels; Acts 3:13; 7:32.

132 See particularly Epp, "Jewish-Christian Continuity," 84.

133 Epp, "Jewish-Christian Continuity," 84, unfortunately concludes that "this continuity of patriarchal faith and of the acceptance of the Messiah who issued from them has been broken."

134 Käsemann, 259; Kuss, 3:677; Dunn, 2:528; Fitzmyer, 547; Hurtado, *Lord Jesus Christ*, 100. In contrast, Walter Grundmann, "The Christ Statements of the New Testament," *TDNT* 9 (1974) 540, maintains that the article makes no difference in the meaning, and that 9:4 could refer either to Jesus or to the messianic title. As BDF §§252–54 explains, the article can be interpreted either as individual or generic, so the context becomes decisive in assessing the nuance of a particular formulation.

135 For an account of Jewish messianism, see Nils A. Dahl, "The Messiahship of Jesus in Paul," in *The Crucified Messiah and Other Essays* (Minneapolis: Augsburg, 1974) 37–47; Martinus de Jonge, "Messiah," *ABD* 4 (1992) 777–88.

136 Commentators favoring simple derivation include Godet, 341; Zahn, 452; Schmidt, 157; Murray, 2:6. In contrast, Kuss, 3:677; Haacker, 180; Moo, 565, wrongly perceive a polemical note in this formulation—that Israel has not accepted its messiah.

137 Cranfield, 2:464, and Dunn, 2:528, both refer to BDF §266.2, "where the addition of the article strongly emphasizes the limitation ('insofar as the physical is concerned')." The neuter article τό is employed here instead of the masculine article ὁ, which would normally follow the masculine expres-

descended from Esau who seek election through "works" are not viewed as part of the authentic Israel.[138] The word "flesh" in this context evokes the realm of self-justification by works as opposed to a neutral reference to human limitations. At one level, this critical note seems to undermine the honorific thrust of Paul's *exsuscitatio*, but his intent is to introduce the full, tragic depth of Israel's dilemma. This reference, and the third proof as a whole, offers a dialectic that verges on contradiction: Israel's legacy is ineluctable for Christian faith, yet the continued rejection of the Messiah by some Israelites reflects a distortion that Paul explains as seeking to establish their righteousness and failing to submit to the righteousness of God (10:3).

The extensive discussion about the grammatical and theological implications of the final line in this pericope is closely related to the dialectic implicit in "the Christ insofar as the flesh is concerned." Two different punctuations of v. 5b-c have been debated for centuries, each with an array of translation options.[139] Since the Greek manuscripts rarely contain punctuation marks,[140] contextual and theological considerations have been followed to decide between these options, which are simply stated as follows:

1. καὶ ἐξ ὧν ὁ Χριστὸς τὸ κατὰ σάρκα, ὁ ὢν ἐπὶ πάντων θεὸς εὐλογητὸς εἰς τοὺς αἰῶνας ("and

from whom is the Christ inasmuch as the flesh is concerned, the one who is God over all, blessed forever").

2. καὶ ἐξ ὧν ὁ Χριστὸς τὸ κατὰ σάρκα. ὁ ὢν ἐπὶ πάντων θεὸς, εὐλογητὸς εἰς τοὺς αἰῶνας ("and from whom is the Christ inasmuch as the flesh is concerned. God who is over all, be blessed forever").

The principal reasons that many scholars[141] prefer option 2 are the following: (a) Paul elsewhere allegedly does not refer to Jesus as God[142]—but Phil 2:6 is a prominent example of his doing so and in many of the 180 instances where Paul refers to Jesus as "Lord," divinity is implied.[143] (b) The phrase "God over all things" is too extensive a claim to make for Christ[144]—yet there are instances in which Paul makes such a claim for Christ by referring to him as "Lord" over all (Rom 10:12; 14:9; 1 Cor 8:6; Phil 2:10). (c) Εὐλογητὸς ("blessed") is always directed toward God in the NT[145]—which is true, including Rom 1:25 and 2 Cor 1:3; 11:31, and if this option is selected, this last detail must be explained.[146]

The principal weaknesses with option 2 are the following: (1) the awkward word order, in that (a) εὐλογητός should appear before the word "God," as in other blessing formulas (Luke 1:68; 2 Cor 1:3; Gen 9:26; 14:20; Exod 18:10; Ps 17:47, etc.);[147] (b) the natural

---

sion ὁ Χριστός if one wished to say "the Christ who is by flesh." In this instance, the phrase κατὰ σάρκα is being set up as a kind of technical expression, which should be taken into account in the interpretation.

138 Jewett, *Terms*, 160–63.

139 See the articles listed under note h above; Moo, 565, counts no fewer than eight variations within two basic punctuation options. Further options are discussed by Ezra Abbot, "On the Construction of Romans ix.5," *JBL* 1 (1881) 87–154, and idem, "Recent Discussions of Romans ix.5," *JBL* 2 (1883) 90–112. See also Murray J. Harris, *Jesus as God: The New Testament Use of Theos in Reference to Jesus* (Grand Rapids: Baker, 1992) 150–51.

140 Cuthbert Lattey discovered a small cross between σάρκα and ὁ ὢν in Codex Ephraemi, which matches the comma in the Nestle-Aland text, and in my translation as noted above.

141 Meyer, 2:120, with earlier advocates listed on 117–18; Abbot, "Construction," 87–90; Jülicher,

292; Lietzmann, 90; Dodd, 152; Käsemann, 260; Kuss, 3:678; Wilckens, 2:189; Ziesler, 239; Zeller, 174; Dunn, 2:528–29; Stuhlmacher, 146; Johnson, 147; and Byrne, 288.

142 Meyer, 2:118–19; Jülicher, 292; Käsemann, 260; Kuss, 3:678; Dunn, 2:529.

143 Hurtado, *Lord Jesus Christ*, 108–18.

144 Meyer, 2:120.

145 Schreiner, 487.

146 It is possible that Hurtado's analysis in *Lord Jesus Christ*, 135–51, of "binitarian worship" in Pauline Christianity would provide an explanation for "blessing the Lord" being understood as "blessing Christ."

147 Ernst Bröse, "Wird Christus Röm. 9,5 Θεός genannt?" *NKZ* 10 (1899) 649.

antecedent of ὁ ὤν ("the one who is") is the immediately preceding noun, that is, Christ, and a change in reference would need to be indicated by δέ ("but") or a different word order;[148] (2) the participle ὤν ("who is, who really is") is inappropriate in reference to God, whose divinity was not in dispute;[149] (3) the proper Greek formulation of an independent clause, "God who is over all things," would be ὁ ἐπὶ πάντων θεός, without ὤν;[150] and finally (4), that there would be a contextual problem with concluding 9:1-5 with a doxology to God because it would then appear that Jewish unbelief is pleasing to God, whereas a doxology to Christ places the christological issue that provokes Jewish resistance on center stage.

In support of option 1, preferred by an even larger number of scholars,[151] is the matter just described: (a) The ascription of divinity to Christ was the principal barrier against Jewish acceptance of Jesus as the Messiah, so a doxology to him as God is relevant to Paul's argument. (b) The participle ὤν makes excellent sense in reference to Christ, with the connotation "who is really God," reflecting the controversial point.[152] (c) The preceding reference to Christ as stemming from Israel "insofar as the flesh is concerned" is a delimitation that invites an antithesis, which the doxology to Christ provides, thus bringing this passage into correlation with the opening confession: "from David's seed according to the flesh, appointed son of God in power according to the Spirit of holiness" (1:3-4).[153] (d) Finally, the syntactical difficulties in option 2 are all avoided by option 1, which flows in a natural way.[154]

Therefore, although certainty is not possible in a complicated issue like this, the doxology is more likely to have been directed at Christ than at God. This completes the dialectic that we discerned in the reference to Christ "according to the flesh." On the one hand, there is no denying the roots of the messianic expectation and the cultural origins of Jesus; but, on the other hand, resistance to recognizing Jesus as the Christ involved the question of his divinity, which Paul boldly claims at the end of this introduction to the third proof. This sets the stage for arguing in 10:9 that confessing Jesus as "Lord" leads to salvation, and in 10:11 that Jesus is Lord of all. If salvation results from calling on the "name of the Lord" (10:13), then the salvation of "all Israel" in 11:26 would entail their recognition that Jesus is "really God over all things" (9:5).

If Christ is to be "blessed for the ages," then the doxology typical for the OT and Hebrew worship[155] is extended to him as God. The εὐλογητός formula is a direct translation of the Hebrew word for blessing, běrākâ,[156] which glorifies God as the source of all benefits.[157] Virtually the same formulation occurs as the ending of Ps 88:52, εὐλογητὸς Κύριος εἰς τὸν αἰῶνα. γένοιτο, γένοιτο ("blessed be the Lord for ever. Amen, amen."). In the Shema 1.2, a similar formula appears: "Blessed be Adonai, who is to be blessed for ever and ever." The blessing formulas were employed in the Jewish temple and synagogue worship,[158] whereby the reference to αἰών extends the blessing into the endless future.[159] The expression is typical for Hebrew worship, but there are also Greco-Roman parallels in the acclamations of Caesar εἰς αἰῶνα.[160] In the context of 9:5, the

148 Godet, 342; Bröse, "Röm. 9,5," 650–55.
149 Godet, 343.
150 Bröse, "Röm. 9,5," 650; Cranfield, 2:468.
151 Godet, 341–44; Weiss, 396; Bröse, "Röm. 9,5," 645–57; Zahn, 342–43; Sanday and Headlam, 233–38, with an extensive list of earlier advocates; Kühl, 315; Schmidt, 158; Schlatter, 202; Murray, 2:6; Michel, 296–98; Schlier, 287–88; Cranfield, 2:465–70; Morris, 349–50; Fitzmyer, 548–49; Haacker, 186–87; Moo, 565–67; Schreiner, 486–89; Witherington, 251–52; Harris, *Jesus as God*, 154–65.
152 Godet, 343.
153 See particularly Moo, 567; Schreiner, 487–88.
154 Cranfield, 2:468.
155 Hermann Patsch, "εὐλογέω κτλ.," *EDNT* 2 (1991) 80.
156 Hermann W. Beyer, "εὐλογέω κτλ.," *TDNT* 2 (1964) 764; Heckel, *Segen*, 48–51.
157 William J. Urbock, "Blessings and Curses," *ABD* 1 (1992) 755.
158 Ibid., 758–59.
159 Hermann Saase, "αἰών, αἰώνιος," *TDNT* 1 (1964) 200; Traugott Holtz, "αἰών," *EDNT* 1 (1990) 44; as Barr, *Time*, 70, points out, there is no distinction in meaning between the singular and the plural forms of αἰών.
160 See G. H. R. Horsley, "An Acclamation to 'the Lord, forever,'" *NDIEC* 2 (1982) 35, for a discussion of *SEG* 27. Nr. 853, "For good fortune. (Extol) forever (εἰς αἰῶνα) the unconquered one."

blessing of Christ as Lord of all points forward to an eschatological future[161] in which the triumph of the gospel is anticipated, so that in the end all Israelites will lend their voices to the chorus of praise (9:6; 10:14-18; 11:15-32; 15:9-13). The "Amen" at the end of this provocative but hopeful blessing invites the congregation to make it "operative" by its assent.[162] The triumph of Christ over "all things" for which Paul hopes, in contrast to Caesar's triumph and also in contrast to the military triumph some messianic Jews hoped to see, comes by persuasion and requires the free response of faith and praise. By uttering their assent, the congregations in Rome take the first step to overcome their cultural chauvinism and open themselves to the mission that Paul wishes to advance, whose "mystery" he reveals at the end of this third proof (11:25).

---

161 Saase, "αἰών, αἰώνιος," 205–7; Holtz, "αἰών," 45.
162 Heinrich Schlier, "ἀμήν," *TDNT* 1 (19964) 336;
     Heckel, *Segen*, 308–12.

9

The Second Pericope

Thesis and the First Part of a Midrash on Israel and the Righteousness of Divine Election

6/ But it is not such that[a] the word of God has fallen short. For not all who [are] from Israel these [are] Israel;[b] 7/ nor [is it] that[c] all [his] children are Abraham's seed, but "in Isaac shall your seed be called." 8/ That is,[d] those who [are] the children of the flesh, these [are] not the children of God, but the children of the promise are reckoned as seed. 9/ For the word of promise [is] this, "About this time I shall return and there shall be for Sarah a son." 10/ Not only so, but also Rebecca [received a promise], having intercourse with one man, Isaac our father; 11/ for when they were not yet born and had not done anything good or worthless,[e] in order that God's selective purpose may continue, 12/ not from works but from the one calling, it was said to her[f] that "The elder will serve the younger." 13/ Just as[g] it has been written, "Jacob I loved, but Esau I hated."

14/ What then shall we say? There is no injustice with God, is there? By no means! 15/ For he says to Moses, "I will have mercy on whomever I am merciful, and I will have compassion on whomever I am compassionate." 16/ So then [it is a matter] neither of him who wills nor of him who runs, but of God who shows mercy.[h] 17/ For the Writing says to Pharaoh, "For this very purpose I raised you up, so that I might demonstrate my power in you, and so that my name might also be proclaimed in all the earth." 18/So then he[i] has mercy on whom he wills, and he hardens whom he wills.

a P[46] it sy[p]; Ambst delete ὅτι ("that") to make the awkward expression conform to the colloquial usage, according to Cranfield, 2:472.

b The plural form Ἰσραηλῖται ("Israelites") found in D F G 88 (330) 614 629 1881[c] *pc* vg[ww] appears to be a secondary, stylistic improvement.

c In place of ὅτι ("because") Origen provides ὅσοι ("as many as"), while a b vg[cl] provide *qui* ("who"), both of which appear to be efforts at stylistic improvement.

d The addition of ὅτι ("that") by ℵ[2] B[1] Ψ 69 104 330 365 614 1319 1505 1506 1573 2495 *pc* appears to be a stylistic improvement.

e The substitution of the frequently used word κακόν ("bad") in P[46] D F G K L Ψ 88 104 323 326 330 424* 614 945[(acc. to Swanson)] 1175 1241 1735 1836 1874 2344 2464 *Maj* for the infrequently used synonym φαῦλον, which is strongly attested by ℵ A B 6 69 81 365 424[c] 630 945[(acc. to N-A)] 1243 1319 1506 1573 1739 1881 *al* Or appears to be a secondary and easier reading. See Cranfield, 2:477. Wilckens, 2:194, observes that the variant κακόν brings Paul's usage into conformity with his usual antithesis between good and bad.

f The word αὐτῇ ("to her") is deleted in P[46] D* vg[mss] sy[p] Or Ambst, which makes this the less difficult and thus secondary reading.

g Nestle-Aland[27] follows the stronger evidence in support of καθώς ("as") found in P[46] ℵ A D F G K L P Ψ 6 33 69 88 104 323 326 330 365 424 614 945 1175 1241 1243 1319 1505 1506 1573 1735 1739 1836 1874 1881 2464 2495 *Maj*, in contrast to Nestle-Aland[25], which followed B Or in reading here καθάπερ ("just as").

h The minor variant in L, εὐδοκοῦντος ("well pleased"), may be an effort to avoid the unusual spelling of ἐλεῶντος ("merciful"); Cranfield, 2:484, notes that "a number of MSS have the more regular ἐλεοῦντος"; in fact the TR reads ἐλεοῦντος at this point, but this variant is not listed in Nestle-Aland[27]. The more difficult reading, ἐλεῶντος ("merciful") in P[40vid, 46] ℵ A B* D* F G P 326 1735, is undoubtedly original.

i The addition of ὁ θεός ("God") by D *pc* ar mon vg[ms] Ambst appears to be explanatory; it is clearly secondary.

Analysis

The connection of this pericope with the preceding introduction appears nonexistent to some,[1] while the link between the theme of election, stated explicitly in v. 11, and the earlier development of the theme in 8:28f., is clearly visible.[2] A particularly strong link is established between the "Israelites" of v. 4 and "Israel"

---

1 Michel, 298.

2 Ibid.

in v. 6, as well as between "flesh" in v. 3 and v. 8. The connection seems logical when one recalls the reason for Paul's grief. The tragic disbelief of Israel in the messianic proclamation raises the central question of chaps. 9–11, one that derives from the *propositio* in 1:16-17, namely, whether the gospel is the "power of God for salvation." The antithetical connection in 9:6, οὐχ οἷον δέ ("but not as if"), relates to a potentially false implication of Paul's grief, namely, that he would not be grieving if indeed God's word had been successful. The thesis in v. 6a[3] that God's word has not failed is developed first by an extensive midrashic discourse,[4] in which Gen 21:12 provides the initial text and Gen 18:10; Gen 25:23; Mal 1:2-3; Exod 33:19; and Exod 9:16 provide the supplemental texts. This midrash creates a logical proof of the thesis in v. 6a by developing a distinction in the paradoxical *sententia* of v. 6b[5] between the elected true Israel and Israel as a whole.[6] Divine selectivity is seen to be at work in the designations of Isaac and Jacob as the recipients of mercy, and those who resist this long-standing purpose of God place themselves in the position of Pharaoh.[7] As Otfried Hofius has shown, two lines of argument in the next three chapters develop the thesis of v. 6a, namely, that 9:6—11:10 shows that God's promise aimed at saving the remnant of Israel—the Jewish Christians—while 11:11-32 deals with the non-Christian majority of Israel, for whom there still remains the hope of salvation in the mysterious plan of God.[8]

An important disagreement among commentators is whether this pericope properly ends with v. 13,[9] or continues through the end of v. 18,[10] or through v. 29.[11] The question in part depends on how one understands the use of the midrashic argument, which in fact is not completed until the reiteration in v. 29 of the "seed" motif of v. 7. But since Paul moves at v. 19 from the initial midrashic development into first person singular diatribe,[12] answering objections to the conclusions he has drawn from his exegesis, it seems more appropriate to hold the material in vv. 6-18 together. If a division between v. 18 and v. 19 is not compelling, it would appear more appropriate to hold the entire section from v. 6 to v. 29[13] together than to divide it into two sections (vv. 6-13; vv. 14-29)[14] or into three sections (vv. 6-13; vv. 14-23; vv. 24-29).[15]

The pericope of 9:6-18 consists of three clusters of sentences,[16] the first of which (vv. 6-8) deals with the question of the reliability of God's word concerning the true children of Abraham. The initial proof text from Gen 21:12 is cited to prove that not all of the physical descendants of Abraham are his true children. This cluster opens with the thesis stated in a single line, consistent with earlier thesis statements in Romans such as 8:1,

---

3 Kim, *Romans 9–11*, 123–24, refers to this declaration as the "propositio" of chaps. 9–11.

4 Ellis, *Prophecy*, 218–20; R. Vincent, "Derash homilético en Romanos 9–11," *Sal* 42 (1980) 751–88; and Stegner, "Midrash," 37–52, discuss Paul's use of midrashic patterns of exegesis. Robin Scroggs, "Paul as Rhetorician: Two Homilies in Romans 1–11," in Robert Hamerton-Kelly and Robin Scroggs, eds., *Jews, Greeks, and Christians: Religious Cultures in Late Antiquity: Essays in Honor of William David Davies* (Leiden: Brill, 1976) 278, argues against the application of the technical term "midrash"; see Sass, *Verheißungen*, 435.

5 Holloway, "Paul's Pointed Prose," 51.

6 See Mesner, "Rhetoric," 284–308, for an analysis of the formal enthymeme.

7 Ibid., 387–88.

8 Hofius, "Evangelium und Israel," 300–310.

9 See Michel, 298–304; Käsemann, 260–67; Cranfield, 2:471; Wilckens, 2:191–97; Schlier, 289–93; Fitzmyer, 558–63; see also Winkel, "Argumenta-

tionsanalyse," 68; Aageson, "Scripture," 268f.; and Siegert, *Argumentation*, 123–27.

10 See Louw, 2:99–100.

11 See Aletti, "Argumentation," 42–43; Dunn, 2:536–37, refers to vv. 6-29 as the "Call of God," but then goes on to treat the pericope 9:6-13 as if it were an independent unit within this topic.

12 See Stowers, *Diatribe*, 98.

13 Aletti, "Argumentation," 43–45, discerns a chiastic development holding vv. 6-29 together, but the scheme appears artificially thematic and awkwardly related to the midrashic structure of the argument.

14 Schlier, 289–305; Wilckens, 2:191–209; Michel, 298–319.

15 Käsemann, 260.

16 Louw, 1:21, suggests four clusters, dividing what I perceive to be the middle cluster of 9:9-13 into two parts, vv. 9-10 and vv. 11-13. This division would cause the division of what appears to be a single, rambling sentence from v. 9 to v. 13; see Godet, 348, and Cranfield, 2:470.

18.[17] The following sentences are in parallel form, with the citation from Genesis falling out of the pattern.[18] The second cluster (vv. 9-13) provides the supplemental text and two supporting texts to show that a selection of only one son was intended by God, which means that not all of the descendants of Abraham are truly included in the promise. The proof text and the supplementary text provide the three catchwords, "call," "seed," and "children," which are used to link the various supporting texts.[19] The threefold reduplication of $\sigma\pi\acute{\epsilon}\rho\mu\alpha$ ("seed") in vv. 7-8 enhances the visibility of the first catchword. The pattern of parallelism is continued in this cluster in vv. 10-12, with the citations from the OT again falling out of the structure and thus gaining emphasis. The third and final cluster (9:14-18) provides two more supporting texts to answer the question of whether the election of certain descendants threatens the justice of God. This cluster is opened by a triple-line diatribal exchange, matching 6:1, 15 and 7:7, in which a false conclusion concerning the justice of God is stated.[20] The denial is supported by discourse arranged for the most part in synthetic and antithetical parallelism.[21] The antithesis in 9:16 is enhanced by homeoptoton in the repetition of the three participle endings $-\nu\tau\sigma\varsigma$. The final antithetical parallelism in the pericope contains a reduplication of $\vartheta\acute{\epsilon}\lambda\epsilon\iota$ ("he wills"),[22] providing emphasis on the sovereignty of God, which contrasts with the will of humans referred to in 9:16.

Rhetorical Disposition

IV.	The *probatio*
9:1—11:36	The third proof: The triumph of divine righteousness in the gospel's mission to Israel and the Gentiles
9:6-18	2. Thesis and the first part of a midrash on Israel and the righteousness of divine election
9:6a	a. The general thesis for the third proof: The reliability of God's word
9:6b-8	b. The initial phase of the midrashic argument concerning the true children of Abraham
9:6b	1) The contention that not all Israelites "belong to Israel," that is, are true children of Abraham
9:7a	2) The contention that not all of the $\sigma\pi\acute{\epsilon}\rho\mu\alpha$ Ἀβραάμ ("seed of Abraham") are his true children
9:7b	3) The citation of the initial proof text from Gen 21:12
	a) First catchword: $\kappa\alpha\lambda\acute{\epsilon}\omega$ ("call, name")
	b) Second catchword: $\sigma\pi\acute{\epsilon}\rho\mu\alpha$ ("seed, descendant")
9:8	4) The initial explanation of the proof text, identifying the true $\sigma\pi\acute{\epsilon}\rho\mu\alpha$
9:8a	a) Formula of explanation: "that is"
9:8a	b) Negative explanation: not "children of flesh"
9:8b	c) Positive explanation: but "children of the promise are reckoned as the seed" ($\sigma\pi\acute{\epsilon}\rho\mu\alpha$; cf. 9:7)
9:9-13	c. The divine election of one son as the content of the promise
9:9	1) The supplemental text clarifying the promise
9:9a	a) The interpretive formula: "the promise is this"
9:9b	b) The citation from Gen 18:10 + 14 concerning the promise of a son to Sarah, containing the catchword $\upsilon\acute{\iota}\acute{o}\varsigma$ ("son")
9:10-12	2) The first supporting text clarifying the promise
9:10-12a	a) The circumstances surrounding the promise to Rebecca
9:10	(1) The situation of Rebecca's pregnancy
9:11a	(2) The situation of the twins prior to birth,
9:11b-12a	(3) The circumstances indicate the way divine election works
9:11b	(a) Purpose clause: "that God's purpose of election might continue"
9:12a	(b) The nature of divine election i. "Not from works" ii. But from God's calling ($\kappa\alpha\lambda\sigma\hat{\upsilon}\nu\tau\sigma\varsigma$; see 9:7)
9:12b	b) The citation of the first supporting text (1) The introduction of the citation (2) The citation of Gen 25:23 concerning Jacob serving Esau with the contextual catchword: $\upsilon\acute{\iota}\acute{o}\varsigma$ ("son" in Gen 25:25; cf. Rom 9:9)

17 See Weiss, "Beiträge," 238.
18 See ibid.
19 See Stegner, "Midrash," 40–41.
20 See Stowers, *Diatribe*, 121.
21 The citation from Exod 9:15 is an example of synthetical parallelism, while the Pauline formulations of 9:16a + 16b and 9:18a + 18b are antithetical parallels. Both parallelism and the midrashic structure are disregarded in Sass's theory in *Verheißungen*, 436–37, of a chiastic structure of A (9:6-9); B (9:10-13); C (9:14-18); C' (9:19-23); B' (9:24-26); and A' (9:27-29).
22 Bullinger, *Figures*, 319, inaccurately refers to this as an example of paronomasia.

9:13	3) The second supporting text
	a) The citation formula
	b) The citation of Mal 1:2-3 concerning God loving Jacob and hating Esau with the contextual catchword: καλέω (in Mal 1:4; cf. Rom 9:7)
9:14-18	d. The answer to an objection concerning the justice of God
9:14	1) A diatribal exchange concerning the justice of God
9:14a	a) The introductory question of general inference
9:14b	b) The question about whether God is unjust
9:14c	c) The emphatic denial: "By no means!"
9:15-17	2) The scriptural proofs
9:15	a) The third supporting text
9:15a	(1) The introduction of the citation
9:15b-c	(2) The citation of Exod 33:19 concerning the sovereignty of God's mercy and compassion with the contextual catchword: καλέω (in portion of Exod 33:19 not cited; cf. Rom 9:7)
9:16	(3) The explanation of election
9:16a	(a) Election depends not on human action
9:16b	(b) Election depends on God's mercy
9:17	b) The fourth supporting text
9:17a	(1) The introduction of the citation
9:17b-d	(2) The citation of Exod 9:16 concerning God using Pharaoh to demonstrate God's power with the contextual catchword: υἱοί ("sons" in Exod 9:26; cf. Rom 9:9)

9:18	3) Conclusion about the selectivity of the divine promise
9:18a	a) God has mercy on whom God wills
9:18b	b) God hardens whom God wills

Exegesis

■ **6** The thesis of the third proof is introduced by a rather unusual denial form, οὐχ οἷον δέ ("but it is not such that")[23] followed by ὅτι ("that"), which some have seen to be an ellipse between two colloquial expressions of denial.[24] The focus of the denial is not on the impossibility of God's word failing[25] but on avoiding a potential misunderstanding of Paul's grief as justifying the inference that God's word had in fact failed.[26] The verb used for this failure, ἐκπίπτω, means to drop off, fall through, drift off course, or come up short in a financial sense.[27] In rhetoric, ἐκπίπτειν τοῦ λόγου refers to someone who "suddenly went silent and was at an utter loss; and stopping, he suffers a failure in his speech (ἐκπίπτει τοῦ λόγου)."[28] This expression can also mean "to digress,"[29] and the verb ἐκπίπτειν can refer to a lack of success.[30] In the context of Paul's argument, ἐκπίπτειν τοῦ λόγου refers to the failure of the gospel message to persuade.[31] As Berger has shown, there is a well-established tradition in the LXX that links πίπτω and its cognates with the promises of God,[32] so that ὁ λόγος τοῦ θεοῦ in this instance is defined by the refer-

---

23   The ordinary formulation in classical Greek is οὐχ οἷόν τε, occurring hundreds of times. It appears more than twenty-five times in Plato, sixteen times in Demosthenes, five times in Lucian, etc. Οὐχ οἷον does not occur elsewhere in the NT or the LXX; among classical Greek authors, the precise wording found in Rom 9:6 appears only in Epicurus *Epistula ad Herodotum* 69.4, with δέ [= Diogenes Laertius *Vitae philos.* 10.69]; Polybius *Hist.* 18.35.11; Chrysippus *Frag. mor.* 643.1 [Stobaeus *Anth.* 2.7.109.5]; Stobaeus *Anth.* 2.4.11m.41; and the Suda *Lex.* π 2055.7.

24   Cranfield, 2:472, and Dunn, 2:538, cite BDF §§304, 480(5), the latter dealing with ellipses of the formulaic type. Zahn, 435–36, denies the ellipse by arguing that the expression is tantamount to οὐχ ὅτι, meaning "I will thereby not have said that. . . ."

25   *NEB,* "It is impossible. . . ." For a critique of older commentators holding this view, see Meyer, 2:123.

26   See Zahn, 435f.; Lübking, *Paulus,* 61f.; Berger, "Abraham," 78. Cranfield, 2:472, offers the apt paraphrase, "But what I have just said about my

grief for my fellow-Jews is not to be understood as meaning that. . . ." See also Sass, *Verheißungen,* 442–44.

27   See BAGD 243–44; also Danker, "Under Contract," 107.

28   Aeschines *Fals. leg.* 34.10.

29   LSJM, *s.v.* 9b.

30   The new LSJMRevSuppl (1996) adds the examples of ἐκπίπτω, "to lose one's case" (δίκης ἐκπίπτειν; Latin, *causa cadere*) in Justinianus *Cod. Just.* 2.2.4.2; for a wrestler to be thrown (*SEG* 35. Nr. 213.8); for a lover to be unsuccessful (*SEG* 35. Nr. 219.10).

31   See R[oy] David Kotansky, "A Note on Romans 9:6: ὁ λόγος τοῦ θεοῦ as the Proclamation of the Gospel," *StBT* 7 (April 1977) 24–30.

32   Berger, "Abraham," 79f., shows that Josh 21:45; 23:14; 1 Kgs 3:19; 2 Kgs 10:10; 3 Kgdms 8:56; Ruth 8:18; Tob 14:14; Jdt 6:9; Esth 6:10 refer principally to the nonfailure of divine promises to Israel.

ence to the promises in 9:4. Yet in contrast to the plural forms of "promises" given to Israel in 9:4 and of the "oracles" and "words" of God in 3:2, 4, Paul uses here the singular, which implies that the issue is broader than the status of Israel's advantages.[33] It seems more likely that "the word of God" in this context is roughly synonymous with "gospel."[34] The question raised here is the fundamental matter of divine reliability,[35] thus related to the doxology in 9:5, namely, whether God in Christ is powerful enough to be "over all." In this sense the thesis of Rom 9–11 is a direct expression of the main thesis of Rom 1:16-17 concerning the gospel as the "power of God" capable of setting right the entire world. The failure of Israel to respond to the gospel appears to invalidate this main thesis—hence the contention of v. 6a that provides the thesis for the entirety of this third proof.[36]

The translation of v. 6b is something of a paraphrase, because the word order literally means "for not all who are from Israel, these [are] Israel." Piper proposes that the οὐ ("not") in the anterior position should be taken to modify the clause at the end of v. 6b, οὗτοι Ἰσραήλ ("these [are] Israel"), following the pattern of Rom 7:15.[37] This would produce the translation "For all those from Israel, these are not Israel,"[38] but a strict construal of this reading would be to extend Paul's claim too widely by implying that none of those descended from Israel belong to the true Israel.[39] Paul has already established the distinction between those descendants of Abraham who follow the law and those who follow faith (Rom 4:13-16), insisting that only the latter are recipients of the divine promise. A similar distinction is intended here, using the term "Israel" to refer not to the patriarch[40] but to his descendants, the "members of the people Israel by birth."[41] By speaking of an "Israel within Israel,"[42] there

---

33   Dunn, 2:539, construes the "word of God" as the "specific promise" given to Israel, following Munck, *Christ*, 34; Barrett, 180; Käsemann, 262; Müller, *Gottes Gerechtigkeit*, 29; Zeller, *Juden*, 113–15; Kümmel, "Probleme," 20, and others.

34   Erhardt Güttgemanns interprets this expression more broadly as the proclamation of the gospel in Paul's ministry in "Heilsgeschichte bei Paulus oder Dynamik des Evangeliums: Zur strukturellen Relevanz von Röm 9–11 für die Theologie des Römerbriefes," in E. Güttgemanns, *Studia linguistica Neotestamentica* (BEvTh 60; Munich: Kaiser, 1971) 40ff. For a similar view, see Kotansky, "Romans 9:6," 24, and Mesner, "Rhetoric," 292. Zeller, *Juden*, 114, denies the identification of "word of God" with "gospel" but admits a close association of the two concepts.

35   See Lübking, *Paulus*, 62. Piper, *Justification*, 32–33, states this point in Calvinist language as the "electing purpose of God," which derives from divine intentionality. Hübner defines the fundamental issue as the divinity of God in *Gottes Ich und Israel*, 16, quoting Luz *Geschichtsverständnis*, 28, concerning the reliability of God.

36   Dunn, 2:539, notes that the advocates of a restricted reference of the thesis to a section of chapter includes Aageson, "Scripture," 286; Zeller, *Juden*, 114–16, though he admits that v. 6a serves as a caption for the entirety of Rom 9–11; Zeller's position is more ambiguous in *Römer*, 176; and Brandenburger, "Paulinische Schriftauslegung," 10, 16–20. Aletti, "Argumentation," 43, suggests that v. 6a is the *propositio* for 9:6-29. The majority support the

use of the thesis in v. 6a as developed in the entirety of Rom 9–11, including Kühl, 318; Käsemann, 261; Dahl, *Studies*, 155; Cranfield, 2:473; Wilckens, 2:191; Rainer Schmitt, *Gottesgerechtigkeit-Heilsgeschichte: Israel in der Theologie des Paulus* (Frankfurt: Lang, 1984) 72–77; Siegert, *Argumentation*, 124, 174, is ambiguous on this point; Martin Rese, "Die Rettung der Juden nach Römer 11," in A. Vanhoye, ed., *L'Apôtre Paul* (BETL 73; Leuven: Leuven University Press, 1986) 423; Hofius, "Evangelium und Israel," 300; Mary Ann Getty, "Paul and the Salvation of Israel: A Perspective on Romans 9–11," *CBQ* 50 (1988) 465.

37   Piper, *Justification*, 47–48.

38   Accepted as the accurate translation by Dunn, 2:539.

39   If from "all those who are from Israel," *none* are truly Israel, then the distinction that Piper wishes to maintain in *Justification*, 48–52, between the Israel according to the flesh and the true Israel is undermined.

40   Schlatter, 203–4.

41   Walter Gutbrod, "Ἰσραήλ κτλ.," *TDNT* 3 (1965) 383; for a discussion of Jewish efforts to distinguish the true elect of Israel from others who do not conform to the law, see Gottlob Schrenk, "ἐκλεκτός," *TDNT* 4 (1967) 184. Although appearing only here in the NT, the phrase ἐξ Ἰσραήλ is used twenty-eight times in the LXX, always in reference to the commonwealth of Israel. The phrase οὗτοι Ἰσραήλ is not found in the LXX, Philo, or Josephus.

42   Cranfield, 2:471; Johnson, *Function*, 148, cites Ps 83:6; *Jub.* 15.28-32; 20.11-13, and other texts to show

is no indication in this verse that Paul is denying Israel's election[43] or claiming the church to be the true Israel replacing the ancient people of Jewish descent.[44] The distinction refers not just to Jewish Christians as the true Israel within the larger circle of the Jewish people[45] for whose salvation Paul continues to hope (Rom 11:26).[46] Since all believers in the messianic proclamation are part of the true Israel, the distinction is finally "between believing and physical Israel" as determined by their response to the "word of God."[47] If the distinction between Israel and the true Israel can be sustained on the basis of the scriptural tradition on which Israel rests, the "word of God" cannot be held to have failed.

■ **7** The grammatical pattern of denial continues in this verse,[48] substantiating the claim in v. 6b by shifting the reference to the broader term "the children of Abraham," which includes Jacob, Isaac, Ishmael, Esau, and others[49] in contrast to "Israel," which involved only Jacob and his descendants.[50] The expression $\sigma\pi\acute{\epsilon}\rho\mu\alpha$ $\grave{A}\beta\rho\alpha\acute{\alpha}\mu$ ("seed/descendants of Abraham") occurs in the LXX of 2 Chr 20:7; Ps 104:6; *Ps. Sol.* 9.9; 18.3; Isa 41:8 and is used by Paul in 2 Cor 11:22. The Greek word order is ambiguous, however, and one cannot be certain in following Barrett's argument that "all the children" should be construed as the subject parallel to the "all" in the preceding verse.[51] Most commentaries, along with Byrne's monograph on this subject, take the opposite tack, that "the seed of Abraham" is the subject, with

"children" as the more limited category including only Isaac and his descendents.[52] The position of "seed of Abraham" becomes emphatic with Barrett's construal,[53] which comports well with the midrashic development concentrating on that phrase.[54] This translation also eliminates the alleged discrepancy between "seed" as the unrestricted term in v. 7a and as the restricted term in v. 7b.[55] What Paul denies here is that the covenantal promise extended to all of Abraham's children. It was the child of Sarah (Gen 21:1-3), not the children of Hagar and Keturah (Gen 16:15; 25:2), who would bear the promise of becoming the people of Israel (cf. Gal 4:22-31). The distinction between the broader category "children" and the restricted term "seed" thus corresponds exactly to that between all Israel and the true Israel in v. 6b.[56] That there was a kind of "divine exclusionary process"[57] in Israel's history was developed in Gal 3:16 to prove that Jesus was the single heir,[58] but here Paul takes the more traditional path of Jewish exegesis, claiming that the line of Abraham, Isaac, and Jacob received the promised inheritance.[59] His point is that from the beginning of Israel's history, physical descent alone was incapable of guaranteeing inclusion in the promise. As Piper has shown, this establishes an "ongoing principle" of selective election that restricts the sphere within which the word of God must be held to be effective, thus advancing the distinction between the true Israel and "all Israel" in v. 6.[60]

---

that "even Jews know that not all Abraham's descendents are his heirs."

43 See Heikki Räisänen, "Römer 9–11" 2900; Watson, *Paul*, 163, 227; Johnson, *Function*, 148. Gaston is so intent on denying a replacement of Jews that he denies the distinction between the true Israel and all Israel in 9:6b, in *Paul*, 6, 92; for a critique of Gaston, see Harvey, *True Israel*, 77–78. Ellison, *Mystery of Israel*, 43–44, develops the theme of "the delusion of national election."

44 See Wright, "Messiah," 193–97.

45 See Hübner, *Gottes Ich und Israel*, 17, citing Erich Dinkler, "Prädestination bei Paulus: Exegetische Bemerkungen zum Römerbrief," in *Signum Crucis: Aufsätze zum Neuen Testament und zur christlichen Archäologie* (Tübingen: Mohr Siebeck, 1967) 267.

46 See Mesner, "Rhetoric," 297.

47 See ibid., 297–301; and Fitzmyer, 560.

48 See Meyer, 2:125.

49 See Fitzmyer, 560.

50 See Cranfield, 2:473.

51 Barrett, 180–81.

52 Byrne, *Sons*, 130–31.

53 Followed by Dunn, 2:540, and Hays, *Echoes*, 206.

54 Stegner, "Midrash," 40.

55 See Berger, "Abraham," 81; Lübking, *Paulus*, 63; Aageson, "Scripture," 269.

56 For a discussion of the logic of this argument, see Mesner, "Rhetoric," 300–305.

57 Michel, 300.

58 See Betz, *Galatians*, 157.

59 Siegfried Schulz and Gottfried Quell, "$\sigma\pi\acute{\epsilon}\rho\mu\alpha$ $\kappa\tau\lambda$.," *TDNT* 7 (1971) 545.

60 Piper, *Justification*, 48; but he extends this argument too far in a Calvinist direction (49) by insisting that 9:6-8 deals with "election unto eternal salvation." As Dunn insists (2:540), it is the "mode, not the objective, of the promise" that is in view here. See also Lübking, *Paulus*, 63.

The quotation of the initial text in Paul's midrashic argument is drawn verbatim from Gen 21:12, without an introductory formula: ἐν Ἰσαὰκ κληθήσεταί σοι σπέρμα ("through Isaac shall your seed be called"). For readers unfamiliar with Genesis, the only indication of a quotation is the syntactic disparity of referring to "your seed" in a discourse dealing with the topic in the third person.[61] The quotation confirms that "seed" is the restricted category in v. 7a, as Barrett suggests, proving that the patriarchal tradition supports the kind of distinction Paul wishes to draw between the various children of Abraham. Only the descendants of Isaac receive the promised inheritance. The preposition ἐν ("through, in") was understood by Paul[62] and the later rabbinic tradition[63] in a restrictive sense of "only through Isaac." This initial text contains two catchwords that Paul develops in the rest of this midrash: "seed" and "call," picked up in vv. 8, 12, 24, 25, 26, and 29.[64] The future passive form of καλεῖν ("call") found in the LXX of Gen 21:12 is particularly crucial in the development of Paul's argument, suggesting that the future inheritance depends not on physical descent but on the promise of God.[65] While the resonance of the creative call in 4:17 would still be heard in this text, the nuance is legal, defining the true heirs of the promise.[66] The argumentative function of the Genesis citation, therefore, is to extend the principle of a distinction between Israel and the true Israel from v. 6b.[67] The importance of this initial text for Paul's argument is shown by the fact that it is the only verse in the midrash "that is the subject of a direct explanation,"[68] in the following verse.

■ **8** The explanatory formula τοῦτ᾽ ἔστιν ("that is") marks the end of the quotation in v. 7b and the beginning of a brief explanation of this crucial initial text. As in v. 6b the construction begins with the negative οὐ and contains a demonstrative pronoun ταῦτα ("these"), indicating that the explanation pertains not only to the text from Gen 21:12 but also to the distinction between the true Israel and all Israel.[69] The phrase ταῦτα τέκνα τοῦ θεοῦ can be best explained as an independent phrase breaking into the sentence to make clear that although the children of flesh are God's children, it is only the children of the promise who are reckoned as "seed." The true Israel corresponds not to the "children of the flesh" but to the "children of the promise." In Fitzmyer's words, "Paul now reverts to the terminology of 8:21, implying that Christians, Jewish and Gentile, are the true children of Abraham."[70] But it must be acknowledged that "these children of God" in v. 8 are initially defined as the Jewish descendants of Isaac; within the midrash itself, there is no hint that this expression refers to Christians,[71] which raises questions about the origin of this material.

In the antithetical context of this verse, the term σάρξ ("flesh") has a negative connotation strongly reminiscent of Gal 4:21-31, where slavery, hostility, the old age, and exclusion from the realm of the Spirit are the characteristics of those born of the flesh.[72] In contrast to the fully developed antithesis between flesh and Spirit in 8:4-8, the antithesis here is dominated by the initial text from Gen 21:12 and therefore uses "promise" in place of "Spirit." The association between "promise" and "reck-

---

61   Koch, *Schrift*, 13.

62   See Dunn, 2:540.

63   Stegner, "Midrash," 45, cites Midrash *Gen. Rab.* 53.12, n. 2, as insisting on this restrictive sense of Gen 21:12: "Without the IN, it would indicate that *all* Isaac's descendants will count as Abraham's descendants; the IN, however, limits it: only *some*, not all, Esau and his descendants being excluded" (italics in original).

64   See Stegner, "Midrash," 40; Aageson, "Scripture," 269.

65   Kühl, 319, and Lübking, *Paulus*, 63.

66   See Zeller, *Juden*, 119.

67   See Mesner, "Scripture," 324–26.

68   Aageson, "Scripture," 269.

69   Piper, *Justification*, 49; Mesner, "Scripture," 324–26.

70   Fitzmyer, 561; see also Esler, *Conflict and Identity*, 279.

71   For example, Gerhard Schneider, "τέκνον," *EDNT* 3 (1993) 341, maintains that the "children of God" in v. 8 are "Christians." If the "children of the promise" are Christians, this would have "tremendous significance" in the Roman community, which has "so many women church members," as pointed out by McGinn, "Feminist Approaches," 175.

72   See Jewett, *Terms*, 161; Dunn's attempt to pare back the polemical quality of σάρξ as "not strongly negative, as though constituting a *disqualifying* factor in itself, but as *not* constituting a qualifying factor in itself" (2:541, italics in original) may be theologically appealing but it is exegetically unsupportable. See also Sass, *Verheißungen*, 448–49.

oned" recalls 4:13-25, where Paul had shown that the divine blessing came not because of Abraham's conformity to the law but rather because of his faith. Paul thus reiterates his denial of a fundamental assumption of contemporary Judaism, that there was "a direct linkage and equation between their nationhood, the covenant, and the law . . . ."[73] The implication of this historical example is that only a small portion of contemporary Israel, those who have accepted the gospel, are called to be the true Israel.[74]

■ **9** The second cluster of sentences in this pericope opens with the term "promise," reiterating the key term in the preceding verse. The content of the promise is a conflated and altered quotation drawn from the LXX of Gen 18:10 + 14.[75] The source of Paul's phrasing may be demonstrated as follows, with the relevant portions underlined:

> Gen 18:10 . . . ἐπαναστρέφων ἥξω πρός σε κατὰ <u>τὸν καιρὸν τοῦτον εἰς ὥρας, καὶ ἕξει υἱὸν Σάρρα ἡ γυνή σου</u> . . . (". . . I will return to you <u>about this time</u> seasonably and Sara your wife shall have a son").
>
> Gen 18:14 . . . εἰς τὸν καιρὸν τοῦτον ἀναστρέφω πρός σε εἰς ὥρας, <u>καὶ ἔσται τῇ Σάρρα υἱός</u> ("at this time I will return to you seasonably <u>and there shall be for Sara a son</u>").
>
> Rom 9:9 <u>*Κατὰ τὸν καιρὸν τοῦτον* ἐλεύσομαι *καὶ ἔσται τῇ Σάρρα υἱός*</u> ("<u>About this time</u> I shall come and <u>there shall be for Sarah a son</u>").

There is a fairly wide consensus that the choice of the verb "I shall come" in place of the LXX in Gen 18:14 "I shall return" is a deliberate Pauline alteration, probably to avoid a functionless reference to an earlier visitation,[76] rather than to express the divine authority to define Israel[77] or to allude to some future epiphany.[78] This composite verse functions as the supplemental text in Paul's midrashic exegesis, elaborating the primary text from Gen 21:12 quoted in 9:7.[79] The supplementary text provides the catchword "son," which will be alliterated in the later quotations of vv. 26 and 27. It confirms through Hebrew Scripture that Israel's election as sons or children of God had always depended not on natural descent but on a selective divine promise. God is confirmed in this verse as the reliable one who comes to make the word of promise come true, thus addressing the issue in v. 6 as to whether "the word of God has fallen short."

■ **10** The next four verses comprise a loose syntactic unit whose subject is Rebecca and whose finite verb must be supplied from the preceding argument.[80] The elaborate opening formula οὐ μόνον δέ, ἀλλὰ καί ("not only so, but also")[81] suggests that the same point can be made about Rebecca as was established concerning Sarah. The divine word rather than physical lineage determines the heir of the promise. I thus propose the verbal completion of the sentence beginning in 9:10 as "received a promise,"[82] thus allowing this verse to stand as an independent clause, elaborated by the citations in vv. 12 and 13 concerning Isaac as the promised heir.

The expression κοίτην ἔχουσα ("having intercourse") combined with ἐξ ἑνός ("from one man"),

73 Dunn, 2:548.
74 Hübner, *Gottes Ich und Israel*, 21.
75 Stanley, *Scripture*, 103–4, rejects the idea that the phrase κατὰ τὸν καιρὸν τοῦτον ("about this time") was drawn from Gen 18:10, because only the preposition κατά differentiates this from Gen 18:14, but he provides no other explanation. A conflation of the two Genesis texts remains likely.
76 Koch, *Schrift*, 142, 172; Stanley, *Scripture*, 104.
77 Hübner, *Gottes Ich und Israel*, 24, 31.
78 Byrne, *Sons*, 133; Dunn, 2:542.
79 Stegner, "Midrash," 47f., shows that Gen 18:10 was also used as a supplementary text in the midrash of *Gen. Rab.* 53.4, demonstrating "the theme of God's steadfastness to his word."
80 For a discussion of nineteenth-century suggestions of the grammatical completion of 9:10-13, see

Weiss, 405. Godet, 348, suggests that the verb to be supplied was that Rebecca "was treated in the same manner, or had to undergo the same lot. . . ." Zahn, 440, also holds 9:10-13 together as a syntactical unit, denying that it is an incomplete sentence in the technical sense. See also Schmidt, 163f., who views vv. 10-13 as a sentence with a semicolon after v. 10. A recent resolution of the grammatical problem, in support of the line of argument in this commentary, may be found in Fitzmyer, 561–62.
81 This phrase appeared in Rom 5:3, 11; 8:23; and 2 Cor 8:19; it is not attested before the first century C.E. and may reflect Koine usage: *Ceb. tab.* 31.5; Justin *1 Apol.* 49.5; Vettius Valens *Anth.* 9.338.9.
82 Lübking, *Paulus*, 65, suggests that the verb "call" derived from v. 7b as the completion of vv. 10-13.

emphasizes that the twins Jacob and Esau had the same mother and father as well as "the same moment of conception."[83] The relevance of this point becomes clear in vv. 11-13, where Paul shows the absolute independence of the divine call from any human qualification or accomplishment,[84] for no distinction could be made in the fleshly origin of these two sons of Rebecca and Isaac. The reference to Isaac as "our father" probably refers to his status as a patriarch of the Jewish people rather than as a parent of all later believers,[85] because the context of the current discussion is Jewish unbelief in the messianic fulfillment.

■ **11** Paul's stress on the absolute freedom and reliability of the divine word continues in this verse with inferences drawn from the status of the twin sons of Isaac and Rebecca. The participles in the genitive absolute expression γεννηθέντων . . . πραξάντων ("born . . . done") refer to the implicit offspring Jacob and Esau[86] and are dependent on the verb in the next verse, "it was said to her."[87] The promise of inheritance came before the twins could achieve or lose divine favor through their own actions. The wording of the antithesis "anything good or worthless" is perhaps an allusion to the rather trashy quality of their later behavior, with Jacob cheating his brother and Esau selling his birthright for a bowl of soup. Dunn observes that Paul here replaces the ἀγαθός/κακός ("good/bad") antithesis used in 2:9-10;

3:8; 7:19; 12:21; 13:3-4; 16:19 with the ἀγαθός/φαῦλος ("good/worthless") categories that allow the negative pole to be understood as "good-for-nothingness,"[88] suggesting the twin's later behavior. Paul's point is that nothing they did disallowed the word of promise, which prevailed despite human corruption.

The final clause beginning with ἵνα ("in order that")[89] in v. 11b shows the theological meaning of the story of Jacob and Esau lies in "God's selective purpose." This expression combines a colloquial expression κατ᾽ ἐκλογήν ("by selection") with the term πρόθεσις ("purpose"), which was employed in 8:28. The idea of divine purpose played a large role in Jewish theology, which appears to be reflected here.[90] Although the word ἐκλογή was a technical term in Pharisaism for freedom of choice,[91] the phrase κατ᾽ ἐκλογήν was so well established in military and governmental contexts to depict selections for special roles that it is likely to be understood in that sense here by a Roman audience.[92] That "God's selective purpose" should continue, that is, be carried through in the destinies of Jacob and Esau, directly answers the issue in v. 6.[93] The verb μένω, used here for the only time in Romans, appears frequently in the LXX in the context of God's immutable being and counsel.[94] A particularly close echo to the usage here is the well-known passage from Isa 14:24, where Yahweh declares Ὃν τρόπον εἴρηκα, οὕτως ἔσται, καὶ ὃν

---

83 Cranfield, 2:476–77.

84 See Berger, "Abraham," 82; Sass, *Verheißungen,* 452–580.

85 Cranfield, 2:477, stresses the context of 9:3, "my kinsmen by race," which would limit Jacob's parentage to persons of Jewish descent. Fitzmyer rightly observes (562) that Paul "identifies himself with ethnic Israel" in this formulation.

86 Wilckens, 2:194, suggests that "sons" is the antecedent but that they do not have to be mentioned because Paul's readers know the biblical story.

87 See Cranfield, 2:477.

88 Dunn, 2:542, citing Trench, *Synonyms,* 315–18. See Prov 5:3; 13:6; 29:9.

89 See Cranfield, 2:478.

90 See Michel, 302, who cites *Apoc. Ab.* 22.2-3 and 26.5-6 as conceptual parallels.

91 Maier, *Mensch,* 335–38, 361, refers to *Ps. Sol.* 9.4-5 and Josephus *Bell.* 2.165 as examples of the Pharasaic doctrine of free will. This doctrine hardly

seems relevant for discussing divine sovereignty, which is Paul's topic in this pericope. Maier is followed by Dunn, 2:542f., who separates the expression in Romans into its two component parts, "that the purpose of God should stand in terms of his free choice," thus erroneously linking ἐκλογή with the verb rather than with the nominative phrase.

92 Gottlob Schrenk, "ἐκλογή," *TDNT* 4 (1967) 176, mentions several occurrences of this colloquial expression in Polybius *Hist.,* of which 1.61.3.6; 6.4.3.3; 6.10.9.3; 6.34.8.5; 10.12.8.3; 31.12.12.1; 38.10.8.4 prove to be relevant. Schlier, 292, observes that "the apposition κατ᾽ ἐκλογήν qualifies the πρόθεσις as one that occurs in a selection or choice."

93 Cranfield, 2:478, observes that "remain" is the opposite of "fallen short" in v. 6.

94 Friedrich Hauck, "μένω," *TDNT* 4 (1967) 575, refers to Pss 9:7; 101:12; Isa 40:8; Dan 6:27; Sir 44:13 as examples of the immutability of God.

τρόπον βεβούλευμαι, οὕτως μενεῖ . . . ("In the manner I have said, so shall it be; and in the manner I have purposed, so shall it remain . . ."). Paul's choice of the present subjunctive (μένη, "may stand") rather than the aorist subjunctive (μείνη, "might stand") implies that God's purpose continues forward from the time of the patriarchs to the events of the current generation.[95]

■ **12** The elliptical clause at the beginning of v. 12 stands in apposition to v. 11b,[96] explaining that God's purpose proceeds not from human works but from divine election. The rather strained antithesis between "works" and "the one calling" is understandable in the context of Paul's midrashic discourse. His initial proof text in v. 7 had contained the term καλέω ("call, name"), to which Paul alludes here.[97] The term also evokes the powerful argument of 4:17 that correlated justification and resurrection with the divine act of "calling" into existence.[98] The contrast between calling and works is crucial for Paul's argument that the continuation of God's purpose from the patriarchs to the present "depends on nothing the elect can do, but only on God's continual call. . . ."[99] This denies several important premises in Jewish theology: that obedience to the law is required for the maintenance of election[100] and that divine election presupposes God's foreknowledge of human works of obedience.[101] The sharp antithesis is consistent with the earlier argument of Romans, indicat-

ing a polemical intention that should not be distorted by theological rationalizing.[102]

The first finite verb in the rambling sentence of vv. 10-13 occurs in v. 12b with reference to the word spoken to Rebecca. The aorist passive ἐρρέθη ("it was said") is an introductory formula[103] indicating the divine source of the oracle. The quotation is derived exactly from the LXX of Gen 25:23, referring to Esau as the "greater" or firstborn child serving Jacob, the "lesser" or second-born of the twins.[104] The oracle illustrates the principle of "God's selective purpose" (v. 11b), which extends to all children of God (vv. 6-7).[105] This selectivity is what links the Esau/Jacob distinction with the distinction in v. 6b between Israel and the true Israel.[106] One should not get sidetracked by speculations about Paul's alleged interest in the nations deriving from Jacob and Esau[107] or in the establishment of a timeless principle.[108] The implications for sonship are rendered more apparent when Stegner's observation is taken into account that the term "son" is located in Gen 25:25. He shows that in midrashic discourse, often supporting texts are cited only partially because the writer or speaker assumes that the audience knows the rest by heart and can identify the catchword connections by themselves.[109] The implication is that the sonship in grace is a matter not of fleshly privilege but of divine selection.

---

95 Godet, 349.
96 See Zahn, 442.
97 Although not exploring the midrashic issue, Aageson, "Scripture," 269–70, points to this connection: "It is evident that the verb καλεῖν and the image of God's call to Isaac have been influential in shaping the distinction in 9:12."
98 See Käsemann, 123.
99 Dunn, 2:543.
100 For example, CD A 1:3-5 explains that God hid his face from Israel "when they were unfaithful in forsaking him," but that God "remembered the covenant with the forefathers" and "saved a remnant for Israel," identified by CD A 4:3-4 as the "sons of Zadok" who are "the chosen ones of Israel those called by name." That ἔργα is employed here as an "abbreviated form" of "deeds of the law" is shown by Fitzmyer, According to Paul, 20.
101 Dunn, 2:543, citing Philo Leg. 3.88.
102 Zahn, 445–49, speaks with regret of the distortion caused by inserting the issue of individual salvation

into the discussion of this verse, or by concluding that Paul was motivated by hostility toward the Jewish people. Wilckens, 2:195, follows Kuss, 3:709, in insisting that the antithesis between works and calling should not be understood as the hermeneutical criterion in the interpretation of justification.
103 Koch, Schrift, 25. It should be noted that aside from Rom 9:26, where it appears in a LXX citation, ἐρρέθη is used as a citation formula only in Matt 5:21, 27, 31, 33, 38, 43; the strangely restricted use of this formula has not been explained.
104 Fitzmyer, 563, observes that the LXX provides a contextually clearer reading of the ambiguous Hebrew expression, which could mean either "the greater will serve the smaller" or "the smaller will serve the greater."
105 See Piper, Justification, 38–40.
106 Mesner, "Rhetoric," 115.
107 Maier, Mensch, 28; Michel, 303.
108 Käsemann, 264.
109 Stegner, "Midrash," 40–41. He cites Eugene Mihaly,

■ 13 The second supporting text is introduced by the traditional formula used in 1:17 and many other passages, "just as it has been written."[110] The quotation is adapted from Mal 1:2-3, with Paul's inversion of word order resulting in a sharper antithesis through the creation of exact antithetic parallelism.[111] The comparison of the LXX wording is easily seen as follows:

> Mal 1:2-3 καὶ ἠγάπησα τὸν Ἰακώβ, τὸν δὲ Ἡσαῦ ἐμίσησα. ("I loved Jacob, but Esau I hated.")
> Rom 9:13 Τὸν Ἰακὼβ ἠγάπησα, τὸν δὲ Ἡσαῦ ἐμίσησα. ("Jacob I loved, but Esau I hated.")

The deletion of the initial "and" in the LXX text is consistent with Paul's citation practice in many other instances,[112] and the reversal of verb and object in the first clause is rhetorically effective. While the original text in Malachi referred to the nations of Israel and Edom, Paul's interest in this context is strictly related to the selective quality of God's purpose.[113] As in the preceding verse, the distinction between Jacob and Esau provides exemplary proof for Paul's distinction in v. 6b that "not all who are from Israel are Israel."[114] Given the historical issue under discussion in Rom 9–11, the figure of Esau as the father of the Edomites is used here "to designate the great majority of Israelites in Paul's day, those who have not responded in belief to the gospel."[115] Most of the scholarly discussion, however, has missed the argumentative thrust of the quotation and concentrated on the problematic wording of the Malachi text. The extraordinary arbitrariness of double predestination in Mal 1:2-3,[116] combined with the use of the allegedly "un-Christian" word "hate,"[117] has led commentators to tone down as far as possible what Paul is saying here.[118] Since Paul moves on in vv. 14-18 to stress the loving side of this antithesis, it appears likely that he is conscious of the problematic quality of the Malachi quotation.[119] In order for Paul's later qualification to have an effect, it would be better to allow the words from Malachi to stand as an extreme statement of Paul's basic point—to confirm the reliability of the divine promise in the face of human rejection of the gospel.[120] The quotation fulfills a vital rhetorical function of sharpening to an excruciating degree the focus on the selectivity of God's word. This basic point may well have been better understood by the original audience, insofar as the midrashic argumentative techniques would have been understood and accepted. As Stegner has noted, the contextual catchword "call" appears in the following verse of Malachi.[121] Although not cited by Paul, it would

---

"A Rabbinic Defense of the Election of Israel," *HUCA* 35 (1964) 104, on this point.

110 For the traditional Jewish background of the formula, "as it has been written," see on 1:17. The formula appears also in Rom 2:24; 3:4, 10; 4:17; 8:36; 9:33; 10:15; 1l:8, 26; 15:3, 21.

111 Koch, *Schrift*, 107; Stanley, *Scripture*, 106.

112 Stanley, *Scripture*, 105.

113 See Cranfield, 2:480, for a wider extension of the argument to "the peoples descended" from Esau and Jacob.

114 Mesner, "Rhetoric," 354–57.

115 Ibid., 357; see U. Hübner, "Esau," *ABD* 2 (1992) 574f., for a list of Greek and rabbinic references to the negative role of Esau in Jewish literature.

116 Dinkler, "Prädestination bei Paulus," 92, observes that this is the clearest example of double predestination in the letter. Piper, *Justification*, 34–54, develops an extensive case that Paul is arguing for the eternal predestination of individuals in this passage.

117 Kuss, 3:714, observes that the Hebrew term behind the Greek word for hate could be used in the sense of "find unacceptable" or "reject." Morris, 357,

makes the improbable suggestion that "hate" should be understood as "love less" or "reject," quoting Calvin. There are precedents for this reference to God's hatred in Qumran, as, for example, *CD* A 2:13, "But those whom he hated he caused to stray." See also *CD* A 8:18; 1QS 9:16, 21.

118 Cranfield, 2:479–81, and Dunn, 2:544–46, offer the most extensive qualifications of the implications of the Malachi quotation for the contemporary discussion. Fitzmyer, 563, refers to "hated" as "ancient Near Eastern hyperbole" for "loved less." Weiss, 410–11, provides an account of nineteenth-century efforts along this apologetic line, to which Colenso, 216, could be added.

119 Mesner, "Rhetoric," 357–58, also points out the opposite intention of Paul's argument. Malachi advocates a turning away from the pagan nations, while Paul is asserting divine selectivity for the sake of a "universal rule of God."

120 See Kühl, 323–24.

121 Stegner, "Midrash," 41.

probably have been understood as pointing to the basic contention that salvation depends on the divine call rather than on any personal qualifications of persons like Jacob and Esau.[122]

■ **14** The shift to diatribal style is signaled by the rhetorical question, $\tau i \ o \hat{v} \nu \ \dot{\epsilon} \rho o \hat{v} \mu \epsilon \nu$ ("What then shall we say"), which indicates a possible false conclusion, as in the expression $\tau i \ \dot{\epsilon} \rho o \hat{v} \mu \epsilon \nu$ ("What shall we say") in 3:5; 4:1; 6:1; 7:7; 8:31; and 9:30.[123] The form of the rhetorical question beginning with $\mu \dot{\eta}$ ("not") requires the hearers to provide a negative answer[124] to the query about whether God is unjust. The question does not presuppose a hostile inquirer, traditionally identified as an unbelieving Jew.[125] The style of the question is clearly Jewish, with the expression $\pi \alpha \rho \dot{\alpha} \ \tau \hat{\omega} \ \vartheta \epsilon \hat{\omega}$ ("before God/with God") being a Hebraism.[126] But as we have learned from Stowers, a diatribal exchange presupposes a friendly audience, raising questions that advance the pedagogical enterprise.[127] This question relates to the entire preceding argument in vv. 6-13,[128] but is particularly provoked by the harsh arbitrariness of the quotation from Malachi. In this sense the rhetorical interaction between v. 13 and v. 14 is extraordinarily effective.

The choice of the noun "injustice" rather than the adjective "unjust" avoids posing a question about God's nature.[129] The precise connotation of the wide-ranging term $\dot{\alpha} \delta \iota \kappa \acute{\iota} \alpha$ ("injustice") in this verse should be inferred contextually. It is not a matter of denying the truth of God[130] or questioning the covenant loyalty of God,[131] which may fit other passages in Romans. If one were to follow the rhetorical clues in this argument, the question is surely that of the basic fairness of God's dealings.[132] Why should God choose to love Jacob and hate Esau? Is "God's purpose of election" a "miscarriage of justice?"[133]

The emphatic answer $\mu \dot{\eta} \ \gamma \acute{\epsilon} \nu o \iota \tau o$ ("By no means!") indicates the depth of Paul's contention, reflected in the entire argument of the letter up to this point. If justice/righteousness is the theme of Romans (1:17) and if the essence of human rebellion against God is understood to be "injustice" (1:18, 29; 2:8; 3:5), then any admission of unjust behavior on the part of God is unacceptable. The issue is not merely one of pitting human standards against the divine,[134] but rather whether the divine purpose of election to salvation is righteous and just. As Paul goes on to show, divine justice is primarily a matter of mercy.

■ **15** The third supporting text is introduced by an unusual formula in which Yahweh is said to speak to Moses. Although there are many instances in which God

---

122 Lübking, *Paulus*, 66, stresses the defining role of "selection, purpose and calling" in this passage.

123 Cranfield, 2:481f.; Stowers, *Diatribe*, 121; Schmeller, *Diatribe*, 327. It should be noted, however, that a *TLG* search indicates that the exact wording, $\tau i \ o \hat{v} \nu \ \dot{\epsilon} \rho o \hat{v} \mu \epsilon \nu$, appears only here in the NT. It does not appear in any Greek writing before Paul's time; thereafter it occurs in the *Sch. Dem.* 2.79b7 and the later *Sch. Iso.* 10.1.5; Aelius Herodianus $\Pi \alpha \rho \omega \nu$. 3,2.866.43.

124 Godet, 351; Dunn, 2:551; BDF §427; BAGD (2000), 646.

125 Godet, 351–52: "This opponent is a Jew . . . [who] was accustomed to consider God's dealings with man as entirely dependent on human merit or demerit." For a contemporary restatement of this approach, see Piper, *Justification*, 70–73.

126 See Michel, 307, and Wilckens, 2:199, both citing Str-B, 3:79f., which discusses *m. 'Abot* from 2 Chr 19:7; Sir 35:15; *Jub.* 5.16 and *'Abot.* 4.22.

127 Stowers, *Diatribe*, 117. In contrast, Kim, *Romans 9–11*, 126, returns to the traditional view of vv. 14-18 as a courtroom defense against a false charge

made by Jewish "opponents" as advocated by Michel, 307, and Schmidt, 164.

128 Wilckens, 2:199; the connection of vv. 14-18 to the preceding paragraph is played down by Brandenburger, "Paulinische Schriftauslegung," 11, who construes the diatribal question as starting a new argument. See the critique in Mesner, "Rhetoric," 361–63.

129 Morris, 359: "Perhaps this way of putting it is due to motives of reverence: Paul asks, 'Is there injustice with God?' rather than 'Is God unjust?'"

130 Piper, *Justification*, 71–73.

131 Wilckens, 2:199; Wright, "Messiah," 211.

132 Zeller, 177, refers to the question of *iustitia distributiva*, fairness and impartiality in judgment. Mesner, "Rhetoric," 363, refers to the "perceived injustice of God's actions toward Jacob and Esau," with the latter being as much in view as the former.

133 Black, 130.

134 Schlier, 295.

is implicitly the speaker, only here and in 9:25 does Paul state the matter explicitly.[135] This thus forms a nexus with "the word of God" in 9:6. The word order indicates an emphasis on Moses the lawgiver, which helps to sustain Paul's point because "according to Jewish perspective Moses is competent in the highest degree concerning the question of the essence of 'righteousness.'"[136]

The supporting text is derived verbatim[137] from a portion of Exod 33:19 where Yahweh accedes to the request of divine manifestation by passing before Moses and uttering the words about the mercy and compassion of his saving glory. The terminology of mercy is the absolutely crucial "key-note"[138] for the subsequent argument in this third proof, appearing in 9:16, 23; 10:20; 11:30, 31, 32. The quotation from Exodus addresses the issue of fairness by showing that divine selectivity is not "the freedom of an unqualified will of God, but of the freedom of God's mercy."[139] The term "compassion" in the quotation appears here for the only time in the NT, but its associated term οἰκτιρμός ("compassion/mercy") recurs later in the crucial location of 12:1. The point in the quotation is that divine benefits are bestowed on whomever God calls to be God's children. It is a matter not of human earning or privilege but of divine decision. In the context of Paul's discussion, the benefits come to those counted among the true Israel of Rom 9:6.[140] While the entire scene in Exodus was full of motifs of potential significance for the theology of Romans,[141] the midrashic framing provided by the initial text of Rom 9:7 would have focused any extraneous echo on the catchword "call," which appears in a portion of the verse from Exod 33:19 that Paul does not cite.[142] By quoting only the final portion of the verse, however, Paul concentrates attention on the mercy of divine selectivity, disallowing any consideration of the role or qualifications of the human partner, in this instance, Moses.

■ **16** The inference from the Exodus citation is drawn with ἄρα οὖν ("so then"),[143] confirming why Paul cites only a portion of 33:19. He wishes to insist on the absolute freedom of divine mercy[144] as the basis not only for understanding predestination but also for understanding the first eight chapters of the letter. "It is because God is merciful that justification by faith is possible . . . indeed, if he treated them otherwise none would survive."[145] The theological principle is formulated in memorable, rhythmic style which my translation attempts to pick up by rendering the parallel participles with "him who wills . . . him who runs . . . God who shows mercy." The structure of antithetical parallelism indicates that no contrast was intended between willing and running;[146] both are juxtaposed with God's showing mercy. Clearly it is human willpower and effort that are set aside as irrelevant factors when compared with the merciful selection of God's children. The connotation of the term θέλειν ("to will") in this context is heavily influenced by its previous use in Rom 7:15, 16, 18, 19, 20, and 21 to depict the incapacity of legalistic willpower to achieve the desired good.[147] As Paul showed in that pericope, neither the will nor the accomplishment of the law prevents the legalist from achieving the opposite of what is intended, thereby coming into conflict with the mercy of God as revealed in Christ.

---

135 See Koch, *Schrift*, 31.
136 Schmidt, 164.
137 Only an insignificant spelling discrepancy separates the LXX from Paul's quotation in v. 15. The LXX has οἰκτειρμήσω/οἰκτειρῶ ("I will have compassion / am compassionate") whereas Romans has οἰκτιρήσω/οἰκτίρω. Mesner, "Rhetoric," 368, cites BDF §23 and BAGD 561f. on the spelling confusion between ει and ι.
138 Barrett, 185.
139 Cranfield, 2:483; it is therefore inappropriate to conclude as Siegert does in *Argumentation*, 128–29, that the quotation from Exod 33:19 is a tautologous exercise in the proposition that God's mercy is just because it is God's.
140 Mesner, "Rhetoric," 373–76.
141 See Piper, *Justification*, 63–68; Dunn, 2:552.
142 Stegner, "Midrash," 41.
143 Hübner, *Gottes Ich und Israel*, 39, argues that ἄρα οὖν is a strengthening of the simple term ἄρα ("so"), requiring a translation like "therefore it is undeniable," which recurs in v. 18.
144 Schmidt, 164.
145 Barrett, 186.
146 See Dunn, 1:353.
147 Gottlob Schrenk, "θέλω κτλ.," *TDNT* 3 (1965) 52.

With the legalistic connotation of "willing" in mind, the hearer of this sentence who knew Hebrew Scripture would naturally associate the metaphor of running with the effort of the devout Jew in Ps 119:32: "I ran the path of your commandments, when you enlarged my understanding."[148] In contrast to the affirmative use of the athletic metaphor of running in 1 Cor 9:24-26; Heb 12:1,[149] the repeated negation οὐδὲ τοῦ τρέχοντος ("nor of he who runs") calls attention to the incapacity of human effort to influence the mercy of God.[150] The contrast with Pharisaic Judaism is particularly stark, as Maier has pointed out by reference to *Ps. Sol.* 9.4-5:[151] "Our works are subject to our own choice and power; To do right or wrong in the works of our hands; And in your righteousness you visit the sons of men. He that does righteousness lays up life for himself with the Lord; And he that does wrong forfeits his life to destruction; For the judgments of the Lord are (given) in righteousness to (every) man and (his) house." Similarly Sir 15:15, 17 refer to the capacity of human willpower to achieve the good and thus assure the blessing of life: If you (so) desire, you can keep the commandment, And (it is) wisdom to do His good pleasure . . . Life and death (are) before man, That which he desires shall be given to him." The polemical antithesis that Paul intends to draw

in this verse does not focus on some alleged inability of Jewish loyalists to obey the law, on some alleged Jewish character flaw of works righteousness,[152] on an erroneous Jewish doctrine of human freedom,[153] or on a more generalized sense of the inefficacy of religious effort.[154] The antithesis relates to the logic implicit in the objection in 9:14, namely, that God is unfair in offering mercy to whomever he wills.[155] In this entire passage, divine mercy is sovereign:[156] "God calls and God is merciful; he is the one who in his mercy elects."[157]

■ **17** The introduction of the fourth supporting text in Paul's midrashic argument is formulaic and characteristically Jewish in viewing "scripture" (γραφή) as "saying" (λέγει) something directly to persons.[158] That this was intended to avoid a direct address from God to the pagan Pharaoh[159] seems unlikely in view of the frequency of such formulaic introductions and the rarity of introductions referring explicitly to God as the speaker.[160] The figure of Pharaoh is archetypal for Jewish literature, symbolizing cruel oppression and hardness of heart. The word itself is a Hebrew construct based on the Egyptian words for "great house" or royal palace, which came to be used for the name of a king around 1500 B.C.E.[161] While Egyptians would attach the name of a king to their form of this term, the absolute

148 Otto Bauernfeind, "τρέχω κτλ.," *TDNT* 8 (1972) 229, refers to the importance of this phrase for the later development of Judaism, indicating that it depicts "the readiness for zealous obedience . . . ." But he does not refer to this verse in explaining Rom 9:16 where the verb "occurs quote unexpectedly" (232). The effort by J. Duncan M. Derrett, "Running in Paul: The Midrashic Potential of Hab 2:2," *Bib* 66 (1985) 566, to explain the use of τρέχω in this verse on the basis of Hab 2:3 is strained because "running" in a missional sense is irrelevant for the context.

149 See Pfitzner, *Paul and the Agon Motif,* 135f.

150 Bauernfeind, "τρέχω κτλ." 232.

151 Maier, *Mensch,* 368–69.

152 Kühl, 327, Kuss, 3.722.

153 See Dunn, 2:553, for a critique of Maier, *Mensch,* 363–69, on this point.

154 See Käsemann, 267.

155 Jülicher, 295, claims that Paul's argument does not directly answer the question of "injustice with God," since it rests merely on an arbitrary proof text from Exodus. However, the inference from that text in

9:16 is fully consistent with the earlier argument of Romans. The parallel to this verse in 1QS 11:10-11 cited by Maier, *Mensch,* 369, stressing that perfect obedience comes from God's decision rather than from human decision, does not exactly correlate with Paul's stress here on divine mercy freely given to the undeserving.

156 See Paul W. Gooch, "Sovereignty and Freedom: Some Pauline Compatibilisms," *SJT* 40 (1987) 537.

157 Aageson, "Scripture," 271; see also Anthony T. Hanson, "The Oracle in Romans xi. 4," *NTS* 19 (1972–73) 301–2.

158 Koch, *Schrift,* 25, noting that the same formula is found in Rom 4:3; 10:11; 11:2; and Gal 4:30. Koch (26–27) discusses the references to "scripture" and "saying."

159 Michel, 309; Schlier, 296.

160 Koch, *Schrift,* 31; see also the rebuttal by Cranfield, 2:485.

161 James M. Weinstein, "Pharaoh," *HBD* (1985) 781.

use of "Pharaoh" as a kind of proper name in a passage like this makes it into a negative symbol that in this instance correlates with "all Israel" and Esau in the preceding argument.[162] Pharaoh serves as "an exemplar of the rejectors who serve God's plan . . . of salvation because his resistance enabled God to display his saving power and to spread abroad the knowledge of it."[163]

The supporting text is drawn from Exod 9:16, which was altered at several decisive points to sharpen up the meaning Paul intends to convey. The underlining below marks the changes:

> Exod 9:16 *Καὶ ἕνεκεν τούτου διετηρήθης, ἵνα ἐνδείξωμαι ἐν σοὶ τὴν ἰσχύν μου, καὶ ὅπως διαγγελῇ τὸ ὄνομά μου ἐν πάσῃ τῇ γῇ* ("And for this purpose you have been preserved, in order that I might demonstrate my strength in you, so that my name might also be proclaimed in all the earth").

> Rom 9:17 *Εἰς αὐτὸ τοῦτο ἐξήγειρά σε ὅπως ἐνδείξωμαι ἐν σοὶ τὴν δύναμίν μου καὶ ὅπως διαγγελῇ τὸ ὄνομά μου ἐν πάσῃ τῇ γῇ* ("For this very purpose I raised you up, so that I might demonstrate my power in you, so that my name might also be proclaimed in all the earth . . .").

In place of the LXX version of the preliminary clause, "and for this purpose you have been preserved," Paul creates an active expression of divine intentionality: *εἰς αὐτὸ τοῦτο ἐξήγειρά σε* ("for this very purpose I raised you up"). The altered clause is somewhat closer to the MT and provides a clearer expression of "the idea of purpose"[164] by focusing attention on the single (*αὐτό,* "very") goal of Yahweh.[165] Even more significant is the alteration of the passive verb "you have been preserved" to the active expression "I raised you up," which strengthens the impression of the sovereign quality of "God's elective purpose."[166] The change from *ἵνα* ("in order that") to *ὅπως* ("so that") enhances the poetic parallelism between the two final clauses by reduplicating the opening conjunction.[167] The immediate aim of Yahweh to demonstrate power in the first clause is thereby brought into consistency with the more distant aim of proclaiming the divine name in the second clause.[168] This brings the Pharaoh incident into exact conformity with God's present behavior toward "vessels" of wrath and mercy as described in the next pericope (9:22).[169] It also strengthens the element of divine intentionality through repetition.[170] The most significant of the alterations, from the rhetorical point of view, is the replacement of *ἰσχύς* ("strength") by its synonym *δύναμις* ("power"), because this relates the quotation directly to the thesis of the letter concerning the gospel as the *δύναμις θεοῦ,* "power of God").[171] The use of this word in 1:4 and 1:20 has likewise been shown to play a crucial role in developing Paul's thesis. Given the reference in Exod 9:16 to proclaiming (*διαγγέλειν*) the message of God's triumph, this alteration sustains the larger missional purpose of the letter. The function of the change is that of a rhetorical echo of an absolutely crucial term, so it is unnecessary to press the definition of *δύναμις* in this quotation into an overly specific mold of "creator in

---

162 See Munck, *Christ,* 50, 59; Hübner, *Gottes Ich und Israel,* 45; and Mesner, "Rhetoric," 384.

163 Hamerton-Kelly, *Cross,* 243 (typescript).

164 Cranfield, 2:485–86.

165 Morris, 360, "*εἰς αὐτὸ τοῦτο* . . . means 'just this (and nothing else),'" citing BDF §290.

166 Sanday and Headlam, 256; Lagrange, 234; Luz, *Geschichtsverständnis,* 77; Michel, 309; Cranfield, 2:486; Koch, *Schrift,* 150–51. Zahn, 451, expresses the significance of the first two alterations by showing that "God made this Pharaoh the king of Egypt for no other purpose than . . . to allow his power to be further seen and felt." Stanley, *Scripture,* 107–8, finds all explanations of this change "dubious" because the Pauline adaptation brings the text closer to the Hebrew original, but the question of

why Paul may have preferred such a translation still needs to be answered.

167 In contrast, Stanley, *Scripture,* 108, rejects any explanation of these changes, which "remain difficult to comprehend."

168 See Wilckens, 2:200.

169 Kühl, 326.

170 Michel, 309; Koch, *Schrift,* 151.

171 Cranfield, 2:487, makes this observation without drawing an appropriate rhetorical conclusion, having argued (486) that the substitution was aimed at avoiding *ἰσχύς,* which "is relatively rare in Greek usage generally." This seems implausible because a *TLG* search turned up more than 150 instances of *ἰσχύς* in Josephus alone, and, furthermore, Paul does not hesitate to use rare words in other quota-

judgment"[172] or "saving power."[173] The means by which Israel was saved in the exodus remain very different from the means revealed in the cross and resurrection of Christ. The similarity for which Paul contends in this pericope is that of the divinely selective purpose of demonstrating mercy to the very ones seeking to oppose it.

Much of the rest of the original wording of Exod 9:16 is also closely integrated into the logical network of Pauline rhetoric in this letter. The verb ἐνδείκνυσθαι ("demonstrate") is the verbal form of ἔνδειξις ("demonstration") used in 3:25 to refer to the manifestation of divine righteousness in the Christ event. Thus the pattern of divine action is seen to be consistent from the Mosaic period to Christ: God acts in behalf of the undeserving to demonstrate redemptive power. The reference to proclaiming God's name (ὄνομα) is a classic theme in biblical theology,[174] related in 1:5; 10:13; and 15:9 to the gospel mission. When the divine name is proclaimed "in all the earth," the hope expressed by the prophets and the psalms of global recognition of Yahweh as the source of salvation would be fulfilled (Ezek 20:9, 14, 22; Ps 79:9-10). The phrase ἐν πάσῃ τῇ γῇ ("in all the earth") resonates with the global sweep of the gospel seen throughout Romans.[175] An additional link with the midrashic argument beginning in 9:4 is that the contextual catchword "sons" is found in the same pericope in Exodus 9 as that cited by Paul.[176]

■ **18** Paul's conclusion is drawn, as in v. 16, with the doubly emphatic ἄρα οὖν ("so then"), which has the sense of "so it is undeniable."[177] The reduplication of θέλει ("he wills") in the carefully crafted parallel sentence rivets attention onto the central issue of divine selectivity. The objection to the gospel in terms of its alleged allowance of divine "injustice" implies a curtailing of this divine freedom. Thus, the reiteration of God's active "will" not only stands in contrast to the impotence of human willing (v. 16) but also carries forward the logic of "God's selective purpose" (v. 11). When this argumentative thrust is taken into account, it becomes clear that the truly scandalous form of selectivity was that God "has mercy on whom he wills," namely, on those who did not deserve it. This matter of honor and shame was the nub of the issue, both in Paul's former persecution of the church and in current Jewish repudiations of the gospel. It is also the point repeatedly discussed in this pericope—that none of the patriarchs earned the blessing in any way.

Well-meaning theologians have expended far more ink in dealing with the hardening side of this antithesis,[178] even though that was widely accepted throughout biblical literature.[179] That Yahweh would harden Pharaoh's heart was repeatedly stated in the exodus narrative (Exod 4:21; 7:3; 9:12; 10:1, 20, 27; 11:10; 14:8), along with the counterbalancing claim that he hardened his own heart (Exod 7:13, 14, 22; 8:15, 19, 32; 9:7, 34, 35).[180] Exodus shows that Pharaoh was caught "in a hardening nexus from which he could not escape nor exercise any *totally independent* self-determining actions, since Yahweh was the ultimate cause of the hardening."[181] There was no scandal in reiterating this theme for Paul's audience, and its avoidance would hardly have

tions throughout Romans. Hübner, *Gottes Ich und Israel*, 40, provides a more adequate explanation by pointing to the decisive role of δύναμις in 1:16-17.

172 Käsemann, 268.

173 Cranfield, 2:487.

174 Hans Bietenhard, "ὄνομα κτλ.," *TDNT* 5 (1967) 255–61.

175 See Rom 1:5, 16, 18; 2:1, 9, 10; 3:4, 9, 12, 19, 20, 22, 23; 5:12, 18; 8:22, 28; 9:5; 10:12, 13, 18; 11:32, 36; 12:18; 14:11; 15:11, where the universal scope of divine sovereignty advanced by the gospel is lifted up.

176 Stegner, "Midrash," 41, argues that the reference to "sons" (of Israel) found in Exod 9:26 is the catchword linking the citation of Exod 9:16 to Paul's midrashic discourse.

177 Hübner, *Gottes Ich und Israel*, 39.

178 For orientation, see G. K. Beale, "An Exegetical and Theological Consideration of the Hardening of Pharaoh's Heart in Exodus 4–14 and Romans 9," *TrinJ* 5 (1984) 129–54. See the extensive apologies for Paul's language in Meyer, 2:140–43; Zahn, 452–55; Lagrange, 235–36; Leenhardt, 144–45; Morris, 361–62; Cranfield, 2:488–89; Dunn, 2:554–55.

179 See F. Hesse, *Das Verstockungsproblem im Alten Testament* (BZAW 74; Berlin: Töpelmann, 1955); Fitzmyer, 567–68.

180 See the discussion in Morris, 361, and the detailed exegesis of the exodus passages in Beale, "Hardening," 133–49.

181 Beale, "Hardening," 149, italics in original.

done justice to the citation from Exod 9:16. Dodd offers a critique of this traditional scriptural view, suggesting on the basis of liberal theology that Paul takes a "false step" in v. 18b that falls short of "a fully ethical conception of God."[182] However, this mistakes the thrust of Paul's argument; it is not that Paul drives "an unethical determinism to its logical extreme, in order to force his opponent to confess the absolute and arbitrary sovereignty of God.[183] It would be more appropriate to conclude that Paul applies the widely shared teaching about Pharaoh's hardening in order to make the much more controversial case that God's mercy is sovereign. Paul was convinced that the refusal of this sovereign grace revealed in the gospel placed his Jewish compatriots in "the position of Pharaoh," incredibly reversing their status before God.[184] Yet human resistance against impartial grace is not the last word, and in the end, according to the Pauline midrash, the "word of God" will not only prevail but will be "proclaimed in all the earth."

---

182 Dodd, 157–58.
183 Ibid., 158.

184 See Mesner, "Rhetoric," 388.

9

The Third Pericope

Diatribe and the Second Half of a Midrash Refuting Objections

19/ You will say to me then, "Why then[a] does he still find fault? For who has resisted her design?" 20/ O human, on the contrary,[b] who are you to talk back to God? What is molded does not say to the molder, "Why have you made[c] me thus?" 21/ Or has the potter no power over the clay to make from the same lump one vessel for honor and the other for dishonor? 22/ Now if God, willing to demonstrate his wrath and make known her power, endures[d] with great patience[e] vessels of wrath prepared for destruction, 23/ even[f] in order that he might make known the riches of his glory[g] upon vessels of mercy, which she prepared beforehand for glory[h]—24/ us whom she also called, not only from among Jews but also from among Gentiles,[i] 25/ as he also says in[j] Hosea,

> "I shall call 'my people' those who are not my people,
> > and her who was not beloved
> > [I will call] 'beloved.'

26/ And there will be in the place where[k] it was said[l] to them,[m] 'you[n] are not my people,'
> there they will be called 'sons of the living God.'"

27/ But Isaiah cries out concerning Israel,
> "Though the number of the sons of Israel be as the sand of the sea,
> [it is] the remnant[o] [that] will be saved,"

28/ "for the Lord will execute his word with rigor and dispatch[p] upon the earth."

29/ And just as Isaiah has foretold,
> "If the Lord of hosts had not left us seed,
> we would have become like Sodom and been made like Gomorrah."

a The omission of οὖν ("then") by ℵ A K L P Ψ 6 33 69 88 104 323 326 330 365 424 614 945 1175 1241 1243 1319 1505 1506 1573 1735 1739 1836 1874 1881 2464 2495 *Maj* vg sy is roughly counterbalanced in the weight of the texts including it, P46 B D F G it vgmss. The older Nestle25 text omitted it and Nestle-Aland26/27 brackets it, indicating "the preference of the editors" but reflecting "a great deal of difficulty in determining the text" (Nestle-Aland27 49*-50*). Cranfield, 2:489, argues for omission on grounds that the frequent repetition of τί οὖν

("what then?") in Romans would have provoked a copyist's error. On the other hand, the deletion of οὖν would seem to be likely on stylistic grounds because of its occurrence in the preceding question. It is a borderline judgment, but the omission is more easily explainable than the addition, so the inclusion of οὖν seems more likely.

b The deletion of μενοῦνγε ("on the contrary") by P46 D* F G 629 latt and the reversal of sequence to μενοῦνγε ὦ ἄνθρωπε ("on the contrary, O human") in ℵ2 D2 K L P Ψ 6 33 88 104 323 326 330 365 424 614 945 1175 1241 1243 1319 1505 1573 1735 1836 1874 2464 2495 *Maj* syh appear to be efforts to simplify the surprising use of μενοῦνγε after the vocative, according to Cranfield, 2:490. The reading ὦ ἄνθρωπε μενοῦνγε in ℵ* A (B) 69 81 630 1506 1739 1881 *pc* Or1739mg is to be preferred as the more difficult option.

c The use of ἔπλασας ("mold") in place of ἐποίησας ("make") in D syp follows the wording of the LXX of Isaiah.

d The verb ἤνεγκεν ("he endured") is omitted by F G it (syp) Ambst in place of their addition of εἰς described in the next note.

e The addition of εἰς ("toward") by F G it (syp) Ambst was required syntactically because of the deletion of the verb "he endured" by the same texts earlier in the sentence; it is clearly secondary.

f The omission of καί ("and") by B 6 69 326 424c 436 1739mg 1912 *pc* ar b vg sa bopt arm Orgr, lat(+1739mg) Severian Hier appears to be an effort to eliminate one of the awkward components in the incomplete sentence of Rom 9:22-24. The inclusion of "and" is strongly supported by P46vid ℵ A D F G K L P Ψ 33 81 88 104 181 256 263 323 330 365 424*b 451 459 614 629 945 1175 1241 1243 1319 1505 1506 1573 1735 1739 1836 1852 1874 1877 1881 1962 2127 2200 2344 2464 2492 2495 *Lect* d f g mon o vgms syp, h bopt eth geo slav Chr Ambst Pel Aug Julian-Eclanum.

g The replacement of δόξης ("glory") by χρηστότητος ("kindness") by P (syp) is inexplicable on the basis of normal rules of textual criticism; although too weakly attested to be considered original, it is hard to explain as an accidental or arbitrary change by later copyists.

h For a discussion of the problem of punctuating vv. 23 and 24, see Cranfield, 2:497–98.

i On the question of the punctuation at the end of v. 24 and the beginning of v. 25, see Cranfield, 2:498–99.

j The deletion of ἐν ("in, by") by P46vid B appears to be a stylistic improvement, since the dative case does not require a preposition. It is not discussed by the commentators.

k   In place of οὗ ("of which") ℵ* Ir^lat vid have ᾧ ("in which") and, according to Cranfield, 2:499, so does P⁴⁶, but not so in Nestle-Aland²⁷ and Aland et al., *Ergänzungsliste,* 79. While each form is acceptable Greek, the replacement of οὗ may be a stylistic improvement or it may have been motivated by a desire to avoid confusion with οὐ ("not") earlier in the sentence. Despite the early witnesses, it is probably secondary.

l   While there is strong support in ℵ A (B omits αὐτοῖς) D K L P (Ψ) 6 33 69 88 104 323 326 330 365 424 614 945 1175 1241 1243 1319 1505 1506 1573 1735 1739 1836 1874 1881 2344 2464 2495 *Maj* vg sy^h cop (Ir^lat vid omits αὐτοῖς) for ἐρρέθη αὐτοῖς ("it was said to them"), P⁴⁶ F G ar b d* sy^p have a strikingly divergent reading, ἐὰν (ἄν) κληθήσονται ("if they are called"), which is probably an assimilation to the wording later in v. 26.

m   The deletion of αὐτοῖς ("to them") by B Ir^lat vid, with Cranfield, 2:499, adding f sy^p Aug, is probably a stylistic improvement or a transcription error. Cranfield suggests that it may be the more difficult reading, since the LXX includes αὐτοῖς, hence explaining why it might have been added, but it is hard to understand why the deletion would have seemed obtrusive.

n   The deletion of ὑμεῖς ("you") by P⁴⁶ it sy^p Ir^lat vid is hard to explain except as originating in a scribal error.

o   The synonym for ὑπόλειμμα ("remnant"),

κατάλειμμα is provided by P⁴⁶ ℵ¹ D F G K L P Ψ 5 6 33 61 69 88 104 181 218 256 263 323 326 330 365 424 436 451 459 614 621 623 629 630 720 917 945 1175 1241 1243 1319 1398 1505 1563 1573 1678 1718 1735 1739* 1751 1836 1838 1845 1852 1874 1875 1877 1881 1912 1942 1962 2127 2138 2197 2200 2344 2464 2492 2495 2516 2523 2544 *Maj*, but the application of the rule of the "more difficult reading" leads most to accept ὑπόλειμμα in ℵ* A B 81 1739^c Eus as original. The fact that the LXX has κατάλειμμα could explain the change.

p   The words ἐν δικαιοσύνῃ ὅτι λόγον συντετμημένον ("in righteousness, because the word is shortened") were probably added by ℵ² D F G K L P Ψ 33 5 61 69 88 104 181 256 263 323 326 330 365 424* 441 451 459 467 614 621 623 629 630 720 915 917 945 1175 1241 1243 1319 1398 1505 1563^c 1573 1678 1735 1751 1836 1838 1845 1874 1875 1877 1908^c 1912 1942 1959 1962 2127 2138 2197 2200 2344 2464 2492 2495 2516 2544 2718 *Maj Lect* ar b d f g mon² o vg sy^h goth arm geo slav Or^lat Chr (Eus^{1/3}) Ambst Hier^{2/4} Pel to make the text conform to the LXX version of Isa 10:23. See Metzger, *Textual Commentary,* 462. Only the first two words were added by 81 436 1852 *pc* Hier^{1/4}, which are also clearly secondary. The better-attested and more difficult text does not have these words: P⁴⁶ ℵ* A B 6 218 424^c 1319 1506 1563* 1718 1739 1881 1908* 2110 2127 *pc* mon* sy^p sa bo eth Eus^{2/3} Cyr (Thret^lem) Ps-Cyp Ambr Gaudentius Hier^{1/4} Aug.

Analysis

The fusion of a formal diatribe into the framework of an extended midrashic exegesis resumes with v. 19. As in 9:1-5 the first person singular μοι ("to me") again refers to Paul, and the switch from the more collective plural of v. 14 focuses attention on Paul as the one responsible for the answer to the rhetorical question of 9:19. The imaginary interlocutor responds to the hard statement of divine sovereignty that concluded the preceding pericope with two closely related objections, which are answered in v. 20a.[1] In the view of current analysis, the identity of this interlocutor is vague as compared with the identity of the Jewish bigot in chap. 2,[2] so that in Tobin's analysis, the diatribe "serves only to raise the questions Paul wants to deal with."[3] The image of the wily scoffer may have been adapted from Jewish wisdom literature,[4] and it seems likely that Paul employs this stereotype in order to differentiate the interlocutor from the audience[5] while making use of the traditional arguments from the wisdom literature about the inscrutable judgments of God. The technique of responding to ques-

---

1   Stowers presents this passage both in the context of the "Imaginary Interlocutor" (*Diatribe,* 113–14) and in the discussion of "Objections and False Conclusions" (121).

2   See Stowers, *Diatribe,* 113–14; idem, *Rereading,* 300; Heil, 105; the question is not discussed by Elliott in *Liberating Paul* or *Rhetoric of Romans.*

3   Tobin, *Paul's Rhetoric,* 332.

4   In Prov 30:1-4 the five rhetorical questions posed by a character with the pseudonym "Agur" comprise sophisticated scoffing with some similarity to the character Paul develops. See W. T. Davison, "Agur," *DBH* 1 (1901) 51; R. B. Y. Scott, *The Way of Wisdom in the Old Testament* (New York: Macmillan, 1971)

tions with rhetorical counterquestions was called *anteisa-goge*, of which vv. 20a-21 are an excellent example.[6]

The argument and quotations from vv. 20-29 answer the objections in v. 19,[7] while elaborating the distinction between all Israel and the true Israel that was stated in v. 6b.[8] The refutation of the objections is substantiated by four scriptural proofs, several of which are ingeniously combined out of fragments of biblical material to make a coherent argument. The fifth supporting text concerning the potter having power over the clay is cited in v. 20b from Isa 29:16, combined with several other texts and interpreted in the following verse. There is a rhetorical inversion in the topic of "vessels for honor and for dishonor" in v. 21, taken up in reverse sequence in vv. 22-23.[9] In vv. 22-24 there is a potent *anantapodoton* (intentionally incomplete syntax), in which the elaborate "if" clause is not followed by the "then" clause at the end of v. 23.[10] The "then" clause must be supplied from vv. 20-21 with one of the rhetorical questions concerning the right of the creature to challenge the creator. Despite the syntactical confusion, v. 23 stands in antithetical parallelism with v. 22, marked by the reduplication of γνωρίζω ("make known") and σκεῦος ("vessel"). The parallelism is followed in v. 24 by a more straightforward statement about the election of Jews and Gentiles. The following verses invert the sequence of "Jew . . . Gentile" in v. 24, taking up the Gentiles in v. 25 and Israel in v. 27.[11]

The sixth, seventh, and eighth supporting texts in vv. 25-28 show that God's promise concerning the election of Gentiles and Jews as God's children has been confirmed. The reference to Jews and Gentiles in v. 24 is developed into a chiasm by means of texts relating to Gentiles in vv. 25-26 and to Jews in vv. 27-29,[12] although both categories are developed in an inclusive manner. The final citation in v. 29 provides an inclusio back to the primary proof text from Gen 21:12 concerning the "seed," thus completing in combination with the supplementary text from Gen 18:10 an effective series of ten texts proving the propriety of divine election and answering the question of the reliability of God's word in v. 6 and the objections in vv. 14 and 19.

Rhetorical Disposition

IV.	The *probatio*
9:1–11:36	The third proof: The triumph of divine righteousness in the gospel's mission to Israel and the Gentiles
9:19-29	3. Diatribe and the second half of a midrash refuting objections
9:19	a. The objection to Paul's doctrine of God's selective purpose
9:19a	1) The introduction of the imaginary interlocutor
9:19b	2) The first objection, about whether God's judgment is fair
9:19c	3) The second objection, about whether humans can be held accountable
9:20-29	b. The answer to the objections
9:20a-21	1) The *anteisagoge* showing that the objections are untenable
	a) The first counterquestion, condemning humans talking back to God

---

165–69; Donald K. Berry, "Agur," *ABD* 1 (1992) 10; Michael V. Fox, "Words for Folly," *ZAH* 10 (1997) 6–8. James Crenshaw, *Old Testament Wisdom: An Introduction* (Louisville: Westminster John Knox, 1998) 68, shows that the wisdom literature identifies eight types of fools, including the "*sakal*—the one who persists in folly," which would fit the Agur character.

5   Stowers, *Diatribe*, 114, perceives a polemical element in this interlocutor: "It is a form of censure for the addressees of the letter who might react to the problems Paul is rehearsing with impious attitudes." Dunn, 2:555, suggests that Paul views the interlocutor "as an expression of Jewish theological sensitivity over the harsher-sounding corollaries to their own doctrine of election." In a similar way, Fitzmyer, 568, summarizes the viewpoint of the

interlocutor: "why blame me, if I, a Jew, do not accept God's offer in Christ." None of these suggestions is plausible rhetorically because throughout this pericope Paul keeps the audience on his side in opposition to the wily scoffer. As Haacker, 195, observes, the interlocutor identifies himself with Pharaoh, who seemed to suffer an arbitrary fate in 9:17-18. White, *Apostle*, 80, is correct in arguing that 9:19-24 "is not polemical."

6   Bullinger, *Figures*, 964.
7   See Siegert, *Argumentation*, 132.
8   See Mesner, "Rhetoric," 389.
9   See Harvey, *Listening*, 200.
10 Bullinger, *Figures*, 54.
11 See Harvey, *Listening*, 200–201.
12 Aletti, "Argumentation," 48. Winkel's proposal in "Argumentationsnanalyse," 71, that a new section

9:20b   b) The second counterquestion, showing the inappropriateness of clay questioning the potter, using the fifth combination of supporting texts from Isa 29:16

9:21   c) The third counterquestion, interpreting the citation by asserting the right of the potter—
           (1) To use clay to make fine ware
           (2) To use clay to make common ware

9:22-23   2) The *anantapodoton* about the divine demonstration of wrath and mercy

9:22a   a) God has a right to demonstrate wrath and power

9:22b   b) God has been patient with "vessels of wrath"

9:23a   c) God desires to reveal "riches" to "vessels of mercy"

9:23b   d) Vessels of mercy are elected beforehand "for glory"
         e) [The apodosis supplied from 9:20-21: "creatures cannot dispute with their Creator"]

9:24   3) The argument about the calling of believers as "vessels of mercy"

9:24a   a) Believers are among the "vessels of mercy" that are "called" ($\dot{\epsilon}\kappa\dot{\alpha}\lambda\epsilon\sigma\epsilon\nu$; see also 9:7)

9:24b   b) The "identity of the vessels of mercy"
           (1) "Not only from the Jews"
           (2) "But also from the Gentiles"

9:25-26   4) The sixth combination of supporting texts, showing that God elects those who were not originally God's beloved

9:25a   a) The introduction of the citation

9:25b   b) The citation from Hos 2:25
           (1) First catchword: $\kappa\alpha\lambda\dot{\epsilon}\sigma\omega$ ("I will call"; cf. 9:7)
           (2) Second catchword: $\dot{\eta}\gamma\alpha\pi\eta\mu\dot{\epsilon}\nu\eta\nu$ ("beloved"; cf. 9:13)

9:26   c) The citation from Hos 2:1
           (1) First catchword: $\kappa\lambda\eta\vartheta\dot{\eta}\sigma\nu\tau\alpha\iota$ ("they shall be called"; cf. 9:7)
           (2) Second catchword: $\nu\iota o\dot{\iota}$ ("sons"; cf. 9:9)

9:27-28   5) The seventh abbreviation of a supporting text, showing that only a remnant will be saved from judgment

9:27a   a) The introduction of the citation

9:27b-28   b) The citation from Isa 10:22-23 + Hos 2:1; Catchword: $\nu\iota\hat{\omega}\nu$ ("sons"; cf. 9:9)

9:29   6) The eighth supporting text, showing that the seed will be preserved by God

9:29a   a) The introduction of the citation

9:29b   b) The citation from Isa 1:9; Catchword: $\sigma\pi\dot{\epsilon}\rho\mu\alpha$ ("seed"; cf. 9:7)

Exegesis

■ **19** The pericope opens with Paul's address to an imaginary interlocutor who raises the logical questions arising from the first half of the pericope. Since the diatribe presupposes a friendly exchange between Paul and his audience,[13] it is not necessary to imagine "the Jewish opponent"[14] as responsible for raising these questions. This person is different from the interlocutor in chap. 2 and fits perfectly into the stereotype in the wisdom literature of the wily scoffer. In a shrewd manner, the interlocutor raises the obviously logical objections to Paul's depiction of God's selective purpose. The sharply formulated conclusion of the preceding verse, in fact, was intended to provoke these questions and thus to move Paul's argument forward. The use of $\dot{\epsilon}\rho\epsilon\hat{\iota}\varsigma$ ("you [sg.] will say") to express objections in a diatribe is not as rare as supposed,[15] and it could be that the extent of skeptical arrogance implied by the questions[16] made it unpalatable to state them in the inclusive first person plural style of 9:14.[17] Paul places these skeptical—and from the perspective of Jewish orthodoxy unacceptable—questions in the words of a single imaginary interlocutor addressing Paul ($\mu o\iota$ = "to me"), thus intensifying the

---

begins with v. 27 would break up the midrashic argument and destroy the chiastic development of v. 24 in vv. 25-29.

13   Stowers, *Diatribe*, 180–84.

14   Michel, 311; Schlier, 298; Ellison, *Mystery of Israel*, 51; Dunn, 2:555; Fitzmyer, 568.

15   Stowers, *Diatribe*, 134, found only one example, but it is not formally similar to Paul's formulation here. A *TLG* search discovered 1,545 examples, including Euripides *Hec.* 1272: "Or, what will you say of me ($\hat{\eta}$ $\tau\dot{\iota}$, $\tau\hat{\eta}\varsigma$ $\dot{\epsilon}\mu\hat{\eta}\varsigma$ $\dot{\epsilon}\rho\epsilon\hat{\iota}\varsigma$)?" Sophocles *Oed. col.* 1036 captures the sense of Rom 9:19 particularly well, "You,

being here, shall say to me nothing blameworthy ($\dot{o}\upsilon\delta\dot{\epsilon}\nu$ $\sigma\dot{\upsilon}$ $\mu\epsilon\mu\pi\tau\dot{o}\nu$ $\dot{\epsilon}\nu\vartheta\dot{\alpha}\delta'$ $\dot{\omega}\nu$ $\dot{\epsilon}\rho\epsilon\hat{\iota}\varsigma$ $\dot{\epsilon}\mu o\dot{\iota}$)." Epictetus *Diss.* 2.25 has "What will you say ($\tau\dot{\iota}$ $\dot{\epsilon}\rho\epsilon\hat{\iota}\varsigma$)?" and there are many other examples. The rhetorical $\dot{\epsilon}\rho\epsilon\hat{\iota}\varsigma$ occurs elsewhere in the NT in Matt 7:4; Acts 23:5; Rom 11:9.

16   Stowers, *Diatribe*, 114: "He is pretentious and arrogant like the types in 2:1-5 and 17-24 but this time he even directly questions God." See also Piper, *Justification*, 165–66.

17   See the discussion in Zahn, 453; Sanday and Headlam, 258. Schmeller, *Diatribe*, 328, considers the

element of dialogue (= *sermocinatio*).[18] The exchange is fictive, yet strikingly concrete[19] in the context of Paul's agonizing over the disbelief of his fellow Jews. The avoidance of the first person plural or the second person plural allows the audience to participate in the exchange without feeling accused of having placed themselves in the position of Pharaoh's advocates,[20] because both questions spring directly from the Exodus quotation and its elaboration in 9:17-18 as indicated by the conjunction οὖν ("then"). The emphatic word order in the phrase ἐρεῖς μοι οὖν ("to me you will say then")[21] also indicates a measure of overstatement that allows the audience to participate in a nonthreatening fashion. They would enjoy the repartee between the wily interlocutor and the Apostle to the Gentiles.

The first question, τί οὖν ἔτι μέμφεται; ("Why then does he still find fault?"), bears directly on the divine selectivity that manifested itself in the treatment of Pharaoh. If God "hardens whom she wills," how was it fair for Pharaoh to be condemned? The question of "injustice" on the part of God (9:14) continues to hover in the background of this question.[22] The word μέμφομαι is used here for the only time in the Pauline letters in its typical meaning of "find fault with, blame,"[23] presupposing a failure measured by some standard of justice. The word appears in similar rhetorical questions in Diogenes Laertius *Vitae philos.* 2.77, τί οὖν ἐμέμφου

("Why then did you blame?") and in Aelius Aristides Ἀθην. 402.17, τί μέμφονται ("Why are they blamed?").[24] The adverb "still" refers to the temporal continuity between the initial hardening of Pharaoh and the subsequent condemnation.[25]

The second question is explanatory of the first (γάρ, "for"), augmenting the supposition that no hardened person can be held accountable if he or she is unable to resist such selectivity on the part of God. The expression βούλημα αὐτοῦ ("his purpose, intention") echoes the theme of God's will in 9:18.[26] Rather than rendering this as "his will,"[27] the abstraction implies "purpose," "intention,"[28] or, more aptly, "plan" or "design."[29] The question is posed with the gnomic perfect of ἀνθίστημι ("resist"),[30] which carries the sense of "who has ever resisted" God's will. The form implies a general rule, which some translators try to capture by the present tense[31] or by augmenting the expression to "can resist."[32] The thought appears very close to Wis 12:12, which uses the same verb: ἢ τίς ἀντιστήσεται τῷ κρίματί σου ("or who will resist your judgment?").[33] Similarly, Job 9:19 asks, τίς οὖν κρίματι αὐτοῦ ἀντιστήσεται ("Who therefore will resist your judgment?"). The assumption that Paul shares with the wisdom tradition is that no one can ultimately resist the judgment of God, so the wily scoffer asks, in effect, if predestination is irresistible, then no one can fairly be held accountable for playing

---

possibility that the second person style alludes to specific voices in the Roman congregation, but he denies the possibility of precise identification.

18 Siegert, *Argumentation*, 133.

19 See Brandenburger, "Paulinische Schriftauslegung," 11.

20 See Piper, *Justification*, 166.

21 Noted by Mesner, "Rhetoric," 390, citing BDF §475.2.

22 Schlier, 298.

23 BAGD 502; it is used elsewhere in the NT only in Heb 8:8.

24 Other examples in Strabo *Geogr.* 12.3.27.2, "Why would anyone find fault (τί ἄν τις μέμφοιτο)?" and Lucian of Samosata *Sacr.* 7.7, "So that how would anyone still find fault (ὥστε πῶς ἂν ἔτι μέμφοιτό τις)?" See also BAGD (2000) 629.

25 Sanday and Headlam, 258.

26 Schlier, 298.

27 Dodd, 158; Barrett, 187; Dunn, 2:556; Hans-Joachim Ritz, "βουλή κτλ.," *EDNT* 1 (1990) 225: "forcible will of God."

28 Gottlob Schrenk, "βούλομαι κτλ.," *TDNT* 1 (1964) 637: "the purposeful intention of God . . . "

29 The use of βουλήματι αὐτοῦ to refer to the design or plan of God is found neither in the NT nor in the LXX, but see Philo *Mos.* 1.287–88: "Besides, he had realized that the purpose of the king who had hired him was not in harmony with the plan of God (οὐ συνάδιε τῷ τοῦ θεοῦ βουλήματι)." In 1QM 14:14 we read, "For great [is] your glorious plan."

30 Wilckens, 2:201.

31 Sanday and Headlam, 259; Lagrange, 236; Cranfield, 2:490.

32 Michel, 304; Barrett, 187; Dodd, 158; Byrne, *Reckoning*, 187.

33 Cranfield, 2:490, makes an overly sharp distinction between Wisdom's reference to the impossibility of resisting divine judgment and Paul's contention "that no man does, as a matter of fact, resist."

the role of Pharaoh. By formulating the second question in this way, Paul associates the imaginary critic of his doctrine of undeserved mercy, grounded on the selective will of God, with Esau, Pharaoh, and the scoffer. This sets up the rhetorical framework for the strongly stated counterquestions in the next verses.

■ **20** The first of three counterquestions[34] is introduced with deeply emotive language of direct address, ὦ ἄνθρωπε ("O human") which dominates the rest of the sentence.[35] There is an unmistakable tone of grief and warning in these opening words, which are far from the polite connotation of "my dear sir."[36] Many commentators have observed the rhetorical contrast between the first and last nouns in this sentence: "human . . . God,"[37] which strengthens the tone of reproach. It elegantly matches the contrast in the subsequent citation between "what is molded" and "the molder." The use of the intensified particle μενοῦνγε meaning "on the contrary"[38] conveys the same tone and prepares for the sharp correction in the following denunciation, which expresses the Jewish as well as the Greco-Roman premise about the need to avoid arrogance before God. The question σὺ τίς εἶ ὁ ἀνταποκρινόμενος τῷ θεῷ; ("Who are you to talk back to God?") has a diatribal quality that echoes the colloquial expression[39] that appears in Job 35:2, where Elihu challenges Job's presumption in claiming to be righteous before God: σὺ τίς εἶ, ὅτι εἶπας, Δίκαιός εἰμι ἔναντι κυρίου; ("Who are you that you have said, I am righteous before the Lord?") Paul's question resonates with Jewish warnings about the fear of God[40] and with Greco-Roman warnings about the dangers of pride before the deity.[41] The widely shared assumption is stated in Pindar's maxim, χρὴ δὲ πρὸς θεὸν οὐκ ἐρίζειν ("one must not contend against God").[42] The nominal form of the compound verb ἀνταποκρίνομαι ("talk back, reply")[43] is used where Job is warned to "no longer give a reply [to God] as fools do (μὴ δῷς ἔτι ἀνταπόκρισιν ὥσπερ οἱ ἄφρονες)."[44] Thus, the sophisticated questioner of the divine selectivity implied by Paul's scandalous doctrine of mercy to the undeserving ends up in the position of the insolent and the foolish, scorned by Greek and Jew alike. Given the earlier argument of Romans, which decries arrogance against God as the root problem of the human race (1:18-32), the position of the challenger in this verse is shown to be untenable by the formulation of this first counterquestion.[45]

The second counterquestion is created from an adaptation of Isa 29:16. The first clause is quoted exactly, and the second clause is adapted so as to echo Isa 45:9; Wis 12:12; and Job 9:12.[46] The source of the citation may be seen as follows:

---

34   Winkel, "Argumentationsanalyse," 69, refers to the three rhetorical questions without using the technical rhetorical category of *anteisagoge*.

35   See BDF §146 for the proof that ὦ conveys "very strong emotion . . . ," noted by Mesner, "Rhetoric," 394.

36   Barrett, 187. The same address, "O human," was found in Rom 2:1, 3. The phrase occurs in Epictetus *Diss.* 2.17.33 in a diametrically opposite sense: "You are a god, O human (ὦ ἄνθρωπε)! You have great plans!"

37   Zahn, 454; Cranfield, 2:490; Wilckens, 2:201; Dunn, 2:556.

38   See BDF §146.1b; 450.4; and BAGD 503; cf. Rom 10:18; Phil 3:8.

39   See BAGD 819: "(just) who are you? What sort of man are you?"

40   Deut 10:12; Job 28:28; Ps 111:10; Prov 1:7; 9:10; Eccl 5:7, etc. See also 4Q381, frg. 77.10, "Who among you will reply a word, and [who] will stand in controversy wi[th him . . .]?

41   Sophocles *Trach.* 280; *Oed. tyr.* 895–910; etc.

42   Cited by BAGD 73 from Pindar *Pyth.* 2.88.

43   Compounds in ἀνταποκριν- are quite rare; the only other place this verb is found in the NT is Luke 14:6. The lexicographer Hesychius *Lex.* α5761.1 glosses this word with ἀπαβειμένος ("to answer back, reply").

44   Job 34:36; cf 1QS 11:20-22, "Who can grasp your glory? What, indeed, is the son of Adam among your wondrous works? . . . What can clay and that which is shaped by hand dispute? And what counsel does it comprehend?"

45   The consistency of this verse with the earlier argument of the letter indicates that Paul is not merely attempting "to dismiss the legitimacy of the question and in that way to eliminate the theological problem," as claimed by Aageson, "Scripture," 272.

46   Cranfield, 2:491; Hays, *Echoes*, 65f.; Shum, *Paul's Use of Isaiah*, 204–6.

592

Romans 9:20	Isaiah 29:16b-e
Μὴ ἐρεῖ τὸ πλάσμα τῷ πλάσαντι	μὴ ἐρεῖ τὸ πλάσμα τῷ πλάσαντι
("What is molded does not say to the molder")	("What is molded does not say to the molder")
τί με ἐποίησας οὕτως;	οὐ σύ με ἔπλασας;
("'Why did you make me thus?'")	("'Did you not mold me?'")
	ἢ τὸ ποίημα τῷ ποιήσαντι,
	("Or the work to the maker,")
	οὐ συνετῶς με ἐποίησας.
	("'You did not make me wisely.'")

As Koch has shown, Paul's verb ποιέω ("make") appears in Isa 29:16e, rendering unnecessary the premise that he quoted it from Isa 45:9.[47] Paul's alteration of the second line in the citation brings it into stylistic conformity with the first objection in 9:19b and thus makes it answer the objection more directly.[48] Since Paul wishes to concentrate on human resistance to divine selectivity, Isaiah's concerns about whether the clay was molded at all (v. 16c), or was molded wisely (v. 16e), are extraneous. In that sense one could say that Paul's alteration allows a more precise grasp of his point in using the Isaiah citation.[49] The terms πλάσμα and πλάσσειν mean "that which is molded" and "to mold," respectively, referring to a wide range of materials and processes used by artisans or artists.[50] The story of God making Adam in Gen 2:7-8 is phrased with the same language: καὶ ἔπλασεν ὁ θεὸς τὸν ἄνθρωπον χοῦν ἀπὸ τῆς γῆς.... Καὶ ἐφύτευσεν κύριος ὁ θεὸς παράδεισον ... καὶ ἔθετο ἐκεῖ τὸν ἄνθρωπον, ὃν ἔπλασεν. ("And God molded the human of dust from the earth.... And the Lord God planted a garden ... and placed there the person he had molded.")

This terminology is widely used by other biblical writers[51] to describe God's shaping of humans in general,[52] or the prophet in particular,[53] the earth and all within it,[54] Israel and its destiny,[55] as well as the other nations.[56] The assumption of this usage is the absolute sovereignty of the molder over what is molded to provide whatever shape God desires.[57] Hence, Paul introduces the question with μή ("not"), indicating the impossibility of any molded object speaking thus to its creator.[58]

Given this broad biblical tradition of understanding the creation as molded by God, the presumption of the question is raised to the intolerable level: "Why have you made me thus?" As Siegert points out, the logical answer to such a question is that if you were not made thus and so, you would not have been made at all; you would not even exist![59] The question thus addresses the objection that God should not hold persons accountable since his purposes are selective, showing that such an objection is an absurdly presumptuous statement of a creature questioning the creator. The rhetorical effectiveness of this verse, supported by so broad a tradition of using the language of molding for divine sovereignty in creation, renders it unlikely that the original audience would have retorted with Dodd, "But the trouble is that a man is not a pot; he *will* ask, 'Why did you make me like this?' and he will not be bludgeoned into silence."[60] The deft hand that reformulated the question τί με ἐποίησας οὕτως; ("Why did you make me thus?") is not swinging a blackjack but stating the obvious absurdity of "talking back" to the Creator in this manner, a point on which his audience is sure to agree. The question throws light on "the

47 Koch, *Schrift*, 144; see also Herbert Braun, "πλάσσω κτλ.," *TDNT* 6 (1968) 260, followed by Dunn, 2:556. Wilk, *Bedeutung des Jesajabuches*, 304–7, and Wagner, *Heralds*, 58–68, argue for the citation of Isa 45:9.
48 Mesner, "Rhetoric," 410–11.
49 Siegert, *Argumentation*, 134; Koch, *Schrift*, 144.
50 Braun, "πλάσσω κτλ.," 255; BAGD 660.
51 See Braun, "πλάσσω κτλ.," 256–58; Wagner, *Heralds*, 68–71, also points to 1QS 11:22b as a close parallel: "What will the clay reply, and the one shaped by hand? And what advice will he be able to understand?"
52 Pss 33:15; 94:9; 119:73; 138:5; Prov 24:12; Isa 44:2, 24; 49:5; 53:11; 2 Macc 7:23; Zech 12:1; Job 10:8f.; Wis 15:11.
53 Isa 49:5; 53:11; Jer 1:5.
54 Ps 74:17; 95:5; 104:26; Isa 45:18; Jer 10:16; 33:2; 51:19; Job 38:14.
55 Deut 32:6; Isa 27:11; 43:1; 44:2, 21, 24.
56 Hab 1:12.
57 Braun, "πλάσσω κτλ.," 257; Erich Seitz, "λόγον συντέμνων—eine Gerichtsankündigung? (Zu Römer 9,27/28)," *BN* 109 (2001) 77–80.
58 Siegert, *Argumentation*, 135.
59 Ibid.
60 Dodd, 159, italics in original. That this "is the weakest point in the whole epistle" is rightly rejected by Dunn, 2:557.

paradox of Israel's continued resistance to God's purposes for them."[61]

■ **21** The third counterquestion turns to the other half of the Creator–creation relationship, referring not to the response of the creature but the ἐξουσία ("power")[62] of the Creator. The analogy of the potter and clay is associated in biblical materials with the language of molder/molded, with a notable example appearing in the very passage from which the previous verse draws its quotation (Isa 29:16; see also Ps 2:9; Isa 41:25; 45:9; Jer 18:1-6; and Sir 33:13). In Wis 15:7-8 this analogy appears with specific reference to clay vessels of various classes: Καὶ γὰρ κεραμεὺς ἀπαλὴν γῆν θλίβων ἐπίμοχθον πλάσσει πρὸς ὑπηρεσίαν ἡμῶν ἓν ἕκαστον· ἀλλ' ἐκ τοῦ αὐτοῦ πηλοῦ ἀνεπλάσατο τά τε τῶν καθαρῶν ἔργων δοῦλα σκεύη τά τε ἐναντία, πάντα ὁμοίως· τούτων δὲ ἑτέρου τίς ἑκάστου ἐστὶν ἡ χρῆσις, κριτὴς ὁ πηλουργός. καὶ κακόμοχθος θεὸν μάταιον ἐκ τοῦ αὐτοῦ πλάσσει πηλοῦ.... ("For a potter, kneading soft dirt, laboriously molds each vessel for our service: but from the same clay he makes both vessels that serve clean purposes and those serving the opposite, all in the same way; but what shall be the use of each, the maker is the judge. And the one who works perversely fashions a vain god from the same clay . . ."). The analogy Paul draws in this passage appears to be an allusion to the Wisdom quotation,[63] which contains several of the key words in v. 21, κεραμεύς ("potter"),[64] πηλός ("clay")[65] and σκεῦος ("vessel")[66] as well as πλάσσειν ("to mold"), which appeared as the key term in v. 20. With the phrase ἐκ τοῦ αὐτοῦ φυράματος ("from the same lump"), Paul also expresses the theme found in the Wisdom quotation, "from the same clay." Paul's formulation of the analogy is both more succinct[67] and more apt than the formulation in Wis 15:7, stressing the power of the potter over the clay and strengthening the antithesis between fine ware and common ware. While there are limits to any such analogy,[68] this one clearly serves Paul's purpose of sustaining the legitimacy of the divine distinction between the true Israel and all Israel that Paul has been following since 9:6b.[69] It would therefore be inappropriate to conclude from Paul's use of the sharply formulated antithesis between "honorable" and "dishonorable" vessels that he is dealing here with the predestination of individuals.[70] If the same lump of clay can produce an elegant decanter for wine[71] or a com-

61 Wagner, *Heralds*, 71; see also Wilk, *Bedeutung des Jesajabuches*, 306–7.

62 Werner Foerster, "ἐξουσία," *TDNT* 2 (1964) 567, understands the basic connotation in this verse as referring to "the absolute power of God"; Dunn, 2:557, argues that this passage stresses the aspect of "right" rather than the power, citing parallels in 1 Cor 7:37; 9:4-6; 2 Thess 3:9. See also Mark 11:28.

63 See Cranfield, 2:491–92. Piper, *Justification*, 176, observes that the idolatrous context of the potter analogy in Wis 15:7 is missing from Rom 9, which leads him to suggest Sir 33:13 as a closer parallel that sustains his theory that Paul is dealing with individual predestination. The Sirach passage has three out of the five key terms or ideas in Rom 9:21 that recur in Wis 15:7: "vessel," "potter," and "clay." See also Johnson, *Function*, 149.

64 See BAGD 428; it is a hapax legomenon in the NT; since the phrase ὁ πηλὸς τοῦ κεραμέυς ("the clay of the potter") is found in Isa 29:16, one wonders whether Paul has simply changed the word order to produce ὁ κεραμεὺς τοῦ πηλοῦ ("the potter of the clay").

65 Karl Heinrich Rengstorf, "πηλός," *TDNT* 6 (1968) 118, translates with "loam" or "clay."

66 Christian Maurer, "σκεῦος," *TDNT* 7 (1971) 362–64.

67 Rom 9:21 has twenty-two words, while Wis 15:7 expresses virtually the same thought with forty-two words.

68 Gale, *Analogy*, 199, points out that clay is a material object while humans are thinking beings capable of a genuine relationship to their Creator.

69 See Mesner, "Rhetoric," 413. Dunn, 2:557–58, refers to the implicit irony of linking unbelieving Israel with a dishonorable vessel, but Paul does not develop this theme.

70 Piper, *Justification*, 183, argues that the analogy refers "to individuals and eternal destinies."

71 The phrase εἰς τιμὴν σκεῦος refers to an expensive vessel, as in Lydus *Magistr.* 126.4, describing the gold and silver booty of Trajan as including "expensive vessels" (σκεύων τιμῆς); the *Historia Alexandri Magni Rec.* λ 63.29 refers to "a very expensive vessel" (πολύτιμον σκεῦος).

mon "chamber pot,"[72] the emphasis remains on the selectivity of the potter to meet practical needs.[73] It would extend the analogy in a false direction to draw conclusions about the "despotic, tyrannical, Sultanic" quality of arbitrariness in the potter's work.[74] The rhetorical question simply requires the answer, "Yes, the potter has such power."[75] Any further inference from the analogy should be deferred until the next two verses when Paul elaborates the intention of God in creating vessels of wrath and mercy.

■ **22** Verses 22 and 23 provide the "if clause" of an incomplete sentence whose logical but ungrammatical conclusion is found in v. 24.[76] The protasis invites the reader to supply the apodosis to the if clause, "If . . . , then it is proper. . . ."[77] These verses apply the analogy of the potter's vessel to the issue of Israel's rejection of the gospel.[78] Thus it would be inappropriate to construe the particle δέ ("now, and, but") in an adversative sense to express the idea "that God's ways are not just like the potter's."[79] It fits the argumentative context better to render δέ as "now."[80] Given the argumentative thrust and the parallelism between v. 22 and v. 23, it is better to construe the participial clause[81] beginning with θέλων ("willing, wanting")[82] in a purposive[83] rather than a causal[84] or concessive sense.[85] The expressions "to demonstrate his wrath" and "make known his power" extend key terms of the propositio (δύναμις, "power," in 1:16) and the opening of the first proof (ὀργή, "wrath," in 1:18) in the letter. The verb ἐνδείκνυσθαι ("demonstrate") links this sentence with the demonstration of "righteousness" in 3:25-26 and the divine self-revelation in 2:15 and 9:17, perhaps echoing Exod 9:16.[86] The second formulation, concerning "making known his power" (γνωρίσαι τὸ δυνατὸν αὐτοῦ), is typical of the OT. For example, Jer 16:21 writes, "I . . . will make known to them my power; and they shall know that my name is the Lord (καὶ γνωριῶ αὐτοῖς τὴν δύναμίν μου, καὶ γνώσονται, ὅτι ὄνομά μοι Κύριος)."[87] In this instance

---

72   Dunn, 2:557; Siegert, *Argumentation*, 136. Epictetus develops the concept of someone as a "worthless vessel (σκεύαριον. . . σαπρόν. . . σκεῦος ἄχρηστον)" in *Diss.* 2.4.4, 6; 3.24.33.

73   Godet, 358.

74   See Kuss, 3:730; Wilckens, 2:202; and the rebuttal in Cranfield, 2:492.

75   See Johnson, *Function*, 149.

76   The older commentators such as Tholuck, 336, and Weiss, 421, referred to this with the classical grammatical category of aposiopesis, explained in BDF §482 as "omission of the apodosis." For a more recent discussion, see Bornkamm, "Anakoluthe," 90–92; Cranfield, 2:492–98. Siegert, *Argumentation*, 136–37, argues in contrast for 9:22 as the protasis and 9:23 as an apodosis, which seems implausible because v. 23 begins with καὶ ἵνα ("and in order that"), which does not match the style of an apodosis. Zeller, *Juden*, 203–8, and *Römer*, 179, follows Maier, *Israel*, 44, in taking v. 22 and v. 23 as parallel lines of a protasis, with v. 24 as the apodosis, which fails to take the broken quality of the syntax into account. See Kuss, 3:731–32, for an account of earlier discussion of the grammatical problem. The problems in this sentence remain unresolved.

77   Lietzmann, 93.

78   Godet, 359.

79   Cranfield, 2:493.

80   See Godet, 359.

81   See the extensive discussions in Bornkamm, "Anakoluthe," 90–92; Luz, *Geschichtsverständnis*, 242–45; Cranfield, 2:493–95.

82   Although it would be more idiomatically appropriate to translate θέλων here as "wanting," its use in 9:18 requires the more theologically appropriate translation, "willing." Gottlob Schrenk, "θέλω κτλ.," *TDNT* 3 (1965) 47, discusses θέλειν "as commanding will . . . Expressly of God and His purposes and rule," citing the classical expression ἐὰν θεὸς θέλῃ ("if God wills") in Xenophon *Cyr.* 2.4.19; Plato *Phaed.* 80d; etc.

83   Lietzmann, 92f.; Schmidt, 167; Luz, *Geschichtsverständnis*, 242–44.

84   Kühl, 333–34; Michel, 305; Barrett, 189f.; Cranfield, 2:494. Luz, *Geschichtsverständnis*, 243, points out that the causal interpretation is merely a strengthening of the purposive construal without adding anything new.

85   Weiss, 421–22; Sanday and Headlam, 261; Leenhardt, 258; Black, 132. Luz, *Geschichtsverständnis*, 244, points out that the concessive sense erodes the parallelism between v. 22 and v. 23 and disregards the earlier argument of Romans that prevents a vague dissociation between wrath and grace.

86   Dunn, 2:558.

87   See also Ps 76:14, "you made known your power among the nations (ἐγνώρισας ἐν τοῖς λαοῖς τὴν δύναμίν σου)." See Rudolf Bultmann, "γνωρίζω," *TDNT* 1 (1964) 718: "The NT use of γνωρίζω corresponds to that of the LXX."

the ultimate purpose of divine wrath and power, as Rom 9:23 and 11:26-32 will show, is to change "vessels of wrath" into "vessels of mercy" through the power of the gospel.[88]

The predominance of mercy over wrath in Paul's elaboration of the metaphor of the potter and the vessel is conveyed by the wording that God "endures with great patience (ἤνεγκεν ἐν πολλῇ μακροθυμίᾳ)"[89] those who deserve wrath. Given the crucial reference to the "patience of God" in 2:5, the implication here is that God delays the enactment of wrath so that the scope of repentance and mercy is widened as far as possible.[90] Paul paraphrases a well-established formula from Exod 34:6 that "echoes again and again through the biblical writings and into later Judaism:"[91] κύριος ὁ θεὸς οἰκτίρμων καὶ ἐλεήμων, μακρόθυμος καὶ πολυέλεος ("The Lord God is piteous and merciful, patient and very compassionate"). Given the context in Exodus, it is clear that divine patience implies no abandonment of the grounds for wrath but rather "postpones its operation until something takes place in man which justifies the postponement."[92] The use of this concept shows the extent to which Paul is willing to bend the analogy of the potter and the vessel into the dissimilar arena of human responsibility, for one would not ordinarily speak of

being "patient" with a clay pot on the premise that it will have time to change its shape.[93]

The reference to "the vessels of wrath prepared for destruction" is thus qualified from the outset by the expression of divine patience that waits for human responses.[94] Such patient endurance on the part of God renders illogical the possibility that σκεῦος should be rendered "instrument" rather than "vessel," following the use in the LXX of Jer 27:25 and the Symmachus version of Isa 13:5, for why should God be "patient" with an "instrument of wrath" designed to punish evildoers?[95] The context indicates that the construction of σκεύη ὀργῆς ("vessels of wrath") should be understood as a genitive of quality[96] rather than a genitive of origin. Paul does not mean "vessels destined to be broken by wrath."[97] The choice of the verb "prepared" in the perfect passive form (κατηρτισμένα) implies action subsequent to the original creation of the vessels, in contrast to the more predestinarian term "made beforehand" used in the following verse.[98] The responsibility for actions punished by wrath remains unstated in this passive form.[99] As in other Pauline passages (Phil 1:29; 3:19; 2 Thess 2:3) the expression εἰς ἀπώλειαν implies annihilation in the last judgment,[100] but as the subsequent argument will demonstrate, God will in fact not reject

---

88   Cranfield, 2:497.

89   Seitz, "λόγον συντέμνων," 80, argues for a gnomic aorist, "endures with great patience," because Paul is here applying the metaphor of the vessel to the situation of Israel.

90   Dunn, 2:559.

91   Johannes Horst, "μακροθυμία κτλ.," *TDNT* 4 (1967) 376; see, e.g., 4QDibHam 1 ii 7-11.

92   Horst, "μακροθυμία κτλ.," 377; he denies, however (382–83), that Rom 9:22 implies the provision of time for repentance.

93   See Gale, *Analogy,* 198–205.

94   See Maurer, "σκεῦος," 363–64; Hanson, *Wrath,* 90–92.

95   See Hanson, *Wrath,* 90–92, and A. T. Hanson, "Vessels of Wrath or Instruments of Wrath? Romans xi. 22-3," *JTS* 32 (1981) 433–43, which disregards the context of divine patience while arguing that Paul is using σκεῦος in a deliberately ambiguous way, including both "instrument" and "vessel," which wrongly imposes the ambiguity of contemporary alternatives onto a clearly defined antithesis. This also forces Hanson to interpret the phrase εἰς

ἀπώλειαν in a strained manner as "for destroying," whereby it remains unclear who the targets of such clay instruments might be. Munck, *Christ,* 67–68, and Dahl, *Studies,* 145, make similar suggestions.

96   Tholuck, 338; Meyer, 2:149; Maurer, "σκεῦος," 364; Godet's suggestion (360–61) that the genitive implies the wrathful contents of the vessel, which are to be "tasted" by the vessel itself, is too elaborate for the simple genitive construction.

97   See the critique of this view in Sanday and Headlam, 261.

98   For the predestinarian construal, see Piper, *Justification,* 192–96; the case for maintaining the basic sense of καταρτίζω as "fit together, prepare," is presented by Ceslas Spicq, "καταρτίζω," *TLNT* 2 (1994) 271, and Dunn, 2:559.

99   See Cranfield, 2:496. Godet, 361, argues that subsequent behavior prepares the path toward destruction; most commentators, however, insist that this must be understood as a "divine passive," in which divine wrath remains predominant. See Maier, *Mensch,* 381; Mayer, *Gottes Heilsratschluß,* 208–9; Dunn, 2:560.

the Jewish people (11:1-2), who stand in the position of the "vessels of wrath" at the present time.[101] Even in this verse Paul is going as far as he possibly can to reconcile human responsibility and divine prerogative with the prospect of the ultimate triumph of mercy.[102]

■ **23** The second half of the garbled "if" clause in Paul's incomplete sentence begins with καὶ ἵνα ("and in order that"), suggesting an ultimately merciful purpose in the divine creation and patience over vessels. As Tobin observes, at this point "Paul moves beyond the traditional discussions of the issue of God's patience and forbearance to claim an additional reason for this patience and forbearance, the inclusion not only of Jews but also of Gentiles as vessels of mercy."[103] The parallelism between v. 23 and v. 22 is carefully contrived, despite the syntactical confusion. The purpose of "making known the riches of his glory" (v. 23) stands parallel to "demonstrate his wrath and make known his power" (v. 22), with the verb γνωρίζω ("make known") reduplicated in each clause; the "vessels of mercy prepared for glory" (v. 23) correspond to the "vessels of wrath prepared for destruction" in the preceding verse, with a reduplication of σκεῦος ("vessel"). Yet the parallelism is not complete,[104] because Paul makes unmistakably clear that the demonstration of mercy in this verse is God's dominant purpose as compared with the demonstration of wrath.[105]

The expression "the riches of his glory" (τὸν πλοῦτον τῆς δόξης αὐτοῦ)[106] appears to be drawn from the tradition of liturgical participation in the numinous cloud or bright fire that was thought to surround the divine tabernacle (Exod 40:34f.) or throne (Ezek 1:26-28).[107] That early Christian worship was thought to be a participation in the riches of divine glory is suggested by the use of this expression in the liturgically formulated references in Phil 4:19; Col 1:27; and Eph 3:16.[108] As Paul had argued in Rom 8:18, 30, believers anticipate the restoration of their participation in the divine glory. Here they are described as having been "prepared beforehand for glory," with the word προετοιμάζω conveying a strong statement of predetermination.[109] Wis 9:8 uses this verb to describe God's primordial design for "the holy tabernacle which you prepared beforehand from the beginning (σκηνῆς ἁγίας ἣν προητοίμασας ἀπ᾽ ἀρχῆς)." The *Thanksgiving Scroll* from Qumran refers to God's predetermina-

---

100   Wilckens, 2:203. See Matt 7:13; Acts 8:20; Rev 17:8, 11. The idea is decidedly Hebrew, going to a place of destruction such as Sheol or Abaddon: see Herbert G. Grether, "Abaddon," *ABD* 1 (1972) 6.

101   See Dunn, 2:559: "Paul's treatment would also provoke a more devastating 'double take' when his readers came to realize that Paul saw the bulk of Israel as the 'vessels of wrath'. . . ."

102   Maurer, "σκεῦος," 364: "The point of this is that the people should turn from its wickedness and be made into a new pot. This means that according to the divine if not the human order there is the possibility that the present σκεῦος ὀργῆς may be received again into the superabundant divine mercy."

103   Tobin, *Paul's Rhetoric*, 336.

104   Zeller's argument in *Juden*, 203–8, and *Römer*, 179, for a complete parallelism that avoids any subordination of v. 22 to v. 23 fails to do justice to the opening words of v. 23. Zeller's construction seeks to avoid implicit contradictions between vv. 17-18 and vv. 22-23, but it is better to allow the tensions in Paul's development of the potter/pot analogy to remain.

105   Godet, 263; Bornkamm, "Anakoluthe," 91; Luz, *Geschichtsverständnis*, 247–50.

106   Newman and Nida, 189, advocate the translation "his rich glory" on the premise that "the abstract noun should be interpreted as a qualifier of the noun which appears in the genitive."

107   See Gerhard von Rad, "δόξα," *TDNT* 2 (1964) 240–41; Zeller, 179, suggests that there are "numerous" Qumran parallels to the liturgical use of this expression, but he does not list them. Cf. 4QDibHam 1-2 iii 4–6, "Only your name have we [acknow]ledged, and for your glory you have created us and [as] sons you have established us for yourself before the eyes of all nations. . . ." Maier, *Mensch*, 381, refers to the "rich peace" and the "crown of glory" enjoyed by the "sons of truth" in 1QS 4:7.

108   See Michel, 316; Schlier, 302, and H. M. Dion, "La notion paulinienne de richesse de Dieu," *ScEc* 18 (1966) 139–48.

109   Dunn, 2:560; Zeller, 179–80. See the close parallel in Sir 49:19 of Joshua raising up a temple to the Lord, "prepared for eternal glory (ἡτοιμασμένον εἰς δόξαν αἰῶνος)."

tion of the saints from their mothers' wombs to receive divine mercy and glory through adherence to the law (1QH 15:15-17), while the *Manual of Discipline* describes the saints as those whom "God has elected to the eternal covenant and to whom belongs all the glory of Adam" (1QS 4:22f.). Paul's repeated use of the prefix προ- to convey the prior decisions of God in the earlier argument of Romans (Rom 1:2; 8:28-30; 9:11) leaves no doubt about the predestination theme here.[110] It is noteworthy, however, that Paul chooses the active aorist form to convey this divine predestination of "vessels of mercy" to participate in glory, while using the more vaguely determined passive form in the preceding verse to describe the vessels "prepared for destruction."[111] The passage is carefully designed to suggest the priority of mercy,[112] which addresses precisely the question in 9:14 about whether God's mercy to the undeserving is justified or not. The antithesis between "vessels of mercy" and "vessels of wrath" appears to be a Pauline innovation.[113] While parallels to the derogatory use of "vessel" have been discovered in *Apoc. Mos.* 16, 26 and 4QTest 25,[114] the idea of a "vessel of mercy"[115] is a unique Pauline expression of the implication of the

gospel concerning the direction of predestination: not toward "destruction" but toward "glory."[116]

■ **24** The awkward phrasing of this verse makes unmistakably clear that Paul wishes the "vessels of mercy" to be understood as contemporary Christian believers.[117] The incomplete sentence in vv. 22-23 would force the attentive reader to pause, as Dunn observes,[118] thus giving the peculiar rhetoric of οὓς καὶ ἐκάλεσεν ἡμᾶς ("whom he also called, us") more force.[119] The ἡμᾶς stands in apposition to οὓς,[120] thus emphatically identifying those being called as fellow believers with Paul.[121] This moves the argument beyond the awkward terrain of a strained analogy concerning different kinds of pots into the straightforward arena of divine calling,[122] which has echoed throughout the midrash (9:7, 11, 12) and which was established earlier as the concomitant of predestination (8:30). The inclusive nature of the Christian community is emphatically restated here,[123] echoing the discussions in 1:16; 3:29; and 4:11-16 and reiterated in 10:11-13. In the logic of the midrashic argument, the term "Gentiles" is now associated with the positive terminology of "seed," "Isaac," "Jacob," "those on whom God shows mercy," the "honorable vessel," and the

---

110 See Schlier, 302. Qumran parallels include 4Q181 1 ii 2f. and 4Q180 frg. 1, line 2, "Before he created them he established their deeds."

111 See Godet, 363; Dunn, 2:561.

112 The *anakoluth* conveys a high level of passionate involvement on the part of a speaker, and draws the audience's attention to the point about vessels of mercy, as shown by Seitz, "λόγον συντέμνων," 81.

113 Maier, *Mensch*, 380–81, claims that the antithesis is Essene, but this is acceptable only in a general sense, because the evidence supports only a predestinarian construal of the doctrine of two paths, not a use of an antithesis between two types of vessels.

114 See Maurer, "σκεῦος," 360, for these and later rabbinic parallels, none of which precisely matches the expression "vessel of wrath."

115 That Paul intended σκεῦος ἐλέους to be understood as "instruments of mercy," as Hanson argues in "Vessels," 441, assumes that they would play an active role in extending mercy to others, whereas the grammar of 9:23 demands that they be understood as passive recipients of divine revelation.

116 See Seitz, "λόγον συντέμνων," 82.

117 See Gignac, *Romans 9–11*, 189; Tobin, *Paul's Rhetoric*, 335–36.

118 Dunn, 2:570.

119 Bornkamm, "Anakoluthe," 91–92, argues in fact that this verse is the reason for the incomplete sentence in vv. 22-23, abandoning the abstract possibilities of divine election for the concrete reality of God's calling of Gentiles and Jews alike.

120 See Cranfield, 2:498.

121 Nida and Newman, 189, translate "We are the ones whom he called."

122 See Karl Ludwig Schmidt, "καλέω κτλ.," *TDNT* 3 (1965) 488, for the extensive listing of passages in which Paul uses this term to designate the status change that marks Christian believers. Dodd, 160, refers to Paul's abstract argument suddenly at this point touching the "concrete reality" of the Christian community. A similar view is present in Qumran, with CD A 4:3-4 claiming that "the sons of Zadok are the chosen ones of Israel, those called by name, who stand in the end of days. See also CD A 2:11.

123 Moxnes, *Theology in Conflict*, 83: "Paul points to his integrated congregations of Jews and non-Jews as an illustration of his thesis."

124 See Mesner, "Rhetoric," 402.

125 The importance of this theme in the argument is exaggerated as the "climax" of Paul's argument by Gaston, *Paul*, 96–97. See the critique by Räisänen,

"vessel of mercy."[124] The "not only . . . but also" formula prohibits any foreshortening of the scope of God's inclusive call.[125] As Elizabeth Johnson points out, Paul redefines Israel "by *in*cluding believing Gentiles rather than *ex*cluding unbelieving Israel."[126] The sequence of mentioning "Jews" first and "Gentiles" (or "Greeks") second is consistent with 1:16; 3:29; and 10:12, providing in this instance a chiasm with the subsequent catena of scriptural citations that deal with the Gentiles in vv. 25-26 and with Jews in vv. 27-29.[127] It remains puzzling that Paul uses the seemingly prejudicial term ἔθνη to convey his inclusive doctrine (as, for example, in 3:29); the translation "non-Jew" is preferred by Ralf Dabelstein to either "Gentile" or "nation" in this verse,[128] but I would prefer to allow the disparity to stand.

■ **25-26** The introduction to the catena of quotations that closes the pericope is loosely attached to the foregoing by ὡς καί ("as also"), suggesting that the claim in v. 24 concerning the calling of Gentiles as well as Jews is to be demonstrated.[129] The verb λέγει should not be translated with the neutral expression "it says"[130] but with "he says," corresponding to "he calls" in v. 24. The first person singular form of an oracle spoken by Yahweh is thus introduced here as a direct, personal confirmation of the calling of believers. The oracle is found "in Hosea," probably meaning that it derived from the Hosea section of the prophetic scroll.[131] Although the material from the book of Hosea is a composite, it is introduced here as a single citation,[132] making this the sixth supporting text in the midrash that began with 9:6. The creation of the composite citation may be visualized as in the chart below, with the first two clauses in Hosea reversed by Paul:[133]

Hosea 2:25b-c[134]	Romans 9:25b-26
25b καὶ ἀγαπήσω τὴν οὐκ ἠγαπημένην, ("and I will love her who was not loved,")[135]	25b καλέσω τὸν οὐ λαόν μου λαόν μου, (I will call 'my people' those who are not my people,")
25c καὶ ἐρῶ τῷ οὐ λαῷ μου, λαός μου εἶ σύ. ("and I will say to those who are not my people, 'You are my people.'")	25c καὶ τὴν οὐκ ἠγαπημένην ἠγαπημένην. ("and her who was not beloved [I will call] 'beloved'")
Hos 2:1b-c[136]	
1b καὶ ἔσται ἐν τῷ τόπῳ οὗ ἐρρέθη αὐτοῖς Οὐ λαός μου ὑμεῖς. ("and there will be in the place where it was said to them, 'You are not my people,'")	26α καὶ ἔσται ἐν τῷ τόπῳ οὗ ἐρρέθη αὐτοῖς, Οὐ λαός μου ὑμεῖς, ("and there will be in the place where it was said to them, 'You are not my people,'")
1c ἐκεῖ κληθήσονται υἱοὶ θεοῦ ζῶντος. ("there they will be called 'sons of the living God.'")	26b ἐκεῖ κληθήσονται υἱοὶ θεοῦ ζῶντος. ("there they will be called 'sons of the living God.'")

"Römer 9–11," 2905, and Johnson, *Function*, 149, who observes that the "not only . . . but also" formula included Jews and Gentiles in 3:29; 4:12, 16.

126 Johnson, *Function*, 149; italics in original.

127 See Jeremias, "Chiasmus," 150, and Koch, *Schrift*, 279.

128 Dabelstein, *Beurteilung*, 37.

129 See Cranfield, 2:498, and Dunn, 2:571.

130 Black, 134, prefers an impersonal formulation such as "as is said," or "as one says."

131 Christoph Burchard, "Römer 9:25 ἐν τῷ Ὡσέ," *ZNW* 76 (1985) 131.

132 See Koch, *Schrift*, 173.

133 Stanley, *Scripture*, 110; Wagner, *Heralds*, 81.

134 Note that the versification of the LXX and the MT differs from the tradition of English translation, which numbers this verse as 2:23.

135 This wording is found in the LXX textual variant BV, while the probable original wording was καὶ ἐλεήσω τὴν οὐκ ἠλεημένην ("and I will have mercy on her who [was called] 'not mercy.'" While it is usually assumed that the variant shows the influence of Rom 9:25, Koch, *Schrift*, 55, argues that the word "love" is inappropriate for the context and thus may be original. In view of the reference to "Jacob I loved" in 9:13, within the same midrashic argument, this argument is not persuasive. Dunn, 2:571, is probably right in suggesting that Paul wished to avoid a negative use of "mercy," since it is so crucial for the immediate context.

136 This verse, 2:1 in the LXX and the MT, corresponds to 1:10 in the standard English translations.

There is a consensus that Paul intentionally altered the wording of Hos 2:25 from ἐρῶ ("I will say") to καλέσω ("I will call"),[137] thus linking the citation directly to the divine calling of Jews and Gentiles in v. 24 and providing a connection with the catchword "call" in the initial proof text of Gen 21:12.[138] The emphatic placement of the verb "call" at the beginning of the citation also required the reversal of the clauses in Hos 2:25b-c,[139] allowing the clause with the most direct connection with the Jew/Gentile theme in the preceding verse to open the Hosea quotation. Those who are "not my people," usually understood to be the Gentiles in this context,[140] are called by God to be λαός μου ("my people"). Here an expression that Hosea had employed to refer explicitly to Israel is used to designate the new Christian community containing both Jews and Gentiles as God's people.[141] Rather than conceiving this narrowly as "Gentile Christians,"[142] both the context of the preceding verse and the framework of the midrashic argument starting in 9:6 suggest that "my people" is the mixed community of the church.[143] The reduplication of the participle ἠγαπημένη ("beloved") brings the second clause in Paul's reversal of the Hosea quotation into exact parallelism with the first clause, requiring the verb "I will call" to be supplied by the hearers. By picking up the catchword from 9:13,[144] this clause brings the Christian community into direct correlation with the love of God for Jacob/Israel, receiving divine favor despite being initially "not beloved."[145] The reversal of favor implicit in the belief of the Christian community, the unbelief of some of the fleshly descendants of Abraham and Jacob, and the ultimate hope of the redemption of all are thus seen to be consistent with God's love toward the northern kingdom during Hosea's time.[146]

As may be seen above, v. 26 is a precise quotation of the LXX of Hos 2:1,[147] which had strong thematic links with Hos 2:25, including the phrase "not my people." It is likely that the joining of the two verses was Pauline rather than traditional,[148] allowing him to create a

---

137 Kühl, 337; Wilckens, 2:199; Dunn, 2:571; Koch, *Schrift*, 167; Stanley, *Scripture*, 110; Barbara Fuß, *"Dies ist die Zeit von der geschrieben ist . . .": Die expliziten Zitate aus dem Buch Hosea in den Handschriften von Qumran und im Neuen Testament* (NTAbh 37; Münster: Aschendorff, 2000) 175.

138 While not operating within the context of midrashic discourse, Aageson, "Scripture," 272, suggests that Paul's alteration "has resulted in a verbal connection in Paul's text between the two Hosea passages in 9:25-26 which is not found in the text of the LXX." Gignac, *Romains 9–11,* 190, refers to 9:25-29 as an instance of "a subversive reading of scripture."

139 Hübner, *Gottes Ich und Israel,* 56.

140 See Schlier, 304; Käsemann, 274; Wilckens, 2:206; Hays, *Echoes,* 67; Tobin, *Paul's Rhetoric,* 336–37. Barrett, 191, and Dunn, 2:571, see a potential double reference here both to Gentiles and to currently unbelieving Jews, which is an unsound allowance of a theologically appealing ambiguity that the text itself does not suggest.

141 For a discussion of the minor shifts from dative to accusative in "not my people" and the deletion of εἶ σύ ("you are") in the Hosea text, see Stanley, *Scripture,* 110–11. Fuß, *Zitate aus dem Buch Hosea,* 178–79, rejects the theory of Paul's redefinition of "my people," but this is strongly suggested by his framing the citation in 9:24 with "not only from

among Jews but also from among Gentiles."

142 See Hermann Strathmann and Rudolf Meyer, "λαός," *TDNT* 4 (1967) 54: "Hence the Gentile Christians are for him 'my people.'" Similarly, Ellis, *Paul's Use,* 138; Schlier, 304; Wilckens, 2:206; Morris, 370–71.

143 Leenhardt, 260; Dahl, *Studies,* 146; Mesner, "Rhetoric," 452–54.

144 Hübner, *Gottes Ich und Israel,* 53; Tobin, *Paul's Rhetoric,* 337.

145 See Wagner, *Heralds,* 82; Stanley, *Arguing,* 159–60.

146 See Cranfield, 2:499–500, and Mesner, "Rhetoric," 415–36.

147 Stanley, *Scripture,* 113, notes that the LXX texts are divided on whether ἐκεῖ ("there") belongs at the beginning of Hos 2:1c and whether καὶ αὐτοί ("and they themselves") belongs before κληθήσονται ("they will be called"). Since no motivation can be discerned for Paul to make these changes and since LXX versions existed without them, Stanley concedes that the matter "is probably best left open."

148 Käsemann, 273–74, offers a solid critique of the proposal by Luz, *Geschichtsverständnis,* 96–98, of a pre-Pauline fusion of these texts. See also Koch, *Schrift,* 167, 174; Zeller, 180. Michel, 317, takes an ambiguous position concerning the source of the composite quotation.

600

coherent two-verse composite marked by synthetic parallelism in each verse that ends with a potent inclusio through the reiteration of the crucial term "calling." The opening clause that Paul quotes from Hos 2:1b, καὶ ἔσται ἐν τῷ τόπῳ οὗ ἐρρέθη αὐτοῖς ("and there will be in the place where it was said to them"), has a theological rather than a spatial connotation in the context of Paul's argument.[149] While the original context in Hosea implied the land of Israel as the "place" where the divine reversal would occur,[150] it is extraneous in the context of this argument for Paul to allude to Jerusalem as the goal of Gentile pilgrimage and the "place" where the Gentile offering will be delivered.[151] This suggestion has been sustained by the assumption that Paul may have inserted ἐκεῖ ("there") in v. 26b, since some versions of the Hosea quotation lack this word,[152] but the text-critical evidence is too ambiguous to make a conclusive case. It is best to assume that the two clauses were cited by Paul in the LXX form known to him in order to retain the symmetry of synthetic parallelism and that the meaning of the first clause is "instead of saying, 'you are not my people.'" The title "sons of the living God" is reminiscent of Paul's claim in 8:14 and 19 that with the gift of the Spirit, believers demonstrate their sonship (8:15, 23), understood inclusively as including both males and females. The Hebrew Scriptures frequently refer to Israel as Yahweh's sons and daughters,[153] which correlates nicely with the argument from 9:6 that the true Israel consists of those now being called from both Jews and Gentiles to participate in the new community of faith.[154] That the Hosea wording refers to God as θεὸς ζῶν ("a living God") resonates nicely with Paul's claim in 4:17 that God is the one who "calls the things that do not exist" into life. There as here the prime example of God's life-giving power is the calling of those who are "not my people" into the exalted status of sonship/daughtership.

■ **27** The introduction of the seventh supporting text in the extended midrash is a dramatic reference to Isaiah's ecstatic, prophetic speech:[155] "but Isaiah cries out. . . ." The verb κράζειν was used in 8:15 to refer to the ecstatic cry of believers under the power of the spirit. Perhaps Paul used this unusually powerful term because of its association with Isaiah's vision of the seraphim "crying to one another, 'Holy, Holy, Holy!'" (Isa 6:3).[156] The choice of the present tense extends the inspired utterance to the present moment in the mission to Jews as well as Gentiles.[157] In combination with the mildly adversative δέ ("but"), this introduction calls particular attention to the Isaiah quotation, though not intending a contrast between the positive word concerning the Gentiles in 9:26 compared with an allegedly negative word concerning the Jews in this verse.[158] The use of the expression ὑπὲρ τοῦ Ἰσραηλ ("for the sake of Israel") "raises the expectation that Isaiah's message will proclaim good news to Israel."[159] It has frequently been observed that Paul's citation of Isa 10:22 is conflated with its close parallel in Hos 2:1.[160] Here are the two texts conflated in 9:27b:

Hos 1:10a LXX (= MT 2:1a) καὶ ἦν ὁ ἀριθμὸς τῶν υἱῶν Ισραηλ ὡς ἡ ἄμμος τῆς θαλάσσης ("and the number of the sons of Israel was as the sand of the sea")

Isa 10:22 καὶ ἐὰν γένηται ὁ λαὸι Ισραηλ ὡς ἡ ἄμμος τῆς θαλάσσης ("and though the people of Israel be as the sand of the sea")

Rom 9:27 ἐὰν ἦ ὁ ἀριθμὸς τῶν υἱῶν Ἰσραὴλ ὡς ἡ ἄμμος τῆς θαλάσσης ("though the number of the sons of Israel be as the sand of the sea")

---

149 See Cranfield, 2:500; Dunn, 2:572.

150 Fuß, *Zitate aus dem Buch Hosea*, 184–85.

151 Sanday and Headlam, 264; Munck, *Christ*, 12f.; Dahl, *Studies*, 146; Michel, 318; Wagner, *Heralds*, 85; see the critique in Koch, *Schrift*, 174.

152 See Sanday and Headlam, 264; Wilckens, 2.206.

153 Georg Fohrer, "υἱός κτλ.," *TDNT* 8 (1972) 351, refers to Deut 14:1; 32:5, 19; Isa 43:6; 45:11; as well as Hos 2:1; see also Isa 63:8 and Jer 4:22.

154 See Johnson, *Function*, 150; Fuß, *Zitate aus dem Buch Hosea*, 188–98.

155 See Wilckens, 2:206.

156 As Walter Grundmann points out in "κράζω κτλ.," *TDNT* 3 (1965) 900, rabbinic Judaism typically referred to Isaiah as crying out before God (e.g., *Tanh.* 14.19), while inspired speech in general was expressed with such language.

157 See Mesner, "Rhetoric," 463; Wagner, *Heralds*, 92.

158 See Godet, 365; Cranfield, 2:501.

159 Wagner, *Heralds*, 93.

160 Käsemann, 275; Dunn, 2:573; Koch, *Schrift*, 167–68; Wagner, *Heralds*, 90–98. Shum, *Paul's Use of Isaiah*, 206–10, disregards the parallels to the Hosea passage.

As so frequently with Pauline citation, the initial "and" found in both Isaiah and Hosea has been eliminated in order to make a smoother transition to the new context.[161] It is clear that the catchword υἱῶν Ἰσραήλ ("sons of Israel), which allows Paul to connect this passage to his supplementary text in 9:9, is derived from Hosea rather than Isaiah.[162] The wording of Isaiah would not have provided the link that Paul's midrashic discourse required, and as Koch has pointed out, it would have contradicted the claim in 9:25 that Israel as a whole is not God's people.[163] Neither text has the precise opening that Paul provides for the quotation, ἐὰν ᾖ ("though, if"), which brings out the contrast between the vast number of the people of Israel and the relative smallness of the "remnant." Both Hos 2:1 and Isa 10:22 have the phrase ὡς ἡ ἄμμος τῆς θαλάσσης ("as the sand of the sea") that Paul uses, the traditional Hebraic reference to the numberless offspring of Abraham.[164]

The variation in 9:27c is harder to explain, though there is little doubt that the changes were intentional:

Isa 10:22 τὸ κατάλειμμα αὐτῶν σωθήσεται ("the remnant of them will be saved")

Romans τὸ ὑπόλειμμα σωθήσεται ("the remnant will be saved")

Since the terms κατάλειμμα and ὑπόλειμμα are synonyms, both being used to translate the same term in the LXX,[165] it remains a mystery why Paul altered the text in his quotation.[166] An examination of the grammatical significance of the prefixes κατά ("down, against") and ὑπό ("by, under") suggests that the latter may have lacked the antithetical, judgmental quality of the former.[167] The alteration may have been intended to soften the potentially judgmental quality of the remnant idea. But the lack of a broadly understood motivation leads one to suspect that the strongly supported textual variant κατάλειμμα may have been original, even though this would violate the accepted principle of preferring the more difficult reading.[168] The deletion of αὐτῶν ("of them") from the Isaiah text may have been motivated by Paul's desire to apply the text directly to the contemporary situation, suggesting that the remnant from the "sons of Israel" are current believers in Christ, not those ancient Israelites who escaped the Assyrian catastrophe discussed by Isaiah.[169] While most commentators take the remnant reference to be a threatening comment on Israel,[170] even inserting the interpretive term "only" in their translations,[171] a primarily positive interpretation of v. 27c is suggested by the link with "will be saved" as well as by the context established in vv. 6-8

---

161 See Stanley, *Scripture*, 114.

162 See Aageson, "Scripture," 273; and Stegner, "Midrash," 40.

163 Koch, *Schrift*, 168, followed by Stanley, *Scripture*, 115; Wilk's skepticism in *Bedeutung des Jesajabuches*, 52, does not seem to be justified.

164 See Gen 22:17; 32:12; Isa 10:22; 48:19.

165 Volkmar Herntrich et al., "λεῖμμα κτλ.," *TDNT* 4 (1967) 196.

166 No Romans commentary suggests an explanation for the change, and even Koch, *Schrift*, 142, and Stanley, *Scripture*, 116, admit the question remains unanswered. Wagner, *Heralds*, 96, follows Joseph Ziegler, "Textkritische Notizen zu den jüngeren griechischen Übersetzungen des Buches Isaias," in J. Ziegler, *Sylloge: Gesammelte Aufsätze zur Septuaginta* (SeptArb 1; MSU 10; Göttingen: Vandenhoeck & Ruprecht, 1971) 68–69, who observes that variations in initial prepositions of compounds in the LXX often imply "no significant change in meaning," but this does not explain Paul's motivation. See also the discussion in Mesner, "Rhetoric," 239-40.

167 Moulton and Howard, *Grammar II*, 316–17, 327–28.

168 See note o above.

169 Similarly, the Qumran community considered its current members to be the divinely selected "remnant." See 1QH 6:7-8, "For I know that in a short time you will raise up survivors among your people and a remnant within your inheritance," cited by Fitzmyer, 574. That salvation is conceived as "communal" in these passages is suggested by Luke Timothy Johnson, "The Social Dimensions of *Sōtēria* in Luke-Acts and Paul," in E. H. Lovering, Jr., ed., *Society of Biblical Literature 1993 Seminar Papers* (SBLSP 32; Atlanta: Scholars Press, 1993) 531. For general background, see Lester V. Meyer, "Remnant," *ABD* 5 (1992) 669–71.

170 Kühl, 337–38; Schlier, 304; Cranfield, 2:502; Michel, 318; Aageson, "Typology," 57. Dunn, 2:573, presents a more balanced view of the positive and negative potential of the "remnant" language in the OT and Qumran.

171 For a critique of this tradition of English translation, see Hays, *Echoes*, 328.

and v. 24.[172] Despite current unbelief in the gospel, this quotation from Isaiah expresses Paul's conviction that the gospel of salvation will not ultimately fail, because the elected "remnant" will receive it in faith and be brought thereby to salvation.[173]

■ **28** A predominantly positive construal of the remnant reference in v. 27 clears the way to understanding Paul's puzzling abbreviation of the next line in the Isaiah quotation. As one can see from a comparison with the original Hebrew text, the Pauline alterations move the meaning even further than the LXX has already done, downplaying the element of annihilating judgment:

Isa 10:22f. (MT): "Destruction is decreed, overflowing with righteousness, for the Lord, the Lord of hosts, will make a full end, as decreed, in the midst of all the earth."

Isa 10:22f. (LXX): "He will complete the word and dispatch it in righteousness, because God will execute the word with dispatch in the whole inhabited world." (λόγον γὰρ συντελῶν καὶ συντέμνων ἐν δικαιοσύνῃ, ²³ὅτι λόγον συντετμημένον ποιήσει ὁ θεὸς ἐν τῇ οἰκουμένῃ ὅλῃ.)

Rom 9:28: "For the Lord will execute the word with completion and dispatch upon the earth" (λόγον γὰρ συντελῶν καὶ συντέμνων ποιήσει κύριος ἐπὶ τῆς γῆς.)

Whether intentionally or not, the LXX translated a somewhat baffling MT in such a way as to weaken the link between Israel's destruction and the completion of God's word.[174] Paul moves further along this path, eliminating the phrase "in righteousness," which would connote judicial judgment in this context,[175] and the clause "execute the word with dispatch," which reinforces the foreshortening of the time before final judgment, as intended in the original MT. That these deletions are simply the result of "haplography," that is, the elimination of reduplication in the LXX version that Paul was citing,[176] is plausible only if Paul's own motivation of transforming judgment into mercy is denied. In effect, Paul transforms the quotation into a comment on the future tense of the preceding verse, "a remnant will be saved."[177] By changing "God" into "Lord" as the subject of this salvatory action, Paul alludes to the role of Christ in this scenario and creates a tighter connection with "Lord" in the citation of v. 29.[178] The participles συντελῶν καὶ συντέμνων are usually understood as "rigor and dispatch" with which apocalyptic judgment is coming with urgent proximity.[179] In this instance, however, these participles are reduced to adverbial qualifications of how and when the divine word will be "executed." In the context of Paul's argument, the accent is on divine mercy rather than wrath.[180] In this context the participle

---

172 See Zahn, 466; Tobin, *Paul's Rhetoric*, 337. Herntrich et al., "λεῖμμα κτλ.," 196, argues that the "remnant" concept in Hebrew Scripture "implies both judgment and salvation," yet concludes (210) that in the light of the reference in v. 28 to "stern and pitiless cutting off" that "Paul effectively emphasizes the thought of judgment." Mesner, "Rhetoric," 471, acknowledges the negative connotations but argues that Paul's "primary interest is in the positive dimensions of the term" remnant.

173 See Wilk, *Bedeutung des Jesajabuches*, 129; Seitz, "λόγον συντέμνων," 60–61.

174 Cranfield, 2:502, claims that the LXX translators "were apparently baffled" by the MT, but concludes that both the LXX and Paul, "though differing considerably from the MT, give the general idea of the original quite correctly."

175 Meyer, 2:160. Wilckens, 2:207, assumes instead that "righteousness" would have been useful in pursuing Paul's theme from 9:14, suggesting that this indicates a pre-Pauline shortening of the text.

176 Kühl, 338; Koch, 83. Stanley, *Scripture*, 117, rightly rejects this suggestion because the words συντέμνων ("dispatch") and συντετμημένον ("execute") "are only loosely similar in appearance," and because the retention of "righteousness" would have inserted a connotation inconsistent with Paul's normal use.

177 Seitz, "λόγον συντέμνων," 62–66.

178 See Wagner, *Heralds*, 97. Stanley's argument in *Scripture*, 118, that the word "Lord" appeared in the LXX version Paul was employing is not plausible in view of the weak support of this reading in BV and a few other later texts.

179 See Käsemann, 275, citing the appearance of the formula in Dan 5:26-28 and 9:24 (Theod.); BAGD 792; most commentaries take this as an expression of irrevocable and swift judgment; Schmidt, 170; Michel, 318; Wilckens, 2:207; Dunn, 2:573; Moo, 615.

180 A contextual interpretation in relation to the triumph of mercy is argued by Weiss, 431; Kühl, 338;

συντελῶν has the sense of "bring to completion,"[181] and the participle συντέμνων means "finish quickly, with dispatch."[182] The expression λόγον ποιεῖν is a typical biblical formula for bringing a prophecy into fulfillment, making a message effective.[183] The "word" in this new setting picks up the catchword from v. 6, understood as the promise of salvation through the gospel[184] rather than the decree of final judgment as in the original Isaiah citation.[185] That the fulfillment of the divine promise to save the faithful remnant in Israel was in view by Paul is confirmed by his alteration of the phrase "in the whole inhabited world" to the simple phrase "upon the earth," thus directing attention away from peoples other than Israel.[186]

■ **29** The final supporting text in the Pauline midrash is introduced by a reiteration of Isaiah's authorship of oracles pertaining to eschatological events.[187] The technical term for such prophecy, προεῖπον ("foretell"), was also used in 1:2. The perfect tense "has foretold" selected by Paul in this introduction serves to make the citation directly relevant for the present situation.[188] In this instance, Paul is able to quote Isa 1:9 without alteration because it fits his purpose precisely and contains the crucial catchword "seed" that the midrash had developed in 9:7. The reiteration of the term σπέρμα ("seed") from the initial proof text of Gen 21:12 provides an inclusio that brings the midrash to an effective conclusion.[189] The point of the quotation in this new context is that the true Israel as the seed of Abraham will pass through judgment and be "left to us,"[190] implying participation through God's mercy in the faith community of Jews and Gentiles described in 9:24.[191] The implication in the context of the midrash is more reassuring than threatening,[192] because with the "quite peculiar exercise of grace on the part of the Lord,"[193] the true Israel will escape the fate of Sodom and Gomorrah, the archetypal biblical examples of irrevocable divine judgment.[194] The action in the Isaiah citation lies

---

Koch, *Schrift*, 149; and Seitz, "λόγον συντέμνων," 66–74.

181 Gerhard Delling, "συντελέω," *TDNT* 8 (1972) 62–64; BAGD (2000) 975.

182 BAGD (2000) 975: "put a limit to something . . . cut short, shorten, limit." In rhetoric, the expression λόγον συντέμνειν has the technical sense of bringing a speech to a rapid, concise conclusion, according to Aristotle *Rhet.* 3.6; other examples are listed in BAGD and Seitz, "λόγον συντέμνων," 67. Seitz (66–71) argues for the translation "enact, establish," which seems beyond the normal semantic range of the verb.

183 See Wilckens, 2:207, referring to 2 Kgs 20:9, καὶ εἶπεν Ησαιας Τοῦτο τὸ σημεῖον παρὰ κυρίου ὅτι ποιήσει κύριος τὸν λόγον, ὃν ἐλάλησεν ("And Isaiah said, 'This is the sign from the Lord, that the Lord will execute the word which he has spoken"); see also the LXX of Exod 35:1; Lev 8:36; Deut 12:28; 31:12; 32:46; Jdg 11:37; 21:11; 2 Sam 14:22; 2 Kgs 11:5; 2 Chr 23:4; Esth 5:5; Job 22:4; Jer 22:4f.; 51:17; 1 Macc 2:34; 2 Macc 7:24.

184 Kühl, 338, 467; Seitz, "λόγον συντέμνων," 60–73; Johnson, *Function*, 150.

185 Godet, 266.

186 Koch, *Schrift*, 149, understands Paul as wishing to avoid weakening the contrast between the large number of Israelites and the small number of the remnant. But the Isaianic expression ἐν τῇ οἰκουμένῃ ὅλῃ ("in the whole world") implies loca-

tion rather than scale, referring to the fulfillment of God's promise among the Gentiles as well as in Judah. Stanley, *Scripture*, 119, suggests another possibility—that Paul adapts the wording of Isa 28:22, but that still leaves open the question of Paul's motivation in making the change.

187 See Koch, *Schrift*, 327f.

188 See ibid., 318.

189 Stegner, "Midrash," 40; Siegert, *Argumentation*, 140; Hays, *Echoes*, 65–68.

190 For the "contemporized" implication of the personal pronoun ἡμῖν ("to us"), see Mesner, "Rhetoric," 491. Wilk, *Bedeutung des Jesajabuches*, 188–89, overlooks the reference to being "left *us* seed" in arguing that the purpose of this citation is that the remnant of Jewish converts guarantees the future salvation of the entire people of God.

191 Schlier, 305; Gaston, *Paul*, 97.

192 For the threatening construal, see Michel, 319; Hübner, *Gottes Ich und Israel*, 58.

193 Godet, 366; see also Brandenburger, "Paulinische Schriftauslegung," 31–33, and Aletti, "Argumentation," 51–52.

194 See BAGD 759, and Wilckens, 2:207; Dunn, 2:574, referring to Jer 23:14; Ezek 16:46, 49; Deut 32:32-35; *Jub.* 16.5-6, as well as NT parallels; also Wagner, *Heralds*, 111–16.

entirely within the initiative of God: "If the Lord of hosts had not left us seed. . . ."[195] With this Paul completes the answer to the question about whether the minimal response to the gospel on the part of Jews indicates that "God's word has fallen short" (9:6).[196] No, says Paul, because the "children of the promise" in the new faith community are showing in Dunn's words that the "'seed' can embrace all nations, Gentile as well as Jew."[197] In Paul's view, divine mercy remains steadfast and triumphant despite the temporary hardness of the human heart.

195 See Lübking, *Paulus*, 77f.

196 See Shum, *Paul's Use of Isaiah*, 212.

197 Dunn, 2:576; see also Tobin, *Paul's Rhetoric*, 339; Esler, *Conflict and Identity*, 280–81.

9

The Fourth Pericope

Diatribe on the Failure to Submit to Divine Righteousness, Which Is Caused by Misguided Zeal

30/ What shall we say, then? Gentiles who were not pursuing[a] righteousness obtained righteousness, but a righteousness that is through faith; 31/ but that Israel which was pursuing the law of righteousness did not attain a law[b]. 32/ Why so? Because it [is] not from faith, but as if from works.[c] They have stumbled over the stumbling stone. 33/ As it has been written,
"Behold, I am laying in Zion a stumbling stone and a rock of falling, and he[d] who has faith in it will not[e] be put to shame."

10:1/ Brothers, my heart's good pleasure and my request to God for them[f] [are] for salvation. 2/ For I bear them witness that they have zeal for God, but without acknowledgment. 3/ For being ignorant of the righteousness of God, and seeking to validate their own righteousness,[g] they did not submit to the righteousness of God. 4/ For Christ is the goal of the law as a means to righteousness for all those having faith.

a The definite article τήν is found before "righteousness" in P[46] G, probably a stylistic improvement.

b The expression νόμον δικαιοσύνης ("law of righteousness") is found in א[2] F K L P Ψ 69 88 104 323 326 330 365 424* 1175 1241 1243 1319 1505 1573 1735 1836 1874 1881 2344 2464[(acc. to Swanson)] 2495 *Maj* lat sy in place of the more likely reading νόμον ("law") alone, which is strongly supported by P[46vid] א* A B D G 6 81 424[c] 945 1506 1739 2464[(acc. to N-A)] *pc* b mon cop Ambst. The addition of "righteousness" appears to be a secondary, theological clarification. There is a highly unlikely omission of εἰς νόμον in 33 and a few other minuscules.

c In place of ἔργων ("works") in P[46vid] א* A B F G 6 424[c] 629 630 1739 1881 2200 *pc* ar b f g mon o vg sa bo Or[lat] Ambst Hier Pel Aug, the expression ἔργων νόμου ("works of law") is found in א[2] D K L P Ψ 33 69 81 88 104 181 256 263 323 326 330 365 424* 436 451 459 614 945 1175 1241 1243 1319 1505 1506 1573 1735 1836 1852 1874 1877 1912 1962 2127 2344 2464 2492 2495 *Maj Lect* d vg[ms] sy[p,h,pal]

goth arm eth geo slav Diodore[vid] Chr. The latter is less strongly attested (see Metzger, *Textual Commentary*, 462–63) and is easily explainable as a theological clarification conforming to Paul's use of "works of law" in Rom 3:20, 28, etc.

d The word πᾶς ("all, everyone") is provided by K L P Ψ 6 33 69 88 104 181 256 263 323 326 330 365 424 436 451 459 614 629 945 1175 1241 1243 1319 1505 1573 1735 1739 1836 1852 1874 1877 1912 1962 2127 2200 2344 2464 2492 2495 *Maj Lect* ar d[2] o vg sy[h] arm[ms] geo slav Did[dub] Chr Theodore Pel, too weakly attested to be original, and easily understandable as a theological clarification. The absence of "all" in this location is supported by א A B D F G 81 1506 1881 *pc* b d* f g mon sy[p,pal] sa bo arm[ms] goth eth Or[gr,lat] Cyr Ambst Aug.

e D F G have οὐ μὴ καταισχύνθη ("he is not shamed") in place of οὐ καταισχυνθήσεται ("he will not be shamed"), which appears to be an assimilation to the exact text of LXX Isa 28:16. The reading with οὐ καταισχυνθήσεται is overwhelmingly supported by all of the other texts.

f The reading αὐτῶν ("for them") is widely attested by P[46] א* A B D F G 6 256 365 1319* (1506) 1573 1739 1881 1912 1962 2127 *l* 249 *pc* d* f g mon sy[p,pal] sa bo goth Cyr Ambst Aug[5/9]. In place of "for them" the words τοῦ Ἰσραήλ ἐστιν ("for Israel is") appear in K L 69 81 104 181 323 326 330 424 436 451 459 614 (629 omits ἐστιν) 945 1175 1241 1243 (1319[c] omits ἐστιν) 1735 1836 1874 1877 2200 2464 2492 *Lect* (eth) geo[2] slav (Mcion[acc. to Tert]), while א[2] [K] P Ψ 33 88 263 1505 1852 2344 2495 ar b d[2] o vg arm geo[1] Or[lat] Chr Pel Aug[4/9] provide αὐτῶν ἐστιν ("for them is"). These latter variants appear to be later clarifications according to Metzger, *Textual Commentary*, 463.

g The term "righteousness" is omitted by A B D P 81 256 365 629 630 1319 1506 1573 1739 1852 1881 1908* 2110 2127 2200 *pc* ar vg cop Cl, but the evidence for its inclusion is considerably stronger in P[46] א F G K L Ψ 5 6 33 61 (69) 88 104 181 218 253 323 326 330 424 436 441 451 459 467 614 621 623 (635) 720 915 917 945 1175 1241 1243 1398 1505 1563 1678 1718 1735 1751 1838 1845 1874 1875 1877 1908[c] 1912 1942 1959 1962 2138 2197 2344 2464 2492 2495 2516 2523 2544 2718 *Maj* (b) d* Ir[lat]. It was omitted in the earlier Nestle[25] but included with brackets in Nestle-Aland[26/27]. The omission is probably an instance of scribal haplography.

Analysis

While J. P. Louw perceives the semantic links that join 9:30—10:4,[1] many current commentators identify 9:30-33 as an independent section concluding the argument of chap. 9,[2] while placing the opening verses of chap. 10 in the next pericope, which extends to 10:4, 13, or 21.[3] There is ambiguity in this decision, however, because it is widely admitted that 9:30-33 provides the "theme" discussed in chap. 10,[4] and the summary of 10:4 requires the references to "righteousness" and "law" in 9:30-31.[5] That the address "brothers" in 10:1 requires the inauguration of a new pericope[6] is belied by the frequent use of this term in the middle of other sections of Romans (1:13; 7:4; 8:12; 15:30). The insights of semantic discourse analysis can be confirmed by argumentative analysis to sustain the conclusion that 9:30—10:4 constitutes an independent pericope. As Mesner has shown, the formation of the enthymeme in 9:6-29 is shifted in 9:30 by the replacement of "word" by "righteousness" as the minor premise.[7] This draws the argument beginning in 9:30 closely to the climax of the argument in 10:4, which contains the seventh reduplication of δικαιοσύνη. This connects the pericope and the third proof as a whole to the thesis of 1:16-17.

The pericope of 9:30—10:4 opens with a rhetorical exchange that draws inferences from the midrashic discourse earlier in chap. 9 and also from the first proof (3:21—4:29). The two rhetorical questions of 9:30 and 32 are each answered by three succinct clauses, supported by the citation in 9:33, and explained in the subsequent verses down to the conclusion in 10:4. There is a well-developed antithetical parallelism in the description of Gentiles and Israel in vv. 30b-31.[8] The theme of "righteousness" is emphasized by the sevenfold reduplication of δικαιοσύνη, in which the second and third references in v. 30 constitute an *anadiplosis*, since the term is used to end and begin successive clauses.[9] Verse 31 contains a panalepsis, a rhetorical figure that in this case shifts the nominative and the genitive forms of the same term so as to lend special emphasis to the shifted component; in this case "law of righteousness" = righteousness through law, with law again repeated in the expression, "did not attain a law."[10] An emphasis on causality is conveyed by the fourfold repetition of γάρ ("for") in 9:2, 3, 4, and 5.[11] The scriptural proof of 9:33, a conflation of Isa 28:16 and 8:14, confirms Paul's contention about unbelieving Jews stumbling over the stone. Paul comments on the citation with the interjection of 10:1, expressing the desire that his fellow Jews should not fall over the stone. This is explained in 10:2-4 with the argument concerning zeal without acknowledgment.

Rhetorical Disposition

IV.	The *probatio*
9:1—11:36	The third proof: The triumph of divine righteousness in the gospel's mission to Israel and the Gentiles
9:30—10:4	4. Diatribe on the failure to submit to divine righteousness, which is caused by misguided zeal
9:30-31	a. The rhetorical exchange about righteousness in relation to Jews and Gentiles
9:30a	1) The question of general inference from the foregoing argument
9:30b-31	2) The answer to the rhetorical question
9:30b-c	a) The inference regarding the Gentiles

1 Louw, 2:103–4. Commentators holding 9:30—10:4 together as a single pericope include Dunn, 2:578–98; Byrne, 308–16; and Schreiner, 534–49. Commentators holding 9:30—10:3 together include Weiss, 436–43; Jülicher, 298–99; and Schmidt, 171–73.

2 Michel, 319-23; Käsemann, 277-79; Wilckens, 3:210-16; Schlier, 305-8; Siegert, *Argumentation*, 141. However, as Dunn, 2:579, observes, "The impression that vv 30-33 are transitional is probably in large part due to the modern chapter division."

3 Badenas, *Christ*, 243, observes that most current scholars have abandoned the idea that 10:1 "starts a new theme," citing only Kühl, 347, and Dahl, *Studies*, 143, as advancing this view.

4 Wilckens, 3:211; Käsemann, 277–78, refers to Weiss, "Beiträge," 239, and Müller, *Gottes Gerechtigkeit*, 37, in this assessment, placing the title of "the theme" over 9:30-33. See also Hübner, *Gottes Ich und Israel*, 60; Lübking, *Paulus*, 80.

5 See Wilckens, 3:222.

6 So Michel, 320.

7 Mesner, "Rhetoric," 501–4.

8 See the schematic analysis in Siegert, *Argumentation*, 141-42.

9 Bullinger, *Figures*, 255.

10 Hofius, *Paulusstudien*, 162, following a suggestion by Calvin.

11 See Gignac, *Romans 9-11*, 200.

Exegesis

■ **30** The rhetorical question that opens this pericope is the exact expression we have found in 4:1; 6:1; 7:7; 8:31; 9:14, 30. As in 8:31, Paul appears to use τί οὖν ἐροῦμεν ("What shall we say, then?") to invite his hearers to share the inference drawn from the preceding argument.[12] Rather than dealing with a false inference as in 9:14, where the same question is used, Paul states the true and consistent inference from the midrashic proof that a faithful remnant will be saved, expecting his hearers to assent. The word fields of "Jew/Gentile," "righteousness," "faith," and "law" that Paul employs in stating the inference provide a close correlation with both the propositio and the first proof of the letter in 1:16— 4:29.[13] The ironic antithesis between those Gentiles "not pursuing" (μὴ διώκοντα) righteousness, yet receiving it, and those Israelites "pursuing" (διώκων) righteousness, yet not achieving it, is enhanced by the association of διώκω ("chase, pursue") with τρέχω ("run"), which was used in 9:16 to describe Pharaoh's futile exertion.[14] If divine mercy is sovereign as 9:14-18 showed, and if God wishes to select a remnant to become "vessels of mercy" as 9:22-29 indicated, then the achievement of righteousness cannot result entirely from human effort. The choice of the word διώκω in this context also evokes associations with persecution and with zealously promoting a cause or pursuing a project,[15] thus preparing for the development of the theme of religious zeal in succeeding verses of this pericope. The entire argument deals with the "present situation of Israel" in failing "to recognize Christ as the goal of the law, in whom there is

12   For the comparison with 8:31, see Siegert, *Argumentation*, 141.

13   Siegert, *Argumentation*, 141, notes the correlation with 1:16-17.

14   See ibid.

15   Albrecht Oepke, "διώκω," *TDNT* 2 (1964) 229f., mentions Matt 10:23 and 23:34; John 5:16; 15:20; Acts 7:52; 9:4 as characteristic examples. Paul himself uses διώκω in Gal 1:13 to refer to his persecution of the early church. The connotation of zealously or vigorously following someone is found in LXX 4 Kgdms 5:21, Καὶ ἐδίωξε Γιεζὶ τοῦ Ναιμάν ("And Giezi pursued Naiman"); Xenophon *Mem.* 2.8.6, Χρὴ . . . τοὺς εὐγνώμενος διώκειν

righteousness for everyone who has faith."[16] The expression διώκειν δικαιοσύνην or δίκαιον ("pursue righteousness or right") is a distinctive expression for Hebrew piety, defined by an explicit relationship to the law;[17] for example, Sir 27:8 assures the faithful, Ἐὰν διώκῃς τὸ δίκαιον, καταλήμψῃ καὶ ἐνδύσῃ αὐτὸ ὡς ποδήρη δόξης ("If you pursue righteousness, you shall attain it and put it on as a glorious garment").

Paul could easily gain the assent of his hearers in claiming that "Gentiles" characteristically do not pursue righteousness in the same manner.[18] The present participial phrase τὸ μὴ διώκοντα has a progressive temporal sense that, when combined with the aorist verb κατέλαβεν ("attained"), requires a description of Gentiles with an imperfect tense, "those who were not pursuing"[19] righteousness under the law. Moreover, as Hübner shows, Rom 9:30-31 resonates with the wider context of Isa 51:1, Ἀκούσατέ μου, οἱ διώκοντες τὸ δίκαιον καὶ ζητοῦντες τὸν κύριον ("listen to me, those who pursue justice and seek the Lord"), which refers to divine righteousness drawing near to fill the promise of becoming a light to the Gentiles (Isa 51:4-5).[20] Now the promised fulfillment for Gentiles has occurred, through the preaching of the gospel. To "obtain righteousness"[21] in this context is to find "righteous status in God's sight,"[22] that is, to respond positively to the gospel of grace and find a place among the remnant whom God has selected.

The carefully developed antithetical parallelism between Gentiles and Jews is stretched by the inclusion of the phrase, "that is, righteousness through faith," which receives emphasis by virtue not only of its intrusion into the parallelism but also by the *anadiplosis* in the reduplication of δικαιοσύνη ("righteousness") as the beginning and end of successive clauses. The crucial importance of this phrase is confirmed by its being picked up for development in the explanation of the paradoxical failure of Israel to achieve its intended goal in 9:32.[23] The reference to "righteousness through faith" recalls both the *propositio* of the letter in 1:16-17 and decisive themes in the first proof (3:21-31; 4:1-25), which defined being set right as coming through faith in Christ rather than through human achievement. God honors the ungodly through evoking faith in the gospel, establishing a new community that belongs to the seed of Abraham.

■ **31** The ironic contrast is that Israel failed to attain the very "law of righteousness" that it so assiduously pursued. The word choice is surprising, as Räisänen points out, because one "would have expected Paul to write that Israel was striving for 'the righteousness of the law,' but did not attain 'righteousness.'"[24] The focus here is on law,[25] which Israel failed to achieve despite zealous striv-

---

("Try . . . to pursue generous masters"); Plato *Theaet.* 168, ἂν μὲν γὰρ οὕτω ποιῇς . . . σὲ μὲν διώξονται καὶ φιλήσουσιν ("For if you act in this manner . . . they will chase after you and love you"). The connotation of zealously promoting a cause or project is present in Thucydides *Hist.* 2.63.1: "And not to flee pains nor to pursue honors (τὰς τιμὰς διώκειν)"; B. P. Grenfell, A. S. Hunt, and D. G. Hogarth, eds., *Fayûm Towns and Their Papyri* (London: Egypt Exploration Society, 1900) 111, 20 (95–96 C.E.), "zealously pursue (διόξον) the irrigation of all the olive-yards"; see MM 166.

16 Tobin, *Paul's Rhetoric*, 341.

17 See Michel, 320; examples are Deut 16:20: "Justly pursue (διώξῃ) justice and you shall live"; Prov 15:9: "The ways of impious ones are an abomination to the Lord, but he loves those that pursue (διώκοντας) righteousness." The closest non-Jewish parallel lacks the verb διώκω: Isocrates *Pac.* 33.2 refers to "those who strive to persevere (καρτερεῖν) and abide in piety and righteousness."

18 Lietzmann, 94. The use of this technical expression mitigates the potential conflict with 2:14-16. To have the law "written on the heart" is not the same as consciously pursuing it; see Schlier, 306.

19 BDF §174f.; Cranfield, 2:507. Most English language commentaries carelessly translate this with "Gentiles who do (or did) not pursue righteousness have attained it," as found in Ziesler, 249, 252; Morris, 374; Dunn, 2:580.

20 Hübner, *Gottes Ich und Israel*, 63–65.

21 The choice of "obtain" for καταλαμβάνω seems more appropriate than "attain," which implies a measure of conscious striving.

22 Cranfield, 2:506.

23 See Siegert, *Argumentation*, 142.

24 Räisänen, *Law*, 53; as Dunn, 2:582, observes, many commentators assume that the emphasis here is on "righteousness" rather than "law," although the latter is emphatically repeated.

25 Kuss, 3:744, refutes the construal of νόμος as "norm" or "order," showing that the connotation of

ing.[26] The ironic use of the expression νόμος τῆς δικαιοσύνης ("law of righteousness") echoes that of the Wisdom of Solomon, where it describes the perversion of the law for political purposes.[27] Unjust Greco-Roman rulers are heard to conspire with the following words: καταδυναστεύσωμεν πένητα δίκαιον, μὴ φεισώμεθα χήρας μηδὲ πρεσβύτου ἐντραπῶμεν πολιὰς πολυχρονίους· ἔστω δὲ ἡμῶν ἡ ἰσχὺς νόμος τῆς δικαιοσύνης, τὸ γὰρ ἀσθενὲς ἄχρηστον ἐλέγχεται. ("Let us overpower the poor righteous man, let us not spare a widow, nor reverence the old grey hairs of the aged. Let our strength be a law of righteousness, for that which is weak proves useless"; Wis 2:10-11.) The expression "law of righteousness" appears to be employed in this passage to depict what a propagandist would understand to be the essence of Jewish piety, which the rulers planned to replace by brute strength. Although this expression was not used elsewhere in Romans, its use in this particular context means that what Israel failed to achieve was the righteousness it sought through obedience to the law.[28] Paul's use of this phrase to depict typical Jewish striving also has an autobiographical resonance, evoking Paul's own zealous pursuance of the law prior to his conversion, which ended up as the choice of the term διώκειν ("to pursue, persecute") suggests, in persecuting the early church (Gal 1:13, 23). There is a close parallel to such pursuance in Phil 3:5-6, where Paul is describing his former life: "as to the law a Pharisee, as to zeal a persecutor of the church, as to righteousness under the law blameless."[29] Paul's discussion of the law in Rom 7:7-25 indicates the way one should interpret νόμον οὐκ ἔφθασεν ("he did not attain a law") here.[30] It is not merely a problem of trusting in one's accomplishment of the good;[31] insofar as the law embodied the divine will to be accomplished by the faithful, any religious system that ended up in opposition to Christ failed to attain its intent. But as Dunn notes, it remains unclear in v. 31 precisely why the ironic failure occurred.[32] The irony is so outrageous, from the perspective of Jewish orthodoxy of the Pharisaic type, that it drives the argument forward to the underlying reason stated in the following verse.

■ **32** The statement of the outrageous irony in vv. 30-31 evokes the abruptly stated question, διὰ τί ("Why so?"), implying "on account of what?" rather than "for what end?"[33] In this instance, the diatribal use of the imaginary interlocutor responds to the difficulty in explaining[34] the extraordinary circumstance of pursuing the law but failing to achieve it. The reason is explained with the succinct theological antithesis "not through faith but as if from works," to which the verb "pursue" needs to be understood from the preceding verse.[35] The expression ὡς ἐξ ἔργων ("as if from works") implies an erroneous subjective assessment on the part of Israel to the effect that the law could really be fulfilled by human works.[36]

---

the Jewish "law" is crucial; see also Siegert, *Argumentation*, 142.

26 Aageson, "Typology," 62, argues that the wording of this verse reveals the setting of conflict between Jews and Gentiles over the place of the law; for a skeptical appraisal of this claim, see Mesner, "Rhetoric," 518.

27 See Dieter Georgi, *Weisheit Salomos,* in *Jüdische Schriften aus hellenistisch-römischer Zeit* (Gütersloh: Gerd Mohn, 1980) 3:408.

28 Hofius, *Paulusstudien,* 163; Westerholm, *Law,* 126–30.

29 The verb διώκειν also appears in Greco-Roman legal contexts in reference to prosecuting a case: "the one pursuing the case of the murderer" (ὁ διώκων τὴν δίκην τοῦ φόνου, Antiphon *Caed. Her.* 11.5; cf. Plato *Leg.* 956d8).

30 Gottfried Fitzer, "φθάνω κτλ.," *TDNT* 9 (1974) 90, discusses the sense of "attain to."

31 As argued by Michel, 321; Lübking, *Paulus,* 80, referring to 7:10 as describing the illusion of gaining "life" through self-reliant works.

32 Dunn, 2:581.

33 See Dunn, 2:582, and Godet, 368.

34 Although Schmeller does not discuss this passage, it fits his concept of using diatribe to explain a difficult theological concept (*Diatribe,* 435).

35 For a discussion of the alternative verbs to be supplied, see Zahn, 470–71, concluding with the choice of "pursue," which most current commentators accept. An exception is Wilckens, 2:212, who prefers "attain" for theological reasons to strengthen the emphasis on the reception of righteousness as a pure gift.

36 Kuss, 3:745; Wilckens, 2:212, and BAGD, 898, cite Radermacher, *Neutestamentliche Grammatik,* 26–27, to support the subjective construal of ὡς ("as if"). The appropriate parallel in the Pauline corpus for this use of ὡς to suggest an erroneous subjective assessment is 2 Thess 2:2 ("either by spirit or word or letter as if from us"), not 2 Cor 2:17 and 11:16, as suggested by Michel, 332, and Dunn, 2:583. See also Bring, *Bedeutung des Gesetzes,* 40–42.

The crucial term "works" cannot be omitted from Israel's erroneous assessment, as suggested by Sanders and Räisänen, reducing the scope of Paul's answer to the simple proposition that Israel's error was the refusal to accept faith in Christ.[37] But it is not appropriate to create an abusive construal of Israel's subjective error, to the effect that their obedience aimed at placing "God under an obligation to themselves," resulting in "imprisonment in one's own self-centredness . . ."[38] or "boasting in one's achievements."[39] Watson suggests that "law" and "works" in this context refer to "the Jewish way of life," which cannot be accepted by Gentiles,[40] and Dunn refers to "the requirements of the law which mark off Jew from Gentile," focusing on the divisive element of ethnocentrism.[41] However, this verse seeks to explain why Israel rejected the message about Christ rather than to discuss its attitude toward Gentiles. Believing erroneously that righteousness could only be reached through performing the works required by the law, they repudiated Christ as a Sabbath breaker and a companion of sinners. As Godet observed, if Israel had pursued righteousness as Abraham did, through faith (Rom 4:1-22), "they would have avoided stumbling at the Messianic righteousness."[42]

The statement of this point in 9:32b is introduced without any connecting particle, which conveys "a special solemnity"[43] to the claim that "they have stumbled over the stumbling stone." While the metaphor of a stumbling block was used in Greek sources,[44] there was a particularly well-developed tradition in the OT and Judaism of referring to divine punishment as stumbling.[45] If Israel sins, Deut 28:25 warns that "the Lord will cause you to stumble before your enemies (προσκόπτοντα ἐναντίον τῶν ἐχθρῶν σου)." Paul's unambiguous declaration resonates with somber biblical echoes of Israel's earlier missteps described in Exod 23:33; Isa 8:14; 29:21; and Ps 91:12.[46] Now the irony of Israel's situation is redoubled: "the stone of salvation becomes for them the stone of falling."[47] Committed to an erroneous perception that righteousness could only be gained "from works,"[48] the bulk of Israel refused to accept Christ. Whether the scandal was the gospel about Christ[49] or Christ himself[50] is difficult to determine. On argumentative grounds, the "stumbling stone" corresponds to "gospel" and "word of God" in the discourse starting in 9:6. Yet the offense did not consist of a "gospel" as such, which could refer to any proclamation, but rather to the gospel of Jesus as the christological stone. So the offense remains christological with either interpretation.[51] The reason for Paul's grief concerning

37 Räisänen, *Law*, 174–76.

38 Cranfield, 2:510.

39 Schlier, 307.

40 Watson, *Paul*, 165.

41 Dunn, 2:582; Kim, *Romans 9–11*, 130, follows this lead in identifying Israel's error as seeking "ethnic privileges."

42 Godet, 369.

43 Cranfield, 2:510.

44 The plural, τὰ προσκόμμα is found as early as Hippocrates *Flat.* 6.3 with the meaning "bruises." Speusippus, writing in the fourth century B.C.E., urges in *Frag.* 63e that the "disregarded argument" should not be passed by "like a certain stumbling-stone lying as an impediment to the progress of knowledge (ὥσπερ τι πρόσκομμα κείμενον εἰς ἐμποδισμὸν τῆς κατὰ τὴν ἐπιστήμην προόδου)."

45 Gustav Stählin, "προσκόπτο κτλ.," *TDNT* 6 (1968) 749–51.

46 See Müller, *Anstoß und Gericht*, 32–45; Shum, *Paul's Use of Isaiah*, 213–19.

47 Stählin, "προσκόπτο κτλ.," 755; also Cranfield, 2:511; Horst Balz, "πρόσομμα," *EDNT* 3 (1993) 173.

48 Paul W. Meyer, "Romans 10:4 and the 'End' of the Law," in J. L. Crenshaw and S. Sandmel, eds., *The Divine Helmsman: Studies on God's Control of Human Events, Presented to Lou H. Silberman* (New York: Ktav, 1980) 66, follows Charles Kingsley Barrett, "Rom 9:30–10:21: Fall and Responsibility of Israel," in De Lorenzi, ed., *Israelfrage*, 112, in identifying the stumbling block as the law itself.

49 Mesner, "Rhetoric," 521–22, follows Paul E. Dinter, "Paul and the Prophet Isaiah," *BTB* 13 (1983) 50, in interpreting the stumbling stone as the gospel rather than as Christ himself. Fitzmyer, 579, writes, "they stumbled over the gospel." See also Tobin, *Paul's Rhetoric*, 342.

50 Cranfield, 2:510–11; Moo, 628–30; Esler, *Conflict and Identity*, 282.

51 See Gustav Stählin's discussion of this christological "high point" in the development of the stumbling block concept in *Skandalon*, 188–92.

his fellow Israelites expressed in 9:2 now becomes explicit for the first time.[52]

■ **33** The citation formula καθὼς γέγραπται ("as it has been written")[53] gives no hint of the composite nature of the quotation Paul provides to sustain the contention that Israel has stumbled on the messianic stone. Since it is possible that Paul adapts the composite quotation from a pre-Pauline citation that appears also in 1 Peter, the following printout of the parallels provides the data to evaluate the issues.

Isaiah 28:16	1 Peter 2:6	Romans 9:33	Isaiah 8:14
ἰδοὺ ἐγὼ ἐμβάλλω εἰς τὰ θεμέλια Σιὼν λίθον πολυτελῆ ἐκλεκτὸν ἀκρογωνιαῖον ἔντιμον εἰς τὰ θεμέλια αὐτῆς καὶ ὁ πιστεύων ἐπ᾽ αὐτῷ οὐ μὴ καταισχυνθῇ	ἰδοὺ τίθημι ἐν Σιὼν ἀκρογωνιαῖον ἐκλεκτὸν ἔντιμον καὶ ὁ πιστεύων ἐπ᾽ αὐτῷ οὐ μὴ καταισχυνθῇ	ἰδοὺ τίθημι ἐν Σιὼν λίθον προσκόμματος καὶ πέτραν σκανδάλου, καὶ ὁ πιστεύων ἐπ᾽ αὐτῷ οὐ καταισχυνθήσεται	ἔσται σοι εἰς ἁγίασμα, καὶ οὐχ ὡς λίθου προσκόμματι συναντήσεσθε αὐτῷ οὐδὲ ὡς πέτρας πτώματι
("behold, I set for the foundation of Zion a costly stone, an elect cornerstone, a precious foundation, and he who believes in it/him would not be put to shame")	("behold I am laying in Zion a cornerstone elect, precious and he who believes in it/him would not be put to shame")	("behold I am laying in Zion a stone of stumbling and a rock of scandal/falling, and he who believes in it/him will not be put to shame")	("and he will be to you a sanctuary, and not as a stone of stumbling will you encounter him, or as a rock of falling")

The arguments for Paul's use of an early Christian version of Isa 28:16,[54] perhaps contained in an early Christian anthology of OT quotations,[55] are convincing as far as the opening and closing of the Pauline quotation are concerned. It is easy to observe that the first five words and the last seven words in Paul's citation almost exactly replicate the quotation in 1 Peter; compared with 1 Peter's precise citation of the final line from Isa 28:16, Paul alters the verb form and drops μή ("not"). The likelihood of a single, pre-Pauline source for the Isa 28:16 portion of Paul's quotation is indicated by the commonalities as compared with the LXX, while the possibility that 1 Peter may be dependent on Romans at this point is unlikely because it would have required both a disentangling of the conflation with Isa 8:14 and an augmenting of additional details from Isa 28:16 in wording that varies from the LXX.[56] A crucial observation is that 1 Peter does not incorporate the motif of the "stone of stumbling" from the second Isaiah text of 8:14. Conversely Paul does not use Ps 117:22, a crucial component

52   See Käsemann, 278.
53   For the Jewish background of the formula, see on 1:17.
54   The argument developed by Koch, "Beobachtungen," 178–84, is reiterated in *Schrift*, 69–71, 160–62.
55   The proposal of an early Christian anthology of quotations was developed by Rendell Harris in *Testimonies* (Cambridge: Cambridge University Press, 1916, 1920) 1:26ff. and elaborated by C. H. Dodd with regard to Rom 9:33 in *According to the Scriptures: The Sub-structure of New Testament Theology* (London: Nisbet, 1952) 35–36, 41–43. Affirmative discussions of the issue are available in Luz, *Geschichtsverständnis*, 95–99, and Ellis, *Paul's Use*, 89–91. The second edition of Otto Michel, *Paulus und seine Bibel* (Darmstadt: Wissenschaftliche Buchgesellschaft, 1972) 213–14, incorporates evidence from florilegia found at Qumran. For critical evaluations that render the hypothesis quite implausible, see Albert C. Sundberg, Jr., "On Testimonies," *NovT* 3 (1959) 268–81; J. P. Audet, "L'hypothèse des Testimonia," *RB* 70 (1963) 381–405; and Koch, *Schrift*, 247–55.

of the quotation in 1 Peter.[57] The text in 1 Peter is explicitly christological in glorifying the stone as an elect and precious cornerstone, whereas Romans presents the stone as a provocation to stumble and fall. So the fusion of the early Christian rendition of Isa 28:16 with Isa 8:14 is probably Pauline,[58] with his version of the latter text freely paraphrasing the LXX or derived from another Greek translation.[59]

Whatever the source, Paul's citation from Isa 8:14 is a more apt translation of the Hebrew text than the LXX provides,[60] eliminating the erroneous negative and using λίθος προσκόμματος ("stone of stumbling") for ולאבן נגף ("and a stone of offense") and πέτρας σκανδάλου ("rock of scandal") for ולצור מכשול ("and a rock of stumbling"). The unique Pauline fusion of the two Isaiah texts produces the christological ambivalence required for Paul's argument. The very Christ for whom Israel yearned became its potential nemesis. This holds true whether the stone corresponds to Christ or to the gospel. While the pre-Pauline form of the Isa 28:16 quotation probably understood the expression "he who believes ἐπ' αὐτῷ" ("in him") in a christological sense,[61] and the later Jewish Targum construed the stone as a

symbol of royal messianic fulfillment,[62] it remains possible that the "stone/rock" of scandal in the context of Rom 9 was intended to be the gospel about Christ rather than Christ himself.[63] The offense to a community committed to righteousness through the law remains the same whether the reference is to Christ or to the gospel about Christ. There is no doubt, however, that when this clause is again quoted in Rom 10:11, ἐπ' αὐτῷ means "in him/Christ."[64] The scandal is that the Messiah appeared as one who reversed the boundaries of honor and shame as defined by a competitive view of Israel's law.

The fused quotation from Isaiah sustains Paul's argument commencing in 9:6 that Jewish repudiation of the gospel does not indicate that God's word has failed. If it is God who has "laid" the messianic stone "in Zion,"[65] there is a "divine purpose"[66] in Israel's current stumbling that will become fully apparent in the revelation of the mystery of the inclusion of the Gentiles in 11:7-12, 25-32. Meanwhile the "twofold meaning of the stone" remains, in that the one "who is placed there for faith Himself becomes an 'obstacle to faith.'"[67] By fusing these two antithetical interpretations of the stone, Paul

---

56 See Dodd, *Scriptures*, 43; and Koch, "Beobachtungen," 180–81; idem, *Schrift*, 161–62.

57 See Dugandzig, *Ja Gottes*, 288.

58 See the compelling arguments by Koch, *Schrift*, 161f., 250; Wilk, *Bedeutung des Jesajabuches*, 23, 34; and Wagner, *Heralds*, 132–35. Stanley, *Scripture*, 121–25, opts for Paul's adaptation of an earlier Christian source, but he cites Jan de Waard, *A Comparative Study of the Old Testament Text in the Dead Sea Scrolls and in the New Testament* (Leiden: Brill, 1965) 69, that the church fathers always cite Isa 28:16 from the LXX rather than from Paul or 1 Peter, which makes any form of the testimonia hypothesis improbable. Others are skeptical that the precise origin of the fused text can be known: Dugandzig, *Ja Gottes*, 289; Hübner, *Gottes Ich und Israel*, 68.

59 Dunn, 2:584, shows that Paul's quotation from Isa 8:14 stands closer to Aquila's and Theodotion's formulation than to the LXX. See also Koch, *Schrift*, 58–60, 162; and Wilk, *Bedeutung des Jesajabuches*, 34.

60 See Koch, *Schrift*, 60.

61 The textual variant in the LXX may indicate that ἐπ' αὐτῷ was added prior to the Christian era, since the B version does not contain it. Joachim Jeremias argues for this construal of the text critical evidence in "λίθος, λίθινος," *TDNT* 4 (1967) 272.

See also Koch, "Beobachtungen," 179; idem, *Schrift*, 70.

62 Str-B 3:276 quotes the Targum for Isa 28:16 as explaining, "Behold, I have set in Zion a king, a mighty king, mighty and terrible. . . ." For other references to this statement, see Jeremias, "λίθος, λίθινος," 272.

63 See Mesner, "Rhetoric," 521–22; and Dinter, "Paul," 50. Wagner, *Heralds*, 157, and Wright, *Climax*, 244, argue that Paul intentionally leaves open whether the stone refers to God, as in the original Isaiah passage, or to Christ, or to the covenant plan of God.

64 See the compelling analysis by Badenas, *Christ*, 106, followed by Dunn, 2:585.

65 Georg Fohrer, "Σιών κτλ.," *TDNT* 7 (1971) 312–17, shows that Zion was expected to be the center of eschatological fulfillment as the place where the messiah would appear and subsequently rule.

66 Dunn, 2:584, consistent with Wilckens, 2:214. See also Stählin, *Skandalon*, 197, cited by Käsemann, 279; Hofius, *Paulusstudien*, 165–66.

67 Gustav Stählin, "σκάνδαλον κτλ.," *TDNT* 7 (1971) 352.

placed into the mouth of Isaiah the thought that the Apostle had expressed in more controversial style in Gal 5:11 and 1 Cor 1:23, referring to the "scandal of the cross" as perceived by Jewish religionists. The two expressions that Paul adapts from Isaiah, "stone of stumbling"[68] and "rock of scandal/falling,"[69] are virtually synonymous in meaning,[70] both referring to items intentionally placed in the path of victims to trap them or cause them to fall down.[71] In Hebrew materials where these terms are used far more prominently than in the non-Jewish world, they often function as metaphors for moral, economic, or political ruin.[72] In this instance ruin can be avoided only by placing one's faith in Christ.

In place of the aorist subjunctive of Isaiah ("he would not be put to shame"), Paul chooses the future form of the verb,[73] οὐ καταισχυνθήσεται ("he/she will not be put to shame"), thus pointing not only to the eschatological context of the last judgment[74] but also to any form of testing to be experienced in the future by the believers in Rome. By placing their lives on the line for the sake of the shameful gospel (see Rom 1:16), they demonstrate that their formerly shameful status has been overcome. Having been freed from a system of honor and shame dependent on conformity to the law and to the acceptance of inherited or earned status, those who rely

on the scandal of Christ crucified have a new basis of honor through sheer grace. Although the principalities and powers will probably continue to cast shame on the "stone of stumbling and the rock of scandal" on which they place their hopes, these believers will no longer be "put to shame," either in their present life or the life to come.

■ **10:1** The abrupt address of this verse, "Brothers," introduced with asyndeton, that is, without punctuation or conjunction, conveys the "emotion with which the apostle's heart is filled."[75] For the first time since 9:1-5 Paul resumes the personal tone, with the term "brothers" signaling his personal relationship with "Israel." Paul places the entire Roman audience, whether Jew or Greek, within a rubric of solidarity as his siblings while introducing the divisive issue of Israel's rejection of the gospel. The particle μέν appears here without the usual δέ in the succeeding clause, implying a restrictive sense that, as far Paul is concerned, nothing but the salvation of his kinsmen is wanted.[76] Although εὐδοκία is usually translated "desire,"[77] this is actually beyond the semantic range of this term, which ordinarily means "good plea sure."[78] The most apt translation for this term, which is used most frequently in Hellenistic Jewish sources,[79] is

---

68 This translation takes the expression λίθος προσκόμματος as a *nomen actionis*, meaning "the stone on which there is the stumbling, which leads to a fall," according to Stählin, "προσκόπτω κτλ.," 746.

69 See Stählin, "σκάνδαλον κτλ.," 341, which describes Isa 8:14 as "an obstacle on the path over which one falls."

70 See Stählin, *Skandalon*, 95ff., 261ff., cited by Käsemann, 279.

71 Stählin, "σκάνδαλον κτλ.," 339–41; idem, "προσκόπτω κτλ.," 745–47.

72 See Stählin, "σκάνδαλον κτλ.," 341, 353; idem, "προσκόπτω κτλ.," 754–55.

73 See Wilk, *Bedeutung des Jesajabuches,* 45. Stanley, *Scripture,* 125, argues again for Paul's citation of a pre-Christian source, whose exact wording he admits is impossible to ascertain. He assumes that there was no "contextual motive" for the future verb, either here or in 10:11, but he does not consider the relevance of overcoming shameful status through Christ.

74 See Käsemann, 279; Rudolf Bultmann, "αἰσχύνω

κτλ.," *TDNT* 1 (1964) 189: "Its primary reference is to the shame brought by the divine judgment."

75 Godet, 374; see also Fitzmyer, 582.

76 See Cranfield, 2:513.

77 See ibid.; BAGD 319; Fitzmyer, 582.

78 Sir 18:31 is sometimes cited in favor of this option, but "if you give your soul the desires that please you (ἐὰν χορηγήσῃς τῇ ψυχῇ σου εὐδοκίαν ἐπιθυμίας)" requires the noun ἐπιθυμία ("desire") to carry this sense, while εὐδοκία continues to carry its usual meaning of "good pleasure." Ps 144:16 is also cited, ἐμπιπλᾷς πᾶν ζῷον εὐδοκίας, which does not require the translation "you satisfy the desire of every living thing"; it can also be translated "you fill every living thing with pleasure." See Gottlob Schrenk, "εὐδοκέω, εὐδοκία," *TDNT* 2 (1964) 746; Robert Mahoney, "εὐδοκία," *EDNT* 2 (1991) 75.

79 A *TLG* search for εὐδοκία and εὐδοκίη, its early Ionic form, shows the dominance of Hellenistic Jewish usage. This word appears sixteen times in Sirach, eight times in the Psalms, and two other places in the LXX as well as nine times in the NT. The

offered by Godet, "my heart's good pleasure."[80] The use of this word is rhetorically effective in avoiding any appearance of hostility to his fellow Israelites, even though they have treated him as a renegade. The prospect of the triumphant gospel transforms the "great pain and unceasing pain in my heart" (9:2) to "my heart's good pleasure" in 10:1. The wording of this verse is a vivid example of Paul's missionary commitment to be "indebted" to Jews as well as Gentiles (Rom 1:14).

In addition to the changed condition of his heart, Paul alludes to his "prayer to God for them" as evidence of his passionate love for his fellow Jews, even when they reject the gospel. The word δέησις implies a specific petition[81] that Paul has made, and the peculiar, generalized wording[82] makes it clear that this was a specific aspect of his prayer life. On the basis of 1 Thess 2:13; 5:17; and Phil 1:4, it is clear that frequent prayer was a feature of Paul's religiosity,[83] and from this verse in Romans and other places we can see that these prayers related to his missionary goals.[84] His prayers were εἰς σωτηρίαν ("for salvation") not just for Gentiles but also for his fellow Jews, to whom he had already shown he

was indebted (Rom 1:14); this precise expression "for salvation" occurred in 1:16. Despite his earlier discussion of "vessels of wrath," Paul prays for his people's participation in the "eschatological salvation of the whole world."[85] While insisting on human responsibility, and thus on the possibility of remaining under wrath, Paul's prayer reveals his refusal "to reduce the sovereignty of the gracious God who has already decided and acted for all human beings" in Christ.[86]

■ **2** It is significant that Paul addresses himself to his unbelieving fellow Jews with the juridical expression "I bear them witness."[87] Since they are undoubtedly not present among the Roman believers addressed in this letter, Paul "seems to be alluding to his conduct of other days"[88] in which open confrontations had occurred. The verb μαρτυρέω ("bear witness") is used here as a public assertion[89] in which Paul gives testimony to his basic critique of a form of Jewish piety of his time. This verb is used in secular writings as well as the LXX to refer to witnessing in a law court or openly affirming a matter of

---

underlying Hebrew word means "pleasure, what is pleasing, or will," according to the lexicon of L. Koehler, W. Baumgartner, and J. J. Stamm, *The Hebrew and Aramaic Lexicon of the Old Testament* (trans. and ed. under the supervision of M. E. J. Richardson; Leiden: Brill, 1994–99) 3;1282. See also Schrenk, "εὐδοκέω, εὐδοκία," 742.

80 Godet, 374; the translation "loving well" suggested by Adolf von Harnack has the right impulse, but is unsatisfactory since εὐδοκία otherwise does not bear the connotation of love. See Harnack, "Über den Spruch 'Ehre sei Gott in der Höhe' und das Wort 'Eudokia,'" in *Studien zur Geschichte des Neuen Testaments und der Alten Kirche, I, Zur neutestamentlichen Textkritik* (AKG 19; Berlin: de Gruyter, 1931) 170.

81 Ulrich Schoenborn, "δέομαι, δέησις," *EDNT* 1 (1990) 287. Since δέησις can also refer to a secular request, the religious context is often made explicit, as in Josephus *C. Ap.* 2.197.1, "let there be a request to God (δέησις δ᾽ ἔστω πρὸς τὸν θεόν)." Similarly *Historia Alexandri Magni Rec.* φ 69.t refers to the "request (δέησις) of the Romans to the god Apollo."

82 There are no parallels in the NT or the LXX for Paul's expression δέησις πρὸς τὸν θεόν ("prayer to God").

83 See Harder, *Gebet,* 8–19; Stanislas Lyonnet, "Un aspect de la 'prière apostolique' d'après saint Paul," *Christus* 5 (1958) 223–24.

84 See Gebauer, *Gebet,* 203.

85 Karl Hermann Schelkle, "σωτηρία," *EDNT* 3 (1993) 327; see also Werner Foerster and Georg Fohrer, "σῴζω κτλ.," *TDNT* 7 (1971) 992. In the *T. Abr.* recension A 14.4-5 Abraham and the archangel Michael make a "request" (δέησιν) for a threatened soul that "was saved through your righteous prayer (σέσωται διὰ τῆς εὐχῆς σου τῆς δικαίας)," that is, granted access to paradise.

86 M. Eugene Boring, "The Language of Universal Salvation in Paul," *JBL* 105 (1986) 291; see also Brendan Byrne, "Universal Need of Salvation and Universal Salvation by Faith in the Letter to the Romans," *Pacifica* 8 (1995) 123–39.

87 The first person usage occurs in forensic orations, e.g., Demosthenes *Mid.* 22; Isaeus *Euph.* 12.7.

88 Godet, 375.

89 Johannes Beutler, "μαρτυρέω κτλ.," *EDNT* 2 (1991) 390; Otto Michel, "Zeuge und Zeugnis," in H. Baltensweiler and B. Reicke, eds., *Neues Testament und Geschichte: Historisches Geschehen und Deutung im Neuen Testament: Oscar Cullmann zum 70. Geburtstag* (Zurich: Theologischer Verlag; Tübingen: Mohr Siebeck, 1972) 15–31.

fact.[90] An example from everyday life is in a papyrus requesting hospitality πρὸς ἐπανελθόντα αὐτὸν μαρτυρῆσαί μοι ("so that after returning he may bear witness of it to me").[91]

"Zeal for God" is a technical expression for Jewish piety,[92] implying a "passionate, consuming" desire to do God's will and to defend God's honor "in face of the ungodly acts of men and nations."[93] Elijah was an archetype of this kind of zeal, complaining that "with zeal I have been zealous for the Lord almighty" (Ζηλῶν ἐζήλωκα τῷ κυρίῳ παντοκράτορι), while others have forsaken the covenant (1 Kgs 19:10, 14). This is characteristically linked with adherence to the law, as in 1 Macc 2:58: Ἐλίας ἐν τῷ ζηλῶσαι ζῆλον νόμου, ἀνελήφθη εἰς τὸν οὐρανόν ("Being zealous with zeal for the law, Elijah was taken up into heaven").[94] Paul's expression "zeal for God" is close to the wording found in T. Ash. 4:5, which describes the righteous as follows: ὅτι ἐν ζήλῳ κυρίου πορεύονται, ἀπεχόμενοι ὧν καὶ ὁ Θεὸς διὰ τῶν ἐντολῶν μισῶν ἀπαγορεύει, ἀπείργων τὸ κακὸν τοῦ ἀγαθοῦ ("because they live by zeal for the Lord, avoiding what God hates and has prohibited through his commandments, warding off evil by the good"). The great examples of zealous fervor in the Jewish tradition are Elijah, Phinehas, Simeon, Levi and Mattathias, with violence against violators explicitly sanctioned in a number of texts.[95] The prophetic leader of the Qumran community claims that "according to the measure of my closeness [to God], I was zealous against all evil-doers and men of deceit."[96] In Donaldson's words, "Zeal was more than just a fervent commitment to the Torah; it denoted a willingness to use violence against any—Jews, Gentiles, or the wicked in general— who were contravening, opposing, or subverting the Torah."[97] Paul describes his former life in Judaism in similar terms as "extremely zealous for the traditions of my fathers" (Gal 1:14) and "as to zeal, a persecutor of the church" (Phil 3:6).[98] Here Paul is dealing with a primary element both in his own previous piety and also in the experience of the Roman believers, whose experience had been so recently shaped by conflicts with Jewish zealots, resulting in the ban under Claudius in 49 C.E.

Although there are no linguistic parallels to this technical, religious usage of zeal outside of the Jewish tradition,[99] the critique of zeal that Paul develops in this passage has some distant echoes in the Greco-Roman world. For example, the sophist Polemo distinguishes between healthy eagerness (σπουδή) and unhealthy jealousy (ζῆλος) in describing the motivations of the great warriors in the Battle of Marathon: Cynegirus "probably [was spurred on] both by jealousy toward Callimachus and by ambition (ἴσως καὶ ζήλῳ τῷ πρὸς Καλλίμαρχον καὶ φιλοτιμίᾳ)" whereas "Callimachus [was] not spurred on by another nor desirous to emulate someone else but [was spurred on] by independent eagerness (Καλλίμαρχος δὲ οὐχ ὑπ᾽ ἄλλου παρωξυμμένος οὐδὲ πρὸς ἕτερον φιλοτιμούμενος ἀλλ᾽ αὐθαιρέτῳ σπουδῇ)."[100] This contrast between behavior motivated by competition for honor and that which stems from an inward state of being has some bearing on Paul's critique of zeal that lacks recognition of the poisonous residue of competition. In a similar vein, in Cor. 15.7.2

---

90 See Hermann Strathmann, "μάρτυς κτλ.," TDNT 4 (1967) 476–83.

91 MM 389, citing P.Oxy. 8. Nr. 1068.19, a papyrus of the third century C.E.

92 The argument in this section is adapted from Jewett, "The Basic Human Dilemma: Weakness or Zealous Violence (Romans 7:7-25 and 10:1-18)," ExAud 13 (1997) 96–109; See also Peace, Conversion, 42–43.

93 See Albrecht Stumpff, "ζῆλος κτλ.," TDNT 2 (1964) 878; Wiard Popkes, "ζῆλος κτλ.," EDNT 2 (1991) 100; Hengel, Judaism and Hellenism, 1:287–309. Significant parallels are found in 1 Macc 2:44f.; 1QS 4:4, 10, 17; 1QH 1:5; 2:15, 31; 4:23; 9:3; 14:14.

94 The expression "zeal for the law" or for divine "ordinances" is found in 1 Macc 2:26, 27, 50, 58;

2 Macc 4:2; 1QS 4:4 ("zeal for righteous precepts"); 9:23 ("zealous for the statute"); 1QH 14:14; see Hengel, Judaism and Hellenism, 1:305–14.

95 See Hengel, Zealots, 147–228.

96 1QH 14:14, cited by Hengel, Zealots, 179.

97 Donaldson, "Zealot and Convert," 673; see also Smiles, "Concept of 'Zeal,'" 285–92.

98 See Ellison, Mystery of Israel, 59, and especially Klaus Haacker, "Paulus und das Judentum," Judaica 33 (1977) 167.

99 Stumpff, "ζῆλος κτλ.," 877–78; Dunn, 2:586.

100 This translation of Polemo Decl. B32 is adapted from William W. Reader, with A. J. Chvala-Smith, The Severed Hand and the Upright Corpse: The Declamations of Marcus Antonius Polemo (TT 42; Atlanta: Scholars Press, 1996) 151.

Plutarch advocates "a zeal for virtue (ζῆλον ἀρετῆς) without envy (φθόνου) for one another." This competitive note is prominent in Paul's references to the zeal that characterized his behavior prior to his conversion. In Gal 1:14 he boasts of having "advanced in Judaism beyond many of my own age" in zeal for the law, a contention that is echoed in this pericope, that unbelieving Jews were seeking "to establish their own righteousness" (Rom 10:3).

Paul's expression "zeal for God, but without acknowledgment," picks up the distinction of 1:28 between "knowing and acknowledging" God, between "cognition and recognition."[101] Since the phrase κατ᾿ ἐπιγνῶσιν is attested here for the first time in Greek literature and is found thereafter only in patristic writers, it seems appropriate to define it in the context of Paul's argument. In light of the previous argument of Romans, it can be claimed that whereas Gentiles have knowledge of God but do not honor him (1:28), the Jews have zeal for God but do not know her (10:2). Whereas the Gentiles have cognizance of God's invisible attributes (1:20), the Jews lack cognizance of divine righteousness (10:3). The intensive aspect of ἐπίγνωσις ("acknowledgment") is reflected in Dunn's comment that the hostile attitude of unbelieving Jews was "not based on a recognition of how God's righteousness is bestowed."[102] Such zeal misapprehends God's will as revealed in Christ.[103] This wording places unbelieving Jews squarely in the context of Paul's earlier argument concerning the universal human tendency to suppress the truth, developed in 1:18-32. Dunn aptly refers to the practical consequence of such misunderstanding as "defending prerogative by killing, rather than fulfilling the law by loving one's neighbor—13:8."[104]

■ **3** Paul's explanation of Jewish unbelievers' lack of recognition begins with the expression "being ignorant of the righteousness of God." Although some have suggested that ἀγνοέω in this context has the connotation of "disregarding,"[105] its earlier use in Romans in the more neutral sense of "not knowing" (1:13; 2:4; 6:3; 7:1)[106] leads me to reject this option. It also seems unlikely, as Munck contends, that Paul is referring here to Jewish ignorance of Jesus' status during his earthly life.[107] In the context of a religion oriented to the righteousness of God, this is a "fatefully inadequate knowledge of God."[108] While a typical pagan can be criticized "because he knew not his Maker" (ὅτι ἠγνόησεν τὸν πλάσαντα αὐτόν, Wis 15:11), to make this charge against people raised in the Jewish tradition of Yahweh's righteousness implies "a delusion under which Israel unknowingly stands. . . ."[109] In the light of Paul's earlier argument that the "righteousness of God" is defined and revealed in revolutionary terms by the gospel (1:17; 3:1-26), this kind of ignorance involves a fundamental misperception of what God wills for the world, indeed, of who God is, as revealed in Christ.[110]

The explanation that unbelieving Jews were "seeking to validate their own righteousness" implies a competitive stance in which one's "own" accomplishment is being compared with others'. The only parallel to the expression ζητοῦντες στῆσαι ("seeking to validate") in Greek literature is the *Sch. Dem.* 18.220a5, in which an account was being ascertained or validated. The verb στῆσαι is used here with the nuance "make or consider valid,"[111] rather than "establish," which would falsely imply that Jewish believers had not already been granted a firm relationship within the covenant. As E. P. Sanders and George Howard have shown, conformity to the law

---

101 Johnson, 158.

102 Dunn, 2:586; see also Schlier, 310; Rudolf Bultmann, "γινώσκω κτλ.," *TDNT* 1 (1964) 703–4; Sullivan, "*ΕΠΙΓΝΩΣΙΣ*," 405–16; Wolfgang Hackenberg, "ἐπίγνωσις," *EDNT* 2 (1991) 25. Colenso, 226: unbelieving Jews "turned this grace of God into a ground for their own self-exaltation, instead of regarding it as a declaration of His Favour, indeed, first, but through them to all mankind."

103 See Badenas, *Christ*, 109, following Dupont, *Gnosis*, 6, who insists that the issue was conscious refusal to obey.

104 Dunn, 2:587.

105 See BAGD 11; Dunn, 2:587; Zahn, 474; Rudolf Bultmann, "ἀγνοέω κτλ.," *TDNT* 1 (1964) 116.

106 See Walter Schmithals, "ἀγνοέω κτλ.," *EDNT* 1 (1990) 20–21.

107 Munck, *Christ*, 83.

108 Käsemann, 280, citing Stuhlmacher, *Gerechtigkeit*, 93.

109 Stuhlmacher, 154.

110 Hofius, *Paulusstudien*, 164.

111 BAGD 382.

was viewed by Jewish teachers not as an "entrance requirement"[112] but as a confirmation of the Jewish community's "collective righteousness, to the exclusion of Gentiles."[113] Although the reference to $\tau\grave{\eta}\nu$ $\grave{\iota}\delta\acute{\iota}\alpha\nu$ $\delta\iota\kappa\alpha\iota\sigma\acute{\upsilon}\nu\eta\nu$ ("their own righteousness") has often been construed in an individualistic manner as the sin of "self-righteousness" and pride in one's religious accomplishments,[114] it is more likely a reference to the sense of ethnic or sectarian righteousness claimed by Jewish groups[115] as well as by various other groups in the Mediterranean world. In the case of first-century Judaism, a number of sectarian groups vied for the loyalty of the nation, each claiming to have the key to the righteousness of God. The zealot movement sought to achieve righteousness by violent warfare against Jewish collaborators and Romans.[116] The Pharisees taught that perfect obedience to the written and oral law would usher in the righteous messianic era; their efforts to reform society led to competition with other groups and to sectarian strife between the Shammai and Hillel groups.[117] The Essenes argued that adherence to their calendar and cultic regulations for the temple would satisfy the conditions of righteousness, opposing other Jewish groups engaged in a "corrupted way" and being led by a "spouter of lies," a "wicked priest," and "instruments of violence."[118] The Sadducees believed that maintaining the purity of the temple and following the laws of the Pentateuch would achieve righteousness, disputing particularly with the Pharisees over questions of purity.[119] In their sectarian competition with each other, and their sense of superiority over the corrupt Gentile world, each of these groups sought to "validate their own righteousness."[120]

The failure to "submit to the righteousness of God" as revealed in Christ is the corollary of attempting to confirm the superiority of one's group through adherence to the law. $\Upsilon\pi\sigma\tau\acute{\alpha}\sigma\sigma\omega$ in the middle voice used here implies voluntary submission or subordination of oneself to a superior,[121] but not the technical sense of "obedience."[122] For example, an orator during the Jewish–Roman war exhorted his faltering troops by asking "whether submission were a heritage from our fathers ($\H{\omega}\sigma\pi\epsilon\rho$ $\grave{\epsilon}\kappa$ $\pi\rho\sigma\gamma\acute{\sigma}\nu\omega\nu$ $\tau\grave{\sigma}$ $\acute{\upsilon}\pi\sigma\tau\acute{\alpha}\sigma\sigma\epsilon\sigma\vartheta\alpha\iota$ $\pi\alpha\rho\alpha\lambda\alpha\beta\acute{\sigma}\nu\tau\epsilon\varsigma$)."[123] The magical papyri employ this verb in spells such as the following: "Yes, Lord, for to you, the God in heaven, all things are subject" ($\pi\acute{\alpha}\nu\tau\alpha$ $\acute{\upsilon}\pi\sigma\tau\acute{\epsilon}\tau\alpha\kappa\tau\alpha\iota$, PGM II. Nr. 12.261). The Psalmist urges, "Submit yourself to the Lord and make supplications to him" ($\Upsilon\pi\sigma\tau\acute{\alpha}\gamma\eta\vartheta\iota$ $\tau\hat{\omega}$ $K\upsilon\rho\acute{\iota}\omega$, $\kappa\alpha\grave{\iota}$ $\grave{\iota}\kappa\acute{\epsilon}\tau\epsilon\upsilon\sigma\sigma\nu$ $\alpha\grave{\upsilon}\tau\acute{\sigma}\nu$, Ps 36:7), but Paul has something more specific in mind than bowing before deity. The designation of the "righteousness of God" as that to which submission should now be granted indicates that the revolutionary revelation of Christ crucified remains at the center of this thought. By overturning the system of honor and shame by which superiority in righteousness could be gained through various forms of adherence to the law, Christ countered the universal human tendency to validate the status of one's group. To submit to this gospel requires abandoning the superiority claims of one's group, no matter what these may entail. For the Jewish sectarians who took offense at the gospel, such submission would lead

---

112 Sanders, *Law*, 36–39.

113 George E. Howard, "Christ the End of the Law: The Meaning of Romans 10:4ff," *JBL* 88 (1969) 336.

114 Michel, 325; Moo, 634–36; Beker, *Paul*, 247.

115 See Ziesler, 256; Sanders, *Law*, 44–45; François Refoulé, "Romains, x,4: Encore une fois," *RB* 91 (1984) 339–40.

116 For an account of the hostility of the zealot movement toward other Jewish groups, see Hengel, *Zealots*, 227–28, 359–66; Donaldson, "Zealot and Convert," 672–80.

117 See Anthony J. Saldarini, "Pharisees," *ABD* 5 (1992) 294–303.

118 The sectarian nature of the Essene movement is described by John J. Collins in "Essenes," *ABD* 2 (1992) 621–22; see also Vermes's discussion of the polemical allusions to other groups and leaders in *Dead Sea Scrolls*, 30–35. For instance, 1QM 4:6 advises that the Sons of Light should write "righteousness of God" on their battle flags.

119 See Gary G. Porton, "Sadducees," *ABD* 5 (1992) 892–93.

120 See Longenecker, *Eschatology and the Covenant*, 262–65.

121 Roland Bergmeier, "$\acute{\upsilon}\pi\sigma\tau\acute{\alpha}\sigma\sigma\omega$," *EDNT* 3 (1993) 408; Gerhard Delling, "$\tau\acute{\alpha}\sigma\sigma\omega$ $\kappa\tau\lambda$.," *TDNT* 8 (1972) 42–43.

122 Godet, 376; Michel, 326. Spicq, however, in "$\acute{\upsilon}\pi\sigma\tau\acute{\alpha}\sigma\sigma\omega$," *TLNT* 3 (1994) 424, is correct in insisting on the primary sense of "to order oneself under" a leader.

123 Josephus *Bell.* 4.175.

to a new system of righteousness, in which honorable status was granted by grace alone rather than by conformity to the ethos and laws of the group.[124]

■ **4** In contrast to the widespread tendency to take this verse out of context as a radical declaration of law's cessation,[125] it is important to take the γάρ ("for") into account.[126] The words, "For Christ is the goal of the law," serve to explain the misunderstanding about the purpose of the law manifest in the phenomenon of competitive zeal, not to summarize Paul's doctrine of freedom from the law and justification by faith alone.[127] The translation of τέλος as "end," although semantically possible in the sense of reaching a conclusion, fulfillment, completion, perfection or climax,[128] should not be understood in this context as cessation or termination. As Badenas and others have shown, "the final notions of τέλος are never indicative of mere cessation, discontinuation, or suspended action. When finality is incurred, it is accompanied by a hint of innate fulfillment."[129] This fits the basic meaning of the word to designate a high point or turning point to be reached.[130] Thus the normal semantic range of τέλος is from high point, goal, or purpose to climax and completion in the sense of attainment. The examples ordinarily adduced in support of the translation "end" in the sense of cessation usually have this sense of reaching a goal or achieving a purpose. To speak of a person executed according to custom

as τέλος ἔχων ("have an end") means that the expected scenario has reached its fulfillment.[131] The expression εἰς τέλος ("until the end"), used 110 times in the LXX, carries the sense of reaching some intended completion.[132] Plutarch's famous epigram, δίκη μὲν οὖν νόμου τέλος ἐστί, νόμος δ᾽ ἄρχοντος ἔργον, ἄρχων δ᾽ εἰκὼν θεοῦ τοῦ πάντα κοσμοῦντος ("Now justice is the goal of law, but law is the work of the ruler, and the ruler is the image of God who orders everything"),[133] gives no hint that the law ceases to be in force when justice is achieved. When Josephus declares that God "is his own work and the beginning and end of all things (ὃς ἔργον ἐστὶν αὐτοῦ καὶ ἀρχὴ καὶ τέλος τῶν ἁπάντων),"[134] the idea of cessation derives from the idea of an originally intended goal for a finite creation. Similarly Plutarch *Amat.* 750f12 explains, "for the goal (τέλος) of desire is pleasure and enjoyment" and Sextus Empiricus *Math.* 11.179.5 summarizes the view of Epicurus, "For pleasure demonstrates by itself the goal (τέλος) of happiness."

Both on semantic and contextual grounds, therefore, it is preferable to translate τέλος in Rom 10:4 as "fulfillment" or "goal," which means that the "teleological perspective" remains primary in this verse.[135] This is consistent with the phrase εἰς δικαιοσύνην ("toward, as a means to righteousness"), which has a directional

124 For an interpretation of this "misdirected" zeal as a conflict between divine righteousness as revealed in Christ and attaining righteousness through the law, see Smiles, "Concept of 'Zeal,'" 295–96.

125 For example, Rudolf Bultmann, "Christ the End of the Law," in *Essays Philosophical and Theological* (London: SCM, 1955) 36–66; Peter Stuhlmacher, "Das Ende des Gesetzes: Über Ursprung und Ansatz der paulinischen Theologie," *ZThK* 67 (1970) 14–39; repr. in P. Stuhlmacher, *Versöhnung, Gesetz und Gerechtigkeit* (Göttingen: Vandenhoeck & Ruprecht, 1981) 166–91; Käsemann, 282–83; Wilckens, 2:221–24; Franz Mussner, "Christus, des Gesetzes Ende zur Gerechtigkeit für jeden der glaubt (Röm 10,4)," in M. Barth et al., eds., *Paulus–Apostat oder Apostel? Jüdische und christliche Antworten* (Regensburg: Pustet, 1977) 31–44; Hans Hübner, "τέλος," *EDNT* 3 (1993) 347–48.

126 See Kuss, 3:748; Meyer, "Romans 10:4," 65–66; Rhyne, *Faith*, 104; Dunn, 2:589–90; Badenas, *Christ*, 112.

127 For example, Stuhlmacher, 155, argues that 10:4 "is intended to be read from the perspective of (final) justification."

128 See Gerhard Delling, "τέλος κτλ.," *TDNT* 8 (1972) 49–50; Wilckens, 2:221–23.

129 Badenas, *Christ*, 44, cited from Du Plessis, *ΤΕΛΕΙΟΣ*, 41.

130 Badenas, *Christ*, 43; Thielman, *Law*, 207.

131 Josephus *Bell.* 7.155, cited by Delling, "τέλος," 50, as evidence of the meaning "cessation."

132 See Moo, 639, who cites this statistic in favor of temporal cessation.

133 Plutarch *Princ. iner.* 780e.

134 Josephus *Ant.* 8.280, cited by Delling, "τέλος," 50, as evidence of the meaning "cessation."

135 Badenas, *Christ*, 148; see also Rhyne, *Faith*, 146–49; Felix Flückiger, "Christus, des Gesetzes τέλος," *ThZ* 11 (1955) 153–57; Meyer, "Romans 10:4," 66; Lukas Kundert, "Christus als Inkorporation der Torah, τέλος γὰρ νόμου χριστός: Röm 10,4 vor dem Hintergrund einer erstaunlichen rabbinischen Argu-

sense[136] that explains how Christ is the goal of the law.[137] As George Howard shows, this phrase points toward the idea that the "very *aim* and *goal* [of the law] was the ultimate unification of the nations under the God of Abraham according to the promise."[138] In Christ righteousness can be gained without conforming to the mores of any culture. Christ thus reveals and accomplishes the original goal of the law, which had been subverted by competition for honor and by ascribing shame to outsiders. In Dunn's words, "The epoch of Israel's exclusive prerogative is ended; the role of the law as a badge of election is over and done."[139] But the scope of Paul's argument reaches far beyond Jewish zealotism. In Christ "righteousness" is granted not just to a particular in-group, not just to those whose zeal for the law is aggressively advanced, but simply to "all who believe" in the gospel. In view of the fact that this "all" has repeatedly been shown by Paul to transcend ethnic boundaries between Greeks and Jews and barbarians, nothing less than the pacification and unification of the entire world is entailed in this verse.

mentation," *ThZ* 55 (1999) 77–78; Bandstra, *Law and the Elements*, 101–6; Bring, *Bedeutung des Gesetzes*, 42–47; for an extensive list of advocates, see Moo, 639.

136 Badenas, *Christ*, 248 n. 237, observes that Zerwick and Grosvener, *Grammatical Analysis*, 2:482, translate εἰς in this verse as "to bring."

137 See Bring, *Bedeutung des Gesetzes*, 35–40, 62–66. In contrast, Gignac, *Romains 9–11*, 208–10, argues that τέλος has a paradoxical connotation expressing both continuity and discontinuity between Christ and the law. See also Alain Gignac, "Le Christ, τέλος de la Loi (Rom 10,4), une lecture en termes de continuité et de discontinuité, dans le cadre du paradigme paulinien de l'élection," *ScE* 46 (1994) 55–81. This is a sensitive assessment of the larger implication of Paul's argument, but there are no semantic indications in 10:4 of this alleged paradox. Oegema is more on target in *Israel und die Völker*, 217–19, 235–44, that Rom 10:4 deals with the proper understanding of the law, namely a christological view.

138 Howard, "Christ and the End of the Law," 336, italics in original.

139 Dunn, 2:598.

10

The Fifth Pericope

Pesher Confirming Righteousness by Faith

5/ For Moses writes concerning[a] the righteousness that comes from[b] law, that "the person[c] who does these[d] [commandments] shall live by them[e]." 6/ But "the righteousness by faith" says thus:
"Do not say in your heart,
'Who will ascend into heaven?'"
that is, to bring Christ down,
7/ or "Who will descend into the abyss?"
that is, to bring Christ up from the dead.

8/ But what does it[f] say? "Near to you is the word, in your mouth and in your heart," that is, the word of faith that we proclaim, 9/ because if you confess[g] "with your mouth,"[h] "Lord Jesus!"[i] and have faith "in your heart" that God raised him from the dead, you will be saved. 10/ For by heart, faith is evoked toward righteousness, but by mouth confession is evoked toward salvation. 11/ For the scripture says,[j]
all "who have faith in him will not be put to shame."
12/ For there is no distinction between Jews and also Greeks. The same one is Lord of all, [bestowing] riches upon all who call upon him. 13/ For, "every one who calls upon the name of the Lord will be saved."

a The position of ὅτι ("that, concerning") is disputed, with ℵ* (omits τοῦ) A (has πίστεως for τοῦ νόμου) D* (has τῆς ἐκ) 6 33* (omits γὰρ) 81 630 1506 1739 1881 *pc* sa bo placing it right after the verb "writes," thus apparently extending the quotation: γὰρ γράφει ὅτι τὴν δικαιωσύνην τὴν ἐκ τοῦ νόμου ὁ ποιήσας ἄνθρωπος ζήσεται ("for he writes that the person who does righteousness from the law shall live . . ."). P46 (ℵ2 B Ψ (omits τοῦ) D2 F G K L P 33c 69 88 104 181 323 326 330 365 424* 436 451 614 629 (945 *omits* τοῦ) 1175 1241 1243 1319 1505 1573 1735 1836 1874 1877 1962 2127 2464 2492 2495 (*l* 249 omits τοῦ) *Maj* ar d f g (syp) may be more likely original in having ὅτι later in the sentence, before the citation proper: γράφει τὴν δικαιοσύνην τὴν ἐκ τοῦ νόμου, ὅτι ὁ ποιήσας ἄνθρωπος ζήσεται ("he writes [concerning] the righteousness that is from the law, 'that the person who does it shall live . . .'"). Metzger, *Textual Commentary (1975)*, 524, makes a compelling case for the latter reading because of "early and diversi-

fied external support" and because the shifting of ὅτι to the position after "writes" is an understandable scribal improvement. This discussion has been deleted in Metzger, *Textual Commentary*, 463. See also Andreas Lindemann, "Die Gerechtigkeit aus dem Gesetz: Erwägungen zur Auslegung und zur Textgeschichte von Römer 10,5," *ZNW* 73 (1982) 236–97. Minuscules 121c 1827 1984 avoid the issue by omitting ὅτι altogether. An odd variant in A, τὴν ἐκ πίστεως ("which is from faith"), appears to accidentally replace ἐκ νόμου with ἐκ πίστεως, as in v. 6. For an obscure suggestion of an intentional alteration by the scribe of Alexandrinus, see Porter, "Rhetorical Scribe," 414.

b The absence of the article τοῦ ("of the") in ℵ*, 2 B Ψ 945 *l* 249 *al* is sufficiently strong to suggest an original reading, with other texts adding the article for clarity. Since the addition is more easily explained than the deletion, the absence of the article constitutes the more difficult and thus the more likely reading. Nestle-Aland[26/27] and *GNT*[3/4] are so uncertain about the omission of this article that it is placed in brackets.

c The omission of ἄνθρωπος ("person") in F G ar f g syp appears to be an intentional deletion for stylistic reasons, to eliminate the seemingly redundant subject.

d The absence of αὐτά ("these") in ℵ* A D 6 81 424c 630 1506 1739 *pc* is closely matched in weight of evidence by its presence in P46 ℵ2 B F G K L P Ψ 33c (33* 69 have ταῦτα) 88 104 181 323 326 330 365 424* 436 451 614 629 945 1175 1241 1243 1319 1505 1573 1735 1836 1874 1881 1877 1962 2127 2344 2464 2492 2495 *Lect* d* f g, but the former is more easily explained as a deletion since it would eliminate the syntactical flaw in a lack of an antecedent for "these [commandments]," since it is the law (νόμος) that is referred to in the singular earlier in the sentence. See Metzger, *Textual Commentary (1975)*, 525; and Lindemann, "Textgeschichte von Römer 10,5," 236–37. The inclusion of the plural form "these" is clearly the more difficult reading.

e The singular dative object in the prepositional phrase ἐν αὐτῇ ("in/by it") as found in ℵ* A B 33 81 630 1506 1739 1881 *l* 249 *pc* vg cop is probably secondary, if the decisions concerning the earlier variants in this verse are sound. The plural object in the phrase ἐν αὐτοῖς ("in them"), which appears in P46 ℵ2 D F G K L P Ψ 6 69 88 104 181 323 326 330 365 424 451 614 629 945 1175 1241 1243 1319 1505 1573 1735 1836 1874 1877 1962 2127 2344 2464 2492 2495 *Maj* it sy, is the more difficult reading because of the syntactical problem it causes with the singular antecedent earlier in the sentence, "the law."

f   The specification of the subject as ἡ γράφη ("the scripture") by D F G (F G place the subject before λέγει) 33 88 104 326 365 629 1319 1573 1735 2344 *l* 249 *al* (ar vg^cl) bo (Ambst) has an explanatory function and appears to be clearly secondary, a conclusion confirmed by the varying placement before and after the verb.

g   The insertion of τὸ ῥῆμα ("the word") by B 81 1735 (*l* 249) sa (Cl) appears to be a grammatical correction providing an object to the verb "confess" and using the term of the citation in 10:8. The text without "the word" is strongly supported by P^46 ℵ A D F G K L P Ψ 6 33 69 88 104 181 323 326 330 365 424 451 614 629 945 1175 1241 1243 1319 1505 1506 1573 1739 1836 1874 1877 1881 1962 2127

h   2344 2464 2492 2495 *Maj* lat sy bo Ir^lat.

The variant ὅτι κύριος Ἰησοῦς ("that Jesus [is] Lord") in B 81 1506 *l* 249 sa (Cl) CyrJ (add Χριστός) appears to be a secondary effort to render the formulation closer to the standard confessional form, according to Cranfield, 2:527.

i   The word Χριστόν ("Christ") is added by P^46 A t, probably out of "scribal piety," according to Metzger, *Textual Commentary (1975)*, 525. The absence of "Christ" is documented by ℵ B D F G K L P Ψ 6 33 69 81 88 104 181 323 326 330 365 424 436 451 614 629 630 945 1175 1241 1319 1505 1506 1573 1735 1739 1836 1874 1877 1881 1962 2127 2344 2464 2492 2495 *l* 249 *Maj* lat sy sa bo Or^lat.

j   The addition of ὅτι ("that") by 42 *pc* is a scribal effort to clarify where the citation begins.

Analysis

Given the skillful interweaving of Paul's argument, it is a good question whether a new pericope begins at v. 5, or indeed, at v. 14. It is clear that 10:5-13 provides a scriptural continuation of the theme of righteousness mentioned in 9:30f. and 10:3-4.[1] The pericope relates the theme of righteousness to the response of Jews and Gentiles to the gospel, dealing both with the christological grounding of the gospel and its openness to everyone. It therefore seems appropriate to accept Louw's semantic analysis, which holds 10:5-13 together in a single pericope.[2]

The form of this pericope is a fusion between a classical "speech-in-character"[3] and a Hebrew *pesher*,[4] with Lev 18:5 set in contrast with composite citations from five different texts: Deut 9:3; 30:11-14; Ps 106:26; Isa 26:16; and Joel 3:5. Two voices interact in this *pesher*, with Moses "writing" in the initial text from Leviticus, and a personified "righteousness by faith" "speaking" the next five citations.[5] Each citation is interpreted in the light of the "by faith" formula derived from Paul's earlier citation from Hab 2:4 in the thesis statement of Rom 1:16-17. Yet the "speech-in-character" conveys the impression that the recontextualizing of these citations derives not from Paul's authority or voice but from Scripture itself, as defined by Hab 2:4. Interpretive comments in line with the "righteousness by faith" perspective are made following the traditional formula in *pesharim*, τοῦτ᾽ ἔστιν ("that is"),[6] which occurs three times. This auda-

---

1   See Wilckens, 2:218, citing Luz, *Geschichtsverständnis*, 31, and Schmidt, 175, who joins 10:4 as the thesis of 10:5-13. Aageson, "Scripture," 274-75, argues that 10:5-13 does not elaborate or explain the dilemma of zeal in 10:2, but this requires further discussion below.

2   Louw, 2:104-6. Commentators viewing 10:4-13 as a single pericope include Dunn, 2:598-618; Byrne, 316-23; Schreiner, 550-63. Printed texts like Nestle-Aland's produce a noticeable gap between v. 4 and v. 5, but not a full paragraph break as at v. 14.

3   See Bultmann, *Stil*, 87-88; Stowers, *Rereading*, 309, refers to this as an example of "speech-in-character," defined by Theon *Prog.* 2.114.10-11 as "introducing into the discourse" a personified character who speaks "words appropriate both to the character

and the subject matter." See also Kim, *Romans 9–11*, 132.

4   Wilckens, 2:225, citing D. Windfuhr, "Der Apostel Paulus als Haggadist," *ZAW* 44 (1926) 328 (i.e., the Talmud at Berakot 6a and 58a) and Bonsirven, *Exégèse rabbinique*, 38; Hays, *Echoes*, 79. Fitzmyer, 588, refers to the "midrashic fashion" of the argument in this passage. See also T. Baarda, "Het einde van de wet is Christus: Rom 10:4-15 een Midrasj van Paulus over Deut. 30:11-14," *GThT* 88 (1988) 208-48.

5   Tobin, *Paul's Rhetoric*, 343.

6   A *pesher* cites a short section of a biblical text and then intersperses explanatory comments, often with "that is . . ." or "its interpretation is. . . ." See Devorah Dimant, "Pesharim, Qumran," *ABD* 5 (1992)

cious *pesher* shows that the gospel of Christ is indeed "the goal of the law," thus substantiating Rom 10:4.

The symmetrical parallelism in 10:6-10 between bringing "Christ down" and bringing him "up from the dead" has been identified by Johannes Weiss.[7] In vv. 6-8 there is an artful use of the *paronomasia* and *homoioteleuton* in the composite citation, augmented by the repetition of *epitrechon*[8] in Paul's interpretive insertions beginning with τοῦτ᾽ ἔστιν ("namely, that is") and ending with καταγαγεῖν ("bring down") and ἀναγαγεῖν ("bring up"). A construction with synthetic parallelism is visible in vv. 9-10, a section with similar verbal forms, *paronomasia* in the choice of prepositions and *homoioteleuton* at the ends of the first two and last two lines, forming an elaborate chiastic structure in 10:8-13 of "mouth . . . heart . . . mouth . . . heart . . . heart . . . mouth," with "you shall be saved" in 10:9 as the central member.[9]

The final paragraph contains Paul's theological argument concerning the inclusiveness of faith in Christ. Its style is typical of Pauline theological argumentation, but there is an effective use of homoioteleuton at the ends of the first and last lines in the repetition of the third person singular, future passive ending. The artful arrangement of the two citations in this paragraph brings to a close an effective series of five quotations in this pericope, conforming to the frequently expressed preference for Judaic numerical sequences in Romans.

Rhetorical Disposition

IV.	The *probatio*
9:1–11:36	The third proof: The triumph of divine righteousness in the gospel's mission to Israel and the Gentiles
10:5-13	5. *Pesher* confirming righteousness by faith
10:5-7	a. Righteousness through law contrasted with righteousness through faith
10:5	1) The citation from Lev 18:5 of the rule of Moses concerning righteousness from law
10:5a	a) The introduction of the citation
	(1) Designation of speaker: "Moses"
	(2) Identification of theme: "righteousness from the law"
10:5b	b) The citation of Lev 18:5 concerning obedience to the law
10:6-7	2) The citation of texts proving that righteousness through faith does not try to manipulate Christ
10:6a	a) The introduction of the citations
	(1) Designation of speaker: "righteousness"
	(2) Source of righteousness: "through faith"
10:6b	b) The first citation from Deut 8:17 and 9:4, concerning avoidance of presumptuous speaking
10:6c-7	c) The second citation from Deut 30:12f., concerning bringing in the messiah, with explanations
10:6c	(1) The citation about ascending into heaven
10:6d	(2) Explanation: "to bring Christ down"
10:7a	(3) The citation about descending into hell
10:7b	(4) Explanation: "to bring Christ up from the dead"
10:8-10	b. The needlessness of attempting to manipulate Christ when faith suffices
10:8	1) The third citation from Deut 30:14, concerning the word of faith, followed by explanations
10:8a	a) The introduction of the citation with a rhetorical question
10:8b-c	b) The citation about the closeness of the word
	(1) First catchword: "word"
	(2) Second catchword: "mouth"
	(3) Third catchword: "heart"
10:8d	c) Explanation of "word" as Paul's gospel
10:9-10	d) Explanation of "mouth" and "heart" in chiastic form
10:9a	(1) Confess Jesus with "mouth"
10:9b	(2) Have faithful "heart" in the resurrection
10:9c	(3) Salvation assured
10:10a	(4) Faith in "heart" leads to righteousness
10:10b	(5) Confession by "lip" leads to salvation
10:11-13	c. The inclusiveness of faith
10:11	1) The fourth citation from Isa 28:16, concerning faith being sustained
10:11a	a) The citation formula, stressing "no one"

248–49; Maurya P. Horgan, *Pesharim: Qumran Interpretations of Biblical Books* (CBQMS 8; Washington: Catholic Biblical Association of America, 1979) 229–47. Fitzmyer, 590, cites Qumran parallels to the formula "that is" in *CD* 1:13 ("that is, the time"); 7:15 ("that is, the tabernacles"); 10:16 ("that is, what he has said"); 16:15 ("that is, what is said"); 1QS 8:15 ("that is, the study of the law"); 1QpHab 12:3-4

7   ("Lebanon, that is the Council of the Community"); 4QFlor 1:11 ("that is, the seed of David").

  Weiss, "Beiträge," 172, 240.

8   *Epitrechon* is a parenthetical addition that does not make a complete sentence by itself, as in the case of "that is, to bring Christ down . . . " See Bullinger, *Figures*, 474.

9   See Jeremias, "Chiasmus," 149.

Exegesis

■ **5** This passage is a classic instance of Paul's interpretation of Scripture to make his point about the promise of the gospel. In 10:5 he cites "Moses" as the author of citation from Lev 18:5 and then goes on to interpret five subsequent texts in a typical rabbinic fashion.[10] Although the introductory formula γράφει ("he writes") differs from the subsequent formula λέγει ("he/it says") of 10:6, it is so frequently used by Paul and by other Jewish writers[11] that it provides no hint that this was intended to suggest that "the lawgiver Moses stands over against the personified righteousness of faith."[12] The formulation of v. 5 is not polemical,[13] with the present tense of the verb "he writes" indicating the ongoing validity of Moses' authority for those committed to "the righteousness that comes from the law." This is a respectful echo of the description of Jewish piety in 9:31 and of references like the "incense of the righteousness of the law" in *2 Bar.* 67.6 or "the righteousness of the law of

God" in *T. Dan* 6.11. The formulation "Moses said" appears for example in *CD* A 5:8. Only when the genre of Romans is erroneously identified as judicial can the wording of this verse be viewed as polemical in any sense.

The citation from the law is abbreviated in a neutral, nonpolemical manner as follows, showing that everyone doing the law is obligated to live within its strictures:

> Lev 18:5: ποιήσετε αὐτά, ἃ ποιήσας ἄνθρωπος
> ζήσεται ἐν αὐτοῖς ("you do them, which [if] a
> man does them, he shall live in them")
> Rom 10:5: ὁ ποιήσας αὐτὰ ἄνθρωπος ζήσεται ἐν
> αὐτοῖς ("the person who does these [command-
> ments] shall live by them")

There is nothing in the choice and wording of this citation or the manner in which it is presented to indicate that Paul wishes to cast doubt on the ability of his fellow Jews to live by the law,[14] to issue some stern warning,[15] or to denigrate Moses as the advocate of a mistaken doctrine of works righteousness.[16] That Paul intended this citation to be understood in the light of Gal 3:10 and Rom 3:23 as a condemnation of Jewish noncompliance with the law[17] seems far from the rhetorical force of this particular *pesher*. It is also impossible that Christ is intended to be viewed as the one "doing the law" in this verse,[18] because this "would make Jesus an exemplar of Israel's nationalist righteousness."[19]

---

10   See Dunn, 2:603; and Suggs, "Word," 289–312.

11   See Koch, *Schrift,* 28–32; the only times in Romans where Paul employs this formula are 10:5 and 19, which are comparable with "Moses writes" in Mark 12:19/Luke 20:28.

12   Käsemann, 284; see also Schlatter, 214; Stuhlmacher, 256; Tobin, *Paul's Rhetoric,* 343.

13   See particularly Hays, *Echoes,* 76; Wagner, *Heralds,* 160. Bring polemicizes in *Bedeutung des Gesetzes,* 49–55.

14   Str-B 3:278 observes that later rabbinic discussion of this verse from Leviticus concentrated on whether "live in it" referred to eternal life or life in the present; there was no discussion about whether "doing" the law was feasible.

15   Moo, 649: "Paul states this principle here as a warning."

16   Käsemann, 285; Günter Klein, "Sündenverständnis und theologia crucis bei Paulus," in C. Andresen

and G. Klein, eds., *Theologia Crucis – Signum Crucis: Festschrift für Erich Dinkler zum 70. Geburtstag* (Tübingen: Mohr Siebeck, 1972) 279.

17   See Zahn, 477; Wilckens, 2:224; Johannes Sijko Vos, "Die hermeneutische Antinomie bei Paulus (Galater 3.11-12; Römer 10.5-10)," *NTS* 38 (1992) 257–60; Vos, *Kunst der Argumentation,* 120–34. This line of argument is criticized by Koch, *Schrift,* 291–92, and Dunn, 2:601.

18   See Markus Barth, *The People of God* (JSNTSup 5; Sheffield: JSOT Press, 1983) 39; William S. Campbell, "Christ the End of the Law: Romans 10:4," in E. A. Livingstone, ed., *Studia Biblica 1978* (JSNTSup 3; Sheffield: JSOT Press, 1979) 3:39; Cranfield, 2:520–21; Stowers, *Rereading,* 308. For a critique of this view, see Lindemann, "Textgeschichte von Römer 10,5," 245.

19   Dunn, 2:601.

Instead, this verse lays down the premise required for the reinterpretation of Deut 30 in vv. 6-7. At this point, Paul is no longer concerned with the question of whether Jews in fact had complied with the law. He simply reiterates the traditional Jewish premise that Israel was obligated to live by the law. This sets the stage for the *pesher*, which reinterprets the subsequent texts in the light of the "by faith" principle. He thereby shows that the law itself points to faith in Christ and provides no foundation for justification by works.[20] This is one more instance of Paul's skill in becoming "one under the law" in order to win over "those under the law" (1 Cor 9:20).

■ **6** That "the righteousness by faith" is depicted as a character capable of speaking is a personification that carries through to the end of this pericope. There are biblical[21] as well as popular philosophical[22] parallels to such personification. This form of a "speech-in-character" in which a concept is made to speak as a person is typical for ancient rhetoric and would have readily been understood by the audience.[23] The message of this character called Righteousness by Faith is found in 10:6b, 7a and 8:b, while Paul's remarks in clarification are found in 10:6c, 7b and 8c.[24] The unique feature of Paul's characterization is the $\dot{\epsilon}\kappa$ $\pi\dot{\iota}\sigma\tau\epsilon\omega\varsigma$ ("by faith") formula that identifies the viewpoint of the fictitious speaker. Since this formula appeared first in the citation from Habakkuk in the thesis of 1:17 and is practically restricted to Romans (3:26, 30; 4:16; 5:1; 9:30, 32) and Galatians (2:16; 3:7, 8, 9, 11, 12, 22, 24; 5:5), where the

citation of Hab 2:4 is elaborated, the hearers of this letter would gain a clear sense of the scriptural definition of this character called Righteousness by Faith. In view of the speech-in-character that Paul employs here, the $\delta\dot{\epsilon}$ ("but") that opens verse 6 indicates a change of speaker from Moses to the personified Righteousness by Faith.[25] Rather than a "contrast to Moses,"[26] which would undermine the validity of the premise that the law must be performed and would counter the thesis of 9:6 that God's word has not failed,[27] the change of voice substantiates the antithesis between the misguided zeal of 10:2 and the intent of the Mosaic revelation. In order to show that righteousness through faith is consistent with Scripture, the voice of Righteousness by Faith cites passages from Deuteronomy that repudiate efforts to usher in the messiah through zealous campaigns. The rhetorical effect of the *pesher* is thus enhanced because it is not Paul's voice that reinterprets the OT passages but rather the scriptural personage called Righteousness by Faith.[28]

Despite the skepticism of earlier commentators,[29] there is a widespread acknowledgment today that the opening line of the composite citation from Deuteronomy comes verbatim from 8:17 and 9:4:[30]

Deut 8:17: $\mu\dot{\eta}$ $\epsilon\ddot{\iota}\pi\eta\varsigma$ $\dot{\epsilon}\nu$ $\tau\hat{\eta}$ $\kappa\alpha\rho\delta\dot{\iota}\alpha$ $\sigma o\nu$ ("do not say in your heart")
Deut 9:4: $\mu\dot{\eta}$ $\epsilon\ddot{\iota}\pi\eta\varsigma$ $\dot{\epsilon}\nu$ $\tau\hat{\eta}$ $\kappa\alpha\rho\delta\dot{\iota}\alpha$ $\sigma o\nu$ ("do not say in your heart")

20 See Wagner, *Heralds*, 163–64. Lindemann, "Textgeschichte von Römer 10,5," 240–45, argues that the citation from Moses shows that both justification by works and justification by faith are included in Israel's law. His conclusion (246) is more in line with my interpretation, "daß Gerechtigkeit, die Gott entspricht, für Juden wie für Heiden nicht anders zu erlangen ist als durch den Glauben an Christus."
21 Moo, 650, cites Prov 8:21ff. and Isa 55:10-11. A personification of righteousness is evident in Ps 85:10-13 ("righteousness and peace have kissed each other . . . righteousness has looked down from heaven . . . righteousness shall go before him") and Isa 45:8 ("let the clouds rain righteousness").
22 See n. 3 above.
23 Tobin, *Paul's Rhetoric*, 343, cites as examples Hermogenes *Prog.* 9.4–6; *Rhet. Her.* 4.66; Cicero *Inv.* 99–100; Quintilian *Inst.* 9.2.31.
24 See Tobin, *Paul's Rhetoric*, 345.
25 Stowers, *Rereading*, 309, argues that $\delta\dot{\epsilon}$ in this context is "connective, not adversative."
26 Dunn, 2:602; also Munck, *Christ*, 84; Wilckens, 2:224; Cranfield, 2:522; Koch, *Schrift*, 291; Hans-Joachim Eckstein, "'Nahe ist dir das Wort': Exegetische Erwägungen zu Röm 10,8," *ZNW* 79 (1988) 207–8.
27 Badenas, *Christ*, 123.
28 In Richard Hays's memorable formulation in *Echoes*, 82, these rhetorical devices are the means "whereby a historically outrageous reading gains poetic plausibility."
29 See the survey by Suggs, "Word," 300–301.
30 See Dunn, 2:802; Michel, 328; Moo, 651.

Rom 10:6: μὴ εἴπῃς ἐν τῇ καρδίᾳ σου ("do not say in your heart")

Recent scholarship points to the significance of the content of Deuteronomy's warning against thinking that the conquest of the promised land was due to "my righteousness" (Deut 9:4).[31] "Not for your righteousness," the passage goes on, "nor for the holiness of your heart that you go in to inherit their land . . ." (Deut 9:5). Given the charge in 10:3 that zealous Jews were seeking to validate their own righteousness, the resonance of this citation would have been unmistakable for those acquainted with Deuteronomy. Scripture itself stands in opposition to the campaigns to validate Israel's righteousness that were leading to the rejection of Jesus as Messiah. As a zealous Jew prior to his conversion, Paul had participated in such rejection by opposing the Christian movement because it seemed to undermine conformity to the law that would usher in the messianic age. In his view at that time, Jesus was a false messiah because he failed to conform to the law. But the discovery made in Paul's conversion was that such obedience to the law had a self-serving aim, to establish his own righteousness and the righteousness of his party within Judaism (10:3; cf. Gal 1:13-14; Phil 3:4-6). The *pesher* in this pericope provides scriptural support for this discovery.

The selection of Deut 30:12-14 reflects the importance this passage had in contemporary Judaism; it is cited in Bar 3:29-30; Philo *Post.* 84–85; and the *Tg. Neof.* on Deut 30:11-14.[32] In contrast to these parallels, which retain the Deuteronomic context of the commandment that is close and accessible, the citation is recontextualized for Paul's purpose by omitting the introduction in 30:11 concerning the commandment that is not too hard to perform. All of the other allusions to performing the law in this passage are also removed,[33] yet the new context of the Mosaic word about living in the law (Rom 10:5) is retained. This opens the door to reinterpreting the citation from Deuteronomy as an expression of the personified Righteousness by Faith.[34] The intent of this particular series of verses in Deuteronomy 30 seems at first glance to be so completely contravened[35] by Paul's use that scholars have suggested that this was merely a paraphrase of a familiar passage[36] or that vv. 6b-8 are an interpolation.[37] But the evidence of citation is unmistakable, and at a deeper level, Paul's critique of self-serving perversions of the message of Deuteronomy in the religiosity of his time is consistent with that book as a whole.[38] The first citation is as follows:

Deut 30:12b: Τίς ἀναβήσεται ἡμῖν εἰς τὸν οὐρανόν . . . ("Who will ascend for us into heaven . . . ?")

Rom 10:6c: Τίς ἀναβήσεται εἰς τὸν οὐρανόν ("Who will ascend into heaven?")

Paul's deletion of the word "for us" eliminates an ambiguous detail and thus avoids any question about who "us" might mean; Paul intends this passage to speak about "them," the zealous Jews who are rejecting the gospel on the basis of motives that are clarified by Deuteronomy.

In the style of Jewish *pesharim*, the character called Righteousness by Faith comments on each phrase of the Deuteronomic citation, beginning with the traditional formula τοῦτ᾽ ἔστιν ("that is").[39] The reference to ascending to heaven "to bring Christ down" is neither a "fanciful" allusion to "looking high and low for Christ,"[40] nor a warning against spiritual journeys to master heaven's secrets[41] or to gain access even to the inaccessible Wisdom revealed in Christ.[42] It is instead a historically apt depiction of the goals of some of the Jewish parties in Paul's time.[43] They sought to hasten the coming of the divinely appointed Χριστός (= "anointed one,

---

31 Moo, 651; see also Hays, *Echoes*, 78–79.
32 See Dunn, 2:603–5.
33 See Koch, *Schrift*, 129–32, 153.
34 See ibid., 130–31; Hays, *Echoes*, 79.
35 See Schmidt, 176; Dodd, 166.
36 See Sanday and Headlam, 286–87; Zahn, 477–78; Godet, 378–79.
37 O'Neill, 165.
38 Jan Heller, "Himmel- und Höllenfahrt nach Römer

10,6-7," *EvTh* 32 (1972) 483, offers a parallel argument that Deuteronomy rejects extraordinary feats of human spirituality.
39 See n. 6 above and also the discussion on 9:8 above.
40 This is advocated by Hayes, *Echoes*, 79.
41 Heller, "Römer 10,6-7," 478–79.
42 Suggs, "Word," 311.
43 Heller, "Römer 10, 6-7," 484–85, makes a similar case, using evidence from the rabbinic tradition.

king") by religious programs associated with the law.[44] This interpretation is sustained by the use of "Christ" rather than "Jesus Christ" in vv. 6 and 7. Among modern commentators, Barrett has the clearest grasp of this background: "the Messiah has appeared, and it is therefore impossible to hasten his coming (as some devout Jews thought to do) by perfect obedience to the law and penitence for its transgressions."[45] For example, Rabbi Levi taught that "[i]f Israel kept the Sabbath properly even for a single day, the son of David would come."[46] Since observing the Sabbath was regarded as the fulfillment of the entire law, Rabbi Simeon ben Johai taught, "If the Israelites only celebrated two Sabbaths according to the Scriptures, they would immediately be saved."[47] Other rabbis taught that penitence and almsgiving would hasten the coming of the Christ.[48] Some of the revolutionary movements within the Judaism of the first century invited followers to enforce the law through zealous violence in support of Christ figures who would function as kings.[49] The Essenes in Qumran anticipated that a priestly and a political messiah would be ushered in by a holy war when God was satisfied with the preparation of the new priestly community.[50]

By the skillful combination of Lev 18:5; Deut 8:17; 9:4; and 30:12, the character called Righteousness by Faith shows that these zealous programs to usher in the messianic age through obedience to this or that law were repudiated by Scripture itself. These programs produced a lethal mixture of religion and politics under the self-serving goal of validating the righteousness of Israel and achieving its status as the ruler of the world, thus violating the Deuteronomic strictures against assuming that divine actions could be manipulated by the righteousness and holiness of the nation.

■ 7 The next portion of the personified Righteousness by Faith's citation departs from the LXX of Deut 30:13, although it is possible that it mirrors some version of Deuteronomy reflected in the Targums.[51] The artful parallelism of this citation echoes the familiar wording of LXX Ps 106:26. Here are the three texts:

Deut 30:13: Τίς διαπεράσει ἡμῖν εἰς τὸ πέραν τῆς θαλάσσης καὶ λήμψεται ἡμῖν αὐτήν ("Who will cross over to the other side of the sea for us and get it for us?")

Ps 106:26: ἀναβαίνουσιν ἕως τῶν οὐρανῶν καὶ καταβαίνουσιν ἕως τῶν ἀβύσσων ("they ascend to the heavens and descend into the abyss")

Rom 10:7: Τίς καταβήσεται εἰς τὴν ἄβυσσον; ("Who will descend into the abyss?")

From a rhetorical point of view, the version of this text cited by the imaginary character called Righteousness by Faith is more coherent and succinct than Deuteronomy, with a clear vertical contrast between the heights and the depths in place of its muddled antithesis between heaven and the other side of the sea. The extraneous references to "us" are removed, as in the preceding verse, so as to relate the text more clearly to the legalistic motivations of the Jewish opponents of the gospel. The word "abyss" in Ps 106:26 is a translation of the Hebrew word

---

The argument in this section is adapted from Jewett, "The Basic Human Dilemma: Weakness or Zealous Violence (Romans 7:7-25 and 10:1-18)," *ExAud* 13 (1997) 96–109.

44 See Heller, "Römer 10,6-7," 484–85.
45 Barrett, 199.
46 Midrash *Exod. Rab.* 25.12.
47 Reported by Rabbi Johanan in *b. Šabb.* 118b. For other similar statements by later rabbis, see Str-B 1:600.
48 Str-B 1:600. For example, Midrash *Exod. Rab.* 25.12 reports that Rabbi Johanan taught that Yahweh promised: "Though I have set a definite term for the millennium which will come at the appointed time whether Israel returns to me in penitence or not, still if they repent even for one day, I will bring it before its appointed time."

49 Richard A. Horsley, "Messianic Movements in Judaism," *ABD* 4 (1992) 792–95, refers to the revolutionaries, Judas, Simon, and Athronges, who were acclaimed to be messiahs after the death of Herod in 4 B.C.E. as well as Simon bar Giora, who claimed kingship during the Jewish–Roman war; see also Richard A. Horsley and John S. Hanson, *Bandits, Prophets, and Messiahs: Popular Movements in the Time of Jesus* (Minneapolis/Chicago/New York: Winston, 1985) 88–134. See also Hengel, *Zealots*, 290–302.
50 See Martinus de Jonge, "Messiah," *ABD* 4 (1992) 783.
51 Stanislas Lyonnet, "Saint Paul et l'exégèse juive de son temps: A propos de Romains 10,6-8," *Études*, 502–5, argues that both the *Fragmentary Targum* and *Targum Neofiti* have the wording "who would descend into the depths of the great sea and bring

tĕhôm, meaning "flood, deep, abyss."[52] The choice of this term retains the resonance of the Deuteronomy text's reference to the sea while suggesting an allusion to Sheol, the underground prison of the dead in Jewish apocalyptic literature and the NT.[53]

The comment that the character Righteousness by Faith introduces with the *pesher* formula "that is"—"to bring Christ up from the dead"—has led to expositions about the doctrine of Christ's resurrection from the dead[54] or the later doctrine of Christ's descent into hell.[55] Others argue that reaching heaven or the abyss is simply a metaphor for what is impossible for humans in this life.[56] There is a parallel in the magical papyri to this contrast between bringing up and down: "Come to me, O Lord, the one who once draws up the light ($\tau[\grave{o}]\ \varphi\hat{\omega}\varsigma\ \dot{\alpha}\nu\dot{\alpha}[\gamma]\omega\nu$), once brings down the darkness ($\tau\grave{o}\ \sigma\kappa\acute{o}\tau o\varsigma\ \kappa\alpha\tau\acute{\alpha}\gamma\omega\nu$), by your own power" (*PGM* III. 564).[57] In necromancy, the shades are drawn up from the dead as described by Lucian of Samosata *Demon.* 25, "and he said he was a magician and could bring up for him ($\alpha\dot{\upsilon}\tau\hat{\omega}\ \dot{\alpha}\nu\alpha\gamma\alpha\gamma\epsilon\hat{\iota}\nu$) a ghost of the boy."[58] The suggestion has even been made that Paul is polemicizing here against Christian participation in the mystery religions.[59] But to follow these parallels would be to lose track of the flow of Paul's argument in chaps. 7, 9, and 10 about the problem with religious zealotism and legalism. The appropriate point of comparison to bringing the messiah up from the abyss needs to be sought in the messianic expectations being held by the Jewish community that had not accepted "the righteousness that comes from faith" in Jesus as the Christ. There was a widespread expectation that Elijah,[60] Enoch, and other

deceased figures of Israel's history[61] would return from the dead at the inception of the messianic age. Elijah in particular was thought to have extensive experience and knowledge of Hades and its inhabitants.[62] This raises the possibility that Paul had in mind sectarian efforts to hasten the return of these figures in order to ensure the favorable arrival of the Messiah. For the believers in Rome, however, these allusions would have had a transparent reference in their own experience. In their view, the questions that preoccupied some branches of contemporary Judaism, about bringing Christ down from heaven or up from the abyss, were already answered by the life, death, and resurrection of Jesus.

■ **8** Paul finds the Christian answer to the questions of Deut 30:12-13 in 30:14, introduced by the formula, "but what does it say?" The antecedent is clearly the personified "righteousness that comes from faith" (Rom 10:6),[63] while the adversative "but" makes clear "what the righteousness based on faith *does* say, in contrast to what it warns us not to say."[64] The reversal of word order in the virtually verbatim citation from Deut 30:14 places $\dot{\epsilon}\gamma\gamma\acute{\upsilon}\varsigma$ $\sigma o\upsilon$ ("near to you") at the beginning of the phrase, at the point of emphasis. This also necessitated the deletion of $\sigma\varphi\acute{o}\delta\rho\alpha$ ("very") to modify the adjective "near." This insistence on proximity means that there was no need for strenuous religious and political activity designed to usher in the messianic age, because the announcement of its dawning is already present in the gospel message.[65] By deriving this assurance from Deuteronomy itself, Paul's character Righteousness by Faith explains the consistency between the Christian proclamation and the original intent of the law.[66] In

---

up the law for us. . . ." Given the difficulty in ascertaining whether this textual tradition was available in the first century, this hypothesis remains possible but not certain.

52 See Otto Böcher, "$\ddot{\alpha}\beta\upsilon\sigma\sigma o\varsigma$," *EDNT* 1 (1990) 4.

53 Böcher, "$\ddot{\alpha}\beta\upsilon\sigma\sigma o\varsigma$," 4, refers to Luke 8:31; Rev 9:1; 21:1, where the abyss is "a prison for the powers opposed to God." See also Hoffmann, *Toten*, 176–80.

54 Cranfield, 2:525; Fitzmyer, 591.

55 See Michel, 328; Käsemann, 288; Dunn, 2:606.

56 Str-B 3:281; Zeller, 186; Suggs, "Word," 310–11, referring to the "inaccessibility of Wisdom."

57 Cited also by Betz, *Greek Magical Papyri*, 33.

58 See also Lucian of Samosata *Dial. mort.* 28.3.14 (§429); 11.4.11 (§224).

59 Heller, "Römer 10,6-7," 485.

60 See Jerome T. Walsh, "Elijah," *ABD* 2 (1992) 465.

61 See *4 Ezra* 6.26.

62 See Orval S. Wintermute, "Elijah, Apocalypse of," *ABD* 2 (1992) 466; M. E. Stone and J. Strugnell, *The Books of Elijah: Parts 1–2* (Missoula: Scholars Press, 1979) 14–24.

63 Cranfield, 2:525; Hays, *Echoes*, 81.

64 Moo, 656.

65 Eckstein, "'Nahe ist dir das Wort,'" 218.

66 As Johnson, *Function*, 158, shows, this stress on the law's affirmation of the "universal availability of the gospel" explains why Paul chose not to cite the final clause of Deut 30:14, "and in your hands to do it (i.e., the law)."

Hays's words, "The word that was near to Israel in the law is identical with the word that is now near in the Christian kerygma."[67] That this word is in "your mouth" and "your heart" means that the message of Deuteronomy that was treasured by Jewish adherents of the law, proclaimed by them and held with passionate intensity in their innermost being, points away from messianic manipulation and toward Jesus of Nazareth as the embodiment of divine righteousness.

Paul drives home the point by the final explanatory "that is" formula in this *pesher* type of commentary. Picking up the key phrase from Deut 30:14, the personified character called Righteousness by Faith claims that the message of Deuteronomy is τὸ ῥῆμα τῆς πίστεως ὃ κηρύσσομεν ("the word of faith that we proclaim"). The term ῥῆμα is employed here, derived from the citation of Deuteronomy, with a meaning roughly synonymous with λόγος, as one can see from parallel expressions such as λόγος τοῦ Θεοῦ ("word of God," Rom 9:5; 1 Cor 14:36; 2 Cor 2:17; 4:2; Phil 1:14; Col 1:25; 1 Thess 2:13), λόγος τοῦ Χριστοῦ ("word of Christ," Col 3:16) or λόγος τοῦ Κυρίου ("word of the Lord," 1 Thess 1:8; 4:15; 2 Thess 3:1).[68] Here the personified character confirms the legitimacy of the message that Paul and other early missionaries are proclaiming.[69] There is an ambiguity about whether the genitive construction "word of faith" should be understood as the believing response to the word[70] or the word that proclaims faith,[71] and Dunn suggests that the references to "heart" and "mouth" in this passage require that both be included in Paul's formula.[72] When one follows the logic of the speech-in-character, however, this is clearly the word of missionaries that proclaims faith. The threefold reference to "heart" in Rom 10:8-10, the Hebraic term for the motivating center of mind, emotion, experience, and purpose, shows that for Paul faith in the gospel about Christ crucified and resurrected involves a total reorientation of a person and his or her relationships.[73] Thus the "word of faith" is essentially interactive and must be preached by more than one person so that the first person plural form (κηρύσσομεν, "we preach, proclaim") conveys the idea of a "gospel held in common,"[74] proclaiming a faith that can only be conveyed through intense interaction "through faith for faith" (Rom 1.17).

■ **9** The ὅτι that opens v. 9 should be translated as "because" or "for," since this verse opens the chiastic explanation in vv. 9-10 of how the "word" is near to believers.[75] The verb ὁμολογέω appears here in a "specifically Christian religious usage" that affirms Jesus as authoritative and identifies the confessor as his follower.[76] The acclamation "Lord Jesus!" was a very early expression of allegiance to Christ, as the parallels in Phil 2:11; 1 Cor 1:2 and 12:3 indicate.[77] There is a close parallel in Greco-Roman political rhetoric,[78] including the

67 Hays, *Echoes*, 81; see also Badenas, *Christ*, 132.

68 Albert Debrunner et al., "λέγω κτλ.," *TDNT* 4 (1967) 109–19; Walter Radl, "ῥῆμα," *EDNT* 3 (1993) 210–11.

69 Eckstein, "'Nahe ist dir das Wort,'" 218.

70 Zahn, 481; Cranfield, 2:526; Eckstein, "'Nahe ist dir das Wort,'" 220.

71 Michel, 329; Schlier, 312; Käsemann, 290.

72 Dunn, 2:606.

73 Alexander Sand, "Καρδία," *EDNT* 2 (1991) 250, refers to the heart as the place "in which the encounter with God is realized."

74 Dunn, 2:606; Martin Rese, "Israels Unwissen und Ungehorsam und die Verkündigung des Glaubens durch Paulus in Römer 10," in D. A. Koch et al., eds., *Jesu Rede von Gott und ihre Nachgeschichte im frühen Christentum: Festschrift Willi Marxsen* (Gütersloh: Mohn, 1989) 265, argues in contrast that the "we" suggests that Paul alone was not responsible for Jewish rejection of the gospel.

75 See Barrett, 200; Cranfield, 2:526.

76 Otfried Hofius, "ὁμολογέω, ὁμολογία," *EDNT* 2 (1991) 515–16; Hans von Campenhausen, "Das Bekenntnis im Urchristentum," *ZNW* 63 (1972) 211; Otto Michel, "ὁμολογέω κτλ.," *TDNT* 5 (1967) 209; Hurtado, *One God*, 112.

77 Moo, 658, cites Neufeld, *Confessions*, 43–47. Hurtado, *Lord Jesus Christ*, 197–200, argues that this confession originated in the earliest phase of Jewish Christianity in Jerusalem. See also Werner Führer, "'Herr ist Jesus': Die Rezeption der urchristlichen Kyrios-Akklamation durch Paulus Römer 10,9," *KD* 33 (1987) 139–42.

78 Josephus *Bell.* 7.418; see Günther Bornkamm, "Homologia: Zur Geschichte einer politischen Begriffs," in *Geschichte und Glaube* (BEvTh 48; Munich: Kaiser, 1968) 1:140–56, referring to Plato *Crit.* 49a-b; 52d; *Phaed.* 7c; and *Hipp. maj.* 294c; Aristotle *Pol.* 1270b31; 1295b3ff.; Plutarch *Virt. mor.* c. 3. p. 441c.

formula Καίσαρα δεσπότην ὁμολογέω ("acknowledge the emperor as ruler"), which was understood as a loyalty oath.[79] To "confess Jesus as Lord" was therefore not only to make a claim about his divine status[80] but also to reveal one's own identity and commitment. A "confession" in this biblical sense is a "slogan of identification" that marks someone "as belonging to Jesus."[81] Such a confession binds the speaker to someone else in final loyalty.[82] To refer to Jesus as Lord ". . . denotes an attitude of subserviency and sense of belongingness or devotion to the one so named."[83] This kind of confession designates to whom the speaker is committed but does not determine what attitude others should take. In contrast to the later development of formulaic "confessions" in the Christian tradition, Paul had no intention of making this confession into a claim of honorable status that raises the speaker above others, using required language that others must employ to avoid peril. To "confess" in this context is also far removed from the traditional connotation in current culture, in which "confession of sins/guilt" is the dominant usage.

The content of faith's conviction is expressed, as in 4:24; 6:4; and 8:11, in traditional terms,[84] ὅτι ὁ θεὸς αὐτὸν ἤγειρεν ἐκ νεκρῶν ("that God raised him from the dead"). In all of these examples, displayed above at 8:11, the verb ἐγείρω ("waken, raise") occurs in association with the anarthrous phrase ἐκ νεκρῶν ("from [the] dead"). That the conviction about Christ's resurrection was foundational for the early church[85] is elaborated in detail in 1 Cor 15:4-19, and it is linked here with the simple assurance "you will be saved." The future tense is

probably "logical"[86] rather than "temporal,"[87] showing the consequence of the mouth's confession and the heart's conviction. The close association between confession and salvation derives from early Christian missionizing, in which the preached word evokes oral responses from converts.[88] The parallelism between mouth and heart in the citation from Deuteronomy requires the dual formulation in this verse, and again as in the earlier references in this pericope, "heart" refers to the center of humans where the deepest convictions are held.[89] Here as elsewhere in Romans it is clear that faith is primarily a matter of being persuaded by the gospel.[90]

To "have faith 'in your heart' that God raised [Jesus] from the dead" (Rom 10:9) reflects the same distinctions that are found in the use of "confess." If the resurrection of Christ really occurred, it confirms that the shamefully crucified one is the divinely authenticated Lord. But no universal claim about the resurrection is intended here. The faith is "in your heart," therefore indicating that a "deeply motivating belief . . . is in view and not merely a recitation of creedal form."[91] To be persuaded in this way is not to make any claim of superiority. It is rather evidence of having abandoned the traditional systems of earning honor and avoiding shame, because this Lord has the marks of the shameful cross on his resurrected body.

■ **10** The explanatory comment that is offered by the character Righteousness by Faith clarifies the sequence of faith and confession.[92] In v. 9, following the sequence of the citation from Deuteronomy, faith in the heart and confession by mouth were in reverse order from the

79   Josephus *Bell.* 7.418; Hofius, "ὁμολογέω, ὁμολογία," 515.
80   See George E. Howard's argument that κύριος was typically used for יהוה in Jewish and early Christian sources, "The Tetragram and the New Testament," *JBL* 96 (1977) 63–83; see also Joseph A. Fitzmyer, "The Semitic Background of the New Testament *Kyrios*-Title," in J. A. Fitzmyer, *A Wandering Aramean: Collected Aramaic Essays* (Missoula: Scholars Press, 1979) 119–23.
81   Dunn, 2:607.
82   Hofius, "ὁμολογέω, ὁμολογία," 515, cites the close parallel to Pauline usage in the Roman political formula, "acknowledge the emperor as lord," as in Josephus *Bell.* 7.418–19. See also Bornkamm, "Homologia," 140–56.

83   Dunn, 2:608.
84   See Paulsen, *Überlieferung*, 51–55, following Kramer, *Christ*, 19–26; Wengst, *Formeln*, 21ff., and others.
85   See Führer, "'Herr ist Jesus,'" 141–42.
86   See Moo, 658.
87   Cranfield, 2:530, contends that "you will be saved" refers to "eschatological salvation."
88   Führer, "'Herr ist Jesus,'" 143–44; Zeller, 187; Müller, "Glaube aus dem Hören," 423–25.
89   See Jewett, *Terms*, 333.
90   See Kinneavy, *Greek Rhetorical Origins*, 120–30.
91   Dunn, 2:609.
92   See Godet, 383; Cranfield, 2:530; Kuss, 3:762; Dunn, 2:609.

standpoint of Christian missionizing. Moreover, the active verbs "you confess" and "you believe" in v. 9 place the emphasis entirely on the human side. In line with Paul's charismatic view of faith articulated in chap. 8 and reiterated in 15:18-19,[93] the verbs in this verse are passive,[94] leading to my translation: "faith is evoked" and "confession is evoked." The concise, elegant formulation[95] joins the language of 1:16-17 with the details of the Deuteronomy citation, creating a fully plausible statement of the viewpoint of the character called Righteousness by Faith.[96] The distinction between righteousness as the gift of right relationship with God and salvation as deliverance from the threats of sin, death, and the law developed in the earlier sections of Romans is reiterated here.[97] But the emphasis is on "heart" and "mouth,"[98] both of which stand in the emphatic position at the beginning of their clauses. Righteousness by Faith works its miracle first within the heart, convincing it of the love of God (5:5, 8) conveyed to the undeserving in the Christ event, and thereafter evokes the oral confession, "Lord Jesus!" As is the case throughout Romans, Paul's purpose is missional rather than dogmatic. Here the biblical character "Righteousness by Faith" lends full support to the missionary project advanced by this letter.

■ **11** In Rom 10:11 Paul quotes Isa 28:16 about believers not being put to shame, but adds the word $\pi\hat{\alpha}\varsigma$ ("all"), as if it belonged to the original citation.[99] As one can see in the following illustration, this word was not in the version of this verse in Isaiah that Paul used in 9:33:

Isaiah 28:16
$\kappa\alpha\grave{\iota}\ \acute{o}\ \pi\iota\sigma\tau\epsilon\acute{\upsilon}\omega\nu\ \grave{\epsilon}\pi'\ \alpha\grave{\upsilon}\tau\hat{\wp}\ o\grave{\upsilon}\ \mu\grave{\eta}\ \kappa\alpha\tau\alpha\iota\sigma\chi\upsilon\nu\vartheta\hat{\eta}$ ("and he who believes in it/him would not be put to shame")

Romans 9:33
$\kappa\alpha\grave{\iota}\ \acute{o}\ \pi\iota\sigma\tau\epsilon\acute{\upsilon}\omega\nu\ \grave{\epsilon}\pi'\ \alpha\grave{\upsilon}\tau\hat{\wp}\ o\grave{\upsilon}\ \kappa\alpha\tau\alpha\iota\sigma\chi\upsilon\nu\vartheta\hat{\eta}$ ("and he who believes in it/him will not be put to shame")

Romans 10:11
$\pi\hat{\alpha}\varsigma\ \acute{o}\ \pi\iota\sigma\tau\epsilon\acute{\upsilon}\omega\nu\ \grave{\epsilon}\pi'\ \alpha\grave{\upsilon}\tau\hat{\wp}\ o\grave{\upsilon}\ \kappa\alpha\tau\alpha\iota\sigma\chi\upsilon\nu\vartheta\hat{\eta}$ ("all who believe in it/him will not be put to shame")

By introducing this altered citation with the introductory formula, $\lambda\acute{\epsilon}\gamma\epsilon\iota\ \gamma\grave{\alpha}\rho\ \acute{\eta}\ \gamma\rho\alpha\phi\acute{\eta}$ ("for the Scripture says"), which is used elsewhere in the authentic Pauline letters only in Rom 9:17, the authoritative voice of Scripture is enlisted in support of this alteration,[100] which again as in v. 6 is in the spoken voice of "Righteousness by Faith" rather than in Paul's own voice. This alteration is consistent with the earlier locations where "all" are made righteous by faith alone, including all Gentiles and all Jews: 1:16; 3:22, 30; 10:4.[101] No separate path to salvation through law is therefore left for Jewish believers.[102] It is therefore inappropriate to translate $\pi\hat{\alpha}\varsigma$ with "anyone,"[103] which sounds too individualistic to refer to the groups that are in view throughout Romans. With this one word, "all," the smear of shame is removed from the entire human race. Whether Jew or Greek, barbarian or Roman, slave or free, male or female, no persons or

---

93 Kuss, 3:762: "There is no confession that is not evoked by the spirit." See also 1 Thess 1:5; 1 Cor 2:4-5; 2 Cor 12:12; Gal 3:5.

94 Among the few commentaries that discuss the passive verbs, see Murray, 2:56, and Moo, 658.

95 See particularly Kuss, 3:672.

96 Dunn, 2:609, points particularly to the link with 1:16-17.

97 See Murray, 2:56; Karl Hermann Schelkle, "$\sigma\omega\tau\eta\rho\acute{\iota}\alpha$," *EDNT 3* (1993) 327.

98 Schmidt, 167. Kuss, 3:762, and Fitzmyer, 592, properly warn against drawing extensive theological or liturgical inferences from this verse.

99 There is wide acceptance of Ellis's observation in *Paul's Use*, 140, that Paul's inclusive interpretation is built into the citation itself. See Dunn, 2:609; Haacker, 213. Stanley, *Scripture*, 133, observes that

since Paul cited Isa 28:16 in 9:33 without the addition of "all," "he is quite aware of the correct reading of the LXX text." This may be true, but it does not alter the fact that Paul presents the "all" in this citation as if it truly belonged to what "scripture says." See Koch, *Schrift*, 133; Bell, *Provoked to Jealousy*, 83–84; Wagner, *Heralds*, 169.

100 See Cranfield, 2:531; Koch, *Schrift*, 133.

101 Kühl, 356; see also Stanley, *Scripture*, 134; Johnson, *Function*, 153; Wilk, *Bedeutung des Jesajabuches*, 62; Wagner, *Heralds*, 169–70; Shum, *Paul's Use of Isaiah*, 221.

102 Weiss, 450; Godet, 384.

103 Käsemann, 292, following BDF §275, although the latter understands "anyone" in the universal sense of "everyone." For the translation "everyone," see Morris, 386.

groups "who have faith in him will be put to shame."[104] As we noted above, however, such faith is not self-honorific. The right confession and properly defined faith do not earn this triumph of not being "put to shame," despite centuries of twisted, self-serving theology. To "call on the name" of this Lord (Rom 10:13) is to abandon any prior claim of honor and to take one's place alongside the dishonored savior and his disheveled flock.

■ **12** In Rom 10:12 the character "Righteousness by Faith" develops the conviction that Christ has erased the boundaries of honor and shame: "For there is no distinction between Jews or Greeks. The same one is Lord of all, [bestowing] riches upon all who call upon him." This is the fifth and final time that the expression Ἰουδαίου τε καὶ Ἕλληνος ("Jews and also Greeks") appears in Romans, once again avoiding the discriminatory epithet "Gentiles."[105] The overcoming of inequalities visible earlier in Romans comes here to its climactic expression in the formula, "for there is no distinction" (οὐ γάρ ἐστιν διαστολή).[106] Here Paul repeats the wording of 3:22, that the gospel eliminates the prejudicial boundaries between social groups.[107] The honor-shame distinctions that divided the Greco-Roman world have been eliminated by Christ, whose crucifixion and resurrection revealed that he is "Lord of all," a formulation that is even more inclusive than Greek/Jew or Gentile/Jew.[108]

The expression κύριος πάντων ("Lord of all") as an expression of Christ's universal sovereignty appears in Acts 10:36 (οὗτός ἐστιν πάντων κύριος, "this one is Lord of all"),[109] and is also employed in political rhetoric. Plato refers to potentates who "seek to be lord over all" (ζητῶν εἶναι κύριος ἀπάντων, Leg. 922d1) and Demosthenes writes of his adversary Philip of Macedon, who "was himself entirely a despot, ruler, lord over all" (δεσπότης, ἡγεμών, κύριος πάντων, Cor. 236; cf. Orat. 13.31.2; Menander Apsis 171). Dio Chrysostom Orat. 56.11.3 refers to the Roman emperor as being "himself lord over all matters (αὐτὸς ὢν κύριος ἀπάντων τῶν πραγμάτων)" and Dio Cassius Hist. Rom. 56.39 speaks in similar terms about the emperor "becoming alone indisputably lord of all (μόνος ἀναμφιλόγως κύριος ἀπάντων)." The formulation of this verse proclaims Christ as the one replacing the emperor in establishing a new realm of plentitude in which all are treated equally. Here the personified "Righteousness by Faith" confirms not only the addition of "all" in the preceding verse but also the argument of 3:29-30 that God is the Lord both of Gentiles and Jews. The antitheses of honor and shame in 1:14, which set the framework of Paul's letter, are included in this Lordship: Greek/barbarian, and educated/uneducated. Jesus' shameful death on behalf of the shamed, which exposed the pretensions of those whom the world honors, was shown through the resur-

---

104 As noted above with regard to the future verb "will not be put to shame," which occurs also in 9:33, it is likely that Paul intentionally made this alteration of Isa 28:16 in order to fit his context of overcoming shameful status through the gospel. For the alteration, see Wilk, *Bedeutung des Jesajabuches*, 45.

105 As in the earlier passages where this expression appears, commentators tend to overlook the distinction between "Greek" and "Gentile," assuming that "'Greek' here stands in for 'Gentile'" as Byrne states (322); see also Michel, 331; Schlier, 315; Cranfield, 2:531; Wilckens, 2:228; Dunn, 2:610; Stuhlmacher, 157; Moo, 659.

106 Although scholars are agreed in translating διαστολή as "distinction" or "difference," the search for parallels in papyri and classical sources has hitherto produced no exact parallel to Paul's usage; see the assessment by G. H. R. Horsley, "διαστολή," *NDIEC* 2 (1982) 80. Overlooked thus far is the parallel in Philo *Mos.* 2.158.4, "of the distinction (διαστολήν) between things sacred and profane, things human and divine." See also Philo *Spec.* 1.100.

107 See Harvey, *True Israel*, 76. James L. Jaquette, "Paul, Epictetus, and Others on Indifference to Status," *CBQ* 56 (1994) 79, suggests the topos of "no difference" (ἀδιάφορα) as the source of Paul's concept of "no distinction," but aside from the lack of linguistic parallels, the social boundaries between Jews and Greeks could not be overcome by mere indifference.

108 See Fitzmyer, 592; Rese, "Israels Unwissen," 261, citing Jacques Dupont, "'Le Seigneur de tous' (Ac 10:36; Rm 10:12): Arrière-fond scripturaire d'une formule christologique," in G. F. Hawthorne and O. Betz, eds., *Tradition and Interpretation in the New Testament: Essays in Honor of E. Earle Ellis for His 60th Birthday* (Grand Rapids: Eerdmans; Tübingen: Mohr Siebeck, 1987) 230.

109 Fitzmyer, 593, cites 1QapGen 20:13 ("Lord and Master over all"), 4Q409 1:6 ("and bless the Lord of all") as well as the disputed 11QPs 28:17 as Jewish parallels. Moo, 650, argues that this formula may be an early Christian adaptation of the LXX of Joel 3:5, but the link is quite distant.

rection to have revolutionary social consequences. As Franz Leenhardt remarks, "all, whoever they may be, must renounce all claim to their own righteousness. . . ."[110] Social discrimination is now illegitimate. The "riches" of divine favor,[111] which traditional religion has always believed would be bestowed only on the honorable,[112] are now bestowed impartially "upon all who call upon him." The expression ἐπικαλεῖν αὐτόν ("to call upon him, that is, the Lord") is a technical expression for praying and expressing allegiance to God or Christ.[113] This verb appears in locations where the allegiance of converts is in view (Acts 9:14, 21; 1 Cor 1:2), and in this context it has the connotation of "acclamation,"[114] as in the confession of 10:9, "Lord Jesus!"[115] The claim that "all" who make such a confession of Christ receive the same blessings makes it clear that no groups have precedence over others because of theology or culture.

■ **13** To confirm that Christ's mercy comes to all who call upon him, the character "Righteousness by Faith" cites a final line from Joel 3:5. With the exception of the transitional "for," the version selected is identical with the LXX, but the new context gives it a different meaning. The κύριος for Joel was clearly Yahweh, who would destroy Israel's enemies and usher in a new age of spiritual and material abundance. In Romans, however, the word κύριος clearly refers to Jesus,[116] who wrought salvation through his own death and resurrection and thereafter by means of evangelical persuasion that equalizes the honor of the entire human race. It is likely that Joel's formulation of the "name of the Lord" would have been understood in the light of the baptismal formula, "into the name of Jesus."[117] Whereas "salvation" in Joel refers to Israel gaining precedence over other nations, with the word "every one" referring to all Israel, including the returning captives, the new context is fully ecumenical, following the explicit reference to the lack of distinction between Jews and Greeks.[118] In Tobin's words, "Paul's emphasis in these verses is on 'all,' all who have faith, God as the God of all and bestowing riches on all who call upon the name of the Lord."[119] This fundamental reorienting of a crucial prophetic text is presented as the climactic statement of the biblical character, "Righteousness by Faith," rather than as an expression of Paul's distinctive theology. With this brilliant rhetorical device the *pesher* comes to a conclusion that is fully supportive of the missionary project that Paul wishes to promote: to preach the gospel of Christ crucified to the end of the known world and thus to overcome the destructive distinctions and imperial exploitations that had ruined the world.

110 Leenhardt, 272.

111 Helmut Merklein, "πλούσιος κτλ.," *EDNT* 3 (1993) 116: the Lord is "rich for all who call upon him. . . ." See also Rom 2:4, "riches of his kindness and forbearance and mercy," and 9:23, "riches of his glory."

112 See *4 Ezra* 7.133, "he is gracious to those who turn in repentance to his law"; cf. 1QH 4:32; 15:14-16; 1QS 4:1-7.

113 See Karl Ludwig Schmidt, "καλέω κτλ.," *TDNT* 3 (1965) 499–500.

114 Käsemann, 292; see also Godet, 385; Murray, 57; Schlier, 315. Zeller, 187, suggests that such acclamation has its context in baptism. As Moo, 660, observes, that prayerful evocation is here in view (Cranfield, 2:532; Morris, 388) is unlikely although there are many LXX references to prayer in which "call upon the name" is employed.

115 Meyer, 2:183, and Kuss, 3:767, show that "Lord" in this context is clearly Christ rather than God, as often claimed by patristic commentators.

116 Meyer, 2:184; Koch, 87–88; Cranfield, 2:532; Wilckens, 2:228; Fitzmyer, 593; Moo, 600; Haacker, 213; Donald B. Capes, *Old Testament Yahweh Texts in Paul's Christology* (WUNT 2.47; Tübingen: Mohr Siebeck, 1992) 116–23. The argument by Gaston, *Paul,* 131, supported in general by Howard, "Tetragram and the New Testament," 63–83, that κύριος in Rom 10:13 refers to Yahweh is highly unlikely in view of the explicit acclamation "Lord Jesus!" in 10:9.

117 See Lars Hartman, "Into the Name of Jesus: A Suggestion concerning the Earliest Meaning of the Phrase," *NTS* 20 (1973–74) 439, for the conclusion on the basis of the Semitic background that Jesus was "the fundamental reference for baptism . . . it was a 'Jesus baptism.'"

118 See particulary Kuss, 3:768; Bassler, *Impartiality,* 160–61; Aageson, *Biblical Interpretation,* 97.

119 Tobin, *Paul's Rhetoric,* 347; see also Esler, *Conflict and Identitiy,* 287.

10

The Sixth Argument

Syllogism and Citation-Chain
Concerning the Gospel Preached
but Rejected

14/ **How therefore might they call[a] upon
him in whom they have no faith?
And how might they have faith in
someone of whom they have not
heard?
And how might they hear[b] without someone preaching?**
15/ **And how might they preach if they
have not been sent? Just as[c] it is written,
"How timely [are] the feet[d] of those
who preach the gospel of the[e] good
things!"**
16/ **But not all have hearkened to the
gospel. For Isaiah says,
"Lord, who had faith in what was
heard from us?"**
17/ **So faith [is] from hearing, but the
hearing [is] through a word of Christ.[f]**
18/ **But I say, have they not heard?
Indeed they have!
"Into all the earth their voice has
gone out,
and to the ends of the world
their words."**
19/ **But I say, did Israel not know? First
Moses says,
"I shall make you zealous in regard
to what is no nation,
with a senseless nation shall I
provoke you to wrath."**
20/ **But Isaiah is bold[g] and says,
"I was found among[h] those who are
not seeking me,
I was made manifest [to][i] those
who did not ask for me."**
21/ **But to Israel he says,
"All day long I reached out my
hands to[j] a disobedient and disputatious [k] people."**

a   In place of the middle aorist subjunctive,
$\epsilon\pi\iota\kappa\alpha\lambda\acute{\epsilon}\sigma\omega\nu\tau\alpha\iota$ ("they might call for themselves"),
as in ℵ A B D F G, a future indicative, $\epsilon\pi\iota\kappa\alpha\lambda\acute{\epsilon}$-
$\sigma\sigma\nu\tau\alpha\iota$ ("they will call"), appears in P[46] K L P Ψ 6
33 69 88 104 326 424 614 945 1175 1241 1243 1319
1505 1506 1573 1735 1739 1836 1874 1881 2344
(2464) 2495 *Maj*, which is noted in Cranfield, 2:533,
but not in Nestle-Aland[26/27]. The stronger early evidence for the subjunctive form—though lacking in
P[46]—makes this the indisputable choice.
b   In place of the infrequently used aorist subjunctive
form $\dot{\alpha}\kappa\sigma\acute{\upsilon}\sigma\omega\sigma\iota\nu$ ("they might hear"), which is

strongly attested in ℵ[2] A B Ψ 33 69 81 88 330 614
1241 1243 1735 1836 1874 2464 *al*, a number of
variants have arisen, all of which appear to be secondary. ℵ* D F G K P 6 104 326 365 424[c] 1243 1319
1505 1506 1573 1739 1881 2495 *al* have the future
middle form $\dot{\alpha}\kappa\sigma\acute{\upsilon}\sigma\sigma\nu\tau\alpha\iota$ ("they shall hear for
themselves"); P[46] has a middle subjunctive aorist
form $\dot{\alpha}\kappa\sigma\acute{\upsilon}\sigma\omega\nu\tau\alpha\iota$ ("they might hear for themselves"); and L 323 424* 945 1175 2344 Cl *al* have
the simple future form $\dot{\alpha}\kappa\sigma\acute{\upsilon}\sigma\sigma\upsilon\sigma\iota\nu$ ("they shall
hear").

c   The more formal term $\kappa\alpha\vartheta\acute{\alpha}\pi\epsilon\rho$ ("just as") appears
in B 81 in place of the more common $\kappa\alpha\vartheta\acute{\omega}\varsigma$ ("as"),
which is attested in the majority of the witnesses:
P[46] ℵ A C D F G K L P Ψ 6 33 69 88 104 323 326
330 365 424 614 945 1175 1241 1243 1319 1505
1506 1573 1735 1739 1836 1874 1881 2344 2464
2495 *Maj* Cl. Cranfield, 2:534, prefers $\kappa\alpha\vartheta\acute{\alpha}\pi\epsilon\rho$
because there are variants at other points in
Romans where it appears. But in this instance
$\kappa\alpha\vartheta\acute{\alpha}\pi\epsilon\rho$ is more weakly attested than in the case
of the variants in Rom 4:6, 9:13, 11:8, and in con-
trast to Cranfield, 1:182, the variant situation in
12:4 (Swanson notes in *Vaticanus: Romans* that
seventy-four Greek witnesses read $\kappa\alpha\vartheta\acute{\alpha}\pi\epsilon\rho$ and
only D* F G have $\ddot{\omega}\sigma\pi\epsilon\rho$ in 12:4) provides less reason to conclude that in each instance there was "a
natural tendency to substitute a more common for
a rather rare word."
d   A variant that brings the wording of this verse much
closer to the LXX text of Isa 52:7 is found in ℵ[2] D F
G K L P Ψ 5 6 33 61 69 88 104 181 218 256 263 323
326[acc. to Swanson] 330 365 424 436 441 451 459 467 614
621 623 629 720 917 945 1175 1241 1319 1398
1505 1563 1573 1678 1718 1735 1751 1838 1845
1852 1874 1875 1877 1908[c] 1942 1959 1962 2127
2138 2197 2344 2464 2492 2495 2516 2523 2544
Maj Lect b d f g o vg sy[p.h] goth arm geo slav[ms]
Mcion[acc. to Tert] (Ir[lat]) Ad (Eus) Apollinaris Chr Cyr[1/2]
Hes Hil Ambst Ambr Hier Pel Aug, $\tau\tilde{\omega}\nu$ $\epsilon\dot{\upsilon}\alpha\gamma\gamma\epsilon\lambda\iota$-
$\zeta\sigma\mu\acute{\epsilon}\nu\omega\nu$ $\epsilon\dot{\iota}\rho\acute{\eta}\nu\eta\nu$ ("those preaching peace"), but
the well-attested absence of these words in P[46] ℵ* A
B C 81 630 915 1243 1506 1739 1836 1881 1908*
1912 2110 2200 2718 *pc* ar sa bo eth slav[ms] Cl Ps-
Hipp Or[gr.lat] Philo-Carpasia Severian Cyr[1/2] and the
wider disparity from the LXX make the shorter text
in this instance appear more original. Cf. Metzger,
Textual Commentary, 463.
e   The inclusion of $\tau\acute{\alpha}$ ("the") is perhaps as well
attested in P[46] ℵ* D[1] K L Ψ 6 33 69 88 104 323 326
330 365 424 614 945 1175 1241 1243 1319 1573
1735 1836 1874 2344 2464 *Maj* Cl as its omission by
ℵ[2] A B C D* F G P 81 1505 1506 1739 1881 2495 *pc*
Eus but the latter can be explained as an assimila-

tion to the wording of the LXX. See Zuntz, *Text*, 173 n. 4. The divided mind of Nestle-Aland[26/27] is manifest in the placement of τά in brackets. The potential exegetical relevance of the inclusion of τά in this context is discussed by Cranfield, 2:535.

f   In place of Χριστοῦ ("of Christ") found in P[46vid] ℵ* B C[vid] D* 6 81 629 1243 1506 1739 1852 *pc* ar b d vg sa bo fay goth arm Or[lat] Aug, the word θεοῦ appears in ℵ[1] A D[1, 2] K L P Ψ 33 69 88 104 256 263 323 326 330 365 424 436 451 459 614 945 1175 1241 1319 1505 1573 1735 1836 1874 1877 1881 1912 1962 2127 2200 2344 2464 2492 2495 *Maj Lect* sy[p, h] eth[pp] geo slav Cl Bas Chr Theodore Gaudentius Hier Sedulius-Scotus, and neither word is found in F G f g o Hilary Ambst Pel. Since the expression "word of/about Christ" is found nowhere else in the NT while "word of God" occurs frequently, the more difficult text should be preferred. See Metzger, *Textual Commentary*, 463–64.

g   The absence of ἀποτολμᾷ καί ("he is also bold") by D*,c vid F G is too weak to be considered original. This deletion was perhaps motivated by the rarity of the word, which occurs here for the only time in the Greek Bible.

h   The preposition ἐν ("in, by") is found in P[46] B D* F

G 1506[vid] (it vg[cl]), but the witnesses for its omission are quite numerous in ℵ A C D[1] L P Ψ 6 33 69 104 323 326 330 365 424 614 945 1175 1241 1243 1319 1505 1573 1735 1739 1836 1874 1881 2344 2464 2495 *Maj* vg[st] Cl and the omission is explainable as an assimilation to the LXX. The choice for the more difficult reading would lead to the judgment that the "in" is original; cf. Zuntz, *Text*, 173 n. 4.

i   The presence of ἐν ("in, by") is too weakly attested in B D* 1506[vid] to be original and is understandable as a characteristic effort in Hellenistic Greek to strengthen the dative by adding a redundant preposition. The absence of "in" is widely supported by P[46] ℵ A C D[1] F G L P Ψ 6 33 69 88 104 323 326 330 365 424 614 945 1175 1241 1319 1505 1573 1735 1739 1836 1874 1881 2344 2464 2495 *Maj* lat Cl.

j   In place of the widely attested preposition πρός ("to"), D Cl have ἐπί ("upon"), which may be a result of the influence of the Lucianic texts of the LXX, according to Stanley, *Scripture*, 147.

k   The words καὶ ἀντιλέγοντα ("and speaking against") are omitted by F G Ambst, but their inclusion is so broadly attested that they must be original. See also Stanley, *Scripture*, 147.

Analysis

There is a wide consensus that 10:14-21 constitutes a separate pericope,[1] with a shift in rhetorical style to that of diatribe and an inferential οὖν ("therefore") that carries the argument forward from the end of the preceding pericope. The diatribe opens with an elegant rhetorical "climax," sometimes referred to as a *gradatio*,[2] in which each succeeding line of 10:14-15a takes up a motif from the preceding line.[3] The opening rhetorical question takes up the word ἐπικαλέω ("call upon") in the climactic phase of the preceding pericope (10:12-13), but in contrast to the preceding pericope, the voice here is that of Paul rather than of the personified "Righteousness by Faith." The structure of the climax is illustrated below:

πῶς οὖν ἐπικαλέσωνται εἰς ὃν οὐκ ἐπίστευσαν;
πῶς δὲ πιστεύσωσιν οὗ οὐκ ἤκουσαν;
πῶς δὲ ἀκούσωσιν χωρὶς κηρύσσοντος;
πῶς δὲ κηρύξωσιν ἐὰν μὴ ἀποσταλῶσιν;

This series of four rhetorical questions opens a powerful syllogism,[4] starting with the presence of saving faith and moving chronologically backwards through hearing, preaching, and sending of preachers.[5] This climactic series of rhetorical questions provides the framework for the following verses, which contain three additional rhetorical questions, producing the satisfying series of seven. The last motif is taken up first in the subsequent series of six citations. This chiastic structure of diatribe and chain-citation has been discerned by Leenhardt,[6]

1   Meyer, 2:184; Sanday and Headlam, 294; Schmidt, 179–80; Schlier, 315–16; Michel, 332; Kuss, 3:771; Käsemann, 293; Dunn, 2:620; Moo, 662, referring to several minority views that fail to see vv. 14-21 as a separate unit.

2   See Tobin, *Paul's Rhetoric*, 349; Anderson, *Glossary*, 57–58.

3   See BDF §493.

4   Käsemann, 293.

5   See Louw, 2:107.

6   Leenhardt, 265, mentioned by Dunn, 2:620.

and it serves an argumentative rather than a purely decorative purpose.[7] These citations from the LXX constitute a carefully organized "citation-chain"[8] in which the answers to Paul's rhetorical questions are provided by Scripture itself. The argument is effectively concluded in the antithetical climax of v. 17, which replicates the sequence of faith depending on hearing and hearing depending on preaching the gospel found in the opening climax:[9] ἄρα ἡ πίστις ἐξ ἀκοῆς, ἡ δὲ ἀκοὴ διὰ ῥήματος Χριστοῦ. ("So faith [is] from hearing, but the hearing [is] through a word of Christ.") This verse is clearly the rhetorical centerpiece of the passage, given its replication of the opening climax and its use of the catchword ῥῆμα ("word"), which resonates not only with the theme of preaching in this passage but also with 10:8, where the same term appears.[10] The impressive *anadiplosis* in the repetition of ἀκοή at the end of v. 17a and the beginning of v. 17b[11] also picks up the prominent "hearing" motif in the opening climax (v. 14b-c). The following paragraph (vv. 18-21) then applies this conclusion to the issue of Jewish and Gentile responses to the gospel, drawing answers from Scripture to the diatribal questions posed in Paul's voice.

Of the six citations in this passage, the first three refer to the proclamation of the gospel and the last three to the responses of Jews and Gentiles.[12] The third, fourth, and fifth citations have the typical Hebraic form of synonymous parallelism, which lends poetic eloquence to the passage.[13] The second, third, and fourth citations are introduced by parallel assertions with antithetical force, "but" or "but I say," guiding the flow of thought and countering false inferences. The difficult logical connections between 10:16 and its neighboring verses have occasioned suggestions that it really belongs as a conclusion after v. 21,[14] or perhaps between v. 17 and v. 18,[15] or that v. 16 or v. 17 were not written by Paul at all,[16] questions that will have to be discussed in the exegesis below. As a whole, this pericope constitutes a

logical syllogism, with the major premise in vv. 14-15, the minor premise in v. 16, the logical conclusion in v. 17, and the application to the issue of Gentile and Jewish responses to the gospel in vv. 18-21. This pericope thus features a highly creative and original syllogism driven forward by diatribal questions and proven by a chain of citations from authoritative Scripture. The point of the syllogism is effectively captured by Thomas Tobin: "(1) God foretold that God would be found by Gentiles, that is, by those who had not sought him, and (2) by this means, God would make Israel jealous. This sums up much of the argument in 9:30—10:21 in the sense that Israel's present situation in relation to the Gentiles is rooted in, and foretold by, the Scriptures. For this reason, Israel has no excuse for not knowing this. Once again, it is not that God's word has failed. Rather, Israel has failed by not understanding what is found in that word."[17]

Rhetorical Disposition

IV.	The *probatio*
9:1—11:36	The third proof: The triumph of divine righteousness in the gospel's mission to Israel and the Gentiles
10:14-21	6. Syllogism and citation-chain concerning the gospel preached but rejected
10:14-15	a. The major premise: The temporal sequence of conversion moves from preaching to faith
10:14-15a	1) The rhetorical questions about the source of faith, in climactic sequence
10:14a	a) Calling upon God requires faith
10:14b	b) Faith requires hearing
10:14c	c) Hearing requires preaching
10:15a	d) Preaching requires a commission
10:15b-c	2) The scriptural proof of Isa 52:7 concerning the timely, authorized preaching
10:15b	a) The citation formula
10:15c	b) The citation of Isa 52:7
10:16	b. The minor premise: Despite the authentic preaching, not all heed the gospel
10:16a	1) The observation that everyone does not heed the gospel

7 Käsemann, 293–94.
8 Koch, *Schrift*, 281.
9 Louw, 2:107.
10 See Aageson, "Scripture," 277; Tobin, *Paul's Rhetoric*, 349: "Paul's interest is primarily in the conjunction of hearing . . . and preaching. . . ."
11 Bullinger, *Figures*, 255.
12 See Michel, 333.
13 See Adele Berlin, "Parallelism," *ABD* 5 (1992) 156–57.
14 Weiss, "Beiträge," 240.
15 Müller, "Zwei Marginalien," 249–54, as noted by Michel, 333.
16 Bultmann, "Glossen," 197–202. For a rebuttal of the suggestions of marginal glosses, see Käsemann, 295.
17 Tobin, *Paul's Rhetoric*, 351.

10:16b-c	2) The scriptural proof concerning the failure of some to believe
10:16b	a) The citation formula
10:16c	b) The citation of Isa 53:1
10:17	c. The conclusion in the form of an antithetical climax
10:17a	1) Faith comes through hearing
10:17b	2) Hearing depends on the "word of Christ"
10:18-21	d. The application: Gentiles responded to the gospel and some Jews did not
10:18	1) The proof that the Jews have heard the gospel
10:18a-b	(a) Rhetorical introduction
10:18a	(1) The rhetorical question about whether the Jews have heard
10:18b	(2) The affirmative answer
10:18c-d	(b) The scriptural proof from Ps 18:57
10:18c	(1) The voice extends to all the world
10:18d	(2) The word has gone to the ends of the world
10:19	2) The proof that Israel knows of the gospel because of the response of the Gentiles
10:19a	(a) The rhetorical question about Israel really knowing
10:19b-d	(b) The scriptural proof from Deut 32:21
10:19b	(1) The introduction of the citation
10:19c-d	(2) The citation
10:19c	i. Israel made jealous of "a non-people"
10:19c	ii. Israel provoked to wrath
10:20-21	3) The scriptural proof that the Gentiles responded to the gospel while Israel remained disobedient
10:20	(a) The citation of Isa 65:1 that outsiders found God
10:20a	(1) The introduction of the citation
10:20b-c	(2) The citation
10:20b	i. God was found by those not seeking God
10:20c	ii. God revealed God's self to those not seeking

10:21	(b) The citation of Isa 65:2 concerning God remaining open to a disobedient Israel
10:21a	(1) The introduction of the address of the citation: "to Israel"
10:21b	(2) The citation

Exegesis

■ **14** The four rhetorical questions in the climax are framed with the particle πῶς ("How?"), which invite a crescendo of negative responses from the audience: "It is impossible!"[18] The third person plural verbs refer back to vv. 12-13, the "all" who call on the Lord in response to the gospel and are saved, both Greeks and Jews.[19] Apart from 4:10, Paul never otherwise employs the sequence πῶς οὖν,[20] in which "therefore" connects the climax with the final verse of the preceding pericope. The expression "they might call upon him," that is, the Lord, as in 10:12-13, reflects the confessional response to missionary preaching as in Acts 22:16, "Rise up, be baptized, and wash away your sins, calling on his name."[21] By selecting aorist subjunctive verbs, Paul draws attention to the events of missionary activity followed by conversions. The climax deals with this process in reverse order, beginning with the confession that marks the appropriate conclusion of the conversion process. The preceding pericope made it clear that such a "calling" involves confessing Jesus as Lord (10:9-10). But if it is true that faith in Christ necessarily precedes such a public confession (10:10), then it follows that without such faith, it is impossible to make a proper confession. Since the preceding argument has made this principle clear for all persons,[22] Greeks as well as Jews,[23]

---

18 Weiss, 454; Käsemann, 293; Dunn, 2:620, following BDF §366.1 and BAGD (2000) 901.

19 Bell, *Provoked to Jealousy*, 83–87, rightly maintains that this "all" includes Gentiles as well as Jews, thus rejecting Michel, 332–35; Dodd, 168–70; Cranfield, 2:533; Barrett, 203–5; Moo, 662, and others who believe that vv. 14-18 deal only with the mission to Israel.

20 See the discussion in Rom 4:1-12 above.

21 This technical early Christian use of ἐπικαλέω ("call upon") is described in the preceding pericope in notes relating to 10:12-13. This usage is quite different from magical papyri, where the supplicant is instructed to say, "I call upon you in the name of

the one who created the universe" (Kotansky, *Greek Magical Amulets*, I. 13–14, with many other examples). In *PGM* IV. 1209–10 there is the invocation, "I call upon your 100-lettered name that passes through the firmament to the depths of the earth: save me!" (Text also in Betz, *Greek Magical Papyri*, 61.) The more general sense of requesting help from God is seen in Josephus *Bell.* 2.394, "How could you call on God, after intentionally refusing to pay the service due to him?"

22 See Schreiner, 567.

23 It is a mistake to assume with Schmidt, 180; Wilckens, 2:228; Cranfield, 2:533; and others that Paul's syllogism relates only to Jewish converts.

the audience would readily answer in response to the question "How then . . . ?"—"It is impossible!" The first step to establishing the major premise of Paul's syllogism is thereby affirmed by the audience itself, on the basis of the shared experience of conversion.[24]

The second through the fourth questions begin with πῶς δέ, in which the particle has the connective function of linking the parallel questions together, and thus is appropriately translated with "and how"?[25] Moving backwards from the end of the conversion process, Paul asks, "How might they believe in someone whom they have not heard?"[26] The relative pronoun in the genitive case (οὗ, "of whom") is required with the verb "hear,"[27] thus referring to the person rather than the message. The risen Christ is therefore the one who is really being heard in the gospel message,[28] a theme that is taken up in 10:17, where the gospel is referred to as the "word of Christ." Once again, the audience is impelled to answer, "It is indeed impossible to believe in the gospel if it has not been heard!"

The third question in this rhetorical climax deals with the necessity of someone preaching the gospel—or, to state the question as ancients would have heard it, "How can they hear apart from a herald?"[29] The verb κηρύσσειν ("to preach, act as herald") appears four times in this and the preceding pericope, beginning with "the word of faith that we preach" (10:8), and it is clear that this concept of the herald proclaiming the new age was established in the pre-Pauline phase of the Christian

mission.[30] This is a clear reference to the decisive role of oral proclamation in the spread of the gospel in the early period before the publication of the gospels and the Pauline letters.[31] Paul knows that he can count on the Roman audience's assent to this third rhetorical question: "No, it is certainly impossible that anyone can hear the gospel without someone preaching it!"

■ **15** The fourth rhetorical question deals with the authentication of the herald as one who has been "sent" by a higher authority. The biblical formulation of this premise is visible in Isa 61:1, which is cited in Luke 4:18, ἀπέσταλκέν με, κηρύξαι αἰχμαλώτοις ἄφεσιν ("he has sent me to proclaim release to the captives"). In the aorist passive used in 10:15a, the sender is assumed to be Christ, a matter that was explicitly claimed in 1:5.[32] Paul presents himself throughout Romans as the authorized ambassador, the herald of Christ, commissioned to preach the gospel to the end of the world (cf. also 1 Cor 1:17). But the link between sending and proclamation is not unique to Paul; it is widely assumed by other branches of early Christianity,[33] which correlates with Paul's ecumenical purpose in this letter. There is no doubt that all of the groups hearing Paul's letter read in their house and tenement churches would assent to this premise that preaching is legitimized by divine sending. They would reply, "Of course, it is impossible to preach if one has not been sent!"

With the completion of this climax, the audience affirms the major premise of Paul's syllogism, which is

---

24   In contrast Kim, *Romans 9–11*, 133–34, interprets these questions as "the charge of the prosecutor" as a "rebuttal" of Jewish misconceptions. This is an expression of the mistaken notion that Romans is an example of judicial rhetoric as an attack on beliefs held by the audience.

25   BAGD (2000) 213.2.

26   See Kinneavy, *Greek Rhetorical Origins*, 143.

27   BAGD (2000) 38.3b, "the genitive of person . . . 'of whom they have not heard' Rom 10:14a."

28   Meyer, 2:186; Sanday and Headlam, 296; Cranfield, 2:534; Morris, 390; Murray, 2:58; Moo, 663. There is a parallel to this conception in Luke 10:16, "he who hears you hears me."

29   Fitzmyer, 596.

30   Otto Merk, "κηρύσσω κτλ.," *EDNT* 2 (1991) 288; Gerhard Friedrich, "κῆρυξ κτλ.," *TDNT* 3 (1965) 703, argues that the NT usage generally retains the

sense of "to proclaim," which is the task of the herald in the ancient world.

31   Dunn, 2:621; Kelber, *Oral and the Written Gospel*, 140–47, esp. 146: "Spoken words enter the human heart . . . elicit faith and faithful heeding and in turn generate confession. . . . For this reason, what enters the human heart affects a person's whole being."

32   Dunn, 2:621.

33   See, e.g., Luke 13:34; 19:32; John 1:6; 3:28; 1 John 4:9; 4:14; Friedrich, "κῆρυξ κτλ.," 710–17. Friedrich (712) argues that 10:15 "is decisive for our understanding of the preaching office," in that "sending" is linked with "preaching." "Without commissioning and sending there are no preachers. . . ."

actually drawn from their conversion experience. This premise concerns the process that leads to the confession "Lord Jesus!" which stands at the center of the preceding pericope, a confession that most of Paul's fellow Jews have thus far refused to make. Each step requires that a prior step has been taken; the sequence of conversion by the gospel is thus a temporal one. In outline form, the major premise is as follows, with the steps in the four rhetorical questions marked in the reverse sequence:[34]

> Confession in Christ ← (1) Belief in Christ ← (2) Hearing the Gospel ← (3) Preaching the Gospel ← (4) Authorized Herald to Preach the Gospel

Each of these steps is taken up in the subsequent phases of the syllogism, beginning with the scriptural proof of the major premise itself, which links most directly with the fourth question, while the later phases of the argument take up the earlier steps and their logical interrelationships, following a roughly chiastic sequence.

The first citation is introduced by $\kappa\alpha\vartheta\grave{\omega}\varsigma\ \gamma\acute{\epsilon}\gamma\rho\alpha\pi\tau\alpha\iota$ ("just as it is written"), the traditional Jewish formula for a biblical citation used in 1:17; 2:24; 3:4, 10; 4:17; 8:36; 9:13, 33; 11:8, 26; 15:3, 21.[35] Many have argued that Paul's citation of Isa 52:7 stands closer to the MT than to the standard versions of the LXX, yet the alterations from the Hebrew text are also significant. The Lucianic family of LXX texts[36] stands closer to Paul's at several points. The comparison is illustrated below with the closest parallels underlined:

Isa 52:7: מַה־נָּאווּ עַל־הֶהָרִים רַגְלֵי מְבַשֵּׂר מַשְׁמִיעַ שָׁלוֹם מְבַשֵּׂר טוֹב ("How timely upon the mountains are

the feet of him who preaches good news, who publishes peace, who preaches good news of good")

Isa 52:7 A & B versions of LXX: $\dot{\omega}\varsigma\ \ddot{\omega}\rho\alpha\ \dot{\epsilon}\pi\grave{\iota}\ \tau\hat{\omega}\nu\ \dot{o}\rho\acute{\epsilon}\omega\nu,\ \dot{\omega}\varsigma\ \pi\acute{o}\delta\varsigma\ \epsilon\dot{v}\alpha\gamma\gamma\epsilon\lambda\iota\zeta o\mu\acute{\epsilon}\nu o v\ \dot{\alpha}\kappa o\grave{\eta}\nu\ \epsilon\dot{\iota}\rho\acute{\eta}\nu\eta\varsigma,\ \dot{\omega}\varsigma\ \epsilon\dot{v}\alpha\gamma\gamma\epsilon\lambda\iota\zeta\acute{o}\mu\epsilon\nu o\varsigma\ \dot{\alpha}\gamma\alpha\vartheta\acute{\alpha}$ ("How timely upon the mountains are the feet of him who preaches the message of peace, as the one preaching good things")

Isa 52:7 Lucianic family of LXX: $\dot{\omega}\varsigma\ \dot{\omega}\rho\alpha\hat{\iota}o\iota\ \dot{\epsilon}\pi\grave{\iota}\ \tau\hat{\omega}\nu\ \dot{o}\rho\acute{\epsilon}\omega\nu\ [o\iota]^{37}\ \pi\acute{o}\delta\epsilon\varsigma\ \epsilon\dot{v}\alpha\gamma\gamma\epsilon\lambda\iota\zeta o\mu\acute{\epsilon}\nu o v\ \dot{\alpha}\kappa o\grave{\eta}\nu\ \epsilon\dot{\iota}\rho\acute{\eta}\nu\eta\varsigma\ \epsilon\dot{v}\alpha\gamma\gamma\epsilon\lambda\iota\zeta o\mu\acute{\epsilon}\nu o v\ \dot{\alpha}\gamma\alpha\vartheta\acute{\alpha}$. ("How timely upon the mountains are the feet of him who preaches the message of peace, the one preaching good things!")

Rom 10:15b: $\dot{\omega}\varsigma\ \dot{\omega}\rho\alpha\hat{\iota}o\iota\ o\dot{\iota}\ \pi\acute{o}\delta\epsilon\varsigma\ \tau\hat{\omega}\nu\ \epsilon\dot{v}\alpha\gamma\gamma\epsilon\lambda\iota\zeta o\mu\acute{\epsilon}\nu\omega\nu\ \tau\grave{\alpha}\ \dot{\alpha}\gamma\alpha\vartheta\acute{\alpha}$. ("How timely are the feet of those who preach the good things!")

The suggestion by Koch that a Greek translation close to Paul's version of this text was available for citation[38] has been confirmed by Stanley by means of his reconstruction of the Lucianic family of texts, which corrected the LXX by bringing it into closer to the Hebrew text.[39] This explains Paul's choice of the adjective $\dot{\omega}\rho\alpha\hat{\iota}o\varsigma$ ("timely")[40] in place of the "hour" ($\ddot{\omega}\rho\alpha$) found in the standard LXX version, and also the inclusion of the article $o\dot{\iota}$ ("the") in front of $\pi\acute{o}\delta\epsilon\varsigma$ ("feet"). Nevertheless, Pauline alterations of the preexisting forms of this citation are clearly visible. There is a wide consensus that the singular reference to the preacher in the MT and both forms of the LXX, which probably referred to the messiah or his herald, was intentionally altered by Paul to refer to the plurality of preachers of the Christian gospel.[41] It therefore resonates with 10:8, "the word of

---

34   See particularly Haacker, 214–15. It is a mistake to select one of the four steps as the central "point" of Paul's premise, following Murray, 2:59, and Käsemann, 294, who single out the fourth member of the climax as emphatic.

35   See particularly Hans Vollmer, *Die alttestamentlichen Citate bei Paulus textkritisch und biblisch-theologisch gewürdigt nebst einem Anhang über das Verhältnis des Apostels zu Philo* (Freiburg/Leipzig: Mohr Siebeck, 1895) 72.

36   See Stanley, *Scripture*, 135–37; the Lucianic texts analyzed by Stanley are minuscules 88 22 c –62-/II [=

90-130-311]-93-86c-456 403′ [= 403-613] and a quotation from Theodoret.

37   Only MSS 88 22c-93 provide $o\dot{\iota}$ ("the") before $\pi\acute{o}\delta\epsilon\varsigma$ ("feet").

38   Koch, *Schrift*, 68–69.

39   Stanley, *Scripture*, 135–36, followed by Wilk, *Bedeutung des Jesajabuches*, 24, and Wagner, *Heralds*, 171–72.

40   See BAGD (2000) 1103, "opportune point of time, happening at the right time, timely." See Schlier, 315, 317; Dunn, 2:621–22; Fitzmyer, 597.

41   Käsemann, 294; Cranfield, 2:535; Dunn, 2:621;

faith that *we* proclaim" and answers the question in the first half of 10:15, whether the preachers indeed have been "sent." Paul's elimination of the "mountains" that appear in the LXX and the MT texts was probably motivated by the desire to generalize this text by withdrawing it from the context of Mount Zion,[42] where Isaiah expected the fulfillment to be centered. The anti-imperial logic of the gospel allows no hope that an Israelite imperium would be an improvement over the Roman Empire. In keeping with the ecumenical emphasis evident through Romans, the message of Christ offers peaceful coexistence for the entire world (cf. esp. 15:7-13), and it overcomes the barriers between the Greeks and the Jews (cf. 10:12-13) that would remain intact in an Israelite empire. This consideration also explains why Paul deleted εὐαγγελιζομένου ἀκοὴν εἰρήνης ("the one preaching the message of peace") found in all of the LXX versions.[43] The concept of "peace" in the Isaiah citation has the same structure as the Pax Romana, resulting from the subordination of all potential enemies under the imperial capitol in Jerusalem. The adjective ὡραῖος is frequently translated as "beautiful," on account of the parallel in Sir 26:18, but in the present context it more likely means "timely" or "opportune,"[44] that is, at the appropriate "time, hour"

(ὥρα) for the gospel message to be spread. This correlates nicely with Paul's eschatological view of the gospel,[45] as well as with the temporal sequence of the major premise itself.[46] The reference to "the good things" in Paul's translation compares with the singular "good" in the MT text and in comparison with the versions of the LXX, he adds the definite article. This indicates that "the good things" are known to the audience. In the new context in Romans, "the good things" would probably be understood to refer to the superabundant "riches" (10:12), "riches of his kindness and forbearance and patience" (2:4), "riches of his glory" (9:23), and "the mercies of God" (12:1) shown forth in the gospel.[47] Thus, in the context of Paul's syllogism, this citation from Isaiah "takes on the overtones of his [i.e. Paul's] good news, the 'gospel' about Christ and the salvation that is available through him,"[48] while avoiding the imperialistic implications of the original wording of Isaiah.

■ **16** The minor premise in Paul's syllogism is set out in antithesis to the first. The ἀλλά should be translated with "but"[49] or "yet,"[50] indicating an exception to the general principle established in the major premise.[51] It is frequently suggested that οὐ πάντες, those who have refused to accept the gospel, constitute a *litotes*[52] or *meio-*

Fitzmyer, 597; Moo, 664; Stanley, *Scripture,* 140. Wagner, "Heralds of Isaiah," 89. Gerhard Friedrich, "εὐαγγελίζομαι κτλ.," *TDNT* 2 (1964) 719, argues that the change to a plural form follows a rabbinic tradition of heavenly messengers, but the texts cited on 715–16 are all several centuries after Paul's time. Since both Acts 10:36 and Eph 2:17 retain the singular of Isa 52:7, it seems unlikely that such a rabbinic tradition was known in the first century.

42 Käsemann, 294; Koch, *Schrift,* 122; Stanley, *Scripture,* 137; Wagner, *Heralds,* 173.

43 Since they cannot discern an argumentative reason for Paul's deletion, Koch, *Schrift,* 81–83, and Stanley, *Scripture,* 139, resort to a weak theory of haplography to explain this omission. See the critique in Bell, *Provoked to Jealousy,* 88–89.

44 BAGD (2000) 1103.1; Käsemann, 294; Dunn, 2:621–22; Fitzmyer, 597.

45 Käsemann, 294: "the eschatological actualization of the promise"; Schlier, 317; Dunn, 2:622; Moo, 664; Byrne, 326.

46 Haacker, 214.

47 Cranfield, 2:535; Godet, 386: "those well-known foretold blessings which were to constitute the Mes-

sianic kingdom." Wilk, *Bedeutung des Jesajabuches,* 174, sees the "good things" as the grace of God revealed in Christ. Stanley, *Scripture,* 141, overlooks the argumentative context in arguing that the significance of the article "remains obscure."

48 Fitzmyer, 597; see also Hanson, *Studies,* 155; Wagner, *Heralds,* 173; Lieu, *Neither Jew nor Greek,* 203, referring with approval to Graham N. Stanton, *The Gospels and Jesus* (Oxford: Oxford University Press, 1989) 14–33. In contrast, Shum, *Paul's Use of Isaiah,* 224, concludes that the citation serves "to condemn his unbelieving Jewish contemporaries by proving their stubbornness and belief to be inexcusable."

49 Morris, 391.

50 Fitzmyer, 598.

51 Dodd's suggestion (170) that v. 16a should be taken as a question ("They have not all given in to the Gospel of glad news? No.") is not supported by the Greek word order, and the negative answer is not in the Greek text; see the critique by Wilk, *Bedeutung des Jesajabuches,* 77–78.

52 Meyer, 2:187; Weiss, 455; Morris, 391; Moo, 664; a *litotes* is an ironic understatement.

sis[53] meaning "only a very few," but this would be a gratuitous insult to the already large number of Roman converts, and it would weaken the rhetorical connection with "all" in 10:4, 11, 12, and 13.[54] There is no indication in this context that anything but a literal reference to "not all" was intended. Paul's choice of the verb ὑπακούειν ("hearken, obey") allows a wordplay with ἀκούειν ("hear") in 10:14 and 18 and ἀκοή ("hearing") in 10:16-17,[55] which leads me to translate it with "hearken." The choice of ὑπακούειν also resonates with the missionary goal of eliciting "obedience of faith" in 1:5 and the "obedience of the Gentiles" in 15:18. As we have seen in earlier references (5:19; 6:12-17), obedience is understood as a positive response in faith to the gospel.[56] While some interpreters express surprise that Paul did not employ the word "faith" in 10:16a,[57] the choice of ὑπακούειν points to the communication nexus that binds preacher, gospel, hearer, Christ, and community together in the charismatic process of conversion as described in vv. 14-15a.[58] It is clear from the context that the refusal of many Jews to accept the gospel is in view here.[59] In 10:2-3 Paul had explained the motivation behind this failed communication, that is, their misguided zeal for the law that aimed to establish honor. Now he moves on to suggest that such a failure to hearken to the good news was predicted by none other than Isaiah himself. The citation formula, "for Isaiah says," is the third time Paul explicitly mentions this prophet as the voice that speaks the clarifying word (see 9:27, 29).

In contrast to the first text in this citation-chain, which departed from both the MT and the LXX, Paul's quotation of Isa 53:1 is taken verbatim from the LXX, "Lord, who had faith in what was heard from us?" As in the other references to the κύριος in the citations of the preceding pericope, Christ rather than Yahweh is implied by Paul's context.[60] The direct address to this Lord has the feeling of lament,[61] evoking once again Paul's agonized disappointment expressed in 9:1-3 at the refusal of so many of his fellow Jews to accept the gospel.[62] The noun ἀκοή ("what is heard, hearing") correlates with the verb employed in the question in v. 16a, "not all have *hearkened to* (ὑπήκουσαν) the gospel."[63] The citation thus "assumes a fundamental correspondence between Paul's apostolic proclamation and Isaiah's message."[64] The citation from Isaiah thereby confirms where the problem lies: not in the gospel message itself or in its preachers, but in the reception thereof.[65] The argumentative effect of the Isaiah citation, however, is to confirm the minor premise of Paul's syllogism, that not all have set faith in the gospel, a tragic circumstance that was forecast by Isaiah and thus fits into the mysterious plan of God.[66]

■ **17** The conclusion of the syllogism is introduced by the inferential particle ἄρα ("so"), which marks "the result" or consequence of the preceding premises.[67] The failure of earlier commentators to detect the syllogistic structure of this pericope has led to comments about alleged illogical development,[68] along with suggestions

---

53   Sanday and Headlam, 297; Cranfield, 2:536; Murray, 2:60; Käsemann, 295; Stuhlmacher, 160; Schreiner, 569; a *meiosis* makes things smaller.
54   See Michel, 333; Dunn, 2:622.
55   Schlatter, 217; Dunn, 2:622.
56   Gerhard Schneider, "ὑπακοή, ὑπακούω," *EDNT* 3 (1993) 394-95.
57   E.g., Moo, 665.
58   Dobbeler, *Glaube als Teilhabe*, 18-25; Theobald, 2:27-28.
59   See, e.g., Godet, 387; Meyer, 2:187; Kuss, 3:774; Wilckens, 2:229; Bell, *Provoked to Jealousy*, 90-92; Fitzmyer, 598.
60   Johnson, 162-64, suggests that these citations from the Servant Songs of Isaiah make the point "that the good news was quite literally 'pre-promised' to the prophets and the 'message about Messiah' was already proclaimed in Torah," and that such knowledge should have led Israel to accept Christ (163).

      Wilk, *Bedeutung des Jesajabuches*, 182, overlooks the contextual clues in maintaining that Yahweh rather than Christ is addressed here.
61   Käsemann, 295.
62   See Shum, *Paul's Use of Isaiah*, 225.
63   See Wagner, "Heralds of Isaiah," 208; Wilk, *Bedeutung des Jesajabuches*, 182-83.
64   Wagner, *Heralds*, 179.
65   Cranfield, 2:535-36; Fitzmyer, 598.
66   Kuss, 3:774; Cranfield, 2:535-56; Wilk, *Bedeutung des Jesajabuches*, 79.
67   BAGD (2000) 127; Bell, *Provoked to Jealousy*, 92, notes that Peter Stuhlmacher, "'Ex Auditu' and the Theological Interpretation of Holy Scripture," *ExAud* 2 (1986) 2, observes that this verse is comparable to a rabbinic short summary of the preceding argument.
68   Barrett, 205; Michel, 334.

of a marginal note inserted at the wrong spot[69] or a later interpolation.[70] Actually v. 17 is a very effective "summarizing conclusion"[71] that is organized as a succinct climax, following the pattern of vv. 14-15a. Both halves of the antithetical climax have equal weight. That $\pi\acute{\iota}\sigma\tau\iota\varsigma$, that is, faith in the gospel, derives from $\dot{\alpha}\kappa o\acute{\eta}$, that is, hearing the oral proclamation of Christ crucified and resurrected,[72] draws together the argument in vv. 14a-c and 16. It articulates the principle that was basic for early Christian mission activity.[73] Here Paul lays out the foundation of the mission to Spain as well as his prior missionary activity. As von Dobbeler has shown, faith for Paul was not a matter of abstract beliefs but the result of personal encounters between preachers and hearers, followed when successful by joining a new community of speaking and hearing the gospel.[74] Werner Kelber has explained this link between the oral proclamation and the evocation of faith in the context of early Christian groups: "Mouth and heart cooperate in the oral delivery of redemption. . . . The spoken word, emanating from interiority and entering another interiority, creates a deep-set bonding of speaker with audience."[75] To "live by faith" (1:17) in the sense assumed by Paul and other early believers was a matter of hearing and responding to the oral gospel rather than of conforming to some written law. This verse, which serves as the rhetorical centerpiece of this pericope, therefore provides a decisive elaboration of the thesis of Paul's letter from Hab 2:4.

The antithetical second half of Paul's conclusion, "but hearing through the word of Christ," insists on an authoritative preaching that is spoken and heard. This expression $\dot{\rho}\acute{\eta}\mu\alpha\tau o\varsigma$ $X\rho\iota\sigma\tau o\hat{v}$ ("word of Christ") echoes the use of the term $\dot{\rho}\hat{\eta}\mu\alpha$ ("word") in 10:8 and should have a similar meaning here. The genitive construction

is therefore probably objective, referring to the "message of salvation"[76] that Paul and other early missionaries have proclaimed. A consideration of parallel expressions such as "word of Christ," "word of the Lord," or "word of God" in the Pauline letters and elsewhere in early Christian literature[77] makes it likely that this genitive expression refers to a "word that proclaims Christ."[78] That Christ was thought to be spiritually present in such preaching was a widely shared belief in early Christianity (see 10:14b),[79] but it does not justify the interpretation of "word of Christ" as a subjective genitive, that is, a word uttered by Christ himself.[80] The use of the preposition ("through") clearly indicates that the source of the hearing leading to faith is the preaching about Christ, thus lifting up an authoritative element that resonates with 10:15.[81] To reject the gospel is to reject God's Messiah, for the compelling power of the gospel resides not in its preachers but in Christ himself, who becomes present in the preached gospel for those who believe. The hearing that produces faith therefore derives from Christ. On the basis of this succinct, antithetical conclusion, Paul has a firm foundation to move on to deal with the distressing issue of the refusal of some of his fellow Jews to accept the gospel.

■ **18** The application phase of Paul's syllogism opens with a rhetorical question about whether those refusing the gospel have in fact "heard" it preached. The verb $\dot{\alpha}$-$\kappa o\acute{v}\epsilon\iota\nu$ ("to hear") picks up the keyword repeated twice in the climactic conclusion of the preceding verse: $\dot{\alpha}\kappa o\acute{\eta}$ ("hearing"). Whereas the conclusion of v. 17 was formulated in general terms that were widely shared in the various branches of the Christian movement, he begins the application in his own voice, $\dot{\alpha}\lambda\lambda\dot{\alpha}$ $\lambda\acute{\epsilon}\gamma\omega$ ("but I"). This first person singular style picks up the strand of 9:1-3 and 10:2, where Paul expresses his personal agony at the

69   Müller, "Zwei Marginalien," 253–54.
70   Bultmann, "Glossen," 197–202.
71   Morris, 391; Binder, *Glaube*, 66–67.
72   That $\dot{\alpha}\kappa o\acute{\eta}$ appears in v. 17 with reference to the act of hearing whereas it is used in v. 16 with reference to what was heard is widely assumed by commentators; e.g., Barrett, 205; Dunn, 2:623; Moo, 665–66.
73   The only parallel is Gal 3:2, 5, $\dot{\eta}$ $\dot{\epsilon}\xi$ $\dot{\alpha}\kappa o\hat{\eta}\varsigma$ $\pi\acute{\iota}\sigma\tau\epsilon\omega\varsigma$; see Betz, *Galatians*, 132, 136.
74   Dobbeler, *Glaube als Teilhabe*, 19–25.
75   Kelber, *Oral and the Written Gospel*, 146; see also Müller, "Glaube aus dem Hören," 422–25.

76   Walter Radl, "$\dot{\rho}\hat{\eta}\mu\alpha$," *EDNT* 3 (1993) 211.
77   See the note on 10:8.
78   Moo, 666; see also Albert Debrunner et al., "$\lambda\acute{\epsilon}\gamma\omega$ $\kappa\tau\lambda$.," *TDNT* 4 (1967) 116; Godet, 387; Sanday and Headlam, 298; Schmidt, 181; Lietzmann, 100; Zeller, 188; Stuhlmacher, 160; Fitzmyer, 598; Haacker, 215; Byrne, 327.
79   Schlatter, 217; Käsemann, 295; Cranfield, 2:537.
80   Zahn, 488–89; Kühl, 359; Müller, "Glaube aus dem Hören," 425; Munck, *Christ*, 94; Schlier, 318; Murray, 2:61; Wilckens, 2:222; Dunn, 2:623.
81   Weiss, 456–57; Michel, 334; Kuss, 3:776.

rejection of the gospel by so many of his compatriots. The ἀλλὰ λέγω formulation at the beginning of the sentence is an objection posed by the author against the foregoing conclusion in 10:17,[82] thus conveying the impression that Paul wishes momentarily to examine a possible excuse for his fellow Jews.[83] However, the question is formulated with a double negative that requires a positive response from the audience to the rhetorical question: μὴ οὐκ ἤκουσαν; ("Have they not heard?"). The audience must answer, "Yes, they have heard!"[84] In this shrewd rhetorical move, Paul places his audience in the position of responding immediately to close out the possibility of an excuse that he himself has suggested. The potential excuse thereby eliminated by the audience's response is then confirmed by μενοῦνγε ("indeed so!"),[85] reiterating in this context that the Jews had indeed heard the gospel. Without an introductory formula, Paul then moves directly into the citation of a Psalm that he believes would be familiar to his audience.

The third citation in the chain is drawn verbatim from LXX Ps 18:5 (= MT 19:4), and takes up the issue suggested in the initial climax (10:14b). This issue had been explicitly posed in the rhetorical question of 10:18a about whether belief is possible if in fact people have not heard the gospel. The psalm referred to God's revelation in nature, which was clearly visible to people everywhere,[86] but Paul applies this saying to the preaching of the gospel of Christ.[87] It has resounded εἰς πᾶσαν τὴν γῆν ("into all the earth") and εἰς τὰ πέρατα τῆς οἰκουμένης ("to the ends of the world"), echoing the expansive language of the early Christian mission[88] and correlating with the earlier citations from Isaiah.[89] The reference to τὰ ῥήματα αὐτῶν ("their words") also resonates nicely with ῥῆμα Χριστοῦ ("word of Christ") in 10:17 and τὸ ῥῆμα τῆς πίστεως ὃ κηρύσσομεν ("the word of faith that we preach") in 10:8. The historical implication is so sweeping that scholars have exerted considerable effort to diminish Paul's apparent overstatement. That the voice of early Christian preaching had already reached the limits of the known world has been taken as prophetic,[90] as hyperbolic,[91] or as an expression of Paul's missionary enthusiasm.[92] That the reference is restricted to the mission to Jews[93] would counter the emphasis on "all" in the preceding argument of Romans, which explicitly includes Jews and Greeks.[94] Probably none of these explanations is

---

82   Meyer, 2:190: "the quite customary ἀλλά of *objection*"; Weiss, 457, following Chrysostom; Meyer, 189.

83   Wagner, *Heralds*, 180–84, suggests that Paul's rhetorical questions echo Isa 40:21 ("will you not know? Will you not hear?") and 40:28 ("And now, have you not known? Have you not heard?"), which are Isaiah's responses to public skepticism about his message. Although Paul's questions are formulated differently, these echos may have enhanced the effectiveness of his argument.

84   BDF §427.2, "have they not heard?" (Answer: "Indeed they have").

85   BDF §450 shows that μενοῦνγε is used to heighten or correct. Kühl, 361, Käsemann, 295, and Wilckens, 2:229, identify the adversative implication in this context, in which a suggested excuse is foreclosed and thus corrected. The interpretation by Schmidt, 181, and Michel, 335, of μενοῦνγε as an ironic comment on the following citation does not take account of the audience's positive response to the rhetorical question in 10:18a; see also the critiques in Zahn, 489, and Weiss, 458.

86   That this citation was intended by Paul to refer to natural revelation, as advocated by O'Neill, 221, and others, is aptly rejected by Bell, *Provoked to Jealousy*, 94–95.

87   The application to the context of missionary expansion is discussed by Zahn, 489; Kühl, 359; Kuss, 3:776–77; Moo, 667; Haacker, 216; Stanley, *Scripture*, 142. In contrast, Koch, *Schrift*, 23, lists this citation as incongruent with its context in Romans.

88   E.g., Mark 13:10, "the gospel must first be preached to all the nations (εἰς πάντα τὰ ἔθνη)"; Matt 28:19, "make disciples of all nations (πάντα τὰ ἔθνη)"; Acts 1:8, "you shall be my witnesses . . . to the end of the earth (ἕως ἐσχάτου τῆς γῆς)"; Acts 17:6, "these men have turned the world (τὴν οἰκουμένην) upside down." For a discussion of the early Christian appropriation of the imperial concept of the οἰκουμένη, see Heinrich Balz, "οἰκουμένη," *EDNT* 2 (1991) 504.

89   Wagner, *Heralds*, 185.

90   Käsemann, 296; Wilckens, 2:230.

91   Cranfield, 2:537; Moo, 667.

92   Zeller, 188–89.

93   Dunn, 2:624, refers to Munck, *Christ*, 96–99. This restriction counters the emphasis on "all" in the preceding argument of Romans as explicitly including Jews and Greeks.

94   See also Bell, *Provoked to Jealousy*, 94.

required when one takes the rhetorical nature of this syllogism into account. As an answer to the question about whether the gospel has been heard by those who reject it, the scriptural citation serves as adequate warrant.[95] The proof lies not in the correlation between the text and historical reality but rather in the biblical text itself, which for Paul and his audience had unequivocal authority. Moreover, the rhetorical question that introduced this citation in 10:18a had already evoked assent from the audience, so that a predisposition to accept the relevance of Ps 18:5 was assured. From a rhetorical point of view, this verse would have been masterful for its original audience despite the problems it raises for modern interpreters.

■ **19** Paul repeats the formula of personal diatribe, ἀλλὰ λέγω ("but I say"), to introduce the reason for the failure of Paul's countrymen to accept the gospel.[96] The translation of μὴ Ἰσραὴλ οὐκ ἔγνω; with "is it the case that Israel has not known,"[97] is exactly parallel to the double negative in v. 18a.[98] "Yes, that is the case!" the audience must answer. Although Israel had ample opportunity to hear the gospel, it did not "know" it.[99] The use of the verb γινώσκειν ("to know") carries forward the thought of 10:2-3, that Israel has ζῆλον . . . οὐ κατ᾽ ἐπίγνωσιν ("zeal without knowledge") and "is ignorant of the righteousnes of God" (ἀγνοοῦντες γὰρ τὴν τοῦ θεοῦ δικαιοσύνην).[100] As I showed in the exegesis

of this earlier section of chap. 10, what prevented proper "knowledge" of the truth of the gospel was Israel's zeal to maintain its honor through obedience to the law and thus to "establish righteousness" in comparison with others. Paul employed the same verb (γινώσκειν) in 7:15 to depict the strange lack of knowledge on the part of the zealot whose fanatical obedience to the law produces evil rather than good. This is the issue to which Paul turns in the citation that follows.

The citation from Deut 32:21 is introduced with explicit reference to Moses, which lends additional warrant to the argument. The word πρῶτος, used here as in 1:8 without a subsequent "second," probably has the sense of "Moses was the first to say."[101] Since two additional citations from Isaiah follow, the temporal priority of Moses was relevant. The following citation, therefore, is not Paul's voice directed to his Roman audience,[102] but Moses' voice directed to Israel. The dilemma of misguided zeal in the earlier argument of Romans, therefore, was not a fiction invented by Paul but a phenomenon first identified by none other than the primary spokesman of the Jewish law. As visible below, the citation differs from the LXX at several points:

LXX of Deut 32:21: κἀγὼ παραζηλώσω αὐτοὺς ἐπ᾽ οὐκ ἔθνει, ἐπ᾽ ἔθνει ἀσυνέτῳ παροργιῶ αὐτούς. ("And I shall make them zealous in regard to a

---

95   See Wilk, *Bedeutung des Jesajabuches*, 133.

96   Weiss, 458.

97   Dunn, 2:624; Cranfield, 2:538; Hofius, "Evangelium und Israel," 298; Byrne, 327.

98   The rule appears in BDF §427.2, but is usually not followed by commentators; see, e.g., Godet, 388; Meyer, 2:193; Morris, 393; Murray, 2:62; Wilckens, 2:230; Moo, 667–68; Bell, *Provoked to Jealousy*, 99–100; Wolfgang Reinbold, "Israel und das Evangelium: Zur Exegese von Römer 10,19-21," *ZNW* 86 (1995) 122–23. Johnson, 163, suggests the translation, "Israel was not ignorant, was it?" on the mistaken ground that a question beginning with μὴ requires a negative response, but this question, like 10:18a, has a double negative that requires a positive response.

99   Wilk, *Bedeutung des Jesajabuches*, 133.

100   See Cranfield, 2:538; Dunn, 2:624. Bell, *Provoked to Jealousy*, 103, notes the verbal correspondences between v. 2 and v. 19 but overlooks the political dimension of fanatical zeal that lies behind Paul's explanation.

101   Weiss, 459–60; Dunn, 2:625; Kuss, 3:779. Cranfield, 2:539, argues convincingly that the proposal by Bentley, Zahn, 490, and others to place the question mark after the word "first" ("Was not Israel the first to know?") remains implausible. The suggestion by Reinbold, "Römer 10,19-21," 126, that a numerical listing was intended by Paul, who would thereby have presented the following Isaiah citation as the second answer to the question posed in v. 19a, is rendered unlikely by the lack of a "second" in the text. Moreover the δέ ("but") in the introduction of v. 20a suggests an antithesis in relation to vv. 18–19.

102   Reinbold, "Römer 10,19-21," 124–25, overlooks the rhetoric of v. 19a in arguing that the citation from Deuteronomy is directed at Roman Gentile Christians. See the detailed critique on exegetical grounds in Keller, *Gottes Treue*, 183–84.

non-nation, with a senseless nation I shall make them angry.")

Paul: Ἐγὼ παραζηλώσω ὑμᾶς ἐπ᾽ οὐκ ἔθνει, ἐπ᾽ ἔθνει ἀσυνέτῳ παροργιῶ ὑμᾶς. ("I shall make you zealous with regard to a non-nation, with a senseless nation I shall make you angry.")

That Paul altered the citation from Deuteronomy is widely assumed.[103] The deletion of the "and" in Paul's version is required because of the need to place the citation in a new context,[104] but the substitution of "you" for "them" is more significant. In the context of the reference to "Israel" in v. 19a, this alteration makes clear that the targets of Moses' accusation are not the same "they" as mentioned in the preceding citation (v. 18b),

that is, the Christian preachers.[105] The result of this minor alteration is that Moses, the most authoritative voice in Jewish history, addresses his fellow adherents to the law in a direct manner.[106] The emphatic ἐγώ ("I") that opens this citation is Yahweh, speaking through Moses.[107] The key translation problem in this verse is the verb παραζηλόω, which can be rendered in several ways. Since the preposition παρά makes the attached verb transitive,[108] rendered here with "make x" or "provoke to x," the translation issue centers on the verb ζηλόω. In the NT, the terms ζηλόω and ζῆλος have four lines of traditional definition, as Wiard Popkes shows:[109] holy zeal in the sense of Israel's holy war;[110] hostility that derives from zeal or jealousy;[111] jealousy

---

103 Koch, *Schrift*, 119; Reinbold, "Römer 10,19-21," 124; Cranfield, 2:539; Dunn, 2:625; Fitzmyer, 599.

104 See Stanley, *Scripture*, 142.

105 Bell, *Provoked to Jealousy*, 96; Koch, *Schrift*, 110. Stanley, *Scripture*, 143, finds Koch's explanation of the change of object unconvincing because v. 19a makes it sufficiently plain that Israel is being addressed. In this instance, however, Paul apparently wished to be doubly certain that the citation would not be misunderstood. Reinbold, "Römer 10,19-21," 124, makes the implausible suggestion that the "you" refers to Gentile believers, which implies that the "non-nation" refers to Jews rather than Gentiles. For a critique, see Keller, *Gottes Treue*, 173–84.

106 Dunn, 2:625, cites Hübner, *Gottes Ich und Israel*, 97: "Paul alters the citation so that this I of God directs itself to the Thou of Israel." See also Stanley, *Scripture*, 144.

107 Luise Schottroff, "ἐγώ," *EDNT* 1 (1990) 378–79, observes that the personal pronoun is usually emphatic and that it frequently occurs in revelatory discourse such as "I am your God Almighty," e.g., Gen 17:1 (ἐγώ εἰμι ὁ θεός σου).

108 BDF §150.

109 Wiard Popkes, "ζῆλος κτλ.," *EDNT* 2 (1991) 100–101. See also Albrecht Stumpff, "ζῆλος κτλ.," *TDNT* 2 (1964) 880–82, 886–88; Hengel, *Zealots*, 59–75, Chris Seeman, "Zeal/Jealousy," in Pilch and Malina, eds., *Biblical Social Values*, 210, defines zeal/jealousy as the concern for maintaining possession and control over that to which one claims to have honorable and exclusive access." He describes (211) the steps of zeal/jealousy as including emotional "ignition" against perceived threats and a "retaliatory response" in defense of injured honor.

Torrey Seland, *Establishment Violence in Philo and Luke: A Study of Nonconformity to the Torah and the Jewish Vigilante Reactions* (Leiden: Brill, 1995) 37–62, surveys the glorification of Phinehas as a model of zealous vigilantism in defense of the Torah, showing that such violence was directed against persons or groups that "posed a socio-theological threat to Jewish identity and the social coherence of the Jews" (362). The zeal that leads to "social group-vigilantism" (301) is a reaction against perceived violations of Israel's holiness (46–59). Bell, *Provoked to Jealousy*, 39–43, discerns two meanings of παραζηλόω in the Pauline letters, "provoke to zealous anger," and "provoke to jealousy."

110 For example, Phil 3:6: "as to zeal (κατὰ ζῆλος) a persecutor of the church"; Heb 10:27: "a zealous fire (πυρὸς ζῆλος) that will consume the adversaries." This follows OT usage, such as Zeph 1:18: "the whole land shall be destroyed by the fire of his zeal (ἐν πυρὶ ζήλου αὐτοῦ)"; or Ezek 36:6, in explaining the destruction of Edom: "Behold, I have spoken in my zeal (ἐν τῷ ζήλῳ μου) and in my wrath, because you have borne the reproaches of the heathen."

111 For example, in Acts 5:17-18, after the high priest and the Sadducees witnessed the expansion of the early church, "they were filled with zeal (ἐπλήσθησαν ζήλου) and arrested the apostles and put them in the common prison." This follows the paradigm in 1 Macc 1:24-26 after Mattathias saw the pagan sacrifice: "he was inflamed with zeal (ἐζήλωσε), and his veins trembled . . . he ran and slew him upon the altar . . . thus he dealt zealously with the law (ἐζήλωσε τῷ νόμῳ), as did Phineas. . . ." A warning against such violent rage or jealousy aroused by alleged evildoers is found in Ps 36:8: "cease from

itself;[112] and emulation or the desire to attain a goal.[113] Previous commentaries have opted for a translation in terms of "jealousy"[114] that takes insufficient account of the references to violent, religious zeal in Rom 7 and 10 or of the autobiographical clues concerning Paul's former life as a zealot (Gal 1:13-14; Phil 3:4-11).[115] This traditional translation also makes it difficult to conceive how the citation from Deuteronomy explains Israel's lack of "knowledge" in v. 19a, because jealousy could only be provoked if Israel understood that admission to the messianic realm was in fact open to Gentiles.[116] Moreover, neither "make jealous" or "cause to emulate" conforms to the formal requirement of synonymous parallelism in matching "make you angry" in the same way that "non-nation" matches "senseless nation."[117] These

contextual and poetic indications, therefore, lead me to believe that a translation such as "make zealous" or "provoke to zealous rage"[118] is required, with the following prepositional phrase understood as "in regard to"[119] the targets of religio-cultural hostility and competition,[120] that is, the Gentiles. There is a consensus that οὐκ ἔθνος ("no-people") in this citation refers to Gentiles,[121] particularly in the light of the Hosea prophecy cited in 9:25-26 concerning the Gentiles as "not my people."[122] The expression ἔθνος ἀσυνέτῳ ("senseless nation") points in the same direction,[123] because the adjective appeared in 1:21, 31 in reference to pagans whose mind and heart lacked the capacity to perceive God.[124] The verb παροργίζω stands parallel to "make zealous," with the same preposition, παρά, changing the verb meaning

---

anger and forsake wrath: do not become zealous (μὴ παραζήλου) so as to do evil."

112 For example, Acts 7:9: "the patriarchs, jealous of Joseph (ζηλώσαντες τὸν Ἰωσήφ), sold him into Egypt"; or 1 Cor 13:4: "love is not jealous (οὐ ζηλοῖ) or boastful," following usage such as Gen 30:1: "And Rachel, perceiving that she bore Jacob no children, was jealous (ἐζήλωσε) of her sister"; or Sir 37:10: "hide your counsel from those who are jealous (τῶν ζηλούντων) of you."

113 For example, 1 Cor 12:31: "zealously desire (ζηλοῦτε) the higher gifts"; or 2 Cor 9:2 with regard to the offering for Jerusalem: "your zealous eagerness (τὸ ὑμῶν ζῆλος) has stirred up most of them"; or Titus 2:14: "to purify for himself a people of his own who are zealous (ζηλωτής) for good deeds." There are parallels to this more positive sense in Sir 51:18: "I zealously sought (ἐζήλωσα) what is good," but the clear sense of "emulation" for παραζηλόω occurs first in Philo Praem. 89, where animals are said to "grow gentle in emulation (τῇ παραζηλώσει) of the docility and affection for the master."

114 For example, Zahn, 493; Godet, 388-89; Meyer, 2:194; Weiss, 460; Sanday and Headlam, 300; Schlier, 315; Käsemann, 297; Kuss, 3:779; Cranfield, 2:539; Wilckens, 2:231; Dunn, 2:625; Stuhlmacher, 160; Fitzmyer, 599-600; Moo, 668; Schreiner, 573; Byrne, 325; Nanos, *Mystery*, 249-50; Gignac, *Romans 9–11*, 218-22; White, *Apostle*, 45; Keller, *Gottes Treue*, 186-92; Esler, *Conflict and Identity*, 288-91. The only commentary I have found that is ambiguous on this point is Michel who properly translates παραζηλόω as *Eifer* (= "zeal") on 332, but speaks of jealousy on 335.

115 Stuhlmacher, 160-61, followed by Keller, *Gottes Treue*, 185-87, argues for "jealous and angry," which takes better account of Paul's autobiography. The clearest grasp of the issue is available in Donaldson, "Zealot and Convert," 668-82.

116 Nanos, *Mystery*, 249: "Paul assumes that his fellow Jews will see in his success among the gentiles that their own Jewish universalistic hopes are being fulfilled. . . . Hence they would be jealous of Paul's ministry and reconsider his declaration that the hope of Israel has come in Christ Jesus." How this explanation can explain the violence of Jewish reactions to the gospel is hard to imagine.

117 Deut 32:21 has the form of synonymous parallelism with chiastic development, in which (a) make zealous/jealous/emulate; (b) "non-nation," is followed by (b') "senseless nation" and (a') make angry.

118 Bell, *Provoked to Jealousy,* 39, prefers the formulation "provoke to jealous anger." Baker is on target in "Motif of Jealousy," 75: "Paul envisions Israel being provoked to angry jealousy in which it zealously upholds Torah."

119 BAGD (2000) 365.8.

120 See Haacker, 217, for an allusion to the competitive relationship between Israel and the Gentiles.

121 Godet, 389; Cranfield, 2:539; Fitzmyer, 599; Haacker, 217; Moo, 668. In contrast, Reinbold, "Römer 10,19-21," 125, makes the implausible suggestion that ἔθνος refers to non-Christian Jews.

122 Moo, 688.

123 See Michel, 336; Haacker, 217.

124 Hans Conzelmann, "συνίημι κτλ.," *TDNT* 7 (1971) 895.

"be angry" into the word referring to provoking some-one else to anger. The Deuteronomy passage is unusual in that this verb is ordinarily employed in reference to Israel's behavior provoking Yahweh to anger.[125] In the context of this pericope, the words from Moses explain the behavior of Jews rejecting the gospel as deriving from divinely provoked zeal and anger against the Gentile world. Since the Jewish form of the competition for honor that marked the ancient Mediterranean world was to exceed others in righteousness through conformity to the Torah, Israel's zeal turned against Gentiles, who polluted the world. Consequently, Israel angrily rejected any gospel that accepted Gentiles as equals. This rage and violence was predicted by Moses, according to Paul's argument, and will be overcome only at the end of time, when the mercy of God becomes triumphant (11:25-26, 32). In the meanwhile, it remains certain that God's word has not failed (9:6).[126]

■ **20** The "but" in v. 20a suggests that the following citation has a change of address: from the fellow Jews of Moses in v. 19 to the Gentiles of v. 20.[127] The reference to Isaiah's boldness[128] may imply an unusual degree of charismatic authority, similar to what Paul claims in 15:15, where a word associated with this stem, $\tau o \lambda \mu \acute{a} \omega$ ("be bold, dare"), also appears.[129] The substantive issue, however, is that the content of this prophecy concerns God's astounding action of revealing God's self to shameful outsiders, evoking the zealous rage and violence of defenders of traditional views[130] and thus requiring special courage on the part of prophets and preachers, which correlates with Paul's use of $\tau o \lambda \mu \acute{a} \omega$ in Phil 1:19.[131]

The citation from Isa 65:1 appears to reflect the word order found in early septuagintal textual traditions as well as in the original Hebrew text.[132] Other minor differences are illustrated below:

MT translation: "I was ready to be sought by those who did not ask for me; I was ready to be found by those who did not seek me."

LXX S and C versions of Isa 65:1: $\acute{E}\mu\varphi\alpha\nu\grave{\eta}\varsigma$ $\acute{\epsilon}\gamma\epsilon\nu\acute{o}$-$\mu\eta\nu$ $\tau o\hat{\iota}\varsigma$ $\acute{\epsilon}\mu\grave{\epsilon}$ $\mu\grave{\eta}$ $\zeta\eta\tau o\hat{\upsilon}\sigma\iota\nu$, $\epsilon\acute{\upsilon}\rho\acute{\epsilon}\vartheta\eta\nu$ $\tau o\hat{\iota}\varsigma$ $\acute{\epsilon}\mu\grave{\epsilon}$ $\mu\grave{\eta}$ $\acute{\epsilon}\pi\epsilon\rho\omega\tau\hat{\omega}\sigma\iota\nu$ ("I showed myself to those who did not seek me, I was found by those not asking for me").

LXX A and Q versions of Isa 65:1: $E\acute{\upsilon}\rho\acute{\epsilon}\vartheta\eta\nu$ $\acute{\epsilon}\nu$ $\tau o\hat{\iota}\varsigma$ $\acute{\epsilon}\mu\grave{\epsilon}$ $\mu\grave{\eta}$ $\zeta\eta\tau o\hat{\upsilon}\sigma\iota\nu$, $\acute{\epsilon}\mu\varphi\alpha\nu\grave{\eta}\varsigma$ $\acute{\epsilon}\gamma\epsilon\nu\acute{o}\mu\eta\nu$ $\tau o\hat{\iota}\varsigma$ $\acute{\epsilon}\mu\grave{\epsilon}$ $\mu\grave{\eta}$ $\acute{\epsilon}\pi\epsilon\rho\omega\tau\hat{\omega}\sigma\iota\nu$ ("I was found by those who did not seek me, I showed myself to those not asking for me").

Paul: $E\acute{\upsilon}\rho\acute{\epsilon}\vartheta\eta\nu$ $\acute{\epsilon}\nu$ $\tau o\hat{\iota}\varsigma$ $\acute{\epsilon}\mu\grave{\epsilon}$ $\mu\grave{\eta}$ $\zeta\eta\tau o\hat{\upsilon}\sigma\iota\nu$, $\acute{\epsilon}\mu\varphi\alpha\nu\grave{\eta}\varsigma$ $\acute{\epsilon}\gamma\epsilon\nu\acute{o}\mu\eta\nu$ $\tau o\hat{\iota}\varsigma$ $\acute{\epsilon}\mu\grave{\epsilon}$ $\mu\grave{\eta}$ $\acute{\epsilon}\pi\epsilon\rho\omega\tau\hat{\omega}\sigma\iota\nu$ ("I was found among those who did not seek me, I showed myself to those not asking for me").

---

125 Most of the more than fifty occurrences of this verb in the LXX refer to provoking God's anger; Dunn, 2:624, cites *T. Lev.* 3.10: "the sons of men . . . sinning and provoking the anger of the Most High"; *T. Zeb.* 9.9: "You will provoke God to wrath by the wickedness of your deeds"; and *T. Ash.* 2.6: "He who cheats his neighbor provokes God's wrath."

126 See Tobin, *Paul's Rhetoric*, 351.

127 Wilk, *Bedeutung des Jesajabuches*, 137.

128 The verb $\acute{a}\pi o\tau o\lambda\mu\acute{a}\omega$ ("be bold") is used here for the only time in the OT or the NT. Wilk, *Bedeutung des Jesajabuches*, 137, rightly rejects Hanson's comment in *Studies*, 189, that "the boldness belongs to God and not to the prophet."

129 Haacker, 217, citing William L. Schutter, "Philo's Psychology of Prophetic Inspiration and Romans 10:20," *SBLSP* (1989) 624–33. It remains unclear why Hanson, *Studies*, 189, says that the reference to "boldness" shows no "interest in the prophet's psychological state as he uttered the prophecy."

130 Morris, 394, cites Haldane's comment that this prophecy was "most offensive to the Jews."

131 Wilk, *Bedeutung des Jesajabuches*, 137, rejects the relevance of the parallel in Phil 1:19 because the element of "resistance" is lacking in the Isaiah citation. This overlooks the underlying issue of zealous opposition to outsiders that lies at the center of Jewish rejection of the gospel. Wilk also unfortunately rejects Bindemann's suggestion in *Theologie*, 233, that boldness in Rom 10:20 refers to the provocation of God's action in relation to Israel and the Gentiles.

132 See Zahn, 492; Koch, *Schrift*, 49–51; Bell, *Provoked to Jealousy*, 104–5.

Whether the sequence of Paul's citation is due to the existence of the A and Q versions,[133] which may in fact have been influenced by Christian scribes,[134] or to his recollection of the Hebrew word order,[135] or to a faulty memory,[136] the citation as he provides it serves his purpose well. The point of emphasis is shifted from the rather neutral expression, "those not asking for me," to the dramatic contention that "I was found among those who did not seek me."[137] The emphasis is clearly on the Gentile converts who have been found by God through the gospel,[138] thus carrying forward the line in 9:30. This confirms the charge in 10:19 that there is no way a message that was producing such wide-ranging results would not have been heard by Jews. The Gentiles had not only heard the gospel but had responded to it in faith, following the principle of 10:17, and thus are assured of having encountered God. The aorist verbs εὑρέθην ("I was found") and ἐγενόμην ("I showed") in the Isaiah text are retained,[139] whether referring back to the time of Isaiah when the vision of a future Messiah was first emerging,[140]or, as seems more likely, referring to the success of the Gentile mission over the two and a half decades before the writing of Romans.[141] In the context of Paul's reinterpretation of Isa 65:2, the present participle in the dative plural, ζητοῦσιν ("by those [not] seeking") and ἐπερωτῶσιν ("to those [not] asking") refers to Gentiles who are being converted by the gospel.[142] Since the standard versions of the Isaiah citation in the MT or the LXX did not include the preposition ἐν ("in, among") before the phrase "those who did not seek me," it is likely that Paul added it or chose to take it over from the A and Q versions. It suggests that God was in fact to be found "among" or "in the midst of" the groups of Gentile believers.[143] Ross Wagner refers to this "'discovery' of Gentiles in a text originally concerned only with Israel" as a "stunning reversal."[144] With this citation, the shocking turnabout of the gospel is fully manifest, whereby insiders become outsiders and vice versa. The traditional system of honor and shame was overturned by the ultimate source of honor, the Lord God, who spoke through Isaiah and who is manifest in the gospel of Christ crucified. This revolution of divine grace, which comes to those not deserving or seeking it, lies at the heart both of Gentile acceptance of the gospel and Jewish rage against it. This was boldness indeed.

■ **21** The prepositional phrase πρὸς τὸν Ἰσραήλ that introduces the final citation in this pericope should be taken as "in reference to Israel"[145] rather than as a direct address, "to Israel."[146] The particle δέ appears again with the sense of "but," indicating that the address to the Gentiles in v. 20 shifts to Israel in v. 21.[147] Once again, the oral quality of the prophecy is emphasized, as Isaiah "says" these words to Israel. This final citation in

133 Koch, *Schrift*, 49–51. Stanley, *Scripture*, 143, finds Koch's explanation, although "speculative," to be more likely than the alternatives. Wagner, *Heralds*, 210–11, also accepts Koch's view.

134 See Melvin K. H. Peters, "Septuagint," *ABD* 5 (1992) 1098–1100.

135 Zahn, 493; Wilk, *Bedeutung des Jesajabuches*, 35–36.

136 Dunn, 2:626.

137 See Wilk, *Bedeutung des Jesajabuches*, 43. Pancratius C. Beentjes, "Inverted Quotations in the Bible: A Neglected Stylistic Pattern," *Bib* 63 (1982) 516, identifies 10:20-21 as an "inverted quotation," following many examples from the OT, but he does not explain its exegetical significance.

138 Weiss, 460–61; Kühl, 363; Cranfield, 2:540–41.

139 See Koch, *Schrift*, 317–18. Wilk's contention in *Bedeutung des Jesajabuches*, 137, that the aorist verbs refer to events in the present that are not yet completed is a flat contradicion of the grammatical function of the aorist as punctiliar; see BDF §§318, 324B.

140 Johnson, 165.

141 Dunn, 2:626, refers to the prior success of the Pauline mission; Wagner, "Heralds of Isaiah," 222, refers to this use of Isaiah as "missiological."

142 Dunn, 2:626.

143 See Stanley, *Scripture*, 145, who nevertheless remains skeptical that Paul can be proven responsible for this insertion.

144 Wagner, *Heralds*, 213.

145 Meyer, 2:196; Morris, 395; Dunn, 2:626; BAGD (2000) 875e; Wilk, *Bedeutung des Jesajabuches*, 137.

146 Godet, 390; Kuss, 3:780; Käsemann, 293.

147 See Meyer, 2:196; Weiss, 461.

the chain is drawn verbatim from Isa 65:2, with a transposition of the expression "all day long" to the point of emphasis at the beginning of the sentence. The change is illustrated below:

LXX of Isa 65:2: ἐξεπέτασα τὰς χεῖράς μου ὅλην τὴν ἡμέραν πρὸς λαὸν ἀπειθοῦντα καὶ ἀντιλέγοντα ("I reached out my hands all day long to a disobedient and disputatious people").

Paul: Ὅλην τὴν ἡμέραν ἐξεπέτασα τὰς χεῖράς μου πρὸς λαὸν ἀπειθοῦντα καὶ ἀντιλέγοντα ("All day long I reached out my hands to a disobedient and disputatious people").

While it is likely that Paul was responsible for transposing the expression "all day long" to the opening of this citation,[148] the redactional motivation is rarely discussed in the commentaries.[149] The transposition seems to resonate with the poignant question that opens the next pericope, whether God has rejected Israel.[150] The entire argument in the third proof of Romans aims at denying this prejudicial possibility. The transposition reinforces the idea that God's patient mercy remains "continually" in force with regard to his beloved Israel.[151] The expression of reaching out hands also points in this direction: the NT hapax legomenon ἐκπετάννυμι τὰς χεῖράς μου ("reach out, spread out my hands")[152] is a "gesture of appealing welcome and fellowship."[153] The expression

ὅλην τὴν ἡμέραν ("all day long") is a semiticism[154] meaning "uninterruptedly" or "without pause," thus accentuating the extraordinary steadfastness of God's mercy. It stands in tension with the description of Israel as "a disobedient and disputatious people." The verb ἀπειθέω was used in 2:8 to depict persons who "disobey the truth," and it appears elsewhere in Paul's letters in reference to refusing to have faith in the gospel.[155] In the new context of Paul's syllogism, the reference in 10:16 leads to the clear implication that "disobedience" should be understood as rejection of the gospel.[156] The final verb, ἀντιλέγειν ("to speak against"), points in the same direction. It appears in Sir 4:25 in the context of the wise person who learns not "to speak against the truth" (ἀντίλεγε τῇ ἀληθείᾳ) and in Isa 50:5 in the context of not speaking against the prophetic message. In the context of this syllogism, the participle ἀντιλέγοντα has the sense of "disputatious," with particular reference to speaking against the gospel and thereby resisting the outstretched hands of divine mercy.[157] The function of the citation is to draw the final consequence from the syllogism, namely, that while they remain a "disobedient and disputatious people,"[158] God continues to reach out his hands imploringly to Israel.[159] They have been blinded by fanatical zeal, according to Deut 32:21, but that is not the final word, and as the subsequent pericopes will go on to show, divine mercy will in the end rule the day (11:32).

148 See Koch, *Schrift*, 105–6; Stanley, *Scripture*, 146–47; Wilk, *Bedeutung des Jesajabuches*, 44.

149 While most commentaries make no effort to explain the transposition, Schmidt, 182, and Fitzmyer, 600, make the obvious point that it provides "emphasis," but they do not elaborate what it implies.

150 Schreiner, 574, cites Stanley, *Scripture*, 146, in support of the inference that the transposition emphasizes "God's longsuffering." See also Wilk, *Bedeutung des Jesajabuches*, 44, 138.

151 Thus Schmidt, 179–83, entitles this pericope "die open door for Israel." See also Schlatter, 218; Johnson, *Function*, 159.

152 BAGD (2000) 307.

153 Cranfield, 2:541; Fitzmyer, 600.

154 As in the citation of Ps 43:23 in Rom 8:36, ὅλην τὴν ἡμέραν is a semiticism for "continually," according to Michel, 336; Cranfield, 2:541. See also Deut 28:32; Isa 65:5; Jer 20:7, 8.

155 See Rudolf Bultmann, "ἀπειθέω," *TDNT* 6 (1968) 11.

156 See Peter Bläser, "ἀπειθέω," *EDNT* 1 (1990) 118.

157 Godet, 390, refers to "the hair-splitting and sophisms whereby the Israelites seek to justifiy their persevering refusal to return to God."

158 See Koch, *Schrift*, 281.

159 See Esler, *Conflict and Identity*, 293.

11

The Seventh Pericope

Diatribe and Midrash concerning the Status of Israel

1/ I say therefore, "God did not cast off God's people[a], did he?" By no means! For I am also an Israelite, from the seed of Abraham, from the tribe of Benjamin. 2/ "God did not cast off God's people" whom he knew beforehand. Or do you not know what the scripture says concerning Elijah, as he pleads with God against Israel[b]?

> 3/ "Lord, they have killed your prophets,
>> they have demolished your altars,
> and I alone am left,
>> and they are seeking my life."

4/ But what does the oracle say to him?

> "I kept[c] for myself seven thousand men,
>> who have not bowed a knee to Baal."

5/ Therefore in this manner also at the present critical time a remnant has been born by election of grace. 6/ But if by grace, no longer[d] from works, since otherwise the grace ceases to become grace.[e]

7/ What then? What Israel is seeking[f], it failed to attain; but the chosen attained it, but the others were made obtuse. 8/ Just as[g] it has been written:

> "God gave them a spirit of stupor,
>> so that eyes do not see and ears do not hear,
> until the present day."

9/ And David says,

> "Let their table become a snare and a trap,
>> a stumbling block and a retribution for them,
> 10/ Let their eyes be darkened so they cannot see,
>> and bend their backs continually."

a   The variant τὴν κληρονομίαν ("the inheritance") in P[46] F G b f g o goth Ambst Tyc Ambr Sedulius-Scotus brings the wording of this verse closer to the LXX of Ps 94:14 and thus is less credible than the strongly attested τὸν λαόν ("the people") found in ℵ A B C D L P Ψ 6 33 69 81 88 104 181 256 263 323 326 330 365 424 436 451 459 614 629 945 1175 1241 1243 1319 1505 1506 1573 1735 1739 1836 1852 1874 1877 1881 1912 1962 1874 2127 2200 2464 2492 2495 *Maj Lect* ar d vg sy[p,h] sa bo arm eth

geo slav Or[lat] Eus Chr Cyr Hier Pel Aug; cf. Metzger, *Textual Commentary*, 464. In "Restoring the Inheritance in Romans 11:1," *JBL* 118 (1999) 89–96, Mark D. Given argues for the priority of τὴν κληρονομίαν on the uncertain grounds that it is the harder reading and provides superior intertextual echoes. The addition of ὃν προέγνω ("whom he foreknew") by P[46] (but with ἥν[vid]) ℵ[2] A D* appears to be a reduplication of the phrase found in v. 2; it is too weakly attested to be original.

b   The inclusion of λέγων ("saying") by ℵ* L 69 88 104 323 326 330 424* 614 945 1175[(acc. to Swanson)] 1241 1319[c] 1735 1836 1874 2464 *Maj* sy[p] appears to be an editorial improvement that makes clear that the following words are a citation. The absence of "saying" is well supported by ℵ[2] A B C D F G P Ψ 6 81 365 424[c] 1175[(acc. to N-A)] 1243 1319* 1505 1506 1573 1739 1881 2495 *al* latt sy[h] Eus.

c   The second aorist form κατέλιπον ("I kept") is found in ℵ B D Ψ 6 69 323 330 365 424 614 945 1241 1243 1505 1881 2495 *Maj* Did, which appears to be original. The future form κατάλειψα in 81 1506 *pc* appears to be influenced by the LXX of 1 Kgs 19:18. The imperfect form κατέλειπον has much stronger support in P[46] A C F G L P 88 104 326 1175 1319 1573 1735 1739 1836 1874 2464 *al*, but is probably a copyist's error.

d   In place of the rather opaque formulation οὐκέτι ἐξ ἔργων ("no longer from works"), P[46] 614 1881 *pc* d vg[st] sy[p] have οὐκ ἐξ ἔργων ("not from works"), which should be accounted as secondary because of its ease and weaker attestation.

e   The "short" text ἡ χάρις οὐκέτι γίνεται χάρις ("the grace no longer becomes grace") is supported by P[46] ℵ* A C D F G P (81 has χάρις γίνεται) 263 629 630 1506[vid] 1739 1852 1881 1908* 2110 2200 ar b d f g o vg sa bo arm (eth) geo[1] Or[gr, lat] Did[vid] Cyr Ambst Ambr Hier Pel Aug. The "long ending" of this phrase appears in ℵ[2] (B *see below*) L Ψ 5 6 33[vid] (61) 69 88 104 181 256 323 330 (365) 424 436 441 451 459 467 614 621 623 720 917 945 1175 1241 1243 1319 1398 1505 1563 1573 1718 (1735) (1836) 1838 1845 1874 1908[c] 1912 1942 1959 (1962 has ἤ χάρις for ἐστι χάρις) 2127 2138 2197 2464 2492 (2495 has χάρις ἐστίν) (2516) 2523 2544 2718 *Maj Lect* vg[ms] (sy[p,h]) geo[2] slav[ms] Chr, εἰ δὲ ἐξ ἔργων οὐκέτι ἐστι [B lacks ἐστι] χάρις, ἐπεὶ τὸ ἔργον οὐκέτι ἐστὶν ἔργον [B 1678 1962 replace the final ἔργον with χάρις, "grace"] ("but if it is from works, then it is no longer grace, since the work is no longer work" [or "grace" in B]). These various forms of the "long ending" are less strongly supported and appear to be explanatory and therefore unoriginal (see Metzger, *Textual Commentary*, 464),

650

and they reflect similar motivations, as, e.g., in 796 1524 1717 1877 1929* 2816*: . . . χάρις. εἰ δὲ ἐξ ἔργον, οὐκέτι ἐστὶ χάρις (". . . grace. But if from work, there is no grace") and 365 1875 2344 (cf. 915 1751) *al* slav^{ms}: . . . χάρις, ἐπεὶ τὸ ἔργον οὐκέτι ἐστὶ ἔργον ("grace, since the work is not work").

f   The replacement of the widely attested and probably original reading ἐπιζητεῖ ("it seeks") by ἐπεζήτει ("it sought") in F G 104 1836 *pc* latt sy appears to have an explanatory motivation.

g   The reading καθάπερ ("as") is strongly enough attested by ℵ B 81 945$^{(acc. to N-A)}$ *pc* that it stands a good chance of being the original, more difficult reading as compared with καθώς ("as") in P^{46} A C D F G L P Ψ 6 33 69 88 104 323 326 330 365 424 614 945$^{(acc. to Swanson)}$ 1175 1241 1243 1319 1505 1573 1735 1739 1836 1874 1881 2344 2464 2495 *Maj.* In this instance Cranfield's reasoning in 1:182, 2:549 appears more sound than the choice of the Nestle-Aland$^{26/27}$ and *GNT*$^{3/4}$.

Analysis

That 11:1-10 is an integral pericope is widely acknowledged in the commentaries.[1] This passage is a brilliant fusion of diatribe and midrash. It is organized in two lines of argument inaugurated by the rhetorical questions in vv. 1 and 7.[2] Each question is followed by an answer in thesis form, supported with appropriate scriptural proofs in midrashic fashion. The initial proof text in the midrash is in 2a, followed by four supporting texts in the rest of the pericope, producing a series of five that is extended over the two halves of the diatribe. The transitional λέγω οὖν ("I say therefore") opens this pericope, just as it does the next pericope in v. 11.[3] The first rhetorical question takes up the logical consequence from the argument of the preceding pericope: if part of Israel refused to accept the gospel, does this not mean that God has rejected them as a chosen people?[4] This false conclusion[5] receives an immediate repudiation in the rhetorically effective phrase "by no means!" This brief, triple-line sentence, characteristic of earlier rhetorical exchanges in Romans, is followed by a matching three-line description of Paul's personal status showing that he could not conceivably be arguing that God has rejected the Jewish people. This point is flatly stated in v. 2 by citing a brief portion of Ps 94:14 and 1 Sam 12:22 that contains the same words used in the rhetorical question of v. 1. It provides the main text in this midrash that is elaborated by the four additional citations of 1 Kings, Deuteronomy, and the Psalms. The citations from 1 Kings are organized in four-line and two-line sentences, respectively,[6] from which Paul draws his decisive conclusion in vv. 5-6 concerning election through grace alone. This conclusion is expressed in a four-line sentence in which "grace" is repeated four times, an impressive example of reduplication. The use of the antithetical catchwords χάρις ("grace") and ἔργα ("works") in these two verses links vv. 1-6 not only with 9:30-32[7] but also with 4:1-6.

The second rhetorical exchange that begins in 11:7 is formulated in brief, three-line sentences matching the pattern of v. 1, and featuring antithetical parallelism and euphony with the fourfold repetition of ἐπ- in the chiastic climax in v. 7:

---

1   Sanday and Headlam, 307; Schlier, 320–21; Michel, 337; Barrett, 206; Käsemann, 298; Cranfield, 2:542; Kuss, 3:784; Wilckens, 2:234–35; Dunn, 2:632–34; Moo, 670–71; Schreiner, 578–90, proposes two pericopes, vv. 1-6 and vv. 7-10, which match the internal divisions proposed in the rhetorical disposition below. Dan G. Johnson, "The Structure and Meaning of Romans 11," *CBQ* 46 (1984) 91–92, also separates out vv. 1-6, but assigns it to a pericope extending to v. 16, which overlooks the midrashic structure that holds vv. 1-10 together as well as the signal of a new pericope, "I say therefore," in v. 11 that exactly parallels v. 1.

2   In *Romans 9–11*, 223, Gignac notes the thesis statements in vv. 1 and 7 but does not deal with the midrashic structure.

3   See Michel, 337; Weiss, "Beiträge," 240.

4   See Louw, 2:109.

5   See Stowers, *Diatribe*, 148.

6   See Weiss, "Beiträge," 240.

7   See Aageson, "Scripture," 280–81.

A ὃ ἐπιζητεῖ Ἰσραήλ ("What Israel is seeking"),
  B τοῦτο οὐκ ἐπέτυχεν ("it failed to attain"),
  B¹ ἡ δὲ ἐκλογὴ ἐπέτυχεν ("but the chosen attained it"),
A' οἱ δὲ λοιποὶ ἐπωρώθησαν ("but the others were made obtuse").

Similar to the use of the extended climax of 10:14-15a that provided the framework for the subsequent argument, 11:7 asserts a thesis about making unbelieving Israel obtuse, which is confirmed in midrashic fashion by the scriptural proofs in 11:8-10, completing the series of five quotations. The rhetorical impact of the pericope is enhanced by the parallelism in the Hebrew poetry cited in vv. 8-10. The catchword ὀφθαλμός ("eye") not only joins the two scriptural passages cited in vv. 8-10,[8] but also recalls the concluding reference in the catena of citations describing the sins of Jews and Greeks (3:18), "there is no fear of God before their eyes."

Rhetorical Disposition

IV.	The *probatio*
9:1–11:36	The third proof: The triumph of divine righteousness in the gospel's mission to Israel and the Gentiles
11:1-10	7. Diatribe and midrash concerning the status of Israel
11:1-6	a. The first midrash: God has not rejected Israel
11:1a-c	1) The rhetorical exchange concerning whether God has rejected Israel
11:1a	a) The transitional formula
11:1b	b) The rhetorical question
11:1c	c) The denial
11:1d-f	2) The refutation on the basis of Paul's personal status
11:1d	a) National status: "Israelite"
11:1e	b) Family lineage: "seed of Abraham"
11:1	c) Tribal status: "Benjamin"
11:2-4	3) The refutation from Scripture
11:2a	a) The thesis
	(1) The main proof text from 1 Sam 12:22 and Ps 94:14 that God has not rejected "his people"
	(2) The interpretive addition concerning those whom he "knew beforehand"
11:2b-4	b) The scriptural proof
11:2b-c	(1) Rhetorical question introducing the citations concerning Elijah
11:3	(2) The citation of 1 Kgs 19:10 concerning Elijah's charge against Israel
11:3a	(a) Killing the prophets
11:3b	(b) Destroying altars
11:3c	(c) Elijah isolated
11:3d	(d) Elijah's life in danger
11:4	(3) The citation and adaptation of 1 Kgs 19:18 concerning God maintaining a remnant
11:4a	(a) Rhetorical question introducing the citation
11:4b	(b) The citation
11:5-6	4) The conclusion: a remnant saved by grace rather than works
11:5	a) Conclusion about the present circumstances
	(1) Concluding formula
	(2) Temporal reference
	(3) Means by which remnant is saved: "grace"
11:6	b) Antithetical inference
11:6a	(1) Premise of grace
11:6b	(2) Antithetical inference concerning works
11:6c	(3) Consequence of not accepting the inference: "grace would no longer be grace"
11:7-10	b. The second midrash on unperceptive Israel
11:7	1) The rhetorical exchange
11:7a	a) The rhetorical question of general inference from the preceding argument
11:7b-e	b) The thesis about Israel becoming obtuse
11:7b	(1) Israel seeks [righteousness]
11:7c	(2) Israel fails to attain it
11:7d	(3) The elect attain it
11:7e	(4) The others were hardened
11:8-9	2) The scriptural proofs
11:8	a) The citation and adaptation of Deut 29:4 concerning a divinely ordained stupor
11:8a	(1) The introductory formula
11:8b-d	(2) The citation
11:8b	(a) The gift of stupor
11:8c	(b) The disabling of eyes and ears
11:8d	(c) The duration of stupor
11:9-10	b) The citation of Ps 68:23 concerning a curse of reversed advantages
11:9a	(1) The introductory formula
11:9b-10	(2) The citation
11:9b	(a) From table to trap
11:9c	(b) Stumbling block and retribution
11:10a	(c) From eyes to darkness
11:10b	(d) Backs under strain

---

8   Ibid., 282.

Exegesis

■ **1** This pericope opens with λέγω οὖν ("I say therefore"), used only here and in the beginning of the next pericope.[9] It fits the many indications that this letter was intended as verbal communication,[10] in which the trained scribe employed by Phoebe reads the letter to the assemblies of house and tenement churches as if Paul's voice were present. The inferential "therefore" introduces a question that arises from the final words of the preceding pericope, that Israel had behaved as "a disobedient and disputatious people."[11] The rhetorical question begins with μή ("not"), which requires a negative answer, which I translate with "God did not cast off his people, did he?" The verb ἀπωθέομαι ("cast off, push aside, jettison, repudiate") occurs here for the only time in Paul's letters, and since the combination of this verb with "his people" appears in two passages of the LXX, a significant verbal echo is created.[12] As seen in the illustration in v. 2 below, Paul's question is virtually identical to the wording of 1 Kgs 12:22 and Ps 93:14 (οὐκ ἀπώσεται κύριος τὸν λαὸν αὐτοῦ, "he will not cast off his people").[13] By placing the verb at the earliest possible position in the question, the words "God" and "his people" stand next to each other so as to express the inconceivability of God actually turning his back on his chosen people.[14] Numerous passages in the OT express the idea of an absolutely irrevocable commitment of Yahweh to Israel.[15] The exclamation "By no means!" expresses "abhorrence" at this incredible possibility.[16]

Paul immediately goes on to provide the first reason for this vehement denial, and it is interesting to observe which widely available reasons he chooses not to cite. There is nothing here about God's irrevocable covenant, Israel's obedience to the law, or her suffering.[17] Instead Paul uses himself as an example that Israel has not been abandoned, citing proof of his belongingness to the people whom God continues to love. He is an "Israelite," which is an honorific self-designation referring to themselves as the people of God.[18] That Paul descended "from Abraham" implies an unbroken line of succession,[19] while membership in the "tribe of Benjamin" places his family along with the tribe of Judah in "the theocratic core of the nation."[20] The tribe of Benjamin provided Israel's first king, Saul, whose name he bore,[21] and spawned the zealous prophetic Elijah who is mentioned in the next verse. The formulation "for I am also . . ." suggests that these details are meant to present himself "as living evidence that God has not abandoned his people Israel."[22] The oral tradition about this former zealot would surely have been as well known in Rome as in Galatia and Judea: "For you have heard of my former life in Judaism, how I persecuted the church of God vio-

---

9   BAGD (2000) 589 (2.a), "*ask* with direct question following."
10   Kelber, *Oral and the Written Gospel*, 141–83.
11   See Kühl, 366.
12   See Hays, *Echoes*, 68–69; Wagner, *Heralds*, 221–31.
13   Cranfield, 2:543. Paul's wording is "clearly reminiscent" of these two OT passages; see also Schlier, 321; Kuss, 3:784; Fitzmyer, 603; for example, see Josephus *Ant.* 1.260.
14   Weiss, 463.
15   Haacker, 219, cites Amos 9:11-15; 2 Kgs 14:27; Jer 31:37. See also Wagner, *Heralds*, 225–26, 230. Bachman, "*Verus Israel*," 506, confirms that the entire Jewish community is in view.
16   Meyer, 2:200.
17   See Schlier, 322.
18   The choice of "Israelite" instead of "Jew" is reflected also in 9:4; the former was the favorite self-designation as "the people of God," whereas the latter was the name used by others, according to Walter Gutbrod, "Ἰσραήλ κτλ.," *TDNT* 3 (1965)

369–72, 384–88; see also Richard Kugelman, "Hebrew, Israelite, Jew in the New Testament," *Bridge* 1 (1955) 215–18.
19   See Karl-Wilhelm Niebuhr, *Heidenapostel aus Israel. Die jüdische Identität des Paulus nach ihrer Darstellung in seinen Briefen*, WUNT 62 (Tübingen: Mohr [Siebeck], 1992) 169–70, for Paul as an exemplary Jew.
20   Meyer, 2:200; Weiss, 464; Niebuhr, *Heidenapostel*, 106.
21   See Michel, 339; for an account of the prestigious history of the tribe of Benjamin, see K.-D. Schunck, "Benjamin," *ABD* 1 (1992) 671–73. Schunck, 671, observes that Benjamin was a favored son, a kind of "true Israel," being born of Rachel, Joseph's beloved. The wording of Josephus *Ant.* 11.198 acknowledges the distinguished position of this tribe in describing Mordecai as "from the Benjaminite tribe, of the first rank among the Jews (τῶν δὲ πρώτων παρὰ τοῖς Ἰουδαίοις)."
22   Moo, 673, following Godet, 392; Schmidt, 184;

lently and tried to destroy it" (Gal 1:13), while the churches in Judea "heard it said, 'He who once persecuted us is now preaching the faith he once tried to destroy'" (Gal 1:23). Although Paul had been a zealous opponent of the gospel, similar to current zealots who were seeking to "hinder us from speaking to the Gentiles" (1 Thess 2:16), he was not cast off by God. His conversion makes clear that the most fanatical opponents of the gospel can also be redeemed.[23]

■ **2** The question of whether a biblical citation is embedded at the beginning of v. 2 is controversial. Some specialists in Pauline citations are skeptical,[24] in part because of the lack of an introductory formula,[25] but others along with the Nestle-Aland text assume a citation from 1 Kgs 12:22 and LXX Ps 93:14.[26] The comparisons are as follows, with the common words underlined and the allusions marked with dotted underlining:

1 Kgs 12:22 οὐκ ἀπώσεται κύριος τὸν λαὸν αὐτοῦ διὰ τὸ ὄνομα αὐτοῦ τὸ μέγα, ὅτι ἐπιεικέως κύριος προσελάβετο ὑμᾶς αὐτῷ εἰς λαόν ("Lord will not cast off his people for his great name's sake. Because the Lord graciously took you to himself as a people")

Ps 93:14-15a οὐκ ἀπώσεται κύριος τὸν λαὸν αὐτοῦ καὶ τὴν κληρονομίαν αὐτοῦ οὐκ ἐγκαταλείψει, ἕως οὗ δικαιοσύνη ἐπιστρέψῃ εἰς κρίσιν ("Lord will not cast off his people and will not abandon his heritage until righteousness returns for judgment")

Rom 11:2 οὐκ ἀπώσατο ὁ θεὸς τὸν λαὸν αὐτοῦ ὃν προέγνω. ("*God* did not cast off his people whom he knew beforehand")

Three changes need to be taken into account in evaluating this evidence: the tense of the verb in Paul's version replaces the future tense with the aorist, thus making clear that the scriptural promise has in fact not been violated, even in the case of Jewish disbelievers in the gospel. The word "Lord" is changed to "God," to remove the possibility that the Lord Jesus could be thought to have uttered these words.[27] The words "whom he foreknew" are also clearly Pauline, although they express the covenantal idea that is contained both in Ps 93:b and 1 Kgs 12:22b. The verb προγινώσκω ("know beforehand") is repeated from 8:29 where its background in the OT is described; Yahweh knows his people even before they were even born (e.g., Jer 1:5).[28] These redactional alterations are consistent with Paul's editing of earlier citations in Romans, and despite the lack of a citation formula and the brevity of the exact verbal parallels, this should be identified as a citation[29] with "contextual echos" that extend beyond 11:2a.[30] As Richard Hays points out, the verb ἐγκαταλείψει ("abandon") occurred in 9:29 and is "etymologically connected with the verb καταλείπω ("remain") and the noun λεῖμμα ("remnant") used in Rom 11:4-5 to describe the remnant left by God's elective grace."[31] A crucial consideration is that 11:2a functions as the main proof text in the midrash, followed by four supporting texts. The citation in 2a also helps to avoid mere redundancy in Paul's argument, since the words replicate the question in 11:1a, which, as we suggested, would already have been heard as an foreshadowing of these biblical passages. With this impressive biblical foundation, the thesis in the first diatribe is rendered plausible.

Kühl, 368; Barrett, 207; Niebuhr, *Heidenapostel*, 169–71; Kim, *Romans 9–11*, 135–36; Tobin, *Paul's Rhetoric*, 355; Esler, *Conflict and Identity*, 293–94. The skepticism of Käsemann, 299, and Johnson, "Structure," 95, about whether the destiny of Paul as an individual could have a bearing on the collective destiny of Israel is ungrounded. In line with Barth's dogmatics, Cranfield, 2:544, argues that these details point to the irony that he, a Jew, was the apostle chosen for the Gentiles, but this moves far beyond the rhetoric of this passage.

23 See Kasemann, 299.
24 Koch, *Schrift*, 18, denies a citation and Stanley, *Scripture*, 147, passes over this verse without comment.

25 Other instances in Romans where a citation occurs without an introductory formula include 2:6; 9:7, 20; 10:13, 18; 11:3 [textual variant]; 11:34; 12:20; 13:9.
26 Dunn, 2:636; Hays, *Echoes*, 68–69, prefers the term "contextual echo" in this instance.
27 Hays, *Echoes*, 69.
28 See Mayer, *Gottes Heilsratschluß*, 247–48; Johnson, "Structure," 95; Maier, *Mensch*, 394, cites in this connection CD 2:7–8.
29 Haacker, 220; Schreiner, 579.
30 Hays, *Echoes*, 69–70.
31 Ibid., 70.

In support of the thesis that God has not abandoned Israel, Paul introduces the first supporting text by a rhetorical question that assumes the audience knows the story of Elijah. Nowhere else in Paul's letters is a citation introduced in this manner. Whereas οὐκ οἴδατε ("do you not know?") occurred in 6:16 with regard to general knowledge of social circumstances, here it refers to a specific biblical episode ἐν Ἠλίᾳ ("concerning Elijah"),[32] a phrase never again used in the New Testament but placed here in the emphatic position before the words "what the scripture says."[33] The particle "or" (ἤ) that opens this sentence is typical in rhetorical questions (as in 3:29)[34] that raise points in antithesis to the foregoing that should be generally accepted by audiences. In Godet's words, the formulation implies with regard to the denial that God has cast Israel aside, "Or if ye allege the contrary, do ye forget . . . ?"[35] Since Paul had just presented himself as derived from the tribe of Benjamin from whence Elijah originated, he is reminding the audience of an episode that in effect was part of his family history. The form of the question requires a positive answer,[36] "Yes, of course, we know!" The prophet's words are described as ἐντυγχάνειν τῷ θεῷ, which has the sense of appealing to God in a manner typical for religious and secular contexts where someone makes a formal request to a higher authority.[37] In this case, however, ἐντυγχάνειν τινὶ κατά is a technical expression for placing an accusation "against someone" before the court or some other authority.[38] By introducing the citation as a formal complaint "against Israel," thus provid-ing a parallel to "casting off his people," Paul can set up the reply in v. 4 as confirmation that God had in fact not given up on Israel.[39]

■ **3** The citation is from 1 Kgs 19:10 (which is virtually identical with 19:14), but a complicated series of alterations needs to be taken into account, as seen below:

1 Kgs 19:10b τὰ θυσιαστήριά σου κατέσκαψαν καὶ τοὺς προφήτας σου ἀπέκτειναν ἐν ῥομφαίᾳ, καὶ ὑπολέλειμμαι[40] ἐγὼ μονώτατος, καὶ ζητοῦσι τὴν ψυχήν μου λαβεῖν αὐτήν ("They have demolished your altars and killed your prophets with the sword, and I alone have been left and they are seeking my life to take it.")

Rom 11:3 Κύριε, τοὺς προφήτας σου ἀπέκτειναν, τὰ θυσιαστήριά σου κατέσκαψαν, κἀγὼ ὑπελείφθην μόνος καὶ ζητοῦσιν τὴν ψυχήν μου ("Lord, they have killed your prophets, they have demolished your altars, and I alone am left, and they are seeking my life.")

Since none of the LXX versions of this text open with the vocative, Κύριε ("Lord!"), it is clear that Paul has added this personal address to Yahweh, probably to make clear that this citation is a prayer directed to God.[41] This addition also brings the first supporting text into direct correlation with the main proof text, whose subject is ὁ θεός ("God"). Paul's reversal of the first two clauses must also have been intentional, and Koch suggests that this serves to contemporize the text.[42] It is clear from 1 Thess 2:14-16 that Paul understood the vio-

---

32 Käsemann, 300, follows Strack-Billerbeck in perceiving a rabbinic reference here, "in the Elijah narrative," but Michel, 339, rightly observes that to take the ἐν as the talmudic ב would imply that there were an OT writing by Elijah. See also Kuss, 3:786.

33 See Weiss, 468.

34 BAGD (2000) 432 (1.d).

35 Godet, 392.

36 Kuss, 3:786.

37 See A. L. Connolly, "A Slave's Bid for Freedom," *NDIEC* 4 (1987) 101, 104; G. H. R. Horsley, "Petition concerning Ephesian Mysteries," *NDIEC* 4 (1987) 94–95.

38 Käsemann, 300, following Lietzmann, 102; see also BAGD (2000) 341. Meyer, 202, cites 1 Macc 8:32 ("make charges against you") and 2 Macc 4:36; Cranfield, 2:546, cites a third-century B.C.E. papyrus *P.Giess.* 2. Nr. 36.15 as an example of this expression.

39 See Cranfield, 2:546. That Paul intends to set himself up as a parallel figure to Elijah as suggested by Munck, *Christ*, 109, and Zeller, 191, is extraneous to the diatribal argument in vv. 1-6.

40 Stanley, *Scripture*, 150, notes that the LXX Lucianic text has the aorist ὑπελείφθην ("I was left alone") in place of the perfect form, ὑπολέλειμμαι ("I have been left alone").

41 Stanley, *Scripture*, 148, observes that in other instances Elijah always addresses Yahweh with the vocative, "Lord!" (1 Kgs 17:20, 21; 18:36, 37; 19:4). Koch's suggestion in *Schrift*, 87, 139, that Paul added Κύριε here following the model of 10:16 seems less plausible.

42 Koch, *Schrift*, 74, citing Odil H. Steck, *Israel und das gewaltsame Geschick der Propheten. Untersuchungen zur Überlieferung des deuteronomistischen Geschichtsbildes im Alten Testament, Spätjudentum und Urchristentum,*

lent opposition against early Christian evangelists under the category of the "Jews who killed both the Lord Jesus and the prophets," whereas there was nothing in contemporary experience that matched Elijah's complaint about "demolishing your altars." By placing the killing of prophets at the point of emphasis in the citation, Paul enlarges the dimension of grace, because God has not abandoned even those who followed the pattern decried in the Elijah citation by acting violently against the Messiah and his messengers.[43] This is consistent with Paul's omission of the phrase "with the sword,"[44] because none of the early Christian martyrs, including Jesus, had been executed by this means.[45] This deletion also improves the parallelism between 3a and 3b,[46] producing the poetic structure noted by Johannes Weiss.[47] Paul's substitution of the aorist verb ὑπελείφθην ("I was left alone") in place of the perfect form found in the standard LXX versions, ὑπολέλειμμαι ("I have been left alone"), may reflect this contemporizing effort, because the latter implies that Elijah was the last in the line of persecuted prophets, whereas Paul's choice of the aorist places Elijah at a single point in the past, leaving open the possibility of a future line of persecuted prophets.[48] The final change that Paul made was to delete the two words fol-lowing "seeking my life," λαβεῖν αὐτήν ("to take it"), which are both awkward and redundant. This deletion is consistent with earlier examples of Paul's achieving conciseness in biblical citations (see Rom 3:10, 14, 15; 9:25),[49] and serves to enhance the poetic parallelism in the last line of the citation.

■ **4** The next supporting text is introduced by the rhetorical question that again assumes the audience's knowledge of the Elijah story. The initial ἀλλά ("but") introduces the citation as an answer that stands in antithesis to the foregoing.[50] Whereas Elijah obviously hoped that Yahweh would take vengeance on the persecutors, Scripture offers a consoling message. Paul lends authoritative weight to this answer by employing a NT hapax legomenon, χρηματισμός, in the sense of a divine utterance.[51] This requires the translation "But what does the oracle say to him?"[52] In 2 Macc 2:4 this term is used to describe the oracle given to Jeremiah to remove the ark and tabernacle during the fall of Jerusalem,[53] and in an inscription explaining how an oracle that came in a dream ordered that an eagle should be carved on an altar.[54] The use of this term makes clear "that what follows is the word of God, not the best human thought on the matter."[55]

WMANT 23 (Neukirchen-Vluyn: Neukirchener Verlag, 1967) 278 n. 2. Koch's hypothesis is accepted by Moo, 676, and Schreiner, 582. The rejection of this hypothesis by Stanley, *Scripture*, 149, is unconvincing.

43   See Käsemann, 301; Schreiner, 581.

44   Koch, *Schrift*, 75, rightly observes that this deletion is Pauline, although he provides no redactional motivation.

45   See Stanley, *Scripture*, 150.

46   Stanley, *Scripture*, 150.

47   Weiss, "Beiträge," 240.

48   Koch, *Schrift*, 74, and Stanley, *Scripture*, 150–51, suggest the influence of alternate forms of the LXX, including the Lucianic version that has the aorist ὑπελείφθην ("I was left alone") reading. Even if this were accepted, Paul's reason for preferring that reading needs to be explained.

49   See Stanley, *Scripture*, 151.

50   Tobin, *Paul's Rhetoric*, 356.

51   See Kühl, 381; BAGD (2000) 1089, "divine statement, answer"; Anthony T. Hanson, "The Oracle in Romans xi. 4," *NTS* 19 (1972–73) 300–302.

52   Hanson, "Oracle," 300.

53   2 Macc 2:4, "the prophet, being warned by an ora-cle (χρηματισμοῦ γενηθέντος), commanded the tabernacle and ark to accompany him." In this and other instances, χρηματισμός can have the sense of a "divine injunction," according to LSJM 2005, definition 5, with Artemidorus Daldianus *Onir.* 1.2; Vettius Valens *Anth.* 1.7; *PGM.* IV.2206 as examples. The latter, however, reads ἐπὶ χρηματισμοῦ, which should probably be translated "for an oracle," thus matching the nuance of Rom 11:4.

54   "I have dedicated, according to an oracle in a dream, the eagle with the altar (κατὰ χρηματισμόν ὀνίρου τὸν αἰετὸν σὺν τῷ βωμῷ ἀνέθηκα)," from *BE* (1982) 414.16–17, cited by G. H. R. Horsley, "χρηματισμός," *NDIEC* 4 (1987) 176; see also E. A. Judge, "A State Schoolteacher Makes a Salary Bid," *NDIEC* 1 (1981) 77. Hanson, "Oracle," 300–301, also cites LXX Prov 31:1; Josephus *Ant.* 5.1.14; 10.1.3; 11.8.

55   Morris, 400.

The poetic improvements and contextual adaptations that Paul made in the citation in v. 3 are continued in the next citation from the Elijah story, as demonstrated below, where the excisions are underlined and the alterations marked with double underlining.

LXX of 1 Kgs 19:18: καὶ καταλείψεις ἐν Ισραηλ ἑπτὰ χιλιάδας ἀνδρῶν, πάντα γόνατα, ἃ οὐκ ὤκλασαν γόνυ τῷ Βααλ ("And you shall leave in Israel seven thousand of men, all the knees of which did not squat down the knee to Baal")

LXX Lucianic Version of 1 Kgs 19:18:[56] καὶ καταλείψω ἐξ Ισραηλ ἑπτὰ χιλιάδας ἀνδρῶν, πάντα γόνατα, ἃ οὐκ ἔκαμψαν γόνυ τῇ Βάαλ ("And I shall leave from Israel seven thousand of men, all the knees of which did not bow the knee to Baal")

Paul's version of 1 Kgs 19:18: Κατέλιπον ἐμαυτῷ ἑπτακισχιλίους ἄνδρας, οἵτινες οὐκ ἔκαμψαν γόνυ τῇ Βάαλ ("I kept for myself seven thousand men, who did not bow the knee to Baal")

The deletion of "and" at the beginning of the citation[57] improves the antithesis with the preceding citation already suggested by the introductory ἀλλά ("but"). Paul changes the verb from a second person singular future, καταλείψεις ("you shall keep"), to the first person aorist, κατέλιπον ("I kept"), and adds the word ἐμαυτῷ ("for myself") to make it plain that God's merciful action toward God's people is in view.[58] Paul's version thus resonates with 11:1 and 2 where God is the subject of action. This is a substantial revision that cannot be accounted by merely stylistic considerations.[59] The fact that the Lucianic version also has the first person singular form, καταλείψω ("I shall keep"), leads Stanley to suggest that Paul was using that text, but this would explain neither the change to the aorist nor the addition of "to myself."[60] Paul probably chose the aorist form to make this citation consistent with the change to the aorist "I was left alone" in v. 3; it implies that the remnant of seven thousand in Elijah's time does not continue at this scale up to the present. Paul wishes his audience to see the point of comparison in God's saving action, not in some contemporary fulfillment of a certain number of believers. There is no doubt that Paul deleted the reference to Israel that is found in all of the LXX versions and the MT, possibly because he wished to avoid the impression that all of the faithful belonged in fact to Israel, which might have been offensive to the Gentile majority among the believers in Rome.[61] The change in the form of "seven thousand men" from the rather awkward expression, ἑπτὰ χιλιάδας ἀνδρῶν, to the more elegant Greek of ἑπτακισχιλίους ἄνδρας is probably owing to Paul's own stylistic preference rather than to the existence of some form of the LXX, as suggested by Koch and Stanley.[62] The reference to "men" in this oracle derives from the Hebrew method of counting, and there is no doubt that the sacred number of 7,000 had a symbolic significance implying "completeness" and "totality,"[63] possibly even, in Paul's new context, an apocalyptic wholeness[64] that points forward to the success of the global mission in 15:9-12.

---

56 This follows Stanley's reconstruction in *Scripture*, 152, based on LXX MS b c₂ e₂ with the exception that e₂ has the verb spelled as ἔκαψαν.

57 Stanley, *Scripture*, 142, 152, observes that in a quarter of Paul's citations, the introductory "and" is deleted for stylistic reasons.

58 Lietzmann, 103; Morris, 400; Dunn, 2:637; Johnson, *Function*, 160.

59 Koch, *Schrift*, 74–75.

60 Stanley, *Scripture*, 153–54.

61 Koch, *Schrift*, 76, suggests this excision was on grounds of irrelevancy while Stanley, *Scripture*, 155, says its inclusion would have been "problematic" with regard to "the incorporation of the Gentiles into historic 'Israel,'" which I fail to grasp.

62 Koch, *Schrift*, 75–76. Despite minor disagreements,

Stanley, *Scripture*, 156, also concludes that this alteration came from the "Greek text of Kingdoms from which he copied his citation." Since no form of the LXX has been found with this wording, this hypothesis is unprovable.

63 Karl Heinrich Rengstorf, "ἑπτά κτλ.," *TDNT* 2 (1964) 628–30.

64 Michel, 340. Rengstorf, "ἑπτά κτλ.," 629, states that the context of Rom 11:5 makes it unclear "whether Paul connected with the OT number [i.e., 7,000] the thought of the totality of the true Israel."

Paul's superior stylistic sense is probably responsible for replacing the awkward and redundant reference to πάντα γόνατα, ἃ οὐκ ὤκλασαν γόνυ ("all the knees of which did not squat down the knee") with the succinct and graceful formulation οἵτινες οὐκ ἔκαμψαν γόνυ ("who did not bow a knee").[65] Since falling on one's knees was "an expression of homage and of petition toward human beings and gods" in the ancient world,[66] the refusal by so large a group to bend even a single knee[67] is presented as a sign of God's "faithfulness to His purpose of salvation for His people, a declaration that that purpose will continue unchanged and unthwarted to the final goal."[68] In the context of Paul's letter, this faithful remnant is also "a pledge of hope for the future"[69] of Israel and the rest of the world. Finally, in contrast to the grammatically correct masculine article with Baal in the standard LXX versions, Paul uses the feminine τῇ Βάαλ. This may well reflect his dependency on the Lucianic texts where this reading is found,[70] but it may also express Paul's desire to avoid offending Jewish Christians who would have preferred the feminine euphemism "the shame" (ἡ αἰσχύνη) to avoid pronouncing the word "Baal" because of its associ-ation with the divine name[71] as well as in accordance with the prohibition in Hos 2:17.[72] This citation completes the scriptural proof for the thesis in the first diatribe so that Paul can move on to his powerful conclusion about the remnant saved by grace.

■ **5** The conclusion of the first diatribe is marked by the unusually formal series of οὕτως οὖν ("in this manner therefore")[73] followed by καί ("also"), which is attached to the following expression ἐν τῷ νῦν καιρῷ ("also at the present critical time"). This establishes a formal typology[74] between the 7,000 faithful in the Elijah episode and the "remnant" of Israel already converted by divine grace. We encountered this expression "the present critical time" in 3:26, where it served to interpret a traditional Christological hymn, and in 8:18, where it referred to the period of sufferings that mark the eschatological period.[75] Since this expression is found with the distinctive eschatological connotation only in the Pauline letters,[76] it appears to be his expression for "the eschatological present,"[77] which in this instance marks a typological fulfillment of the 7,000 men whom God "kept for God's self" in faithful covenant. Picking up the cognate expression ὑπόλειμμα

---

65   With the exception of the change of the verb from "squat" to "bow," which also appears in the Lucianic text, the suggestion of stylistic improvement made by Koch, *Schrift,* 75 seems appropriate. That Paul here is citing the Lucianic text, as proposed by Stanley, *Scripture,* 156–57, rests on the unlikely assessment that one word must have been taken over, while the other four words were inexplicably deleted.

66   Johannes M. Nützel, "γόνυ," *EDNT* 1 (1990) 258.

67   The singular γόνυ ("knee") is employed here to convey this total refusal, according to Meyer, 2:203.

68   Cranfield, 2:547.

69   Moo, 677.

70   Stanley, *Scripture,* 157–58.

71   See Stanley, *Scripture,* 157–58, for an account of this phenomenon and its frequent impact on the LXX, where the grammatically incorrect feminine article frequently appears with the word "Baal."

72   The oracle in Hos 2:17 ("I shall take the names of the Baals out of her mouth, and their names will be remembered no more," is cited by Haacker, 222.

73   The adverb οὕτως ("so, in this manner") can refer to what follows or what precedes, and in this case probably the former according to BAGD (2000) 742 (1.b); the particle οὖν ("accordingly, therefore")

draws the inference from the preceding scriptural proof. The sequence οὕτως οὖν occurs in Matt 6:9; Luke 14:33, and in the Attic orators (Demosthenes *Cor.* 315.4; *Orat.* 19.340.5; Andocides *Myst.* 105.7; 131.5; Dinarchus *Dem.* 89.4; Hyperides *Dem.* 7.30.6).

74   Goppelt, *Typos,* 67–69, 152–55; Käsemann, 300; Aageson, "Typology," 51–72; Aageson, *Biblical Interpretation,* 94–95; Johnson, "Structure," 94–96.

75   Neuhäusler, "Entscheidende Augenblick," 2–11; Jörg Baumgarten, "καιρός," *EDNT* 2 (1991) 232; Gerhard Delling, "καιρός," *TDNT* 3 (1965) 459–60. In Gen 29:34 and 30:20, this expression lacks the eschatological implication found in all four Pauline passages, including 2 Cor 8:14.

76   Although Tachau, *Einst,* 94–96, shows that various branches of early Christianity employed the eschatological "then . . . now" antithesis, he does not deal with any of the passages that contain the expression ἐν τῷ νῦν καιρῷ.

77   Schlier, 323; Dunn, 2:638; Moo, 677. See particularly Weiss, 468, "the messianic present."

("remnant") from the Isa 10:22 passage cited in Rom 9:27, Paul refers here to this group as a λεῖμμα ("remnant"), an idea developed by the prophets that gained currency with regard to the survivors of the Assyrian and Babylonian conquests of Israel.[78] The basic idea is that the salvation of the remnant consists in their having survived while the rest of the population was killed in battle or disappeared in exile (e.g., Isa 37:4; Jer 8:3; Mic 2:12).[79] The remnant will be restored to a glorious Zion by divine intervention after the majority of Israel has suffered divine punishment (e.g., Isa 4:2-6; 10:20-23). The exiled remnant will be returned by God to their restored homeland (e.g., Jer 23:3; 31:7-14; Mic 2:12; 4:6-7) while their enemies are punished (e.g., Isa 11:11-16; Mic 5:6-8; Zeph 2:3-9). In some instances, survival is granted to the virtuous while Israel's enemies will perish, as, for example, in Zeph 2:1-7; 3:12-13.[80] The Damascus Document 1:3-13 describes how the Babylonian destruction struck the wicked except for a "remnant" who came to acknowledge their sins and follow the Teacher of Righteousness.[81] These motifs of military catastrophe, political restoration, the defeat of enemies, and the survival of the righteous disappear in Paul's new definition of the λεῖμμα κατ᾽ ἐκλογὴν χάριτος γέγονεν ("remnant born by election of grace").[82] The expression κατ᾽ ἐκλογήν appeared earlier in 9:11 with the connotation of "by selection" or "by free choice" of God, and here it refers to "the remnant of Christian believers in Israel . . . chosen according to the principle of grace."[83] A similar use of ἐκλογή appeared in Paul's first letter with reference to converts as "beloved of God, His chosen ones" (1 Thess 1:4).[84] The word χάρις ("grace") recurs here as a genitive attached to "election,"[85] having been defined in 3:24; 4:16; 5:2, 15, 17, 20, 21; 6:1, 14, 15 as divine benefaction in the form of unconditional access to God and specific benefits conveyed to the undeserving through Christ.[86] Whereas ordinary benefactors conveyed their gifts to worthy and honorable recipients, Christ as the dishonored benefactor extends his grace to "the ungodly and ungrateful enemies of God (Rm 5:6, 10)."[87] In contrast to the 7,000 righteous persons in Israel who had not committed idolatry, and thus deserved divine commendation, the regime of grace eliminates all human qualifications.[88] Those who have no claim to honor are given the honor of God's grace and brought into a community in which the honor system has been transformed. By combining this "election of grace" with the perfect tense verb γέγονεν ("it has been born"),[89] it becomes clear that the cre-

---

78 See Gottlob Schrenk and Volkmar Herntrich, "λεῖμμα κτλ.," *TDNT* 4 (1967) 198–209; Ronald E. Clements, "'A Remnant Chosen by Grace' (Romans 11:5): The Old Testament Background and Origin of the Remnant Concept," in D. A. Hagner and M. J. Harris, eds., *Pauline Studies: Essays Presented to Professor F. F. Bruce on His 70th Birthday* (Exeter: Paternoster; Grand Rapids: Eerdmans, 1980) 106–21.

79 Allen Verhey, "Remnant," *ABD* 5 (1992) 669: "what is left of a community after it undergoes a catastrophe." The historian Michael Grant observes in *Jesus* (London: Wiedenfeld and Nicolson, 1977) 20, "It was a vital Jewish belief that, when the end of the world comes and the kingdom of God is fully established, a faithful Remnant, a purified elect core of the chosen people of Israel, will survive and emerge triumphant. It was as that faithful, final Remnant of the 'Elect of God' awaiting redemption that the Qumran community saw itself. And that, too, was how Jesus hopefully saw his band of disciples."

80 See Verhey, "Remnant," 670.

81 See also *2 Bar.* 77.2–10.

82 Godet, 393; Schrenk and Herntrich, "λεῖμμα κτλ.," 212–13.

83 Gottlob Schrenk, "ἐκλογή," *TDNT* 4 (1967) 180; Mayer, *Gottes Heilsratschluß*, 251. Jost Eckert, "ἐκλεκτός, ἐκλογή," *EDNT* 1 (1990) 419, prefers the translation "chosen by grace." See also Maier, *Mensch*, 395–96, for the correlation between this expression and the doctrine of the freedom of God.

84 In a similar manner, Jewish sectarian groups referred to the community of the elect, as in *1 En.* 1.7-10; 62.7-12; *Odes Sol.* 23.2-3; 1QS 8:6; see Käsemann, 300; Fitzmyer, 605.

85 Along with Weiss, 468; Zahn, 499; Schlier, 324; and Käsemann, 300, I take χάριτος ("of grace") as a descriptive genitive attached to ἐκλογήν ("election").

86 See Wobbe, *Charis-Gedanke*, 63–74.

87 Harrison, *Language of Grace*, 224–25.

88 See Schlier, 324.

89 Alternative translations, according to LSJM 349 I.3, are "take place, come to pass, and in the past tenses, to be." I prefer "born" because the primary meaning of γίγνομαι, "come into being . . . to be born" (LSJM 349 I.1), refers to the origin of this particular "remnant."

ation of this new form of remnant remains in effect up until "the present critical time."[90]

■ **6** The conclusion of the first diatribe in v. 5 is followed here by an antithetical enthymeme that clarifies the distinctiveness of the new remnant defined by grace. The premise of the preceding verse is introduced by εἰ δὲ χάριτι ("but if by grace"), referring to the manner by which membership in the elect remnant is achieved.[91] Assuming this premise is correct, the antithetical inference is introduced by οὐκέτι ("not, no longer"), which has a logical rather than a chronological connotation in this context,[92] as in 7:17, 20 and 14:15. The antithesis eliminated by the regime of grace is a community ἐξ ἔργων ("from works"). This succinct antithesis reflects Paul's earlier polemic against seeking to gain honor through works of the law in 3:20, 27-28; 4:2, 6; 9:12, 32,[93] and in particular it eliminates the false inference that might be drawn from the Elijah story about the remnant of 7,000 who had not bowed so much as a single knee to Baal.[94] The final portion of the sentence states the consequence that would follow if the inference concerning the elimination of works were rejected. It is introduced by ἐπεί, which has the sense of "since otherwise."[95] The subject of the final clause is arthrous, ἡ χάρις ("the grace"), which is dropped without discussion by commentators,[96] thus conveying the impression that grace is a doctrinal abstraction rather than a concrete benefac-

tion. The only discussion I have found is by Meyer, who says that the article in "the grace" [11:6c] refers to the "definite grace, which has made the election."[97] In the context of Romans there is no doubt that this "definite grace" was conveyed through Christ and is reflected in arthrous formulations such as "*the* grace of our Lord Jesus be with you all" (16:20; see also 5:2, 15, 17, 20, 21; 6:1). Without the article, this clause would lack logical force, because in most instances in the Greco-Roman and Jewish cultures,[98] grace was granted to the deserving and the honorable and thus provided no antithesis to works. For example, Harrison cites the papyrus from a Neronian official who apportions imperial "complete grace" (ἡ χάρις ὁλόκληρος) according to the measure of service to the empire: "Whilst God's grace in Christ does not discriminate concerning the worth of its recipient, imperial χάρις observes hard and fast distinctions—'you do not all have the same right!'"[99] Only in Christ could it be maintained that in an admixture with works of any kind, "*the* grace would not be grace." As noted above, the adverb οὐκέτι is used here as a "marker of inference in a logical process,"[100] and the verb γίνεται means that grace "ceases, in its concrete manifestation, to become" grace.[101]

■ **7** The second diatribe opens with τί οὖν; ("what then?"), a rhetorical question that opened similar diatribes in 3:9 and 6:15. The particle οὖν suggests that an

---

90   See Weiss, 468; Wilckens, 2:237; Dunn, 2:638.
91   Moo, 678, correctly identifies a "dative of manner" in the form χάριτι ("by grace").
92   Godet, 394; Weiss, 469; Lietzmann, 103; Schlier, 324; Schmidt, 186; Käsemann, 300; Kuss, 3:788; Dunn, 2:639; BAGD (2000) 736 (2). Wilckens, 2:238, argues for a temporal understanding of οὐκέτι, thus marking the boundary between the old dispensation and the new, but Paul's argument throughout Romans is that salvation has always been a matter of grace rather than of works.
93   See Roman Heiligenthal, "ἔργον," EDNT 2 (1991) 50.
94   As a further consideration that seems rather distant from the issue in this pericope, Haacker, 223, suggests that the polemic against "works" prevents linking Jewish resistance against the gospel with Baal worship.
95   Lietzmann, 103; BAGD (2000) 360 (2), "marker of cause or reason, *because, since, for*"; Dunn, 2:639, citing BDF §456 (3), "for otherwise."

96   Godet, 394; Schlier, 320; Barrett, 209; Dodd, 172; Michel, 337; Käsemann, 298; Cranfield, 2:542; Murray, 2:65; Morris, 402; Ziesler, 268; Dunn, 2:639; Fitzmyer, 605; Moo, 670; Byrne, 329; Schreiner, 578, 582. Lietzmann, 102; Weiss, 469; Schmidt, 183; Kuss, 3:784; Zeller, 190; Wilckens, 2:234, and Haacker, 218, translate the article but provide no explanation.
97   Meyer, 2:206.
98   See particularly Harrison, *Language of Grace*, 220–34.
99   Ibid., 88, citing from *P.Fouad* Nr. 21.14.
100   BAGD (2000) 736.
101   Meyer, 2:206, followed by Kühl, 373, insists that γίνεται is not equivalent with the verb "to be," which is employed in most commentaries: Murray, 2:65; Dunn, 2:633; Fitzmyer, 602; Moo, 670; Byrne, 329; Schreiner, 578. See also BAGD (2000) 196–99.

660

inference should be drawn from the preceding argument,[102] that is, if God has not rejected God's people but preserves only a remnant thereof, "What has happened?"[103] Paul answers the rhetorical question by reiterating the argument of 9:30-33 concerning Israel's failure to attain the righteousness it sought because of a misconception that it was based on works. The verb ἐπιζητέω ("I seek")[104] is used here in place of διώκω ("I strive") that Paul used in 9:30 and 31,[105] but the subject remains Ἰσραήλ ("Israel"), which is the focus of attention throughout Rom 9–11. The wording in the present tense,[106] which I translate as a present progressive "is seeking," implies that Israel, with the exception of the remnant, is presently continuing the effort to maintain its status through "works," to use the expression from the preceding verse. The emphatic τοῦτο ("this") at the beginning of the subordinate clause[107] refers to the status of superior honor so assiduously sought but not achieved. The reduplication of the same aorist form of the verb ἐπιτυγχάνω ("I attain, achieve, I gain what I seek"),[108] employed here for the only time in the Pauline letters, places Israel as a whole in an exact antithesis to the remnant. "But the elect attained (ἡ δὲ ἐκλογὴ ἐπέτυχεν)" what Israel sought but failed to achieve. Some have assumed that "the chosen" refers to Gentile Christians,[109] but the context of discussing a remnant within Israel indicates that those born κατ᾽ ἐκλογὴν χάριτος

("by election of grace") are Jewish Christians.[110] In order to avoid confusion with the expression ἐκλεκτοὶ θεοῦ in reference to the community of Jewish and Gentile believers in 8:33, I prefer the translation "chosen" for the closely related term ἐκλογή in 11:7.[111] The Jewish converts had accepted the message of pure grace, conveyed to the unworthy through the shameful death and glorious resurrection of Jesus, and had accepted their place in the church, the community of the "called." What they "attained" was not due to their personal achievement or their group's innate superiority over others, but was purely an "election of grace" as opposed to works.

The final clause of v. 7 is again antithetical to the foregoing, and should be translated "*but* the others were made obtuse (οἱ δὲ λοιποὶ ἐπωρώθησαν)." The "others"[112] are defined in contrast to the remnant of chosen ones, and the expression οἱ λοιποί is in no sense an attempt to disguise the historical fact that the majority of Israelites had hitherto refused to accept the gospel.[113] The passive verb ἐπωρώθησαν ("they were hardened, obtuse, closed-minded, undiscerning")[114] should probably be translated in the metaphorical sense, "made obtuse,"[115] because of the following scriptural citation concerning impeded understanding and in order to maintain a distinction from the verb σκληρύνω

---

102 BAGD (2000) 736 (1.β), "*what, then, are we to conclude?*" For instance, Dio Chrysostom *Orat.* 2.9.1, "What then? (τί οὖν;) Are not these things, he said, useful for men?" See also *Orat.* 4.20.4; 4.62.5; 7.69.4; 7.70.2; 10.7.10; 11.18.1, etc.
103 Godet, 395; K. L. McKay, "Time and Aspect in New Testament Greek," *NovT* 34 (1992) 209–28, cited by Moo, 679.
104 The verb ἐπιζητέω appears here for the only time in Romans, and was also used in Phil 4:17 in the sense of "seek." The connotation "eagerly seek" is suggested by Horst Balz and Gerhard Schneider, "ἐπιζητέω," *EDNT* 2 (1991) 27; Morris, 403; BAGD (2000) 371 (2), "be seriously interested in or have a strong desire for," but Moo, 680, rightly doubts that the intensive meaning conveyed in earlier classical Greek by the prefix ἐπί is conveyed here. See also Meyer, 2:207.
105 See Dunn, 2:639.
106 See Weiss, 470.
107 See ibid.
108 When used with the accusative, as here, ἐπιτυγχάνω means "attain to," "reach," or "gain one's end," according to LSJM 669. For instance, Xenophon *Mem.* 4.2.28, "Even those who know what they may do attain it (καὶ οἱ μὲν εἰδότες ὅ τι ποιοῦσιν ἐπιτυγχάνοντες)."
109 For example, Zahn, 500–501; Barrett, 210.
110 Dodd, 175; Luz, *Geschichtsverständnis*, 82; Ziesler, 271; Wilckens, 2:238; Fitzmyer, 606; Byrne, 331.
111 See BAGD (2000) 306 (2), "that which is chosen/selected."
112 See BAGD (2000) 602 (b).
113 Dunn, 2:640, rejecting the concealment theory advanced by Käsemann, 301.
114 See BAGD (2000) 900; Horst Balz and Gerhard Schneider, "πωρόω," *EDNT* 3 (1993) 202, "to be obtuse." The verb πωρόω occurs here and in 2 Cor 3:14, and the cognate πώρωσις ("obtuseness, hardening") in Rom 11:25.
115 Fitzmyer, 606. Newman and Nida, 211–12, translate appropriately, "the rest grew deaf to God's call."

("harden") in 9:18.[116] In the extensive development of this theme in the OT,[117] divine causation of an obtuse and undiscerning heart was paradoxically mixed with human accountability.[118] Thus, in Romans, Paul implies "not only that this Israel was hardened by God (11:7-10) but also that on its own responsibility it chose the wrong path (9:30—10:3)."[119] This paradox allows Paul to deny that God's word has failed while keeping the door open to the future conversion of Israel.[120] In fact, as Paul goes on to show, this situation of failed communication was predicted by the word of God itself.

■ **8** This verse opens with the traditional citation formula, "just as it has been written," as in 1:17; 2:24; 3:4, 10; 4:17; 8:36; 9:13, 33; 11:8, 26; 15:3, 21, introducing a citation from Deut 29:3 with an insertion from Isa 29:10. The comparisons are illustrated below, with portions underlined to show the Pauline adaptations.

Deut 29:3 καὶ οὐκ ἔδωκεν κύριος ὁ θεὸς ὑμῖν καρδίαν εἰδέναι καὶ ὀφθαλμοὺς βλέπειν καὶ ὦτα ἀκούειν ἕως τῆς ἡμέρας ταύτης ("yet the Lord God did not give you a heart to know and eyes to see and ears to hear until this day")

Isa 29:10 ὅτι πεπότικεν ὑμᾶς κύριος πνεύματι κατανύξεως καὶ καμμύσει τοὺς ὀφθαλμοὺς αὐτῶν καὶ τῶν προφητῶν αὐτῶν καὶ τῶν ἀρχόντων αὐτῶν, οἱ ὁρῶντες τὰ κρυπτά ("for the Lord made you drink a spirit of stupor and he shall shut their eyes and [the eyes] of their prophets and their rulers, who see the secrets")

Paul's version: Ἔδωκεν αὐτοῖς ὁ θεὸς πνεῦμα κατανύξεως, ὀφθαλμοὺς τοῦ μὴ βλέπειν καὶ ὦτα τοῦ μὴ ἀκούειν, ἕως τῆς σήμερον ἡμέρας ("God gave them a spirit of stupor, so that eyes do not see and ears do not hear, until the present day.")

As in earlier citations that we have analyzed, the initial "and" in the citation from Deuteronomy is eliminated to fit the text into the new context. The "you" in Deuteronomy is shifted to "they" by Paul, which correlates with earlier references to Israel in third person style,[121] whereas second person speech is employed for the Gentiles in 11:13.[122] Paul shifts the location of the object of "God gave" to the emphatic location in front of the verb so that αὐτοῖς ("them"), that is, the Israelites, are even more clearly the target of divine action.[123] This correlates with the shift in the location of "not" from the main clause to the subordinate clause. As Christopher Stanley observes, the Deuteronomy text referred to divine reluctance to overcome the uneducated heart of the Israelites in the desert, but Paul's version makes it clear that "God had actually 'hardened' his people for a time," which fits the context of the argument in chapter 11, "in order to give the Gentiles a chance to turn to him through faith in Christ" (11:11, 25-27).[124] Since the gift of "a heart to know" as in the Deuteronomy text would have been confusing in the light of Paul's earlier references to the "senseless heart" of pagans in 1:21 and the "impenitent heart" of the Jewish bigot in 2:5, Paul substitutes the LXX expression found only in Isa 29:10 and 60:3, πνεῦμα κατανύξεως ("a spirit of stupor").[125] This

---

116 Tobin, *Paul's Rhetoric*, 358, explains why Paul uses the term πωρόω ("make obtuse") instead of σκληρύνω ("harden"), but then, following the lead of most commentators, he refers to "this hardening of Israel." An example of the "hardening" interpretation is available in Ellison, *Mystery of Israel*, 77–79.

117 The investigation by Marie-Irma Seewann, "Semantische Untersuchung zu πώρωσις, veranlasst durch Röm 11,25," *FilN* 10.19–20 (1997) 144–56, shows that the Hebrew term שרירות is related to discernment, and that the opposite of "hardness" is not "softness" but "non-discernment." She recommends the translation "Nicht-Erkennen" rather than "Verstockung" or "Verhärtung" for the NT references.

118 See Karl Ludwig Schmidt and Martin Anton Schmidt, "παχύνω, πωρόω κτλ.," *TDNT* 5 (1967)

1024.

119 Ibid., 1027.

120 Cranfield, 2:549, speaks of the "provisional character of the hardening." See also Moo, 681; Johnson, "Structure," 96–97.

121 See Stanley, *Scripture*, 159–60; cf. 9:4-5, 32; 10:1-3.

122 See Koch, *Schrift*, 111.

123 See Wilk, *Bedeutung des Jesajabuches*, 53. For Stanley, *Scripture*, 160, this change "remains clouded in mystery."

124 Stanley, *Scripture*, 159; see also Koch, *Schrift*, 171; Johnson, "Structure," 96–97.

125 Koch, *Schrift*, 170, feels that the change from dative to accusative in the word πνεῦμα ("spirit") points to Paul's dependency on a minority LXX reading, but Stanley, *Scripture*, 161, is rightly skeptical that the

expression may have been selected because it refers to a temporary condition from which one can recover.[126] This appears consistent with the otherwise unexplainable alteration of Deuteronomy's expression ἕως τῆς ἡμέρας ταύτης ("until this day") to ἕως τῆς σήμερον ἡμέρας ("until the present day"). Whereas "this day" could easily have been understood as the time of ancient Israel, Paul's choice of σήμερον ἡμέρας (literally, "today day" or "this very day")[127] evokes the contemporizing thrust of the citation. Paul employed this expression, σήμερον ἡμέρας, in 2 Cor 3:14-15, where Paul maintains that the minds of unbelieving Jews "were hardened, for to *the present day* when they read the old covenant, that same veil remains unlifted, because only through Christ is it taken away. Yes, *to the present day* whenever Moses is read a veil lies over their minds."[128] This condition of torpor that is visible in contemporary Jewish reactions to the gospel results in the incapacity to see and hear despite the fact that eyes and ears are available. Paul's slight alteration of the syntax of Deuteronomy by inserting the possessive article, τοῦ μὴ βλέπειν καὶ ὦτα τοῦ μὴ ἀκούειν, produces succinct articular infinitives in the genitive case that convey purpose,[129] which I translate with "so that eyes do not see and ears do not hear." This communicative failure that was imposed by God, Paul insists on the basis of his editing of the Deuteronomy citation, is manifest in the present period of zealous resistance against the gospel. But as the chapter will go on to demonstrate, this resistance will not last forever.[130]

■ **9-10** The fifth citation in the pericope is introduced again with reference to the oral expression of the Scripture; Ps 68:22-23 is announced with the same words as 4:6, "David says." The changes made in this citation from the LXX are visible in the following illustration that retains the poetic structure, which is an important factor in Paul's redactional work:

Ps 68:22-23:
γενηθήτω ἡ τράπεζα αὐτῶν ἐνώπιον αὐτῶν εἰς παγίδα
καὶ εἰς ἀνταπόδοσιν καὶ εἰς σκάνδαλον·
σκοτισθήτωσαν οἱ ὀφθαλμοὶ αὐτῶν τοῦ μὴ βλέπειν,
καὶ τὸν νῶτον αὐτῶν διὰ παντὸς σύγκαμψον·
("Let their table before them become a snare,
and for retribution a stumbling block.
Let their eyes be darkened so they cannot see,
and bend their backs continually.")

Paul's version:
γενηθήτω ἡ τράπεζα αὐτῶν εἰς παγίδα καὶ εἰς θήραν
καὶ εἰς σκάνδαλον καὶ εἰς ἀνταπόδομα αὐτοῖς,
σκοτισθήτωσαν οἱ ὀφθαλμοὶ αὐτῶν τοῦ μὴ βλέπειν
καὶ τὸν νῶτον αὐτῶν διὰ παντὸς σύγκαμψον·
("Let their table become a snare and a trap,
a stumbling block and a retribution for them,
Let their eyes be darkened so they cannot see,
and bend their backs continually.")

---

evidence supports such an inference; it remains likely that Paul selected the proper accusative form because of his own grammatical sensitivity.

126 Stanley, *Scripture*, 161: "Instead of being consigned to eternal ignorance, Israel is now portrayed as 'stunned,' a condition from which they may be already starting to recover." See also Wilk, *Bedeutung des Jesajabuches*, 54; Shum, *Paul's Use of Isaiah*, 234.

127 The formula "from this very day" (ἀπὸ τῆς σήμερον ἡμέρας) is commonly found in magical spells for healing, as for example, ". . . drive away all harm and all epilepsy . . . from this very day (. . . [ἀ]πὸ τῆς σήμερον ἡμέρας) and from this present hour, for the whole time of her life," cited by Kotansky, *Greek Magical Amulets*, 1:327. See also Daniel

and Maltomini, *Suppl. Mag.* I.14. 9–10; *P. Berol.* 17202, 17218–19.

128 Ernst Fuchs, "σήμερον," *TDNT* 7 (1971) 273–74, classifies this as "theological usage" that "emphasizes the alternative of judgment and fulfilled promise."

129 See Stanley, *Scripture*, 162; BDF §400.

130 Wagner, *Heralds*, 244–54, suggests that Isa 6:9-10 lies behind Paul's fusion of Isa 29:10 and Deut 29.4, but that in the larger context of Isaiah, the hardening of Israel is not "God's final verdict" (253) because Israel's unfaithfulness will finally be overcome. Wilk, *Bedeutung des Jesajabuches*, 145, refers to stupor as a "reversible phenomenon."

A crucial element in this citation is "the table," mentioned in the opening line from Ps 68. Dunn notes the "heavy overtone" of this motif, and recalls that Paul Minear perceived this as a reference to the major bone of contention between the weak and the strong in Rome discussed in 14:1–15:6.[131] The use of "the table" as a reference to a cultic meal is found in Greco-Roman religious texts and also in Luke 22:30; Acts 6:2; and 16:34 has been noted by G. H. R. Horsley.[132] Paul draws a contrast between "the table of the Lord" and the "table of demons" in 1 Cor 11:21. In the citation of Rom 11:9, the "cultic table"[133] that marks a separation with the Gentile world is a problem not just for those pure enough to be welcomed but an even greater problem for those excluded. Thus the reference in Ps 68:23a to the "table before them" was unsuited to Paul's larger purpose.[134] So he resolves the inconcinnity by improving the poetic structure, which the LXX had muddled by the redundant reference to $\alpha\dot{v}\tau\hat{\omega}\nu$ ("their"). By inserting the neat piece of poetic parallelism, $\epsilon\dot{\iota}\varsigma$ $\pi\alpha\gamma\dot{\iota}\delta\alpha$ $\kappa\alpha\dot{\iota}$ $\epsilon\dot{\iota}\varsigma$ $\vartheta\dot{\eta}\rho\alpha\nu$ ("for a snare and a trap"), he gains an additional biblical resonance from the fact that these words occur as a pair in Ps 34:8; 123:6-7; Prov 11:8-9; and Hos 5:1-2.[135]

As in my earlier discussion of the "rock of scandal/stumbling" in 9:33, the table of the hard-hearted ones in Paul's reworked citation causes others to stumble and fall.[136] The fact that Paul returns to this theme in 14:13 makes it likely that $\sigma\kappa\dot{\alpha}\nu\delta\alpha\lambda o\nu$ in 11:9 is directly related to conflicts over the table. The theme of religious offense as developed in Judaism is prominent here.[137] In the same line Paul changes the abstract term $\dot{\alpha}\nu\tau\alpha\pi\dot{o}\delta o\sigma\iota\nu$ ("reward, recompense") to the word indicating the result of an action, $\dot{\alpha}\nu\tau\alpha\pi\dot{o}\delta o\mu\alpha$ ("retribution")[138] followed by $\alpha\dot{v}\tau o\hat{\iota}\varsigma$ ("to them"), which makes it clear that the retribution comes not to outsiders but to the celebrants themselves. Again, Paul achieves his contextual goal while at the same time improving the poetic structure of the citation from the Psalm. The final two lines are taken without change from the LXX, because they aptly elaborate what Paul meant about Israel having been made "obtuse" in v. 7. That their eyes "are darkened" ($\sigma\kappa o\tau\iota\sigma\vartheta\dot{\eta}\tau\omega\sigma\alpha\nu$) is reminiscent of darkening of the heart of the wicked in 1:21 and of the darkness of the lost in 2:19. In the apocalyptic worldview of Paul and other early Christians, this state is tantamount to damnation.[139] That the minds of pagans were deliberately darkened by God is claimed in *1 En.* 99:7f. and *T. Levi* 14:4, but the application of this idea to a portion of God's chosen people would have had a shocking effect. But Paul's experience of many years of hostile opposition against the gospel on the part of his fellow Israelites leads him to see a mysterious divine distortion of the capacity to perceive the light of the truth. The implication of "bend their backs continually" is less clear, and is usually left unclarified by commentaries. It is possible that the reference to unbearable weight alludes to an inner bondage under the weight of the law,[140] an interpretation that would correlate nicely with my interpretation of Rom 7:7-25. There is an emerging consensus,

---

131 Dunn, 2:642–43, referring to Minear, *Obedience*, 78–79, who brought the "table" in 11:9 into connection with "barriers of table-fellowship" between Christian groups in Rome as well as with the "constant pressure from the synagogue to enforce the Torah provisions on foods." See also Barrett, 211, and Esler, *Conflict and Identity*, 295–96. Haacker, 224, is skeptical of any allusion to table fellowship here.

132 G. H. R. Horsley, "A Sacrificial Calender," *NDIEC* 2 (1982) 37. See also the examples discussed in Jameson, Jordan, and Kotansky, *Lex Sacra*, 14f., 64, 75–70.

133 See Koch, *Schrift*, 138, following Müller, *Anstoß und Gericht*, 24–27.

134 Neither Koch, *Schrift*, 138, nor Stanley, *Scripture*, 163–64, provides an explanation for Paul's deletion of "before them."

135 In contrast, Stanley, *Scripture*, 164, can discern "no clear reason" for Paul's altered wording. Wagner, *Heralds*, 259–61, argues that Ps 34:8 is the most likely source of the phrase $\epsilon\dot{\iota}\varsigma$ $\vartheta\dot{\eta}\rho\alpha\nu$.

136 See Stählin, "$\sigma\kappa\dot{\alpha}\nu\delta\alpha\lambda o\nu$," 339–41.

137 See Müller, *Anstoß und Gericht*, 32–45.

138 For the distinction between these two closely related words, see Stanley, *Scripture*, 165, who notes that Paul's choice of $\dot{\alpha}\nu\tau\alpha\pi\dot{o}\delta o\mu\alpha$ "provides a better parallel for the concrete nouns of verse 9."

139 See Hans Conzelmann, "$\sigma\kappa\dot{o}\tau o\varsigma$ $\kappa\tau\lambda.$," *TDNT* 7 (1971) 431, 441–42.

140 Weiss, 474; Meyer, 2:210; Schmidt, 188.

however that the expression διὰ παντός in relation to the bending of backs should be translated "continually"[141] rather than "forever."[142] In Ross Wagner's formulation, "the profound stupor that has been poured out on 'the rest' of Israel represents an intermediate stage in God's plan to redeem Israel."[143] In the end, God's mercy will prevail with regard to "his people."[144] In the next pericope, this mysterious plan will be disclosed to show the reliability of God's promises.

141 Michel, 337; Cranfield, 2:522; Dunn, 2:643; Fitzmyer, 607; Haacker, 218; Moo, 682; Schreiner, 586, 89; Byrne, 329.
142 Schmidt, 183; Barrett, 207; Kuss, 3:784; Morris, 398.
143 Wagner, *Heralds*, 265.
144 See Gignac, *Romans 9–11*, 227.

11

The Eighth Pericope

Diatribe and Allegorical Enthymeme Dealing with the Missional Purpose of Israel's Trespass

11/ I say therefore, "They did not stumble so as to fall, did they?" By no means! But through their trespass the salvation [is coming] for the Gentiles, in order to make them zealous. 12/[a] Now if their trespass [makes] wealth for the world and their loss [makes] wealth for the Gentiles, how much more [wealth will] their full total [make]?

13/ Now[b] I speak to you Gentiles. Inasmuch, notwithstanding,[c] that I am indeed an apostle of Gentiles, I do glorify[d] my service 14/ if somehow I might make my very flesh zealous and might save some of them. 15/ For if their discarding [the gospel were] reconciliation of [the] world, what [would] their welcome [be] if not life from [the] dead?

16/ Now[e] if the first fruit [is] holy, so also [is] the batch of dough; and if[f] the root [is] holy, so also the branches. 17/ But if some of the branches were broken off, and you being a wild olive were grafted among them to become a co-participant in the root[g] of the olive tree with its fatness, 18/ do not brag against the [other] branches. But if you[h] do brag, it is not you that support the root but the root you. 19/ Thus you will say, "Branches[i] were broken off in order that I might be grafted in." 20/ Well said! They were broken off[j] on account of their unfaith, but you have stood on account of faith. Do not be uppity[k]-minded, but fear. 21/ For if God did not spare the natural branches, [l]he will not spare you.

22/ Pay attention therefore to God's[m] kindness and severity: toward those who fell, on the one hand, severity[n]; but toward you on the other hand, the kindness[o] of God[p], if you remain[q] in the kindness, because otherwise you will also be cut off. 23/ And they, if they do not remain[r] in unfaith, will be grafted in. For God is able to graft them in again. 24/ For if you were cut from a natural olive tree and were grafted unnaturally into a cultivated olive tree, how much more [will] those who are natural be grafted back into their own olive tree!

a   The entirety of v. 12 is deleted by A, although this is not marked in the Nestle-Aland text. Porter, "Rhetorical Scribe," 413, suspects a theological motive for this deletion, to downplay "Jewish sinfulness" and concentrate on the "common human predicament." Since this is a concern that emerged with later Protestant orthodoxy, an accidental deletion seems more likely.

b   In place of δέ ("but, now") in ℵ A B P 81 104 630 1243 1506 1735 1739 1874 1881 *pc* sy, secondary efforts to strengthen the connection between v. 13 and the foregoing are visible in C's οὖν ("therefore") and γάρ ("for") in D F G L Ψ 6 33 69 88 323 326 330 365 424 614 945 1175 1241 1319 1505 1573 1836 2344 2464 2495 *Maj* latt.

c   In place of μὲν οὖν ("on the other hand, therefore") in P[46] ℵ A B C P 81 104 1506 *pc*, the texts that replaced δέ in the first part of this verse made logical alterations here: L Ψ 6 33 69 88 323 330 424 614 945 1175 1241 1243 1505 1735 1739 1836 1874 1881 2344 2464 2495 *Maj* lat sy[h] have only μέν and D F G 326 365 1319 1573 *pc* sy[p] Pel delete both μέν and οὖν. Neither variant appears original.

d   The variant δοξάσω ("I will glorify") in P[46] F G Ψ 33 88 1175 1836 1874 2344 *pc* latt appears to have originated as a dictation error.

e   The replacement of the widely attested δέ ("now") by γάρ ("for") in A may have the same motivation as that noted with regard to the variant in v. 13.

f   The deletion of εἰ ("if") by P[46] F G P* 6 88 436 1241 1243 1506 1881 1962 2127 2464 *al* f g appears accidental according to Metzger, *Textual Commentary (1975)*, 526. But the omission could be intentional because it alters the verse's meaning: "Now if the first fruit is holy, the lump [is] also, and the root is holy and the branches." The version that includes "if" is broadly supported by ℵ A B C D L P[c] Ψ 33 69 104 181 323 326 330 365 424 451 614 629 945 1175 1319 1505 1573 (1735) 1739 1836 1874 1877 2344 2492 2495 *Maj* lat sy cop Cl[ex Theodoto] Ambst.

g   The presence of καί ("and") after τῆς ῥίζης ("of the root") in ℵ[2] A D[2] L P 6 33 69 81 88 104 181 256 263 323 326 330 365 424 436 451 459 614 629 945 1241 1243 1319 1505 1573 1735 1739 1836 1852 1874 1877 1881 1962 2127 2200 2344 2464 2492 2495 *Maj Lect* ar vg sy[p.h] arm geo slav Or[lat3/4] Chr Cyr Pel Aug[2/5] and the omission of τῆς ῥίζης ("of the root") in P[46] D* F G d f g bo[ms] fay Ir[lat] Pacian Aug[3/5] are both "suspicious as ameliorating emendations," according to Metzger, *Textual Commentary*, 464, because of the awkward asyndeton of three genitive phrases in sequence, τῆς ῥίζης, τῆς πιότητος τῆς ἐλαίας ("of the root of the olive tree of the fatness") found in ℵ* B C Ψ 1175 1506 1912 2464 *pc* b o sa bo Or^lat3/4 Gildas, which is probably the original wording. An additional effort to clarify the expression is visible in the reversal of "sap" and "root" in sa bo (τῆς πιότητος τῆς ῥίζης), while Pel inserts a καί ("and") in the reversal.

h   The variant σὺ καυχᾶσαι ("you boast") in P^46 D^* F G (330 omits σ?) it Ambst appears to improve the more strongly attested reading that awkwardly repeats the verb used earlier in the verse, κατα-καυχᾶσαι ("you boast"), found in ℵ A B C D^2 L P Ψ 6 (33) 69 88 104 323 326 365 424 614 945 1175 1241 1243 1319 1505 1506 1573 1735 1739 1874 1881 2344 2464 2495 *Maj* vg.

i   The addition of the article οἱ ("the") before "branches" in D^* 88 330 424 630 1501 2495 *al* is a secondary, stylistic improvement.

j   The weakened form ἐκλαύθησαν ("they were broken") in B D^* F G appears to be an effort to avoid repeating the intensified ἐξεκλάσθησαν ("they were broken off") in succeeding verses.

k   The term ὑψηλοφρόνει ("be proud") appears in C D F G L P Ψ 6 33 69 88 104 323 326 330 365 424 614 945 1175 1241 1243 1319 1505 1506 1573 1735 1739 1836 1874 1881 2344 2464 2495 *Maj* in place of the more strongly attested expression typical for Pauline usage elsewhere, ὑψηλὰ φρόνει ("upward, uppity-minded"), found in P^46 ℵ A^vid B 81 *pc*.

l   The inclusion of the ameliorating term μή πως ("perhaps") by P^46 D F G L Ψ 33 69 88 104 181 323 326 330 424* 451 459 614 629 945 1175 1241 1243 1505 1735 1836 1874 1877 1912 1962 2344 2464 2492 2495 *Maj Lect* ar b d f g o vg ⲥy^p,h arm (eth) (geo) slav Ir^lat Chr Severian Cyp Ambst Pel appears to soften the stark contention "he will not spare you." ℵ A B C P 6 81 256 263 365 424^c 436 630 1319 1506 1573 1739 1852 1881 2127 2200 *pc* sa bo fay Or^lat Gregory-Elvira Aug provide strong support for the shorter reading that omits this term. Despite the uncertainty in Nestle-Aland^26/27 and *GNT*^3/4, as shown by the square brackets and the discussion by Metzger, *Textual Commentary*, 464f., the shorter reading should be preferred.

m   The addition of the definite article τοῦ before "God" in P^46 B appears to be a stylistic improvement.

n   The addition of the accusative case ending ν to ἀποτομία ("severity") in ℵ^2 D F G L Ψ 33 69 88 104 323 326 330 365 424* 614 945 1175 1241 1243 1319 1505 1573 1735 1836 1874 1881 2344 2464 *Maj* latt Cl is a grammatical improvement that would make it conform to the first use of this term in v. 21. It is clearly secondary. The text without the accusative ending is found in P^46 ℵ*,c vid A B C 6 81 424^c 630 1506 1739 *pc*.

o   The accusative ending as in note n, χρηστότητα ("goodness"), is found in D^2 F G L Ψ 33 69 88 104 323 326 330 424* 614 945 1175 1241 1319 1505 1735 1874 2464 *Maj* latt Cl. The word χρηστότης ("kindness") is strongly supported by P^46 (ℵ) A B C D^* 6 81 424^c 630 1243 1506 1573 1739 1881 *pc*.

p   The deletion of θεοῦ ("of God") in D^2 F G L Ψ 6 33 69 88 104 323 326 424 614 945 1175 1241 1319 1505 1836 1874 2344 2464 2495 *Maj* it sy Cl Ambst (365 omits θεοῦ by *homoioteleuton*) is consistent with the variants above where the accusative "goodness" does not include God; it is clearly secondary. The inclusion of θεοῦ is supported by P^46 ℵ A B C D^* 81 330 365 630 1243 1506 1573 1735 1739 1881 *pc* vg cop.

q   The subjunctive aorist form ἐπιμείνῃς ("if you remained") in P^46vid A C D^2 F G L 6 33 69 88 104 323 326 330 365 424 945 1175 1241 1319 1506 1573 1739* 1836 1874 1881 2344 *Maj* Cl is not discussed by commentators. The witnesses for the subjunctive present form adopted by Nestle-Aland^26/27 and *GNT*^3/4, ἐπιμένῃς ("if you remain"), are ℵ B D^* Ψ 81 630 1243 (1735 *reads* ἐπιμήνῃς) 1739^c *pc*, appear stronger. The phrase "if you remain in the kindness" is lacking in 614 1505 2464 2495, an unlikely omission.

r   Just as in v. 22, there is an alternate form to the ἐπιμένωσιν ("they remain") found in ℵ* B D^* Ψ 81 365 1739 1881 (1243 2464 read ἐπιμήνωσιν) *pc*, namely, the aorist subjunctive ἐπιμείνωσιν ("they remained") in ℵ^2 A C D^2 F G L 6 33 69 88 104 323 326 330 424 614 945 1175 1241 1319 1505 1506 1573 1735 1836 1874 2344 2495 *Maj* is not discussed by the commentators or Metzger, but it is clearly the inferior reading.

Analysis

Commentators have had difficulty discerning the logical structure and extent of this part of Romans, with Dodd placing all of 11:1-32 in a single pericope[1] and O'Neill extending the pericope from 10:16 to 11:36,[2] while Johnson reduces it to 11:7-36.[3] Among the great majority who view 11:11-24 as a separate pericope, Barrett and others perceive three paragraphs in 11:11-12, 13-16, and 17-24,[4] while Schlier's three paragraphs are somewhat different: 11:11-12, 13-18, and 19-24.[5] Wilckens organizes the material into four paragraphs: 11:11-15, 16-18, 19-21, and 22-24.[6] In contrast, Kuss divides the pericope into two parts, 11:11-12 and 11:13-24;[7] while Michel and others make a division between 11:11-16 and 17-24;[8] and Godet and others divide between 11:11-15 and 16-24.[9] Among the most convincing points of demarcation that have arisen out of this discussion are those between 11:15 and 16 and between 11:21 and 22, but rarely in this discussion, so far as I have been able to tell, has the function of v. 11 been properly understood.

On rhetorical and argumentative grounds, I propose a logical organization of this pericope, with a thesis in 11:11, a logical enthymeme in vv. 12-15, an allegorical enthymeme on the topic of the olive tree in vv. 16-21, and a rhetorically effective conclusion in vv. 22-24. The entire pericope is conspicuous for its lack of scriptural citations, whose argumentative function is taken over by commonsense analogies, including that of the olive trees and branches.[10] Whether this should be called an "allegory" remains unclear in the standard commentaries, which usually interpret the details as if they were allegorical,[11] but often describe it as the olive tree "figure,"[12] "illustration,"[13] "metaphor,"[14] "parable,"[15] or "analogy."[16] The most appropriate category is in fact "allegory,"[17] although it differs from many classical and biblical examples in not interpreting a well-known story. An explicit discussion of the allegorical argument is available in Siegert's study.[18] He takes up the impression that many scholars have that the "comparison" between the olive trees and the situation between Israel and the church is muddled, but that when one reads it as allegory, it makes sense. The discussion of the rhetorical theories of allegory by Anderson[19] makes it clear that this is a figure that says one thing but hints at another.[20] In his discussion of Paul's reference in Gal 4:24,[21]

1   Dodd, 173–74.
2   O'Neill, 175–76; Zeller, 193, places 11:11-36 in a single pericope, while Theobald, 1:292, extends the pericope from 11:1-36.
3   Johnson, 165.
4   Barrett, 211–12, followed by Ziesler, 271–72; Dunn, 2:650–51; Witherington, 242–43; and by Morris, 405, who adds an additional paragraph division between 11:17-21 and 22-24.
5   Schlier, 326–27.
6   Wilckens, 2:241.
7   Kuss, 3:792, 3:798–99.
8   Michel, 343, followed by Byrne, 337; Haacker, 225, 232; and in part by Schreiner, 593, 603.
9   Godet, 398, 404; Sanday and Headlam, 318–19; Kühl, 376, 383; Schmidt, 188–89, 192–93; Murray, 2:75; Moo, 685, 696–97. This division is also followed by Zeller, 193, who assumes a longer pericope from 11:11-36.
10   Bullinger, *Figures*, 750, refers to 11:16-18 as an allegory.
11   See, for example, Michel, 349–50; Kuss, 3:802–4; Schreiner, 604–7.
12   Jülicher, 305; Murray, 2:86; Zeller, 196–97; Wilckens, 2:246.
13   Morris, 412.
14   Sanday and Headlam, 326; M. M. Bourke, *A Study of the Metaphor of the Olive Tree in Romans XI*, SST 2.3 (Washington: Catholic University of America, 1947); Best, 129; Käsemann, 308; Dunn, 2:660; Stuhlmacher, 168; Moo, 702; Witherington, 240; Stowers, *Rereading*, 312–16; Pieter J. Maartens, "Inference and Relevance in Paul's Allegory of the Wild Olive Tree," *HerTS* 3 (1997) 1007–9.
15   Lietzmann, 105; Schmidt, 194; Rengstorf, "Ölbaum-Gleichnis," 127–64; Theobald, 1:298; Bell, *Provoked to Jealousy*, 118; but "metaphor" on 123.
16   Aageson, "Scripture," 284.
17   See Dodd, 179–80; Barrett, 217; O'Neill, 187; Johnson, 169; Haacker, 232; Byrne, 341.
18   Siegert, *Argumentation*, 167–71.
19   Anderson, *Terms*, 14–16.
20   See also Glenn W. Most, "Allegorie/Allegorese. II. Griechisch-römische Antike," *RGG*[4] 1 (1998) 304–5.
21   Anderson, *Paul*, 172–80.

Anderson observes that Paul speaks of the Sarah-Hagar story as an allegory intended by its author: "It seems clear that Paul means to say that this Bible story is *spoken* allegorically."[22] Yet in view of Anderson's impression that Paul's interpretation is exactly the opposite of the literal meaning of this story, he judges that "Paul's use of such an obviously *invented* interpretation comes close to the definition of a *fable*,"[23] strongly suggesting that this is the category that Paul as an uninformed rhetorician should have employed.[24] On the basis of this reasoning Anderson denies that Paul ever employs allegorical interpretation,[25] including Rom 11:17-24, which he defines as a metaphor.[26] The authoritative article by Hans-Josef Klauck is more credible in identifying 11:17-24 as an allegory because it fits the definition of a symbolic text that provides a point-by-point connection with realities beyond the text.[27] Both in Gal 4:24-31 and in Rom 11:17-24 Paul develops a limited number of allegorical points to serve his argumentative purpose, and instead of using terms such as "like" or "be compared to," he flatly identifies current groups or characters with the original story or natural phenomena. It is clear that Paul was not the only early Christian who employed this method of argumentation, because a prominent example of a natural phenomenon employed as an allegory appears in Mark 4:10-20 and Matt 13:36-43, 49-50.[28] In *Abr.* 1.6, Philo uses the grafting of plants as a metaphor for human behavior: "The same thing happens, I may remark, in the case of men, when adopted sons (ὡς τοὺς

θετοὺς παῖδας) by reason of their native good qualities, become congenial to those who by birth are aliens from them, and so become firmly fitted (ἐναρμό-ζεσθαι) into the family."

The thesis of this pericope is stated in 11:11c-d,[29] in answer to a rhetorical question that opens this passage in a manner exactly parallel to 11:1. This is supported in the opening of the first enthymeme by an impressive instance of stating premises in the form of synonymous parallelism v. 12a = v. 12b,[30] which enhances the credibility of these paradoxical premises and strengthens the inference in 11:12c that employs the *a minore ad maius* ("lesser to greater") scheme.[31] This verse is marked with parachesis in the repetition of -μα endings in each of the three lines, παράπτωμα ("trespass"), ἥττημα ("failure"), and πλήρωμα ("fulfillment").[32] In 11:11 and 14 the catchword παραζηλόω ("make zealous") is picked up from the scriptural citation in 10:19.[33] In 11:13-14 Paul develops an *exemplum* of himself[34] as an apostle to the Gentiles in order to show that concern for the conversion of Jews belongs to that office. The hyperbaton in 11:13a-b places the emphasis on "to you" and "apostle" by the unusual first and last positions of those words.[35] This provides definition for the diatribe that had started with the rhetorical question in v. 11, which now continues with an imaginary interlocutor through the end of the pericope.[36] In this case, the "speech-in-character"[37] is made by a blatantly arrogant Gentile Christian whose witty depiction is comparable to that of the insufferable

22 Anderson, *Ancient Rhetorical Theory*, 178, italics in original.
23 Ibid., 180, italics in original.
24 For a more judicious appraisal, see Betz, *Galatians*, 243, who assumes that Paul in fact employs the allegorical method that he derived from Hellenistic Judaism.
25 Anderson, *Paul*, 178.
26 Anderson, *Paul*, 237.
27 Hans-Josef Klauck, "Allegorie/Allegorese. III. Bibel," *RGG⁴* 1 (1998) 305–6.
28 See also the extended allegories of the eagle in *4 Ezra* 11.1–12.35, of the forest, vine, fountain, and cedar in *2 Bar.* 36.1–40.
29 See Käsemann, 304.
30 See Weiss, "Beiträge," 240. He also suggests on 241 that the following verses are in parallel form, 13 + 14; 15a + 15b; 16a + 16b, which is not very compelling.
31 Siegert, *Argumentation*, 166.
32 See Lagrange, 275; Kuss, 3:796; Dunn, 2:652.
33 See Michel, 343.
34 Siegert, *Argumentation*, 166, refers to this as an *argument du prestige* formulated in the "I" style.
35 Bullinger, *Figures*, 696.
36 See Stowers, *Diatribe*, 114–15; *Rereading*, 312–16.
37 See Stowers, *Rereading*, 16–21, for an analysis of the rhetorical technique of προσωποποεία; see also the critical view of Anderson, *Paul*, 201–5. Anderson argues that the classical parallels always identify the character of the imaginary interlocutor, but in the case of Rom 2 and 11, the audience readily identifies these characters from its own experience.

Jewish bigot of chapter 2.[38] The four propositions in 11:12-15 developed in this diatribe form a substantive chiasm:

11:12 A. Jewish trespass and inclusion helps Gentiles
11:13 B. Paul's apostleship to the Gentiles
11:14 B'. Paul's apostleship to the Jews
11:15 A'. Jewish trespass and inclusion helps Gentiles.[39]

This section is linked with the following by a parallel series of chain-link inferences introduced by εἰ ("if"). The first in 11:12 and those in 11:15 and 24 employ the *a minore ad maius* ("from lesser to greater") argument, in 11:21 the *a maiore ad minus* ("from greater to lesser) argument, and the two "if" clauses in 11:16 establish a *locus a simili* ("argument from similarity") scheme. There is a perfect parallelism between the two arguments in 11:16, each including an "if" clause and an inference clause introduced by "so also." This is followed by the extensive argument employing three more "if" clauses concerning the wild olive tree (11:17-24). In the pericope as a whole, a satisfying number of ten "if" clauses is presented.

The allegory of the olive tree functions in part because the order of nature had a high level of authority in the ancient world.[40] A neat, chiastic formula concludes v. 18: "it is not you that support the root but the root supports you."[41] In 11:19 we find a *permissio* statement,[42] in which Paul allows the arrogant boast of the branches to be stated without refutation so that he can deal with the issue of accountability. The next verse provides a "concession" to the viewpoint of the interlocutor followed by a "dissociation" between "unfaith" and "faith."[43] Verse 22 has a chiastic development in that the words "kindness and severity" in 22a are taken up in reverse sequence in 22b and c.[44]

Johannes Weiss has suggested a somewhat irregular, four-sentence arrangement of the material in vv. 17-24,[45] which is refined in the translation above into three sentences of six lines followed by a final sentence of four lines. When one unites this scheme with the preceding four lines of v. 16, the balance between a first and a last sentence of four lines each becomes apparent. The speech-in-character addressed in the second person singular in vv. 17-24 is a Gentile identified as "the personified 'branch' of the wild olive tree grafted onto the cultivated olive tree" of Israel.[46] The revised verse analysis in the allegorical enthymeme of vv. 16-21 and the concluding paragraph of vv. 22-24, more clearly visible in the Greek than in this English translation, is as follows:

1a	16/	Now if the first fruit [of the dough is] holy,
1b		so also [is] the batch of dough;
1c		and if the root [is] holy,
1d		so also [are] the branches.
2a	17/	But if some of the branches were broken off,
2b		and you being a wild olive were grafted into them
2c		to share the sap of the root of the olive,
2d	18/	do not boast concerning the branches.
2e		But if you boast, it is not you that supports the root,
2f		but the root supports you.
3a	19/	Thus you will say, "Branches were broken off in order that I might be grafted in."
3b	20/	Fine. They were broken off for their faithlessness,
3c		but you are standing in faith.
3d		Do not be uppity-minded, but fear.

---

38 See Stowers's description of the "pretentious and arrogant Gentile Christian" in *Diatribe*, 114–17; he does not perceive the humor in Paul's depiction, and in his later *Rereading*, 312–16, he offers a much less plausible analysis of this passage as a footrace between Jews and Gentiles.
39 See Louw, 2:110–11.
40 Siegert, *Argumentation*, 167. Anderson, *Paul*, 237–38, prefers the term "extended metaphor." He discusses ancient theories of allegory in 172–80.
41 See Harvey, *Listening*, 202.
42 See Bullinger, *Figures*, 972. The Greek term for this figure is *epitrope*, which is defined by Anderson, *Glossary*, 54.
43 Siegert, *Argumentation*, 169.
44 See Kuss, 3:805; Fitzmyer, 616.
45 Weiss, "Beiträge," 241.
46 Tobin, *Paul's Rhetoric*, 363.

3e 21/ For if God did not spare the natural branches,

3f   he will not spare you.

4a 22/ Note then the kindness and severity of God;

4b   severity toward those who fell;

4c   but to you the kindness of God,

4d   if you remain in the kindness;

4e   otherwise you will also be cut off.

4f 23/ And they, if they do not remain in faithlessness, will be grafted in.

5a   For God is able to graft them in again.

5b 24/ For if you were cut from a natural olive tree

5c   and were grafted unnaturally into a cultivated olive tree,

5d   how much more [will] these who are natural be grafted back into their own olive tree?

Since the motif of the "root" in 11:16c is picked up in 11:17c and 18b, it is inappropriate to separate the analogies in 11:16 from 11:17-24, as in many commentaries.[47] In fact, v. 16 provides the premise for the enthymeme whose application extends from v. 17 to v. 24. With this arrangement that traces the logical and rhetorical development of the argument from v. 16 through the end of the pericope in v. 24, it is possible to see the correspondence in reference to "branches" being "broken off" in lines 2a (11:17a) and 3a (11:19a), between the imperatives in lines 2d (11:18a) and 3d (11:20c), between the "if" clauses followed by an apodoses in 2e-f (11:18b-c) and 3e-f (11:21a-b), as well as the thematic links in reference to the character of God between 4a (11:22a) and 5a (11:23b). The elegant development in the fourth sentence is also noteworthy, with χρηστότης ("kindness") and ἀποτομία ("severity") taken up in inverted sequence in 4b (11:22b) and 4c (11:22c), and then reversed again as 4e (11:22e) speaks of severity to Gentiles and 4f (11:23a) describes kindness shown to Jews.[48] Weiss notes that the final lines in 11:23a and 11:24c are longer and hence more impressive than the others,[49] which signals in my view an emphasis on the theme of Israel's ultimate inclusion. It is also noteworthy that dia-

tribal elements mark this entire pericope, with rhetorical questions in 11:11, 12, 15, and 24 and addresses to the imaginary interlocutor in the role of a wild olive shoot in 11:17-24,[50] so that the bearing of the argument on the Gentile mission and its beneficiaries becomes unmistakable.

Rhetorical Disposition

IV.	The *probatio*
9:1–11:36	The third proof: The triumph of divine righteousness in the gospel's mission to Israel and the Gentiles
11:11-24	8. Diatribe and allegorical enthymeme dealing with the missional purpose of Israel's trespass
11:11	a. The thesis concerning the hidden purpose of Israel's current unbelief
11:11a	1) The rhetorical question about whether Israel was intended to fall
11:11b	2) The emphatic denial
11:11c-d	3) The reason for the denial: the thesis
11:11c	a) Salvation comes to Gentiles through Israel's trespass
11:11d	b) Israel will subsequently be provoked to zeal
11:12-24	b. The proof of the purpose of Israel's trespass and salvation
11:12-15	1) Logical enthymeme concerning the missional relevance of Israel's trespass and salvation
11:12	a) The *a minore ad maius* proof that Israel's trespass and salvation helps the Gentiles
11:12a	(1) The premise of Israel's trespass enriching the world
11:12b	(2) The parallel premise of Israel's failure enriching Gentiles
11:12c	(3) The inference about how much greater riches will come from Israel's salvation
11:13-14	b) The *exemplum* of Paul's apostolic responsibility both to Gentiles and to Jews
11:13a	(1) Emphatic clarification of address to Gentiles
11:13b	(2) The premise of Paul's identity as an apostle to the Gentiles
11:13c	(3) The statement of missional glorification
11:14	(4) Paul's missional purpose with the Jews
11:14a	(a) The goal of provoking Jewish zeal
11:14b	(b) Paul's purpose of saving Jews

---

47   For example, see Wilckens, 2:241; Michel, 344; Dodd, 173, 179–82; Sanday and Headlam, 326.

48   Bullinger, *Figures*, 361, refers to the introverted parallelism in 11:21-23. The return to the themes of

"kindness" and "severity" from 22a in 22b-d is called *prosapodosis*, according to Bullinger, 395.

49   Weiss, "Beiträge," 242.

50   See Stowers, *Rereading*, 99–100, 114–15.

11:15	c) The *a minore ad maius* proof that Israel's rejection and acceptance brings global reconciliation and life
11:15a	(1) Reiteration of the premise of Israel's rejection leading to global reconciliation
11:15b	(2) The concluding rhetorical question about Israel's conversion as new life
11:16-21	2) Allegorical enthymeme with speech-in-character that aims at acknowledging Israel as the holy foundation of the church
11:16	a) The analogical premise of extended holiness
11:16a-b	(1) The simile of the dough
11:16a	(a) The assumption of holy "first fruit"
11:16b	(b) The inference concerning the loaf made holy by the offering of the "first fruit"
11:16c-d	(2) The correlative simile of the root
11:16c	(a) The assumption of the holy root
11:16d	(b) The inference concerning the branches made holy by the root
11:17-21	b) The allegory of the wild olive branch as the Gentile speech-in-character in relation to Israel that constitutes the domestic olive tree
11:17-18	(1) The rationale for the wild olive not to boast of superiority
11:17a	(a) Broken branches are unbelieving Jews
11:17b	(b) The interlocutor is a wild olive branch grafted in to share the "fatness" of the domestic tree
11:18a	(c) The admonition to the interlocutor not to brag
11:18b	(d) If the interlocutor brags, he overlooks the support of the domestic root
11:19-21	(2) Since faithless branches are broken off, God will not spare faithless Gentiles
11:19	(a) The interlocutor disregards the facts and brags about displacing the domestic branches
11:20a	(b) Paul's acceptance of the foolish interlocutor: "Well said!"
11:20b	(c) The clarification of branches broken because of unfaith

11:20c	(d) The stance of the interlocutor due to faith
11:20d	(e) The warning to the interlocutor i. Do not be uppity-minded ii. Fear (God)
11:21	(f) If God does not spare the natural branches he will not spare the interlocutor
11:22-24	3) Conclusion: the rationale of the kindness and severity of God
11:22-23a	a) Kindness and severity remain in effect for the interlocutor as well as for Jews
11:23b-24	b) Since God grafted in the Gentile interlocutor as a wild olive branch, he will also graft in the Jews who are the natural olive tree

Exegesis

■ **11** The pericope opens with a rhetorical question introduced exactly as in 11:1, λέγω οὖν ("I say therefore"), whereby "therefore" refers back to the dreadful catena of scriptural accusations in 11:7-10 about Israel stumbling blindly in reaction to the gospel of grace. The rhetorical question introduced by μή ("not") requires a negative response from the audience,[51] which leads to my translation, "they did not stumble so as to fall, did they?"[52] The question is exactly in parallel with 11:1, even in employing the same aorist tense in the verb, as seen below:

11:1	Λέγω οὖν, μὴ ἀπώσατο ("I say therefore, he did not cast off")
11:11	Λέγω οὖν, μὴ ἔπταισαν ("I say therefore, they did not stumble")

The wordplay between "stumble" (πταίω) and "fall" (πίπτω) in 11:11 is unique to this passage, so far as I can tell, but the idea of tripping over a rock but not falling on one's face is easily understandable. The verb πταίω that appears here for the only time in the Pauline letters has the basic sense of "stumble against" or "collide with,"[53] and sometimes carries the figurative sense of

---

51 See BAGD (2000) 646 (c), "marker of expectation of a negative answer to a question."

52 Most translations and commentators treat the aorist in this question as a perfect verb, "have stumbled," which implies an action begun in the past and existing to the present, as compared with the "punctiliar" sense of the aorist; see Moulton, *Grammar I*, 109.

53 Karl Ludwig Schmidt, "πταίω," *TDNT* 6 (1968) 883. For example, Xenophon *Cyr.* 3.1.26 reports that Tigranes replied to Cyrus, "It certainly seems to me when a man who in his good fortune proves arrogant, but immediately cowers when fallen (πταίσαντα), will indeed again, when set on foot, prove high-minded and again stir up problems."

making mistakes or errors.[54] This verb therefore evokes the σκάνδαλον ("stumbling block") of Christ in 9:32-33 and 11:9. The more common term in the Pauline letters is πίπτω ("fall"), which appears in 1 Cor 10:12 in reference to "apostasy from God and from Christ"[55] that also entailed separation from the community of faith. We encounter the same connotation in Rom 11:22 and 14:4, which are followed closely in other early Christian writings (Heb 4:11; Rev 2:5). Although there are semantic overlaps between these terms, Paul's formulation conveys the idea of progressing from stumbling to falling,[56] in which the latter has the connotation of "fall to rise no more."[57] Whether ἵνα should be taken as purposive ("in order to")[58] or resultant ("so as to")[59] is a matter on which scholars are evenly divided, but the context and the formulation of the question make the former more likely. The question was not whether a portion of Israel had stumbled and fallen, which it certainly had as indicated by the branches ἐξεκλάσθησαν ("lopped off") in v. 17 and the reference to Israel as τοὺς πεσόντας ("those who fell") in v. 22. While the result of Jewish rejection of the gospel was clear, the divine intention was not, which gave rise to the rhetorical question and the subsequent thesis. The categorical denial is expressed with μὴ γένοιτο ("by no means!"), which appears here for tenth and last time in the letter.[60]

The thesis that Paul sets forth in support of the denial is introduced by ἀλλά ("but"), which sets his contention in an adversative relationship with the question just raised, that is, whether God intended the final destruction of Israel.[61] Israel's stumbling is referred to as "their trespass" (τῷ αὐτῶν παραπτώματι), a term that Paul had employed in 4:25 in the plural reference to "our transgressions" and in 5:15-29 in reference to Adam's sin. Particular transgressions either of law or of other obligations are in view with this term,[62] and in Israel's case the previous argument of Romans would lead the audience to understand παράπτωμα as rejection of the gospel (9:30–10:3, 16-21; 11:7-10).[63] As defined by the previous distinction between stumbling and falling, παράπτωμα is correlated with πταίειν ("stumble"),[64] a serious offense that could be overcome rather than a final lapse into oblivion. An appropriate parallel to this use of παράπτωμα is therefore Gal 6:1, "if a person is overtaken by any trespass, you who are spiritual should restore him in a spirit of gentleness."[65] For, as this pericope goes on to demonstrate, God will ultimately graft back in (11:24) those branches of Israel that had been lopped off because of their unfaith in the gospel (11:20). In the meanwhile, Paul's thesis contends, by means of this trespass, "the salvation [is coming] for the Gentiles."[66] In contrast to the earlier, anarthrous references to σωτηρία ("salvation") in 1:16; 10:1, 10, Paul refers here to "the salvation," as "known, particular, pre-

54   Schmidt, "πταίω," 885, refers to Marcus Aurelius Τὰ εἰς ἑαυτὸν 7.22.1, who refers to loving a "relative and those who make a false step (τοὺς πταίοντας). Now this does occur, if it happens to you at the same time, because even relatives, both willingly and through ignorance, do err."

55   Wilhelm Michaelis, "πίπτω κτλ.," TDNT 6 (1968) 164–65; Elisabeth Palzkill, "πίπτω," EDNT 3 (1993) 90–91.

56   Meyer, 2:211.

57   Dunn, 2:653, citing Isa 24:20, Israel "falls and will not rise again." Morris, 406, refers to "fall beyond recovery." Schmidt, "πταίω," 886, speaks of "eternal ruin" and Meyer, 2:212, of "everlasting destruction," thus evoking eternal damnation that is extraneous to this passage.

58   Weiss, 475; Mayer, Gottes Heilratschluß, 263; Kuss, 3:793; Schlier, 328; Käsemann, 304; Murray, 2:76.

59   Godet, 399; Sanday and Headlam, 321; Lagrange, 275; Cranfield, 2:554; Morris, 406; Dunn, 2:653; Witherington, 266.

60   For a discussion of the use of μὴ γένοιτο in the diatribes of Epictetus, see Malherbe, "Μὴ γένοιτο," 25–33, and note 58 in 3:1-8 above.

61   See Morris, 407.

62   See Wilhelm Michaelis, "παραπίπτω, παράπτωμα," TDNT 6 (1968) 170–72. Michael Wolter, "παράπτωμα," EDNT 3 (1991) 34, stretches the semantic range of this term by contending that in 11:11 παράπτωμα bears the meaning of "fall from the realm of salvation."

63   Michaelis, "παραπίπτω, παράπτωμα," 172; see also Michel, 344; Murray, 2:76; Cranfield, 2:555–56; Wilckens, 2:249; Bell, Provoked to Jealousy, 112.

64   Meyer, 2:212; Weiss, 476. Wolter, "παράπτωμα," 34, stretches the semantic range of this term by contending that in 11:11 παράπτωμα bears the meaning of "fall from the realm of salvation."

65   See also Ps 18:13; Ps. Sol. 3.7; 13.5, 10.

66   The clause ἡ σωτηρία τοῖς ἔθνεσιν should be translated as a dative of benefit, "the salvation for the Gentiles."

viously mentioned"[67] in the earlier argument of Romans and experienced in the life of the Roman congregations. The sequence of conversion by divine power that moves from "faith" to "confession" and then to "salvation" as described in 10:10 is presupposed here, with $\sigma\omega\tau\eta\rho\iota\alpha$ understood as eschatological deliverance.[68] Since the clause is elliptical, commentators ordinarily add a past-tense verb, usually in the perfect, that matches the mistranslation of the aorist in 11b, but a present-progressive verb with its inherently future orientation ("is coming")[69] seems more appropriate in the context of this missional letter in which Paul immediately moves on to "glorify" his ministry to the Gentiles (11:13) in order to stimulate the conversion of the Jews (11:14).

The idea of Jewish resistance providing an opportunity for the gospel to be preached to the Gentiles rests on the premise of an apocalyptic scenario.[70] At the end of time all Israel will be saved (11:26) but this cannot occur until "the fullness of the Gentiles" has been achieved (11:25). Reckoning backwards from this apocalyptic climax, Paul infers that current Jewish resistance against the gospel provides time for the Gentile mission. This is the reasoning behind the Spanish mission project

that this letter seeks to advance, for if the gospel can be brought to the end of the known world, the climactic conversion of Israel can occur and the parousia can come as promised.

The articular infinitive followed by a pronoun, $\epsilon\iota\varsigma$ $\tau\delta$ $\pi\alpha\rho\alpha\zeta\eta\lambda\hat{\omega}\sigma\alpha\iota$ $\alpha\upsilon\tau\omega\varsigma$, indicates the purpose of salvation coming first to the Gentiles,[71] and should be translated "in order to provoke them to zeal/jealousy/emulation."[72] Here Paul refers back to the citation from Deut 32:21 in 10:19, which was translated in my discussion above as "I will make you zealous" in relation to the Gentiles. Admittedly, there are problems with all of the suggested translations of $\pi\alpha\rho\alpha\zeta\eta\lambda\omega$ in this passage. If the traditional translation "jealousy" is selected,[73] the "fantastic" improbability in believing that envy could lead to salvation[74] along with the inherent unworthiness of envy as a motivation for conversion[75] are hard to deny. In view of the fact that Jewish legalists viewed the early Christian proclamation as heretical, no satisfactory explanation has ever been given to explain why they would have been "jealous" when Gentiles accepted this allegedly mistaken doctrine. Moreover, the links with the earlier argument of Romans are weakened by the tradi-

67 BDF §252.

68 See Schelkle, "$\sigma\omega\tau\eta\rho\iota\alpha$," 327.

69 See Barrett, 213; Dunn, 2:653. Witherington, 267, follows Stephen Llewelyn, "Slaves and Masters §9," *NDIEC* 6 (1992) 68, that the omitted verb should always conform to the immediately preceding verb, but the evidence for this is not conclusive in every case, according to BDF §§479, 481.

70 Käsemann, 304, refers to the "salvation-historical aspect" of 11:11; Aageson, "Scripture," 282, refers to "God's plan of salvation," but Terence L. Donaldson, "'Riches for the Gentiles' (Rom 11:12): Israel's Rejection and Paul's Gentile Mission," *JBL* 112 (1993) 92–98, provides the clearest view of Paul's apocalyptic scenario. Commentaries routinely refer to Acts 11:19-21; 13:45-48; 18:6; 28:24-28, but these later theories of Jewish resistance leading to the Gentile mission are not reflected in the Pauline letters, all of which display an apocalyptic orientation. Lagrange, 275, and Ellison, *Mystery of Israel*, 81, claim that Jewish customs would have stood in the way of Gentile conversion, but this plays no role in Romans. Even less plausible is Cranfield's explanation (2:556) on the basis of Barth's theory that Jewish resistance against Christ led to his redemptive death and hence to the salvation of the world; there

is no evidence of christological speculation in this passage. Nor is there a basis to claim with Wright, "Messiah," 180–82, that Israel had to be cast aside in order to conform to the fate of the Messiah.

71 Meyer, 2:212; Morris, 407; Moulton and Turner, *Grammar III*, 143, shows that this construction usually indicates purpose.

72 See Stumpff, "$\zeta\hat{\eta}\lambda o\varsigma$ $\kappa\tau\lambda$.," 881; Popkes, "$\zeta\hat{\eta}\lambda o\varsigma$ $\kappa\tau\lambda$.," 100.

73 Among the almost unanimous voice of commentators favoring "jealousy," Murray, 2:77, and Wilckens, 2:242–43, seem conscious of the problems with this choice. Stuhlmacher, 167, suggests "angry jealousy," which is accepted by Keller, *Gottes Treue*, 185–87. Nanos, *Mystery*, 249–50, argues that Jews were jealous of Paul's successful ministry with Gentiles because he was realizing "their own Jewish universalistic hopes" in a manner superior to their own missionary successes.

74 Käsemann, 304.

75 Fitzmyer, 611.

tional translation, because ζηλόω has the sense of religious zeal and rage rather than jealousy in 10:2, as generally acknowledged, and also in 10:19, as argued above on contextual and poetic grounds.[76] If "emulation" is selected,[77] Bell has a hard time explaining how "jealous anger," his preferred translation for 10:19, could have been thought to shift into the positive desire to emulate the behavior of the previously hated Gentiles.[78] If one selects "provoke to zealous rage" or "make zealous,"[79] thus providing the best continuity with the probable connotation of παραζηλόω in 10:19 and the certain meaning of ζηλόω in 10:2, it remains puzzling that such religious hostility could be thought to lead to their salvation, for which Paul hopes in 11:14.[80] Perhaps he has the model of his own conversion in mind, namely, that when his zeal reached its violent climax in the persecution of the believers in Damascus, the risen Christ was revealed to him and his desire to destroy alleged evildoers turned into its opposite, a desire for coexistence with those whom the Messiah had chosen to accept. Zeal to exclude hated Gentiles turned into a comparable zeal to include them as part of the people of God. It appears that Paul hoped for a similar process of conversion for current Jewish critics of the gospel.[81]

However one chooses to translate παραζηλόω, it is clear that a kind of double thesis has been established in v. 11 for the rest of this pericope. In the enthymeme that follows, Paul goes on to develop the idea that (1) benefits for Gentiles come through the hostile resistance of the Jews, and (2) the conversion of Gentiles will provoke the Jews to a divinely instigated reaction that will result in their conversion as well. In the long history of interpretation, with the exception of a few commentators who are revolted by Paul's alleged trust in jealousy, this

extraordinary thesis has come to seem unremarkable. But in the viewpoint of Paul's original audience in Rome, this thesis must have appeared both improbable and unappealing. Neither the weak nor the strong in Rome, who were damning each other and refusing intercommunion, would have had an interest in increasing the number of their competitors on the other side. And that the mass conversion of potential allies to their competitors would ultimately redound to their own benefit must have appeared preposterous. Those who read this pericope as unproblematic discourse have forgotten that its audience was in Rome, where power politics, alliances, and lethal competition had for centuries been the most engaging aspects of life and conversation. The rhetorical brilliance and wit of the following argument was ingeniously devised to overcome Roman resistance to Paul's missional project.

■ 12 The first proof begins with an eloquent oral ellipse,[82] that is, without verbs, which must be supplied by the hearer. It is widely recognized that this verse provides an *a minore ad maius* ("lesser to greater") argument, employing the "how much more" scheme that we saw in 5:9, 10, 15, 17.[83] The premise of the argument begins with an inferential εἰ ("if") and is formulated as a compelling, synonymous parallelism that restates the first portion of the thesis as expressed in 11:11c. The expression παράπτωμα αὐτῶν ("their trespass") is repeated chiastically from 11c, thus making clear that the *a minore ad maius* argument sustains the thesis already stated. There is an ironic juxtaposition between the terms Paul selects, because "trespass" would ordinarily be thought to lead to failure, but here it brings πλοῦτος κόσμου ("wealth for the world"). Deuteronomy and Proverbs consistently maintain that bad behavior

76 See particularly Baker, "Motif of Jealousy," 475, who rejects a "shift in meaning between Rom 10:19 and 11:11, 14.

77 The only commentary that comes close to this interpretation is Weiss, 476.

78 See Bell, *Provoked to Jealousy*, 113–67.

79 The only commentary close to this translation is O'Neill, 179, who refers to Paul's aim "to stir unbelieving Jews to greater fury." Stuhlmacher, 167, picks up part of this motif with "angry jealousy."

80 Keller, *Gottes Treue*, 186–94, grapples with this problem but suggests that Paul's strategy of "saving some" (11:14) was by normal means of gospel persuasion and that jealous anger would have been ineffective. In the end, actual jealousy of the position of Gentiles as God's people would effect mass Jewish conversion (193).

81 In Murray Baker's formulation, "Although not explicit, the salvation envisaged is surely Christocentric: Christ the redeemer at the *parousia* turning Israel to faith in Christ" (Baker, "Motif of Jealousy," 482)

82 See BDF §481.

83 For example, Meyer, 2:214; Käsemann, 305; Wilckens, 2:243; Siegert, *Argumentation*, 166; Moo, 688.

leads to poverty while righteous behavior leads to wealth.[84] This is also assumed throughout the Greco-Roman world,[85] so the counterintuitive paradox of Paul's argument was evident. The word πλοῦτος connotes both material and spiritual wealth and prosperity,[86] which has led commentators to define it as salvation.[87] The paradoxical quality of Paul's claim is visible in contrast to the conventional piety of Ps 21:2, where "the account of my transgressions (παράπτωμα μου) is far from my salvation."[88] In view of the variety of verbs to be supplied in Pauline ellipses,[89] it is questionable whether the usual "is" would be appropriate in reference to wealth.[90] Since Paul argues that an actual augmentation of wealth, both spiritual and material, will occur as a result of the mission to Jews and Gentiles, it seems more natural to supply a verb that expresses the production thereof: I therefore translate "if their trespass [makes] wealth for the world."

In the synonymous parallel of v. 12b, the rare word ἥττημα stands in the correlative position with "trespass" and enhances the antithesis in 12a because of its connotation of "loss,"[91] falling short,[92] or being defeated.[93] The semantic connotation of "loss" fits the context best,[94] while the usual translations of "failure"[95] or "defeat"[96] ruin the antithesis with "wealth."[97] The divine paradox of the gospel that overturns all human expectations is neatly encapsulated by the thought that Israel's "loss" produces "wealth" for the Gentiles.[98] The correlative formulation "wealth for the Gentiles" in 12b clarifies what was meant by "wealth for the world" in 12a, that is, that spiritual and material prosperity has come to the Gentiles as a result of Israel's repudiation of the gospel that afforded time for the gospel to be preached and new communities of faith formed.[99] Although commentators are inclined to view this as bland and virtually redundant parallelism,[100] the reference to "wealth for the Gentiles" was a relevant clarification in the Roman context, because the Gentile majority

---

84 Deut 8:1-20; 11:8-17; Prov 6:6-13; 10:3-5, 15-16; 11:25-31; 12:11, 27; 13:21, 25; 19:3, 15-16; 21:5-7, 17; 22:4-5, 8; 24:30-34; 28:18-20; 31:10-31; see also Hauck and Kasch, "πλοῦτος κτλ.," 324.

85 For example, see Hesiod *Op.* 225-47, who claims that just and righteous deeds cause a city and her people to prosper, bringing them peace, lack of famine, and plenty in respect to crops and produce in the land, whereas wickedness and violence bring the opposite.

86 Hauck and Kasch, "πλοῦτος κτλ.," 328-29.

87 Godet, 400; Schlier, 329; Murray, 2:77; Cranfield, 2:557; Byrne, 338, all refer to "salvation." Käsemann, 305; Schreiner, 597, refer to "eschatological blessing"; Dunn uses similar language in 2:654.

88 See Sir 3:13; 10:2; also Michaelis, "παραπίπτω, παράπτωμα," 170.

89 See Moulton and Turner, *Grammar III*, 300-303.

90 Commentators often supply verbs other than "is" for the ellipses in 11:12. Lietzmann, 102; Morris, 405; Cranfield, 2:553; Zeller, 193; Ziesler, 274; Dunn, 2:654; Moo, 685, 88; Byrne, 336, supply "means"; Barrett; 211, supplies "has come to mean . . . has led . . . will mean"; Schmidt, 188, and Haacker, 225, supply "make"; Wilckens, 2:241, supplies "has become"; Jülicher, 303, supplies "bring."

91 BAGD (2000) 441, citing 1 Cor 6:7 as an example of ἥττημα, "to have lawsuits with one another is *an utter loss* for you." LSJM 780 renders ἥττημα as "discomfiture, loss." The *Con. Eph.* I.1.6.149.19

refers to ἀνθρωπίνης ἀσθενείας ἥττημα ("loss of human frailty").

92 BAGD (2000) 441 notes that ἡττάομαι means "feel less important, be treated worse," as in 2 Cor 12:13, "for in what were you treated worse than the rest of the churches?"

93 BAGD (2000) 441 says ἡττάομαι can mean "be vanquished, be defeated," as in 2 Pet 2:19-20 and Isa 31:8. MM 282 cites *Chrest.* 1. Nr. 16.7, with regard to the defeat of a Jewish uprising during Hadrian's reign, οἱ ἡμέ[τ]ερο[ι] ἡττ[ή]θησαν καὶ πολλοὶ [α]ὐτῶν συνεκόπ[ησαν ("Ours were worsted, and many of theirs soundly thrashed!")

94 Lietzmann, 103, speaks of a "minus;" Kühl, 379, refers to Israel falling behind the Gentiles and Barrett speaks of "a diminution" of the numbers of Jewish converts; Fitzmyer, 611, translates with "loss," as does Johnson, 168.

95 Dunn, 2:651; Byrne, 336.

96 Michel, 345; Schlier, 329; Cranfield, 2:557; Murray, 2:78; Bell, *Provoked to Jealousy,* 114.

97 See Barrett, 214.

98 See Morris, 408.

99 See Donaldson, "Riches," 92-94.

100 Weiss, 478; Schlier, 329; Morris, 407-8.

in the churches was hostile to Jewish Christians and thus would not have been inclined to welcome their augmentation. While commentaries concentrate exclusively on the spiritual side of this twice-repeated term πλοῦτος, it is important to remember that Paul employed this term with reference to material plentitude in 2 Cor 8:2, describing how the extreme poverty of the Macedonian churches had "overflowed in a wealth of liberality on their part (τὸ πλοῦτος τῆς ἁπλότητος αὐτῶν)" in their contributions to the Jerusalem offering. Also, in Phil 4:19, after thanking this same impoverished congregation for their gift to meet his financial need, Paul promises that "my God will supply every need of yours according to his riches in glory (κατὰ τὸ πλοῦτος αὐτοῦ ἐν δόξῃ) in Christ Jesus." In the common life of early churches, the pooling of resources through koinonia and the augmented morale of members resulted in actual increases of material wealth, as Paul makes clear in 2 Cor 9:8-10.[101] Now Paul creates an argument that a further increase in material as well as spiritual wealth will occur when the mission is completed.

The content of the "how much more" phase of Paul's first argument employs πόσῳ μᾶλλον in place of πολλῷ μᾶλλον ("how much more?") that we saw in chapter 5. The two expressions appear to have a virtually identical meaning,[102] but apparently Paul felt that πόσῳ μᾶλλον was more appropriate in reference to its adjacent reference, πλοῦτος. While most commentaries fail to specify how much more of *what* was intended by this question, Meyer clarifies what the successful Jewish conversion will produce: "how much more will it issue in the enrichment of the Gentiles."[103] I therefore translate, "how much more [wealth will] their full total [make]?" There is an unresolved debate over the interpretation of τὸ πλήρωμα αὐτῶν,[104] which has been taken to refer to Israel's complete acceptance of faith,[105] the fulfillment of the demand of love as in 13:10,[106] the fulfillment of Israel's predestination,[107] the filling up of "the blank in the kingdom of God which arose through their unbelief,"[108] the "fulfillment of God's will,"[109] or, in the assessment of most commentators, "the full and completed number" of Jewish converts.[110] The "most common use" of πλήρωμα in secular literature is "complete, full-total, completeness," according to the survey by P. D. Overfield.[111] A close parallel to Paul's expression is πλήρωμα ἔθνους ("fullness of a people") to describe the entire citizenry in a Greek polis.[112] In the confessional formula that Paul cites in Gal 4:4, the word πλήρωμα refers to the divinely ordained moment when the requisite time had passed: "when the fullness of time had come (ἦλθεν τὸ πλήρωμα τοῦ χρόνου), God sent his son . . . ." As Betz observes, this is the traditional "Jewish and Christian eschatological language which Paul shared."[113] Since the same usage is visible in Mark

---

101 Betz, *2 Corinthians 8 and 9*, 109–11, places this passage in the context of Greco-Roman and Jewish conceptions that material wealth was a gift of God that enables human sharing.

102 BAGD (2000) 849 ב and 855 (1); πόσῳ μᾶλλον appears also in Luke 11:13; 12:24, 28; Heb 9:14, and among the Attic Orators only once in Demosthenes *Orat.* 19.238.5.

103 Meyer, 2:214; see also Käsemann, 305.

104 Dunn cannot decide between the alternative interpretations and offers "fullness" on the grounds that "Paul strives more for effect than for precision."

105 Zahn, 506; similarly, Fritzsche refers to "the fullness of Messianic salvation," as reported by Meyer, 2:214; for a more recent statement, see Plag, *Israels Wege*, 33–34.

106 Lietzmann, 103.

107 Umbreit as described by Meyer, 2:214.

108 Philippi, as reported by Meyer, 2:214–15.

109 Reported by Cranfield, 2:558.

110 Ibid.; see also Godet, 401; Sanday and Headlam,

922, Murray, 2:70; Wilckens, 2:243; Stuhlmann, *Eschatologische Maß*, 186–87; Witherington, 267; Donaldson, "Riches," 94, confirmed by Baker, "Motif of Jealousy," 478–80.

111 Overfield, "Pleroma," 388. In Aristotle *Pol.* 1267b16; 1284a5; Plato *Resp.* 371e7, the πλήρωμα of a πόλις refers to the full population of a city.

112 Aelius Aristides Παν. 160.13. Gerhard Delling, "πλήρης κτλ.," *TDNT* 6 (1968) 299, also cites Aristotle *Pol.* 4.4, 1291a.17 as an example of this use.

113 Betz, *Galatians*, 206, referring to parallels in Mark 1:15; John 7:8; Heb 1:2; 1QS 4:18-19; 1QM 14:14; 1QpHab 7:13. Witherington, 167, adds *2 Bar.* 81.4 ("He made known to me the mystery of the times. And the advent of the hours he showed me") as an example of this idea of the predestined time of fulfillment.

1:15, πεπλήρωται ὁ καιρός ("the time is fulfilled") and John 7:8, ὁ ἐμὸς καιρὸς οὔπω πεπλήρωται ("my time is not yet fulfilled"), there is no doubt that the audience in Rome would have understood Paul's formulation as the divinely appointed full measure.[114] Rainer Stuhlmann has shown that the idea of an eschatological full measure extended also to the predestined number of the saved, as in *4 Ezra* 4.35-37:[115] "And when will come the harvest of our reward?" And Jeremiel the archangel answered them and said, "When the number of those like yourselves is completed; for he has weighed the age in the balance, and measured the times by measure, and numbered the times by number; and he will not move or arouse them until that measure is fulfilled." The interpretation of πλήρωμα as a full measure in 11:12 is confirmed by the same language in 11:25 that clearly describes the full number of Gentile converts.[116] With this rhetorical question that demands a positive response from his audience, Paul completes the first phase of his enthymeme. With a brilliant rhetorical stroke, Paul has made a persuasive start in overturning the inclinations of his audience in Rome to resist missionizing that would benefit their competitors. He gets them to agree with the divine paradox that the very conversions they resist are of the most decisive benefit, both spiritual and material, not just to their competitors but also to themselves.

■ **13** As noted above, many commentators are inclined to take "Now I speak to you Gentiles" as the beginning of a new section,[117] but, as Siegert points out, the connections to both the preceding and following discourse are very tight, and the δέ should not be viewed as adversative but translated as a development of the argument,[118] which leads to my translation with "now." The direct address to Gentiles is not merely an indication of the likely majority of the congregation,[119] but reveals where the strongest resistance to Paul's contention was perceived to lie. The pronoun ὑμῖν is in the emphatic position, which makes it clear that the discourse in this section is primarily directed[120] at Gentile believers.[121] The prejudice of the Gentile Christian majority against the "weak" was the major barrier against the proper development of Paul's missional scheme, because, as I have suggested, they did not welcome the prospect of an increase in the number of their competitors that would come from a mass conversion of Jews. Paul is forced by the rhetorical situation to address the Gentile congregations directly and make it clear that he is on their side of the equation despite his urging them to a course of action that they were inclined to loathe. He thus makes it plain that such a course is intrinsic to the Gentile mission as such, using himself as an *exemplum*.[122] The expression ἐφ᾽ ὅσον ("inasmuch")[123] is followed by the concessive μὲν οὖν, which has the sense of "contrary to what you may be inclined to think."[124] I attempt to render this with "notwithstanding." This is combined with the emphatic εἰμι ἐγώ, which I render as "I am indeed"[125] an apostle appointed by God to missionize among Gentiles. It is important to observe that he does not claim to be "*the* apostle to the Gentiles"; by omitting the article, the unusual expression ἐθνῶν ἀπόστολος ("an apostle to the Gentiles")[126] places his task alongside

---

114 See Delling, "πλήρης κτλ.," 305; Hans Hübner, "πλήρωμα," *EDNT* 3 (1993) 110–11.

115 Stuhlmann, *Eschatologische Maß*, 109–12; other comparable passages include *1 En.* 47:4 and Rev 6:11.

116 Kühl, 379, makes a compelling case that 11:25 requires the concept of the "full number" of Jewish converts; Weiss, 478, rejects the numerical interpretation.

117 Barrett, 211–12; Schlier, 326–27; Ziesler, 271–72; Kuss, 3:792, 798–99; Dunn, 2:650–51; Witherington, 242–43; Morris, 405.

118 Siegert, *Argumentation*, 166; see also Meyer, 2:215.

119 Dunn, 2:655, and Moo, 691, reiterate the view of most commentators on this point.

120 See Cranfield, 2:559.

121 Even Dabelstein, *Beurteilung*, 37, who often trans-

lates ἔθνη as "nations," recognizes that "Gentile believers" are in view. All commentators agree.

122 See Anderson, *Glossary*, 87–88, 109.

123 BAGD (2000) 729 (3), "to the degree that," in this case, "that I am an apostle to the Gentiles." Schlier, 330, cites *Barn.* 4.11 ("so far as in us lies [ἐφ᾽ ὅσον ἐστὶν ἐν ἡμῖν] let us exercise ourselves in the fear of God" and 17.1 ("so far as [ἐφ᾽ ὅσον] possibility and simplicity allow an explanation to be given . . .").

124 See Lagrange, 277; Cranfield, 2:559; Moo, 691; see also Weiss, 479.

125 Meyer, 2:215.

126 See the discussion of the grammatical issue of the anarthrous formulation in Morris, 409 n. 60, and Moo, 691 n. 40, considers the possibility that ἐθνῶν ἀπόστολος may have been titular, but this seems

others and implies that service to the cause of the Jewish mission is a generic obligation of every Gentile apostle. Here Paul alludes back to 1:1 and 1:5 where he claimed to have received a specific calling to missionize among "all the Gentiles." Since this calling derived from Paul's conversion (Gal 1:16) and was recognized by the pillar apostles (Gal 2:7, 9), it would have been seen as indisputable by the audience in Rome. In view of the divine authorization of apostolic service, it would have seemed unobjectionable that Paul glorifies his ministry. The verb δοξάζειν ("to glorify") is an inherent obligation of humans toward God (cf. 1:21; 15:6, 9),[127] so that honoring the agency of apostolic service was a logical extension of this obligation.[128] There is no indication that he believed such glorification is a violation of the fundamental prohibition of boasting in behalf of one's self and one's achievements, as in 3:27; for Paul this is an acceptable form of "boasting in the Lord" (2:17; 5:2, 11; 1 Cor 1:31; 2 Cor 10:17; Phil 3:3).

In 2 Cor 4:1 and 11:23 Paul speaks of apostolic service as a διακονία, which is an "in-between" activity such as speaking or serving in behalf of others,[129] in this case in behalf of the gospel and the formation of communities of faith.[130] That this term referred to a formal church office, as argued by Lietzmann and others,[131] is doubtful at this early stage in the development of the church, but that early Christian leaders of congregations bore this title from the very earliest stage is clear from Phil 1:1 and Rom 16:1. There was nothing in this verse, therefore, that would have seemed problematic to the believers in Rome. What the Gentile Christian audience was not so prepared to accept, however, was the contention in the next verse that serving the cause of Jewish conversion was inextricably bound up with apostolic ministry.

■ **14** Paul's hope in the effect of glorifying his apostolic ministry is stated in a carefully qualified manner. He begins with εἴ πως ("if somehow"), which leaves open the means by which the following is to be achieved.[132] In a formula comparable to English "flesh and blood," Paul refers to his fellow Jews with the typical biblical expression employed in 9:3, "my flesh," as in Gen 29:14 ("Laban said to him, 'Surely you are my bone and my flesh [ἐκ τῆς σαρκός μου]'"; see also Judg 9:2; 2 Sam 5:1).[133] Since this expression appears repeatedly in the OT, this constitutes a clear "echo," even though the emphatic position of "my" in Paul's formulation, μου τὴν σάρκα, requires the translation "my very flesh." There is, in any event, no derogatory implication in this reference.[134] The verbs παραζηλώσω and σώσω can be taken as either future indicative[135] or aorist subjunctive,[136] and the latter seems more likely following εἴ πως. I therefore translate with "might make zealous" and "might save." In line with the definition of παραζηλόω

---

unlikely. BDF §474.4 provides the relevant rule. Sansone, "Article in Greek," 199–201, suggests that the absence of the article indicates "focality."

127 See Walter Grundmann, "δοκέω κτλ.," *TDNT* 2 (1964) 241, 253–54; Ceslas Spicq, "δόξα κτλ.," *TLNT* 1 (1974) 372–73, 376–78.

128 Harald Hegermann, "δοξάζω," *EDNT* 1 (1990) 348. Michel, 347, places this reference in the context of the obligatory *Beraka*, which glorifies God. Cranfield, 2:560, seeks to avoid any implication of boasting and thus adds the thought that Paul fulfills his apostolic calling "with all his might and devotion," which is not germane to this context.

129 See Collins, *Diakonia*, 77–95, 335–36.

130 Alfons Weiser, "διακονέω κτλ.," *EDNT* 1 (1990) 302–3, shows that the organization of table service as well as the ministry of the word were entailed in Paul's use of the term διακονία.

131 Lietzmann, 109; Schlier, 330; Murray, 2:124; Brockhaus, *Charisma*, 98–100. For a critique of this view, see Käsemann, 306.

132 See BDF §375; BAGD (2000) 901, a "marker of undesignated means or manner, somehow, in some way, perhaps." Examples are Josephus *Bell.* 6.423, "*if somehow* he might be able to count their number," and *Ant.* 2.159, "falling at Joseph's feet, *if somehow* he might soften his wrath." See also Acts 27:12; Rom 1:10; and Phil 3:11.

133 Sand, "σάρξ," 231, "In the genealogical sense, *flesh* refers to the people of Israel, to whom a person belongs through conception and birth."

134 Dunn, 2:656, suggests that Paul's choice of "flesh" refers back to the "hardened" quality of his fellow Jews; I made a similar claim in *Terms*, 160, 163, but it now appears to me that the negative connotation of "flesh" is extraneous to this verse.

135 The indicative is selected by Kühl, 381, and Haacker, 226; Kuss, 3:799, seems to favor the indicative, but his translation on 798 reflects the subjunctive.

136 The aorist subjunctive is favored by Zahn, 510; Moo, 685, 692, and most translations.

as "make zealous" or "provoke to zealous anger" in 10:19 and 11:11, this connotation should be assumed here, rather than "make jealous" or "cause to emulate." However one chooses to translate παραζηλόω, it is clear that Deut 32:21, from which this term was drawn, serves as "a charter for his mission to the Gentiles," namely, to serve "God's intention . . . to save Israel along with the entire cosmos."[137] The subjunctive voice of the verbs along with "if somehow" insert a measure of divine mystery in this process. The verb σώζειν ("to save") reflects early Christian missionary language as in 1 Cor 7:16; 9:22; and 1 Thess 2:16,[138] and takes up the theme of "salvation" from 11:11. In the light of Rom 10:8-10, it is clear that Paul functions as an agency in this charismatic process, which involves proclamation of the gospel, a response of faith, a public confession, and becoming part of a house or tenement church. There is also a measure of "diplomatic caution"[139] in his hope to effect the conversion of τινὰς ἐξ αὐτῶν ("some of them"). Particularly in the face of Gentile Christian resistance against augmenting the number of their Jewish Christian competitors, Paul's formulation leaves the effectuation up to God. If the Jews in fact respond positively to Paul's provocation, it will be a result of miraculous divine intervention, not of Paul's persuasive powers. As in the formulation of 11:12, the precise measure of the "full number" of Jewish converts remains in the hands of

God, whose mysterious purpose is acclaimed at the end of this third great proof (11:33-36).

■ **15** It is interesting to observe that after presenting the personal *exemplum* in vv. 13-14, which was bound to be highly controversial, Paul returns in this verse to the safer arena of an extraordinarily exalted *a minore ad maius* ("lesser to greater") argument, which ends with a rhetorical question that forces the audience to make a positive response. This verse has the feel of a recapitulation by beginning as in 11:12 with a protasis introduced by εἰ ("if") followed by an apodosis in the form of a rhetorical question. As in v. 12, the style is that of an eloquent ellipse, for which the verbs must be supplied by the audience. In view of the subjunctive verbs in the preceding sentence, a subjunctive form of γένοιτο, thus echoing v. 11 and translated "would be," seems most natural here.[140] The normal lexical range for ἀποβολή is (1) "throw away, jettison" or (2) "loss," whereas there are no clear examples of the widely popular translation, "reject."[141] The expression ἡ ἀποβολὴ αὐτῶν could be taken as a subjective genitive, "the loss of, or throwing away [the gospel] by the Jews themselves,"[142] or an objective genitive, "their being thrown away [by God]."[143] The subjective genitive is sustained by Fitzmyer's compelling observation that in 11:1 Paul explicitly repudiated the idea that God had rejected his people.[144] In this pericope, he employs the word "trespass" in 11:11, 12, which

---

137 Wagner, *Heralds*, 269.

138 See Wilckens, 2:244, for a complete listing of passages. Radl, "σώζω," 320, confirms that "conversion" is in view with this usage.

139 Käsemann, 306.

140 This is an instance where the principle suggested by Llewelyn, "Slaves," 68, about elisions normally following the immediately previous verbal form appears to be followed.

141 Verena Jegher-Bucher, "Erwählung und Verwerfung im Römerbrief? Eine Untersuchung von Röm 11,11-15," *ThZ* 47 (1991) 329, insists that the LSJM 193 restriction to these two definitions is correct, while BAGD (2000) 108 inappropriately suggests the translation "reject" for Rom 11:15 on the basis of mistranslating Josephus *Ant.* 4.314 as "reject" instead of "yet will they [i.e., temple and city] be lost not once, but often (ἔσεσθαι δὲ τὴν τούτων ἀποβολὴν οὐχ ἅπαξ ἀλλὰ πολλάκις)."

142 Advocated by Zahn, 510–11; Fitzmyer, 612; Donaldson, "Riches," 93; Haacker, 227–29. Haacker suggests parallels to ἀποβολή as "loss" in Acts 27:22;

Josephus *Ant.* 4.314 and 14.377. Classical parallels found via *TLG* include Plutarch *Sol.* 7.1.1, decrying "fear in our loss of possessions (ὁ τῷ φόβῳ τῆς ἀποβολῆς τὴν κτῆσιν)"; and *Sol.* 7.6.2, referring to the "loss of friends (πρὸς φίλων ἀποβολή)." See also Plutarch *Pyrrh.* 30.3.2; *Ant.* 71.1.2; Diodorus Siculus *Hist.* 15.50.2; Dionysius of Halicarnassus *Antiq. Rom.* 9.13.4. Jegher-Bucher, "Erwählung," 334, suggests the temporary "loss" of God's longtime coworkers, the Jews, which seems extraneous to this passage.

143 Godet, 403; Weiss, 481; Sanday and Headlam, 325; Schmidt, 192; Michel, 345–46; Black, 155; Cranfield, 2:562; Murray, 2:81; Kuss, 3:800; Käsemann, 307; Wilckens, 2:245; Heinrich Balz and Gerhard Schneider, "ἀποβολή," *EDNT* 1 (1990) 125; Siegert, *Argumentation*, 166; Dunn, 2:657; Moo, 693. An example of this concept is the gloss on Sir 10:20 ("fear of the Lord is the beginning of acceptance, but the beginning of rejection is obstinacy and arrogance").

144 Fitzmyer, 612.

directs attention to the behavior of the Jews themselves, which also supports the subjective reading. Since "loss" would assume an identical Greek term with v. 12, and "throwing away" is so awkward in English, I suggest that the most appropriate translation is "their discarding [the gospel]."

That the jettisoning of the gospel on the part of the Jews gave space for the mission to Gentiles leads Paul to his dramatic and exalted equation: καταλλαγὴ κόσμου ("reconciliation of [the] world, global reconciliation"). In 5:10-11 Paul had described the gospel's impact in terms of reconciliation, and in 2 Cor 5:18 he had summarized his entire apostolic ministry under this heading: "all this is from God, who through Christ reconciled us to himself and gave us the ministry of reconciliation (τὴν διακονίαν τῆς καταλλαγῆς)." The expression "global reconciliation" echoes themes in the Roman civic cult and its antecedents in the cult of Alexander the Great, as we observed in connection with 5:8-10.[145] This ecstatic language naturally leaves loopholes that the original hearers probably did not have time to notice; in this instance, the global reconciliation visible at the time of Paul's writing did not include overcoming the conflicts between Jews and Gentiles.[146] He comes back to rectify this shortcoming in chapters 14–15. At this point in Romans, however, the mission to the Gentiles that followed from Jewish rejection of the gospel is depicted in grandiose terms as the fulfillment of the Greco-Roman and Jewish visions of global peace under the rule of a single sovereign.[147] This formulation reveals the breathtaking vision that is embodied in Paul's project of extending the circle of Christ's reconciling sovereignty to the end of the known world in Spain.

The rhetorical question that brings the first enthymeme to a close deals with what the ἡ πρόσλημψις ("the acceptance, welcome") might mean. This word is found here for the only time in the OT or NT, but it is associated with the more frequently employed verb προσλαμβάνω, which Paul uses in 14:1, 3; 15:7 in reference to welcoming others into the fellowship of a house or tenement church. This verb has the sense of "to receive hospitably" in Philemon 17 and Acts 28:2.[148] In view of Paul's concern for mutual welcome in the concrete settings of love feasts organized by various churches in Rome, I prefer the translation "welcome" in this context,[149] leaving it open whether such welcome is extended by God or other churches or both.

The formulation of the potential equation with εἰ μὴ ζωὴ ἐκ νεκρῶν ("if not life from [the] dead") leaves the audience only one way to respond: affirmatively. The unparalleled expression "life from the dead" probably refers to the resurrection at the end of time, to which the completion of the mission was thought to lead.[150] Paul's apocalyptic orientation fits the widely accepted scheme of Israel's redemption as the decisive event leading to the eschatological scenario that would climax with the resurrection of deceased saints.[151] Reducing this to a metaphorical reference to spiritual blessing, new life, or restoration of Israel[152] undercuts the rhetorical force of Paul's climactic question. Although the churches could squabble indefinitely over what constitutes "new life," none would have wished to deny the resurrection of the dead at the end of time. Here Paul employs the final trump card in his campaign to persuade the reluctant churches in Rome that the conversion of their adversaries would work to their advantage, despite current tensions. The rhetoric of this question leaves the audience only one way to answer: "Yes, the resurrection!"

■ 16 The enthymeme of vv. 16-24 opens with a principle drawn from Num 15:20-21, that a portion of each

---

145 See particularly Hengel, "Erlösungstat," 75.
146 See Morris, 410.
147 For an interpretation that disregards the political dimension, see Findeis, *Versöhnung*, 295–320.
148 See Gerhard Delling, "λαμβάνω κτλ.," *TDNT* 4 (1967) 15.
149 The stress on "final acceptance" in Wilckens, 2:245, and Dunn, 2:657–58, is a theological qualification that is not justified by the word πρόσλημψις.
150 See Meyer, 2:217; Zahn, 512; Lietzmann, 103; Kühl, 382; Lagrange, 278; Sanday and Headlam, 325; Schmidt, 192; Barrett, 215; Kuss, 3:800; Michel, 346; Käsemann, 307; Cranfield, 2:562–63; Dunn, 2:658; Stuhlmacher, 167; Moo, 694–96; Byrne, 339; Schreiner, 599; Hoffmann, *Toten*, 182–85. In support of this option Moo observes that all but one of the forty-seven occurrences of the phrase ἐκ νεκρῶν in the NT refer to the resurrection.
151 See particularly Dale C. Allison Jr., "The Background of Romans 11:11-15 in Apocalyptic and Rabbinic Literature," *StBT* 10 (1980) 229–34.
152 See Schlatter, 222; Murray, 2:81–83; Morris, 411;

lump of bread prepared for baking must be dedicated to God as a holy offering, thus rendering the entire batch of bread holy. The procedure of handling such an ἀπαρχή ("offering") is as follows: "Of the first of your coarse meal you shall present a cake as an offering; as an offering from the threshing floor, so shall you present it. Of the first of your coarse meal you shall give to the LORD an offering throughout your generations." This small portion of the batch of bread[153] becomes a burnt offering whose smoke is pleasing to Yahweh, who thereupon blesses the whole "batch of dough"[154] as well as the participants in the sacrifice.[155] The same principle pertains with first fruits of the harvest.[156] A holy relationship between supplicants and God is renewed through the offering that removes sins that distort that relationship.[157] There are parallel regulations in Greco-Roman sacrificial systems, in which a sample of the animal or bread is dedicated to the gods, thus assuring their blessing on the whole.[158] This brief introduction concerning yeast bread sets the framework for interpreting the following allegory of the olive tree that begins in 16b and runs to the end of the pericope in v. 24. As K. H.

Rengstorf explains, in such cases the religious quality of the sample guarantees the quality of the whole.[159] Whether or not the OT itself explicitly states that the sample purifies the whole,[160] and regardless of later rabbinic speculation about Adam and Abraham as "first fruits,"[161] Paul introduces this premise as if would be readily accepted by his audience.

The second half of Paul's premise statement develops the idea of the root and the branch, which seems more directly related to the subsequent argument concerning grafting into the wild olive tree. The idea of the dependency of branches on roots is widely used in Jewish sources (Job 18:16; Jer 17:8; Ezek 31:8; Hos 9:16; Sir 1:20; 40:15), and there are many references to Israel having been planted by God (Ps 92:13; Jer 11:17; *Ps.Sol.* 14.3-4; *1 Enoch* 84.6).[162] The references to Israel as the "righteous plant" in *Jub.* 1.16; 7.34; 16.26; 21.24; 36.6; *1 Enoch* 10.16; 93.2-10 are particularly relevant for Paul's reference to the root as "holy." The precise rhetorical parallelism between 16a and 16b conveys the idea that the principle in the one case extends to the other:

Fitzmyer, 613; Ziesler, 277; Wright, *Climax*, 248; Haacker, 229–30; Johnson, 169; Bell, *Provoked to Jealousy*, 117–18; Witherington, 269.

153 See the parallel in Philo *Sacr. AC* 107, "the first fruit of your lump is dough (ἀπαρχὴν φυράματος ὑμῶν ἄρτον)."

154 Alexander Sand, "ἀπαρχή," *EDNT* 1 (1990) 116. Matthias Hartung, "Die kultische bzw. agrartechnisch-biologische Logik der Gleichnisse von der Teighebe und vom Ölbaum in Röm 11.16-24 und die sich daraus ergebenden theologischen Konsequenzen," *NTS* 45 (1999) 128–29, overlooks this sacrificial context in arguing that Paul reverses the Jewish cultic practice with regard to bread.

155 Ceslas Spicq, "ἀπαρχή," *TLNT* 1 (1994) 152; see also Eberhard, *Studien*, 77–88, 293–94.

156 See Richard O. Rigsby, "First Fruits," *ABD* 2 (1992) 797: "The offerings of first fruits provided the redemption of the harvest."

157 See Gary A. Anderson, "Sacrifice and Sacrificial Offerings (OT)," *ABD* 2 (1992) 871–72, 878, citing Job 1:5 and Lev 1:4.

158 Spicq, "ἀπαρχή," 145–46, cites Aristotle *Eth. nic.* (1160a); Plutarch *Pyth. orac.* 16; *I. Magn.* 83.12-13, "first fruits to the goddess Artemis (ἀπαρχὴν τῇ θεᾷ Ἀρτέμιδι)." See also Jameson, Jordan, and Kotansky, *Lex Sacra*, 38–39, 69.

159 Karl Heinrich Rengstorf, "Das Ölbaum-Gleichnis in Rom 11:16ff. Versuch einer weiterführenden Deutung," in E. Bammel et al., eds., *Donum Gentilicium: New Testament Studies in Honour of David Daube* (Oxford: Clarendon Press, 1978) 129. See also Dodd, 178.

160 The OT source of this idea is argued by Weiss, 482–83; Kühl, 383; Käsemann, 307; Bourke, *Olive Tree*, 68–72, but rejected by Lagrange, 279; Dunn, 2:658, and questioned by Lietzmann, 104.

161 The alleged rabbinic background suggestion by Strack-Billerbeck, 4.667–68, and Rengstorf, "Ölbaum-Gleichnis," 130–35, is unprovable since those sources postdate Romans, and even if it could be proven, it is highly unlikely that Paul would be advancing speculation about Adam as the "first fruits" in the light of the link between Adam and original sin developed in Rom 5, as Dunn, 2:659, points out.

162 See Maurer, "ῥίζα κτλ.," 986–88. For an unconvincing attempt to reinterpret the olive tree as Christ the Messiah rather than Israel, see Maria Neubrand and Johannes Seidel, "'Eingepfropft in den edlen Ölbaum' (Röm 11,24): Der Ölbaum ist *nicht* Israel," *BN* 105 (2000) 68–71.

Now if the first fruit [is] holy,
    so also [is] the lump;
and if the root [is] holy,
    so also [are] the branches.

The principle of extended holiness provides the premise for Paul's enthymeme, which means that the basis for acknowledging the continued priority of Israel is that it provided the vehicle by which the holy, righteous community of the church came into the world.[163] Paul's view of the church as an arena of mystical and material wholeness and vitality must therefore be presupposed as the premise of each of the inferences and admonitions in vv. 17-24. When interpreters overlook this argumentative function of v. 16 in the enthymeme of vv. 16-24, they insert perplexing contradictions into the argument as a whole. When v. 16a is taken as directly allegorical, parabolic, or analogical for the subsequent argument, then the "first fruits" become Abraham, the Patriarchs or the prophets,[164] Jewish[165] or Gentile converts,[166] or Christ himself.[167] However, in view of the synonymous parallelism between "first fruit" and "lump" in v. 16a with the "root" and "branches" in v. 16b, each of these allegorical interpretations contradicts the development in subsequent verses in which Israel is the root and a Gentile believer is the branch. This verse provides the absolutely essential premise for the allegory of the wild olive branch, because, as we shall see below, Paul needs to reverse the normal horticultural practice of grafting domestic branches onto wild olive trees.

■ **17** The application phase of the enthymeme begins with reference to God's action in making dull some of Israel's hearts and minds with regard to the gospel as described in the previous pericope. The protasis of a sentence to be completed in v. 18 features the verb ἐξεκλάσθησαν ("they were broken off") that has rightly been construed as a divine passive.[168] The indeterminate expression τινες τῶν κλάδων ("some of the branches")[169] alludes back to οἱ δὲ λοιποὶ ἐπωρώθησαν ("but the others were made obtuse") in 11:7. It implies that only some of the original branches have been removed while others remain in the holy olive tree as intended by God. A discourse of "you" (sg.) as opposed to "them" begins at this point and continues through to the end of the pericope, and it is clear from the context that the "you" (sg.) refers to a Gentile Christian interlocutor and that "they" are the majority of Israel that had thus far disbelieved. The choice of the second person singular σὺ δέ ("but you") in the emphatic position has a lively, exemplary effect that makes a potentially deprecatory allusion acceptable to the audience.[170] Like other examples of speech-in-character in Romans, the playful, humorous quality of this discourse avoids polemic against the audience.[171] The technique of

163 See Nanos, *Mystery*, 251–55; Maartens, "Wild Olive Tree," 1018–19.

164 Meyer, 2:220; Weiss, 483–84; Godet, 405; Zahn, 514–15; Sanday and Headlam, 326; Lagrange, 279; Schmidt, 194; Michel, 348; Murray, 2:85; Schlier, 332; Christian Maurer, "ῥίζα κτλ.," *TDNT* 6 (1968) 989; Angela Palzkill, "ῥίζα," *EDNT* 3 (1993) 212; Wilckens, 2:246; Althaus, 104; Bourke, *Olive Tree*, 75–76; Zeller, 196; Moo, 699–700; Byrne, 346; Haacker, 231; Schreiner, 600–601.

165 Lietzmann, 104; Kühl, 383; Barrett, 216; Cranfield, 2:564; Fitzmyer, 614; Johnson, "Structure," 98–99; Bell, *Provoked to Jealousy*, 118–20.

166 Dunn, 2:659, referring to parallels in Rom 16:15; 1 Cor 16:15; 2 Thess 2:13.

167 Ellison, *Mystery of Israel*, 86–87, following Karl Barth; Hanson, *Studies*, 107–17.

168 Dunn, 2:660, referring to Rom 11:7, 8, 10, 15; the verb ἐκκλάω ("break off, separate by force") appears in this passage for the only time in the NT; see BAGD (2000) 303.

169 The expression εἰ δέ τινες ("but if some") appears here for the only time in the NT.

170 Anderson, *Paul*, 237–38, refers to the "liveliness" achieved by referring to the Gentiles with the second person singular; see also Cranfield, 2:566. Morris, 413, refers to Robertson, *Grammar*, 678, as "the representative sense" of the second person singular pronoun. BDF §281 explains the rhetorical use of the first and second person singular to "illustrate something universal in a vivid manner."

171 Tobin, *Paul's Rhetoric*, 363: "Paul is not directly addressing the Gentile members of the Roman community in 11:13-24." Most interpreters misunderstand this discourse as directly polemical: Kühl, 383; Schmidt, 192–97; Schlier, 333; Dunn, 2:662; Fitzmyer, 614; Haacker, 232; Heil, 123; Byrne, 340–41; Witherington, 270–71; Davies, "Romans 11:13-24," 160–61; Gignac, *Romans 9–11*, 240–43; Kim, *Romans 9–11*, 137; Esler, *Conflict and Identity*, 300, 305.

speech-in-character allows Paul to discuss the issues with an imaginary interlocutor whose traits are sufficiently exaggerated that the audience does not feel attacked, but sufficiently analogous that the audience can grasp the allegorical relevance. The interlocutor is a wild olive tree (ἀγριέλαιος),[172] a small, scraggly bush that produces "nothing useful."[173] Theophrastus *Caus. plant.* 1.6.10 describes the normal process of grafting domestic olive branches into wild olive trees whose roots are stronger but whose fruit never ripens properly:

> It is also reasonable that grafted trees are richer in fine fruit, especially when a scion from a cultivated tree is grafted onto a stock of a wild tree of the same bark, since the scion receives more nourishment from the strength of the stock. This is why people recommend that one should first plant wild olive trees and graft in buds or branches later, for the grafts hold better to the stronger stock, and by attracting more nourishment the tree bears rich fruit. If, on the other hand, someone were to graft a wild scion into a cultivated stock, there will be some difference, but there will be no fine fruit.[174]

That this procedure was actually followed was confirmed by Philip Esler's citation of an inscription from an orchard in Mykonos that provides an inventory of 147 cultivated olive trees, 87 wild olive trees that had been grafted, and 200 wild olive trees that were apparently being grown for future grafting.[175]

The unusual procedure of grafting branches of wild olive trees into already existing cultivated trees is described by Columella *Rust.* 5.9.16 and Palladius *Instit.* 53–54, and also appears to be employed in modern times.[176] Columella, a contemporary of Paul, describes the procedure as follows: "It happens also frequently that, though the trees are thriving well, they fail to bear fruit. It is a good plan to bore them with a Gallic augur and to put tightly into the hole a green slip taken from a wild olive tree; the result is that the tree, being as it were impregnated with fruitful offspring, becomes more productive."[177] According to the study by Baxter and Ziesler, the purpose of such grafting was to rejuvenate domestic trees.[178] Yet the fact remains that Paul does not develop the theme of rejuvenation suggested by Columella,[179] and he develops a profile for the speech-in-character that is the opposite of the standard procedure described by Theophrastus of using domestic olive branches for grafting. This has led to the perception that Paul was an uninformed "town-bred man"[180] or to inferences that the wild olive allegory implied that Gentile believers lacked "spiritual attainments" and were "underprivileged" in comparison with Jewish believers.[181] The premise of Paul's allegory differs from both Columella and Theophrastus in viewing the "root" of the domestic olive tree as fully adequate to produce "fatness" (11:17b) and "holiness" (11:16). Paul's rhetorical finesse leads him to identify the interlocutor as a branch of a "wild olive tree" grafted in among the natural branches of the domestic "olive tree" (ἐλαίας). In Jer 11:16 and Hos 14:6 Israel is referred to as the olive tree, and it is important to remember that the audience would have been

---

172 BAGD (2000) 15 notes that the adjective ἀγριέλαιος is employed here as a noun.

173 Davies, "Romans 11:13-24," 155.

174 Translation from Esler, *Conflict and Identity,* 302.

175 Ibid., 303, cited from Felix Durrbach, ed., *Inscriptions de Délos: Comptes des Hiéropes (Nos. 290–371)* (Paris: Librairie Ancienne Honoré Champion, 1926) 166, Nr. 366 B, lines 8–25. Esler also cites Lin Foxhall, "Olive Cultivation within Greek and Roman Agriculture: The Ancient Economy Revisited" (Ph.D. dissertation, University of Liverpool, 1990) 97–98. See also Hartung, "Agrartechnisch-biologische Logik," 132–35.

176 See Williams, *Paul's Metaphors,* 42.

177 Translation from E. F. Foster and E. H. Heffner, *Lucius Junius Moderatus Columella on Agriculture* (London: Heinemann; Cambridge: Harvard University Press, 1968) 85; passage cited in part by Fitzmyer, 615.

178 A. G. Baxter and John A. Ziesler, "Paul and Arboriculture. Romans 11.17-24," *JSNT* 24 (1985) 27–28. In contrast, Davies, "Romans 11:13-24," 155, writes that "the horticultural process is unthinkable." See the similar comment in Maurer, "ῥίζα κτλ.," 989, and Hartung, "Agrartechnisch-biologische Logik," 138–39.

179 See Esler, *Conflict and Identity,* 303.

180 Dodd, 180.

181 Davies, "Romans 11:13-24," 155, 157.

aware that one of the Jewish synagogues in Rome bore the name συναγωγὴ Ἑλαίας ("Synagogue of the Olive").[182] This could well have been one of the synagogues from which the Christ believers emerged as distinct groups in the decades prior to the writing of Paul's letter. Although Greco-Roman culture was also associated with the olive,[183] Paul develops the theme of the source of holy vitality rather than seeking to overturn claims of cultural superiority.[184]

The grafting of the wild olive shoot ἐν αὐτοῖς ("among them") refers in this context to the branches that had not been broken off, that is, the Jewish Christians.[185] The verb ἐνεκεντρίσθης ("you [sg.] were grafted in") is also in the passive, implying divine action as in the case of the others who were broken off. The wild olive that had no hope of belonging within the sphere of productivity is therefore "a remnant according to the election of grace,"[186] which conforms to the elective climax in 8:29-30. By grace, believers from different ethnic groups now enjoy a "shared lineage" as God's people.[187] Consistent with the holiness premise, Paul picks up the theme of πλοῦτος κόσμου ("riches for the world") from v. 12 by developing the allegory of τῆς ῥίζης τῆς πιότητος τῆς ἐλαίας ("the root of the olive with its fatness"). The construction can be taken as a genitive of quality and thus adjectival, that is, "the fat root of the olive tree,"[188] or as an appositive genitive, that is, "the root of the olive with its fatness."[189] The latter seems more consistent with Paul's stress on the extraordinary privileges of wealth, holiness, and nourishment devolving on the church from the situation of Israel. But

it is clear that Paul's allegory leaves space neither for Theophrastus's observation about the superior strength of the wild olive tree nor for Columella's theory of rejuvenation.[190]

The status of being made a co-participant (συγκοινωνός) in access to the fatness is particularly evocative in view of the use of the koinonia terminology in relation to membership in the holy community (Rom 12:13; 15:26, 27; 1 Cor 1:9; 9:23; 10:16; 2 Cor 1:7; 6:14; 8:4, 23; 9:13; 13:13; Phil 1:5, 7; 2:1; 3:10; 4:14-15; Phlm 6, 17; Gal 2:9; 6:6). The reciprocal theme of "fellowship / partnership (with someone) through (common) participation (in something)" is basic to all of these koinonia terms employed by Paul,[191] and the prefix συν- ("with") enhances the dimension of sharing something equally with others. In this case, the grafted branches become equal sharers with the original branches in the holy, life-sustaining fatness,[192] thus preventing negative inferences being drawn from the potentially pejorative reference to a Gentile believer as an unproductive wild olive tree. The conditional clause in the sentence thus comes to a climax by depicting the extraordinary privilege and benefit bestowed on the elected outsider by divine grace.

■ 18 The protasis in the first application phase of Paul's enthymeme is an imperative in second person singular style consistent with "and you" (sg.) earlier in the sentence. The verb κατακαυχᾶσθαι appears here for the only time in the Pauline letters and when followed by a noun in the genitive it has the connotation of boasting

---

182 For an assessment of the dispute about how to translate ἐλαίος, see W. D. Davies, "Paul and the Gentiles: A Suggestion concerning Romans 11:13-24," in W. D. Davies, *Jewish and Pauline Studies* (Philadelphia: Fortress Press, 1984) 159–60; Leon, *Jews*, 145–47.

183 Siegert, *Argumentation*, 168.

184 Davies, "Romans 11:13-24," 160–63; Dunn, 2:661.

185 Dunn, 2:661, following Cranfield, 2:567. In "Romans 11:13-24," 155, 356, Davies suggests in contrast that Paul refers to grafting "into or among, not instead of the branches lopped off. . . ."

186 Murray, 2:86.

187 Caroline Johnson Hodge, "Olive Trees and Ethnicities: Judeans and Gentiles in Rom. 11.17-24," in J. Zangenberg and M. Labahn, eds., *Christians as a Religious Minority in a Multicultural City: Modes of*

Interaction and Identity Formation in Early Imperial Rome (London / New York: T. & T. Clark, 2004) 84.

188 Weiss, 485; Lietzmann, 105; Barrett, 217; Haacker, 233.

189 Meyer, 2:223; Zahn, 516; Michel, 350; Cranfield, 2:567; BAGD (2000) 814; Fitzmyer, 615.

190 Esler, *Conflict and Identity*, 303–5, makes a compelling case that the hypothesis of Baxter and Ziesler's theory based on Columella and Palladius does not match Paul's allegory, but he is unable to explain the discrepancy between Paul and the normal practice of grafting described by Theophrastus. He does not take account of the speech-in-character developed in this allegory.

191 See Josef Hainz, "κοινωνία κτλ.," *EDNT* 2 (1991) 304.

192 See Cranfield, 2:567; Moo, 702.

or bragging over against others.[193] As Rudolf Bultmann shows, κατακαυχάομαι "brings out strongly the element of comparative superiority expressed in boasting, 'to boast in triumphant comparison with others.'"[194] While such bragging was acceptable in the competitive atmosphere of the Greco-Roman world, it is illegitimate in the community of grace: "Where then is the boast? It is excluded!" (Rom 3:27; cf. 2:17, 23; 4:2). The verb appears also in Jas 3:14 and 4:13 with a negative connotation of inappropriate boasting. These references lead to my translation with the verb "brag." The target of such bragging on the part of the imaginary interlocutor is τῶν κλάδων ("of, in relation to the branches"), which according to the inclusive reference to the branches in v. 17 implies both the Jews that were broken off and those that were already incorporated in the new community of faith.[195] In the light of the fact that such a reference would have been insulting in the allegory if it had no basis in the current behavior of the audience, this is clear evidence of residual anti-Semitism within the Roman churches,[196] which Paul addresses more directly in 14:1—15:7. Here he addresses only the interlocutor, in a nonpolemical manner.[197] The basis of the categorical prohibition, however, is not some theory of tolerance but the believer's experience of grace, unearned and undeserved. The logic of Paul's allegory is that having been elected by God to become a co-participant with Jewish Christian converts in the nourishing fatness of the olive tree, in a movement in which the cultural paradigms of seeking honor and boasting in superiority over

competitors have been overturned, the interlocutor's bragging now must be perceived as illegitimate.

The second conditional sentence in the application phase of the enthymeme begins with "but if" (εἰ δέ), exactly as in the first sentence of v. 17a. The formulation assumes that regardless of the appeal in vv. 17-18a, the Gentile convert playing the role of the imaginary interlocutor is indeed inclined to continue boasting at the expense of Jewish believers and unbelievers.[198] Since the verb κατακαυχάομαι appears again, the context requires a translation such as "but if you *do* brag."[199] In case the imaginative interlocutor does not grasp the evangelical logic of grace expressed in vv. 17-18a, Paul turns to the premise of the enthymeme in v. 16b, that the root supports the branches, not vice versa.[200] With an emphatic word order in which the protasis begins with οὐ ("not"),[201] Paul employs the verb βαστάζειν with the basic sense of "pick up, carry." In this context, βαστάζειν has the allegorical sense of the root bearing the weight of the branches.[202] However, in other passages (Gal 6:2; Rom 15:1), Paul employs βαστάζειν in contexts in which some persons carry burdens for others, which is probably the connotation meant here. The branches do not support the root but vice versa, which means that bragging is a denial of a fundamental reality of the dependency of the one upon the other.[203] The implications for the Gentile Christian majority in Rome are clear: "there is no salvation apart from the history of Israel";[204] "a church which is not drawing upon the sustenance of its Jewish inheritance . . . would be a contradic-

193 See Cranfield, 2:567; Dunn, 2:661–62; Moo, 703.

194 Rudolf Bultmann, "καυχάομαι κτλ.," *TDNT* 3 (1967) 653; according to BAGD (2000) 517, a grave inscription in Asia Minor celebrates a gladiator who boasted over his defeated foe (*SPAW*, 1932, 855).

195 See Godet, 406; Weiss, 486; Sanday and Headlam, 328; Meyer, 2:224; Lagrange, 230; Kühl, 386; Cranfield, 2:567–68; Dunn, 2:662; Moo, 703.

196 See Lütgert, *Römerbrief*, 79–90; Bartsch, "Gegner," 34–43; Minear, *Obedience*, 79; Davies, "Romans 11:13-24," 157–59; Lieu, *Neither Jew nor Greek*, 122–26; Lichtenberger, *Ich Adams*, 7; Schäfer, *Judeophobia*, 180–95. In *Origins*, 225, Gager denies that Paul ever speaks of God as rejecting Israel, but he does not deal with Paul's audience in Rome.

197 See Tobin, *Paul's Rhetoric*, 363. Stowers abandons the claim of diatribe as nonpolemical discourse

with a friendly interlocutor (*Diatribe*, 76–78) by concluding in *Diatribe*, 99, and *Rereading*, 299 and 315, that "Paul sternly warns the gentile audience not to be arrogant toward those Jews (11:18)." Maartens, "Wild Olive Tree," 1023–24, also perceives a direct warning to Gentile Christian members of the audience.

198 Godet, 406; Moo, 704.

199 See Godet, 406, "But if, notwithstanding, thou despisest"; Meyer, 2:225, "But if the case occur, that thou boastest against them"; Fitzmyer, 615, "If you do, remember this."

200 See Weiss, 487.

201 See Dunn, 2:662.

202 Werner Stenger, "βαστάζω," *EDNT* 1 (1990) 208–9.

203 See Ehrensperger, *Mutually Encouraged*, 183.

204 Käsemann, 309–10.

tion in terms for Paul."[205] Such implications remain on the implicit level, however, as Paul moves skillfully forward to deal with the boasting impulse in the imaginary interlocutor.

■ **19** Godet notes that Paul's diatribe places in the mouth of the Gentile Christian interlocutor a further alibi arising from the logic of the preceding verse:[206] granted the dependency of branches on the root, I have been elected to displace the original branches that were removed by God himself! The formulation ἐρεῖς οὖν ("you will say then, therefore") appears only here in the NT, and is also rare in other Greek discourse.[207] Here it formulates a logical inference from the preceding argument that Paul places in the mouth of the interlocutor. In a witty manner that the audience would have enjoyed, the interlocutor throws Paul's words back into his face by employing precisely the same terms that Paul had used in v. 17: "the branches," "broken off," and the wild olive shoots "grafted in." This is an effective example of rhetorical "anticipation and refutation" (προκατάληψις) in the form of *praedictio* as described by Quintilian *Inst.* 9.2.17.[208] An impression of an overly expansive self-image on the part of this braggart is conveyed by the pronoun ἐγώ ("I"), which reduplicates and therefore emphasizes the "I" in the first person singular form of the verb.[209] This interlocutor demonstrates a truly ludicrous degree of competitive incorrigibility. Unmoved by the gospel of boundless grace (vv. 17-18a) or by the natural allegory concerning roots and branches (vv. 16, 18b), he now turns Paul's words to his own egoistic advantage. But in smiling at the foibles of this blatantly unconverted Christian, the Gentile audience gains a measure of awareness about its own behavior.

■ **20** Paul answers the witty objection that he has placed in the mouth of the Gentile interlocutor with a single adverb, καλῶς, which could be taken as a flat rejection ("No, thank you!"),[210] an ironic concession ("Well, well!"),[211] a qualified acceptance ("All right, but!"),[212] or an acceptance of the point ("Well said!").[213] The latter is most likely in this context because it preserves the wit of this discourse, in that Paul accepts the transparently arrogant comment that he himself has invented for the interlocutor from the words of his own previous argument. The audience would enjoy Paul's admission that a sharp riposte was made at his own expense by such an undiscerning Christian blockhead.

The refutation of the interlocutor's claim of having replaced the Jewish branches centers on the concept of faith in response to the gospel. They were broken off τῇ ἀπιστίᾳ, a dative construction in 20a that probably has a causal connotation, "on account of their unbelief,"[214] which is matched by a causal dative τῇ πίστει, "on account of faith" in 20b.[215] Both terms appeared in Paul's earlier description of Abraham in 4:20: "no doubt

205 Dunn, 2:662; see also Hartung, "Agrartechnisch-biologische Logik," 140.
206 Godet, 407.
207 A *TLG* search located examples of ἐρεῖς οὖν from the second century C.E. in Galen *Adv.* 7.494.17 and 7.495.4. Later examples from Christian literature include *Herm. Mand.* 6.6.1; Theophilus Antiochenus *Autol.* 1.3.1, 14; 1.11.3; 2.22.1.
208 See Anderson, *Glossary*, 14, 104.
209 Weiss, 487; Meyer, 2:225; Murray, 2:87: "the egoism and vainglory of this boasting." See BDF §277. For background, see Bartsch, "Gegner," 41; Bartsch, "Historische Situation," 287–88.
210 In Aristophanes *Ran.* 888, in response to the urge to burn incense, Euripides replies, "No, thank you (καλῶς); my vows are paid to other gods than these."
211 Donaldson, "Riches," 85, following T. W. Manson in the *Peake's Commentary on the Bible*, 949; also Zahn, 518; Schmidt, 196; Michel, 351; Morris, 414.
212 Aristophanes *Eccl.* 1092, where καλῶς has the sense of "well and good." See also Aristophanes *Nub.* 488, "O well, it doesn't matter." Lietzmann, 104; Käsemann, 310; Dunn, 2:663; Moo, 705; Schreiner, 607.
213 LSJM 870 C.2.6, approving the words of the former speaker as in Euripides *Orest.* 1216, "'Tis well"; Demosthenes *Orat.* 39.15, "Well said!" In Aristophnes *Eccl.* 149, καὶ καλῶς ἐρεῖς ("and you will speak well") has the verb ἐρεῖς that Paul employed in v. 19 and which should probably be supplied in 20a. Aristophanes *Plut.* 481, "'Tis well." See Meyer, 2:225; Godet, 407; Weiss, 487; Sanday and Headlam, 329; Schlier, 334; Barrett, 218; Cranfield, 2:568; Wilckens, 2:247; Fitzmyer, 615; Byrne, 342; Siegert, *Argumentation*, 169.
214 Meyer, 2:225; Weiss, 488; Kuss, 3:804. Schlier, 334; Käsemann, 310; and Dunn, 2:668, cite BDF §196; see also Moulton and Turner, *Grammar III*, 242.
215 The suggestion by Dunn, 2:633; Moo, 705, following Bultmann, "πιστεύω κτλ.," 218, that the latter is an "instrumental dative" is an overly facile theological assessment rather than a grammatical likelihood; it

made him waver in unfaith, but he was strengthened in his faith." In response to the interlocutor, however, Paul uses the faith/unfaith antithesis in reference to conversion or unconversion in response to the gospel.[216] The perfect verb ἕστηκας ("you [sg.] have stood") in this context refers to the relation of the interlocutor to the gospel and with the community shaped by Christ. As in 5:2, through Christ the believers "also have gained access in faith to this grace in which we have stood."[217] Since Paul had earlier made the case that the principle of faith eliminates boasting (Rom 3:27), the boasting of the imaginary interlocutor is a violation of the new relationship inaugurated by the gospel of unconditional grace. As we have seen throughout Romans, the test of faith is not doctrinal but behavioral. When social or cultural competition remains dominant, faith in Christ crucified has not yet achieved its transforming purpose of equalizing honor.

There is no doubt that the admonition ὑψηλὰ φρονεῖν ("be uppity-minded") has the negative connotation of "haughtiness"[218] instead of the positive connotation "be high-minded" as in the classics and Philo *Ebr.* 128.1, "lofty and sublime thoughts" (ὑψηλὰ φρονῶν λογισμός).[219] Paul's expression deals with the social dimension of claiming superiority over others, consistent with the use of "bragging" in v. 18 and with the focus on honor and shame throughout the rest of the letter. Nei-

ther the individualistic, psychological dimension of feeling proud nor a doctrine of self-righteousness[220] is in view. As in Luke 16:15, ὑψηλός refers to "what is exalted among men" and thus "is an abomination in the sight of God."[221] Similarly, Pyrthos is warned by Agamemnon to avoid outrageous behavior "out of fear of the merciful gods" (*variosque casus tremere metuentem deos*), while using himself as an example of avoiding "raising myself all too high up" *(superbus altius memet tuli)* over others.[222] Although a close parallel to the second person singular formulation ἀλλὰ φοβοῦ ("but fear!") occurs in Prov 24:21, φοβοῦ τὸν θεόν ("fear God!"), Paul states the admonition to "fear" without an object or qualification,[223] in a direct antithesis to being arrogant in relation to Israel.[224] While a proper fear of God was taught by Jewish as well as Greco-Roman cultures,[225] the antithesis with "but" makes it clear that this is a fear concerning the loss of an allegedly superior status.[226] This becomes clear in the next verse that takes up the question of preservation or loss of favored status.

■ **21** The rationale for the admonition to fear in 20b signaled by γάρ ("for") refers to God as the ultimate source of status assignment. The originally favored status of the Israelites that were later broken off from the life-giving root is indicated by the phrase κατὰ φύσιν ("according to nature, natural"), referring to their original "circumstance as determined by birth."[227] The Stoics

---

is also unclear that Bultmann intends an instrumental connotation because he insists that Rom 11:20 "does not mean: 'Thou standest in faith,' but: 'Thou hast attained thy standing through faith.'"

216 See von Dobbeler, *Glaube als Teilhabe,* 184–88; in 184 Dobbeler interprets τῇ πίστει in 11:20b as instrumental but stresses conversion in 188.

217 See Wolter, "ἵστημι," 207; see also Grundmann, "Stehen," 148–51, where "stand" and "fall" appear also in Qumran writings in reference to believers' adherence to the community and its beliefs.

218 BAGD (2000) 1044 (2); Hennig Paulsen, "φρονέω κτλ.," *EDNT* 3 (1993) 440. Paul follows here the biblical tradition of criticizing the proud, as, for example, *1 Reg.* 2:3, "Don't boast and don't speak high-minded things (μὴ καυχᾶσθε καὶ μὴ λαλεῖτε ὑψηλά)." See also Isa 2:12; Prov 16:10.

219 A typical example from Greek literature is Plutarch *Soll. an.* 970e10, who employs ὑψηλὸς φρόνημα in reference to the "high-mindedness" of dogs that do not attack when one is prostrate.

220 Baxter and Ziesler, "Arboriculture," 29.

221 See Horst Balz and Gerhard Schneider, "ὑψηλός," *EDNT* 3 (1993) 409.

222 Seneca *Tro.* 262, 267.

223 See also Eccl 5:6; 12:13; Sir 7:31.

224 Horst Balz, "φοβέομαι," *EDNT* 3 (1993) 431.

225 See ibid., 429; Horst Balz, "φοβέω κτλ.," *TDNT* 9 (1974) 195–203.

226 See Weiss, 488; Fitzmyer, 615; Schreiner, 607. Schlier, 335; Michel, 351; Cranfield, 2:569; Wilckens, 2:247; Dunn, 2:663; Moo, 705, concentrate instead on fearing God, while Barrett, 218, and Morris, 415, speak of "awe" and "reverence . . . before God." The antithesis with regard to social status is also overlooked by the existentialist interpretation of fear as "knowledge of his own insignificance and his constant dependence upon God's grace" (Bultmann, *Theology,* 1:321–22); followed by Käsemann, 310.

227 BAGD (2000) 1069 (1).

made extensive use of the distinction between the favored status κατὰ φύσιν and its antithesis mentioned in 11:24, παρὰ φύσιν ("against nature, unnatural").[228] To use Helmut Koester's summary of Stoic thought, life according to nature was wise, healthy, and good while unnatural life was unhealthy and unwise.[229] The same distinction appears in Philo, who discusses the τῆς κατὰ φύσιν χρήσεως ("the use according to nature")[230] in contrast to ἡ ἄλογος καὶ παρὰ φύσιν κίνησις ὑπαίτιος ("the irrational and unnatural movements of the soul").[231] Thus, that God did not spare "the *natural* branches" establishes a "greater to lesser" logic,[232] which enforces the conclusion that God will not spare the Gentile interlocutor who lacks the inherent honor of being a natural branch from the root of Israel. The verb φείδεσθαι occurs twice in this sentence in the sense of "spare" or "refrain from cutting," and although Paul employed it earlier with respect to Christ (8:32), there is no hint that he intends a christological interpretation of Israel's fate.[233] The parallel in Wis 12:16 is more apt,[234] because with regard both to Gentiles and the sinful inhabitants of the Holy Land, God's "sovereignty over all leads you to spare all" (πάντων φείδεσθαι). Paul's point is simply that the arrogant Gentile interlocutor who claims superiority over Jews is risking expulsion from the arena of grace. The imaginary interlocutor who was earlier untouched by the arguments based on grace, faith, and common sense now faces the ultimate arbitrament of power: God is the final authority in the matter of status and no one who seeks "privileges with God"[235] can escape being cut off. The future form of the verb φείσεται ("he will spare") is gnomic,[236] expressing "that which is to be expected under certain circumstances,"[237] that is, if the Gentile interlocutor persists in being uppity-minded with regard to Israel. The logic of this sentence is reminiscent of 1 Cor 10:12, as Schreiner points out:[238] "The one who thinks he stands should beware lest he fall."

■ **22** The enthymeme and the pericope come to a conclusion with doctrinal reflection on the redemptive action of God, introduced by the aorist imperative, ἴδε οὖν ("notice, pay attention therefore!").[239] This is reminiscent of the opening admonitions in Wis 6:1-2, a passage in which the boasting of the Gentiles is also countered by the threatened severity of God: "hear therefore . . . learn . . . give ear!" The admonition to wake up and pay attention in Romans is directed to the imaginary interlocutor who has just received the shocking news that he will not be spared if he continues to boast of his superiority over others. Since neither "kindness" nor "severity" is introduced with an article, the attention here is on the nature of God's actions rather than his or her character.[240] While scholars have referred to Paul's use of a traditional antithesis from wisdom literature,[241] nowhere else in Jewish writings are these two terms employed in a single passage. In Wis 6:5-6 κρίσις ἀπότομος ("severe judgment") against the exalted and powerful is juxtaposed with divine ἔλεος ("mercy") on those of low estate, but nowhere in the Wisdom of Solomon does the term χρηστότης ("kindness") appear. It surfaces in *Odes Sol.* 11.15 as "kindness of the Lord" and in *Ps. Sol.* 5.13 as "human kindness," but never in

228 See Pohlenz, *Stoa*, 1:116–18; 488.
229 Helmut Koester, "φύσις κτλ.," *TDNT* 9 (1974) 264–65. According to Diogenes Laertius *Vitae philos.* 7.4, the Stoic philosopher Zeno wrote a treatise titled "On Life according to Nature" (Περὶ τοῦ κατὰ φύσιν βίον), which counters passion as "an irrational and unnatural (κατὰ φύσιν) movement of the soul" (7.110). Epictetus *Diss.* 1.11.11 advocates knowing the distinction between "things according to nature and contrary to nature (τῶν κατὰ φύσιν καὶ παρὰ φύσιν)."
230 Philo *Mut.* 112.
231 Philo *Spec.* 4.79.
232 Siegert, *Argumentation*, 170.
233 Hays, *Echoes*, 61, accepted by Donaldson, "Riches," 94.
234 See Dunn, 2:664.
235 Käsemnn, 310.
236 Haacker, 234 n. 17, citing Gundry-Volf, *Paul and Perseverance*, 198.
237 BDF §349.1.
238 Schreiner, 607; see also Morris, 415.
239 BAGD (2000) 720 B2.
240 Weiss, 489.
241 Michel, 351–52; Schlier, 335; Käsemann, 310; Josef Zmejewski, "χρηστότης," *EDNT* 3 (1993) 475. Helmut Koester, "τέμνω κτλ.," *TDNT* 8 (1972) 108, follows Michel, 351–52.

antithesis to ἀποτομία θεοῦ ("God's severity"). Severity is paired with mildness in Pseudo-Plutarch *Lib. ed.* 138d9, in reference to fathers mingling "severity of their rebukes with mildness (ἀποστομίαν τῇ πραότητι μίγνυνσαι)," but no precise parallels to Paul's antithesis have been found. It is significant that Paul avoids the typical biblical antithesis between divine mercy and justice,[242] preferring in this climactic phase of the diatribe with the Gentile interlocutor to employ terminology that was more characteristic of the Greco-Roman environment.

The antithesis is developed chiastically in a neat μὲν . . . δέ ("on the one hand . . . on the other hand") formulation, with "severity" taken up first. It is directed against τοὺς πεσόντας ("those who fell"), which in the context of this enthymeme must refer to the nonbelieving portion of Israel that was cut off from the fruitful olive tree (11:17, 19).[243] The verb πίπτω appears quite often in early Christian writings in the figurative sense of falling out of the community or out of a proper relationship with God (Rom 14:4; 1 Cor 10:12; Heb 4:11; Jas 5:12; Eph 2:5; Rev 2:5).[244] Although there is a natural antithesis between the "falling" of unbelievers and the proper "standing" of believers in 11:20, there is a potential contradiction with 11:11, where Paul had explicitly denied that Israel had stumbled so as to fall (πέσωσιν). As Donaldson has demonstrated, this matter is clarified in 11:24, 26-32 with the temporal logic of delay: while a large part of Israel currently rejects the gospel and has been cut off from the olive tree, this situation will be overcome with the parousia so that Israel in the end will not have fallen.[245] In the present, however, God's response to the ἀπίστια ("faithlessness," 11:20) of those rejecting the gospel is ἀποτομία ("severity"), which appears here alongside χρηστότης ("kindness") as rhetorically effective absolute nominatives.[246] Helmut Koester describes Paul's contention as follows: "Those who do not cleave to God's goodness are threatened by 'the inflexible hardness and severity' of the Judge as the only alternative."[247] The rejection of grace places humans back under the powers of sin, death, and the law, and as Paul argued in the first proof, divine wrath is already visible in the shameful distortions caused thereby. The audience can easily see that the interlocutor disregards this righteous reality at his own peril.

In contrast to the currently desperate fate of "them" in v. 22b, the message for "you" (sg.) in v. 22c is hopeful. In chiastic constructions, the item postponed receives the emphasis so that here "kindness" gains priority over "severity."[248] The expression "God's kindness" is "virtually a substitute for χάρις" ("grace")[249] that is offered to the undeserving through the Christ event (5:2). The earlier portions of the pericope fill out the contours of this "kindness" in terms of undeserved "wealth" (11:12), "reconciliation" (11:15a), "life from the dead" (11:15b), holiness (11:16), and access to the nourishing sap of the olive tree (11:17). Since the Gentile interlocutor was not a "natural" part of the life-giving domestic olive tree (11:21), he has no claim on any of these advantages. Thus χρηστότης θεοῦ ("God's kindness") alone is the source of these undeserved and unearned benefits. In Schreiner's words, "their inclusion in the people of God is all due to grace. They would fail to continue in the faith if they became convinced that they were chosen as Gentiles for their ethnic or moral distinctiveness."[250] The condition under which God's kindness continues to be accessible is described with an "if" clause. The conjunctive particle ἐάν ("if") followed by the subjunctive verb ἐπιμένῃς ("you [sg.] might remain") conveys "what is expected to occur, under certain circumstances,"[251]

242 Fitzmyer, 616, notes that this is a significant point, but fails to explain it. Paul also avoids dealing with Greco-Roman ideas such as Plutarch *Cat. Maj.* 5.2, that "kindness is of broader scope than righteousness (καίτοι τὴν χρηστότητα τῆς δικαιοσύνης πλατύτερον τόπον)."

243 Weiss, 489.

244 See Michaelis, "πίπτω κτλ.," 164–65; Palzkill, "πίπτω," 90–91.

245 Donaldson, "Riches," 92–98.

246 Godet, 408; see BDF §466.2–4.

247 Koester, "τέμνω κτλ.," 108; see also Käsemann, 310.

248 Siegert, *Argumentation*, 170, following Bullinger, *Figures*, 361, 395.

249 Zmejewski, "χρηστότης," 475.

250 Schreiner, 608.

251 BAGD (2000) 267.

that is, that the interlocutor accepts a proper relationship with God and the entire community of faith. The close parallel in Col 1:21-23 indicates that this is a condition that the writer expects to be fulfilled: "And you, who were once estranged . . . he has now reconciled . . . in order to present you holy and blameless and irreproachable before him, *provided that you remain in the faith*" (εἰ γε ἐπιμένετε τῇ πίστει). We encountered ἐπιμένω ("remain, persist") in 6:1 ("Shall we remain in sin?"), and the connotation of continuing "in an activity or state"[252] remains predominant here. To "remain in the kindness" of God is the same as "standing in faith" in 11:20, which in the case of this interlocutor requires an entirely new orientation.[253] To rest one's confidence and pride in God's mercy means abandoning trust and boasting in one's own achievements or cultural status. Divine kindness requires active acceptance that must be maintained by believers.[254] Therefore, as Dunn insists, the condition clause in 22d "should not be underplayed"[255] because it is the line that runs through to chapters 14–16. If my reconstruction is correct, the remarkable reality was that both the Jews and the Gentiles were endangered because of their claims on honor and their persistence in placing their competitors in a position of shame. Despite the clear message of the gospel that such boasting was excluded, this social misbehavior must be cleared away before the Roman house and tenement churches can credibly participate in the mission to the barbarians in Spain. The situation is too delicate for Paul to address directly, which is why the brilliantly crafted diatribe with the imaginary Gentile interlocutor was required. It should be clear, however, in contrast to centuries of misinterpretation of Romans, that the real threat in Paul's view was not theological differences, but social contempt that "proper theology" usually deepens, by providing ever more subtle forms of superiority claims. Only the severity of grace can cure this malady, but it required believers to become self-critical in ways that honor and shame cultures found difficult.

The warning at the end of v. 22 begins with ἐπεί with the sense of "because otherwise,"[256] referring to what will occur if the interlocutor does not "remain in the kindness" of God. The σύ ("you") singular is emphatic, bringing the Gentile believer into the same situation as the "fallen" Jewish unbeliever.[257] The future tense of the verb ἐκκόπτω ("cut off, cut down")[258] conveys this absolute certainty: "otherwise you [sg.] will also be cut off." This is the final threat of divine sanction against an interlocutor prior to chapters 14–16, revealing the seriousness that Paul assigns to what would have been perceived as perfectly normal forms of social competition and contempt. God's kindness and severity eliminate partiality in all of its forms and therefore demand an abandonment of prejudice. Paul makes no ethical appeal, which believers can more or less follow; it is an either/or matter, and the person who persists in boasting loses access to kindness and receives the annihilating severity of God. In a passage that was highly unusual in nineteenth-century commentaries, Godet offers a haunting assessment of the prevailing nonchalance regarding Paul's warning about anti-Semitic prejudice eliminating the possibility of salvation by grace: "It is but too clear to anyone who has eyes to see, that our Gentile Christendom has now reached the point here foreseen by St. Paul. In its pride it tramples under foot the very notion of that grace which has made it what it is. It moves on, therefore, to a judgment of rejection like that of Israel, but which shall not have to soften it a promise like that which accompanied the fall of the Jews."[259]

■ 23 To carry Godet's thought a step further, it becomes clear in v. 23 that Israel's "fall" will be overcome by divine power. "But they also" (κἀκεῖνοι δέ)[260] refers to the Jews who are currently resisting the gospel of Christ crucified, but who will end up as branches alongside the faithful Gentiles in the holy olive tree.[261] As in the preceding verse, the condition to be fulfilled is introduced by ἐάν ("if") followed by the verb ἐπιμένειν ("remain, persist in"). Picking up the motif from v. 20,

---

252 BAGD (2000) 375 (2).
253 See Stachowiak, *Chrestotes*, 77–83.
254 Ibid., 82.
255 Dunn, 2:665.
256 Fitzmyer, 616, following BDF §456.3; see also BAGD (2000) 360 (2).
257 See Morris, 417.
258 This verb appears in Matt 3:10; 7:19; Luke 3:9 in relation to the message of John the Baptist and Jesus concerning the bad tree that will be cut down by divine action.
259 Godet, 408.
260 BAGD (2000) 500 (1b).
261 Meyer, 2:228; Weiss, 491.

the condition is that they no longer persist "in unfaith" ($\tau\hat{\eta}$ $\dot{\alpha}\pi\iota\sigma\tau\acute{\iota}\alpha$).[262] There is a parallel to "remain in unfaith" in *T. Levi* 4.1 that unbelieving persons who remain in their wrongdoing will be punished.

The characteristic paradox of divine action and free human decision that we have observed throughout this pericope is reiterated by placing "unfaith" right next to the divine passive, $\dot{\epsilon}\gamma\kappa\epsilon\nu\tau\rho\iota\sigma\vartheta\acute{\eta}\sigma\sigma\nu\tau\alpha\iota$ ("they will be grafted in"). Without allowing a moment's pause for the audience to question the feasibility of grafting branches that in many instances had been separated for years, Paul states the basis of his confidence: "For God is able ($\delta\upsilon\nu\alpha\tau\grave{o}\varsigma$ $\gamma\acute{\alpha}\rho$ $\dot{\epsilon}\sigma\tau\iota\nu$ $\acute{o}$ $\vartheta\epsilon\acute{o}\varsigma$) to graft them in again." Here Paul employs again the leitmotif of the $\delta\acute{\upsilon}\nu\alpha\mu\iota\varsigma$ $\vartheta\epsilon o\hat{\upsilon}$ ("power of God") that played a decisive role in the thesis of 1:16-17 and surfaces in various formulations in 1:4, 20; 4:21; 9:17, 22; 14:4; 15:13, 19. Just as in the explanation of divine kindness and severity, the final appeal and explanation is God's power.[263] In 2 Cor 9:8 we find a similar connection between abundant grace and divine power: "And God is able ($\delta\upsilon\nu\alpha\tau\epsilon\hat{\iota}$ $\delta\grave{\epsilon}$ $\acute{o}$ $\vartheta\epsilon\acute{o}\varsigma$) to make you flourish in every grace."[264] If God is indeed omnipotent, then the miracle of transforming grace and kindness is plausible, both for Jews and for Gentiles. It is not that "grace is understood as a power which overcomes unbelief and brings to faith," as Käsemann argues,[265] but that God is powerful enough to break through the resistance against grace, which is as formidable a barrier for Gentiles as for Jews.[266] The entire project of this letter and the mission it advances rest on this single premise: God is able.

■ **24** This verse "sums up the main argument" of the pericope[267] and thus provides a compelling conclusion. The final *a minore ad maius* ("from lesser to greater") topos in the pericope supports the proposition that God

is powerful enough to achieve the miraculous grafting of previous unbelievers in Israel.[268] Paul appeals to the amazing miracle of conversion that the Gentile Christian interlocutor had experienced, with "you" (sg.) in the emphatic position:[269] $\epsilon\grave{\iota}$ $\gamma\grave{\alpha}\rho$ $\sigma\grave{\upsilon}$ ("but if *you*") were pruned out of your former environment and grafted into the productive olive tree, how much more likely is a comparable miracle for Jews? Here Paul is able to recapitulate the allegory of the olive trees by bringing the Gentile experience of conversion into precise correlation with Jewish conversion, with both groups ending up as equal branches sharing the holy benefits of a single tree:

Gentiles were cut out from wild olive tree	Jews were cut out from domestic olive tree
Gentiles were grafted in (unnatural status)	Jews will be grafted in (natural status)
Both share in the same olive tree	

The antithesis between "natural" and "unnatural" that surfaced in v. 21 is used again in an ingenious manner to show that the Jews who had formerly rejected the gospel and are the current objects of Gentile contempt actually have a more intrinsic right to belong to the holy olive tree than does the Gentile convert himself. First Paul observes that the Gentile interlocutor belonged $\kappa\alpha\tau\grave{\alpha}$ $\varphi\acute{\upsilon}\sigma\iota\nu$ ("naturally, according to nature") to the unproductive, wild olive tree (11:24a). With the interlocutor's conversion, he was grafted $\pi\alpha\rho\grave{\alpha}$ $\varphi\acute{\upsilon}\sigma\iota\nu$ ("unnaturally, against nature") into the domestic tree. The expression "unnatural" does not imply that such grafting "does not and cannot happen, but rather because it is interfering with nature."[270] If this can occur with a worthless branch of a wild olive tree, "how much more" ($\pi\acute{o}\sigma\omega$ $\mu\hat{\alpha}\lambda\lambda o\nu$)

262 See Plag, *Israels Wege*, 49–54.
263 Siegert, *Argumentation*, 171, cites Wilke, *Neutestamentliche Rhetorik*, 313, on the crucial function of the topos of divine omnipotence.
264 See Walter Grundmann, "$\delta\acute{\upsilon}\nu\alpha\mu\alpha\iota$ $\kappa\tau\lambda.$," *TDNT* 2 (1964) 306.
265 Käsemann's comment in 311 reifies the doctrine of grace and relies on doctrinal instruction to evoke faith, which places those who think they have the right understanding of doctrine on the pedestal of honor and power, thus leaving the prejudices of Gentiles as well as Jews untouched.
266 Murray, 2:89, argues that this emphasis on divine power counters "the assumption entertained by Gentiles . . . the presumptuous confidence . . . that Israel, once disinherited and cast off, cannot again be established in God's covenant favor and blessing."
267 Sanday and Headlam, 330.
268 Meyer, 2:228, shows that v. 24 does not so much demonstrate the power of God as the contention of Jewish engrafting.
269 See Morris, 417.
270 Baxter and Ziesler, "Arboriculture," 29.

likely is it that the "natural" (κατὰ φύσιν) branches will be restored by God?[271] Paul does not allow the difference in honor between natural and unnatural to be the final word, however, because his point is that both kinds of branches will come to share the same sacred tree.[272] The future passive verb, ἐγκεντρισθήσονται ("they will be grafted in"), can be taken as a logical future[273] or as an actual, historical future,[274] which seems more likely in view of the visionary argument in the next pericope. His point is that the Gentile mission does not intend the creation of a separate Gentile church but rather a church of Jews and Gentiles,[275] both of whom will have been enabled by the gospel of "God's kindness and severity" to overcome their cultural prejudices. But Paul was wise enough to know that one cannot deal with such prejudices by frontal assault. So he selects a natural allegory with persuasive power along with a "speech-in-character" by a Gentile interlocutor whose prejudicial inclinations

are exaggerated in a humorous manner. This enables the audience to gain perspective on itself by smiling at the foibles of the interlocutor. In the end, the audience is enabled to recognize that, despite its reluctance to support a mission that would augment the numbers of perceived competitors, there were nine very good reasons to reconsider the matter: the "salvation" (11:11), the "wealth" (11:12), the "reconciliation" (11:15), the "life from the dead" (11:15), the "welcome" (11:15), the "holy" (11:16), the "nourishing sap" (11:17), the "faith" (11:20), and finally, the "kindness and severity of God" (11:22). This passage, which many interpreters have viewed as muddled, turns out to be a brilliant fusion of allegory and diatribe that would have functioned effectively with Paul's audience in Rome, drawing them in the direction of supporting his audacious mission to Spain that would provide a truly inclusive reconciliation of the world.

271 The πόσῳ μᾶλλον ("how much more") figure does not demonstrate the effectiveness of divine power (Meyer, 2:228), or show that Jewish conversion is "easier" than converting Gentiles (Sanday and Headlam, 330; Fitzmyer, 617), or the "Israelitish character of the covenant" (Murray, 2:90), but rather which divine action is more likely (Schmidt, 197), i.e., Jewish conversion along with Gentile conversion. White, *Apostle*, 152, aptly concludes that this passage "assumes that the creator's power transcends even nature's generativity."

272 See Hodge, "Olive Trees," 89: "God has added a branch to the family tree so that both Judeans and gentiles-in-Christ might be saved."

273 Weiss, 492; Kühl, 389.

274 Schmidt, 197; Wilckens, 2:248–49; Donaldson, "Riches," 93–94.

275 See Wilckens, 2:250; Dunn, 2:666; Ziesler, 281.

11

The Ninth Pericope

Oracular Disclosure and Enthymeme on the Mystery of Global Salvation

25/ For I do not want you to be ignorant of this mystery, brothers, "lest you become [wise] minded [in relation to]ᵃ yourselves," that an obtusenessᵇ has occurred in a part of Israel, until which time the full number of the Gentiles might come in, 26/ and in such a manner all Israel shall be saved, as it has been written,

> "The deliverer shall come from Zion;
> He shall turn aside impious
> deeds from Jacob. 27/
> And this, with them, [shall be] myᶜ
> very own covenant,"
> > "when I shall have taken away
> > their sins."

28/ On the one hand in regard to the gospel, [they are] enemies on account of you, but on the other hand in regard to election, [they are] beloved on account of the patriarchs. 29/ For the gifts and the call of God are without regret. 30/ For just asᵈ you were once disobedient to God but nowᵉ have been shown mercy because of their disobedience, 31/ so also have they now been disobedient because of the mercy you received, in order that they themselves may also nowᶠ be shown mercy. 32/ For God confined all personsᵍ in disobedience, in order that he might show mercy to all.

a   A difficult text-critical problem is produced by the "considerable doubt" (Metzger, *Textual Commentary*, 465) concerning whether there should be a preposition in this phrase. P⁴⁶ F G Ψ 6 424ᶜ 1506 1739 *pc* ar d f g o vg sa bo fay Hil Ambst Hier²ᐟ³ Pel Aug have no preposition, which Lagrange, 284, convincingly argues is the original reading; Zahn, 521–22; Käsemann, 312; and Pallas, 131, concur. The inclusion of παρ᾽ ("among, with") in ℵ C D L 33 69 81 104 256 263 323 326 330 365 424* 436 459 614 945 1175 1241 1243 1319 1505 1573 1735 1836 1874 1881 1912 1962 2127 2464 2495 *Maj* b syʰ ⁽ᵃᶜᶜ· ᵗᵒ ᴺ⁻ᴬ⁾ slav Orˡᵃᵗ Chr Theodore Hesˡᵃᵗ Gregory-Elvira Hier¹ᐟ³ could be an assimilation to the wording of Rom 12:16 and LXX Prov 3:7. The inclusion of ἐν ("in") found in A B 630 1506 1852 2200 syᵖ· ʰ ⁽ᵃᶜᶜ· ᵗᵒ ᴳᴺᵀ⁾ arm might be influenced by the wording of LXX Isa 5:21. Nestle-Aland²⁴ᐟ²⁵ and Michel, 354, preferred ἐν; Cranfield, 2:574, prints ἐν but says he is "inclined to agree with Lagrange." Nestle-Aland²⁶ᐟ²⁷ place παρ᾽ in brackets, indicating the divided opinion of the editors. I believe that an original text without a preposition is more likely to have evoked these emendations, and that in view of the parallel wordings in Proverbs and Isaiah, the lack of a preposition constitutes the more difficult reading. The simple dative construction is grammatically understandable and would still require "in" or "in relation to" in an English translation.

b   Nestle-Aland²⁶ᐟ²⁷ provides *caecitas* ("blindness") as an alternate reading to πώρωσις ("hardening") found in latt sy, which is too weakly supported to be original. Nestle-Aland²⁵ suggests this may go back to an original Greek πήρωσις ("blindness").

c   A transposition is evident in P⁴⁶ placing ἡ ("the") after παρ᾽ ἐμοῦ ("with me"), possibly a dictation error.

d   The addition of καί ("also, and") is weakly attested by ℵ² D¹ L Ψ 33 69 424 614 1175 1241 1505 1735 1836 1874 2344 2495 *Maj* lat sy appears to have a theologically apologetic purpose, reminding the Gentile readers that if they have been sinners, the Jews have been also. The absence of καί is strongly supported by P⁴⁶ ℵ¹ (ℵ* omits vs 30) A B C D* F G 81 323 326 330 365 945 1243 1319 1506 1573 1739 1881 *al* cop.

e   B 1243 1505 2495 have νυνί, the emphatic form of νῦν ("now"), which appears to be a secondary heightening of Paul's argument.

f   The stylistic and logical awkwardness of a thrice repeated νῦν ("now") may have elicited the variants present at this point. The word is omitted by P⁴⁶ A D² F G L Ψ 6 69 81 104 181 323 326 330 424 436 451 614 629 945 1175 1241 1243 1505 1739 1836 1874 1877 1881 2200 2344 2492 2495 *Maj Lect* ar b d f g o vg syᵖ arm eth geo Orˡᵃᵗ Diodore Did Chr Ambst Ambr Hier Pel Aug, which conforms to the stylistic tendencies noted earlier in these traditions. The substitution of νῦν by ὕστερον ("later, thereafter") in 33 88 256 263 365 1319 1573 1735 1852 1912 1962 2127 *pc* sa fayᵐˢ slav Ambstᵐˢˢ is a similar logical improvement. The evidence supporting the inclusion of νῦν (ℵ B D*·ᶜ 1506 *pc* bo fayᵐˢ) is not overwhelming, but it is difficult to conceive that these texts gratuitously added a third reference to "now." The inclusion of νῦν is therefore the more difficult reading that should be accepted. See Metzger, *Textual Commentary*, 465.

g   The neuter plural form τὰ πάντα ("all, all things") in P⁴⁶ᵛⁱᵈ D* (F G Ir omit τά) ar b d f g o vg Ir⁽ᵍʳ⁾· ˡᵃᵗ Cyr²ᐟ³ Ambst Prisc Ambr Hier¹²ᐟ¹⁷ Aug¹ᐟ¹⁰ appears to extend the condemnation beyond human agencies referred to in the undoubtedly original masculine form τοὺς πάντας ("all persons"), found in all of the other texts. Metzger, *Textual Commentary*, 465 suggests that the reading τὰ πάντα is a "scribal recollection" of Gal 3:22. The form τοὺς πάντας ("all persons") is strongly supported by ℵ A B D² L Ψ 6 33 69 81 88 104 181 256 263 323 326 330 365 424 436 451 459 614 629 1175 1241 1319 1505 1506 1573 1735 1739 1836 1852 1874 1877 1881 1912 1962 2127 2200 2344 2492 2495 *Lect* sy^{p.h} sa bo fay arm eth geo Or^{lat} Diodore Did Chr Theodore^{lat} Cyr^{1/3} (John-Damascus) Ambst^{mss} Hier^{5/17} Aug^{9/10}.

Analysis

This pericope dealing with the mystery of salvation serves to explain the allusion in 11:23-24 about the future engrafting of Israel alongside Gentile converts into the holy olive tree. Although commentaries usually view this section as concentrated on Israel's salvation,[1] the entire world is in fact in view[2] with respect to the power of the gospel to overcome otherwise irresolvable barriers. The pericope contains two major parts, a disclosure of the mystery with scriptural support (11:25-27) and a theological explanation of its significance for salvation history (11:28-32).[3]

The pericope opens with a stylized disclosure formula that prepares the audience for something significant.[4] The second person singular discourse in the preceding diatribe shifts here to second person plural forms.[5] Two parallel statements about Israel's obtuseness and Gentile salvation in 25c and d are followed by the declaration of the mysterious, future salvation of all Israel in v. 26a, a statement that is often treated as a kind of independent centerpiece of this pericope.[6] The validity of the hope of Israel's salvation is confirmed by the skillful creation of a four-line prophecy in 11:26c-27, assembled from Isa 59:20-21 and Isa 27:9.

The rest of the pericope has the form of a theological enthymeme that explains the relevance of this mystery in terms of the gospel's global mission. The thesis of 11:28 concerning the enmity and election of Israel is stated in the form of an elegant, antithetical parallelism[7] with homoioptoton in the -οι endings of "enemies" and "beloved" and the -ας endings of "you" and "patriarchs,"[8] as well reduplication in the prepositions κατά and διά. Siegert observes that this is a perfect example of *paromoiosis*, an elegant figure with balanced clauses and similar sounding endings.[9]

$$
\begin{aligned}
&\kappa\alpha\tau\grave{\alpha}\ \mu\grave{\epsilon}\nu\ \tau\grave{o}\ \epsilon\grave{\upsilon}\alpha\gamma\gamma\acute{\epsilon}\lambda\iota o\nu \\
&\quad \grave{\epsilon}\chi\vartheta\rho o\grave{\iota} \\
&\qquad \delta\iota'\ \grave{\upsilon}\mu\tilde{\alpha}\varsigma, \\
&\kappa\alpha\tau\grave{\alpha}\ \delta\grave{\epsilon}\ \tau\grave{\eta}\nu\ \grave{\epsilon}\kappa\lambda o\gamma\grave{\eta}\nu \\
&\quad \grave{\alpha}\gamma\alpha\pi\eta\tau o\grave{\iota} \\
&\qquad \delta\iota\grave{\alpha}\ \tau o\grave{\upsilon}\varsigma\ \pi\alpha\tau\acute{\epsilon}\rho\alpha\varsigma
\end{aligned}
$$

This thesis concerning the current hostility and continued election of Israel is explained and elaborated in

---

1   See, for example, the titles for this pericope such as "Israel's redemption" (Käsemann, 311), "Israel's ultimate salvation" (Schlier, 337), "the salvation of all Israel" (Moo, 710); see also Morris, 418; Stuhlmacher, 170; Theobald, 1:302; Fitzmyer, 618; Byrne, 348; Haacker, 235.

2   See the titles for 11:25-32 by Barrett, 221, "God's Plan Complete"; Cranfield, 2:572, "The mystery of God's merciful plan"; Dunn, 2:675, "The Final Mystery Revealed."

3   See Wilckens, 3:251; Tobin, *Paul's Rhetoric,* 368.

4   See Mullins, "Disclosure," 49–50; Siegert, *Argumentation,* 171.

5   Dunn, 2:677.

6   In "Beiträge," 242, Weiss describes the grammatical independence of this clause and refers to it as a kind of "Ruhepunkt" ("resting point") in the argument. That vv. 25-27 form a secondary interpolation, as proposed by Plag, *Israels Wege,* 60, is rightly rejected by Peter Stuhlmacher, "Zur Interpretation von Röm 11,25-32," in H. W. Wolff, ed., *Probleme biblischer Theologie. Festschrift für Gerhard von Rad zum 70. Geburtstag* (Munich: Kaiser, 1971) 557.

7   See Weiss, "Beiträge," 242, and Käsemann, 315: "a hard paradox in which the two lines correspond antithetically in their individual members." See also Siegert, *Argumentation,* 171–72.

8   Siegert, *Argumentation,* 172.

9   Ibid., 174; for a convenient definition of *paromoiosis,* see Anderson, *Glossary,* 91–92.

11:29-32, as revealed in the fourfold repetition of γάρ ("for").[10] There is "an extremely skilful chiasmus" in the "just as . . . so also" figure of 11:30-31,[11] in which the "mercy" and "disobedience" of 11:30b are replicated by the "disobedience" and "mercy" of 11:31a.[12] The situation of Israel and the Gentiles is shown to be parallel in their reception of mercy despite the previous disobedience of each group. In addition, there is a striking paranomasia in the threefold use of νῦν ("now") of the eschatological present in vv. 30-31 that stands in antithesis to the ποτε ("then") of the old age. The verbs "have mercy" and "be disobedient" are also repeated three times in this artful chiasm. The conclusion of the argument in 11:32 takes up the categories of disobedience and mercy in their universal scope so that the mystery of the ultimate conversion of Gentiles and Jews is brought into consistency with the earlier argument about the sinfulness (1:18–3:20) and salvation (3:21–5:21) of all humans. The word πᾶς ("all") is reduplicated in this final verse. In the end, divine mercy will triumph over cultural resistance in its various, destructive forms (11:30-32). The rhetoric of these final verses provides both a summary and a pause before the ecstatic conclusion of 11:33-36.[13]

Rhetorical Disposition

Exegesis

■ **25** The argumentative link with the preceding claim that Israel will be grafted back into the olive tree (11:23-24) is indicated by γάρ ("for") in the opening clause.[14] The disclosure formula, οὐ θέλω ὑμᾶς ἀγνοεῖν, ἀδελφοί ("I do not want you to be ignorant, brothers"), replicates the formula in 1:13, indicating again a topic of

---

10   In contrast, Louw, 2:115–17, separates 11:28 into a separate cluster of cola from 11:29-31.

11   Käsemann, 317; Louw, 2:16, concurs that "a complete parallelism and chiasm is achieved."

12   Käsemann, 316; there is a somewhat confusing analysis of this chiasm in Louw, 2:117, but a clear

and succinct description in Weiss, "Beiträge," 180, 242.

13   See Weiss, "Beiträge," 242–43.

14   The substantiation of the claim of divine engrafting in 11:23-24 is inferred by Meyer, 1:229; Weiss, 493; Moo, 713, but is inappropriately extended to the

"special importance" to the audience.[15] Among examples of such disclosure formulas cited by Terrence Mullins are *P.Oxy.* 12. Nr. 1493.5–9, γινώσκειν σε θέλω, ἀδελφέ, ὅτι κατὰ τὴν τοῦ ὄντος μηνὸς Θὼλ ἐκομισάμην σου τὸν υἱὸν εὐρωστοῦντα καὶ ὁλοκληροῦντα διὰ παντός ("I wish to let you know, O brother, that in the current month of Thôl, I have welcomed your son in complete health and totally robust in every respect").[16] Also as in 1:13, Paul addresses his audience as "brothers,"[17] referring to male and female members of the community[18] that consists of Jews as well as Gentiles.[19] On the basis of the preceding argument, it is clear that everyone in Paul's audience are children of God (8:14, 15, 19, 21; 9:8, 26) whose joint patrimony was assured because Abraham "is the father of us all" (4:16), and whose solidarity with Paul and with each other was conveyed in the formulas "all who have faith" (1:16; 3:22; 4:11; 10:4, 11), "all of you" (1:8), and "all who call upon the name of the Lord" (10:12-13).

The object of the verb "to be ignorant" that Paul wishes to prevent is τὸ μυστήριον τοῦτο ("this mystery"), referring to a divine disclosure that is detailed in the later part of v. 25. The word μυστήριον was widely used in Greco-Roman religion, particularly in the mystery religions,[20] and was equally popular in apocalyptic Judaism and various branches of early Christianity.[21] Common features of these traditions of μυστήριον [22] include the premise of limited access to divine knowledge;[23] the demand to refrain from revealing content to the uninitiated;[24] the role of prophetic or visionary characters in gaining access to such knowledge;[25] and the crucial role of angelic mediation and visionary journeys to otherwise inaccessible realms of divine knowledge.[26] A fundamental disparity between insiders to whom the mysteries were revealed and outsiders whose access is barred[27] is evident in widespread literary references and also in the etymology of μυστήριον, derived from μύειν ("to close"), probably referring to the maintenance of closed lips about secrets.[28] In literature close to the NT, there are frequent demands to avoid disclosure to outsiders. For example, 1QS 4:6 demands "concealment concerning the truth of the mysteries of knowledge," and Ezra is told that "you alone were worthy to learn this secret of the Most High. Therefore write all these things that you have seen in a book, and put it in a hidden place; and you shall teach them to the wise among your people, whose hearts you know are able to comprehend and keep these secrets."[29] The content of the mystery usually favors insiders at the expense of outsiders, as, for example, in *1 En.* 38.3, "When the mysteries of the

---

15 Cranfield, 2:573; Meyer, 2:229; Schmithals, "ἀγνοέω κτλ.," 21; the formulation θέλω / θέλομεν ὑμᾶς ἀγνοεῖν, ἀδελφοί is uniquely Pauline, appearing also in 1 Cor 10:1; 12:1; 2 Cor 1:8; and 1 Thess 4:13, and always introduces a point of great importance.

16 Mullins, "Disclosure," 47.

17 See the references to the investigations of "brother" in connection with 1:13.

18 See BAGD (2000) 18; Beutler, "ἀδελφός," 30.

19 Tobin, *Paul's Rhetoric*, 369, notes that the "you" (pl.) in this verse should not be confused with the "you" of the imaginary interlocutor in 11:13-24.

20 Bornkamm, "μυστήριον, μυέω," 803–13; Krämer, "μυστήριον," 446–47; Wolter, "Verborgene Weisheit," 300–303.

21 Bornkamm, "μυστήριον, μυέω," 814–24; Krämer, "μυστήριον," 447–49; Bockmuehl, *Revelation and Mystery*, 24–126; Johnson, *Function*, 163; Dieter Sänger, "Rettung der Heiden und Erwählung Israels. Einige vorläufige Erwägungen zu Römer 11,25-27," *KD* 32 (1986) 112–15.

The references to the entire preceding pericope by Cranfield, 2:573, and Dunn, 2:677.

22 See Bornkamm, "μυστήριον, μυέω," 816; Marvin W. Meyer, "Mystery Religions," *ABD* 4 (1992) 941–44. Raymond E. Brown, "The Semitic Background of the New Testament Mysterion (I)," *Bib* 39 (1958) 426–48, overlooks these parallels in insisting on "a purely Semitic background" (426) for the NT use of μυστήριον; he is followed by Dunn, 2:678; Fitzmyer, 621; Johnson, 171–72; and Byrne, 354.

23 1 Cor 2:6, 10; 1 Thess 2:6-7.

24 1 Cor 2:14; 2 Cor 12:4.

25 1 Cor 4:1; 7:7; 15:51.

26 2 Cor 12:1-4.

27 See Achtemeier, 187.

28 Meyer, "Mystery Religions," 941–42; Bornkamm, "μυστήριον, μυέω," 803: "the etymology leads only to the fairly certain general conclusion that a μυστήριον is something on which silence must be kept." Keller, *Gottes Treue*, 78, concurs.

29 *4 Ezra.* 12.37-38; see also 14.5-6, 26, 45-47; *2 Bar.* 20.3; 48.3.

Righteous One are revealed, he shall judge the sinners; and the wicked ones will be driven from the presence of the righteous and the elect."

That Paul sought to overcome this insider bias in the use of the term "mystery" is evident not only in the warning against haughty-mindedness in 11:25b but also by first articulating the content of the mystery by means of the carefully constructed diatribe in 11:11-24 with an interlocutor who takes Gentile Christian prejudices against Jewish Christians to a ridiculous extreme. In the light of these rhetorical observations, what Paul discloses here is authoritative "new doctrine,"[30] an oracle whose authority derives from God.[31] Efforts to specify the precise source of this oracle have not been successful. If it derived from spiritual interpretation of Scripture,[32] then why was the term "mystery" not applied to the many previous citations that Paul selected, edited, and in some cases substantially transformed to fit his argumentative purpose? If it was an answer to Paul's prayer for Israel's redemption (Rom 10:1),[33] why does Paul remain in anguish over Israel's unbelief and continue to pray for its redemption?[34] If the mystery was disclosed at the time of Paul's conversion, leading him to evangelize among Gentiles while avoiding Jews,[35] how is one to explain his receiving five times the customary synagogal punishment of 39 stripes (2 Cor 11:24)?[36] Seyoon Kim's theory is based on his interpretation of 1 Cor 1:6-10 concerning the divine plan of salvation, which was a development of the theophanic call patterned after Isaiah 6 and 49.[37] He makes a case against Sandnes, Hofius, and Mussner that this mystery was not derived

from Paul's scriptural work on Isaiah 59, 27, Jeremiah 31 in the period after his conversion, but this case can hardly be compelling with regard to the precise moment of Paul's conversion. Kim is right to rely on Hübner's observation that the mystery is not entirely dependent on scriptural exegesis. The reversed sequence that Paul develops, "the Gentiles first and then the Jews" coming into salvation, seems strongly opposed to the LXX citations. I find the Ulrich B. Müller's suggestion in *Prophetie* more plausible, that the mystery may have originated in connection with 1 Thess 2:14-16.[38]

The strongest argument in favor of Kim's reconstruction is that Paul never appears to have followed the traditional rationale of mission to the Jews first and then to the Gentiles, making the Gentile cities his base of operations and avoiding Jerusalem.[39] The material contained in Isaiah 6 and 49 reflected in Paul's references to his conversion have material concerning the obtuseness of Israel.[40] But Kim observes that Paul does not explicitly cite these passages in describing his conversion, "because they were not the primary sources of the 'mystery,' but only confirmation of it."[41] Kim makes a much less plausible case that this mystery was involved in an allegedly early agreement (ca. 34–35 C.E.) between Paul and Peter concerning a division of the mission fields, suggested by Luedemann.[42] The main point is more compelling, that from the moment of Paul's conversion it was clear to him that Israel had experienced an obtuseness or hardening, and that the Isaianic vision would be fulfilled in reverse order. Could Paul have not identified himself along with those zealous Jews, ren-

---

30 Bockmuehl, *Revelation and Mystery*, 170–75; see also Kühl, 390.

31 Zahn, 521; Luz, *Geschichtsverständnis*, 289.

32 Otto Betz, "Die heilsgeschichtliche Rolle Israels bei Paulus," *ThBei* 9 (1978) 20; Hübner, *Gottes Ich und Israel*, 113, 121; Otfried Hofius, "'All Israel Will Be Saved': Divine Salvation and Israel's Deliverance in Romans 9–11," *PSBSup* 1 (1990) 33–38; Franz Mussner, "'Ganz Israel wird gerettet werden' (Röm 11,26). Versuch einer Auslegung," *Kairos* 18 (1976) 249–51; Sandnes, *Paul*, 180–81; Bockmuehl, *Revelation and Mystery*, 174–75; Keller, *Gottes Treue*, 124.

33 Müller, *Prophetie*, 225–32; Zeller, 198; Sandnes, *Paul*, 178; Wilckens, 2:254.

34 See Seyoon Kim, "The 'Mystery' of Rom 11:25-26 Once More," *NTS* 43 (1997) 417–18.

35 Kim, *Origin*, 74–99; Kim, "Mystery," 412–15, 420–29.

36 See Martin, *2 Corinthians*, 376–77; this historical detail also counters Nanos's explanation in *Mystery*, 249–50, that Jews were actually jealous of Paul's missionary success with Gentiles.

37 Kim, "Mystery," 412–15.

38 Müller, *Prophetie*, 230.

39 Kim, "Mystery," 418–19, 428.

40 Ibid., 421.

41 Ibid., 422.

42 Luedemann, *Chronologie*, 79–83, 97–98.

dered obtuse so as to oppose the Christ? When one takes Rom 10:4 into account, describing the dilemma of zealous Jews who reject Christ, an insight available to Paul at the moment of his conversion could well have been in view.

Despite the discomfort of some interpreters,[43] it is best to acknowledge that Paul's use of the word "mystery" in this context reflects the perspective of a mystic whose "revelation experiences"[44] remain partially beyond analysis. Even though it can be publicly disclosed, its origin and content remain partially "unfathomable and incomprehensible."[45]

Before revealing the content of the "mystery," Paul cites a brief warning from Prov 3:7. The wording of LXX Prov 3:7a is abbreviated[46] and altered from a singular to a plural admonition, as the comparison indicates:

LXX Prov 3:7 μὴ ἴσθι φρόνιμος παρὰ σεαυτῷ ("Do not be [wise] minded in yourself").

Rom 11:25b ἵνα μὴ ἦτε ἑαυτοῖς φρόνιμοι ("lest you [pl.] become [wise] minded in yourselves").

The fact that being "[wise] minded" (φρόνιμος) has a positive connotation in Greco-Roman writings[47] and in most of the NT occurrences (Matt 10:16; 24:45; 25:2, 4, 8, 9; Luke 12:42) strengthens the impression that the negative admonition must be derived from either a citation of Proverbs or at least a strong echo thereof.[48] In this context the reflexive pronoun ἑαυτοῖς in combination with φρόνιμοι implies being wise in your own estimation, implying an unacceptable measure of arro-

gance.[49] The critical tone is similar to that of 1 Cor 4:10 where Paul contrasts the inflated self-image of the proto-Gnostics with the proper humility of the apostles: "We are fools for Christ's sake, but you are wise minded (φρόνιμοι) in Christ" (cf. 2 Cor 11:19, "being wise minded yourselves").[50] The warning of Rom 11:25b in second person plural style makes it clear that the previous discussion with the imaginary interlocutor has implications for the congregation as a whole. The arrogance that Paul so skillfully and humorously depicted in the interlocutor is to some degree characteristic of the congregation as a whole. Paul makes no distinction here between Gentile Christians and Jewish Christians,[51] both of whom may have had reasons to resist evangelization that would result in the conversion of additional Gentiles and previously zealous Jews.[52] But since the majority of Gentile Christians perceived their interests to counter the mystery of Israel's conversion, as evident in the preceding pericope, this is where the main criticism must lie.[53]

It seems clear that the mystery contains three elements that had been introduced earlier in chapter 11: making a portion of Israel obtuse, the conversion of Gentiles, and the subsequent conversion of Jews.[54] The concept of πώρωσις ("obtuseness, hardening") was introduced by its verbal equivalent πωρόω ("make obtuse, hard") in 11:7, which Paul had elaborated by means of scriptural citations as a failure to discern and to see that was simultaneously a willful act and divine punishment.[55] That this condition had fallen only "on a part of Israel" (ἀπὸ μέρους τῷ Ἰσραήλ) is consistent with 9:27,

---

43 Zahn, 521; Sänger, *Verkündigung*, 181-93.
44 Meier, *Mystik*, 295, 99.
45 Wilk, *Bedeutung des Jesajabuches*, 66.
46 See note a above.
47 See Georg Bertram, "φρήν κτλ.," *TDNT* 9 (1974) 221-24.
48 Schlier, 338, speaks of a reminiscence of Prov 3:7; Dunn, 2:679, refers to "an echo of Prov 3:7."
49 Dunn, 2:679; Fitzmyer, 621; Barrett, 222: "wise in your own conceit"; Ziesler, 283: "clever in yourselves."
50 See Paulsen, "φρονέω κτλ.," 440.
51 See Wilckens, 2:252-53; Dunn, 2:679.
52 That Paul's warning counters an ahistorical, charismatic enthusiasm in the Roman congregations as proposed by Otto Glombitza, "Apostolische Sorge.

Welche Sorge treibt den Apostel Paulus zu den Sätzen Röm xi 25ff.?" *NovT* 7 (1964-65) 314-18, followed by Stuhlmacher, "Interpretation," 559, remains unsupported by the evidence in the rest of the letter.
53 Weiss, 493; Michel, 354; Cranfield, 2:574; Morris, 419; Schreiner, 614; Mussner, "'Ganz Israel,'" 254. In "Einige vorwiegend sprachliche Beobachtungen zu Römer 11.25-36," in L. de Lorenzi, ed., *Die Israelfrage nach Röm 9-11*, SMB 3 (Rome: Abbayia S. Paolo, 1977) 193-205, Joachim Jeremias describes the domination and intolerance of the Gentile Christians.
54 Zahn, 523; Michel, 354-55; Fitzmyer, 621; Moo, 716; Keller, *Gottes Treue*, 124-27.
55 Schmidt and Schmidt, "παχύνω, πωρόω κτλ.,"

that "only a remnant will be saved"; with 11:7, that "the chosen" obtained righteousness in Christ, "but the others were made obtuse"; with 11:14, that "some" of Israel has already accepted the gospel; and with 11:17, that only "some" of the branches of Israel had been broken off. It is thus inappropriate to attach the phrase $\dot{\alpha}\pi\dot{o}$ $\mu\acute{e}\rho o\nu\varsigma$ in an adverbial manner to the noun $\pi\acute{\omega}\rho\omega\sigma\iota\varsigma$ ("obtuse, hardening") and the verb $\gamma\acute{e}\gamma o\nu\epsilon\nu$ ("has become") in order to maintain the premise that Paul always refers to Israel "as a unified whole."[56] He usually does so, but the argument in this instance would be fatally flawed with the notion of a "partial obtuseness" and the contextual clues in the earlier argument of Rom 9–11 should be followed. Paul knows that he himself and many of his fellow converts had formerly been afflicted with such obtuseness, and the mystery he now conveys is that only a portion of Israel remains blind and that this malady will ultimately be overcome. The choice of the perfect tense in the verb $\gamma\acute{e}\gamma o\nu\epsilon\nu$ ("has become") implies that this nondiscernment was imposed at a particular time and continues to the present,[57] which matches the circumstance of a portion of Israel's rejection of Jesus as the Christ and its continued hostility to the spread of the gospel.

The reference to the conversion of Gentiles begins with $\ddot{\alpha}\chi\rho\iota\varsigma$ $o\hat{v}$ ("until which [time]"), used elsewhere to mark the "continuous extent of time up to a point,"

"until the time when."[58] Joachim Jeremias shows that $\ddot{\alpha}\chi\rho\iota\varsigma$ $o\hat{v}$ in combination with $\epsilon i\sigma\acute{e}\lambda\vartheta\eta$ ("might come in") functions as a prospective conjunction that points forward to the goal, in this instance, of Gentile conversion.[59] In this instance, it refers to the time period of Israel's obtuseness lasting until the fulfillment of the predestined plan for Gentile conversion.[60] The $\tau\dot{o}$ $\pi\lambda\acute{\eta}$-$\rho\omega\mu\alpha$ $\tau\hat{\omega}\nu$ $\dot{e}\vartheta\nu\hat{\omega}\nu$ ("full total of the Gentiles")[61] refers in this instance to the predestined number of the elect according to an apocalytic scheme.[62] Whether this full number of Gentile converts was larger or smaller than the ultimate number of Jewish converts[63] is impossible to determine on the basis of this succinct reference. It is significant, however, that Paul employs the same term here as in 11:12 for the full number of Jewish converts, which places both groups in a similar status with regard to the completion of a fore-ordained number of converts. In view of the mission proposed in this letter, the full number of Gentile converts was probably thought by Paul to require the inclusion of Spanish converts.

Since the verb $\epsilon i\sigma\acute{e}\rho\chi o\mu\alpha\iota$ ("come in") is left without an object, scholars have either suggested that the converts were conceived as making an eschatological pilgrimage to Jerusalem[64] or entering into the church as the kingdom of God.[65] A less likely option is that the verb implies the engrafting into the olive tree of Israel.[66] In view of the fact that $\epsilon i\sigma\acute{e}\rho\chi o\mu\alpha\iota$ is a technical term

1024; Marie-Irma Seewann, "'Verstockung', 'Verhärtung' oder 'Nicht-Erkennen': Überlegungen zu Röm 11,25," *Kirche und Israel* 12 (1997) 165–70, concludes that "non-discernment" is the appropriate translation, which can result from either incapacity or an unwillingness to understand.

56   Dunn, 2:679.
57   Ibid.
58   BAGD (2000) 160; see also Wilk, *Bedeutung des Jesajabuches,* 68, who cites Mayer, *Gottes Heilsratschluß,* 282.
59   Jeremias, "Römer 11.25-36," 196.
60   Hofius, "All Israel," 33.
61   For the common use of $\pi\lambda\acute{\eta}\rho\omega\mu\alpha$ as "full number," see Overfield, "Pleroma," 384–96.
62   See particularly Stuhlmann, *Eschatologische Maß,* 164–78; Hübner, "$\pi\lambda\acute{\eta}\rho\omega\mu\alpha,$" 110–11; relevant parallel passages are cited under 11:12 above. The proposal by Aus, "Paul's Travel Plans," 251, 257, that this "full number" was thought to include Spanish converts participating in the Jerusalem offering

raises insuperable chronological problems because Paul planned to deliver the offering before traveling to Rome to organize the Spanish mission.

63   Dunn, 2:680, referring to an ambiguous reference in Murray, 2:93.
64   Cf. Plag, *Israels Wege,* 56–58; Aus, "Paul's Travel Plans," 251–52; Schmidt, 110; Räisänen, "Römer 9–11," 2922; Wilk, *Bedeutung des Jesajabuches,* 68–70; Ziesler, 284; Zeller, 198; Wilckens, 2:255; Tobin, *Paul's Rhetoric,* 371–72. For a skeptical assessment, see Haacker, 238.
65   Sanday and Headlam, 335; Michel, 355; Käsemann, 313; Schlier, 339; Cranfield, 2:576; Murray, 2:93; Morris, 420; Stuhlmacher, 272; Fitzmyer, 622.
66   See the critique by Dunn, 2:680, albeit mistakenly attributing this view to Fitzmyer.

for "entering the kingdom" in the gospel tradition and the later reference to the "kingdom of God" in Rom 14:17; and in view of the avoidance of the references to Mount Zion and the "gospel of peace" in the citation of Isa 52:7 in Rom 10:15 as noted above, the implied logic is more likely to be the eschatological church containing the predestined full number of Jews and Gentiles.

■ **26a** The third element in the mystery conveyed to the Romans is the conversion of Israel. By introducing it with καὶ οὕτως ("and in such a manner, and so"), Paul makes plain that the first two components of the mystery are the means by which the final component will be accomplished by God.[67] As he explained in 11:11-14, zealous anger at the conversion of Gentiles and their inclusion as equally honored members of the kingdom of God is expected to provoke the conversion of Israel, in a manner parallel to Paul's own conversion. The logic of the three-step mystery has led some scholars to assume a temporal sequence or to combine the temporal with the modal dimension in the words καὶ οὕτως.[68] In contrast to current opinion,[69] there is lexical support for the temporal sense.[70] For example, Plato reports that Socrates and Hippocrates arrive at Protagoras's house but decide to "finish their discussion and then go into the house" (ἀλλὰ διαπερανάμενοι οὕτως

ἐσίοιμεν, Plato *Prot.* 314c). In *T. Abr.* (rec. A) 7.11, the Archangel Michael tells Abraham, "I have been sent to you in order to tell you not to forget death; but thereafter (εἶθ᾽ οὕτως) I will return to him as he commanded me." Pieter van der Horst observes that "the modal and the temporal senses are not necessarily mutually exclusive.[71] The shift in verb tense from the perfect in the first element of the mystery (11:25c), to the subjunctive in the second (11:25d), and to the future in the third (11:26a), provides grounds for asserting a kind of sequence in the "mystery," but the fact that portions of all three elements had already occurred should make one cautious in asserting "definite stages" in the divine plan.[72]

Some interpreters have proposed that "all Israel" refers to elect believers, whether Jews or Gentiles,[73] but in all of the earlier references to "Israel" in Romans, the ethnic Israel is in view. There is a broad consensus among contemporary exegetes for another interpretation, that πᾶς Ἰσραήλ refers to "Israel as a whole, as a people, whose corporate identity and wholeness could not be lost even if in the event there were some (or indeed many) individual exceptions."[74] This is a shrewd formulation that appears to protect Paul's reputation by paring back his prophecy to a more reasonable level, as

---

67   BAGD (2000) 742.2, "in this way, as follows"; Godet, 411; Kühl, 392; Schmidt, 199; Wilckens, 2:255; Dunn, 2:681; Moo, 720; Jeremias, "Römer 11.25-36," 198-99; Sänger, "Rettung der Heiden," 108; Wright, *Climax,* 249-50; Tobin, *Paul's Rhetoric,* 371.

68   Barrett, 223; Michel, 255; Käsemann, 314. Dunn, 2:681, cites André Feuillet, "L'espérance de la 'conversion' d'Israël en Rom 11,25-32. L'Interprétation des versets 26 et 31," in M. Carrez et al., eds., *De la Tôrah au Messie. Études d'exégèse et d'herméneutique bibliques offertes à Henri Cazelles* (Paris: Desclée, 1981), 486-87. Dunn rightly rejects a reference to the subsequent citation of Isa 59, as proposed by Müller, *Prophetie,* 226-27, and others. The temporal interpretation of καὶ οὕτως is also advocated by Müller, *Gottes Gerechtigkeit,* 43; Plag, *Israels Wege,* 37; Stuhlmacher, "Interpretation," 560.

69   Fitzmyer, 622-23; Luz, *Geschichtsverständnis,* 294, insists that καὶ οὕτως should be translated with "and so," which does not imply the chronology of an apocalyptic plan.

70   See Pieter W. van der Horst, "'Only Then Will All Israel Be Saved': A Short Note on the Meaning of

καὶ οὕτως in Romans 11:26," *JBL* 119 (2000) 521-25, citing earlier studies by Eiliv Skard, "Zum temporal Gebrauch von οὕτως. Eine Bemerkung zu den Asteriostexten," SO 37 (1961) 151-52, and D. Holwerda, "Heel Israel behouden," in Holwerda, *De Schrift opent een vergezicht* (Kampen: Kok-Voorhoeve, 1998) 160-93.

71   Van der Horst, "Romans 11:26," 524.

72   Moo, 710, following Hofius, "Evangelium und Israel," 315, and Bell, *Provoked to Jealousy,* 136. See also Schreiner, 614.

73   Jeremias, "Römer 11.25-36," 200; Hervé Ponsot, "Et ainsi tout Israël sera sauvé. Rom XI,26a: Salut et conversion," *RB* 89 (1982) 413-15; François Refoulé, "'...Et ainsi tout Israël sera sauvés.' Romains 11,25-32," LD 117 (Paris: Cerf, 1984; repr. pp. 39-57 in J. Todd et al., *Israel, the Church and the World Religions Face the Future,* EITRY 1983-84 (Jerusalem: Ecumenical Institute for Theological Research, 1984); other advocates are listed in Moo, 721.

74   Dunn, 2:681; see also Maier, *Israel,* 140; Zeller, *Juden,* 251; Luz, *Geschichtsverständnis,* 292; Mayer,

viewed in the light of subsequent experience. However, the word πᾶς means "all," "any and every entity out of a totality," and thus it does not lend itself to the expression of exceptions.[75] There is also nothing in this context that supports an interpretation of "most, with a few exceptions," because v. 27 goes on to argue that "all" of Israel's sins will be taken away and v. 32 concludes that God will show mercy "to all."[76] It seems most likely that Paul's "mystery" was believed to include all members of the house of Israel, who, without exception, would be saved.[77] As Luke Johnson observes, "Paul's faith . . . is not in human possibility but in 'the God who brings into being that which does not exist and gives life to the dead' (4:17)."[78] Paul's formulation is carried by his missional conviction that God's word has ultimate power,[79] and it is consistent with 1:5; 1:16; 4:16; and 11:32. He returns to this conviction in the final section of the theological argument of the letter in 15:9-13, where the vision of a transformation of all nations is expressed. There is also little doubt that the verb σωθήσεται ("they shall be saved") refers to evangelical conversion, as in 5:9-10; 10:9-13; and 11:14.[80] There is no indication in Paul's formulation that Jewish conversion constitutes a *Sonderweg* ("separate path"),[81] although this remains a legitimate theological option that takes account of post-Pauline

developments. It is, in any event, clear that in Paul's mind the identity of Israel would not be erased by accepting Christ as the Messiah.[82] The missional horizon of Romans must be kept in view, despite all of the difficulties with subsequent interpretation and historical developments. Paul believed that when all the peoples of the earth accept the gospel, they will all for the first time praise God rather than themselves. The competition between nations that had always brought war and destruction will thereby come to an end. The Pauline hope of a world-transforming mission is viewed as a fulfillment of biblical prophecy, that all nations will find in the Messiah a new and peaceful destiny, including solidarity with one another.[83] To whittle back the details of Paul's vision to more "reasonable" levels, reflecting the fact of their nonfulfillment in the twenty centuries past, undercuts the magnificent scope of the "mystery" that Paul believed he had been given.

■ **26b-27** The traditional Jewish background of the formula "as it has been written" was discussed in connection with 1:17, appearing also in 2:24; 3:4, 10; 4:17; 8:36; 9:13, 33; 11:8, 26; 15:3, 21. The final scriptural citation in the third proof is drawn from Isaiah 27 and 59, providing confirmation of Paul's disclosure of the mystery of Israel's future salvation.[84] A coherent, four-line

Gottes Heilsratschluß, 287–89; Hofius, "Evangelium und Israel," 316–18; Zahn, 524; Lagrange, 285; Barrett, 224; Käsemann, 313; Cranfield, 2:576–77; Schlier, 340; Fitzmyer, 623; Moo, 723; Wright, *Climax,* 250; Nanos, *Mystery,* 276–77; Kim, *Romans 9–11,* 138; Tobin, *Paul's Rhetoric,* 372.

75 BAGD (2000) 783; Keller, *Gottes Treue,* 223–41.

76 See particularly Franz Mussner, "Heil für alle. Der Grundgedanke des Römerbriefs," *Kairos* 23 (1981) 208–10.

77 So Jülicher, 307; Kühl, 302; Schmidt, 200–201; Ziesler, 285; Bachmanu, "*Verus Israel,*" 506.

78 Johnson, 172; see also Richard A. Batey, "'So All Israel Will Be Saved': An Interpretation of Romans 11:25-32," *Int* 20 (1966) 227–28.

79 See Keller, *Gottes Treue,* 129–32, with particular reference to 9:6-13.

80 Cranfield, 2:577; Fitzmyer, 623; see also Walter Radl, "σώζω," *EDNT* 3 (1993) 320.

81 See, for example, Mussner, "Heil für alle," 209–13; idem, "Ganz Israel," 245–53; Gager, *Origins,* 261–62; Lloyd Gaston, "Israel's Misstep in the Eyes of Paul," in Gaston, *Paul,* 147–49. For a comprehen-

sive critique, see Reidar Hvalvik, "A 'Sonderweg' for Israel. A Critical Examination of a Current Interpretation of Romans 11.25-27," *JSNT* 38 (1990) 87–107; other critical views include Davies, "Paul and the People of Israel," 228–29; Sänger, "Rettung der Heiden," 117–19. Moo, 725–26, provides an extensive bibliography on various sides of this issue, but the most comprehensive survey is provided by Keller, *Gottes Treue,* 2–67.

82 See particularly Davies, "Paul and the People of Israel," 23.

83 See Juan Escarfuller, "Repudiating Assimilation in Reading Romans 9–11," in Khiok-Khng Yeo, ed., *Navigating Romans through Cultures: Challenging Readings by Charting a New Course* (New York / London: T. & T. Clark International, 2004) 159: "Thus I read Paul's message in Romans 9–11 revealing for a Gentile social movement the role of solidarity with the oppressed as essential to God's ways of deliverance with Israel."

84 Wilk, *Bedeutung des Jesajabuches,* 67, correctly observes that the citation confirms 11:26a but not 11:25.

prophecy is thereby created, which in some ways sub-verts the original meaning of these texts in order to demonstrate the mystery of triumphant grace.[85] The underlining below marks which portions Paul chose to use.

Isa 59.20-21: καὶ ἥξει ἕνεκεν Σιων ὁ ῥυόμενος
καὶ ἀποστρέψει ἀσεβείας ἀπὸ Ιακωβ.
καὶ αὕτη αὐτοῖς ἡ παρ᾽ἐμοῦ διαθήκη, εἶπεν
κύριος·
τὸ πνεῦμα τὸ ἐμόν, ὅ ἐστιν ἐπὶ υοί,
καὶ τὰ ῥήματα, ἃ ἔδωκα εἰς τὸ στόμα σου. . . .
("And the deliverer will come for the sake of Zion,
and shall turn aside impious deeds from Jacob. And
this shall be my very own covenant with them, said
the Lord. My spirit, which is upon you, and my words
that I put into your mouth. . . .")

Isa 27:9: διὰ τοῦτο ἀφαιρεθήσεται ἡ ἀνομία
Ιακωβ,
καὶ τοῦτό ἐστιν ἡ εὐλογία αὐτοῦ,
ὅταν ἀφέλωμαι αὐτοῦ τὴν ἁμαρτίαν ("therefore
shall the lawlessness of Jacob be taken away, and this
is his blessing, when I shall have taken away his sin")

Paul's version: Ἥξει ἐκ Σιὼν ὁ ῥυόμενος,
ἀποστρέψει ἀσεβείας ἀπὸ Ιακώβ·
καὶ αὕτη αὐτοῖς ἡ παρ᾽ἐμοῦ διαθήκη,
ὅταν ἀφέλωμαι τὰς ἁμαρτίας αὐτῶν.

("The deliverer will come from Zion;
He will turn aside impious deeds from Jacob.
27/ And this, with them, [is] my very own covenant,
when I shall have taken away their sins.")

The connective "and" that opens the LXX form of Isa 59:20-21 is deleted by Paul in order to fit it into the new context, following the pattern of earlier citations that I have analyzed in Romans.[86] Much more significant is the change from ἕνεκεν Σιών ("for the sake of Zion") to ἐκ Σιών ("from Zion"). Since this change seems irrelevant for the traditionally doctrinal interpretation of Paul's argument, several important studies have suggested that he cites a hitherto undiscovered form of the Isaiah oracle.[87] When one takes the historical setting and rhetorical quality of Paul's letter into account, however, the reason that he would have had to make this change becomes clear.[88] For an audience with a Gentile Christian majority, and in a letter arguing for a cooperative mission to the barbarians in Spain, Isaiah's formulation that the Messiah came "for the sake of Zion"[89] would have been offensive and misleading. Paul does not want to undercut his contention that "there is no distinction between Jews and also Greeks. The same Lord is Lord of all, [bestowing] riches upon all who call upon him" (10:12). Paul's formulation "from Zion"[90] is consistent with the composite creed that opens this letter concerning Jesus "descended from David" (1:3) and with the reminder that Christ came from the Israelites (9:5) and

---

85 Gignac, *Romans 9–11*, 190–92.
86 See Stanley, *Scripture*, 166.
87 Berndt Schaller, "ΠΕΡΙ ΕΚ ΣΙΩΝ Ο ΡΥΟΜΕΝΟΣ: Zur Textgestalt von Jes 59:20f. in Röm 11:26f.," in A. Pietersma and C. Cox, eds., *De Septuaginta. Studies in Honour of John William Weavers on His Sixty-fifth Birthday* (Mississauga, Ontario: Beuben, 1984) 203, argues that the original wording of Isa 59 with ἕνεκεν would have served Paul's purpose more adequately because he is attempting to prove that Israel would not be excluded, and the christological issue of coming "from Zion" seems irrelevant. Schaller explains the change by an unlikely theory of textual corruption of εἰς Σιών ("to Zion") to ἐκ Σιών. This assessment of argumentative irrelevance is followed by Stanley, *Scripture*, 166–68; Koch, *Schrift*, 176; and Albl, *Scripture*, 167, who conclude that Paul is citing a previously altered adaptation of this oracle. Wilk,

Bedeutung des Jesajabuches, 39–40, follows Schaller, "Röm 11:26f.," 203–4, in the unlikely suggestion of textual corruption.
88 See Shum, *Paul's Use of Isaiah*, 236–45.
89 See BAGD (2000) 334 on ἕνεκεν as "because of, on account of, for the sake of." Wagner, *Heralds*, 284–86, translates ἕνεκεν Σιών as "to Zion" in order to correlate this alteration with the expectation of the Messiah coming (284) *"from* a restored Zion to bring deliverance to his people."
90 The phrase ἐκ Σιών also occurs in LXX Ps 13:7; 52:7; 109:2; Isa 2:3, and although he may have followed this tradition, as Hübner suggests in *Gottes Ich und Israel*, 115–56, Paul's reason for doing so needs to be explained.

that it was in "Zion" that Christ the stone of stumbling was laid (9:33).[91] Zion in this citation appears to be identical with the heavenly Jerusalem ("Jerusalem above," Gal 4:26),[92] the place from which Christ originated and was expected to descend at the parousia.[93] It is also generally recognized that although the Isaiah citation referred to Yahweh as ὁ ῥυόμενος ("the deliverer"), in Paul's context this refers to the Messiah, for whom this verb was used in 7:24 and in 1 Thess 1:10, "Jesus who delivers [Ἰησοῦν τὸν ῥυόμενον] us from the wrath to come."[94] The future verb "will come" is most naturally linked with the parousia,[95] which was the likely context in which Paul expected the miraculous conversion of that portion of Israel which had hitherto resisted the gospel out of hostile zeal. The citation thus explains the means by which Jacob's "impiety" will be overcome, namely, by the parousia of Christ.[96]

The deletion of καί ("and") at the beginning of the second line of the Isaiah citation has a much larger bearing on Paul's interpretation than was the case with the initial "and." It improves the parallelism between the first two lines of the citation and, as Christopher Stanley explains, it eliminates "the possibility that the second clause might be understood as following temporally or logically after the first. This view of the relation between the two clauses is consistent with a Christian interpretation that would see the divine promise to 'turn away ungodly deeds from Jacob' as being fulfilled in the very 'coming' of the 'Redeemer,' Jesus Christ."[97] In this case, however, it is probably the second coming of Christ that is in view rather than earlier references to Jesus' life and death in behalf of the ungodly (1:3-4; 3:24-25; 5:6-10; 8:34).[98]

Jacob's ἀσεβείας ("impious deeds")[99] in this new context must refer to Israel's "stumbling," "trespass," and "unfaith" in relation to the gospel message, as detailed in the preceding pericope. A list of such impious deeds by Jewish zealots is provided in 1 Thess 2:15-16: they "drove us out and displease God and all people by hindering us from speaking to the Gentiles that they may be saved." Although the wording of Rom 11:26 is derived without alteration from Isaiah, "impieties" also has an ironic connotation in Paul's context, not just because ἀσέβεια was condemned in 1:18 as a characteristically pagan abuse, but also because it was Israel's clinging to its own piety that led to the rejection of Christ. In this case, zealous piety had turned into its opposite, a profound insight that was prepared in 7:7-25 and 10:1-4. In the new context of Paul's discussion, the

91 See Aageson, "Scripture," 285; Murray, 2:99; Fitzmyer, 625; Wright, *Climax*, 250–51.
92 Schlier, 341; Haacker, 240.
93 Zahn, 526; Michel, 356; Wilckens, 2:256–57.
94 See, for example, Sanday and Headlam, 337; Kühl, 393; Kuss, 3:816; Wilckens, 2:256; Cranfield, 2:578; Hermann Lichtenberger, "ῥύομαι," *EDNT* 3 (1993) 215; Dunn, 2:682; Moo, 728; Byrne, 355; Kim, *Romans 9–11*, 139; Tobin, *Paul's Rhetoric*, 374. Highly improbable are the suggestions by Gaston in "Israel's Misstep," 143, and Christopher D. Stanley, "'The Redeemer Will Come ἐκ Σιών: Romans 11.26-27 Revisited," in C. A. Evans and J. A. Sanders, eds., *Paul and the Scriptures of Israel*, JSNTSup 83; Studies in Scripture in Early Judaism and Christianity 1 (Sheffield: Academic Press, 1993) 140–42, that the deliverer in this context is God rather than Christ.
95 See Cranfield, 2:578; Käsemann, 314; Wilckens, 2:256; Dunn, 2:682; Moo, 727–28; Theobald, 1:304–5; Schreiner, 619. Without providing evidence to the contrary, this link between the future verb and the parousia is denied by Kühl, 393, and

Schmidt, 199. Zeller, 199, proposes that the future verb be understood as a prophetic future that is already fulfilled, because Christ had already come from Zion and salvation through him could only come through justification by faith, which was already available for Jews. This strained translation is required only if one knows precisely the process Paul had in mind with the reference to the Messiah turning aside Jacob's "impiety."
96 Wilk, *Bedeutung des Jesajabuches*, 67.
97 Stanley, *Scripture*, 168; see also Wilk, *Bedeutung des Jesajabuches*, 57.
98 See Witherington, 276, in contrast to Wright's rejection of the parousia reference in *Climax*, 250.
99 Although recent commentators and translators render this as an abstract singular "impiety," the plural accusative form stands in parallel to the plural "sins" in 27b, as noted by Foerster, "ἀσεβής κτλ.," 189. Commentators who properly translate ἀσεβείας with plural forms include Meyer, 2:236; Weiss, 497; Lietzmann, 104; Kühl, 393; Schmidt, 197; Michel, 353; Barrett, 224; Cranfield, 2:572, 78; Zeller, 194.

Isaiah reference to the deliverer "causing a change"[100] or "converting"[101] Jacob's impieties describes the content of Israel's salvation. This develops the theme that was suggested in the last pericope regarding Paul's expectation that Israel's zeal would be transformed into its opposite at the end of time. Otfried Hofius aptly describes the implications of v. 26b-c, that "Israel will come to faith in the same way as Paul himself!"—that is, through an encounter with Christ the deliverer,[102] which in my view would turn the obtuseness of hostile zeal into urgent attachment to coexistence with former adversaries.

The third line in the oracle constructed by Paul out of the Isaiah passages defines this converting activity of the deliverer as ἡ παρ᾽ ἐμοῦ διαθήκη ("my very own covenant") that will be established between God and Israel. This is the second reference to "covenant" in Romans,[103] and in contrast to the plural form in 9:4 that refers to the various covenants made between God and the patriarchs in the past, this implies a final and ulti-

mate covenant to be enacted in the future.[104] It is possible that allusions to the "new covenant" of Jeremiah 31[105] or the Lord's Supper[106] are in view, but the focus here is on the future transformation of Israel.[107] Wilk makes a plausible case that the verb to be supplied for the ellipse in 27a should be future, in line with the two previous verbs in the future.[108] There is a binding promise in this line to be faithful to the covenant promise made to Israel, which confirms Paul's earlier argument in 11:1, 11, and 24 that God will not abandon his/her people.[109]

Since the continuation of the oracle from Isa 59:20-21 referred to the covenant renewal as consisting in the gift of the spirit and of divine messages, which would have been extraneous to Paul's argumentative purpose in this pericope, he substituted a line from Isa 27:9.[110] Since both oracles referred to removing the guilt from "Jacob," this substitution would have been viewed as acceptable according to the rules of Jewish exegesis.[111]

---

100 BAGD (2000) 123 (2), referring to *Ps. Sol.* 18.4 ("to divert the perceptive person from unintentional sins") and 1 Macc 3:8 ("turning away [ἀπέστρεψεν] wrath from Israel").

101 Gerhard Delling, "στρέφω κτλ.," *TDNT* 7 (1971) 720–21, shows that ἀποστρέφω frequently appears in the LXX with the connotation of "conversion," as in Jer 3:10; 23:22; 37:23; Ezek 3:19; 13:22; 14:6; 18:21, and that it carries this connotation in Rom 11:26.

102 Hofius, "Evangelium und Israel," 319–20, as cited and explained by Dunn, 2:683. Hofius is also cited with approval by Haacker, 241–42.

103 For orientation, see Behm, "διαθήκη," 129–30.

104 Erich Gräßer, *Der Alte Bund im Neuen. Exegetische Studien zur Israelfrage im Neuen Testament*, WUNT 35 (Tübingen: Mohr [Siebeck], 1985) 24–25, overlooks the future verbs in v. 26 that provide the context for interpreting "covenant" in v. 27, and argues on theological grounds that the "old covenant" is in view here, contrasting with a new covenant of justification by faith.

105 Murray, 2:99; Morris, 422; Fitzmyer, 625.

106 Harald Hegermann, "διαθήκη," *EDNT* 1 (1990) 301.

107 See Dunn, "Covenant Theology?" 17–18. Stanley, 169, argues that covenant "plays a surprisingly limited role in Paul's theology," because it is traditional in 1 Cor 11:25 and merely presupposed in 2 Cor 3:6 and Gal 4:24. This may be true, but Paul apparently felt the covenant concept was important for the

present context, because he had a choice of which material to excise. Christiansen, *Covenant*, 225–32, offers a more positive role for covenant in Romans, but interprets the Isaiah citation in 11:26b-27 "both as a fulfilled prophecy with a view back to the Christ events, indirectly stating that Old Testament prophecies of forgiveness are already fulfilled; and . . . as a guarantee for the future." Since there is no reference in the citation to past events and the "covenant" is dependent on a future removal of Israel's zealous sins by divine action, this is a different covenant than the one at Sinai, and Christiansen's elaborate theological structure collapses.

108 Wilk, *Bedeutung des Jesajabuches*, 57.

109 See Christiansen, *Covenant*, 227–28, for the evidence that Paul viewed Israel's covenant as still valid. She counters the view of Wright, *Climax*, 241–43, that Israel's covenant is absorbed into the Christian covenant.

110 See Koch, *Schrift*, 176–77; Wilk, *Bedeutung des Jesajabuches*, 58. Wagner, *Heralds*, 294, suggests that the citation of Isa 27:9 "keeps the focus on the *fact* of Israel's redemption rather than pausing to consider its *effects*" (italics in original). In contrast, Stanley, *Scripture*, 169–70, believes that "another interpreter" may have been responsible for combining the two passages because of the many alleged disparities between both passages and the traditional view of Paul's theology.

111 Dunn, 2:684, citing Plag, *Israel's Wege*, 50–52; see also Wagner, *Heralds*, 293–94.

The citation begins with the temporal particle ὅταν ("when, whenever"), which, in coordination with an aorist subjunctive verb as in this case, implies an action that must precede that of the preceding clause.[112] Until Israel's sins are removed, the final covenant with God will not yet have been enacted. The translation of the aorist subjunctive form, ἀφέλωμαι, is usually placed in the present, "when I take away their sins,"[113] but it more properly should be translated as a future, following the future indicative verbs in the first two lines of the citation. The citation refers to a condition that must be fulfilled before the "covenant" can be restored: "when I shall have taken away their sins."[114] Paul alters the singular "sin" in the Isaiah oracle to the plural "sins," which is interpreted by some as evidence that the citation is inconsistent with Paul's theology in earlier chapters of Romans.[115] However, the plural form was required to refer not to sin in general but rather to particular acts of violent opposition against the gospel and its messengers on the part of zealous Jews. That not all Jews were in view is also confirmed by Paul's change of Isaiah's wording, αὐτοῦ τὴν ἁμαρτίαν ("his, i.e. Jacob's sin"), which would refer to the sins of Israel as a whole, to τὰς ἁμαρτίας αὐτῶν ("their, i.e. the zealous Jews' sins"). The shift in the location of the possessive pronoun to the more natural spot at the end of line 4 is also probably due to Paul's rhetorical acumen.[116]

The verb ἀφαιρέω ("take away, put away, cut off"), which appears here for the only time in the Pauline letters, was used in the LXX for removing sins through atonement rituals. The same formulation appears in

Heb 10:4, which is based on OT formulations such as Num 14:18, the Lord is merciful, "removing (ἀφαιρῶν) transgressions and iniquities and sins"; in Lev 10:17, the atonement ritual is required so that "you might take away (ἀφέλητε) the sin of the congregation." This is usually explained as "forgiveness of sins,"[117] but fanatical zeal does not yield to the promise of forgiveness, which in any case was already sufficiently available in Judaism. Instead, Paul's expectation is that zealous violence will be overcome by the return of the deliverer, which will result in the cessation of such sins. It seems that Paul hopes that such violent acts will be "taken away" just as his own sinful violence against early Christ believers was brought to an end by his encounter with the risen Christ. Consistent with the thesis in 1:16, Paul trusts the power of evangelical persuasion, because when it becomes evident to all that the Crucified One is the designated Messiah, zealous violence to ensure his coming will no longer seem appropriate. Repentance and forgiveness will only be possible when the self-righteous madness of zealous rage is broken by divine power.

■ 28 The theological explanation of the mystery that continues to the end of the pericope is opened with an elegant *paromoiosis*, as noted in the analysis above, whose asyndeton indicates the beginning of a new section.[118] Since each term in this rhetorical form is multivalent, the precise connotation intended by Paul has to be inferred from the context as well as from the internal logic of the *paromoiosis* itself. Interpreters agree that the subject is the currently unbelieving portion of Israel,[119] whose "impiety" and "sins" according to my interpreta-

112 BAGD (2000) 731 (β).

113 For example, Cranfield, 2:572; Dunn, 2:676.

114 BDF §318, 333, 379, 382. BAGD (2000) 731 shows that ὅταν followed by the aorist subjunctive refers to an action that "precedes that of the main clause."

115 See Stanley, *Scripture*, 170, who takes this disparity as evidence that Paul is employing "pre-Pauline Jewish or Christian usage."

116 See Koch, *Schrift*, 109, following the rule stated in Kühner and Gerth, *Grammatik*, 1:619, and BDF §284 that the possessive pronouns are normally placed "after an arthrous substantive."

117 Zahn, 526; Meyer, 2:237; Cranfield, 2:579; Wilckens, 2:257; Dunn, 2:684; Stuhlmacher, 172; Moo, 729; Davies, "Paul and the People of Israel," 26; Christiansen, *Covenant*, 225–27; Gräßer, *Alte Bund*

im Neuen, 22–23. However, since "forgiveness of sins" was readily available for both Jews and Christians, making it more available was ineffectual as a means to overcome zealous violence. This conventional explanation is ill suited for the Isaiah citation, which speaks of the removal of sinful actions. Morris, 422, is more on track: "God will take such action as will remove sins from the scene."

118 See BDF §463; Güting and Mealand, *Asyndeton*, 14.

119 See, for example, Weiss, 499; Michel, 357; Fitzmyer, 625; Moo, 730.

tion of the preceding citation consisted in zealous hostility against the gospel. It is significant that Paul begins with κατὰ μὲν τὸ εὐαγγέλιον ("on the one hand with regard to the gospel"), because resistance to its proclamation and acceptance is the result of the "obtuseness . . . on a part of Israel," in the words of the first component of the mystery (11:25). In this context "the gospel" refers to "the proclamation of salvation"[120] that evokes the obtuse enmity of Israel. That zealous Israelites thereby make themselves into God's "enemies" by warring against the gospel and its proclaimers requires an active[121] rather than a passive[122] definition of ἐχϑροί ("enemies"). This reference to enmity against God is consistent with 5:10 and 8:7, and, as Schmidt points out, there are no NT allusions to "enemies" as hated by God,[123] which means that the currently popular compromise that Paul intended a fusion between hating God and being hated by God[124] is unsupportable. There is, however, a multivalence in the reference to their being enemies δι᾽ ὑμᾶς ("on account of you") because, while the mystery makes plain that Israel's obtuseness provides time for the conversion of the "fullness of the Gentiles,"[125] the reason that zealous Jews rejected the gospel was precisely because it placed Gentiles and Jews on the same footing before God. Zealous resistance against the gospel was directed against Gentiles and all who would accept their polluting presence in the realm of God. Their enmity was thus in both directions "on your account," motivated by hostility against Gentiles while at the same time providing time for the Gentile mission.

The second half of the *paromoiosis* begins with the parallel formulation κατὰ δὲ τὴν ἐκλογήν ("on the other hand in regard to election"), referring not to the election of Christian converts as in 8:33 but of Israel as in 9:11 and 11:8. As Jeremias observed, there is an incongruity in this use of the preposition κατά as compared with that of v. 28a, because it has a causal connotation in v. 28c, "on account of their election,"[126] but this is easily accommodated within the structure of the *paromoiosis*, which requires parallel prepositions. There is no indication in this highly compressed formulation that Paul wishes to call attention to the "character of God's choice of Israel as a free and gracious choice,"[127] because the context of this proof involves the question of whether God has now rejected Israel (11:1-2) and whether Israel in fact will be saved (11:26). Thus it is the status and not the quality of Israel's election that is in view here.[128] The prepositional phase in the expression ἀγαπητοὶ διὰ τοὺς πατέρας can therefore be translated exactly parallel with the first member of the *paromoiosis* as "beloved on account of the fathers."[129] In the OT and related literature, God's love for the patriarchs (e.g., Deut 10:15; 33:12; Isa 41:8; Josephus *Ant.* 1.3.9), for Israel's king (2 Sam 12:24; Neh 13:26), for those who seek wisdom (Wis 7:28) and righteousness (Prov 15:9), and for Israel as a whole (e.g., Deut 7:7, 9-13; Ps 127:2; Isa 63:9; Hos 11:1; 14:4; Prov 3:12; *Ps. Sol.* 18:4) is an important theme. Wischmeyer and Haacker have shown that this remains a crucial axiom for Paul.[130] With few exceptions,[131] such love has nothing to do with the pecu-

120 Käsemann, 315; see also Barrett, 324; Schlier, 341; Michel, 357. Cranfield, 2:580, extends the definition of "gospel" too widely for the present context, including the preaching by Jesus himself and the events of Christ's death and resurrection.

121 Zahn, 526; Lagrange, 287; Kühl, 394; Schmidt, 201; Schlier, 341; Stuhlmacher, "Interpretation," 564-55; Hofius, "Evangelium und Israel," 321; Fitzmyer, 625; Haacker, 242.

122 Meyer, 2:239; Weiss, 499; Sanday and Headlam, 337; Lietzmann, 106; Foerster, "ἐχϑρός, ἔχϑρα," 814; Kuss, 3:816; Cranfield, 2:580; Dunn, 2:693; Wilckens, 2:257.

123 Schmidt, 201; also Wolter, "ἐχϑρός," 93-94.

124 Käsemann, 315; Dunn, 2:685; Moo, 84; Byrne, 356; Schreiner, 625. The problematic implication of this compromise is visible in Jülicher, 307, who imagines

that Paul depicts a struggle between God's hatred and love, which was rightly rejected by Schmidt, 201.

125 Meyer, 2:239; Weiss, 499-500; Cranfield, 2:580; Murray, 2:100; Fitzmyer, 625; Moo, 731.

126 Jeremias, "Römer 11.25-36," 202.

127 Dunn, 2:685.

128 Kühl, 394; Barrett, 225; Murray, 2:101; Zeller, 200; Moo, 732.

129 Dunn, 2:685, claims that "most" exegetes recognize that this phrase should not be translated in an identical manner; he prefers "for the sake of the fathers," which opens the door to the question of the quality of their election.

130 Haacker, "Evangelium," 71, as cited by Dunn, 2:685; Wischmeyer, "ΑΓΑΠΗΤΟΣ," 477-78.

131 *2 Bar.* 84.10 advises prayer for God's mercy, "that

liar virtues of Israel or the patriarchs, but is rather an expression of divine choice, pure and simple. This was Paul's view, in any event, as expressed in 9:11, that Isaac's descendants are beloved as God's elect, although "they were not yet born and had done nothing either good or bad, in order that God's purpose of election might continue, not because of works but because of his call." In support of this view, Paul cited Mal 9:13, "Jacob I loved, but Esau I hated." What Paul maintains in 11:28 is that this love for the patriarchs continues for their descendants, the Israel of the present time. As he goes on to say in the next verse, this choice is "without regret"; it stands firm no matter what enmity Israel currently expresses against God's Messiah and his people.

■ **29** This verse declaring that "the gifts and the call of God are without regret" has been viewed as the summary of Rom 9–11 as a whole,[132] yet very few studies have been devoted to its clarification.[133] Joseph Sievers points to the decisive contribution of Karl Barth in overturning the consensus that the believers were the sole heirs of these promises. In *Church Dogmatics* he argued that this verse expresses the abiding commitment of God to all of God's beloved Jewish people, whether they believe in the gospel or not.[134] Daniel Harrington reflects the newly emerging consensus of Roman Catholic exegesis when he concludes that this verse "is Paul's endorsement of the continuing nature of God's election of Israel, even of those Israelites who have refused to accept the gospel."[135] The exegetical details confirm this assessment. In the context of Paul's statement about Israel's election in v. 28, for which v. 29 provides the reason as indicated by γάρ ("for"), both the gifts and the call of God are directed to Israel.[136] There is a well-grounded consensus that τὰ χαρίσματα ("the gifts") refers back to the formal list of Israel's divinely bestowed attributes in 9:4-5.[137] Although some have suggested that the following words, καὶ ἡ κλῆσις τοῦ θεοῦ ("and the call of God"), constitute a hendiadys meaning the "benefits of calling,"[138] or refer to God's calling as the most important of the gifts,[139] it is likely that the noun κλῆσις ("calling") that appears here for the only time in Romans evokes the verb καλέω ("to call") that was used in connection with Paul's earlier argument that what God called the "the seed of Abraham" came through Isaac and thus constitutes the children of promise (9:7, 11, 24, 25, 26). Although in other contexts Paul employs this noun in reference to the calling of Gentile and Jewish believers (Phil 3:14; 2 Thess 1:11), it is likely that God's specific election of Israel is intended here. This is suggested by the formulation of the preceding verse, referring to Israel's ἐκλογή ("election") on account of the patriarchs.[140]

The adjective ἀμεταμέλητος is usually translated "irrevocable," which implies a legal axiom that cannot be

he not reckon the multitude of your sins, but remember the integrity of the fathers." Philo *Spec.* 4.181 argues, in contrast, that the election of the patriarchs reflected the "righteousness and virtue shown by the founders of the race."

132 Kühl, 394; see Joseph Sievers, "'God's Gifts and Call Are Irrevocable': The Interpretation of Romans 11:29 and Its Uses," *SBLSP* (1997) 338.

133 See Sievers, "Romans 11:29 and Its Uses," 338–39; also Joseph Sievers, "A History of the Interpretation of Romans 11:29," *ASE* 14.2 (1997) 381–442. The only articles devoted to this verse, prior to Sievers's studies, are Ceslas Spicq, "*ΑΜΕΤΑΜΕΛΗΤΟΣ* dans Rom XI,29," *RB* 67 (1960) 210–19, and Alberto Vaccari, "Irrevocabilità dei favori divini. Nota a commente di Rom.11,29," in vol. 1 of P. Hennequin et al., eds., *Mélanges Eugène Tisserant*, StT 231–33 (Vatican City: Vatican Apostolic Library, 1964) 437–42. Kühl, 395, and Ziesler, 286–87, pass over this verse without comment.

134 Karl Barth, *Church Dogmatics* (Edinburgh: T. & T.

Clark, 1936–69) II.2.303; cited by Sievers, "Romans 11:29 and Its Uses," 427–30.

135 Daniel J. Harrington, *Paul on the Mystery of Israel* (Collegeville, Minn: Liturgical Press, 1992) 64.

136 Haacker, 245, properly rejects the proposal by Karl Heim (*Vorlesung von 1924/25*, 188–89) that this verse refers to Gentiles as well as Jews, a contention found also in Bonda, *One Purpose*, 192–93, and Dunn, 2:686.

137 Weiss, 500; Schlier, 342; Kuss, 3:817; Michel, 358; Cranfield, 2:581; Wilckens, 2:258; Dunn, 2:686; Moo, 732; Haacker, 244; Theobald, 1:306; Schreiner, 626.

138 Cranfield, 2:581, cites Calvin as advocating this view; Käsemann, 316, appears to concur.

139 Michel, 358; Schmidt, 202.

140 Moo, 732, observes that κλῆσις ("call") is cognate with ἐκλογή ("election") in v. 28.

repealed,[141] but the basic meaning is "without regret,"[142] as in 2 Cor 7:10, the only other use of this term in the OT or NT: "repentance that leads to salvation and brings no regret." The classical parallels are mostly personal rather than judicial, as, for example, Aesop, "but his coming was without regret" (τοῦ δὲ ἀμεταμελήτως ἐλθόντος, *Fabulae* 83.2.6) or Plato, "of a deed done without regret" (ἀμεταμέλητον, *Leg.* 866e).[143] The formulation thus relates to the rhetorical question in 11:1, whether God has "rejected his people," and reaffirms the continued status of "beloved [by God] on account of the fathers" in 11:28. That the God of biblical faith was in fact frequently depicted as changing his mind[144] provides the background for this denial that she had done so with regard to Israel's distinctive gifts and calling. Although God was free to withdraw such privileges, while humans often come to regret and then to renege on their gifts and commitments, God's faithfulness remains firm.[145] In the end, despite the current rejection of the divinely designated Messiah by a large portion of Israel, the divine gifts and calling will achieve their intended purpose of salvation.

■ **30** The carefully contrived chiasm of vv. 30-31 is embedded in a ὥσπερ ("just as") . . . οὕτως ("so also") argumentative structure that moves from what is known and accepted by the audience to the logical inference that Paul wishes to demonstrate.[146] The exact parallelism between the elements of this figure serves the argumentative purpose of showing that just as the believing community was formerly disobedient and now has received God's merciful salvation, so also Israel's current disobedience will be overcome by divine mercy. A conclusion that the Gentile audience might otherwise be inclined to resist thus can be avoided only at the price of denying their own experience of conversion. Ulrich Wilckens has provided a lucid display of the parallelism between these antithetical elements of once/now, you/them, disobedience/receiving mercy and the concluding dative phrases that include yet another antithesis between disobedience and mercy:[147]

ὥσπερ γὰρ	ὑμεῖς	ποτε	ἠπειθήσατε	τῷ θεῷ
νῦν δὲ	ἠλεήθητε	τῇ τούτων ἀπειθείᾳ,		
οὕτως καὶ	οὗτοι	νῦν	ἠπείθησαν	τῷ ὑμετέρῳ ἐλέει,
ἵνα καὶ		αὐτοὶ	νῦν	ἐλεηθῶσιν·
For just as	you	once	were disobedient	to God
		but now	you have been shown mercy	
	so also	they	now	because of their disobedience, have been disobedient because of the mercy you received,
in order that	they	now		may also be shown mercy.

That Paul refers to the formerly unconverted status of believers with the verb "to be disobedient" was somewhat inappropriate for Gentiles who did not have the Torah to disobey, but the parallelism with Israel's disobedience required its use on rhetorical grounds.[148]

Moreover, the earlier argument of Romans provided adequate precedence for the use of ἀπειθέω ("to disobey") here. Gentiles had the law written on their hearts (2:15) and inherit Adam's "disobedience" (παρακοή, 5:19), while Gentiles as well as Jews who "do

141 Ceslas Spicq, "ἀμεταμέλητος," *TLNT* 1 (1994) 92–94.
142 BAGD (2000) 53.
143 See further examples in Spicq, "ἀμεταμέλητος," 93.
144 For example, Gen 6:6-7; Exod 32:14; Deut 32:26; 1 Sam 15:11, 35; Jer 18:8, 10; 26:13; Jonah 3:10; see also Dunn, 2:686, who denies that this is the appropriate context for interpreting ἀμεταμέλητος.
145 Zeller, 200; Haacker, 244.
146 See Weiss, 500–502; Cranfield, 2:582–86; Wilckens, 2:259.
147 Wilckens, 2:259; see also Tachau, *Einst,* 87, 110–12, 133.
148 See Cranfield, 2:582–85; Käsemann, 316; Moo, 733.

not obey the truth" will receive divine "wrath and fury" (2:8).[149]

To describe the salvation of believers as a matter of receiving mercy returns to what Barrett has called the "key-note"[150] for this third proof, which received extensive development in 9:15-18 beginning with a citation from Exod 33:19 and ending with the claim that God has mercy on whomever God wills. God's mercy is absolutely sovereign, which means that salvation is entirely a matter of grace rather than any form of human achievement. In 9:23-24 Paul shows that Gentile believers join with Jewish converts as "vessels of mercy" and in 15:9 he returns to this theme in explaining that Christ's ministry aimed at Gentiles coming to "glorify God for his mercy." The ironic exchange in this formulation is that the message of divine mercy, which overcame the disobedience of Gentiles, could be preached only because Israel's rejection of the gospel granted time for the Gentile mission. Thus the Roman audience's reception of mercy came τῇ τούτων ἀπειθείᾳ ("because of their disobedience"), that is, the disobedience of Israel with regard to the gospel as in the "mystery" of 11:25. The implication is that Gentile believers should be thankful for rather than critical of Israel's temporary disobedience. Here Paul seeks to reverse the hostility that sectarian believers ordinarily feel toward those who reject their message and to transform it into grateful respect.[151]

■ **31** The explanation of Israel's disbelief on grounds of its benefit to Gentiles is continued in the "so also" portion of the chiasm. The debate about whether the dative phrase τῷ ὑμετέρῳ ἐλέει ("because of your mercy") is attached to the immediately preceding verb ἠπείθησαν ("they have been disobedient") or with the subsequent ἵνα ("so that") clause has been resolved by Siegert, Dunn, and others on the basis of following the logic of

the chiastic rhetoric and taking the phrase as a dative of advantage: "so also have they now been disobedient *because of the mercy you received*."[152] Israel's rejection of the gospel is thus explained not on the basis of some alleged incorrigibility on the part of Israel, as Gentile prejudice was likely to assume, but rather for the sake of extending mercy to the Gentiles themselves. Once again Paul reverses the trajectory of cultural hostility and bias by showing the benefit Israel's disobedience provided for the Gentile audience. The logic of the chiastic οὕτως καί ("so also") clause is ineluctable because the preceding clause describing the Gentiles' conversion was rooted so deeply in their experience; the argumentative inference in the somewhat more problematic second clause derives its force from the clause that the Gentiles have already accepted as true. Paul's intent is not to "shock his fellow Jews into a recognition" that what they understood as "obedience" to the Torah "is in fact disobedience to the word of faith," as Dunn formulates the matter,[153] but to overcome Gentile bias. This explains why the dative expression "because of the mercy you received" was placed at the point of emphasis at the end of 11:31a. Israel's disobedience served the cause of "*your*" salvation, by which the Gentile converts in the Roman congregation who were most likely to feel contempt for Jews are directly addressed. The demonstrative rhetoric of Romans that concentrates on honor and advantage surfaces with particular clarity in this brilliant chiasm.

The purpose clause that follows the chiasm elaborates the final point in the mystery of 11:25-26, that "all Israel will be saved." Israel will receive salvation in exactly the form that the Gentiles have already received, as "mercy" that they will not have earned but which places all humans on an appropriately equal level before God.[154] The invidious distinctions of human honor and shame

149 See Rudolf Bultmann, "ἀπειθέω," *TDNT* 6 (1968) 11; Peter Bläser, "ἀπειθέω," *EDNT* 1 (1990) 118–19.
150 Barrett, 185.
151 The opposite implication is imposed by Dunn, 2:695, that the "Jewish assumption of monopoly on divine mercy and of gentile disobedience did *not* disqualify from mercy, and, irony of ironies, what did 'qualify' the Gentiles was *Jewish* disobedience." (Italics in original.)

152 Siegert, *Argumentation*, 174; Dunn, 2:688. See also Schlier, 343; Käsemann, 316; Wilckens, 2:260; BDF §196. Advocates of attaching τῷ ὑμετέρῳ ἐλέει ("because of your mercy") to the subsequent "so that" clause include Sanday and Headlam, 338; Lagrange, 288.
153 Dunn, 2:695.
154 See Sänger, "Rettung der Heiden," 110–11.

will have been overcome along with claims of cultural superiority. Grace alone will unite the varied children of Adam once the legacy of his fall is finally overcome. The final "now" in the threefold series stands in peculiar tension with this futuristic expectation, which may well have been a factor in its deletion in several textual traditions. I believe this reference to the eschatological present[155] lends urgent emphasis to the missionary project that the letter is currently proposing for the support of the Roman house and tenement churches. In cooperating in the Spanish mission by which the circle of the known world would be completed and the "fullness of the Gentiles" brought into the faith, the stage would be set for Israel's conversion, according to the mystery Paul has announced. The time for involvement in this historically culminating project is "now," the urgent eschatological present ordained by the Spirit.

■ **32** The forceful epigram that concludes this pericope employs the terms of the preceding chiasm, "disobedience" and "mercy," while stressing their universal scope for "all" persons. The strikingly dramatic verb συγκλείω appears here with the meaning "to confine to specific limits, imprison,"[156] as in Gal 3:22-23: "But the scripture confined (συνέκλεισεν) all things to sin, that what was promised to faith in Jesus Christ might be given to those who believe. Now before faith came, we were imprisoned under the law, kept under restraint until faith should be revealed."[157] When followed by the prepositional phrase εἰς ἀπείθειαν ("to disobedience"), this verb is employed in a typical manner to express the idea of confining someone in something.[158] As Jeremias observed, the Septuagintal parallels have this same structure, as, for example, Ps 30:9, "you have not confined me into the hands of the enemy" (οὐ συνέκλεισάς με εἰς χεῖρας ἐχθροῦ; see also Ps 77:50, 62; Amos 1:6).[159] The earlier

argument of Romans provides the basis for this paradoxical claim of divine imprisonment within the consequences of sin: the threefold reiteration of God "delivered them" to the web of sin in 1:24, 26, 28; the proof that all humans are under the power of sin in 3:9-23; the universal reign of sin because each person repeats Adam's fall in 5:12-14; the divine creation of "vessels of wrath" whose voluntary involvement in sin provokes the patience of God in 9:20-22; the creation of a stone of stumbling that will make Israel fall in 9:33, along with the claim that Israel was responsible for rejecting the gospel in 10:16-21; the argument in 11:7-25 that God made Israel's heart obtuse so it would reject the gospel; and finally the mystery in 11:25-26 that Israel's obtuseness served the purpose of Gentile conversion.[160]

With this climactic reference to God's mercy, sounding the keynote of the third proof for the ninth and final time, Paul not only expresses the essence of the gospel but also makes clear that no remnant of claims of cultural superiority or personal entitlement through piety, social status, or other achievement can remain legitimate.[161] In the Roman context, mercy was reserved for the worthy among captives and vanquished enemies. Nowhere in the ancient world, outside of this text, was mercy granted in so indiscriminate and impartial a manner to "all." The reduplication of πᾶς ("all, i.e., all persons") in this verse is the climactic expression of one of the most important themes of the letter, salvation for all, found in 1:5, 7, 8, 16, 18; 2:9-10; 3:9, 12, 19, 20, 22, 23; 4:11, 16; 5:12, 18; 6:3; 8:14; 9:5, 6, 7, 17; 10:11-13, 18, 26.[162]

As Dunn observes, this extraordinary epigram manages in only twelve words to sum up what he takes to be "the principal themes of the whole letter,"[163] climaxing

155 Käsemann, 316; Dunn, 2:695; Moo, 735; Neuhäusler, "Entscheidende Augenblick," 4–8.
156 BAGD (2000) 952.
157 See Betz, *Galatians*, 175.
158 BAGD (2000) 952, with examples of the verb with εἰς in Polybius *Hist.* 3.63.3; Diodorus Siculus *Hist.* 2.34.5; 19.19.8, etc.
159 Jeremias, "Römer 11.25-36," 203.
160 See also the reviews of the preceding argument in Godet, 415; Schlier, 343; Cranfield, 1:386–87; Dunn, 2:688–89.
161 See Davies, "Paul and the People of Israel," 30–38.
162 See Byrne, 356; Mussner, "Heil für alle," 213–14; Marianne Meye Thompson, "'Mercy upon All': God as Father in the Epistle to the Romans," in S. K. Soderlund and N. T. Wright, eds., *Romans the People of God: Essays in Honor of Gordon D. Fee on the Occasion of His 65th Birthday* (Grand Rapids / Cambridge: Eerdmans, 1999) 215–16.
163 Dunn, 2:696.

in the "final reconciliation of the whole world to God through the triumph of mercy."[164] The expectation of universal salvation in this verse is indisputable, regardless of the logical problems it poses for systematic theologians. What Dunn and other commentators fail to observe, however, is how this doctrinal summary serves the purpose of overcoming cultural biases so as to clear the way to support the Spanish mission as the means of this global reconciliation.[165] If God confines all to sin, then there is no basis for superiority claims, and if she has mercy on all, then the conversion of other groups serves the interests of all.

---

164 Ibid., 697; see also Achtemeier, 189; Kim, *Romans 9–11*, 139.

165 See Wright, *Climax*, 251: "These themes . . . result in the clear message to the Roman church: here, and nowhere else, is the basis of the mission of the church, the mission in which Paul is engaged and for which he now enlists their support."

11

The Tenth Pericope

Conclusion: A Hymn on the Majesty of God as Revealed in the Mysterious Plan of Global Salvation

33/ O depth
   of riches
      and[a] of wisdom
         and of knowledge of God!
   How unfathomable his judgments,
      and inscrutable his ways!
34/ For "who has known the mind of the Lord,
      or who has become his counselor?"
35/ "Or who gave first to him,
      so he shall receive recompense?"

36/ Because from him
      and through him
         and unto him
            [are] all things,
               to him be the glory forever! Amen.

a   The absence of καί ("and") in 321 lat may be a dictation mistake, but it enhances the coherence of the hymn by attaching "riches" to wisdom and knowledge, i.e., that God is rich in wisdom and knowledge.

Analysis

The poetic quality of this composition has been widely accepted, suggesting a hymn of nine or ten lines with triple structuring within several lines.[1] The Nestle-Aland 26th and 27th editions print the hymn out in strophic form, placing the words "and wisdom and knowledge of God" into a separate line that results in a ten-line hymn. The recent investigation of early Christian hymns by Gunter Kennel prefers for Rom 11:33-36 the vague category of a "universal text" with a doxological function, but most of the criteria he develops to define hymnic material are present in the original form of this passage.[2] The anomaly in this hymn appears not to have been taken into account by Fennel, and it is usually overlooked by commentators. The scriptural citations in vv. 34-35 are not only unparalleled in hymnic material, but their removal produces a more coherent hymn to God in which the fourth line beginning with "because" provides a rationale for the foregoing.

<11:33> Ὦ βάθος πλούτου καὶ σοφίας καὶ γνώσεως θεοῦ·

ὡς ἀνεξεραύνητα τὰ κρίματα αὐτοῦ
καὶ ἀνεξιχνίαστοι αἱ ὁδοὶ αὐτοῦ.
   <11:36> ὅτι ἐξ αὐτοῦ καὶ δι᾽ αὐτοῦ καὶ εἰς
   αὐτὸν τὰ πάντα·
αὐτῷ ἡ δόξα εἰς τοὺς αἰῶνας, ἀμήν.

The removal of the citations produces a hymn in the style of ellipsis that concentrates entirely on God. Two eloquent exclamations, beginning with identical sounds, ὦ ("O!") and ὡς ("How!"), open the hymn. The threefold attributes of God in the first line are echoed in the fourth line by the threefold formula of "from . . . through . . . for him."[3] The two adjectives in the second exclamation have the poetic alpha-privative and display *parachesis* in their similar sounds: ἀνεξεραύνητα and ἀνεξιχνίαστοι ("unsearchable" and "inscrutable").[4] Lines 2 and 3 end with αὐτοῦ ("his"), which is reduplicated by the end of the next line. The hymn concludes with a poetic confession and doxology. The confessional line (11:35) has a threefold elaboration concerning the origin of τὰ πάντα ("all things"), alluding back to the expression ἐπὶ πάντων ("over all") in the rhetorical counterpart to this section, 11:5. The doxology to God

1   Käsemann, 318, refers to Norden's *Agnostos Theos*, 240ff. Michel, 354, refers to Harder, *Gebet*, 51–55, 79ff. Cranfield, 2:589, refers to Bornkamm, *Experience*, 105–11. See also Deichgräber, *Gotteshymnus*, 61–64; Gloer, "Homologies and Hymns," 123; Johnson, *Function*, 164–68.

2   Gunter Kennel, *Frühchristliche Hymnen? Gattungskri-

tische Studien zur Frage nach den Liedern der frühen Christenheit*, WMANT 71 (Neukirchen-Vluyn: Neukirchener Verlag, 1995) 281.

3   See Deichgräber, *Gotteshymnus*, 62. On the triadic structure of the hymn, see Tobin, *Paul's Rhetoric*, 377.

4   These distinctive six-syllable adjectives match

in 11:36 is the counterpart to the doxology to Christ as God in 9:5. Since the removal of the citations produces a hymn of superior coherence and stylistic conformity, it is likely that they were added at a later stage.[5] Since there are no explicitly Christian references in the hymn, it could well have arisen in a Hellenistic Jewish setting,[6] but its citation in this critical location of Paul's letter strongly suggests that it was known and used by believers in Rome. It has also been suggested that Paul himself is the author of the original hymn,[7] but the lack of explicitly Christian elements and the indications of later redaction make this seem unlikely.[8]

The insertion of the citations from Isaiah and Job in vv. 34-35 is likely to have come from Paul's hand, transforming the original hymn into a suitable climax for the third proof. The choice and redaction of the citations are very skillfully accomplished,[9] matching Pauline citations earlier in the letter. The triple elaboration of the first exclamation provides a chiastic series that is replicated in reverse sequence by the three questions of vv. 34-35a.[10] "Riches . . . wisdom . . . knowledge" are taken up in reverse order by the scriptural citations describing divine knowledge in v. 34a, wisdom in v. 34b, and riches in v. 35.[11] The techniques of editing biblical texts to fit Paul's argumentative purpose are visible not only in the choice of these citations but also in the manner of their redaction, analyzed in the exegesis below. There are solid reasons, therefore, to infer that Paul himself was responsible for the insertion of the citations, in order to transform the hymn into a suitable climax of the argument in the third proof.

The thought progression in the redacted hymn comprises three phases: the acclamation of the greatness of God, the rhetorical questions about the incapacity of humans to grasp such majesty, and the ascription of glory to God alone.[12] The passage thus leads to a suitable rectification of the human pretension and unwillingness to glorify God as developed in 1:18-25, and of cultural feelings of superiority and prejudice against others that Paul counters in 9:20; 10:2-3; 11:20, 25.

There are Jewish hymns probably deriving in part from worship settings that share some of the characteristics of the original hymn in Rom 11:33-36. Michael Lattke has surveyed a large number of such hymns and hymnic fragments, including *1 En.* 84.2-3 that addresses God as creator:[13]

> Blessed are you, O Great King,
> you are mighty in your greatness.
> O Lord of all the creation of heaven,
> King of kings and God of the whole world.
> Your authority and kingdom abide forever and ever;
> and your dominion throughout all the generations of generations;
> all the heavens are your throne forever,
> and the whole earth is your footstool forever and ever and ever. . . .
> Everything you know, you see, and you hear;
> nothing exists that can be hidden from you, for everything you expose.

ἀμεταμέλητα ("without regret") in 11:29, lending a sense of grandeur to the final sections of this proof.

5   The hymn without the citations focuses entirely on God's attributes with no gesture of human response, no human involvement. The LXX citations baldly introduce human responses vis-à-vis God's greatness and raise the question about whether God would require a counselor or recompense.

6   Deichgräber, *Gotteshymnus,* 62–63; Johnson, *Function,* 172. Among Hellenistic elements in the hymn are the acclamation ὦ ("O!"), which occurs only here in the NT and never in the LXX, because there is no Hebrew equivalent, according to Michel, 360.

7   Bornkamm, *Experience,* 105; Käsemann, 318; Cran-

field, 2:589; Dunn, 2:698; Fitzmyer, 633; Byrne, 59; Moo, 740.

8   See Gloer, "Homologies and Hymns," 123.

9   For example, the citations are not introduced with standard formulas such as "as it is written," which would destroy the hymnic quality; the citations are well embedded in the text.

10   Although the chiasmus was noted by Bengel, *Gnomon,* 134, Käsemann, 319, refers to Günther Bornkamm, *Experience,* 107, and Deichgräber, *Gotteshymnus,* 62. See also Jeremias, "Chiasmus in den Paulusbriefen," *ZNW* 49 (1958) 145–56; Lund, *Chiasmus,* 222.

11   Harvey, *Listening,* 203; Siegert, *Argumentation,* 178.

12   See Louw, 2:118; Tobin, *Paul's Rhetoric,* 377.

13   Michael Lattke, *Hymnus. Materialien zu einer*

The Hebrew hymn that concludes 1QS[14] contains some thematic links with the redacted form of the hymn in Rom 11:33-36:

> Blessed be you, my God, who opens the heart of your servant to knowledge! Establish all his deeds in justice, and raise up the son of your handmaid to stand everlastingly in your presence. . . . You have taught all knowledge and all that exists is so by your will. Beyond you there is no-one to oppose your counsel, to understand any of your holy thoughts, or to gaze into the abyss of your mysteries, to fathom all your marvels or the strength of your might. Who can endure your glory? (1QS 11:15b-20)

Thomas Tobin cites the thanksgiving hymn from Qumran as "the most enlightening passage for understanding Rom 11:33-36" because it contains three rhetorical questions about the possibility of humans understanding the divine mysteries:[15]

> I give you [thanks, Lord,]
> because you have taught me your truth,
> you have made me know your wonderful mysteries,
> your kindness with [sinful] men,
> your bountiful compassion with the depraved of
>   heart.
> Who is like you, Lord, among the gods?
> Who is like your truth?
> Who, before you, is just when judged?
> No spirit can reply to your reproach,
> no one can stand up against your anger.
> All the sons of your truth
> you take to forgiveness in your presence,
> you purify them from their sins
> by the greatness of your goodness,
> and in your bountiful mercy,
> to make them stand in your presence,
> for ever and ever.
> For you are an eternal God

> and all your paths remain from eternity to eternity.
> And there is no one apart from you.
> What is empty man, owner of futility,
> to understand your wondrous deeds?[16]

As the detailed analysis below demonstrates, the hymn of 11:33-36 provides an eloquent conclusion for the third proof.[17]

Rhetorical Disposition

IV.	The *probatio*	
9:1—11:36	The third proof: The triumph of divine righteousness in the gospel's mission to Israel and the Gentiles	
11:33-36	10. Conclusion: a hymn on the majesty of God as revealed in the mysterious plan of global salvation	
11:33	a. The mysterious majesty of God	
11:33a	1. An exclamation about the depth of God	
	a) "Of riches"	
	b) "Of wisdom"	
	c) "Of knowledge"	
11:33b-c	2. An exclamation about the mysteries of God	
11:33b	a) God's judgments are "unsearchable"	
11:33c	b) God's ways are "inscrutable"	
11:34-35	b. The scriptural proof of the inability of humans to control the mystery of God	
11:34a	1. The citation of Isa 40:13, a rhetorical question about knowing "the mind of God"	
11:34b	2. Continuation of Isa 40:13, a rhetorical question about being God's "counselor"	
11:35a	3. The emended citation of Job 41:3, a rhetorical question about paying off God	
11:35b	4. Continuation of Job 41:3, a rhetorical question about placing God in debt	
11:36	c. The praise of God's majesty	
11:36a	1. The confession of omnipotence: "the all" (cf. Rom 9:5) was created—	
	a) "From God"	
	b) "Through God"	
	c) "For God"	
11:36b	2. The doxology	
	a) The ascription of glory to God	
	b) The "Amen"	

Geschichte der antiken Hymnologie, NTOA 19 (Freiburg: Universitätsverlag; Göttingen: Vandenhoeck & Ruprecht, 1991) 118.

14 See Lattke, *Hymnus,* 126.

15 Tobin, *Paul's Rhetoric,* 377.

16 Cited by Tobin, *Paul's Rhetoric,* 377–78, from Flor-

intino García Martínez, *The Dead Sea Scrolls Translated: The Qumran Texts in English,* 2d ed.(Leiden: Brill, 1996) 344–45.

17 Kim, *Romans 9–11,* 139–41, identifies this as a peroration for the whole of Rom 9–11.

Exegesis

■ **33** The hymn opens with an exclamation about the mysterious depth of divinity: the word $\tilde{\omega}$ conveys awe and wonder, and is used in the negative sense by Isa 6:5, "O wretched me!" ($\tilde{\omega}$ τάλας ἐγώ), and in the positive sense by Philo *Fug.* 149, "O admirable assay! O sacred test!"[18] The word βάθος ("depth") is formulated in asyndeton (without the article) that lends eloquence to the hymnic style. That the hymn was addressed to "the depth" itself therefore seems unlikely.[19] Such an address is unlikely to have been in Paul's mind, in view of 8:39 where he denied the power of the "depth" to separate believers from Christ.[20] The "depth" in the Romans hymn is perceived to convey "the thought of the inexhaustible and unsearchable 'fullness'" of God.[21] Philo refers to the "depth of knowledge" (βάθους. . . ἐπιστήμης) in *Post.* 130 and extols the "depth" of wisdom in *Ebr.* 112, "For wisdom lies deep below the surface and gives forth a sweet stream of true nobility for thirsty souls." As an example of the utter limit in the negative sense, Prov 18:3 says that "when impiety reaches to the depth of evil" (ὅταν ἔλθῃ ἀσεβὴς εἰς βάθος κακῶν), it will be scorned. The connotation is probably close to the use of βάθος in 1 Cor 2:10, which suggests the limit of divine profundity that is barred to humans except with divine assistance: "For the Spirit searches everything, even the depths of God."

The reference to "riches" in the possessive seems peculiar at first glance (how can riches be deep?), but the formulation would not have seemed odd in the ancient world, in which riches were conceived as precious metal piled in mounds that are βαθύς ("deep" or "high"), depending on one's viewing position.[22] There is a classical parallel to this link between "depth" and "riches" in Sophocles *Aj.* 130, in which Athena warns Odysseus against arrogance because one's adversary

might prove "mightier in hand or in depth of great wealth (ἢ μακροῦ πλοῦτον βάθει)." The reference to "riches" makes special sense in the context of Paul's earlier discourse that described the spiritual as well as material blessings that accrue to participants in the new age. In 2:4 he referred to the "riches of God's kindness and forbearance and patience"; in 9:23 "the riches of his glory" are granted to "the vessels of mercy"; in 11:12, Paul refers to "riches for the world" and "riches for the Gentiles" that would come as a result of global conversion; in 11:17 converts are promised a share in "the richness of the olive tree." In the context of Romans, the word πλοῦτος ("riches") is thus not a mere modifier of the following references to wisdom and knowledge,[23] but rather an explicit reminder of the material and spiritual benefits that the enactment of God's "mystery" (11:25) will bring.[24] That Paul intended the term "riches" to be understood in this manner is also suggested by the citation of Job 41:3 in 11:35 involving "payment" and "gift," as well as by the final line of the hymn that claims that "all things," which would include everything both material and spiritual, are from God, through God, and for God.

The second divine attribute in the hymn is σοφία ("wisdom"), which resonates with a broad stream of biblical, apocalyptic, and Hellenistic Jewish thought.[25] In the context of creation, Wis 7:21 insists, for example, that σοφία provides "certain knowledge of the things that are, namely to know how the world was made and the operation of its elements." Sir 1:4 claims that σοφία "was created before all things" (1:4) and was active in the creation itself (24:1-6). Σοφία occurs here for the only time in Romans, in contrast to 1 Corinthians, where it is a major theme involving the contrast between human arrogance and the realm of divine mystery known only to those who receive the Spirit of God. As I noted with regard to 11:25, the same antithesis was

---

18 See BDF §146.2 and BAGD (2000) 1100 with other examples.

19 Dunn, 2:699, rightly rejects this suggestion by Deichgräber, *Gotteshymnus*, 62, but Dunn does not explain the significance of asyndeton in the hymn.

20 See Adolf Strobel, "βάθος," *EDNT* 1 (1990) 190; Heinrich Schlier, "βάθος," *TDNT* 1 (1964) 517–18.

21 Strobel, "βάθος," 190; see also Schlier, "βάθος," 517.

22 See LSJM 301.

23 Godet, 416; Murray, 300; Morris, 427–28; for a correct grammatical assessment, see Weiss, 505.

24 See Kühl, 400; Schlier, 345; Michel, 360.

25 See Georg Fohrer and Ulrich Wilckens, "σοφία," *TDNT* 7 (1971) 489–509.

stated with regard to the mystery of the plan of salvation. Some commentators thus assume that wisdom in the context of this proof is intended to refer to "the mystery of God's saving purpose for all" disclosed in 11:25-26.[26] That this mystery has "depth" that no human can penetrate without mystical disclosure is self-evident, not just because of the limitation of finite intelligence but also because of cultural biases that the preceding argument of Romans has sought to overcome. If Paul's gospel is accepted by the Roman believers, that God's mercy is wide enough to cover habitual antagonisms between Jews and Gentiles, Greco-Romans and barbarians, educated and uneducated, they will be able to join him in praising God for this "depth of wisdom" that offers an end to lethal human conflict.

The third attribute cited in the hymn is the "depth of . . . knowledge." Although the γνώσεως θεοῦ ("knowledge of God") was usually understood as an objective genitive, namely, human knowledge about God (e.g., Hos 4:1; 6:6; Isa 11:2, 9),[27] there are in fact no other references in the NT to God's own knowledge.[28] It is quite possible, therefore, that the Hellenistic Jewish context of the original hymn understood γνώσεως θεοῦ as knowledge about God granted to the righteous. In the context of Paul's argument, however, divine "knowledge" probably would have been understood in the light of the previous references to God's foreknowledge about Israel in 11:2 and about those who would accept the gospel and enter the realm of grace in 8:29-30.[29] That God alone knew the murky hearts of Israel and the various Gentile peoples is an unspoken premise of the mystery disclosed in 11:25-26 and its preceding argument, because it is anything but self-evident that a mission to convert Gentiles in Spain would ultimately have a positive effect on Israel. In the words of the Psalm found at Qumran,

"who can discern your thoughts, O God?" (4Q381, frg. 31.5), except for the disclosure of this astounding mystery.

The following exclamation beginning with ὡς ("how!") is typical for biblical hymns.[30] For example, Ps 8:2, 10 exclaim, "How wonderful (ὡς θαυμαστόν) is your name in all the earth!"[31] After extolling the depths of divine riches, wisdom, and knowledge, it follows logically that the unfathomability of God's judgment should be named. The adjective ἀνεξεραύνητος ("unfathomable, unassertainable") appears in biblical Greek only in two textual variants (Symmachus of Prov 25:3 and Jer 17:9) and is also rarely found in classical texts.[32] It correlates in an elegant fashion with the word "depth" in the preceding sentence and, in the context of Paul's argument, it carries forward the theme of the divine mystery that is accessible only through special revelation. In Hellenistic Judaism where this hymn probably originated, "God's judgments" (τὰ κρίματα αὐτοῦ) comprise actions against oppressors and in behalf of the oppressed that are extolled as "true and righteous altogether" (Ps 18:10).[33] Sirach 21:5 promises that in response to a "poor man's prayer," God's judgment "comes speedily." In the context of conflicts between nations, Wis 12:12 asks, "Who shall withstand your judgment?" As in the hymn, which originally flowed directly from v. 35 to the theme of creation in v. 36, Ps 104:6 calls the faithful to remember the wonders that God made, "his marvels and the judgments of his mouth (τὰ τέρατα αὐτοῦ καὶ τὰ κρίματα τοῦ στόματος αὐτοῦ)." In the context of Romans, the "judgments" of God are concentrated in the sphere of establishing righteousness through grace alone. In 2:16 in response to the hypocritical piety of a Jewish interlocutor, Paul insists that "God judges the secrets of men by Christ Jesus," for God's

26 Dunn, 2:699. Other scholars on this track include Kuss, 3:827; Schlier, 345; Dupont, *Gnosis*, 91–93.
27 See particularly Bultmann, "γινώσκω κτλ.," 700–703.
28 See Cranfield, 2:590.
29 Godet, 417; Dunn, 2:699; Moo, 741–42; Bultmann, "γινώσκω κτλ.," 706–7; Schmithals, γινώσκω κτλ.," 249; Tobin, *Paul's Rhetoric*, 378.
30 Deichgräber, *Gotteshymnus*, 61; Dunn, 2:699.
31 See also Ps 66:3; 83:2; 103:24; Sir 17:29.
32 BAGD (2000) 77 lists Heraclitus Ephesius *Frag.* 18

and Dio Cassius *Hist. Rom.* 69.14, "For the multitude of those who perished by famine, disease, and fire was unascertainable (ἀνεξερεύνητον ἦν)." The Heraclitus citation comes from Clement of Alexandria *Stro.* II, 17.4, "If one does not expect the unexpected one will not find it, since it is not to be ascertained (ἀνεξερεύνητον) and difficult to locate."
33 Büchsel and Herntrich, "κρίνω κτλ.," 942.

judgment is impartial (2:2; 3:6). The righteous judgment of God is extended in Christ to those who have faith in the gospel (3:21-26). Abraham was reckoned as righteous on the basis of faith alone (4:3-5), and his true descendants are made righteous by grace rather than through the performance of works (4:13-16). In the third proof, for which this hymn provides the conclusion, the theme of God's righteous judgment is extensively developed in the metaphor of the potter's right to shape the clay into varied objects of judgment (9:20-23); in the analysis that Israel's quest for righteousness was ruined by the quest for status that was repudiated by impartial judgment (9:30—10:3); in the insistence that although God has broken off some Jewish branches of the olive tree, God's judgment allows no favoritism for the engrafted Gentile branches (11:21), and thus that no person or group should dare to be "wise in their own eyes" (11:25). Particularly unfathomable was the idea of a divinely imposed obtuseness of Israel that provided time for the Gentile mission, combined with the expectation that its completion would provoke a transformation of Israel's rejection of the gospel (11:11-14, 25-26). Indeed, as the later history of Christian–Jewish relations after the death of Paul revealed, it appears that God's judgments were also unfathomable for the apostle himself.

The reference to God's inscrutable ways employs the Semitic term ὁδός ("path, way") as a metaphor for acting. In particular, as Dunn points out,[34] the expression "the way of the Lord" is a characteristic biblical expression (Gen 18:19; Exod 33:13; Deut 26:17-18; Ps 81:13; 103:7; Prov 8:22; Jer 32:30; Ezek 18:25-29). Ordinarily, the ὁδοί κυρίου refers to the path of the commandments that the faithful should follow,[35] and this was probably the connotation intended in the original hymn. The adjective ἀνεξιχνίαστος ("inscrutable, incomprehensible") appears three times in Job (5:9; 9:10; 34:24) and elsewhere in Greek and Hebrew literature to depict the transcendence of God.[36] In 4Q381, frg. 35.3 God's wisdom is "unsearchable," and in the *Odes Sol.* 12.6 the "mercy of God's promise" is extolled as "immeasurable and inscrutable" (ἀμέτητριόν τε καὶ ἀνεξιχνίαστός).

The *Prayer of Manasseh* 6 states that the "promised mercies" of God are "unending and immeasurable." In the context of Paul's argument, God's "ways" of dealing with Israel and the Gentiles can be understood only on the basis of the disclosure of the "mystery," which pertains to a salvation through response to the gospel rather than through conformity to the commandments. In a parallel manner, the reversal of traditional expectations that God will favor the in-group and that salvation can be gained by good performance or the achievement of honorable status by other means remains incomprehensible, except for the revelation of divine righteousness in the Christ event.

■ **34** The citation from Isa 40:13 and the following citation from Job 41:3 were carefully selected to produce a chiastic development of "riches and wisdom and knowledge of God" in 11:33.[37] As one can see from the illustration below, in which the correspondence is underlined, the citation related to "knowledge" and "wisdom" is virtually verbatim:

Isa 40:13 Τίς ἔγνω νοῦν κυρίου; καὶ τίς σύμβουλος αὐτοῦ ἐγένετο; ("Who has known the mind of the Lord, and who has become his counselor?")

Rom 11:34 Τίς γὰρ ἔγνω νοῦν κυρίου; ἢ τίς σύμβουλος αὐτοῦ ἐγένετο; ("For 'who has known the mind of the Lord, or who has become his counselor?'")

The insertion of γάρ ("for") was required as a transitional device,[38] showing that the following citation confirms the hymnic celebration of unsearchability and inscrutability of God. The replacement of καί ("and") by ἤ ("or") augments the stylistic unity of the hymn by bringing the beginning of v. 34b into conformity with the ἤ at the beginning of v. 35a. The two successive "or's" intensify the "negativity" of the citation by insisting that no human being is in the position of trumping the wisdom and riches of God as demonstrated in the previous three chapters concerning the mysterious course of the

---

34   Dunn, 2:699; see also Wilhelm Michaelis, "ὁδός κτλ.," *TDNT* 5 (1967) 48–65.

35   Michaelis, "ὁδος κτλ." 51–53.

36   BAGD (2000) 77.

37   Bornkamm, *Experience,* 107–8; Koch, *Schrift,* 178; Wilk, *Bedeutung des Jesajabuches,* 307–8.

38   Koch, *Schrift,* 178.

gospel mission with regard to Israel.[39] The function of this citation is therefore quite different from Paul's citation of the same verse in 1 Cor 2:16.[40] Since the mystery of God's plan has just been disclosed in vv. 25-26, the rhetorical questions in the citation are not intended to evoke the generic response "No one!"[41] In the original context of Isaiah's discourse, the rhetorical questions countered skepticism and disbelief regarding God's bringing Israel back home to Zion.[42] In the context of the closing pericope of the third proof of Romans 9–11, the $νοῦς κυρίου$ ("mind of the Lord") now relates to God's disposition and purpose that includes an unbreakable promise to Israel.[43]

The $σύμβουλος$ ("counselor") reference[44] is similar to Philo's criticism in *Migr.* 136 of those who pretend to be "self-wise" to the degree that they think they know what happened at creation; they delude themselves into thinking that "they were counselors ($σύμβουλοι$) with the Creator concerning the things he was fashioning." In the context of the third proof, this reference evokes the mysterious strategy of making Israel's heart obtuse so as to cause a delay in their conversion that would allow time for the Gentile mission, at the fulfillment of which

Israel's zeal would be transformed and Israel thereby saved.[45] The issue here is not whether God's plan was known or not, because Paul has just revealed the mystery of its threefold strategy. The rhetorical questions drive home the discourse of the entire third proof, which aimed to overcome the cultural superiority and prejudice that resisted this divinely disclosed scheme that would redeem the entire world, including the antagonistic groups of converts in Rome. The "who" in the rhetorical questions therefore includes the Christian congregations in Rome that continue to be "haughty-minded" with regard to other cultural groups. In this context, the rhetorical questions constitute a direct challenge to the Christian groups in Rome: 'Now that God's plan has been revealed, do you dare to oppose it? Do you think you are in a position to advise God to suit your preferences?' The answer required by these first two rhetorical questions, therefore, is suggested by the earlier warning: 'No, we had better not be haughty-minded!'

■ **35** The citation from this verse appears to come from a version of Job 41:3 that is quite different from the LXX and the Hebrew texts, as visible below where the exact parallel is marked with underlining:

39   Ibid., 270, elaborated by Wilk, *Bedeutung des Jesajabuches*, 309.

40   See Wilk, *Bedeutung des Jesajabuches*, 287–92, 309. Lim, *Holy Scripture*, 159–60, suggests that Paul knew two versions of the Isaiah citation (visible in 1QIsaᵃ), which might explain the different use in 1 Corinthians as compared with Romans.

41   See Haacker, 247. A generic response of "No one!" is advocated by Schlier, 347; Moo, 743; Shum, *Paul's Use of Isaiah*, 246, and would match the rhetorical questions in *2 Bar.* 14.8-9 ("O Lord, my Lord, who can understand your judgment? Or who can explore the depth of your way? Or who can discern the majesty of your path? Or who can discern your incomprehensible counsel? Or who of those who are born has ever discovered the beginning and the end of your wisdom?").

42   Wagner, *Heralds*, 302–3.

43   See Johannes Behm, "$νοῦς$," *TDNT* 4 (1967) 959, "the saving purpose of God in which Paul finds the solution to the problem of R. 9-11 . . . the hidden plan of salvation." A *TLG* search turns up no examples of the expression, but Philo *Migr.* 134, maintains that "the limit of knowledge is to realize that nothing can be known, since God alone is wise, who

      is also God alone ($ἑνὸς ὄντος μόνου σόφου τοῦ καὶ μόνου θεοῦ$)."

44   BAGD (2000) 957 makes clear that the verbal form of $σύμβουλος$ ($συμβουλεύω$) depicts tactical and strategic "advice on a course of action," "plotting a course of action," as in Philo *Mut.* 104.3; *Fug.* 6.5; *Jos.* 60.3; *Legat.* 203.4. The noun $σύμβουλος$ occurs here for the only time in the NT and is not adequately analyzed by the commentaries. The self-delusion of counselors is depicted by Philo *Legat.* 203.4, as Caligula's problematic scheme to erect a gold statue in the temple at Jerusalem was made "on the consent of his most excellent and wise counselors ($συμβούλοις χρησάμενος τοῖς ἀρίστοις καὶ σοφωτάτοις$)." Philo *Migr.* 204.4 and 206.2, sarcastically identifies these "wise counselors" as Helikon, a former slave, and Apelles, a former stage actor, both of whom later fell victim to Caligula for their "impiety" ($ἀσεβείᾳ$).

45   The rhetorical question does not turn on the question of whether any human can serve as God's counselor (as in Haacker, 247, citing Isa 55:8-9), but whether the plan as announced in the "mystery" of 11:33 necessarily conforms to human preferences.

Job 41:3 MT מִי הִקְדִּמַנִי וַאֲשַׁלֵּם ("Will he make requests of you and speak ingratiatingly to you?")

Job 41:3 LXX ἢ τίς ἀντιστήσεταί μοι καὶ ὑπομενεῖ; ("Or who will resist me, and abide?")

Rom 11:35 ἢ τίς προέδωκεν αὐτῷ, καὶ ἀνταποδοθήσεται αὐτῷ; ("<u>Or who</u> gave first to him, so he shall receive recompense?")

Although there is a broad consensus that Paul is citing Job 41:3, the differences are so great that caution is required.[46] A further allusion to Job 35:7 has been suggested[47] ("what will you give him [τί δώσεις αὐτῷ], or what shall he receive from your hand"), which comes closer to providing a basis for the distinctive verbs προδίδωμι or ἀνταποδίδομαι. Paul's opening ἢ τίς ("or who?") matches the LXX of Job 41:3,[48] but there are no correspondences thereafter. Since the LXX misses the irony of the Job query, it appears certain that Paul's ironic version returns in one way or another to the spirit, if not the precise wording, of the original Hebrew text. The syntax of Paul's version includes a καί ("and, so") in the second line that probably has the sense of "a result that comes from what precedes,"[49] so that earning the repayment from God rests on indebtedness incurred when someone gives a gift to God.[50] An explanation of this wording derived from Strack-Billerbeck is that Paul cites an early form of the Targum on Job 41:3, but the formulation is not close enough to be very plausible: "Who comes before me in the works of creation, that I must repay him."[51] Berndt Schaller argues that Paul is probably citing from a corrected version of the LXX that brings it closer to the Hebrew text. This line of reasoning was first developed by Adolf Deissmann in 1905 with

regard to other citations, and it has been partially confirmed by Qumran texts.[52] It is plausible that an earlier corrector of the LXX or Paul himself selected ἀνταποδιδόναι ("recompense, pay back") as a translation of the Hebrew שׁלם, which occurred in two other locations in Job, in 21:19, 31.[53] But there is no parallel for προδιδόναι ("give in advance, first") as a translation of the rare Hebrew verb קדם, which occurs only in Job 41:3 and Amos 9:10. Moreover, in the other textually clear passages in the LXX (4 Kgs 6:11; 2 Macc 7:37; 4 Macc 4.1), προδιδόναι occurs with the alternative definition of "betray" or "turn over" rather than "give in advance." Although Schaller's suggestion is cited with approval,[54] no evidence has yet appeared of this hypothetical pre-Christian correction of the Job text, and it is more plausible to conclude that Paul himself is responsible for the corrected translation.

However one explains the origin of this citation, its succinct wit surpasses both the Hebrew and the LXX versions. That one could provide a gift that would place God in one's debt,[55] requiring God in accordance with the ancient laws of reciprocity to provide a healthy recompense, is preposterous within the framework of Jewish and Christian monotheism.[56] Moreover, as Dahl observed, "That no [one] holds God in his debt, so that what he receives from God is never merited, is a fundamental idea which underlies all of Romans."[57] The revised citation aptly picks up the theme of God's "riches" from 11:33, and carries forward the crucial theme of Israel's trespass and ultimate conversion providing "riches for the world . . . and for the Gentiles" in 11:12, 17. Although commentators restrict this to the spiritual riches of "saving grace,"[58] there is nothing in this context to eliminate the inclusion of material riches

---

46 Nestle-Aland prints the entire verse in italics as if the entirety were from Job 41:3, which seems rather audacious since only ἢ τίς is actually cited.

47 Fitzmyer, 635; Johnson, 174.

48 The expression ἢ τίς appears in other biblical texts, such as Job 6:11; 9:12; Isa 40:14; Wis 9:13; 12:12; 19:15; Sir 2:10; Jer 15:5; 21:13.

49 BAGD (2000) 495; see also Wilckens, 2:268, followed by Moo, 743.

50 That this verse refers to the preexistent Christ as the one "to whom God disclosed his whole mind" (Hanson, Interpretation, 91) is properly rejected by Johnson, Function, 167–68.

51 Str-B 3:295, cited by Käsemann, 318, and Wilckens, 2:271.

52 Berndt Schaller, "Zum Textcharakter der Hiobzitate im paulinischen Schrifttum," ZNW 71 (1980) 23–26.

53 Ibid., 25.

54 Koch, Schrift, 72–73; Wilk, Bedeutung des Jesajabuches, 270, 309–10.

55 See Newman and Nida, 230–31.

56 See Bornkamm, Experience, 107; Haacker, 248, citing Mott, "Hellenistic Benevolence," 64–67.

57 Dahl, Studies, 157, cited with approval by Johnson, Function, 174.

58 Byrne, 359; see also Wilckens, 2:272; Moo, 743.

as well. The implication of the two citations is that to question the "mystery" is to reverse the system of unmerited grace that has redeemed the congregations in Rome and placed them in the position to enjoy both material and spiritual benefits. Do the splintered congregations in Rome really wish to throw away these immense benefits by opposing the mission to Spain?

■ **36** The hymn originally continued from v. 33 to this series of prepositional phrases with God as the source of τὰ πάντα ("all things"), following a style that was widespread in the Greco-Roman and Hellenistic Jewish environments. In 1 Cor 8:6 there is a closely related example of such hymnic material in an explicitly Christian form, with Christ playing a crucial role in the divine drama that is missing in the Roman example: "But for us there is one God, the Father, from whom (ἐξ οὗ) are all things (τὰ πάντα), and we [exist] for him (εἰς αὐτόν), and one Lord, Jesus Christ, through whom are all things (τὰ πάντα) and we [exist] through him (δι' αὐτοῦ)." The preposition ἐξ ("from") appears in both hymns, with ἐξ αὐτοῦ ("from him") in Romans and ἐξ οὗ ("from whom") in 1 Corinthians emphasizing that God is the source of the entire creation and everything in it.[59] The phrase δι' αὐτοῦ ("through him") claims that God's own wisdom and power were the means by which the universe was created. Both of these phrases repudiate a deistic view of God as one who remains uninvolved in the created order.[60] Both claims are found in Philo *Cher.* 125–26:

> For in order for there to be a genesis to anything, it is necessary for many things to come together: something that comes "by which"; something that comes "from which"; something that comes "through which"; something that comes "on account of which" (τὸ ὑφ' οὗ, τὸ ἐξ οὗ, τὸ δι' οὗ, τὸ δι' οὗ), and the first of these is the cause, the second the material, the third the means, and the fourth the end or object.

Although not sharing the Jewish doctrine of creation, there is a similar formulation with the prepositions ἐκ ("from") and διά ("through") in the Stoic text of Pseudo-Aristotle *Mund.* 6, ὅτι ἐκ θεοῦ πάντα καὶ διὰ θεοῦ συνέστηκε ("because everything comes from God and is sustained by God"). *Asclepius* 34 contains a similar series of prepositional phrases in Latin: *omnia enim ab eo et in ipso et per ipsum* ("For everything is from him, and in itself, and through itself") However, in the context of the third proof, the phrases "from him" and "through him" refer not to creation itself but rather to salvation by faith (10:9-13) defined as mercy (9:16-18, 23; 11:32) and global reconciliation (11:15), and resulting in material and spiritual gifts of "wealth for the world" (11:12) and the "fatness" of the olive tree (11:17).

That the universe goes "to him" (εἰς αὐτόν), as the third phrase in the Roman hymn claims, implies a historical concept of creation that begins and ends with a purposeful God. Philo makes a similar claim in *Spec.* 1.208, ἓν τὰ πάντα ἦ ὅτι ἐξ ἑνός τε καὶ εἰς ἕν . . . ("all things are one, or that they come from one and return to one . . ."). There are also Stoic texts that include the "from" and "to" God formulas, while lacking the "through" formula: Marcus Aurelius Τὰ εἰς ἑαυτὸν 4.23, writes, ἐκ σοῦ πάντα, ἐν σοὶ πάντα, εἰς σὲ πάντα ("all things [are] from you; all things [are] in you; all things [are] for you"), and Seneca *Ep.* 65.8, has the Latin equivalent, *Quinque ergo causae sunt, ut Plato dicit: id ex quo, id a quo, id in quo, id ad quo, id propter quod* ("Therefore there are five causes, as Plato says: 'What comes out of which, that which comes from which, what is in which, what is to which, and what is near which'"). In the Pauline context, this third phrase reiterates earlier claims of salvation for Jews and Gentiles alike (3:22; 11:23-24, 32). Jan Bonda has discerned this universalistic dimension most clearly: "These two words, 'to him,' exclude the possibility that any creature could be created by God for the purpose of being and remaining far from him . . . eternal destruction is not the final word. For even those who are eternally far from him, are created 'to him.' That they remain. Therefore, their destiny is that eventually they come, from their

---

59　See also Col 1:16-17.
60　See Haacker, 249, citing Gustav Stählin, "Das Schicksal im Neuen Testament und bei Josephus," in O. Betz et al., eds., *Josephus-Studien. Untersuchungen zu Josephus, dem antiken Judentum und dem Neuen Testament. Otto Michel zum 70. Geburtstag gewidmet* (Göttingen: Vandenhoeck & Ruprecht, 1974) 329: in the NT there is no such thing as accident because "it all comes from God."

eternal destruction, 'to him.'"[61] Paul's purpose, however, was more missional than doctrinal. In the context of the third proof, that "all things" will return to God, despite their current distance from the gospel, reinforces the claim that Israel's sins will be "removed" (11:27), that the full number of Jews as well as Gentiles will come into the realm of grace (11:12, 25), and that all humans will thereby be shown "mercy" (11:30-32).

In view of the language employed, as we have seen, the creation theology in the original hymn cited was typical for Hellenistic Judaism. The riches, wisdom, and knowledge of God are visible in the created order that originated "from God" and was created through his divine power, and will serve her purpose in the end. The unfathomability and inscrutability of God are thus primarily manifest in the creation.

In the context of the third proof, however, and particularly in the light of the immediately preceding scriptural insertions, the three prepositional phrases no longer primarily express a doctrine of creation. Instead, they reinforce the mystery of salvation disclosed in 11:25-26 as derived from the absolute transcendence of God over the entire created order and over all forms of cultural resistance and prejudice.[62] To resist the mystery[63] on the grounds of defending culturally shaped advantages in power and status is to deprive one's group of the far greater benefits that come from the Lord of all creation. While no group or person is in the position of placing the Creator in their debt, they all are granted access through grace to the largesse of "the all."

The conclusion of the original hymn is unchanged in this Pauline version, giving suitable glory to God. In the original context of Hellenistic Judaism, this doxology ascribes all glory to God for all eternity.[64] The wording but not the form is reminiscent of Ps 85:12, "I will glo-

rify your name forever," and *1 En.* 63.3, "your glory is forever and ever." While echoing the conclusion of many Psalms,[65] the form of the NT doxologies appears to derive from Judaism,[66] as reflected in *3 Ezra* 4.40, "Glory be to the God of truth," referring to truth as revealed in *3 Ezra*. There is a virtually identical formulation in the closing words of 4 Macc 18:24, $\hat{\Omega}$ ἡ δόξα εἰς τοὺς αἰῶνας τῶν αἰώνων, ἀμήν ("To him be the glory for ever and ever, Amen"). Here again the deity praised grants blessings only on those who unfailingly obey the Torah (4 Macc 4:16—6:30; 16:14—17:23; 18:23).

Paul employs this kind of doxology in Phil 4:20, "To our God and Father be the glory for ever and ever," bringing the argument of that letter to a formal conclusion.[67] In the earlier argument of Romans, this doxology was prepared by the claim that sinful humans do not "glorify God as God" (1:21) but that the mysterious process of salvation for both Jews and Gentiles demonstrates the "riches of God's glory" (9:23). The αὐτῷ ("to him") in the doxology is therefore not the God of the Jews or the Gentiles, as shown in 3:29, but the one God (3:30) proclaimed by the gospel. This doxology therefore prepares the way for the climactic vision of 15:9-12, in which all nations join in the chorus of glorifying God,[68] picking up an important motif in traditional Jewish and early Christian worship of augmenting divine glory by human praise.[69] Only in the Pauline doxologies, however, can it be said that cultural chauvinism is explicitly eliminated.

The "Amen" at the end of the doxology conforms to a pattern established in the Psalms, "to attest the praise of God in response to a doxology."[70] In LXX Ps 41:13; 72:19; 89:52; 106:48 the Hebrew "Amen" is translated with γένοιτο, γένοιτο ("so be it, so be it!"), which captures the intended validation. Other Hellenistic Jewish

61 Bonda, *One Purpose*, 195.
62 See Tobin, *Paul's Rhetoric*, 379.
63 See Kühl, 402.
64 See Deichgräber, *Gotteshymnus*, 35–40, 64.
65 Ernst Jenni, "Zu den doxologischen Schlussformeln des Psalters," *ThZ* 40 (1984) 114–20.
66 See Alfred Stuiber, "Doxologie," *RAC* 4 (1959) 212–14, and Samuel Vollenweider, "Doxologie. I. Formgeschichtlich. 2. Neues Testament," *RGG⁴* 2 (1999) 963. G. H. R. Horsley, "An Acclamation to 'the Lord, Forever,'" *NDIEC* 2 (1982) 35, discusses the parallel formulations in the Roman civic cult.
67 See Fee, *Philippians*, 455; O'Brien, *Philippians*, 549–50.
68 See du Toit, "Doxologische Gemeinschaft," 75.
69 Champion, *Benedictions and Doxologies*, 95–97.
70 Heinrich Schlier, "ἀμήν," *TDNT* 1 (1964) 335. Jenni, "Schlussformeln des Psalters," 16–20, argues that the concluding "Amen" was probably spoken by the believing community rather than sung.

writings simply transliterate the Hebrew with the Greek ἀμήν,[71] which Paul always employs. In synagogue worship, the congregation affirms its "concurrence" in the praise of God by uttering "Amen!"[72] In the original doxology, the creation theology expressed therein is thereby affirmed by the believing community.

As in the two earlier occurrences of "Amen" in Rom 1:25 and 9:5, Paul expects the congregation to confirm the specific theological point of his argument; there is explicit confirmation of such a liturgical expectation in 1 Cor 14:16 where Paul asks, "how can anyone in the position of an outsider say the 'Amen' to your thanksgiving when he does not know what you are saying?"[73] So, in Rom 11:36, the congregation is invited to assent to the entire argument of the third proof, including the controversial "mystery" of Gentile and Jewish conversion that counters the prejudicial inclinations in the various house and tenement churches in Rome. By concurring in glorifying this one God of both Jews and Gentiles, they take decisive steps against their own chauvinistic tendencies and open themselves to the challenging project of the Spanish mission for which the entire letter provides a rationale.

---

71   See BAGD (2000) 53.
72   Schlier, "ἀμήν," 336; Bruce Chilton, "Amen," *ABD* 1 (1992) 184–85.
73   Schlier, "ἀμήν," 336; Heckel, *Segen*, 308–12; Conzelmann, *1 Corinthians*, 239.

12:1-2 The Fourth Proof

12

The First Pericope

Introduction: The Thesis concerning the Motivation and Assessment of Praiseworthy Behavior

1/ **I urge you therefore, brothers, through the mercies of God, to present your bodies as a sacrifice, living, holy [and] acceptable to God[a]—your reasonable worship. 2/ Also, do not be conformed[b] to this aeon, but be transformed[c] by the renewal of the mind,[d] that you may ascertain what the will of God is,—the good and acceptable and perfect.**

a   The sequence εὐάρεστον τῷ θεῷ ("acceptable / well pleasing to God") is found in P⁴⁶ (omits τῷ) ℵ² B D F G L Ψ 6 33 69 88 104 323 326 330 365 424 614 945 1175 1241 1243 1319 1505 1573 1735 1739 1836 1874 1881 (τῷ κυρίῳ for τῷ θεῷ) 2344 2495 *Maj* Tert. Sanday and Headlam, 352, comment that this is the "more usual expression" but that Paul "may well have written τῷ θεῷ εὐάρεστον to prevent ambiguity" as found in ℵ*A P 81 1506 *pc* lat Spec. The former sequence allows the term "God" to be connected with the verb "present yourselves," which would leave "acceptable" dangling in an awkward manner. It seems unlikely that such ambiguity would have been created by later copyists to create

stylistic conformity with other Pauline expressions. The ambiguity is more likely to have been eliminated by the latter sequence, which would therefore be secondary.

b   In place of the imperative in P⁴⁶ ℵ B* L P 6 69 104 365 424 614 945ᶜ 1241 1319 1573 1739 1874 1881 2344 *pm* Cl, the infinitive form συσχηματίζεσθαι ("to be conformed") is found in A B² D* F G Ψ 33 81 88 323 326 330 630 945* 1175 1243 1505 1506 1735 1836 2495 *pm*. The infinitive form may be a phonetic error, according to Cranfield, 2:605.

c   Many of the same manuscripts listed in textual note b provide a secondary infinitive form μεταμορφοῦσθαι ("be transformed") as earlier in this verse, probably also a phonetic error, namely, A B² D* F G Ψ 323 326 330 945 1175 1243 1505 1506 1735 2495, but the second infinitive is supported also by ℵ (6) 1319 1881 1874* 2344. Both imperatives occur in P⁴⁶ B* L P 69 104 365 424 1241 1573 1739 Cl, but μεταμορφοῦσθε here also finds support in D¹ 33 88 1836 1874ᶜ.

d   The addition of ὑμῶν ("your") after "mind" by ℵ D¹ L P Ψ 33 69 88 104 323 326 330 365 424* 614 945 1175 1241 1243 1319 1505 1506 1573 1735 1836 1874 2344 2495 *Maj* latt sy appears to be a secondary clarification; the reading of P⁴⁶ A B D* F G 6 424ᶜ 630 1739 1881 *pc* Cl Cyp that omits this word is to be preferred.

Analysis

There is a consensus among current exegetes that these two verses provide the main theme,[1] the introduction,[2] summary,[3] or a kind of title paragraph[4] for the subsequent chapters of moral exhortation that I am calling the fourth proof of the letter. Unfortunately, this is usually presented as if Paul were setting forth an ethic for the ages, which overlooks the eschatological urgency of his thought and the specific purpose for writing Romans. Here Paul sets forth the premises of his ethic in a manner that sustains the missional imperative of the letter as a whole. The metaphors of bodily sacrifice and

reasonable worship as a fitting response to grace received by the Roman believers suggest the basis of their cooperation with Paul, the "minister of Christ Jesus to the Gentiles, in priestly service to the gospel of God, in order that the offering of the Gentiles might become acceptable, made holy in the Holy Spirit" (Rom 15:16). The appeal on the basis of the "mercies of God" links this passage not only with 9:15-23; 11:30-32, but also with the entire earlier argument of Romans concerning the mercy/grace of God that comes to those who do not deserve it.[5] In this sense, the *exhortatio* grows

---

1   Käsemann, 323.
2   Cranfield, 2:595.
3   Dunn, 2:707, following Grabner-Haider, *Paraklese*, 116–17.
4   Michel, 365; Wilckens, 3:1; Ortkemper, *Leben*, 19.
5   See Hans Dieter Betz, "Das Problem der Grundlagen der paulinischen Ethik," *ZThK* 85 (1988) 210f.

out of the thesis of Romans in 1:17, just as did the earlier theological proofs about the "righteousness of God" revealed in the gospel of Christ. In response to mercy received, believers are here called to respond with ethical worship involving nonconformity with the present evil age and transformation of the mind, expressing the restoration of righteousness that Christ provides. The theme of responding to God's mercy by praising God also closes this fourth proof, a praise that reappears in 15:9-11 to reaffirm the missional impulse of bringing all nations into proper worship.

This introductory pericope opens in a direct address to the Roman believers with a sentence reminiscent of the dialogical and rhetorical exchanges at the beginning of earlier sections of Romans; this is followed by a rhythmically formulated exhortation[6] that contrasts conformity with the present aeon with transformation of the mind. Verse 2 defines praiseworthy behavior and the second warns against incurring blame, thus placing the rhetoric of the fourth proof squarely within the parameters of the demonstrative genre.[7] The prominent use of παρακαλῶ ("I exhort") as the opening word in the pericope evokes the frequent parallels in ambassadorial and administrative rhetoric,[8] thus fitting the demonstrative genre, and expressing Paul's earlier self-introduction as the representative of the gospel as the power of God.[9] Each verse begins with an imperative and ends with an appositional line in the accusative, resulting in a parallelism that is rendered more attractive by the threefold homoioteleuton of τὸν ἀγαθὸν καὶ εὐάρεστον καὶ τέλειον ("the good and acceptable and perfect") in the second strophe. This triadic figure echoes the triad of the "living, holy [and] acceptable" sacrifice in 12:1, resulting in a thesis of remarkable coherence.

Rhetorical Disposition

IV.	The *probatio*
12:1–15:13	The fourth proof: Living together according to the gospel so as to sustain the hope of global transformation
12:1-2	1. Introduction: the thesis concerning the motivation and assessment of praiseworthy behavior
12:1	a. The positive appeal to reasonable worship through bodily service
12:1a	1) Status of the audience: "brothers"
12:1b	2) The theological basis of the appeal: "the mercies of God"
12:1c	3) The locus and rationale of the ethic of gratitude: "bodily sacrifice"
	a) First attribute of sacrifice: "living"
	b) Second attribute of sacrifice: "holy"
	c) Third attribute of sacrifice: "acceptable to God"
12:1d	4) Apposition to sacrifice: "reasonable worship"
12:2	b. The appeal to replace conformity with authentic ethical assessment
12:2a	1) The negative command: nonconformity "to this aeon"
12:2b	2) The positive command: transformation by "renewal of the mind"
12:2c	3) The consequence: collective discernment of God's will
12:2d	4) Apposition of God's will as "the good, acceptable and perfect"

Exegesis

■ **1** The controversy over the use of παρακαλῶ ("I urge, exhort, encourage") is linked with the misconception of Romans as establishing timeless doctrine, with Schlier and Grabner-Haider arguing for a distinctive early Christian concept of moral and theological admonition from the apostle which replaces law as the basis for life.[10] Elab-

---

6   See Weiss, "Beiträge," 243.
7   Aristotle *Rhet.* 1.3.3: "The epideictic kind has for its subject praise or blame." 1.3.5: "The end of those who praise or blame is the honorable and disgraceful. . . ." See also Quintilian *Inst.* 3.7.1.
8   Carl J. Bjerkelung, *PARAKALÔ: Form, Funktion und Sinn der parakalô-Sätze in den paulinischen Briefen* (Oslo: Universitetsvorlaget, 1967).
9   Rom 1:1-2, 16-17; see Jewett, "Ambassadorial Letter," 11–12.
10   Heinrich Schlier, "Vom Wesen der apostolischen Ermahnung nach Römerbrief 12,1-2," in *Die Zeit der Kirche. Exegetische Aufsätze und Vorträge* (Freiburg: Herder, 1962) 78–89; Schlier works out the eschatological implications of Pauline exhortation in "Die Eigenart der christlichen Mahnung nach dem Apostel Paulus," in *Besinnung auf das neue Testament. Exegetische Aufsätze und Vorträge II* (Freiburg: Herder, 1964) 340–57. Anton Grabner-Haider stresses the unity of eschatological exhortation and proclamation in *Paraklese*, discussing Rom 12:1 in 116–28. Along with most contemporary Romans commenta-

orate theories of the ethical imperative resting on the theological indicative were developed, with this verse as foundational.[11] It was widely assumed that Paul's purpose in writing Rom 12 was to create such a theological ethic on an authoritative basis.[12] Bjerkelund sought to reverse this trend by pointing out the typically epistolary function of παρακαλῶ as a request formula, particularly prominent in diplomatic correspondence.[13] In place of commands that might offend the sensitivities of allied groups, παρακαλεῖν was used to urge compliance with some aim or policy of the sovereign. For instance, King Ptolemy II wrote to Miletus to remind them of his benefactions and their previous loyalty, requesting a continuation of the same: παρακαλοῦμεν δὲ καὶ εἰς τὸν λοιπὸν χρόνον τὴν αὐτὴν ἔχειν αἵρεσιν πρὸς ὑμᾶς ("we urge you for the future to maintain the same policy of friendship toward us . . .").[14] An exact parallel to the first three words of Paul's formulation was easily accessible to readers of the LXX in 2 Macc 9:26 where King Antiochus writes the Jewish people to remind them of their relationship: παρακαλῶ οὖν ὑμᾶς καὶ ἀξιῶ μεμνημένους τῶν εὐεργεσιῶν κοινῇ καὶ κατ' ἰδίαν ἕκαστον συντηρεῖν τὴν οὖσαν εὔνοιαν εἰς ἐμὲ καὶ τὸν υἱόν ("I therefore urge and implore you to remain mindful of the public and private benefits you have received and to preserve, each of you, your present goodwill toward me and my son").[15] Bjerkelund pointed out

the similarity between these diplomatic appeals and the situation of Paul writing to independent congregations.[16] He concludes that "The significance of this passage is therefore not on the theological but on the level of personal, brotherly encounter."[17] The first half of this conclusion is more compelling than the second, which leads some scholars to dismiss Bjerkelund's contribution.[18] Paul's purpose in Rom 12 was not primarily personal and brotherly but, in the view of this commentary, diplomatic and missional. While it seems clear that Pauline usage derives from this epistolary convention, the terms παρακαλέω and παράκλησις appear in his various letters with some distinctive connotations influenced by his missionary practice.[19] It is thus unnecessary to follow Bjerkelund in denying the ethical and theological framework in which Paul chooses to cast his appeal. I believe Bjerkelund is on the right track, however, in seeing Paul's epistolary purpose rather than some abstract theological framework as the key to understanding what precisely is being urged.[20] In George Smiga's words, "Romans 12:1-2 is not paraenesis but a request."[21] In the effort to gain the cooperation of the Roman house churches for Paul's missionary project, the language of command is avoided; hence my translation "urge" that conveys something of the original meaning of παρακαλέω as to "call to one's side,"[22] while avoiding the technical contemporary connotation of

tors, Otto Schmitz follows the line developed by Schlier without stressing the replacement of the law in "παρακαλέω and παράκλησις in the NT," *TDNT* 5 (1967) 793–99.

11   For an overview of this discussion, stimulated by Rudolf Bultmann's article "Das Problem der Ethik bei Paulus," *ZNW* 23 (1924) 123–40, see R. Hasenstab, *Modelle paulinischer Ethik. Beiträge zu einem Autonomie-Model aus paulinischen Geist* (Mainz: Matthias-Grünewald, 1977) 67–147. See also Ortkemper, *Leben*, 150–56; Schrage, *Ethics*, 167–72; Furnish, *Theology*, 224–27.

12   See K. Arvid Tångberg, "Romerbrevet 12,1-2 og parenesebegrepet i nytestamentlig forskning," *TTKi* 2 (1986) 81–91.

13   Bjerkelund, *PARAKALÔ*, 59–87, 109–11.

14   *P.Milet.* 1.3. #139, discussed by Bjerkelund, *PARAKALÔ*, 60f., translation adapted from Welles, *Royal Correspondence*, 72–73.

15   See the discussion by Bjerkelund, *PARAKALÔ*, 91–92.

16   Ibid., 66.

17   Ibid., 173; my translation.

18   See Ortkemper, *Leben*, 21; Dunn, 2:708.

19   Especially significant are the descriptions of Paul's missionary practice in 1 Thess 2:12; 3:2; 4:1, 18; 5:11. The exact phrase παρακαλῶ οὖν ὑμᾶς also appears in 1 Cor 14:16; Eph 4:1. It should be admitted, however, that παρακαλῶ is common in rhetorical speech outside of epistolary contexts: Isocrates *Evag.* 77.5; *Antid.* 65.5; Xenophon *Mem.* 2.10.2; Plato *Phaed.* 89c; *Prot.* 340a; *Gorg.* 526e; Demosthenes *Epitaph.* 1.10.1, 7; Aeschines *Tim.* 107.9; *Fals. leg.* 180; 184; etc. The closest to the formulation in Rom 12:1 occurs in Plutarch *Def. orac.* 438d: καὶ ὑμᾶς παρακαλῶ καὶ ἐμαυτόν ("I exhort both you and myself").

20   Bjerkelund, *PARAKALÔ*, 173.

21   Smiga, "Occasion of the Letter," 267.

22   BAGD 617.

"exhort" and the demeaning connotation of "admonish." As the ambassador of the power of God (1:17), Paul issues an appeal in language consistent with his earlier admission that he has as much to gain from their faith as they from his (Rom 1:12). Παρακαλεῖν is modulated by the previously mentioned συμπαρακαλεῖν (Rom 1:12). Given the long tradition of construing Paul's ethic as if it were addressed primarily to individuals, it is also important to observe that the appeal is to "you" in the plural, identified as "brothers," thus strengthening the familial ethos[23] by which all of the members of the various house churches are addressed together.

The use of οὖν ("therefore") in connection with οἰκτιρμοὶ τοῦ θεοῦ ("mercies of God") indicates that the earlier argument of Romans provides the basis and force of the ethical appeal.[24] The plural form of "mercies" is typical of LXX usage[25] and evokes earlier references to the grace and love of God (Rom 1:5, 7; 3:24; 4:4, 16; 5:2,15-21; 6:1, 14-17; 11:5-6), as well as the specific references to mercy in 9:15-23 and 11:30-32. The appeal of this reference is sustained by pagan as well as Jewish religion, which assumed that the reception of divine benefaction placed a person or group under obligation to the deity.[26] Yet, as Betz points out, only in Romans does Paul use this concept as the basis of his ethic.[27] In the case of the Roman believers, the primary form of divine mercy received was the gift of salvation through the gospel, as the earlier argument of Romans reiterated. He thus avoids the pitfalls of ethical systems based on the law or the Spirit.[28] The instrumental use of διά ("through")[29] seems to be a Pauline peculiarity,[30] repeated in 12:3, 15:30, 1 Cor 1:10, 2 Cor 10:1, and elsewhere. Although the phrase "through the mercies of God" could be linked with the process of sacrifice, it seems more likely that it was intended to be linked with the preceding verb, "I urge you," providing the rationale for Paul's appeal.

There is a broad consensus that "to present . . . a sacrifice" is "drawn from the technical language of sacrifice" in Greek religion,[31] and that Paul follows a tradition in Greco-Roman religion by using sacrifice as a metaphor of personal devotion.[32] One thinks of the classic statement of Isocrates: "In the worship of the gods, follow the example of your ancestors, but consider that the noblest sacrifice and greatest service (ϑῦμα τοῦτο κάλλιστον εἶναι καὶ θεραπείαν μεγίστην) is to show

---

23 See Ortkemper, *Leben*, 20.

24 See Söding, *Liebesgebot*, 240–41; Strom, *Reframing Paul*, 124. While Kühl, 415, insists that "therefore" draws consequences from the entire earlier argument of the letter, Lietzmann, 107, downplays its significance. Bjerkelund, *PARAKALÔ*, 162, rejects the logical consequence theory because it had been used to support a purely theological construal of παρακαλῶ. Schlier, 351, interprets οὖν as a signal of a return to the main theme of Rom 5–8.

25 BAGD 561 cites 2 Kgs 24:14; Ps 24:6; Isa 63:15, and *T. Jos.* 2.3 as examples of οἰκτιρμοί translating the Hebrew plural *raḥᵃmim*. The plural implies specific deeds of mercy rather than the abstract concept of mercy. Bjerkelund, *PARAKALÔ*, 161, cites Dehn, *Leben*, 11, to the effect that the plural "mercies" should be translated "Barmherzigkeitserweisungen," a suggestion paralleled by Betz's translation "angesichts der Erweise göttlichen Erbarmens" ("in face of the proofs of divine mercies") in "Ethik," 208–9.

26 See H. W. Pleket, "Religious History as the History of Mentality: The 'Believer' as Servant of the Deity in the Greek World," in H. S. Versnel, ed., *Faith, Hope and Worship: Aspects of Religious Mentality in the Ancient World* (Leiden: Brill, 1981) 183–89. In

"Philosophers, Intellectuals and Religion in Hellas," also in *Faith, Hope and Worship*, 253, P. A. Meijer describes the ideal of Theophrastus, who advocated "the deepest veneration for the deity as benefactor . . . [which] leaves no room for the contractual element so characteristic of Greek religious feelings."

27 See Betz, "Ethik," 211. In "Religious History," 153, Pleket shows that a continuous aspect of Greco-Roman religion, even prior to Hellenistic times, was "a close affective relationship between deity and worshipper."

28 See Tobin, *Paul's Rhetoric*, 387–88.

29 BAGD 180; Dunn, 2:709.

30 Since the normal preposition with παρακαλεῖν is πρός with the genitive, Zahn, 534, suspects a Latinism in which διά stands in place of *per*. Bjerkelund discusses the preposition in *PARAKALÔ*, 162–68, concluding with the implausible suggestion that it denotes an oath.

31 BAGD 628; Klauck, "Kultische Symbolsprache," 113; Dunn, 2:709. In contrast, Calvin J. Roetzel attempts to explain Paul's metaphor on the basis of his Pharisaic background in "Sacrifice in Romans 12–15," *WW* 6 (1986) 414–16.

32 A classic statement is found in Odo Casel, "Die Λογικὴ θυσία der antiken Mystik in christlich-

yourself the best and most righteous person, for such persons have greater hope of enjoying a blessing from the gods than those who slaughter many victims."[33] However, to present "your bodies" as the form of sacrifice is unique in several ways.[34] Rather than offering a sacrificial object distinct from the self or the group,[35] or even a depiction of the portion of the body healed by the deity,[36] Paul refers here to placing the audience's own bodies on the altar.[37] Only in this way can the "mortal bodies" of 8:11 be "made alive," through self-giving actions performed by the community in response to the mercies of God shown in Christ. In contrast to the "individualized mysticism of late antiquity" that spoke of replacing blood sacrifices with divine knowledge, virtue, and prayer,[38] Paul refers here to the collective devotion of the Roman believers as a group. As Smiga shows, Paul asks for "a sacrifice which is communal rather than factional," which fits the context of "the tensions between Jewish-Christians and Gentile Christians in the house-

churches."[39] In using the verb παραστῆναι ("to present"), he picks up the terminology of 6:13-19, which urged believers to present themselves to God as weapons of righteousness.[40] Paul's unusual description of believers as σώματα ("bodies), which implies the basis of relationship and identity,[41] surfaces here, which has given rise to frequent celebrations of the ideal of worldly service in submission to the Lordship of Christ.[42] But in emphasizing the totality, earthiness, and quotidian aspects of such obedience,[43] the dramatic urgency of Paul's language is obscured by vaguely uplifting sentiments. A sacrifice killed or burned on the altar[44] is hardly the appropriate metaphor for mopping the floor. Surely an element of communal risk is envisioned when one speaks of placing the entire membership of house churches on the altar.[45] The aorist infinitive παραστῆσαι ("to present") is also inappropriate for continuous service in daily life, pointing rather to some specific

liturgischer Umdeutung," *JLW* 4 (1924) 37–47. See also Hans Wenschkewitz, "Die Spiritualisierung der Kultusbegriffe Tempel, Priester und Opfer im Neuen Testament," *Angelos* 4 (1932) 71–230; Raymond Corriveau builds on this work in *The Liturgy of Life: A Study of the Ethical Thought of St. Paul in His Letters to the Early Christian Communities*, STR 25 (Paris: Desclée de Brouwer; Montreal: Bellarmin, 1970) 159–69. See also Everett Ferguson, "Spiritual Sacrifice in Early Christianity and Its Environment," *ANRW* II 23.2 (1980) 1151–61; Wick, *Gottesdienste*, 180–81.

33   Isocrates *Nic.* 20, cited by Ferguson, "Spiritual Sacrifice," 1153.

34   See Wenschkewitz, "Spiritualisierung," 71–230, esp. 191.

35   See Zahn, 535.

36   In "Ethik," 211, Betz points to the parallel within the Asklepios cult in which persons healed by the deity presented votive offerings in the form of replicas of the diseased limb. See F. T. Straten, "Gifts for the Gods," in Versnel, *Faith, Hope and Worship*, 149–51.

37   Josef Blank describes the Pauline transformation of spiritual to somatic categories in "Zum Begriff des Opfers nach Röm 12:1-2," in *Paulus. Von Jesus zum Urchristentum* (Munich: Kösel, 1982) 184. Similarly Roetzel writes in "Sacrifice," 416: "Calling on and transposing the cultic language from his Pharisaism into a new key Paul appeals to his readers to make a

living sacrifice of their bodies and in the most radical sense to become both patron and victim."

38   Casel, "Umdeutung," 38.

39   Smiga, "Occasion of the Letter," 270.

40   See Heil, 137; Esler, *Conflict and Identity*, 311; Tobin, *Paul's Rhetoric*, 388.

41   See Jewett, *Terms*, 301–4.

42   The classic statement is by Ernst Käsemann, "Worship in Everyday Life: A Note on Romans 12," in *New Testament Questions of Today* (London: SCM, 1969) 188–95. Other examples are Ortkemper, *Leben*, 23f.; Schlier, *Zeit*, 82f.; Furnish, *Theology*, 101–6.

43   See esp. Käsemann, "Worship," 191, 194; Schrage, *Einzelgebote*, 49; Peter Seidensticker, *Lebendiges Opfer (Röm 12:1)* (Münster: Aschendorff, 1954) 256–63; Radl, "Kult und Evangelium," 62; Bauer, *Leiblichkeit*, 177–81; Bindemann, *Hoffnung*, 99–105.

44   See Jewett, *Terms*, 301–2: The sacrifice would be "not only used but used up, for normally that which was offered was either burnt on the altar or consumed in the temple by the priests. Paul apparently has something like this in mind, for he often refers to the deterioration of his body under the impact of persecutions and/missionary exertions."

45   The fact that Paul makes no distinction between slaves and free persons in formulating this admonition confirms Gülzow's assessment in *Christentum und Sklaverei*, 56, that in comparison with Judaism, the Roman households, and colleges, early Chris-

"transaction"[46] that Paul has in mind. The fact that Paul's other use of priestly language in Rom 15:16 is in the context of the conversion of the Gentiles indicates the scope of the transaction called for in Romans 12.[47] But in whatever arena this sacrifice occurs for the various house and tenement churches, its beneficial effect can come only "through his Spirit dwelling in your midst," according to the argument already laid down in 8:11.

The three attributes of sacrifice—"living, holy, acceptable"—somewhat obscured by translations that speak of a "living sacrifice,"[48] seem appropriate for a cultic setting, although no parallels to this triad have been found in connection with sacrifice outside of the NT and church fathers. The term "living" implies a sacrifice that is not bloody.[49] It thus modulates and softens the shocking metaphor of placing the life of believers on the altar. In contrast to 8:23 where the singular σῶμα refers to the collective body of believers, here the plural τὰ σώματα ὑμῶν clearly refers to "your bodies," each of which is to be sacrificed individually.[50] Paul wants their active partic-

ipation in the mission, expressing "newness of life" (Rom 6:4),[51] not some symbolic self-sacrifice along the lines of 1 Cor 13:3. The term "holy" designates the sacrifice as set apart from the profane realm for the sole purpose of God.[52] In this letter, that purpose is the enlisting of the bodies of the Romans for the cause of righteousness and holiness (cf. Rom 6:19) for a mission project. Paul returns to this motif in 15:16, referring to converted Gentiles as "sanctified by the Holy Spirit." "Acceptable to God" is a Koine expression[53] used infrequently in the LXX (Wis 4:10; 9:10) but employed elsewhere by Paul to depict actions consistent with the divine will (Rom 14:18; Phil 4:18; cf. "acceptable to the Lord" in Col 3:20). In substance, the term addresses the key question in Jewish cultic theory: what God wills and what God despises.[54] As Hamerton-Kelly observes, this view of sacrifice reverses the scapegoating that escapes responsibility.[55] The form of bodily sacrifice that Paul wishes to elicit from the Roman house churches should fulfill this divine assessment.

The expression τὴν λογικὴν λατρείαν ὑμῶν ("your

tianity held each person, whether slave or free, to the same ethical standard. This stance also entailed a measure of risk. See Patte, *Paul*, 295.

46 Cranfield, 2:598 n. 4, "very tentatively" suggests that Paul should have selected the present infinitive to express "the essentially continuous character of the action contemplated," i.e., the worldly service envisioned by contemporary exegetes and ethicists. This is the interpretation favored by Viagulamuthu, *Offering*, 286–88. However, the cultic framework of presenting a sacrifice is appropriately expressed with the aorist.

47 In "θύω," *TDNT* 3 (1965) 185, Johannes Behm also draws Rom 12:1 within the context of Paul's mission: "All that faith does (cf. Gal 5:6), whether it be ministry in the spread of the Gospel (Phil 2:17b; cf. 16a; also the apostle's own work and calling, R. 15:16; Phil 2:17a; 2 Tim 4:6), or the giving of material assistance (Phil 4:18), becomes θυσία and λειτουργία." Viagulamuthu, *Offering*, 214–18, 285–92, 365–468, overlooks the specific missional project promoted by Romans in his effort to interpret Rom 12:1-1 in line with timeless Catholic theology and ethics.

48 Cranfield, 2:600, observes that the *AV, RV, RSV, NEB*, and Moffatt separate ζῶσαν ("living") from the second and third attributes.

49 In "Ethik," 212, Betz cites *T. Levi* 3.6 and Athenago-

ras *Leg.* 13:2 as evidence that the term "living" means an "unbloody" sacrifice, i.e., a grain or vegetable offering. An early opponent of blood sacrifice was Theophrastus, whose work *On Piety* is discussed by Meijer, "Philosophers," 250–58. He advocated sacrifices "of a bloodless and pure kind," in Philostratus *Vit. Apoll.* 4.11. See also the discussion by Ferguson, "Spiritual Sacrifice," 1154.

50 This is not an appropriate text on which to decry the language of Christian individualism, as, for instance, in Cranfield, 2:600; Ortkemper, *Leben*, 24.

51 See Corriveau, *Liturgy of Life*, 170.

52 See Ortkemper, *Leben*, 25, who draws on the standard treatments of holiness in the OT and Qumran.

53 Werner Foerster, "εὐάρεστος, εὐαρεστέω," *TDNT* 1 (1964) 456f.

54 Dunn, 2:711, tentatively suggests the relation to the prophetic critique of sacrifices in Hos 8:13; Amos 5:22; Mic 6:7; Mal 1:8, 10, 13. For an overview of Hebrew sacramental theory, see J. Milgrom, "Sacrifices and Offerings, OT," *IDBS* (1976) 763–71.

55 Hamerton-Kelly, "Sacred Violence," 50–51: "Romans 12:1-2 opens the ethical section of the letter by placing the image of sacrifice as a rubric over the discussion. . . . Sacrifice is a metaphor for moral self-dedication and not a ruse for shifting responsibility on to a substitute. Thus the logic of substitution has been reversed."

reasonable worship") stands in apposition to the entire preceding clause, "to present your bodies. . . ."[56] While the term λατρείαν is used in Rom 9:4 and in the LXX for cultic service,[57] there has been considerable consternation in the commentaries over Paul's choice of the adjective λογικός, which means "rational, reasonable" and does appear in the LXX.[58] Most commentators and translators opt for the connotation "spiritual," based on the parallels in Rom 1:9 and 1 Pet 2:2, 5.[59] But the use of λογικός as a "favorite expression" of the Greek philosophers,[60] denoting the rational faculty in humans, should warn against assimilation to later Christian and Neoplatonic spirituality.[61] Particularly in Stoicism one finds the idea that worship should conform to reason, which resonates to the divine Logos.[62] Reacting against the anthropomorphic superstition of Greco-Roman religion, philosophers sought to transform cultic practices into intellectual and spiritual concepts.[63] Philo applies these ideas to Hellenistic Judaism, using λογικός to depict genuine worship and sacrifice,[64] while *T. Levi* 3.6 refers to angelic worship in language strikingly close to Romans: προσφέροντες τῷ Κυρίῳ ὀσμὴν εὐωδίας λογικὴν καὶ ἀναίμακτον θυσίαν ("offering to the Lord a sweet-smelling savor, a reasonable and bloodless offering.") Equally prominent is the use of "reasonable sacrifice" in the later Hermetic literature, where the mystic prays: Δέξαι λογικὰς θυσίας ἁγνὰς

ἀπὸ ψυχῆς καὶ καρδίας πρὸς σὲ ἀνετεταμένης, ἀνεκλάλητε, ἄρρητε, σιωπῇ φωνούμενε ("Accept my reasonable sacrifices, pure from soul and heart always stretched up to You . . . whose name nothing but silence can express").[65] In another location a Hermetic hymn celebrates the mystical union between the divine Logos and the individual mystic, which constitutes a "reasonable sacrifice": ὁ σὸς Λόγος δι᾽ ἐμοῦ ὑμνεῖ σέ. δι᾽ ἐμοῦ δέξαι τὸ πᾶν λόγῳ, λογικὴν θυσίαν ("Your reason sings through me your praises. Take back through me the All into Reason—a reasonable sacrifice"). [66] These parallels from the *Corpus hermeticum* were written a century or more after Romans and provide a substantial contrast in orientation: their individualistic, mystical, and escapist qualities contrast greatly with the sober realism and eschatological urgency of the Pauline ethic.[67] One could make similar comparisons with Hebrew and Greek philosophical efforts to transform worship.[68] But Paul does not indulge in polemical contrasts. His use of "reasonable worship," even though it may have been mediated by the Hellenistic synagogue,[69] signals the desire to set claim to a broad tradition of Greco-Roman as well as Jewish philosophy of religion. In place of the λατρεία of the Jewish cult (9:24) or the worship of finite images in Greco-Roman cults (1:23), Paul presents the bodily service of a community for the sake of world transformation and unification as the ful-

56 See Cranfield, 2:601; Dunn, 2:711.

57 Hermann Strathmann, "λατρεύω, λατρεία," *TDNT* 4 (1967) 61.

58 Cranfield, 2:604.

59 Barrett, 231; Cranfield, 2:604f.; Ferguson, "Spiritual Sacrifice," 1165; Ortkemper, *Leben*, 27.

60 BAGD 476, derived from Lietzmann, 108. Typical references are Epictetus *Diss.* 2.9.2; Marcus Aurelius Τὰ εἰς ἑαυτὸν 2.16.6; also the Latin equivalent in Seneca *Ep.* 95.50; *Ben.* 1.6.3; *Frag.* 123. See Nordon, *Agnostos Theos*, 37ff.; Sevenster, *Paul and Seneca*, 46; and Gerhard Kittel, "λογικός," *TDNT* 4 (1967) 142–43.

61 For an account of the problematic use of "spiritualization" by Wenschkewitz and others, see Georg Klinzing, *Die Umdeutung des Kultus in der Qumrangemeinde und im Neuen Testament* (Göttingen: Vandenhoeck & Ruprecht, 1971) 143–47. Betz, "Ethik," 212, cites H. W. Bartsch, "λογικός," *EWNT* 2 (1981) 877, as rejecting the translation "spiritual."

62 See Wenschkewitz, "Spiritualisierung," 125; Cran-

field, 2:602, mentions Epictetus *Diss.* 1.16.20; 2.9.2 and Marcus Aurelius Τὰ εἰς ἑαυτὸν 2.16 as examples of humans as "reasonable beings" who praise the divine source of reason. Engberg-Pedersen, *Stoics*, 262, maintains that Paul "aims to develop the meaning and impact of the Christ event in the logical categories of the understanding."

63 See esp. Meijer, "Philosophers," passim.

64 Kittel, "λογικός," 142. Dunn, 2:711, cites Philo *Opif.* 119; *Leg.* 1.141,70–72; 2.22–23; *Det.* 82–83; *Spec.* 1.201, 277.

65 *Corp. herm.* 1.31; translation adapted from Ferguson, "Spiritual Sacrifice," 1154. See also Klauck, "Kultische Symbolsprache," 114.

66 *Corp. herm.* 13.18–19; translation adapted from Ferguson, "Spiritual Sacrifice," 1154.

67 See Ortkemper, *Leben*, 32–33.

68 See Klinzig, *Umdeutung*, 214–17, and Radl, "Kult und Evangelium," 60–62.

69 So Dunn, 2:711, quoting Barrett, 232.

fillment of the vision of worship that would be truly reasonable.[70] In place of the enlightened individual, touted by Greco-Roman philosophers, there now stands the rationality of a redeemed community[71] committed to world mission.[72] Collective "reason," not some vague spiritual sentiment,[73] was the crucial requirement of the Spanish mission project with its wide range of intellectual, logistical, and political challenges. With this final phrase, "your [pl.] reasonable worship," a smooth transition is provided to the theme of the next verse.

■ **2** While the first premise of the ethic deals with somatic relations, the second concentrates on mental outlook. This echoes the first proof of the letter, where σώματα (1:24) is contrasted with νοούμενα (1:20). Two imperatives concerning nonconformity and transformation are developed in antithetical fashion, allegedly contrasting "external and fleeting fashion" and "inmost nature."[74] This distinction is inappropriate, as Cranfield and Dunn have shown, not because the two terms are synonymous,[75] but because our individualizing exegetical tradition makes such a distinction unclear and inappropriate. When the social dimension of Paul's rhetoric is taken into account,[76] a distinction surfaces between conformity to social and political pressure on the one hand and transformation of a group's ethical understanding on the other. Nonconformity with the present world order, suggested already by Paul's allusion to risky bodily sacrifices and his new definition of "reasonable worship," is urged by means of the root σχῆμα ("form, scheme, outward appearance") popularized by Greek history, philosophy, rhetoric, and science.[77] The term συσχηματίζω in the passive voice means to "be formed like, be conformed to,"[78] as the parallel in Plutarch's *Virt. vit.* 100f. indicates: μεθ' ἡμέραν μὲν γὰρ ἔξω βλέπουσα καὶ συσχηματιζομένη πρὸς ἑτέρους ἡ κακία δυσωπεῖται καὶ παρακαλύπτει τὰ πάθη . . . ("Vice, looking outside during the day and conforming itself to others, is ashamed and disguises its passions

---

70 Radl provides an overly generalized reference to "somatization" and "ethicization" in "Kult und Evangelium," 62, and relates the formulation in Romans to the proclamation of the gospel, though in 65–66 without explicit reference to the Spanish mission. Wick, *Gottesdienste*, 182, also overlooks the missional imperative that aims to create a worldwide chorus of praise (15:6-12) and defines λογικὴ λατρεία as "verbally appropriate worship" ("wortgemäßer Kultgottesdienst").

71 The second person plural pronoun is prominently linked with "reasonable worship," a point overlooked in the commentaries and studies like Corriveau, *Liturgy of Life*, 179–80. Even the penetrating study by Blank appears to have only individual rationality in mind in "Begriff des Opfers," 185–87. Engberg-Pedersen, *Stoics*, 264, also has the enlightened individual who overcomes "I-directedness" in mind when he explains, "The bodily self that has been removed in the total directedness towards God *not only* prevented a proper relation to God *but also* to others" (italics in original).

72 For an alternative view, see Nikolaus Walter, "Christusglaube und heidnische Religiosität in paulinischen Gemeinden," *NTS* 25 (1978–79) 422–42. Although Walter urges cognizance of the pagan background of Paul's language in the present post-Christian era (442), he defines "reasonable worship" as a matter of theological consistency with justification by faith (438), giving no hint of a missional imperative.

73 While he overlooks the communal and missional dimensions of the text, Betz, in "Ethik," 212, interprets "reasonable worship" as "ethical, eschatological and open to reason. It is an enlightened religion, not an irrational, diffuse superstition."

74 Sanday and Headlam, 353, refers to J. B. Lightfoot's study, "Recent Editions of St. Paul's Epistles," *JCSP* 3 (1856) 114, for the distinction between σχῆμα and μορφή. Lightfoot translates as follows: "Follow not the fleeting *fashion* of this world, but undergo a complete change (assume a new *form*, become new beings) in the renewal of your mind" (italics and parentheses in original). See also Michel, 371.

75 Cranfield, 2:605–8; Dunn, 2:712–13. While the terms μεταμορφόω and μετασχηματίζω are used as virtual synonyms in 2 Cor 3:18 and Phil 3:21, respectively, the same cannot be said for the term used here: συσχηματίζω has an inherently derivative sense—formed *by* something else.

76 Both imperatives are second person plural, which seems to be overlooked by commentators bound by the individualizing ethical tradition of the Western world.

77 Johannes Schneider, "σχῆμα, μετασχηματίζω," *TDNT* 7 (1971) 955.

78 BAGD 795.

. . ."). The link in Paul's rhetoric with "this aeon"[79] evokes the apocalyptic orientation that distinguishes Pauline thought from that of the moralist Plutarch. As the use of the passive form indicates, Paul views "this aeon" as an evil power seeking to extend its tentacles once again about those set free by Christ. A close parallel is 1 Cor 7:31, where Paul reiterates the apocalyptic urgency underlying his ethic: "the form ($\sigma\chi\tilde{\eta}\mu\alpha$) of this world is passing away."[80] In the case of the audience of Romans, these words would have had an immediate and painful resonance, for they had recently experienced the effort of the leading power of "this aeon" to make them conform. Since the Edict of Claudius had aimed at curtailing disorders provoked by Christian missionizing in Rome, this admonition has a direct bearing on the main purpose of Paul's letter. If the Roman house churches are reluctant to cooperate with the risky Spanish mission on grounds that it might once again endanger their existence, they will violate this imperative that is congruent with their own self-understanding as members of the new age. This verse also provides a crucial premise for our interpretation of Rom 13:1-7, which has often been taken as if Paul promoted servile acquiescence to Roman rule.

Paul's use of $\mu\epsilon\tau\alpha\mu\rho\varphi\rho\tilde{\upsilon}\sigma\vartheta\alpha\iota$ ("be transformed") is, like "rational worship," an effort to claim a Greco-Roman religious ideal for the new ethic. With a basic meaning of "remodel" and "change into another form,"[81] it was widely used in pagan religious contexts to depict the changing of gods into visible forms;[82] the movement of initiates in the mystery religions through various stages toward apotheosis;[83] the change of humans through the use of magical imprecations into divine beings capable of miracles;[84] and religious alteration through mystical vision.[85] In Seneca there is an even closer parallel, in which wisdom and the influence of a friend effect a transformation of one's moral and spiritual nature: *Intelligo, Lucili, non emendari me tantum, sed transfigurari . . . Et hoc ipsum argumentum est in melius translati animi, quod vitia sua, quae adhue ignorabat, videt.* ("I feel, my dear Lucilius, that I am not only being reformed but transformed . . . And indeed this very fact is proof that my spirit is altered into something better—that it can see its own faults, of which it was previously ignorant.")[86] Another use of the Latin equivalent of $\mu\epsilon\tau\alpha\mu\rho\varphi\acute{o}\omega$ in the passive along with a reference to the "mind" is found in Seneca's reflections about consistency: *Philosophia . . . dividitur in haec, scientiam and habitum animi. Nom qui didicit et facienda ac vitanda percepit, nondum sapiens est, nisi in ea, quae didicit, animus eius transfiguratus est.* ("Philosophy . . . is divided into knowledge and state of mind. For one who has learned and understood what he should do and avoid is not a wise man until his mind is transformed into the shape of that which he has learned.")[87] More distant parallels are available in late Jewish apocalyptic, in which the saints are expected to be "transformed . . . into the glory of angels" after death (*2 Bar.* 51.5) and Enoch is transformed in the process of his vision (*1 En.* 71.11).[88]

---

79   See Barr, *Time,* 121; Nils A. Dahl, "Neutestamentliche Ansätze zur Lehre von den zwei Regimenten," in H. H. Schrey, ed., *Reich Gottes und Welt,* WF 107 (Darmstadt: Wissenschaftliche Buchgesellschaft, 1969) 3–29; Gerhard Delling, *Zeit und Endzeit,* BibS(N) 58 (Neukirchen: Neukirchener, 1970) 24–82.

80   See Fee, *1 Corinthians,* 342: "it is not simply the 'outward form' that is on its way out, but the total 'scheme' of things as they currently exist." It is also clear from 1 Cor 2:6 that "this aeon" is easily linked with political authorities in Paul's mind.

81   Johannes Behm, "$\mu\epsilon\tau\alpha\mu\rho\varphi\acute{o}\omega$," *TDNT* 4 (1967) 755.

82   Typical representatives of the metamorphosis genre of religious literature are Ovid *Metam.* 8.626–724; Apuleius *Metam.* passim; Pseudo-Lucian *Asin.* 11–15, 56.

83   The classic study is Richard Reitzenstein, *The Hellenistic Mystery-Religions: Their Basic Ideas and Significance,* trans. J. E. Steely (Pittsburgh: Pickwick Press, 1978) 333–36, as exhibited in Apuleius *Metam.* 11.23–30, with "transformation" explicitly mentioned in 11.27; *Corp. herm.* 13.3, 14; 10.6.

84   Behm, "$\mu\epsilon\tau\alpha\mu\rho\varphi\acute{o}\omega$," 757: "magic brings it about that the human soul reflects the immortal form of deity," citing *PGM* XIII.270–74, 581–82; see also VII.560–65.

85   See Schlier, 359.

86   Seneca *Ep.* 6.1; translation from R. A. Gummere, *Seneca: ad lucilium epistulae morales* (Cambridge: Harvard, 1917) 1:25; for interpretation, see Sevenster, *Paul and Seneca,* 127.

87   Seneca *Ep.* 94.48; translation adapted from Gummere, *Seneca,* 3.43.

88   Dunn, 2:713, exaggerates the scale of this tradition,

The Pauline concept of transformation is oriented to this life rather than the next, and in contrast to the philosophers and mystery religions, it is corporate rather than individual.[89] As the context of Rom 1:18-32 and the subsequent discussion in 12:3-8 indicate, μετα-μορφοῦσθαι for Paul contains no element of apotheosis (see also 2 Cor 3:18). The means of the transformation is set forth clearly in the expression "by the renewal of the mind," which evokes the restoration of the twisted human mind in Rom 1–8, elaborating the meaning of λογικός ("reasonable") in 12:1. The term ἀνακαίνωσις ("renewal") appears in this verse for the first time in Greek literature.[90] Given the prominence of the term καινότης ("newness") in Rom 6:4 and 7:6 as denoting the restoration of humans through the power of Christ[91] and the later Christian use of ἀνακαινίζω ("to make new") for baptismal regeneration,[92] there is no doubt that Paul has in mind the basic recovery of righteousness and rationality through conversion. The original capacity of the human race to recognize and respond to the truth (Rom 1:20), which was distorted as a result of sin (Rom 1:28; 7:23, 25), has now been recovered and restored.[93] The word "mind" is used here in the singular,

parallel to the expression "reprobate mind" in 1:28, implying a complex of assumptions and mental abilities characteristic of a group rather than an individual.[94] The most significant parallel in Paul's writing is 1 Cor 2:16, where the Christian community is said to share the "mind of Christ," a formulation that counters the philosophical tradition of νοῦς as the rational capacity in individuals.[95] "The gospel does not make one more intelligent."[96] The transformation Paul has in view here is shaped by the recovery of a realistic appraisal of ethical choices in the light of the converted community's experience of the "new creation" brought by Christ.

The focus on group decision making[97] in this introductory pericope is sharpened by the unequivocal phrasing "that you (pl.) may ascertain what is the will of God." The basic sense of δοκιμάζειν is "to test," "to try," usually in a public arena.[98] An example of this public approval is given by Socrates to Alcibiades, who wants to know what a law is: πάντες γὰρ οὗτοι νόμοι εἰσίν, οὓς τὸ πλῆθος συνελθὸν καὶ δοκιμάσαν, ἔγραφε, φράζον ἅ τε δεῖ ποιεῖν καὶ ἃ μή ("For all these laws are in existence since the majority having convened, approved and wrote them up, declaring what things must and

---

including references to *1 En.* 104.6, where the concept is missing entirely. In Dan 12:3, *2 En.* 22.8, *4 Ezra* 7.97, and *Asc. Isa.* 9.9, the righteous will appear in glory in the next life, but without the term "transformation" being used.

89 This is more than a matter of each individual Christian having the same experience, as Behm suggests in "μεταμορφόω," 758–59. "The initiate has no aristocratic claim to a special experience of God; all Believers participate in the miracle of transformation." The transformation in Rom 12:2 involves the group mind, represented by individual house and tenement churches and Roman Christianity as a whole.

90 The word occurs later in Titus 3:5 and in *Herm. Vis.* 16.9, "Let this reminder and the renewal of your spirits (ἀνακαίνωσις τῶν πνευμάτων ὑμῶν) be sufficient for you and the saints."

91 Tobin, *Paul's Rhetoric*, 389; see also Paul's use of καινὴ κτίσις ("new creation") in Gal 6:15 and 2 Cor 5:17.

92 Johannes Behm, "ἀνακαινίζω," *TDNT* 3 (1965) 451; see esp. Titus 3:5.

93 See Betz, "Ethik," 214–15.

94 Jewett, *Terms*, 386–87. See in 360–61 the critique of Johannes Behm, "νοῦς," *TDNT* 4 (1967) 951–60.

My suggestion that νοῦς in Paul is a "constellation of thoughts and beliefs which provides the criteria for judgments and actions" (361) was stimulated by Adolf Schlatter, *Die Theologie des Judentums nach dem Bericht des Josephus* (Gütersloh: Bertelsmann, 1932) 27. H. E. Stoessel, "Notes on Romans 12:1-2: The Renewal of the Mind and Internalizing Truth," *Int* 17 (1963) 164–66, refers to the "collective usage" of νοῦς as descriptive of a "common mind," whether Pagan or Christian.

95 Sanday and Headlam, 354; Betz, "Ethik," 214–15.

96 Jewett, *Terms*, 385.

97 The first commentator to explicitly identify the corporate dimension is Dunn, 2:715, citing Ortkemper, *Leben*, 39. In "Das Zusammenkommen der Gemeinde und ihr 'Gottesdienst' nach Paulus," *EvTh* 33 (1973) 548–53, Klaus Wengst insists that the assembled congregation hears this exhortation and is given the task to determine the will of God in concrete situations. Schnabel, *Law*, 306, refers to a broad consensus on this point that includes studies by Wolfgang Schrage, Otto Merk, H. D. Wendland, H. Schürmann, P. Grech, J. F. Collange, and T. J. Deidun.

98 Walter Grundmann, "δόκιμος," *TDNT* 2 (1964) 256. See also Therrien, *Discernement*, 15.

must not be done").[99] Precisely the same phrase is found in Phil 1:10, εἰς τὸ δοκιμάζειν ὑμᾶς, referring to the congregation's discernment of appropriate behavior in preparation for the return of Christ (see also 1 Thess 5:21). In the case of Romans, it is the "will of God"[100] that is to be discerned, namely, what God desires the community to do in a particular situation. In place of definitions of praiseworthy behavior on the basis of the law and casuistry,[101] or of natural reason, or of public consensus, or of authoritarian decree,[102] it is clear that Paul understands the early Christian community in Rome as needing to weigh alternatives in the light of the "renewed mind" given by Christ—and also in the light of this letter, which sets forth an agenda of the divine will to resolve disputes and cooperate in a missionary venture of great significance.

Paul's effort to incorporate leading concepts of Greco-Roman and Jewish ethics is visible in the remarkable threefold apposition of "good," "acceptable," "perfect" that ends the pericope. Two of the three terms were ordinarily far removed from the Hebraic concept of the "will of God" with which they are correlated here.[103] But Paul's goal is not to provide an ethic sufficiently broad and general as to be suitable for later Christian individuals.[104] The context of Rom 12:1-2 provides a dramatic transformation of these traditional concepts. Zahn showed that "the good and acceptable and perfect" should not be understood as three attributes of the will of God but rather as an apposition providing traditional guidelines to evaluate alternate courses of action as consistent or inconsistent with the divine will.[105] The three terms never appear together in a sequence like this and thus cannot be viewed as a traditional formulation.[106] They evoke disparate and at times overlapping fields of discourse in the Greco-Roman and Jewish world and thus function in an inclusive manner to take account of the various orientations in the Roman house and tenement churches in defining the will of God. Ἀγαθόν ("good") is the generic term for the highest moral quality in the Hebrew wisdom tradition and rabbinic ethics, in Hellenistic Judaism, in classical and later Greek philosophy, and in the Roman value system, with definitions that fluctuate according to those intellectual contexts.[107] The term εὐάρεστος ("acceptable, satisfactory"), used here without the attribution "to God" as in 12:1,[108] evokes the realm of sophistic and

99 This parallel from Xenophon *Mem.* 1.2.42 was suggested by Wengst, "Zusammenkommen," 549.

100 Gottlob Schrenk discusses the distinctively biblical concept of the will of God in "ϑέλω, ϑέλημα," *TDNT* 3 (1965) 47–59. K.-W. Niebuhr shows how Jewish paraenesis in the pre-Christian period understood the law as the expression of the will of God: *Gesetz und Paränese: Katechismusartige Weisungsreihen in der frühjüdischen Literatur* (Tübingen: Mohr-Siebeck, 1987) 239–42.

101 Tobin, *Paul's Rhetoric*, 388, shows that the "will of God" is not identical here with "the Mosaic law."

102 See Wengst, "Zusammenkommen," 548; Dunn, 2:715, particularly points to the contrast with Jewish ethics as described in Rom 2:18.

103 The index of Greek words in Niebuhr, *Gesetz und Paränese*, shows that while ἀγαθός ("good") appears in early Jewish exhortations as a correlate with the law, there are no parallels to "acceptable" and "perfect."

104 For illustrations of the exclusively individualistic construal of this passage, along with the assumption that Paul aimed to create an ethic for the ages, see Cranfield, 2:609–10; Michel, 371–73; Leenhart, 172; Achtemeier, 195; Therrien, *Discernement*, 294–99.

105 Zahn, 539–40, argued that "acceptable" would be a redundant attribute to the "will of God" and that "perfect" would be inappropriate as an attribute because it evokes the absurd possibility of imagining an imperfect will of God. See also Cranfield, 2:610. Arguing for the attribute theory are Godet, 429; Barrett, 233; Morris, 436; Betz, "Ethik," 215.

106 See Leenhardt, 172. Michel, 372 n. 24, notes the proximity of these terms in Stoic popular ethics in the expressions τὸ ἀγαθὸν εὐάρεστον ("the acceptable good") and τὸ τέλειον ἀγαθόν ("the perfect good").

107 Walter Grundmann, "ἀγαθός," *TDNT* 1 (1964) 10–15. See also Dodd, 192: the term "good . . . is the most general expression for what is of absolute worth in and for itself, and as such is common to all philosophies." For the Roman value system, see Meister, "Tugenden," 16–17.

108 Dodd, 193, repudiates the connotation "acceptable to God" as a tautology of the previous expression "the will of God" and concludes that it refers to "the kind of action which in itself gives satisfaction to all concerned." The effort by Therrien, *Discernement*, 147, to refute Dodd is unconvincing.

public ethics, which advocate whatever is widely approved,[109] or in business, in which the satisfactory quality of a product is touted.[110] It also is used in slavery ethics, as in "giving satisfaction" to masters (Titus 2:9),[111] and in Roman popular ethics, as the rough equivalent of *satis* ("sufficient, satisfactory"). In contrast to the rather mundane connotation of "acceptable," the final term τέλειος ("perfect") evokes the exalted realms of the initiate in mysteries, the seer capable of divine vision, the mature in judgment or knowledge, the philosopher with fully developed character, or the hero possessing genuine virtue.[112] The term and its equivalents were used by Hebrew, Greek, and Latin writers to depict the highest realm of moral and spiritual insight, with Paul making particularly prominent use of it in the dialogue with gnostically inclined believers in 1 Corinthians.[113] To list the "good and acceptable and perfect" in the context of nonconformity with this world and of determining the will of God is to legitimize as well as challenge the behavioral standards of the various groups of Roman believers and the cultural arenas from which they were drawn. The broad inclusivity of this threefold list precludes the polemical intent suspected by commentators.[114] Yet every ethical category requires transformation on the basis of the "mercies of God" and the "renewal of the mind" revealed in Christ.[115] To provide guidance in this task with specific reference to the decision making of the Roman house and tenement churches is the goal of the fourth proof, whose introduction is now complete.

---

109 See E. A. Judge, "Moral Terms in the Eulogistic Tradition," *NDIEC* 2 (1982) 105–6.

110 MM 259.

111 BAGD 318.

112 See Gerhard Delling, "τέλειος," *TDNT* 8 (1972) 67–72, and BAGD 809; Ch. Guignebert, "Quelques remarques sur la Perfection et ses voies dans le mystère paulinien," *RHPhR* 8 (1928) 415–19; Du Plessis, ΤΕΛΕΙΟΣ, 73–121; Karl Prümm, "Das neutestamentliche Sprach- und Begriffsproblem der Vollkommenheit," *Bib* 44 (1963) 76–92, esp. 89; B. Schwank, "Was versteht die Bibel unter Vollkommenheit?" in *Der "vollkommene" Mensch*, BBKW 75 (1963) 7–28; Martin Winter, *Pneumatiker und Psychiker in Korinth: Zum religionsgeschichtlichen Hinter-grund von 1. Kor. 2,6–3,4*, MTS 12 (Marburg: Elwert, 1975) 21–25, 45–49, 98–143.

113 1 Cor 1:28; 13:10; 14:20. See esp. Winter, *Pneumatiker und Psychiker*, 45–49, 98–143, 212–26.

114 Käsemann, 315, detects an "anti-enthusiastic" intent in the listing of the sober virtues of the good, acceptable, and perfect, while Cranfield, 2:610, sees warnings against those valuing "spectacular charismatic gifts" and inclined toward "Gentile paganism."

115 In ΤΕΛΕΙΟΣ, 177, Du Plessis appears to overlook this transformational framework when he defines "perfection" in 12:2 as "an unblemished character in a kinship regulated by divine initiative."

12

The Second Pericope

The Elaboration of Sober Self-Assessment and the Exercise of Charismatic Gifts

3/ For I say through the grace[a] given to me to every one who is[b] among you, do not be superminded above what one ought to be minded, but set your mind on being sober-minded, according to the measuring rod of faith that God dealt out[c] to each. 4/ For as in one body we have many members,[d] but all members do not have the same use, 5/ so we the many are[e] one body in Christ, each[f] one a member of others, 6/ yet having charismatic gifts that differ according to the grace given to us,
    whether prophecy—according to the analogy of faith,
        7/ or service[g]—in the serving,
        or the one who teaches[h]—in the teaching,
            8/ or[i] the exhorter—in the exhortation,
            the sharer—with generosity,
                the leader[j]—with diligence,
                the one showing mercy—with cheer.

a   The addition of τοῦ θεοῦ ("of God") by L 69 81 323 330 424 945 1241 1506 1735 *al* t vg^ms sy^h is clearly a secondary expansion.
b   Nestle-Aland[26/27] cites a conjecture by Hermannus Venema (1697–1787) to add τι ("who, what, something") after ὄντι (participle meaning "who is / being") that has the effect of isolating a particular type of person as the target of this passage. Dodd, 194, finds this plausible, but the basis of the conjecture is a mistaken view of Romans as polemicizing against heretics. The conjecture is rejected by Cranfield, 2:612.
c   In "ΕΜΕΤΡΕΣΕΝ in Rom. XII.3," *JTS* 14 (1963) 103–4, J. Neville Birdsall discusses the variant ἐμέτρησεν ("he measured") found (usually as ἐμέτρισεν) in 489 491 1739 (supralinear reading by its scribe) 1881 1908* Or^lat (once) Chrys^(?cat)) as "a secondary reading due to the influence of the following μέτρον."
d   The reversal in sequence of "many" and "members" by A L P Ψ 6 33 69 88 104 323 326 424 614 1175 1243 1319 1505 1506 1573 1739 1836 1874 1881 2344 2495 *Maj* appears to be a secondary stylistic improvement that does not change the meaning. The sequence πολλὰ μέλη ἔχομεν ("many members we have") is strongly supported by P[31,46] ℵ B D F G 629 1241 *pc* latt.
e   The omission of ἐσμεν ("we are") by F G appears to be a simple, scribal error.
f   The minor variant in D[2] L Ψ 33 69 88 104 323 326 424 614 945 1175 1241 1505 1735 1836 1874 1881 2495 *Maj* that reads ὁ, the masculine definite article, for τό, the neuter definite article, is a secondary grammatical improvement, perhaps revealing that the "idiomatic expression" (Sanday-Headlam, 355) with the neuter was no longer in use. The neuter article is found in P[31,46] ℵ A B D* F G P 6 81 365 1243 1319 1506 1573 1739 *pc*. (2344 reads οἱ.)
g   The substitution ὁ διακονῶν in ℵ[2] 69 330 1241 1506 *pc* is likely an "assimilation" to the following form of "he who teaches," according to Cranfield, 2:621.
h   The variant found in A, διδασκαλίαν ("teaching"), is an assimilation to the preceding forms "serving" and "prophesying."
i   The omission of εἴτε ("whether") by P[46vid] D* F G latt assimilates this phrase to the ones that follow in v. 8.
j   The variant spelling of "he who leads" as found in P[31] ℵ appears to be an example of reduplication; cf. Moulton and Howard, *Grammar II*, 192–93.

Analysis

This pericope is organized in a rhythmic fashion, with the first sentence composed of four nicely balanced clauses and the next with six similar clauses.[1] In the first sentence there is an elaborate paronomasia,[2] with the element φρονεῖν ("to be minded") repeated four times, with the first and last in the antithetical constructions of

---

1   See Michel, 374. In "Beiträge," 243–44, Weiss identifies four strophes in 12:4-5 but suggests that 12:3 is a three-line strophe, which has the disadvantage of combining the antithetical material concerning supermindedness and sober-mindedness in the same overly long line.

2   Bullinger, *Figures*, 305, refers to this as a "paregmenon; or derivation," a figure in which words are derived from the same root.

"superminded" and "sober-minded" conveying the guideline for a proper self-understanding. The first three lines of this first sentence conclude with homoioteleuton in the form of -ιν and -ειν endings. The second sentence also contains a paronomasia involving the word μέλη ("members") which is repeated in three of the four lines, with the fourth containing the associated word "body." Verse 3 thus provides the basis for a proper self-understanding in the context of the Christian community as the body of Christ.

Verses 4 through 6 deal with the charismatic gifts that mark the church as "one body in Christ." There is a paronomasia that links the congregational χαρίσματα ("charismatic gifts") to the divinely granted χάρις ("gift of grace") received by each Christian in 12:6. Verses 6 through 8 feature an artfully constructed series of seven charismatic gifts, arranged in four parallel εἴτε ("whether, or") clauses followed by three clauses with participles and prepositional phrases with ἐν ("in") without the article. The last three clauses all begin with ὁ ("the"), resulting in an anaphora that parallels the anaphora in the first four clauses beginning with εἴτε. The anaphora with ὁ is anticipated by the shift from nouns describing the gifts in the first two clauses to nouns describing the gifted persons in the subsequent five clauses beginning with ὁ διδάσκων ("he who teaches") in v. 7. The polysyndeton in the first four clauses "produces the impression of the extensiveness and abundance by means of an exhausting summary," while the asyndeton in the final three clauses "produces a vivid and impassioned effect."[3] Three pairs of identical word stems in different forms and cases provide an intriguing paronomasia in the references to the second through fourth charismatic gifts. Grammatically speaking, vv. 6-7 are dependent on the finite verbs ἔχομεν ("we have") and ἐσμεν ("we are") in 12:4-5, providing therefore a graceful and definitive description of the body of Christ. It has a mildly imperative connotation only insofar as so artful and impassioned a description of the ethos of the church provides an appealing vision.

The rhetorical flair in this passage leads one to admire the congruence between subject matter and style: Paul speaks charismatically on the subject of the charismatic gifts.[4]

Rhetorical Disposition

IV.	The *probatio*
12:1–15:13	The fourth proof: Living together according to the gospel so as to sustain the hope of global transformation
12:3-8	2. The elaboration of sober self-assessment and the exercise of charismatic gifts
12:3	a. The admonition concerning proper self-understanding
12:3a	1) The basis of the appeal to "every one": "the grace given to me"
12:3b	2) The repudiation of supermindedness
12:3c	3) The affirmation of sober-mindedness
12:3d	4) The criterion of the "measuring rod consisting of faith"
12:4-5	b. A *similitudo* ("similitude") that demonstrates a proper self-understanding
12:4	1) The similitude of "one body"
12:4a	a) First premise: bodies have "many members"
12:4b	b) Second premise: differentiation in the use of members
12:5	2) The inferences from the similitude
12:5a	a) Believers are "one body in Christ"
12:5b	b) Each Christian is "a member of others"
12:6-8	c. The exercise of charismatic gifts within the Christian community
12:6a	1) The charismatic criterion of individual impartations of grace
12:6b-8	2) Description of seven charismatic gifts in the congregation
12:6b	a) For prophecy: "analogy of faith"
12:7a	b) For service: "in serving"
12:7b	c) For teaching: "in teaching"
12:8a	d) For exhortation: "in exhortation"
12:8b	e) For philanthropy: "with generosity"
12:8c	f) For leadership: "with diligence"
12:8d	g) For social service: "with cheer"

3   W. C. van Unnik, "The Interpretation of Romans 12:8: ὁ μεταδιδοὺς ἐν ἁπλότατι," in M. Black and W. A. Smalley, eds., *On Language, Culture and Religion: In Honor of Eugene A. Nida* (The Hague: Mouton, 1974) 181, quoting from BDF §460.

4   See Schlier, 365.

Exegesis

■ **3** The opening of the second pericope is surprisingly formal, with Paul's charismatic authority as an apostle emphasized and the scope of his injunction widened to include each member of each congregation in Rome. Clearly, what he says here is of fundamental importance in the furtherance of Paul's missionary plan. Commentators recognize the γάρ ("for") as linking this pericope closely to the foregoing,[5] with the suggestion that the introduction has a particular bearing on the issue of charismatics.[6] I think we can identify the element in the introduction that has a particular bearing here: the issue of communal discernment of God's will, which involves the exercise of the charismatically renewed mind of the Christian community. The use of λέγω ("I say, enjoin") in the emphatic position as the opening word of the pericope is reminiscent of the introductory formula in prophetic and apocalyptic literature,[7] an impression which is strengthened by the formal declaration of Paul's charismatic authority in διὰ τῆς χάριτος τῆς δοθείσης μοι ("through the grace given to me"). But in view of the references in Rom 1:5 and 15:15 to the specific grace of an apostolic vocation, it is clear that prophecy as such is not implied.[8] It is rather an authoritative, oral declaration,[9] conveyed by Phoebe's scribe as the letter is read aloud to the house and tenement churches, and validated by Paul's own apostolic charisma.[10] The reference to grace in v. 6 indicates "that his 'grace' is no different in kind from the 'grace given' to them too. . . . Paul speaks as a charismatic to charismatics."[11] The use of the passive participle δοθείσης ("given") seems formulaic because of its recurrence in 12:6 and 15:5 (also 1 Cor 3:10; Gal 2:9; Eph 3:2, 7, 8),[12] thereby placing Paul's utterance, his apostolic vocation, and the charismatic gifts of the Roman congregations under the structure of divine gift.[13] The ethic of obligation, a distinctive feature of Romans,[14] rests on the foundation of grace that is given but never earned.[15] This foundation is of particular importance in the discussion of the dangers of charismatic pride.[16]

The emphatic placement[17] of "every one who is among you" is so peculiar[18] that it is often explained with suggestions that Paul wished to polemicize against

---

5   Cranfield, 2:611; Wilckens, 3:10.
6   Michel, 374.
7   See Müller, *Prophetie*, 132–33.
8   See Ortkemper, *Leben*, 42, for a critique of Müller's contention in *Prophetie*, 135–36, that the introductory formula marks this pericope as "prophetic."
9   The direct speaking of the apostle is conveyed in this formulation, because λέγω has the rhetorical force of speech making. Among the "classic" ten Attic orators, Demosthenes uses λέγω some 258 times; Aeschines 49 times; Lysias 26 times; Isaeus 23 times; Isocrates 22 times; Andocides 10 times; Antiphon 7 times; Hyperides 5 times; Lycurgus 1 time; and Dinarchus never.
10   Note that the instrumental use of διά ("through") parallels that in 12:1. See note 30 in the preceding pericope.
11   Dunn, 2:720. However, Akari Satake notes in "Apostolat und Gnade," 100, that whenever Paul speaks of having received "grace," it is in connection with his apostolic service. He goes on to argue (102–6) for a sharp distinction between Paul's apostolic χάρις ("grace") and the χαρίσματα ("charismatic gifts") shared by congregational leaders. This raises a terminological nuance to the level of an authoritarian principle that contrasts greatly with Paul's argument in Romans. Wobbe, *Charis-Gedanke*, 74, develops a precedent to Satake's case.
12   Michel, 374.
13   See Ortkemper, *Leben*, 42: "The gift-character of grace, which is in implied by the concept itself, is further underlined through the passive δοθείσης."
14   See Betz, "Ethik," 215.
15   See Hans Conzelmann, "χάρις κτλ.," *TDNT* 9 (1974) 394f. See also Wobbe, *Charis-Gedanke*, 15–17, 40–69. Berger, "Gnade," 14–17, deals with the background of this theme in Jewish texts.
16   Doughty, "Priority," 178–79: "The grace-character of the spiritual gifts excludes their appropriation by man for his own glorification; that which comes to man from God as a 'gift of grace' can never be a ground for human boasting. . . . Where life in the Spirit is not understood as a gift of grace the result is spiritual anarchy."
17   See Cranfield, 2:612.
18   The peculiarity of this expression is indicated by Venema's emendation, noted in note b above. A *TLG* search yields no occurrence of the phrase παντὶ τῷ ὄντι apart from two very late philosophers, Themistius and Syrianus, both using the phrase in a different philosophical sense.

charismatics who might feel exempt from his warning,[19] or that he wishes to include various Christian groups in Romans.[20] The extreme expression of the polemical approach was suggested by several nineteenth-century commentators who followed the logic of the Venema conjecture to translate "to every one who thinks himself to be something among you."[21] The absence of directly polemical details in this pericope[22] and the correlation with the inclusive address of 1:7 lead me to the conclusion that Paul's urgency is motivated by his knowledge of the role of charismatic gifts in the splintered house churches in Rome. He does not wish to single anyone out for blame here, particularly not charismatics, among whom he has explicitly identified himself by reference to his own "grace." Operating on the premise that every Christian has charismatic gifts (12:6),[23] Paul wishes to include everyone in the scope of his authoritative discourse.

The content of the admonition[24] is provided in a witty wordplay based on a fourfold paronomasia with the stem φρον- ("think, be minded"), which had been used in 11:20 and 25 to warn against Gentile Christian claims of superiority over Jews. There are frequent examples of this particular wordplay in Greek literature,[25] so that Paul's formulation would have evoked delight and immediate comprehension in his hearers. In the first example given below, Socrates explains why one ought to avoid curiosity about how the gods created the heavenly bodies. The wordplay developed by Socrates is underlined below:

Κινδυνεῦσαι δ' ἂν ἔφη καὶ παραφρονῆσαι τὸν ταῦτα μεριμνῶντα οὐδὲν ἧττον ἢ Ἀναξαγόρας παρεφρόνησεν ὁ μέγιστον φρονήσας ἐπὶ τῷ τὰς τῶν θεῶν μηχανὰς ἐξηγεῖσθαι ("He said that the one who meddles with these matters also risks <u>mental illness</u> as completely as Anaxagoras, who went <u>mentally ill</u> as the grandee was <u>minded</u> to explain the machinery of the gods.")[26]

The association of the wordplay with the Odyssean tradition of moderate heroism is indicated by Penelope's response to the announcement that he had returned:

Μαῖα φίλη, μάργην σε θεοὶ θέσαν, οἵ τε δύνανται ἄφρονα ποιῆσαι καὶ ἐπίφρονά περ μάλ' ἐόντα, καί τε χαλιφρονέοντα σαοφροσύνης ἐπέβησαν.
("Dear nurse, the gods have made you mad, the gods who can make <u>silly-minded</u> even one who is exceedingly <u>sensibly minded</u> and who have brought the <u>light-minded</u> to <u>moderate mindedness</u>.")[27]

The classical background of these terms is unmistakable, illuminated particularly by Helen North.[28] Her work should relieve complaints concerning the alleged ambiguity of Paul's usage.[29] The poets, orators, and philosophers of the fifth to fourth centuries BCE drew on epic poetry to create the distinction between the moderate hero, the σώφρων ἀνήρ who lived within limits, and the

---

19   Michel, 374; additional references in Ortkemper, *Leben*, 43.
20   Zahn, 541; Dunn, 2:720.
21   Meyer, 2:255, cites Koppe and Baumgarten-Crucius. The Venema conjecture is discussed in note b above.
22   Ortkemper, *Leben*, 43.
23   See Koenig, *Charismata*, 93–127; Schatzmann, *Charismata*, 70–80; Brockhaus, *Charisma*, 197f.; and Joachim Herten, "Charisma—Signal einer Gemeindetheologie des Paulus," in J. Hainz, ed., *Kirche im Werden* (Munich: Schöningh, 1976) 80.
24   The admonition is expressed by the negative infinitive (μὴ ὑπερφρονεῖν), which, when following after "for I say," tends to place the whole into indirect discourse, thus softening its effect ("I say to you [that you] not be superminded . . .").
25   See BAGD 802, 842. An additional, more extensive example is quoted by Helen North, *SOPHROSYNE: Self-Knowledge and Self-Restraint in Greek Literature* (Ithaca, N.Y.: Cornell University Press, 1966) 3–4.
26   Xenophon *Mem.* 4.7.6. A less elaborate wordplay associated with the Socratic tradition is *Soc. Ep.* 36 σωφρονέω . . . συσσωφρονέω ("I am sober . . . I am sober with another").
27   Homer *Od.* 23.11–13; translation adapted from North, *SOPHROSYNE*, 3f. Three other locations where the element φρον- is used in smaller scale paronomasias are Maximus Tyrius *Phil.* 18.1c, ἐσωφρόνει . . . ὑπερφρόνει ("innerminded . . . superminded"); Demetrius Phalereus *Frag.* 92, ὑπερφρον- καταφρον- ("superminded . . . contemptuous"); and Plutarch *Mor.* 776d, φρονεῖν καὶ σωφρονεῖν ("wise-minded and sober-minded").
28   Bibliographic details in note 22.
29   Cranfield, 2:612; Ortkemper, *Leben*, 44f.

"high-minded" heroes like Achilles and Ajax who broke such limits.[30] In the context of the Greek democracies, σωφροσύνη ("sober-mindedness") was the virtue of mature civility and submission to law while its opposite, pride or high-mindedness, was the vice of tyrants.[31] "The *polis* by its very nature required a much greater exercise of restraint (*aidôs, sôphrosyne*) than had the loosely organized Homeric society. . . . In Finley's words, only by taming the hero could the community grow."[32] Moderation was associated with *aidôs* ("reverence") and *metron* ("limit"),[33] the latter being used in precisely this relationship in Rom 12:3. The virtue of moderation was anchored in the religious ethos of Apollo and Delphi that stressed "Know thyself that thou art but mortal," "Think mortal thoughts," and "Not too much of anything" or the "Golden Mean,"[34] all of which were associated with accepting limits. These ideas were correlated in Greek poetry and drama, with Aechylus and Sophocles placing sober-mindedness in conflict with superheroic self-assertion that loses touch with limitations.[35] The Attic orators such as Lysias and Demosthenes reiterated the association of sober-mindedness as readiness to respect democractic authority while standing in opposition to oligarchy which pridefully breaches limits.[36] Socrates embodied these ideals for later generations, influencing the ascetic development of sober-mindedness as self-sufficiency and self-control.[37] From the classical age down through the later Stoics and popular philosophers, echoed in the prescribed school exercises of the Hellenistic and the Greco-Roman eras, moderation was listed as one of the cardinal virtues.[38]

The philosophical treatment of sober-mindedness was decisively shaped by Plato and Aristotle, moving it in a direction diametrically opposed to Pauline usage. Plato takes up the themes in the earlier development, solidifying the position of sober-mindedness as a cardinal virtue. The problematic new direction was Plato's association of sober-mindedness with the divine. In the *Laws*, sobriety makes a person similar to God: "God would be for us the measure of all things . . . and the one who would be dear to God must become like God, so far as possible. According to the present reasoning, the sober-minded among us (ὁ μὲν σώφρων ἡμῶν) is dear to God, for he/she is like God, and the one who is not sober-minded (ὁ δὲ μὴ σώφρων) is not like God, but different and unjust."[39] Aristotle echoes this theme by insisting that humans should make themselves immortal through the exercise of reason, which is the divine element in humankind.[40] The Stoics during the Greco-Roman period picked up this line by urging imitation of the sobriety of God so that the person marked by sober-mindedness is expressing divine kinship.[41] Philo assimilated these ideas to biblical paradigms of virtue, suggesting that sober-mindedness originates in the

---

30 North, *SOPHROSYNE*, 2.

31 Ibid., 14.

32 Ibid., 12; the reference is to M. I. Finley, *The World of Odysseus* (New York: Viking, 1954) 129.

33 North, *SOPHROSYNE*, 6, 10, 16; she quotes Cleobulus in Diehls and Kranz, *Vorsokratiker*, 10.1, "*Metron* is best."

34 North, *SOPHROSYNE*, 4–5; also 10: "The great development of the influence of the Delphic oracle belongs to this same period—a time during which the priests of Apollo preached measure and restraint in public and private life and encouraged decency and civilized behavior in religious rites. It was at this time that sophrosyne acquired a strongly religious flavor." See also Hans Dieter Betz, "The Delphic Maxim, 'ΓΝΩΘΙ ΣΑΥΤΟΝ' in Hermetic Interpretation," *HTR* 63 (1970) 465–84.

35 North, *SOPHROSYNE*, 32–33, 35: "The observance of limits is the essence of Aeschylean sophrosyne." Typical in the plays of Sophocles is the "insistence on human responsibility and his habit of finding the cause of tragedy in some violation of sophrosyne" (68).

36 Ibid., 135–42.

37 Ibid., 117–21.

38 Ulrich Luck, "σώφρων κτλ.," *TDNT* 7 (1971) 1099; North, *SOPHROSYNE*, 246, 271.

39 Translation of Plato *Leg.* 716c-d adapted from North, *SOPHROSYNE*, 194, where Plato *Gorg.* 507bff. is cited as a parallel passage. She notes the contrast with classical—and, I would add, Pauline—usage: "The imitation to God, which is the aim of Plato's legislation, is actually a contradiction of those traditional warnings against likening oneself to God which were among the earliest themes of sophrosyne. The conflict between *hybris* and sophrosyne, which had provided tragedy with one of its most fruitful subjects, has now largely lost its meaning."

40 Aristotle *Eth. nic.* 1177b33; *Metaph.* 982b30ff; Plato *Theaet.* 176b, cited by North, *SOPHROSYNE*, 211.

divine realm to provide the basis of the beatific vision of God.[42] This association of sober-mindedness with the divine eroded the classical contrast with "high-mindedness"[43] or "pride" and rendered less plausible its definition in terms of respecting one's "measure" or "limit."[44]

It is significant that Paul recovers the classical usage[45] rather than employing σωφρονεῖν ("to be sober minded") in a manner typical for his era, which opened too large a door to religious and philosophical arrogance. Having argued in Rom 1:18-32 that the loss of rationality comes from a confusion of oneself or one's group with God, Paul avoids any illusion of God-likeness here by recovering a contrast with "supermindedness," understood in a pejorative sense[46] as a violation of divinely established limits.[47] The expression παρ᾽ ὃ δεῖ means "beyond what one ought, or is necessary."[48] The "ought" has been defined in Romans as the "will of God,"[49] which should determine the shape of one's self-image; to take the earlier argument of Romans seriously, it must be that of sinners formerly in enmity with God but now saved by grace alone.[50] To be "superminded above what one ought to be minded" is to fall back into the primal lie (1:18, 22, 25), to abandon the Abrahamic promise of inheritance through faith (4:11-16), and to fall back into sin and death (5:12—6:23). Paul's formulation addresses the fundamental tendency in his era, to strive for superior status and honor in every arena. As Tacitus remarks of the arrogant philosopher Helvildus Priscus, "Even among wise men the lust for glory (cupidio gloriae) is the last one rooted out."[51]

Paul's recovery of the classical concept of sobriety is confirmed by its association with μέτρον ("measure") in 12:3d.[52] The standard of "sober-mindedness," Paul suggests, is the "measure consisting of faith that God dealt out to each."[53] There is an element of ambiguity, however, because μέτρον has roughly the same range of meanings in Greek as the term "measure" in English, implying an instrument or scale of measurement, the result of measurement in terms of quantity, size, or meter, or a limit or proportion derived by comparison with an instrument of measurement.[54] The primary meaning is "that by which anything is measured,"[55] which is reflected in most NT usages[56] and in my translation that is intended to avoid ambiguity: "measuring rod." That Paul intends the connotation "amount" or "quantity" of miracle-working faith[57] seems unlikely

---

41 North, SOPHROSYNE, 217–31.

42 Luck, "σώφρων κτλ.," 1101, citing Philo Leg. 1.63–73, 2.81, and Somn. 2.100 sic (probably 2.200).

43 Aristotle eliminated the pejorative connotation of μεγαλοψυχία by redefining it as "greatness of soul," the mark of the virtuous person emulating the divine. See North, SOPHROSYNE, 204.

44 North, SOPHROSYNE, 185, 200, 216, 226.

45 See also Dehn, Leben, 29; Luck, "σώφρων κτλ.," 1102.

46 Georg Bertram, "φρήν κτλ.," TDNT 9 (1974) 232; Dunn, 2:721.

47 See the exploration of the Greek precedents and later church historical development of this theme by Walter Magass, "Die Paradigmatik einer Paränese am Beispiel von Röm 12,3: 'er soll nicht höher von sich denken, als er denken darf.' Ein Beitrag zum Häresieverdacht als Τέρμα Verdacht," LingB 35 (1975) 1–16.

48 This expression is found in Plutarch, Quo. quis 83F 9, describing how we are inclined to be "praiseworthy of people and words beyond what is necessary (παρ᾽ ὃ δεῖ) rather than contemptuous."

49 Walter Grundmann, "δεῖ κτλ.," TDNT 2 (1964) 25.

50 That this admonition is "fundamentally anti-cultural" in contrast to status gained "on the basis of class or education," as argued by Winter, "Romans 12–15," 78–79, is worth weighing. However, none of the rest of the evidence about tensions between congregations in Rome appears to derive primarily from class differences.

51 Cited by Lendon, Empire of Honour, 92, from Tacitus Hist. 4.6.

52 See North, SOPHROSYNE, in notes 30 and 41 above, and Johanna Schmidt, "ΜΕΤΡΟΝ ΑΠΙΣΤΟΝ—Mass und Harmonie. Hellenischer Ursprung einer abendländischen Ideologie," EEPS 15 (1964–65) 515–17.

53 For the argument in favor of understanding μέτρον πίστεως as an appositive genitive, "measuring rod consisting of faith," see Cranfield, 2:615. This is the form of genitive demanded by the classical use of μέτρον.

54 See C. E. B. Cranfield, "μέτρον πίστεως in Romans 12:3," NTS 8 (1961–62) 346, and Kurt Deissner, "μέτρον κτλ.," TDNT 4 (1967) 632.

55 LSJM 1123. See particularly Plato Leg. 716c and Xenophon Cyr. 1.3.18.

56 Cranfield, 2:615, cites Matt 7:2; Mark 4:24; Rev 21:15; 2 Cor 10:13.

57 Lagrange, 296; Zahn, 542; Barrett, 235; Ortkemper, Leben, 45f.; Schlier, 367; Brockhaus, Charisma, 199;

because such gifts are only given to some (1 Cor 12:8-11), whereas Paul is here addressing παντὶ τῷ ὄντι ἐν ὑμῖν ("every one who is among you / every single one of you"). Moreover, if one's self-image depends on the amount of faith one has, then one would be entitled to think of oneself more highly than of others who have less faith, which would be fundamentally at variance with the line of argument in Romans.[58] While Cranfield is closer to the mark in maintaining the sense of μέτρον as a standard by which a Christian is "to measure, estimate himself," he softens the indications of unique individuation by insisting on a kind of uniformity of faith in the form of "his God-given relation to Christ" which does not include "subjective feelings."[59] However, that each believer has a unique μέτρον πίστεως is strongly suggested by the choice of the verb μερίζω ("deal out, distribute")[60] and the emphatic position of ἑκάστῳ ("to each") at the beginning of 12:3d. A differentiation between various "measuring rods" is also suggested by the only parallel in the Pauline corpus: in 2 Cor 10:13-15 Paul distinguishes between the "measure" or boundary of his missionary responsibilities and that of others.[61] It seems that Paul has developed an innovative twist on Protagoras's famous dictum, "Man is the measure of all things" (πάντων χρημάτων μέτρον ἐστὶν ἄνθρωπος).[62] Paul's μέτρον is "the norm that each person is provided in the appropriation of the grace of God.

Although faith in its proper sense is the relationship of holding fast to the grace of God, it includes a measuring rod that allows for differentiation."[63] And in the light of the subsequent argument about preserving the integrity of faith in both the weak and the strong (Rom 14:1–15:6), it is clear that for Paul, "There are political, ideological, racial, and temperamental components that are legitimately connected with faith, comprising the peculiar 'measuring rod' that each person in the church has been given."[64] By making these unique faith relationships the "measure of all things," so to speak, Paul defines "sober-mindedness" as the refusal to impose the standard of one's own relationship with God onto others. The same thought is reiterated in 14:4, 22-23 in the admonition not to interfere with the faith relationships that other believers have with the Lord.[65] This verse therefore stands as a bulwark against elitist conceptions of "divine-men," superleaders and geniuses who claim precedence over others because of their gifts and benefactions.[66]

■ **4-5** The metaphor of the body in vv. 4-5 is framed in classical fashion by καθάπερ . . . οὕτως ("just as . . . so"),[67] reflecting the parallel passage of 1 Cor 12:12. In classical rhetoric, a *similitudo* ("similitude") is a type of argument drawn from everyday experience, as contrasted with an *exemplum* ("example") drawn from history or literature.[68] A similitude like that of the body

---

other advocates of this view are listed in Cranfield, "μέτρον," 346.

58 See Cranfield, "μέτρον," 348f.; *Romans*, 614. The same objection would rule out the possibility that Black weighs in 169, taking πίστις to mean "responsibility." Acknowledging the difficulty with this suggestion, he considers the possibility of a scribal error in which πνεύματος was changed to πίστεως, which seems highly unlikely.

59 Cranfield, 2:614; similarly, Wilckens, 3:2, and Morris, 438.

60 BAGD 504; Dunn, 2:721; see particularly the parallel in 2 Cor 10:13. The expression ἐμέρισεν μέτρον does not occur at all in Greek literature before Paul's use, and thereafter is restricted to the handful of patristic writers who quote Rom 12:3, with the single exception of Damascius *Par.* 18.1, "The Entirety, it is said, is the measure of all things that have been dealt out (μέτρον ἐστιν τῶν μεριζομένων), but Eternity is the measure of all things that have been dealt out and multiplied."

61 See Betz, *Sokratische Tradition*, 130–31.

62 Protagoras *Frag.* 1, in Diehls and Kranz, *Vorsokratiker*, 2.263, 3ff. See also Deissner, "μέτρον κτλ.," 632. For a discussion of the philosophical efforts to overcome the subjectivity of Protagoras's position, see Schmidt, "μέτρον κτλ.," 544–50.

63 Jewett, *Tolerance*, 62.

64 Ibid.; accepted by Campbell, "Identity," 82, and Yeo, "Messianic Predestination," 276–77.

65 See Fitzmyer, 646.

66 This verse supports what Helmut Koester described in "The Divine Human Being," *HTR* 78 (1985) 252, as a "fundamental rejection, of the elements which constitute the concept of the divine man and the genius." For a discussion of the congregational relevance of this warning, see Lütgert, *Römerbrief*, 98–100.

67 Classical parallels provided by BAGD 387.

68 See Lausberg, *Handbuch*, 232–34, and D. M. Coffee, "The Function of Homeric Simile," *AJP* 78 (1957) 113–32.

therefore ordinarily requires no specialized knowledge or education to be effective. The two premises Paul sets forth are indisputable from the perspective of everyday experience: that a body has "many members, but all members do not have the same use. The formulation of these premises moves beyond any universal definition of common sense, however, by referring to Paul's audience as belonging to the "we" that are joined together ἐν ἑνὶ σώματι ("in one body/in a single body"). Given the emphasis on unity in the use of this metaphor as an expression of political and cosmic solidarity in the Greco-Roman world, this may have appeared to be commonsensical to Paul's audience.[69] The aim of uniting the Greek city-states had been described by Plutarch with the very words used by Paul: ἐν σῶμα ("one body").[70] The fables of Aesop and Menenius Agrippa were widely known in the Greco-Roman world, referring to the state as a σῶμα in which some members revolted against the stomach until they faced starvation and rediscovered their organic unity.[71] This idea plays an important role in the Sophist doctrine of society, with Dionysius of Halicarnassus claiming the state is like a body with interdependent members: ἔοικέ πως ἀνθρωπείῳ σώματι πόλις. σύνθετον γὰρ ἐκ πολλῶν μερῶν ἐστιν ἑκάτερον ("How like a human body is a city. For it is also put together from many different parts").[72] A parallel tradition is that of the universe as the body of God, advocated by the Orphics and Stoics.[73] Seneca reflects this pantheistic tradition when he claims that humans are part of the world body: . . . *omne hoc, quod vides, quo divina atque humana conclusa sunt, unum est; membra sumus corporis magni. Natura nos cognatos edidit, cum ex isdem et in eadem gigneret. Haec nobis amorem indibit mutuum et sociabiles fecit* (". . . all that you behold, that which comprises both god and man, is one—we are the parts of one great body. Nature produced us related to one another, since she created us from the same source and to the same end. She engendered in us mutual affection, and made us prone to friendships").[74] However, Seneca can also refer to the classical distinction between "a composite body" and "a separated body" in the social sphere: *Quaedam continua corpora esse, ut hominem; quaedam esse composita, ut navem, domum, omnia denique, quorum diversae partes iunctura in unum coactae sunt; quaedam ex distantibus, quorum adhuc membra separata sunt, tamquam exercitus, populus, senatus* ("There are certain continuous bodies, such as a man; there are certain composite bodies,—as ships, houses, and everything which is the result of joining separate parts into one sum total: there are certain others made up of things that are distinct, each member remaining separate—like an army, a populace, or a senate").[75] This last example reflects the widespread use of σῶμα to refer to social bodies such as legislatures. Paul had used the expression "body of Christ" in 1 Cor 12:12-27 in a description of the church, moving beyond these Greco-Roman precedents by linking the σῶμα with a particular person while retaining the emphasis on unity.[76] The extensive debate over the origin of this expression[77] does not need to be reviewed here because Paul avoids the realistic identification of the Christian community with Christ and remains on the metaphorical level.[78] Here the emphasis is on the

---

69 Eduard Schweizer, "σῶμα κτλ.," *TDNT* 7 (1971) 1069: "Paul says [the church] . . . is a body. This does not go beyond widespread Greek usage." See also Tobin, *Paul's Rhetoric*, 391.

70 Plutarch, *Phil.* 8, as cited by Schweizer, "σῶμα κτλ.," 1041.

71 Aesop *Fab.* 132; Dio Chrysostom *Orat.* 33.16; Livy *Hist.* 2.32; Epictetus *Diss.* 2.10.4–5; see Johannes Horst, "μέλος," *TDNT* 4 (1967) 556, 562f., and W. Nestle, "Die Fabel des Menenius Agrippa," *Klio* 21 (1927) 350–60.

72 Dionysius Halicarnassus *Antiq. Rom.* 6.86.1; for a discussion of the wide dispersion of this idea, see Horst, "μέλος," 556, and Arnold A. T. Ehrhardt, *Politische Metaphysik von Solon bis Augustin* (Tübingen: Mohr-Siebeck, 1959) 2:10–12, and idem, "Das Corpus Christi und die Korporationen," *ZRG* (1953) 299–300; (1954) 25–26.

73 Schweizer, "σῶμα κτλ.," 1037–38.

74 Seneca *Ep.* 95.52; translation from Gummere, *Seneca Ep.* 3.91; see Sevenster, *Paul and Seneca*, 170–71.

75 Seneca *Ep.* 102.6; translation from Gummere, *Seneca*, 3.171; see Schweizer, "σῶμα κτλ.," 1034f.

76 For a discussion of the evolution of Paul's usage in 1 Corinthians, see Jewett, *Terms*, 279–87.

77 See ibid., 227–50; also Dunn, 2:722–24.

78 Jewett, *Terms*, 303; for a skeptical comment that this distinction "should not be overemphasized," see Dunn, 2:723.

unity of the community "in Christ," with the subsequent line driving home the point that "each one [is] a member of others." Although it is conceivable that Paul's formulation in Romans seeks to counter enthusiastic misuse of the "body of Christ" concept,[79] it is more certain that the emphasis here is on "horizontal unity and relationship."[80] Countering the divisive forces within and between the Roman house and tenement churches and the refugees returning from the exile of the Edict of Claudius,[81] this expression stresses the solidarity between Christian groups as a single body "in Christ." Their common "participation" in Christ results in the characteristic Pauline form of "mysticism."[82] In selecting the expression τὸ δὲ καθ᾽ εἷς ("each one, individually")[83] Paul stresses that each Christian is actually an interdependent "member" along with all others. The unity is not organic as in the case of the Greco-Roman pantheists[84] but historical and confessional, shaped by the "in Christ" relationship.[85] Christ is the larger reality within which the various congregations and individual members are to find their unity.

■ **6** Most translations and commentaries assume that the participle ἔχοντες ("having") should be taken as the beginning of a new sentence, with the subsequent list of charismatic gifts understood in an imperatival sense.[86] But, as Dunn has shown, it is more appropriate grammatically and in terms of the content of the subsequent verses to take vv. 6-8 as a continuation of the body metaphor in vv. 4-5,[87] which means that the list of gifts is descriptive[88] and exemplary.[89] I therefore prefer to take the particle δέ in a mildly contrasting sense of "yet," implying that while each Christian is a member of the body along with others, there is no uniformity or lack of responsibility, since each has a peculiar gift. While some interpreters have limited the scope of such gifts to specific officeholders in the church,[90] the grammar of the particle "having"[91] as well as the contextual details involving the body with many members, the stress on "the many" and "each" (12:5), and the coordination with "the grace given to us" (12:6) require the conclusion that each Christian has some χάρισμα ("charismatic gift").[92] As 3:24; 5:2, 15, 17; 6:14 show, every single Christian has received God's χάρις ("grace"), of which the particular χαρίσματα ("charismatic gifts") are congregationally useful manifestations.[93] This rhetorically effective wordplay between

79 Jewett, *Terms*, 303–4, and James L. Breed, "The Church as the 'Body of Christ': A Pauline Analogy," *NETR* 6 (1985) 14.

80 Jewett, *Terms*, 304.

81 See Fitzmyer, 646.

82 See Luz, "Mystic," 143; Shantz, "Paul in Ecstasy," 173: "Paul felt himself to be 'gloriously' transformed through his religious ecstasy and . . . those experiences inspired his thinking about a corporate body of Christ."

83 See Fitzmyer, 646, citing BDF §305.

84 See Horst, "μέλος," 563.

85 See Neugebauer, *In Christus*, 104, and A. J. M. Wedderburn, "Some Observations on Paul's Use of the Phrases 'in Christ' and 'with Christ,'" *JSNT* 25 (1985) 83–97.

86 For example, Wilckens, 3:10; Cranfield, 2:618; Leenhardt, 174; Michel, 377; Morris, 439.

87 Dunn, 2:725; Norbert Baumert also argues against viewing 12:6 as an independent sentence, citing patristic evidence in "Zur 'Unterscheidung der Geister,'" *ZKTh* 111 (1989) 187f.

88 Dunn, 2:725; see also Schlier, 369: "In any event verse 6a is carried not by an imperative but by an indicative. We have *charismata*."

89 Brockhaus, *Charisma*, 201, and Ortkemper, *Leben*, 59.

90 Wilckens, 3:14, cites F. Grau, "Der neutestamentliche Begriff charisma, seine Geschichte und seine Theologie" (dissertation, University of Tübingen, 1946) 188ff., and Merk, *Handeln*, 160, as holding the more restricted view. In fact, the contrast between the broad dispersion of charismatic gifts in Pauline writings and the limitation of such a gift to the Teacher of Righteousness in the Qumran community is shown by Josef Schreiner, "Geistbegabung in der Gemeinde und Qumran," *BZ* 9 (1965) 179–80.

91 Cranfield, 2:619, notes that the subject of ἔχοντες ("having") must be the "we" in the previous sentence.

92 See Käsemann, 334–36; Wilckens, 3:13f.; Dunn, 2:726. A *TLG* search indicates the link between χαρίσματα and gifts is probably inherent in Greek usage, indicated by the *Sch. Aristoph., Scholia in nubes recentiora* 305.1, which glosses it with δωρήματα ("gifts, presents"), δωρεαί ("gifts, bounties, grants"); similarly, *Sch. Opp., Scholia et glossae in halieutica* 2.23.7 glosses it with δῶρα ("presents, gifts").

93 See Herten, "Charisma," 84. The plural χαρίσματα is rare outside of biblical contexts, according to a *TLG* search. It appears to correspond to the

χάρις and χαρίσματα[94] replaces the coordination between charismatic gifts and πνευματικά ("spiritual gifts") as found in 1 Cor 12:1-31,[95] resulting in a shift of emphasis away from the more spectacularly ecstatic manifestations such as glossolalia to the sober expressions of congregational leadership mentioned in Romans.[96] There is no reference to "Spirit" in the discussion of this issue in Romans. That Paul intended this verse to have an "anti-enthusiastic thrust,"[97] however, is an overly broad inference to be drawn from so slight a change of terminology from 1 Corinthians to Romans. There is no denying that Paul's conception of the Christian community in Rome remains fundamentally charismatic, in contrast to the main streams of ecclesiology in more recent times.[98] Since the χαρίσματα are illustrated in 12:6-8 by functions in which unique talents of individuals are activated, they are more than simple "gifts"[99] but certainly not regularized ecclesiastical offices such as developed toward the end of the century in Pauline churches.[100]

The emphatic position of διάφορα ("different")[101] at the end of the first clause of v. 6 correlates with the emphasis on "many members" of the body in v. 4 and the warning against "supermindedness" in v. 3, signaling that Paul wishes to overcome claims of superiority or autonomous adequacy that the Christian groups in Rome were inclined to make.[102] The contributions of discriminated groups and persons, mentioned in the later discussion of the "weak" (14:1–15:6), are here ranked as "charismatic gifts" on the same level as all others while differing in their scope and function.[103] Consistent with this emphasis, the charismatic gifts in vv. 6-8 are listed in random sequence,[104] lacking the hierarchical structure of 1 Cor 12–14.[105] The avoidance of technical terms for early Christian leaders in this list sidesteps any possible disagreements among house and tenement churches concerning the status of particular roles. The selection of a series of seven gifts, Israel's holy number implying

---

Hebrew word חסדים as in Isaiah 55:3, translated by Holladay, *Concise Hebrew and Aramaic Lexicon*, as "evidences of [God's] grace" or by the Koehler-Baumgartner dictionary as "[God's] proofs of mercy."

94   See Brockhaus, *Charisma*, 200.

95   See Siegfried Schulz, "Die Charismenlehre des Paulus," in J. Friedrich et al., eds., *Rechtfertigung: Festschrift für Ernst Käsemann zum 70. Geburtstag* (Tübingen: Mohr-Siebeck, 1976) 455, and Ortkemper, *Leben*, 63.

96   Schütz, "Charisma," 691, notes that the Corinthian problem of pneumatic enthusiasm was not present in Rome; Conzelmann overlooks this change of emphasis by assimilating the Roman's usage into that of 1 Corinthians in "χάρισμα κτλ.," *TDNT* 9 (1974) 404f.

97   Käsemann, 333.

98   See Schulz, "Charismenlehre," 447; Brockhaus, *Charisma*, 89–94, 198–202; Dunn, 2:726.

99   Norbert Baumert seeks to replace the vocational understanding of "charismatic gift" by the simple term "gift" in "'Unterscheidung,'" 185–89. See also his study "Zur Begriffsgeschichte von *charisma* im griechischen Sprachraum," *ThPh* 65 (1990) 79–80. His case rests on the slim foundation of alleged logical shortcomings in Paul's reference to the gifts of interpreting and distinguishing in 1 Cor 12:10, but the application to Rom 12 is unconvincing.

100   For a survey of the consensus on this point, see W. G. Kümmel, "Das Urchristentum. II. Arbeiten zu

Spezialproblem. d. Ämter und Amtsverständnis," *ThR* 52 (1987) 111–54.

101   See Brockhaus, *Charisma*, 204. The term διάφορα ("difference") is used here for the only time in the Pauline corpus, indicating an emphasis unparalleled in the other letters.

102   See Lütgert, *Römerbrief*, 98–100.

103   See the stress on mutual admission of legitimate charismatic gifts in Brockhaus, *Charisma*, 200; also Herten, "Charisma," 81: "All members are equal in principle despite the inequality of their function."

104   Lagrange, 300, distinguishes between the first four gifts as pastoral and the last three as public while Schulz, "Charismenlehre," 446–47, distinguishes between charismatic, diaconal, pneumatic, and leadership gifts. Neither system of distinctions holds up under close examination. For critiques of these proposals, see Ortkemper, *Leben*, 66–67, and Brockhaus, *Charisma*, 207. Wilckens, 3:15, suggests that "service" implies the office here and that the final three of the seven gifts develop its dimensions, just as the two before that relate to prophecy. But teaching is no more directly related to prophecy than is leading with service. The list lacks internal indices showing such a structuring principle. The choice of a random sequence appears deliberate.

105   Hainz, *Ekklesia*, 185; Brockhaus, *Charisma*, 203–10. Ortkemper, *Leben*, 66f., acknowledges the unsystematic nature of the list, but retains an unfortunate element of hierarchy based on Paul's listing of prophecy first.

perfection and totality,[106] also conveys the sense of exemplary universality. The poetic balance and equality of gifts are conveyed by the grammatical construction εἴτε . . . εἴτε ("whether . . . whether").[107] Some of the gifts mentioned have particular relevance for the Spanish mission project, but their main function is to stand for the hitherto unacknowledged range and significance of the charismatic gifts collectively present in the various Roman congregations.[108]

The first of the seven gifts mentioned by Paul is prophecy, which should not lead to inferences about this as the most important gift,[109] since the list as a whole reflects a random sequence. All one can say is that this gift, like the other six, was sufficiently important for the Roman house churches to be mentioned here. Characteristic for early Christianity, in fact, was the remarkably broad dispersion of prophetic gifts as a sign of the new age and the high prestige attached to prophets.[110] Dautzenberg has shown that the basic meaning of prophecy should be derived from the normal usage of this term in Judaism and Hellenism, which involves the revelation and interpretation of divine secrets.[111] According to Forbes, "Christian prophecy was the reception and . . . public declaration of spontaneous, (usually) verbal revelation, conceived of as revealed truth. . . . It might include, but was not limited to, the prediction of the future: it might equally be unsolicited guidance, exhorta-tion, or remonstration."[112] Since Paul himself functioned at times as a prophet,[113] this role could involve a prophetic call (Gal 1:12-16), revelatory experiences (2 Cor 12:1-10), oracles and pronouncements (1 Thess 4:15-17; Gal 5:19-21),[114] or miracle working (Rom 15:19; 2 Cor 12:12; 1 Thess 1:5; Gal 3:5; 1 Cor 2:1-5). The usual scope of early Christian oracles was pastoral rather than esoteric, as the discussion in 1 Cor 14:24-25 indicates.[115] Since Paul has already provided an example of such revelation of the "mystery" of Israel's salvation in connection with the Gentile mission (Rom 11:25-26),[116] the relevance of this gift to missionary activity such as Paul will propose to Spain will become clear to the Roman house churches.[117] But the self-evident manner of Paul's reference to this charismatic gift indicates that it was already a typical part of early Christian worship.[118] There are indications that particular persons bearing the title of "prophet" worked in local congregations (1 Cor 12:28-29; 14:37), despite the ideal that every charismatic Christian should prophesy (1 Cor 14:1, 5, 12, 39). However, Paul refers here to their function rather than their office.[119] He thus sidesteps any potential controversy about the legitimacy of individual prophets in competing Roman house churches; this formulation also avoids the status gradation implied in "first apostles, second prophets, third teachers . . ." (1 Cor 12:28), which may have been an issue of contention between congregations.

106 Karl Heinrich Rengstorf, "ἑπτά κτλ.," *TDNT* 2 (1964) 628, 632f.

107 See BDF §454.3.

108 That the peculiar list of charismatic gifts takes account of the situation in Rome is argued by Michel, 378.

109 The primacy of prophecy is maintained by many scholars, including Ortkemper, *Leben*, 67, and Dunn, 2:727. In the more categorical list of χαρίσματα in 1 Cor 12, primacy is accorded to the apostles and secondly to prophets (12:28), but the congregational situation requiring this hierarchy is evidently not present in Rome.

110 Helmut Krämer et al., "προφήτης κτλ.," *TDNT* 6 (1968) 849f.

111 Gerhard Dautzenberg, *Urchristliche Prophetie: Ihre Erforschung, ihre Voraussetzungen im Judentum und ihre Struktur im ersten Korintherbrief*, BWANT 104 (Stuttgart: Kohlhammer, 1975).

112 Christopher Forbes, *Prophecy and Inspired Speech in Early Christianity and Its Hellenistic Environment*,

WUNT 75 (Tübingen: Mohr-Siebeck, 1995) 236, citing with approval Max Turner, "Spirtual Gifts Then and Now," *VoxEv* 15 (1985) 7–64.

113 David E. Aune, *Prophecy in Early Christianity and the Ancient Mediterranean World* (Grand Rapids: Eerdmans, 1983) 248–49.

114 See ibid., 249–62.

115 See David Hill, "Christian Prophets," in J. Panagopoulos, *Prophetic Vocation in the New Testament and Today* (Leiden: Brill, 1977) 108–30, and Müller, *Prophetie*, 57–100.

116 See Hill, "Christian Prophets," 117–18; Aune, *Prophecy*, 252–53.

117 For a succinct description of Paul as a prophetic, charismatic thinker who viewed his mission to Spain as the fulfillment of an apocalyptic plan, see Schulz, "Charismenlehre," 443.

118 See Johannes Panagopoulos, "Die urchristliche Prophetie: Ihr Charakter und ihre Funktion," in Panagopoulos, *Prophetic Vocation in the New Testament and Today*, 11–12; also Aune, *Prophecy*, 204.

That early Christian prophecy was generally distinguishable from pagan prophecy by a less ecstatic form[120] has been questioned by more recent studies.[121] Rather than qualifying its form, Paul suggests a correlation with "faith." The expression κατὰ τὴν ἀναλογίαν τῆς πίστεως ("according to the analogy of faith") has provoked intensive debate between advocates of dogmatic theological standards[122] and advocates of individual faith.[123] Without disputing that the term "analogy" is derived from Greek mathematics and logic, indicating the right ratio or proportion of one thing to another,[124] the question is how the criterion of faith functions. In the context of this verse, which stresses the differentiation of charismatic gifts within the congregation, the individuated measuring rods of faith are most likely in view. To speak of a *regula fidei* ("rule of faith") here is an anachronistic imposition of later ecclesiastical developments.[125] What protects Paul's formulation from arbitrary individualism and subjectivism is the thesis in 12:1-2, referring to the collective assessment of the will of God. The faith of each member of the Roman house churches would be employed as the community weighs the validity of a particular prophecy.[126] Neither hierarchical authority nor isolated charisma is allowed

supremacy by this formulation.[127] In an informal kind of charismatic democracy, the "measuring rods of faith" within all the members comprise the substance of the analogy or ratio by which any new oracle should be evaluated. A similar model is found in 1 Cor 14:29 and 1 Thess 5:19-22, where the members of house and tenement churches are called upon to "weigh" and "test" what their prophets and prophetesses say.[128] Despite the prestige and indispensable presence of prophecy in the church, Paul remains true to the principle enunciated in 1 Cor 13:9, "our prophecy is imperfect."

■ **7** According to the comprehensive recent study by John N. Collins, the term διακονία ("service/ministry") and its cognates retained the basic sense of "in-between" activities such as errand running, speaking or acting in behalf of others, or attending someone to perform a task.[129] The διακον- words are used for household servants, waiters, priests, statesmen, tradesmen, retailers, attendants in religious ceremonies, messengers, and even ambassadors. While "waiting at table . . . provision for bodily sustenance"[130] was a prominent example of such ministry in the context of early Christianity,[131] the stem itself does not imply menial subordination.[132] These terms are more frequently found in literary and

119 Dunn, 2:727.

120 See Krämer et al., "προφήτης κτλ.," 851.

121 Aune, *Prophecy*, 230–31, and Forbes, *Prophecy*, 219–21.

122 For example, see Heinrich Greeven, "Propheten, Lehrer, Vorsteher bei Paulus: Zur Frage der 'Ämter' im Urchristentum," *ZNW* 44 (1952) 9–10; Käsemann, 341–42; Ortkemper, *Leben*, 73–74; Müller, *Prophetie*, 214; Schlier, 370; Zeller, 209; Aune, *Prophecy*, 204–5, 235.

123 See Zahn, 544; Schlatter, 234; Lietzmann, 109; Kühl, 423–23; Schmidt, 211; Hainz, *Ekklesia*, 185; Michel, 377–78; Cranfield, 2:620–21; Dunn, 2:727.

124 See Michel, 377; LSJM 111, referring to Cleomedes *Motu* 1.7; Aristotle *Rhet. Alex.* 1443b15; Plato *Tim.* 31c, 32c. The phrase κατὰ τὴν ἀναλογίαν means "according to the mathematical proportion" in Aristotle *Eth. nic.* 1132a; 1133a10; *Phys.* 215b3; *Pol.* 1282b39. Plato has Socrates say (*Pol.* 257b3), "With men, though each is appointed equal worth, some are weighed down with more honor than others, or according to the proportion, that is, according to your skill (ἡ κατὰ τὴν ἀναλογίαν τὴν τῆς ὑμετέρας τέχνης)."

125 See Fitzmyer's reference in 648 to L. Scheffczyk, "Analogy of Faith," in vol. 1 of *Sacramentum Mundi* (New York: Herder & Herder, 1968–70) 25–27.

126 See Morris, 441.

127 The contrast with the orientation of the book of Revelation is unmistakable, for there the prophetic oracle simply derives from the spirit and is beyond criticism. See Krämer et al., "προφήτης κτλ.," 849f.

128 See Jewett, *Apostle to America*, chapter 9.

129 Collins, *Diakonia*, 77–95, 335–36. For a survey of the earlier discussion, see C. Tatton, "Some Studies of New Testament *Diakonia*," *SJT* 25 (1972) 423–34.

130 Hermann Wolfgang Beyer, "διακονέω κτλ.," *TDNT* 2 (1964) 87.

131 See Collins, *Diakonia*, 150–68.

132 The allegedly menial quality of διακον- plays a crucial role in Beyer's definitive article in "διακονέω κτλ.," 82–87, which is followed by Schweizer, Colson, Lemaire, Guerra, and others. See Schweizer, *Church Order*, 171–80; Jean Colson, "Der Diakonat im Neuen Testament," pp. 3–22 in Karl Rahner and H. Vorgrimler, eds., *Diaconia in Christo über die Erneurung des Diakonates*, QD 15–16 (Freiburg: Herder, 1962), esp. 3–4, 14–19; André Lemaire, *Les*

religious contexts than in the vernacular, where menial usage would be expected.[133] The term is of marginal interest to Jewish writers, the verb διακονεῖν not even appearing in the Septuagint.[134] It is therefore a significant example of cultural selectivity when early Christianity exalted διακον- to a position of great importance.[135] While Hudson counts ninety references to "service" and its cognates in the NT, the other seven terms for leadership and service such as "bishop," "slave," and "minister" appear only thirty-eight times.[136] A wide range of activities is encompassed within the Pauline letters by διακονία and its cognates, from apostolic calling (2 Cor 6:4; 11:23; Rom 11:13) to fund-raising (Rom 15:25, 21; 2 Cor 8:4, 19-20; 9:1, 12-13) and meeting the daily needs of fellow believers (1 Cor 16:15). Paul's contribution is to ground such activities in christological motivation (Rom 15:8; 2 Cor 4:5) and spiritual endowment (1 Cor 12:1-11) and to develop a theory of their relationship to ecclesiology (1 Cor 12:12-31).[137]

Given the wide range of semantic associations this term has for the early church, the puzzle is how to define "service" when used absolutely in this verse. An exclusive definition in terms of preaching the gospel[138] seems arbitrary and redundant in its overlapping with prophecy, teaching, and exhortation. The suggestion that διακονία is the qualifying concept for the following gifts is unsupported by the grammar of the verse.[139]

Dunn defines "service" in the "middle of the spectrum" from lifelong ministry to individual acts.[140] This is no better than the conclusion of Ortkemper that in light of the wide range of usage in Pauline letters, one cannot provide a precise translation.[141] In fact, there is no way to determine why the middle of a spectrum is what Paul had in mind; despite its reasonable sound, this invites a subjective judgment. If semantic principles were followed, an unqualified noun like διακονία would normally revert to its basic meaning—which in this instance would be the "in-between" activity that was most characteristic of the Roman congregations being addressed here, that is, service, especially serving meals. As Roloff has shown, the diaconal role in early Christianity developed from functions related to the common meal.[142] Given the social structure of several of the Roman house and tenement churches,[143] this was probably a role of absolutely fundamental importance. The eucharistic celebration, probably celebrated as a daily, common meal by many of the congregations, was the center of their common life. Bo Reicke has demonstrated that the remarkably rich development of διακον- terminology in Pauline thought rests on this vital foundation in the experience of "love feasts" in early churches.[144]

Whether διακονία implies an ecclesiastical office, as argued by Lietzmann and others,[145] is doubtful at this early stage in church development.[146] The evidence sug-

---

ministères aux origines de l'Église: Naissance de la triple hiérarchie: évêques, presbytres, diacres, LD 68 (Paris: du Cerf, 1971) 31–33; Manuel Guerra y Gómez, "Diáconos hellénicos y biblicos," Burg 4 (1963) 9–143.

133 Collins, Diakonia, 177–91.

134 Διακονία occurs in Esth 6:3, 5 and 1 Macc 11:58.

135 The evidence in Acts 6 suggests that the priority granted to the διακον- stem emerged at the very beginning of what we ordinarily identify as "Hellenistic Christianity," with the selection of Stephen and his six colleagues as leaders called "deacons."

136 Hudson, "Diakonia," 142.

137 See Jürgen Roloff, "Amt / Ämter / Amtsverständnis IV: Neues Testament," ThRE 2 (1978) 518–20.

138 J. S. Bosch, "Le Corps du Christ et les charismes dans l'épître aux Romains," in Lorenzo de Lorenzi, ed., Dimensions de la vie chrétienne (Rm 12–13), SMB 4 (Rome: Abbaye de S. Paul, 1979) 64f. In Diakonia, 233, Collins defines διακονία in 12:7 as "delivering the word" because of its proximity to prophecy,

teaching, and exhortation, disregarding the random sequence of the charismatic gifts.

139 Heinz Schürmann, "Die geistlichen Gnadengaben in den paulinischen Gemeinden," in H. Schürmann, Ursprung und Gestalt. Erörterungen und Besinnungen zum Neuen Testament (Düsseldorf: Patmos, 1970) 240; for a critique, see Ortkemper, Leben, 74.

140 Dunn, 2:728.

141 Ortkemper, Leben, 76.

142 Roloff, "Amt," 522.

143 See the Introduction, section 7.

144 Reicke, Agapenfeier, 31–38; see also Pervo, "Panta Koina," 187–94.

145 Lietzmann, 109; Murray, 2:124; and Brockhaus, Charisma, 98–100, argue that both Phil 1:1 and Rom 16:1 indicate such an office existed in Paul's time.

146 See Ortkemper, Leben, 74; Hainz, Ekklesia, 187f.; Roloff, "Amt," 510, 518–23. However, Haacker, 256, observes that Phoebe is described as a "deacon" in Rom 16:2; see also Moo, 766.

gests that some, but not all, congregations used this as an informal term for congregational leadership.[147] This may throw light on why Paul does not mention the functionary here, but rather the function. This formulation allows him to affirm ministry as a charismatic gift without taking sides in the Roman controversies over the legitimacy of particular leadership roles.

The expression ἐν τῇ διακονίᾳ is interpreted by Cranfield as an exhortation for "wholehearted" engagement and the use of the gift "for the purpose for which it was given," which also entails not undertaking a task for which one is not equipped.[148] Only the second point appears germane. The criterion theme from Rom 12:6b is followed here, which appears more satisfactory than Dunn's abstract comment that the phrase "underlines the basic character of a charism for Paul as grace."[149] Such underlining is not needed for those who could follow the rhetorical flow of this letter, and is in any event not clearly conveyed by this phrase, which says nothing about charisma. Paul insists that the criteria for the exercise of "ministry" are to be derived from ministry itself,[150] an arena of regular eucharistic activity that played a much larger and more self-evident role in charismatic early churches than in most contemporary Christian groups.

The wording of ὁ διδάσκων ἐν τῇ διδασκαλίᾳ ("the one teaching—in the teaching") has occasioned considerable debate because Paul chooses not to continue the series of functions from "prophecy" and "service," selecting instead the participial form indicating the person teaching.[151] In principle, this formulation refers to anyone who is teaching in any context; it does not imply a fixed office of teacher. Paul's formulation entails an avoidance of the technical term διδάσκαλος, used frequently in the gospels for Jesus and others playing the role of "teacher," even though it would have produced a forceful reduplication (ὁ διδάσκαλος ἐν τῇ διδασκαλίᾳ) that would exactly parallel vv. 7a and 8a. Rengstorf hinted that the reluctance to use διδάσκαλος for early Christian teachers expresses the sense that there could be no real successors to Jesus the teacher,[152] a theory that Filson seems to find questionable because of widespread evidence of teaching activities in the NT.[153] Alfred Zimmermann argues for Paul's principled avoidance of διδάσκαλος in Rom 12:7 on church political grounds,[154] arguing that the only other place Paul uses the term, in 1 Cor 12:28, is a concessionary quotation from the Petrine faction.[155] Although overstretching his case by contending that Acts 13:1 and Matt 23:8 show that an early Christian-Pharisaic circle of teachers was displaced around 50, leaving the church without explicitly acknowledged teachers during Paul's missionary period,[156] the evidence indicates the likelihood that the Pauline and Petrine churches differed in the author-

147 Ortkemper, *Leben*, 75; Collins, *Diakonia*, 228–30, 235–38.

148 Cranfield, 2:623.

149 Dunn, 2:729.

150 Moo, 767: using the deaconal gift "in accordance with its true nature."

151 Josef Brosch, *Charismen und Ämter in der Urkirche* (Bonn: Hanstein, 1951) 112–15, argued that the participial form revealed that the teaching office was undeveloped, while Dunn, 2:729, suggests the opposite, "that Paul saw teaching here as a more regular ministry." Neither inference can be supported with other evidence about the evolution of early Christian leadership. In "Propheten, Lehrer, Vorsteher bei Paulus: Zur Frage der 'Ämter' im Urchristentum," *ZNW* 44 (1952) 16, Heinrich Greeven tried to explain the participial usage on grammatical grounds, arguing that διδαχή ("teaching") could not be used to refer to a teaching role in a manner parallel to "prophecy" and "service," but the distinction does not hold.

152 Karl Heinrich Rengstorf, "διδάσκω κτλ.," *TDNT* 2 (1964) 146, 56; idem, "μανθάνω κτλ.," *TDNT* 4 (1967) 448f. Floyd V. Filson took Rengstorf to imply that the avoidance of "teacher" resulted "from the feeling that there could be no real successor to Jesus" ("The Christian Teacher in the First Century," *JBL* 60 [1941] 321).

153 Filson, "Christian Teacher," 321f. He concludes that in the early church, "every leader was a teacher, because teaching was indispensable" (322). See also Dunn, 2:729.

154 Alfred F. Zimmermann, *Die urchristlichen Lehrer: Studien zum Tradentenkreis der διδάσκαλοι im frühen Urchristentum*, WUNT 2 (Tübingen: Mohr-Siebeck, 1984) 110.

155 Ibid., 106–13, 216; the indications of a quotation or allusion do not, however, prove that Pauline churches had no legitimate place for teachers.

156 Ibid., 217–19. This point is challenged by Werner Georg Kümmel, "Das Urchristentum: II. Arbeiten

ity given to teachers. Even if Ellis and others are wrong in suggesting that the logion criticizing the honorific title "teacher" in Matt 23:8 was known in Pauline churches,[157] the retention of the saying indicates conflicting assessments of authority.[158] Since competitive ecclesiastical systems were represented in Rome, the avoidance of the disputed term διδάσκαλος probably reflects Paul's desire to avoid exacerbating the conflicts over leadership that are evident elsewhere in the letter.

While some have tried to delimit the role of the early Christian teachers to the exposition of tradition[159] or Scripture,[160] the evidence in the Pauline tradition suggests that their activities included general paraenesis (1 Cor 4:17; Col 1:28; 2:6f.; 3:16), theological instruction derived from early Christian tradition (Gal 1:12; 2 Thess 2:15; Col 2:7; Rom 6:17), as well as exposition of Scripture (Rom 2:21).[161] Such formal and informal educational activities overlapped with those of prophets[162] and apostles.[163] When one places such activities within the context of the transforming thesis of Rom 12:1-2, the Pauline ideal takes on differentiated contours. In contrast to scribal leaders who concentrated on the memorizing of tradition or Greco-Roman teachers who passed on a specific subject matter and engaged in philosophical speculation, the defining feature of early Christian teachers according to this ideal was the interaction between spirit and tradition.[164] That Paul was conscious of the distance between ideal and reality is suggested by the expression "in the teaching," which points to a criterion of performance within the taught material itself.[165] Paul insists that Christian teachers adhere to the rule that marked the fall of certain Jewish teachers in Rom 2:20—living up to the teaching one advocates.

■ 8 The expression ὁ παρακαλῶν ("the exhorter or comforter") is associated with the Greco-Roman tradition of the "care of souls."[166] A formidable literature of reproof, admonition, and exhortation emerged to deal with the psychological, social, and intellectual difficulties faced by persons associated with philosophical communities or movements; in addition, there was a literature of consolation to comfort and exhort the bereaved, the dying, the exiled, and the victims of injustice or misfortune.[167] While a distinction was sometimes made between consolation and admonition, the two aspects of παρακαλέω tended to blend in a cultural tradition that devised multitudinous reasons to admonish the bereaved to stop weeping.[168] In principle, everyone was expected to play the role of comforter, but the philosopher and poet in particular undertook this task.[169] Judaism also produced a substantial literature of consolation, including Lamentations, Job, some of the Psalms and Proverbs, as well as prophetic material like Isa 40. Prophets, teachers, family members, and neighbors played the role of comforters but the ultimate

zu Spezialproblemen. d. Ämter und Amtsverständnis," *ThR* 52 (1987) 151.

157 Ellis, *Prophecy*, 21.

158 Zimmermann, *Lehrer*, 110–13.

159 See ibid., 62–66, for references; a prominent advocate is Greeven, "Propheten," 330–42.

160 Rengstorf, "διδάσκω κτλ.," 146.

161 Greeven, "Propheten," 18–22.

162 Hill, "Christian Prophets," 123.

163 Heinrich Schürmann, ". . . und Lehrer: Die geistliche Eigenart des Lehrdienstes und sein Verhältnis zu anderen geistlichen Diensten im neutestamentlichen Zeitalter," in Wilhelm Ernst et al., eds., *Dienst der Vermittlung: Festschrift zum 25. jährigen Bestehen des philosophisch-theologischen Studiums im Priesterseminar Erfurt*, EThSt 37 (Leipzig: St. Benno, 1977) 141–47.

164 Schürmann, "Lehrer," 121, 147.

165 That ἐν τῇ διδασκαλίᾳ simply places "primary emphasis on the act of teaching" as a charismatic activity (Dunn, 2:729) makes sense only if Paul

aimed to undercut ecclesiastical offices, which would be anachronistic in this period of informal development of the church. The precedent of mentioning the formal criterion of faith in the first of the seven examples of charismatic gifts leads the hearer to understand the prepositional phrase as providing a similar criterion. See Zahn, 546.

166 See Otto Schmitz and Gustav Stählin, "παρακαλέω κτλ.," *TDNT* 5 (1967) 779–88. For general orientation on psychagogy, see Malherbe, *Paul and the Thessalonians*, 81–88; he makes use of P. Rabbow, *Seelenführung. Methodik der Exerzitien in der Antike* (Munich: Kösel, 1954), and P. Hadot, *Exercices spirituels et philosophie antique* (Paris: Études Augustiniennes, 1981).

167 Schmitz and Stählin, "παρακαλέω κτλ.," 780f.

168 Ibid., 780.

169 Ibid., 781.

source of consolation was thought to be God (Ps 71:21; 86:17; 94:19; Isa 51:12).[170] The wording of the blessing in Rom 15:5, "the God of steadfastness and exhortation," confirms that Paul stands firmly within this biblical tradition. Although some scholars cannot understand such a task on the same level as teaching or prophesying,[171] it was evidently important for most early Christian groups,[172] and it clearly involved general moral exhortation as well as consolation for the suffering. There is certainly no indication in this pericope that Paul thought of exhortation as a less important charismatic gift for the church. Paul refers to the role of himself (1 Thess 2:3, 11f.), his missionary colleagues (1 Thess 3:2), and other congregational members (1 Thess 4:18) as exhorters, grounding such activities finally in divine exhortation (2 Cor 5:20).[173] Given the cultural dissonance that early believers had to face[174] and the adversities suffered by the Roman congregations in connection with the Edict of Claudius, it seems likely that they would understand "the exhorter" as providing comfort and consolation as well as exhortation.[175]

That the criterion to be employed by exhorters is "exhortation" itself, following the pattern of the preceding two charismatic gifts, would be easily comprehensible in a culture with such elaborate philosophical and religious traditions about the care of souls under stress. A person involved, the care of souls was expected "to give attention to individuals and to vary his exhortation according to the condition he addresses."[176] Such a person was expected to be courageous, incorruptible, sensitive, gentle, and more devoted to his charges than to his own family. Consolers were expected to visit the bereaved or afflicted, to join their laments, and to offer condolences by means of philosophical or religious reasoning.[177] In the case of Pauline Christianity, the criterion was defined by the models of nurse and parent (1 Thess 2:7, 11)[178] and grounded finally in the "demonstration of the comfort of God" in the Christ event.[179]

The translation of ὁ μεταδιδούς could be "the contributor,"[180] "the distributor,"[181] "the giver or almsgiver,"[182] or "the sharer."[183] The latter is the more accurate translation because of the prefix μετα-, implying "with" or "among." The verb μεταδίδωμι is also used by Paul to imply sharing in Rom 1:11 and 1 Thess 2:8. Since van Unnik has shown that μεταδίδωμι requires a particular context to imply almsgiving,[184] the sharing that Paul has in mind is probably associated with contributions to the daily love feasts that formed the center of the common life in early Christianity.[185] The idea of distributing the resources of the community does not correlate as well with the expression ἐν ἁπλότητι ("with simplicity/generosity") as with sharing one's own resources.[186] It remains likely, however, that the sharing in this instance relates to material rather than spiritual

170 See Ibid., 789–90.
171 Hainz, *Ekklesia*, 188; Schmitz and Stählin subordinate "exhortation" to "prophecy," using 1 Cor 14:3, 31 as evidence, in "παρακαλέω κτλ.," 789–90.
172 Schmitz and Stählin, "παρακαλέω κτλ.," 793–99.
173 Heinrich Schlier, "Die Eigenart der christlichen Mahnung nach dem Apostel Paulus," *GuL* 36 (1963) 327–40; repr. in *Besinnung auf das Neuen Testament: Exegetische Aufsätze und Vorträge II* (Herder: Freiburg, 1964), esp. 344.
174 See Malherbe, *Paul and the Thessalonians*, 46–52.
175 Ortkemper, *Leben*, 79, concludes this on the basis of the semantic range of the term. It seems quite inappropriate to limit ὁ παρακαλῶν to the proclamation of the gospel, as suggested by Bjerkelund, *PARAKALÔ*, 26.
176 Malherbe, *Paul*, 55.
177 Schmitz and Stählin, "παρακαλέω κτλ.," 782–89.
178 See Malherbe, *Paul*, 35–48, 67–77.
179 Schlier, "Eigenart," 344–52.
180 Moffatt and *RSV* both translate with "contribute."
181 Calvin's reference to the person distributing church property is discussed by Cranfield, 2:624f. Käsemann, 342, refers to the distribution of "community alms."
182 The translation "he who gives" is favored by BAGD 511; almsgiving is advocated by Lagrange, 300; Lietzmann, 109; Joseph Amstutz, *ΑΠΛΟΤΗΣ: Eine begriffsgeschichtliche Studie zum jüdisch-christlichen Griechisch* (Bonn: Hanstein, 1960) 108–9.
183 W. C. van Unnik has in mind sharing the gospel as well as material resources in "Interpretation of Romans 12:8," 177–78; see also Dunn, 2:730.
184 Unnik, "Interpretation of Romans 12:8," 173–76.
185 See Jewett, "Tenement Churches," 23–43; idem, *Apostle to America*, chapter 6.
186 See Dunn, 2:730.

possessions because generosity is hardly relevant to the communication of ideas.[187] The term used here is a virtual synonym for κοινωνόω ("share"), which Paul frequently employs to denote the sharing of material possessions that was characteristic of the early church (Rom 12:13, 15:27; 1 Cor 9:11; 2 Cor 8:4, 9:13; Phil 4:15). What is in view is not so much making contributions to the poor who remain separate from one's own group, as sharing things in common, probably starting with the common meal of early house churches. As the profile of the Roman house and tenement churches indicates, the poor were represented there in large numbers.[188]

The criterion for exercising this charisma is ἁπλότης, meaning basically "simplicity," and secondarily, "generosity."[189] Paul uses the term elsewhere to describe dedication and purity of heart (2 Cor 11:3; Col 3:22), as well as generosity (2 Cor 8:2; 9:11, 13). The term is associated with the philosophical ideal of the simple life[190] and with the Judaic ideal of integrity.[191] These ideals play an important role in the *Testament of Issachar*[192] and appear in Paul's characterization of the Macedonian believers as poor, simple, and generous.[193] The term ἁπλότης is difficult to translate into English,

because "generosity" does not necessarily imply single-mindedness or integrity and may even contain patronizing connotations. Simplicity, on the other hand, does not necessarily imply liberality. Some commentators attempt to fuse the connotations, with little success.[194] On the whole, "generosity" is the best translation so long as its motivation is kept clearly in mind. For Paul, generosity arises from the generosity of God as revealed in Christ (2 Cor 9:10-15), so that house and tenement church members are "God-taught" in the love of the brethren (1 Thess 4:9). They have no further need for ulterior motives[195] such as "selfish calculation . . . haughtiness,"[196] "ostentation or reward."[197] These typical elements of the Greco-Roman system of patronage and benefaction[198] are to be overcome as resources are shared by those made equal in honor by the impartial grace of God in Christ.

The allusive style of avoiding some of the technical terms for early Christian leaders is particularly evident in the sixth charismatic gift. Rather than referring to the head of a congregation with technical terms like "bishop" or "elder,"[199] Paul uses the bland expression ὁ προϊστάμενος ("the leader/presider").[200] The passive participle describes someone being "set over or at the

---

187 See the strained argument in favor of sharing "religious knowledge" in Unnik, "Interpretation of Romans 12:8," 178–79. Zahn, 547, argues for sharing both spiritual and material resources.

188 See Introduction, section 6.

189 Otto Baurenfeind, "ἁπλοῦς, ἁπλότης," *TDNT* 1 (1964) 386–87.

190 See Heinrich Bacht, "Einfalt," *RAC* 4 (1959) 821–40, and idem, "Einfalt des Herzens, eine vergessene Tugend?" *GuL* 29 (1956) 416–26.

191 Ceslas Spicq, "La vertu de simplicité dans l'Ancien et le Nouveau Testament," *RSPhTh* 22 (1933) 5–26; Amstutz, *ΑΠΛΟΤΗΣ*, 40f.

192 Ortkemper, *Leben*, 80, and Dunn, 2:730, refer to *T. Iss.* 3.2; 4.6, 7, 8; 4.1, 6; 5.1, 8; 6.1; 7.7, and with regard to the theme of "generosity," esp. 3.8.

193 See Betz, *2 Corinthians 8 and 9*, 44–45.

194 Baurenfeind, "ἁπλοῦς, ἁπλότης," 387, speaks of "sacrificial 'liberality,'" which loses sight of simplicity; Dunn, 2:730, translates the word "in sincere concern," which stresses singleness of heart but does not imply generosity; Amstutz, *ΑΠΛΟΤΗΣ*, 103, speaks of "simplicity in giving," while 108–9 refers to "spontaneous freedom without anxious

concerns," which also seems to lose sight of liberality.

195 Black, 171.

196 Godet, 433.

197 Sanday and Headlam, 357.

198 See Joubert, *Benefactor*, 58–70.

199 Schlatter, 234, says flatly, "Here the episcopate is in view" without "legal ordinances." Greeven, "Propheten," 38, points out that the terms "bishop" and "leader" are virtually interchangeable because each comes from the same realm of administrative language in the Greco-Roman culture. He observes (40–41) that Paul entirely avoids the use of "elder," although this office is mentioned in Pauline congregations by Acts 14:23 and 20:17 and becomes a favorite term in the Pastorals.

200 See Greeven, "Propheten," 32. Ortkemper, *Leben*, 83, notes that προϊστημι is also used in the Pastorals in a nontechnical sense. The general sense of leadership conveyed by προϊστάμενος is conveyed in Demosthenes' description of his administration in *Epitaph.* 2.9.3–6), that he had "acted as a leader (προϊστάμενος) without any anger nor ill-will nor unjust venality."

head of" a group,[201] a usage reflected in the collective leadership that had been put in charge of the Thessalonian congregation (1 Thess 5:12).[202] This appointed role is different from the cognate term προστάτις ("patron"), which is an upper-class designation of someone who can provide support and protection.[203] The passive form of the expression "the leader" renders unlikely that it merely refers to someone financially or societally capable of giving aid to clients.[204] That ὁ προϊστάμενος implies the more general sense of "the one giving care"[205] also seems unlikely because it would then become completely redundant with regard to the gifts of serving and exhorting, which encompass the scope of care in the ancient world. The expression probably implies appointment to a leadership role in an early house or tenement church, whether as presider,[206] administrator of charitable work,[207] or pastoral supervisor.[208]

The semantic resonance of the phrase ἐν σπουδῇ ("with diligence, zeal") correlates with a leadership role in an administrative sense. Both uses of the verbal form of this word in the Pauline letters are in connection with vigorous pursuit of congregational responsibilities (Gal 2:10; 1 Thess 2:17),[209] while 2 Cor 8:7-8 uses σπουδή to denote "the aggressiveness and efficiency needed to get things done, a virtue one would expect of a good administrator."[210] The use of σπουδαῖος ("zeal, earnestness")

in 2 Cor 8:17, 22 also refers to the diligent pursuit of administrative responsibilities.[211] To avoid the "element of ruthlessness" implied by the term "zeal" in a religious context (ζῆλος in Rom 10:2),[212] the word "diligence" is the appropriate translation. This criterion for the pursuance of administrative responsibilities would have had clear implications in the Roman setting, related to bureaucratic conscientiousness, efficiency, honest effort, goodwill, and vigor.[213] Paul himself had embodied this administrative criterion, resolutely fulfilling his commitment to promote the Jerusalem offering (Rom 15:25-28; 2 Cor 8-9; Gal 2:10) and eagerly endeavoring to meet the needs of his congregations (1 Thess 2:17).

The final charismatic gift—mercy—appears to relate the ministry of the church as much to outsiders as to insiders, particularly if redundancy with the fifth gift of sharing is to be avoided.[214] It is used elsewhere in the Pauline letters exclusively in connection with God's mercy to undeserving humans,[215] but its opposite, "merciless," is used in Rom 1:31 to describe the reprobate mind. Particularly in Judaism, this language is used for "human kindness and pity"[216] shown to persons in physical pain or deprivation, whether within one's family or with enemy groups. Tobit claims to have "walked in the ways of truth and in acts of righteousness all the days of my life, and I did many deeds of mercy (ἐλεημοσύνας πολλὰς ἐποίησα) to my brethren and my nation" (Tob

201 LSJM 1482.

202 See Marshall, *Thessalonians*, 147–48.

203 See Michel, 379, and the discussion below on Rom 16:2.

204 Dunn, 2:731, argues (1) that such a theory is required by the allegedly subordinate placement of the leadership role in the sixth position in the series of charismatic gifts, and (2) that προϊστάμενος should be defined in relation to the neighboring gifts of sharing and showing mercy. The first argument is advanced also by Ortkemper, *Leben*, 82–83. Neither argument is compelling in a random series like this. Fitzmyer, 649, applies the coup de grâce to this theory by posing the decisive question of redundancy: "What is the difference between this charism and ὁ μεταδιδούς or διακονία?"

205 Bo Reicke, "προΐστημι," *TDNT* 6 (1968) 701; followed by Malherbe, *Paul and the Thessalonians*, 90.

206 This alternative is suggested by Barrett's translation "president," in 239.

207 Lagrange, 300; Kühl, 424–25.

208 See the discussion of προϊστάμενος in 1 Thess 5:12-13 in Malherbe, *Paul and the Thessalonians*, 90.

209 Günther Harder, "σπουδάζω κτλ.," *TDNT* 7 (1971) 565; Ceslas Spicq, "σπουδάζω κτλ.," *TLNT* 3 (1994) 276–85.

210 Betz, *2 Corinthians 8 and 9*, 58.

211 Ibid., 70, 77.

212 See Dunn, 2:731; however, he uses the term "zest," which places the accent on the pleasure derived in the pursuance of duties rather than the diligence and efficiency with which they are performed.

213 See the discussion of first-century bureaucratic inscriptions in Spicq, "σπουδάζω κτλ.," 284. Betz, *2 Corinthians 8 and 9*, 58, provides the equivalent terms in Latin bureaucratic language: *studium, observantia*, and *officiosus*.

214 See Zahn, 547.

215 See Rudolf Bultmann, "ἔλεος κτλ.," *TDNT* 2 (1964) 482–85.

216 Ibid., 481.

1:3).[217] The Good Samaritan story expresses this obligation in classic form, referring to him as ὁ ποιήσας τὸ ἔλεος ("the one who does mercy," Luke 10:37). In principle, actions to meet human need would include care for the sick, burial of the dead, or giving alms.[218] In contrast to "sharing with generosity," whose arena was primarily the early house or tenement church, the gift of "mercy with cheer" would have been expressed both inside and outside of the faith community.

There is a clear scriptural echo when Paul connects mercy with "cheer," as the parallel in the LXX version of Prov 22:8 suggests: ἄνδρα ἱλαρὸν καὶ δότην εὐλογεῖ ὁ Θεός ("God blesses a cheerful and generous man"). Whether directly derived from the LXX or from a Greco-Roman proverb,[219] the same association between ἱλαρο- and acts of charity is found in 2 Cor 9:7. Sir 35:8 uses this stem to describe the cheerful countenance of the benevolent saint, while the later rabbis linked almsgiving with cheer: "He who gives alms, let him do so with a cheerful heart."[220] The term ἱλαρότης is connected with the English word "hilarity," suggesting the "joyful eagerness, the amiable grace, the affability going the length of gayety"[221] of those who demonstrate the "freedom and authenticity of generous giving."[222] The ideal itself was supported throughout the Greco-Roman world.[223] But as in the exercise of the other six charismatic gifts, the origin of such cheerful mercy within the framework of Romans is finally the generous "mercies of God" experienced in the Christ event.[224] Within this framework, all of the charismatic gifts of the church can be exercised with sober-mindedness, with due respect for the contributions of others.

---

217 See Fitzmyer, 649, referring also to Tob 4:7.
218 See Michel, 379.
219 See the discussion in Betz, *2 Corinthians 8 and 9*, 106f.
220 Cited by Rudolf Bultmann, "ἱλαρός, ἱλαρότης," *TDNT* 3 (1965) 298, from *Leviticus Rabbah* 34, on Lev 25:39.
221 Godet, 433.
222 Bultmann, "ἱλαρός, ἱλαρότης," 299.
223 Ibid., 297–300.
224 See Ortkemper, *Leben*, 84.

12

The Third Pericope

The Elaboration of Guidelines for Genuine Love

9/ The love [is] without pretense: abhorring[a] the evil, cleaving to the good; 10/ [having] affection for one another with brotherly love, taking the lead in honoring one another, 11/ not flagging in diligence, remaining effervescent in Spirit, serving the Lord,[b] 12/ rejoicing in hope, persevering in affliction, persisting in prayer, 13/ sharing in the needs[c] of the saints, pursuing hospitality to strangers.

14/ Bless the persecutors,[d] bless[e] and do not curse. 15/ Rejoice with those who rejoice,[f] weep with those who weep; 16/ being of the same mind toward one another,[g] not setting your minds on the heights, but being drawn toward lowly people.

"Do not be [wise] minded in yourselves!"

17/ Do not "pay back evil for evil," "taking into consideration excellent things in the sight[h] of" all[i] persons. 18/ If possible, so far as it depends on you, being at peace with all persons; 19/ not avenging yourselves, beloved, but give way to His wrath, for it is written,

"Vengeance is for me, I will repay," says the Lord.

20/ But "if[j] your enemy is hungry, feed him; if[k] he is thirsty, give him drink; for by doing this you will pile up coals of fire upon his[l] head." 21/ Do not be conquered by what is evil, but conquer the evil with the good.

---

a F G lat sy have μισοῦντες ("hating") in place of the infrequently used, but probably original, ἀποστυγοῦντες ("abhorring"), possibly influenced by the Latin tradition, as Lietzmann, 100, suggests.

b The variant τῷ καιρῷ ("the appointed time") in place of τῷ κυρίῳ ("the Lord") found in D*,3 F G 5 d* g Or^{lat 1/2} Latin mss^{acc. to Or(lat) and Hier} Cyp Ambst Hier^{1/2}, has been accepted by Schlatter, Michel, Käsemann, Lagrange, Schmidt, Leenhardt, and Pallas as the more difficult reading. However, the use of the expression "serve the time, be an opportunist" in Plutarch *Arat.* 43.2 and later writers undercuts this argument. Cranfield, 2:634–36, rightly calls this variant a *lectio impossibilis* and shows its inappropriateness in Pauline material. Metzger, *Textual Commentary*, 466, suggests the variant arose from a confusion of the contractions of κυρίῳ and καιρῷ, that is, *if* the contraction of καί was applied

to that portion of καιρῷ, but this possibility does not seem very likely. More likely is a simple visual error because of the similar appearance of καιρῷ and κυρίῳ in cursive; at any event, the latter is strongly supported by P^{46} ℵ A B D^2 L P Ψ 6 33 69 81 88 104 181 256 263 323 326 330 365 424 436 451 459 614 629 945 1175 1241 1243 1319 1505 1506 1573 1735 1739 1836 1852 1874 1877 1881 1962 2127 2200 2344 2492 *Maj Lect* ar b d^2 f o s (t *deo*) vg sy^{p,h,pal} sa bo fay arm eth geo slav Cl Or^{lat 1/2} Greek mss^{acc. to Or(lat)} Bas Chr Greek mss^{acc. to Ambst and Hier} Hier^{1/2} Pel Aug. The phrase is lacking in 1912.

c Zahn, Kühl, Kallas, and others prefer the reading μνείαις ("remembrance"), as found in D* F G t vg^{mss} Ambst. This is an inferior reading to χρείαις ("needs") found in every other MS; its dispersion is understandable in the later church that afforded a large place to the commemoration of the saints. See Zahn, 550f.; Sanday and Headlam, 362; also Käsemann, 346; Lagrange, 305; and Dunn, 2:737. Note, however, the similarity to the visual copyist error I discussed in v. 11.

d There is strong support for ὑμᾶς ("you") in ℵ A D (but with an intervening clause) L P Ψ 33^{vid} 69 81 88 104 181 256 263 323 326 330 365 424* 436 451 459 614 629 945 1175 1241 1243 1319 1505 1506 1573 1836 1852 1874 1877 1881 1912 1962 2127 2200 2344 2492 2495 *Maj Lect* (b) d s t vg^{cl} sy^{p,h} sa bo fay arm eth geo slav Or^{lat 1/4} Bas Chr Ambr Pel Aug^{2/6}. However, the more difficult reading that omits "you" in P^{46} B 6 424^c 1739 *pc* vg^{ww, st} Cl is to be preferred in this instance because the addition can be explained on the basis of the influence of Matt 5:44. See Cranfield, 2:640. In contrast, a deletion of this word "in order to extend the range of the exhortation," as Metzger, *Textual Commentary (1975)*, 528, suggests, is not plausible because to bless all persecutors would appear irresponsible for parties that are not involved. In place of "persecutors," Or has the variant ἐχθροὺς ὑμᾶς ("your enemies"), which also has no claim on originality. The whole clause is lacking in F G and several other witnesses, perhaps due to homoioteleuton.

e The omission of εὐλογεῖτε by P^{46} (bo^{ms}) is probably an example of accidental haplography. Dunn, 2:737, suggests "an understandable attempt to polish."

f The variant that adds καί ("and") between 15a and b is found in A D^2 L P 69 88 104 323 326 365 424* 614 945 1175 1241 1243 1319 1506 1573 1836 1874 2344 *Maj* sy^p Tert. The weight of the early textual tradition favors the absence of "and" in P^{46} ℵ B D* F G 6 330 424^c 1505 (1735) 1739 1881 2495 *pc* latt sy^h, and its addition is more easily explained than its deletion. Dunn, 2:737, suggests the motive of adding "and" to polish the Greek.

g   The inclusion of $\mathring{\alpha}\gamma\alpha\pi\eta\tau o\acute{\iota}$ ("beloved") in the original hand of the ninth-century uncial P has insufficient warrant to be seriously considered.

h   Several poorly attested variants provide qualifications of Paul's statement, bringing it into closer conformity with 2 Cor 8:21 and Prov 3:4. A[1] reads $\mathring{\epsilon}\nu\acute{\omega}\pi\iota o\nu$ $\tau o\hat{\upsilon}$ $\vartheta\epsilon o\hat{\upsilon}$ $\kappa\alpha\grave{\iota}$ $\pi\acute{\alpha}\nu\tau\omega\nu$ $\mathring{\alpha}\nu\vartheta\rho\acute{\omega}\pi\omega\nu$ ("before God and all persons"), while F G 629 lat read, $o\mathring{\upsilon}$ $\mu\acute{o}\nu o\nu$ $\mathring{\epsilon}\nu\acute{\omega}\pi\iota o\nu$ $\tau o\hat{\upsilon}$ $\vartheta\epsilon o\hat{\upsilon}$ $\mathring{\alpha}\lambda\lambda\grave{\alpha}$ $\kappa\alpha\grave{\iota}$. . . ("not only before God but also all persons"). A harmonizing motive in these variants is suggested by Dunn, 2:737.

i   The substitution of $\tau\hat{\omega}\nu$ ("of the") for $\pi\acute{\alpha}\nu\tau\omega\nu$ ("of all"), and the omission of $\pi\alpha\nu$ (leaving only $\tau\omega\nu$) in P[46] A[1] D* F[gr] G 181 436 d g Lcf Ambst *pc*, appear to be efforts to delimit ethical obligations, reflecting a stance of later generations.

j   The reading $\mathring{\alpha}\lambda\lambda\grave{\alpha}$ $\mathring{\epsilon}\acute{\alpha}\nu$ ("but if") is strongly supported by ℵ A B P 6(+ $o\mathring{\upsilon}\nu$) 5 69 81 218 256 263 330 365 424[c](+ $o\mathring{\upsilon}\nu$) 441 451 467 614 621 623 630 1243 1319 1506 1563 1573 1718 1739 1852 1881 1959 1962 2110 2127 2200 2492 *pc* lat. The variant $\mathring{\epsilon}\grave{\alpha}\nu$ $o\mathring{\upsilon}\nu$ ("if therefore") in D[2] L 33 61 88 104 181 326 424* 459 614 629 915 917 945 1175 1241 1505 1678 1735 1751 1836 1838 1845 1874 1875 1877 1908 1912 1942 2138 2197 2344 2495 2718 *Maj pm* sy[h] and the use of $\mathring{\epsilon}\grave{\alpha}\nu$ alone in P[46vid] D* F G Ψ 323 436 720 pc it Ambst Spec appear to be stylistic improvements by softening the sharply antithetical "but" at the beginning of this citation from Prov 25:21-22.

k   The addition of $\kappa\alpha\acute{\iota}$ ("and") by D* and the addition of $\delta\acute{\epsilon}$ ("and, now") to an original $\mathring{\epsilon}\acute{\alpha}\nu$ ("if") alone, supplied by all other manuscripts, by D[2] Ψ 1505 1735 2495 *pc* sy[h] are secondary stylistic improvements.

l   The substitution of the genitive $\tau\hat{\eta}\varsigma$ $\kappa\epsilon\varphi\alpha\lambda\hat{\eta}\varsigma$ in place of the accusative with $\mathring{\epsilon}\pi\acute{\iota}$ for "his head," in B, is a secondary grammatical improvement.

Analysis

Despite the tendency of exegetes to view this section as "a series of loosely connected items of exhortation,"[1] it is artfully constructed for rhetorical impact and closely related to the tensions between Christian groups in Rome. When the copulative $\mathring{\epsilon}\sigma\tau\acute{\iota}\nu$ is supplied[2] to the first clause of v. 9, "the love [is] without pretense" serves as the thesis statement for the pericope.[3] The subsequent pair of participial phrases coordinate such love with the discrimination between good and evil. Ten neatly balanced phrases follow in vv. 10-13,[4] beginning with $\varphi\iota\lambda\alpha\delta\epsilon\lambda\varphi\acute{\iota}\alpha$ ("brotherly love") and ending with $\varphi\iota\lambda o\xi\epsilon\nu\acute{\iota}\alpha\nu$ ("love for strangers, hospitality"),[5] which would have been understood as relating to congregational problems in Rome. David Black has detected a regularly developed chiastic structure from 12:9b through 12c.[6] The imperative expressions have parallel structures, beginning with the articles and ending with participles. The rhetorical device of anaphora is used to link these participial phrases into a compelling chiastic series, with the article $\tau\hat{\eta}$ opening lines 10a, 10b, and

---

1   Cranfield, 2:628; see Barrett, 239–43; Charles H. Talbert, "Tradition and Redaction in Romans 12:9-21," *NTS* 16 (1969) 83–93; Gordon Zerbe, "Paul's Ethic of Nonretaliation and Peace," in W. M. Swartley, ed., *The Love of Enemy and Nonretaliation in the New Testament* (Louisville: Westminster/Knox, 1992) 184. His study is a reprinted and expanded chapter 6 of G. Zerbe, *Non-Retaliation in Early Jewish and New Testament Texts: Ethical Themes in Social Contexts*, JSNTSup (Sheffield: Academic, 1993).

2   Moulton and Turner, *Grammar III*, 303, and all other commentators supply the imperative verb, but that seems to lack grammatical warrant.

3   Schlier, 373–74, refers to this as a heading, followed by Dunn, 2:739. Walter T. Wilson, *Love without Pretense: Romans 12.9-21 and Hellenistic-Jewish Wisdom Literature*, WUNT 46 (Tübingen: Mohr-Siebeck, 1991) 150, demonstrates more precisely that 12:9a is a maxim serving as a "thesis statement."

4   In *Love without Pretense*, 165, Wilson suggests that this tenfold series may be a formal enumeration, conveying "a sense of completion or fulfillment." But the two admonitions in v. 9b-c are linked to this series grammatically and substantively, requiring reflection on the meaning of series of twelve. For general orientation, see Jewett, "Numerical Sequences," 227–45.

5   See Michel, 302.

6   David A. Black, "The Pauline Love Command: Structure, Style, and Ethics in Romans 12:9-21," *FilN* 2 (1989) 5–9. His chiastic scheme is accepted by Fitzmyer, 652; a similar, less convincing rhetorical disposition is suggested by Dunn, 2:738.

11a; the article τῷ opening lines 11b and 11c; and the article τῇ opening lines 12a, 12b, and 12c; while the articles ταῖς and τήν round off the A/B/C/B'/A' series. Homoioptoton is achieved by the participial endings of each line, the first series of three ending with -οι and the next seven with -τες. The focus of this symmetrically constructed series of admonitions is on relationships within the Roman congregations, in contrast to the next series (14-21) that deals with relations with insiders as well as outsiders.[7]

In vv. 14-21 the sequence of participial expressions gives way to imperative and infinitive forms. Walter Wilson has proposed a chiastic structure in these verses, but some flaws in the analysis render this implausible.[8] It seems more likely that Paul sought to group the exhortations in thematic series of fours and twos. These verses are linked to the previous series with a wordplay on διώκοντες ("pursuing") in v. 13 and διώκοντας ("persecuting") in v. 14,[9] so that the admonitions to the ostracized and the ostracizing are closely coordinated.[10] Paronomasia is used quite prominently in these verses, with εὐλογεῖτε ("bless") repeated in v. 14, the stem φρον- ("minded") repeated three times in v. 16, and the word νικῶ ("conquer") varied with νίκα in v. 21. The figure of pleonism is found in v. 14b, in which the admonition to "bless" is amplified by its opposite, "do not curse."[11] There is a brilliant example of polyptoton in the strictly parallel structure of v. 15:[12]

χαίρειν μετὰ χαιρόντων
κλαίειν μετὰ κλαιόντων

The themes of good versus evil in vv. 17 and 21 develop the motif in 12:2, while the discussion of haughty-mindedness in v. 16 (with a citation from Prov

3:7) develops that in 12:3. Both themes relate to the question of in-group definitions of good and evil and to the expressions of mutual spite and arrogance taken up in 14:1—15:13. Peaceful interaction with the outside world is enjoined by means of allusions or quotations skillfully adapted from *Jos. Asen.* 28:4 in v. 17a; from Prov 34 in v. 17b; from Ps 33:15 in 12:18b; from Lev 19:18 in v. 19a; from Deut 32:35 in v. 19b; and from Prov 25:21-22 in v. 20. The inclusive range of such interaction with enemies as well as the general public is stressed by the reduplication of πάντων ἀνθρώπων ("all persons") in vv. 17 and 18. The pericope concludes with a culminating exclamation[13] formulated with antithetical parallelism and marked with paranomasia in the wordplay with "conquer" as well as with reduplication in the use of "evil."

Rhetorical Disposition

IV.	The *probatio*
12:1—15:13	The fourth proof: Living together according to the gospel so as to sustain the hope of global transformation
12:9-21	3. Elaboration of guidelines for genuine love
12:9a	a. The thesis concerning genuine love
12:9b-13	b. The chiastic development of love in relation to congregational life
12:9b-c	1) Part A: the antithesis defining genuine love
12:9b	a) Relation to evil: "abhorrence"
12:9c	b) Relation to good: "cleaving"
12:10a-11a	2) Part B: three lines beginning with τῇ
12:10a	a) Reference to "brotherly love"
12:10b	b) Reference to mutual honor
12:11a	c) Reference to spiritual zeal
12:11b-c	3) Part C: two lines beginning with τῷ
12:11b	a) Reference to spiritual intensity
12:11c	b) Reference to serving the Lord

---

7   See Dunn, 2:738.
8   Wilson, *Love without Pretense*, 176, suggests A = v. 14; B = v. 15; C = v. 16; D = vv. 17-19a; C' = v. 19b-c; B' = v. 20; A' = v. 21. The material in sections C and C' does not seem to be parallel and the alleged center of the ring composition in vv. 17-19a (section D) is arbitrarily concluded in the middle of a sentence that contains clear antithetical parallelism linked with ἀλλά ("but"). Similarly, the mini-ring composition that Wilson proposes in section D results in identifying v. 18a as the "focal center of the ring," which is implausible because this again is the prota-

sis of a coherent, longer sentence that needs to be kept together. Finally, although v. 21 is included in Wilson's proposed chiasm, its proper correspondence is with v. 9, since the terms "good" and "evil" appear in both.
9   Bullinger, *Figures*, 291, lists this as an example of antanaclasis, in which the same word is used in a sentence with clashing definitions.
10   See Minear, *Obedience*, 87; Käsemann 331.
11   Bullinger, *Figures*, 418.
12   See ibid., 274.
13   Wilson, *Love without Pretense*, 197, shows that this

12:12a-c	4)	Part B': three lines beginning with τῇ
12:12a		a) Reference to hope
12:12b		b) Reference to persecution
12:12c		c) Reference to prayer
12:13a-b	5)	Part A': sharing with members and strangers
12:13a		a) Reference to sharing inside the Christian community
12:13b		b) Reference to sharing outside the Christian community
12:14-20	c.	Guidelines for responding to hostility inside and outside the Christian community
12:14-15	1)	Four admonitions in response to persecution and adversity
12:16	2)	Four admonitions to avoid hostile competition
12:17-19	3)	Four admonitions concerning retaliation and vengeance
12:20	4)	Two admonitions concerning reconciliation with enemies
12:21	d.	Recapitulation of commands in relation to good and evil
12:21a	1)	Negative guideline: not to be conquered by evil
12:21b	2)	Positive guideline: conquer evil with good

Exegesis

■ **9** The pericope opens with a succinct maxim that serves as a heading for the entire section: "the love [is] without pretense."[14] In a gnomic form consisting only of a noun and an adjective, there is no need or justification for supplying an imperative verb, a translation habit universally followed by contemporary translations and commentaries.[15] Having laid out a basis for a charismatic ethic in which each Christian responds to the gift of salvation with grateful, bodily service in 12:1-2, Paul assumes the presence of "the love" in v. 9.[16] The subsequent discourse establishes the dimensions and implications of such love. The use of the definite article indicates that it is not love in general[17] but specifically Christian love already manifest in the Roman churches that now comes under discussion.[18] The social context of the early Christian "love feast" would probably have provided the primary resonance of this term for the Roman believers,[19] although its range extends beyond the Christian community, as the later discussion of strangers and persecutors indicates (12:13-14). *Agapê* is the spiritual "gift which is at the root of all the rest,"[20] that needs to be refined rather than evoked. It is the nature of such love, poured into the heart (5:5) of each beloved member of the community (1:7), to be both spontaneous and indiscriminatingly generous. Hence Paul defines ἀγάπη ("love") as ἀνυπόκριτος, objectively "genuine," "without pretense" rather than "sincere" or "unhypocritical" in the modern sense of that term.[21] However, since the

sentence is an ἐπιφώνημα ("concluding exclamation") as defined by the classical rhetorical handbooks: Aristotle *Rhet. Alex.* 39ª8–39ᵇ2, and Demetrius Phalereus *Eloc.* 2.106–10. Holloway identifies this verse as a formal *sententia* in "Paul's Pointed Prose," 49.

14   In *Love without Pretense*, 150–51, Wilson shows that the form of 12:9a is that of a gnomic saying that provides a definition of love rather than urging the performance of love; but he inconsistently retains the traditional translation "let love be without pretense."

15   For instance, the famous Delphic maxim is verbless and nounless: μηδὲν ἄγαν, "Nothing to excess." Wilson, *Love without Pretense*, 151, provides a list of similar sayings in Cleobulus *Epig.* 1; Solon *Epig.* 1; Thales *Epig. ded.* 11–13; Pittacus *Epig.* 11; Periander *Ep.* 11.

16   See Wilson, *Love without Pretense*, 155; Moo, 775.

17   The tradition of dropping the definite article in modern translations and commentaries serves to generalize and decontextualize Paul's statement. Even the excellent study by Wilson treats this statement as a generalizing maxim, translated without reference to the article in *Love without Pretense*, 150.

18   There is a broad consensus that early Christians used the term ἀγάπη more frequently and with greater significance than earlier writers; see Warnach, *Agape*, 106–44; Ceslas Spicq, *Agapè dans le Nouveau Testament. Analyse des Textes*, ÉtBib (Paris: Gabalda, 1958–59) 1:208–315, 2:9–305; Furnish, *Love*, 102–11; John Piper, *"Love Your Enemies": Jesus' Love Command in the Synoptic Gospels and the Early Christian Paraenesis*, SNTSMS 38 (Cambridge: Cambridge University Press, 1979) 4–18, 102–8; Wilson, *Love without Pretense*, 151.

19   Dunn, 2:739, is the only commentator to mention the "love feast," in the context of "subsequent" usage in the early church. It is likely, however, that the language of the "love feast" was being used from the beginning of Christianity in Rome and elsewhere; see Reicke, *Agapenfeier*, 9–18.

20   Godet, 433.

21   Ulrich Wilckens, "ὑποκρίνομαι κτλ.," *TDNT* 8 (1972) 559–71, implies that "genuine" is the appropriate translation because pre-Christian usage did

adjective is derived from ὑποκριτής ("actor"), this formulation contains an implicit "warning against pretense and deception in love."[22] A somewhat similar maxim is found in Prov 27:5, again with the copulative to be supplied: κρείσσους ἔλεγχοι ἀποκεκαλυμμένοι κρυπτομένης φιλίας ("Open rebukes [are] better than disguised love"), dealing with friends who refrain from frank comment even when necessary. There are similar maxims among the pre-Socratic philosophers: "Many who seem to be friends are not, and many who do not seem to be are" (πολλοὶ δοκέοντες εἶναι φίλοι οὐκ εἰσί, καὶ οὐ δοκέοντες εἰσίν);[23] "It is difficult for an enemy to deceive his foe, Cyrnus, but easy for friend to deceive friend" (ἐχθρὸν μὲν χαλεπὸν καὶ δυσμενῆ ἐξαπατῆσαι, Κύρνε, φίλον δὲ φίλωι ῥαιδίον ἐξαπατᾶν).[24] These parallels all deal with friendship rather than communal solidarity and they do not use the specific terms Paul employs here. The closest parallel is Paul's own wording of 2 Cor 6:6, ἐν ἀγάπη ἀνυποκρίτῳ ("with genuine love"), formulated out of the controversy with the superapostles who in Paul's view had used gifts like love for the sake of power and status. To remain "genuine" in love requires a disciplined commitment to honesty and the respect of limits, as the rest of this passage will demonstrate.[25]

While earlier interpreters had mistakenly conceived the connection between 12:9a and b-c as aiming to avoid the danger of insincerity,[26] the tendency among scholars in recent decades is to deny any logical connection at all and to assume that Paul simply cites a traditional ethical catalog haphazardly formulated in participial style.[27] On both substantive and grammatical grounds, it seems likely that v. 9b-c should be understood as a protreptic maxim that serves to elaborate v. 9a[28] and to forecast the argument in the section: "cleaving to the good" is elaborated in vv. 10-16 and "abhorring the evil" in vv. 17-21. There has been a substantial debate over the imperatival connotation of the participles in v. 9b-c, in Hellenistic Greek,[29] and in Aramaic ethical catalogs.[30] The least problematic approach is to assume with Funk that "the

---

not have the psychological connotation of "insincerity" or "hypocrisy." On 3:571, Wilckens specifically rejects the psychological construal by Schlatter, 235. Günther Bornkamm, "Heuchelei," *RGG³* 3 (1959) 305–6, argues for the basic meaning of ὑπόκρισις as "objective self-contradiction." In the LXX the substantive is used in a negative sense, translating חָנֵף, the impious person whose deeds are alienated from God (Wilckens, 3:565). But Wilckens's discussion of 12:9 is somewhat prolix, concluding on the basis of parallels in Wis 5:18 and 18:16 that ἀνυπόκριτος implies the "unfeigned simplicity of that which is irrevocable and definitive" (3:570). Actually, these parallels have more nearly the meaning of "unfeigned" enactment of divine judgment, as the discussion by R. H. Charles makes plain, *APOT* 1:543, 565. The lexicographer Hesychius *Lex* α5569 glosses ὑπόκρισις with ἄδολος ("guileness, genuine") and ἀπροσωπόληπτος ("impartial, unbiased").

22 Wilson, *Love without Pretense*, 152. For an extensive treatment of the background of the term, see Bruno Zucchelli, ΥΠΟΚΡΙΤΗΣ. *Origine e storia del termine* (Breschia: Paideia, 1963). In *Clothed with Christ*, 92–94, Michael Thompson argues that Paul's critical use of the ὑπόκρισις terminology is rooted in the Jesus tradition. A particularly significant parallel is Philo *QG* 3.29: "The unhypocritical habit is worthy of praise but truth an object of desire (Τὸ

ἀνυπόκριτον ἦθος ἐπαινετόν, καὶ φίλον ἡ ἀλήθεια)." See also Söding, *Liebesgebot*, 243.

23 *Gnomologium Democrateum* 97; translation by Wilson, *Love without Pretense*, 153.

24 Theognis *Eleg.* 1219–20; translation by Wilson, *Love without Pretense*, 153.

25 See Jewett, *Tolerance*, 92–120, and Ortkemper, *Leben*, 86.

26 Godet, 434; Lagrange, 301; Dodd, 198.

27 Cranfield, 2:631: "it is . . . a mistake to connect v. 9b specially closely with v. 9a." Käsemann, 330; Talbert, "Tradition and Redaction," 88–91.

28 See Wilson, *Love without Pretense*, 154.

29 H. G. Meecham, "The Use of the Participle for the Imperative in the New Testament," *ExpT* 58 (1947) 207–8; A. P. Salom, "The Imperatival Use of the Participle in the New Testament," *ABR* 11 (1963) 41–49; David Daube, "Appended Note: Participle and Imperative in 1 Peter," in Edward Gordon Selwyn, *The First Epistle of St. Peter* (London: MacMillan & Co., 1964) 467–88; Charles Kingsley Barrett, "The Imperatival Participle," *ExpT* 59 (1948) 165–66.

30 David Daube, "Jewish Missionary Maxims in Paul," *StTh* 1 (1948) 158–69; Daube, "Appended Note," 467–88; Barrett, "The Imperatival Participle," 165–66.

participle derives its mood from an associated finite form,"[31] in this instance the copulative ἐστίν supplied to v. 9a. The first-century hearers of Romans would probably have perceived a qualifying connection between the participial phrases in v. 9b and c with the admonition in v. 9a,[32] so that distinguishing between the "evil" and the "good" is the means by which love is kept "genuine." Congregational involvement in making such distinctions links this pericope very closely with 12:1-2, where the term τὸ ἀγαθόν ("the good") was also used.[33] The highly emotional terms ἀποστυγοῦντες ("abhorring")[34] and κολλώμενοι ("cleaving")[35] imply a passionate commitment to the objective good of the fellow members of one's congregation. The language is reminiscent of Amos 5:15, "we have hated evils and loved good things (μεμισήκαμεν τὰ πονηρὰ, καὶ ἠγαπήσαμεν τὰ καλά)." The Qumran community is exhorted "to love all that He has chosen and hate all that He has despised; to depart from all evil and cling to all good works" (1QS 1:4-5). A similar use of "cling" is found in T. Benj. 8.1, "Do away with evil, envy, and hatred of brothers, and cling to goodness and love."[36] A somewhat more distant parallel in the context of friendship appears in Isocrates:

"Scrutinize your actions and believe that they are evil (πονηράς) when you wish to hide from me what you do, and useful (χρηστάς) when my knowledge of them will be likely to make me think better of you."[37]

Paul's formulation brings love far beyond the mild "live and let live" stance of Greco-Roman humanitarian ideals.[38] The choice of the expression "genuine love" suggests a derivation in Paul's struggle with opponents such as those reflected in 2 Cor 6:6, who tended to obscure the objectivity of good and evil by concentrating on the inspired quality of action that stands beyond normal ethical strictures.[39] Similarly, the gnostic view of love tended to assume that "only by human opinion are actions good or bad."[40] Rom 12:10-21 moves on to counter such tendencies by elaborating the way genuine love manifests itself in the face of congregational conflict and political adversity.

■ **10** The congregational focus of Paul's description of love is confirmed by the expression εἰς ἀλλήλους ("for one another") in this verse.[41] Klaus Schäfer has shown that φιλαδελφία ("brotherly love") had been used primarily for affection between family members prior to its employment in early Christianity.[42] In the first appear-

---

31 BDF §647.

32 See Godet, 434.

33 Wilson, *Love without Pretense*, 154, refers to the "rational ability of . . . members to determine their ethical responsibilities and to discriminate between what is good and evil."

34 The word ἀποστυγέω ("abhor") is a hapax legomenon in the NT; in classical Greek it means "hate violently, abhor," according to LSJM 220. For example, Euripides *Ion* 448 has the chorus declare, "I abhor the bereavement of children (τὸν ἄπαιδα δ᾿ ἀποστυγῶ)." Sanday and Headlam, 360, aptly remark: "the word expresses a strong feeling of horror."

35 This term is used otherwise by Paul only in the context of sexual intercourse (1 Cor 6:16f.); see Karl Ludwig Schmidt, "κολλάω," *TDNT* 3 (1965) 822.

36 See Fitzmyer, 653.

37 Isocrates *Nic.* 52; cited by Wilson, *Love without Pretense*, 155.

38 See W. Rüegg, "Humanität," *RGG³* 3:482–84; Ulrich Luck, "φιλανθρωπία," *TDNT* 9 (1947) 107–10. In "ἀγαπάω κτλ.," *TDNT* 1 (1964) 40, Ethelbert Stauffer suggests on the basis of Philo *Virt.* 51ff., and Josephus *C. Ap.* 2.290ff., that Hellenistic Judaism developed a traditional, apologetic ethic incorporat-

ing this humanitarian ideal, so it is unlikely that Paul derived his ethical urgency from this quarter. Compare Ceslas Spicq, "La Philanthropie hellénistique, vertu divine et royale (à propos de Tit. III,4)," *StTh* 12 (1958) 169–91.

39 See Georgi, *Opponents*, 258–64, 315–19.

40 Hans Jonas, *The Gnostic Religion*, 3d ed. (Boston: Beacon Press, 1970) 272; cf. also 46, 89, 273–78.

41 See Söding, *Liebesgebot*, 244–45.

42 Schäfer, *Bruderschaft*, 135–58; see also H. Sedlaczek, "Ἡ φιλαδελφία nach den Schriften des heiligen Apostels Paulus," *TQ* 76 (1897) 274, 277–78. Dunn, 2:740–41, argues that while φιλαδελφία refers initially to familial love, it extends beyond the family to members of a religious or political association. For instance, in 2 Macc 15:14 Onias commends Jeremias as "a lover of the brethren" (ὁ φιλάδελφος) when he extends to Judas Maccabeus the golden sword.

ance of this term in a Pauline letter (1 Thess 4:10), φιλαδελφία is used as if had already been employed for material and emotional sharing within the congregation.[43] Both in 1 Thess and this reference in Romans, it is evident that congregational members are viewed as constituting a fictive family.[44] That "brotherly love" would normally be perceived to include each other within the congregation would seem to be so self-evident[45] as to make this expression unnecessary, but the peculiar historical circumstances in Rome demanded the emphatic inclusion of other fellow believers. The congregational focus, in fact, continues from 12:10 through 12:13a. The use of the NT hapax legomenon, φιλόστοργος ("affection"), augments this appeal with a concept widely used in Hellenistic ethics.[46] The solicitude typical for family and friendship is seen here as characteristic for the Christian community,[47] a matter confirmed by later writers.[48] The implications of this social reality for opposing cliques within Roman house and tenement churches are developed in chapters 14–15.

The same term ἀλλήλους ("another") is used in v. 10b so that congregational relations remain in the forefront. None of the prevailing translations of προηγούμενοι has proven satisfactory. "Preferring" or "esteeming" one another lack lexicographic support[49] and appear to be influenced by theological reflections based on Phil 2:3, where this difficult term does not appear.[50] "Surpassing" one another[51] is also unsupported by lexicographical evidence, as Zahn has shown,[52] and is grammatically difficult because one would expect the genitive or dative rather than the accusative in such a construction.[53] The same grammatical difficulty weakens the translation "anticipating" one another.[54] And "conducting others before you"[55] makes little sense. The straightforward option that remains may not have been considered before because the audience situation has usually not been taken sufficiently into account at this point. "Taking the lead in honoring one another" fits the basic meaning of the verb[56] and meets the requirement of the accusative ἀλλήλους in the context of τιμή ("honor").[57] It takes account of the social context of honor that marked the ancient Mediterranean world, in which pub-

43 Schäfer, *Bruderschaft*, 160–62.

44 See Bartchy, "Siblings," 68–70.

45 Hans Freiherr von Soden, "ἀδελφός κτλ.," *TDNT* 1 (1964) 146.

46 For example, Plutarch *Brut.* 13.4.1 describes Porcia, the wife of Brutus, as being "affectionate and loving her husband" (φιλόστοργος δ᾽ ἡ Πορκία καὶ φίλανδρος οὖσα). Diogenes Laertius reports in *Vita philos.* 2.121.1 that Crito was "most especially affectionate (μάλιστα φιλοστοργότατα)" toward Socrates. This becomes a cosmopolitan philosophical term in the first century B.C.E., with 13 occurrences in Philo Judaeus and Diodorus Siculus; in the first century C.E., 36 times in Plutarch, 21 in Josephus, 28 times in Epictetus, who devoted an entire chapter to the topic, Περὶ φιλοστοργίας (*Diss* 1.11). See Ceslas Spicq, "ΦΙΛΟΣΤΟΡΓΟΣ (À Propos de Rom., 12.10)," *RB* (1955) 497–510; G. H. R. Horsley, "A Personalised Aretalogy of Isis," *NDIEC* 1 (1981) 20; idem, "φιλοστοργία in epitaphs from Asia Minor," *NDIEC* 2 (1982) 100–103; idem, "A Woman's Virtues," *NDIEC* 3 (1983) 40–43.

47 See Godet, 434.

48 That mutual affection in fact became characteristic of early Christians is indicated by the second-century *Diogn.* 1.1.8, where they are said to "have a certain affection towards one another (καὶ τίνα τὴν φιλοστοργίαν ἔχουσιν πρὸς ἀλλήλους)."

49 Friedrich Büchsel, in "ἡγέομαι κτλ.," *TDNT* 2 (1964) 909, adduces 2 Macc 10:12 in favor of the prevailing translation "prefer, esteem more highly," but the context clearly favors the less strained translation of the Maccabean passage, "Ptolemy . . . took the lead in showing justice to the Jews," as in the *RSV* translation. See also Charles, *APOT*, 2:144.

50 See Cranfield, 2:632–33. The verb ἡγέομαι used in Phil 2:3 does have the sense of "consider, think, esteem," but the compound employed in Romans, προηγέομαι, requires the sense of "go before and show the way (to) somebody," according to BAGD 706.

51 Cranfield, 2:632, provides the Greek text of Chrysostom, *PG*, col. 605, in support of this translation. Fitzmyer, 654, is on a similar track with "outdo one another."

52 Zahn, 548 n. 41.

53 Compare Godet, 434.

54 Cranfield, 2:632, provides the texts from the Vulgate, Oecumenius, and Theophylact in support of this translation. Dunn, 2:741, follows a version of this option in his translation "show the way."

55 Godet, 435.

56 See BAGD 712; LSJM 1480.

57 Johannes Schneider, "τιμή κτλ.," *TDNT* 8 (1972) 169–80.

lic recognition was the essential basis of personal identity.[58] This alternative matches the Hebraic idiom mentioned by Michel, namely, the virtue of taking the lead in greeting others.[59] This translation matches the congregation situation in Rome, in that members of competing groups were refusing to accept each other in their love feasts. As Lendon observes, "a Roman dinner party was an honorific event *par excellence.*"[60] If each side now "takes the lead" in showing honor to their competitors, the imbalance in honor due to social stratification and group competition would be transformed in a way that matched "genuine love."[61] The countercultural quality of this admonition is demonstrated by Scott Bartchy, who cites Anonymous Iamblici, *fragmenta* 2.8: "People do not find it pleasant to give honor to someone else, for they suppose that they themselves are being deprived of something (οὐ γὰρ ἡδὺ τοῖς ἀνθρώποις ἄλλον τινὰ τιμᾶν [αὐτοὶ γὰρ στερίκεσθαί τινος ἡγοῦνται])."[62]

■ **11** The three exhortations in this verse would seem to begin with a tautology except for the context of a charismatic ethic as established in 12:3-8. Translators over-

come this in part by selecting verbal forms like "flagging"[63] for the noun ὀκνηρός ("indolence"), the antithesis of σπουδή ("eagerness, diligence").[64] The premise of the exhortation is an already active enthusiasm that derives from an extrahuman stimulus, but which can be stifled or allowed to become inactive. Since enthusiasm is usually maintained in contexts of mutual support for one's cause and beliefs, the actions suggested in 12:10 could have a dampening effect. To honor those who follow a different ethos could easily promote relativism, which would make enthusiasm appear inappropriate. This is countered by an exhortation phrased with a term typically used to warn against worthless indolence on the part of slaves or employees.[65] The contempt felt for the indolent, shared both by the classical and the Hebraic tradition, is expressed in the following examples:[66]

ὀνειδιζόμενος ὀκνηρὸς οὐκ αἰσχύνεται . . . ("A slothful person is not ashamed when admonished . . ." Prov 20:4)

58 For general orientation, see Malina, *New Testament World,* 25–50; Jewett, "Honor and Shame," 257–72. For the application of this scheme with regard to equalizing the effects of social stratification in Rom 12:10, see Moxnes, "Honour and Righteousness," 73–74. A theological assessment of this topic is available in Otto Hennig Nebe, *Die Ehre als theologisches Problem,* FurSt 12 (Berlin: Furche, 1936). See also Bartchy, "Siblings," 71–72.

59 Michel, 384, mentions *P. 'Abot* 4:15 and *Ber* 6b in this context. In *'Abot* 4:15 Rabbi Eleazar ben Shammua said, "Let the honor of your disciple be dear to you as the honor of your associate, and the honor of your associate as the fear of your teacher, and the fear of your teacher as the fear of Heaven." In *'Abot* 4:20 the second-century rabbi Mattia ben Harash taught, "Be first in greeting every man. . . ."

60 Lendon, *Empire of Honour,* 133, italics in original.

61 See Moxnes, "Honour and Righteousness," 74–75: "Paul here introduces an idea of equality with respect to honour which must have created tensions within the community. . . . In a challenging way Paul breaks with the competition inherent in an honor society. In a transformation of values, Paul claims that honour is now to be freely granted on the basis of love, regardless of status and merit." Similarly, Dehn, *Leben,* 47, speaks of every member of the congregation being worthy of the same "honor."

62 Bartchy, "Siblings," 71; the citation appears in Diehls and Kranz, *Vorsokratiker,* 2:400. In "Paul and Stoicism: Romans 12 as a Test Case," *NTS* 50 (2004) 123–24, Philip F. Esler argues that Stoic teachers would not support Paul's admonition. This assessment is criticized by Troels Engberg-Pedersen, "The Relationship with Others: Similarities and Differences between Paul and Stoicism," *ZNW* 96 (2005) 54–57, who nevertheless concludes that Paul differed from the Stoics in "forgetting *completely* about oneself, thinking *instead* and *only* of others" (57, italics in original). Strom is more on target in *Reframing Paul,* 202: Paul shaped the life of the early church "around a radical break with rank and status. These early groups thus began one of the most radical social experiments of all time."

63 Moffatt and the *RSV* select this term.

64 See Günther Harder, "σπουδάζω κτλ.," *TDNT* 7 (1971) 566, who interprets this reference in terms of "holy zeal . . . full dedication to serving the community." On 561, Harder shows that this usage derived from Hellenistic political and military contexts where serious, expeditious engagement was demanded.

65 Friedrich Hauck, "ὀκνηρός," *TDNT* 5 (1967) 166–67; Ceslas Spicq, "ὀκνέω, ὀκνηρός," *TLNT* 2 (1994) 577. Matt 25:26 uses this term to refer to a "slothful slave."

66 See Dunn, 2:741–42.

Λίθῳ ἠρδαλωμένῳ συνεβλήθη ὀκνηρός, καὶ πᾶς ἐκσυριεῖ ἐπὶ τῇ ἀτιμίᾳ αὐτοῦ. βολβίτῳ κοπρίων συνεβλήθη ὀκνηρός, πᾶς ὁ ἀναιρούμενος αὐτὸν ἐκτινάξει χεῖρα. ("A slothful person is like a filthy stone, and every one will sweep him out in his dishonor. A slothful person is like the filth of a dunghill; everyone who takes it up will shake his hand." Sir 22:1-2)

μετὰ ὀκνηροῦ περὶ παντὸς ἔργου . . . οἰκέτῃ ἀργῷ περὶ πολλῆς ἐργασίας, μὴ ἔπεχε ἐπὶ τούτοις περὶ πάσης συμβουλίας· ("[Do not discuss] with a slothful person concerning any work . . . nor with an idle servant concerning much business; do not heed such persons concerning any matters of counsel." Sir 37:11)

Paul's striking juxtaposition of indolence and diligence serves notice that the energies of love, stimulated by the Spirit, must be allowed to flow freely or be lost. The spiritual basis of this "diligence" is reiterated in the middle phrase of the verse.[67] It has been suggested that *τῷ πνεύματι ζέοντες* ("remaining effervescent in Spirit") is a unique, early Christian expression.[68] The verb means to bubble, boil, ferment, seethe, and was frequently used in a metaphorical sense to describe high emotion.[69] The use of this precise expression in a traditional description of the preacher Apollos (Acts 18:25) leads one to infer that it was probably developed by the first generation of charismatic Christianity.[70] That the apportioned Holy Spirit was in view in this expression is generally assumed.[71] This is consistent with the subsequent clause, "serving the Lord." For Paul the Spirit was the Lord's presence in believers, evoking obedience.[72] The logic of Rom 6 is being employed here, with believers being urged to exercise their gifts of love within the context of the lordship of Christ. There may be a defense against self-serving forms of spiritual enthusiasm in this expression, for, as Käsemann insists, the gift of the Spirit in Pauline theology is inseparable from its divine giver who extends lordship through his gifts.[73] Taken as a whole, v. 11 reveals that for Pauline ethics, service is the natural expression of spiritual enthusiasm, not the consequence of dutiful obedience to moral obligations or a violation of freedom.[74] The task of Christian ethics is to keep the spiritual current flowing in responsible channels. The intent of that current is not merely to uplift believers with an exalted mood. Spiritual enthusiasm is not an end in itself, aiming at an emotional peak experience similar to a drug-induced state, but rather extends the Lord's rule over a formerly disobedient creation. The reference to "serving the Lord" at the end of the verse brings the discussion of ethical guidelines within the parameters of the general thesis of the letter concerning the "righteousness of God."

■ **12** Although the term *χαίρω* ("rejoice") is used here for the first time in Romans, the formula "rejoicing in hope" encapsulates the paradoxical argument of 5:1-5.[75] The Spirit evokes hope in spite of persecution and other adversities because it communicates the love of God that is experienced with particular clarity when all other supports fail. Joy in the specific early Christian sense was distinct from happy moods or victorious exultations. As the dative *τῇ ἐλπίδι* ("in hope") makes clear, it is not a matter of joy *concerning* the future accomplishment of what is hoped for[76] but joy *in* the eschatological hope evoked by the Spirit in the present difficult circumstances.[77] This gives one the power to "persevere in affliction" in that the faithful status of resting one's

---

67 This section is adapted from Jewett, "Apportioned Spirit," 205–6.

68 Albrecht Oepke, "*ζέω κτλ.*," *TDNT* 2 (1964) 876.

69 See BAGD 337; Dunn, 2:742.

70 See the discussion by Ernst Käsemann in "Die Johannesjünger von Ephesus," *ZThK* 49 (1952) 150; Herbert Preisker argues that the expression *ζέων τῷ πνεύματι* ("effervescent in spirit") in Acts 18:25 refers to the Holy Spirit: "Apollos und die Johannesjünger in Acts 18²⁴-19⁶," *ZNW* 30 (1931) 301–2.

71 See Käsemann, 330; Cranfield, 2:634; Barrett, 240.

72 See Rom 6:12-23; Cor 3:17; also Bertil E. Gärtner and Gerhard Krodel, "The Lordship of Christ in the New Testament," in Martin J. Heinecken, ed., *Christian Hope and the Lordship of Christ* (Minneapolis: Augsburg, 1969) 7–18.

73 Käsemann, *Perspectives*, 75. This interpretation is not developed in the Käsemann commentary in relation to this verse because he appears to be preoccupied with the text-critical problem discussed above.

74 See Ortkemper, *Leben*, 94–96.

75 See Dunn, 2:742; Zeller, 210.

76 Barrett, 240.

77 Hans Conzelmann, "*χαίρω κτλ.*," *TDNT* 9 (1974) 369 n. 91.

being in the love of God provides sustenance in the midst of adversity. To paraphrase the fuller development of this theme in Rom 5:4-5, endurance comes from the constant reassurance by the Spirit of the love of God. It is the vital relationship with the "God of patience" (Rom 15:5), not the actual prospects of surviving a particular persecution, that allows one to endure patiently. The recent experience of persecution related to the Edict of Claudius provided a concrete focus for the Roman congregations, but the term θλίψις would also include the wide range of adversity experienced by house and tenement churches in a hostile environment.[78]

The theme of remaining faithful in adversity in 12:12b prepares for the relational stress in the following clause, "persisting in prayer." As Walter Grundmann showed, there was an unprecedented concentration on the ongoing relationship with God through prayer in early Christianity.[79] Verse 12c is reminiscent of Acts 1:14, 2:42, and 6:4, which depicts how the early Christian community persisted in the life of prayer taught by Jesus, placing all cares and thanksgivings before God. The verb προσκαρτερέω ("persist, remain loyal to") was used in all of these passages to refer to communal prayer, making it something of a technical term in early Lukan Christianity.[80] In contrast to the legally prescribed prayer periods of Judaism—or later Islam—it was a matter of constant relationship, led and sustained by the Spirit. The theme of unceasing prayer also appears in earlier Pauline letters (1 Thess 5:17; Col 1:9), and in this context the link with the Spirit established in Rom 8 and reiterated in 12:11 remains crucial.[81]

■ **13** The final series of participial clauses draws attention back to the tensions aroused by the return to the Roman house churches of Jewish Christian leaders expelled by the Edict of Claudius. The reference to fellow believers as "the saints" (τῶν ἁγίων), a term that elsewhere refers explicitly to Jewish Christians in Judea (Rom 15:25, 26, 31), led Theodor Zahn to suggest that this verse refers explicitly and exclusively to the Jerusalem offering.[82] This appears unlikely because of the generality of the reference in 12:13[83] and, more important, one would have to overlook the experience of hearing a letter read sequentially, as Romans was, to believe that the Roman audience would know ahead of time about the Jerusalem offering which is announced in chapter 15. It appears more likely that the wording in 12:13 evokes the situation of the edict, which appears to have banned Jewish Christian leaders while leaving other believers alone.[84] This may explain the choice of κοινωνοῦντες ("sharing") rather than μεταδοῦντες ("contributing") as in 12:8.[85] The "needs of the saints" are not to be viewed from a distance as evidence of misfortunes that the more favored are spared. Instead, those who have just been reminded that they are constantly sustained in affliction by the love of Christ are led here to identify with others who are in need. In Bauer's felicitous description of the connotation of κοινωνοῦντες in this passage, "participation in something can reach such a degree that one claims a part of it for oneself."[86] Those who escaped the deportation under Claudius are thus to participate fully in the plight of the returnees, which in this context would imply the actual sharing of economic resources.[87] In every other instance where the verb κοινωνέω appears in Paul's letters (Rom 15:27; Gal 6:6; Phil 4:15), it carries this sense of making financial contributions and sharing other resources.

---

78 See Heinrich Schlier, "θλίβω," *TDNT* 3 (1965) 146–48.

79 Walter Grundmann, "προσκαρτερέω," *TDNT* 3 (1965) 181f. For references to prayer in Jewish and Greco-Roman contexts, see Wilson, *Love without Pretense*, 164.

80 See Grundmann, "προσκαρτερέω," 618; the close Lukan parallels are Acts 1:14; 2:42, 46.

81 See Gebauer, *Gebet*, 217.

82 Zahn, 550–51. His case rests in part on the inferior textual variant ταῖς μνείας that is discussed in note c above.

83 See Barrett, 240, and Hainz, *Koinonia*, 115–16.

84 See Introduction, Section 6.

85 The *RSV* and Moffatt translations confuse this distinction by rendering both passages with "contribute."

86 BAGD 439. This admonition also resonates with the Delphic Precept, κοινὸς γίνου ("Be communal!" *Precepta Delphica* I.19, in *SIG* 1268), and with Epicurus's advice regarding "what is expedient in the needs of sharing with one another" (ἐν ταῖς χρείαις τῆς πρὸς ἀλλήλους κοινωνίας, cited by Diogenes Laertius *Vitae philos.* 10.152.2).

87 See Friedrich Hauck, "κοινός κτλ.," *TDNT* 3 (1965) 808. In *Koinonia*, 116, Hainz explicitly rejects any implication concerning a "community of goods" in this verse. A broader and more appropriate con-

The same focus on local conditions is visible in v. 13b, in which hospitality is to be "pursued." This unusual use of διώκω ("persecute, pursue") was noted by Origen,[88] and while it cannot include the precise connotation of "seeking out" strangers,[89] it certainly implies vigorous intentionality.[90] This verse therefore picks up the nuance of 12:10b; rather than waiting for strangers to beg for help, one is to "take the lead" in meeting their requirements. That the term φιλοξενία should be translated "hospitality" in this context is widely acknowledged.[91] The early Christian revitalization of the Greco-Roman and Jewish ethics of hospitality[92] is visible here, in that no references to subsequent pecuniary rewards, requirements of good behavior on the part of recipients, or distinctions between Jew/Gentile or Greek/barbarian are allowed.[93] No subsidiary motivation for "hospitality to strangers" is included in this verse, probably because the context of the charismatic love ethic renders it unnecessary. Also, given the importance of the cultural ideal of

the *ius hospitii* ("custom of hospitality") and its association with *pietas* ("religious devotion, respect") in the Roman cultural environment,[94] Paul could count on simple acceptance of this description of love's implication.[95] Although cast in general terms, consistent with the demonstrative rhetoric of Romans, some specific implications for the Roman church situation are plain.[96] With a large number of Jewish Christian and other leaders returning to Rome after the lapse of the Edict of Claudius, evoking conflicts and hostilities, there was a concrete need for the kind of hospitality that marked the Jesus movement and subsequent Christianity.[97]

■ **14** With v. 14 the citation of traditional paranetic material begins,[98] as indicated by the varied style, the extensive parallels, and the presence of a Pauline hapax legomenon in the use of the word "curse."[99] The theme that links the material from vv. 14-20 together is the response to hostility, which in the Roman situation has been experienced both inside and outside the Christian community.[100]

strual of participating in a helpful manner in the material needs of the church is suggested by Seesemann, *KOINΩNIA*, 26. See also Campbell, "*KOINΩNIA*," 368, who suggests the translation "making common cause with the needs of the saints," implying "practical helpfulness." Similarly, Ortkemper, *Leben*, 99–100, makes a case for practical forms of sharing.

88 Compare Cranfield's citation of Origin in 2:640.
89 See, in 2:477, Meyer's refutation of Origen and Bengel.
90 Albrecht Oepke, "διώκω," *TDNT* 2 (1964) 230. One thinks of the Delphic precept δόξαν δίωκε ("Pursue good repute!" *Precepta Delphica* I.11, in *SIG* 1268), which also implies active engagement.
91 Dunn, 2:743; Fitzmyer, 655; John Koenig, *New Testament Hospitality: A Partnership with Strangers as Promise and Mission*, OBT 17 (Minneapolis: Augsburg, 1985) 13.
92 See the discussion of Greek, Roman, and Jewish traditions of hospitality in Dunn, 2:743–44. Donald W. Riddle traces the continuity of hospitality through the late NT and later sources in "Early Christian Hospitality: A Factor in the Gospel Transmission," *JBL* 57 (1938) 141–54, suggesting its social significance. See also John T. Fitzgerald, "Hospitality," *DNTB* (2000) 522–25. The study by Ladislaus J. Bolchazy, *Hospitality in Early Rome: Livy's Concept of Its Humanizing Force* (Chicago: Ares, 1977) 40–41, suggests that Christian revitalization of the Roman

ius hospitii ("custom of hospitality") was an important factor in its success in the Roman environment.
93 Gustav Stählin, "ξένος κτλ.," *TDNT* 5 (1967) 16–23. See the discussion of Greco-Roman and Jewish traditions of hospitality in Dunn, 2:743–44.
94 On *pietas* as one of the three cardinal principles in the Roman value system, see Meister, "Tugenden," 6–8.
95 See Bolchazy, *Hospitality in Early Rome*, 43–82.
96 Ortkemper refers to Rome as a center of travel, receiving Christians from the rest of the empire, in *Leben*, 101.
97 See the studies by Riddle, "Early Christian Hospitality," 141–54; John Dominic Crossan, *The Historical Jesus: The Life of a Mediterranean Jewish Peasant* (San Francisco: Harpers, 1991) 261–64, 332–48; and Theissen, *Social Setting*, 28–34; Theissen, *Social Reality*, 33–59.
98 See Söding, *Liebesgebot*, 246–47.
99 Daube, "Jewish Missionary Maxims," 158–69; Talbert, "Tradition and Redaction," 87–91; Michel, 305; Jürgen Sauer, "Traditionsgeschichtliche Erwägungen zu den synoptischen und paulinischen Aussagen über Feindesliebe und Wiedervergeltungsverzicht," *ZNW* 76 (1985) 19.
100 See Dunn, 2:739; Zerbe, "Paul's Ethic of Nonretaliation," 186–89.

Although v. 14 introduces this theme, it is inappropriate to think of it as a kind of thesis for the paragraph.[101] Much of the scholarly debate on this verse has centered on the question of whether it is a quotation. The widespread emendation of the original reading that lacked "you" or "your"[102] may well reflect the form that this saying took in the early church. It certainly fits Matt 5:44, "pray for those who persecute you (προσεύχεσθε ὑπὲρ τῶν διωκόντων ὑμᾶς)"; Luke 6:28, "bless those who curse you (εὐλογεῖτε τοὺς καταρωμένους ὑμᾶς)"; and Did. 1.3b, "bless those who curse you and pray for your enemies (εὐλογεῖτε τοὺς καραρωμένους ὑμῖν καὶ προσεύχεσθε ὑπὲρ τῶν ἐχθρῶν ὑμῶν)." The fact that the characteristic "you" or "your" is missing in Romans may indicate Paul's editing of cited material, whether from the Jesus tradition or some other tradition of Jewish or early Christian ethics.[103] The generic formulation "bless the persecutors" implies that all persecutors are to be blessed, whether they have persecuted you or not. This has a direct bearing on the Roman situation after 54 C.E., because it extends the scope of the reference to include those in the Roman church situation who had not experienced the deportation under Claudius.[104] Compared with the traditional formulation, Paul's wording provides a superior transition from v. 13, which dealt with the deportees. The link between vv. 13 and 14 with the word διώκω, meaning "pursue" in the former and "persecute" in the latter, is rendered more smooth by the deletion of "you/your," and a possible squabble between the persecuted and those whose inclination may have been to sympathize with the persecutors[105] is avoided. For the Gentile Christians who remained in Rome, to "bless and not curse" was not to condone the deportation, but to convey divine aid and concern for the well-being of the authorities. For the Jewish Christians who had been deported, it means refraining from the natural desire to place their adversaries under divine wrath.

In biblical thought, a curse deriving from a holy person was perceived to inaugurate the process of divine judgment on a sinner,[106] while the blessing concretely conveyed well-being and strength deriving from divine power.[107] In the context of a pericope headed by "the love [is] genuine," blessing implies seeking the well-being

---

101 In *Love without Pretense*, 172, Wilson argues that v. 14 "presides over the chapter's remaining verses." Excluded from this generalization would be the content of vv. 15-16.

102 See note d above.

103 Dunn argues in 2:745 and "Jesus Tradition," 201, that Paul is quoting from the Jesus tradition. Peter Stuhlmacher in "Jesustradition im Römerbrief? Eine Skizze," *ThBei* 14 (1983) 240–50, and Allison, "Parallels," 11–12, also argue for dependency on a Jesus saying in the Sermon on the Mount or Plain. See also Thompson, *Clothed with Christ*, 96–105. A cautious appraisal of this question is available in Neirynck, "Paul and the Sayings of Jesus," 265–321, and Nikolaus Walter, "Paulus und die urchristlichen Tradition," *NTS* 31 (1985) 501–2. Wilson's extensive discussion of this issue in *Love without Pretense*, 165–71, concludes that Paul was quoting "an anonymous part of traditional Jewish (or Jewish-Christian) wisdom" (171) reflected in the Didache and elsewhere. Gordon Zerbe takes a similar position in "Paul's Ethic," 207–8. Zeller, 210, argues for an allusion to a common early Christian catechism. None of these discussions deals with the apparent Pauline deletion of "you." William Klassen takes up this matter in *Love of Enemies: The Way to Peace*, OBT 15 (Philadelphia: Fortress, 1984) 114–15, noting that no modern English translation accurately reflects the omission of "you" in the Greek text.

104 The treatment of this verse by Söding, *Liebesgebot*, 247, takes no account of the historical situation of the Roman audience.

105 Compare Wiefel, "Roman Christianity," 94–101, for the details concerning tensions in the congregations and anti-Semitism in Rome. Bartsch, "Gegner," 30–39, builds his case concerning anti-Semitism on details from Rom 9–11, 14–15, passing over those in this passage on the premise that they derive from traditional paranesis unrelated to the concrete congregational situation. He does not therefore account for the peculiar wording of 12:14 as suggested here.

106 Friedrich Büchsel, "ἀρά . . . κατάρα κτλ.," *TDNT* 1 (1964) 449; Dunn, 2:745. See also Igor Kišš's discussion of the curse as separating people from God in "Der Begriff 'Fluch' im Neuen Testament," *CV* 7 (1964) 88–90; a comprehensive survey is available in W. Speyer, "Fluch," *RAC* 7 (1969) 1160–1288, esp. 1233–45. The apocalyptic context of blessing and cursing in the NT is lifted up by Helmut Koester, "Segen und Fluch. III. Im NT," *RGG³* 5 (1961) 1651–52.

107 Hermann Wolfgang Beyer, "εὐλογέω κτλ.," *TDNT* 2 (1964) 755–59; see also R. Trevijano, "Estudio

of persecutors, treating them with care, and interceding for them before God.[108] As Wilson has shown, the prohibition of cursing enemies eliminates any possibility "of blessing now and cursing later, or of blessing publicly and then cursing privately. . . . In this way the admonition serves not only as a call for love in the face of adversity but also as an indirect warning against insincerity and hypocrisy."[109] The antithesis between blessing and cursing serves to indicate the capacity of love to embody the "transformation" (Rom 12:2) that Paul had shown was evoked by the gospel.[110] The ethical risk in this description of how genuine love behaves, manifest in the subsequent history of Christian nonviolence, is that it can be misunderstood as a command of passivity once the power of such transformation is no longer experienced.[111]

■ **15** The stylistic shift in v. 15 from imperatives to infinitives, followed by participles in v. 16, indicates the varying origins of these paraenetic traditions.[112] The theme of creative response to adversity, particularly as experienced by others, is continued from the preceding verse, however. The close Hebraic parallels to this exhortation concerning emotional responsiveness are noteworthy. Sir 7:34 admonishes the wise person: μὴ ὑστέρει ἀπὸ κλαιόντων, καὶ μετὰ πενθούντων πένθησον ("Do not withdraw yourself from weepers, and mourn with the mourners"). A Greek maxim by Menander establishes the same point: λυποῦντα λύπει, καὶ φιλοῦνθ᾿ ὑπερφίλει ("Return grief for grief, and more

than love for love"; Menander *Sent. Byz.* 448). A somewhat more reluctant and morally critical involvement in celebration is visible is Epictetus's dictum: ὅπου γὰρ τὸ χαίρειν εὐλόγως, ἐκεῖ καὶ τὸ συγχαίρειν ("For where a man rejoices with good reason, there others may rejoice with him," *Diss.* 2.5.23).[113] *Testament of Joseph* 17:7-8 offers a more extensive parallel to Rom 12:15-16. Joseph describes his attitude toward his brothers and their families after their betrayal came to light: ". . . their life was my life, and all their suffering was my suffering, and all their sickness was my infirmity (ἡ ψυχὴ αὐτῶν ψυχή μου, καὶ πᾶν ἄλγημα αὐτῶν μου, καὶ πᾶσα μαλακία αὐτῶν ἀσθένεια μου). My land was their land, and their counsel my counsel. And I exalted not myself among them in arrogance (ἐν ἀλαζονείᾳ) because of my worldly glory, but I was among them as one of the least." Although Jesus was reported to have shared both in celebrations and mourning, the only parallel saying that we have about the former derives from much later rabbinic material: "man should not take pleasure among those who weep, nor should he weep among those who take pleasure.[114]

The fact that v. 15 not only includes "rejoicing with those who rejoice" but also places it in the spot of emphasis has led interpreters to see this as the main point.[115] But Paul cites it in a context that allows both clauses equal standing. Whether among fellow believers or outsiders, the person of faith is to sympathize and share in joys and sorrows.[116] This requires a break from

sobre la eulogia paulina," *Burg* 10 (1969) 29–53, and Dunn, 2:744; Claus Westermann, *Blessing in the Bible and the Life of the Church* (Philadelphia: Fortress, 1978) 90–99.

108 See Schenk, *Segen*, 73–79.

109 Wilson, *Love without Pretense*, 172.

110 See Gaugler, 1:261, as cited by Cranfield, 2:640–41.

111 See Klaasen, *Love of Enemies*, 133–36; Jürgen Becker, "Feindesliebe—Nächstenliebe—Bruderliebe. Exegetische Betrachtungen als Anfrage an ein ethisches Problemfeld," *ZEE* 25 (1981) 5–18; Luise Schottroff, "Non-violence and the Love of Enemies," in L. Schottroff, *Essays on the Love Commandment*, trans. Reginald H. and Ilse Fuller (Philadelphia: Fortress, 1978) 9–39; Dorothy Jean Weaver, "Transforming Nonresistance: From *Lex Talionis* to 'Do Not Resist the Evil One,'" in W. M. Swartley, ed., *The Love of Enemy and Nonretailiation*

in the New Testament (Louisville: Westminster/Knox, 1992) 54–58.

112 See Michel, 387; Daube, "Jewish Missionary Maxims," 162–63; Talbert, "Tradition and Redaction," 88; Dunn, 2:738–39.

113 A similarly critical admonition appears in Sextus *Sent.* 414, χαίρειν ἔθιζέ σου τὴν ψυχὴν ἐφ᾿ οἷς καλὸν χαίρειν ("Accustom your soul to rejoice over whatever/whomever it is good to rejoice!").

114 *Der. Er. Rab.* 6.

115 See Sanday and Headlam's citation of Chrysostom in 363; also Lagrange, 306; Huby, 425–26; Fitzmyer, 655.

116 See the extensive discussion of this admonition by Cranfield, 2:642, who follows Barth in affirming that "the Christian is to take his stand beside his fellow-man (whoever he may be)." Dunn, 2:746, follows Furnish, *Love*, 106, in viewing this admonition

the Cynic-Stoic ideals of "apathy" and "impassiveness,"[117] thus constituting another arena in which the admonition concerning nonconformity with the world in 12:2 was to be carried through.

In the Roman church situation the burden of sharing sorrow would fall on those who had not suffered persecution and exile, while the burden of rejoicing was perhaps more evenly divided. The returnees would need to rejoice with the reports of successful expansion of the house and tenement churches in their absence, while those who had remained in Rome would need to share in the joy of those returning. The mutuality, empathy, and solidarity required by this traditional saying[118] differentiates it from the paradoxical wording and eschatological emphasis in Paul's characteristic sayings about joy, noted by Conzelmann.[119] To follow the admonition in v. 15 in the Roman context would have the effect of overcoming divisions at the deepest level and building the basis of a genuine solidarity that must rest not on mental assent alone but also on shared emotional experiences.

■ **16** As in 12:3 where I analyzed the fourfold play on the word φρονέω ("be minded"), here are three distinct sayings with the same component. The thematic progression is usually disguised by translators' preferences for graceful English expressions. Wilson has shown that the progression is marked by an opening maxim (v. 16a) followed by a two-part explanation (v. 16b-c), and concluded with a "direct application to the audience."[120] That the individual sayings originated elsewhere is indicated by the close parallels in other Pauline letters. The expression τὸ αὐτὸ εἰς ἀλλήλους φρονοῦντες ("be of the same mind toward one another") is found with slight variations in 2 Cor 13:11; Phil 2:2; 4:2, but without the "toward one another" phrase that is typical for Romans (see esp. Rom 15:5). The admonition to "set the mind on exalted things," τὰ ὑψηλὰ φρονοῦντες, is closely paralleled by Rom 11:20 as well as by Phil 3:19 and Col 3:2, the latter two of which are directed against claims to possess superior mindedness.[121] The exhortation not to be φρόνιμοι παρ᾽ ἑαυτοῖς ("wise-minded in yourselves") reflects the Corinthian radicals' self-designation as οἱ φρόνιμοι ("the wise-minded ones," 1 Cor 4:10; 10:16; 2 Cor 11:19).[122] After a consideration of this evidence, Michel properly concludes that v. 16 is a warning formed by Paul out of his struggles with ecstatics.[123] The connections between this background and the Roman situation are most easily grasped if the components of v. 16 are considered in reverse sequence, beginning with the element of final emphasis.

To be "wise-minded" (φρόνιμος) is a positive trait in Hellenistic sources[124] and in most of the NT occurrences (Matt 10:16; 24:45; 25:2, 4, 8, 9; Luke 12:42), but here it has the negative valence found in 1 and 2 Corinthians.[125] In the view of first-century Proto-Gnosticism, wise-minded "in oneself" would have implied the self-sufficiency of a mind that believes itself divine. It raises conceit to a philosophical level, justifying it ontologically by the premise of a spark of divinity embedded in true Gnostics, and producing a profound distain for the unenlightened. The wording of Paul's admonition in v. 16c is adapted from Prov 3:7 by changing the singular to plural and dropping the antithesis about fearing God: μὴ ἴσθι φρόνιμος παρὰ σεαυτῷ, φοβοῦ δὲ τὸν θεὸν καὶ ἔκκλινε ἀπὸ παντὸς κακοῦ: ("Do not be wise in yourself, but fear God and refrain from all evil").[126]

---

as extending both to congregational members and outsiders.

117 See Käsemann's reference to ἀταραξία ("impassiveness") in 347. See also the articles by H. Reiner, "Ataraxie," *HWP* 1 (1971) 593, and M.-P. Engelmeier, "Apathie," *HWP* 1 (1971) 429–33.

118 See Wilson, *Love without Pretense*, 179.

119 Conzelmann, "χαίρω κτλ.," 369–70.

120 Wilson, *Love without Pretense*, 179–80.

121 See Jewett, "Conflicting Movements," 378–79; Eduard Schweizer, *The Letter to the Colossians*, trans. A. Chester (Minneapolis: Augsburg, 1982) 125–33, 175.

122 See Walter Schmithals, *Gnosticism in Corinth: An*

Investigation of the Letter to the Corinthians, trans. J. E. Steeley (Nashville: Abingdon Press, 1971) 182–83; see also Barrett, *1 Corinthians*, 231; Henning Paulsen, "φρονέω κτλ.," *EDNT* 3 (1993) 440.

123 Michel, 388.

124 See Georg Bertram, "φρήν κτλ.," *TDNT* 9 (1974) 221–24.

125 Paulsen, "φρονέω κτλ.," 440.

126 See the discussion of rabbinic versions of this saying in Str-B 3:299 and note also that the antithesis of Prov 3:7 was retained in Rom 11:20.

The effect of these minor alterations is to relate the citation more closely to the congregational situation in Rome, dealing with the superiority claims of congregations and ethnic groups.[127] The critique of pride would have resonated positively with the mainstream of both Jewish and Greco-Roman ethics, but the shift to plural forms makes clear that Paul wishes to place an additional bulwark against the prideful tendencies in various house and tenement churches.[128] The connection between conceit and community is specified by the antithesis between "exalted things"[129] and associating with "lowly people"[130] in v. 16b. Only by repudiating the sense of superiority is it possible to achieve genuine solidarity, and if the argument of Romans is accepted, all persons are "the lowly" because all have sinned and fallen short of the glory of God. A similar statement, with somewhat different premises, is found in Didache 3:9b: οὐ κολλη-θήσεται ἡ ψυχή σου μετὰ ὑψηλῶν, ἀλλὰ μετὰ δικαίων καὶ ταπεινῶν ἀναστραφήσῃ ("Let your soul not cleave to those who are proud, but associate with the just and humble"). The most curious feature of Paul's admonition is the use of the verb συναπάγω ("lead away

with/together").[131] Kühl views the participle as a passive, which might imply that the lowly are to be allowed to compel others into compliance,[132] but Michel has shown how implausible this is.[133] The participle could also have a middle connotation so that the action of choosing to go along with others is in view. Schlatter suggests that the participle implies "that fellowship with the lowly always implies renunciation,"[134] but this misses the nuance of almost involuntary movement. That συνα-παγόμενοι is a mistranslation of a Hebrew original, as Cheyne and Talbert suggest,[135] seems highly unlikely. It is noteworthy that no classical Greek parallel to this use of συναπάγω has been found.[136] Hans Dieter Betz offers the most intriguing clue in observing that the use of this term in Gal 2:13 "has a strong connotation of irrationality . . . [of being] carried away by emotions."[137] The Corinthians who called themselves "the wise ones" proudly exhibited gifts like glossalalia, in which they were "moved" by the power of the divine.[138] Walter Grundmann infers from the use of this term ἀπάγω ("lead") in 1 Cor 12:2 that "ecstatic rapture" is in view,[139] so that in this verse in Romans, being drawn "to lowly

127 See Dunn, 2:747. Wilson contends in *Love without Pretense*, 183, that a connection with the "fear of God" motif in the Prov 3:7 citation was intended by Paul, as shown by the parallel citation in Rom 11:25. But the theme of fear is also deleted from that citation. I think it is more likely that Paul's redaction of Proverbs intentionally passed over the fear-of-God motif because there was now a new foundation for the ethic in 12:1-2.
128 See the discussion of the Greco-Roman and Jewish background in Wilson, *Love without Pretense*, 179–83. A particularly apt parallel is the LXX version of 1 Kgs 2:10: "Let not the wise man (φρόνι-μος) boast in his wisdom."
129 See Ortkemper, *Leben*, 105.
130 I follow Karl Thieme, "Die ταπεινοφροσύνη Philipper 2 und Römer 12," *ZNW* 8 (1907) 24–25; Godet, 437; Lagrange, 306–7; Cranfield, 2:644; Ragnar Leivestad, "*ΤΑΠΕΙΝΟΣ-ΤΑΠΕΙΝΟΦΡΩΝ*," *NovT* 8 (1966) 46, and Thompson, *Clothed with Christ*, 106–7, in viewing τοῖς ταπεινοῖς as a masculine plural ("the lowly people"). As Leivestad points out, the somewhat negative connotation of "common, poor people" is retained in the whole context and it is inappropriate to transfer the more positive valence of Christian humility derived from Phil 2 and elsewhere. See also Bartchy, "Siblings," 71–72.
131 LSJM 1696. Sauer concludes in "Feindesliebe," 19, that the distinctively Pauline use of this verb συνα-πάγομαι in Rom 12:16 and Gal 2:13, and its use only one other time in the NT (2 Pet 3:17), points to the Pauline provenance of this saying.
132 Kühl, 429.
133 Michel, 388.
134 Schlatter, 239.
135 Talbert, "Tradition and Redaction," 91, cites T. K. Cheyne, "The Rendering of Rom. xii. 16," *Exp* 2.6 (1883) 469–72.
136 BAGD 784 cites only the modern commentators in support of their translation "associate." LSJM 1696 views the use in Rom 12:16 as synonymous with συμπεριπέρομαι ("go about with, have intercourse with"), but provides no classical parallels. No other dictionary that I have consulted goes beyond such philological guesswork at this point.
137 Betz, *Galatians*, 110.
138 See Conzelmann, *1 Corinthians*, 205–6, for a discussion of the philological evidence on this point.
139 Walter Grundmann, "ταπεινός κτλ.," *TDNT* 8 (1972) 20.

people" would be the antithesis of the self-containment of the religious or gnostic visionary who feels caught up in the divinity of her or his own mind.

The context of visionary experience connects closely with τὰ ὑψηλά ("the exalted things, heights"), used both here and in Rom 11:20. Whereas some interpreters construe this as a kind of adverb qualifying the verb "to be minded," producing translations like "do not be haughty,"[140] the neuter plural needs to be taken into account.[141] Both in the LXX and in Hellenism, τὰ ὑψηλά connotes the cultic high places or the heavenly realms.[142] Philo gives "the heights" a theological significance as the "highest level of the knowledge of God"[143] and the Epistle to the Hebrews refers to it as the location of the throne of God above the heavens (Heb 1:3; 7:26).[144] This background leads one to expect that "to set one's mind on exalted things" would be desirable; here it is not. Since the negative connotation of "the heights" in Rom 12:16b is unparalleled,[145] I am inclined to suggest its context in Paul's polemic against an early form of Proto-Gnosticism which held that the mind, being divine, had an affinity for the sublime realms that could be experienced in ecstasy. The emergence of the later gnostic sect in Asia Minor that called its members the "Hypsistarians," the "dwellers in the heights,"[146] lends credence to this suggestion. Whereas Gnostics believed their minds were drawn inexorably to their sublime homeland above all earthly cares and responsibilities,[147] Paul is demanding here that love (12:9) be allowed to draw one into association with the less enlightened. Superiority is replaced by equality, condescension by solidarity.

If I have accurately traced back the line of reasoning and caught the peculiar nuances that v. 16b and c would have had for the original audience, the admonition in v. 16a can be fit into place. To be "of the same mind toward one another" does not imply agreeing on particulars or achieving a consensus on general points that overcomes disagreements.[148] It implies, rather, the admission of mental equality that might allow people to work with each other. As Godet saw even without grasping the gnostic background of Paul's choice of terms, the attack is against "every sort of spiritual aristocracy."[149] The literal sense of εἰς, "toward" others in the congregation, must be kept in view here.[150] If love is to be genuine, it must eschew any claim of possessing superior insight or status, lest competition between believers and their congregations be encouraged to assume destructive dimensions.

The antithesis between these admonitions and the Roman social environment has been lifted up by Bruce Winter: "Roman class distinctions bred strife and jealousy both between and within different classes. Private conflicts spilt over into the arena of *poleteia* and resulted

---

140 See Cranfield, 2:644; *RSV* and Moffatt have "never be conceived."

141 Barrett, 241, offers the best translation: "Do not set your mind on exalted things." Similarly, Wilson, *Love without Pretense*, 179, suggests "not thinking proud thoughts."

142 See BAGD 850.

143 Georg Bertram, "ὕψος κτλ.," *TDNT* 8 (1972) 604.

144 See ibid., 605. For a discussion of the significance of "the heights" in the heresy being combated in Hebrews, see Jewett, *Letter to Pilgrims: A Commentary on the Epistle to the Hebrews* (Philadelphia: United Church Press, 1981) 26, 128.

145 Plutarch's formulation lacks the critical view of "lofty places," while warning against conceit in *Quo. adul.* 65E.25. "It is true that lofty places (τὰ ὑψηλά) are difficult of approach and access for those who propose to capture them, but loftiness or conceit (ὕψος καὶ φρόνημα) in a mind that lacks sense because of the favors of Fortune or Nature, lies at the mercy of the insignificant and mean (τοῖς μικροῖς καὶ ταπεινοῖς)."

146 See Willem C. van Unnik, "Hypsistarier," *RGG³* 3:506–7.

147 See Rudolf, *Gnosis*, 86–91, 171–80.

148 See Schlier, 380.

149 Godet, 437; see also Hofman, 528–30.

150 Cranfield, 2:643, tones down the distinctive use of εἰς in order to coordinate this verse more closely with other Pauline usage and retain the relevance of the verse for those outside the church. That it implies "outward conduct" is unfounded and that Paul "has in mind specially the effect which their agreement will have on those outside" misses the reciprocal connotation of ἀλλήλους ("each other"), as noted by BAGD 39. That "agreement among themselves is something which Christians owe to the world," as Cranfield states it, may in some sense be true, but it is not Paul's point here.

in vexatious litigation, which was played out in the civil courts and was a powerful aspect of life in Rome endorsed by Roman law. The stated offense was simply the excuse for legal action, but the reason was the public humiliation of one's opponents. Romans dreaded such action being mounted against them, knowing that the judge and the jury were required to pronounce judgement on the basis of the rank and status of the plaintiff and the accused. They were aware that the verdict could create a new set of inimical relationships and that it was not the awarding of damages, but the public shame that most hurt the one against whom the judgement went. Judges and juries in civil litigation were corrupt in their judgements and Roman law provided a legal context to be vindictive and to secure revenge."[151] To refuse to humiliate "lowly people" by vaunting superiority over others is thus an expression of the countercultural social reality in Christ, which reflects the impartial righteousness of God.

■ **17** The warning against retaliation reflects a broad tradition[152] that includes the legacy of ancient Egypt and Babylon[153] and that of the classical and biblical worlds: the book of Proverbs,[154] the Wisdom of Sirach,[155] Pseudo-Phocylides,[156] Hesiod,[157] Theognis,[158] Menander,[159] the *Apocalypse of Sedrach*,[160] and other writings. Both here and in 1 Thess 5:15 Paul virtually cites a version of this saying found in *Jos. Asen.*[161] The exact parallels in the use of the verb "pay back," in the expression "evil for evil," and the similarities in the inclusive pronouns translated "anyone" or "no one" are illustrated below:

μὴ ἀποδιδόντες κακὸν ἀντὶ κακοῦ τινι ἀνθρώπῳ ("do not pay back evil for evil to any person," *Jos. Asen.* 28:14)
μὴ τις κακὸν ἀντὶ κακοῦ τινι ἀποδῷ ("let no one pay back evil for evil to anyone," 1 Thess 5:15)
μὴ ἀποδιδόντες κακὸν ἀντὶ κακοῦ. . . ("do not return evil for evil . . . ," 1 Pet 3:9)
μηδενὶ κακὸν ἀντὶ κακοῦ ἀποδιδόντες. . . ("pay back no one evil for evil . . . ," Rom 12:17)

The adaptation of this quotation reflects the effort seen throughout Romans to find common ground between differing groups in Rome. The slight variation in wording from *Joseph and Aseneth* and 1 Thess reflects the demonstrative genre of Romans, which generally refrains from direct commands and prefers the more generalizing, polite formulation with participial forms.[162] But given the wide range of choices of citations available to Paul, it is perhaps significant that he selects a text from Hellenistic Judaism that would likely have been known to the Jewish Christian branches of the Roman church. Since they were the ones who had suffered the most under the Edict of Claudius, Paul would be appealing to them with their own ethical tradition.

151 Winter, "Romans 12–15," 79–80; see also Lendon, *Empire of Honour*, 50–55.
152 See Piper, *Love Command*, 19–48; Wilson, *Love without Pretense*, 187f.
153 Sauer, "Feindesliebe," 20, refers to the parallels in the "Counsels of Wisdom" found in *ANET* 426 and in Ahikar sayings found in *APOT* 2:730.
154 See Prov 17:13: ὃς ἀποδίδωσιν κακὰ ἀντὶ ἀγαθῶν, οὐ κινηθήσεται κακὰ ἐκ τοῦ οἴκου αὐτοῦ. ("Whoever pays back evil for evil, evil shall not be removed from his house.") See the comprehensive listing of Jewish wisdom material with this theme in Wilson, *Love without Pretense*, 188.
155 Sirach collects a number of sayings concerning non-retaliation in 27:22–28:26.
156 Pseudo-Phocylides *Sent.* 32–34, 63–64, 74–75, 77, 142–43, 151.
157 Hesiod *Op.* 265–66, 327.
158 Theognis *Eleg.* 279–82, 325–28, 365–66, 833–36, 1029–30, 1051–54, 1133–34, 1223–24.
159 Menander *Mon.* 5, 19, 46, 99, 269, 604, 675.
160 Sauer, "Feindesliebe," 20, refers to *Apoc. Sedr.* 7.7, πῶς ἔπας, κύριε, κακὸν ἀντὶ κανοῦ μὴ ἀποδώσῃς ("How can you say, Lord, 'do not pay back evil for evil'?").
161 The expression "evil for evil" is also found in *Jos. Asen.* 23.9 and 28.14. See the discussions in Sauer, "Feindesliebe," 20; Neirynck, "Paul and the Sayings of Jesus," 300; Wilson, *Love without Pretense*, 187. Piper argues in *Love Command*, 39, against a direct quotation, suggesting that Paul is quoting some other "previously existing Jewish paraenetic tradition."
162 See Wilson, *Love without Pretense*, 163.

But the choice and adaptation are subtle and unobtrusive: the wording is universal, applying equally to everyone in the various Roman communities.[163]

Verse 17b appears to be a further adaptation of a verse from Proverbs that Paul had used in 2 Cor 8:21. A comparison of the three texts allows us to discern a deliberate pattern of adaptation:[164]

προνοοῦ καλὰ ἐνώπιον κυρίου καὶ ἀνθρώπων ("consider what is good in the sight of the Lord and humans," Prov 3:4)
προνοοῦμεν γὰρ καλὰ οὐ μόνον ἐνώπιον κυρίου ἀλλὰ καὶ ἐνώπιον ἀνθρώπων ("for we consider what is good not only in the sight of the Lord but also in the sight of humans," 2 Cor 8:21)
προοούμενοι καλὰ ἐνώπιον πάντων ἀνθρώπων ("taking into consideration what is good in the sight of all persons," Rom 12:17b)

The alterations in this verse are quite significant and fit tightly into the flow of Paul's discourse in this pericope. The addition of "all" extends the scope of this polite admonition[165] beyond the congregation to the larger society, including enemies.[166] It takes account of the "good" in the values of human beings everywhere, the *communis sensus* of the human race.[167] This involves "community recognition" of what was perceived to be honorable,[168] a crucial element in Greco-Roman and Jewish cultures. The deletion of the reference to the "sight of the Lord" restricts the scope of the saying to understanding the motivations and values of fellow humans. More specifically, this alteration provides a crucial foundation for chapters 14–15, particularly because the question of divine standards is eliminated for a time, which allows Paul to build the later case that each group in Rome is pursuing its particular style of worship in honor of the same Lord; what a particular group is convinced God wants is not to be used as the standard for evaluating others. Instead, consideration is to be given to what they think is good, taking account of this in shaping one's own actions. The two halves of v. 17 are brought into close harmony with this formulation, because creative nonretaliation requires both an understanding of the motivations of the enemy and a desire to respond appropriately. The practice of Christian tolerance is also receiving here one of its crucial foundations.[169] However, without the framework provided by the earlier argument of Romans, particularly including that of Rom 12:1-2 and 12:9, this maxim would seem to be an invitation to relativism.[170] The verb προνοέω used here in its participial form does not imply accepting or enacting what others think is right,[171] but rather "taking into consideration" what they perceive as the good.[172] As a verb of perception προνοέω differs from the preceding φρονέω cognates and harks back to the νοούμενα of 1:20. It is clear that the preposition ἐνώπιον should be translated "in the sight of,"[173] rather than taken as a dative implying a Christian obligation to

163 For the contrast with Stoic ethics, see Esler, "Paul and Stoicism," 123.
164 See Koch, *Schrift*, 18; Wilson, *Love without Pretense*, 188f.; Zerbe, "Paul's Ethic of Nonretaliation," 190. Fitzmyer, 656, is more circumspect, referring to the "echo" of Prov 3:4 in this verse.
165 The change in the verbal form to a participle fits the polite discourse visible throughout this passage; see Wilson, *Love without Pretense*, 188.
166 See Fitzmyer, 656.
167 See Zahn, 552, and P. Rossano, "L'ideale del Bello (*kalos*) nell'etica di S. Paolo," *SPCIC* 2 (1963) 373–82.
168 Lendon, *Empire of Honour*, 36; see also 37–43, 267–69.
169 This aspect of Romans is overlooked by Carl Schneider, "Ursprung und Ursachen der christlichen Intoleranz," *ZRGG* 30 (1978) 203–8.
170 Cranfield, 2:646, attempts to preclude this implication by a forced construal: "The meaning is rather that Christians are to take thought for, aim at, seek, in the sight of all men those things which (whether they recognize it or not) are good, the arbiter of what is good being not a moral *communis sensus* of mankind, but the gospel." See the critique by Dunn, 2:748.
171 Zerbe overlooks this distinction in "Paul's Ethic of Nonretaliation," 190, when he translates "Take forethought for noble conduct in the sight of all."
172 See Dunn, 2:747.
173 Kühl, 429; Althaus, 114; Morris, 451; Dunn, 2:748; Moo, 785. In this instance, the connotation "in the sight of" (BAGD [2000] 342.2) is close to the etymology which implies "in" (ἐν) + "face."

do good to all persons.[174] In the context of the situation in Rome, gaining some understanding of the motivations of the government and of pagan neighbors,[175] involved in various forms of harassment from public to private, would be an appropriate expression of "genuine love." Within the context provided in Romans, a saying that otherwise seems to demand social conformity and ethical relativism is lifted up into the service of divine righteousness.

■ **18** The theme of insightful interaction with a hostile world is carried forward in the admonition to be at peace "with all persons" (μετὰ πάντων ἀνθρώπων), an expression nearly reduplicated from the preceding verse. This rhetorical device provides a clear indication of the inclusive range of Paul's argument: peace is to be sought with those outside as well as inside of the Christian community. There is a discernible shift in this formulation from the strictly internal ethic of 12:10-13a. Now the Christian community sees itself as standing vis-à-vis the world at large. The double qualification, εἰ δυνατόν ("if possible") and τὸ ἐξ ὑμῶν ("so far as it depends on you"), makes it clear that with regard to outsiders, peace may only be possible under certain circumstances.[176] This is not an "escape clause," as Wilson points out, but an indication that the ethic "rests upon the courage and imagination of the Romans. They must make a realistic assessment of the problems to be addressed and be aware of how much each of them can do and what sorts of things they can change."[177] What Paul urges is that believers, committed to the principle of "genuine love," should do all in their power to achieve it.[178]

Although it has been suggested that Paul is quoting from Ps 33:15 in this admonition to peacemaking,[179] the differences between Paul's succinct wording of εἰρηνεύοντες ("being at peace") and the Psalmist's admonition ζήτησον εἰρήνην καὶ δίωξον αὐτήν ("seek peace and pursue it") indicate that we have an allusion rather than a citation here.[180] There is also a possible allusion to Mark 9:50, εἰρηνεύετε ἐν ἀλλήλοις ("be at peace with one another").[181] Paul had made similar admonishments, using the verb εἰρηνεύω ("make peace"), in the context of congregational conflicts in 1 Thess 5:13 and 2 Cor 13:11. While there was a broad affirmation of the value of peace in the Jewish and Greco-Roman cultures,[182] there is a close verbal parallel to Paul's wording in a Greco-Roman writer who is discussing how the true philosopher should respond to public pressures: οὐχὶ δὲ παραλθὼν εἰς μέσον κηρύσσεις, ὅτι εἰρήνην ἄγεις πρὸς πάντας ἀνθρώπους ὅ τι ἂν ἐκεῖνοι ποιῶσι . . . ("Why do you not come forth with the announcement that you are at peace with all persons, no matter what they do . . . ?" Epictetus, *Diss.* 4.5.24). Paul's admonition is more robust and communal, dealing with much more serious problems of persecution and public ostracism than Epictetus had in mind. But the broadly based parallels indicate that Paul could count on assent from the Roman believers concerning the need for peacemaking, and there is no doubt that their recent experience with an abusive deportation under Claudius provided a context for understanding the qualification "if possible, so far as it depends on you."

174 See Lietzmann, 110; Michel, 390; Ortkemper, *Leben*, 107; Wilckens, 3:24.
175 See Unnik, "Reaktion der Nicht-Christen," 498–522.
176 See Ortkemper, *Leben*, 108; Dunn, 2:748. Wilson, *Love without Pretense*, 189–90, argues that v. 18a is the central element in an elaborate ring structure, but this seems unlikely in light of its syntactical relationship with v. 18b and the problems with his chiastic hypothesis, noted above in note 8. More useful is his gathering of some parallels to this unique Pauline expression. Pythagoras *Carm.* 6–8a urges, "Yield to gentle words and useful deeds, and do not hate your friend for a small fault, for as long as you can (ὄφρα δύνηι)." Sextus Phil. *Sent.* 381 states that "He honors God best who conforms his mind to God, as far as possible (εἰς δύνατον)."

177 Wilson, *Love without Pretense*, 190–91.
178 See Zerbe, "Paul's Ethic of Nonretaliation," 190: "What we have here is a realistic acknowledgment that hostility from the opponent may preclude the establishment of true peace. Nevertheless the proviso implies a unilateral readiness to be at or to pursue peace with all."
179 Piper, *Love Command*, 112.
180 See Thompson, *Clothed with Christ*, 108.
181 Fitzmyer, 657.
182 See Wilson, *Love without Pretense*, 191; also Erich Dinkler and Erika Dinkler-von Schubert, "Friede," *RAC* 8 (1972) 434–505, and Hans-Werner Gensichen, Hans Heinrich Schmid, Werner Theissen, Gerhard Delling, and Wolfgang Huber, "Frieden," *ThRE* 11 (1983) 599–646.

■ 19 The polite form of participial imperatives continues through the first clause of this verse, urging the congregations to avoid personal revenge. The verb ἐκδικέω involves taking revenge, executing judgment.[183] The use of the reflexive pronoun in μὴ ἑαυτοὺς ἐκδικοῦντες ("not avenging yourselves") points more clearly to individual than to collective revenge.[184] But the plural form also rules out a popular form of peacemaking through the vengeful destruction of adversaries,[185] represented by the zealous stream of the Hebrew tradition[186] as well as in the Roman civic cult[187] or the court system that adjudicated lawsuits over insults to honor.[188] Paul stands at this point with the more pacific side of Greco-Roman and Jewish cultures, as the following examples make clear:[189]

μὴ εἴπῃς Τείσωμαι τὸν ἐχθρόν. Ἀλλὰ ὑπόμεινον τὸν κύριον, ἵνα σοι βοηθήσῃ ("Do not say, 'I shall take vengeance on the enemy'; but wait for the Lord so he may help you," Prov 20:9)

ὁ ἐδικῶν παρὰ κυρίου εὑρήσει ἐκδίκησιν ("The vengeful will suffer vengeance from the Lord," Sir 28:1)

μὴ μιμοῦ κακότητα, δίκῃ δ᾽ ἀπόλειψον ἄμυναν ("Do not mimic evil, but leave vengeance to justice," Pseudo-Phocylides 77; cf. *Carmen Aureum* 70).

A unique feature of Paul's admonition, compared with these examples, is the addition of the personal epithet "beloved," shifting the style from polite discourse into personal address.[190] Neither the commentaries[191] nor the specialized studies[192] on this passage provide a satisfactory explanation for the suddenly personal note that Paul inserts at this point. The remarkable frequency of this epithet in Rom 16:5, 8, 9, and 12 may provide a clue, because it is used with reference to the refugees

---

183 See Horst Goldstein, "ἐκδίκησις κτλ.," *EDNT* 1 (1990) 408; Gottlob Schrenk, "ἐκδικέω κτλ.," *TDNT* 2 (1964) 444.

184 See Zerbe, "Paul's Ethic of Nonretaliation," 191; also Simon Légasse, "Vengeance humaine et vengeance divine en Romains 12,14-21," in *La vie de la Parole. De l'Ancien au Nouveau Testament. Études d'exégèse et d'herméneutique bibliques offertes à Pierre Grelot professeur à l'Institut Catholique de Paris* (Paris: Desclée, 1987) 281-91.

185 Dunn, 2:749, discusses the relation to potential zealotism in Rome, but neither he nor other commentators link this with the preceding verse.

186 See Gerhard von Rad, *Der heilige Krieg im alten Israel,* 2d ed. (Göttingen: Vandenhoeck & Ruprecht, 1965) 26ff.; Hengel showed how Phinehas became the model of Jewish zealotism, because his lynching of a lawbreaker averted a plague and instituted "a covenant of peace" in Num 25:12. See *Zealots,* 149-76, 302-12.

187 See Fears, "Cult of Jupiter," 34-55, which shows that Jupiter was thought to guarantee peace through sanctioning treaties after military victories (Livy *Hist.* 1.24.7); that Jupiter the God of War sanctioned military campaigns to extend the empire and preserve the peace; and that in the later Republic he was celebrated as "a warrior god who conquered to bring universal peace and prosperity" (43-44). The representation of Jupiter hurling thunderbolts to bring chaos under control became "symbolic of a higher purpose of such warfare, the protection and spread of civilization, law, and peace." The Roman

ideology picked up the Stoic theme of "Zeus' power to bring order out of chaos, to transform hate into love, and to unite all things under universal justice," of course, through Roman military power (46, referring to the words of Cleanthes in *SVF* 1.547). See also Georgi, *Theocracy,* 101; Wengst, *Pax Romana,* 23-31.

188 Lendon, *Empire of Honour,* 50, describes the *sponsio,* "consecrated to legal battles over honour" in which Roman aristocrats responded to insults. The courts were inclined to decide such cases in view of equity or justice but on the basis of which contestant demonstrated the higher social prestige, as Lendon shows on 209-22.

189 See Wilson, *Love without Pretense,* 193-94.

190 Wilson, *Love without Pretense,* 192, refers to the "unexpected" quality of this vocative statement, noting that it "creates something of an interrruption."

191 See Dunn, 2:749: "The ἀγαπητοί functions both as an encouragement to those who might easily find themselves under extreme provocation . . . and as a reminder that it is none other than God who is their champion." But why is such encouragement required at this specific point? And how does the address "beloved" serve as a reminder? Morris, 453, suggests that the personal address is required in an admonition that "runs counter to a strong natural urge." But this would pertain to most of the admonitions in 12:9-21. See also Lagrange, 308, and Murray, 2:140.

192 This detail is not discussed by Söding, *Liebesgebot,* 247-50. Wischmeyer, "ΑΓΑΠΗΤΟΣ," 478, refers to

from Rome that Paul had met in his earlier missionary activities. These persons had suffered directly from the Roman deportation, both psychically and materially, and their situation was being made worse by the prejudices of fellow believers who had remained in Rome during the banning, who were now refusing to welcome them back into their house and tenement churches. Could Paul be making a personal appeal to these persons who have multiple reasons for desiring revenge, lending both ethos and pathos to the admonition that is prepared by the references to their status as "beloved" both in 1:7 and 12:9? However it is explained, the personal reference to the "beloved" in Rome marks a stylistic transition between the somewhat indirect admonitions in participial style and the direct imperative that follows in 12:19b.

The imperative in the second half of the antithesis is formulated with an aorist form, providing a forceful statement: ἀλλὰ δότε τόπον τῇ ὀργῇ ("but give place to the wrath"). The Greek background of the idiom "give way/give place" is widely acknowledged,[193] but the context of a Hebraic kind of divine wrath apparently leads some to insist that Paul is following a Hellenistic Jewish tradition at this point.[194] There are several similar expressions in Greek that could be compared to this metaphorical usage. Plutarch's essay on anger has the following injunction, which is the only example we have of "give place" in connection with wrath, in this instance, human anger that threatens to destroy per-

sonal friendship: Δεῖ δὲ μήτε παίζοντας αὐτῇ διδόναι τόπον, ἔχθραν γὰρ ἐπάγει τῇ φιλοφροσύνῃ ("Surely we should give no place [to anger] even in jest, for that brings enmity in where friendship was," Plutarch Cohib. ira 14). At the conclusion of a trial before Emperor Claudius, a fellow convict tells an Alexandrian agitator after the death sentence was pronounced: Τί γὰρ ἄλλο ἔχομεν ἢ παραφροῦντι βασιλεῖ τόπον διδόναι ("For what else can we do but give place to a demented king?").[195] Sirach uses the idiom "give place" in the context of becoming an unwelcome recipient of the wrath of another: Ἀπὸ δεομένου μὴ ἀποστρέψῃς ὀφθαλμόν, καὶ μὴ δῷς τόπον ἀνθρώπῳ καταράσασθαί σε ("Do not turn your eye away from the needy, and give a person no place to curse you," Sirach 4:5; see also 13:22; 16:14; 19:17; 38:12). The Wisdom of Solomon refers to God "giving a place for repentance" to sinners (ἐδίδους τόπον μετανοίας, Wis 12:10; see also 12:20).

These examples illustrate the typical range of the idiom "give place," showing that it appeared both in pagan and Jewish materials, but never in the context of divine wrath. It appears to me that Paul was the first to combine this typical Greek idiom with the theme of divine wrath, indicated clearly by the presence of the article (τῇ ὀργῇ; "the wrath").[196] This opens up a perspective on vengeance that may be unique to Romans. If refraining from personal vengeance gives space for divine wrath against evildoers, both present and

---

the word "beloved" as expressing the parental relationship Paul has with his congregation, but that hardly would pertain in the Roman situation. That God's election is conveyed by this address is true in a general sense but throws no light on Rom 12:19. Wilson, *Love without Pretense*, 192, tries to explain the word "beloved" as (1) a kind of "inclusio (of sorts)" relating back to 12:9a and (2) showing the center of a chiastic structure. The first is more plausible than the second, but why an inclusio was required at this particular moment is not explained.

193 BAGD 822; Ortkemper, *Leben*, 109; Helmut Koester, "τόπος," *TDNT* 8 (1972) 190, 205–6. Koester rejects the effort to interpret this expression in the light of a modern Greek idiom "to calm down," as proposed by Donald Blythe Durham, "Acts xv, 9; Romans xii, 19," *ClW* 36 (October 19, 1942) 29–30.

194 Dunn, 2:749; Wilson, *Love without Pretense*, 194. As

shown by the examples below, there are actually no Hellenistic Jewish examples of "give place" in the context of divine wrath.

195 Cited by Edgar R. Smothers, "Give Place to the Wrath (Rom 12:19): An Essay in Verbal Exegesis," *CBQ* 6 (1944) 211, from *BGU* 2. Nr. 511.

196 While some patristic writers opt for human wrath in this context, as shown by Smothers, "Give Place to the Wrath," 206–9, Romans commentators have concluded that divine wrath is in view. Ortkemper states the consensus in *Leben*, 109–10, citing Gutjahr's argument that reference to accommodating the "wrath of the enemy" would be nonsensical in the context. This verse is thus consistent with the use throughout the rest of the letter. See Hanson, *Wrath*, 92–93.

future,[197] then it must follow that the exercise of human vengeance takes up that same space. In the light of Rom 1:18-32, this points to an element of presumption in human retaliation; it is a matter of usurping God's place.[198] If this insight is correct, it places both the Jewish and Roman rationales for vengeance in the cause of peace[199] in a very critical light. It places Paul even more firmly on the side of the nonjudgmental tradition in Judaism, which assumes that God alone should be the final avenger. For example: "And if he be shameless and persist in his wrongdoing, even so forgive him from the heart, and leave to God the avenging" (ἄφες αὐτοῦ καὶ δὸς τῷ θεῷ τὴν ἐκδίκησιν, *T. Gad* 6.7). If God is the only one capable of legitimate vengeance, the theological thrust of the similar argument in Rom 12:19b may help to explain why it is formulated so much more directly than the foregoing.

The significance of Paul's prohibition of personal vengeance is enhanced by a formal quotation from Deut 32:35, introduced by the citation formula γέγραπται γάρ ("for it is written").[200] The citation differs from the Greek, Hebrew, and Targumic texts of Deut 32:35:[201]

Rom 12:19 ἐμοὶ ἐκδίκησις ἐγὼ ἀνταποδώσω, λέγει κύριος ("For to me is judgment, I will repay, says the Lord")

LXX ἐν ἡμέρα ἐκδικήσεως ἀνταποδώσω ("on the day of judgment, I will repay")

MT לִי נָקָם וְשִׁלֵּם ("mine is vengeance and recompense")

Tg. Neof. דידי היא נקמתא ואנא די משלים ("Vengeance is mine, and I am he who will repay")

Tg. Onq. קדמי פורענותא ואנא אשלים ("Punishment is before me; and I, even I, will repay")

Since the first part of the Pauline version of this citation is found in Heb 10:30, it is generally assumed that a different version of the Septuagint or an oral form of this saying was current in the first century.[202] But Paul's motivation in preferring the version that begins (as do the MT and the *Tg. Neof.* texts) by reference to God's prerogative in vengeance has not been clarified.[203] It fits precisely into the logical connection suggested above for v. 19b, namely, that human vengeance invades the sole divine right to such judgment. The stress is on ἐμοί, placed in the emphatic position at the beginning of the maxim: "for me, reserved to me, i.e., for God" is the matter of vengeance. God alone is the one who will "repay," who is entitled to retaliate for wrongdoing. In Koch's words, "It becomes a statement about the sovereignty of God as the only judge."[204] The Pauline addition of the phrase λέγει κύριος ("says the Lord"), found in none of the other versions of this saying, enhances this stress on divine authority and sovereignty.[205]

The meaning of divine wrath and vengeance in the context of Romans needs to be clarified. In the light of the earlier argument of the letter, it is advisable to go beyond traditional considerations concerning the nature of the future judgment.[206] In "Sacred Violence," Robert Hamerton-Kelly argues that references to a future wrath such as Rom 12:19 should be interpreted in the light of 1:18-32: "In the eschaton there will simply be a climax and a conclusion of the process of self-destruction that has been going on all the time, and end of the possibil-

---

197 Schlier, 382. Dunn, 2:749, is on track in insisting on both present and future wrath, in the light of Rom 1:18-32.

198 Compare Klassen, *Love of Enemies*, 119: "To God alone belongs vengeance. We must believe that God will repay. To preempt God's act is to put ourselves in the place of God. It is the ultimate act of unbelief."

199 See notes 87 and 88 above.

200 See Koch, *Schrift*, 25.

201 See Dunn, 2:749; Koch, *Schrift*, 77.

202 See Godet, 438; Lagrange, 308; Dunn, 2:749f.; Morris, 454; Koch, *Schrift*, 77.

203 See Käsemann, 349. See also Nieder, *Ethik*, 70.

204 Koch, *Schrift*, 78 (translation by RJ).

205 See Koch, *Schrift*, 139; Ellis, *Paul's Use*, 109-11, calls this phrase "the badge of prophetic pronouncement" that reflects the prophetic testimony of the early church.

206 For instance, Morris, 454, rejects the idea that God is presented as "vindictive" in this passage: "Whenever his wrath is seen in punishment, this is an activity in which justice is done." In "ὀργή κτλ.," *TDNT* 5 (1967) 425, Gustav Stählin argues that "Only he who knows the greatness of wrath will be mastered by the greatness of mercy. The converse is also true: Only he who has experienced the greatness of mercy can measure how great wrath must be. For the wrath of God arises from His love and mercy."

ity of repentance and restoration."[207] He goes on to explain: "The wrath works by self-inflicted harm. God gives sinners up to the consequences of their self-destructive actions. . . . Thus there is no actual violence in God, and the quotation, 'vengeance is mine, I shall repay' must, therefore, be taken loosely. The vengeance of God is to give sinners their own way and not to mitigate the consequences of their freely chosen desires."[208] The appeal of this approach is that it takes the distinctive argument of Romans seriously, breaking away from traditional parameters in considering the question. Whether or not this provides a satisfactory approach to the issue of divine judgment in Romans, it at least remains clear from Rom 12:19 that the divine wrath requires no human vindictiveness, that it remains a divine prerogative, and thus that it belongs in that arena of unsearchable mystery celebrated at the end of Rom 11.

■ **20** The citation of Prov 25:21-22a is straight out of the LXX, with the exception of a variation in the verb used for "feed" ($\psi\acute{\omega}\mu\iota\zeta\epsilon$), which is found in Manuscript B of the LXX.[209] Moreover, Paul refrains from citing the final words from Prov 25:22b that refer to a divine reward for those who treat their enemies humanely.[210] The citation is introduced by Paul's word $\grave{\alpha}\lambda\lambda\acute{\alpha}$ ("but"), which places it in contrast to the opening line of the preceding verse since both deal with human responses to enmity.[211] The debate on this verse has centered on the interpretation of 20c, which must be clarified before the rest of the verse can be understood. To heap up $\check{\alpha}\nu\vartheta\rho\alpha\kappa\alpha\varsigma$ $\pi\nu\rho\acute{o}\varsigma$ ("coals of fire") on the head of an adversary has been explained as a mistaken metaphor due to ambiguities in the Hebrew text;[212] as a metaphor for "burning pangs of shame" felt by an adversary moved by the generosity of the persecuted;[213] as a sophisticated form of revenge by increasing the guilt of the persecutor;[214] and—what is most consistent with a context—a reference to an Egyptian ritual of a sinner carrying a dish of hot coals on the head to symbolize repentence.[215] None of these options is fully satisfactory, but the congruity with the synoptic tradition of loving the enemy and Paul's argumentative context of "genuine love" and overcoming evil with good makes it likely that he had the impace of hospitality in mind. Given the context of the house and tenement churches of Rome, and the fact that hospitality and benevolence were expressed through the system of love feasts that each of these small communities sponsored,[216]

207 Hamerton-Kelly, "Sacred Violence," 103.
208 Ibid., 152.
209 Dunn, 2:750, and Fitzmyer, 657, suggest that this variant in the LXX may have stemmed from Paul's use here in Romans.
210 See Koch, *Schrift,* 271.
211 Zeller, 212, shows the antithesis is to v. 19a, not to v. 19b-c as advocated by Wilckens, 3:26. Despite some confusion, Dunn, 2:750, appears to follow Wilckens on this point. See also Godet, 438. Piper, *Love Command,* 115, argues convincingly that there is an antithesis between actively doing good in v. 20a and passive renunciation of vengeance in v. 19.
212 See T. K. Cheyne, "The Rendering of Rom. xii. 16," *Exp* 2.6 (1883) 469-72; M. J. Dahood, "Two Pauline Quotations from the Old Testament," *CBQ* 17 (1955) 19-24; Léonard Ramaroson, "'Charbons ardents': 'sur la tête' ou 'pour le feu'? (Prov 25,22a—Rom 12,20b)," *Bib* 51 (1970) 230-34. Fitzmyer, 657-58, refutes this theory on grounds that Paul is citing the LXX text, which eliminates this possible misunderstanding.
213 See Fitzmyer, 658, who cites Origen, Pelagius, Augustine, Jerome, and Käsemann, among others who adopt this view. He notes that the only textual support for this alternative is the much later Tar-

gum Prov 25:21-22, "If your enemy is famished, give him bread to eat; if he is thirsty, give him water to drink, for you will bring coals of fire upon his head, and God will deliver him to you."
214 See Fitzmyer, 658, who cites Chrysostom and Theophylact as ancient advocates of this option, with Stendahl providing a modern adaption based on 1QS 1:9-11; 9:21-22; 10:17-20; and possibly *4 Ezra* 16.54. See also Piper, *Love Command,* 118.
215 Siegfried Morenz, "Feurige Kohlen auf dem Haupt," *ThLZ* 78 (1953) 187-92, followed by William Klassen, "Coals of Fire: Sign of Repentance or Revenge?" *NTS* 9 (1962-63) 337-50. Klassen notes that this Egyptian ceremony has biblical parallels in the ashes of repentence (2 Sam 13:19) but admits (347) that Paul probably would not have known about the Egyptian ceremony. On contextual grounds he concludes that Paul used the metaphor to convey the hope of the conversion of the adversary, which presupposes some understanding of the pacific nature of the metaphor. See also Klassen, *Love of Enemies,* 120.
216 See Reicke, *Agapenfeier,* 21-50.

this admonition should not be understood in terms of "contributing to your local charity" in which care for the needy is accomplished with a minimal level of personal involvement. If Paul's social context is kept in mind, the implication for the Roman believers can be understood in a straightforward way: they are to invite hostile neighbors and other enemies to their common meals.

The admonition to give food and drink to the enemy, derived from the prudential framework of the wisdom tradition,[217] gains a new motivation in the Pauline context.[218] In place of a divine reward for good behavior promised by Prov 25:22, which Paul had deleted, there is a new motivation in a love ethic resting on God's love for the undeserving, developed in earlier sections of Romans. There is no guarantee that giving food and drink will necessarily make a friend out of an enemy[219] or that such actions will always produce the conversion of enemies, thus freeing them from the prospect of divine wrath;[220] it is particularly unlikely that Paul hopes such deeds will increase the inevitability of wrath against those who refuse to respond positively.[221] The actions of kindness to enemies flow from the transformed community (12:1-2), set right by the power of the gospel concerning God's love for the ungodly. This involves being motivated by "genuine love" (12:9), and is consistent with "hospitality to strangers" (12:13). This verse therefore illustrates what might be involved in being "at peace with all persons" (12:18).[222]

■ **21** Given the fact that Paul had deleted the final line of the well-known maxim from Prov 25:22 (i.e., "and the Lord will reward you"), this concluding maxim serves to interpret the saying from Proverbs and to provide a conclusion for the pericope as a whole. It would clearly have been felt as a correction by an audience acquainted with the custom of rhetors and moralists employing quotations "as a foil against which to highlight their own positions." Walter Wilson goes on to show that the replacement of Prov 25:22b with the memorable saying in Rom 12:21 "also dramatizes the absence in the prescriptive section of any promise of personal benefits for those who accept instruction. In this respect, Rom 12 is distinguished from all of the Hellenistic-Jewish texts" that Wilson has surveyed.[223] In place of the promise of rewards from heaven, Romans offers a transformative ethic motivated by a reward already received, namely, the grace of God conveyed by the gospel that restores right relationships everywhere.

There are significant parallels to the use of "conquer" in maxims such as Paul creates in this location,[224] and also to the theme of overcoming evil with good.[225] But

---

217 Proverbs offers the prospects of long life, worldly success, harmonious relationships, and other rewards from God for those who follow wisdom. See Georg Fohrer, "σοφία κτλ.," *TDNT* 7 (1971) 494. Note that Paul's citation of Prov 25:21-22 deletes the final line, "and the Lord will reward you."

218 Herbert Preisker offers a memorable critique of the motivation of this ethic, assuming as he does that v. 20c offers an ulterior motive; see *Das Ethos des Urchristentums*, 2d ed. (Darmstadt: Wissenschaftliche, 1968) 184; translation in Piper, *Love Command*, 116.

219 Wilckens, 3:26, notes that this is the prospect mentioned in a Targum on Prov 25.

220 Wilckens, 3:26, cites Jeremias for this suggestion.

221 See Krister Stendahl, "Hate, Non-Retaliation, and Love. 1QS x, 17-20 and Rom. 12:19-21," *HTR* 55 (1962) 346–48; repr. pp. 137–49 in K. Stendahl, *Meanings: The Bible as Document and as Guide* (Philadelphia: Fortress, 1984). For a critique, see Dunn, 2:750–71.

222 See Winter, "Romans 12–15," 80, which suggests that this passage "provided a counter-cultural response to the lack of harmony and the undercurrent of strife and jealousy that pervaded relationships in Roman society."

223 Wilson, *Love without Pretense*, 196.

224 Wilson, *Love without Pretense*, 197, cites Sextus Phil. *Sent.* 165b: ὁ νικῶν τῷ ἀπατᾶν νικᾶται ἐν ἤθει ("whoever conquers with deception is conquered in integrity"). One could add Menander *Sent. Byz.* 419, καλὸν τὸ νικᾶν, ἀλλ᾽ ὑπερνικᾶν κακόν ("conquer good, but super-conquer evil").

225 Commentators often cite the *T. Benj.* 4.3 in which a good man is described as one who shows mercy even to enemies, because "by doing good he overcomes the evil, being protected by the good" (οὗτος ἀγαθοποιῶν νικᾷ τὸ κακόν, σκεπαζόμενος ὑπὸ τοῦ ἀγαθοῦ). In a pre-Christian Hellenistic text (Polyaenus *Strat.* 5.12; cited by Michel, 393), the Carthaginian Gisco explains his policy: "I did not defend evil with evil, but evil with good (οὐ κακῷ κακὸν ἠμυνάμην, ἀλλὰ ἀγαθῷ κακόν)." Similar wordplays on good and evil may also be found in 1QS 10:17-18 and CD 9.2-5.

nowhere else in his letters, except in the citation from Ps 51:6 in Rom 3:4, does Paul employ the verb for conquering and being victorious (νικάω) that was so widely popularized in the celebrations of the Greek goddess Nike and of the Roman goddess Victoria.[226] The imperial authorities celebrated Victoria in monuments, coins, public inscriptions, triumphal parades, public games, and other propaganda as the key to world peace: "Pax was thus the blessed condition brought about by Augustus' labor. It rested upon Victoria; and Augustan propaganda constantly and intimately linked the imperial virtues of Pax and Victoria. Pax could only be achieved through Victoria; and the promise of permanent Pax lay entirely in the guarantee of perpetual Victoria. Victory was thus the essential prerequisite for peace."[227] The subtle interaction with the Roman cultural context that I have traced throughout the letter thus surfaces again in the wording of this crucial verse, contrasting triumph over evil by love and hospitality rather than by force.[228]

In the immediate context of the citation from Proverbs, for which this verse provides such an effective rhetorical climax, treating enemies as fellow humans who require basic necessities is the path to overcoming enmity.[229]

As the "culminating exclamation"[230] at the end of a discourse on "genuine love," this verse places the Christian ethic within a transformative framework that is universal in scope but local in operation. The thought of overcoming "evil" through everyday acts of solidarity would be grandiose except for the framework of a global mission in behalf of the righteousness of God, which is the theme and purpose of Romans. Within that framework, even a cup of water given to the thirsty becomes a means of expressing the love of Christ and thus extending the realm of divine righteousness. Given the beleaguered and marginalized circumstances of the Roman believers, it is no exaggeration to name this verse "the bravest statement in the world."[231]

---

226 See Otto Bauernfeind, "νικάω κτλ.," *TDNT* 4 (1967) 942–43; Fears, "Theology of Victory," 748–49: "Victoria in her various forms was an integral part of Roman cult, a supernatural power which had manifested itself to the Roman People and was capable of rendering benefits to the community of worshippers. . . . Victoria came to be the center of a rich and complex political mythology, the most critical element in an ideology to support the immense and fragile fabric of empire."

227 Fears, "Theology of Victory," 807; he refers also to the studies by S. Weinstock, "Pax and the Ara Pacis," *JRS* 50 (1960) 44–58, and H. Stier, "Augustusfriede und römische Klassik," *ANRW* II, 2 (1975) 13–40.

228 See Klassen, *Love of Enemies*, 123: "In a society which boasted of the Pax Romana ("the peace of Rome"), which was maintained by force, Paul does

not reject the military metaphor. He simply transforms it into the battle language of the Christian church." Klassen notes the contrast with the Roman use of the slogan "If you want peace, prepare for war," described by Wolfgang Haase, "'Si vis pacem, para bellum.' Zur Beurteilung militärischer Stärke in der römischen Kaiserzeit," in *Akten des XI. Internationalen Limeskongresses* (Budapest: Hungarian Academy of Sciences, 1977) 721–55.

229 See Godet, 439: "The true victory over evil consists in transforming a hostile relation into one of love by the magnanimity of the benefits bestowed."

230 See Wilson, *Love without Pretense*, 197.

231 Cited by Ortkemper, *Leben*, 124, from H. Weinel, *Paulus. Der Mensch und Sein Werk: Die Anfänge des Christentums, der Kirche und des Dogmas*, 2d ed. (Tübingen: Mohr, 1915) 253.

13

The Fourth Pericope

Diatribe concerning Fulfilling Obligations to the Governing Authorities

1/ **Let every soul ^a subject himself to the governing authorities. For there is^b no authority except that by^c God and those that are^d have been appointed by^e God. 2/ So that the one^f resisting the authority has opposed^g what God has appointed,**

> **and the resisters will receive a verdict against themselves. 3/ For the rulers are not a [cause of] fear to the good^h work but to the bad.ⁱ**

Now, do you (sg.) wish not to fear the authority? Do the good, and you (sg.) will have praise from her. 4/ For she is God's servant to you^j (sg.) for the^k good. But if you (sg.) do the bad, be afraid, for she does not carry the sword to no purpose. For she is God's servant, an avenger^l [bringing] wrath upon the one practicing the bad.

5/ Therefore it is necessary^m to subject yourself, not only on account of the wrath but also on account of your conscience-pang.

6/ **For this reason you (pl.) also pay tributes, for they are ministers of God diligently devoting themselves to this very thing. 7/ You (pl.) should render to all what is obligated:**

> **to the one [owed] the tribute, the tribute,**
>> **to the one [owed] the custom tax, the custom tax,**
>>> **to the one [owed] the fear, the fear,**
>>>> **to the one [owed] the honor, the honor.**

---

a The absence of ψυχή ("soul/person"), the grammatical alteration of the nominative πᾶσα ("all") to the dative plural πάσαις, and the use of the imperative ὑποτασσέσθω ("let be subject") in the second person plural form in P⁴⁶ D* F G ar b d* f g t vg^mss (eth) Ir^lat Hipp (Tert) Ambst Spec^1/2 Cassiodorus Sedulius-Scotus may originate in an early scribal error and subsequent grammatical correlations, as Cranfield, 2:656, suggests. However, the differences may represent intentional efforts to strengthen the command of subordination as binding in respect of "every authority" (πάσαις ἐξουσίαις). The inclusion of "soul" is strongly supported by ℵ A B D² L P Ψ 5 6 33 61 69 81 88 104 181 218 256 263 323 326 330 365 424 436 441 451 459 467 614 621 623 629

630 720 915 917 945 1175 1241 1243 1319 1398 1505 1506 1563 1573 1678 1718 1735 1739 1751 1836 1838 1845 1852 1874 1875 1877 1881 1908 1912 1942 1959 1962 2110 2127 2138 2197 2200 2344 2492 2495 2516 2523 2544 2718 *Maj Lect* d² gue o vg sy^p,h,pal sa (bo) arm geo slav Or Acacius Bas Did Chr Hier Pel Aug Spec^1/2.

b A different accentuation, typical of Greek New Testaments until the late nineteenth century, appeared in Bernhard Weiss's Greek New Testament (1894–1900) and was noted in Nestle-Aland²⁴/²⁵, οὐ γάρ ἐστιν ("for an authority *does not exist*"); this stands in place of the virtually universal accentuation from Tischendorf on, οὐ γὰρ ἔστιν ("*there is* no authority").

c The substitution of ἀπό ("from") for ὑπό ("by") in D* F G 69^c 88 323 629 945 1506 1573 *pc* appears to be a secondary, conceptual improvement, but it is accepted by Godet, 441, for precisely this reason, and that it is more suitably joined with 8:1b.

d The addition of ἐξουσίαι ("authorities") in D² L P Ψ 33 69 104 323 326 424* 614 945 1175 1241 1243 1505 1735 1836 1874 2344 2495 *Maj* sy is a secondary explanation. The text without "authorities" is strongly supported by ℵ A B D* F G 0285^vid 6 81 88 330 365 424^c 1319 1506 1573 1739 1881 *al* latt cop Ir^lat Or.

e The addition of the article τοῦ before θεοῦ by ℵ^c L 6 33 323 326 330 424 614 945 1175 1241 1505 1735 1836 1874 2344 2495 *Maj* Ir is a secondary, stylistic improvement. The omission of the article is strongly supported by ℵ* A B D F G P 0285^vid 69 81 88 104 365 1243 1319 1506 1573 1739 1881 *al* Or.

f Origen *Cels.* 8.65.10 has the perfect participle οἱ ἀνθεστηκότες ("they who have resisted") in place of the present singular ὁ ἀντιτασσόμενος in all of the other witnesses. If there were other support for Origen's reading, one would be inclined to follow it because it reflects an early third-century tradition, even though it is the easier reading on the grounds that it would produce consistency in the plural subject between v. 2a and 2b.

g Origen *Cels.* 8.65.10 has plural verb ἀνθίστανται ("they resist"), matching the variant described in note f.

h The variant found in F*, τῷ ἀγαθοεργῷ ("to the one doing good"), and the provision of plural forms, τῶν ἀγαθῶν ἔργων ("of good works"), by D² L Ψ 5 33 61 69 81 88 104 181 218 263 323 326 330 365 424* 436 441 451 459 467 614 621 623 629 720 915 917 945 1175 1241 1398 1505 1563 1678 1718 1735 1751 1836 1838 1845 1874 1875 1877 1908 1912 1942 1959 1962 2127 2138 2200 2344 2492 2495 (2516) 2544 2718 *Maj* (sy) appear "to be merely attempted improvements," according to Cranfield, 2:664. The expression $\tau\hat{\omega}\ \dot{\alpha}\gamma\alpha\vartheta\hat{\omega}\ \ddot{\epsilon}\rho\gamma\omega$ ("to the good work") is well supported by P[46] ℵ A B D* F[c] G P 0285 6 256 424[c] 630 (1243) 1319 1506 1573 1739 1852 1881 2110 2523 *pc* (lat) cop Ir[lat] Cl.

i   The plural $\tau\hat{\omega}\nu\ \kappa\alpha\kappa\hat{\omega}\nu$ ("bad works"), found in the same witnesses as for the plural "good works" above, is much more weakly attested than the singular "bad work," as in the same witnesses, above, for "good work".

j   The deletion of $\sigma o\acute{\iota}$ ("to you") by F G 2344 bo[ms] is probably a stylistic improvement.

k   The deletion of the article by B *pc* is probably a scribal error.

l   There are several variants at this point, none of which has strong support. The words $\epsilon\grave{\iota}\varsigma\ \dot{o}\rho\gamma\acute{\eta}\nu$ ("for wrath") are deleted by D* F G; the word order is given as $\epsilon\grave{\iota}\varsigma\ \dot{o}\rho\gamma\grave{\eta}\nu\ \ddot{\epsilon}\kappa\delta\iota\kappa o\varsigma$ in ℵ* D[2] Ψ[c] 33 323 424 614 945 1175 1241 1319[c] 1735 1836 1874 2344

pm. The word order of $\ddot{\epsilon}\kappa\delta\iota\kappa o\varsigma\ \epsilon\grave{\iota}\varsigma\ \dot{o}\rho\gamma\acute{\eta}\nu$ ("avenger [bringing] wrath") is strongly supported by P[46] ℵ[c] A B L P Ψ* 048 6 69 81 88 104 326 330 365 630 1243 1319* 1505 1506 1573 1739 1881 2495 *pm* Ir[lat].

m   P[46] D F G it Ir[lat] Ambst have in lieu of "it is necessary to be subjected" the imperative $\dot{v}\pi o\tau\acute{\alpha}\sigma\sigma\epsilon\sigma\vartheta\epsilon$ ("be subject!"); this "Western" reading does not appear to be an interpolation and deserves a measure of respect. Similarly, 6 69 1243 1319 1874 2344 read $\dot{\alpha}\nu\acute{\alpha}\gamma\kappa\eta\ \dot{v}\pi o\tau\acute{\alpha}\sigma\sigma\epsilon\sigma\vartheta\epsilon$. P[46] and Ir[lat] also have $\kappa\alpha\acute{\iota}$ ("and/also") before the imperative form: "therefore *also* be subject." Neither reading has as much support as the very terse formulation $\dot{\alpha}\nu\acute{\alpha}\gamma\kappa\eta\ \dot{v}\pi o\tau\acute{\alpha}\sigma\sigma\epsilon\sigma\vartheta\alpha\iota$ ("necessary to subject oneself") in ℵ A B L P Ψ 048 33 81 88 104 181 323 326 330 365 424 436 451 614 629 630 945 1175 1241 1505 1506 1573 1735 1739 1836 1877 1881 1962 2127 2492 2495 *Maj Lect* (vg) sy cop.

Analysis

This passage starts afresh, with no transitional links to the preceding pericope. It is important to realize that apart from the late division of Scripture into verses and chapters, 13:1-7 joins directly onto the gnomic collection of sayings that ends what we call chapter 12. The gnomic style of the preceding pericope continues in 13:1a without transition. There are elements of diatribe in this pericope, however, with 13:3b-5 addressed to a single imaginary conversation partner and vv. 6-7 addressed in second person plural style to the congregation as a whole, with a rhetorical question in the middle of v. 3.[1] The thematic exhortation of 13:1a is followed by three coherently phrased arguments and a concluding ethical application concerning the payment of taxes.[2] The first argument opens with two statements of two lines each, providing a chain-link parallelism that portrays a doctrine of the divine institution of earthly authority and

---

1   The following analysis is adapted from Tobin, *Paul's Rhetoric*, 396.

2   See Wilckens, 3:29–30, for a good overview of this structure, but without reference to the number of arguments. See also Roland Bergmeier, "Loyalität als Gegenstand paulinischer Paraklese. Eine religionsgeschichtliche Untersuchung zu Röm 13,1ff und Jos. B. J. 2, 140," *Theok* 1 (1967–69) 59. An alternative structure is proposed by Helmut Merklein, "Sinn und Zweck von Röm 13, 1-7. Zur semantischen und pragmatischen Struktur eines umstrittenen Textes," in H. Merklein, ed., *Neues Testament und Ethik. Für Rudolf Schnackenburg* (Freiburg: Herder, 1989) 241–43, with two arguments (13:1-2; 13:3-4) followed by a conclusion in 13:5 and an application to the readers in 13:6-7. Ulrich Duchrow, *Christenheit und Weltverantwortung. Tradi-*

tionsgeschichte und systematische Struktur der Zweireichelehre, FBESG 25 (Stuttgart: Klett, 1970) 138–40, proposes a thesis in 13:1a, a theological rationale in vv. 1b-2, a practical rationale in vv. 3-4, an inference from the main thesis in v. 5, an additional practical rationale in v. 6, and a special paranesis in v. 7; see also Vilho Riekkinen, *Römer 13. Aufzeichnung und Weiterführung der exegetischen Diskussion*, AASF 23 (Helsinki: Suomalainen Tiedeakatemia, 1980) 42. A similar structure is proposed by Stefan Schreiber, "Imperium Romanum und römische Gemeinde. Dimensionen politische Sprechweise in Röm 13," in U. Busse, ed., *Die Bedeutung der Exegese für Theologie und Kirche*, QD 215 (Freiburg: Herder, 2005) 140–41. Robert H. Stein, "The Argument of Romans 13:1-7," *NovT* 31 (1989) 339, argues for a chiastic structure; 13:1b-2 = A; 13:3-4 = B; 13:5b =

the resultant necessity to avoid resistance.[3] The antithetical wordplay between the ὑποτάσσεσθαι ("to subject oneself") of v. 1a and the ἀντιτασσόμενος ("the one resisting") of v. 2a[4] and the paronomasia of the repeated ἀνθίστημι ("oppose") in v. 2a and 2b, along with the synthetic parallelism in v. 2, lend a compelling coherence to this first argument not to resist the authorities. The word ἐξουσία ("power") is also repeated four times in the first three verses, while the τασσ- stem ("appoint") appears five times, the prefixal ἀντι- appears three times, the φοβ-stem three times, and the phrase ὑπὸ θεοῦ ("under God") twice. In v. 4 the word "servant" (διάκονος) occurs twice. In the pericope as a whole, the word "God" appears no less than six times. These instances of paranomasia provide a potent rhetorical force to the pericope.

The second argument in 13:3b-5 is addressed to the imaginary conversation partner. It is organized in groups of short sentences[5] of which v. 4a and 4c contain γάρ ("for") and provide the rationale why persons opposing the authorities bring judgment upon themselves.[6] Verses 13:4a and 4d define the ruler's relation to good and evil, while 13:3b-c and 4b-c apply the arguments with rhetorical questions and exhortations to the situation of the imaginary conversation partner.[7] The theme of "fear" appears in vv. 3a-b and 4b, a motif picked up in the reference to "conscience-pang" in v. 5b.[8] The

reiteration of ὑποτάσσεσθαι ("to subject oneself") in v. 5a serves to fuse these arguments very effectively with the opening thematic exhortation.[9]

The third argument in 13:6-7 is addressed to the congregation as a whole and draws out the practical implications of the foregoing discourse. The reference to the payment of taxes is followed by an artfully constructed exhortation about rendering whatever is owed. The asyndetic style of the imperative in v. 7 matches that of 13:1a, and thus provides an effective inclusio for the passage.[10] The four final parallel expressions heightened by paronomasia in the repetition of "taxes," "customs," "fear," and "honor" provide a compelling conclusion to the passage. Hearers would have picked up the rhyming and parallelism between φόρον/φόβον and τέλος/τιμήν ("tribute–fear; custom tax–honor").[11] In addition, each of the final four lines begins with the article τῷ ("to the"), providing a poetic symmetry for this conclusion. While the suggestion has been made that the pericope extends to 13:8a,[12] there is practically universal agreement among commentators that it ends with v. 7.

The Question of Glosses or Interpolations

The suggestions that 13:5 is a gloss intended to provide an additional rationale for paying taxes in 13:6,[13] or an

---

B'; 13:5c = A', which does not seem plausible; his summary of the argument on 34 is more helpful.

3   See Weiss, "Beiträge," 244. Bullinger, *Figures*, 462, refers to 13:1b as an *epitasis* or amplification, but I would prefer more frequently used terms such as "rationale" or "argument."

4   See Michel, 394.

5   Weiss, "Beiträge," 244–45, organizes vv. 3-4c into two strophes of three lines each, but allows v. 4d to stand alone, with double-lined strophes following. This overlooks the parallelism between v. 4a and 4d, in both of which the governor is identified as God's servant in relation to the good and bad. Verse 5a and b are therefore the second and third lines of the final, three-line strophe.

6   See Stein, "Argument," 332–36.

7   See Merklein, "Sinn," 243.

8   See Wilckens, 3:30.

9   See Stein, "Argument," 336.

10 Ibid., 33–34.

11 Ibid., 33.

12 Bernhard Bonsack develops this suggestion in "Rohmaterialien zu Röm. 13, 1-8a. Dankesschrift an das Sozialethische Institut der theologischen Fakultät in Zürich" (Typescript: Zurich, 1977) in order to contend that in view of the sole commitment to love, obligations to the state are nonbinding. This is supported by reconceiving the imperative in 13:1 as an indicative and rearranging 13:6-7 to read "For they are ministers of God. Keeping this in mind, render to all what is obligated. . . ." While this reading is appealing on contemporary ethical grounds, it requires too many strained exegetical choices, and the only scholar to accept it is Riekkinen, *Römer 13*, 35–39, 42–43, 203–19.

13 Bultmann, "Glossen," 281–82.

"early Catholic" augmentation of Paul's command of subordination to the state,[14] rest on the observation that the argument from wrath in the earlier verses is here supplanted by a new consideration of "conscience." While this may match the pattern of ancient glosses, these suggestions have been widely rejected because the style and some of the vocabulary in this verse seem consistent with the rest of the passage.[15] Even less plausible is the suggestion that 13:6a and 7c are apologetic glosses from the end of the first century.[16] While several scholars have suggested that the entire pericope is a non-Pauline interpolation,[17] the case is not as strong as in the case of several sections toward the end of chapter 16. When one reviews the usual criteria for determining whether an interpolation is present,[18] the evidence provides only marginal support for interpolation despite the resolution it would afford for interpretive difficulties in a passage that seems to provide "support for tyrants."[19] Distaste for a passage has no bearing on its authenticity. The four criteria follow.

(a) The most serious reason for an interpolation is the abrupt transition between 12:21 and 13:1, compared with an allegedly smoother transition between 12:21 and 13:8.[20] The shift from the second person plural admonitions of 12:9-21 to third person singular style in 13:1 is indisputable and there is no conjunction in 13:1 to mark the transition to the new pericope. The impression that 13:1-7 is an "independent block" that is somewhat "alien" to its context is hard to deny;[21] it may reflect the compositional circumstances of this letter dictated by Paul over a period of time while incorporating materials that may have originated earlier. However, the inclusion of ethical issues concerning relations with nonbelievers in 12:17-21, including the concept of "wrath" that recurs in 13:4 and the distinction between "good" and "evil" that recurs in 13:3, makes the thematic transition to the subject of the state at 13:1 plausible.[22] Moreover, the theme of "obligation" in 13:7 is picked up in 13:8, producing a much stronger transition than between 12:21 and 13:8.[23]

(b) Another significant issue is the disparity between apocalyptic hostility against the old age and its institutions throughout the Pauline corpus and the acknowledgment of the state as an abiding institution to which absolute obedience is owed in 13:1-7.[24] While Paul speaks of the "rulers of this age" with bitter resistance in 1 Cor 2:8 and views the "principalities and powers" as opponents in Rom 8:38, this passage seems to reflect a time when the church has made peace with the world.[25] But, as Valentin Zsifkovits and Vilho Riekkinen have

---

14 Schulz, *Mitte der Schrift*, 129–30.

15 See Schmithals, *Römerbrief*, 207; Ernst Käsemann, "Grundsätzliches zur Interpretation von Röm 13," in vol. 2 of *Exegetische Versuche*, 219; Riekkinen, *Römer 13*, 30–32.

16 Pier F. Beatrice, "Il giudizio secondo le opere della Legge e l'amore compimento della Legge. Contributo all' esegesi di Rm 13, 1-10," *StPat* 20 (1973) 518–22, 540–42; see the critique by Riekkinen, *Römer 13*, 34.

17 I know of seven scholars who have proposed that Rom 13:1-7 is an interpolation: Pallis, 141; Christian Eggenberger, "Der Sinn der Argumentation in Röm 13,2-5," *KRS* 100 (1944) 54–70, 118–30, 101 (1945) 243–44; idem, "Neue Gesichtspunkte zur neutestamentlichen Einstellung gegenüber dem Staate," *Neue Wege* 44 (1950) 245–54; Ernst Barnikol, "Römer 13. Der nichtpaulinische Ursprung der absoluten Obrigkeitsbejahung von Römer 13,1-7," in *Studien zum Neuen Testament & zur Patristik. Erich Klostermann zum 90. Geburtstag dargebracht*, TU 77 (Berlin: Akademie, 1961) 65–133; James Kallas, "Romans 13:1-7: An Interpolation," *NTS* 11

(1964–65) 365–74; Schmithals, *Römerbrief*, 191–97; O'Neill, 209; Munro, *Authority*, 56–67; idem, "Romans 13:1-7: Apartheid's Last Biblical Refuge," *BTB* 20 (1990) 161–68.

18 See Nash, "Interpolations," 23. Winsome Munro relies primarily on thematic and stylistic observations in the argument for interpolation in *Authority*, 56–67; see also Munro's discussion of nine proposed criteria in "Interpolation in the Epistles," 432–41.

19 O'Neill, 209.

20 On 393, 395, Michel frankly admits both the abruptness and the superior link between 12:21 and 13:8.

21 Käsemann, 352; yet on 351, Käsemann finds "no reason" to support theories of interpolation.

22 See Riekkinen, *Römer 13*, 45–48; Dunn, 2:758.

23 See especially Riekkinen, *Römer 13*, 48, 50–51, referring to Merk, *Handeln*, 165.

24 See particularly Kallas, "Romans 13:1-7," 36ff.; Barnikol, "Römer 13," 75–76.

25 Kallas, "Romans 13:1-7," 374.

pointed out,[26] this disparity is caused in part by exaggerating the notion of absolute, unqualified obedience to a timeless government. Actually, there is nothing in 13:1-7 to preclude the view that government is an interim institution established by God until the parousia.

(c) Non-Pauline vocabulary and rhetoric have been alleged by Barnikol,[27] but the seemingly most significant points are the Pauline hapax legomena διαταγή ("commandment") and ἀντιστάσσεσθαι ("resist commandment"), which seem quite unproblematic in view of Paul's use of διατάσσω ("command") in 1 Cor 7:17; 9:14; 11:32; 16:1; Gal 3:19 and τάσσω in Gal 1:7; 5:10.[28] That the style of this passage is that of a legally binding decree is accurate enough,[29] but so are many other Pauline passages (e.g., 1 Cor 6:1-11; 11:2-16; 2 Thess 3:6-13). Further, Paul himself may have incorporated traditional material into his composition. In contrast to the likely interpolation of 16:17-20, which has an entirely different style, tenor, and rhetorical disposition, the tone of this passage seems consistent with most of the rest of Romans. There are also other passages in Romans that, when viewed in isolation, appear to lack specific Christian content (e.g., Rom 1:18–2:11; 9:6-18), which is a key contention in Schmithal's evaluation of this issue.[30] However, a strong indication of non-Pauline provenance could be the references in 13:3 to having fear of and receiving "praise" (ἔπαινος) from the government, which contrasts strongly with Paul's statements in other letters (Gal 1:10; 1 Thess 2:4), as well as with the formulation of Rom 8:15.

(d) For an interpolation to be plausible, a convincing redactional motivation must be present. While Eggenberger made a case for a later extension of a nonconfrontational attitude toward Rome as in Luke-Acts and 1 Clement,[31] and Pallis proposed a motivation for the interpolation after 133 C.E. to distance Christians from Jewish zealotism,[32] no redactional rationale for an insertion of such material at this precise location in Romans has been proposed. Moreover, the transition between 13:8-10 and the final verse of this pericope, 13:7, is far superior to the link that would result if 13:8-10 followed immediately after 12:21. The thematic links between "good" and "bad" in 12:21 are direct and plausible with the same terms appearing in 13:3-4 but nonexistent with the next two pericopes, 13:8-10 or 13:11-14.

Whereas all four criteria should be fulfilled to prove an interpolation, only one has proven to be partially compelling in this case. Despite the problems it causes for later interpreters who would prefer a seemingly less subservient attitude toward the state, it remains highly likely that 13:1-7 is an authentic and original portion of Paul's letter.

Rhetorical Disposition

IV.	The *probatio*
12:1—15:13	The fourth proof: Living together according to the gospel so as to sustain the hope of global transformation
13:1-7	4. Diatribe concerning fulfilling obligations to the governing authorities
13:1a	a. The gnomic admonition concerning voluntary subjection to the authorities
13:1b-3a	b. The first argument concerning the basic need for subjection to the authorities
13:1b-c	1) Rationale: the divine origin of governmental authority
13:1b	a) No authority exists except from God (understood as the righteous deity revealed in the crucified Christ)
13:1c	b) Current governmental authorities are "appointed by God"

26   Valentin Zsifkovits, *Der Staatsgedanke nach Paulus in Röm. 13,1-7 mit besonderer Berücksichtigung der Umwelt und der patristischen Auslegung*, WBTh 8 (Vienna: Herder & Herder, 1964) 106ff., cited by Riekkinen, *Römer 13*, 12–13.

27   Barnikol, "Römer 13," 74–80.

28   Gerhard Delling makes a case in *Römer 13:1-7 innerhalb der Briefe des Neuen Testament* (Berlin: Evangelische Verlagsanstalt, 1962) 41ff. that all of the words with the stem ταγ- are typical for Pauline usage.

29   Barnikol, "Römer 13," 75.

30   Schmithals, *Römerbrief*, 192, citing Martin Dibelius, "Rom und die Christen im ersten Jahrhundert," *SHAW* (1941–42); repr. in vol. 2 of M. Dibelius, *Botschaft und Geschichte* (Tübingen: Mohr [Siebeck], 1956) 234.

31   Eggenberger, "Neue Gesichtspunkte," 246–54.

32   Pallis, 141.

13:2	2) Inference: the awesome consequences of resisting governmental authority	13:6a	a) The congregation's previous payment of tributes
13:2a	a) Resisting the authorioties is resisting God	13:6b	b) Reason: tax collectors are "ministers of God"
13:2b	b) Resisting the authorities brings divine judgment	13:7	2) Meeting various governmental obligations
13:3	3) The relation of officials to good and evil	13:7a	a) The command to render "what is obligated" (τὰ ὀφειλάς)
13:3a	a) No terror for those who do good (ἀγαθός; cf. 12:9, 21)	13:7b-e	b) Specification of governmental obligations
	b) Terror for those who do bad (κακός; cf. 12:9, 21)	13:7b	(1) Tributes to whomever is due
13:3b-5	c. The second argument: diatribe on practical reasons for conforming to the admonition	13:7c	(2) Custom taxes to whomever is due
		13:7d	(3) Fear to whomever is due
13:2b-c	1) Diatribal exchange with the imaginary conversation partner	13:7e	(4) Honor to whomever is due
13:3b	c) Rhetorical question from Paul as the interlocutor about avoiding fear of the authorities		
13:3c	d) Answer in terms of "doing good"		
13:4	2) The official as "the servant of God"		
13:4a	a) The relation of the "servant" to "the good"		
13:4b	b) The warning that anyone doing bad should fear		
13:4c	c) The rationale for fear: the coercion through fear of capital punishment		
13:4d	d) The rationale that "God's servant" brings wrath to the one doing "bad"		
13:5	3) The recapitulation of the need to be subject to governmental authorities		
13:5a	a) Reiteration of the requirement to submit himself to the authorities		
13:5b	b) Reminder of the reasons for submission		
	i) The negative reason: "wrath"		
	ii) The positive reason: "conscience"		
13:6-7	d. The third argument: general diatribe on proper subjection to the authorities by believers		
13:6	1) Payment of tributes and custom taxes		

Exegesis

■ **1** The interpretation of this pericope has swung from abject subservience to political authorities viewed as virtually divine to critical submission on the basis of their advancement of justice. The endless stream of studies has been marked by advocacy of various appraisals of the role of government shaped by denominational traditions and by modern ethical considerations.[33] The passage has been interpreted as a warning not to participate in Jewish zealotism,[34] in revolutionary agitation,[35] or, as seems even less likely, not to create unrest that would jeopardize "the already vulnerable situation of the beleaguered Jewish population in Rome."[36] It has been seen as a warning against Christian enthusiasm that believed the requirement of a state was incommensurate with the new age, which hardly matches the details in the passage.[37] The quiet early years of the Nero regime are depicted as the background of this positive

---

33 See Fritzhermann Keienburg, *Die Geschichte der Auslegung von Römer 13, 1-7* (Gelsenkirchen: Kommissionsverlag W. Hertel, 1956) 140–45; Ernst Käsemann, "Römer 13,1-7 in unserer Generation," *ZThK* (1959) 316–76; Gerta Scharffenorth, "Römer 13 in der Geschichte des politischen Denkens. Ein Beitrag zur Klärung der politischen Traditionen in Deutschland seit dem 15. Jahrhundert" (dissertation, University of Heidelberg, 1964); Riekkinen, *Römer 13*, 118–202; Lutz Pohle, *Die Christen und der Staat nach Röm 13, 1-7 in der neueren deutschsprachigen Schriftauslegung* (Mainz: Grünewald, 1984) 159–76.

34 Dodd, 203; Ernst Bammel, "Ein Beitrag zur paulinischen Staatsanschauung," *ThLZ* 85 (1960) 837–40; idem, "Romans 13," in E. Bammel and C. F. D. Moule, eds., *Jesus and the Politics of His Day* (Cam-

bridge: Cambridge University Press, 1984) 365–83; Marcus Borg, "A New Context for Romans 13," *NTS* 19 (1972–73) 205–18.

35 Lütgert, *Römerbrief*, 98–111.

36 Neil Elliott, "Romans 13:1-7 in the Context of Imperial Propaganda," in R. A. Horsley, ed., *Paul and Empire: Religion and Power in Roman Imperial Society* (Harrisburg: Trinity Press International, 1997) 196; see also Elliott, *Liberating Paul*, 221–26. In a similar vein, Alexander F. C. Webster, "St. Paul's Political Advice to the Haughty Gentile Christians in Rome: An Exegesis of Romans 13:1-7," *VTQ* 25 (1981) 281–82, suggests that this passage struggles against "intolerance and haughtiness" felt by Gentile Christians toward Jews and Jewish Christians.

37 Ernst Käsemann, "Principles for the Interpretation of Romans 13," in Käsemann, *Questions*, 196–216;

view of the state,[38] and Paul wished to avoid any gesture of disloyalty[39] that might jeopardize the peaceful extension of the Christian mission.[40] According to the comprehensive survey by Vilho Riekkinen, investigations of the background of Paul's view of the governing authorities have sifted biblical Hebrew,[41] Hellenistic Jewish,[42] Greco-Roman,[43] and early Christian sources.[44] Since no single tradition or source contains all of the material in 13:1-7, it appears that Paul has incorporated terminology and ideas from a variety of directions.[45] Only recently have scholars begun to view this passage in the light of the Roman civic cult,[46] which could be a step toward taking fuller account of the political and cultural context of Paul's letter and its missional purpose.[47]

My approach is to interpret the verbal details in view of their rhetorical significance for the Roman audience whom Paul is attempting to recruit in support of his Spanish mission.[48] Romans 13:1-7 was not intended to create the foundation of a political ethic for all times and places in succeeding generations—a task for which it has proven to be singularly ill-suited.[49] Believing himself to be a member of the end-time generation, Paul had no

idem, *Romans*, 357; Rolf Walker, *Studie zu Römer 13,1-7*, TEH 132 (Munich: Kaiser, 1966) 7–9.

38 Theobald, 2:88; Walter E. Pilgrim, *Uneasy Neighbors: Church and State in the New Testament* (Minnneapolis: Fortress, 1999) 28–29.

39 Wengst, *Pax Romana*, 102–4; Bergmeier, "Loyalität," 51–63.

40 Haacker, "Friedensmemorandum," 25–41; Cineira, *Religionspolitik*, 403.

41 In *Römer 13*, 76, Riekkinen discusses the work of Willy Böld, *Obrigkeit von Gott? Studien zum staatstheologischen Aspekt des Neuen Testamentes* (Hamburg: Friedrich Wittig, 1962). Critics of this view include Fritz Neugebauer, "Zur Auslegung von Röm 13:1-7," *KD* 8 (1962) 153–59.

42 Riekkinen, *Römer 13*, 78–82, discusses the proposals of Duchrow, *Christenheit*, 16–19; Wolfgang Schrage, *Die Christen und der Staat nach dem Neuen Testament* (Gütersloh: Mohn, 1971) 25–26; Ulrich Wilckens, "Röm 13:1-7," in U. Wilckens, *Rechtfertigung als Freiheit: Paulusstudien* (Neukirchen-Vluyn: Neukirchener, 1974) 225–26; Hans-Werner Bartsch, "Auslegung von Römer XIII, 1-7," *Kirche in der Zeit* 13 (1958) 404–5; Käsemann, "Grundsätzliches," 215; Bergmeier, "Loyalität," 53–56.

43 Riekkinen, *Römer 13*, 61–65, discusses the work of Zsifkovits, *Staatsgedanke*, 28–30; see also August Strobel, "Röm 13," 67–93; Strobel, "Furcht, wem Furcht gebührt. Zum profangriechischen Hintergrund von Rm 13:7," *ZNW* 55 (1964) 58–62.

44 Riekkinen, *Römer 13*, 83–94, discusses the suggestions of Duchrow, *Christenheit*, 154–55; Wilckens, "Röm 13:1-7," 211ff.; Johannes Friedrich, Wolfgang Pöhlmann, and Peter Stuhlmacher, "Zur historischen Situation und Intention von Röm 13:1-7," *ZThK* 73 (1976) 134–35; Delling, *Römer 13:1-7*, 12–17; Gerhard Kittel, "Das Urteil des Neuen Testaments über den Staat," *ZSTh* 14 (1937) 655; Leonhard Goppelt, "Die Freiheit zur Kaisersteuer: Zu Mark 12:17 und Röm 13:1-7," in G. Kretschmar and B. Lohse, eds., *Ecclesia und Res publica. Kurt Dietrich Schmidt zum 65. Geburtstag* (Göttingen: Vandenhoeck & Ruprecht, 1961) 40–50; repr. pp. 208–19 in Goppelt, *Christologie und Ethik*, esp. 211–17. The more recent study by Thompson, *Clothed with Christ*, 119, concludes that the evidence of derivation from the Jesus tradition is "indecisive. A dominical echo is probable; an allusion, possible at best."

45 See Riekkinen, *Römer 13*, 95.

46 Steps in this direction were taken by Wengst, *Pax Romana*, 80–84, 137–38, and Jost Eckert, "Das Imperium Romanum im Neuen Testament. Ein Beitrag zum Thema 'Kirche und Gesellschaft,'" *TThZ* 96 (1987) 256, 264; more substantial contributions were made by Georgi, *Theocracy*, 81–102; Elliott, "Romans 13:1-7," 184–204.

47 Roman Heiligenthal, "Strategien konformer Ethik im Neuen Testament am Beispiel von Röm 13.1-7," *NTS* 29 (1983) 59, argues that this passage opens the door to mission, but does not have the Spanish mission in view. Philip H. Towner argues for a more active motive of political transformation in "Romans 13:1-7 and Paul's Missiological Perspective: A Call to Political Quietism or Transformation?" in S. K. Soderlund and N. T. Wright, eds., *Romans and the People of God: Essays in Honor of Gordon D. Fee on the Occasion of His 65th Birthday* (Grand Rapids/Cambridge: Eerdmans, 1999) 149–69. Schreiber, "Imperium," 142–46, takes the social and political circumstances of the imperial context into account.

48 Paul's purpose to gain support for the mission, along with the demonstrative genre of the letter, lead me to be skeptical of the actant analysis developed by Merklein, "Röm 13, 1-7," 254–59, which assumes an antithesis at each point between Paul's view and that of his audience. He discusses on 267 why Paul does not critique the viewpoint of the audience, and finds no satisfactory answer.

49 Schreiber, "Imperium," 131–33, shows that Paul in this passage has no interest in political theory.

interest in the concerns that would later burden Christian ethics, and which continue to dominate the exegetical discussion. His goal was to appeal to the Roman audience as he conceived it, addressing their concerns in a manner that fit the occasion of his forthcoming visit.

The passage opens in gnomic style with an admonition in 13:1a that sets the tone for the entire pericope. The expression πᾶσα ψυχή ("every soul") is a semiticism (כל נפש) that echoes the language of the LXX[50] and Qumran[51] where "soul" denotes a person.[52] This expression is particularly frequent in legal materials that sometimes begin the same way. For example, Πᾶσα ψυχὴ ἣ φάγῃ αἷμα, ἀπολεῖται ἡ ψυχὴ ἐκείνη ἀπὸ τοῦ λαοῦ αὐτῆς ("Every soul who eats blood, that soul shall perish from his people," Lev 7:17).[53] Here the word

ψυχή has the sense that "every individual person,"[54] without exception, must subject himself or herself to the authorities. No differentiation is allowed by this formula between believers and nonbelievers, between lower and higher ranks of citizens.[55] Paul's unusual combination of ἐξουσίαις ὑπερεχούσαις ("governing authorities")[56] and the desire to avoid abject subservience to dictators have led to elaborate theories about respecting the angelic powers that lie behind political authorities[57] or about personal interactions with noninstitutionalized, governmental agents.[58] While the context does not support either option, the angelic theory in particular is contradicted by Paul's belief that Christ has triumphed over the demonic principalities and powers (Phil 2:10-11; 1 Cor 15:24-25; Rom 8:38-39).[59] It is also significant

---

50 See Daniel Lys, "Israelite Soul according to the LXX," *VT* 16 (1966) 181–228; Gerhard Dautzenberg, "Seele (naefaeš -psyche) im biblischen Denken sowie das Verhältnis von Unsterblichkeit und Auferstehung," in K. Kremer, ed., *Seele, ihre Wirklichkeit, ihr Verhältnis zum Leib und zur menschlichen Person*, SPGAP 10 (Leiden: Brill, 1984) 186–203.

51 Hendrik Antonie Brongers, "Das Wort NFŠ in den Qumranschriften," *RevQ* 4 (1963) 407–15.

52 Georg Bertram, Albert Dihle, et al., "ψυχή κτλ.," *TDNT* 9 (1974), note that while there are occasional classical parallels to this usage (617), the NT expression πᾶσα ψυχή is used "as in the OT" for every man or each man (639, 632). This was confirmed by a TLG search, which discovered a few examples of πᾶσα ψυχή as every person (Plato *Leg.* 731b7; 791b5; 831c6; 839c4), but many references assume the Greek concept of the soul, as, for instance, Plutarch *Gen. Socr.* 591d4, "every soul shares in mind (ψυχὴ πᾶσα νοῦ μετέσχειν);" and Epictetus *Diss.* 3.3.2, "just as every soul by nature (πέφυκεν δὲ πᾶσα ψυχή) assents to the truth."

53 See also Exod 12:16; Lev 17:14, 15; 20:11; 23:29, 30; Num 35:11, 15.

54 Alexander Sand, "ψυχή," *EDNT* 3 (1993) 501; see also Jewett, *Terms*, 356–57.

55 See Walker, *Römer 13,1-7*, 11–12. A more cautious ethic emerged in Rabbinic Judaism, "Be ye guarded in your relations with the ruling power; for they who exercise it draw no man near to them except for their own interests" (*Sayings of the Fathers* [West Orange: Behrman House, 1945] 31).

56 The only other example found thus far is the eleventh-century C.E. writer, Syntipas *Fab.* p. 127.4, noted by BAGD 841.

57 According to Lutz Pohle, *Römer 13*, 89, the first elaborations of the angelic interpretation were developed by Karl Ludwig Schmidt, "Das Gegenüber von Kirche und Staat in der Gemeinde des Neuen Testaments," *ThBl* 16 (1937) 1–16, and Günther Dehn, "Engel und Obrigkeit: Ein Beitrag zum Verständnis von Römer 13,1-7," in E. Wolf, ed., *Theologische Aufsätze, Karl Barth, zum 50. Geburtstag* (Munich: Kaiser, 1936) 100–109. See also Dehn's later study, *Vom christlichen Leben. Auslegung des 12. und 13. Kapitels des Briefes an die Römer*, BibS(N) 6–7 (Neukirchen-Vluyn: Neukirchener, 1954); the most influential advocate of this interpretation was Oscar Cullmann, *The State in the New Testament* (New York: Scribner's, 1956; London: SCM, 1957, 1961) 95–114, followed by Clinton D. Morrison, *The Powers That Be: Earthly Rulers and Demonic Powers in Romans 13:1-7*, SBT 29 (London: SCM; Naperville: Allenson, 1960), and others.

58 See Pohle's apt description in *Römer 13*, 89, of the personal, noninstitutional understanding of ἐξουσίαις ὑπερεχούσαις developed by Käsemann, 355–56; idem, "Grundsätzliches," 208–9; Hans-Werner Bartsch, "Die neutestamentlichen Aussagen über den Staat. Zu Karl Barths Brief an einen Pfarrer in der DDR," *EvTh* 19 (1959) 387–90.

59 See the summaries of the critiques in Pohle, *Römer 13*, 99–103, and Riekkinen, *Römer 13*, 166–70; also Carr, *Angels and Principalities*, 115–18; Frederick F. Bruce, "Paul and the 'Powers That Be,'" *BJRL* 66 (1983–84) 88–90; Dunn, 2:760.

that Paul refrains from employing any of the terms for cosmic powers that appeared in 8:38-39. He picks up instead the term employed in 9:21 for the potter's "power" over the clay. Ἐξουσία has a wide semantic range, including individual freedom of choice, capability, authority in an individual as well as a governmental sphere, dominion, and power.[60] August Strobel showed that the plural expression "governing authorities" used in Rom 13:1 encompasses a variety of imperial and local offices such as *proconsulare imperium*/ἡ ἀνθυπατικὴ ἐξουσία ("proconsular authority"); *tribunicia potestas*/ἡ δημαρχικὴ ἐξουσία ("tribunal authority"); *praefectura praetorii*/ἡ ἐπαρχικὴ ἐξουσία ("pretorian authority"); *quaestoria potestas*/ἡ ταμιεντικὴ ἐξουσία ("fiscal authority").[61] The Augustan development of an elaborate system of local officials in Rome and the provinces is reflected in Paul's wording.[62] Since the participle οἱ ὑπερέχοντες,[63] as well as the noun ἐξουσίαι,[64] can be used to refer to governmental officials, their somewhat redundant combination here has a cumulative sense that encompasses a range of officials placed in superior positions of political authority,[65] duly appointed to their tasks[66] and currently exercising their power.[67] In contrast

to the premise of "church–state" debate based on this passage,[68] this reference is "not of the state as such but of political and civil authority as it would actually bear upon his readers,"[69] that is, the local magistrates in Rome. Since two of the Christian groups Paul knows to be in Rome consist of imperial slaves working in behalf of such officials, the implication of Paul's wording is that they would not be exercising their power without divine appointment.

The verb ὑποτασσέσθω, translated here with "subject himself," is in the middle or passive voice and in this context has the middle sense of subjecting oneself to someone else. It can have the sense of "to submit voluntarily," which has been lifted up as characteristic for early Christian ethics[70] in contrast to "obedience."[71] For example, this verb is employed in 1 Cor 16:16 in reference to believers voluntarily subjecting themselves to their congregational leaders, a matter of their willing decision since legal, coercive powers had not yet arisen in the church.[72] In Porter's view, Paul "uses an imperative to reiterate the call for a willing subordination, since use of the imperative implies ability to refuse on the reader's part."[73] It should also be kept in mind that the

60   BAGD 277-79; Werner Foerster, "ἔξιστιν κτλ.," *TDNT* 2 (1964) 562-66; G. H. R. Horsley, "Ἐξουσία," *NDIEC* 2 (1982) 83-84.

61   Strobel, "Röm 13," 79; cf. Blumenfeld, *Political Paul*, 389-90.

62   See Judge, "Cultural Conformity," 9-10; Zsifkovits, *Staatsgedanke*, 64-65; White, *Apostle*, 124, referring to Andrew Wallace-Hadrill, *Augustan Rome* (London: Bristol Classical Press, 1993) 47-50, and Zanker, *Power of Images*, 129-35. Mason, *Greek Terms*, 132-34, shows that the Latin equivalent to ἐξουσία is *imperium*.

63   See Gerhard Delling, "ὑπερέχω κτλ.," *TDNT* 8 (1972) 524. For example, Diodorus Siculus employs ὑπερέχοντες for "those in authority" in *Hist.* 20.8.3.6; 23.23.2.20.

64   For example, Isocrates *Panath.* 40.6 refers to "all governments and authorities (πάσαις ἀρχαῖς καὶ ἐξουσίαις)"; Dionysius Halicarnassus *Antiq. Rom.* 31.36.1 speaks of "honoring those existing in authoritative positions (τιμῶντες τοὺς ἐν ἐξουσίαις ὄντας)."

65   Ingo Broer, "ἐξουσία," *EDNT* 2 (1981) 11.

66   See Cranfield, 1:259-60. The argument by Stanley E. Porter, "Romans 13:1-7 as Pauline Political Rhetoric," *FilN* 3 (1990) 123, that ὑπερέχω implies

"superiority not of position but of quality," seems unlikely in view of Paul's strenuous argument earlier in this letter that no one is superior in virtue or accomplishment so that all boasting is excluded (Rom 3:27).

67   See Walker, *Römer 13*, 112-13; Wilckens, 3:32.

68   See, for example, the flat identification of the "powers" with the "state" itself in Johannes Koch-Mehrin, "Die Stellung des Christen zum Staat nach Röm. 13 und Apok. 13," *EvTh* 7 (1947-48) 381-83.

69   Dunn, 2:759.

70   Gerhard Delling, "τάσσω κτλ.," *TDNT* 8 (1972) 39-44, esp. 40; Kähler, *Unterordnung*, 176-78; Ceslas Spicq, "ὑποτάσσω," *TLNT* 3 (1994) 424. Porter, "Romans 13:1-7," 121, shows that the majority of instances of ὑποτάσσω in the NT in ethical contexts "speak of voluntary submission."

71   Roland Bergmeier, "ὑποτάσσω," *EDNT* 3 (1993) 408, prefers this sense of "subordination, obedience." See the critique of this "loyal obedience" construal by Walker, *Römer 13*, 14-15.

72   See Leenhardt, 326; Wilckens, 3:33; Morris, 461; Murray, 2:148.

73   Porter, "Romans 13:1-7," 122.

decisions Paul encourages the believers in Rome to make in accordance with this guideline of willing subordination are subject to the premises set forth in the introductory pericope of the fourth proof (12:1-2), not to "be conformed to this world" but to be "transformed" as the congregation assesses "what is the will of God" in particular situations. This is an ethic requiring public discussion and spiritual insight and it is far removed from an authoritarian ethic of obedience. But Paul's formulation would have had a significant appeal to Christian bureaucrats in two of the congregations mentioned in chapter 16, indicating that public acceptance of their administration was consistent with the faith.

The first argument in 13:1b-3a provides a basic rationale for the foregoing admonition. There is no ambiguity about the wording of v. 1b-c or its background in the Jewish wisdom tradition. It opens the first argument for submission, that governmental authority has a divine origin, a point made first negatively in v. 1b and then positively in 1c. The word "authority" is repeated in the claim that it is ὑπὸ θεοῦ ("by God").[74] Since this same expression appears in both v. 1b and 1c, it appears to be a formula for designating the source of governmental power.[75] Thus, no matter what Roman officials may claim as their authority, it really comes from the God of Jewish and Christian faith.[76] We find basically the same idea in the OT (Jer 27:5-6; Dan 4:17, 25, 32; 5:21) and in Hellenistic Judaism. For example, Sir 10:4 uses the key term ἐξουσία in claiming that "the power of the earth is in the hands of the Lord (ἐν χειρὶ κυρίου ἡ ἐξουσία τῆς γῆς)." The Wisdom of Solomon 6:3 formulates this with different terminology: ὅτι ἐδόθη παρὰ κυρίου ἡ κράτησις ὑμῖν καὶ ἡ δυναστεία παρὰ ὑψίστου ("your dominion was given to you from the Lord, and your power from the Most High"). The verb τάσσω, appearing in v. 1c in the perfect passive participle, τεταγμέναι, derives from military use, meaning arranged in rank and file;[77] an associated concept is to be placed in command of others in the order of battle,[78] and then in the political sphere.[79] The same verb is employed in the LXX for political appointments (2 Sam 7:11; Tob 1:21).[80]

The key to understanding the revolutionary implications of this argument is the twice-repeated formula, "by God" in v. 1b c, echoed and reinforced by 1a, v. 4a & d, and v. 6b referring to governmental agents as servants of God. That all such officials are divinely appointed needs to be understood rhetorically. The range of interest of the Roman audience would not have extended to the question of whether officials beyond the boundaries of the empire, or whether governments arising in later centuries, were appointed by God; the relevant question was the status of the Roman government. The issue usually not raised in the scholarly discussion is precisely who this God is. The relevance of this question is most easily grasped when one compares Paul's statement with the Roman civic cult and takes account of the twelve chapters of argument that precede this pericope. The God who grants authority to governmental agencies in Paul's argument is not Mars or Jupiter, as in the Roman civic cult; nor is he represented by the pantheon of Greco-Roman deities that had been assimilated into the civic cult since the time of Augustus.

---

74 BAGD (2000) 1035a, occurring with the genitive, "marker of agency or cause, by." See also Porter, "Romans 13:1-7," 125, citing Pohle, *Christen*, 112–13. The expression "by God" (ὑπὸ θεοῦ) occurs only here and in Gal 3:9 in the NT, but is common elsewhere, occurring 879 times in a *TLG* search. For instance, Philo *Leg.* 1.41 says that "some things come into existence by God and through God (ὑπὸ θεοῦ γίνεται καὶ δι᾽ αὐτοῦ)."

75 For instance, the *Acts John* 8.4-5 tells the emperor, "Even you will rule for many periods granted to you by God (ὑπὸ θεοῦ), and after you, very many others."

76 See Walker, *Römer 13*, 16–17.

77 See Delling, "τάσσω κτλ.," 27; LSJM 1759: "draw up in order of battle," as, for example, Xenophon *Anab.* 1.2.15 reports that Cyrus ordered the troops "to be drawn up in four lines (ἐπὶ τεττάρων ταχθῆναι)" to demonstrate their prowess to the Cilician queen.

78 For example, Xenophon *Hell.* 7.2.34 describes how the Arcadian troops "appointed as their leaders (ἄρχοντας ἔταττον) whomever he [Lycomedes] directed them to appoint."

79 For example, Plato *Leg.* 952e: strangers are received "by the officials in charge thereof (ἄρχοντας τεταγμένους)."

80 See Bergmeier, "τάσσω," 337: "instituted by God"; idem, "Die Loyalitätsparänese Röm 13:1-7 im Rahmen von Römer 12 und 13," *ThBei* 27 (1996) 60–61.

The God of whom Paul speaks here is the same as announced in chapter 1 whose righteousness was elaborated for the next twelve chapters; it is the God embodied in the crucified Christ that is in view here, which turns this passage into a massive act of political co-optation.[81] If the Roman authorities had understood this argument, it would have been viewed as thoroughly subversive.[82] That the Roman authorities were appointed by the God and Father of Jesus Christ turns the entire Roman civic cult on its head, exposing its suppression of the truth. Its involvement in the martyrdom of Christ, crucified under Pontius Pilate, cannot have been forgotten by the readers of chapter 13, who knew from firsthand experience of the Edict of Claudius the hollowness of Rome's claim to have established a benign rule of law. The critique of the law in all its forms in the first eight chapters of this letter cannot have been forgotten, which explains why the proudest institution of the Pax Romana, the rule of law, goes unmentioned here. Nothing remains of the claim in Roman propaganda that its law-enforcement system was redemptive, producing a kind of messianic peace under the rule of the gods Justitia and Clementia. Christ alone is the fulfillment of the law (10:4), not the emperor or the Roman gods. And nothing remains of the specious claim in the civic cult that the empire had been given to Rome because of its superior virtue and piety, a matter that had been demolished by 1:18–3:20. What remains is the simple fact of divine appointment, a matter justified not by the virtue of the appointee but by the mysterious mind of God who

elects whom she will as the agents of her purpose (9:14-33; 11:17-32). Submission to the governmental authorities is therefore an expression of respect not for the authorities themselves but for the crucified deity who stands behind them. That this argument would have had an appeal to Christian groups working within the Roman administration is self-evident.

■ **2** The inferential nature of this verse is indicated by ὥστε ("so that, accordingly"),[83] the same conjunction used in 7:4. This verse thus belongs with v. 1a-b in clarifying why the Roman churches should subject themselves to the political authorities. The verb ἀντιτάσσομαι ("resist, oppose")[84] is used here for the only time in the Pauline letters, but it is used elsewhere in the sense of resistance to duly constituted authority. For example, Vettius Valens uses this language in referring to a slave "in accordance of the command of the one ordering it, not resisting . . . (κατὰ τὴν τοῦ κελεύοντος διαταγὴν μὴ ἀντιτασσόμενος)."[85] This verb is the opposite of ὑποτάσσεσθαι ("to submit oneself"), used in v. 1, and a virtual synonym of ἀνθίστημι ("oppose"),[86] used twice in this sentence and also in 9:19 with the same sense of opposing the Creator.[87] Although we have no examples outside of the NT of this verb being employed in the context of opposing God, its use in the LXX generally depicts futile resistance against forces of superior strength.[88] Paul's inference is that since the authorities were appointed by God, to resist them is to resist that divine appointment, a futile endeavor indeed. But again, the power does not reside in the political authorities

81   Preliminary steps in this direction were taken by Jacob Taubes, *Die politische Theologie des Paulus. Vorträge gehalten an der Forschungsstätte der evangelischen Studiengemeinschaft in Heidelberg, 23–27 Februar 1987*, ed. A. Assmann et al. (Munich: Wilhelm Fink Verlag, 1995) 24–27, 73–75, and Schreiber, "Imperium," 160–64.

82   This was perceived by Jacques Ellul, "Petite note complémentaire sur Romains 13,1," *FV* 89 (1990) 81–82, which recalls that Seneca cites Nero's statement, "I . . . have been chosen to serve on earth as vicar of the gods" (*deorum vice*, in *Clem.* 1.2) and thereupon is celebrated as a god himself, the embodiment of Jupiter and Apollo. Paul's argument is that Nero "is not God. He is not the center of the world. He is not the master of nature: if he has power, it was given to him by the God of Jesus Christ."

83   BAGD 899.1a; BDF §391.3; Moule, *Idiom-Book*, 144. In contrast, Stein, "Argument," 330, argues for "logical result or consequence" from 13:1b.

84   BAGD 76.

85   Vettius Valens *Anth.* 9.355.16; see also LXX 2 Esd 4:11; *Historia Alexandri Magni, rec. β* 1.33.38 = *Rec. γ* 33.46; *Rec. Byz.* 4494; 5888.

86   Ἀνθίστημι appears here in the middle voice, implying setting oneself against something; see BAGD 67. Michel, 400, fails to make a convincing case that these terms have a virtually synonymous meaning.

87   See Horst Balz and Gerhard Schneider, eds., "ἀνθίστημι," *EDNT* 1 (1990) 99.

88   Dunn, 2:762, citing Lev 26:37; Deut 7:24; 9:2; 11:25; Josh 1:5; 7:13; 23:9; Judg 2:14; 2 Chron 13:7; Jdt 6:4; 11:8.

themselves, but in their appointment by a God whose name they do not yet know and acknowledge.

The use of διαταγή in this verse has occasioned some controversy, because Deissmann and Strobel cited it in support of their theory that Paul employed technical governmental language in this passage.[89] The key evidence was a partially extant inscription that was read τῶν θείων δια[ταγ]ῶν ("of divine appointment"), but more recent readings fill in the text to read τῶν θείων δια[ταμάτ]ῶν ("of divine ordinances").[90] Johannes Friedrich, Wolfgang Pöhlmann, and Peter Stuhlmacher argued that διαταγή was actually not used for official decrees and appointments, but that closely associated terms such as διατάξις or διάταγμα were used instead, and that therefore the entire case for Paul's use of Roman and Hellenistic administrative language collapses.[91] More recently, G. H. R. Horsley cited a Trajan inscription that employed the abstract form of this "standard terminology" in settling a dispute over an estate boundary: "in accordance with the ordinance (διάταγμα) of the emperor Nerva Trajan. . . ."[92] While it appears clear that Paul chooses not to use a technical term for governmental appointments, the fact remains that the verb τάσσω and the stem ταγ- were typically used in this connection, as noted above, and in the rhetoric of this pericope the noun in v. 2 echoes the verb in v. 1 and is defined by it. That Paul wished to avoid glorifying the Roman state may be true, but not from the use of the isolated word διαταγή;[93] it is suggested, rather, from Paul's argument that Roman rule is from the God and Father of our Lord Jesus Christ. It is safe to conclude that v. 2a refers to "the actual basis of submission under governmental authority as an *order* willed by God even for Christians."[94] The relevance of this point for Paul's original audience is transparent.

In v. 2b, the rhetoric shifts from the third person singular to the plural. The perfect participle οἱ ἀνθεστηκότες ("those who have resisted") implies that the problem of opposition against Roman authorities was a matter of the past with continuing present relevance, which is usually overlooked by commentators and translators, but whether it also has the connotation of a "determined and established policy" of resistance to governmental authority, that is, the issue of "anarchy," is debatable.[95] Paul either had in mind past events of biblical history in which rebels were condemned, or, as seems more likely in view of the rhetorical situation, the formulation evokes events in Roman history where this had occurred. In either case, the wordplay between ὑποτάσσομαι ("submit oneself") and ἀντιτάσσομαι ("resist") in this passage clarifies the alternatives open to the audience, and the verse as a whole indicates the consequences of the latter.[96]

The expression "receive judgment on themselves" is Semitic, reflecting the wording of Ezek 4:5; Job 9:19; Wis 12:12.[97] The position of ἑαυτοῖς ("in relation to themselves") is emphatic, which conveys the sense that those opposing the authorities bring a penalty upon themselves.[98] The word κρίμα itself has the basic connotation of a "verdict," but in Romans it seems always to be used to refer to a negative verdict, thus "condemnation."[99] In view of the earlier references in Romans to

89 Deissman, *Light*, 86–88, in reference to "imperial ordinances" such as that found in an inscription from Hierapolis (C. Humann et al., eds., *Altertümer von Hierapolis*, 100, no. 78): "if anyone acts contrary to my ordinance (εἴ τις παρὰ τὴν διαταγὴν τὴν ἐμὴν ποιήσι)." See also Strobel, "Röm 13," 86.

90 The inscription is from the second century C.E., *CIG* 4300.6. Friedrich, Pöhlmann, and Stuhlmacher, "Röm 13,1-7," 137, point out this correction, citing M. Guarducci, *Epigrafie greca II* (Florence, 1969) 71ff., and Mason, *Greek Terms*, 126–51; see also Fitzmyer, 667.

91 Friedrich, Pöhlmann, and Stuhlmacher, "Röm 13,1-7," 136–40.

92 G. H. R. Horsley, "Giving Thanks to Artemis," *NDIEC* 4 (1987) 129.

93 Friedrich, Pöhlmann, and Stuhlmacher, "Röm 13,1-7," 140, followed by Riekkinen, *Römer 13*, 206.

94 Lorenz Oberlinner, "διατάσσω, διαταγή," *EDNT* 1 (1990) 314, italics in original; see also Delling, "τάσσω κτλ.," 34–36.

95 Leenhardt, 329; Dunn, 2:762; Moo, 799.

96 Heiligental, "Strategien," 57.

97 Michel, 400; Black, 182, citing Ezek 4:5; Dunn, 2:762.

98 Weiss, 530; Kühl, 432.

99 Friedrich Büchsel and Volkmar Herntrich, "κρίνω κτλ.," *TDNT* 3 (1965) 942; Mathias Rissi, "κρίμα," *EDNT* 2 (1991) 317.

divine judgment (2:2, 3; 3:8; 5:16), it seems likely that Paul had in mind the threat of facing God's tribunal,[100] as well as governmental verdicts.[101] The latter is strongly implied by the immediate context, referring to the frightful prospect of civil judgment (13:3-4).[102] The future verb λήμψονται ("they will receive") conveys the sense of a certain, negative outcome of resistance. Some have inferred that this formulation implies that God's future judgment is present in the penalties imposed by these civil authorities.[103] This is a point of genuine significance for the members of Paul's audience whose employment involved them in such legal administration. One way or another, even if civil authorities overlook one's resistance, the verdict is assured. This adds a significant pragmatic consideration to the issue of a group submitting itself to governmental authority. Even if the Roman gods do not exist, from whom the state officials believed they derived their powers, the God of the universe will not be thwarted. Since at least two of the Christian groups in Rome were probably members of governmental bureaucracies,[104] these two verses provide a significant sanction for their activities. It is clear that, in Paul's view, they are not "working for the other side," no matter what the Roman civic cult and administrative system assumed about their service to the gods.

■ **3** The practical argument in support of the admonition in 13:1 begins in this verse,[105] namely, that the civil authorities conform to the standards of good and bad set forth in the preceding pericopes (12:2, 9, 21). That οἱ ἄρχοντες refers to public officials is indicated by the context and supported by the close parallel in 1 Cor 2:6, 8, the "rulers of this age" who crucified Christ.[106] That these officials are not a φόβος τῷ ἀγαθῷ ἔργῳ, literally "a fear/terror to good work," is consistent with Greco-Roman usage.[107] For example, Appian *Bell. Civ.* 3:4.27, 20–22, reports that when Mark Antony in 44 B.C.E. wanted to pressure the Senate to grant him control of a province, "he immediately ordered Gaius to bring his army across the Ionian Sea to Brindisium to bring fear in the Senate (ἐς φόβον τῆς βουλῆς)." In order to maintain consistency in the translation of φόβος, which appeared in 3:18 and 8:15, I follow recent commentators with the formulation "a [cause of] fear."[108] The expression "good work" (ἔργον ἀγαθόν) appeared in 2:7 in the context of discussing divine approbation of good behavior whether it occurs with Jews or Gentiles.[109] Closer at hand, both "good" (ἀγαθός) and "bad" (κάκος) appeared at the beginning and closing of the preceding pericope (12:9, 21), referring to the universally acknowledged ethical standards that guide the expression of love. This correlates with a widespread Greco-Roman consensus that governmental authorities should mete out "censure and chastisement according to law for wrong-doers [and] praise and honour for all well-doers, again, according to the law," in Philo's words.[110] There is no escaping the conclusion that this formulation in 13:3 implies that governmental officials were guided by the same standards.[111]

100 Michel, 400, finds that this formulation supports only divine judgment, and not governmental coercion.

101 Mathias Rissi opts for both civil and divine penalty in "κρίμα," 317; see also Barrett, 245; Black, 182. Weiss, 530; Leenhardt, 329; and Riekkinen, *Römer 13*, 206–7, argue that only state sanctions are in view here.

102 The verdict in question is probably related to taxes, which 13:6-7 reveal to be the heart of the issue facing the Roman congregation. Thomas M. Coleman, "Binding Obligations in Romans 13:7: A Semantic Field and Social Context," *TynB* 48 (1997) 326, observes that "tax evasion was a criminal offense," citing Robinson, *Criminal Law*, 90–91.

103 Zsifkovits, *Staatsgedanke*, 72–73; Merklein, "Röm 13,1-7," 245.

104 See Introduction and 16:3-16.

105 Stein, "Argument," 332–33, following Käsemann,

355, and Reikkinen, *Römer 13*, 207–11, argues that v. 3a is a second, practical argument.

106 Barrett, *1 Corinthians*, 357; Wesley Carr, "The Rulers of this Age—I Corinthians II.6-8," *NTS* 23 (1976–77) 20–35; Carr, *Angels and Principalities*, 118–20.

107 Horst Balz and Günther Wanke, "φοβέω κτλ.," *TDNT* 9 (1974) 190.2b.

108 Dunn, 2:763; Moo, 800.

109 See also G. H. R. Horsley, "Family Terminology for Social Relationships," *NDIEC* 1 (1981) 59–60, where καλῶς ποιήσις, ἄδελφοι ("you will act rightly, brother") refers to meeting family obligations.

110 Philo *Mos.* 1.154, cited by Coleman, "Binding Obligations," 308.

111 This formulation is an implicit critique of the totalitarian claims of an emperor like Caligula, who, according to Barrett, *Caligula*, 56, had claimed the right to exercise "every power over every person"

Paul's second argument begins with a rhetorical question by an interlocutor in 13:3b. Although this shift to diatribe has been noted by a few scholars,[112] its argumentative function has not been clarified and the profile of the interlocutor has not been identified. The question "Do you wish not to fear the authority?" seems to be in Paul's own voice and it addresses anxiety on the part of the audience concerning the governmental "verdict" (13:2) that might be enacted. With "you" (sg.) being addressed, a member of the audience, in effect, is made into the second imaginary character in this exchange, whose anxiety Paul is able to address. I suggest that this second imaginary character stands for members of the congregations who had experienced the unfair burden of such verdicts in connection with their banning in C.E. 49. Many others had probably witnessed or experienced governmental brutality in other contexts, because Rome ruled with an iron hand. By conversing with a fearful believer with a different profile than conversation partners and interlocutors earlier in the letter, Paul appeals to congregations with close ties to the government that harbored concerns that his project would entail public disturbances like those in his earlier career. The oral traditions later used in the book of Acts concerning Paul's involvement in riots and imprisonments would have been known at least in part in Rome, and, by Paul's own admission, he had often experienced "beatings, imprisonments, tumults" (2 Cor 6:5) and was three times "beaten with rods" (2 Cor 11:25) by Roman authorities.[113] Now he advises a fearful imaginary conversation partner how to avoid such threatening encounters with the authorities: "do the good and you will have praise" from Roman officials (13:3c). This advice was not entirely hollow, because August Strobel and Willem van Unnik have made a case that many civic authorities consciously sought to conform to the ethical standards of good and evil.[114] They offered ἔπαινος ("praise, commendation") in the form of public recognition to those performing good deeds in behalf of their communities. Strobel points to the practice of placing commendations of good deeds performed by citizens in public monuments. Van Unnik traces the public patterns both of punishing evil deeds and rewarding good deeds.[115] Bruce Winter provides examples of inscriptions praising benefactors with the word ἀγαθός ("good"), which Paul employs here.[116] The fact that Romans was drafted during a period of exemplary Roman administration led by Seneca and Burrus augments the likelihood that Paul's formulation would have resonated positively in Rome.[117] However, before and after that period, Paul's unqualified formulation that officials punish the bad and praise the good seems far from accurate. Moreover, there are many indications in Paul's earlier career when no such assessment would have been possible, including his judgment about the authorities' mistaken judgment in Christ's crucifixion (1 Cor 2:6-8). Even more problematic is that Paul here conforms to the tradition of desiring ἔπαινος ("praise, commendation") from human officials.[118] Paul's wording clearly implies that within the Roman churches "there must have been Christians of very considerable means" who could play the role of public benefactors and gain such recognition.[119] Yet, in his earlier letters, such praise is considered legitimate only if it comes from God, and emphatically not from foreign governmental authorities. These disparities should not be overlooked, because they cannot be eliminated by an interpolation theory.

(*omnia in omnes licere*), cited from Suetonius *Cal.* 14.1.

112 Schlier, 389; Dunn, 2:763; Byrne, 391; Tobin, *Paul's Rhetoric*, 396.

113 See Martin, *2 Corinthians*, 171, 377.

114 August Strobel, "Furcht, wem Furcht gebührt. Zum profangriechischen Hintergrund von Rm 13:7," *ZNW* 55 (1964) 58–60; Willem C. van Unnik, "Lob und Strafe durch die Obrigkeit. Hellenistisches zu Röm 13,3-4," in E. E. Ellis and E. Grässer, eds., *Jesus und Paulus. Festschrift für Werner Georg Kümmel zum 70. Geburtstag* (Göttingen: Vandenhoeck & Ruprecht, 1975) 334–43.

115 Unnik, "Lob und Strafe," 334–43.

116 Bruce W. Winter, "The Public Honouring of Christian Benefactors: Romans 13.3-4 and 1 Peter 2.14-15," *JSNT* 34 (1988) 91–92; see also Winter, "Romans 12–15," 83.

117 See Zahn, 558.

118 Otfried Hofius, "ἔπαινος, ἐπαινέω," *EDNT* 2 (1991) 16, accepts the evidence adduced by Strobel and van Unnik concerning civic recognition as the appropriate background for 13:3.

119 Winter, "Christian Benefactors," 94.

The most plausible explanation of the problematic wording of this verse is to see Paul's argument as missional rather than theoretical. He overlooks other problematic aspects of governmental behavior in times past in order to appeal to the groups of believers within the imperial bureaucracy whose cooperation was perceived to be absolutely vital in the Spanish mission.[120] These particular bureaucrats, being Christian, would be responsive to the ethical rationale of praising the good and punishing the evil that Paul had developed in 12:9-21. Thus the aim of this diatribe is to support their vocational aims by urging subservience to their kind of administration; if Paul can thereby attract their goodwill, they will perhaps cooperate with his mission project, which in some respects could be interpreted as evil by non-Christian Roman officials concerned about maintaining imperial interests in Spain. Paul hopes that for the Christian bureaucrats, such concerns can be overcome. In this diatribe, he places an effective argument at their service: he whose reputation as a subversive troublemaker was in fact an advocate of good public order, and his plans for the Spanish venture should, therefore, not be thwarted.

■ **4** The diatribe with the fearful conversation partner continues in this verse with reassurance about the reliable identity of governmental agents. With the possessive of "God" in the emphatic position,[121] Paul contends that a governmental official is a διάκονος ("servant"), the same root he had used for his own office in 11:13 and treated as a church service in 12:7. This extraordinarily high position of "God's servant,"[122] given the early Christian choice of the term διάκονος for an important leadership role in local churches (see Rom 16:1; 2 Cor 11:23),[123] has some precedence in Greco-Roman governmental theory. While the servant generally was granted

only a menial role with minimal honor, service to the state was prestigious. For example, in *Laws* 12.c, Plato claims that friendship and honor are due to anyone who serves the state and that to prevent base motives, "those who are performing any act of service (διακονοῦντας) to the state must do it without gifts." A statesman thus becomes a "servant of the state."[124] For example, Demosthenes *Cor.* 311.1 asks, "Which is the ambassadorship? What is the service (τίς διακονία) by which the polis is more honored?" There is a first-century B.C.E. inscription where the city officials dedicating a statue to Hermes are described as διάκονοι, while another inscription from the same period refers to temple officials with this title.[125] The use of this title "servants of God" would correspond to Roman official titles such as the *ministri* who served municipal cults and formed part of the imperial bureaucracy.[126] It is nevertheless noteworthy that Paul selected none of the more prestigious titles for public officials currently employed in Rome, preferring one that had profound Christian resonance: even Christ in 15:8 is referred to as a διάκονος. Especially when one considers that the God in question is the father of Jesus Christ instead of Zeus or Hermes or Apollo, the co-optation is clear. To think of themselves in the fullest Christian sense as "servants of God," dedicated to serving "you" as a church member as well as the general public in achieving "the good," would be highly appealing to the two groups of believers within the imperial bureaucracy. That this title is mentioned twice in the same verse augments its effect.

Verse 13:4b-d develops the theme of wrongdoers rightfully fearing the servants of God, which reiterates the thought of v. 3a-b. An essential component of the task of a διάκονος θεοῦ is to provide a threat against the imaginary conversation partner if he does "the bad."

120 Overlooking the issue of the Spanish mission, Towner's assessment in "Romans 13:1-7," 168, 160, of "Paul's missiological perspective" in this verse involves urging the Roman Christians to "transforming engagement in the world," which includes the modern-sounding formulation "to participate proactively in public life."

121 Black, 183.

122 For a discussion of the problematic application of this concept in the modern world, particularly with a totalitarian state, see Jean Héring, "'Serviteurs de

Dieu': Contributions à l'exégèse pratique de Romains 13,3-4," *RHPhR* 30 (1950) 31–40.

123 See Alfons Weiser, "διακονέω κτλ.," *EDNT* 1 (1990) 302–3.

124 See Hermann W. Beyer, "διακονέω κτλ.," *TDNT* 2 (1964) 82.

125 MM 149, citing *I.Magn.* Nrs. 109.5; 217.4–5.

126 See Rostovtzeff, *Empire*, 104, 583 n. 32, referring to Boehm's article in *PW* 12.810 and G. Grether, "Pompeian Ministri," *CP* 27 (1932) 59ff.

This is why Paul denies that the threat of punishment is εἰκῆ ("in vain").[127] Since it proved to be a mistake for interpreters to limit "bear the sword" to the *ius gladii*, the right of provincial governers to execute Roman citizens convicted of crimes,[128] it now appears more likely that it refers to police powers and governmental coercion in a broader sense.[129] Neil Elliott[130] has pointed to Neronian propaganda as the immediate background for this reference, because Nero had allegedly replaced the sword with peace, in the words of his spokesman Calpurnius Siculus in *Eclogue* 1.45–65: "Clemency has . . . broken every maddened sword-blade. . . . Peace in her fullness shall come; knowing not the drawn sword, she shall renew once more the reign of Saturn in Latium, once more the reign of Numa who first taught the tasks of peace to armies that rejoiced in slaughter." Seneca, who served in the Nero administration, boasted that the present emperor proclaimed, "the sword is hidden, nay is sheathed; I am sparing to the utmost of even the meanest blood."[131] This was, of course, all propaganda, because during Nero's administration, while the execution of citizens was carefully restricted by law, noncitizens and slaves were routinely killed,[132] often as a form of public entertainment. Roland Auguet reports how *noxii ad gladium ludi damnati* ("criminals condemned to the sword in the games") would be driven en masse into the amphitheater during a noontime lull and forced to kill each other until the last was dispatched by an official.[133] The μάχαιρα in Romans was not a ceremonial dagger worn by high public officials but the military sword, the classic symbol for governmental coercion as noted with regard to 8:35. The present tense of the verb φορέω in the present tense implies "a lasting, continuing, repeated, or customary action" of carrying something, in this instance the routine wearing of the sword by law-enforcement officials,[134] who in the Roman setting were specially trained soldiers. There are papyri, some from the period of Paul's Roman letter, referring to police officers as μαχαιροφόροι ("sword-bearers").[135] For the audience of Paul's letter, few of whom were Roman citizens with a degree of protection against the sword of the state, this reference allowed no illusions about the fate of evildoers. Despite imperial propaganda, the sword "continues to threaten destruction and bloodshed."[136]

After the repetition of "he is God's servant," Paul places in apposition the expression ἔκδικος εἰς ὀργήν, which can be translated either "an avenger for wrath"[137] or "a legal officer for a court."[138] The former seems more plausible because 12:19; 2 Cor 7:11; 10:6; 1 Thess

---

127 BAGD 222; Paul's use of this adverb in 1 Cor 15:2; Gal 3:4; 4:11 has the sense of "in vain," but some commentators and BAGD prefer the sense of "for no purpose," reflecting the intention of governmental force but not its actual effectiveness (Kühl, 432; Michel, 401; Dunn, 2:762; Fitzmyer, 668). Since Paul is arguing for submission on pragmatic grounds, the matter of effectiveness is more crucial (Weiss, 531; Schlier, 390). The inscription on a sarcophagus that begins with εἰκῆ οὐ δύνῃ ἀνῦξε ("In vain, you cannot open [it]") points in the same direction (G. H. R. Horsley, "Εἰκῆ," *NDIEC* 2 (1982) 81, citing *I.Tyre* 1.17).

128 Lagrange, 313; Michel, 401; Leenhardt, 333; Barrett, 247; Black, 160. The use of the expression *ius gladii* in provincial administration is discussed by Mommsen, *Römisches Staatsrecht*, 1.433–35; Sherwin-White, *Roman Society*, 8–11; see the critique by Friedrich, Pöhlmann, and Stuhlmacher, "Römer 13, 1-7," 140–45; Dunn, 2:764; Fitzmyer, 668.

129 See Friedrich, Pöhlmann, and Stuhlmacher, "Römer 13, 1-7," 144; Fitzmyer, 668. Eckhart Plümacher, "μάχαιρα," *EDNT* 2 (1991) 398, questions this judgment for unclear reasons.

130 Elliott, "Romans 13:1-7," 202–3; see also Witherington, 305–6.

131 Seneca *Clem.* 1.4; see also *Clem.* 11.3 and 13.5.

132 See Robinson, *Criminal Law*. This renders implausible the suggestion by Borg, "Romans 13," 216–17, that "sword" refers to "war-making" powers; or Walker, *Römer 13,1-3*, 40–41, that it refers to apocalyptic judgment.

133 Auguet, *Cruelty and Civilization*, 65–68.

134 Konrad Weiss, "φέρω κτλ.," *TDNT* 9 (1974) 83–84.

135 *CPJ* 2. Nr. 152.5; *PSI* 10.1100.9; *P.Tebt.* 2. Nr. 391.20; *P.Mich.* 10 Nr. 577.8; other references listed by MM 391 are *P.Amh.* 2. Nr. 38.3; *P.Oxy.* 2. Nr. 294.20.

136 Elliott, "Romans 13:1-7," 203.

137 Gottlob Schrenk, "ἐκδικέω, ἔκδικος, ἐκδίκησις," *TDNT* 2 (1964) 445; Michel, 402; Dunn, 2:764. For example, Plutarch *Garr.* 509f = *Mor.* 409f; Herodianus *Mar.* 1.14.3; 7.4.5; LXX Ps 98:8; 4 Macc 15.29.

138 Strobel, "Röm 13," 89–90; Zsifkovits, *Staatsgedanke*, 88; Horst Goldstein, "ἐκδίκησις, ἐκδικέω, ἔκδικος," *EDNT* 1 (1990) 408. Examples of "legal officer" are *I.Magn.* Nr. 93.15; Cicero *Fam.* 13.56; of "legal adviser," *P.Oxy.* 2. Nr. 261.14.

4:6; 2 Thess 1:8 have words on this stem in the basic meaning of vengeance; also, this does not require a special translation for this appearance of "wrath," which was a prominent theme in earlier chapters of Romans (1:18; 2:5, 8; 3:5; 4:15; 5:9; 9:22; 12:19).[139] The idea here is that governmental law enforcement carries out divine wrath against evildoers.[140] Paul legitimates for these governmental "servants of God" the task of vengeance that is explicitly forbidden to believers acting on their own behalf (12:17, 19).[141]

The target of wrath is the "one practicing the bad," a conventional expression for evil behavior that I discussed in 7:19. For example, LXX Prov 13:10 says "a bad man does evil ($\pi\rho\acute{\alpha}\sigma\sigma\epsilon\iota$ $\kappa\alpha\kappa\acute{\alpha}$) with insolence." The verb $\pi\rho\acute{\alpha}\sigma\sigma\omega$ ("perform, practice") usually appears in the LXX with a negative connotation,[142] which is certainly the case here. The Latin equivalent *malefacere* is a technical expression in Roman law enforcement, from which the English term "malefactor" is derived. Paul clearly implies that only criminals would be targets of such governmental vengeance, but within a few years after writing this letter a fateful travesty occurred. Tacitus reports what happened to the audience receiving Paul's letter after the terrible Roman fire in the summer of 64 C.E.: "Nero substituted as culprits (*subdidit reos*), and punished with the utmost refinements of cruelty, a class of men, loathed for their vices, whom the crowd called Christians. . . . First, then, the confessed members of the sect were arrested; next, on their disclosures, vast numbers were convicted, not so much on the count of arson as for hatred of the human race (*odio humani generis convicti sunt*). And derision accompanied their end: they were covered with wild beasts' skins and torn to death by dogs; or they were fastened on crosses, and, when daylight failed were burned to serve as lamps by night. Nero had offered his Gardens for the spectacle, and gave an exhibition in his Circus."[143] It is obvious from Paul's formulation of 13:4 that no such travesty of law enforcement was envisioned as even remotely possible. Persons other than malefactors have in fact repeatedly been targeted, so the problem with Paul's formulation should not be overlooked. Paul's clever co-optation notwithstanding, the Neronian administration showed itself to be the servant of Jupiter and Mars. Yet the rhetorical force of Paul's argument was clear for the original audience: the Spanish mission will not encourage illegal subversion against the empire, because Paul accepts the doctrine that imperial officers are divinely appointed avengers for wrath against malefactors. This formulation would have been particularly well received by the two churches situated within the imperial bureaucracy. The missional motivation of Paul's discourse may be commendable, but one cannot say the same of his assessment of the evil potential of totalitarian regimes, including the Neronian government then in power.

■ **5** Paul completes the second argument with the timid conversation partner by recapitulating the admonition to voluntary submission, in a sentence beginning with the inferential conjunction $\delta\iota\acute{o}$ ("therefore"), which I analyzed in 1:24; 2:1; and 4:22, the latter of which functions as here to draw a conclusion in the middle of an argument. In view of what has been demonstrated in the preceding verses, Paul concludes that "it is necessary to subject yourself." The word $\acute{\alpha}\nu\acute{\alpha}\gamma\kappa\eta$ is employed here in the idiomatic sense of "what is necessary" rather than in the sense of a personalized, magical fate.[144] It has the sense that subjection "is indispensable."[145] Whereas in his earlier letters Paul had used $\acute{\alpha}\nu\acute{\alpha}\gamma\kappa\eta$ as grim necessity that should be replaced by free decisions reflecting the new life in Christ (1 Cor 7:37; 2 Cor 9:7; Phlm 14),

139 See Gustav Stählin, "$\grave{o}\rho\gamma\acute{\eta}$, in the NT," *TDNT* 5 (1967) 440–41; Wilhelm Pesch, "$\grave{o}\rho\gamma\acute{\eta}$," *EDNT* 2 (1991) 530.
140 See, for example, Morris, 464.
141 Dunn, 2:765; Moo, 802.
142 Christian Maurer, "$\pi\rho\acute{\alpha}\sigma\sigma\omega$ $\kappa\tau\lambda$.," *TDNT* 6 (1968) 634, 636–37.
143 Tacitus *Ann.* 15.44; for interpretation, see Christensen, *Christus oder Jupiter*, 46–47.
144 See Walter Grundmann, "$\grave{\alpha}\nu\alpha\gamma\kappa\acute{\alpha}\zeta\omega$ $\kappa\tau\lambda$.," *TDNT* 1 (1964) 345–47; August Strobel, "$\grave{\alpha}\nu\acute{\alpha}\gamma\kappa\eta$ $\kappa\tau\lambda$.,"
EDNT 1 (1990) 77–79; Ernst Baasland, "$\grave{\alpha}\nu\acute{\alpha}\gamma\kappa\eta$ bei Paulus im Lichte eines stoischen Paradoxes," in H. Cancik, H. Lichtenberger, and P. Schäfer, eds., *Geschichte–Tradition–Reflexion. Festschrift für Martin Hengel zum 70. Geburtstag*, vol. 3, *Frühes Christentum* (Tübingen: Mohr [Siebeck], 1996) 361–65.
145 Strobel, "$\grave{\alpha}\nu\acute{\alpha}\gamma\kappa\eta$ $\kappa\tau\lambda$.," 79.

here he employs it to convey a binding necessity. Although the middle voice of the verb ὑποτάσσεσθαι is again employed, implying willing subjection as in 13:1, the combination with ἀνάγκη effectively eliminates choice or debate on the essential point.

Two considerations are offered as explanations within the framework of a "not only . . . but also" framework, employed here for the ninth and final time in the letter.[146] The first consideration is well prepared by the preceding argument: διὰ τὴν ὀργήν ("on account of the wrath") refers back to the preceding verse that described governmental authorities as servants of divine wrath. To avoid divine displeasure, conveyed in the form of official sanctions, one must submit to such authorities. The second expression διὰ τὴν συνείδησιν ("on account of the conscience") seems unmotivated in this passage and has attracted a large amount of scholarly debate. Those who understand conscience in the traditional manner of Western culture explain this expression as referring to a sense of moral responsibility,[147] to a mental agency that provides guidance to moral choice,[148] or to an understanding of the theological significance of government.[149] These options overlap and it is difficult to choose between them without recourse to one's own theological and ethical presuppositions. Moreover, these traditional explanations presuppose that συνείδησις in 13:5 is identical with that of 2:15 and 9:1. But the formulation and the context point to a very different connotation that reaches back to the beginnings of the discovery of conscience in Greco-Roman thought (ca. sixth century B.C.E.). The phrase διὰ τὴν συνείδησιν occurred in the Corinthians' letter to Paul, inquiring about whether food offered to idols should be examined "on account of the conscience" (1 Cor 10:25, 27).[150] C. A. Pierce's discovery of the "moral bad absolute" use of συνείδησις and related terms as a conscience-pang whose very presence is painful is essential to understanding this Corinthian question as well as Rom 13:5.[151] For example, Plutarch writes: "The soul of every wicked person will probably meditate thus upon the empty joylessness of vice and take counsel with itself how it may escape the memory of its ill-deeds, cast out conscience (τὸ συνειδός) and, having become pure, live another life over again from the beginning."[152] This reflects the basic phenomenon of conscience when it was first articulated, which is visible in the makeup of the words for conscience in Greek and Latin. Both συν + εἰδησις and con + science refer to the spontaneous knowledge one has *with* oneself that a deed performed is bad; such painful knowledge should be avoided, which leads to the peculiar formulations in ancient literature about avoiding "conscience" altogether, understood as the painful "conscience-pang." For instance, Diodorus Siculus *Hist.* 4.65.7 writes that after murdering his mother, Alcmaeon "on account of his conscience (διὰ τὴν συνείδησιν) over the defilement went mad." Similarly Heron *Bel.* 1.27 reports that "because of conscience (κατὰ συνείδησιν)" they remained troubled. In both of these instances, what I call the "conscience-pang" is in view. In the case of Rom 13:5, therefore, Paul is referring to the avoidance of such painful knowledge by acting in a manner consistent with the audience's grasp of the divinely appointed function of governmental authorities.[153] Whether the audience's sense of obligation with regard to these authorities

---

146 See Rom 1:32; 4:12, 16; 5:3, 11; 8:23; 9:10; 9:24; see also the use of μόνον with another antithetical formulation in 3:29.

147 Eckstein, *Syneidesis*, 287–300; Murray, 2:154; Byrne, 388.

148 Johannes Stelzenberger, *Syneidesis im Neuen Testament*, AMT 1 (Paderborn: Schöningh, 1961) 33; Margaret E. Thrall, "The Pauline Use of Συνείδησις," *NTS* 14 (1967–68) 124; Ceslas Spicq, "συνείδησις," *TLNT* 3 (1994) 335; Leenhardt, 335; Morris, 465; Ziesler, 313; Gerd Lüdemann, "συνείδησις," *EDNT* 3 (1993) 302.

149 Gutbrod, *Anthropologie*, 62; Karl H. Neufeldt, "Das Gewissen. Ein Deutungsversuch im Anschluss an Röm 13, 1-7," *BibLeb* 12 (1971) 432–45; Christian

Maurer, "σύνοιδα, συνείδησις," *TDNT* 7 (1971) 916; Walker, *Römer 13,1-7*, 46–49; Cranfield, 2:668; Wilckens, 3:36–37; Merklein, "Röm 13, 1-7," 250; Moo, 803.

150 See Jewett, *Terms*, 426–32.

151 Pierce, *Conscience*, 34–38.

152 Plutarch *Sera* 556a (Ex 5,1); translation from Pierce, *Conscience*, 34. Additional examples are Vettius Valens *Anth.* 5.1; *P.Ryl.* 2. Nr. 116.9–10; *P.Flor.* 3. Nr. 338.17.

153 Jewett, *Terms*, 440; Pierce, *Conscience*, 71 (see the critique of his formulation in Jewett, *Terms*, 412); Dunn, 3:765; see also Schlatter, 243. For a critique of my view of the "conscience-pang," see Stein, "Argument," 337–38.

derived from their background, which seems quite likely, or was decisively shaped by Paul's discourse, avoidance of a conscience-pang caused by violation was desirable. Thus Paul offers an external,[154] pragmatic motivation of avoiding wrath and an internal motivation of avoiding the conscience-pang, however it may have been socially conditioned. In the light of this background and the diatribal style of second person singular discourse, I translate the article with συνείδησις as "your [sg.] conscience." Despite the problems it caused in later ethics,[155] this verse provided additional grounds for the churches associated with the imperial bureaucracy to be willing to support Paul's project.

■ **6** In this third argument Paul addresses himself directly to the congregations in Rome with second person plural forms.[156] Having laid a foundation through the preceding discourse, he turns to the concrete issue the congregation is confronting, introduced by διὰ τοῦτο γάρ ("for this reason"), which refers back to the discussion in the previous verse[157] or verses.[158] What Paul provides are not mere illustrations[159] but the practical point of the entire discourse, namely, that despite pressures to the contrary the tribute taxes should continue to be paid.[160] The expression φόρους τελεῖτε could be translated either as an imperative, "pay tributes!"[161] or as an indicative, "you [pl.] pay tributes."[162] The word order[163] and the presence of the connective γάρ ("for")[164] point to the latter. Paul draws from the Romans' own experience the fact that the considerations of avoiding conscience-pangs and wrath mentioned in the preceding verse are already operative: the Christian audience does in fact pay the tribute taxes, and this implies that they accept the corollary that governmental officials engaged in tax collection are λειτουργοὶ θεοῦ ("ministers of God").[165] The background of this discussion of φόρους ("tribute taxes")[166] has been related by Friedrich, Pöhlmann, and Stuhlmacher[167] to the unrest in the period before 58 C.E. when a formal tax protest was brought to Nero, as reported by Tacitus *Ann.* 13.50–51:

> In the same year, as a consequence of repeated demands from the public, which complained of the exactions of the revenue-farmers (*publicanorum*), Nero hesitated whether he ought not to decree the abolition of all indirect taxation (*vectigalia*). . . . His impulse, however . . . was checked by his older advisors, who pointed out that the dissolution of the empire was certain if the revenues on which the state subsisted were to be curtailed: —"For, the moment the duties on imports (*portoriis*) were removed, the logical sequel would be a demand for the abrogation of the direct taxes (*tributorum*)." . . . The emperor, therefore, issued an edict that the regulations with regard to each tax, hitherto kept secret, should be posted for public inspection. . . . The annulment, however, of the "fortieth," "fiftieth," and other irregular exactions, for which the publicans had invented titles, is still in force.

Friedrich, Pöhlmann, and Stuhlmacher have noted that the Latin equivalent of φόρος (*tributum*) was employed by Tacitus, in distinction from import taxes (τέλος, *vecti-*

---

154 See Riekkinen, *Römer 13*, 211.

155 Leenhardt, 324, offers the most succinct summary of Paul's position: he speaks "of obedience but not of collaboration."

156 Tobin, *Paul's Rhetoric*, 396.

157 Weiss, 533; Walker, *Römer 13,1-7*, 49; Merklein, "Röm 13,1-7," 251; Riekkinen, *Römer 13*, 214.

158 See Porter, "Romans 13:1-7," 134: "because of this discussion."

159 Barrett, 247; Käsemann, 359; Porter, "Romans 13:1-7," 134.

160 Dunn, 2:766, referring to Furnish, *Moral Teaching*, 126, 131–35; Winter, "Romans 12–15," 83.

161 Meyer, 2:282, cites Tholuck, Klee, Reiche, Köllner, and Hoffman as favoring an imperative reading; see also Zahn, 559.

162 For example, Fitzmyer, 669, following most commentators.

163 Schlier, 391, points out that the imperative word order should be διὰ τοῦτο τελεῖτε καὶ φόρους.

164 See Cranfield, 2:668. Meyer, 2:282, says γάρ "might certainly be taken with the imperative," citing Rom 6:19.

165 See Merklein, "Röm 13, 1-7," 251–52; however, this assessment contradicts his actant analysis on 257 that implies the audience rejected paying their taxes.

166 Konrad Weiss, "φέρω κτλ.," *TDNT* 9 (1974) 78, notes that the φόρος is essentially "tribute to be paid by subject peoples"; Walter Rebell, "φόρος," *EDNT* 3 (1993) 436, defines this as "the direct tribute (property- or head-tax)."

gal) mentioned in 13:7c.[168] The Tacitus citation indicates, however, that the controversy in Rome concerned the import taxes rather than the tribute taxes which were imposed on captive peoples and were in principle not to be paid by Roman citizens living in certain areas outside of Rome or on the general population of Rome itself.[169]

An advance in our understanding of Rom 13:6-7 has recently been made by Thomas Coleman, who pointed out that immigrants to Rome were being compelled by the Nero administration to pay the tribute levied by the provinces in which they resided at the previous census, which would have been in 54/53 C.E.,[170] prior to the writing of Romans. This means that the tribute tax could have been levied on all those exiled from Rome by the Edict of Claudius in 49 C.E., because they were elsewhere in the empire at the time of the last census.[171] Whether this administrative crackdown included other emigrants who had resided for continuous periods in Rome still remains unclear, but there is other evidence of measures taken against people fleeing their localities to avoid onerous taxes during this period.[172] Paul's formulation clearly implies that the hearers of his letter were in fact paying the tribute tax and the fact that Paul repeats φόρος in the next verse confirms that this was the nub of the issue for the Roman congregation, consisting mainly of emigrants and noncitizens, some of whom were apparently subject to the tribute tax. However, the situation is even clearer in Spain, whose horizon is distantly visible at so many points in Romans. While it remains unclear how many participants in the Roman churches were subject to the tribute tax, the entire population of Spain carried this burden. Given the crucial importance of Spanish revenues,[173] it would have jeopardized the entire mission project if the church in Rome were to become involved in the emerging conflict over tax resistance. Inasmuch as the conflict involved resentment about Roman administration, Paul's stance would undoubtedly have been welcomed by the churches within the bureaucracy.

That the Roman tax authorities are λειτουργοὶ θεοῦ ("ministers of God") is a most surprising claim,[174] even though this word was used to refer to public officials and private citizens rendering service to the state.[175] The Latin equivalents (*ministrum, lictores, munus*) were widely employed to refer to public officials.[176] In his other letters (Phil 2:17, 25, 30; 2 Cor 9:12) and later in Romans (15:16), Paul uses "minister" and its semantic equivalents only in connection with services performed in behalf of the church. There are examples of the expression "ministers of God" in the context of cultic activities in Greco-Roman temples, as, for example, Dionysius of Halicarnassus's reference to "magistrates or the ministers of the gods" (ἄρχουσι καὶ λειτουργοῖς θεῶν) whose duties were prescribed by the Ordinances of Numa.[177] LXX Isa 61:6 promises Israel's restoration with the words, "You shall be called priests of the Lord, the ministers of God (ἱερεῖς Κυρίου κληθήσεσθε,

167 Friedrich, Pöhlmann, and Stuhlmacher, "Röm 13, 1-7," 156–60.
168 Friedrich, Pöhlmann, and Stuhlmacher, "Röm 13, 1-7," 157–59, followed by Dunn, 2:766; Byrne, 13, 388; Tobin, *Paul's Rhetoric*, 399.
169 See Coleman, "Binding Obligations," 309–13, citing P. A. Brunt, "The Revenues of Rome," in *Roman Imperial Themes* (Oxford: Clarendon, 1990) 327.
170 Coleman, "Binding Obligations," 312; S. R. Llewelyn, "Roman Administration §15," *NDIEC* 6 (1992) 113, refers to H. Braunert, "*ΙΔΙΑ*: Studien zur Bevölkerungsgeschichte des ptolemäischen und römischen Ägyptiens," *JJP* 9–10 (1955–56) 211–328, which pointed out that the Neronian administration introduced "the concept of *idia*, i.e. a person's fiscal/legal domicile or the community in which he was registered. So defined, the *idia* became the place where the individual fulfilled his obligations to the state." In "Roman Administration §16," 125–26, Llewelyn further cites Braunert, 311, to show that taxes were levied on the basis of residence at the time of the census in 54–55 C.E. or 61–62 C.E.
171 Coleman, "Binding Obligations," 313.
172 See S. R. Llewelyn, "Flight from Personal Obligations to the State," *NDIEC* 8 (1998) 97–105.
173 See Richardson, *Romans in Spain*, 70–75, 86–88, 312.
174 Schlier, 391, refers to λειτουργὸς θεοῦ as a "paradoxical, grotesque" title for a tax official.
175 Lewis, "*Leitourgia*," 175–82; Hermann Strathmann and Rudolf Meyer, "λειτουργέω κτλ.," *TDNT* 4 (1967) 229–30; Ceslas Spicq, "λειτουργέω κτλ.," *TLNT* 2 (1994) 378–80.
176 Strathmann and Meyer, "λειτουργέω κτλ.," 229, refer to Plutarch *Rom.* 26.4 (I.34b).
177 Dionysius Halicarnassus *Antiq. Rom.* 2.73.2.

λειτουργοὶ Θεοῦ)." But to refer to the tax officials of Rome as the "ministers of God" remains surprising, because the *publicani* ("revenue-farmers") mentioned in the Tacitus citation were semipublic agents who bought taxing rights at yearly auctions and earned their profit by raising more than the amounts specified in their contracts, a system notoriously subject to abuse despite the elaborate regulations developed by the imperial authorities.[178] Moreover, the gods Jupiter, Mars, Apollo, or Diana are, in Paul's formulation, not in view as assumed by the Roman civic cult, but the God and Father of Jesus Christ. That the true and only God made the *publicani* and their bureaucratic overseers into his "ministers" was an audacious act of co-optation. Whether this amounts to a sacralizing of their role[179] is debatable,[180] since all Roman public officials nominally enacted cultic functions, but Paul leaves no doubt that they are actually serving the true God. In view of the historical circumstances, it remains a breathtaking claim.

Since the phrase εἰς αὐτὸ τοῦτο ("for this very thing") in v. 6b is not in the dative to match the verb,[181] it could refer back to the details in vv. 3-4,[182] to the preceding διὰ τοῦτο in v. 6a referring to the grounds for paying taxes,[183] or qualify "ministers of God" in terms of righteous behavior.[184] None of these options provides a very smooth sense, and the suggestion that the phrase marks a transition to the imperatives in v. 7 is difficult grammatically.[185] The most plausible option was suggested by Stanley Porter, that the phrase is employed periphrastically to provide the "completive" of the participle προσκαρτεροῦντες; this would produce the translation,

the ministers of God "are devoting themselves to this very thing."[186] The verb προσκαρτερέω occurs in a variety of contexts and here has the meaning "occupy oneself diligently/eagerly,"[187] of which there are some cultic examples. For instance, Antiochos I of Kommagene commanded the priest responsible for the preservation of his burial site as follows: "Let him in liberation from all other duties or obligations, and without evasion, eagerly occupy himself at this sacred burial place and give thought to his service and the appropriate adornment of these sacred images."[188] The same sense is captured in Diodorus Siculus *Hist.* 3.12.3 in describing condemned prisoners who "are diligently devoted to their tasks (προσκαρτεροῦσι τοῖς ἔργοις συνεχῶς) day and night without cease."[189] The implication of Paul's wording is that taxes must be paid because the imperial agents entrusted with this task are eagerly pursuing their vocation. Whether this carries the covert implication that public officials "ought to behave in a way worthy of God's 'officials,'"[190] or that Paul wishes to promote "the ideal . . . of dedicated public service,"[191] seems doubtful in view of Paul's missional goals in this letter and his apocalyptic expectation of a quick end to world history. However, this formulation would have been rhetorically appealing to the portion of his audience engaged in the imperial bureaucracy. As a *captatio benevolentio*, it is understandable as serving Paul's immediate purpose, but in view of the eager depredations of Roman tax farmers, it remains problematic. The vivid description by Naphtali Lewis of conditions in Egypt, based on extensive papyri evidence not available elsewhere in the

---

178 See S. R. Llewelyn, "Tax Collection and the τελῶναι of the New Testament," *NDIEC* 8 (1998) 47–76.

179 See Meyer, 282; Romeo, "ΛΕΙΤΟΥΡΓΙΑ," 184–85, citing A. van Veldhuizen, "Wie zijn λειτουργοὶ ϑεοῦ in Rom 13,6," *ThSt*(U) 32 (1914) 302–11; Walker, *Römer 13, 1-7*, 51–54; Black, 183.

180 Strobel, "Röm 13," 86–87; Riekkinen, *Römer 13,* 214.

181 See Dunn, 2:767.

182 Barrett, 247.

183 Walker, *Römer 13,1-7*, 53, citing Otto, 395; Tholuck, 692–93.

184 Walter Grundmann, "προσκαρτερέω," *TDNT* 3 (1965) 618; Ludwig Gaugusch, "Die Staatslehre des Apostels Paulus nach Röm 13," *ThGl* 26 (1934) 544.

185 Riekkinen, *Römer 13*, 215; see the critique in Dunn, 2:767.

186 Porter, "Romans 13:1-7," 135; this appears close to Cranfield's preference (2:669) that the phrase refers "to the receiving of taxes." See also Murray, 2:155; Fitzmyer, 669.

187 Grundmann, "προσκαρτερέω," 618; Horst Balz and Gerhard Schneider, eds., "προσκαρτερέω," *EDNT* 3 (1993) 172.

188 Cited by Danker, *Benefactor*, 240, from *SIG* 383.130.

189 See also Diodorus Siculus *Hist.* 3.13.3; 3.17.1; Plutarch *Frag.* 43.13.

190 Cranfield, 2:699; Porter, "Romans 13:1-7," 135.

191 Dunn, 2:767.

empire, throws light on what προσκαρτεροῦντες ("diligently devoting themselves") actually implied for the situation in Rome: "The system of farming out the collection of taxes to the highest bidder . . . was an open invitation to corruption. Once his bid had been accepted and he had contracted to pay the government the proffered lump sum, the first aim and overriding purpose of every tax-farmer was to show a profit in his enterprise. . . . once the contract was safely in his pocket he did not hesitate to employ any and all means, illegal as well as legal, to maximize his profit by wrestling excessive and extortionate payments from his hapless and helpless victims. Such overbearing and violent behaviour was facilitated by the fact that collectors were frequently accompanied, ostensibly for their protection, by soldiers or armed guards, whom they could and did use to intimidate and maltreat the taxpayers."[192]

■ **7** The final verse in the pericope is in asyndetic style, a highly compressed gnomic saying that summarizes the basic contention of the passage.[193] The imperative ἀπόδοτε, which I discussed in 12:17 with the literal sense of "give back" in kind, is here employed in the sense of "pay, pay back," which implies a response to social obligations such as taxes and respect.[194] This verb is often used in the Gospels to depict payment of debts or taxes (Matt 5:26; 18:25-34; Mark 12:17; Luke 7:42; 10:35; 12:59; 19:8), with the most-discussed parallel being "Give back to Caesar what is Caesar's" (Mark 12:17 and parallels). Direct dependency on this logion[195] is not required,[196] in part because this verb is a typical word choice carried over from the classical world. Menander

Mon. 1.3.7 teaches, "Receive, give back (ἀπόδος), and you will receive again." In *Op.* 349, Hesiod urges, "Receive fairly from your neighbor, and give back fairly with the same measure (ἀποδοῦναι αὐτῷ τῷ μέτρῳ), and more, if you are able." In *Vitae philos.* 1.785, Diogenes Laertius advises, "What you have received in deposit, give back (ἀποδοῦναι)," and he reports in *Vit.* 3.83 that Plato taught, "Those paying back (ἀποδιδόντες) debts and deposits practice justice in respect of people." The implication in Romans is that since the governmental authorities serve "you" (13:4) as God's ministers, reciprocity is required by those receiving such benefits. We shall encounter the same logic in 15:27, that since the Gentile Christians are in debt to the Jewish Christians for "their spiritual blessings," it is right that they should reciprocate "in material blessings" in the form of the Jerusalem offering. The noun ὀφειλή ("obligation, debt") fits into this reciprocity framework, implying something owed in return for something already received.[197] To whom this indebtedness is owed remains a matter of dispute, with πᾶσιν ("to all") implying, as earlier in Romans, everyone everywhere,[198] or, as seems much more likely, every governmental officer as specified in the fourfold description in v. 7b.[199] To take "everyone" literally here reaches beyond the scope of this passage and implies the absurdity of owing tribute and import taxes to someone other than the governmental authorities. Furthermore, to propose that "everyone" includes God, on the grounds that fear and honor are only properly due to him,[200] is a theological assessment that is far removed from the logic of this passage. Paul's

---

192 Llewelyn, "Tax Collection," 68, cited from Naphtali Lewis, *Life in Egypt under Roman Rule* (Oxford, 1983) 160–61. Lewis, 69, provides an example (*P.Oxy* 2. Nr. 393 = *SB* 14. Nr. 11902.7–9) of a petition to the emperor Claudius by a man who claims, "I have suffered extortion by Damis, former tax collector (Διεσίσθην ὑπὸ Δάμιτος γενομένου πράκτορος) . . . to the amount of sixteen silver drachmae. . . ."

193 Schlier, 392.

194 See Friedrich Büchsel, "δίδωμι κτλ.," *TDNT* 2 (1964) 167; Alexander Sand, "ἀποδίδωμι," *EDNT* 1 (1990) 128.

195 Michel, 403; Black, 161; Neugebauer, "Röm 13,1-7," 165; Cranfield, 2:669; Wilckens, 3:38; Stuhlmacher, 204; Thompson, *Clothed with Christ*, 112–16.

196 Käsemann, 352; Riekkinen, 89–90; Neirynck, "Paul and the Sayings of Jesus," 291.

197 See Friedrich Hauck, "ὀφείλω κτλ.," *TDNT* 5 (1967) 560, 564; Michael Wolter, "ὀφειλέτης κτλ.," *EDNT* 2 (1991) 550.

198 Weiss, 535, following Reiche and others; see also Lipsius, 170.

199 Meyer, 283; Godet, 445; Walker, *Römer 13,1-7*, 54; Murray, 2:155; Merklein, "Röm 13,1-7," 252; Moo, 805.

200 Cranfield, 1:267–72; with qualifications, Porter, "Romans 13:1-7," 136.

admonition is simply that believers are obligated to pay whatever is owed to the authorities who serve as God's ministers.

The form of the final lines in this pericope is compressed, succinct, and correlative. In each of four examples, governmental obligations are to be paid to those who qualify. Helmut Merklein aptly refers to the "conditionality" of this formulation.[201] Instead of absolute subservience, obligations are to be met if they prove legitimate. The formulation leaves space for assessments of appropriateness made by the community, as defined in 12:1-2. The first two examples are ὁ φόρος ("the tribute tax") and τὸ τέλος ("the custom tax"), which come out of the preceding discussion. In contrast to ὁ φόρος, which was imposed as tribute to be carried to Rome by captive peoples,[202] τὸ τέλος is a generic term referring to a wide range of import and use taxes levied by the government.[203] S. L. Llewelyn refers to more than a hundred different taxes "on land, grain, animal, capitation, trade, customs, transport, manumission etc."[204] Paul's formulation implies that these taxes were to be paid to whomever they were due, reflecting the various tax farmers and civic administrators responsible for each type of tax. While the poetic structure of v. 7b is quite elegant, the terminology is characteristic of everyday usage. For example, Josephus reports that Gaius required the inhabitants of Judea "to pay tribute" (τὸν φόρον ἀποδιδῶσι) consisting of one-fourth of the agricultural product.[205]

The last two examples are φόβος ("fear, respect") and τιμή ("honor"), the first repeating the term from v. 3, but with a different connotation. A distinction between two types of fear appears to surface here. Here is the section of Pseudo-Aristotle first cited in this connection by August Strobel where the distinction was made:[206] "There are two forms of fear: the one that honorable and respectful sons display to their fathers and honorable, decent citizens display to right-minded rulers; but the other comes from enmity and hate, such as slaves feel about their masters and citizens about unjust and unworthy rulers." In contrast to v. 3 where subordinate fear is required, v. 7 appears to reflect Aristotle's first type of φόβος. It is similar to the respect recommended by Prov 24:21, φοβοῦ τὸν Θεὸν υἱέ, καὶ βασιλέα ("My son, fear God and king"). Similarly, Paul uses "fear of the Lord" (2 Cor 5:11) in a positive sense with reference to his own apostolic motivation,[207] but Rom 13:7 is the only instance where such respectful φόβος is recommended by him toward humans. Strobel argues that respect for imperial agents had become a matter of law in the closing years of the Claudius administration when financial administrators were given judicial powers equal to that of the emperor.[208] In the period after this ruling (53 C.E.), citizens were required to have the same φόβος for imperial administrators as for Caesar himself,[209] so Paul's wording becomes understandable when compared with other references restricting such fear to divine forces.[210] "Respect" in this sense is the acknowledgment of legitimate jurisdiction, which in the context of governmental powers of taxation meant accepting the right of the "ministers of God" to assess and collect what was due.

201 Merklein, "Röm 13, 1-7," 266.
202 An example from earlier Greek culture is reported by Isocrates *Panath.* 116.8f., that the Athenians were forcing other Greek cities "to pay contributions and tribute monies (συντάξεις καὶ φόρους ἀποτελεῖν)."
203 See LSJM 1773.6: "dues exacted by the state"; Gerhard Delling, "τέλος κτλ.," *TDNT* 8 (1972) 51: "obligation to do certain things for the state . . . tax"; Hans Hübner, "τέλος," *EDNT* 3 (1993) 347.
204 Llewelyn, "Roman Administration §15," 113; Llewelyn, "Tax Collection," 67–68, describes the administrative methods used to collect these various taxes. See also Ramsay MacMullen, "Tax-Pressure in the Roman Empire," *Lat* 46 (1978) 737–54.
205 Josephus *Ant.* 14.203; see also Josephus *C. Ap.* 1.119 and Thucydides *Hist.* 5.18.
206 Strobel, "Furcht," 60, cited from Pseudo-Aristotle *Oec.* 3.3. See also Balz and Wanke, "φοβέω κτλ.," 194; Coleman, "Binding Obligations," 316–17.
207 Balz, "φόβος," 433.
208 Strobel, "Furcht," 61, citing Tacitus *Ann.* 12.60; Suetonius *Claud.* 12.
209 See Lendon, *Empire of Honour*, 34, cited by Coleman, "Binding Obligations," 318.
210 For example, Rom 3:18; 11:20; 2 Cor 5:11; 7:1, 11; Phil 2:12. See Cranfield's extensive discussion of this problem (2:669–73), resulting in the suggestion criticized above that φόβος in this verse was intended to be reserved only for God. Others are troubled by the seeming contradiction in Paul's recommendation of "fear" for governmental authorities: Lenski, 801; Byrne, 389.

This would have been a matter of considerable significance for the Christian groups in Rome.

In contrast, τιμή ("honor") is a matter not of acknowledging jurisdiction but of recognizing superior status and good performance. That it was thought to be due to the emperor and his subordinates was self-evident in the honor–shame system that unified the Greco-Roman world,[211] so long as the good was being achieved and benefits received.[212] Honor was earned by "virtue, kinship, public service," according to Plutarch, and to fail to grant τιμή in such cases is to deprive a person "of his accustomed honor" (τῆς συνήθους τιμῆς).[213] With regard to the honors due to Roman emperors, Philo claimed that they "are superior to the Ptolemies in prestige and fortune and deserve to receive superior honors (μειζόνων δὲ καὶ τιμῶν τυγχάνειν ὀφείλουσιν).[214] Richard Shaller and J. E. Lendon have shown that the granting of honors stood at the center of Rome's imperial system, and that honoring emperors and their representatives was a crucial social obligation.[215] It was also a means to influence the government in favor of the subjects granting such honor.[216] The wording of the final line in 13:7 seems particularly to embody the voluntary component of ὑποτάσσεσθαι ("to subject oneself to"); only those worthy of honor are to be granted it and honor is to be granted only when it serves the interest of the subject. The element of discretion implicit in this entire ethic is informed by 12:1-2, which assigns early church groups the task as ascertaining the will of God by weighing "the good, the acceptable, and the perfect." However, it remains noteworthy that at this point, Paul reverts to the cultural stereotypes, and abandons the revolutionary approach to honor visible in the preceding chapters, where in the light of Christ, the dishonored receive honor and the socially inferior are granted precedence. If Paul's motivation for this discourse was missional, as we have attempted to show, the irony is particularly acute. For the sake of the proclamation of Christ crucified, who overturned the honor system and rendered Paul a debtor to "Greeks as well as barbarians, educated as well as uneducated" (1:14), in Rome as well as Spain, Paul was willing to accept the system that demanded honor for the emperor and his officials whether they deserved it or not. It seems that in his view, the mission would have no chance of extending its transformation of the sinful system of honor clear to the end of the known world without giving honor to whomever honor was due. This pericope is an excruciating example of Paul's willingness to be in the world but not of the world, to reside between the ages,[217] to be all things to all people, all for the sake of the gospel. But the paradox needs to be named and acknowledged that Rom 13:1-7 has provided the basis for propaganda by which the policies of Mars and Jupiter have frequently been disguised as serving the cause of Christ, thus evoking the ongoing controversy that the exegetical literature has reflected.

---

211 See Danker, *Benefactor*, 30–44, 213–33, 467–68; Lendon, *Empire of Honour*, 73.

212 See Johannes Schneider, "τιμή, τιμάω," *TDNT* 8 (1972) 170–72.

213 Plutarch *Quaest. conv.* 617C; see also Plutarch *Phil.* 21.12.6.

214 Philo *Legat.* 10.140, cited by Coleman, "Binding Obligations," 321.

215 Richard Saller, "Poverty, Honor and Obligation in Imperial Rome," *Criterion* [University of Chicago] 37 (1998) 12–20; Lendon, *Empire of Honour*, 30–175.

216 Lendon, *Empire of Honour*, 201–22.

217 Käsemann, 359; Sampley, *Walking*, 26, 111–12.

13

The Fifth Pericope

The Admonition to Fulfill Law through the Agape Meal

8/ **Owe[a] no one anything, except to love one another; for the one who loves the other has fulfilled the law.[b] 9/ For[c] [there is] the [commandment],**
> **"You shall not commit adultery,**
> **You shall not murder,**
> **You shall not steal,[d]**
> **You shall not covet,"**

and if [there is] any other commandment it is summed up in[e] the [saying][f]
> **"You shall love your neighbor as yourself."[g]**

10/ **The agape does[h] no evil to the neighbor; therefore the agape is law's fulfillment.**

a   In place of the strongly attested imperative form ὀφείλετε ("to owe, be obligated to do"), there are several variants that reflect efforts at stylistic improvement: ℵ² has the subjunctive form ὀφείλητε, which carries the sense of "you ought not owe," a slight orthographic variation, while ℵ* Ψ 945 *pc* have the participle ὀφείλοντες ("owing"), which subordinates v. 8 to the command to be obligated to pay taxes in Rom 13:7.

b   An alternate translation, to be weighed below, is "the one who loves fulfills the other law."

c   In place of the article τό ("the [commandment]"), F G b provide the word γέγραπται ("it has been written"), an obvious effort at stylistic improvement.

d   The addition of οὐ ψευδομαρτυρήσεις ("you shall not bear false witness") found in ℵ (P has the subjunctive, οὐ ψευδομαρτυρήσῃς, here and in the other three verbs) 048 69 81 88 104 256 263 323 326 330 365 424 436 451 459 629 945 1243 1319 1506 1573 1852 1912 1962 2127 (1505 2495 place οὐ ψευδομαρτυρήσεις after οὐκ ἐπιθυμήσεις) *pm* ar b vg^cl sy^(h),pal bo arm eth slav Or^lat1/6 appears to be a later addition to bring Paul's text into conformity with OT formulations of the commandments.

See Metzger, *Textual Commentary*, 467; Cranfield, 2:677. The text without the addition is strongly supported by P⁴⁶ A B D F G L Ψ 6 33 181 614 630 1175 1241 1735 1739 1836 1874 1877 1881 2200 2344 2492 *pm Lect* d f g o vg^ww, st sy^p sa geo Cl^1/2 Bas Ambst Ambr Hier^1/2 Pel Aug^8/15. Additional minor variants are the omission of οὐκ ἐπιθυμήσεις by 1734 1984* Chr^1/2 Hier^1/2; the omission of οὐκ ἐπιθυμήσεις by Or^lat1/6 Hes^lat Aug^7/15; and the lack of both phrases in Chr^1/2.

e   The reversal of "this" and "word" in A L P Ψ 048 6 33 88 323 326 424 614 945 1175 1241 1506^(acc. to Swanson) 1735 1836 2344 *Maj* lat Cl is not strongly enough attested to be original. The sequence ἐν τῷ λόγῳ τούτῳ ("in word this") is strongly supported by P⁴⁶ ℵ B D F G 69 81 104 330 365 630 1243 1319 1505 1506^(acc. to N-A) 1573 1739 1881 2495 *al* ar.

f   The deletion of ἐν τῷ ("in the") by P^46vid B F G would eliminate a redundancy. This reading is favored by Michel, 327, and Cranfield, 2:677, while the Nestle-Aland^26/27 text is undecided, placing the words in brackets. On grounds of favoring the more difficult and awkward reading, and since it is hard to imagine a motivation for these words to be added later, it seems more likely that they are original. The inclusion of "in the" is supported by ℵ A D L P Ψ 048 6 33 69 88 104 323 326 330 365 424 614 945 1175 1241 1243 1319 1505 1506 1573 1735 1739 1836 1874 1881 2344 2495 *Maj* sy^h cop Cl.

g   The reading ἑαυτόν ("oneself") in F G L P Ψ 33 69 104^(acc. to N-A) 330 365 614 945* 1175 1241 1243 1319 1506 1573 1881 2344 *pm* appears to reflect a stylistic preference discussed by BAGD 212, section 2; it is clearly an inferior reading. The word σεαυτόν ("yourself") is strongly supported by P⁴⁶ ℵ A B D 048 6 81 88 104^(acc. to Swanson) 323 326 424 945^c 1505 1735 1739 1836 1874 2495 *pm* Cl.

h   The reading οὐ κατεργάζεται ("it does not accomplish") in D* 33 365 945 1243 1505 1739 1881 2495 *al* appears to be a secondary refinement produced by making a compound verb out of the original text οὐκ ἐργάζεται ("it does not do") as found in all the other manuscripts.

Analysis

This brief section is a symmetrically constructed, self-contained admonition concerning love as law's fulfillment. Although the opening maxim is linked with the foregoing verse by the term "obligation" in 13:8, and with the earlier admonition to genuine love in 12:9, this pericope is quite independent in structure and rationale.[1] The double-lined strophes of vv. 8 and 10 are exactly parallel to each other, with the first lines stressing love to the neighbor and the second lines clarifying love as the "fulfillment of law."[2] Verse 9 contains five quotations from the law, in which the last sums up the first four as well as the entire law. Four symmetrically expressed commandments from the LXX are selected for this series, lending a high degree of coherence by the paronomasia of the repeated $οὐ$ ("not"). This pentadic series honors "Judaic stylistic preferences"[3] by constituting a demi-decalogue, a Christian embodiment of the whole law. The final verse provides a formal recapitulation in chiastic form, moving from $ἡ ἀγάπη$ ("the agape/love feast") in the opening words to $ἡ ἀγάπη$ in the final words,[4] redefining love in relation to law. The logic of this passage fits the repeated contention in Romans that believers are to fulfill the law even though they cannot be saved by virtue of conforming to it.

Rhetorical Disposition

IV.	The *probatio*
12:1–15:13	The fourth proof: Living together according to the gospel so as to sustain the hope of global transformation
13:8-10	5. The admonition to fulfill the law through the agape meal
13:8	a. Law and the obligation of mutual love
13:8a	1) The admonition to follow the obligation to love one another
13:8b	2) The rationale concerning love of the "other" as fulfillment of the law
13:9	b. Elaboration of the definition by means of commandments
13:9a-e	1) Examples of commandments
13:9a	(a) The first citation of the commandment about adultery
13:9b	(b) The second citation of the commandment about murder
13:9c	(c) The third citation of the commandment about stealing
13:9d	(d) The fourth citation of the commandment about coveting
13:9e-f	(e) All commandments are summed up in the fifth citation of the commandment about love of the neighbor
13:10	c. Recapitulation of the ethical definition
13:10a	1) The agape does nothing bad ($κακός$; see 12:9, 21; 13:3) to the neighbor
13:10b	2) The agape meal is law's fulfillment

Exegesis

■ **8** The admonition to love one another begins with the theme of obligation developed in 13:7. The maxims in these two verses follow the pattern of "antilogical $γνῶμαι$" found in classical Greek collections.[5] Whereas 13:7 urged "Render to all what is obligated," 13:8 insists that believers should "owe no one anything." The expression $μηδενὶ μηδὲν ὀφείλετε$ ("owe no one anything") employs a conventional expression for monetary or social indebtedness, as the parallels indicate.[6] The expression $ὀφείλω τινί$ was the typical expression for "I have debts with someone"[7] while $μηδὲν ὀφείλω$ meant "he owes nothing."[8] Adolf Strobel pointed to a striking parallel in a grave inscription that celebrated a Roman woman of pagan background who "lived well and owed no one anything" ($καλῶς βιώσασα, μηδενὶ μηδὲν ὀφείλουσα$).[9] This widely shared value of being free of debts is also expressed in a letter from a young man to his mother: "Don't you know that I would rather become a cripple than to owe a man even an obolos?"[10] The famous saying of Philemon Comic was "I ask first, health, then success, third, to be happy, last to owe nobody ($ὀφείλειν μηδενί$)."[11] Paul's admonition extends this traditional reluctance to incur debt into all areas of life with the word $μηδέν$ ("anything"), which

1   See Michel, 408.
2   See Weiss, "Beiträge," 245. Louw, 2:125, argues in contrast for a chiastic structure beginning with 13:8b matching 13:10b, with the material in between reiterating love of the neighbor, but this appears to overlook the parallel structure within 13:8 and 10.
3   See Jewett, "Numerical Sequences," 234–35.
4   See Ortkemper, *Leben*, 131, and Dunn, 2:775; Anselm L. Bencze, "An Analysis of 'Romans xiii. 8-10,'" *NTS* 20 (1973–74) 91.
5   See John Barns, "A New Gnomologium: With Some Remarks on Gnomic Anthologies, II," *CQ* 45 (1951) 3, discusses Plutarch *Quo. adoles.* §4 (20c), who presents "opposite points of view on a given subject" as an educational technique.
6   See Friedrich Hauck, "$ὀφείλω κτλ.$," *TDNT* 5 (1967) 559–60; BAGD 598–99.
7   *BGU* 1. Nr. 36,6; also Matt 18:28-30; Phlm 18.
8   MM 468, citing from *P.Oxy.* 7. Nr. 1067.13–14.
9   Cited by Strobel, "Röm 13," 92, from *IGRom,* 1.104.
10 Cited from *BGU* 3. Nr. 846.15–16 by Wilckens, 3:67.
11 Cited in Lucian of Samosata *Laps.* 6.17.

includes the list of taxes, customs, respect, and honor owed in v. 7. These and all other obligations are to be met, taken care of, paid off, so that believers are free to devote themselves to their new obligations.[12] This implies the avoidance of falling under the control of creditors or remaining entangled with patrons that might erode the capacity of the members of house and tenement churches to shape their common life in Christ. This counsel is consistent with Paul's preference to avoid dependency relations, except for radical dependency as a slave of Christ, visible in 1 Corinthians 9, 1 and 2 Thessalonians, and Philippians 4.[13] He wants believers to be slaves of no human, if they can avoid it,[14] indebted only to mutual love. Their former social obligations are to be replaced by a single new obligation to meet the needs of fellow members in the church.

The puzzle about the admonition in 13:8a is whether the exception clause (ϵi μὴ τὸ ἀλλήλους ἀγαπᾶν) was meant to be understood antithetically ("but you ought to love one another")[15] or inclusively ("except to love one another"), which is the more natural and convincing option.[16] A new obligation is to replace the social dependency on patrons or families, namely, ἀλλήλους ἀγαπᾶν ("to love one another"). The succinct formulation signifies a well-known command,[17] which has numerous parallels in Greek, Jewish, and Apocalyptic literature.[18] For instance, Zebulun urges his descendants to follow the example of Joseph being reconciled with his brothers: ". . . do you also, my children, approve yourselves without malice, and love one another (ἀγαπᾶτε ἀλλήλους); and do not set down in account, each one of you, evil against his brother" (T. Zeb. 8:5).[19] Similarly, the Damascus document found at Qumran exhorts the members of the community to show mutual love: "Each one should love his brother as himself (לאהוב איש את אחיהו כמהו). Accept the suffering and poor and strangers. Let each one seek the well-being of his brothers" (CD 6:20–21).[20] The Greek parallels use ἀγαπᾶν in the sense of "cherish" in the context of friendship, as, for instance, Appian's maxim φίλους ἀγάπα [variant σχεῖν] ἐσθλοὺς ἢ χρήματα ("cherish fine friends rather than money," 2.2.20). An example in which "love/cherish" between friends appears in close proximity with "another" (ἀλλήλους) is Isocrates Dem. 1: πολὺ δὲ μέγιστην διαφερὰν εἰλήφασιν ἐν ταῖς πρὸς ἀλλήλους συνηθείαις. οἱ μὲν γὰρ φίλους

---

12 Morris, 467, observes that the present imperative form of the verb "will have a continuous force: 'Don't continue owing. Pay your debts.'" The status of debt, however, places one under a continuous state of owing, which requires the present imperative.

13 See Martin's discussion of this issue in *Slavery as Salvation*, 126–35.

14 See Jewett, *Apostle to America*, chapter 6.

15 Fridrichsen provides a penetrating analysis of the issue in "Paulusbriefen," 294–97, concluding that Theodoret, Fritzsche, and Bernhard Weiß were correct in perceiving a subjective obligation in v. 8b as opposed to the objective indebtedness in v. 8a. The verse thus contains "a simple and natural wordplay" on the term "obligation" (297). He was followed by Willi Marxsen, "Der ἕτερος νόμος Röm 13,8," *ThZ* 11 (1955) 235–36; Barrett, 250; Hauck, "ὀφείλω κτλ.," 564; and Ortkemper, *Leben*, 126f. Schlier, 294, also appears to favor this option.

16 Most commentators since Origen, Chrysostom, Pelagius, and Bengel have accepted this alternative that retains the ordinary translation of εἰ μή as "except" (BDF §376, 423.3). The most cogent argument for this is in Cranfield, 2:674, who shows that the antithetical option requires the verb ὀφειλέω to be supplied in v. 8b in a different sense and mood, which is highly improbable: it would appear in 8a as "owe" and in v. 8b as "ought to be obligated." For the articular infinitive clause τὸ ἀλλήλους ἀγαπᾶν, see BDF §§398–99.

17 BDF §399.1; see also Thompson, *Clothed with Christ*, 123.

18 See Thompson, *Clothed with Christ*, 123–24.

19 See also T. Sim. 4.7, Καὶ ὑμεῖς, τέκνα μου, ἀγαπήσατε ἕκαστος τὸν ἀδελφὸν αὐτοῦ ἐν ἀγαθῇ καρδίᾳ ("So also, my children, love each one his brother with a good heart"); T. Gad 6.1, ἀγαπᾶτε ἕκαστος τὸν πλησίον αὐτοῦ ("love each one his neighbor"); 7.7, "love one another (ἀγαπήσατε ἀλλήλους) with uprightness of heart"; T. Jos. 17.2, "Also therefore love one another (ἀγαπήσατε ἀλλήλους) and with long-suffering hide one another's shortcomings."

20 See also 1QS 8:2; Josephus *Bell.* 2.119 describes the Essenes as showing "a greater attachment to each other (φιλάλληλοι) than do the other sects."

παρόντασμόνον τιμῶσιν, οἱ δὲ καὶ μακρὰν ἀπόντας ἀγαπῶσι ("... in our social affairs toward one another can be perceived. For one group honors only friends who are present, the other loves/cherishes them even when they are quite far away.")

Particularly in comparison with the classical Greek examples, it is crucial for the interpretation of this pericope to clarify the social context of Paul's formulaic obligation. That Paul has in mind the new obligation to love the members of one's house or tenement church as the new fictive family in which believers are embedded is strongly indicated by the wording of this verse and close parallels elsewhere in the Pauline letters (1 Thess 3:12; 2 Thess 1:3; 4:9; Gal 5:13).[21] "One another" clearly refers to fellow believers, as Zahn, Lietzmann, and others have shown.[22] We have encountered such "one another" sayings repeatedly in Romans (1:12; 12:5, 10, 16), referring to fellow believers,[23] as in the later sayings (Rom 14:13, 19; 15:5, 7, 14; 16:16). Most commentators are inclined to improve Paul's ethic by including "all with whom the Roman Christians would come in contact," to use Dunn's expansive phrasing.[24] This overlooks the transparent meaning of the expression "one another." When Paul wishes to address the attitude of believers toward outsiders, he refers to strangers (12:13), persecutors (12:14), "all" (12:18), or "enemies" (12:20). No, the appropriate social context of the love ethic in this section is the small Christian congregations in Rome, and, more concretely, the love feasts and sacramental celebra-

tions in which members shared resources.[25] This context, which was natural and close at hand for the early church—but alien and unacknowledged in the orientation of most later scholars—renders it unnecessary to theorize about a *debitum immortale* ("eternal debt")[26] that can never be paid since it is owed to all people everywhere.[27] There is no indication in any of Paul's references to love that it was a boundless and thus impossible burden. That misconception is due to the social decontextualization of Paul's ethic in the mainstream of the interpretive tradition, replacing it with elaborate intellectual constructs that have boundless implications and hence contain the convenient corollary of never being capable of actualization. There is not a shred of support in this pericope for this expansive and finally evasive understanding of love. The obligation to love fellow believers is advocated in a self-evident and unambiguous manner, on the presumption that its motivation was understood by the hearers. It had been reiterated by the earlier chapters of Romans; Paul refers, in Dunn's words, to "a responsive obligation . . . which arises from what those addressed have received" from God,[28] namely, love shown to the ungodly through the gospel that calls hearers into new communities based on love.[29]

There is a translation problem in v. 8b, which provides a rationale for the preceding clause as indicated by the presence of γάρ ("for"). It is possible to translate τὸν ἕτερον νόμον in an adjectival sense referring to "the other law." The problem is where to place the pause or

21 There is a need for a study that traces the trajectory of these sayings concerning the obligation to love one another, including 1 John 4:11 and the admonitions without the word "obligation" in John 13:34; 1 John 3:11, 23; 4:7; 1 Pet 1:22. For a start in this direction, see Bartchy, "Siblings," 68–78.

22 Zahn, 562; Lietzmann, 112; Lagrange, 315; Wilckens, 3:68.

23 The single pejorative use of a "one another" sayings was analyzed in 1:27, where pagans are accused of mutual passion.

24 Dunn, 2:776; he acknowledges, however, that "the exhortation elsewhere would normally refer to fellow Christians" and concludes that "it would be best to say that Paul has fellow believers particularly in view but not in any exclusive way." Fitzmyer, 678, takes the same line, apparently in an attempt to make Paul appear less narrowly sectarian.

25 See Pervo, "Panta Koina," 192.

26 The concept of an "eternal debt" is from Bengel, *Gnomon*, 144.

27 See Marxsen, "Röm 13,8," 236, referring to Gaugler, 2:295; Cranfield, 2:675; Morris, 467f.

28 Dunn, 2:776. Fitzmyer, 677, argues that Paul's formulation is an "oxymoron, for love cannot be 'owed,'" but this overlooks the earlier argument of the letter that the love of Christ places believers under a mutual obligation to love one another, to redeem the love debt, so to speak.

29 See also Furnish's somewhat more individualistic statement of this point in *Love*, 100: "Rather, the obligation to 'love one another' inheres in what God has done, in the new life he has granted the believer in Christ."

comma, whether after τὸν ἕτερον, producing the translation "the one who loves the other," or after ἀγαπῶν, resulting in the translation "the one who loves, fulfills the other law." The latter translation could refer to the Mosaic covenant, compared either with the law of love to be mentioned in 13:10,[30] or with Roman law alluded to in 13:1-7.[31] Some identify the "other law" as the law of love in v. 8a.[32] Since the term "law" does not appear in 13:1-7, some commentators assume that the reference in 13:8 must refer to the Jewish Torah because the context does not clearly indicate otherwise.[33] The reference to the "other law in my members" (7:23), referring to the law of sin, would make a confusing counterpart to any reference to "another law" here in 13:8. Although either translation is possible, I prefer "the one who loves the other has fulfilled the law."[34] Since Paul frequently refers to other people with the term ἕτερος,[35] it is likely that he wished to refer to the person being loved, with the expression τὸν ἕτερον ("the other") functioning as the object of the participial expression ὁ ἀγαπῶν ("the one who loves").[36] A further consideration was pointed out by Zahn, that the expected object of the verb ἀγαπάω is either "brother" or "neighbor,"[37] which raises the question about the nuance that Paul intends in the odd choice

of the term "other." That it refers to a fellow believer is indicated by the expression "love one another" in v. 8a, for which v. 8b provides the justification.

Paul's choice of the word "other," rather than "neighbor" or "brother," opens the door to consider the obligation to love believers beyond one's small circle[38] of the house or tenement church. This fits perfectly into the context, because mutual acceptance of members and leaders from other Christian groups was a significant problem in Rome. This subtle widening of the love command to include the "other" Christian in v. 8b thus opens the door to the topic directly addressed in 14:1–16:23, the welcome of persons identified as the "weak."

Love between believers is presented in v. 8b as the law's fulfillment, which is usually assumed to be a typically Jewish expression for Torah observance.[39] Paul had used a similar expression in Gal 5:14, "For the whole law is fulfilled in one word: 'you shall love your neighbor as yourself.'"[40] The use of πληρόω ("fulfill") in this context, however, appears to be distinctively early Christian, probably shaped by a polemical interaction with Jewish demands to "do" or "perform" the Torah.[41] The closest parallels to the use of "fulfill" both in Pauline rhetoric and in Matt 5:17 are in Greco-Roman rather than in

---

30 Hofman, 542–43; Zahn, 562–63.

31 The most extensive case has been developed by Willi Marxsen in "Der ἕτερος νόμος Röm 13,8," ThZ 11 (1955) 230–37. He argues that the word "other" is never used as the object of the verb "love" in the other Pauline letters and is more frequently used in the adjectival than the substantive sense. Leenhardt, 337–38, modifies this by perceiving a contrast between the Mosaic law, summed up in love, and the Roman law of 13:1-7.

32 See Walter Gutbrod, "νόμος κτλ.," TDNT 4 (1967) 1071.

33 See Cranfield, 2:675; Michel, 409; Wilckens, 3:68; Ortkemper, Leben, 128f.; Dunn, 2:776–77.

34 This translation is more natural because ἀγαπᾶν all but requires a direct object, since love is an emotion directed toward another. See Zahn, 562.

35 Ortkemper, Leben, 128, points to Rom 2:1, 21; 1 Cor 6:1; 10:24, 29; 14:17; Gal 6:4; Phil 2:4, but it should be acknowledged that Paul uses ἕτερος in Rom 7:3, 4 to refer to "others" who are not members of the community.

36 See Daniel García Hughes, "Nota breve. Rom. 13,8b," EstBib 2 (1943) 308.

37 Zahn, 562. In contrast, the Delphic Precept, φιλίαν

ἀγάπα ("Love friendship!" Precepta Delphica I.9, in SIG 1268), advises love between friends.

38 See Barrett, 250, followed by Thompson, Clothed with Christ, 125.

39 See Michel, 410, citing Str.-B.'s claim in 1:241; 3:306 that πληρόω is equivalent to the Aramaic word מקים. This is based on a quotation from Rabbi Jonathan around 140 C.E., "Whoever fulfills the law in poverty will finally fulfill it in riches." But Henrik Ljungman has shown that this is a mistranslation, that the Aramaic term should be rendered "hold" or "stand"; see Das Gesetz erfüllen. Matth. 5,17ff. und 3,15 Untersucht, LUÅ 50.6 (Lund: Gleerup, 1954) 26–33. Nevertheless, most commentators understand "fulfill" as equivalent to Hebraic expressions for "doing," "performing," or "keeping" the Torah. See Barrett, 251; Wilckens, 3:68, 71; Heinrich Schlier, Der Brief an die Galater, KEK 7, 14th ed. (Göttingen: Vandenhoeck & Ruprecht, 1971) 244; Schnabel, Law, 274.

40 See Söding, Liebesgebot, 255–57.

41 See Betz, Galatians, 275; Dunn, 2:777.

Hebraic material.[42] For instance, Augustus is celebrated in an official inscription as the divinely appointed regent who "fulfilled" what all people had hoped for: οὗ ἡ πρόνοια τὰς πάντων εὐχὰς . . . ἐπλήρωσε ("by whose foresight you fulfilled all aspirations").[43] The use of πληρόω to express ideas of accomplishing duties or completing the tasks required by an office is illustrated by these typical citations from papyri of the first and second centuries C.E.

ὃς ἕξει καὶ τὴν τοῦ ξυστάρχου τειμήν, πληρῶν τὰ εἰθισμέν[α] ("who also held the honor of the presidency, discharging the customary procedures").[44]

ἵνα . . . τὴν συνήθη [οἰ]κονομίαν τῆ[ς ἀπο]γραφῆς πληρώσωσιν ("in order that they may accomplish the regular administration of the census").[45]

That this usage could be taken over by Hellenistic Judaism is evident in Philo's approbation of the nation that "has fulfilled the words [of the moral law] with honorable deeds (πληρῶσαι τοὺς λόγους ἔργοις ἐπαινετοῖς)."[46] Just as in the parallel usage by Matthew, to "fulfill" the law means to accomplish its original intent and purpose.[47] The scope of Paul's argument moves beyond the Torah, however, because νόμος is used here without the article, and should be translated "law" in the

generic sense.[48] The formulation includes both Jewish and Roman law, and indeed any other law that could be mentioned. Law in general is fulfilled, according to this context, not by performing every duty prescribed in Leviticus or Deuteronomy or some other code but by following the lead of the Spirit[49] in loving one's fellow believers in a local house or tenement church. It is not love in general, or in the abstract, but rather love in the everyday experience of the love feast and other intense interactions of small groups of urban believers that is in view here. The contrast in tenses between the present participle, "the one who loves," and the perfect verb, "he has fulfilled,"[50] points in the direction of the steady, everyday work of love on the local level that is seen here as the fulfillment of divine law. Marxsen refers in this context to the "continuous activity" of love that constitutes the fulfillment,[51] but he and other commentators overlook the social setting of this formulation. It is not some theology of love or law that fulfills the divine intent, but love as practiced among members of small church groups, with particular reference in this verse to their extension of hospitality to "the other," to members of other groups whose orientation and background may differ substantially.

■ **9** Paul cites five commandments to illustrate his contention about loving one another as the fulfillment of law. The first four prohibitions are drawn from the LXX

42 See BAGD 671.
43 Cited by Gerhard Delling, "πληρόω κτλ.," *TDNT* 6 (1968) 287, from *B. Mus. In.* 4.1. Nr. 894.12.
44 Cited by MM 520 from a first-century Spartan inscription in *ABSA* 12 (1905–6) 452. See also *CIG* 2:2236.
45 MM 520 cites this papyrus from *P.Lond.* 3. Nr. 904.24–26.
46 Philo *Praem.* 83.
47 See Georg Strecker, *Die Bergpredigt. Ein exegetischer Kommentar* (Göttingen: Vandenhoeck & Ruprecht, 1984) 57. Jan Lambrecht, *The Sermon on the Mount: Proclamation and Exhortation* (Wilmington: Glazier, 1985) 84. Schnabel, *Law*, 275, argues in contrast that fulfillment implies "concentrated reference of the various individual commandments to one point of reference," citing Stanislas Lyonnet, "La charité plénitude de la loi (Rom 13,8-10)," in L. de Lorenzi, *Dimensions*, 156.
48 Commentaries routinely translate νόμος in 13:8 as "the law," as, for example, Lagrange, 315; Schlier,

394; Barrett, 250; Cranfield, 2.673, 2.676; Morris, 468; Dunn, 2:774, 2:777; Fitzmyer, 676; Moo, 810, 814.
49 See Betz, *Galatians*, 275: "the prescriptions and prohibitions of the Jewish Torah stand before the Jew as demands 'to be done' by him, while love is the result of liberation and the gift of the Spirit." The context in Romans does not have the polemical antithesis found in Galatians, which disturbs a commentator like Käsemann, 361. In the light of cultural expectations and their implications for local groups of Christians, both passages are equally revolutionary. Hans Hübner offers a partially satisfactory analysis of the differences between the two in "πληρόω κτλ.," *EDNT* 3 (1993) 109.
50 See Zahn, 563.
51 Marxsen, "Röm. 13,8," 236.

of Exod 20:13-17 and Deut 5:17-21. These commandments concerning adultery, murder, theft, and coveting may well be in a sequence used in the diaspora, as argued by Berger and Dunn.[52] The more interesting question, from the perspective of Paul's audience in this letter, is why these four commandments were selected and the other commandments mentioned in those other lists were not.[53] We can omit the first two of the Ten Commandments from consideration, since they were dealt with indirectly in Rom 1:18-32. The last two commandments, concerning coveting a wife and coveting property, were effectively fused with the wording οὐκ ἐπιθυμήσεις ("you shall not covet"), a step that was prepared in the use of this commandment in Rom 7:7.[54] One of the laws not mentioned was controversial among the Roman congregations, namely, the Sabbath law of Exod 20:8-11; Deut 5:12-15.[55] Another law not mentioned demands honor to parents (Exod 20:12; Deut 5:16), which would have been problematic in the new fictive families of house and tenement churches with a painful sense of separation from unconverted relatives.[56] The issue of bearing false witness (Exod 20:16; Deut 5:20) would have been irrelevant for most church members, whose social status eliminated the possibility of their appearing in the Roman court system.[57]

The four commandments that Paul selects would have been particularly relevant for life in the urban environment of Rome, where interpersonal relations, especially in the slums where most of the Christian cells were located, were tense, volatile, and full of temptations and provocations. The command οὐ μοιχεύσεις ("do not commit adultery") protects the sanctity of marriage, and the unconditional, unqualified formulation is probably meant to include both men and women in the admonition.[58] The egalitarian ethos of early Christianity surfaces in the prominence given to protecting the sexual rights and responsibilities of both men and women. Neither the Jewish nor the Greco-Roman culture shares this strict prohibition of sexual relations for both males and females outside of covenantal boundaries.[59] The *lex de adulteriis* promulgated by Augustus had prescribed severe penalties for adultery, but allowed husbands to have sexual relations with other unmarried women.[60] Early Christianity was probably shaped in this regard by the teachings of Jesus, which held both men and women to high standards (e.g., Matt 5:32; 19:8; Mark 10:11-12).[61] The sensitivity of early Christian writers concerning the erotic implications of the "holy kiss" in congregational gatherings[62] and the charges of promiscuity raised by nonbelievers suggest that adultery was a significant problem in the ecstatic and closely knit communities of men and women from different families that made up early churches. The current urgency of this issue may account for Paul's following a tradition in which the commandment on adultery was listed before the others he selects.

There is a curious lack of interest among NT commentators in the commandment οὐ φονεύσεις ("you

52   See Berger, *Gesetzesauslegung Jesus*, 275–76; and Dunn, 2:777; the sequence here is found in the Nash papyrus of Deut 5; in Philo *Dec.* 29, Luke 18:20, Jas 2:11, and elsewhere.

53   Dunn, 2:778, offers a preliminary answer to this question in suggesting that the prohibitions selected "were of broader appeal and less distinctively Jewish than the earlier commandments."

54   See Wilckens, 3:69.

55   See the commentary below on Rom 14:5.

56   See Meeks, *Urban Christians*, 84–96.

57   Koch, *Schrift*, 116–17, discusses the omission of this commandment as an ad hoc decision by Paul, offering no suggestion about its motivation.

58   See Friedrich Hauck, "μοιχεύω κτλ.," *TDNT* 4 (1967) 733: "A mark of the NT is the sharp intensifying of the concept of adultery. The right of a man to sexual freedom is denied. Like the wife, the husband is under an obligation of fidelity." See also Gerhard Delling, "Ehebruch," *RAC* 4 (1959) 675.

59   Hauck, "μοιχεύω κτλ.," 730, 732, 734.

60   See the discussion in Gugliermo Gerrero, *The Greatness and Decline of Rome. 5. The Republic of Augustus*, trans. H. J. Chaytor (London: Heinemann, 1909) 70–72.

61   See J. M. D. Derrett, "The Teaching of Jesus on Marriage and Divorce," in Derrett, *Law and the New Testament* (London: Darton, Longman & Todd, 1970) 377–88, and Fiorenza, *In Memory of Her*, 140–54.

62   See Benko, *Early Christians*, 79–102, which discusses Athenagoras's reference to the "very carefully guarded" kiss in *Legatio pro Christianis* around 177 C.E., and other similar references.

shall not murder").[63] The prominent place given to this problem in the OT,[64] the reiteration of the prohibition of murder in Matt 19:18, and the listing of murder in the catalog of vices discussed above in Rom 1:29 confirm the high value accorded to the preservation of human life in the biblical tradition as a whole.[65] Greek and Roman laws prohibiting murder indicate that in the ancient world as a whole, murder was taken very seriously;[66] in Rome it was punished with ferocious zeal.[67] It is safe to assume that the distinctions found in the OT as well as in the Greco-Roman penal codes between murder as a premeditated act and other forms of accidental or justifiable homicide are presupposed in this formulation drawn from Exod 20:15.[68] Given the high incidence of crime and vigilantism in the slums of Rome, especially at night,[69] and the violent conflicts that had

already led to the banning of Christian and Jewish leaders under Claudius, this topic was a significant one for the audience of the letter.

The prohibition οὐ κλέψεις relates to secretive theft rather than robbery, which has the connotation of violent assault.[70] Hebrew law made no distinction between theft and robbery as modern systems of jurisprudence do,[71] but the audience in Rome would probably have assumed their own system of justice in the wording of the prohibition.[72] The prohibition against theft in both the OT and the NT[73] rested more on the significance of individual work and the sanctity of life than on the value of ownership as such.[74] While some Jewish laws allowed theft from criminals or unbelievers such as Samaritans,[75] and Horace satirized a pious Roman who would sacrifice "to Laverna, the goddess of theft, for the power to com-

63 There is no article on φονεύω in the *TDNT* but *EDNT* provides brief surveys by Heinrich Balz, "φονεύς κτλ.," *EDNT* 3 (1993) 435–36. BAGD 864 provides no indication of studies on this topic and the commentators I have checked all pass over the topic of murder without discussion.

64 See Bernard S. Jackson, "Murder," *HBD* (1985) 663–64.

65 J. Poucher, "Crimes and Punishments," *DBH* 1 (1901) 522: "Murder, according to the divine word, is a crime against which all nature revolts (Gn 4^{10.23.24}). The sanctity of human life is founded on the fact that man was made in the image of God (Gn 9^6)."

66 See Kurt Latte's survey of Greek laws in "Mord," *PW* 16 (1935) 278–89. He notes on 285 the early Greek distinction between three classes of homicide: premeditated murder, killing without premeditation, and official execution. A survey of Roman laws and attitudes is provided by Pfaff, "Homicilium," *PW* 8 (1913) 2248–50. See also Theodor Mommsen's discussion of how murder came to be viewed as a crime against the community as a whole in *Römisches Strafrecht*, 612–51, esp. 614. For a more recent discussion, see D. G. Cracknoll and C. H. Wilson, *Roman Law, Origins and Influence* (London: HCT, 1990).

67 Pfaff reports in "Homicilium," 2249, that in the first century there were three levels of penalty for murderers: for *altiores*, banishment; for *honestiores*, execution by decapitation; and for *humiliores*, execution by wild animals in the Colosseum or by crucifixion. For Roman laws about murder, see Robinson, *Criminal Law*, 41–47.

68 See Jackson's discussion of the provisions for manslaughter and justified homicide found in the "Covenant Code" in "Murder," 664.

69 See Stambaugh, *Ancient Roman City*, 125–27.

70 See Herbert Preisker, "κλέπτω, κλέπτης," *TDNT* 3 (1965) 754; the Greek verb "to rob" is ἁρπάζω rather than κλέπτω. See also Bernard S. Jackson, "Robbery," *HBD* (1985) 873.

71 See Jackson, "Robbery," 873.

72 In *Ancient Roman City*, 126–27, Stambaugh refers to the seven *cohortes vigilum* that served as a police force in Rome at night, but noted that rich people hired their own bodyguards to prevent theft. Criminal trials were conducted before appointed praetors, or, in some instances, before the emperor. Punishment for most crimes, especially for the lower classes, was public and often horrific, as detailed in *Ancient Roman City*, 126–27. See also Robinson, *Criminal Law*, 23–32.

73 See the references in BAGD 434.

74 R. Gnuse, *You Shall Not Steal: Community and Property in Biblical Tradition* (Maryknoll, N.Y.: Orbis, 1985) 48. He observes that "the commandment not to steal meant that no individual had the right to deprive another person of possessions necessary for meaningful existence" (10).

75 See Poucher, "Crimes and Punishment," 522.

mit fraud and robbery while retaining his good reputation,"[76] the biblical prohibition against theft as quoted in this verse was unconditional.[77] It had a direct bearing on church members living in close proximity in the city of Rome, where the slum conditions made preservation of property difficult and the widespread poverty made theft appealing as well as damaging.

The prohibition against coveting, οὐκ ἐπιθυμήσεις, dealt with extensively above in connection with Rom 7:7, was derived from a selective compression of Deut 5:21, reducing it to its verbal essential:

> You shall not covet (οὐκ ἐπιθυμήσεις) your neighbor's wife; you shall not covet (οὐκ ἐπιθυμήσεις) your neighbor's house, nor his field, nor his manservant, nor his maid, nor his ox, nor his ass, nor any beast of his, nor any thing that is your neighbor's.

Although it is clear that an initial step toward this compression on the theoretical but not the literary level was made by 4 Macc 2:4-6,[78] and that the simple two-word prohibition used by Paul is found in Samaritan inscriptions of the Decalogue,[79] it is worth observing that much of the material in the original wording of the ninth and tenth commandments would have been ill-suited to the house and tenement churches in Rome. The chauvinistic language about "his wife" might have offended churches with such prominent feminine leadership, and was inconsistent with Paul's egalitarian ethos; the references to the neighbor's slaves would not be appropriate in congregations consisting largely of slaves

and former slaves; and the agricultural references to the farm animals would have been inappropriate in the urban setting. But the most important consideration about the relevance of this prohibition relates to the emerging solidarity of the communal systems of eating together in the house and tenement churches in Rome and elsewhere: the threat to agapaic sharing is the desire for possessions under one's own control. This commandment is effectively recontextualized in this pericope to relate to the question of "loving one another," in a passage that climaxes with two explicit references to "the agape," probably referring to the love feast. In short, all four of these issues—adultery, murder, theft, and coveting—would have been of crucial importance for small believing groups attempting to carve out decent spaces for common life in Rome. The selection of four prohibitions is accomplished without polemical emphasis or explanation, making an inclusive case that would appeal to the Roman audience, especially when followed by the open-ended formulation, καὶ εἴ τις ἑτέρα ἐντολή ("and if [there is] any other commandment"). This formulation may seem awkward to the contemporary audience, and is ordinarily smoothed out in contemporary translations, but it served a crucial purpose of including any commandment stressed by any group of believers in Rome, even a law coming from outside of Scripture.[80] This is consistent with the wording of 13:8, where "law" appears anarthrously, implying law in general.

The summing up[81] of the commandments is drawn not from the Decalogue but from "this word"[82] of Lev 19:18, ἀγαπήσεις τὸν πλησίον σου ὡς σεαυτόν ("you

---

76 Ferrero, *Republic of Augustus*, 51.

77 See Preisker, "κλέπτω," 754.

78 See Joachim Jeremias, "θυμός, ἐπιθυμία κτλ.," *TDNT* 2 (1964) 171. The text of the 4 Macc 2:4-6 citation is as follows: "And it is . . . every desire that reasoning is able to master. For instance, the law says, 'You shall not covet your neighbor's wife, nor anything that belongs to your neighbor.' Now, then, since it is the law that has forbidden us to desire (ἐπιθυμεῖν), I shall more easily persuade you that reasoning is able to govern our lusts."

79 Klaus Berger discusses the exegetical tradition that seems to prepare the way for Paul's wording in *Gesetzesauslegung Jesus*, 346–49, including a reference to the prohibition in Samaritan inscriptions. His conclusion has been accepted by Koch, *Schrift*, 117.

80 See Ortkemper, *Leben*, 130, and, more explicitly, Fitzmyer, 679. Michel, 410, restricts the commands to those in Scripture.

81 See Heinrich Schlier's discussion of this Greek word that has no parallel in Hebrew thought: "κεφαλή, ἀνακεφαλαιόομαι," *TDNT* 3 (1965) 681f. It means to "sum up" in a rhetorical sense. In "ἀνακεφαλαιόω," *EDNT* 1 (1990) 82, Helmut Merklein suggests that the summary means in this instance that the Commandments "are brought together in a single major and fundamental statement from which they can be deduced or to which they can be reduced."

82 Dunn, 2:778, notes that the expression ἐν τῷ λόγῳ τούτῳ ("in this word") refers to a revealed word, as in Isa 10:23, and might remind some of Paul's audi-

shall love your neighbor as yourself"). The grafting of the rule from Leviticus to the previous four commandments is unparalleled, resulting in a distinctive Pauline pentad. While not combining this summary with other commandments, some teachers in the Jewish tradition offered similar summaries of the law, with Hillel selecting the golden rule, and Akiba selecting the same verse that Paul uses here. However, as Wischmeyer has pointed out, there are no citations at all from Lev 19:18 in Jewish literature prior to Paul's letters,[83] and the later rabbinic emphases on single verses did not eliminate the need to learn and obey the entire Torah.[84] While some would argue that Paul follows the traditions of Hellenistic Judaism in this emphasis,[85] the frequent citations of Lev 19:18 by early Christian writers makes it likely that Paul is following a tradition established by Jesus, who gave unique importance to the law of love, as Mark 12:31 and parallels indicate.[86] Paul takes an independent line with this tradition, as usual, treating it as no other NT writer did as a summary of the law,[87] and contextualizing it within the local Christian community by the peculiar wording of 13:8. This results in a redefinition of τὸν πλησίον ("the neighbor"), which in Leviticus as well as the later Jewish tradition was restricted to a fellow Jew.[88] Here it refers concretely to the Christian neighbor of whatever cultural background, ordinarily a member of one's small house or tenement church,[89] but also including the "other" of v. 8 who may belong to another congregation. In this context, the reference in Lev 19:18 to loving others "as yourself" should not be interpreted as a concession to human sinfulness[90] and requires no rationalizing about the need for decent self-respect.[91] In the ongoing messianic banquet that marked the group life of early Christianity, in which food and resources were shared "in common," there was no question about one's own needs being met. The command to love aims at mutuality, with each aiming to meet the needs of others as well as oneself, as the wording of 13:8 concerning "love one another" makes plain.

■ **10** A proper interpretation of this verse should continue the focus on local church relations that I have followed throughout this pericope.[92] However, the persistent deletion by commentators and translators of the article "the" in connection with love in this verse serves to generalize the admonition and drive it in a theoretical, legalistic direction not intended by Paul. This entails a significant misunderstanding of the function of the article in Greek, which serves "to distinguish the subject noun from the predicate noun," thus establishing the topic of the sentence.[93] There are two means of

---

ence that the Ten Commandments were often referred to as "the ten words."

83 Oda Wischmeyer, "Das Gebot der Nächstenliebe bei Paulus. Eine traditionsgeschichtliche Untersuchung," *BZ* 30 (1986) 164. She concludes on 168 that "a summary of the Torah in the form of the decalogue and the law of loving the neighbor lay outside of the viewpoint of the various forms of Jewish theology prior to Paul's time."

84 Ibid., 166–68; Thompson, *Clothed with Christ*, 136. Andreas Nissen goes on to point out, in *Gott und der Nächste im antiken Judentum. Untersuchungen zum Doppelgebot der Liebe*, WUNT 15 (Tübingen: Mohr-Siebeck, 1974) 389–415, that later rabbinic summaries are not summaries in the true sense of "summing up."

85 See Wischmeyer, "Gebot der Nächstenliebe," 181–85, largely following Berger, *Gesetzesauslegung Jesu*, 100–142; also Merklein, "ἀνακεφαλαιόω," 82.

86 See Dunn, 2:779; also his study, "Jesus Tradition," 202. The most extensive case concerning Paul's use of a tradition from the historical Jesus is in Thompson, *Clothed with Christ*, 132–40.

87 See Wischmeyer, "Gebot der Nächstenliebe," 181.

88 Fitzmyer, 679, points to the explicit reference to "the sons of your own people" in Lev 19:18. See also the extensive discussion in Nissen, *Gott und der Nächste*, 285–308, showing that the command to love a neighbor was limited to fellow Jews, and was never applied to enemies. Dunn's effort (2:779–80) to extend the "neighbor" to non-Jews is not convincing.

89 See Heinrich Greeven's critique of the generalized construal of "neighbor" to mean "one's fellow man" rather than a specific person one encounters, so to speak, in the "neighborhood": "πλησίον," *TDNT* 6 (1968) 317. Ortkemper, *Leben*, 131, quotes with approval the explanation by Martin Noth that the neighbor in the OT context was a person with whom one associates and lives closely, but he does not relate this to local house churches.

90 See Cranfield, 2:677.

91 Dunn, 2:780.

92 This section is adapted from Jewett, "Love Feast," 265–78.

93 Sansone, "Article in Greek," 200.

establishing topicalization in Greek: the article and word order. As Sansone points out, "Often these two means will coincide and reinforce one another,"[94] as in Rom 13:10. By the emphatic positioning of ἡ ἀγάπη ("the love") as the first and last words in the sentence, and by repeating the article twice in this carefully constructed verse, Paul makes clear that the specific and distinctive form of love as experienced by early house and tenement churches is the topic.[95] The logical social corollary to "the love" in this verse is the agape meal otherwise known as the love feast, the common meal shared by most sectors of the early church in connection with the Lord's Supper. The repeated arthrous use of "love" in this verse justifies the translation "the agape." Only when this social context is kept in view does v. 10a rise above the level of a conventional truism,[96] as the parallels make plain.

That "the love" does no "evil" to neighbors echoes passages such as Ps 15:3, which defines the blameless person with these same words: ἐποίησε τῷ πλησίον αὐτοῦ κακόν ("does no evil to his neighbor").[97] The typical expression for inquiring into a misdemeanor in Greek sources is εἴ τις ἢ βεβούλευται κακὸν ἢ πεποίηκεν ("whether anyone has planned or committed evil").[98] Although the admonition to do no evil to the neighbor was frequently used,[99] none of these references speak of "the love" in such specific terms as Paul does here. By employing a conventional moral rule ("doing no evil") that was sure to gain assent in Rome, Paul is able to

place "the agape" as practiced by the Roman congregations within the context of the discrimination between good and evil stated in 12:9 and thereby to make a subtle point concerning the "other" that still echoes from 13:8. What is ordinarily not explained, however, is why Paul would have to deny that "the agape" harms the neighbor. Why does he couch this admonition in such a defensive manner? It makes rhetorical sense only if there were in fact charges that it did such harm. The love-feast hypothesis provides a context for such charges, not only in the occasional reemergence of social discrimination within the meals themselves (1 Cor 11:20-22) but also in the hostility of non-Christian families whose members had joined the new meal system. Such charges provide the background of Paul's insistence that the love feast is the πλήρωμα οὖν νόμου ("fulfillment therefore of law"). It is not just any love that is in view here, but "the love" within the Christian congregation. The greatest barrier against such love in the Roman situation was conformity to various forms of law, which insisted that family members should always eat together, which divided the weak from the strong and prevented the celebration of the love feast together. It is essential therefore to recognize that νόμος appears without the article here, in opposition to the usual formulation in commentaries and modern versions.[100] It is law as a principle, in its multifarious forms, that is fulfilled in the agape meal. The meaning of πλήρωμα in this sentence is the entire completion of

---

94 Ibid., 201.

95 See BDF §252, where ἡ ἀγάπη is rendered "Christian Love," with reference to John 1:21. For a discussion of the fact that the Greek article derived from the demonstrative pronoun, and retains its deictic quality of pointing to a specific or previously named topic, see Robert W. Funk, "The Syntax of the Greek Article: Its Importance for Critical Pauline Problems" (dissertation, Vanderbilt University, 1953) 31–56. He discusses the arthrous use of ἀγάπη as "a good example of an abstract that has been thoroughly Christianized" on 106–12.

96 Furnish, *Love*, 111, accepts Ceslas Spicq's view in *Agape in the New Testament* (St. Louis, 1965) 2:60 that 13:10a serves as a rhetorical *litotes*, "an understatement for the sake of emphasis."

97 Koch, *Schrift*, 297, does not consider this reference in Rom 13:10 as a citation, but an "intertextual

echo" as defined by Hays, *Echoes*, 14–21, seems to be present. See also Sir 10:6; *Ep. Arist.* 168, 207; Tob 4:15; and especially Zech 8:17, "let none of you devise evil in his heart against his neighbor."

98 Plutarch *Curios.* 523a. See also Peder Borgen's discussion of the reciprocal form of this command in "The Golden Rule: With Emphasis on Its Use in the Gospels," in P. Borgen, *Paul Preaches Circumcision and Pleases Men and Other Essays on Christian Origins* (Trondheim: Tapir, 1983) 100–104.

99 For example, Diogenes Laertius *Vitae philos.* 1.69, μὴ κακολόγειν τοὺς πλησίον ("Don't 'badmouth' your neighbors"); or Isocrates *Dem.* 30, Γίγνου πρὸς τοὺς πλησιάζοντας ὁμιλητικός, ἀλλὰ μὴ σεμνός ("Be affable towards your neighbors, not austere").

100 Most commentaries and translations translate νόμος in 13:10 as "the law": for example, Lagrange,

law, not the sum total of its individual demands.[101] In effect, Paul is claiming that the final goal of law, in whatever culture or family it manifests itself,[102] is achieved in the love feasts of early Christian communities. This concrete social context helps to avoid "a sentimental but unrealistic idealism"[103] that so frequently afflicts the NT doctrine of love. In this discussion, "the call to love the other is in fact *limited* to the neighbor."[104] But I would like to go beyond this insight to insist on the precise social context in which such love was expressing itself: in the agape meals of house and tenement churches of Rome, previously separated by ideological and cultural conflicts, and challenged now to live up to their inherent ethos.

317; Schlier, 395; Barrett, 251; Cranfield, 2:673; Morris, 469; Dunn, 2:780; Fitzmyer, 677; Moo, 817; the only exception I have found is Johnson, 193.

101 See BAGD 672 and Ortkemper, *Leben*, 132, who follows Gerhard Delling on this point in "πλήρωμα," *TDNT* 6 (1968) 305. Delling shows that the translation "complete fulfillment" is required here rather than "sum," which would be redundant with "sum up" in 13:9. André Feuillet rejects this active sense of "fulfillment" in "Loi ancienne et morale chrétienne d'après l'épître aux Romains," *NRTh* 92 (1970) 797: "la seule vertu de charité se trouve renfermée la totalité des préceptes de la Loi." C. F. D. Moule is ambivalent on this point in "'Fulness' and 'Fill' in the New Testament," *SJT* 4 (1951) 83.

102 See Leenhardt, 338: Paul takes "πλήρωμα νόμου in the double meaning of fulfilling the law of God and fulfilling the civil law."

103 Dunn, 2:783.

104 Ibid., italics in original.

13

The Sixth Pericope

The Admonition to Moral Alertness in the Last Days

11/   **And knowing this [hymn], The Critical Time,**
    "The hour [is] already [past] for us[a]
    to be roused from sleep" (for now is our salvation nearer than when we came to faith.)
        12/ **"The night is far advanced, the day is drawn near.**
    Let us therefore cast off[b] the works of darkness
        And[c] let us step into the armor[d] of light."
    13/ **As by day, let us walk in a seemly manner,**
        Not in carousings and drunken bouts,
            Not in bouts of sex and indecencies,
                Not in strife[e] and zealotry.
    14/ **But put on the Lord[f] Jesus Christ and make no provision for the flesh [to gratify] its desires.[g]**

a   Although there is a fairly wide consensus that ἡμᾶς ("us") is the inferior reading, it is impressively supported by P[46vid] ℵ[c] D (1505) 1506 1243 1573 1739 (2495), which read ἤδη ἡμᾶς, and by F G L Ψ 6 33 88 104 323 424 614 945 1175 1241 1735 1836 1874 1912 2344, which read ἡμᾶς ἤδη, and by 181 256 263 436 459 629 1877 2200 (sequence undetermined) *Maj* latt sy[p,pal] sa arm geo Chr. Cranfield, 2:680, and Fitzmyer, 682, explain this reading as an assimilation to the "us" of the following sentence; Metzger, *Textual Commentary*, 467, describes the majority opinion to this effect. However, it seems equally likely that ὑμᾶς ("you") in ℵ[*] A B C (P) 69 81 326 330 365 (451 ὑμεῖς) 1319 1852 (1881 omits ἤδη) (1962 ὑμᾶς ἤδη) 2127 2492 *al* ar b d f g o vg bo slav Cl Pachomius[lat] Cyr Ambst Hier Pel Aug was influenced by the vowel and rough breathing of the following word ὕπνου ("sleep"). There is an additional rhetorical consideration, in that "for us to be roused from sleep" is consistent with hymnic style, matching the first person plural imperative forms in vv. 12-13. None of the previous discussions of this text-critical issue has taken the hymnic citation into account. The translation above therefore opts for the reading "for us." Witnesses that omit the word entirely are sy[h] eth Or[lat].

b   The reading ἀποβαλώμεθα ("let us cast off") in P[46] D[*.2] F G eth is reasonably well attested and vivid, but the use of ἀποθώμεθα ("let us put off, renounce") in "formulas of renunciation" led the UBS committee to favor it, according to Metzger, *Textual Commentary*, 467. The support for "let us put off" is strong, in ℵ A B C D[1] L P Ψ 048 0285[vid] 6 33 69 81 88 104 181 218 256 263 323 326 365 424 436 441 451 459 467 614 621 623 629 630 720 915 917 945 1175 1241 1243 1319 1398 1505 1506 1563 1573 1678 1718 1735 1739 1751 1836 1838 1845 1852 1874 1875 1877 (1881 ἀποθέμενοι) 1908 1912 1942 1959 1962 2110 2127 2138 2197 2200 2344 2492 2495 2516 2523 2544 2718 *Maj Lect* slav Cl Pacomius[lat] (GrNy) Did Chr Cyr Proclus Thret Qu. Actually, the text-critical rule of accepting the "harder reading" should have led to a judgment in favor of ἀποβαλώμεθα. Zuntz, *Text*, 94–95, argues convincingly that the Pauline hapax legomenon ἀποβαλώμεθα was the original formulation that was later "ousted by a verb which was familiar from many similar passages," including Eph 4:22, 25 and Col 3:8. See also the arguments in favor of ἀποβαλώμεθα by Cranfield, 2:685, and in commentary below.

c   In place of the particle δέ ("but, and"), ℵ[c] C[3] D[2] F G L Ψ 33 69 88 104 323 326 365 424 614 945 1175 1241 1243 1319 1505 1573 1836 1735 1874 2344 2495 *Maj* latt sy provide καί ("but, also") in front of the verb, as do 330 1506, which also retain δέ after the verb; P[46c] ℵ[*] 6 omit δέ (though P[46*] provides οὖν ["therefore"]). These variants appear to be secondary because they smooth out the awkwardness of the transition between the two independent clauses. Despite the fact that both Nestle-Aland[26/27] and the UBS committee decided to place δέ in brackets "in view of wide variation involving the connective" (Metzger, *Textual Commentary (1975)*, 530), a strict application of text-critical method leads me to accept δέ as the original reading. It is strongly supported by A B C[*] D[*] P 048 630 1739 1881 *pc* Cl, and by 330 1506, which also have καί (see above).

d   A D 88 *pc* eliminate the awkward metaphor of "weapons of light" by substituting ἔργα ("works of light"), thus providing a symmetrical parallelism to the earlier expression, "works of darkness." See Michel, 415.

e   The plural form of "strife and zealotry" found in B (424[c] 1739—with singular for "zealotry") sy[h] sa Cl Cyp is a weakly attested effort to bring the final pair of sins into correspondence with the plurals of the first two pairs.

f   Several insignificant alterations of the sequence of "the Lord Jesus Christ," as found in ℵ A C D F G L P Ψ 0285[vid] 6 33 69 104 330 326 365 424 1175 1241 1243 1319 1505 1506 1573 1735 1836 1874 2344

2495 *Maj* lat sy, are present at this point. "Christ Jesus" appears in B Cl; "the Lord Jesus" in 323 630 1739 1881 *pc*; and "Jesus Christ our Lord" in P⁴⁶ (629) ar t. These variations look like later pietistic embellishments.

g   The accusative singular εἰς ἐπιθυμίαν in P⁴⁶* A C 1243 1506 1735 *pc* and the plural formula ἐν ἐπιθυμίαις in F G are too weakly attested to be original.

Analysis

Current commentators agree that this is a separate pericope, linked to the foregoing material but having a distinct structure and theme of its own.[1] The phrase καὶ τοῦτο ("and this")[2] introduces the following cited material.[3] The verb εἰδότες ("knowing") signals that the citation is known to the audience.[4] The cited material in the new pericope provides the eschatological rationale for performing the ethic in the preceding as well as the present pericope.[5] The passage is carefully constructed with synthetic and antithetical parallelisms. The first and last strophes of two lines apiece contain synthetic parallelism,[6] while the four-line strophes of 13:12 and 13 have strikingly formal characteristics. There is an elegant paranomasia in the repetition of ἐγγύτερον ("closer") in 13:11 and ἤγγικεν ("it drew closer") in 13:13.

Heinrich Schlier has suggested that some of these rhetorical features reflect a baptismal hymn being quoted in 13:11-12.[7] He proposed the following strophic pattern, which I print out with text-critical decisions made above:

11b Ὥρα ἤδη ὑμᾶς ἐξ ὕπνου ἐγερθῆναι
12a-b Ἡ νὺξ προέκοψεν, ἡ δὲ ἡμέρα ἤγγικεν.
12c Ἀποβαλώμεθα οὖν τὰ ἔργα τοῦ σκότους,
12d Ἐνδυσώμεθα δὲ τὰ ὅπλα τοῦ φωτός.

This hypothesis has been criticized because the prose material in 11c was left out of the analysis,[8] but Schlier appropriately identifies this as explanatory.[9] Other early Christian hymns cited by Paul have similar additions. The proposed hymn has impressive homoioptoton in the identical verbal forms with -μεθα in the beginnings of lines 12c and d, with parechesis in the assonance of "o" sounds in the conclusions of these two lines that echo the "o" sound of the opening syllable of 11b. There is an appealing rhythmic symmetry in the proposed hymn, with each line containing five beats. However, the second line of the hymn contains an antithetical parallelism that is not matched by the other lines; the subsequent two lines echo this parallelism in an A + B: A' + B' pattern. The content and rhetoric of the hymn seem more suited for the Agape meal than for a baptismal service, particularly in the first person plural exhortative forms that seem to fit the context of repetitive actions by the

1 See Cranfield, 2:679; Dunn, 2:784–85; Fitzmyer, 681–82; Moo, 817; Stuhlmacher, 211; Johnson, 193.
2 See the discussion of the grammatical problem in Godet, 448–49. BDF §553.9 refers to καὶ τοῦτο as "emphatic," while §290 translates "and at that, and especially."
3 See BDF §§290–91; there οὗτος/τοῦτω ("this") refers to the topic "under immediate consideration" and ἐκεῖνος ("that") refers to a topic or person previously mentioned in a more distant context.
4 See the use of εἰδότες ὅτι in Rom 5:3; 6:9; 1 Cor 1:7; 15:58; 2 Cor 4:14; 5:6; Gal 2:16.
5 Michel, 412, argues more broadly that this eschatological intensification applies to all of the ethical material in chapters 12–13. So also Ortkemper, *Leben*, 132; Thompson, *Clothed with Christ*, 141.

6 Weiss identifies the parallelism but does not designate it as synthetic in "Beiträge," 245.
7 Schlier, 395–97; Michel, 414, also refers to the liturgical quality of this discourse.
8 Fitzmyer, 682.
9 Whether the entirety of v. 11c is an explanatory addition by Paul needs to be weighed. If the first six words belonged to the hymn, they would also contain five beats, admirably matching the rhetoric of the rest of the hymn: νῦν γὰρ ἐγγύτερον ἡμῶν ἡ σωτηρία. With this construal, the Pauline addition would clarify the point of comparison: "than when we came to faith."

community. It also seems clear from the addition of 11c that Paul thought an Agape rather than a baptismal hymn was in view, with the reference to the current experience of salvation and the allusion to the time "when we came to faith." Perhaps it would be better to say that this is an Agape hymn with a secondary use in baptism contexts. Since this proposed hymn is not included in the standard treatments of early Christian hymns,[10] there is a need for a detailed investigation to determine whether these matters can be resolved. In the meanwhile, the Schlier proposal is plausible enough to test in this commentary.

The antithesis between "works of darkness" and "weapons of light" in 12c-d is carried forward in the succeeding two verses. Verse 13 opens with an exhortation that is followed by three pairs of evil works in parallel syntactical structures of a repeated $\mu\grave{\eta} \ldots \kappa\alpha\acute{\iota}$ ("not . . . and"). The first nouns of the first two pairs of plurals are linked by parechesis: $\kappa\acute{\omega}\mu\omicron\iota\varsigma \ldots \kappa\omicron\acute{\iota}\tau\alpha\iota\varsigma$ ("carousings . . . affairs"), whereas the final pair of vices breaks out of the plural pattern,[11] thus providing a point of emphasis that may link the vices with congregational conflicts characteristic of Rome.[12] In v. 14, the positive alternative of the "weapons of light" is sketched in the synthetic parallelism concerning putting on Christ and overcoming the desires of the flesh. The verb $\acute{\epsilon}\nu\delta\acute{\upsilon}\sigma\alpha\sigma\vartheta\epsilon$ ("put on") has a paranomastic resonance with "put on" in 12d. This passage thus serves as an effective climax of the general ethic set forth in 12:1–13:7, preparing the way for the specific ethical admonitions in 14:1–15:6.

Rhetorical Disposition

IV.	The *probatio*
12:1–15:13	The fourth proof: Living together according to the gospel so as to sustain the hope of global transformation

13:11-14	6. The admonition to moral alertness in the last days
13:11-12a	a. The citation of the Agape/baptismal hymn
13:11a	1) Introductory formula and name of hymn, "The Critical Time"
13:11b	2) The first line about being "roused from sleep"
13:11c	3) Explanation about the proximity of "salvation"
13:12a	4) The second line with antithetical parallelism between light and darkness
13:12b	5) The third line with exhortation to repudiate the "works of darkness"
13:12c	6) The fourth line with exhortation to put on "armor of light"
13:13	b. Elaborating the exhortation to repudiate the works of darkness
13:13a	1) The exhortation to behave in accordance with the eschatological day
13:13b	2) First pair of negative examples: "carousings and drunkenness"
13:13c	3) Second pair of negative examples: "affairs and indecencies"
13:13d	4) Third pair of negative examples: "strife and zealotry"
13:14	c. The antithesis of Christ mysticism
13:14a	1) The Pauline exhortation to "put on the Lord Jesus Christ"
13:14b	2) The exhortation to "make no provision for the flesh"

Exegesis

■ **11** The opening of this pericope is difficult to translate into English and its relevance has been obscured by the lack of awareness of cited material in the hymn of vv. 11-12. It is therefore unnecessary to supply $\pi\omicron\iota\epsilon\hat{\iota}\tau\epsilon$ ("you should do") to overcome the seeming awkwardness of v. 11a,[13] which disappears when the eschatological relevance of the Agape hymn is taken into account. The expression $\tau\omicron\hat{\upsilon}\tau\omicron \ \epsilon\grave{\iota}\delta\acute{\omicron}\tau\epsilon\varsigma$ ("knowing this") is used in an indicative sense, since it does not follow a finite verb in this sentence.[14] This is a typical formula for cited mater-

---

10 See Amos N. Wilder, *Early Christian Rhetoric*, 2d ed. (Cambridge: Harvard University Press, 1971) 107–17; Schille, *Frühchristliche Hymnen*; idem, "Katechese und Taufliturgie," *ZNW* 51 (1960) 113–21; Deichgräber, *Gotteshymnus*; Gloer, "Homologies and Hymns," 115–32; Quasten, *Music and Worship*; Schattenmann, *Prosahymnus*.

11 Weiss observed in "Beiträge," 245, that the third pair of vices breaks out of the formal series and does not fit into the theme of the succeeding verse

dealing with gratification of the flesh, but this overlooks the social setting of the love feast in which quarrels could easily arise.

12 Reicke, *Agapenfeier*, 248–51, deals with the parallel passage in Gal 5:18-21 as an expression of boundless celebration and zealotism in a congregation motivated by eschatological excitement. For the argument that Rom 13:13 warns against similar dangers in the Roman churches, see below.

ial in other Pauline letters,[15] indicating something that Paul is confident that the Roman believers fully understand.[16] In view of the hymn to be cited, it is not necessary to survey the entire range of the apocalyptic tradition to determine what was most likely to be present in Paul's mind or in Rome.[17] The context makes it likely that Paul is alluding to the premise widely shared in early Christianity that the messianic feast, referred to in the previous sentence as "the agape," reflected the dawning of the final age. The καιρός ("time") mentioned here is "the eschatological time that began with the sending of Christ," in Baumgarten's words,[18] but its present context includes the expectation of the Messiah's return in the eschatological love feast. Bo Reicke traced the emergence of this eschatological expectation in which justice would be restored and the poor would be fed in a great and joyous banquet (Isa 25:6-10; 65:13-19; Joel 2:15-26); the early church felt this expectation was fulfilled in its breaking of bread (e.g., Acts 2).[19] The word τὸν καιρόν functions here as a kind of double

accusative, providing the likely title of the hymn: "The Critical Time."[20] Paul plans to build on the eschatological premise of this hymn, nourished by the joyous celebrations of early congregations, in order to make a case about ethics that will provide leverage to deal with the conflicted situation in Rome.[21]

The first line in the hymn announces that "the hour" has already come for believers to live in the new reality of Christ's realm. In contrast to Paul's other uses of ὥρα ("hour") in a noneschatological sense as a past (2 Cor 7:8; Gal 2:5; 1 Thess 2:17; Phlm 15), present (1 Cor 4:11), or recurrent (1 Cor 15:30) moment in time, here it "refers to the eschatological hour of decision in which Christians must prove themselves."[22] The connotation is close to 1 John 2:18; Rev 3:3, 10, which may provide a hint about the source of this hymnic material; it does not appear to derive from the Pauline circle. The combination of ὥρα ἤδη ("hour [has come] already") is a colloquial expression for indicating that the appropriate time has long since arrived.[23] If Schlier were correct about

---

13   For example, Louw, 2:125; Leenhardt, 338; Schlier, 389; Fitzmyer, 682; *NIV*.

14   For a discussion of the participle used as an indicative, see Moulton, *Grammar I*, 182.

15   The most relevant parallels are καὶ τοῦτο προσεύχομαι ("And this do I pray") in Phil 1:9, 25; the Christ hymn is introduced by τοῦτο φρονεῖτε in Phil 2:5.

16   See Dunn, 2:785.

17   See Gerhard Dautzenberg, "Was bleibt von der Naherwartung? Zu Röm 13:11-14," in H. Merklein and J. Lange, eds., *Biblische Randbemerkungen: Schülerfestschrift Rudolf Schnackenburg . . .* (Würzburg: Echter, 1974) 365–67; and Anton Vögtle, "Röm 13:11-14 und die 'Nah'-Erwartung," in J. Friedrich et al., eds., *Rechtfertigung. Festschrift für Ernst Käsemann zum 70. Geburtstag* (Tübingen: Mohr-Siebeck, 1976) 562–68. Thompson also enters into this discussion, suggesting a dominical source for the end-time doctrine alluded to in this verse (*Clothed with Christ*, 143–44).

18   Jörg Baumgarten, "καιρός," *EDNT* 2 (1991) 333. Gerhard Delling, "καιρός," *TDNT* 3 (1965) 460, points out that the particular requirement of the present "time" in this passage of Romans is to fulfill the "exercise of brotherly love." The closest parallels are 2 Cor 6:2; 7:29; Gal 6:9-10. See also R. B. Onians, *The Origins of European Thought* (Cambridge: Cambridge University Press, 1951) 343–48.

19   Reicke, *Agapenfeier*, 186–206.

20   The use of words to indicate the titles of hymns or poems can be illustrated by Orphic titles such as Δίκτυον ("Net" in Orphica *Frag.* 289); Πέπλος ("Mantle" in Orphica *Frag.* 289); Κρατήρ ("Mixing Bowl" in Orphica *Frag.* 21); Σφαῖρα ("Globe" in Orphica *Frag.* 27). In the magical papyri there are titles such as Ἀφροδίτης Ὄνομα ("Aphrodite's Name" in *PGM* IV. 1265); Ξίφος Δαρδάνου ("Dardanos' Sword" in *PGM* IV. 1716); Ἀγωγή ("Fetching" in *PGM* IV. 2890); Ποτήριον ("Cup" in *PGM* VII. 643); Διάκοπος ("Breach" in *PGM* XII. 365), etc. In *Christologie*, 99, Schade identifies 13:11a as a kind of title for the following.

21   We find a similar combination of eschatological hymn followed by moral exhortation in Eph 5:14-20.

22   Heinz Giesen, "ὥρα," *EDNT* 3 (1993) 508; see 1 Thess 5:1; Eph 5:16.

23   Although Gerhard Delling cites no precise parallels in "ὥρα," *TDNT* 9 (1974) 675–81, the colloquial expression is found in Plato *Prot.* 361e6: νῦν δ' ὥρα ἤδη κατ' ἐπ' ἄλλο τι τρέπεσθαι ("But now it's past time to even turn to another matter"); Arrian *Tact.* 33.6.4: ὥρα ἤδη λέγειν ("it is past time to speak"); also Lucian of Samosata *Pseudol.* 32:12; Polybius *Hist.* 10.40.12; Pausanias *Graec. descr.* 9.13.5; Matt 14:15.

this hymm as baptismal, this wording would recollect the eschatological situation of the baptisand and reiterate the admonition to behave accordingly.[24] If, as seems more likely, the hymn was agapaic, it claims that the hour of the eschatological meal has already arrived; the eschatology is intensely realized because the "critical time" has come. In the context of the love feast, the hymn celebrates the new age as fully present in the meal itself.[25]

The image of being "roused from sleep" (ἐξ ὕπνου ἐγερθῆναι)[26] must be interpreted in the eschatological context rather than following the tradition of "the disparagement of sleep" that runs through Greco-Roman philosophy and the Jewish wisdom tradition.[27] Epictetus argued that if you are convinced that the good is a matter of pleasure, you should "go to bed and sleep, and lead the life of a worm . . . eat and drink and copulate and defecate and snore (βαλὼν κάθευδε καὶ τὰ τοῦ σκώληκος ποίει . . . ἔσθιε καὶ πῖνε καὶ συνουσίαζε καὶ ἀφόδευε καὶ ῥέγκε)." In contrast, he describes the heroic philosopher as "being raised from slumbers (τὸ ἐγεῖρον αὐτὸν ἐκ τῶν ὕπνων)" to do his writing, drawn by his higher nature to transcend base desires (Epictetus *Diss.* 2.20.10–11, 15). Similarly, the later *Corp. herm.* 1.15.23 links sleep with the fallen material world, referring to the Gnostic as one "who is exempt from sleep since he comes from a sleepless God (ἐξ ἀρρενοθήλεος ὢν πατρὸς καὶ ἄϋπνος ἀπὸ ἀϋπνου)." Thus Poimandres admonishes potential converts to the gnostic gospel with language reminiscent of our verse: "O you people, earth-born folk, you who have given yourselves to drunkenness and sleep and ignorance of God, be sober, cease from your surfeit, cease to be glamoured by irrational sleep (θελγόμενοι ὕπνῳ ἀλόγῳ)!" (*Corp.*

herm. 1.27.23).[28] While most Judaic materials have a more balanced appreciation of sleep, Prov 6:4-11 links it with sloth and resultant poverty, while Sir 22:8 associates sleep with an inability to concentrate the mind so as to understand wisdom. The NT shares this critical perspective (Mark 13:36; Matt 25:5-7; 1 Thess 5:5-8).[29] This wide range of negative connotations suggests that the wording of Rom 13:11b would place a heavy blame on persons oblivious to the arrival of the new age. The connection of ἤδη ("already") with ὥρα ("hour") has a mildly scolding quality, implying that "it is high time"[30] to wake up. The infinitive ἐγερθῆναι ("to be roused, awakened") is used elsewhere in the NT only in the context of Christ's resurrection, but here in the sense of "waken, stand up."[31] The sentence could easily be understood to imply that the audience is still inclined to sleep, even though it knows the eschatological crisis has arrived.[32] This rhetorical problem, which is not discussed in the recent commentaries and specialized investigations,[33] would be resolved if Schlier's hypothesis about a hymn being cited in 11b were accepted. Paul would then be reminding the Roman believers of the hymn in which they had regularly reminded themselves to wake from sleep so as to enjoy the messianic banquet. No remnant of scolding on Paul's part would then remain.

Following the Schlier hypothesis, I am taking v. 11c as an explanatory addition to the hymn written by Paul. The νῦν ("now") of v. 11c is in the emphatic position at the beginning of the clause, referring to "the eschatological now"[34] just as it had in 3:21 and 5:9. But there is a clear sense in this verse of "a moving on of the eschatological clock"[35] that was ticking according to a divine plan from the death and resurrection of Christ to the

24 Schlier, 396.
25 For the utopian background of such meals, see Pervo, "Panta Koina," 175–87.
26 For this translation of the idiom, see Fitzmyer, 682.
27 Heinrich Balz, "ὕπνος κτλ.," *TDNT* 8 (1972) 547–53.
28 Reference and ET from Evald Lövestam, *Spiritual Wakefulness in the New Testament*, LUÅ 55.3 (Lund: Gleerup, 1963) 26; see also *Acts Thom.* 110:43–44; 111:65 and various references in later Mandaean writings listed by Lövestam on 26 n. 5. Sleep as a gnostic symbol of "total abandonment to the world" is discussed by Jonas in *Gnostic Religion*, 70, while

the divine calling is typically expressed as awakening from sleep (81).
29 See Thompson, *Clothed with Christ*, 145.
30 Cranfield, 2:681, referring to Sanday and Headlam, 378.
31 Mark 14:28; Matt 16:21; 26:32; Luke 9:22; see Jakob Kremer, "ἐγείρω," *EDNT* 1 (1990) 372.
32 See Jülicher, 318.
33 See, for example, Lövestam, *Spiritual Wakefulness*, 37–39.
34 See Dunn, 1:257, 2:786.
35 Gustav Stählin, "νῦν," *TDNT* 4 (1967) 1120.

time of his parousia. Given the argument of Rom 8:19-25, "our salvation" (ἡμῶν ἡ σωτηρία) implies that the parousia will be "a universal eschatological event"[36] that includes the restoration of the entire creation. It will include the salvation of Jews (11:26) as well as Gentiles (11:11), thus comprising the hope that all nations will come to praise God (15:11), including even the barbarians in Spain situated at the end of the civilized world (1:14; 15:24, 28). That this cosmic event was perceived to be "closer" (ἐγγύτερον)[37] to its scheduled fulfillment reflects the expectation that Christ would return within the lifetime of the first generation of Christian converts. The comparative form "closer" is nevertheless unique in eschatological literature[38] and a hapax legomenon in the NT. The point of reference for the comparison is ἢ ὅτε ἐπιστεύσαμεν ("than when we came to faith"), referring to the conversion of Paul and his audience.[39] Rather than merely reminding the audience of shortened time left to believers in order to intensify the admonition to wakefulness in 11b,[40] this Pauline insertion extends the horizon beyond local love feasts to the missional purpose of cosmic salvation. While "salvation" was indisputably embodied in such Agape meals, it was not fulfilled therein. What the Roman house and tenement churches experience "now" is a step toward the ultimate event of cosmic restoration. When the ecstatic cry "Maranatha" ("Our Lord come!") was heard in the sacramental love feasts,[41] Paul wished to ensure that the future as well as the present coming of Christ remained in view. Without such a future eschatology, neither ethical accountability nor missional imperative could be maintained.

■ **12** The second line in the hymn that Paul is probably citing in this verse[42] employs an unusual expression for the night progressing toward its end: ἡ νὺξ προέκοψεν ("the night has far advanced").[43] The lack of a connective between 11c and 12a[44] reflects material being cited. The wording is reminiscent of the colloquial expression found in Josephus: "the night advanced (τῆς νύκτης προκοπτούσης) and the storm approached its climax," *Bell.* 4.298).[45] Gustav Stählin suggests that the aorist verb "has advanced, pushed forward" implies "the time of night when especially deep darkness holds sway just before the dawn."[46] In contrast to other Pauline passages where the change of the aeons has already occurred (2 Cor 5:17; 1 Cor 7:31), or where the old and new aeons coincide in tension with each other (1 Cor 7:29-31; 2 Cor 6:8-10), interpreters feel that this verse implies a turn from night to day in the present or near future.[47] Although the rhetorical use of a contrast between night and day has some biblical precedents (Ps 139:12; Isa 21:11-12), it is most fully developed by Paul in 1 Thess 5:4-7, which contrasts those who belong to the day and those to the night. But the metaphor of night yielding to day and bringing the reign of God is not found there; it appears to be a distinctive feature of the hymn that Paul is citing. It provides the reason why the participant in the Agape meal should recognize that it is "already the hour" to wake from the sleep of the old age and to take part in the celebration of the new age.

---

36 Barrett, 253. Similarly, Ziesler, 319, refers to "the cosmic consummation of the divine purposes."

37 Herbert Preisker, "ἐγγύς κτλ.," *TNDT* 2 (1964) 331, shows that the various forms of this word "express the characteristic aspect of the early Christian situation, being used of the eschatological fulfillment, of the great turning point in world history, of the coming of the kingdom of God." See Detlev Dormeyer, "ἐγγίζω," *EDNT* 1 (1991) 370, for an analysis of the idea of "the decisive day" in the NT.

38 Vögtle, "'Nah'-Erwartung," 564.

39 Godet, 450. Gerhard Barth, "πίστις, πιστεύω," *EDNT* 3 (1993) 93–94, confirms that the aorist of πιστεύω is a technical term for "becoming a Christian," referring to Luke 8:12; Acts 4:4; 8:13, etc.; 1 Cor 3:5; 15:2, 11; Gal 2:16. Paul uses the aorist of πιστεύω in reference to his converts coming to faith in 1 Cor 3:5 and 15:2, 11; Gal 2:16.

40 Vögtle, "'Nah'-Erwartung," 562, 565.

41 See Max Wilcox, "Maranatha," *ABD* 4 (1992) 514.

42 See the introduction to this chapter, notes 7–10.

43 Except for several patristic quotations, this exact expression is not found elsewhere in Greek literature. Pseudo-Galen *De rem. par.* 14.567.10 has a similar expression: "for you are not unaware how great a period had passed by (ὅσον χρόνον προέκοψεν)"; similarly, Damascius *Par.* 236.13 refers to the "passing of time (προκόπτει ὁ χρόνος)."

44 See Morris, 471.

45 See Wolfgang Schrenk, "προκόπτω, προκοπή," *EDNT* 3 (1993) 157–58.

46 Stählin, "προσκοπή κτλ.," *TDNT* 6 (1968) 716; see also Lövestam, *Spiritual Wakefulness*, 30.

47 See Lövestam, *Spiritual Wakefulness*, 3–33; Vögtle, "'Nah'-Erwartung," 566.

The final portion of the second line of the hymn echoes the word "closer" in the preceding verse: "the day is drawn near." The nearest echo of this wording seems to be the synoptic saying καὶ ἤγγικεν ἡ βασιλεία τοῦ θεοῦ ("and the kingdom of God draws near," Mark 1:15 and parallels). Whereas Paul uses "the day" (ἡ ἡμέρα) elsewhere in the absolute sense without attributes to refer to the day of judgment (1 Thess 5:5; 1 Cor 3:13), this hymnic reference is to "the epoch since the resurrection of Jesus Christ"[48] that is experienced in the love feast itself. In contrast to the usually threatening tone of most early Christian discourse about the "day of the Lord,"[49] this verse has a joyous, celebrative quality. For the believer who has accepted the gospel, the period of hopeless darkness is over and the daylight of a new era has dawned. The impression of a thoroughly realized eschatology in this Agape hymn is reinforced by this wording.

In the third line of the hymn, the first person plural style in the hortatory subjunctive ἀποβαλώμεθα ("let us cast off")[50] of 12c places the congregation in solidarity with fellow believers. The use of a word not otherwise used by Paul points to cited material. The closest parallel is Hermas's description of converts who "cast aside desires" (ἀποβάλωσι τὰς ἐπιθυμίας) for "these women"; males can only enter God's house if they "cast aside the deeds" (ἀποβάλωσι τὰ ἔργα) of such temptresses.[51] The middle voice of this verb, found here, is used in the sense of discarding objects rather than undressing, as required for the Schlier hypothesis of a baptismal ceremony. This wording carries forward the motif of line 1 in the hymn, rising from sleep and casting off the bed covering. In the baptismal material of the Pauline tradition, the more conventional verb for

taking off clothing (ἀποτίθεμαι) is employed (Eph 4:22, 25; Col 3:8); it is also employed by Greek moralists for putting off vices.[52] What the hymn urges to be tossed off are the "works of darkness." While Galatians counseled an ongoing struggle against the "works of the flesh" (Gal 5:19), and 2 Cor 6:14 rejects any "partnership" with "darkness," the closest parallels to this expression in the hymn come from Judaism.[53] In *T. Levi* 19.1, we find a call to decisive action that associates "darkness" with satanic works:[54] "And now, my children, you have heard everything. Choose either the light or the darkness (τὸ σκότος), the law of the Lord or the works of Beliar (τὰ ἔργα τοῦ Βελίαρ)." This antithesis between "the Law of the Lord" and "the works of Beliar" is reminiscent of the antithesis in Rom 13:12c-d. An inherent opposition between "darkness" and "good works" is found in *T. Benj.* 5.3: "For where someone has a respect for good works (ἀγαθῶν ἔργων) . . . the darkness (τὸ σκότος) will flee from him."[55] The likely reason for this association is that darkness cloaks activities understood to be shameful or unlawful; in the words of the War Scroll that are strongly reminiscent of the phrase in Rom 13:12c, "they are the congregation of wickedness *and all their works occur in the darkness* (ובחושך כול מעשיהם)."[56] In the context of Romans, this reference to works of darkness in the hymn would evoke associations with Paul's earlier critique of the "works of law" (3:20, 28) that contrast with "good works" (2:7; 13:3).

The final line in the cited hymn urges converts to gird themselves for battle. The expression "let us step into the armor of light" reflects the verb ἐνδύω that implies a garment like a tunic or a suit of armor that one "steps into" or "sinks into."[57] For example, Herodotus

---

48 See Gerhard Delling, "ἡμέρα," *TDNT* 2 (1964) 952–53.

49 See Wolfgang Trilling, "ἡμέρα," *EDNT* 2 (1991) 121: "the center of gravity in NT use of ἡμέρα is in reference to the eschatological *day*, the day of judgment and redemption . . . derived from the OT and Jewish tradition of 'the day of Yahweh.'"

50 See note b for the basis of the text-critical choice of ἀποβαλώμεθα.

51 *Herm. Sim.* 91.1–2; see also *Herm. Mand.* 42.4: "Therefore cast off grief from yourself and all shall live to God who cast away (ἀποβάλωσιν) grief from themselves, and put on (ἐνδύσωνται) all joy."

52 Demosthenes *Orat.* 8.46; Plutarch *Cor.* 19.4; see also *Ep. Arist.* 122.

53 See Hans Conzelmann, "σκότος κτλ.," *TDNT* 7 (1971) 442; Heiligenthal, *Werke*, 225–27.

54 See also *T. Naph.* 2.10; 1QM 15:9; for other references, see Conzelmann, "σκότος κτλ.," *TDNT* 7 (1971) 432.

55 See also *T. Levi* 18.4; 1QH 18:28; 1QM 1:8.

56 1QM 15.9, cited by Thompson, *Clothed with Christ*, 148.

57 See the *OCD³* article on "dress," 497–98: "most classical garments belonged either to the category of mantles or cloaks that were 'thrown around' . . . or

Hist. 7.218 refers to "men dressed in armor" (ἐνδυομέ-νους ὅπλα) and Xenophon *Cyr.* 1.4.18 describes Cyrus "then stepping into armor for the first time" (αὐτὸς πρῶτον τότε ὅπλα ἐνδύς).[58] In contrast to the hymn's reference to ὅπλον as armor, Paul's earlier use of this term in Rom 6:13 clearly referred to the weapons themselves. The translation with "weapons" is required for 2 Cor 6:7 (τῶν ὅπλων τῶν δικαιοσύνης, "weapons of righteousness") and 10:4 (τὰ ὅπλα τῆς στρατείας ἡμῶν, "the weapons of our warfare"). As in this hymn, Paul uses the verb ἐνδύω ("put on") in the figurative sense in 2 Cor 5:3; 1 Thess 5:8, and Col 3:12. There are significant precedents for this metaphorical use of clothing oneself[59] in references such as "to put on righteousness" (δικαιοσύνην δὲ ἐνεδεδύκειν, Job 29:14; also Ps 131:9; Wis 5:18) or "a high priest putting on doctrine and truth" (ἀρχιερεὺς ἐνδεδυμένος τὴν δήλωσιν καὶ τὴν ἀλήθειαν, 1 Esdr 5:40). Isa 52:1 cries out, "Awake, awake Zion, put on your strength . . . and put on your glory, Jerusalem" (Ἐξεγείρου ἐξεγείρου Σιών, ἔνδυσαι τὴν ἰσχύν σου . . . καὶ σὺ ἔνδυσαι τὴν δόξαν σου Ἰερουσαλήμ). The liturgical background of this metaphorical use is indicated by the description of the priestly raiment of Aaron: "He [God] exalted Aaron . . . beautified him with lovely ornaments and clothed him with a robe of glory. He put on him a proud consummation (Ἐνέδυσεν αὐτὸν συντέλειαν καυχήματος) and strengthened him with rich garments, with breeches, a long robe, and the ephod" (Sir 45:6-8). As Edgar Haulotte has shown,[60] the priestly garments symbolize the sanctification and consecration of someone to temple service. Throughout the ancient world, forms of clothing signified specific tribal and social identities, whether slave or free, common, royal, or priestly.[61] In the NT era, the metaphors of clothing are used to symbolize the new identity in Christ.[62] Haulotte observes that while the LXX tends to use active verbs for such raiment, the metaphorical uses of ἐνδύω in the NT, including Rom 13:12, employ the middle voice to convey the idea of individual (and, I would add, group) transformation.[63]

While the expression "armor of light" appears to be unique to the hymn, the association of "light" with weapons and armor appears to derive from Jewish apocalyptic literature.[64] Although φῶς ("light") is employed in Greek poetry and drama,[65] in moral discourse by Greco-Roman philosophers,[66] in descriptions of initiations offered by mystery religions,[67] in the OT,[68] in Hel-

---

to those items, including tunics, that were 'entered into.'"

58 See also Dionysius Halicarnassus *Antiq. Rom.* 9.34.4; Pausanias *Graec. descr.* 4.28.7; 8.5.9; 8.53.10.

59 See the extensive list in Albrecht Oepke, "δύω κτλ.," *TDNT* 2 (1964) 319.

60 Edgar Haulotte, *Symbolique du vêtement selon la Bible*, Theologie 65 (Paris: Aubier, 1966) 44–54.

61 Ibid., 76–79.

62 Ibid., 210–21.

63 Ibid., 212–13.

64 See Hans Conzelmann, "φῶς κτλ.," *TDNT* 9 (1974) 312; Dunn, 2:788.

65 See Rudolf Bultmann, "Zur Geschichte der Lichtsymbolik im Altertum," 323–35, in R. Bultmann, *Exegetica.*

66 For example, Plato says that the philosopher kings would be required "to turn the vision of their souls upwards and fix their gaze on what sheds light on all (τὸ πᾶσι φῶς παρέχον) and when they have beheld the good itself (τὸ ἀγαθὸν αὐτό), they shall employ it as the pattern for the proper ordering of the state" (*Resp.* 540a). See Bultmann, "Lichtsymbolik," 336–48; D. Bremer, "Hinweise zum griechi-schen Ursprung und zur europäischen Geschichte der Lichtmetaphysik," *ABG* 17 (1973) 7–35; D. Torrent, "Greek Metaphors of Light," *CQ* 54 (1960) 181–87.

67 For example, Apuleius *Metam.* 11.23 describes the initiate's experience: "I came to the boundary of death, and having passed through the threshold of Proserpina, I traveled through all the elements and returned. In the middle of the night I saw the sun flashing with light (*vidi solem candido coruscantem lumine*). I came face to face with the gods below and the gods above and worshipped them." See Martin Dibelius, "Die Vorstellung vom göttlichen Licht. Ein Kapitel aus der hellenistischen Religionsgeschichte," *DLZ* 36 (1915) 1469–83.

68 For example, Ps 119:105 declares, "Your law is a lamp to my feet and a light (φῶς) to my paths," while 19:8 confesses, "the commandment of the Lord is bright, enlightening (φωτίζουσα) the eyes." Prov 4:18 says, "But the paths of the righteous shine like light (ὁμοίως φωτὶ λάμπουσιν); they go on and make light (φωτίζουσιν) until the day has fully come." See also Sverre Aalen, *Die Begriffe "Licht" und "Finsternis" im Alten Testament, Spätjudentum*

lenistic Judaism,[69] and in Gnosticism,[70] the martial association is found only in Qumran. The War Scroll opens with the words "the beginning of the attack of the Sons of Light against the company of the Sons of Darkness, the army of Satan" (1QM 1:1). It continues to describe the battle against the "Kittim," probably the Romans, in which "the Sons of Light" fight against "iniquity" and annihilate the Sons of Darkness (1QM 1:10-11). The enemies of the community are "the company of darkness, but the company of God belongs to the Light" (אל לאור וגורל, 1QM 13:5). The community is given this assurance:

> You have decreed for us a destiny of light (אור הפלתגו ובגורל) according to your truth. And the Prince of Light you have appointed from of old to come to our aid, and all the spirits of truth are under his dominion. But Satan, the angel of malevolence, you have created for Sheol; his realm is in darkness and his purpose is to bring about wickedness and iniquity. . . . You have appointed the day of battle from ancient times to come to the aid of truth and to destroy iniquity, to bring down darkness and to magnify light (חושך ולהגביר אור), to stand forever, and to destroy all the sons of darkness. (1QM 13:9-15)

This language is adopted by Paul in 1 Thess 5:5-8, which refers to believers as υἱοὶ φωτός ("sons of light") who should clothe themselves with the "breastplate of faith and love" and "the helmet of the hope of salvation" in order to participate in the eschatological battle.[71] These parallels suggest that the expression "weapons of light," although not found elsewhere, implies that believers should engage in the struggle between light and darkness.[72] Neufeld's conclusion about the divine warrior metaphor appears apt for Rom 13:12: "Paul lays the groundwork for a critical and confrontative ethic vis-à-vis the security state and its ideology, even if the means of that confrontation are faith, love, and hope."[73] In view of the placement of this material after Rom 13:1-7, it certainly appears that any martial implications are ruled out. Whatever its precise source, this liturgical fragment serves Paul's purpose by reinforcing the stance of believers in struggling against the forces of the old age not with the traditional weapons used by Rome but with the armor of the new age.

■ **13** In the next two verses, Paul provides his own elaboration of the moral implications of the Agape hymn. The rhythmic disparity between this material and the five-beat structure of the hymn indicates that Paul's own voice is surfacing again. The exhortation to live in the day rather than the night concentrates in an unusual manner on activities associated with symposia, which matches the contextualization of the love ethic within the system of early Christian love feasts, shown in the preceding pericope. The precise formulation of "as by day" (ὡς ἐν ἡμέρᾳ) does not recur in the NT, the closest parallels being in the LXX.[74] There is a debate about

---

und im Rabbinismus, SNVAO 1951.1 (Oslo: Dybwad, 1951); S. Agrelo, "El tema bíblico de la luz," *Ant* 50 (1975) 353–417.

69 For example, Philo teaches that "wisdom is not only, in the manner of light (φωτὸς τρόπον), a means of sight, but is able to see its own self besides. Wisdom is God's archetypal radiance (ἀρχέτυπον φέγγος) and the sun is a copy and image of it" (*Migr.* 40). See Erwin Ramsdell Goodenough, *By Light, Light: The Mystic Gospel of Hellenistic Judaism* (New Haven: Yale University Press, 1935; repr. Amsterdam: Philo Press, 1969); Franz-Norbert Klein, *Die Lichtterminologie bei Philon von Alexandrien und in den hermetischen Schriften. Untersuchungen zur Struktur der religiösen Sprache der hellenistischen Mystik* (Leiden: Brill, 1962).

70 For example, in the *Corp. herm.* 1.6, Poimandres urges believers to "understand the light (νόει τὸ φῶς), then, and recognize it." He explains in 1:17

that "from life and light the man became soul and mind; from life came soul, but from light came mind (ἐκ δὲ φωτὸς νοῦν)." See Dibelius, "Vorstellung vom göttlichen Licht," 1469–83; Wilson, *Gnosis and the New Testament*, 49; Rudolf, *Gnosis*, 84–87, 335–39.

71 See also Phil 2:15; 1 Cor 4:5; 2 Cor 4:4-6; 6:7; 10:4; Eph 6:13-17; and Lech Remigius Stachowiak, "Die Antithese Licht–Finsternis, ein Thema der paulinischen Paränese," *ThQ* 143 (1963) 385–421; Thomas R. Yoder Neufeld, *Put on the Armour of God: The Divine Warrior from Isaiah to Ephesians*, JSNTSup 140 (Sheffield: Sheffield Academic Press, 1997) 84–93.

72 See Murray, 2:170; Wilckens, 3:77.

73 Neufeld, *Put on the Armour of God*, 92.

74 See ὡς ἐν ἡμέρᾳ σκοπιᾶς ("as in a day of keeping watch") in Sir 40:6 and ὡς ἐν ἡμέρᾳ ἑορτῆς ("as in a day of feasting") in Zeph 3:17 and Lam 2:7.

whether the "as" in ὡς ἐν ἡμέρα depicts the real conditions of the new age currently present,[75] proleptic conditions, that is, living as if the new age were present whereas it is in fact "not yet here,"[76] or the ongoing tension between the "Already" and the "Not-yet."[77] The former appears more likely, because Paul is developing a contrast between two forms of behavior, the one associated with the evil darkness of night and the other with the righteous light of day, both of which are present realities for the Roman believers. This discussion gained cogency because the sacramental love feasts of early Christianity occurred mostly at night, which opened the movement to charges of secret, nocturnal orgies that had been leveled against earlier cults throughout Greco-Roman culture. So Paul is urging the Roman house and tenement churches to walk "as by day" in the metaphorical sense even though they meet at night.

The moral theme in εὐσχημόνως περιπατήσωμεν ("let us walk decently") employs an adverbial form of an adjective that ordinarily refers to "conventional respectability."[78] It is a Greco-Roman moral concept concerning the avoidance of public shame by outwardly conforming to accepted standards,[79] a concept infrequently represented in the Jewish sources.[80] For example, Socrates is reported to have accepted the death penalty of the court rather than taking the opportunity to escape because "he regards what is decent" (τὸ εὔσχημον σκοπεῖ) in the sense of publicly accepted "virtue and moral excellence."[81] Public inscriptions used this term to applaud the decent behavior of honorees, as, for example, in the second-century B.C.E. inscription at Magnesia: ἐποίησαν[τ]ο δὲ καὶ τὴν παρεπιδημίαν καλὴν καὶ εὐσχήμονα καὶ ἀξίαν ἀμφοτέρων τῶν πόλεων ("And they have made an excellent and decent and worthwhile residency in both cities").[82] A new defin-

ition of decency is suggested, however, by the coordination with the luminous reality of the new age. As in other Pauline passages where the idea of decency appears (1 Thess 4:12; 1 Cor 7:35; 12:23-24; 14:40), a public impression on outsiders is in view,[83] but its moral shape is provided by the new standard of behavior brought by Christ.[84] The use of περιπατέω for behavior or conduct occurred also in Rom 6:4, but here we find the ingressive aorist subjunctive, conveying an imperative that reveals a "contrast with prior conduct."[85] This continues the antithesis to the "works of darkness" that characterize the old age (13:12), and the admonition, although coming from Paul rather than from the hymn, flows directly out of the latter and thus does not depend entirely on Paul's authority.

The ethical antitheses that follow are primarily a reflection of the dangers of excesses associated with nocturnal feastings in the Greco-Roman world. These dangers were particularly threatening at night when public controls were not available. The cultural and political environment also diminished the scope of internalized moral limitations, because, as Lagrange pointed out, "it was believed among the Romans that during the night everything was permitted."[86] For example, the following was reported of Nero: "No sooner was twilight over (*post crepusculum statim*) than he would catch up a cap or a wig and go to the taverns and range about the streets playing pranks, which however were very far from harmless; for he used to beat men as they came home from dinner, stabbing any who resisted him and throwing them into the sewers" (Suetonius *Nero* 26). The indecent behavior typical of the night was therefore a matter of public discussion during this period in Rome, particularly for those likely to become victims of such abuse, thus providing vivid background for Paul's admonitions. But the

---

75   Schlier, 398; Cranfield, 2:686–87; Käsemann, 363; Wilckens, 3:77; Moo, 824.

76   Barrett, 254; see also Lietzmann, 113.

77   Dunn, 2:789; see also Sampley, *Walking*, 13–17.

78   Dunn, 2:789.

79   See particularly Ceslas Spicq, "εὐσχημόνως κτλ.," *TLNT* 2 (1994) 139–42. Key references are in Plutarch *Quaest. conv.* 746d1; Epictetus *Diss.* 2.5.23; Xenophon *Mem.* 3.12.4; *Cyr.* 1.3.8–9; Aristotle *Eth. nic.* 1101a1.

80   See Heinrich Greeven, "εὐσχήμων," *TDNT* 2 (1964)

771, noting that this word appears in the LXX only at Prov 11:25 and 4 Macc 6.2.

81   Epictetus *Diss.* 4.1.163–65.

82   *I.Magn.* Nr. 101 14-15, cited by Greeven, "εὐσχήμων," 771.

83   See Unnik, "Reaktion der Nicht-Christen," 498–522.

84   See Zahn, 566; Wilckens, 3:77; Morris, 472.

85   BDF §337, 173: "Thus R 13:13 περιπατήσωμεν with reference to the commencement of this way of life."

86   Cited from Dunn, 2:789, from Lagrange, 318.

content of these admonitions seems to concentrate on indoor activities associated with symposia rather than on activities on the city streets.

The first of three rhetorically effective pairs of negative examples, μὴ κώμοις καὶ μέθαις ("not in carousings and drunkenesses"), indicates frequent or habitual behavior that would be particularly troubling when occurring in the context of the love feast, or simply in the buildings where Christian groups reside. The plural forms signify habitual behavior, with frequent episodes.[87] Κῶμος originally had religious connotations.[88] It was associated with the Anthesteria celebrations, parodies of official processions in which ribald masks, dances, and invective were used, and with Dionysian celebrations in which devotees danced and celebrated in an uncontrollable, ecstatic manner in the belief that the god Dionysius had taken them over. It later came to be used for carousings of other sorts, looked on with disapproval by some Jewish and Greco-Roman moralists.[89] Despite such protests, carousing remained typical for Roman dinners, as Bruce Winter reports: tables were reserved for drinking bouts and activities with prostitutes.[90] Cicero describes how young men behaved in the parties celebrating their coming-of-age (toga virilis): "If there is anyone who thinks that youth should be forbidden affairs even with courtesans, he is doubtless eminently austere; but his view is not only contrary to the license of this age, but also to the custom and concessions of our ancestors. For when was this not a common practice? When was it blamed? When was it forbidden? When, in fact, was it, that "what is allowed" was not allowed?"[91] In the vice catalog of Gal 5:21, Paul lists κῶμοι as well as μέθαι, both in the plural, which suggests that these are regular features of the unseemly behavior that marks the old age. Μέθη is the common word for drunkenness, which has a negative connotation in the LXX[92] and is treated with ambivalence in Hellenistic Judaism.[93] The association of drunkenness with night and the present age is developed in 1 Thess 5:5-8.[94]

The second pair of "works of darkness" relates to sexual excesses and was associated with the drunken dining pleasures of revelry typical of Greco-Roman symposia.[95] Ἡ κοίτη ("the bed") is a euphemism for sexual intercourse. Adultery was thought of as "defiling the bed," as expressed by the wife of Potiphar who accuses Joseph as "this wicked slave who tried to defile your bed" (κοίτην μιᾶναι τὴν σὴν, Josephus Ant. 2.55). The singular form of this word was used in a positive sense in Rom 9:10 with reference to the intercourse between Rebecca and Jacob, resulting in the child of promise, Isaac. However, the plural implies a series of sexual affairs, illicit in Jewish and Christian eyes because it violates the monogamous ideal. The negative connotation of the word "beddings" is reinforced by its association with ἀσέλγεια, a "comprehensive expression for evil and perversion."[96] "Debauchery" and "sexual excess" are implied by this word, especially when it occurs in the plural.[97] Such activities are condemned throughout the NT (Mark 7:22; 2 Cor 12:21; Gal 5:19; 1 Pet 4:3) and by Hellenistic Judaism (Wis 14:26; Philo Mos. 1.305); they are associated with Sodom and Gomorrah (2 Pet 2:7).

---

87 Dunn, 2:789.
88 See Ceslas Spicq, "κῶμος," TLNT 2 (1994) 353.
89 See Wis 14:23; 2 Macc 6:4; Diodorus Siculus Hist. 17.72; Philo Cher. 92; Dio Chrysostom Orat. 4.110. Sib. Or. 8.118 warns against "getting drunk at lawless carousels" (κώμοις μεθύοντες ἀθέσμοις). Josephus charges that Archelaus seemed to grieve by day, but "at night was getting drunk to the point of all out carousings" (νύκτωρ δὲ μέχρις κώμων μετυσκόμενος, Bell. 2.29.3).
90 Winter, "Romans 12–15," 86.
91 Translation taken from Winter, "Romans 12–15," 86, citing Cicero Cael. 20.48.
92 See Herbert Preisker, "μέθη κτλ.," TDNT 4 (1967) 546, referring to Isa 28:7; Prov 20:1; Sir 31:30.
93 Preisker, "μέθη κτλ.," 546–47, referring to Philo Plant. 162–65; Leg. 1.84, etc.

94 The suggestion has been made by Dunn, 2:789, and Cranfield that the two words belong together as a hendiadys "drunken bout" or "drunken revelry," but this seems unlikely. As noted above, the two words are closely associated because of the symposia background.
95 A particularly clear illustration of the association between carousing and debauchery may be found in Dio Chrysostom Orat. 4.110.3, describing someone "who carouses by day in licentious carousel" (κωμάζοντι μεθ᾽ ἡμέραν ἀσελγῆ κῶμον).
96 Horst Goldstein, "ἀσέλγεια," EDNT 1 (1990) 169.
97 See Otto Bauernfeind, "ἀσέλγεια," TDNT 1 (1964) 490.

The final pair of nightly actions relates to partisanship that was characteristic of the Greco-Roman world, and, according to many clues in Romans, was surfacing in the relationships between Christian groups in Rome. That both words are in the singular suggests that Paul does not have in mind repetitive actions so much as a stance of partisanship. We encountered ἔρις ("strife") in 1:29 and ζῆλος in 10:2. Both words were used by Paul in 1 Cor 3:3 and 2 Cor 12:20 in connection with partisan conflict that was threatening the unity of the Corinthian churches.[98] But this negative connotation was not typical of the Greco-Roman world as a whole, which celebrated a virtual "cult of rivalry."[99] In Spicq's description, "The Greeks divinized Dispute or Emulation, which they considered the energizing spirit of the world and one of the primordial forces."[100] Winter notes that strife was a regular feature of Roman dinner parties, because, as Athenaeus reported, "after drinking comes mockery, after mockery filthy insults, after insults a law-suit, after the lawsuit a verdict."[101] The early Christian revolution in the honor and shame system turned this tendency upside down, viewing "strife" and "dispute" as factors of the old age—the deeds of darkness—that eroded the equality of believers and destroyed the faith community.

In connection with 10:2 I described the distinctively Jewish background of religious zeal.[102] Here is partisanship in a broader Greco-Roman context, aimed at "personal advancement" in the competition over honor.[103] Since the expression ζῆλος καὶ ἔρις appears in 1 Cor 3:3 in description of partisanship in Corinth and the words stand next to each other in the vice catalogs of 2 Cor 12:20 and Gal 5:20, it is clear that Paul ranks these features of social competition along with the two previous pairs of vices as marks of the old age of darkness that the new form of Christian decency should avoid.

■ **14** In contrast to v. 13, where Paul conforms to the first person plural rhetoric of the Agape hymn, here he moves into a second person plural imperatival style. With ἀλλά ("but") indicating an antithesis with the works of darkness described in the preceding verse, Paul exhorts the Roman house and tenement churches to "put on" (ἐνδύσασθε) Christ, a powerful expression of early Christian mysticism.[104] Some have identified this language as baptismal,[105] which is certainly the context of the close parallel in Gal 3:27, ὅσοι γὰρ εἰς Χριστὸν ἐβαπτίσθητε, Χριστὸν ἐνεδύσασθε ("For as you were all baptized into Christ, you put on Christ").[106] But the most one could contend is that Paul is here reminding the Roman believers of earlier baptismal experiences. It is unlikely that he is calling for a further baptism.[107] The same idiom occurs in the context of acting in Dionysius of Halicarnassus *Antiq. Rom.* 11.5.2, ἀλλὰ τὸν Ταρκύνιον ἐκεῖνον ἐνδυόμενοι ("but they dressing the role of that Tarquin"). There are also parallels, though from a later period, in the mystery religions and Gnosticism.[108] These parallels reinforce the impression that Paul has a profound form of Christian mysticism in view here, in which the divine righteousness revealed in Christ transforms believers and communities, freeing them from the compulsions of the old age of darkness with its sensuality and competitive strife, and enabling them to live under the lordship of Christ. Although this admonition

98 See Heinz Giesen, "ἔρις," *EDNT* 2 (1991) 52–53.
99 Ceslas Spicq, "ἐριθίζω κτλ.," *TLNT* 2 (1994) 71, citing J. Delorme, *Gymnasion* (Paris, 1960) 460: "For any instance in which it was possible to make a comparison between two people on some particular point, the Greeks set up a contest and established rankings, if not prizes. If a battle took place, they compared the individual or collective valor of the combatants. If there were dramatic productions at the theater, a jury rated the poets, the actors, the chorus leaders. They went so far as to compare deaths." This characteristic was not restricted to Greece; Spicq (72) refers to other areas of the Mediterranean world where nations were described by Strabo *Geogr.* 5.1.10 as having invaded each other "out of a spirit of rivalry (ἔρις)."
100 Spicq, "ἐριθίζω κτλ.," 71.
101 Citation from Winter, "Romans 12–15," 88, from Athenaeus *Deipn.* 2.36.
102 See Stumpff, "ζῆλος κτλ.," 877–80.
103 Ibid., 881–82.
104 See Schmidt, 225; Lövestam, *Spiritual Wakefulness*, 41–45; Jost Eckert, "'Zieht den Herrn Jesus Christus an . . . ! (Röm 13, 14). Zu einer enthusiastischen Metapher der neutestamentlichen Verkündigung," *TThZ* 105 (1996) 99–60.
105 See Schlier, 399; Michel, 417; Käsemann, 363–64; Müller, *Prophetie*, 147; Ortkempter, *Leben*, 146.
106 See Jung Hoon Kim, *The Significance of Clothing Imagery in the Pauline Corpus*, JSNTSup 268 (London / New York: T. & T. Clark, 2004) 150–51.
107 Dunn, 2:791.
108 See Betz, *Galatians*, 187; Oepke, "δύω κτλ.,"

appears to flow directly out of the Agape hymn, and has no signs of polemical intent, it is actually a more fully Christianized formulation than the hymn's reference to putting on the "armor of light," which could have been derived from Qumran and other branches of apocalyptic Judaism. The formula "Lord Jesus Christ" recurs here from 1:7, placing lordship in the place of emphasis; in Käsemann's words, "Paul is concerned about the lordship of Christ which must be confirmed and passed on by every Christian and which stands in sharp opposition to the powers that rule the world."[109] The One whose lordship climaxed in shameful death in behalf of the shamed rules a new community in which the competition for pleasure and honor is no longer dominant. Christian mysticism of the Pauline type places the transformed community under obedience to the Lord who rules the day and overcomes the shameful legacy of night.

The idiom πρόνοιαν ποιεῖσθαι ("make provision") is found in legal, administrative, and business contexts but employed only here in the Pauline letters. For example, a second-century B.C.E. papyrus letter contains the explanation, "therefore as you had made no provision for your interests (ὅθεν ὑμῶν μηδεμίαν πρόνοιαν ποησαμένων) . . . I was obliged to remove Arius."[110] The concept of fleshly passions was developed in 7:5-8, having surfaced years earlier in the context of the Judaizer crisis (Gal 5:16, 24), where it depicts not the lures of the lower nature as in Hellenistic dualism, but rather the desire for honor through competitive performance.[111] The desires of the flesh are to gain dominance, pleasure, and prestige, to act in self-centered ways that demonstrate superior honor.[112] These perverse expressions of twisted systems of honor and shame, whose successes and failures produce the "works of darkness," are countered by the shameful death of Christ in behalf of the shamed, and by the incorporation of the transformed community under the lordship of Christ. Therefore, no "provision" is to be granted to such works. The new ethos of light replaces the competition and exploitation of the darkling night with the mutuality of grace. But this ethos must be hallowed and preserved in the new community's constant battle against the "works of darkness" within and without. Thus the final admonition sets the framework for understanding the following pericopes, in which Paul takes up the issues within Roman Christianity where competitive and domineering "desires of the flesh" are surfacing in hostility between the house and tenement churches. It will soon become clear that the decisive act of putting on Christ and opposing the flesh will be to "welcome one another as Christ has welcomed you" (Rom 15:7).

319–20; and especially the judicious assessment of Wedderburn, *Baptism and Resurrection*, 338–40.

109 Käsemann, 363.

110 *P.Amh.* 2. Nr. 40.12–18, cited along with other references in MM 543.

111 See Jewett, *Terms*, 99–108.

112 In the context of Paul's argument, the interpretation of "desires" in terms of "lust" as in Räisänen, "ἐπιθυμία and ἐπιθυμεῖν," 108–9, seems inappropriate.

14

The Seventh Pericope

Exemplary Guidelines for the Weak and the Strong

1/ Welcome the one who is weak in his faith, but not for disputes over opinions.[a] 2/ The one has faith to eat everything, while the weak person eats[b] leafy vegetables. 3/ Let the one who eats not despise the one who does not eat; let the[c] one who does not eat not judge the one who eats; for God has welcomed him. 4/ Who are you to be judging another's house slave? It is in relation to his own Lord that he stands or falls. He will be made to stand because the Lord[d] has the power[e] to enable him to stand.

5/ Now[f] the one person judges one day better than another, while the other judges all days [alike]. Let each be fully convinced in his own thinking. 6/ The one setting his mind on the day sets his mind in relation to a Lord,[g] and[h] the one eating eats in relation to the Lord, since he is giving thanks to God. And he who does not eat does so in relation to a Lord, and he gives thanks to God. 7/ For none of us lives in relation to himself, and none dies in relation to himself. 8/ For if we live, we live in relation to the Lord, and if we die,[i] we die[j] in relation to the Lord. So whether we live or die, we belong to the Lord. 9/ For it was to this end that Christ[k] died and lived[l] in order that he might be Lord over both the dead and the living.

10/ But who are you to judge your brother? Or also who are you to despise your brother? For all shall stand before the judicial bench of God.[m] 11/ For it is written,
   "As I live, says the Lord,
      that[n] to me shall every knee bow
   and every tongue shall acknowledge God."
         12/ So[o] each of us shall give[p] account of himself.[q]

a   The minor variant λογισμῶν ("thoughts") in 69 81 1175 1874 2344 pc in place of διαλογισμῶν ("opinions") may be due to haplography caused by the replication of δια- / δια- at the end of the sentence.

b   The imperative form ἐσθιέτω ("let him eat") found in P46 D* F G it vgww Ambst is too weakly attested to be original and does not fit the context. Cranfield,

2:701, offers a plausible suggestion that it arose as an assimilation to the imperative forms in the next verse. There is stronger support for ἐσθίει ("he eats") in ℵ A B C D2 L P Ψ 048 6 69 33 104 323 326 330 365 424 614 945 1175 1241 1243 1319 1505 1506 1573 1735 1739 1836 1874 1881 2344 2495 Maj vgst sy cop Tert Cl.

c   Several variant readings of the opening words of this clause are found. Καὶ ὁ ("also the") in ℵc D2 L P Ψ 0285 6 33 61 69 81 88 181 104 218 256 263 323 326 330 365 424 436 441 451 459 467 614 621 629 630 720 915 917 945 1175 1241 1243 1398 1505 1563 1573 1678 1718 1735 1739 (1751 lacks μή) 1836 1838 1845 1852 1874 1875 1877 1881 1908 1912 1942 1959 1962 (2127 lacks μή) 2138 2197 2200 2344 2492 2495 2516 2523 2455 2718 Maj lat syh is an improved, secondary reading. F and G offer οὐδὲ ὁ ("nor the"), which would also be an improvement, but is weakly attested and secondary. The third variant appears to be the earliest, ὁ δέ ("and/but the") in P46 ℵ* A B C D* 048vid 5 623 1506 2110 pc Cl, because it is rougher and more strongly attested.

d   In place of κύριος ("lord") in P46 ℵ A B C P Ψ 1852 pc (syp has κύριος αὐτοῦ ["his Lord"]) sa bo arm geo1 slavms Severian Optatus Aug1/6, the reading Θεός ("God") is found in D F G L 048 6 33 69 81 88 104 181 256 263 323 326 330 365 424 436 451 459 614 629 945 1175 1241 1243 1319 1505 1506 1573 1735 1739 1836 1874 1877vid 1881 1912 1962 2127 2200 2344 2492 2495 Maj Lect ar b d f g o vg syh geo2 slavms Orlat Bas Chr Cyp Ps-Cyp Ambst Pacian Hier Pel Aug5/6. The former reading is better attested and the latter can be explained as an assimilation to the wording of v. 3, according to Metzger, Textual Commentary, 530, and Cranfield, 2:704.

e   The reading δυνατεῖ γάρ ("for he has the power/ is strong") in ℵ A B C D* F G 1962c is to be preferred because it is better attested, more awkward, and contains the rarer word δυνατέω ("be strong"). The readings δυνατός γάρ ("for strong") in P46 D1 P Ψ 256 263 330 365 441 451 623* 1319 1505 1573 1678* 1735 1739 1838 1852 1912 1942 1962* 2127 2344 2495 2523 2544 and δυνατός γάρ ἐστιν ("for he is strong") in L 5 6 33 61 69 81 88 104 181 218 323 326 424 436 459 467 614 621 623c 629 630 720 915 917 945 1175 1241 1243 1398 1506 1563 1678c 1718 1751 1836 1845 1874 1875 1877 1881 1908 1959 2110 2138 2197 2200 2492 2516 2718 Maj both fit Cranfield's description in 2:704 of "the substitution of a familiar expression for an unfamiliar."

f   The particle γάρ ("for") is omitted in P46 ℵc B D F G L Ψ 048 6 33 81 88 181 330 424 436 451 614 629 1175 1241 1739 1877 1881 1912 1962 2200 2492 Maj syp.h sa arm ethpp geo slav Orlat Adamantius Chr

829

Severian Hier Aug$^{2/3}$, while it appears in ℵ* A C^2 (C* illegible) P 104 256 263 326 365 459 1319 1506 1573 1852 2127 *pc* ar b d f g o vg bo ethTH Bas Ambst Pel Aug$^{1/3}$. Nestle-Aland$^{26/27}$ and *GNT*$^{3/4}$ include this word in brackets, indicating a difficult choice. It appears that the weight of the textual evidence for omitting it is "slightly superior," in Metzger's words, *Textual Commentary*, 530. See also Cranfield, 2:704. The word "for" is also syntactically extraneous in a sentence with the μὲν . . . δέ antithesis.

g The parallel addition of καὶ ὁ μὴ φρονῶν τὴν ἡμέραν κυρίῳ οὐ φρονεῖ ("and the one who does not set his mind on the day does not do so in relation to a Lord") in C^3 L P Ψ 5 33 61 69 81 88 104 181 256 263 323 326 330 365 424* 436 441 451 459 467 614 621 623 629^c 720 915 917 945 1175 1241 1243 1319 1505 1506 1563 1573 1678 1718 1735 1751 1836 1838 1845 1874 1875 1877 1908 1912 1942 1959 1962 2110 2127 2138 2197 (2200^c) 2492 2495 2516 2523 2544 2718 *Maj* sy appears to be a redundant gloss. There is strong support for the text without such an addition in P^{46} ℵ A B C^{2vid} D F G 048 6 218 424^c 629* 630 1398 1739 1852 1874^{mg} 1881 2200* 2344 *pc* latt. (C* is illegible.)

h The deletion of καί ("also/and") by P^{46} *pc* is explained by Cranfield, 2:706, as "a tidying up after the addition" of the long variant described in the note above, which is difficult to understand since P^{46} does not contain the long variant (Nestle-Aland$^{26/27}$ fail to note this, but see Junack et al., *Neue Testament auf Papyrus*, 118). At any event, the deletion is too weakly attested to be original, and something is required to connect the first two sentences in v. 6.

i The weakly attested variant ἀποθάνωμεν ("we died") in C L 6 33 88 323 424 945 1175 1241 1836 1874 *pm* serves to relate the argument to symbolic death in baptism, which is extraneous to the passage.

j The subjunctive ἀποθνήσκωμεν ("we might / should die") in ℵ C L 33 81 326 365 1175 1243 1319 1505 1506 1735 1874 2495 *pm* is less strongly attested than the indicative, which is more appropriate for the context. The indicative "we die" is found in A B D F G P Ψ 048 6 69 88 323 330 424 614 630 945 1241 1573 1739 1836 1881 2344 *pm*. Ian A. Moir suggests in "Orthography and Theology: The Omicron-Omega Interchange in Romans 5:1 and Elsewhere," in Eldon Jay Epp and Gordon Fee, eds., *New Testament Textual Criticism: Its Significance for Exegesis* (Oxford: Clarendon, 1981) 172, that the omega may have been understood as an omicron, denoting the indicative. But if it was understood as a subjunctive, the variant interjects an exhortative

element that is inappropriate at this point in the argument; see Cranfield, 2:707.

k The addition of καί ("and") before ἀπέθανεν ("he died") and of καὶ ἀνέστη ("and he was raised"), in ℵ^c C^3 D^1 L 0209^{vid} 6 69 81 104 263 323 424^c 436 459 614 945 1175 1241 1243 1505 1735 1836 1874 1881 1912 2344 2495 *Maj* (*Lect*) ar d vgst sy^h geo^2 slav^{ms} (Asterius) Diodore Chr$^{1/2}$ (Ir^{lat}), which would result in the translation "Christ both died and was raised," appears to be a secondary, stylistic improvement. Essentially the same reading without the initial καί, namely, ἀπέθανεν καὶ ἀνέστη, occurs in P Ψ 33 88 326 330 424* 2200 (see also on F G, below). These two formulations produce Χριστός (καὶ) ἀπέθανεν καὶ ἀνέστη καὶ ἔζησεν ("Christ [both] died and was raised and lived"). Note that D^{*,2} (ar b d* o Ir^{lat} Ambst Gaudentius Aug$^{1/6}$ Sedulius-Scotus) have ἔζησεν before καὶ ἀπέθανεν. The absence of καί preceding ἀπέθανεν and of καὶ ἀνέστη following it—that is, the reading ἀπέθανεν καὶ ἔζησεν—is convincingly supported in ℵ* A B C* (C^c has the first καί) 256 365 630 1319 1506 1573 1739 1852 (1881 has the first καί) 2127 *al* vg$^{cl, (st)}$ sa bo arm eth slav^{ms} Or$^{lat\ 1/2}$ Hipp^{slav} Ps-Dion CyrJ Chr$^{1/2}$ Cyr$^{9/10}$ (Aug$^{2/6}$ omits καὶ ἔζησεν).

l The decision in the preceding note leaves the somewhat awkward, but undoubtedly original formulation ἀπέθανεν καὶ ἔζησεν ("he died and lived")—see the attestation above. The numerous variants remaining appear to be efforts to eliminate the awkwardness of referring to the resurrection as mere "living." The replacement of ἔζησεν by ἀνέστη ("he was raised"), hence only ἀπέθανεν καὶ ἀνέστη, in F G 629 (d^2) f g vg$^{cl, ww}$ geo^1 Or^{gr} Titus-Bostra Cyr$^{1/10}$ (Niceta) (Pel) Aug$^{3/6}$ is an obvious theological correction, typical of the tradition reflected in F and G elsewhere in Romans. Witnesses for the addition of ἀνέστη to the original expression (resulting in ἀπέθανεν καὶ ἀνέστη καὶ ἔζησεν, "he died and was raised and lived") are given in the preceding note. It appears to be a conflation of the first two readings. Additional variants show further theological improvements: ἀπέθανεν καὶ ἀνέστη καὶ ἀνέζησεν ("he died and was raised and lived again") in 056 0142; ἔζησεν καὶ ἀπέθανεν καὶ ἀνέστη ("he lived and died and was raised") in D^{*,2} (ar b d* o Ir^{lat} Ambst Gaudentius Aug$^{1/6}$ Sedulius-Scotus); and finally ἀπέθανεν καὶ ἔζησεν καὶ ἀνέστη ("he died and lived and was raised") in 1962 sy^p. Metzger, *Textual Commentary*, 531, notes the influence of 1 Thess 4:14 ("Jesus died and was raised") on these variants. The wide range of variants may reflect extensive liturgical use of christological formulas.

m In place of θεοῦ ("of God"), strongly attested by ℵ*

A B C* D F G 630 1506 1739 1852 1908ᶜ 2110 2200 ar b d f g o vgʷʷ, ˢᵗ sa bo armᵐˢ slavᵐˢ Orˡᵃᵗ5/6 Cyr Hier¹/³ Aug¹/⁶, Χριστοῦ appears in ℵ² C² L P Ψ 048 0209 5 6 33 69 81 88 104 181 218 256 263 323 326 330 365 424 436 441 451 467 459 614 621 623 629 720 915 917 945 1175 1241 1243 1319 1398 1505 1563 1573 1678 1718 1735 1751 1836 1838 1845 1874 1875 1877 1881 1912 1942 1959 1962 2127 2138 2197 2344 2492 2495 2516 2523 2544 2718 *Maj Lect* gue r vgᶜˡ syᵖ,ʰ armᵐˢ eth geo slavᵐˢ Polyc Mcion McionᵀᵉʳᵗOrˡᵃᵗ1/⁶ Amphilochiusᵛⁱᵈ Didᵈᵘᵇ Chr Severian Cyp Ambst Ambr Hier²/³ Aug⁵/⁶, possibly an assimilation to 2 Cor 5:10 or Rom 2:16.

n The replacement of the widely attested though rather awkward ὅτι ("that") by εἰ μή ("if not") in D*ᵛⁱᵈ F G appears to be a minor stylistic improvement, removing a possible indication of indirect discourse in this verse.

o An evenly balanced attestation for ἄρα ("so") in B D* F G P* 6 424ᶜ 630 1739 1881 *pc* lat and for ἄρα οὖν ("so therefore") in ℵ A C D² L Pᶜ Ψ 0209 33 69 88 104 323 326 330 365 424* 614 945 1175 1241 1243 1319 1505 1506 1573 1735 1836 1874 2344 2495 *Maj* syʰ leads Nestle-Aland²⁶/²⁷ to place οὖν in square brackets. Metzger does not discuss this reading, and Cranfield, 2:711, concludes that the question "can hardly be answered with confidence." Since ἄρα οὖν is grammatically more acceptable at the beginning of a sentence, it seems likely that οὖν would have been added and that ἄρα alone is the more difficult reading. This appears to be an instance where B and the so-called Western text preserved a more original reading.

p In place of δώσει ("he will give") found in ℵ A C D²

L P* (δώσει λόγον) Ψ 0209 6 33 69 88 104 323 330 365 424 614 945 (δώσει λόγον) 1175 1241 1243 1319 1505 1506 1573 1735 1739 1836 1874 1881 2344 2495 *Maj*, the more technical term ἀποδώσει ("he will give back, render account") appears in B D* F G Pᶜ 326 *pc*. The simpler verb is more likely to be original.

q The phrase τῷ θεῷ ("to God"), found in ℵ A C D L P Ψ 048 0209 33 69 81 88 104 181 256 263 323 326 330 365 424* 436 451 459 614 629 945 1175 1241 1243 1319 1505 1506 1573 1735 1836 1852 1874 1877 1912 1962 2127 2344 2492 2495 *Maj Lect* ar b d gue vg syᵖ,ʰ sa bo armᵐˢ eth geo slav Orˡᵃᵗ Bas Chr Ps-Cyp Pel Aug²/⁸, is omitted by B F G 6 424ᶜ 630 1739 1881 2200 f g o r armᵐˢ Polyc Cyp Ambst Aug⁶/⁸ Salvian. Although there is strong external evidence favoring the inclusion of the phrase, early evidence for omission (Polycarp and Cyprian) and weighty internal factors make it understandable that Nestle-Aland²⁶/²⁷ should have placed it in square brackets, a decision defended by Metzger, *Textual Commentary*, 531. Cranfield, 2:711, admits that the omission should be favored as the "more difficult reading" but opts for the inclusion on argumentative and rhetorical grounds. I would add that the omission should also be preferred as the shorter reading. Since it is very difficult to believe that the phrase would have been intentionally omitted if it were originally present, the reading preserved in B G et al. should be favored. As Cranfield remarks, "there can be no doubt about Paul's meaning" of this sentence without the graceful and theologically satisfying concluding expression "to God."

Analysis

The pericope of 14:1-12[1] opens with a thematic exhortation in the form of a typical Pauline dystich, set off from the previous pericope by the particle δέ ("and/but/now"), which in this case is not translated.[2] This "heading"[3] is followed by five lines linked by anaphora, each beginning with ὅς ("one") or ὁ ("the").[4] The first two pairs of lines are carefully constructed antithetical parallelisms describing the positions of the weak and the strong, while the final line expresses the divine assessment of the situation: "God has welcomed him" (14:3c).

---

1 Most commentators treat vv. 1-12 as a single pericope: Godet, 454; Michel, 418, 421; Dunn, 2:796; Morris, 476; Moo, 833–35.

2 See Cranfield, 2:699.

3 See Parunak, "Transitional Techniques," 534–36, for a discussion of the parallel headings in 14:1 and 15:7, leading him to group the material of 14:1–15:6 in a single unit that stands parallel to 15:7-13.

4 Weiss, "Beiträge," 246, suggests a similar structure, except that he joins 14:2a and 2b into a single line, designating the two halves (?) and (ß). In all, ὅς or ὁ occurs here for a combined total of twelve times in vv. 2-6, lending the whole a sort of gnomic style.

Verse 4 opens with a question to the imaginary interlocutor[5] similar to the earlier rhetorical questions in Romans. Just as in the preceding sentence, the divine assessment of the situation appears in the third line (14:4c). The word κύριος ("lord") runs from this point as a leitmotif through the passage, appearing nine times in addition to the verb κυριεύω ("be lord over").[6] An additional paranomasia that lends coherence to this pericope is the fivefold use of κρινεῖν ("to judge"), the first two appearing in addition to the compound διακρίσις ("dispute") in this first paragraph.[7]

The second paragraph (14:5-9) applies the principle of mutual welcome to the issue of the sacred calendar, featuring once again a series of lines marked by anaphora in the rough breathing of ὅς ("he") or ὁ ("the"). The two triple-lined sentences are organized in parallel fashion, with the first two lines in antithetical parallelism and the third lines (14:5c, 6c) providing a theological exhortation or clarification. The following double-lined sentence (14:6d-e) stands exactly parallel to the final two lines of the preceding sentence, providing a satisfying symmetry in a five-lined combination of sentences that completes the illustration of the attitudes of the weak and the strong in relation to both eating and honoring the calendar.[8]

This is followed in 14:7-8 by another five-lined combination in an intricately organized syllogism concerning life and death in Christ. Two pairs of antithetical parallelisms state the premises and counterpremises of living and dying in relation to the Lord, followed by the inference in 14:8c that whether one dies or lives, the believer is with the Lord.[9] This structure is linked by paronomasia in the repetition of οὐδείς ("none") in the first two lines and of ἐάν ("if") in the final three lines. The christological premise of this syllogism is stated in a neatly balanced[10] christological statement (14:9) that reiterates the themes of Christ's lordship over life and death. This brings the paragraph to its conclusion with the last of five pairs of alternations between life and death that began in v. 7.[11] The suggestions that vv. 7-9 originated as a baptismal confession,[12] a Christ hymn,[13] or in part as a message of consolation[14] have been taken up by Michael Theobald, who has shown that it is a Pauline composition that originated prior to the writing of Romans.[15] Its original context was probably his reflection on the problem of the death of believers in the wake of the Thessalonian controversy, reflecting a mature eschatology that affirms belongingness to the Lord whether or not believers die before his return.

The final paragraph (14:10-12) opens with questions to the imaginary interlocutor, with a theological comment in the final line.[16] Verse 10 contains an inclusio with 14:3 in the inverse-ordered references to judging and despising.[17] The questions are carefully constructed in parallel fashion so that the comparability between the opposing attitudes of the weak and the strong is expressed. The theological comment about each person facing final judgment is sustained by a composite scriptural citation (14:11-12). The last line of the final sentence stands parallel to the theological comment in the final line of v. 10, emphasizing individual accountability and providing a reprise of the argument in 14:1-4.

5   See Stowers, *Diatribe*, 100, 115. Schmeller, *Diatribe*, 406–7, speaks of a distant analogy to diatribe in the second person singular references in this verse and vv. 10-13.

6   See Moo, 840.

7   As pointed out in private correspondence with Mark Reasoner, D. G. Bradley, "The Origin of the Hortatory Materials in the Letters of Paul" (Ph.D. dissertation, Yale University, 1947) 163, shows that the use of κρινεῖν and cognates as key words continues into the next pericope, 14:13-23.

8   Weiss, "Beiträge," 246, in contrast organizes 14:6 into three lines, of which the last two are overly extended with the clauses I have designated as 6c and 6e.

9   Weiss, "Beiträge," 180, discusses this passage under the rubric of antithetical parallelism, but he places 14:7a and 7b in a single line that disguises their symmetrical parallelism to each other.

10   Ibid., 246.

11   Harvey, *Listening*, 206.

12   Michel, 143.

13   Schlier, 409.

14   Schmithals, 500–501, excluding v. 7 from the original form.

15   Theobald, 2:138–40, and *Studien*, 158–60.

16   See Weiss, "Beiträge," 246, who sees the structure a/a/b in 14:10.

17   Harvey, *Listening*, 206.

The discourse in this pericope is typical for the demonstrative genre in remaining at the level of generalities and not providing highly specific advice. As Nababan observes, "the concrete situation is lifted up into the typical and fundamental. Paul does not lose himself in the details but lifts up the fundamental insights of the earlier controversies reflected in 1 Cor 8 and 10."[18]

Rhetorical Disposition

IV.	The *probatio*
12:1–15:13	The fourth proof: Living together according to the gospel so as to sustain the hope of global transformation
14:1-12	7. Exemplary guidelines for the weak and the strong
14:1	a. Thematic admonition to welcoming the weak without ulterior motives
14:2-4	b. Application of the principle of welcome to the issue of eating
14:2	1) Definition of the issue of eating
14:2a	a) One person eats "everything"
14:2b	b) The "weak person" eats "vegetables"
14:3	2) Admonitions to the strong and the weak
14:3a	a) For the strong: do not "despise"
14:3b	b) For the weak: do not "judge"
14:3c	c) Theological justification: divine welcome
14:4	3) The argument concerning inviolable relations
14:4a	a) Rhetorical question about judging the member of another's household
14:4b	b) Refutation on the premise of householders subordinate only to their own lord
14:4c	c) Assurance that members of the Lord's household will "stand"
14:5-9	c. Extending the principle of mutual welcome to the issues of sacred days and sacred foods
14:5a-b	1) The definition of the issue of sacred days
14:5a	a) The weak person believes one day is "better than another"
14:5b	b) The strong person believes all days are alike
14:5c	2) The admonition to act from full assurance of one's own views
14:6-9	3) The theological justification of responsibility to one's own Lord
14:6a	a) The weak respond to the Lord by respecting sacred days
14:6b	b) The strong respond to the Lord by eating
14:6c	c) The strong give thanks
14:6d	d) The weak give thanks
14:7-9	e) A syllogism of life and death in the Lord
14:7a	(1) First premise: no believer lives to himself/herself
14:7b	(2) Second premise: no believer dies to himself/herself
14:8a	(3) First counterpremise: believers live "in relation to the Lord"
14:8b	(4) Second counterpremise: believers die "in relation to the Lord"
14:8c	(5) The inferential conclusion: whether believers live or die, they are the Lord's
14:9	(6) The christological rationale: the death and resurrection of Christ that establishes lordship over the living and the dead
14:10-12	d. The challenge to avoid violating the principle of mutual welcome
14:10a	1) Rhetorical question for the weak: "why judge?"
14:10b	2) Rhetorical question for the strong: "why despise?"
14:10c	3) Eschatological rationale for avoiding such actions
14:11	4) Scripture proof
14:11a	a) Citation formula
14:11b	b) Citation from Isa 49:18
14:11c	c) Citation from Isa 45:23
14:12	5) Conclusion: individual accountability

Exegesis

■ **1** A gnomic admonition, lightly set off from the previous pericope by the untranslated particle δέ,[19] opens the "special exhortation"[20] that takes up the conflicts

---

18 Nababan, "Bekenntnis," 25.
19 BAGD (2000) 213 and BDF §447 indicate that δέ may occasionally remain untranslated when no clear antithesis is present. Cranfield, 2:699, argues that δέ marks the beginning of a new pericope; Murray, 2:141, is one of the few commentators who translates it as "but." Dunn, 2:797, makes an elaborate case that Paul intended an adversative link with the previous reference to the desires of the flesh understood as a false Jewish trust in their "ethnic identity," but nowhere in 14:1–15:7 does Paul argue against maintenance of such identity and the admonitions to both sides make it clear that he does wish to identify Jewish ethnicity as the main problem. Paul appears to feel instead that all parties in Rome are at fault in excluding each other. The other reasons Dunn advances for the adversative rendering of δέ suggest continuity rather than antithesis to the preceding argument, thus undermining his case.
20 Käsemann, 364.

between groups in Rome. The singular object of the verb that opens the sentence is clearly gnomic,[21] referring to the "one weak in faith" as an abstract entity representing a group or series of groups in Rome.[22] This indirect, covert, oblique style of reference[23] is consistent with the advice of ancient rhetoricians in addressing sensitive circumstances requiring good taste or arousing a fear of retribution.[24] There is wide agreement that Paul employs the "current jargon"[25] of a community dominated by the "strong," because no group in the early church would have enjoyed the epithet "weak in faith" and because Paul's argument counters the kind of prejudicial assessment that the expression implies. It is certainly unlikely that this epithet originated with him. The verb ἀσθενέω was used for physical illness, social or economic inferiority, and powerlessness of any kind.[26] There is a rare indication of the moral potential of the term in Epictetus's warning about persons of weak character gaining too much philosophical and rhetorical training: ὅτι καὶ ἐν τῷ καθόλου πᾶσα δύναμις ἐπισφαλὴς τοῖς ἀπαιδεύτοις καὶ ἀσθενέσι προσγενομένη πρὸς τὸ ἐπᾶραι καὶ χαυνῶσαι ἐπ' αὐτῇ ("The reason is that usually every power that is acquired by the uneducated and weak is apt to make them conceited and boastful over it").[27] In the Roman context, the comparable Latin adjectives *tenuis* and *infirmus* carried a servile connotation, involving low economic, social, and political status.[28] A combination of social and religious inferiority is conveyed in Horace's witty depiction of a man who admits he is "weak" because he cannot converse at length on the Sabbath:

"Certainly you know more than I do about this secret."
"I remember it very well but can only speak at a better time; today is a sabbath on the thirtieth; do you really want to insult the Jews?"
"That means nothing to me," I say, "it is a religious scruple."
"It does to me; I am a small man of weakness, one of many (*sum paulo infirmior, unus multorum*). Pardon me, we'll speak another time."[29]

This is a suggestive parallel to Rom 14:1 because it shows that "the person excessively observant in a foreign religion who matched the 'weak' caricature was known to Horace's audience" in the Latin world.[30] This requires a modification of the judgment that only in the NT do we find this term implying "an ethical-religious weakness."[31] The caricature was effective because the Roman public was inclined to view strength as an indication of honor and weakness as a term of contempt.[32] It is very likely that Paul's audience in Rome felt the same way, and that the epithet "weak in faith" had been imposed

---

21   Schlier, 402, followed by Reasoner, "The 'Strong' and the 'Weak' in Rome," 48.

22   In contrast, Starnitzke, *Struktur*, 411–20, interprets this passage under the rubric of the responsibility of the individual before God.

23   See Barclay, "Undermine the Law," 3: "the theme is discussed with a degree of generality and obliqueness (e.g. 14:5, 15, 21), but this is easily explained on rhetorical grounds."

24   See Sampley, "Weak and Strong," 43–45. He builds his case on Plutarch *Mor.* 69e and Demetrius *On Style*, 287–94, following the work of Frederick Ahl, "The Art of Safe Criticism in Greece and Rome," *AJP* 105 (1984) 174–208. Unfortunately, Sampley draws a false conclusion from this rhetorical tradition, that the terms "weak and strong have no objective referents in the Roman congregations" (48). If the Roman churches were not able to see the links between Paul's gnomic references and their situation, the argument would be ineffective, failing to achieve what Plutarch and Demetrius recommend.

25   Käsemann, 369; Cranfield, 2:700; Dunn, 2:797.

26   See BAGD 115; Gustav Stählin, "ἀσθενής κτλ.," *TDNT* 1 (1964) 490–93.

27   Epictetus *Diss.* 1.8.8–9.

28   See Reasoner, *The Strong*, 49–55; for a skeptical appraisal of Reasoner's argument, see Pitta, "Strong," 94–97.

29   Horace *Sat.* 1.9.67–72, cited by Reasoner, *The Strong*, 53–54.

30   Reasoner, *The Strong*, 54.

31   Stählin, "ἀσθενής κτλ.," 492; see also Josef Zmijewski, "ἀσθενής κτλ.," *EDNT* 1 (1990) 171; BAGD refers to "religious and moral weakness" in this verse.

32   See Reasoner, *The Strong*, 58–61.

on the subordinate group by an opposing group that was in a more dominant position.[33] The epithet seems to imply a defect in the subordinate group's πίστις,[34] which probably reflects the assessment of their opponents,[35] the "powerful" (15:1), regarding ascetic or legalistic tendencies.[36] However, as Paul's admonition in this verse reveals, he assumes that the "faith" of the weak fully qualifies them for membership in the church and admission to its sacramental meals.[37] The negative epithet imposed on the subordinate members of the congregation by the "powerful" appears to have involved their religious scruples, leading most scholars to identify them as including Jewish Christians who remain committed to kosher regulations[38] or to an ascetic vegetarianism.[39] However, in view of Greco-Roman ascetic ideals present in Rome, it is altogether possible that the "weak" also included ascetics from pagan background.[40]

The plural imperative verb Paul uses, προσλαμβάνεσθε ("you [pl.] should welcome"), links this verse very closely with the plural imperative of 13:14. The extensive study of Ceslas Spicq has shown that this verb often carried the sense of "take part in an enterprise, come to the aid of, assist."[41] When people are received into a group, they take up the common cause, such as joining a military expedition. Thus, for instance, an officer of Ptolemy VI in 157 B.C.E. orders Demetrius as follows: προσλαμβέσθαι τὸν προωνομασμένον μου ἀδελφὸν Ἀπολλώνιον εἰς τὴν Δεξειλάου σημέαν ("Welcome my previously named brother, Apollonius the Macedonian, into Dexilaos' company").[42] This verb is also used for receiving cities in confederations and taking partners into marital relations.[43] As in the case of the other three Pauline occurrences (14:3, 15:7, twice), always in the middle voice as elsewhere in the NT, προσλαμβάνειν in 14:1 has a technical sense of "welcome someone" into a "home or circle of acquaintances."[44] A characteristic expression of this idiom appears in a papyrus of 14 B.C.E.: δὶς προσελαβόμην αὐτὸν εἰς οἶκον παρ᾽ ἐμέ ("Twice I welcomed him home, by my side").[45] Welcoming others into one's social space in the sense of offering hospitality is conveyed by this verb in early Christian texts such as Acts 18:27, 28:2, and Phlm 17, all of which evoke "the hospitality which was the first manifestation of brotherly agapê in the primitive church."[46] The Philemon parallel is particularly close to the usage in Romans, involving both hospitality and the fellowship of equals: "So if you have me as your partner, welcome him [i.e., the slave Onesimus] as you would welcome me" (εἰ οὖν με ἔχεις κοινωνόν, προσλαβοῦ αὐτὸν ὡς ἐμέ, Phlm 17). Especially in the light of the earlier references to "hospitality" (Rom 12:13) and the Agape meal (Rom 13:10), "welcome" in this context carries the technical sense of reception into the fellowship of the congregation, that is, to the common meal.[47] Those who partici-

---

33 See ibid., 60; Marcus, "Circumcision and Uncircumcision," 73; Esler, *Conflict and Community*, 341.

34 Cf. Dunn's discussion in 2:798 of "weakness in trust . . . which leans on the crutches of particular customs," a description that assumes Paul shares this negative assessment.

35 Wilckens, 3:81; Käsemann, 369; Tobin, *Paul's Rhetoric*, 408–9.

36 Nanos, *Mystery*, 945; Elliott, "Asceticism," 237–38.

37 Calvert-Koyzis, *Paul*, 138, argues in contrast that obedience to the law on the part of the weak "is actually a denial of the oneness of God . . . a kind of idolatry" that would presumably disqualify them from church membership.

38 See Lütgert, *Römerbrief*, 90–96; Michel, 422; Cranfield, 2:700; Reasoner, *The Strong*, 6–16; Stuhlmacher, 195–97; Lampe, *Paul to Valentinus*, 72–74; Schneider, "Schwachen," 122–23; Tomson, *Paul and the Jewish Law*, 195; Barclay, "Undermine the Law," 294–308.

39 Reasoner, *The Strong*, 130–38; Elliott, "Asceticism,"

40 Reasoner, *The Strong*, 75–84, 137–38.

41 Ceslas Spicq, "προσλαμβάνομαι," *TLNT* 3 (1994) 195.

42 *P.Lond.* 1. Nr. 23.21–23 (p. 38), cited in MM 549–50.

43 Spicq, "προσλαμβάνομαι," 197.

44 BAGD 717; see also Esler, *Conflict and Identity*, 347.

45 *BGU* 4. Nr. 1141.37.

46 Spicq, "προσλαμβάνομαι," 199. See also Gerhard Delling, "προσλαμβάνω, πρόσλημψις," *TDNT* 4 (1967) 15; Horst Balz and Gerhard Schneider, eds., "προσλαμβάνομαι," *EDNT* 3 (1993) 175.

47 See particularly Schlatter, 249–52; Michel, 422. That the issues concerning welcome and eating were related to commensality is argued by Barclay, "Undermine the Law," 291; Tobin, *Paul's Rhetoric*, 407, 413.

231–51. Nanos, 119–44, argues in contrast that the "weak" are non-Christian Jews.

pate in the common meal become part of the body of Christ, brothers and sisters with each other, and partners in a common cause. In view of this social context, it is misleading to make a distinction between "an official act of reception" and "everyday recognition and practice of brotherhood," as if the church had already developed elaborate regulations.[48] To welcome the "weak" into the love feast was to treat them as brothers and sisters in Christ, as equal beneficiaries of God's grace, as the formerly shamed who are now equally honored by the blood of Christ. From the opening words of this pericope, therefore, it must have been apparent to Paul's audience that he intended to reverse the shameful status of the "weak." Such a reversal required Paul to employ the discriminatory epithet evidently created and employed by groups opposing the "weak in faith."

Paul's refusal to allow any loophole in the reversal of shameful status is signaled by the final clause in the admonitory heading: "but not for disputes over opinions." The word διάκρισις was used by Paul in a positive sense of "interpret" or "explain" in the context of revelations of the spirit in 1 Cor 12:10, but the plural form used here seems to imply "quarrels," "disputes,"[49] or "discriminations."[50] Polybius uses the verbal cognate to depict the Carthaginian determination to concentrate their resources on winning the military conflict with Rome: νομίζοντες συμφέρειν σφίσι τὸ διακριθῆναι πρὸς τούτους ("considering the dispute with them their main interest").[51] The assumption that such a διάκρισις would be resolved in favor of the dominant party, implied in the Polybius citation,[52] is visible in Dio Chrysostom's appeal to Nicomedia to avoid a war that lacks the prospect of τὸ τάχος τῆς διακρίσεως ("the speed of its decision").[53] These parallels and the address of v. 1 to the strong rather than to the weak render implausible the suggestion that disputes initiated by both sides are in view.[54] In these verses it is the opinions/reasoning (διαλογισμοί) of the "weak" that are under scrutiny by the dominant group.[55] While classical and septuagintal usage of this word can include "thought, opinion, reasoning, design . . . plan," as well as balancing accounts, disputes, and arguments,[56] the NT ordinarily employs it in a negative sense, as I noted with reference to 1:21.[57] In chapter 14, however, Paul does not cast doubt on the legitimacy of such opinions. In the context of welcoming fellow believers to love feasts, he flatly repudiates the ulterior motive of doing so in order to induce the weak to adopt the opinions of the strong.[58] In the sectarian atmosphere of the early house and tenement churches, and in a cultural setting where intellectual competition was the order of the day, this was an extraordinary prohibition.[59] It legitimates a "certain diversity of opinion and practice"[60] and does not seek "to erase subgroup identities."[61]

---

48 Dunn, 2:798, referring to Rauer's repudiation of the official recognition concept in *Schwachen*, 81–82.

49 Gerhard Dautzenberg, "διακρίνω . . . διάκρισις," *EDNT* 1 (1990) 306.

50 Glad, *Paul and Philodemus*, 223.

51 Polybius *Hist.* 2.22.11; see also 18.28.3.

52 In *Polybius, The Histories* (New York: Putnam, 1922) 6:297, W. R. Paton translates as follows: "considering it their main interest to bring this to a decisive conclusion."

53 Dio Chrysostom *Orat.* 38.21, translated by H. Lamar Crosby, *Dio Chrysostom* (Cambridge: Harvard University Press, 1936) 4:69.

54 See Käsemann, 367, referring to Zahn, Lagrange, and Ridderbos. Cranfield's critique of this in 2:701 is compelling.

55 See Wilckens, 3:81; Gerd Petzke, "διαλογίζομαι . . . διαλογισμός," *EDNT* 1 (1990) 308.

56 BAGD 186; G. D. Kilpatrick, "Διαλέγεσθαι and διαλογίζεσθαι in the New Testament," *JTS* 11

(1960) 339. Esler, *Conflict and Identity*, 349, interprets διαλογισμοί on the part of a dominant group as having the "likely consequence" of "schism rather than consensus."

57 Gottlob Schrenk, "διαλέγομαι κτλ.," *TDNT* 2 (1964) 97.

58 See Schneider, "Schwachen," 135.

59 Michel, 523, followed by Dunn, 2:799, undercuts the radicality of Paul's argument by insisting that "healthy congregations" must engage in some forms of dispute. Paul clearly makes such concessions in other locations (e.g., 1 Cor 11:19), but in Romans he wishes to counter the domination of the weak by the strong, overturning the social system of honor and status. Calvert-Koyzis, *Paul*, 144, counters Paul's argument by insisting that the weak "support a kind of idolatry that is contrary to the fulfilled monotheistic faith."

60 Viard, 283; see also Campbell, "Identity," 74–82.

61 Esler, *Conflict and Identity*, 352.

■ **2** The gnomic style of reference to the congregational situation continues with antithetical parallelism marked by correlative particles μέν . . . δέ ("on the one hand . . . on the other hand"). A singular subject is employed, as in the preceding verse, to refer to a group's behavior: "the one has faith to eat everything." The verb πιστεύ-ειν ("to have faith") followed by an infinitive is used here in the sense of "believe that," as in Acts 15:11:[62] ἀλλὰ διὰ τῆς χάριτος τοῦ κυρίου Ἰησοῦ πιστεύομεν σωθῆναι καθ᾽ ὃν τρόπον κἀκεῖνοι ("But through the grace of the Lord Jesus we believe that we are saved just as they are"). Current commentators agree that the formulation is unusual for Paul, but provide inventive paraphrases to force this clause to conform to the usual Pauline parameters. Cranfield refers to "the assurance that his faith permits him to eat,"[63] while Dunn describes "trust in God" that sets one free from the food laws.[64] It would be better to allow the disparity with Paul's earlier use of "faith" in Romans to stand, admitting that he is creating an exaggerated and somewhat ludicrous paraphrase of the position of the "strong" in Rome. The formulation of eating everything is broadly drawn,[65] including everything edible, which probably extended considerably past actual practices in Rome. Consistent with the requirements of demonstrative rhetoric, and matching the requirements of the oblique style, Paul creates abstractions that are recognizable by his audience, but that not precisely match any of the groups in Rome. The use of πάντα may well have evoked smiles among the hearers of Romans,[66] not only at the thought of eating obscure foods but also at the reduction of the concept of faith, which had received so profound a development in the earlier chapters of the letter, into mere license for uncritical consumption.

The depiction of the eating habits of the "weak" is equally simplistic, which seems to be overlooked in the extensive discussion of the rationale and extent of vegetarianism in the Roman churches.[67] Ancient vegetarians did not restrict their diet to green leafy vegetables and herbs grown in the garden, as implied by Paul's choice of the word λάχανα.[68] The primitive ideal was stated by Empedocles, that the virtuous original humans avoided violence and refrained from eating living creatures: ἀλλὰ μύσος τοῦτ᾽ ἔσκεν ἐν ἀνθρώποισι μέγιστον, θυμὸν ἀπορραίσαντας ἐνέδμεναι ἠέα γυῖα (". . . but this was the greatest abomination among humans, to snatch out the life and eat the goodly limbs").[69] The ancient Orphics ate all ordinary foods with the exception of meat, beans, and eggs,[70] while the Pythagoreans usually avoided wine, meat, and fish.[71] Roman philosophers such as Attalus, Sotion, Quintus Sextius, Seneca, and Musonius Rufus advocated vegetarianism as a form of self-control but did not restrict consumption to λάχανα ("lettuce, leafy vegetables").[72] Plutarch reports that the austere statesman Marcus Cato recommended that the sick should eat "vegetables," but he did not disallow eating "tidbits of duck, pigeon, or rabbit" (τρέφων δὲ λαχάνοις καὶ σαρκιδίοις νήσσης ἢ φάσσης ἢ λαγώ).[73] The Jews of Rome were well known for avoiding pork,[74] but their other kosher regulations did not

---

62 See Michel, 423.

63 Cranfield, 2:698.

64 Dunn, 2:799.

65 Elliott, "Asceticism," 238, overlooks this detail in arguing that "there is no reason to connect being 'strong' with a particular diet (or lack of one)."

66 In *The Strong*, 66, Reasoner argues against the exaggerated, humorous construal of this detail.

67 See Eduard Riggenbach, "Die Starken und Schwachen in der römischen Gemeinde," *ThStK* 66 (1893) 655–68; Hermann Strathmann, *Geschichte der frühchristlichen Askese bis zur Entstehung des Mönchtums im religionsgeschichtlichen Zusammenhange*, vol. 1, *Die Askese in der Umgebung des werdenden Christentums* (Leipzig: Deichert, 1914) 1–13; Rauer, *Schwachen*, 138–69; Johannes Behm, "ἐσθίω," *TDNT* 2 (1964) 694; Dunn, 2:799–802; Elliott, "Asceticism," 239–45.

68 See BAGD 467; LSJM 1032: "garden herbs, opposite wild plants."

69 Fragment 128, with translation adapted from Lovejoy and Boas, *Primitivism*, 33.

70 Haußleiter, *Vegetarismus*, 83–87.

71 Ibid., 99–111; see also Robert M. Grant, "Dietary Laws among Pythagoreans, Jews, and Christians," *HTR* 73 (1980) 299–302.

72 See Reasoner's discussion in *The Strong*, 75–84, citing Seneca *Ep.* 108.13–21 and Musonius Rufus Περὶ τροφῆς 18A.

73 Plutarch *Cat. Maj.* 23.4.

74 See Barclay, "Undermine the Law," 8–9. He cites Augustus's quip reported by Macrobius *Sat.* 2.4.11 that in view of Herod's execution of his sons, *melius est Herodis porcum esse quam filium* ("I would rather be Herod's pig than Herod's son"). Text from Menahem Stern, *Greek and Latin Authors on Jews and*

require a restriction of diet to green leafy vegetables.[75] There was no ancient prohibition against eating fruits and grains, which the term λάχανα definitely excludes, while the practical vegetarianism of the Cynic movement avoided all domesticated agricultural products such as λάχανα.[76] Paul's formulation echoes the lampoon of the Pythagoreans cited by Diogenes Laertius: "they only consume greens (λάχανα τε καὶ πίνουσιν) . . . and their lack of a bath . . . and their old threadbare coats stink so badly that nobody else will come near them."[77] The exaggeration in Paul's depiction might be somewhat more aptly rendered by translating, "the weak only eat lettuce."

In view of the cultural evidence, the likelihood of any group in Rome actually practicing so extreme an asceticism is on the same level as to imagine a group actually eating everything.[78] The rhetorical effect of placing these parameters so far beyond the likely, actual behavior of groups in Rome is to enable each group to smile and feel included in the subsequent argument. Since it is impossible to imagine any group in Rome that would not fit somewhere along the scale between the uncritical omnivores and the leaf mongers of Rom 14:2, Paul's argument becomes relevant for "all the positions inside this range."[79] In this way a series of critical issues relating to ethnic identity expressed in eating habits,[80] as well as the configuration of common meals,[81] could be dealt

with at a level of generality that includes all while leaving the resolution of details up to the Roman churches. It appears clear to most interpreters, however, that the "weak" who eat only vegetables probably included Jewish Christians who refrained from meat because of concern over kosher regulations.[82] Bruce Winter has made a case that the privilege of buying "suitable" (ἐπιπήδεια), that is, kosher, meat in the Roman markets had been suspended as a result of the Edict of Claudius, which resulted in enforced vegetarianism on the part of the "weak."[83] There is evidence that conservative Jewish Christians such as James refrained from meat and wine,[84] and that other Jewish leaders and writings of this period advocated such abstinence,[85] perhaps also because of unavailability of kosher products.

■ **3** Paul's admonition to both of the abstract extremes on the eating scale in Rome is to break the culturally formed habit of shaming nonconformists. The position of the majority group in Rome, "the strong," is taken up first, the "ones who eat" without compunction and have contempt on those who scrupulously abstain. The prohibition μὴ ἐξουθενέω ("do not despise") likely refers to the feeling of superiority on the part of the majority toward a minority that bore the double disability of derivation from a different ethnic group and also being overly scrupulous in areas that the majority felt were irrelevant for the faith.[86] As Morris observes, the verb is

Judaism (Jerusalem: Israel Academy of Sciences and Humanities, 1974, 1980) Nr. 543, on 2.665. Other indications of Roman awareness of the Jewish avoidance of pork are Petronius *Frag.* 37 in Stern Nr. 195, on 1.444; Philo *Legat.* 361–62; Juvenal *Sat.* 6.160; 14.99; Tacitus *Hist.* 5.4.

75 See S. Safrai's discussion of food in "Home and Family," in S. Safrai and M. Stern, eds., *The Jewish People in the First Century*, CRINT 1 (Philadelphia: Fortress, 1976) 2:746–48.

76 Haußleiter, *Vegetarismus*, 167–84; Lovejoy and Boas, *Primitivism*, 117–52.

77 Diogenes Laertius *Vitae philos.* 8.38, citing a lost comedy by Aristophon, *The Pythagorist.*

78 See Schneider, "Schwachen," 131.

79 Jewett, *Tolerance*, 30.

80 See Dunn, 2:801.

81 See Barclay, "Undermine the Law," 5, 16–17.

82 See Dunn, 2:799–802; Moo, 837; Roger L. Omanson, "The 'Weak' and the 'Strong' and Paul's Letter to the Roman Christians," *BT* 33 (1982) 108; Heil,

Ablehnung der Speisegebote, 258; Elliott, "Asceticism," 239–40.

83 Winter, "Romans 12–15," 90–91, citing Zeev, *Jewish Rights,* 381–408.

84 Reasoner, *The Strong,* 130, cites Eusebius *Hist.* 2.23.5 referring to Hegesippus's testimony about James's vegetarianism.

85 Reasoner, *The Strong,* 130–31, cites Josephus *Vita* 14 for the account of the Jewish priests imprisoned in Rome around 61 C.E. who abstained from meat on kosher grounds. *T. Isaac* 4.5 also claims that the paragon of spirituality "would not eat meat or drink wine all his life long. He also would not enjoy the taste of fruit."

86 See Kühl, 449; Schmidt, 227; Dunn, 2:803; Esler, *Conflict and Identity*, 350. Ziesler resists this mirror reading in 329: "Certainly there is no hint in Rom. 14 that those who did observe days were censorious or aggressive, just as there is no hint that non-observers of days regarded observers with contempt." Ziesler overlooks the pejorative language

constructed from οὐθέν ("nothing") and the prefix ἐξ, resulting in the meaning "to make absolutely nothing of."[87] To hold a group in contempt in this sense was to treat them as nobodies, as devoid of honor despite any claim they might make to the contrary. Paul himself had experienced such contempt on the part of the Corinthians, because of his inelegant style of speaking (2 Cor 10:10). The experience of such social contempt by persons of minority status is visible in Jonathan's prayer in 2 Macc 1:27 for the Jewish exiles scattered among the Gentiles: . . . ἐλευθέρωσον τοὺς δουλεύοντας ἐν τοῖς ἔθνεσιν, τοὺς ἐξουθενημένους καὶ βδελυκτοὺς ἔπιδε, καὶ γνώτωσαν τὰ ἔθνη ὅτι σὺ εἶ ὁ Θεὸς ἡμῶν (". . . deliver those who are enslaved among the Gentiles, look upon them that are despised and abhorred, and let the Gentiles know that you are our God"). Given the intense competition for superior status in the Roman world, whose class system relegated the vast majority to the position of despicable nonentities, Paul's admonition is strikingly countercultural. The disdainful smile[88] of social and theological contempt is no longer to remain in the repertoire of Christian group life.

With precisely parallel wording in 14:3b, Paul turns to the behavior of the weak who are refraining from eating certain foods and are apparently judgmental about those who feel free to eat.[89] When members of a religious community judge their fellows, this places them in the shameful status of moral condemnation that God is expected to inflict. As Dunn explains, "The one who does not eat evidently regards *not* eating as of crucial importance in maintaining the relationship with God, so that *eating* becomes an act unacceptable to God, an act, that is to say, which merits divine condemnation."[90] The use of κρίνειν in the sense of "pass an unfavorable judgment upon"[91] is found in Epictetus's denunciation of immature students who come to his lectures with a judgmental attitude whose basis is contradicted by their behavior at home:[92] Ἄνθρωπ᾽, ἐν οἴκῳ διαπεπύκτευκας τῷ δουλαρίῳ, τὴν οἰκίαν ἀνάστατον πεποίηκας, τοὺς γείτονας συντετάραχας. καὶ ἔρχῃ μοι καταστολὰς ποιήσας ὡς σοφὸς καὶ καθήμενος κρίνεις, πῶς ἐξηγησάμην τὴν λέξιν . . . (" Man, at home you had fisticuffs with your slave, you got your household thrown out, you have disturbed your neighbors. And now you come to me putting on a dignified look, like a wise man, and sit down to pass judgment on how I exegeted the text. . . . ")

The pejorative use of the κρίνειν stem noted in 14:1 is picked up here with the flat command, μὴ κρινέτω ("do not judge"). This goes against the grain of the Greco-Roman culture, whose educational system aimed to encourage informed, critical judgments of issues and persons; it seems to counter the need to judge people who have done wrong[93] or judges in athletic or musical contests.[94] Given the important role of judging in the OT[95] and particularly in contemporary Judaism, whose community life centered on the process of judging which actions were consistent with the law and which defined one as a sinner,[96] this admonition is clearly countercul-

---

Paul employs in this verse as well as 14:1, which would have been offensive unless there were actual conflicts among the Roman congregations.

87   Morris, 479. Note that there is no study of this term or its closely related partner, ἐξουδενέω, in the *TDNT* or *EDNT*. Significant occurrences of these terms of social contempt may be found in Sir 34:31; *Vi. Aes.* 26.5; *Historia Alexandri Magni, Rec.* γ 38.43; and Aelius Herodianus 3.2.10, p. 508.

88   See Murray, 2:175.

89   See Meyer, 2:303; Zeller, 225; Morris, 479. Elliott, "Asceticism," 238, denies any critique of the "weak" in these verses.

90   Dunn, 2:802, italics in original; see also Glad, *Paul and Philodemus*, 219–21.

91   BAGD 452.

92   Epictetus *Diss.* 2.2.11.

93   See the absolute use of κρινεῖν in the sense of making a judgment about an unidentified wrong in Aristophanes *Frag.* 489 (473): "Indeed, do listen, O woman, apart from wrath, and judge yourself (κρῖνον αὐτή), without fretfulness."

94   Aristophanes *Ran.* 873: ἀγῶνα κρῖναι τόνδε μουσικώτατα ὑμεῖς δὲ ταῖς Μούσαις τι μέλος ὑπᾴσατε ("but to judge a competition of the most musical of songs, what phrase you dart under!").

95   See Friedrich Büchsel and Volkmar Herntrich, "κρίνω κτλ.," *TDNT* 3 (1965) 921–35; Temba L. J. Mafico, "Judge, Judging," *ABD* 3 (1992) 1104–6.

96   For example, the Pharisee program included the admonition "be deliberate in judgment," *P. 'Abot* 1.4; see also 1.18. The *Ps. Sol.* 17.26, 29 declares that the Messiah "shall judge the tribes of the holy people (κρινεῖ φυλὰς λαοῦ ἡγιασμένου)" and

tural. This Pauline theologomenon[97] is probably derived from the categorical prohibition of judging (Matt 7:1; Luke 6:37),[98] which was a distinctive aspect of the "ethical radicalism of Jesus":[99] Μὴ κρίνετε, ἵνα μὴ κριθῆτε ("judge not, that you be not judged"). There are no exact parallels outside of early Christianity to this prohibition,[100] although Jewish sources frequently urge fair and sympathetic judgment. For example, Pseudo-Phocylides 10–11 exhorts its diaspora audience as follows: μὴ ῥιψῃς πενίην ἀδίκως, μὴ κρῖνε πρόσωπον. ἢν σὺ κακῶς δικάσησις, σὲ θεὸς μετέπειτα δικάσσει ("Do not cast down the poor unjustly or judge partially. If you judge unfairly, God will judge you thereafter.") Rabbi Hillel comes closer to the rationale behind Paul's admonition: "judge not your associate until you come to his place" (*Pirkê Aboth* 2:5).

The categorical admonition not to judge persons who feel free to eat forbidden food seems to contradict Paul's call in 1 Cor 5 for the community to issue judgments on such matters. Roetzel argues that "Paul's intention in Romans 14 is not so much to discourage judgment altogether as it is to call for a new concern for the brother,"[101] an assessment that appears consistent with the rationale for ascertaining the will of God in Rom 12:1-2. The distinction may be between judgment as a form of conformity to the world, which in this instance involves conforming to the eating habits of a particular cultural group, and developing a more balanced appraisal of God's will, using the criteria of the "mercies of God," the "good and acceptable and perfect" (Rom 12:1-2). At any rate, in the case of eating or not eating, Paul's prohibitions against scorning and judging are absolute.[102] The treatment of the weak and the strong is thus "equivalent,"[103] and Paul's evenhandedness is unmistakable even though he otherwise identifies himself primarily with the strong.[104] The frown of the legalist is just as inappropriate for the realm of Christ as the disdainful smile of the liberated.[105]

As the conjunction γάρ ("for") indicates, the rationale for Paul's evenhanded ethic is that God "welcomes" sinners without regard to their prior status or performance. This verse recapitulates the argument of the first four chapters of the letter, stating that welcome is unconditional and impartial, unrelated to prior performance or social status. Those whom God welcomes are thereby declared righteous and acceptable, thus reversing their status in the culture as well as in the Roman church conflicts. Since Paul employs the same welcoming terminology in v. 3c as in v. 1a, it is not enough to claim that "'God has received' the other precisely as the ultimate judge."[106] Welcome to the banquet is the crucial issue here, and Paul probably relies on the widely shared tradition of Christ as the host of the Lord's Supper, the master of the love feast, acting in behalf of God to wel-

"judge peoples and nations in the wisdom of his righteousness (κρινεῖ λαοὺς καὶ ἔθνη ἐν σοφίᾳ δικαιοσύνης αὐτοῦ)." See Adolf Schlatter, *Der Evangelist Matthäus* (Stuttgart: Calwer, 1963) 238; James D. G. Dunn, "Pharisees, Sinners and Jesus," in Neusner, *Social World*, 276–83; idem, "Jesus and Ritual Purity: A Study of the Tradition History of Mk 7,15," in R. Gantoy, ed., *À Cause de L'Évangile: Études sur les Synoptiques et les Actes offertes au P. Jacques Dupont, O.S.B. à l'occasion de son 70ᵉ anniversaire*, LD 123 (Paris: Cerf, 1985) 269–73.

97 See Rom 2:1-3; 1 Cor 4:5.
98 See Dunn, "Jesus Tradition," 203; Thompson, *Clothed with Christ*, 163–67.
99 Georg Strecker, *The Sermon on the Mount: An Exegetical Commentary*, trans. O. C. Dean Jr. (Nashville: Abingdon, 1988) 143. For a less radical interpretation, see Hans Dieter Betz, *The Sermon on the Mount* (Minneapolis: Augsburg Fortress, 1995) 489–90.
100 See Thompson, *Clothed with Christ*, 170–71. Jas 4:11-12 stands in this tradition.

101 Roetzel, *Judgement*, 134.
102 See Barrett, 261.
103 Wayne A. Meeks, "Judgment and the Brother: Romans 14:1–15:13," in G. F. Hawthorne and O. Betz, eds., *Tradition and Interpretation in the New Testament: New Testament Essays in Honor of E. Earle Ellis* (Grand Rapids: Eerdmans; Tübingen: Mohr [Siebeck], 1987) 295.
104 Dunn, 2:803, insists, in contrast, that Paul comes down harder in criticizing "the condemnatory attitude of the weak," an assessment based not on the wording of 14:3 but on Dunn's grasp of the element of damnation in "judging." But the "strong" in Rome were equally damning, holding their opponents to be "nothing" with regard to faith in Christ, and thus, effectively, outside of the Christian circle.
105 Murray, 2:175.
106 Meeks, "Judgment and the Brother," 295.

come the faithful into the messianic banquet in fulfillment of the ancient prophecies.[107] As Michel paraphrases, "God has received him into the fellowship of his house (familia dei)."[108]

The crucial issue in this verse is who receives such welcome. It seems clear that the αὐτόν ("him") in 14:3c is a generic reference to welcoming both to the weak and the strong[109] rather than being directed solely to the weak.[110] The formulation is typical of the Psalms: ὁ δὲ κύριος προσελάβετο με ("the Lord has welcomed me") (LXX Ps 26:10; see also 64:4; 72:24). But this type of reference to God's acceptance of worshipers in the context of the Jewish temple is recontextualized by the references to the Christian love feast in Rom 12:13; 13:10; and 14:1; it is theologically anchored in God's grace granted to sinners and enemies, whether Jew or Gentile, through the earlier argument of Romans concerning the revelation of divine righteousness in the Christ event. As Spicq explains, God "has chosen him as his own, taking

him from the world to make him a believer and bring him into his church. How can this divinely established brotherhood be refused?"[111]

■ **4** The theme of God's acceptance of both weak and strong into God's household is carried forward with the indictment of v. 4a. In diatribe style[112] marked by the colloquial expression σὺ τίς εἶ ("who are you?")[113] Paul challenges the pretension of anyone involved in judging members of other masters' households. Given the virtually absolute authority of masters over all the members of their households in the Greco-Roman world,[114] the question would elicit embarrassment from its audience. The expression ἀλλότριος οἰκέτης is usually translated "someone else's slave/servant,"[115] but this overlooks the distinction between οἰκέτης and δοῦλος.[116] The former denotes a normally inalienable member of the household, including slaves[117] who function almost as family members,[118] whereas the latter is ordinarily limited to slaves and hired servants, whether in the household or

---

107 Schlier, 406, relates this welcome to baptism, but the association with hospitality lends stronger support to the link with the Lord's Supper.

108 Michel, 423.

109 See Käsemann, 369; Parunak, "Transitional Techniques," 535; Meeks, "Judgment and the Brother," 295.

110 Dunn argues for this in 2:803 on grounds that only the Jewish Christian "weak" would believe that the other side was not acceptable to God, but there is no reason to suppose that the contempt felt by the Gentile Christians for those perceived to be "weak in faith" was any less condemnatory.

111 Spicq, "προσλαμβάνομαι," 199; Michel, 423: "God has welcomed him into the fellowship of his house."

112 See Stowers, Diatribe, 115.

113 See BAGD 819: "(just) who are you? What sort of man are you?" The same expression appeared in Rom 9:20. Epictetus Diss. 3.1.22 reports a similar response of Athenians to Socrates' moral inquiries by the put-down question, σὺ οὖν τίς εἶ; ("So who are you?").

114 Dio Chrysostom Orat. 31.34.1 uses some of the terms of Paul's formulation in describing the cultural premise of the exclusive authority of masters over slaves: . . . ἀλλ᾽ ἐὰν οἰκέτην τις ἀλλότριον ἢ σκεῦος ἀποδῶνται ψευσάμενος ὡς ἑαυτοῦ, σφόδρα ἕκατος ἀγανακτεῖ τῶν ἠπατημένων, καὶ θαυμάζοιμ᾽ ἄν, εἰ μὴ κἂν [θανάτῳ] ἐζημιοῦτε τοῦτον ὑμεῖς (". . . but if someone sells the slave or

chattel of another, falsely claiming as his own, anyone so defrauded is exceedingly vexed, and it would not amaze me if you applied the death penalty to such a one").

115 NRSV: "servants of another;" Cranfield, 2:698; Dunn, 2:803; Moo, 839.

116 Black, 191, claims the two terms are "synonymous," but LSJM 1202 notes that while οἰκέτης sometimes implies "servitude," it also can be used in distinction to slavery, as in Plato's distinction in Leg. 663a between οἰκέται ("house slaves") and δοῦλοι ("slaves") in describing the refusal of ideal rulers to be served by others.

117 The second-century philosopher Athenaeus defines the distinction in terms of householders being permanently attached to the household without the possibility of being sold: διαφέρειν δὲ φησι Χρύσιππος δοῦλον οἰκέτου, γράφων ἐν δευτέρῳ περὶ ὁμονοίας, διὰ τὸ τοὺς ἀπελευθέρους μὲν δούλους ἔτι εἶναι, οἰκέτας δὲ τοὺς μὴ τῆς κτήσεως ἀφειμένους. ὁ γὰρ οἰκέτης (φησι) δοῦλος ἐστι κτήσει κατατεταγμένος ("Chrysippus describes the difference between a slave and a house slave, writing later concerning concord, that the slaves can be set free while the house slaves cannot be let go as property. 'For the house slave, he says, is a slave appointed as property'") SVF 86 (Nr. 353).

118 Aeschylus clearly includes house slaves as part of a household when the chorus of Ag. 732 declares: αἵματι δ᾽ οἶκος ἐφύρθη, ἄμαχον ἄλγος

in other service.[119] Of modern commentators, Theodor Zahn has the most contextual grasp of the nuance of *Hausgenossenschaft* ("membership in the household") intended by Paul's choice.[120] This would include all persons in a typical Greco-Roman household who are dependent on the master of the house, including children, house slaves, freedpersons, clients, and spouses.[121] The close of the preceding sentence demands this broader, familial nuance, because slaves are not "welcomed" by masters. In this admonition, hospitality extends a form of equality of status. The household connotation is also suggested by the previous argument of the letter, which has defined believers as "beloved of God" (1:7), "children of God" (8:16), "heirs of God . . . joint heirs with Christ" (8:17), "the elect of God" (8:33), "the children of the promise" (9:8), and finally as "one body in Christ" (12:5). Paul's word choice in this verse is reminiscent of Gal 6:10 ("household of faith"), which continued its honorific connotations in the later Pauline tradition (Eph 2:19). Paul avoids the more subordinate term for slave at this point in Romans, because his intent is not to undermine the status of the members of Roman house and tenement churches but to establish their equality with each other in relation to the authority of their κύριος ("lord/master"). The rhetorical question reveals that the culturally shaped judging and despising is an arrogant attempt to place themselves in the superior role, displacing the role of God.[122] As Mathias Rissi

formulates the matter, "Because judging is God's right alone, human judging is forbidden."[123]

The expression τῷ ἰδίῳ κυρίῳ ("to/for his own lord/master") is often taken as a dative of advantage, suggesting that the master's "interest" is at issue here.[124] But Dunn has made a compelling case for a dative of reference because "the master's benefit does not seem to be in view. The issue is rather whether the master regards the slave's conduct as acceptable or unacceptable."[125] In the Roman slave and family system, only the master of the household had the right to make such a judgment. To "stand" or "fall" in this context would be entirely at the discretion of the slave owner, who alone had the authority to assess whether a house slave had met expectations or not. The verb στήκω ("stand"), a formation from the verb ἵστημι ("set up, stand"), appears for the first time in variant readings of the LXX and in the NT, primarily in the Pauline letters.[126] To "stand in the Lord" (Phil 4:1); "stand firm in the Lord" (1 Thess 3:8); "stand in the faith" (1 Cor 16:13); or "stand in one spirit" (Phil 1:27) is technical Pauline language for eschatological perseverance.[127] Correspondingly, the verb πίπτω ("fall") has the same metaphorical connotation as in Rom 11:11, to lose the approbation of a powerful lord. The relation between such loss of status and resultant shame is visible in Sir 1:30: Μὴ ἐξύψου σεαυτὸν, ἵνα μὴ πέσῃς, καὶ ἐπαγάγῃς τῇ ψυχῇ σου ἀτιμίαν, καὶ ἀποκαλύψει Κύριος τὰ κρυπτά σου, καὶ

οἰκέταις ("But the house was defiled with blood, and the house slaves had irresistible grief"); see also Herodotus *Hist.* 8.4, 106, 142.

119 Ceslas Spicq, "Le vocabulaire de l'esclavage dans le Nouveau Testament," *RB* 85 (1978) 204–14, 218–20.

120 Zahn, 571–72, citing Eph 2:19 (συμπολῖται τῶν ἁγίων καὶ οἰκεῖοι τοῦ θεοῦ, "citizens with the saints and members of the household of God") and Gal 6:10 (τοὺς οἰκείους τῆς πίστεως, "house slaves of faith"). Esler also emphasizes this definition in *Conflict and Identity*, 347–48.

121 See Peter Lampe's synthesis of research in "'Family' in Church and Society in New Testament Times," *Affirmation* 5.1 (1992) 3.

122 See Jülicher, 321; Wilckens, 3:82.

123 Mathias Rissi, "κρίνω, κρίσις," *EDNT* 2 (1991) 320. Thompson notes that the rhetorical question in Jas 4:12, "Who are you that you judge your neighbor?" is similar to Rom 14:4 both in motivation and in

categorical quality, allowing no exception. James, like Paul, was probably influenced by the historical Jesus on this point; *Clothed with Christ*, 171.

124 See Lagrange, 324; Cranfield, 2:703.

125 Dunn, 2:804, followed by Moo, 840. For all earlier advocacy of this view, see Hermann, *Kyrios und Pneuma*, 89–91.

126 BDF §73 "virtually confined to Paul"; BAGD 767; LSJM 1643 notes that this is a "late form" but that it appears first in 3 Kgdms 8:11. Walter Grundmann suggests in "στήκω, ἵστημι," *TDNT* 7 (1971) 636, that the textual variants in the LXX indicate that "Christian redactors put it in place of forms of ἵστημι." The parallels in the Hebrew of Qumran such as 1QH 4:21-22 and 1QS 11:15-17 are discussed by Grundmann, "Stehen," 156–57.

127 See Grundmann, "στήκω, ἵστημι," 648–49; Wolter, *Röm 5,1-11*, 122; Volf, *Paul and Perserverance*, 52–53, 72–74.

ἐν μέσῳ συναγωγῆς καταβαλεῖ σε . . . ("Do not exalt yourself, lest you fall and bring dishonor on your soul, and the Lord discover your secrets and cast you down in the midst of the congregation . . . "). The typical association between falling and being judged in apocalyptic literature is visible in *T. Gad* 4.3: Ἐὰν γὰρ πέσῃ ὁ ἀδελφός, σπουδάζει εὐθὺς ἀναγγεῖλαι τοῖς πᾶσιν, καὶ σπεύδει περὶ αὐτοῦ ἵνα κριθεὶς καὶ κολοσθεὶς ἀποθάνῃ . . . ("For if a brother falls, it [hatred] wants to proclaim it immediately to everyone and urges that he should be judged for it, be punished and should die . . ."). Both standing and falling are used in Paul's memorable warning of 1 Cor 10:12, ὁ δοκῶν ἑστάναι βλεπέτω μὴ πέσῃ ("the one who thinks he is standing should look out lest he fall"). To "fall" in this context seems to entail "loss of faith and separation from grace" as well as "apostasy from God and from Christ."[128] Both "stand" and "fall" thus have a multivalent reference in this passage, reflecting social relations between patrons and householders and at the same time echoing distinctive early Christian language concerning the eschatological situation of believers in relation to their Lord as the agent of divine judgment both in the present and in the future. The choice of κύριος is also multivalent, with connotations ranging from master of a household, owner, slaveholder, to explicit Christian references to Jesus or God.[129] Since Paul did not choose to use

δεσπότης ("master, owner") in this passage, it must have been clear to his Roman audience that the "Lord" who determines whether believers are welcome in the love feast[130] is the divine one, whether God or Christ.[131]

In v. 4b the verb σταθήσεται can be taken as either a middle ("he shall stand")[132] or a passive ("he shall be made to stand"), but the latter seems more likely because the logic of the passage depends on the power and authority of the lord to determine the status of house slaves. In Käsemann's words, "Paul is announcing his confidence that the Lord of the community, having once received a member, can cause him to stand. . . . Grace is stronger than human frailty."[133] The emphasis in this passage is on the power of the κύριος, which is accentuated in v. 4c. With the verb δύναμαι ("be able, be powerful") there is an echo of the thesis of Romans concerning the gospel as the "power of God" (1:16). That God is powerful was a premise shared with Judaism as well as the other religions of the Greco-Roman world.[134] In the context of the Roman society, where power was so widely celebrated,[135] to claim that the Lord has the power to make his householders stand would have particular resonance. Thus I prefer the somewhat redundant translation suggested by the *NEB*, "has power to enable him to stand."[136] The double valence of the passage makes the argument indisputable, because while every master of a Roman house had the power to make his

---

128 Wilhelm Michaelis, "πίπτω κτλ.," *TDNT* 6 (1968) 164. Unfortunately, Michaelis places this passage under the rubric "Falling as Becoming Guilty," which is a typical attempt to assimilate this biblical language into the post-Augustinian theology of guilt. See also Elizabeth Palzkill, "πίπτω," *EDNT* 3 (1993) 90.

129 See BAGD 458–60.

130 See Godet, 455.

131 See Moo's listing in 840 of the ten references to κύριος or its verbal counterpart in this passage, some identified with Christ and others identified with God, concluding that Paul thought of "Christ, Lord, and God on equal terms." See also Thüsing, *Per Christum,* 34–36.

132 Cranfield, 2:703, argues for the middle voice of the verb in order to retain "a satisfactory progression of thought," but the middle voice would imply that a person stands himself up (Funk, *Grammar,* §306.1), which would undercut Paul's argument for the divine dependence of members of competing churches.

133 Käsemann, 370, following Kühl, 449, and in contrast to Leenhardt, 348. See also Schlier, 407. Dunn, 2:804, corrects Käsemann's implication that "a fall has preceded" the standing up.

134 See Otto Schmitz, "Der Begriff δύναμις bei Paulus," in *Festgabe für Adolf Deissmann zum 60. Geburtstag 7. November 1926* (Tübingen: Mohr [Siebeck], 1927) 150–54; Walter Grundmann, *Der Begriff der Kraft in der neutestamentlichen Gedankenwelt,* BWANT 4.8 (Stuttgart: Kohlhammer, 1932) 11–38; Erich Fascher, "Dynamis," *RAC* 4 (1959) 416–34; Prümm, "Dynamis," 400–419.

135 See Wagenvoort, *Roman Dynamism,* 12–72; Fascher, "Dynamis," 426–27.

136 See Black, 192.

householders stand or fall, the recipients of Paul's letter believed the Lord of the church surpassed all others in power.[137] In Harrison's words, "Paul ultimately subverts the patronal system . . . by subjecting everyone to a common Master who outshines all."[138] As in the preceding verse, the object of the verb (αὐτόν, "him") pertains to both the weak and the strong.[139]

■ **5** When Paul turns to the Roman controversy over sacred days, he employs the verb κρίνειν again, with the connotation of "judge to be preferable." There is a close parallel to this use in Plato's argument that simple musical instruments are more appropriate for the ideal republic than instruments that arouse dangerous emotions: Οὐδέν γε, ἦν δ᾽ ἐγώ, καινὸν ποιοῦμεν, ὦ φίλε, κρίνοντες τὸν Ἀπόλλω καὶ τὰ τοῦ Ἀπόλλωνος ὄργανα πρὸ Μαρσύου τε καὶ τῶν ἐκείνου ὀργάνων ("We are not innovating, O friend, in judging Apollo and the instruments of Apollo preferable to Marsyas and his instruments," *Resp.* 399e1). Whereas Plato qualifies the word "judge" with the preposition πρό ("before, in

front of"), Paul uses παρά with an accusative in the sense of "in comparison with, superior to."[140] Thus some groups hold certain days to be preferable to other days while the second half of the antithetical statement indicated by μέν . . . δέ shows that their opponents judge πᾶσαν ἡμέραν ("all days") to be alike.[141] By using "judge" for both sides of this controversy, Paul equalizes the religious and moral foundation of each position. Yet what is even more striking about his formulation is that the technical terms for the various forms of sanctifying time are avoided. In keeping with the "oblique style" of rhetoric employed throughout this pericope, the argument is generic, incorporating a wide variety of possible viewpoints and practices in Paul's audience. While scholars have argued that Paul had in mind the early development of Sunday as a day of worship,[142] the Jewish Sabbath,[143] and/or the Jewish festivals,[144] fast days,[145] the lucky days of Greco-Roman astrological calculation,[146] or Roman feast days,[147] his generic formulation prevents a more precise determination of these alterna-

137 See L. A. Rood, "Le Christ comme δύναμις Θεοῦ," in A. Descamps et al. *Littérature et Théologie Pauliniennes*, RechBib 4 (Leuven: Desclée de Brouwer, 1960) 100–106.

138 Harrison, *Language of Grace*, 322.

139 See Meeks, "Judgment and the Brother," 295. Dunn, 2:805, suggests a possible connection with Rom 10:3, which should be repudiated because it would relate the passage only to the Jewish Christian wing of the congregation.

140 BAGD 611; see also Harald Riesenfeld, "παρά," *TDNT* 5 (1967) 734: "comparative sense. . . . Superiority over the thing denoted by παρά is expressed."

141 Cranfield, 2:705.

142 Schlatter, 255; Willi Rordorf, *Sunday: The History of the Day of Rest and Worship in the Earliest Centuries of the Christian Church*, trans. A. A. K. Graham (London: SCM; Philadelphia: Westminster, 1968) 137–38; Richard J. Bauckham surveys the NT use of κυριακὴ ἡμέρα ("Lord's Day"), concluding that "Sunday worship began at an early stage of Christian history" in "The Lord's Day," in D. A. Carson, ed., *From Sabbath Day to Lord's Day: A Biblical, Historical, and Theological Investigation* (Grand Rapids: Zondervan, 1982) 221–50, 240. Samuele Bacchiocchi argues less plausibly that Sunday observance began in second-century Roman Christianity; *From Sabbath to Sunday: A Historical Investigation of the Rise of Sunday Observance in Early Christianity* (Rome:

Pontifical Gregorian University, 1977); "How It Came About: From Saturday to Sunday," *BAR* 4.3 (1978) 32–40.

143 Dunn, 2:805–6; Douglas R. de Lacey, "The Sabbath/Sunday Question and the Law in the Pauline Corpus," in Carson, *From Sabbath Day to Lord's Day*, 172, 181–82; for general orientation, see Robert Goldenberg, "The Jewish Sabbath in the Roman World up to the Time of Constantine the Great," *ANRW* 2.19.1 (1979) 414–47; Christopher Rowland, "A Summary of Sabbath Observance in Judaism at the Beginning of the Christian Era," in Carson, *From Sabbath Day to Lord's Day*, 43–56. For evidence about the widespread observance of the Sabbath by Jews in the Diaspora, see Lutz Doering, *Schabbat. Sabbat halacha und -praxis im antiken Judentum und Urchristentum*, TSAJ 78 (Tübingen: Mohr Siebeck, 1999) 283–386, esp. 383–84. In "Undermine the Law," 11, Barclay points to the confluence of the Jewish Sabbath and "the seven-day planetary week, which was coming into vogue at just this time."

144 Murray, 2:177–78, 2:257–59.

145 Rauer, *Schwachen*, 181–83; Lagrange, 325; Leenhardt, 349; Bacchiocchi, *Sabbath to Sunday*, 364–65; Raoul Dederen, "On Esteeming One Day Better Than Another—Romans 14:5,6," *AUSS* 9 (1971) 31; for recent literature, see John Muddiman, "Fast, Fasting," *ABD* 2 (1992) 773–76.

146 Käsemann, 370; O'Neill, 224; Zeller, 225.

tives. He may well have intended to address controversies concerning several of the above, and the variety of Roman Christianity evident in the first three centuries of its existence renders several of them more or less plausible. Although the argument of Rom 12:1 implied that "there are no longer holy days, since the entire existence of Christians is holy and thus the right time for worship,"[148] no precedence is granted in this formulation. While Paul's seemingly nonchalant acceptance of all options is disturbing for commentators,[149] it seems to be a fitting expression of his missionary principle of being "all things to all people."

The sole admonition that Paul makes concerning special days pertains to individual conviction. Just as in the description of Abraham's faith in 4:21, the rare verb πληροφορέω is used in a passive form that means "be fully convinced/assured."[150] The closest parallels to this usage are in early Christian materials describing certitude of belief (Col 4:12; Ignatius *Mag.* 8.2; *Smyrn.* 1.1). For example, Clement uses both the passive verb and the corresponding noun to describe the certainty with which the apostles proclaimed the gospel: παραγγελίας οὖν λαβόντες καὶ πληροφορηθέντες διὰ τῆς ἀναστάσεως τοῦ κυρίου ἡμῶν Ἰησοῦ Χριστοῦ καὶ πιστωθέντες ἐν τῷ λόγῳ τοῦ θεοῦ μετὰ πληροφορίας πνεύματος ἁγίου ἐξῆλθον εὐαγγελιζόμενοι, τὴν βασιλείαν τοῦ θεοῦ μέλλειν ἔρχεσθαι ("Having received commands therefore and being fully assured through the resurrection of our Lord Jesus Christ and having been entrusted with oracles of God and full assurance of the Holy Spirit, they went out preaching the gospel that the Kingdom of God was about to come"; *1 Clem.* 42.3; see also Clement *Hom.* 11.17.2.3) This formulaic passage, and the distinctive use of the language of "full conviction/assurance" by other early Christian sources, raise the possibility that Paul is employing a verb in 14:5 that was on the way of becoming a technical term for charismatic assurance. There is pre-Christian precedent in using this word in the context of religious certainty, as evident in a somewhat more distant parallel that does not employ the passive; the following epitaph on a sarcophagus assures a wife that her initiation assures a welcome from Isis:[151] "χαῖρε καλλιφενής," εἴποι σοι, "πληροφοροῦ ψυχή." ("Hail, O shining one," may she [the goddess Isis] say to you, "be fully assured, O soul.") That "each" member of the house and tenement churches in Rome is to be fully convinced ἐν τῷ ἰδίῳ νοΐ ("in his own thinking") therefore reflects the extraordinary confidence in the power and appropriateness of individual conviction that became characteristic of early Christianity.[152] Νοῦς is used here in as in Rom 12:2 to refer to the "constellation of thoughts and assumptions" that a person holds, in this case in response to the gospel.[153] Paul is encouraging the Christians of Rome, whether they belong to the majority or the minority, to avoid "indecision and vacillation"[154] that could result from the conforming pressures reflected in 14:1-3. He wants them to grasp their "charismatic freedom" that "sanctions different attitudes" and legitimates an "infinite breadth of possibilities" for cultural variation in belief and practice.[155]

147 While Reasoner's dissertation concluded that Roman feast days cannot "be totally excluded" ("The 'Strong' and the 'Weak' in Rome," 285), he now believes that an astrological motivation is "most likely off the mark" (*The Strong*, 148).

148 Zeller, 225.

149 For example, Dederen argues in "On Esteeming," 28, that "the seventh-day Sabbath" cannot be in view because he would not "trifle" with a commandment; a similar case is presented by Murray, 2:257–59, and Morris, 480.

150 See Gerhard Delling, "πληροφορέω," *TDNT* 6 (1968) 309. A *TLG* search indicates only two occurrences prior to the NT: Aesop *Prov.* 69.3 and Ctesias *Frag.* 3c,688, F.14.75, while it occurs in first-century C.E. Christian literature eighty-eight times. Joachim

Becker argues for the sense of "abound" in "Quid πληροφορεῖσθαι in Rom 14,5 significet," *VD* 45 (1967) 11–18, and "Zu πληροφορεῖσθαι in Röm 14,5," *Bib* 65 (1984) 364.

151 Ceslas Spicq, "πληροφορέω, πληροφορία," *TLNT* 3 (1994) 121, citing the text from Franz Valerie Marie Cumont, *Recherches sur le symbolisme funérier des romains* (BAH 35; Paris: Geuthner, 1942), 299.

152 See Schlatter, 257–60; Barclay, "Undermine the Law," 14–15.

153 Jewett, *Terms*, 385.

154 Cranfield, 2:705.

155 Käsemann, 370.

■ **6** This verse opens the argument that runs through v. 9, explaining the theological basis of differing approaches to sacred days and sacred foods. It spells out the content of the "full assurance" that various groups in Rome should have. To set one's "mind on the day" (φρονεῖν τὴν ἡμέραν) is an unusual expression for liturgical observance, but it echoes the language of Rom 8 concerning the mind that is directed either toward the spirit or toward the flesh.[156] By selecting the verb "be minded," used twice in this compact wordplay, Paul can link liturgical behavior with devotion κυρίῳ ("in respect of a lord").[157] Given the distinction between "super-minded" and "sober-minded" established in the wordplay on φρονεῖν in 12:3, Paul places the liturgical practices of the "weak" minority in Rome[158] within the parameters of responsible Christian behavior. This has a legitimating[159] rather than a restricting function,[160] acknowledging the Christian motivation of practices previously scorned by the majority. Since φρόνιμοι ("wise ones") may well have been a self-appellation of the strong, as suggested by my exegesis of Rom 11:25 and 12:16, linking this term with the behavior of the weak serves the same legitimizing function.

In a parallel formulation, Paul turns in v. 6b to authenticate the behavior of the "strong." Their eating of foods prohibited by the "weak" is κυρίῳ ("in respect for a lord") and therefore an expression of legitimate discipleship.[161] The verb "eat" is used here in the absolute, which in the strict sense would pertain to the "weak" minority as well as the "powerful" majority, but its restricted reference to the "powerful" (15:1) would have been unmistakable to the audience because of the formulation in 14:2 that they eat "everything" while the "weak" abstain. The additional justification that the eaters "give thanks to God" refers to grace at meals,[162] which believers could have taken over from either Greco-Roman[163] or Jewish custom.[164] The NT contains frequent references to such blessings at mealtimes (Matt 15:36; Mark 8:6; John 6:11, 23; Acts 27:35; 1 Tim 4:3-5), including the Lord's Supper (1 Cor 11:24; Matt 26:27; Mark 14:23; Luke 22:17, 19), and Paul uses the custom as an argumentative premise in 1 Cor 10:30: εἰ ἐγὼ χάριτι μετέχω, τί βλασφημοῦμαι ὑπὲρ οὗ ἐγὼ εὐχαριστῶ; ("If I partake with gratitude, why should I be denounced because of that for which I give thanks?"). That such table blessings with formulas like εὐχαριστοῦμεν σοι, πάτερ ἡμῶν ("we give you thanks, our father") remained customary with early Christians is evident from *Did.* 9.2-3; 10.1-4 and *Herm. Sim.* 2.6; 5.1. The allusion to this custom serves to justify the behavior of the "powerful," whose lack of scruples was being condemned by the "weak" as a violation of religious law; if they give thanks to God while eating, they are engaged in religious devotion to the same God being worshiped by the "weak."

---

156 Other examples of φρόνιμοι with the accusative are noted in BAGD 866.

157 See Georg Bertram, "φρήν κτλ.," *TDNT* 9 (1974) 233: "responsibility to the Lord."

158 Cranfield, 2:706; Wilckens, 3:83; Dunn, 2:806.

159 See Käsemann, 371: "If we live to please the Lord, no one has any right to restrict our freedom, to establish norms for our judgment."

160 For example, Leenhardt, 349: "it is not enough for a conviction to be sincere to be true. The Christian is not free because he thinks in honour of the Lord." See also Henning Paulsen, "φρονέω," *EDNT* 3 (1993) 439.

161 See Murray, 2:179: the "threefold repetition of the words 'unto the Lord' in verse 6 expresses the religious conviction. . . ."

162 See Goltz, *Gebet*, 103; Theodor Schermann, "Εὐχαριστία und εὐχαριστεῖν," in ihren Bedeutungswandel bis 200 n. Chr," *Philol* 69 (1910) 375–410; Harder, *Gebet*, 121; Hans Conzelmann,

"εὐχαριστέω κτλ.," *TDNT* 9 (1974) 412; A. Stuiber, "Eulogia," *RAC* 6 (1966) 911–12.

163 Schubert, *Thanksgivings*, 85, 138–39; Klauck, *Herrenmahl*, 278–79; Dennis E. Smith, "Meal Customs," *ABD* 4 (1992) 651, 653. Plato's *Symp.* 176a refers to a traditional act of devotion between the supper and the symposium: τε σφᾶς ποιήσασθαι καὶ ᾄσαντας τὸν θεὸν καὶ τἆλλα τὰ νομιζόμενα . . . (". . . they made libation and sang a chant to the god and so forth, as custom bids . . ."). Epictetus provides a general exhortation to give thanks for food in *Diss.* 2.23.5: "for dry fruits, for wine, for olive oil, give thanks to God (εὐχαρίστει τῷ θεῷ)." See also 2.20.32 and 4.1.105–6. See also Schermann, "Εὐχαριστία und εὐχαριστεῖν," 379, 390.

164 Commentators usually stress only the Jewish tradition of table blessing, for example, Tholuck, 418; Michel, 427; Stuhlmacher, 224; Moo, 843; Harder, *Gebet*, 121; Conzelmann, "εὐχαριστέω κτλ.," 412; Hermann Patsch, "εὐχαριστέω," *EDNT* 2 (1991)

The symmetry between v. 6a, which deals with the "weak," and v. 6b, which deals with the "powerful," is thrown off balance by what appears to be a Pauline afterthought in v. 6c.[165] That those who refrain from eating do so in relation to the same Lord while offering thanks to God is articulated in v. 6c with the same terminology used in v. 6b, placing the religious devotion of both sides on precisely the same level. The only change is replacing γάρ ("for, since") in v. 6b with καί ("and, also") in v. 6c, which equalizes the status of the two thanksgivings.[166] The motivation for the afterthought was probably to ensure that the religious devotion of the "weak" be given equal honor.[167] If each group can acknowledge the devotion of the other, directed to the same Lord Jesus Christ, and giving thanks to the same God, they will be able to share their meals with each other without insisting on uniformity.[168]

■ **7** In vv. 7-9 Paul presents a formal syllogism[169] in support of the principle enunciated in v. 6 that Christians act "in relation to the Lord/God."[170] The first two premises stated in v. 7 are that οὐδεὶς ἡμῶν ("none of us"), which would exclude all members of the various house and tenement churches in Rome, lives or dies ἑαυτῷ ("in relation to himself/herself"). Interpreters are inclined to place this reference under categories such as "selfishness," or "self-centeredness,"[171] terminology that first emerged in the seventeenth century. At first glance, some ancient references appear to support this view. Plutarch cites the hero Cleomenes, who resists suicide in

the face of inevitable defeat on the ground that αἰσχρὸν γὰρ καὶ ζῆν μόνοις ἑαυτοῖς καὶ ἀποθνήσκειν ("it is shameful to die, as well as to live, for one's own self alone").[172] Similarly, Terence describes in highly ironic tones a shiftless brother who "lived for himself and spent his money on himself" (sibi vixit, sibi sumptum fecit), yet "all the world speaks well of him and loves him" (omnes bene dicunt, amant).[173] But the same expression can be used by Diodorus Siculus in a positive sense to describe the self-reliant courage of the Spartans who risk dying for freedom while facing the Persian hordes: Παραλαμβάνουσι γὰρ οἱ Σπαρτιᾶται παρὰ τῶν πατέρων οὐχ ὥσπερ οἱ λοιποὶ πλοῦτον, ἀλλὰ προθύμως τελευτᾶν περὶ τῆς ἐλευθερίας. . . . Παρειλήφασι γὰρ ὑπὸ τῶν πατέρων ζῆν μὲν ἑαυτοῖς, τελευτᾶν δ᾽ ὅταν χρεία ταῖς πατρίσιν ἐπῇ ("For the inheritance that the Spartans receive from their fathers is not wealth as with all other peoples, but a willingness to die for the sake of liberty. . . . For the inheritance they have received from their fathers is to live for themselves, and to die in response to their country's need," Diodorus Siculus Hist. 10.34.8, 11–12). It appears to me, therefore, that the reference to not living or dying for oneself reflects group identity, which in the case of Romans rested on distinctively Christian foundations set forth in Rom 6:8-11. Since all the members of this group had died to sin and the old self, and had been baptized into Christ's death, they all live now "in relation to God in Christ Jesus."[174] A close parallel to this Pauline theologumenon is 2 Cor

---

88; Stuiber, "Eulogia," 912. B.Ber 35a states, "It is forbidden man to enjoy anything of this world without benediction." In Spec. 2.175 Philo refers to the Jewish custom of blessing food: . . . οὐθ᾽ ὅσιον ἀπολαῦσαι καὶ μετασχεῖν τινος τῶν πρὸς ἐδωδὴν μὴ ἐν οἷς εὐπρεπὲς καὶ θέμις εὐχαριστήσαντας . . . ("it is also not right to enjoy and partake of any kind of food for which thanks had not been offered in the proper and right manner").

165 See Jülicher, 322; Lagrange, 325; Cranfield, 2:706.

166 Murray, 2:179, points to this "striking" distinction but resists interpretive options that disparage either side.

167 Jülicher, 211; Zahn, 573; Kühl, 450–51; Cranfield, 2:706–7.

168 See Schlatter, 258–60; Michel, 427.

169 For the distinction between a syllogism and an enthymeme, see Moores, Wrestling, 33–37. That this syllogism originated as a Pauline composition cre-

ated before the writing of Romans has been shown by Theobald, 2:138–40, in part because the life-and-death theme is somewhat extraneous to the context of chapter 15.

170 Moule, "Death," 151, suggests that the datives in this and the following verse should be understood as datives of advantage, but his expression dative "of relation" (152, 157) seems more appropriate.

171 See Black, 194; Dunn, 2:807; Murray, 2:180; Morris, 482.

172 Plutarch Ag. Cleom. 31.5, cited by Leenhardt, 350; Cranfield, 2:707; and Black, 194. See also the saying found several times in Menander Frag. 506–7; 646.1: τοῦτ᾽ ἔστι τὸ ζῆν, οὐχ ἑαυτῷ ζῆν μόνον ("This is the life, not to live for oneself alone").

173 Terence Ad. 865.

174 Rom 6:11; see Viard, 285–86; Nababan, "Bekenntnis," 27.

5:15, which proclaims that Christ "died for all, so that those who live might no longer live for themselves, but for him who died and was raised for them." Therefore, whether the believer dies or lives in a physical sense, one's life as a "household slave" is not one's own.[175] This framework provides a link with the life and death metaphors in 14:7-8, which otherwise seem too drastic to be derived merely from the conflict over eating;[176] whether one eats meat or lettuce hardly seems to be a life-and-death matter. Yet for Paul the mystical relationship of living and dying with Christ provides a new context for all other issues.

■ **8** In a precisely parallel manner this verse sets forth the counterpremises of Paul's syllogism of life and death in the Lord. That those who live and die $\tau\hat{\omega}$ $\kappa\upsilon\rho\acute{\iota}\omega$ ("in relation to the Lord") are believers is indicated by the first person plural verbal forms, "we live . . . we die."[177] The paranomasia on "in relation to the Lord" and "to God," beginning in v. 4 and continuing in vv. 6 and 8 with seven additional repetitions, reinforces the point that the various groups in Rome are finally accountable only to their divine partner.[178] This passage is a clear example of collective mysticism, drawing every aspect of the community's existence from life to death into the relationship with their Lord.[179] Ernst Käsemann rightly refers to this as "the central statement of the passage from which all else naturally flows."[180] Albert Schweitzer has a clear grasp of the encompassing nature of this relationship, even though formulating it in too individualistic a manner. It involves "the believer's whole being, down to his most ordinary everyday thoughts and

actions," a relationship that has "a breadth, a permanence, a practicability, and a strength almost unexampled elsewhere in mysticism."[181] It is not the kind of mysticism that absorbs the self into the divine but rather provides "a sense of continuous communion."[182] Paul understands the liberated life of the congregation as determined by the "logic of the relationship of dominion,"[183] in which the lordship of Christ is all-important. The inference of the syllogism marked by "therefore" ($o\hat{\upsilon}\nu$) in v. 8c places this relationship in the possessive: $\tauo\hat{\upsilon}$ $\kappa\upsilon\rho\acute{\iota}o\upsilon$ $\dot{\epsilon}\sigma\mu\acute{\epsilon}\nu$ ("we are of the Lord / belong to the Lord"). This means that believers are "in every state of the case the Lord's *property*."[184] This is the basic barrier against judging or despising fellow believers, which is the issue at hand. In Michel's words, "the important behavior patterns of both groups (verses 5,6) appear small and unimportant in face of the fundamental lordship of Jesus Christ over the life of every single one."[185] This lordship is a gracious rather than a domineering one, as indicated by the welcome of household members into the Lord's banquet stated in 14:3. Although all the members of the Roman house and tenement churches belong to Christ, they are not to be treated as menial slaves but rather as the "beloved of God" (1:7), the "children of God" (8:16), "joint heirs with Christ" (8:17), and, as the next pericope will declare, "your brother[s] . . . for whom Christ died" (14:15) and "the work of God" (14:20).

■ **9** To conclude the syllogism based on the collective, mystical experience of life and death in Christ (14:7-8), Paul articulates its theological foundation in v. 9.

---

175 For example, Phil 1:21, "For me to live is Christ and to die is gain." See also 2 Cor 5:9 and the analyses by Rudolf Bultmann, "ζάω . . . The Concept of Life in the NT," *TDNT* 2 (1964) 865–69, and Luise Schottroff, "ζῶ," *EDNT* 2 (1991) 106–7.

176 See Theobald, *Studien*, 155–58; James L. Jaquette, *Discerning What Counts: The Function of the Adiaphora Topos in Paul's Letters*, SBLDS 146 (Atlanta: Scholars, 1995) 126–36; idem, "Life and Death, Adiaphora, and Paul's Rhetorical Strategies," *NovT* 38 (1996) 30–54.

177 Barrett, 260. Godet, 458, notes that ζῶμεν and ἀποθνῄσκωμεν must be taken as subjunctives following ἐάν ("if"), but that the second ζῶμεν in v. 8a should be understood as an indicative rather than an imperative.

178 Synofzik, *Vergeltungsaussagen*, 45, 123.

179 See H. Clavier, "Le drame de la mort et la vie dans le Nouveau Testament," *Studia Evangelica III*, TU 88 (1964) 175–77; J. N. Sevenster, *Leven en dood in de brieven van Paulus*, VerV 9 (Amsterdam: Uitgeversmaatschappij Holland, 1954) 30–40.

180 Käsemann, 371.

181 Schweitzer, *Mysticism*, 125.

182 Helmer Ringgren, "Mysticism," *ABD* 4 (1992) 946.

183 Schottroff, "ζῶ," 106.

184 Godet, 453, italics in original; see also Meyer, 2:309; Schlier, 409–10.

185 Michel, 427.

Whereas in many earlier syllogisms in Romans the theological foundation of the death and resurrection of Christ remains an unstated premise,[186] Paul now makes it explicit. The prepositional phrase εἰς τοῦτο γάρ ("for toward this") describes the purpose of the redemptive life and death of Christ as foundational for the preceding syllogism.[187] Paul adapts the traditional confessional formula, "Christ died and was raised" (Rom 8:34; 1 Cor 15:3-4; 2 Cor 5:15; see also Gal 1:4; 1 Thess 4:14),[188] bringing it into the life-and-death framework of his previous syllogism by the verb ἔζησεν ("he lived").[189] The aorist form may be ingressive, meaning Jesus "came to life"[190] after being crucified.[191] Paul's formulation is, in any event, a reversal of the usual career of famous people celebrated in Greco-Roman biography, moving from living to dying.[192]

The purpose clause in v. 9b marked by ἵνα ("in order that") employs κυριεύειν ("to rule"), the verbal form in addition to the other nine references to the lordship of Christ in this pericope. The aorist subjunctive κυριεύσῃ indicates the purpose was "that he might become/act as Lord."[193] The reversal of the normal sequence, "living and dead," appears to match the sequence of v. 9a and

there is no hint that Jesus' death is correlated only with the dead and his life only with the living.[194] The καὶ . . . καί construction of v. 9b clearly implies that both[195] the dead and the living are encompassed by the lordship of Christ. The sequence lends emphasis to the limitless reach of Christ's lordship, indicating, in Schlier's words, "the breadth and depth of his rule. This Lord, in whom we live and die, admits no boundaries as the one who died and now lives forever."[196] The logical conclusion from Paul's wording was drawn by Jan Bonda: "That the dead fall under Christ's lordship means that he can reach them,"[197] so that salvation will ultimately become universal. But there is an implication that lies closer to Paul's immediate purpose in writing Romans: if Christ rules over everything from life to death, he certainly is the final arbiter in matters of calendar and diet. This eliminates the final shred of credibility on the part of either the weak or the powerful in their attempts to lord it over each other.

■ **10** The final section of the pericope opens as 14:4 did with a direct challenge to the audience: Σὺ δὲ τί κρίνεις ("But who are you to judge?"). The diatribal question challenges the habit of arrogant judgment,[198]

---

186 See Moores, *Wrestling*, 67, 159.
187 See Käsemann, 372.
188 See Kegel, *Auferstehung*, 126; Wengst, *Formeln*, 45–46; Nababan, "Bekenntnis," 54–72; Schlier, 410.
189 See Dunn, 2:808, referring to Kramer, *Christ*, 29–30.
190 BDF §331; see Kühl, 451; Schlier, 410.
191 Murray, 2:182, shows conclusively that the reference here is to the resurrection, noting that Rom 5:10 and 2 Cor 4:10 also used the word "life" in this sense.
192 See also Gibson, "Dying Formula," 28–40, who shows that the Christian formula is also the antithesis to the tradition of the heroic warrior who dies to preserve his country's superior status.
193 See Werner Foerster, "κυριεύω," *TDNT* 3 (1965) 1097. That the aorist is again ingressive is shown by Moo, 845, indicating that Christ's lordship is conceived as beginning with his death and resurrection. Kenneth W. Clark shows that there is no inherent negative implication in this verb, as suggested by a translation such as "to lord it over"; "The Meaning of (*KATA*) *KYPIEYEIN*," in J. K. Elliott, ed., *Studies in New Testament Language and Text: Essays in Honour of George D. Kilpatrick on the Occasion of His Sixty-fifth Birthday*, NovTSup 44 (Leiden: Brill, 1976) 103–5.

194 Cf. Moule, *Idiom-Book*, 195; this option is properly rejected by Meyer, 2:369; Kramer, *Christ*, 193; and Moo, 846.
195 See BAGD 393; BDF §444; Moulton and Turner, *Grammar III*, 335.
196 Schlier, 410; see also D. M. Stanley, *Christ's Resurrection in Pauline Soteriology*, AnBib 13 (Rome: Pontifical Biblical Institute, 1961) 199.
197 Bonda, *One Purpose*, 108. He goes on in 110 to insist that "God wants all people to be saved, and that remains his desire even after their death. We therefore know that he cannot possibly desire their eternal destruction."
198 See Käsemann, 372; Schlier, 410; Stowers, *Diatribe*, 115. The use of this kind of question to challenge presumptuous behavior is also visible in Menander *Epitr.* 174: σὺ δ᾽ εἶ τίς; ("But who are you?"). Text from Alfredus Körte, ed., *Menander Reliquiae* (Leipzig: Teubner, 1938), 1.20.

with δέ ("but") indicating the antithesis to the universal authority of the Lord articulated in the preceding verse.[199] The emphatic position of σύ[200] lifts up the element of pretension,[201] which is all the more embarrassing to the audience because the argument since the last emphatic question of 14:4 eliminates any justification for mutual judging. Jas 4:12 has a similar question, σὺ δὲ τὶς εἶ, ὁ κρίνων τὸν πλησίον; ("But who are you that judges your neighbor?") and it is likely that both sayings are influenced by words of Jesus reported by Matt 7:3: τὶ δὲ βλέπεις τὸ κάρφος τὸ ἐν τῷ ὀφθαλμῷ τοῦ ἀδελφοῦ σου. . . ; ("Why do you see the speck that is in your brother's eye . . . ?").[202] Although it would be possible to understand ἀδελφός in 14:10 along the lines of James as "neighbor,"[203] most commentators agree that its sudden reappearance after being used last at 12:1, and its fivefold repetition in this and the next pericope, indicate "not a mere acquaintance but a brother in Christ."[204] This inference flows directly out of the preceding argument, because if all believers belong to the Lord, they must all be part of the "spiritual brotherhood" of believers.[205] The "house slaves" of the early part of this pericope have now become honored brothers and sisters.

Whereas the first challenge refers to the "weak" who are judging others for not following the law on food and calendar,[206] the second is directed to the "strong" who are holding others to be "nothing." The order is reversed from 14:3, thus equalizing the force of Paul's indictment. The expression ἢ καί ("or also") is characteristic of comparisons,[207] while καὶ σύ ("you also") or its Latin equivalent *et tu* were the colloquial expressions in countless depictions of the evil eye placed opposite the entrances of Greco-Roman residences, threatening the same evil on intruders that they intend to inflict upon the household.[208] Both this and the preceding question require the answer "Not I," thus delegitimizing the accusations that have hitherto burdened the relationship between the weak and the strong in Rome. Referring to the scorned as "your brother" reinforces the parallelism between the two groups, implying that despite differences in practice each is "in the fullest sense a fellow-believer, one who belongs altogether to the same Lord."[209]

The emphatic position of πάντες ("all") in v. 10c corresponds to the emphasis on σύ ("you") in v. 10a and 10b,[210] making clear that no one can escape accountability to God. By using technical juridical language of "standing before a judgment seat," Paul reiterates the theme of universal, impartial judgment by God that had been established in 2:5-16.[211] The verb παρίστημι ("place, stand before") is a legal technical term for appearing before a judge.[212] For example, in a first-century papyrus the leaders of a guild of weavers acknowledge to a judge

199 See Meyer, 2:310; Godet, 358; Lagrange, 326–27.
200 See BDF §277.1.
201 Thompson, *Clothed with Christ*, 166.
202 See ibid., 165–66.
203 Johannes Beutler, "ἀδελφός," *EDNT* 1 (1990) 30.
204 Morris, 483; see also Wilckens, 3:84; K. H. Schelke, "Bruder," *RAC* 2 (1954) 636–38.
205 Hans Freiherr von Soden, "ἀδελφός κτλ.," *TDNT* 1 (1964) 145; see also Stöger, "Brüderliche Ordnung," 187, and Cranfield, 2:709.
206 See Omanson, "Weak," 113.
207 See Kühner-Gerth, *Grammatik*, 2:256; Lagrange, 327. Lietzmann's comment in 116 that the καί is redundant fails to grasp the rhetorical need to include both sides of the Roman controversy in the diatribe.
208 See John H. Elliott, "The Evil Eye and the Sermon on the Mount: Contours of a Pervasive Belief in Social Scientific Perspective," *BibInt* 2 (1994) 51–84; idem, "Paul, Galatians and the Evil Eyes," *CurTM* 17 (1990) 262–73; Matthew W. Dickie and

Katherine M. D. Dunbabin, "Invida Rumpantur Pectora: The Iconography of Phthonos/Invidia in Graeco-Roman Art," *JAC* 26 (1983) 7–37; Matthew W. Dickie, "Heliodorus and Plutarch on the Evil Eye," *CP* 86 (1991) 17–29; Frederick E. Brenk, "The ΚΑΙ ΣΥ Stele in the Fitzwilliam Museum, Cambridge," *ZPE* 126 (1999) 172–73, with extensive bibliography; Brenk translates the gravestone formula, in Greek (χαῖρε καὶ σύ) and Latin (*uale et tu*), as "best wishes to you too," whereas it probably means "Good-bye! Even you [are mortal]!"
209 Cranfield, 2:709.
210 Synofzik, *Vergeltungsaussagen*, 123.
211 See Murray, 2:184; Bassler, *Impartiality*, 163.
212 BAGD 628; MM 494–95; Michel, 340, refers to this usage as *Gerichtssprache* ("court language").

that "it is our obligation to place them [i.e., the accused guild members] before you whenever you choose, to answer the claims stated in the petition of Paninoutis (ἐπάνανκον παραστῆοι(ν) υυι αὐτοὺ(ς) ὁπηνίκα ἐὰν ἐρῇ ἐδικοῦντες τὰ διὰ τοῦ ὑπομνήματος Πανινούντιος)."[213] The word βῆμα is likewise a technical expression for a tribunal or judicial bench,[214] the raised podium on which the judge or presiding ruler sits to issue official judgments that come ἐπὶ βήματος ("from the bench").[215] This term appears routinely in references to divine judgment such as the Sibylline prediction that "all the souls of men" will be led "to the tribunal of the great, immortal god (ἐπὶ βῆμα θεοῖο ἀθανάτου μεγάλου)."[216] Paul uses this term in 2 Cor 5:10 to insist that τοὺς γὰρ πάντας ἡμᾶς φανερωθῆναι δεῖ ἔμπροσθεν τοῦ βήματος τοῦ Χριστοῦ ("it is necessary for all of us to appear before the judicial bench of Christ"). Although there is a textual variant, "judicial bench of Christ," that appears to assimilate the wording of 2 Corinthians,[217] it appears that Paul sees "no essential difference" between the βῆμα of God or Christ.[218] That Christ was understood by early Christians to occupy the divine seat of judgment remains highly likely.[219] The accountability of believers to Christ in this passage is presented as identical with accountability to God.

■ **11** With the formula "for it is written," Paul introduces a composite citation from Isaiah to sustain the claim of v. 10c, that all persons, whether weak or strong, will confront divine judgment. The words cited are underlined below, with the material from Isaiah 45 marked with double underlining:

Isa 49:18 ζῶ ἐγώ, λέγει κύριος, ὅτι πάντας αὐτοὺς ἐνδύσῃ καὶ περιθήσῃ αὐτοὺς ὡς κόσμον νύμφης. ("As I live, says the Lord, that you shall dress and adorn yourself as a bride.")

Isa 45:23 κατ᾽ ἐμαυτοῦ ὀμνύω Ἦ μὴν ἐξελεύσεται ἐκ τοῦ στόματός μου δικαιοσύνη, οἱ λόγοι μου οὐκ ἀποστραφήσονται ὅτι ἐμοὶ κάμψει πᾶν γόνυ καὶ ἐξομολογήσεται πᾶσα γλῶσσα τῷ θεῷ ("By myself I swear, righteousness shall surely come out of my mouth, my words shall not be obviated, because to me shall every knee bow and every tongue shall acknowledge God.")

Rom 14:11 Ζῶ ἐγώ, λέγει. κύριος, ὅτι ἐμοὶ κάμψει πᾶν γόνυ καὶ πᾶσα γλῶσσα ἐξομολογήσεται τῷ θεῷ. ("As I live, says the Lord, because to me shall every knee bow and every tongue shall acknowledge God.")

The citation opens with a typical prophetic oath formula,[220] ζῶ ἐγώ, λέγει κύριος ("as I live, says the Lord"), probably drawn from Isa 49:18,[221] which lends authority to the citation. By a reversal of "every tongue" and "confess," Paul adapts Isa 45:23 to bring it into conformity with the early Christian requirement of "verbal 'confession' before God"[222] that each group of believers in Rome has made. This harks back to the reference in 14:10c about each believer standing "before the judgment seat of God."[223] In contrast to the original context of Isa 45, it is not God's saving power but her exclusive and final authority in judgment that is in view.[224] The reiteration of πᾶς ("every, all"), which was used in v. 10c, is particularly striking[225] because it lends impressive sup-

---

213 *P.Ryl.* 2. Nr. 94.11–13; translation adapted from MM 495.

214 MM 109; Berndt Schaller, "βῆμα," *EDNT* 1 (1990) 216.

215 See A. M. Schneider, "Bema," *RAC* 2 (1954) 129.

216 *Sib. Or.* 2.218.

217 See Michel, 428; Cranfield, 2:709; and note m above.

218 Dunn, 2:809.

219 See Godet, 459; Synofzik, *Vergeltungsaussagen,* 45; Hurtado, *Lord Jesus Christ,* 108–17.

220 See Michel, 428, referring to Num 14:21, 28; Dan 12:7, etc.

221 Koch, *Schrift,* 184–85; Wilk, *Bedeutung des Jesajabuches,* 48; Wagner, *Heralds,* 337. The formula is

also found in Num 14:28; Zeph 2:9; Jer 22:24; 26:18; and eleven times in Ezekiel. Since Isa 49:18 has "almost nothing in common" with Isa 45:23 or Rom 14:11, Stanley, *Scripture,* 177, maintains this is simply typical biblical language rather than a citation from Isaiah.

222 Stanley, *Scripture,* 178.

223 Wilk, *Bedeutung des Jesajabuches,* 48.

224 Koch, *Schrift,* 184; Wilk, *Bedeutung des Jesajabuches,* 64; Wagner, *Heralds,* 337.

225 See Zahn, 575.

port to Paul's contention that all of the house and tenement churches in Rome, whether weak or strong, are accountable to God rather than to each other. To bend the knee[226] and to utter public praise and acknowledgment[227] are typical expressions of homage and obeisance in the ancient world. The implication is that those who continue to judge and despise their competitors "are usurping the authority of God alone, falling into the same old trap of idolatry and putting themselves in the place of God."[228] They are in effect denying the universal implication of the gospel, "that God's salvation includes all people,"[229] even their competitors in the church of whose theology and practices they disapprove. This quotation from Isaiah therefore sets the stage for the climactic vision in 15:6, 9-12 of a global participation in the praise of God.

■ **12** The pericope concludes with a generalization initiated by the inferential particle ἄρα ("so then"), including both the weak and the strong in the inclusive "each of us" who must be accountable to God. The emphatic position of "each"[230] makes clear that there will be no exemption or privilege granted by the divine court. As in 14:10c, the emphasis here is that none can escape accountability to God. The stipulation περὶ ἑαυτοῦ ("of himself") makes clear that, contrary to the mutual accusations between groups in Rome, each will in fact be called upon to account for his or her own behavior, not for the behavior of their competitors. In keeping with the demonstrative genre of Romans, Paul contents himself with generalities here, apparently assuming that the Roman believers will make the proper decisions about how to follow the general guidelines.[231]

The clause λόγον δίδωμι ("give account") is a technical expression from the administrative realm of accounting for one's actions as a subordinate, handing in the account books for audit, and so on.[232] For example, the young Cyrus is described by Xenophon as having been required by his teacher "to give an account of what he was doing and to obtain an account from others whenever he was judge . . ." (διδόναι λόγον ὧν ἐποίει καὶ λαμβάνειν παρ᾽ ἄλλων, ὁπότε δικάζοι . . . , Xenophon *Cyr.* 4.3). A papyrus from Egypt calls for financial accountability: ὡς σοῦ μέλλοντος λόγον διδόναι τῷ λαμπροτάτῳ ἡγεμόνι ("as you will be giving account to the magnanimous leader").[233] Some of the NT parallels (Matt 12:36; 1 Pet 4:5) and the context of this argument indicate clearly that the account will be rendered to God, even though the secondary textual variant is not admitted.[234] As Morris comments, "A reminder of the judgment we all face is a fitting conclusion to this stage of the discussion. The fact that each will render account for himself leaves no room for despising and judging others. The verdict on them is for God" and not for humans to make.[235] If the Roman believers would accept this premise and act upon it, they would cease their squabbles and be in the position to cooperate effectively in Paul's missionary project in behalf of the righteousness of God.

---

226 See J. M. Nützel, "γόνυ," *EDNT* 1 (1990) 258.

227 See BAGD 277; Dunn, 2:809, noting that the other Pauline uses of ἐξομολογέω in Rom 15:9 and Phil 2:11 have the sense of "acknowledge, confess, praise." The suggestion by Otto Michel, "ὁμολογέω κτλ.," *TDNT* 5 (1967) 215, and Otto Hofius, "ὁμολογέω," *EDNT* 2 (1991) 9, that the verb has the technical sense of "confession of sins" in this context is implausible because of the context.

228 Dunn, 2:809; see also Shum, *Paul's Use of Isaiah*, 250.

229 Bonda, *One Purpose*, 221. He goes on (228) to develop the theme that "The judgment of the godless will be the end. All who are lost will one day come to conversion and return to the Father, the God of love; *together with* the church they will kneel and join in their hymn of praise for the salvation he extends to all in the name of Jesus" (italics in original).

230 See Meyer, 2:312; that all of the words in this sentence are emphatic, as suggested by Denney, 704; Cranfield, 2:711, is syntactically implausible.

231 See Schneider, "Schwachen," 157.

232 See BAGD 478; MM 379.

233 *BGU* 1. Nr. 164.20–23.

234 See note q above.

235 Morris, 484.

14

The Eighth Pericope

Exemplary Guidelines for Mutual Upbuilding in Pluralistic Congregations

13/ Let us therefore no longer judge one another, but on the contrary you should make this judgment, "not to place a stumbling block or hindrance[a] before a brother." 14/ I know and am persuaded by Lord Jesus that, "Nothing is profane in itself,[b]" except that if a person reckons it profane, it is profane for that one. 15/ For if your brother is grieved by food, you are no longer walking according to love. Do not by means of your food continue to destroy that one "for whom Christ died." 16/ Therefore,[c] do not let the good thing of yours[d] be discredited. 17/ For the kingdom of God is not eating or drinking, but righteousness and peace and joy in [the] Holy Spirit. 18/ For he who in this[e] [matter] enslaves [himself] to the Christ [is] pleasing to God and acceptable[f] to people.

19/ We therefore pursue[g] what makes for peace and what makes for the edification of each other.[h] 20/ Do not keep on tearing down[i] the work of God for the sake of food. "All things [are] indeed clean,"[j] but [it is] bad for a person who eats with stumbling. 21/ [It is] good neither to eat meat nor drink wine nor [do] anything else by[k] which your brother [l]stumbles.[m] 22/ Keep the faith that[n] you have in accordance with yourself in the presence of God.[o] Blessed is the one who does not condemn himself by what he approves. 23/ But the one who doubts has been condemned, if he does eat, because it is not "out of faith." Everything not [done] "out of faith" is a sin.[p]

a   The words "stumbling block" and "or" are deleted by B (365), apparently an attempt to eliminate a seemingly awkward redundancy that mentions "hindrance" as a kind of afterthought.

b   In place of ἑαυτοῦ ("of himself/itself") convincingly attested in ℵ B C² 048 6 69 81 104 330 365 1319 1505 1506 1573 1739 2495 *al*, some of the Alexandrian and the "Western" texts, A C* D F G L P Ψ 0209 33 88 323 326 424 614 945 1175 1241 1243 1735 1836 1874 1881 2344 *Maj*, offer an improvement with αὐτοῦ ("of it/him") with the intention to suggest that "because of Jesus" nothing is unclean. See Cranfield, 2:713.

c   The omission of οὖν ("so, therefore") by F G 1319

sy^p appears to be a stylistic improvement. Its inclusion is strongly supported by P^46 ℵ A B C D L P Ψ 048 6 33 69 88 104 323 326 330 365 424 614 945 1175 1241 1243 1505 1506 1573 1735 1739 1836 1874 1881 2344 2495 *Maj* lat sy^h cop Cl Ambst.

d   A "Western" text "improvement" surfaces in the replacement of the widely attested ὑμῶν ("your"), found in ℵ A B C L P 048 0209 6 33 69 81 88 104 181 323 326 330 365 424 436 451 614 629 945 1175 1241 1243 1319 1505 1573 1735 1739 1836 1874 1877 1881 1962 2127 2344 2492 *Maj* f, by ἡμῶν ("our") in D F G Ψ 1506 *pc* lat sy^p sa Cl Ambst, which identifies the "good" of freedom from the law with all Christians.

e   In place of the ambiguous but probably original τούτῳ ("in this") found in ℵ* A B C D* F G P 048 0209 81 326 330 1243 1506 1739 1881 *pc* lat, τούτοις ("in these matters") appears in ℵ¹ D² L Ψ 6 33 69 88 104 323 365 424 614 945 1175 1241 1319 1505 1573 1735 1836 1874 2344 2495 *Maj* b vg^mss sy. This is probably an interpretive improvement of the text, since it was unclear in Paul's original formulation what the antecedent of "this" might be, especially in light of three potential antecedents at the end of the preceding sentence.

f   In place of the widely attested singular δόκιμος ("acceptable") in the phrase δόκιμος τοῖς ἀνθρώποις ("acceptable to people") (though 131 reads τοῖς ἀνθρώποις δόκιμος Swanson, *Vaticanus: Romans,* 223; Cranfield, 2:720, implies that 131 reads δοκίμοις), B G* (*pc*) have the dative plural δοκίμοις with τοῖς ἀνθρώποις ("to acceptable people"). Cranfield suggests it "may be a clumsy attempt to take account of the fact that not all men will actually approve of those of whom they ought to approve." It seems more likely that the plural form was a clerical error, assimilating to the next two word endings (-οις).

g   A difficult instance of the countervailing pressures of context and text-critical evidence confronts us at this point. The strong attestation of ℵ A B F G^gr L P 048 0209 6 88 263 326 330 451 629 1836 1874 2200*^vid supports the indicative διώκομεν ("we pursue"), while there is weak support in C D Ψ 33 69 81 104 181 256 323 365 424 436 459 614 945 1175 1241 1243 1319 1505 1506 1573 1735 1739 1852 1877 1881 1912 1962 2127 2200^c vid 2344 2492 2495 *Maj Lect* ar b d f g gue o r vg sy^pal sa bo arm eth geo² Or^lat Chr Ambst Pel Aug Spec for the contextually more appropriate subjunctive διώκωμεν ("let us pursue"). Ian Moir is convinced in "Orthography and Theology," 172, that the omicron could easily have been understood as an omega, denoting the subjunctive, but this can never be more than a hypothesis. Metzger, *Textual Commentary,* 532, reveals that the committee opted for the subjunctive on contextual grounds despite the evidence to the contrary, including the fact that ἄρα οὖν is always followed by the indicative in Romans. Nestle-Aland[26/27] concurs with the *GNT*[3/4] in this decision. Michel, 436, makes the more appropriate decision in following the stronger evidence supporting the indicative. He mentions that Zahn, 583 n. 34, suggests the indicative was an early dictation error.

h The inclusion of the verb φυλάξωμεν ("we might, should guard") by D* F G (629) it vg[ww] appears to be an intended stylistic improvement, supplying a separate verb for the construction "the edification of each other" and clearly understanding the text as an exhortation.

i The minor variant ἀπόλλυε ("you ruin, destroy") in ℵ* in place of the widely attested κατάλυε ("you destroy") may be an assimilation to the wording of 14:15, according to Cranfield, 2:723.

j The minor variant that adds τοῖς καθαροῖς ("to the clean") in ℵ[2] appears to be a stylistic improvement.

k The conjectures by Hofmann and Zahn that ἐν ("in") should be read as ἕν ("one thing which"), and by Mangey that ἕν should be supplied before ἐν (= "one thing by which"), do not appear plausible; see the critical discussions in Meyer, 2:320; Cranfield, 2:725 n. 1; and Reasoner, "The 'Strong' and the 'Weak' in Rome," 83. But these conjectures reflect the sense that something is amiss with the text at this point, a matter that deserves more thorough examination.

l In place of the widely attested προσκόπτει ("stumbles"), ℵ* P have λυπεῖται ("is grieved") (see the following note), apparently another assimilation to Rom 14:15.

m The words ἢ σκανδαλίζεται ἢ ἀσθενεῖ ("or is scandalized or is weak") appear at this point in P[46vid] (Swanson to the contrary) ℵ[2] B D F G L Ψ 0209 5 33 61 69 88 104 181 218 256 263 323 326 330 365 424* 436 441 451 459 467 614 621 623 629 630 (720) 915 917 945 1175 1241 (1243 lacks ἢ ἀσθενεῖ) 1319 1398 1505 1563 1573 1678 1718 1735 1751 1836 1838 1845 1874 1875 1877 1881 1908 1912 1942 1959 1962 2127 (2197) 2200 2344 2492 2495 2516 2523[c] 2544 2718 *Maj Lect* ar b d f g o vg sy[h,pal] sa arm geo[2] slav Bas Chr[1/2 (1/2)] Ps-Cyp Ambst Gaudentius Pel Aug[2/5] Spec. Additional variants include λυπεῖται ("grieve") for προσκόπτει in ℵ*, λυπεῖται ἢ σκανδαλίζεται ἢ ἀσθενεῖ ("grieve or scandalize or weaken") in P, and σκανδαλίζεται ἢ προσκόπτει ἢ ἀσθενεῖ ("scandalize or offend or weaken") in 1827 1984 1985 mon. These variants appear to be influenced by 1 Cor 8:11-13, since the omission of ἢ σκανδαλίζεται ἢ ἀσθενεῖ in ℵ* A C 048 6 81 424[c] 1506 1739 1852 2110 *pc* r sy[p] bo eth geo[1] Mcion Or[gr,lat] Aug[3/5] seems more likely to be original. But this is a very difficult decision that deserves further investigation.

n The omission of the relative pronoun ἥν ("that") in D F G L P Ψ 0209[vid] 6 69 81 88 104 181 256 263 323 326 330 365 424 436 451 459 614 629 945 1175 1241 1243 1319 1505 1506 1573 1735 1739 1836 1852 1874 1877 1881 1912 1962 2127 2200 2344 2492 2495 *Maj Lect* b d f g o sa bo arm eth geo slav Chr Ambst Aug[1/4] appears to be a stylistic improvement, resulting in making the first four words of this verse into a question, according to Cranfield, 2:726, and Käsemann, 378. The inclusion of the relative pronoun is adequately attested in a few strong witnesses, ℵ A B C 048 *pc* ar r vg[mss] Or[lat] Pel Aug[3/4] to be considered original, although Nestle-Aland[26/27] places it in square brackets, indicating a difficult choice.

o The omission of ἐνώπιον τοῦ θεοῦ ("in the presence of God") in ℵ* *pc* appears to be a scribal error.

p For a discussion of the extensive variants, placing portions of Rom 16 at this point, see Introduction, Section 2.

Analysis

That 14:13-23 is a self-contained pericope is widely assumed,[1] but suggestions that it has a chiastic structure are not compelling.[2] The admonition of 14:13 provides the theme of avoiding destructive behavior with three balanced clauses.[3] The admonitory style is continued throughout the pericope.[4] The admonitions are sup-

---

1 Michel, 429–30; Käsemann, 374–75; Dunn, 2:816; Morris, 485; Moo, 849–50.

2 In "Transitional Techniques," 536, Parunak proposes a chiasm from vv. 13 through 21, which Thompson, *Clothed with Christ*, 201–2, accepts even though it is "not exact." Bruce Robert Magee sees a

chiastic structure running from 14:13 through 23, with v. 17 at the center; "A Rhetorical Analysis of First Corinthians 8:1–11:1 and Romans 14:1–15:13" (dissertation, New Orleans Baptist Theological Seminary, 1988) 165.

3 See Weiss, "Beiträge," 246; on 14:13 as a kind of

ported by authoritative quotations from dominical and biblical sources, identified by quotation marks in vv. 13, 14, 15, 20, and 23. A word chain in polyptoton with κρίνωμεν ("we judge") and κρίνατε ("you judge")[5] marks the antithesis in this verse between destructive and constructive assessment.[6] This is followed by four sentences that provide the theological rationale for the avoidance of antagonism related to food laws.[7] An antithesis between κοινὸν δι᾽ ἑαυτοῦ ("unclean in itself") and ἐκείνῳ κοινόν ("unclean to him") marks the antithetical parallelism in 14:14. Reduplication occurs again in the next sentence with "food" in v. 15a and 15b, in a formal *sententia*.[8] In vv. 16-17[9] there is an antithesis between a common double expression βρῶσις καὶ πόσις ("eating and drinking")[10] marked by parechesis in v. 17a and the triad of "righteousness and peace and joy" in v. 17b. Verse 17 has also been identified as a formal *sententia*, in antithetical style.[11] Another double expression occurs in 14:18, "pleasing to God and acceptable to people," consistent with other Hebraic-sounding double expressions throughout this pericope: "stumbling block or hindrance" in v. 13, "know and am persuaded" in v. 14, and "actions of peace and actions of edification" in v. 19.[12] The style in this paragraph is abstract and generalizing, which is typical for demonstrative rhetoric, lifting up the fundamental dimensions of the congregational issue.[13]

The final paragraph in this pericope clarifies Paul's idea of behaving so as to protect the integrity of both the weak and the strong. Verse 19 contains synonymous parallelism in the objects of the verb "pursue," with "what makes for peace" replicating the syntax of "what makes for the edification."[14] The actions promoting "peace" and "edification" in this verse stand in thematic antithesis to "tear down the work of God" in v. 20a, while a bad kind of eating in v. 20b is contrasted to a good kind of abstinence from eating in v. 21. The final two sentences form a chiasm in which "faith" in v. 22a corresponds to "faith" in v. 23b, while the defense of integrity in v. 22b corresponds to the avoidance of condemnation in v. 23a.[15] There is a "conscious paronomasia" with κρίνω in v. 22b followed by διακρίνω and κατακρίνομαι in v. 23.[16] The final *sententia* in v. 23b[17] about everything not done out of faith as sin links this pericope very closely with the earlier theological argument of Romans.

Rhetorical Disposition

IV.	The *probatio*
12:1—15:13	The fourth proof: Living together according to the gospel so as to sustain the hope of global transformation
14:13-23	8. Exemplary guidelines for mutual upbuilding in pluralistic congregations
14:13	a. The thematic admonition to avoid destructive behavior in the congregation
14:13a	1) Avoid judging others
14:13b	2) Make a contrary judgment
14:13c	3) Avoid placing stumbling blocks or hindrances before others

---

"heading" for the passage, see Theobald, *Studien*, 484.

4   The prohibition μή is repeated ten times in the pericope, in v. 13a with μηκέτι, in 21 twice with μηδέ, and in vv. 13b, 14, 15, 16, 20, 21, and 22 with μή standing alone. The prohibition οὐ or οὐκ occurs in v. 17 and twice in v. 22, in v. 14 with οὐδέν, and in v. 15 with οὐκέτι, a total of five times. See Parunak, "Transitional Techniques," 535; Theobald, *Studien*, 481.

5   See Weiss, "Beiträge," 246.

6   See also Bengel, *Gnomon*, 149.

7   See Wilckens, 3:90.

8   See Holloway, "Paul's Pointed Prose," 48–49.

9   Weiss, "Beiträge," 246, allows 14:16 to stand alone as an "application" of the preceding admonition, but it appears to be linked with the following verse by the γάρ ("for") in v. 17a.

10 For example, see Polybius *Hist.* 6.7.5: "neither in respect of food and drink (μήτε περὶ τὴν βρῶσιν καὶ πόσιν)"; also Philo *Jos.* 154.6; *Mos.* 1.184; Plutarch *Tu. san.* 126c13; 991a12; Dioscorides Pedanius *Eup.* 2.122.1; Xenophon *Mem.* 1.3.5; Hippocrates *Diaet. m.* i–iv 18.1; Diodorus Siculus *Hist.* 1.45.2.

11 Holloway, "Paul's Pointed Prose," 48–49, 51. It is possible that this verse was preformed by Paul in another context, as argued by Theobald, *Studien*, 487–88.

12 See Weiss, "Beiträge," 246.

13 See Nababan, "Bekenntnis," 97.

14 See Kitzberger, *Bau der Gemeinde*, 41.

15 See Louw, 2:133; note also that Weiss, "Beiträge," 246, organizes vv. 22-23 into a four-line unit matching this chiastic pattern.

16 Gerhard Dautzenberg, "διακρίνω," *EDNT* 1 (1990) 306.

17 Holloway, "Paul's Pointed Prose," 50.

Exegesis

■ **13** The argumentative function of v. 13 is to provide a thematic admonition to both the weak and the strong, which is elaborated and explained through the rest of the pericope. This leads me to modify the current consensus that while v. 13a refers both to the "weak" and the "strong,"[18] v. 13b is directed only to the latter.[19] This consensus has a superficial plausibility because vv. 14-18 focus on avoiding abusive behavior against the "weak," but 14:19 urges mutual edification and v. 22 deals with maintaining the integrity of the "strong" who are being criticized by the weak. Since the "but" clause of v. 13b contains ἀλλά, which introduces a contast,[20] the syntax of this verse requires a straightforward antithesis between the prohibitions in v. 13a and 13c,[21] not a change of subject as the current consensus supposes. The peculiar nature of the subsequent argument was required by the rhetorical situation. While the larger and more difficult form of intolerance in the Roman churches was caused by the group identified as the "strong," which required the bulk of Paul's subsequent argument, he is careful in this verse to generalize. Whereas the tendency on the part of the "weak" to judge the "strong" was criticized in

---

18   Käsemann, 374; Lagrange, 328; Dunn, 2:817; Moo, 850.

19   Lagrange, 328; Michel, 431; Dunn, 2:817; Moo, 850–51; Stählin, *Skandalon*, 172; Nanos, *Mystery*, 149–50.

20   See BAGD 38.

21   See Käsemann, 374: "The comparative in v. 13b is adversative."

14:3, here he broadens the concept as in 14:4 to include both the "weak" and the "strong," using the present hortatory subjunctive to indicate a continuous activity that must now "no longer" ($μηκέτι$)[22] continue.[23] The object of the verb is $ἀλλήλους$ ("one another"), which makes it clear that the admonition pertains to both sides.[24] This is followed by a wordplay in which $κρίνειν$ ("judge") is used in the aorist, second person plural to describe a "specific judgment" that both sides are now to make, in the light of the argument of Romans.[25] Calvin Roetzel argues that the wordplay on $κρίνειν$ in this verse shows that Paul is not attempting to eliminate judgment entirely, but to eliminate "contemptuous" and "disdainful" judgments and to promote "a new concern for the brother."[26] Clarence Glad goes further to contend on the basis of 15:14 that Paul "does not aim at abrogating that practice [of moral evaluation] but attempts rather to rectify a social praxis gone awry. . . . Judgment among members should continue but in a way that guards against mutual caricature and arrogance."[27] That $ὁ ἀδελφός$ in Paul's formulation includes every believer in Paul's circle of hearers just as it did in 14:10 is clearly implied by Büchsel and Herntrich: "What is unconditionally demanded is that such evaluations should be subject to the certainty that God's judgment falls also on those who judge, so that superiority, hardness and blindness to one's own faults are excluded, and a readiness to forgive and to intercede is safeguarded."[28]

I follow Reasoner in denying that Paul wishes to allow "some sort of continuing education between 'strong' and 'weak.'"[29] In contrast to his earlier argument in 1 Corinthians, the Roman circumstances lead him to forbid mutual conversion between these theological and ethnic adversaries. His view is closer to the admonition found in Sophocles Ajax 583: $μὴ κρῖνε, μὴ ξέταζε. σωφρονεῖν καλόν$ ("Don't judge; don't scrutinize; it is good to be soberminded").

The measure that Paul urges is for either side to avoid placing "a stumbling block ($πρόσκομμα$) or hindrance ($σκάνδαλον$) before a brother" (14:13c). The formulation is introduced as if it were a quotation introduced by "this judgment" in v. 13b. Although the words related to stumbling were broadly used in Greco-Roman culture, the metaphorical sense of religious offense is distinctively Jewish.[30] This was visible in the earlier citation of Isa 8:14 in Rom 9:32-33, referring to Christ as a stone of stumbling. An admonition to avoid such a danger is stated in Exod 34:12: $Πρόσεχε σεαυτῷ, μήποτε θῇς διαθήκην τοῖς ἐγκαθημένοις ἐπὶ τῆς γῆς . . . μή σοι γένηται πρόσκομμα ἐν ὑμῖν$ ("Take heed to yourself, lest you ever make a covenant with the inhabitants of the land . . . lest it be a stumbling block among you"). Jeremiah hears Yahweh condemn Israel because "you retained many shepherds as a stumbling-block to yourself" ($ἔσχες ποιμένας πολλοὺς εἰς πρόσκομμα σεαυτῇ$, Jer 3:3). The NT picks up this metaphor of the stumbling block in 1 Cor 8:9; 10:32; 2 Cor 6:3; Phil 1:10, and 1 Pet 2:8.

Similarly, the word $σκάνδαλον$, which may have originally referred to the stick on which bait was placed in a trap,[31] develops the metaphorical sense of "cause of ruin" or "occasion of misfortune" in the LXX.[32] This

---

22 BAGD 518.

23 BDF §336.

24 Godet, 460; Kühl, 455; Lagrange, 328; Schlier, 413; Cranfield, 2:711; Dunn, 2:817; Helmut Krämer, "$ἀλλήλων$," EDNT 1 (1990) 63: "Of theological relevance here is the use of $ἀλλήλων$ primarily in the description of the (obligatory) conduct of Christians in the community toward each other, with emphasis on mutuality."

25 See Barrett, 262.

26 Roetzel, Judgement, 134.

27 Glad, Paul and Philodemus, 217; see the critique by Reasoner, The Strong, 196–97.

28 Friedrich Büchsel and Volkmar Herntrich, "$κρίνω κτλ.$," TDNT 3 (1965) 939.

29 Reasoner, The Strong, 197; in contrast, Nanos, Mystery, 151, contends that "Paul's intention toward the 'weak' was to change their 'faith' to faith in Jesus as the Christ," while Watson, Paul, 97, maintains that Paul "wishes to convert the Jewish Christian congregation to Paulinism."

30 See Müller, Anstoß und Gericht, 32–45. For $πρόσκομμα$, see the classical references and commentary at Rom 9:32.

31 See Gustav Stählin, "$σκάνδαλον, σκανδαλίζω$," TDNT 7 (1971) 339.

32 Ibid., 341–43.

biblical usage completely dominates the use of σκάν-δαλον in the NT,[33] and was reflected in Paul's earlier use in the citation from Isaiah in Rom 9:32-33. The use of this word in combination with a form of the verb τίθημι ("put, place") is found in Lev 19:14, ἀπέναντι τυφλοῦ οὐ προσθήσεις σκάνδαλον ("you shall not place a hindrance in the path of the blind"). Sir 7:6 warns against legal activity in which θήσεις σκάνδαλον ἐν εὐθύτητί σου ("you will lay a hindrance in the path of your uprightness"). Hos 4:17 charges that μέτοχος εἰδώλων Ἐφραὶμ ἔθηκεν ἑαυτῷ σκάνδαλον ("having joined with idols, Ephraim laid his own hindrance").

The use of "stumbling block" and "hindrance" in Rom 9:32-33 evidently influenced the choice of these two nearly synonymous terms[34] in a rhetorical hendiadys linked with ἤ ("or") used in a syndetic sense,[35] which includes both in a single, comprehensive frame.[36] The formulation in the context of "one another" is that no stumbling block or hindrance whatsoever is to be placed in the path of any Christian brother.[37] Efforts to split this expression into separate allusions to the "weak" and the "strong,"[38] or to a less serious "wound" as compared with a more serious "fall,"[39] have rightly been repudiated.[40] Käsemann and Barrett are correct in applying this inclusive reference to both sides: "We should avoid putting stumbling blocks or obstacles in each other's way."[41]

That Paul alludes here to the Jesus tradition lying behind Mark 9:42 and parallels is quite possible, as the careful analyses by Dodd, Davies, Allison, Müller, and Thompson have suggested.[42] Whereas the synoptic saying is concerned only with persons in power and authority hindering the "little ones," Paul broadens the warning to include both the "weak" and the "strong." Moreover, there is nothing in the synoptic tradition that prepares one for the double reference to "stumbling block or hindrance," which, as I have concluded, seems to be shaped by the citation from Isaiah in Rom 9:33. So, if there is an allusion to the gospel tradition in this verse,[43] it is significantly adapted to fit the new social circumstance not envisioned in the original sayings of Jesus.

■ **14** This parenthetical verse explains the circumstances in which the recommendation in the preceding verse was to be understood.[44] The solemn asseveration with its emphatic subject,[45] "I know and am persuaded by Lord Jesus," seems to imply that "Paul intends to be understood as referring to a teaching of Jesus."[46] This is indicated by the reference to the "Lord Jesus" rather than to Christ or the word "Lord" alone.[47] While the preposition ἐν ("in") implies "union and fellowship with Christ,"[48] there is no necessity of deciding between the historical and the mystical dimensions of this phrase. Paul's formulation requires that both be taken into

33   Ibid., 344; Heinz Giesen, "σκάνδαλον," EDNT 3 (1993) 249-50.

34   Gustav Stählin, "προσκόπτω κτλ.," 753; idem, Skandalon, 172; Balz, "πρόσκομμα," 173; Giesen, "σκάνδαλον," 249; Müller, Anstoß und Gericht, 32-33.

35   See Müller, Anstoß und Gericht, 33-34, citing BDF §446.

36   Sählin, Skandalon, 172.

37   That ἀδελφός in this context should be translated "brother," rather than "another" as in the NRSV, is noted by Bartchy, "Siblings," 70.

38   See Zahn, 580; Cranfield, 2:711; Murray, 2:187; Jewett, Tolerance, 135; Nanos, Mystery, 123-24, 150.

39   Godet, 460.

40   Stählin, Skandalon, 261-63; Kühl, 455; Dunn, 2:817.

41   Käsemann, 374; Barrett, 262.

42   Dodd, 218; Davies, Paul, 138; Allison, "Parallels," 14-15; Müller, Anstoß und Gericht, 42-45; Thompson, Clothed with Christ, 174-84. These arguments for dependency on the synoptic tradition are accepted by Dunn, 2:818.

43   See the judicious conclusion by Thompson, Clothed with Christ, 184: "Paul has probably been influenced by the teaching of Jesus, but he does not draw attention to the origin of the thought."

44   Cranfield, 2:714: "a parenthesis inserted asyndetically, introduced for the purpose of making clear both Paul's own acceptance of the basic assumption of the strong and at the same time the fact that there is an important qualification of that assumption which must not be forgotten. . . ."

45   See Cranfield, 2:712.

46   Leenhardt, 352.

47   Lagrange, 329; Dunn, 2:818; Thompson, Clothed with Christ, 194, referring to 1 Cor 11:23; 9:1; 1 Thess 2:15; 2 Cor 4:14; 11:31. Werner Foerster, "Ἰησοῦς," TDNT 3 (1965) 289, claims that the use of Ἰησοῦς in these contexts "makes it plain that Paul is thinking especially of the historical Jesus." See also Gerhard Schneider, "Ἰησοῦς," EDNT 2 (1991) 184.

account.[49] There is an unusual use of two verbs οἶδα ("I know") and πείθομαι ("I am convinced") linked with the copulative καί ("and"), which expresses an extraordinary level of conviction on Paul's part.[50] The first verb deals with "a rational, theoretical conviction"[51] often conveyed by rhetorical discourse,[52] while the second, πέπεισμαι—a perfect passive form of a verb also frequently used in the arena of rhetoric—refers to being persuaded or convinced by proofs.[53] There are several examples in Paul's letters of the expression πέπεισμαι ἐν κυρίῳ ("I am persuaded/confident in [the] Lord," Gal 5:10; Phil 2:24; 2 Thess 3:4). The classical parallels to the use of these two verbs in close proximity feature πείθειν in the active voice, as, for example, Adrastus's reply to King Theseus, οὐκ οἶδα πλὴν ἕν, σοῖσι πείθεσθαι λόγοις ("I know nothing except one thing: to obey your words").[54] When πείθειν appears here in the passive, the sequence that one would expect, with persuasion preceding knowledge, is reversed by Paul. In his mind the certain "knowledge" that a believer has "by [the] Lord Jesus" produces persuasion that convinces. In this case, the entirety of v. 14 is included within the realm of Paul's certainty.[55]

In the light of the close parallel to Mark 7:15, it seems quite likely that the clause "nothing is unclean in itself"

is a citation from the dominical tradition.[56] It is introduced with ὅτι-recitativum,[57] represented by the quotation marks in my translation. The saying also reflects the conflicts over the common meal in the first decades of the Christian movement (Gal 2:11-13; Acts 10:9-16; 11:1-18) which were thought to be resolved by the heavenly voice, "What God has cleansed you must not call profane" (ἃ ὁ θεὸς ἐκαθάρισεν, σὺ μὴ κοίνου, Acts 11:9).[58] The use of the term κοινός ("common") in the cultic sense of "profane" reflects distinctively Jewish usage in passages like 1 Macc 1:62, describing the commitment of loyal Jews μὴ φαγεῖν κοινά ("not to eat anything profane"). While there are no clear parallels to this usage in Greco-Roman literature,[59] it is found in the NT (Mark 7:2, 5; Acts 10:14; 11:8-9), and Wilfred Pascher goes so far as to speak of κοινός in such contexts as an "anti-Hellenistic actualization" of OT purity laws that originated during the Maccabean crisis.[60] The food laws "expressed an understanding of holiness, and of Israel's special status as the holy people of God. The division into clean (edible) foods and unclean (inedible) foods corresponded to the division between holy Israel and the Gentile world."[61] This rationale was rigidified under "the increasing purity concerns of the Maccabean and

48 Murray, 2:188; see also Morris, 486.
49 See Cranfield, 2:712.
50 Cranfield, 2:712, refers to the "strikingly emphatic" formulation.
51 Godet, 460. For the classical sense of οἶδα as denoting assured knowledge, see Burdick, "Οἶδα and γινώσκω," 347; also Axel Horstmann, "οἶδα," EDNT 2 (1991) 494.
52 Among the Ten Attic Orators, Demosthenes uses οἶδα 42 times, Isocrates 17 times, Aeschines 4 times; Andocides 4 times, Antiphon 4 times, etc.
53 See Rudolf Bultmann, "πείθω κτλ.," TDNT 6 (1968) 3; Alexander Sand, "πείθω," EDNT 3 (1993) 63. Lausberg discusses the technical rhetorical term πείθω ("persuade") in Handbuch, §257.
54 Euripides Suppl., 933. See also Euripides Frag. 795.5, οὐδέν τι μᾶλλον οἶδεν ἢ πείθειν λέγων; Sophocles Oed. col. 797; Xenophon Apol. 20.2; Cyr. 2.2.10.7.
55 See Owen E. Evans, "What God Requires of Man—Romans xiv.14," ExpT 69 (1957-58) 201-2.
56 See Pascher, Rein und Unrein, 171; Lagrange, 329; Michel, 431; Dunn, 2:818-19; Thompson, Clothed

with Christ, 185-99; Theobald, Studien, 491-95. Critics of the theory of an allusion in this verse include Lietzmann, 117; Zeller, 227; and Neirynck, "Paul and the Sayings of Jesus," 308.
57 See BAGD (2000) 732.
58 See Pascher, Rein und Unrein, 171-72.
59 The Greek proverbs containing κοινός are unrelated to foods or religious laws; for example, in Leuc. Clit. 5.22 Achilles Tatius has Melitte say in respect to someone mistaken for her husband, οὐδὲν κοινὸν ἐστιν ἢ τοῖς λίθοις ("He has nothing more common than with stones"). In Plato's Leg., the Athenian stranger says of the despised Persians, οὐδὲν κοινὸν ἐν αὐτοῖς ("there is nothing common among them") when it comes to battle (Leg. 697d7). See also Friedrich Hauck, "κοινός κτλ.," TDNT 3 (1965) 791.
60 Pascher, Rein und Unrein, 165-68; see also B. W. Dombrowski, "היחד in 1QS and τὸ κοινόν. An Instance of Early Greek and Jewish Synthesis," HTR 59 (1966) 294-307.
61 Gordon J. Wenham, "The Theology of Unclean Food," EvQ 53 (1981) 11; see also Dunn, 2:818-19.

post-Maccabean period,"[62] so Paul's position stands as part of the countercultural tradition of early Christian commensality.[63] He had termed the reemergence of purity laws that prevented open commensality within the Antioch church as "not walking straight in accordance with the gospel" (Gal 2:14).[64] Since this is the only occurrence of "profane" in the Pauline letters, Paul is likely to have selected this traditional formulation because of its prominence in the Roman controversy.[65] He carried over the premise from the Corinthian controversy over food offered to idols that although nothing was "profane in itself," it was so "if a person reckons it profane."[66] The verb λογίζομαι is used here, as in 3:28 and 8:18, to refer to a well-grounded belief "based on a reality that claims validity and from which the individual believer may not depart without harm."[67] The use of this term in philosophical discourse to refer to objective reasoning based on evidence[68] eliminates the possibility that Paul is referring here merely to the "subjective reaction" of the weak in Rome[69] or to an issue that is *adiaphora*, that is, inconsequential.[70] As the preceding pericope demonstrated, the weak are acting in "honor of the Lord," so their devotion is to be respected even if Paul disagrees with the theological and ethical implications of their behavior. The idea of differing "measuring rods" of faith that Paul developed in 12:3 comes to expression here, and it is once again clear that Paul does not want to encourage either side to continue the effort to convert the other.

■ **15** There is a consensus that γάρ ("for") refers back to v. 13b, explaining the circumstances of the "stumbling block or hindrance" that each side was in danger of placing before the other.[71] The word βρῶμα ("food"), used twice in this verse, refers to whatever a person or group chooses to eat[72] in the context of the "full love-feast."[73] Although this context is overlooked by recent commentators, it is clear that what a Roman Christian consumed in his or her private lodging would not be expected to give offense to a "brother." In referring to the parallel in 1 Cor 8, commentators[74] are tacitly assuming a conflict in connection with the common meal of early Christian groups.

Ceslas Spicq suggests that a strand of the biblical usage of λυπέω influences the NT where "irritation, indignation, disgust" or "outrage" is implied.[75] For example, the fellow workers of the unmerciful servant in Jesus' parable were "greatly outraged" (ἐλυπήθησαν σφόδρα) at his refusal to forgive a pittance when he had been forgiven so great a debt (Matt 18:31). One thinks also of the description of the "good man" in *T. Benj.* 6.3: "he does not gaze passionately upon corruptible things . . . he does not grieve his neighbor (οὐ λυπεῖ τὸν πλησίον), he does not sate himself with luxuries." Spicq suggests that the verb is used here in a euphemistic way to indicate the "weak" would be "shocked, hurt."[76] But Käsemann rightly observes that Rom 14:15, viewed in its entirety, cannot be taken to refer to "irritation" or "provocation" caused by breaking conventions that the weaker brother favors.[77] As v. 15b makes clear, the issue is allowing the freedom of the strong with regard to eat-

62 Dunn, 2:818; Newton, *Concept of Purity*, chapter 2.
63 Newton, *Concept of Purity*, 102, concludes that in Rom 14 Paul abandons both the kosher food laws and prohibitions about food associated with idolatry. See also Atkins, *Egalitarian Community*, 141–42.
64 See Jewett, "Gospel and Commensality," 240–52.
65 See Reasoner, *The Strong*, 99, citing Schneider, "Schwachen," 113, 129.
66 See Wendell L. Willis, *Idol Meat in Corinth: The Pauline Argument in 1 Corinthians 8 and 10*, SBLDS 68 (Chico: Scholars, 1985) 89–96; Khiok-Khng Yeo, *Rhetorical Interaction in 1 Corinthians 8 and 10: A Formal Analysis with Implications for a Cross-Cultural, Chinese Hermeneutic*, BibIntSer 9 (Leiden: Brill, 1995) 192–98.
67 Michel, 432; BAGD 476; W. H. Heidland, "λογίζομαι, λογισμός," *TDNT* 4 (1967) 288.

68 For example, in *Mag. mor.* 1201a20 Aristotle describes a person "whose reasoning is mistaken and leads him to reckon what is good to be bad (αὐτῷ λογιζομένῳ τὰ καλὰ εἶναι φαύλα)." See also Hans-Werner Bartsch, "λογίζομαι," *EDNT* 2 (1991) 354.
69 Fitzmyer, 696; see also Ziesler, 332; Dodd, 216.
70 See Käsemann's critique of this option in 375.
71 See Lagrange, 330; Schlier, 414; Cranfield, 2:714; Dunn, 2:820; Moo, 852.
72 Hans-Jürgen van der Minde, "βρῶμα," *EDNT* 1 (1990) 228.
73 Godet, 461.
74 See Sanday and Headlam, 391; Lagrange, 330; O'Neill, 228; Dunn, 2:820.
75 Ceslas Spicq, "λυπέω," *TLNT* 2 (1994) 421.
76 Ibid., 422.
77 Käsemann, 376; see also Murray, 2:190; Dunn,

ing food to lead a weak member of the community to violate his or her conscience and thereby to "continue to destroy that one for whom Christ died." Here Paul employs the pronoun ἐκείνῳ, "to that one," that is, a fellow believer for whom Christ died, in the emphatic position before the verb. Paul uses the powerful verb ἀπόλλυμι ("annihilate, destroy, ruin") in the present imperative, which implies an ongoing process rather than once and for all "being lost before God."[78] Here, as in the parallel passage of 1 Cor 8:11, Paul charges that by the aggressive behavior of the strong in urging the weak to violate their conscience, ἀπόλλυται . . . ὁ ἀσθενῶν ("the weak one is destroyed/ruined").[79] Since conscience is the "guardian of personal integrity,"[80] its violation can result in a fatal loss in the ability to respond to God.[81] Horst Balz is therefore closer to the nuance required by this context in suggesting the translation of λυπέω in this verse as "injured/deeply troubled," which implies an ongoing state.[82] The "earnestness" of Paul's admonition is enhanced by the second person singular that marks this verse with you (sg.) destroying your "brother."[83]

In explaining the implication of leading believers to violate their integrity, Paul employs the term περιπατεῖς ("you walk"), a characteristic Pauline expression of the Christian ethic, adapted from LXX usage.[84] For instance, the upright man of Prov 8:20 says, Ἐν ὁδοῖς δικαιοσύνης περιπατῶ ("I walk in the paths of righteousness"). From his earliest to his latest letters, Paul

urges his congregations περιπατεῖν ὑμᾶς ἀξίως τοῦ θεοῦ ("to walk/behave worthily of God," 1 Thess 2:12; see also 2 Cor 4:2; Phil 3:17). In this instance, Paul had already assumed that the Romans were living according to the distinctive Christian ethic of love (Rom 12:9) which "does no harm to the neighbor" (Rom 13:10). Here he defines a certain form of abusive behavior as inconsistent with this "norm."[85] The formulation is distinctive: the phrase κατὰ ἀγαπήν is a hapax legomenon in the NT. Sigfred Pedersen argues that not "walking according to love" is an eschatological sin, because it signals that the "love of God through Christ" has not achieved its intended goal of creating a "new eschatological reality" in the midst of a fallen world.[86]

The direct command that follows the clarification of v. 15a is extraordinarily severe in depicting the consequence of leading a fellow Christian to violate conscience on account of "your food."[87] This is a reference to the food being consumed at a love feast, which in the case of the presence of the "weak" who are committed to kosher regulations would have a devastating effect.[88] That "that"[89] person is "being destroyed" is clearly a "metaphorical" use of the word,[90] but it does not imply the temptation to apostasy except in a secondary sense.[91] It should be noted that Paul selects the present rather than the aorist imperative, implying a sustained and continuous action of wrecking someone. Thus I translate, "continue to ruin." References in the commentaries to "eschatological ruin"[92] or "spiritual ruin"[93] not

2:820.

78 Armin Kretzer, "ἀπόλλυμι," EDNT 1 (1990) 136; see also Dunn, 2:821, who observes that "all recent commentators" agree that "final eschatological ruin" is in view. But this does not appear to take the force of the present imperative form into account.

79 See Murray, 2:190–91.

80 Jewett, "Conscience," IDB Supplement (Nashville: Abingdon, 1976) 174.

81 In "ἀπόλλυμι κτλ.," TDNT 1 (1964) 395, Albrecht Oepke refers to the aggressor in this verse acting as a "destroyer of souls."

82 Horst Balz, "λύπη," EDNT 2 (1991) 363. An example of being placed in the status of injured distress is provided by the Magical Papyri, which contain a love spell designed to inflict a woman with "terrible worry and fearful distress" (στυγερὰν μέριμναν καὶ φοβερὰν λύπην, PGM IV.1428; cf. PGM

IV.1769). Rudolf Bultmann, "λύπη κτλ.," TDNT 4 (1967) 320, suggests the less severe expression "cause sorrow to our brethren."

83 Cranfield, 2:715.

84 See Georg Bertram and Heinrich Seesemann, "πατέω κτλ.," TDNT 5 (1967) 544.

85 Bergmeier, "περιπατέω," 75; see also Schlier, 414; Wilckens, 3:92.

86 Pedersen, "Agape," 167.

87 See Hans Jürgen van der Minde, "βρῶμα," EDNT 1 (1990) 228.

88 See Schneider, "Schwachen," 142–48.

89 Morris, 487, observes that ἐκεῖνον ("that one") is emphatic.

90 O'Neill, 229.

91 Murray, 2:192, refutes this possibility.

92 Dunn, 2:821; Schlier, 414.

93 Cranfield, 2:714; Moo, 854–55.

only overlook the tense of the verb but also provide scant explanation of the effects of conscience violation. When people are impelled to act in violation of their individual conscience, no matter how it has been formed in their familial and cultural tradition, they lose their integrity and their capacity to act as moral agents. "To act without regard to one's own conscience is to enter into destruction through the dissolution of the self," through a loss of "personal unity" and integrity.[94] The priority ascribed to personal unity is a prominent feature of Hebrew thought that evil comes from "the divided heart" (בלב ולב),[95] that individual integrity must be preserved against all assaults.[96] That the person thus being destroyed of one "for whom Christ died" evokes the most profound sanction available in early Christianity. Since Christ died for all, as the formulas in Rom 5:6, 8 reminded the Romans,[97] the life of each believer is infinitely valued. To disregard this is to hold Christ's death on the cross in contempt.[98] Thus Paul advocates a peculiar form of asceticism on the part of the "strong,"[99] aimed not at gaining self-control or access to spiritual resources, but rather at protecting the integrity of members of the community whose conscience structure differs from that of the majority.

■ **16** Paul now opens the inferential issue of protecting the integrity of the strong in the context of a cross-cultural community of faith, in which differing theological and liturgical preferences and traditions give rise to conflict. The prohibition of allowing ὑμῶν τὸ ἀγαθόν ("the good thing of yours") to be brought into disrepute because it causes harm to others has occasioned significant debate. That the "good" constitutes the broad blessings of salvation is argued on the basis of the pronoun "your," which could include both the "weak" and the "strong."[100] This, however, is inherently ambiguous, since the "you" addressed in the preceding verse is a representative of the "strong." A narrower construal of τὸ ἀγαθόν as referring to the freedom of the strong is much more widely supported on contextual grounds,[101] which means that it refers to the freedom to partake of any food in the sacramental meal, regardless of legal prohibitions. The verb βλασφημέω in this context means "slandered"[102] and brought into disrepute and dishonor. A classical example of this usage is Isocrates *Hel.* 45.4: ἤδη τινὲς ἐλοιδόρησαν αὐτὸν, ὧν τὴν ἄνοιαν, ἐξ ὧν ἐβλασφήμησαν περὶ ἐκείνου, ῥάδιον ἅπασι καταμαθεῖν ("Already some have reviled him [Alexander]; their ignorance can easily be discerned by all from the slanders they throw at him"). By misusing freedom from food laws so that others are destroyed, the freedom from the law and from corruption that Paul had extolled in Rom 6:20; 7:3; 8:21 would be discredited as erroneous and morally irresponsible.[103] The damage to the weak would be visible both within and outside the church;[104] and the very ethos of the "strong" would thereby be discredited.

■ **17** The antithetical *sententia* about the "kingdom of God" is introduced by γάρ ("for"), indicating that it provides support for the preceding admonition.[105] It is widely thought that the kingdom of God is "only a mar-

---

94 See Jewett, *Tolerance*, 55.
95 1QH 4:14; see also 1QpHab 12:4 and the studies by Ceslas Spicq, "La vertu de simplicité dans l'Ancien et le Nouveau Testament," *RSPhTh* 22 (1933) 5–26, esp. 15, 22; Heinrich Bacht, "Einfalt," *RAC* 4 (1959) 821–40; idem, "Einfalt des Herzens—eine vergessene Tugend?" *GuL* 29 (1956) 418–19, 424–26; O. G. F. Seitz, "Antecedents and Signification of the Term ΔΙΨΥΧΗΣ," *JBL* 66 (1947) 211–19; idem, "Afterthoughts on the Term 'Dipsychos,'" *NTS* 4 (1957–58) 327–34.
96 See Job 31:1-39.
97 See the analysis of the formulas with "Christ," "die," and "for" us in the section on 5:8 above, which leads to my placing quotation marks around the formula in 14:15.
98 See Schlier, 414.
99 Elliott, "Asceticism," 237–45; although Elliott does not employ this term, one could even speak of a distinctive form of situational asceticism implicit in Paul's advice.
100 Schmidt, 333; Dunn, 2:821; Heil, 151.
101 Sanday and Headlam, 391; Lagrange, 330; Michel, 433; Barrett, 264; Cranfield, 2:715–17; Murray, 2:193; Käsemann, 377; Wilckens, 3:93; Ziesler, 333.
102 Otfried Hofius, "βλασφημέω κτλ.," *EDNT* 1 (1990) 220.
103 See Murray, 2:193.
104 See Reasoner, "The 'Strong' and the 'Weak' in Rome," 71–73.
105 See Michel, 434. Schlier, 415, and Cranfield, 2:717, think instead of "for" relating to both vv. 15 and 16.

ginal concept for Paul,"[106] because of its relative rarity as compared with the Synoptic Gospels.[107] However, its use as a formal thesis in this verse,[108] with close verbal similarities to 1 Cor 4:20, indicates that Paul assumes its understandability with the Roman audience. It appears to refer to the church realm where God presently reigns,[109] manifesting salvation in the form of the righteousness of God.[110] Although that congregation had not been founded by Paul, he appears to assume that the "kingdom of God" was a standard part of foundational preaching and baptismal instruction, as shown by Günter Haufe's analysis; the antithetical formulation in 14:17 indicates that he wishes to downplay the overly high value placed on dietary questions in the Roman congregation.[111] The use of the well-worn combination βρῶσις καὶ πόσις[112] has a mildly deprecatory resonance, reducing the distinctions in eating habits that are dividing the Roman house and tenement churches to a quotidian level. While a literal exclusion of all consumption of victuals from the love feast would be "surprising,"[113] Paul's point is that "being able to eat or drink more or less freely and regardlessly toward our neighbor"[114] is not the essence of the "kingdom of God." Less plausible is Roman Garrison's suggestion that Paul is seeking to "correct" a rather hedonistic "concept of the kingdom as

a virtual banquet table at which liquid refreshment would be enjoyed."[115] That Paul is unconcerned in this passage with excesses in charismatic excitement is evident in the formulation of v. 17b, which places "joy" in the emphatic position. The triad of "righteousness and peace and joy," possibly echoing Ps 84:4, is used to describe the new life of Christian congregations "in [the] Holy Spirit,"[116] in which love overcomes social distinctions and barriers.[117] The interest evident throughout Romans in overcoming discrimination on the basis of honor and shame surfaces when one compares this passage with Gal 5:22, where "joy" is the second in a series of nine fruits of the Spirit; here it is the climactic evidence that in the Spirit, traditional claims of superior "righteousness" have been overcome by divine power[118] so that "peace"[119] is created in a formerly competitive social environment. The "eschatological and paradoxical element" in this reference to joy[120] consists in the reconciliation promised for the end time (Isa 11:6-9; 25:6-8)[121] being experienced in the present moment when groups lay aside their superiority claims and prejudices and welcome each other as equals. Given the close parallel in 1 Thess 1:6, μετὰ χαρᾶς πνεύματος ἁγίου ("with joy [given by] the Holy Spirit"), it seems more likely that the phrase "in [the] Holy Spirit" should be attached to "joy,"[122] rather than

---

106 Ulrich Luz, "βασιλεία," EDNT 1 (1990) 204. Schulz, Mitte der Schrift, 128, goes so far as to maintain that this verse is an "early Catholic" interpolation, but I know of no others who have this opinion. The standard criteria for identifying an interpolation are not present in this case.

107 See the statistical chart concerning the fourteen uses of "kingdom" in the Pauline corpus in Dunn, 2:822.

108 See Michel, 434; Holloway, "Paul's Pointed Prose," 48–49, 51.

109 George Johnston, "'Kingdom of God' Sayings in Paul's Letters," in P. Richardson and J. C. Hurd Jr. eds., From Jesus to Paul: Studies in Honour of Francis Wright Beare (Waterloo: Wilfrid Laurier University, 1984) 153.

110 Luz, "βασιλεία," 204.

111 Günter Haufe, "Reich Gottes bei Paulus und in der Jesus Tradition," NTS 31 (1985) 472.

112 See Homer Od. 1.191; 15.490, βρῶσιν τε πόσιν ("eating and drinking"); other references are listed in BAGD 148; LSJM 332, including Col 2:16.

113 Hans-Jürgen van der Minde, "βρῶσις," EDNT 1

(1990) 229.

114 Godet, 461.

115 Roman Garrison, The Graeco-Roman Context of Early Christian Literature, JSNTSup 137 (Sheffield: Academic Press, 1997) 90–91.

116 See particularly Murray, 2:194, who shows that the theological terms in this verse "should be taken as the rectitude and harmony that must govern the attitude and behaviour of the believer within the fellowship of the church."

117 The links between "joy" and "love" are worked out by E. G. Gulin, Die Freude im Neuen Testament, AASF 26/2, 37/3 (Helsinki: Suomalainen Tiedeakatemia, 1932, 1936) 179–81.

118 See Schlier, 415, referring to Rom 5:21.

119 See Käsemann, 377: "peace is openness toward everyone."

120 Hans Conzelmann, "χαίρω, χαρά, συγχαίρω," TDNT 9 (1972) 369.

121 Nababan, "Bekenntnis," 96, stresses the eschatological dimension of this formulation.

122 See Zahn, 581; Michel, 435, argues that the spirit preserves "joy" from falsification; I would prefer to

qualifying the triad of "righteousness and peace and joy."[123]

■ **18** In this verse Paul goes on to clarify the status of those who follow his admonition with regard to overcoming the barriers to commensality in the Lord's Supper, with ἐν τούτῳ ("in this [matter]") referring to the issue under discussion rather than to one or more details from the preceding verse.[124] Although the only close parallel to δουλεύειν τῷ Χριστῷ ("to be enslaved to the Christ") is Acts 20:15, this usage appears to echo the LXX references to God as the object of cultic service on the part of Israel.[125] Although the ordinary translations employ "serve," the verb actually requires a more menial expression such as "enslave oneself to." For example, 2 Chron 30:8 and 33:16 refer to the admonitions that "you are enslaved to the Lord your God" (δουλεύσατε τῷ κυρίῳ θεῷ ὑμῶν) and "enslaved to the Lord God of Israel" (δουλεύειν κυρίῳ θεῷ Ἰσραήλ). The use of this cultic language is particularly striking in a discussion about relativizing cultic standards in the common meal; Paul claims it is precisely the one who overlooks differences in "eating and drinking," performed in good conscience in relation to the same Lord as 14:6 acknowledged, who properly "is enslaved" to Christ. The use of the definite article with "Christ," which continues through 15:3 and 7, may be "a deliberate attempt to express himself in terms closest to those of the Jewish Christian minority," which views "the Christ" as the annointed one, the "Messiah."[126]

That a person conforming to Paul's counsel is εὐάρεστος τῷ θεῷ ("pleasing to God") places adherents in the same status as the wise and righteous man of Wis 4:10, Εὐάρεστος τῷ θεῷ γενόμενος ἠγαπήθη . . . ("He was pleasing to God and beloved by him . . .").[127] In the biblical worldview, the goal of an ideal servant is to satisfy the master. By using the same adjective as in 12:1, Paul provides an apt example of what it means to "present your bodies as a sacrifice," extending the welcome that comes from Christ beyond the borders of convention and social restriction, thus acting in a manner consistent with Christ who gave himself for others.

To be δόκιμος τοῖς ἀνθρώποις ("acceptable to people") uses a typical term for persons who are "respected, esteemed" by others,[128] a widely desired social attribute in the ancient world.[129] This is the only location in Paul's letters where δοκιμός refers to recognition from humans.[130] An example of typical usage appears in a second-century C.E. inscription from Ephesus that recognizes Priscus, who had served as the benefactor of the Festival of Artemesia, as a "man very well thought of" (ἀνδρὸς δοκιματάτου) and therefore "worthy of all honor and acceptance" by the city.[131] Paul does not specify who is meant by ἄνθρωποι ("persons, people"), used here in the generic sense of men and women generally,[132] but it would definitely include those involved on various sides of the boundary of discredited freedom mentioned in 14:16.[133] The formulation also includes society at large, as the expression δόκιμος τοῖς ἀνθρώποις implies. That "pleasing God" can so easily be combined with being "acceptable to people" seems odd, in light of Paul's characteristic admonition not to be conformed to this world (e.g., Rom 12:1). Apparently, to be

---

place in social rather than individual terms the observation by Cranfield, 2:719, that attaching "holy spirit" to joy distinguishes it "from any joy which is merely the temporary result of the satisfaction of one's own selfish desires."

123 Käsemann, 377; Wilckens, 3:93; Fitzmyer, 697; Moo, 857.

124 See Michel, 435–36; Dunn, 2:824, citing the parallel in 1 Cor 11:22, ἐν τούτῳ οὐκ ἐπαινῶ ("In this I will not commend you"). The other options weighed by Cranfield, 2:719–20, do not appear to rest on solid parallels in Pauline usage.

125 See Newton, *Concept of Purity*, 68–69; Karl Heinrich Rengstorf, "δοῦλος κτλ.," *TDNT* 2 (1964) 267: "In the LXX δουλεύειν is the most common term for

the service of God . . . in that of total commitment to the Godhead."

126 Dunn, 2:827.

127 In contrast, in Ἑρμην. 41.6, Pseudo-Hippocrates describes an amulet that makes the wearer "pleasing to and beloved by all people" (πᾶσιν ἀνθρώποις ἔσται εὐάρεστος καὶ ἠγαπημένος).

128 BAGD 203.

129 See Malina, *New Testament World*, 54–55; Pilch and Malina, *Biblical Social Values*, 88–91.

130 See Wilckens, 3:94.

131 G. H. R. Horsley, "Holy Days in Honor of Artemis," *NDIEC* 4 (1987) 74–77.

132 See Dunn, 2:824.

133 See Cranfield, 2:720.

respected in the world does not require conformity to its practices, but it does require attention to issues of honor and dishonor that would be exhibited in unseemly conflicts over food. There is a later rabbinic saying that appears to move in the same direction:[134] "So do what is good and right in the eyes of Yahweh, i.e. what is good in the eyes of God and what is right in the eyes of men."

■ **19** Beginning with this verse, Paul draws inferences (ἄρα οὖν, "so then") showing that his advice concerning the Roman situation fit into the strategy he and his colleagues followed in dealing with church conflict. Despite the fact that the textual variant διώκωμεν ("let us pursue") would be more appropriate in this context, and may well have been originally intended as Paul dictated this letter, I decided in note g above to follow the preponderant evidence for the indicative "we pursue." As Kitzberger points out, however, the argumentative function of this verse is clearly imperatival even in the indicative, because the actions described are obviously in contrast with the past behavior of the Roman churches.[135] The shift from the third person singular in 14:18 to the first person plural form in this verse places Paul and his missionary associates in the position of models that both the weak and the strong congregations should follow to "pursue" (διώκειν)[136] "peace" and the "edification" of others.

To "pursue peace" is a biblical phrase describing the righteous person, as in Ps 34:14 (LXX 33:14), ζήτουσον εἰρήνην, καὶ δίωξον αὐτήν ("seek peace, and pursue it"), but the plural formulation τὰ τῆς εἰρήνης ("the

things of peace") retains the focus on the variety of local circumstances that Paul and his colleagues habitually took into account in seeking concord.[137] The policy of becoming a Jew to the Jews, a weak person to the weak, "all things to all people" (1 Cor 9:19-23) lies behind this usage. The parallel expression τὰ τῆς οἰκοδομῆς ("the things of edification") "should probably be understood as serving more to fill out and clarify the significance which τὰ τῆς εἰρήνης has in this context."[138] The use of οἰκοδομή for congregational edification is a typical Pauline metaphor for congregational work (1 Cor 3:9-10; 14:3, 5, 12, 26; 2 Cor 10:8; 12:19; 13:10). While the LXX uses this metaphor to describe God's building of Israel (Jer 12:16; 38:4, 28; 40:7; 49:10; 45:4; 51:34), the clearest parallels to the idea of building a congregation of believers are found in Qumran.[139] For example, in 1QS 8:5-10 the Qumran community is described as the "eternal planting of a holy house for Israel and a circle of the Most High" whose task is to witness to the truth of the law, to "make atonement for the land and to judge the Godless." In the pesher on Ps 37 found at Qumran, it is the Teacher of Righteousness whom God "appointed to build for him the congregation" (הכינו לבנות לו עדת, 4QpPs37 III.16). Although the metaphor is the same, the nature of the early Christian communities is very different and the responsibility for upbuilding is much more widely shared than in Qumran.[140] Clarence Glad has discovered the closest parallels to Paul's idea of mutual upbuilding of congregations in the

---

134 Rabbi Akiba, from *Sheq.* 2.1, cited by Walter Grundmann, "δοκιμός κτλ.," *TDNT* 2 (1964) 260.

135 Kitzberger, *Bau der Gemeinde*, 38, citing Sickenberger, 289, and Schmidt, 233.

136 See Albrecht Oepke, "διώκω," *TDNT* 2 (1964) 230: "earnestly to pursue or promote a cause" as in Thucydides *Hist.* 2.63, where Pericles urges the Athenians to "pursue the honor" (τὰς τιμὰς διώκειν) of maintaining its imperial rule over other cities. See also the administrative texts in B. P. Grenfell, A. S. Hunt, and D. G. Hogarth, eds., *Fayûm Towns and Their Papyri* (London, 1900) 111, 20 (95–96 C.E.) τὸν λ[ι]μνασμ[ὸν] δ[ι]ξον τῶν [ἐ]λα[ι] ών[ων τ] ῶν πάντον ("zealously pursue the irrigation of all the olive-yards"); idem, 112, 2 (99 C.E.) εὖ πυήσις διώξαι τοὺς σκαφήτρους τῶν

ἐλαιώνον ("please pursue the digging of the olive-yards"); see MM 166 and Otto Knoch, "διώκω, διωγμός," *EDNT* 1 (1990) 339.

137 See Günther Baumbach, "Das Verständnis von εἰρήνη im Neuen Testament," *ThV* 5 (1975) 39. While no commentator explains the plural form τά ("the things"), some recognize the focus on congregational relations; e.g., Moo, 859: "peace with other Christians"; Morris, 490: "It is the responsibility of those at peace with God to pursue the kind of conduct that will promote peace with people."

138 Cranfield, 2:721.

139 Pfammatter, *Kirche als Bau*, 155–64.

140 See the section titled "οἰκοδομεῖν as a Spiritual Task of the Community" in Otto Michel, "οἰκοδομέω κτλ.," *TDNT* 5 (1967) 140–42.

Epicurian philosophical communities.[141] To build up "one another" clearly implies that both the weak and the strong are to undertake this task of edifying the other side.[142] The use of the ἀλλήλους ("others") formula that we encountered earlier in this pericope (14:13) amplifies the urge to unite competitive factions. As each group supports the integrity of the other and encourages growth in others, a "mutually nurturing community" flourishes.[143] As usual through Romans, Paul has the whole community of God in mind,[144] and the formulation here should prevent the "individualistic misunderstandings" that have marked the traditional interpretation of this passage.[145] If mutual upbuilding replaces hostile competition and mutual shaming between the Roman house and tenement churches, the kind of "peace" that is reiterated in 14:17 and 19 will be advanced. The synonymous parallelism between "things that make for peace" and "things that make for edification" drives this point home.[146]

■ 20 The clarification of Paul's congregational strategy concludes with the exhortation in v. 20a. The building metaphor in the previous verse is carried over in the reference to the congregations of Rome as τὸ ἔργον τοῦ θεοῦ ("the work of God").[147] That "work" is used here in the sense of a structure, a building erected by God, is suggested by the parallels in 1 Cor 3:9-14 and 9:1, as well as by inscriptions found on ancient buildings. For example, an inscription in Tralles refers to a building contributed by a philanthropist as his ἔργον: Γάιος ὁ πραγματευτὴς τὸν ἀνδριάντα ἀνέστησεν ἐν τῷ ἔργῳ τῷ ἰδίῳ αὐτῆς ("Gaius the guild official

erected this statue in the building paid by his own means").[148]

It thus seems inappropriate to think of the "work of God" in this verse as the salvation event,[149] the individual "Christian personality,"[150] the "weak believer,"[151] or the fate of individual believers in general.[152] Rather, it is the divine edifice of apostolic work through the gospel, as 1 Cor 3:10-15 indicates. While the admonition is formulated with the second person singular form, μὴ . . . κατάλυε ("you [sg.] should not continually tear down, destroy"),[153] as in 14:15, which strongly suggests that "the plea is addressed to 'the strong,'"[154] the structure thereby impaired is the entire congregation.[155] Paul's assumption is that the weak are just as essential to the congregation as the strong, since a building will collapse when either part of its structure is removed. It is a remarkably pluralistic view of the church, whose integrity can only be preserved when each group takes responsibility for the growth toward maturity of the other side.

In v. 20b, Paul opens a discussion of the distinction between good and bad with regard to eating that runs through the end of v. 21.[156] The evangelical, situational redefinition of good and evil that appears in chapters 7, 12, and 13 comes to expression here. The motto πάντα μὲν καθαρά ("all things are indeed clean") differs in formulation from Paul's statements in 1 Cor 6:12 and 10:23, "all things are allowed," which probably reflected his own teaching of freedom from the law. Here he uses the term καθαρός[157] for the only time in the Pauline corpus, probably echoing the language found in Luke

141 Glad, *Paul and Philodemus*, 124–32.

142 Kitzberger, *Bau der Gemeinde*, 41; Leenhardt, 355–56.

143 Jewett, *Tolerance*, 139; Kruse, *Paul*, 238–39.

144 See Schlatter, 258; Michel, 436; Pfammatter, "οἰκοδομή," 496; idem, *Kirche als Bau*, 57–60.

145 Vielhauer, *ΟΙΚΟΔΟΜΗ*, 94.

146 Ibid.

147 Georg Bertram, "ἔργον κτλ.," *TDNT* 2 (1964) 643: "The ἔργον τοῦ θεοῦ in R. 14:20 is the οἰκοδομή of the community."

148 Text from *Athenische Mitteilungen* (1896) 113.16–19, cited by Erik Peterson, "ΈΡΓΟΝ in der Bedeutung 'Bau' bei Paulus," *Bib* 22 (1941) 439.

149 Michel, 437; Schmidt, 234.

150 Meyer, 2:318; Godet, 462: "the *work of God* in the person." (Italics in original.)

151 Lagrange, 332; Murray, 2:195; Cranfield, 2:723.

152 Zahn, 583; Kühl, 457.

153 The present imperative form implies ongoing activity, which is overlooked by current commentators: e.g., Dunn, 2:825; Moo, 859.

154 Dunn, 2:825.

155 See Barrett, 265; Schlier, 417; Dunn, 2:825; Moo, 860; Peterson, "'Bau' bei Paulus," 441; Pfammatter, *Kirche als Bau*, 61–66.

156 See Käsemann, 328.

157 See Hartwig Thyen, "καθαρός κτλ.," *EDNT* 2 (1990) 218–19, for a summary of anthropological insights into the role of "pure" and "impure" as the supreme categories in Israel's symbolic universe. He argues (220) that Paul made the most radical break with this tradition by insisting "that God has acted eschatologically to declare the impure Gentiles pure

11:41, πάντα καθαρὰ ὑμῖν ἐστιν ("every [food] is clean to you") and Mark 7:19, καθαρίζων πάντα τὰ βρώματα ("making all foods clean") that was current in oral tradition in Rome.[158] The motto declares a complete break from the purity laws that bound both Judaism and the Greco-Roman world.[159]

While Paul concedes[160] the legitimacy of this motto, he qualifies it in a manner that remains audacious[161] even though its cogency is fully prepared by the preceding argument. Such eating is "bad for a person who eats with stumbling," which picks up some of the language of 14:13-15.[162] As Gustav Stählin notes, the formulation of v. 20b "does not fit too smoothly into the use of πρόσκομμα" ("stumbling-block") elsewhere in Paul, where falling under divine judgment is more clearly in view.[163] The prepositional phrase διὰ προσκόμματος ("with stumbling, with offense") should be understood as describing attendant circumstances related to the eating,[164] but there are no precedents to this combination of preposition and noun.[165] A unique situation was required in which this unusual, virtually untranslatable, combination would be meaningful. Some have taken this phrase to refer to the weak violating their conscience in eating unkosher food[166] and others see the strong causing offense in urging such violation.[167] The most plausible approach is that the ambiguity inherent in διὰ προσκόμματος was intentional, allowing both the weak and the strong to apply it to their own situation.[168] As 14:4 had made clear, standing or falling is a possibility for either group, and the same Lord has the "power" to preserve both; each group will be held responsible for its own actions (14:12), whether stumbling or standing firm in the "conviction" of their own mind (14:5).

■ 21 This verse begins with the word καλός ("good") without the article, which conveys the sense of an "authoritative pronouncement,"[169] or, to be more precise, of a *Tobspruch* ("good-saying") beginning with the word "good" or "better" such as Prov 15:16, 17; 19:22; 27:10; Eccl 7:1, 2, 3, 5, 8; 8:13.[170] An example of such a pronouncement in the NT is 1 Cor 7:1, καλὸν ἀνθρώπῳ γυναικὸς μὴ ἅπτεσθαι ("It is good for a man not to touch a woman"). In contrast to most sayings of this type,[171] this one is in the aorist rather than the present tense; the shift from the present tense of v. 20b seems to suggest that "Paul does not envisage the strong abstaining permanently" from their freedom to eat meat and

---

'without the law'. . . ." Moo, 860, lists Gen 7:2-3, 8; 8:20; Lev 4:12; 6:11; 7:19; Ezra 6:20; Mal 1:11 as typical examples of ritually "clean" food. See also Pascher, *Rein und Unrein,* and Wenham, "Unclean Food," 6–15.

158 Reasoner, "The 'Strong' and the 'Weak' in Rome," 80, citing Nababan, "Bekenntnis," 100; Dunn, 2:825, suggests that this may be "a slogan of 'the strong'" but says "we cannot assume that Paul had that much detailed information" about the situation in Rome. The linguistic evidence suggests, however, that this formulation was atypical of Paul and typical of the synoptic tradition that otherwise has been shown to have been brought to Rome by early evangelists. There is no reason to doubt that Paul selects this formulation with an anticipation that it will be recognized in Rome. Pascher, *Rein und Unrein,* 170-73, shows that Paul's discussion reflects interaction with the saying of Jesus about food being clean.

159 Friedrich Hauck and Rudolf Mayer, "καθαρός κτλ.," *TDNT* 3 (1965) 413–23, show the important role of purity for Greco-Roman as well as Jewish religion.

160 *Μέν* is used here in a concessive sense; see BAGD 502; Cranfield, 2:723.

161 Michel, 438: "yet Paul dares to add a new delimitation to this saying of Jesus."

162 The use of the generic τῷ ἀνθρώπῳ ("for a person") rather than τῷ ἀδελφῷ ("for a brother") that was used in 14:13-15 may point to a less contextual source, or perhaps a broader bearing, of Paul's formulation.

163 Stählin, "προσκόπτω κτλ.," 756; see also Balz, "πρόσκομμα," 173.

164 BDF §223.3; Cranfield, 2:723; Dunn, 2:826.

165 A *TLG* search from the eithth century B.C.E. to the first century C.E. turned up no examples before Rom 14:20.

166 Stählin, "προσκόπτω κτλ.," 757; Meyer, 2:318–19; Godet, 463; Murray, 2:195; Wilckens, 3:393.

167 Balz, "πρόσκομμα," 173; Sanday and Headlam, 392–93; Zahn, 583; Lagrange, 332; Michel, 437; Fitzmyer, 698; Moo, 860.

168 Barrett, 266; Morris, 491; Dunn, 2:826.

169 Cranfield, 2:724; see also Michel, 437.

170 See Graydon F. Snyder, "The *Tobspruch* in the New Testament," *NTS* 23 (1976–77) 117–20.

171 Ibid., 120.

drink wine.[172] Moreover, while the usual gnomic contrast is κακόν/ἀγαθόν ("bad/good"), Paul here uses the contrast κακόν/καλόν ("bad/good or beautiful"), thus suggesting appearance over moral substance; it is the public display that provides the offense, something visible at the love feast and not the deed itself, that is problematic. The social context for this situational renunciation is provided by the series of admonitions in Rom 16, which were to be extended to representatives of other groups, including those that practiced abstinence. Given the restricted circumstances of space and resources available to early Christian love feasts, some of which met in the poorest slums of Rome, there was no possibility of envisioning the permanent joining of groups of weak and strong churches. Nevertheless, when a member of an abstaining group was invited, the host group is here encouraged to view their "conscious self-limitation of personal liberty for the sake of the 'weak,'" as "good," that is, matching the high standards of the Christian ethic (12:2; 16:16).[173]

The references to "meat" and "wine" in this verse provide essential details to identify the background of the ascetic impulses within the Roman churches. Although there were Greco-Roman religious and philosophical traditions favoring vegetarianism[174] and Roman laws limiting the consumption of meat,[175] nowhere outside of Jewish and Christian sources is this linked with κοινός as profane/unkosher as in this pericope. The fact that the cheapest meat available in Rome was pork,[176] which was an item of particular concern for persons of Jewish background,[177] throws light on this detail. Much of the meat consumed by the lower classes in Rome was distributed by the state during festivals in honor of the gods, and most meat purchased in the market had been sacrificed to the gods. These circumstances would have caused problems for anyone sensitive to the kosher laws. Moreover, Bruce Winter has developed the plausible theory that the privilege of buying kosher products had been suspended with the banning of Jewish and Jewish Christian agitators by Claudius in 49 C.E.[178] Another possibility is developed by Reasoner: "eclectic asceticism," which allows a variety of motives to be covered by Paul's formulation in this verse.[179]

A similar case could be made about the renunciation of wine. In general, wine had a sacred significance in Greco-Roman culture,[180] so advocacy of abstinence was rare. Some sources advocated abstinence on the grounds of moderation,[181] which is paralleled in Jewish sources that warn against drunkenness.[182] When Apollonius Tyanensis describes his renunciation of wine and "animal

---

172 Dunn, 2:826.

173 Reasoner, "The 'Strong' and the 'Weak' in Rome," 81.

174 See Haußleiter, *Vegetarismus*, 3–356; Reasoner, *The Strong*, 75–84; Vincent L. Wimbush, ed., *Ascetic Behavior in Greco-Roman Antiquity: A Sourcebook* (Minneapolis: Fortress, 1990); Wimbush and R. Valantasis, eds., *Asceticism* (Oxford: Oxford University Press, 1995).

175 Reasoner, *The Strong*, 77–79; Mireille Corbier, "The Ambiguous Status of Meat in Ancient Rome," trans. R. Saller, *Food and Foodways* 3 (1989) 240–45.

176 See Heil, *Ablehnung der Speisegebote*, 258, citing T. J. Leary, "Of Paul and Pork and Proselytes," *NovT* 35.3 (1993) 292.

177 Barclay lays out the evidence that "the Jews in Rome were particularly well known for their abstinence from pork," in "Undermine the Law," 8–9, citing Macrobius *Sat.* 2.4.11; Philo *Legat.* 361; Juvenal *Sat.* 6.160; 14.98–99; Tacitus *Hist.* 5.4.2.

178 Winter, "Romans 12–15," 90–91.

179 Reasoner, *The Strong*, 138. Elliott, "Asceticism," 237–39, appears to consider only the kosher regulations as a background for Paul's argument.

180 See Karl Kircher, *Die sakrale Bedeutung des Weines im Altertum*, RVV 9 (Gießen: Töpelmann, 1910; repr. Berlin: de Gruyter, 1970) 4–47; Heinz Schmitz, "Heiliger Wein. Religionsgeschichtliche Anmerkungen zu einigen Trinksitten," *ZPE* 28 (1978) 288–94. Dionysius/Bacchus was, of course, the god of wine, and intoxication was viewed as divine possession (Kircher, *Die sakrale Bedeutung des Weines im Altertum*, 87–90; Ferguson, *Backgrounds*, 243–44). Wine was used in the regular libations to the good daimon of the house in the Greek domestic cult and in local mystery cults (Ferguson, *Backgrounds*, 166, 237), understood as communion with the gods (Kircher, *Die sakrale Bedeutung des Weines im Altertum*, 45–47).

181 See Reasoner, "The 'Strong' and the 'Weak' in Rome," 83, citing Seneca *Ep.* 108.14–16, which places abstinence from wine under the rubric of "moderation in diet" (*sobriam mensam*).

182 See Heinrich Seesemann, "οἶνος," *TDNT* 5 (1967) 162; Everett Ferguson, "Wine," *EEC*, 2d ed. 2 (1997) 1179–80; Jack M. Sasson, "The Blood of Grapes: Viticulture and Intoxication in the Hebrew Bible," in L. Milano, ed., *Drinking in Ancient Societies: His-*

food," it is to follow the wisdom of the ancient Pythagoras.[183] On the Jewish side, wine was ordinarily a self-evident part of family meals and Passover celebrations,[184] although it was avoided in temple ceremonies.[185] Some of the rare instances of Jewish advocacy of total abstinence seem to reflect a fear of involvement with pagan ceremonies.[186] In the case of the ancient Rechabites described in texts like Jer 35:6-7, abstinence from wine and the refusal to plant vineyards expressed a commitment to the desert ideals of early Yahwism[187] or perhaps aimed to avoid inadvertent disclosures of technological secrets.[188]

In *T. Jud.* 15.4, the patriarch describes his ascetic life with almost the same terms found in Romans: οἶνον καὶ κρέα οὐκ ἔφαγον ἕως γήρους μου ("neither wine nor meat did I eat until my old age"). The wording of the parallel passage in *T. Reub.* 1.9–10 is somewhat more distant from Romans, but it reveals the rationale of such abstinence within apocalyptic Jewish circles as an extreme expression of repentance:[189] Καὶ μετὰ τοῦτο ἐν προαιρέσει ψυχῆς μου ἑπτὰ ἔτη μετενόησα ἐνώπιον Κυρίου. Καὶ οἶνον καὶ σίκερα οὐκ ἔπιον, καὶ κρέας οὐκ εἰσῆλθεν ἐν τῷ στόματί μου. Καὶ πᾶν ἄρτον ἐπιθυμίας οὐκ ἔφαγον ἀλλ᾽ ἤμων πενθῶν ἐπὶ τῇ ἁμαρτίᾳ μου, μεγάλη γὰρ ἦν, οἷα οὐ γέγονεν ἐν

Ἰσραὴλ οὕτως. ("After this in the deliberate choice of my soul for seven years I repented before the Lord. Neither wine nor liquor did I drink and meat did not enter my mouth. I did not eat any desirable food but was mourning over my sin, since it was so great. Never had anything like this been done in Israel.") The fact that a similar renunciation of meat and wine is reported of Daniel (Dan 10:3; 1:10-16)[190] and of the Jewish Therapeutae of Upper Egypt[191] indicates that traditions of such "ascetic practices . . . in peripheral groups within later Judaism" based on "eschatological dualism" probably "offered a pattern for the ascetic impulse of early Jewish Christianity."[192] These details point to a Jewish rather than a Greco-Roman background of the asceticism in Roman churches.

The third clause of the *Tobspruch* urges the avoidance of "anything else" that might cause the member of another house church to stumble. Sirach contains a similar admonition: Ἐπίστρεφε ἐπὶ Κύριον καὶ ἀπόλειπε ἁμαρτίας . . . καὶ σμίκρυνον πρόσκομμα ("Return to the Lord and forsake sins . . . and stumble less," Sir 16:25). While some have suggested Paul had in mind the avoidance of other foods or drinks that presumably might trouble the "weak,"[193] Wilckens has forthrightly acknowledged the difficulty this produces in identifying

tory and Culture of Drink in the Ancient Near East: Papers of a Symposium held in Rome, May 17–19 1990, HANES 6 (Padua: Sargon, 1994); Vincenz Zapletal, Der Wein in der Bibel. Kulturgeschichtliche und exegetische Studie, BibS(F) 20.1 (Freiburg: Herder, 1920) 50–57, 399–419.

183 Philostratus *Vit. Apoll.* 1.32.

184 See Arnold A. Wieder, "Ben Sira and the Praises of Wine," *JQR* 61 (1970) 156–58.

185 Zapletal, *Wein*, 42, observes that the use of wine by priests during their official service was forbidden under the threat of death (Lev 10:9; Ezek 44:21). See also F. Stolz, "Rausch, Religion und Realität in Israel und seiner Umwelt," *VT* 26 (1976) 179–86.

186 See Reasoner, "The 'Strong' and the 'Weak' in Rome," 82–83, Heil, *Ablehnung der Speisegebote*, 259. Zapletal, *Wein*, 42, notes that no wine could be used that had any connection with pagan cults, according to Deut 32:38, a prohibition later continued in the Mishnah. Schmitz, "Heiliger Wein," 290–91, describes the pagan customs of linking wine with communion with the gods.

187 Hans Bardke, "Rekabiter," *RGG*³ 5 (1961) 951.

188 See Frank W. Frick, "Rechab," *ABD* 5 (1992) 631; idem, "Rechabites Reconsidered," *JBL* 90 (1971) 284–87.

189 See H. W. Hollander, H. J. de Jonge, and Th. Kortenweg, *The Testaments of the Twelve Patriarchs: A Critical Edition of the Greek Text*, PVTG 1.2 (Leiden: Brill, 1978) 90.

190 See Daud H. Soesilo, "Why Did Daniel Reject the King's Delicacies? (Daniel 1.8)," *BT* 45 (1994) 441–44.

191 Philo *Cont.* 37, 73–74; for a critical evaluation of Philo's views, see Hans Gottfried Schönfeld, "Zum Begriff 'Therapeutai' bei Philo von Alexandrien," *RevQ* 3 (1961) 219–40; Roger T. Beckwith, "The Vegetarianism of the Therapeutai, and the Motives for Vegetarianism in Early Jewish and Christian Circles," *RevQ* 13 (1988) 407–10.

192 James E. Goehring, "Asceticism," *EAC*, 2d ed. (1997) 1:127.

193 Reasoner, "The 'Strong' and the 'Weak' in Rome," 84, cites Rauer, "Schwachen," 100, and others. Other commentators also assume that the weak are in view here: Lagrange, 333; Murray, 2:195; Dunn, 2:827.

their grounds beyond what has been mentioned earlier in the pericope; but that they worried about food offered to idols is not indicated anywhere in the letter.[194] Paul's sweeping formulation of "anything else" includes both the strong and weak within its purview, that is, everything that might violate the faith of any church in Rome.[195] Consistent with the admonitions in the preceding pericope to treat both the weak and the strong as brothers (14:10), the object of attention here is "your brother," which extends the familial bonds in both directions. It is therefore essential to interpret προσκόπτει ("he stumbles") in the broadest sense of any Christian group being brought into a situation of "stumbling in faith or conscience,"[196] rather than restricting it to the "weak" minority as in 1 Cor 8.[197] Although the concept of a stumbling block derives from Jewish culture, as noted above,[198] its connotation in this context includes both Gentile and Jewish Christian groups. There is a need for mutual responsibility in preserving a healthy faith in each group, and none are capable of maintaining such health by their own efforts alone. The "weak" need the "strong" just as the "strong" need the "weak."

■ **22** This verse goes on to suggest a strategy of avoiding damage to either side in the Roman dispute. It has already been established that the "faith that you have" is somewhat different for the "weak" or the "strong" factions in Rome; as in the reference to the "measuring rod of faith" in 12:3, πίστις ἣν ἔχεις ("faith that you have") is used here to designate the peculiar form of faith that

each group has been given by God, which includes the cultural and theological factors that govern each group's service to its Lord (see Rom 14:4-6).[199] The emphatic position of the pronoun "you" and the second person singular form of the verb direct this rule to each person in the Roman church, not just to the "strong."[200] Faith refers here to a trusting, obedient response to the gospel that a particular group has made in response to the Spirit; it thus includes an element of group adherence. To hold such faith κατὰ σεαυτόν should thus be translated "in accordance with yourself."[201] The issue is integrity, not privacy or discreet silence, as in the ordinary translation, "keep your faith to yourself."[202] This preservation of consistency between belief and action in a social context of pluralism in values is similar to the advice of Epictetus: τήρει τὸ ἀγαθὸν τὸ σαυτοῦ ἐν παντί ("Guard your own good in everything").[203] While Epictetus viewed God as the somewhat distant guarantor of the laws that guide the wise person (*Diss.* 4.3.12), Paul employs the intensive relational term from the Hebrew Scriptures, ἐνώπιον τοῦ θεοῦ ("in the presence of/eyes of God").[204] "David did right in the eyes of the Lord" (ἐνώπιον Κυρίου, 3 Kgdms 15:5, 11; 22:42) is typical of hundreds of examples in the LXX. It is the direct relationship that each group has before God, each serving its Lord in ways that are culturally informed (Rom 14:3-9, 18), which provides the final, authenticating horizon of faith.[205]

---

194 Wilckens, 3:96.

195 Although he individualizes and contemporizes the matter, Morris, 491, comes the closest to grasping the inclusive formulation: "The important thing is to take such action that we do not lead anyone to stumble . . . to perform actions they can only do in defiance of their conscience."

196 Balz, "πρόσκομμα," 173.

197 See Stählin, "προσκόπτω κτλ.," 757; *Skandalon*, 255–65.

198 Müller, *Anstoß und Gericht*, 32–45.

199 See Käsemann, 378: "faith is imparted to each only in a limited horizon. . . ."

200 As in Dunn, 2:826; Murray, 2:195.

201 In place of meaning II.1c in BAGD as proposed by Dunn, 2:826, I am translating this with II.5a, "according to, in accordance with, in conformity with . . . to introduce the norm which governs something."

202 See Cranfield, 2:726; Fitzmyer, 698; Morris, 492. Reasoner, "The 'Strong' and the 'Weak' in Rome," 85, cites W. K. C. Guthrie, *Orpheus and Greek Religion: A Study of the Orphic Movement* (New York: Norton, 1966) 201, which cites *Ety. mag.* "τελετή" (= Chrysippus, *Frag. log.* 1008.1), that Chrysippus held μέγα γὰρ εἶναι τὸ ἆθλον ὑπὲρ θεῶν ἀκοῦσαί τε ὀρθὰ καὶ ἐγκρατεῖς γενέσαι αὐτῶν ("it is a great reward to hear the truth about the gods and to be capable of keeping it to oneself").

203 Cited by O'Neill, 323, from Epictetus *Diss.* 4.3.11.

204 See Helmut Krämer, "ἐνώπιον," *EDNT* 1 (1990) 462, for the argument that this reference in Romans retains the sense of standing "before the eyes, i.e., in the presence of . . . God."

205 See Michel, 438; Schlier, 417–18.

Consistency between faith and action is the focus of the beatitude that concludes this verse. In a rare use of this form that announces the "distinctive religious joy" of participating in "the salvation of the kingdom of God,"[206] Paul pronounces a blessing on the person ὁ μὴ κρίνων ἑαυτὸν ἐν ᾧ δοκιμάζει ("the one who does not condemn himself by what he approves"). We encountered the verb δοκιμάζειν in 1:28, 2:18, and 12:2 with the same connotation found here, to ascertain or approve in a public setting.[207] The verb κρίνειν is used here with the connotation "condemn" that it bears in 14:3,[208] describing the judgmental reactions of the "weak," but in this verse it appears to relate to both the weak and the strong.[209] The party of the "strong" would be condemned if they abandoned their freedom from the law or if they exercised this freedom in a manner that destroyed the "weak"; the latter would be condemned if they allowed themselves to act against their conscience in eating food that they considered unclean. The blessing in this case comes to everyone who maintains integrity with the faith as they received it from God, whether it is consistent with the preferences of other groups or not.

■ 23 The final explanation in this pericope drives home the necessity of integrity measured as consistency with internalized standards of behavior. The participle διακρινόμενος in the middle voice has the sense of having "misgivings, doubts," a connotation that probably developed out of Greek vernacular usage, although it appears for the first time in early Christian writings.[210] The wordplay with κατακέκριται, a perfect passive form that means "has been condemned," suggests that the person or group acting against the standards of con-science is not just subjectively feeling that "an irrevocable breach in the covenant" has been made.[211] If the "weak"[212] actually eat (ἐὰν φάγῃ) food that their conscience forbids, they stand under divine condemnation because they have violated the faith with which they were entrusted: ὅτι οὐκ ἐκ πίστεως ("because it is not out of faith"). As Leenhardt explains, in overly individualistic terms, "the wrong lies in not obeying one's own sincere conviction, in a divided personality which agrees to act in contradiction to an inner persuasion."[213] In effect, they are rendering final loyalty to a lord other than the Lord who saved them and called them to the distinctive form of service described in 14:4-8.[214]

Paul's concern about the barrier that doubts and misgivings erected against consistent action was shared by Roman thinkers who condemn not the doubt itself but the acting thereon. For example, Cicero *Off.* 1.30 writes:[215] *Quocirca bene parecipiunt, qui vetant quicquam agere, quod dubites aequum sit an iniquum. Aequites enim lucet ipsa per se, dubitatio cogitationem significat iniuriae* ("It is, therefore, excellent that they urge us not to something when there is doubt about its being right or wrong; for righteousness shines with a brilliance of its own, but doubt is a sign that we are thinking of a possible wrong"). The Jewish tradition also saw the problem of acting in a manner inconsistent with one's doubts. For example, the *Apocalypse of Elijah* 24.3–4 warns, "None should go to the holy place who doubts in his heart. He who doubts in prayer is his own enemy, and the angels do not add their assent."[216]

The formal *sententia* in v. 23b establishes a norm[217] whose general applicability is reinforced by the sweeping πᾶν ("all"), which appears to imply that all actions every-

206 Friedrich Hauck, "μακάριος κτλ.," *TDNT* 4 (1967) 367, 369.
207 See the discussion on 12:2 above.
208 See Dunn, 2:828.
209 While Leenhardt, 358–59, sees both sides addressed by the beatitude, most commentators relate it only to the strong, e.g., Schlier, 418; Dunn, 2:828; Fitzmyer, 699.
210 See Dautzenberg, "διακρίνω," 305, who rejects the suggestion of a unique early Christian development by Friedrich Büchsel and Volkmar Herntrich, "κρίνω κτλ.," *TDNT* 3 (1965) 948. See also BAGD (2000) 231.
211 Dunn, 2:828.

212 That ὁ διακρινόμενος refers here to the "weak" is universally affirmed by commentators; that a party of "doubters" is hereby proven, as proposed by Minear, *Obedience*, 12–13, is not compelling.
213 Leenhardt, 358.
214 See Michel, 439.
215 Noted by Reasoner, "The 'Strong' and the 'Weak' in Rome," 88; he cites a shorter version of the saying in Pliny *Ep.* 1.18.5: *quod dubites ne feceris* ("if you doubt, don't do it!").
216 Cited by Büchsel and Herntrich, "κρίνω κτλ.," 948.
217 Michel, 440.

where are "sin" if they do not spring "out of faith." Since the phrase ἐκ πίστεως ("out of faith") that appears twice in this verse also occurs twice in the thesis of 1:17, twice in 4:16, and also in 3:26, 30; 5:1; 9:30, 32; 10:16, I now place it in quotation marks as a citation. The quest for parallels to this maxim has turned up only one relevant example, so far as I know. Philo offers a general statement about divine guidance that opens with "everything":[218] Πᾶν γὰρ τὸ σὺν θεῷ καλὸν καὶ συμφέρον πάντως, ἐπεὶ καὶ τὸ ἄνευ θείας ἐπιφρονσύνης ἀλυσιτελές ("For everything that has to do with God is in every respect also beneficial, since what is done apart from divine mindfulness is unprofitable").

Paul's maxim has been under debate at least since the time of Augustine.[219] That all actions not derived from faith are sin seems "absurd" from a commonsense point of view,[220] leading commentators to claim "it is not a general maxim concerning faith."[221] Others achieve the same end by insisting on a strictly contextual interpretation in relation to the controversy between the "weak" and the "strong."[222] They tend to reduce the scope of the maxim to "whatever proceeds not from conviction is sin."[223] Others reformulate the *sententia* as "whoever violates his conscience sins,"[224] which goes considerably beyond the normal semantic range for πίστις. Wilckens avoids accounting for the "all," and restricts the meaning of v. 23b to the situation of the "weak," who eat in violation of their understanding of the law, and thus sin in the "strict sense of breaking the law."[225] Similarly, Barrett restricts the relevance of the maxim to the situation

when a "waverer eats meat," explaining that "to eat, therefore, *in these circumstances*, is sin."[226] Cranfield adjusts the meaning of all three of the key terms in the maxim: "all" refers only to the "weak" and the "strong"; "faith" has the special sense of "*confidence that* one's Christian faith *allows one* to do something"; and "sin" is not a "power controlling man" but an "individual sinful" act.[227] Dunn is among the few commentators who take the maxim at face value, contending "that *whatever* is not an expression of dependence on and trust in God (whether Jewish or Gentile or 'Christian' or 'non-Christian') is marked by that fatal flaw of human presumption and/or self-indulgence."[228] That such a statement had relevance to both the "weak" and the "strong" is clear, in that both sides were attempting to achieve "uniformity" by converting the others to their views.[229] The maxim has a particularly sharp bearing on the issue raised in 14:1, welcoming the weak in faith "for disputes over opinions," because if the weak were to give halfhearted consent to the arguments of the strong, they would be led back into the state of "sin," under that demonic power that has enslaved the world since Adam.[230] They must act according to the "measuring rod of faith" that they have been given through their encounter with the gospel.[231] The maxim thus raises the stakes beyond the ethical and theological categories used earlier in the pericope: the realm of righteousness is counterposed to the realm of sin. The sweeping nature of the maxim thus had a significant, rhetorical purpose,[232] even though when taken out of context and pressed to its logical lim-

---

218 Philo *Abr.* 18, cited by Lietzmann, 118.
219 See Augustine *C. Jul.* 4.32 and the survey of patristic opinion in Fitzmyer, 699–700.
220 See Ziesler, 335.
221 Sanday and Headlam, 394.
222 Cranfield, 2:728–29.
223 Fitzmyer, 699. See also Sanday and Headlam, 393; Lagrange, 334; Lietzmann, 113; Black, 198; Murray, 2:196; Bardenhewer, Best, Gutjahr are also listed as following this line. A compelling critique of this construal is provided by Dobbeler, *Glaube als Teilhabe*, 219–20.
224 Zeller, 228; see also Jülicher, 325, who views the maxim as suitable for mature Christians but not for others.
225 Wilckens, 3:97; see also Moo, 863.

226 Barrett, 267, italics in original.
227 Cranfield, 2:728–30; for a similar construal, see Meyer, 2:322.
228 Dunn, 2:829, italics in original; see also Käsemann, 378–80; Morris, 492; Dobbeler, *Glaube als Teilhabe*, 220.
229 See Dunn, 2:829.
230 See the exposition by Peter Fiedler, "ἁμαρτία κτλ.," *EDNT* 1 (1990) 67–69.
231 See Käsemann, 379.
232 In particular, Schneider, "Schwachen," 157, observes that Paul remains at the level of generalities and refrains from offering highly specific advice. This is consistent with demonstrative rhetoric.

its by later interpreters, it retains the potential to cause problems. It is particularly ironic that Augustine's use of this dictum to declare the Pelagians heretics and thus worthy of death went in precisely the opposite direction of Paul's extraordinary defense of Christian tolerance, with particular reference to a vulnerable minority. The opening admonition in this pericope must therefore be held in concert with the final verse: "not to place a stumbling block or hindrance before a brother."

15

The Ninth Pericope

The Obligation to Follow Christ's Example in Edifying Each Other

1/ **Now we the powerful ones are obliged to bear the weaknesses of the powerless ones and not to please ourselves. 2/ Let each of us[a] please the neighbor for the good, toward upbuilding. 3/ For even the Christ did not please himself, but as it has been written,**
  "The reproaches of those who reproach you fell upon me."
4/ For whatever was previously[b] written[c] was written[d] for our instruction, in order that through the steadfastness and through[e] the encouragement of the scripture we might have[f] the hope.
5/ **Now may the God of this steadfastness and encouragement give you the same mind among one another, according to Jesus Christ,[g] 6/ in order that unanimously with one mouth you might glorify the God and Father of our Lord Jesus Christ.**

a   In place of ἡμῶν ("of us") found in the earlier and more reliable texts, D[1] F G P 048 0209[vid] 69 104 326 330 365 424 614 630 1505 1506[(acc. to N-A)] 1881 2495 *al* lat bo provide the reading ὑμῶν ("your"), perhaps in an effort to avoid a contradiction with Paul's identification of himself only with the "strong" in the preceding verse. Another possibility is that the variant reflects an effort to augment Paul's authority. The support for the more likely reading of ἡμῶν is found in ℵ A B C D[*.2] L Ψ 6 33 88 323 945 1175 1241 1243 1319 1506[(acc. to Swanson)] 1573 1739 1836 1874 2344 *Maj* r sy sa bo[ms].

b   The term "written previously" is reduced to "written," ἐγράφη, by B lat Cl, perhaps as an assimilation to the succeeding clause.

c   The addition at this point of πάντα ("all") by B P Ψ 33 69 330 436 451 1678* 1718 1735 1962 *pc* sy appears to be a secondary, doctrinal qualification to reinforce the "unlimited scope" of Paul's statement, as suggested by Leander E. Keck, "Romans 15:4—An

Interpolation?" in J. T. Carroll, C. H. Cosgrove, and E. E. Johnson, eds., *Faith and History: Essays in Honor of Paul W. Meyer* (Atlanta: Scholars, 1990) 129. See also Schlier, 421.

d   The reading προεγράφη ("written before") in ℵ[2] A L P Ψ 048 33 69 88 104 323 326 330 365 424* 614 945 1175 1241 1319 1505 1506[(acc. to Swanson)] 1573 1735 1836 1874 2344 2495 *Maj* sy[h] is a weakly attested assimilation to the preceding verb. The word ἐγράφη ("written") is supported by ℵ[*,c vid] B C D F G 6 81 424[c] 630 1243 1506[(acc. to N-A)] 1739 1881 *pc* latt sy[p] Cl.

e   The omission of διά ("through") by C[c] D F G P Ψ 6 33 69 81 88 104 323 326 365 630 945 1175 1243 1319 1505 1506 1573 1836 1874 1881 2344 2495 *pm* lat Cl constitutes an easier but later reading because it eliminates the seeming redundancy with the previous use of διά in the sentence. An overly elaborate theory is offered by Michael, "Phenomenon," 150–54, who regards the "omission" as reflecting an intermediate stage through dittography by the insertion of the phrase "steadfastness and encouragement" found in 15:5. The inclusion of "through" is convincingly supported by ℵ A B C* L 048 330 424 614 1241 1735 1739 *pm* d*.

f   B vg[ms] Cl add τῆς παρακλήσεως ("of encouragement"), apparently an example of dittography, repeating this phrase from earlier in the sentence; cf. Cranfield, 2:734.

g   In place of "Christ Jesus," the "Jesus Christ" in ℵ A C* F P 048 69 104 330 629 1505 2495 *al* lat sy is not accepted by Nestle-Aland[26/27], *GNT*[3/4], Cranfield, or the other commentators, even though this reading has higher quality of support. Perhaps the usage of the Koine predisposes people to prefer the traditional sequence, suggesting that "Jesus Christ" is secondary; on the other hand, since the sequence "Jesus Christ" is used at the end of v. 6, the alternate sequence sounds more graceful in v. 5, rendering "Christ Jesus" secondary. Support for the sequence "Christ Jesus" is found in B C[c] D G L Ψ 6 33 88 323 326 365 424 614 945 1175 1241 1243 1319 1506 1573 1735 1739 1836 1874 1881 2344 *Maj* vg[mss] Ambst.

Analysis

This pericope is a self-contained unit,[1] opening with an ethical declaration that moves beyond the theological generalization at the end the preceding pericope,[2] and closes with a homiletical benediction urging conformity with Christ's example in dealing with congregational differences.[3] Scriptural proofs replace the dialogical style of theological admonition and reasoning in the preceding two pericopes.[4] The opening line contains an inclusio with 14:1 in the reference to the weak.[5] The sentences are linked with impressive elements of paranomasia. The term ἀρέσκειν ("to please") in 15:1a is repeated in vv. 2 and 3a, effectively joining the first two sentences. The citation from Ps 69:9 in v. 3 contains an internal paranomasia with the repetition of "reproach" in nominal and verbal forms. There is also a form of paranomasia in v. 4a in the wordplay between προεγράφη ("written beforehand") and ἐγράφη ("it was written"). Finally, the Hebraicizing pair of "steadfastness and encouragement" in the parallel διά ("through") phrases in v. 4b is repeated in the benediction of v. 5a, providing an impressive double paranomasia. The expression ὁμοθυμαδὸν ἐν ἑνὶ στόματι in v. 6 is particularly alliterative, with the repetition of o-sounds, producing a harmonious euphony when read aloud. The benediction ends with an effective clausula in the extended line "the God and Father of our Lord Jesus Christ."[6]

Rhetorical Disposition

IV.	The *probatio*
12:1—15:13	The fourth proof: Living together according to the gospel so as to sustain the hope of global transformation
15:1-6	9. The obligation to follow Christ's example in edifying each other
15:1-2	a. Admonitions concerning the proper way of "pleasing"
15:1	1) Declaration concerning the moral obligation of the strong
	a) The positive obligation: bear with weaknesses
15:1b	b) The negative obligation: do not please yourselves
15:2	2) The admonition to both the weak and the strong
	a) The address: "each of us"
	b) The recipients of action: "neighbors"
	c) The form of action: "pleasing"
	d) The ethical criterion: "the good"
	e) The purpose: "upbuilding"
15:3-4	b. The theological rationale
15:3a	1) The *exemplum* of Christ with regard to "pleasing"
15:3b-4	2) The scriptural proof
15:3b	a) The citation formula
15:3c	b) The citation from Ps 69:9
15:4	c) The reason to accept the scriptural proof as applicable in Rome
15:4a	(1) The purpose of Scripture: "for our instruction"
15:4b	(2) The means of scriptural impact: "steadfastness and encouragement"
	(3) The purpose of Scripture: to create hope in the community of faith
15:5-6	c. The homiletical benediction
15:5a	1) The source of benediction: the "God of steadfastness and encouragement"
15:5b	2) The content and scope of the benediction
	a) The recipients: "you" (plural)
	b) The benefit: "the same mind" (see Rom 12:3, 16)
	c) The criterion of the mind: "Jesus Christ"
15:6	3) The purpose of the benediction
	a) The means of accomplishment: the unanimous mouth of congregational members in Rome
	b) The action: giving glory
	c) The appropriate objects to glorify, in a concluding clausula: "the God and Father of our Lord Jesus Christ"

Exegesis

■ **1** Although the rationale for relations between the weak and the strong was laid down in the preceding two pericopes, the declaration of obligation that opens this

---

1   See Wilckens, 3:100. Michel, 441–42, places 15:1-13 in a larger pericope but acknowledges that vv. 1-6 and 7-13 are self-contained thought units ending with benedictions. In contrast, Parunak, "Transitional Techniques," 535–36, places this paragraph at the end of an argument commencing in 14:1.

2   Dunn, 2:836, argues that the "chapter break is poorly located" because 15:1-6 "clearly continues the theme of chap. 14," but he tacitly acknowledges the change of subject by titling this section "Christ as Exemplar."

3   See Louw, 2:134–35.

4   See Michel, 442.

5   See Harvey, *Listening*, 205.

6   In light of the rhetorical brilliance of this pericope, it is puzzling that Weiss, Beiträge," 247, comments: "Chapter 15 contains for our purposes [of rhetorical analysis] nothing of importance."

verse resonates with the "ethic of reciprocity" that was considered binding in the Roman world.[7] In Cicero's words,[8] "For no duty is more imperative than that of proving one's gratitude (*nullum enim officium referenda gratia magia necessarium est*)." Having received the supreme gift of salvation, granted freely to the undeserving, each recipient has the reciprocal obligation of gratitude to the divine Giver and of passing on the gift with similar generosity to others who are equally undeserving. The verb ὀφείλειν echoes the earlier passages in Romans where Paul confesses his obligation to "Greeks and barbarians" (1:14) and where fellow believers were obligated to the Spirit (8:12), which created the further obligation "to love one another" in the social context of house and tenement churches (13:8).[9] The use of ὀφείλομεν ("we are obligated") in the indicative followed by infinitives therefore should not be translated as an imperative, "we ought,"[10] but as an objective statement of a "duty"[11] derived from faith in the gospel, the gift of the Spirit, and membership in the community of faith. Paul is not admonishing in 15:1; he is declaring a social obligation that derives from a particular relationship in which benefits have already been received, that is, the new life in Christ.[12] It is not until the next verse that the admonition begins. The use of ὀφείλειν in this verse is analogous to Philo's description of high-priestly obligation, derived from a previously granted divine election to an exclusive group: Καὶ γὰρ ἄλλως προσκεκληρωμένος θεῷ καὶ τῆς ἱερᾶς τάξεως γεγενὼς ταξίαρχος ὀφείλει πάντων ἀλλοτριοῦσθαι τῶν ἐν γενέσει . . . ("And being otherwise dedicated to God and made leader of the sacred order, he is obligated to be estranged from all ties of birth . . .").[13] The subject of this obligation explicitly includes Paul along with the Gentile Christian majority of the Roman churches: ἡμεῖς οἱ δυνατοί ("we the powerful ones"). This has the rhetorical effect of placing Paul on the same level and under the same burden as the dominant members of his audience. The language of weak and strong appears to have been adapted from Roman congregational usage, reflecting the socioeconomic, political, and probably numerical predominance of the Gentile Christians.[14] It certainly does not reflect Paul's assessment of actual theological insight or spiritual endowment,[15] because 15:27 refers to the spiritual blessings granted to Gentile Christians from their Jewish Christian partners. "The powerful" is a typical expression of social and political prominence, describing, for instance, the occupants of the few houses left standing during the Persian occupation of Athens, which ended in 478 B.C.E.: ἐν αἷς αὐτοὶ ἐσκήνωσαν οἱ δυνατοὶ τῶν Περσῶν ("which the powerful among the Persians had reserved for their shelter").[16] Josephus uses the expression Ἰουδαίων οἱ δυνατοί ("the powerful among the Jews") to refer to the leaders complaining to Roman authorities about Herod's activities.[17] Paul uses the same word in 1 Cor 1:26 to depict the contrast with the social status of most of the believers in Corinth: οὐ πολλοὶ δυνατοί ("not many powerful").[18] By ranking himself among the dominant Gentile Christians, Paul places himself under the same obligation "to bear the weaknesses of the powerless ones and not to please ourselves."

The word ἀσθενήματα ("weaknesses") clearly alludes to the related term used in 14:1, "the ones who are weak in faith," and it probably refers to deficits that are perceived to be both theological[19] and social.[20] Paul's reference to "the weaker members" (τὰ μέλη ἀσθενέστερα) in 1 Cor 12:22 is primarily social in its connotation, associated with a lack of honor (12:23-26).

---

7   See Reasoner, *The Strong*, 176–86.
8   Cicero *Off.* 1.47, cited by Reasoner, *The Strong*, 178.
9   See Michel, 442.
10 Michael Wolter, "ὀφείλω," *EDNT* 2 (1991) 551; Dunn, 2:836; Moo, 864.
11 Friedrich Hauck, "ὀφείλω κτλ.," *TDNT* 5 (1967) 564.
12 See Reasoner, *The Strong*, 192.
13 Philo *Spec.* 1.114; translation adapted from F. H. Colson, *Philo with an English Translation* (Cambridge: Harvard University Press, 1937) 7:165.
14 See Reasoner, *The Strong*, 218–20.
15 Michel, 443; Dunn, 2:837. Schmidt, 237, also overlooks the social connotation and associates "strong" with Paul's doctrine of freedom in faith.
16 Thucydides *Hist.* 1.89.3.
17 Josephus *Bell.* 1.242.
18 See Theissen, *Social Setting*, 72: "The 'powerful' would be influential people."
19 See Josef Zmijewski, "ἀσθενής κτλ.," *EDNT* 1 (1990) 171; Reasoner, *The Strong*, 218–19.
20 Reasoner, *The Strong*, 50–55, 218–19.

Early Christian writers also use this word in the social sense, involving a lack of wealth, status, and power, as, for example, in Diognetus 10:5:[21] Οὐ γὰρ κατακυνασ-τεύειν τῶν πλησίον οὐδὲ το πλέον ἔχειν βούλεσθαι τῶν ἀσθενεστέρων οὐδὲ τὸ πλουτεῖν καὶ βιάζεσθαι τοὺς ὑποδεστέρους εὐδαιμονεῖν ἐστιν ("For happiness does not consist of domination over neighbors, nor in wishing to have more than the weak [i.e., the poor], nor in being wealthy, and having power to compel those who are below you"). The use of the expression τῶν ἀδυνάτων ("the powerless ones") also points toward persons of low socioeconomic status and power. In a similar manner, Job 5:11, 15-16 extols God as the powerful savior for the underclass:[22] τὸν ποιοῦντα ταπεινοὺς εἰς ὕψος . . . ἀδύνατος δὲ ἐξέλθοι ἐκ χειρὸς δυνάστου· εἴη δὲ ἀδυνάτῳ ἐλπίς, ἀδίκου δὲ στόμα ἐμφραχθείη ("the one who [raises] the weak ones to the heights . . . [and] the powerless one escape from the hand of the powerful. But there is hope for the powerless ones, but the mouth of the unjust will be stopped"). Ziesler makes an important observation with regard to this social language: "It is extraordinary that he can use such prejudicial language in a passage that is aimed at reconciliation."[23] The key is that while using the social language of honor and shame being employed in Rome, which had a specific link to the Jewish Christian minority as well as an association with lower-class and slave members of tenement churches, Paul reverses the ordinary structure of obligation. Rather than the weak being forced to submit to the strong as was typical in Greco-Roman culture, the powerful are here under obligation to "bear / carry" (βαστάζειν) the weaknesses of the powerless. Although this verb might be used in a somewhat grudging sense of putting up with other people's "vagaries,"[24] it more likely conveys the straightforward sense of carrying their loads,[25] as in Gal 6:2: Ἀλλήλων τὰ βάρη βαστάζετε καὶ οὕτως ἀναπληρώσετε τὸν νόμον τοῦ Χριστοῦ ("Bear one another's burdens and thus fulfill the law of Christ"). The only parallel that has been found that links "bear" with "weaknesses" in a single sentence is the altered citation of Isa 53:4 in Matt 8:17: αὐτὸς τὰς ἀσθενείας ἡμῶν ἔλαβεν καὶ τὰς νόσους ἐβάστασεν ("he took our weaknesses and bore our diseases").[26] Mutual assistance between house and tenement churches, involving material as well as theological and spiritual resources, appears to be in view with Paul's formulation. The crossing of difficult ethnic and theological barriers, such as those that stood between the "weak" and the "strong" in Rome,[27] seems particularly to be implied by the antithesis καὶ μὴ ἑαυτοῖς ἀρέσκειν ("and not to please ourselves"). The reflexive pronoun was used in a similar way in 14:7, which brings this formulation into close proximity with the preceding argument,[28] while the verb implies accommodating oneself to someone.[29] Epictetus offers the opposite counsel from Paul, in the context of avoiding domination by the opinions of others: θέλησον ἀρέσαι αὐτός ποτε σεαυτῷ. θέλησον καλὸς φανῆναι τῷ θεῷ ("Make it your wish then to please your own self, and you will be pleasing to god!").[30] As. Mos. 7.4 is closer to Paul in viewing self-pleasing in a highly negative light, describing impious, pagan rulers as homines dolosi, sibi placentes, ficti in omnibus suis ("deceitful men, self-pleasing, hypocrites in all their affairs").[31] Both Epictetus and the author of the Assumption of Moses share the cultural premise presupposed in Paul's argument that it is the strong who have the capability of pleasing themselves; slaves and members of the urban underclass could only

21 See BAGD 115 and 1 Clem. 10.2.

22 See Walter Grundmann, "δύναμαι κτλ.," TDNT 2 (1964) 285; other close parallels are Job 24:4; 29:16.

23 Ziesler, 337.

24 BAGD 137; Barrett, 269. Both appear to be influenced by the modern concept of tolerance because precise ancient parallels have not been adduced for this connotation.

25 See Käsemann, 381, and Werner Stenger, "βαστάζω," EDNT 1 (1990) 208.

26 See Thompson, Clothed with Christ, 211; he develops Michel's suggestion in 443 that Paul intended an allusion to Isaiah in this verse.

27 See Ehrensperger, Mutually Encouraged, 185.

28 Käsemann, 381.

29 BAGD 105.

30 Epictetus Diss. 2.18.19.

31 Translation adapted from Johannes Tromp, The Assumption of Moses: A Critical Edition with Commentary (Leiden: Brill, 1993) 16–17; his commentary (211) links this expression with φιλαυτία ("self-love"), viewed as a great evil by Philo Sacr. 3; Det. 32, 68, 78; and 2 Tim 3:2.

hope to please their masters. The point in 15:1 is to reverse this cultural premise, showing that in Christ it is the powerful who are obliged to serve the powerless. In the context of Romans, the matter of pleasing others rather than themselves must at least include "not destroying the fellow Christian/work of God (14:15, 20), pursuing peace and the upbuilding of community members (14:19), and abstaining from meat and anything else offensive (14:21)."[32] That it moves beyond such parameters into the broader arena of mutual assistance between house and tenement churches with differing resources becomes clear in the following sentence.

■ **2** It is striking that having identified himself with the strong, reversing the normal pattern of obligation in the patronage system, Paul now imposes the same admonition on both the strong and the weak.[33] He includes himself now with the weak as well as the strong with the formulation ἕκαστος ἡμῶν ("each of us"). As in Rom 12:3-8, each member of the charismatic community is a moral actor, capable of providing resources for others, capable of serving the good, of upbuilding the others and the church itself. This is a remarkable admonition in the Roman social system that assumed only the powerful had the capacity to act independently. To "please the neighbor" is a formulation that combines the verb of the preceding sentence with Paul's earlier reference to the πλησίον of 13:9-10, in which "neighbor" refers to members of Roman house and tenement churches. When Paul spoke in 1 Cor 10:33 of his apostolic strategy to "please all people in all he does" (πάντα πᾶσιν ἀρέσκω), he was referring to church members as well as prospective converts, but the immediate occasion of his formulation was the conflict between the "weak" and the "strong" in Corinth.[34] Although studies of "neighbor" continue to define πλησίον quite broadly as "one's

fellow human being,"[35] it is better to take this as a fellow believer.[36] The verb ἀρέσκω occasionally appeared in monumental inscriptions that celebrate significant service that pleases the city.[37] For example, a third-century C.E. inscription from Palmyra celebrates a benefaction as follows: Ἰούλιον Αὐρήλιον . . . οἱ σὺν αὐτῷ κατελθόντες εἰς Ὀλογενιάδα . . . ἀνέστησαν ἀρέσαντα αὐτοις τειμῆς χάριν . . . ("Julius Aurelius . . . [and] those coming down with him into Ologenias . . . raised [this] honorable gift which pleased them . . .").[38] Another inscription from the same time period refers to a benefaction that was ἀρέσαντα τῇ τε αὐτῇ βουλῇ καὶ τῷ δήμῳ ("pleasing to the same council and to the people").[39] Paul uses the word in a similar sense here, but since he otherwise was highly critical of "pleasing" the crowd or persons in authority (Gal 1:10; 1 Thess 2:4) for self-serving purposes, it seems likely that the double phrase εἰς τὸ ἀγαθὸν πρὸς οἰκοδομήν ("for the good, toward upbuilding") was intended as an ethical qualification.[40] The first phrase is a restatement of 13:10a, "the love does no evil to the neighbor"; it stipulates that the ethical category of "the good" to which believers should "cling" (12:9) and which according to 12:21 was to "overcome evil," should guide every effort to meet the needs of neighbors. Undiscriminating efforts to interact with fellow believers and their expectations that result in "good being spoken of as evil" (14:16) would violate this proviso. The distinctively Christian definition of "the good" is implied by the final qualification, "toward upbuilding." The term οἰκοδομή had been used in 14:19 in the distinctive sense of mutual edification within the context of the house or tenement church, which establishes the parameters of its interpretation here. As Ingrid Kitzberger has shown,[41] this word always relates to congregational life, and does not focus

32 Reasoner, *The Strong*, 192; see also Ziesler, 337.

33 See Godet, 468; Lagrange, 342; Michel, 444. Reasoner, *The Strong*, 191–93, overlooks the important shift between 15:1 and 2 in suggesting that "each" includes only the strong, as in the preceding verse.

34 See Thompson, *Clothed with Christ*, 212–13; Schneider, "Schwachen," 154–55.

35 Klaus Haacker, "πλησίον," *EDNT* 3 (1993) 113; see also Morris, 498.

36 See Heinrich Greeven, "πλησίον in the New Testament," *TDNT* 6 (1968) 317: "brother Christian."

37 See MM 75.

38 *SIG* Nr. 641, vol. 2:348.

39 *SIG* Nr. 646.12 in vol. 2:353.

40 Cranfield, 2:732; Dunn, 2:838.

41 Kitzberger, *Bau der Gemeinde*, 55–57, 305.

on individual edification and perfection, as our interpretive tradition often maintains.[42] As noted earlier, the idea of mutual upbuilding of congregations seems to have originated with the Pauline movement because no exact precedents have been found.[43] The wording here is somewhat reminiscent of the very first written evidence of this idea, in 1 Thess 5:11, where Paul admonishes the congregation to "build up each one" ($οἰκοδομεῖτε\ εἰς$ $τὸν\ ἕνα$).[44] Interpreting this in the light of Rom 14:19, each group has the responsibility of building up the other, thus reversing the cultural habit of seeking honor for one's own group by heaping dishonor on competitors. Although Pfammatter remains at the level of individual "selflessness in place of self-seeking,"[45] his formulation points toward this kind of fundamental reversal. If each group seeks constructively to encourage the development of integrity and maturity in other groups,[46] rather than trying to force them to conform to a single viewpoint, the ethnic and theological diversity in Rome would no longer be divisive and destructive.

■ 3 The crucial importance of Paul's admonition is grounded in the redemptive action of the Messiah who did not "please himself." As Michel observes, this verse has the titular form ὁ Χριστός ("the Christ"), referring to Jesus' messianic role.[47] The aorist verb in the expression οὐχ ἑαυτῷ ἤρεσεν ("he did not please himself") has been taken as complexive/constative,[48] which would include the entire ministry of Jesus as the arena of this selfless service to others,[49] but this would have been better stated if Paul had selected an imperfect verb, implying continual effort. The aspect of Christ's ministry that Paul has in mind is defined by an exact quotation from LXX Ps 68:10. It is introduced with the expression "but as it has been written,"[50] bringing the citation into antithetical relation with the negative statement of 15:3a: rather than "pleasing himself," he accepted reproaches. In a typical christological adaptation, Paul places the words of the psalmist on the lips of Jesus. The reproaches falling on the "me" of the beleaguered and shamed temple enthusiast in the Psalm now fall on Christ.[51] The hermeneutical adaptation is striking, in part because this is the only instance in the Pauline letters where a biblical precedent is cited for Jesus' passion.[52] The usual construal of "reproaches" is in relation to Christ's atoning death for others,[53] which would be sustained if the σε in the expression "reproach *you*" refers to a human victim rather than to God as in the original psalm. A distinguished group of earlier commentators insisted that Paul recontextualized the citation so that Christ takes up the burden of human humiliation,[54] with the key observation most clearly stated by Kühl: "otherwise the inner connection with verse 2 would be completely lost."[55] While most contemporary commentators are more concerned with theological cor-

---

42 Many commentaries err in the direction of individualizing this exhortation; see Meyer, 2:331; Leenhardt, 361–62; Dodd, 219–20; Cranfield, 2:732.

43 See Otto Michel, "οἰκοδομέω κτλ.," *TDNT* 5 (1967) 137–38.

44 See O. Semmelroth, "'Erbauet einer den anderen' 1 Thess 5,11)," *GuL* 30 (1957) 362–71.

45 Pfammatter, *Kirche als Bau*, 60–61.

46 See Fitzmyer's critique (70) of pietistic, sanctimonious understandings of "upbuilding," relating it to "spiritual growth" in a corporate sense that contributes to "Christian solidarity."

47 Michel, 444, followed by Dunn, 2:838.

48 See BDF §332.1 "in his whole earthly life," cited by Thompson, *Clothed with Christ*, 221.

49 See Barrett, 296; Cranfield, 2:732. Kleinknecht, *Gerechtfertigte*, 358, points particularly to the "selflessness of the messiah."

50 For the traditional Jewish background of the formula "as it has been written," see on 1:17. The formula appears also in Rom 2:24; 3:4, 10; 4:17; 8:36; 9:13, 33; 11:8, 26; 15:21.

51 This adaptation disturbed Jülicher, 325, who complained that the choice of Ps 68:10 was "not particularly apt."

52 See Koch, *Schrift*, 324, who notes the difference between this use of Ps 69 and the citation of Deut 21:23 in Gal 3:13. In *Jesus Christ in the Old Testament* (London: SPCK, 1965) 153–55, Anthony T. Hanson attempts to broaden the messianic reading by arguing that the citation refers both to Christ's preexistent activities and his passion because of the larger context of Ps 68, which does not seem plausible; see also idem, *Interpretation*, 115; idem, *Studies*, 15–16.

53 See Wilckens, 3:101–2; Kleinknecht, *Gerechtfertigte*, 359–60.

54 Meyer, 2:332; Sanday and Headlam, 395; Jülicher, 325; Lietzmann, 119; Lagrange, 342; Nieder, *Ethik*, 76–77.

55 Kühl, 461.

rectness than with the direct application of Paul's argument to the Roman audience,[56] it remains likely that Paul is attempting in this citation to correlate the shameful insults that both Christ and his followers bear. The shame they suffer falls on him. Otherwise, Paul would have chosen what some have suggested would have been a more obvious text such as Isa 53:4.[57]

The basic meaning of the noun ὄνειδος is "disgrace, shame, scandal . . . abuse,"[58] and the abstract term ὀνειδισμός used in the psalm citation means "insult, abuse, reproach" in passages like Sir 23:15 and Lam 3:30.[59] The verb ὀνειδίζειν ("to reproach/insult") appears in the passion narratives (Mark 15:32; Matt 27:44) that depict the insults Jesus received while on the cross. Christ died the most shameful of deaths in behalf of the shamed. In the context of Rom 15, the selection of this quotation serves perfectly to sustain a mutually accepting attitude between the "weak" and the "strong."[60] Since the former tended to "judge" and the latter to "despise" their competitors (14:3), both strategies of shaming are captured by the word "reproach/insult." This has the stunning implication that the contempt and judging going on between the Roman congregations add to the shameful reproach that Christ bore on the cross for the sake of all. Whenever one of the believers hearing this letter is shamed, Christ absorbs it. This lends a tremendous force to the admonition that the competing house churches should seek to "please the neighbor" in 15:2, adding to the other group's honor and integrity rather than participating in mutual shaming.[61]

■ **4** The focus on congregational relations is continued in 15:4 with a pointedly situational description of the function of Scripture. That all of Scripture is written "for our instruction" is consistent with other Pauline passages (1 Cor 9:10; 10:11; Rom 4:23-25),[62] but only here do we find Scripture explicitly linked to a congregation's "steadfastness," "encouragement," and "hope." The unusual expression ὅσα γὰρ προεγράφη ("for whatever was previously written")[63] refers to the entirety of Scripture, which, of course, includes the verse just cited from Ps 68:10.[64] The intent is to justify Paul's use of Scripture,[65] using a formula that may have been adapted from Jewish Christian usage.[66] The formula εἰς τὴν ἡμετέραν διδασκαλίαν ἐγράφη appears to reflect the rabbinic expression "in order to teach you."[67] The question is why Paul provides this rationale, which strikes

---

56   Scholars opting for σε as referring to God include Käsemann, 382; Cranfield, 2:733; Dunn, 2:839; Thompson, *Clothed with Christ*, 222; Fitzmyer, 703; Moo, 868; Koch, *Schrift*, 326. In "The Interpretation of the Second Person Singular in Quotations from the Psalms in the New Testament: A Note on Romans XV,3," *Her* 73 (1949) 73, Anthony T. Hanson argues for this option on the grounds that "every other quotation from the Psalms in the N.T. where the second person singular [pronoun] occurs it is understood as applying either to the Father or to the Son," but this does not address the question of precisely how this particular citation was intended to fit into Paul's argument.

57   Thompson, *Clothed with Christ*, 223–24, citing Chrysostom. Schweizer shows that the choice of Ps 68:10 in place of Isa 53 allows a more direct connection with the audience; "Röm 15,1-13," 81.

58   Johannes Schneider, "ὄνειδος κτλ.," *TDNT* 5 (1967) 238.

59   See Schneider, "ὄνειδος κτλ.," 241.

60   See Lagrange, 342; Kleinknecht, *Gerechtfertigte*, 361–64; Reasoner, *The Strong*, 192–93.

61   Cranfield, 2:733, argues against reducing the bearing of the LXX quotation "to encourage the strong Christians in Rome to imitate this particular ele-

ment of Christ's endurance," but he acknowledges this as a primary implication.

62   See Ellis, *Paul's Use*, 147–58; Koch, *Schrift*, 322–24.

63   The surveys by Gottlob Schrenk, "γράφω κτλ.," *TDNT* 1 (1964) 742–73; Hans Hübner, "γραφή," *EDNT* 1 (1990) 260–64; and Horst Balz, "προγράφω," *EDNT* 3 (1993) 154, make it clear that the verb Paul employs here, προγράφω, is never used elsewhere in reference to Scripture. Whether this is an indication of an interpolation, as argued by Keck, "Romans 15:4," 129, seems questionable because an interpolator would probably use more conventional language.

64   Morris, 499, cites Denis M. Farkasfalvy in W. R. Farmer and D. M. Farkasfalvy, *The Formation of the New Testament Canon: An Ecumenical Approach* (New York: Paulist, 1983) 105: "This statement is a bold generalization expropriating all Scriptures for the infant church."

65   See Käsemann, 382; Dunn, 2:829.

66   Michel, 445, points to the similar Hebrew expression, referring to Bruce M. Metzger, "The Formulas Introducing Quotations of Scripture in the New Testament and the Mishnah," *JBL* 70 (1951) 297–307; see especially 300–301.

67   Michel, 445; Keck, "Romans 15:4," 129, notes that

some commentators as a digression[68] more closely linked with the scriptural citations in 15:9-12 than with the current context.[69] Some have even suggested that this verse is an interpolation,[70] since it seems to reiterate the message of Rom 4:23-25 redundantly[71] and is so "all-encompassing" that it seems to "overshoot" the context.[72] It was certainly not required because of the christological adaptation of the psalm text,[73] because such christological readings are the norm in Paul's letters. Leander Keck has provided a compelling critique of suggestions that this verse "points back to the Old Testament to the recurring pattern of suffering of God's faithful down the centuries"[74] or that it affirms "a unity in the spiritual history of man."[75] However, Keck's critique overlooks the clue that Paul explicitly lifts up: "for *our* instruction," which matches the first person plural reference in 15:2 and includes the "you" in 15:3. The scandal in Paul's recontextualizing of Ps 68:10 is precisely what most contemporary scholars have avoided, namely, the understanding of σε ("you") as referring to the audience of his letter. To shift from an address to God, clearly intended by the "you" in the psalm, was a gigantic, virtually heretical step for Paul as well as his audience, requiring an explicit statement of his hermeneutic.[76] Just as in the Qumran community, Scripture is being "modernized" here, adapted under the power of the Spirit to the current situation of the audience regardless of its original meaning in the OT.[77]

There is a syntactical ambiguity in v. 4b, whether the two parallel phrases "through steadfastness" and "through encouragement" should be subordinated to "Scripture" or understood independently.[78] Subordinating both ὑπομονή ("steadfastness") and παράκλησις ("encouragement") to τῶν γραφῶν ("of the Scriptures") correlates well with the topic of scriptural authority in this sentence and matches the parallelism between these two words in the homiletic benediction in the next verse.[79] Most current commentators opt for the somewhat less coherent approach of separating the clauses because of the repeated διά,[80] so that the first phrase uses "through" in the sense of attendant circumstance while the second is causal. Certainty is not possible in this case, thus justifying a vague grammatical link in the translation above. However, since the advocates of the separating option undercut their point by correlating both ὑπομονή ("steadfastness") and παράκλησις

διδασκαλία means "instruction" rather than the activity of teaching as in Rom 12:7 or the "thing taught" as in 1 Tim 4:13, 16; 2 Tim 3:10; Titus 2:7. See also BAGD 191.

68 See Weiss, 570; Michel, 445; Ziesler, 338; Thompson, *Clothed with Christ*, 225. Moo, 869, refers to a "brief detour."

69 See Käsemann, 383. In "Zu Röm. 15,4.7.8," *ThStK* 86 (1913) 109–12, Friedrich Spitta argues that 15:4 relates more closely with 15:8-13 than with its immediate context, which allegedly supports a puzzling literary-critical theory that these verses belong with chapter 11.

70 Keck, "Romans 15:4," 125–36. In an earlier era, F. C. Baur had cast doubt on the authenticity of this section because the claims of scriptural authorization seemed too broad to be credible; see Godet's allusion in 469.

71 See Zahn, 592; Keck, "Romans 15:4," 126: "Why did Paul, having audaciously adduced many OT quotations without justification (apart from 4:24), provide a legitimation for this one precisely here?"

72 Keck, "Romans 15:4," 129.

73 See Koch's argument in *Schrift*, 324–26, that this rationale points to an interpretation of Ps 68:10 solely in terms of Christ's passion.

74 Wedderburn, *Reasons*, 86.

75 Dodd, 222.

76 This answers the main objection shared by Zahn, 592, and Keck, "Romans 15:4," 126, that "there is actually no substantial connection between v. 3 and v. 4."

77 See Fitzmyer, "Old Testament Quotations," 315. Dunn, 2:839, refers to Gaugler, 2:364–65, for a discussion of Paul's view of Scripture as the living word of God.

78 In "Phenomenon," 154, Michael proposes an elimination of the entire problem by deleting τῆς ὑπομονῆς καὶ διὰ τῆς παρακλήσεως from 15:4, assuming dittography from 15:5, but that would eliminate the definition of these terms by their coordination with Scripture as noted below.

79 See Meyer, 2:333; Godet, 469; Zahn, 592; Kühl, 462; Lagrange, 343; and Murray, 2:200.

80 See especially Michel, 445–46; Schmidt, 238; Käsemann, 383; Cranfield, 2:735; Schmidt, 238; Schlier, 421; Dunn, 2:839; Moo, 870.

("encouragement") closely with Scripture,[81] it seems preferable to subordinate both phrases in a parallel manner.[82] Paul seems to be contending that both "the steadfastness" and "the encouragement" are contained and authorized in a specific manner by Scripture,[83] which may explain the use of the definite article in both cases. Paul is not interested in steadfastness or encouragement in general, as all current translations seem to assume in deleting the article. By defining ἡ ὑπομονή in scriptural terms, he differentiates it from soldierly courage[84] and Stoic endurance,[85] because biblical encouragement characteristically depends on God.[86] Similarly, ἡ παράκλησις is quite different in the biblical tradition where the final source of comfort is God as compared with the Greek philosophical tradition of consolation that ordinarily remains within a human framework.[87] Moreover, by linking "the endurance" with "the encouragement," Paul broadens the claim of biblical reliance in 1 Macc 12:9, which is frequently mentioned as a close parallel.[88] In response to Spartan overtures, Jonathan the High Priest writes as follows:

ἡμεῖς οὖν ἀποσδεεῖς τούτων ὄντες, παράκλησιν ἔχοντες τὰ βιβλία τὰ ἅγια τὰ ἐν ταῖς χερσὶν ἡμῶν . . . ("while we need none of these [ties of alliance and friendship] since we have as our source of encouragement the holy books in our possession . . .").[89]

Both moral qualities that Paul derives from Scripture are highly relevant for the congregational situation: divinely granted steadfastness in bearing one another's burdens while living in the midst of reproaches;[90] godly encouragement to seek responsible forms of upbuilding through pleasing others.[91] Both qualities are grounded in the work of Christ in bearing reproaches for others, which the scriptural citation has just affirmed, through Paul's daring recontextualization, to the Roman setting. Facing insults and reproaches, within and without, the steadfastness and the encouragement of Scripture will sustain the Roman believers in a world-uniting hope.

The conclusion of v. 4 has produced puzzlement[92] because it states that the purpose of Scripture is that "we

81 See Käsemann, 383: "Scripture gives comfort and leads to patience"; Cranfield, 2:736: "with patient endurance and strengthened by the comfort and encouragement which the scriptures give. . . ."

82 This brings Paul's formulation in 15:4 into close correlation with 2 Cor 1:6, as noted by Walter Radl, "ὑπομονή," EDNT 3 (1993) 406.

83 Lagrange, 343.

84 Ceslas Spicq, "ὑπομονέω, ὑπομονή," TLNT 3 (1994) 415–16, shows that for Plato and Aristotle manly courage is visible when one expects no help from others. For example, Aristotle argues in Eth. nic. 1104b.1, ὁμοίως δὲ καὶ ἐπὶ τῆς ἀνδρείας. ἐθιζόμενοι γὰρ καταφρονεῖν τῶν φοβερῶν καὶ ὑπομένειν αὐτὰ γινόμεθα ἀνδρεῖοι, καὶ γενόμενοι μάλιστα δυνησόμεθα ὑπομένειν τὰ φοβερά ("And so with manliness: we become brave by training ourselves to despise and be steadfast against terrors, and we shall be best able to be steadfast against terrors when we have become brave"). See also Festugière, "ΥΠΟΜΟΝΗ," 477–83; M. Spanneut, "Geduld," RAC 9 (1976) 245–47.

85 Spicq, "ὄνειδος κτλ.," 415–16, cites Pseudo-Plato Def. 413c: "Constancy is the enduring of pain on account of the good and distress on account of the good (καρτερία ὑπομονὴ λύπης ἕνεκα τοῦ καλοῦ, ὑπομονὴ πόνων ἕνεκα τοῦ καλοῦ)." See also Seneca

Ep. 67.10 and Musonius Rufus 25.8–9, 12–13, and the discussion in Spanneut, "Geduld," 247–52.

86 Spicq, "ὄνειδος κτλ.," 418; Spicq notes that with the LXX, on which Paul's usage is dependent, "one enters a different semantic world altogether. . . . For the believer hope comes from God." See also P. M. Goicoechia, "De conceptu ὑπομονή apud S Paulum," dissertation, Rome, 1965; Friedrich Hauck, "ὑπομονέω, ὑπομονή," TDNT 4 (1967) 583, 585–86; P. Ortiz Valdisieso, "La hypomone en el Nuevo Testamento," dissertation, Rome, 1965; repr. as "ΥΠΟΜΟΝΗ en el Nuevo Testamento," EX (1967) 51–161; (1969) 115–205; Spanneut, "Geduld," 253–60.

87 See Otto Schmitz and Gustav Stählin, "παρακαλέω κτλ.," TDNT 5 (1967) 786–90, 797; Malherbe, Paul and the Thessalonians, 81–88.

88 Käsemann, 386; Dunn, 2:840; Fitzmyer, 603.

89 Translation adapted from Goldstein, 1 Maccabees, 453; consistent with the military context, he suggests "courage" for παράκλησις.

90 See Leenhardt, 363; Schmidt, 238.

91 See the application of this passage to modern issues of Christian disunity by Yves Congar, "La Consolation des Écritures (Rom 15,2-6)," in G. Casalis and F. Refoulé, eds., La Bible, chemin de l'Unite?, CTOB 1 (Paris: Cerf, 1967) 69–79.

92 See Cranfield, 2:735.

might have hope," rather than perhaps "faith." Although there is a tendency to interpret this verse in terms of hope in general,[93] or hope of "eternal salvation,"[94] the use of the definite article and the following discussion indicate that a specific form of hope is in view here. It is the hope in the conversion of the nations,[95] which will involve "the eschatological uniting of the church of Jews and Gentiles."[96] The use of the subjunctive, ἔχωμεν ("that we might have"), indicates that such hope is not currently present among all included in the first person plural, but that the logic of the Christ event and of Scripture will produce this missional expectation.

■ 5 The homiletic benediction that opens in this verse, which some prefer to call a "wish-prayer,"[97] "ties together major themes of the letter, particularly the parenetic themes, and also serves as a transition to the final paragraph of the parenesis."[98] The liturgical tone has frequently been observed, with Barrett suggesting that Paul may be drawing on "a liturgical doxology,"[99] and others indicating that it was designed for public reading in worship.[100] As in the other benedictions of this type in the Pauline corpus, it begins with the subject, God, linked to the foregoing by the particle δέ used in a connective sense.[101] The subject is defined with attributes that reiterate the details in the preceding verse, echoing the references to steadfastness in 2:7; 5:3-4; 8:24-25; and 12:11, and to encouragement in 1:12 and

12:1-8. While he did not find precise parallels to Paul's formulation in Greco-Roman or Jewish prayers, Günther Harder pointed to the similarity in genitive attributions to God in Septuagintal prayers such as ὁ θεὸς τῆς δικαιοσύνης μου ("the God of my righteousness") in Ps 4:1 and Κύριε ὁ θεὸς τῆς ἀληθείας ("O Lord God of truth") in Ps 30:5.[102] The definition of ἡ παράκλησις and ἡ ὑπομονή is provided by the preceding sentence, following the scriptural parameters that lead one to expect that their source would be God alone. To make this reference clear in English, I translate the articles with a single demonstrative pronoun, "this."[103] In the light of Christ, God is in fact the God of a specific form of steadfastness and encouragement, providing resources for the congregation to overcome their conflicts and reproaches[104] so they will be able to participate responsibly in the mission to the end of the world.

As in other homiletic benedictions, the verb is in the optative mood, δῴη ("may he give"), which was typical of LXX prayers and wishes[105] even though its more general usage was becoming obsolete in the first century.[106] The optative in this kind of context denotes "an attainable wish"[107] which in fact can only be attained if God wills. It does not have an imperatival sense, as suggested by Van Elderen and Murray,[108] yet this is typical of biblical benedictions in having a performative function. As the blessing is uttered by an authorized person, acting in a

93 Ibid.
94 Meyer, 2:334.
95 See Meyer's reference in 2:334 that hope in this verse refers to the "conversion of the world of nations."
96 Bernhard Mayer, "ἐλπίς κτλ.," *EDNT* 1 (1990) 439; see also Dunn, 2:840.
97 Wiles, *Paul's Intercessory Prayers*, 79; Weima, *Neglected Endings*, 144; Moo, 871. The inappropriateness of the term "prayer-wish" is captured by Cranfield, 2:736, who observes that it is "formally a wish and not a prayer (since in it God is not directly addressed, but the church)."
98 Jewett, "Homiletic Benediction," 26; see also Sanday and Headlam, 396; Lietzmann, 113.
99 Barrett, 270; see also Schlier, 421; Dunn, 2:840. In the strict sense, 15:5 is not doxological because it conveys a blessing to believers rather than expressing praise of God.
100 See Asmussen, 289; Käsemann, 383. Schnider and Stenger doubt that benedictions like this originated

in worship settings, insisting that they are "brief-spezifisch" in *Briefformular*, 89.
101 See Jewett, "Homiletic Benediction," 23.
102 Harder, *Gebet*, 65.
103 See BDF §249 for a discussion of the original function of the article as a demonstrative pronoun, and §252 referring to "the known, particular, previously mentioned" item.
104 See Wiles, *Paul's Intercessory Prayers*, 79–81. Karl Wennemer observes that the active quality of steadfastness in view here requires a divine source, alluded to in this reference; "Die Geduld in neutestamentlicher Sicht," *GuL* 36 (1963) 41; see also Schneider, "Schwachen," 157.
105 See Robertson, *Grammar*, 327.
106 See Moulton, *Grammar I*, 194–99; BDF §65.
107 BDF §384.
108 Murray, 2:200. Bastiaan Van Elderen develops the idea of an "imperatival optative," expressing a strong confidence in fulfillment; "The Verb in the Epistolary Invocation," *CTJ* 2 (1967) 48. While

manner deemed appropriate, it conveys divine power for its own fulfillment.[109] In this case the gift is to be granted to ὑμῖν ("you" [pl.]), which extends the singular σε ("you") in the psalm citation of 15:3 in order to address "all the Christians in Rome alike and together."[110] As in 15:2, the "weak" as well as the "strong" are included in the blessing, each having a need and responsibility to participate in the "same mind among one another" in the task of mutual upbuilding.

The expression τὸ αὐτὸ φρονεῖν ("the same mind/ thinking") was used in 12:16 in the sense of mental equality between different groups and persons that allows cooperation; it was defined by being drawn "toward" the lowly and avoiding being wise-minded in oneself. It did not involve agreeing on particulars or eliminating cultural conflicts, because the argument in Rom 14 explicitly rejected the ideal of ideological conformity.[111] To have the same mind "among"[112] one another is therefore to acknowledge every group's obedience to the same Lord and hence their legitimacy. It is therefore crucial to take the phrase κατὰ Χριστὸν Ἰησοῦν as meaning "according to Jesus Christ" whose example of bearing reproaches for others has just been affirmed in 15:3.[113] This produces a distinctive form of same-mindedness because the focus is no longer on achieving unanimity in doctrine or practice but rather on bearing abuse for each other and pleasing each other

as Christ did. This allows the theological, liturgical, cultural, and ethical differences between the "weak" and the "strong" to remain in force within a broader community of mutual respect and love.

■ **6** The purpose clause in the homiletic benediction focuses the attention of the audience on their common object of praise, which replaces the group glory that each congregation in Rome had been pursuing. The adverb ὁμοθυμαδόν, literally ὁμο meaning "same" and –θυμός meaning "emotion,"[114] was ordinarily used in the political sense of a unanimous decision or passion of a group. For instance, Aristophanes uses it in an ironic sense to depict the Spartan impulse to expel troublemakers: ὁμοθυμαδὸν σποδεῖν ἅπαντας τοὺς ἀλαζόντας δοκεῖ ("unanimously they're all resolved to beat up every imposter").[115] Philo uses it in a context closer to Romans, as God tells Moses: καὶ γὰρ <οἶδ᾽> ἰδίᾳ ἕκαστον καὶ πάντας ὁμοθυμαδὸν ἐφ᾽ ἱκετείας καὶ λιτὰς τραπομένους ἐλπίζειν τὴν ἐξ ἐμοῦ βοήθειαν ("For I know that each individually and all unanimously have devoted themselves to prayers and supplications hoping to gain help from me").[116] On the basis of its tenfold use in Acts as well as in this passage, "unanimous" appears to be a "technical term" for prayerful unity in the early church,[117] just as the comparable Hebrew word יחד was used as a technical term for unity in the Qumran materials.[118] While the idiom ἓν στόμα ("one mouth/voice") is

---

accepted by Weima, *Neglected Endings*, 84, this is a problematic category because Greco-Roman and Jewish religious leaders would not have approved of issuing commands to God.

109 See William J. Urbrock, "Blessings and Curses," *ABD* 1 (1992) 755.

110 Cranfield, 2:737.

111 The difficulty with Wiles's formulation in *Paul's Intercessory Prayers*, 81—"overcome their dissensions and to live in harmony with one another"—is that this admission of legitimate differences seems to be overlooked.

112 Weiss, 571, observes that while 12:16 uses the expression "be of the same mind" with "toward one another," in 15:5 it is qualified with "among one another."

113 See Dunn, 2:840, in contrast to Lagrange, 344, and others who downplay the aspect of moral example by referring to the "will of Christ."

114 See Hans Wolfgang Heidland, "ὁμοθυμαδόν," *TDNT* 5 (1967) 185.

115 Aristophanes *Av.* 1015; translation adapted from Benjamin Bickley Rogers, *Aristophanes* (New York: Putnam, 1927) 2:229. The ordinary political sense of the word may be found in Demosthenes' exhortation to resist Philip of Macedonia in *Orat.* 10.59; see Heidland, "ὁμοθυμαδόν," 186.

116 Philo *Mos.* 1.72. Other examples of Hellenistic-Jewish uses are Josephus *Ant.* 15.277 and *Ep. Aris.* 178.

117 Ceslas Spicq, "ὁμοθυμαδόν, ὁμόφρων," *TLNT* 2 (1994) 581.

118 Michel, 447. See the adverbial use of יחד to depict the unity of the Qumran community in 1QS 6:2–3: "They shall eat in common, pray in common and deliberate in common" (translation from Vermes, *Dead Sea Scrolls*, 69). See also 1QS 5:3, 10; 6:24; 1QH 4:24; 5:22, 30; 6:13; 11:25. The technical sense of military unity is visible in 1QM 1:11; 2:9; 7:6; 10:6; 12:4.

a typical expression of unanimity in classical Greek writers,[119] the closest parallel to ἐν ἑνὶ στόματι ("in one mouth/voice") in the context of worship is the description of the singing of Shadrach, Meshach, and Abednego in the fiery furnace: Ἀναλαβόντες δὲ τότε οἱ τρεῖς ὡς ἐξ ἑνὸς στόματος ὕμνουν καὶ ἐδόξαζον καὶ εὐλόγουν καὶ ἐξύψουν τὸν θεὸν . . . ("As with one mouth the three took up singing and glorifying and blessing and exalting God . . .").[120] The reference in Romans also "presupposes the picture of a chorus,"[121] in which formerly competitive groups in Rome are enabled to express their unity through "united liturgical worship of their hymns."[122] Johannes Quasten pursues this line through the later development of Christian hymnody: "With the understanding that unity and harmony stood in opposition to duality and disharmony the primitive Church rejected all heterophony and polyphony."[123] Although the love-feast settings in disparate and separated house and tenement churches would not have allowed this music to be united under a single roof, thus eliminating all polyphony, Paul nevertheless envisions that their voices in various locations would join in a harmonious chorus that gives glory to God rather than to their particular group. Since the object of their worship is "the God and Father of our Lord Jesus Christ," they would together be celebrating the transformation of the honor system of each nation and group in the light of the cross of Christ, adding their voices to a cosmic chorus of praise.[124] Since the expression δοξάζητε τὸν θεόν ("to glorify God") derives from traditional Jewish doxologies,[125] it seems quite likely that liturgical formulas derived from the Jewish liturgy such as the threefold "Holy, Holy, Holy" of Isa 6:3 sung by the angelic choir are in view here.[126] As humans participate in this chorus of praise, sharing the pleasing euphony of the benediction itself, God's glory is extended and increased.[127] The lordship of Christ is lifted up in this final clausula,[128] echoing the ten references to Jesus as the κύριος that played such a decisive role in the preceding chapter, thus indicating that the God to be praised "is none other than the Father of our Lord Jesus Christ, who creates and demands such unity."[129] But unlike the imperialistic unity previously sought by the Roman house and tenement churches, requiring that others conform to the practices and beliefs of a particular in-group, this is a chorus that encourages diversity to flourish, under the same blessed Lord.

119 See BAGD 770; Peterson, *ΕΙΣ ΘΕΟΣ*, 192–93.

120 This reference to the LXX of Dan 3:51 was pointed out by Harder, *Gebet*, 57. See also Sir 39:35.

121 Käsemann, 383; see also William Sheppard Smith, "Musical Aspects of the New Testament" (dissertation, Free University, Amsterdam, 1962); printed as *Musical Aspects of the New Testament* (Amsterdam: Uitgeverij W. ten have N. V., 1962) 162: "the musical performance of the church is above all else praise, the worship of God."

122 Wiles, *Paul's Intercessory Prayers*, 82.

123 Quasten, *Music and Worship*, 67.

124 Smith observes in "Musical Aspects," 163, that the singing of the church was conceived as joining "the heavenly hosts in praise of God and the Lamb, singing of the mighty acts of divine redemption. . . . When the church on earth sings 'Hallelujah!' she participates even now, as it were, in the mighty eschatological anthem which celebrates the ultimate salvation and judgment, the absolute reign of God."

125 See Harald Hegermann, "δοξάζω," *EDNT* 1 (1990) 348. Quasten traces the antipathy of early Christian worship to pagan liturgical forms in *Music and Worship*, 59–62.

126 See the survey of Jewish and early Christian liturgical materials in David Flusser, "Sanktus und Gloria," in Otto Betz et al., eds., *Abraham unser Vater. Juden und Christen im Gespräch über die Bibel. Festschrift für Otto Michel*, AGSU 5 (Leiden: Brill, 1963) 129–52.

127 In "Thanksgiving," 78, 81, Boobjer showed that by human praise "the glory of God received actual increase or was made stronger."

128 See Dunn, 2:841.

129 Schlier, 422; see also Hultgren, *Gospel*, 144–45.

15

The Tenth Pericope

Conclusion: Recapitulating the Inclusive Ethic That Will Contribute to the Mission of Global Transformation

7/ Therefore welcome one another, just as the Christ has also welcomed you,[a] to [the] glory of God. 8/ For I declare that Christ has become[b] a servant of "circumcision" for the sake of God's truth, in order to confirm the promises to the fathers, 9/ and at the same time [in order that] for the sake of mercy the Gentiles would glorify God, just as it is written:

> "On account of this shall I confess you among the Gentiles[c],
>> and to your name I shall sing praise."

10/ And again it says, "Rejoice, O Gentiles, with his people."

>> 11/ And again,[d] "Praise the Lord, all the Gentiles,
>> and let[e] all the peoples praise him."

>> 12/ And again Isaiah says, "The shoot of Jesse will come,
>> and he who rises up to rule the Gentiles,
>>> in him will the Gentiles hope."

13/ Now may the God of hope fill[f] you with all joy and peace in[g] having faith, so[h] that you may abound in this hope by the power of the Holy Spirit.

a   The reading $\dot{\eta}\mu\tilde{\alpha}\varsigma$ ("us") is strongly attested in B D* P 048 104 323 459 614 629 945 1506 1852 1877 2127[c] 2492* *al* ar b d* r o vg[ms] sa Thret[lem], but it has a limiting effect that is not congruent with Paul's argument. Cranfield, 2:739, observes that the reading $\dot{\upsilon}\mu\tilde{\alpha}\varsigma$ ("you") is "more pointed" in including both the weak and the strong, but he does not provide the full listing of support, which includes ℵ A C D[2] F G L Ψ *Maj* 6 33 69 81 88 181 256 263 326 330 365 424 436 451 1175 1241 1243 1319 1505 1573 1735 1739 1836 1874 1881 1912 1962 2200 2344 2492[c] 2495 *Maj* d[2] f g gue vg sy[p,h] bo arm eth geo slav Or[lat] Chr Cyr Ambst Pel Spec. Metzger, *Textual Commentary*, 536, accepts this latter reading, "which has superior and more diversified support."

b   The replacement of the widely attested perfect verb "has become" with the aorist $\gamma\dot{\epsilon}\nu\epsilon\sigma\vartheta\alpha\iota$ ("became") in B C* D* F G Ψ 630 1739 1881 *pc* appears to be a secondary, theological emendation that serves to drop the implication of the original reading that

Christ remains the servant of the Jews; see Barrett, 271. Zahn, 503, is the only commentator I found who argues for the aorist, on theological grounds, while Cranfield, 2:741, makes a plausible case that the perfect is the more difficult, and thus more original, reading. The perfect form $\gamma\epsilon\gamma\epsilon\nu\tilde{\eta}\sigma\vartheta\alpha\iota$ is supported by ℵ A C[2] D[1] L P 048 6 33 69 88 104 323 326 330 ($\delta\iota\dot{\alpha}\kappa\sigma\nu\sigma\nu$ follows rather than precedes the verb) 365 424 614 945 1175 1241 1243 1319 1505 1506 1573 1735 1836 1874 2344 2495 *Maj* Epiph.

c   The addition of the $\kappa\dot{\upsilon}\rho\iota\epsilon$ ("O Lord") by ℵ[2] 33 104 326 330 1505 1874 2495 *al* ar gue t vg[cl] sy[h] bo[mss] probably derives from the LXX where it was originally a part of LXX Ps 17:50. Paul apparently deleted it to carry through with his placement of the citation in the mouth of Jesus. See Cranfield, 2:745; Lagrange, 347.

d   B D F G 1505 1735 2495 *pc* it sy Ambst add the verb $\lambda\dot{\epsilon}\gamma\epsilon\iota$ ("he / it says") at this point. With the early evidence so equally divided on this variant, text critics prefer the majority text without this word, found in ℵ A C L P Ψ 6 33 69 88 104 323 326 330 365 424 614 945 1175 1241 1243 1319 1506 1573 1739 1836 1874 1881 2344 *Maj* ar t vg. It seems more likely to have been added than deleted, since $\lambda\dot{\epsilon}\gamma\epsilon\iota$ is found in the introduction of the preceding and succeeding citations.

e   F G L P 6 33 69 104 323 330 424 614 945 1175 1241 1243 1735 1836 1874 2344 *Maj* latt sy have the second person plural imperative, $\dot{\epsilon}\pi\alpha\iota\nu\dot{\epsilon}\sigma\alpha\tau\epsilon$ ("you [pl.] should praise") instead of the third person plural imperative found in the earlier and more reliable witnesses P[46] ℵ A B C D Ψ 81 88 326 365 1319 1505 1506 1573 1739 1881 2495 *pc*. The variant conforms to the wording of LXX Ps 116:1.

f   In place of $\pi\lambda\eta\rho\dot{\omega}\sigma\alpha\iota$ $\dot{\upsilon}\mu\tilde{\alpha}\varsigma$ $\pi\dot{\alpha}\sigma\eta\varsigma$ $\chi\alpha\rho\tilde{\alpha}\varsigma$ $\kappa\alpha\grave{\iota}$ $\epsilon\dot{\iota}\rho\dot{\eta}\nu\eta\varsigma$ ("fill you with all joy and peace"), B F G read $\pi\lambda\eta\rho\sigma\phi\sigma\rho\tilde{\eta}\sigma\alpha\iota$ $\dot{\upsilon}\mu\tilde{\alpha}\varsigma$ (B adds $\dot{\epsilon}\nu$) $\pi\dot{\alpha}\sigma\eta$ $\chi\alpha\rho\tilde{\alpha}$ $\kappa\alpha\grave{\iota}$ $\epsilon\dot{\iota}\rho\dot{\eta}\nu\eta$ ("give you full assurance in all joy and peace")—the dative case instead of the genitive. Commentators express puzzlement about this variant (Cranfield, 2:748). It has little chance of being original.

g   The omission of "in believing/being faithful" by D F G 1912 1962 b m Spec appears to be a mistake in the so called "Western" text.

h   The deletion of $\epsilon\dot{\iota}\varsigma$ $\tau\grave{\sigma}$ $\pi\epsilon\rho\iota\sigma\sigma\epsilon\dot{\upsilon}\epsilon\iota\nu$ ("so as to abound") by B 218 263 945 1243 1505 1874 1877 2495 *pc* is a mistake that requires explanation. Junack et al., *Neue Testament auf Papyrus*, 130, suggest that it might be due to homoioteleuton: skipping from $\pi\iota\sigma\tau\epsilon\dot{\upsilon}\epsilon\iota\nu$ to what follows $\pi\epsilon\rho\iota\sigma\sigma\epsilon\dot{\upsilon}\epsilon\iota\nu$.

Analysis

Although some commentators link 15:7-13 with 15:1-6,[1] most current commentators separate them into two separate units because of the parallel benedictions in 15:5-6 and 15:13 and because of the shift in terminology from "weak-strong" in the former and "Jew-Gentile" in the latter.[2] This pericope roughly matches the structure of the preceding paragraph, opening with an admonition followed by a scriptural proof and concluding with a homiletic benediction.[3] The actions of Christ in behalf of Jews and Gentiles draws together the themes of the fourth proof and provides a "coda" for the entire preceding argument of the letter.[4] The double use of $\pi\rho o\sigma\lambda\alpha\mu\beta\acute{\alpha}\nu\omega$ ("welcome") in 15:7 provides an inclusio with 14:1 and 3. The expression $\dot{\alpha}\lambda\acute{\eta}\vartheta\epsilon\iota\alpha\ \vartheta\epsilon o\hat{\upsilon}$ ("truth of God") in 15:8 reiterates 1:25 and 8:7. The "promise to the fathers" in 15:8 picks up the argument of 4:9-22 and 9:4, 8-9, while God's "mercy" to the Gentiles reiterates the theme of 9:15-18, 23, and 11:30-32.[5] The reference to $\pi\acute{\iota}\sigma\tau\iota\varsigma$ ("faith") in 15:13 reiterates that of 14:1, 2, 22, 23,[6] as well as the thesis of the letter in 1:16-17 and in the first proof of 1:18—4:25. The scriptural citations are drawn from five different passages representing all three divisions of the Hebrew Scriptures.[7] Paranomasia is repeatedly employed to fuse the pericope into a coherent whole. Continuing the glory-of-God-theme that provided the climax of the preceding pericope, the term $\delta\acute{o}\xi\alpha$ ("glory") in v. 7b is repeated in v. 9a as well as in the citation in v. 9b. The theme of glorifying God is elaborated in v. 11a and b by the repetition of the term "praise." The term "welcome" in 15:7a is repeated in the parallel line of 7b. The term "Gentiles" is repeated so frequently (15:9a, 9b, 10, 11, 12b, 12c) that it virtually provides the theme of the passage in coordination with the "people" of Israel (15:10, 11b).[8] Finally, the term "hope," which played a crucial role in the preceding pericope (15:4), recurs in 15:12c and is repeated in the closing benediction of v. 13a and 13b. The benediction concludes with a clausula of modest length, "by the power of the Holy Spirit." The result of these carefully crafted rhetorical devices is that this final pericope in the fourth proof assumes a heightened eloquence and compelling power, bringing the argument of the fourth proof to an effective conclusion.

Rhetorical Disposition

IV.	The *probatio*
12:1—15:13	The fourth proof: Living together according to the gospel so as to sustain the hope of global transformation
15:7-13	10. Conclusion: recapitulating the inclusive ethic that will contribute to the mission of global transformation
15:7	a. The ethical recapitulation to welcome others in a manner consistent with Christ's welcome of outsiders
15:7a	1) The summary of the preceding exhortation
	a) The action: "welcome"
	b) The actors: "you" (pl.)
	c) The recipients: "one another"
15:7b	2) The summary of the rationale
	a) The analogy to Christ's action of welcoming outsiders
	b) The analogy to the recipients of Christ's action: "you" (pl.)
	3) The purpose: glorifying God
15:8-12	b. The theological recapitulation of the relation between mutual welcome and world mission
15:8-9a	1) Christological recapitulation
15:8a	a) Christ as servant to the circumcised
15:8b	b) Christ's confirmation of the promise to the patriarchs
15:9a	c) Recapitulation of the purpose: that the nations might glorify God in response to mercy received
15:9b-12	2) Scriptural confirmation
15:9b-c	a) The first scriptural proof
15:9b	(1) The citation formula
15:9c	(2) The citation of Ps 17:50 and 2 Sam 22:50 concerning glorifying God among the nations
15:10	b) The second scriptural proof

1 See Godet, 466; Lagrange, 341; Morris, 495–96; Louw, 2:134.
2 See Dodd, 223; Althaus, 131; Käsemann, 380; Parunak, "Transitional Techniques," 535–36.
3 See Louw, 2:136.
4 Dunn, 2:844–45. See also Sass, *Verheißungen*, 462–65.
5 See Dunn, 2:845.
6 See Harvey, *Listening*, 205.
7 See Wilckens, 3:104. This supports the contention in our interpretation of 15:4 that $\ddot{o}\sigma\alpha\ \pi\rho o\epsilon\gamma\rho\acute{\alpha}\varphi\eta$ ("whatever was previously written") refers to the entirety of Scripture.
8 See Michel, 442.

15:10a	(1) The citation formula
15:10b	(2) The citation of Deut 32:43 concerning the nations rejoicing with Israel
15:11	c) The third scriptural proof
15:11a	(1) The citation formula
15:11b	(2) The citation of Ps 117:1 concerning all peoples praising God
15:12	d) The fourth scriptural proof
15:12a	(1) The citation formula
15:12b	(2) The citation of Isa 11:10 concerning the nations hoping for Christ
15:13	c. The homiletical benediction
15:13a	1) The source of benediction: the "God of hope"
	2) The recipients of benediction: "you" (pl.)
	3) The benefit: to be filled
	a) The content of filling: "all joy and peace"
	b) The means of filling: through faith
15:13b	4) The purpose of the benediction
	a) So that the congregation will "abound in hope"
	b) The means of abounding: "by the power of the Holy Spirit"

Exegesis

■ **7** The final pericope in the fourth proof begins with the inferential conjunction διό ("therefore") that draws together the argument commencing in 14:1.[9] As in the earlier use of προσλαμβάνομαι in 14:1, to "welcome" others implies to "receive or accept in one's society, in(to) one's home or circle of acquaintances."[10] In the context of early Christian literature, the home in view is the house or tenement church and the occasion is most likely the love feast, since this was the format of the assembly that turned the secular space of a house or portion of a tenement or shop into an arena of sacred welcome. While most commentators overlook this social context, reducing Paul's reference to vague sentiments of "mutual acceptance" and the like that seem more appropriate for the modern than the early church,[11] Schlatter, Michel, and Black have pointed quite properly to the common meal as the setting for this particular kind of welcome.[12] In a similar manner, Dupont associates this exhortation primarily with hospitality, welcoming people into one's home.[13] What is most striking about this admonition, however, is that the focus on the actions of the "strong" that marked 14:1 is now broadened to "one another," which implicitly includes the "weak."[14] This is consistent with the prohibition of judging "one another" in 14:13, where the "weak" are viewed as "brothers" who are equally obliged to "edify" the other side (14:19). While "the tensions and debates vanish completely from view" in this formulation as compared with chapter 14, it is wrong to infer that the admonition to welcome one another "cannot be oriented" to the conflicts in Rome.[15] Both the congregations of the "weak" and the "strong" are called upon here[16] to invite and welcome members of the other groups into their congregational meetings. If all of the groups in Rome participate in this extension of hospitality to outsiders, it will serve "to put an end to the hostile competition, and to admit the basic legitimacy of the other sides."[17] The hostility cannot be overcome if only one side participates in this breaking down of barriers, and the barriers themselves can most effectively be dismantled by sharing in sacramental love feasts in which Christ's inclusion of insiders and outsiders is recalled and celebrated.

In a comparative formulation introduced by καθώς

9 See Cranfield, 2:739; for the inferential use, see BAGD 198 and Molland, "Διό," 43–52.
10 BAGD 717; Glad, *Paul and Philodemus*, 224.
11 See, for instance, Dunn, 2:845: "mutual acceptance"; Murray, 2:203: "acceptance of believers"; Morris, 502: "wholehearted acceptance"; Stuhlmacher, 232: "accept one another."
12 Schlatter, 260; Michel, 447; Black, 200: "welcoming one another to common meals."
13 Jacques Dupont, "Accueillants à tous: Rm 15,4-9," *AsSeign* 6 (1969) 17.
14 See particularly Jülicher, 326; Weiss, 572; Schmidt, 239; Heil, 156; Moo, 873; Reasoner, *The Strong*, 194; Esler, *Conflict and Community*, 354.
15 Käsemann, 384, suggests that the new focus is "the acceptance of the Gentiles as an eschatological miracle," which overlooks the formulation of 15:10, which includes Jews as well as Gentiles in the chorus of praise.
16 See Reasoner, *The Strong*, 195; Hendrikus Boers, "The Problem of Jews and Gentiles in the Macro-Structure of Romans," *Neot* 15 (1981) 8–9.
17 Jewett, *Tolerance*, 29; see also de Silva, *Introduction*, 628, 636–38.

("as"),[18] Paul describes the basis of his innovative concept of mutual welcome.[19] Christ has acted toward each member of the Christian community in Rome precisely as they are to act toward each other: he "welcomed you." In the love feasts where Christ played the role of host and in the kerygma in which Christ's death for sinners was declared, each member of the various congregations had experienced such unearned welcome. A reminder of this basis was provided in 15:3 and will be reiterated in 15:8, but it also needs to be recognized that this clause "succinctly summarizes the main argument of Romans, namely, that God accepts sinners who formerly made themselves into his enemies. . . . The essence of the Christ event, as Paul depicts it in Romans, was 'welcome' shown to God's enemies."[20] It should also be clear that in the experience of first-generation believers, whose common life centered in sacramental love feasts, Christ's welcome to the feast echoed his behavior of welcoming sinners to share the messianic banquet during his earthly ministry. It is no accident that Paul uses the same verb, $\pi\rho\sigma\lambda\alpha\mu\beta\acute{\alpha}\nu\sigma\mu\alpha\iota$, to describe Christ's redemptive actions and the welcome to be extended by the congregations to each other. The use of the definite article with Christ, $\acute{o}$ $X\rho\iota\sigma\tau\acute{o}\varsigma$, is a subtle reminder that the Jewish Messiah is their redeemer, which places an additional bulwark against the discrimination the Gentile "strong" groups in Rome had been expressing to the predominately Jewish "weak" groups. Yet the $\acute{v}\mu\tilde{\alpha}\varsigma$ ("you" plural) is as inclusive of the various competitive groups in Rome as the word "one another," used in the preceding clause.[21] The Messiah welcomes both insiders and outsiders to his banquet, crossing in his resurrected ministry of the Lord's Supper the ethnic barriers between Jews and Gentiles as well as the theological and social barriers between the "weak" and the "strong." This provides the foundation of an ethic of inclusivity that is far more radical and wide-reaching than the grudging tolerance promoted by the later Enlightenment and the liberal churches of the present day, because it rests not on the inaccessibility of truth and the relativity of human viewpoints but on the welcoming action of Christ himself, as experienced in faith.[22] It is an ethic of obligation, anchored in ancient views of reciprocity, in which "Christ's acceptance of the believer forms the basis for the obligation to accept a fellow member."[23]

The adverbial phrase $\epsilon\acute{\iota}\varsigma$ $\delta\acute{o}\xi\alpha\nu$ $\tau\sigma\tilde{v}$ $\vartheta\epsilon\sigma\tilde{v}$ ("to [the] glory of God") should be attached to the main clause of v. 7 concerning mutual welcome,[24] continuing the theme of the chorus of divine praise in 15:6 and providing the theological basis for the subsequent argument in this pericope about all nations glorifying God.[25] As various groups of believers overcome the formerly hostile ethnic and theological diversity and welcome each other into their love feasts, this will reverse the competitive pattern

---

18 Käsemann, 385, following Nabadan, "Bekenntnis," 112, and followed by Cranfield, 2:739, suggests a causal construal of $\kappa\alpha\vartheta\acute{\omega}\varsigma$, which in fact occurs only when this conjunction is used at the beginning of a sentence. See BAGD 391; BDF §453. Although this alternative seems theologically superior to a comparative construal understood as a mere model for correct behavior, Paul's formulation requires no such improvement. That Christ's action of welcoming shameful outsiders provides a genuinely transforming basis of the congregations' ethic is adequately conveyed in 15:3 and 8.

19 See Smiga, "Occasion of the Letter," 269.

20 Jewett, *Tolerance*, 36. Thompson, *Clothed with Christ*, 231, points out that this "reception of the readers is rooted in and inseparable from the salvific death of the historical Jesus."

21 As noted in text-critical note a, the variant reading $\acute{\eta}\mu\tilde{\alpha}\varsigma$ ("us") is far less inclusive than the probably original reading $\acute{v}\mu\tilde{\alpha}\varsigma$. Lietzmann, 119, and Zeller, *Juden*, 219, restrict $\acute{v}\mu\tilde{\alpha}\varsigma$ to Gentiles, but this is rightly refuted by Reasoner, "The 'Strong' and the 'Weak' in Rome," 104.

22 See Jewett, *Tolerance*, 36–40.

23 Reasoner, *The Strong*, 194.

24 See Cranfield, 2:739–40.

25 This construes $\delta\acute{o}\xi\alpha$ as roughly equivalent to $\delta\sigma\xi-\acute{\alpha}\zeta\epsilon\iota\nu$ ("to glorify"), as Weiss, 573, and Moo, 875, suggest, bringing this statement into conformity with 15:9, "to glorify God for the sake of mercy." Another option is to take $\epsilon\acute{\iota}\varsigma$ $\delta\acute{o}\xi\alpha\nu$ in a local sense as entering into God's glory, as Tholuck, 425, suggests. This would be similar to the wording of Exod 24:16-18, where glory is a radiant cloud into which one enters. See also Kotansky, *Greek Magical Amulets*, I.137.

of glorifying one's group through the exclusion of others. As Moxnes shows, this also reverses the age-old pattern of humans usurping the central place of God, allowing history to reach its fulfillment when God receives "the praise and glory that are his due."[26] Paul's usage at this point reflects that of the OT, which ascribed the highest level of glory to God's "divine radiance," "his sovereign rule over nature and history," and the "majesty of his historical acts of salvation and judgment."[27] The preposition $\epsilon i \varsigma$ therefore conveys the "purpose"[28] of mutual welcome based on the welcome of Christ, overcoming the tensions between Jews and Gentiles, conservatives and liberals, that marked the Roman church. In Kühl's words, "The work of Christ for Jews and Gentiles alike served the glory of God, in order that both, Jews and Gentiles, would be able to praise God in the same congregation, with one accord and one voice."[29] It is particularly significant that this passage overturns a triumphalist biblical tradition, echoed in the Roman civic cult, that assumed that divine glory would be manifest only in the total victory of one side over the other. In Ps 149, for instance, "the Lord is celebrated as the one who adorns his humble people with victory so that they can 'exult in glory.' They are to take 'two-edged swords in their hands, to wreak vengeance on the nations and chastisement on the peoples . . . to execute on them the judgment written, 'This is glory for all his faithful ones.' . . ." This is precisely what Paul reverses in

Rom 15:7. It is not in the victory of the "weak" over the "strong," or vice versa, says Paul, but in their mutual, tolerant welcome that the glory of God is manifest. "To give glory to God is to place humans in their rightful place as creatures whom it is always dangerous to glorify."[30] By celebrating the glorious diversity of God's creation in sacramental love feasts based on Christ's sacrificial welcome of insiders and outsiders, the Roman house and tenement churches would find the proper way to join that cosmic chorus of praise, mentioned in the preceding verse, which Paul hopes will soon encompass the earth.

■ **8** With a solemn introduction, $\lambda \acute{\epsilon} \gamma \omega \ \gamma \acute{\alpha} \rho$ ("for I declare"),[31] Paul reiterates the doctrinal basis of his ethic of mutual welcome,[32] recapitulating several themes developed earlier in Romans.[33] This loosely structured sentence, which continues on into v. 9a, opens with a main subject and verb, "I declare," followed by an accusative with infinitive construction translated with "Christ became a servant," and then by a purpose clause, "in order to confirm the promises. . . ." That Christ "has become a servant of circumcision" reflects the formulation of 3:30 and 4:12 in which $\pi \epsilon \rho \iota \tau o \mu \acute{\eta}$ ("circumcision") denotes the Jewish people as a whole.[34] That this rather offensive formulation derives from the Roman congregational conflict as an epithet hurled by the strong against the weak has been made plausible by Joel Marcus.[35] As an example of such hostile usage, Marcus

26 Moxnes, *Theology in Conflict*, 87.
27 See Harald Hegermann, "δόξα," *EDNT* 1 (1990) 345. Everett F. Harrison points out the concentration of the glory language in Romans almost entirely on God; "The Use of Doxa in Greek Literature with Special Reference to the New Testament" (dissertation, University of Pennsylvania, 1950) 155; for an older account, see August Freiherrn von Gall, *Die Herrlichkeit Gottes. Eine biblisch theologische Untersuchung ausgedehnt über das alte Testament, die Targume, Apokryphen, Apokalypsen und das neue Testament* (Giessen: Ricker [Töpelmann], 1900) 61–66. Boobjer emphasizes the amplication of divine "light-substance" through human worship, in "Thanksgiving," 7–15, 81.
28 BAGD 229, describing $\epsilon i \varsigma$ as indicating the "goal . . . to denote purpose."
29 Kühl, 464; my translation appeared first in Jewett, *Tolerance*, 40–41. See also Maurice Carrez, *De la souffrance à la gloire. De la* δόξα *dans la pensée paulin-*

ienne, Bibliothèque théologique (Neuchâtel/Paris: Delachaux et Niestlé, 1976) 89, 97–98.
30 Jewett, *Tolerance*, 41–42, citing Ps 149:4-5, 9.
31 See Michel, 448; Käsemann, 385; Cranfield, 2:740.
32 Cranfield, 2:740, argues correctly that the $\gamma \acute{\alpha} \rho$ is intended to link the entirety of 15:8-12 with the main clause of 15:7.
33 See Ljungman, *PISTIS*, 48.
34 See Sanday and Headlam, 397–98; Fitzmyer, 706; Reasoner, *The Strong*, 230.
35 Marcus, "Circumcision and Uncircumcision," 78–81.

cites Josephus's report that the pagan polemicist Apion "mocks the practice of circumcision" (τὴν τῶν αἰδοίων χλευάζει περιτομήν).[36] Similarly, Philo acknowledges that circumcision was "an object of laughter among many people (ἀπὸ γελωμένου παρὰ τοῖς πολλοῖς)."[37] The use of this epithet evokes the argument in Rom 3–4 about the status of circumcision, providing a framework to claim that the Messiah's service to the "circumcision . . . includes the receiving of the Gentiles,"[38] as v. 9 goes on to show. The choice of the term "servant," unusual for Paul's view of Christ,[39] seems to reflect the early synoptic tradition that crystallized in Mark 10:45 (parallel to Matt 20:28), "for the Son of Man came not to be served but to serve (διακονηθῆναι ἀλλὰ διακονῆσαι) and to give his life as a ransom for many."[40] The priority granted here to Jewish Christian usage[41] is consistent with the formula reiterated throughout Romans, "the Jews first and then the Gentiles." In the context of the admonition to welcome the shamed, it is particularly

striking that Paul insists that Christ "has become" such a servant to the group stereotyped as "weak" in Rome,[42] using the perfect infinitive that implies Christ remains active in this role even in his resurrected state.[43] This formula resonates with the confession in 1:3-4, which depicted Jesus as Israel's Messiah, the "son of David."[44]

On the other hand, Paul's formulation allows no basis for Jewish chauvinism by insisting that the "truth of God" (see 3:4, 7) and the confirmation of the "promise to the Fathers" (see 4:16; 9:4; 11:28) open the path of divine mercy for the Gentiles (15:9).[45] In the light of Rom 3, to qualify Jesus' servanthood as expressing the "truth" of God's mercy to all without works of the law as disclosed in Christ means that any claim of Jewish advantage is radically delimited.[46] To follow Käsemann, Dunn, Hübner, and others[47] in rendering "truth of God" as a generalized theological abstraction of "covenant faithfulness" undercuts the direct relevance to the social context and to Paul's earlier argument in Romans. In contrast to

36 Josephus *C. Ap.* 2.137.

37 Philo *Spec.* 1.1.

38 See Ljungman, *Pistis*, 51.

39 Only in Gal 2:17 does Paul use διάκονος for Christ, posing a rhetorical question whether he was a "servant of sin," which requires a negative answer.

40 See Alfons Weiser, "διακονέω," *EDNT* 1 (1990) 303; Thompson, *Clothed with Christ*, 233. It is tempting to suggest that the use of "servant" points also to the "servant songs" in Deutero-Isaiah, as suggested by Cranfield, 2:741; for general background, see also Alexander Kerrigan, "Echoes of Themes from the Servant Songs in Pauline Theology," *SPCIC* 2 (1963) 217–19. But the LXX of Isaiah never uses the word διάκονος in this context and, as Morna D. Hooker observes in *Jesus and the Servant: The Influence of the Servant Concept of Deutero-Isaiah in the New Testament* (London: SPCK, 1959) 75, the figure in Deutero-Isaiah is Yahweh's servant rather than the servant of Israel. However one answers this question, Grieb, *Story of Romans*, 131, aptly observes "that the Jesus who died for others is a paradigm for Christian obedience."

41 Reasoner, "The 'Strong' and the 'Weak' in Rome," 106, goes further to suggest the possibility that "Christ became a servant to the circumcised" was a slogan created by the weak, but this seems implausible because the epithet "circumcised" was more likely employed by the strong. The Jewish Christian usage was probably restricted to "servant." In the

revised form of his dissertation, Reasoner simply claims that this reference points to "an interest in the Jewishness of Jesus." *The Strong*, 194.

42 See especially Leenhardt, 365: "Christ . . . has welcomed both groups and especially those who were the weakest, the most underprivileged, the most remote."

43 See Barrett, 271; Cranfield, 2:741; Schlier, 424. Note that the textual variant discussed above in note b weakens the claim that Christ remains the servant of the Jewish people. The theological and ethical implications concerning the ongoing priority that should be granted to Jews is worked out by Hans L. Reichrath, "Juden und Christen—Eine Frage von 'Ökumene'? Was uns Römer 15,7-13 dazu lehrt," *Judaica* 47 (1991) 25–27.

44 See Whitsett, "Son of God," 665–68.

45 See Ljungman, *Pistis*, 50–51; Donaldson, *Paul and the Gentiles*, 96–100; Jan Lambrecht, "Syntactical and Logical Remarks on Romans 15,8-9a," in Lambrecht, *Collected Studies*, 30–32; Sass, *Verheißungen*, 467–69.

46 See Ljungman, *Pistis*, 52. It would be extraneous to Paul's argument to see an allusion here to Isa 61:8-9 as suggested by Reasoner, "The 'Strong' and the 'Weak' in Rome," 107.

47 Käsemann, 385; Dunn, 2:847; Hans Hübner, "ἀλήθεια," *EDNT* 1 (1990) 59.

the blessing on "the Lord God of my master Abraham . . . who has not suffered his righteousness or truth to fail (ὃς οὐκ ἐγκατέλιπε τὴν δικαιοσύνην αὐτοῦ καὶ τὴν ἀλήθειαν)," pronounced by the servant after finding the beautiful Rachel as a wife for Isaac (Gen 24:27), Paul's view of God's truth extends beyond the ethnic boundaries of Abraham and his descendants. While the use of βεβαιοῦν with the connotation of "confirm" points in the same direction, Michel and others suggest that this verb implies both confirmation and fulfillment.[48] An example of the use of βεβαιόω as "fulfill" in connection with "promises" is Hannibal's oration to his army that "deeds" rather than "words" are now needed and that by the "will of the gods I am confident that I shall fulfill my promises forthwith (θεῶν γὰρ βουλομένων ὅσον οὔπω βεβαιώσειν ὑμῖν πέπεισμαι τὰς ἐπαγγελίας)."[49] The more typical sense of βεβαιόω to describe something that is firm and reliable is found in General Nicias's speech to the Athenians, warning about the illusion of thinking "that the truce that you have made will be firm (τὰς γενομένας ὑμῖν σπονδὰς ἔχειν τι βέβαιον)."[50] However, there are no instances of a double meaning in the same expression in the classical Greek and biblical parallels.[51] The primary sense of "make firm, establish, guarantee" remains most likely for this verse;[52] the "fulfillment" of the promises, in the context of Romans, is dependent on the future mission to Spain. In the light of Rom 4 and 11, to confirm "the promise to the fathers" means that they will most assuredly become a blessing to "many nations" (Rom 4:18) and thus contribute to the conversion of the world.[53] This careful description of Christ's relation to

Israel not only clears away any possibility of justifiable hostility and competition between the ethnic groups in Rome but also prepares the way for the completion of the global mission on the Spanish peninsula, which is the primary purpose of the letter as a whole.

■ **9** The compressed, elliptical style of this completion of the sentence begun in v. 8 requires grammatical choices unless one is content to produce a vague and open-ended translation such as that offered by Dunn, who refrains from tightening up the syntax.[54] After sorting through the grammatical investigations by Lagrange, Barrett, Cranfield, Williams, Ljungmann, Zeller, Wilckens, Dunn, Donaldson, and Lambrecht, I conclude that the infinitive δοξάσαι ("to glorify") in v. 9a was most likely intended to be dependent on the εἰς τό clause at the end of v. 8,[55] meaning that the Gentiles glorifying God runs as a sequential parallel to confirming the promise to the fathers.[56] The main sentence, on which all else is dependent, thus remains v. 8a, the declaration of Christ as the servant of circumcision. Although this entails "a harsh change of subjects,"[57] from "promises to the fathers" in v. 8b to "Gentiles glorifying God" in v. 9a, it is superior to making v. 9 dependent on the "I declare" at the beginning of v. 8[58] because that would make the "confirm the promise" clause into a parenthesis and would separate the christological center of the sentence in v. 8a from the conversion of the Gentiles in v. 9a. I therefore accept the view that the two ὑπέρ phrases, "for the sake of the truth of God" and "for the sake of mercy," were intended to stand in antithesis to one another.[59] I take the δέ at the beginning of v. 9 as an additive that connects the truth of God's promises to the

---

48 Michel, 448; see also Käsemann, 385; Albert Fuchs, "βεβαιόω," *EDNT* 1 (1990) 210.

49 Polybius *Hist.* 3.111.10–11.

50 Thucydides *Hist.* 6.10.2.

51 See Heinrich Schlier, "βέβαιος," *TDNT* 1 (1964) 600–601.

52 BAGD 138; Reasoner, "The 'Strong' and the 'Weak' in Rome," 108.

53 See particularly Williams, "Righteousness," 285–89; Wright, *Climax*, 234–35. Ljungman argues rightly in *Pistis*, 53, that the emphasis in 15:8 "lies in the receiving of the Gentiles together with the circumcised as one people, the true Israel." See also Harvey, *True Israel*, 78.

54 Dunn, 2:847: "Christ became a servant for the truth

of God . . . [elision in original] but the Gentiles glorify God for his mercy— [dash in original]."

55 The infinitive δοξάσαι in v. 9 is therefore one of result (BDF §391.4). Lambrecht, *Collected Studies*, 32, observes on contextual grounds that "the Gentiles' glorification of God is also considered an aim, a purpose."

56 See Barrett, 271; Ljungman, *Pistis*, 52; Moo, 876; Donaldson, *Paul and the Gentiles*, 99.

57 Cranfield, 2:743.

58 Cf. Lagrange, 346–47; Cranfield, 2:743; Zeller, *Juden*, 218–19; Wilckens, 3:106.

59 As advocated by Wilckens, 3:106, and Donaldson, *Paul and the Gentiles*, 99. The contrast between ὑπὲρ ἀληθείας and ὑπὲρ ἐλέους is also recognized by

patriarchs in v. 8 that will be fulfilled with the completion of the global mission with the mercy of God that is already being experienced by Gentile believers in v. 9a.[60]

The result of this grammatical conclusion is that v. 9a places Gentile conversion as the consequence of Christ's becoming a servant to Israel and therefore as the logical fulfillment of the promises to the Jewish patriarchs that their blessing would extend to the whole world.[61] While the Gentiles who have not heard the gospel remain caught in sin, glorifying themselves rather than God, Paul expects that they will be led to a reorientation by the "mercy" revealed in the gospel, thus fulfilling the hope expressed in 11:30-32 that all humankind may now receive mercy. In Dunn's words, "Paul's whole point is that Christ became servant of the circumcised *not* with a view to their salvation alone, but to confirm *both* phases of God's saving purpose: to Jew first and also to Gentile."[62] All will join in glorifying God, which will globalize the chorus that is already being heard in Christian worship.[63] The scriptural confirmation that follows serves to confirm the vision of the Gentiles joining the Jews in a cosmic chorus of praise, which Roman participation in the Spanish mission will promote, provided that the mutual welcome within Rome itself makes such participation feasible. There is a direct line in the argument from 15:7 to 15:9, linking the inclusive ethic to the missional vision.

In the interest of clarifying the congregational situation, it is worth observing that the antithesis of "circumcision . . . Gentile" in this pericope stands parallel to the antithesis of "weak . . . powerful" in the preceding three pericopes.[64] The shifting parallelism provides a substantial barrier against the view of Nanos, who argues that the "weak . . . are those Jews who do not yet believe in Jesus as the Christ of Israel . . . the non-Christian Jews in Rome."[65] While it was clear in 15:2 that the weak "neighbor" was a fellow Christian, there is little doubt that those of the "circumcision" in 15:8 are the original Jewish audience of the historical Jesus and that they along with some Jewish Christians in Rome will constitute "his people" in the citation from Deut 32:43 in 15:10.

The introductory formula in 15:9, $\kappa\alpha\vartheta\grave{\omega}\varsigma\ \gamma\acute{\epsilon}\gamma\rho\alpha\pi\tau\alpha\iota$ ("just as it is written"), opens a catena of citations, just as it had in 3:10 and 11:8.[66] Following the rabbinic custom of the הרז (*haraz*/"chain quotation") while avoiding technical rabbinic language,[67] Paul selects citations from all three branches of Jewish Scripture, the law, the prophets, and the writings, each one referring to the Gentiles and the praise of God.[68] In contrast to rabbinic custom, which always begins the *haraz* with a Pentateuch citation, Paul's first quotation is from the identically worded passages in LXX Ps 17:50 and 2 Sam 22:50. With the exception of deleting the word "Lord" in the vocative,[69] found in both LXX texts in slightly different locations, the quotation is verbatim. In the original context of 2 Sam, King David confesses God before the Gentile nations, initiating the praise of God that later scriptural voices suggest will be joined by the Gentiles themselves (Ps 117:1; Deut 32:43; Isa 11:10).[70] In the original context of Ps 18, it is either the believer or—in

---

Lambrecht, *Collected Studies*, 30, although he is sharply critical of Wilckens. On theological grounds, Dunn, 2:848, criticizes the strongly antithetical reading of δέ required by the Cranfield and Wilckens approaches.

60   The translation of δέ as "and at the same time" follows BAGD (2000) 213 (4), "a marker with an additive relation . . . *at the same time*." As an example BAGD cites Titus 1:1, "Paul, God's slave, and at the same time apostle of Jesus Christ."

61   See Williams, "Righteousness," 289; Whitsett, "Son of God," 668–70; Lambrecht, *Collected Studies*, 32; Sass, *Verheißungen*, 472–73.

62   Dunn, 2:848, with italics in the original, referring to Nabadan, "Bekenntnis," 115–18.

63   See Schlier, *Besinnung*, 315.

64   See Michel, 442.

65   Nanos, *Mystery*, 143.

66   Fitzmyer discusses the Qumran parallel to this introductory formula in "Old Testament Quotations," 301.

67   See Ellis, *Paul's Use*, 49–50: "The apostle never introduces his *haraz* in the explicit rabbinical manner, i.e. The Law says. . . ."

68   Michel, 449, based on his earlier study, *Bibel*, 54; see also Ernst von Dobschütz, "Zum paulinischen Schriftbeweis," *ZNW* 24 (1925) 307.

69   Koch, *Schrift*, 87, suggests that the deletion prevents misunderstanding "Lord" in this citation as Christ, an explanation that Stanley, *Scripture*, 180, finds implausible since "Lord" is retained in the parallel citation of Rom 15:11.

70   See Michel, 449. Leenhardt, 365, and Dunn, 2:849, argue that the Davidic voice is intended by Paul.

Christian imagination—Christ who lifts the voice of praise, in which case the deletion of "O Lord" might be understandable.[71] The christological interpretation[72] is not very consistent with the passage, because Christ is referred to in the third person in v. 8 and now would suddenly speak in the first person; the content of the citations also does not fit Christ very well, because he did not confess God in the midst of the Gentiles, having confined his ministry largely to the Jewish population, as reiterated in 15:8. The appropriate method in this instance is not to dwell on the original meanings of the citation or their surrounding contexts[73] but to attend to the rhetorical clues that Paul provides in introducing this catena of citations. In the context of the argument in this pericope, διὰ τοῦτο ("for this reason") appears to refer back to Christ's having become a servant to the Jews in order to extend mercy to the Gentiles, and in consequence, the "I" who is making the divine confession among the Gentiles must be the Christian evangelist bearing the news of this mercy. The "I" of 15:8 is thus identical with the "I" of 15:9. Ernst Käsemann draws the appropriate conclusion: "If so, the apostle to the Gentiles finds his own task delineated in Scripture."[74] This interpretation offers the most precise correlation with the missional purpose of Romans.[75] As in 14:1, the verb ἐξομολογέω would thus carry the distinctively Christian connotation of confessing faith in relation to the gospel,[76] in a cosmic liturgical context similar to the Christ hymn in Phil 2:11:

καὶ πᾶσα γλῶσσαι ἐξομολογήσηται ὅτι κύριος Ἰησοῦς Χριστὸς εἰς δόξαν θεοῦ πατρὸς ("and every tongue confess that Jesus Christ is Lord, to the glory of God the father").

The use of ψάλλω ("sing, sing praise, make melody"),[77] which originally referred to plucking the strings of musical instruments,[78] but which Paul ordinarily uses for singing aloud in the church,[79] resonates with the chorus of voices within the Christian congregations mentioned in 15:6. In this formulation, the evangelist himself is responsible for extending the psalmody into the Gentile world: I, Paul, "shall sing praise to your name!" If it is the name of "the God and Father of our Lord Jesus Christ" (15:6) that will be confessed and sung, it is understandable that the potentially confusing vocative, "O Lord," would have been deleted.[80] That ἐν ἔθνεσιν in this citation should be construed as "among the nations," thus including Israel,[81] seems unlikely in the light of v. 9a, which explicitly mentions Gentiles in contrast to Jews in the preceding sentence. In this first citation in the catena, Paul places himself in the role of the eschatological agent whose task is to initiate the crescendo of praise that will sweep over the Gentile world, responding to the conversion and pacification of the world evoked by the gospel.[82]

---

71   Michel, 449; Lagrange, 347; Cranfield, 2:745; Hays, *Echoes*, 72; Moo, 879.

72   Advocates of the christological interpretation include Cranfield, 2:742–43; Wilckens, 3:106–8; Moo, 879; Wagner, *Heralds*, 312; Whitsett, "Son of God," 670; Byrne, 432.

73   See Hays, *Echoes*, 71–72.

74   Käsemann, 387, adopting the view of Nababan, "Bekenntnis," 118–21. Wilk, *Bedeutung des Jesajabuches*, 154–55, and Sass, *Verheißungen*, 478, defend Käsemann's interpretation.

75   For example, Dunn, 2:848, says that the details of this verse evoke the travel plans mentioned in 1:5, 13; 15:16, 18, 27; 16:4.

76   This passage recalls the use of ὁμολογεῖν in Rom 10:9-10, where the "connection between confession and faith" is explicitly in view; see Otto Michel, "ὁμολογέω," *TDNT* 5 (1967) 209.

77   See BAGD 891.

78   See Gerhard Delling, "ὕμνος κτλ.," *TDNT* 8 (1972) 490–91.

79   Horst Balz argues on the basis of 1 Cor 14:15 and 26 that this term implies "collective singing in the assembly"; "ψάλλω," *EDNT* 3 (1992) 495. In *Music and Worship*, 66, Quasten refers to the prohibition of instrumental music in early Christian worship because it had been "so closely connected with idolatry"; see also C. H. Robertson, "The Meaning and Use of *Psallo*," *RestQ* 6 (1962) 19–31.

80   See Koch, *Schrift*, 121. Käsemann, 387, suggests that "the object of exhomologesis is the exalted Christ" but notes that this would not explain the deletion of "Lord."

81   Schlier, 425.

82   See Michel's allusion to the "Vorbeter" who initiates the prayer and praise of others in 449. In *Mission*, 108, Ferdinand Hahn grasps the distinctive thrust of this passage, referring to "the eschatological glorifying of God, which is the last and true goal of history." See also Hultgren, *Gospel*, 144–45.

■ **10** With an introductory formula that links the catena together, "and again it says," the LXX version of Deut 32:43 is cited[83] to show how the Gentiles will take up the melody of the cosmic chorus of praise. As Dunn points out, the LXX had expanded the Hebrew wording of the song of Moses and mitigated the triumph over the Gentiles with the phrase Paul cites here: μετὰ τοῦ λαοῦ αὐτοῦ ("with his people"),[84] implying that both Jews and Gentiles will join in the same chorus. The Masoretic text, in contrast, has "O Gentiles, praise his people" (הרנינו גוים עמו). By selecting this line from the LXX and avoiding the other references in Deut 32:43 to avenging "the blood of his children, and . . . vengeance on his adversaries" among the Gentiles, Paul drives forward his thesis of ethnic mutuality in Christ.[85] Consistent with his avoidance of the rabbinic custom of giving precedence in a *Haruz* to Pentateuch texts, Paul not only places Deuteronomy after a psalm text but recontextualizes and reinterprets it in the light of Christ's welcome of Jews and Gentiles alike (15:7), which entails the redemption of "the entire world."[86] Furthermore, in contrast to the broad tradition of anticipating Gentile conversion as a form of social and political subordination to Israel, bringing their gifts to the Jerusalem temple,[87] Paul envisions all nations rejoicing together, *with* each other rather than *above or below* each other with respect to honor, lending their varied voices to the cosmic chorus of praise.[88]

■ **11** The theme of inclusive praise is reinforced by the citation of Ps 117:1 (LXX 116:1), which includes parallel references to "all the Gentiles" and "all the nations." As Cranfield observes, "With its repeated use of πᾶς, it stresses the fact that no people is to be excluded from this common praise of God."[89] The citation is slightly altered by moving the first phrase ahead in the sentence, lending additional emphasis on the inclusion of the Gentiles.[90] It is possible that Paul changed the verb from the imperative used in the LXX, ἐπαινέσατε ("praise"), to the third person imperative ἐπαινεσάτωσαν ("let them praise"),[91] but it is also possible that he simply cited from the Symmachus version of this sentence that has the verbal form found here in Romans.[92] In either case, the form Paul uses matches the need of his citation chain, which refers to the Gentiles in the third person because the missionary goal of reaching beyond the already converted Gentiles in Rome to the yet unconverted Gentiles in Spain is in view. Their voices will be added to the voices of Jewish Christians in the eschatological chorus, as the wording of 15:11b makes plain. In the context of Paul's argument, the phrase πάντες οἱ λαοί ("all the peoples") includes the Jews among the other peoples of the world, as Kühl, Zahn, and Dabelstein have shown.[93] This scriptural warrant reinforces the emphasis of the preceding citation concerning ethnic groups rejoicing *with* each other rather than at each other's expense.[94] Their chorus of praise augments the glory of God and thus fulfills an ideal of Jewish and early Christian worship.[95]

■ **12** It is highly significant that the citation of Isa 11:10 in Paul's catena is placed last in the series, because while Isaiah may well be his favorite prophet,[96] and the larger context of Isa 11 conveys the eschatological vision of the lost tribes of Israel being restored,[97] the chauvinistic potential of Israel's military dominance over the Gentiles in Isaiah's wording needed to be eliminated by the placement and content of the three preceding citations.

---

83 See Stanley, *Scripture*, 180–81; Wagner, *Heralds*, 315–17.

84 Dunn, 2:849. Wilk, *Bedeutung des Jesajabuches*, 155, confirms that "his people" refers to Israel.

85 See Wilckens, 3:107–8; Sass, *Verheißungen*, 479.

86 Wagner, *Heralds*, 317.

87 Ps 68:29; 76:11-12; Zeph 3:9-10; Isa 18:7; 56:6-7; Tob 13:11; see Zeller, *Juden*, 223.

88 As Hays shows in *Echoes*, 71, this passage embodies "his vision for a church composed of Jews and Gentiles glorifying God together."

89 Cranfield, 2:746.

90 See Stanley, *Scripture*, 181–82.

91 Käsemann, 386.

92 Koch, *Schrift*, 111; Stanley, *Scripture*, 182.

93 Kühl, 464; Zahn, 595; Dabelstein, *Beurteilung*, 193.

94 Dunn, 2:850; Hays, *Echoes*, 71–72; and Moo, 879, turn the attention away from Paul's inclusive argument in this catena by commenting on what he does *not* cite in this verse, namely, the references in Ps 117:2 to God's mercy and truth.

95 See Champion, *Benedictions and Doxologies*, 95–97; du Toit, "Doxologische Gemeinschaft," 74–76.

96 See Dunn, 2:850.

97 See especially Hays, *Echoes*, 73.

The citation is virtually verbatim from the LXX, with the usual deletion of the initial "and"[98] as well as the elimination of the phrase "in that day." If the latter deletion was motivated by the desire to preserve "that day" as a reference to the final judgment as in 2:5, 16, and 13:12,[99] it also allows a recontextualizing of the citation as a prophecy of missionary fulfillment[100] rather than a threatened day of judgment in which the Gentiles would be forced to acknowledge their subordination under Israel's Messiah. The Masoretic text, once again, was much less suitable for Paul's purpose,[101] referring to the shoot of David standing as an "ensign" to the Gentiles, that is, as a battle flag symbolizing Israel's military predominance.[102] While ῥίζα meant "root" in Rom 11:16-18, here it seems to refer to a "shoot" that springs up from the root.[103] In Maurer's words, "From the pitiable remnant of the house of Jesse there will come forth, as from the remaining stump of a tree, a new shoot which will establish the coming kingdom."[104] It appears likely that "shoot of Jesse" was a traditional messianic title, both for Judaism and for early Christianity.[105] Here Paul returns to the same Jewish Christian creedal tradition with which the letter began, referring to Jesus as "born of the seed of David" (1:3). Even the expression ἐξ ἀναστάσεως νεκρῶν ("from the resurrection of the dead") (1:4) is echoed in the wording the LXX supplied

for the shoot of Jesse, ὁ ἀνιστάμενος ("who rises up") to fulfill his messianic role.[106] The expression ἄρχειν ἐθνῶν is a typical Hellenistic Jewish expression for ruling the Gentiles. The *Ep. Arist.* refers to "the multitudes whom you rule (ὧν ἄρχεις ὄχλων)," while Mark 10:42 refers to "the ones recognized to rule the Gentiles (οἱ δοκοῦντες ἄρχειν τῶν ἐθνῶν)." The same verb was used to describe the goddess Isis as "having great power and ruling in the world (κράτος ἔχουσα με[γ]ιστον καὶ ἐν τῷ κόσμοι ἄρχουσα)."[107] Without the recontextualizing provided by the preceding citations, which insist on mutual welcome between ethnic groups, and indeed, by the entire earlier argument of Romans that eliminates any basis for cultural or political predominance, this reference would simply remain an expression of Jewish cultural and political imperialism. But if Jesus is the long-expected "shoot of Jesse," his lordship has the quality of servanthood that 15:8 reinforced by means of the term διάκονος ("servant"). Christ died for his enemies rather than subjugating them by force. On the basis of this transformation of Jewish messianism, Paul is able to cite the final line of Isa 11:10, ἐπ᾽ αὐτῷ ἔθνη ἐλπιοῦσιν ("in him will the Gentiles hope"), because the rule of Christ is not simply another form of despotism.[108] The Gentiles hope for their own conversion in the context of global pacification, an eschatological

---

98   See Stanley, *Scripture*, 183.

99   Dunn, 2:850. Dietrich-Alex Koch makes the implausible suggestion in "Beobachtungen zum christologischen Schriftgebrauch in den vorpaulinischen Gemeinden," *ZNW* 71 (1980) 185, that the phrase was deleted because Paul did not wish to refer to a future event. Nebe seems more on target in suggesting in *Hoffnung*, 164, that Paul's christological reinterpretation of the citation led to the deletion. In "Jesaja und Paulus in Röm 15:12," *BZ* 27 (1983) 241, Bo Frid makes an implausible case that Paul did not intend to delete "in that day," so that the ἔσται ("it will be") at the beginning of 15:12 should not be connected with the "shoot of Jesse."

100   Wagner, *Heralds*, 318.

101   Dunn, 2:850, overlooks this militaristic detail in concluding that the LXX is "an acceptable paraphrase which does not significantly alter" the Hebrew text.

102   See the discussion of this predominately military symbol by Heinz-Josef Fabry, "*nes*," *TDOT* 5 (1985) 468–73. Typical OT parallels are Exod 17:6; Num

26:10; Isa 5:26; 18:3; 30:17; 31:9; Zech 9:16; Ps 74:4. If the Hebrew text had been used here, it probably would have evoked the battle flags of the Roman legions familiar to the hearers of Paul's letter in Rome.

103   See BAGD 736: "shoot or scion growing from the root"; Cranfield, 2:747.

104   Christian Maurer, "ῥίζα," *TDNT* 6 (1968) 986.

105   Other messianic uses of this expression may be found in Sir 47:22 and, in the expression "shoot of David," in 4QPat 3–4; 4QFlor 1:11; 4QpIsa 3:10ff.; 1QSb 5:26; Rev 5:5 and 22:16. See Koch, "Christologischer Schriftgebrauch," 185–86; Wagner, *Heralds*, 320–28; and Dunn, 2:850.

106   See Schlier, 425; Dunn, 2:850.

107   A shorter form of this was cited by BAGD 113 from Ulrich Wilckens, ed., *Urkunden der Ptolemäerzeit. Ältere Funde* (Berlin: de Gruyter, 1927–35) #81, col. 2.18.

108   See Dunn, 2:853: "Paul takes OT language, which might more naturally hold out hope of . . . Israel's ultimate dominance over the Gentiles (under the

---

hope centered in Christ.[109] Since Paul's purpose is to elicit support for the Gentile mission, he ends the citation at this point, rather than continuing on to the ingathering of Jewish exiles in Isa 11:11.[110]

Looking back over the catena of citations, one cannot help but be impressed with the careful selection and coherent editing, which effectively recontextualizes the meaning of each verse. Käsemann was right in noting that Paul has now demonstrated that the "Old Testament foreshadowed this message" of the inclusion of Jews and Gentiles,[111] and Hays properly remarks about how the catena embodies Paul's claim in 1:2 that the gospel was "promised beforehand through his prophets in holy texts."[112] However, this claim could only be properly fulfilled, in Paul's view, by reinterpreting the scriptural promises in the light of the Christ event, eliminating the toxic residues of chauvinism and imperialism that apparently still held considerable appeal to the Christian factions in Rome. The mission to the Spaniards, who had remained restive and rebellious under Roman imperialism, would be credible only if the gospel could shed the ethnic distortions of Jewish messianism.

■ **13** The homiletic benediction that concludes this final pericope of the fourth proof draws together the themes of the pericope as well as the central thesis of the letter.[113] In particular, 15:4 prepared the way by claiming that the inclusive purpose of Scripture was to produce hope. The hope of the Gentiles in their redemption through Christ foretold in the Isaiah citation in 15:12 is picked up in the double reference to hope in the benediction. This stress on hope, including the claim that God as revealed in Christ is ὁ θεὸς τῆς ἐλπίδος ("the God of hope"), appears opaque to those who view Romans as primarily a doctrinal treatise on the theme of faith.[114] As defined by the Isaiah citation that provides warrant for the missional purpose of the letter as a whole, this unprecedented expression[115] implies more than confidence in God as the one who in a general way fulfills promises,[116] or becomes the source of a positive outlook[117] that distinguishes "the authentic Christian from his pagan neighbours."[118] A more situational nuance is intended than is conveyed in Bultmann's claim that hope "constitutes Christian existence,"[119] as true as that may be. Paul's formulation also moves beyond the prospect of uniting the factions

---

royal messiah) . . . and by setting it in different sequence and in the different light cast by the Christ event, he transforms it into an expression of the idea of a humanity (Gentile with Jew) united in worship of the same God and by hope in the same Christ."

109 See Nebe, *Hoffnung,* 165; Wilk, *Bedeutung des Jesajabuches,* 158.

110 Hays, *Echoes,* 73, followed by Moo, 880, draws attention to this material that Paul decided not to quote, which diverts attention from Paul's "hope" to arouse support for the Gentile mission, which he expects would reach the end of the known world in Spain.

111 Käsemann, 387; he goes on to refer to Paul's letter as an "apology," which is wide of the mark.

112 Hays, *Echoes,* 71.

113 See Jewett, "Homiletic Benediction," 26–27.

114 This is the only verse of Romans that Zahn (595) cites without comment or explanation in his extensive commentary; Ziesler also passes over this verse without comment in 339, as does Nygren, 451. Fitzmyer, 708, defines the "God of hope" as the "one in whom both Jews and Gentiles believe and find their justification and salvation." Harrisville goes the farthest in subsuming hope under faith in 237 by

claiming that the benediction "does not take up the theme of the section it concludes," but summarizes the entire discourse starting in 12:3, which "is all a believing!" [exclamation point in the original]. This latter expression is repeated with emphasis, explaining 15:7: "It is *all* a believing" (italics in original).

115 Neither of the standard articles on ἐλπίς provides parallels to Paul's formulation in 15:13; see Rudolf Bultmann, "ἐλπίς κτλ.," *TDNT* 2 (1964) 532; and B. Mayer, "ἐλπίς κτλ.," *EDNT* 1 (1990) 439. No occurrence of "the God of hope" aside from Romans appeared in a *TLG* search of Greek materials from the eighth century B.C.E. to the first century C.E. As noted with reference to 15:5-6, there are similar ascriptions to God in Jewish and pagan prayers, as assembled by Harder, *Gebet,* 42–46, 64–66.

116 Wilhelm Thüsing, "Der Gott der Hoffnung (Röm 15,13)," in W. Heinen and J. Schreiner, eds., *Erwartung-Verheissung-Erfüllung* (Würzburg: Echter, 1969) 63–85.

117 See Murray, 2:207: "God is the God of hope because he generates hope in us."

118 Cranfield, 2:738; see also Reasoner, "The 'Strong' and the 'Weak' in Rome," 114.

119 Bultmann, "ἐλπίς κτλ.," *TDNT* 2 (1964) 532.

of the "weak" and the "strong" in the Roman church.[120] The context of Paul's argument points primarily to God as the source of the Isaianic vision of the future conversion of the Gentiles cited in the preceding verse, which was expected as the prelude to their joining with Israel as pacified equals before the throne of the one true God. This is the "cosmic goal of redemption"[121] which the Spanish mission will advance, because with the conversion of the Gentiles at the end of the known world and the concomitant conversion of hitherto unbelieving Jews, the goal of history will have been reached, the conflicts between the nations adjudicated, and the "revelation of the glory of the sons of God" (Rom 8:21) for which the whole creation groans will have occurred.

The powerful action that the benediction requests is that God, the source and ground of eschatological hope, "may fill you [pl.] with all joy and peace in believing," in order that this hope might "abound." The language is ecstatic,[122] reaching far beyond the bounds of human capability either to produce or to describe. The charismatic piety that Paul shared with the early church expresses itself in this "overflowing style."[123] The verb $\pi\lambda\eta\rho\delta\omega$, used here in the optative as is typical for homiletic benedictions elsewhere in the NT,[124] means "to fill something completely." The expression claims, in Delling's words, that "the joy, knowledge, etc. which fill the Christian shape his whole existence and imperiously claim his whole being."[125] The problem in Delling's formulation, typical of modern commentary on this verse,[126] is that Paul does not have primarily the Christian individual in view: the recipients are explicitly identified as $\dot{\nu}\mu\hat{\alpha}\varsigma$, "you" plural. The ecstatic piety is social rather than individual. To be filled in this way is for the

Roman congregations to have all other concerns crowded out, so that the missional vision completely captures their collective imagination and subsequent activity. The expansive formulation, "filled with *all* joy and peace," includes the rejoicing of the Gentiles mentioned in 15:10 as well as the peaceful harmony between the previously hostile factions in Rome mentioned in 15:5.[127] The inclusive formulation includes all of the earlier references to peace in the letter (1:7; 2:10; 3:17; 5:1; 8:6), and particularly 14:17 where both joy and peace are described as constitutive of the "kingdom of God," the social and spiritual realm of the church. Paul's ecstatic formulation seems to transcend limits: the $\pi\hat{\alpha}\varsigma$ ("all") makes the Roman house and tenement churches partners with the rejoicing of the whole creation at the prospect of peace in the form of redemption from the burden of sin (Rom 8:22-25); it also joins the churches' liturgies with those of the angelic creatures that converts believed were rejoicing about the throne of God,[128] embodying the dynamic quality of heavenly peace. The only qualification is that such joy and peace be $\dot{\epsilon}\nu$ $\tau\hat{\omega}$ $\pi\iota\sigma\tau\epsilon\dot{\nu}\epsilon\iota\nu$ ("in having faith"), an infinitive phrase whose peculiarity gives weight to its importance.[129] As Cranfield observes, "There are sorts of joy and peace which Paul certainly does not desire for the Christians in Rome: what he does desire is all the joy and peace which result from true faith in Christ."[130] Although there are suspicions that $\dot{\epsilon}\nu$ $\tau\hat{\omega}$ $\pi\iota\sigma\tau\epsilon\nu\epsilon\iota\nu$ ("in having faith") may have been a later addition to the text,[131] it seems clear that faith in this verse provides a necessary recapitulation of the earlier argument of Romans. Having faith in this context should not be restricted to doctrinal assent to justification by faith; it has to do with the accepting the gospel and join-

120 See Schmidt, 241; Moo, 880.

121 Käsemann, 387.

122 See Dunn, 2:853: "The language is rich and immoderate, like all uninhibited devotion."

123 Wiles, *Paul's Intercessory Prayers*, 85.

124 See Jewett, "Homiletic Benediction," 23–24.

125 Gerhard Delling, "$\pi\lambda\dot{\eta}\rho\eta\varsigma$ $\kappa\tau\lambda$.," *TDNT* 6 (1968) 291.

126 See Sanday and Headlam's restriction of the reference to the individual "Christian's heart" in 399; also Godet, 473; Cranfield, 2:748.

127 Recent commentators tend to restrict the reference to the congregational difficulties, overlooking the joy of the Gentiles mentioned in the immediate con-

text; see Michel, 451; Wiles, *Paul's Intercessory Prayers*, 86: "In asking for 'joy' and 'peace,' he selects graces which would be most endangered by their unfortunate divisions."

128 See Duane F. Watson, "Angels, New Testament," *ABD* 1 (1992) 253–55.

129 See Dobbeler, *Glaube als Teilhabe*, 205.

130 Cranfield, 2:748.

131 Michel, 451; Pallis, 154; Nababan, "Bekenntnis," 123; Wilckens argues for haplography in 3:109; Black, 201, rejects the suggestion of "in believing" as a gloss. See the text-critical note g above.

ing a house or tenement church whose distinctive forms of peace and joy are being shaped by Christ.[132] Chauvinistic joy in peace achieved through triumph over enemies, which the careful selection and editing of the previous citations seemed intended to avoid, would therefore not be included in the "all" that Paul has in mind because it is inconsistent with faith in Jesus as the Christ.

The purpose of the divine action of filling believers with hope and peace in believing is that "you [pl.] may abound in this hope." The verb $\pi\epsilon\rho\iota\sigma\sigma\epsilon\acute{u}\epsilon\iota\nu$ means to overflow, to be rich, to have more than enough, transcending all boundaries,[133] a meaning that we encountered in 5:15 with reference to "abundantly sharing in Christ's sufferings." The use of this verb in combination with "fill" to convey the "exuberant" quality of the prayer life of the apostle[134] is closely paralleled in Phil 1:9-11 where Paul petitions that their love "may overflow ($\pi\epsilon\rho\iota\sigma\sigma\epsilon\acute{u}\eta$) more and more with knowledge and full insight . . . filling out ($\pi\epsilon\pi\lambda\eta\rho\omega\mu\acute{e}\nu\omicron\iota$) the fruit of righteousness." While Paul's ecstatic, "superabundant" piety is manifest in this formulation,[135] following a charismatic, eschatological "law of excess,"[136] it is usually overlooked that the hope which overflows here is stated with the definite article: $\acute{e}\nu$ $\tau\hat{\eta}$ $\acute{e}\lambda\pi\acute{\iota}\delta\iota$ ("in the hope"). Paul is not requesting hope in general but the specific hope of the conversion of the nations toward which the entire letter points, which the Isaiah citation had articulated in the immediate context. I therefore translate the phrase as "in this hope," taking the article as a kind of demonstrative pronoun.[137]

The final phrase, "in the power of the Holy Spirit," needs to be interpreted in the light of the thesis in 1:16, that the gospel embodies the power of God. The benediction thus points forward to the detailing of the "power of the Holy Spirit" in 15:19, which includes the signs and wonders of evangelistic activity. It is therefore inadequate to suggest that Paul's interest was in observing "that the existence of this hope in men is no human possibility but the creation of the Spirit of God"[138] or that terms like "Spirit" and "power" simply overlap in Pauline thought.[139] The missional goal remains in sharp focus right to the end of this eloquent benediction,[140] while the concluding phrase makes it a performative blessing, conveyed and empowered by the spirit as the letter is being read aloud in the worship services of the Roman congregations.[141] With this magnificent ending of the formal argumentation in the letter, Paul can now move into his peroration, taking up the practical steps that are required to bring this world-transforming mission to fulfillment.

132 Wiles, *Paul's Intercessory Prayers*, 86, points particularly to 14:1-2, 22-23 to define what "faith" means in this context, noting that it also reiterates "a primary theme in the letter." See also Dobbeler, *Glaube als Teilhabe*, 205–6.

133 See especially Theobald, *Gnade*, 49–50.

134 See Wiles's discussion of Phil 1:9-11 and 4:19 in *Paul's Intercessory Prayers*, 101–7, esp. 104.

135 Wilhelm Hauck, "$\pi\epsilon\rho\iota\sigma\sigma\epsilon\acute{u}\omega$ $\kappa\tau\lambda$.," *TDNT* 6 (1968) 60; Gerhard Schneider, "$\pi\epsilon\rho\iota\sigma\sigma\epsilon\acute{u}\omega$," *EDNT* 3 (1993) 77.

136 See Theobald, *Gnade*, 332–44.

137 See BDF §249.

138 Cranfield, 2:748; see also Käsemann, 387; Gräbe, *Power of God*, 200–201.

139 Dunn, 2:851.

140 See Wiles, *Paul's Intercessory Prayers*, 88: "So the prayer functions partly in redirecting the message of the letter towards those practical missionary purposes with which it had begun." In "Röm 15,1-13," 83, Eduard Schweizer lifts up the connections to the Gentile mission announced in 1:5, 13-15, concluding that "here as in the entire letter to the Romans it is a matter of the establishment of nothing less than the reign of God in the world."

141 See Wiles, *Paul's Intercessory Prayers*, 90.

15:14-21 The *Peroratio*

15

The First Pericope

Recapitulation of Paul's Missionary Calling and Strategy

14/ Now as far as I personally am concerned, I am confident concerning you, my[a] brothers, that you yourselves[b] are also full of goodness,[c] having been filled with every kind of[d] knowledge, capable also to admonish one another.[e] 15/ Now I have written rather boldly[f] to you,[g] in part as a mere reminder to you on account of the grace given to me by[h] God, 16/ to[i] be a minister of Christ Jesus to the Gentiles,[j] in priestly service to the gospel of God, in order that the offering of the Gentiles might become[k] acceptable,[l] made holy in the Holy Spirit.

17/ [m] I have therefore the boast in Christ Jesus[n] before God; 18/ for I shall[o] not make bold to say anything[p] except what Christ has performed through me,[q] toward the obedience[r] of the Gentiles, by word and deed, 19/ in [the][s] power of signs and[t] wonders, in [the] power of the Spirit,[u] so that from Jerusalem[v] also as far round as Illyricum, I have fulfilled the gospel of Christ, 20/ thus aspiring[w] not to preach where Christ has already been named, lest I might build on another's foundation, 21/ but as it has been written,
"They shall see,[x] who have never been informed about him,
    and those who have never heard of him shall understand."

a   The absence of μου ("my") in P[46] D* F G 1739 1881 *pc* it Ambst is more than counterbalanced by its inclusion in ℵ A B C D⁹ L P Ψ 6 33 69 88 104 323 326 330 365 424 614 945 1175 1241 1243 1319 1505 1506 1573 1735 1836 1874 2344 2495 *Maj* mon vg sy. This omission appears to be an effort to generalize the message of Romans by eliminating the appearance of special ties between Paul and the Roman Christians.

b   The absence of the widely attested καὶ αὐτοί ("also yourselves") in P[46] D F G it Spec has little likelihood of being original, and may fit into the pattern discerned earlier of paring back the indications of special Roman status.

c   In place of the solidly attested ἀγαθωσύνης ("of goodness") there are some minor variants that may

have arisen from the similar appearance of the Greek terms: F G latt have ἀγάπης ("of love") and 629 *pc* have ἁγιωσύνης ("of holiness").

d   The article τῆς ("of the") is omitted by P[46] A C D F G L 33 69 88 104 323 326 365 424 614 945 1175 1241 1319 1505 1573 1735 1836 1874 2495 *Maj* and is included by ℵ B P Ψ 6 330 1243 1506 1739 1881 2344 *pc* Cl. The evidence is so evenly divided that Nestle-Aland[26/27] *GNT*[3/4] places the article in square brackets; Metzger fails to discuss it. The resultant phrase would be "with all knowledge," if the article is included, and "with every kind of knowledge," if it is omitted; see Cranfield, 2:753. On the basis of the rules favoring the more difficult and shorter reading, the article is more likely to have been absent in the original text.

e   In place of ἀλλήλους ("one another") attested overwhelmingly by P[46] ℵ A B C D F G P Ψ 88 326 630 1175 1243 1505 1506 1739 1881 2495 *al* latt sy[h], a minor variant, ἄλλους ("others"), in L 6 33 69 104 323 330 365 424 614 945 1175 1241 1319 1573 1735 1836 1874 2344 *Maj* sy[p], tends to generalize the relevance of the text and also amplify the authority of the Roman church. Zahn, 596, argues unconvincingly for the priority of this variant.

f   While the adjective τολμηρότερον ("rather boldly") is found in P[46] ℵ C D F G L P Ψ 6 33 69 88 104 323 326 365 424 614 945 1175 1241 1243 1319 1505 1573 1735 1739 1836 1874 1881 2344 2495 *Maj*, the adverbial form τολμηροτερῶς ("rather boldly") appears in A B 330 629 1506 *pc*. The former is surely to be preferred as more broadly attested, despite the judgment of Cranfield, 2:753.

g   The appearance of ἀδελφοί ("brothers") in P[46] ℵ[2] D F G L P Ψ 5 6 33 61 69 88 104 181 256 263 323 326 330 365 424 436 441 451 459 467 614 621 623 629 720 915 917 945 1175 1241 1243 1319 1398 1505 1506 1573 1678 1718 1735 1751 1836 1845 1852 1874 1875 1877 1908 1912 1942 1959 2110 2127 2138 2197 2344 2492 2495 2516 2523 2544 2718 *Maj* d g vg sy[p.h.pal] sa[mss] arm may be influenced by lectionary use, according to Metzger, *Textual Commentary*, 473. The shorter version without "brothers," as found in ℵ* A B C 81 218 630 1563 1739 1881 1962 2200 2495 *al* ar b sa bo eth Or Cyp Chr Aug, is to be preferred. The argument for the inclusion of "brothers" by Aasgaard, "Brothers in Brackets," 317–18, is unconvincing because of the weighty support for deletion.

h   The evidence is rather evenly balanced between ℵ* B F with the reading ἀπό ("from") and P[46] ℵ[2] A C D

G L P Ψ 6 33 69 88 323 326 330 365 424 614 945 1175 1241 1243 1319 1505 1506 1573 1735 1739 1836 1874 1881 2344 2495 *Maj* with the reading ὑπό ("by"). The latter has a slightly better chance of being original, in part because the tendency in Koine Greek was for ἀπό to replace ὑπό, according to BAGD 88. For a contrary assessment, see Cranfield, 2:754.

i   A single text, P⁴⁰, has διά ("on account of") in place of εἰς ("to, for"). It is clearly a scribal error, and Cranfield, 2:754, suggests the replication of a phrase with διά earlier in the sentence.

j   The omission of εἰς τὰ ἔθνη ("to the Gentiles") in B appears to be accidental.

k   In place of the widely attested aorist subjunctive γένηται ("it might become"), the aorist passive form γενήθη ("it became") is found in B 1881*, which is perhaps a retrospective correction about the outcome of the Gentile mission.

l   The omission of εὐπρόσδεκτος ("well-pleasing, acceptable") in F G appears to be a grammatical smoothing of the text, allowing ἡ προσφορὰ τῶν ἐθνῶν ("the offering of the nations") to be linked directly with ἁγιασμένη ("sanctified").

m   In place of ἔχω οὖν τὴν καύχησιν ("I have therefore the boast") that is adequately attested in B C^vid D F G 69 81 330 365 1319 1506 1573 1735 *pc*, there are two major variants. P⁴⁶ has ἣν ἔχω καύχησιν ("which boast I have") and ℵ A L P Ψ 6 33 (88 + μέν) 104 323 326 424 614 945 1175 1241 1243 1505 1739 1836 1874 1881 2495 *Maj* have ἔχω οὖν καύχησιν ("I have therefore a boast"). The first option is more likely to have been original since the use of the article with "boast" is a somewhat more difficult reading because of the vague antecedent. See Cranfield, 2:757.

n   The omission of "Jesus" in P⁴⁶ 323* *pc* Ambst is difficult to explain, but in view of the weak attestation, unlikely to be original.

o   The future verb τολμήσω ("I shall make bold") found in all of the major groups of texts is replaced in ℵ² B with the present verb τόλμω ("I make bold"), which is probably secondary not only because of narrow attestation, but also because the odd dissonance of the future tense compared with the present and past verbs used otherwise in this pericope would thereby be eliminated. The present verb could easily have been caused by haplography. Thus τολμήσω is to be preferred as the more difficult reading.

p   The wording τολμήσω τι λαλεῖν ("bold to say anything") found in ℵ* (ℵ² B have τόλμω—see preceding note) A C P 69 81 326 365 629 630 1243 1319 1506 1735 1739 *pc* lat is so broadly attested by the Alexandrian and Western traditions that it is likely original. P⁴⁶ has the sequence τι τολμήσω λαλεῖν

and L Ψ 6 33 88 104 323 330 424 614 945 1175 1241 1836 1874 *Maj* b have τολμήσω λαλεῖν τι. D F G Spec have τολμήσω τι ἐπεῖν. 1505 1881 2495 *pc* provide, in differing sequences, the aorist verb λαλῆσαι ("to [have] said anything"). All of these variants appear to be intended as stylistic improvements.

q   In place of the widely attested δι᾿ ἐμοῦ ("through me"), B has an obvious theological improvement of δι᾿ ἐμοῦ λόγων ("through my words"). The explanation offered by Cranfield, 2:758, that B sought an antecedent for ὧν ("of which") earlier in the sentence, is also plausible.

r   Another variant in B, apparently associated with the addition of "words" earlier in the sentence, is ἀκοήν ("hearing") in place of the broadly attested ὑποκοήν ("obedience").

s   The reading of αὐτοῦ ("his") in P⁴⁶ D* F G mon Spec looks like an interpretive addition, specifying that the power of miracle working is Christ's. The version without the addition of "his" has stronger support in ℵ A B C D¹ L P Ψ 6 33 69 88 104 323 326 330 365 424 614 945 1175 1241 1243 1319 1505 1506 1573 1735 1739 1836 1881 2495 *Maj* lat sy cop Ambst.

t   The addition of the particle τε (in combination with καί, "and") by P⁴⁶ is apparently a stylistic improvement closely related to several other eccentric P⁴⁶ readings in vv. 16-19.

u   The earlier editions of Nestle¹⁶⁻²¹ and Nestle-Aland²²⁻²⁵ manifested a sharp critical assessment in following B, which alone lacks qualifications to the expression ἐν δυνάμει πνεύματος ("in [the] power of [the] spirit," while Nestle-Aland²⁶⁾²⁷ GNT³⁾⁴ hedge by adding θεοῦ ("of God") in square brackets, following P⁴⁶ ℵ (C illegible) D¹ L P Ψ 6 88 181 323 326 424 436 614 629 945 1175 1241 1505 1506 1735 1836 1874 1877 1912 2492 2495 *Maj Lect* b syr^{p,h} geo² slav Or^{lat2/3} Did^{dub1/3} Chr Cyr^{1/2}. In *Textual Commentary*, 473, Metzger acknowledges that this was a "compromise" between the purists willing to follow B and the "majority of the committee . . . unwilling to adopt a reading based on such slender Greek evidence." The fact that there are additional variants that add the completions to the bare expression found in B lends credence to its superiority in this instance. The reference to ἁγίου ("holy"), resulting in "holy spirit," occurs in A D^{+,2} F G 33 69 81 104 256 263 365 459 630 1243 1319 1573 1739 1852 1881 1962 2127 2200 *pc* ar d f g mon o vg sy^{hmg,pal} sa bo arm eth geo¹ Or^{lat1/3} Ath Ps-Ath Apollinaris Did^{dub1/3} Cyr^{1/2} Ambst Pel Aug Spec Ps-Vig Varimadum. A combination of the several completions is found in 330 451 with πνεύματος θεοῦ ἁγίου ("holy spirit of God"). For support of the seemingly daring choice of the B reading, see Michel, 459; Cranfield, 2:758.

v   D F G mon substitute the expression $\pi\epsilon\pi\lambda\eta\rho\hat{\omega}\sigma\vartheta\alpha\iota$ $\dot{\alpha}\pi\dot{o}$ $\text{'}I\epsilon\rho\text{ο}\upsilon\sigma\alpha\lambda\dot{\eta}\mu$ $\mu\dot{\epsilon}\chi\rho\iota$ $\tau\text{ο}\hat{\upsilon}$ $I\lambda\lambda\upsilon\rho\iota\kappa\text{ο}\hat{\upsilon}$ $\kappa\alpha\dot{\iota}$ $\kappa\dot{\upsilon}\kappa\lambda\omega$ ("to be completed/fulfilled from Jerusalem to Illyricum and around"), which appears to be a secondary correction of the original text, implying a broader scope for Paul's mission. The same interest is visible in the D text of Acts.

w   In place of the rather awkward neuter participle $\varphi\iota\lambda\text{ο}\tau\iota\mu\text{ο}\dot{\upsilon}\mu\epsilon\nu\text{ο}\nu$ ("aspiring"), attested in ℵ A C D[2] L P Ψ 6 33 69 88 104 323 326 330 365 424 614 945 1175 1241 1243 1319 1505 1506 1573 1735 1739 1836 1874 1881 2495 *Maj* sy[h], the finite verb $\varphi\iota\lambda\text{ο}\tau\iota\mu\text{ο}\dot{\upsilon}\mu\alpha\iota$ ("I aspire") appears in P[46] B D* F G b sy[p] as a grammatical improvement, according to Cranfield, 2:763.

x   The placement of the verb $\ddot{\text{ο}}\psi\text{ο}\nu\tau\alpha\iota$ ("they shall see") in B 69 330 1243 *pc* Ambst prior to $\text{ο}\hat{\iota}\varsigma$ at the beginning of the line rather than after $\alpha\dot{\upsilon}\tau\text{ο}\hat{\upsilon}$ ("him") at the end of the line is another instance where the minority witness is methodologically correct as the more difficult reading. Nestle-Aland[26/27] and *GNT*[3/4] have in this instance fallen away from the methodological clarity of the earlier Nestle[16-21] and Nestle-Aland[22-25] text, which followed this reading despite the slender evidence. The placement of $\ddot{\text{ο}}\psi\text{ο}\nu\tau\alpha\iota$ at the end of the line in P[46] ℵ A C D F G L P Ψ 6 33 88 104 323 326 365 424 614 945 1175 1241 1319 1505 1506 1573 1735 1739 1836 1874 1881 2344 2495 *Maj* latt sy is a clear assimilation to the LXX, which should be rejected as the easier reading.

Analysis

This passage corresponds in style and content to Rom 1:1-12,[1] providing a sober recapitulation of Paul's earlier argument.[2] Review does not lend itself to eloquence, here or elsewhere. In his survey of classical references to recapitulation, Josef Martin observes that the "simple, plain" style can become a "dry occasion" which the rhetor must counter.[3] The infrequency of parallelism or other rhetorical devices[4] matches this simple style, differentiating this pericope substantially from most of the rest of Romans.[5] There are occasional parallel formulations such as the three successive participial phrases in 15:14 or the three roughly parallel phrases in 15:18-19 describing the powerful signs accompanying Paul's mission. However, the sentences in which these phrases occur do not appear to be organized in rhythmic style and hence would likely be read aloud in a straightforward, discursive manner, suitable for recapitulation. Only at the end of this pericope, in the citation of Isa 52:15, does the style shift into the synthetic parallelism of Hebrew poetry.

The "carefully composed"[6] material in this pericope is organized into two topics, an ingratiating review of Paul's rationale in writing to the Romans (15:14-16) and a vivid description of his strategy of Gentile mission that concludes with the citation from Isaiah (15:17-21). In the first topic, Paul expresses confidence in the maturity of the Roman converts, recapitulating the themes of 1:8 and 1:12 and referring to his letter as a "reminder" of the faith they hold in common. In the second, Paul reiterates the apostolic urgency that had been announced in 1:1, 5-6, 13-15, referring to himself as an agent of Christ's work of converting the Gentile world. From a rhetorical point of view, it is clear that Paul fulfills the admonition of Quintilian concerning the difficult task of recapitulation:

Quae autem enumeranda videntur, cum pondere aliquo dicenda sunt et aptis excitanda sententiis et figuris utique varianda; alioqui nihil est odiosius recta illa repetitione. . . . ("On the other hand the points selected for enumeration must be treated with weight and dignity, enlivened by apt reflexions and diversified by suitable figures; for there is nothing more tiresome than a dry repetition of facts. . . ." *Inst.* 6.1.2–3)

---

1   See Michel, 454; Dunn, 2:857; Harvey, *Listening*, 207.
2   See Wuellner, "Paul's Rhetoric," 136–37.
3   Martin, *Antike Rhetorik*, 150.
4   The suggestion by Bengel, 564; Cornely, 754–55; Kühl, 470; Michel, 459; Black, 203, of a chiastic development in v. 19, reversing the sequence of

$\lambda\dot{o}\gamma\omega$ $\kappa\alpha\dot{\iota}$ $\ddot{\epsilon}\rho\gamma\omega$ at the end of v. 18, is effectively refuted by Cranfield, 2:759.
5   This portion of chapter 15 sustains Weiss's assessment of the lack of rhetorical interest in "Beiträge," 247.
6   See Käsemann, 391.

Rhetorical Disposition

Exegesis

■ **14** The peroration of the letter opens with a typical, epistolary form of a *captatio benevolentiae.* Although he resists referring to a "confidence formula," Stanley N. Olson has shown that papyrus letters often contain polite apologies for making requests on the grounds that the recipient is already predisposed by excellent character to perform the duty anyway.[7] For instance, a petitioner writes the following apology to an Egyptian official in requesting help, claiming that the official already knows his duties: Καὶ ἄνευ γραμμάτων οἶδ᾽, ὅτι ἀφ᾽ ἑαυτῆς ἐστιν ἡ σὴ ἀρετὴ καὶ οὐ χρήζει (α) ὑπομνησθῆναι εἰς τὰ κατ᾽ ἐμέ, ἀλλὰ . . . ἀναγκαῖον ἡγησάμην . . . ("I know well that without any letter from me, your Excellence can rely upon himself and has no need to be reminded of my affairs, but . . . I consider it necessary . . . to urge you . . . to look after my affairs," *SB* 7656 = *Papyrus Berlin* 2753). The typicality of this confidence formula renders unnecessary any explanation of Paul's "flattery" of the Roman congregation.[8] This is "Christian courtesy"[9] only in the sense that the content of Paul's polite confidence is redefined by the earlier argument of the letter. As in earlier parts of the letter, the audience is addressed as "my brothers," indicating mutual respect and a shared status.[10] The reference to the "goodness"[11] of the Roman congregations would have sounded unexceptional for readers of Greco-

---

7   Stanley N. Olson, "Pauline Expressions of Confidence in His Addressees," *CBQ* 47 (1985) 291. He criticizes John White for referring to a confidence "formula" in *Body of the Greek Letter*, 103–4, but the evidence rather clearly points toward formulaic use.

8   See Lagrange, 350; Zeller, 237; Käsemann, 391.

9   Cranfield, 2:752.

10   See Schäfer, *Bruderschaft,* 348–50.

11   Although ἀγαθωσύνη is used only in biblical contexts, according to Ceslas Spicq, "ἀγαθοποιέω, ἀγαθωσύνη," *TLNT* 1 (1994) 3–4, it is closely paralleled by the use of ἀγαθός in the papyrus letters analyzed by Stanley N. Olson. See *P.Oxy.* 7 Nr. 1021.8; Pliny *Ep.* 10.12.

Roman letters, except for the term "full," μεστοὶ ἀγαθωσύνης ("full of goodness"), which provides a neat, rhetorical antithesis to the wording of Paul's earlier description of the unredeemed human race in 1:29 as "full of envy, murder, strife, etc."[12] This expression implies the restoration of righteousness[13] that the gospel under the power of the Holy Spirit has achieved. Similarly, the expression πεπληρωμένοι πάσας γνώσεως ("filled with every kind of knowledge") provides a precisely antithetical echo to "filled with every manner of evil, greed, etc.," in 1:29. While there is doubtless an element of hyperbole in this expression,[14] it conveys Paul's theological conviction that while the old age fills life with the evil that comes from a corrupt corporate and individual mind, the new age that dawned with Christ restores every form of knowledge to its rightful vitality. Whereas the mind dominated by the old age worshiped the creature and fell into every form of distorted folly (1:21-25), those who have been given the knowledge of the love of Christ are set free to grapple honestly and freely with "every kind" of knowledge. This includes but is not restricted to knowledge of God's saving purpose[15] or of the ethical wisdom required to resolve difficulties in Rome.[16] Paul believes that those who have been granted the "mind of Christ" (1 Cor 2:16) are free to use their minds in an aptly liberated and self-critical manner, so that "all knowledge" is literally at their disposal (1 Cor 13:2). The proximity of this extraordinary optimism to later gnostic thought should not lead interpreters to downplay the sweeping scope of Paul's

confidence; he speaks here as the harbinger of genuine, Christian enlightenment that later provided one of the foundations of scientific objectivity in the truest and broadest sense. The wording of this verse, and indeed of the entire argument of Romans, resists the multitudinous forms of obscurantism and fundamentalism that have sought to constrict the investigations of believers from Paul's time to our own.

The capability of the faithful in Rome is lifted up by the term δυνάμενοι ("those empowered, capable"), which again echoes the opening verses of the argument of Romans, referring to the gospel as the δύναμις θεοῦ ("power of God").[17] It also carries forward the theme of the "power of the Holy Spirit" in 15:13 and prepares the way for the allusions to the powerful signs and wonders that attend the early Christian mission in 15:19. In this letter, it is the gospel, empowered by the Spirit, that gives power to believers. The wording makes plain that it is not merely given to selected leaders but to every member of the congregation. The restoration of "goodness" on the part of the converted, along with the restoration of their minds so as to make genuine knowledge accessible to them, enables the Roman believers to participate in that crucial communal effort not merely to dispense information but "to correct the mind, to put right what is wrong, to improve the spiritual attitude."[18] This fundamental task of Greco-Roman pedagogy in its broadest sense is not limited by Paul to the role of a teacher to students,[19] a parent to a child,[20] or a master toward a slave.[21] In a manner that has similarities to Epicurean

---

12 In "A Family Feud," *NDIEC* 3 (1983) 149-55, G. H. R. Horsley discusses a similar phrase, ἀπονοίας μεστόν ("full of rebelliousness"), in an early fourth-century C.E. papyrus from Egypt, in which the writer complains to a local official about the behavior of a neighbor.

13 See Michel, 455; Käsemann, 391.

14 See Cranfield, 2:752.

15 Michel, 455; Dunn, 2:858.

16 Zeller, 237; Dunn, 2:858: "I am sure you know how to handle the situation."

17 See Walter Grundmann, "δύναμαι, δύναμις," *TDNT* 4 (1964) 310-12.

18 Johannes Behm, "νουθετέω, νουθεσία," *TDNT* 4 (1967) 1019.

19 Plutarch *Quo. adoles.* 20b links a philosopher's "admonishment" directly with pedagogy: οἱ γνοῦν φιλόσοφοι παραδείγμασι χρῶνται, νουθε-

τοῦντες καὶ παιδεύοντες ἐξ ὑποκειμένων ("Philosophers, at any rate, for admonition and instruction, use examples taken from known facts").

20 Philo *Spec.* 2.232 states the commonplace premise of the Greco-Roman world concerning the authority of parents over children: διὰ τοῦτ᾽ ἔξεστι τοῖς πατράσι καὶ κακηγορεῖν πρὸς τοὺς παῖδας καὶ ἐμβριθέστερον νουθετεῖν καὶ, εἰ μὴ ταῖς δι᾽ ἀκοῶν ἀπειλαῖς ὑπείκουσι, τύπτειν καὶ προπηλακίζειν καὶ καταδεῖν ("And therefore fathers have the right to upbraid their children and admonish them severely and if they do not submit to threats conveyed in words to beat and degrade them and put them in bonds").

21 For example, in *Pol.* 1260b9 Aristotle affirms the need of masters to instruct slaves who, unlike children, have the capacity of reason: νουθετητέον

communities in which "members admonish and censure each other in friendship,"[22] Paul extends this power of admonishment to each member of the community. The accusative pronoun ἀλλήλους ("one another") thus carries forward the argument supporting mutual upbuilding that dominated the preceding pericopes in Romans. But in view of 14:1–15:13, it seems unlikely that Paul had "rebuke and censure" in mind, "focusing on behavior modification and attitude change through admonition and blame in the reformation of others," as Glad suggests.[23] In place of attempts to convert others to an in-group point of view, Paul suggests a form of admonishment that upbuilds others in the integrity of their own orientations. Rather than "mature members" evaluating "their erring co-members,"[24] Paul assigns the "weak" a responsibility to admonish the "strong" and vice versa, thus undercutting the superiority claims that each side was making in Rome.[25] It is a countercultural strategy of corporate psychagogy, reversing the hierarchical and elitist premises of the Mediterranean world.[26]

■ **15** The polite apology for Paul's "boldness" is consistent with the confidence formula in the preceding sentence, admitting his audacity in intervening in the affairs of the congregation he had not founded while relying on the traditional motif of a reminder.[27] The comparative τολμηρότερος may be translated "more boldly" or "rather boldly,"[28] implying "more freely than it seemed I

should do in the case of such a church."[29] It appears, however, that he immediately qualifies this apology by adding ἀπὸ μέρους ("in part"), which could qualify either "more boldly,"[30] "I have written,"[31] or "reminder."[32] If attached to the verb, it remains unclear which part of the letter is intended, whether the sections dealing with the internal situation in Rome[33] or the entire letter,[34] which, as we have demonstrated in contrast to earlier commentaries, was related in its entirety to the congregational situation. To connect "in part" with "more boldly" seems strained grammatically and unsupported by the word order; it is also both illogical and impolite in that Paul would simultaneously be admitting that he has written more boldly than he really ought—yet only partially so, which implies he should really have been even more bold and offensive. The proximity of ἀπὸ μέρους to ὡς ἐπαναμιμνῄσκων ("as a reminder") and the polite tone of the passage inclines me to the option advocated by Godet and Fitzmyer, that Paul's discourse is "partially" a reminder of what the Roman converts already know and believe.[35] Paul's choice of the rare term ἐπαναμιμνήσκω ("remind, call to mind"), used here for the only time in the Bible, accents the formal politeness of Paul's discourse[36] and coordinates well with the qualification: "in part as a mere reminder." The polite discourse does not disguise, however, that a substantial part of what Paul has written in this letter coordinates and develops commonly held

---

γὰρ μᾶλλον τοὺς δούλους ἤ τοὺς παῖδας ("for admonition is more for slaves than for children").

22   Glad, *Paul and Philodemus*, 108; see his chapter "Epicurean Communal Psychagogy," 101–60.

23   Ibid., 232–33.

24   Ibid., 217.

25   Johannes Behm refers appropriately in "νουθετέω, νουθεσία," *TDNT* 4 (1967) 1022, to "the reciprocal brotherly ministry of the members" in this verse.

26   Even Philodemus, whose writings come closest to Pauline mutuality (see Περί Παρρησίας, discussed by Glad, *Paul and Philodemus*, 124–32), would not be prepared to assign equal roles to both the "weak" and the "strong," or to extend mutuality to "barbarians" and "uneducated" (Rom 1:14).

27   See the citation from *SB* 7656 above.

28   See Cranfield, 2:753. Zahn's argument in 596–97 in favor of a superlative translation of τολμηρότερον is not compelling; see BDF §§60, 244. The word is a hapax legomenon for the NT as a whole.

29   Godet, 476.

30   See Schlier, 428, following Ludwig Gaugusch, "Untersuchungen zum Römerbrief. Der Epilog (15,14—16,27). Eine exegetische Studie," *BZ* (1938–39) 164–84, 252–66, esp. 165. Murray, 209, follows this line with the translation "boldly in some measure."

31   Cranfield, 2:753.

32   See Godet, 477; Fitzmyer, 711.

33   Meyer, 2:343; Cranfield, 2:753.

34   Dunn, 2:859; Brendan Byrne, "'Rather Boldly' (Rom 15,15): Paul's Prophetic Bid to Win the Allegiance of Christians in Rome," *Bib* 74 (1993) 83–96.

35   See also Kettunen, *Abfassungszweck*, 151.

36   See Sanday and Headlam, 404; Chrysostom commented that the word "means putting you in mind in a quiet way," as Morris notes in 510.

beliefs in innovative ways that, if accepted, will move the Romans toward attitudes and actions that counter their current stance. Honest and effective rhetoric requires Paul to admit that part of his letter moves beyond reminder toward a timely, prophetic claim against their present and future behavior, a claim consistent with the grace of God shown in the Christ event.

There is nothing apologetic, therefore, in the rest of v. 15, where Paul claims to be writing "on account of the grace given to me by God."[37] This reiterates the claim of Paul's apostolic calling in 1:5 as a specific vocation of ministry to the Gentiles. The preposition $\delta\iota\acute{\alpha}$ with the accusative implies "the reason why something happens, results, exists,"[38] which in this context has a formal, diplomatic connotation in introducing the office that Paul was given. The aorist participle $\delta o\vartheta\epsilon\hat{\iota}\sigma\alpha\nu$ ("given") implies a gift of grace at a specific time in the past, in this case at the time of his conversion when unconditional acceptance came to him from Christ simultaneously with his call to Gentile ministry.[39] He insists that this gift was given to him "by God," so that his ministry constitutes a direct expression of divine power.[40] Paul is not writing in his own behalf, but as an expression of his

particular calling to missionize among the Gentiles, toward which end the Romans are shortly to be asked to take a decisive responsibility. As one can see from Paul's use of this same expression in 1 Cor 3:10 and Gal 2:9, his entire existence grows out of this grace-filled calling to an ecumenical ministry.[41]

■ **16** The recapitulation of Paul's worshipful evangelism described in 1:9 takes the form of "highly unusual" terminology as far as Paul's previous letters are concerned.[42] Here he refers to himself as the $\lambda\epsilon\iota\tau o\nu\rho\gamma\grave{o}\varsigma$ $X\rho\iota\sigma\tau o\hat{\nu}$ $I\eta\sigma o\hat{\nu}\varsigma$ $\epsilon\grave{\iota}\varsigma$ $\tau\grave{\alpha}$ $\check{\epsilon}\vartheta\nu\eta$ ("minister of Christ Jesus to the Gentiles"), which has led to the development of elaborate priestly theories that end up restricting Paul's revolutionary mission within institutional boundaries that are contrasted with Judaism and associated with later, established churches.[43] The use of this term in 13:6, however, points more clearly to the role of a "public functionary"[44] of a city, regent, or God, an agent who provides benefaction without remuneration in a particular role.[45] Of particular interest is Spicq's reference to $\lambda\epsilon\iota\tau o\nu\rho\gamma o\acute{\iota}$ who serve as ambassadors sent from particular Greek cities.[46] For instance, Orthagoras of Araxa is celebrated in an inscription of the second century B.C.E.

37 See Käsemann's discussion of the shift from apology to authoritative claim in 392. Note, however, that in contrast to 1:5, Paul does not mention here his apostolicity but only the grace that produced it. The polite, nonauthoritarian tone continues to predominate in the second half of 15:15.

38 BAGD 181.

39 See Morris, 510.

40 See Schlier, 429, who observes that the expression in this verse is exactly correlated with the wording of 1:5, where grace given was "received."

41 Heinrich Schlier offers the most detailed and penetrating discussion of the theology in this sentence; see particularly his study "Die 'Liturgie' des apostolischen Evangeliums (Röm 15, 14-21)," in H. Schlier, *Ende*, 169–83.

42 Käsemann, 392; the closest parallel is Phil 2:17.

43 See Schlier, 430; Konrad Weiss, "Paulus—Priester der christlichen Kultgemeinde," *TLZ* 79 (1954) 355–64; Karl Hermann Schelkle, "Der Apostel als Priester," *ThQ* 136 (1956) 257–83, esp. 178; Albert-Marie Denis, "La fonction apostolique et la liturgie nouvelle en esprit. Étude thématique des métaphores pauliniennes du cult nouveau," *RSPhTh* 42 (1958) 401–36, 617–56, esp. 403–8; Robert M. Cooper, "Leitourgos Christou Iesou: Toward a The-

ology of Christian Prayer," *ATR* 47 (1965) 263–75. Michael Newton expresses enthusiasm for Konrad Weiss's work in *Concept of Purity*, 62–63. For a balanced appraisal of the debate, see Claude Wiéner, "$I\epsilon\rho o\nu\rho\gamma\epsilon\hat{\iota}\nu$ (Rm 15,16)," *SPCIC* 2:399–404; Zmijewski, *Paulus–Knecht*, 132–34; Corriveau, *Liturgy of Life*, 150–51.

44 Godet, 477; Danker, *Benefactor*, 330–31; see also the explicit rejection of a priestly construal by Zahn, 597. A comprehensive discussion of classical and biblical usage is provided by Romeo, "$\Lambda EITO\Upsilon P-\Gamma IA$," 467–519. Naphtali Lewis provides a survey of the variant spelling, etymology, and semantics of "compulsory public service" in "Leitourgia," (1960) 175–84; (1965) 227–30.

45 H. Strathmann and R. Meyer in "$\lambda\epsilon\iota\tau o\nu\rho\gamma\epsilon\acute{\omega}$ $\kappa\tau\lambda$.," *TDNT* 4 (1967) 216, refer to the basic etymology and meaning of the term $\lambda\epsilon\iota\tau o\nu\rho\gamma\acute{o}\varsigma$ as coming from $\lambda\acute{\eta}\ddot{\iota}\tau o\varsigma$ ("concerning the people") and $\check{\epsilon}\rho\gamma$- ("work, do"). They discuss the political and public use of these terms on 216–18.

46 Ceslas Spicq, "$\lambda\epsilon\iota\tau o\nu\rho\gamma\epsilon\acute{\omega}$ $\kappa\tau\lambda$.," *TLNT* 2 (1994) 382.

as having "accomplished well other embassies, without demanding the cost of travel" (ἄλλας τε πολλὰς πρε[σ]βείας ἄνευ μεθοδίων λελειτούργηκεν).[47] The expression λειτουργὸς Χριστοῦ Ἰησοῦς gracefully reiterates Paul's claim to be δοῦλος Χριστοῦ Ἰησοῦ in 1:1 and resonates with the theme of the preceding verse, in that Paul also serves free of charge, impelled by grace already received rather than seeking a reward.[48] The specification of Paul's ministry as directed εἰς τὰ ἔθνη ("to the Gentiles") is more suitable for the ambassadorial role than for the priestly role, which the term λειτουργός carries in other contexts such as Neh 10:39; Isa 61:6; Sir 7:30.[49] As an ambassador, Paul is sent by God *to* the Gentiles. Although Dabelstein recommends the translation of ἔθνη as "Gentile Christians,"[50] it seems more likely that "Gentiles" in the sense of the non-Jewish nations is intended here; clearly, the "universal, almost cosmic breadth of his missionary program,"[51] directed to those who have not yet heard the gospel, comes to expression in this verse.

The participial clause with an accusative of relation, ἱερουργοῦντα τὸ εὐαγγέλιον τοῦ θεοῦ ("in priestly service related to the gospel of God") modifies the preceding clause and characterizes Paul's ambassadorship as a "verbalized" form of priesthood.[52] This reiterates 1:9 while continuing the transformation of cultic terminology announced in 12:1. Rather than bringing a sacrifice to the altar as would have been typical for Jewish as well as Greco-Roman worship,[53] Paul's evangelistic proclamation results in a transformation of the Gentiles into "an acceptable offering" in the fulfillment of an end-time scheme announced in 11:11, 25 and derived from Isa 66:20.[54] Paul uses a term for a sacrificial or votive offering, προσφορά,[55] a word with a technical liturgical meaning in the LXX that appears here for the only time in the authentic Pauline letters.[56] The "offering" is used here in a way that both fulfills and reverses Isaiah,[57] thus continuing the transformation-of-sacrifice scheme stated in 12:1. Gentiles who were formerly kept at a distance from the altar in Yahweh's temple are now brought near[58] to a sacrifice that is "well-pleasing"

47 Ibid., cited from Jean Pouilloux, *Choix d'Inscriptions grecques. Textes, traductions et notes* (Paris: Belles Lettres, 1960) 34.

48 Zahn, 597–98, points to the relevance of 1 Cor 9:18 in this connection.

49 For a discussion of the LXX use of the λειτουργ- stem in cultic contexts, see Suzanne Daniel, *Recherches sur le vocabulaire du culte dans la Septante*, EeC 61 (Paris: Klincksieck, 1966) 76–78, 82–92, 101–7.

50 Dabelstein, *Beurteilung*, 37.

51 Klauck, "Kultische Symbolsprache," 115; see also Dewey, "Σπανίαν," 345–46.

52 See the discussion of the grammatical construction and its interpretation by Radl, "Kult und Evangelium," 64–68, esp. 65: "Service of the gospel as service of the cult." The verb ἱερουργέω is a hapax legomenon in the NT.

53 See Gottlob Schrenk, "ἱερουργέω," *TDNT* 3 (1965) 251–52. For instance, Jewish usage is reflected in Josephus *Ant.* 7.333, which describes how Oronnas, "having built the altar, consecrated it and offered burnt offerings and peace offerings (καὶ οἰκοδομήσας τὸν βωμὸν ἱερούργησε καὶ ὡλοκαύτωσε καὶ θυσίας ἀνήκεγκεν εἰρηνικάς)." Typical Greco-Roman usage may be found in Plutarch's description of King Numa: "After he established and regulated the priestly orders, he built, near the Temple of Vesta, the so-called Regia or royal house.

Here he passed most of his time, performing priestly functions . . . (Ἐπεὶ δὲ διεκόσμησε τὰς ἱερωσύνας, ἐδείματο πλησίον τοῦ τῆς Ἑστίας ἱεροῦ τὴν καλουμένην Ῥηγίαν, οἷόν τι βασίλειον οἴκημα. καὶ τὸ πλεῖστον αὐτόθι τοῦ χρόνου διέτριβεν ἱερουργῶν . . . *Num.* 15.1)."

54 Godet, 477; Aus, "Paul's Travel Plans," 241.

55 See BAGD 720; Daniel, *Vocabulaire du culte*, 122, 129–30, 219–22.

56 In "προσφέρω, προσφορά," *TDNT* 9 (1974) 68, Konrad Weiss shows that προσφορά always appears in the NT with the meaning "sacrifice," a connotation not found in classical sources. It appears first in the LXX. He cites Ps 39:6; Dan 3:38; numerous occurrences in Sirach; and Josephus *Ant.* 11.77 as examples. See also Wolfgang Schenk, "προσφορά," *EDNT* 3 (1993) 178.

57 Whereas Isa 66:20 expects that the Gentiles will bring the Jews back from exile as an offering to God, Paul is bringing the converted Gentiles themselves as the offering.

58 See Dunn, 2:860–61. Another option would be to construe προσφορὰ τῶν ἐθνῶν as a subjective genitive, referring either to the offering being brought by the Gentiles to Jerusalem, a matter discussed in the next pericope (15:26-28), or to an offering of praise and obedience on the part of Gentiles. See Denis, "La fonction apostolique et la liturgie nouvelle en esprit," 405–6; Dabelstein, *Beurteilung*,

($εὐπρόσδεκτος$)[59] to God, thus reiterating the theme of the sacrifice "acceptable to God" in 12:1.[60]

The clause $ἡγιασμένη$ $ἐν$ $πνεύματι$ $ἁγίῳ$ ("made holy in/by the Holy Spirit") recapitulates the references to holiness in 1:4 and 7. The set-apartness and purity of God's chosen people,[61] separated from the degenerate Gentile world, comprising an island of vitality and decency, are now extended to the Gentiles. The association of the Spirit with conversion and charismatic experience in 5:5, 8:9-16, 12:1, 14:17, and 15:13 makes clear that the context in which this phrase should be understood is the evangelistic gospel that extends holiness to the Gentile congregations. In contrast to the individualistic tradition of interpreting this passage,[62] it is the presence of the Holy Spirit within Christian communities that makes them holy. As the wording makes plain, these house and tenement churches are "*in* the Holy Spirit." It is the transformation of their social life that requires the appellation "holy." The characteristically Hebraic paranomasia involving the stem $ἁγια$- in this compressed

expression[63] implies that God's holy presence is the wonder-working, transforming, converting power that maintains holiness in these small groups of believers in their common life. Paul's metaphor envisions the Gentile world, symbolized by representative groups rather than by an array of isolated individuals, as the singular "offering" that he is commissioned to bring.[64] This collective interpretation will be confirmed by the geographic scheme of mission articulated in 15:19.

■ **17** Most recent commentators convey a vague sense of the function of this verse, attaching it loosely to the foregoing verses.[65] Godet and Cranfield are on more solid ground in allowing this verse to serve as a transition that opens the second topic in the pericope;[66] it explains the boldness of Paul's claims as a "minister of Christ Jesus to the Gentiles" as derived from the power and authority of his regent. The ambassador makes claims for his ruler, not for himself. This boasting is of a different order than that decried in 3:27. Rather than competing with God as ultimate forms of boasting tend to do, this boast will

112–14. D. W. B. Robinson develops the idea of the Gentiles' own priestly ministry constituting the offering in "The Priesthood of Paul in the Gospel of Hope," in R. J. Banks, ed., *Reconciliation and Hope: New Testament Essays on Atonement and Eschatology Presented to L. L. Morris on His 60th Birthday* (Exeter: Paternoster; Grand Rapids: Eerdmans, 1974) 231–45. The first option seems unlikely, because Paul would then be explaining his entire ministry in 15:16 as aimed at collecting this single offering.

59 The compound adjective $εὐπρόσδεκτος$ ("well-pleasing") is not found in Jewish literature but is used with some frequency by Paul: Rom 15:31; 2 Cor 6:2; 8:12. It was a familiar term in Greco-Roman cults, with Aristophanes referring in *Pax* 1054 to a "sacrifice as well-pleasing" ($εὐπρόσδεκτος$ $ἡ$ $θυσία$). The concept, expressed in simpler language, surfaces frequently in biblical materials: Lev 1:3; 19:5; Jer 6:20, etc. See Walter Grundmann, "$δεκτός$ $κτλ$.," *TDNT* 2 (1964) 59.

60 See Nils A. Dahl, "The Missionary Theology in the Epistle to the Romans," in Dahl, *Studies,* 87.

61 See the extensive discussion in Dunn, 2:861, with special reference to the holiness of Israel in Exod 19:14; Lev 11:44; 20:8; 22:32; Deut 33:3; Ezek 20:41; 28:25; 37:28; 39:27; Jud 6:19; Sir 36:3; 3 Macc 6.3.

62 See Godet, 478; Murray, 2:211. In Fee, *Empowering Presence*, 627, the individualistic and moralistic construal of holiness unfortunately remains predominant. The recent survey by Horst Balz, "$ἅγιος$ $κτλ$.," *EDNT* 1 (1990) 16–20, also does not move beyond the traditional individualism. The study of the spirit by Ragnar Asting in *Die Heiligkeit im Urchristentum*, FRLANT 46 (Göttingen: Vandenhoeck & Ruprecht, 1930), presents sanctification as individual striving toward high ethical ideals (202–34), while explaining the distinctiveness of Paul's view on the basis of his individual conversion experience rather than the communal experience of his charismatic churches (191).

63 The paranomasia in the clause $ἡγιασμένη$ $ἐν$ $πνεύματι$ $ἁγίῳ$ ("made holy in the Holy Spirit") is somewhat similar to that of Rev 22:11 ("let the holy still be holy!" $καὶ$ $ὁ$ $ἅγιος$ $ἁγιασθήτω$ $ἔτι$) and is reminiscent of LXX passages such as 1 Chr 23:13 ("and Aaron was appointed to make holy the holy of holies," $καὶ$ $διεστάλη$ $Ἀαρὼν$ $τοῦ$ $ἁγιασθῆναι$ $ἅγια$ $ἁγίων$), and 2 Chr 31:18 ("for in faith they made holy the holy place," $ὅτι$ $ἐν$ $πίστει$ $ἥγνισαν$ $τὸ$ $ἅγιον$). See also Lev 11:44; 21:8; 22:3; Num 18:9; 27:14; 1 Chr 26:26; 30:8; Neh 12:47.

64 See Käsemann, 393: "the Gentile world itself is the offering."

65 See Dunn, 2:861; Fitzmyer, 712.

66 Godet, 479; Cranfield, 2:757; see also Morris, 512; Zeller, 238; Murray, 2:211.

concern τὰ πρὸς τὸν θεόν ("what pertains to God"),[67] that is, what God has accomplished in Paul's mission.[68]

On the basis of a parallel pointed out by Stanley N. Olson, it becomes clear that modestly boastful statements similar to the one commencing in this verse have an honored place in Greco-Roman, ambassadorial rhetoric.[69] For instance, Dio Chrysostom addresses the council at Apameia in behalf of his own city of Prusa, hoping to ratify an agreement to overcome a conflict that probably arose over commercial relations. Fearing that the audience may "discount or reject his advice on the basis of their feelings about him,"[70] Dio begins with the following self-commendation, which is considerably more elaborate than Paul's: "Members of the Council and you other fair-minded persons here present, I believe I know that you are kindly and amiably disposed toward me. For I am sure I myself esteem highly your favorable regard and have never said or done anything against you. . . . For not only cities wherever I have been, but even most of those which are of equal rank with yourselves, have presented me with citizenship, with membership in the Council, and with highest honors without my asking it, believing me to be not unserviceable to themselves or unworthy to be honored" (*Orat.* 41.1–2). While the conventions of ambassadorial rhetoric allowed such boasting, it is clear that Paul's manner of developing the subject was theologically consistent with the rest of the argument of Romans and thus would have been particularly effective with his audience in Rome, where the ubiquity of various forms of governmental boasting and propaganda would have rendered most such language somewhat transparent. The accom-

plishments to be touted are "in Christ"[71] and, as the next verse will show, they have been performed by Christ rather than by Paul himself. The one to be accorded "highest honors," as 15:6 made clear, is not Paul but "the God and Father of our Lord Jesus Christ."

■ **18** In a rather involuted sentence,[72] which is partially explained by Paul's polite style of self-commendation,[73] we find an elaboration of the boasting announced in the preceding verse as being "in Christ Jesus before God."[74] Using the verb τολμάω ("be bold, make bold"), reminiscent of the wording of v. 15, Paul again qualifies the basis of his "boldness" as derived from nothing ὧν οὐ κατειργάσατο Χριστὸς δι' ἐμοῦ εἰς ὑπακοὴν ἐθνῶν ("except what Christ has performed through me toward the obedience of the Gentiles"). Paul denies being the agent capable of boasting in and of himself, preferring as he does in 2 Corinthians to stress his agency, with himself as the means by which Christ performed the ministry of the gospel.[75] The phrase δι' ἐμοῦ ("through me") is a perfect expression of Paul's instrumentality. The choice of the compound verb κατεργάζομαι in place of the more simple ἐργάζομαι ("work, do, accomplish") is deliberate, implying the achievement, the working out, the performance of a complex task.

The pregnant phrase εἰς ὑπακοὴν ἐθνῶν ("toward the obedience of the Gentiles") recapitulates the formulation of 1:5 concerning "the obedience of faith among all the Gentiles." Indeed, as Michel observed, this formulation recapitulates the entire preceding argument of Romans.[76] This use of the term "obedience," which was so characteristically related to biblical religion,[77] entails the claim that "in Christ" all converted Gentiles "could

67 For the grammatical construction, see BDF §160.
68 Note the similar wording in 2 Cor 1:12.
69 Stanley N. Olson, "Epistolary Uses of Expressions of Self-Confidence," *JBL* 103 (1984) 585–97, esp. 588.
70 Ibid., 589.
71 Bouttier, *En Christ*, 58.
72 See Cranfield, 2:758, citing Cornely, 753–54.
73 See the discussion in the verse above. The discovery of these self-commendation forms helps to resolve the interpretive dilemma of defining the two things that Paul is allegedly trying to combine in this sentence; see the differing attempts to define these in Lietzmann, 120; Lagrange, 352; Barrett, 276.
74 See Cranfield, 2:757; Dacquino, "In Christo," 282–85. Despite the close parallels to 2 Cor 10:2, 12; 11:21 where Paul is criticizing the boasting of

superapostles, there is no indication that his line of argument here is intended as a defense against the charge of being an irresponsible charismatic, as Michel, 459, suggests.
75 See Jeffrey A. Crafton, *The Agency of the Apostle: A Dramatistic Analysis of Paul's Responses to Conflict in 2 Corinthians*, JSNTSup 51 (Sheffield: Sheffield Academic Press, 1991) 59–102. See also Hermann, *Kyrios und Pneuma*, 122.
76 Michel, 439.
77 See Kuss, "Begriff des Gehorsams," 695–702; Bernhard W. Anderson, "The Biblical Ethic of Obedience," *Christian Scholar* 39 (1956) 66–71; E. A. McNamara, "Obedience in the Scriptures," *AER* 15 (1964) 332–42.

now enter into covenant relation with the God of Israel and be accounted faithful by him apart from the necessity of first becoming and then remaining Jewish."[78] Being granted righteousness through faith, thus being made holy through the power of the Spirit, these Gentile communities have been brought to a new form of obedience through Paul's gospel.

The means by which obedience was being achieved are articulated in the first of two sets of terms, λόγῳ καὶ ἔργῳ ("by word and deed"), which seem to reflect "the Greek distinction between speech and action."[79] The same terms are found in the first-century philosopher Cebes' allusion to a foreigner who came to study and adopt the ancient model of wisdom: ἀνὴρ ἔμφρων καὶ δεινὸς περὶ σοφίαν, λόγῳ καὶ ἔργῳ Πυθαγό-ρειος τινα καὶ Παρμενίδειον ἐζηλωκὼς βίον ("a sensible man and outstanding in wisdom, who was emulating in word and deed a Pythagorean and Parmenidian way of life," *Ceb. tab.* 2.2). The reverse sequence appears in Hellenistically influenced writings of Judaism, as, for instance, in the admonition of Sir 3:8: Ἐν ἔργῳ καὶ λόγῳ τίμα τὸν πατέρα σου . . . ("In deed and word honor your father . . .").[80] The appearance of these two terms in the sequence of "word and deed" in 2 Thess 2:17, Col 3:17, along with the more distant parallel in 2 Cor 10:11, suggests habitual usage in the Pauline tradition, referring on the one hand to words spoken in preaching and teaching, and on the other hand to missionary actions, labors, sufferings, travels, and so on. While Paul provides the agency through which these

words and deeds were accomplished, their agent remains Christ, according to the wording of this verse.[81]

■ **19** Traditional language from the Jewish rather than the Greco-Roman realm surfaces in the next pair of phrases elaborating how the obedience of the Gentiles has been achieved in Paul's mission. As Fritz Stolz has shown, the formula σημείων καὶ τεράτων ("signs and wonders") was used to authenticate the divinely appointed status and role of prophets (Deut 13:1-2; Isa 20:3), to describe the divine intervention in the exodus (Exod 7:3; Deut 7:19; 29:3; 34:11; Ps 135:9), and to prove God's presence in the miraculous experience of the early church (Acts 4:30; 5:12; 6:8; 14:3; 15:12).[82] The two terms appear to have overlapping meanings that cannot be sharply distinguished.[83] The legitimating function of many of these references[84] correlates well with the self-commending context of Paul's discourse in this pericope,[85] even though no defensiveness is evident in the formulation.[86] This reference to "signs and wonders" places Paul's work within the "continuity of God's redemptive activity" from the exodus through the Christian mission.[87] To subordinate these "signs and wonders" to the divine δύναμις ("power") in this verse continues an important theme in ambassadorial rhetoric that I first detected in the thesis statement of 1:16. For Paul such miracles point to their divine source in the δύναμις θεοῦ,[88] and there is no hint at this point that Paul is worried about Greco-Roman suspicions of superstition[89] or about giving too much encouragement to

78 Garlington, *Obedience*, 255.

79 Käsemann, 394.

80 See the other parallels listed in BAGD 307.

81 See Leenhardt, 369: "it is Christ who is the hidden author. . . ." See also Alkier, *Wunder*, 278–79.

82 Fritz Stolz, "Zeichen und Wunder. Die prophetischen Legitimation und ihre Geschichte," *ZThK* 69 (1972) 125–44; see also Gräbe, *Power of God*, 209–10.

83 Newman and Nida, 281, followed by Gräbe, *Power of God*, 210.

84 Stolz, "Zeichen," 143–44.

85 Gerhard Delling refers to the wonders in Rom 15:19 "as confirmation of Paul's commission and thereby of the proclamation of the inbreaking of the new age," in "Das Verständnis des Wunders im Neuen Testament," in G. Delling, *Studien zum Neuen Testament und zum hellenistischen Judentum. Gesammelte*

Aufsätze 1950–1968, ed. F. Hahn, T. Holtz, and N. Walter (Göttingen: Vandenhoeck & Ruprecht, 1970) 147.

86 See Helge Kjær Nielsen, "Paulus' Verwendung des Begriffes Δύναμις. Eine Replik zur Kreuzestheologie," in S. Pedersen, ed., *Die Paulinische Literatur und Theologie. Anlässlich der 50. jährigen Gründungs-Feier der Universität Aarhus*, TSt 7 (Aarhus: Aros; Göttingen: Vandenhoeck & Ruprecht, 1980) 152.

87 Stefan Schreiber, *Paulus als Wundertäter. Redaktionsgeschichtliche Untersuchungen zur Apostelgeschichte und den authentischen Paulusbriefen*, BZNW 79 (Berlin/New York: de Gruyter, 1996) 202.

88 Alkier, *Wunder*, 278–79.

89 Karl Heinrich Rengstorf, "σημεῖον κτλ.," *TDNT* 7 (1971) 206–7, cites, among other examples, Polybius's sarcastic account of the superstitions to which the Roman population fell prey after a threatening

charismatics in Rome.[90] Given the Roman preoccupation with power, which led Wagenvoort to investigate the links with the Austronesian concept of "mana," it is clear that Paul is interacting positively with the Roman audience in this emphasis on the power of God.[91] There are enough references to charismatic signs and wonders in the other letters (2 Cor 12:12; 1 Thess 1:5; Gal 3:5; 1 Cor 2:1-5) to make clear the central role this divine activity played in Paul's churches.[92] This includes glossolalia, healings, and conversions.[93] In the parallel phrase this motif of divine power is again emphasized: $\dot{\epsilon}\nu$ $\delta\upsilon\nu\acute{\alpha}\mu\epsilon\iota$ $\pi\nu\epsilon\acute{\upsilon}\mu\alpha\tau\sigma\varsigma$ ("in [the] power of [the] Spirit"). The genitive construction indicates that the source of the power is the Spirit, while the parallel expression in the preceding verse shows that Christ is the agent in such exhibitions of power, as Walter Grundmann explains: "The Spirit is the One who dispenses and mediates power. The Pauline concept of power is constructed from two different standpoints. On the one side $\pi\nu\epsilon\hat{\upsilon}\mu\alpha$ ("spirit") expresses the mode in which the exalted Lord is present and there is identification with Him. On the other, it expresses the corresponding mode of existence of believers. The unity of the two is to be seen in the synonymous use of $\dot{\epsilon}\nu$ $\pi\nu\epsilon\acute{\upsilon}\mu\alpha\tau\iota$ ("in spirit") and $\dot{\epsilon}\nu$ $X\rho\iota\sigma\tau\hat{\omega}$ ("in Christ"). When we grasp this, it is evident that in the combination of $\delta\acute{\upsilon}\nu\alpha\mu\iota\varsigma$ ("power") and $\pi\nu\epsilon\hat{\upsilon}\mu\alpha$ ("spirit") there is expressed the power with which the risen Lord is present to his people as $\pi\nu\epsilon\hat{\upsilon}\mu\alpha$ ("spirit")."[94] The "matter-of-fact" character of this double reference to divine $\delta\acute{\upsilon}\nu\alpha\mu\iota\varsigma$ is quite striking,[95] particularly in a letter addressed to the center of the Roman imperium,[96] and it is clear that both Paul and his audience in Rome assume that such manifestations of miracle-working power are routine features in every authentic house and tenement church.[97] They are signs that Christ is present and active in the new, eschatological community (15:17-18), evoking "obedience" to the gospel (15:18), setting relationships right, and thereby producing social "holiness" (15:16). Insofar as they demonstrate the power of Paul's regent, these signs authenticate his ambassadorial role, and the appropriateness of his addressing the varied Christian communities in Rome.

The final clause in v. 19 begins with the conjunction $\ddot{\omega}\sigma\tau\epsilon$ ("so that"), which introduces the result of foregoing exhibitions of power. While most translations use this word to initiate a separate sentence, it is more appropriate to see this final, independent clause as reaching back to include all the material from v. 17 on, and elaborating the scope of Paul's "ministry . . . to the Gentiles" mentioned in v. 16.[98] It has progressed thus far from

defeat by Hannibal: $\pi\acute{\alpha}\nu\tau\epsilon$ δ' $\mathring{\eta}\nu$ $\tau\grave{\alpha}$ $\pi\alpha\rho$' $\alpha\mathring{\upsilon}\tauο\hat{\iota}\varsigma$ $\lambda\acute{o}\gamma\iota\alpha$ $\pi\hat{\alpha}\sigma\iota$ $\tau\acute{o}\tau\epsilon$ $\delta\iota\grave{\alpha}$ $\sigma\tau\acute{o}\mu\alpha\tau\sigma\varsigma$, $\sigma\eta\mu\epsilon\hat{\iota}ο\nu$ $\delta\grave{\epsilon}$ $\kappa\alpha\grave{\iota}$ $\tau\epsilon\rho\acute{\alpha}\tau\omega\nu$ $\pi\hat{\alpha}\nu$ $\mu\grave{\epsilon}\nu$ $\iota\epsilon\rho\acute{o}\nu$, $\pi\hat{\alpha}\sigma\alpha$ δ' $\mathring{\eta}\nu$ $ο\iota\kappa\acute{\iota}\alpha$ $\pi\lambda\acute{\eta}\rho\eta\varsigma$ ("All the oracles that had ever been delivered to them were in men's mouths, every temple and every house was full of signs and wonders," *Hist.* 3.112.8).

90   See Dunn, 2:863. For an extensive discussion of unapologetic role of miracles in Philo, see Gerhard Delling, "Wunder—Allegorie—Mythus bei Philon von Alexandreia," in Delling, *Studien zum Neuen Testament und zum hellenistischen Judentum*, 72–129. Gräbe, *Power of God*, 209: "It is notable how unrestrained Paul can speak of the extraordinary signs and wonders which accompany his ministry."

91   Wagenvoort, *Roman Dynamism*, 6; of particular relevance is the discussion of triumphal processions in Rome on 163–68, in which the victor wears the clothes of Jupiter and paints his face red to match the image of Jupiter, thus claiming to embody the god's power.

92   See Prümm, "Dynamische," 657–58; Paul-Émile Langevin, "La signification du miracle dans le mes-

sage du Nouveau Testament," *ScE* 27 (1975) 163–64; Schreiber, *Paulus als Wundertäter*, 176, 204, argues that the "signs and wonders" terminology was already well known to the Christian audience of Romans.

93   See Shantz, "Paul in Ecstasy," 229–35.

94   Walter Grundmann, "$\delta\acute{\upsilon}\nu\alpha\mu\alpha\iota/\delta\acute{\upsilon}\nu\alpha\mu\iota\varsigma$," *TDNT* 2 (1964) 311–12; see also Käsemann, 394; Schreiber, *Paulus als Wundertäter*, 205–7; Gräbe, *Power of God*, 211. For the "latent Trinitarianism" in this text, see Fee, *Empowering Presence*, 630.

95   Fee, *Empowering Presence*, 630.

96   Wagenvoort, *Roman Dynamism*, shows that "*imperium* originally meant 'chief's mana'" or power, with the ruler giving such powers to his subordinates (66). The adjective *imperiosus* means "full of *imperium*," or "mighty, powerful," (68) "full of war-chief's mana" (69).

97   The use of the concept of power in Hellenistic religion and philosophy is surveyed by Karl Prümm, providing general background for this passage: "Dynamis," 393–430.

98   See Lietzmann, 121.

Jerusalem to Illyricum, the district across the Adriatic Sea to the east of Italy that had become an imperial province in 11 B.C.E.[99] The curious expression καὶ κύκλῳ μέχρι ("also as far round as") provides a clue to the odd geographic details in this account of Paul's mission. World maps from the Roman period placed the circle of the Mediterranean at the center of the four quarters of the world.[100] While land survey maps, city plans, and engineering drawings provided relatively accurate spatial representations,[101] travelers in the Roman period sometimes carried measured itineraries or narrow strip maps of routes that were easy to carry while rolled up.[102] The strip maps either circle the Mediterranean or radiate out from it in various directions. As one can observe in the Peutinger map, a fourth-century map[103] that was probably based on a model reaching back sometime before 79 C.E.,[104] or perhaps back to Marcus Vipsanius

Agrippa (64–12 B.C.E.), the friend of Augustus whose worldmap was later placed in marble in the Porticus Vipsania,[105] these maps were not organized spatially like modern road maps, but depicted north–south distances on a much smaller scale than east–west. Major barriers such as rivers and mountains were marked along with left and right turns, but the spatial relations on the Peutinger map were very different from what the modern eye might expect. Thus the section on Illyricum shows an elongated Balkan Peninsula with sea above and below, with the Danube toward the top of the land strip, and with Italy at the bottom across a narrow-appearing strait.[106] This strip map connects on one end to the map of Italy,[107] with Rome at the center of the world,[108] and on the other end to strips that run through Macedonia[109] and Asia Minor,[110] along the coast to Antioch[111] and literally circling around the eastern coast of the

99   BAGD 376 notes that Illyricum consisted of two Roman provinces, Dalmatia and Pannonia, and that both were closely associated in literary references to Macedonia, where Paul had missionized in Philippi, Thessalonica, and Beroea. For geographic and cultural orientation, see the studies by János Szilágyi, "Illyricum," *Der Kleine Pauly. Lexikon der Antike* (Stuttgart: Müller, 1967) 1365–69; Géza Anföldy, with a contribution by András Mócsy, *Bevölkerung und Gesellschaft der römischen Provinz Dalmatien* (Budapest: Akadémiai Kiadó, 1965). John Wilkes makes it clear that "Illyricum" was the name the Romans were using for their Adriatic territories by the middle of the first century: *The Illyrians* (Oxford/Cambridge, Mass.: Blackwell, 1992) 208; see 182–219.

100 See Konrad Miller, *Mappaemundi. Die ältesten Weltkarten* (Stuttgart: Roth, 1895–98) 6, 145–47; O. A. W. Dilke, "Maps in the Service of the State: Roman Cartography to the End of the Augustan Era," in J. B. Harley and D. Woodward, eds., *The History of Cartography*, vol. 1, *Cartography in Prehistoric, Ancient, and Medieval Europe and the Mediterranean* (Chicago: University of Chicago Press, 1987) 205–9.

101 See O. W. A. Dilke, "Roman Large-Scale Mapping in the Early Empire," in Harley and Woodward, *Cartography in Prehistoric, Ancient, and Medieval Europe and the Mediterranean*, 212–33.

102 See O. A. W. Dilke, "Itineraries and Geographical Maps in the Early and Late Roman Empires," in Harley and Woodward, *Cartography in Prehistoric, Ancient, and Medieval Europe and the Mediterranean*, 234–57.

103 See Richard Talbert, "Cartography and Taste in

Peutinger's Roman Map," in R. Talbert and K. Brodersen, eds., *Space in the Roman World: Its Perception and Presentation*, Antike Kultur und Geschichte 5 (Münster: LIT Verlag, 2004) 128–31.

104 Konrad Miller, *Itineraria Romana. Römische Reisewege an der Hand der Tabula Peutingeriana* (Rome: Bretschneider, 1964) xxxvi–xxxix. For a discussion of the Peutinger maps, see Dilke, "Itineraries and Geographical Maps," 234, 238–42. Talbert, "Cartography," 132–41, provides an account of subsequent publications of the map, some of them based on photographic copies.

105 Web site www.livius.org/pen-pg/peutinger/map.html.

106 Miller, *Itineraria*, 415–18.

107 Ibid., 191–94.

108 Talbert, "Cartography," 121, observes that when the missing parchments on the western end of the map are restored, Rome appears "precisely at the center of the entire map."

109 Ibid., 495–98.

110 Ibid., 631–34, 693–94. The geographic "distortion" in comparison with modern maps is seen in the depiction of Alexandria Troas on a straight stretch that runs toward Antioch, with Africa shown a short distance toward the bottom of the strip across a narrow Mediterranean Sea. Anatolia is compressed into a narrow series of horizontal roads below the Black Sea toward the top of the strip. Around the circle of the narrow Mediterranean at the bottom of the strip is Palestine, with Tyre, for example, depicted just below Phaselis on the central, southern coast of what is now Turkey.

Mediterranean to Jerusalem.[112] James M. Scott has pointed to the Jewish variety of this circular image of the world, centered in Jerusalem as seen particularly in Ezek 5:5.[113] The word κύκλος is used in this verse and elsewhere in the OT with reference to Jerusalem: Τάδε λέγει κύριος. Αὕτη ἡ Ἰερουσάλημ ἐν μέσῳ τῶν ἐθνῶν τέθεικα αὐτὴν καὶ τὰς κύκλῳ αὐτῆς χώρας ("Thus says the Lord, 'This is Jerusalem; I have placed her in the midst of the Gentiles and in the circle of the nations,'" Ezek 5:5). With this geographic framework, it is not at all mysterious[114] that Paul would have thought of Illyricum as lying on a circle from Jerusalem, and that Illyricum was the closest point he had reached on the route to Rome. His framework is not chronological but, given his worldview, geographic—and eschatological, for the early Christian mission aimed at completing the circle around the known world centered in the Mediterranean,[115] before the parousia.[116] The strip map of Palestine, in fact, depicts all of the locations of Paul's ministry from Damascus, Arabia, Cilicia, Antioch, Cyprus, Galatia, Asia, Macedonia, and Greece as lying along the arc of the northern side of the Mediterranean between Jerusalem and Illyricum.[117]

That Paul did not engage in a Gentile mission on his first visit to Jerusalem is clear on the basis of Gal 1.18-22,[118] but there is no doubt from his account of the second visit to Jerusalem at the time of the Apostolic Conference in Gal 2:1-2 that he "submitted before them the gospel which I preach among the Gentiles," which means that he reiterated and defended his message.[119] We have no evidence aside from this reference in Romans of a ministry in Illyricum,[120] but my chronology allows several months for this in the summer and fall of

111 Ibid., 635–36.

112 Ibid., 803–4. Palestine is depicted as a strip of land with sea at the top and bottom, with the Jordan River system flowing horizontally and Jerusalem located above the Dead Sea. The disparity from our contemporary geographic conception is particularly evident in the placement of the island of Rhodes a short distance above Caesearea while the island of Crete is a short distance above Damascus, with the land route between Palestine and what we would now think of as Turkey circling the end of a narrowly depicted Mediterranean through Antioch.

113 James M. Scott, *Paul and the Nations: The Old Testament and Jewish Background of Paul's Mission to the Nations with Special Reference to the Destination of Galatians*, WUNT 84 (Tübingen: Mohr-Siebeck, 1995) 5–56. He cites Gen 10 and 1 Chr 1:1–2:2, which place Israel at the center of the world, a conception reflected in Ezek 38–39 and Isa 66:18-20. The later impact of this conception of the world is reflected in *Jub.* 8–9 and Josephus *Ant.* 1.120–47, describing travels to the surrounding nations, using the schemes of the Garden of Eden and the locations of the sons of Jacob, retaining the idea of Israel's centrality, and describing cities in Spain as the furthermost point in the world.

114 For example, A. S. Geyser argues in "Un essai d'explication de Rom xv.19," *NTS* 6 (1959–60) 156–59, that Paul is only speaking symbolically when referring to travels "from Jerusalem to Illyricum" in order to claim equal status with the twelve disciples. Ferdinand Hahn in *Mission*, 96, suggests that Paul refers to Illyricum as the boundary between the two halves of the empire, but this seems too vague a connotation without more explicit evidence somewhere in the Pauline corpus.

115 See John Knox, "Rom 15:14-33 and Paul's Conception of His Apostolic Mission," *JBL* 83 (1964) 11. The worldwide scope of Paul's mission to the Gentiles is also lifted up by Peter Müller in "Grundlinien paulinischer Theologie (Röm 15,14-33)," *KD* 35 (1989) 216–21.

116 See Oscar Cullmann, "Le caractère eschatologique de devoir missionnaire et de la conscience apostolique de S. Paul," *RHPhR* 16 (1936) 235–39; Munck, *Paul*, 48–55; C. K. Barrett, "New Testament Eschatology," *SJT* 6 (1953) 228, 235–30; Barrett, *Romans*, 276–77.

117 See note 95 describing the depiction of Palestine in Miller, *Itineraria*, 803–4. While modern atlases lead us to the assumption that Damascus, for instance, is off the direct route from Jerusalem to Antioch and Asia Minor, the strip map places Damascus to the right of Jerusalem on one of the two main roads to Antioch.

118 See Cranfield, 2:760.

119 See Betz, *Galatians*, 84–88.

120 To conclude that Paul never visited Illyricum, because Acts fails to mention it, overlooks the primacy that should be granted to the primary evidence found in the Pauline letters. Hence, I do not find plausible the suggestion of Morris, 514, that Paul "had preached from the boundary of Jerusalem to the boundary of Illyricum," which means that he never reached the latter.

56 C.E. after meeting Titus in Macedonia (2 Cor 7:5-16);[121] the later tradition of the Pauline school associated Titus with Dalmatia, which is part of Illyricum (2 Tim 4:10). The founding visit to Illyricum would have immediately preceded Paul's return for the final winter in Corinth—when Romans was written. Since Paul usually missionized in important urban centers, it is likely that he worked in Epetium, Salona, Tragurium, or Scodra, of which the latter would have been most easily accessible from Macedonia.[122]

The choice of the verb πεπληρωκέναι ("I have fulfilled") to describe Paul's achievement has elicited explanations of his allegedly astonishing exaggeration,[123] but the geographic framework and Paul's strategy of regional missionizing[124] explain why he would use this term in a bureaucratic sense of executing a mission.[125] The use of πληρόω for accomplishing duties of a particular office frequently surfaces in the papyri and other sources.[126] In the following example, the Roman prefect writes to the official at Oxyrhynchus to reiterate an order; while the lacuna at the beginning of each line obscures the content of the order, the use of πληρόω is instructive: Καὶ νῦν [τ]οῦτο ἐπιστέλλω . . . πλήρωσον τὸ κεκελευσμένον ("and now I send this . . . fulfill what is ordered . . ."; P.Oxy. 10.252, recto 8–10). Another governmental document from 104 C.E. uses πληρόω in reference to officials carrying out a census: ἵνα . . . τὴν συνήθη [οἰ]κονομίαν τῆ[ς ἀπο]γραφῆς πληρώσωσιν ("in order that they may carry out the regular adminis-

tration of the census," P.Lond. 3. Nr. 904.24–26). In a first-century C.E. Spartan inscription, the following regulation refers to an officer in charge of training athletes for a contest, again using πληρόω in reference to discharging responsibilities: ὃς ἕξει καὶ τὴν τοῦ ξυστάρχου τειμήν, πληρῶν τὰ εἰθισμέν[α] ("who also held the honor of the official, discharging the customary procedures").[127] We even have an example of this verb in association with "ministry," the term that Paul had applied to his ambassadorial vocation in 15:16: Ἡ βουλὴ καὶ ὁ δῆμος Σάτυρον Φιλεί[ν]ου, [π]ληρώσαντα πασᾶν ἀρχὴν καὶ λ[ε]τουργίαν . . . ("The council and the people of Satyr Phileinos, having fulfilled every office and ministry . . ."; CIG II. 2336.1–3).

What Paul claims is not that he has preached the gospel in every conceivable location but that he had fulfilled his specific calling to establish churches in a sufficient number of important centers to make the subsequent missionizing of their regional hinterlands by local colleagues feasible.[128] He has now discharged his responsibilities in the East and is ready to move on. The use of τὸ εὐαγγέλιον as the object of the verb confirms that "the gospel" connotes the act of proclamation as well as the content to be preached.[129] Whether the expression "gospel of Christ" should be viewed as an objective genitive, the "gospel about Christ,"[130] is impossible to determine with certainty,[131] but there is no doubt that the "good news"[132] Paul proclaims relates in a variety of ways to, and is derived from, Christ. In con-

---

121 Jewett, Chronology, Graph of Dates and Time Spans at the end of the publication of 1979.

122 See János Szilágyi's listing of the major commercial centers of Illyricum in the article "Illyricum," in Der Kleine Pauly. Lexikon der Antike (Stuttgart: Müller, 1967) 1369. He notes (69) that there is evidence of Christian communities in Illyricum by the second century, with larger congregations emerging in the third. Scodra would have been easily accessible about fifty miles north of the western terminus of the Egnatian Way at Dyrrhachium. Scodra was an important, walled city that became a colony with additional Italian settlers under Augustus, according to Anföldy, Dalmatien, 143, 184. The most important city was Salona, described by Anföldy on 99, in which there was evidence of Christianity in the second half of the third century (115, 187). See also Wilkes, Illyrians, Map 4, xxiii, 213–18.

123 See Käsemann, 395; Dunn, 2:864; Fitzmyer, 713;

also most of the earlier commentaries.

124 See Schille, Kollegialmission, 71–80, 100–109.

125 See Gerhard Delling, "πλήρης κτλ.," TDNT 6 (1968) 297: "to execute . . . a commanded action."

126 See MM 520.

127 Cited by MM 520 from the ABSA 12 (1905–6) 452.

128 See Schille, Kollegialmission, 97–104; Knox, "Apostolic Mission," 3.

129 Gerhard Friedrich, "εὐαγγελίζομαι κτλ.," TDNT 2 (1964) 729.

130 See Zmijewski, Paulus–Knecht, 136–37, italics in original.

131 See Friedrich, "εὐαγγελίζομαι κτλ.," 731, citing Kühner and Gerth, Grammatik, 2:333–34.

132 G. H. R. Horsley discusses a late-second- or early-third-century C.E. papyrus letter that uses this term in response to a wedding invitation: χαρᾶς ἡμᾶς ἐπλήρωσας εὐαγγελισαμένη τὸν γάμον τοῦ κρατίστου Σαραπίωνος ("You filled us with joy

trast to the modern tendency to understand evangelization as individual conversion, Paul Bowers has shown that this terminology implies founding and nurturing congregations: "Paul's familiar formula 'proclaiming the gospel' is . . . not simply an initial preaching mission but the full sequence of activities resulting in settled churches. All of this involved the application of the gospel and its full elaboration."[133]

■ **20** Although the opening words in this verse could be taken in several ways,[134] I think that οὕτως δέ ("thus, so that") points both forward and backward, linking the claim to have fulfilled the gospel with the ambition not to preach in locations evangelized by others.[135] Paul's apostolic ambition is expressed with the verb φιλοτιμέομαι, which no longer was restricted to the technical sense of striving after civic honors,[136] and was being used to describe vocational goals[137] or the willingness to carry out a task set by a superior.[138] The choice of terms is consistent with an ambassadorial construal of Paul's task, appointed as the delegate of Christ to the Gentiles and acting out of gratitude for benefits already received.[139]

The shape of Paul's aspiration is "not to preach where Christ has already been named," that is, in regions that had not yet been evangelized. The use of the aorist passive ὠνομάσθη indicates making a person known,[140] in this case, introducing Christ to persons and regions that had not yet heard of him.[141] A close parallel to this usage is 1 Macc 3:9, which describes how well known Judas Maccabeus became after carrying out his purge in Israel: Καὶ ὠνομάσθη ἕως ἐσχάτου τῆς γῆς ("So he was even named to the ends of the earth").[142] Similarly, the *Ep. Arist.* 124 describes the ambition of Eleazar to attract well-trained followers about whose reputations he had heard: "For he knew how the king in his love of excellence regarded it a very great gain, whenever a man surpassing others in culture and intellect was made known (ὠνομασθῇ) to him, to summon him to himself." The use of the word "name" in these contexts refers to making someone known for the first time, which is Paul's particular calling as an apostle of Christ. Paul's rule of not building on another's foundation is laid out in definitive detail in 2 Cor 10:12-18; in 1 Cor 3:6-15 he refers to his calling to θεμέλιον τιθέναι ("to establish foundations") of congregations.[143] Although there are distant

when you announced the good news of most noble Sarapion's marriage"). A number of other joyous citations are provided in "The 'Good News' of a Wedding," *NDIEC* 3 (1983) 10–15.

133 Paul Bowers, "Fulfilling the Gospel: The Scope of the Pauline Mission," *JETS* 30 (1987) 185–98, esp. 198.

134 See Cranfield's argument for a forward reference in 2:763; Käsemann, 395, appears to reject this.

135 See Dunn, 2:865, citing BAGD 597–98 and 1 Cor 9:24.

136 Lendon, *Empire of Honour*, 86, explains the use of φιλοτιμία in reference to public service and philanthropy: "It was in honour terms that the rich man's motivation, involving so much trouble and expense, was chiefly understood: he devoted to the city his money and effort and got honor in return." MM 672 notes that the technical sense of this word erodes in later Greek, so that it "means little more than 'am zealous,' 'strive eagerly.'" See also G. H. R. Horsley, "φιλοτιμία," *NDIEC* 1 (1981) 88.

137 For example, Herod is described by Josephus as being "ambitious to leave behind to posterity still greater monuments of his reign than cities" (φιλοτιμούμενος μείζω τὰ μνεῖα τῆς ἀρχῆς τῶν πόλεων ἐκεκίνητο, *Ant.* 15.330).

138 MM 672 mentions a third-century B.C.E. papyrus that declares willingness to carry out a travel command: ἐφιλοτιμοῦ με παραγέσθαι σοι καὶ ἦλθον ("being myself eager to be sent to you and also to come," *P.Petr.* 3. Nr. 42.H.8.f.3–4). Similarly, Paul describes his desire to please the Lord in all circumstances in 2 Cor 5:9: διὸ καὶ φιλοτιμούμεθα, εἴτε ἐνδημοῦντες εἴτε ἐκδημουντες, εὐάρεστοι αὐτῷ εἶναι ("So whether we are at home or away, we aspire to please Him").

139 Lendon, *Empire of Honour*, 87, describes the typical motivation: "Gratitude to one's town, whether for upbringing, services, honour, or office, also played its role in inspiring public benefaction." It was natural to extend this social concept into the realm of service to Christ.

140 See BAGD 574. Dunn, 2:865, prefers the "more pregnant sense of 'be named in worship . . . ,'" which appears strained in this context. Fitzmyer, 715, concurs.

141 Käsemann, 395, suggests that this usage may "come from the vocabulary of mission."

142 The same formulation is found in 2 Macc 14:10.

143 See Vielhauer, *OIKODOMH*, 82–83; Pfammatter, *Kirche als Bau*, 61–62.

parallels in Epictetus,[144] Paul's metaphorical use of οἰκοδομεῖν ("to build") probably was influenced by the LXX and Jewish Hellenism.[145] An example of this usage is the word to Israel in Jer 38:4, in which the nation is "built" by God: Ὅτι οἰκοδομήσω σε, καὶ οἰκοδο-μηθήσῃ παρθένος Ἰσραήλ ("For I will build you and you shall be built, O virgin of Israel"). More exact examples of building a small group of believers could be drawn from Qumran,[146] where the term "foundation" appears as a metaphor for the rule on which the sect was established: והאיש אשר ילון על יסוד היחד ישלחתהו ולוא ישוב ("Anyone who murmurs against the foundation of the community shall be expelled and shall not return," 1QS 7:17; for a more extended use of the metaphors of building and foundation for the Qumran community, see 8:4-9). In Paul's formulation, building only on his own foundation implies avoidance of areas where either Gentile congregations or Jewish Christian congregations were already in existence, as in Rome.[147] His calling is that of a pioneer.[148] Future missionizing was to be done in an area thus far untouched by the gospel and, as 15:24, 28 reveal, the area Paul has in mind is Spain. The puzzle of coordinating Paul's rule of working only in churches he has established with his purpose in visiting Rome as announced in 1:13-15 has led to radical resolutions,[149] which are rendered unnecessary by a straightforward comprehension of Paul's plan to visit Rome only briefly in order to gain support for the mission to Spain, which had not yet been evangelized.[150] The adversative construction in 20b-21a, ἵνα μὴ . . . ἀλλά ("in order not . . . but"), brings into contrast preaching where churches have already been established and preaching to those who have not yet heard; the central concern here is not Paul's status but the situation of Gentiles who have not yet gained access to Christ.[151]

■ **21** The citation from Isaiah provides the scriptural basis of Paul's apostolic rule in 15:20 while offering an effective reprise of 1:1-15 and the earlier use of Isa 52 in 10:15-17.[152] The quotation is introduced with the traditional formula[153] that I analyzed in 1:17, καθὼς γέ-γραπται ("it has been written"), denoting a citation drawn from Scripture. The initial ὅτι ("that") is deleted because it would have disrupted the transition from this introduction to the citation itself.[154] If my reading of the text-critical evidence is correct, Paul's citation alters the wording of the LXX version of Isa 52:15c-d by placing the verb at the beginning of 15c,[155] thus accentuating the eschatological promise. In Cranfield's words, "Paul sees the words of the prophet as a promise which is even now being fulfilled by the spreading of the knowledge of

---

144 Epictetus uses "foundation" as a more individualistic metaphor, urging that the basis of ethical choices should be sound in *Diss.* 2.15.8: οὐ θέλεις τὴν ἀρχὴν στῆσαι καὶ τὸν θεμέλιον, τὸ κρίμα σκέψασθαι πότερον ὑγιὲς ἢ οὐκ ὑγιές . . . ("Do you not wish to make your beginning and foundation firm, to consider whether your decision is sound or unsound . . . ?").

145 See Otto Michel, "οἰκοτομέω," *TDNT* 5 (1967) 140. Jürgen Roloff argues in *Apostolat* 105–11 that early Christian use of the metaphor of building and foundation derives from the Jesus tradition, but in passages like Mark 12:10, Acts 4:11, etc., developed from Isa 18:16 and Ps 118:22-23, it is Christ who is himself the cornerstone whom God set in Israel; it is unclear that Paul thought of himself laying the foundation in quite the same sense.

146 See Pfammatter, *Kirche als Bau*, 152–64, and Henryk Muszyński, *Fundament, Bild und Metapher in den Handschriften aus Qumran. Studie zur Vorgeschichte des neutestamentlichen Begriffs ΘΕΜΕΛΙΟΣ*, AnBib 61 (Rome: Biblical Institute Press, 1975) 121–68; the link with Rom 15:20 is briefly discussed on 231.

147 See Vielhauer, *ΟΙΚΟΔΟΜΗ*, 83.

148 Schmidt, 245; Kitzberger, *Bau der Gemeinde*, 60.

149 See Sigfred Pedersen's survey of the various solutions to the "Gordian knot" of the Pauline rule in "Isagogik des Römerbriefes," 51. He refers to Günter Klein's argument that Paul intends to provide an apostolic foundation for the church in Rome in "Paul's Purpose," 29–43. Schmithals's division hypothesis (*Römerbrief*, 129–44) separates the references in chapters 1 and 15 to avoid this alleged conflict.

150 See Pedersen, "Isagogik des Römerbriefes," 63–67.

151 See ibid., 62 n. 44.

152 See Zeller, 239.

153 See Koch, *Schrift*, 25.

154 See Stanley, *Scripture*, 184.

155 Dunn, 2:865; Cranfield, 2:765; and Murray, 2:215, correctly see that Paul moved ὄψονται to the beginning of 15:5c. Koch's discussion of the text in *Schrift*, 102, 318, follows Nestle-Aland[26/27] in believing that Paul conformed precisely to the LXX.

916

Christ."[156] Those who have "never been informed about him" and "never heard of him," in Shum's view, "no doubt fit well with the apostle's next target group of mission, i.e., the people(s) in Spain and beyond."[157] His non-intervention rule of 15:20b is therefore not a matter of arrogant independence from others but an obedient constraint in response to a scriptural warrant. In contrast to the MT, the LXX version adds περὶ αὐτοῦ ("about him"), which serves Paul's purpose in making it plain that the proclamation involves the suffering servant of Yahweh. Although some have argued that Paul saw himself in the role of this servant,[158] it seems clear that the "him" in this citation refers to Christ[159] and that the accent lies on the explanation of Paul's peculiar rule of not missionizing where the message about Christ has

already been heard. As Pedersen points out, the adversative introduction of the citation with ἀλλά ("but") coordinates it directly with Paul's evangelistic rule in 15:20b.[160] Paul's mission seeks to fulfill this eschatological promise of enlightenment to the Gentiles,[161] so they can "be informed" (ἀνηγγέλη) and "understand" (συνήσουσιν) the transforming message about the righteousness of God revealed in Christ.[162] The reversal of the formerly shameful status of the Gentiles echoes other passages earlier in Romans; Paul sees Scripture as a witness to the impact of divine grace in their conversion. With this scriptural authentication of his mission,[163] which would have evoked a measure of emotional appeal in the Roman audience suitable for the peroration,[164] Paul is ready to set forth his plans in the next pericope.

156 Cranfield, 2:765; see also Schlier, 433.
157 Shum, *Paul's Use of Isaiah*, 257; parenthesis in original.
158 See Alexander Kerrigan, "Echoes of Themes from the Servant Songs in Pauline Theology," *SPCIC* 2:217–28; Walter Radl, "Alle Mühe umsonst? Paulus und der Gottsknecht," in A. Vanhoye, ed., *L'Apôtre Paul. Personnalité, Style et Conception du Ministère*, BETL 73 (Louvain: Leuven University, 1986) 144–49, with reference to Isa 49:4; Dunn, 2:866.
159 Wagner, *Heralds*, 333.
160 Pederson, "Isagogik des Römerbriefes," 62.
161 The ἔθνη ("Gentiles") are the antecedent of "they" in the LXX citation, and by implication carried forward from 15:18, also in Romans.
162 Wagner, *Herald*, 333–34, points out that the preceding half-verse in Isaiah not cited also supports his mission.
163 Wilk, *Bedeutung des Jesajabuches*, 81–82.
164 See Zeller's discussion of the crucial role of the Isaiah prophecy for the early Christian mission in 239; the audience in Rome would therefore have already been the beneficiaries of this prophecy, which was being confirmed by the spread of the gospel in Rome. Quintilian's *Inst.* 6.1.7; 6.2.1–24 discusses the role of emotional appeals in perorations.

15

The Second Pericope

The Report on Travel Plans and an Appeal to Participate in Present and Future Missionary Activities

22/ Therefore I was also often[a] hindered in coming to you. 23/ But now, having no more room in these regions, but having[b] the desire to come to you for many[c] years, 24/ when I travel to Spain[d] (for I hope to see you while traveling through[e] and to be sent there with your help,[f] after I first have the full pleasure of your company for a while)— 25/ But now I am traveling to Jerusalem, serving[g] the saints. 26/ For Macedonia[h] was well pleased[i], also Achaia, to establish a particular fellowship for the poor among the saints in Jerusalem. 27/ For they were well pleased and are their debtors.[j] For if the Gentiles shared their spiritual things, they ought also to minister to them in fleshly things. 28/ Therefore when[k] I have completed this, sealing this fruit[l], I shall be off by way of you to Spain. 29/ But I know[m] that coming to you, I shall come in the fullness[n] of Christ's blessing[o].

30/ Now I urge you brothers,[p] through[q] our Lord Jesus Christ and through the love of the Spirit, to join in my struggle by praying in my behalf[r] before God, 31/ in order that I might be delivered from the disobedient ones in Judea, and[s] my service[t] to[u] Jerusalem might be acceptable to the saints, 32/ in order that in coming[v] to you in joy[w] through [the] will of God,[x] I may be refreshed together[y] with you.[z]

33/ The God of peace [be] with all of you. Amen.[aa]

---

a The support for τὰ πολλά ("many times") in ℵ A C L P Ψ 6 33 69 88 104 323 326 365 424 614 945 1175 1241 1243 1319 1505 1506 1573 1735 1739 1836 1881 2344 2495 *Maj* is no stronger than for that of πολλάκις ("frequently, many times") in P[46] B D F G 330, but the fact that the latter is used in a similar context in Rom 1:13 leads one to judge the former as the more difficult and thus the more likely original text.

b In place of the widely attested and probably original participle ἔχων ("having"), found in P[46] ℵ A D[1] B L P Ψ 6 33 88 104 323 330 365 424 614[(acc. to N-A)] 945 1175 1241 1505 1573 1735 1739 1836 1874 1881 2495 *Maj*, the variant, ἔχω ("I have"), appears in D* F G 69 614[(acc. to Swanson)] 1243 1506 *pc* it, perhaps as

Cranfield, 2:768, suggests, in an attempt to eliminate the incomplete sentence by replacing the second participle with a finite verb.

c The earlier text of the Nestle-Aland[24/25] editions favored ἱκανῶν ("sufficient, many") found in B C P 69 81 326 365 1243 1319 1506 1573 1962 2127 *pc*, but Nestle-Aland[26/27] and *GNT*[3/4] favor πολλῶν ("many") found in P[46] ℵ A D (F—see v. 22) G L Ψ 6 33 88 104 181 323 330 424 436 451 629 630 945 1175[(according to Swanson)] 1241 1505 1735 1739 1836 1874 1877 1881 2492 2495 *Maj Lect*. Metzger, *Textual Commentary (1975)*, 537, refers to "the early and diversified evidence supporting πολλῶν" and to the likelihood that it was replaced by a more polished term that curtails the exaggeration. In this instance, the latest editions of Nestle-Aland appear to have solid reasons for accepting πολλῶν as the superior reading.

d The completion ἐλεύσομαι πρὸς ὑμᾶς ("I shall come to you") in ℵ[2] L 5 6 33 61 69 88 104 181 218 256 263 323 326 330 365 424 436 441 451 459 467 621 623[c] 629 630 720 915 917 945 1175 1241 1319 1398 1505 1563 1573 1678 1718 1735 1751 1836 1838 1845 1874 1875 1877 1908 1912 1942 1959 2127 2138 2197 2200 2344 2492 2495 2516 2523 2544 2718 *Maj Lect* sy[h] geo[2] slav appears to be a secondary clarification because some readers might gain the impression that the Roman congregation was in Spain. The omission of these words is strongly and widely attested by P[46] ℵ* A B C D F G P Ψ 81 614 623* 1243 1506 1739 1852 1881 1962 2110 *pc* ar (b) d f g mon o vg sy[p] sa bo arm eth geo[1] Or[lat] Chr Ambst Hier Pel. See the discussion of the grammatical issues related to the various formulations in Godet, 482–83.

e A minor variant to the broadly attested διαπορευόμενος ("traveling through") is found in P[46] A 630 1506 1739 1881 *pc*: πορευόμενος ("traveling"). Cranfield, 2:769, suggests that the variant was influenced by πορεύωμαι ("I travel") in 15:24.

f As in Rom 15:15 there is a confusion between ἀφ᾽ (ἀπό = "from, with the help of"; see BAGD 87) in P[46] B D F G 330 629 630 *pc* and ὑφ᾽ (ὑπό = "by") in the rest of the texts. In this instance, a different and stronger array of Alexandrian and Western witnesses favor the former, which also seems more appropriate for what we now know about the logistical requirements for the Spanish mission. In addition, the latter is the easier reading because it would have seemed odd to later scribes for Paul to require the help of the Romans to travel to Spain. For a contrary assessment that supports the choice of ὑφ᾽ in Nestle-Aland[26/27] and *GNT*[3/4], see Cranfield, 2:769.

g In place of the rather awkward but probably original present participle διακονῶν ("serving") found

918

in ℵ^c A B C L P Ψ 6 33 69 88 104 323 326 330 365 424 614 945 1175 1241 1243 1319 1505 1506 1573 1735 1739 1836 1874 1881 2344 2495 *Maj*, P^46 and the "Western" texts D F G latt have the aorist infinitive διακονῆσαι ("to serve") and ℵ* has διακονῆσων ("having served"). Neither variant has a strong possibility of originality.

h   A minor variation in F G it sy^p Ambst has Μακεδόνες ("Macedonians") in place of the widely attested Μακεδονία ("Macedonia"). The plural form may well have been influenced by the change to the plural form of the verb εὐδόκησαν ("they were pleased"), discussed in the next note.

i   In place of the widely attested plural aorist εὐδόκησαν ("they were pleased"), the singular form εὐδόκησεν ("he/she was pleased) appears in P^46 B 1241 *pc* Spec. The variant is not discussed by Metzger or any of the commentaries, but it seems possible that there was a grammatical link between a singular verb and the word "Macedonia" at an early level of the history of the text. The awkwardness of this wording was corrected by what appears to be an easier reading—the plural εὐδόκησαν coordinated with both "Macedonia and Achaia" that is adopted by Nestle-Aland^26/27 and *GNT*^3/4. This appears to be an example similar to Rom 15:19, 21 where the Vaticanus reading (B) preserves the most ancient and reliable version of the text, despite its inferior quality in the rest of the Pauline letters as noted by Aland and Aland, *Text*, 50.

j   In place of the rather awkward, but probably original, expression εὐδόκησαν γὰρ καὶ ὀφειλέται εἰσίν ("For they were pleased and were debtors") strongly attested in ℵ A B C L P Ψ 6 33 69 88 104 323 326 330 365 424 614 945 1175 1241 1319 1505 1506 1573 1243 1735 1739 1836 1874 1881 2344 2495 *Maj* ar vg sy cop, several variants arose to eliminate the roughness. D has simply ὀφειλέται εἰσίν ("they were debtors") and P^46 F G it Ambst Spec have ὀφειλέται γὰρ εἰσὶν ("for they were debtors").

k   The addition of the particle ἄρα (following οὖν "so then") by F G appears to be an intended stylistic improvement.

l   A difficult textual variant at this point, strongly attested in P^46 B *pc* vg^mss Ambst, omits αὐτοῖς ("to them"). Neither Nestle-Aland^26/27 nor *GNT*^3/4 accepts this omission. But given the trustworthiness of B, as recently seen in Rom 15:19, 21, 24, 26, this variant in combination with the other witnesses deserves serious consideration. It is hard to discern a motivation for omitting αὐτοῖς if it were original, because the sentence would become rather vague without it. Hence, the omission would appear to be the harder reading. Also, the possibility of an assimi-

lation of the αὐτοῖς from the end of v. 27 seems likely. For the rather lame suggestion that the omission was "probably accidental," see Cranfield, 2:774.

m   In place of the widely attested οἶδα δέ ("but I know, understand"), F G mon vg^mss Ambst have the more technical expression γινώσκω γάρ ("for I know, perceive"), which appears to be a secondary effort to eliminate the puzzling antithesis with "but" and to remove the slight indications of uncertainty about how Paul would be received in Rome.

n   Showing a similar thematic interest evident in the elaborate variant observed in Rom 15:13, D* (reads -ίας) F G offer a theological improvement of πληροφορία ("in full assurance") in place of πληρώματι ("in fullness").

o   Another theological qualification, this time by later traditions represented in ℵ^2 L Ψ 5 33 61 69 88 104 181 218 256 323 326 330 365 424* 436 441 451 459 467 614 621 623 720^c 915 (917 Ἰησοῦ for Χριστοῦ) 945 1175 1241 1319 1398 1505 (1506 2110 (Χριστοῦ placed first) 1563 1573 1678 1718 1735 1751 1836 1838 1845 1846 1874 1875 1877 1908 1912 1942 1959 1962 2127 2138 2344 2492 2495 2523 2544 2718 *Maj Lect* vg^cl sy^p.h geo^2 slav Chr, adds τοῦ εὐαγγελίου τοῦ ("of the gospel of") before "Christ." The version lacking these words is convincingly supported in P^46 ℵ* A B C D F G P 6 81 263 424^c 629 630 720* 1243 1506 1739 1881 2200 *pc* ar b d f g mon o vg^ww, st sa bo geo^1 Cl Or^lat Ambst Pel.

p   The omission of ἀδελφοί ("brethren") by P^46 B is so difficult to explain that Nestle-Aland^26/27 and *GNT*^3/4 place it in square brackets. The support for the inclusion of "brothers" is found in ℵ A C D F G L P Ψ 6 33 69 88 104 323 326 330 365 424 614 945 1175 1241 1243 1319 1505 1506 1573 1735 1739 1836 1874 1881 2344 2495 *Maj* lat sy cop. The issue is not discussed by Metzger. Cranfield, 2:775–76, makes a case for inclusion on the basis that "I exhort you, brothers" was typical of Pauline usage elsewhere, which seems contrary to generally accepted text-critical principles, that a copyist would more likely add than delete a typical feature. Westcott, as well as Zuntz, *Text*, 175, accepted the omission. However, in "Brothers in Brackets," 311–13, Aasgaard has shown that P^46 B are both susceptible to omission and that in view of the stronger witness for inclusion, the word ἀδελφοί should be considered original.

q   The inclusion of ὀνόματος τοῦ ("of the name of") in L 1881 *pc* appears to be a secondary theological correction.

r   Several minor variants replace the ecclesiologically awkward but undoubtedly original reference to "the prayers" ὑπὲρ ἐμοῦ ("for me"). F G d* mon replace it with ὑμῶν ("your"), producing the simplified expression "in your prayers." D vg^cl conflate the two readings in ὑμῶν ὑπὲρ ἐμοῦ, which would result in the translation "your prayers for me."

s   An obvious grammatical improvement is offered by the addition of ἵνα in ℵ² D¹ L Ψ 33 69 88 104 323 326 330 365 424* 614 945 1175 1241 1319 1505 1573 1735 1836 1874 2344 2495 *Maj* f g syʰ Ambst. The absence of ἵνα is more strongly supported by P⁴⁶ ℵ* A B C D* F G P 6 81 424ᶜ 630 1243 1506 1739 1881 *pc* lat.

t   In place of the term διακονία ("service") in P⁴⁶ ℵ A C D¹ L P Ψ 6 33 69 81 88 104 181 256 263 323 326 330 365 424 436 451 459 614 629 945 1175 1241 1243 1319 1505 1506 1573 1735 1739 1836 1852 1874 1877 1881 1912 1962 2127 2200 2344 2492 2495 *Maj Lect* d² f g vgᵐˢˢ syᵖ·ʰ sa bo arm geo slav Orˡᵃᵗ Chr, a reading that implies Paul's subordination to Jerusalem, B D* F G ar b d* *(remuneration)* mon o (vg *obsequii mei oblatio*) Ambst Pel substitute the less problematic term δωροφορία ("gift bringing"). It is a clear case of correction for ecclesiastical purposes.

u   In place of εἰς ("to"), which in this context carries out the same unwanted element of subordination to Jerusalem, the same Greek majuscules involved in the change from "service" to "gift bringing" earlier in the sentence, B D* F G substitute ἐν ("in"). They are joined by 1505 2495 *pc*. The reading with εἰς in P⁴⁶ ℵ A C D² L P Ψ 6 33 69 88 104 323 326 330 365 424 614 945 1175 1241 1243 1319 1573 1735 1739 1836 1874 1881 2344 *Maj* is undoubtedly correct.

v   In place of the participle ἐλθών ("coming") found in ℵ* A C 6 33 81 88 181* 256 263 326* 365 424ᶜ 630 1243 1319 1505 1506⁽ᵃᶜᶜ· ᵗᵒ ᴺᴬ; ᵛⁱᵈ ᴳᴺᵀ⁾ 1573 1739 1852 1881 2127 2200 2495 *pc* sa arm Orˡᵃᵗ, the finite verb ἐλθῶ ("I come") appears in P⁴⁶ ℵ² B D F G L P Ψ 69 104 181ᶜ 323 326* 330 424* 436 451 459 614 629 945 1175 1241 1506⁽ᵃᶜᶜᵒʳᵈⁱⁿᵍ ᵗᵒ ˢʷᵃⁿˢᵒⁿ⁾ 1735 1836 1874 1877 1912 1962 2344 2492 *Maj Lect*ᵖᵗ· ᴬᴰ ar b d f g mon o vg syᵖ·ʰ bo eth geo slav Chr Ambst, apparently in an effort to clear up the awkward construction of the sentence, particularly for those texts omitting the rare verb "refreshed together," discussed below.

w   *GNT*³/⁴ mention several minor variants concerning the order of the clause "coming to you with joy" (see the preceding note), which are not discussed in the standard commentaries. There is a reversal of ἐν χαρᾷ ἐλθών to ἐλθών ἐν χαρᾷ in ℵ* and a shifting of ἐν χαρᾷ to create the reading ἐλθὼ πρὸς ὑμᾶς ἐν χαρᾷ in 629. Both appear to be efforts at stylistic improvement.

x   In place of θεοῦ ("of God"), a reading well attested in P⁴⁶ ℵ² A C D² L P Ψ 6 33 69 88 104 323 326 330 365 424 614 945 1175 1241 1243 1319 1505 1506 1573 1735 1739 1836 1874 1881 2344 2495 *Maj* vg sy, there are several apparent substitutions. B has

κυρίου Ἰησοῦ ("of [the] Lord Jesus"), D* F G it Ambst have Χριστοῦ Ἰησοῦ ("of Christ Jesus"), and ℵ* *pc* (b) have Ἰησοῦ Χριστοῦ ("of Jesus Christ").

y   While the rare compound verb συναναπαύσωμαι ("I might be refreshed together") is strongly attested by ℵ* A C 6 ⁽ᵃᶜᶜᵒʳᵈⁱⁿᵍ ᵗᵒ ᴺ⁻ᴬ, ᴳᴺᵀ⁾ 81 181* 256 263 365 424ᶜ 630 1243 1505 1506 ⁽ᵃᶜᶜᵒʳᵈⁱⁿᵍ ᵗᵒ ᴺ⁻ᴬ, ᵛⁱᵈ ᴳᴺᵀ⁾ 1573 1739 1852 1881ᶜ⁽ᵃᶜᶜᵒʳᵈⁱⁿᵍ ᵗᵒ ᴳᴺᵀ⁾ 2200 2495 *pc* sa arm Orˡᵃᵗ, appearing also in context preceded by καί ("and") in ℵ² L⁽ᵃᶜᶜᵒʳᵈⁱⁿᵍ ᵗᵒ ᴳᴺᵀ⁾ 33 69 181ᶜ 323 424* 436 451 614 945 1175 1735 1874 1877 1962 2492 *Maj Lect*ᵖᵗ· ᴬᴰ vg syᵖ·ʰ bo eth geo slav Chr, it is omitted in P⁴⁶ and B. The omission may be the result of a transcription error (Metzger, *Textual Commentary*, 474), but more likely is an effort to avoid a rare and ambiguous term (Sanday and Headlam, 415; Cranfield, 2:779). Other indications of the tendency to remove this difficult term are found in the substitution of ἀναψύξω ("I shall be refreshed") by D*·² ar b d f g mon o vgᵐˢ Ambst; ἀναψύχω ("I am refreshed") by F G; ἀναπαύσομαι ("I shall be rested") in 1881*; and συναναπαύσομαι ("I shall be rested with someone") in 6⁽ᵃᶜᶜ· ᵗᵒ ˢʷᵃⁿˢᵒⁿ⁾ 1319 1506⁽ᵃᶜᶜ· ᵗᵒ ˢʷᵃⁿˢᵒⁿ⁾ 1881ᶜ⁽ᵃᶜᶜ· ᵗᵒ ˢʷᵃⁿˢᵒⁿ⁾ 2127 *Lect*ᵖᵗ, and with a preceding καί in L⁽ᵃᶜᶜ· ᵗᵒ ˢʷᵃⁿˢᵒⁿ⁾ P Ψ⁽ᵃᶜᶜ· ᵗᵒ ᴳᴺᵀ, ˢʷᵃⁿˢᵒⁿ⁾ 88 104 326 330 459 1241 1836 1912 2344.

z   A variant reading in D F G has μεθ' ὑμῶν ("with you") in place of the widely attested ὑμῖν ("with you"), apparently another attempt at stylistic improvement.

aa The omission of "Amen" by P⁴⁶ A F G 330 436 451 630 1506 1739 1881 2200 *pc* f g mon o vgᵐˢ is understandable in the case of P⁴⁶ and 1506 because they place the doxology of 16:25-27 here. Whether the omission in the Alexandrian as well as some of the other texts is influenced by P⁴⁶ is difficult to say, but otherwise nobody seems to be able to explain it. The evidence for the inclusion of "Amen" in ℵ B C D L P Ψ 6 33 69 81 88 104 181 256 263 323 326 365 424 459 614 629 945 1175 1241 1243 1319 1505 1573 1735 1836 1852 1874 1877 1912 1962 2127 2344 2492 2495 *Maj Lect* ar b d vg syᵖ·ʰ sa bo arm eth geo slav Orˡᵃᵗ Chr Ambst Pel appears to be equally strong, so there are grounds for Metzger's argument that Nestle-Aland²⁶/²⁷ and *GNT*³/⁴ should place ἀμήν in square brackets (though they did not do so); *Textual Commentary*, 538. This would at least reflect consistency in text-critical methodology, although I would prefer to avoid ambiguous brackets altogether. Since the inclusion of "Amen" has broad support from a variety of textual groups, it is probably original. For a discussion of the placement of the doxology and other portions of chapter 16 at this point, see the Introduction, section 2.

Analysis

In this pericope Paul shifts from the recapitulation of his apostolic calling and strategy into a discussion of current and future plans, carefully opening the door to potential cooperation with the Roman churches. The shift from a review of church-building activities with others to a visit πρὸς ὑμᾶς ("to you") in the opening verse of this pericope indicates a change of subject and focus.[1] Here Paul elaborates the reasons for the impending visit to Rome that was announced in 1:11-13, thus continuing the reiteration of material from the introduction that is characteristic of well-designed perorations. A carefully diplomatic, discursive style continues in this pericope. Repetitions, corrections, and parenthetical comments suggest the unliterary style of typical Greco-Roman letters.[2] Only on occasion in this section does Paul rise to the eloquence in the rest of Romans, such as that found in the antithesis between τοῖς πνευματικοῖς ("in spiritual things") and τοῖς σαρκικοῖς ("in fleshly things") in the parallel clauses of 15:17b-c. Also, in 15:30 we encounter parallel phrases, "through our Lord Jesus Christ" and "through the love of the Spirit." However, the passage as a whole is not organized in rhythmic sentences. Its style reflects the urgency and immediacy of circumstantial details not found in the earlier sections of the letter.

In 15:22-29 Paul provides a review of his current missionary activities and his plans to visit Jerusalem, Rome, and Spain. In the context of a *peroratio*, particularly following the scriptural warrant of 15:21, this review contains subtle appeals to the Roman congregations to lend assistance in these eschatologically motivated missionary plans. As Brandt and Kennedy remind us, the peroration provides the climax of discourse by inciting the audience to action,[3] and it is logical for demonstrative discourse, especially in its ambassadorial form, to incite gently and indirectly. The review of present plans is followed by a more explicitly stated appeal for prayerful support in the delivery of the Jerusalem offering (15:30-32), whose impassioned quality would have been perceived as particularly appropriate for a *peroratio*.[4] The pericope is completed by a brief benediction (15:33).

Rhetorical Disposition

15:14–16:24	V. The *peroratio*: An appeal for cooperation in missionary activities in Jerusalem, Rome, and Spain
15:22-33	B. The report on travel plans and an appeal to participate in present and future missionary activities
15:22-29	1. A review of present and planned missionary activities
15:22-24	a. The plan for the visits to Rome and Spain
15:22	1) Paul's previous frustration in visiting Rome
15:23-24	2) The background of the current plan to visit Rome
15:23a	a) The reason Paul is now free to visit: "no more room" in the East
15:23b	b) Reiteration of Paul's long-standing desire to visit Rome
15:24	3) The plan to visit Rome on the way to Spain
15:24a	a) The plan to travel to Spain
15:24b	b) The hope to visit Rome in transit to Spain
15:24c	c) The hope to receive Roman help
15:24c	d) The plan to enjoy the company of the Roman believers
15:25-29	b. The plan to deliver the Jerusalem offering before traveling to Rome
15:25	1) The imminent departure for Jerusalem
15:26-27	2) The participation in and rationale for the Jerusalem offering
15:26a-b	a) Participants in the offering: Macedonia and Achaia
15:26c	b) The purpose of the offering: to aid the poor in Jerusalem
15:27	c) The participation in the offering and its theological justification

---

1   The assessment that 15:22-33 comprises a separate pericope is found in Michel, 461–62; Schlier, 433–34; Käsemann, 396–97; Wilckens, 3:123; Morris, 516–17; Dunn, 2:870–71.

2   See Michel, 462; White, *Light*, 190–91.

3   Brandt, *Rhetoric of Argumentation*, 68–69; Kennedy, *New Testament Interpretation*, 48: "At the end of a speech there is commonly an epilogue; in classical theory its primary functions are to recapitulate the points the speaker has made and to arouse the emotions of the audience toward action."

4   See Quintilian *Inst.* 6.1.9; 2.1; in 2.8–24 Quintilian discusses the two basic forms of emotional appeal, pathos and ethos, of which the latter is being evoked here.

15:27a	(1) Macedonia and Achaia "pleased" to participate
15:27b	(2) Macedonia and Achaia "obligated" to participate
15:27c-d	(3) The theological appropriateness of such obligation
15:27c	(a) Gentiles shared spiritual blessings of Jews
15:27d	(b) Therefore Gentiles should reciprocate with material gifts
15:28-29	3) Recapitulation of travel plans
15:28	a) The plan to travel to Rome and Spain after completing the delivery of the offering
15:29	b) Paul's confidence in coming with the "blessing of Christ"
15:30-32	2. The appeal for prayer support in the Jerusalem offering
15:30a	a. The formula of appeal
15:30b-c	b. The basis of the appeal
15:30b	1) Through Christ
15:30c	2) Through the "love of the Spirit"
15:30d	c. The requested action: urgent prayers
15:31-32	d. The content of the requested prayers
15:31a	1) Preservation from zealots in Judea
15:31b	2) Acceptance of Gentile offering by the Jerusalem church
15:32	3) The desired consequences of answered prayers for Paul's missionary plans
15:32a	a) The fulfillment of Paul's plans to travel to Rome
15:32b	b) The fulfillment of Paul's hopes for a sustaining relationship with Rome
15:33	3. The benediction
	a. The source of benediction: the "God of peace"
	b. The recipients of benediction: "all of you"
	c. The benefit: to be with you in Rome
	d. The Amen formula

Exegesis

■ **22** The opening words of the pericope refer back to Paul's extensive efforts to proclaim Christ to the Gentiles described in 15:19-21,[5] as well as to his long-standing desire to visit Rome (Rom 1:10-13),[6] explaining why he had been hitherto prevented. The two conjunctions, διὸ καί ("therefore also"), provide a swift transition to the new pericope by implying that the following inference is "self-evident"[7] on the basis of the factors mentioned at the end of the preceding pericope. The evocative verb ἐγκόπτω (literally: "cut down; impede, hinder") is derived from the military practice of digging ditches in the street to hold up a pursuing enemy; the delay is temporary but effective.[8] Paul used the same verb in Gal 5:7 and 1 Thess 2:18 to refer to satanic hindrances to the advance of his mission. When combined with τὰ πολλά ("frequently, often"), this expression refers not to a general hindrance or any ongoing personal reluctance but a series of specific hindrances such as those mentioned in Paul's catalog of missional impediments and disasters in 2 Cor 11:24-29. These include imprisonments, injuries, shipwrecks, travel delays due to weather and danger, threats to the unity and health of his congregations, and the need to labor with his hands to provide food and shelter. When we reconstruct the events of the two to three years immediately preceding the writing of Romans, the hindrances to his advancing further along the arc from Jerusalem to Illyricum are obvious. In my sketch of Paul's career,[9] I count several imprisonments (1 Cor 15:32; 2 Cor 1:8; Phlm 1; Phil 1:14); congregational problems in Colossae (Col 2:8-23), Laodicia (Col 2:1), Philippi (Phil 3:1-21), and Corinth (all of 1 and 2 Corinthians); postponed plans to deliver the Jerusalem offering because of congregational conflicts and threats from zealots (2 Cor 8–9; Acts 20:3); and extensive travels such as the abortive trip to Corinth (2 Cor 2:1; 12:14; 13:1) and the anxious trip to Troas in search of Titus bearing news about his alienated congregation (2 Cor 2:12-13; 7:5-16). While there is considerable disagreement about the precise dating of these hindrances, all biographies of Paul assume a series of problems in the period prior to the writing of Romans.[10]

5   See Käsemann, 397, referring to Noack, "Current," 160–61; see also Dunn, 2:871.
6   See Fitzmyer, 716.
7   BAGD 198.
8   Gustav Stählin, "ἐγκοπή, ἐγκόπτω," *TDNT* 3 (1965) 855–56.
9   Jewett, "Paul the Apostle," *EncR* 11:212–21.

10 See William M. Ramsay, *St. Paul the Traveller and the Roman Citizen* (London: Hodder & Stoughton, 1920) 270–89; Sabatier, *Apostle Paul*, 165–84; Bornkamm, *Paul*, 68–87; Herold Weiss, *Paul of Tarsus: His Gospel and Life* (Berrien Springs: Andrews University Press, 1986) 28–36; Becker, *Paul*, 216–39, 257–73.

This reference to frequent hindrances is therefore no exaggeration, although it is understandable for political reasons why Paul does not elaborate in detail. His goal is to convince the Romans that he is a plausible candidate to carry the gospel to Spain, despite repeated delays, not to raise suspicions about his chronic troubles.

■ **23** The incomplete sentence that stands in antithesis to the hindered journey opens with νυνὶ δέ ("but now"), which has an almost eschatological tone in view of the fulfillment of the Isaianic prophecy in Paul's mission and in view of the frequent use of this term earlier in the letter.[11] The hindrances, whatever their satanic or circumstantial origins might be, are now at an end. Paul's mission in the East has now reached the fulfillment alluded to in 15:19, so that, μηκέτι τόπον ἔχων ἐν τοῖς κλίμασι τούτοις ("having no more room in these regions"), he is free to travel west to Rome. As in Gal 1:21 and 2 Cor 11:10, Paul refers here to "regions" rather than Roman provinces,[12] referring to the areas to the east of Illyricum on the arc toward Jerusalem where mission centers had already been established. This "astounding statement" reveals not just that "representative churches had finally been so well established that they would, with the help of God, be able to prepare themselves for the day of the Lord, without the supervision of the apostle,"[13] but that the scope for founding new congregations in crucial urban areas on the circle for which Paul feels called to minister is exhausted.[14]

The second half of Paul's incomplete sentence, which lacks a finite verb, reiterates 1:11-15. The anacoluthon conveys an informal, conversational tone[15] that invites clarification and negotiation with the congregation. "Having the desire to come to you" is formulated with a term not yet found elsewhere in Greek literature, ἐπιποθία ("desire"),[16] which is based on the polite verb that Paul had used in his first reference to visiting Rome (1:11). The stylistic preference to avoid an exact replication of the wording in the introduction may have led to his choice of this unusual form of ἐπιπόθησις. The reference to the length of time this yearning to visit Rome has matured, ἀπὸ πολλῶν ἐτῶν ("for many years"), implies a missionary goal of long standing. This provides a subtle claim on a relationship with the Roman congregations that reaches back to an earlier phase of his apostolic ministry, even though he has never been granted the opportunity of seeing them face-to-face. There is an element of *captatio benevolentiae* in this statement that prepares the way for the missional collaboration suggested in the subsequent verses.

■ **24** The incomplete sentence that began in 15:23 continues with the clause introduced by ὡς ἄν ("when, as soon as").[17] This is a favorite conjunction for Pauline travel plans, as 1 Cor 11:34 and Phil 2:23 indicate. The papyri have numerous examples such as the request in this letter of 253 B.C.E., ὡς ἄν οὖν λάβῃς τὴν ἐπιστολὴν . . . ἀπόστειλον ("as soon as you receive the letter . . . send");[18] or this promise in a letter of 228 B.C.E.: ὡ[ς δ'] ἄν παραγένωμαι . . . συνλαλήσω σοι ("as soon as I arrive . . . I will converse with you").[19] The verb used for travel, πορεύομαι, is also the usual word in the travelogue sections of Paul's letters.[20] The subjunctive is employed here in reference to a future plan whose precise details need to be worked out,[21] but it does not indicate doubt about Paul's intention.[22] So, only the destination of Spain would have caught the attention of the hearers of this letter in Rome, making clear for the

---

11 See the earlier discussions of "now" in Rom 3:21, 26; 5:9, 11; 6:19, 21, 22; 7:6, 17; 8:1, 18, 22; 11:5, 30, 31; 13:11.

12 See Betz, *Galatians*, 79; BAGD 436.

13 See Dahl, *Studies*, 76.

14 See Barrett, 277; Cranfield's exasperated rebuttal in 2:766–67, by citing geographic regions that Paul would have surely known in other directions from Jerusalem, fails to take account of Paul's specific circle of responsibility or the eschatological basis of Paul's drive toward what he perceives as the end of the world, in Spain. See Käsemann, 397.

15 See BDF §458.

16 See LSJM 652; BAGD 298; whether this is a Pauline coinage, or a slang term used in the vernacular but not appearing in written form, is unclear, but the meaning is not in doubt.

17 See BDF §455.2, "on my imminent journey to Spain"; BAGD 898.

18 MM 703 provides this example from *P.Hib.* 1. Nr. 44.5–6.

19 MM 703, citing from *P.Hib.* 1. Nr. 66.4.

20 See 1 Cor 10:27; 16:4, 6.

21 See Sanday and Headlam, 411; Schmidt, 246–47.

22 Lagrange, 356; see also Moulton and Turner, *Grammar III*, 112: "of a definite action occurring in the future: *when*."

first time that Paul's intent was not to remain in Rome for an extended visit. The diplomatic finesse of Paul's formulation is accurately grasped by Käsemann: "Paul must avoid the suspicion that he wants to make the world capital his own domain, and he does not want to say brusquely that he regards it merely as a bridgehead."[23]

The references to Spain in 15:24 and 28 remain somewhat puzzling for most modern commentaries,[24] in part because of mistaken historical and cultural information[25] that dominated the interpretation of Romans until Fitzmyer took account of the new evidence in 1993.[26] The introduction above surveys the decisive factors of the lack of Jewish settlement,[27] the cultural, economic, and linguistic barriers to Christian missionizing, and the bearing these conditions have on the purpose of Romans. As for the choice of Spain as Paul's next missionary target, three factors can be adduced. First of all, as the recent studies have shown, Spain was both Gentile and barbarian, par excellence. It lacked any Jewish population and remained stubbornly resistant to Greco-Roman culture, so it was a logical goal for the apostle to the Gentiles who felt "indebted both to Greeks and to barbarians" (1:15). Second, Spain lies at the conclusion of the northern circuit of the Mediterranean on the strip maps of antiquity,[28] thus completing the arc from Jerusalem through Illyricum and Rome, and on to the

end of the earth as discussed in 15:19 above.[29] Finally, as Roger D. Aus has shown, it is very likely that Paul interpreted Isa 66:19 as indicating that Tarshish at the western end of the Mediterranean would provide the final "offering of the Gentiles" (Rom 15:16) and thus complete the eschatological mission before the parousia.[30] There is no doubt that Tarshish was the city of Tartessos in Spain, near the Pillars of Hercules (i.e., the Straits of Gibraltar) that in antiquity were considered the end(s) of the earth. For example, *Ps. Sol.* 8.16 refers to Pompey as coming to Jerusalem ἀπ᾽ ἐσχάτου τῆς γῆς ("from the end of the earth") in Spain.[31] Biblical and rabbinic references also show that the end of the earth was identified with Tarshish, as, for example, LXX Ps 71:8, 10:[32] καὶ κατακυριεύσει ἀπὸ θαλάσσης ἕως θαλάσσης καὶ ἀπὸ ποταμοῦ ἕως περάτων τῆς οἰκουμένης . . . βασιλεῖς Θαρσις καὶ αἱ νῆσοι δῶρα προσοίσουσιν ("And may he have dominion from sea to sea, and from the river [i.e., the Euphrates] to the ends of the earth. . . . May the kings of Tarshish and the isles bring him presents").

The parenthetical remark loosely attached to the incomplete sentence provides three explanations of Paul's travel plans, echoing and elaborating the references in 1:10-15. The anacolouthon is typical for Paul in that the parenthetical remarks in 24:b-d begin with a finite verb that "causes the author to forget the original

---

23 Käsemann, 397.

24 The argument in this section is adapted from Jewett, "Spanish Mission," 144–64.

25 For example, Ernst Barnikol finds the Spanish references so puzzling and improbable that they were likely a fiction of the later editor of Romans; see *Römer 15. Letzte Reiseziele des Paulus, Jerusalem, Rom, und Antiochien. Eine Voruntersuchung zur Entstehung des sogenannten Römerbriefes*, vol. 4 of E. Barnikol, *Forschungen zur Entstehung des Urchristentums* (Kiel: Muhlau, 1931) 13–20. As pointed out by Klein, "Paul's Purpose," 30–31, Lipsius, 75, 85–86, 195, deletes the references to Spain as extraneous to Paul's purpose in writing the letter.

26 Fitzmyer, 717. My article, "Spanish Mission," which takes the same line as Fitzmyer, was published in 1988.

27 A breakthrough in understanding the relevance of the Spanish situation came from Bowers, "Jewish Communities in Spain," 395–402; the short study by T. C. G. Thornton, "St. Paul's Missionary Intentions

in Spain," *ExpT* 86 (1974–75) 120, points in the same direction.

28 The Miller edition of the Peutinger map, *Itineraria*, 147–49, depicts Spain as an elongated peninsula at the end of strip maps that continue through Gaul (27–30) and Italy (189–94).

29 See also Dunn, 2:872.

30 Aus, "Paul's Travel Plans," 240–41.

31 Cited by Aus, "Paul's Travel Plans," 244. On the equation of Cádiz and Tartessos in Spain with Tarshish in popular thinking, see M. E. Aubert, *The Phoenicians and the West: Politics, Colonies, and Trade* (Cambridge: Cambridge University Press, 1993) 176–79; on the possibility of an early Christian missionary impulse to Spain, see Kotansky, "Jesus and Heracles in Cádiz," 229.

32 In "Paul's Travel Plans," 245, Aus also cites Jonah 1:3; Ps 48:7-10; and the saying of Rabbi Simlai in *B. Nid.* 30b, all of which show that Tarshish in Spain was considered the end of the world.

construction and substitute another for it in resuming."[33] But I do not think this anacolouthon is unintentional; it fits Paul's diplomatic strategy of leaving his missionary plans and their potential support by the Roman congregations open to their response. Moreover, as we shall see in 15:25-32, the fulfillment of these plans depends on the successful delivery and reception of the Jerusalem offering.[34] The first explanation is stated as a polite hope: ἐλπίζω γὰρ διαπορευόμενος θεάσασθαι ὑμᾶς ("for I hope to see you while passing through"). The choice of ἐλπίζειν is particularly pregnant in the light of Paul's definition in 8:24 and the benediction of 15:13;[35] it acknowledges the uncertainty of future plans and diplomatically leaves the door open for the Roman congregations to decide whether to receive Paul or not. The technical term for passing through a location (διαπορεύομαι)[36] is used here in the absolute, making it clear that Paul does not intend to missionize in Rome. The principle of not building on someone else's foundation (15:20) will be respected. The word "see" (θεάομαι), is used here in the sense of "visit, greet,"[37] rather than "get acquainted,"[38] which would have required the use of ἱστορεῖν as in Gal 1:18.[39] Θεάομαι is sometimes employed in the context of official visits for the purpose of acquaintance and consultation, which is similar to the use in Romans. For example, Appian describes a Roman consul's voyage of inspection in 282 B.C.E. as follows: "With ten decked ships Cornelius visited (ἐθεᾶτο) the coast of Magna Graecia, and at Tarentum there was a demagogue named Philocharis . . ." (Appian Samn. 7.1). Similarly, the parable in Matt 22:11 says "the king came in to see the guests" (εἰσελθὼν δὲ ὁ βασιλεὺς θεάσασθαι τοὺς ἀνακειμένους), which implies extending official greetings. Other references deal with family visits in which greetings and friendly discourse are implied (Josephus Ant. 16.6; 2 Chron 22:6). Paul's choice of terms opens up the possibility of polite acquaintance and consultation with the Roman churches within the restricted scope of a short visit,[40] which could hardly have been objectionable under the rules of hospitality in the ancient world.

Somewhat more suggestive in terms of its potential burden on the churches is Paul's hope "to be sent on with your help" (ἀφ' ὑμῶν προπεμφθῆναι). There is broad consensus among commentators that this verb implies "the provision of rations, money, means of transport, letters of introduction, and escort for some part of the way" to Spain,[41] but some uses of this verb merely imply escorting someone part way on their journey.[42] Seven of the nine occurrences of προπέμπω in the NT imply some sort of equipping or provisioning for travelers who are sent off without escort (1 Cor 16:6, 11; 2 Cor 1:16; Titus 3:13; 3 John 6; Acts 15:3; and Rom 15:24), which justifies Dodd's observation that "the expression seems to have been almost a technical term with a well-understood meaning among missionaries."[43] In a similar vein, 1 Macc 12:4 reports that the Romans sent Jonathan's ambassadors back to Israel with letters

33 BDF §467.

34 See the discussion by Lagrange, 356–57.

35 See Rudolf Bultmann, "ἐλπίς," TDNT 2 (1964) 531–32.

36 See BAGD 187; an example of the participial use is in Xenophon Anab. 2.2.11, which explains why the Greeks retreated along a different route in order to find sustenance because "we consumed it entirely while marching through (ἡμεῖς διαπορευόμενοι κατεδαπανήσαμεν)." The same usage is found in Mark 2:23; Luke 6:1. In Acts 16:4, passing through was combined with congregational consultations: ὡς δὲ διεπορεύοντο τὰς πόλεις, παρεδίδοσαν αὐτοῖς φυλάσσειν τὰ δόγματα τὰ κεκριμένα . . . ("As they passed through the cities, they delivered to them for observations the decisions which had been reached . . .").

37 See BAGD 353; Kettunen, Abfassungszweck, 162.

38 See Michel, 463; Schmidt, 246; Käsemann, 398.

39 See Kettunen, Abfassungszweck, 162.

40 In contrast, Kettunen, Abfassungszweck, 162, understands "see you" to imply a kind of inspection tour, to see if everything is "in order."

41 Cranfield, 2:769; see also Dodd, 220; Michel, 463; Black, 204; Schlier, 435; Wilckens, 3:124; Dunn, 2:872; Peter Müller, "Grundlinien paulinischer Theologie (Röm 15,14-33)," KD 35 (1989) 222. See also BAGD 709.

42 Ollrog contends in Mitarbeiter, 124, that all the NT references deal with escort rather than provision, but the article on "προπέμπω" by Heinrich Balz and Gerhard Schneider in EDNT 3 (1993) 160 more properly identifies escorting in Acts 20:38 and 21:5.

43 Dodd, 229; see also Michel, 463.

that would provide for their safety and provisioning: καὶ ἔδωκαν ἐπιστολὰς αὐτοῖς πρὸς αὐτοὺς κατὰ τόπον, οὕτως προπέμπωσιν αὐτοὺς εἰς γῆν Ἰούδα μετ᾽ εἰρήνης ("And the Romans gave them letters to those in every place, that they should send them on to the land of Judea with peace").[44] There is more explicit reference to provisioning in a third-century C.E. papyrus authorizing that "in sending on the fourteen camels that form the convoy of Polycarpus and Protys, [you should] supply the customary foods (τοῖς προπέμπουσι καμήλοις οὖσι τὸν ἀριθμὸν ιδ᾽ Πολύκαρπον καὶ Πρωτῦν παράσχες τὰς συνήθεις τροφάς)."[45]

It seems likely that Paul wished to leave the precise requirements of his "send-off" to Spain up to the Roman congregations in negotiation with Phoebe, who had agreed to function as the patron of the Spanish mission.[46] With the sponsorship of this generous patron, the churches of Rome would not have had to provide travel funds or provisions, but an array of other resources such as translators, letters to local contacts, and including perhaps escorts, would have been needed to mount this expedition. By refraining at this point from making specific demands, Paul conveys his willingness to trust the hospitality of the Roman churches and to receive whatever they deemed appropriate.[47]

The third part of Paul's explanation moves back from the delicate issues of logistical support and advice, implying that such matters could be decided after they had enjoyed each other's company for a while. Zeller refers to the "courteous formulation" of Paul's reference to a cordial but temporary relationship, which avoids placing pressure on the congregation.[48] The translation of this expression is difficult in English because the verb ἐμπίμπλημι ("have one's fill of")[49] in the aorist passive subjunctive would produce a translation like "that I might have my fill" of you, which sounds derisive in English. Given the parallels in having the eyes (Homer *Od.* 11.451) or appetite (Appian *Bell. civ.* 2.64) sated, one might translate "that I might be sated" of you, which seems even more awkward. Dunn comes fairly close to the literal meaning of the clause in "once I have had the full pleasure of being with you for a time."[50] The inclusion of the words πρῶτον ἀπὸ μέρους ("first for a time") makes clear that the discussion of logistics will not occur until a personal relationship is established between Paul and the Roman congregations, allowing time for the "mutual encouragement by each other's faith," to use the echoing expression in 1:12. On the other hand, Paul indicates that he and his colleagues will not become a long-term burden to their hospitality.

■ **25** Moving from the open-endedness of the anacoluthon in 15:23-24, Paul shifts into a more direct and coherent style in announcing his travel plans to deliver the offering to Jerusalem.[51] The νυνὶ δὲ that is repeated from the beginning of v. 23 suggests to Dunn "the momentous junction which Paul sensed his work to have reached, with something at least of the eschatological overtone which is a regular feature of Paul's usage."[52] In contrast to v. 23, the "but" seems more clearly adversative, introducing the obstacle of the Jerusalem journey that must be removed before the plans to visit to Rome can materialize.[53] However, the use of exactly the same conjunctions routinizes the material in vv. 25-31, which might otherwise appear to be a contradiction of Paul's hope to visit Rome. The present indicative πορεύομαι ("I am traveling"), contrasted with the subjective form of this verb used in v. 24, conveys without equivocation "that he is on the point of departure for Jerusalem."[54] It must have been a surprising turn for the Roman audience, because Jerusalem is hardly on the route between

44   See also 1 Esdr 4:47; *Ep. Arist.* 172.
45   MM 544 provides this citation from *P.Flor.* 2. Nr. 206.2–7.
46   See the Introduction and Jewett, "Spanish Mission."
47   See Kettunen, *Abfassungszweck*, 167–68.
48   Zeller, 240. Kettunen argues in contrast that this expression suggests quite directly that Paul wants something from the congregation; *Abfassungszweck*, 163.
49   BAGD 256.
50   Dunn, 2:873.
51   See Michel, 464.
52   Dunn, 2:873.
53   Lagrange, 357.
54   Fitzmyer, 721; see also Kühl, 474; Cranfield, 2:771; Morris, 518.

Corinth and Rome.[55] Does it not raise questions about his independence from the authorities in Jerusalem?[56] About the sincerity of his desire to visit Rome and enjoy the company of believers there? No occasion is allowed for such questions in the straightforward, matter-of-fact flow of v. 25.

The expression διακονῶν τοῖς ἁγίοις ("serving the saints") appears to be a shorthand version of the title that was probably devised for the Jerusalem offering, ἡ διακονία ἡ εἰς τοὺς ἁγίους ("the service that is for the saints").[57] On the basis of my analysis of διακον- in relation to 12:7,[58] it is likely that the "in-between" activity relates to the provision of resources to be used for the sustenance of the Jerusalem believers. The frequent use of this term for ministry in early Christianity[59] made it likely that the "unpretentious"[60] statement in 15:25 would have had a positive resonance among the Roman converts even if they had no information about the particular offering Paul had been collecting. The present participial use of διακονῶν in behalf of the "saints"[61] indicates the purpose of Paul's journey being undertaken to Jerusalem,[62] which was in "the general service of love which Christians evince to one another as saints."[63] As the next verse will make plain, this service involved sharing of material resources needed for the common life and sustenance of Christian groups in and around Jerusalem, fulfilling the commitment Paul had made at the time of the Apostolic Conference (Gal 2:10), which is considerably more concrete than contemporary understandings of the "general service of love" might be.

■ **26** Some of the details describing the Jerusalem offering are rather puzzling, particularly if the text-critical decision made above is correct concerning the third person singular expression in εὐδόκησεν γὰρ Μακεδονία ("for Macedonia was pleased"). In addition to the absence of reference to other churches that probably participated in the Jerusalem offering,[64] it appears that Paul initially intended to mention only Macedonia as contributing, and then added Achaia as an afterthought. The addition is understandable enough, since Paul was dictating in Corinth, which was the capital of Achaia, and his colleagues involved in the production of the letter could naturally have raised objections out of local pride. This could have led to the appending of καὶ Ἀχαΐα ("also Achaia") without the alteration of the verb to a plural form. But what could have led Paul to the initial intention of mentioning only Macedonia? This question has not been faced in the discussion concerning the Jerusalem offering, because text critics and commentators have never followed the more difficult, and thus more reliable, reading in this instance.

The clue may be found in the effort to answer the more frequently posed question about why Paul mentions only two provinces as involved in the offering. On the basis of 2 Cor 8:1-5, Betz has confirmed that the Macedonians completed the Jerusalem offering first, with exemplary motivation despite the depth of their

---

55   This discrepancy was fundamental to the reconstruction by Barnikol, *Römer 15*, 15, that chapter 15 was directed to Ephesus to inform the church there of his plans to travel from Jerusalem to Ephesus and then on to Rome.

56   See Zeller, 240.

57   See Betz, *2 Corinthians 8 and 9*, 90.

58   See particularly Collins, *Diakonia*, 77–95, and Reicke, *Agapenfeier*, 31–38.

59   See Hudson, "Diakonia," 142; Hermann W. Beyer, "διακονέω κτλ.," *TDNT* 2 (1964) 84–87.

60   Georgi, *Remembering the Poor*, 115.

61   Lietzmann's excursus in 121–23 showed that although "saints" is the usual NT term for Christians, it is the particular self-designation of the original Jerusalem congregation (1 Cor 16:1-14; 2 Cor 8:4; 9:12). See also Lucien Cerfaux, "'Les Saints' de Jérusalem," *ETL* 2 (1925): 510–29; repr. pp.

389–413 in vol. 2 of *Receuil Lucien Cerfaux*, BETL 6–7, 18 (Gembloux: Duculot, 1954–85); Keck, "Saints in Jewish Christianity and Qumran," 118–22.

62   See John J. O'Rourke, "The Participle in Rom 15:25," *CBQ* 29 (1967) 116–18, and BDF §339.2c. A durative sense in this participle as suggested by Michel, 464, seems less likely; if present, it relates to the process of delivering the offering, not gathering it; see Käsemann, 398.

63   Beyer, "διακονέω κτλ.," 87.

64   Käsemann, 399, goes so far as to suggest that Paul was "intentionally concealing" the broad scope of participation in the offering; see Dunn, 2:875; Georgi, *Remembering the Poor*, 122–27.

poverty,[65] so that Paul does not hesitate to use their good example to urge the Corinthians into action. It was the Macedonian church, not the Corinthians whose participation was long delayed by the church conflicts reflected in both 1 and 2 Corinthians, that actually would have deserved the formulation εὐδόκησεν ("was well pleased"), a verb that implies a freely chosen and well-motivated resolve.[66] While Paul writes positively about the "willingness" of Achaians, that is, provincial churches outside of Corinth, to participate in the offering (2 Cor 9:2),[67] it is not clear from 2 Cor 8 or Rom 15 that either the Achaian or the Corinthian funds were already on hand for the departure to Jerusalem. On the basis of Georgi's analysis of the travel details in Acts 20 and the Pauline letters, it appears that the original plan had been to rendezvous in Corinth with the church delegates bringing the Jerusalem funds and to depart from there by ship, probably with a number of other Jewish pilgrims.[68] Given the original scheme of arriving in Jerusalem by Pentecost (Acts 20:6), it is likely that none of the delegates would have arrived in Corinth by the time Paul wrote Romans in the winter of 56–57. So, at this point the only funds he is certain of taking along are those already on hand from Macedonia. The contribution from Achaia, which, according to 2 Cor 9:2, had been essentially ready for delivery a year before writing that section of the Corinthian correspondence, also had probably not yet arrived in Corinth with their accompanying envoys.[69]

Sometime after dispatching the letter to Rome, Paul discovered the plot that would interrupt the sea journey from Corinth to Israel (Acts 20:3) and decided to travel overland from Corinth through Thessalonica to Macedonia. There the delegates from the churches mentioned in Acts 20:5-6 are reported to divide into two parties, one going directly to Troas and the other coming later with Paul, who remained in Philippi until after the festival of unleavened bread. The large group of delegates, probably representing churches from Galatia to Corinth, then assembled in Troas for the trip south and later shifted to a larger vessel sailing from Patara to Phoenicia (Acts 20:5—21:1), probably arriving in Jerusalem after Pentecost (Acts 21:15-17).[70]

Georgi's reconstruction therefore provides the basis for a possible explanation of the odd references to Macedonia and Achaia: Paul probably wished initially only to refer to the Macedonian funds that were on hand, about which he could make the unequivocal claim that they reflected authentic generosity and readiness to enter into κοινωνία ("fellowship, sharing"). At this point he was reminded that the Achaian funds were also available to be delivered. Not yet knowing the precise level or motivation of the participation of the other churches that had agreed to send delegates to the rendezvous in the early spring, Paul wanted to make the best case he could on the basis of the funding known with certainty to be available at the moment of writing.

The usual translation of κοινωνίαν τινὰ ποιήσασθαι as "make a contribution" has recently been shown to be problematic.[71] It is a fairly apt semantic equivalent because the passage deals with funds to be shared with the Jerusalem church. However, the transla-

---

65 Betz, *2 Corinthians 8 and 9*, 42–49.

66 BAGD 319 refers to Polybius *Hist.* 1.78.8, in which the Carthaginian king was impressed with the courage of Naravas, who strode into their camp unarmed offering to aid their campaign: "Hamilcar, on hearing this, was so delighted at the young man's courage in coming to him and his simple frankness at their interview that not only was he well pleased (εὐδόκησε) to join his undertakings but swore to give him his daughter in marriage if he remained loyal to Carthage." For a discussion of the extensive NT use of this term in passages such as Matt 3:17; Col 1:19; 2 Cor 12:10; and 2 Thess 2:12, see Gottlob Schrenk, "εὐδοκέω, εὐδοκία," *TDNT* 2 (1964) 740–42, who interprets Rom 15:26 in terms of "free decision."

67 See Betz, *2 Corinthians 8 and 9*, 52–53, 91–92.

68 Georgi, *Remembering the Poor*, 124; see also the similar reconstruction in Barnikol, *Römer 15*, 15–17.

69 See Betz, *2 Corinthians 8 and 9*, 92–93.

70 See Georgi, *Remembering the Poor*, 122–24, for this reconstruction.

71 See G. W. Peterman, "Romans 15.26: Make a Contribution or Establish Fellowship," *NTS* 40 (1994) 457–63. The traditional view is supported by Heinrich Seesemann, who argues for a specific aspect of *Mitteilsamkeit*, which is the "collection" itself, in *KOINΩNIA*, 29; see also Michael McDermott, "The Biblical Doctrine of *KOINΩNIA*," *BZ* 19 (1975) 71–72.

tion "fellowship" is preferable, because, while no instances of a concrete sense of the term as "contribution" have been found,[72] there are at least two examples of "make fellowship" or "reach an agreement" in political contexts that seem close to some aspects of the Jerusalem offering. Polybius reported that the deposed ruler of Sparta, Cleomenes, "made a pragmatic agreement (ἐποιήσατο τὴν κοινωνίαν τῶν πραγμάτων)" with Ptolemy Euergetes in order to gain help to recover his throne (*Hist.* 5.35.1). Plato writes that Socrates showed how sharing the products of labor comprises the reason that by "making fellowship we establish a city" (κοινωνίαν ποιησάμενοι πόλιν ᾠκίσαμεν, *Resp.* 371b). Another factor in the translation is the connotation of τινά, which qualifies κοινωνία; it appears to delimit the fellowship as a specific effort to aid to the poor,[73] perhaps in contrast with local and regional partnerships being established in support of love feasts[74] and mission projects[75] throughout the area of Pauline influence. I prefer the translation "to establish a particular fellowship for the poor among the saints in Jerusalem,"[76] because it retains the element of commonality in the word κοινωνέω, which was so crucial a concept for the

early church,[77] and it avoids the contemporary implications of the word "contribution," in which the rich sometimes demonstrate their superior status by being charitable to the poor.[78] As the next verse indicates, there was a substantial rationale of mutual indebtedness that guided Paul's understanding of the Jerusalem offering.

The precise connotation of the expression εἰς τοὺς πτωχοὺς τῶν ἁγίων τῶν ἐν Ἰερουσαλήμ ("for the poor among the saints in Jerusalem") is disputed. Karl Holl and others argued that "the poor" was an honorific title claimed by the Jerusalem Christians along with the title "saints,"[79] and thus that the genitive construction should be translated epexegetically, that is, "the poor who are the saints."[80] It is clear that Qumran[81] and probably also the later Ebionite movement[82] used "poor" as a designation of the elect. Nevertheless, Leander E. Keck has argued on historical and grammatical grounds that "Paul does not designate the recipients as 'the Poor' but thinks of them as saints who are now distressingly poor."[83] This requires the more normal partitive genitive, "the poor among the saints,"[84] which implies a continuation of the adverse economic circumstances

---

72 Keith P. Nickle argues in *The Collection: A Study in the Strategy of Paul*, SBT 48 (London: SCM; Naperville: Allenson, 1966) 124 that the verb ποιέω ("make, do") requires a concrete translation of κοινωνία as gift or contribution, but Peterman, "Romans 15.26," 457–63, found two instances in Polybius *Hist.* 5.35.1 and Plato *Resp.* 371b5–6 (cited above) where the combination of these terms clearly means "establish fellowship."

73 See Hainz, *Koinonia*, 147, where the alternative construals of τινά are discussed.

74 See Jewett, *Apostle to America*, 73–86.

75 Sampley, *Pauline Partnership*, 81–87.

76 In *Koinonia*, 147, Hainz offers a similar translation: "ein gewisses Gemeinschaftswerk zu betreiben."

77 See particularly J. Y. Campbell, "*KOINΩNIA*," 352–80, who argues for the basic meaning of common participation with others; Josef Hainz goes farther to define the specifically Christian concept in *Koinonia*, 111–12, 173–76.

78 See Judge, *Rank and Status*, 26: "Giving money to others was not a mark of subordination but of superiority."

79 Karl Holl, "Der Kirchenbegriff des Paulus in seinem Verhältnis zu dem der Urgemeinde," *SPAW* (1921) 920–47; repr. pp. 44–67 in vol. 2 of K. Holl,

Gesammelte Aufsätze zur Kirchengeschichte (Tübingen: Mohr, 1928); see also Ernst Bammel and Friedrich Hauck, "πτωχός κτλ.," *TDNT* 6 (1968) 909.

80 Lietzmann, 122–23; Althaus, 134; Schlier, 436; Cerfaux, "'Les Saints' de Jérusalem."

81 See Keck, "Saints in Jewish Christianity and Qumran," 66–78; H.-J. Kandler, "Die Bedeutung der Armut im Schrifttum von Chirbet Qumran," *Judaica* 13 (1957) 193–209. A clear example of the use of "poor" as a designation of the Qumran community is 1QM 11:13: "For you will deliver into the hands of the poor the enemies from all the lands" (see also 1QM 11:8; 4QpPsa 1–2 ii 9; 1,3– iii 10).

82 See Bammel and Hauck, "πτωχός κτλ.," 913; for a skeptical review of this link, see Keck, "Saints in Jewish Christianity and Qumran," 54–65.

83 Keck, "Saints in Jewish Christianity and Qumran," 122.

84 See BDF §164.1; Leander E. Keck, "The Poor among the Saints in the New Testament," *ZNW* 56 (1965) 119; Michel, 465; Lagrange, 358; Cranfield, 2:772; Käsemann, 401; Wilckens, 3:125; Dunn, 2:875; Fitzmyer, 722.

associated with Paul's initial agreement at the time of the Apostolic Conference to raise funds for "the poor" in Judea (Gal 2:10).[85] However one chooses to interpret the genitive construction, these particular ἅγιοι appear to be the Jewish Christian group in Judea, which correlates this reference closely with the reference to the "saints" in 1:7. The ethical assumption lying behind this reference is also plain: both in Judaism and early Christianity, it was the obligation of the righteous to share resources with the poor and thereby to demonstrate solidarity.[86] Despite subsidiary motives, this obligation remains central in all of Paul's discussions of the Jerusalem offering.

■ **27** Paul goes on to describe the motivation and rationale for the Jerusalem offering as a combination of freely chosen goodwill on the part of Gentile churches and of their obligation to repay the original Jewish churches for spiritual benefits. To the ancient mind there was no necessary contradiction between goodwill and obligation. In the light of the early chapters of Romans, this reiteration of being "well pleased, glad" (εὐδόκησαν) lifts up the element of an uncoerced decision that derives from grateful hearts, transformed by divine righteousness, rather than from any form of social or political pressure.[87] In Paul's mind it was natural to coordinate free decision with reciprocity by a simple καί, which should be translated "and" rather

than "and indeed,"[88] as if reciprocity were an extraneous or politically motivated afterthought.[89] The concept of indebtedness is basic to Romans,[90] for, as Minear showed, "faith in Christ inevitably creates a mutuality of indebtedness."[91] The Greco-Roman shared a more general form of this premise;[92] in Seneca's words, *Non referre beneficiis gratiam et est turpe et apud omnes habetur* ("not to return gratitude for benefits is a disgrace and everyone counts it as such," *Ben.* 3.1.1). This produces a widely shared concept of mutual indebtedness, described by Seneca within the context of friendship and patron–client relations: *Illi beneficio, quod actio perficit, relata gratia est, si illud benevole excipimus; illus alterum, quod re continetur, nondum reddidimus, sed volemus reddere. Voluntati voluntate satis fecimus; rei rem debemus. Itaque, quamvis rettulisse illum gratiam dicamus, qui beneficium libenter accipit, iubemus tamen et simile aliquid ei, quod accepit, reddere* ("For the benefit that is accomplished by an act has been repaid by our gratitude if we accept it willingly; the other, which consists of some object, we have not yet returned, but we shall have the desire to return it. Goodwill we have repaid with goodwill; for the object we still owe an object. And so, although we say that he who receives a benefit gladly has repaid it, nevertheless, we also urge him return some gift similar to the one he received," *Ben.* 2.35.1).

The distinctive framework of reciprocal obligation

---

85   See Betz, *Galatians*, 102. In contrast to other studies of the Jerusalem offering, Nicholas Taylor develops the implausible argument in *Paul, Antioch and Jerusalem: A Study in Relationships and Authority in Earliest Christianity*, JSNTSup 66 (Sheffield: JSOT, 1989) 194–99, that the collection reflected in Romans was not a result of the commitment Paul refers to in Gal 2:10. This removes some tensions in the evidence but restricts the Galatians agreement to the Antiochenes and the Jerusalem church, whereas Paul explicitly states in 2:10, "which very thing *I* was eager to do." Since these words were written after the confrontation at Antioch, where tensions with the Jerusalem authorities surfaced, it is fallacious to reason that "Paul was no longer a member of the Antiochene church and therefore no longer party to that κοινωνία" (195).

86   See Klaus Berger, "Almosen für Israel. Zum historischen Kontext der paulinischen Kollekte," *NTS* 23 (1976–77) 183–95.

87   The political dimensions of the original agreement

to gather an offering for Jerusalem as reported in Gal 2:10 are undeniable, and there is no doubt that Paul was the reluctant, inferior partner in the negotiations; see Holmberg, *Paul and Power*, 35–56, and Betz, *Galatians*, 101–3. Note that this verse insists that such an offering was "the very thing I was eager to do," which reflects the effort one sees in Romans to place the offering within the context of mutual obligation owed because of grace.

88   Cranfield, 2:750; Dunn, 2:876, referring to an ambiguous discussion in BDF §452.2; Fitzmyer, 722.

89   See Schlier, 436.

90   See the exegesis of 1:14; 8:12; 13:8; 15:1 and Michael Wolter, "ὀφειλέτης, ὀφείλημα," *EDNT* 2 (1991) 550; idem, "ὀφείλω," *EDNT* 2 (1991) 551.

91   Minear, *Obedience*, 104.

92   See Mott, "Hellenistic Benevolence," 60–72.

within the Christian community surfaces in v. 27b, referring to the receipt of "spiritual things" that came to the Gentiles by way of the Jewish Christians in Judea, who were the first converts to the faith. However, the earlier argument of Romans demonstrated the impartiality of the grace of God that is given without anyone deserving or earning it. Paul presents the Jerusalem offering as neither a quid pro quo in line with the cultural tradition as reflected in Seneca nor an acknowledgment of the superiority of the Jerusalem church,[93] but as an expression of mutual indebtedness that binds the ethnic branches of the church together.[94] Within this framework, $τὰ πνευματικά$ ("the spiritual things") should be understood as an echo of 1:11 with reference to the gospel and of 8:2-27 with reference to the work of the Spirit in the life of the Christian community. The prior argument of Romans made plain that the "things belonging to the new creation"[95] include ethics as well as doctrine, mission to the outsiders as well as faith development of congregations already in existence. It seems unlikely in this context that the polemical sense of $σαρκικός$ ("thing belonging to flesh") visible elsewhere in the Pauline letters (1 Cor 3:3; 9:11; 2 Cor 1:12; 10:4) was intended in this passage.[96] The antithesis is effective rhetorically, but, as in 1 Cor 9:11, the realm of the flesh remains neutral as long as it does not vaunt itself. If the "things of the flesh" were innately evil, none of them could reciprocate a spiritual gift or be associated with so positive a verb as $λειτουργεῖν$ ("to minister"), which had been used with the same connotation of providing benefaction in 15:16.[97] This secular sense of "ministering" through the provision of material resources is illustrated by a regulation under Tiberius that required local authorities in Asia Minor to provide the following transport for official travelers: $Σαγαλασσεῖς λειτουργεῖν δεῖ μέχρι δέκα κάρρων ...$ ("The Sagalassenes are obliged to supply a service of up to ten carts ...").[98] Since Paul uses $λειτουργία$ in this sense in Phil 2:30, referring to Epaphroditus as risking his life in bringing a material gift to Paul, it is likely that "minister" has the more practical sense here of meeting the material needs of the poor[99] and does not require a theory of breaking the boundary between the cultic and the secular.[100]

■ **28** The language of this verse is consistent with secular, material usage in the Greco-Roman world. Paul refers to "completing" the task of gathering and delivering the Jerusalem collection with the verb $ἐπιτελεῖν$, which was typically used in administrative settings to refer to the completion of assigned tasks.[101] For instance, in a papyrus of 163 B.C.E. a subordinate official is exhorted as follows: $ἕκαστα δ' ἐπιτελεσθῇ κατὰ τὸν ὑποδεδειγμένον ἐν τῷ πεμφθέντι σοι παρ' ἡμῶν ὑπομνήματι τρόπον$ ("... that everything be completed according to the example laid down in the reminder sent to you by us ...").[102] Paul uses this verb in the same sense of completing an apostolic task in Phil 1:6 and 2 Cor 8:6, 11, the latter two with regard to the Jerusalem offering.

An expression with close associations with the completion of a delivery task is joined with the connective $καί$, namely, $σφραγισάμενος τὸν καρπὸν τοῦτον$ ("sealing this fruit"). This verb is frequently used in the shipping business to denote products or letters from a particular person or firm that are closed and secured with a wax seal bearing the name of the owner or producer.[103] For example, a late-second-century C.E. papyrus

---

93 Wilckens, 3:127, stresses that the obligation is placed only on the Gentile Christians, which seems to imply superior status; Cranfield, 2:773, places this in the context of "Jews first, then the Gentiles."

94 See Minear, *Obedience*, 105; Berger, "Almosen," 198–202; Peterman, "Romans 15:26," 460–61; Müller, "Grundlinien," 230–32.

95 Georgi links this particularly with the doctrine of the resurrection in *Remembering the Poor*, 116.

96 See Jewett, *Terms*, 165–66.

97 See Danker, *Benefactor*, 330–31.

98 See E. A. Judge, "The Regional *kanon* for Requisitioned Transport," *NDIEC* 1 (1981) 36–45.

99 H. Strathmann, H. and R. Meyer, "λειτουργέω κτλ.," *TDNT* 4 (1967) 227.

100 See Dunn, 2:876.

101 See Gerhard Delling, "ἐπιτελέω," *TDNT* 8 (1972) 61–62; Betz, *2 Corinthians 8 and 9*, 54.

102 Cited by MM 247–48 from *P.Par.* Nr. 63.16; see also *P.Par.* Nr. 26.28. Three additional examples of ἐπιτελεῖν for completing administrative tasks are provided by Welles, *Royal Correspondence*, 54.11; 65.11; 67.11.

103 This was first suggested by Deissmann, *Studies*, 95–96, followed shortly by Franz Josef Dölger,

contains this routine order: ἂν ἔρχῃ ἄφες ἀρτάβας ἐξ
εἰς τοὺς σάκκους σφραγίσας λαχανοσπέρρου ἵνα
πρόχιροι ὦσι ("When you come, take out six artabae of
vegetable seed, sealing it in the sacks in order that they
may be ready").[104] Another papyrus contains a governmental regulation referring to sealed grain that is probably reserved for military use: διὰ δὸν [σῖ]τον τὸν
σφραγισθέντα εἰς τὴν συνωνὴν . . . ("because of the
corn that has been sealed for the obligatory sale . . .").[105]
The association of σφραγίζω with preparation for delivery is illustrated by the instructions about a grain ship-
ment on a governmental ship, including a receipt written
by the shipmaster along with the command δεῖγμα
σφραγισάσ[θ]ω ("let him seal a sample"), to guarantee
that no tampering could occur in transit.[106] Similarly, a
second-century C.E. papyrus announces an imminent
delivery of fruit, sealed against nibbling by transport
workers: ἔπεμψα ὑμεῖν . . . κτ[ί]στην σταφυλῆς λείαν
μάχης καὶ σφυρίδα φοίνικος καλοῦ ἐσφραγί
[σμενας] ("I sent you . . . a box of very excellent grapes
and a basket of excellent dates under seal").[107] These
routine examples of shipping terminology show that one
does not have to resort to Eduard Norden's suggestion
of derivation from Jewish cultic usage and Hellenistic
mystery religions in this verse,[108] nor construe the καρπός ("fruit") that Paul is delivering as the faith of Gentile converts that Paul needs to certify.[109] To seal the
fruit of the Jerusalem offering is rather to guarantee its
delivery against theft and embezzlement,[110] which conforms to the arrangements Paul made in 2 Cor 8:20-23
to ensure that the Corinthian contribution would be

securely delivered.[111] Paul evidently feels that such delivery requires his personal presence, thus causing him to
journey east before he can undertake the journey west to
Rome and Spain. His explanation says in effect, "when I
am completely finished with this matter,"[112] I will be free
to fulfill the long-standing plan to visit Rome.

The unadorned formulation, "I shall be off by way of
you to Spain,"[113] uses conventional language for departing on a trip[114] while planning to make a visit under
way.[115] Conforming to diplomatic style, Paul does not
specify precisely what he wishes to accomplish in the
brief visit to Rome. Nevertheless, he makes it clear once
again that the purpose of his journey is not to establish a
long-term ministry in Rome, but to travel west into
Spain. Without making any specific demands, this formulation invites the Roman congregations to participate
in some way in his missionary travels. If my interpretation of the purpose of Romans is correct, all of the previous argument of the letter has aimed to provide a
rationale for a visit that would be productive in this
sense. Diplomatic sensitivity forbids specification at this
point, either of Paul's precise hopes or of the extensive
requirements of a successful mission to Spain. Yet the
weight Paul attaches to this simple announcement of an
impending arrival is confirmed by the surprising turn in
the next verse.

■ 29 The theme of Paul's confidence in sharing the
"fullness of Christ's blessing" with the Roman congregations completes the thought of 15:24 and echoes the
hope of mutual enrichment expressed in 1:11-12.[116] The
hesitant awkwardness of this formulation, which a tex-

*Sphragis. Eine altchristliche Taufbezeichnung in ihren
Beziehungen zur profanen und religiösen Kultur des Alter-
tums,* SGKA 5 (Paderborn: Schöningh, 1911; repr.
New York: Johnson Reprint Company, 1967) 11, 15.

104 Cited by MM 617 from *P.Oxy.* 6. Nr. 932.5-6.
105 See the discussion and translation by G. H. R. Hors-
     ley, "The Trial of Bishop Phileas," *NDIEC* 2 (1982)
     191; the source is *P.Mich.* 13. Nr. 661.19.
106 See MM 617, cited from *P.Hib.* 1. Nr. 39.15-16 from
     265 B.C.E.
107 MM 617-18, cited from *P.Oxy.* 1. Nr. 116.17-20; see
     also *P.Oxy.* 3. Nr. 528.16.
108 Eduard Norden, *Die Antike Kunstprosa vom VI.
     Jahrhundert v. Chr. bis in die Zeit der Renaissance*
     (Leipzig/Berlin: Teubner, 1898), 2:477.
109 Hans-Werner Bartsch, ". . . wenn ich ihnen diese

     Frucht versiegelt habe. Röm 15:28. Ein Beitrag zum
     Verständnis der paulinischen Mission," *ZNW* 63
     (1972) 96-107.
110 See Ludwig Radermacher, "Σφραγιζέσθαι: Rm
     15,28," *ZNW* 32 (1933) 87-88.
111 See Zeller, 241, and Betz, *2 Corinthians 8 and 9,*
     72-82.
112 See Gaugler, 2:386-87, cited by Cranfield, 2:775.
113 For the translation, see Barrett, 279.
114 BAGD 84 cites Mark 1:35, Matt 28:10, and a num-
     ber of other uses of the conventional expression
     ἀπέρχομαι εἰς ("depart, go to").
115 BAGD 179 suggests the translation of δι᾽ ὑμῶν as
     "through your city on the way," with parallels in
     Acts 9:32; 2 Cor 1:16.
116 See Kühl, 475; Lietzmann, 123; Barrett, 279.

tual variant sought to remove,[117] has not been explained by commentators. The verse begins with the mild antithesis of οἶδα δέ ("but I know"), usually translated as "and I know," which eliminates the slight contrast between this and the foregoing sentence, a contrast which in this instance is indeed "scarcely discernible."[118] This formulation conveys a note of hesitancy about whether the arrival in Rome announced in 15:28 will be successful, while maintaining that, despite possible conditions to the contrary, Paul is nevertheless confident of divine blessing. Michel discerns a note of boasting in this sentence, which he explains as an expression of Paul's spiritual gifts,[119] but this does not explain why Paul would suddenly and unexpectedly reassert his apostolic claims at this particular point, especially in the context of a mild antithesis. The proper approach is to be found in Georgi's assessment of the hope "that the disbursement of the collection will contribute to the success of his future work."[120] The conflicts between Jewish and Gentile Christians in Rome are related to the ethnic and theological tensions that Paul had hoped to overcome by the successful completion of the Jerusalem offering. However, in view of the political risks that the offering might reawaken zealot pressures on the Jerusalem church, increasing the provocative aspects of Paul's theological rationale, there was a chance that the offering could turn out disastrously, a concern that the wording of 15:30-32 reveals. This would clearly jeopardize any prospect of overcoming the ethnic tensions between house and tenement churches in Rome, which the earlier argument of Romans seeks to achieve, and which the mounting of a credible, cross-cultural mission to Spain requires. The formulation of this verse is thus not "a sigh of relief" that Paul's tasks in the East are almost completed,[121] but a statement of confidence that Christ will prevail despite serious odds.

The formulation ἐν πληρώματι εὐλογίας Χριστοῦ ("in the fullness of Christ's blessing") indicates that Paul's confidence rests not in his own calling or his apostolic powers, but finally in the expansive power of Christ as described in 15:18-19.[122] Christ is clearly the subject of the blessing in this genitive expression,[123] which I translate "Christ's blessing." The use of πλήρωμα in this context cannot help but recall to the audience the evocative references to the "fullness" to be enjoyed by the Gentiles (11:12), to "the full number of the Gentiles" that are to be converted before the parousia (11:25), and to Christian love as "law's fulfillment" (13:10). Paul had referred to the offering as a "blessing" in 2 Cor 9:5, linking it with the expectation of bountiful, expansive fulfillment. The background of this allusion to an expanding blessing is visible in the proverb Paul composed in 2 Cor 9:6: Τοῦτο δέ, ὁ σπείρων φειδομένως φειδομένως καὶ θερίσει, καὶ ὁ σπείρων ἐπ᾽ εὐλογίαις ἐπ᾽ εὐλογίαις καὶ θερίσει ("Consider this, 'He who sows sparingly, sparingly will he also reap, and he who sows upon blessings, upon blessings will he also reap'").[124] When believers respond generously to the blessings they have received from Christ, their sharing with one another in occasions like the Jerusalem offering will produce increased blessings for all concerned. Thus Paul explains the rationale for generous participation in 2 Cor 9:8, "God is able to make every benefit abundant for you, so that always having enough of everything, you may also share abundantly in every good work." Georgi is correct in seeing in this rationale "a circular movement so strong that it sweeps everyone along with it."[125] As the Jerusalem church accepts the generous offering from the Gentile churches, this will incite the Jerusalem Christians to a crescendo of gratitude, which in turn will stimulate an expansive cycle of blessing and harmony between the ethnic groups throughout the church,[126] redounding to Rome and beyond. Given the earlier references to πλήρωμα in connection with the Gentile mission,[127] this expansion of the blessing points beyond Paul and beyond Rome itself; it alludes to the conver-

---

117 See note m above.
118 See BAGD 171.
119 Michel, 466, followed by Schlier, 437.
120 Georgi, *Remembering the Poor*, 121.
121 Käsemann, 402, followed by Dunn, 2:877.
122 Heckel, *Segen*, 111.
123 See Schenk, *Segen*, 48; Zeller, *Juden*, 234.
124 For a discussion of the translation and the parallels

to this proverb, with the conclusion concerning Paul's formulation, see Betz, *2 Corinthians 8 and 9*, 101–3.
125 Georgi, *Remembering the Poor*, 121.
126 See Nickle, *Collection*, 141; Keck, "Saints in Jewish Christianity and Qumran," 126; Zeller, *Juden*, 235.
127 See Schenck, *Segen*, 48.

sion of the whole world through the gospel, which was the theme that concluded the final proof of the letter in 15:7-13. The "fullness of Christ's blessing" therefore refers to the expansive triumph of the gospel that Paul's letter and travel aim to advance. Although Paul's hopes for the Jerusalem offering, the visit to Rome, and the subsequent mission to Spain remained unfulfilled, as we now know, "the fact remains," as Ferdinand Hahn points out, that Paul "more than any other before him gave the signal for the gathering together of all the nations on earth."[128]

■ **30** The typical request formula used in ambassadorial rhetoric,[129] παρακαλῶ δὲ ὑμᾶς ("But I urge you" [pl.]), indicates the importance of these verses in the purpose of Romans.[130] On the basis of the preceding fifteen chapters of argumentation, Paul hopes to gain the prayerful support of the Roman churches in the delicate political project of delivering the Jerusalem offering. The audience is addressed as "brothers," members of the same holy family and thus, Paul hopes, equal partners in a common enterprise.[131] The solemnity of the exhortation is enhanced by the double use of διά, "*through* our Lord Jesus Christ and *through* the love of the Spirit."[132] Murray argues convincingly that more than the mediations of Christ and the Spirit are involved here: "It is rather that he makes Christ Jesus his plea for compliance with his request."[133] The lordship of Christ demands mutual acceptance between ethnic branches of the church, as 14:4-9 had shown; the love of God poured into the heart of believers by the Spirit (5:5) made clear

that Jewish and Gentile Christians alike are "joint heirs with Christ" (8:17). Paul wants the Romans to understand that the project of unifying the church through the Jerusalem offering is grounded in the action of God through Christ and the Spirit, therefore deserving the prayerful intercession of the Roman congregations.

The choice of the verb συναγωνίζομαι ("join in struggle, struggle together"), a military and athletic expression[134] found only here in the NT, points to the urgent need for assistance. The use of this term in a team competition is illustrated by Aristophanes' lines: ἥπερ πέρουσιν ἐν τῷδε ταὐτῷ χωρίῳ, Εὐριπίδη καὐτὴ ξυνηγωνιζόμην ("I who last year, in these same lists contended, A faithful friend, beside Euripides").[135] In a military context, the term is used to refer to persons fighting on the same side; for instance, Josephus explains the valor of the Roman legionnaires as follows: "For when Caesar was with them struggling together (συναγωνιζομένου), cowardice seemed monstrous, while the one who struggled well (τῷ καλῶς ἀγωνισαμένῳ) had as witness one who would also reward it" (*Bell.* 5.311). An Athenian inscription honors Ptolemy I for struggling alongside the city in a nonmilitary type of crisis: "He also took care of provisions of wheat for the people that he provided safely, struggling together in the preservation of the people (συναγωνιζό[μενος τῆς τοῦ δήμ]ου σωτηρίαι)."[136] Of particular interest is the honorific decree for Kallias of Sphettos for his ambassadorial work in 287 B.C.E. . . . ταῖς πρεσβείας ταῖς

---

128 Hahn, *Verständnis der Mission*, 110.

129 See the discussion of Bjerkelund, *PARAKALÔ*, 59–87, 109–11, in connection with Rom 12:1 above. The use in 15:30 is discussed on 157–60. For example, Antiochus II exhorts the city of Erythrae to comply with his request in the words: παρακαλοῦμεν δὲ καὶ ὑμᾶς μνημονεύοντας ἡμῶν . . . ("and we exhort you also, remembering that we . . ." Welles, *Royal Correspondence*, 79–80; see also 141–42).

130 See Bjerkelund, *PARAKALÔ*, 158–59, following a suggestion by Nils A. Dahl, "Hovedsak og bisetninger," in *Festschrift til biskop A. Fjellbu* (Oslo: Gyldendal Norsk Forlag, 1960) 57–66; see also Dahl, *Studies*, 77. George Smiga provides a convincing case that Bjerkelund exaggerated the primacy of 15:30-32 in the purpose of Romans in "Occasion of the Letter," 260.

131 See Aasgaard, *Siblingship in Paul*, 275–78.

132 See Schettler, *Durch Christus*, 50, 54.

133 Murray, 2:221. Unfortunately Murray decontextualizes and individualizes this grounding of the argument in Christ and the Spirit by referring to what they accomplish "in us" rather than in the conflicted congregations of the first century. See also Cranfield, 2:776; Hermann, *Kyrios und Pneuma*, 93.

134 See BAGD 783; Gerhard Dautzenberg, "ἀγών κτλ.," *EDNT* 1 (1990) 25; the definitive study of struggle in athletic contexts is provided by Pfitzner, *Paul and the Agon Motif*, 109–29.

135 Aristophanes *Thesm.* 1060–61; translation by Benjamin Bickley Rogers, *Aristophanes III*, Loeb Classical Library (New York: Putnam, 1927) 225.

136 *SIG* 367.16–20.

ἀποστελλουμέναις ὑπὸ τοῦ δημοῦ συναγωνιζόμενος εἰς πάντα καὶ συνεργὼν εἰς τὰ συμφέροντα τεῖ πόλει ("... with the embassies dispatched by the people, striving together in every way, working for what was in the city's interests").[137]

To "struggle together in prayers" implies sharing Paul's intercessions for the success of the Jerusalem offering,[138] not a struggle against God similar to Jacob's wrestling with the angel.[139] Given the situation Paul is facing, the use of this expression for strenuous exertion evokes the kind of spiritual battle with the principalities and powers depicted in Romans 8.[140] To describe Paul's intent as merely requesting earnestness in prayer[141] is to overlook the seriousness of the threats to these endeavors[142] and the very real dangers he foresees.[143] The unusual double reference to "my" (μοι) struggle and "in my behalf" (ὑπὲρ ἐμοῦ) in this sentence shows that Paul is recruiting the Roman congregations to his side in the spiritual battle against "opposition from Judea and the Jerusalem church"[144] that opposes the cross-cultural reconciliation that Paul has placed at the center of the gospel. The intercessory prayers are, of course, directed

πρὸς τὸν θεόν ("before God"),[145] whose righteous purpose is expressed in the gospel mission.

■ **31** Paul mentions two immediate outcomes that he hopes for as a result of the prayers shared between himself and the Roman churches. The first involves the mortal danger of assassination by zealots in Judea: ἵνα ῥυσθῶ ἀπὸ τῶν ἀπειθούντων ἐν τῇ Ἰουδαίᾳ ("in order that I might be delivered from the disobedient ones in Judea"). The verb ῥύομαι is used here in its root meaning of "guard, protect, deliver,"[146] referring not to final redemption as in 7:24 and 11:26[147] but to "deliverance from enemies, mortal danger, perils and persecutions."[148] The expression ῥύεσθαι ἀπό ("to be delivered from") also appears in 2 Thess 3:2, as well as in the Lord's Prayer (Matt 6:13; Luke 11:4), and seems to reflect LXX usage such as Isa 25:4, ἀπὸ ἀνθρώπων πονηρῶν ῥύσῃ αὐτούς ("from evil persons you shall deliver them").[149] The participle οἱ ἀπειθοῦντες ("the disobedient ones") is used in a similar way in the finite verb of Rom 2:8 to refer to persons rejecting the truth, and in a polemical way in 10:21; 11:30-31[150] to refer to Paul's fellow Jews who have rejected the gospel about

---

137 G. H. R. Horsley, "συναγωνίζομαι," *NDIEC* 3 (1983) 84.

138 For this conclusion and a comprehensive analysis of the discussion, see Gebauer, *Gebet*, 172–75. See also the similar conclusion in Wiles, *Paul's Intercessory Prayers*, 269–70.

139 Michel, 467; Schlier, 438; Black, 205; F. Zimmer, "Das Gebet nach den Paulinischen Schriften," *Theologische Studien und Skizzen aus Ostpreussen* 1 (1887) 138–39; Stanislas Lyonnet, "Un aspect de la 'prière apostolique' d'après saint Paul," *Christus* 5 (1958) 224–26; P.-Y. Emery, "Prayer in Saint Paul," *LV* 24 (1969) 606. See the critique of this position in Pfitzner, *Paul and the Agon Motif*, 123.

140 Sanday and Headlam, 415; Werner Bieder, "Gebetswirklichkeit und Gebetsmöglichkeit bei Paulus. Das Beten des Geistes und das Beten im Geist," *ThZ* 4 (1948) 23.

141 See Cranfield, 2:777.

142 See Dunn, 2:878; Pfitzner, *Paul and the Agon Motif*, 121–22.

143 Käsemann, 406; S. Zedda, "La preghiera apostolica in Paolo," *Parola Spirito e Vita* 3 (1981) 174–75; Dautzenberg, "ἀγών κτλ.," 26; Wiles, *Paul's Intercessory Prayers*, 268.

144 Dunn, 2:878; see also Pfitzner, *Paul and the Agon Motif*, 122.

145 Gebauer, *Gebet*, 107, lifts up the typical quality of Jewish faith in Paul's addressing prayers to God, citing Adalbert Hamman, *La Prière*, vol. 1, *Le Nouveau Testament*, BT.B (Tournai: Desclée, 1959) 264–70.

146 See Wilhelm Kasch, "ῥύομαι," *TDNT* 6 (1968) 998–99.

147 See Dunn, 2:878.

148 Hermann Lichtenberger, "ῥύομαι," *EDNT* 3 (1993) 214; see also Gebauer, *Gebet*, 328 n. 532.

149 See Kasch, "ῥύομαι," 1000, and also 1 Esdr 8:16; 2 Esdr 8:31; Job 33:17; Ps 16:13; 17:29, 48; 21:20; 38:8; 42:1; 139:1, 4; Prov 2:12; 11:4; Ezek 37:23; Dan 8:7; 1 Macc 12:15; 3 Macc 6.10. The verb also frequently appears in late-Christian magical spells requesting deliverance from evil; for a non-Christian usage, cf. *PGM* IV.1167, "A stele useful for everything, it even delivers from death (ῥύεται καὶ ἐκ θανάτου)." Further, cf. Roy Kotansky, "Two Amulets in the Getty Museum," *JPGMJ* 8 (1980) 181–87. A close thematic parallel from Homer uses the preposition ὑπό rather than ἀπό, as Ajax prays, "Father Zeus, but save the sons of the Achaians from this fog . . ." (Ζεῦ πάτερ, ἀλλὰ σὺ ῥῦσαι ὑπ' ἠέρος υἷας Ἀχαιῶν . . , *Il.* 17.645). Most other references both in the LXX and in secular Greek use the preposition ἐκ.

150 See Michel, 468; Schlier, 438.

Jesus as the Christ.[151] Only in Romans does Paul use this language, reflecting in part his struggle with the problem of Jewish rejection of the gospel, and also his desire to find common ground in the usage of the LXX[152] as well as Greco-Roman religion.[153] The assumption in this usage is that persons who are "disobedient to God" will endanger the lives of those who obey; in this instance, as in 2 Thess 3:2, it is expected that those who do not have "faith" in Christ will be hostile to those who do.

The specification of the threat against Paul's life as centered ἐν τῇ Ἰουδαίᾳ ("in Judea") refers to what was commonly described as "the Jewish land," namely, the areas of Palestine primarily inhabited by Jews.[154] It is clear from this formulation that he did not anticipate the assassination plot en route to Judea (Acts 20:2) that later caused him to change travel plans.[155] As in 1 Thess 2:14, he anticipates the possibility of anti-Christian persecution occurring in Judea, in this instance probably motivated by hostility against his missionizing and particularly against his goal of unifying the Gentile and Jewish branches of the church, which in the eyes of zealous revolutionaries would further pollute Israel. Such hostility could only be increased by Paul's missionary rationale expressed in 11:11-24, converting Gentiles in order to provoke Jews to zeal.[156] Moreover, as Georgi points out, the "provocative nature of Paul's plan to convey the collection must have been tremendous, especially if Paul were to arrive in Jerusalem—as he probably originally planned—during the Passover festival."[157]

The resultant outcome for which Paul hopes is that "my service to Jerusalem" would be welcomed by the church.[158] Stephan Joubert explains the situation on the basis of the Greco-Roman system of benefaction: Paul and his communities "had officially fulfilled their responsibilities" as benefactors and "it is now up to Jerusalem to either accept their gift, and thus ensure the continuance of the reciprocal relationship, or to reject it, and thereby threaten the unity of the early Christian movement. Rejection of the collection would be a flagrant insult to Paul and his communities."[159] The wording I investigated in connection with 15:25 is employed again, including "service," "Jerusalem," and "saints," probably reflecting the title used for the Jerusalem offering[160] as well as the usage of early Christianity in general for sharing resources in the common life of house and tenement churches. The level of Paul's own investment in the task of organizing and delivering the offering is evident in the personalized expression ἡ διακονία μου ("my service"); it is not only that he was party to the agreement at the Apostolic Conference to raise such funds (Gal 2:10) but that he construed the offering as integral to his task as a Gentile missionary.[161] In Paul's view, both the collection and reception of the offering would give expression to the pacification and cooperation of ethnic groups whose former hostilities have been overcome by the gospel of Christ. So Paul uses the same term he had employed in 15:16 with reference to the offering as "acceptable," hoping now that with the help of the Romans prayers, the offering would be εὐπρόσκδεκτος τοῖς ἁγίοις ("acceptable to the saints"). This has been interpreted as suggesting that the Jerusalem church might reject the collection outright,[162]

151 See Rudolf Bultmann, "ἀπειθέω," TDNT 6 (1968) 10–11; Peter Bläser, "ἀπειθέω," EDNT 1 (1990) 118: "Unbelief is disobedience against God."

152 Among scores of examples of "disobedience" in the LXX, see, for example, the absolute use in Isa 1:25, τοὺς δὲ ἀπειθοῦντας ἀπολέσω ("the disobedient ones I will destroy").

153 See Bultmann, "ἀπειθέω," 10, referring to disobedience "against the deity" in passages like Euripides Orest. 31, ὅμως δ' ἀπέκτειν οὐκ ἀπειθήσας θεῷ ("Though he did not slay in disobedience to God").

154 See Walter Gutbrod, "Ἰουδαῖος, Ἰσραήλ, Ἑβραῖος in Greek Hellenistic Literature," TDNT 3 (1965) 382; Otto Betz, "Ἰουδαία, ας," EDNT 2 (1991) 191–92; Dunn, 2:879: "the whole national territory of the Jews."

155 See Gebauer, Gebet, 328 n. 532.

156 See Georgi, Remembering the Poor, 118.

157 Ibid., 120.

158 As Walter Schmithals points out in Paul and James, trans. D. M. Barton, SBT 46 (Naperville: Allenson; London: SCM, 1965) 81–82, the widespread acceptance of the inferior reading ἵνα ("that") in v. 31b leads commentators falsely to infer that Paul seeks two ends in Jerusalem; see note s above.

159 Joubert, Benefactor, 207.

160 See Betz, 2 Corinthians 8 and 9, 90.

161 See Joubert, Benefactor, 208.

162 Wilckens, 3:129; Käsemann, 407; Zeller, 241. Haacker places the possible rejection of Gentile philanthropy in the context of the revolutionary campaign against Rome in "Probleme," 3–4.

that they would receive the offering without appropriate welcoming,[163] that there might be difficulties in passing over the funds,[164] or that Paul merely wishes to express his "freedom from self-centered complacency" in anticipating how the offering will be received.[165] Schmithals correctly infers that "the more sharply the Jews reacted to Paul's arrival the less welcome to the Jewish Christians could the contributions be which Paul had brought them."[166] This means that the political circumstances might encourage an outright rejection. Given the environment of violent, anti-Gentile hostility in Palestine, it seems likely that Paul's concern was that the offering would either be refused or that it would be received under auspices that would not express the cross-cultural solidarity that he believed was central to the gospel. When one examines the "remarkable silence" of Acts about the delivering of the offering[167] and the strange story about Paul paying for a Nazarite vow (Acts 21:23-24), it appears that a kind of religious money-laundering scheme was in fact adopted that sanctified the Jerusalem offering by assimilating it into legalistic devotion.[168] It is very likely that Paul's fears about the acceptability of the offering to the Jerusalem church, under extreme pressure from nationalistic zealots, were fully justified.

■ **32** The second purpose clause initiated by ἵνα ("in order that") subordinates the successful delivery of the Jerusalem offering to Paul's "coming to you in joy through the will of God."[169] This second result that Paul hopes for is dependent on the successful delivery of the Jerusalem offering (15:31), which means that the prayers of the Romans for Paul's safe journey[170] invite

their support for the larger issue. Unless Paul is successful in unifying the Gentile and Jewish Christian wings of the church, the missional goal of the intended visit to Rome can hardly be accomplished. In view of Paul's use of χάρα ("joy") in connection with the present and future triumph of divine righteousness through the gospel (Rom 14:17; 15:13), joy functions here as "a primary mode of the appropriation of the eschatological event of salvation by human beings."[171] The combination of joy with the preposition "in," which is avoided in secular usage,[172] points to biblical scenes of festal triumph when salvation is celebrated. In such moments, the saved community is in a collective state of exultant joy.[173] Particularly memorable is the double use of the phrase ἐν χαρᾷ in connection with Yahweh's promise in Deutero-Isaiah to the exiles who will be brought back in triumph: Ἐν γὰρ εὐφροσύνῃ ἐξελεύσεσθε, καὶ ἐν χαρᾷ διδαχθήσεσθε, τὰ γὰρ ὄρη καὶ οἱ βουνοὶ ἐξαλοῦνται προσδεχόμενοι ὑμᾶς ἐν χαρᾷ . . . ("For in exaltation you shall go forth, and shall be taught in joy, for the mountains and the hills shall leap up welcoming you in joy . . ." Isa 55:12). Similarly, the king who trusts Yahweh is given the promise by the psalmist: Ὅτι δώσεις αὐτῷ εὐλογίαν εἰς αἰῶνα αἰώνων εὐφρανεῖς αὐτὸν ἐν χαρᾷ μετὰ τοῦ προσώπου σου ("You will give him a blessing for ever and ever, you will gladden him in joy with your countenance," Ps 20:6).[174] Paul's reference to joy διὰ θελήματος θεοῦ ("through [the] will of God") echoes the wording of the *exordium* in 1:10, making clear that the travel arrangements and hopes being shared with the Romans are an expression

---

163 Gebauer, *Gebet*, 177.

164 Kettunen, *Abfassungszweck*, 173–74; Michel, 468.

165 Cranfield, 2:778.

166 Schmithals, *Paul and James*, 82.

167 Holmberg, *Paul and Power*, 43. The only reference to the purpose of Paul's final journey to Jerusalem surfaces incidentally in Paul's later speech to Felix in Acts 24:17. See also the discussion by Taylor, *Paul, Antioch and Jerusalem*, 216.

168 See Holmberg, *Paul and Power*, 42–43; Georgi, *Remembering the Poor*, 125; Murphy-O'Connor, *Paul*, 349–51; Joubert, *Benefactor*, 213–15.

169 That the purpose clause is dependent on v. 31 is argued by Käsemann, 407; Dunn, 2:880.

170 See Lagrange, 360; Kühl, 475; Schlier, 438; Morris, 524; Sminga, "Occasion of the Letter," 271.

171 Klaus Berger, "χαρά, ᾶς," *EDNT* 3 (1993) 454.

172 See LSJM 1977 and MM 683, where the preferred preposition is μετά ("with") and no examples are given for the use of joy with ἐν. Käsemann's reference to "the profane sense" of "a cheerful, relieved heart" in 407 does not take the distinctively Hebraic background of this phrase into account. Dunn, 2:880, follows this mistaken line in referring to a primary sense of "relief" in Paul's expression.

173 See Hans Conzelmann, "χαίρω κτλ.," *TDNT* 9 (1972) 363: "Most common, however, is the use in a cultic relation, joy as festal joy and its expression." See also Julius Schniewind, "Die Freude im Neuen Testament," in J. Schniewind, *Nachgelassene Reden und Aufsätzen*, ThBT 1 (Berlin: Töpelmann, 1952) 75.

174 See also 1 Macc 5:54; Prov 29:6.

of a divine plan.[175] With all the dangers that Paul faces, the use of this classic expression of the Judeo-Christian concept of God conveys "the recognition that God is sovereign and that the coming to pass of these events is dependent upon his sovereign will."[176] The placement of this phrase indicates that both the safe arrival in Rome and the mutual refreshment of the succeeding words are determined by this divine will.[177]

The interpretation of the odd expression συναναπαύσωμαι ὑμῖν ("I may be refreshed together with you") depends on the context of Paul's visit to Rome, which I have been showing was aimed at gaining support and guidance for the difficult mission to Spain. Therefore, it seems unlikely that Paul merely seeks a rest stop after a difficult journey to Jerusalem and Rome,[178] requiring respite from physical exertions[179] or time to gather strength for the journey to Spain.[180] As Kettunen points out, other references to such "refreshment" in the Pauline letters involve the resolution of conflicts and problems affecting the mission of the gospel (1 Cor 7:13-15; 16:18; Phlm 7, 20). Therefore, Paul's choice of this expression relates in part to the ethnic tensions that might thwart the unifying purpose of the Jerusalem offering,[181] and in larger part to the role such tensions might play in frustrating the plans for the Spanish mission. Unless Phoebe is successful in her diplomatic venture of reconciling the competitive Roman house churches on the basis of the theological and ethical platform set forth in the letter, such mutual refreshment would be unlikely.[182] Therefore, I think it is significant that Paul chose the unusual compound form of συν + ἀναπαύομαι, used otherwise in the Bible only in Isa 11:6 in the context of the eschatological vision of former enemies coexisting together in harmony: Καὶ συμβοσκηθήσεται λύκος μετὰ ὀρνὸς, καὶ πάρδαλις συναναπαύσεται ἐρίφῳ. . . . ("And the wolf shall feed with the lamb, and the leopard shall be refreshed with the kid. . . .") Since this verb was used by secular writers in sexual contexts extraneous to the context of this discussion,[183] and since Paul cited this passage from Isaiah in 15:12, it seems likely that Paul and at least part of his audience would have been aware of the rhetorical echo of Isaianic coexistence.[184] Paul hopes for "refreshment" along "*with*" the Romans, because unless the competitive house and tenement churches can find refreshment with each other, the leopard lying down with the calf, they will not be able to cooperate with the Spanish mission in a credible manner. This hope for peace in the new creation of the Christian community leads naturally to the final verse in the pericope.

■ **33** The appeal to participate in Paul's missionary struggle to unify the church and pacify the world through the gospel is effectively concluded with a benediction concerning the peace of God.[185] Jeffrey Weima

---

175 See Meinrad Limbeck, "θέλημα, ατος, τό," *EDNT* 2 (1991) 137.

176 Murray, 2:223; see also Morris, 524.

177 See Schlier, 439; also John A. Allan, "The Will of God III: In Paul," *ExpT* 72 (1960–61) 143.

178 Lietzmann, 123.

179 Käsemann, 408; Morris, 525: "rest in general." See the critique of this interpretation by Kettunen, *Abfassungszweck*, 165.

180 Zeller, 241.

181 Kettunen, *Abfassungszweck*, 165–66.

182 Sanday and Headlam reflect an inadequate grasp of tensions in Rome in 415: "he hopes to find rest in a community as yet untroubled by such strife and distraction." Dunn, 2:880, expresses a similar view.

183 The secular usage refers to gaining mutual relief in sleeping with someone, usually in the marital context; see BAGD 784; LSJM 1695. For instance, Plutarch *Mor.* 125a describes gaining sexual satisfaction with one's wife as compared with "notorious women": "There are times when they gain quiet refreshment (συναναπαυώμενοι) with their own wives who are both lovely and loving, but when they have paid money to a Phryne or a Laïs, although their body is in sorry state and is inclined to shirk its task, they rouse it forthwith to action."

184 Although Hays, *Echoes*, 70–73, does not mention this particular echo, it fits the criteria he lays out in 29–32.

185 C. J. Cuming argues in "Service-Endings in the Epistles," *NTS* 22 (1975–76) 110–13, that this is the first portion of the three-folding ending of early Christian services. James M. Gibbs, "Canon Cumings' 'Service-Endings in the Epistles': A Rejoinder," *NTS* 24 (1977–78) 545–47, argues instead that a letter like Romans may have been intended to be read prior to the eucharistic celebration. In view of the scarcity of information about worship patterns in the first century, and the risk of reading later church conditions back into the Pauline letters, neither alternative is likely to be demonstrable.

has argued that the particle δέ ("but, and") in the peace benediction signals the beginning of the letter closing,[186] but, as in 1 Thess 5:23 and 2 Thess 3:16, the benediction appears to summarize and conclude the preceding discussion while having a less direct relationship with the immediately succeeding recommendation of Phoebe.[187] The argumentative function of the benediction was aptly described by Godet as "suggested to him by his conviction of the hostilities and dangers lying before himself, and by the need of soon being in full peace in the midst of his readers."[188] The expression "the God of peace"[189] indicates the divine "source and giver of peace" and conveys the wish that such peace be given to the Roman believers.[190] The wish is implicit, however, and the lack of a finite verb differentiates this benediction from LXX forms such as 2 Kgs 24:23, Κύριος ὁ θεός σου εὐλογήσαι σε ("the Lord your God bless you").[191] Outside of the NT, the only occurrence of this expression "the God of Peace" is in *T. Dan* 5.1-2,[192] where it deals with conflicts within the faith community: Φυλάξατε οὖν, τέκνα μου, τὴν ἐντολὴν τοῦ κυρίου . . . Ἀλήθειαν φθέγγεσθε ἕκαστος πρὸς τὸν πλησίον αὐτοῦ καὶ οὐ μὴ ἐμπέσητε εἰς μῆνιν καὶ ταραχάς, ἀλλ᾿ ἔσεσθε ἐν εἰρήνῃ ἔχοντες τὸν θεὸν τῆς εἰρήνης. Καὶ οὐ μὴ κατισχύσει ὑμῶν πόλεμος ("Observe the Lord's commandments, then, my children. . . . Each of you speak truth clearly to his neighbor, and do not fall into pleasure and troublemaking, but be at peace, holding to the God of peace. Thus no conflict will overwhelm you"). In contrast to the suggestion in *T. Dan* that conflicts should be resolved by following the law more carefully, Paul understands peace as the activity of God through the gospel, which transforms antagonists and makes cooperation possible. The inclusive reference to πάντων ὑμῶν ("all of you"), unique to this particular peace benediction as compared with the rest of the NT letters,[193] echoes the inclusive address in 1:6-7, where the theme of peace for all is also found. In this context, at the conclusion of Paul's plea for prayer concerning the Jerusalem offering that was intended to unify the ethnic branches of the early church, the "all" would be understood to include the Jewish as well as the Gentile branches of the church in Rome.[194]

The typical Jewish conclusion of a blessing or curse provides the final punctuation of this pericope.[195] In Deut 27:15-26, for instance, each of the twelve curses is

---

186 Weima, *Neglected Endings*, 88–90, 220. Weima makes a good point that the connective καί is used with the peace benedictions of 2 Cor 13:11; Phil 4:9; and Gal 6:16, indicating a distinction from benedictions introduced by δέ. But he cannot make a consistent case because no adversative significance is claimed for the peace benediction introduced by δέ in 16:20 (see 228–29).

187 See Roller, *Formular*, 196; Jewett, "Homiletic Benediction," 22–23. The adversative force of δέ that Weima takes as the sign of a new pericope is substantially undercut by the fact that the pericope of 15:22-33 has four other occurrences of this particle, none of which indicates the beginning of a new pericope. Most Romans commentators perceive that 15:33 concludes the preceding pericope; Cranfield, 2:779–80, provides the exception, but, unlike Weima, he does not understand v. 33 as opening a new section of the letter.

188 Godet, 486. In contrast, Lagrange, 361, denies any link with the congregational situation.

189 The argument in this section is adapted from Robert Jewett, "The God of Peace in Romans: Reflections on Crucial Lutheran Texts," *CTM* 25.3 (1998) 186–94.

190 See Weima, *Neglected Endings*, 91–92; Fitzmyer, 727.

Gerhard Delling places this benediction in the context of the argument of Romans, which defined peace in 5:1; 8:6; and 14:17 in terms of "salvation in its fullness" in "Die Bezeichnung 'Gott des Friedens' und ähnliche Wendungen in den Paulusbriefen," in E. E. Ellis and E. Grässer, eds., *Jesus und Paulus Festschrift für Werner Georg Kümmel zum 70. Geburtstag* (Göttingen: Vandenhoeck & Ruprecht, 1975) 79. This appears to overlook the context of ethnic tensions that are the immediate context of 15:33.

191 This appears to be overlooked in Terrence Y. Mullins, "Benediction as a NT Form," *AUSS* 15 (1977) 61–63.

192 See Delling, "Gott des Friedens," 77–78; for a discussion of the broader Jewish background of this expression, see Michel, 468.

193 See Weima's useful chart of the seven Pauline peace benedictions in *Neglected Endings*, 89.

194 See ibid., 95–96.

195 See Joachim Jeremias, "Amen," *ThRE* 2.386–87.

followed by an "amen." The "amen" in Rom 15:33 has a function similar to the use earlier in the letter (1:25), inviting the Roman audience to add its concurrence by a liturgical response to what Paul has just said.[196] They are expected to reply to Paul's "amen" with an "amen" of their own.[197] The "so be it" function of this liturgical formula[198] confirms God's peace as uniting both the Roman believers and their fellow members from various ethnic traditions throughout the world. The benediction followed by "amen" thus provides an appropriate transition to the introduction of Phoebe and the requests for mutual greetings in the rest of chapter 16, affirming the need of God's peace within the church so that the gospel may be able to extend the realm of divine concord to the end of the known world.

196 See Heinrich Schlier, "ἀμήν," *TDNT* 1 (1964) 336; Jeremias, "Amen," 2.390; see also H.-W. Kuhn, "ἀμήν," *EDNT* 1 (1990) 70.

197 See Schlier, "ἀμήν," 336–37; M. Alamo, "La acla-mación litúrgica 'Amen' en S Pablo," *Liturgia* 1 (1946) 197–200, 227–32; Heckel, *Segen*, 308–12.

198 See Gustav Stählin, "Zum Gebrauch von Beteure-rungsformeln im NT," *NovT* 5 (1962) 115–43.

16

The Third Pericope

The Recommendation of Phoebe as Missionary Patroness

1/ Now[a] I recommend to you Phoebe, our[b] sister, since she also[c] acts as a deacon of the church in Kenchreia, 2/ that you receive her[d] in the Lord in a manner worthy of the saints and provide her whatever she might need from you in the matter, for she herself[e] became a patroness to many[f] and to myself as well.

a The deletion of δέ ("now, but") by D* F G mon appears to be a secondary, stylistic improvement. See Ollrog, "Abfassungsverhältnisse," 226.

b The pronoun ἡμῶν ("our") is strongly attested by ℵ B C D L Ψ 6 33 69 88 104 323 326 330 365 424 614 945 1175 1241 1243 1319c [1319* lacking] 1505 1573 1735 1739 1836 1874 1881 2344 2495 *Maj* f vg sy Ambst and is probably original. The variant reading of ὑμῶν ("your") in P46 A F G P *pc* it boms Pel is identified as "a mistake" by Cranfield, 2:780; a similar shift from ἡμῶν ("our") in F G P is also found in Rom 15:2. In this instance, the variant attempts to specify whose sister Phoebe was.

c The textual evidence for the inclusion of καί ("and, also") is so evenly divided that Nestle-Aland26/27 *GNT*3/4 place it in brackets. P46 ℵ2 B C* 81 1243 1319c [1319* lacking] *pc* bo provide this reading while ℵ* A C2 D F G L P Ψ 6 33 69 88 104 323 326 330 365 424 614 945 1175 1241 1505 1573 1735 1739 1836 1874 1881 2344 2495 *Maj* latt sy sa do not. Cranfield, 2:781, and Michel, 473, argue for its inclusion because it makes good sense, but they provide no explanation for its deletion. Since καί in this clause lends weight to Phoebe's qualifications, its deletion may well have been motivated by the desire to downplay the leadership role of women in the early church.

d The reversal of αὐτὴν προσδέξησθε ("her you receive") to προσδέξησθε αὐτήν ("you receive her") in B C D F G ar mon is rather strongly attested, though probably secondary. The reversal would move the pronoun "her" to a point of lesser emphasis, which may have served the same purpose of de-emphasizing the role of Phoebe that was noted in the deletion of καί by most of the same witnesses in v. 1. In support of the sequence "you receive her" are ℵ A L P Ψ 6 33 69 88 104 323 326 330 365 424 614 945 1175 1241 1243 1319 1505 1573 1735 1739 1836 1874 1881 2344 2495 *Maj* b vg Ambst. P46vid appears to show only προσδέξησθε, with the pronoun to be understood.

e An obscure textual variant found in B2 D2 L Ψ 6 33 69 104 323 330 424 614 629 630 945 1175 1243 1505 1739 1881 2344 2495 *al* articulates the αυτη of the early unaccented majuscules P46 ℵ A B* C D* F G P (though accents later were inserted by some correctors) as αὕτη ("this one," i.e., "this woman") rather than as αὐτή ("she" or "she herself"), which is supported by most of the remaining textual tradition. The variant is unlikely to be original, and it may be an effort to de-emphasize Phoebe by avoiding the emphatic pronoun, translated here as "she herself." See Cranfield, 2:782.

f There are several variants to the clause προστάτις πολλῶν ἐγενήθη καὶ ἐμοῦ αὐτοῦ ("[she] became a patroness to many and to myself as well"), as found in the most likely original form in A B Cvid L P 33vid 69 (88) 104 365 1241 1243 1319 1573 2344 *Maj* vg sy cop Ambst, but with τε after ἐμοῦ in A; with ἐμοῦ και αὐτοῦ in 330; with αὐτοῦ καὶ ἐμοῦ instead of ἐμοῦ αὐτοῦ in ℵ; and with the order αὐτοῦ ἐμοῦ in Ψ 6 323 326 424 614 945 1175 1505 1735 1739 1836 1874 1881 2495. D* provides καὶ ἐμοῦ καὶ ἀλλῶν προστάτις ἐγένετο ("both to myself and others she was a patroness"), as do F G, but with παραστάτις ("helper") in place of προστάτις ("patroness"); D2 places πολλῶν ("many") after ἀλλῶν to produce "and many others," as does P46 in its fragmentary text: καὶ ἀλλῶν πολλῶν. While F and G's παραστάτις ("helper") fits into the pattern of downplaying the status of Phoebe that was detected in earlier variants provided by F G, the others appear to be efforts to correct the loose syntax of the original, according to Cranfield, 2:782.

Analysis

That 16:1-2 comprises a separate pericope is frequently noted by commentators[1] but its relation to the rest of the *peroratio*, including particularly the succeeding greetings, deserves careful attention. The inclusion of the transitional particle δέ ("now") relates these verses to the foregoing in a manner that precludes the possibility

1 Godet, 487–88; Dodd, 234–35; Barrett, 282–83; Michel, 472; Wilckens, 3:131–32. Louw, 2:141, includes 16:1-2 with 16:3-16 as part of the same pericope but admits that "it is quite possible to divide this pericope into two pericopes . . ." because the two sections have "little in common."

of the recommendation standing alone.[2] This brief pericope contains the typical structural elements found in other epistolary commendations in the Pauline letters (Phil 4:2-3; 1 Cor 16:15-18; 1 Thess 5:12-13a; Phlm 10-17). Chan-Hie Kim shows that these commendations include (a) an introduction, (b) credentials, and (c) a desired action, which appears to match what we have in Rom 16:1-2.[3] The use of the transitional particle δέ ("now") in the opening of such a recommendation is also typical in Pauline usage.[4] The only oddity of this structure is that Paul seems to return to (b) credentials in 16:2b,[5] but, as we shall argue, this clause actually suggests the scope of the aid requested from the Roman house churches.

Rhetorical Disposition

15:14—16:24	V.	The *peroratio:* An appeal for cooperation in missionary activities in Jerusalem, Rome, and Spain
16:1-2	C.	The recommendation of Phoebe as missionary patroness
16:1a	1.	The formula of recommendation
16:1b	2.	Phoebe's credentials
		a. Formula of relationship: "our sister"
		b. Official status: "deacon of church in Kenchreia"
16:2a-b	3.	The desired action
16:2a		a. Suitable reception in Rome "with full hospitality . . . worthy of the saints"
16:2b		b. The formula of requested aid: "provide whatever she needs from you in the matter"
16:2c	4.	The scope and rationale of the desired action
		a. Phoebe's past patronage of other missionaries
		b. Phoebe's patronage of Paul

Exegesis

■ 1 The verb συνίστημι was used in 3:5 and 5:8 with the connotation of to prove or demonstrate, but here it bears the sense of "commend" or "introduce."[6] An example of this verb in introducing someone in a social situation is Socrates' comment in Xenophon *Mem.* 1.6.14: "And if I have any good thing, I teach (them) and recommend (them) to others (διδάσκω καὶ ἄλλοις συνίστημι) from whom I consider that they might derive some benefit toward virtue." In a period shortly after Paul's, Chariton writes, "I introduce to you (συνίστημί σοι) my child whom you also gladly know."[7] "I recommend" and its cognates are typically associated with letters of recommendation, but in view of the tendency toward periphrastic use of this term in the Roman period,[8] the forthrightness of Paul's commendation is striking.[9] It has frequently been asserted that this formula of recommendation implies that Phoebe was in fact the bearer of the letter to the Romans.[10] The likelihood of this assertion as well as the confidential role played by letter bearers are sustained and illustrated by Pseudo-Demetrius's example of a typical letter of recommendation:

Τὸν δεῖνα τὸν παρακομίζοντά σοι τὴν ἐπιστολὴν καὶ ἡμῖν κεκριμένον καὶ δι᾽ ἣν ἔχει πίστιν ἀγαπώμενον καλῶς ποιήσεις ἀποδοχῆς ἀξιώσας καὶ δι᾽ τὰ ἐμὲ καὶ δι᾽ αὐτόν, ἔτι δὲ καὶ διὰ σαυτόν. οὐ μεταμελήσῃ γάρ ἐν οἷς θέλεις εἴτε λόγον ἀπόρρητον εἴτε πρᾶξιν εἰπεῖν. ἀλλὰ καὶ σὺ πρὸς ἑτέρους ἐπαινέσεις αὐτὸν αἰσθόμενος ἣν ἐν

---

2   See Ollrog, "Abfassungsverhältnisse," 226–27.

3   Kim, *Recommendation*, 126.

4   Ibid., 133.

5   Ibid., 132, identifies the clause "for she has been a patroness . . ." as ". . . not directly related to" the earlier credentials although it "certainly strengthens" them "by disclosing Phoebe's help given to some members of the congregation and particularly to Paul himself."

6   Armin Kretzer, "συνίστημι, συνιστάνω," *EDNT* 3 (1993) 308.

7   Chariton *Chaer.* 8.4.8.5. See also Libanius *Ep.* 761.1; 832.1; 1198.1; Vettius Valens *Anth.* 9.225.3, recommending something "tried and true."

8   Kim, *Recommendation*, 68–70, 132–33. The expression συστατικὴ ἐπιστολή ("letter of recommendation") is widely used, also by Paul in 2 Cor 3:1; see also BAGD 795.

9   This material is adapted from Jewett, "Spanish Mission," 144–64.

10   See Cranfield, 2:780: "It is highly probable that Phoebe was to be the bearer of Paul's letter to Rome." Most commentators who believe chapter 16 originally belonged to the letter draw a similar conclusion. See Godet, 488; Michel, 473; Wilckens, 3:131.

παντὶ δυνατός ἐστι χρείαν παρασκέσθαι. ("So-and-so, who is conveying this letter to you, has been tested by us and is loved on account of his trustworthiness. You will do well if you deem him worthy of approval both for my sake and his, and indeed for your own. For you will not be sorry if you entrust to him, in any manner you wish, either confidential words or matters. Indeed, you will also praise him to others when you notice how useful he can be in everything.")[11]

Ancient epistolary practice would therefore assume that the recommendation of Phoebe was related to her task of conveying and interpreting the letter in Rome as well as in carrying out the business entailed in the letter.[12]

On the basis of the mythological background of her name,[13] it appears that Phoebe was a Gentile Christian,[14] probably a freed slave,[15] in light of the various indications to be discussed below of her high social status and wealth. She came from Kenchreia, most probably to be identified as the eastern port of Corinth.[16] The excavation of Kenchreia, which lies on the Saronic Gulf approximately eleven kilometers southeast of Corinth, indicates a relatively extensive development of the harbor and the adjacent urban areas during the Roman period.[17] A few Greek inscriptions were found along with evidence of immigration from Italy in the first century,[18] but no indications of the presence of a Jewish population were detected.[19] Pausanius refers to temples of Artemis, Asklepios, Aphrodite, and Isis in or around Kenchreia, of which the latter two have been confirmed by excavation.[20] As in the case of other urban areas, no

---

11   Greek text derived from, and translation adapted from, Malherbe, "Ancient Epistolary Theorists," 30–31.

12   See White, *Light*, 216.

13   Fitzmyer, 729, refers to Hesiod *Theog.* 136, which indicates that the mythical Phoebe was the daughter of Heaven and Earth, the wife of Koios, and the grandmother of Apollo and Artemis. She was a titaness, according to Theognis *Eleg.* 404–9; Aeschylus *Eum.* 4–8; Apollodorus *Biblio.* 1.8; see Timothy Gantz, *Early Greek Myth: A Guide to Literary and Artistic Sources* (Baltimore: Johns Hopkins University Press, 1993) 37. Phoebe was a Peloponnesian heroine, according to *OCD*, 3d ed., 1173. The frequency of this name in the Greco-Roman world is indicated by *SIG* 805.10, where a first-century example is found.

14   Cranfield, 2:780: "That she was a Gentile Christian may be inferred from her name; for a Jewess would scarcely have had a name deriving from pagan mythology." This is a problematic generalization, since many Jews had Greek names and a Jewish slave would have been named by the master, who could easily have chosen this name. See also M. D. Gibson, "Phöbe," *ExpT* 23 (1912) 281.

15   See Schlier, 441, followed by Fitzmyer, 729.

16   Given the six possible towns with the name Kenchreia, the most prominent and closely associated with the Pauline mission at the time of writing Romans was the port of Corinth. See *PW* 11.1.165–70. Wilhelm Michaelis argues for the Kenchreia in Asia Minor in "Kenchreä: Zur Frage des Abfassungsortes des Rm," *ZNW* 25 (1926) 149–50, but this cannot be correlated with the

chronology of Paul's travels. For a discussion of the efforts to locate Kenchreia in the Troad, with locations quite distant in time and space from the first-century city of Troas associated with Paul's mission, see J. M. Cook, *The Troad: An Archaeological and Topographical Study* (Oxford: Clarendon, 1973) 288–89. Fitzmyer, 730, has gathered some references to the port of Kenchreia near Corinth, including Strabo *Geogr.* 8.6.4; 8.6.22; Pausanias *Graec. descr.* 2.1.5; 2.2.3; 7.6.7; Apuleius *Metam.* 10.35. Other references are found in Polybius *Hist.* 2.60.8.3; 4.19.7.6; 5.101.4.2; 18.16.4.1; Phylarchus *Frag.* 2a, 81, F.54.4; Diodorus Siculus *Hist.* 19.63.4.3; 19.64.5.1; Plutarch *Demetr.* 23.3.2; *Arat.* 23.5.4; 29.2.2; 44.6.1. Philo *Flacc.* 155.3 refers to Kenchreia as "the Corinthian harbor (τὸ Κορίνθιον ἐπίνειον)."

17   Robert Scranton et al., *Kenchreia: Eastern Port of Corinth: Results of Investigations by the University of Chicago and Indiana University for the American School of Classical Studies at Athens* (Leiden: Brill, 1978–81) 5 vols; esp. 1:37–90 and Figure 5, "Schematic Restoration of Roman Harbor Area." A convenient summary is available in G. H. R. Horsley, "Kenchreai's Architecture," *NDIEC* 4 (1987) 139–40.

18   Scranton et al., *Kenchreia*, 1:36–37.

19   Excavators found no evidence of Jewish synagogues and the only potentially Jewish artifact discovered was from the fifth century; ibid., 5:80.

20   Pausanias describes the locations of the temples in *Graec. descr.* 1. 2, 3 and the discovery of the harborside sanctuaries is described by Scranton et al., *Kenchreia*, 1:53–90.

archeological evidence has been found that would identify a house or tenement church in Kenchreia during the first century. On the basis of Paul's reference to such a church in 16:1, we must assume that it was a church in Phoebe's residence that had been founded by Paul or his colleagues operating out of Corinth[21] some time between Paul's arrival at that center in 50 C.E. and the writing of Romans in 56–57.[22]

The reference to Phoebe as "our sister" indicates what Cranfield describes as "membership in the Christian community."[23] This expression carries the nuance of her solidarity with Paul as well as with all other believers in Rome or elsewhere. The participle phrase with οὖσαν states her position or occupation in life. In this context, it has an explanatory function: "since she lives as a deacon of the church in Kenchreia." We encountered an earlier use of this participle in 1:7,

"those who live in Rome." Although earlier commentaries interpret the term διάκονος as a subordinate role,[24] it now appears more likely that she functioned as the leader of the congregation.[25] That διάκονος was an official title of leadership has been shown by Brockhaus and Holmberg,[26] and is strongly indicated by earlier references in Rom 11:13; 12:7; and 13:4. In the light of its use in 1 Cor 3:5; 2 Cor 3:6; 6:4; 11:15 and 23 to refer to missionaries, including Paul himself, it is no longer plausible to limit her role to philanthropic activities.[27] Fiorenza contends that the "*diakonos*, like the *synergos*, therefore, is a missionary entrusted with preaching and tending churches. . . . It can be concluded, therefore, that Phoebe is recommended as an official teacher and missionary in the church of Kenchreia."[28] However, in the light of the possessive qualification, "deacon *of the* church in Kenchreia," it seems more likely that she

---

21 See Ollrog, *Paulus und seine Mitarbeiter*, 128f.

22 Jewett, *Chronology*, 161.

23 Cranfield, 2:780; Wilckens, 3:131; Viard, 307. See also Johannes Beutler, "ἀδελφός," *EDNT* 1 (1991) 30: "The prevailing sense in Paul is that of *fellow Christian* . . . "; Meeks, *Urban Christians*, 86: "Especially striking is the language that speaks of the members of the Pauline groups as if they were a family."

24 For instance, see Hodge, 704: Phoebe was "a *servant* . . . i.e., *deaconess*. It appears that in the apostolic church, elderly females were selected to attend upon the poor and sick of their own sex." See also Sanday and Headlam, 417; Lietzmann, *History of the Early Church* (London: Lutterworth, 1963) 1:146, and Michel, 377. Many commentaries follow this general line, limiting Phoebe's activities to "the practical service of the needy" (Cranfield, 2:781) and "charitable care of the poor, sick, widows, orphans . . ." (Käsemann, 410). Kazimierz Romaniuk tries to downplay Phoebe's role in "Was Phoebe in Romans 16:1 a Deaconess?" *ZNW* 81 (1990) 132–34, suggesting that Paul was making a "courteous exaggeration" of her role, but he does not deal with the recently discovered linguistic and sociological evidence. Clarke, "Romans 16," 115–17, insists on the "servile" connotations of διάκονος. Jülicher, 330, was among the first to correctly reject this subordinate interpretation. Caroline F. Whelan showed in "Amica Pauli: The Role of Phoebe in the Early Church," *JSNT* 49 (1993) 68, that the term διακόνισσα ("deaconess") did not develop until the late third century C.E. See also Flo-

rence Morgan Gillman, "Phoebe," *ABD* 5 (1992) 348–49.

25 Fitzmyer, 729–30, reflects the current consensus by translating διάκονος as "minister," implying an important leadership position in the church. The argument against this by Michaelis in "Kenchreä . . ." (*ZNW* 25 [1926] 146) appears to be based on an outdated conception of the possibility of feminine leadership in the early church. See the more adequate assessment by D. C. Arichea, "Who Was Phoebe? Translating *diakonos* in Romans 16:1," *BT* 39 (1988) 409: "a person with special functions in the pastoral and administrative life of the church." Ray R. Schulz opts for a leadership position based on the affinities between the Greek terms for "patron" and "leader" in "A Case for 'President' Phoebe in Romans 16:2," *LTJ* 24 (1990) 124–27; Gillman, "Phoebe," 349.

26 Brockhaus, *Charisma*, 100; Holmberg, *Paul and Power*, 99–102.

27 See Ollrog, *Paulus und seine Mitarbeiter*, 31, 73–74, for the evidence linking the διάκονος role with "missionarische Verkündigungstätigkeit im weitesten Sinn." Aloys Funk, *Status und Rollen in den Paulusbriefen: Eine inhaltsanalytische Untersuchung zur Religionssoziologie* (Innsbruck: Tyrolia, 1981) 86, 112, refers to the "positiv bewertete institutionalisierte Rolle" that Phoebe exercised as the leader of the congregation.

28 Fiorenza, *In Memory of Her*, 171.

functioned as a local leader rather than as a traveling missionary.[29]

■ **2** The key question in relation to Phoebe's recommendation is how to understand what Paul requests in her behalf. The expression αὐτὴν προσδέξησθε ἐν κυρίῳ ἀξίως τῶν ἁγίων implies welcoming her to Rome with full hospitality. Käsemann refers to "the secular sense" of προσδέχεσθαι "of welcoming and offering lodging and help."[30] Cranfield protests against this secular interpretation on grounds of the prominent use of "in the Lord,"[31] but feels that the expression "worthy of the saints" is redundant. The fact that προσδέχεσθαι often appears in secular letters of recommendation with the connotation of hospitality for the bearer of a letter[32] indicates that Käsemann was on the right track. I think that the expression as a whole should be interpreted in light of Phil 2:29, where προσδέχεσθαι is used in reference to welcoming back the beloved Epaphroditus with suitable honor and celebration. Goodspeed suggested that Phoebe's welcome consisted primarily in the provision of respectable housing, but this would probably not have been essential for a person of her means and status.[33] The expression ἀξίως τῶν ἁγίων ("worthy of the saints")[34] suggests how Phoebe is to be welcomed: "as a fellow believer should be received"[35] by believers adhering to the standard of hospitality defined by "holiness."[36] Ἀξίως and its cognates were important hon-

orific terms in the Roman environment, equivalent to the Latin term *dignitas,* that is, "worthiness, excellence, rank, office, esteem, honour," as defined by Lendon.[37] Phoebe should be welcomed with honors suitable to her position as a congregational leader, her previous contributions to the Christian mission, and her role in the missionary project envisioned in Romans; the latter point is yet to be mentioned, but the Roman churches would have heard the entirety of 16:2 long before Paul's arrival in Rome, giving them time to reflect on the role she was intended to play.

The second half of the request in behalf of Phoebe is to "provide her whatever she might need from you in the matter . . ." (Rom 16:2). The expression ᾧ ἂν χρῄζη πράγματι ("she might need in the matter") occurs here for the only time in Greek literature, apart from a few patristic writers. The closest parallel to the verb with an indeterminate object is Athenaeus *Deipn.* 10.74.10, "to do whatever one might wish (ὅ τι ἂν χρήσῃ)." Paul's request is either interpreted in light of the use of πρᾶγμα as referring to a personal transaction in business or law that brings Phoebe to Rome,[38] or in view of the indeterminate expression ἐν ᾧ ἂν ὑμῶν χρῄζη ("whatever she might need from you"), as an open-ended request for aid.[39] The latter is far more plausible in view of the frequent use of similarly conditional expressions in typical letters of recommendation.[40] For example, in a

---

29 See Susanne Heine, "Diakoninnen—Frauen und Ämter in den ersten christlichen Jahrhunderten," *IKZ* 78 (1988), 222; Roman Garrison, "Phoebe, the Servant-Benefactor and Gospel Traditions," in S. G. Wilson and M. Desjardins, eds., *Text and Artifact in the Religions in Mediterranean Antiquity: Essays in Honour of Peter Richardson,* StCJ 9 (Waterloo: Wilfrid Laurier University Press, 2000) 63–65.

30 Käsemann, 411.

31 Cranfield, 2:781–82.

32 See Kim, *Recommendation,* 76–77, 133.

33 The inattention to the class implications of προστάτις leads several commentators to follow Goodspeed in suggesting that the provision of housing was the major need that the congregation in Rome would have to meet; Edgar J. Goodspeed, "Phoebe's Letter of Introduction," *HTR* 44 (1951) 55–57.

34 See Peter Trummer, "ἄξιος, ἀξίως," *EDNT* 1 (1991) 114: "appropriately, worthily, suitably."

35 Murray, 2:226.

36 See Horst Balz, "ἅγιος," *EDNT* 1 (1990) 17; see also P. R. Raabe, "The Law and Christian Sanctification: A Look at Romans," *CJ* 22 (1996) 178–85.

37 See Lendon, *Empire of Honour,* 274; see also 275–79.

38 Michel, 378, and Dunn, 2:888, infer from the parallel in 1 Cor 6:1 that Phoebe's "matter" is probably a lawsuit in Rome; see also Feine, *Abfassung,* 148. The vague expression "whatever she may need from you" seems inappropriate for a legal conflict; this theory also seems unlikely because most of the churches in Rome would not have been in a position to help Phoebe out in such a legal situation, given their low social status.

39 Käsemann, 411; the subjunctive χρῄζη ("he might need") leaves the precise requirements open for discussion.

40 See Kim, *Recommendation,* 78f., 133.

letter of the first century B.C.E., there is a similar reference to providing whatever help the emissary requires: "Achilleus to Seleucus: greetings and be well! We have recommended (καθεστάκαμεν) Archedamos from our own people along with Diocles, in respect of the patronage (πρὸ τῆι προστασίαι) of all the customary matters. Concerning which things, if he has any need of you (ἐν οἷς ἐὰν σοῦ προσδέ[ητ]αι), assist him most generously (συνέργ[ει] φιλωτειμότερον) so that there be nothing lacking in us. Take care of yourself, friend."[41] It is clear from this and other examples that requests are placed in a conditional form because appropriate measures are more easily decided by the recipient than by the letter writer. Cranfield interprets Paul's open-ended request in far too personal a manner, explaining that "in widely varying matters Phoebe could stand in need of their help; and in all such matters they are loyally to stand by their fellow-Christian."[42] It is more likely that the "matter" that Phoebe will bring to Rome has an integral relation to the purpose of the letter, and Paul requests that the congregation provide whatever she needs to accomplish it. That Phoebe needs help with her business or legal affairs hardly seems plausible, given her stature as a patron capable of giving aid to a number of early Christian missionaries. Her wealth and social status belie the pathetic descriptions by imaginative exegetes of her need for Paul's intercession in the face of dire necessity.[43] However, if such fantasies are abandoned, what is the content of Paul's request? It must have significance,

or else it would hardly have been mentioned as the opening request in the final series of personal greetings.

I believe a case can be made that Paul provides a direct hint in the wording of Rom 16:2c, "for she became a patron to many, and also to me." The explanatory words καὶ γάρ ("also for") follow immediately after the vague term πρᾶγμα, thus specifying what is meant by the "matter." It is the matter of Phoebe's patronage. The aorist passive verb used here, ἐγενήθη ("she became"), suggests that Phoebe functioned as a patron on a specific occasion for each of the persons named. She provided resources in concrete acts of patronage, implying the employment of substantial resources. The term προστάτις means "protectress, patroness, helper" and its masculine counterpart took on the technical sense of a legal patron.[44] Although the upper-class connotation of "patroness" runs counter to the subordinate implication traditionally seen in the term "deaconess," several commentators have pointed to its relevance in this context.[45] Käsemann argued, on the basis of an alleged lack of precise parallels to the legal use of the feminine term, προστάτης, that "women could not take on legal functions,"[46] but this does not stand up under the weight of evidence discovered since 1981. E. A. Judge was one of the first to point out the relevance of the papyrus from 142 B.C.E. that was published in 1981, referring to a woman being appointed the legal προστάτις of her fatherless son.[47] Subsequently, the third-century C.E. inscription discovered at Aphrodisias

---

41 Cited by Kim, *Recommendation*, 197, from *PSI* 969; see also Kim, *Recommendation*, 192, no. 37.

42 Cranfield, 2:782.

43 Godet, 448, cites Renan's romantic speculation that "this poor woman started on a wild winter journey across the Archipelago without any other resource than Paul's recommendation."

44 BAGD 718. The social function of προστάτις figures in Plutarch is instructive. *Cor.* 8.1 refers to the Roman Senate "electing five men as *patrons of those who needed help* (προστάτας τῶν δεομένων βοηθείας)." At the time of Solon's reforms, the Athenian poor "began to join together and exhort one another not to submit to their wrongs, but to elect *a faithful man as their patron, to set free the condemned debtors . . .* (ἕνα προστάτην ἄνδραν πιστὸν ἀφελέσθαι τοὺς ὑπερημέρους . . . Plutarch *Sol.* 13.3). Theseus's tomb in Athens became a place of

refuge for runaway slaves and impoverished citizens since he had been "patron (προστατικοῦ) of such during his life, and graciously received the supplications of the poor and needy" (Plutarch *Thes.* 36.2). The same word can be used to describe foreign kings who provide funds and military protection (Plutarch *Phil.* 8.3) and a god such as Harpocrates who functions as a patron (προστάτην) of the human race in Plutarch *Is. Os.* 378c.

45 Jülicher, 330; Deissmann, *Paul*, 216–17; Schumacher, *Letzten Kapitel*, 50; Michel, 377; Marco Zappella, "A proposito di Febe *ΠΡΟΣΤΑΤΙΣ* (Rm 16,2)," *RivB* 37 (1989) 167–71.

46 Käsemann, 411.

47 Edwin A. Judge, "Cultural Conformity and Innovation in Paul: Some Clues from Contemporary Documents," *TynB* 35 (1984) 21. The papyrus was published by Orsolina Montevecchi, "Una donna

has been published with a reference to a Jewish woman by the name of Jael as the προστάτις of a synagogue, clearly indicating a patronage role.[48]

It is now clear that the patronage role played by Phoebe was not unique. Ramsay MacMullen's survey showed that women made up "a fifth of all rescript-addresses" in the Roman period and that "perhaps a tenth of the protectors and donors that *collegia* sought out were women. Honors paid to a patroness *ob merita*, or some similar hint, indicate how the game was played."[49] He concludes that "as a general rule, then, women as benefactors should be imagined playing their part personally and visibly, out in the open."[50] Other investigations of the archeological and cultural evidence confirm this picture.[51] Recent studies by Theissen,[52] Holmberg,[53] Funk,[54] Murphy-O'Connor,[55] Meeks,[56] Kearsley,[57] Trebilco,[58] and Garrison[59] of the leading role played by upper-class benefactors, both male and female, in early Christian communities provide the social background of the description of Phoebe's status. The host or hostess of house churches was usually a person of high social standing and means, with a residence large enough for the church to gather, who presided over the eucharistic celebrations and was responsible for the ordering of the congregation. The fact that Paul mentions Phoebe as a patroness "to many, and also to me" indicates the level of material resources that would support this kind of leadership role. In light of her high social standing, and Paul's relatively subordinate social position as her client,[60] it is mistaken to render προστάτις as "helper" or to infer some kind of subordinate role.[61]

I infer that Phoebe had agreed to underwrite a project of vital significance to Paul and to the letter he is writing.[62] The Roman recipients of the letter would understand her to be recommended as the patroness of the Spanish mission, which Paul had announced in the preceding chapter. As a missionary patroness "of many"

'prostatis' del figlio minorenne in un papiro del II$_a$," *Aeg* 61 (1981) 103–15. Montevecchi prints the legal petition on 103 and discusses the Phoebe parallel on 106. A more recent statement of his discovery is in "Phoebe prostatis (Rom. 16,2)," in *Miscellània papirològica Ramon Roca-Puig enel seuvuitantè anaiversari*, ed. S. Janeras (Barcelona: Fund.S. Vives Casajuana, 1987) 205–16.

48 Joyce Reynolds and Robert Tannenbaum, *Jews and God-Fearers at Aphrodisias: Greek Inscriptions with Commentary*, CPSSV 12 (Cambridge: Cambridge University Press, 1987) 41. Perhaps in part because of what was perceived to be an unusual social role for a woman, Reynolds and Tannenbaum believe "Jael" may be a masculine name, although they admit on 101 that "no other examples" have been found of the masculine use.

49 Ramsay MacMullen, "Women in Public in the Roman Empire," *Hist* 29 (1980) 211.

50 Ibid., 212.

51 E. Lyding Will, "Women's Roles in Antiquity: New Archeological Views," *SDig* (March 1980) 35–39; Matthews, *Rich Pagan Women*, 29–42. G. H. R. Horsley, "A Freedman's Dedication for his Patroness," *NDIEC* 2 (1982) 60–61, provides the text of a second- to third-century inscription in Rome in honor of a "patroness." Horsley provides an extensive discussion of the evidence concerning patronesses in "Sophia, 'the second Phoibe,'" *NDIEC* 4 (1987) 239–44.

52 Theissen, *Social Setting*, 69–120.

53 Holmberg, *Paul and Power*, 103–6.

54 Funk, *Status und Rollen*, 206–15.

55 Murphy-O'Connor, *St. Paul's Corinth*, 153–66.

56 Meeks, *Urban Christians*, 51–73.

57 R. A. Kearsley, "Women in Public Life in the Roman East: Iunia Theodora, Clauda Metrodora and Phoibe, Benefactress of Paul," *ASRT* 15 (1985) 124–37.

58 Paul Trebilco, "Women as Co-Workers and Leaders in Paul's Letters," *JCBRF* 122 (1990) 27–36.

59 Garrison, "Phoebe," 65–71.

60 See Judge, "Cultural Conformity," 21: "Paul is acknowledging his social dependence upon Phoebe."

61 The *RSV* translated προστάτις as "helper" but the *NRSV* corrects matters by "benefactor." A modern commentator who comes close to conveying the nuance of προστάτις in his translation is Barrett, 283, "a protectress of many, and of me myself," but he insists that Paul could not have been her client because he was freeborn, so that "the more general sense" of protectress is to be preferred to patron.

62 Fiorenza suggests that the rationale of Paul's request was the "exchange law" of Greco-Roman patronage in which he "asks that the community of Rome repay Phoebe for the assistance and favors, which Paul owed her as her client." See *In Memory of Her*, 182, citing Mott, "Hellenistic Benevolence," 60–72. It is not clear, however, why Paul would have expected that the Roman house churches, who owed nothing to him for their formation and

and therefore a person of substantial wealth, the churches of Rome would have no fear that cooperation with her would require onerous financial obligations on their part. They would be honored by the prospect of involvement with a person of this high social status. Her patronage would involve gaining the cooperation of the Roman house churches in creating the logistical base and arranging for the translators that would be required for the Spanish mission.[63] This means that the persons being greeted in the subsequent pericope would understand that they are being recruited as advisers and supporters of Paul's and Phoebe's "matter,"[64] a project of supreme importance in the eschatologically motivated scheme of the early Christian mission.

---

growth, could have felt obligated to repay Phoebe in his behalf.

63 For the detailed development of this hypothesis, see Jewett, "Paul, Phoebe, and the Spanish Mission," in Peter Borgen et al., eds., *The Social World of Formative Christianity and Judaism: Essays in Tribute to Howard Clark Kee* (Philadelphia: Fortress Press, 1988) 144–64; cited with approval by Müller, *Schluß*, 215–16.

64 In "Amica Pauli," 84, Caroline F. Whelan suggests an alternative theory, based on the premise of the Ephesian provenance of Rom 16, that "the Ephesians would enter into a patron-client relationship with Phoebe. This double relationship will secure Paul's interests in the east." Aside from the unlikelihood of an Ephesian audience for the chapter as a whole, this theory seems to contradict Paul's plan in 15:20 to relinquish responsibility for the eastern mission field.

16

The Fourth Pericope

Greetings and Commendations between Ministerial Leaders

1. Greetings to Congregational Leaders in Rome

3/ Greet Prisca[a] and Aquila, my co-workers in Christ Jesus,[b] 4/ who risked their own necks for my life, for whom not only I give thanks but also all of the churches of the Gentiles; 5/ also [greet] the church in their house. Greet my beloved Epainetos, who is the first fruit[c] in Asia[d] for[e] Christ. 6/ Greet Miriam,[f] who has labored much for[g] you. 7/ Greet Andronikos and Junia,[h] my compatriots and my fellow prisoners,[i] who are outstanding among the apostles, who[j] were begotten in Christ even before me. 8/ Greet Ampliatus,[k] my[l] beloved in [the] Lord. 9/ Greet Urbanus, our co-worker in Christ,[m] and my beloved Stachys. 10/ Greet Apelles, the approved one in Christ. Greet those from among the [slaves] of Aristoboulos. 11/ Greet my compatriot Herodion. Greet those from among the [slaves] of Narkissos who are in [the] Lord. 12/ Greet Tryphaina and Tryphosa, the laborers in [the] Lord. Greet the beloved Persis, who has labored much in [the] Lord. 13/ Greet Rufus, the chosen in [the] Lord, and also his mother and mine. 14/ Greet Asynkritos, Phlegon, Hermes, Patrobas, Hermas, and the brothers with them. 15/ Greet Philologos and Julia,[n] Nereus[o] and his sister, and Olympas,[p] and all the saints with them. 16/ Greet one another with a holy kiss.

a   The diminuitive form, Πρίσκιλλαν ("Priscilla"), is found in the *TR* as evidenced in 81 104 256 323 365 614 629 630 945 1319 1505 1573 1735 1852 1881[c] 2495, as well as ar mon vg[mss] sy (bo[pt]) *al* Ambst, but it is clearly a secondary convention consistent with the variants in 1 Cor 16:19, 2 Tim 4:19 as well as the usage in Acts 18:2, 18, 26. All of the earlier texts have the proper name, Πρίσκαν, with P[46] and B* offering the insignificant variation in spelling of Πρείσκαν.

b   D[*.2] F G ar mon have the phrase καὶ τὴν κατ᾽ οἶκον αὐτῶν ἐκκλησίαν ("and the church in their house") here rather than at 16:5a, where—in the other witnesses—it appears as a kind of afterthought. The phrase may well have been a corrector's addition placed after v. 4, due to the verbal connection of

ἐκκλησίαν with v. 4's αἱ ἐκκλησίαι. In P the phrase has been omitted both at v. 3 and at v. 5.

c   The variant ἀπ᾽ ἀρχῆς ("from [the] beginning") in P[46] D* 1837* g mon appears to be a transcription error of the almost identically sounding word ἀπαρχή ("first fruit").

d   The weakly attested variant (in spite of wide minuscule support), Ἀχαΐας ("Achaia"), found in D[1] L P Ψ 5 33 61 69 88 104 181 218 330 323 326 424* 436 441 451 459 467 614 621 623 629 720 915* 917 945 1175 1241 1243 1398 1505 1563 1678 1718 1751 1836 1838 1845 1846 1874 1875 1877 1881 1908 1942 1959 1962 2138 2197 2344 2492 2495 2516 2523 2544 2718 *Maj* sy, may be an assimilation to the identical expression, "first fruit of Achaia," in 1 Cor 16:15. The support for Ἀσίας ("Asia") is found in P[46] ℵ A B C D* F G 6 81 256 263 365 424[v.l.] 630 915[v.l.] 1319 1573 1739 1852 1912 2110 2127 2200 *pc* latt.

e   The variant found in D F G 323 1505 1881 *pc*, ἐν Χριστῷ ("in Christ"), is probably an assimilation of the common Pauline expression in place of the unusual expression εἰς Χριστόν ("for Christ") found in all of the other MSS.

f   The textual evidence in the earliest and most reliable MSS is evenly divided between the spelling Μαρίαν ("Mary") in A B C P Ψ 104 365 1505 1573 1735 1739 2495 *pc* cop and Μαριάμ ("Miriam") in P[46] ℵ D F G L 6 69 88 323 326 330 424 614 945 1175 1241 1243 1319 1836 1874 1881 2344 *Maj* Chr, so that Nestle-Aland[16-25] selected the former and *GNT*[1/2] the latter, though Nestle-Aland[26/27] and *GNT*[3/4] all have Μαρίαν. Most commentators provide no clear grounds for making a decision (see Sanday and Headlam, 422; Cranfield, 2.787, Dunn, 2:890). Metzger, *Textual Commentary*, fails to discuss this variant, but the Semiticized Μαριάμ should be preferred as the more difficult reading since Μαριά is the more common Greek spelling. Zahn, 607, supports this choice on grounds that Μαριάμ is more strongly attested and could more easily have been changed to Μαρίαν than vice versa.

g   The weakly attested variant ἐν ὑμῖν ("in/among you"), found in D F G, appears to be a stylistic improvement. The text εἰς ὑμᾶς ("for you") is strongly supported by P[46] ℵ A B C* P Ψ 6 61 81 256 263[c] 326 330 365[c] 424 451 1243 1319 1505 1573 1718 1739 1852 1881 1908 1942 2110 2127 2197 2495 *al*. An additional variant of εἰς ἡμᾶς ("for us") is found in C[2] L 5 33 69 88 104 181 218 263* 323 365* 436 441 459 467 614 621 623 629 630 720 915 917 945 1175 1241 1398 1563 1678 1735 1751 1836 1838 1845 1846 1874 1875 1877 1912 1959 1962 2138 2200 2344 2492 2516 2523 2544 2718 *Maj* ar vg[s].

h There is an editorial as well as a textual variant related to the name Junia. If the circumflex is provided as in the medieval miniscules, resulting in Ἰουνιᾶν as in Nestle[13-21], Nestle-Aland[22-27 (4th printing 1996)], GNT[1-4 (2d printing 1994)], and some older commentaries, it would be a contracted form ("Junias"), in the accusative, of the common masculine name Junianus. However, as Epp points out in *Junia*, 40–48, there never was a shred of text-critical evidence for this masculine reading, nor is there any evidence to date for the name "Junias" and hence no evidence that the name Junianus was ever contracted. If the acute accenting of Ἰουνίαν is supplied as in Nestle-Aland[27 (5th printing 1998)], GNT[4 (3d printing 1998)], it would be in the first declension accusative of the common feminine name, "Junia." According to Epp, *Junia*, 45–46, this accent is supported by B² D² L Ψ[vid] 0150 33 81 104 256 263 365 424 436 459 1175 1241 1319 1573 1739 1852 1881 1912 1962 2127 2200 *Maj Lect* Chr sa and some 55 other minuscules—in fact, by all that have been examined and reported to date (Epp, *Junia*, 100). Since the original uncial manuscripts of the NT were unaccented before the seventh century, and an acute accent was provided in this location by later editors of B and D, the decision in favor of the circumflex is an editorial judgment. Cranfield, 2:788, made a compelling case that the female form should be preferred since the masculine name, Junias, (as noted above) is not found elsewhere and must be assumed to be an undiscovered or nonexistent short form of Junianus. See also Bernadette J. Brooten, "'Junia . . . Outstanding among the Apostles' (Romans 16:7)," in L. Swidler and A. Swidler, eds., *Women Priests: A Catholic Commentary on the Vatican Declaration* (New York: Paulist, 1977) 141–44, and Epp, "Romans 16,7," 167, 251–63; *Junia*, 32–44. In "War Junia(s), der hervorragende Apostel (Röm 16,7), eine Frau?" *JAC* 27–28 (1984–85) 53–64, Valentin Fàbrega shows that patristic interpreters consistently viewed Junia as a woman. This is confirmed by the independent survey by Epp, *Junia*, 32–36. The authoritative study of the linguistic evidence by Richard S. Cervin, "A Note regarding the Name 'Junia(s)' in Romans 16.7," *NTS* 40 (1994) 464–70, shows that the name is feminine. In "Romans xvi.7: Junia or Junias?" *ExpT* 98 (1987) 108–10, Ray R. Schulz shows that the text-critical evidence is overwhelmingly in favor of the acute accent and Metzger, *Textual Commentary*, 475–76, appears to agree. P[46] 6 1718 ar b vg[mss] bo eth Ambst Hier have Ἰουλίαν ("Julia"), perhaps because the identical female name appears in Rom 16:15, but "Junia" is far better attested. The variant indicates that ancient copyists, in contrast to

modern commentators and editors, showed no bias against women being qualified as apostles.

i The addition of the definite article, τούς, before "fellow prisoners" in P[46] B is a secondary, stylistic improvement. On this and the next note, see Eldon J. Epp, "Minor Textual Variants in Romans 16:7," in J. W. Childers and D. C. Parker, eds., *Transmission and Reception: New Testament Text-Critical and Exegetical Studies*, Texts and Studies, Series Three, 4 (Piscataway: Gorgias, 2006) 123–41.

j A tangle of textual variants arises with this awkwardly appended clause, of which οἳ καὶ πρὸ ἐμοῦ γέγοναν ("who were begotten even before me") is the best attested in ℵ (but omits οἵ [who], added in ℵᶜ) A B 630 1739 1881 *pc* f vg sy. An alternative but clearly secondary reading is found in C L P Ψ 6 33 69 81 88 104 181 323 326 330 365 424 436 451 614 629 945 1175 1241 1243 1319 1505 1573 1735 1836 1874 1877 1962 2127 2344 2492 2495 *Maj*, with the perfect form of the verb γεγόνασιν ("they were"); see Moulton and Howard, *Grammar II*, 221. A variant deserving to be taken more seriously is found in D F G it vg[mss] Ambst, τοῖς πρὸ ἐμοῦ ("those before me"). It is the shorter as well as the more difficult reading, entailing the implication that the other apostles preceded Paul not only in chronology but also in rank; see Metzger, *Textual Commentary (1975)*, 539. The origin of this variant has not been satisfactorily explained either as "a careless abridgment" (Metzger, *Textual Commentary (1975)*, 539) or "an attempted improvement by someone who wrongly understood οἵ to refer, not to Ἀνδρόνικον καὶ Ἰουνίαν . . . , but to τοῖς ἀποστόλοις (cf. Gal 1:17)," as proposed by Cranfield, 2:790.

k The full spelling of this name "Ampliatus" (Ἀμπλιᾶτον) is more strongly attested by P[46] ℵ A B* C[vid] F G (ὁ Ἀπλιᾶτον) 424ᶜ 1739* *pc* lat bo than the abbreviated form Ἀμπλιᾶν ("Amplian") found in B² D L P Ψ 33 69 88 104 323 326 330 424* 614 945 1175 1241 1243 1735 1739ᶜ 1836 1874 1881 2344 (Ἀπλίαν 365 1319 1505 1573 2495) *Maj* vg[ms] sy sa.

l The word μου ("my") is deleted in P[46] B F bo[mss], probably because "my beloved in the Lord" seemed odd as compared with "the beloved in the Lord." Otherwise Paul refers either to "my beloved" or "in the Lord beloved," but only here do we find both expressions combined.

m A rather strongly attested variant in C D F G Ψ 69 81 326 365 630 1319 *al* it bo[ms] provides κυρίῳ ("Lord") in place of "Christ," probably to provide consistency with the expression "in the Lord" in 16:2, 11, 12 (twice), 13. The more strongly attested word χριστῷ ("Christ") in P[46] ℵ A B L P 6 33 88 104 323 330 424 614 945 1175 1241 1243 1505

1573 1735 1739 1836 1874 1881 2344 2495 *Maj* b vg sy sa^ms bo Ambst is probably original.

n   A minor variant in C* F G reads Ἰουνιαν ("Junia," but unaccented) in place of Julia, which is strongly supported by ℵ A B C² D L P Ψ 6 33 69 81 88 104 181 256 263 323 326 330 365 424 436 451 459 614 629 945 1175 1241 1243 1319 1505 1573 1735 1739 1836 1852 1874 1877 1881 1912 1962 2127 2200 2344 2464 2492 2495 *Maj Lect* ar b d f g mon o vg sy^{p,h} sa bo arm (eth) geo slav Or^lat Chr Pel. This is the opposite scribal mistake from that in 16:7; see Metzger, *Textual Commentary*, 476. As in 16:7, it is also possible to accentuate the variant Ἰουνιαν as a masculine or feminine form, but the latter is more frequent and thus to be preferred; see Cranfield, 2:795; Michel, 478; Wilckens, 3:132; BAGD 380.

o   It is curious that neither Metzger's 1975/1994 edi-

tions of *Textual Commentary* nor other commentators explain the reversal of sequence and garbling of the first letters of the names of Julia and Nereus in P⁴⁶, substituting Βηρέα καὶ Ἀουλίαν ("Bereus and Aoulia"). It appears to fit the pattern of a rather extensive and hitherto unexplained effort visible in P⁴⁶ to alter the names in Rom 16. There is strong support for the wording "Julia, Nereus" in ℵ A B C² D L P Ψ 6 33 69 81 88 104 181 323 326 330 365 424 436 451 614 629 630 945 1175 1241 1243 1319 1505 1573 1735 1739 1836 1874 1877 1881 1962 2127 2464 2492 2495 *Maj* latt sy cop.

p   The weakly attested variant spelling of the shortened name, Olympas, is provided by F G, Ὀλυμπιδᾶ, perhaps to lend an element of formality. The Latin versions move in the same direction with "Olympiadem" in place of the short form.

Analysis

Greetings typically are placed at the end of personal letters in antiquity[1] and appear much more frequently in the period after 70 C.E.[2] They appear in three types: the first person greeting is extended directly from the author to the recipient; the second person greeting asks the recipient to greet someone else; and the third person greeting is extended from someone other than the author to the recipient.[3] The greetings in this pericope fit the second type, whose normal form is in the second person singular rather than in the plural.[4] For instance, the recipient of *P.Tebt.* 2. Nr. 412.4 is asked, ἀσπάζου τὴν μητέρα καὶ τὸν πατέρα σου ("greet your mother and father"). A private letter in *P.Köln.* 1. Nr. 56.9–12 requests Valerius Maximus to "greet (ἀσπάζου) Amas, Paulina, Publius, Diodoros, Granias, and Tyche."[5] Most frequently, the greeting is a brief and formulaic ἔρρωσθε ("be well!").[6] The combination of greetings to so large a number of persons and the use of the second person plural form in Romans is unparalleled, contributing to the establishment of a precedent that popularizes greetings in subsequent Christian letters.[7] Since no other Pauline letter carries so many greetings, "this indicates that the situation under which Romans was written differed in some significant way,"[8] which my hypothesis concerning the purpose and audience of Romans attempts to clarify and which the exegesis below will elaborate. The second person plural imperative ἀσπάσασθε ("you [pl.] greet!") is repeated fifteen times in this pericope. In the next pericope beginning in v. 16b the form shifts to the third person indicative, ἀσπάζονται ("they greet"), which is continued in 16:21-23 that originally followed immediately, prior to the creation of the interpolation in 16:17-20a.[9]

Paul's selection of the second person plural imperative form was surely intentional and should not be translated as "I send greetings to. . . ."[10] The use of this

---

1   See MM 85–86; Mullins, "Greeting," 418–26; Koskenniemi, *Studien*, 148–51; White, *Light*, 196–97.

2   See Roller, *Formular*, 473–74.

3   See Mullins, "Greeting," 418.

4   See ibid., 420–21. The only examples of a second person plural greeting that I have been able to find are in the second- to third-century C.E. *P.Oxy.* 3. Nr. 533.26–27.

5   Discussed by G. H. R. Horsley, "Personal News and Greetings in a Letter," *NDIEC* 1 (1981) 54–56.

6   Roller, *Formular*, 69.

7   See ibid., 474. Mullins, "Greeting," 425, refers to the numerous greetings in *P.Oxy.* 3. Nr. 533.26–27, but these are in the second person singular style.

8   Mullins, "Greeting," 425. It is highly improbable that these greetings constitute covert references to Greco-Roman deities and rulers, as suggested by Gerleman, *Heidenapostel*, 86–95.

9   See Introduction, section 2 and the chapter on 16:17-20a below.

10 Newman and Nida, 291. The contention by Gamble in *Textual History*, 93, that "the imperative form of the greeting verb functions here as a surrogate for

second person form of greeting asks the hearers of the letter to extend Paul's greetings to persons belonging to other groups in Rome, thus establishing "a series of close and friendly bonds."[11] As Michel points out, "The ones being greeted are at the same time those whom the Roman congregation should grant recognition."[12] When one observes the random sequence of the requested greetings and the interweaving of established congregations (16:3-5, 10b, 11b, 14, 15) and isolated Christian leaders, it becomes clear that the recognition is to be mutual. Paul wants every believer in Rome to greet every other believer. In view of the fact that so many women are included in this list, it is clear that this mutuality extends across sexual barriers.[13] In this context, to greet is to honor and welcome one another, probably with the hug, kiss, handshaking, or bowing that gave expression to greeting in the ancient world; the original meaning of the Greek term ἀσπάζομαι ("greet") was "to embrace" by wrapping one's arms around another.[14] As Hans Windisch observes, the Pauline command to greet one another "expresses and strengthens the bond of fellowship with those who are engaged in the same task, and who serve the same Lord, i.e., with saints and brothers."[15] J. E. Lendon explains the crucial role of such greetings in the honor-and-shame environment of Paul's letter: "When one man honoured another in the Roman world, he granted him a quantum of honour, which, provided that the bestower was sufficiently distinguished himself, the aristocratic community at large then accepted that the recipient possessed . . . a great man's laudatory remarks—or speeches—in public, his greetings on the street, prompt admission at his levee, his kisses, all such things were honours, closely watched by contemporaries, and added to the recipients' honour. . . . To be known to be such a man's intimate, that was indeed worth boasting about, as it conferred an *ornamentum*, a quantum of honour, upon one. . . . Favours and honours mingle and cling in the ancient mind: even the most ordinary acts of men toward one another might not be wholly devoid of honorific quality."[16] Thus Paul's greetings had a double function that served as the climax of his letter, honoring leaders of various congregations as known to him, the famous and honorable apostle, but, even more important, encouraging them to honor each other and thereby extend the principle of the impartial righteousness of God, which is the theme of the letter.

The effort by Ollrog and others[17] to perceive an orderly sequence in the greetings, moving from close personal friends in vv. 3-9, 10a, 11a, 12b, and 13 to more distant and less known individuals and groups in the rest of the passage, is rendered implausible by the presence of the general references in vv. 10b and 11b, which reveal that Paul had no personal acquaintance with leaders or members of the Christian circles among the slaves of Narkissos and Aristoboulos. The perception that the greetings are in a rather random sequence[18] is correct, revealing an intent to place all the Christian persons and groups in Rome on an equal footing.

The names and groups included in these greetings can be classified under several categories:

(a) Close personal friends and coworkers in the Pauline and other mission fields who now reside in Rome. Judging from the personal references and individual details, these persons include:

1. Prisca	6. Junia	11. Tryphaina
2. Aquila	7. Ampliatus	12. Tryphosa
3. Epainetos	8. Urbanus	13. Persis
4. Miriam	9. Stachys	14. Rufus
5. Adronicus	10. Apelles	15. Rufus's mother

the first person indicative form, and so represents a direct personal greeting of the writer himself to the addressees" is unsupported by any evidence. Nevertheless, it has been accepted by Dunn, 2:891, and Weima, *Neglected Endings*, 105, 108. Moo, 919, comes to a similarly erroneous conclusion that "Paul is asking the Roman Christians to convey his own greetings to the respective individuals and groups."

11 Mullins, "Greeting," 420; see also Ollrog, "Abfassungsverhältnisse," 221–44; Schnider and Stenger, *Briefformular*, 124; Müller, *Schluß*, 220.

12 Michel, 474.

13 See McGinn, "Feminist Approaches," 169.

14 See Windisch, "ἀσπάζομαι κτλ.," 497; Witherington, 380.

15 Windisch, "ἀσπάζομαι κτλ.," 501.

16 Lendon, *Empire of Honour*, 48–49.

17 Ollrog, "Abfassungsverhältnisse," 236; see also the unsuccessful attempts to discern a structured sequence of greetings by Schille, *Kollegialmission*, 51–52; Wilckens, 3:133; Stuhlmacher, 247.

18 See Althaus, 150. Käsemann, 413, notes that Prisca and Aquila are mentioned first as "the most promi-

(b) Leaders of Roman house churches whose identity appears to be known to Paul only through hearsay. On the basis of observations by Erbes[19] and Ollrog,[20] it appears that many of the persons greeted had not been in personal contact with him. These leaders include the following:

1. Herodian	5. Patrobas	9. Nereus
2. Asynkritos	6. Hermas	10. Nereus's sister
3. Phlegon	7. Philologos	11. Olympas
4. Hermes	8. Julia	

(c) Five house or tenement churches whose members Paul does not know,[21] though in several instances he knows the names of leaders:

1. the church in the house of Prisca and Aquila (16:5a)
2. those among the slaves of Aristoboulus (16:10b)
3. those among the slaves of Narkissos (16:11b)
4. the brothers who are with Asynkritos et al. (16:14b)
5. the saints who are with Philologos et al. (16:15b).

At shown in the exegesis below, the requests for greetings to these diverse leaders and congregations serve a significant purpose that is integral to the project proposed in this letter. As Markus Müller observes, "Clearly, Paul incorporates these persons in his plan in the hope that the free members of the house churches will provide the economic and logistical support necessary for its realization."[22] The emotional and affectional bonds created and expressed through such greetings, particularly when extended across the barriers erected by previous conflicts, carry forward Paul's gospel concerning the impartial grace of God, and thus provide a suitable peroration for the letter as a whole.

The Cultural Implications of Names

There is a tendency in recent years for classical scholars not to "Latinize" Greek names, which has long been the tradition in Western scholarship. In view of the argument of Romans, this tendency warrants approval, because Paul is struggling against cultural chauvinism in all its forms. Particularly in the imperial context of Rome, where the majority of Greek-speaking persons, including most of those with Jewish background, were slaves or former slaves, respect for original cultural origins and identity was a matter of importance. Since Paul refers to the persons in this chapter with Greek, Latin, and Jewish names,[23] I have decided to break with the Latinized tradition of commentaries and translations in order to present the names in a manner that reflects their distinctive cultural identities. If I have correctly identified the cultural identity of these names, they fall into three categories, with a number of the persons bearing Greek and Latin names explicitly identified by Paul as Jewish. I place the one Jewish name and the Jewish identities in the middle column, with the latter identified by italics:

19 Greek Names:	Jewish Name: Miriam	8 Latin Names:
	Jewish Identity:	
Andronikos→	*Andronikos*	Ampliatus
Apelles		
Aristoboulos	*Aquila*	←Aquila
Asynkritos	*Junia*	←Junia
Epainetos		
Hermas		Julia
Hermes		Prisca
Herodion→	*Herodion*	
Narkissos	*Rufus*	←Rufus
Nereus	*Rufus's Mother*	←Rufus's mother
(Nereus's sister)		
Olympas		Urbanus
Patrobas		
Persis		
Pflegon		
Philologos		
Stachys		
Tryphaina		
Tryphosa 1		

nent members of the community," but offers no other principle of sequence.

19 Karl Erbes, "Zeit und Ziel der Grüsse Röm 16,3-15 und der Mitteilungen 2. Tim 4,9-21," *ZNW* 10 (1909) 128–47, esp. 142.
20 Ollrog, "Abfassungsverhältnisse," 236–241.
21 See Minear, *Obedience*, 7; Dunn, 2:891. Lampe agrees with this identification of five groupings, but suggests the rest of the names in Rom 16 imply at least two further groups, and that when Paul arrived in Rome, he founded an eighth group; see "Roman Christians," 229–30.
22 Müller, *Schluß*, 217.
23 For identification, see Solin, *Beiträge*, passim; *Namenbuch*, passim; E. A. Judge, "Greek Names of Latin Origin," *NDIEC* 2 (1982) 106–8.

Rhetorical Disposition

15:14—16:24 V. The *peroratio*: An appeal for cooperation in missionary activities in Jerusalem, Rome, and Spain

16:3-16, 21-23 D. Greetings and commendations between ministerial leaders

16:3-16b 1. Greetings to congregational leaders in Rome

16:3-5a a. Prisca and Aquila

16:3a 1) The formula of greeting

16:3b 2) Official status: "my co-workers in Christ Jesus"

16:4a 3) Noteworthy accomplishment and relation to Paul: "risked their necks for my life"

16:4b 4) The formula of appreciation
  a) Source of thanks: Paul
  b) Source of thanks: "all the churches of the nations"

16:5a 5) The renewed formula of greeting: to "the church in their house"

16:5b b. Epainetos
  1) The formula of greeting
  2) Relation to Paul: "beloved"
  3) Official status: first convert in Asia

16:6 c. Mary
  1) The formula of greeting
  2) Official status: past missionary in Rome

16:7 d. Andronikos and Junia

16:7a 1) The formula of greeting

16:7b 2) Noteworthy accomplishment and relation to Paul: fellow Jews and prisoners

16:7c 3) Official rank and status: "outstanding among the apostles"

16:7d 4) Tenure in the faith: "in Christ before me"

16:8 e. Ampliatus
  1) The formula of greeting
  2) Relation to Paul: "beloved"
  3) Official status: "in the Lord"

16:9a-b f. Urbanus

16:9a 1) The formula of greeting

16:9b 2) Relation to Paul: missionary colleague

16:9b 3) Official status: "co-worker in Christ"

16:9c g. Stachys
  1) [The formula of greeting]
  2) Relation to Paul: "beloved"

16:10a h. Apelles
  1) The formula of greeting
  2) Rank in the church: "approved in Christ"

16:10b i. Those belonging to Aristoboulos
  1) The formula of greeting
  2) Location of believers: "among the slaves of Aristoboulos"

16:11a j. Herodion
  1) The formula of greeting
  2) Relation to Paul: "fellow countryman"

116:11b k. Those belonging to Narkissos
  1) The formula of greeting
  2) Location of believers: "among the slaves of Narkissos"

16:12a l. Tryphaina and Tryphosa
  1) The formula of greeting
  2) Official status: "laborers in the Lord"

16:12b m. Persis
  1) The formula of greeting
  2) Relation to Paul: "beloved"
  3) Official rank and status: "labored much in the Lord"

16:13a n. Rufus
  1) The formula of greeting
  2) Rank in the church: "chosen in the Lord"

16:13b o. Rufus's mother
  1) [The formula of greeting]
  2) Relation to Paul: metaphorical "mother"

16:14 p. Asynkritos, Phlegon, Hermes, Patrobas, Hermas
  1) The formula of greeting
  2) Extended greetings to "brothers" with them

16:15 q. Philologos, Julia, Nereus and sister, Olympas
  1) The formula of greeting
  2) Extended greetings to "saints" with them

16:16a-b r. The request for mutual greetings

16:16a 1) The revised formula of greeting: "greet one another"
  2) The means of greeting: "the holy kiss"

Exegesis

■ **3** The first persons to be greeted are Prisca and Aquila, who had worked with Paul in his earlier missions in Corinth and Ephesus. It is clear from Acts 18:2 that both of them were banned from Rome at the time of the Edict of Claudius in 49 C.E., which means that they were not Pauline converts in Corinth but had been leaders in the Roman church prior to meeting Paul for the first time. At the time of writing 1 Cor 16:19, Paul sent greetings to the Corinthians from Prisca and Aquila's church in Ephesus. The greeting in Romans makes it clear that they have now returned to Rome, probably after the lapse of the Edict of Claudius in 54. The names "Prisca" and "Aquila" are Latin,[24] both being used occasionally by slaves and former slaves.[25] In the case of Aquila, the evidence in Acts indicates that he was probably a freedman of Jewish origin.[26] The fact that Aquila, not his wife, was identified as a Jew from Pontus (Acts 18:1-2) has led some researchers to infer that she was not a Jew. Her name and other details point to freeborn origin[27] in the noble Roman family of Acilius.[28] The fact that Prisca's name is mentioned first indicates her higher social status in the Roman context.[29] A less plausible suggestion is that her precedence indicates that she was the more active partner in leading the house church.[30] The inference that Prisca came from a noble background is consistent with the ancient naming of the Santa Prisca parish in the Aventine district of Rome, probably on the site of the original house church that was named after her rather than after Aquila.[31] The *Titulus Priscae* address strongly suggests that this expensive property was originally registered in Prisca's name, reverting to church ownership centuries later. Under the Santa Prisca church archeologists found two private homes, one of which containing a "large Nymphaeum with an apse" dating from the early second century[32] that was later turned into a magnificently decorated Mithraeum.[33] Since Mithraism was "especially popular among soldiers and the imperial personnel," including some persons "of the equestrian order who rose to high military positions,"[34] there is reason to believe that this property was expropriated and turned into a military shrine after the discovery that Prisca and her husband were believers. The Catacomb of Priscilla was located in the country estate of the Acilian family, which further confirms her noble origin. That the Acilius family was associated with Christianity at an early date is confirmed by the details in Tacitus *Ann.* 67.14 and Dio Cassius *Hist. Rom.* 67.14

---

24 See Judge's discussion in "Greek Names," 106–8, of the high ratio of Latin names within early Christian writings as indications of persons who had gained Roman citizenship through emancipation.

25 Lampe, *Paul to Valentinus*, 181.

26 See ibid., 187–95.

27 See Peter Lampe, "Prisca/Priscilla," *ABD* 5 (1992) 467.

28 See Sanday and Headlam, 420, and the somewhat skeptical assessment of Cranfield, 2:784.

29 The first reference I have found to this inference is Plumptre, *Studies,* 423. See also the authoritative assessment by Judge, "Scholastic Community," 129: "The fact that Priscilla (or Prisca) is more often named first implies either that she was of higher rank, or more probably that it was she rather than her husband who was Paul's sponsor." Meeks, *Urban Christians*, 59, concludes that Prisca had "higher status than her husband." Stowers concurs in *Rereading*, 75. For background, see also Sanday and Headlam, 419–20. Of the six references to this couple in the NT, four list Prisca/Priscilla first (Acts 18:18, 26; 2 Tim 4:19; and Rom 16:3). Aquila is mentioned first in Acts 18:2 and 1 Cor 16:19, conforming to the ordinary usage that gives precedence to the male name in a married couple. The precedence of the female name in Rom 16:3 appears to reflect Paul's knowledge of a Roman perception of Prisca's higher status, a perception that was apparently not present in Ephesus or Corinth, as reflected in the 1 Cor 16:19 usage.

30 See Adolf von Harnack, "Über die beiden Recensionen der Geschichte der Prisca und des Aquila in Act. Apost. 18,1-27," *SPAW* (1900) 2–13; his suggestion is followed by Michel, 474; Ollrog, *Mitarbeiter*, 25; Schlier, 443; Wilckens, 3:134; Cineira, *Religionspolitik*, 218. This line of thought appears to be based on a modern conception of active and inactive church membership; no such distinctions are visible in first-generation Christianity. In contrast to Harnack and others, Matthews, *Rich Pagan Women*, 53–54, shows that the author of Acts limits the role of Prisca and other women so as to "diminish their contributions to early Christian communities."

31 For a discussion of the title churches, most of which originated in the private homes of early church patrons, see Lampe, *Paul to Valentinus*, 360–65. The most comprehensive treatment of these parishes and their historical background is to be found in Kirsch, *Titelkirchen*, 101–4, 127–37. See the discussion in section 6 of the "Introduction" above.

32 Lampe, *Paul to Valentinus*, 59.

33 Ibid., 61.

34 E. Merkelbach, "Mithras, Mithraism," *ABD* 4 (1992) 877.

that M. Acilius Glabrio, who was elected consul in 91 C.E., was executed when his allegiance to the faith was discovered.[35]

There is unclarity about the name Aquila at the moment, because Peter Lampe claims it was an animal name,[36] presumably an eagle, while the comprehensive Liddell-Scott dictionary lists ἄκυλος as "acorn."[37] The older supposition that Ἀκύλας was a Greek form of the Latin family name Acilius[38] is a possibility. The Latin name *Aculius*/Aquila appears twenty-eight times in Roman sources, none of which can be dated to the period of Paul's letter, with four of the references pointing to the status of slavery.[39] The standard Greek grammars identify the name Ἀκύλας in Rom 16:3 as derived not from the word "eagle" but from the Roman name *Aculius*/Aquila.[40] If this is indeed a derivation from the family name of Acilius,[41] reflecting the status of slavery in some branch of that family, this could explain the remarkable coincidence that his name was associated with the family name of his wife, Prisca. However, Lampe passes over this possibility without comment while stating that "Aquila was probably freeborn" because so few Roman references point to the status of slavery.[42] The matter remains open, because the standard articles on Aquila are content to cite Acts 18:2, 18 concerning his being a tent-making Jew from Pontus, which actually could be easily coordinated with his having served as a slave or the descendant of a slave in the Acilian family, someone who later gained the status of freedman and Roman citizen.

The skeptical claim that there is no "proof" of a connection between the Prisca of Rom 16:3 and the Priscan church or catacomb[43] rests on the expectation of historical explicitness not available in most ancient circumstances and also on general laws of probability that are not fully applicable to historical events where there is evidence of unusual conditions. Of course, it was unlikely that a noble Roman woman would become a believer and marry a Jewish handworker, who might have served as a slave in her family. It was equally unlikely that any group in the Greco-Roman world would have developed the expectation that in Christ the normal separations between male and female, Greek and Jew, slave and free would be overcome (Gal 3:28). One cannot use general laws of historical probability to disallow evidence as suggestive as that available concerning Prisca and Aquila. A mixed marriage between a Roman noblewoman and a Jewish Christian freedman is the only circumstance that explains all the evidence about this couple.

The question of the social status of Prisca and Aquila is debated, with Judge, Theissen, Ollrog, Meeks, and Stowers inclining toward relatively high status because of their patronage of Paul, their frequent travels, and the capacity to own property in Corinth, Ephesus, and Rome large enough for house churches.[44] Peter Lampe is skeptical, in part because of the lower-status connotations of Aquila's trade. He calculates the cost of their travels in precise detail, showing that lower-class status is possible.[45] His case is not compelling, however, and does not account for all the evidence. The likelihood that Prisca's house was in the elegant Aventine quarter of

35 See Sanday and Headlam, 419–20; Stowers, *Rereading*, 75. "M. Acilius Glabrio," *PW* I.1.257; Dio Cassius *Hist. Rom.* 67.14.3, referring to the banning, after he successfully defended himself against a lion in the Coliseum, on the charge of "atheism (ἀθεότητος), a charge on which many others who drifted into Jewish ways were condemned." Suetonius *Dom.* 10 refers to Glabrio's execution while in exile.

36 Lampe, *Paul to Valentinus*, 181; he does not specify which animal is in view, but G. Milligan, "Aquila," *DBH* 1 (1901) 129, identifies this with Latin, "eagle," but there are no examples of the Latin word *acula* being used as a personal name. The Latin examples of this name all have the spelling *Acilius*.

37 LSJM 59, ὁ ἄκυλος, "acorn" or "ornament," but in any case a noun of the second declension that could not have an accusative single ending -αν as in Rom 16:3, Ἀκύλαν.

38 For example, Gore, 194.

39 Lampe, *Paul to Valentinus*, 169, 181.

40 BDF §54; Moulton and Howard, *Grammar II*, §60.6.

41 Sanday and Headlam, 420.

42 Peter Lampe, "Aquila," *ABD* 1 (1992) 319.

43 See Cranfield, 2:784, and Peter Lampe, "Prisca/Priscilla," *ABD* 5 (1992) 468.

44 Judge, "Scholastic Community," 29; Ollrog, *Mitarbeiter*, 26; Meeks, *Urban Christians*, 59; Theissen, *Social Setting*, 90; Stowers, *Rereading*, 75.

45 Lampe, *Paul to Valentinus*, 195.

Rome[46] and that the names of Prisca and possibly also Aquila were associated with the noble Acilius family indicates a higher social niveau.[47]

Paul refers to Prisca and Aquila as τοὺς συνεργούς μου ἐν Χριστῷ Ἰησοῦ ("my co-workers in Christ Jesus"), which is technical language for missionary colleagues.[48] Wolf-Hennig Ollrog has shown that συνεργός is a distinctive and unique Pauline expression referring to a person "who works together with Paul as an agent of God in the common 'work' of missionary proclamation."[49] His analysis of the expression used frequently in the Pauline letters shows that it implies (1) sharing a divine commission,[50] (2) working in a collegial manner with Paul in congregational activities,[51] and (3) including specifically missionary proclamation.[52] Nowhere else in the early or later church is this word used in quite this way, revealing a distinctive Pauline approach to missional collegiality, referring both to himself and to others with this egalitarian term. The use of this term does not imply that Prisca and Aquila are "helpers of the apostle";[53] the clear implication is that each functions as "a missionary who becomes a colleague and co-worker with Paul, who is called to the same task and in the same service of proclamation: to awaken faith in the . . . congregation."[54] That they func-

tioned, among other things, as theological teachers is indicated by the account of their instructing Apollos in Acts 18:26.[55] The use of this term "coworker," along with the fact that Paul worked closely with Prisca and Aquila in Ephesus and Corinth, makes it likely that they shared a theological and congregational orientation compatible with that of the apostle. They would probably have been classified among the "strong," to use the category developed in Rom 14.

■ 4 The reference to Prisca and Aquila risking their life for Paul's sake, whether in Ephesus or Corinth where they had ministered together, implies sufficient clout for political effectiveness. Most commentators assume that they came to Paul's aid during the Ephesian crisis referred to in 1 Cor 15:32 and Acts 19:23-31.[56] If they were merely impoverished handworkers who had recently immigrated to Ephesus, it is scarcely possible that they would have been in the position to intervene effectively with the authorities on Paul's behalf. Their ability to save Paul's life in a threatening situation reveals a patronal capacity that derived from high social status.[57] The language Paul employs to describe this intervention points in the same direction. The reference to endangering "one's neck" is a colloquialism for risking execution,[58] although plainly figurative for risking

---

46   For a description of the elite Aventine region of Rome, see ibid., 58–61.

47   See Stowers, *Rereading*, 75–76.

48   See Bouttier, *En Christ*, 59.

49   Ollrog, *Mitarbeiter*, 67; Ollrog, "συνεργός, συνεργέω," 303–4; Elisabeth Schüssler Fiorenza, "Missionaries, Apostles, Co-workers: Romans 16 and the Reconstruction of Women's Early Christian History," *WW* 6 (1986) 430. Rudolf Schumacher followed a mistaken conception of female leadership in the early church in denying that Prisca could have functioned as a "coworker" in "Aquila und Priscilla," *ThGl* 12 (1920) 97. The use of the term "coworker" and their earlier banning under the Edict of Claudius render implausible the inference by Marcel Devis, "Aquila et Priscille," *L'Anneau d'or* 65 (1955) 395, that they had received all their Christian training from Paul.

50   Ollrog, *Mitarbeiter*, 68–69, drawing inferences from 1 Cor 3:5-9; 2 Cor 1:24; 6:1-4; and 1 Thess 3:2.

51   Ollrog, *Mitarbeiter*, 70–71, referring to 1 Cor 3:5-9; 15:48; 16:10; 2 Cor 1:26; 6:1; 8:17, 23; Phil 2:30; 1 Thess 3:2.

52   Ibid., 71–72, based on the close association with διάκονος ("service") and κοπιᾶν ("labor") in 1 Cor 3:8-9; 16:15-18; 1 Thess 3:2.

53   Ollrog, "συνεργός, συνεργέω," 304.

54   Ollrog, *Mitarbeiter*, 72.

55   Eisen, *Amtsträgerinnen*, 107–8.

56   Michel, 474; Wilckens, 3:134; Zeller, 246–47.

57   See Norbert Rouland's description of the role of patrons in providing judicial assistance, in *Pouvoir*, 524–27, 605–6.

58   See BADG 825, citing Anonymus Epicureus V. Phil. 951 and Deissmann, *Light*, 94–95; *LAE* 117–18. The expression for risking the neck is found in Diogenes Laertius *Vitae. philos.* 4.11: Εἰπόντος δὲ Διονυσίου πρὸς Πλάτωνα ὡς ἀφαιρήσεται αὐτοῦ τὸν τράχηλον, παρὼν οὗτος καὶ δείξας τὸ ἴδιον, οὐκ ἄν γε, ἔφη, τίς πρότερον τούτου ("When Dionysius told Plato that he would cut off his neck, Xenocrates, who was present, pointed to his own and said, 'No one shall touch it till he cuts off mine'").

one's life in general. The specific verbal expression Paul selects in this instance, however, alludes explicitly to death by decapitation.[59] Since this form of quick execution was normally the privilege of Roman citizens,[60] avoiding crucifixion, strangulation, burning at the stake, or the various terrors of the arena, the expression provides additional confirmation of the high social status of Prisca and Aquila.

Paul conveys his sense of indebtedness to Prisca and Aquila with the εὐχαριστῶ formula. An example of the widespread use of this formula may be seen in an imperial inscription found in Ephesus, "I give thanks to you (εὐχαριστῶ σοι), Lady Artemis."[61] That Paul expresses his thankfulness for Prisca's and Aquila's services is understandable, but the intention of the seemingly effusive claim that πᾶσαι αἱ ἐκκλησίαι τῶν ἐθνῶν ("all the churches of the Gentiles") share Paul's appreciation has been difficult for scholars to discern. Cranfield suggests that the Gentiles' share of thanksgiving is primarily due to saving the life of the apostle to the Gentiles, but that would seem to shift the attention to Paul himself, which could hardly be the intention in a sentence aiming to honor Prisca and Aquila.[62] Zahn and Schlier lift up the oddity of a couple with Jewish Christian background receiving universal praise from Gentiles.[63] Ollrog observes that their shifting of location from Corinth to Ephesus and now back to Rome in cooperation with Paul's missionizing may have entailed financial sacrifices for which the Gentile churches were thankful.[64] These observations correlate with the theme of unity between Jewish and Gentile Christians that was extensively developed in Rom 14:1—15:13 and exemplified in the description of the Jerusalem offering as an expression of mutual indebtedness between Jews and Gentiles (Rom 15:27). That "all the Gentiles" give thanks to the Jewish Christian Aquila and his Roman wife Prisca conveys this sense of unity and mutuality, and it seems clear that Paul had made it known to his other churches what they had done in his behalf. The effusiveness of claiming gratefulness on the part of "all" the Gentile Christians constitutes an implicit invitation for the Roman house churches to provide similarly audacious and perhaps risky aid to the Pauline mission just as Prisca and Aquila had, so that they may also become recipients of the universal thanks and praise of others. To excel in benefaction is to gain an appropriate fame and honor.[65] Paul may therefore be using the first greeting to advance the agenda that Phoebe is to pursue in the Roman congregations, encouraging the contribution of various forms of support for the difficult venture of the Spanish mission.

■ **5** The reference to the church in the house of Prisca and Aquila is clear evidence that at least one of the Roman congregations had the form of a house church. The word ἐκκλησία means "assembly," and was used for political as well as religious groups.[66] It becomes "a fixed Christian term" that should be translated "congregation, congregational assembly or church," according to Jürgen Roloff.[67] Paul often speaks of the "church of God" (1 Cor 1:2; 10:32; 11:22; 15:9; 2 Cor 1:1; Gal 1:13) or "churches of God" (1 Cor 11:16, 22; 1 Thess 2:14; 2 Thess 1:4), referring to congregations as God's elect.[68] This appears nowhere in Romans, whereas the word ἐκλησία is the usual name for Christian congregations elsewhere, in Kenchreia (16:1), in Corinth (16:23), and in all other locations (16:4, 16). In contrast to modern usage, the word "church" did not refer to a distinctive building until centuries after the writing of Romans.[69] The definitive study of house congregations and house churches by Hans-Josef Klauck opens with a citation from Heinz Schürmann, "The living space of the con-

---

59 See Godet, 490; Morris, 532. The verb ὑποτίθημι means to lay something down, and in this context it implies the willingness to place one's neck on the chopping block.

60 See Mommsen, *Römisches Strafrecht*, 924; Levick, *Government*, 193.

61 See G. H. R. Horsley, "Giving Thanks to Artemis," *NDIEC* 4 (1987) 127–29.

62 Cranfield, 2:786; similarly, see Michel, 475.

63 Zahn, 605–6; Schlier, 443.

64 Ollrog, *Mitarbeiter*, 27, followed by Zeller, 247.

65 For the general framework of benefaction earning fame, gratitude, and enhanced social status, see Danker, *Benefactor*, 436–71.

66 Roloff, "ἐκκλησία," 411; examples of ἐκκλησίαι as political assemblies are in Acts 19:39 and Josephus *Ant.* 12.164, where Joseph calls the people together "in assembly" (εἰς ἐκκλησίαν).

67 Roloff, "ἐκκλησία," 411.

68 Ibid., 412.

69 See Halton, "Church," 253.

gregation is the house."[70] These and other widely accepted studies investigate the references to houses as the meeting places of early Christian congregations and usually assume a freestanding building owned or rented by the patron or patroness of a house church.[71] Although the term οἶκος can refer not only to a Roman atrium, a Greek peristyle home, a Hellenistic style of courtyard with adjoining rooms, or even an apartment in an insula building that has shops on the ground floor,[72] the standard conclusion is that "Private houses were the first centers of church life."[73] Carolyn Osiek and David Balch state their conclusion as follows: "the atrium-house is surely not the exclusive but is the primary setting for Pauline *ekklesiai*, which did not meet primarily in apartment buildings."[74] Hans-Josef Klauck remains more open than most scholars on this question, concluding that congregations of ten to forty members could function in any of the four options,[75] but he does not entertain the possibility that a different structure of leadership and a different style of community life would necessarily result from meeting in a space not provided by a patron. It is therefore crucial for understanding the situation in Rome to recognize that the congregation led by Prisca and Aquila is the only one known to Paul that is called a "church" and meets in the private home of

patrons.[76] In his definitive analysis of the expression "the church in so-and-so's house" found in Rom 16:5; 1 Cor 16:19; Phlm 2; Col 4:15, Marlis Gielen has shown that a particular congregation is in view because the expression κατ᾽ οἶκον has a predominately local significance.[77] The fact that this congregation meets in the house of Prisca and Aquila has a significant social implication, that this congregation was probably marked by what Ernst Troelsch and Gerd Theissen have identified as "love patriarchalism" that accepted the hierarchal structure of the Greco-Roman house while ameliorating its social inequality "through an obligation of respect and love."[78] In contrast to the other groups of believers greeted in this chapter, the church in Prisca and Aquila's house would have integrated members of different strata, including slaves and children. Paul carries forward the revolutionary pattern of social equality in Christ by greeting the members of this diverse community of believers along with their patrons, Prisca and Aquila.

Without a transition, Paul moves on to greet an individual believer. The name Epainetos is Greek, found three times in the Rome of the first century, of which one is also an immigrant from Ephesus.[79] In the Roman context, a Greek name like this would point to a social

---

70   Klauck, *Hausgemeinde*, 11; citation from Heinz Schürmann, "Gemeinde," 68–69.

71   See Strobel, "Begriff des 'Hauses'," 91–100; Petersen, "House Churches," 264–72; Dassmann and Schöllgen, "Haus II (Hausgemeinschaft)," 801–905; Lorenzen, "Hauskirche," 333–52; Branick, *House Church*; Joseph Pathrapankal, "Church and 'Churches' in corpus Paulinum," in J. E. Martins et al., eds., *Unité et diversité dans l'église: text officiel de la Commission Biblique Pontificale et travaux personels des membres* (Vatican City: Libreria Editrice Vaticana, 1989) 175–82; White, *Building God's House*, 21–22; White, *Texts and Monuments*, 18–24.

72   See Klauck's discussion of the semantic range of οἶκος and οἰκία in *Hausgemeinde*, 15–20.

73   Murphy-O'Connor, *St. Paul's Corinth*, 153.

74   Osiek and Balch, *Families*, 16–17, 21. They make the unwarranted claim (24) that insula buildings were "just beginning to be built in Roman cities in Paul's decade," discounting the literary references in Strabo *Geogr.* 5.3.7 and Seneca *Ira* 3.35.5. In "Pauline House Churches," 28–37, Balch modifies this claim by taking account of shop spaces and

large apartments in tenement buildings, but he retains the traditional view that the social structure was exclusively that of "house church" with a normal patron. For information concerning insula in Rome during the first century B.C.E., see Yavetz, "Living Conditions," 500–517, and Kunst, "Wohnen," 4–19.

75   See also White, *Building God's House*, 105–7.

76   See Banks, *Community*, 32–33.

77   Marlis Gielen, "Zur Interpretation der Formel ἡ κατ᾽ οἶκον αὐτῶν ἐκκλησία," ZNW 77 (1986) 111–12, 120, 124–25.

78   Theissen, *Social Setting*, 107, developing the idea of Ernst Troeltsch, *The Social Teaching of the Christian Churches* (New York, 1931) 1:69–89.

79   See Lampe, *Paul to Valentinus*, 180. Sanday and Headlam print the striking parallel found in *CIL* 6 Nr. 17171 referring to an Epainetos from Ephesus whose family resides in Rome during the first century. No one has suggested that this is the same person as mentioned in Rom 16, but this remains a possibility.

status of slave or freedman,[80] since the name means "praiseworthy." The fact that this person who had been converted in Ephesus is now in Rome along with Prisca and Aquila has been taken to indicate that he may have been either their slave or a freedman in their employ.[81] But this is rendered unlikely by Paul's reference to him as ἀπαρχὴ τῆς Ἀσίας εἰς Χριστόν ("first fruit of Asia for Christ"), which places Epainetos in the same status as the household of Stephanos in 1 Cor 16:15, the earliest and thus most honored convert in the province.[82] In the Jewish tradition, the "first fruit" was the first part of a harvest to ripen to maturity, so desirable that it should be sacrificed to Yahweh.[83] The word ἀπαρχή is also common in Greek sacrifices.[84] The expression "for Christ" clearly indicates to whom the choice offering was brought,[85] indicating the kind of cultic veneration that led to the early development of Christology.[86] The expression is clearly honorific, providing a compelling reason why Epainetos should be greeted by the believers in Rome. Since Paul worked with Prisca and Aquila, who were missionizing in Ephesus prior to his arrival in circa 53 C.E. (Acts 18:26),[87] the early conversion of Epainetos provides grounds for associating him with their ministry. Since their slaves and family would undoubtedly have become members of their house church, and would have accompanied them to Ephesus, no such person would be likely to be described as the "first fruits of Asia." Since he was a resident in "Asia," presumably from Ephesus,

there is no reason to associate him with the status of slavery; he was probably a freeman.

These considerations confirm the inference that Epainetos was probably associated with Prisca and Aquila's house church on the basis of his conversion during the period of their Ephesian residence.[88] Since he is in Rome at the time of Paul's letter, it also seems likely that he "may have moved from Ephesus to Rome together with Prisca and Aquila."[89] Paul's reference to Epainetos as τὸν ἀγαπητόν μου ("my beloved") indicates a significant measure of personal attachment even though he was probably not a Pauline convert;[90] there is no reason to doubt that the expression implies he was in some sense a "Pauline Christian,"[91] inclined to support Paul's theological and pastoral position in a similar way that one would expect from Prisca and Aquila on the basis of their long-standing cooperation in ministry.

■ **6** The assessment of the greeting to be extended to Miriam/Maria in this verse depends on a text-critical judgment. If the usual alternative is followed, "Maria" is probably to be identified as a woman of pagan-Latin background whose name was derived from some branch of the Marius family.[92] If the stricter assessment of the text-critical evidence is followed, as I propose in note f above, "Miriam" would be identified as a woman of Jewish background[93] whose name was derived from that of Moses' sister (Exod 15:20).[94] Since the Jewish community in Rome began primarily with "the enslaved prison-

---

80   Solin, *Beiträge,* 135–38.
81   See Michel, 475.
82   See Spicq, "ἀπαρχή," 150.
83   See Delling, "ἀπαρχή," 485, and Sand, "ἀπαρχή," *EDNT* 1 (1990) 116–17. Typical references to the "first fruits" are Deut 18:4; 26:2, 10; Num 18:8-12; Neh 10:37; Ezek 44:30; 45:13-16.
84   Delling, "ἀπαρχή," 484; BAGD (2000) 98.
85   See Delling, "ἀπαρχή," 495.
86   See Hurtado, *One God,* 93–124.
87   Jewett, *Chronology,* 161.
88   See Zahn, 606-7; Wilckens, 3:134; Ollrog, *Mitarbeiter,* 38.
89   Lampe, "Roman Christians," 221.
90   See Zahn, 606.
91   Ziesler, 351.
92   Judge, *Rank and Status,* 36. Lampe, *Paul to Valentinus,* 175–76, reports that 108 examples of the Latin name Mary have been found in Roman records, and that she is likely to have been a slave or former slave

in the Marius family. In ". . . a problem like Maria," *NDIEC* 4 (1987) 229–30, G. H. R. Horsley examines other examples of this name and concludes that whether she was "a Jew or a Roman cannot be determined with certainty." Horsley discusses the epitaph of a later, Byzantine Mary in "Maria the diakonos," *NDIEC* 2 (1982) 193–95.
93   See Solin, "Juden und Syrer," 665.
94   See Black, 208; Fitzmyer, 737; and BAGD 191–92; also Otto Bardenhewer, *Der Name Maria. Geschichte der Deutung desselben,* BibS(F) 1 (Freiburg: Herder, 1895) 1–17; Manfred Görg discusses the Semitic and Egyptian forms of this name in "Mirjam—ein weiterer Versuch," *BZ* 23 (1979) 285–89.

ers of war" brought by Pompey in 62 B.C.E.,[95] Miriam probably derived from a family of slave background. Her name indicates derivation from a family that retained a strong Jewish identity in Rome.[96] After her conversion, Miriam functioned as an evangelist in Rome, as indicated by Paul's use of the technical expression ἐκοπία-σεν εἰς ὑμᾶς ("labor for you").[97] Harnack's analysis of the twenty-three instances of the verb "labor" and the eighteen occurrences of the noun "labor" in early Christian sources showed the technical meaning of missionary and congregational work.[98] That Miriam had done "much" (πολλά) of this kind of work in Rome suggests that she was therefore "one of the earliest members of the church at Rome and its organization could have been largely due to her influence."[99] Since Paul's personal acquaintance with Miriam most likely occurred during her exile after the Edict of Claudius, there is additional reason to believe that her congregational work commenced long enough before 49 C.E. to justify the adverb πολλά, that is, "much" work. The Jewish origin of the Christian community in Rome is strongly indicated by the details in this verse, and the crucial role of feminine leadership visible elsewhere in Rom 16 is an impressive indication of the social revolution associated with the early church, quite apart from the influence of the Pauline missionary movement.

■ **7** Paul asks the Roman tenement and house churches

to greet Andronikos and Junia, providing a fourfold rationale whose motivation becomes clear when the details are analyzed. The names are revealing: Andronikos is a prestigious Greek name frequently given to slaves or freedmen during the Greco-Roman period.[100] Junia is a Latin feminine name,[101] ordinarily given to slaves or freedwomen of the Junia family, of which some 250 examples have been found in Roman evidence.[102] The modern scholarly controversy over this name rests on the presumption that no woman could rank as an apostle, and thus that the accusative form must refer to a male by the name of Junias or Junianus.[103] However, the evidence in favor of the feminine name "Junia" is overwhelming.[104] Not a single example of a masculine name "Junias" has been found.[105] The patristic evidence investigated by Fàbrega and Fitzmyer indicates that commentators down through the twelfth century refer to Junia as a woman, often commenting on the extraordinary gifts that ranked her among the apostles.[106] The traditional feast of Saints Andronikos and Junia celebrates *admirabilem feminam Juniam* ("the admirable woman Junia"),[107] which suggests that while some medieval copyists of Romans assumed a male name,[108] the church as a whole had no difficulty on this point until later, particularly after Luther popularized the masculine option.[109] Despite its impact on modern translations based on Nestle-Aland and the UBS,[110] it

---

95 See Leon, *Jews*, 4; La Piana, "Foreign Groups," 345. For an account of the social status of Jewish slaves, see Hengel, *Juden, Griechen und Barbaren*, 119–26.

96 Leon, *Jews*, 105, lists eight examples of women with this name buried in Jewish catacombs.

97 See Schille, *Kollegialmission*, 50.

98 Adolf von Harnack, "Κοπιᾶν (Οἱ Κοπιῶντες) im frühchristlichen Sprachgebrauch," *ZNW* 27 (1928) 1–10; see also Ollrog's reference to the "technical term" used by Paul in this verse in *Mitarbeiter*, 71; Hauck refers to "missionary and pastoral work" in "κόπος, κοπιάω," 829.

99 Murray, 2:229.

100 Solin, *Beiträge*, 91; Lampe, *Paul to Valentinus*, 178, Lampe, "Andronicus," *ABD* 1 (1992) 247–48.

101 See Judge, *Rank and Status*, 36.

102 Lampe, *Paul to Valentinus*, 176.

103 See Zahn, 607, and Lietzmann, 125, followed by BAGD 380; also Schlatter, 399; Althaus, 137; Schmidt, 253; Michel, 475; Schlier, 444–45; Murray, 2:229, and the discussion of the text-critical evi-

dence in note h above. A complete survey of Greek editions, modern translations, and commentaries is provided by Epp, "Romans 16,7," 267–84; *Junia*, 45–59.

104 See the analysis of the debate in Walters, "'Phoebe' and 'Junia(s),'" 185–87, and Epp, "Romans 16,7," 242–84.

105 The exhaustive search by Brooten reported in "Junia," 142–43, discovered no examples of the masculine name "Junias," thus confirming the assessment of numerous earlier scholars, such as Lagrange, 366.

106 Fàbrega, "Junia(s)," 53–64; Fitzmyer, 737–38.

107 See Fitzmyer, 738.

108 See Peter Lampe, "Iunia/Iunias. Sklavenherkunft im Kreise der vorpaulinischen Apostel (Röm 16:7)," *ZNW* 76 (1985) 132.

109 See Brooten, "Junia," 142.

110 See for example *RSV*, *NEB*, and *NJB*.

appears that the name "Junias" is a figment of chauvinistic imagination.[111] Given the pairing with the male name first, it is likely that Andronikos and Junia are a married couple.[112] Paul refers to them as τοὺς συγγενεῖς μου ("my kinsmen"), which probably indicates Jewish origins for both, as the parallel in Rom 9:3 suggests.[113] That "kinsmen" in this instance refers to fellow Benjaminites[114] or "close companions,"[115] swings from over- to underinterpreting this straightforward reference, in order to explain the oddity of identifying some of the names in this chapter as Jewish. My audience theory explains such details as Paul's effort to affirm the legitimacy of some of the Jewish Christians currently being discriminated against by the Gentile Christian majority in the Roman house and tenement churches.[116] By placing himself in solidarity with Andronikos and Junia, Paul counters the prejudicial treatment about which he apparently was well informed.

Andronikos and Junia are not only compatriots, but also "my fellow prisoners," probably indicating they had shared a particular prison experience with Paul.[117] Since the possessive pronoun "my" along with the prefix συν- ("with, fellow") indicate shared experience,[118] and since

the parallels to the use of συναιχμαλώτος ("fellow prisoner/prisoner of war") in Phlm 23 and Col 4:10 refer to persons who were evidently sharing Paul's imprisonments at the times of writing, it seems gratuitous to suggest with Sanday and Headlam that Andronikos and Junia simply "had like him been imprisoned for Christ's sake" but not necessarily at the same time.[119] That "fellow prisoner" was merely a metaphor in reference to militant struggle, as argued by Gerhard Kittel,[120] seems most unlikely because it would then remain unclear why all the other early Christian evangelists mentioned in this chapter were not also so designated.[121]

Studies of the Roman prison system indicate that incarceration was ordinarily not used as punishment as in modern jurisprudence but was designed to secure arrested persons until they could be tried, to coerce confessions and other forms of cooperation with magistrates, or to confine condemned persons until they could be punished.[122] Prisoners were typically kept together in confined spaces where the conditions of crowding, inadequate ventilation and sanitation, deprivation of nourishment and sleep, as well as violence among inmates were frequent causes of complaints.[123] The use of iron

111 See Walters, "'Phoebe' and 'Junia(s),'" 187; Epp, "Romans 16,7," 283–84, 290–91; *Junia*, 53–59.

112 See Lagrange, 366; Stuhlmacher, 249: "Andronicus and (his wife?) Junia."

113 See Michel, 475; Dunn, 2:894; BAGD (2000) 950.

114 Lagrange, 366.

115 Wilhelm Michaelis, "συγγενής, συγγένεια," *TDNT* 7 (1971) 742.

116 See Watson, "Two Roman Congregations," 210–11.

117 See Black, 209; Wilckens, 3:135; Zeller, 248. The recent survey of the scholarly debate over a metaphorical as opposed to a real imprisonment by Jean-Marie Salamito concludes that the latter is more likely: "*ΣΥΝΑΙΧΜΑΛΩΤΟΙ* : Les 'Compagnons de Captivité' de l'Apôtre Paul," in C. Betrand-Dagenbach et al., eds., *Carcer. Prison et privation de liberté dans l'antiquité classique* (Paris: De Boccard, 1999) 207–8.

118 The only literary parallel to συναιχμαλώτος listed in LSJM is Pseudo-Lucian *Asin.* 27, which is a clear reference to shared experience: "The maiden showed me great consideration as was right for my sharing with her imprisonment (συναιχμαλώτου)."

119 Sanday and Headlam, 423, followed by Schlier, 444, and Fitzmyer, 739. This interpretation disregards the μου ("my"), which is explicitly repeated in con-

nection with "prisoner," indicating that Andronikos and Junia had not merely been partners with Paul in one of his prison experiences.

120 Gerhard Kittel, "αἰχμάλωτος κτλ.," *TDNT* 1 (1964) 196–97. See the evaluation of this approach by Teodorico da Castel S. Pietro, "Συναιχμάλωτος: Campagno di prigionia o conquistato assieme? (Rom. 16,7; Col. 4,10; Filem 23)," *SPCIC* 2 (1963) 417–28.

121 Sanday and Headlam, 423, aptly characterized this approach: "Metaphorical explanations of the words are too far-fetched to be probable."

122 The most comprehensive studies are by F. A. Karl Krauss, *Im Kerker vor und nach Christus* (Freiburg/Tübingen: Mohr, 1895); Craig S. Wansink, *Chained in Christ: The Experience and Rhetoric of Paul's Imprisonments,* JSNTSup 130 (Sheffield: Sheffield Academic Press, 1996) 27–95; Brian Rapske, *The Book of Acts in Its First Century Setting,* vol. 3, *The Book of Acts and Paul in Roman Custody* (Grand Rapids: Eerdmans; Carlisle: Paternoster, 1994) 9–37, 313–22. The legal details are reviewed in S. Arbandt, W. Macheiner, and C. Colpe, "Gefangenschaft," *RAC* 9 (1976) 318–45.

123 See H. Hitzig, "Carcer," *PW* 3 (1899) 1581; Wansink, "Imprisonment," 33–55; Rapske, *Roman Custody,* 195–226.

chains and stocks typically added a significant measure of torturous punishment to Roman imprisonment.[124] Since the prison system was administered largely by military authorities,[125] it was natural for Paul to refer to himself and his colleagues as συναιχμαλώτοι ("fellow prisoners of war"), which was probably understood within the context of the conflict between Christ and the principalities and powers alluded to in Rom 8:38-39 and 2 Cor 10:3-5.[126] Since most of the Jewish community had been brought to Rome as prisoners of war to be purchased as slaves, the choice of this expression would have had an evocative connotation for some of Paul's audience.

The honorific expression ἐπίσημοι ἐν τοῖς ἀποστόλοις should be translated "outstanding among the apostles"[127] rather than "remarkable in the judgment of the apostles,"[198] because the adjective ἐπίσημος lifts up a person or thing as distinguished or marked in comparison with other representatives of the same class, in this instance with the other apostles.[129] The Latin equivalent is honoratus, the acknowledgment of the distinction and honor earned by another.[130] Thus τὸ ἐπίσημον was used to refer to the badge distinguishing one shield from another (Herodotus *Hist.* 9.74), the flag or figure-head that identifies one ship in comparison with an otherwise identical ship in the same class (Herodotus 8.88), or the device stamped on a coin to distinguish it from another (Plutarch *Thes.* 6.1).[131] The adjective is used by 3 Macc 6:1 to identify Eleazar as ἐπίσημος τῶν ἀπὸ τῆς χώρας ἱερέων ("remarkable among the priests of the country") and by Josephus to describe Mary of Bethezuba as "remarkable (ἐπίσημος) by reason of family and fortune" (*Bell.* 6.201). A striking confirmation of this interpretation is provided by Chrysostom's comment about Junia: "Even to be an apostle is great, but also to be prominent among them—consider how wonderful a song of honor that is!"[132] A more debatable question is whether Andronikos and Junia functioned as evangelists or emissaries of a particular congregation,[133] or as witnesses to the resurrection.[134] Since Paul gives no evidence that they had been associated with a particular congregation, in contrast to Phoebe in 16:1-2, and since his usage of "apostle" is oriented to resurrection witness unless otherwise indicated, it seems likely that he ranked them among "all the apostles" who laid claim to being witnesses of the resurrection.[135] With regard to the locations where Andronikos and Junia served as evangelists, all we can say with certainty is that they had functioned

---

124 See Rapske, *Roman Custody*, 206–9.

125 Hitzig, "Carcer," 1580; Wansink, *Chained*, 75–79; Rapske, *Roman Custody*, 252–54.

126 See Kittel, "αἰχμάλωτος κτλ.," 196–97, and especially Castel S. Picton, "Συναιχμάλωτος," 2:117–28.

127 See Colenso, 265; Sanday and Headlam, 423, following the lead of all patristic commentators; also Cranfield, 2:789; Käsemann, 414; Rengstorf, "ἐπίσημος," 268; Epp, "Romans 16,7," 284–85, 289; *Junia*, 69–78.

128 Cornely, 776–77; Zahn, 608, argues for this option on grounds that nothing more is reported about these two missionaries in the NT, but our information about early missionaries beyond Peter and Paul is too sketchy for this conclusion; see Fabrèga, "Junia(a)," 52. In "Was Junia Really an Apostle? A Re-examination of Rom. 16.7," *NTS* (2001) 76–91, Michael H. Burer and Daniel B. Wallace attempt to restore the "remarkable in the judgment of the apostles" reading, but their examples are not compelling, as shown by Epp, "Romans 16,7," 285–89; *Junia*, 72–78.

129 See Karl Heinrich Rengstorf, "ἐπίσημος," *TDNT* 7 (1971) 267 and Fàbrega, "Junia(s)," 52.

130 See Lendon, *Empire of Honour*, 274–78.

131 See LSJM 655–56 for these and numerous other examples.

132 Cited by Epp, "Romans 16,7," 389–90; *Junia*, 33, from John Chrysostom *Hom. Rom.* 31.2.

133 For example, Schlier, 444, restricts Andronikos and Junia to the role of congregational emissaries as in 2 Cor 8:23; Phil 2:25; Acts 13:1-3; 14:4, 14, or as traveling missionaries as in 1 Cor 15:7; 2 Cor 11:5, 13; 12:11.

134 Schmithals, *Office of Apostle*, 62, places Andronikos and Junia within the framework of 1 Cor 15:5-7 as witnesses to the resurrection.

135 See Fàbrega, "Junia(s)," 53, rejecting the groundless assertion of Rudolf Schnackenburg, "Apostles before and during Paul's Time," in W. W. Gasque and R. P. Martin, eds., *Apostolic History and the Gospel: Biblical and Historical Essays Presented to F. F. Bruce . . .* (Exeter: Paternoster; Grand Rapids: Eerdmans, 1970) 294, that they were not "able to lay claim to an appearance of the risen Lord." See also Dunn, 2:894–95; Stuhlmacher, 249.

somewhere in the eastern mission during the time of shared imprisonment with Paul, and that they are now in Rome. That Andronikos was identical with the Ephesian civic leader of that name whose house was used by John in the apocryphal *Acts of John* 31 and 62[136] seems unlikely because the Johannine traditions were associated with the history of the Ephesian church several decades after Paul's ministry. Lampe discovered some twenty-nine references to persons with the name of Andronikos in Rome,[137] so there is no reason to suspect he was not a resident there. It seems quite likely that they had missionized in Rome prior to the banishment under Claudius, and had returned to their earlier residence there after the lapse of the Edict.[138] That they were καὶ πρὸ ἐμοῦ γέγοναν ἐν Χριστῷ ("also in Christ before me") means that they were converted prior to 34 C.E.,[139] which correlates well with the earlier reference to their apostolic status, because Paul thought of himself as the last in the series of witnesses to the resurrection (1 Cor 15:8). This means that Andronikos and Junia could easily have been among the "visitors from Rome" identified in Acts 2:10 as part of the Pentecost crowd.[140] They could well have been among the Hellenists in Jerusalem (Acts 6:1),[141] who were later scattered to various locations outside of Jerusalem, according Acts 11:19.[142] The supposition that they were part of the Antioch church[143] seems less plausible in view of their very early origin as Christian missionaries. All we can

say with certainty is that this couple had functioned as Christian apostles for more than two decades before Paul wrote this letter to Rome requesting that they be greeted by other believers in Rome who evidently were not inclined to acknowledge their accomplishments and status.[144]

■ **8** The name "Ampliatus" was coined as a slave name with the meaning "ample" during the Augustan period, and it is highly likely that he was a slave or freedman.[145] The most intriguing evidence comes from the Domitilla Catacombs in Rome where this name appears twice, of which one can be dated to the first century C.E.[146] Although this detail is disputed,[147] it would point to a link between this person and the senatorial family from which the Flavian Domitilla came, who was exiled as a believer during Domitian's reign (81–96 C.E.).[148] The catacomb on her family estate is the earliest Christian cemetery in Rome. If Ampliatus were a slave or freedman under the patronage of Domitilla, this could explain why he was free to travel to the east, where he met Paul, and now has returned to Rome. Although certainty is impossible at this stage in the interpretation of the details in the Domitillan Catacombs,[149] it is clear that Ampliatus stands along with Epainetos in a particularly close relationship to Paul.[150] The translation "my dear friend"[151] would certainly be appropriate. The reference to his status "in the Lord" refers to Ampliatus's membership in the body of Christ.

136 In "Andronicus," *ExpT* 42 (1930–31) 300–304, Benjamin W. Bacon made this suggestion on the premise that Rom 16 was addressed to Ephesus.
137 Lampe, *Paul to Valentinus*, 178.
138 See Erbes, "Zeit und Ziel," 139–40.
139 See Jewett, *Chronology*, 29–30, 99–100.
140 See Erbes, "Zeit und Ziel," 140. Lagrange, 368, places them in the earliest Jerusalem congregation after Pentecost.
141 Zeller, 247.
142 Sanday and Headlam, 423–24.
143 Ollrog, *Mitarbeiter*, 51–52.
144 See Eisen, *Amtsträgerinnen*, 54–55.
145 See Michel, 476; Lampe, *Paul to Valentinus*, 173, citing J. Baumgart, "Die römischen Sklavennamen" (dissertation, University of Breslau, 1936) 30–31.
146 See Sanday and Headlam, 424–25; Michel, 476; Cranfield, 2:790.
147 This detail is flatly rejected by Peter Lampe, "Ampliatus," *ABD* 1 (1992) 217, referring to pages

20–21 in the German edition of *Paul to Valentinus*, but absent in the English edition. This is a matter deserving further clarification, because the inscriptions were apparently clearly visible in the 1880s when the discussion of this matter began.
148 For a resolution of the conflicts within the sources concerning Domitilla, see Lampe, *Paul to Valentinus*, 198–203.
149 For orientation, see J. Stevenson, *The Catacombs* (London: Thames & Hudson, 1978).
150 Zahn, 609; Morris, 535. This detail is watered down by Dunn, 2:893, on grounds that all believers are beloved, but this does not explain why only four persons in chapter 16 are singled out with this epithet.
151 Fitzmyer, 740.

■ **9** The greeting requested for Urbanus relates to some-one Paul definitely knows personally, because, along with Prisca and Aquilla, he is identified as "our co-worker in Christ," that is, a missionary colleague.[152] He had worked with Paul somewhere in the eastern mission field.[153] The name is Latin, which ordinarily would indicate an origin in Rome, and there are ninety-five instances of this name in Roman inscriptions and papyri.[154] Yet both Lampe and Solin deny that the name Urbanus points to Roman origin.[155] Perhaps the fact that Urbanus had met Paul in the east, indicating his freedom to travel, contributed to their decision. The facts that this is a "wish-name" with the meaning "refined, cultivated, ingenious" that usually was given to slaves, and that twenty-five of the Roman references are definitely to slaves while all of the feminine form, Urbana, are slaves,[156] leads me to believe that this particular Urbanus was likely a freedman of Roman origin.[157] There are two examples of the names Urbanus as imperial freedmen that illustrate this possibility.[158] The details make it likely that the Urbanus greeted by Paul was among the exiles driven out of Rome in 49 after involvement in the synagogue riots. He has now returned to his home city of Rome. The reference to him as "our co-worker" indicates that he had freely cooperated in the Pauline mission,[159] and that this Gentile believer shared a theological and missional outlook congenial to Paul. In this instance, the request for greetings would have been particularly hard for the "weak," who, according to 14:3-4, 10, were inclined to pass judgment on those who like Paul were free from the law. Urbanus is honored by Paul with the request that all other converts in Rome greet him as an equal.

The request for greetings to "my beloved Stachys" indicates a close personal relationship with Paul, as in the cases of Epainetos, Ampliatus, and Persis discussed below.[160] The male name Stachys is a Greek derivation from the term for an ear of corn, probably indicating servile status.[161] Although Lampe believes it is unlikely that Stachys was a slave, because only three of thirteen occurrences in Roman records clearly indicate servile origin,[162] the fact that this Greek name was in the Roman context indicates the likelihood of a slave background.[163] In *CIL* 6 Nr. 26732 there is a reference to a Stachys as a slave in the imperial household and in *CIL* 6 Nr. 4452 a physician with freedman status.[164] In view of his Roman origin, it is likely that Stachys was part of the Gentile majority in the Roman congregations, but his personal acquaintance with Paul indicates that he had traveled in the east, and had perhaps also been banned along with other Christ believers in 49 C.E.

■ **10a** Apelles is also a Greek name, which indicates immigration from the east. This name appears only twenty-seven times in Roman materials.[165] Although most of the persons with Greek names living in Rome were either slaves or freedmen, the social and ethnic status of Apelles is difficult to determine. There is, for example, an Apelles who was a Roman nobleman who originated in Pergamon[166] and an "Apella the Jew" mentioned by Horace *Sat.* 1.5.100 that leads some to conclude that "the name was common among Jews."[167] In view of inscriptions linking persons with this name with

152 Schille, *Kollegialmission*, 50.
153 Meeks, *Urban Christians*, 56; Peter Lampe, "Urbanus," *ABD* 6 (1992) 767.
154 Lampe, *Paul to Valentinus*, 181.
155 Solin, *Beiträge*, 152 n. 2; Lampe, "Urbanus," 767, and *Paul to Valentinus*, 168.
156 Lampe, *Paul to Valentinus*, 181.
157 See also Sanday and Headlam, 425; Cranfield, 2:790–91; Dunn, 2:895; Fitzmyer, 740; Moo, 924.
158 See *CIL* 6. Nrs. 33764 and 4237 and the discussion in Lightfoot, "Caesar's Household," 174.
159 Ollrog, *Mitarbeiter*, 63–72, cited with approval by Wilckens, 3:136. See also Haacker, 321. Michel, 476, and Cranfield, 2:791, mistakenly infer that the "our" indicates "perhaps that Urbanus had not been a colleague of Paul personally" but was "a colleague of all gospel-workers generally."
160 Zahn, 609; Godet, 492; Morris, 535.
161 Solin, *Beiträge*, 120.
162 Peter Lampe, "Stachys," *ABD* 6 (1992) 183.
163 See Lampe, *Paul to Valentinus*, 171: "a first rule of thumb says that bearers of Greek names in first century Rome were mostly descendents of slaves."
164 Noted by Lampe, *Paul to Valentinus*, 180; Lightfoot, "Caesar's Household," 174, argues for "some connection with the court."
165 Peter Lampe, "Apelles," *ABD* 1 (1992) 275; *Paul to Valentinus*, 166–71.
166 Solin, *Beiträge*, 139.
167 BAGD (2000) 101; Dunn, 2:896.

imperial service, Lightfoot concludes that Apelles "is a name belonging to the imperial household."[168] The reference to him as "(the) approved in Christ" (τὸν δόκιμον ἐν Χριστῷ), in contrast to the expression "acceptable to people" in 14:18, has the sense of having been tested and found to be genuine.[169] In 1 Cor 11:19 Paul employs δόκιμος to refer to believers who are found to be "genuine," and in 2 Cor 13:5-7, where the test of genuineness is doing "what is right." It is likely, therefore, that Apelles was known to have had his status "in Christ" tested in some particular manner,[170] resulting, so to speak, in a stamp of approval. It seems likely from this commendation that Paul was personally acquainted with Apelles, because it would not have been rhetorically convincing to recommend someone as genuine whom one had never met. It is, in any event, clear that Paul wished all other believers in Rome to greet him as an honored equal.

■ **10b** Paul's request that greetings be extended to "those from among the [slaves] of Aristoboulos" is a probable reference to a congregation among the slaves of his household. It is significant that Aristoboulos is not greeted by Paul, indicating that it is not he but the members of his household who were believers. It is also clear from the formulation that not all of the Aristoboulos group belong to this group of believers.[171] Since no name of a patron is provided, and the members are associated with a particular household, this group probably constituted a tenement church.[172] The name Aristoboulos is found only twice in Roman records and inscriptions, and likely belongs to someone not born in

Rome.[173] We know of an Aristoboulos who came to Rome as a hostage along with his brother, Herod Agrippa, that they were educated with the future emperor Claudius, and that Aristoboulos later appeared before the procurator Petronius to protest Caligula's placement of his statue in the Jerusalem temple (Josephus *Ant.* 18.273–76). It is plausible, therefore, that this particular Aristoboulos was the grandson of Herod the Great, who died sometime after 45 C.E.,[174] having apparently willed his household to his friend the emperor Claudius, who thereupon incorporated the administrative slaves into his imperial bureaucracy.[175] If so, the strategic setting of this congregation within the bureaucracy indicates not only how far Christianity had penetrated into governmental circles but also how they could have been helpful in clearing the way for the Spanish mission. Another possibility is that this group belonged to some other Aristoboulos. In either case, their role as administrative slaves entailed a measure of education and independence.[176] Since Paul makes no personal reference to them, it is clear that his knowledge is secondhand. He had probably heard of this remarkable group from other Roman believers whom he had met during their exile between 49 and 54 C.E. If the link to the Herodian family is valid, their association with their now deceased Jewish patron, Aristoboulos, who had forcefully interceded in behalf of his compatriots in the Caligula incident, undoubtedly means that they were sympathetic to the viewpoint of the Jewish Christians within Rome. It is significant that Paul honors them here as worthy of the same acceptance as the members of the

---

168 Lightfoot, "Caesar's Household," 174.

169 See Grundmann, "δόκιμος κτλ.," 259; BAGD (2000) 256.1, "genuine on the basis of testing . . . genuine."

170 See Godet, 492; Wilckens, 3:136; Dunn, 2:896.

171 See Lampe, "Roman Christians," 222.

172 Lampe, *Paul to Valentinus,* 359, refers to this group as a "concentration" and "Christian island" in Rome.

173 Lampe, *Paul to Valentinus,* 167; this inference is not a mere "supposition," as suggested by Clarke, "Romans 16," 114, because it is based on an examination of the relevant evidence.

174 Lightfoot, "Caesar's Household," 174–75; see also the article with no author named, "Aristobulos. 5," *Neue Pauly* 1 (1996) 1106.

175 See Stowers, *Rereading,* 76–78; see also Scott T. Carroll, "Aristobulus (Person)," *ADB* 1 (1992) 383, section 7, for the account of the Aristobulus who was educated with Claudius in Rome. Judge, *Rank and Status,* 20, argues on the basis of *P.Oxy.* 46. Nr. 3312.10–13 ("you should know then, that Herminus went off to Rome and became a freedman of Caesar to take up official appointments [ὀπίκια λάβ(η)]") that nonslaves sometimes had enough "leverage" to find their way into lucrative public service, referred in the papyrus as ὀπίκια (Latin: *officiium*), the technical term for a career appointment.

176 See Gülzow, *Christentum und Sklaverei,* 48–49.

church of Prisca and Aquila, who would have been more sympathetic to Paul's mission to the Gentiles.

■ **11a** The next person greeted is Herodion, identified as Paul's compatriot,[177] which lends credence that this Aristoboulos was a member of the Herodian family.[178] Herodion may well have been a member of the congregation among the slaves of Aristoboulos. The name is otherwise unattested in Rome and was likely given to a slave or freedman who had been in the service of a member of the Herodian family.[179] Lampe suggests that "Herodion was an imperial freedman and had Roman citizenship."[180] There may have been a synagogue of the Herodians in Rome, which would have been founded by members of the Herodian family in Rome or their slaves and freedmen.[181] If so, this synagogue would have been closed by Claudius in 49 C.E. and some members of this congregation including Herodion would have founded the "tenement church" in their workplace or dwelling. Again, the fact that Paul adds no personal commendation indicates that he knows of Herodion's role by hearsay. As an indisputably Jewish Christian, Herodion is honored by Paul with the request that all other converts greet him as a member of their family.

■ **11b** The greeting to "those belonging to Narkissos who are in the Lord" is among the most intriguing in chapter 16. As in the case of Aristoboulos, the wording here indicates that the patron himself is not a believer, but that a group of his household slaves are known to have become a congregation. As Lampe points out, the formulation τοὺς ἐκ τῶν Ναρκίσσου ("those belonging to Narkissos") indicates that some, but not all, of the slaves in his household belonged to this group of believers, and the wording of τοὺς ὄντας ἐν κυρίῳ ("who are in the Lord") distinguishes between those belonging to Narkissos who are believers and those who are not.[182] The name Narkissos was frequently used in Rome for slaves and freedmen.[183] We know of an influential freedman of Claudius by this name;[184] also one from the administration of Nero.[185] Another freedman with the name of Narkissos is mentioned as owning slaves.[186] I accept the assessment that the Claudian Narkissos is most likely in view here.[187] He exercised immense political and economic power during Claudius's reign, serving *ab epistulis* in charge of Caesarean correspondence.[188] Like other freedmen in Claudius's burgeoning bureaucracy, he amassed an immense fortune before his execution in 54,[189] when his estates and administrators were apparently confiscated and incorporated into the imperial possessions. This means that the bureaucratic studies concerning the formation of the enlarged imper-

---

177 That τὸν συγγενῆ μου should be understood as "my relative" is semantically possible, as suggested by Murrray, 2:231; Witherington, 394; Clarke, "Romans 16," 112, but in this case unlikely because five others are identified in the same way in 16:7 and 21, none of whom is a possible relative, and because the lack of personal commendation indicates that Paul is not well acquainted with Herodion. See Weiss, 600; Sanday and Headlam, 425; Kühl, 479; Schlier, 445; Morris, 535; Ziesler, 353; Johnson, 218; Schreiner, 791; Michaelis, "συγγενής, συγγένεια," 741.

178 Peter Lampe, "Herodion," *ABD* 3 (1992) 176.

179 Lampe, "Roman Christians," 226; cited with approval by Moo, 925. See also Stowers, *Rereading*, 77; Lightfoot, "Caesar's Household," 175.

180 Lampe, "Herodion," 176.

181 Leon, *Jews*, 159–62, argues against the inscriptional reconstruction of *CIL* 6 Nr. 9005 that results in the word "Herodian," preferring a reference to the "Synagogue of the Rhodians." The question remains unresolved.

182 Lampe, "Roman Christians," 222.

183 Lampe, *Paul to Valentinus*, 165.

184 Suetonius *Claud.* 28.

185 Dio Cassius *Hist. Rom.* 64.3.

186 *CIL* 6 Nr. 9035.

187 Lightfoot, "Caesar's Household," 175; Stein, "Narcissus. 1," *PW* 16.2 (1935) 1704–5; Sanday and Headlam, 426; Zahn, 609; Cranfield, 2:792–93, citing Lightfoot, "Caesar's Household," 175; Wedderburn, *Reasons*, 16, referring to the Claudian Narkissos whose household "may have been absorbed into the imperial household, not so much by bequest this time as by confiscation," citing *CIL* 3 Nr. 3973; 6 Nrs. 9035, 15640, where the epithet Narcissianus is found. See also *CIL* 15 Nr. 7500; Stowers, *Rereading*, 78–79. For a skeptical assessment that Narkissos can be more closely identified, see Peter Lampe, "Narcissus," *ABD* 4 (1992) 1022–23.

188 Eck, *Verwaltung*, 1:176; 1:148, citing *CIL* 15 Nr. 7500.

189 Stein, "Narcissus," 1704–5; "Narcissus," *Neue Pauly* 8 (2000) 710–11.

ial administration under Claudius and Nero would be relevant for this group of household slaves.[190] These imperial bureaucrats were well educated and comfortably maintained,[191] with prospects of advancement and ultimately freedom after years of faithful service.[192] Since there was no link between Narkissos and Judaism, it is likely that this group of enslaved administrators would have been strongly Roman in outlook, and thus belonging among the Gentile Christian majority in Rome.

■ **12** The feminine Tryphaina is a Greek slave name derived from the masculine name, Tryphon,[193] with the meaning "dainty."[194] In addition to examples found in Rome, this name has been found in inscriptions and papyri from Lydia and Egypt.[195] The name Tryphosa means "luscious,"[196] and a reference to this name has been found in a Lydian inscription concerning honors of gold crowns granted to Appios's "foster-sister Tryphosa and her husband Theophilos," which reflects free status and relatively high social rank.[197] On the basis of thirty-two examples of Tryphosa and sixty examples of Traephena found in Roman inscriptions and papyri, Peter Lampe concludes that they were probably Gentile Christians from slave background,[198] but cannot say whether they were sisters,[199] which seems likely to other scholars because of the similarity in their names and because the καί ("and") indicates that they belonged together.[200] Some even suggest they were identical twins, which might explain why they remained together.[201] The reference to their being "laborers in the Lord" (τὰς κοπιώσας ἐν κυρίῳ) indicates that they were either missionaries or local church leaders.[202] The personal commendation could not have been given if Paul were not personally acquainted with Tryphaina and Tryphosa, which probably indicates that they were among the leaders banned by Claudius in 49 C.E. for involvement in the conflicts in the Roman synagogues. This would explain how Paul had met them in the eastern mission field along with Prisca, Aquila, and others. The fact that the name Tryphaina appears as a Jewish woman in a papyrus of 73 C.E.[203] indicates the possibility that the Tryphaina greeted by Paul had been a slave of Roman owners who named the children of Jewish slave parents in a non-Jewish manner. The two women are, at any event, now in Rome playing the role of church leaders whom Paul wishes all other believers in Rome to greet with honor.

The name "Persis" is a typical name for a feminine slave originating in Persia, a name occurring six times in Roman epigraphic and literary sources.[204] She may be a Gentile believer of ethnic Persian origin, or perhaps a believer of Jewish background whose family had lived in the large Persian-Babylonian diaspora. The reference to Persis as "beloved" indicates a close relationship with Paul, but slightly more distant than Epainetos, identified in v. 5 as "my beloved." Paul had met her in the eastern mission area, and her current location in Rome indicates that she was probably among the exiles whom Paul met after 49 C.E. That Persis had "labored much in the Lord" indicates a very intensive involvement in congregational and missionary leadership.[205] Whether she comes from Gentile or Jewish background, Paul urges all of the other believers in Rome to honor her with appropriate greetings as an important leader.

■ **13** The Latin name Rufus is a color designation,[206] "redhead," and was used for slaves as well as freeborn children in the century prior to the Roman letter. Of

190 See Eck, *Verwaltung*, 2:147–65.
191 See Gülzow, *Christentum und Sklaverei*, 48–49.
192 Brockmeyer, *Antike Sklaverei*, 178–82; see also Martin, *Slavery as Salvation*, 15–22.
193 Solin, *Beiträge*, 73.
194 BAGD (2000) 1018.
195 G. H. R. Horsley, "Tryphaina," *NDIEC* 3 (1983) 93.
196 BAGD (2000) 1018.
197 See G. H. R. Horsley, "A Tribute from a *syntrophos*, and Others," *NDIEC* 3 (1983) 37–39.
198 Lampe, *Paul to Valentinus*, 169, 183.
199 Peter Lampe, "Tryphaena and Tryphosa," *ABD* 6 (1992) 669.
200 Lightfoot, "Caesar's Household," 175–76; Lagrange,

368; Käsemann, 414–15, although the German edition expresses skepticism; Dunn, 2:879: "quite possible that they were sisters"; Fitzmyer, 741.
201 Wilckens, 3:136.
202 Schille, *Kollegialmission*, 50; Lampe, "Tryphaena and Tryphosa," 669.
203 *CPJ* 2. Nr. 421.183.
204 Peter Lampe, "Persis," *ABD* 5 (1992) 244; BAGD (2000) 808.
205 Schille, *Kollegialmission*, 50–52.
206 Solin, *Beiträge*, 19 n. 4.

374 occurrences of Rufus or Rufa in the *CIL*, only 30 are male slaves and 50 female slaves, which leads Lampe to the conclusion that he was probably a freeborn Gentile.[207] The other details in this verse tend to confirm the assessment of this man as a Gentile believer of considerable means and reputation. The reference to him as τὸν ἐκλεκτὸν ἐν κυρίῳ ("chosen in the Lord") is a designation that could be borne by all believers, according to Rom 1:6-7; 8:33; 9:24, but in this instance it distinguishes Rufus from all of the other persons greeted and must therefore refer to his particular status "in the Lord."[208] This is not a typical Pauline designation for individual believers and is likely to have been a mark of distinction granted by the community. The use of ἐκλεκτός in reference to handpicked soldiers (*Ep. Arist.* 13; *Sib. Or.* 3.521) or especially gifted religious figures (Wis 3:14; 2 John 1; Ignatius *Phld.* 11.1) sustains the impression that a specific calling or biographical distinction was attached to Rufus,[209] which Paul assumes was known to the Roman audience. This is what makes the hypothesis developed by Lightfoot plausible, that the Rufus referred to in Mark 15:21 was in fact this particular man. Simon of Cyrene, who was forced to carry Jesus' cross, is identified as the "father of Alexander and Rufus," indicating clearly that these sons were well known to the initial audience of Mark's gospel,[210] which most scholars have identified as Rome.[211] To dismiss this inference as "pious speculation"[212] is to overlook the rhetorical significance in the Roman setting of referring to this particular Rufus as the "elect/chosen in the Lord."[213] If Lightfoot's hypothesis is correct, "chosen" could well refer to a class of believers who had a direct link with the historical Jesus. That Paul had met Rufus and his mother in the eastern mission area and that they are now back in Rome where they are well known to the audience indicates that they had probably belonged to the exiles resulting from the Edict of Claudius in 49 C.E.[214] To refer to Rufus's mother as "mine" indicates that she had provided hospitality and patronage[215] in such a manner that Paul at some point in his career became virtually a member of their family.[216] This detail confirms the impression that Rufus was a person of considerable means, because he and his mother were in the position of providing hospitality in their dwelling. If the identification with the family of Simon of Cyrene is correct, there is also evidence of considerable mobility and thus a measure of economic power in their travels between Africa, Jerusalem, Rome, and somewhere in Paul's eastern mission areas.[217]

■ **14** In this verse a group of believers is identified as "the brothers," who are together with five named leaders.[218] Although it is clear that Paul is not personally acquainted with any of these persons, the names are quite revealing.[219]

207 Lampe, *Paul to Valentinus*, 181–82; he notes that *CIL* 6 Nr. 13208 reveals a Rufus who was an imperial freedman and there are patrons in *CIL* 6 Nrs. 11220, 16087, 16744, 18321, 21590, 23484, 23702, 25585, 35702.

208 Cranfield, 2:794.

209 See Dunn, 2:897; Haacker, 322.

210 Incigneri, *Gospel to the Romans*, 100.

211 Lightfoot, "Caesar's Household," 176; see the survey of research in Incigneri, *Gospel to the Romans*, 59, 96–115.

212 Käsemann, 414; Fitzmyer, 741.

213 Sanday and Headlam, 427; Lagrange, 369.

214 The suggestions that Rufus's mother had provided hospitality during Paul's alleged early years in Jerusalem (Acts 22:3) as surveyed by Haacker, 322, are less probable because Paul claims in Gal 1:22 that he was not acquainted with believers in Jerusalem and because this would not explain the personal acquaintance with Rufus and his mother on the part of the Roman audience.

215 See Lietzmann, 127; Schlier, 445; Moo, 926.

216 The readiness to refer to nonfamily members in parental terms was not unusual, as noted by McDonald, "Separate Letter," 370, in the letter of Aurelius Dius to his own father and mother as well as to "my father Melanus and my mother Timpesouris." See also *P.Oxy.* 1296.8, 15; 1678; John 19:27. G. H. R. Horsley, "Dearer Than My Mother," *NDIEC* 4 (1987) 33–35, discusses a Roman epitaph that refers to the patroness Faustina as "dearer than my mother."

217 See Meeks, *Urban Christians*, 57.

218 See Lampe, *Paul to Valentinus*, 359.

219 This section is adapted from Jewett, "Tenement Churches," 23–43.

According to Solin and Lampe,[220] "Asynkritos" is found only twice in the Roman evidence, of which one comes from the second half of the first century. A royal freedman by this name is mentioned in *CIL* 6 Nr. 12565. The name is Greek with the meaning "incomparable," which one would expect to have been used for slaves or freedmen. But G. H. R. Horsley points to other probable examples of the name Asynkritos that reflect higher social status, including a name appearing in a report of senatorial proceedings (*P.Oxy.* 12 Nr. 1413.22) and another instance in a list of tax allotments (*P.Lips.* 1 Nr. 98 col. 1.2), which suggests that an originally servile name had passed over to use "by those of higher status."[221] However, the fact that this particular Asynkritos belongs with a group of other persons whose servile status is indisputable leads me to concur with Lampe that he is probably a slave or freedman.[222]

"Phlegon" appears nine times in Roman records, of which seven come from the first century. Three of these references are for persons of slave background. The name is Greek, and was used in earlier times as a dog's name,[223] which likewise indicates servile status. Although Lampe maintains that this particular Phlegon was probably a Gentile of free background,[224] it seems more likely that he was either a slave or a freedman.[225] Examples of persons with the name Phlegon that clearly reflect servile status include *CIL* 6 Nr. 8965, a slave of the Caesarean household assigned to accompany children to school, and *CIL* 6 Nr. 15202, a freedman living in Rome. Although Paul was not personally acquainted with Phlegon, he requests that others greet him.

The name "Hermes" is very frequently found at Rome,[226] being often used for slaves or freedmen. Named after the god, Hermes was, in Lampe's words, "the Roman name for slaves." A strikingly large number of persons with this name are found among Claudian freedmen.[227] Lampe points to several such persons who owned numerous slaves and freedmen, indicating a measure of economic and social status.[228] It remains likely, however, that even these wealthy persons with the name of Hermes originated as slaves or freedmen themselves.[229] Again, it is clear from the lack of personal attribution that Paul was personally unacquainted with Hermes, and has probably heard about him from exiles from Rome during the period 49–54 C.E.

"Patrobas" is not found at all in Rome, but a similar name, Patrobius, occurs eight times, of which four are in the NT period. Lampe identifies Patrobas as a Greek name; the Latinized ending "ius" on associated names may indicate an effort to avoid the social status of slaves and freedmen. Three of the eight persons with the name Patrobius are explicitly of slave background. Several prominent freedmen are mentioned in close proximity to the imperial administration: an indicted royal freedman in Martial's fiction whose name is spelled "Patrobas" as in Paul's greeting;[230] a freedman of the Nero administration;[231] and a M. Aemilius Patrobius Libertus.[232] However, in view of the grouping with other colleagues of servile status, the Greek Patrobas found in this verse probably refers to a person of less prominent social status.[233] He was a Gentile Christian whose family stemmed from the east,[234] although he had never met Paul and

220 Solin, *Namenbuch*, 1274; Lampe, *Paul to Valentinus*, 169, 182–83; Peter Lampe, "Asyncretus," *ABD* 1 (1992) 508.
221 G. H. R. Horsley, "Asyncretus," *NDIEC* 2 (1982) 108.
222 Lampe, *Paul to Valentinus*, 183.
223 Michel, 478, cites Xenophon *Cyr.* 7.5 on this point; see also Lampe, *Paul to Valentinus*, 180; Peter Lampe, "Phlegon," *ABD* 5 (1992) 347.
224 Lampe, "Phlegon," 347, although in *Paul to Valentinus*, 183, Lampe more circumspectly observes that "no statement is presently possible" concerning social status because Phlegon was an immigrant from the east. However, the "rule of thumb" cited from Lampe, *Paul to Valentinus,* 171, in n. 163 indicates the likelihood of servile background.
225 See Cranfield, 2:795; Dunn, 2:898; Fitzmyer, 741.
226 Lampe, *Paul to Valentinus*, 173–74, refers to 841 examples, of which 640 are from the first century.
227 Lightfoot, "Caesar's Household," 176; Lampe, *Paul to Valentinus*, 174, cites *CIL* 6 Nrs. 15097–15110; Nr. 12642; Nr. 15557.
228 Lampe, *Paul to Valentinus*, 174.
229 Solin, *Beiträge*, 108–11.
230 Martial 3.32, noted by Lampe, *Paul to Valentinus*, 178.
231 Suetonius *Galb.* 20, noted by Lampe, *Paul to Valentinus*, 178.
232 *CIL* 6 Nr. 11095, noted by Lampe, *Paul to Valentinus*, 178.
233 See Cranfield, 2:795.
234 Peter Lampe, "Patrobas," *ABD* 5 (1992) 186.

very well may have been a slave or freedman who resided in Rome all his life. Whatever his social status or personal history, Paul requests greetings that place him on a level with the most distinguished members of the Roman churches.

"Hermas" is found six times in Roman records, of which three are from the NT period.[235] This particular Hermas is not to be confused with the author of the Shepherd of Hermas from the mid-second-century C.E.[236] The name is Greek, derived from the god Hermes, and probably was borne by eastern immigrants to Rome. One of the three references from the NT period is to a slave,[237] and in view of his association with others from slave background in this list of five congregational leaders, it is best to assume a menial social status for Hermas.[238]

The reference to "the brothers with them" indicate that the five persons named are the leaders of this group. Judging from the background of the names, a Gentile membership and ethos, with a mix of slave, freedmen, and lower-class Greeks, is evident. As Heikki Solin has shown, persons with Greek names in Rome reflect a social background that was almost exclusively slave or former slave.[239] Since all five names are Greek, it is likely that this church consisted entirely of persons with low social status associated with slavery. The fact that Asynkritos is mentioned first may indicate his leading status in the congregation, but there is no indication that he or others of the five played the role of patron. Although there is a consensus among exegetes that this group constitutes a separate congregation, it is inappropriate to refer to them as a "house church."[240] This group is an example of what I have identified as a "tene-ment church," meeting somewhere in one of the multi-storied dwellings where slaves and lower-class handworkers and laborers lived in rented spaces in the upper floors.[241] Having no patron to provide space and food, their common life around the love feast would have been an example of "agapaic communalism," in which the members shared their space and provisions with one another. The selection of the epithet "brothers" for this group may indicate an egalitarian ethos.[242]

■ 15 The congregation greeted in this verse is identified with the sobriquet "the saints," indicating a possible affinity with the moral legacy of conservative Jewish Christianity. Although all Christians can be called "saints,"[243] Paul referred to the Jewish Christians in Judea as "the saints" in Rom 15:25; 1 Cor 16:1; 2 Cor 8:4; 9:12.[244] There are no indications of Jewish background, however, in the names of the leaders of this group.

"Philologos," a Greek name, is found twenty-three times in Roman materials, of which eighteen references are from the NT period. Half of the references are explicitly to slaves or freedmen. Several persons with this name are mentioned as lower officials in the Roman bureaucracy.[245] There is a Philologos who is a freedman of the emperor Claudius (*CIL* 6 Nr. 8601) and a Philologos who functioned as an *aeditus*, a low-level temple official (*CIL* 6 Nr. 2215). Since this name "carried connotations of a slave name in Rome,"[246] it is likely that he was a slave or freedman who had originated outside of Rome.

"Julia" is the most frequently used of any of the names in Rom 16, being found more than 1,400 times in Roman records, mostly for persons of unfree back-

235 Peter Lampe, "Hermas," *ABD* 3 (1992) 147–48; *Paul to Valentinus*, 180.
236 See Godet, 493; Fitzmyer, 742; Graydon F. Snyder, "Hermas the Shepherd," *ABD* 3 (1992) 148–49.
237 *CIL* 15 Nr. 6476, noted by Lampe, *Paul to Valentinus*, 180; another slave with this name mentioned in *CIL* 6 Nr. 8121 is listed by Michel, 478.
238 Michel, 478; Dunn, 2:898.
239 Solin, *Beiträge*, 135–38.
240 For example, Fitzmyer, 742; Moo, 926.
241 Jewett, "Tenement Churches," 23–43.
242 For the egalitarian implications of "brothers," see Johannes Beutler, "ἀδελφός," *EDNT* 1 (1990) 28–30; Meeks, *Urban Christians*, 165–68; Schüssler

Fiorenza, *Memory*, 160–98; Aasgaard, *Siblingship in Paul*, 306–12. Ebel, *Attraktivität*, 211–13, has demonstrated the uniqueness of this early Christian view of community when compared with membership in other associations.
243 See Horst Balz, "ἅγιος," *EDNT* 1 (1990) 17.
244 See the discussion of 15:25 above and esp. Lietzmann, 121–23; Keck, "Saints in Jewish Christianity and Qumran," 54–78.
245 Lampe, *Paul to Valentinus*, 178–79.
246 Ibid., 179.

ground.[247] The name was often given to slaves and other members of the Julian households who usually received Roman citizenship.[248] It is a Latin rather than a Greek name,[249] but of course could be given to a noble member of the Julian house or to a Greek or Jewish slave belonging to a Julian family.[250] If she were part of the nobility, it seems incredible that she is not listed as the patron of the church, rather than, as in v. 14, part of a group of five leaders. She is likely a slave or freedwoman. The fact that Julia is connected with Philologos with καί ("and") probably indicates that they were a married couple, or possibly brother and sister.[251] The facts that the five names in the previous verse were listed without the connective, that the male name is ordinarily listed before the name of his wife, and that the following reference to Nereus's sister would seem strange if Julia were also a sister of Philologos lead me to conclude that she was probably married to Philologos.[252]

"Nereus" was a name typically given to slaves, named after the god of the ocean, and carried by thirty-six persons in Roman materials, of which twenty-eight are of the NT period. A majority of those so named are clearly identified as slaves or freedmen.[253] It is a Greek name, which ordinarily indicates an origin outside of Rome. Examples of persons with this name include a slave of Tiberius (*CIL* 6 Nr. 5248), imperial slaves (*CIL* 6 Nr. 8117–19), and a bodyguard among the slaves of Claudius (*CIL* 6 Nr. 4344).[254]

The sister of Nereus is not known by Paul and his associates, but she is reputed to have played a leading role in the church, so Paul mentions her. He has evidently not heard her name mentioned, except that she is Nereus's sister. That she and Nereus are the children of Philologos and Julia has frequently been suggested,[255] but there is no indication in the text that this is the case.

It is noteworthy, however, that she and Julia comprise two-fifths of the leadership of this congregation, which in all probability should be classified as a "tenement church," because of the lack of a single patron.

"Olympas" is found only twice in Roman records, of which no examples are from the NT period. This masculine name is a short form of a name like Olympiodorus, Olympianus, and so on.[256] The origin of the word and the menial status of associated names in the empire point to the likelihood of unfree background.[257] An example of an Olympas in the status of an imperial freedman is found in *CIL* 6 Nr. 536.[258] Like the other Greek names we have discussed, Olympas points to an origin outside of Rome; he was a slave or freedman originating somewhere in the eastern part of the empire, but now resident in Rome. As in the case of the other four names in this group, it is clear that Paul has not met Olympas, but has heard of his leadership from other Roman exiles that Paul had met between 49 and 54 C.E.

This congregation, like that mentioned in the preceding verse, fits the profile of a tenement church. Instead of a patron there is collective leadership by five persons. This group probably meets for its love feasts somewhere in an insula building where the majority of Rome's underclass lived. In lieu of a patron who could provide the means for the common meal, this group, like many others in the early church, would have to rely on "agapaic communalism" by pooling resources from the earnings of the members.[259] Although its structure and ethos were very different from a standard house church such as that led by Prisca and Aquila, Paul asks for them to be greeted and welcomed as equals.

■ **16a** Although treated routinely by many commentators as a typical closing formula in early Christian letters (1 Cor 16:20; 2 Cor 13:12; 1 Thess 5:26; 1 Pet 5:13),[260]

247 Ibid., 169, 175.
248 Peter Lampe, "Julia," *ABD* 3 (1992) 1125.
249 See Judge, *Rank and Status*, 36.
250 Leon, *Jews*, 98, lists three persons with the name of Julian buried in Jewish catacombs.
251 Lightfoot, "Caesar's Household," 177.
252 See Godet, 493: "Julia is undoubtedly the wife of Philologus"; Meyer, 2:376; Sanday and Headlam, 427; Weiss, 602; Cranfield, 2:795; Dunn, 2:898; Peter Lampe, "Julia," *ABD* 3 (1992) 1125, says the indication of marriage is "only a possibility," but I believe this reflects an unwarranted skepticism.
253 Lampe, *Paul to Valentinus*, 174.
254 Examples drawn from ibid.
255 Cranfield, 2:795; Fitzmyer, 742; Moo, 926. Dunn, 2:898, is correct in saying that this is nothing more than "a possibility."
256 Peter Lampe, "Olympas," *ABD* 5 (1992) 15.
257 Lampe, *Paul to Valentinus*, 179.
258 See Michel, 478.
259 See Jewett, "Tenement Churches," 43–58.
260 For example, see the brief references in Ziesler, 353; Zeller, 248; Fitzmyer, 742.

the climactic location of the command to share a φίλημα ἅγιον ("holy kiss") at the end of the extensive list of requested greetings functions as an expression of familial intimacy between members of disparate house and tenement churches.[261] The evidence from the Jewish as well as the Greco-Roman environments indicates that "Kisses are for relatives," while other contexts, including the erotic, are secondary.[262] Returning family members are greeted "by kisses and streaming tears" (διὰ φιλημάτων ἰὼν δάκρυά τε, Euripides *Andr.* 416–17). Friends are described as "greeting one another with kisses" (φιλήμασιν ἠσπάζοντο ἀλλήλους, Pseudo Lucian *Asin.* 17). This is also the Jewish custom,[263] as evident in the request of Isaac to his son Jacob in Gen 27:26, "Draw nigh to me and kiss me, son." When guests are kissed, it marks them as members of the extended family.[264] Thus Jesus accuses Simon the Pharisee of not extending the normal greeting: "You gave me no kiss" (Luke 7:45). The social occasions of such kissing include "meeting and salutation," "parting, making contracts, reconciliation."[265] Similarly, in Acts 20:37-38 the Ephesian elders "all wept and embraced Paul and kissed him," knowing that "they would see his face no more."

A distinctive feature of early Christianity is the connection between holiness and the kiss of greeting. As William Klassen observes, "nothing analogous to it is to be found among any Greco-Roman societies, nor indeed at Qumran."[266] That such kisses belong to God[267] and thus partake of his ethical holiness[268] needs to be under-stood in the context of the wide circle that was included in early congregations, including members of various families—men, women, children, slaves, and free—who under normal circumstances would not kiss one another. As Klassen observes, "The holy kiss is to be seen in a living context of people who are building a new social reality. . . . The 'holy kiss' is a public declaration of the affirmation of faith: 'In Christ there is neither male nor female, Jew nor Greek, slave nor free' (Gal 3:28)."[269] There was an indisputably promiscuous element in such kissing beyond the circle of one's own family, especially when it included both men and women of various families, which was probably one of the sources of the early pagan accusation that converts were sexually irresponsible.[270] Since the kiss may well have been mouth to mouth, in order to pass the spirit from one to another,[271] the possibility of abuse was obvious. As Stephen Benko concludes, "In the kiss the Spirit was mingled, and the church became in a proleptic way a unity, the living body of Christ."[272] In the post-NT period, when the church was attempting to conform to the society, "the men kissed the men and the women the women,"[273] thus avoiding the appearance of promiscuity. It is therefore likely that the adjective "holy" was attached to this inclusive greeting in response to sexual promiscuity encouraged by such kissing.[274] As Murray observes, "Paul characterizes the kiss as 'holy' and thus distinguishes it from all that is erotic or sensual."[275]

The extensive debate over the liturgical use of the

---

261 See Michel, 478; Gamble, *Textual History*, 78; Weima, *Neglected Endings*, 114.

262 Gustav Stählin, "φιλέω κτλ.," *TDNT* 9 (1974) 119; extensive examples are provided on 119–27. See also W. Kroll, "Kuss," PWSup 5 (1931) 511–20.

263 August Wünsche, *Der Kuss in Bibel, Talmud, und Midrasch* (Breslau: Marcus, 1911) 3–8; Immanuel Löw, "Der Kuss," *MGWJ* 65 (1921) 259–61.

264 For example, Apuleius *Metam.* 4.1.1, "we stopped in a village at the house of some old men. They were friends and acquaintances of the robbers, as even an ass could understand from their initial reception and . . . their mutual kisses (*et oscula mutua*)."

265 Stählin, "φιλέω κτλ.," 121. For example, Pseudo-Lucian *Asin.* 17.

266 William Klassen, "Kiss (NT)," *ABD* 4 (1992) 91.

267 Angela Standhartinger, "Kuss. II," *RGG*[4] 4 (2001) 1907.

268 Stählin, "φιλέω κτλ.," 139.

269 Klassen, "Kiss (NT)," 92.

270 See Benko, *Early Christians*, 84–86, 98.

271 See Nicholas James Perella, *Kiss Sacred and Profane: An Interpretative History of Kiss Symbolism and Related Religio-Erotic Themes* (Berkeley: University of California Press, 1969) 15; Benko, *Early Christians*, 82–83.

272 Benko, *Early Christians*, 86.

273 A. Grieve, "Kiss," *DBH* 3 (1901) 6. Both Hippolytes *Trad. ap.* 2.18 and *Apost. Con.* 2.7.57; 8.2.11 insist on same-sex kissing in the church.

274 Clement of Alexandria *Paed.* 3.12 refers to the "shameless use of a kiss" that gives rise to "foul suspicions and evil reports" about Christian assemblies.

275 Murray, 2:232.

kiss[276] has disguised to a substantial degree the imperatival context of Rom 16:16a. As William Klassen shrewdly asks, if the kiss were simply customary in the early Christian congregations, "why command it?"[277] In view of the condemnation and contempt that were flying between the various Roman congregations, according to Rom 14, this admonition is the climax of Paul's campaign to establish an active form of mutual acceptance. Since the holy kiss was associated with the celebration of the love feast,[278] which probably occurred each time congregations met, the admonition entails the obligation to welcome one another into full fellowship and worship, despite the hindrances of various customs of eating and liturgy. The key to Paul's admonition is therefore ἀλλήλους ("one another"), which extends the greeting beyond the small family circle of the house or tenement churches to the members of other groups. The men and women mentioned as leaders in the earlier verses of chapter 16 are to be kissed as equals, despite the fact that they represented separate branches of the believing community in Rome. It is significant that the other instances of such admonitions in the Pauline letters (1 Cor 16:20; 2 Cor 13:12; 1 Thess 5:26) are in contexts of divided or conflicted congregations, which explains why not every Pauline letter contains this command. The admonition to extend the holy kiss to members of other congregations thus becomes the climactic exhortation of impartial righteousness, embodying "rightwising" by faith that overcomes the barriers of shame and extends honor to all who stand under the lordship of Christ. While in general the kiss remained within one's own family, which meant that it was considered aberrant or promiscuous to extend the kiss beyond the familial boundary, that boundary is now extended to all members of the body of Christ, no matter what their custom, family, or culture may be. This is the climactic point in Paul's peroration, summing up the tolerant implication of the gospel of the inclusive, holy righteousness of God. The holy kiss overcomes shameful discrimination and celebrates the glorious freedom of the children of God.

---

276 Beyond earlier studies that alluded to the liturgical use of the "holy kiss," Karl-Martin Hofmann presented the first book-length argument on the basis of NT usage and extensive parallels that the kiss occurred in the context of worship: *Philema hagion*, BFCTh 38 (Gütersloh: Bertelsmann, 1938) 23–26. He is followed by Benko, *Early Christians*, 79–102, and Perella, *Kiss Sacred and Profane*, 13–18. Klaus Thraede developed an extensive critique of this liturgical explanation in "Ursprünge und Formen des 'Heiligen Kusses' im frühen Christentum," *JAC* 11–12 (1968–69), 124–80, arguing for the primacy of the epistolary context in 132–38.

277 William Klassen, "The Sacred Kiss in the New Testament," *NTS* 39 (1993) 134.

278 Stählin, "φιλέω κτλ.," 138, cited with approval by Haacker, 323. See also Cranfield, 2:795–96. In Justin Martyr *1 Apol.* 65 there is an explicit reference to the holy kiss in the context of the Eucharist.

16

The Fourth Pericope

Greetings and Commendations between Ministerial Leaders

2. Greetings from Congregational Leaders in Corinth and Elsewhere

16b/ **All the churches of Christ greet you [pl.].ᵃ 21/ Timothy, myᵇ co-worker, greetsᶜ you [pl.], also Lucius and Jason and Sosipatros, my compatriots.ᵈ 22/ I, Tertius,ᵉ the one who wrote this letter in [the service of the] Lord, greet you [pl.]. 23/ Gaius, my host and [the host of] the whole church,ᶠ greets you [pl.]. Erastos, the city administrator, greets you [pl.], also his brother Quartus [greets you (pl.)].ᵍ**

a   An abbreviated version of Rom 16:16b (καὶ αἱ ἐκκλησίαι πᾶσαι τοῦ Χριστοῦ ["and all the churches of Christ"]) appears in D* F G ar mon Pel at the end of 16:21, which seems to be a secondary movement to smooth out the ending of the letter after the insertion of the interpolation of 16:17-20.

b   The omission of μου ("my") in B 6 424ᶜ 1739 1881 *pc* appears to be a transcriptional error due to haplography.

c   The third person singular verb ἀσπάζεται ("[he] greets"), convincingly attested by P⁴⁶ ℵ A B C D* F G P Ψ 6 69 81 365 424ᶜ 630 1243 1319 1505 1573

1739 1881 2495 *al* lat syʰ, is replaced in D² L 33 88 104 323 326 330 424* 614 945 1175 1241 1735 1836 1874 2344 2464 *Maj* vgᵐˢ syᵖ with the plural ἀσπάζονται ("they greet"), which corrects the grammatical agreement with the plural subject. Paul apparently dictated "Timothy greets you" and then added "Lucius and Jason," without changing the verb form.

d   As observed above in note a, the final words of Rom 16:16, "and all the churches of Christ," appear at this point in D* F G ar mon Pel, a logical but clearly secondary improvement of the disposition of the greetings. See Cranfield, 2:805.

e   A variant to Τέρτιος ("Tertius") is found in a single manuscript, 7, Τερέντιος ("Terentius"). The overwhelming support for "Tertius" leaves no question about this as the best reading. The minuscule 337 concludes with a reference to Tertius, ἐγράφη διὰ Τερτίου ἐπέμφθη διὰ Φοίβης ("written by Tertius [and] sent by Phoebe"), which reflects an accurate later tradition about the transmission of the letter.

f   In place of the widely attested singular construction, ὅλης τῆς ἐκκλησίας or τῆς ἐκκλησίας ὅλης ("the whole church"), F G ar b vgᶜˡ Pel provide a secondary correction, ὅλαι αἱ ἐκκλησίαι ("all the churches [greet you]"), which in effect moves the greetings from v. 16b to this location.

g   For a discussion of the textual variants, some of which place a version of Rom 16:20b in this location, see Introduction, section 2.

Analysis

The impression of a somewhat random sequence of greetings that marked 16:3-16a is continued here, yet each has a significant bearing on Paul's missionary project.[1] When the rhetorical function of these greetings is understood, it becomes clear that this is by no means a "feeble conclusion" to Paul's magnificent letter.[2] The list begins with an inclusive greeting from all of the churches of Christ followed by individual greetings, producing an effective paronomasia in the fivefold repeti-

tion of the expression ἀσπάζεται ὑμᾶς ("to greet you [pl.]"). Since there are eleven earlier instances of such series in this letter that reflect the Jewish perception of this as a holy number,[3] it can hardly have been accidental and it points again to Paul's desire to find common ground with the Jewish Christian minority in Rome. In the probably original form of the letter, the statement "All the churches of Christ greet you" would have followed immediately after the admonition "Greet one another with a holy kiss," thus continuing the stress on mutual acceptance by all of the believers in Christ.

---

1   Müller, *Schluß*, 220.

2   Käsemann, 420. Although he dislikes Käsemann's formulation, Fitzmyer, 748, also overlooks the rhetorical function of this section by commenting that these greetings "have really nothing to do with the theme or subject of chaps. 1–15." The case

against the Pauline authorship of these verses presented by Lucht, *Untersuchung*, 119–26, is not persuasive.

3   Jewett, "Numerical Sequences," 231–36.

There are two groupings of names within this pericope, each series internally linked with "and," which suggests that they belong in the same categories. In both series, the first person named sends greetings with the third person singular form of ἀσπάζεται, followed by the other names connected with "and" in a way that makes clear that they each also send greetings to all of the believers in Rome, as required by the plural pronoun, ὑμᾶς ("you"). The four persons listed in v. 21, Timothy, Lucius, Jason, and Sosipatros, are in all probability representatives who have gathered in Corinth to deliver the Jerusalem offering. The fact that the last three are identified as Jews conveys support for the cooperation between Jewish Christian and Gentile Christian congregations that Paul had advocated in 14:1—15:13.[4] The final pair of names, Erastos and Quartus, are probably socially prominent brothers, as demonstrated in the exegesis below. All of these names of Pauline colleagues present at the place of writing—Corinth—were associated with his mission in the east and their greetings lend support to the proposed extension of that mission west to Spain.[5]

The placement of greetings from the place of writing after greetings or special messages to individual recipients follows the pattern in 1 Cor 16:15-20 and Phil 4:21-22, whereas in Col 4:10-17 the greetings to recipients and from the place of writing are intermixed. In Phlm 23-24, the greetings from colleagues in the place of writing are at the end of the letter. In Romans, this final list of greetings provides a powerful rhetorical endorsement of Paul's project of completing the circle of the known world by the mission to Spain and thus constitutes a suitable conclusion to the *peroratio*.[6]

Rhetorical Disposition

15:14—16:24   V. The *peroratio*
16:3-16, 21-23   D. Greetings and commendations between ministerial leaders

16:16b, 21-23   Greetings from congregational leaders in Corinth and elsewhere
16:16b   a. Comprehensive greetings from "all the churches of Christ"
16:21a   b. Timothy
         1) The formula of greeting
         2) Relation to Paul: "my . . ."
         3) Official status: "fellow worker"
16:21b   c. Lucius, Jason, Sosipatros
         1) The formula of greeting
         2) Relation to Paul: fellow Jews
16:22   d. Tertius
         1) Scribal formula of greeting
         2) Relation to Paul: amanuensis
         3) Status: "in the Lord"
16:23a   e. Gaius
         1) The formula of greeting
         2) Significant role and relation to Paul: "host" to Paul and "whole church"
16:23b   f. Erastus
         1) The formula of greeting
         2) Civil status: "city administrator"
16:23c   g. Quartus
         1) [The formula of greeting]
         2) Relationship to the preceding name: "brother"

Exegesis

■ **16b** The extension of greetings from "all of the churches of Christ" at the end of a letter is unique in both form and extension.[7] Since his usual reference to the ἐκκλησία θεοῦ ("church of God"; 1 Cor 1:2; 10:32; 11:22; 15:9; 2 Cor 1:1; Gal 1:13; 1 Thess 2:14; 2 Thess 1:4) or to the ἐκκλησία ἐν θεῷ ("church in God"; 1 Thess 1:1; 2 Thess 1:1) could have been misunderstood as a reference to Jewish assemblies,[8] here he makes clear that Christian congregations are extending the greetings to their believing brothers and sisters in Rome.[9] That "all" of the churches send greetings was not a euphemism because it reflects the situation of the initial rendezvous in Corinth with representatives of churches

---

4   Müller, *Schluß*, 20; also Schnider and Stenger, *Briefformular*, 128.
5   Müller, *Schluß*, 220.
6   See Schnider and Stenger, *Briefformular*, 128.
7   See Cranfield, 2:796; Dunn, 2:899.
8   Karl Ludwig Schmidt, "καλέω κτλ.," *TDNT* 3 (1965) 527, observes that of the one hundred occur-

rences of ἐκκλησία in the LXX, there are references to the "congregation of the Lord" in Deut 23:2ff.; 1 Chr 28:8; Neh 13:1; Mic 2:5 and that in many other instances "the addition τοῦ θεοῦ ('of God') is either explicit or implicit." The Hebrew equivalent, "God's assembly," was used in Qumran (1QM 4:10; see also 1QSa 1:25, "the congrega-

participating in the Jerusalem offering, which occurred at approximately the time of writing Romans (Acts 20:3-4).[10] As I shall show from the analysis of the names listed in 16:21-23, some of them were likely representatives of churches outside of Corinth. In addition to these representatives who happened to be at hand when the letter was completed, the expression "all the churches of Christ" implies that Paul had discussed with his other churches the plan to travel to Rome to organize support for the Spanish mission. Their greeting lends weight to Paul's venture.[11] As Weima shows, in this inclusive greeting, "Paul presents himself to the Romans as one who has the official backing of all of the churches in Achaia, Macedonia, Asia, Galatia, Syria and elsewhere in the eastern part of the empire."[12]

■ **21** Following the collective greetings from churches, Paul turns to the colleagues closest at hand and extends their personal greetings to the Roman congregations. First and foremost, he mentions Timothy as ὁ συνεργὸς μου, which means "my co-worker."[13] This introductory epithet suggests that Paul feels Timothy may be unknown to the Roman congregations.[14] Timothy is introduced in Acts 16:1-2 as the son of a Jewish mother and a Greek father in Lystra who subsequently accompanied Paul on his missionary journeys and frequently served as an emissary. He is named as coauthor in 1 Thess 1:1; 2 Thess 1:1; 2 Cor 1:1; Phil 1:1; Col 1:1; Phlm 1) and travels back and forth between Corinth, Thessalonica, Troas, and Ephesus.[15] He was among Paul's most trusted coworkers. According to Acts 20:4,

Timothy had returned to Corinth along with other church representatives gathering on the occasion of delivering the Jerusalem offering, which explains why he was present at the end of the process but not mentioned at the beginning of the letter as a coauthor.[16]

The three persons mentioned at the end of v. 21 also send greetings, which justifies the translation of the first καί ("and") in front of Lucius's name with "also." Along with Timothy, they also send greetings to the Roman congregations. Lucius is a Latin name,[17] but as Paul's "compatriot" he must have been a convert of Jewish origin. Although Lucius has been identified as Lucius of Cyrene who was active in the Antioch church (Acts 13:1), this seems unlikely because such a distinguished leader would have deserved a fuller commendation.[18] That he was the Luke mentioned in Phlm 24 and Col 4:14 as a companion of Paul, and possibly the author of Luke's gospel, is unlikely because the name is spelled here with Λούκιος ("Lucius") and in those letters and elsewhere as Λούκας ("Lucas").[19] While it is possible that he was a leader in the Corinthian church despite his not having been mentioned in the Corinthian correspondence itself, his mention in a series of four names of which two are definitely delegates for the Jerusalem offering makes it more likely that he was a representative of one of the other Pauline churches.[20]

Jason is quite likely the person who hosted Paul in Thessalonia (Acts 17:7) and posted a bond to release him from detention there (Acts 17:9).[21] In support of this identification are the Jewish identity of this particu-

tion"). I have not found examples of synagogues referred to as ἐκκλησίαι.

9   See Dunn, 2:899.

10 See Dodd, 240; Morris, 538; Haacker, 323. For a reconstruction of the circumstances, see Ollrog, *Mitarbeiter*, 58, and Georgi, *Remembering the Poor*, 111, 122–23.

11 Zeller, 248.

12 Weima, *Neglected Endings*, 277; see also Schnider and Stenger, *Briefformular*, 127.

13 Schille, *Kollegialmission*, 49; John Gillman, "Timothy," *ABD* 6 (1992) 559. Käsemann, 420, refers to this expression as a "matchless claim." See also Ollrog, *Mitarbeiter*, 20–23.

14 Schmidt, 259.

15 See the detailed reconstruction of Timothy's travels in Gillman, "Timothy," 558–59.

16 See Dunn, 2:909.

17 See BDF §41.1 BAGD (2000) 603.

18 Dunn, 2:909.

19 Fitzmyer, 748, followed by John Gillman, "Lucius," *ABD* 4 (1992) 397, who further notes that the Luke associated with Paul's travels was a Gentile, whereas this Lucius is identified as a Jewish Christian.

20 See Godet, 500–501; Ollrog, *Mitarbeiter*, 58; Wilckens, 3:146; Moo, 934.

21 See Florence Morgan Gillman, "Jason," *ABD* 3 (1992) 649; commentators supporting the possibility of this identification include Dodd, 244; Cranfield, 2:805; Fitzmyer, 749; Haacker, 329.

lar Jason and the listing of Jason's name next to the name of Sosipatros, who is identified in Acts 20:4 as representing the neighboring church at Beroea in traveling with Paul to deliver the Jerusalem offering. That the Macedonian churches of Thessalonica and Beroea participated in the Jerusalem offering is clear from 2 Cor 8:1, and that their representatives would have brought their contribution to the rendezvous is highly likely,[22] thus confirming the probable link between Jason and Thessalonica.

Sosipatros is the longer form of the name Sopater, a Greek name with the meaning "of sound parentage."[23] He is probably the "Sopater the son of Pyrrhus" mentioned in Acts 20:4 as the delegate bringing the Jerusalem offering from Beroea.[24] As in the case of the other two names listed in 16:21, there is nothing to link him with Corinth. In all probability he had arrived along with Jason as representatives of the Macedonian churches with the contributions for Jerusalem. All three are identified as Paul's συγγενεῖς, which has the connotation of fellow Jews, as in the cases of 9:3; 16:7 and 11. That they were relatives of Paul, as occasionally suggested by commentators because συγγενής allows that connotation,[25] is as unlikely here as for the three persons so identified in the list of greetings to Roman leaders.[26] The word συγγενής appears here with the same sense of 9:3 as "fellow Jews." Although there is some discussion about whether all three names or only the last two are included with this designation,[27] commentators

have not explained why Paul should have included this detail, now for the third time in chapter 16. I believe it is part of his campaign to grant equal honor to the Jewish Christian minority in Rome. By explicitly identifying these persons as his fellow Jews, he makes plain that although he identified himself with the "strong" Gentile majority in Rome, he maintains respectful, collegial relationships with Jewish Christian leaders. Moreover, these Jewish Christian leaders had been entrusted with the Jerusalem offering donated by churches with Gentile majorities, which means that their greetings to all of the congregations in Rome embodies the mutuality that derives from their common life in Christ (Rom 15:26-27).[28] Greetings from and to such leaders solidify Paul's effort to provide a basis for mutuality across ethnic lines, which was a crucial requirement for the mission project to the "barbarians" in Spain.

■ **22** There follows a direct greeting to the believers in Rome from Tertius, the amanuensis who wrote Paul's letter. The name is Latin meaning "third," and was often used as a name for slaves.[29] In this instance the name belongs to a Christian, judging from his greeting "in the Lord." The phrase ἐν κυρίῳ ("in [the] Lord") appears at the end of v. 22 and could be attached to the verb "I greet"[30] or to the adjacent participial phrase "who wrote."[31] Heinrich Schlier posed the decisive objection to the widely accepted view of "greeting in the Lord" that he himself adopted: "But all greetings to the con-

22 See Georgi, *Remembering the Poor*, 122–23; Betz, *2 Corinthians 8 and 9*, 72–79.

23 Joe E. Lunceford, "Sopater," *EDB* (2000) 1244.

24 Lietzmann, 128; Dodd, 244; Cranfield, 2:806; Dunn, 2:909; Haacker, 329; Moo, 934; Byrne, 460; Florence Morgan Gillman, "Sosipater," *ABD* 6 (1992) 160.

25 Meyer, 2:81–82; Murray, 2:238; Ceslas Spicq, "συγγένεια," *TLNT* 3 (1994) 306; Clarke, "Romans 16," 112. BAGD (2000) 950 lists "belonging to the same extended family or clan . . . akin to" as a possible translation of συγγενής, but places the references in Rom 16:7, 11, 21 under the category of "compatriot."

26 See Godet, 501; Sanday-Headlam, 432; Michaelis, "συγγενής, συγγένεια," 741: "the narrower sense of relatives may be ruled out, since it is most improbable that there would have been six mem-

bers of Paul's immediate family among those mentioned in R. 16."

27 Cranfield, 2:805.

28 See Müller, *Schluß*, 220.

29 Michel, 483.

30 Meyer, 2:383; Weiss, 606, citing the precedent of 1 Cor 16:19, "hearty greetings in the Lord." This is adopted by most modern commentators: Schmidt, 260; Dodd, 243; Schlier, 450; Murray, 2:288; Cranfield, 2:806; Dunn, 2:910; Byrne, 460; Schreiner, 807.

31 Morris, 543; Stuhlmacher, 254; Wilckens, 3:145; Fitzmyer, 749, observes that Origen understood ἐν κυρίῳ ("in Lord") as attached to the service of writing, commenting that Tertius writes for the glory of God (Origen, *PG* 14.1289).

gregation proceed ἐν κυρίῳ."[32] In view of the routine ritual of greeting fellow believers at the beginning of love feasts, it would have been redundant to speak of "greeting in the Lord," an expression that, moreover, is unparalleled in Pauline or early Christian usage. The more appropriate translation concerning "writing in the Lord" also follows the more natural syntax of word order in that the prepositional phrase follows immediately after the participial expression, "the one who wrote this letter." In view of this probability, ἐν κυρίῳ could refer either to the slave's master[33] or to Christ.[34] The latter is more likely,[35] and this provides an answer to a puzzling feature of this greeting. In Käsemann's words, "Oddly the secretary, too, sends greetings to the church,"[36] which makes sense to Käsemann only if Tertius were known to the recipients.[37] While travel back and forth between Corinth and Rome seems improbable for a slave, it would fit perfectly with the hypothesis developed above concerning Phoebe's patronage of the Roman journey and the Spanish mission project. While it is clear from 16:23 that Paul is currently lodging with Gaius in Corinth rather than with Phoebe in Cenchraea, I suggest that part of her patronage consisted in placing her highly skilled scribe, Tertius, at Paul's disposal for the long period required for planning, refining, and drafting this letter. As a person of patronage status whose likely business in Cenchraea was in shipping, she

had in all likelihood traveled with her staff back and forth to Rome, where Tertius could have easily become acquainted with fellow believers. As Richards suggests, he may actually have originated in Rome, where secretaries using shorthand were frequently trained and available.[38] The identification of this particular amanuensis was therefore an integral part of the strategy of this letter, because Tertius was to accompany his owner Phoebe to Rome, where a skilled reading was required for each of the house and tenement churches. As the amanuensis of this letter, he was in the best position to present this complicated text orally, taking advantage of each stylistic nuance.[39] The writing of this letter ἐν κυρίῳ thus not only reveals that Tertius understood his work "as a piece of service to his Lord,"[40] but it also introduces him as the appropriately informed, Christian scribe who could present Paul's message to the Roman congregations in a credible manner.[41]

Amanuenses were often slaves, as, for example, in a legal agreement between heirs in Egypt concerning the distribution of slaves belonging to the deceased Tiberius Julius Theon; the document mentions two amanuenses (προχειροφόροι) and five shorthand writers (νωτάριοι), which leads G. H. R. Horsley to pose the question whether Tertius was a slave.[42] If he was part of Phoebe's staff, a status of slave or freedman is likely. Whatever his social status, Tertius speaks here with a

---

32 Schlier, 451.
33 Gordon J. Bahr, "Paul and Letter Writing in the First Century," *CBQ* 28 (1966) 465, assuming that the "lord" in this instance was Paul. See also Chris Ukachukwu Manus, "'Amanuensis Hypothesis': A Key to the Understanding of Paul's Epistles in the New Testament," *BBH* 10 (1984) 169.
34 Morris, 543; Longenecker, "Ancient Amanuenses," 289; Richards, *Secretary*, 172, with a detailed critique of Bahr's interpretation.
35 Longenecker, "Ancient Amanuenses," 297, suggests that the expression ἐν κυρίῳ had "become through Paul's influence" a kind of early Christian jargon that was sometimes used "somewhat ambiguously."
36 Käsemann, 420, referring to Windisch, "ἀσπάζομαι κτλ.," 501.
37 At this point Käsemann, 421, relies on Zahn, 613; Schumacher, *Letzten Kapitel*, 102. That Tertius was known in Rome is accepted by Cranfield, 2:806; Schreiner, 808; Richards, *Secretary*, 170.
38 Richards, *Secretary*, 171; see 26-43 for the evidence

of Latin and Greek systems of shorthand by the time of the first century C.E.
39 Richards, *Secretary*, 171, observes that Romans "contains the strongest oral features" of any Pauline letter, a judgment that the commentary above documents in great detail.
40 Morris, 543.
41 This reconstruction confirms the suggestion by Schille, *Kollegialmission*, 49, that Tertius was a missionary coworker who participated actively in the creation of the letter.
42 G. H. R. Horsley, "The Distribution of a Deceased Man's Slaves," *NDIEC* 1 (1981) 69–70, discussing *P.Oxy.* Nr. 3179, dated 111 C.E. Solin, *Sklavennamen*, 152–53, lists many examples of Tertius as a slave name.

self-assurance that is unusual for amanuenses, who, when revealing their identity, usually provided a reason for their secretarial work by employing formulas concerning disability or illiteracy.[43] For instance, a letter from Thebes concludes with the words, "Written for him by Eumelus the son of Herma . . . being desired to do so because he writes somewhat slowly," and in other instances the formula "written for him because he is illiterate" appears.[44] No such explanation appears here or anywhere else in Paul's letters. The fact that Tertius's comment is inserted into the letter itself rather than being attached as an independent note at the end reveals that he does so with Paul's approval and that he enjoys Paul's trust.[45] Whether he was an independent secretary or a slave, the self-introduction of Tertius reveals the remarkable equality "in Christ" that was characteristic for the first generation of Pauline Christianity. Along with many other persons in chapter 16 who have served as Paul's partners, including some of the patron class, Tertius is honored by the apostle, who allows him to speak on his own behalf.

■ **23** The Gaius who sends greetings to all of the believers in Rome is probably Gaius Titius Justus,[46] who is mentioned in Acts 18:7 and 1 Cor 1:14 as a leader in the Corinthian movement of believers and one baptized by Paul. According to Acts, his house was located next to the synagogue. His Latin name suggests connection with the prestigious Titian family mentioned by Horace and Cicero,[47] whether as a person of noble rank or a freedman previously in their service and probably now enjoy-

ing Roman citizenship. It is unlikely that this Gaius should be identified as the Macedonian who traveled with Paul (Acts 19:29), the Gaius who represents the congregation in Derbe in delivering the Jerusalem offering (Acts 20:4), or the "beloved Gaius" who receives the later letter from John the Elder (3 John 1).[48]

Paul refers to the Gaius of Corinth as his host and the host of the whole church, by which the Greek term ξένος carries the connotation of the person granting hospitality[49] rather than of "stranger."[50] Gaius is prosperous enough to own a house and to provide hospitality for traveling Christians, which leads John Gillman to conclude that he "belonged to the class of Roman freedman who had come to Corinth and had apparently prospered economically."[51] While there is no doubt that Paul is currently lodging with Gaius, the reference to his being host to ὅλης τῆς ἐκκλησίας ("the whole church") has elicited considerable discussion. That this means the entire membership of the church in the eastern empire would turn this reference into a vast hyperbole that overshadows the patronage of Phoebe and Prisca with Aquila in a shameful manner that is highly unlikely here.[52] That it refers to all of the believers in Corinth[53] is also unlikely because of the presence of other house churches and groupings mentioned in the Corinthian correspondence that are too numerous to be accommodated in a single house,[54] and also because the Corinthians would hardly qualify as strangers needing hospitality.[55] The more likely interpretation is that Gaius had the reputation of extending hospitality to Christian

43   Richards, *Secretary*, 73–76.
44   Cited by Richards, *Secretary*, 74.
45   Ibid., 170.
46   For an analysis of the triple name and the identification with the Gaius in Rom 16:23, see Edgar J. Goodspeed, "Gaius Titius Justus," *JBL* 69 (1950) 382; John Gillman, "Gaius," *ABD* 2 (1992) 869.
47   Cranfield, 2:807, observes that "since 'Titius' is a Roman nomen . . . the person is likely to have had also a praenomen, which might easily have been Gaius." See *PW* VI.8.2.1531–35 for an account of members of this family.
48   See Gillman, "Gaius," 869.
49   Gustav Stählin, "ξένος κτλ.," *TDNT* 5 (1967) 20.
50   See BAGD (2000) 684.
51   Gillman, "Gaius," 869.
52   Dunn, 2:910.

53   Jülicher, 333; Althaus, 137; Dunn, 2:911; Haacker, 329; Schreiner, 808.
54   I count between six and ten groups of believers in Corinth that are reflected in NT evidence: Crispus's house (Acts 18:8); Stephanus's house (1 Cor 1:16; 16:15-18); the house of "Chloe's people" (1 Cor 1:11); Phoebe's church in neighboring Cenchraea (Rom 16:1-2); the house of Erastus (Rom 16:23); the members of Prisca and Aquila's church that remained in Corinth after their departure; those who say "I belong to Paul" (1 Cor 1:12); those who say "I belong to Apollos" (1 Cor 1:12); those who say "I belong to Cephas" (1 Cor 1:12); and those who say "I belong to Christ" (1 Cor 1:12). See Alfred Schreiber, *Die Gemeinde in Korinth. Versuch einer gruppendynamischen Betrachtung der Entwicklung der Gemeinde von Korinth auf der Basis des ersten*

travelers from all over the world, an inference supported by most commentaries.[56] Two factors render this description of Gaius's hospitality plausible for the audience: the presence of delegates of the Jerusalem offering in his house at the time of writing Romans, as represented by the aforementioned Lucius, Jason, and Sosipatros; and the likelihood that some of the Roman refugees between 49 and 54, as well as later travelers from Rome, had found shelter for a time in his house. Since this hospitality was extended to Jewish Christians and Gentile Christians alike, the greeting from this distinguished and generous convert lends additional weight to Paul's project. There is an "ecumenical" scope in Gaius's hospitality[57] that was consonant with the theology and ethic of this letter, so that his greeting provides an endorsement thereof.

Among the eight names of colleagues present at the time of finishing this letter, Erastus has evoked the most debate. There is no doubt that this is a Latin name that correlates with a civic office that Erastus holds in Corinth, because after the refounding of Corinth as a Roman colony in 44 B.C.E., it was dominated by Roman freedmen. The name does not appear frequently, but there are examples from Corinth and Athens of public officers with this name in the second century B.C.E.[58] Although much of the populace continued to speak Greek, the official language in Corinth was Latin, which

is reflected in the public inscriptions of this period.[59] The debate centers on two matters: the Latin equivalent of Paul's description of Erastus's office, ὁ οἰκονόμος τῆς πόλεως ("the city administrator/treasurer"), and the correlation with the discovery of an inscription with the name Erastus linked with an office that might be the Latin form of this expression. There are many references to οἰκονόμοι who play the role of stewards or estate managers in Greco-Roman inscriptions and papyri, including "an honorific decree in which the oikonomos Phanodikos is assigned the task of seeing to the erection" of a public stele, which indicates he is a civic officer.[60] The analyses of the linguistic question by Henry Cadbury, Gerd Theissen, and others indicate that ὁ οἰκονόμος τῆς πόλεως can refer to the slave or freedman in charge of city works, arcarius rei publicae,[61] but also that it can also refer to a civic office of high status responsible for management of the material resources of a city.[62] Theissen concludes that Paul's expression probably refers to the office of quaestor that was normally held before the appointment as aedilis,[63] but the authoritative study by Hugh Mason lists aedelis coloniae as one of the standard equivalents of οἰκονόμος τῆς πόλεως.[64] In either case, the career of a civic administrator in a Roman city would require some form of philanthropy given to a city in return for the honor of an office.

The Corinthian inscription mentioning an Erastus

Korintherbriefes, NTAbh 12 (Münster: Aschendorff, 1977) 130–34. That all of these converts could have been accommodated in Gaius's house with a potential capacity of "about 40" (Murphy-O'Connor, St. Paul's Corinth, 156–61; Dunn, 2:911) is implausible, as seen by Kühl, 485, and Michel, 483.

55 Godet, 501.

56 Zahl, 614; Godet, 501; Lietzmanm, 128; Lagrange, 376–77; Schmidt, 260; Schlier, 451; Käsemann, 421; Michel, 483; Wilckens, 3:146; Stuhlmacher, 255; Moo, 935.

57 Wilckens, 3:146.

58 See Andrew D. Clarke, "Another Corinthian Erastus Inscription," TynB 42 (1991) 1:49–50; the second-century C.E. inscription (SEG 29 [1979] 301) referring to the Vitellii brothers, "[Fro]ntinus [and E]rastus," is shown by Clarke (146–48, 151) to be unconnected with Rom 16:23. Solin, Sklavennamen, 456, lists six examples of Erastius as a slave name in Rome, including four from the first century, which supports the impression that Erastus was a freedman.

59 See Jerome Murphy-O'Connor, "Corinth," ADB 1 (1992) 1138–39; Richard A. Horsley, 1 Corinthians (Nashville: Abingdon Press, 1998) 22–25.

60 G. H. R. Horsley, "οἰκονόμος," NDIEC 4 (1987) 161, discussing I.Lamp. 33.29.

61 Henry J. Cadbury, "Erastus of Corinth," JBL 50 (1931) 51–52, citing examples from other cities (CIL 9, p. 787; 10, p. 1155) but none from Corinth. The alternative of slave status is difficult to correlate with the honorific status suggested by Paul's formulation, at the point of emphasis at the end of the series of greetings; see Theissen, Social Setting, 76.

62 Theissen, Social Setting, 76–83, cites a series of inscriptions from western Asia Minor drawn from the study by P. Landvogt, "Epigraphische Untersuchungen über den οἰκονόμος. Ein Beitrag zum hellenistischen Beamtenwesen" (dissertation, University of Strasbourg, 1908).

63 Theissen, Social Setting, 82–83.

64 Mason, Greek Terms, 71, refers to the inscription

was discovered by the archeologist J. H. Kent and his colleagues in 1929.[65] A paving block reused at the level of the theater in the mid-second century had an inscription that made it clear that Erastus paid for the original paving of a street in return for the office of *aedile*. The wording of this famous inscription was reconstructed by Kent as follows, with the missing portions marked with [−] where the inscription is broken, indicating space for the first two names of Erastus: [−] *Erastus pro aedilit[at]e s(ua) p(ecunia) stravit*. Since the initials s. p. refer to "his own expense," the translation is "[−] Erastus, in return for the aedileship, laid the pavement at his own expense."[66] Since the reuse of this stone must have occurred after the death of Erastus, Kent and others placed the original paving in the middle of the first century, which would correlate closely with the reference to the Erastus in Romans. Although the dating remains controversial,[67] this assessment fits reasonably well with the archeological record of the reconstruction of Corinth after its establishment as a Roman colony in the first century B.C.E. The facts that no other inscriptions or literary references to a Corinthian Erastus in the first century have been found, and that both the inscription and Rom 16:23 refer to his civic office in roughly identical terms, enhance the likelihood that the same person was in view.[68] The office mentioned in the inscription was part of the Roman constitution of Corinth that called for the yearly election of four *duoviri* ("magistrates"), under whose direction there were two *aediles*

who functioned as city business managers.[69] There are other examples that confirm the custom of making a substantial contribution to the city in return for the office of *aedile*.[70]

The evidence thus points to the Christian Erastus of 16:23 as a rich freedman with Roman citizenship who held a responsible office in the city administration. Gerd Theissen points out that this is the only instance in which Paul refers to the worldly office of a church member, which contrasts with other references in chapter 16 to service in the church.[71] He draws an important inference that "an exceptional instance in which the worldly status of one member of the community is mentioned probably indicates status *worth* mentioning, that is, relatively high status."[72] This important insight has been cited with approval,[73] but the rhetorical implications remain to be explained. Why Paul places this reference to Erastus the city administrator at the emphatic conclusion of a carefully constructed series of five greetings must have a significant bearing on the project that the entire letter seeks to advance. My suggestion is that this greeting from a Roman official implies his support for the mission project that Paul wishes to organize from Rome. The introduction above to the situation in Spain offers a possible explanation, namely, that Spain was the most sensitive colony in the empire, not only because of its frequent rebellions but also because its silver mines and other economic resources were under the direct control of the government and were essential for the

found in Corinth, with other examples from Hierapolis, Philadelphia, and Smyrna. On 145, Mason lists οἰκονόμος as a standard equivalent of the Latin office of *aedilis munumcipii*. Andrew D. Clarke, "Another Corinthian Erastus Inscription," *TynB* 42 (1991) 151, concludes that *quaestor* and *aedelis* "*may* have been identical" (italics in original).

65 J. H. Kent, *Corinth 8.3. The Inscriptions 1926–1950* (Princeton: American School of Classical Studies at Athens, 1966) 99–100.

66 See Theissen, *Social Setting*, 80; Murphy-O'Connor, *St. Paul's Corinth*, 37; Fitzmyer, 750.

67 See, for example, the skeptical assessment of Justin J. Meggitt, "The Social Status of Erastus (Rom. 16:23)," *NovT* 38 (1996) 220–21, following Henry J. Cadbury, "Erastus of Corinth," *JBL* 50 (1931) n. 17.

68 See the assessments of Victor P. Furnish, "Corinth in Paul's Time: What Can Archaeology Tell Us?"

BARev 15.3 (1988) 20, and Winter, *Seek the Welfare*, 192.

69 See Murphy-O'Connor, "Corinth," 1137–38, referring to details in Kent, *Corinth 8.3*, 24–27, including the names of sixty-nine such officers found in various Corinthian inscriptions.

70 A. G. Roos, "De titulo quodam latino Corinthi nuper reperto," *Mnemosyne* 58 (1930) 160–65, refers to *aediles* in Venusia and Timgad who contributed the paving of streets in return for the honor of their office (*CIL* 9. Nr. 442; 8. Nr. 17834).

71 Theissen, *Social Setting*, 75–76.

72 Ibid., 76, italics in original.

73 Florence Morgan Gillman, "Erastus," *ABD* 2 (1992) 571.

financial viability of the empire as a whole. A mission to convert the barbarians in Spain to a religion whose subversive qualities had already come to the attention of imperial authorities might endanger the congregations in Rome. There was no more effective way to allay such concerns than by sending greetings from Erastus, a Roman official in Corinth.[74] It was not merely his eminent social status but, more important, his public office held despite his Christian identity that carried the rhetorical force in this situation.

The last person to send greetings to the believers in Rome has in some ways been the most puzzling. Quartus is a Latin name meaning "Fourth," which was common among slaves and freedmen,[75] but the identification of him as "the brother" is quite peculiar. Why should he be thus singled out when all other male believers were routinely called "brothers"?[76] And why is the series of greetings concluded on such a note, in which a singular verb of greeting is attached to Erastus, and Quartus's name follows as if an afterthought? The same expression appears in 1 Cor 1:1, where Σωσθένης ὁ ἀδελφός, usually translated "Sosthenes our brother," appears as the coauthor of the letter. The article appears in the genitive in 1 Cor 16:12, employed to raise the topic of Ἀπολλῶ τοῦ ἀδελφοῦ, whereby the article is routinely translated as "Apollos our brother." If these precedents are followed, the most likely translation would be "Quartus our brother," as in the reference to Phoebe as "our sister" in

16:1. The problem is that this translation produces an anticlimactic impression that is hardly improved by the theory that Quartus was known in Rome, because the neutral expression ὁ ἀδελφός would have been perceived as insufficiently honorific when the appropriate formulation would be something like "your beloved brother." If this is merely a reference to "our brother," the peroration would thereby close with a faintly resounding thud that seems totally out of place in the most rhetorically sophisticated and carefully composed letter in the career of one of the greatest letter writers in history.

There are three clues that lead to a potential resolution of this interpretive anomaly. (1) The preceding reference to Erastus was intended to lend maximum public prestige to Paul's project, especially among those circles in Rome that were within the imperial administration, which leads one to expect that the reference to Quartus in the same sentence must also have been honorific in some way. (2) The connection with καί ("and") between two names is ordinarily understood as linking persons who have a relationship with each other, as in "Prisca and Aquila" (16:3), "Andronicas and Junia" (16:7), and "Nereus and his sister" (16:15). (3) The article between "Quartus" and "brother" can readily be translated with the possessive "his,"[77] because the article often functions as a possessive in Greek.[78] For example, Josephus Ant. 2.183 refers to "Judas his brother (Ἰούδας ὁ ἀδελφός),"

74 Schnider and Stenger, Briefformular, 128, point to the influence that the Roman colonists in Corinth would have in Rome, including the possibility that they were known there.

75 Solin, Sklavennamen, 154, lists two examples of Quartus as the name of slaves in Rome.

76 See Bruce, 281; John Gillman, "Quartus," ABD 5 (1992) 583.

77 Lagrange, 377, and Bruce, 281, support the translation of the article with "his," but draw a problematic inference from the meaning of Quartus as "fourth," interpreting the "and" as linking his name with his alleged brother "Tertius," meaning "third." The fact that the names of Gaius and Erastus occur between Tertius and Quartus makes this interpretation of "and" extremely unlikely, as pointed out by Gillman, "Quartus," 583. The objection by Cranfield, 2:808, and Dunn, 2:911, that if Paul intended the meaning "his," he would have used the possessive pronoun αὐτοῦ, overlooks the fact that καί

Κούαρτος ὁ ἀδελφός would readily have been understood as "and his brother Quartus." The objection is valid only if καὶ Κούαρτος ὁ ἀδελφός lacks the semantic possibility of referring to Erastus's brother, which it clearly contains.

78 Smyth, Grammar, §1121, says that the article may take the place of the pronoun, the "weak possessive," "when there is no doubt as to the possessor." He cites Xenophon Anab. 1.8.3, where both ἀπὸ τοῦ ἅρματος ("from his chariot") and τὸν θώρακα ἐνδέδυ ("put on his breastplate") refer to Cyrus. Indeed, as here with Quartus's brother, it seems that common filial terms especially do not require the possessive since the possessor is invariably unmistakable. For example, Dionysius Halicarnassus refers in Antiq. Rom. 73.3 to "his brothers" with πρὸς τοὺς ἀδελφούς and in 1.76.4 to "his elder brother Numitor (τὸν πρεσβύτερον ἀδελφόν Νεμέτορα)"; see also 1.76.4; 1.78.2; Plutarch Cim. 15.3.

and *Ant.* 2.279 speaks of "his brother Aaron (ὁ ἀδελφὸς Ἀαρών)."[79]

The translation "and his brother Quartus [sends greetings]," referring to Quartus as the brother of Erastus, eliminates the impression of an afterthought, because it was natural to mention the office held by Erastus before referring to his sibling. Moreover, this translation satisfies the rhetorical requirement of ending the list of greetings on a positive and honorific note, because if Quartus is Erastus's brother, he shares the same high social status and prestige within the circle of Roman citizens that had colonized Corinth. That both brothers in this Roman family send greetings to the house and tenement churches in Rome, and thereby endorse Paul's project, addresses one of the major barriers that could have been felt to jeopardize the mission that this letter promotes, namely, whether it would threaten the fragile relations between believers and the state, because Spain was so sensitive an area of imperial administration. This tension would have been most acutely felt by the Christian slaves of Narcissus and Aristobulus, if my hypothesis is correct that they were part of the Neronian bureaucracy. The sponsorship by the rich patroness Phoebe at the beginning of chapter 16 and the support of the influential Roman brothers Erastus and Quartus at the end of the chapter are the rhetorical trump cards that finally render Paul's project politically plausible. With this reading, there is nothing lame or awkward about the greeting from the Roman administrator of Corinth and his brother Quartus. For this particular audience in Rome, where public honors were supremely valued, there was no more effective way for Paul to conclude his peroration.

---

79   See also Josephus *Ant.* 7.285.3; 9.27.2; 12.234.3; 14.361; 20.243.

16

The First Interpolation

The Church's Campaign
against Heretics

17/ Now I exhort[a] you, brothers, to look
out[h] for those causing[c] dissensions and
hindrances in opposition to the teaching that you learned, and[d] steer away[e]
from them. 18/ For such persons are
not enslaved to our Lord, Christ, but to
their own belly, and by sweet talk and
fine language[f] they deceive the hearts
of the simple. 19/ For your obedience
has reached to all. Therefore I rejoice[g]
in you, but I want[h] you to be wise[i] in
what is good, but innocent in what is
bad. 20a/ And the God of peace will
speedily crush[j] Satan under your feet.

a   In place of the broadly attested παρακαλῶ ("I
    exhort"), D* latt have ἐρωτῶ ("I ask"), which seems
    unlikely to be original, although as a nonbiblical
    term the latter is clearly the more difficult reading.
    Παρακαλῶ is not the sort of reading that one
    would expect to be replaced because of its typicality
    in Pauline materials.

b   The "Western" group of texts, which appears to
    have a particular interest in this pericope, offers a
    variant that strengthens the severity of the warning:
    ἀσφαλῶς σκοπεῖτε ("firmly mark") in D F G (ar)
    mon Spec. The simpler text without ἀσφαλῶς, and
    with the infinitive, is to be preferred.

c   As a modification and strengthening of the partici-
    ple ποιοῦντας ("doing/causing") convincingly
    attested in ℵ A B C L P Ψ 6 33 69 88 104 323 326
    330 365 424 614 945 1175 1241 1243 1319 1505
    1573 1735 1739 1836 1874 1881 2344 2464 2495
    Maj lat sy cop Ambst, the "Western" text as repre-
    sented by D F G (ar) mon Spec adds λέγοντας ἤ
    ("saying or [making]") and P46 goes one step further
    to add ἤ λέγοντας ἤ ("either saying or [making]").
    For a discussion of the illogic of these variants, see
    Cranfield, 2:797.

d   The omission of καί in P46 1175 1836 1874 pc Spec
    appears to be an effort to smooth out the rhetoric
    of this verse.

e   In place of ἐκκλίνετε ("keep withdrawing/steer
    clear!") in ℵ* B C Ψ 6 69 424c 630 1505 1739 1881
    2464 2495 pc, a present imperative, P46 ℵ2 A D F G
    L P 33 88 104 323 326 330 365 424* 614 945 1175
    1241 1243 1319 1573 1735 1836 1874 2344 Maj
    have ἐκκλίνατε ("withdraw/steer clear once and
    for all!"), an aorist imperative. Given the involve-
    ment of the "Western" tradition in earlier alter-
    ations in these verses, and the weightier support for
    ἐκκλίνετε, a case can be made that the latter is

more likely original. See the extensive discussion in
Cranfield, 2:798–99. It is possible that ἐκκλίνατε
arose from a false anticipation of the subsequent
alpha of the adjacent ἀπό.

f   In place of the widely attested καὶ εὐλογίας ("and
    well-chosen words, praise"), 460 618 1738 have
    εὐγλωττίας ("and glibness"), while the "Western"
    texts D F G 33 81 1319 pc mon lack the entire
    phrase, which is unusual because "Western" texts
    are usually expansions and paraphrases. J. Lionel
    North suggests that these alterations reflect dissatis-
    faction with the "uniquely pejorative εὐλογίας.
    "'Good Wordes and Faire Speeches' (Rom 16.18
    AV): More Materials and a Pauline Pun," NTS 42
    (1996) 601.

g   In contrast to the word order with emphasis on the
    virtue of the Roman readers, ἐφ᾽ ὑμῖν οὖν χαίρω
    ("concerning you therefore I rejoice") found in ℵ* A
    B C L P (69) 81 365 1243 1319 1573 pc, several ver-
    sions including the "Western" texts have a more
    prosaic word order that tends to make the warning
    about heretics relevant to all churches, χαίρω οὖν
    ἐφ᾽ ὑμῖν ("I rejoice therefore concerning you") in
    P46 D* F G 323(acc. to N-A) 330* 1881 pc latt. Another
    possible step in the direction of generalizing the
    wording is found in ℵ2 D2 Ψ 6 33 88 104 323(according
    to Swanson) 326 330c 424 614 945 1175 1241 1505 1735
    1739 1836 1874 2344 2464 2495 Maj syh with χαίρω
    οὖν τὸ ἐφ᾽ ὑμῖν ("I rejoice therefore about the
    "matter" concerning you"). Whatever the precise
    motivation of these transpositions, neither of these
    variants has a claim on originality.

h   The well-attested reading θέλω δέ ("now I want")
    stands in contrast to the "Western" texts D* F G
    mon vgmss Spec with the reading καί θέλω ("also I
    want"); in P46 one finds both readings combined in
    καὶ θέλω δε ("and I also want").

i   In ℵ A C P 6(according to Swanson) 33 69 88 104 323 326
    424 614 945 1175 1241 1243 1735 1739 1836 1874
    1881 2344 2464 Maj syh Cl there is a fairly well-
    supported addition of μέν ("on the one hand") that
    matches the context quite well. The attestation for
    the omission of μέν is somewhat stronger with P46
    B D F G L Ψ 6(acc. to N-A) 330 365 1319 1505 1573
    2495 al latt. It is likely that μέν was added to lend
    rhetorical precision by forming a μέν . . . δέ con-
    struction; see Zuntz, Text, 197–98.

j   A minor variant in A 365 630 1319 1573 pc f g t vgcl
    Spec shifts the widely supported future tense συν-
    τρίψει ("he will crush") to the optative, thus mak-
    ing it into a prayer request συντρίψαι ("may he
    crush"), clearly a secondary improvement of the
    text.

Analysis

The rhetoric of this passage is different both in style and in logical development[1] from the rest of Romans. The distinctively Pauline parallelisms, antitheses, and other flourishes are absent. The awkwardly related admonitions of 16:17b and c are justified not by a theological rationale, as in the rest of Romans, but by a stereotypical description of the heretics in 16:18. Verses 19-20a are oddly related to the foregoing in that the material introduced by γάρ ("for") does not really provide a rationale for the actions urged in 16:17. These verses describe the nature of the true church in terms of obedience to apostolic teaching and offer a benediction which, in contrast to other Pauline blessings, is a kind of curse related to the crushing of demonic heretics under the feet of true believers.[2] This curse is replete with non-Pauline terminology, as the commentary below demonstrates.

A remarkable formulation of a peace benediction closes the pericope:[3] this is the only instance in the Pauline letters where such a benediction is repeated, in this case, from 15:33; the only instance where a grace benediction follows immediately, in 16:20b; and the only closing benediction in the Pauline letters that promises that God will act against the audience's enemies. Weima observes that if 16:17-20a were understood as a separate section, a Pauline postscript, this could account for the "unique occurrence, placement and form" of the benediction.[4] These odd features are explained more adequately by a theory of non-Pauline interpolation.

The Case for Interpolation

While most commentators view this passage as a peculiar, Pauline postscript, a small group of scholars has correctly identified it as a non-Pauline interpolation.[5] In order to avoid undue repetition in discussing the exegetical details, reserved for the commentary below, the main reasons for viewing 16:17-20a as an interpolation[6] may be stated briefly:

(a) These verses produce an egregious break in the flow and tone of Paul's series of greetings to honored leaders of the Roman churches.[7] The personal comments that dominate Rom 16:1-16 are marked by collegiality and inclusiveness, a tone that is picked up again in vv. 21-23. The commentators who insist on the authenticity of vv. 17-20 find it impossible to explain the extreme change of mood, the angry tone of denunciation, and the sharp breaks in the flow at the beginning and end of this section.[8] Even the defenders of authen-

---

1   See Louw, 2:142: "The structure is rather loosely knit. . . ."
2   See Käsemann, 418.
3   For the following, see Weima, *Neglected Endings*, 96.
4   Ibid., 96.
5   See Baur, *Zweck*, 148–49; Erbes, "Zeit und Ziel," 146; John Knox, "Romans," 664; Walter Schmithals, "The False Teachers of Romans 16:17-20," pp. 219–38 in Walter Schmithals, *Paul and the Gnostics* (Nashville: Abingdon, 1972); Ollrog, "Abfassungsverhältnisse," 230–34; Ollrog, *Mitarbeiter*, 226–34; Jewett, *Tolerance*, 17–23. Among commentators, see O'Neill, 252–53; Byrne, 446, 455–56; Brändle and Stegemann, "Formation," 124. In "Rm 16,17-20: Vocabulaire et Style," *RB* 107 (2000) 548–57, Marie-Émile Boismard makes a case that 16:17-18a are glosses from an editor of the Lukan school.
6   For the definition of an "interpolation" as "an insertion in a document with the object of obtaining backing for the interpolator's opinion or project," see Nash, "Interpolations," 23. A study of interpolations in the legal material of the OT has been writ-
    ten by Bernard M. Levinson, "The Case for Revision and Interpolation within the Biblical Legal Corpora," in B. M. Levinson, ed., *Theory and Method in Biblical and Cuneiform Law: Revision, Interpolation and Development*, JSOTSup 181 (Sheffield: Sheffield Academic Press, 1994) 37–59. In *The Manuscript Evidence for Interpolation in Homer* (Heidelberg: Winter, 1980), M. J. Athorp makes a compelling case that at least one classical text from the ancient world contains numerous interpolations. Walker, *Interpolations*, 26–36, surveys other classical texts that show interpolations and cites Zenodotus's four principles in identifying interpolations (27), which are adapted below.
7   For the assessment that this passage is contextually "atypical," see Müller, *Schluß*, 218.
8   See particularly Kühl, 482–83, who finds the disparities between this pericope and the rest of Romans impossible to explain, suggesting in the end that it lends plausibility to the hypothesis that the entirety of Rom 16 may have been addressed to another audience.

ticity, such as Douglas Moo, acknowledge the "abrupt interruption" of these verses,[9] while Joseph Fitzmyer admits that "there is nothing in the immediately preceding context that calls for" this material.[10]

(b) These verses contain direct contradictions to the preceding argument of Romans. Whereas 6:17 acknowledges that the Roman Christians were "obedient to the form of teaching with which you were entrusted," 16:17 warns against a group within Rome that opposes such teaching.[11] Whereas 14:1 calls for unconditionally welcoming members of other Christian groups who differ in theology and liturgy, 16:17 flatly demands that such people be "avoided." Whereas 12:1-2 affirms the presence of transformed intellect in the congregation, capable of "rational worship," 16:18 stereotypes intellectual gifts as "fair and flattering words." Whereas Rom 1:12 had referred to the Romans and Paul mutually strengthening each other, acknowledging in 15:14 that they are "full of goodness, filled with all knowledge, and able to instruct one another," in 16:20 there is a demand for absolute "obedience" to apostolic authority. This reference stands in considerable tension with the distinctive expression used twice in Romans, the "obedience of faith" (Rom 1:5; 16:26). Whereas Rom 1:18–3:9 offered definitive proof that "all have sinned and fallen short of the glory of God," and Rom 7:7-25 shows the ambiguity of all human motivations, 16:19 expects the audience to be "innocent as far as evil is concerned." Furthermore, as sketched below, the expression "God of peace" is used here with a connotation that is directly opposed to its use in 15:33.

(c) The rhetoric and vocabulary of this section are non-Pauline. Wolf-Hennig Ollrog counts seven Pauline hapax legomena in this short section, strongly suggesting non-Pauline provenance.[12] Other words are used in this passage with definitions that are atypical for his ordinary usage.[13] The formula "serve our Lord Christ" (16:18) is unparalleled in the authentic Pauline letters, which refer to "serving Christ,"[14] "serving the Lord,"[15] or being a "slave of Christ Jesus";[16] only in Col 3:24 is the wording of this interpolation replicated. The typical blessing formula in Paul's letters uses the optative verb, as in 15:13, "May the God of hope fill you . . . ," but in 15:20 we have an unparalleled future verb: "God will crush Satan under your feet." Historical certainty here replaces the mysterious sovereignty of God whose judgments are "unsearchable" and whose ways are "inscrutable," according to the hymn of Rom 11:33-36. Moreover, in the authentic Pauline letters, it is Christ rather than believers who defeats the demonic forces (1 Cor 15:23-26; 2 Thess 2:8). The rhetoric and argumentative style of this paragraph are very different from other Pauline passages that interact with heresy: there is no discussion of doctrinal or ethical issues; the ad hominem references are generic and lack the kind of argumentation typical of Pauline letters. As Ziesler observes, "The most unexpected thing about vv. 17-20 is . . . the fact that in them Paul does not argue. He simply denounces. It could hardly be farther from the mutual acceptance of differences in 14[1-12] and 15[7]."[17] The style of antiheretical discourse matches the Pastoral Epistles and Ignatian letters rather than the other authentic Pauline letters.[18] In contrast to other authentic Pauline critiques of heretics, the details are so "broad and non specific"[19] that most current commentators give up the attempt at precise identification of these opponents as "almost impossible."[20]

9 Moo, 929.
10 Fitzmyer, 745.
11 See Lucht, *Untersuchung*, 152–53.
12 Ollrog, "Abfassungsverhältnisse," 230, lists ἐκκλίνειν ("keep away, shun," used otherwise only in a citation by Paul), χρηστολογία ("smooth speech"), ἄκακος ("innocent"), ἀφικνέομαι ("reach"), συντρίβειν ("crush"), ἐν τάχει ("quickly"), εὐλογία (in the sense of "well-chosen words, false eloquence").
13 Ollrog, "Abfassungsverhältnisse," 230, refers to διδαχή ("teaching"), used here not in the sense of a charismatic gift (1 Cor 14:6, 26) but as an established doctrine. I would add that the word σκάν-δαλον ("offense"), used by Paul always in the singular, appears in v. 17 in the plural and in the sense of "word traps." Furthermore, as North points out in "Pun," 600, only in Rom 16:18 is εὐλογία used by Paul "disparagingly."
14 Rom 14:18; see also 1 Cor 7:22; Gal 1:10.
15 Rom 12:11.
16 Rom 1:1; Phil 1:1.
17 Ziesler, 353.
18 See Ollrog, "Abfassungsverhältnisse," 231.
19 Dunn, 2:904; see also Lucht, *Untersuchung*, 155–57.
20 Moo, 929; see also Fitzmyer, 745; Johnson, 222; Theobald, 2:250; Müller, *Schluß*, 218.

(d) Finally, there is a plausible redactional rationale for an interpolation at this precise location, even though it obviously interrupts the series of greetings. Verse 16 had urged the Romans to adopt a widely inclusive policy: "Greet one another with a holy kiss. All the churches of Christ greet you." Although the broad inclusivity of this "ecumenical greeting"[21] is consistent with the final three chapters of Romans, it is radically restricted by vv. 17-20. These verses set a firm limit on those who should be greeted as legitimate members of the Christian family, which was the original significance of the kiss.[22]

The provenance of this interpolation should probably be assigned to the group that produced the Pastoral Epistles toward the end of the first century.[23] They share the strategy of demanding a complete separation from heretics (2 Tim 3:5; Titus 3:10-11); the emphasis on doctrinal instruction that has been learned and must be preserved (1 Tim 2:11; 5:4; 2 Tim 3:14; 4:2-4; Titus 1:9); the demand for submission to authority (1 Tim 2:11-12; 3:4; 4:11-16; 5:17-22; 6:2; 2 Tim 4:1-5; Titus 1:5-11; 2:2-9; 3:1-2); and the rhetorical strategy of ad hominem invective (1 Tim 1:3-7; 4:1-3; 2 Tim 2:16-19; 3:1-9; Titus 1:10-16).

Rhetorical Disposition

16:17-20a	The first interpolation: the church's campaign against heretics
16:17-18	A. The avoidance of heretics
16:17	1. The admonition
16:17a	a. The formula of admonition
16:17b	b. The admonition to be on guard
16:17b	c. The stereotype of heretics
	1) Those making "dissensions"
	2) Those making "scandals"
	3) Those opposed to traditional teaching
16:17c	d. The admonition of separation
16:18	2. The rationale for responding harshly to heretics
16:18a	a. The allegations concerning the perverse allegiance of heretics
	1) They do not serve the Lord
	2) They serve "their own bellies"
16:18b	b. The allegation concerning the heretics' deception
	1) The means of deception
	a) "Sweet talk"
	b) Flattery
	2) The targets of deception: "simple" Christians
16:19-20a	B. The alleged relation of Paul to the true church
16:19	1. The behavior of the true church
16:19a	a. Obedience that is publicly manifest
16:19b	b. Paul rejoices over the true church
16:19c	c. The proper attitude of the true church
	1) Wise in relation to the good
	2) Guileless in relation to evil
16:20a	2. The apostolic benediction
	a. The source of the benediction: "the God of peace"
	b. The benefit: prompt crushing of "Satan"
	c. The means of benediction: the "feet" of the true church

Exegesis

■ **17** This passage begins with the exhortative formula παρακαλῶ δὲ ὑμᾶς ("now I exhort you"), with δέ carrying the same adversative force[24] as in 15:30, from which the first four words may actually be copied verbatim.[25] In contrast to the other passages in the Pauline letters where this formula is used, this material "abruptly separates"[26] the prior and subsequent material in the letter. If ἐρωτῶ ("I ask/request") is taken as the original reading,[27] the change of subject would be equally forceful. The placement of this demand of quarantine from heretics immediately follows the request in 16:16 to extend the holy kiss to all other members of the church,

21 Müller, *Schluß*, 217.
22 See Thraede, "Heiligen Kusses," 123–43; Benko, *Early Christians*, 98.
23 Ollrog suggests a provenance in the same period in "Abfassungsverhältnisse," 234.
24 See Michel, 480.
25 The formula "but I exhort you brethren" is found also in 1 Cor 1:10 and 1 Thess 4:10. The first two words in this formula are common in Greek rhetoric, as, for example, in Plato *Gorg.* 526e 1–3: παρακαλῶ δὲ καὶ ἄλλους πάντας ἀνθρώπους

("now I also exhort all people"). In a warning context, the verb appears in Polybius *Hist.* 15.7.5: "Concerning what you see, I exhort you (παρακαλῶ σε) not to contemplate grand schemes but to plan by human design regarding what's at hand."
26 Käsemann, 416. This accurate observation, shared by Lagrange, 372, is refuted by weak and apologetic considerations by Cranfield, 2:797, followed by Dunn, 2:902.
27 See note a above.

and to receive the greetings from all the churches of Christ. The author of the interpolation, probably writing at the end of the first century, was in conflict with congregations calling themselves Christian whom he did not approve. Whether gnostic Christians on the left or extreme, apocalyptic groups on the right, the author demands of the Roman Christians that they neither extend them the holy kiss nor receive their greetings.

The warning to "look out" ($\sigma\kappa o\pi\epsilon\hat{\iota}\nu$) for allegedly dangerous persons is the antithesis of the reminder in Phil 3:17, $\sigma\kappa o\pi\epsilon\hat{\iota}\tau\epsilon$ $\tau o\hat{\upsilon}\varsigma$ $o\check{\upsilon}\tau\omega$ $\pi\epsilon\rho\iota\pi\alpha\tau o\hat{\upsilon}\nu\tau\alpha\varsigma$ $\kappa\alpha\vartheta\dot{\omega}\varsigma$ $\check{\epsilon}\chi\epsilon\tau\epsilon$ $\tau\acute{\upsilon}\pi o\nu$ $\acute{\eta}\mu\hat{\alpha}\varsigma$ ("look for those who behave in this way as you have an example from us"), which is followed by the warning about heretics in 3:18. In Philippians the verb has the sense "to look at critically" or "consider something critically,"[28] as in the rest of the authentic Pauline letters where it is used with "a positive nuance."[29] (2 Cor 4:18; Gal 6:1; Phil 2:4). In this case the nuance is strongly negative, warning against persons making trouble in the community.[30] The plural "dissensions" ($\delta\iota\chi o\sigma\tau\alpha\sigma\acute{\iota}\alpha\varsigma$) is drawn from Greek political discourse,[31] in contrast to the ideal of civic unity. It appears in the vice list of Gal 5:20 in the sequence "quarrels, dissensions, and factions" and becomes a stock motif in early Christian denunciations of heresy (*1 Clem.* 20.4; 46.5; 51.1).[32]

In contrast to the three earlier uses of "hindrance" in Romans (9:33; 11:9; 14:13), here the word appears in the plural ($\sigma\kappa\acute{\alpha}\nu\delta\alpha\lambda\alpha$)[33] and is defined as is $\delta\iota\chi o\sigma\tau\alpha\sigma\acute{\iota}\alpha$ by the phrase "in opposition to the teaching that you received." This link between teaching and heretical opposition thereto is found also in Qumran; in 1QH 16:15 the member of the community prays to be preserved from נגע מכשול מחוקי בריתך ("a hindrance to fall away from the laws of your covenant"), usage which becomes quite typical in the early rabbinic tradition.[34] In this development, the "scandal" is defined as violation of a particular group's teaching about the law. There are also striking Greek parallels to this combination of $\sigma\kappa\acute{\alpha}\nu\delta\alpha\lambda\alpha$ and $\delta\iota\chi o\sigma\tau\alpha\sigma\acute{\iota}\alpha\iota\varsigma$ within the framework of partisan vituperation. For example, the comic sayings of Aristophanes include the warning: "Setting little word traps ($\sigma\kappa\alpha\nu\delta\acute{\alpha}\lambda\eta\vartheta\rho$') with double-talk ($\delta\iota\chi o\sigma\tau\alpha\sigma\acute{\iota}\eta$), even the certain polemarch, Androcles, has blinded you."[35] In the *Testament of Solomon* one of the demons identifies himself by employing these two terms: "I'm called Saphthorael. I cast dissensions ($\delta\iota\chi o\sigma\tau\alpha\sigma\acute{\iota}\alpha\varsigma$) among men and take delight in causing them to stumble ($\sigma\kappa\alpha\nu\delta\alpha\lambda\acute{\iota}\zeta\omega\nu$)."[36] These parallels evoke the "sectarian, heretical resonance"[37] that differentiates this verse from the earlier argument of Romans. Moreover, in place of the typical biblical expression with $\tau\acute{\iota}\vartheta\eta\mu\iota$ $\sigma\kappa\acute{\alpha}\nu\delta\alpha\lambda o\nu$ ("to place a hindrance"), this verse uses the verb $\pi o\iota\acute{\epsilon}\omega$ ("make, do, cause"), which implies not just that one per-

---

28 Ernst Fuchs, "$\sigma\kappa o\pi\acute{\epsilon}\omega$," *TDNT* 7 (1971) 414–15. A *TLG* search indicates the frequency of this term in warning discourse, 78 times in Demosthenes; 25 in Isocrates; 86 in Plato; 134 in Aristotle; 22 in Xenophon; 46 in Plutarch; and 14 in Dio Chrysostom. A good example is Xenophon *Mem.* 3.7.9, "Many rush to look out for the affairs of others ($\epsilon\pi\grave{\iota}$ $\tau\grave{o}$ $\sigma\kappa o\pi\epsilon\hat{\iota}\nu$ $\tau\grave{\alpha}$ $\tau\hat{\omega}\nu$ $\check{\alpha}\lambda\lambda\omega\nu$ $\pi\rho\acute{\alpha}\gamma\mu\alpha\tau\alpha$) but never turn aside to examine themselves."

29 Moo, 930.

30 William J. Hassold, "'Avoid Them': Another Look at Romans 16:17-20," *CurTM* 27 (2000) 201, argues for a generic interpretation of the article $\tau o\acute{\upsilon}\varsigma$ ("them"), referring to "dissensionists in general."

31 For example, Demosthenes *Orat.* 19.255 reported that Solon celebrated Eunomia because "she ends the deeds of sedition/discord ($\pi\alpha\acute{\upsilon}\epsilon\iota$ δ' $\check{\epsilon}\rho\gamma\alpha$ $\delta\iota\chi o\sigma\tau\alpha\sigma\acute{\iota}\eta\varsigma$). 1 Macc 3:29 refers to the "dissension" ($\delta\iota\chi o\sigma\tau\alpha\sigma\acute{\iota}\alpha$) that Antiochus Epiphanes provoked by assaulting Israel's law. See also Heinrich Schlier, "$\delta\iota\chi o\sigma\tau\alpha\sigma\acute{\iota}\alpha$," *TDNT* 1 (1964) 514. It

seems very unlikely that in this context $\delta\iota\chi o\sigma\tau\alpha\sigma\acute{\iota}\alpha$ has the connotation of "doubts," as found in its verbal cognate, $\delta\iota\chi o\sigma\tau\alpha\tau\acute{\epsilon}\omega$ ("feel doubts," according to BAGD).

32 Given the association of *1 Clement* with Rome, the use of this term may point to Clement's involvement in creating the interpolation of Rom 16:17-20 sometime in the 90s C.E.

33 While this word appears only in the singular in the other Pauline letters, the plural is found in Matt 13:41; 18:7; Luke 17:1.

34 See the discussion in Müller, *Anstoß*, 49–50; rabbinic parallels are discussed on 50–60. Hebrew citation from the Sukenik edition.

35 Cratinus *Frag.* 457–59; see also Aristophanes *Ach.* 687. LSJM 1604 explains "word traps" as "throwing out words which one's adversary will catch at, and so be caught himself."

36 *T. Sol.* 18.16; see Busch, *Testament Salomos*, 225.

37 Müller, *Anstoß*, 67.

son's actions inadvertently place a hindrance in front of a brother, but rather that culprits create these "dissensions and hindrances," with demonic energy and intentionality (see 16:20).[38] In Gustav Stählin's words, 16:17 definitely "takes up an isolated place" in comparison with the other references to "hindrance" in Romans.[39] Although scholars often deny specific reference in the "dissensions and scandals,"[40] the plural form of these abstracts points to "concrete phenomena"[41] in the view of the interpolator, that is, trends in the church toward the end of the first century that are believed to be heretical.

The phrase παρὰ τὴν διδαχήν ("in opposition to the teaching") is unique in all of Greek literature, apart from a few patristic writers on Paul. The preposition παρά appears here with the connotation of "contrary to/in opposition to," as in Gal 1:8, "But even if we, or an angel from heaven, should preach to you a gospel contrary to that which we preached to you (παρ᾽ ὅ εὐηγγελισάμεθα ὑμῖν), let him be accursed."[42] In contrast to Galatians, however, Rom 16 refers to "teaching" as a matter of "firmly established . . . definite traditions of faith that one is to learn."[43] In place of a transforming gospel that provokes conversions under the power of the Spirit, religion now consists of doctrine that one must learn, which is a clear indication that the rhetoric in these verses stems from a time after Paul. The use of the verb ἐμάθετε ("you have learned") points to an established catechetical system in which the audience is assumed to have received "instruction about a doctrine,"[44] perhaps in the form of baptismal catechism.[45] In none of the other letters does Paul refer to learning in this indoctrinating sense (1 Cor 4:6; 14:31, 35; Gal 3:2; Phil 4:9, 11); the closest parallels are in the Pastorals (1 Tim 2:11; 5:4; 2 Tim 3:14).[46] In contrast to Paul's ordinary usage, which employs διδαχή as a charismatic gift (e.g., Rom 12:7), this phrase is consistent with OT and rabbinic understandings of traditional religious teachings.[47] The closest parallels in the NT are in the Pastoral Epistles: The bishop "must hold firm to the true word as taught (κατὰ τὴν διδαχήν), so that he may be able to give instruction in sound teaching (ἐν τῇ διδασκαλίᾳ τῇ ὑγιαινούσῃ) and refute those who contradict it" (Titus 1:9). Timothy is exhorted to "convince, rebuke, and exhort, be unfailing in patience and in teaching (καὶ διδαχῇ). For the time is coming when people will not endure sound teaching (τῆς ὑγιαινούσης διδασκαλίας), but with itching ears they will draw teachers to themselves to suit their own liking and will turn away from listening to the truth" (2 Tim 4:2-4).

The command ἐκκλίνετε ἀπ᾽ αὐτῶν ("steer clear from/avoid them") uses language employed for shunning fools[48] or sinners.[49] The verb becomes part of the stock repertoire for dealing with heretics in early Christianity.[50] For example, it appears in Ignatius's command in *Eph.* 7.1: "For there are some who make a practice of carrying about the Name with wicked guile, and do certain other things unworthy of God; these you must shun as wild beasts (ὡς θηρία ἐκκλίνειν), for they are ravenous dogs, who bite secretly, and you must be upon your guard against them, for they are scarcely to be cured."[51] In contrast to the insistence repeated throughout Rom

38 Ibid., 61–66; Stählin, "σκάνδαλον κτλ.," 336: "indirectly a work of Satan." See also Heinz Giesen, "σκάνδαλον," *EDNT* 3 (1993) 249. The combination of ποιοῦντας and τὰς διχοστασίας is echoed in the phrase of Dionysius Halicarnassus *Antiq. Rom.* 5.66.4: "these are the same things that cause dissensions (τὰ ποιοῦντα διχοστασίας) in the cities." See also 8.72.4.

39 Stählin, *Skandalon*, 183.

40 See Müller, *Anstoß*, 47.

41 BDF §142.

42 See Zeller, 249; BAGD (2000) 758.6 "against, contrary to."

43 Hans-Friedrich Weiss, "διδαχή," *EDNT* 1 (1990) 20.

44 See Gottfried Nebe, "μανθάνω," *EDNT* 2 (1991) 384.

45 Dunn, 2:902.

46 For the role of μανθάνειν in the Pastorals, see Karl Heinrich Rengstorf, "μανθάνω κτλ.," *TDNT* 4 (1967) 410.

47 See Karl Heinrich Rengstorf, "διδαχή," *TDNT* 2 (1964) 164.

48 Sir 22:13, ἔκκλινον ἀπ᾽ αὐτοῦ καὶ εὑρήσεις ἀνάπαυσιν ("steer clear from him [the fool] and you shall find rest").

49 Prov 1:15, "Do not go in the path with them [sinners], but turn away your foot (ἔκκλινον δὲ τὸν πόδα σου) from their paths."

50 It appears in *1 Clem.* 22.4; also it appears seventeen times in Clement of Alexandria, and 89 times in Origen.

51 Translation from Kirsopp Lake, *Apostolic Fathers I*, LCL (Cambridge: Harvard University Press, 1912, repr. 1985) 181.

14:1–16:16 that Christians of different orientation are to be welcomed and greeted, this section demands exclusion and separation, which has made this pericope particularly appealing to later Christian groups maintaining a separatist ethos.[52]

■ **18** The anonymous opponents are characterized as οἱ τοιοῦτοι ("such persons"), thus placing them in a class of persons bearing "certain definite qualities"[53] suggested in the preceding verse. This is the style of "heretical caricature,"[54] condemning people by class and type rather than according to individual deeds. For example, in universally condemning his opponents, Isocrates writes that "all such persons (πάντες οἱ τοιοῦτοι) despise the established laws,"[55] which thereby places them categorically in an undesirable class. The wording "our Lord, Christ" is different from Paul's usual references to "Jesus Christ our Lord";[56] the use of "Christ" without Jesus indicates Χριστός is used as a title, which shows some similarity to the titular preference in the Pastorals for the sequence "Christ Jesus."[57] The idea of "serving as slave" or "not serving as slave" (οὐ δουλεύουσιν) the Lord Christ is a formulation of the later Pauline tradition, with an exact parallel in Col 3:24, τῷ κυρίῳ Χριστῷ δουλεύετε ("serving the Lord Christ").[58] The nuance in the interpolator's formulation was caught by Lagrange: "such persons do not serve *our* Lord Christ";[59] they are under an alien lordship, so to speak.

The allegation that the heretics "serve their own belly" is a stock complaint in antiheretical discourse. For example, in Phil 3:19, Paul charges that for the libertinists threatening the congregation,[60] "their God is the belly (ὧν θεὸς ἡ κοιλία) and they glory in their shame." The κοιλία is ordinarily the abdominal cavity into which food enters, but at times it refers to the womb, the male sexual organ, or the inner self.[61] To serve the belly implies that the opponents are slaves to their appetite and to other bodily pleasures.[62] None of these nuances surfaced in the discussion of the conflicts over foods in Rom 14. Dualistic Greek thought appears to lie behind this polemical usage, viewing the κοιλία as the seat of desire, often with a strongly sexual connotation. Philo cites the Platonic philosophical tradition in his assessment: Τῷ δὲ ἐπιθυμητικῷ τὸν περὶ τὸ ἦτρον καὶ τὴν κοιλίαν τόπον, ἐνταῦθα γὰρ κατοικεῖ ἐπιθυμία, ὄρεξις ἄλογος ("To the lustful portion of the soul [they assign] the area around the abdomen and the belly, for there desire dwells, an irrational impulse"; Philo *Leg.* 3.115). A functional equivalent of the charge of "serving the belly" in this dualistic sense is the Greek word κοιλιοδαίμων ("one who makes a god of his belly").[63] A more lengthy description of heretics perceived to be enslaved to passion in this manner is found in 2 Tim 3:2-5.

The charge that the heretics are involved in χρηστολογία καὶ εὐλογίας ("sweet talk and well-chosen

---

52 See P. E. Kretzmann, "Zu Röm. 16, 17f.," *CTM* 4 (1933) 413–24; Karl Koehler, "The Battle for Romans 16:17-20," *Faith-Life* 15.5 (May 1942) 11–15; 15.6 (June 1942) 1, 12–16; 15.7 (July 1942) 1, 12–15; Edward W. A. Koehler, *Romans 16:17-20* (Milwaukee: Northwestern Publishing House, 1946); Martin H. Franzmann, "Exegesis on Romans 16:17ff.," *ConJ* 7 (1981) 13–20; Richard W. Kraemer, "The Interpretation of Romans 16:17-20 in Ecclesiology," mimeographed research paper (St. Louis: Concordia Seminary, 1968); other mimeographed writings on this topic are listed by Robert George Hoerber, *A Grammatical Study of Romans 16:17* (Milwaukee: Northwestern Publishing House, 1948) 3. An effort to moderate these interpretations is available in Hassold, "'Avoid Them,'" 207–8.

53 BAGD 821.

54 Zeller, 249; see also Kühl, 484; Michel, 480: "οἱ τοιοῦτοι klingt verächtlich und abwehrend."

55 Isocrates *Loch.* 22; see also Isocrates *Pac* 121.5.

56 Rom 4:1; 5:1, 11, 21; 6:23; 7:25; 8:39; 13:14; 15:6, 30, 16:20b, 24.

57 See Ferdinand Hahn, "Χριστός," *EDNT* 3 (1993) 484.

58 See Fitzmyer, 746: "to lead a Christian life in an ecclesial, everyday setting." See also Eph 6:7.

59 Lagrange, 374, italics in original; he views the heretics as Jewish Christians adhering to the Jewish law.

60 See Jewett, "Conflicting Movements," 376–82; O'Brien, *Philippians*, 455–56.

61 See Johannes Behm, "κοιλία," *TDNT* 3 (1965) 786. The ordinary Greek word for "stomach" is γαστήρ, not κοιλία.

62 See Franz Georg Untergassmair, "κοιλία," *EDNT* 2 (1991) 301.

63 Eupolis Comic *Frag.* 172; Claudius Aelianus *Frag.* 109. Behm, "κοιλία," 788 n. 11, refers also to the later ecclesiastical terms for heretics as κοιλιόδουλος ("belly servant") and κοιλιολάτρης ("belly server").

words") implies that the "'friendly speeches and fine words' by which the recipients of the letter are deceitfully wooed are simply a mask for fraudulent purposes."[64] The word χρηστολογία appears here for the first time in ancient literature,[65] and there is an intriguing parallel in the nickname attached to the Roman emperor Pertinax who was assassinated in 193 C.E. when he failed to provide the bonus anticipated from his elevation: *nec multum tamen amatus est, si quidem omnes, qui libere fabular conferebant, male Pertinacem loquebantur, chrestologun eum appellantes qui bene loqueretur et male faceret* ("Nevertheless he was not much loved, if indeed everyone openly joined in speaking badly of Pertinax, calling him Chrestologus—'well speaking, but ill-working'").[66] While we encountered εὐλογία ("blessing, well-chosen words") as a theologically significant sense of "blessing" in Rom 15:29, there is no doubt that the word is used here in the pejorative sense,[67] the only examples of which come from Greek sources.[68] For example, Lucian of Samosata *Lex.* 1.25 ridicules Lucinus's "demonstrating too much fine language (πολλὴν τὴν εὐλογίαν) and good choice of words."

Taken together, the expression "sweet talk and well-chosen words" is a rhetorical hendiadys[69] that reinforces the idea of misusing rhetorical gifts to mislead and corrupt others. The standard word for "deceive" (ἐξαπατάω)[70] is used here as it was in Rom 7:11; for instance, in 2 Cor 11:3 Paul reminds the congregation that "the serpent deceived Eve by his cunning" (ὁ ὄφις ἐξηπάτησεν Εὕαν ἐν τῇ πανουργίᾳ αὐτοῦ; see also the deutero-Pauline texts, Eph 5:6 and Titus 1:10). Similarly,

Isocrates *Nic.* 2.6 warns of men who unjustly use words to deceive (τῶν ἀνθρώπων . . . τοῖς λόγοις ἐξαπατώντων) and in the period closer to Paul, Dio Chrysostom *Orat.* 33.23 warns, "For these people are deceiving you (ἐξαπατῶσιν ὑμᾶς) and inducing folly just like young children (ὥσπερ νηπίους παῖδας)." The interpolator's contention that the "hearts of the simple" (τὰς καρδίας τῶν ἀκάκων) are particularly vulnerable to such propaganda reflects a patronizing anthropology; the ἀκάκοι in this instance are "guileless" and "simple."[71] They are like the unintelligent fools in Prov 14:15: "The simple believes everything." Diodorus Siculus refers to the Spartan naval leader Callicratidas as a "very young man, innocent and straightforward in character (ἄκακος καὶ τὴν ψυχὴν ἁπλοῦς), since he had had as yet no experience of the ways of foreign peoples" (*Hist.* 13.76.2). Paul never otherwise uses this term "innocence," which is fundamentally incompatible with his anthropology, as Rom 3 and 7 clearly indicate. But naïveté is an important idea in the Pastorals, which warns against heretics "who make their way into households and capture weak women, burdened with sins and swayed by various impulses who will listen to anybody" (2 Tim 3:6-7). Titus 1:15 maintains the possibility of moral and intellectual innocence that the authentic Paul has repudiated: "To the pure all things are pure. . . ." It serves the purpose of the interpolator to contend that the heretics pose a genuine danger to naive branches of the church.

■ **19** The link between this verse and the foregoing verse is puzzling, since it is introduced with γάρ ("for") which indicates that v. 19 provides the proof for the pre-

64 Konrad Weiss, "χρηστολογία," *TDNT* 9 (1974) 492.

65 Origen *Frag. Lam.* 56.5; *Exp. Prov.* 17.173.11. See also North, "Pun," 602–3.

66 *Hist. Aug.* 13, quoted by North, "Pun," 604. North suggests the innovative but rather implausible hypothesis that χρηστολογία derives from Pliny's report that wild endives smeared on the body "would make one more popular and more likely to achieve one's aims" (606), and that the term refers to "endive-pickers, who would prefer to use magic to get their own way and woo away from Paul his supporters" (613).

67 See Boismard, "Rm 16,17-20," 553. Ramón M. Trevijano Etcheverría, "*Εὐλογία* in St. Paul and the Text of Rom. 16,18," *StEv* 6.540, suggests in con-

trast that Paul is "denouncing eulogies with a sectarian christological content," which seems implausible in light of the hendiadys with χρηστολογία.

68 Hermann W. Beyer argues in contrast that the NT usage of this word derives from Hebrew background; "εὐλογέω κτλ.," *TDNT* 2 (1964) 754, 763, but no parallel Hebrew texts are suggested.

69 Käsemann, 398; Dunn, 2:903.

70 See Albrecht Oepke, "ἀπατάω κτλ.," *TDNT* 1 (1964) 384–85; G. H. R. Horsley, "A Prefect's Circular Forbidding Magic," *NDIEC* 1 (1981) 47–49: "[I have come across many people] who consider themselves to be beguiled (ἐξαπατᾶσθ[αι]) by means of divination," which the Egyptian prefect Q. Aemilius Saturninus goes on to condemn.

71 Walter Grundmann, "ἄκακος," *TDNT* 1 (1964) 482.

ceding.[72] Douglas Moo suggests that there may be "an intentional play on the idea of 'innocence'" in that while the Romans are innocent (ἀκεραίους) in the sense of "freedom from sin as a result of their obedience to the gospel message," Paul wants them to "combine this innocence with 'wisdom.'"[73] But such an antithetical word-play should have been introduced by "but" rather than "for." Somehow the author believes that the "obedience" of the audience confirms the evil character of the heretics. Elsewhere in the Pauline letters, ὑπακοή ("obedience") is contextualized as the "obedience of faith" (Rom 1:5; 16:26), the "obedience of the Gentiles" (Rom 15:18), "obedience unto righteousness" (Rom 6:16), "the obedience of Christ" (2 Cor 10:5);[74] it is fundamentally a matter of positive response to the gospel of salvation by grace alone. When "obedience" is used in the absolute, as in this verse, its social context of personal indebtedness to Paul's apostolic work is visible (2 Cor 7:15; Phil 2:12; Phlm 21). The striking features about obedience in Rom 16:19 are not only that the context remains unstated, making it unclear whether obedience to Paul's authority, or to the authority of other teachers, or to God is intended, but also the exaggerated statement of how widely such obedience is a matter of public knowledge: it has "reached to all."[75] The interpolator goes on to state, "concerning you therefore I rejoice." As Dunn remarks, "After the (over-)dramatic warning, here is a compensating word of lavish praise."[76] One gains the impression that the interpolator is going overboard to support submission to authority as the mark of the true church, the decisive defense against heresy. The Pastoral

Epistles, again, seem to provide the closest parallels to this preference.[77]

The interpolator's desire that the congregation σοφοὺς εἶναι εἰς τὸ ἀγαθόν ("be wise toward the good") needs to be defined contextually,[78] as achieved through the obedience celebrated in the first part of v. 19. The critical attitude toward persons achieving wisdom through education[79] expressed in Rom 1:22 ("claiming to be wise, they became witless;" see also Rom 11:34) and 1 Cor 1:20 ("Where is the wise man? . . . Has not God made foolish the wisdom of the world?")[80] is replaced here with a socially conformist understanding of wisdom defined as adherence to authoritative teaching, probably about what is "morally good."[81] The brilliant, transformative dialectic between "good" and "evil" developed earlier in the letter (12:2, 21; 14:16) is brought down to a pedestrian level in this verse, especially by the use of ἀκέραιος ("innocent, pure"). It is used here in the sense of "integrity which they have kept in face of evil,"[82] not being "admixed with evil."[83] While the Matthean parallel, "be therefore wise as serpents and innocent as doves" (Matt 10:16), contains dialectical and metaphorical dimensions that prevent a definition of innocence as naïveté, a closer parallel is available Plato Resp. 409a, who argues that only the person who is "inexperienced with bad habits (ἀκέραιοι κακῶν ἠθῶν) and uncontaminated by them while young" is likely to be a good judge. This view of "innocence" is the opposite of Paul's view that humans discover the depth of their own evil in the light of the gospel (Rom 1:18–3:20; 7:7-25) and henceforth are given a new, righteous relation-

G. H. R. Horsley, "In Brief (c)," *NDIEC* 4 (1987) 186, cites a grave inscription for a twelve-year-old who was a "child, young and innocent" (παῖς νέος ὢν ἄκακος).

72 Cranfield, 2:802, claims that v. 19 "supports the exhortation of v. 17f." but does not explain how.

73 Moo, 931–32.

74 See Gerhard Schneider, "ὑπακοή, ὑπακούω," *EDNT* 3 (1993) 394–95.

75 The Greek expression is awkward and fragmentary, since the usual idiom is that "a word" or report has "reached" someone; Aristotle *Eth. nic.* 1097a.24; Sir 47:16; Josephus *Ant.* 17.155; 19.127; other examples in BAGD 126. In Rom 16:19 it is the "obedience" of the Romans that has "reached" everyone, which must imply that a report about their obedience has gone out.

76 Dunn, 2:904.

77 1 Tim 2:11-12; 3:4; 4:11-16; 5:17-22; 6:2; 2 Tim 4:1-5; Titus 1:5-11; 2:2-9; 3:1-2.

78 That this expression is a hapax legomenon in the NT is noted by Boismard, "Rm 16,17-20," 554.

79 See Harald Hegermann, "σόφος," *EDNT* 3 (1993) 261.

80 See especially Ulrich Wilckens's section of the article "σοφία," *TDNT* 7 (1971) 517–22.

81 Cranfield, 2:802; it seems less likely, in view of the context, that the wisdom concerns salvation, as suggested by Schmidt, 258; Schlier, 449.

82 Gerhard Kittel, "ἀκέραιος," *TDNT* 1 (1964) 210.

83 Zahn, 612.

ship with God that requires them continually to reassess the boundaries between good and evil (Rom 12:1-2). This is the sense in which ἀκέραιος was used in Phil 2:15, referring to the Christians' *"present* innocence"[84] as persons reshaped by Christ. There is no hint of such transformation in Rom 16:19.

■ **20a** The characteristic early Christian phrase, ὁ δὲ θεὸς τῆς εἰρήνης ("but the God of peace"), appears at the climax of the interpolation with a definition antithetical to that in 15:33.[85] Instead of referring to mutuality and coexistence between ethnic groups within the church, this passage promises the kind of peace that follows a holy war that annihilates opponents.[86] The metaphor of crushing a foe underfoot evokes martial victory both in the Hebrew and in the Greco-Roman traditions.[87] The familiar refrains from Ps 110 of making enemies a "footstool" and Ps 8 of placing all things "under his feet" echo through the NT.[88] Ps 91:13 promises that with God's assistance, the elect will tread on dangerous serpents and wild beasts, fulfilling the promise of Gen 3:15.[89] *T. Levi* 18.12 promises that after the apocalyptic battle, the Lord "shall grant to his children the authority to trample on wicked spirits (καὶ δώσει ἐξουσίαν τοῖς τέκνοις αὐτοῦ πατεῖν ἐπὶ τὰ πονηρὰ πνεύματα)."[90] In the great frieze at the temple in Pergamon, Aphrodite is shown with her foot on the face of the opponent she has just killed.[91] Similarly, Isis is depicted with the entire globe under her foot.[92] The familiar scene in Roman arenas throughout the empire was the victorious gladiator placing his foot on the neck of a vanquished opponent and waiting for the signal either to dispatch him or allow him to go free.[93] Roman coinage celebrated the emperors as peacemakers through military means.[94]

The choice of the verb συντρίβω ("shatter, crush") leaves no doubt about the violent means required to subdue the church's enemies.[95] The word is used in connection with mistreating people, beating them severely, bruising them, or annihilating them.[96] There are numerous parallels to this usage of the verb in the context of holy war, as, for example, when Judas Macabbeus reassures his followers when facing a numerically superior foe, καὶ αὐτὸς συντρίψει αὐτοὺς πρὸ προσώπου ἡμῶν ("And [the Lord] himself will crush them before our face").[97] Only after the crushing of satanic forces in an apocalyptic battle is peace possible, according to this passage,[98] and there is no doubt that the reference to Satan implies that the church's enemies are perceived to be his evil minions, as in other antiheretical passages.[99] That this victory will occur ἐν τάχει ("speedily/

---

84 O'Brien, *Philippians*, 293, italics in original.

85 See also Phil 4:9; 1 Thess 5:23; Heb 13:20.

86 The argument in this section is adapted from Robert Jewett, "The God of Peace in Romans: Reflections on Crucial Lutheran Texts," *CTM* 25.3 (1998) 186–94.

87 Konrad Weiss, "πούς," *TDNT* 6 (1968) 624–28.

88 See Hay, *Glory at the Right Hand*, 34–103; Georg Bertram, "συντρίβω κτλ.," *TDNT* 7 (1971) 923–24.

89 See Bertram, "συντρίβω κτλ.," 924.

90 See also *T. Sim* 6.6.

91 Weiss, "πούς," 625, refers to A. Gotsmich's description in "Die 'grausame' Aphrodite am Gigantenfries des Pergamener Altars," *AA* 56 (1941) 844–79.

92 Roland Bergmeier, "πούς, ποδός," *EDNT* 3 (1993) 144, refers to the depiction of Isis in Michel Malaise, *Les conditions de pénétration et de diffusion des cultes Égyptiens en Italie*, EPRO 22 (Leiden: Brill, 1972) 179–80.

93 See also the account of a duel during the time of Alexander the Great in Diodorus Siculus *Hist.* 17.100.8.

94 See Kreitzer, *Striking New Images*, 120–25.

95 See Bertram, "συντρίβω κτλ.," 920: "There is no doubt that when συντρίβω is used for שׁבר in the Bible it denotes processes of destruction even to radical obliteration, Ezek 26:2, 30:8."

96 See BAGD 793.

97 1 Macc 3:22; although overlooked by the few studies available, one could make a case that this is a technical expression for violent, military triumph in 1 Macc 3:23; 4:10, 30, 36; 5:7, 21, 43; 7:42, 43; 8:4, 5, 6; 9:7, 15, 16, 68; 10:52, 53, 82; 13:51; 14:13.

98 The apocalyptic violence implied in this formulation is particularly visible in Käsemann's description (418–19) of how the Christian victors set their "feet on the vanquished and trample him, thus seizing eschatological power. . . . Since the parousia is directly at hand, this will take place very soon." See also Michel, 482–83; Bergmeier, "πούς," 144.

99 See, for example, 2 Cor 11:14-15; 1 Tim 4:1; 2 Tim 2:26 and the discussion in Bertram, "συντρίβω κτλ.," 924; Werner Foerster, "σατανᾶς," *TDNT* 7 (1971) 161. Foerster points out (158) that the NT usually refers to Satan as ὁ σατανᾶς (except for Mark 3:23 and Luke 22:3 and a few vocative refer-

quickly")[100] has led to considerable debate over whether the author expects the victory to occur only in the context of the parousia[101] or in the church's act of excommunicating heretics in the near future.[102] The shift from the traditional wording of "placing enemies under his [Christ's] feet" to ὑπὸ τοὺς πόδος ὑμῶν ("under your feet") makes it clear that the author of this formula has the action of the current church in mind,[103] which will quickly result in a defeat of demonic heresy if the interpolator's advice is followed.[104] That ἐν τάχει carries magical overtones has been overlooked thus far in the scholarly debate, but it fits this context quite well. One of the most common formulas in the magical texts is ἤδη, ἤδη, τάχυ, τάχυ ("now, now; quickly, quickly"), always in reference to the expedience of performing a magical request. In one instance, the formula used in Rom 16 is employed· ἄκουε καὶ ποίησον ἄπαντα ἐν τάχει δρᾶσαι μηδὲν ἐναντιωθεὶς ἐμοί. ὑμεῖς γὰρ ἐστε τῆς γαίης ἀγχηρύται ("Listen and do everything quickly, in no way opposing me in the performance of this action, for you are the governors of the earth").[105] In view of this background, the interpolator promises divine dispatch in the execution of wrath against Satan's minions, once the believers' "innocence" is established. Verses 19-20a suggest a cause-and-effect relationship in which the believers' wise obedience in shunning heretics brings about a quick defeat of satanic power.

While the invective of this pericope was doubtless felt to be required in the period after the death of Paul, when the church lacked the intellectual resources to cope with threats of Gnosticism, apocalypticism, and asceticism and was forced to resort to exclusion of dissidents in order to maintain the faith, this pericope should not be confused with the rest of the argument of Romans. Rom 16:17-20a was intended as a refutation of tolerance within the church that was advocated in chapters 14–16 as the social corollary of the impartial divine righteousness revealed in Christ. In Paul's view, this interpolation is an unsuitable foundation for the normal course of ecumenical relations.[106] Yet, for most commentators, this pericope is presented as consistent with Pauline argumentation elsewhere and thus appropriate at the end of Romans.[107] Peter Stuhlmacher states this assessment in the clearest manner, thus revealing how the entirety of this letter is to be understood:

> Moreover, if one takes into consideration that, from 2:16 on, Paul is constantly taking up and refuting arguments which his Jewish-Christian opponents have brought up against him, this warning against false

ences), so it does not seem appropriate to translate "the Satan" as suggested by Dunn, 2:905. Paul always refers to Satan with the definite article, yet appears to view him as a named entity. See also Otto Böcher, "σατανᾶς, ᾶ, ὁ," *EDNT* 3 (1993) 234; Bent Noack, *Satanás und Sotería. Untersuchungen zur neutestamentlichen Dämonologie* (Copenhagen: Gads, 1948); and K. Schubert, "Versuchung oder Versucher? Der Teufel als Begriff oder Person in den biblischen und ausserbiblischen Texten," *BLit* 50 (1977) 104–13.

100 For the translation of "speedily," see BAGD (2000) 992; MM 627; Schlier, 450; Kühl, 482, argue for eschatological proximity. The phrase ἐν τάχει is typically Lukan: Luke 18:8; Acts 12:7; 22:18; 25:4; it also occurs in Rev 1:1; 22:6 with an apocalyptic flavor similar to Rom 16:20a.

101 See Michel, 483; Schmidt, 258–59; Käsemann, 419; Cranfield, 2:803.

102 Lietzmann, 128; Schmithals, "Irrlehre von Rm 16,17-20," 66; Baumgarten, *Paulus*, 216; Morris, 541; Dunn, 2:905.

103 See Foerster, "σατανᾶς," 161: "God will do it, but He does it through the community."

104 Baumgarten refers to the "de-eschatologizing" of the blessing (*Paulus*, 216), which overlooks the end-time scheme associated with denunciations of heretics in the Pastorals (1 Tim 6:3-14; 2 Tim 1:15-18, 3:1-9), which stand close to the wording of this passage. He is right, however, in sensing the difference from the Pauline approach to apocalyptic. Bertram attempts to fuse the apocalyptic and anti-heretical moments in "συντρίβω κτλ.," 924. The eschatological context of the campaign against heresy is discussed by Günther Bornkamm, "Das Anathema in der urchristlichen Abendmahlsliturgie," *ThLZ* 75 (1950) 227–30.

105 Cited by Daniel and Maltomini, *Suppl. Mag.* I.42.7-8; translation p. 138.

106 See Jewett, "God of Peace in Romans," 186–94.

107 See, for example, Lietzmann, 127; Schmidt, 256–57; Cranfield, 2:797–98; Käsemann, 417; Achtemeier, 238; Dunn, 2:901-2; Fitzmyer, 745; Johnson, 221–23; Moo, 929–30; Schreiner, 801; Witherington, 396–98.

teachers no longer in any way appears unmotivated. Rather, in it Paul summarizes the criticism of his opponents, which the apostle has already had in mind up until now and which he has already previously expressed in 3:8.[108]

The only current commentary I have found that takes a more critical stance is by Byrne, which concludes that "the case for regarding this warning as deutero-Pauline, while not a majority view, remains strong. In view of this the following commentary will speak of 'Paul' rather than Paul."[109] The sad reality is that the Paul with quotation marks has so often been taken as the author of the letter as a whole, which results in a fundamental distortion of its message. A case in point is one of the most remarkable episodes in Romans research, that Bishop John Colenso was declared a heretic in part for his commentary on Romans, which presented Paul's message of intercultural tolerance with incomparable clarity. His book was pulped so that only a few copies of the Cambridge publication are still extant.[110] In such a way, Paul's vision of the impartial righteousness of God and of the inclusive holy kiss have repeatedly been crushed under the church's feet, as if the very idea of agapaic coexistence were Satan's offspring.

---

108 Stuhlmacher, 252.
109 Byrne, 456; the O'Neill commentary of 1975 (258) takes a similar line.

110 See Draper's introduction to the Colenso commentary on Romans, ix–x, xxxii–xxxiii.

16

The Second Interpolation

The Supersessionist Doxology

25/ **Now[a] to the one who is able to confirm you according to my gospel and the proclamation of Jesus Christ, according to a revelation of a mystery kept secret for eternal periods 26/ but now having been disclosed, and[b] through prophetic writings,[c] according to the command of the eternal God, having been made known for obedience of faith to all the Gentiles, 27/ to God only wise, through Jesus Christ, to whom[d] [be] glory for aeons of aeons.[e] Amen.[f]**

a   For a discussion of the various locations of this doxology, see Introduction, section 2.

b   Cranfield, 2:811–12, reports that τέ ("and, both") is missing in D lat sy Chr, a matter overlooked by Nestle-Aland and UBS texts but recorded in Merk, *Novum Testamentum*, 11, and Swanson, *Vaticanus: Romans*, 270. Lagrange, 380, notes that the Vulgate has *et* ("and") but that it is missing in the Old Latin version. Godet, 504, suggests that copyists connected "by prophetic writings" with the preceding participle φανερωθέντος ("manifest") rather than with the following participle γνωρισθέντος ("made known"), which caused the suppression of τέ.

c   A minor variant in Or Hier^mss adds the phrase καὶ τῆς ἐπιφανείας τοῦ κυρίου ἡμῶν Ἰησοῦ Χρίστου ("and through the appearance of our Lord Jesus Christ"), but there is no likelihood of its originality. For a discussion of its implications, see Cranfield, 2:811.

d   In place of the widely attested though somewhat ambiguous ᾧ ("to whom"), P 81 104 436 1243 1962 2492 *pc* provide αὐτῷ ("to him") and B 323 630 f sy^p omit it altogether. Both variants appear to be efforts to resolve the ambiguity of the relative pronoun, eliminating the anacoluthon (Fitzmyer, 754).

e   The evidence for the two variants is rather closely divided, yet the support for inclusion of the genitive τῶν αἰώνων ("of aeons") is sufficiently broad in P^61 ℵ A^{1/2} D P^{1/2} 5 81 104^{1/2} 436 459^{1/2} 1243^{2/2} 623 1243^{2/2} 1852 1962 2110 2464^{1/2} 2492 2523 *pc* ur b d* f o vg sy^p bo arm eth geo Or^lat Hil Pel Aug that the judgment of the earlier editions of Nestle^{16-25} to include it in the text was justified. The omission of this seemingly redundant expression in P^46 (only after 15:33) B C L^{2/2} Ψ^{2/2} 6^{2/2} 33^{2/2} 61^{2/2} 69^{2/2} 88^{(extant only at 14:33)} 104^{1/2} 181 218 256 263 323^{2/2} 326^{2/2} 330^{2/2} 365 424^{2/2} 441 451 459^{1/2} 467 614^{2/2} 621 630 720 915 917 945^{2/2} 1175^{2/2} 1241^{2/2} 1319 1398 1505^{2/2} 1506^{2/2} 1563 1573 1678 1718 1735^{2/2} 1751 1739 1836^{2/2} 1838 1845 1846^{(not extant at 14:23)} 1874 1881^{2/2} 1908 1912 1942 1959 2127 2138 2197 2200 2495^{2/2} 2516 2544 2718 *Maj* sy^h sa slav Eus Chr Cyr Thret Ambst may well be "an assimilation to the simpler formula . . . predominant in most of the NT," according to Cranfield, 2:813. But Metzger, *Textual Commentary*, 477, feels it is more likely that the ascription was expanded with the second reference to "aeons." (Manuscripts listed above with fractions [^{1/2}, etc.] have the doxology both following 14:23 and at 16:27; P^46 has it only after 15:33.)

f   The benediction discussed above under Rom 16:20b is found at this point in P 33 104 256 263 365 436 441 459 1319 1573 1852 1962 *pc* vg^ms sy^p bo^ms arm eth geo^1 Ambst. For a comprehensive discussion, see the Introduction, section 2. See also Aland, *Text*, 295–96, 301, 304.

Analysis

The structure of this short pericope is that of a sprawling nominal sentence without an active verb, with the object of the acclamation in the dative. None of the distinctive features of Pauline style are visible, such as parallelism, assonance, or chiasm. J. K. Elliott's comprehensive analysis of its style is therefore forced to restrict itself to grammatical observations: "Three prepositional phrases depend on the infinitive στηρίξαι; three participles in apposition qualify μυστηρίου; two prepositional phrases illuminate φανερωθέντος and two amplify γνωρισθέντος. There are three indirect objects including one relative. There is one dative of time. Διά appears twice, κατά three times and εἰς three times."[1] The nominal structure without the copula suggests that this originated as a Semitic doxology,[2] with the verb to be supplied in the indicative.[3] The sentence is very difficult to analyze because of its loose structure and lack of logical development.[4]

---

1   J. K. Elliott, "The Language and Style of the Concluding Doxology of the Epistle to the Romans," *ZNW* 72 (1981) 129.

2   Deichgräber, *Gotteshymnus*, 30.
3   Ibid., 32.
4   See Louw, 1, pericope 43.

The Case for Interpolation

It has long been recognized that this doxology has many traits of a post-Pauline interpolation. While the list of those favoring interpolation is about as long[5] as that of defenders of its authenticity as a Pauline creation designed for the end of chapter 16,[6] the evidence more strongly supports the former. Bacon proposed another alternative, accepting it as a Pauline fragment deriving from another context, which was later attached to Romans.[7] Those who believe this to be an interpolation generally agree that it was originally created to provide a conclusion to the fourteen-chapter version of Romans associated with Marcion.[8] It is unclear from Origen's statement whether the doxology was present in the version of Romans that Marcion mutilated or whether he was responsible for adding it. We followed the text-critical analysis by Peter Lampe, who showed that Marcion deleted chapters 15–16 in their entirety; and that the new ending of 16:25-27 was added later.[9] The following considerations support the theory of an interpolation.

1. The textual history of this doxology makes it highly unlikely that it was originally a part of Paul's letter to the Romans.[10] While one group of texts lacks the doxology entirely, others place it in a variety of other locations.[11]

2. The transitions between doxology and the text of Romans in any of the extant locations, after 15:33, 16:23, and 16:24, are extremely rough and implausible. With the greetings in chapter 16 interrupted by the interpolation in vv. 17-20a, followed by the greetings of 16:21-23, the change of subject between these greetings and the doxology is abrupt and graceless. After the "Amen" at the end of 15:33, the doxology is anticlimactic. These transitions are all the more problematic in view of the thoughtful organization of the rest of the letter, with plausible transitions between pericopes and proofs.

3. There are significant disparities in content between the doxology and the rest of Romans or other Pauline letters.

---

5   Könnecke, *Emendationen*, 28; Lucht, *Untersuchung*, 92–118; Corssen, "Überlieferungsgeschichte," 32–34; Jülicher, 334; Lietzmann, 130–31; Norden, *Agnostos Theos*, 255; Kühl, 490–92; Champion, *Benedictions and Doxologies*, 123–24; Gaugler, 1:7–8; 2:416–17; Manson, "Romans—and Others," 8–11; Barrett, 10–13; Kümmel, *Introduction*, 314–17; Gamble, 107–10; Dodd, 245–46; Schlier, 451–55; Black, 215–16; O'Neill, 259–63; Cranfield, 1:6–9; Käsemann, 409, 22–23; Wilckens, 1:22–24; Elliott, "Concluding Doxology," 124–30; Lampe, "Textgeschichte," 274; Schmithals, *Römerbrief*, 566–70; Munro, "Interpolation in the Epistles," 441–43; Karl Paul Donfried, "A Short Note on Romans 16," in K. P. Donfried, ed., *The Romans Debate: Revised and Expanded Edition* (Peabody: Hendrickson, 1991) 50; Trobisch, *Entstehung*, 1, 8; Zeller, 250–51; Dunn, 2:912–17; Fitzmyer, 753; Byrne, 461–62; Collins, "Wandering Doxology," 293–303; Walker, *Interpolations*, 67–68, 194–99; Brändle and Stegemann, "Formation," 124.

6   F. J. A. Hort, "On the End of the Epistle to the Romans," in J. B. Lightfoot, ed., *Biblical Essays*, repr. of 2d ed. (Peabody: Hendrickson, 1994) 321–29; Eduard Riggenbach, "Die Textgeschichte der Doxologie Röm. 16,25–27," *NJDTh* 1 (1892) 603–5; Sanday and Headlam, 432–36; Parke-Taylor, "Romans i.5 and xvi.26," 305–6; Larry W. Hurtado, "The Doxology at the End of Romans," in E. J. Epp and G. D. Fee, eds., *New Testament Textual Criticism: Its Significance for Exegesis: Essays in Honor of Bruce M. Metzger* (Oxford: Clarendon, 1981) 185–99; Schmidt, 265–66; Murray, 2:262–68; Bruce, 281–82; K.-H. Walkenhorst, "The Concluding Doxology of the Letter to the Romans and Its Theology," [in Japanese, with English summary] *Katorikku Kenkyu* 27 (1988) 99–132; Don B. Garlington, "The Obedience of Faith in the Letter to the Romans. Part I: The Meaning of ὑπακοὴ πίστεως (Rom 1:5; 16:26)," *WTJ* 52 (1990) 201; Weima, *Neglected Endings*, 142–44, 218–20; Stuhlmacher, 244–45; Johnson, 221, 223; Moo, 936–37; Schreiner, 810–11; I. Howard Marshall, "Romans 16:25-27—An Apt Conclusion," in S. K. Soderlund and N. T. Wright, eds., *Romans and the People of God: Essays in Honor of Gordon D. Fee on the Occasion of His 65th Birthday* (Grand Rapids/Cambridge: Eerdmans, 1999) 170–84.

7   Benjamin W. Bacon, "The Doxology at the End of Romans," *JBL* 18 (1899) 172–75.

8   See section 2 in the Introduction above.

9   Lampe, "Textgeschichte," 273–75.

10 See the Introduction, section 2; see also Knox, "A Note," 191–93; Wilckens, 3:147; Käsemann, 423.

11 See Lampe, "Textgeschichte," 275; Collins, "Wandering Doxology," 295–97.

a. The studies of the content of the benediction by Kamlah[12] as well as a comparison with other benedictions and doxologies in Romans[13] or other authentic letters[14] make Pauline authorship seem unlikely. Kamlah[15] and Deichgräber[16] have identified it as belonging to an enabling type of doxology, found also in Eph 3:20-21; Jude 24-25; *Mart. Pol.* 20.2, but not elsewhere in the indisputably Pauline letters. The function of the doxology also differs from all others in the Pauline letters. In no other letter does Paul conclude with a doxology; its normal position is at the end or middle of proofs, usually in the context of discussing some aspect of the "inexpressible greatness" of God,[17] as, for example, Rom 1:25; 9:5; 11:33-36; 2 Cor 9:15; Gal 1:5; Phil 4:20.

b. The μυστήριον ("mystery") of the conversion of the Jews (11:25) that forms such an impressive part of chapters 9–11 is replaced in the doxology by the mystery of the favored status now granted to Gentiles (16:26). The doxology thus counters a crucial theme in Romans, expressed throughout the letter in the formula "to the Jew first, then to the Gentile."

c. The prophetic scriptures (1:2) that led to the confession shaped by Jewish and Gentile Christian groups in 1:3-4, and pointed to impartial righteousness (3:21) that showed God was a God both of Jews and Gentiles (3:29-30), now confirm the mystery of the salvation of the Gentiles alone (16:23). Paul's extensive use of scriptural citations as proof of his doctrine of the impartiality of God, of salvation through faith alone, and of God's irrevocable promises to Israel is countered by the doxology, which claims the Jews never understood the message of salvation that was silenced at God's command so that the Gentiles alone could inherit their promises.

d. The "obedience of faith to all the Gentiles" in 1:5, which entails faith as the means of access to grace for Jews as well as Gentiles, is shifted to the "obedience of faith for all the Gentiles" in 16:26. It is for them, but not for the Jews. This radically transforms the content and implications of the formula ὑπακοὴ πίστεως which embodies the inclusive theology of Romans that offers salvation in equal measure to Greeks and Jews.

e. The missional goal of Romans to extend the gospel to the end of the known world, including all the Gentile nations, is contained in the doxology, but without its correlate of the conversion of the Jews as an essential element of global reconciliation.

f. The central theme in Romans of God rectifying the human race through faith in Christ crucified in behalf of the shamed, thus equalizing the position of all peoples before God and requiring all to recognize that they are shamed and sinful and must rely on grace alone for salvation, is here reduced to believing in the mystery of salvation for the Gentiles.

These significant disparities point very strongly toward the conclusion that hands other than Paul's were at work in the creation of the doxology.

4. The style of the doxology is close to that of Ephesians, Colossians, and the Pastorals but lacks the parallelism and syntactical coherence of Pauline discourse.[18] A considerable portion of the vocabulary in these three verses is either non-Pauline or has non-Pauline nuances.

a. In 16:25 the "to him who is able" scheme is typical of the doxologies in Eph 3:20; Jude 24; *Mart.Pol.* 20.2, but does not occur in any of Paul's doxologies, blessings, or benedictions.

b. τὸ κήρυγμα Ἰησοῦ Χριστοῦ ("the proclamation of Jesus Christ") is never found elsewhere in Paul's

---

12 Ehrhard Kamlah, "Traditionsgeschichtliche Untersuchungen zur Schlußdoxologie des Römerbriefes" (dissertation, University of Tübingen, 1955) 127–30.

13 See above the discussion of Rom 1:25, 11:36, 15:5-6, and 15:13.

14 See Jewett, "Homiletic Benediction," 20–27.

15 Kamlah, "Schlußdoxologie," 77; see also Lucht, *Untersuchung*, 95–97.

16 Deichgräber, *Gotteshymnus*, 39.

17 Bacon, "Doxology," 173.

18 See Lucht, *Untersuchung*, 99–102; Elliott, "Concluding Doxology," 129; Collins, "Wandering Doxology," 298–300.

writings; he consistently refers to the "Gospel of Christ" in Rom 15:19; 1 Cor 9:12; 2 Cor 2:12; 9:13; 10:14; Gal 1:7; Phil 1:27; 1 Thess 3:2. "Jesus Christ" appears to be employed here in a Gentile manner, as a proper name. Similar references to the kerygma of Jesus Christ are found in the patristic period,[19] so the assessment is warranted that this expression "indicates a later date" than the Pauline period.[20] A similar expression appears in Titus 1:3, "through the proclamation (ἐν κηρύγματι ὃ ἐπιστεύθην) with which I have been entrusted" and in 2 Tim 4:17, "to proclaim the word fully."[21]

c. The words ἀποκάλυψις ("revelation") and μυστήριον ("mystery") are not directly linked with each other anywhere else in the NT, although the notion of mysteries being revealed is found in 1 Cor 2:6-10, Eph 3:3-9, and Col 1:26-27.[22]

d. The expression "secret for eternal periods" (χρόνοις αἰωνίοις σεσιγημένου) is peculiar; although Paul uses both χρόνος and αἰών, he never combines them in this peculiar expression that is found also in the Pastorals: 2 Tim 1:9 and Titus 1:2 refer to πρὸ χρόνων αἰωνίων ("for eternal periods").[23] The three preceding doxological formulas in Rom 1:25; 9:5; 11:36 all have the singular of αἰών and the only other times he uses the plural are in the stereotypical LXX formulas, "before the ages" (πρὸ τῶν αἰώνων, 1 Cor 2:7) and "for ages of ages" (εἰς τοὺς αἰῶνας τῶν αἰώνων, Gal 1:5; Phil 4:20). It is therefore likely that "secret for eternal periods" is "non-Pauline."[24]

e. In 16:26 the expression "prophetic writings" (γραφῶν προφητικῶν) is never otherwise used by Paul, and does not occur elsewhere in the NT.[25] Paul either uses γραφή in the absolute to refer to Scripture as a whole (Rom 4:3; 9:17; 10:11; 11:2; 15:4; 1 Cor 15:3-4; Gal 3:8, 22; 4:30) or speaks of "holy writings" (Rom 1:2).[26] He never uses προφητικός ("prophetic") or the adverb προφητικῶς ("prophetically"), although such terminology is at home in 2 Pet 1:19 and the Apostolic Fathers (*Herm. Mand.* 11.9; *2 Clem.* 11.2; *Mart. Pol.* 12.3; 16.2; also *3 Cor.* 2.10). This expression, "prophetic writings," is therefore probably non-Pauline.[27]

f. The reference to "the eternal God" (τοῦ αἰωνίου θεοῦ) is a non-Pauline expression and is out of step with his emphasis on God's self-revelation in the death and resurrection of Christ. In fact, aside from this verse the adjective αἰώνιος is never attached as a predicate to God in the NT, while it occurs in the LXX and remains characteristic for Hellenistic Judaism.[28] For example, Gen 21:33 says that the name of the Lord is Θεὸς αἰώνιος ("God eternal") and Isa 40:28 employs the same expression. Philo explains the significance of this title from Genesis as follows: "The title "God eternal" (Θεὸς αἰώνιος) is equivalent to 'He that is, not sometimes gracious and sometimes not so, but continuously and always; He that without intermission bestows benefits; He that causes His gifts to follow each other in ceaseless flow; He who makes His boons come round in unbroken cycle, knitting them together by unifying forces; He who lets no opportunity of doing good go by; He who is Lord, and so is able to hurt also'" (*Plant.* 89). An association between this expression and the revelation of

19 *Herm. Sim.* 92.4 refers to "The forty apostles and teachers of the kerygma of the son of God (διδάσκαλοι τοῦ κηρύγματος τοῦ υἱοῦ τοῦ θεοῦ)" and Origen *Com. Joan.* 6.44.229.3 refers to "the gospel proclamation of Jesus the Christ (τῷ εὐαγγελικῷ κηρύγματι Ἰησοῦ τοῦ Χριστοῦ)."

20 Elliott, "Concluding Doxology," 129; also Walker, *Interpolations*, 196.

21 See Kamlah, "Schlußdoxologie des Römerbriefes," 63–65; Collins, "Wandering Doxology," 302.

22 See Elliott, "Concluding Doxology," 126.

23 See Hans Hübner, "χρόνος," *EDNT* 3 (1993) 488.

24 Elliott, "Concluding Doxology," 129; also Walker, *Interpolations*, 196.

25 See Kamlah, "Schlußdoxologie des Römerbriefes," 45–52; Collins, "Wandering Doxology," 301.

26 See Hans Hübner, "γραφή, γράφω," *EDNT* 1 (1990) 262–63.

27 Elliott, "Concluding Doxology," 129; also Walker, *Interpolations*, 196.

28 See Horst Balz, "αἰώνιος," *EDNT* 1 (1990) 47.

mysteries is evident in Sus 42, "the eternal God (ὁ θεὸς ὁ αἰώνιος), the knower of hidden things." *1 En.* 75.3 refers to the Lord as "the God of eternal glory." The blessing given to Terah in *Jub.* 12.29 contains the line, "May God eternal make straight your path" (see also *Jub.* 13.8).

g. The word ἐπιταγή ("command") does not appear elsewhere in Romans, and is otherwise employed in Paul's letters only in the context of congregational regulations (1 Cor 7:6, 25; 2 Cor 8:8). This use in the doxology reappears with exactly the same connotation in 1 Tim 1:1 and Titus 1:3, and with an authoritarian ethical implication in Titus 2:15.[29] This term, which originated in the Hellenistic period to refer to the ordinance or command of an emperor whose power was considered to be absolute,[30] is consistent with the usage of Hellenistic Judaism. For example, the Wisdom of Solomon depicts "God's almighty word leaping from heaven out of God's royal throne," resulting in an "unmistakable command like a sharp sword" (ξίφος ὀξὺ τὴν ἀνυπόκριτον ἐπιταγήν, Wis 18:15–16) that destroys wickedness. *Ps. Sol.* 18.23 refers to God sending out orders "by command of his servants (ἐν ἐπιταγῇ δούλων αὐτοῦ)." While such usage is consistent with references to pagan deities,[31] it remains uncharacteristic of Paul.[32] The adherence to "the command of the eternal God" is strongly at variance with Rom 3:21–5:21, where Paul argues against salvation through obedience to the law of God, and with 12:1-2, which contends that God's

will must be ascertained by discernment and discussion within Christian communities.

h. The verb γνωρίζω ("make known") is always used by Paul in the active voice, referring to direct disclosure to his congregations (1 Cor 12:3; 2 Cor 8:1; Gal 1:11; Phil 1:22), to his proclamation of the gospel (1 Cor 15:1), and to making significant facts known directly to God and by God (Phil 4:6; Rom 9:22, 23).[33] In deutero-Pauline literature, this term occurs in the passive in Eph 3:3, 5, 10, referring as in the doxology to the disclosure of mysteries through divine action. It implies a mysterious communication process that does not involve normal human agency.

i. The formula "God only wise" (μόνῳ σοφῷ θεῷ) in 16:27 is not found elsewhere in the NT and seems unlikely to have been coined by Paul.[34] The idea of only one God appears in Greco-Roman and Jewish sources as well as early Christian documents, so identifying the specific source of this theme is difficult.[35] While the idea of God's wisdom occurs in the OT (Isa 31:32; Jer 10:12; Ps 104:24; Job 26:12; Prov 3:19-20),[36] and the Socratic tradition contends that "the god is wise (ὁ θεὸς σοφὸς εἶναι) . . . [while] human wisdom is of little or no value,"[37] the combination of wisdom, oneness, and God occurs only in Hellenistic Jewish texts such as Pseudo-Phocylides *Sent.* 54, and *Sib. Or.* 2*.126; 5.356 refer to "the only God is wise" (εἷς θεός ἐστι σοφός).[38] Philo follows this tradition in refer-

29 See W. Grimm, "ἐπιτάσσω, ἐπταγή," *EDNT* 2 (1991) 41; Collins, "Wandering Doxology," 301, also discusses the link to Titus 1:3.

30 Gerhard Delling, "τάσσω κτλ.," *TDNT* 8 (1972) 36, refers to *OGIS* 2. Nr. 674.1; *SIG* 2. Nr. 821.D.2.

31 For example, *PGM* III. Nr. 80: "By order of the great god Neouphneioth (κατ᾽ ὑποταγὴ[ν] τοῦ μ[ε]γάλου θε[οῦ] Νεουφνείωθ)."

32 See Elliott, "Concluding Doxology," 129; also Walker, *Interpolations*, 196.

33 See Otto Knoch, "γνωρίζω," *EDNT* 1 (1990) 256; F. Gaboriau, "Enquête sur la signification biblique de connaître," *Ang* 45 (1968) 18–25.

34 Paul's characteristic formulation is "wisdom of God" in Rom 11:33; 1 Cor 1:21-24; 1:7; see Elliott, "Concluding Doxology," 128.

35 See Gerhard Delling, "ΜΟΝΟΣ ΘΕΟΣ," *ThLZ* 77 (1952) 469–76; Joseph A. Fitzmyer, "μόνος," *EDNT* 2 (1991) 441, traces the background of the monotheistic claim in this verse back to the OT and intertestamental Jewish writers; see also Fitzmyer, 755.

36 See Georg Fohrer and Ulrich Wilckens, "σοφία," *TDNT* 7 (1971) 489.

37 Plato *Apol.* 23a, linked to Rom 16:27 by Jacques Dupont, "ΜΟΝΩΙ ΣΟΦΩΙ ΘΕΩΙ (Rom., xvi, 27)," *EThL* 22 (1946) 363–64.

38 See Dupont, "ΜΟΝΩΙ ΣΟΦΩΙ ΘΕΩΙ," 365–66.

ring to God as "the only wise being" ($\tau\grave{\eta}\nu\ \tau o\hat{v}$ $\mu\acute{o}\nu o\upsilon\ \sigma o\varphi o\hat{v}\ \sigma\upsilon\mu\mu\alpha\rho\chi\acute{\iota}\alpha\nu$, *Conf.* 39): "He alone being wise, who is also alone God" ($\acute{\epsilon}\nu\grave{o}\varsigma\ \acute{o}\nu\tau o\varsigma$ $\mu\acute{o}\nu o\upsilon\ \sigma o\varphi o\hat{v}\ \tau o\hat{v}\ \kappa\alpha\grave{\iota}\ \mu\acute{o}\nu o\upsilon\ \vartheta\epsilon o\hat{v}$, *Migr.* 134).[39] It therefore seems likely that the phrase "God only wise" derived from Hellenistic Judaism; aside from the doxology in Rom 16:27, it is employed otherwise in early Christianity only by Clement of Alexandria *Paed.* 1.10.93.3: $\sigma o\varphi\grave{o}\varsigma\ \delta\grave{\epsilon}\ \acute{o}\ \vartheta\epsilon\grave{o}\varsigma$ $\mu\acute{o}\nu o\varsigma$ ("and God alone is wise"). The usefulness of this expression in Jewish critiques of Christians as ditheists, and its resonance with Gnosticism,[40] may account for its lack of wider use in subsequent Christianity.

j. With the plural of "aeons," the acclamation "to him be glory for aeons of aeons" could easily have come from Paul. I discussed virtually the same formulation in 11:36, $\alpha\grave{\upsilon}\tau\hat{\omega}\ \acute{\eta}\ \delta\acute{o}\xi\alpha\ \epsilon\grave{\iota}\varsigma\ \tau o\grave{\upsilon}\varsigma\ \alpha\grave{\iota}\hat{\omega}\nu\alpha\varsigma,\ \grave{\alpha}\mu\acute{\eta}\nu$ ("to him be glory for aeons, Amen"). Since an exact parallel occurs in Gal 1:5; 2 Tim 4:18; Heb 13:21; and 4 Macc 18:24 ($\hat{\omega}\ \acute{\eta}\ \delta\acute{o}\xi\alpha\ \epsilon\grave{\iota}\varsigma\ \tau o\grave{\upsilon}\varsigma\ \alpha\grave{\iota}\hat{\omega}\nu\alpha\varsigma,$ $\grave{\alpha}\mu\acute{\eta}\nu$), and since ascription of glory to God is virtually omnipresent in biblical and apocalyptic materials,[41] this line could have come from any of these sources, including Paul himself.

5. There is a plausible redactional motivation in the creation and original placement of the doxology. There is a widely shared scholarly assessment that Marcion's aim in eliminating chapter 15 was to avoid the OT citations in 15:1-13 as well as the view of Scripture as authoritative in 15:4, and that he decided to close the argument on the theme congenial to his theology in 14:23, that "whatever is not of faith is sin."[42] The resultant fourteen-chapter letter had no appropriate ending, especially for liturgical purposes.[43] The doxology shared some of the Marcionite interests in eliminating the theme of coexistence between Jewish Christians and Gentile Christians and particularly the idea of Christ serving the Jewish people in 15:8. The supersessionist line in the fourteen-chapter letter that expresses a Marcionite interest is well embodied by the redacted doxology that claims the mystery was hidden to Jews but disclosed to Gentile believers.

These five factors are most easily accommodated by a theory of interpolation and of an original placement of the doxology after 14:23. The subsequent popularity of the doxology, reflecting many of the interests of patristic Christianity, explains why it appears in thirteen of the fifteen text types. In the exegetical analysis that follows, I shall attempt to analyze the significance of the details in this original setting after 14:23 and in its currently more widely accepted location at the end of the letter.

Doxological Analysis

The basic dilemma is that the doxology is lumbering, redundant, and somewhat contradictory in its theological impulses, particularly in the context of a post-Marcionite ending. These dilemmas can all be resolved by accepting a theory of redaction in several stages, only the final of which occurred in response to Marcion's mutilation. Two lines of scholarship contribute to the proposed resolution. Adolf von Harnack argued that an originally Marcionite doxology was catholicized by the addition of the phrases "and the proclamation of Jesus Christ," "through the prophetic writings," and "made known."[44] While the doxology only faintly reflects Mar-

---

39 See ibid., 366.

40 See Fohrer and Wilckens, "$\sigma o\varphi\acute{\iota}\alpha$," 508, 520.

41 For example, 2 Chr 30:8, "give glory to the Lord God"; Ps 28:1, "Bring to the Lord glory due to his name"; *Apoc. Ez.* 33.4–6, "To whom is glory . . . now and always and forever and ever, Amen ($\nu\hat{\upsilon}\nu\ \kappa\alpha\grave{\iota}$ $\grave{\alpha}\epsilon\grave{\iota}\ \kappa\alpha\grave{\iota}\ \epsilon\grave{\iota}\varsigma\ \tau o\grave{\upsilon}\varsigma\ \alpha\grave{\iota}\hat{\omega}\nu\alpha\varsigma\ \tau\hat{\omega}\nu\ \alpha\grave{\iota}\acute{\omega}\nu\omega\nu,\ \grave{\alpha}\mu\acute{\eta}\nu$); *Vi. Ad.* 43.8, "Holy, holy, holy is the Lord, for the glory of God [the] Father, because to him is fitting glory and honor and obeisance now and always and forever and ever, Amen ($\nu\hat{\upsilon}\nu\ \kappa\alpha\grave{\iota}\ \grave{\alpha}\epsilon\grave{\iota}\ \kappa\alpha\grave{\iota}\ \epsilon\grave{\iota}\varsigma\ \tau o\grave{\upsilon}\varsigma$ $\alpha\grave{\iota}\acute{\omega}\nu\omega\nu\ \tau\hat{\omega}\nu\ \alpha\grave{\iota}\acute{\omega}\nu\omega\nu,\ \grave{\alpha}\mu\acute{\eta}\nu$)." For further examples,

see Gerhard Kittel and Gerhard von Rad, "$\delta o\kappa\acute{\epsilon}\omega$ $\kappa\tau\lambda$.," *TDNT* 2 (1964) 238–47.

42 Manson, "Romans—and Others," 11. In contrast Schmidt, *Marcion*, 289–94, argues that the fourteen-chapter version of Romans was created before Marcion's time, following Trobisch, *Entstehung*, 75–79, that the deletion of chapters 15–16 resulted from an early textual defect.

43 See Champion, *Benedictions and Doxologies*, 26–28, 96–97, 106.

44 Adolf von Harnack, *Marcion*, 2d ed., TU 14 (Berlin:

---

cionite interest, and is assumed by recent scholarship to be a post-Marcionite product, the elimination of these phrases from the doxology reduces its redundancy. Moreover, a theory of a two-stage redaction following the creation of the fourteen-chapter letter is undermined by the fact that in all its varied locations, the doxology never appears without these seemingly orthodox phrases. It seems much more likely that these phrases were in the doxology before its attachment to Romans. A second line of inquiry was opened by John O'Neill, who reconstructed an originally Jewish doxology to which later Christian interpolations were added, noted in brackets below.[45]

To him who is able to strengthen you
   [according to my gospel
   and the preaching of Jesus Christ]
According to the revelation of the mystery
Kept silent for long ages;
   [now manifest through the prophetic writings]
According to the command of the eternal God
Made known to the obedience of faith;
   [to all Gentiles]
To the only wise God
   [through Jesus Christ]
To him be glory for ever. Amen.

Although there are some minor discrepancies in this assignment of interpolations, the reconstructed original form of this doxology matches some examples in Hellenistic Judaism, as noted by Richard Deichgräber.[46] For example, as noted above, 4 Macc 18:24 is virtually identical with the final line of the doxology: ᾧ ἡ δόξα εἰς τοὺς αἰῶνας τῶν αἰώνων. Ἀμήν. ("to whom be glory for ever and ever. Amen").

The insights developed by these previous hypotheses suggest the possibility of a three-step creation and redaction of the doxology, two of which occurred before the Marcionite mutilation of Romans:

Step One

The text of a Hellenistic Jewish doxology can be reconstructed by eliminating the redactional elements identified by Harnack and O'Neill. The result is as follows:

Τῷ δὲ δυναμένῳ ὑμᾶς στηρίξαι	25a
κατὰ ἀποκάλυψιν μυστηρίου	25c
χρόνοις αἰωνίοις σεσιγημένου	25d
κατ᾽ ἐπιταγὴν τοῦ αἰωνίου θεοῦ	26b
μόνῳ σοφῷ θεῷ	27a
ᾧ ἡ δόξα εἰς τοὺς αἰῶνας. ἀμήν.	27b-c

In contrast to the sprawling form of the final doxology in Rom 16:25-27, this has six lines of three beats apiece, with the second through the fourth marked by a poetic homoioptoton and the fifth and sixth lines containing a sixfold homoioteleuton with the repetition of o-sounds, thus rendering it plausible in liturgical use. This doxology matches the "revelation scheme" identified by Nils Dahl[47] and developed by Michael Wolter and others,[48] in which hidden wisdom is revealed by divine decree. Wolter has demonstrated the correlation between this material and *As. Mos.* 1.12–14,[49] in which the great lawgiver declares that God did not want to "manifest this purpose of creation from the foundation of the world, in order that the Gentiles might thereby be convicted," so he "designed and devised me and He prepared me before the foundation of the world, that I should be the mediator of His covenant." God is glorified in this benediction for keeping the mystery of the law hidden from

---

Töpelmann, 1924) 165. Black, 216, cites E. C. Blackman, *Marcion and His Influence* (London: SPCK, 1948) 49, as confirming this assessment.

45   See Kamlah, "Schlußdoxologie des Römerbriefes," 77–82; O'Neill, 260; Käsemann, 423.

46   Deichgräber, *Gotteshymnus*, 37–38, followed by Samuel Vollenweider, "Doxologie," *RGG⁴* 2 (1999) 963, listing *Pr. Man.* 15; 4 Macc 18:24.

47   Nils A. Dahl, "Formgeschichtliche Beobachtungen zur Christusverkündigung in der Gemeindepredigt," in F.-W. Eltester, ed., *Neutestamentliche Stu-*

dien für Rudolf Bultmann zu seinem siebzigsten Geburtstag am 20. August 1954, 2d ed., BZNW 21 (Berlin: de Gruyter, 1957) 4–5.

48   Wolter, "Verborgene Weisheit," 297–319, following up on work by Dieter Lührmann, *Offenbarungsverständnis*, 113–40, and others.

49   Wolter, "Verborgene Weisheit," 316.

Gentiles and revealed to Jews through Moses. The "Amen" was undoubtedly included in the original Jewish doxology, following the model in 4 Macc 18:24, etc.[50] All of the terminology in this original doxology is consistent with Hellenistic Judaism. The final line is cited from 4 Macc 18:24, including the relative pronoun $\hat{\omega}$ ("to whom"), which originally referred to God and, with the Christianized redaction in step two, refers to Jesus Christ.

Step Two

Prior to the Marcionite mutilation of Romans in the middle of the second century, this Hellenistic Jewish doxology was transformed into a Christian counterpart in a manner similar to Col 1:26-27 and Eph 6:19. It employs some of the same vocabulary: $\nu\hat{\nu}\nu$ $\delta\acute{\epsilon}$ ("but now") shared with Colossians; and $\varphi\alpha\nu\epsilon\rho\acute{o}\omega$ ("reveal"), $\gamma\nu\omega\rho\acute{\iota}\zeta\omega$ ("make known"), $\acute{\epsilon}\vartheta\nu\epsilon\sigma\iota\nu$ ("Gentiles"), and $\mu\nu\sigma\tau\acute{\eta}\rho\iota\nu$ ("mystery") shared with both Ephesians and Colossians. Both letters present the idea of Paul as the one conveying the gospel of this revelation to the Gentiles. The expression "prophetic writings" has its closest counterparts in 2 Peter and the Apostolic Fathers, and functioned very well to assert both the validity of the OT prophecies about Jesus and the prophetic, inspired nature of early Christian writings. The expression "proclamation of Jesus Christ" redefines the standard on which believers are "confirmed," and is employed in a similar way by *Herm. Sim.* 92.4. This redactional step inserted verbal redundancy, with $\varphi\alpha\nu\epsilon\rho\acute{o}\omega$ ("disclosed") and $\gamma\nu\omega\rho\acute{\iota}\zeta\omega$ ("made known") functioning as virtual synonyms of the word $\grave{\alpha}\pi o\kappa\acute{\alpha}\lambda\upsilon\psi\iota\varsigma$ ("revelation") in the original doxology. Its addition of $\tau\acute{\epsilon}$ ("and") in 26a forces no less than four subsequent phrases ("through prophetic writings," "according to the command of the eternal God," "for obedience of faith," and "for all the Gentiles") to be attached to the participle "made known" in 26d, creating a rambling syntax that is difficult to follow with precision. To the final line concerning the "one wise God" was added the phrase $\delta\iota\grave{\alpha}$ $\emptyset \eta\sigma o\hat{\nu}$ $X\rho\iota\sigma\tau o\hat{\nu}$ ("through Jesus Christ"). While this addition counters the charge that Christians were ditheists who no longer believed in one God, it remains awkward and somewhat unclear: is it God's wisdom that comes through Christ? Or the oneness of God?

This Christianized doxology was probably used in worship by circles sympathetic with the theology of Colossians and Ephesians, interested in the theme of a distinctive revelation to the Gentiles that supersedes the revelation of the law through Moses.

Step Three

In the period after Marcion's redaction, the Christianized doxology was adapted to provide a suitable conclusion for the fourteen-chapter version of the letter extant in Rome. The phrases $\tau\grave{o}$ $\epsilon\grave{\upsilon}\alpha\gamma\gamma\acute{\epsilon}\lambda\iota\nu$ $\mu o\nu$ ("my gospel") and $\epsilon\grave{\iota}\varsigma$ $\grave{\upsilon}\pi\alpha\kappa o\grave{\eta}\nu$ $\pi\acute{\iota}\sigma\tau\epsilon\omega\varsigma$ ("for the obedience of faith") were added at this time, both being characteristic expressions from Romans that served to bind the doxology to its new, epistolary setting. An additional redundancy is thereby created between "my gospel" and the "proclamation of Jesus Christ." The interpolated phrases are both used in the doxology in ways that reflect that the Pauline connotations are no longer fully understood, but they express the reaction of later Paulinists to the threat posed by Marcion. In this new context, the Christianized expression "prophetic writings" in 26a would counter Marcionite contempt for the OT prophetic legacy, and the phrase "the proclamation of Jesus Christ" in 25b would counter his denigration of the gospel traditions.[51] This final redaction created the lumbering, somewhat redundant doxology currently found in Romans, printed out below with the initial Christianization marked with single underlining, and the post-Marcionite redaction with double underlining. The original form of the Hellenistic Jewish doxology appears in normal type.

$T\hat{\omega}$ $\delta\grave{\epsilon}$ $\delta\nu\nu\alpha\mu\acute{\epsilon}\nu\hat{\omega}$ $\grave{\upsilon}\mu\hat{\alpha}\varsigma$ $\sigma\tau\eta\rho\acute{\iota}\xi\alpha\iota$	25a
<u>$\kappa\alpha\tau\grave{\alpha}$</u> <u>$\tau\grave{o}$ $\epsilon\grave{\upsilon}\alpha\gamma\gamma\acute{\epsilon}\lambda\iota\nu$ $\mu o\nu$ $\kappa\alpha\iota$</u>	
$\tau\grave{o}$ $\kappa\acute{\eta}\rho\nu\gamma\mu\alpha$ $\emptyset \eta\sigma o\hat{\nu}$ $X\rho\iota\sigma\tau o\hat{\nu}$	25b
$\kappa\alpha\tau\grave{\alpha}$ $\grave{\alpha}\pi o\kappa\acute{\alpha}\lambda\upsilon\psi\iota\nu$ $\mu\nu\sigma\tau\eta\rho\acute{\iota}\nu$	25c
$\chi\rho\acute{o}\nu\iota\varsigma$ $\alpha\grave{\iota}\omega\nu\acute{\iota}\iota\varsigma$ $\sigma\epsilon\sigma\iota\gamma\eta\mu\acute{\epsilon}\nu\nu$	25d
$\varphi\alpha\nu\epsilon\rho\omega\vartheta\acute{\epsilon}\nu\tau o\varsigma$ $\delta\grave{\epsilon}$ $\nu\hat{\nu}\nu$ $\delta\iota\acute{\alpha}$ $\tau\epsilon$	
$\gamma\rho\alpha\varphi\hat{\omega}\nu$ $\pi\rho o\varphi\eta\tau\iota\kappa\hat{\omega}\nu$	26a

---

50   See H. -W. Kuhn, "$\grave{\alpha}\mu\acute{\eta}\nu$," *EDNT* 1 (1990) 69–70.

51   For Marcion's views on these matters, see Hendrik F. Stander, "Marcion," *EEC* 2 (1997) 715–17.

κατ᾽ ἐπιταγὴν τοῦ αἰωνίου θεοῦ   26b
εἰς ὑπακοὴν πίστεως   26c
εἰς πάντα τὰ ἔθνη γνωρισθέντος   26d
μόνῳ σοφῷ θεῷ   27a
διὰ Ἰησοῦ Χριστοῦ   27b
ᾧ ἡ δόξα εἰς τοὺς αἰῶνας τῶν αἰώνων.   27c
ἀμήν.   27d

In view of the evolution of this doxology, it is understandable that its current form should be perceived to have a "beautiful solemnity"[52] that repeats well-known Pauline phrases. It is open-ended, evocative, lacking in precise syntactical articulation, but eminently suited for liturgical use. The analysis below is a rather unsatisfactory effort to impose a measure of order on this sprawling construction.

Rhetorical Disposition

16:25-27   The second interpolation: the supersessionist doxology
16:25-26   A. The capability of God to confirm Gentile believers
16:25a   1. The recipients of divine action: you Gentiles
         2. The nature of divine action: confirming Gentile believers
           a. The means of confirmation: Paul's gospel to the Gentiles
             1) Clarification of "gospel" as "the preaching of Jesus Christ"
16:25b   2) The revelation of the "mystery" kept silent from the Jews
16:26   3) The disclosure of the gospel in Scripture
           b. The communication of confirmation through the gospel
             1) The scope of the communication: "to all the Gentiles"
             2) The goal of communication: to evoke "obedience of faith" on the part of Gentiles
16:27   B. The ascription of glory
         1. The God of the Gentiles as the "only wise"
         2. The agency through whom God is glorified: "Jesus Christ"
         3. The eternal extent of glory
         4. The "amen"

Exegesis

■ **25** The doxology to the "one who is able to confirm you" opens with a formulation that at first glance seems congenial to Romans. The theme of divine power is crucial for the preceding argument, related to the gospel (1:16), to the demonstrations of divine sovereignty (8:38; 9:17), and to the converting work of the Spirit in 15:13, 19. However, nowhere else in Romans is the δυν-stem employed to refer to strengthening believers in the face of adversity. The verb στηρίζω is used in 1 Thess 3:2-4, 13; 2 Thess 2:17, 3:3 in the context of providing encouragement "under assault" by eschatological woes.[53] The threat of persecution is reflected in the similar doxology found in *Mart. Pol.* 20.2: "And to him who is able to bring us all into his grace and bounty (Τῷ δὲ δυναμένῳ πάντας ἡμᾶς εἰσαγαγεῖν ἐν τῇ αὐτοῦ χάριτι καὶ δωρεᾷ), to his heavenly kingdom . . . be glory, honor, might, and majesty for ever (εἰς τοὺς αἰῶνας)." The use of στηρίζω in Rom 16:25 not only lacks this context of persecution but is also somewhat different from the context of its earlier appearance in 1:11, where it referred to mutual encouragement by means of sharing one another's insights about the faith. Since the semantic range of this term is from "set up, fix" to "confirm, establish, strengthen,"[54] it seems likely in view of the wording of the original Hellenistic Jewish doxology that the sense of doctrinal and ethical consolidation under the rule of the law was in view. It is similar to Sir 6:37: "Let your mind be upon the ordinances of the Lord, and meditate continually on his commandments; he shall establish your heart (αὐτὸς στηριεῖ τὴν καρδίαν σου) and give you the desired wisdom at all times." The same sense carries over into the redacted doxology, denoting "corroboration . . . in sound doctrine and sure convictions."[55] This connotation becomes dominant in the late NT writing associated with Rome, which reminds believers "of these things, though you know them and are confirmed in the truth that you have (ἐστηριγμένους ἐν τῇ παρούσῃ ἀληθείᾳ," 2 Pet 1:12).[56] The nominal counter-

52   Leenhardt, 388.
53   Günther Harder, "στηρίζω κτλ.," *TDNT* 7 (1971) 656; see also Michel, 486–87; Dunn, 2:914.
54   BAGD 768; Gerhard Schneider, "στηρίζω," *EDNT* 3 (1993) 276.
55   Black, 216.
56   For the Roman connections with 2 Peter, see John H. Elliott, "Peter, Second Epistle of," *ABD* 5 (1992) 287.

part στηριγμός appears for the first time in the NT in 2 Pet 3:17, referring to "perseverance" in the "orthodox teaching" of 1:12, while ἀστηρικός in 2 Pet 2:14; 3:16 refers to the "unstable" teaching of heretics.[57] The στηριγ-stem plays an important role among the church fathers of the second century C.E. when the doxology was probably attached to Romans. Clement of Rome argues that membership among the elect can be guaranteed only "if our mind is established (ἐστηριγμένη) faithfully towards God"[58] while Ignatius refers to believers as "established in Christ (ἐστηριγμένοι ἐν Χριστῷ)."[59] The *Mart. Pet.* 36.5 promises that "the Lord is able to establish you in His faith (στηρίξαι δυνατός ἐστιν εἰς τὴν πίστην αὐτοῦ)."[60]

The phrase κατὰ τὸ εὐαγγελιόν μου ("according to my gospel") is distinctively Pauline,[61] found in 2:16 and with the plural pronoun "our" and without the preposition "according to" in 2 Cor 4:3; 1 Thess 1:5; 2 Thess 2:14. The context and the later use of this phrase in 2 Tim 2:8 strongly suggest that κατά with the accusative should be taken as "according to, in accordance with, in conformity with, corresponding to,"[62] implying that Paul's message is the standard by which the divine confirmation occurs.[63] The parallel expression found in the Christianized doxology before its redaction for inclusion in Romans had the parallel expression κατὰ τὸ κήρυγμα Ἰησοῦ Χριστοῦ ("according to the proclamation of Jesus Christ"), found nowhere else in the NT. While cautioning about pressing the distinction between subjective and objective genitive constructions in this kind of expression, Gerhard Friedrich suggests the former for this verse, that Christ "is the author . . . in his earthly manifestation (R. 16:25)."[64] However, most commentators find the objective genitive more plausible in this context, that is, the preaching *about* Jesus Christ,[65]

and with the formula "Jesus Christ" used as a double name, the implication is that the entire life of Jesus of Nazareth is in view. Paul's emphasis, in contrast, is on Christ crucified and resurrected.[66] In its redacted form, the double reference to the theological basis of confirmation reflects a vague grasp of Paul's original gospel; the two expressions "my gospel" and "proclamation of Jesus Christ" are linked with an ambiguous καί ("and"). There is an obvious contrast here to an authentic Pauline expression such as Rom 2:16, κατὰ τὸ εὐαγγελιόν μου διὰ Χριστοῦ Ἰησοῦ ("according to my gospel through Jesus Christ") in which it is clear that a dynamic action is expected of Christ. The major themes of Paul's gospel in Romans, the righteousness of God and righteousness through faith alone, are no longer in view, replaced by theological formulas that are no longer understood as they were originally intended. It is clear from this composite formulation that either in its original location after 14:23 or at 16:25, this doxology commences a long tradition of interpreting Romans as a doctrinal treatise, summing up the gist of orthodox theology in one form or another. In contrast to 1:11-12 where στηρίζω implies mutual enrichment, on the premise that neither Paul nor the Roman Christians have the whole truth, here a theological canon is consolidated by fusing the traditions about Jesus' life story with a formulaic grasp of Paul's gospel.

The phrase "according to the revelation of the mystery" belonged to the original, Hellenistic-Jewish doxology and reflected an interest in the disclosure of religious and mystical secrets found in apocalyptic Judaism and some other arenas of Greco-Roman religion.[67] For example, *1 En.* 49.2 proclaims that the "Elect One" has mastery over "all the mysteries of righteousness," and in 93.2 Enoch himself reveals to the

---

57 Harder, "στηρίζω κτλ.," 657.

58 *1 Clem.* 35.5.2.

59 Ignatius *Ep. interp.* 11.12.1.2; see also Irenaeus *Adv. haer.* 11.3, 6; Origen *Com. Joan.* 6.32.189.4; *Acts John* 87.4.

60 See also *Mart. Pet.* 30.4; 40.16; *Acts John* 106.6; *AcPlTh* 41.3; Epiphanius *Adv. haer.* 2.520.14.

61 See Georg Strecker, "Εὐαγγέλιον," *EDNT* 2 (1991) 72.

62 BAGD 407.5?; see Lagrange, 377; Schlier, 452–53; Cranfield, 2:809.

63 See Marshall, "Apt Conclusion," 179.

64 Gerhard Friedrich, "εὐαγγελίζομαι κτλ.," *TDNT* 2 (1964) 731; idem, "κῆρυξ κτλ.," *TDNT* 3 (1965) 716.

65 Weiss, 609, referring to Köllner, Reitmayer, Goebel, Godet, Philippi, and critiquing Meyer, 2:385, who argued for a subjective genitive; more recent advocates of the objective reading include Cranfield, 2:810; Black, 216; Murray, 2:241; Wilckens, 3:148; Moo, 938.

66 See Otto Merk, "κηρύσσω κτλ.," *EDNT* 2 (1991) 288.

67 See Günther Bornkamm, "μυστήριον, νυέω,"

"children of righteousness . . . that which was revealed to me from the heavenly vision." The connections between the wording of the doxology and Qumran materials are particularly close. The Teacher of Righteousness has seen with his own eyes "wisdom that has been hidden from mankind" (1QS 11:6); he is the one "to whom God has made known all the mysteries (כול רזי) of the words of his servants, the prophets" (1QpHab 7:4–5). While a number of NT passages have a similar revelation scheme,[68] the most exact parallel in terminology, if not in syntactical relationships, is provided by Eph 3:3, where the pseudonymous Paul claims that "according to revelation the mystery was made known to me (κατὰ ἀποκάλυψιν ἐγνωρίσθη μοι τὸ μυστήριον)."[69] Here we find the same passive verbal form that dominates the doxology in Romans: σεσιγημένου . . . φανερωθέντος . . . γνωρισθέντος, in which divine confirmation is provided by the gospel preached by the Pauline tradition and by the revelation of the mystery contained therein.

The expression "kept silent for eternal periods" is unique in several respects. Ordinarily, χρόνος ("time") and αἰών ("eternity") are separate, somewhat overlapping terms that would not be combined in standard Greek.[70] Αἰών represents an indefinitely extended epoch of time as opposed to χρόνος, the minute-by-minute, day-to-day calculation of time.[71] This distinction was explained by Plato in *Tim.* 37d that describes the demiurgic Father's creating a "certain dynamic image of Eternity (εἰκὼ . . . κινητόν τινα αἰῶνος)" that abides unchanging in heaven in contrast to the calculation of

days, months, and years "which we designate as time (τοῦτον ὃν δὴ χρόνον ὠνομάκαμεν)." The LXX appears to confuse this distinction in translating several Hebrew expressions for time, creating the pleonastic expression in the singular, εἰς τὸ αἰῶνα χρόνον ("for an eternal period"), which appears in Exod 14:13; Isa 9:6; 13:20; 14:20; 18:7; 33:20; 34:17; 3 Macc 3:29. A similar expression, ἀπ᾽ αἰῶνος χρόνου ("from an eternal period"), appears in Bar 3:32; 3 Macc 5:11. A plural expression similar to that used in the doxology appears in 3 Macc 7:23, "Blessed be the Redeemer of Israel for continual periods (εἰς τοὺς ἀεὶ χρόνους)." It thus appears likely that the pleonastic expression "eternal periods" had its home in Hellenistic Judaism and that the unique expression found in the doxology was picked up in the Pastorals (2 Tim 1:9; Titus 1:2) as "a variant of αἰῶνες in the eternity formulae" such as "ages of ages."[72] I discussed the simple plural of αἰών in Paul's doxology of Rom 1:25. Hermann Saase contends that the uniquely pleonastic expression in 16:25 weakens the "concept of eternity,"[73] by which he presumably means that it refers to periods that are less than eternal, that is, historical periods of immense but not infinite length. Given the Judeo-Christian concept of creation at a particular point in time, this expression appears to mean "from the beginning of time,"[74] that is, from the moment of creation.

The perfect passive participle σεσιγημένος[75] attached to the pleonastic expression "for eternal periods" has the sense of something intentionally kept silent.

TDNT 4 (1967) 808–16; Helmut Krämer, "μυστήριον," *EDNT* 2 (1991) 446–47; Wolter, "Verborgene Weisheit," 300–303.

68 See Bornkamm, "μυστήριον, μυέω," 821.

69 See Traugott Holtz, "ἀποκαλύπτω, ἀποκάλυψις," *EDNT* 1 (1990) 131. This theme from the doxology and Ephesians is carried forward by Irenaeus *Adv. haer.* 21.6: "This is the mystery that he tells, according to the revelation made known to him, that the one who suffered under Pontius Pilate, this one is Lord of all and King and God and Judge." See also *Adv. haer.* 1.1.1.42, 48; 1.6.3.16; 1.1.17.31.

70 See Gerhard Delling, "χρόνος," *TDNT* 9 (1974) 581–85; Hermann Saase, "αἰών, αἰώνιος," *TDNT* 1 (1964) 197–200.

71 See *OCD³*, 48; Kotansky, *Greek Magical Amulets*, 1:115.

72 Saase, "αἰών, αἰώνιος," 209.

73 Ibid.

74 Dunn, 2:915; see also Meyer, 2:387; Barr, *Time*, 120–21; Balz, "αἰώνιος," 47. Lagrange, 378, and Murray, 2:241, suggest "eternity of God," and Delling, "χρόνος," 592–93, suggests "before unimaginable times," neither of which seems to be implied.

75 Apart from this verse, the perfect participle σεσιγημέν- is unattested before the second century C.E., but Irenaeus *Adv. haer.* 1.1.1.43 refers to the twelve aeons that are οἱ σεσιγημένοι καὶ μὴ γινωσκόμενοι ("kept secret and unknown").

This is the only appearance of σιγάω ("make silent") in Romans, and it is employed elsewhere by Paul only in the context of keeping silent in worship situations (1 Cor 14:28, 30, 34). Helmut Krämer argues that σεσιγη-μένος implies "an intensification of 'hidden'" messages referred to in Colossians and Ephesians.[76] But while Col 1:26-27 and Eph 3:5-6, 9 speak of the hidden mystery (τὸ μυστήριον τὸ ἀποκεκρυμμένον), inaccessible because human finitude cannot grasp the transcendence of God, the doxology refers to silencing,[77] which implies that insiders knew the truth but concealed it from others.[78] Moreover, only those with superior power can enforce silence.[79] These observations fit my hypothesis that this portion of the doxology belonged to the Hellenistic Jewish doxology sharing the view of *As. Mos.*1.12–14, that the truth about God and his law was intentionally hidden from the Gentiles by divine power. In the Christianized version of the doxology, of course, this claim was reversed: God's truth was kept silent from Jewish interpreters but is now revealed, as the next verse claims, to the Gentile believers.[80] Michael Wolter lifts up the polemical implication of these details, that the wisdom of God was expressed not in the law and the election of Israel but for the first time in the Pauline gospel proclaimed among the Gentiles.[81] This theme was taken up by Ignatius, who polemicizes against Jewish doctrines and claims that God's word "proceeds from silence" (ἀπὸ σιγῆς προελθών, *Mag.* 8.2; cf. *Eph.* 19.1); it is stated in *Diogn.* 3.1–5 and 8.9–11;[82] it is also "to be found in Valentinian Gnosticism."[83]

In the original location of this benediction, after 14:23, the possession of the great divine mystery replaces the hope of global transformation that joins Jews and Gentiles into one chorus of praise. By the time the doxology was attached to Romans, the Jewish population had been reduced and discredited, with the survivors of the Jewish-Roman Wars of 66–70 and 132–35 working in slave-labor camps building pagan temples, their wives and children being used for prostitution and pederasty. The hope of converting the great Jewish people to the gospel, which could have avoided this holocaust, has been abandoned by the circle that added the doxology. In place of a gospel that overcomes the boundaries of honor and shame, there is now the possession of a gospel and of preaching that no Jewish interpreter had been able to understand, and which therefore places the Gentile Christian interpreter in a unique and supremely honored location. A new system of acquiring honor and avoiding shame thereby arises that has an implicit supersessionism at its heart. This system entails an abandonment of Paul's vision of global transformation that includes the Jews. At its more widely accepted location at the end of chapter 16, these polemical implications are somewhat muted. But the claim of Gentile supersession remains.

■ **26** The language of 16:26a contains Pauline terminology that sounds quite familiar, with φανερόω ("make known") employed here as a virtual synonym of ἀποκαλύπτω ("reveal") just as in 1:18-19; 3:21;[84] and νῦν marking the current phase of eschatological fulfillment.[85] Although it would be natural to connect "through prophetic writings" to the participle φανε-ρωθέντος ("made manifest"),[86] the presence of τέ

76 Krämer, "μυστήριον," 488; see also L.-M. Dewailly, "Mystère et silence dans Rom xvi. 25," *NTS* 14 (1967–68) 113–18; Walter Radl, "σιγάω, σιγή," *EDNT* 3 (1993) 242.

77 For the distinction, see Wolter, "Verborgene Weisheit," 310.

78 See Corssen, "Überlieferungsgeschichte," 32–33, which Cranfield, 2:810, dismisses as pedantic.

79 For example, magical formulas were used to enforce silence; *PGM* IV.557–59 says, "You immediately place your right finger to your mouth and say, 'Silence! Silence! Silence!' (σιγή, σιγή, σιγή), a symbol of the Living God Incorrupt."

80 See Marshall, "Apt Conclusion," 181: "The Gentile readers are assured that there is almost a divine 'bias toward the Gentiles.'"

81 Wolter, "Verborgene Weisheit," 317.

82 See Marshall, "Apt Conclusion," 182.

83 O'Neill, 261.

84 Paul-Gerd Müller, "φανερόω," *EDNT* 3 (1993) 41; for a discussion of the relation between φανερόω and ἀποκαλύπτω, see Bockmuehl, "Verb φανερόω," 93–99.

85 Walter Radl, "νῦν, νυνί," *EDNT* 2 (1991) 480, citing Luz, *Geschichtsverständnis*, 88.

86 See Barrett, 286–87; Käsemann, 421.

("and") in the middle of the prepositional phrase "through prophetic writings" indicates that this phrase belongs with the following verb.[87] Whether these writings are by the Hebrew prophets[88] or early Christian writers[89] remains debatable. If the doxology had been written by Paul, one would surely opt for the former. But in the second-century context, the latter seems equally germane. This is the period when Christian leaders are referred to as "prophets" (Eph 2:20; 3:5; 4:11; Rev 18:20; *Mart. Pol.* 16.2) and 2 Pet 3:16 refers to Paul's letters as γραφαί ("writings, scriptures").[90] Similarly, *2 Clem.* 2.4 refers to a saying of Jesus as γραφή ("writing, scripture," see also 45.2) and Irenaeus *Adv. haer* 1.1.3 and 2.28.3 employs it in reference to inspired writings. Moreover, Godet argues convincingly that διά in connection with the writings implies that the disclosure occurred "through these writings," which is contradicted by the claim that their meaning was silenced until the gospel proclamation began.[91]

The phrase "according to the command of the eternal God," employing terminology characteristic of Hellenistic Judaism as noted above, fits the original doxology as a qualifier to the silencing of the mystery. It was commanded by none other than the transcendent deity whose will cannot be questioned. In the context of the Christianized doxology, since it follows the phrase "according to the proclamation of Jesus Christ" and precedes the phrase "for obedience of faith," it places the divine imprimatur on the revelation of this new form of faith to the Gentiles, bringing to an end the era of divinely imposed silence. It therefore follows that ὑπακοὴ πίστεως is defined contextually in an authoritarian, legalistic manner that is alien to Paul's general orientation and is quite different from the earlier use of this expression in 1:5.[92] Moreover, the supersessionist impulse comes to expression here with the "obedience of faith" available now to "all the Gentiles," but no longer to "the Jew first and then to the Greek." The key question in this connection is whether the phrase εἰς πάντα τὰ ἔθνη should be translated "for all the nations"[93] or "for all the Gentiles."[94] In view of the close parallel in Eph 3:3-5, it seems that the technical sense of "Gentiles" is in view. Certainly, the original hearers of Romans, which uses ἔθνοι consistently to refer to "Gentiles,"[95] would understand it this way. It is also important to keep the nuance of εἰς in view, indicating purpose, advantage, or reference to,[96] because the phrases with this preposition in v. 26c and 26d should be translated alike: "for obedience of faith" and "for all the Gentiles."

With a translation of "for all the Gentiles," the disparity with Paul's earlier view of the "obedience of faith" can be set forth more clearly. As Don Garlington's study of this expression shows, "Paul has chosen to apply to Jews and Gentiles indiscriminately terms evocative of

---

87 See Meyer, 2:389; Godet, 504; Cranfield, 2:811–12, followed by Dunn, 2:915; Moo, 939.

88 Meyer, 2:389, implies that this was the universal view of commentators up until his time; for more recent advocacy of this traditional view, see Morris, 547; Murray, 2:242; Dunn, 2:915; Stuhlmacher, 257; Fitzmyer, 754; Moo, 940. Theophilus Antiochenus *Autol.*1.14 links "the prophetic writings" (αἱ προφητικαὶ γραφαί) with "the sacred scriptures of the holy prophets," and Origen refers in the same manner to τῶν προφητικῶν γραφῶν ("of the prophetic writings") in *Cels.* 1.43; see also *Cels.* 2.76 and Origen *Exc. Ps.* 17.109.12.

89 Godet, 504–5; Corssen, "Überlieferungsgeschichte," 33–34; Schmithals, *Römerbrief*, 121–22; Lührmann, *Offenbarungsverständnis*, 123–24; Schlier, 454; Wilckens, 3:150, referring to 2 Pet 1:19, which speaks of Christian writings as "the prophetic word" (τὸν προφητικὸν λόγον). See also Horst Balz and Gerhard Schneider, eds., "προφητικός," *EDNT* 3 (1993) 186. See Clement of Alexandria *Stro.*

5.14.126.3; Clement of Alexandria *Ex. The.* 3.50.3.4; Justin Martyr *1 Apol.* 32.2.10f. According to Clement of Alexandria *Pro.* 8.77.1, the expression προφητικαὶ γραφαί can also refer to pagan hexametric oracles; see also *Stro.* 1.21.148.1.

90 See Schmithals, *Römerbrief*, 122.

91 Godet, 504–5.

92 This contextual difference is overlooked by Parke-Taylor, "Romans i.5 and xvi.26," 305–6. Since Miller, *Obedience of Faith*, 184–86, views 16:25-27 as a Pauline benediction, he sees no problem in defining ὑπακοή πίστεως in 16:26 as identical with 1:5.

93 "Nations" is favored by Meyer, 2:390; Käsemann, 427; Dunn, 2:916; Byrne, 464.

94 "Gentiles" is favored by Godet, 505; Barrett, 287; Cranfield, 2:812; Fitzmyer, 755.

95 See Nikolaus Walter, "ἔθνος," *EDNT* 1 (1990) 382–83.

96 BAGD 229–30.

Yahweh's relation to Israel."[97] The phrase "obedience of faith" encapsulates the claim that Israel's privileges and burdens are now "available to the nations simply by faith in Jesus the Risen Christ, in whom God's eschatological design for his ancient people had been fulfilled."[98] Although the formula contains a polemical implication that Gentiles do not have to become Jews to inherit the promises, in its context of 1:5 it provided no basis for excluding Jewish believers. In the doxology, however, the very cultural prejudices that Paul had struggled against for sixteen chapters now come to expression: the prophetic message is accessible only through Gentile believers. Only they know the command of God. The Jews have turned away, and have been shattered in the great zealotic wars against which Jesus had warned, and which the Christian movement had tried to avert. So now the Gentiles alone inherit the promise of Israel and the key to its prophetic legacy. They are the new elite, who alone have access to the mystery hidden for ages. In this regard, the doxology breathes the spirit of Melito of Sardis rather than of Ephesians, with which it is often compared.

These implications would have been intensified at the original location of the doxology after 14:23, because the entire discussion of Christ becoming a servant to the Jewish people, and their joint participation with Gentile Christians in mutual welcome and cooperative mission in the last two chapters of Romans, would have been deleted. That inclusive hope was replaced by this doxology, which places the mastery of the mystery in the hands of Gentiles alone. Like the interpolation of 16:17-20a, this one seeks to reverse a major emphasis in the letter, namely, the irreducible presence of Jewish believers in the church, and the unbroken promises to Israel. In the location after 14:23, the doxology provides this reversal in a masterful manner. The matter is more adequately in balance at the end of chapter 16, but the tension with Paul's original vision still remains tangible.

■ **27** The ascription of praise to "God only wise" (μόνῳ σοφῷ θεῷ) links the biblical traditions of monotheism and wisdom with the preceding claim that the concealed mystery is now being disclosed to the Gentiles. In contrast, the original Hellenistic Jewish doxology had employed this formula to sustain its claim that the mystery had been concealed from the Gentiles and revealed only to Jews maintaining the divine law. By adding the phrase "through Jesus Christ," the Christian antithesis was powerfully expressed in the claim that the revelation of God's wisdom came through him. As Paul had contended in 1 Cor 1:24, 30, through Christ both the "power of God and the wisdom of God" are accessible.[99] In the original context of the Christianized doxology at the end of 14:23, both wisdom and monotheism are modified. If wisdom is epitomized by the saying "whatever is not of faith is sin" (14:23), which sustains the ethos of the Gentile "strong," and if there is no subsequent celebration of the conversion of all nations in 15:7-13 which includes both Jews and Gentiles, then Paul's earlier reference to divine wisdom (11:33) in the context of the mystery of Jewish conversion is reinterpreted. The wisdom of God now stands behind the reality of Gentile dominance. The monotheistic theme of 3:28-31 is also modified; in place of God who is God both of Jews and Gentiles, now the "only God" sustains the Gentile supersession of Jewish prerogatives. These implications are softened somewhat by the placement of the doxology at the end of chapter 16, but they still remain in force and have influenced the interpretation of this letter in every subsequent generation.

The final lines of the doxology glorify God forever, and are consistent, except at one point, with the theme of 15:1-13, where the church is viewed as a doxological fellowship.[100] The difference is that whereas the praise in chapter 15 comes from Jewish Christians and Gentile Christians who unite with one voice,[101] here it comes from Gentiles alone. This distinction was rendered even acute at the original location of the doxology, because chapters 15 and 16 would have been absent. However, in either location, the congregation responds with ἀμήν ("Amen!"), the "liturgical concluding word" carried over from Jewish worship.[102]

---

97 Garlington, *Obedience*, 242.
98 Ibid., 253.
99 See Harald Hegermann, "σοφία," *EDNT* 3 (1993) 260.
100 Du Toit, "Doxologische Gemeinschaft," 72–75.
101 Ibid., 74.
102 See Kuhn, "ἀμήν," 70.

Wherever the doxology is located in the various editions of Romans, it remains clear that the time line has now shifted. In place of the eschatological urgency of 13:11-14, and of the benedictions of 15:5-6, 13 with their emphasis on the hope of the global mission's completion, now there is praise "for aeons of aeons," carried forward by the Gentile church. Romans is now a book for the ages, its original context lost from memory. With the death of Paul in 62, the devastation of the Roman house and tenement churches in 64, the disaster of the Jewish-Roman war in 66–70, and the widespread disappointment of hopes for a rapid end to world history in the last decades of the first century, the Spanish mission was no longer plausible. Instead of supporting strenuous efforts to cross cultural and linguistic barriers, Romans becomes an instrument of consolidation for those who claim that they alone understand the mystery and can ascribe requisite glory to God. But whether "the God and Father of our Lord Jesus Christ" (15:6) is thereby properly glorified is a matter on which the rest of this magnificent letter gives reason to doubt. As Bishop John William Colenso realized more than 140 years ago, chauvinism does not easily comport with the righteousness of God.

16

The Epistolary Benediction

24/ **The grace of our Lord Jesus Christ be with you all. Amen.**[a]

20b[b]/ **The grace of our Lord Jesus[c] be with you.**[d]

a   The entirety of v. 24 is absent here (but with 16:25-27 following v. 23) in P⁶¹ ℵ A B C 5 81 621 623 (1506 but omits 16:1-24) 1739 1838 1962 2110 2127 2464 *pc* b vg^{ww, st} sa bo Or^{lat}, while P⁴⁶ has 16:25-27 after 15:33, but lacks 16:24. However, this benediction is included in three places and in various contexts in the manuscript tradition: (a) after 16:23 (= 16:24) in 566 MSS (of which 50 read ἡμῶν for the second ὑμῶν, and 8 lack ἀμήν) (ar) d (f) (g) mon o vg^{cl} sy^h slav Thret (Pel); (b) after 16:23 as the conclusion of the letter in F G 629, but omitting "Jesus Christ"; (c) after 16:27 in 441 459 *pc* vg^{ms} sy^p bo^{ms} arm eth geo¹ Ambst; and after 16:27 but also at 16:20b in P 33 104 256 263 365 436 1319 1573 1852 1962 *pc*; (d) at 16:20b, supported by nearly 600 MSS (25 MSS have πάντων; only MS 2400 has ἀμήν), with the benediction omitted here only by D F G; (e) at both 16:20b and 16:24 in 48 MSS (with minor variations). See Aland et al., *Ergänzungsliste*, 439–41, 443–47.

b   The entirety of 20b is absent before v. 21 in D*^{vid} F G d* f g mon o vg^{ms} Ambst Sedulius Scotus, though D F G have it after 16:23 (as v. 24); it is found before 16:21 in 593 MSS (25 MSS have πάντων; only MS 2400 has ἀμήν), with the benediction omitted in Greek MSS at this point only by D F G, which leads most text critics to believe that this is the spot the benediction occupied in the earliest published form of Romans that included chapter 16. See the Introduction, section 2, and the analysis below.

c   The word "Christ" appears here in A C L P Ψ *Maj* 6 33 61 69 81 88 104 181 218 256 263 323 326 330 365 424 436 441 451 459 467 614 623 629 630 720 915 917 945 1175 1241 1243 1319 1398 1505 1563 1573 1678 1718 1735 1739 1751 1836 1838 1845 1846 1852 1874 1875 1877 1908 1912 1942 1959 1962 1984 1985 2110 2127 2138 2197 2200 2344 2464 2492 2495 2516 2523 2544 2718 *Maj Lect* ar b (d²) vg sy^{p.h} sa bo arm eth geo (slav) Or^{lat} Chr, but Metzger, *Textual Commentary*, 476, argues that it would hardly have been deleted and that consequently the shorter form, featuring "Jesus" without "Christ" as found in P⁴⁶ ℵ B 1881 *pc*, is "more primitive."

d   The unlikely variant μεθ᾽ ἡμῶν ("with us") is found in 326 1838 1846 *pc*.

Rhetorical Disposition

Exegesis

With current text-critical studies and standard critical texts supporting for the most part two locations for the benediction, it would be wise to explain its significance in both locations: at the end of 16:20, and after 16:23.

When located at the end of the interpolation of 16:17-20a, the benediction of 16:20b has the effect of blessing the church as it takes steps against heretics. It functions not as a letter closing but as an eschatological promise to those who act as the interpolation commands,[1] placing Satan and his minions under their feet.[2] It is significant in this context that the formulation of 16:20b does not include the words "you all." Since the interpolation of 16:17-20a was originally intended to reduce the scope of ecclesiastical inclusivity, placed immediately after Paul's command to "greet one another with the holy kiss" and "all the churches of Christ greet you," the blessing is now restricted to those who conform to the antiheretical stance. The blessing thus stands in tension with the rest of the argument of Romans, especially 14:1—5:13.

---

1   See Müller, *Schluß*, 219.
2   Haacker, 328, shows that this form of blessing fits smoothly with the tradition of holy war embodied in the preceding verses.

The implications of the longer form of the benediction after 16:23, assuming the absence of both interpolations, are entirely different, and completely consistent with the earlier argument of Romans. As demonstrated in section 2 of the introduction above, this verse has the strongest claim to be the original ending of Paul's letter. The wording of 16:24 contains the formula $\mu\epsilon\tau\grave{\alpha}\ \pi\acute{\alpha}\nu\tau\omega\nu\ \acute{\upsilon}\mu\hat{\omega}\nu$ ("with you all"), which is missing in 16:20b. As in the earlier instances of this formula in Romans, the "all" includes both the "weak" and the "strong," the Greeks and barbarians, the educated and uneducated, the Jews and Gentiles. All of the competitive antitheses that Paul seeks to overcome in the argument of Romans are hereby encompassed: God's grace is extended to each, without reservation or discrimination. God's impartial love, demonstrated on the cross for all of the human race (3:21-26; 5:6-17), is maintained through to the final words of the letter as the proper embodiment of the impartial righteousness of God.

The gift of grace in this final greeting is the logical conclusion of Romans, providing the proper echo to the greeting of 1:7. It is far more germane to the preceding argument than the material in the doxology of 16:25-27. The theme of grace appears twenty times in the preceding chapters of Romans, and is particularly developed in 3:24; 5:15-21; 6:14-23; 11:5-6; and 15:15. The burden of Christ's redemptive work is captured by this term $\chi\acute{\alpha}\rho\iota\varsigma$, involving unconditional love to enemies, outsiders, and the godless.[3] In Christ, acceptance is no longer a matter of performance or previous status, but of sheer grace, which "abounds" and overflows in a superabundant fashion (5:15, 20; 6:1).[4] Since the source of grace is Christ,[5] the gift of grace is simultaneously the gift of Christ himself: to say "grace be with you" is identical in meaning with "the Lord be with you." To "stand" in grace (5:2) is to be "in Christ" (6:11, 23; 8:1; 12:5) and to experience the love of God as revealed in Christ (8:39).

The theme of "you all" is one of the most prominent in the letter, appearing no less than thirty-six times, and receiving extensive, congregational emphasis in 16:4, 15, 16, 19, along with repeated references to "one another" in 14:13, 19; 15:5, 7, 14; it climaxes in the mutuality of the holy kiss in 16:16. This confirms the contention made throughout this commentary that issues of social status relating to honor and shame have priority over the issue of individual forgiveness that has dominated the interpretation of Romans since the time of Augustine. Grace is unconnected with forgiveness of sins, either in the linguistic tradition of the wisdom writings of the NT or in Pauline usage.[6] The central question of this letter is whether divine favor is shown to the shameful representatives of the human race, the barbarians and the uneducated, the formerly excluded Gentiles, and the Jews now being viewed in the prejudicial status of "the weak." The missional impulse motivating this letter rests on the foundation of inclusive grace, an expression of the impartial righteousness of God revealed in Christ.

In contrast to 16:20b, the benediction at 16:24 concludes with the traditional "Amen," which appears at the end of such benedictions in 1 Cor 16:24; Gal 6:18. It appears to have a liturgical function, evoking the response of the congregation,[7] just as in the earlier instances of its use in Rom 1:25; 9:5; 11:36; and 15:33. It confirms the truth of what has been said,[8] in this case, that the grace of Christ is with all groups of the Roman congregation. If the Roman house and tenement churches join in this response, Paul will have gained acceptance of the gist of his message and the congregations will be able to set about the tasks of mutual reconciliation and missional preparation that this letter hopes to evoke. They will demonstrate thereby that the "grace of our Lord Jesus Christ" flows through them toward others, welcoming outsiders into their fellowship and thus extending the righteousness of God.

The various altered endings of Romans reveal that this foundation of grace came to appear unsatisfactory to the later church. After the interpolation of 16:17-20 that radically curtailed the extension of grace, the doxology in 16:25-27 was added with its claim of confirmation in the Gentile believers' possession of the secret of

3 See Berger, "Gnade," 17.
4 Klaus Berger, "$\chi\acute{\alpha}\rho\iota\varsigma$," *EDNT* 3 (1993) 459.
5 Wobbe, *Charis-Gedanke*, 21–27.
6 See Berger, "Gnade," 3–4.
7 Champion, *Benedictions and Doxologies*, 94–96; Hein-

rich Schlier, "$\grave{\alpha}\mu\acute{\eta}\nu$," *TDNT* 1 (1964) 336; H.-W. Kuhn, "$\grave{\alpha}\mu\acute{\eta}\nu$," *EDNT* 1 (1990) 70.
8 See Mateo del Alamo, "La aclamación litúrgica 'Amen' en S Pablo," *Liturgia* 1 (1946) 229.

divine favoritism, and in radical Marcionite circles, this led to the excision of chapters 15–16. With 16:25-27, supersession of Jewish prerogatives thus emerged at the center of the Christian faith, creating a new form of mission that entailed cultural and theological domination and a destructive legacy of anti-Semitism. These changes in the ending of Romans were fateful, influencing the future of world history by distorting the way the Christian faith was understood. Anti-Semitism was thereby reinforced, but the issue is actually much broader than that. Resistance against grace for all, generous and unbounded, capable of overcoming shameful status in every society, thwarted the proper understanding of Romans and therewith the understanding of the faith

itself. The violent impulse of identifying heretics and destroying them, as embodied in 16:17-20, was an even more serious restriction of the range of grace. What this letter actually calls for is not newly refined doctrines such as "faith alone," "justice alone," "correctness alone," or "Christ and the law," allegedly eliminating heresy while sustaining the superiority of those with doctrinal conformity, but rather effective forms of mutual welcome. It is chapter 16:3-16, 21-23 that reveals the social means by which Paul believes that God's boundless grace for all needs to be shared and extended. Until the believers hearing and reading Romans get that right, any effort to pursue Paul's program by missionizing among the "barbarians" will remain a travesty.

Glossary of Rhetorical and Exegetical Terms

Rhetorical terms are defined somewhat differently in reference works such as Bullinger, *Figures,* Anderson, *Glossary,* and Lausberg, *Handbuch,* and the same can be said of standard studies of exegetical terminology. Therefore, the following list makes no claim to be definitive and simply reflects how the terms are employed in this commentary.

A fortiori
  argument from the greater.
Allegory
  argumentative figure that says one thing but hints at another.
Ambitus sive circuitus
  reference to an earlier phase of argument.
A maiore ad minus
  argument from a greater reality to a lesser.
A minore ad maius
  an argument that if the lesser reality is true, how much more the greater.
Amplification, *amplificatio*
  the development of an argument through heightening, disjunction, enumeration, illustration, etc.
Anakolouthon
  a sentence that is grammatically incomplete.
Antanaclasis
  the use of the same word with different definitions in the same sentence.
Antithetical parallelism
  parallel formulation in style of Hebrew poetry, with lines in opposition to one another.
Anantapodoton
  syntax that is left intentionally incomplete for rhetorical effect.
Anaphora
  the identity of initial words in each member of parallel formulations.
Anarthrous
  a word or phrase lacking a definite or indefinite article.
Antanaclasis
  repetition of terms in the same sentence with different meanings.

Anteisagoge
  response to questions with counter questions or the compensation of a statement by an opposite.
Antistrophe
  repetition of similar sounding endings in close proximity.
Apodosis
  the main portion of a complex sentence, usually the second half.
Apology
  discourse in judicial rhetoric that excuses or defends the accused.
Apostrophe
  turning toward someone to address him or her specifically in an argument.
Approbation
  seeking or gaining approval by a higher authority.
Arthrous
  a noun or phrase with a definite or indefinite article.
Assonance
  pleasing sound achieved through word choice.
Asyndeton
  words listed one after another without punctuation or conjunction.
Captatio benevolentiae
  discourse aimed at ingratiation of the audience.
Catchword
  references in quoted material that are picked up and developed later, a typical device in midrashic exegesis.
Catena
  a series of citations organized into a meaningful discourse
Causa
  the issue discussed in a letter or speech, indicating what the speaker intends to achieve
Chiasm
  discourse organized in a crossing pattern such as A, B, C, B^1, A^1
Chain-citation
  a series of quotations linked thematically.

Chain-link parallelism
   an argumentative form in which thought advances step by step through parallel expressions.
Clausula
   the ending of a paragraph or larger unit with an extended, formal phrase.
Climax
   repetition of key words in parallel phrases.
Coda
   formal ending of a paragraph or longer discourse designed for rhetorical impact.
Deliberative genre
   discourse with advisory function that concentrates on advantage and disadvantage.
Demonstrative genre
   discourse with celebrative function that concentrates on honor and shame.
Denunciatio
   accusatory discourse.
Diatribe
   argument in dialogue style.
Diatribal exchange
   questions and answers between a writer and an imaginary interlocutor.
Disclosure formula
   a standardized way of saying, "I want you to know. . ."
Dispositio
   the organization of discourse.
Dystich
   sentence with two roughly equal parts.
Ellipse, elliptical style
   verbal absence, style in which the verbs must be supplied.
Enthymeme
   an argument in which a major premise is supported by a minor premise, either of which may be deleteld on the assumtion that the audience will supply it.
Enumeratio
   a sequential listing of terms, often in Romans with totals of 5, 7 or 10.
Epanadiplosis
   An identical word appears both at the beginning and at the end of a sentence.
Epanalepsis
   the emphatic use of the same word within a sentence.

Epistolography
   the study of the form and function of letters.
Epitrechon
   parenthetical addition with brief explanatory comments.
Epitrope
   temporary acceptance of a problematic statement for a rhetorical purpose.
Erotesis
   an interrogative series with animated questions.
Excursus
   section dealing with an issue beyond that of the main topic.
Exemplum
   an example or illustration drawn from history or literature.
Exhortatio
   a parenetic/exhortative portion of an argument.
Exordium
   the introduction of a speech or writing.
Exsuscitatio
   discourse aim at arousal of sympathy in the audience.
Form criticism
   the study of the form of discourse with the aim of discovering its original context and function.
Gloss
   comment inserted by a later writer, usually serving an explanatory purpose.
Gradatio
   rhetorical climax with the repetition of key words in parallel phrases.
Grand style
   complex sentence and paragraph development that makes a stately, ornate impression.
Hapax legomenon
   a word appearing only once in the New Testament or the Bible as a whole.
Historical-critical methods
   techniques employed to discover the likely course of past events and the meaning of writings for their original audiences.
Homoioptoton
   the use of similar sounding word endings for pleasing rhetorical effect.

Homoioteleuton
  identical endings in successive lines.
Homiletical benediction
  a blessing at the end of a section of homiletical discourse.
Hymn
  a song whose lyrics can be discerned by means of stylistic analysis.
Imaginary interlocutor
  a character created by a writer to enter into dialogue for an argumentative purpose.
Inclusio
  recapitulation of a term or theme at the end of discourse that had been employed at the beginning.
Interlocutor
  a character created by a writer to pose questions that advance the argument.
Interpolation
  a later insertion into a document with the intent to change its meaning.
Invention
  the choice of argumentative means within a discourse.
Isocolic reduplication
  repitition of words in a sentence.
Judicial genre
  rhetoric characteristic of court settings, in which persons are accused or defended.
Kerygma
  the proclamation of a message, used by NT scholars to refer to the early preaching about Jesus.
Lesser to greater
  an argument that if the lesser is true, how much more is the greater.
Litote
  the creation of an understatement for the sake of emphasis.
Locus a simili
  an argument based on the similarity between realities.
Maranatha
  the liturgical formula, "May the Lord come!"
Merismos
  the division or enumeration of aspects of the whole in an argumentative form.

Midrash
  Jewish argumentative style with a main text interpreted by subsequent texts
Mishnah
  an carly collection of rabbinic sayings.
Narratio
  an account of the background of a case or project that is ordinarily placed toward the beginnng of discourse.
New Perspective
  viewpoint developed by J. D. G.Dunn that Paul's critique of the law related to problematic dimentions of Jewish ethnicity.
Parablepsis
  the creation of similar wording in successive sentences.
Paria ex paribus
  comparison between equals employed as an argumentatve form.
Parallelismus, Parallelismus membrorum
  each line having parallel, though slightly differing features, a typical expression of Hebrew poetry.
Parecbasis, sometimes called *parabasis*
  a digression, deviation or embellishment that halts the main flow of an argument.
Parechesis
  the selection of similar sounding words in close proximity for rhetorical effect.
Paregmenon
  the use of different words derived from the same root in a sentence or paragraph.
Parenthesis
  explanatory material that disrupts the flow of argument.
Paromoiosis
  a figure with balanced clauses and similar sounding word endings.
Paronomasia
  repitition of the same word or stem in successive phrases or sentences.
Pars pro toto
  the argumentative technique that what pertains to the part also pertains to the whole.
Partitio
  a short statement of the thesis in a larger body of

discourse or an enumeration of the issues to be discusssed.

Pericope
a term employed by biblical scholars for an internally coherent section within a larger discourse.

Period
a grammatically and syntactically coherent and independent portion of Greek prose.

Peristasis, peristasis catalogue
some form of suffering, and a listing of various forms.

Permissio
temporary acceptance of a problematic statement for a rhetorical purpose.

Peroratio, peroration
conclusion of discourse that often recapitulates the argument and requests some action from the audience.

Pesher
Jewish argumentative form in which biblical texts are interpreted with the "that is, . . . formula.

Polemic, polemicize
discourse aimed at refuting adverse opinion, ordinarily employed in the judicial genre of rhetoric.

Polysyndeton
listing of items with articles.

Polyptoton
word play that uses different endings on the same word or stem.

Probatio
the proof portion of discourse.

Propositio
the theme or thesis that is usually stated at the beginning of a proof.

Prosopopeia
a "speech-in-character" in which an imaginary person speaks of his personal experience.

Protasis
the first, subordinate clause in a complex sentence.

Qal wahomer
the Hebrew term for a lesser to greater argument.

Ratiocinatio
the Latin term for an argument with a major premise, one or more minor premises, and a conclusion; sometimes referring simply to logical discourse in general.

Recitativum
quotation of a word, phrase, or larger discourse, often introduced by "that. . ."

Redaction, redaction criticism
editing of material to fit a new context, and the study of its method.

Reenactment
a process by which believers replicate the fate of their savior, in the Christian context normally through religious ritual such as baptism.

Refutatio
discourse aimed to repudiate contrary opinion, often characteristic of discourse in the judicial genre.

Rhetoric
the study of the various means of persuasion.

Rhetorical question
an interrogative aimed at exposing error or advancing an argument.

Rhetorical situation
the historical exigency requiring discourse of a particular type.

Ring-composition
discourse organized in a circular manner that returns in the end to its starting poiint.

Sententia
a formal saying that can stand alone and be readily cited.

Sententia ex inopinato
a paradoxical formulation employed as an argumentative device.

Sermocinatio
argumentative discourse marked by dialogical elements.

Servant Songs
material in Isaiah referring to Israel as Yahweh's suffering servant.

Shekinah
the Hebrew term for the presence of God.

Shema
the Hebrew confession of the oneness of God.

Signum
a nickname.

Similitudo
an example drawn from everyday experience.

Speech-in-character

    discourse in which an imaginary person speaks of his personal experience.

Syllogism

    a logical argument with a major premise, one or more minor premises, and a conclusion.

Symploce

    successive clauses or phrases with the same beginnings and endings, i.e. both anaphora and antistrophe together.

Synonymous parallelism

    a Hebrew poetic form in which successive lines of similar length have identical meaning.

Synthetic parallelism

    a Hebrew poetic form in which successive lines of similar length convey a single thought.

Targum

    interpretation and translation of Hebrew material into contemporary vernacular.

Text criticism

    the analysis of variant forms of texts to determine which reading is most likely to be original.

Textus Receptus

    the standardized Byzantine version of the Old and New Testament.

Topos

    a traditional theme or topic employed in argumentative discourse.

Torah

    the Hebrew law and/or the first five books of the Hebrew scripture.

Tobspruch

    a beatitude that states what is "good".

Transitus

    material providing a transition between major sections of discourse.

Tricola

    a three-part formulation.

Type, typology

    a reality that provides the pattern for a later reality, and the employment of this thought in argumentative discourse.

Vice catalogue

    a listing of evils or types of evil persons.

Index

1024

4.207	229
4.237	201n71
4.314	680n141; 142
5.1	656n54
5.14	656n54
5.107	211
5.132	211
6.26	335n145
6.143	365n214
6.144	201n71
6.164	489n144
6.275-80	113n181
6.353	365n207
7.185	365n208
7.196	365n208
7.285.3	984n79
7.333	907n53
8.129	230
8.142	214n206
8.280	619n134
8.350	486n114
9.27.2	984n79
9.243	230; 328n60
10.1	656n54
10.3	656n54
10.48	398n65
10.213	243n34
10.265	129n24
11.77	907n56
11.8	656n54
11.55	246n71
11.195	365n208
11.198	653n21
11.207	222n24
11.233.5	510n30
11.300	418
12.51	97n10
12.27	283n134
12.118	209n160
12.164	958n66
12.234.3	984n79
12.399	397n57
12.418	245
13.69	328n60
13.78	224n45
13.88	488n135
13.257	232
13.289-90	489n144
13.318-19	232
13.397	232
14.77-79	55n349
14.167	230
14.203	802n205
14.225	97n9
14.235	97n9
14.361	984n79
14.377	680n142
15.48	289n206
15.277	884n116
15.330	915n137
16.6	925
16.212	406n169
17.155	993n75
17.324	222n24
18.14-15	333
18.81	230; 328n60
18.103	222n24
18.268	230; 328n60
18.273-76	966
19.127	993n75
19.154	500n291
20.5.2	21
20.6.2	21
20.44	232n114
20.90	201n71
20.108	207n141
20.117	222n24
20.125-133	21
20.134-137	21
20.139	232
20.144	201n71
20.145	232
20.158-162	20
20.158-165	20
20.179	21
20.243	984n79
71.1.2	680n142
182	20

De bello Judaico

1.44	335n145
1.173	291
1.204	525n180
1.242	876n17
1.355	327n39
2.29.3	826n89
2.101	222n24
2.119	806n20
2.138	354
2.165	578n91
2.261-63	20
2.288.1	510n30
2.394	637n21
3.183	335n143
4.175	618n123
4.358	487n124; 525n180
4.298	821
5.311	934
6.102	222n24
6.201	963
6.411	405n157
6.414-19	471n138
6.423	679n132
7.112	450n96
7.155	619n131
7.254-55	233n121
7.346	153n522
7.418	629n78; 630n79
7.418-19	630n82

Contra Apionem

1.119	802n205
1.165	222
1.222	186n242
2.80	154n59
2.137	891n36
2.148	154n59
2.167	153n52
2.173	224n45
2.178	451n98
2.197.1	615n81
2.273-75	175n118
2.290-95	760n38
2.291-95	225
179	222n24

Athenaeus (*cont.*)

2.36	827n101; 106n102
10.444b	248n99
10.74.10	945
13.84n605d)	175n118

Caelius Aurelianus
Morb.

4.9.131-35	177n131

Calpurnius Siculus
Ecl.

1.33–99	509n27; 516n87; 517n94
1.45-65	795

Ceb. tab.

2.2	910
31.5	352n72; 577n81

Chariton
Chaer.

4.2.4–5	179n148
8.4.8.5	942n7

Chrest.

1.16.7	676n93

Chrysippus 183; 257; 841n117

Frag. log.

355.6	111n165
902.48	274n52
1008.1	870n202
1021	332n107

Frag. mor.

1.121	172n90
3.443–55	172n90
643.1	573n23

Cicero 49; 51; 56; 77; 269; 482; 980

Arch.

26	367n233

Att.

10.8	189n294
12.8	77n530

Cael.

20.48	826n91

Clu.

58.159	216n228

De or.

2.50	25n150
3.202-5	25n150
97	269n4

Fam.

2.1	198n41
13.56	795n138

Fin.

215	130n40

Flacc.

24	154n59 130n39

Inv.

1.22.31– 1.23.33	135n11
1.7.9	39n225
2.66	110n151
99-100	625n23

Leg.

3.32	205n118

Mil.

98	120n27

Nat. d.

1.4	152n39
1.18.44	156n74 51n306
49	162n136
104	162n136

Off.

1.130	871
1.147	876n8
1.150	53
1.160	493n205
3.20	183n202

Parad.

34	462

Planc.

34.84	77n530

Prov. cons. 154n59

Quint. fratr.

1.1.27	131n47

Claudius Aelianus

Frag,	243n41
109	991n63

Cleanthes 375
Frag.

547	774n187

Cleobulus
Epig.

1	758n15
10.1	740n33

Cleomedes
Motu

1.7	747n124

Cornutus
Nat. d.

16	483n76
55.8	518n105

Corp. herm. 730

1.6	824n70
820	
1.27.23	820
730n65	
10.6	732n83
11.14	493
497	
13.3; 14	732n83
538n61	
13.18-19	730n66
34-37	471n142

Cratinus
Frag.

457-59	989n35

Ctesias
Frag.

3c,688;	
F.14.75	845n150

Damascius
Par.

18.1	742n60
236.13	821n43

Herodotus
Hist.

2.58	350n45
3.137.22	459
5.5.7	398n64
5.20.17	58n30
5.62.4	418n36
5.111	245n62
6.75	547n145
7.218	823
8.4; 106; 142	842n118
8.73.5	130n37
8.88	963
9.74	963
9.88	550

Heron
Bel.

1.27	797

Hesiod
Op.

109-201	516n85
225-47	676n85
265-66	771n157
327	771n157
349	801

Theog.

126	943n13
240	501n297
366	501n297
444	405n158
766	488n131

Hesychius	189

Lex.

Π-Ω πι.3444.1	256n13
a5569	759n21
5761.1	592n43

Hipparchus	461n41

Hippocrates	701

Aphor.

624	400n94

Diaet. m.

i-iv 18.1	855n10

Epist.

11.19	373-74n35

Flat.

6.3	611n44

Morb.

6.3.1	420n60

Off.

17.1	179n156

Praec.

9	179n155

Septim.

50.17	549n161

Hist. Aug.

13	992n66

Historia Alexandri

Magni	374n36

Rec. β

1.33-38	700n85

Rec. γ

21.45	549n159
38.43	839n87

Rec. ε

15.2.18	549n159

Rec. byz.

21	549n159
512-16	553n204
4494	700n85
5888	700n85

Rec. λ

63.29	594n71

Rec. φ

69.t	615n81

Homer
Il.

5.501	210n174
8.234	508n21
9.49	405n158
14.106	403n125
17.355	256n16
17.645	935n149

Od.

1.191	863n112
1.335	409n202
1.395	403n125
11.451	926
15.490	863n112
23.11-13	739n27

Horace	811-12; 834; 980

Carm.

2.13.5	175n116
4.9.10	175n115

Ep.

1.19.28	175n115

Sat.

1.5.100	965
1.9.67-72	834n29

Hyperides	738n9

Dem.

7.30.6	658n73

Isaeus	272n19; 738n9

Euph.

12.7	615n87

Orat.

10.21.2	297
39.7	137n21
111.22.9	224

Isocrates	118n9; 129n20; 738n9; 859n52; 989n28

Antid.

19.4	127na
33.1	553n204
65.5	726n19
147.7	460n32
153.2	559n45
167.4	553n204
171.3	127na
272.7	137n21
299.1	127na

Antipat.

9	128n12

Arch.

39.3	127na

Plato (*cont.*)
Symp.
176a   846n163
200c8   196n27
Theaet.
168   609n15
176b   740n40
Tim.
31c; 32c   747n124
37d   1007
42a6   400n93
92c   155n70

Plautus
Curc.
23   180n170

Pliny   77
Ep.
1.18.5   871n215
8.24.4   131n47
8.24.9   137n27
10.12   903n11
10.57   21n117

Pliny the Elder   992n66
Nat.
7.25.91   22n127

Plotinus   185; 202
Enn.
2.9.12   374n36

Plutarch   175-76; 185;
    243n36;
    257n22;
    487n125;
    732; 989n28
Adul. amic.
64c13   500n291
Adv. Col.
1125b3   106n102
Aem.
27.4   310n44
Aet. Rom.
288a   180n170

Ag. Cleom.
17.2 (802d)   261n70
31.5   847n172
Amat.
750c-d   179n149
750e2   178n144
750f12   619
751c; e   175n118
759b   179n148
761e   176n120
763a   178n148
Ant.
71.1.2   680n142
Arat.
23.5.4   943n16
29.2.2;   943n16
43.2   755nb
44.4.1   376
44.6.1   943n16
Brut.
13.4.1   761n46
Cat. Maj.
5.2   690n242
23.4   837n73
Cic.
18.1   537n45
Cim.
2.1.3   374n35
15.3   983n78
Cohib. Ira
14   775
Comp. Thes.
6.4.2 (I,39b)   216n231
Cor.
8.1   946n44
15.7.2   616
19.4   822n52
23.1   387n220
Curios.
523a   814n98
Def. orac.
438b   523n165
438d   726n19
Demetr.
23.3.2   943n16
38.3   503n319

E. Delph.
319e9   508n20
388-89   162n136
393   162n136
Fat.
570d9   104n84
Frag.
43.13   800n189
Garr.
14 (2.509f)   795n137
Gen. Socr.
596a   387n220
581e   496n231
586a   496n231
591d4   787n52
Is. Os.
378c   946n44
Luc.
33.2.7   508n20
Lyc.
12.4.3   226n55
18   174n108
27.1.9   398n65
Mor.
69e   834n24
125a   938n183
329c   365
398a   156n74
398e   279n96
402e   279n96
409f   795n137
479e3; 4   352n72
549b   279n96
486b   205n117
665a   156n74
776d   739n27
1038d   257
Non pos.
2.1100d   189n294
Num.   905n53
Pel.
21.5   332n107
Phil.
8   743n70
8.3   946n44
21.12.6   803n213

Solon 946n44; 989n31

Epig.
1 758n15

Sophocles 740n35
Aj.
130 716
162-63 226n56
583 857
589-90 133
761 248n99
769 550n172
777 248n99
1378 398n65
Ant.
30 256n16
945 161n119
El.
1207 210n174
Oed. col.
598 248n99
797 859n54
1036 590n15
Oed. tyr.
895–910 592n41.
Trach.
280 592n41

Soranus 257n22
Gyn.
3.20.1.3 503n319

Speusippus
Frag.
63e 611n44

Stobaeus
Anth.
16 188n270
2.4.11m41 573n23
2.59 184n213
2.7.109.5 573n23
3.20.67 202n95
3.36.1.3 523n164
4.2.29 156n74
4.20 184n213

4.960.15h 461n41
5.4.1 523n164
6.65 489n145
95 188n270

Strabo 131
Geog.
1.21.33 508n20
1.4.9 120n39
3.4.13 77n529
5.1.10 827n99
5.3.7 959n74
8.6.4 943n16
8.6.22 943n16
10.3.10 521n130
12.3.27.2 591n24
12.3.34.12 335n145
14.1.31 119
16.2.10 226n55

Suda
Lex.
π 2055.7 573n23

Suetonius 59-60
Aug.
76.2 56n358
94.4 497n240
Cal.
14.1 47n273; 293n111
Claud.
12 802n208
25 19
28 967n184
Dom.
10 956n35
16 120n27
Galb.
14.1 144n88
20 970n231
Nero
26 825
Περὶ βλασ.
8.6 439n85
SVF
1.121 172n90

1.547 774n187
3.181.21-22 179n149
3.382-83 184n214
3.443-55 172n90
86.353 841n117

Syntipas
Fab.
127.4 787n56

Syrianus 738n18

Tacitus 62; 799-800
Ann.
4.11 188n273
4.38.20 50n295
6.7 186n252
12.60 802n208
13.50-51 798
14.8 61n400
15.44 796n143
15.44.4 61
67.14 955
Dial.
19 83n202
Hist.
4.6 741n51
5.4 838n74
5.4.2 868n177

Teles
Rel.
2.39 (SH) 379n118
3.24 (25H) 379n118
108 379n118
115 (26H) 379n118
207 (19H) 379n118

Terence
Ad.
865 847n173

Thales
Epig. ded.
11-13 758n15

P.Par.	
Nr. 26.28	931n102
Nr. 63.16	931n102

P.Petr.	
3.Nr. 42.H.8.f.3-4	915n138

P.Rein	
1.Nr. 18.40	386n210

P.Ryl.	
2.Nr. 94.11-13	851n213
2.Nr. 116.9-10	797n152
2.Nr. 128.8-12	486n119
2.Nr. 243.11	376n81

PSI	
5.Nr. 525.9	438n73
10.1100.9	795n135
969	946n41
1337.17	201n83

P.Tebt.	
2.Nr. 242.4-5	394n21
2.Nr. 391.20	795n135
2.Nr. 412.4	951
2.331.11	410n211

SIG	
Nr. 641,vol.2:348	878n38
Nr. 646.12 vol.2.353	878n39

2. Nr.438.8	279n91
2. Nr.821.D.2	1001n30
2.250.7	521n133
90.4	113n176
367.16-20	934n136
383.130	800n188
805.10	13n943
867.31	156n74
1268	764n86;
	765n90;
	808n37

SupplMag	
I 13,8	438n74

2. Greek Words

ἀγαθός
204; 204n108; 360;
453; 578; 734; 793

ἀγαπάω, ἀγάπη
113; 356; 543; 758-
59; 805; 814

ἁγιασμός
421

ἁγιωσύνη
106

ἀδιαλείπτως
121; 559

ἀδικία
149; 152; 410; 581

αἷμα
287; 363

αἰχμαλωτίζω
470

αἰών
172; 205; 389; 425;
568-69; 1000-1001;
1002; 1007

ἀκαθαρσία
168; 420

ἀκροβυστία
232-34; 301; 317-20

ἀλαζόναι
188

ἀλήθεια
153; 227; 557; 891-
92

ἀλλάσσω
160; 265

ἁμαρτάνω, ἁμαρτία
210; 258-59; 279;
290; 316; 361; 374;
379; 382; 388-89;
395; 403-5; 410;
415; 417; 436; 446;
459; 461-62; 467-68;
483-84; 491; 706

ἁμαρτωλός
249-50; 361; 386

ἀμετανόητος
202

ἀμήν
172; 569; 722-23;
940; 1010; 1013

ἀνάγκη
431; 796-97

ἀνακαίνωσις
733

ἀναπολόγητος
156; 196

ἀνελεήμων
189-90

ἄνθρωπος
218; 248; 298; 402-
3; 439; 864

ἀνομία
316; 420-21

ἀνοχή
201

ἀντιμισθία
180

ἀντιστρατεύομαι
470

ἀπαρχή
518; 618; 682; 960

ἀπεδέχομαι
507

ἀποβολή
680

ἀποκαλύπτω
142-43; 144; 146;
150-51; 154; 1007-8

ἀποκαραδοκία
507; 511

ἀπόλλυμι
210-11; 861

ἀποστέλλω
101

ἀπόστολος
44; 101; 678-79

ἀπολύτρωσις
283; 519

ἄρα
385; 432; 457; 473;
479; 493; 582; 585;
641; 852; 865

ἀπωθέομαι
653

ἀρέσκω
489-90; 879

ἀσεβής, ἀσέβεια
152; 313-14; 358-
59; 361; 704

ἀσθενέω, ἀσθενής,
ἀσθένεια
336; 358-59; 522;
834; 876-77

ἄστοργος
189

ἀσύνετος
31; 189; 646

ἀσυνθέντος
189

ἀσχημοσύνη
179

ἀτιμάζω
229-30

ἀτιμία
172-73; 178; 229-30

ἄφεσις, ἀφίημι
289; 316

ἀφορίζω
102

ἀφορμή
449

βάθος
553-54; 716

βαπτίζω
397-98

βασιλεύω, βασιλεία
377-78; 383-84;
389; 409; 893

βέβαιος
330; 892

βδελύσσομαι
228

γενεῦσιν ἀπειθεῖς
188

γινώσκω
157; 227; 263; 446;
462-63; 717; 859

γράφω
103; 144; 310; 340-
41; 880

διαστολή
279; 632

διαφέροντος
223-24

διδάσκω
226-27; 749-50

δικαιοκρισία
203

δικαίωμα, δικαίωσις
190-91; 196; 233;
343; 382-83; 385;
485

διακρίνω
337; 832; 836; 871

διότι
265

δοκιμάζω
181; 223-24; 354;
733-34; 871

δοκιμή, δόκιμος
354; 733

δόλος
186; 261

δοξάζω, δοξά
503; 563; 679

δουλεία
404; 417-18; 438;
497; 515; 864; 991

δύναμαι, δύναμις
137-38; 156; 224;
338; 399; 553; 584;
595; 692; 843; 904;
910-11

δωρεάν, δώρημα
282; 381; 383-84;
744

ἐγείρω
341; 343; 399; 477;
492; 542; 630; 820

ἐγκαλεῖν
539

ἐγκόπτω
922

ὑστερεῖν
280

φαίνομαι
273; 459

φανερόω, φανερός
149; 154; 234-35;
273; 997; 1004;
1007-8

φθόνος
31; 185-86; 617

φιλοτιμία
137; 205; 367; 616;
915

φοβέω
263; 498; 688; 792;
802

φρονέω, φρόνημα
476; 486-87; 592;
688; 699; 736; 739;
768; 772; 846; 884

φυλάσσω
232-34

φύσις
175-76; 214; 234;
688-89; 692-93

φῶς
225; 823-24

χάρις
96; 98; 109; 115;
124; 157; 282; 313;
329; 350; 372; 379-
84; 388; 412; 415;
417; 426; 472-73;
538; 651; 659-61;
690; 737; 738; 744-
45; 846; 1005; 1013

χάρισμα
124; 372; 379-80;
382; 426; 744

χρηστότης
194; 200-201; 261;
671; 689-90

χωρίς
273; 298; 451

ψεῦσμα, ψεύστη
246; 249

ψιθυριστής
183; 186

χρηστολογία
991-92

χρηστότης
194; 200-201; 261;
671; 689-90

ὡραῖος
639-40

ὥσπερ
371-73; 399; 420;
709

ὠφέλεια
242

ὠφελέω
231

3. Subjects

Abba
116; 315; 476;
479; 484; 499-500;
521; 525-26; 565

Abraham
27; 34; 37; 84; 87;
113; 157; 224;
243; 304-21; 323-
43; 350; 352; 536;
538; 557; 563;
564; 565; 566;
571-72; 574; 575-
77; 600; 602; 604;
609; 611; 653;
682-83; 687; 697;
701; 718; 845;
892

Abundance
383; 388-89; 633

Acceptance
109; 110; 120;
144-45; 151; 218;
276; 301; 311;
316; 329; 348;
361; 384; 388;
401; 434; 442;

486; 526; 614;
648; 672; 677;
681; 691; 808;
841; 888-89; 906;
922; 934; 966;
974-75; 987;
1013

Acclamation
498-99; 525-26;
568; 628; 633;
714; 997; 1002

Adam
29; 177; 182; 184;
186; 191; 211;
280; 327; 343;
370-89; 395; 402-
3; 409; 423; 426;
442; 447-48; 451-
53; 472; 480; 483;
491; 494; 506;
513-14; 517; 538;
593; 598; 673;
682; 709; 711;
872

Adultery
34; 220; 228; 250;
314; 428-29; 432-
33; 448; 805; 810;
812; 826

A fortiori
363

Agapaic communal-
ism
66; 812; 971-72

Agape Hymn
25; 66; 818; 820;
822; 824; 827-28

Agape meal (love
feast)
66; 68-69; 72; 215;
326; 362; 408;
435; 490; 491;
494; 511; 681;
748; 751; 758;
762; 777; 804-5;
807; 809; 812;

814-15; 817; 819-
22; 824-26; 835-
36; 840-41; 843;
860; 861; 863;
868; 885; 888-90;
929; 971-72; 974;
979

Allegory
668-70; 672; 682-
87; 692-93

Aquila
19; 55; 59-61; 63-
64; 85; 949; 952-
60; 967; 968; 972;
980; 983

A maiore ad minus
670

Ambassadorial letter
44; 46; 74; 108;
109; 725; 907;
909-11; 914; 915;
921; 934

Ambitus sive circuitus
346n9

A minore ad maius
29; 669-72; 675;
692

Amplification
33n197; 39; 42;
165; 479; 782n3

Anakolouthon
221n16; 373n29;
376n73; 387n219;
453n120;
597n105;
598nn112, 119;
997nb

Ananias ben
Nedebaeus
20-21

Anantapodoton
589; 590

Ellipse, elliptical style
(*cont.*)
401; 417; 573;
579; 674-76; 680;
705; 713; 892

Enthymeme
viii, ix, 24; 28-29;
323-28; 362; 372;
390; 392-94; 400;
402; 404-8; 607;
660; 666; 668-72;
675; 678; 681;
683; 685-86; 689-
90; 694-96; 847

Enumeratio
32; 535

Epanadiplosis
507; 507n10

Epanalepsis
476n9; 607

Epistolography
42; 90

Epitrechon
623

Epitrope
670n42

Erotesis
533-34; 543

Eschatology
66; 84; 820-22; 832

Ecstasy
73; 74; 247; 491;
496; 770

Egypt
20-21; 113; 115;
128; 161-62; 207;
222; 242; 410;
583; 771; 777;
800; 852; 869;
903; 968; 979

Eleazar
97; 232; 286; 365;
485; 564; 915;
963

Electra
487

Elijah
35; 616; 628; 650;
652; 653; 655-60

Enoch
489; 628; 732;
1006

Enthusiasm
74; 133; 380; 402;
491; 518; 520;
551; 643; 762;
763; 785

Ephesian hypothesis
9

Ephesus
8; 9; 18; 19; 59;
64; 74; 81; 90;
119; 359; 433;
473; 543; 545-46;
864; 954-60; 977

Essene
114; 275; 349;
354; 486; 528;
618; 627

Eternal life
146; 192; 195;
205-6; 212; 229;
367; 372; 389;
414-15; 425-26;
494; 565

Eucharist
66; 104; 158; 434;
536; 748-49; 947

Eve
191; 280; 327;
374; 386; 448;
451-52; 514; 992

Evil, evildoers
31; 38-39; 101;
165; 170; 183-91;
202-3; 207-9; 232;
248; 251; 254;
259; 263; 327;
371; 373; 376-77;
388; 410-11; 417;
423; 437; 442;
448-53; 460-72;

484; 494-95; 511;
514; 521; 526;
545; 596; 616;
644; 675; 732;
756-79; 793-96;
814; 825-27; 850;
862; 866; 878;
904; 931; 987;
993-94

Exclusion
67-68; 86; 260;
296; 483; 490;
575-76; 618; 890;
991; 995

Excursus
157; 174; 315;
440

Exemplum
27; 29; 173; 306;
669; 671; 678;
680; 742; 875

Exhortatio
724

Exordium
24; 29-30; 43; 96-
100; 108-9; 112-
13; 117-19; 124;
137; 139; 243; 937

Expiation
270; 284-85; 288;
404; 561

Exsuscitatio
556; 558; 560-63;
567

Extended holiness
672; 683

Faith
Passim

Father
96; 99; 115-16;
188; 307-43; 393;
399; 485; 499;
538; 562-66; 578;
580; 707-9; 721;
790-91; 794; 800;

885; 891-94; 909;
1011

Felix
20; 198

Festus
20-21

Fool
131; 150; 160;
254; 259; 260; 557

Forbearance
37; 192; 194-95;
201; 268; 270-71;
283; 290; 291;
597; 533; 640; 716

Foreskin
232-34; 236; 301;
304; 306-7; 317-20

Form criticism
1; 24; 68

Gaius (Caligula)
44; 58; 792; 802;
866

Gaius Titius Justus
21-22; 65; 975-76;
979-81

Gallio inscription
19

Gentile
Passim

Gloss
217; 345; 354;
359; 414; 417-19;
455; 458; 473;
476; 782; 830

Glossolalia
73-74; 523-25;
551; 745; 911

Gnostic, Gnosticism
66; 374; 379; 470;
487; 514; 531;
699; 735; 760;
768; 770; 820;
824; 827; 904;
989; 995; 1002;
1008

Golden Age
47-49; 279; 509;
512-13; 516-17;
520

Gradatio
31; 346; 635

Grand style
270-71; 294

Hapax legomenon
125; 270; 409;
649; 656; 761;
765; 784; 816;
861; 987

Heart
116; 150; 158;
167-68; 180; 189;
202; 213-18; 236-
37; 241-42; 320;
356-57; 361; 417-
18; 423; 434; 446;
489; 518; 524-26;
559; 583; 585;
605; 614-15; 625-
31; 646; 662-64;
683; 709; 711;
717; 719; 752;
754; 758; 862;
930; 934; 992;
1004

Heir
341; 430; 501-2;
575; 577

Hellenistic Christian
24; 106; 107-8;
287

Hillel
306; 317; 362;
618; 813; 840

Historical-critical
methods
xiii, 1; 2-3; 18; 70

Homoioptoton
31; 149; 359; 456;
695; 757; 817;
1003

Homoioteleuton
31; 149; 165; 194;
323; 346; 370-71;
392; 454; 456;
476; 532; 555-56;
623; 667; 725;
737; 755; 886;
1003

Homiletical benedic-
tion
874-75; 888

Homosexuality
173-80

Honor
xv; 1-2; 26-27; 46-
53; 72; 86-89; 103;
110-11; 115; 120;
123; 133-34; 136-
39; 149-53; 158;
165-91; 194; 205-
9; 212; 229-37;
261; 266; 272;
278-82; 290-93;
295-303; 307; 310-
17; 329-31; 339-
43; 348-57;
361-63; 367-68;
384; 388-89; 398-
401; 408-9; 412;
422-24; 427; 434-
39; 449-53; 459-
73; 481-97;
500-503; 510; 526;
536; 542; 545;
551; 554; 562-67;
585; 594-98; 609;
613-20; 630-33;
641-48; 653; 659-
61; 679; 686-93;
710-11; 741; 761-
62; 772-74; 794;
801-3; 827-36; 839;
847; 860; 865; 876-
85; 909; 929; 945-
48; 952-74; 978-84;
1008; 1013

Hope
142; 223; 323-40;
346-57; 387; 492;
504-30; 565; 569;
658; 675; 679-80;
695; 702; 706;
763; 880-83; 887-
99

House church
35; 54; 59; 63-66;
68-70; 90-91; 113-
14; 143; 726-29;
732; 739; 746;
747; 752; 764;
869; 880; 942;
947-48; 952-53;
955-56; 958-61;
971 72; 980

Human, humanity
Passim

Hybris
181n179;
187n260; 516n85;
740n39

Hymn
24-25; 37; 43; 66;
71; 158; 270; 283-
93; 327; 343; 384;
530-36; 658; 713-
23; 813-28; 832;
885

Hypocrisy
26; 199; 228; 251;
366; 759n21; 767

Illyricum
42; 130; 900; 902;
903; 912-14; 922-
24

Imaginary interlocu-
tor
25-26; 34; 193-96;
219-20; 222; 227-
28; 230; 232; 235;
239-40; 242; 249;
252; 254; 347;

359; 360; 371;
393-94; 588-90;
610; 669; 671;
684; 686-89; 699;
832

Imperialism
513; 539; 549;
550; 896-97

Incarnation
327; 374; 483

Inclusion, inclusivity
26; 67; 86-87; 272;
301; 331; 334;
394; 550; 575;
597; 613; 670-71;
690; 700; 701;
761; 889; 895;
897

Inclusio
35; 165; 255-56;
263; 589; 601;
604; 782; 832;
887

Inheritance
227; 323; 325-26;
331; 431; 479;
498; 501-2; 539;
575-76; 578; 650;
686; 741; 847

Interlocutor
25-28; 34; 193-
267; 295-303; 310;
347; 359-60; 371;
395; 407; 588-610

Interpolation
3; 6-7; 17-18; 30;
43; 418; 456-58;
626; 642; 782-84;
793; 881; 951;
985-1011

Invention
23-25

Isis
397; 845; 896;
943; 994

Narcissus
47; 100; 984

Narratio
29; 30; 82; 117; 127; 128; 135; 148

Natural revelation
155

Nature
154; 168; 175-77; 182; 214; 301; 375; 437; 448; 484; 512-17; 643; 670; 689; 693; 820; 828; 890

Neighbor
27; 65; 110; 197; 350; 447; 617; 750; 773; 778; 801; 805; 808; 812-15; 839; 850; 860-61; 863; 877-78; 880; 893; 939; 978

Nero
20-21; 47-49; 61-63; 78; 115; 139; 173; 178; 190; 497; 509; 517; 785; 795-96; 798-99; 825; 967; 968; 970

New Perspective
296n15; 310

Obedience, disobedi-
ence
27; 49; 53; 100; 110-11; 121-23; 141; 151; 182; 188; 205; 212; 220; 233-36; 250; 267; 311; 325; 328; 385-89; 409; 412; 416-21; 431; 437-38; 452-53; 463-69; 495; 526; 579; 610-11; 618;

626-27; 641; 644; 649; 653; 696-711; 728; 763; 783-89; 828; 884; 909-11; 985-95; 999-1010

Obligation
38; 82; 106-7; 114; 128; 130; 132-34; 157; 182-83; 189; 203; 214; 230; 313; 348; 412; 431-32; 451; 459; 465; 478; 493-94; 497; 513; 611; 624-25; 673; 679; 727; 738; 754; 763; 772; 783; 797; 800-808; 851; 875-78; 889; 930; 948; 959; 974

Orphic
24; 300; 494; 743; 837

Osiris
397-98

Pallas
20; 47

Parablepsis
390

Parallelism
30-31; 98; 136; 149; 159; 165; 194; 209; 220; 260; 295; 305; 323; 342-43; 346-47; 358-59; 371-72; 381; 385; 393; 407; 414; 417; 455-56; 476-78; 487; 492; 506; 541; 556; 572; 580-84; 589; 595-97; 600-601; 607-9; 623; 627; 630; 636; 646; 652; 656; 664; 669-70;

675-76; 682-83; 695-96; 704; 709; 725; 757; 781-82; 817-18; 831-32; 837; 850; 855; 866; 881; 893; 902; 986; 999

Paria ex paribus
385n195

*Parallelismus membro-
rum*
30; 136; 165

Parecbasis
96n3

Parechesis
31; 165; 186; 817-18; 855

Paregmenon
371; 736n2

Parenthesis
217; 269; 279; 281; 288; 377; 379; 892

Paromoiosis
31; 695; 696; 706-7

Paronomasia
31; 35; 38; 97; 149; 165; 193-94; 240; 250; 255; 269; 370; 372; 392; 393; 440-41; 455; 477; 478; 507; 534; 553; 556; 623; 736-37; 739; 757; 782; 805; 832; 855; 975

Pars pro toto
191

Partitio
29; 135

Paradise
38; 300; 381; 426; 509; 514

Parousia
39; 82; 356-67; 384-85; 519; 530;

674; 690; 704; 784; 821; 913; 924; 933; 995

Partiality, impartiality
1; 26; 31; 42; 79; 86-89; 113; 150; 153; 166; 190-97; 203-4; 207-13; 219-20; 238-41; 248; 255; 266; 271; 257; 278-79; 289; 291; 293; 295; 300; 306; 324; 350-51; 382; 453; 539; 557; 586; 633; 711; 718; 752; 771; 840; 850; 931; 952-53; 974; 995-96; 999; 1013

Participation
40; 42; 66; 111; 120-21; 125; 133; 145; 162; 212; 267; 276-78; 313; 315; 329; 353; 362; 375; 393; 481; 491; 497; 503; 517; 529; 539; 551; 564; 597; 604; 615; 628; 685; 729; 744; 764; 852; 893; 921; 928; 933; 1010

Partisanship
141; 206; 275; 827; 989

Passover
21; 564; 869; 936

Patron, patronage
17; 23; 47; 49; 52; 57; 62-70; 75; 79; 81; 88-91; 129; 132; 181; 416; 423; 436; 493-94; 536; 752-53; 806;

Title church
63-64; 69-70; 955

Tobspruch
867; 869

Topos
202; 221; 226;
692

Torah
30; 33-34; 86-87;
138; 142; 145;
154; 158-59; 190;
210-14; 222; 227;
229; 232-33; 243-
44; 251; 297-99;
314; 325-27; 377;
386-87; 412; 430-
33; 436; 445-47;
450-53; 461; 463;
468-69; 480-81;
488; 616; 647;
709-10; 722; 808-
9; 813

Tolerance, intolerance
28; 80; 197; 201;
233; 303; 686;
699; 772; 785;
856; 873; 877; 888

Transitus
43; 323; 346n3

Trap, entrapment
158-60; 202-3;
206; 211; 217;
223; 473; 613;
650; 652; 663-64;
852; 857; 987;
989

Trastevere
55; 57; 62-65; 69-
70

Travel plans
87; 128-29; 700;
894; 907; 913;
915; 921-28; 932;
934; 936-37; 943;
956; 977-81

Trespass
382-88; 446; 666;

669-71; 673; 675-
76; 680; 704; 720

Tricola
35; 255; 262

Type, typology
46; 131; 250; 330;
340; 369; 378;
402; 418; 443;
610; 828

Uneducated
55; 88; 115; 132-
33; 136; 142; 160;
267; 296; 336;
632; 717; 803;
834; 905; 1013

Vice catalogue
31; 165-66; 174;
184-89

Weak
Passim

Weapon
216; 390; 393;
410-12; 421; 423-
24; 437; 512; 728;
816; 818; 823-24

Wily scoffer
588-591

Work, works
28; 68; 73; 111;
119; 155; 192;
194-95; 202; 204-
6; 212; 224-25;
235-36; 253; 255;
266; 272-77; 294-
99; 303-6; 308-10;
312-13; 315; 317-
18; 326; 348; 421;
424-28; 436-37;
439; 444; 449;
480; 495; 497;
509; 516; 521;
527; 530; 567;
570; 572; 579;
583; 595; 602;

606; 610-11; 619;
624; 650-52; 660-
61; 708; 718; 760;
780-81; 792; 809;
811; 816; 818;
822; 825; 865;
866; 878; 891;
909; 957; 961;
979-80

Wrath
Passim

Zeal
26; 133; 240; 443-
44; 450; 460; 468;
471; 607-8; 610;
616-17; 619-20;
625; 641; 644-47;
649; 674-75; 704-
6; 719; 753; 811;
827

Zealot, zealotism
28; 83; 411; 422;
444-45; 449; 451;
453; 455; 457-58;
463; 466-67; 469-
73; 556; 616; 618;
620; 628; 644;
646; 653-54; 704;
784-85; 922; 933;
935; 937

4. Modern Authors, Editors, Translators

Baur, Ferdinand
  Christian
  xxxv; 70; 81n566;
  526n202; 881n70;
  986n5
Baxter, A. G.
  684; 684n178;
  685n190; 688n220;
  692n270
Beale, G. K.
  585nn178, 180, 181
Beard, Mary
  xxxv; 48n284;
  511nn46, 49;
  517n93
Beare, Francis Wright
  537n41; 863n109
Beasley-Murray, G. R.
  396n48
Beatrice, Pier F.
  783n16
Beaujeu, J.
  61n401
Beck, Johann Tobias
  xxxv; 112n168;
  485n110; 519n112
Beck, Norman A.
  xxxv
Becker, Joachim
  338n181; 845n150
Becker, Jürgen
  xxxv; 98n19;
  104nn77, 89;
  105n95; 767n111;
  922n10
Beckwith, Roger T.
  869n191
Beentjes, Pancratius
  C.
  648n137
Behm, Johannes
  8n48; 9n51;
  132n55; 202n88;
  226n61; 227;
  227n65; 356n110;
  363n189; 399n87;
  438n77; 542n97;

560n68; 563n106;
  705n103; 719n43;
  729n47; 732nn81,
  84; 733nn89, 92,
  94; 837n67;
  904n18; 905n25;
  991nn61, 63
Behrens, Achin
  311nn52, 55, 56;
  312n57
Beilner, Wolfgang
  275n54
Béjin, A.
  181n174
Beker, J. Christiaan
  xxxv; 84n611;
  373n24; 387n222;
  394n20; 440n2;
  618n114
Beld, A. van den
  470n127
Bell, Richard H.
  xxxv; 631n99;
  637n19; 640n43;
  641nn59, 67;
  643nn86, 94;
  644nn98, 100;
  645nn105, 109;
  646n118; 647n132;
  668n15; 673n63;
  675; 675n78;
  676n96; 682n152;
  683n165; 701n72
Bencze, Anselm L.
  805n4
Benecke, William
  xxxv; 256n15;
  277n75
Benekert, H.
  110n143
Bengel, J. A.
  xxxv; 12; 135n10;
  219n2; 378n100;
  408n184; 422n81;
  476n9; 552n192;
  714n10; 765n89;
  806n16; 807n26;

855n6; 902n4
Benko, Stephen
  xxxv; 19n98;
  60nn386, 388;
  810n62; 973;
  973nn270-72;
  974n276; 988n22
Benoit, A.
  254n3
Berger, Klaus
  xxxv; 24n144;
  67nn439, 444;
  96n2; 109nn134-
  36; 115nn195, 198,
  204; 124nn82, 84;
  209nn165, 169;
  282n128; 289n198;
  295n9; 309n31;
  313n72; 318n145;
  319n146; 320n166;
  329n77; 380n127;
  384n179; 392n10;
  426nn117, 121;
  447n65; 473n159;
  481n45; 538nn56,
  59; 573; 573nn26,
  32; 575n55;
  578n84; 738n15;
  810; 810n52;
  812n79; 813n85;
  930n86; 931n94;
  937n171; 1013nn3,
  4, 6
Bergmeier, Roland
  xxxv; 213n199;
  214n206; 399n85;
  618n121; 781n2;
  786nn39, 42;
  788n71; 789n80;
  861n85; 994nn92,
  98
Berkley, Timothy W.
  xxxv; 207n143;
  225n49; 230n94;
  231n99; 236n153
Berlin, Adele
  30n169; 636n13

Berry, Donald K.
  589n4
Bertman, Stephen
  188n280
Bertram, Georg
  111n152; 160n111;
  187nn261, 264,
  266; 207nn144,
  146; 208nn148,
  154; 226n55;
  233n124; 327n51;
  353n83; 399n85;
  437n65; 449nn84,
  85; 486nn111,
  118; 487n122;
  511nn47, 48;
  545n129, 553n214;
  699n47; 741n46;
  768n124; 770n143;
  787n52; 846n157;
  861n84; 866n147;
  994nn88, 89, 95,
  99; 995n104
Betrand-Dagenbach,
  C.
  962n117
Best, Ernest
  xxxvi; 18n90; 103;
  103n76; 135n6;
  448n73; 668n14;
  872n223
Betz, Hans Dieter
  xxxvi; 28; 43n244;
  102n58; 109n127;
  127; 127n5;
  174n105; 211n183;
  232n117; 248n99;
  264n98; 266;
  266n121; 300nn58,
  61, 65; 378n97;
  396n48; 397;
  397nn48, 52, 60;
  398nn61, 71;
  400n93; 401nn100,
  104; 470nn127,
  129; 494n212;
  496n230;

Brockhaus, Ulrich
xxxvii; 679n131;
739n23; 741n57;
744n89; 745nn94,
98, 101, 103-5;
748n145; 944;
944n26
Brockmeyer, Norbert
xxxvii; 51n307;
416n18; 968n192
Broughton,
T. Robert S.
76n515
Brinton, A.
41; 41n236
Broer, Ingo
551n190; 788n65
Brose, Ernst
567n147;
568nn148, 150,
151
Brongers, Hendrik
Antonie
32n195; 787n51
Brooten, Bernadette J.
xxxvii; 174;
175nn112, 115,
116; 176nn124,
128, 129;
177nn131, 135;
178n145;
179nn150, 152;
950nh; 961nn105,
109
Brosch, Josef
749n151
Brown, A.
xlviii
Brown, Michael
Joseph
100; 100nn37, 41
Brown, Raymond E.
xxxvii; 1n1; 2n10;
58; 58nn377, 378;
60n390; 61n403;
83n600; 101n56;
697n22

Bruce, Frederick F.
xxxviii; 18n87;
32n183; 119n23;
151n31; 152n36;
244n52; 246n80;
285n164; 360n149;
375n65; 405n162;
435n51; 448n73;
480n35; 523n162;
527n203; 548n157;
787n59; 983nn76,
77; 998n6
Brun, Lyder
561n71
Brunt, P. A.
xxxviii; 276n66;
799n169
Bruston, C.
378n98
Bryskog, Samuel
xxxviii; 29n164; 97;
97n6; 108n120
Büchler, J.
21n115
Büchsel, Friedrich
xxxviii; 160n116;
168n27; 170n53;
197n34; 198n48;
204n104; 207nn139,
141; 211n185; 248;
249n107; 251n133;
283n139; 284n149;
365n213; 382nn157,
160; 408n188;
447n65; 448nn68,
69; 468n112;
480n38; 486n114;
519n114; 717n33;
761n49; 766n106;
791n99; 801n194;
839n95; 857;
857n28; 871nn210,
216
Bühlmann, Walter
32; 32n185
Bühner, Jan-Adolf
101n56; 386n209

Bullinger, Ernest W.
xxxviii; 96n3;
165n9; 194nn7, 10;
195n15; 219n1;
220nn5, 6, 11;
269n8; 323n4;
370n4; 371n18;
372n19; 428n1;
476n11; 478nn21,
23, 24; 507n10;
533nn7, 11;
556n17; 572n22;
589nn6, 10; 607n9;
623n8; 636n11;
668n10; 669n35;
670n42; 671n48;
690n248; 736n2;
757nn9, 11; 782n3
Bultmann, Rudolph
xxxviii; 8n48;
25n148; 105;
105n99; 106n101;
108n118; 120n25;
141; 141n65;
142n78; 153n50;
154n60; 157n83;
190n300; 205n123;
206n136; 207n138;
212n192; 217;
217nn248, 249;
223n34; 227n63;
230n87; 235n143;
244n52; 270;
270nn13, 16;
273n37; 277n74;
280n113; 289n202;
292n229; 296nn13,
14; 329nn67, 69,
71; 333n127;
334n128;
335nn144, 148,
337n158; 351;
351nn61, 62;
355n100; 357n121;
358n129; 360n149;
364n202; 373nn25,
29; 375n60; 376n78;

378n98; 379n110;
384n190; 386nn211,
212; 406n165;
417n30; 418n38;
433n36; 440n3; 448;
448n80; 449;
449n81; 450n91;
456n11; 457;
457n16; 459n25;
462n55; 463n62;
476n2; 491n184;
492nn193, 195;
493n196; 496n233;
530n237; 543n113;
550n170; 559n48;
595n87; 614n74;
617nn102, 105;
619n125; 622n3;
636n16; 642n70;
649n155; 686;
686n194; 687n215;
688nn215, 226;
710n149; 717nn27,
29; 726n11;
753n215;
754nn220, 222;
782n13; 823nn65,
66; 848n175;
859n53; 861n82;
897; 897nn115,
119; 925n35;
936nn151, 153
Burdick, Donald W.
xxxviii; 198n46;
264; 264n99;
353n82; 406n173;
859n51
Burger, Christoph
xxxviii; 24n143;
98n21; 104n78;
107n109
Burchard, Christoph
428n1; 430n13;
432n29; 437n68;
599n134

Burer, Michael H.
963n128

Burgess, S.
425n106

Burgess, Theodore C.
43; 43nn246, 247;
44; 44n250

Burke, Trevor J.
498nn258, 260

Burnett, Gary W.
xxxviii; 140n56;
275n60; 445n44

Burns, J. B.
494n210

Bushnell, Horace
280n113

Busse, Ulrich
374n54; 781n2

Bussmann, Claus
xxxviii, 154n57;
156n82; 183n211

Byrne, Brendan, S. J.
Passim 115 times

Cadbury, Henry J.
981; 981n61;
982n87

Cambiano, Giuseppe
52n316

Cambier, Jules–M.
xxxviii; 213n197;
291n224; 375n61

Campbell, Alastair
xxxviii; 394n20;
396n41; 401;
401n110; 403n138

Campbell, Douglas A.
xxxviii; 141n62;
142n74; 144n89;
269; 269nn3-5;
270n10; 271n18;
274nn49, 51;
275n55; 277n75;
279; 280n113; 281;
281n115; 282n133;
284n149; 285n164;
288; 288n194;

289n195; 291n222;
292nn229, 237, 238;
305n1; 308n20;
310n44; 324n13;
325n18; 326n38;
333n119; 342n218

Campbell, J. Y.
xxxviii; 765n87;
929n77

Campbell, William S.
xxxviii-xxxix; 84;
84nn614-18; 85;
85n619; 89;
145n110; 240n9;
270n9; 281;
281n122; 624n18;
742n64; 836n60

Cantarelli, Eva
174n111;
181nn174, 175,
177, 178

Capes, Donald B.
633n116

Caragounis, Chrys C.
153n49; 371;
371n13; 379;
379nn115, 119;
381; 382n153

Caratelli, Giovanni
Pugliese
494n212

Carcopino, Jérôme
76n515

Carmignac, Jean
545n129

Carney,Thomas F.
59; 59n382

Carpenter, Rhys
76n517

Carr, Wesley
xxxix; 550nn176,
178; 552nn191,
196; 553n212;
554nn214, 215;
787n59; 792n106

Carras, George P.
197n36

Carrez, Maurice
701n68; 890n29

Carroll, J. T.
305n5; 874nc

Carroll, Scott T.
73n485; 966n175

Casel, Odo
727n32; 728n38

Carson, D. A.
lvii; 307n9;
844nn142, 143

Carter, T. L.
xxxix; 140n58;
197n39; 254n6;
258n36; 352n64;
384n191; 449n81;
463n60; 471n140;
486n115

Carter, Warren C.
281n123

Casalis, G.
882n91

Cassien, Bp.
530n239

Castel S. Pietro,
Teodorico da
962n120; 963n126

Castriota, David
511n46; 512;
512n54; 516n85

Cavalin, H. C. C.
146; 146n114

Cavallin, Anders
130n35

Cazelles, Henri
lix

Cerfaux, Lucien
316n117; 320n162;
375n61; 927n61;
929n80

Cervin, Richard S.
950nh

Chadwick, Henry
45; 45n263

Chae, Daniel Jong-
Sang
xxxix; 87n646

Champion, L. G.
xxxix; 8n45;
24n144; 722n69;
895n95; 998n5;
1002n43; 1013n7

Chang, Hae-Kyung
504nd; 506nn1, 6;
507n9; 511nn44,
47, 48, 50; 512n52;
513n63; 514nn66,
68, 71; 515n82;
517nn88, 91;
518n98

Charles, R. H.
115n196; 759n21;
761n49

Chaytor, H. J.
xliii; 810n60

Chester, A.
786n121

Cheyne, T. K.
769; 769n135;
777n212

Chilton, Bruce D.
537nn38, 41;
723n72

Christensen, Torben
xxxix; 48n282;
796n143

Christiansen, Ellen
Juhl
xxxix; 555ne;
705nn107, 109;
706n117

Christoffersson, Olle
511; 512nn51, 52;
523; 523n154;
525n192

Chvala-Smith, A. J.
616n100

Clark, Kenneth W.
327n43; 849n193

Clarke, Andrew D.
xxxix; 360nn150,
151, 159; 944n24;

Goppelt, Leonhard
xliv; 340n195; 365;
365n212;
378nn101, 102;
658n74; 786n44

Gordon, Richard
138; 138n34

Gore, Charles
xliv; 282n130;
956n38

Gorman, Michael J.
xliv; 28n158;
282n129;
544n115;
546n133

Goshen-Gottstein,
Moshe
340n202

Gotsmich, A.
994n91

Gowan, Donald E.
187n264; 512;
512n56; 514n73

Grabbe, Leslie L.
xliv; 19nn99, 103;
20nn108, 111, 112;
21n114

Gräbe, Petrus J.
xliv; 137n30;
156n72; 899n138;
910nn82, 83;
911nn90, 94

Grabner-Haider,
Anton
xliv; 724n3; 725;
725n10

Gräßer, Erich
310n41; 705n104;
706n117

Graham, A. A. K.
844n142

Grande, C. del
187n261

Grant, Michael
xlii; 47n276;
174n109; 178n141;

180n172; 539n72;
659n79

Grant, Robert M.
62n407; 837n71

Grappe, Christian
xliv; 442nn21, 23;
472n149; 480n42

Grassi, J. A.
499n268

Grau, F.
744n90

Green, D. E.
xliv; lxi

Green, Joel B.
20nn`112, 113;
41n237; 397n50

Greenlee, J. Harold
xliv; 164ni

Greenwood, David
214nn207, 209

Greeven, Heinrich
524nn169, 170;
560n59; 747n122;
749n151;
750nn159, 161;
752nn199, 200;
813n89; 825nn80,
82; 878n36

Grelot, Pierre
774n184

Grene, David
44n252; 187n263

Grenfell, B. P.
609n15; 865n136

Grether, G.
794n126

Grether, Herbert G.
597n100

Grieb, Katherine A.
xliv; 80n556;
81n564; 891n40

Grieve, A.
973n273

Griffin, Miriam T.
xliv; 47nn276, 277;
48nn280, 281;

61nn393, 399;
173n100; 517n94

Griffith, Terry
229n78

Grimm, W.
1001n29

Grobel, Kendrick
xxxviii; 194n6;
280n113

Grossouw, W. K.
445n44

Grosvener, Mary
lxviii; 112n169;
620n136

Grundmann, Walter
xlv; 112; 112n172;
138n32; 181n182;
182n190; 185n229;
223nn38, 39; 258;
259n42; 338n172;
339n186; 350nn51,
52; 354n90;
360nn149, 152;
398nn67, 68;
453n123; 467;
467n108; 498n262;
499; 499nn265, 268;
502; 502n310;
551n190; 553n212;
566n134; 601n156;
679n127; 688n217;
692n264; 733n98;
734n107; 741n49;
764; 764nn79, 80;
769; 769n139;
796n144; 800nn184,
187; 842nn126, 127;
843n134; 865n134;
877n22; 904n17;
908n59; 911,
911n94; 966n169;
992n71

Guardini, Romano
529n224

Guarducci, M.
791n90

Gubler, Marie-Louise
270n11

Guelich, Robert A.
286n169; 36n205

Guerra, Anthony J.
xlv; 312n63;
334n135; 341n204;
747n132

Guerra y Gómez,
Manuel
748n132

Gülzow, Henneke
xlv; 51n307;
416n18; 728n45;
966n176; 968n191

Güttgemanns, Erhardt
574n34

Güting, Eberhard W.
xlv; xlix; 194n10;
706n18

Guignebert, Ch.
735n112

Gulin, E. G.
863n117

Gummere, R. A.
732nn86, 87;
743nn74, 75

Gundry, Robert H.
xlv; 169n42;
380n125;
383nn166, 174;
403n129; 448;
448n74; 465;
465nn87, 90, 92;
472n154; 495n217

Gunkel, Hermann
73; 73n488;
74n493

Gutbrod, Walter
210n173; 222n21;
264n103; 316n114;
420; 420n66;
561n82; 562;
562nn86, 91;

Herntrich, Volkmar
198n48; 211n184;
602n165; 603n172;
659nn78, 82;
717n33; 791n99;
839n95; 857;
857n28; 871nn210,
216
Herold, Gerhard
xlvi; 151n22
Herring, H.
155n68
Herrmann, Johannes
284n149; 501;
501nn300, 303;
502nn309, 312;
524nn169, 170
Herten, Joachim
739n23; 744n93;
745n103
Hertling, L.
56n360
Hertz, Joseph H.
544n118;
545n128
Hervas, José Manuel
Roldán
76n515
Hester, James D.
xlvi; 100n42;
109n126; 128n7;
326n25;
501n302
Heyken, Enno
349n34
Higgins, A. J. B.
104n78
Hilgenfeld, Adolf
73n492
Hill, David
xlvi; 746nn115,
116; 750n162
Hills, J. V.
xlviii
Hirschberger,
Johannes
487n119

Hitchcock, F. R.
Montgomery
517n96
Hitzig, H.
962n123; 963n125
Hock, Ronald F.
xlvi; 75; 75n510
Hodge, Caroline
Johnson
245; 308n24;
360n150; 491n180;
685n187; 693n272;
944n24
Hodges, Z. C.
12n65
Hoekema, A. A.
445n44
Hoerber, Robert
George
991n52
Hoffman, C. D. F.
xliii
Hoffmann, Paul
xlvi; 628n53;
681n150
Hofius, Otfried
xlvi; 237n165;
251n126; 280n103;
365; 366n216;
370n3; 373n27;
374n47; 374n53;
376nn72, 80; 377;
377nn82, 84;
382n155;
387nn219, 221;
442n21; 470n131;
571; 571n8;
574n36; 607n10;
610n28; 613n66;
617n110; 629n76;
630nn79, 82;
644n97; 698;
698n32; 700n60;
701n72; 702n74;
705; 705n102;
707n121; 793n118;
852n227; 862n102

Hofmann, J. C. K. von
xlvi; 111n162;
112n170; 312n59;
335n148; 348n28;
355n104; 373n23;
381n137; 408n184;
454na; 485n110;
497n248; 525n187;
552n191; 800n183;
854nk
Hofmann, Karl-
Martin
974n276
Hogarth, D. G.
609n15; 865n136
Hodgson, Robert, Jr.
425; 425n106;
543n113; 545n127
Holl, Karl
929; 929n79
Hollander, H. W.
201n77; 207n139;
869n189
Holloway, Paul A.
xlvii; 194n12;
270n10; 323n7;
392nn6, 8; 478n22;
494n209; 507n13;
571n5; 758n13;
855nn8, 11, 17;
863n108
Holmberg, Bengt
xlvii; 44; 45n258;
930n87; 937nn167,
168; 944; 944n26;
947; 947n53
Holst, H.
lv
Holst, Richard
312n58
Holter-Stavanger,
Knut
174n104; 177n138
Holtz, Traugott
143n82; 160n118;
378n96; 401n103;
484; 484n89;

515n77; 568n159;
569n161; 910n85;
1007n69
Holtzmann, H. J.
217n251
Holwerda, D.
701n70
Hommel, Hildebrecht
xlvii; 462nn58, 59;
472nn153, 155;
509n26; 516n87
Hooke, S. H.
105n95
Hooker, Morna D.
xlvii; 161nn121,
126, 131; 182n187;
253nb; 256n15;
287n181; 891n40
Horgan, Maurya P.
623n6
Horn, Friedrich
Wilhelm
xlvii; 499n267
Horsley, G. H. R.
xlvii; 119n15;
122n52; 203n99;
320n170; 337n158;
365n214; 411n228;
416n21; 468n112;
473n163; 498;
498n256;
502nn306, 309;
519n109; 563n99;
568n160; 632n106;
655n37; 656n54;
664; 664n132;
722n66; 761n46;
788n60; 791;
791n92; 792n109;
795n127; 864n131;
904n12; 914n132;
915n136; 932n105;
935n137; 943n17;
947n51; 951n5;
958n61; 960n92;
968nn195, 197;
969n216; 970;

Horsley, G. H. R.
(cont.)
970n221; 979;
979n42; 981n60;
992n70; 993n71
Horsley, Richard A.
xxxviii; xliv; xlvii;
lviii; 48n282;
138n34; 627n49;
785n36; 981n59
Horst, Johannes
410n209; 437n64;
470n134; 596nn91,
92; 743nn71, 72;
744n84
Horstmann, Axel
136n15; 263n85;
264n99; 423n92;
859n51
Hort, F. J. A.
lxvi; 12; 13;
80n554; 305nk;
998n6
Horton, Fred L., Jr.
145n101
Howard, George
277n75; 298n39;
301; 301n71; 617;
618n113; 620;
620n138; 630n80;
633n116
Howard, David M., Jr.
315n104
Howard, Wilbert
Francis
lv; 322nb; 451n104;
602n167; 736nj;
950nj; 956n40
Hubbard, Moyer V.
xlvii; 41n109;
431n14; 438n81;
481n50
Huber, Wolfgang
773n182
Huby, Joseph
xlvii; 112n163;
217n251; 375n65;

498n254; 529n224;
767n115
Hudson, D. F.
xlvii; 748; 748n136;
927n59
Hübner, Hans
xlvii; 25n145;
103n71; 141n65;
205n117; 230n89;
234nn133, 138;
244n58; 264n102;
302n81; 310nn46,
47; 327n43;
389n253; 404n139;
409n201; 423n93;
425n109; 447n66;
481n45; 574n35;
575n45; 577nn74,
77; 582n143;
584n162; 585n177;
585n171; 600nn139,
144; 604n192;
607n4; 609; 609n20;
613n58; 619n125;
645n106; 678n114;
698n32; 700n62;
703n90; 802n203;
809n49; 880n63;
891; 891n47;
1000nn23, 26
Hübner, U.
580n115
Huggins, Ronald V.
463n60
Hughes, Daniel
García
808n36
Hultgren, Arlan J.
xlvii; 58n378;
140n58; 251n130;
270n11; 278n79;
284n149; 885n129;
894n92
Hunter, Archibald M.
98; 98n26; 103;
103n76; 270n16;
491n180; 523n159

Hunt, A. S.
609n15; 865n136
Hunt, Lynn
1; 1nn3, 6, 7; 2;
2nn9, 12
Hurd, John C., Jr.
537n41; 863n109
Hurtado, Larry W.
xlvii; 7n36; 24n143;
104n87; 119n18;
119n20; 537n40;
566n134; 567n143,
146; 629nn76, 77;
851n219; 960n86;
998n6
Hvalvik, Reidar
702n81
Hyldahl, Niels
161nn119, 132

Incigneri, Brian J.
xlvii; 60nn384, 387;
61n400; 152n39;
162n139;
969nn210, 211
Inwood, B.
172n90

Jackson, Bernard S.
67n442; 811nn64,
68, 70, 71
Jacob, Margaret
1; 1nn3, 6, 7; 2nn9,
12
Jacobelli, Luciana
174; 174n110
Jacobs, P. J.
528n218
Jaeger, Werner
xlvii; 132nn53, 54;
187n261
Jameson, M. H.
xlvii; 518n105;
664n132; 682n158
Janowski, Bernd
102n63; 284n150;
285nn154, 163

Janzen, J. Gerald
145n102
Jaquette, James L.
632n107; 848n176
Jeffers, James S.
xlvii; 19n103;
48n282; 51; 51n308;
53n334; 56n360;
62n405; 69nn455,
456; 70; 70n463;
88n656; 431n20
Jegher-Bucher, Verena
680nn141, 142
Jenni, Ernst
722nn65, 70
Jeremias, Joachim
xlvii; xlviii;
116n213; 149;
149n9; 162n142;
165; 165n1;
166n15; 172nn79,
80; 240; 240n16;
248n100; 250n122;
305n5; 308n26;
315n108; 317n118;
380n134; 499;
499n272; 536n29;
599n130; 613nn61,
62; 623n9; 699n53;
700; 700n59;
701nn67, 73; 707;
707n126; 711;
711n159; 714n10;
760n42; 778n220;
812n78; 939n195;
940n196
Jervell, Jacob
xlviii; xlix; 42; 83;
83nn592, 595, 601,
602; 161nn121,
131; 327n41;
374n45; 528n220;
529n222
Jervis, L. Ann
xlviii; lxvi; 8n40;
80; 80n554; 82;
82nn585, 586, 588;

Michael, J. Hugh
liv; 144n92; 345nd;
347n15; 874ne;
881n78
Michaelis, Wilhelm
8n48; 155nn67, 68;
172n86; 173nn91,
94; 263n95;
342n227; 343n228;
379n122; 346n61;
503n320; 510n28;
529n231; 547n147;
561n77; 673nn55,
62, 63; 676n88;
690n244; 718nn34,
35; 843n128;
943n16; 944n25;
962n115; 967n177;
978n26
Michel, Otto
Passim 455 times
Michl, J.
361n168
Middendorf, Michael
Paul
liv; 442n18;
460n28; 462n52
Mihaly, Eugene
579n109
Milgrom, J.
729n54
Millard, Alan Ralph
308n25
Miller, James C.
liv; 110n146;
174n111; 176n127;
177n140;
1009n92
Miller, Konrad
912nn100, 104,
106; 913n177
Milligan, G.
956n36
Minde, Hans-Jürgen
van der
liv; 25n145; 103;
103n72; 265n117;

270n11; 271n18;
305n5; 326n36;
340n200; 860n72;
861n87; 863n113
Minear, Paul S.
liv; 42; 80n558;
84n611; 132;
132n60; 133n63;
198n40; 384n191;
385n199; 389n251;
494n208; 558n28;
664; 664n131;
686n196; 757n10;
871n212; 930;
930n91; 931n94;
953n21
Mitchell, Christopher
Wright
liv; 171n74
Mócsy, András
912n99
Mohrmann, Christine
157n87
Moir, Ian A.
lv; 344na; 390na;
830nj; 853ng
Moiser, J.
67n443
Molland, Einar
lv; 166n14; 196n19;
339n189; 888n9
Mollaun, Romuald
Alphonse
284n149; 286n168
Momigliano, Arnaldo
lv; 19nn94, 103;
47n275; 60n388;
162n135
Mommsen, Theodor
lv; 795n128;
811n66; 958n60
Montevecchi, Orsolina
946n47; 947n47
Montgomery, James
523n162
Montgomery, W.
lxi

Moo, Douglas J.
Passim 370 times
Moody, R. M.
146; 146n114
Moores, John D.
lv; 28; 28nn154,
155, 158-61; 125;
126nn105, 106;
362n181; 406n167;
535n20; 536n34;
550n171; 554n222;
847n169; 849n186
Moral, A. Garcia del
224n43
Morenz, Siegfried
104n86; 777n215
Morgan, Robert
lv; 401n100
Morison, James
lv; 245; 245n65;
256n15
Morris, Leon
Passim 222 times
Morrison, Clinton D.
787n57
Most, Glenn W.
668n20
Mott, Stephen C.
lv; 720n56; 930n92;
947n62
Moule, Charles
Francis Digby
lv; lxiii; 103n66;
150n17; 193nj;
202n86; 215n226;
257n24; 395n32,
36; 407n177;
421n76; 433n34;
495n224; 525n187;
535n21; 555nh;
561n81; 785n34;
790n83; 815n101;
847n170;
849n194
Moulton, James Hope
lv; 197n31; 202n86;
233n127; 244n50;

264n105; 277n78;
288n188; 292n228;
293n239; 322nb;
336n150; 386n211;
404n142; 409n195;
410n218; 432n23;
446n55; 451n104;
602n167; 672n52;
674n71; 676n89;
687n214; 736nj;
756n2; 819n14;
849n195; 883n106;
923n22; 950nj;
956n40
Moxnes, Halvor
lv; 49n293; 50n301;
102; 102nn64, 65;
249n112; 282;
282n131; 295n8;
296; 296n17; 301;
302; 302n76;
305n5; 334n137;
598n123; 762nn58,
61; 890; 890n26
Muddiman, John
844n145
Müller, Christian
lv, 247n83;
292n229; 574n33;
607n4; 701n68
Müller, Friedrich
lv; 456n11; 459n22;
476n1; 636n15;
642n69
Müller, Heinrich
lv; 29n162;
362n182; 363n183;
380n136;
383nn172, 173
Müller, Karlheinz
lv; 325n25; 611n46;
664nn133, 137;
857n30; 858;
858nn34, 35, 42;
870n198; 989nn34,
37; 990n40

Räisänen, Heikki
(*cont.*)
449n81; 455n4;
481nn44, 45;
485n106; 495n222;
556n11; 575n43;
599n128; 609;
609n24; 611;
611n37; 700n64;
828n112
Rahner, Karl
747n132
Ramaroson, Léonard
777n212
Ramsay, William
Mitchell
20n113; 21n118;
922n10
Rapske, Brian
962nn122, 123;
963nn124, 125
Rath, Mansetus
289n202
Rauer, Max
lix; 42; 836n48;
837n67; 844n145;
869n193
Rawson, Beryl
188n280
Reader, William W.
616n100
Reasoner, Mark
lix; 71n475;
132n57; 336n156;
493nn203-5;
832n7; 834nn21,
28-30, 32; 835nn38-
40; 837nn66, 72;
838nn84, 85;
845n147; 854nk;
857; 857nn27, 29;
860n65; 862n104;
867n158; 868;
868nn173-75, 179,
181; 869nn186, 193;
870n202; 871n215;
876nn7, 8, 12, 14,

19, 20; 878nn32, 33;
880n60; 888nn14,
16; 889nn21, 23;
890n34; 891nn41,
46; 892n52;
897n118
Rebell, Walter
798n166
Redalié, Yann
liv
Reed, Jeffrey T.
30n166; 118nn12,
13; 370n1; 422;
422n84; 424n99
Rees, Wilhelm
560n69
Refoulé, François
8n48; 618n115;
701n73; 882n91
Reichardt, Michael
465n86
Reiche, Johann Georg
lix; 133n65;
274n39; 314n85;
335n148; 373n24;
381n137; 386n212;
400n100; 454na;
485n110; 798n161;
801n198
Reichert, Angelika
80; 80nn555, 558;
86; 86nn635-37; 89
Reichrath, Hans L.
891n43
Reicke, Bo Ivar
lix; 66; 66n434;
98n25; 113n175;
215n223; 409n204;
615n89; 748;
748n144; 753n205;
758n19; 777n216;
818n12; 819;
819n19; 927n58
Reid, J. K. S.
xxxix
Reid, Marty L.
lix; 41n237; 117n5;

124; 124n77;
125n101; 346nn2,
9-11; 347nn17, 18,
20; 348nn22, 31;
349n33; 351n56
Reid, Marty L.
353nn76, 78, 81;
355n100; 357n119;
360n160; 370n1;
371n18; 373n30;
375n61; 377n88;
382n161; 384n182;
389n255
Reinbold, Wolfgang
644nn98, 101, 102;
645nn103, 105;
646n121
Reiner, H.
768n117
Reiterer, F. V.
275n54
Reitzenstein, Richard
732n83
Rendtorff, Rolf
103n69
Renehan, Robert
462n59; 463n69
Rengstorf, Karl
Heinrich
lix; 32; 32n190;
35nn204, 207; 44;
44n257; 100n34;
101; 101nn51, 53;
124n76; 133n69;
226n58; 250nn121,
122; 279n98;
361nn163, 165;
460; 460n30;
594n65; 657nn63,
64; 668n15; 682;
682nn159, 161;
746n106; 749;
749n152;
750n160;
864n125; 910n89;
963nn127, 129;
990nn46, 47

Rese, Martin
341n214; 574n36;
629n74; 632n108
Reumann, John
Henry Paul
lix; 141n61;
142n74; 272n23;
290n216; 292n232
Reventlow, Henning
Graf
lix
Reynolds, Joyce
947n48
Rhyne, C. Thomas
lix; 619nn126, 135
Richard, Earl J.
121n48
Richards, E.
Randolph
lix; 22nn125, 128-
33; 23n134; 979;
979nn34, 37-39;
980nn43-45
Richards, Kent
Harold
315; 315n106;
316n109
Richardson, John S.
74n501; 77nn526,
528, 530-33; 78;
78nn534, 535;
79n547; 799n173
Richardson, M. E. J.
615n79
Richardson, Peter
xxxvii; xli; xlvii;
xlviii; lix; lxvi;
53n331; 57nn363-
66, 368, 370;
537n41; 863n109
Richlin, Amy
175n114;
178nn141, 142;
179n158
Ridderbos, Herman
lix; 836n54

1128

ΚΑΙΚΟΥΑ ΠΡΟϹΟΛΔΕΛΦΟϹ

ΠΟΛΥΜΕΡΩϹ ΚΑΙΠΟΛΥΤΡΟΠΩϹ
ΠΑΛΑΙ Ο ΘΕΟϹ ΛΑΛΗϹΑϹΤΟΙϹΠΑΤΡΑϹΙΝ ΗΜΩΝ
ΤΟΙϹ ΠΡΟΦΗΤΑΙϹ ΕΠΗϹΧΑΤΟΥΤΩΝΗΜΕ
ΡΩΝΤΟΥΤΩΝ ΕΛΑΛΗϹΕΝΗΜΙΝ ΕΝ
ΥΙΩ ΟΝ ΕΘΗΚΕΝ ΚΛΗΡΟΝΟΜΟΝ ΠΑΝΤΩ
ΔΙΟΥ ΕΠΟΙΗϹΕΝΤΟΥϹΑΙΩΝΑϹ ΟϹΩΝ
ΑΠΑΥΓΑϹΜΑ ΤΗϹΔΟΞΗϹ ΚΑΙΧΑΡΑ
ΚΤΗΡΤΗϹΥΠΟϹΤΑϹΕΩϹΑΥΤΟΥ ΦΕΡΩΝΤ
ΤΑΠΑΝΤΑΤΩΡΗΜΑΤΙΤΗϹΔΥΝΑΜΕΩϹ
ΔΙΑΛ̣ΑΥΤΟΥ ΚΑΘΑΡΙϹΜΟΝΠΟΙΩϹΑΜΕΝΟϹΤΩΝ ΑΜΑΡΤΙΩΝ